MW00562131

The Descendants of Nicholas Holt of Andover Through Six Generations

Including Male and Female Lines of Descent from Generation One to Generation Six

Compiled by:

Patricia A. Abbott

ISBN- 978-1-7351258-0-0 (Patricia A. Abbott)

Dedication: For my millions of Holt cousins everywhere

Introduction

This compilation is an attempt to provide as complete information as possible of the descendants of Nicholas Holt and his wives Elizabeth and Hannah including complete families through five generations and all the children that comprise the sixth generation. This includes coverage of more than 1,000 complete families. Both the male and female lines are included so there are many Abbotts, Farnums, Johnsons, Grays, Chandlers, Ingalls, Ballards, Russells, and many more names.

Within these pages you will find the full range of human behavior: individuals with great accomplishments, those with humble, ordinary lives, and those who faced incredible hardship and tragedy. There are personal struggles including poverty and reliance on almshouses for subsistence, out-of-wedlock children, and persons who wrestled with alcoholism, depression, and other mental illness. There are also Harvard graduates, attorneys, physicians, and clergymen. There are women pioneers persevering in the face of tremendous challenges. There are the first settlers of many communities in Massachusetts, Connecticut, New Hampshire, Maine, Vermont, Pennsylvania, and upstate New York. Moving into the fifth generation who will find more descendants who made their way to Canada and into Ohio and Michigan and the southern states. By the sixth generation, descendants can be found in most of the continental United States.

Although this is a genealogical compilation, I hope that the presentation of the individual families will allow at least some sense of the humanity of these individuals and their contributions to the founding and development of the country.

Why this book?

While working on a compilation of the descendants of Robert Russell and Mary Marshall (which is still in the works), I encountered many Holts who are prominently represented among the descendants of Robert Russell. The Holt Association of America has a very well-done genealogy of the first three generations of Holts, but I was looking to go much further than the first three generations. Durrie's *Genealogical History of the Holt Family in the United States*, although providing multiple generations of descendants and much detail, seemed to have some important inaccuracies in the lineage and gaps in information. It just seemed that it might be time to attempt a more complete compilation of descendants of Nicholas Holt. This compilation includes the male and female lines which provides a fuller appreciation of the complex kinship patterns that occurred in colonial America.

I aimed to verify each piece of information with documents (birth, death, and marriage records; wills and probate records; and land transactions) to the degree that these could be accessed online. Admittedly this is a quite limited record access, but even within these limits, a large amount of information was able to be verified. Vital records present their own problems as what are mostly available are transcriptions of records, not original records. There are doubtless errors that crept into the transcriptions. Undoubtedly, I also made errors entering my data from the transcriptions. There are inconsistencies in records. For example, there are birth records for a single family in which one child is listed as born in April and a second child is recorded as being born in October of the same year. Often, birth records were recorded in more than one location (for example, when a family had their family information recorded in the town records after moving to the town), so it is not possible to *really* know where the person was born unless it can be certainly established where the family was living at the time of the birth. But within the limits of available records, I have done my best to be accurate.

Of course, there are not available records for all events (certainly not yet online), or even any records for some persons. For that, I have relied on previously published and unpublished genealogical material and town and county histories. You will find a complete list of references at the end of the book. Sources are also noted in footnotes. Even in those cases in which previously published work was used, I attempted to verify the information contained in those sources. In several cases, there was information that conflicted with available vital records, wills, or land records and I have noted those discrepancies and how they were resolved.

A note about the spelling of names

There tend not to be many variations of spelling for Holt, although earlier records may use Hoult, Holte, or some other variant. But I have chosen to use Holt uniformly. There are other surnames that are less consistent such as Abbot/Abbott, Farnham/Farnum, Coburn/Colburn. Groo/Grow, Payn/Paine, and several others that are prominent in this book. Variations of spelling occur among different documents for the same person, and often these variations occur on the same page of a document. As far as possible, I have tried to use the variation used by that family if one spelling was used consistently, but I am sure I have missed some of those. If you are a Farnham rather than a Farnum, and I spelled the name of your ancestor not the way you would spell it, I can only apologize.

How the book is organized

The book is divided into chapters based on generations. When an individual is first introduced, if that person married and had children, you will see a number at the start of the entry that will allow you to know where to look for the next generation for that person. For example, you will see this type of entry when a person is first introduced:

2) i ELIZABETH HOLT, b. at Newbury, 30 Mar 1636; d. at Andover, 14 Oct 1710; m. at Andover, 26 Oct 1657, RALPH FARNUM, baptized at St. Nicholas, Rochester, Kent, 4 Aug 1633 son of Ralph and Alice (Harris) Farnum; Ralph d. at Andover, 8 Jan 1692/3.

The "2)" indicates that you will find follow-up information later in the book. (The "i" indicates that this is the first child in that family.) Of course, there are complications. There are many instances in which descendants of the immigrant Nicholas Holt married each other. In those cases, I have cross-referenced the information, so you hopefully will be able to find what you are looking for from either side of the couple.

The book is organized by generations. All the second generation, followed by all the third generation, then all the fourth, and then all the fifth. There are some complications with this, for example when a descendant from the second generation married a descendant from the third generation. In those cases, that couple and their children are included in the generation that appears first.

When moving down the generations, you will find in parentheses the track back to Nicholas Holt. For example, Nehemiah Holt son of George and Mary (Bixby) Holt married Anna Farnum daughter of Nathaniel and Hannah (Preston) Farnum and also a descendant of Nicholas Holt. When the family is introduced, you will see this.

92) NEHEMIAH HOLT (*George*^{3}*, Henry*^{2}*, Nicholas*^{1}), b. at Andover, 3 Apr 1723 son of George and Mary (Bixby) Holt; d. at Chaplin, CT, 17 Apr 1799; m. ANNA FARNUM (*Nathaniel Farnum*^{4}*, Ralph Farnum*^{3}*, Elizabeth Holt Farnum*^{2}*, Nicholas*^{1}), b. at Windham, 26 Apr 1726 daughter of Nathaniel and Hannah (Preston) Farnum; Anna d. at Chaplin, 1 Apr 1810.

When just the first name is given within the parentheses, the last name is Holt. For many individuals, there are several paths of descent from Nicholas Holt, in some cases as many as five paths. For simplicity, just one path is listed.

Table of Contents

The Descendants of Nicholas Holt of Andover Through Six Generations

Generation One

1) NICHOLAS HOLT, of Romsey, Hampshire, b. about 1608; d. at Andover, 30 Jan 1685/6; m. 1st by 1636 ELIZABETH who is not definitively identified;[1] Elizabeth d. at Andover, 9 Nov 1656. Nicholas m. 2nd at Ipswich, 20 Jun 1658, HANNAH BRADSTREET, b. about 1625 daughter of Humphrey and Bridget (-) Bradstreet; Hannah d. at Andover, 20 Jun 1665. Nicholas m. 3rd at Andover, 21 May 1666 MARTHA the widow of Roger Preston, b. about 1622. Martha d. at Andover, 21 Mar 1702/3.

On 6 April 1635 (or 5 April 1635), "Nicholas Holte of Romsey, tanner" embarked from Southampton on the *James* of London commanded by Mr. William Cooper, bound for New England.[2] The *James* arrived in Boston on 6 June 1635 and soon after Nicholas Holt was in Newbury where he resided for approximately eight years.[3]

Nicholas likely married Elizabeth soon after arrival in Newbury, although it has also been suggested that he married in England prior to emigration but that is not known. The three eldest children of Nicholas and Elizabeth were born in Newbury.

Nicholas Holt took the oath as freeman of the colony on 17 May 1637. This occurred at Newe Towne (Cambridge) at the same time John Winthrop was elected governor of the colony.[4] From the start, Nicholas was active in civic affairs. In June 1638, Nicholas Holt was named as commander of one of the four militia companies formed in Newbury along with John Pike, John Baker, and Edmund Greenleafe.[5] On 19 April 1638, Holt and John Baker were named surveyors of highways. However, at the quarterly court for the colony in June 1638, the town was fined six shillings four pence due to defects in the highway.[6]

Around 1643, Nicholas Holt was one of those who accompanied the Rev. John Woodbridge to the newly incorporated town of Cochichwicke (later named Andover) in Essex County which was formed 10 May 1643. The exact date of arrival of the Woodbridge settlers in Cochichwicke is not certain as negotiations for this new settlement had begun by 1640 with final arrangements made by 1642.[7] The church at Andover was organized 24 October 1645 and Nicholas Holt was one of the ten required freeholders to form the church that was headed by Rev. John Woodbridge.[8]

After he made the move from Newbury to Andover, Nicholas Holt substantially increased his land holdings from what they had been in Newbury becoming the third-largest land holder in Andover with 457 acres. As an indication of his prominence in the new town, house lots were assigned to those accepted as townsmen, the sizes of the lots proportional to the estate of each. Nicholas Holt's house lot of 15 acres was second only to the lots of Simon Bradstreet and John Osgood.[9]

The Holt homestead was established on what was known as Holt Hill, later Prospect Hill and then reverted to Holt Hill, which at 423 feet above sea level is the highest point in Essex County. This property is now part of the 704-acre Ward Reservation in Andover.[10]

In a series of land transactions, Nicholas disposed on his property to his children. On 10 March 1679/80, five acres was deeded to Robert Gray (who married daughter Hannah on 8 March 1668/9). Rogers Marks husband of daughter Sarah received twenty acres of upland and two acres of meadow on 1 September 1680. Eldest son Samuel Holt received substantial holdings of one-half of three score acres of upland, 130 acres of upland Nicholas received in the great division of 1661, and several areas of meadows on 14 February 1680/1. Second son Henry Holt also received 130 acres of upland and parcels of meadows on 15 December 1681. On 16 June 1682, third son Nicholas Holt received his deed in return for providing maintenance for his father and his wife Martha. Nicholas's deed included one third of the homestead farm, parcels of meadows, and the dwelling, well, and orchard. Fourth son James Holt received one-third of the farm, one-third of Great Meadow, and three acres of the common lands in town, this transaction on 15 April 1681 also in return for maintenance of Nicholas. On 19 June 1685, son John received a parcel lying easterly of the dwelling house, parcels of meadow, and 15 acres of upland.[11]

Nicholas Holt and his first wife Elizabeth were parents of nine children. After Elizabeth's death, Nicholas married Hannah Bradstreet who was daughter of Humphrey Bradstreet and the widow of Daniel Rolfe. Humphrey Bradstreet had come on the *Elizabeth* in 1634 and settled in Ipswich. Hannah was born in England and at age nine accompanied her parents to New England.[12]

---

[1] It is most often suggested that Elizabeth was Elizabeth Short but that has not been established.

[2] Coldham, *The Complete Book of Emigrants: 1607-1660*, pp 133-134

[3] Currier, *The History of Newbury*, p 32

[4] Currier, *History of Newbury*, p 41

[5] Currier, *History of Newbury*, p 62

[6] Currier, *History of Newbury*, p 413

[7] Currier, *History of Newbury*, p 74

[8] Bailey, *Historical Sketches of Andover*, p 416

[9] Greven, *Four Generations: Population, Land, and Family in Colonial Andover, Massachusetts*, p 60, pp 45-46

[10] The Trustees, Ward Reservation, http://www.thetrustees.org/places-to-visit/northeast/ward-reservation.html

[11] Anderson, *The Great Migration*, volume III, pp 398-399

[12] Anderson, *The Great Migration*, volume I, p 384

2) i ELIZABETH HOLT, b. at Newbury, 30 Mar 1636; d. at Andover, 14 Oct 1710; m. at Andover, 26 Oct 1657, RALPH FARNUM, baptized at St. Nicholas, Rochester, Kent, 4 Aug 1633 son of Ralph and Alice (Harris) Farnum; Ralph d. at Andover, 8 Jan 1692/3.

3) ii MARY HOLT, b. at Newbury, 7 Oct 1638; d. at Andover, 15 Nov 1700; m. by Mr. Bradstreet at Andover, 5 Jul 1657, THOMAS JOHNSON, baptized at Strood, Kent, 28 Jul 1633 son of John and Susannah (Asherst) Johnson;[13] Thomas d. at Andover, 15 Feb 1718/9. Thomas was second married to Damaris, widow of John Marshall.

4) iii SAMUEL HOLT, b. at Andover, 6 Oct 1641; d. at Andover, 7 Nov 1703; m. before 1670, SARAH ALLEN, b. at Andover 1646 daughter of Andrew and Faith (Ingalls) Allen;[14] Sarah d. at Andover, 3 Apr 1716.

5) iv HENRY HOLT, b. at Andover, 1643; d. at Andover, 13 Jan 1718/9; m. at Andover, 24 Feb 1669/70, SARAH BALLARD, b. at Andover, about 1652 daughter of William and Grace (-) Ballard; Sarah d. at Andover, 25 Nov 1733.

6) v NICHOLAS HOLT, b. at Andover, 1645; d. at Andover, 8 Oct 1715; m. 8 Jan 1679/80, MARY RUSSELL, b. at Andover, 14 Jan 1661 daughter of Robert and Mary (Marshall) Russell; Mary d. at Andover, 1 Apr 1717.

7) vi HANNAH HOLT, b. at Andover, 1648; d. at Andover, 30 Mar 1728; m. at Salem, 8 Mar 1668/9, ROBERT GRAY, b. about 1634. Robert d. at Andover, 5 Sep 1718.

8) vii JAMES HOLT, b. at Andover, 1650; d. at Andover, 14 Dec 1690; m. at Andover, 12 Oct 1675, HANNAH ALLEN, b. at Andover, 28 Oct 1652 daughter of Andrew and Faith (Ingalls) Allen; Hannah d. at Andover, 30 Sep 1698.

viii PRISCILLA HOLT, b. 20 Jun 1653; d. 16 Oct 1653.

ix SARAH HOLT, birth uncertain but likely between 1640 and 1655; d. at Andover, 22 Dec 1690; m. 1680, ROBERT MARKS. Sarah and Robert did not have children.

Nicholas Holt and Hannah Bradstreet were parents of two children.

i REBECCA HOLT, b. 14 Nov 1662; nothing further known.

9) ii JOHN HOLT, b. at Andover, 11 Jan 1663/4; d. at Andover, 10 Mar 1686/7; m. at Andover, 3 Jul 1685, SARAH GEARY, b. at Roxbury, 3 Jul 1665 daughter of Nathaniel and Anne (Douglas) Geary. Sarah married second John Preston.

Generation Two

2) ELIZABETH HOLT (*Nicholas*[1]), b. at Newbury, 30 Mar 1636; d. at Andover, 14 Oct 1710; m. at Andover, 26 Oct 1657, RALPH FARNUM, baptized at St. Nicholas, Rochester, Kent, 4 Aug 1633 son of Ralph and Alice (Harris)[15] Farnum; Ralph d. at Andover, 8 Jan 1692/3.

Ralph Farnum at age two years traveled with his parents on the ship *James* enrolled to travel on 13 July 1635.[16] The family was initially in Ipswich and Ralph and his family later settled in Andover.

Ralph Farnum did not leave a will and his estate entered probate 29 March 1693.[17] Real estate was valued at £167 and personal estate at £66.17.3 which included cattle valued at £31. Debts were £14.10.0.

Elizabeth Holt and Ralph Farnum were parents of ten children born at Andover.

10) i SARAH FARNUM, b. at Andover, 14 Jan 1661; d. before 1726; m. at Andover, 22 Apr 1685, BENJAMIN ABBOTT, b. at Andover, 20 Dec 1661 son of George and Hannah (Chandler) Abbott; Benjamin d. at Andover, 30 Mar 1703.

---

[13] Anderson, *The Great Migration*, volume IV, p 79. It is not certain that the surname of Thomas's mother was Asherst.

[14] The 1690 will (probate 31 March 1691) of Andrew Allin of Andover includes a bequest to his daughter Sarah Holt.

[15] It is not certain that Alice's name was Harris, but this is the name most often given.

[16] Anderson, *The Great Migration*, volume II, p 494.

[17] *Essex County, MA: Probate File Papers, 1638-1881.*Online database. *AmericanAncestors.org.* New England Historic Genealogical Society, 2014. Case 9251

11) ii RALPH FARNUM, b. at Andover, 1 Jun 1662; d. likely at Rumford, 3 Jan 1737/8;[18] m. at Andover, 9 Oct 1685, SARAH STERLING, b. at Haverhill, 4 May 1669 daughter of William and Elizabeth (Sawtelle) Sterling; Sarah d. at Andover, 12 Apr 1732.

12) iii JOHN FARNUM, b. at Andover, 1 Apr 1664; d. at Andover, 10 Jan 1728/9; m. at Andover, 10 Apr 1684, ELIZABETH PARKER, b. at Andover, 20 Jan 1663 daughter of Nathan and Mary (Ayer) Parker.

13) iv SAMUEL FARNUM, b. at Andover, about 1665; d. at Andover, 20 Dec 1754; m. 4 Jan 1697/8, his first cousin, HANNAH HOLT, b. at Andover, 10 Aug 1677 daughter of James and Hannah (Allen) Holt; Hannah d. at Andover, 11 Apr 1747.

14) v MARY FARNUM,[19] b. at Andover, estimate 1660; d. at Andover, 25 Dec 1739; m. 29 Nov 1680, WILLIAM LOVEJOY, b. at Andover, 21 Apr 1657 son of John and Mary (Osgood) Lovejoy; William d. at Andover, 9 Jul 1748.

vi HENRY FARNUM, b. 7 Dec 1666; d. 7 May 1683.

15) vii HANNAH FARNUM, b. at Andover, 7 Dec 1668; d. at Andover, 30 Jun 1758; m. 1693, her first cousin, SAMUEL HOLT, b. at Andover, 3 Aug 1671 son of Samuel and Sarah (Allen) Holt; Samuel d. at Andover, 20 Jul 1747.

16) viii THOMAS FARNUM, b. at Andover, 14 Jul 1670; d. at Andover, 24 Apr 1744; m. 1st at Andover, 14 May 1693, HANNAH HUTCHINSON, b. about 1675 daughter of Samuel and Hannah (Johnson) Hutchinson; Hannah d. at Andover, 19 May 1716 in her 41st year. Thomas m. 2nd at Andover, 3 Aug 1720, DOROTHY LACY, b. about 1677; Dorothy d. at Andover 10 Oct 1747 in her 71st year.

17) ix ELIZABETH FARNUM, b. at Andover, about 1672; d. at Andover, 28 Sep 1714; m. 10 May 1698, her first cousin, GEORGE HOLT, b. at Andover, 17 Mar 1676 son of Henry and Sarah (Ballard) Holt; George d. at Windham, CT, 29 Jun 1748. George married second Priscilla Preston and married third Mary Bixby.

18) x EPHRAIM FARNUM, b. at Andover, 1 Oct 1676; d. at Andover, 9 Jun 1744; m. at Andover, 20 Mar 1699/1700, his first cousin, PRISCILLA HOLT, b. at Andover, 13 Aug 1679 daughter of James and Hannah (Allen) Holt. Widow Priscilla Farnum married Stephen Johnson of Hampstead, NH on 28 Aug 1750. Samuel Johnson was born about 1678 and died at Hampstead 8 Jan 1769 at age 91. It is not clear whether this is the widow Priscilla Farnum who married Samuel Johnson. There is a younger Priscilla Ingalls Farnum (wife of Ephraim's nephew Ebenezer) and she is another possibility; Ebenezer Farnum died in 1741.

3) MARY HOLT (*Nicholas*[1]), b. at Newbury, 7 Oct 1638; d. at Andover, 15 Nov 1700; m. at Andover, 5 Jul 1657, THOMAS JOHNSON, baptized at Strood, Kent, 28 Jul 1633 son of John and Susannah (Asherst) Johnson; Thomas d. at Andover, 15 Feb 1718/9. Thomas was second married to Damaris, widow of John Marshall.

Thomas Johnson's final estate division was 22 January 1724.[20] There is a brief record of the personal estate division with eldest son John receiving a double share and the remaining shares to Thomas, James, Josiah, Susannah, Phebe, and Jemima.

Mary Holt and Thomas Johnson were parents of nine children born at Andover.

19) i MARY JOHNSON, b. 11 May 1659; d. at Medfield, 1713 (probate 1713); m. at Andover, 6 Sep 1673, RETURN JOHNSON, b. about 1653 (based on age 25 in 1678 when took oath of allegiance); d. at Medfield, 15 Mar 1706/7. Mary is not included in the 1724 division of her father's estate. Return is reported to have been the first physician in Medfield.[21][22]

ii SUSANNA JOHNSON, b. at Andover, 4 Oct 1662; she was living in 1724 but nothing further is known.

20) iii PHEBE JOHNSON, b. at Andover, 3 Jan 1664; d. at Andover, 4 Feb 1738; m. about 1685, THOMAS RUSSELL, b. at Andover, 16 Dec 1663 son of Robert and Mary (Marshall) Russell; Thomas d. at Andover, 30 Aug 1731.

---

[18] Ralph's death is recorded at Andover, but he had moved to Rumford with his son Barachias by 1733 and most likely died there.

[19] Although Farnham, Descendants of Ralph Farnum states that it was Mary daughter of Thomas Farnum who married William Lovejoy, it can be demonstrated through deeds that Mary daughter of Thomas married John Johnson (Essex Deeds 37:190 and 38:158 in which Mary and John Johnson quitclaim property from honored father Thomas Farnum to John Frie who was the spouse of Mary's sister Tabitha Farnum daughter of Thomas).

[20] *Essex County, MA: Probate File Papers, 1638-1881.*Online database. *AmericanAncestors.org.* New England Historic Genealogical Society, 2014. Case 15138

[21] Abbott, "Abbott Genealogies" Johnson Family

[22] Tilden, *History of the Town of Medfield*, p 97

21) iv JOHN JOHNSON, b. at Andover, 28 Feb 1667; d. at Andover, 26 May 1741; m. 1st 13 Sep 1689, ELLENOR BALLARD, b. at Andover, 24 Aug 1672 daughter of Joseph and Elizabeth (Phelps) Ballard; Ellenor d. 21 Nov 1707. John m. 2nd 1708, MARY FARNUM, b. at Andover, 24 Mar 1665/6 daughter of Thomas and Elizabeth (Sibborn) Farnum; Mary d. 17 May 1723. John m. 3rd 24 Aug 1723, ANNE FARNUM (widow of Thomas Russ), b. about 1677 daughter of John and Rebecca (Kent) Farnum.

22) v THOMAS JOHNSON, b. at Andover, 19 Oct 1670; d. at Andover, 22 Oct 1733;[23] m. at Andover, 24 Jul 1701, HANNAH STONE, b. 23 Mar 1679/80 daughter of Hugh and Hannah (Foster) Stone; Hannah d. at Andover, 5 Feb 1744/5.

23) vi JAMES JOHNSON, b. at Andover, 4 Feb 1672; d. 14 Oct 1748; m. 1st at Andover, 26 Apr 1692, ELIZABETH FARNUM (widow of Andrew Peters), b. 19 Feb 1661 daughter of Thomas and Elizabeth (Sibborn) Farnum; Elizabeth d. 31 Jan 1716. James m. 2nd at Andover, 23 Aug 1716, SARAH PEABODY (widow of Benjamin Smith), b. at Boxford, 4 Sep 1676 daughter of Joseph and Bethiah (Bridges) Peabody.

vii PETER JOHNSON, b. at Andover, 8 Aug 1675; m. at Andover, 29 Nov 1693, MEHITABLE FARNUM, b. 25 Feb 1673 daughter of Thomas and Elizabeth (Sibborn) Farnum. Peter and Mehitable are said to have left Andover soon after marriage, and the last record of them there was related to a land transaction in 1713. No children were located for them. Peter is not included in the 1724 division of his father's estate.

24) viii JEMIMA JOHNSON, b. at Andover, 1 Jan 1678; d. at Watertown, 4 Mar 1754; m. 1st at Watertown, 1697, JOHN ABBOTT, b. at Andover, 26 Aug 1662 son of George and Sarah (Farnum) Abbott; John d. at Watertown, 24 Mar 1718. Jemima m. 2nd at Boston, 1 Sep 1719, JOHN BEAKS.

25) ix JOSIAH JOHNSON, b. at Andover, 29 Oct 1683; d. at Lancaster, 15 Oct 1727; m. 19 Jun 1711, ANNIS CHANDLER, b. at Andover, 24 Mar 1689 daughter of Thomas and Mary (Peters) Chandler. After Josiah's death, Annis married Benjamin Robbins.

4) SAMUEL HOLT (*Nicholas*[1]), b. at Andover, 6 Oct 1641; d. at Andover, 7 Nov 1703; m. before 1670, SARAH ALLEN, b. at Andover 1646 daughter of Andrew and Faith (Ingalls) Allen; Sarah d. at Andover, 3 Apr 1716.

Samuel Holt was a farmer in Andover. He served his community as a militia corporal and served on the grand jury in 1685. He was one of the town citizens who made the oath of allegiance to the king in 1678.[24]

Sarah Allen was the second oldest child of Andrew and Faith Allen. Her older sister Martha Allen Carrier was hung as a witch at Salem on 19 August 1692.

In his will written 22 March 1702/3 (probate 6 December 1703), Samuel Holt, bequeathed to dear and loving wife Sarah a portion of the house while she is a widow and she is to be cared for by their two sons Samuel and John. He provides lengthy specifications for her maintenance by her sons. Son Samuel receives the house, barn and half the land. Son John receives half the land and the stock animals.[25]

15) i SAMUEL HOLT, b. at Andover, 3 Aug 1671; d. at Andover, 20 Jul 1747, his first cousin, HANNAH FARNUM, b. at Andover, 7 Dec 1668 daughter of Ralph and Elizabeth (Holt) Farnum; Hannah d. at Andover, 30 Jun 1758.

26) ii JOHN HOLT, b. at Andover, about 1672; d. at Andover, after 1753; m. 1st at Andover, 16 Jan 1705/6, ELIZABETH PRESTON, b. 14 Feb 1682 daughter of Samuel and Susanna (Gutterson) Preston; Elizabeth d. by 1712. John m. 2nd at Andover, 17 Jul 1712, MEHITABLE WILSON who d. at Andover, 1732.

5) HENRY HOLT (*Nicholas*[1]), b. at Andover, 1643; d. at Andover, 13 Jan 1718/9; m. at Andover, 24 Feb 1669/70, SARAH BALLARD, b. at Andover, about 1652 daughter of William and Grace (-) Ballard; Sarah d. at Andover, 25 Nov 1733.

Henry Holt was a prominent man in Andover often serving on committees, on the grand jury, and as selectman. In 1686, he was given the right to set up a sawmill on Ladle-Meadow Brook.[26]

On 25 March 1719, the surviving children of Henry Holt quitclaimed their rights to property of their honored father Henry Holt to their honored mother Sarah Holt to be for her only sole use, benefit, and disposal. The children signing this quitclaim were Oliver Holt, Henry Holt, James Holt, George Holt, Josiah Holt, Paul Holt, William Holt, Humphrey Holt, Benjamin Harnden and Elizabeth his wife, Daniel Pierce and Dinah his wife, John Cram and Sarah his wife, Jonathan Abbot and Zerviah his wife, and Keturah Holt.[27]

Sarah Ballard and Henry Holt were parents of fourteen children born at Andover.

---

[23] Thomas, "in the flames of his House that was Burnt with fier," Oct. 22, 1733.

[24] Bailey, *Historical Sketches of Andover*

[25] *Essex County, MA: Probate File Papers, 1638-1881.*Online database. *AmericanAncestors.org.* New England Historic Genealogical Society, 2014. Case 13687

[26] Bailey, *Historical Sketches of Andover*, p 575

[27] Massachusetts Land Records 1620-1986, Essex County, 36:253; accessed through familysearch.org.

i ELIZABETH HOLT, b. 29 Dec 1670; d. at Wilmington, 21 Dec 1734; m. 14 Jun 1711, BENJAMIN HARNDEN, b. at Reading, 24 Apr 1671 son of Richard and Mary (-) Harnden; Benjamin d. at Wilmington, 30 May 1740. Benjamin and Elizabeth were parents of one child, Susanna, who died at Wilmington 12 Aug 1735 without marrying.[28] Benjamin was first married to Mary. The will of Benjamin Harnden written 2 May 1740 has bequests to son Benjamin and daughters Elizabeth Preston and Hannah Wright who were children from his first marriage.

27) ii OLIVER HOLT, b. 14 Jan 1671/2; d. at Andover, 24 Dec 1747; m. 1st, 9 Mar 1697/8, HANNAH RUSSELL, b. at Andover, 28 Jun 1679 daughter of Robert and Mary (Marshall) Russell; Hannah d. at Andover, 16 May 1715. Oliver m. 2nd, 10 Jul 1716, MARY HUSE, b. at Newbury, 23 Mar 1690/1 daughter of Thomas and Hannah (Webster) Huse;[29] Mary d. 1 Sep 1778.

28) iii HENRY HOLT, b. 24 Jan 1673/4; d. at Andover, 7 Jun 1751; m. about 1700, MARTHA MARSTON, b. at Andover, 28 Jan 1679 daughter of John and Martha (Fuller) Marston; Martha d. at Andover, 15 Nov 1754.

29) iv JAMES HOLT, b. 3 Sep 1675; d. at Andover, 1732 (probate 6 Nov 1732); m. 24 May 1705, SUSANNA PRESTON, b. at Andover, 30 Mar 1677 daughter of Samuel and Susanna (Gutterson) Preston; Susanna d. at Andover, 20 Feb 1741/2.

17) v GEORGE HOLT, b. 17 Mar 1676; d. at Windham, CT, 29 Jun 1748; m. 1st, 10 May 1698, his first cousin, ELIZABETH FARNUM b. about 1672 daughter of Ralph and Elizabeth (Holt) Farnum; Elizabeth d. at Andover, 28 Sep 1714. George m. 2nd, about 1715, PRISCILLA PRESTON daughter of Samuel and Susanna (Gutterson) Preston; Priscilla d. 29 Jan 1716. George m. 3rd, by 1717, MARY BIXBY, b. at Andover, 10 Apr 1693 daughter of Daniel and Hannah (Chandler) Bixby.

30) vi SARAH HOLT, b. 17 Jun 1678; d. at Lyndeborough, NH, 1 Oct 1757; m. 18 Feb 1707, JOHN CRAM, b. at Hampton Falls, 12 Jan 1685 son of Thomas and Elizabeth (Weare) Cram; John d. at Amherst, NH, 1759.[30]

vii JOSIAH HOLT, b. 13 Dec 1679; d. at Andover, 23 Oct 1754; m. 1st, 8 Jun 1710, MARY LOVEJOY, b. at Andover, 15 Nov 1685 daughter of William and Mary (Farnum) Lovejoy; Mary d. 5 Jul 1724. Josiah m. 2nd, 22 Dec 1726, HEPHZIBAH BARKER, b. at Andover, 24 Mar 1686/7 daughter of William and Mary (Dix) Barker; Hephzibah d. at Andover, 7 May 1769. Josiah did not have children of his own but took in John Fiske who lived with him for many years. In his 1748 will, after providing for his wife Hephzibah, Josiah left his estate to John Fiske. In her will, Hephzibah Barker Holt left her possessions to her brothers and sisters and their children.

31) viii DINAH HOLT, b. 23 May 1681; d. at Wilmington, MA, 7 Jan 1738; m. at Woburn, 3 Jul 1705, DANIEL PIERCE, b. at Woburn, 7 Oct 1676 son of John and Deborah (Converse) Pierce; Daniel d. at Harvard, MA, 14 Mar 1754.

32) ix PAUL HOLT, b. 7 Feb 1684; d. at Hampton, CT, 6 May 1742; m.10 Jan 1711/2 his first cousin, ABIGAIL HOLT, b. at Andover, 23 Nov 1688 daughter of Nicholas and Mary (Russell) Holt; Abigail d. at Hampton, 12 Aug 1742.

x WILLIAM HOLT, b. 3 Feb 1687; d. 22 Dec 1719. William did not have children. In his will dated 15 October 1719, he left his mother the use of all his lands and house during her life and after her death, the property would go to his brother Humphrey. This is provided that Humphrey stay in the house with his mother if she chooses that. Each of the other siblings singed a quitclaim for William's property.

33) xi ZERVIAH HOLT, b. 24 Mar 1688; d. at Andover, 26 Mar 1768; m. 6 May 1713, her first cousin once removed, JONATHAN ABBOTT (*Sarah Farnum Abbott[3], Elizabeth Holt Farnum[2], Nicholas[1]*), b. at Andover, Sep 1687 son of Benjamin and Sarah (Farnum) Abbott; Jonathan d. at Andover, 21 Mar 1770.

34) xii KETURAH HOLT, b. 15 Dec 1690; d. at Hampton, CT, 2 Oct 1781; m. 16 Feb 1725/5, her first cousin, JOSHUA HOLT, b. at Andover, 1703 son of Nicholas and Mary (Russell) Holt; Joshua d. at Hampton, 26 Jan 1787.

---

[28] Wilmington Vital Records; deaths; Susanna, d. of Benjamin and Elizabeth. Aug. 12, 1735.

[29] The 1737 will of widow Hannah Huse includes a bequest to her daughter Mary Holt.

[30] Donovan, *History of Lyndeborough*, p 710

35) xiii HUMPHREY HOLT, b. 22 Sep 1693; d. at Andover, 8 Aug 1754; m. 30 Dec 1715, ABIGAIL FIFIELD, b. at Hampton, NH, about 1695 possibly the daughter of Benjamin and Mary (Calcord) Fifield;[31] Abigail d. after 1754.

xiv BENJAMIN HOLT, b. 8 Jul 1696; d. 15 Sep 1703.

6) NICHOLAS HOLT (*Nicholas*[1]), b. at Andover, 1645; d. at Andover, 8 Oct 1715; m. 8 Jan 1679/80, MARY RUSSELL, b. at Andover, 14 Jan 1661 daughter of Robert and Mary (Marshall) Russell; Mary d. at Andover, 1 Apr 1717.

Mary Russell was the daughter of Robert Russell an immigrant of Scottish heritage. Robert accumulated a considerable estate in Andover which was known as Scotland Yard. In his will, Robert Russell included a bequest for his grandson Robert Holt who was named for him.

On 1 March 1710/11, Nicholas Holt, signed also by Mary his wife, transferred property in Andover for love and affection to his sons Nicholas Holt and Thomas Holt, this land generally to be equally divided although Nicholas was to receive three more acres than Thomas. It was noted that sons Nicholas and Thomas had obliged themselves to do several things for their father. The property granted to the sons included the property where father Nicholas then resided. In a deed recorded 15 June 1715, Nicholas conveyed to his two eldest sons Nicholas and Thomas his rights to all the common land in Andover.[32]

Nicholas Holt and Mary Russell were parents of eleven children born at Andover.

36) i MARY HOLT, b. at Andover, 13 Feb 1680/1; d. at Andover, 9 Feb 1714/5; m. at Andover, 19 Sep 1705, JOSIAH INGALLS, b. at Andover, 28 Feb 1676 son of Henry and Mary (Osgood) Ingalls. Josiah d. at Andover, 14 Aug 1755. After Mary's death, Josiah married Esther Frye.

37) ii NICHOLAS HOLT, b. at Andover, 21 Dec 1683; d. at Andover, 1 Dec 1756; m. 1st, 16 Sep 1708, MARY MANNING; Mary d. at Andover, 3 Mar 1715/6. Nicholas m. 2nd, 12 Apr 1717, DORCAS ABBOTT, b. at Andover, 25 Apr 1698 daughter of Timothy and Hannah (Graves) Abbott; Dorcas d. at Andover, 25 Oct 1758.

38) iii THOMAS HOLT, b. at Andover, 16 Aug 1686; d. at Andover, 12 Jan 1767; m. 1st, at Andover, 14 Dec 1708, ALICE PEABODY, b. at Andover, 5 Jan 1685 daughter of Joseph and Bethiah (Bridges) Peabody; Alice d. at Andover, 29 Jul 1726. Thomas m. 2nd, at Boxford, 16 Nov 1727, ABIGAIL POORE (widow of John Fiske), b. at Newbury, 9 Sep 1680 daughter of Henry and Abigail (Hale) Poore; Abigail d. at Andover, 20 Nov 1766.

32) iv ABIGAIL HOLT, b. at Andover, 23 Nov 1688; d. at Hampton, 12 Aug 1742; m. at Andover, 10 Jan 1711/2, her first cousin, PAUL HOLT, b. 7 Feb 1684 son of Henry and Sarah (Ballard) Holt; Paul d. at Hampton, 6 May 1742.

v SARAH HOLT, b. 10 Mar 1690/1; d. at Andover, 26 Oct 1761. Sarah did not marry.

vi JAMES HOLT, b. 23 Jul 1693; d. 12 Dec 1722.

39) vii ROBERT HOLT, b. at Andover, 23 Jan 1695/6; d. at Windham, CT, 1768 (probate 4 May 1768); m. 1st, 22 May 1718, REBECCA PRESTON (widow of her cousin Joseph Preston), b. at Andover, 23 Jan 1688/9 daughter of John and Sarah (Gear) Preston; Rebecca d. at Windham, 1 May 1727. Robert m. 2nd, 13 Dec 1727, BETHIAH PEABODY, b. at Boxford, 3 Apr 1681 daughter of Joseph and Bethiah (Bridges) Peabody; Bethiah d. 6 Feb 1742. Robert m. 3rd, at Hampton, 28 Mar 1743, HANNAH ADROSS who has not been identified; Hannah was living in 1767.

40) viii ABIEL HOLT, b. at Andover, 28 Jun 1698; d. at Willington, 10 Nov 1772; m. 1st, at Andover, 21 Feb 1721, HANNAH ABBOTT, b. at Andover, 5 Apr 1701 daughter of William and Elizabeth (Geary) Abbott; Hannah d. at Windham, 11 Feb 1751/2. Abiel m. 2nd, at Willington, 19 Dec 1752, SARAH DOWNER, b. about 1699; Sarah d. 15 Apr 1784.

41) ix DEBORAH HOLT, b. at Andover, 16 Nov 1700; d. at Willington, 26 Nov 1784; m. at Windham, 5 May 1727, BENJAMIN PRESTON, b. at Andover, 1705 son of Jacob and Sarah (Wilson) Preston; Benjamin d. at Willington, 26 Nov 1784.[33]

34) x JOSHUA HOLT, b. at Andover, 1703; d. at Hampton, 26 Jan 1787; m. at Windham, 16 Feb 1724/5, his first cousin, KETURAH HOLT, b. at Andover, 15 Dec 1690 daughter of Henry and Sarah (Ballard) Holt; Keturah d. at Hampton, 2 Oct 1781.

---

[31] Dow and Dow, *History of the Town of Hampton*, p 708; Abigail is described as "of Hampton, NH" at the time of marriage; Benjamin and Mary Fifield of Hampton are reported to have a daughter Abigail.

[32] Massachusetts Land Records 1620-1986, Essex County, 23:88; 28:49

[33] The deaths of Deborah and Benjamin are recorded as occurring on the same day.

42) xi DANIEL HOLT, b. at Andover, 1705; d. at Pomfret, 5 Nov 1773; m. 1st, 31 Mar 1731, ABIGAIL SMITH, b. at Lebanon, CT, 22 Jun 1706 daughter of John and Abigail (-) Smith; Abigail d. at Pomfret, CT, 9 Feb 1752. Daniel m. 2nd, at Pomfret, Dec 1752, KEZIA STRONG (widow of Noah Rust), b. at Northampton, MA, 1 Dec 1709 daughter of Joseph and Sarah (Allen) Strong;[34] Kezia d. at Cherry Valley, NY, 1796.

7) HANNAH HOLT (*Nicholas1*), b. at Andover, 1648; d. at Andover, 30 Mar 1728; m. at Salem, 8 Mar 1668/9, ROBERT GRAY, b. about 1634. Robert d. at Andover, 5 Sep 1718.

Hannah and Robert lived in Salem in the first years of their marriage and births of the four oldest children are recorded there. Robert was fined in Salem for attending a Quaker meeting the same year he was married.[35]

Robert Gray is described as a mariner in land records. He transferred his land to his sons in a series of transactions from 1712 to 1718. On 3 December 1712, he transferred to son Henry for love and affection twenty-five acres of pasture and upland and followed this with land transfers to sons Robert, Braviter, and Edward.[36]

Hannah Holt and Robert Gray were parents of nine children.

i KATHERINE GRAY, b. at Salem, 15 Jul 1670; d. at Andover, 28 Sep 1751. Katherine did not marry.

43) ii HENRY GRAY, b. at Salem, 17 Jan 1671/2; d. at Andover, 1 Jul 1741; m. at Andover, 3 May 1699, MARY BLUNT, b. at Andover, 28 Sep 1679 daughter of William and Elizabeth (Ballard) Blunt; Mary d. at Andover, 7 Aug 1733.

iii JEMIMA GRAY, b. at Salem, Dec 1673; d. 1674.

44) iv HANNAH GRAY, b. at Salem, 30 Jan 1674/5; d. at Andover, 25 Jan 1763; m. at Andover, 7 Dec 1697, THOMAS ABBOTT, b. at Andover, 6 May 1666 son of George and Hannah (Chandler) Abbott; Thomas d. at Andover, 28 Apr 1728.

45) v ROBERT GRAY, b. about 1677; d. at Andover, Mar 1718; m. at Andover, 29 Nov 1705, MIRIAM LOVEJOY, b. at Andover, 11 Aug 1686 daughter of Christopher and Sarah (Russ) Lovejoy; Miriam d. 21 Apr 1770. Miriam married second Richard Nutting on 17 Jun 1718.

46) vi EDWARD GRAY, b. at Andover, 12 Sep 1679; d. at Andover, 15 Sep 1759; m. 1st at Andover, 2 Dec 1702, SARAH OSGOOD, b. at Andover, 19 Feb 1682 daughter of Christopher and Hannah (Barker) Osgood; Sarah d. at Andover, 14 May 1718. Edward m. 2nd 27 Oct 1719, HANNAH BARKER, b. at Andover, 5 Sep 1681 daughter of William and Mary (Dix) Barker; Hannah d. at Andover, 27 Jan 1762.

vii THOMAS GRAY, b. at Andover, 16 Sep 1681; m. at Andover, 24 Dec 1703, SUSANNA BATCHELDER. Nothing further is known of him. He is not included among the deeds of land that Robert Gray made to his sons Henry, Robert, Edward, and Braviter in 1711 and 1712.

47) viii BRAVITER GRAY, b. at Andover, 29 Sep 1685; d. at Andover, 10 Nov 1724; m. at Andover, 21 Nov 1710, DOROTHY ABBOTT, b. at Andover, about 1683 daughter of Thomas and Sarah (Stewart) Abbott; Dorothy d. at Andover, 22 Oct 1743. Dorothy was second married to Benjamin Holt son of Oliver and Hannah (Russell) Holt.

ix AARON GRAY, b. 14 Apr 1692; d. 20 Dec 1711.

8) JAMES HOLT (*Nicholas1*), b. at Andover, 1650; d. at Andover, 14 Dec 1690; m. at Andover, 12 Oct 1675, HANNAH ALLEN, b. at Andover, 28 Oct 1652 daughter of Andrew and Faith (Ingalls) Allen; Hannah d. at Andover, 30 Sep 1698.

James and Hannah resided in Andover and James took the oath of allegiance there on 11 February 1678.[37] In a deed dated 15 April 1681 and recorded 6 November 1685, Nicholas Hoult senior, dish turner of Andover, conveyed to his fourth son James Hoult of Andover in consideration of "natural love and affection" and for "diverse other good causes and considerations" one-third part of the farm on the section where James's house stood. James in turn is to pay his father the sum of £3 a year, and after Nicholas's death, to pay Nicholas's widow forty shillings per year as long as she is a widow.[38]

James Holt did not leave a will and his estate entered probate 23 March 1691 with inventory showing real estate valued at £120.[39] On 31 March 1712 (deed recorded 19 July 1717), son Joseph Holt of York conveyed to his brother Timothy for the sum of £20 his rights to lands from the estate of James Holt.[40]

---

[34] Dwight, *History of the Descendants of Elder John Strong*, p 310

[35] Holt Association of America, *The First Three Generations of Holts*, p 191

[36] Massachusetts Land Records 1620-1986, Essex County, 26:42, 28:97, 30:76, and 34:182; accessed through familysearch.org.

[37] Bailey, *Historical Sketches of Andover*, p 107

[38] Massachusetts Land Records 1620-1986, Essex County, 7:292-296; accessed through familyseach.org

[39] *Essex County, MA: Probate File Papers, 1638-1881.*Online database. *AmericanAncestors.org.* New England Historic Genealogical Society, 2014. Case 13647

[40] Massachusetts Land Records 1620-1986, Essex County, 32:83; accessed through familysearch.org.

James Holt and Hannah Allen were parents of seven children born at Andover. James and his son James both died in the 1690 smallpox epidemic.

13) i HANNAH HOLT, b. at Andover, 10 Aug 1667; m. at Andover, 4 Jan 1697/8, her first cousin, SAMUEL FARNUM, b. at Andover, about 1665 son of Ralph and Elizabeth (Holt) Farnum;[41] Samuel d. at Andover, 20 Dec 1754.

18) ii PRISCILLA HOLT, b. at Andover, 13 Aug 1679; m. at Andover, 20 Mar 1699/1700, her first cousin, EPHRAIM FARNUM, b. at Andover, 1 Oct 1676 son of Ralph and Elizabeth (Holt) Farnum; Ephraim d. at Andover, 9 Jun 1744.

48) iii LYDIA HOLT, b. at Andover, 27 Sep 1681; d. at Andover, 10 Oct 1741; m. at Andover, 27 Jan 1701/2, SAMUEL PEABODY, b. at Boxford, 8 Apr 1678 son of Joseph and Bethiah (Bridges) Peabody; Samuel d. at Andover, 1 May 1706.

49) iv TIMOTHY HOLT, b. at Andover, 25 Jan 1683; d. at Andover, 4 Mar 1758; m. at Andover, 19 Apr 1705, RHODA CHANDLER, b. at Andover, 26 Sep 1684 daughter of William and Bridget (Henchman) Chandler; Rhoda d. at Andover, 14 Aug 1765.

50) v JOSEPH HOLT, b. at Andover, 5 Mar 1686; d. at York, ME, 26 Apr 1774;[42] m. at York, 28 Dec 1709, as her second husband, MARY HARMON, b. at York, about 1682 daughter of John and Deborah (Johnson) Harmon;[43] Mary d. at York, 15 Nov 1760. Mary was first married to Benjamin Donnell. Joseph was a deacon in York.

51) vi REBEKAH HOLT, b. at Andover, 29 Mar 1688; d. at Pomfret, CT, 9 Sep 1762; m. at Andover, 1 Jul 1710, THOMAS GROW,[44] b. at Ipswich, 20 Feb 1684 son of John and Hannah (Lord) Grove; Thomas d. at Pomfret, 13 Jan 1753.

vii JAMES HOLT, b. 1690 and d. 13 Dec 1690 in the smallpox epidemic.

9) JOHN HOLT (*Nicholas*[1]), b. at Andover, 11 Jan 1663/4; d. at Andover, 10 Mar 1686/7; m. at Andover, 3 Jul 1685, SARAH GEARY, b. at Roxbury, 3 Jul 1665 daughter of Nathaniel and Anne (Douglas) Geary. Sarah married second John Preston.

In his will written 22 February 1686/7, John bequeathed to his beloved wife Sarah all the moveable estate both indoors and out, a piece of meadow, and the use of all the housing and land until his son comes of age. Only son Moses Holt will receive the housing and land when he comes of age. If Moses dies before adulthood, then the estate will go to loving brother Daniel Rolfe (his half-brother). Wife Sarah was named executrix.[45] The personal estate was valued at £41 and it was also noted there were a total of fifty acres of land, but the value was not listed.

John Holt and Sarah Geary were parents of two children born at Andover.

i AARON HOLT, b. 7 Jun 1686; died young.

52) ii MOSES HOLT, b. at Andover, 7 Jun 1686; d. at Andover, 7 Nov 1730; m. at Andover, 31 Jan 1715/6, ELIZABETH RUSSELL, b. at Andover, 16 Jul 1687 daughter of Robert and Mary (Marshall) Russell; Elizabeth d. at Andover, 3 Nov 1772.

---

[41] Samuel's parentage is not certain, but he is most often listed as a child of Ralph and Elizabeth.

[42] *Here lies the Body of Elder Joseph Holt who departed this Life April 26th 1774 in the 89th Year of his Age*. Findagrave ID: 63730374. There had been disagreement about two Joseph Holts, this one and Joseph born 1702 son of Henry and Martha (Marston) Holt. The evidence supports that Joseph born 1686 went to York, Maine, and Joseph b. 1702 settled in Reading and married Abigail Rich. Of note is the age at death of Joseph Holt which matches with the year of birth for Joseph born 1686.

[43] Harmon, *The Harmon Genealogy*, p 145

[44] The name is sometimes given as Grove.

[45] *Suffolk County, MA: Probate File Papers.* Online database. *AmericanAncestors.org.* New England Historic Genealogical Society, 2017-2019. Case 1529

Generation Three

Children of Elizabeth Holt and Ralph Farnum

10) SARAH FARNUM (*Elizabeth Holt Farnum^2, Nicholas^1*), b. at Andover, 14 Jan 1661 daughter of Ralph and Elizabeth (Holt) Farnum; d. before 1726;[46] m. at Andover, 22 Apr 1685, BENJAMIN ABBOTT, b. at Andover, 20 Dec 1661 son of George and Hannah (Chandler) Abbott; Benjamin d. at Andover, 30 Mar 1703. Benjamin had an out-of-wedlock relationship with NAOMI HOYT in 1683.

Although Benjamin made important contributions to his community, he is also known as being the accuser of Martha Carrier for witchcraft. There was a property dispute that may also have been a factor in the accusations of witchery. Martha Carrier and her husband Thomas owned a property adjacent to Benjamin Abbot. There was dispute about the property line and, during an argument between Martha and Benjamin, she cursed him for seven years. At some point following this, Benjamin developed a series of maladies including a swollen foot and a pustule on his side. He attributed this to Martha's witchery. Martha was arrested and jailed, the first accused witch from Andover. She was also accused of witchcraft by the infamous Salem girls who fell in hysterics during her trial. Martha was tried, convicted, and hanged in Salem on August 19, 1692.[47]

Benjamin Abbot was the builder of what is now one of the two oldest houses in Andover located at 9 Andover Street. The house was placed on the National Register in 1976.[48]

Benjamin Abbot's estate entered probate 26 April 1703.[49] He did not leave a will, and Sarah Abbott was administratrix of the estate. Sarah Abbott was named guardian for the minor children Benjamin, David, Jonathan, and Samuel Abbott.

Benjamin Abbot had a relationship with Naomi Hoyt Lovejoy when he was about age 22 and she was a young widow about age 28. There was a daughter born of this relationship recorded in the Andover vital records: "Abbot, Ben Naomie, d. illegitimate, Benjamin and Naomie Lovejoy, 1684." It is not known what became of this child.

Benjamin Abbot and Sarah Farnum had four children whose births are recorded at Andover.

53) i BENJAMIN ABBOTT, b. 11 Jul 1686; d. before 5 Dec 1748; m. 1st, 24 Dec 1716 ELIZABETH ABBOTT, b. 25 Jul 1690 daughter of George and Dorcas (Graves) Abbott. Benjamin m. 2nd, 23 Oct 1722 MARY CARLETON, b. 7 Apr 1700 daughter of John and Hannah (Osgood) Carleton; Mary died 19 Jan 1725/6. BENJAMIN m. 3rd 1729, ABIGAIL ABBOTT, b. 7 Oct 1699 daughter of Nehemiah and Abigail (Lovejoy) Abbott; Abigail d. 8 Dec 1753.

33) ii JONATHAN ABBOTT, b. Sep 1687; death reported as 21 Mar 1770 although record was not located;[50] m. 6 May 1713, ZERVIAH HOLT, b. 24 Mar 1688/9 daughter of Henry and Sarah (Ballard) Holt; Zerviah d. 26 Mar 1768.

54) iii DAVID ABBOTT, b. 18 Jan 1688/9; d. 14 Nov 1753; m. 20 Mar 1717/8, HANNAH DANFORTH, b. at Billerica, 20 Aug 1698 daughter of Samuel and Hannah (Crosby) Danforth; Hannah d. 8 Jan 1788.

iv SAMUEL ABBOTT, b. 19 May 1694; d. 29 Oct 1762; m. 8 Aug 1735, MARY PRESTON, widow of Christopher Lovejoy; Mary b. 31 Mar 1699 daughter of Samuel and Sarah (Bridges) Preston; Mary d. 15 Apr 1754. Samuel and Mary had no children. In his will, Samuel makes bequests to his three "sons-in-law" (stepsons) who were the sons of his deceased wife Mary (the sons of Mary with first husband Christopher Lovejoy): Christopher, Nathan, and Isaac Lovejoy, and a bequest to Nathan's wife Apphia. He also makes bequests to the six daughters of his deceased brother Benjamin (Sarah, Mary, Abigail, Elizabeth, Anna, and Dorcas), three sons of his brother Benjamin (Benjamin, Daniel, and Abiel), the sons of his brother Jonathan (Jonathan, David, Nathaniel, and Samuel), three sons of his deceased brother David (David, Solomon, and Jonathan), Zuriah daughter of brother Jonathan, Hannah and Sarah daughters of brother David, and the children of deceased Job Abbott (Job being a son of Samuel's brother Jonathan).

11) RALPH FARNUM (*Elizabeth Holt Farnum^2, Nicholas^1*), b. at Andover, 1 Jun 1662 son of Ralph and Elizabeth (Holt) Farnum; d. likely at Rumford, 3 Jan 1737/8 (death record at Andover; m. at Andover, 9 Oct 1685, SARAH STERLING, b. at Haverhill, 4 May 1669 daughter of William and Elizabeth (Sawtelle) Sterling; Sarah d. at Andover, 12 Apr 1732.

---

[46] Abbott, "Early Notes and Records of the Farnum Family of Andover," undated manuscript. Retried from https://www.mhl.org/sites/default/files/files/Abbott/Farnum%20Family.pdf

[47] Information summarized from Bill Dalton, 2010, Witches and Switches: The Benjamin Abbot House, The Andover Townsman Online, Retrieved from http://www.andovertownsman.com/community/dalton-column-witches-and-switches-the-benjamin-abbot-house/article_6954f4c3-c022-5274-814e-a15d94ac99d5.html

[48] Andover Historic Preservation, 9 Andover Street, Retrieved from https://preservation.mhl.org/9-andover-st

[49] *Essex County, MA: Probate File Papers, 1638-1881, Probate of Benjamin Abbot, 26 Apr 1703, Case number 21.*

[50] Holt Association of America, *First Three Generations of Holts in America*, (Newburgh, NY: Moore, 1930), 316

Ralph Farnum was one of those, along with several other Holt descendants and their spouses, who were called to testify in the witchcraft trial of Martha Allen Carrier. Ralph Farnum, Jr., his brother John Farnum, Benjamin Abbott (husband of Sarah Farnum just above), and Samuel Holt (husband of Sarah Allen) were all summoned.[51]

Ralph and Sarah were parents of twelve children born at Andover. They raised their children in Andover where Sarah died, and Ralph's death is also recorded there. Sons Barachias and Ralph relocated to Rumford prior to their father's death.

55) i SARAH FARNUM, b. at Andover, 5 May 1686; d. 1766; m. 14 Feb 1712, her first cousin, HENRY LOVEJOY (*Mary Farnum Lovejoy[3], Elizabeth Holt Farnum[2], Nicholas[1]*), b. at Andover, 27 Nov 1683 son of William and Mary (Farnum) Lovejoy; Henry d. at Andover, 1 Feb 1776.

56) ii HENRY FARNUM, b. at Andover, 15 Sep 1687; d. at Windham, 25 Jul 1732; m. at Andover, 12 Jun 1712, PHEBE RUSSELL, b. at Andover, 21 Jan 1689/90 daughter of Thomas and Phebe (Johnson) Russell; Phebe d. after 1753. Phebe m. 2nd at Canterbury, 3 Jan 1734, NATHANIEL ROBBINS; Nathaniel d. at Windham, 7 Apr 1753.

57) iii RALPH FARNUM, b. at Andover, 25 May 1689; d. at York, ME, 1758; m. about 1712, ELIZABETH AUSTIN, b. at York, about 1687 daughter of Matthew and Mary (Littlefield) Austin.

58) iv DANIEL FARNUM, b. at Andover, 21 Jan 1690/1; d. at Georgetown, ME, 1746; m. 1st about 1719, HANNAH BRAGDON, b. at York, 25 May 1697 daughter of Arthur and Sarah (Came) Bragdon; Hannah d. at York, 2 Nov 1729. Daniel m. 2nd at York, 21 Aug 1733, PATIENCE HUBBARD (widow of William Card), b. at South Berwick, 30 Mar 1704 daughter of Philip and Elizabeth (Goodwin) Card; Patience d. at Georgetown, ME.

59) v ABIGAIL FARNUM, b. at Andover, 3 May 1692; m. at Andover, 6 Jan 1713/4, JAMES ABBOTT, b. at Andover, 12 Feb 1694/5 son of William and Elizabeth (Geary) Abbott; James d. at Concord, NH, 26 Dec 1787.

60) vi WILLIAM FARNUM, b. at Andover, 5 Aug 1693; d. at Windham, 1742 (probate 1742); m. at Andover, 2 Apr 1715, ANNE FLINT, b. at Salem, 3 Aug 1693 daughter of Joseph and Abigail (Howard) Flint; Anne d. at Windham, about 1755.

61) vii NATHANIEL FARNUM, b. at Andover, 25 Jul 1695; d. at Windham, 9 Jul 1760; m. at Andover, 19 May 1719, HANNAH PRESTON, b. at Andover, 17 Jun 1698 daughter of John and Sarah (Geary) Preston; Hannah d. at Windham, about 1766 (redistribution of her widow thirds to the children).

62) viii BARACHIAS FARNUM, b. at Andover, 16 Mar 1696/7; d. at Haverhill, MA, 22 Aug 1767; m. at Reading, 1 Jan 1722/3, HEPHZIBAH HARNDEN, b. at Reading, 25 May 1705 daughter of John and Susanna (-) Harnden; Hephzibah d. after 1748. Barachias m. 2nd SUSANNAH who has not been identified.

ix BENJAMIN FARNUM, b. 14 Mar 1698/9; it is not certain what became of him.

63) x JOSEPH FARNUM, b. at Andover, 4 Feb 1700/1; m. at Windham, 24 Dec 1724, LYDIA HOWARD.

64) xi STEPHEN FARNUM, b. at Andover, 1703; d. at Lake George, NY, 1 Sep 1756; m. at Andover, 8 Nov 1726, HANNAH RICHARDSON, b. at Woburn, 8 Jan 1707 daughter of Joshua and Hannah (-) Richardson.[52]

xii ZEBADIAH FARNUM, b. 1705; d. 5 Feb 1706/7.

12) JOHN FARNUM (*Elizabeth Holt Farnum[2], Nicholas[1]*), b. at Andover, 1 Apr 1664 son of Ralph and Elizabeth (Holt) Farnum; d. at Andover, 10 Jan 1728/9; m. at Andover, 10 Apr 1684, ELIZABETH PARKER, b. at Andover, 20 Jan 1663 daughter of Nathan and Mary (Ayer) Parker.

Elizabeth's mother Mary Ayer Parker was one of those hanged as a witch at Salem on 22 September 1692. Elizabeth's sister Sarah was also imprisoned after being accused of witchcraft. John's brother Ralph Farnum was one of those supposed afflicted by the witches.[53]

John Farnum was a wheelwright in Andover. On 6 February 1717/8 (recorded 28 January 1719/20), John Farnum conveyed property to his son James for love and affection with certain provisions including making payments to his sisters Mary, Phebe, Sarah, Deborah, and Tabitha when they reach to age of marriage. There were other provisions including that James would have half of the land at the time of the deed for his improvement and the remainder after the decease of his father. John also reserved to right to sell portions of the land if he chose to do so.[54]

John Farnum and Elizabeth Parker were parents of nine children born at Andover.

---

[51] Sterling, *The Sterling Genealogy*, volume 1, p 266

[52] The 1748 will of Joshua Richardson of Woburn includes a bequest to his daughter Hannah "Varnum".

[53] Kelly, Jacqueline, "The Untold Story of Mary Ayer Parker: Gossip and Confusion in 1692," 2005, Salem Witch Trials Documentary Archive and Transcription Project, http://salem.lib.virginia.edu/people/?group.num=&mbio.num=mb42

[54] Massachusetts Land Records 1620-1986, Essex County, 36:225, accessed through familysearch.org

65) i JOHN FARNUM, b. at Andover, 13 Feb 1684/5; d. at Andover, 22 Oct 1762; m. 10 Feb 1710, JOANNA BARKER, b. at Andover, 7 Jul 1687 daughter of John and Mary (Stevens) Barker; Joanna d. at Andover, 4 Jan 1785.

66) ii ELIZABETH FARNUM, b. at Andover, 7 Jun 1687; d. at Andover, 23 May 1753; m. at Andover, 23 Dec 1708, EBENEZER FRYE, b. 16 Feb 1686 son of Samuel and Mary (Aslett) Frye; Ebenezer d. at Andover, 16 May 1725.

67) iii JAMES FARNUM, b. at Andover, 17 Oct 1691; d. at Andover, 17 Jun 1748; m. at Andover, 10 Jul 1722, JOHANNA GRAINGER, b. at Andover, 4 Feb 1691/2 daughter of John and Martha (Poor) Grainger; Johanna d. at Andover, 3 Dec 1745.

68) iv HANNAH FARNUM, b. at Andover, 31 Dec 1693; d. at Andover, 11 Nov 1784; m. at Andover, 18 Apr 1717, BENJAMIN STEVENS, b. at Andover, 14 Mar 1684/5 son of John and Esther (Barker) Stevens; Benjamin d. at Andover, 26 Mar 1748.

v MARY FARNUM, b. about 1696; she was living and unmarried in 1718 at the time of the deed from John Farnum to son James; nothing further known. She might have married Solomon Wood but that cannot be confirmed.

69) vi PHEBE FARNUM, b. at Andover, 24 Jun 1698; d. at Andover, 18 Feb 1760; m. at Andover, 29 Dec 1720, JOSEPH INGALLS, b. at Andover, 17 Apr 1697 son of Henry and Abigail (Emery) Ingalls; Joseph d. at Andover, 29 Dec 1757.

70) vii SARAH FARNUM, b. at Andover, 23 Oct 1700; d. 23 May 1745; m. at Andover, 13 May 1725, SAMUEL BARKER, b. at Andover, 13 Feb 1691/2 son of William and Mary (Dix) Barker; Samuel d. at Andover, 13 May 1770. Samuel married second Sarah Robinson on 10 Apr 1746.

71) viii DEBORAH FARNUM, b. at Andover, about 1702; m. at Andover, 4 Feb 1729/30, TIMOTHY FAULKNER, b. at Andover, about 1705 son of John and Sarah (Abbott) Faulkner; d. likely at Sturbridge, 1784. "Faulkner, ___ "an old man" May 16, 1784."

72) ix TABITHA FARNUM, b. at Andover, 1706; d. at Rindge, NH, 18 Feb 1804; m. 20 Mar 1733, ISRAEL ADAMS,[55] b. at Newbury, 24 Feb 1707/8 son of Sarah Adams; Israel d. at Rindge, 16 Oct 1789.

13) SAMUEL FARNUM (*Elizabeth Holt Farnum*[2], *Nicholas*[1]), b. at Andover, about 1665 son of Ralph and Elizabeth (Holt) Farnum; d. at Andover, 20 Dec 1754; m. 4 Jan 1697/8, his first cousin, HANNAH HOLT (*James*[2], *Nicholas*[1]), b. at Andover, 10 Aug 1677 daughter of James and Hannah (Allen) Holt; Hannah d. at Andover, 11 Apr 1747.

Samuel and Hannah resided in Andover where they kept a farm and Samuel was a weaver.

In 1730 (deeds recorded 9 March 1730), Samuel Farnum, with consent of his wife Hannah, conveyed one-half of his homestead to his son Samuel and the other half to his son David. Each son was to pay a sum of £500 for the property. The conveyance to David included the provision that David provide for Samuel and his wife Hannah "all things needful and convenient for their maintenance and subsistence in sickness and in health."[56]

Samuel and Hannah were parents of nine children born at Andover.

73) i LYDIA FARNUM, b. at Andover, 15 Oct 1699; d. at Andover, 21 Mar 1745/6; m. at Andover, 29 Aug 1716, as his second wife, DAVID FOSTER, b. 1694 son of Ephraim and Sarah (Eams) Foster; David d. at Boxford, 22 Jun 1759. David was first married to Elizabeth Abbott and third married to Judith Norton.

74) ii SAMUEL FARNUM, b. May 1701; d. at Louisburg, 27 Aug 1745; m. at Middleton, 13 Jan 1731, MARY HOW who has not been identified; Mary seems to be living in Andover as a widow on the tax lists in the 1760's and 1770's.

75) iii HANNAH FARNUM, b. at Andover, 1703; m. at Andover, 11 Nov 1720, DAVID BEVERLY, likely b. at Hingham, 18 Jul 1689 son of Lenox and Mary (Farrow) Beverly.

iv TABITHA FARNUM, b. 1706; d. 3 Jan 1740/1. Tabitha did not marry.

v DAVID FARNUM, b. 1708. David does not seem to have married. He may have died in a house fire in 1762.[57]

---

[55] Israel Adams's origins are murky. He may have been the out-of-wedlock child of Sarah Adams who later married John Hutchinson. He went by the name Israel Adams although some genealogies call his Israel Hutchinson.

[56] Massachusetts Land Records, Essex County, 55: 219 and 220; accessed through familysearch.org

[57] Abbott, "Abbott Genealogies" Farnum Family

vi ELIZABETH FARNUM, b. Mar 1720; no further clear record. She is not the Elizabeth that married Robert Swan; that was Elizabeth the daughter of Jonathan which is confirmed by probate records.

vii ALICE FARNUM, b. 4 May 1712. Alice had an out-of-wedlock child, Rachel, born about 1733 and baptized in 1737. *Rachel "gradd. Samuel Farnum by his Daughter Alice," bp. —— —, 1737.* It is possible that daughter Rachel Farnum married either James Burch or as the second wife of John Holt. If she married James Burch (perhaps the more likely option), Rachel died at the almshouse in Andover as the widow Rachel Burch. James Burch died in 1760 ("from home in ye army"). James and Rachel Burch were parents of two identified children both of whom seem to have died as infants.

viii BRIDGET FARNUM, b. 28 May 1714; northing further known.

14) MARY FARNUM[58] (*Elizabeth Holt Farnum², Nicholas¹*), b. at Andover, about 1660 daughter of Ralph and Elizabeth (Holt) Farnum; d. at Andover, 25 Dec 1739; m. 29 Nov 1680, WILLIAM LOVEJOY, b. at Andover, 21 Apr 1657 son of John and Mary (Osgood) Lovejoy; William d. at Andover, 9 Jul 1748.

William and Mary resided in the south precinct of Andover and William was one of the first deacons of South Church in 1711. William also served as selectman.[59]

William and Mary were parents of nine children born at Andover.

76) i WILLIAM LOVEJOY, b. at Andover, 22 Nov 1681; d. at Andover, 8 Mar 1762; m. 1st 1704/5, SARAH FRYE, b. at Andover, 27 Feb 1684 daughter of James and Lydia (Osgood) Frye; Sarah d. at Andover, 17 Oct 1747. William m. 2nd 28 Nov 1749, SARAH PAINE (widow of Jonathan Blanchard), b. at Charlestown, 3 Feb 1688 daughter of Edward and Bethia (Sweetser) Paine; Sarah d. at Andover, 9 Oct 1772.

55) ii HENRY LOVEJOY, b. at Andover, 27 Feb 1683; d. at Andover, 21Feb 1776; m. 14 Feb 1712, his first cousin, SARAH FARNUM (*Ralph Farnum³, Elizabeth Holt Farnum², Nicholas¹*), b. at Andover, 5 May 1686 daughter of Ralph and Sarah (Sterling) Farnum.

iii MARY LOVEJOY, b. at Andover, 15 Nov 1685; d. at Andover, 5 Jul 1724; m. 8 Jun 1710, her second cousin, JOSIAH HOLT (*Henry², Nicholas¹*), b. at Andover, 13 Dec 1679 son of Henry and Sarah (Ballard) Holt; Josiah d. at Andover, 23 Oct 1754. Josiah and Mary did not have children.

iv ALICE LOVEJOY, b. 23 Aug 1687; d. 25 Jul 1741. Alice did not marry.

v CALEB LOVEJOY, b. 29 Mar 1691; d. 26 Apr 1691.

77) vi SAMUEL LOVEJOY, b. at Andover, 10 Apr 1693; d. at Andover, 3 Dec 1749; m. at Andover, 23 Apr 1717, HANNAH STEVENS, b. at Andover, 28 Jul 1692 daughter of John and Ruth (Poor) Stevens; Hannah d. at Andover, 11 May 1767.

78) vii ABIGAIL LOVEJOY, b. at Andover, 11 Jun 1695; d. at Andover, 5 Sep 1759; m. 8 Dec 1718, HENRY PHELPS, b at Andover, 24 Sep 1693 son of Samuel and Sarah (Chandler) Phelps; Henry d. at Andover, 18 Oct 1766. After Abigail's death, Henry married the widow Susanna Kittredge.

79) viii LYDIA LOVEJOY, b. at Andover, 26 Apr 1699; m. at Andover, 3 Dec 1718, her first cousin, CALEB JOHNSON, b. at Andover, 19 Oct 1694 son of William and Sarah (Lovejoy) Johnson; Caleb d. at Willington, CT, 18 May 1760. Caleb was first married to Mary Turner and was third married to Sarah who has not been identified.

ix SARAH LOVEJOY, b. 6 Aug 1701; d. 15 Jul 1775. Sarah did not marry.

15) HANNAH FARNUM (*Elizabeth Holt Farnum², Nicholas¹*), b. at Andover, 7 Dec 1668 daughter of Ralph and Elizabeth (Holt) Farnum; d. at Andover, 30 Jun 1758; m. 1693, her first cousin, SAMUEL HOLT (*Samuel², Nicholas¹*), b. at Andover, 3 Aug 1671 son of Samuel and Sarah (Allen) Holt; Samuel d. at Andover, 20 Jul 1747.

Samuel was a farmer in Andover, and the eight children of Hannah and Samuel were born there. Hannah Farnum Holt was one of the thirty-five founding member of Andover south church in 1711, although husband Samuel did not join at that time.[60]

---

[58] Although Farnham, Descendants of Ralph Farnum states that it was Mary daughter of Thomas Farnum who married William Lovejoy, it can be demonstrated through deeds that Mary daughter of Thomas married John Johnson (Essex Deeds 37:190 and 38:158 in which Mary and John Johnson quitclaim property from honored father Thomas Farnum to John Frie who was the spouse of Mary's sister Tabitha Farnum daughter of Thomas).

[59] Bailey, *Historical Sketches of Andover*

[60] "South Parish's 35 Founding Members and Their Homes", http://www.southchurch.com/images/EarlySCHistory.pdf

i HANNAH HOLT, b. 11 Feb 1693/4; died young.

80) ii SAMUEL HOLT, b. at Andover, 1697; d. at Andover, 25 Nov 1758; m. 12 Jan 1724, his second cousin, JEMIMA GRAY (*Henry Gray*[3], *Hannah Holt Gray*[2], *Nicholas*[1]), b. at Andover, 28 Aug 1701 daughter of Henry and Mary (Blunt) Gray; Jemima d. at Andover, 27 Aug 1775.

81) iii OBADIAH HOLT, b. at Andover, 8 Dec 1700; d. 24 Jan 1739 when he drowned in the Kennebec River; m. 14 Nov 1726, his first cousin, REBECCA FARNUM (*Thomas Farnum*[3], *Elizabeth Holt Farnum*[2], *Nicholas*[1]), b. at Andover, 1705 daughter of Thomas and Hannah (Hutchinson) Farnum. Rebecca m. 2nd, 22 Jun 1742, JOSEPH BERRY son of John and Rachel (-) Berry. Rebecca also had an out-of-wedlock relationship with Edward Farrington in 1723 which produced a daughter Mary.

82) iv HANNAH HOLT, b. at Andover, 30 Nov 1702; d. at Reading, 3 Apr 1749; m. at Andover, 2 Jan 1727/8 as his second wife, ROBERT RUSSELL, b. at Andover, about 1690 son of Thomas and Phebe (Johnson) Russell; Robert d. at Reading, 1759 (probate 1759). Robert was first married to Abigail Flint, third married to the widow Elizabeth Manning and fourth married to the widow Martha Johnosn Parker.

83) v MARTHA HOLT, b. at Andover, 8 Mar 1705; m. 3 Mar 1725/6, SOMERS PIERCE, b. at Woburn, 16 Feb 1697 son of William and Abigail (Somers) Pierce.

84) vi EBENEZER HOLT, b. at Andover, 8 Apr 1705; m. at Andover, 4 Dec 1729, MEHITABLE STEVENS, b. about 1708 of undetermined parents.

85) vii JOHN HOLT, b. at Andover, 1707; d. at Wilton, NH, before 1786; m. at Andover, 8 Oct 1731, MARY LEWIS, b. about 1710; Mary d. at Wilton, 15 May 1786.[61]

viii REBECCA HOLT, b. 1713; d. 28 May 1714.

16) THOMAS FARNUM (*Elizabeth Holt Farnum*[2], *Nicholas*[1]), b. at Andover, 14 Jul 1670 son of Ralph and Elizabeth (Holt) Farnum; d. at Andover, 24 Apr 1744; m. 1st at Andover, 14 May 1693, HANNAH HUTCHINSON, b. about 1675 daughter of Samuel and Hannah (Johnson) Hutchinson; Hannah d. at Andover, 19 May 1716 in her 41st year. Thomas m. 2nd at Andover, 3 Aug 1720, DOROTHY LACY, b. about 1677 and likely the daughter of Lawrence and Mary (Foster) Lacy; Dorothy d. at Andover 10 Oct 1747 in her 71st year.

In his will written 4 March 1736/7 (probate 28 May 1744), Thomas Farnum bequeathed to beloved wife Dorothy the use of the west end of the dwelling house while she is a widow and the household items she brought with her at the marriage to be at her disposal. Other provisions for her support are specified. Daughter Dinah is to receive £30 within six years of his decease and daughter Rebecah receives twenty shillings as she has already received her portion. Son Ebenezer receives all the homestead lands. Son Thomas receives nothing additional as he has received his portion. All the other materials of the homestead (stock animals, tools, etc.) go to Ephraim who is also named executor.[62]

Thomas and Hannah were parents of six children born at Andover.

i HANNAH FARNUM, b. 24 Jan 1694/5; d. at Andover, 9 Dec 1716. Hannah did not marry.

ii DINAH FARNUM, b. at Andover, 1703. She was living and unmarried in 1737. Nothing further is known.

81) iii REBECCA FARNUM, b. at Andover, 1705; living in 1758; m. 1st 14 Nov 1726, her first cousin, OBADIAH HOLT (*Samuel*[3], *Samuel*[2], *Nicholas*[1]), b. at Andover, 8 Dec 1700 son of Samuel and Hannah (Farnum) Holt; Obadiah d. by drowning in the Kennebec River, 24 Jan 1739. Rebecca m. 2nd 22 Jun 1742, JOSEPH BERRY, b. at Andover, about 1695 son of John and Rachel (-) Berry; Joseph d. at Middleton, 1757 (probate 9 Jan 1758). Before her first marriage, Rebecca had an out-of-wedlock daughter with EDWARD FARRINGTON.

86) iv THOMAS FARNUM, b. at Andover, 16 May 1709; m. at Andover, 23 Nov 1733, PHEBE TOWNE, b. at Topsfield, 30 Jul 1714 daughter of Nathan and Phebe (Curtis) Towne;[63] Phebe d. 9 Jul 1763.

87) v EBENEZER FARNUM, b. at Andover, 1711; m. 12 Feb 1732/3, his second cousin, PRISCILLA INGALLS, b. at Andover, 1706 daughter of James and Hannah (Abbott) Ingalls.

vi MEHITABLE FARNUM, d. at Andover, 29 Dec 1716. "Mehitabel, d. Thomas and Hannah, Dec. 29, 1716." No birth record was located.

---

[61] Mary Holt, widow of John, died at age 76. "New Hampshire Death Records, 1654–1947." Index. FamilySearch, Salt Lake City, Utah, 2010. New Hampshire Bureau of Vital Records. "Death Records, 1654–1947." Bureau of Vital Records, Concord, New Hampshire. Film 15345

[62] *Essex County, MA: Probate File Papers, 1638-1881.*Online database. *AmericanAncestors.org.* New England Historic Genealogical Society, 2014. Case 9255

[63] Towne, *The Descendants of William Towne*, p 27

17) ELIZABETH FARNUM (*Elizabeth Holt Farnum²*, *Nicholas¹*), b. at Andover, about 1672 daughter of Ralph and Elizabeth (Holt) Farnum; d. at Andover, 28 Sep 1714; m. 10 May 1698, her first cousin, GEORGE HOLT (*Henry²*, *Nicholas¹*), b. at Andover, 17 Mar 1676 son of Henry and Sarah (Ballard) Holt; George d. at Windham, CT, 29 Jun 1748. George m. 2nd, about 1715, PRISCILLA PRESTON daughter of Samuel and Susanna (Gutterson) Preston; Priscilla d. 29 Jan 1716. George m. 3rd, by 1717, MARY BIXBY, b. at Andover, 10 Apr 1693 daughter of Daniel and Hannah (Chandler) Bixby.

George Holt's property in Andover was along what was later known as the Essex Turnpike and today is Route 28.[64]

In his will written 7 March 1746 (proved 29 June 1748), George Holt bequeaths to beloved wife Mary the dowry thirds during her widowhood. If she marries and quits his estate, she receives her clothing and a bed and furniture and £5. Son Zebadiah Holt receives ten shillings as he has received his portion by deed. Son George receives £15 and son Nathaniel receives £110 at age 21. Daughters Elizabeth Coburn and Dinah Ford each receives £10. Daughter Priscilla Rogers receives ten shillings. Daughters Hannah Holt and Sarah Holt each receives £30 at age eighteen or at marriage. Sons Jonathan and Nehemiah receive all the real estate not otherwise disposed of and are named executors.[65]

George Holt and Elizabeth Farnum were parents of five children born at Andover.

88) i ZEBADIAH HOLT, b. at Andover, 25 Jan 1700; d. at Windham, CT, about 1760 (estate inventory 3 Apr 1760); m. at Windham, 14 Aug 1732, SARAH FLINT, b. at Windham, 12 Jan 1717 daughter of Nathaniel and Sarah (Cutler) Flint.[66]

ii ELIZABETH HOLT, b. and d. 1703.

89) iii ELIZABETH HOLT, b. 1706; m. at Windham, 16 Nov 1727, SAMUEL COBURN, b. 1700 son of Edward and Sarah (Hayward) Coburn.

90) iv DINAH HOLT, b. at Andover, 1710; d. at Hampton, CT, 12 Jan 1763; m. at Windham, 1 Oct 1730, NATHANIEL FORD, b. at Windham, 3 Jun 1707 son of Joseph and Elizabeth (Hovey) Ford; Nathaniel d. at Hampton, 25 Oct 1779. Nathaniel married second Hannah Brigham on 7 Jul 1763.

91) v GEORGE HOLT, b. 2 Jan 1713; m. at Windham, 4 Jul 1743, MARY ALLEN.

George Holt and Priscilla Preston had one child.

i ELIAS HOLT, b. 16 Jan 1716; d. 25 Jan 1716.

George Holt and Mary Bixby were parents of eight children, the first five children born at Andover and the three youngest children at Hampton.

Son Jonathan Holt married Mary Parker, but they did not have children of their own. Jonathan and Mary cared for the children of Jonathan's brother Nathaniel who died in 1763. In his will dated 22 March 1794, Jonathan Holt has bequests to his siblings and his nieces and nephews. Jonathan bequeathed five shillings each to his siblings: brother Nehemiah five, the heirs of sister Elizabeth Coburn, Priscilla Rogers, the heirs of Dinah Ford, the heirs of Hannah Rogers, the heirs of George Holt, and the heirs of Zebadiah Holt. Niece Cynthia Staples (daughter of Nathaniel) receives five pounds, and Lucy Holt and Mary Holt the daughters of his nephew Jonathan Holt, Jr. receive the indoor moveable estate. Nephew Jonathan Holt receives the remainder of the estate and is named executor.[67]

i MARY HOLT, b. 4 Mar 1716/7; likely died young.

ii JONATHAN HOLT baptized 28 Dec 1718; d. 10 Dec 1800; m. 12 Apr 1738, MARY PARKER. Jonathan and Mary did not have children of their own but adopted son Jonathan of Jonathan's brother Nathaniel.

iii JOSIAH HOLT, b. 2 Jul 1721; likely died young.

92) iv NEHEMIAH HOLT, b. at Andover, 3 Apr 1723; d. at Chaplin, CT, 17 Apr 1799; m. ANNA FARNUM (*Nathaniel Farnum⁴*, *Ralph Farnum³*, *Elizabeth Holt Farnum²*, *Nicholas¹*), b. at Windham, 26 Apr 1726 daughter of Nathaniel and Hannah (Preston) Farnum; Anna d. at Chaplin, 1 Apr 1810.

93) v PRISCILLA HOLT, b. at Andover, 4 Sep 1725; d. at Wales, MA, m. at Hampton, CT, 10 Nov 1743, ICHABOD ROGERS, b. at Windham, 19 Jan 1718/9 son of Hope and Esther (Meacham) Rogers; Ichabod d. at Wales, 19 Jan 1800.

---

64 "A Plan for Andover Taken for the Town", Norman B. Leventhal Map and Education Center, https://collections.leventhalmap.org/search/commonwealth:8336h340s#image. Abbott, Charlotte Helen, "Early Records of the Holt Family"

65 *Connecticut State Library (Hartford, Connecticut);* Probate Place: *Hartford, Connecticut, Probate Packets, Hicks-Hovey, Elisha, 1719-1880,* George Holt, 1748, Case 1941

66 The 1754 will of Nathaniel Flint includes a bequest to his daughter Sarah Holt.

67 *Connecticut State Library (Hartford, Connecticut);* Probate Place: *Hartford, Connecticut, Probate Packets, Hicks-Hovey, Elisha, 1719-1880, Estate of Jonathan Holt, Case 1944*

94) vi HANNAH HOLT, b. at Hampton, 11 Mar 1730; m. at Hampton, 8 Oct 1747, JETHRO ROGERS, b. at Windham, 14 Apr 1722 son of Hope and Esther (Meacham) Rogers.

vii SARAH HOLT, b. at Hampton, 7 Mar 1732; d. 26 Oct 1761.

95) viii NATHANIEL HOLT, b. at Hampton, 18 Mar 1734; d. at Windham, 1763; m. 16 Dec 1756, PHEBE CANADY, b. at Hampton, 1735 daughter of Isaac and Phebe (Leonard) Canady. Phebe married second Israel Litchfield on 14 Jan 1766.[68]

18) EPHRAIM FARNUM (*Elizabeth Holt Farnum[2], Nicholas[1]*), b. at Andover, 1 Oct 1676 son of Ralph and Elizabeth (Holt) Farnum; d. at Andover, 9 Jun 1744; m. at Andover, 20 Mar 1699/1700, his first cousin, PRISCILLA HOLT (*James[2], Nicholas[1]*), b. at Andover, 13 Aug 1679 daughter of James and Hannah (Allen) Holt.

Ephraim and Priscilla were parents of nine children born at Andover. Most of the children in the family relocated to Concord. Second son Timothy remained in Andover. In 1726 (deed recorded 4 November 1751), Ephraim Farnum conveyed to his son Timothy for love and good will a 25-acre lot of land in the area known as Boston hill.[69]

96) i EPHRAIM FARNUM, b. at Andover, 12 Oct 1700; d. at Concord, NH, 1775; m. at Andover, 12 Nov 1728, MARY INGALLS, b. at Andover, 27 Mar 1705 daughter of John and Sarah (Russell) Ingalls.

97) ii TIMOTHY FARNUM, b. at Andover, 4 May 1702; d. at Andover, 25 Jul 1780; m. 18 Jan 1727, DINAH INGALLS, b. at Andover, about 1705 daughter of James and Hannah (Abbott) Ingalls; Dinah d. at Andover, 22 Nov 1781.

98) iii JAMES FARNUM, b. at Andover, 1705; d. at Concord, after 1769; m. at Haverhill, MA, 7 Dec 1732, ELIZABETH WILSON, b. about 1709 daughter of Joseph and Mary (Richardson) Wilson.[70]

iv MARY FARNUM, b. 25 Mar 1708; nothing further known.

99) v PRISCILLA FARNUM, b. at Andover, 1709/10; d. at Andover, 19 May 1790;[71] m. at Andover, 25 Jul 1732, her second cousin, JOHN RUSS, b. at Andover, 1706 son of Thomas and Anne (Farnum) Russ; John d. at Rumford, NH, by Dec 1743 (date of mother's will and posthumous child born Apr 1744).

100) vi ZEBADIAH FARNUM, b. at Andover, about 1710; d. at Concord, 17 Apr 1799; m. at Concord, 22 Mar 1738, MARY WALKER.

101) vii JOSIAH FARNUM, b. at Andover, 19 Jul 1712; d. at Concord, about 1790 (probate Feb 1790); m. his first cousin once removed, MARY FRYE (*Elizabeth Farnum Frye[4], John Farnum[3], Elizabeth Holt Farnum[2], Nicholas[1]*), b. at Andover, 6 Nov 1712 daughter of Ebenezer and Elizabeth (Farnum) Frye.

102) viii JOSEPH FARNUM, b. at Andover, 1714/5; d. at Concord, 1 Nov 1792; m. about 1740, ZERVIAH HOIT, b. about 1720 daughter of Abner and Mary (Blaisdell) Hoit;[72] Zerviah d. at Concord, 29 Dec 1794.[73]

103) ix ELIZABETH FARNUM, b. at Andover, 1718; m. at Andover, 31 Dec 1736, JAMES PETERS, b. about 1711 son of Seborne and Mary (-) Peters; James d. at Salisbury, NH, 16 Oct 1801.

Children of Mary Holt and Thomas Johnson

19) MARY JOHNSON (*Mary Holt Johnson[2], Nicholas[1]*), b. 11 May 1659 daughter of Thomas and Mary (Holt) Johnson; d. at Medfield, 1713 (probate 1713); m. at Andover, 6 Sep 1673, RETURN JOHNSON, b. about 1653 (based on age 25 in 1678 when took oath of allegiance); d. at Medfield, 15 Mar 1706/7. Mary is not included in the 1724 division of her father's estate.

---

[68] There is disagreement as to whether the Phebe Holt who married Israel Litchfield was Phebe Holt daughter of Joshua and Keturah Holt or Phebe Canady Holt the widow of Nathaniel Holt who died in 1763. The sequence of the marriages for the two Phebe Holts that are of issue make is more likely that the Phebe who married Israel Litchfield was Phebe Canady Holt and that Phebe Holt who married Ebenezer Goodale was the daughter of Joshua and Keturah. Phebe Holt and Ebenezer Goodale were married in 1755 and Phebe Canady married Nathaniel Holt in 1756, so she cannot be the Phebe Holt that married Ebenezer Goodale. The two Phebes were born the same year so that does not help differentiate them. But one of the children of Phebe and Israel was named Leonard and Phebe Canady was the daughter of Isaac Canady and Phebe Leonard.

[69] Massachusetts Land Records 1620-1986, Essex County, 97:107; accessed through familysearch.org

[70] The 1742 will of Joseph Wilson, cooper, of Haverhill, includes a bequest to his daughter Elizabeth Farnum.

[71] Priscilla, wid., old age, bur. May 19, 1790, a. 86 y. C.R.2.

[72] Hoyt, *A Genealogical History of the Hoyt Families*, p 140

[73] One record gives the date of Zerviah's death as 20 Dec 1792.

Return Johnson arrived in Medfield about 1679 and was the first physician there.[74] He and Mary were parents of four daughters. Return also fathered an out-of-wedlock child with Priscilla Pratt, a son Roger born in 1696 who died as a young child.

In her will proved 13 February 1713, Mary Johnson relict of Doctor Return Johnson bequeathed to her daughter Mary a note worth £25 which is owed to Mary by her brother James Johnson. Mary is to pay £3 of the amount to daughter Sarah. Daughter Elizabeth receives "all my debts in Canterbury." Daughter Jemima receives a scarf and coat. Grandchild Mary Arnold receives bed and bedding. Daughter Mary is named sole executrix.[75]

104) i MARY JOHNSON, b. at Medfield, about 1675; d. at Medfield, 18 Dec 1763; m. 1st at Andover, 25 Jul 1701, BARACHIAS HARNDEN whose parentage is not determined; Barachias d. at Andover, 8 Feb 1702/3. Mary m. 2nd at Andover, 25 Sep 1704, SAMUEL SADEY, b. at Boston, 8 Feb 1681 son of John and Elizabeth (Peters) Sadey; Samuel d. at Medfield, 8 Oct 1744.

105) ii ELIZABETH JOHNSON, b. at Medfield, 16 Aug 1681; m. JEREMIAH PLIMPTON, b. at Medfield, 8 Nov 1683 son of Joseph and Marie (Morse) Plimpton.

106) iii JEMIMA JOHNSON, b. at Medfield, 16 Sep 1683; d. at Middletown, CT, 4 Oct 1753; m. at Medfield, 4 Feb 1704/5, JOHN PELTON, b. at Dorchester, 9 Jan 1682 son of Samuel and Mary (Smith) Pelton; John d. at Essex, CT, 15 Jul 1735.

107) iv SARAH JOHNSON, b. at Medfield, about 1688; m. at Medfield, 4 Sep 1710 JOHN ALLEN.

20) PHEBE JOHNSON (*Mary Holt Johnson[2], Nicholas[1]*), b. at Andover, 3 Jan 1664 daughter of Thomas and Mary (Holt) Johnson; d. at Andover, 4 Feb 1738; m. about 1685, THOMAS RUSSELL, b. at Andover, 16 Dec 1663 son of Robert and Mary (Marshall) Russell; Thomas d. at Andover, 30 Aug 1731.

Phebe Johnson and Thomas Russell were parents of ten children born at Andover. On 21 February 1727 (recorded 31 May 1727), Thomas and Phebe Russell for love and affection deeded the homestead property in Andover to beloved son Joseph Russell. This deed covered all the estate including stock animals and tools, although Phebe and Thomas reserved for themselves the use and improvement of one-half of the estate during their lives and a room in the homestead dwelling.[76]

i THOMAS RUSSELL, b. at Andover, 13 Aug 1687. Nothing definitive is known of Thomas.

108) ii MEHITABLE RUSSELL, b. at Andover, about 1688; d. at Andover, 18 Dec 1733; m. at Andover, 10 Jun 1708, JOSEPH CHANDLER, b. at Andover, 17 Jul 1682 son of William and Bridget (Henchman) Chandler; Joseph d. at Andover, 22 Apr 1734.

81) iii ROBERT RUSSELL, b. at Andover, about 1690; d. at Reading, 1759 (probate 1759); m. 1st at Andover, 22 Jun 1716, ABIGAIL FLINT; Abigail d. at Andover, 10 May 1723. Robert m. 2nd at Andover, 2 Jan 1727/8, his second cousin, HANNAH HOLT (*Hannah Farnum Holt[3], Elizabeth Holt Farnum[2], Nicholas[1]*), b. at Andover, 30 Nov 1702 daughter of Samuel and Hannah (Farnum) Holt; Hannah d. at Reading, 3 Apr 1749. Robert m. 3rd at Andover, 23 Dec 1749, widow ELIZABETH MANNING. Robert m. 4th at Andover, 17 Apr 1755, widow MARTHA PARKER.

56) iv PHEBE RUSSELL, b. at Andover, 21 Jan 1689/90; d. at Windham, CT, after 1753 (distribution of widow's dower to Phebe Farnum aka Robins 13 Apr 1753 from the estate of Henry Farnum); m. at Andover, 12 Jun 1712, her second cousin, HENRY FARNUM (*Ralph Farnum[3], Elizabeth Holt Farnum[2], Nicholas[1]*), b. at Andover, 15 Sep 1687 son of Ralph and Sarah (Sterling) Farnum; Henry d. at Windham, 23 Jul 1732. Phebe m. 2nd at Canterbury, 3 Jan 1734, NATHANIEL ROBBINS; Nathaniel d. at Windham, 7 Apr 1753.

109) v MARY RUSSELL, b. at Andover, 10 Feb 1692/3; d. at Andover, 1778 (probate 3 Feb 1778); m. at Andover, 10 May 1716, TIMOTHY OSGOOD, b. at Andover, 22 Aug 1693 son of Timothy and Deborah (Poor) Osgood; Timothy d. 1772 (probate 24 Nov 1772).

110) vi SARAH RUSSELL, b. at Andover, about 1695; m. at Andover, 9 Sep 1715, JOHN ROSS, b. at Billerica, 18 Jan 1686/7 son of Thomas and Seeth (Holman) Ross.

111) vii PETER RUSSELL, b. at Andover, 23 Apr 1700; d. at Litchfield, NH, Nov 1759 (will 3 Nov, proved 28 Nov 1759); m. 31 Mar 1727, DEBORAH CROSBY, b. at Billerica, 13 Jul 1709 daughter of Joseph and Sarah (French) Crosby.

---

[74] Tilden, *History of Medfield*, p 420

[75] *Suffolk County (Massachusetts) Probate Records, 1636-1899;* Author: *Massachusetts. Probate Court (Suffolk County), Probate Records volume 17-18, volume 18, p 59*

[76] Massachusetts land records 1620-1986, Essex County, 48:264; accessed through familysearch.org.

112) viii JOSEPH RUSSELL, b. at Andover, Apr 1702; m. 1st at Reading, 26 Nov 1728, HEPSIBAH EATON; Hepsibah d. at Andover, 14 Mar 1742/3. Joseph m. 2nd at Andover, 24 Nov 1746, HANNAH PERKINS, b. at Andover, 15 Nov 1720 daughter of Timothy and Hannah (Buxton) Perkins; Hannah d. at Andover, 22 Mar 1775.

113) ix JEMIMA RUSSELL, b. at Andover, 18 Jul 1704; d. at Littleton, MA, 20 Sep 1790; m. at Andover, 16 Jul 1724, JOSEPH HUNT, b. at Billerica, 21 Sep 1694 son of Samuel and Mary (-) Hunt; Joseph d. at Andover, 1743 (probate 7 Nov 1743). Jemima m. 2nd, 13 Dec 1743, CHRISTOPHER TEMPLE, b. 1690 and d. at Littleton, 8 May 1782.

114) x JAMES RUSSELL, b. at Andover, 15 Jun 1706; m. at Amesbury, 3 Jun 1729, RHODA CHANDLER, b. at Andover, 1705 daughter of Joseph and Sarah (Abbott) Chandler.

21) JOHN JOHNSON (*Mary Holt Johnson*[2], *Nicholas*[1]), b. at Andover, 28 Feb 1667 son of Thomas and Mary (Holt) Johnson; d. at Andover, 26 May 1741; m. 1st 13 Sep 1689, ELLENOR BALLARD, b. at Andover, 24 Aug 1672 daughter of Joseph and Elizabeth (Phelps) Ballard; Ellenor d. 21 Nov 1707. John m. 2nd 1708, MARY FARNUM, b. at Andover, 24 Mar 1665/6 daughter of Thomas and Elizabeth (Sibborn) Farnum; Mary d. 17 May 1723. John m. 3rd 24 Aug 1723, ANNE FARNUM (widow of Thomas Russ), b. about 1677 daughter of John and Rebecca (Kent) Farnum.

Ellenor Ballard's parents Joseph and Elizabeth (Phelps) Ballard played a role in the Salem witch hysteria. In 1692, Elizabeth became ill and doctors were baffled by her illness and suspected witchcraft. Joseph sought assistance for this and brought Anne Putnam, who was twelve years old, and Mary Walcott from Salem. These two girls identified Elizabeth's illness as the result of witchcraft and named Ann Alcock Foster after the two girls fell into fits at the sight of Ann. Soon after, Ann's daughter, Mary Foster Lacey, and her granddaughter, Mary Lacey, also came under suspicion. Mary Foster Lacey and her daughter Mary are referred to as Mary Lacey, Sr. and Mary Lacey, Jr. in the records. The two Mary's were promptly arrested and charged with witchcraft. Mary Lacey, Sr. confessed to being a witch and stated her mother was also, claiming they had ridden upon a pole to a witch meeting in Salem. Mary, Sr. also implicated several others including Rebecca Nurse, Richard Carrier, and Andrew Carrier. Mary, Sr. and her mother Ann Alcock Foster were tried and convicted of being witches and were sentenced to execution. However, their trials came at the end of the witch trials and their executions were not carried out. All three women were imprisoned. Ann Foster died while she was in prison on 6 December 1692. Her daughter Mary, Sr. was released in 1693. Mary, Jr. was later found to be not guilty and was released.[77]

Ellenor Ballard and John Johnson were parents of nine children born at Andover.[78] In his will written 28 January 1735/6, John Johnson bequeathed to beloved wife Anne the dwelling house from the cellar to the top as long as she is a widow. She also receives the use and improvement of one-third of the real estate. No household items are left to her as she reserved to herself the household goods she brought to the marriage. Anne also receives other provisions for her support. Son John Johnson receives the westerly side of the homestead lands and these are detailed in the will. John also receives one-half of the common right lands. Son Zebadiah Johnson receives the easterly half of the homestead and other lands as detailed in the will and the other half of the common rights land. Daughter Tabitha receives £30 and she has already received the largest part of her portion. Son Joshua Johnson has received his portion by deed of gift. Sons John and Zebadiah are named executors.[79] Daughter Tabitha Danforth and son Joshua Johnson signed quitclaims to their brothers John and Zebadiah. The homestead property of about 100 acres with buildings was valued at £1,200. Joshua mentioned in the will is a child from John Johnson's second marriage to Mary Farnum.

i JOHN JOHNSON, b. 24 Feb 1690/1; d. at Andover, 14 Nov 1756. He does not seem to have married.

115) ii TABITHA JOHNSON, b. 4 Apr 1693; m. 17 Sep 1726, JOHN DANFORTH, b. at Billerica, 3 Jun 1703 son of Jonathan and Rebecca (Parker) Danforth;[80] John d. at Westborough, 1737 (will 8 Nov 1737; proved 4 Jan 1737/8).

iii LYDIA JOHNSON, b. 26 May 1695; d. 16 Nov 1718; m. 1718, JOSEPH DANE, b. at Andover, 5 Apr 1696 son of Francis and Hannah (Poor) Dane; Joseph d. 27 Dec 1721. Lydia and Joseph had an infant, Joseph, who died 30 Nov 1718.

iv ELLENOR JOHNSON, b. 26 Dec 1697; no further record.

v PHEBE JOHNSON, b. 2 Feb 1699/1700; d. 29 Mar 1718.

116) vi ZEBADIAH JOHNSON, b. about 1701; d. at Andover, 1770 (probate 3 Feb 1770); m. 8 Jun 1723, HANNAH ROBBINS, b. at Charlestown, 30 Jun 1705 daughter of Nathaniel and Hannah (Chandler) Robbins.

---

[77] University of Virginia, Salem Witch Trials Documentary Archive and Transcription Project

[78] There is perhaps another son James in this family who died before adulthood.

[79] Essex County, MA: Probate File Papers, 1638-1881.Online database. AmericanAncestors.org. New England Historic Genealogical Society, 2014. Case 15063

[80] May, *Danforth Genealogy*, p 19

vii JOSEPH JOHNSON, d. at Andover 5 Mar 1701/2.

ix SARAH JOHNSON, d. at Andover, 2 Aug 1707.

Child of John Johnson and Mary Farnum:

i JOSHUA JOHNSON, b. 1708; nothing further known. He is in his father's will. It is reported by Charlotte Helen Abbott that Joshua was dissatisfied with the settlement of the estate and left town to parts unknown.

22) THOMAS JOHNSON (*Mary Holt Johnson*[2], *Nicholas*[1]), b. at Andover, 19 Oct 1670 son of Thomas and Mary (Holt) Johnson; d. at Andover, 22 Oct 1733;[81] m. at Andover, 24 Jul 1701, HANNAH STONE, b. 23 Mar 1679/80 daughter of Hugh and Hannah (Foster) Stone; Hannah d. at Andover, 5 Feb 1744/5.

Thomas and Hannah lived in Andover where their three children were born. Thomas was killed in a fire at his house: *Thomas, "in the flames of his House that was Burnt with fier," Oct. 22, 1733.*

Thomas Johnson did not leave a will and his estate entered probate 29 October 1733 with widow Hannah declining administration and requesting that this be assumed by her sons-in-law John Wright and Joseph Faulkner. One-third of the estate was set-off to Hannah for use during her natural life. The estate was valued at £1331. The remaining two-thirds of the estate were divided into two equal portions to be settled on daughter Hannah and heirs of Damaris.[82]

i ABIEL JOHNSON, b. 1702; d. 20 Jun 1703.

117) ii DAMARIS JOHNSON, b. at Andover, 1704; d. at Andover, 13 Nov 1728; m. 16 Jan 1727/8, JOSEPH FAULKNER, b. at Andover, 1 Mar 1695/6 son of John and Sarah (Abbott) Faulkner; Joseph d. at Andover, 28 Dec 1780. Joseph married second Mary Parker and married third Rebecca Barnard.

118) iii HANNAH JOHNSON, b. at Andover, 13 Jan 1705/6; m. at Andover, 27 Jul 1725, JOHN WRIGHT, b. at Andover, Mar 1701/2 son of John and Mary (Wardwell) Wright.

23) JAMES JOHNSON (*Mary Holt Johnson*[2], *Nicholas*[1]), b. at Andover, 4 Feb 1672 son of Thomas and Mary (Holt) Johnson; d. 14 Oct 1748; m. 1st at Andover, 26 Apr 1692, ELIZABETH FARNUM (widow of Andrew Peters), b. 19 Feb 1661 daughter of Thomas and Elizabeth (Sibborn) Farnum; Elizabeth d. 31 Jan 1716. James m. 2nd at Andover, 23 Aug 1716, SARAH PEABODY (widow of Benjamin Smith), b. at Boxford, 4 Sep 1676 daughter of Joseph and Bethiah (Bridges) Peabody.

In his will written 15 February 1745 (21 November 1748), James Johnson bequeathed to eldest, well-beloved son Andrew a piece of land running from his dwelling house to the property of Uriah Ballard which is described in detail. Son Obadiah receives all of the old division of land. Youngest son Joseph receives land on the southerly side of Wardwell meadow. Daughter Mary receives a bond which her husband Joseph Chamberlain was bound to James in the amount of £47 and some personal items (e.g., brass kettle) and this constitutes her full portion. His two grandchildren, the children of daughter Mehitable who is deceased, each receives £5. Sons Andrew and Obadiah were named executors. Real estate was valued at £875.[83]

James Johnson and Elizabeth Farnum were parents of eight children born at Andover.

i ELIZABETH JOHNSON, b. 17 Jan 1692/3; d. at Billerica, 20 Apr 1717. *Elizabeth, d. James and Elizabeth, "drowned in Concord River at Bildrekey," Apr. 20, 1717.*

ii JAMES JOHNSON, b. 4 Feb 1693/4; d. 13 Oct 1714.

119) iii ANDREW JOHNSON, b. at Andover, Oct 1695; d. at Andover, 4 Feb 1757; m. 21 Aug 1723, HANNAH CHANDLER, b. at Andover, 23 Aug 1700 daughter of Thomas and Mary (Peters) Chandler.

iv PETER JOHNSON, b. about 1697; d. 10 Feb 1715/6.

120) v OBADIAH JOHNSON, b. at Andover, about 1700; d. at Andover, 8 Jul 1780; m. 1st 12 Feb 1724/5, HANNAH OSGOOD, b. at Andover, 4 Mar 1701/2 daughter of Stephen and Hannah (Blanchard) Osgood; Hannah d. 11 Mar 1729. Obadiah m. 2nd about 1740, DEBORAH RUSS daughter of Thomas and Anne (Farnum) Russ; Deborah d. at Andover, 18 Jul 1745. Obadiah m. 3rd 26 Sep 1748, DOROTHY BALLARD, b. at Andover, 26 Jan 1714/5 daughter of Joseph and Rebecca (Johnson) Ballard; Dorothy was living in 1780. Dorothy Ballard was first married to Benjamin Smith.

---

81 Thomas, "in the flames of his House that was Burnt with fier," Oct. 22, 1733.

82 *Essex County, MA: Probate File Papers, 1638-1881.* Online database. *AmericanAncestors.org.* New England Historic Genealogical Society, 2014. Case 15139

83 *Essex County, MA: Probate File Papers, 1638-1881.* Online database. *AmericanAncestors.org.* New England Historic Genealogical Society, 2014. Case 15051

121) vi MARY JOHNSON, b. at Andover, Feb 1701/2; d. at Amenia, NY, 1 May 1783; m. 1720, JOSEPH CHAMBERLAIN, b. at Billerica, Nov 1696 son of Clement and Mary (-) Chamberlain; Joseph d. at Amenia, NY, 8 Apr 1765.

122) vii MEHITABLE JOHNSON, b. at Andover, about 1703; d. at Mansfield, CT, 28 Apr 1740; m. at Andover, 4 Apr 1733, THOMAS HUNTINGTON, b. at Norwich, CT, 22 Apr 1688 son of Thomas and Elizabeth (Backus) Huntington; Thomas d. at Mansfield, 18 Jan 1755. Thomas was first married to Elizabeth Arnold.

viii JOSEPH JOHNSON, b. about 1704; d. 7 Feb 1715/6.

James Johnson and Sarah Peabody were parents of three children.

i JOSEPH JOHNSON, baptized at Andover, 19 May 1717; living in 1748; nothing further known.

ii JAMES JOHNSON, b. Apt 1718; died young.

iii PETER JOHNSON, b. 9 Sep 1719; likely died young as is not mentioned in father's will.

24) JEMIMA JOHNSON[84] (*Mary Holt Johnson*[2], *Nicholas*[1]), b. at Andover, 1 Jan 1678 daughter of Thomas and Mary (Holt) Johnson; d. at Watertown, 4 Mar 1754; m. 1st at Watertown, 1697, JOHN ABBOT, b. at Andover, 26 Aug 1662 son of George and Sarah (Farnum) Abbot; John d. at Watertown, 24 Mar 1718. Jemima m. 2nd at Boston, 1 Sep 1719, JOHN BEAKS.

John Abbot enjoyed relative prosperity. He lived in Sudbury and Watertown where he was a husbandman, carpenter, and owner of a grist mill. He was a selectman in Sudbury and served as constable in 1706-1707.[85]

John Abbot did not leave a will and his estate entered probate 28 April 1718 administered by widow Jemima Abbot later named as Jemima wife of John Becks. Real estate was valued at £750 including a grist mill.[86] In her will written 28 May 1747 (proved 18 March 1754), Jemima Beaks requested that her estate be divided in three equal shares and divided among daughter Jemima Norcross, daughter Hannah Cadee, and the heirs of daughter Mary Wheeler. David Livermore was executor.[87]

Jemima and John were parents of five children born at Sudbury. Son John Abbott made his way to the southern colonies and has been referred to as the "pioneer of the Southern Abbotts."[88]

123) i JEMIMA ABBOT, b. at Sudbury, 10 Oct 1699; m. 12 Dec 1717, NATHANIEL NORCROSS, b. at Watertown, 20 Dec 1695 son of Nathaniel and Susannah (Shattuck) Norcross; Nathaniel d. at Watertown, 9 Apr 1749.

124) ii JOHN ABBOTT, b. at Sudbury, 3 Oct 1702; d. after 1738 likely in North Carolina; m. 18 Oct 1721, ELIZABETH PHIPPS, b. at Lexington, MA, 10 Sep 1701 daughter of Samuel and Elizabeth (Stevens) Phipps.

125) iii MARY ABBOTT, b. at Sudbury, 10 Sep 1704; d. at Tolland, 12 Mar 1740; m. at Boston, 17 Dec 1725, NATHAN WHEELER, b. at Concord, MA, 2 Mar 1700 son of Edward and Sarah (Merriam) Wheeler; Nathan d. at Amenia, NY, 10 Jan 1766. Nathan second married Rachel Paulk on 23 Apr 1741.

iv SARAH ABBOTT, b. at Sudbury, 1 Feb 1706/7; d. at Cambridge, by 1737; m. at Watertown, 19 Mar 1723/4, NATHANIEL WILLIAMS, b. at Cambridge, 31 Oct 1699 son of John and Mary (-) Williams; Nathaniel d. at Arlington, 20 Jul 1748. Nathaniel married second 30 Jul 1738, Anna Davis. Sarah and Nathaniel do not seem to have children. At the probate of the estate, Nathaniel's father John asks that Nathaniel's brother Jason administer the estate with the concurrence of widow Anna. Mention is made of providing for the widow, but there is no mention of children or heirs.

126) v HANNAH ABBOTT, b. at Sudbury, Jul 1710; m. at Watertown, 6 May 1729, JOHN CADY, b. at Old Groton, CT, 9 Aug 1699 son of John and Elizabeth (-) Cady.

---

[84] Lemuel Abbott in the Descendants of George Abbott of Rowley questions whether it was Jemima Gray or Jemima Johnson that married John Abbot and which of the two married Samuel Holt. There is a marriage record for the marriage of Jemima Gray to Samuel Holt leaving Jemima Johnson as the wife of John Abbot.

[85] Abbott, *Descendants of George Abbott of Rowley*, p 55

[86] *Middlesex County, MA: Probate File Papers, 1648-1871.*Online database. *AmericanAncestors.org.* New England Historic Genealogical Society, 2014. Case 26

[87] *Middlesex County, MA: Probate File Papers, 1648-1871.*Online database. *AmericanAncestors.org.* New England Historic Genealogical Society, 2014. Case 1418

[88] Abbott, *Descendants of George Abbott of Rowley*

25) JOSIAH JOHNSON (*Mary Holt Johnson*[2], *Nicholas*[1]), b. at Andover, 29 Oct 1683 son of Thomas and Mary (Holt) Johnson; d. at Lancaster, 15 Oct 1727; m. 19 Jun 1711, ANNIS CHANDLER, b. at Andover, 24 Mar 1689 daughter of Thomas and Mary (Peters) Chandler. After Josiah's death, Annis married Benjamin Robbins.

Josiah and Annis had their oldest six children in Andover and relocated to Lancaster where their youngest son was born.

Josiah Johnson did not leave a will and his estate entered probate 24 October 1727[89] with Annis alias Agnes Johnson (and later named as Annis Robbins) as administratrix. The homestead consisting of 140 acres with buildings was valued at £578 and two additional parcels were valued at £22. Personal estate was valued at £116.9.0. The widow's dower was set off to Annis, and when the dower reverted to the estate at her remarriage, that part of the estate was distributed to eldest son David or his assignee Joseph Temple. David was then to pay £79.8 to each of the other children, named as Annis, Mary, Isaac, and Josiah.[90]

Josiah Johnson and Annis Chandler were parents of seven children.

127) i ANNIS JOHNSON, b. at Andover, 29 Aug 1712; d. at Templeton, MA, 31 Jul 1792; m. at Lancaster, 19 Nov 1728, JOSHUA CHURCH, b. at Watertown, 4 Mar 1708/9 son of Isaac and Mary (Hitchin) Church; Joshua d. at Watertown, 1 Apr 1766.

128) ii DAVID JOHNSON, b. at Andover, 20 Aug 1715; d. at Leominster, 10 Nov 1799; m. 1st at Lancaster, 22 Feb 1738/9, MARY WARNER, b. at Lancaster, 1716 daughter of John Warner; Mary d. at Leominster about 1795. David m. 2nd at Leominster, 5 Nov 1796, PRUDENCE DIVOL, b. at Lancaster, 24 Jan 1756 daughter of Ephraim and Elizabeth (Woods) Divol.

iii Daughter, b. 17 Dec 1717

129) iv MARY JOHNSON, b. at Andover, 10 Nov 1719; d. at Westmoreland, NH, 7 Apr 1793; m. at Lancaster, Oct 1741, JONATHAN KNIGHT, b. at Woburn, 19 Sep 1722 son of Amos and Elizabeth (Kendall) Knight; Jonathan d. at Westmoreland, 14 Jan 1809. Jonathan married second Anna Dean on 7 Nov 1793.

v JOSIAH JOHNSON, b. 2 Apr 1722; d. 4 Dec 1724.

130) vi ISAAC JOHNSON, b. at Andover, 17 Jul 1724; m. 1st a Leominster, 2 Jul 1746, LYDIA PIERCE, b. about 1729; Lydia d. at Walpole, NH, about 1779. Isaac m. 2nd at Walpole, 26 Jul 1780, ELIZABETH DEAN.

131) vii JOSIAH JOHNSON, b. at Lancaster, 5 Jun 1726; m. at Westford, 7 Mar 1750, SARAH HUNT, b. at Billerica, 23 Dec 1725 daughter of Joseph and Jemima (Russell) Hunt.

Children of Samuel Holt and Sarah Allen

Note: Samuel Holt son of Samuel and Sarah (Allen) Holt is covered in Family 15 with his wife Hannah Farnum.

26) JOHN HOLT (*Samuel*[2], *Nicholas*[1]), b. at Andover, about 1672 son of Samuel and Sarah (Allen) Holt; d. at Andover, after 1753; m. 1st at Andover, 16 Jan 1705/6, ELIZABETH PRESTON, b. 14 Feb 1682 daughter of Samuel and Susanna (Gutterson) Preston; Elizabeth d. by 1712. John m. 2nd at Andover, 17 Jul 1712, MEHITABLE WILSON who d. at Andover, 1732.[91]

John Holt was a husbandman in Andover and built his homestead on the corner of what is now Wildwood Road and Holt Road in Andover. John had inherited one-half of his father Samuel's 100-acre estate. On 12 March 1745 (recorded 12 January 1747), John Holt conveyed to his son John (called John 3rd in the records), one-half of his estate including the easterly half of the dwelling house. On 22 March 1753 (recorded 26 November 1761), John Holt conveyed to his eldest son John the third, for consideration of £12, remaining portions of the estate.[92]

There are no children known for John Holt and his first wife Elizabeth Preston. John Holt and Mehitable Wilson were parents of six children born at Andover.

132) i JOHN HOLT, baptized at Andover, May 1713; d. at Andover, 10 May 1794;[93] m. at Andover, 22 Jan 1746/7, DEBORAH STEVENS, b. about 1721 perhaps the daughter of John and Elizabeth (Chandler) Stevens; Deborah d. at Andover, 24 Jan 1809. [Genealogies report John had a first marriage to Rachel Fletcher of Chelmsford, but no record of the marriage or any children from the marriage was found. At least two of the

[89] The first probate document is dated 24 October 1728, but the inventory was taken 12 Jan 1727/8, so the October 1728 must be an error.

[90] *Middlesex County, MA: Probate File Papers, 1648-1871.*Online database. *AmericanAncestors.org.* New England Historic Genealogical Society, 2014. Case 12709

[91] The date of death for Mehitable Wilson Holt is that given by the Andover Historic Preservation web site. https://preservation.mhl.org/24-wildwood-road

[92] Massachusetts Land Records 1620-1986, Essex County, 90:130, 107:239

[93] Genealogies report his dying when he fell from a wagon while going to Wilton, but the town records report he died at Andover of old age. John [old age. CR2], May 10, 1794. [a. 81 y. CR2]

children attributed in genealogies to that marriage were the children of John Holt's nephew John Holt and his wife Rachel Farnum. Other children attributed to that marriage were children of John Holt and Mary Lewis in the records.]

ii MEHITABLE HOLT, baptized at Andover, 23 Oct 1715; nothing further known.

133) iii ELIZABETH HOLT, baptized at Andover, 8 Jun 1718; d. at Wilton, NH, 21 Mar 1776; m. at Andover, 18 Nov 1744, her second cousin, TIMOTHY HOLT (*Nicholas³, Nicholas², Nicholas¹*), b. at Andover, 17 Jan 1720/1 son of Nicholas and Dorcas (Abbott) Holt; Timothy d. at Wilton, Nov 1801.

iv ISAAC HOLT, b. 22 Jul 1721; d. 26 Jul 1724.

134) v JOSHUA HOLT, b. at Andover, 11 Jun 1724; m. 4 Feb 1748/9, RUTH BURNAP, b. at Reading, 18 Dec 1727 daughter of Samuel and Ruth (Huse) Burnap.[94]

135) vi DANIEL HOLT, b. at Andover, 1726; d. at Townsend, 1798 (probate 17 Nov 1798); m. about 1748, his second cousin, MEHITABLE HOLT (*Humphrey³, Henry², Nicholas¹*), baptized at Andover, 7 Feb 1725 daughter of Humphrey and Abigail (Fifield) Holt; Mehitable d. at Townsend, after 1810.

Children of Henry Holt and Sarah Ballard

Note: George Holt son of Henry and Sarah (Ballard) Holt is covered in Family 17 with his wife Elizabeth Farnum.

27) OLIVER HOLT (*Henry², Nicholas¹*), b. 14 Jan 1671/2 son of Henry and Sarah (Ballard) Holt; d. at Andover, 24 Dec 1747; m. 1st, 9 Mar 1697/8, HANNAH RUSSELL, b. at Andover, 28 Jun 1679 daughter of Robert and Mary (Marshall) Russell; Hannah d. at Andover, 16 May 1715. Oliver m. 2nd, 10 Jul 1716, MARY HUSE, b. at Newbury, 23 Mar 1690/1 daughter of Thomas and Hannah (Webster) Huse;[95] Mary d. 1 Sep 1778.

Oliver Holt was a farmer and blacksmith in Andover and lived in what was known as the Scotland district. Hannah Russell's father Robert was from Scotland. Oliver and Hannah were members of the South Church. Oliver and Hannah were parents of nine children before Hannah's death at age 35. Oliver then married Mary Huse of Newbury and they had four children.

There was a smallpox epidemic at the end of 1760 and two of the children and their spouses died in the epidemic: son Oliver and his wife Susannah Wright and son Jacob and his wife Margaret Dolliver.

Oliver Holt and Hannah Russell were parents of nine children.[96]

136) i OLIVER HOLT, b. at Andover, 26 Dec 1698; d. of smallpox, at Andover, 11 Nov 1760; m. 5 Jul 1722, SUSANNAH WRIGHT, b. at Andover, 24 Jul 1700 daughter of John and Mary (Wardwell) Wright; Susannah d. of smallpox, 1 Dec 1760.

137) ii URIAH HOLT, b. at Andover, 25 Jun 1701; d. at Lancaster, MA, 24 Aug 1741; m. 28 Sep 1725, SARAH WRIGHT, b. at Andover, 20 Mar 1696 daughter of Walter and Elizabeth (Peters) Wright. Sarah m. 2nd, at Harvard, 24 Jun 1747, Jonathan Cole (1696-1780).

iii ZEBADIAH HOLT, b. 30 Dec 1702; d. 17 Mar 1704.

47) iv BENJAMIN HOLT, b. at Andover, Jan 1704; d. at Andover, 1783 (probate 4 Nov 1783); m. 1st 6 Dec 1728, DOROTHY ABBOTT (widow of Braviter Gray who is also a Holt descendant), b. at Andover, about 1683 daughter of Thomas and Sarah (Stewart) Abbott; Dorothy d. at Andover, 22 Oct 1743. Benjamin m. 2nd 11 Apr 1745, ELIZABETH WILSON, b. at Hampton, NH, 1 Jul 1708 daughter of William and Elizabeth (Andrews) Wilson; Elizabeth d. at Andover, 28 Feb 1788.[97] Elizabeth was first married to Ezekiel Lovejoy.

v HANNAH HOLT, b. 9 May 1707; d. 1708.

---

[94] Belknap, *The Burnap Genealogy*, p 78

[95] The 1737 will of widow Hannah Huse includes a bequest to her daughter Mary Holt.

[96] All published genealogies include a daughter Priscilla for Oliver and Hannah and report that she married Nathan Chandler. It seems more likely that Priscilla was a daughter of Timothy Holt and Rhoda Chandler. There are two reasons for this. First, the 1758 will of Timothy Holt includes a bequest for his daughter Priscilla and notes that she is married (without providing the last names of his married daughters). Previously, Timothy's daughter Priscilla was described as having an unknown outcome, but it can be confirmed that she was married and living in 1758. Second, Benjamin Holt the son of Oliver Holt and Hannah Russell wrote a will (probate 1783) in which he names all his other living siblings and half-siblings and there is no sister Priscilla in his will. This at least suggests that he did not have a sister Priscilla, or not living at that time. I have chosen to list Priscilla Holt who married Nathan Chandler with the family of Timothy Holt and Rhoda Chandler.

[97] Elisabeth, wid., schirrous, bur. Feb. 28, 1788, a. 79 y. 8 m. CR2

138) vi DAVID HOLT, b. 5 Jun 1708; d. at Andover, 21 Aug 1747; m. 14 Sep 1732, SARAH RUSSELL, b. 5 Apr 1713 daughter of John and Sarah (Chandler) Russell; Sarah d. at Andover, 27 Apr 1781.

139) vii JONATHAN HOLT, b. 29 Aug 1711; d. at Andover, 14 Oct 1791; m. 10 Feb 1734/5, LYDIA BLANCHARD, b. at Andover, 21 Aug 1714 daughter of Thomas and Rose (Holmes) Blanchard; Lydia d. at Andover, 17 Dec 1788.

viii JOSEPH HOLT, b. 9 Feb 1713; d. 1714.

140) ix JACOB HOLT, b. 30 Mar 1714; d. 25 Dec 1760; m. 1st 29 Dec 1737, MARY OSGOOD, b. at Andover, 1706 daughter of Stephen and Hannah (Blanchard) Osgood; Mary d. 4 Nov 1745. Jacob m. 2nd 25 May 1747, MARGARET DOLLIVER; Margaret d. 22 Dec 1760.

Oliver Holt and Mary Huse were parents of four children born at Andover.

141) i THOMAS HOLT, b. at Andover, 23 Aug 1717; d. at Lancaster, MA, 3 Jul 1791; m. 1st at Lancaster, 21 Apr 1744, SUSANNAH PARKER, baptized at Wakefield, 2 Jun 1723 daughter of Stephen and Elizabeth (Batchelder) Parker;[98] Susannah d. by 1769. Thomas m. 2nd, intention at Lancaster, 17 Feb 1770, DINAH FOWLER (widow of Samuel Corey), b. at Rowley, 16 Jul 1739 daughter of Philip and Abigail (-) Fowler; Dinah d. at Lancaster, 9 Nov 1803.

142) ii MARY HOLT, b. at Andover, 29 Jul 1720; m. at Andover, 29 Oct 1745, DANIEL LOVEJOY, b. at Andover, Mar 1710 son of Nathaniel and Dorothy (Hoyt) Lovejoy.

143) iii WILLIAM HOLT, b. at Andover, 1 Apr 1727; d. at Lyndeborough; m. about 1759, BEULAH who has not been identified.

iv JUDITH HOLT, b. at Andover, 9 Apr 1731; d. by 1788; m. at Andover, 11 Jun 1777, as his second wife, JOSEPH BATCHELDER, b. about 1716 son of John and Bethia (Woodbury) Batchelder. Joseph was first married to Judith Rea and married third Anne Jenkins in 1789.

28) HENRY HOLT (*Henry2, Nicholas1*), b. 24 Jan 1673/4 son of Henry and Sarah (Ballard) Holt; d. at Andover, 7 Jun 1751; m. about 1700, MARTHA MARSTON, b. at Andover, 28 Jan 1679 daughter of John and Martha (Fuller) Marston; Martha d. at Andover, 15 Nov 1754.

Henry Holt and Martha Marston were parents of nine children born at Andover.

144) i JOSEPH HOLT, b. at Andover, 28 Nov 1702; d. at Reading, 1774 (probate); m. 1st at Reading, 7 Apr 1726, ABIGAIL RICH, b. at Reading 14 Jul 1708 daughter of John and Martha (-) Rich; Martha d. perhaps by 1755. Joseph was married either second or third to ELIZABETH CROSBY at Reading on 28 Apr 1763.[99]

145) ii BENJAMIN HOLT, b. at Andover, 1704; d. at Andover, 17 Mar 1779; m. at Andover, 30 Jan 1734/5, his second cousin, LYDIA HOLT (*Thomas3, Nicholas2, Nicholas1*), b. 2 Jan 1713/4 daughter of Thomas and Alice (Peabody) Holt; Lydia d. at Andover, 10 Sep 1778.

146) iii HENRY HOLT, b. at Andover, 1706; d. at Andover, 25 Sep 1754; m. at Andover, 6 Jan 1735/6, his second cousin, REBECCA GRAY (*Henry Gray3, Hannah Holt Gray2, Nicholas1*), b. at Andover, 1708 daughter of Henry and Mary (Blunt) Gray; Rebecca d. at Andover, Aug 1775.

147) iv SARAH HOLT, b. at Andover, 3 Jul 1707; m. at Andover, 12 Jun 1728, her second cousin MOSES PEABODY (*Lydia3, James2, Nicholas1*), b. 1706 son of Samuel and Lydia (Holt) Peabody; Moses d. at Andover, 13 Nov 1746.

148) v EPHRAIM HOLT, b. at Andover, May 1713; d. at Andover, 31 Dec 1749; m. 13 Feb 1735, PHEBE RUSSELL, b. at Andover, Jun 1716 daughter of John and Sarah (Chandler) Russell. Phebe married second Abraham Sheldon.

---

[98] The inventory of the estate of Stephen Parker in 1749 includes a note owed by Thomas Holt for £12.

[99] There has been disagreement about which Joseph Holt married whom, although that seems now resolved. The confusion is between this Joseph and Joseph born in 1686 son of James and Hannah (Allen) Holt. Some sources report one Joseph or the other married Abigail Rich and then Zerviah. Others suggest one or the other married Mary Harmon and went to York, Maine. Mary Harmon was born about 1686 and was a widow when she married Joseph Holt 28 Dec 1709 which would rule out Joseph born in 1702 as her husband. There is also documentary evidence in the form of deeds that establishes that Joseph the son of James went to York. The children of Joseph and Abigail Holt were born in Reading and are in the 1774 will of Joseph Holt. Although it is possible that he had a marriage between Abigail Rich and Elizabeth Crosby to a woman named Zerviah, no record of that was located. Joseph's widow at his death was Elizabeth and the children in the will are children with Abigail.

149) vi KETURAH HOLT, b. at Andover, Feb 1715; d. at Amherst, NH, 16 Jan 1797; m. at Andover, 17 Dec 1741, JOHN STEWART, b. about 1714 son of Robert Stewart; John d. at Amherst, after 1790.

150) vii MARY HOLT, b. at Andover, 28 Mar 1717; m. at Andover, 24 Oct 1744, JOSEPH PEABODY, b. at Boxford, 18 Dec 1718 son of Jonathan and Alice (Pearl) Peabody; Joseph d. at Boxford, 1751 (probate 5 May 1751).

viii HANNAH HOLT, b. at Andover, Aug 1719. She is perhaps the Hannah Holt who died at Andover, 27 Jan 1784 at age 64.

ix BETHIAH HOLT, b. Mar 1721; d. at Andover, 20 Jan 1805. Bethiah did not marry.

29) JAMES HOLT (*Henry*[2], *Nicholas*[1]), b. at Andover, 3 Sep 1675 son of Henry and Sarah (Ballard) Holt; d. at Andover, 1732 (probate 6 Nov 1732); m. 24 May 1705, SUSANNA PRESTON, b. at Andover, 30 Mar 1677 daughter of Samuel and Susanna (Gutterson) Preston; Susanna d. at Andover, 20 Feb 1741/2.

James Holt did not leave a will and his estate entered probate 6 November 1732 with James Holt as administrator. Real estate was valued at £277. The probate record includes a statement from Barzillai in 1738 that he has received payment from his brother James for his portion of the estate.[100]

James and Susanna were parents of four children born at Andover.[101]

i ABIGAIL HOLT, b. 20 Mar 1705/6; d. 10 Nov 1716.

151) ii JAMES HOLT, b. 1707; d. at Andover, 1751 (probate 16 Dec 1751); m. 22 Oct 1733, MARY CHANDLER (*Mehitable Russell Chandler*[4], *Phebe Johnson Russell*[3], *Mary Holt Johnson*[2], *Nicholas*[1]), b. at Andover, 4 Mar 1713 daughter of Joseph and Mehitable (Russell) Chandler; Mary d. at Andover, 10 Feb 1751.

iii ZERVIAH HOLT, b. Mar 1711/2; d. 9 Oct 1715.

152) iv BARZILLAI HOLT, b. 25 Oct 1716; d. at Boylston, MA, 7 Sep 1774; m. 1st 27 Aug 1738, ELIZABETH GOSS who has not been identified, Elizabeth d. about 1756. Barzillai m. 2nd at Lancaster, 22 Feb 1759, LOIS PIKE (widow of Isaac Allard).

30) SARAH HOLT (*Henry*[2], *Nicholas*[1]), b. at Andover, 17 Jun 1678 daughter of Henry and Sarah (Ballard) Holt; d. at Lyndeborough, NH, 1 Oct 1757; m. 18 Feb 1707, JOHN CRAM, b. at Hampton Falls, 12 Jan 1685 son of Thomas and Elizabeth (Weare) Cram; John d. at Amherst, NH, 1759.[102]

John Cram is believed to be the first official settler of Salem-Canada which became Lyndeborough. The family including the children, spouses of children, and grandchildren arrived in 1737. John and Sarah started their family in Hampton Falls where their first three children were born. In 1712, the family moved to Woburn where their youngest seven children, including two sets of twins, were born. On 16 May 1727, John Cram sold his property in Woburn to Benjamin Abbott and John and Sarah went to Wilmington, Massachusetts where they joined the church in 1733. They were then finally in Salem-Canada.

As an early settler in Salem-Canada, John was active in completing clearing for the roads and building the meeting house. In 1738, he began the process of building a sawmill which was operational by 1740.[103]

Sarah Holt and John Cram were parents of ten children.

153) i JONATHAN CRAM, b. at Wilmington, MA, 21 Feb 1708; d. at Lyndeborough, 23 Jan 1790; m. 1 Dec 1732, MARY CHAMBERLAIN, b. at Billerica, 20 Jan 1706 daughter of Daniel and Mary (-) Chamberlain; Mary d. at Lyndeborough, 5 Jan 1770.

154) ii HUMPHREY CRAM, b. at Hampton Falls, 8 Nov 1710; m. at Lisbon, CT, 22 Feb 1733, his second cousin, HANNAH BLUNT, b. at Andover, Jul 1710 daughter of Ambrose and Mehitable (Johnson) Blunt; Hannah d. at Holland, MA, 17 Jun 1776.

155) iii PHEBE CRAM, b. at Hampton, NH, 8 Jul 1712; m. at Hampton, 8 Jan 1735, MOSES STILES, b. at Boxford, 10 Feb 1705 son of Samuel and Elizabeth (Cary) Stiles.

iv JOSEPH CRAM, b. 23 Sep 1713; d. at Lyndeborough, 24 Dec 1794. No information on a marriage for Joseph was found.

---

[100] *Essex County, MA: Probate File Papers, 1638-1881.*Online database. *AmericanAncestors.org.* New England Historic Genealogical Society, 2014. Case 13648

[101] Durrie's Holt genealogy adds a second daughter Abigail who died unmarried reported as 1756. There is no birth or death record. I believe this to be Abigail daughter of James and Susanna (Nurs) Holt born in 1736 and died in 1750.

[102] Donovan, *History of Lyndeborough*, p 710

[103] Donovan, *History of Lyndeborough*, pp 597-599

156) v HULDAH CRAM, b. at Hampton, NH, 5 May 1715; d. at Brooklyn, CT, 21 Aug 1810; m. 22 Jul 1742, as his second wife, EPHRAIM WOODWARD, b. 8 Jan 1710 son of John and Hannah (Hyde) Woodward; Ephraim d. at Canterbury, CT, 15 Jan 1782. Ephraim was first married to Hannah Williams.

157) vi JOHN CRAM, b. at Hampton, NH, 10 Apr 1717; m. about 1740, SARAH who has not been identified. John and Sarah lived in Wilton where the births of eleven children are recorded.

158) vii SARAH CRAM, b. at Hampton, NH, 27 Jun 1719; d. at Lyndeborough, 15 Oct 1777; m. EPHRAIM PUTNAM, b. at Danvers, 10 Feb 1719 son of Nathaniel and Hannah (Roberts) Putnam; Ephraim d. At Lyndeborough, 13 Nov 1777.

159) viii ELIZABETH CRAM, b. at Hampton, NH, 27 Jun 1719; d. at Lyndeborough, 30 Apr 1806; m. about 1741, JONATHAN CHAMBERLAIN, b. at Chelmsford, 11 Feb 1711/2 son of Samuel and Abigail (Hill) Chamberlain.

ix ELI CRAM, b. 10 Mar 1721

160) x BENJAMIN CRAM, b. at Hampton, NH, 10 Mar 1721; d. at Lyndeborough, 1823; m. about 1747, ELIZABETH who has not been identified.

31) DINAH HOLT (*Henry*[2], *Nicholas*[1]), b. at Andover, 23 May 1681 daughter of Henry and Sarah (Ballard) Holt; d. at Wilmington, MA, 7 Jan 1738; m. at Woburn, 3 Jul 1705, DANIEL PIERCE, b. at Woburn, 7 Oct 1676 son of John and Deborah (Converse) Pierce; Daniel d. at Harvard, MA, 14 Mar 1754.

Daniel and Dinah resided in Woburn. Daniel was a legislator of the General Court.[104] Dinah and Daniel were parents of eight children born at Woburn.

i ABIGAIL PIERCE, b. 18 May 1706; m. at Woburn, 26 Jul 1726, EPHRAIM BUCK. Abigail likely died in the first year of marriage without children. Ephraim remarried on 9 May 1728 to Mary Wood.

161) ii THOMAS PIERCE, b. at Woburn, 30 Oct 1707; d. at Wilmington, MA, 19 May 1790; m. at Woburn, 27 Jul 1732, HANNAH THOMPSON, b. at Woburn, 10 Jan 1705 daughter of Joshua and Martha (Dale) Thompson; Hannah d. at Wilmington, 10 Aug 1767.

iii SARAH PIERCE, b. 30 May 1709; d. at Boylston, 20 Nov 1794; m. at Harvard, 19 May 1746, DANIEL ALBERT, b. about 1701; Daniel d. at Lancaster, 22 Jan 1769. Sarah and Daniel do not seem to have had children.

162) iv JOSEPH PIERCE, b. 5 May 1711;[105] m. by 1734, DEBORAH who has not been identified but who may be Deborah Frost daughter of Thomas Frost.

163) v DANIEL PIERCE, b. 23 Jun 1714; d. at Leominster, May 1759 (probate Jun 1759); m. at Wilmington, 23 Dec 1741, SARAH BUCK, b. at Woburn, 16 Apr 1716 daughter of Samuel and Hannah (-) Buck; Sarah d. about 1768 (reversion of dower to the estate).

164) vi JOHN PIERCE, b. at Woburn, 23 May 1716; d. about 1779;[106] m. 1st at Harvard, 22 Nov 1744, HANNAH STONE, b. at Groton, 18 Apr 1726 daughter of Simon and Sarah (Turner) Stone;[107] Hannah d. about 1746. John m. 2nd at Harvard, 10 Mar 1747, HANNAH HOUGHTON, b. about 1727 daughter of Thomas and Meriah (Moore) Houghton;[108] Hannah d. at Harvard, 16 Apr 1811.

vii DINAH PIERCE, b. at Woburn, 2 Nov 1719; nothing further known.

---

[104] Massachusetts: Legislators of the General Court, 1691-1780 (Online database: *AmericanAncestors.org*, New England Historic Genealogical Society, 2002)

[105] Pierce's *Pierce Genealogy*, and other sources, report that this Joseph married Abigail Green and had four children. However, Joseph who married Abigail Green and second Susannah Gleason was likely Joseph born at Woburn in 1714 son of Joseph and Mary (-) Pierce. Joseph Pierce who had married Abigail and then Susannah died in 1754. His probate documents include a statement dated 14 Jan 1754 signed by two of Joseph's unmarried sisters, Mary and Elizabeth, agreeing to the appointment of John Gleason as administrator of the estate. "Pray you appoint Mr. John Gleason to administer upon the estate of our brother Joseph Pierce deceased." This is signed (by mark) by Elizabeth Pierce and Mary Pierce. These two single ladies are the daughters of Joseph and Mary (-) Pierce (which can be established by birth and death records). As Daniel Pierce and Dinah Holt did not have daughters Mary and Elizabeth, Joseph who married Abigail Green is not this Joseph. The probate records do confirm that Joseph Pierce who died in 1754 was not only the brother of Elizabeth and Mary but the father of five children by his two wives.

[106] Pierce, *Pierce Genealogy* reports that John is reported to have left home during the Revolutionary War and is believed to have been killed in New York.

[107] The 1746 probate of Simon Stone of Harvard includes John Pierce signing as an heir agreeing to the distribution.

[108] The 1764 will of Thomas Houghton includes a bequest to "my daughter Pierce."

165) viii KEZIA PIERCE, b. at Woburn, 9 May 1723; d. likely at Westmoreland, NH, after 1780 when she signed probate records as Kezia Robbins; m. at Harvard, 16 Apr 1744, ISAAC STONE, b. at Groton, 17 May 1723 son of Simon and Sarah (Turner) Stone; Isaac d. at Westmoreland, 1776 (probate 1776). Kezia m. 2nd Mr. Robbins who has not been identified.

32) PAUL HOLT, b. at Andover, 7 Feb 1684 son of Henry and Sarah (Ballard) Holt; d. at Hampton, CT, 6 May 1742; m.10 Jan 1711/2 his first cousin, ABIGAIL HOLT (*Nicholas[2], Nicholas[1]*), b. at Andover, 23 Nov 1688 daughter of Nicholas and Mary (Russell) Holt; Abigail d. at Hampton, 12 Aug 1742.

Paul and Abigail had their two children in Andover and then relocated to Hampton, Connecticut in 1726 along with Paul's brother George.

166) i ABIGAIL HOLT, b. 21 Aug 1716; d. at Hampton, CT, 3 Nov 1749; m. 3 Dec 1736, JONATHAN KINGSBURY, b. 1712 son of Thomas and Margaret (Haines) Kingsbury; Jonathan d. at Hampton, 28 Dec 1770. Jonathan married second Hannah Clark on 9 Jan 1751 and married third Sarah *How* Ballard the widow of John Ballard.

167) ii PAUL HOLT, b. Aug 1720; d. at Hampton, CT, 21 Dec 1804; m. 20 Jan 1742, MEHITABLE CHANDLER, b. 12 Apr 1719 daughter of Philemon and Hannah (Clary) Chandler; Mehitable d. at Hampton, 10 May 1773. Paul m. 2nd, 4 Jan 1774, MARY SPENCER.

33) ZERVIAH HOLT (*Henry[2], Nicholas[1]*), b. at Andover, 24 Mar 1688 daughter of Henry and Sarah (Ballard) Holt; d. at Andover, 26 Mar 1768; m. 6 May 1713, her first cousin once removed, JONATHAN ABBOTT (*Sarah Farnum Abbott[3], Elizabeth Holt Farnum[2], Nicholas[1]*), b. at Andover, Sep 1687 son of Benjamin and Sarah (Farnum) Abbott; Jonathan d. at Andover, 21 Mar 1770.

The births of eight children of Jonathan Abbott and Zerviah Holt are recorded at Andover. Published genealogies include a daughter Mary in this family, but no record of her was found.

168) i JONATHAN ABBOT, b. at Andover, Dec 1714; d. 31 May 1794; m. 1st 8 Oct 1739, his second cousin, MARTHA LOVEJOY (*Henry Lovejoy[4], Mary Farnum Lovejoy[3], Elizabeth Holt Farnum[2], Nicholas[1]*), b. 2 Nov 1720 daughter of Henry and Sarah (Farnum) Lovejoy; Martha d. about 1768. Jonathan m. 2nd as her second husband, his second cousin MARY ABBOTT, b. at Andover, 12 Mar 1722/3 daughter of George and Mary (Phillips) Abbott; Mary d. at Andover, 8 Aug 1792. Mary Abbott was first married to Stephen Abbott.

169) ii DAVID ABBOTT, b. at Andover, Dec 1716; d. 1777 at Rockingham, NH (probate 31 Dec 1777); m. 10 Aug 1741, his second cousin, once removed, HANNAH CHANDLER (*Mehitable Russell Chandler[4], Phebe Johnson Russell[3], Mary Holt Johnson[2], Nicholas[1]*), b. 1724 daughter of Joseph and Mehitable (Russell) Chandler; Hannah's death not known but she was living at the time of her husband's will.

iii NATHAN ABBOTT, b. Apr 1719; d. 28 Jun 1798; m. 12 Mar 1744/5, his second cousin, ABIGAIL AMES, b. about 1722 daughter of Samuel and Hannah (Stevens) Ames; Abigail d. 27 Aug 1812. Nathan Abbott and Abigail Ames did not have any children. Nathan Abbott wrote his will 21 March 1776 and the estate entered probate 3 September 1798. Dearly beloved wife Abigail receives "all my household stuff proper for woman's use." She receives other provisions for her support and the use and improvements of one-third of the real property. He makes a bequest to his "cousin" Nathan Abbott who is the son of his brother Job who is deceased. The nephew Nathan is named executor and has the remainder of the estate bequeathed to him.

170) iv ZERVIAH ABBOTT, b. at Andover, Aug 1722; d. likely at Pembroke, NH; m. 17 Sep 1745, EPHRAIM BLUNT, b. 5 Feb 1720/1 son of William and Sarah (Foster) Blunt.

171) v JOB ABBOTT, b. at Andover, 3 Oct 1724; d. likely at Pembroke, NH; m. about 1751, his second cousin, SARAH ABBOTT (*Abigail Farnum Abbott[4], Ralph Farnum[3], Elizabeth Holt Farnum[2], Nicholas[1]*), b. 13 Aug 1730 daughter of James and Abigail (Farnum) Abbott. Sarah m. 2nd about 1765, RICHARD EASTMAN, b. at Haverhill, 9 Aug 1712 son of Jonathan and Hannah (Green) Eastman; Richard d. at Lovell, ME, 29 Dec 1807. Richard Eastman m. 1st 15 Nov 1737, MARY LOVEJOY (*Henry Lovejoy[4], Mary Farnum Lovejoy[3], Elizabeth Holt Farnum[2], Nicholas[1]*), b. at Andover, Dec 1718 daughter of Henry and Sarah (Farnum) Lovejoy.

172) vi SAMUEL ABBOTT, b. at Andover, 20 Sep 1727; m. 12 Jul 1749, MIRIAM STEVENS whose origins are undetermined but may be the Miriam baptized in 1730 at Newbury.

vii JEREMIAH ABBOTT, b. 30 Sep 1733; d. 1755 in the French and Indian War.

34) KETURAH HOLT (*Henry², Nicholas¹*), b. at Andover, 15 Dec 1690 daughter of Henry and Sarah (Ballard) Holt; d. at Hampton, CT, 2 Oct 1781; m. 16 Feb 1725/5, her first cousin, JOSHUA HOLT (*Nicholas², Nicholas¹*), b. at Andover, 1703 son of Nicholas and Mary (Russell) Holt; Joshua d. at Hampton, 26 Jan 1787.

Keturah and Joshua Holt settled in Windham around the time of their marriage, and their four children were born there.

173) i DINAH HOLT, b. at Windham, 17 Mar 1725/6; d. at Willington, 25 Sep 1805; m. at Windham, 6 Nov 1746, TIMOTHY PEARL, b. at Windham, 24 Oct 1723 son of Timothy and Elizabeth (Stevens) Pearl; Timothy d. at Willington, 19 Oct 1789.

174) ii JOSHUA HOLT, b. at Windham, 19 Mar 1728; d. at Hampton, 5 Jul 1791; m. 1st 28 Jun 1749, MARY ABBOTT, b. at Pomfret, 3 Mar 1728 daughter of Paul and Elizabeth (Gray) Abbott; Mary d. at Windham, 10 Aug 1769. Joshua m. 2nd, 26 Apr 1770, SUSANNA GOODELL, b. at Pomfret, 22 Jan 1728 daughter of Zachariah and Hannah (Cheney) Goodell; Susanna d. at Windham, 28 Jun 1812. Susanna was first married to Samuel Darby.

iii KETURAH HOLT, b. at Windham, 22 Nov 1729; d. at Willington, 1805; m. at Willington, 17 Jun 1750, JOHN PEARL, b. at Windham, 20 Jan 1725/6 son of Timothy and Elizabeth (Stevens) Pearl. There do not seem to be any children for this couple. There is a probate record for Keturah from 1805. The distributions of the estate of Keturah Holt Pearl are to the following persons: sister Dinah Pearl; sister Phebe Goodale; and heirs of brother Joshua Holt who is deceased.

175) iv PHEBE HOLT, b. at Windham, 16 Aug 1734; d. at South Windsor, CT, 7 Feb 1808; m. at Pomfret, 13 Feb 1755, EBENEZER GOODALE, b. at Pomfret, 12 Sep 1729 son of Ebenezer and Experience (Lyon) Goodale; Ebenezer d. at East Windsor, 1794.

35) HUMPHREY HOLT (*Henry², Nicholas¹*), b. at Andover, 22 Sep 1693 son of Henry and Sarah (Ballard) Holt; d. at Andover, 8 Aug 1754; m. 30 Dec 1715, ABIGAIL FIFIELD, b. at Hampton, NH, about 1695 possibly the daughter of Benjamin and Mary (Calcord) Fifield;[109] Abigail d. after 1754.

Humphrey Holt was a farmer in Andover where he and Abigail were parents of eight children.

In his will written 25 July 1754 (probate 14 October 1754), Humphrey Holt bequeaths to beloved wife Abigail the use of the east room of the new dwelling house, chamber above, and the cellar. There are also specific provisions for her support, a lengthy list which includes eight pounds of good tobacco per year. Oldest son Fifield receives all the lands in Suncook and all the stock of brute creatures. Son William receives five shillings, which together with the tract of land at Lunenburg, constitutes his full portion. Son Humphrey receives five shillings in addition to the £186.13.4 he has received. Son Jonathan receives two shillings in addition to the tract of land in Lunenburg he received. Daughter Mehitable Holt wife of Daniel Holt receives £4 in addition to £9.6.8 she has received. Daughter Shua Holt receives £13.6.8. Clothing is to be divided among his four sons and the household items between his two daughters after the decease of their mother. Son Fifield Holt was named sole executor.[110] Real estate was valued at £265.6.8

176) i FIFIELD HOLT, b. at Andover, 28 Jul 1717; d. at Wilton, NH, after 1776; m. at Salem, 31 Aug 1741, ABIGAIL TAYLOR who has not been identified.

ii ANNE HOLT, b. 29 Apr 1719; d. 18 Oct 1741.

177) iii WILLIAM HOLT, baptized at Andover, 11 Jun 1721; d. at Lunenburg, 14 Nov 1759; m. at Lunenburg, 30 Jul 1744, MARY MARTIN, b. at Ipswich, 24 Sep 1720 daughter of John and Jane (Durkee) Martin;[111] Mary d. after 1760.

178) iv HUMPHREY HOLT, baptized at Andover, 19 May 1723; d. at Andover, 29 Mar 1785; m. 1st at Andover, 1 Jan 1745, ELIZABETH KIMBALL, baptized at Boxford, Aug 1724 daughter of John and Elizabeth (Chapman) Kimball; Elizabeth d. 30 Jan 1749. Humphrey m. 2nd 30 Nov 1749, MARY HOLTON, b. about 1729; Mary d. at Andover, 13 Jul 1774. Humphrey m. 3rd at Danvers, 21 Sep 1775, ABIGAIL VERY, b. about 1727; Abigail d. at Andover, 15 Apr 1808.

[109] Dow and Dow, *History of the Town of Hampton*, p 708; Abigail is described as "of Hampton, NH" at the time of marriage; Benjamin and Mary Fifield of Hampton are reported to have a daughter Abigail.

[110] Essex County, MA: Probate File Papers, 1638-1881.Online database. AmericanAncestors.org. New England Historic Genealogical Society, 2014. Case 13643

[111] The 1757 will of John Martin of Ipswich (with wife named Jane) includes a bequest to his daughter Mary Holt.

135) v MEHITABLE HOLT, baptized at Andover, 7 Feb 1725; d. at Townsend, MA, after 1810; m. about 1748, her second cousin, DANIEL HOLT (*John³, Samuel², Nicholas¹*), b. at Andover, 1726 son of John and Mehitable (Wilson) Holt; Daniel d. at Townsend, 1798 (probate 17 Nov 1798).

vi SARAH HOLT baptized 13 Nov 1726; d. 6 May 1729.

179) vii JONATHAN HOLT, b. at Andover, about 1727; d. at Lunenburg, 17 Mar 1805; m. 1st 25 Feb 1752, RACHEL TAYLOR; Rachel d. at Fitchburg, 25 Apr 1753. Jonathan m. 2nd at Andover, 14 Nov 1753, his second cousin once removed, SUSANNA HOLT (*James⁴, Timothy³, James², Nicholas¹*), likely b. at Andover, 18 Apr 1737 daughter of James and Susanna (Nurs) Holt; Susanna d. 11 Jul 1801. Jonathan m. 3rd, 13 Jan 1802, AZUBA BUTTERFIELD, b. at Townsend, 13 Nov 1767 daughter of Eleazer and Mary (Wright) Butterfield; Azuba d. at Fitchburg, 24 Jan 1852.

180) viii SHUAH HOLT, b. at Andover, 21 Mar 1728/9; d. at Andover, 9 Jan 1766; m. 6 Nov 1754, her second cousin once removed, JONATHAN HOLT (*Samuel⁴, Samuel³, Samuel², Nicholas¹*), b. at Andover, 5 Feb 1728/9 son of Samuel and Jemima (Gray) Holt; Jonathan d. at Andover, 23 Sep 1792. Jonathan m. 2nd 24 Sep 1766, BETTY GOULD; Betty d. at Andover, 16 Feb 1774. Jonathan m. 3rd 23 May 1775, ELEANOR JOHNSON.

Children of Nicholas Holt and Mary Russell

Note: Two of the children of Nicholas Holt and Mary Russel are covered earlier. Daughter Abigail Holt is covered in Family 32 with her husband Paul Holt. Son Joshua Holt is covered in Family 34 with his wife Keturah Holt.

36) MARY HOLT (*Nicholas², Nicholas¹*), b. at Andover, 13 Feb 1680/1 daughter of Nicholas and Mary (Russell) Holt; d. at Andover, 9 Feb 1714/5; m. at Andover, 19 Sep 1705, JOSIAH INGALLS, b. at Andover, 28 Feb 1676 son of Henry and Mary (Osgood) Ingalls. Josiah d. at Andover, 14 Aug 1755.[112] After Mary's death, Josiah married Esther Frye.

Mary Holt and Josiah Ingalls were parents of five children born at Andover. Josiah had two children with his second wife Esther Frye, a daughter Anne born 6 June 1717 and a son Josiah born 4 August 1719. On 30 December 1743, Josiah Ingalls conveyed to his son Josiah Ingalls, one-half of his property and dwelling house in Andover. On 6 January 1742 (executed 30 December 1743), Josiah conveyed to his son Josiah his full right to grant land known as Rowley Cannada.[113]

i Son b. 15 Mar 1706

181) ii PHEBE INGALLS, b. at Andover 1708; d. after 1784 perhaps in Poland, ME;[114] m. at Andover, 12 Aug 1731, JAMES PARKER, b. at Andover, 12 Oct 1696 son of John and Hannah (Brown) Parker; James d. at Andover, 1782 (will 1773; probate 1782).

iii ABIGAIL INGALLS, b. 1710; nothing further known.

iv Child, perhaps Josiah, b. 22 May 1712; died young.

v RACHEL INGALLS, b. 3 Sep 1713; nothing further known.

37) NICHOLAS HOLT (*Nicholas², Nicholas¹*), b. at Andover, 21 Dec 1683 son of Nicholas and Mary (Russell) Holt; d. at Andover, 1 Dec 1756; m. 1st, 16 Sep 1708, MARY MANNING; Mary d. at Andover, 3 Mar 1715/6. Nicholas m. 2nd, 12 Apr 1717, DORCAS ABBOTT, b. at Andover, 25 Apr 1698 daughter of Timothy and Hannah (Graves) Abbott; Dorcas d. at Andover, 25 Oct 1758.

Nicholas Holt was a yeoman in Andover. In his will written 29 December 1752 (probate 27 December 1756), Nicholas Holt makes bequests to the following persons: dearly beloved wife Dorcas, eldest and well-beloved son Benjamin, well-beloved son Stephen, well-beloved son Nicholas, well-beloved son Timothy, well-beloved son James, well-beloved son Nathan, well-beloved son Joshua, well-beloved son Daniel, eldest and well-beloved daughter Mary, and well-beloved daughter Dorcas. Real property included the homestead valued at £266.13.4 and several other tracts of land with an additional value of about £340.[115]

Nicholas Holt and Mary Manning were parents of four children.

---

[112] Josiah, Aug. 14, 1755, in his 79th y.

[113] Massachusetts Land Records, Essex County, 93:18, 93:19

[114] Phebe was living in November 1784 when she consented to the sale of the dwelling house and land in Andover by her son James Parker, then of Poland, ME. It seems possible that Phebe and her daughter accompanied James to Poland.

[115] *Essex County, MA: Probate File Papers, 1638-1881. Probate of Nicholas Holt, 27 Dec 1756, Case number 13680.*

182) i BENJAMIN HOLT, b. at Andover, 23 Jul 1709; d. at Pembroke, NH, 1774 (probate 26 Oct 1774); m. at Andover, 7 Apr 1737, SARAH FRYE, b. May 1717 daughter of Nathan and Sarah (Bridges) Frye; Sarah d. at Pembroke, 1804.

183) ii MARY HOLT, b. at Andover, 1 Aug 1711; m. 1st at Andover, 4 Mar 1735/6, WILLIAM CHANDLER, b. 14 Jul 1704 son of Thomas and Mary (Stevens) Chandler; William d. at Andover, 15 Apr 1741. William Chandler was first married to Elizabeth Blanchard. Mary Holt m. 2nd, 29 May 1745, JEREMIAH OSGOOD, b. at Andover, 1702 son of Christopher and Sarah (-) Osgood. Jeremiah was first married to Lydia Poor.

184) iii STEPHEN HOLT, b. at Andover, 14 Apr 1713; d. at Andover, 25 Apr 1798; m. 12 Jul 1739, his second cousin once removed, MARY FARNUM (*John Farnum4, John Farnum3, Elizabeth Holt Farnum2, Nicholas1*), b. at Andover, 21 May 1714 daughter of John and Joanna (Barker) Farnum; Mary d. at Andover, 9 Aug 1802.

185) iv NICHOLAS HOLT, b. at Andover, 29 Feb 1716; d. at Blue Hill, ME, 16 Mar 1798; m. 1st at Andover, 26 Apr 1739, HANNAH OSGOOD, baptized at Andover, 1 Jun 1718 daughter of Ezekiel and Rebecca (Wardwell) Osgood;[116] Hannah d. at Andover, 1 Sep 1744. Nicholas m. 2nd at Andover, 7 Feb 1750/1, LOIS PHELPS, b. at Reading, about 1720 daughter of Samuel and Elizabeth (Bare) Phelps; Lois d. Jan 1814.

Nicholas and Dorcas had six children all born at Andover.

133) i TIMOTHY HOLT, b. 17 Jan 1720/1; d. at Wilton, NH, Nov 1801; m. 18 Sep 1744, his second cousin, ELIZABETH HOLT (*John3, Samuel2, Nicholas1*), b. Jun 1718 daughter of John and Mehitable (Wilson) Holt; Elizabeth d. at Wilton 21 Mar 1776.

186) ii JAMES HOLT, b. 13 Jan 1722/3; d. 22 Aug 1812; m. 1st, SARAH ABBOTT, b. 2 Aug 1718 daughter of Benjamin and Elizabeth (Abbott) Abbott; Sarah d. 5 Mar 1778. James m. 2nd, 22 Jun 1779, PHEBE BALLARD, b. at Andover, 25 Jul 1738 daughter of Josiah and Mary (Chandler) Ballard and widow of Abiel Abbot; Phebe d. 9 Jun 1815. Phebe Ballard was first married to ABIEL ABBOTT, b. at Andover, 24 Jul 1735 son of Benjamin and Abigail (Abbott) Abbott; Abiel d. at Andover, 24 Jun 1764.

187) iii NATHAN HOLT, b. 28 Feb 1725; d. at Danvers, 2 Aug 1792; m. 4 Aug 1757, SARAH ABBOTT, b. 14 Jan 1729/30 daughter of George and Mary (Phillips) Abbott; Sarah d. 29 Dec 1797.

188) iv DORCAS HOLT, b. 4 Sep 1727; death unknown but may have been at Wilton, NH; m. 26 Jan 1749, as his second wife, her first cousin, THOMAS HOLT (*Thomas3, Nicholas2, Nicholas1*), b. Mar 1711/2 son of Thomas and Alice (Peabody) Holt; Thomas d. at Andover, 21 Nov 1776. Thomas m. 1st, 15 Oct 1734, HANNAH KIMBALL, baptized at Boxford, 7 Sep 1712 daughter of John and Elizabeth (Chapman) Kimball; Hannah d. at Andover, 12 Jun 1748.

189) v JOSHUA HOLT, b. 30 Jun 1730; d. 24 Jul 1810; m. 2 Dec 1755, his second cousin once removed, PHEBE FARNUM (*Timothy Farnum4, Ephraim Farnum3, Elizabeth Holt Farnum2, Nicholas1*), b. 10 Oct 1731 daughter of Timothy and Dinah (Ingalls) Farnum; Phebe d. 26 Jan 1806.

190) vi DANIEL HOLT, b. 10 Feb 1732/3; d. at Andover, 15 Feb 1796; m. 29 Nov 1759, his first cousin once removed, HANNAH HOLT (*Thomas4, Thomas3, Nicholas2, Nicholas1*), b. 11 Feb 1738/9 daughter of Thomas and Hannah (Kimball) Holt; Hannah d. at Andover, 2 Aug 1831.

38) THOMAS HOLT (*Nicholas2, Nicholas1*), b. at Andover, 16 Aug 1686 son of Nicholas and Mary (Russell) Holt; d. at Andover, 12 Jan 1767; m. 1st, at Andover, 14 Dec 1708, ALICE PEABODY, b. at Andover, 5 Jan 1685 daughter of Joseph and Bethiah (Bridges) Peabody; Alice d. at Andover, 29 Jul 1726. Thomas m. 2nd, at Boxford, 16 Nov 1727, ABIGAIL POORE (widow of John Fiske), b. at Newbury, 9 Sep 1680 daughter of Henry and Abigail (Hale) Poore; Abigail d. at Andover, 20 Nov 1766.

Thomas Holt was a farmer in Andover. He and his wife Alice were received into Andover south church on 7 July 1723.[117]

In his will written 11 February 1766, Thomas Holt makes bequests to the following persons: eldest and well beloved son Thomas, two grandsons Abiel and Joseph Holt who are the sons of his deceased son Joseph, his fourth son William, his fifth and well beloved son Daniel, well beloved daughter Allace, and well beloved daughter Lydia. Clothing is divided among three sons: Thomas, William, and Daniel. He also makes son Thomas responsible for the care of his mother-in-law (stepmother Abigail) and after her death to return household items to her two children John Fisk and Phebe Abbott.

Thomas Holt and Alice Peabody were parents of eight children born at Andover.

---

[116] The 1740 will of Ezekiel Osgood includes a bequest to his daughter Hannah Osgood alias Holt.

[117] South Church, *Historical Manual of South Church in Andover*, p 128

188) i THOMAS HOLT, b. at Andover, Mar 1711/2; d. at Andover, 21 Nov 1776; m. 1st, 15 Oct 1734, HANNAH KIMBALL, baptized at Boxford, 7 Sep 1712 daughter of John and Elizabeth (Chapman) Kimball; Hannah d. at Andover, 12 Jun 1748. Thomas m. 2nd, 26 Jan 1749, his first cousin, DORCAS HOLT (*Nicholas[3], Nicholas[2], Nicholas[1]*), b. at Andover, 4 Sep 1727 daughter of Nicholas and Dorcas (Abbott) Holt.

145) ii LYDIA HOLT, b. at Andover, 2 Jan 1713/4; d. 10 Sep 1778; m. at Andover, 30 Jan 1734/5, her second cousin BENJAMIN HOLT (*Henry[3], Henry[2], Nicholas[1]*), b. 1704 son of Henry and Mary (Marston) Holt; Benjamin d. at Andover, 17 Mar 1779.

191) iii JOSEPH HOLT, b. at Andover, 28 Feb 1715/6; d. at Lunenburg, 1754; m. 1st 14 Aug 1742, MARY ABBOTT, b. at Andover, 4 Aug 1713 daughter of Stephen and Sarah (Stevens) Abbott; Mary d. at Lunenburg, 5 Aug 1748. Joseph m. 2nd at Lunenburg, 20 May 1749, DORCAS BOYNTON, b. at Groton, MA, 21 Dec 1715 daughter of Benoni and Anna (Mighill) Boynton; Dorcas d. at Lunenburg, 11 Jun 1775. Dorcas Boynton was first married to Thomas Frost.

iv ABIEL HOLT, b. 25 Apr 1718; d. 11 Sep 1744.

192) v WILLIAM HOLT, b. at Andover, 10 Dec 1720; d. at Hampton, CT, 2 Aug 1793; m. 1st at Hampton, 14 Jul 1742, his first cousin, HANNAH HOLT (*Abiel[3], Nicholas[2], Nicholas[1]*), b. at Windham, CT, 17 Apr 1723 daughter of Abiel and Hannah (Abbott) Holt; Hannah d. at Windham, 25 Jan 1750/1. William m. 2nd at Windham, 14 May 1752, SYBEL DURKEE, b. at Windham, 10 Jan 1731 daughter of Stephen and Lois (Moulton) Durkee;[118] Sybel d. at Hampton, 11 Jan 1794.

193) vi ALICE HOLT, b. at Andover, about 1722; d. at Andover, 1762 (probate 22 Nov 1762); m. 13 Mar 1739/40, as his third wife, JOHN BARNARD, b. at Andover, 16 Apr 1697 son of John and Naomi (Hoyt) Barnard; John d. at Andover, 1752 (probate 15 Jun 1752). John was first married to Sarah Osgood and second married to Mehitable Stiles.

vii DANIEL HOLT, b. 18 Sep 1723; living in 1767 but nothing further known.

viii JONATHAN HOLT, b. 18 May 1726; d. 2 Jun 1726.

39) ROBERT HOLT (*Nicholas[2], Nicholas[1]*), b. at Andover, 23 Jan 1695/6 son of Nicholas and Mary (Russell) Holt; d. at Windham, CT, 1768 (probate 4 May 1768); m. 1st, 22 May 1718, REBECCA PRESTON (widow of her cousin Joseph Preston), b. at Andover, 23 Jan 1688/9 daughter of John and Sarah (Gear) Preston; Rebecca d. at Windham, 1 May 1727. Robert m. 2nd, 13 Dec 1727, BETHIAH PEABODY, b. at Boxford, 3 Apr 1681 daughter of Joseph and Bethiah (Bridges) Peabody; Bethiah d. 6 Feb 1742. Robert m. 3rd, at Hampton, 28 Mar 1743, HANNAH ADROSS who has not been identified; Hannah was living in 1767.

Robert Holt was part of the migration to Windham. He and Rebecca had their first children in Andover before relocating to Connecticut.

In his will written 27 February 1767 (proved 4 May 1768), Robert Holt bequeaths to beloved wife Hannah the dwelling house with an acre of land, all the stock animals, and the household furnishings to be hers forever. Son Ezekiel receives five shillings and a fifth part of the wearing apparel. Grandson Robert Lyon receives £4 and one-fourth of the remaining estate not otherwise disposed of. Daughter Abigail Kendall receives a fourth part and daughter Mary Truesdell receives a fourth part. His grandchildren Reuben Richardson, Sarah Richardson, and Stephen Richardson the children of daughter Martha Richardson deceased receive the remining fourth. Friend Mr. Joseph Burnam of Windham was named executor.[119]

Robert Holt and Rebecca Preston were parents of seven children.

i ABIGAIL HOLT, b. at Andover, 12 Aug 1719; died young.

ii SARAH HOLT, b. at Andover, 18 Jan 1720/1; died young.

194) iii ABIGAIL HOLT, b. at Windham, 20 Feb 1722; m. at Windham, 5 Nov 1741, DAVID KENDALL; David d. at Ashford, 16 Dec 1777.

195) iv SARAH HOLT, b. at Windham, 20 Feb 1722; d. at Pomfret, 11 Oct 1743; m. at Pomfret, 2 Feb 1741/2, PELETIAH LYON, b. at Pomfret, 20 Sep 1711 son of Abiel and Judith (Farrington) Lyon.

196) v MARY HOLT, b. at Windham, 7 Feb 1725; m. at Pomfret, 15 Jun 1742, JOSEPH TRUESDELL, b. at Pomfret, 24 Jun 1719 son of Ebenezer and Rachel (Davis) Truesdell; Joseph d. at Havana, 8 Oct 1762.

197) vi MARTHA HOLT, b. at Windham, 11 Apr 1725; d. at Pomfret, 4 Oct 1759; m. 1 Jan 1754, JOHN RICHARDSON.

---

[118] The 1766 will of Stephen Durkee of Windham includes a bequest to his daughter Sibbel Holt.

[119] *Connecticut. Probate Court (Windham District)*; Probate Place: *Windham, Connecticut, Probate Records, Vol 7-8, 1764-1775, Folio 394*

vii EZEKIEL HOLT, b. at Windham, 21 Apr 1727; d. 6 Jan 1807; m. 1st 5 Nov 1746, LUCY DURKEE, b. at Windham, 6 Jan 1728 daughter of William and Rebecca (Gould) Durkee; Lucy d. at Windham, 11 Aug 1747. Ezekiel m. 2nd, 2 May 1748, ABIAH SESSIONS; Abiah d. 23 May 1811. Ezekiel did not have children.

40) ABIEL HOLT (*Nicholas*^{2}, *Nicholas*^{1}), b. at Andover, 28 Jun 1698 son of Nicholas and Mary (Russell) Holt; d. at Willington, 10 Nov 1772; m. 1st, at Andover, 21 Feb 1721, HANNAH ABBOTT, b. at Andover, 5 Apr 1701 daughter of William and Elizabeth (Geary) Abbott; Hannah d. at Windham, 11 Feb 1751/2. Abiel m. 2nd, at Willington, 19 Dec 1752, SARAH DOWNER, b. about 1699; Sarah d. 15 Apr 1784.

Hannah and Abiel were part of the migration of several Andover families to Windham. There are records for ten children, all born at Windham, Connecticut. Most of the children in this family relocated to Willington.

192) i HANNAH HOLT, b. 17 Apr 1723; d. 25 Jan 1750/1; m. 14 Jul 1742, her first cousin WILLIAM HOLT (*Thomas*^{3}, *Nicholas*^{2}, *Nicholas*^{1}), b. at Andover 10 Dec 1720 son of Thomas and Alice (Peabody) Holt; William d. at Hampton 2 Aug 1793. William m. 2nd at Windham, 14 May 1752, SYBEL DURKEE, b. at Windham, 10 Jan 1731 daughter of Stephen and Lois (Moulton) Durkee;[120] Sybel d. at Hampton, 11 Jan 1794.

198) ii ELIZABETH HOLT, b. 16 Feb 1724/5; d. about 1753; m. 10 Jun 1746, FRANCIS FENTON, b. at Willington, b. 16 Mar 1718 son of Francis and Ann (Berry) Fenton;[121] Francis d. at Willington, 1781 (date of probate). Francis m. 2nd Ann Newcomb.

199) iii ABIEL HOLT, b. 1 Feb 1726/7; d. 2 Oct 1785; m. 1st 22 Apr 1755, MARY DOWNER whose origins are unknown; Mary d. 28 Jan 1766. Abiel m. 2nd 2 Apr 1767, EUNICE KINGSBURY (widow of John Marshall), b. 17 Feb 1733/4 daughter of John and Deborah (Spalding) Kingsbury;[122] Eunice d. at Willington, 2 Jun 1784.

200) iv CALEB HOLT, b. 6 Mar 1729; d. 18 Aug 1810; m. 29 Jan 1755, MARY MERRICK, b. 6 Dec 1726 daughter of John and Sarah (Parsons) Merrick; Mary d. 4 Jun 1790. Caleb m. 2nd 17 May 1791, CHLOE HATCH; Chloe d. at Willington, 21 Feb 1815.

201) v NATHAN HOLT, b. 18 Apr 1733; d. 31 May 1800; m. 1st 19 Jan 1758, ABIGAIL MERRICK, b. 17 Jun 1737 daughter of John and Sarah (Parsons) Merrick; Abigail d. 1 Dec 1765. Nathan m. 2nd 26 Nov 1766, BATHSHEBA WILLIAMS, b. at Lebanon, 22 Mar 1737 daughter of Samuel and Deborah (Throope) Williams; Bathsheba d. 1 Aug 1769. Nathan m. 3rd 6 Jun 1770, LYDIA KINGSBURY, b. at Bolton, 1737 daughter of John and Deborah (Spaulding) Kingsbury; Lydia d. 22 Mar 1776.

202) vi ANNA HOLT, b. 14 Jan 1735; d. 10 Oct 1806; m. 29 Jan 1755, JOSEPH MERRICK, b. 17 Oct 1733 son of John and Sarah (Parsons) Merrick; Joseph d. 9 Apr 1787.

203) vii ISAAC HOLT, b. 2 Mar 1737/8; d. 14 Oct 1822; m. 26 May 1762, SARAH ORCUTT, b. at Stafford, 7 Nov 1740 daughter of William and Sarah (Leonard) Orcutt; Sarah d. 30 Mar 1816.

204) viii TIMOTHY HOLT, b. 2 Dec 1739; d. 7 May 1807; m. 7 May 1761 as her 2nd husband, REBECCA CHAMBERLAIN (widow of Nathaniel Fenton);[123] Rebecca was b. about 1730 probably the daughter of Edmund and Sarah (Furbush) Chamberlain; Rebecca d. 11 Apr 1809.

205) ix MARY HOLT, b. 4 May 1742; d. 13 Jan 1823; m. 27 Nov 1760, JOSEPH PERSONS, birth record not found but son of Joseph and Hannah (-) Persons; Joseph d. at Willington, 4 Nov 1812.

206) x JAMES HOLT, b. 27 Aug 1746; d. 30 Sep 1818; m. 1st 20 Apr 1769, ESTHER OWENS, b. 20 Feb 1747 son of Eleazer and Jerusha (Russ) Owens; Esther d. 5 Dec 1774. JAMES m. 2nd LUCE SAWINS, b. 28 Sep 1740 daughter of George and Anne (Farrar) Sawins; Luce d. 25 Dec 1824.

41) DEBORAH HOLT (*Nicholas*^{2}, *Nicholas*^{1}), b. at Andover, 16 Nov 1700 daughter of Nicholas and Mary (Russell) Holt; d. at Willington, 26 Nov 1784; m. at Windham, 5 May 1727, BENJAMIN PRESTON, b. at Andover, 1705 son of Jacob and Sarah (Wilson) Preston; Benjamin d. at Willington, 26 Nov 1784.[124]

---

[120] The 1766 will of Stephen Durkee of Windham includes a bequest to his daughter Sibbel Holt.

[121] William Weaver, *Genealogy of the Fenton Family*. (Willimantic, CT, 1867).

[122] Kingsbury, *Genealogy of the Descendants of Henry Kingsbury*, p 224

[123] This information is confirmed by the 1809 probate record of Rebecca Holt which includes heirs from her first marriage to Nathaniel Fenton.

[124] The deaths of Deborah and Benjamin are recorded as occurring on the same day. It is reported they died in the same hour and are buried in the same grave. J. H. Beers, Commemorative and Biographical Record of Hartford County, Connecticut, volume I, p 211

Benjamin traveled with his parents to Connecticut the family arriving about 1723. Benjamin was an early settler in Willington and had a tanning business.[125] Deborah and Benjamin were parents of eight children born at Windham.

207) i BENJAMIN PRESTON, b. at Windham, 31 Dec 1727; d. at Ashford, 1 Dec 1798; m. at Ashford, 17 Nov 1763, BATHSHEBA SNOW, b. at Bridgewater, about 1732 daughter of Solomon and Bathsheba (Mahurin) Snow;[126] Bathsheba d. at Ashford, 22 Jan 1813.

208) ii DANIEL PRESTON, b. at Windham, 16 Mar 1729; m. at Windham, 4 Mar 1756, his second cousin once removed, DINAH FORD (*Dinah Holt Ford⁴, George³, Henry², Nicholas¹*), b. at Windham, 17 Sep 1735 daughter of Nathaniel and Daniel (Holt) Ford.

209) iii DARIUS PRESTON, b. at Windham, 3 Mar 1731/2; d. at Willington, 30 May 1821; m. at Willington, 15 Nov 1759, HANNAH FISKE, b. at Willington, 26 Mar 1740 daughter of William and Mary (Blancher) Fiske; Hannah d. at Willington, 12 Jan 1813.

iv MARY PRESTON, b. 2 Apr 1734; d. 31 Aug 1742.

210) v JERUSHA PRESTON, b. at Windham, 29 Jul 1736; m. at Ashford, 25 Aug 1767, as his third wife, JOHN PECK, b. at Uxbridge, MA, 30 Dec 1726 son of Simon and Sarah (-) Peck; John d. in VT, 1805.[127] John was first married to Mary Bowen and second married to Elizabeth Dennerson.

vi AMOS PRESTON, b. 27 Jan 1738; d. 5 Nov 1756.

211) vii DEBORAH PRESTON, b. at Windham, 10 Dec 1740; d. at Willington, 6 Mar 1822; m. at Willington, 19 Oct 1763, TIMOTHY POOL, b. at Willington, 11 Jun 1739 son of John and Mary (Parker) Pool; Timothy d. at Willington, 16 Jul 1821.

viii MARY PRESTON, baptized at Hampton 4 Nov 1744. She is *perhaps* the Mary who married Stevens Chandler as his second wife. Stevens Chandler's family is Family 813.

42) DANIEL HOLT (*Nicholas², Nicholas¹*), b. at Andover, 1705 son of Nicholas and Mary (Russell) Holt; d. at Pomfret, 5 Nov 1773; m. 1st, 31 Mar 1731, ABIGAIL SMITH, b. at Lebanon, CT, 22 Jun 1706 daughter of John and Abigail (-) Smith; Abigail d. at Pomfret, CT, 9 Feb 1752. Daniel m. 2nd, at Pomfret, Dec 1752, KEZIA STRONG (widow of Noah Rust), b. at Northampton, MA, 1 Dec 1709 daughter of Joseph and Sarah (Allen) Strong;[128] Kezia d. at Cherry Valley, NY, 1796.

In his will written 23 October 1773 (proved 7 December 1773), Daniel Holt bequeathed to beloved wife Kezia use of the north great room, part of the cellar, and other provisions for her support while she is a widow. Son Daniel receives all the real and personal estate in Pomfret. The outlands, particularly those in the Delaware purchase, are to be divided among sons Daniel and Asa and the male heirs of son Silas. Daughters Abigail, Lois, Eunice, and Lucy each receives £1.[129]

Daniel and Abigail were parents of seven children born at Windham.

212) i DANIEL HOLT, b. at Windham, 5 Apr 1731; d. at Cherry Valley, NY, 21 Jan 1796; m. at Pomfret, 26 Dec 1753, his stepsister, KEZIA RUST, b. at Coventry, 16 Aug 1735 daughter of Noah and Kezia (Strong) Rust;[130] Kezia d. at Cherry Valley, 23 Dec 1825.

213) ii ABIGAIL HOLT, b. at Windham, 20 Feb 1732; d. at Abington, 11 Oct 1774; m. RICHARD KIMBALL, b. at Bradford, MA, 18 Jul 1722 son of Samuel and Sarah (Spofford) Kimball; Richard d. at Ames, NY, 30 Apr 1810.

214) iii SILAS HOLT, b. at Windham, 29 Dec 1735; d. at Ashford, 23 Oct 1773; m. at Pomfret, 20 Jan 1757, MARY BROOKS, b. at Pomfret, 14 Oct 1735 daughter of John and Phebe (Richardson) Brooks.

215) iv LOIS HOLT, b. at Windham, 4 Feb 1739; d. at Ashford, Oct 1792; m. at Pomfret, 26 Sep 1758, MOSES ROGERS, b. at Billerica, 24 Feb 1730/1 son of Nathaniel and Mary (Haggit) Rogers; Moses d. at Ashford, 1797 (probate 1797).

---

[125] Preston, *Descendants of Roger Preston*, p 60

[126] *Mayflower Families Fifth Generation Descendants, 1700-1880*. (Online database: *AmericanAncestors.org*, New England Historic Genealogical Society, 2017). John Alden, volume 16, part 3, p 207

[127] Peck, *Genealogical History of the Descendants of Joseph Peck*, p 279

[128] Dwight, *History of the Descendants of Elder John Strong*, p 310

[129] *Connecticut. Probate Court (Pomfret District);* Probate Place: *Windham, Connecticut, Probate Records, Vol 3-4, 1762-1778, volume 3, pp 391-392*

[130] The distribution of the estate of Noah Russ includes distribution to daughter Keziah Holt. Distribution is 27 December 1753 the day after the wedding of Daniel and Kezia.

216) v EUNICE HOLT, b. at Pomfret, 22 Aug 1741; m. at Pomfret, 28 Nov 1760, JOSIAH WHEELER, b. at Pomfret, 21 Mar 1737/8 son of Josiah and Anna (Grosvenor) Wheeler.

217) vi ASA HOLT, b. at Pomfret, 7 Jun 1745; d. at Springfield, VT, 1 Mar 1813; m. at Pomfret, 20 Nov 1766, MARGARET HAMMOND, baptized at Woodstock, 9 Dec 1744 daughter of Jonathan and Katherine (Davis) Hammond; Margaret d. at Springfield, 28 Sep 1834.

218) vii LUCY HOLT, b. at Pomfret, 10 Oct 1747; m. at Brooklyn, CT, 27 Nov 1770, JEDEDIAH DANA, b. at Ashford, 9 Aug 1739 son of Jedediah and Elizabeth (Barnard) Dana; Jedediah d. at German Flatts, NY, 1809 (probate 31 Jan 1809).

Children of Hannah Holt and Robert Gray

43) HENRY GRAY (*Hannah Holt Gray*[2], *Nicholas*[1]), b. at Salem, 17 Jan 1671/2 son of Robert and Hannah (Holt) Gray; d. at Andover, 1 Jul 1741; m. at Andover, 3 May 1699, MARY BLUNT, b. at Andover, 28 Sep 1679 daughter of William and Elizabeth (Ballard) Blunt; Mary d. at Andover, 7 Aug 1733.

In his will written 13 May 1740 (probate 20 July 1741), Henry Gray bequeathed to eldest son Henry all the lands in the township of Andover, all the stock animals, husbandry tools, and weaving loom. Son Samuel receives 20 shillings and the right of land to a property in Suncook that has already been conveyed to him. Samuel also received assistance from his father in entering the carpenter trade. Son Aaron is to receive 25 pounds, a gun, and he has already received 140 pounds. Youngest son William is lately deceased and left a widow, and if his widow has a child begotten by William, then that child will receive 20 pounds at age 21. Eldest daughter Elizabeth receives 20 shillings and household items she received before and since her marriage. Daughters Jemima, Mary, Rebecca, and Hannah receive a similar bequest. Youngest daughter Sarah receives 71 pounds when she comes of age. His books are to be equally divided among his six daughters. Real estate included several parcels with total value of £1,650.[131]

Henry and Mary were parents of twelve children born at Andover.

219) i ELIZABETH GRAY, b. 28 Mar 1700; d. at Pomfret, CT, 9 Jul 1765; m. 8 Feb 1719/20. PAUL ABBOTT, b. at Andover, 28 Mar 1697 son of William and Elizabeth (Geary) Abbott; Paul d. at Hampton, CT, 8 May 1752.

80) ii JEMIMA GRAY, b. 1701; buried at Andover, 27 Aug 1775; m. 12 Jan 1724, her second cousin, SAMUEL HOLT (*Samuel*[3], *Samuel*[2], *Nicholas*[1]), b. 1697 son of Samuel and Hannah (Farnum) Holt; Samuel d. at Andover, 25 Nov 1758.

iii MARY GRAY, b. 1703; d. 1706.

220) iv HENRY GRAY, b. 1706; d. at Andover, 18 Sep 1754; m. 1736, ALICE PEABODY, b. about 1709 daughter of Jonathan and Alice (Pearl) Peabody;[132] Alice d. at Andover, 13 Nov 1797.

221) v MARY GRAY, b. about 1707; d. likely at Pembroke; m. 26 Nov 1730, as his second wife, MOSES FOSTER, b. at Andover, 27 Sep 1696 son of Ephraim and Hannah (Eams) Foster; Moses d. at Pembroke, about 1770 (will 12 Mar 1766; probate 7 Dec 1770). Moses was first married to Elizabeth Rogers who died in 1729.

146) vi REBECCA GRAY, b. 1708; d. at Andover, Aug 1775; m. at Andover, 6 Jan 1735/6, HENRY HOLT, b. at Andover, 1706 son of Henry and Martha (Marston) Holt; Henry d. at Andover, 22 Sep 1754.

222) vii SAMUEL GRAY, b. Jul 1711; d. at Amherst, NH, 3 Oct 1769; m. at Andover, 8 Sep 1736, SARAH ABBOTT, b. at Andover, 25 Jan 1715/6 daughter of Ephraim and Sarah (Crosby) Abbott.[133]

viii AARON GRAY, b. 15 Oct 1712; died young.

223) ix HANNAH GRAY, b. at Andover 4 Jan 1714/5; m. 1st, about 1740, SAMUEL SESSIONS, b. about 1710 son of Samuel and Mary (Cox) Sessions; Samuel d. of fever,[134] at Andover, 24 Apr 1746. Hannah m. 2nd, at Andover, 31 May 1750, DAVID FOSTER, b. at Boxford, 17 Aug 1704 son of Timothy and Mary (Dorman) Foster;[135] David d. at Keene, NH 1779 (probate 1779).

---

[131] Essex County, MA: Probate File Papers, 1638-1881.Online database. AmericanAncestors.org. New England Historic Genealogical Society, 2014. Case 11603

[132] The 1741 probate record of Jonathan Peabody includes acknowledgment from Henry Gray and Alice Gray that they have received settlement from the estate of "our father" Jonathan Peabody.

[133] The 1761 will of Daniel Abbott (who is a son of Ephraim Abbott and Sarah Crosby) includes a bequest to his sister Sarah Gray.

[134] Sessions, *History of the Sessions Family*

[135] Griffin, *History of the Town of Keene*, p 599

224) x AARON GRAY, b. 24 Mar 1715/6; d. at Keene, NH, 30 Mar 1799; m. at Boxford, 18 Jul 1744, BETHIA PEABODY, b. at Boxford, about 1716 daughter of Jonathan and Alice (Pearl) Peabody;[136] Bethia d. 21 Jan 1788.

xi WILLIAM GRAY, b. 1718; d. at Andover, 27 Nov 1739; m. at Andover, 26 Apr 1739, MARGARET MCCUTCHEN who has not been identified. William did not have children.

xii SARAH GRAY, b. 5 Mar 1722/3; living in 1754 and unmarried when her brother Henry wrote his will.

44) HANNAH GRAY (*Hannah Holt Gray[2], Nicholas[1]*), b. at Salem, 30 Jan 1674/5 daughter of Robert and Hannah (Holt) Gray; d. at Andover, 25 Jan 1763; m. at Andover, 7 Dec 1697, THOMAS ABBOTT, b. at Andover, 6 May 1666 son of George and Hannah (Chandler) Abbott; Thomas d. at Andover, 28 Apr 1728.

A probate record for Thomas Abbott was not located. Thomas Abbott and Hannah Gray had ten children all born at Andover.

225) i THOMAS ABBOTT, b. at Andover, 3 Jan 1698/9; d. 11 Jul 1774; m. 28 Jan 1724/5, ELIZABETH BALLARD, b. 14 Jan 1700/1 daughter of Joseph and Rebecca (Johnson) Ballard; Elizabeth d. 31 Jul 1782.

ii HANNAH ABBOTT, b. 11 Sep 1700; d. at Rumford, NH, 22 Jul 1746; Hannah did not marry but accompanied some of her siblings to New Hampshire.

226) iii EDWARD ABBOTT, b. at Andover, 9 Jun 1702; d. at Concord, NH, 14 Apr 1759; m. 15 Jul 1728, DORCAS CHANDLER, b. about 1705 daughter of Thomas and Mary (Peters) Chandler; Dorcas d. 16 May 1748. Edward married 2nd, 23 Jan 1748/9, MEHITABLE EASTMAN, b. at Haverhill 17 Nov 1707 daughter of Jonathan and Hannah (Green) Eastman.

227) iv DEBORAH ABBOTT, b. at Andover, 1 Dec 1704; d. at Concord, NH, 25 Oct 1801; m. at Andover 5 Jul 1736, JOSEPH HALL, b. 15 Dec 1707 son of Joseph and Sarah (Kimball) Hall; Joseph d. 8 Apr 1784 at Concord.[137]

228) v GEORGE ABBOTT, b. at Andover, 7 Nov 1706; d. at Concord, NH, 6 Oct 1785; m. 1 Feb 1737, SARAH ABBOTT (who was his first cousin, once removed), b. Oct 1711 daughter of Samuel and Sarah (Stevens) Abbott; Sarah d. at Concord 14 Jun 1769.

vi ZEBADIAH ABBOTT, b. 25 Jan 1708/9; d. 17 May 1745 in the siege of Louisburg.

229) vii BENJAMIN ABBOTT, b. at Andover, 31 Mar 1710; d. at Concord, NH, 8 Mar 1794; m. 23 Jun 1742, HANNAH ABBOTT (who was his first cousin once removed), b. 30 Jul 1716 daughter of Samuel and Sarah (Stevens) Abbott and granddaughter of John and Sarah (Barker) Abbott; Hannah d. at Concord 27 Jul 1786.

viii CATHERINE ABBOTT, b. 31 Mar 1710; d. at Andover, 14 Sep 1744; Catherine did not marry.

ix AARON ABBOTT, b. 8 Aug 1714; d. 9 Apr 1730.

x ISAACK ABBOTT, b. 13 Feb 1715/6; d. 3 Nov 1745 in the siege of Louisburg from illness; Isaac, s. Thomas and Hannah, "sickness in ye Kings Service at Lewisburg," Nov. 3, 1745, a. 28 y. 8m. 21 d.[138]

45) ROBERT GRAY (*Hannah Holt Gray[2], Nicholas[1]*), b. at Andover, about 1677 son of Robert and Hannah (Holt) Gray; d. at Andover, Mar 1718; m. at Andover, 29 Nov 1705, MIRIAM LOVEJOY, b. at Andover, 11 Aug 1686 daughter of Christopher and Sarah (Russ) Lovejoy; Miriam d. 21 Apr 1770. Miriam married second Richard Nutting on 17 Jun 1718.

Robert and Miriam resided in Andover where they were members of the South Church.

In her will written 24 July 1767 (proved 8 May 1770), Miriam Nutting bequeathed to her granddaughter Percy Snow daughter of her late son Jonathan Gray, six shillings to complete her portion as her father received his full portion during his lifetime. Grandson David Gray Nutting son of her late son Joseph Nutting also receives six shillings. Sons Abiel Gray and Robert Gray also receive six shillings. The remainder of the estate is to be divided in four equal portions among her children and grandchildren named: son Isaac Gray, daughter Miriam Fitch, grandson Robert Gray son of Robert Gray, and granddaughter Sarah Gray daughter of David Gray. She also expresses that her grandson Robert Gray should provide what is necessary for his mother Lydia Gray as she has no other estate to support her. Grandson Robert Gray is named sole executor.[139]

Robert and Miriam were parents of eight children born at Andover.

---

[136] Although there is not a birth record for Bethia, there is a distribution to daughter Bethia in the 1741 probate record of Jonathan Peabody.

[137] New Hampshire Death and Disinterment Records, 1754-1947, accessed through ancestry.com

[138] Massachusetts: Vital Records, 1620-1850

[139] *Essex County, Massachusetts, Probate Records and Indexes 1638-1916, volumes 345-346, Book 45-46, 1768-1771, p 109*

230) i ROBERT GRAY, b. at Andover 1706; m. at Andover, 1 May 1728, his second cousin, LYDIA PEABODY (*Lydia Holt Peabody[3], James[2], Nicholas[1]*), b. at Andover, 13 Feb 1703 daughter of Samuel and Lydia (Holt) Peabody; Lydia d. at Andover, 24 Aug 1775.

ii MIRIAM GRAY, b. 3 Jul 1707; d. 9 Nov 1708.

231) iii ISAAC GRAY, b. at Andover, 6 Sep 1709; d. at Tewksbury, 4 Oct 1770; m. at Andover, 20 Nov 1733, REBECCA FROST (widow of David Blanchard), b. at Billerica, 9 Aug 1701 daughter of Thomas and Rebecca (Farley) Frost; Rebecca d. at Tewksbury, 1 Feb 1782.[140]

iv AARON GRAY, b. 31 Jul 1712; d. 12 Aug 1712.

232) v MIRIAM GRAY, b. at Andover, 4 Sep 1713; m. at Andover, 28 Feb 1731/2, BENJAMIN FITCH, b. at Billerica, 30 Jul 1703 son of Samuel and Elizabeth (Walker) Fitch; Benjamin d. at Bedford, MA, 7 Jul 1770.

233) vi ABIEL GRAY, b. at Andover, 26 Jan 1714/5;[141] d. at Tolland, CT, 14 Apr 1805; m. 1st about 1737, ZERVIAH HATCH, b. at Tolland, 3 Oct 1715 daughter of Ichabod and Abigail (Weeks) Hatch; Zerviah d. at Tolland, 8 May 1754. Abiel m. 2nd about 1755, LOIS PALMER, b. at Stonington, 3 Mar 1721/2 daughter of Moses and Abigail (Allen) Palmer; Lois d. at West Hartford, 11 Nov 1786. Abiel m. 3rd at Hartford, 12 Nov 1787, LUCY FULLER of Willington, b. about 1735; Lucy d. at West Hartford, 16 Aug 1793.

234) vii JONATHAN GRAY, b. at Andover, 21 Mar 1715/6; m. at Woburn, 20 Feb 1738, PERSIS REED, b. at Woburn, 21 Jul 1711 daughter of Timothy and Persis (Kendall) Reed.[142]

235) viii DAVID GRAY, b. at Andover, 22 Oct 1717; d. at Andover 1767 (by suicide); m. at Andover, 3 Jun 1756, his first cousin once removed, REBECCA HOLT (*Samuel[4], Samuel[3], Samuel[2], Nicholas[1]*), baptized at Andover 31 Oct 1725 daughter of Samuel and Jemima (Gray) Holt; Rebecca d. at Andover, 10 Jul 1800.

46) EDWARD GRAY (*Hannah Holt Gray[2], Nicholas[1]*), b. at Andover, 12 Sep 1679 son of Robert and Hannah (Holt) Gray; d. at Andover, 15 Sep 1759; m. 1st at Andover, 2 Dec 1702, SARAH OSGOOD, b. at Andover, 19 Feb 1682 daughter of Christopher and Hannah (Barker) Osgood; Sarah d. at Andover, 14 May 1718. Edward m. 2nd 27 Oct 1719, HANNAH BARKER, b. at Andover, 5 Sep 1681 daughter of William and Mary (Dix) Barker; Hannah d. at Andover, 27 Jan 1762.

On 22 July 1729, Edward Gray conveyed to his son Edward for love and affection three parcels of land in Andover. On 3 April 1746, Edward conveyed several parcels of land in Andover to his son Thomas for love and affection.[143]

In his will written 22 February 1759 (probate 13 November 1759), Edward Gray bequeathed to Hannah "my dear and well-beloved wife all my household goods such as belongs to woman's use to be at her disposal." Edward also provides a lengthy list of annual provisions which are in lieu of her dower. Eldest son Edward receives all the lands and buildings in Andover except four acres at the south end of the homestead. Edward also receives all the tools and every other part of the estate and is to make payments to the other children. Son Thomas receives the four acres at the south end of the homestead which completes his portion. Daughters Hannah Colbe, Margery Wardwell, Priscilla Carlton, Abigail Wardwell, Lydia Stevens, Elizabeth Kimbal, and Sarah Stevens each receives £13.6.8. Son Edward was named executor.[144] Real estate was valued at £305. There was conflict related to the will son Thomas being dissatisfied. On 11 October 1759, daughter Margery wife of William Wardwell wrote to the probate judge describing some of the conflict in the family. She traced this to "one and forty years" since the two brothers and five former sisters were "bereaved of their own natural mother." The two brothers were apparently not able to get along in the house together and the older son Edward had stayed there caring for his father and working until age twenty-three. It was Margery's belief that her younger brother had been made more than equal by the provisions of the will. All the sisters and their husbands signed a statement that they had received their portion from the estate and were satisfied.

Edward Gray and Sarah Osgood were parents of nine children born at Andover.

i SARAH GRAY, b. about 1703; d. at Boston of smallpox, 10 Oct 1721.[145]

236) ii EDWARD GRAY, b. at Andover, Nov 1705; d. after 1773 perhaps in Maine; m. by 1742, SARAH who has not been identified.[146]

---

[140] Rebecca [wid., somewhat sudden. CR1], Feb. 1, 1782, a. 81 y.

[141] In the Tolland records, there is also listed Abiel's information on his birthdate giving birth as 26 Jan 1714/5 and parents as Robert and Miriam.

[142] Jonathan Gray and Persis Reed were parents of a daughter Persis who married James Snow. She is the granddaughter Percy Snow in the will of Jonathan's mother.

[143] Massachusetts Land Records 1620-1986, Essex County Deeds, 56:207, 89:12; accessed through familysearch.org

[144] *Essex County, MA: Probate File Papers, 1638-1881.*Online database. *AmericanAncestors.org.* New England Historic Genealogical Society, 2014. Case 11595

[145] Sarah, d. Edward and Sarah, smallpox, at Boston, Oct. 10, 1721. Died at age 18 years.

[146] It is possible that this is Sarah Coombs who married Edward Gray in Tolland, CT in 1741. Edward's first cousin Abiel Gray was in Tolland at that time and there are no other Gray families there during that period.

237) iii HANNAH GRAY, b. at Andover, about 1707; d. after 1783 (husband's will); m. at Andover, 2 Sep 1730, DANIEL COLBY, b. at Amesbury perhaps the son of John and Mary (Frame) Colby; Daniel d. at Dracut, 1785 (probate).

238) iv MARGERY GRAY, b. about 1708; d. at Andover, 31 Oct 1795; m. at Andover, 17 May 1739, WILLIAM WARDWELL, b. at Andover, 3 May 1709 son of William and Dorothy (Wright) Wardwell; William d. at Andover, 24 Mar 1790.

239) v THOMAS GRAY, b. at Andover, 22 Jul 1709; d. at Andover, 5 Feb 1796; m. 1st 21 Jun 1739, ELIZABETH HUTCHINSON, b. at Andover, 4 Aug 1715 daughter of John and Sarah (Adams) Hutchinson; Elizabeth d. at Andover, 22 Mar 1739/40. Thomas m. 2nd 19 Mar 1757, LYDIA GRAVES, b. at Reading, 1732 daughter of Daniel and Martha (Coats) Graves; Lydia d. at Andover, 21 Apr 1793.

240) vi PRISCILLA GRAY, b. at Andover, 10 Jan 1712/3; m. 4 Dec 1735, DANIEL CARLETON, b. at Andover, May 1708 son of John and Hannah (Osgood) Carleton; Daniel d. at Andover, 2 May 1795.

241) vii ABIGAIL GRAY, b. at Andover, 13 Aug 1714; d. at Andover, 16 Oct 1778; m. 11 Dec 1735, THOMAS WARDWELL, b. at Andover, 3 May 1709 son of William and Dorothy (Wright) Wardwell; Thomas d. at Andover, 29 Feb 1776.

242) viii LYDIA GRAY, b. at Andover, 22 Aug 1716; d. after 1792;[147] m. 7 Apr 1737, JOHN STEVENS, b. 1711 son of Abiel and Deborah (Barker) Stevens.

ix JOHN GRAY, b. 2 Apr 1718; d. 4 Jun 1720.

Edward Gray and Hannah Barker were parents of two children born at Andover.

243) i ELIZABETH GRAY, b. at Andover, Nov 1720; m. at Boxford, 3 Dec 1747, EPHRAIM KIMBALL, b. at Boxford, 11 Apr 1721 son of Richard and Hannah (Dorman) Kimball.[148]

244) ii SARAH GRAY, b. at Andover, 18 Mar 1723; m. 14 Jan 1747/8, THOMAS STEVENS, b. at Andover, 9 Aug 1724 son of John and Elizabeth (Chandler) Stevens; Thomas d. in PA during the Revolution on 29 Dec 1777.

47) BRAVITER GRAY (*Hannah Holt Gray*[2], *Nicholas*[1]), b. at Andover, 29 Sep 1685 son of Robert and Hannah (Holt) Gray; d. at Andover, 10 Nov 1724; m. at Andover, 21 Nov 1710, DOROTHY ABBOTT, b. at Andover, about 1683 daughter of Thomas and Sarah (Stewart) Abbott; Dorothy d. at Andover, 22 Oct 1743. Dorothy m. 2nd 6 Dec 1728, BENJAMIN HOLT (*Oliver*[3], *Henry*[2], *Nicholas*[1]), b. at Andover, Jan 1704 son of Oliver and Hannah (Russell) Holt; Benjamin d. at Andover, 1783 (probate 1783). Benjamin m. 2nd 11 Apr 1745, ELIZABETH WILSON, b. at Hampton, NH, 1 Jul 1708 daughter of William and Elizabeth (Andrews) Wilson; Elizabeth d. at Andover, 28 Feb 1788.[149] Elizabeth was first married to Ezekiel Lovejoy.

In deeds recorded 7 October 1747, Braviter Gray, Timothy Gray, and Dorothy Gray quitclaimed their rights in the estate of their honored father Braviter Gray transferring this to their honored father-in-law Benjamin Holt.[150]

While a young man, Benjamin Holt married the widow Dorothy Abbott Gray who was about twenty years his senior. After, Dorothy's death, he married the widow Elizabeth Wilson Lovejoy. Benjamin and his second wife Elizabeth Wilson had one daughter who died at age 17. Benjamin names some of his stepchildren in his will.

In his will written 6 January 1779 (proved 4 November 1783), Benjamin Holt left to his dearly beloved wife Elisabeth all the household stuff proper for woman's use. She also receives the use and improvement on one-third of the real estate while a widow. Beloved son-in-law James Holt, Jr. receives all the real estate except for the following bequests. He bequeaths one pound 10 shillings to his brothers and sisters to be equally divided among them: Jonathan Holt, Thomas Holt, William Holt, Mary Holt, and Judith Batchelder. Beloved son Phineas Lovejoy receives twelve pounds. Beloved daughter-in-law Dorothy Hagget receives one pound and daughter-in-law Elizabeth Brown receives three pounds. Six beloved cousins receive one pound sixteen shillings to divide equally: Nathaniel Holt, Uriah Holt, Joseph Holt, David Holt, Jacob Holt, and Timothy Russell. Beloved cousin Timothy Gray, Jr. receives the firelock. His wife receives all the books except the great bible. She has use of the bible during her life, but it then goes to his granddaughter Dorothy Holt. Son-in-law James Holt, Jr. was named sole executor.[151] James Holt, Jr. was the husband of Benjamin's stepdaughter Dorothy Lovejoy. [James Holt and Dorothy Lovejoy are Family 1015.]

Braviter Gray and Dorothy Abbott were parents of six children.

---

[147] In 1792, widow Lydia Stevens (John) was dismissed from the church in Andover to church in Thetford, Vermont. Historical Manual of the South Church of Andover, p 142

[148] Morrison and Sharples, *History of the Kimball Family in America*

[149] Elisabeth, wid., schirrous, bur. Feb. 28, 1788, a. 79 y. 8 m. CR2

[150] Massachusetts Land Records 1620-1986, Essex County Deeds, 91:76, 91:77, 91:83; accessed through familysearch.org

[151] *Essex County, MA: Probate File Papers, 1638-1881.*Online database. *AmericanAncestors.org.* New England Historic Genealogical Society, 2014. Case 13625

i BRAVITER GRAY, b. Apr 1711; d. 13 Apr 1711.

ii DOROTHY GRAY, b. at Andover, 5 Jun 1712; d. at Andover, 10 Apr 1779; m. at Andover, 16 May 1754, as perhaps his second wife, THOMAS HAGGETT, b. 1713; Thomas d. at Andover, 15 Apr 1778.

iii JOSEPH GRAY, b. 28 Mar 1714; d. 31 Jan 1736/7.

245) iv BRAVITER GRAY, b. at Andover, 19 Jul 1717; d. at Billerica, 1768 (probate 1768); m. 1st at Charlestown, 6 Jul 1743, BETHIAH HILL, b. at Billerica, 16 Jul 1718 daughter of Jonathan and Mary (Bracket) Hill; Bethiah d. at Billerica, 30 Jan 1754. Braviter m. 2nd at Billerica, 14 Jul 1757, ANNE DANFORTH, b. at Billerica, 28 Feb 1729 daughter of Jonathan and Elizabeth (Manning) Danforth; Anne d. 10 Aug 1757. Braviter m. 3rd ELIZABETH RICHARDSON (widow of John Blanchard), b. at Billerica, 9 Dec 1719 daughter of Andrew and Hannah (Jefts) Richardson; Elizabeth d. at Billerica, 1768 (probate Oct 1768).

246) v TIMOTHY GRAY, b. at Andover, 19 Jul 1721; d. at Wilton, 17 Nov 1793; m. 1st at Andover, 3 May 1748, ELINOR BEST, b. at Boston, 25 Aug 1724 daughter of James and Mary (Frye) Best; Elinor d. at Wilton, 22 Sep 1775. Timothy m. 2nd ABIGAIL who d. at Wilton, 20 May 1801.

vi MARY GRAY, b. 1723; d. 26 Feb 1734/5.

Benjamin Holt and Elizabeth Wilson were parents of one child.

i HANNAH HOLT, b. at Andover, 15 Nov 1749; d. 24 Jun 1767.

Children of James Holt and Hannah Allen

Note: Two of the children of James Holt and Hannah Allen are covered earlier. Daughter Hannah Holt is in Family 13 with her husband Samuel Farnum. Daughter Priscilla Holt is in Family 18 with her husband Ephraim Farnum.

48) LYDIA HOLT (*James*[2], *Nicholas*[1]), b. at Andover, 27 Sep 1681 daughter of James and Hannah (Allen) Holt; d. at Andover, 10 Oct 1741; m. at Andover, 27 Jan 1701/2, SAMUEL PEABODY, b. at Boxford, 8 Apr 1678 son of Joseph and Bethiah (Bridges) Peabody; Samuel d. at Andover, 1 May 1706.

Lydia and Samuel were parents of two children.

230) i LYDIA PEABODY, b. at Andover, 13 Feb 1703; d. at Andover, 24 Aug 1775; m. at Andover, 1 May 1728, her second cousin, ROBERT GRAY (*Robert Gray*[3], *Hannah Holt Gray*[2], *Nicholas*[1]), b. at Andover, 1706 son of Robert and Miriam (Lovejoy) Gray.

147) ii MOSES PEABODY, b. at Andover, 1705; d. at Andover, 13 Nov 1746; m. at Andover, 12 Jun 1728, his second cousin, SARAH HOLT (*Henry*[3], *Henry*[2], *Nicholas*[1]), b. at Andover, 3 Jul 1707 daughter of Henry and Martha (Marston) Holt.

49) TIMOTHY HOLT (*James*[2], *Nicholas*[1]), b. at Andover, 25 Jan 1683 son of James and Hannah (Allen) Holt; d. at Andover, 4 Mar 1758; m. at Andover, 19 Apr 1705, RHODA CHANDLER, b. at Andover, 26 Sep 1684 daughter of William and Bridget (Henchman) Chandler; Rhoda d. at Andover, 14 Aug 1765.

In his will written 6 June 1754 (probate 27 March 1758), Timothy Holt bequeathed to beloved wife Rhoda the east end of the dwelling house from the bottom of the cellar to the top of the chimney. She also receives the improvement on all his money and notes and a lengthy list of other provisions for her support. The provisioning of wife Rhoda is entrusted to his son Timothy. Son James receives all the lands and buildings where he now dwells. Son Timothy receives the homestead land and buildings where father Timothy now dwells. Youngest son Joseph receives £16 with what he has received for his learning is his full portion. Daughters Rhoda, Priscilla, Hannah, and Phebe each receives thirteen shillings four pence together with what each received at time of marriage is their full portion. James and Timothy were named executors. Real estate was valued at £792.12.8 and personal estate £109.8.6.[152]

The problem of Priscilla Holt: All published genealogies note the daughter Priscilla in this family, but universally suggest nothing is known about her. From the will of Timothy Holt, we know there was a daughter Priscilla, she likely falls between Rhoda and Hannah in birth order so born about 1708, and that she did marry. But who is her husband? Published genealogies universally accept that Oliver and Hannah (Russell) Holt had a daughter Priscilla that married Nathan Chandler, although without noting the documentation that supports this. There is some evidence to suggest that Oliver and Hannah did not have a daughter Priscilla, or at least she was not living in 1779. Benjamin Holt son of Oliver and Hannah (Russell) Holt

[152] *Essex County, MA: Probate File Papers, 1638-1881.* Online database. *AmericanAncestors.org.* New England Historic Genealogical Society, 2014. Case 13700

wrote his will in 1779 (probate 1783) in which he has bequests for his brothers and sisters and names all other living siblings and half-siblings, but no Priscilla is mentioned.[153]

Timothy and Rhoda were parents of nine children born at Andover.[154]

i JOSEPH HOLT, b. 8 Apr 1706; died young.

247) ii RHODA HOLT, b. at Andover, about 1707; d. likely at Concord; m. at Boston, 13 Nov 1728, ELIAS WHITTEMORE, b. likely at Malden, 1702 son of John and Ruth (Bassett) Whittemore;[155] Elias d. at Concord, NH, Dec 1792.[156]

248) iii PRISCILLA HOLT, b. about 1708; d. at Andover, 25 Nov 1803; m. 14 May 1729, NATHAN CHANDLER, b. at Andover, 31 Jan 1708 son of John and Hannah (Frye) Chandler; Nathan d. at Andover, 31 Jul 1784.

249) iv HANNAH HOLT, b. at Andover, 18 Dec 1709; d. at Andover, 2 Aug 1775; m. 22 Mar 1733, BARACHIAS ABBOTT, b. at Andover, 14 May 1707 son of John and Elizabeth (Harnden) Abbott; Barachias d. at Andover, 2 Oct 1784.

250) v JAMES HOLT, b. at Andover, 11 Dec 1711; d. at Andover, 2 Sep 1775;[157] m. 1st at Wilmington, 11 Jan 1734/5, SUSANNA NURS, b. at Reading, 14 Aug 1714 daughter of Jonathan and Abigail (Hornden) Nurs; Susanna d. at Andover, 20 Feb 1742. James m. 2nd at Wilmington, 22 Oct 1742, MARTHA WINN; Martha d. at Andover, 30 Mar 1753. James m. 3rd 6 Aug 1767, MARY CARROLL (widow of Phineas McIntire) who was his widow at the probate of his estate.

251) vi TIMOTHY HOLT, b. at Andover, 16 Apr 1714; d. at Andover, 27 Jul 1798; m. 13 Feb 1739, HANNAH DANE, b. at Andover, 14 Dec 1718 daughter of John and Sarah (Chandler) Dane; Hannah d. 6 Feb 1802.

vii JOSEPH HOLT, b. 16 Apr 1714; d. 20 Aug 1714.

252) viii JOSEPH HOLT, b. at Andover, 14 Feb 1718; d. at Wilton, Aug 1789; m. 1st 17 Jan 1744/5, DOROTHY "DOLLY" JOHNSON, b. at Andover, 3 May 1719 daughter of John and Phebe (Robinson) Johnson; Dolly d. at Andover, 30 Dec 1753. Joseph m. 2nd 1755, MARY RUSSELL, b. at Andover, 10 Feb 1728/9 daughter of John and Sarah (Chandler) Russell.

253) ix PHEBE HOLT, b. at Andover, 1 Jun 1722; d. at Tewksbury, 15 Jan 1779;[158] m. 1st 11 Feb 1742, FRANCIS PHELPS, b. at Andover, 11 Jan 1720 son of Samuel and Hannah (Dane) Phelps; Francis d. at Pepperell, 1758 (probate 1758). Phebe m. 2nd at Tewksbury, 8 Aug 1771, THOMAS MARSHALL.

50) JOSEPH HOLT (*James*[2], *Nicholas*[1]), b. at Andover, 5 Mar 1686 son of James and Hannah (Allen) Holt; d. at York, ME, 26 Apr 1774;[159] m. at York, 28 Dec 1709, as her second husband, MARY HARMON, b. at York, about 1682 daughter of John and Deborah (Johnson) Harmon;[160] Mary d. at York, 15 Nov 1760. Mary was first married to Benjamin Donnell.

Elder Joseph Holt was in York by 1709 where he served as deacon of the church for fifty years. He and wife Mary are buried in South Side Cemetery in York. Mary Holt's stone bears this inscription: *wife of Elder Joseph Holt/ She was a good Wife/ an affectionate Mother/ a very kind Neighbour/ and exemplary Christian/ lived desired, and died lamented.* The stone of Joseph Holt bears this inscription: *a plain reprover/ and a steadfast Christian/ one who joined the Church/ in the first Parish in York/ in which he serv'd as an officer upwards/ of fifty years.*[161]

The home built by Joseph Holt in 1717 still stands in York at 1 Old Seabury Road and is part of the York Historical District.

---

[153] The will of Benjamin Holt has bequests to beloved wife Elizabeth; son-in-law James Holt, Jr. (husband of Dorothy Lovejoy who was a daughter of Elizabeth Wilson and her first husband Ezekiel Lovejoy); "my beloved brothers and sisters namely Jonathan Holt, Thomas Holt, Mary Holt, and Judath Batchelder"; son Phineas Lovejoy (a son of Elizabeth and Ezekiel Lovejoy); daughter-in-law Dorothy Hagget; daughter-in-law Elizabeth Brown; six beloved cousins namely Nathaniel Holt, Uriah Holt, Jacob Holt, Timothy Holt, Joseph Holt, and Timothy Russell; and Timothy Gray, Jr. *Essex County, MA: Probate File Papers, 1638-1881.*Online database. *AmericanAncestors.org.* New England Historic Genealogical Society, 2014. Case 13625

[154] Published genealogies also report a daughter Rebecca, but there are no records for her, and she is not in her father's will and so is not included here.

[155] Whittemore, *A Genealogy of Several Branches of the Whittemore Family*, p 62

[156] U.S., Newspaper Extractions from the Northeast, 1704-1930

[157] James, bur. Sept. 2, 1775, a. 63 y. CR2

[158] Phebe, wid. [Thomas, formerly w. Francis Phelps of Pepperell. G. R. 1; apoplexy, C. R. 1.], Jan. 15, 1779, in her 57th y.

[159] *Here lies the Body of Elder Joseph Holt who departed this Life April 26th 1774 in the 89th Year of his Age*. Findagrave ID: 63730374.

[160] Harmon, *The Harmon Genealogy*, p 145

[161] Mitoraj, Suzanne O., "A Tale of Two Cemeteries: Gravestones as Community Artifacts", *The English Journal*, vol 90, no 5, pp 82-87

On 19 July 1717, Joseph Holt of York in the county of York in the province of Massachusetts Bay sold to Timothy Holt of Andover for £20 "my share of the lands of my father James Holt" lying in Andover. The deed is signed by Joseph Holt and Mary Holt (by her mark).[162]

On 4 February 1722/3, Nathan Donnell for himself and on behalf of his two sisters Sarah and Hannah Donnell of Boston, quitclaimed to Joseph Holt of York property related to the estate of Thomas Donnell father of Nathan, Sarah, and Hannah. Joseph Holt was representative of a daughter late the wife of Nathan's brother Benjamin Donnell.[163]

On 20 December 1726, John Harmon of York conveyed to Joseph Holt of York one full nineteenth part of a sawmill and of a gristmill standing on a creek called Meeting House Creek. Joseph has paid already £38 which is one-nineteenth of the cost of building the mills and he will also be responsible for one-nineteenth of cost related to running of the mills.[164]

In his will written 12 April 1758 (proved 8 June 1774), Joseph Holt bequeathed to his beloved wife, in addition to her thirds in the real estate, all the household goods. Eldest son Joseph Holt receives a small lot on the homestead where his dwelling house now stands and other specified lots. Youngest son Benjamin Holt receives a lot of land on the homestead. His two sons Joseph and Benjamin receive all the remainder of the homestead to be equally divided. This includes the stock animals, buildings, and personal estate not otherwise disposed of. His two daughters Mary the wife of Jacob Booker and Hannah the wife of Nathan Raynes receive, to be equally divided, a 46-acre tract of farmland in York that he purchased of Stephen Greenleaf. Daughter Lydia wife of Edward Ingraham receives £32 and all the outlands and meadows on the northeast side of the York River. His two grandchildren Samuel and Dorcas Holt the children of his son James deceased receive £20 when they arrive at age twenty-one.[165]

Joseph and Mary were parents of eight children born at York, Maine.

254) i JOSEPH HOLT, b. at York, 27 Aug 1710; d. at York, 1784 (probate 11 Jun 1784); m. his second cousin once removed, MARY FARNUM (*Ralph Farnum⁴, Ralph Farnum³, Elizabeth Holt Farnum², Nicholas¹*), b. at York, 14 May 1717 daughter of Ralph and Elizabeth (Austin) Farnum. Joseph had a second marriage to JERUSHA HARMON (widow of Rev. Edward Pell), b. at York, 6 Mar 1716 daughter of John and Mehitable (Parker) Harmon;[166] Jerusha was living in Berwick, ME in 1798.

ii MARY HOLT, b. 30 Oct 1713; m. JACOB BOOKER, b. at York, 17 Oct 1719 son of John and Hester (Adams) Booker. No children have been identified.

255) iii JAMES HOLT, b. at York, 17 Jul 1716; d. about 1742; m. about 1737, ALICE MOULTON, b. at Portsmouth, NH, 4 Jun 1715 daughter of Joseph and Abigail (Ayers) Moulton.

256) iv BENJAMIN HOLT, b. at York, 13 Jan 1717/8; d. at York, 19 Aug 1772; m. at York, 28 Feb 1740, HANNAH MOULTON, b. at Portsmouth, NH, 7 Feb 1720 daughter of Jeremiah and Hannah (Ballard) Moulton.

257) v HANNAH HOLT, b. at York, 4 Apr 1719; m. at York, 8 May 1740, NATHAN RAYNES, b. at York, 9 Jun 1712 son of Nathan and Elizabeth (Payne) Raynes; Nathan d. at York, 1774 (probate 10 Dec 1774).

vi DORCAS HOLT, b. at York, 17 Mar 1721; since she is not in the estate distribution, she may not have married or died young

258) vii LYDIA HOLT, b. at York, 23 Oct 1723; m. at York, 17 Apr 1742, EDWARD INGRAHAM son of Moses Ingraham.

viii SAMUEL HOLT, b. at York, 8 Jul 1726; nothing further known.

51) REBEKAH HOLT (*James², Nicholas¹*), b. at Andover, 29 Mar 1688 daughter of James and Hannah (Allen) Holt; d. at Pomfret, CT, 9 Sep 1762; m. at Andover, 1 Jul 1710, THOMAS GROW,[167] b. at Ipswich, 20 Feb 1684 son of John and Hannah (Lord) Grove; Thomas d. at Pomfret, 13 Jan 1753.

Rebekah and Thomas married in Andover and the births of six children are recorded there. They then relocated to Pomfret perhaps precipitated by the birth of an out-of-wedlock child born to Thomas and Elizabeth Nichols in 1728 (John Grow baptized in 1728).[168] Thomas and Rebekah traveled with their children to Pomfret where they were first settlers.

259) i REBEKAH GROW, b. at Andover, 21 Apr 1712; d. at Pomfret, 30 Jan 1762; m. at Pomfret, 16 Jan 1734, STEPHEN INGALLS, b. at Andover, 24 Jul 1710 son of John and Sarah (Russell) Ingalls; Stephen d. at Pomfret 10 Dec 1771.

---

[162] Massachusetts Land Records 1620-1986, Essex County, Deeds 1717-1718, volume 32, page 83, accessed through familysearch.org. https://www.familysearch.org/ark:/61903/3:1:3QSQ-G9ZZ-19VL?i=91&wc=MCBG-76D%3A361613201%2C361874101&cc=2106411

[163] Maine Genealogical Society, York Deeds, volume 11, folio 57

[164] Maine Genealogical Society, York Deeds, volume 12, part 1, folio 85

[165] Maine, York County Probate Estate Files, 1690-1917, Case 9643, Estate of Joseph Holt

[166] Farnham, *Descendants of Ralph Farnum*, p 194

[167] The name is sometimes given as Grove.

[168] Massachusetts Vital Records Project; John, s. Elizabeth Nichols "and servant to Nath Frie," bp. ——, 1728. CR1

260) ii THOMAS GROW, b. at Andover, 7 Nov 1714; d. at Guilford, VT, 10 Aug 1806; m. at Pomfret, 26 Jan 1738/9, SUSANNA EATON, b. Apr 1715 daughter of Jonathan and Lydia (Starr) Eaton;[169] Susanna d. at Pomfret, 17 May 1786. Thomas m. 2nd at Hampton, 10 Nov 1786, MARTHA WINTER.

261) iii JOSEPH GROW, b. at Andover, 16 Oct 1717; d. at Newbury, VT, 3 May 1782; m. at Pomfret, 4 Feb 1741/2, ABIGAIL DANA, b. Apr 1722 daughter of Samuel and Susanna (Starr) Dana.

262) iv RUTH GROW, b. at Andover, 2 Aug 1720; d. at Amherst, MA, after 1781; m. at Pomfret, 4 Nov 1740, JOSEPH WILLIAMS likely the son of Joseph and Mary (Goad) Williams; Joseph d. at Amherst, MA, 1781 (probate 1781).

263) v HANNAH GROW, b. at Andover, 8 Nov 1723; d. at Windham, 29 Jul 1765; m. at Pomfret, 27 Feb 1752, EPHRAIM BARKER, b. at Andover, 23 May 1730 son of William and Martha (Ingalls) Barker.

264) vi JAMES GROW, b. at Andover, 25 Oct 1727; d. at Norwich, VT, 27 Oct 1799; m. 6 Mar 1754, ANNA ADAMS, b. 9 Jan 1735; Anna d. at Greensboro, VT, 11 Feb 1813.

Children of John Holt and Sarah Geary

52) MOSES HOLT (*John², Nicholas¹*), b. at Andover, 7 Jun 1686 son of John and Sarah (Geary) Holt; d. at Andover, 7 Nov 1730; m. at Andover, 31 Jan 1715/6, ELIZABETH RUSSELL, b. at Andover, 16 Jul 1687 daughter of Robert and Mary (Marshall) Russell; Elizabeth d. at Andover, 3 Nov 1772.

Moses Holt did not leave a will and his estate entered probate on 14 December 1730 with Nicholas Holt and Timothy Holt as administrators. The final division of the estate occurred 16 November 1743 which was after the death of son Moses. In the division, one-third was set off to the widow and the other two-thirds were divided in four parts. Two-fourths were distributed to the heirs of son Moses deceased and one-fourth each to daughters Mary and Elizabeth.[170]

Moses Holt and Elizabeth Russell were parents of four children.

265) i MOSES HOLT, b. at Andover, 21 Oct 1716; d. at Andover, 6 Jul 1743; m. 9 Jul 1741, his first cousin once removed, PRUDENCE RUSSELL (*Robert Russell⁴, Phebe Johnson Russell³, Mary Holt Johnson², Nicholas¹*), baptized at Andover, 31 Jul 1720 daughter of Robert and Abigail (Flint) Russell; Prudence d. at Andover, 15 Nov 1745. Prudence Russell m. 2nd, 11 Mar 1744/5, her first cousin, JOHN CHANDLER (*Mehitable Russell Chandler⁴, Phebe Johnson Russell³, Mary Holt Johnson², Nicholas¹*), b. 17 Andover, 19 Jan 1722 son of Joseph and Mehitable (Russell) Chandler; John d. at Andover, 11 May 1759. John Chandler m. 2nd, at Andover, 15 Oct 1747, HANNAH PHELPS, b. at Andover, 1709 daughter of Samuel and Hannah (Dane) Phelps; Hannah d. at Andover, 5 Aug 1781.

ii ELIZABETH HOLT, b. at Andover, 12 Mar 1719/20; d. 19 Aug 1744; m. 4 Oct 1743, BENJAMIN BLANCHARD, b. at Andover, 19 Mar 1720/1 son of Benjamin and Mary (Abbott) Blanchard; Benjamin d. at Canterbury, NH, 7 Mar 1791. Benjamin had two further marriages to Keziah Hastings on 27 Dec 1744 and Sarah Burbank on 9 Jul 1778. Elizabeth Holt and Benjamin Blanchard had one son, Benjamin who was born 2 Jul 1744 and died 2 Oct 1744.

iii MARY HOLT, b. at Andover, 4 Jul 1722; Mary was living in 1744 at the final division of her father's estate. Nothing further in known.

iv SARAH HOLT, baptized 22 Mar 1724; d. 23 Jan 1737/8.

[169] Jordan, *Genealogical and Personal History of the Alleghany Valley*, volume 1, p 144

[170] *Essex County, MA: Probate File Papers, 1638-1881.*Online database. *AmericanAncestors.org.* New England Historic Genealogical Society, 2014. Case 13674

Generation Four Families

Grandchildren of Elizabeth Holt and Ralph Farnum

53) BENJAMIN ABBOTT (*Sarah Farnum Abbott[3], Elizabeth Holt Farnum[2], Nicholas[1]*), b. 11 Jul 1686 son of Benjamin and Sarah (Abbott) Farnum; d. before 5 Dec 1748 (probate date); m. 1st 24 Dec 1716, his first cousin, ELIZABETH ABBOTT, b. 25 Jul 1690 daughter of George and Dorcas (Graves) Abbott. Benjamin m. 2nd 23 Oct 1722 MARY CARLETON, b. 7 Apr 1700 daughter of John and Hannah (Osgood) Carleton; Mary died 19 Jan 1725/6. Benjamin m. 3rd 1729, ABIGAIL ABBOTT, b. 7 Oct 1699 daughter of Nehemiah and Abigail (Lovejoy) Abbott; Abigail d. 8 Dec 1753.

As the oldest son, Benjamin assumed ownership of his father's farm. His father died when Benjamin was about 17.

Benjamin did not leave a will. His estate entered probate 5 December 1748 and includes an 81-page probate document. The probate settlement dated 18 February 1754 includes the following heirs: eldest son Benjamin, second son Daniel, daughter Mary, daughter Sarah the wife of James Holt, daughter Abigail, son Abiel, son Jacob, daughter Elizabeth, daughter Anna, and daughter Dorcas. Jacob, Elizabeth, Anna, and Dorcas have guardians who represent their interests.[171]

Benjamin and Elizabeth were parents of one child.

186) i SARAH ABBOTT, b. 2 Aug 1718; d. 5 Mar 1778; m. 10 Apr 1746, her second cousin, JAMES HOLT (*Nicholas[3], Nicholas[2], Nicholas[1]*), b. 13 Jan 1722/3 son of Nicholas and Dorcas (Abbott) Holt. James m. 2nd Phebe Ballard who was the widow of Abiel Abbott son of Benjamin and Abigail (Abbott) Abbott; James Holt d. 22 Aug 1812.

Children of Benjamin Abbott and his second wife, Mary Carleton, born at Andover:

266) i BENJAMIN ABBOT, b. 21 Oct 1723; d. at Hollis, NH, 1771;[172] m. 2 Apr 1747, his second cousin, ELIZABETH ABBOTT, b. 5 Nov 1727 daughter of George and Mary (Phillips) Abbott. Elizabeth m. 2nd, 22 Mar 1775, James Pollard.[173] Elizabeth m. 3rd, Josiah Bowers of Billerica who died in 1794. Elizabeth died about 1802 at Westford (date of will 10 Aug 1802). There is a 1790 deed from Josiah Bowers of Billerica to his son Benjamin and named in the deed record is Josiah's wife Elizabeth.[174]

267) ii DANIEL ABBOTT, b. 29 Dec 1725; d. Apr 1793;[175] m. 3 Apr 1756, LUCY PARKER, b. 5 Jun 1732 daughter of Thomas and Lydia (Richardson) Parker; the date of death of Lucy is not known.

Benjamin Abbott and third wife, Abigail Abbott, had nine children born at Andover.

i ABIGAIL ABBOTT, b. 28 Mar 1731; d. 21 Oct 1733.

268) ii MARY ABBOTT, b. 21 Jul 1732; d. at Milford, NH, 9 Aug 1798; m. 13 Nov 1759, NEHEMIAH BARKER, b. at Methuen, 11 Feb 1734 son of Ebenezer and Abigail (Morse) Barker; Nehemiah d. 20 Jan 1810.

269) iii ABIGAIL ABBOTT, b. 13 Jan 1733/4; d. 1 Feb 1807; m. 1 Jun 1758, her second cousin, once removed, JOHN ABBOT, b. 12 Sep 1735 son of John and Phebe (Fiske) Abbott; John d. 24 Apr 1818.

186) iv ABIEL ABBOT, b. 24 Jul 1735; d. 24 Jun 1764; m. 5 Feb 1761, his third cousin PHEBE BALLARD, b. 25 Jul 1738 daughter of Josiah and Mary (Chandler) Ballard. Phebe m. 2nd as his second wife, her third cousin, JAMES HOLT son of Nicholas and Dorcas (Abbott) Holt; Phebe d. 9 Jun 1815. James Holt was first married to Abiel Abbot's half-sister, SARAH ABBOTT, b. at Andover, 2 Aug 1718 daughter of Benjamin and Elizabeth (Abbott) Abbott; Sarah d. at Andover, 5 Mar 1778.

v JACOB ABBOTT, b. 2 Feb 1736/7; d. at Albany while in the army "of cold and fatigue" Feb 1760.[176]

---

[171] *Essex County, MA: Probate File Papers, 1638-1881. Probate of Benjamin Abbott, 5 Dec 1748, Case number 23.*

[172] There is a probate record in Middlesex County, MA in 1771 related to Benjamin's estate and includes information about Benjamin being a mortgagee of Samuel Abbott. Twenty-three acres were set off to widow Elizabeth Abbott. Perley's article in the Essex Antiquarian gives a date of 5 Jan 1770.

[173] This marriage may not be accurate. There is a record for a marriage in Hollis 22 Mar 1775 for "Captain Jonas Pollard" of Westford and Mrs. Elizabeth Abbott. There is a Captain James Pollard of Westford who died in 1781 with a widow Elizabeth named in the will. James Pollard was born about 1708 and he was widowed in 1774. I believe the marriage transcription in the Hollis records is an error and the spouse is James Pollard.

[174] Middlesex County Deeds, 1792-1827, volumes 110-112, Images 85-86, Familysearch.org.

[175] Abbot and Abbot, *Genealogical Record of Descendants*

[176] Abbot and Abbot, *Genealogical Record of Descendants*

270) vi ELIZABETH ABBOTT, b. 27 Oct 1738; d. at Conway, NH, 12 Oct 1789;[177] m. 1st 1 Jun 1758, EBENEZER CUMMINGS, b. at Groton, 17 Apr 1735 son of William and Lucy (Colburn) Cummings; Ebenezer d. 1 Jun 1778. Elizabeth m. 2nd as his fourth wife, THOMAS MERRILL, b. at Haverhill, 5 Feb 1723/4 son of John and Lydia (Haynes) Merrill. Thomas had married as his first wife, Phebe Abbott; Thomas Merrill d. at Conway, NH, 21 Jul 1788.

271) vii ANNA ABBOTT, b. 13 Oct 1740; d. at Hollis, NH, 15 Jan 1810; m. Jan 1762, EPHRAIM BURGE, b. at Westford, 1 May 1738 son of Josiah and Susannah (Jaquith) Burge; Ephraim d. 20 Jul 1784.

viii JOEL ABBOTT, b. 20 Oct 1742; d. 23 Mar 1742/3.

272) ix DORCAS ABBOT, b. 1 Aug 1744; d. at Wilton, NH, 23 Feb 1829;[178] m. 20 Nov 1764, her second cousin, once removed, ABIEL ABBOT, b. 19 Apr 1741 son of John and Phebe (Fiske) Abbott; Abiel d. 19 Aug 1809.

54) DAVID ABBOT (*Sarah Farnum Abbott*[3], *Elizabeth Holt Farnum*[2], *Nicholas*[1]), b. 18 Jan 1688/9 son of Benjamin and Sarah (Abbott) Farnum; d. 14 Nov 1753; m. 20 Mar 1717/8, HANNAH DANFORTH, b. at Billerica 20 Aug 1698 daughter of Samuel and Hannah (Crosby) Danforth; Hannah d. 8 Jan 1788.

David had a farm at Merrimack Corner in Andover. He and his wife Hannah had nine children all born at Andover.

The will of David Abbot, written 7 November 1753, has the following bequests: beloved wife Hannah receives the widow's third; beloved son Solomon receives land and meadows above the brook, and "all the rest" of the children receive the rest of the estate. These children are David, Josiah, Jonathan, Benjamin, Hannah, and Sarah. The four boys share equally while the two daughters get half as much as each of the boys. The bequests to the younger children do include bequests of land. David calls on his "trusty friends" Ebenezer Abbot, Samuel Abbot, and Thomas Abbot to divide the land and the sons are to buy out the value of the portion of the daughters.[179]

Two of the sons, Josiah and Benjamin, died within a week after the death of their father. A third child, daughter Elizabeth, died two months before her father. The family might have been a victim of one of the several epidemics that came through the colonies. In 1753, some areas of Massachusetts had an outbreak of "putrid fever"[180] and there was also a smallpox outbreak. The causes of death are not given on the death records for these four family members.

i HANNAH ABBOT, b. 21 Oct 1721; d. 25 Feb 1721/2.

ii HANNAH ABBOT, b. 23 Dec 1723; d. 12 Mar 1813; Hannah did not marry.

273) iii SARAH ABBOT, b. 7 Apr 1726; d. at Bedford, 5 Mar 1814; m. 1st 30 Jan 1753, ROBERT HILDRETH, b. at Dracut, 18 May 1713 son of Ephraim and Mercy (Richardson) Hildreth; Robert d. 1760. Sarah m. 2nd 28 May 1761, JOHN LANE, b. at Bedford, 2 Oct 1720 son of Job and Martha (Ruggles) Lane; John d. 7 Dec 1789. Sarah m. 3rd 14 Jul 1791, Benjamin Parker.

274) iv DAVID ABBOT, b. 28 Mar 1728; d. at Billerica 1 Nov 1798; m. 28 Dec 1752, PRUDENCE SHELDON, b. at Billerica 31 Aug 1732 daughter of Samuel and Sarah[181] (Hutchinson) Richardson. A death record for Prudence was not located, although she was living at the time of her husband's death and she was on the tax rolls in Billerica for 1798.

275) v SOLOMON ABBOT, b. 14 Feb 1730/1; d. probably at Dracut 17 Dec 1797;[182] m. 3 May 1756, HANNAH COLBY (*Hannah Gray Colby*[4], *Edward Gray*[3], *Hannah Holt Gray*[2], *Nicholas*[1]), b. 22 Oct 1735 daughter of Daniel and Hannah (Gray) Colby; Hannah's date of death is not known.

vi ELIZABETH ABBOT, b. 2 Aug 1733; d. 31 Aug 1753.

vii JOSIAH ABBOT, b. 1735; d. 26 Nov 1753.

276) viii JONATHAN ABBOT, b. 24 Oct 1739; d. 10 Apr 1817; m. 13 Nov 1759, his second cousin once removed, MARY CHANDLER (*Priscilla Holt Chandler*[4], *Timothy*[3], *James*[2], *Nicholas*[1]), b. 15 Jun 1740 daughter of Nathan and Priscilla (Holt) Chandler; Mary d. 1 Apr 1824.

ix BENJAMIN ABBOT, b. 16 Jan 1743; d. 20 Nov 1753.

---

[177] *New Hampshire, Death and Disinterment Records, 1754-1947*

[178] *New Hampshire: Births, Deaths and Marriages, 1654-1969.* (From microfilmed records. Online database: *AmericanAncestors.org*, New England Historic Genealogical Society, 2014.)

[179] *Essex County, MA: Probate File Papers, 1638-1881. Probate of David Abbot, 26 Nov 1753, Case number 28.*

[180] Ernest Caulfield (1950, January). The Pursuit of a Pestilence. In *Proceedings of the American Antiquarian Society* (Vol. 60, No. 1, p. 21). American Antiquarian Society

[181] The marriage record lists her name as Mary Hutchinson, but all the births of the children, including a daughter Sarah born in 1719, list the mother's name as Sarah.

[182] Abbot and Abbot, *Genealogical Record of Descendants* gives this date of death; a death record or probate record was not located.

55) SARAH FARNUM (*Ralph Farnum[3], Elizabeth Holt Farnum[2], Nicholas[1]*), b. at Andover, 5 May 1686 daughter of Ralph and Sarah (Sterling) Farnum; d. 1766; m. 14 Feb 1712, her first cousin, HENRY LOVEJOY (*Mary Farnum Lovejoy[3], Elizabeth Holt Farnum[2], Nicholas[1]*), b. at Andover, 27 Nov 1683 son of William and Mary (Farnum) Lovejoy; Henry d. at Andover, 1 Feb 1776.

Henry Lovejoy owned an iron works and grist mill in Andover. In a deed recorded 4 February 1742, son Henry Lovejoy and his wife Phebe sold to his father Henry for "___ hundred pounds" his interest in the iron works and grist mill at Andover. It was about this time that Henry and Phebe relocated to Concord, New Hampshire.[183] On 13 September 1746, father Henry Lovejoy sold one-half of his grist mill to son Joshua for £250 and the other half to son William. On that same date, Henry sold two parcels of land to his son William, described as a saddler, for £400. On 13 July 1762 Henry sold three parcels of land to son Joshua for £150.[184]

Sarah Farnum and Henry Lovejoy were parents of twelve children born at Andover.

277) i SARAH LOVEJOY, baptized at Andover, 30 Nov 1712; d. at Andover, 11 Aug 1767; m. at Andover, 27 Nov 1736, BENJAMIN SMITH, b. about 1707 likely the son of Samuel and Sarah (-) Smith; Benjamin d. at Andover, 24 Jan 1779.

278) ii HENRY LOVEJOY, b. at Andover, 14 Aug 1714; d. at Concord, NH, 15 Mar 1793; m. 1 Jan 1735, PHEBE CHANDLER, b. at Andover, 2 Jan 1714/5 daughter of John and Hannah (Frye) Chandler; Phebe d. at Concord, Jan 1805.

279) iii DAVID LOVEJOY, b. at Andover, 10 Oct 1715; d. at Pembroke, NH, 18 Feb 1819; m. at Andover, 26 Mar 1741, ELIZABETH CHANDLER, b. at Andover, 5 Feb 1721 daughter of Zebadiah and Sarah (Abbott) Chandler.

280) iv CALEB LOVEJOY, b. at Andover, 28 Dec 1716; d. at Pembroke, 1781;[185] m. at Andover, 26 Jan 1738, MEHITABLE CHANDLER, b. at Andover, 1717 daughter of Zebadiah and Sarah (Abbott) Chandler; Mehitable d. at Andover, 26 Jan 1786.

171) v MARY LOVEJOY, baptized at Andover, 14 Dec 1718; d. about 1765; m. at Andover, 15 Nov 1737, RICHARD EASTMAN, b. at Haverhill, 9 Aug 1712 son of Jonathan and Hannah (Green) Eastman; Richard d. at Lovell, ME, 29 Dec 1807. Richard Eastman m. 2nd, SARAH ABBOTT (*Abigail Farnum Abbott[4], Ralph Farnum[3], Elizabeth Holt Farnum[2], Nicholas[1]*), b. at Andover, 13 Aug 1730 daughter of James and Abigail (Farnum) Abbott. Sarah Abbott was 1st married to JOB ABBOTT (*Zerviah Holt Abbott[3], Henry[2], Nicholas[1]*), b. at Andover 3 Oct 1724 son of Jonathan and Zerviah (Holt) Abbott.

281) vi JOSHUA LOVEJOY, b. at Andover, 2 Dec 1719; d. at Andover, 2 Feb 1812; m. at Andover, 24 Mar 1742/3, LYDEA ABBOTT, b. at Andover, 10 Feb 1722/3 daughter of Henry and Mary (Platts) Abbott; Lydea d. at Andover, 11 Sep 1807.

168) vii MARTHA LOVEJOY, b. at Andover, 2 Nov 1720; d. at Andover, 1768; m. at Andover, 8 Oct 1739, her second cousin, JONATHAN ABBOTT (*Zerviah Holt Abbott[3], Henry[2], Nicholas[1]*), baptized at Andover, 12 Dec 1714 son of Jonathan and Zerviah (Holt) Abbott; Jonathan d. at Andover, 31 May 1794. Jonathan was second married to Mary Abbott.

viii WILLIAM LOVEJOY, b. 31 Jan 1722; d. 15 Apr 1722.

282) ix WILLIAM LOVEJOY, b. at Andover, 10 Apr 1723; d. at Andover, 1759 (probate 13 Nov 1759); m. at Andover, 13 Feb 1744, HANNAH EVANS.

283) x STEPHEN LOVEJOY, b. at Andover, 7 Jun 1724; m. at York, ME, 26 Jun 1749, OLIVE TRAFTON, b. at York, 4 Dec 1725 daughter of Zacchaeus and Annabel (Allen) Trafton.

xi JERUSHA LOVEJOY, b. 5 Jul 1725; d. 15 Jul 1725.

xii ABIEL LOVEJOY, b. 24 Feb 1731; d. 8 Feb 1732.

56) HENRY FARNUM (*Ralph Farnum[3], Elizabeth Holt Farnum[2], Nicholas[1]*), b. at Andover, 15 Sep 1687 son of Ralph and Sarah (Sterling) Farnum; d. at Windham, 25 Jul 1732; m. at Andover, 12 Jun 1712, PHEBE RUSSELL, b. at Andover, 21 Jan 1689/90 daughter of Thomas and Phebe (Johnson) Russell; Phebe d. after 1753. Phebe m. 2nd at Canterbury, 3 Jan 1734, NATHANIEL ROBBINS; Nathaniel d. at Windham, 7 Apr 1753.

---

183 Massachusetts Land Records 1620-1986, Essex County Deeds, 84:167

184 Massachusetts Land Records 1620-1986, Essex County Deeds, 88:187, 88:188, 112:54

185 This is the date of death used by the DAR; a record was not located.

Henry and Phebe began their family in Andover. Henry purchased land in Windham County, Connecticut in 1725 and the family relocated there. Henry committed suicide by hanging.[186] Phebe remarried, and her second husband died in 1753. In 1753, the dower from the estate of Henry Farnum was set off to his widow Phebe Farnum alias Robens.[187]

Phebe Russell and Henry Farnum were parents of nine children, all but the youngest two children born perhaps at Andover, although most of the births are recorded both at Andover and at Windham.

284) i PHEBE FARNUM, b. at Andover, 4 Jul 1713; d. at Windham, 1750 (probate Apr 1750); m. at Windham, 9 May 1735, JOSEPH PRESTON, b. at Andover, 22 Aug 1713 son of Joseph and Rebecca (Preston) Preston; Joseph d. at Windham, 24 Feb 1738.

285) ii HENRY FARNUM, b. at Andover, 8 Apr 1715; d. at Sprague, CT, 20 Jun 1799; m. 3 Nov 1741, SARAH READ (widow of Joseph Knight), b. at Norwich, 28 Dec 1711 daughter of William and Ann (Stark) Read; Sarah d. at Sprague, 24 Feb 1781.

286) iii MANASSEH FARNUM, b. at Windham, 15 Feb 1717; d. at Ashford, 1768 (probate 1768); m. at Windham, 23 Apr 1739, KEZIAH FORD, b. at Windham, 27 Mar 1721 daughter of Joseph and Elizabeth (Hovey) Ford; Keziah was living in 1768.

iv JEMIMA FARNUM, b. at Windham, 6 Feb 1719; m. 7 Feb 1746, NATHANIEL JOHNSON. No children have been located for Jemima and Nathaniel.

287) v EPHRAIM FARNUM, b. at Windham, 20 Mar 1721; d. at Norwich, about 1750 (probate 17 Jan 1751); m. 1 Nov 1744, CHENEY ANNE WHITE, b. at Marshfield, MA, 16 Jul 1722 daughter of Ebenezer and Hannah (Doggett) White. Cheney Anne second married John Louden.

288) vi JOSHUA FARNUM, b. at Windham, 29 Mar 1723; d. at Scotland, CT, 3 Feb 1797; m. at Hampton, 6 Jun 1748, SARAH FORD, b. at Windham, 20 Dec 1714 daughter of Joseph and Elizabeth (Hovey) Ford; Sarah d. at Scotland, 28 Apr 1789.

289) vii ELIPHALET FARNUM, b. at Windham, 21 Mar 1725; m. 1st at Canterbury, 11 Oct 1750, MARY ROGERS, possibly Mary b. at Windham, 6 Oct 1727 daughter of Hope and Esther (Meacham) Rogers; Mary d. at Canterbury, 1 May 1753. Eliphalet m. 2nd at Canterbury, 1 Feb 1757, MARY ADAMS.

viii STEPHEN FARNUM, b. at Windham, 27 Mar 1728. He perhaps m. at Pomfret, 2 Mar 1752, JOANNA WARNER. No children were located for Stephen with his possible marriage to Joanna.

290) ix ELIAB FARNUM, b. at Windham, 24 Jul 1731; d. at Otisville, NY, 9 Jun 1806; m. at Preston, 19 Jun 1754, ABIGAIL KILLAM, b. at Norwich, 19 Aug 1736 daughter of John and Abigail (Kimball) Killam; Abigail d. at Otisville, about 1782. Eliab m. 2nd EUNICE NICHOLS, b. about 1739. Eunice had two previous marriages to John Osborne and Samuel Bouton.

57) RALPH FARNUM (*Ralph Farnum³, Elizabeth Holt Farnum², Nicholas¹*), b. at Andover, 25 May 1689 son of Ralph and Sarah (Sterling) Farnum; d. at York, ME, 1758; m. about 1712, ELIZABETH AUSTIN, b. at York, about 1687 daughter of Matthew and Mary (Littlefield) Austin.

Ralph and Elizabeth resided in York where Ralph was a cordwainer by trade in addition to farming. It is reported that Elizabeth Austin's sister Mary, then age five years, was taken by the Indians in 1692 during the York massacre. Mary was never returned to her family and was raised by a French family in Québec.[188]

In his will written 24 August 1756 (presented 16 March 1758), Ralph Farnum bequeathed to his son Joseph, besides what he has received, £2.13.4 and son Matthew the same bequest. Son Jonathan receives the house where he now lives and one-third of the land that lies between the river and the highway. Son Paul receives £2.13.4. Sons Nathaniel and John receive the house in which Henry now lives and two-thirds of the land lying between the river and the highway. Daughter Betty Jakes receives £1.6.8 and granddaughter Elizabeth Farnum daughter of son Ralph deceased receives thirteen shillings four pence. Son Nathaniel was named sole executor. Although Nathaniel was named executor, the estate was administered by Jonathan Farnum and son-in-law Joseph Holt.[189] This was a consequence of the will being disallowed due to inadequate witnesses to the will and lack of clarity in parts of the will.

Ralph and Elizabeth were parents of eleven children born at York, Maine.[190]

---

[186] Farnham, *The New England Descendants of Immigrant Ralph Farnum*, p 91

[187] *Connecticut State Library (Hartford, Connecticut);* Probate Place: *Hartford, Connecticut, Probate Packets, Durkee, P-Fitch, Eleazer, 1719-1880, Estate of Henry Farnam, Case 1312*

[188] Farnham, The New England Descendants of Ralph Farnum, p 94. A lengthy detailing of Ralph's land transactions and other details can be found in the Farnham genealogy.

[189] Maine, York County Probate Estate Files, Estate of Ralph Farnum, Case 5570

[190] Bragdon, Vital Records of York, Maine, NEHGS, 1956, volume 110, p 59

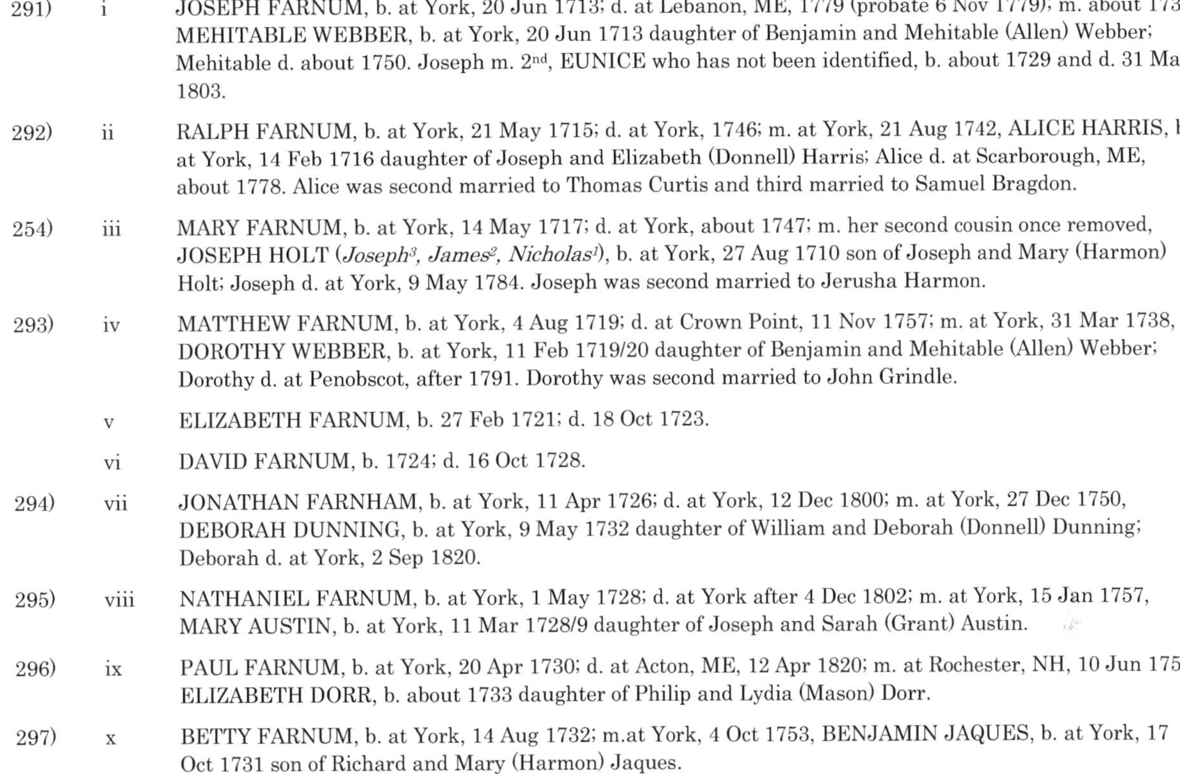

291) i JOSEPH FARNUM, b. at York, 20 Jun 1713; d. at Lebanon, ME, 1779 (probate 6 Nov 1779); m. about 1734, MEHITABLE WEBBER, b. at York, 20 Jun 1713 daughter of Benjamin and Mehitable (Allen) Webber; Mehitable d. about 1750. Joseph m. 2nd, EUNICE who has not been identified, b. about 1729 and d. 31 May 1803.

292) ii RALPH FARNUM, b. at York, 21 May 1715; d. at York, 1746; m. at York, 21 Aug 1742, ALICE HARRIS, b. at York, 14 Feb 1716 daughter of Joseph and Elizabeth (Donnell) Harris; Alice d. at Scarborough, ME, about 1778. Alice was second married to Thomas Curtis and third married to Samuel Bragdon.

254) iii MARY FARNUM, b. at York, 14 May 1717; d. at York, about 1747; m. her second cousin once removed, JOSEPH HOLT (*Joseph^3, James^2, Nicholas^1*), b. at York, 27 Aug 1710 son of Joseph and Mary (Harmon) Holt; Joseph d. at York, 9 May 1784. Joseph was second married to Jerusha Harmon.

293) iv MATTHEW FARNUM, b. at York, 4 Aug 1719; d. at Crown Point, 11 Nov 1757; m. at York, 31 Mar 1738, DOROTHY WEBBER, b. at York, 11 Feb 1719/20 daughter of Benjamin and Mehitable (Allen) Webber; Dorothy d. at Penobscot, after 1791. Dorothy was second married to John Grindle.

v ELIZABETH FARNUM, b. 27 Feb 1721; d. 18 Oct 1723.

vi DAVID FARNUM, b. 1724; d. 16 Oct 1728.

294) vii JONATHAN FARNHAM, b. at York, 11 Apr 1726; d. at York, 12 Dec 1800; m. at York, 27 Dec 1750, DEBORAH DUNNING, b. at York, 9 May 1732 daughter of William and Deborah (Donnell) Dunning; Deborah d. at York, 2 Sep 1820.

295) viii NATHANIEL FARNUM, b. at York, 1 May 1728; d. at York after 4 Dec 1802; m. at York, 15 Jan 1757, MARY AUSTIN, b. at York, 11 Mar 1728/9 daughter of Joseph and Sarah (Grant) Austin.

296) ix PAUL FARNUM, b. at York, 20 Apr 1730; d. at Acton, ME, 12 Apr 1820; m. at Rochester, NH, 10 Jun 1753; ELIZABETH DORR, b. about 1733 daughter of Philip and Lydia (Mason) Dorr.

297) x BETTY FARNUM, b. at York, 14 Aug 1732; m.at York, 4 Oct 1753, BENJAMIN JAQUES, b. at York, 17 Oct 1731 son of Richard and Mary (Harmon) Jaques.

298) xi JOHN FARNUM, b. at York, 26 May 1735; d. at Bowdoin, 24 Nov 1819; m. about 1762, ABIGAIL STOVER,[191] b. at York, 19 Sep 1732 daughter of John and Miriam (Harmon) Stover.

58) DANIEL FARNUM (*Ralph Farnum^3, Elizabeth Holt Farnum^2, Nicholas^1*), b. at Andover, 21 Jan 1690/1 son of Ralph and Sarah (Sterling) Farnum; d. at Georgetown, ME, 1746 (probate April 1746); m. 1st about 1719, HANNAH BRAGDON, b. at York, 25 May 1697 daughter of Arthur and Sarah (Came) Bragdon; Hannah d. at York, 2 Nov 1729. Daniel m. 2nd at York, 21 Aug 1733, PATIENCE HUBBARD (widow of William Card), b. at South Berwick, 30 Mar 1704 daughter of Philip and Elizabeth (Goodwin) Card; Patience d. at Georgetown, ME.

Daniel Farnum was born in Andover and settled in the area of York, Maine where the births of his children are recorded. About 1734 he was in Georgetown. Ralph was a carpenter by trade and he also owned part of a sawmill which he operated. He held property along the York River.

Son Daniel Farnum petitioned the Court 7 April 1746 requesting that he be named administrator of his father's estate. Part of the reason for this was that the widow was very prejudiced against the children by Daniel's first wife. This included that she had intimated to son Daniel that if it were within her power as administratrix that she would keep him from having any part of the estate. Daniel also claimed that his father had built and improved a valuable gristmill and that since his father's death, Benjamin Webber had taken over the mill without any right. Son Daniel was named administrator. Real estate was valued at £495 with about 300 acres of land and part of a sawmill. Personal estate was valued at £773.[192] Administrative costs included clothing for two minor children John and Jeremiah and a payment of £2.8.0 "to costs in getting negro Scipio belonging to the estate out of the hands of Andrew Bordman who detained him."

There are records for four children of Daniel Farnum and Hannah Bragdon born at York, Maine.[193]

299) i DANIEL FARNHAM, b. at York, 15 Nov 1719; d. at Newburyport, MA, 18 Mar 1776; m. at Cambridge, 11 Jul 1740, SYBIL ANGIER, b. 5 Sep 1718 daughter of Samuel and Dorothy (Avery) Angier; Sybil d. at Newburyport, Jun 1797.

300) ii ZEBADIAH FARNUM, b. at York, 19 Feb 1722; m. at York, 15 Jun 1748, LUCY WEARE, b. at York, 2 Sep 1724 daughter of Elias and Elizabeth (Sayword) Weare.

---

[191] Some records also give the name of this family as Storer.

[192] Maine, York County Estate Files, Estate of Daniel Farnum, Case 5552, accessed through familysearch.org

[193] Bragdon, Vital Records of York, Maine, NEHGS, 1956, volume 110, p 95

301) iii OLIVE FARNUM, b. at York, 5 Jul 1725; m. at York, 11 Nov 1747, EDWARD GROW, b. at York, 27 Oct 1722 son of William and Joanna (Poor) Grow; Edward d. at York, 5 May 1785.

302) iv JOSHUA FARNHAM, b. at York, Nov 1728; d. at Woolwich, ME, 15 Jan 1803; m. at York, 13 Feb 1749/50, MARY GROW, b. at York, 13 Sep 1732 daughter of William and Joanna (Poor) Grow.[194]

Daniel Farnum and Patience Hubbard were parents of three children.

303) i JOHN FARNUM, b. at Georgetown, ME, about 1735; d. in service and recorded at Woolwich, 7 May 1778; m. 4 Oct 1763, HANNAH CARD, b. at Georgetown, about 1746 daughter of Winchester and Elizabeth (Grow) Card; Hannah d. at Bowdoinham, Jan 1827.

304) ii DAVID FARNHAM, b. at Georgetown, ME, about 1737; d. at Woolwich, 1 Sep 1773; m. at Woolwich, 4 Jul 1763, MARTHA CARD, b. at Georgetown, about 1743 daughter of Winchester and Elizabeth (Grow) Card; Martha d. at Woolwich, 27 May 1831.

iii JEREMIAH FARNUM, b. at Georgetown, about 1740. He was likely living in 1790 at Woolwich but nothing definitive has been located on his family.

59) ABIGAIL FARNUM (*Ralph Farnum³, Elizabeth Holt Farnum², Nicholas¹*), b. at Andover, 3 May 1692 daughter of Ralph and Sarah (Sterling) Farnum; m. at Andover, 6 Jan 1713/4, JAMES ABBOTT, b. at Andover, 12 Feb 1694/5 son of William and Elizabeth (Geary) Abbott; James d. at Concord, NH, 26 Dec 1787.

James was a farmer. He and Abigail married and had all their fifteen children in Andover. The family then relocated to New Hampshire about 1735. They lived for a time in one of the garrison houses of early Concord.[195]

305) i ABIGAIL ABBOTT, b. 1 Jan 1714/5; d. at Charlestown about 1737; m. 13 May 1734, JOHN KIDDER, b. at Charlestown 13 Feb 1709 son of Stephen and Mary (Johnson) Kidder. John married second Anna Walker and third Mary Snow.

306) ii JAMES ABBOTT, b. 12 Jan 1716/7; d. at Newbury, VT, 27 Dec 1803; m. about 1742, SARAH BANCROFT, b. 19 Feb 1722 daughter of Samuel and Sarah (Lampson) Bancroft; Sarah d. 1765.[196]

iii ELIZABETH ABBOTT, b. 24 Jun 1718.

iv WILLIAM ABBOTT, b. 8 Sep 1719; d. 29 Oct 1741.

v RACHEL ABBOTT, b. 17 Nov 1720; (little other information yet). The Abbot genealogy states she had husbands named Manning and Russell and a daughter named Phebe. She was also reported to have gone to Londonderry, but no information has been found for her.

vi EZRA ABBOTT, b. 11 Mar 1721/2; d. 5 Dec 1741.

307) vii REUBEN ABBOTT, b. 4 Apr 1723; d. at Concord, NH, 13 May 1822; m. 1st RHODA WHITTEMORE, b. at Malden, 18 Aug 1729 daughter of Elias and Rhoda (Holt) Whittemore; d. 29 Jan 1785. Reuben m. 2nd DINAH BLANCHARD, b. at Andover, 28 Dec 1731 daughter of Stephen and Deborah (Phelps) Blanchard; Dinah d. 11 Mar 1826. Dinah Blanchard had first been married to her cousin Joseph Blanchard.

viii SIMEON ABBOTT, b. 18 Sep 1724; d. 15 Nov 1741.

308) ix AMOS ABBOTT, b. 18 Feb 1725/6; d. at Concord 3 Dec 1821; m. by 1754, as her 2nd husband, REBECCA ABBOTT (widow of ABIEL CHANDLER), b. 24 Apr 1717 daughter of Nathaniel and Dorcas (Hibbert) Abbott; Rebecca d. 13 Feb 1803.

309) x PHEBE ABBOTT, b. 22 Nov 1727; d. at Conway NH, 29 Sep 1754; m. 5 Nov 1747, as his 1st wife, THOMAS MERRILL, b. 5 Feb 1723/4 at Haverhill son of John and Lydia (Haynes) Merrill. Thomas had a total of four marriages, his 2nd to Mehitable Harriman, 3rd to Abigail Goodhue, and 4th to Elizabeth Abbott daughter of Benjamin and Abigail (Abbott) Abbott. Thomas Merrill d. at Conway 21 Jun 1788.

xi Son ABBOTT, b. and d. 1729.

310) xii REBECCA ABBOTT, b. 13 Aug 1730; d. at NH date unknown; m. 1750, ENOCH EASTMAN, b. at Salisbury, 1 Jun 1725 son of Joseph and Abigail (Merrill) Eastman.

---

[194] Davis, *John Grow of Ipswich*

[195] Bouton, *History of Concord*, p 627

[196] A gravestone engraved with the names James Abbott and Sarah Bancroft is in Oxbow Cemetery in Newbury, VT.

171) xiii SARAH ABBOTT, twin of Rebecca, b. 13 Aug 1730; m. about 1751, as her 1st husband, her second cousin, JOB ABBOTT (*Zerviah Holt Abbott*[3], *Henry*[2], *Nicholas*[1]), b. 3 Oct 724 son of Jonathan and Zerviah (Holt) Abbott. Sarah m. 2nd about 1765, RICHARD EASTMAN, b. at Haverhill, 9 Aug 1712 son of Jonathan and Hannah (Green) Eastman; Richard d. at Lovell, ME, 29 Dec 1807. Richard Eastman m. 1st 15 Nov 1737, MARY LOVEJOY (*Henry Lovejoy*[4], *Mary Farnum Lovejoy*[3], *Elizabeth Holt Farnum*[2], *Nicholas*[1]), b. at Andover, Dec 1718 daughter of Henry and Sarah (Farnum) Lovejoy.

311) xiv MARY ABBOTT, b. 12 Oct 1732; d, about 1780; m. by 1760 ADONIJAH TYLER, b. 26 Nov 1738[197] son of Moses and Miriam (Bailey) Tyler; Adonijah d. 12 Oct 1812 at Hopkinton, NH.

xv HANNAH ABBOTT, b. 12 Jan 1734/5; d. 10 Sep 1736.

60) WILLIAM FARNUM (*Ralph Farnum*[3], *Elizabeth Holt Farnum*[2], *Nicholas*[1]), b. at Andover, 5 Aug 1693 son of Ralph and Sarah (Sterling) Farnum; d. at Windham, 1742 (probate 1742); m. at Andover, 2 Apr 1715, ANNE FLINT, b. at Salem, 3 Aug 1693 daughter of Joseph and Abigail (Howard) Flint; Anne d. at Windham, about 1755.

William was born in Ashford, but as a young man was part of the migration of families from Andover to new settlements in Windham County, Connecticut including Ashford. The migration from Andover to Windham County in the 1720's included William and three of his brothers, Henry, Nathaniel, and Joseph.

William Farnum did not leave a will. On 10 May 1742, William Farnum, Jr. signed that he received 40 acres of land in Canterbury by deed of gift from his honored father as his full portion of the estate. On 17 June 1755, the portion of the estate that had been set off for the widow's thirds was distributed to the heirs of the estate. William Farnum of Canterbury received two-sevenths as his double portion and the remaining sevenths to Zebadiah Farnum, Anna Rogers, Elijah Farnum, Isaiah Farnum, and Eunice Farnum. On 26 April 1756, the final distribution included the heirs of Eunice Farnum who was then deceased.[198] The estate of Eunice Farnum was in probate in 1756. The 1759 will of son Isaiah Farnum includes bequests to Isaiah Farnum the son of his brother William and to his brothers and sisters William Farnum, Zebadiah Farnum, Elijah Farnum, and Anna Rogers.

William Farnum and Anne Flint were parents of seven children born at Windham.

312) i WILLIAM FARNUM, b. at Windham, 15 Aug 1718; d. at Windham, 29 Oct 1800; m. at Windham, 23 Jun 1742, MARTHA FULLER, b. at Windham, 7 Sep 1724 daughter of Stephen and Hannah (Moulton) Fuller; Martha d. at Hampton, 16 Apr 1792.

313) ii ZEBADIAH FARNUM, b. at Windham 18 Jun 1721; d. at Hampton, 8 Sep 1814; m. at Windham, 27 Jul 1743, MARY FULLER, b. at Windham, 9 Mar 1726/7 daughter of Stephen and Hannah (Moulton0 Fuller; Mary d. at Hampton, 20 Jul 1802.

314) iii ANNA FARNUM, b. at Windham, 27 Oct 1723; d. at Windham, 30 Dec 1762; m. at Windham, 21 Oct 1747, JEDUTHUN ROGERS, b. at Windham, 17 Feb 1723/4 son of Hope and Esther (Meacham) Rogers; Jeduthun d. at Hampton, 19 Nov 1800. Jeduthun second married Hannah Knight on 12 Oct 1763.

iv ISAIAH FARNUM, b. 1 Jul 1726; d. 1 Nov 1729.

v ELIJAH FARNUM, b. at Windham, 10 Jan 1728/9; d. at Hampton, 1 Mar 1780. Elijah does not seem to have married. His estate was administered by Zebadiah Farnum, Jr. who was his nephew. Elijah died of smallpox.

vi ISAIAH FARNUM, b. at Windham, 7 Apr 1731; d. at Windham, 11 Nov 1759. Isaiah did not marry.

vii EUNICE FARNUM, b. 13 Feb 1735/6; d. at Windham, 1756.

61) NATHANIEL FARNUM (*Ralph Farnum*[3], *Elizabeth Holt Farnum*[2], *Nicholas*[1]), b. at Andover, 25 Jul 1695 son of Ralph and Sarah (Sterling) Farnum; d. at Windham, 9 Jul 1760; m. at Andover, 19 May 1719, HANNAH PRESTON, b. at Andover, 17 Jun 1698 daughter of John and Sarah (Geary) Preston; Hannah d. at Windham, about 1766 (redistribution of her widow thirds to the children).

Nathaniel Farnum and his wife Hannah Preston made the move from Andover to Windham, Connecticut. Three of Nathaniel's brothers also made the move to Windham County, and this mini-migration also included several Preston families.

Nathaniel Farnum did not leave a will. The first distribution 28 April 1761 included the widow's thirds to Hannah and heirs: son John, daughter Rebecca Robbins, daughter Martha Clark, son Asa, legatees of Solomon deceased, Jeremiah Farnum, Aaron Farnum, heirs of Hannah Robbins, Sarah Fisk, Anna Holt, son Asa Farnum, and Nathaniel Farnum. The final distribution of the estate including the widow's thirds distributed to the children was 4 April 1767 and the heirs receiving portions were as follows: the heirs of Solomon deceased, the heirs of John deceased, Nathaniel who receives a double portion,

[197] New Hampshire: Births, Deaths and Marriages, 1654-1969 (accessed through americanancestors.org)

[198] *Connecticut State Library (Hartford, Connecticut)*; Probate Place: *Hartford, Connecticut, Probate Packets, Durkee, P-Fitch, Eleazer, 1719-1880, Estate of William Farnam, Case 1318 and Case 1319*

heirs of Hannah deceased, son Aaron, daughter Sarah, daughter Anna, daughter Rebecca, daughter Martha, son Jeremiah, and son Asa.[199]

Nathaniel and Hannah were parents of eleven children born at Windham.

i NATHANIEL FARNUM, b. at Windham, 9 May 1720; d. at Hampton, 9 Oct 1781; m. at Windham, 18 Nov 1762, HANNAH KNOWLTON, b. about 1720 daughter of Robert and Hannah (Robinson) Knowlton.[200] Nathaniel and Hannah did not have children.

ii HANNAH FARNUM, b. at Windham, 19 Jan 1721/2; d. at Windham, May 1748; m. at Windham, 31 Jan 1744, JEHIEL ROBBINS, b. at Canterbury, 27 Apr 1719 son of Nathaniel and Elizabeth (Levins) Robbins. Jehiel married second the widow Mary Bennett. Hannah and Jehiel had three children all of whom died in early childhood (Enos, Hannah, and Nathaniel).

315) iii SARAH FARNUM, b. at Windham, 27 Mar 1724; d. at Hampton, 9 Sep 1813; m. at Windham, 26 Mar 1747, DAVID FISKE, b. at Windham, 17 Dec 1726 son of David and Elizabeth (Durkee) Fiske; David d. at Hampton, 3 Oct 1809.

92) iv ANNA FARNUM, b. at Windham, 26 Apr 1726; d. at Chaplin, CT, 1 Apr 1810; m. about 1746, her second cousin once removed, NEHEMIAH HOLT (*George*[3], *Henry*[2], *Nicholas*[1]), b. at Andover, 3 Apr 1723 son of George and Mary (Bixby) Holt; Nehemiah d. at Chaplin, 17 Apr 1799.

v SOLOMON FARNUM, b. at Windham, 10 Jan 1727/8; d. before 1761. No marriage was located for Solomon.

316) vi REBEKAH FARNUM, b. at Windham, 12 Apr 1730; d. at Hampton, 1814; m. at Windham, 21 Jan 1748/9, JOHN ROBBINS, b. at Canterbury, 12 Jul 1721 son of Nathaniel and Elizabeth (Levins) Robbins; John d. about 1774.

317) vii ASA FARNUM, b. at Windham, 11 Nov 1731; d. at Ashford, 11 Jul 1807; m. at Windham, 2 Mar 1746, LYDIA BIDLACK, b. at Windham, 8 Jan 1736/7 daughter of Benjamin and Lydia (Abbe) Bidlack; Lydia d. at Ashford, 16 Apr 1811.

318) viii JEREMIAH FARNUM, b. at Windham, 31 Jul 1733; d. at Hampton, 18 Mar 1827; m. at Hampton, 8 Oct 1774, LUCY DURKEE, b. at Windham, 9 Aug 1747 daughter of Henry and Relief (Adams) Durkee;[201] Lucy d. at Hampton, 2 Sep 1809.

ix JOHN FARNUM, b. at Windham, 28 Mar 1735; d. at Windham, 29 Jan 1763. John served in the French and Indian War in Colonel Fitch's Regiment.[202]

319) x MARTHA FARNUM, b. at Windham, 17 Dec 1736; d. at Hampton, 10 Nov 1815; m. at Windham, 6 Apr 1759, JONATHAN CLARK, b. at Windham, 12 Sep 1734 son of John and Ruth (Haskell) Clark; Jonathan d. at Hampton, 21 Oct 1797.

320) xi AARON FARNUM, b. at Windham, 30 May 1742; d. about 1777 (perhaps at Otter Creek during the war); m. RELIEF DURKEE, b. at Windham, 3 Apr 1743 daughter of Henry and Relief (Adams) Durkee.[203]

62) BARACHIAS FARNUM (*Ralph Farnum*[3], *Elizabeth Holt Farnum*[2], *Nicholas*[1]), b. at Andover, 16 Mar 1696/7 son of Ralph and Sarah (Sterling) Farnum; d. at Haverhill, MA, 22 Aug 1767; m. at Reading, 1 Jan 1722/3, HEPHZIBAH HARNDEN, b. at Reading, 25 May 1705 daughter of John and Susanna (-) Harnden; Hephzibah d. after 1748. Barachias m. 2nd SUSANNAH who has not been identified.

Barachias was a wheelwright. He and Hephzibah started their family in Andover. They were perhaps in Rumford for a time as the births of the two youngest children are recorded there. They were finally in Haverhill, Massachusetts where Barachias died. There are records of ten children of Barachias and Hephzibah.

The indenture to settle the estate of Barachias Farnum was signed 6 June 1768.[204] Those entering into the agreement were John Farnum yeoman, Jonathan Dustin housewright, Isaac Bradley yeoman and Rachel his wife, Josiah Fulsom yeoman and Abigail his wife, Ephraim Marsh yeoman and Sarah his wife, all of Haverhill in Massachusetts, and Ebenezer Hall, Jr. yeoman of Concord in New Hampshire. The settlement notes that during his life that Barachias had granted by deed of gift to John Farnum half of his homestead lands and half the buildings, daughter Hephzibah Hall in her lifetime and Ebenezer Hall

---

199 *Connecticut State Library (Hartford, Connecticut)*; Probate Place: *Hartford, Connecticut, Probate Packets, Durkee, P-Fitch, Eleazer, 1719-1880, Estate of Nathaniel Farnam, Case 1315*

200 The 1765 will (probate 1775) of Robert Knowlton includes a bequest to his daughter Hannah Farnum.

201 The 1785 will of Henry Durkee includes a bequest to his daughter Lucy Farnum.

202 Connecticut Soldiers, French and Indian War, 1755-62

203 The 1785 will of Henry Durkee includes a bequest to his daughter Relief Farnum which consists of forgiving the debt that her deceased husband Aaron Farnum owed to Henry.

204 Massachusetts Land Records, 1620-1986, Essex County, Deeds 1765-1770, 125:77-79

since her death had received sixty pounds, daughter Susanna Dustin in her lifetime received the value of thirty-three pounds, and Susanna's daughter Mehitable on her marriage to Thomas Shepard received five pounds six shillings. It was planned to provide to each of the other grandchildren who were children of Susanna the sum of five pounds six shillings to bring the total bequest to Susanna to sixty pounds, the other grandchildren being Jesse, Susanna, Tamer, and Jonathan Dustin. The amounts to daughters Sarah and Abigail would be adjusted so that each daughter receives sixty pounds. The whole of the homestead will go to John Farnum which includes a gristmill. The dower will be set off to Susanna widow of Barachias. John Farnum will then grant to each of the other children various parcels of other land which are described in detail in the deed.

Barachias Farnum and Hephzibah Harnden were parents of ten children.

321) i HEPHZIBAH FARNUM, b. at Andover, 3 Oct 1723; d. likely at Rumford, NH, about 1744; m. about 1744, EBENEZER HALL, b. at Bradford, MA, 19 Sep 1721 son of Joseph and Sarah (Kimball) Hall; Ebenezer d. at Concord, 24 Apr 1801. Ebenezer was second married to Dorcas Abbott.

ii SARAH FARNUM, b. at Andover, 22 Mar 1724/5; death recorded at Rumford, 16 Oct 1736.

322) iii RACHEL FARNUM, b. at Andover, 31 Jan 1726/7; d. at Haverhill, Feb 1805; m. 1st at Haverhill, 23 Jul 1747, SAMUEL AYER, b. at Haverhill, 13 Feb 1726/7 son of Samuel and Rachel (Kimball) Ayer; Samuel d. about 1761. Rachel m. 2nd at Haverhill, 23 Nov 1762, ISAAC BRADLEY, b. at Haverhill, 10 Jan 1718/9 son of Isaac and Elizabeth (Clement) Bradley; Isaac d. at Haverhill, 14 Jan 1802. Isaac was first married to Lydia Kimball.

iv BARACHIAS FARNUM, b. 11 Mar 1728/9; d. 2 Apr 1729.

323) v SUSANNA FARNUM, b. at Andover, 9 Apr 1730; d. at Haverhill, 22 Aug 1757; m. at Haverhill, 17 Feb 1746/7, JONATHAN DUSTIN, b. at Haverhill, 4 Jul 1719 son of Jonathan and Elizabeth (Watts) Dustin. Jonathan d. at Canaan, NH, 4 July 1812

vi MARY FARNUM, b. at Andover, 22 Apr 1732; d. recorded at Rumford and Andover, 13 Oct 1736.

324) vii ABIGAIL FARNUM, b. at Andover, 27 May 1734; m. at Haverhill, 26 Mar 1755, JOSIAH FOLSOM, b. at Exeter, NH, 1725 son of John and Mary (Sewall) Folsom. Josiah was first married to Elizabeth Bradley.

viii BARACHIAS FARNUM, b. 8 Apr 1736; likely died before adulthood.

325) ix SARAH FARNUM, b. recorded at Rumford, 20 Apr 1738; d. at Cabot, VT, 30 Jun 1823; m. at Plaistow, NH, 7 Mar 1759, EPHRAIM MARSH, b. at Londonderry, 2 Apr 1738 son of Ephraim and Hannah (Smith) Marsh; Ephraim d. at Cabot, 6 Nov 1825.

326) x JOHN FARNUM, b. recorded at Rumford, 6 Apr 1740; m. at Haverhill, MA, 1762, HANNAH EASTMAN, baptized at Haverhill, Dec 1740 daughter of Jonathan and Hannah (Ingalls) Eastman.

63) JOSEPH FARNUM (*Ralph Farnum³, Elizabeth Holt Farnum², Nicholas¹*), b. at Andover, 4 Feb 1700/1 son of Ralph and Sarah (Sterling) Farnum; m. at Windham, 24 Dec 1724, LYDIA HOWARD.[205]

Joseph settled in Windham where his brothers Henry, William, and Nathaniel also settled. Joseph Farnum and Lydia Howard were parents of eleven children.

327) i LYDIA FARNUM, b. at Windham, 3 Oct 1728; d. at Walpole, NH, 15 Jan 1791; m. at Killingworth, 22 May 1754, JOSEPH GRISWOLD, b. at Killingworth, 22 Oct 1716 son of Joseph and Temperance (Lay) Griswold; Joseph d. at Walpole, 13 Jul 1791. Joseph was first married to Rebecca Ruttey.

328) ii MARY FARNUM, b. at Windham, 28 Jan 1729/30; d. at Norwich, 13 Apr 1775; m. at Plainfield, 20 Mar 1753, JAMES LONGBOTTOM, b. 27 Dec 1729 son of James and Priscilla (Lovett) Longbottom; James d. at Hanover, CT, Feb 1814. James married second Sarah Averell.

329) iii JOSEPH FARNUM, b. at Windham, 2 Dec 1731; d. at Plainfield, 1803; m. at Canterbury, 10 Jul 1764, LYDIA WHEELER, b. at Plainfield, 18 Nov 1740 daughter of Benjamin and Prudence (Huet) Wheeler.

---

[205] Both the Sterling genealogy and the Farnum genealogy report that Joseph went first to Portsmouth, New Hampshire and had a first marriage to Elizabeth Huse or Elizabeth Hussey and three children from that marriage. However, as court records related to a deposition summons in 1733 for Joseph and Elizabeth Farnum suggest that the Joseph Farnum who married Elizabeth Huse was alive in 1733, it seems unlikely that the same Joseph Farnum had both these marriages. This would also require that Joseph first married before age 20, which although possible, would not be a common occurrence for this era. In any case, no outcomes are known for the three children attributed to Joseph Farnum and Elizabeth Huse. Please refer to Farnham's *Descendants of Ralph Farnum*, p 123 and Sterling's *The Sterling Genealogy*, volume 1, p 267.

330) iv SARAH FARNUM, b. at Canterbury, 28 Nov 1734; d. at Jewett City, CT, 17 May 1798; m. about 1754, ELEAZER JEWETT, b. at Norwich, 31 Aug 1731 son of Eleazer and Elizabeth (Griggs) Jewett; Eleazer d. at Jewett City, CT, 7 Dec 1817. Eleazer married second Elizabeth.

331) v BENJAMIN FARNHAM, b. at Canterbury, 3 Jan 1736; d. at Barkhamsted, CT, 12 Nov 1809; m. at Simsbury, 8 Dec 1777, ABIGAIL ROBE, b. at Simsbury, 7 Jun 1754 daughter of Andrew and Hannah (Miller) Robe; Abigail d. at West Granby, 5 Sep 1837.

vi ABIGAIL FARNUM, b. at Canterbury, 5 Nov 1738.

vii HANNAH FARNUM, b. at Canterbury, 10 Nov 1740.[206]

332) viii STEPHEN FARNUM, b. at Canterbury, 16 Oct 1741; d. about 1779; m. at Plainfield, 10 Mar 1768, OLIVE WHEELER, b. at Plainfield, 11 Sep 1750 daughter of Benjamin and Prudence (Huet) Wheeler; Olive d. at Hampton, 18 Oct 1835. Olive second married Philip Pearl in 1780.

333) ix LUCY FARNUM, b. at Canterbury, 1 Feb 1744; d. at Plainfield, 7 Apr 1766; m. at Plainfield, 9 Feb 1764, ROBERT WASHBURN, b. Apr 1739 (calculated from death age of 92 years 9 days); Robert d. at Wilton, NY, 24 Apr 1831. Robert married second Adah Bennett.

x WILLIAM FARNUM, b. at Canterbury, 6 May 1747; m. at Preston, 13 Apr 1768, JERUSHA STARKWEATHER, b. at Preston, 4 May 1747 daughter of Daniel and Mary (Geer) Starkweather. There is no clear evidence of children for William and Jerusha.

xi EUNICE FARNUM, b. at Canterbury, 4 Aug 1748.

64) STEPHEN FARNUM (*Ralph Farnum*[3], *Elizabeth Holt Farnum*[2], *Nicholas*[1]), b. at Andover, 1703 son of Ralph and Sarah (Sterling) Farnum; d. at Lake George, NY, 1 Sep 1756; m. at Andover, 8 Nov 1726, HANNAH RICHARDSON, b. at Woburn, 8 Jan 1707 daughter of Joshua and Hannah (-) Richardson.[207]

Stephen and Hannah started their family in Andover but relocated to Dracut by 1734. Stephen was a militia member killed at Lake George.

Stephen Farnum did not leave a will and widow Hannah Farnum was admitted as administratrix on 22 April 1757. The inventory of the estate included two parcels of land in Pelham, New Hampshire with a total value of £85. Property in Dracut including the dwelling house was valued at £140. In a real estate distribution on 4 May 1761, the dower was set off to widow Hannah. There was also distribution to eldest surviving son Stephen who was also the only son of age to assume responsibility and it was felt that property could not be divided without prejudice to the value of the property. On 19 September 1769, there was a distribution from the estate with a payment of £6.13.11 to the widow. The assignee of this last distribution was son William who was to make payment to each of his brothers and sisters or their representatives: to the lawful heirs of elder brother Joshua, two shillings two pence; to Stephen Farnum, twenty-three shillings two pence; to Hannah, eight shillings six pence; to Martha, twenty-nine shillings ten pence; to Benjamin, William, Sarah, Mary, Phebe, Abigail, and Rachel each three pounds one shilling two pence.[208]

Stephen Farnum and Hannah Richardson were parents of twelve children.

334) i JOSHUA FARNUM, b. at Andover, 24 Jul 1727; d. at Dracut about 1759 (probate 28 Jan 1760); m. about 1751, MILLICENT PERRY, likely b. at Lexington, 10 May 1726 daughter of John and Deborah (Wilson) Perry. Millicent was second married to Richard Bradden.

335) ii HANNAH FARNUM, b. at Andover, 17 Jan 1728/9; d. at Methuen, 5 May 1804; m. about1748, NATHAN AUSTIN, b. at Methuen, 25 Jan 1725 son of Thomas and Sarah (Lovejoy) Austin; Nathan d. at Methuen, 1755.

336) iii MARTHA FARNUM, b. at Andover, 22 Jan 1730/1; m. at Woburn, 15 Dec 1753, ZEBULON MAY.

SARAH FARNUM, b. about 1732. Sarah was unmarried in 1767 (described as a spinster on a deed).[209]

337) v STEPHEN FARNUM, b. at Dracut, 19 Jan 1734; d. at Manchester, VT, 13 Jan 1813; m. at Chelmsford, 12 Feb 1765, KEZIA SKIDMORE, b. at Worcester, 23 Jul 1736 daughter of Richard and Jemima (Gould) Skidmore.

---

[206] Farnham's New England Descendants of Ralph Farnum reports that Hannah married Eleazer Hubbard. However, the Hannah who married Eleazer died in 1842 at age 96 which does not fit with this Hannah. The Hannah who married Eleazer Hubbard was more likely the daughter of William and Martha Farnum born at Canterbury in 1746.

[207] The 1748 will of Joshua Richardson of Woburn includes a bequest to his daughter Hannan "Varnum".

[208] *Middlesex County, MA: Probate File Papers, 1648-1871.*Online database. *AmericanAncestors.org.* New England Historic Genealogical Society, 2014. Case 7270

[209] Farnham, *New England Descendants of Ralph Farnum*, p 128

vi MARY FARNUM, b. at Dracut, 12 Feb 1736; d. at Dracut, 7 Apr 1766. Mary did not marry.

338) vii PHEBE FARNUM, b. at Dracut, 27 Jan 1739; m. at Andover, 1 Sep 1757, THOMAS RICHARDSON, likely b. at Andover, 15 Feb 1732 son of Thomas and Elizabeth (-) Richardson.

339) viii ABIGAIL FARNUM, b. at Dracut, 22 Dec 1741; d. at Dracut, 5 Sep 1826; m. at Dracut, 12 Sep 1761, DANIEL CLOUGH, b. 1737 son of Daniel and Ruth (Wright) Clough; Daniel d. at Dracut, 1805 (probate 3 Dec 1805).

ix BENJAMIN FARNUM, b. 24 Mar 1743/4; d. at Dracut, 19 Apr 1765.

340) x RACHEL FARNUM, b. at Dracut, 4 Mar 1746/7; d. at Andover, 8 Apr 1826; m. at Andover, 4 May 1775, JOHN STICKNEY, b. 16 May 1744 son of Moses and Hannah (Style) Stickney; John d. at Andover, 12 Aug 1807.

341) xi WILLIAM FARNUM, b. at Dracut, 23 Apr 1748; d. after 1814;[210] m. at Pelham, 29 Oct 1772, HANNAH MARSH, b. at Bradford, MA, 13 Feb 1753 daughter of John and Martha (Rolfe) Marsh; Hannah d. 12 Mar 1821 (buried in the Marsh family plot in Pelham).

xii EUNICE FARNUM, b. 1 Oct 1750; d. 27 Dec 1754.

65) JOHN FARNUM (*John Farnum[3], Elizabeth Holt Farnum[2], Nicholas[1]*), b. at Andover, 13 Feb 1684/5 son of John and Elizabeth (Parker) Farnum; d. at Andover, 22 Oct 1762; m. 10 Feb 1710, JOANNA BARKER, b. at Andover, 7 Jul 1687 daughter of John and Mary (Stevens) Barker; Joanna d. at Andover, 4 Jan 1785.

Deacon John Farnum and his wife Joanna Barker raised their five children in Andover where John was a wheelwright.

In his will written 25 June 1762 (probate 15 November 1762), John Farnum bequeaths to beloved wife Joanna the dwelling house while she is a widow which is to be kept in good repair by the executor. She also receives the use of all the household movables which will be equally divided among his four daughters after his decease. There are also detailed specific provisions for her support to be provided by the executor. Daughter Joanna Stevens widow of Ebenezer Stevens receives £10. Bequests of £10 each are made to his other daughters Mary the wife of Stephen Holt, Elizabeth the wife of Samuel Barker, and Mehitable the widow of Asa Stevens. The wearing apparel and books are to be equally divided among his five children. Son John Farnum receives all of the estate both real and personal and is named executor.[211]

John and Joanna were parents of five children born at Andover.

342) i JOHN FARNUM, b. at Andover, 1 Apr 1711; d. at Andover, 21 Oct 1786; m. at Andover, 26 Dec 1738, SARAH FRYE, b. at Andover, 25 Mar 1721 daughter of Samuel and Sarah (Osgood) Frye); Sarah d. at Andover, 24 Jul 1816.

343) ii JOHANNA FARNUM, b. at Andover, 1712; d. at Andover, 27 Dec 1787; m. at Andover, 2 Apr 1741, EBENEZER STEVENS, b. at Andover, 1713/4 son of Ebenezer and Sarah (Sprague) Stevens; Ebenezer d. at Andover, 6 Aug 1754.

184) iii MARY FARNUM, b. at Andover, 21 May 1714; d. at Andover, 9 Aug 1802; m. 12 Jul 1739, her second cousin once removed, STEPHEN HOLT (*Nicholas[3], Nicholas[2], Nicholas[1]*), b. at Andover, 14 Apr 1713 son of Nicholas and Mary (Manning) Holt; Stephen d. at Andover, 25 Apr 1798.

344) iv ELIZABETH FARNUM, b. at Andover, 10 Oct 1714; d. at Andover, 17 Jun 1799; m. 2 Apr 1741, SAMUEL BARKER, b. at Andover, 10 Oct 1714 son of Samuel and Sarah (Gage) Barker; Samuel d. at Andover, 11 Nov 1796.

345) v MEHITABLE FARNUM, b. at Andover, 1720; m. 1st 9 Sep 1742, ASA STEVENS, b. at Andover, 14 Dec 1717 son of Ebenezer and Sarah (Sprague) Stevens; Asa d. at Albany, 20 Dec 1755.[212] Mehitable m. 2nd 5 Jan 1768, SAMUEL CHICKERING, b. at Charlestown, 10 Jul 1704 son of John and Susanna (Symmes) Chickering; Samuel d. at Andover, 1787. Samuel was first married to Hannah Osgood.

66) ELIZABETH FARNUM (*John Farnum[3], Elizabeth Holt Farnum[2], Nicholas[1]*), b. at Andover, 7 Jun 1687 daughter of John and Elizabeth (Parker) Farnum; d. at Andover, 23 May 1753; m. at Andover, 23 Dec 1708, EBENEZER FRYE, b. 16 Feb 1686 son of Samuel and Mary (Aslett) Frye; Ebenezer d. at Andover, 16 May 1725.

---

210 On 5 Mar 1814 (recorded 6 Apr 1814), William transferred his homestead farm to his son Jacob Marsh Farnum for $1800. Massachusetts Land Records 1620-1986, Essex County, volume 203, p 77, accessed through familysearch.org.

211 *Essex County, MA: Probate File Papers, 1638-1881.* Online database. *AmericanAncestors.org.* New England Historic Genealogical Society, 2014. Case 9245

212 Asa, Capt., "at Albany on his Return from Lake George," Dec. 20, 1755, a 38 y. 6 d.

In his will written 23 June 1724 (probate 22 Jan 1725/6), Ebenezer Frye bequeathed to beloved wife Elizabeth all his stock and moveable estate to be at her own disposal and the use of all the real estate while she is a widow. Afterwards, the estate is to be divided among his children as his wife and brother-in-law John Farnum shall think best. His wife and brother-in-law may as they think best bind out the children to trades as they come of age. Wife Elizabeth and John Farnum are named executors.[213]

Elizabeth and Ebenezer were parents of nine children born at Andover.

i JOSEPH FRYE, b. and d. 14 Sep 1709.

ii ELIZABETH FRYE, b. at Andover, 1711; d. at Pembroke, NH, about 1798 (probate 9 Dec 1798); m. at Andover, 11 Jan 1732, AMBROSE GOULD who has not been identified but perhaps the Ambrose baptized at Salem in 1714 son of James and Deborah (-) Gould; Ambrose d. at Pembroke, 22 May 1780. Elizabeth and Ambrose do not seem to have had children. In his will written at Pembroke 20 Apr 1780, Ambrose Gould left his estate to his loving wife Elizabeth and named his beloved nephew Captain Ebenezer Frye as executor. In her will written 17 Aug 1797, Elizabeth bequeathed $100 to James Gould Frye and the remainder of the estate to her nephew Captain Ebenezer Frye.

101) iii MARY FRYE, b. at Andover, 6 Nov 1712; m. 30 Oct 1733, her first cousin once removed, JOSIAH FARNUM (*Ephraim Farnum[3], Elizabeth Holt Farnum[2], Nicholas[1]*), b. at Andover, 19 Jul 1712 son of Ephraim and Priscilla (Holt) Farnum; Josiah d. at Concord, before 1790 (probate).

346) iv EBENEZER FRYE, b. at Andover, 2 Oct 1714; d. at Lake George, 27 Sep 1755; m. at Andover, 22 Nov 1744, ELIZABETH KIMBALL, b. about 1724 who has not been identified; Elizabeth d. at Andover, 20 Oct 1812.

347) v JONATHAN FRYE, b. at Andover, 3 Mar 1716/7; d. at Andover, 2 Feb 1788; m. 1st at Andover, 24 Jan 1744, SARAH WILSON; Sarah d. at Andover, 3 Jun 1747. Jonathan m. 2nd at Andover, 13 Nov 1753, his third cousin, SARAH PEABODY (*Moses Peabody[4], Lydia Holt Peabody[3], James[2], Nicholas[1]*), b. at Andover, 31 Mar 1729 daughter of Moses and Sarah (Holt) Peabody; Sarah d. at Andover, 12 Oct 1802.

vi DAVID FRYE, b. 3 Mar 1716/7; reported to have sailed for England and was never heard from again.

348) vii JOHN FRYE, b. at Andover, 7 Apr 1719; d. at Royalston, MA, 19 Mar 1814; m. at Sutton, 2 Nov 1748, ELIZABETH WOODBURY, likely b. 28 Oct 1728 daughter of Benjamin and Ruth (Conant) Woodbury; Elizabeth d. at Royalston, 23 Jan 1814.

viii DEBORAH FRYE, b. 20 Apr 1722; d. at Andover, 18 Jul 1738.

349) ix HANNAH FRYE, b. at Andover, 4 Jul 1725; d. at Andover, 30 Oct 1803; m. 25 Mar 1742, JOHN WILSON, b. about 1720 whose parents are not clearly identified; John d. at Andover, 23 Sep 1774. John may be the son of Joshua and Mary (Wright) Wilson or John and Mercy (Wright) Wilson.

67) JAMES FARNUM (*John Farnum[3], Elizabeth Holt Farnum[2], Nicholas[1]*), b. at Andover, 17 Oct 1691 son of John and Elizabeth (Parker) Farnum; d. at Andover, 17 Jun 1748; m. at Andover, 10 Jul 1722, JOHANNA GRAINGER, b. at Andover, 4 Feb 1691/2 daughter of John and Martha (Poor) Grainger; Johanna d. at Andover, 3 Dec 1745.

James was a weaver in Andover and also a large land holder. In his will written 14 March 1744 (probate 4 July 1748), James Farnum bequeaths to beloved wife Joanna the improvement of one comfortable room in the dwelling house and a lengthy list of provisions for her support. Daughter Martha receives £150; daughter Joanna wife of John Flint, ten shillings; daughter Elizabeth Farnum, £150; daughter Deborah, £150; and daughter Deborah, £150. Son James receives all the lands in Andover and the remainder of the estate and is named executor. Real estate was valued at £1,060.[214]

James Farnum and Johanna Grainger were parents of seven children born at Andover.

i JAMES FARNUM, b. at Andover, 24 Apr 1723; d. at Andover, 27 Feb 1749/50; m. at Andover, 27 Dec 1748, LYDIA KIMBALL, b. at Wenham 13 Dec 1730 daughter of Josiah and Elizabeth (Bragg) Kimball; Lydia d. at Andover, 7 May 1756. Lydia married second, JOHN HOLT (1732-1765). James and Lydia did not have children. In his will after providing for his wife, James left all his lands to his sisters Joanna and Tabitha. John Holt and Lydia Kimball are Family 402.

ii MARTHA FARNUM, b. 16 May 1724; d. 8 Sep 1747.

[213] *Essex County, MA: Probate File Papers, 1638-1881.*Online database. *AmericanAncestors.org.* New England Historic Genealogical Society, 2014. Case 10286

[214] *Essex County, MA: Probate File Papers, 1638-1881.*Online database. *AmericanAncestors.org.* New England Historic Genealogical Society, 2014. Case 9239

350) iii JOANNA FARNUM, b. at Andover, 22 May 1725; d. at Reading, 22 Feb 1753; m. at Andover, 6 Jun 1744, JOHN FLINT, baptized at Wakefield, 30 Aug 1719 son of Ebenezer and Tabitha (Burnap) Flint; John d. at Reading, 15 Feb 1802. John married second Tamer Kimball on 30 Apr 1761.

iv Daughter, b. 18 Nov 1726

v ELIZABETH FARNUM, b. 19 Jan 1727/8; d. 9 Jan 1745/6.

vi DEBORAH FARNUM, b. 13 Jan 1728/9; d. 18 Feb 1747/8.

351) vii TABITHA FARNUM, b. at Andover, 18 Mar 1729/30; m. at Andover, 7 Dec 1748, JACOB STEVENS, b. at Andover, 7 Nov 1725 son of Ebenezer and Sarah (Sprague) Stevens.

68) HANNAH FARNUM (*John Farnum*[3], *Elizabeth Holt Farnum*[2], *Nicholas*[1]), b. at Andover, 31 Dec 1693 son of John and Elizabeth (Parker) Farnum; d. at Andover, 11 Nov 1784; m. at Andover, 18 Apr 1717, BENJAMIN STEVENS, b. at Andover, 14 Mar 1684/5 son of John and Esther (Barker) Stevens; Benjamin d. at Andover, 26 Mar 1748.

Benjamin Stevens served as representative from Andover to the Massachusetts General Court in 1728 and 1729. He was a selectman in Andover and served as town clerk 1735 to 1748.[215]

Benjamin Stevens did not leave a will and his estate entered probate 2 May 1748 with Hannah Stevens as administratrix.[216] Real estate was valued at £2,423. The distribution of the personal estate included payments to only son Benjamin who received a double payment of £48.10.7, daughters Esther, Deborah, Phebe, and Sarah receiving £245.3 ½, daughter Hannah Stevens alias Gage has received her full portion of £378, and daughter Elizabeth Stevens has received £220. Hannah Stevens was named as guardian to Phebe, Sarah, and Benjamin Stevens.

Benjamin and Hannah were parents of seven children born at Andover.

352) i HANNAH STEVENS, b. at Andover, 1 Oct 1720; d. at Bradford, 15 Dec 1749; m. at Andover, 16 May 1745, AARON GAGE, b. ay Bradford, 24 Feb 1717/8 son of John and Susanna (Ross) Gage; Aaron d. at Merrimack, NH, 12 Mar 1797.[217] Aaron married second Sarah Hall.

352a ii ELIZABETH STEVENS, b. at Andover, 12 Jan 1722/3; d. at Andover, 5 Nov 1804; m. at Andover, Dec 1748, CHRISTOPHER CARLTON,[218] b. at Andover, 31 Dec 1717 son of Christopher and Martha (Barker) Carlton; Christopher d. at Andover, 15 Dec 1800.

353) iii ESTHER STEVENS, b. at Andover, Feb 1724/5; d. at Andover, 15 Apr 1803; m. at Andover, 20 Feb 1754, as his second wife, JOHN JOHNSON, b. at Andover about 1711 son of John and Phebe (Robinson) Johnson; John d. at Andover, 26 Jul 1775. John was first married to Lydia Osgood who died in 1750.

354) iv DEBORAH STEVENS, b. at Andover, 4 Feb 1726/7; d. at Andover, 15 Feb 1781; m. at Andover, 8 May 1755, JOHN INGALLS, b. at Andover, 25 Apr 1728 son of Henry and Hannah (Martin) Ingalls; John d. at Andover, 26 Aug 1810.

v PHEBE STEVENS, b. 9 May 1729; d. 12 Sep 1760. Phebe did not marry.

355) vi SARAH STEVENS, b. at Andover, 14 Aug 1731; d. at Methuen, 19 Dec 1803; m. at Andover, 3 Mar 1757, JOSIAH OSGOOD, b. at Andover, 20 Nov 1732 son of Josiah and Abigail (Day) Osgood; Josiah d. at Methuen, 10 Dec 1788.

356) vii BENJAMIN STEVENS, b. at Andover, 14 May 1734; d. at Andover, 6 Feb 1800; m. at Andover, 21 Jul 1783, his first cousin once removed LYDIA FRYE (*Ebenezer Frye*[5], *Elizabeth Farnum Frye*[4], *John Farnum*[3], *Elizabeth Holt Farnum*[2], *Nicholas*[1]), b. at Andover, 23 May 1752 daughter of Ebenezer and Elizabeth (Kimball) Frye; Lydia d. about 1806 (probate 6 May 1806).

69) PHEBE FARNUM (*John Farnum*[3], *Elizabeth Holt Farnum*[2], *Nicholas*[1]), b. at Andover, 24 Jun 1698 daughter of John and Elizabeth (Parker) Farnum; d. at Andover, 18 Feb 1760; m. at Andover, 29 Dec 1720, JOSEPH INGALLS, b. at Andover, 17 Apr 1697 son of Henry and Abigail (Emery) Ingalls; Joseph d. at Andover, 29 Dec 1757.

---

[215] Massachusetts: Legislators of the General Court, 1691-1780 (Online database: *AmericanAncestors.org*, New England Historic Genealogical Society, 2002)

[216] *Essex County, MA: Probate File Papers, 1638-1881.*Online database. *AmericanAncestors.org.* New England Historic Genealogical Society, 2014. Case 26295

[217] Aaron is buried at Turkey Hill Road Cemetery in Merrimack, NH.

[218] Some sources suggest that it was Elizabeth daughter of John Stevens and Elizabeth Chandler that married Christopher Carlton but there is a death record for their daughter Elizabeth (born in 1723) at about age one year. John Stevens and Elizabeth Chandler had a second daughter Elizabeth born in 1730 who married Nathaniel Holt.

In his will written 9 October 1752 (probate 17 Apr 1758), Joseph Ingalls bequeathed to beloved wife Phebe a lower room in the house while she lives his widow. Annual provisions to be provided by the executor are detailed. Son Joseph Ingalls receives six shillings as he has already received a large portion of the estate. Daughter Phebe wife of Joshua Abbot receives six shillings which completes her full portion. The lands he still has will be divided equally between sons Joshua and Stephen except for two acres that he purchased from his beloved mother Abigail Ingalls which son Stephen shall have over and above his share. Daughter Tabitha receives £42 and may remain in the dwelling house while she is unmarried. John Farnum, Jr. and son Joshua Ingalls were named executors, although John Farnum, Jr. declined this responsibility at probate. Real estate was valued at £476.9.4 On 1 July 1758, widow Phebe Ingalls signed that she accepted what was given her in the will as her full portion of the estate.[219]

Joseph Ingalls and Phebe Farnum were parents of twelve children born at Andover.

i JOSEPH INGALLS, b. Jan 1721/2; d. 20 Feb 1721/2.

357) ii JOSEPH INGALLS, b. at Andover, 9 Aug 1723; d. at Pomfret, 26 Oct 1790, SARAH ABBOTT, b. at Pomfret, 15 Oct 1730 daughter of Paul and Elizabeth (Gray) Abbott; Sarah d. at Pomfret, 17 Dec 1811.

iii PHEBE INGALLS, b. 7 Jul 1725; d. 13 Feb 1728/9.

iv TABITHA INGALLS, b. 23 Mar 1726/7; d. 13 Mar 1728/9.

v DEBORAH INGALLS, baptized 1728; she was not living at time of father's will.

vi JOSHUA INGALLS, b. 30 Jan 1728/9; d. 15 Feb 1728/9.

358) vii PHEBE INGALLS, b. at Andover, 10 Aug 1730; d. after 1772; m. at Andover, 20 Nov 1749, JOSHUA ABBOTT, b. at Andover, 25 Sep 1722 son of Ephraim and Sarah (Crosby) Abbott; Joshua d. at Amherst, NH, about 1772 (will 2 Mar 1772).

359) viii JOSHUA INGALLS, b. at Andover, 13 Aug 1732; d. at Andover, 1785 (probate 5 Jul 1785); m. at Andover, 9 Sep 1760, ELIZABETH STEEL, b. at Andover, 21 Feb 1737 daughter of Nicholas and Phebe (Stevens) Steel.

360) ix TABITHA INGALLS, b. at Andover, 14 Mar 1734/5; d. at Amherst, NH, 8 May 1794; m. at Andover, 14 Feb 1755, SOLOMON KITTREDGE, b. at Billerica, 9 Jun 1736 son of Francis and Lydia (-) Kittredge;[220] Solomon d. at Amherst, 24 Aug 1792.

x STEPHEN INGALLS, b. 23 Apr 1737; he was living in 1752 but nothing further known by me.

xi ELIZABETH INGALLS, b. 21 Aug 1739; d. 13 May 1752.

xii PETER INGALLS, b. 28 Oct 1741; d. 10 Dec 1741.

70) SARAH FARNUM (*John Farnum³, Elizabeth Holt Farnum², Nicholas¹*), b. at Andover, 23 Oct 1700 daughter of John and Elizabeth (Parker) Farnum; d. 23 May 1745; m. at Andover, 13 May 1725, SAMUEL BARKER, b. at Andover, 13 Feb 1691/2 son of William and Mary (Dix) Barker; Samuel d. at Andover, 13 May 1770. Samuel married second Sarah Robinson on 10 Apr 1746.

In his will written 26 November 1767 (probate 4 June 1770), Samuel Barker bequeaths to beloved wife Sarah the use and improvement of one-third of the real and personal estate and also the household goods and movables she brought to the marriage. She will receive a payment of £13.6.8 on the date of her marriage if she remarries. Son-in-law Jedediah Holt and his wife Phebe receive all the estate both real and personal and Jedediah is also named executor.[221] Phebe was Samuel's daughter from his marriage to Sarah Robinson.

Samuel and Sarah had two children who died in infancy.

i JOSHUA BARKER, b. 7 Aug 1727; d. 3 Oct 1727.

ii JOSHUA BARKER, b. 23 Dec 1728; d. 28 Aug 1730.

71) DEBORAH FARNUM (*John Farnum³, Elizabeth Holt Farnum², Nicholas¹*), b. at Andover, about 1702 daughter of John and Elizabeth (Parker) Farnum; m. at Andover, 4 Feb 1729/30, TIMOTHY FAULKNER, b. at Andover, about 1705 son of John and Sarah (Abbott) Faulkner; d. likely at Sturbridge, 1784. "Faulkner, ___ "an old man" May 16, 1784."

---

[219] *Essex County, MA: Probate File Papers, 1638-1881.*Online database. *AmericanAncestors.org.* New England Historic Genealogical Society, 2014. Case 14533

[220] Kittredge, *The Kittredge Family in America*, p 26

[221] *Essex County, MA: Probate File Papers, 1638-1881.*Online database. *AmericanAncestors.org.* New England Historic Genealogical Society, 2014. Case 1712

Timothy Faulkner was a joiner and Timothy and Deborah lived in Andover, Littleton, and then Chelmsford. They then traveled back to Andover, and Timothy and at least two of the children were then in Sturbridge. Deborah and Timothy were parents of seven children, but marriages were located for just two of the children, both at Sturbridge.

i TIMOTHY FAULKNER, b. at Andover, 14 Sep 1730

ii JOHN FAULKNER, b. at Littleton, 7 Nov 1731

361) iii DEBORAH FAULKNER, b. at Littleton, 26 Aug 1735; d. at Sturbridge, 31 Jul 1828; m. at Sturbridge, 11 Jul 1764, as his second wife, MOSES WELD, b. at Roxbury, 27 Mar 1722 son of John and Mehitable (Child) Weld; Moses d. at Sturbridge, 10 May 1806. Moses was first married to Elizabeth Holbrook.

iv SARAH FAULKNER, b. at Chelmsford, 17 Sep 1737; d. 20 Aug 1740.

v ELIZABETH FAULKNER, b, at Chelmsford, 4 Dec 1739

vi SARAH FAULKNER, b. at Andover, 3 May 1742

362) vii PETER FAULKNER, b. at Andover, 5 Nov 1743; d. at Lancaster, NH, 11 Dec 1829; m. at Sturbridge, 10 Dec 1768, his third cousin, CHLOE CRAM (*Humphrey Cram[4], Sarah Holt Cram[3], Henry[2], Nicholas[1]*), b. at Union, CT, 25 Nov 1750 daughter of Humphrey and Hannah (Blunt) Cram.

72) TABITHA FARNUM (*John Farnum[3], Elizabeth Holt Farnum[2], Nicholas[1]*), b. at Andover, 1706 son of John and Elizabeth (Parker) Farnum; d. at Rindge, NH, 18 Feb 1804; m. 20 Mar 1733, ISRAEL ADAMS,[222] b. at Newbury, 24 Feb 1707/8 son of Sarah Adams; Israel d. at Rindge, 16 Oct 1789.

Tabitha and Israel resided in Andover where all their children were born. Late in life, they relocated to Rindge, New Hampshire arriving there by 1772.[223] Oldest son Israel located in Rindge within a few years of his marriage. On 25 August 1766, Israel Adams and Israel Adams. Jr. and their wives Tabitha and Elizabeth sold a tract of land in Andover consisting of about fourteen acres to Joshua Stevens. The property of Andover was more fully disposed of on 25 April 1772 (deed recorded 13 November 1798) when Israel and Israel, Jr. along with wives Tabitha and Elizabeth sold three tracts of land and all the buildings on the lands to Daniel Page for £350.[224]

Israel and Tabitha were parents of seven children born at Andover.

363) i ISRAEL ADAMS, b. at Andover, 26 Jun 1733/4; d. at Rindge, NH, 1 Aug 1808; m. at Andover, 20 Nov 1760, his third cousin, ELIZABETH STEVENS, b. at Andover, 22 May 1738 daughter of Samuel and Hephzibah (Ingalls) Stevens; Elizabeth d. at Rindge, 9 Nov 1809.

364) ii JOHN ADAMS, b. at Andover, 3 Jul 1735; d. at Andover, 27 Jun 1813; m. 1st at Andover, 23 Nov 1758, his third cousin, HANNAH OSGOOD (*Mary Russell Osgood[4], Phebe Johnson Russell[3], Mary Holt Johnson[2], Nicholas[1]*), b. at Andover, 31 Jul 1735 daughter of Timothy and Mary (Osgood) Russell; Hannah d. about 1771. John m. 2nd at Rowley, 24 Jun 1773, HANNAH THURSTON, b. at Rowley, 25 Dec 1743 daughter of Richard and Mehitable (Jewett) Thurston; Hannah d. at Andover, 22 Jan 1774. John m. 3rd at Andover, 21 May 1776, his first cousin once removed, MARY HOLT (*Stephen[4], Nicholas[3], Nicholas[2], Nicholas[1]*), b. at Suncook, 15 Dec 1741 daughter of Stephen and Mary (Farnum) Holt; Mary d. at Andover, 9 Nov 1829.

365) iii ELIZABETH ADAMS, b. at Andover, 24 Dec 1737; d. at Andover, 27 Sep 1779; m. at Andover, 29 Nov 1759, MICHAEL CARLTON, b. at Andover, 22 Nov 1737 son of Ezekiel and Marcy (Kimball) Carleton; Michael d. at Andover, 1785 (probate 5 Dec 1785). Michael married second the widow Phebe Porter.

iv JOSHUA ADAMS, b. 9 Nov 1739; d. at Andover, 7 Dec 1757.

366) v DAVID ADAMS, b. at Andover, 2 May 1742; d. at Londonderry, NH, 12 Apr 1815; m. 1st 1 May 1766, ABIAH ORDWAY, b. at Methuen, 7 Mar 1744 daughter of James and Meribah (Morse) Ordway; Abiah d. 29 Jul 1776. David m. 2nd at Dracut, 20 Dec 1777, MARTHA MARSH, b. at Bradford, 12 Jan 1743 daughter of John and Martha (Rolfe) Marsh; Martha d. at Londonderry, 9 Apr 1812.

vi SARAH ADAMS, b. 26 Jul 1744; d. 30 Aug 1746.

vii Twin of Sarah, b. and d. 26 Jul 1744

---

[222] Israel Adams's origins are murky. He may have been, and perhaps he was likely, the out-of-wedlock child of Sarah Adams who later married John Hutchinson. He went by the name Israel Adams although some genealogies call him Israel Hutchinson. Adams, *Genealogical History of Robert Adams* reports him as the son of Sarah Adams born out-of-wedlock. The Adams genealogy also notes there is an alternative theory of his origins, that being he was the son of Abraham O. Adams of Quincy and Hannah La Grasse and born in Quincy in 1706.

[223] Stearns, *History of the Town of Rindge*, p 426

[224] Massachusetts Land Records, Essex County, 123:101; 164:166

73) LYDIA FARNUM (*Samuel Farnum³, Elizabeth Holt Farnum², Nicholas¹*), b. at Andover, 15 Oct 1699 daughter of Samuel and Hannah (Holt) Farnum; d. at Andover, 21 Mar 1745/6; m. at Andover, 29 Aug 1716, as his second wife, DAVID FOSTER, b. 1694 son of Ephraim and Sarah (Eams) Foster; David d. at Boxford, 22 Jun 1759. David was first married to Elizabeth Abbott and third married to Judith Norton.

In his will written 22 October 1754 (probate 23 July 1759), David Foster bequeathed to beloved wife Judith in addition to her dower of thirds the following items: a decent suit of mourning apparel, the use of one-half of the house, a riding horse, and use of the garden while she is a widow. She also has use and improvement of "my negro boy Simon." She also receives annual provisions for her support. Daughter Rebekah Foster, as an equivalent to what her sisters who are married have received, is bequeathed a list of specific household items and the sum of £13.6.8. Son-in-law Benjamin Porter receives £1.6.8 in consideration of his kindness in David's time of sickness. Grandson Foster Stiles receives a heifer. The Rev. John Cushing of Boxford receives one good cow and the Second Church of Boxford receives a pewter tankard for the communion table. All the remainder of the estate, real and personal is to be divided among his four daughters: Elizabeth Stiles, Ruth Porter, Mehitabel Andross, and Rebekah Foster. Wife Judith and brother-in-law Israel Adams were named executors. Real estate was valued at £391.13.4 and personal estate at £230. The final division of the real estate occurred 14 May 1779 after reversion of the dower to the estate. Distributions were made to Rebekah Johnson widow of Benjamin Johnson, the heirs of Ruth Porter deceased, to widow Elizabeth Stiles, and to the heirs of Mehitable Andrews deceased.[225]

There are records for five children of Lydia Farnum and David Foster.[226] David also had two children with his first wife Elizabeth Abbott, daughter Elizabeth and son Ebenezer who died young. Grandson Foster Stiles referred to in the will was the son of David's daughter with Elizabeth Abbott, Elizabeth Foster who married Benjamin Stiles.

i DAVID FOSTER, b. 29 Nov 1717; d. 22 Dec 1736.

ii LYDIA FOSTER, b. 21 Jul 1720; d. 24 Aug 1736.

367) iii RUTH FOSTER, b. at Andover, 31 Oct 1722; d. at Boxford, 7 Nov 1760; m. at Andover, 8 Nov 1744, BENJAMIN PORTER, b. at Boxford, 6 Oct 1721 son of Benjamin and Sarah (Tyler) Porter; Benjamin d. at Boxford, 15 May 1784. Benjamin married second Mary Sherwin on 28 Apr 1763.

368) iv MEHITABLE FOSTER, b. at Andover, 21 May 1730; d. at Boxford, 25 Jan 1760; m. at Boxford, 23 Apr 1751, NATHAN ANDREWS, b. at Boxford, 25 May 1726 son of Robert and Deborah (Frye) Andrews; Nathan d. at Boxford, 29 Mar 1806. Nathan married second the widow Sarah Symonds on 6 Feb 1764.

v REBECCA FOSTER, b. at Andover, 25 Jul 1732; d. after 1779. At the final estate division in 1779, she was Rebecca Johnson widow of Benjamin Johnson. It seems probable that she was the widow Rebecca Poland that married Benjamin Johnson at Andover 30 Nov 1769. Benjamin was born at Andover 1729 son of Francis and Mary (Fiske) Johnson. In his 1773 will, Benjamin left his estate to his wife Rebecca and to his siblings and other kinsmen. It is possible that Rebecca was a wife of Samuel Poland who died in Ipswich in 1767, but she would be a later wife and had no children. A record of a marriage of Rebecca Foster to a Mr. Poland was not located.

74) SAMUEL FARNUM (*Samuel Farnum³, Elizabeth Holt Farnum², Nicholas¹*), b. May 1701 son of Samuel and Hannah (Holt) Farnum; d. at Louisburg, 27 Aug 1745; m. at Middleton, 13 Jan 1731, MARY HOW who has not been identified; Mary seems to be living in Andover as a widow on the tax lists in the 1760's and 1770's.

Samuel Farnum and Mary How were parents of three known children.

369) i MARY FARNUM, b. at Andover, 13 Aug 1731; d. at Boxford, 29 Jun 1819; m. 2 Jan 1754, JOSEPH WOOD, b. at Boxford, 29 Mar 1734 son of Daniel and Sarah (Peabody) Wood; Joseph d. at Boxford, 4 May 1801.

ii CUMMINGS FARNUM, b. 22 Jan 1732/3; d. 22 Nov 1735.

iii JEREMIAH FARNUM, b. 27 Jul 1735; nothing further known.

75) HANNAH FARNUM (*Samuel Farnum³, Elizabeth Holt Farnum², Nicholas¹*), b. at Andover, 1703 daughter of Samuel and Hannah (Holt) Farnum; m. at Andover, 11 Nov 1720, DAVID BEVERLY, likely b. at Hingham, 18 Jul 1689 son of Lenox and Mary (Farrow) Beverly.

Hannah Farnum and David Beverly were parents of ten children born at Andover.

i JAMES BEVERLY, b. 19 Jan 1723/4

ii HANNAH BEVERLY, b. 24 Jan 1725/6; d. 2 Mar 1728/9.

---

[225] *Essex County, MA: Probate File Papers, 1638-1881.*Online database. *AmericanAncestors.org.* New England Historic Genealogical Society, 2014. Case 9833

[226] It is possible there were two or three other children that died young but there are no records.

370) iii MARY BEVERLY, b. at Andover, 5 Feb 1728; m. 1st at Andover, 6 Apr 1750, ASA TOWNE, b. at Boxford, 25 Aug 1729 son of Nathan and Phebe (Curtis) Towne; Asa d. at Andover, 9 Sep 1764.

371) iv HANNAH BEVERLY, b. at Andover, 11 Sep 1731; m. at Andover, 15 Oct 1755, AARON TOWNE, b. at Andover, 25 Jul 1734 son of Nathan and Phebe (Curtis) Towne; Aaron d. at Andover, 26 Feb 1822, at the almshouse.

v DAVID BEVERLY, b. 12 Feb 1733/4; d. 9 Jun 1738.

vi JOHN BEVERLY, b. 22 Nov 1737; d. 26 May 1738.

372) vii DAVID BEVERLY, b. at Andover, 2 Aug 1739; m. at Andover, 7 Jul 1763, RUTH CLOUGH.

viii TABITHA BEVERLY, b. at Andover, 7 May 1742; m. at Andover, 13 Aug 1763, STEPHEN WYATT. Nothing further was located for this couple.

373) ix JOHN BEVERLY, b. at Andover, 19 Apr 1744; d. at Andover, 12 Dec 1811; m. at Andover, 13 Nov 1777, LYDIA HILDRETH, b. 1754; d. at Andover, 5 Apr 1821.

374) x SAMUEL BEVERLY, b. at Andover, 8 Aug 1748; d. after 1810 when he was living in Boscawen; m. at Salisbury, MA, 8 Apr 1775, RUTH CONNOR, b. at Salisbury, 1 Aug 1755 daughter of Gideon and Dorothy (Bracy) Connor.

76) WILLIAM LOVEJOY (*Mary Farnum Lovejoy[3], Elizabeth Holt Farnum[2], Nicholas[1]*), b. at Andover, 22 Nov 1681 son of William and Mary (Farnum)Lovejoy; d. at Andover, 8 Mar 1762; m. 1st 1704/5, SARAH FRYE, b. at Andover, 27 Feb 1684 daughter of James and Lydia (Osgood) Frye; Sarah d. at Andover, 17 Oct 1747. William m. 2nd 28 Nov 1749, SARAH PAINE (widow of Jonathan Blanchard), b. at Charlestown, 3 Feb 1688 daughter of Edward and Bethia (Sweetser) Paine; Sarah d. at Andover, 9 Oct 1772.

Capt. William Lovejoy was active in the community of Andover serving in the militia, was a selectman, and served as deacon of the church.[227]

In his will written 14 January 1762 (probate 5 April 1762), William Lovejoy bequeaths to beloved wife Sarah £13.6.8 and also confirms the contract they made at the time of their marriage. Beloved daughter Anne Abbot receives the silver tankard and half the real and personal estate. His grandchildren William, Isaac, Phebe, and Sarah who are the children of daughter Phebe Abbot deceased receive the other half of the estate to equally divide. Negro man Pompey is granted his freedom "from all slavery and servitude". Son-in-law Isaac Abbot and grandson Nehemiah Abbot were named joint executors. Real estate was valued at £471.3.4 and personal estate at £251.5.7.[228]

Pompey Lovejoy, the slave of William Lovejoy who was freed in 1762, continued to live in Andover, married, and had a family. William Lovejoy provided him a 31-acre lot along with his freedom. Pomp's Pond in Andover is named for Pompey.[229]

William Lovejoy and Sarah Frye were parents of two children.

375) i ANNE LOVEJOY, b. at Andover, 4 Nov 1711; d. at Andover, 5 Sep 1770; m. at Andover, 20 Jun 1728, ZEBADIAH ABBOT, b. at Andover, 6 Apr 1695 son of Nehemiah and Abigail (Lovejoy) Abbot; Zebadiah Abbot d. at Andover, 9 Sep 1767.

376) ii PHEBE LOVEJOY, b. at Andover, 20 Jan 1715; d. at Andover, 17 Dec 1751; m. at Andover, 29 Nov 1739, ISAAC ABBOT, b. at Andover, 4 Apr 1699 son of George and Dorcas (Graves) Abbott; Isaac d. at Andover, 9 Aug 1784. Isaac married second Lydia Stimson widow of Robert Calley.

77) SAMUEL LOVEJOY (*Mary Farnum Lovejoy[3], Elizabeth Holt Farnum[2], Nicholas[1]*), b. at Andover, 10 Apr 1693 son of William and Mary (Farnum) Lovejoy; d. at Andover, 3 Dec 1749; m. at Andover, 23 Apr 1717, HANNAH STEVENS, b. at Andover, 28 Jul 1692 daughter of John and Ruth (Poor) Stevens; Hannah d. at Andover, 11 May 1767.

In his will written 5 November 1749 (probate 19 February 1750), Samuel Lovejoy bequeaths to beloved wife Hannah the use of one-third of the estate during her widowhood unless Hannah and his three sons agree on an annual payment to Hannah for her support. Eldest son Isaac receives two-thirds part of all of the homestead, all the stock of brute animals, and all the husbandry tools. Isaac will be obliged to care for his brothers Peter and James in sickness and in health and all things necessary for their support until they are capable of supporting themselves. The other one-third of the estate will be divided between Peter and James. A portion of the house will be reserved for the use of his four daughters Hannah, Elizabeth, Mary,

227 Lovejoy, *Lovejoy Genealogy*, p 61

228 *Essex County, MA: Probate File Papers, 1638-1881.*Online database. *AmericanAncestors.org.* New England Historic Genealogical Society, 2014., Case 17081

229 Bailey, *Historical Sketches of Andover*

and Phebe while they are unmarried. Each of these four daughters receives £100 and daughter Deborah receives £5. Son Isaac was named executor. Buildings were valued at £175, land and meadows at £1454 and personal estate at £508.14.6.[230]

Samuel Lovejoy and Hannah Stevens were parents of ten children born at Andover.

377) i HANNAH LOVEJOY, b. at Andover, 1 Mar 1717/8; d. at Andover, 28 Mar 1776; m. at Andover, 27 Dec 1752, as his second wife, HEZEKIAH STILES, baptized at Boxford, 1 May 1711 son of Ebenezer and Dorothy (Dalton) Stiles. Hezekiah was first married to Hannah Barnard.

378) ii DEBORAH LOVEJOY, b. at Andover, 17 Feb 1718/9; d. at Hollis, NH; m. at Andover, 16 Dec 1740, JOHN PHELPS, b. at Andover, 12 Mar 1718 son of John and Sarah (Andrews) Phelps.

iii ELIZABETH LOVEJOY, b. at Andover, 8 Aug 1720. Elizabeth was living and unmarried in 1749.

iv SAMUEL LOVEJOY, b. 2 Feb 1722; d. 29 Jul 1736.

379) v ISAAC LOVEJOY, b. at Andover, 9 Feb 1723; d. at Andover, 3 Dec 1799; m. at Billerica, 28 Feb 1750, DEBORAH SHELDON, b at Billerica, 23 Oct 1723 daughter of Samuel and Sarah/Mary[231] (Hutchinson) Sheldon; Deborah d. at Andover, 25 May 1813.

vi PETER LOVEJOY, b. at Andover, 5 Nov 1725; d. at Andover, 5 Feb 1774. Peter did not marry.

vii JAMES LOVEJOY, b. at Andover, 28 Dec 1727; he is perhaps the James that died at Andover on 14 Jan 1816. James did not marry.

380) viii MARY LOVEJOY, b. at Andover, 23 Jul 1730; d. at Jaffrey, NH, 25 Oct 1802; m. at Andover, 25 Mar 1752, ISAAC BAILEY, b. at Andover, 8 Aug 1729 son of Josiah and Elizabeth (Stevens) Bailey; Isaac d. at Jaffrey, NH, 7 Jun 1812. After Mary's death, Isaac married Susannah Stevens.

ix WILLIAM LOVEJOY, b. 28 Dec 1727; d. 8 Feb 1739/40.

x PHEBE LOVEJOY, b. 8 Mar 1734/5; she was living at the time of her father's will, but nothing further found.

78) ABIGAIL LOVEJOY (*Mary Farnum Lovejoy[3], Elizabeth Holt Farnum[2], Nicholas[1]*), b. at Andover, 11 Jun 1695 daughter of William and Mary (Farnum) Lovejoy; d. at Andover, 5 Sep 1759; m. 8 Dec 1718, HENRY PHELPS, b at Andover, 24 Sep 1693 son of Samuel and Sarah (Chandler) Phelps; Henry d. at Andover, 18 Oct 1766. After Abigail's death, Henry married the widow Susanna Kittredge.

In his will written 6 September 1766 (proved 11 November 1766), Henry Phelps bequeaths to beloved wife Susannah the use of the easterly part of the house and other provisions for her support including a horse and two cows. She also receives one of his swarms of bees which she may choose. He gives the poor of Andover £5.13.4. He also makes monetary bequests to his sister Deborah Blanchard, the heirs of his brother John Phelps, the heirs of his brother Thomas Phelps, and the heirs of his sister Anna Stevens late the wife of John Stevens. There are bequests to various kinsmen and kinswomen including widow Hannah Chandler daughter of his late brother Samuel Phelps, wife of Thomas Austin the daughter of his late sister Elizabeth Lovejoy, kinsman Benjamin Stevens, Sarah Lovejoy spinster sister of his first wife, Abigail Phelps the daughter of his kinsman John Phelps, and kinswomen wife of Mr. Abraham Moore and wife of Mr. Hezekiah Lovejoy. "I give to my Negro Servant Man named Pompey his Freedom and my will is that at my decease the said Pompey shall be freed from all Servitude and shall go without Control and have his Time and Freedom at his own dispose." The remainder of the estate goes to kinsman Samuel Shields who is also named executor. Real estate was valued at £507.17.6.[232]

Abigail and Henry had two children both of whom died in childhood.

i ABIGAIL PHELPS, b. 10 Jun 1730; d. 17 Nov 1739.

ii HENRY PHELPS, b. 4 Apr 1732; d. 18 Apr 1732.

79) LYDIA LOVEJOY (*Mary Farnum Lovejoy[3], Elizabeth Holt Farnum[2], Nicholas[1]*), b. at Andover, 26 Apr 1699 daughter of William and Mary (Farnum) Lovejoy; m. at Andover, 3 Dec 1718, her first cousin, CALEB JOHNSON, b. at Andover, 19 Oct 1694 son of William and Sarah (Lovejoy) Johnson; Caleb d. at Willington, CT, 18 May 1760. Caleb was first married to Mary Turner and was third married to Sarah who has not been identified.

Lydia and Caleb lived in Andover and their first six children were born there. On 11 March 1728/9 (recorded 13 May 1747), Caleb Johnson, with the consent of his wife Lydia, conveyed to William Foster for the sum of £400, several tracts of land

[230] *Essex County, MA: Probate File Papers, 1638-1881.*Online database. *AmericanAncestors.org.* New England Historic Genealogical Society, 2014. Case 17078

[231] Records are inconsistent in reporting the first name of Deborah's mother.

[232] *Essex County, Massachusetts, Probate Records and Indexes 1638-1916, volumes 342-344, Book 42-44, 1764-1768, pp 289-292*

including Caleb's homestead property.[233] The family then relocated to Windham and their six youngest children were born there.

In his will written 20 February 1760, Caleb Johnson bequeathed to his well-beloved wife Sarah the use and improvement of one-third of the estate during the time she is a widow. Son Caleb receives three shillings. The remainder of the estate goes to son William who is also responsible for the debts and paying the other legacies. Son Isaac receives five shillings and son Stephen, £70. His daughters each receives five shillings. Daughters named are Mary Thomas, Mehitable Sparks, Sarah Bugbee, and Alice Abbe. William is the sole executor. Real estate was valued at £245 and the total value of the estate was £331.[234]

Lydia and Caleb were parents of twelve children.

i LYDIA JOHNSON, b. at Andover, 4 Sep 1719; perhaps married John Frame at Windham in 1746 and died soon after without children. She is not mentioned in her father's will.

381) ii MARY JOHNSON, b. at Andover, 26 Jun 1721; m. at Windham, 10 Oct 1739, DAVID THOMAS.

iii WILLIAM JOHNSON, b. at Andover, 5 Nov 1722; died young.

iv SARAH JOHNSON, b. at Andover, 19 May 1724; d. 21 Nov 1728.

382) v MEHITABLE JOHNSON, b. at Andover, 27 Jan 1725/6; m. 29 Apr 1747, JOSEPH SPARKS; Joseph d. at Fort La Presentation, 10 Sep 1760 (probate 24 Nov 1760).

vi BENJAMIN JOHNSON, b. at Andover, 2 Nov 1727; d. 13 Dec 1728.

383) vii SARAH JOHNSON, b. at Windham, 29 Jul 1729; d. at Hartford, VT, 18 Mar 1815; m. 22 Jan 1746, NATHANIEL BUGBEE, b. at Ashford, 5 Apr 1721 son of Josiah and Sarah (Hubbard) Bugbee; Nathaniel d. at Hartford, 23 Jul 1808.

384) viii ALICE JOHNSON, b. at Windham, 27 Dec 1730; m. at Willington, 16 Apr 1752, JONATHAN ABBE, b. 1725 son of Jonathan and Mary (Johnson) Abbe.

385) ix WILLIAM JOHNSON, b. at Windham, 26 Aug 1732; d. at Willington, 6 Jun 1764; m. at Willington, 3 Jan 1754, EUNICE FISKE, b. at Willington, 29 Mar 1737 daughter of William and Mary (Blancher) Fiske.

x ABIGAIL JOHNSON, b. at Windham, 11 Mar 1733/4; nothing further known and not mentioned in her father's will.

386) xi ISAAC JOHNSON, b. at Windham, 5 Dec 1735; d. at Hadley, MA, 14 Sep 1808; m. at Willington, 15 Jul 1756, ELIZABETH BEAL, b. at Willington, 16 Jun 1734 daughter of William and Rachel (Heath) Beal; Elizabeth d. at Hadley, 5 Apr 1803.

xii STEPHEN JOHNSON, b. at Windham, 26 Dec 1737; d. at Willington, 5 Oct 1761. Stephen did not marry. His brother William was administrator of his estate.

80) SAMUEL HOLT (*Hannah Farnum Holt*[3], *Elizabeth Holt Farnum*[2], *Nicholas*[1]), b. at Andover, 1697 son of Samuel and Hannah (Farnum) Holt; d. at Andover, 25 Nov 1758; m. 12 Jan 1724, his second cousin, JEMIMA GRAY (*Henry Gray*[3], *Hannah Holt Gray*[2], *Nicholas*[1]), b. at Andover, 28 Aug 1701 daughter of Henry and Mary (Blunt) Gray; Jemima d. at Andover, 27 Aug 1775.

Samuel and Jemima resided in Andover throughout their lives. On 20 June 1762, Jemima Gray Holt was received into the South Church in Andover.[235]

Samuel Holt did not leave a will and his estate entered probate 4 December 1748. At the estate settlement on 24 September 1759, one-third was set-off to the widow. Oldest son Jonathan gets two-thirds of the real estate as it cannot be divided without prejudice to the value. He pays thirteen pounds eight shillings to each of the other children: Samuel Holt, David Holt, Ambrose Holt, Rebekah Gray wife of David Gray, Mary Holt, Jemimah Holt, Dinah Holt, and legal representative of Zebadiah Holt deceased.[236]

Samuel Holt and Jemima Gray were parents of ten children born at Andover.

235) i REBECCA HOLT, baptized at Andover, 31 Oct 1725; d. at Andover, 10 Jul 1800;[237] m. at Andover, 3 Jun 1756, her first cousin once removed, DAVID GRAY (*Robert Gray*[3], *Hannah Holt Gray*[2], *Nicholas*[1]), b. at Andover, 22 Oct 1717 son of Robert and Miriam (Lovejoy) Gray; David d. at Andover, 1767 (probate 1767).

[233] Massachusetts Land Records, Essex County, 91:84

[234] *Connecticut State Library (Hartford, Connecticut), Probate Packets, Jennings, Betsy-Kellogg, Ebenezer, 1759-1880, Caleb Johnson, Case 1214.*

[235] South Church, *Historical Manual*, p 136

[236] Essex County, MA: Probate File Papers, 1638-1881.Online database. AmericanAncestors.org. New England Historic Genealogical Society, 2014. Case 13688

[237] Rebecca, wid., general decay of nature, bur. July 10, 1800, a. 75 y. 10 m. CR2 [Aug. 8, 1800, in 75th y. GR2].

ii MARY HOLT, b. 5 Nov 1727; d. 18 Apr 1735.

180) iii JONATHAN HOLT, b. at Andover, 5 Feb 1728/9; d. at Andover, 23 Sep 1792; m. 1st 6 Nov 1754, his second cousin once removed, SHUAH HOLT (*Humphrey*[3], *Henry*[2], *Nicholas*[1]), b. at Andover, 21 Mar 1728/9 daughter of Humphrey and Abigail (Fifield) Holt; Shuah d. at Andover, 9 Jan 1766. Jonathan m. 2nd 24 Sep 1766, BETTY GOULD. Jonathan m. 3rd 23 May 1775, ELEANOR JOHNSON.

387) iv SAMUEL HOLT, b. at Andover, 18 Dec 1730; d. at Andover 3 Feb 1803; m. at Andover, 14 Feb 1760, ABIGAIL BLANCHARD, b. 1734 daughter of Josiah and Sarah (Blanchard) Blanchard; Abigail d. 1 Nov 1814.

v ZEBADIAH HOLT, b. 1 Jun 1733; d. 7 Dec 1758.

vi MARY HOLT, b. at Andover 7 Jul 1735; was living and unmarried in 1759; nothing further known.

388) vii DAVID HOLT, b. at Andover, 28 Aug 1737; d. at Andover, 1813 (probate 8 Dec 1813); m. 26 Jun 1764, HANNAH MARTIN, b. at Andover, 11 Apr 1738 daughter of John and Hannah (Steele) Martin; Hannah d. at Andover, Aug 1831.

viii JEMIMA HOLT, b. 16 Mov 1739; d. at Andover, 31 Jan 1829. Jemima was a teacher. She did not marry.

ix AMBROSE HOLT, b. at Andover, 20 Sep 1742. Ambrose selected Barachias Abbot for his guardian in 1759; nothing further known.

389) x DINAH HOLT, b. at Andover, 6 Nov 1744; d. at Andover, 20 Nov 1780; m. 10 Sep 1765, her third cousin, ASA HOLT (*Thomas*[4], *Thomas*[3], *Nicholas*[2], *Nicholas*[1]), b. at Andover, 3 May 1742 son of Thomas and Hannah (Kimball) Holt; [3]Asa d. at Andover, 20 Feb 1793. After Dinah's death, Asa married 5 Jul 1781, LYDIA STEVENS (widow of Elijah Patten), b. at Andover, 15 Nov 1753 daughter of Jonathan and Lydia (Felch) Stevens.

81) OBADIAH HOLT (*Hannah Farnum Holt*[3], *Elizabeth Holt Farnum*[2], *Nicholas*[1]), b. at Andover, 8 Dec 1700 son of Samuel and Hannah (Farnum) Holt; d. 24 Jan 1739 when he drowned in the Kennebec River; m. 14 Nov 1726, his first cousin, REBECCA FARNUM (*Thomas Farnum*[3], *Elizabeth Holt Farnum*[2], *Nicholas*[1]), b. at Andover, 1705 daughter of Thomas and Hannah (Hutchinson) Farnum. Rebecca m. 2nd, 22 Jun 1742, JOSEPH BERRY son of John and Rachel (-) Berry. Rebecca also had an out-of-wedlock relationship with Edward Farrington in 1723 which produced a daughter Mary.

Obadiah drowned in the Kennebec River before the birth of his youngest child: "Obediah, drowned in 'Canebeck River,' Jan. 24, 1738-9." Rebecca remarried Joseph Berry and had two further children.

Obadiah Holt and Rebecca Farnum were parents of nine children born at Andover, the youngest child born after Obadiah's death.

i HANNAH HOLT, b. 24 May 1727

ii MEHITABLE HOLT, b. at Andover, 21 Aug 1728; likely m. at Middleton, 11 Dec 1750, BENJAMIN CLARK. Nothing further was found.

390) iii ISAAC HOLT, b. at Andover, 30 Oct 1729; d. 1780; m. at Danvers, 26 Dec 1757, MARY MARBLE.

iv OBADIAH HOLT, b. 6 May 1731

391) v SARAH HOLT, baptized at Andover, 25 Feb 1733; d. likely at Annapolis, Nova Scotia, about 1773; m. at Andover, 30 Mar 1758, SAMUEL BANCROFT, b. at Reading, 12 Jul 1736 son of Samuel and Lydia (Parker) Bancroft. Samuel married second widow Mercy *Foster* Whitman.

392) vi JAMES HOLT, b. at Andover, 18 Feb 1732/3; m. 2 Jan 1755, his first cousin, MEHITABLE HOLT (*Ebenezer*[4], *Samuel*[3], *Samuel*[2], *Nicholas*[1]), b. at Andover, 3 Sep 1733 daughter of Ebenezer and Mehitable (Stevens) Holt; Mehitable d. at Andover, 4 Mar 1767. James m. 2nd 6 Aug 1767 widow MARY MCINTIRE.

vii JOB HOLT, b. 25 May 1735; d. 15 Jul 1735.

viii REBECCA HOLT, b. 22 Jun 1736

ix JOB HOLT, b. at Andover, 28 Feb 1738/9; m. 1st at Danvers, 3 May 1762, MEHITABLE ANDREW. Job m. 2nd at Danvers, 21 Nov 1767, MARY BURRELL. There is a record for one daughter Mehitable baptized at Danvers in 1779, but nothing further was found for her. There is a William Holt born 1765 in Danvers (according to his Revolutionary War pension application) who was later in Maine and he is thought to be a son of Job, but there were no records found to support that. That William Holt married Lucy Hutchins and they were grandparents of William Greely Holt pioneer of the Australia Holts.

Prior to her marriage to Obadiah, Rebecca had an out-of-wedlock child with Edward Farrington. Rebecca appeared before the General Court of Essex County 16 Jul 1723 and confessed to having given birth to an illegitimate child and was fined £12.10.0.

393) i MARY FARRINGTON, b. at Andover, 31 Jan 1722/3: "Mary, d. Rebeca and "Reputed,", d. Edward Farington, jr., Jan. 31, 1722-3."[238] Mary m. at Andover, 26 Oct 1742, JOHN GROW, perhaps the John born at Andover, 15 Sep 1721 (baptized in 1728),[239] the out-of-wedlock child of Elizabeth Nichols and an unknown Mr. Grow. John d. at Dudley, MA, 17 Oct 1775.

In his will written 13 October 1757 (probate 9 January 1758), Joseph Berry bequeathed to beloved wife Rebecca all the indoor movables, the right to a room in the house while she is a widow, and specific provisions for her support. Son Bartholomew receives all the lands lying in Middleton. Son John Berry receives £25.13.4. There are also bequests to daughters Sarah Parker, Mary, and Abigail.[240] Bartholomew, Sarah, and Mary are children from his marriage to Sarah.

Rebecca had two children with Joseph Berry.

i JOHN BERRY, b. at Andover, 23 May 1743. Samuel Berry was named as guardian to John Berry, a minor above age 14, on 9 January 1758.

ii ABIGAIL BERRY, baptized at Andover, 11 Dec 1748. Bartholomew Berry was named as guardian to Abigail, minor under fourteen, on 9 January 1758.[241]

82) HANNAH HOLT (*Hannah Farnum Holt, Elizabeth Holt Farnum[2], Nicholas[1]*), b. at Andover, 30 Nov 1702 daughter of Samuel and Hannah (Farnum) Holt; d. at Reading, 3 Apr 1749; m. at Andover, 2 Jan 1727/8 as his second wife, ROBERT RUSSELL (*Phebe Johnson Russell[3], Mary Holt Johnson[2], Nicholas[1]*), b. at Andover, about 1690 son of Thomas and Phebe (Johnson) Russell; Robert d. at Reading, 1759 (probate 1759). Robert was first married on 22 Jun 1716 to ABIGAIL FLINT, b. 1691; Abigail d. at Andover, 10 May 1723. Robert married third on 23 Dec 1749, the widow ELIZABETH MANNING. Robert married fourth on 17 Apr 1755, the widow MARTHA (JOHNSON) PARKER.

Robert Russell resided in Reading where he served on a committee to find a suitable place to keep school.[242]

In his will written 8 June 1757 (probate 31 December 1759), Robert Russell bequeathed to beloved wife Martha the income of one-third part of the real estate during her natural life as well house one-third of the household goods. Son Ezekiel receives £3.6.8 which makes his full portion. Son Timothy receives all the lands and buildings in Reading and Andover. Daughter Hannah Peirce receives £3.6.8 and daughters Mary, Eunice, Phebe, and Elizabeth each receives £13.6.8. Granddaughter Abigail Bachelor receives six shillings as does grandson Phineas Holt. Household goods are to be equally divided among his five daughters and clothing divided between his two sons. Son Timothy was named sole executor.[243] Personal estate was valued at £21.8.11. Son Timothy Russell married but did not have children. In his will, he includes small bequests to brother Ezekiel Russell, sister Pierce, sister Mary Levis, sister Eunice Brown, sister Phebe Cheney, and sister Elizabeth Perley.[244]

Robert Russell and Abigail Flint were parents of three children born at Andover.

394) i ABIGAIL RUSSELL, b. at Andover, 4 Oct 1717; d. at Reading, 1746 (probate Sep 1746); m. at Reading, 23 Sep 1735, EBENEZER EATON; Ebenezer d. at Reading, 1738 (probate 1738).

265) ii PRUDENCE RUSSELL, baptized at Andover, 31 Jul 1720; d. at Andover, 15 Nov 1745; m. 1st 9 Jul 1741, her first cousin once removed, MOSES HOLT (*Moses[3], John[2], Nicholas[1]*), b. at Andover, 21 Oct 1716 son of Moses and Elizabeth (Russell) Holt; Moses d. at Andover, 6 Ju; 1743. Prudence m. 2nd 11 Mar 1744/5, her first cousin, JOHN CHANDLER (*Mehitable Russell Chandler[4], Phebe Johnson Russell[3], Mary Holt*

---

[238] Mary is listed both as Mary Farnum and Mary Farrington in the town records.

[239] The parentage of John Grow is not certain, but can be established through town records that a John Grow out-of-wedlock child of Elizabeth Nichols was born at Andover 15 Sep 1721 and was baptized in 1728 at age seven when he is described as the son of Elizabeth Nichols and servant to Nathaniel Frye: John, s. Elizabeth Nichols "and servant to Nath Frie," bp. ——, 1728. For further discussion of this topic, see Davis, *John Grow of Ipswich*, p 72 and Charlotte Helen Abbott's notes on the Grow Family of Andover.

[240] *Essex County, MA: Probate File Papers, 1638-1881.*Online database. *AmericanAncestors.org.* New England Historic Genealogical Society, 2014. Case 2400

[241] *Essex County, MA: Probate File Papers, 1638-1881.*Online database. *AmericanAncestors.org.* New England Historic Genealogical Society, 2014. Case 2392

[242] Eaton, *Genealogical History of the Town of Reading*, p 146

[243] *Middlesex County, MA: Probate File Papers, 1648-1871.*Online database. *AmericanAncestors.org.* New England Historic Genealogical Society, 2014. Case 19690

[244] *Essex County, MA: Probate File Papers, 1638-1881.*Online database. *AmericanAncestors.org.* New England Historic Genealogical Society, 2014. Case 24431

Johnson[2], Nicholas[1]), b. at Andover, 19 Jan 1721/2 son of Joseph and Mehitable (Russell) Chandler; John d. at Andover, 11 May 1759. John married second HANNAH PHELPS.

395) iii EZEKIEL RUSSELL, b. at Andover, 10 Jun 1722; d. at Wilbraham, MA, 3 Jan 1802; m. TABATHA FLINT, b. at Reading, 18 May 1721 daughter of Ebenezer and Tabitha (Burnap) Flint; Tabitha d. at Wilbraham, 4 Jan 1808.[245]

Robert Russell and Hannah Holt were parents of seven children born at Reading.

i HANNAH RUSSELL, b. 20 Apr 1730; not mentioned in father's will.

ii MARY RUSSELL, b. 1731; died young.

iii TIMOTHY RUSSELL, b. at Reading, 11 Aug 1733; d. at Boxford, 1818 (probate 20 Oct 1818); m. MARGARET who has not been identified. Timothy and Margaret did not have children.

iv BENJAMIN RUSSELL, b. 1735; not mentioned in father's will.

v MARY RUSSELL, b. at Andover, 7 Jun 1740. She perhaps married John Lovis in 1781. If so, she did not have children.

vi ASA RUSSELL, b. 28 Sep 1744; not mentioned in father's will.

vii EUNICE RUSSELL, b. at Andover, 23 Feb 1746; m. at Reading, 29 Nov 1764, JONATHAN BROWN. No children were identified for Eunice and Jonathan.

Robert and Elizabeth Russell were parents of two children born at Reading.

396) i PHEBE RUSSELL, b. 1751; m. at Andover, 19 Nov 1776, DAVID CHENEY, b. at Boxford, 11 Sep 1750 son of Ichabod and Rebekah (Smith) Cheney. Phebe is perhaps the widow Phebe Cheney who married John Perley in Rowley in 1805.

397) ii ELIZABETH RUSSELL, b. at Reading, 1752; d. at Boxford, 12 Mar 1840; m. 1st at Danvers, 12 Dec 1776, ELIJAH MOULTON, b. at Danvers, 5 Dec 1748 son of Benjamin and Sarah (Smith) Moulton; Elijah d. at Danvers, 1782 (probate 7 Oct 1782). Elizabeth m. 2nd at Boxford, 10 Jun 1788, JESSE PERLEY, b. at Boxford, 20 Jun 1761 son of Nathaniel and Mehitable (Perley) Perley; Jesse d. at Boxford, 18 Apr 1846.

83) MARTHA HOLT (*Hannah Farnum Holt[3], Elizabeth Holt Farnum[2], Nicholas[1]*), b. at Andover, 8 Mar 1705 daughter of Samuel and Hannah (Farnum) Holt; m. 3 Mar 1725/6, SOMERS PIERCE, b. at Woburn, 16 Feb 1697 son of William and Abigail (Somers) Pierce.

Little is known of the family of Martha and Somers. The birth of son William is reported at both Andover and Pomfret. There is a presumed second son Somers who was in Ashford at the same time as William and who was the father of a daughter Martha born in 1755.

398) i WILLIAM PIERCE, b. at Pomfret, 16 Mar 1727/8; d. at Andover, VT, 22 Jul 1818;[246] m. by 1750, HANNAH who has not been identified.

ii SOMERS PIERCE, b. about 1730 (a presumed child). He is the father of a daughter Martha born at Ashford 20 Apr 1755. Nothing further is known.

84) EBENEZER HOLT (*Hannah Farnum Holt[3], Elizabeth Holt Farnum[2], Nicholas[1]*), b. at Andover, 8 Apr 1705 son of Samuel and Hannah (Farnum) Holt; m. at Andover, 4 Dec 1729, MEHITABLE STEVENS, b. about 1708 of undetermined parents.[247]

This family is believed to have relocated to New Hampshire and records related to the latter part of their lives have not been located.[248] Mehitable and Ebenezer were parents of nine children born at Andover.[249]

---

[245] Ezekiel and Tabatha are buried at the Old Hampden Cemetery in Hampden. Find A Grave 43582031 and 43582032

[246] Pierce, *Pierce Genealogy*, p 61

[247] Published genealogies give a death date for Mehitable of May 1805 at the age of 97 which would make her born about 1708. Mehitable is consistently reported as being the daughter of Ephraim Stevens and Sarah Abbott, but their daughter Mehitable born in 1700 can be demonstrated through multiple deeds to be living and unmarried in Andover in 1742.

[248] Durrie, *A Genealogical History of the Holt Family*

[249] Both Secomb's History of Amherst, New Hampshire and Durrie's Holt genealogy give a daughter Mary in this family and list her as marrying Darius Abbott. However, the probate record of Henry Holt (*Essex County, MA: Probate File Papers, 1638-1881. Probate of Henry Holt, 14 Oct*

399) i EBENEZER HOLT, b. 7 Sep 1730; d. at Mount Vernon, NH, Apr 1805;[250] m. 15 Feb 1753, LYDIA PEABODY (*Sarah Holt Peabody[4], Henry[3], Henry[2], Nicholas[1]*), b. 5 Jul 1731 daughter of Moses and Sarah (Holt) Peabody; Lydia's date of death is not known.

392) ii MEHITABLE HOLT, b. 3 Sep 1733; d. 4 Mar 1767; m. 2 Jan 1755, her first cousin JAMES HOLT (*Obadiah[4], Samuel[3], Samuel[2], Nicholas[1]*), b. 18 Feb 1732/3 son of Obadiah and Rebecca (Farnum) Holt.

iii RACHEL HOLT (twin), b. 15 Jun 1737; d. 14 Jul 1737.

iv PRISCILLA HOLT (twin), b. 15 Jun 1737; no further record.

400) v EZEKIEL HOLT (twin), b. 7 Jul 1741; d. at Amherst, NH date unknown; m. by 1772, MARY STEWART, b. 2 Sep 1749 daughter of Samuel and Sarah (Tarbell) Stewart.

vi RACHEL HOLT (twin), b. 7 Jul 1741; no further record.

401) vii REUBEN HOLT, b. 27 Jun 1744; d. at Landgrove, VT 2 Mar 1836;[251] m. at Amherst, NH, 6 Feb 1772, LYDIA SMALL, b. Mar 1745[252] daughter of William and Sarah (Clark) Small; Lydia d. at Amherst, NH, 9 Mar 1795.

viii HEPHZIBAH HOLT, b. 13 Jun 1748; d. at Amherst, NH, 11 Jan 1851;[253] m. at Amherst, 27 Apr 1790, WILLIAM HARTSHORN, b. at Reading, 1753 son of Benjamin and Mary (Swain) Hartshorn; William d. 22 Jun 1831 at Amherst.[254] Hephzibah and William do not seem to have had children.

ix HANNAH HOLT, b. 27 Oct 1749; no further record.

85) JOHN HOLT (*Hannah Farnum Holt[3], Elizabeth Holt Farnum[2], Nicholas[1]*), b. at Andover, 1707 son of Samuel and Hannah (Farnum) Holt; d. at Wilton, NH, before 1786; m. at Andover, 8 Oct 1731, MARY LEWIS, b. about 1710; Mary d. at Wilton, 15 May 1786.[255]

John Holt and Mary Lewis were parents of eight children born at Andover. They then relocated to Wilton where four of their children settled.

402) i JOHN HOLT, b. at Andover, 16 Mar 1732; d. at Andover, 12 Jun 1765; m. 1st 28 Nov 1753, LYDIA KIMBALL (widow of James Farnum), baptized at Wenham, 13 Dec 1730 daughter of Josiah and Elizabeth (Bragg) Kimball; Lydia d. at Andover, 7 May 1756. John m. 2nd 5 Feb 1757, RACHEL FARNUM (or Varnum) who has not been identified. Rachel was living at the probate of her husband's estate, but no information for her after that time was located. Lydia Kimball m. 1st, 27 Dec 1748, JAMES FARNUM (*James Farnum[4], John Farnum[3], Elizabeth Holt Farnum[2], Nicholas[1]*), b. at Andover, 24 Apr 1723 son of James and Johanna (Grainger) Farnum; James d. at Andover, 27 Feb 1749/50.

403) ii JEREMIAH HOLT, b. at Andover, 31 Mar 1734; d. at Wilton, 1816; m. at Andover, 21 Apr 1756, his third cousin, HANNAH ABBOTT (*Hannah Holt Abbott[4], Timothy[3], James[2], Nicholas[1]*), b. at Andover, 18 May 1737 daughter of Barachias and Hannah (Holt) Abbott; Hannah d. at Wilton, Nov 1812.

404) iii MARY HOLT, b, at Andover, 12 Apr 1737; d. at Wilton, 1821; m. at Andover, 4 Nov 1756, SAMUEL PETTENGILL, b. at Andover, 16 Mar 1731/2 son of Nathaniel and Sarah (Abbott) Pettengill; Samuel died in the Ticonderoga campaign in 1776. Mary m. 2nd at Wilton, 10 Feb 1780, JOHN WRIGHT.

405) iv AMOS HOLT, b. at Andover, 9 May 1740; d. at Wilton, 29 Nov 1820; m. at Andover, 29 Jun 1762, JEMIMA INGALLS, b. at Andover, 27 Jul 1740 daughter of Francis and Lydia (Ingalls) Ingalls; Jemima d. at Wilton, 4 Dec 1816.

406) v ELEANOR "NELLY" HOLT, b. at Andover, 27 Jun 1743; m. 5 Jan 1762, AARON BLANCHARD, b. at Andover, 27 Jun 1740 son of Thomas and Elizabeth (Johnson) Blanchard; Aaron d. at Hartford, NY, 28 Oct 1801. Aaron married second Mehitable Mooar (widow of Emery Chase) on 21 Sep 1789.

1754, Case number 13640), husband of Rebecca Gray, support that Mary who married Darius Abbott was their daughter. Although Henry Holt died in 1754, the final settlement of his estate in 1762 includes the settlement of one lot on Mary wife of Darius Abbot

250 Secomb, *History of the Town of Amherst*

251 *Vermont, Vital Records, 1720-1908* (Provo, UT, USA: Ancestry.com Operations, Inc., 2013).

252 Lydia was baptized at Salem but may have been born at Andover.

253 Hephzibah's longevity is confirmed by her listing in the 1850 US Census as being at age 103 on the census report.

254 William Hartshorn is listed in the 1810 US Census of Amherst but is not in the 1820 census.

255 Mary Holt, widow of John, died at age 76. "New Hampshire Death Records, 1654–1947." Index. FamilySearch, Salt Lake City, Utah, 2010. New Hampshire Bureau of Vital Records. "Death Records, 1654–1947." Bureau of Vital Records, Concord, New Hampshire. Film 15345

vi REUBEN HOLT, b. 27 May 1744; nothing further known.

407) vii DANIEL HOLT, b. at Andover, 10 Jan 1745/6; d. at Wilton, 5 Nov 1777;[256] m. about 1766, MEHITABLE PUTNAM, b. at Wilton, 25 Dec 1745 daughter of Jacob and Susannah (Stiles) Putnam; Mehitable d. at Wilton 20 Jan 1800.

408) viii SAMUEL HOLT, baptized at Andover, 7 May 1749; d. at Temple, NH, 5 Dec 1799;[257] m. about 1771, LYDIA ADAMS, b. at Dunstable, NH, 27 Jul 1749 daughter of Ephraim and Thankful (Blodgett) Adams; Lydia d. at Wilton, 24 Jun 1844.

86) THOMAS FARNUM (*Thomas Farnum³, Elizabeth Holt Farnum², Nicholas¹*), b. at Andover, 16 May 1709 son of Thomas and Hannah (Hutchinson) Farnum; m. at Andover, 23 Nov 1733, PHEBE TOWNE, b. at Topsfield, 30 Jul 1714 daughter of Nathan and Phebe (Curtis) Towne;[258] Phebe d. 9 Jul 1763.

Thomas and Phebe resided in Andover. On 10 December 1736 (deed recorded 22 June 1757), Thomas received three pieces of land and meadow from his father Thomas "in consideration of that parental love good will & affection that I have a do bear towards my well beloved and dutiful son Thomas Farnaum Junior."[259] There are records for four children of Thomas and Phebe born at Andover.

409) i THOMAS FARNUM, b. at Andover, 6 Sep 1734; d. perhaps at Greenfield, NH; m. at Andover, 13 Jan 1757, LYDIA ABBOTT, b. at Andover, 28 Mar 1733 daughter of Timothy and Mary (Foster) Abbott; Lydia d. at Andover, 13 Mar 1816.

410) ii ASA FARNUM, b. at Andover, 11 May 1736; m. at Topsfield, 16 Mar 1758, SUSANNAH TOWNE, b. at Topsfield, 6 Sep 1733 daughter of Benjamin and Susanna (Wilds) Towne.[260]

411) iii JOSEPH FARNUM, b. at Andover, 18 Jun 1745; d. at Mont Vernon, NH, 10 May 1824; m. 1st about 1766, MARY LYON, b. about 1747 likely the daughter of Ebenezer and Abigail (Bullard) Lyon; Mary d. 1787. Joseph m. 2nd at Amherst, 17 Sep 1794, TABITHA WESTON (widow of Daniel Wilkins and Jesse Baldwin), b. at Wakefield, MA, 31 Mar 1748 daughter of Ebenezer and Mehitable (Sutherick) Weston; Tabitha d. at Mont Vernon, Jan 1820. Joseph m. 3rd, EDITH SMITH, b. about 1774; Edith d. at Mont Vernon, 12 Nov 1862.

iv PHEBE FARNUM, b. at Andover, 1749/50

87) EBENEZER FARNUM (*Thomas Farnum³, Elizabeth Holt Farnum², Nicholas¹*), b. at Andover, 1711 son of Thomas and Hannah (Hutchinson) Farnum; m. 12 Feb 1732/3, his second cousin, PRISCILLA INGALLS, b. at Andover, 1706 daughter of James and Hannah (Abbott) Ingalls.[261]

Ebenezer Farnum and Priscilla Ingalls were parents of eight children born at Andover.

412) i HANNAH FARNUM, b. at Andover, 9 Sep 1733; m. at Andover, 13 Nov 1753; DANIEL FARRINGTON, b. at Andover, Jun 1732 son of Daniel and Elizabeth (Putnam) Farrington; Daniel d. at Fryeburg, ME, about 1818.

413) ii SUSANNAH FARNUM, b. at Andover, 31 Aug 1735; d. at Fryeburg, ME; m. at Andover, 29 May 1753, ISAAC ABBOTT, b. at Andover, 30 Jun 1728 son of Ebenezer and Hannah (Turner) Abbott; Isaac d. at Fryeburg, after 1790.

iii EBENEZER FARNUM, b. 13 Nov 1737; d. 9 Aug 1741.

414) iv PRISCILLA FARNUM, b. at Andover, 24 Mar 1740/1; d. at Andover, 25 Oct 1784; m. 4 Sep 1760, JONATHAN BALLARD, b. 25 Nov 1729 son of Sherebiah and Lydia (Osgood) Ballard; Jonathan d. at Middleton, 1 Feb 1764.

v SARAH FARNUM, b. 21 Oct 1742; d. 8 Aug 1760.

---

[256] Daniel died in the 32nd year of his age according to his gravestone making it likely that it is Daniel the son of John and Mary who married Mehitable Putnam. Some sources suggest he was the son of the proposed marriage of John Holt (born 1713) and Rachel Fletcher but there are no records of that marriage or records for any children from that marriage.

[257] Samuel's death record lists his parents as John and Mary Holt.

[258] Towne, *The Descendants of William Towne*, p 27

[259] Massachusetts Land Records, Essex County, 106:61

[260] The 1772 will of Benjamin Towne includes a bequest to his daughter Susanna Varnum.

[261] There is uncertainty about the parentage of Priscilla Ingalls. It has also been suggested that she was a daughter of John and Sarah (Russell) Ingalls. Farnham, *Descendants of Ralph Farnum*, p 144. However, the family of John Ingalls and Sarah Russell went to Connecticut and they seem the less likely choice as parents for Priscilla.

415) vi DOROTHY "DOLLY" FARNUM, b. at Andover, 21 Jan 1744/5; d. 1820; m. at Andover, 10 Mar 1774, JOHN FOWLER, b. at Ipswich, 1748 son of Joseph and Elizabeth (Perkins) Fowler;[262] John d. about 1778 at Mill Prison in England where he was a prisoner after being captured during the Revolution.[263]

416) vii ABIAH FARNUM, b. at Andover, 13 Feb 1746/7; d. at Tamworth, NH, 22 Jun 1823; m. 4 Apr 1769, JOHN AYER; John d. at Pembroke, NH, 1802 (probate 19 May 1802). Abiah m. 2nd at Pembroke, 8 Nov 1810, as his third wife, Col. DAVID GILMAN, b. at Exeter, NH, 9 Jun 1735 son of Israel and Deborah (Thwing) Gilman; David d. at Tamworth, 11 May 1826. David Gilman was first married to Betsy Gilman and second married to Sarah Smith.

417) viii PHEBE FARNUM, b. at Andover, 15 Dec 1750; likely m. about 1771, JOB ABBOTT,[264] b. at Pembroke, about 1742 son of David and Hannah (Chandler) Abbott; Job d. at West Barnet, VT, 15 Dec 1815.

88) ZEBADIAH HOLT (*Elizabeth Farnum Holt*[3]*, Elizabeth Holt Farnum*[2]*, Nicholas*[1]), b. at Andover, 25 Jan 1700 son of George and Elizabeth (Farnum) Holt; d. at Windham, CT, about 1760 (estate inventory 3 Apr 1760); m. at Windham, 14 Aug 1732, SARAH FLINT, b. at Windham, 12 Jan 1717 daughter of Nathaniel and Sarah (Cutler) Flint.[265]

Zebadiah Holt did not leave a will and his estate was inventoried 3 April 1760. There was some dispute related to the settlement of the estate and the portion that should be received by eldest son Zebadiah being questioned by other of the heirs and then all parties agreeing to arbitration. The dispute centered on the amount that Zebadiah should receive for his labor on his father's farm between the time he had come of age and his father's decease. Those heirs or representatives agreeing to the arbitration were Zebadiah Holt, Isaac Burnam, George Martin, Ichabod Downing, Sarah Holt, Aaron Fuller, and Thomas Butler. Isaac Burnam, Aaron Fuller, and Thomas Butler signed on behalf of themselves and their respective wives, George Martin signed as guardian to Josiah Holt, Ichabod Downing as guardian for Marcy Holt, and widow Sarah Holt signing as guardian for Abigail Holt.[266] The distribution from the estate was made in 1760.

418) i EUNICE HOLT, b. at Windham, 8 Oct 1732; d. at Ashford, 16 Feb 1776; m. at Windham, 22 Mar 1747, ISAAC BURNHAM, b. at Ipswich, Dec 1729 son of Ebenezer and Dorothy (Andrews) Burnham; Isaac d. at Ashford, 14 Oct 1807.

419) ii ZEBADIAH HOLT, b. at Windham, 13 Sep 1734; d. at Hampton, 15 Dec 1811; m. at Ashford, 16 Feb 1758, JEMIMA SIMONS, b. at Windham, 6 Apr 1729 daughter of Jacob and Mary (Crane) Simons;[267] Jemima d. at Hampton, 12 May 1807.

420) iii SARAH HOLT, b. at Windham, 13 Feb 1737; d. at Hampton, 16 Mar 1806; m. at Windham, 15 Mar 1755, AARON FULLER, b. at Windham, 26 Jan 1734 son of Stephen and Hannah (Moulton) Fuller; Aaron d. at Hampton, 27 Feb 1809.

421) iv ELIZABETH HOLT, b. at Windham, 10 Jan 1738/9; d. at Ashford, 9 Jun 1814; m. at Windham, 19 Jan 1757, THOMAS BUTLER, b. at Windham, 23 Jun 1734 son of Thomas and Abigail (Craft) Butler; Thomas d. at Ashford, 29 Nov 1787.

422) v MERCY HOLT, b. at Windham, 14 Feb 1740/1; d. at Hampton, 15 Sep 1799; m. at Windham, 8 Sep 1763, her third cousin, WILLIAM HOLT (*William*[4]*, Thomas*[3]*, Nicholas*[2]*, Nicholas*[1]), b. at Windham, 15 Jul 1743 son of William and Hannah (Holt) Holt; William d. at Hampton, 6 Aug 1815.

vi JOSIAH HOLT, b. at Windham, 19 Nov 1743. Josiah was living in 1760 but nothing further was found.

vii JONATHAN HOLT, baptized at Windham, 8 Apr 1750; nothing further known and likely died young as he is not mentioned in his father's estate distribution.[268]

viii ABIGAIL HOLT, b. at Windham, 26 Aug 1753. She was living in 1760 but nothing further was found.

---

[262] Stickney, *The Fowler Family*

[263] Cards Concerning Revolutionary War Service and Imprisonment, NEHGR, 1947

[264] There are at least five Phebe Farnums born in a ten-year period at Andover with little or no record evidence that would discriminate one from the other in terms of marriages. This marriage seems the most likely for this Phebe.

[265] The 1754 will of Nathaniel Flint includes a bequest to his daughter Sarah Holt.

[266] *Connecticut State Library (Hartford, Connecticut);* Probate Place: *Hartford, Connecticut, Probate Packets, Hicks-Hovey, Elisha, 1719-1880, estate of Zebadiah Holt, Case 1960*

[267] The 1765 estate distribution of Jacob Simonds (Simmons) includes a distribution to daughter Jemima Holt.

[268] Published genealogies report that this Jonathan was adopted by his uncle Jonathan (Zebadiah's half-brother) but those same genealogies report his birth as 1758 and the Jonathan son of Zebadiah was born in 1750. There is no son Jonathan in the estate distribution of Zebadiah Holt. It is much more likely that it is Jonathan the son of Nathaniel and Phebe (Canada) Holt who was adopted by Uncle Jonathan. Nathaniel Holt (the uncle's full brother) died in 1763.

89) ELIZABETH HOLT (*Elizabeth Farnum Holt*[3], *Elizabeth Holt Farnum*[2], *Nicholas*[1]), b. 1706 daughter of George and Elizabeth (Farnum) Holt; m. at Windham, 16 Nov 1727, SAMUEL COBURN, b. 1700 son of Edward and Sarah (Hayward) Coburn.[269]

Elizabeth and Samuel resided in Windham. They were admitted as members of the church at Hampton on 14 December 1735 and most of their children were baptized there.[270] Elizabeth and Samuel were parents of fifteen children born at Windham.

423) i SAMUEL COBURN, b. at Windham, 29 Sep 1728; m. at Windham, 23 Jan 1751, JUDAH WEBSTER, baptized at Beverly, MA, 8 Mar 1719 daughter of Benjamin and Ruth (Hibbard) Webster.[271]

424) ii EDWARD COBURN, b. at Windham, 5 Apr 1730; d. at Hampton, 28 Jul 1791; m. 17 Oct 1751, PRUDENCE WEAKLEY, b. at Preston, 13 Apr 1731 daughter of William and Prudence (Randall) Weakley; Prudence d. at Windham, 19 Oct 1772. Edward m. 2nd at Windham, 22 Feb 1774, SARAH WYMAN, b. about 1736; Sarah d. at Hampton, 28 Jul 1791.

425) iii ZEBADIAH COBURN, b. at Windham, 26 Feb 1732; d. about 1814 location unknown; m. 22 Jan 1754, ELIZABETH DURKEE, b. at Hampton, 28 Nov 1737 daughter of William and Elizabeth (Ford) Durkee.[272]

426) iv CORNELIUS COBURN, b. at Windham, 1 Jan 1734; d. at Rome, NY, 20 Jun 1824; m. 1st 20 Apr 1757, ABIGAIL GREENSLIT, b. at Preston, 17 Nov 1736 daughter of John and Sarah (Manning) Greenslit; Abigail d. at Windham, 21 Apr 1778. Cornelius m. 2nd 5 Apr 1780, RACHEL ROBINSON, b. at Windham, 30 Mar 1744 daughter of Peter and Ruth (Fuller) Robinson; Rachel d. at Rome, 12 Jun 1828.

427) v SARAH COBURN, b. at Windham, 17 Apr 1736; d. at Rutland, VT, 25 Feb 1802; m. 1756, EZEKIEL ORMSBY, b. at Hampton, 19 Mar 1738 son of John and Mehitable (Way) Ormsby; Ezekiel d. at Rutland, 26 Mar 1802.

428) vi GEORGE COBURN, b. at Windham, 5 Sep 1737; d. at Wilton, NH, 25 Jan 1812; m. 19 Nov 1764, MARY ADAMS, b. 13 Apr 1744 daughter of Ephraim and Thankful (Blodgett) Adams; Mary d. at Wilton, 28 Mar 1842.

429) vii MARY COBURN, b. at Windham, Apr 1740; m. at Windham, 28 Aug 1761, WILLIAM NEFF, b. at Windham, 14 May 1739 son of William and Grace (Webster) Neff; William d. at Hampton, 14 Jan 1818.

430) viii NATHANIEL COBURN, b. at Windham, 28 Apr 1742; d. at Hampton, 6 Dec 1788; m. HANNAH BURNHAM, b. at Hampton, 27 Nov 1746 daughter of Eben and Martha (Hibbard) Burnham; Hannah d. at Williamstown, VT, 17 Dec 1834.

ix ELIZABETH COBURN, b. 27 Aug 1743

x LYDIA COBURN, b. 13 Apr 1745

xi DINAH COBURN, b. 20 Sep 1746

xii PRISCILLA COBURN, b. 16 Sep 1748

431) xiii HEZEKIAH COBURN, baptized at Windham, 15 Apr 1750; d. at Lewis, NY, 1835; m. at Hampton, 17 Jan 1771, MARY BILL, b. at Lebanon, CT, 6 May 1750 daughter of Jonathan and Esther (Owen) Bill; Mary d. at Lewis, 1802.

432) xiv EBENEZER COBURN, b. at Windham, 28 Jun 1752; m. at Scotland, CT, 20 Nov 1777, SYBIL ROBINSON, b. at Scotland, 14 Sep 1755 daughter of Samuel and Sarah (Kimball) Robinson.

433) xv STEPHEN COLBURN, b. at Windham, 20 Jul 1755; d at Lebanon, NH, 20 Jun 1820; m. Dec 1779, MIRIAM WOOD, b. at Mansfield, CT, 1755 daughter of Joseph and Anna (Palmer) Wood; Miriam d. at Lebanon, 21 Oct 1851.

90) DINAH HOLT (*Elizabeth Farnum Holt*[3], *Elizabeth Holt Farnum*[2], *Nicholas*[1]), b. at Andover, 1710 daughter of George and Elizabeth (Farnum) Holt; d. at Hampton, CT, 12 Jan 1763; m. at Windham, 1 Oct 1730, NATHANIEL FORD, b. at Windham, 3 Jun 1707 son of Joseph and Elizabeth (Hovey) Ford; Nathaniel d. at Hampton, 25 Oct 1779. Nathaniel married second Hannah Brigham on 7 Jul 1763.

---

[269] Coburn, *Genealogy of the Descendants of Edward Colburn*, p 30

[270] Ancestry.com. *Connecticut, Church Record Abstracts, 1630-1920* [database on-line]. Volume 050, Hampton, p 47

[271] The 1762 will of Benjamin Webster of Windham includes a bequest to his daughter Judah Coburn.

[272] The 1757 estate distribution of William Durkee included a set-off to daughter Elizabeth wife of Zebadiah Coburn.

Nathaniel Ford did not leave a will and the division of his estate was made 12 September 1780 with two-eighths settled on eldest son Amos and one-eighth each to Dinah, Abraham, Jonathan, Phineas, Sarah, and the heirs of daughter Elizabeth deceased. The final accounting of the estate was made by son Amos in 1786.[273]

Dinah Holt and Nathaniel Ford were parents of eleven children born at Windham.

434) i ELIZABETH FORD, b. at Windham, 4 June 1733; d. at Windham, 1764; m. at Windham, 17 Oct 1751, JOSEPH MARTIN, b. at Windham, 29 Mar 1730 son of Ebenezer and Jerusha (Durkee) Martin. Joseph second married Elizabeth Coy at Windham on 3 Jan 1765.

208) ii DINAH FORD, b. at Windham, 17 Sep 1735; m. at Windham, 4 Mar 1756, her second cousin once removed, DANIEL PRESTON (*Deborah Holt Preston[3], Nicholas[2], Nicholas[1]*), b. at Windham, 16 Mar 1729 son of Benjamin and Deborah (Holt) Preston.

iii EUNICE FORD, b. 25 May 1737; d. at Windham, 21 Oct 1754.

iv NATHANIEL FORD, b. at Windham, 7 Nov 1739; d. at Greenbush, NY, 9 Oct 1758.

435) v AMOS FORD, b. at Windham, 2 Aug 1742; d. at Hampton, 21 Dec 1834; m. at Windham, 25 May 1761, LYDIA DAVISON, b. at Preston, 1 Jan 1738/9 daughter of Thomas and Lydia (Herrick) Davison; Lydia d. at Hampton, 15 May 1829.

436) vi ABRAHAM FORD, b. at Windham, 29 Aug 1744; d. at Brookfield, VT, 19 Mar 1832; m. at Windham, 8 Nov 1763, ABIGAIL WOODWARD, b. at Hampton, 1 May 1740 daughter of Jacob and Abigail (Flint) Woodward;[274] Abigail d. at Brookfield, 23 Mar 1826.

437) vii JONATHAN FORD, b. at Windham, 20 Sep 1746; d. at Alexander, NY, 28 Nov 1833; m. 1st 1772, ANNA FRENCH. Jonathan m. 2nd 1782, MARY WHALING; Mary d. 23 Mar 1820.

viii GEORGE FORD, b. 7 Mar 1748/9; d. 14 Jul 1750.

438) ix SARAH FORD, b. at Windham, 2 Jul 1751; m. at Hampton, 21 May 1772, THOMAS MOSELEY, b. at Windham, 7 May 1749 son of Nathaniel and Sarah (Capon) Moseley;[275] Thomas died "in public service at New York" 8 Sep 1776.[276]

x PHINEAS FORD, b. at Windham, 26 Mar 1753; d. at Chaplin, 7 Jun 1837; m. at Hampton, 22 Feb 1774, MARY MARTIN, b. at Windham, 9 May 1749 daughter of John and Sarah (Parker) Martin; Mary d. at Chaplin, 9 Dec 1827. Phineas and Mary did not have children. In his will written 15 August 1835 (probate 27 June 1837), Phineas left his household possessions and anything that might be due him from the government of the United States to his nephew Stephen Ford of Chaplin. Phineas was a Revolutionary War pensioner.

xi EUNICE FORD, b. 21 Aug 1758; not living at the estate division.

91) GEORGE HOLT (*Elizabeth Farnum Holt[3], Elizabeth Holt Farnum[2], Nicholas[1]*), b. 2 Jan 1713 son of George and Elizabeth (Farnum) Holt; m. at Windham, 4 Jul 1743, MARY ALLEN.

There are records for the births of three children of George and Mary born at Hampton.

439) i MARY HOLT, b. at Hampton, 25 Apr 1746; d. at Canterbury, 20 Sep 1807; m. about 1766, JONATHAN WHEELER, b. about 1741; Jonathan d. at Canterbury, 29 Jul 1796.

440) ii BENJAMIN HOLT, b. at Hampton, 8 Sep 1748; d. at Windham, 22 Jun 1809; m. about 1769, ESTHER WEBB, baptized at Scotland, CT, 28 Oct 1750 daughter of Timothy and Sarah (Howard) Webb.

iii ELIZABETH HOLT, b. 25 May 1751

92) NEHEMIAH HOLT (*George[3], Henry[2], Nicholas[1]*), b. at Andover, 3 Apr 1723 son of George and Mary (Bixby) Holt; d. at Chaplin, CT, 17 Apr 1799; m. at Windham, 25 Nov 1745, ANNA FARNUM, b. at Windham, 26 Apr 1726 daughter of Nathaniel and Hannah (Preston) Farnum; Anna d. at Chaplin, 1 Apr 1810.

Nehemiah left home to serve in the French and Indian War leaving Anna and five children at home. While he was away, all five of his children died from throat distemper. Anna and Nehemiah went on the have six more children. The births of the children are recorded at Windham.

---

[273] *Connecticut State Library (Hartford, Connecticut);* Probate Place: *Hartford, Connecticut, Probate Packets, Fitch, Eleazer-Frink, E, 1719-1889*

[274] The 1768 estate distribution of Jacob Woodward includes a payment to Abraham Ford on behalf of his wife.

[275] The 1788 will on Nathaniel Moseley includes a bequest to his granddaughter Sarah Moseley the only heir of his son Thomas.

[276] Dimock, *Births, Baptisms, Marriages and Deaths from the Records of the Town and Churches in Mansfield, Connecticut*, p 333

i NEHEMIAH HOLT, b. 24 Oct 1746; d. 8 Sep 1754.

ii ELIPHALET HOLT, b. 1 Apr 1749; d. 4 Sep 1754.

iii JONATHAN HOLT, b. 20 Aug 1750; d. 1 Jul 1754.

iv SARAH HOLT, b. 30 Aug 1752; d. 30 Aug 1754.

v NATHANIEL HOLT, b. 3 Mar 1754; d. 3 Sep 1754.

441) vi NEHEMIAH HOLT, b. at Windham, 28 Nov 1756; d. at Chaplin, CT, 5 Jun 1824; m. 1st 11 Jun 1782, MARY LAMPHEAR, b. about 1755; Mary d. at Chaplin, 11 Dec 1799. Nehemiah m. 2nd 1 Jan 1801, SARAH DUNLAP, b. 1766 daughter of Joshua and Elizabeth (Kennedy) Dunlap;[277] Sarah d. at Chaplin, 7 Nov 1808. Nehemiah m. 3rd 10 Sep 1809, his first cousin once removed, EUNICE FULLER (*Sarah Holt Fuller[5], Zebadiah Holt[4], Elizabeth Farnum Holt[3], Elizabeth Holt Farnum[2], Nicholas[1]*), b. at Windham, 5 May 1773 daughter of Aaron and Sarah (Holt) Fuller; Eunice d. at Chaplin, 31 Dec 1846.

442) vii SARAH HOLT, b. at Windham, 12 Oct 1758; d. at Leicester, VT, 26 Sep 1843. m. by 1783, her third cousin once removed, STEPHEN SPARKS (*Mehitable Johnson Sparks[5], Lydia Lovejoy Johnson[4], Mary Farnum Lovejoy[3], Elizabeth Holt Farnum[2], Nicholas[1]*), b. at Tolland, 24 Apr 1759 son of Joseph and Mehitable (Johnson) Sparks; Stephen d. at Leicester, 25 Jun 1827.

443) viii MARTHA HOLT, b. at Windham, 20 Sep 1760; d. at Mansfield, CT, 24 Apr 1849; m. 1st 1785, JOSEPH CLARK. Martha m. 2nd 28 Apr 1791, NATHAN MARTIN, b. at Mansfield, 28 Jun 1760 son of John and Hannah (Spofford) Martin; Nathan d. 2 Jun 1812.

444) ix ROXERENE HOLT, b. at Windham, 6 Apr 1762; d. at Leicester, VT, 13 Mar 1825; m. at Ludlow, MA, 12 May 1783, EBENEZER MORRIS HITCHCOCK, b. at Springfield, MA, 13 Nov 1762 son of Joseph and Sarah (Morris) Hitchcock; Morris d. at Leicester, 24 Oct 1833.

445) x ANNA HOLT, b. at Windham, 6 Jul 1765; d. at Hampton, 10 Oct 1806; m. at Hampton, 22 Jun 1786, AMOS FORD, b. at Windham, 24 Aug 1763 son of Amos and Lydia (Davison) Ford. Amos married second Abigail Snow on 4 Oct 1807.

xi SABRA HOLT, b. at Windham, 12 Jan 1768; m. 1796, her third cousin once removed, JUSTUS SNOW (*Mary Chandler Snow[5], Mary Holt Chandler[4], Nicholas[3], Nicholas[2], Nicholas[1]*), b. at Ashford, 26 Mar 1769 son of Joseph and Mary (Chandler) Snow. No children were located for Sabra and Justus.

93) PRISCILLA HOLT (*George[3], Henry[2], Nicholas[1]*), b. at Andover, 4 Sep 1725 daughter of George and Mary (Bixby) Holt; d. at Wales, MA, m. at Hampton, CT, 10 Nov 1743, ICHABOD ROGERS, b. at Windham, 19 Jan 1718/9 son of Hope and Esther (Meacham) Rogers; Ichabod d. at Wales, 19 Jan 1800.

Priscilla and Ichabod were in Ashford in their early marriage, but were in Wales, Massachusetts about 1748. The homestead in Wales was on the road to Stafford. Family records from the town of Wales describe Ichabod as being a "hard-laboring, steady, stable-minded man."[278]

Priscilla Holt and Ichabod Rogers were parents of fourteen children.

446) i JOSEPH ROGERS, b. at Ashford, 4 Aug 1744; m. at Wales, MA, 25 Dec 1765, SARAH JORDAN, b. at Brimfield, 30 Mar 1748 daughter of Richard and Isabel (-) Jordan.

447) ii ISHMAEL ROGERS, b. at Ashford, about 1746; d. at Shaftsbury, VT, 27 Mar 1813; m. at Wales, 30 Oct 1766, MARY JORDAN, b. at Brimfield, 28 Oct 1744 daughter of Richard and Isabel (-) Jordan; Mary d. at Shaftsbury, 26 Apr 1809.

448) iii SARAH ROGERS, b. at Ashford, 12 Feb 1747/8; d. at Hawley, MA, 4 Feb 1814; m. at Wales, 29 May 1768, JOHN BURROUGHS, b. at Windsor, CT, 30 Apr 1748 son of Simon and Lydia (Porter) Burroughs; John d. at Hawley, 21 Mar 1821.[279]

449) iv ROBERT ROGERS, b. at Brimfield, 4 Dec 1749; d. at Stafford, CT, 25 Mar 1813; m. 1st at Wales, 2 Apr 1769, ELEANOR NELSON, b. at Brimfield, 11 Feb 1743 daughter of John and Elizabeth (Nelson) Nelson;

---

[277] The 1810 estate settlement of Joshua Dunlap includes payment of a legacy to Nehemiah Holt.

[278] Ancestry.com. *Massachusetts, Town and Vital Records, 1620-1988,* Town of Wales, Family Records, p 414

[279] Information on this family obtained from Onondaga County Family Bible pages, in this case a transcription of the bible records of Porter Burroughs a child of Sarah and John Burroughs. http://www.rootsweb.com/~nyononda/BIBLE/BURROUGH.HTM. Information posted by Victor Burroughs who reports the original bible is in the possession of Frank Burroughs of Seneca Falls, NY.

Eleanor d. at Stafford, about 1790. Robert m. 2nd about 1792, HULDAH ORCUTT, b. at Stafford, 9 May 1767 daughter of Simeon and Elizabeth (Rockwell) Orcutt; Huldah d. at Stafford, 19 Mar 1863.

450) v NATHANIEL ROGERS, b. at Brimfield, 18 May 1752; d. at Stafford, CT, 23 Jun 1836; m. at Ware, 3 Nov 1773, ABIGAIL KELSEE, b. about 1756 of Ware; Abigail d. after 1840 when she was living at Stafford.

vi JONATHAN ROGERS, b. at Wales, 17 Apr 1754; nothing further known.

451) vii NEHEMIAH ROGERS, b. at Wales, 7 Jul 1756; d. at Wallingford, VT, 1813 (probate 1813); m. 1st at Wales, 2 Jul 1778, RHODA MUNGER, b. at Wales, about 1758 daughter of Samuel and Abigail (Bester) Munger; Rhoda d. at Wallingford, about 1801. Nehemiah m. 2nd at Wallingford, 3 Oct 1802, widow JUDITH ROUNDS.

452) viii EBENEZER ROGERS, b. at Wales, 11 Apr 1759; m. at Wales, 4 Dec 1777, CATHERINE RENOLDS, b. at Stafford, CT, 27 May 1757 daughter of James and Sarah (Fargo) Renolds; Catherine d. at Shaftsbury, VT, 23 Dec 1785.

ix PRISCILLA ROGERS, b. 31 Dec 1760; d. 17 Jan 1761.

x MARY ROGERS, b. at Wales, 12 Aug 1762; d. at Wales, Aug 1786; m. 3 Jun 1784, EBENEZER MOULTON, b. at Brimfield, 8 Mar 1756 son of Jonathan and Annah (Flint) Moulton; Ebenezer d. at Wales, 24 Feb 1816. Ebenezer married second Mehitable Needham. Mary and Ebenezer had one child, daughter Mary who b. and d. Aug 1786.

xi ESTHER ROGERS, b. at Wales, 27 Feb 1764; nothing further known.

453) xii ROCKSANA ROGERS, b. at Wales, 30 Dec 1765; d. at Monroe, MI, after 1820; m. at Wales, 31 Mar 1785, GIDEON BADGER, b. at Union, CT, 24 Feb 1765 son of Daniel and Phillipi (Hale) Badger; Gideon d. at Monroe, 26 Mar 1826.

454) xiii JERUSHA ROGERS, b. at Wales, 25 Oct 1767; m. at Wales, 17 Nov 1796, DANIEL MOULTON, b. at Wales, 17 Nov 1773 son of Jonathan Moulton.

xiv ICHABOD ROGERS, b. at Wales, 10 Sep 1770; m. at Wales, 16 Jun 1791, HANNAH DAVISON, b. at Wales, 27 Mar 1775 daughter of Dominicus and Hannah (Twist) Davison; Hannah d. at Wales, 18 Mar 1853. Ichabod was reported to be a shiftless character who abandoned his family about five years after marriage and it is not known what became of him. No children are recorded at Wales.[280] Hannah married second Stephen Johnson presenting herself as a widow although there was no firm confirmation that she was, in fact, a widow.

94) HANNAH HOLT (*George*[3], *Henry*[2], *Nicholas*[1]), b. at Hampton, 11 Mar 1730 daughter of George and Mary (Bixby) Holt; m. at Hampton, 8 Oct 1747, JETHRO ROGERS, b. at Windham, 14 Apr 1722 son of Hope and Esther (Meacham) Rogers.

Hannah Holt and Jethro Rogers were parents of eight children.

455) i OLIVER ROGERS, b. at Windham, 14 Apr 1748; d. at Chaplin, Apr 1829; m. at Windham, 11 Feb 1770, HANNAH COBURN, b. at Windham, 11 Oct 1750 daughter of Robert and Mary (Gennings) Coburn.

ii BIXBY ROGERS, b. at Windham, 18 Dec 1749; d. 27 Dec 1749.

iii MARY ROGERS, b. at Canterbury, 23 Nov 1750

iv HANNAH ROGERS, b. at Canterbury, 19 Dec 1752

v SARAH ROGERS, b. at Canterbury, 13 Oct 1754

456) vi BIXBEE ROGERS, b. at Canterbury, 9 Nov 1758; d. at Galena, OH, 10 Sep 1831; m. ESTHER, b. about 1769 who has not been identified; Esther d. at Galena, 27 Nov 1817.

457) vii JOSIAH ROGERS, b at Canterbury, 14 Nov 1760; d. at Washington, PA, 14 Aug 1841; m. 2 Oct 1786,[281] RUTH HARRIS, b. at Canterbury, 26 Mar 1764 daughter of Paul and Mary (Herrington) Harris; Ruth d. at Mehoopany, PA, 22 Sep 1844.

viii JOSEPH WRIGHT ROGERS, b. at Canterbury, 10 Jun 1764; d. after 1830 when he was living in Plymouth, PA.

---

[280] Town and City Clerks of Massachusetts. *Massachusetts Vital and Town Records*. Provo, UT: Holbrook Research Institute (Jay and Delene Holbrook). Town of Wales Family Records. Accessed through ancestry.com.

[281] This is the date of marriage given by Ruth in her widow's pension application file.

95) NATHANIEL HOLT (*George³, Henry², Nicholas¹*), b. at Hampton, 18 Mar 1734 son of George and Mary (Bixby) Holt; d. at Windham, 1763; m. 16 Dec 1756, PHEBE CANADY, b. at Hampton, 1735 daughter of Isaac and Phebe (Leonard) Canady. Phebe married second Israel Litchfield on 14 Jan 1766.[282]

Nathaniel Holt did not leave a will and the inventory of his estate was taken 5 April 1763 and had a total value of £28.11.3.[283]

Nathaniel and Phebe were parents of three children all baptized at Hampton on 14 November 1762, so their order of birth is not known.

i LUCY HOLT, b. about 1757; nothing further found.

458) ii JONATHAN HOLT, b. at Hampton, about 1758; d. at Hampton, 11 Aug 1833; m. 19 Oct 1780, ANNA FAULKNER,[284] b. 23 Nov 1761 daughter of Caleb and Esther (Morse) Faulkner; Anna d. at Hampton, 31 Aug 1842.

459) iii CYNTHIA HOLT, b. at Hampton, 27 Sep 1759; m. at Brooklyn, CT, 5 Aug 1837, ABEL STAPLES,[285] b. at Pomfret, 30 Aug 1757 son of Jacob and Eunice (Cady) Staples; Abel d. at Brooklyn, 5 Aug 1837. Abel had a second marriage to Elizabeth who has not been identified but was his widow in the probate record.

96) EPHRAIM FARNUM (*Ephraim Farnum³, Elizabeth Holt Farnum², Nicholas¹*), b. at Andover, 12 Oct 1700 son of Ephraim and Priscilla (Holt) Farnum; d. at Concord, NH, 1775; m. at Andover, 12 Nov 1728, MARY INGALLS, b. at Andover, 27 Mar 1705 daughter of John and Sarah (Russell) Ingalls.

Ephraim and Mary had their first child in Andover, but then relocated to Concord (Rumford) where Ephraim and four of his brothers were first settlers.[286] Ephraim and Mary were parents of six children.

i MARY FARNUM, b. at Andover, 16 Sep 1729; d. at Concord, 13 Jun 1736.

460) ii EPHRAIM FARNUM, b. at Rumford, 21 Sep 1733; d. at Concord, 12 May 1827; m. at Bradford, MA, 23 Mar 1758, JUDITH HALL, b. at Bradford, 12 Apr 1739 daughter of David and Naomi (Gage) Hall; Judith d. at Concord, 13 Jul 1809.

461) iii MARY FARNUM, b. at Rumford, 8 Aug 1737; d. at Sanbornton, NH, 14 Feb 1805; m. about 1760, JONATHAN MERRILL, b. at Rumford, 10 Feb 1733 son of John and Lydia (Haynes) Merrill; Jonathan d. at New Chester, NH, 1795 (probate 21 Feb 1795).

462) iv BENJAMIN FARNUM, b. at Rumford, 21 Mar 1739; d. at Concord, 18 Mar 1812; m. ANNA MERRILL, b. at Rumford, 20 Dec 1743 daughter of John and Lydia (Haynes) Merrill;[287] Anna d. at Concord, 7 Mar 1803.

v JOHN FARNUM, b. at Rumford, 1 May 1743; d. 4 Sep 1746.

463) vi SARAH FARNUM, b. at Concord, 26 Jul 1747; d. at Fryeburg, ME, Mar 1829; m. WILLIAM EATON, b. at Hampstead, NH, 21 Apr 1743 son of Jeremiah and Hannah (Osgood) Eaton; William d. about 1780.

97) TIMOTHY FARNUM (*Ephraim Farnum³, Elizabeth Holt Farnum², Nicholas¹*), b. at Andover, 4 May 1702 son of Ephraim and Priscilla (Holt) Farnum; d. at Andover, 25 Jul 1780; m. 18 Jan 1727, DINAH INGALLS, b. at Andover, about 1705 daughter of James and Hannah (Abbott) Ingalls; Dinah d. at Andover, 22 Nov 1781.

In his will written 8 March 1765 (probate 3 October 1780), Timothy Farnum bequeathed to beloved wife Dinah the improvement on one-third of all his lands and buildings during her natural life. She also has use of all the household movables

---

[282] There is disagreement as to whether the Phebe Holt who married Israel Litchfield was Phebe Holt daughter of Joshua and Keturah Holt or Phebe Canady Holt the widow of Nathaniel Holt who died in 1763. The sequence of the marriages for the two Phebe Holts that are of issue make is more likely that the Phebe who married Israel Litchfield was Phebe Canady Holt and that Phebe Holt who married Ebenezer Goodale was the daughter of Joshua and Keturah. Phebe Holt and Ebenezer Goodale were married in 1755 and Phebe Canady married Nathaniel Holt in 1756, so she cannot be the Phebe Holt that married Ebenezer Goodale. The two Phebes were born the same year so that does not help differentiate them. But one of the children of Phebe and Israel was named Leonard and Phebe Canady was the daughter of Isaac Canady and Phebe Leonard.

[283] *Connecticut State Library (Hartford, Connecticut);* Probate Place: *Hartford, Connecticut, Probate Packets, Hall, Stephen-Hopkins, L, 1747-1880, Estate of Nathaniel Holt, Case 1094*

[284] Durries's Holt genealogy and other published sources state that Jonathan Holt who married Anna Faulkner was the son of Zebadiah and Sarah (Flint) Holt. But Zebadiah's son Jonathan was deceased before 1760 as evidenced by his absence from the distribution in the settlement of Zebadiah's estate.

[285] The 1800 will of Jonathan Holt the brother of Cynthia's father Nathaniel includes a bequest to his niece Cynthia Staples.

[286] Bouton, *History of Concord*, p 655

[287] The 1773 will of John Merrill includes a bequest to his daughter Ann Farnham.

and these will go to daughter Phebe wife of Joshua Holt after Dinah's decease. Daughter Phebe receives £8. Son Benjamin receives all of the estate and is named sole executor. Real estate was valued at £910.10.0 and personal estate at £103.9.0.[288]

Timothy and Dinah were parents of seven children born at Andover.

i ABIAH FARNUM, b. 15 Sep 1729; d. 29 Aug 1736.

189) ii PHEBE FARNUM, b. at Andover, 10 Oct 1731; d. at Andover, 26 Jan 1806; m. 2 Dec 1755, her second cousin once removed, JOSHUA HOLT (*Nicholas³, Nicholas², Nicholas¹*), b. at Andover, 30 Jun 1730 son of Nicholas and Dorcas (Abbott) Holt; Joshua d. at Andover, 24 Jul 1810.

iii TIMOTHY FARNUM, b. 18 Sep 1736; d. 1 Jul 1738.

iv BENJAMIN FARNUM, b. 16 Sep 1738; d. 20 Sep 1746.

v PETER FARNUM, b. 8 Nov 1740; no further record and not in father's will.

vi ABIAH FARNUM, b. 15 Oct 1742; d. 23 Sep 1746.

464) vii BENJAMIN FARNUM, b. at Andover, 16 Dec 1746; d. at Andover, 4 Dec 1833; m. 26 Nov 1767, his second cousin, DOROTHY "DOLLY" HOLT (*Joseph⁴, Timothy³, James², Nicholas¹*) perhaps the daughter of Joseph and Dolly (Johnson) Holt;[289] Dolly d. at Andover, 25 Jul 1815.

98) JAMES FARNUM (*Ephraim Farnum³, Elizabeth Holt Farnum², Nicholas¹*), b. at Andover, 1705 son of Ephraim and Priscilla (Holt) Farnum; d. at Concord, after 1769; m. at Haverhill, MA, 7 Dec 1732, ELIZABETH WILSON, b. about 1709 daughter of Joseph and Mary (Richardson) Wilson.[290]

James held several positions in Concord serving as fence-viewer in multiple years from 1733 to 1738, tythingman, and hogreeve.[291]

There are records for seven children of James and Elizabeth born at Rumford/Concord, New Hampshire. A marriage was located for just one of the children.

i ELIZABETH FARNUM, b. 19 Aug 1734

ii DEBORAH FARNUM, b. 29 Dec 1735

iii PHEBE FARNUM, b. 23 Dec 1737

iv JAMES FARNUM, b. at Rumford, 23 Oct 1739; d. at Concord, Apr 1804. James does not seem to have married.

v HANNAH FARNUM, b. 14 Sep 1747

vi EBENEZER FARNUM, b. 19 May 1749

465) vii JOHN FARNUM, b. at Concord, 1 Aug 1753; d. at Salisbury, NH, 17 Feb 1820; m. 22 May 1772, his first cousin, SARAH PETERS (*Elizabeth Farnum Peters⁴, Ephraim Farnum³, Elizabeth Holt Farnum², Nicholas¹*), b. about 1750 daughter of James and Elizabeth (Farnum) Peters; Sarah d. at Salisbury, 7 Oct 1818.

99) PRISCILLA FARNUM (*Ephraim Farnum³, Elizabeth Holt Farnum², Nicholas¹*), b. at Andover, 1709/10 daughter of Ephraim and Priscilla (Holt) Farnum; d. at Andover, 19 May 1790;[292] m. at Andover, 25 Jul 1732, her second cousin, JOHN RUSS, b. at Andover, 1706 son of Thomas and Anne (Farnum) Russ; John d. at Rumford, NH, by Dec 1743 (date of mother's will and posthumous child born Apr 1744).

Priscilla and John lived in Rumford in the Penacook plantation where four of their children were born. John held positions as a field-driver and tythingman.[293] John died by December 1743 (when his mother wrote her will) and Priscilla returned to Andover where their fifth child was born after John's death.[294]

---

[288] *Essex County, MA: Probate File Papers, 1638-1881.*Online database. *AmericanAncestors.org.* New England Historic Genealogical Society, 2014. Case 9256

[289] These are the parents of Dolly identified in the History of Wilton and in Durrie's Holt genealogy. However, the Dolly daughter of Joseph and Dolly is reported as born in 1751 and Dolly the wife of Benjamin Farnum died in 1815 at age 68 giving her a birth year of 1747. No other Dolly Holt was identified who might fit better, so it will be left as is.

[290] The 1742 will of Joseph Wilson, cooper, of Haverhill, includes a bequest to his daughter Elizabeth Farnum.

[291] Bouton, *History of Concord*

[292] Priscilla, wid., old age, bur. May 19, 1790, a. 86 y. C.R.2.

[293] Bouton, *History of Concord*

[294] Deborah, d. John, deceased and Priscilla, Apr. 30, 1744.

John Russ's mother, Ann Russ Johnson wrote her will at Andover on 17 December 1743. In her will she bequeaths to her granddaughters Priscilla and Ann Russ two pewter plates and to her grandson John Russ, one bible.[295]

On 3 April 1762, Deborah Russ daughter of John, a minor over the age of fourteen, made choice of her brother-in-law Ebenezer Rand as her guardian.

466) i PRISCILLA RUSS, b. at Rumford, 3 Jun 1733; d. at Andover, 1 Aug 1818; m. 1st at Andover, 17 Nov 1757, THOMAS BLANCHARD, b. at Andover, 20 Jan 1734/5 son of Thomas and Elizabeth (Johnson) Blanchard; Thomas d. at Lake George, 9 Oct 1758. Priscilla m. 2nd at Andover, 10 Jan 1760, EBENEZER RAND *perhaps* the son of Waffe and Elizabeth (Orne) Rand of Boston; Ebenezer d. at Andover, 1813 (probate 1813).

ii ANNA RUSS, b. 19 Jun 1734; d. 4 May 1738.

iii JOHN RUSS, b. at Rumford, 2 Nov 1736; he is known to be living in 1755, but nothing further known, and no marriage was located for him.

iv ANNA RUSS, b. 13 Dec 1740; d. at Andover, 6 Oct 1746.

467) v DEBORAH RUSS, b. at Andover, 30 Apr 1744; m. 1st about 1765 in a Native American ceremony, Almonoch (aka Peter Bridges) of the Narragansett tribe; reported as having divorced.[296] Deborah m. 2nd at Tewksbury, 23 Jun 1768, JOHN HOYT; John d. at Tewksbury, 6 Mar 1769 when felling a tree.[297] Deborah m. 3rd at Tewksbury, 12 Mar 1778, EBENEZER KITTREDGE.

100) ZEBADIAH FARNUM (*Ephraim Farnum³, Elizabeth Holt Farnum², Nicholas¹*), b. at Andover, about 1710 son of Ephraim and Priscilla (Holt) Farnum; d. at Concord, 17 Apr 1799; m. at Concord, 22 Mar 1738, MARY WALKER.

Zebadiah and Mary resided in Concord and lived in Henry Lovejoy's garrison house. Zebadiah was named hogreeve in 1735. He served a period of 7 months 17 days in the militia company of Capt. John Goffe that was raised for the expedition to Crown Point in 1756.[298]

Zebadiah and Mary were parents of eight children.

468) i TIMOTHY FARNUM, b. at Concord, about 1739; m. at Hopkinton, NH, 8 May 1763, SUSANNAH SCALES, b. at Canterbury, NH, 26 Oct 1744 daughter of Rev. James and Susannah (Hovey) Scales.[299]

469) ii SAMUEL FARNUM, b. at Concord, 10 Feb 1743; d. at Essex, NY, 25 Jan 1813; m. at Hopkinton, NH, 1 Dec 1764, SARAH ABBOTT, b. at Concord, 3 Dec 1748 daughter of Nathaniel and Penelope (Ballard) Abbott; Sarah d. at Elizabethtown, NY, 2 Apr 1841.

470) iii JOHN FARNUM, b. at Concord, 1 Feb 1750; d. likely at Rumford, ME; m. about 1772, SARAH "SALLY" WEST, b. at Concord, 8 Nov 1745 daughter of Nathaniel and Sarah (Burbank) West; Sally d. at Concord, 17 Dec 1800.

iv MARY FARNUM, b. at Concord, about 1752; m. about 1775, NATHAN ABBOTT who is not yet identified. Farnham's Farnum genealogy (p. 155) reports four children for this family: Samuel, David, William, and Orance. However, no further information on this couple or their children was located.

v MARGARET FARNUM, b. at Concord, about 1754; m. NATHANIEL HART. Margaret and Nathaniel are reported as having one child, but no records were found.

471) vi LYDIA FARNUM, b. at Concord, about 1756; m. at Pembroke, 14 Oct 1783, ASA HARDY

472) vii ANN FARNUM, b. at Concord, about 1758; d. at Bow, NH, before 1835; m. 1st about 1780, NOAH WEST, b. at Rumford, 1 Oct 1756 son of Nathaniel and Sarah (Fairbank) West; Noah d. about 1785. Ann m. 2nd at Pembroke, 6 Feb 1787, JONATHAN CLOUGH, baptized 8 Oct 1749 son of Elisha and Mary (Welch) Clough; Jonathan d. at Bow, 7 Jun 1835. Jonathan Clough was first married to Abigail Buswell.

viii ZEBADIAH FARNUM, b. about 1760; nothing further known.

---

[295] *Massachusetts, Essex County, Probate Records;* Author: *Massachusetts. Supreme Judicial Court (Essex County), Case 14993*

[296] Abbott, Abbott Genealogies, Russ Family of Andover

[297] John, "with ye fall of a tree," Mar. 6, 1769. CR1

[298] Bouton, *History of Concord*, pp 155, 183, and 191

[299] Although published genealogies report her name as Searles, she seems to be the daughter of Rev. James Scales. For example, a deed from James *Seals* to Timothy and Susannah Farnham mentions the education that has been provided to James's son Stephen and this would be Rev. Stephen Scales. Rev. Scales and his wife Susannah were living in Hopkinton where James was the long-time minister.

101) JOSIAH FARNUM (*Ephraim Farnum³, Elizabeth Holt Farnum², Nicholas¹*), b. at Andover, 19 Jul 1712 son of Ephraim and Priscilla (Holt) Farnum; d. at Concord, about 1790 (probate Feb 1790); m. his first cousin once removed, MARY FRYE (*Elizabeth Farnum Frye⁴, John Farnum³, Elizabeth Holt Farnum², Nicholas¹*), b. at Andover, 6 Nov 1712 daughter of Ebenezer and Elizabeth (Farnum) Frye.

Josiah and Mary had their children in Andover and then headed to Concord where they lived in Henry Lovejoy's garrison house.[300]

Josiah Farnum did not leave a will and his estate was in probate in February 1790, although the inventory and estate division were in December 1789. Real estate of about 200 acres was divided into three parcels which were set-off to the heirs of Theodore Farnum, Ephraim Farnum, Jr., and Ebenezer Farnum. There is no mention in the available records of any payments made to the daughters and no mention of the oldest son Josiah although he was living at the time, but pages of the record are missing.[301]

Josiah and Mary were parents of ten children born at Andover.

i MARY FARNUM, b. 28 Dec 1734; Mary did not marry.

ii JOSIAH FARNUM, b. 19 Dec 1736; d. 11 May 1738.

473) iii JOSIAH FARNUM, b. at Andover, 4 Aug 1739; d. at Concord, 1809; m. 1st at Andover, 25 Sep 1766, MEHITABLE KIMBALL, b. at Andover, 4 May 1738 daughter of Daniel and Mehitable (Ingalls) Kimball; Mehitable d. about 1779. Josiah m. 2nd, 29 Feb 1780, SARAH SAWYER,[302] b. about 1747 (based on age 80 at death); Sarah d. at Concord, 16 Jul 1827. Sarah married second Capt. Benjamin Emery on 17 Dec 1812 (his first wife Sarah Bailey died in 1811).

iv THEODORE FARNUM, b. 13 Apr 1742; d. 25 Sep 1746.

v EPHRAIM FARNUM, b. 3 Jul 1744; d. 27 Sep 1746.

vi ELIZABETH FARNUM, b. at Andover, 4 Sep 1746; Elizabeth did not marry.

474) vii THEODORE FARNUM, b. at Andover, 24 Jan 1748/9; d. at Concord, 1789; m. about 1772, SARAH LOVEJOY, b. at Rumford, 8 Jun 1752 daughter of Henry and Phebe (Chandler) Lovejoy; Sarah d. at Concord, 1815. Sarah second married Jedediah Hoit on 28 Feb 1796.

475) viii EPHRAIM FARNUM, b. at Andover, 13 Oct 1751; d. at Concord, 19 Sep 1803; m. at Concord, 3 Oct 1776, ABIGAIL STEVENS; Abigail d. after 1815 when she transferred property to her two daughters.

476) ix EBENEZER FARNUM, b. at Andover, 4 Aug 1754; d. at Concord, 11 Mar 1829; m. about 1776, DOROTHY "DOLLY" CARTER, b. about 1755; Dolly d. at Concord, 2 Dec 1827.

477) x JOANNA FARNUM, b. at Andover, 27 Sep 1757; d. at Concord, 17 Nov 1832; m. about 1781, JOSEPH RUNNELS, b. at Boxford, 19 Oct 1758 son of Samuel and Joanna (Platts) Runnels; Joseph d. at Concord, 18 Dec 1843.

102) JOSEPH FARNUM (*Ephraim Farnum³, Elizabeth Holt Farnum², Nicholas¹*), b. at Andover, 1714/5 son of Ephraim and Priscilla (Holt) Farnum; d. at Concord, 1 Nov 1792; m. about 1740, ZERVIAH HOIT, b. about 1720 daughter of Abner and Mary (Blaisdell) Hoit;[303] Zerviah d. at Concord, 29 Dec 1794.[304]

Joseph Farnum settled in Concord in the area of Penacook Lake which was also known as Long Pond. He had a farm of about 200 acres.[305] Joseph and Zerviah were also residents of the Lovejoy garrison house in Concord as were his siblings Elizabeth and Josiah. He filled various tasks in the town such as hogreeve, fence viewer, and field driver. Joseph was also part of the committee that laid out Main street.[306]

Joseph and Zerviah were parents of ten children born at Rumford/Concord.

478) i JOSEPH FARNUM, b. at Rumford, 27 Nov 1740; d. at Concord, 1 Nov 1837; m. about 1768, RUTH WALKER, b. about 1750 whose parents have not been identified; Ruth d. at Concord, 15 Jun 1829.

---

300 Bouton, *History of Concord*

301 *New Hampshire. Probate Court (Rockingham County);* Probate Place: *Rockingham, New Hampshire, Estate Papers, No 5512-5600, 1790, Estate of Josiah Farnum, Case 5517*

302 Farnham, *The Descendants of Ralph Farnum*, p 293. The Farnum genealogy states she was the widow of Benjamin Emery, but that seems to be the other way around and Sarah married Capt. Benjamin Emery in 1812 after Josiah's death. It is not clear that her name was Sarah Sawyer.

303 Hoyt, *A Genealogical History of the Hoyt Families*, p 140

304 One record gives the date of Zerviah's death as 20 Dec 1792.

305 Farnham, *Descendants of Ralph Farnum*, p 157

306 Bouton, *History of Concord*

479) ii STEPHEN FARNUM, b. at Rumford, 24 Aug 1742; d. at Concord, 15 Feb 1832; m. at Bradford, MA, 25 Sep 1766, MARTHA HALL, b. at Bradford, 27 Dec 1743 daughter of David and Naomi (Gage) Hall; Martha d. at Concord, 25 Aug 1825.

480) iii BETTY FARNUM, b. at Concord, about 1743; d. at Concord, 11 Nov 1821; m. about 1766, NATHAN ABBOTT, b. at Andover, 7 Feb 1736/7 son of Thomas and Elizabeth (Ballard) Abbott; Nathan d. at Concord, 18 Jan 1805.

481) iv ABNER FARNUM, b. at Concord about 1746; d. at Concord, 2 Aug 1820; m. 1st about 1769, REBECCA MERRILL, b. at Rumford, 16 Aug 1751 daughter of John and Rebecca (Abbott) Merrill; Rebecca d. about 1777. Abner m. 2nd about 1778, SARAH ELLIOT, b. about 1743 (age at death 73); Sarah d. at Concord, 13 Dec 1816.

v DANIEL FARNUM, b. at Concord, about 1748; d. at Canaan, NH, 29 Aug 1810; m. about 1770, MARY WALKER, b. about 1752; Mary d. at Concord, 10 Apr 1833. Daniel and Mary did not have children.

vi AFFIA FARNUM, b. about 1750

482) vii ZERVIAH FARNUM, b. at Concord, 1752; d. at Concord, Dec 1818; m. 24 Sep 1776, her second cousin once removed, REUBEN ABBOTT (*Reuben Abbott5, Abigail Farnum Abbott4, Ralph Farnum3, Elizabeth Holt Farnum2, Nicholas1*), b. at Concord, 5 Feb 1754 son of Reuben and Rhoda (Whittemore) Abbott; Reuben d. at Concord, 12 Dec 1834.

viii MARY FARNUM, b. about 1754

483) ix SUSAN FARNUM, b. at Concord, about 1759; d. at Loudon, NH, 23 Oct 1850; m. about 1786, WILLIAM WHEELER, b. at Concord, MA, 31 Mar 1760 son of Jeremiah and Esther (Russell) Wheeler; William d. at Loudon, NH, 26 Nov 1852.

484) x JACOB FARNUM, b. at Concord, about 1758; d. at Rumford, ME, 1 Sep 1836; m. about 1794, BETSEY WHEELER, b. at Concord, MA, 7 Mar 1766 daughter of Jeremiah and Esther (Russell) Wheeler; Betsey d. at Rumford, 8 Nov 1858.

103) ELIZABETH FARNUM (*Ephraim Farnum3, Elizabeth Holt Farnum2, Nicholas1*), b. at Andover, 1718 daughter of Ephraim and Priscilla (Holt) Farnum; m. at Andover, 31 Dec 1736, JAMES PETERS, b. about 1711 son of Seborne and Mary (-) Peters; James d. at Salisbury, NH, 16 Oct 1801.

Elizabeth and James lived in Concord at the garrison house of Henry Lovejoy. A total of ten families lived in the garrison house.[307] Elizabeth and James were parents of four children born at Concord. There are records for three of the children and daughter Sarah is given in Farnham's *The New England Descendants of Immigrant Ralph Farnum.* A fifth child may have been born at Hopkinton.

James and his family arrived in Henniker from Hopkinton about 1761 where they were early settlers. It is believed that James and Elizabeth stayed in Henniker a few years, then returned to Hopkinton, and then went on to Vermont where they died.[308] On the other hand, the Farnum genealogy reports that James died in Salisbury, New Hampshire.

i JAMES PETERS, b. 19 Jan 1738

485) ii WILLIAM PETERS, b. at Rumford, 7 Dec 1740; d. at Henniker, 5 Jul 1775 when a tree fell on him; m. at Hopkinton, NH, 25 Oct 1766, SARAH JEWELL; Sarah d. at Henniker, 1812.

iii OBADIAH PETERS, b. 8 Oct 1747

465) iv SARAH PETERS, b. about 1750; d. at Salisbury, NH, 7 Oct 1818; m. 22 May 1772, her first cousin, JOHN FARNUM (*James Farnum4, Ephraim Farnum3, Elizabeth Holt Farnum2, Nicholas1*), b. at Concord, 1 Aug 1753 son of James and Elizabeth (Wilson) Farnum; John d. at Salisbury, 17 Feb 1820.

v SIBBONS PETERS, b. about 1755; d. about 1771.

Grandchildren of Mary Holt and Thomas Johnson

104) MARY JOHNSON (*Mary Johnson Johnson3, Mary Holt Johnson2, Nicholas1*), b. at Medfield, about 1675 daughter of Return and Mary (Johnson) Johnson; d. at Medfield, 18 Dec 1763; m. 1st at Andover, 25 Jul 1701, BARACHIAS HARNDEN whose parentage is not determined; Barachias d. at Andover, 8 Feb 1702/3. Mary m. 2nd at Andover, 25 Sep 1704, SAMUEL SADEY, b. at Boston, 8 Feb 1681 son of John and Elizabeth (Peters) Sadey; Samuel d. at Medfield, 8 Oct 1744.

---

307 Bouton, *History of Concord*

308 Cogswell, *History of Henniker*, p 55

Mary and Barachias were parents of one child. There are no known children from her second marriage to Samuel Sadey.

Samuel Sadey did not leave a will and his estate entered probate 23 December 1744 with widow Mary Sadey as administratrix. The probate record includes a statement from Joshua Morse of Medfield attesting that he heard Capt. Samuel Sadey say that he purchased a colt for his grandson Barachias Mason, and a similar statement was made by Joseph Morse. Joshua Boyden made a statement that Samuel Sadey gave his "trooping tracken" to his grandson Sadey Mason. Personal estate was valued at £1004.17.2 and real estate at £966.[309] Barachias Mason and Sadey Mason were children of Mary Harnden and Thomas Mason.

486) i MARY HARNDEN, b. at Andover, 1702; d. at Medfield, 1798; m. at Boston, 6 Sep 1722, THOMAS MASON, b. at Medfield, 22 Aug 1699 son of Ebenezer and Hannah (Clark) Mason; Thomas d. at Medfield, 26 Dec 1789.

105) ELIZABETH JOHNSON (*Mary Johnson Johnson[3], Mary Holt Johnson[2], Nicholas[1]*), b. at Medfield, 16 Aug 1681 daughter of Return and Mary (Johnson) Johnson; m. JEREMIAH PLIMPTON, b. at Medfield, 8 Nov 1683 son of Joseph and Marie (Morse) Plimpton.

Jeremiah and Elizabeth were parents of three children. The family apparently left Connecticut after the children were born, but it is not known where they went.

i SARAH PLIMPTON, b. at Canterbury, 17 Oct 1709

ii SIBBILATH PLIMPTON, b. at Canterbury, 20 Aug 1712

iii BETTE PLIMPTON, b. at Plainfield, 20 Sep 1720

106) JEMIMA JOHNSON (*Mary Johnson Johnson[3], Mary Holt Johnson[2], Nicholas[1]*), b. at Medfield, 16 Sep 1683 daughter of Return and Mary (Johnson) Johnson; d. at Middletown, CT, 4 Oct 1753; m. at Medfield, 4 Feb 1704/5, JOHN PELTON, b. at Dorchester, 9 Jan 1682 son of Samuel and Mary (Smith) Pelton; John d. at Essex, CT, 15 Jul 1735.

John Pelton was from Dorchester and he and Jemima married at Medfield. They were very soon after in Canterbury where John purchased land in 1706 and 1708. They family was then in Lyme by 1713 where a house was built and then in nearby Haddam. The family was finally settled at Middletown.[310][311]

In his will written July 1735 (proved 20 August 1735), John Pelton of Middletown bequeaths to beloved wife Jemima all the household goods to be hers forever and the use of one-half of the house at Middletown and the improvement on one-third part of the 400-acre farm in Middletown called the "school lot". Eldest son John receives additional tracts of land in addition to what he has received. Son James receives five shillings in addition to what he has received. On condition that he discharge the executor from any further claims against the estate, the mortgage that father holds for a yoke of oxen that James has will be resigned and he will also receive £40. Sons Johnson and Phineas receive one-half of the 400-acre so called "school lot" and one-half of the dwelling house. His two other sons Joseph and Josiah and daughter Mary receive the other half of the "school lot". Daughter Jemima receives £20 within two years. His three other daughters Sarah, Elizabeth, and Keturah each receives £20 when they arrive at the age of eighteen. Wife Jemima and son Phineas were named executors.[312]

Jemima and John were parents of eleven children with birth records for the oldest three children. Other birth years are estimated based on age of death and/or year of marriage.

487) i MARY PELTON, b. at Canterbury, 21 Oct 1706; d. at Middletown, CT, 12 Dec 1740; m. at Middletown, 11 Dec 1735, THOMAS MCCLAVE son of Scottish immigrants John and Joanna (McCornach) McClave; Thomas d. at Middletown, 23 Mar 1756, Thomas married second Mary Burr on 9 Jul 1741 and third Elizabeth Bigelow.

488) ii JOHN PELTON, b. at Canterbury, 29 Feb 1708; d. at Saybrook, 29 Jan 1786; m. 1st at Saybrook, 9 Dec 1731, ELIZABETH CHAMPION, b. at Lyme, 13 Mar 1710 daughter of Thomas and Elizabeth (Wade) Champion; Elizabeth d. at Saybrook, 10 Jul 1755. John m. 2nd, 1756, MARTHA SHIPMAN. b. about 1733 daughter of John and Ruth (Hungerford) Shipman; Martha d. at Essex, CT, 4 Sep 1787. After John's death, Martha married Dr. Joseph Bishop on 28 Sep 1786.

489) iii JAMES PELTON, b. at Canterbury, 21 Jul 1710; d. at Haddam, 1795 (probate 1795); m. at Middletown, 14 Jan 1735/6, ELIZABETH BURR, b. at Middletown, 23 Apr 1719 daughter of Jonathan and Abigail (Hubbard) Burr; Elizabeth d. at Haddam, 12 Nov 1804..

---

309 *Suffolk County, MA: Probate File Papers.* Online database. *AmericanAncestors.org.* New England Historic Genealogical Society, 2017-2019. Case 8142

310 Harvey, *The Harvey Book*, p 611

311 Cutter, *New England Families*, volume 3, p 1270

312 *Connecticut. Probate Court (Hartford District);* Probate Place: *Hartford, Connecticut, volume 12, pp 321-323*

490) iv PHINEAS PELTON, b. about 1712; d. at Chatham, 30 May 1799; m. at Middletown, 22 May 1740, MARY MCKEE, b. about 1724 daughter of Andrew and Jerusha (-) McKee;[313] Mary d. at Portland, CT, 28 Sep 1749.

491) v JOSIAH PELTON, b. about 1714; d. at Portland, CT, 2 Feb 1792; m. HANNAH CHURCHILL, b. at Portland, Apr 1731 daughter of John and Bethiah (Stocking) Churchill;[314] Bethiah d. 12 Jun 1810.

492) vi JOHNSON PELTON (twin of Josiah), b. about 1714; d. at Portland, CT, 13 Dec 1804; m. at Chatham, 3 Mar 1748, KEZIAH FREEMAN, b. about 1724; Keziah d. at Chatham, Mar 1814.

493) vii JEMIMA PELTON, b. about 1716; m. at Saybrook, Jan 1732/3, GIDEON BUCKINGHAM, b. at Saybrook, 22 Feb 1707/8 son of Hezekiah and Sarah (Lay) Buckingham.

494) viii SARAH PELTON, b. about 1718; d. at Saybrook, 20 Sep 1745; m. at Saybrook, 18 Jan 1738/9, DANIEL COMSTOCK, b. at Saybrook, 20 Sep 1713 son of Samuel and Martha (Pratt) Comstock. Daniel married second Annah Brockway.

495) ix ELIZABETH PELTON, b. about 1720; d. at Lyme, CT, 3 Dec 1771; m. 1745, BENJAMIN HARVEY, b. at Lyme, 28 Jul 1722 son of John and Sarah (-) Harvey; Benjamin d. at Plymouth, PA, 27 Nov 1795.

x KETURAH PELTON, b. about 1721; baptized as an adult at Portland, CT on 1 Sep 1751. She was unmarried in 1751 and no marriage record was located for her.[315]

496) xi JOSEPH PELTON, b. 15 Apr 1722; d. at Portland, CT, 31 Dec 1804; m. at Middletown, 27 Sep 1744, ANNA PENFIELD, b. at Middletown, 26 Oct 1728 daughter of John and Anne (Cornwell) Penfield; Anna d. at Portland, 19 May 1797.

107) SARAH JOHNSON (*Mary Johnson Johnson*[3], *Mary Holt Johnson*[2], *Nicholas*[1]), b. at Medfield, about 1688 daughter of Return and Mary (Johnson) Johnson; m. at Medfield, 4 Sep 1710 JOHN ALLEN.

Almost no information was located for this family. The birth of one child is recorded at Medfield and nothing further is known.

i SARAH ALLEN, b. at Medfield, 12 Dec 1710

108) MEHITABLE RUSSELL (*Phebe Johnson Russell*[3], *Mary Holt Johnson*[2], *Nicholas*[1]), b. at Andover, about 1688 daughter of Thomas and Phebe (Johnson) Russell; d. at Andover, 18 Dec 1733; m. at Andover, 10 Jun 1708, JOSEPH CHANDLER, b. at Andover, 17 Jul 1682 son of William and Bridget (Henchman) Chandler; Joseph d. at Andover, 22 Apr 1734.

Mehitable Russell and Joseph Chandler resided in Andover and were members of South Church, admitted on profession of faith on 5 June 1720.[316]

In his will written 18 December 1732 (probate 20 May 1734), Joseph Chandler bequeaths to beloved wife Mehitable all the beds and bedding, and the brass, pewter, and iron ware that are household items. Son Thomas Chandler receives all the lands and buildings in Andover, particularly the homestead. He also receives the husbandry tools. Son Joseph Chandler receives £20 in the current money of New England to be paid by Thomas. Son John Chandler also receives £20. Daughter Mebitabel Crosby receives five shillings as she received her portion at her marriage. Daughter Mary Chandler receives £20. Daughters Bridget, Phebe, and Hannah each also receives £20. Thomas Chandler is named sole executor.[317]

497) i MEHITABLE CHANDLER, b. at Andover, about 1709; d. at Townsend, MA, Jul 1768;[318] m. 1st at Andover, 7 Feb 1731/2, ROBERT CROSBY, b. at Billerica, 20 Jul 1711 son of Joseph and Sarah (French) Crosby; Robert d. at Townsend, 10 Feb 1743. Mehitable m. 2nd 26 Nov 1745, ANDREW SPALDING, b. at Chelmsford, 8 Dec 1701 son of Andrew and Abigail (Waring) Spalding. Andrew was first married to Hannah Wright.

[313] The 1765 will of Andrew McKee includes bequests to his grandchildren Ithamar and Mary Pelton.

[314] Roberts, *Genealogies of Connecticut Families: From the New England Historical and Genealogical Register*, volume 1, p 410

[315] Connecticut, Church Record Abstracts, 1630-1920

[316] South Church of Andover, *Historical Manual*, p 128

[317] *Essex County, MA: Probate File Papers, 1638-1881.*Online database. *AmericanAncestors.org.* New England Historic Genealogical Society, 2014. Case 4945

[318] Mehetabel Spalding the wife of Andrew Spalding deceast this life July the . . . 1768 (Townsend, MA town records)

498) ii THOMAS CHANDLER, b. at Andover, 22 Apr 1711; d. at Andover, about 1761 (probate 13 Sep 1761); m. at Andover, 15 Feb 1739, ELIZABETH WALCOTT perhaps the daughter of Ebenezer and Elizabeth (Wiley) Walcott.[319]

151) iii MARY CHANDLER, b. at Andover, 4 Mar 1712/3; d. at Andover, 10 Feb 1751; m. at Andover, 22 Oct 1733, JAMES HOLT (*James³, Henry², Nicholas¹*), b. at Andover, 1707 son of James and Susanna (Preston) Holt; James d. at Andover, 1751 (probate 16 Dec 1751).

iv PHEBE CHANDLER, b. about 1717; d. at Andover, 13 May 1737.

499) v JOSEPH CHANDLER, b. at Andover, 13 Feb 1716/7; m. 30 Dec 1741, SARAH RICHARDSON, b. at Bradford, 26 Sep 1719 daughter of Joseph and Hannah (Nelson) Richardson.[320]

vi BRIDGET CHANDLER, b. 19 Sep 1719; d. 20 Aug 1736.

265) vii JOHN CHANDLER, b. at Andover, 19 Jan 1721/2; d. at Andover, 11 May 1759; m. 1st at Andover, 11 Mar 1744/5, his first cousin, PRUDENCE RUSSELL (*Robert Russell⁴, Phebe Johnson Russell³, Mary Holt Johnson², Nicholas¹*), baptized at Andover 11 Jul 1720 daughter of Robert and Abigail (Flint) Russell; Prudence d. 15 Nov 1745. John m. 2nd at Andover, 15 Oct 1757, HANNAH PHELPS, b. at Andover, 1709 daughter of Samuel and Hannah (Dane) Phelps; Hannah d. at Andover, 5 Aug 1781. Hannah was first married to Ephraim Abbott. Prudence Russell was first married to Moses Holt.

169) viii HANNAH CHANDLER, baptized at Andover, 2 Feb 1724; m. at Andover, 10 Aug 1741, DAVID ABBOTT (*Zerviah Holt Abbott³, Henry², Nicholas¹*), b. at Andover, Dec 1716 son of Jonathan and Zerviah (Holt) Abbott; David d. at Pembroke, NH, 1777 (probate 31 Dec 1777).

ix Son b. 10 Sep 1726 and d. 16 Sep 1726.

109) MARY RUSSELL (*Phebe Johnson Russell³, Mary Holt Johnson², Nicholas¹*), b. at Andover, 10 Feb 1692/3 daughter of Thomas and Phebe (Johnson) Russell; d. at Andover, 1778 (probate 3 Feb 1778); m. at Andover, 10 May 1716, TIMOTHY OSGOOD, b. at Andover, 22 Aug 1693 son of Timothy and Deborah (Poor) Osgood; Timothy d. 1772 (probate 24 Nov 1772).

In his will written 13 June 1769 (probate 24 November 1772), Timothy Osgood bequeaths to beloved wife Mary all the household goods and one-third of the personal estate to be at her disposal. She also receives the improvement on one-third of the real estate. Son Peter receives the dwelling house and the tanner house on the land where Peter now lives which completes his portion. Son Isaac receives £67 to complete his portion. Grandchildren who are the children of Timothy deceased receive five shillings and no more as Timothy received his full portion. The grandchildren are Timothy, Phebe, Abiah, and Asa. Daughter Deborah wife of Obadiah Wood receives £90. Daughter Phebe wife of Thomas Poor receives forty shillings and daughter Hannah wife of John Adams receives £107. Son Thomas Osgood receives all the real and personal estate in Andover as well as the money and bonds. Thomas is named executor. Real property was valued at £883 and personal estate at £155.[321]

In her will written 30 January 1775 (probate 3 February 1778), Mary Osgood made bequests of six shillings each to her children and the grandchildren of those children who were deceased as named: son Peter Osgood; son Timothy Osgood; son Thomas Osgood; son Isaac Osgood; the children of son Timothy Osgood who are Timothy, Phebe, Abiah, and Asa; granddaughter Susannah Kittredge; grandsons John Adams and Isaac Adams the children of Hannah the late wife of John Adams. Daughters Phebe Poor wife of Thomas Poor and Deborah Wood wife of Obadiah Wood receive all the household goods. Son-in-law Thomas Poor was named executor.[322] Susanna Kittredge named in the will is a daughter of Peter; she married Thomas Kittredge.

Mary Russell and Timothy Osgood were parents of eight children born at Andover.

500) i PETER OSGOOD, b. at Andover, 14 Nov 1717; d. at Andover, 17 Nov 1801; m. at Andover, 8 Sep 1743, SARAH JOHNSON, b. at Andover, Nov 1719 daughter of Timothy and Katherine (Sprague) Johnson; Sarah d. at Andover, 1 Aug 1804.

501) ii TIMOTHY OSGOOD, b. at Andover, 27 Aug 1719; d. at Andover, 31 Aug 1753; m. 6 Jan 1742, PHEBE FRYE, b. at Andover, 19 Mar 1721 daughter of Nathan and Hannah (Bridges) Frye; Phebe d. at Andover, after 1783 (living at time of daughter's will).

---

319 The historic property at 102 Gould Road in Andover is reported as being obtained by Thomas Chandler from Ebenezer Walcott. https://preservation.mhl.org/102-gould-rd

320 The 1746 will of Joseph Richardson of Bradford includes a bequest to his daughter Sarah wife of Joseph Chandler.

321 *Essex County, MA: Probate File Papers, 1638-1881.*Online database. *AmericanAncestors.org.* New England Historic Genealogical Society, 2014. Case 20285

322 *Essex County, MA: Probate File Papers, 1638-1881.*Online database. *AmericanAncestors.org.* New England Historic Genealogical Society, 2014. Case 20245

502) iii THOMAS OSGOOD, b. at Andover, 2 Nov 1721; d. at Andover, 3 Nov 1798; m. 3 Dec 1747, SARAH HUTCHINSON, b. at Andover, 24 Sep 1719 daughter of John and Sarah (Adams) Hutchinson; Sarah d. 3 Nov 1798.

503) iv ISAAC OSGOOD, b. at Andover, 4 Aug 1724; d. at Haverhill, 17 May 1791; m. 18 Jun 1752, ABIGAIL BAILEY, b. at Haverhill, 10 Jan 1730 daughter of Joshua and Elizabeth (Johnson) Bailey; Abigail d. at Haverhill, 25 Jan 1801 of black jaundice.

v MARY OSGOOD, b. 21 Feb 1726; likely died young.

504) vi DEBORAH OSGOOD, b. at Andover, 28 Apr 1730; d. about 1793; m. 2 Jan 1759, OBADIAH WOOD, b. about 1734 likely the son of Nathaniel and Elizabeth (Powell) Wood; Obadiah d. at Andover, 23 Oct 1810. Obadiah m. 2nd 8 May 1794 widow Lydia Blanchard.

505) vii PHEBE OSGOOD, b. at Andover, 26 May 1733; d. at Methuen, 2 Mar 1797; m. about 1757, THOMAS POOR, b. at Andover 19 Jul 1732 son of Thomas and Mary (Adams) Poor; Thomas d. at Methuen, 23 Sep 1804. Thomas married second Miriam Sargent.

364) viii HANNAH OSGOOD, b. at Andover, 31 Jul 1735; d. at Andover, 22 Oct 1771; m. at Andover, 23 Nov 1758, JOHN ADAMS (*Tabitha Farnum Adams[4], John Farnum[3], Elizabeth Holt Farnum[2], Nicholas[1]*), b. at Andover, 3 Jul 1735 son of Israel and Tabitha (Farnum) Adams; John d. at Andover, 27 Jun 1813. John married second Hannah Thurston. John m. 3rd, 21 May 1776, MARY HOLT (*Stephen[4], Nicholas[3], Nicholas[2], Nicholas[1]*), b. at Andover, 15 Dec 1741 daughter of Stephen and Mary (Farnum) Holt; Mary d. at Andover, 9 Nov 1829.

110) SARAH RUSSELL (*Phebe Johnson Russell[3], Mary Holt Johnson[2], Nicholas[1]*), b. at Andover, about 1695 daughter of Thomas and Phebe (Johnson) Russell; m. at Andover, 9 Sep 1715, JOHN ROSS, b. at Billerica, 18 Jan 1686/7 son of Thomas and Seeth (Holman) Ross.

Births of three children are recorded. It is not known what became of this family.

i JOHN ROSS, b. at Billerica, 23 Dec 1716

ii THOMAS ROSS, b. at Andover, 5 Oct 1718; d. 19 Dec 1719.

iii SARAH ROSS, b. at Andover, 3 Nov 1720

111) PETER RUSSELL (*Phebe Johnson Russell[3], Mary Holt Johnson[2], Nicholas[1]*), b. at Andover, 23 Apr 1700 son of Thomas and Phebe (Johnson) Russell; d. at Litchfield, NH, Nov 1759 (will 3 Nov, proved 28 Nov 1759); m. 31 Mar 1727, DEBORAH CROSBY, b. at Billerica, 13 Jul 1709 daughter of Joseph and Sarah (French) Crosby.

Peter and Deborah had their first four children in Andover and then settled in Litchfield, New Hampshire.

In his will written 3 November 1759 (proved 28 November 1759), Peter Russell bequeaths to beloved wife Deborah the income from one-third of the real estate and one-half of the house. The heirs of son Peletiah who is deceased receive five shillings and daughter Rachel also receives five shillings which completed her portion. There are bequests to other daughters Rebackah (three pounds five shillings), Phebe (four pounds), Deborah (five shillings), Hannah (four pounds), and Sarah (four pounds). His four sons will divide the rest of the estate and these are Peter, Joseph, James, and Thomas.[323]

Peter Russell and Deborah Crosby were parents of eleven children.

506) i PELETIAH RUSSELL, b. at Andover, 27 Dec 1727; d. in Nova Scotia in 1757 during the French and Indian War; m. about 1752, OLIVE MOORE, b. at Westford, 27 Dec 1729 daughter of Samuel and Deborah (Butterfield) Moore; Olive d. at Bath, NH, 11 Oct 1807. Olive m. 2nd Timothy Barron.

507) ii RACHEL RUSSELL, b. at Andover, 1 Nov 1730; d. 28 Nov 1802; m. about 1747; TIMOTHY UNDERWOOD, b. about 1725 son of Joseph and Susannah (Parker) Underwood; Timothy d. at Putney, VT, about 1804.

iii REBECCA RUSSELL, b. at Andover, 29 Aug 1734; living in 1759 but nothing further certain known.

508) iv PHEBE RUSSELL, b. at Andover, 16 May 1736; d. at Goffstown, NH, Nov 1836; m. 1st about 1752, JOHN BUTTERFIELD, b. at Chelmsford, 20 Feb 1731 son of John and Anne (Hildreth) Butterfield; John d. at Goffstown, 1765. Phebe m. 2nd, 774, SAMUEL ROBIE, b. at Hampton, NH, 17 Oct 1717 son of Ichabod and Sarah (Cass) Robie; Samuel d. at Goffstown, 18 Oct 1793.

[323] Ancestry.com. *New Hampshire, Wills and Probate Records, 1643-1982* [database on-line]. Otis G. Hammond, New Hampshire Wills, volumes 35-38, pp 488-489

508a) v PETER RUSSELL, b. at Litchfield, NH, 6 Aug 1738; d. at Peeling (later Woodstock), NH, 20 Aug 1815; m. about 1760, MEHITABLE STILES, b. at Middleton, MA, 10 Jun 1739 daughter of Caleb and Sarah (Walton) Stiles; Mehitable d. at Peeling, NH, 27 May 1811.

509) vi DEBORAH RUSSELL, b. at Litchfield, NH, 3 Jun 1740; d. at Merrimack, NH, 9 Sep 1820; m. about 1758, JONATHAN CUMMINGS, b. at Dunstable, 5 Jun 1729 son of Jonathan and Elizabeth (Blanchard) Cummings; Jonathan d. at Merrimack, 10 Jul 1787.

vii HANNAH RUSSELL, b. at Litchfield, about 1742; living in 1759; nothing further known.

viii SARAH RUSSELL, b. about 1743; living in 1759; nothing further known.

ix JOSEPH RUSSELL, b. at Litchfield, about 1744; d. at Litchfield, 23 Jun 1762.

510) x JAMES RUSSELL, b. at Litchfield, 31 May 1746; d. at Belpre, OH, 1821; m. 1st about 1774, MARY FRENCH, b. at Dunstable, NH, 18 Oct 1755 daughter of Benjamin and Mary (Lovewell) French; Mary d. at Woodstock, VT, about 1790. James m. 2nd at Ross, OH, 9 Aug 1814 the widow JUDAH O'NEAL.

xi THOMAS RUSSELL, b. at Litchfield, 13 Dec 1749; living in 1759; nothing further known.

112) JOSEPH RUSSELL (*Phebe Johnson Russell*[3], *Mary Holt Johnson*[2], *Nicholas*[1]), b. at Andover, Apr 1702 son of Thomas and Phebe (Johnson) Russell; m. 1st at Reading, 26 Nov 1728, HEPSIBAH EATON; Hepsibah d. at Andover, 14 Mar 1742/3. Joseph m. 2nd at Andover, 24 Nov 1746, HANNAH PERKINS, b. at Andover, 15 Nov 1720 daughter of Timothy and Hannah (Buxton) Perkins; Hannah d. at Andover, 22 Mar 1775.

Joseph Russell and Hepsibah Eaton were parents of five children born at Andover.

i JOSEPH RUSSELL, b. 9 Jan 1729/30; d. at Andover, 1758 (probate 4 Dec 1758). Joseph did not marry. In his will, he left his entire estate to his brother Thomas "for the love, good will and affection I bear for him above the rest of my friends and relations."

511) ii THOMAS RUSSELL, b. at Andover, 5 Jun 1732; d. at Wilton, 30 Mar 1818; m. at Andover, 15 May 1760, his second cousin, BETHIAH HOLT (*Ephraim*[4], *Henry*[3], *Henry*[2], *Nicholas*[1]), b. at Andover, 20 Mar 1743 daughter of Ephraim and Phebe (Russell) Holt; Bethiah d. at Wilton, 20 Aug 1817.

512) iii HEPHZIBAH RUSSELL, baptized at Andover, 30 Jun 1734; m. at Andover, 26 Feb 1756, her first cousin once removed, JOSEPH RUSSELL, b. at Andover, 8 Jan 1719/20 son of John and Sarah (Chandler) Russell; Joseph d. at Andover, 31 Aug 1783.

iv HANNAH RUSSELL, b. 11 Jan 1739/40; likely died young.

v DANIEL RUSSELL, baptized 17 Oct 1742; d. 3 Feb 1743.

Joseph Russell and Hannah Perkins were parents of eight children born at Andover.

i PERKINS RUSSELL, b. 7 May 1748; *perhaps* d. at Middleton, 23 Aug 1765.

513) ii JONATHAN RUSSELL, b. 14 Oct 1749; d. after 1820 when he was living in Pamelia, NY; m. at Middleton, 17 Jan 1771, RUTH HUTCHINSON, baptized 16 Sep 1750 daughter of Josiah and Sarah (Dean) Hutchinson; Ruth d. after 1820.

514) iii SARAH RUSSELL, b. 29 Oct 1750; d. at Middleton, MA, 2 Jan 1844; m. at Middleton, 12 Aug 1772, NEHEMIAH WILKINS, b. at Middleton, 14 Aug 1752 son of Ichabod and Mary (Clark) Wilkins; Nehemiah d. at Middleton, 17 Jun 1811.

515) iv JAMES RUSSELL, b. at Andover, 7 Jan 1753; d. at Boxford, 24 Apr 1830; m. about 1782, REBECCA PEABODY, b. at Middleton, 24 Mar 1763 daughter of Joseph and Mary (-) Peabody; Rebecca d. at Middleton, 11 Oct 1844.

v DANIEL RUSSELL, b. 21 Aug 1754

vi ELIJAH RUSSELL, b. 8 Mar 1756

516) vii RACHEL RUSSELL, b. at Andover, 23 Feb 1757; d. after 1830 when she as living at Hillsborough; m. at Middleton, 29 Jan 1784, JONATHAN DWINELLS, b. at Lynn, 4 May 1759 son of David and Keziah (Ramsdell) Dunnel; Jonathan d. after 1830.

517) viii HANNAH RUSSELL, b. at Andover, 11 Oct 1760; d. at Newburyport, 24 Aug 1840; m. at Middleton, 10 May 1784, CALEB PUTNAM, b. at Danvers, 24 Nov 1763 son of Archelaus and Abigail (Goodrich) Putnam; Caleb d. at Newburyport, 6 Mar 1826.

113) JEMIMA RUSSELL (*Phebe Johnson Russell[3], Mary Holt Johnson[2], Nicholas[1]*), b. at Andover, 18 Jul 1704 daughter of Thomas and Phebe (Johnson) Russell; d. at Littleton, MA, 20 Sep 1790; m. at Andover, 16 Jul 1724, JOSEPH HUNT, b. at Billerica, 21 Sep 1694 son of Samuel and Mary (-) Hunt; Joseph d. at Andover, 1743 (probate 7 Nov 1743). Jemima m. 2nd, 13 Dec 1743, CHRISTOPHER TEMPLE, b. 1690 and d. at Littleton, 8 May 1782.

Joseph Hunt did not leave a will and his estate entered probate 7 November 1743 with widow Jemima as administratrix and Joseph Russell and Robert Russell as sureties.[324] Personal estate was valued at £10.10.7.

Jemima and Joseph were parents of five children born at Billerica.

518) i SARAH HUNT, b. at Billerica, 23 Dec 1725; m. at Westford, 7 Mar 1750, JOSIAH JOHNSON, b. at Lancaster, 5 Jun 1726 son of Josiah and Annis (Chandler) Johnson.

ii JOSEPH HUNT, b. 11 May 1728; nothing further known.

iii AMOS HUNT, b. 25 Nov 1729; nothing further known.

519) iv ROBERT HUNT, b. at Billerica, 20 Jan 1731/2; m. at Canaan, CT, 26 Dec 1753, REBEKAH PECK, b. at Litchfield, 15 Dec 1736 daughter of Isaac and Ruth (Tomlinson) Peck; Rebekah d. at Salisbury, CT, 1812.

520) v RUSSELL HUNT, b. at Billerica, about 1733; d. at Canaan, CT, 18 Oct 1806; m. at Canaan, 3 May 1758, LYDIA PECK, b. about 1738 likely the daughter of Isaac and Ruth (Tomlinson) Peck; Lydia d. at Canaan, 18 Feb 1818.

114) JAMES RUSSELL (*Phebe Johnson Russell[3], Mary Holt Johnson[2], Nicholas[1]*), b. at Andover, 15 Jun 1706 son of Thomas and Phebe (Johnson) Russell; m. at Amesbury, 3 Jun 1729, RHODA CHANDLER, b. at Andover, 1705 daughter of Joseph and Sarah (Abbott) Chandler.

Although James and Rhoda likely had more than the three children listed, that cannot be confirmed as yet. Sons James Russell and Thomas Chandler Russell are confirmed with birth records and Joseph is a likely son of this family.

521) i JAMES RUSSELL, b. at North Yarmouth, 7 Aug 1737; m. at North Yarmouth, 5 Jun 1760, LYDIA MITCHELL.

522) ii THOMAS CHANDLER RUSSELL, b. at Cumberland, 9 Oct 1740; m. about 1767, SARAH GOOCH, b. 17 Oct 1751 daughter of John and Elizabeth (Boothbay) Gooch.

523) iii JOSEPH RUSSELL, b. about 1742; d. 1775; m. at Cumberland, 22 Oct 1765, MIRIAM BROWN, b. at Cumberland, 10 Jun 1746 daughter of Jacob and Lydia (Weare) Brown.

115) TABITHA JOHNSON (*John Johnson[3], Mary Holt Johnson[2], Nicholas[1]*), b. 4 Apr 1693 daughter of John and Ellenor (Ballard) Johnson; m. 17 Sep 1726, JOHN DANFORTH, b. at Billerica, 3 Jun 1703 son of Jonathan and Rebecca (Parker) Danforth;[325] John d. at Westborough, 1737 (will 8 Nov 1737; proved 4 Jan 1737/8).

In his will written 28 November 1737, John Danforth bequeaths to beloved wife Tabitha all the within doors moveable estate and the use and improvement of one-third of the lands. To daughter Hannah now living in Lexington, he leaves all the movables that were her mother's. Only son John Danforth receives a double share of the estate. Daughter Lydia Danforth receives the remaining part of the estate. Father-in-law John Johnson of Andover was named sole executor.[326]

The daughter Hannah mentioned in the will was born about 1721 and was from an earlier marriage, or perhaps an out-of-wedlock relationship, of John Danforth and Miss Poulter. In 1735 at her fourteenth year, Hannah was placed in the guardianship of Joseph Loring of Lexington. In her guardianship packet, she is described as a granddaughter of Jonathan Poulter.[327]

Tabitha Johnson and John Danforth were parents of two children born at Westborough.

---

[324] *Essex County, MA: Probate File Papers, 1638-1881.*Online database. *AmericanAncestors.org.* New England Historic Genealogical Society, 2014. Case 14255.

[325] May, *Danforth Genealogy*, p 19

[326] *Probate Records (Worcester County, Massachusetts); Index 1731-1881*, Probate Records volume 1, pp 293-294, will of John Danforth

[327] *Middlesex County, MA: Probate File Papers, 1648-1871.*Online database. *AmericanAncestors.org.* New England Historic Genealogical Society, 2014. Case 5888

524) i LYDIA DANFORTH, b. at Westborough, 29 Jun 1729; m. at Andover, 24 Jan 1754, her first cousin once removed, URIAH BALLARD, b. at Andover, 28 Apr 1715 son of Uriah and Elizabeth (Henshaw) Ballard; Uriah d. at Wilton, 1803. Uriah was first married to Sarah Dane and second married to Mehitable Barker.

525) ii JOHN DANFORTH, b. at Westborough, 25 Mar 1731; d. at Greenbush, 29 Sep 1758; m. 6 Mar 1755, ELIZABETH WILSON, likely b. at Billerica, 10 Oct 1732 daughter of John and Jemima (Shed) Wilson; Elizabeth d. at Concord, NH, 27 Jun 1804. Elizabeth married second Ebenezer Dow on 12 Jun 1760.

116) ZEBADIAH JOHNSON (*John Johnson³, Mary Holt Johnson², Nicholas¹*), b. at Andover, about 1701 son of John and Ellenor (Ballard) Johnson; d. at Andover, 1770 (probate 3 Feb 1770); m. 8 Jun 1723, HANNAH ROBBINS, b. at Charlestown, 30 Jun 1705 daughter of Nathaniel and Hannah (Chandler) Robbins.

In his will written 18 November 1769 (probate 6 February 1770), Zebadiah Johnson bequeathed to beloved wife Hannah the use and improvement of one-third of the real and personal estate while she is a widow and she receives all the moveable estate. Son John receives the real and personal estate including the one-third dower after the decease of his mother. Daughter Hannah Thurston wife of Moses Thurston receives five shillings. Daughter Lydia Dinsmore wife of Abraham Dinsmore receives thirteen shillings. Daughter Ellenor Johnson receives £13.6.8. Granddaughter Sarah Townsend receives two pounds. Son John was named sole executor.[328]

Zebadiah Johnson and Hannah Robbins were parents of nine children born at Andover.

526) i HANNAH JOHNSON, b. at Andover, 31 Mar 1724; d. about 1773; m. at Andover, 29 May 1744, MOSES THURSTON, b. about 1721 son of Abner and Shua (Gilman) Thurston; Moses d. at Hollis, 6 Apr 1800. Moses was second married to Katherine Emerson.

ii LYDIA JOHNSON, b. 14 Nov 1725; d. 26 Dec 1726.

iii MARY JOHNSON, baptized at Andover, 25 May 1729; nothing further known; she is not in father's will.

iv SARAH JOHNSON, b. at Andover, 18 Dec 1731; d. before 1769; m. at Andover, 21 May 1751, NATHANIEL TOWNSEND. Little is known of this family. They perhaps had one daughter Sarah, but no further concrete information was found.

v PHEBE JOHNSON, b. at Andover, 16 Mar 1733/4; nothing further known; she is not in father's will.

527) vi LYDIA JOHNSON, b. at Andover, 27 Feb 1735/6; d. at Temple, NH, 13 Sep 1774; m. at Andover, 13 Aug 1752, ABRAHAM DINSMORE, b. at Bedford, NH, 22 Feb 1730 son of Thomas and Hannah (Whitaker) Dinsmore.

vii ELINOR JOHNSON, b. at Andover, 10 Jun 1738; she was living and unmarried at the time of her father's will in 1769.

528) viii ZEBADIAH JOHNSON, b. at Andover, 20 Sep 1742; d. likely at Temple, NH; m. at Reading, 1 Sep 1761, LYDIA BANCROFT, b. at Reading, 8 Sep 1738 daughter of Samuel and Lydia (Parker) Bancroft.[329]

529) ix JOHN JOHNSON, baptized at Andover, 28 Jun 1747; m. at Reading, 9 Jul 1767, MARGARET MCINTIRE

117) DAMARIS JOHNSON (*Thomas Johnson³, Mary Holt Johnson², Nicholas¹*), b. at Andover, 1704 daughter of Thomas and Hannah (Stone) Johnson; d. at Andover, 13 Nov 1728; m. 16 Jan 1727/8, JOSEPH FAULKNER, b. at Andover, 1 Mar 1695/6 son of John and Sarah (Abbott) Faulkner; Joseph d. at Andover, 28 Dec 1780. Joseph married second Mary Parker and married third Rebecca Barnard.

The will of Joseph Faulkner written 11 January1765 has bequests to the following persons: wife Rebecca, daughter Damaris the wife of David Farnum, daughters Mary and Hannah, grandson Abiel Faulkner, granddaughter Damaris Faulkner, and two sons Joseph Faulkner and Daniel Faulkner.

Damaris Johnson and Joseph Faulkner were parents of one child, Damaris dying two weeks following the birth.

530) i ABIEL FAULKNER, b. at Andover, 30 Oct 1728; d. at Andover, 4 Jul 1756; m. at Andover, 4 Mar 1752, MARY POOR, b. at Andover, 6 Apr 1734 daughter of Thomas and Mary (Adams) Poor; Mary d. at Andover, 20 Apr 1791.

---

[328] *Essex County, MA: Probate File Papers, 1638-1881.*Online database. *AmericanAncestors.org.* New England Historic Genealogical Society, 2014. Case 15165

[329] Zebadiah is not mentioned in his father's 1769 will, although he was clearly living at that time. It may be that Zebadiah had received already his portion. There may also have been a family falling out. The family records of Lydia's father, Deacon Samuel Bancroft of Reading, makes note on 5 Mar 1769 of traveling to Andover: "Monday 5 up this day to Andover: Johnson haveing again abused his wife. I reconciled them again. Came home at Eleven at Night." Bancroft, *Family Record of Dea. Samuel Bancroft*, p 23. It was about this time (1769-1770) that Zebadiah and his wife Lydia relocated to Temple, New Hampshire.

118) HANNAH JOHNSON (*Thomas Johnson³, Mary Holt Johnson², Nicholas¹*), b. at Andover, 13 Jan 1705/6 daughter of Thomas and Hannah (Stone) Johnson; m. at Andover, 27 Jul 1725, JOHN WRIGHT, b. at Andover, Mar 1701/2 son of John and Mary (Wardwell) Wright.

The births of ten children are recorded at Andover. Marriages were located for just two of the children.

531) i JOHN WRIGHT, b. at Andover, 9 Apr 1726; d. at Woolwich, ME, 19 May 1809; m. at Andover, 7 Apr 1748, MARY ELLOYT; Mary d. about 1751. John m. 2nd, by 1754, MARY BOWEN, b. about 1737 and d. at Woolwich, ME, 1798.

ii Daughter, b. 9 May 1730

iii JOSEPH WRIGHT, b. 15 Mar 1731/2

iv MARY WRIGHT, b. 25 Mar 1734

532) v SARAH WRIGHT, b. at Andover, 25 Jan 1735/6; d. at Pelham, NH, about 1774; m. at Andover, 26 Apr 1757, URIAH ABBOTT, b. at Andover, 29 Sep 1735 son of Uriah and Sarah (Mitchell) Abbott; Uriah d. at Pelham, about 1808 (probate 1808). Uriah married second Sarah Perry.

vi SUSANNAH WRIGHT, b. 14 Dec 1737

vii PHEBE WRIGHT, b. 17 Feb 1739/40

viii BENJAMIN WRIGHT, b. 22 Jun 1742

ix ELIZABETH WRIGHT, b. 22 Jan 17744/5

x JAMES WRIGHT, b. 21 Mar 1746/7; d. 18 Jun 1749.

119) ANDREW JOHNSON (*James Johnson³, Mary Holt Johnson², Nicholas¹*), b. at Andover, Oct 1695 son of James and Elizabeth (Farnum) Johnson; d. at Andover, 4 Feb 1757; m. 21 Aug 1723, HANNAH CHANDLER, b. at Andover, 23 Aug 1700 daughter of Thomas and Mary (Peters) Chandler.

Andrew had a farm in Andover and also owned property in York, Maine. He participated in the excursion to Crown Point during the French and Indian Wars and was ill upon his return hastening his death. Hannah petitioned for assistance related to this.[330] Two of the sons in the family died at the siege of Louisburg in 1745.[331]

Andrew Johnson did not leave a will and his estate entered probate 21 February 1757 with widow Hannah requesting that son Jonathan be named administrator. Real estate was valued at £315.[332]

Andrew and Hannah were parents of ten children born at Andover.

i ANDREW JOHNSON, b. 16 Jan 1723/4; d. 18 Jan 1723/4.

ii ANDREW JOHNSON, b. 1 Feb 1724/5; d. at Louisburg, 1 Oct 1745.

iii THOMAS JOHNSON, b. 23 Apr 1727; d. 18 Jun 1744.

iv DAVID JOHNSON, b. 1 Jun 1729; d. at Louisburg, 29 Oct 1745.

533) v JONATHAN JOHNSON, b. at Andover, 27 Jan 1731/2; d. at Westford, MA, 1789 (probate 12 Nov 1789); m. 11 Jul 1754, SARAH BATES, b. at Westford, 29 Aug 1733 daughter of Edward and Mary (Snow) Bates;[333] Sarah d. at Westford, 27 Feb 1813.

vi JOSIAH JOHNSON, b. 31 Aug 1734; nothing further known.

534) vii ELIZABETH JOHNSON, b. at Andover, 18 Apr 1737; d. about 1777; m. at Andover, 30 May 1765, SAMUEL FARLEY, b. at Reading, 1 May 1741 son of Samuel and Mary (Adams) Farley. Samuel married second Hannah Chandler on 5 Mar 1778.

viii EPHRAIM JOHNSON, b. 21 Dec 1739; d. 11 Jan 1739/40.

---

[330] Chandler, *Descendants of William and Annis Chandler*, p 75

[331] Andrew, s. Andrew and Hannah, "at Lewesbug in the Kings Service," Oct. 1, 1745. David, s. Andrew and Hannah, "in the Kings Service at Lewesbug," Oct. 29, 1745.

[332] *Essex County, MA: Probate File Papers, 1638-1881.*Online database. *AmericanAncestors.org.* New England Historic Genealogical Society, 2014. Case 14992

[333] In 1781, Jonathan Johnson served as administrator of the estate of Edward Bates of Westford.

535) ix EPHRAIM JOHNSON, b. at Andover, 31 Mar 1742; d. at Wilton, NH, 27 Dec 1834; m. (intention) 23 Mar 1765, MARY FARLEY, b. at Reading, 28 Apr 1743 daughter of Samuel and Mary (Adams) Farley; Mary d. at Wilton, 24 Apr 1834.

536) x JAMES JOHNSON, b. at Andover, 15 Oct 1743; m. at Andover, 16 Aug 1768, ANNIS COREY, b. at Chelmsford, 4 Nov 1735 daughter of Ephraim and Hannah (Merrill) Corey.

120) OBADIAH JOHNSON (*James Johnson³, Mary Holt Johnson², Nicholas¹*), b. at Andover, about 1700 son of James and Elizabeth (Farnum) Johnson; d. at Andover, 8 Jul 1780; m. 1st 12 Feb 1724/5, HANNAH OSGOOD, b. at Andover, 4 Mar 1701/2 daughter of Stephen and Hannah (Blanchard) Osgood; Hannah d. 11 Mar 1729. Obadiah m. 2nd about 1740, DEBORAH RUSS daughter of Thomas and Anne (Farnum) Russ; Deborah d. at Andover, 18 Jul 1745. Obadiah m. 3rd 26 Sep 1748, DOROTHY BALLARD, b. at Andover, 26 Jan 1714/5 daughter of Joseph and Rebecca (Johnson) Ballard; Dorothy was living in 1780. Dorothy Ballard was first married to Benjamin Smith.

In his will written 6 March 1777 (proved 5 September 1780), Obadiah Johnson bequeaths to beloved wife Dorothy the improvement of as much of the house and cellar as she deems reasonable. Son Peter who has received a valuable portion of the estate is responsible for her support. Dorothy also receives all the moveable estate to be hers except for the money and the clock. Son Obadiah receives the largest blacksmith anvil and vise and £3. Son Jacob receives a piece of plowing and mowing land of about seven acres in Andover and a piece of woodland of about ten acres also in Andover. Daughter Deborah the wife of Nathan Baly receives twelve shillings. Daughter Hannah wife of Timothy Holt receives £4. Son Peter receives all the remainder of the lands and the dwelling house plus the stock animals. Sons Peter and Jacob are named executors. The value of the estate was £509.[334]

Obadiah Johnson and Hannah Osgood were parents of four children.

537) i OBADIAH JOHNSON, b. at Andover, 20 Nov 1725; m. 29 Dec 1748, LYDEA BALLARD, b. at Andover, 12 Mar 1727/8 daughter of Josiah and Mary (Chandler) Ballard; Lydea d. at Andover, 6 Jul 1779.

538) ii JACOB JOHNSON, b. at Andover, 19 May 1727; d. at Andover, 31 May 1803; m. at Andover, 16 May 1758, SARAH DOLIVER, b. about 1740; Sarah d. at Andover, 4 Apr 1807.

iii ELIZABETH JOHNSON, b. 27 Feb 1729; d. 1 Mar 1729.

iv HANNAH JOHNSON, b. 27 Feb 1729; d. 8 Mar 1729.

Obadiah Johnson and Deborah Ruse were parents of one child.

539) i DEBORAH JOHNSON, b. at Andover, 5 Jul 1742; d. at Haverhill, 30 Mar 1812; m. at Andover,12 Nov 1761, NATHAN BAILEY, b. at Bradford, 17 Jul 1740 son of Nathan and Mary (Palmer) Bailey; Nathan d. at Haverhill, 25 Aug 1806.

Obadiah Johnson and Dorothy Ballard were parents of three children.

i PHINEAS JOHNSON, b. 26 Jul 1749; d. 3 Mar 1753.

540) ii PETER JOHNSON, b. at Andover, 26 Jul 1749; d. at Andover, 3 Nov 1798; m. at Andover, 26 Aug 1773, EUNICE BLANCHARD, b. at Andover, 12 Aug 1755 daughter of Samuel and Ruth (Tenney) Blanchard; Eunice d. at Wayland, MA, 6 Oct 1846.[335]

541) iii HANNAH JOHNSON, b. at Andover, 8 Feb 1753; m. at Andover, 8 Apr 1773, her third cousin, TIMOTHY HOLT (*Elizabeth Holt Holt⁴, John³, Samuel², Nicholas¹*), b. at Andover, 19 May 1746 son of Timothy and Elizabeth (Holt) Holt; Timothy d. at Weston, VT, 3 May 1836.

121) MARY JOHNSON (*James Johnson³, Mary Holt Johnson², Nicholas¹*), b. at Andover, Feb 1701/2 daughter of James and Elizabeth (Farnum) Johnson; d. at Amenia, NY, 1 May 1783; m. 1720, JOSEPH CHAMBERLAIN, b. at Billerica, Nov 1696 son of Clement and Mary (-) Chamberlain; Joseph d. at Amenia, NY, 8 Apr 1765.[336]

Mary and Joseph started in Billerica, were briefly in Lebanon, Connecticut and then Mansfield and Tolland. They finally located in Amenia where at least five of the children settled. Joseph built a home in Amenia that was purchased by Sylvanus Nye in 1774 and was one of the last historic homes standing in Amenia.[337]

---

334 *Essex County, MA: Probate File Papers, 1638-1881.*Online database. *AmericanAncestors.org.* New England Historic Genealogical Society, 2014. Case 15104

335 Eunice, b. Andover, wid. Peter, dropsy, Oct. 6, 1846, a. 91.

336 *Connecticut, Hale Collection of Cemetery Inscriptions and Newspaper Notices, 1629-1934*

337 Read, *Early History of Amenia*, p 144

Joseph and Mary were parents of twelve children.[338]

542) i ELIZABETH CHAMBERLAIN, b. at Billerica, 5 Apr 1720; d. at Mansfield, CT, 19 Mar 1809; m. 30 Mar 1738, PETER DIMMOCK, baptized at Mansfield, 15 Sep 1717 son of Benjamin and Mary (Thatcher) Dimmock; Peter d. at Mansfield, 30 Jul 1810.

543) ii JOSEPH CHAMBERLAIN, b. at Billerica, 24 Feb 1721/2; m. at Stafford, CT, 3 Jul 1744, ELIZABETH DELANO, b. at Dartmouth, MA, 15 May 1722 daughter of Jonathan and Amy (Hatch) Delano.[339]

iii MARY CHAMBERLAIN, b. at Billerica, 27 Jan 1723/4; nothing further definite known; perhaps died at Amenia.

544) iv MEHITABLE CHAMBERLAIN, b. at Lebanon, CT, 19 Aug 1727; likely d. at Surry, NH; m. at Tolland, 25 Mar 1751, ELIJAH BENTON, b. at Tolland, 30 Jun 1728 son of Daniel and Mary (Skinner) Benton; Elijah d. at Surry, NH, 1786 (probate 1786).

545) v JOHN CHAMBERLAIN, baptized at Tolland, 21 Jun 1730; m. 1st about 1758, MARGARET, b. about 1733 who has not been identified; Margaret d. at Amenia, 29 Dec 1772. John m. 2nd about 1773, ABIGAIL FENTON (widow of Abiel Abbot), b. at Willington, 27 Aug 1730 daughter of Francis and Ann (Berry) Fenton; Abigail d. at Amenia, 14 Aug 1776. John m. 3rd about 1777, LYDIA LATHROP (widow of Timothy Delano), b. at Tolland, 21 Jun 1736 daughter of John and Ann (Thatcher) Lathrop.

546) vi ABIAL CHAMBERLAIN, b. at Mansfield, Mar 1732; d. at Mansfield, 15 May 1771; m. at Mansfield, 10 Dec 1751, JAMES ROYSE, baptized at Mansfield, 15 Apr 1722 son of James and Mehitable (Arnold) Royse. James was first married to Abigail Scripture on 10 Dec 1742 and third married on 12 Nov 1771 to Rachel Kidder (widow of Jesse Dimmock).

547) vii JAMES CHAMBERLAIN, b. at Mansfield, 11 Feb 1734; d. at Amherst, MA, 28 Apr 1812; m. 27 Jan 1757, ABIGAIL BOYNTON (widow of John Palmer), b. at Coventry, 17 Jun 1729 daughter of Zachariah and Sarah (Wyckham) Boynton; Abigail d. at Amherst, 5 Mar 1814.

548) viii PHEBE CHAMBERLAIN, baptized at Mansfield, 7 Aug 1737; m. at Amenia, NY, 4 Mar 1762, ELIHU BEARDSLEY, baptized at Stratford, CT, 31 Oct 1736 son of David and Sarah (Wells) Beardsley;[340] d. after 1800 when he was in Amenia.

549) ix COLBE CHAMBERLAIN, b. at Tolland, 2 Dec 1738; d. at Amenia, NY, 11 Sep 1796; m. at Amenia, 14 Nov 1765, CATHERINE WINEGAR, b. 2 Mar 1749 daughter of Conrad and Ann (Rauh) Winegar;[341] Catherine d. at Amenia, 26 May 1808.

x JACOB CHAMBERLAIN, b. at Tolland, 21 Jan 1740/1; d. at Amenia, 14 Nov 1762.

550) xi WILLIAM CHAMBERLAIN, b. at Tolland, 25 Jan 1744/5; d. at Amenia, 27 Nov 1810; m. at Amenia, 12 Mar 1767, ABIGAIL HATCH, b. at Kent, CT, Dec 1742 daughter of Barnabas and Phebe (Cushman) Hatch;[342] Abigail d. at Amenia, 4 Apr 1812.

551) xii REBECCA CHAMBERLAIN, b. at Tolland, 25 Jan 1744/5; d. at Amenia, 10 Dec 1777; m. at Amenia, 25 Jan 1765, SOLOMON CHASE, b. at Groton, MA, 9 Sep 1743 son of Benjamin and Rachel (Hartwell) Chase; Solomon d. at Westerlo, NY, 4 Nov 1828. Solomon married Mercy Oldridge on 18 Aug 1779.

122) MEHITABLE JOHNSON (*James Johnson[3], Mary Holt Johnson[2], Nicholas[1]*), b. at Andover, about 1703 daughter of James and Elizabeth (Farnum) Johnson; d. at Mansfield, CT, 28 Apr 1740; m. at Andover, 4 Apr 1733, THOMAS HUNTINGTON, b. at Norwich, CT, 22 Apr 1688 son of Thomas and Elizabeth (Backus) Huntington; Thomas d. at Mansfield, 18 Jan 1755. Thomas was first married to Elizabeth Arnold.

Mehitable Johnson and Thomas Huntington were parents of three children born at Mansfield, Connecticut.

i ELIZABETH HUNTINGTON, b. 19 May 1735; d. 24 May 1735.

---

338 Some sources list two daughters Mehitable, one born Aug 1727 and one Aug 1729, but the birth and baptism records are for 1727 and a record for the second Mehitable was not found, but there may well be two daughters Mehitable.

339 The March 1751 will of Jonathan Delano of Tolland includes bequests to his wife Amy and to his daughter Elizabeth Chamberlain.

340 Holt, *Beardsley Genealogy*, p 40

341 Reed, *Early History of Amenia*, p 19

342 The 1778 will of Barnabas Hatch includes a bequest to his daughter Abigail Chamberlain.

ii THOMAS HUNTINGTON, b. at Mansfield, 5 Jun 1736; d. at Washington County, NY, about 1805.[343] The Huntington genealogy reports that Thomas located in Fort Miller, married, and had a son James. There is a Thomas Huntington in the 1800 census for Argyle, NY and a James Huntington there on the tax lists for Argyle in 1802. Nothing further has been learned of this family.

552) iii CHRISTOPHER HUNTINGTON, b. at Mansfield, 7 Jul 1738; d. at Compton, Québec, 14 Dec 1810; m. at Mansfield, 7 May 1761, MARY DIMOCK, b. at Mansfield, 9 Oct 1739 son of Perez and Mary (Bailey) Dimock; Mary d. 1833.[344]

123) JEMIMA ABBOT (*Jemima Johnson Abbot[4], Mary Holt Johnson[2], Nicholas[1]*), b. at Sudbury, 10 Oct 1699 daughter of John and Jemima (Johnson) Abbot; m. 12 Dec 1717, NATHANIEL NORCROSS, b. at Watertown, 20 Dec 1695 son of Nathaniel and Susannah (Shattuck) Norcross; Nathaniel d. at Watertown, 9 Apr 1749.

In his will written 28 December 1748, Nathaniel Norcross bequeaths to his beloved wife the use and improvement of one-third of the estate. She also has the use of the other portion of the estate until son Uriah comes of age. Son Josiah receives a pair of steer. Lame son Nehemiah receives £100. Daughter Jemima Robbins has received her portion but will share which is to be considered to the division of the residue of the estate. The remainder of the estate to be divided among his eight children: Uriah, Jemima, Mercy, Josiah, Mary, Asa, Nehemiah, and Susannah. His wife is named executrix, but her name is not stated. Jemima Norcross is named as executrix in the probate documents.[345]

Jemima and Nathaniel were parents of thirteen children born at Watertown.

553) i JEMIMA NORCROSS, b. at Watertown, 24 May 1720; d. at Cambridge by 1776; m. at Watertown, 30 Apr 1741, ELIPHALET ROBBINS, baptized at Cambridge, 16 Jan 1718 son of John and Abigail (Adams) Robbins; Eliphalet d. at Cambridge, 1795 (probate 1795). Eliphalet was second married to Mrs. Sarah Whiting on 13 Mar 1777.

ii NATHANIEL NORCROSS, b. 6 Mar 1721/2; died young.

iii SUSANNAH NORCROSS, b. 9 Apr 1724; died young.

iv URIAH NORCROSS, b. 20 Oct 1726; died young.

v NATHANIEL NORCROSS, b. at Watertown, 25 Jun 1727; d. at sea, 5 Aug 1744. Nathaniel Norcross was named administrator of his son's estate.

vi JOSIAH NORCROSS, baptized 13 Oct 1728; died young.

554) vii MERCY NORCROSS, baptized at Watertown, 9 Aug 1730; d. at Cambridge, MA (now Brighton), 28 Jun 1791; m. at Cambridge, 3 May 1749, JOHN STRATTON, b. at Cambridge, 9 Aug 1727 son of Ebenezer and Lydia (Fuller) Stratton; John d. at Cambridge, 21 Nov 1791.

555) viii URIAH NORCROSS, b. at Watertown, 23 Jul 1732; d. at Boston, 23 Jun 1797; m. 1st at Boston, 15 Apr 1754, MERCY WATTS, b. at Hull, MA, 19 Jan 1734/5 daughter of Joseph and Hannah (Paine) Watts; Mercy d. at Boston, 6 Jan 1779.[346][347] Uriah m. 2nd at Boston, 25 Aug 1779, ABIGAIL DINSDALE who has not been identified.

556) ix JOSIAH NORCROSS, b. at Watertown, about 1734; d. at Newton, 13 Dec 1801; m. at Watertown, 6 Jan 1757, ELIZABETH CHILD, b. at Watertown, 1 Jan 1737/8 daughter of Jonathan and Elizabeth (-) Child; Elizabeth d. at Newton, 30 Jul 1801.

557) x MARY NORCROSS, baptized at Watertown, 16 Apr 1738; m. at Cambridge, 1 Jun 1755, DANIEL ROBBINS, b. at Newton, 10 Jan 1733 son of Daniel and Hannah (Trowbridge) Robbins.

558) xi ASA NORCROSS, b. at Watertown, 9 Mar 1740/1; d. at Holliston, MA, 25 Aug 1830; m. 1st at Newton, MA, 20 Apr 1760, ELIZABETH GREENWOOD, b. at Newton, 21 Nov 1740 daughter of Josiah and Phebe (Stearns) Greenwood; Elizabeth d. by 1774. Asa m. 2nd 10 Nov 1774, ELIZABETH FAIRBANKS, b. at Medway, MA, 11 Aug 1749 daughter of George and Jerusha (Twitchell) Fairbanks; Elizabeth d. at Holliston, Sep 1829.

---

[343] Huntington Family Association, *The Huntington Family in America*, p 308, reports Thomas was at Fort Miller, NY which is in Washington County.

[344] Huntington, *The Huntington Family in America*

[345] *Middlesex County, MA: Probate File Papers, 1648-1871.*Online database. *AmericanAncestors.org.* New England Historic Genealogical Society, 2014. Case 16032

[346] Reports of Cases Argued in the Supreme Judicial Court of the Commonwealth of Massachusetts, volume I, p 324; date of death of Mercy Watts is given in part of court case documents related to a dispute of the estate of Mercy Watts's father.

[347] There is a 1779 guardianship case for the minor children of Uriah Norcross who are the grandchildren of Joseph Watts related to his estate.

559) xii NEHEMIAH NORCROSS, baptized at Watertown, 7 Feb 1741/2; m. at Roxbury, 26 Jun 1764, RUTH BUGBEE.

560) xiii SUSANNAH NORCROSS, b. at Watertown, 27 Jul 1746; m. 10 Oct 1765, JONATHAN WHITNEY, b. at Watertown, 12 Apr 1743 son of Joseph and Mary (Child) Whitney; Jonathan d. at Watertown, 3 Jun 1802.[348]

124) JOHN ABBOTT (*Jemima Johnson Abbot[4], Mary Holt Johnson[2], Nicholas[1]*), b. at Sudbury, 3 Oct 1702 son of John and Jemima (Johnson) Abbot; d. after 1738 likely in North Carolina; m. 18 Oct 1721, ELIZABETH PHIPPS, b. at Lexington, MA, 10 Sep 1701 daughter of Samuel and Elizabeth (Stevens) Phipps.

John Abbott has been characterized as the "pioneer of the Southern Abbotts."[349] He spent his early adulthood in Connecticut and Massachusetts where his children were born. He was then in South Carolina and later North Carolina, but his final whereabouts are unknown. Although described as the pioneer of Southern Abbotts that is perhaps a misnomer as none of his children seem to have settled there.

John Abbott and Elizabeth Phipps were parents of five children.

i ELIZABETH ABBOTT, b. at Stow, MA, 13 Nov 1722; d. 16 Nov 1722.

561) ii JOHN ABBOTT, b. at Stow, MA, 2 Apr 1724; d. at Sempronius, NY, 21 May 1814; m. at Lyme, CT, 1747, SARAH BAKER; Sarah d. at Hoosick, NY, 1777.

562) iii SAMUEL ABBOTT, b. at Windham, CT, 18 Sep 1726; d. at Norwich, 1788; m. at Norwich, 4 Oct 1749, PHEBE EDGERTON, b. at Norwich, 8 Feb 1732 daughter of John and Phebe (Harris) Edgerton; Phebe d. at Norwich, 1793.

iv SARAH ABBOTT, b. about 1727. She is a child reported in Lemuel Abbott's genealogy about whom nothing else is known.

563) v JEMIMA ABBOTT, b. perhaps at Windham, 23 Mar 1729; d. at Bridgeport, VA (current WVA), 1815; m. at Windham, 14 Mar 1751, JOHN WALDO, b. at Windham, 18 Oct 1728 son of Edward and Thankful (Dimock) Waldo; John d. at Bridgeport, 23 Aug 1814.

125) MARY ABBOTT (*Jemima Johnson Abbot[4], Mary Holt Johnson[2], Nicholas[1]*), b. at Sudbury, 10 Sep 1704; d. at Tolland, 12 Mar 1740 daughter of John and Jemima (Johnson) Abbot; m. at Boston, 17 Dec 1725, NATHAN WHEELER, b. at Concord, MA, 2 Mar 1700 son of Edward and Sarah (Merriam) Wheeler; Nathan d. at Amenia, NY, 10 Jan 1766. Nathan second married Rachel Paulk on 23 Apr 1741.

Nathan Wheeler was a cooper in Boston. The first child of Mary and Nathan was born in Boston, and the family relocated to Connecticut where seven more children were born. Mary died after the stillbirth of the youngest child. Nathan remarried and had at least four more children. The family relocated to the Amenia district in Dutchess County.

In his will written 6 January 1766, Nathan Wheeler of Amenia bequeaths to his true and loving wife (not named) the household movables which now remain of "what she brought to me" or family possessed. Daughter Mary Benton receives one twenty-third part of the whole estate as do daughters Jerusha and Sarah. The remainder of the estate is to be divided into one-fourth parts with each of four sons receiving one-fourth. The sons are Elijah, Eliphalet, Samuel, and Edward. Samuel and Eliphalet were named executors.[350] Sarah, Samuel, and Edward are children from Nathan's second marriage.

i MARY WHEELER, b. at Boston, 19 Sep 1726; died young.

564) ii MARY WHEELER, b. at Norwich, 12 Jun 1728; d. at Tolland, about 1808 (final estate division for Daniel Benton in Oct 1808 was made after her death); m. at Tolland, 3 Nov 1747, DANIEL BENTON, b. at Tolland 6 Jan 1723/4 son of Daniel and Mary (Skinner) Benton; Daniel d. at Tolland, 4 Dec 1777.

iii NATHAN WHEELER, b. at Norwich, 22 Mar 1730

565) iv ELIJAH WHEELER, b. at Norwich, 22 Feb 1731; d. at Amenia, 3 Sep 1774; m. at Kent, CT, 27 Nov 1760, SARAH MARSH, b. at Kent, 9 Feb 1740/1 daughter of Cyrus and Margaret (Kinsman) Marsh.

v JERUSHA WHEELER, b. at Norwich, 7 Apr 1734. She perhaps married Elihu Curtis, but that is not certain.

vi BEULAH WHEELER, b. 10 Oct 1736; d. 24 Oct 1738.

566) vii ELIPHALET WHEELER, b. at Tolland, 3 Jul 1738; d. at Amenia, NY, 5 Sep 1788; m. 10 Nov 1767, ABIGAIL COLE, b. at Sharon, 10 Sep 1751 daughter of Caleb and Anne (St. John) Cole.

---

348 Bartley, "Watertown, Massachusetts, Marriages, Deaths, and Other Events, 1797-1837," NEHGR, volume 165, 2011, p 202

349 Abbott, *Descendants of George Abbott of Rowley*, pp 88-93; please refer to this source for a lengthy biography.

350 *New York, Dutchess County Wills, 1751-1903; Index, 1790-1905, Wills, Vol Aa, A, 1751-1796, pp 50-51*

viii Son, b. and d. 7 Mar 1740

126) HANNAH ABBOTT (*Jemima Johnson Abbot⁴, Mary Holt Johnson², Nicholas¹*), b. at Sudbury, Jul 1710 daughter of John and Jemima (Johnson) Abbot; m. at Watertown, 6 May 1729, JOHN CADY, b. at Old Groton, CT, 9 Aug 1699 son of John and Elizabeth (-) Cady.

John and Hannah resided in Tolland where their seven children were born.

i JOHN CADY, b. 29 Jun 1730; d. 25 Oct 1737.

567) ii HANNAH CADY, b. at Tolland, 24 Jun 1732; d. at Chesterfield, NH, 21 Jun 1803; m. Nov 1753, WILLIAM SHURTLEFF, b. at Plympton, MA, 7 Apr 1730 son of John and Sarah (Lucas) Shurtleff; William d. at Chesterfield, 25 Dec 1801.

iii Son b. and d. 22 May 1734

568) iv ELIZABETH CADY, b. at Tolland, 6 Jun 1736; d. at Columbia, CT, 5 Sep 1813; m. 30 Aug 1770, SOLOMON DEWEY, b. at Lebanon, 29 Apr 1724 son of Josiah and Sarah (Hutchinson) Dewey; Solomon d. at Columbia, CT, 2 May 1819. Solomon was first married to Anna Downer.

v JOHN CADY, b. an d. 31 Jan 1739/40

569) vi NAHUM CADY, b. at Tolland, 14 Mar 1743; d. at East Windsor, 14 Oct 1834; m. Jan 1771, DEBORAH FITCH, b. about 1752 likely the daughter of Elisha and Priscilla (Patten) Fitch; Deborah d. at South Windsor, 17 Apr 1826.

570) vii AMOS CADY, b. at Tolland, 3 Sep 1747; d. at Vernon, CT, 5 Aug 1843; m. 1st 16 Jul 1771, HANNAH KINGSBURY, b. at Tolland, 5 Apr 1752 daughter of Simon and Deliverance (Cady) Kingsbury;[351] Hannah d. 7 Nov 1786. Amos m. 2nd 10 Dec 1789, ESTHER TUTHILL, b. in Maryland, about 1757 daughter of Moses and Martha (Edwards) Tuthill; Esther d. at Vernon, 27 Jan 1857.

127) ANNIS JOHNSON (*Josiah Johnson³, Mary Holt Johnson², Nicholas¹*), b. at Andover, 29 Aug 1712 daughter of Josiah and Annis (Chandler) Johnson; d. at Templeton, MA, 31 Jul 1792; m. at Lancaster, 19 Nov 1728, JOSHUA CHURCH, b. at Watertown, 4 Mar 1708/9 son of Isaac and Mary (Hitchin) Church; Joshua d. at Watertown, 1 Apr 1766.

Annis and Joshua seem to have struggled financially and were "warned out" of Templeton along with their children Silas and Huldah on 8 May 1764.[352] They seemed to have stayed there, however, as Joshua died there in 1766. Joshua did not leave a will and widow Annis was administratrix of the estate on 13 May 1766. An inventory taken 27 May 1767 totaled £45.10. Accounting was made 18 April 1768 and after payments of debts of the estate, Annis had a total of £11.16.1 left in her hands.[353]

Annis and Joshua were parents of eleven children, most of the births recorded at both Harvard and Lancaster.

i JOSEPH CHURCH, b. 22 Jul 1729

571) ii ANNIS CHURCH, b. at Lancaster, 6 Jul 1731; d. at Sterling, 6 Apr 1807; m. at Harvard, 16 Nov 1749, CALEB WHITNEY, b. at Lancaster, 4 Oct 1729 son of Jonathan and Alice (Willard) Whitney; Caleb d. at Sterling, 28 Mar 1822.

iii MARY CHURCH, b. at Harvard, 1 Jan 1733

iv VASHTI CHURCH, b. at Harvard, 2 Oct 1736

572) v PRUDENCE CHURCH, b. at Lancaster, 5 Apr 1739; m. at Harvard, 19 Oct 1758, EBENEZER KNIGHT, b. at Lancaster, 12 Jan 1730/1 son of Amos and Elizabeth (Kendall) Knight; Ebenezer d. at Lancaster, 1776 (probate 5 Apr 1776).

573) vi CALEB CHURCH, b. at Lancaster, 3 Jun 1741; m. 1st at Harvard, 11 May 1762, TAMER WARNER, b. at Harvard, 3 Dec 1738 daughter of Nathan and Nathan (Goodenough) Warner; Tamer d. at Harvard, 22 Feb 1763. Caleb m. 2nd, at Bolton, 11 Jul 1764, ELIZABETH WALKER.

574) vii JOSHUA CHURCH, b. at Lancaster, 6 Apr 1743; d. at Chester, VT, about 1829; m. at Lancaster, 21 Feb 1765, KEZIAH GOSS.

---

[351] The 1793 will of Simon Kingsbury includes a bequest to the heirs of daughter Hannah Cady deceased.

[352] *Mayflower Families Fifth Generation Descendants, 1700-1880*. (Online database: *AmericanAncestors.org*, New England Historic Genealogical Society, 2017). From *Mayflower Families Through Five Generations: Descendants of the Pilgrims who landed at Plymouth, Mass., December 1620*. Plymouth, MA: General Society of Mayflower Descendants, 1975-2015. Descendants of Richard Warren, volume 18, part 2, p 309

[353] *Worcester County, MA: Probate File Papers, 1731-1881.* Online database. AmericanAncestors.org. New England Historic Genealogical Society, 2015. Case 11799

viii SILAS CHURCH, b. 18 Jun 1745; died young

575) ix OLIVE CHURCH, baptized at Harvard, 10 Apr 1748; d. at Templeton, 2 Jul 1822; m. at Templeton, 29 Nov 1764, JOSHUA WRIGHT, b. about 1737 (age 74 at death); Joshua d. at Templeton, 27 Nov 1811.

576) x SILAS CHURCH, b. at Harvard, 23 Oct 1751; d. at Templeton, 27 Oct 1845; m. at Lancaster, 25 Nov 1771, MARY OSGOOD, b. at Lancaster, 23 Apr 1751 daughter of Jonathan and Asenath (Sawyer) Osgood; Mary d. at Templeton, 16 Feb 1817.

577) xi HULDAH CHURCH, b. at Harvard, 20 Apr 1754; m. at Templeton, 20 Oct 1769, JOSEPH OSGOOD, b. at Lancaster, 18 Oct 1742 son of Jonathan and Asenath (Sawyer) Osgood; Joseph d. at Canaan, ME, 29 May 1822.

128) DAVID JOHNSON (*Josiah Johnson[3], Mary Holt Johnson[2], Nicholas[1]*), b. at Andover, 20 Aug 1715 son of Josiah and Annis (Chandler) Johnson; d. of consumption, at Leominster, 10 Nov 1799; m. 1st at Lancaster, 22 Feb 1738/9, MARY WARNER, b. at Lancaster, 1716 daughter of John Warner; Mary d. at Leominster about 1795. David m. 2nd at Leominster, 5 Nov 1796, PRUDENCE DIVOL, b. at Lancaster, 24 Jan 1756 daughter of Ephraim and Elizabeth (Woods) Divol.

David and Mary settled in Leominster soon after their marriage having been first in Lancaster. David purchased 80 acres of land in Lancaster on 6 March 1737/8 with an additional purchase from Ebenezer Wilder on 27 October 1739. On 10 May 1786, David Johnson of Leominster conveyed a tract of land to Luke Johnson for the payment of £60. On 5 March 1794, a second parcel was sold to Luke for £55.[354]

In his will written 30 July 1798 (probate 19 November 1799), David Johnson states that wife Prudence should receive whatever is agreeable to her according to the marriage contract dated 8 February 1797 and several household items listed. Son Josiah receives his two best suits and two best hats, tools including shoemaker tools, and one-fifth part of the estate that is not otherwise disposed of. Son Luke receives tools and household items. Son David receives one of the best feather beds, one of the best blue quilts, and listed clothing, tools, and household items including the ivory-headed cane. David also receives one-fifth part of the estate. Daughter Lucy now the wife of Henry Sweetser receives pewter items, bed and bedding, and one-fifth part of the estate. Daughter Elizabeth now the wife of Samuel Evans receives pewter, bed and bedding, and one-fifth of the estate. Granddaughter Annice wife of Nathaniel Low, Jr. receives the same bequest as Elizabeth and Lucy. Asa Johnson, gentleman of Leominster, was named executor for which he should receive reasonable compensation.[355]

David and Mary were parents of eight children.

578) i LUCY JOHNSON, b. at Lancaster, 21 Oct 1739; d. at Wendell, 16 Feb 1833; m. at Leominster, 5 Oct 1763, HENRY SWEETSER, b. at Malden, 25 Mar 1738 son of Phillips and Mary (Green) Sweetser; Henry d. at Wendell, 18 Jun 1827.

579) ii ELIZABETH JOHNSON, b. at Leominster, 5 Mar 1744; d. at Dunbarton, NH, 1818; m. at Leominster, 29 Sep 1766, SAMUEL EVANS, b. at Woburn, 1742 son of Andrew and Mary (Richardson) Evans; Samuel d. at Leominster, 9 Dec 1811.

580) iii JOSIAH JOHNSON, b. at Leominster, 7 Mar 1746; d. at Buckland, 21 Feb 1827; m. 1774, MARTHA TAYLOR, b. 21 Dec 1756 daughter of Orthniel and Martha (Arms) Taylor; Martha d. 27 Oct 1825.

581) iv ANNIS JOHNSON, b. at Leominster, 28 Mar 1750; d. at Leominster, 5 Apr 1777; m. at Leominster, 17 Jan 1771, DAVID KENDALL, b. at Leominster, 5 Dec 1746 son of Amos and Mary (Hart) Kendall; David d. at Leominster, 15 Sep 1825. David married second Prudence.

v EUNICE JOHNSON, baptized at Leominster, 26 Jan 1752; likely died young.

vi DAVID JOHNSON, baptized at Leominster, 18 Mar 1753; died young.

582) vii LUKE JOHNSON, b. at Leominster, 26 Aug 1755; d. at Leominster, 26 Feb 1828; m. 1st 26 Nov 1789, SARAH BOWERS ROGERS, b. at Leominster, 6 Jun 1762 daughter of John and Relief (Prentice) Rogers; Sarah d. 2 Jul 1794. Luke m. 2nd 5 Mar 1796, BEULAH LELAND, b. at Holliston, 17 May 1754 daughter of Asaph and Beulah (Littlefield) Leland; Beulah d. at Leominster, 16 Sep 1831.

583) viii DAVID JOHNSON, b. at Leominster, 8 Apr 1758; d. at Sempronius, NY, 22 Jun 1840; m. PRUDENCE COLBURN, b. at Buckland, 13 Nov 1765 daughter of Ebenezer and Prudence (Carter) Colburn; Prudence d. 12 Feb 1849.

129) MARY JOHNSON (*Josiah Johnson[3], Mary Holt Johnson[2], Nicholas[1]*), b. at Andover, 10 Nov 1719 daughter of Josiah and Annis (Chandler) Johnson; d. at Westmoreland, NH, 7 Apr 1793; m. at Lancaster, Oct 1741, JONATHAN KNIGHT, b. at

---

[354] Massachusetts Land Records, Worcester County, 28:531; 28:533; 99:547; 120:475

[355] *Worcester County, MA: Probate File Papers, 1731-1881.* Online database. AmericanAncestors.org. New England Historic Genealogical Society, 2015. Case 33331

Woburn, 19 Sep 1722 son of Amos and Elizabeth (Kendall) Knight; Jonathan d. at Westmoreland, 14 Jan 1809. Jonathan married second Anna Dean on 7 Nov 1793.

Jonathan Knight was a physician. Mary and Jonathan had their children in Lancaster, and they relocated to Westmoreland in their middle-age, admitted to the church in Westmoreland in 1779.[356]

Jonathan Knight did not leave a will and his estate entered probate 18 January 1809 with Jonathan Knight as administrator. The estate was valued at $22.70.[357]

Mary Johnson and Jonathan Knight were parents of eight children born at Lancaster.

i DAMARIS KNIGHT, b. at Lancaster, 10 Oct 1742; m. at Groton, MA, 10 Mar 1766, PAUL DICKENSON, b. at Rowley, 14 May 1742 son of James and Sarah (Stickney) Dickenson. Damaris was dismissed from the church at Lancaster to the Church of Christ at Pepperell (undated but seems around 1771). They were perhaps living in Harvard in 1790 with Paul head of household and one female in the home. No records for children were located.

ii MARY KNIGHT, b. 21 Apr 1744; d. 5 Feb 1747.

584) iii MARY KNIGHT, b. at Lancaster, 1 Apr 1748; m. at Lancaster, 18 Sep 1766, WILLIAM KENDALL *possibly* the son of Jonathan and Admonition (Tucker) Kendall; William d. after 1822 when he was living in Westmoreland.

585) iv ANNIS KNIGHT, baptized at Lancaster, 24 Mar 1751; d. at Canton, PA, 14 Sep 1833; m. 29 May 1770, JOSEPH BROWN, b. at Lancaster, MA, 5 Jul 1746 son of Josiah and Prudence (Prentice) Brown.

586) v RUTH KNIGHT, b. at Lancaster, 18 Jan 1753; d. at Chester, VT, 6 Aug 1826; m. at Leominster, 15 May 1773, JOSEPH WHITMORE, b. at Leominster, 6 Jun 1749 son of Joseph and Mary (Marion) Whitmore;[358] Joseph d. at Chester, VT, 30 Aug 1830.

587) vi ELIZABETH KNIGHT, b. at Lancaster, 10 Apr 1756; d. 1801; m. 30 May 1775, EPHRAIM KENDALL, b. at Lancaster, 16 Feb 1756 son of Jonathan and Admonition (Tucker) Kendall, Ephraim d. at Sandy Creek, NY, 1842. Ephraim m. 2nd Experience Coleman.

588) vii SIBBEL KNIGHT, b. at Lancaster, 22 Aug 1759; m. at Lancaster, 16 Jul 1776, HENRY WILLARD FARMER, b. at Worcester, 7 Feb 1753 son of William and Ruth (Willard) Farmer; Henry d. at Herkimer, NY, about 1814 (probate 8 Jan 1814)

589) viii JONATHAN KNIGHT, b. at Lancaster, 12 Jan 1761; d. at Piermont, NH, 15 Dec 1836; m. 1st OBEDIENCE ROOT, b. 1755; Obedience d. 12 Feb 1789. Jonathan m. 2nd, ELIZABETH DUDLEY, b. at Groton, MA, 31 Oct 1763 daughter of John and Sybil (Russell) Dudley; Elizabeth d. at Westmoreland, NH, 29 Apr 1866.

130) ISAAC JOHNSON (*Josiah Johnson³, Mary Holt Johnson², Nicholas¹*), b. at Andover, 17 Jul 1724 son of Josiah and Annis (Chandler) Johnson; m. 1st a Leominster, 2 Jul 1746, LYDIA PIERCE,[359] b. about 1729; Lydia d. at Walpole, NH, about 1779. Isaac m. 2nd at Walpole, 26 Jul 1780, ELIZABETH DEAN.

Isaac and his family were in several locations and births and baptisms of the children are recorded at Leominster, Montague, and New Salem. Those baptisms recorded at New Salem indicate they were living at what was then known as Erving's Grant. The family then relocated to Walpole, New Hampshire where they were by 1769. Several deeds involving Isaac and his sons are recorded in Cheshire County. Marriages of six of the children are recorded in Walpole and Isaac's second marriage is also at Walpole. Isaac's brother Josiah was in Walpole for a time. The last record of Isaac in Walpole is in 1786 when he had two property transactions with his son David Johnson.[360] Some of the children moved on the Vermont. The date or place of Isaac's death is not known. In June 1805, Elizabeth wife of Isaac Johnson was dismissed from the church at Walpole and recommended to the church at Grafton.[361]

One history of Walpole (*Walpole As It Was and As It Is*) notes that Isaac Johnson had a large farm there. He tended to be "overly joyful" in his use of alcohol and on 18 November 1769, James Bundy complained of Isaac's intemperance.[362]

---

[356] Westmoreland Historical Committee, *History of Westmoreland*, p 476

[357] *New Hampshire. Probate Court (Cheshire County);* Probate Place: *Cheshire, New Hampshire, Estate Files, K26-K78, 1805-1821, Case 34*

[358] Stearns, *History of Ashburnham*, p 954

[359] There is disagreement about the identity of Isaac's wife Lydia, some suggesting she is Lydia Deane. The town records clearly give her name as Lydia Pearce (Leominster, "A Copy of the First Volume of the Records of the Town of Leominster Commencing with the First Town Meeting July 9th 1740 and Ending December 27th 1779", p 529); accessed through ancestry.com. On the other hand, Massachusetts Compile Marriages 1633-1850 gives the name Lydia Deane.

[360] New Hampshire, Cheshire County Deeds, 21:313 and 5:305; FHL Film # 007919204

[361] New Hampshire, Town Clerk Vital and Town Records, Cheshire County, Walpole, Town Records 1814-1850, volume 3, p 432; image 218 of 287; accessed through familysearch.org

[362] Aldrich, *Walpole As It Was*, p 132 and p 296

There are records for nine children of Isaac and Lydia and those are reported here. There are perhaps one or two other children, but none that were clearly identified as belonging to this family.

Isaac and Lydia were parents of nine children.

590) i ISAAC JOHNSON, b. at Leominster, 9 Nov 1746; m. at Walpole, NH, 1771, MARY MESSER, b. at Willington, 9 Nov 1748 daughter and Timothy and Hannah (Marble) Messer.[363]

591) ii SARAH JOHNSON, b. at Leominster, 18 Apr 1749; d. at Walpole, NH, 26 Dec 1787; m. about 1769, as his second wife, ISAAC BUNDY, b. at Preston, CT, 9 Jun 1745 son of James and Sarah (Jameson) Bundy; Isaac d. at Columbia, NH, 1825. Isaac was married first to Mehitable Brown and married third the widow Amelia Fowler.

592) iii LYDIA JOHNSON, b. at Leominster, 22 Oct 1751; d. at Westminster, VT, 11 Feb 1787; m. at Walpole, NH, 21 Dec 1771, EPHRAIM RANNEY, b. at Middletown, CT, 27 Oct 1749 son of Ephraim and Silence (Wilcox) Ranney; Ephraim d. at Westminster, 30 Jul 1835. Ephraim married second Rhoda Harlow.

iv SUSANNAH JOHNSON, b. at Leominster, 25 May 1754; nothing further known.

593) v DAVID JOHNSON, b. at Montague, MA, 16 Feb 1757; d. at Saratoga, NY, 22 Feb 1839; m. at Walpole, NH, 14 Nov 1783, MARY JOINER likely the daughter of William and Hannah (Bowker) Joiner who were in Walpole in the 1770's; Mary d. at Day Center, NY, 5 Jan 1844.

vi LUCRETIA JOHNSON, baptized as New Salem, 18 Nov 1759; died young.

594) vii LUCRETIA JOHNSON, baptized at New Salem, 13 Jun 1762; d. at Cambridge, VT, 9 Mar 1841; m. at Walpole, NH, 20 Aug 1780, THOMAS PARKER, b. at Salem, NH, 20 Mar 1754 son of Samuel and Sarah (Messer) Parker; Thomas d. at Cambridge, VT, 29 Jun 1829.

595) viii ELISHA JOHNSON, baptized at Ervings Grant, MA, 18 Jun 1764; d. at Shrewsbury, VT, 15 Sep 1845; m. at Walpole, NH, 5 Nov 1789, OLIVE ASHLEY, b. 1765 likely the daughter of Martin and Sarah (Root) Ashley; Olive d. at Shrewsbury, 4 Apr 1813. Elisha m. 2nd at Shrewsbury, ELIZABETH KILBURN (widow of Willard Colburn), b. at Walpole, 3 Feb 1770 daughter of John and Content (Carpenter) Kilburn; Elizabeth d. at Shrewsbury, 4 Aug 1826. Elisha m. 3rd BETSEY who has not been identified.

596) ix ANNIS JOHNSON, b. at Ervings Grant, MA, 27 Oct 1766; d. at Putney, VT, 20 May 1851; m. 26 Oct 1788, THEOPHILUS CRAWFORD, b. at Union, CT, 25 Apr 1764 son of James and Grace (Carpenter) Crawford; Theophilus d. at Putney, 10 Jan 1856.

131) JOSIAH JOHNSON (*Josiah Johnson³, Mary Holt Johnson², Nicholas¹*), b. at Lancaster, 5 Jun 1726 son of Josiah and Annis (Chandler) Johnson; m. at Westford, 7 Mar 1750, SARAH HUNT, b. at Billerica, 23 Dec 1725 daughter of Joseph and Jemima (Russell) Hunt.

There are records for births of five children of Josiah and Sarah, but nothing further is known.

i JOSIAH JOHNSON, b. at Leominster, 20 Jan 1752

ii JEMIMA JOHNSON, b at Montague, 2 May 1757

iii JOSEPH JOHNSON, b. at Montague, 21 Jan 1761

iv JEREMIAH JOHNSON, b. at Montague, 16 Sep 1763

v SARAH JOHNSON, b. at Montague, 24 Apr 1766

Grandchildren of Samuel Holt and Sarah Allen

132) JOHN HOLT (*John³, Samuel², Nicholas¹*), baptized at Andover, May 1713 son of John and Mehitable (Wilson) Holt; d. at Andover, 10 May 1794;[364] m. at Andover, 22 Jan 1746/7, DEBORAH STEVENS, b. about 1721 perhaps the daughter of John and Elizabeth (Chandler) Stevens; Deborah d. at Andover, 24 Jan 1809. [Genealogies, such as Durrie's Holt genealogy, report John had a first marriage to Rachel Fletcher of Chelmsford, but no record of the marriage or any children from the marriage was found. At least two of the children attributed in genealogies to that marriage were the children of John Holt's nephew John

[363] Frizzell, *A History of Walpole, New Hampshire*, volume 2, p 164

[364] Genealogies report his dying when he fell from a wagon while going to Wilton, but the town records report he died at Andover of old age. John [old age. CR2], May 10, 1794. [a. 81 y. CR2]

Holt and his wife Rachel Farnum. Other children attributed to that marriage were children of John Holt and Mary Lewis in the records.]

The births of four children are recorded at Andover for John Holt and Deborah Stevens.

i DEBORAH HOLT, b. 17 Nov 1747; d. 23 Feb 1769.

ii JOHN HOLT, b. at Andover, 29 Apr 1749; nothing further known. He may be the John who died at Andover 21 Oct 1815.

597) iii PETER HOLT, b. at Andover, 30 Sep 1752; d. at Andover, 9 Jan 1830; m. 28 Dec 1776, HEPHZIBAH STEVENS (*Sarah Gray Stevens⁴, Edward Gray³, Hannah Holt Gray², Nicholas¹*), b. at Andover, 15 Jan 1757 daughter of Thomas and Sarah (Gray) Stevens.

iv PHEBE HOLT, b. at Andover, 3 Feb 1757; d. at Andover, 3 Aug 1777.

133) ELIZABETH HOLT (*John³, Samuel², Nicholas¹*), baptized at Andover, 8 Jun 1718 daughter of John and Mehitable (Wilson) Holt; d. at Wilton, NH, 21 Mar 1776; m. at Andover, 18 Nov 1744, her second cousin, TIMOTHY HOLT (*Nicholas³, Nicholas², Nicholas¹*), b. at Andover, 17 Jan 1720/1 son of Nicholas and Dorcas (Abbott) Holt; Timothy d. at Wilton, Nov 1801.

Timothy Holt and Elizabeth Holt had four children whose births are recorded at Andover. The family relocated to Wilton.

541) i TIMOTHY HOLT, b. 19 May 1746; d. at Weston, VT, 3 May 1836; m. at Andover, 8 Apr 1773, his third cousin, HANNAH JOHNSON (*Obadiah Johnson⁴, James Johnson³, Mary Holt Johnson², Nicholas¹*), b. at Andover, 8 Feb 1753 daughter of Obadiah and Dorothy (Ballard) Johnson.[365]

598) ii ELIZABETH HOLT, b. 25 Nov 1748; m. 1 Jun 1769, ISAAC FRYE, b. at Andover, 6 Feb 1748 son of Abiel and Abigail (Emery) Frye; Isaac d. at Wilton, NH, 3 Nov 1791.

599) iii HANNAH HOLT, b. 18 Jan 1754; d. at Brookline, VT, Apr 1833; m. about 1774, as his second wife, RICHARD WHITNEY, b. at Oxford, MA, 22 Apr 1743 son of Israel and Hannah (Blodgett) Whitney Richard d. at Brookline, 20 Apr 1816. Richard was first married to Sarah Butterfield who died in 1773.

600) iv SARAH HOLT, b. at Andover, 31 May 1757; m. at Wilton, 30 Mar 1780, her second cousin once removed, WILLIAM PIERCE (*William Pierce⁵, Martha Holt Pierce⁴, Hannah Farnum Holt³, Elizabeth Holt Farnum², Nicholas¹*), b. at Ashford, CT, 28 Jun 1759 son of William and Hannah (-) Pierce of Wilton, NH.[366][367]

134) JOSHUA HOLT (*John³, Samuel², Nicholas¹*), b. at Andover, 11 Jun 1724 son of John and Mehitable (Wilson) Holt; m. 4 Feb 1748/9, RUTH BURNAP, b. at Reading, 18 Dec 1727 daughter of Samuel and Ruth (Huse) Burnap.[368]

Joshua and Ruth resided in Andover, and it is possible that they left Andover later in life but that is not clear and at least four of their children remained in Andover. Ruth was admitted to South Church in Andover on 31 March 1751 on profession of faith. Date of removal is not given but noted as "probably by death."[369]

Joshua and Ruth were parents of ten children born at Andover.

i SAMUEL HOLT, baptized 18 May 1750; likely died young.

601) ii ISAAC HOLT, b. at Andover, 15 May 1752; d. at Andover, 11 Oct 1821; m. at Andover, 8 Jan 1778, HANNAH STEVENS, b. at Andover, 22 May 1754 daughter of Samuel and Hannah (Shattuck) Stevens; Hannah d. at Andover, 15 Jun 1814.

iii ISRAEL HOLT, baptized 19 May 1754; d, at Greenfield, NH, 1819; m. 18 Mar 1783, ABIGAIL BAILEY. No children were located for this couple.

iv RUTH HOLT, baptized 25 Jul 1756; d. 29 Jun 1757.

v RUTH HOLT, b. at Andover, 11 May 1758; Ruth d. at Andover, 17 Aug 1835. Ruth did not marry.

vi UZZIEL HOLT, baptized 1 Mar 1761; d. 19 Feb 1762.

---

365 There are two Timothy Holts of similar age, one who married Hannah Johnson and one who married Ede McIntire. It is generally accepted in published genealogies that this Timothy married Hannah Johnson.

366 Livermore, *History of Wilton*, p 470

367 Littlefield, *Genealogies of the Early Settlers of Weston*

368 Belknap, *The Burnap Genealogy*, p 78

369 South Church, *Historical Manual*, p 134

602) vii HANNAH HOLT, b. at Andover, 17 Mar 1764; d. at Salem by 1792; m. 4 Jan 1781, WILLIAM PHELPS, b. 1747 perhaps the son of Jonathan and Judith (Cox) Phelps;[370] William d. at Salem, 8 Sep 1812. William second married Sally Punchard on 29 Dec 1792.

603) viii UZZIEL HOLT, b. 12 Apr 1766; d. at Sharon, VT, after 1840; m. by 1801, SARAH who may be SARAH STILES, b. at Lyndeborough, 24 Mar 1762 daughter of Moses and Sarah (-) Stiles. There is a record of one child for Uzziel and Sarah Holt, Jacob H. Holt born at Lyndeborough in 1801. Uzziel served in the Vermont militia during the War of 1812 as a private and suffered a broken leg. He ultimately received a pension. Uzziel Holt, age 75 and a veteran, was living in Sharon, VT in 1840. It is known from the 1811 will of Moses Stiles that his daughter Sarah married a Holt and no other marriage was found for her. It is speculation at this point that Uzziel is the Holt that she married.

ix MICAH HOLT, b. at Andover, 31 Mar 1768; d. at Andover, 5 Sep 1840; m. at Boston, 15 Apr 1798, RACHEL COOK. There is a record for one child of Micah and Rachel, Emily Burnap Holt born at Boston on 19 Jul 1800 and died at Cambridge on 24 Mar 1872. Emily did not marry.

x TABITHA HOLT, b. 28 Feb 1770; d. at Andover, 17 Mar 1849. Tabitha did not marry.

135) DANIEL HOLT (*John*[3], *Samuel*[2], *Nicholas*[1]), b. at Andover, 1726 son of John and Mehitable (Wilson) Holt; d. at Townsend, 1798 (probate 17 Nov 1798); m. about 1748, his second cousin, MEHITABLE HOLT (*Humphrey*[3], *Henry*[2], *Nicholas*[1]), baptized at Andover, 7 Feb 1725 daughter of Humphrey and Abigail (Fifield) Holt; Mehitable d. at Townsend, after 1810.

Soon after marrying, Mehitable and Daniel were in Lunenburg where six children were born.[371] They were members of the church there and were discharged to the church in Townsend 29 March 1770.[372] In is not known when Mehitable died, but she was listed as head of household in Townsend in the 1810 census with household of two females over age 45. The other woman in the home is assumed to be daughter Sybil who did not marry.

Daniel Holt did not leave a will and his estate was in probate by 17 November 1798 when there were directions to the committee to complete an inventory and to set-off the dower to widow Mehitable., that task completed 5 April 1799.[373]

i ELIZABETH HOLT, b. at Lunenburg, 7 Nov 1749; m. at Townsend, 26 Dec 1777, as his second wife, JACOB BALDWIN, b. about 1737. Jacob was first married to Elizabeth Lewes who died in 1776. There are no children known for Elizabeth Holt and Jacob Baldwin.

604) ii MEHITABLE HOLT, b. at Lunenburg, 20 Sep 1751; d. at Amherst, NH, 1827; m. about 1778, BENJAMIN STEARNS, b. at Lunenburg, 3 Dec 1754 son of Benjamin and Ann (Taylor) Stearns; Benjamin d. at Amherst, NH, 1808.

605) iii ABIGAIL HOLT, b. at Lunenburg, 9 Mar 1753; m. at Townsend, 28 Oct 1776, WILLIAM BLOOD, b. at Pepperell, 14 Sep 1748 son of William and Lucy (Fletcher) Blood.

606) iv DANIEL HOLT, b. at Lunenburg, 26 Mar 1756; d. at Townsend, 31 Aug 1798; m. at Townsend, 13 Dec 1781, his third cousin once removed, MARY BUTTERFIELD, b. at Townsend, 17 Jan 1756 daughter of Eleazer and Mary (Wright) Butterfield; Mary d. at Lunenburg, 29 Jun 1849. Mary second married, at Townsend, 28 Apr 1803, SILAS CARLY who d. at Townsend in 1805.

v SYBIL HOLT, b. at Lunenburg, 6 Apr 1758; d. likely after 1810 at Townsend. Sybil did not marry.

607) vi SARAH HOLT, b. at Lunenburg, 2 Sep 1762; d. at Townsend, 2 May 1837; m. at Townsend, Dec 1783, JONATHAN BAILEY, b. at Bradford, MA, 27 Aug 1758 son of Nathaniel and Mary (Spofford) Bailey; Jonathan d. at Townsend, 27 Dec 1844.[374]

Grandchildren of Henry Holt and Sarah Ballard

136) OLIVER HOLT (*Oliver*[3], *Henry*[2], *Nicholas*[1]), b. at Andover, 26 Dec 1698 son of Oliver and Hannah (Russell) Holt; d. of smallpox, at Andover, 11 Nov 1760; m. 5 Jul 1722, SUSANNAH WRIGHT, b. at Andover, 24 Jul 1700 daughter of John and Mary (Wardwell) Wright; Susannah d. of smallpox, 1 Dec 1760.

---

[370] Phelps, *The Phelps Family of America*, volume 2, p 1593

[371] The birth of the youngest child is recorded at Lunenburg and Townsend although the family were still with the church in Lunenburg at that time.

[372] Cunningham, *Cunningham's History of the Town of Lunenburg*

[373] *Middlesex County, MA: Probate File Papers, 1648-1871.*Online database. *AmericanAncestors.org.* New England Historic Genealogical Society, 2014. Case 11773

[374] Jona Bailey; Male; Widower; Age 86; Laborer; Died Dec 27 1844; Buried in Townsend; Old Age; (A Pauper).

Oliver was a blacksmith in Andover. He and Susannah died in a smallpox epidemic.

In his will written 2 May 1760 (probate 9 March 1761), Oliver Holt bequeaths to beloved wife Susannah the use of the east end of the house and a lengthy list of provisions, and the household goods. Eldest son Nathaniel receives all the lands and buildings. Second son Oliver receives £13.6.8. Only surviving daughter Bula receives £6.13.4 when she arrives at age twenty-one or marries. Nathaniel was named executor. Real estate was valued at £190.8.0.[375]

Oliver and Susannah were parents of eight children born at Andover.

i OLIVER HOLT, b. 1 Jan 1723; d. 15 Apr 1738.

608) ii NATHANIEL HOLT, b. at Andover, 23 Nov 1725; d. at Andover, Feb 1806; m. 1 Aug 1751, ELIZABETH STEVENS, b. at Andover, 21 Oct 1730 daughter of John and Elizabeth (Chandler) Stevens; Elizabeth d. Dec 1807.

iii HANNAH HOLT, b. at Andover, 29 Aug 1728; d. at Boxford, about 1756; m. 16 Nov 1752, JOHN STILES, b. at Boxford, 17 Mar 1724/5 son of John and Eleanor (Pearl) Stiles. John married second Hannah Deney on 14 Mar 1757. There are no known children of Hannah and John.

iv SUSANNAH HOLT, b. 6 Apr 1731; d. 16 Jan 1747/8.

v URIAH HOLT, b. 1 Dec 1733; he was not living in 1760.

vi ASA HOLT, b. 4 Aug 1736; d. 25 Jan 1737/8.

609) vii OLIVER HOLT, b. at Andover, 24 Jan 1739/40; m. at Andover, 8 Oct 1761, EUNICE RAYMOND, b. at Beverly, 30 Apr 1744 daughter of Boanerges and Jemima (Meacham) Raymond. Oliver and Eunice lived in Wilton, NH.

610) viii BEULAH HOLT, b. at Andover, 12 Apr 1744; m. at Andover, 26 Apr 1770, her third cousin, JOHN GRAY (*Edward Gray^4, Edward Gray^3, Hannah Holt Gray^2, Nicholas^1*), b. at Andover, 26 Dec 1745 son of Edward and Sarah (-) Gray.

137) URIAH HOLT (*Oliver^3, Henry^2, Nicholas^1*), b. at Andover, 25 Jun 1701 son of Oliver and Hannah (Russell) Holt; d. at Lancaster, MA, 24 Aug 1741; m. 28 Sep 1725, SARAH WRIGHT, b. at Andover, 20 Mar 1696 daughter of Walter and Elizabeth (Peters) Wright. Sarah m. 2nd, at Harvard, 24 Jun 1747, Jonathan Cole (1696-1780).

Uriah Holt was a blacksmith in Lancaster. After Uriah's early death, Sarah and her children relocated to Harvard where the children married and where Sarah remarried.

Uriah Holt did not leave a will and his estate entered probate 7 September 1741 with Sarah as administratrix.[376] His personal estate including blacksmith tools and materials was appraised at £338.

Uriah and Sarah were parents of seven children born at Lancaster.

i URIAH HOLT, b. 10 May 1726; died young.

611) ii SARAH HOLT, b. at Lancaster, 18 Mar 1727; d. at Harvard, 29 Oct 1769; m. at Harvard, 27 Nov 1746, JONATHAN WHITNEY, b. 1724 son of Jonathan and Alice (Willard) Whitney;[377] Jonathan d. at Harvard, 20 Jan 1770.

612) iii URIAH HOLT, b. at Lancaster, 7 Feb 1729; d. at Woodstock, VT, 1812; m. at Harvard, 20 Feb 1752, ANNESS WILLARD, b. at Harvard, 20 Jun 1730 daughter of Henry and Abigail (Fairbanks) Willard; Anness d. at Ashburnham, 28 Nov 1779. Uriah m. 2nd, at Ashburnham, 6 Jun 1785, SARAH GOODRIDGE.

iv JOSHUA HOLT, b. 18 May 1733; nothing further known.

v HANNAH HOLT, b. at Lancaster, 6 Oct 1735; m. at Harvard, 22 Feb 1770, as his second wife, WILLIAM FARMER, b. about 1720. William was first married to Ruth Willard. Hannah and William do not seem to have had children.

vi LEMUEL HOLT, b. 10 Feb 1737; nothing further known.

613) vii MARY HOLT, b. at Lancaster, 5 Apr 1740; m. at Harvard, 7 Sep 1764, THOMAS DARBY, b. at Harvard, 22 Sep 1739 son of Simon and Mercy (Wilson) Darby; Thomas d. at Westminster, VT, 7 Dec 1833.[378]

---

[375] *Essex County, MA: Probate File Papers, 1638-1881.*Online database. *AmericanAncestors.org.* New England Historic Genealogical Society, 2014. Case 13681

[376] *Worcester County, MA: Probate File Papers, 1731-1881.* Online database. AmericanAncestors.org. New England Historic Genealogical Society, 2015. Case 30680

[377] Although there is not a birth record for Jonathan, he can be established as the son of Jonathan and Alice through probate records.

[378] Thomas Darby, age 95, born about 1738, died 7 Dec 1833.

138) DAVID HOLT (*Oliver³, Henry², Nicholas¹*), b. at Andover, 5 Jun 1708 son of Oliver and Hannah (Russell) Holt; d. at Andover, 21 Aug 1747; m. 14 Sep 1732, SARAH RUSSELL, b. 5 Apr 1713 daughter of John and Sarah (Chandler) Russell; Sarah d. at Andover, 27 Apr 1781.

David Holt did not leave a will and his estate entered probate 5 October 1747 with widow Sarah as administratrix. Real estate was valued at £158 which included a house and barn with 30 acres and a separate 2-acre parcel.[379]

David Holt and Sarah Russell were parents of six children born at Andover.

614) i SARAH HOLT, b. at Andover, 20 Nov 1733; d. at Andover, 30 Sep 1769; m. 26 May 1757, JAMES BARNARD, b. at Andover, 24 Sep 1727 son of James and Abigail (Wilson) Barnard. James m. 2nd, 11 Mar 1775 widow Mary Barker.

ii DORCAS HOLT, b. 31 Jan 1735/6; d. 8 Sep 1736.

615) iii DORCAS HOLT,[380] baptized at Andover 31 Jul 1737; m. at Andover, 22 Mar 1759, THOMAS PEAVEY, b. at Andover, 14 Mar 1736 son of Peter and Esther (Barker) Peavey.

616) iv DAVID HOLT, b. at Andover, 4 Jul 1740; m. at Andover, 22 Jun 1769, REBECCA OSGOOD, b. at Andover, 6 Feb 1739/40 daughter of Samuel and Dorothy (Wardwell) Osgood; Rebecca d. at Andover, 21 May 1790.

v LOIS HOLT, b. 28 Jun 1743; d. at Andover, 20 Aug 1812. Lois did not marry.

vi EUNICE HOLT, b. 22 May 1747; d. at Andover, 27 Nov 1774. Eunice did not marry.

139) JONATHAN HOLT (*Oliver³, Henry², Nicholas¹*), b. at Andover, 29 Aug 1711 son of Oliver and Hannah (Russell) Holt; d. at Andover, 14 Oct 1791; m. 10 Feb 1734/5, LYDIA BLANCHARD, b. at Andover, 21 Aug 1714 daughter of Thomas and Rose (Holmes) Blanchard; Lydia d. at Andover, 17 Dec 1788.

Jonathan is referred to as Lt. Jonathan Holt on his death record. Jonathan and Lydia were parents of six children born at Andover.

i LYDIA HOLT, b. 7 Mar 1735/6; died young.

617) ii JONATHAN HOLT, b. 29 Sep 1738; d. at Albany, ME, 1810 (probate 1810); m. at Andover, 31 Dec 1761, RUTH KIMBALL, baptized 30 Mar 1739 daughter of Josiah and Elizabeth (Bragg) Kimball;[381] Ruth d. at Albany, ME, 5 Mar 1823.

iii LYDIA HOLT, b. 16 Mar 1739/40; d. 20 Mar 1758.

iv ROSE HOLT, b. 5 Jan 1742; d. at Andover, Mar 1784. Rose did not marry.

v MOSES HOLT, b. at Andover, 19 Jan 1743/4; d. at Portland, ME, 26 Jan 1772;[382] m. 1771, MARY COTTON, b. about 1753 daughter of William and Sarah (Fletcher) Cotton; Mary d. at Portland, 27 Jul 1808. Mary married second Stephen Hall on 4 Jul 1778. Moses received the A.M. degree from Harvard in 1767.[383] He was a preacher for a time, then a teacher and involved in business in Portland. He did not have children.

618) vi HANNAH HOLT, b. at Andover, 19 Dec 1745; d. at Concord, NH, 1 Dec 1818; m. at Andover, 1763, NATHAN BALLARD, b. at Andover, 1 Nov 1744 son of Timothy and Hannah (Chandler) Ballard; Nathan d. at Concord, 14 Jan 1835.

140) JACOB HOLT (*Oliver³, Henry², Nicholas¹*), b. at Andover, 30 Mar 1714 son of Oliver and Hannah (Russell) Holt; d. 25 Dec 1760; m. 1st 29 Dec 1737, MARY OSGOOD, b. at Andover, 1706 daughter of Stephen and Hannah (Blanchard) Osgood; Mary d. 4 Nov 1745. Jacob m. 2nd 25 May 1747, MARGARET DOLLIVER; Margaret d. 22 Dec 1760.

---

379 *Essex County, MA: Probate File Papers, 1638-1881.*Online database. *AmericanAncestors.org.* New England Historic Genealogical Society, 2014. Case 13631

380 Although sources (Durrie's Holt genealogy and Charlotte Helen Abbott's Andover notes) state that Dorcas who married Thomas Peavey was the daughter of Ephraim Holt and Phebe Russell, there is no evidence that Ephraim and Phebe had a daughter Dorcas. The 1759 distribution of the estate of Ephraim Russell has only the following children as heirs: eldest son Ephraim, Phebe Houghton, Bethiah Holt, Asenath Holt, and Mastin Holt. These are also the only children of Ephraim and Phebe for whom there are birth records.

381 Morrison and Sharples, *History of the Kimball Family*, p 113

382 Grave Inscription: Here lies buried the Body of Mr. Moses Holt, who departed this life the 26th January, 1772, aged 28 years

383 Harvard University, *Quinquennial Catalogue,* p 130

Jacob Holt did not leave a will and his estate entered probate 9 March 1761 with son Jacob Holt as administrator. Real estate was valued at £269.10.0 and personal estate at £113.1.9. Debts were £85.13.3. Part of the estate accounting is money for the support of Mary Holt.[384]

Jacob Holt and Mary Osgood were parents of four children born at Andover.

619) i JACOB HOLT, b. at Andover, 29 Mar 1739; d. at Albany, ME, 12 May 1816; m. at Andover, 22 Mar 1764, RHODA ABBOTT, b. at Andover, 22 Jun 1741 daughter of Ephraim and Hannah (Phelps) Abbott; Rhoda d. at Albany, 12 Jan 1821.

620) ii NEHEMIAH HOLT, b. at Andover, 24 Oct 1740; d. at Salem, MA, 1786 (probate 1786); m. at Salem, 21 Jul 1771, ESTHER VARNUM, b. 21 May 1747; Esther d. at Salem, 12 Feb 1822.

iii MARY HOLT, baptized at Andover, 25 Mar 1744

iv MARY HOLT, baptized at Andover, 1 Sep 1745; death unknown. Part of the accounting in father's probate is for payments made for the support of Mary Holt.

Jacob Holt and Margaret Dolliver were parents of four children born at Andover.

621) i ELIZABETH HOLT, b. at Andover, 24 Jan 1747/8; d. at Chelmsford, 8 Aug 1794; m. at Andover, 28 Feb 1771, FRANCIS BOWERS, baptized at Chelmsford, 22 Jul 1744 son of Jonathan and Mary (Grimes) Bowers.

ii DAVID HOLT, b. 13 Jul 1749; d. 18 Dec 1749.

iii DAVID HOLT, b. at Andover, 4 Oct 1751; d. at Peterborough, NH, 24 Apr 1835; m. at Topsfield, 13 Dec 1781, RUTH DWINELL, baptized at Topsfield, 17 Oct 1756 daughter of Jacob and Keziah (Gould) Dwinell;[385] Ruth d. at Peterborough, 24 Jun 1833. No children were identified for David and Ruth.

622) iv TABITHA HOLT, b. at Andover, 19 May 1753; d. at Andover, 23 Sep 1778; m. at Andover, 16 May 1769, her third cousin, ABIEL STEVENS (*Lydia Gray Stevens⁴, Edward Gray³, Hannah Holt Gray², Nicholas¹*), b. at Andover, 24 Mar 1749/50 son of John and Lydia (Gray) Stevens; Abiel d. at Strafford, VT, 1806 (probate 31 Mar 1806). Abiel m. 2nd 7 Jan 1779, his second cousin once removed, ELIZABETH HOLT (*Nathaniel⁵, Oliver⁴, Oliver³, Henry², Nicholas¹*), b. at Andover, 14 Nov 1752 daughter of Nathaniel and Elizabeth (Stevens) Holt.

141) THOMAS HOLT (*Oliver³, Henry², Nicholas¹*), b. at Andover, 23 Aug 1717 son of Oliver and Mary (Huse) Holt; d. at Lancaster, MA, 3 Jul 1791; m. 1st at Lancaster, 21 Apr 1744, SUSANNAH PARKER, baptized at Wakefield, 2 Jun 1723 daughter of Stephen and Elizabeth (Batchelder) Parker;[386] Susannah d. by 1769. Thomas m. 2nd, intention at Lancaster, 17 Feb 1770, DINAH FOWLER (widow of Samuel Corey), b. at Rowley, 16 Jul 1739 daughter of Philip and Abigail (-) Fowler; Dinah d. at Lancaster, 9 Nov 1803.

Thomas Holt and Susannah Parker resided in Lancaster and were parents of seven children.

i LOIS HOLT, b. at Lancaster, 12 Sep 1744; m. 26 Nov 1778, as his second wife, HENRY RICE. Lois and Henry do not seem to have had children. Henry may have first been married to Sarah Boynton.

ii LUCY HOLT, b. at Lancaster, 2 Aug 1746

623) iii THOMAS HOLT, b. at Lancaster, 1 Mar 1749; d. at Bolton, Sep 1808; m. at Bolton, Dec 1770, MARY COREY, b. about 1748; Mary d. at Bolton, 18 Jan 1803. Thomas m. 2nd 20 May 1806, ABIGAIL FLETCHER.

iv DAVID HOLT, b. 22 Feb 1752; died young.

v MARY HOLT, b. 17 Feb 1753

vi SUSANNAH HOLT, b. 8 Aug 1755

vii JABEZ HOLT, b. 10 Feb 1758

Thomas Holt and Dinah Fowler were parents of one child.

---

[384] *Essex County, MA: Probate File Papers, 1638-1881.* Online database. *AmericanAncestors.org.* New England Historic Genealogical Society, 2014. Case 13645

[385] The 1784 will of Jacob Dwinell of Topsfield includes a bequest to his daughter Ruth Holt.

[386] The inventory of the estate of Stephen Parker in 1749 includes a note owed by Thomas Holt for £12.

i DAVID HOLT, b. at Lancaster, 22 Jul 1772

142) MARY HOLT (*Oliver³, Henry², Nicholas¹*), b. at Andover, 29 Jul 1720 daughter of Oliver and Mary (Huse) Holt; m. at Andover, 29 Oct 1745, DANIEL LOVEJOY, b. at Andover, Mar 1710 son of Nathaniel and Dorothy (Hoyt) Lovejoy.

Mary and Daniel were first in Methuen but relocated to Andover where their youngest two children were born. On 20 July 1775 (deed recorded 22 November 1799), Daniel Lovejoy and his wife Mary of Andover conveyed certain tracts of swampland and upland, which had been previously part of the homestead of Capt. Timothy Holt, to son Daniel Lovejoy, Jr. for "true parental love and regard."[387]

Mary and Daniel were parents of eight children.

i ELIZABETH LOVEJOY, b. at Andover, 9 Jun 1747; nothing further known.

624) ii DANIEL LOVEJOY, b. at Methuen, 28 May 1749; d. at Wilton, NH, Apr 1808 (will Mar 1808; probate May 1808); m. at Andover, 25 Jul 1770, ABIGAIL CUMMINS whose parents have not been identified; Abigail was living in 1808.

625) iii MOSES LOVEJOY, b. at Methuen, 9 Sep 1751; d. at Wilton, 19 Mar 1807; m. at Andover, 25 Nov 1773, his third cousin, DORCAS HOLT (*Thomas⁴, Thomas³, Nicholas², Nicholas¹*), b. at Andover, 19 Mar 1753 daughter of Thomas and Dorcas (Holt) Holt.

626) iv JONATHAN LOVEJOY, b. at Methuen, 11 Apr 1754; d. at Milford, 3 Jun 1830; m. at Andover, 31 Jul 1777, TABITHA UPTON, b. at Reading, 26 Jul 1751 daughter of Isaac and Tabitha (-) Upton; Tabitha d. 12 Apr 1824.

v MARY LOVEJOY, b. at Methuen, 3 Oct 1756; nothing further known.

627) vi SARAH LOVEJOY, b. at Methuen, 5 Jun 1759; d. at Temple, NH, 19 Jun 1830; m. at Amherst, NH, 19 Apr 1781, SILAS KEYES, b. at Shrewsbury, 7 Aug 1757 son of John and Abigail (-) Keyes; Silas d. 18 Aug 1840.

628) vii DORCAS LOVEJOY, b. at Methuen, 16 Apr 1762; d. at Andover, VT, 15 Aug 1817; m. at Wilton, 27 Oct 1785, her third cousin once removed, BENJAMIN PIERCE (*William Pierce⁵, Martha Holt Pierce⁴, Hannah Farnum Holt³, Elizabeth Holt Farnum², Nicholas¹*), b. at Wilton, 18 May 1762 son of William and Hannah (-) Pierce; d. at Londonderry, VT, 9 May 1847.

629) viii DOROTHY LOVEJOY, b. at Andover, MA, 26 Sep 1764; d. at Andover, VT, 4 Aug 1807; m. at Wilton, NH, 5 Feb 1793, JACOB SHELDON, b. at Wilton, about 1764 son of Samuel and Sarah (Wellman) Sheldon.

143) WILLIAM HOLT (*Oliver³, Henry², Nicholas¹*), b. at Andover, 1 Apr 1727 son of Oliver and Mary (Huse) Holt; d. at Lyndeborough; m. about 1759, BEULAH who has not been identified.

William Holt was an early settler in Lyndeborough, and his arrival there is not known certainly, but was prior to 1760 when the birth of his son William is recorded there. The History of the Town of Lyndeborough reports that he may have been in that area as early as 1745 and that he took deed for a farm on 9 August 1753.[388]

William and Beulah were parents of five known children, although there may have been others.

630) i WILLIAM HOLT, b. at Lyndeborough, 23 Mar 1760; m. about 1784, BETSEY SPAULDING, b. at Lyndeborough, 18 Nov 1759 daughter of Levi and Anna (Burns) Spaulding.

631) ii OLIVER HOLT, b. at Lyndeborough, about 1761; d. at Lyndeborough, after 1850;[389] m. at Lyndeborough, 31 Dec 1789, JANE KARR, b. 1768; Jane d. at Goshen, 1 Sep 1844.

632) iii BENJAMIN HOLT, b. at Lyndeborough, about 1765; m. at Lyndeborough, 19 Aug 1788, BATHSHEBA BARKER, b. at Wilton, 6 Sep 1769 daughter of Daniel and Bathsheba (Blanchard) Barker.

633) iv MARY HOLT, b. at Lyndeborough, about 1767; m. at Lyndeborough, 9 Aug 1790, her second cousin once removed, MOSES STILES (*Moses Stiles⁵, Phebe Cram Stiles⁴, Sarah Holt Cram³, Henry², Nicholas¹*), b. at Lyndeborough, 6 Jun 1765 son of Moses and Sarah (-) Stiles.

634) v JUDITH HOLT, b. at Lyndeborough, about 1769; d. at Northfield, VT, 28 Sep 1843; m. at Lyndeborough, 12 Nov 1793, her second cousin once removed, ABIEL CRAM (*John Cram⁵, John Cram⁴, Sarah Holt Cram³,*

---

[387] Massachusetts Land Records, Essex County, 165:166; Daniel and Mary appeared to verify the transaction on 7 March 1777.

[388] Donovan, *The History of the Town of Lyndeborough*, p 773

[389] Oliver was living with his son David in Lyndeborough in 1850.

Henry[2]*, Nicholas*[1]), b. at Wilton, 28 Aug 1770 son of John and Susanna Cram; Abiel d. at Tunbridge, VT between 1820 and 1830.[390]

144) JOSEPH HOLT (*Henry*[3]*, Henry*[2]*, Nicholas*[1]), b. at Andover, 28 Nov 1702 son of Henry and Martha (Marston) Holt; d. at Reading, 1774 (probate); m. 1st at Reading, 7 Apr 1726, ABIGAIL RICH, b. at Reading 14 Jul 1708 daughter of John and Martha (-) Rich; Martha d. perhaps by 1755. Joseph was married either second or third to ELIZABETH CROSBY at Reading on 28 Apr 1763.[391]

In his will written 20 September 1773, Joseph Holt bequeaths to daughter Abigail wife of Obed Johnson £13.6.8 and an equal bequest to the heirs of daughter Phebe wife of Jonathan Batchelder which daughter is deceased, daughter Elizabeth Abbot wife of Peter Abbot, and daughter Rachel Upton wife of James Upton. Son Joseph Holt receives all the lands and buildings except for the part which use and improvement of has been given to wife Elizabeth while she is a widow.[392]

Joseph Holt and Abigail Rich were parents of five children.

635) i JOSEPH HOLT, b. at Andover, 16 Jan 1726/7; d. at Reading, 1787 (probate 1787); m. ABIGAIL BEAN (or Bourn), b. about 1730; Abigail was living in 1787.

636) ii ABIGAIL HOLT, b. at Andover, 16 Jan 1726/7; d. at Andover, 12 Dec 1767; m. at Andover, 15 Jul 1749, OBED JOHNSON, b. at Haverhill, 30 Dec 1727 son of Cornelius and Lydia (Clement) Johnson; Obed d. at Reading, Dec 1773 (probate 20 Dec 1773). Obed was second married to Eleanor Upton.

637) iii PHEBE HOLT, b. at Reading, 22 Jun 1731; d. at Reading, 3 Nov 1754; m. at Reading, about 1751, JONATHAN BATCHELDER, b. at Reading, 22 Mar 1730 son of Jonathan and Sarah (Lewis) Batchelder; Jonathan d. at Reading, 6 Oct 1817. Jonathan m. 2nd, 1755, ABIGAIL EATON (*Abigail Russell Eaton*[5]*, Robert Russell*[4]*, Phebe Johnson Russell*[3]*, Mary Holt Johnson*[2]*, Nicholas*[1]), b. at Reading, about 1736 daughter of Ebenezer and Abigail (Russell) Eaton; Abigail d. at Reading, Nov 1817.

638) iv ELIZABETH HOLT, b. about 1733; d. at Kingston, NH, after 1774; m. 1st, about 1750, EDMUND DAMON, b. at Reading, 1728 son of Ebenezer and Elizabeth (-) Damon; Edmund d. at Reading, 23 Jun 1754. Elizabeth m. 2nd, at Reading, 22 Sep 1757, PETER ABBOTT, b. at Andover, 8 May 1734 son of Ephraim and Sarah (Crosby) Abbott; Peter d. at Kingston, 18 Apr 1774.

639) v RACHEL HOLT, b. about 1740; m. at Billerica, 9 Apr 1764, JAMES UPTON, b. 26 Mar 1733 son of William and Hannah (Felton) Upton.

145) BENJAMIN HOLT (*Henry*[3]*, Henry*[2]*, Nicholas*[1]), b. at Andover, 1704 son of Henry and Martha (Marston) Holt; d. at Andover, 17 Mar 1779; m. at Andover, 30 Jan 1734/5, his second cousin, LYDIA HOLT (*Thomas*[3]*, Nicholas*[2]*, Nicholas*[1]), b. 2 Jan 1713/4 daughter of Thomas and Alice (Peabody) Holt; Lydia d. at Andover, 10 Sep 1778.

Benjamin and Lydia resided in Andover where they kept a farm. On 31 May 1749, Henry Holt of Andover, in consideration of £2,000 in bills of credit, conveyed to his son Benjamin Holt, Jr. husbandman of Andover 35 acres of tillage and woodland in Andover, this being land that Benjamin had been improving for some years.[393]

On 26 April 1762, Benjamin Holt, Jr. yeoman of Andover, in consideration of £100, conveyed to Joseph Holt, Jr. all his lands lying in Falls meadow containing about 16 acres with half the dwelling house. On 22 February 1765, Benjamin Holt, Jr., yeoman of Andover, in consideration of £113 lawful money, conveyed to his son Joseph Holt, Jr. parcels of land in Andover containing 36 acres, one 6-acre tract and a 30-acre tract (this latter tract described in a manner similar to the property conveyed to Benjamin by his father Henry).[394]

Benjamin and Lydia were parents of nine children born at Andover.

i LYDIA HOLT, b. 18 Dec 1735; d. 18 Dec 1765.

ii BENJAMIN HOLT, b. 4 Apr 1737; d. 22 Nov 1741.

---

[390] In the 1820 census, Abial Cram is head of household in Tunbridge. In the 1830 census, the head of household is widow Judith Cram.

[391] There is disagreement about which Joseph Holt married whom. The confusion is between this Joseph and Joseph born in 1686 son of James and Hannah (Allen) Holt. Some sources report one Joseph or the other married Abigail Rich and then Zerviah. Others suggest one or the other married Mary Harmon and went to York, Maine. Mary Harmon was born about 1686 and was a widow when she married Joseph Holt 28 Dec 1709 which would rule out Joseph born in 1702 as her husband. There is also documentary evidence in the form of deeds that establishes that Joseph the son of James went to York. The children of Joseph and Abigail Holt were born in Reading and are in the 1774 will of Joseph Holt. Although it is possible that he had a marriage between Abigail Rich and Elizabeth Crosby to a woman named Zerviah, no record of that was located. Joseph's widow at his death was Elizabeth and the children in the will are children with Abigail.

[392] *Middlesex County, MA: Probate File Papers, 1648-1871.*Online database. *AmericanAncestors.org.* New England Historic Genealogical Society, 2014. Case 11785

[393] Massachusetts Land Records, Essex County, 94:212

[394] Massachusetts Land Records, Essex County, 110:159, 117:62

640) iii JOSEPH HOLT, b. at Andover, 20 Aug 1740; d. at Andover, 15 Dec 1801; m. at Andover, 1 Jun 1762, RUTH JOHNSON, b. at Haverhill, 27 Oct 1744 daughter of Cornelius and Eleanor (Currier) Johnson;[395] Ruth d. at Andover, 18 May 1827.

641) iv ALICE HOLT, b. at Andover, 13 Nov 1742; d. at Morrisville, NY, 7 Mar 1826; m. at Andover, 3 Dec 1761, her first cousin, DANIEL HOLT (*Thomas[4], Thomas[3], Nicholas[2], Nicholas[1]*), b. at Andover, 11 Sep 1740 son of Thomas and Hannah (Kimball) Holt.

642) v BETHIAH HOLT, b. at Andover, 3 Aug 1744; d. at Nelson, NH, 13 Apr 1812; m. at Andover, 20 Oct 1767, her third cousin, SOLOMON WARDWELL (*Abigail Gray Wardwell[4], Edward Gray[3], Hannah Holt Gray[2], Nicholas[1]*),[396] b. at Andover, 14 Jul 1743 son of Thomas and Abigail (Gray) Wardwell; Solomon d. at Nelson, 20 Sep 1825.

vi BENJAMIN HOLT, b. 6 Dec 1746; d. 31 Aug 1748.

vii BENJAMIN HOLT, b. May 1749; d. at Andover, 12 Apr 1822. Benjamin likely did not marry.

643) viii MARY HOLT, b. at Andover, 19 Sep 1751; m. at Andover, 13 Apr 1772, JAMES LARRABEE[397] perhaps the son of Joseph and Elizabeth (Trask) Larrabee.

644) ix MARTHA HOLT, b. at Andover, 15 Oct 1754; d. at Smithville, NY, 9 Oct 1829; m. at Andover, 23 Nov 1775, JONATHAN FELT, b. at Temple, NH, 8 Apr 1753 son of Aaron and Mary (Wyatt) Felt; Jonathan d. at Packersfield (Nelson), NH, 17 Feb 1807 (probate 1807).

146) HENRY HOLT (*Henry[3], Henry[2], Nicholas[1]*), b. at Andover, 1706 son of Henry and Martha (Marston) Holt; d. at Andover, 25 Sep 1754; m. at Andover, 6 Jan 1735/6, his second cousin, REBECCA GRAY (*Henry Gray[3], Hannah Holt Gray[2], Nicholas[1]*), b. at Andover, 1708 daughter of Henry and Mary (Blunt) Gray; Rebecca d. at Andover, Aug 1775.

Henry Holt did not leave a will and his estate entered probate 14 October 1754. Real estate was valued at £552.18.2. The following distributions were made at the final estate settlement on 18 October 1762: one-third of the real estate set-off to the widow Rebecca during her life; the remaining two-thirds settled on Mary wife of Darias Abbot[398] and Elizabeth wife of Moses Abbot.[399]

Rebecca Gray and Henry Holt were parents of five children born at Andover.[400]

i HENRY HOLT, b. 1 Oct 1736; d. 13 Feb 1737/8.

645) ii MARY HOLT, b. at Andover, 30 Apr 1739; d. at Amherst, NH, 1787; m. at Andover, 1 Nov 1757, her first cousin, DARIUS ABBOTT (*Elizabeth Gray Abbott[4], Henry Gray[3], Hannah Holt Gray[2], Nicholas[1]*), b. at Pomfret, CT, 16 Oct 1734 son of Paul and Elizabeth (Gray) Abbott; Darius d. 1817.

iii REBECCA HOLT, b. 5 May 1741; d. 25 Apr 1751.

646) iv ELIZABETH HOLT, b. at Andover, 8 Jun 1743; d. at Andover, 25 Sep 1838; m. at Andover, 31 Dec 1761, her third cousin, MOSES ABBOTT (*Hannah Holt Abbott[4], Timothy[3], James[2], Nicholas[1]*), b. at Andover, 9 Aug 1735 son of Barachias and Hannah (Holt) Abbott; Moses d. at Andover, 23 Feb 1826.

v ANNE HOLT, b. 3 Jan 1746/7; d. 18 Apr 1751.

147) SARAH HOLT (*Henry[3], Henry[2], Nicholas[1]*), b. at Andover, 3 Jul 1707 daughter of Henry and Martha (Marston) Holt; m. at Andover, 12 Jun 1728, her second cousin MOSES PEABODY (*Lydia[3], James[2], Nicholas[1]*), b. 1706 son of Samuel and Lydia (Holt) Peabody; Moses d. at Andover, 13 Nov 1746.

Sarah Holt and Moses Peabody were parents of six children born at Andover.

---

[395] The 1774 will of Cornelius Johnson of Concord includes a bequest to his daughter Ruth Holt.

[396] There are two Bethiah Holts near in age, one of whom married Solomon Wardwell and one who married Thomas Russell. There do not seem to be any records that clearly establish which was which, and I have chosen this arrangement: Bethiah daughter of Benjamin married Solomon Wardwell and Bethiah daughter of Ephraim Holt and Phebe Russell married Thomas Russell. It could well be the other way around.

[397] Name is also spelled Leatherby

[398] Durrie's Holt genealogy lists Mary daughter of Ebenezer Holt and Mehitable Stevens as the wife of Darius Abbott, but this probate distributions demonstrates that Mary wife of Darius was a daughter of Henry Holt.

[399] *Essex County, MA: Probate File Papers, 1638-1881.*Online database. *AmericanAncestors.org.* New England Historic Genealogical Society, 2014. Case 13640

[400] Durrie's Holt genealogy lists a second son Henry with wife Ruth with widow Ruth deceased in 1827. Although the Andover records list Ruth widow of Henry dying in 1827, Ruth Holt who died in 1827 was the widow of Joseph Holt. That can be established by the 1827 probate record of Ruth Holt widow of Andover which includes a will that describes legacies to children and grandchildren who are the children and grandchildren of Joseph Holt and Ruth Johnson. The death transcription listing Ruth as the widow of Henry may just be an error.

347) i SARAH PEABODY, b. at Andover, 31 Mar 1729; d. at Andover, 12 Oct 1802; m. at Andover, 13 Nov 1753, as his second wife, JONATHAN FRYE, b. at Andover, 3 Mar 1716/7 son of Ebenezer and Elizabeth (Farnum) Frye; Jonathan d. at Andover, 2 Feb 1788. Jonathan was first married to Sarah Wilson.

399) ii LYDIA PEABODY, b. at Andover, 5 Jul 1731; m. at Andover, 15 Feb 1753, her third cousin, EBENEZER HOLT (*Ebenezer*[4], *Hannah Farnum Holt*[3], *Elizabeth Holt Farnum*[2], *Nicholas*[1]), b. at Andover, 7 Sep 1730 son of Ebenezer and Mehitable (Stevens) Holt; Ebenezer d. at Mont Vernon, NH, Apr 1805.

iii SAMUEL PEABODY, b. 6 May 1734; died young

iv HANNAH PEABODY, b. 9 Aug 1739

647) v SAMUEL PEABODY, b. at Andover, 1 Sep 1741; d. at Mont Vernon, 6 Aug 1814; m. at Reading, 26 Sep 1765, ELIZABETH WILKINS, baptized at Middleton, 1743 daughter of Joseph and Abigail (Burtt) Wilkins.

vi REBECCA PEABODY, b. at Andover, 5 Jan 1744/5; d. at Boxford, 4 Jan 1817; m. at Boxford, 20 Dec 1770, JOHN STILES, b. about 1747 *perhaps* the son of Daniel and Elizabeth (Booth) Peabody;[401] John d. at Boxford, 3 Jun 1804. No children have been identified for Rebecca and John.

148) EPHRAIM HOLT (*Henry*[3], *Henry*[2], *Nicholas*[1]), b. at Andover, May 1713 son of Henry and Martha (Marston) Holt; d. at Andover, 31 Dec 1749; m. 13 Feb 1735, PHEBE RUSSELL, b. at Andover, Jun 1716 daughter of John and Sarah (Chandler) Russell. Phebe married second Abraham Sheldon.

The estate of Ephraim Holt entered probate 2 April 1750. The real estate distribution on 9 April 1759 included one-third to the widow for her use during her lifetime and the other two-thirds to eldest son Ephraim Holt. Ephraim is to make payments of £19.6.8 to sister Phebe Houghton, sister Bethiah Holt, sister Asenath, and brother Marston Holt.[402]

Phebe Russell and Ephraim Holt were parents of five children born at Andover.[403]

648) i PHEBE HOLT, b. at Andover, Apr 1735; m. at Andover, 11 Sep 1755, JAMES HOUGHTON, b. at Pomfret, 13 Sep 1728 son of Edward and Abigail (Coy) Houghton.

649) ii EPHRAIM HOLT, b. at Andover, Jan 1736/7; d. at Holden, MA, 25 May 1816;[404] m. at Boxford, 7 Jan 1762, SARAH BLACK, baptized at Boxford, 24 Jul 1743 daughter of Daniel and Sarah (Symonds) Black.[405]

511) iii BETHIAH HOLT, b. at Andover, 20 Mar 1743; d. at Wilton, NH, 20 Aug 1817; m. at Andover, 15 May 1760, her second cousin, THOMAS RUSSELL (*Joseph Russell*[4], *Phebe Johnson Russell*[3], *Mary Holt Johnson*[2], *Nicholas*[1]), b. at Andover, 5 Jun 1732 son of Joseph and Hepsibah (Eaton) Russell; Thomas d. at Wilton 30 Mar 1818.

650) iv ASENATH HOLT, b. at Andover, 31 Mar 1743; d. at Reading, 8 Nov 1785; m. at Reading, 7 Jun 1764, EBENEZER FLINT, b. at Reading, 17 Jun 1742 son of Ebenezer and Abigail (Sawyer) Flint; Ebenezer d. at Wilton, 29 Apr 1829. After Asenath's death, Ebenezer married Mary Damon (widow Mrs. Taylor) on 29 Nov 1789.

651) v MARSTIN HOLT, b. at Andover, 13 Aug 1747; m. at Holden, 13 Feb 1772, ABIGAIL WHEELER, b. at Holden, 20 Sep 1746 daughter of Moses and Abigail (Godin) Wheeler.

149) KETURAH HOLT (*Henry*[3], *Henry*[2], *Nicholas*[1]), b. at Andover, Feb 1715 daughter of Henry and Martha (Marston) Holt; d. at Amherst, NH, 16 Jan 1797; m. at Andover, 17 Dec 1741, JOHN STEWART, b. about 1714 son of Robert Stewart; John d. at Amherst, after 1790.

John Stewart was perhaps born in Scotland (or is at least of Scottish origins) and as a boy emigrated with his brother and father. The family was first in Andover where his father Robert had a second wife. John and Keturah started their family in Andover and their six children were born there. They relocated to Amherst, New Hampshire by 1749. They were living there together in 1790 and John died between 1790 and 1797 when Keturah was a widow.[406]

---

401 John Stiles of Boxford was the executor of the estate of his father Daniel Stiles of Middleton in 1789.

402 *Essex County, MA: Probate File Papers, 1638-1881.*Online database. *AmericanAncestors.org.* New England Historic Genealogical Society, 2014. Case 13637

403 Although sources (Charlotte Helen Abbott and Durrie's Holt genealogy) state that Dorcas who married Thomas Peavey is the daughter of Ephraim Holt, Ephraim Holt did not have a daughter Dorcas. This can be established by the 1759 estate distribution of Ephraim Holt with heir eldest son Ephraim who receives two-thirds of the estate and makes payments to his sister Phebe Houghton, sister Bethiah Holt, sister Asenath, and brother Marston.

404 U.S., Newspaper Extractions from the Northeast, 1704-1930

405 Perley, *Essex Antiquarian*, volume 9, p 187

406 Edson, *Stewart Clan Magazine*, p 185

i JOHN STEWART, baptized at Andover, 25 Apr 1742; nothing further certain known.

652) ii KETURAH STEWART, baptized at Andover, 16 Sep 1744; m. about 1773, AMOS GREEN, b. at Reading, 16 May 1740 son of Thomas and Mary (Green) Green.

653) iii WILLIAM STEWART, baptized at Andover, 9 Aug 1747; d. at Londonderry, VT, 12 May 1837; m. SARAH KIMBALL,[407] b. 1752; Sarah d. at Londonderry, 28 Feb 1828.

654) iv SIMPSON STEWART, baptized at Andover, 5 Feb 1749; d. at Berlin, VT, 13 Jun 1841; m. about 1774, HANNAH,[408] b. about 1752 who has not been clearly identified; Hannah d. at Berlin, VT, 13 Jan 1813.

655) v HENRY STEWART, baptized at Andover, 8 Mar 1752; d. at Kingsbury, NY, 16 May 1835 (probate 1835); m. 1st, about 1772, SARAH who has not been identified; Sarah d. at Dublin, NH, 5 Jan 1785. Henry m. 2nd, MARTHA WEATHERBY who was living in 1827 when Henry wrote his will.

656) vi MARTHA STEWART, baptized at Andover, 6 Nov 1757; d. at Reading, MA, 19 Apr 1843; m. 1st, about 1775, JAMES HARTSHORN, b. at Amherst, 17 Mar 1755 son of James and Tabitha (Pratt) Hartshorn; James d. about 1780. Martha m. 2nd, at Amherst, AMOS ELLIOTT, b. at Amherst, 17 Jun 1755 son of Francis and Phebe (Wilkins) Elliott; Amos d. at Amherst, 7 Apr 1807. Martha m. 3rd, at Reading, MA, 2 Feb 1812, JONATHAN WESTON, b. 1 Mar 1757 son of Jonathan and Ruth (Flint) Weston; Jonathan d. at Reading, 23 Apr 1839.

150) MARY HOLT (*Henry³, Henry², Nicholas¹*), b. at Andover, 28 Mar 1717 daughter of Henry and Martha (Marston) Holt; m. at Andover, 24 Oct 1744, JOSEPH PEABODY, b. at Boxford, 18 Dec 1718 son of Jonathan and Alice (Pearl) Peabody; Joseph d. at Boxford, 1751 (probate 5 May 1751).

Joseph and Mary resided in Boxford where their two children were born. Joseph Peabody did not leave a will and his estate entered probate 27 May 1751 with Mary as administratrix.[409] A third part of the real estate was set off to widow Mary on 30 April 1776. The set off occurred after the death of her son Henry.

i MARY PEABODY, b. 21 Feb 1746; nothing further known.

657) ii HENRY PEABODY, b. at Boxford, 25 May 1749; d. 1776 while serving in the Army (probate 5 Mar 1776); m. 17 Apr 1769, LYDIA REA, b. at Beverly, 8 Oct 1750 daughter of Joshua and Sarah (Prince) Rea.[410] Lydia's date of death not found, but she was living in 1783 and had not remarried.

151) JAMES HOLT (*James³, Henry², Nicholas¹*), b. at Andover, 1707 son of James and Susanna (Preston) Holt; d. at Andover, 1751 (probate 16 Dec 1751); m. 22 Oct 1733, MARY CHANDLER, b. at Andover, 4 Mar 1713 daughter of Joseph and Mehitable (Russell) Chandler; Mary d. at Andover, 10 Feb 1751.

In his will written 21 November 1751, James Holt ordered that all his real estate be sold. Eldest beloved son Zelah Holt receives £20, second son Jesse receives £13, and third son Lemuel receives £17. Daughters Mary and Bridget each receives £8. The personal estate is also to be sold except the books will be divided among the five children. The proceeds from the sale of his shoemaker and carpenter tools is to be divided among his sons. His brother Barzilai Holt of Lancaster was named executor. The value of the farm was £217.5.1, and the total estate value was £236.1.9.[411]

James and Mary were parents of five children born at Andover.

658) i MARY HOLT, baptized at Andover, 18 May 1735; m. 1st, 3 Sep 1754, NATHANIEL ANDREWS likely the son of Thomas and Ruth (Bixbee) Andrews; Nathaniel d. at Boxford, 1759 (probate 1759). Mary m. 2nd, 19 Nov 1761, JACOB ANDREWS; Jacob d. at Boxford, 1786 (probate 1786).

659) ii BRIDGET HOLT, baptized at Andover, 16 Jan 1737; m. at Boxford, 16 Oct 1757, LEVI ANDREWS, b. at Boxford, 27 Aug 1727 son of Thomas and Ruth (Bixbee) Andrews.

660) iii ZELA HOLT, b. at Andover, 29 Dec 1738; d. likely at Bethel, ME; m. at Andover, 16 Nov 1762, his second cousin, PRISCILLA ABBOTT (*Hannah Holt Abbott⁴, Timothy³, James², Nicholas¹*), b. at Andover, 13 Feb 1742/3 daughter of Barachias and Hannah (Holt) Abbott.

---

[407] Sarah's last name is given as Kimball on the death record of her son Robert Kimball (1793-1865).

[408] Hannah's name is variously reported as Hannah Rollins or Hannah Delano but not record of a marriage for Simpson and Hannah has been located.

[409] *Essex County, MA: Probate File Papers, 1638-1881.*Online database. *AmericanAncestors.org.* New England Historic Genealogical Society, 2014. Case 20857

[410] The 1783 will of Joshua Rea includes a bequest to his daughter Lydia Peabody.

[411] Essex County, MA: Probate File Papers, 1638-1881.Online database. AmericanAncestors.org. New England Historic Genealogical Society, 2014. Case 13649

661) iv JESSE HOLT, b. at Andover, 8 Oct 1739; d. at Tewksbury, Feb 1817; m. at Tewksbury, 30 Aug 1781, MARY CLARK, b. at Tewksbury, 26 May 1745 daughter of Nathaniel and Mary (Wyman) Clark . Mary was first married at Tewksbury, 29 Jun 1769 to MOSES GRAY (*Robert Gray⁴, Robert Gray³, Hannah Holt Gray², Nicholas¹*), baptized at Andover, 11 Jan 1747 son of Robert and Lydia (Peabody) Gray; Moses d. at Tewksbury, 11 Sep 1775.

v LEMUEL HOLT, baptized at Andover, 24 Jan 1748; m. at Andover, 19 Oct 1769, MEHITABLE LOVEJOY, b. at Andover, 20 May 1742 daughter of Joseph and Mehitable (Foster) Lovejoy; Lemuel d. at Andover, 1782 (probate 1782). Lemuel and Mehitable did not have children. In his will written 5 Mar 1776, Lemuel made bequests to wife Mehitable, brother Zela, brother Jesse, sister Mary, and sister Bridget.

152) BARZILLAI HOLT (*James³, Henry², Nicholas¹*), b. at Andover, 25 Oct 1716 son of James and Susanna (Preston) Holt; d. at Boylston, MA, 7 Sep 1774; m. 1st 27 Aug 1738, ELIZABETH GOSS who has not been identified, Elizabeth d. about 1756. Barzillai m. 2nd at Lancaster, 22 Feb 1759, LOIS PIKE (widow of Isaac Allard).

In his will written 21 January 1774, Barzillai Holt includes lengthy, specific provisions for his wife Lois. Sons Abel Holt, Barzillai Holt, James Holt, Silas Holt, daughter Elizabeth wife of Jedediah Boynton, son Levi Holt, son Abiel Holt, and son Jotham Holt receive money bequests of varying amounts. Trusty friend Aaron Sawyer was named executor. Aaron Sawyer is directed to sell the estate and to make divisions of the money following the guidelines in the will.[412]

Barzillai and Elizabeth were parents of five children.

662) i ABEL HOLT, b. at Marlborough, 14 Jun 1740; d. at Boylston, MA, Feb 1815; m. 21 Oct 1765, EUNICE KEYES, b. at Shrewsbury, 19 Apr 1745 daughter of Henry and Ruth (Moore) Keyes; Eunice d. 21 Oct 1840.

663) ii BARZILLAI HOLT, b. at Marlborough, 12 May 1745; d. at Plattsburgh, NY, 1819' m. at Shrewsbury, 9 Nov 1770, LUCY WILLIAMS, b. about 1748 of undetermined parents.

iii JAMES HOLT, b. at Marlborough, 6 Jun 1746. He was living in 1774 but no further record was found for him.

664) iv SILAS HOLT, b. at Marlborough, about 1752; d. at Sempronius, NY, 1 Jan 1823;[413] m. at Lunenburg, 25 Jan 1772, SARAH HARRINGTON, b. at Westminster, MA, 10 Nov 1752 daughter of Seth and Abigail (-) Harrington.

665) v ELIZABETH HOLT, b. at Marlborough, 29 Aug 1753; d. at Shutesbury, MA, 28 Feb 1842; m. 1st at Lancaster, 10 Feb 1772, JEDEDIAH BOYNTON, baptized at Rowley, 22 Jan 1743/4 son of Ephraim and Sarah (Stewart) Boynton; Jedediah d. at Royalston, 1774 (probate 15 Jun 1774). Elizabeth m. 2nd JOSIAH WHITE BEAMAN, b. at Lancaster, 4 Oct 1752 son of Phineas H. and Joanna (White) Beaman; Josiah d. at Shelburne, MA, 2 Dec 1841.

Barzillai and Lois were parents of three children.

i LEVI HOLT, b. at Marlborough, 6 May 1760; d. about 1776 of illness while in an Army camp.

666) ii ABIEL HOLT, b. at Marlborough, 11 May 1763; d. at West Boylston, 29 Jun 1845; m. at Sterling, 16 Nov 1785, DOLLY FAIRBANK, b. at Lancaster, 8 Feb 1769 daughter of Silas and Lydia (Prouty) Fairbank. Abiel married 2nd at Grafton, 27 Feb 1828, MIRIAM WOOD (widow of Reuben Jenks), b. at Grafton, 4 Nov 1779 daughter of Dr. Joseph and Miriam (Collester) Wood; Miriam d. at West Boylston, 14 Dec 1842.

667) iii JOTHAM HOLT, b. at Lancaster, 10 Jan 1765; d. at Barre, NY, 3 Jan 1839; m. at Sterling, 3 Jan 1788, LYDIA FAIRBANK, b. at Lancaster, 3 Mar 1770 daughter of Silas and Lydia (Prouty) Fairbank; Lydia d. at Pitcher, NY, 23 Sep 1856.

153) JONATHAN CRAM (*Sarah Holt Cram³, Henry², Nicholas¹*), b. at Wilmington, MA, 21 Feb 1708 son of John and Sarah (Holt) Cram; d. at Lyndeborough, 23 Jan 1790; m. 1 Dec 1732, MARY CHAMBERLAIN, b. at Billerica, 20 Jan 1706 daughter of Daniel and Mary (-) Chamberlain; Mary d. at Lyndeborough, 5 Jan 1770.

Jonathan and Mary started their family in Wilmington, Massachusetts but were settled in Lyndeborough about 1743. They were parents of eight children.

---

[412] *Probate Records (Worcester County, Massachusetts); Index 1731-1881, Probate Records, Vol 11-12, 1769-1774, volume 12, pp 511-512*

[413] U.S., The Pension Roll of 1835, Volume 2, New York, p 514

668) i JONATHAN CRAM, b. at Wilmington, MA, 8 Jun 1733; d. at Wilton, NH, 24 Oct 1810; m. about 1759, SARAH PUTNAM, b. at Salem, 28 Jun 1736 daughter of Jacob and Susannah (Stiles) Putnam; Sarah d. at Wilton, 26 May 1805.

ii MARY CRAM, b. 6 Jun 1735; d. 5 Jun 1738.

669) iii DAVID CRAM, b. at Wilmington, MA, 26 Jun 1737; d. at Lyndeborough, NH, 25 Jun 1825; m. about 1760, MARY BADGER, b. 1739 daughter of John and Mary (McFarland) Badger; David d. at Lyndeborough, 10 Mar 1825.

670) iv JACOB CRAM, b. at Wilmington, 4 Oct 1739; d. at Lyndeborough, 1819 (probate 6 Aug 1819); m. about 1762, ISABELLA HUTCHINSON, b. Dec 1739; Isabella d. at Lyndeborough, 3 Feb 1812.

671) v ELIZABETH CRAM, b. at Wilmington, 4 Nov 1741; d. at Lyndeborough, 10 Nov 1829; m. about 1764, JOHN CARKIN, b. at Nottingham, 18 Dec 1735 son of John and Esther (Wines) Carkin; John d. at Lyndeborough, 2 Mar 1799.

672) vi RACHEL CRAM, b. at Lyndeborough, 16 Apr 1744; d. at Lyndeborough, 29 Apr 1833; m. 1769, EPHRAIM PUTNAM, b. at Salem, 30 Sep 1744 son of Archelaus and Mehitable (Putnam) Putnam; Ephraim d. at Lyndeborough, 11 May 1821.

673) vii SOLOMON CRAM, b. at Lyndeborough, about 1746; d. at Lyndeborough, 1 May 1825; m. about 1771, MARY, b. about 1740; Mary d. at Lyndeborough, 21 Apr 1819.

674) viii URIAH CRAM, b. about 1750; d. at Lyndeborough, 2 Oct 1831; m. about 1779, EUNICE ELLENWOOD, b. 1745; Eunice d. at Lyndeborough, 1 Dec 1831.

154) HUMPHREY CRAM (*Sarah Holt Cram[3], Henry[2], Nicholas[1]*), b. at Hampton Falls, 8 Nov 1710 son of John and Sarah (Holt) Cram; m. at Lisbon, CT, 22 Feb 1733, his second cousin, HANNAH BLUNT, b. at Andover, Jul 1710 daughter of Ambrose and Mehitable (Johnson) Blunt; Hannah d. at Holland, MA, 17 Jun 1776.

Humphrey and Hannah lived in Union, Connecticut but relocated to Holland, Massachusetts where Humphrey served as deacon. When the family arrived in Holland is not clear as Humphrey held land in Holland while the family was still members of the church in Union. Humphrey was elected deacon in Holland in 1766. He also served in the French and Indian War.[414] Hannah and Humphrey were parents of seven children.

i HANNAH CRAM, baptized at Hampton, 22 Jul 1733

ii HUMPHREY CRAM, b. at Windham, 12 Mar 1735; d. at Wales, MA, 12 Nov 1759.

675) iii DINAH CRAM, b. at Windham, 10 Dec 1737; d. at Hartland, VT, 13 Oct 1821; m. 1st at Windham, 1 May 1755, THOMAS PARKE ROOD, b. 23 May 1732 son of David and Joanna (Parke) Rood; Thomas d. at Hartland, 10 Oct 1795. Dinah m. 2nd about 1796, WILLIAM BENJAMIN, b. at Watertown, 16 Jun 1738 son of Jonathan and Hannah (Cunnable) Benjamin; William d. at Hartland, Dec 1816. William's first wife was Sarah Child.

676) iv SARAH CRAM, b. at Hampton, about 1740; m. at Union, CT, 10 Apr 1760, JOHN ROSEBROOK, b. at Grafton, 24 May 1738 son of James and Margaret (MacCoy) Rosebrooks; John d. at Fabyan, NH, 25 Sep 1817.

677) v MEHITABLE CRAM, b. at Union, CT, 15 Apr 1745; d. at Milton, VT, about 1781; m. at Union, 29 Nov 1764, JONAH LOOMIS, b. at Windsor, CT, 5 May 1743 son of Daniel and Sarah (Enos) Loomis; Jonah d. at Georgia, VT, 22 Apr 1813. Jonah was second married to Martha Post.

678) vi JONATHAN CRAM, b. at Union, 9 Mar 1746; d. at Lancaster, NH, 28 Aug 1811; m. at Wales, MA, 15 Jan 1770, ABIGAIL WEBBER, b. at Brimfield, 15 May 1749 daughter of Edward and Abigail (Haynes) Webber.

362) vii CHLOE CRAM, b. at Union, 25 Nov 1750; m. at Sturbridge, MA, 10 Dec 1768, her third cousin, PETER FAULKNER (*Deborah Farnum Faulkner[4], John Farnum[3], Elizabeth Holt Farnum[2], Nicholas[1]*), b. at Andover, 5 Nov 1743 son of Timothy and Deborah (Farnum) Faulkner; Peter d. at Lancaster, NH, 11 Dec 1829.

155) PHEBE CRAM (*Sarah Holt Cram[3], Henry[2], Nicholas[1]*), b. at Hampton, NH, 8 Jul 1712 daughter of John and Sarah (Holt) Cram; m. at Hampton, 8 Jan 1735, MOSES STILES, b. at Boxford, 10 Feb 1705 son of Samuel and Elizabeth (Cary) Stiles.

---

[414] Lovering and Chase, *History of the Town of Holland, Massachusetts*

Phebe and Moses were in Ashford but relocated to Lyndeborough by 1749 residing on what was known as the Lakin place.[415] There are records for eight children of Phebe Cram and Moses Stiles.

679) i MOSES STILES, b. at Ashford, 17 Oct 1735; d. at Greenfield, NH, 1811 (probate 1811); m. by 1761, SARAH who has not been identified.

ii PHEBE STILES, b. at Ashford, 11 Jan 1737/8

680) iii ASAHEL STILES, b. at Ashford, 21 May 1739; d. at Addison, NY; m. by 1768, SARAH DUTTON, b. at Nottingham, NH, 18 Apr 1744 daughter of Josiah and Sarah (Parker) Dutton.

681) iv JOHN STILES, b. at Ashford, 19 Aug 1740; m. at Pepperell, 30 Sep 1774, SUSANNAH CHAMBERLAIN, b. at Pepperell, 1752 daughter of Phineas and Lydia (Williams) Chamberlain.

v MARY STILES, b. at Ashford, 31 Oct 1742

vi SAMUEL STILES, b. at Ashford, 1 Feb 1745/6

682) vii SARAH STILES, b. at Ashford, 24 Jul 1747; m. by 1770, BENJAMIN DUTTON, b. at Nottingham, 27 Apr 1743 son of Josiah and Sarah (Parker) Dutton; Benjamin d. at Lyndeborough, 3 Sep 1803.

viii REUBEN STILES, b. at Lyndeborough, 13 Jun 1749; d. at Wilton, 7 Sep 1773 when killed by a falling beam while building the meeting house at Wilton.[416]

156) HULDAH CRAM (*Sarah Holt Cram*[3], *Henry*[2], *Nicholas*[1]), b. at Hampton, NH, 5 May 1715 daughter of John and Sarah (Holt) Cram; d. at Brooklyn, CT, 21 Aug 1810; m. 22 Jul 1742, as his second wife, EPHRAIM WOODWARD, b. 8 Jan 1710 son of John and Hannah (Hyde) Woodward; Ephraim d. at Canterbury, CT, 15 Jan 1782. Ephraim was first married to Hannah Williams.

In his will written 15 September 1775 (proved 5 February 1782), Ephraim Cram bequeathed to beloved wife Huldah the improvement of one-third of the real estate during her life and one-third of the moveable estate to be hers forever. Third son Ward Woodward receives one-half of the real estate. Daughter Elizabeth Griggs receives ten shillings as does daughter Abigail Davison. Daughter Hannah Woodward receives £26. The other half of the real estate is to be divided equally among sons Eleazer, Ithamar, and John. Wife Huldah and son Ward were named executors.[417] Eleazer and Elizabeth are children from Ephraim's marriage with Hannah Williams.

Huldah and Ephraim were parents of six children born at Canterbury.

683) i ABIGAIL WOODWARD, b. at Canterbury, 24 Mar 1742/3; d. at Brooklyn CT, 28 May 1786; m. at Canterbury, 28 Apr 1768, PETER DAVISON, b. at Pomfret, 15 May 1739 son of Joseph and Mary (Warner) Davison; Peter d. at Brooklyn, CT, 29 May 1800. Peter married second Susannah Hammett (widow of Benjamin Weaver) on 6 Nov 1786.

ii HULDAH WOODWARD, b. 1746; d. 26 Jun 1751.

684) iii ITHAMAR WOODWARD, b. at Canterbury, 21 Jan 1748/9; d. at Francestown, NH, 9 Jan 1839; m. at Canterbury, 23 Nov 1773, HULDAH SHARP, b. at Pomfret, 3 Oct 1749 daughter of Solomon and Sarah (Goodell) Sharp; Huldah d. at Francestown, 12 Jun 1823.

685) iv WARD WOODWARD, b. at Canterbury, 5 Apr 1751; d. at Brooklyn, CT, 12 Apr 1810; m. 19 Oct 1780, his first cousin, REBECCA PUTNAM (*Sarah Cram Putnam*[4], *Sarah Holt Cram*[3], *Henry*[2], *Nicholas*[1]), b. at Lyndeborough, 17 Mar 1761 daughter of Ephraim and Sarah (Cram) Putnam; Rebecca d. 18 Oct 1848.

686) v JOHN WOODWARD, b. at Canterbury, 10 Jun 1753; d. at Lyndeborough, 14 Oct 1825; m. about 1777, JUDITH FOSTER, b. 13 Nov 1753; Judith d. at Lyndeborough, 1 Jun 1835.

vi HANNAH WOODWARD, b. at Canterbury, Jan 1757. Hannah went with her brothers to Lyndeborough. No record of a marriage was found for her.

157) JOHN CRAM (*Sarah Holt Cram*[3], *Henry*[2], *Nicholas*[1]), b. at Hampton, NH, 10 Apr 1717 son of John and Sarah (Holt) Cram; m. about 1740, SARAH who has not been identified.

---

[415] Donovan, *The History of the Town of Lyndeborough*, volume 1, p 864

[416] Donovan, *The History of the Town of Lyndeborough*, volume 1, p 864

[417] *Connecticut. Probate Court (Plainfield District)*; Probate Place: *Windham, Connecticut, Probate Records, Vol 5-7, 1762-1790, volume 6, pp 472-473*

John and Sarah Cram were parents of eleven children born at Wilton. Most of the children relocated to Andover, Vermont. While they were in Wilton, John and Sarah had their place on lot No. 14 of the fifth range, but are thought to have gone to Lyndeborough after the births of their children.[418]

i SARAH CRAM, b. at Wilton, 18 May 1741. Nothing further certain is known. She perhaps married Leonard Judkins.

687) ii JOHN CRAM, b. at Wilton, 28 Sep 1743; m. 1st by 1767, SUSANNA who is *likely* SUSANNA FULLER, b. at Middleton, MA, 11 Mar 1747 daughter of Amos and Hannah (Putnam) Fuller; Susanna d. at Wilton, 1779. John m. 2nd at Wilton, 9 Dec 1779, MARY JAQUITH.

688) iii ASA CRAM, b. at Wilton, 4 Apr 1746; d. 16 Jul 1775; m. 25 Jul 1771, SYBIL MCLANE, b. at Chelmsford, 22 Mar 1749 daughter of Charles and Susanna (Farmer) McLane.

689) iv JOSEPH CRAM, b. at Wilton, 21 Apr 1748; m. 13 Dec 1773, ABIGAIL FARMER.

690) v LYDIA CRAM, b. at Wilton, 28 May 1750; d. at Andover, VT, 2 Jul 1818; m. NATHANIEL GREELEY, b. at Hudson, 28 Oct 1744 son of Samuel and Abigail (Blodgett) Greeley; Nathaniel d. at Andover, VT, 16 Dec 1819.

vi PHEBE CRAM, b. 10 Aug 1752; d. 29 Aug 1752.

691) vii EBENEZER CRAM, b. at Wilton, 19 Sep 1754; d. at Chester, VT, 23 Feb 1835; m. about 1774, his second cousin, RACHEL HOLT (*Jonathan[4], Humphrey[3], Henry[2], Nicholas[1]*), b. at Lunenburg, 20 Apr 1753 daughter of Jonathan and Rachel (Taylor) Holt. Ebenezer married second SARAH who has not been identified but who was his widow at probate.

viii HUMPHREY CRAM, b. at Wilton, 10 Jan 1755; d. at Weston, VT, 15 Jan 1825; m. at Temple, NH, 12 Dec 1782, MARY FULLER. Humphrey and Mary may not have had children. In the 1800 Census, they are in Andover, Vermont and there are no children in the home. Humphrey was a Revolutionary War veteran for which he received a pension.

ix PHEBE CRAM, b. 11 Apr 1757

692) x ZEBULON CRAM, b. at Wilton, 30 Jun 1760; d. at Clarendon, VT, 27 Jan 1850; m. about 1783, ESTHER who has not been identified.

693) xi HANNAH CRAM, b. at Wilton, 5 Jun 1764; d. at Wallingford, VT, 16 Jun 1840; m. 19 Jun 1782, DAVID HASELTINE, b. at Haverhill, MA, 15 Dec 1759 son of Nathan and Elizabeth (Follensbee) Haseltine; d. at Wallingford, VT, 17 Apr 1840.

158) SARAH CRAM (*Sarah Holt Cram[3], Henry[2], Nicholas[1]*), b. at Hampton, NH, 27 Jun 1719 daughter of John and Sarah (Holt) Cram; d. at Lyndeborough, 15 Oct 1777; m. EPHRAIM PUTNAM, b. at Danvers, 10 Feb 1719 son of Nathaniel and Hannah (Roberts) Putnam; Ephraim d. at Lyndeborough, 13 Nov 1777.

Sarah and Ephraim resided in Lyndeborough where Ephraim was a deacon of the Congregationalist church. He contributed to the efforts of the Revolution by fitting out other men for service and paying bounties for service. For a time, Ephraim and Sarah were on the homestead of Ephraim's father, but in 1753 they received through deed the homestead of Sarah's father John Cram.[419]

Ephraim Putnam did not leave a will and the administration of the estate was granted to his eldest son Ephraim Putnam. Real estate of his homestead land and buildings was valued at £600. The personal estate included several books with religious themes. The personal estate was valued at £367.7.2.[420]

Ephraim and Sarah were parents of ten children whose births are all recorded at Lyndeborough.

694) i HANNAH PUTNAM, b. at Lyndeborough, 9 Mar 1742/3; d. at Lyndeborough, 5 Oct 1811; m. about 1764, ELEAZER WOODWARD, b. at Brooklyn, CT, 8 Jan 1738 son of Ephraim and Hannah (Williams) Woodward; Eleazer d. at Lyndeborough, 19 Dec 1815.

695) ii EPHRAIM PUTNAM, b. at Danvers, 15 Jun 1744; d. at Lyndeborough, 2 Mar 1799; m. about 1767, LUCY SPALDING.

---

[418] Livermore, *History of the Town of Wilton*, p 353

[419] Donovan, *History of the Town of Lyndeborough*, p 196, p 607

[420] New Hampshire County Probate Records, Hillsborough, Probate records 1777-1791, volume 3-4, volume 3, pp 87-90. Accessed through familysearch.org.

696) iii SARAH PUTNAM, b. at Lyndeborough, 8 Jun 1746; d. at Hancock, NH, 27 Apr 1822; m. about 1768, JOHN BRADFORD, b. 1744 son of Andrew and Rebecca (Cole) Bradford;[421][422] John d. at Hancock, 27 Jun 1836.

697) iv HULDAH PUTNAM, b. at Lyndeborough, 15 May 1748; d. at Lyndeborough, 13 Jan 1778; m. at Lyndeborough, 26 Nov 1768, JONAS KIDDER, b. at Hudson, NH, 16 Nov 1743 son of Jonas and Hannah (Proctor) Kidder; Jonas d. at Hudson, 1 Nov 1837. Jonas was second married to Alice Taylor on 20 May 1778 and third to Abigail Carleton on 5 Jul 1827. Abigail Carleton was the widow of Huldah's brother David.

v JESSE PUTNAM, b. 21 Sep 1750; died young.

698) vi DAVID PUTNAM, b. at Lyndeborough, 6 May 1753; d. at Lyndeborough, 3 Jul 1826; m. at Lyndeborough, 18 Jun 1778, ABIGAIL CARLETON, b. about 1751 daughter of Jeremiah and Eunice (Taylor) Carleton; Abigail d. at Lyndeborough, 5 Jan 1835. Abigail was first married to Adam Johnson and was third married to Jonas Kidder who had been married to David's sister Huldah.

699) vii KETURAH PUTNAM, b. at Lyndeborough, 29 Jun 1756; m. about 1776, JOHN SMITH, b. at Amherst, NH, 8 Dec 1751 son of John and Ann (Davis) Smith.

700) viii AARON PUTNAM, b. about 1758; m. 1st at Lyndeborough, 28 Dec 1780, SARAH LEE who has not been identified. Aaron m. 2nd at Lyndeborough, 28 Apr 1789, PHEBE FARNUM (*Stephen Farnum⁵, Stephen Farnum⁴, Ralph Farnum³, Elizabeth Holt Farnum², Nicholas¹*) *likely* b. about 1768 daughter of Stephen and Kezia (Skidmore) Farnum.[423]

685) ix REBECCA PUTNAM, b. at Lyndeborough, 17 Mar 1761; d. 18 Oct 1848; m. 19 Oct 1780, her first cousin, WARD WOODWARD (*Huldah Cram Woodward⁴, Sarah Holt Cram³, Henry², Nicholas¹*), b. at Canterbury, CT, 5 Apr 1751 son of Ephraim and Huldah (Cram) Woodward; Ward d. at Brooklyn, CT, 12 Apr 1810.

701) x JOHN PUTNAM, b. at Lyndeborough, about 1762; d. at Hyde Park, VT, 5 Nov 1837; m. at Lyndeborough, 30 Nov 1784, OLIVE BARRON, b. at Lyndeborough, 17 Feb 1765 daughter of William and Olive (Johnson) Barron; Olive d. at Hartford, VT, 24 May 1858.

159) ELIZABETH CRAM (*Sarah Holt Cram³, Henry², Nicholas¹*), b. at Hampton, NH, 27 Jun 1719 daughter of John and Sarah (Holt) Cram; d. at Lyndeborough, 30 Apr 1806; m. about 1741, JONATHAN CHAMBERLAIN, b. at Chelmsford, 11 Feb 1711/2 son of Samuel and Abigail (Hill) Chamberlain.

Early in their married life, Elizabeth and Jonathan were in Salem-Canada, but perhaps returned to Chelmsford at some point. It is not certain where the children were born, although the births of most of the children are recorded in Chelmsford perhaps when the family was registered there. In 1768, Jonathan received a deed of land from the heirs of Joseph Cram in consideration of providing care for Joseph. Joseph Cram was Elizabeth's brother. Both Jonathan and his son Jonathan enlisted in Captain Peter Clark's Company during the Revolution.[424]

Jonathan and Elizabeth were parents of eight children.

i ELIZABETH CHAMBERLAIN, b. 30 Apr 1742

702) ii JONATHAN CHAMBERLAIN, b. (recorded at Lyndeborough), 23 Feb 1743/4; d. at Lyndeborough, 26 Apr 1815; m. 13 Jul 1768, his first cousin, MARGARET CRAM (*Benjamin Cram⁴, Sarah Holt Cram³, Henry², Nicholas¹*), b. at Lyndeborough, 1748 daughter of Benjamin and Elizabeth (-) Cram.

703) iii SAMUEL CHAMBERLAIN, b. 4 Apr 1745 (recorded at Chelmsford); d. at Lyndeborough, about 1812; m. 1st about 1774, HANNAH ABBOTT, b. at Amherst, NH, 18 Sep 1755 daughter of Josiah and Hannah (Hobbs) Abbott; Hannah d. at Lyndeborough, 25 Sep 1784. Samuel m. 2nd 8 Nov 1785, NAOMI RICHARDSON, b. about 1762; Naomi d. about 1850.[425]

704) iv OLIVE CHAMBERLAIN, b. recorded at Chelmsford, 16 Aug 1750; m. about 1774, her first cousin, BENJAMIN CRAM (*Benjamin Cram⁴, Sarah Holt Cram³, Henry², Nicholas¹*), b. at Lyndeborough, 1754 son of Benjamin and Elizabeth (-) Cram; Benjamin d. at Lyndeborough, 31 Jul 1836.

v SARAH CHAMBERLAIN, b. 6 Apr 1753; d. at Lyndeborough, 5 Jan 1797. Sarah did not marry.

---

421 Hayward, *The History of Hancock*, p 385

422 Browne, *History of Hillsborough*, p 77

423 Farnham, *The New England Descendants of the Immigrant Ralph Farnum*

424 Donovan, *History of Lyndeborough*, pp 690-691

425 Donovan, *History of Lyndeborough*, p 692

705) vi MOLLY CHAMBERLAIN, b. recorded at Chelmsford, 10 May 1756; d. at Albion, ME; m. at Lyndeborough, 18 Jan 1780, JOHN KIDDER, b. at Lyndeborough, 4 Mar 1757 son of John and Tryphena (Powers) Kidder.

706) vii JOHN CHAMBERLAIN, b. recorded at Chelmsford, 16 Sep 1759; d. at Waterford, VT, about 1825 (probate Feb 1826); m. about 1782, MOLLY POWERS, b. at Acton, MA, 7 Feb 1762 daughter of Elliot and Mary (Cragin) Powers.

viii ABIGAIL CHAMBERLAIN, b. 8 Jul 1763

160) BENJAMIN CRAM (*Sarah Holt Cram³, Henry², Nicholas¹*), b. at Hampton, NH, 10 Mar 1721 son of John and Sarah (Holt) Cram; d. at Lyndeborough, 1823; m. about 1747, ELIZABETH who has not been identified.

There are six children of Benjamin and Elizabeth listed in the History of Lyndeborough.

702) i MARGARET CRAM, b. at Lyndeborough, 1748; m. 13 Jul 1768, his first cousin, JONATHAN CHAMBERLAIN (*Elizabeth Cram Chamberlain⁴, Sarah Holt Cram³, Henry², Nicholas¹*), b. at Lyndeborough, 26 Feb 1743/4 son of Jonathan and Elizabeth (Cram) Chamberlain; Jonathan d. at Lyndeborough, 26 Apr 1815.

707) ii NATHAN CRAM, b. at Lyndeborough, 5 Apr 1752; d. at Hancock, NH, 21 Jan 1851; m. RACHEL DUTTON, b. at Nottingham, NH, 9 Sep 1757 daughter of Joseph and Sarah (Dutton); Rachel d. at Hancock, 15 Aug 1835.

704) iii BENJAMIN CRAM, b. at Lyndeborough, 1754; d. at Lyndeborough, 31 Jul 1836; m. about 1774, his first cousin, OLIVE CHAMBERLAIN (*Elizabeth Cram Chamberlain⁴, Sarah Holt Cram³, Henry², Nicholas¹*), b. at Chelmsford, 16 Aug 1750 daughter of Jonathan and Elizabeth (Cram) Chamberlain.

iv HULDAH CRAM, b. about 1756

v JONAH CRAM, b. about 1762

vi DAVID CRAM, b. about 1768; d. May 1838. There is no clear information on David. *The History of the Town of Lyndeborough* reports him dying in 1838, but it is not clear if he married. There is a David Cram who died at Deerfield in 1838 and he had a wife Naomi in his probate record, but that seems to be a different David.

161) THOMAS PIERCE (*Dinah Holt Pierce³, Henry², Nicholas¹*), b. at Woburn, 30 Oct 1707 son of Daniel and Dinah (Holt) Pierce; d. at Wilmington, MA, 19 May 1790; m. at Woburn, 27 Jul 1732, HANNAH THOMPSON, b. at Woburn, 10 Jan 1705 daughter of Joshua and Martha (Dale) Thompson; Hannah d. at Wilmington, 10 Aug 1767.

Thomas and Hannah were parents of three children born at Wilmington.

708) i HANNAH PIERCE, b. at Wilmington, 16 Dec 1733; d. at Marblehead, 23 Jul 1797; m. at Wilmington, 7 Feb 1754, PETER DOLIVER[426], b; at Marblehead, 1726 son of Peter and Mary (Dennis) Doliver; Peter d. at Marblehead, 28 Sep 1807. Peter married second Jane Girdler (widow of Joseph Doliver) on 13 Jul 1800.

ii JACOB PIERCE, b. 18 Nov 1738; d. 9 Dec 1750.

709) iii ESTHER PIERCE, b. at Wilmington, 27 Aug 1741; d. at Wilmington, 6 Sep 1821; m. 1st at Wilmington, 26 Dec 1759, JOSEPH HARNDEN;[427] Joseph d. about 1777 (probate 3 Feb 1778).[428] Esther m. 2nd 18 Feb 1778, SAMUEL EAMS, b. at Wilmington, 14 Oct 1755 son of John and Mary (Jaquith) Eams; Samuel d. at Wilmington, 21 Jan 1834.

162) JOSEPH PIERCE (*Dinah Holt Pierce³, Henry², Nicholas¹*), b. 5 May 1711 son of Daniel and Dinah (Holt) Pierce;[429] m. by 1734, DEBORAH who has not been identified but who may be Deborah Frost daughter of Thomas Frost.

---

[426] Name is also given as Doliber.

[427] Joseph might be the son of John and Mary (Jaquith) Harnden born in 1736. One issue is discrepancies in dates. The death transcription for Joseph son of John and Mary is Dec 1775. The last child of Joseph and Esther was Jan 1777 and the probate of his estate was Feb 1778.

[428] The probate case and the guardianship cases for the children are in 1778 two weeks before Esther's second marriage.

[429] Pierce's *Pierce Genealogy*, and other sources, report that this Joseph married Abigail Green and had four children. However, Joseph who married Abigail Green and second Susannah Gleason was likely Joseph born at Woburn in 1714 son of Joseph and Mary (-) Pierce. Joseph Pierce who had married Abigail and then Susannah died in 1754. His probate documents include a statement dated 14 Jan 1754 signed by two of Joseph's unmarried sisters, Mary and Elizabeth, agreeing to the appointment of John Gleason as administrator of the estate. "Pray you appoint Mr. John Gleason to administer upon the estate of our brother Joseph Pierce deceased." This is signed (by mark) by Elizabeth Pierce and Mary Pierce. These two single ladies are the daughters of Joseph and Mary (-) Pierce (which can be established by birth and death records). As Daniel

On 20 January 1746/7 (deed recorded 20 March 1754), Joseph Pierce obtained from his father Daniel the family homestead property in Harvard.[430] On that same day, the elder Daniel made a sale of property to Joseph's brother Daniel. On 12 June 1756 (recorded 1761), Joseph Pierce and his wife Deborah sold this homestead property to Ephraim Stone for £173.[431]

There are records for the births of ten children of Joseph and Deborah. As Joseph and Deborah sold their property in Harvard in 1756, it is assumed that the family left Harvard around that time. It is not known where they went and no marriages for the children were identified.

i TIMOTHY PIERCE, b. at Wilmington, 13 Oct 1734; d. 21 Oct 1737.

ii JOSEPH PIERCE, b. 2 Oct 1736; d. 26 Nov 1737.

iii ELIZABETH PIERCE, b. at Wilmington, 28 Oct 1738

iv DINAH PIERCE, b. at Harvard, 22 Apr 1741; d. 16 Apr 1758.

v DEBORAH PIERCE, b. at Harvard, 24 Dec 1742

vi RUTH PIERCE, b. at Harvard, 24 Nov 1745

vii JOSEPH PIERCE, b. at Harvard, 26 Aug 1748

viii TIMOTHY PIERCE, b. at Harvard, 22 May 1750

ix THOMAS PIERCE, b. at Harvard, 27 Dec 1752

x HANNAH PIERCE, b. at Harvard, 15 Sep 1755

163) DANIEL PIERCE (*Dinah Holt Pierce[3], Henry[2], Nicholas[1]*), b. 23 Jun 1714 son of Daniel and Dinah (Holt) Pierce; d. at Leominster, May 1759 (probate Jun 1759); m. at Wilmington, 23 Dec 1741, SARAH BUCK, b. at Woburn, 16 Apr 1716 daughter of Samuel and Hannah (-) Buck; Sarah d. about 1768 (reversion of dower to the estate).

Daniel Pierce did not leave a will and his estate entered probate on 5 June 1759 with widow Sarah as administratrix. Real estate was valued at £219. The initial division of the real estate was in 1759 with the dower set off to the widow, eldest son Daniel receiving a double portion, and portions to the other children Reuben, Samuel, Jacob, Sarah, Abigail, and Keziah. Benjamin Whitcomb served as guardian for the five youngest children. The final division of the estate after the reversion of the dower was in 1768.[432]

Daniel Pierce and Sarah Buck were parents of eight children.

710) i DANIEL PIERCE, b. at Harvard, 3 Oct 1742; d. at St. Johnsbury, VT, 1821; m. at Leominster, 11 Dec 1766, MARCY GATES, b. about 1747 likely the daughter of Paul and Submit (Howe) Gates; Marcy d. 1827.[433]

ii ABIGAIL PIERCE, b. at Harvard, 5 Nov 1744; d. 6 Sep 1746.

711) iii REUBEN PIERCE, b. at Harvard, 17 Mar 1747; d. at Leominster, 30 Dec 1801; m. at Leominster, 1 Jan 1771, MARY WOOD, b. about 1748 *perhaps* the daughter of Nehemiah and Mary (Johnson) Wood; Mary d. at Jaffrey, 22 Aug 1833.

712) iv SAMUEL PIERCE, b. at Harvard, 21 May 1749; d. at Jaffrey, 27 Dec 1824; m. 1st 10 Jun 1774, ABIGAIL CARTER, b. 1751; Abigail d. 28 Feb 1777. Samuel m. 2nd at Lancaster, 13 Mar 1778, his third cousin once removed, ELIZABETH WHITNEY (*Annis Church Whitney[5], Annis Johnson Church[4], Josiah Johnson[3], Mary Holt Johnson[2], Nicholas[1]*), b. at Harvard, 27 Jun 1751 daughter of Caleb and Annis (Church) Whitney; Elizabeth d. at Jaffrey, 23 Oct 1823.

Pierce and Dinah Holt did not have daughters Mary and Elizabeth, Joseph who married Abigail Green is not this Joseph. The probate records do confirm that Joseph Pierce who died in 1754 was not only the brother of Elizabeth and Mary but the father of five children by his two wives.

[430] Massachusetts Land Records, Worcester County, 34:264

[431] Massachusetts Land Records, Worcester County, 43:491

[432] *Worcester County, MA: Probate File Papers, 1731-1881.* Online database. AmericanAncestors.org. New England Historic Genealogical Society, 2015. Case 46616

[433] Pierce's *Pierce Genealogy* varies from this information in two ways. First, Pierce states this son of Daniel was named David and married Sarah Mainer but that is not correct. This son is clearly Daniel which can be established with birth, probate, and land records. A David Pierce did marry Sarah Mainer but that is another person. Secondly, Pierce states it was Daniel a son of John Pierce that married Marcy Gates and that Daniel was a resident of New Hampshire at the time of his marriage. However, the Leominster records clearly state that Daniel and Marcy were both residents of Leominster at the time of marriage. Their first child was born in Leominster in 1768. On 5 Nov 1768, Daniel Pierce and wife Marcy of Leominster sold the lands set off to him from his honored father's estate, the description of the land being the same as the land distributed to Daniel Pierce eldest son of Daniel Pierce, to James Richardson, and after that time Daniel and Marcy were in Westmoreland where their other children were born.

713) v JACOB PIERCE, b. at Harvard, 2 Aug 1751; d. at Jaffrey, 9 Aug 1826; m. at Leominster, 19 Feb 1777, REBECCA WHITCOMB, b. at Leominster, 19 Mar 1754 daughter of Benjamin and Dorothy (White) Whitcomb; Rebecca d. at Jaffrey, 3 Mar 1843.

vi SARAH PIERCE, b. at Leominster, 2 Aug 1754; d. 3 Mar 1771.

vii ABIGAIL PIERCE, b. at Leominster, 1 Apr 1756; she was living in 1768 but nothing further found.

viii KEZIAH PIERCE, b. at Leominster, 13 May 1759; m. at Leominster, 20 Jul 1781, JONATHAN HOLT who has not been identified. Nothing further was found for this couple.

164) JOHN PIERCE (*Dinah Holt Pierce³, Henry², Nicholas¹*), b. at Woburn, 23 May 1716 son of Daniel and Dinah (Holt) Pierce; d. about 1779;[434] m. 1st at Harvard, 22 Nov 1744, HANNAH STONE, b. at Groton, 18 Apr 1726 daughter of Simon and Sarah (Turner) Stone;[435] Hannah d. about 1746. John m. 2nd at Harvard, 10 Mar 1747, HANNAH HOUGHTON, b. about 1727 daughter of Thomas and Meriah (Moore) Houghton;[436] Hannah d. at Harvard, 16 Apr 1811.

Child of John Pierce and Hannah Stone:

i HANNAH PIERCE, b. at Harvard, Aug 1745; d. 21 Oct 1745.

John Pierce and Hannah Houghton were parents of seven children.

714) i MERIAH PIERCE, b. at Harvard, 19 Oct 1748; d. at Harvard, 12 Apr 1781; m. at Bolton, 30 Nov 1768, ELISHA HOUGHTON, baptized at Harvard, 5 Jun 1748 son of Ephraim and Sarah (-) Houghton; Elisha d. at Shaftsbury, VT, 18 Nov 1826. Elisha married second Elizabeth Rice, intention 28 Sep 1781.

ii HANNAH PIERCE, b. 6 May 1750; d. 4 Oct 1750.

715) iii HANNAH PIERCE, b. at Harvard, 25 Aug 1751; m. at Bolton, 28 Jun 1769, LEMUEL BURNHAM

iv THOMAS PIERCE, b. 2 Oct 1754; d. 14 Jun 1757.

716) v JOHN PIERCE, b. at Bolton, 22 May 1759; d. at Harvard, 12 Sep 1828; m. 1st 16 May 1799, DINAH SAWYER, b. 1772; Dinah d. at Harvard, 12 Jun 1825.

vi LUTHER PIERCE, b. at Bolton, 16 Jun 1764; d. at Bolton, 1832. Luther did not marry.

717) vii CALVIN PIERCE, b. at Bolton, 1 Mar 1766; d. at Bolton, after 1832; m. 1st 12 Jan 1786, BETSEY BROWN, b. 1771; Betsey d. at Bolton, 1817. Calvin m. 2nd 31 Mar 1818, Mrs. LUCY BRIDE of Berlin, MA; Lucy d. after 1832.

165) KEZIA PIERCE (*Dinah Holt Pierce³, Henry², Nicholas¹*), b. at Woburn, 9 May 1723 daughter of Daniel and Dinah (Holt) Pierce; d. likely at Westmoreland, NH, after 1780 when she signed probate records as Kezia Robbins; m. at Harvard, 16 Apr 1744, ISAAC STONE, b. at Groton, 17 May 1723 son of Simon and Sarah (Turner) Stone; Isaac d. at Westmoreland, 1776 (probate 1776). Kezia m. 2nd Mr. Robbins who has not been identified.

Kezia and Isaac had their children in Harvard, Massachusetts and about 1767 relocated to Westmoreland, New Hampshire. Lieutenant Isaac Stone served as a Corporal during the French and Indian War in the expedition to Crown Point. He served as First Lieutenant Jacob Hinds Company from May to August 1775 and was at the Battle of Bunker Hill.[437]

Isaac Stone did not leave a will and his estate was in probate in 1776 with the inventory taken in October 1776.[438] Real estate was valued at £125. Ephraim Stone was named administrator. In 1791, George Pierce filed a petition with the Court as he was a creditor of the estate and learned that the estate was declared insolvent and also that payment from the estate had been made to the heirs meaning it was not insolvent and he wanted his money. In August 1777, Ephraim Stone had petitioned to sell part of the real estate as the personal estate was not sufficient to pay claims against the estate. Keziah Stone in 1776 was allowed as guardian to the minor children. In 1780, daughter Abigail Stone selected Kezia Robbins of Westmoreland as her guardian.

Kezia and Isaac were parents of eight children whose births were recorded at Harvard, Massachusetts.

---

[434] Pierce, *Pierce Genealogy* reports that John is reported to have left home during the Revolutionary War and is believed to have been killed in New York.

[435] The 1746 probate of Simon Stone of Harvard includes John Pierce signing as an heir agreeing to the distribution.

[436] The 1764 will of Thomas Houghton includes a bequest to "my daughter Pierce."

[437] Bartlett, *Simon Stone Genealogy*, pp 107-108

[438] *New Hampshire. Probate Court (Cheshire County)*; Probate Place: *Cheshire, New Hampshire, Estate Files, R536-R570, 1882-1885; Estate Files, S1-S57, 1771-1790, Estate of Isaac Stone, Case number 6*

718) i EPHRAIM STONE, b. at Harvard, 22 Jan 1745; d. at Brome, Québec, 15 Jun 1820; m. 12 Aug 1768, LUCINDA CHAMBERLAIN, b. at Bridgewater, MA, 20 Mar 1751 daughter of Henry and Susannah (Hinds) Chamberlain; Lucinda d. at Brome, 1 Apr 1821.

ii ISAAC STONE, b. 22 Jan 1746

719) iii DINAH STONE, b. at Harvard, 3 Aug 1749; d. at Westmoreland, NH, 26 Oct 1811; m. at Westmoreland, 25 Dec 1766, MOSES WHITE, b. at Brookfield, MA, 2 Aug 1743 son of Cornelius and Hannah (Gilbert) White; Moses d. at Westmoreland, 6 Mar 1829.

720) iv DANIEL STONE, b. at Harvard, 10 Jul 1754; d. at Lower Canada, 9 May 1842; m. 27 Oct 1779, ABIGAIL ELLIS, b. at Keene, NH, 1 May 1755 daughter of Gideon and Elizabeth (Metcalf) Ellis; Abigail d. at Lower Canada, 20 Jul 1847.

721) v JACOB STONE, b. at Harvard, 26 Jul 1756; d. likely at Ogdensburg, NY; m. about 1782, ABIGAIL HOWE, b. at Sudbury, 28 Mar 1751 daughter of Edward and Lois (Maynard) Howe.[439]

vi KEZIA STONE, b. 6 Apr 1760

vii SARAH STONE, b. 20 Mar 1762

722) viii ABIGAIL STONE, b at Harvard, 19 Feb 1765; m. at Westmoreland, 11 Dec 1783, SETH GARY, b. 1764 son of Seth and Hannah (Briggs) Gary;[440] Seth was living in Charlotte, VT in 1810.

166) ABIGAIL HOLT (*Paul*[3], *Henry*[2], *Nicholas*[1]), b. at Andover, 21 Aug 1716 daughter of Paul and Abigail (Holt) Holt; d. at Hampton, CT, 3 Nov 1749; m. 3 Dec 1736, JONATHAN KINGSBURY, b. 1712 son of Thomas and Margaret (Haines) Kingsbury; Jonathan d. at Hampton, 28 Dec 1770. Jonathan married second Hannah Clark on 9 Jan 1751 and married third Sarah *How* Ballard the widow of John Ballard.

In his will written 12 October 1770 (proved 17 January 1771), Jonathan Kingsbury bequeaths to beloved wife Sarah the household items that she had when they married, £8, other household items, a saddle and bridle, and other provisions for her support including improvements on a portion of the real estate. Beloved daughter Abigail Abbot receives a piece of land with house and barn in Ashford that he holds by deed from William Knowlton. Beloved son Jonathan receives the remainder of the estate real and personal provided he pay the other legacies in the will. These legacies are £200 each to daughters Hannah Kingsbury, Elizabeth Kingsbury, Mary Kingsbury, and Esther Kingsbury when arriving at the age of twenty with provision for land valued at £220 each if Jonathan refuses to pay the legacies. Grandsons John Goold and Jonathan Goold each receives £10. Son Jonathan is sole executor. The total value of the estate was £1755.6.4 which included one farm in Ashford with 434 acres and a second farm of 41 acres.[441]

Abigail Holt and Jonathan Kingsbury were parents of two children born at Hampton.

723) i ABIGAIL KINGSBURY, b. at Hampton, 17 May 1742; d. at Lima, NY, 1791; m. 1st, at Windham, 13 Nov 1759, JOHN GOULD, b. 1731 son of Henry and Rebecca (Cole) Gould; John d. at Hampton, 29 Oct 1764 (probate Nov 1764). Abigail m. 2nd, at Hampton, 11 Sep 1770, JOHN ABBOTT. On 14 Mar 1791, Abigail filed for divorce from John Abbott on grounds of desertion.[442]

724) ii JONATHAN KINGSBURY, b. at Hampton, 25 Apr 1745; d. at Hampton, 25 Sep 1802; m. 1st, 14 Jan 1768, ANNE GEER, b. at Preston, 22 Dec 1745 daughter of Aaron and Mercy (Fisher) Geer;[443] Anne d. 23 Oct 1773. Jonathan m. 2nd, 21 Jun 1775, LODEMA RANSOM, b. at Kent, 8 Mar 1752 daughter of John and Bethia (Lewis) Ransom;[444] Lodema d. 24 Mar 1814.

167) PAUL HOLT (*Paul*[3], *Henry*[2], *Nicholas*[1]), b. at Andover, Aug 1720 son of Paul and Abigail (Holt) Holt; d. at Hampton, CT, 21 Dec 1804; m. 20 Jan 1742, MEHITABLE CHANDLER, b. 12 Apr 1719 daughter of Philemon and Hannah (Clary) Chandler; Mehitable d. at Hampton, 10 May 1773. Paul m. 2nd, 4 Jan 1774, MARY SPENCER.

Paul was born in Andover but migrated to Hampton with his father. It is reported that Mehitable died while doing her washing at a tub.[445]

Paul Holt did not leave a will and son Paul Holt was named administrator 18 January 1805. The inventory was taken 31 December 1804 with a total value of $2,061.76 including a farm of 104 acres. The widow's dower was set off to Mary Holt.

---

439 Westmoreland Historical Committee, *History of Westmoreland*, p 459

440 Brainerd, *Gary Genealogy*, p 174

441 *Connecticut. Probate Court (Windham District), Probate records volume 8, pp 131-138*

442 Knox and Ferris, Connecticut Divorces: Superior Court Records for the Counties of Tolland, New London & Windham 1719-1910, p 259; John, Wrentham, MA m. Abigail Gould, Windham, 11 Sep 1770; desertion 14 Mar 1791

443 The 1797 will of Aaron Geer includes a bequest to the heirs of Anne Kingsbury wife of Jonathan Kingsbury.

444 The 1791 will of John Ransom of Kent includes a bequest to his daughter Lodema Kingsbury.

445 Chandler, *The Chandler Family: The Descendants of William and Annis* Chandler, p 99

Other heirs receiving distribution from the estate were Paul Holt, Philemon Holt, Ebenezer Holt, Stephen Holt, James Holt, Josiah Holt, and Mahitabel Phelps wife of Jeremiah Phelps.[446]

725) i PAUL HOLT, b. at Windham, 4 Jan 1742/3; d. at Hampton, 26 Oct 1827; m. 1st, 20 Aug 1767, SARAH WELCH, b. at Norwich, 6 Jul 1742 daughter of Joseph and Lydia (Rudd) Welch; Sarah d. 26 Dec 1784. Paul m. 2nd, 15 Jan 1789, PHEBE WELCH CADY, b. 1754 daughter of Gideon and Sarah (Hutchins) Cady;[447] Phebe d. at Hampton, 31 May 1800. Paul m. 3rd, 27 Nov 1800, his second cousin, DINAH HOLT (*Joshua4, Joshua3, Nicholas2, Nicholas1*) (widow of Seth Stowell), b. at Windham, 22 Mar 1750 daughter of Joshua and Mary (Abbott) Holt; Dinah d. 21 Feb 1826.

726) ii PHILEMON HOLT, b. at Hampton, 22 Jun 1744; d. at Willington, 31 Jul 1818; m. at Willington, 27 Aug 1771, JEMIMA ELDREDGE, b. at Willington, 28 Mar 1755 daughter of Jesse and Abigail (Smith) Eldredge; Jemima d. at Willington, 3 Oct 1821.

727) iii EBENEZER HOLT, b. recorded at Windham, 23 Feb 1745/6; m. at Somers, 29 Aug 1771, MARY COLLINS.

728) iv STEPHEN HOLT, b. 12 Mar 1748; d. at Pittsfield, VT, 31 Dec 1838; m. 20 Nov 1774, HANNAH GEER, b. 2 Nov 1755 daughter of Aaron and Mercy (Fisher) Geer;[448] Hannah d. at Chaplin, CT, 1858.

729) v JAMES HOLT, b. at Hampton, 21 May 1750; d. at Bristol, CT, 29 Mar 1826; m. 1st, 31 Dec 1769, HULDAH STILES, b. at Hampton, 18 Sep 1736 daughter of Samuel and Huldah (Durkee) Stiles; Huldah d. at Hampton, 12 Jul 1799.[449] James m. 2nd, 29 Jun 1800, CHLOE STILES (niece of Huldah), b. 4 May 1781 daughter of Isaac and Abigail (Case) Stiles. Chloe Holt was living in Bristol in 1850 with her son James.

vi THOMAS HOLT, b. 25 Feb 1752; d. 17 Aug 1754.

vii JOSIAH HOLT, b. at Windham, 28 May 1754; d. at Burlington, CT, 14 Jan 1810; m. at Medfield, MA, 28 May 1777, KEZIAH ADAMS, b. at Medfield, 31 Mar 1747 daughter of Henry and Jemima (Morse) Adams;[450] Keziah d. at Bristol, CT, 7 Apr 1811. No children were identified for Josiah Holt and Keziah Adams.

730) viii MEHITABLE HOLT, b. at Windham, 1 May 1757; d. at Hampton, 27 Oct 1819; m. at Pomfret, 27 Nov 1789, JEREMIAH PHELPS, b. at Hebron, 13 Jul 1729 son of Timothy and Hannah (Calkins) Phelps.[451]

168) JONATHAN ABBOT (*Zerviah Holt Abbott3, Henry2, Nicholas1*), b. at Andover, Dec 1714 son of Jonathan and Zerviah (Holt) Abbott; d. 31 May 1794; m. 1st 8 Oct 1739, MARTHA LOVEJOY (*Henry Lovejoy4, Mary Farnum Lovejoy3, Elizabeth Holt Farnum2, Nicholas1*), b. 2 Nov 1720 daughter of Henry and Sarah (Farnum) Lovejoy; Martha d. about 1768. Jonathan m. 2nd as her second husband, his second cousin, MARY ABBOTT, b. at Andover, 12 Mar 1722/3 daughter of George and Mary (Phillips) Abbott; Mary d. at Andover, 8 Aug 1792.

In his will written 13 November 1787 (probate 9 July 1794), Jonathan Abbot has bequests to the following persons: well beloved wife Mary, son William Abbot, daughter Martha Whiting, and son Jonathan Abbot who is named executor.[452]

Jonathan Abbot and Martha Lovejoy had four children. The births of the three oldest children are recorded at Lunenburg. The birth of the youngest child was recorded at Andover.

731) i JONATHAN ABBOT, b. at Lunenburg, 20 Aug 1740; d. at Andover, 26 Dec 1821; m. 1st, about 1762, his third cousin, MEHITABLE ABBOTT, b. at Andover 11 Aug 1736 daughter of Ephraim and Hannah (Phelps) Abbott; Mehitable d. 1 Jan 1777. Jonathan m. 2nd, 17 Dec 1778, his third cousin, DORCAS ABBOTT, b. 23 Sep 1758 daughter of Stephen and Mary (Abbott) Abbott; Dorcas d. 3 Mar 1844.

ii NATHAN ABBOT, b. Jan 1743/4; died young.

732) iii WILLIAM ABBOT, b. at Lunenburg, 24 Nov 1745; d. Wilton, NH, Oct 1807;[453] m. 26 Aug 1766, his third cousin, SARA HOLT (*Timothy4, Timothy3, James2, Nicholas1*), b. 11 Aug 1746 daughter of Timothy and Hannah (Dane) Holt.

---

[446] *Connecticut State Library (Hartford, Connecticut), Probate Packets, Hicks-Hovey, Elisha, 1719-1880, Estate of Paul Holt 1804, number 1952*

[447] The 1799 will of Gideon Cady includes a bequest to his daughter Phebe Holt.

[448] The 1797 will of Aaron Geer includes a bequest to daughter Hannah Holt wife of Stephen Holt.

[449] Huldah the wife of James Holt died at age 63.

[450] Adams, *A Genealogical History of Henry Adams of Braintree*, p 15

[451] Phelps and Servin, *The Phelps Family in America*, volume 1, p 211

[452] *Essex County, MA: Probate File Papers, 1638-1881. Probate of Jonathan Abbot, 9 Jul 1794, Case number 81.*

[453] Livermore, *History of the Town of Wilton*, p 550; no death record was located to support this information.

733) iv MARTHA ABBOT, b. at Andover, 23 Jan 1749/50; d. at Temple, NH, 10 Jan 1842; m. 3 May 1774; OLIVER WHITING, b. at Pelham, NH, 6 Apr 1750 son of Eleazer and Dorothy (Crosby) Whiting; Oliver d. 28 Sep 1829.

169) DAVID ABBOT (*Zerviah Holt Abbott*[3], *Henry*[2], *Nicholas*[1]), b. at Andover, Dec 1716 son of Jonathan and Zerviah (Holt) Abbott; d. 1777 at Rockingham, NH (probate 31 Dec 1777); m. 10 Aug 1741, his second cousin, once removed, HANNAH CHANDLER (*Mehitable Russell Chandler*[4], *Phebe Johnson Russell*[3], *Mary Holt Johnson*[2], *Nicholas*[1]), b. 1724 daughter of Joseph and Mehitable (Russell) Chandler; Hannah's death not known but she was living at the time of her husband's will.

The will of David Abbot, written 11 June 1771, includes bequests to the following persons: son John Abbot receives a pair of three year old steers, one cow and all his wearing apparel; daughter Hannah Holt receives 5 shillings; daughter Bridget Abbot receives 15 pounds and a yearling heifer; daughter Mehitable also get 15 pounds and a heifer at marriage or the age of 21; son Job Abbot is to be the sole executor; beloved wife Hannah has use of all the household during her widowhood; son Job receives remainder of real and personal estate, although noting that certain tracts of land have been granted to son John by warrantee deed.[454]

The five children listed in the will are given here. *The History of Pembroke* and other sources list a son Benjamin with this family. However, it seems more likely that Benjamin was the son of David Abbott and Hannah Danforth, and as he is not mentioned/living at the time of the will, he is not included here. Five children were born at Pembroke.

417) i JOB ABBOT, b. about 1742; d. at West Barnet, VT, 15 Dec 1815; m. about 1771, PHEBE FARNUM, likely the daughter of Ebenezer and Phebe (Ingalls) Farnum, b. at Andover, 15 Dec 1750.

734) ii HANNAH ABBOT, b. 7 Sep 1743; d. at Pembroke, 17 Mar 1813; m. her third cousin, BENJAMIN HOLT (*Benjamin*[4], *Nicholas*[3], *Nicholas*[2], *Nicholas*[1]), b. 28 Feb 1741 son of Benjamin and Sarah (Frye) Holt.

iii JOHN ABBOT, b. about 1752 (although he may be the oldest child in this family born in the early 1740's); still living in 1771. There are no records located yet for him. As he was an adult at the time of his father's will having already received land through deed, it is possible that he married although clear evidence not found yet.

735) iv BRIDGET ABBOT, b. about 1761; m. 24 Dec 1787, her third cousin, PHINEAS AMES, b. 7 Sep 1764 son of Samuel and Elizabeth (Stevens) Ames; Phineas d. about 1792. Bridget m. 2nd, 17 Dec 1793, STEPHEN HARRIMAN, b. at Haverhill, 10 Mar 1757 son of Stephen and Sarah (Mascraft) Harriman; Stephen d. at Lisbon, OH, 25 Feb 1828. Stephen was first married to Lucy Story.

v MEHITABLE ABBOT, b. about 1762; still living in 1771.

170) ZERVIAH ABBOTT (*Zerviah Holt Abbott*[3], *Henry*[2], *Nicholas*[1]), b. at Andover, Aug 1722 daughter of Jonathan and Zerviah (Holt) Abbott; d. likely at Pembroke, NH; m. 17 Sep 1745, EPHRAIM BLUNT, b. 5 Feb 1720/1 son of William and Sarah (Foster) Blunt.

There is record evidence for three children of Zerviah Abbott and Ephraim Holt. This family seems to have moved several times and were at various times in Massachusetts, New Hampshire, and Vermont.

i EPHRAIM BLUNT, b. at Andover, 9 Aug 1747; died young.

736) ii EPHRAIM BLUNT, b. at Danville, VT, 20 Jun 1754; d. at Danville, 15 Feb 1829; m. 21 Nov 1776, MARTHA ORDWAY, b. at Amesbury, 28 Mar 1753 daughter of Moses and Anna (-) Ordway.

737) iii ZERVIAH BLUNT, b. at Suncook, NH, 1759;[455] d. at Calais, VT, 18 Jan 1860; m. at Canterbury, NH, 26 Feb 1778, AARON HARTSHORN, b. at Reading, 1754 son of Thomas and Abia (-) Hartshorn; Aaron d. at Danville, VT, 19 Jun 1799.

171) JOB ABBOTT (*Zerviah Holt Abbott*[3], *Henry*[2], *Nicholas*[1]), b. at Andover, 3 Oct 1724 son of Jonathan and Zerviah (Holt) Abbott; d. likely at Pembroke, NH; m. about 1751, his second cousin, SARAH ABBOTT (*Abigail Farnum Abbott*[4], *Ralph Farnum*[3], *Elizabeth Holt Farnum*[2], *Nicholas*[1]), b. 13 Aug 1730 daughter of James and Abigail (Farnum) Abbott. Sarah m. 2nd about 1765, RICHARD EASTMAN, b. at Haverhill, 9 Aug 1712 son of Jonathan and Hannah (Green) Eastman; Richard d. at Lovell, ME, 29 Dec 1807. Richard Eastman m. 1st 15 Nov 1737, MARY LOVEJOY (*Henry Lovejoy*[4], *Mary Farnum Lovejoy*[3], *Elizabeth Holt Farnum*[2], *Nicholas*[1]), b. at Andover, Dec 1718 daughter of Henry and Sarah (Farnum) Lovejoy; Mary d. at Pembroke, 14 Jun 1764.

---

[454] *New Hampshire Wills and Probate Records 1643-1982*, Probate of David Abbott, Rockingham, 31 Dec 1777, Case number 4406.

[455] Zerviah Hartshorn's death record lists her parents as Zerviah Blunt and Ephraim "Hartshorn" although this seems just to be a confusion of the name of her spouse and the name of her father. Her age on the death record is 100 years, 11 months, 21 days. *Vermont Vital Records 1720-1908*

Sarah Abbott and Job Abbott had four children. Three of the children of the second child, Nathan, married three of the children of the third child, Job.

738) i SARAH ABBOTT, b. 1751 at Suncook; d. at Temple, NH, 9 Oct 1854;[456] m. 25 Nov 1773, her third cousin, ABIEL HOLT (*Joseph[4], Thomas[3], Nicholas[2], Nicholas[1]*), b. at Lunenburg, 14 Jul 1748 son of Joseph and Mary (Abbott) Holt; Abiel d. 7 Jan 1811.

739) ii NATHAN ABBOTT, b. at Pembroke 4 Sep 1753; d. at Andover 1801 (probate of will 31 Mar 1801); m. 8 May 1777, his third cousin, SARAH BALLARD, b. 28 Dec 1755 daughter of Hezekiah and Lydia (Chandler) Ballard; Sarah d. 20 Aug 1825.

740) iii JOB ABBOTT, b. about 1755 at Pembroke; d. at Wilton 12 Jul 1805; m. at Andover, 12 Dec 1780, his third cousin once removed, ANNA BALLARD (*Sarah Abbott Ballard[6], Anne Lovejoy Abbott[5], William Lovejoy[4], Mary Farnum Lovejoy[3], Elizabeth Holt Farnum[2], Nicholas[1]*), b. 15 Nov 1762 daughter of Timothy and Sarah (Abbott) Ballard; Anna d. at Wilton, 7 Apr 1805.[457]

741) iv ABIGAIL ABBOTT, b. about 1757; d. 1 May 1845 at Lovell, ME;[458] m. by 1778, STEPHEN DRESSER, b. at Andover, 25 Oct 1754 son of Jonathan and Sarah (Foster) Dresser; Stephen d. at Frye, ME, 28 Sep 1829.

Richard Eastman and Mary Lovejoy were parents of thirteen children,[459] some of whom were born at Pembroke, but at least one of the births recorded at Conway.

i CALEB EASTMAN, b. 27 Oct 1738; d. 25 Aug 1739.

ii JONATHAN EASTMAN, b. 13 Sep 1739; d. 23 Feb 1761 during military in the French war.

742) iii MARY EASTMAN, b. at Pembroke, 22 May 1742; d. at Andover, 26 Jul 1801; m. at Andover, 4 Jul 1766, JONATHAN CUMMINGS, b. at Topsfield, 14 Oct 1743 son of David and Sarah (Goodhue) Cummings; Jonathan d. at Andover, 1805. After Mary's death, Jonathan m. 30 Dec 1802, MARY LOVEJOY (*Joshua Lovejoy[5], Henry Lovejoy[4], Mary Farnum Lovejoy[3], Elizabeth Holt Farnum[2], Nicholas[1]*) (widow of James Parker), b. at Andover, 13 Aug 1745 daughter of Joshua and Lydea (Abbott) Lovejoy; Mary Lovejoy d. at Andover, 15 Apr 1826.

743) iv ABIATHAR EASTMAN, b. at Pembroke, 29 Apr 1745; d. at North Conway, 10 Jan 1815; m. at Conway, 3 Dec 1775, his second cousin, PHEBE MERRILL (*Phebe Abbott Merrill[5], Abigail Farnum Abbott[4], Ralph Farnum[3], Elizabeth Holt Farnum[2], Nicholas[1]*), b. at Conway, Dec 1753 daughter of Thomas and Phebe (Abbott) Merrill; Phebe d. at North Conway, 9 Oct 1839.

744) v RICHARD EASTMAN, b. at Pembroke, 20 Apr 1747; d. at North Conway, NH (buried at Conway), 6 Dec 1826; m. 1st about 1766, his third cousin once removed, ABIAH HOLT (*Benjamin[4], Nicholas[3], Nicholas[2], Nicholas[1]*), b. about 1747 daughter of Benjamin and Sarah (Frye) Holt; Abiah d. at North Conway, 1 May 1790. Richard m. 2nd 27 Aug 1791, SUSANNAH RUNNELS (widow of Benjamin Durgin), b. 1765 daughter of Jonathan and Keziah (Carter) Runnels;[460] Susannah d. at North Conway, 29 May 1849.

745) vi SARAH EASTMAN, b. at Pembroke, 6 May 1749; d. at Conway, 29 Dec 1836; m. 1767, THOMAS RUSSELL, b. at Andover, 12 Feb 1746/7 son of Thomas and Abigail (Ballard) Russell; Thomas d. at Conway, 15 Jul 1823.

vii JOB EASTMAN, b. 26 Jul 1751; d. at Norway, ME, 24 Feb 1845. Job married but the name of his wife has not been found. He and his wife did not have children. Job was Justice of the Peace in Norway, ME for nearly 50 years. Job was reported to have married "a sister of the proprietor of the Cummings tract" in Norway, ME.[461]

746) viii NOAH EASTMAN, b. at Pembroke, 20 Mar 1753; d. 28 Aug 1829; m. his third cousin once removed, HANNAH HOLT (*Benjamin[4], Nicholas[3], Nicholas[2], Nicholas[1]*), b. 28 Feb 1758 daughter of Benjamin and Sarah (Frye) Holt; Hannah d. 15 Apr 1820.

---

456 Gravestone inscription: Aged 103 yrs. 2 ms. & 25 ds.

457 Date of death obtained from her gravestone which has the following inscription: Erected to the memory of Mrs. Anne Abbott, consort of Mr. Job Abbott, who died April 7, 1805, in the 43 year of her age. Findagrave Memorial ID: 34218725

458 Ancestry.com, *U.S., Find A Grave Index, 1600s-Current* (Provo, UT, USA: Ancestry.com Operations, Inc., 2012).

459 Rix, *History and Genealogy of the Eastman Family*, pp 82-83

460 Runnels, *Genealogy of the Runnels and Reynolds Families in America*, p 131

461 Whitman, *A History of Norway, Maine*, p 139

ix HANNAH EASTMAN, b. 7 Apr 1755; d. 8 Aug 1757.

x MARTHA EASTMAN, b. 8 Aug 1757; nothing further known.

xi Twin 1, b. and d. 1759

xii Twin 2, b. and d. 1759

747) xiii ESTHER EASTMAN, b. at Pembroke, 6 May 1761; d. at Sherbrooke, Québec, 30 Dec 1846; m. 26 Oct 1781, EPHRAIM ABBOTT, b. at Andover, 18 Mar 1759 son of Ebenezer and Lydia (Farrington) Abbott; Ephraim d. at Sherbrooke, 1 Jan 1834.[462]

172) SAMUEL ABBOTT (*Zerviah Holt Abbott[3], Henry[2], Nicholas[1]*), b. 20 Sep 1727 son of Jonathan and Zerviah (Holt) Abbott; m. 12 Jul 1749, MIRIAM STEVENS whose origins are undetermined but may be the Miriam baptized in 1730 at Newbury.

Samuel Abbott and Miriam Stevens had eleven children whose births are recorded at Pembroke, New Hampshire.

748) i SAMUEL ABBOTT, b. 16 Apr 1750; d. at North Pembroke, 11 Mar 1836; m. 22 Mar 1781, LYDIA PERRIN, b. about 1752 (based on age at time of death) parents not yet certain; Lydia d. 1 Apr 1829.

ii EBENEZER ABBOTT, b. 18 Oct 1751; no further record.

749) iii ABIGAIL ABBOTT, b. 6 Sep 1753; d. likely at Salisbury, NH; m. 23 Nov 1773, BENJAMIN WHITTEMORE, b. 4 Dec 1750 son of Aaron and Abigail (Coffin) Whittemore.

iv JUDITH ABBOTT, b. 28 Jul 1755; m. 18 Apr 1791, perhaps as his third wife, HEZEKIAH YOUNG. Published genealogies report that Judith was Hezekiah's first wife, but the available records are that Judith married Hezekiah in 1791 as his second, or perhaps even his third, wife. He married Mary Kimball in 1783 and Judith Abbott in 1791 at Pembroke. There is another marriage for Hezekiah Young and Mary Young in 1777 at Canterbury, but that may be a different Hezekiah. There are no records for any children for Judith and Hezekiah.[463]

750) v JEREMIAH ABBOTT, b. 9 May 1757; d. at Montville, ME, 27 Jan 1816; m. 29 Nov 1787, ELIZABETH "BETSEY" FRYE, b. 18 Feb 1767 daughter of Ebenezer and Hannah (Baker) Frye; Betsey d. 27 Aug 1841.

751) vi SARAH ABBOTT, b. 21 Jul 1759; m. 4 Nov 1790, as his second wife, JEREMIAH WHEELER, b. at Concord, MA, Feb 1745 son of Jeremiah and Esther (Russell) Wheeler; Jeremiah d. at Concord, NH, 17 Oct 1827.

752) vii LYDIA ABBOTT, b. 14 Jul 1761; d. at Bethel, VT, 9 Dec 1840; m. 29 Mar 1787, NATHANIEL MORRILL, b. at South Hampton, NH, 11 Jan 1761 son of Paul and Martha (Worthen) Morrill; Nathaniel d. 17 Nov 1832.

753) viii EZRA ABBOTT, b. 4 Aug 1763; d. at Sanbornton, NH, 16 Nov 1824; m. 30 Nov 1794, MOLLY BROWN daughter of William and Ruth (McDuffee) Brown;[464] Molly d. at Cabot, VT, 1836.

754) ix WILLIAM ABBOTT, b. 10 Sep 1765; d. at Pembroke, 22 Jul 1838; m. his third cousin, DORCAS PARKER, b. at Andover, 17 Feb 1769 daughter of Joseph and Hannah (Abbott) Parker; Dorcas d. 9 Nov 1853.

755) x RACHEL ABBOTT, b. 15 Jun 1768; d. at Pembroke, 28 Dec 1854; m. 30 Dec 1789, JOHN KELLEY, b. 22 Jul 1764 son of Samuel and Sarah (Barker) Kelley.

756) xi MARIAM ABBOTT, b. 5 Sep 1771; d. at Randolph, VT, 21 Jun 1820; m. JOHN MORRILL, b. 17 Jan 1759 son of Paul and Martha (Worthen) Morrill; John d. 21 Sep 1849.

173) DINAH HOLT (*Keturah Holt Holt[3], Henry[2], Nicholas[1]*), b. at Windham, 17 Mar 1725/6 daughter of Joshua and Keturah (Holt) Holt; d. at Willington, 25 Sep 1805; m. at Windham, 6 Nov 1746, TIMOTHY PEARL, b. at Windham, 24 Oct 1723 son of Timothy and Elizabeth (Stevens) Pearl; Timothy d. at Willington, 19 Oct 1789.

There are some double-birth records at Windham which have children (Hannah, Phineas) of the same names and birthdates with one attributed to Timothy and Dinah and one attributed to Timothy's father Timothy and his second wife Mary. [Phineas, s. of Timothy and Mary, b. 2 Aug 1753; Phineas, s. of Timothy and Dinah, b. 2 Aug 1753.] These children are all named in the will of the elder Timothy. Also, they are recorded at Windham and Timothy and Dinah were at Willington soon after their marriage. Therefore, they are not included here as it seems more likely they are the children of Timothy and Mary.

---

[462] *Quebec, Canada, Vital and Church Records (Drouin Collection), 1621-1968.*

[463] Ancestry.com, New Hampshire, Marriage Records Index, 1637-1947

[464] Chase, *History of Old Chester*, p 478

There are births of nine children recorded for Timothy and Dinah, the oldest at Windham and the rest of the children at Willington.

i ALICE PEARL, b. 6 Sep 1747; d. 10 Sep 1747.

757) ii ALICE PEARL, b. 6 Jul 1748. The birth transcription says 6 Jul 1743, but this seems an error and Durrie's Holt genealogy says 1748; her age at death in 1826 was 76. Alice d. Dec 1826; m. at Willington, 10 Oct 1767, ELEAZER SCRIPTURE, b. at Willington, 10 May 1742 son of John and Hannah (Wells) Scripture; Eleazer d. at Willington, 1813 (estate inventory 13 Oct 1813).

758) iii OLIVER PEARL, b. 9 Oct 1749; d. 4 Nov 1831; m. 1st, 1 Jan 1772, MERCY HINCKLEY, b. 1749 daughter of John and Susanna (Harris) Hinckley;[465]; Mercy d. at Willington, 15 Nov 1781. Oliver m. 2nd, 24 Apr 1782, his second cousin, HANNAH HOLT (*Abiel⁴, Abiel³, Nicholas², Nicholas¹*), b. 14 Mar 1756 daughter of Abiel and Mary (Downer) Holt; Hannah d. 20 Nov 1832.

759) iv JOSHUA PEARL, b. 15 Sep 1752; d. at Vernon, 11 Oct 1837; m. 14 Jan 1773, DEBORAH MARSHALL, b. at Bolton, 1755 daughter of John and Eunice (Kingsbury) Marshall; Deborah d. at Vernon, 11 May 1818.

760) v LOIS PEARL, b. 21 Apr 1753; d. at Willington, 15 Jul 1788; m. 6 Aug 1771, SAMUEL DUNTON, b. at Wrentham, MA, 10 Nov 1748 son of Samuel and Sarah (Bennet) Dunton; Samuel d. at Willington, 1 May 1813. After Lois's death, Samuel married Lovina Marcy.

761) vi ELIZABETH PEARL, b. 15 Jan 1756; d. at Willington, 8 Jan 1779; m. 6 Aug 1771, ZOETH ELDRIDGE, b. at Willington, about 1751 son of Jesse and Abigail (Smith) Eldridge; Zoeth d. at Willington, 18 Mar 1828. Zoeth m. 2nd, Bethiah Hinkley.[466]

762) vii SARAH PEARL, b. 16 Nov 1758; d. at Willington, 11 Oct 1826; m. 17 Nov 1776, SAMUEL JOHNSON, b. 1751 (based on age 92 at time of death); Samuel d. at Willington, 22 Mar 1843. Samuel is likely the son of Daniel and Keziah (Dodge) Johnson born at Lebanon 10 Jun 1751.

763) viii TIMOTHY PEARL, b. 6 Jun 1760; d. at Willington, 2 Jul 1834; m. 9 Jan 1783, LOIS CROCKER, b. 9 Dec 1763 daughter of Joseph and Anne (Fenton) Crocker; Lois d. 24 Sep 1850.

764) ix PHEBE PEARL, b. 27 Nov 1765; d. at Willington, 10 Apr 1816; m. 24 Mar 1785, ZEBADIAH MARCY, b. at Woodstock, 2 Jul 1761 son of Zebadiah and Priscilla (Morris) Marcy; Zebadiah d. 24 Sep 1851.

174) JOSHUA HOLT (*Keturah Holt Holt³, Henry², Nicholas¹*), b. at Windham, 19 Mar 1728 son of Joshua and Keturah (Holt) Holt; d. at Hampton, 5 Jul 1791; m. 1st 28 Jun 1749, his second cousin once removed, MARY ABBOTT (*Elizabeth Gray Abbott⁴, Henry Gray³, Hannah Holt Gray², Nicholas¹*), b. at Pomfret, 3 Mar 1728 daughter of Paul and Elizabeth (Gray) Abbott; Mary d. at Windham, 10 Aug 1769. Joshua m. 2nd, 26 Apr 1770, SUSANNA GOODELL, b. at Pomfret, 22 Jan 1728 daughter of Zachariah and Hannah (Cheney) Goodell; Susanna d. at Windham, 28 Jun 1812. Susanna was first married to Samuel Darby.

In his will written 13 April 1791,[467] Joshua Holt has bequests for the following persons: dear and loving wife Susannah, daughter Dinah Stoel, daughter Mary Fuller, son Uriah, son Lemuel, daughter Keturah Amidown, daughter Sarah Durkee (although there are other last names for Sarah crossed out, one of them Holt), daughter Hannah Carpenter, daughter Dorcas Fuller, daughter Zilphia, and sons Samuel and Oliver who divide equally everything not given to the other children.

Mary Abbott and Joshua Holt had eight children whose births are recorded at Windham.

725) i DINAH HOLT, b. 22 Mar 1750; d. 21 Feb 1826; m. 30 Jun 1778, SETH STOWELL, b. 29 May 1742 son of Nathaniel and Margaret (Trowbridge) Stowell; Seth d. about 1798 (when estate went to probate). Dinah m. 2nd, 27 Nov 1800, PAUL HOLT (*Paul⁴, Paul³, Henry², Nicholas¹*), b. at Windham, 4 Jan 1742/3 son of Paul and Mehitable (Chandler) Holt; Paul d. at Hampton, 26 Oct 1827. Dinah was Paul Holt's third wife.

765) ii MARY HOLT, b. 11 Jul 1752; d. at Hampton, 23 Oct 1824; m. 7 Nov 1771, JOSEPH FULLER, b. at Ipswich, 1738 son of John and Hannah (Lord) Fuller; Joseph d. 29 Jan 1805.

766) iii URIAH HOLT, b. 23 Mar 1754; d. at West Springfield, MA, 22 Sep 1828; m. at Ashford, 11 Nov 1779, MARGARET MASON, b. at Ashford, 13 Aug 1754 daughter of Ebenezer and Mehitable (Holmes) Mason; Margaret d. 1817. Uriah m. 2nd, at West Springfield, 15 Oct 1818, EUNICE CHAPIN (widow of Charles Ferry), b. at Springfield, 22 Feb 1769 daughter of Elisha and Eunice (Jones) Chapin; Eunice d. at West Springfield, 1843.

---

465 The 1788 Connecticut probate record of John Hinckley (widow Susanna) includes as heirs grandsons Daniel Pearl and Oliver Pearl the children of Mercy who is deceased.

466 Eldredge, *Eldredge Genealogy*, p 8

467 *Connecticut Wills and Probate, 1609-1999*, Probate of Joshua Holt, Hartford, 1791, Case number 1945.

767) iv LEMUEL HOLT, b. 28 Feb 1756; d. at Lyme, NH, 1 Aug 1836; m. 1778, his first cousin, MARY ABBOTT (*Isaac Abbott*[5], *Elizabeth Gray Abbott*[4], *Henry Gray*[3], *Hannah Holt Gray*[2], *Nicholas*[1]), b. 20 Jan 1757 daughter of Isaac and Mary (Barker) Abbott; Mary d. 8 Sep 1849.

768) v KETURAH HOLT, b. 21 Aug 1758; d. at Randolph, VT, 25 Jul 1839;[468] m. 29 Jan 1784, JONATHAN AMIDON, b. 7 Feb 1759 son of Henry and Sarah (Doubleday) Amidon; Jonathan d. at Randolph, 15 Apr 1838.

769) vi SARAH HOLT, b. 26 Oct 1761; d. at Stockbridge, VT, 19 Feb 1813; m. 1783, JOHN DURKEE, b. at Windham, 2 Jul 1762 son of Joseph and Elizabeth (Fiske) Durkee; John d. at Stockbridge, 2 May 1838.

770) vii HANNAH HOLT, b. 24 May 1764; d. in Vermont, 7 Aug 1855; m. at Clarendon, VT, 21 Jan 1788, AARON CARPENTER, b. at Rehoboth, 9 May 1763 son of Jabez and Abigail (Dyer) Carpenter; Aaron d. 26 Sep 1836.[469]

771) viii DORCAS HOLT, b. 30 Mar 1767; d. at Middlebury, VT, 1 Jul 1800; m. JOSIAH FULLER, b. 30 Oct 1764 son of David and Hannah (Fuller) Fuller; Josiah d. Potsdam, NY, 4 Dec 1835.

Joshua Holt and Susanna Goodell were parents of three children.

772) i SAMUEL HOLT, b. at Windham, 16 May 1771; d. at Hampton, 22 Jun 1846; m. at Hampton, 28 Nov 1799, HANNAH BENNETT, b. at Windham, 5 Jan 1775 daughter of Isaac and Sarah (Cady) Bennett;[470] Hannah d. at Hampton, 5 Oct 1862.

773) ii OLIVER HOLT, baptized at Windham, 9 May1773; d. at Pomfret, CT, 1 Nov 1821; m. at Eastford, 26 May 1803, SIDNEY BEDOLPH CLAPP, b. 1784 daughter of Seth and Charlotte (Borden) Clapp;[471] Sidney d. at Pomfret, 6 Sep 1837.

774) iii ZILPHA HOLT, b. at Windham, 2 Fen 1776 and baptized at Hampton, 28 Apr 1776; d. at Stockbridge, VT, 8 Mar 1830; m. at Stockbridge, VT, 17 Mar 1808, as the third of his four wives, JONATHAN WHITNEY, b. at Willington, 20 Feb 1766 son of Peter and Marcy (Case) Whitney; Jonathan d. at Tunbridge, VT, 12 Apr 1853. Jonathan was first married to Eunice Story, second married to Dora Marsh, and fourth married to Betsey Goodell.

175) PHEBE HOLT (*Keturah Holt Holt*[3], *Henry*[2], *Nicholas*[1]), b. at Windham, 16 Aug 1734 daughter of Joshua and Keturah (Holt) Holt; d. at South Windsor, CT, 7 Feb 1808; m. at Pomfret, 13 Feb 1755, EBENEZER GOODALE, b. at Pomfret, 12 Sep 1729 son of Ebenezer and Experience (Lyon) Goodale; Ebenezer d. at East Windsor, 8 Sep 1794 (probate 19 Dec 1794).

Ebenezer Goodale did not leave a will and his estate entered probate 19 December 1794 with Phebe as administratrix and surety provided by Walter Goodale. Personal estate was valued at £34.10.3.[472]

Phebe Holt and Ebenezer Goodale were parents of thirteen children.

775) i CHLOE GOODALE, b. at Pomfret, 28 Dec 1755; d. at New Haven, Oct 1833; m. at Willington, 25 May 1775, her second cousin, FRANCIS FENTON (*Elizabeth Holt Fenton*[4], *Abiel*[3], *Nicholas*[2], *Nicholas*[1]), b. at Willington, 13 Feb 1750/1 son of Francis and Elizabeth (Holt) Fenton.

776) ii RHODA GOODALE, b. at Pomfret, 28 Feb 1758; d. at South Windsor, CT, 17 Nov 1841; m. at Willington, JOSEPH ELDREDGE, b. at Willington, 28 Feb 1759 son of Joseph and Abigail (Smith) Eldredge.[473]

iii SARAH GOODALE, b. 19 May 1759; d. 20 Jun 1759.

777) iv SARAH GOODALE, b. at Pomfret, 10 Jul 1760; d. at Willington, 4 Oct 1831; m. at Willington, 8 Jan 1783, her second cousin, CALEB HOLT (*Caleb*[4], *Abiel*[3], *Nicholas*[2], *Nicholas*[1]), b. at Willington, 23 Apr 1759 son of Caleb and Mary (Merrick) Holt; Caleb d. at Willington, 8 Sep 1826.

---

[468] Ancestry.com, *Vermont, Vital Records, 1720-1908* (Provo, UT, USA: Ancestry.com Operations, Inc., 2013).

[469] Ancestry.com, Vermont, Vital Records, 1720-1908

[470] The 1817 probate of Isaac Bennett includes a distribution to Hannah Holt and spouse Samuel Holt.

[471] Clapp, *The Clapp Memorial*, p 165

[472] *Connecticut State Library (Hartford, Connecticut)*, Estate of Ebenezer Goodale, case 1303

[473] Eldredge, *Eldredge Genealogy*

778) v CHESTER GOODALE, b. at Pomfret, 3 Sep 1762; d. at Egremont, MA, 29 Jan 1835; m. at Richmond, MA, 10 Jul 1790, ASENATH COOK, b. at Goshen, CT, 11 Oct 1769 daughter of Walter and Ruhamah (Collins) Cook;[474] Asenath d. at Egremont, 7 May 1858.

779) vi LOIS GOODALE, b. at Pomfret, 31 Jul 1764; d. at Willington, 20 May 1842; m. at Willington, 6 Feb 1783, her second cousin, NATHAN HOLT (*Nathan⁴, Abiel³, Nicholas², Nicholas¹*), b. at Windham, 29 Aug 1761 son of Nathan and Abigail (Merrick) Holt; Nathan d. at Willington, 5 Sep 1820.

780) vii WALTER GOODALE, b. at Pomfret, 6 Apr 1766; d. at South Windsor, 20 Jul 1820; m. about 1787, SABRA BISSELL (widow of John Loomis), b. at Windsor, 25 May 1763 daughter of Hezekiah and Sabra (Trumbull) Bissell; Sabra d. at East Windsor, 17 Nov 1834.

781) viii WILLARD GOODALE, b. at Pomfret, 8 Mar 1768; d. at Perry, NY, 11 Nov 1858; m. MARY ANN MCLEAN, b. 1772; Mary Ann d. at Perry, 2 Oct 1752.

ix LUTHER GOODALE, b. at Pomfret, 21 Feb 1770; d. at East Windsor, CT, 1816; m. at East Windsor, 23 Apr 1795, ELIZABETH GRANT b. about 1770 daughter of Samuel Rockwell and Mabel (Loomis) Grant.[475] Luther and Elizabeth may not have had children. At the 1800 census, the household consists of one male 26-44 and one female 26-44.[476] Luther seems to have had a second marriage as the widow on the probate record is Dosha Goodale. No children were identified for Luther Goodale and Elizabeth Grant.

x OLIVER GOODALE, b. 4 Nov 1771; d. 4 Feb 1773.

xi PHEBE GOODALE, b. 4 Nov 1773; d. 7 Jan 1774.

xii OLIVER GOODALE, b. about 1774 (record for birth of second Oliver in the family has an unreadable date); m. at Pomfret, 10 Apr 1796, his second cousin once removed, JERUSHA TRUESDELL (*Seth Truesdell⁵, Mary Holt Truesdell⁴, Robert³, Nicholas², Nicholas¹*), b. at Pomfret, 6 Apr 1776 daughter of Seth and Esther (West) Truesdell. Nothing further was found for this couple. No children were identified for Oliver Goodale and Jerusha Truesdell.

782) xiii PHEBE GOODALE, b. at Willington, 29 Aug 1775; d. at South Windsor, 6 Nov 1856; m. as his third wife, GUSTAVUS GRANT, b at East Windsor, 1759 son of Samuel Rockwell and Mabel (Loomis) Grant;[477] Gustavus d. at South Windsor, 11 Mar 1841. Gustavus was first married to Lucina Grant and second married to Electa Goodwin.

176) FIFIELD HOLT (*Humphrey³, Henry², Nicholas¹*), b. at Andover, 28 Jul 1717 son of Humphrey and Abigail (Fifield) Holt; d. at Wilton, NH, after 1776; m. at Salem, 31 Aug 1741, ABIGAIL TAYLOR who has not been identified.

Little is known of this family. Fifield and Abigail had three children in Andover and relocated to Wilton where Fifield was still in residence in 1776.

i ANNA HOLT, b. 26 Sep 1742

783) ii FIFIELD HOLT, b. at Andover, 29 Oct 1744; d. at Hollis, 6 Apr 1819; m. ANNA LAKIN, b. at Groton, MA, 16 Jan 1746 daughter of Robinson and Hannah (Dodge) Lakin; Anna d. at Hollis, 29 Jun 1811.

iii ABIGAIL HOLT, b. 11 Apr 1748

177) WILLIAM HOLT (*Humphrey³, Henry², Nicholas¹*), baptized at Andover, 11 Jun 1721 son of Humphrey and Abigail (Fifield) Holt; d. at Lunenburg, 14 Nov 1759; m. at Lunenburg, 30 Jul 1744, MARY MARTIN,[478] b. at Ipswich, 24 Sep 1720 daughter of John and Jane (Durkee) Martin;[479] Mary d. after 1760.

---

474 Hibbard, *A History of the Town of Goshen*, p 450

475 Grant, *The Grant Family*, p 48

476 Year: 1800; Census Place: East Windsor, Hartford, Connecticut; Series: M32; Roll: 1; Page: 366; Image: 198; Family History Library Film: 205618

477 Cutter, *New England Families, Genealogical and Memorial*, volume 3, p 1304

478 There are discrepancies in published sources regarding which William Holt married Mary Martin and lived in Lunenburg and which married Beulah and settled in Lyndeborough. The two Williams in question are William born June 1721 son of Humphrey and William born 1 Apr 1727 son of Oliver. Sone sources give the birth date of William son of Oliver as 11 Sep 1721, but the currently available transcriptions have a 1727 year. As William Holt and Mary Martin married in 1744, and if the birth dates of 1721 for William son of Humphrey and 1727 for William son of Oliver are correct, then it must be the son of Humphrey that married Mary Martin. William Holt and Mary Martin have a son Humphrey and William and Beulah Holt have a son Oliver. In addition, the will of Humphrey Holt specifies that his son William has received a tract of land in Lunenburg as his inheritance. In any case, I have placed William son of Humphrey with Mary Martin and William son of Oliver with Beulah.

479 The 1757 will of John Martin of Ipswich (with wife named Jane) includes a bequest to his daughter Mary Holt.

William Holt did not leave a will and the inventory of his estate was made 13 March 1760. The probate records described him as of Ipswich Canada (plantation in the town of Winchenden) although the probate is in Lunenburg, Worcester County. Mary Holt was administratrix.[480]

William Holt and Mary Martin were parents of six children.

784) i WILLIAM HOLT, b. at Lunenburg, 16 Feb 1744; d. at New Salem, MA, 7 Jan 1805; m. 2 Mar 1769, HANNAH PIKE, b. 17 Sep 1748 likely daughter of Thomas and Lois (Perley) Pike.[481]

785) ii DAVID HOLT, b. at Lunenburg, 26 Sep 1746; d. at New Salem, 1792; m. at Lancaster, 30 Oct 1770, HANNAH KENDALL, b. at Lancaster, 10 Dec 1747 daughter of Ebenezer and Hannah (Thompson) Kendall.

786) iii JONATHAN HOLT, b. at Lunenburg, 22 Jan 1748; d. at New Salem, 22 Sep 1831; m. at New Salem, 12 Dec 1772, MARIA WHEELER, baptized at New Salem, 28 Oct 1750 daughter of Samuel and Ruth (Wheeler) Wheeler; Maria d. at New Salem, 29 Mar 1813.

787) iv HUMPHREY HOLT, b. at Lunenburg, 1 Jan 1750; m. likely EDITH CHASE, b. at Sutton, MA, 27 Aug 1753 daughter of Ambrose and Thankful (Robbins) Chase.

788) v MARY HOLT, b. at Winchendon, 8 Nov 1754; d. at Royalston, MA, 26 Jan 1847; m. JONATHAN BOSWORTH, b. at Bellingham, MA, Sep 1748 son of Jonathan and Susanna (Chilson) Bosworth; Jonathan d. at Royalston, 1 Dec 1818.

vi SARAH HOLT, b. at Winchendon, 30 May 1756; m. SAMUEL CASS. Sarah and Samuel are reported as going to Pennsylvania[482] but no further record of them was found.

178) HUMPHREY HOLT (*Humphrey³, Henry², Nicholas¹*), baptized at Andover, 19 May 1723 son of Humphrey and Abigail (Fifield) Holt; d. at Andover, 29 Mar 1785; m. 1st at Andover, 1 Jan 1745, ELIZABETH KIMBALL, baptized at Boxford, Aug 1724 daughter of John and Elizabeth (Chapman) Kimball;[483] Elizabeth d. 30 Jan 1749. Humphrey m. 2nd 30 Nov 1749, MARY HOLTON, b. about 1729; Mary d. at Andover, 13 Jul 1774. Humphrey m. 3rd at Danvers, 21 Sep 1775, ABIGAIL VERY, b. about 1727; Abigail d. at Andover, 15 Apr 1808.

Elizabeth Kimball Holt was admitted to Andover South Church on 5 April 1747 coming from second church at Boxford. Humphrey was also a member of South Church.[484]

Humphrey Holt did not leave a will and his estate entered probate 3 May 1785. Widow Abigail Holt and son Simeon Holt resigned any rights to administer the estate and requested that this be assumed by James Holt, Jr. Land and buildings were valued at £9 and personal estate at £18.10.1.[485]

Humphrey Holt and Elizabeth Kimball were parents of one child.

789) i SIMEON HOLT, b. at Andover, 26 Jan 1747; d. at Andover, 5 Jan 1828; m. at Wilmington, 31 Mar 1767, SARAH READ who has not been identified; Sarah d. at Andover, 20 Aug 1827. Both Simeon and Sarah died at the almshouse.[486]

Humphrey Holt and Mary Holton were parents of eight children.

i ELIZABETH HOLT, b. at Andover, 29 Oct 1750

790) ii HUMPHREY HOLT, baptized at Andover, 18 Feb 1753; d. at Londonderry, NH, 1826 (probate 5 Sep 1826); m. 1st at Andover, 12 May 1774, PHEBE CURTIS (widow Fish). Humphrey m. 2nd, perhaps in Maine, JERUSHA who has not been identified. Humphrey m. 3rd at Londonderry, 11 Sep 1817, SARAH BATCHELDER who survived him.

---

[480] *Worcester County, MA: Probate File Papers, 1731-1881.* Online database. AmericanAncestors.org. New England Historic Genealogical Society, 2015. Case 30683

[481] Cunningham's History of Lunenburg gives Hannah's parents as Perley and Elizabeth Pike, but Perley's other children are born between 1767 and 1772 and it is more likely that Hannah is Perley's sister.

[482] Durrie's Holt genealogy, p 33

[483] The 1757 (probate 1763) will of John Kimball of Boxford includes a bequest to his grandson Simeon Holt who was the son of Humphrey and Elizabeth. John Kimball's will has a separate bequest to his granddaughter Hannah Holt who was the daughter of Thomas Holt and another of John's daughters Hannah Kimball (Family 188).

[484] South Church of Andover, *Historical Manual*, p 134

[485] *Essex County, MA: Probate File Papers, 1638-1881.*Online database. *AmericanAncestors.org.* New England Historic Genealogical Society, 2014. Case 13644

[486] Simeon, at the almshouse, Jan. 5, 1828.

iii MARY HOLT, b. at Andover, 11 Jan 1755

iv LYDIA HOLT, b. at Tewksbury, 7 Feb 1758

791) v WILLIAM HOLT, b. at Tewksbury, 29 Jul 1761; d. at Fryeburg, ME, 4 May 1827; m. about 1792, ESTHER FRYE, b. at Fryeburg, 11 Jul 1773 daughter of Simon and Hannah (Johnson) Frye; Esther d. at Fryeburg, 21 Jan 1863.

vi JOHN HOLT, b. 26 Apr 1763; d. 23 Dec 1763.

792) vii JOHN HOLT, b. at Andover, 12 May 1764; d. at Bethel, ME, 16 Jul 1830; m. 7 Jun 1787, his third cousin once removed, LYDIA RUSSELL (*Hephzibah Russell Russell*[5], *Joseph Russell*[4], *Phebe Johnson Russell*[3], *Mary Holt Johnson*[2], *Nicholas*[1]), b. at Andover, 17 May 1764 daughter of Joseph and Hephzibah (Russell) Russell; Lydia d. at Bethel, 12 Sep 1847.

viii NATHANIEL HOLT, baptized at Andover, 27 Sep 1767; d. at Boston, 11 Feb 1795; m. at Boston, 2 Dec 1789, SARAH NEWELL. No records of children were located.

179) JONATHAN HOLT (*Humphrey*[3], *Henry*[2], *Nicholas*[1]), b. at Andover, about 1727 son of Humphrey and Abigail (Fifield) Holt; d. at Lunenburg, 17 Mar 1805; m. 1st 25 Feb 1752, RACHEL TAYLOR; Rachel d. at Fitchburg, 25 Apr 1753. Jonathan m. 2nd at Andover, 14 Nov 1753, his second cousin once removed, SUSANNA HOLT (*James*[4], *Timothy*[3], *James*[2], *Nicholas*[1]), likely b. at Andover, 18 Apr 1737 daughter of James and Susanna (Nurs) Holt; Susanna d. 11 Jul 1801. Jonathan m. 3rd, 13 Jan 1802, AZUBA BUTTERFIELD, b. at Townsend, 13 Nov 1767 daughter of Eleazer and Mary (Wright) Butterfield; Azuba d. at Fitchburg, 24 Jan 1852.

Jonathan Holt was a farmer in Lunenburg with his property partly in the area that is now Fitchburg. In the Revolutionary War, Jonathan served as Sergeant in Captain Ebenezer Bridge's Company which was part of Whetcomb's Brigade which "marched at the alarm." He was credited with fourteen days of service.[487]

In his will 13 July 1804 (proved 27 Mar 1805), Jonathan Holt bequeathed to beloved wife Azubah one-half of his real estate. Sons Jonathan, Elijah, William, and James receive fifty cents each. Daughters Rachel wife of Ebenezer Cram, Susanna wife of Cotton Whiting, Abigail wife of Joshua Whitney, and Rachel wife of Nathan Taylor each receives fifty cents. One-half of the real and personal estate goes to youngest daughter Roxana. The remainder of the estate goes to wife Azubah who is also named executrix.[488]

Child of Jonathan Holt and Rachel Taylor.

691) i RACHEL HOLT, b. at Lunenburg, 20 Apr 1753; m. about 1774, her second cousin, EBENEZER CRAM (*John Cram*[4], *Sarah Holt Cram*[3], *Henry*[2], *Nicholas*[1]), b. at Wilton, NH, 19 Sep 1754 son of John and Sarah(-) Cram; Ebenezer d. at Chester, VT, 23 Feb 1835.

Jonathan and Susanna Holt were parents of eight children whose birth are in the Lunenburg town records, but some of the births are recorded in Fitchburg (although at the time Jonathan's location was part of Lunenburg).

793) i JONATHAN HOLT, b. at Lunenburg, 16 May 1756; d. at Clinton, ME, 12 Dec 1832; m. at Jaffrey, NH, 12 Dec 1782, MARY "POLLY" BAILEY, b. at Lunenburg, 14 Feb 1753 daughter of Isaac and Mary (Lovejoy) Bailey.

794) ii SUSANNA HOLT, b. at Lunenburg, 29 May 1758; m. at Leominster, MA, 26 Nov 1779, COTTON WHITING, b. at Concord, MA, 27 Oct 1752 son of Stephen and Mary (Grover) Whiting; Cotton d. at Chester, VT, 1815 (probate 6 Apr 1815).

795) iii ELIJAH HOLT, b. at Lunenburg, 23 Oct 1759; d. at Jamaica, VT, before 1815; m. at Oakham, 1 Feb 1781, LUCY PARMENTER, b. 1757 daughter of Solomon and Elizabeth (Craig) Parmenter;[489] d. at Elk Creek, PA, after 1840.

796) iv WILLIAM HOLT, b. at Lunenburg, 11 Apr 1761; d. at Chester, VT, 27 Jul 1827; m. 20 Apr 1782, ELIZABETH HUTCHINSON, b. at Lunenburg, 22 Oct 1763 daughter of Samuel and Elizabeth (Fessenden) Hutchinson.

---

[487] Massachusetts Soldiers and Sailors in the Revolution, volume 8, p 192

[488] *Worcester County, MA: Probate File Papers, 1731-1881.* Online database. AmericanAncestors.org. New England Historic Genealogical Society, 2015. Case 30652

[489] The will of Solomon Parmenter includes a bequest to his daughter Lucy Holt wife of Elijah Holt.

797) v JAMES HOLT, b. at Lunenburg, 2 May 1764; d. at Warsaw, NY, 22 Jul 1837; m. at Jaffrey, 28 Jan 1783,[490] OLIVE DEAN, b. at Wilmington, MA, 27 Aug 1755[491] daughter of William and Sarah (Underwood) Dean; Olive was living in Attica, NY in 1848.

vi ABIGAIL HOLT, b. at Lunenburg, 2 May 1766; m. at Fitchburg, 22 Mar 1790, JOSHUA WHITNEY. Nothing further was found for this family.

798) vii RHODA HOLT, b. at Lunenburg, 22 Feb 1768; d. at Norridgewock, ME, 21 Sep 1848; m. 1st at Fitchburg, 12 Oct 1784, NATHAN TAYLOR, b. at Dorchester, MA, 18 Feb 1760 son of Nathan and Submit (Blackman) Taylor; Nathan d. at Canaan, ME by drowning on 10 Jun 1804. Rhoda m. 2nd 19 Jul 1812, Capt. ASA LONGLEY, b. at Groton, Jul 1762; Asa d. at Corinna, ME, 21 May 1845. Asa Longley was first married to Betsey Parker who died in 1811.

viii AMASA HOLT, b. 7 Oct 1769; d. 18 Mar 1770.

Jonathan Holt and Azuba Butterfield were parents of two children.

799) i ROXANNA HOLT, b. at Lunenburg, 10 Jul 1802; d. at Mercer County, IL, after 1870; m. at Mason, NH, 15 Mar 1820, JAIRUS ROBINSON, b. at Weathersfield, VT, 7 Aug 1793 son of Benjamin and Ruth (Johnson) Robinson; Jairus d. at Weathersfield, 28 May 1828.

800) ii IRA HOLT, b. at Lunenburg, 21 Mar 1805; d. at Arlington, MA, 14 May 1880; m. 13 May 1827, HANNAH ROBBINS daughter of Abram and Hannah (-) Robbins.

180) SHUAH HOLT (*Humphrey³, Henry², Nicholas¹*), b. at Andover, 21 Mar 1728/9 daughter of Humphrey and Abigail (Fifield) Holt; d. at Andover, 9 Jan 1766; m. 6 Nov 1754, her second cousin once removed, JONATHAN HOLT (*Samuel⁴, Samuel³, Samuel², Nicholas¹*), b. at Andover, 5 Feb 1728/9 son of Samuel and Jemima (Gray) Holt; Jonathan d. at Andover, 23 Sep 1792. Jonathan m. 2nd 24 Sep 1766, BETTY GOULD; Betty d. at Andover, 16 Feb 1774. Jonathan m. 3rd 23 May 1775, ELEANOR JOHNSON.

In his will written 24 June 1791 (probate 4 December 1792), Jonathan Holt left improvement on one-third part of the real estate to beloved wife Eleanor. She also receives the household items that she brought to the marriage and the value of three notes that he holds. Son George Holt receives £12 which completes his portion. Son Jonathan Holt also receives £12. Son William Holt, if he is still living and if he returns to Andover, receives £6. Daughter Rebecca receives a bed, furniture, all the pewter not disposed of, and £6. Daughter Phebe wife of Levi Fletcher receives the large brass kettle. Daughter Sarah wife of Jonathan Baker receives six shillings which completes her portion. Son Zebadiah Holt receives all the lands and buildings and is named executor.[492]

Shuah and Jonathan were parents of seven children born at Andover.

i REBECCA HOLT, b. at Andover, 5 Feb 1755; d. at Andover, 5 Dec 1837. Rebecca did not marry.

801) ii GEORGE HOLT, b. at Andover, 21 Feb 1756; m. NANCY FISH, b. at Andover, 6 Jan 1758 daughter of Benjamin and Mary (Johnson) Fish.

802) iii SARAH HOLT, b. at Andover, 3 Feb 1757; d. at Sullivan, NH, 12 Apr 1844; m. at Andover, 21 May 1776, JONATHAN BAKER, b. at Topsfield, 25 Jun 1749 son of Thomas and Sarah (Wade) Baker; Jonathan d. at Sullivan, 12 Oct 1833.

803) iv ZEBADIAH HOLT, b. at Andover, 28 Jul 1759; d. 15 Mar 1817; m. at Billerica, 23 Dec 1784, SARAH LEWES. Sarah married second Jotham Blanchard.

804) v PHEBE HOLT, b. at Andover, 31 Jan 1761; d. 20 Sep 1848; m. at Chelmsford, 11 Jan 1790, LEVI FLETCHER, b. at Chelmsford, 3 Mar 1757 son of William and Mary (Blodgett) Fletcher; Levi d. at Lowell, 2 Nov 1832.

vi JONATHAN HOLT, b. 28 Jun 1762. He was living in 1791, but nothing further definite known. Durrie's Holt genealogy reports he died 1 Dec 1829. There is a Jonathan Holt that died at Andover 1 Dec 1827 but that is a different Jonathan (his nephew son of Zebadiah born 1793).

vii WILLIAM HOLT, b. at Andover, 21 Dec 1763; likely died at sea.

---

490 This is the date of marriage given by Olive Dean Holt in the pension application file of James Holt. It varies by five years from the transcription at Jaffrey, NH, but the daughter in this family was born in 1784 according to the family bible records.

491 Olive Dean Holt gives her birth date as August 1755 in the pension application file of James Holt.

492 *Essex County, MA: Probate File Papers, 1638-1881.*Online database. *AmericanAncestors.org.* New England Historic Genealogical Society, 2014. Case 13657

Grandchildren of Nicholas Holt and Mary Russell

181) PHEBE INGALLS (*Mary Holt Ingalls[3], Nicholas[2], Nicholas[1]*), b. at Andover 1708 daughter of Josiah and Mary (Holt) Ingalls; d. after 1784 perhaps in Poland, ME;[493] m. at Andover, 12 Aug 1731, JAMES PARKER, b. at Andover, 12 Oct 1696 son of John and Hannah (Brown) Parker; James d. at Andover, 1782 (will 1773; probate 1782).

James Parker was a tailor in Andover and farmed.

In his will dated 9 October 1773 (probate 2 December 1782), James Parker bequeaths to beloved wife Phebe a lengthy list of yearly provisions to be provided by son James Parker. Phebe also has use and improvement of as much of the dwelling house and cellar as she needs for her natural life. Son James is to meet all the needs of his mother during her life. These provisions are in lieu of her dower. Daughter Anne Bragg receives all the household furniture after her mother's decease and the sum of £3.6.8. Anne also has the use of the east room of the house and use of the cellar and oven. Anne has use of the house while she is a single woman, but the furniture and money are hers forever. Son James receives all the remaining personal and real estate and is named executor. Real estate was valued at £417 and personal estate at £60.16.0.[494]

On 8 July 1784, son James Parker now residing in the new town of Bakerstown (later Poland) in Cumberland County of the Commonwealth of Massachusetts (current day Maine) sold land and dwelling house in Andover to Samuel Johnson for £60. The said James Parker, his mother Phebe Parker, and sister Anne Bragg give their consent to the conveyance.[495]

Phebe Ingalls and James Parker were parents of six children born at Andover.

i PHEBE PARKER, b. 12 Jul 1734; d. 14 Aug 1737.

ii ANNE PARKER, b. at Andover, 9 Apr 1736; d. after 1784; m. at Andover, 8 May 1753, JOHN BRAGG who has not been identified. John was a cordwainer, resident of Andover and deed records suggest he was related to Thomas Bragg innholder at Andover. John was living in 1762 when he was involved in three land transactions including the gift of land from James Parker to John and Anne Bragg for "love, good will, and affection."[496] No children were identified for Anne and John.

iii JESSE PARKER, b. 25 Oct 1738. Jesse was captured during the French and Indian War and taken to prison in Canada and is believed to have died in prison. There were attempts to ransom Jesse and other prisoners.[497]

805) iv JAMES PARKER, b. at Andover, 30 Aug 1746; d. at Livermore, ME, 26 Apr 1815;[498] m. at New Gloucester, ME, 16 Aug 1783, PHEBE NOYES, b. 13 Apr 1763 daughter of Simon and Elizabeth (Eaton) Noyes; Phebe d. at Livermore, 23 Jul 1848.

v PHEBE PARKER, b. 7 Dec 1748; not living in 1773.

vi MARY PARKER, b. 3 Jul 1751; d. 20 Feb 1752.

182) BENJAMIN HOLT (*Nicholas[3], Nicholas[2], Nicholas[1]*), b. at Andover, 23 Jul 1709 son of Nicholas and Mary (Manning) Holt; d. at Pembroke, NH, 1774 (probate 26 Oct 1774); m. at Andover, 7 Apr 1737, SARAH FRYE, b. May 1717 daughter of Nathan and Sarah (Bridges) Frye; Sarah d. at Pembroke, 1804.

Benjamin and Sarah started their family in Andover and settled in Suncook about 1745. They were parents of twelve children.

Benjamin Holt did not leave a will and his estate entered probate 26 October 1774 with widow Sarah Holt as administratrix. Real estate was valued at £145 and Benjamin also held multiple notes owed to him totaling £1051 and debts of the estate £104.7.9. Debts of the estate were more than the personal estate and a portion of the real estate was sold to settle the debts. The widow's thirds were set off to Sarah 7 Mar 1775.[499]

806) i WILLIAM HOLT, b. at Andover, Oct 1737; d. at Allenstown, NH, 28 Aug 1816; m. at Andover, 2 Sep 1769, ELIZABETH "BETSEY" AMES, perhaps b. at Andover, 13 Jan 1744/5 daughter of Samuel and Elizabeth (Stevens) Ames.

---

[493] Phebe was living in November 1784 when she consented to the sale of the dwelling house and land in Andover by her son James Parker, then of Poland, ME. It seems possible that Phebe and her daughter accompanied James to Poland.

[494] *Essex County, MA: Probate File Papers, 1638-1881.*Online database. *AmericanAncestors.org.* New England Historic Genealogical Society, 2014. Case 20508

[495] Massachusetts Land Records 1620-1986, Essex County, volume 142, p 233, Film #007463322; accessed through familysearch.org. https://www.familysearch.org/ark:/61903/3:1:3QS7-89ZZ-1S6Q?i=519&cc=2106411&cat=209907

[496] Massachusetts Land Records 1620-1986, Essex County, volume 110, p 113, accessed through familysearch.org.

[497] Bailey, Historical Sketches of Andover, p 266

[498] Livermore Vital Records, p 269; accessed through familysearch,org

[499] *New Hampshire. Probate Court (Rockingham County), Estate Papers, Estate of Benjamin Holt, Case 4128*

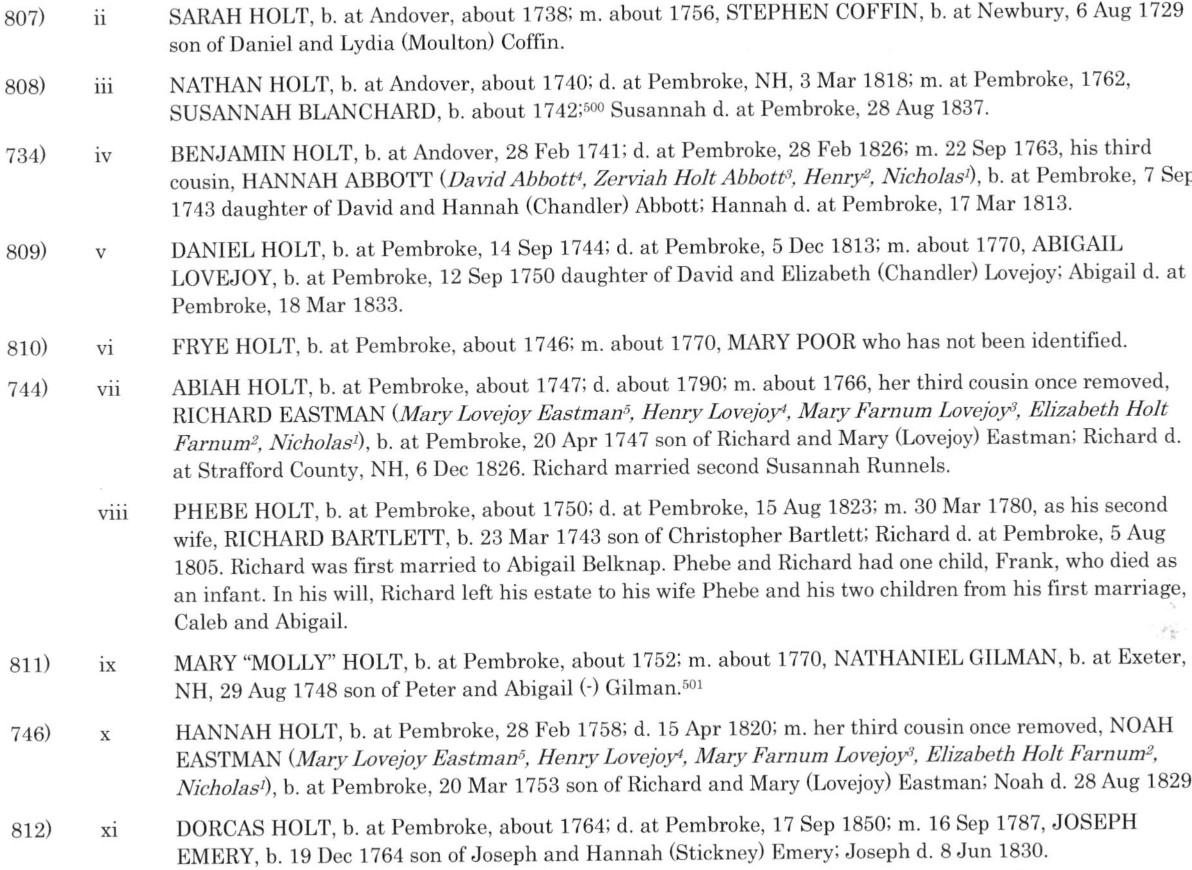

807) ii SARAH HOLT, b. at Andover, about 1738; m. about 1756, STEPHEN COFFIN, b. at Newbury, 6 Aug 1729 son of Daniel and Lydia (Moulton) Coffin.

808) iii NATHAN HOLT, b. at Andover, about 1740; d. at Pembroke, NH, 3 Mar 1818; m. at Pembroke, 1762, SUSANNAH BLANCHARD, b. about 1742;[500] Susannah d. at Pembroke, 28 Aug 1837.

734) iv BENJAMIN HOLT, b. at Andover, 28 Feb 1741; d. at Pembroke, 28 Feb 1826; m. 22 Sep 1763, his third cousin, HANNAH ABBOTT (*David Abbott[4], Zerviah Holt Abbott[3], Henry[2], Nicholas[1]*), b. at Pembroke, 7 Sep 1743 daughter of David and Hannah (Chandler) Abbott; Hannah d. at Pembroke, 17 Mar 1813.

809) v DANIEL HOLT, b. at Pembroke, 14 Sep 1744; d. at Pembroke, 5 Dec 1813; m. about 1770, ABIGAIL LOVEJOY, b. at Pembroke, 12 Sep 1750 daughter of David and Elizabeth (Chandler) Lovejoy; Abigail d. at Pembroke, 18 Mar 1833.

810) vi FRYE HOLT, b. at Pembroke, about 1746; m. about 1770, MARY POOR who has not been identified.

744) vii ABIAH HOLT, b. at Pembroke, about 1747; d. about 1790; m. about 1766, her third cousin once removed, RICHARD EASTMAN (*Mary Lovejoy Eastman[5], Henry Lovejoy[4], Mary Farnum Lovejoy[3], Elizabeth Holt Farnum[2], Nicholas[1]*), b. at Pembroke, 20 Apr 1747 son of Richard and Mary (Lovejoy) Eastman; Richard d. at Strafford County, NH, 6 Dec 1826. Richard married second Susannah Runnels.

viii PHEBE HOLT, b. at Pembroke, about 1750; d. at Pembroke, 15 Aug 1823; m. 30 Mar 1780, as his second wife, RICHARD BARTLETT, b. 23 Mar 1743 son of Christopher Bartlett; Richard d. at Pembroke, 5 Aug 1805. Richard was first married to Abigail Belknap. Phebe and Richard had one child, Frank, who died as an infant. In his will, Richard left his estate to his wife Phebe and his two children from his first marriage, Caleb and Abigail.

811) ix MARY "MOLLY" HOLT, b. at Pembroke, about 1752; m. about 1770, NATHANIEL GILMAN, b. at Exeter, NH, 29 Aug 1748 son of Peter and Abigail (-) Gilman.[501]

746) x HANNAH HOLT, b. at Pembroke, 28 Feb 1758; d. 15 Apr 1820; m. her third cousin once removed, NOAH EASTMAN (*Mary Lovejoy Eastman[5], Henry Lovejoy[4], Mary Farnum Lovejoy[3], Elizabeth Holt Farnum[2], Nicholas[1]*), b. at Pembroke, 20 Mar 1753 son of Richard and Mary (Lovejoy) Eastman; Noah d. 28 Aug 1829.

812) xi DORCAS HOLT, b. at Pembroke, about 1764; d. at Pembroke, 17 Sep 1850; m. 16 Sep 1787, JOSEPH EMERY, b. 19 Dec 1764 son of Joseph and Hannah (Stickney) Emery; Joseph d. 8 Jun 1830.

xii NICHOLAS HOLT, reported as being unmarried in published genealogies.

183) MARY HOLT (Nicholas[3], Nicholas[2], Nicholas[1]), b. at Andover, 1 Aug 1711 daughter of Nicholas and Mary (Manning) Holt; m. 1st at Andover, 4 Mar 1735/6, WILLIAM CHANDLER, b. 14 Jul 1704 son of Thomas and Mary (Stevens) Chandler; William d. at Andover, 15 Apr 1741. William Chandler was first married to Elizabeth Blanchard. Mary Holt m. 2nd 29 May 1745, JEREMIAH OSGOOD, b. at Andover, 1702 son of Christopher and Sarah (-) Osgood. Jeremiah was first married to Lydia Poor.

William Chandler was a miller in Andover. He did not leave a will and his estate entered probate June 1741. Real estate at inventory was valued at £150. On 30 May 1748, the division of the estate occurred, and it was determined that division of the real estate could not be done without harm to its value. The real estate was settled on eldest son Thomas Chandler with Thomas to pay his brothers and sisters their proportional shares. Thomas was to make payments of £8.5.10 to each of the following brothers and sisters: Rose Chandler, William Chandler, James Chandler, Stevens Chandler, and Mary Chandler.[502] Thomas, Rose, and William were children of William and his first wife Elizabeth Blanchard.

On 19 April 1742, Mary Chandler was granted guardianship of her three minor children James, Stevens, and Mary. On 28 May 1753, James made choice of his uncle Nicholas Holt of Andover as his guardian and Stevens made choice of his uncle the Rev. James Chandler of Rowley as his guardian.

Mary Holt was second married to Jeremiah Osgood and they had two children in Andover, but then relocated to Pomfret where Jeremiah purchased a farm of 148 acres in 1748.[503]

The three children of Mary Holt that married each married a child of Joseph and Sarah (Cornell) Snow.

---

[500] Although several published genealogies report the name of Nathan's wife as Sarah Chamberlain, the pension file for Nathan clearly establishes that Nathan married Susannah Blanchard at Pembroke in 1762 and she is the mother of his children.

[501] Ames, *The Story of the Gilmans*, p 110

[502] *Essex County, MA: Probate File Papers, 1638-1881.* Online database. *AmericanAncestors.org.* New England Historic Genealogical Society, 2014. Case 4981

[503] Osgood, *A Genealogy of the Descendants of John, Christopher, and William Osgood*, p 262

i JAMES CHANDLER, b. 13 Dec 1736; d. between 1753 and 1763. In 1763, Mary and Jeremiah Osgood acknowledged receipt from son-in-law Thomas Chandler, the one-sixth portion of the estate of "our late son James Chandler" from the estate of his father William Chandler.[504]

813) ii STEVENS CHANDLER, b. at Andover, 15 Dec 1738; d. at Andover, Nov 1814 (buried 10 Nov 1814); m. 1st at Ashford, about 1762, ALICE SNOW, b. at Ashford, 23 Sep 1741 daughter of Joseph and Sarah (Cornell) Snow; Alice d. at Ashford, 17 Jan 1782. Stevens m. 2nd at Ashford, Jun 1784, MARY PRESTON; Mary d. 10 Mar 1787. Stevens m. 3rd at Ashford, 3 Jul 1790, SARAH ROGERS; Sarah d. at Andover, 26 Aug 1817.

814) iii MARY CHANDLER, b. at Andover, 8 Feb 1740/1; d. at Ashford, 11 Mar 1787; m. at Ashford, 18 Nov 1762, JOSEPH SNOW, b. at Ashford, 15 Nov 1738 son of Joseph and Sarah (Cornell) Snow.

Mary Holt and Jeremiah Osgood were parents of two children.

i DORCAS OSGOOD, b. 14 Jul 1746; died young.

815) ii DORCAS OSGOOD, b. at Andover, 11 Aug 1748; d. at Westport, NY, 31 Aug 1811; m. at Ashford, CT, 5 Jul 1764, BENJAMIN SNOW, b. at Ashford, 23 Jan 1743/4 son of Joseph and Sarah (Cornell) Snow.

184) STEPHEN HOLT (*Nicholas³, Nicholas², Nicholas¹*), b. at Andover, 14 Apr 1713 son of Nicholas and Mary (Manning) Holt; d. at Andover, 25 Apr 1798; m. 12 Jul 1739, his second cousin once removed, MARY FARNUM (*John Farnum⁴, John Farnum³, Elizabeth Holt Farnum², Nicholas¹*), b. at Andover, 21 May 1714 daughter of John and Joanna (Barker) Farnum; Mary d. at Andover, 9 Aug 1802.

Stephen and Mary were in Suncook after their marriage and their children were born there. However, they returned to Andover with their children.

In his will written 9 December 1793 (probate 7 May 1798), Stephen Holt bequeathed to beloved wife Mary all the household goods to be at her disposal except the clock. Mary also has use of all the personal and real estate and is not to want for anything. Daughter Mary wife of John Adams receives the pew in the north meeting house. Daughter Mary also receives the clock and the buildings that Stephen owns that are on the property of John Adams. Grandsons Samuel and Stephen Holt the sons of Jedediah receive two-thirds of the estate that remains after his wife's decease. Daughter-in-law Lydia Lary receives twenty shillings. Mr. William Frost is named executor.[505] Real estate was valued at $60 and personal estate at $503.98.

Stephen and Mary were parents of four children born at Suncook.

364) i MARY HOLT, b. at Suncook, 15 Dec 1741; m. at Andover, 21 May 1776, her first cousin once removed, Lt. JOHN ADAMS (*Tabitha Farnum Adams⁴, John Farnum³, Elizabeth Holt Farnum², Nicholas¹*), b. 3 Jul 1735 son of Israel and Tabitha (Farnum) Adams; John d. at Andover, 27 Jun 1813. John was first married to Hannah Osgood and second married to Hannah Thurston. Mary and John did not have children.

ii STEPHEN HOLT, b. 23 Feb 1743/4; d. at Andover, 8 Mar 1771; m. 21 Jan 1768, LYDIA JOHNSON. Lydia married second Jonathan Larey. Stephen and Lydia did not have children.

816) iii JEDEDIAH HOLT, b. at Suncook, 23 Feb 1743/4; d. at Andover, 12 Feb 1790; m. at Andover, 19 Jun 1766, PHEBE BARKER, b. at Andover, 2 Jan 1749/50 daughter of Samuel and Sarah (Robinson) Barker.

iv PETER HOLT, b. 8 Feb 1749/50; d. 3 Mar 1749/50.

185) NICHOLAS HOLT (*Nicholas³, Nicholas², Nicholas¹*), b. at Andover, 29 Feb 1716 son of Nicholas and Mary (Manning) Holt; d. at Blue Hill, ME, 16 Mar 1798; m. 1st at Andover, 26 Apr 1739, HANNAH OSGOOD, baptized at Andover, 1 Jun 1718 daughter of Ezekiel and Rebecca (Wardwell) Osgood;[506] Hannah d. at Andover, 1 Sep 1744. Nicholas m. 2nd at Andover, 7 Feb 1750/1, LOIS PHELPS, b. at Reading, about 1720 daughter of Samuel and Elizabeth (Bare) Phelps; Lois d. Jan 1814.

Nicholas was in Andover where his children were born. He relocated to Blue Hill Maine about 1765. He was prominent in the town of Blue Hill serving in positions such as justice of the peace, Colonel in the local militia, town clerk, and foreman of the coroner's jury.[507][508]

Nicholas Holt and Hannah Osgood were parents of two children.

---

[504] *Essex County, MA: Probate File Papers, 1638-1881.*Online database. *AmericanAncestors.org.* New England Historic Genealogical Society, 2014. Case 4981

[505] *Essex County, MA: Probate File Papers, 1638-1881.*Online database. *AmericanAncestors.org.* New England Historic Genealogical Society, 2014. Case 13696

[506] The 1740 will of Ezekiel Osgood includes a bequest to his daughter Hannah Osgood alias Holt.

[507] Durrie, Holt Genealogy

[508] *Blue Hill, ME: Vital Records, 1766-1809.* (Online database: *AmericanAncestors.org*, New England Historic Genealogical Society, 2012)

i JEDEDIAH HOLT, b. 19 Apr 1740; d. 8 Sep 1740.

817) ii HANNAH HOLT, b. at Andover, 16 Nov 1741; d. at Blue Hill, ME, 31 Dec 1826; m. at Andover, 15 Sep 1763, JONATHAN DARLING, baptized at Salem, 11 Jul 1742 son of Jonathan and Sarah (Wardwell) Darling; Jonathan d. at Blue Hill, 26 Feb 1828.

Nicholas Holt and Lois Phelps were parents of three children.

818) i PHEBE HOLT, b. at Andover, 29 Jan 1752; d. at Blue Hill, 12 Feb 1831; m. about 1769, ISRAEL WOOD, b. at Beverly, MA, 17 Oct 1744 son of Joseph and Ruth (Haskell) Wood; Israel d. at Blue Hill, 13 Nov 1800.

819) ii JEDEDIAH HOLT, b. at Andover, 12 Mar 1754; d. at Blue Hill, 17 Aug 1847; m. at Beverly, 24 Feb 1778, SARAH THORNDIKE, b. at Beverly, Sep 1751 (baptized 4 Jul 1756) daughter of Hezekiah and Sarah (Prince) Thorndike; Sarah d, at Blue Hill, 15 Jan 1836.

820) iii NICHOLAS HOLT, b. at Andover, Feb 1756; d. at Blue Hill, 8 Mar 1833; m. 1st at Reading, 26 Nov 1782, his third cousin once removed, PHEBE BATCHELDER (*Phebe Holt Batchelder[5], Joseph[4], Henry[3], Henry[2], Nicholas[1]*), b. at North Reading, 3 Nov 1754 daughter of Jonathan and Phebe (Holt) Batchelder; Phebe d. at Blue Hill, about 1790. Nicholas m. 2nd at Blue Hill 13 Apr 1795, MARY "MOLLY" WORMWOOD, b. about 1765; Mary d. at Blue Hill, 30 Nov 1831.

186) JAMES HOLT (*Nicholas[3], Nicholas[2], Nicholas[1]*), b. at Andover, 13 Jan 1722/3 son of Nicholas and Dorcas (Abbott) Holt; d. 22 Aug 1812; m. 1st, SARAH ABBOTT, b. 2 Aug 1718 daughter of Benjamin and Elizabeth (Abbott) Abbott; Sarah d. 5 Mar 1778. James m. 2nd, 22 Jun 1779, PHEBE BALLARD, b. 25 Jul 1738 daughter of Josiah and Mary (Chandler) Ballard and widow of Abiel Abbot; Phebe d. 9 Jun 1815. Phebe Ballard was first married to ABIEL ABBOTT, b. at Andover, 24 Jul 1735 son of Benjamin and Abigail (Abbott) Abbott; Abiel d. at Andover, 24 Jun 1764.

In his will written 24 March 1804, James Holt has bequests to the following persons: well beloved wife Phebe, grandson James Abbot (who has lived with him for 10 years), beloved daughter Sarah wife of Barachias Abbott, beloved daughter Abigail wife of Isaac Chandler, and his two sons-in-law Barachias Abbott and Isaac Chandler. Grandson James Abbot is named executor.[509]

James Holt elaborates on his bequest to his grandson: "For special and weighty reasons in my mind, I give to my beloved grandson, James Abbot, who has lived with me about ten years, and to his heirs and assigns, all my estate, both real and personal, not herein disposed of." He goes on to list several household items that are to go to him stating these were mostly items that had belonged to James Abbot's uncle. We can only imagine the nature of these "special and weighty reasons."

Sarah and James had seven children, all born at Andover.

i JAMES HOLT, b. 16 Apr 1749; d. 26 Nov 1800; m. 5 Jun 1778, HANNAH FOSTER, b. 23 Jul 1754 daughter of Jacob and Abigail (Frost) Foster; Hannah died from consumption 24 Oct 1794. They do not seem to have had any children that lived to adulthood. There is a daughter Hannah baptized in 1777 who is perhaps their child, but there is no further record for her and since she is not mentioned in the wills of either of her grandfathers, she likely died young. James is not mentioned in his father's will. Likewise, Hannah Foster is not mentioned in the will of her father Jacob who died in 1806.

ii ELIZABETH HOLT, b. 10 Mar 1750/1; d. 12 Nov 1777; Elizabeth did not marry.

iii JOEL HOLT, b. 7 Aug 1753; d. 20 Mar 1755.

iv DORCAS HOLT, b. 6 May 1756; d. 16 May 1778; Dorcas did not marry.

821) v ABIGAIL HOLT, b. 18 Jun 1758; d. 2 Oct 1824; m. 7 Dec 1780, her fourth cousin, ISAAC CHANDLER, b. 4 Oct 1754 son of William and Rebecca (Lovejoy) Chandler; Isaac d. 12 Jan 1832. After Abigail's death, Isaac married Elizabeth Upton.

822) vi SARAH HOLT, b. 7 Mar 1746/7; d. 11 Feb 1808; m. 6 Dec 1770, her third cousin, BARACHIAS ABBOTT (*Hannah Holt Abbott[4], Timothy[3], James[2], Nicholas[1]*), b. 22 May 1739 son of Barachias and Hannah (Holt) Abbott; Barachias d. 29 Jan 1812.

vii SUSANNA HOLT, b. 27 Oct 1760; d. 26 Nov 1760.

187) NATHAN HOLT (*Nicholas[3], Nicholas[2], Nicholas[1]*), b. at Andover, 28 Feb 1725 son of Nicholas and Dorcas (Abbott) Holt; d. at Danvers, 2 Aug 1792; m. 4 Aug 1757, SARAH ABBOTT, b. 14 Jan 1729/30 daughter of George and Mary (Phillips) Abbott; Sarah d. 29 Dec 1797.

---

[509] *Essex County, MA: Probate File Papers, 1638-1881. Probate of James Holt, 5 Nov 1812, Case number 13653.*

Sarah and Nathan had four children. The births of the three daughters are recorded at Danvers. The son James is attributed to this family in Durrie's Holt genealogy.[510] Nathan did not leave a will. The administrator of the estate was his son-in-law William Frost.

823) i SARAH HOLT, b. 29 Oct 1758; d. 17 Sep 1841; m. at Danvers, 2 Dec 1777, WILLIAM FROST, b. at New Castle, NH, 15 Nov 1754 son of William and Elizabeth (Prescott) Frost; William d. at Andover 28 Sep 1836. Sarah and William are second great grandparents of Robert Frost.

824) ii MARY HOLT, b. 3 Oct 1761; d. at Beverly, 7 Jan 1850; m. 1 Nov 1781, ROBERT ENDICOTT, b. 29 Oct 1756 son of John and Elizabeth (Jacobs) Endicott; Robert d. at Beverly, 6 Mar 1819.

825) iii HANNAH HOLT, b. 11 May 1769; d. at Beverly 26 Jul 1857; m. 23 Jan 1793, her first cousin, PETER HOLT (*Joshua*[4], *Nicholas*[3], *Nicholas*[2], *Nicholas*[1]), b. at Andover 12 Jun 1763 son of Joshua and Phebe (Farnum) Holt; Peter d. at Greenfield, NH 25 Apr 1851. Two of the daughters of Hannah and Peter married Samuel Endicott son of Mary Holt and Robert Endicott (Hannah's sister Mary just above).

826) iv JAMES HOLT, b. 1772; d. in India, Aug 1807;[511] m. 30 Aug 1796, LUCY WHIPPLE, b. 8 Mar 1778; Lucy d. at Danvers, 6 Mar 1839. Although James's death is reported as August 1807, the probate of his estate was April 1807.

188) DORCAS HOLT (*Nicholas*[3], *Nicholas*[2], *Nicholas*[1]), b. at Andover, 4 Sep 1727 daughter of Nicholas and Dorcas (Abbott) Holt; death unknown but may have been at Wilton, NH; m. 26 Jan 1749, as his second wife, her first cousin, THOMAS HOLT (*Thomas*[3], *Nicholas*[2], *Nicholas*[1]), b. Mar 1711/2 son of Thomas and Alice (Peabody) Holt; Thomas d. at Andover, 21 Nov 1776. Thomas m. 1st, 15 Oct 1734, HANNAH KIMBALL, baptized at Boxford, 7 Sep 1712 daughter of John and Elizabeth (Chapman) Kimball; Hannah d. at Andover, 12 Jun 1748.

Thomas's first marriage was to Hannah Kimball with whom he had six children. Following her death, Thomas married his cousin Dorcas and they had six children. The story is that Thomas Holt was the largest landholder in Andover at that time. Dorcas was also a horse lover and is supposed to have had the first horse gig in town.[512] After the death of her husband, Dorcas went with one, or perhaps more, of her children to Wilton and she is believed to have died there.

Thomas wrote his will 8 Oct 1774. Dorcas was named executrix of the estate in Thomas's will, but she requested that this duty be assumed by her brother Joshua Holt. In his will, Thomas Holt has bequests for the following persons: dearly beloved wife Dorcas who receives use of the West end of the dwelling house as well as other provisions for her support and son William is charged with seeing to her support and care; well-beloved son Nathan receives a token bequest of six shillings to make up his total portion; well-beloved son Daniel receives £13; well-beloved son Asa, six shillings; well-beloved son Thomas, a tract of land that was purchased from Samuel Ames; well-beloved son William, real and personal estate not otherwise disposed of; well-beloved son Joseph, a tract of land lying south of the land of the widow Rebecca Gray; beloved daughters Hannah and Mehitable receive six shillings each; beloved daughter Dorcas receives a piece of pasture land; beloved daughter Mary, £53; beloved daughter Lois, £53; daughters Lois and Mary also allowed use of a bed and chest in the house where they might stay in times of sickness as long as they are unmarried.[513] Hannah, Mehitable, Nathan, Daniel, and Asa are children from Thomas's first marriage.

There are birth records for six children of Dorcas Holt and Thomas Holt recorded at Andover.

826a) i THOMAS HOLT, b. 15 Jun 1750; m. 27 Oct 1774, his second cousin, LYDIA FARNUM (*Thomas Farnum*[5], *Thomas Farnum*[4], *Thomas, Farnum*[3], *Elizabeth Holt Farnum*[2], *Nicholas*[1]), b. 10 Nov 1756 daughter of Thomas and Lydia (Abbott) Farnum.

625) ii DORCAS HOLT, b. 19 Mar 1753; m. 25 Nov 1773, her third cousin, MOSES LOVEJOY (*Mary Holt Lovejoy*[4], *Oliver*[3], *Henry*[2], *Nicholas*[1]), b. 9 Sep 1751 son of Daniel and Mary (Holt) Lovejoy; Moses d. at Wilton, 19 Mar 1807.

827) iii MARY HOLT, b. 11 Mar 1758; d. at Andover, 20 Mar 1830; m. at Andover, 7 Dec 1780, her third cousin, THOMAS GRAY (*Thomas Gray*[4], *Edward Gray*[3], *Hannah Holt Gray*[2], *Nicholas*[1]), b. at Andover, 23 Mary 1758 son of Thomas and Lydia (Graves) Gray; Thomas d. at Andover, 5 Sep 1823.[514] Although it is not certain this Mary Holt married Thomas Gray, that seems currently the most likely option.

---

[510] Durrie, *Genealogical History of the Holt Family*, p 44

[511] James, h. Lucy (Whipple), at India, Aug. —, 1807.

[512] Livermore, *History of the Town of Wilton*, p 404

[513] *Essex County, MA: Probate File Papers, 1638-1881. Probate of Thomas Holt, 3 Feb 1777, Case number 13699.*

[514] Durrie's Holt genealogy lists Mary as the Mary Holt that married John Adams in 1776 (his third marriage). However, John Adams's Mary died in 1829 at age 89, meaning she was born about 1740 so that is not this Mary.

828) iv LOIS HOLT, b. 29 Oct 1760; d. at Andover, 17 Apr 1852; m. 4 Jan 1785, MOSES PEARSON, b. at Wilmington, about 1752 son of Nathan and Mary (Wilson) Pearson; Moses d. at Andover 11 Aug 1835.

829) v WILLIAM HOLT, b. 7 Sep 1763; m. 29 Jul 1784, ELIZABETH JONES daughter of Jacob and Mary (Winn) Jones; Elizabeth d. at Weld, ME, 1829.

830) vi JOSEPH HOLT, b. 29 Sep 1766; d. at Andover, 8 Jun 1791; m. 27 Nov 1788, his third cousin once removed, ABIGAIL HOLT (*Samuel⁵, Samuel⁴, Samuel³, Samuel², Nicholas¹*), b. 19 May 1767 daughter of Samuel and Abigail (Blanchard) Holt; Abigail d. 13 May 1821.

Thomas Holt and Hannah Kimball were parents of six children.

i NATHAN HOLT, b. at Andover, 17 Jul 1735; d. at Andover, 26 Aug 1785. Nathan did not marry.

190) ii HANNAH HOLT, b. at Andover, 11 Feb 1738/9; d. at Andover, 2 Aug 1831; m. at Andover, 29 Nov 1759, her first cousin once removed, DANIEL HOLT (*Nicholas³, Nicholas², Nicholas¹*), b. at Andover, 10 Feb 1732/3 son of Nicholas and Dorcas (Abbott) Holt; Daniel d. at Andover, 15 Feb 1796.

641) iii DANIEL HOLT, b. at Andover, 11 Sep 1740; m. at Andover, 3 Dec 1761, his first cousin, ALICE HOLT (*Benjamin⁴, Henry³, Henry², Nicholas¹*), b. at Andover, 13 Nov 1742 daughter of Benjamin and Lydia (Holt) Holt; Alice d. at Morrisville, NY, 7 Mar 1826.

389) iv ASA HOLT, b. at Andover, 3 May 1742; d. at Andover, 20 Feb 1793; m. 1st 10 Sep 1765, his third cousin, DINAH HOLT (*Samuel⁴, Samuel³, Samuel², Nicholas¹*), b. at Andover, 6 Nov 1744 daughter of Samuel and Jemima (Gray) Holt; Dinah d. at Andover, 20 Nov 1780. Asa m. 2nd at Andover, 5 Jul 1781, LYDIA STEVENS, b. at Andover, 15 Nov 1753 daughter of Jonathan and Lydia (Felch) Stevens.

831) v MEHITABLE HOLT, b. at Andover, 8 Feb 1743/4; d. at Hillsborough, 20 Oct 1816; m. 1st 28 May 1761, SAMUEL LUFKIN son of Samuel Lufkin; Samuel d. 30 Apr 1777. Mehitable m. 2nd at Andover, 14 Jul 1785, ABNER WILKINS, b. 1 Jul 1743; Abner d. at Middleton, 17 Aug 1820. Abner was first married to Eunice Smith.

832) vi ABIEL HOLT, b. at Andover, 3 Apr 1746; d. at Andover, 17 Nov 1824; m. 23 Jun 1767, his third cousin once removed, LYDIA LOVEJOY (*Joshua Lovejoy⁵, Henry Lovejoy⁴, Mary Farnum Lovejoy³, Elizabeth Holt Farnum², Nicholas¹*), b. at Andover, 21 Jul 1747 daughter of Joshua and Lydea (Abbott) Lovejoy; Lydia d. at Haverhill, 3 Jan 1838.

189) JOSHUA HOLT (*Nicholas³, Nicholas², Nicholas¹*), b. 30 Jun 1730 son of Nicholas and Dorcas (Abbott) Holt; d. 24 Jul 1810; m. 2 Dec 1755, his second cousin once removed, PHEBE FARNUM (*Timothy Farnum⁴, Ephraim Farnum³, Elizabeth Holt Farnum², Nicholas¹*), b. 10 Oct 1731 daughter of Timothy and Dinah (Ingalls) Farnum; Phebe d. 26 Jan 1806.

Joshua Holt and Phebe Farnum had as their homestead what is now 111 Reservation Road in Andover, known as the Solomon Holt farm. Joshua is believed to have built this homestead in 1790. His son Solomon, as noted in the will, received the homestead from his father.[515]

Joshua was deacon of the South Parish church in Andover for 34 years. He also served in the Revolutionary War as a member of the 4th Essex County militia.[516]

Joshua Holt revised his will 24 May 1807 in response to "great alterations" that had taken place in his family. Perhaps these "great alterations" related to the death of his wife Phebe in 1806. Four sons, John, Joshua, Timothy, and Stephen, each receive $40. Son Peter receives $110. Each of his daughters receive $33.34. These daughters are Phebe the wife of Joseph Batchelder, Mary the wife of Isaac Foster, Abiah the wife of Deacon Daniel Kimbal, Hannah the wife of Ephraim Holt, and Chloe the wife of Francis Bowers. The daughters also receive all the household goods and furniture. Son Solomon receives all the lands and buildings that Joshua still holds at the time as his death as well as his pew in the meeting house. His six sons will divide his wearing apparel, although Solomon is free to select what items he wants. Solomon is named sole executor.[517]

Solomon was the only child in this family that remained in Andover. All the other children moved to New Hampshire and settled in towns in Hillsborough County.

Joshua Holt and Phebe Farnum had eleven children whose births are recorded at Andover. Some sources (e. g., Durrie's *A Genealogical History of the Holt Family*) also list a child Ruth in this family, but there was another Joshua Holt married to Ruth Burnap who was in Andover at the same time and rearing a family. There were records for two girls named Ruth in Andover, one baptized in January 1756 and the other born 11 May 1758; both these dates conflict with births of other children of Joshua and Phebe, and Ruth is likely the daughter of Joshua and Ruth (Family 134).

515 Andover Historic Preservation. https://preservation.mhl.org/111-reservation-road

516 Massachusetts Soldiers and Sailors, volume 8, p 193

517 *Essex County, MA: Probate File Papers, 1638-1881. Probate of Joshua Holt, 9 Aug 1810, Case number 13666.*

833) i PHEBE HOLT, b. 28 Nov 1756; d. at Greenfield, 1849; m. 11 Dec 1778, JOSEPH BATCHELDER, b. 6 Mar 1748 son of Joseph and Judith (Rea) Batchelder; Joseph d. 1826.

834) ii JOSHUA HOLT, b. 17 Jan 1758; d at Greenfield, 14 Mar 1835; m. 31 Oct 1782, HANNAH INGALLS, b. 20 Feb 1759 daughter of David and Priscilla (Howe) Ingalls; Hannah d. 1 Dec 1838.

835) iii MARY HOLT, b. 5 Dec 1759; d. at Greenfield, 9 Jul 1819; m. 26 Aug 1784, ISAAC FOSTER, b. 23 Dec 1751 son of Jacob and Abigail (Frost) Foster.

836) iv ABIAH HOLT, b. 16 Apr 1761; d. at Hancock, NH, 4 May 1841; m. 21 Jun 1791, as his second wife, DANIEL KIMBALL, b. at Ipswich, 20 Oct 1755 son of Daniel and Hephzibah (Howe) Kimball; d. 24 May 1843. Daniel's first wife was Elizabeth Osgood.

825) v PETER HOLT, b. 12 Jun 1763; d. at Greenfield, 25 Apr 1851; m. 23 Jan 1793, his first cousin, HANNAH HOLT (*Nathan*^{4}*, Nicholas*^{3}*, Nicholas*^{2}*, Nicholas*^{1}), b. at Danvers, 11 May 1769 daughter of Nathan and Sarah (Abbott) Holt; Hannah d. at Beverly, 26 Jul 1857.

837) vi JOHN HOLT, b. 12 Jan 1765; d, at Greenfield, 11 Feb 1835; m. 6 Jan 1792, his third cousin, DORCAS ABBOTT, b. Dec 1766 daughter of George and Hannah (Lovejoy) Abbott; Dorcas d. 15 Mar 1841.

838) vii TIMOTHY HOLT, b. Apr 1767; d. at Peterborough, 22 Oct 1856; m. 7 Nov 1793, his second cousin once removed, LYDIA HOLT (*Joseph*^{5}*, Benjamin*^{4}*, Henry*^{3}*, Henry*^{2}*, Nicholas*^{1}), b. 18 Apr 1767 daughter of Joseph and Ruth (Johnson) Holt; Lydia d. 22 Nov 1825. Timothy m. 2nd, 11 Mar 1830, CHARITY SAVAGE, b. 1779 and d. at Peterborough, 28 Feb 1846.

839) viii SOLOMON HOLT, b. Dec 1768; d. 15 Apr 1830; m. 22 May 1798, MARY CUMMINGS, b. at Andover, 1 Nov 1774 daughter of Jonathan and Mary (Eastman) Cummings; Mary d. 8 Oct 1852.

840) ix HANNAH HOLT, b. Jun 1771; d. at Greenfield, 21 Apr 1842; m. 27 Nov 1794, her third cousin once removed, EPHRAIM HOLT (*Jacob*^{5}*, Jacob*^{4}*, Oliver*^{3}*, Henry*^{2}*, Nicholas*^{1}), b. 19 Mar 1769 son of Jacob and Rhoda (Abbott) Holt; Ephraim d. 24 Oct 1836.

841) x STEPHEN HOLT, b. May 1773; d. at Greenfield, 26 Mar 1868; m. 1799, his third cousin once removed, FANNY BOWERS (*Elizabeth Holt Bowers*^{5}*, Jacob*^{4}*, Oliver*^{3}*, Henry*^{2}*, Nicholas*^{1}), b. at Chelmsford, Jun 1773 daughter of Francis and Elizabeth (Holt) Bowers; Fanny d. 18 Apr 1828. Stephen married in 1831, MARGARET BATCHELDER, b. 1784 and d. at Greenfield, 17 Aug 1867.

842) xi CHLOE HOLT, b. Jun 1775; d. at Peterborough, 6 Nov 1849; m. 23 Oct 1798, her third cousin once removed, FRANCIS BOWERS (*Elizabeth Holt Bowers*^{5}*, Jacob*^{4}*, Oliver*^{3}*, Henry*^{2}*, Nicholas*^{1}), b. at Chelmsford, 20 May 1775 son of Francis and Elizabeth (Holt) Bowers; Francis d. 15 Oct 1835.

190) DANIEL HOLT (*Nicholas*^{3}*, Nicholas*^{2}*, Nicholas*^{1}), b. 10 Feb 1732/3; d. at Andover, 15 Feb 1796 son of Nicholas and Dorcas (Abbott) Holt; m. 29 Nov 1759, his first cousin once removed, HANNAH HOLT (*Thomas*^{4}*, Thomas*^{3}*, Nicholas*^{2}*, Nicholas*^{1}), b. 11 Feb 1738/9 daughter of Thomas and Hannah (Kimball) Holt; Hannah d. at Andover, 2 Aug 1831.

There are births for three children in this family that are recorded at Andover. A probate record was not located, and no other specific information about this couple.

843) i DANIEL HOLT, b. Dec 1761; d. at Fitchburg, 27 Nov 1830; m. 5 Jan 1790, MARY JONES, b. at Andover, about 1769 daughter of Jacob and Mary (Winn) Jones.[518]

844) ii ABIEL HOLT, b. 8 Jun 1765; d. at Rindge, NH, 18 Jun 1825; m. 26 Jul 1791, PHEBE PUTNAM, b. at Fitchburg, 20 Sep 1770 daughter of Daniel and Rachel (-) Putnam; Phebe d. at Fitchburg, 12 Nov 1827.

iii NATHAN HOLT, b. 13 Jul 1767; d. 1 Sep 1778.

191) JOSEPH HOLT (*Thomas*^{3}*, Nicholas*^{2}*, Nicholas*^{1}), b. at Andover, 28 Feb 1715/6 son of Thomas and Alice (Peabody) Holt; d. at Lunenburg, 1754; m. 1st 14 Aug 1742, MARY ABBOTT, b. at Andover, 4 Aug 1713 daughter of Stephen and Sarah (Stevens) Abbott; Mary d. at Lunenburg, 5 Aug 1748. Joseph m. 2nd at Lunenburg, 20 May 1749, DORCAS BOYNTON, b. at Groton, MA, 21 Dec 1715 daughter of Benoni and Anna (Mighill) Boynton; Dorcas d. at Lunenburg, 11 Jun 1775. Dorcas Boynton was first married to Thomas Frost.

In his will written 16 February 1754 (probate 26 Apr 1754), Joseph Holt bequeaths to beloved wife Dorcas the use of all the real estate, mansion house, and barn until his youngest son Joseph reaches age seven years four months old. He adds several stipulations related Dorcas keeping the farm and barn in good repair. After son Joseph reaches age seven, Dorcas will

---

[518] The will of Jacob Jones includes a bequest to his granddaughter Mary Holt the child of his daughter Mary who is deceased.

have the use of one-third of the estate. Dorcas receives all the husbandry tools, smith tools, and smith shop which are hers forever except that part of the estate that he leaves to his two daughters Mary Holt and Sarah Holt. He bequeaths to Dorcas's daughter Dorcas Frost £3.6.8 for her service while she was with the family. His two sons Abiel and Joseph are to receive two-thirds of the real estate and are to pay to their sister Mary and Sarah £13.6.8 when they reach age twenty-one. He also bequeaths to his two daughters household items that belonged to their mother which are currently in the care of Stephen Abbott in Andover. His four children will equally divide the books. Wife Dorcas and brother Thomas Holt are named executors. Real estate was valued at £200.[519]

Mary Abbott and Joseph Holt had four children all born at Lunenburg.

i JOSEPH HOLT, b. 4 Apr 1744; d. in infancy.

845) ii MARY HOLT, b. 17 Aug 1745; m. 26 Jun 1766, BENJAMIN DARLING, b. 28 Apr 1728 son of John and Lois (Gowing) Darling; Benjamin d. at Lunenburg, about 1783 based on date of probate.

846) iii SARAH HOLT, baptized at Lunenburg 14 Dec 1746; m. at Lunenburg, 1 Feb 1767, BARNABAS WOOD, b. at Lunenburg, 21 May 1746 son of Jonathan and Sarah (Whitney) Wood; Barnabas d. at Windsor, VT, 5 Apr 1822.

738) iv ABIEL HOLT, b. 14 Jul 1748; d. at Temple, NH, 7 Jan 1811; m. 25 Nov 1773, his third cousin, SARAH ABBOTT (*Job Abbott[4], Zerviah Holt Abbott[3], Henry[2], Nicholas[1]*), b. at Suncook, 1751 daughter of Job and Sarah (Abbott) Abbott; Sarah d. 9 Oct 1854 (age at death inscribed as 103 years, 2 months, 25 days on her gravestone).[520]

Joseph Holt and Dorcas Boynton were parents of one child.

847) i JOSEPH HOLT, b. at Lunenburg, 18 Dec 1752; d. at Fitchburg, 3 Sep 1803 (suicide by hanging); m. 30 Jan 1777, ELIZABETH STRATTON.

192) WILLIAM HOLT (*Thomas[3], Nicholas[2], Nicholas[1]*), b. at Andover, 10 Dec 1720 son of Thomas and Alice (Peabody) Holt; d. at Hampton, CT, 2 Aug 1793; m. 1st at Hampton, 14 Jul 1742, his first cousin, HANNAH HOLT (*Abiel[3], Nicholas[2], Nicholas[1]*), b. at Windham, CT, 17 Apr 1723 daughter of Abiel and Hannah (Abbott) Holt; Hannah d. at Windham, 25 Jan 1750/1. William m. 2nd at Windham, 14 May 1752, SYBEL DURKEE, b. at Windham, 10 Jan 1731 daughter of Stephen and Lois (Moulton) Durkee;[521] Sybel d. at Hampton, 11 Jan 1794.

Hannah Holt and William Holt had four children whose births are recorded at Windham.

422) i WILLIAM HOLT, b. 15 Jul 1743; d. at Hampton, 6 Aug 1815;[522] m. 8 Sep 1763, his third cousin, MERCY HOLT (*Zebadiah[4], Elizabeth Farnum Holt[3], Elizabeth Holt Farnum[2], Nicholas[1]*), b. 14 Feb 1740/1 daughter of Zebadiah and Sarah (Flint) Holt; Mercy d. 15 Sep 1799.

ii HANNAH HOLT, b. 26 Jan 1744/5; d. 30 Aug 1754.

848) iii ALICE HOLT, b. 26 Apr 1747; d. at Stockbridge, VT, 28 Nov 1814;[523] m. 13 Nov 1764, her second cousin, ROBERT LYON (*Sarah Holt Lyon[4], Robert[3], Nicholas[2], Nicholas[1]*), b. at Pomfret, 30 Sep 1743 son of Peletiah and Sarah (Holt) Lyon; Robert d. 12 Feb 1809.

849) iv SARAH HOLT, b. 21 Jun 1748; d. at Hampton, 7 Apr 1777; m. 16 Nov 1769, HENRY DURKEE, b. 29 Sep 1749 son of Henry and Relief (Adams) Durkee. Henry m. 2nd, Sarah Loomis; Henry d. 22 Apr 1820.

William Holt and Sybel Durkee were parents of four children born and Windham.

i BETHIAH HOLT, b. and d. 16 Aug 1754

ii ABIEL HOLT, b. 8 Jul 1755; m. at Windham, 18 Jul 1776, ABIGAIL DURKEE, b. at Windham, 11 Feb 1756 daughter of Joseph and Elizabeth (Fiske) Durkee. Abiel and Abigail had one son Abiel Holt who was born at Windham on 24 Oct 1790. Nothing further that is certain is known of the son Abiel.

iii HANNAH HOLT, b. 25 Apr 1756; d. 10 Sep 1774.

---

519 *Worcester County, MA: Probate File Papers, 1731-1881.* Online database. AmericanAncestors.org. New England Historic Genealogical Society, 2015. Case 30653

520 Findagrave.com

521 The 1766 will of Stephen Durkee of Windham includes a bequest to his daughter Sibbel Holt.

522 *Connecticut, Deaths and Burials Index, 1650-1934.*

523 *Vermont, Vital Records, 1720-1908.*

iv AMASA HOLT, b. at Windham, 24 May 1759; perhaps the Amasa who d. at Waterford, CT, 23 Jul 1847 at age 88.

193) ALICE HOLT (*Thomas*[3], *Nicholas*[2], *Nicholas*[1]), b. at Andover, about 1722 daughter of Thomas and Alice (Peabody) Holt; d. at Andover, 1762 (probate 22 Nov 1762); m. 13 Mar 1739/40, as his third wife, JOHN BARNARD, b. at Andover, 16 Apr 1697 son of John and Naomi (Hoyt) Barnard; John d. at Andover, 1752 (probate 15 Jun 1752). John was first married to Sarah Osgood and second married to Mehitable Stiles.

John Barnard did not leave a will and his estate entered probate 15 Jun 1752 with widow Alice declining administration which was assumed by John Barnard. The dower was set off to widow Alice which was for life. The other real estate was settled on eldest son John who received the double portion and daughter Sarah Kidder who were children from John's first marriage to Sarah Osgood. The children of Alice and Abigail receiving portions in the settlement were Mehitable, Allis, Jacob, Abigail, Lidia, and Rebecca.[524]

Alice's estate entered probate 22 November 1762.[525] The value of her estate consisting of clothing and household items was £16.4.9.

Alice Holt and John Barnard were parents of seven children born at Andover.

i MEHITABLE BARNARD, b. at Andover, 17 Dec 1740; d. at Andover, 23 Apr 1824. Mehitable did not marry. She did have an out-of-wedlock child Josiah Sawyer born in 1773.

ii ALICE BARNARD, b. at Andover, 28 Jul 1742. Alice was living in 1762 at the estate settlement, but no marriage or death record was located.

850) iii ABIGAIL BARNARD, b. at Andover, 15 May 1744; m. at Andover, 22 Mar 1764, SAMUEL DOWNING, baptized at Salem, 2 May 1742 son of Richard and Temperance (Derby) Downing; Samuel d. at Minot, ME, 13 Dec 1812.

851) iv LYDIA BARNARD, b. at Andover, 23 Jan 1745/6; d. at Sharon, NH, 9 Feb 1829; m. at Andover, 3 Sep 1767, JOSIAH SAWYER, b. at Reading, 17 Sep 1744 son of Josiah and Hannah (Gowing) Sawyer; Josiah d. at Sharon, 3 Oct 1829.

v MARY BARNARD, b. 21 Jan and d. 29 Jan 1747/8.

vi REBECCA BARNARD, b. at Andover, 21 Jan 1747/8; m. at Wilmington, 27 Jan 1791, as his second wife, THOMAS EVANS, likely b. at Salisbury, 15 Oct 1725 son of Thomas and Dorothy (Stockman) Evans; Thomas d. at Wilmington, 1802 (probate). Thomas was first married to Ruth Ballard. Rebecca did not have children.

vii JACOB BARNARD, b. at Andover, 20 Jul 1750. Jacob served in the Revolution in 1775 in Capt. Benjamin Farnum's company.

194) ABIGAIL HOLT (*Robert*[3], *Nicholas*[2], *Nicholas*[1]), b. at Windham, 20 Feb 1722 daughter of Robert and Rebecca (Preston) Holt; m. at Windham, 5 Nov 1741, DAVID KENDALL; David d. at Ashford, 16 Dec 1777.

There are records of five children of Abigail Holt and David Kendall.

852) i ABIGAIL KENDALL, b. at Windham, 21 Oct 1742; d. at Ashford, 8 Nov 1781; m. 28 May 1771, ENOS PRESTON, b. at Windham, 7 Jun 1737 son of John and Sarah (Foster) Preston. Enos married second Hannah Stiles on 12 Nov 1783.

853) ii DAVID KENDALL, b. at Windham, 13 Nov 1744; m. at Ashford, 23 Feb 1775, MEHITABLE STILES, b. at Windham, 15 Nov 1740 daughter of Samuel and Huldah (Durkee) Stiles; Mehitable d. at Ashford, 27 Jan 1827.

iii ALICE KENDALL, b. at Windham, 18 Jan 1746; d. at Ashford, 16 Apr 1798.

iv REBECCA KENDALL, baptized at Hampton, 22 Jan 1749

v EZEKIEL KENDALL, baptized at Hampton, 30 Jun 1751

---

[524] *Essex County, MA: Probate File Papers, 1638-1881.*Online database. *AmericanAncestors.org.* New England Historic Genealogical Society, 2014. Case 1745

[525] *Essex County, MA: Probate File Papers, 1638-1881.*Online database. *AmericanAncestors.org.* New England Historic Genealogical Society, 2014. Case 1732

195) SARAH HOLT (*Robert*[3], *Nicholas*[2], *Nicholas*[1]), b. at Windham, 20 Feb 1722 daughter of Robert and Rebecca (Preston) Holt; d. at Pomfret, 11 Oct 1743; m. at Pomfret, 2 Feb 1741/2, PELETIAH LYON, b. at Pomfret, 20 Sep 1711 son of Abiel and Judith (Farrington) Lyon.

Sarah Holt and Peletiah Lyon were parents of one child.

848) i ROBERT LYON, b. at Pomfret, 30 Sep 1743; d. at Stockbridge, VT, 12 Feb 1809; m. 13 Nov 1764, his second cousin, ALICE HOLT (*William*[4], *Thomas*[3], *Nicholas*[2], *Nicholas*[1]), b. at Windham, 26 Apr 1747 daughter of William and Hannah (Holt) Holt; Alice d. at Stockbridge, 28 Nov 1814.

196) MARY HOLT (*Robert*[3], *Nicholas*[2], *Nicholas*[1]), b. at Windham, 7 Feb 1725 daughter of Robert and Rebecca (Preston) Holt; m. at Pomfret, 15 Jun 1742, JOSEPH TRUESDELL, b. at Pomfret, 24 Jun 1719 son of Ebenezer and Rachel (Davis) Truesdell; Joseph d. at Havana, 8 Oct 1762.

Joseph Truesdell did not leave a will and his estate entered probate 4 January 1763 with Samuel Craft as administrator. The total value of the estate was £16.6.4 with debts exceeding its value.[526]

The births of eight children are recorded for Joseph Truesdell and Mary Holt.

i JERUSHA TRUESDELL, b. at Pomfret, 4 Apr 1743; d. 30 Jun 177__ in the death transcription. Jerusha did not marry.

ii ASA TRUESDELL, b. at Pomfret, 16 Aug 1744; d. at Suffield, CT, 1796; perhaps m. in 1778, SYBIL CARRINGTON. No children were identified.

854) iii SETH TRUESDELL, b. at Pomfret, 23 Mar 1746; d. at Pomfret, 19 Oct 1776; m. at Pomfret, 10 Jan 1771, ESTHER WEST.

855) iv JEDUTHUN TRUESDELL, b. recorded at Killingly, 21 Jan 1748; d. at Pomfret, 12 Apr 1801; m. at Pomfret, 20 Jan 1774; ABIGAIL WHITE.

v RACHEL TRUESDELL, b. 17 Oct 1750; d. 29 Jan 1767.

856) vi DARIUS TRUESDELL, b. at Pomfret, 16 Jan 1752; d. at Woodstock, 6 May 1808; m. at Woodstock, 10 Oct 1772, RHODA CHAFFEE, b. at Woodstock, 10 May 1751 daughter of Thomas and Dorcas (Abbott) Chaffee; Rhoda d. at Woodstock, 19 Nov 1834.

vii SARAH TRUESDELL, b. at Pomfret, 20 Aug 1753; d. at Pomfret, 27 Mar 1787. Sarah did not marry.

viii MOLLY TRUESDELL, b. at Pomfret, 9 Jul 1756. Molly is not known to have married but had an out-of-wedlock child, Hannah Abbott b. at Pomfret 12 Oct 1779. It is not known what became of daughter Hannah.

197) MARTHA HOLT (*Robert*[3], *Nicholas*[2], *Nicholas*[1]), b. at Windham, 11 Apr 1725 daughter of Robert and Rebecca (Preston) Holt; d. at Pomfret, 4 Oct 1759; m. 1 Jan 1754, JOHN RICHARDSON.

Martha and John had three children in Windham County and Martha died after the birth of her third child. John remarried and took his family to Yarmouth, Nova Scotia where he was by 1761.[527]

857) i REUBEN RICHARDSON, b. at Windham, 7 Dec 1754; m. at Yarmouth, 24 Aug 1775, MARY BURGESS daughter of Joshua Burgess.

ii SARAH RICHARDSON, b. at Pomfret, 22 Apr 1758

858) iii STEPHEN RICHARDSON, b. at Pomfret, 26 Sep 1759; d. at Middletown, VT, 3 Jan 1834;[528] m. at Norwich, CT, 21 Dec 1786, HANNAH RUDD, b. about 1767; Hannah d. at Middletown, about 1848.

198) ELIZABETH HOLT (*Abiel*[3], *Nicholas*[2], *Nicholas*[1]), b. at Windham, 16 Feb 1724/5 daughter of Abiel and Hannah (Abbott) Holt; d. about 1753; m. 10 Jun 1746, FRANCIS FENTON, b. at Willington, b. 16 Mar 1718 son of Francis and Ann (Berry) Fenton;[529] Francis d. at Willington, 1781 (date of probate). Francis m. 2nd Ann Newcomb on 31 Oct 1754.

Elizabeth Holt and Francis Fenton had two children whose births are recorded at Willington.

859) i MARY FENTON, b. at Willington, 13 Apr 1749; d. at Willington, 14 Apr 1822; m. 1st, 21 May 1770, ISAAC SAWIN, b. 23 Sep 1748 son of George and Anna (Farrar) Sawin; Isaac d. 29 Oct 1776. Mary m. 2nd, 2 Jul

---

526 *Connecticut State Library (Hartford, Connecticut)*; Probate Place: *Hartford, Connecticut, Probate Packets, Thayer, E-Tyler, Septimus, 1752-1880, Estate of Joseph Truesdell, Case 4064*

527 Campbell, *A History of the County of Yarmouth, Nova Scotia*

528 *U.S., Revolutionary War Pension and Bounty-Land Warrant Application Files, 1800-1900* [database on-line].

529 William Weaver, *Genealogy of the Fenton Family*. (Willimantic, CT, 1867).

1778, as his second wife, JAMES NILES, b. at Braintree, 2 Apr 1747 son of John and Dorothy (Reynolds) Niles; James d. 18 Jan 1822.

775) ii FRANCIS FENTON, b. at Willington, 13 Feb 1750/1; m. 25 May 1775, CHLOE GOODALE (*Phebe Holt Goodale⁴, Keturah Holt Holt³, Henry², Nicholas¹*), b. at Pomfret, 28 Dec 1755 daughter of Ebenezer and Phebe (Holt) Goodale; Chloe d. at New Haven, Oct 1833.[530]

199) ABIEL HOLT (*Abiel³, Nicholas², Nicholas¹*), b. at Windham, 1 Feb 1726/7 son of Abiel and Hannah (Abbott) Holt; d. at Willington, 2 Oct 1785; m. 1st 22 Apr 1755, MARY DOWNER whose origins are unknown; Mary d. 28 Jan 1766. Abiel m. 2nd 2 Apr 1767, EUNICE KINGSBURY (widow of John Marshall), b. 17 Feb 1733/4 daughter of John and Deborah (Spalding) Kingsbury; Eunice d. 2 Jun 1784.

Abiel resided in Willington where he served as deacon.

The distributions from the estate of Abiel Holt were made 19 December 1785 to the following heirs: Hannah Pearl, eldest daughter; Sarah Crocker, second daughter; Mary Needham, third daughter; Abial Holt, eldest son; Bethiah Holt, fourth daughter; Andrew Holt, second son; Abel Holt, third son; and Eunice Holt, youngest daughter. The first five children are from Abiel's marriage to Mary Downer; Eunice Kingsbury is the mother of the three youngest children.[531]

Abiel Holt and Mary Downer had six children born at Willington.

758) i HANNAH HOLT, b. 14 Mar 1756; d. 20 Nov 1832; m. 24 Apr 1782, as his second wife, her second cousin, OLIVER PEARL (*Dinah Holt Pearl⁴, Joshua³, Nicholas², Nicholas¹*), b. 9 Oct 1749 son of Timothy and Dinah (Holt) Pearl. Oliver was married first to Mercy Hinkley.

860) ii SARAH HOLT, b. 8 Dec 1757; d. at Willington, 1856;[532] m. 24 Oct 1782, ZEBULON CROCKER, b. at Willington, 5 Mar 1757 son of Ebenezer and Hannah (Hatch) Crocker; Zebulon d. at Willington, 17 Jan 1826.

iii MARY HOLT, b. 13 Jul 1759; d. 4 Feb 1760.

861) iv MARY HOLT, b. 8 Dec 1760; m. at Charlton, MA, 17 Feb 1783,[533] DANIEL NEEDHAM possibly the son of Daniel and Hannah (Allen) Needham; Daniel d. at Paxton, MA 1801 (date of probate 6 Oct 1801; will written 4 Mar 1801).

862) v ABIEL HOLT, b. 12 Jul 1762; d. at Fairfax, VT, 6 Jun 1829; m. by 1787, MARY MOSHER, b. 21 Jul 1762 daughter of Nathaniel and Elizabeth (Crandall) Mosher; Mary d. 6 Sep 1827.

vi BETHIAH HOLT, b. 26 Mar 1764; d. 1833. Bethiah did not marry.

Abiel Holt and Eunice Kingsbury had three children born at Willington.

i ANDREW HOLT, b. 3 May 1768; d. at Hadley, MA, 21 Sep 1853;[534] m. HANNAH SMITH, b. at Hadley, 28 Aug 1775, daughter of Joseph and Nancy (Day) Smith; Hannah d. 28 Jul 1855. Andrew and Hannah did not have children.

863) ii ABEL HOLT, b. 1770; m. 1st, 17 Nov 1793, ANNA ABEL, b. at Norwich, 8 Jul 1771 daughter of Thomas and Zerviah (Hyde) Abel; Anna d. at Sharon, VT 13 Apr 1798. Abel m. 2nd, by 1798, RUTH KING, b. at Wilbraham, MA, 13 Feb 1779 daughter of Oliver and Ruth (Cooley) King. This family had nine children born in Vermont and then seem to have relocated to Oneida, New York.

iii EUNICE HOLT, b. 5 Mar 1772. She was living at the time of her father's will, but no record found following that.

200) CALEB HOLT (*Abiel³, Nicholas², Nicholas¹*), b. at Windham, 6 Mar 1729 son of Abiel and Hannah (Abbott) Holt; d. at Willington, 18 Aug 1810; m. 29 Jan 1755, MARY MERRICK, b. 6 Dec 1726 daughter of John and Sarah (Parsons) Merrick; Mary d. 4 Jun 1790. Caleb m. 2nd 17 May 1791, CHLOE HATCH; Chloe d. at Willington, 21 Feb 1815.

---

[530] Connecticut, Deaths and Burials Index, 1650-1934

[531] *Connecticut Wills and Probate, 1609-1999*, Probate of Abial Holt, Hartford, 1785, Case number 1057.

[532] In the 1850 U.S. Census, 92-year old widow Sarah Crocker was living at the home of her daughter Bethiah Hull. Probate of estate was 1856 with Joseph Hull as administrator.

[533] *Massachusetts, Compiled Marriages, 1633-1850*. Daniel and Mary Holt of Willington, int. Feb. 17, 1783.

[534] *Massachusetts, Death Records, 1841-1915*, New England Historic Genealogical Society; Boston, Massachusetts; Massachusetts Vital Records, 1840–1911. Parents are listed on the death record as Abiel and Eunice Holt.

Caleb wrote a will 11 Apr 1793.[535] There are bequests for wife Chloe, sons Elijah and Caleb, and daughter Elizabeth Howe(?). He wrote a codicil 4 April 1798, it which he bequeathed to his wife Chloe the whole of a farm that he purchased from Samuel Dunham so long as she gives up rights to property she brought with her into the marriage. There are no other changes to heirs. The estate entered probate 29 August 1810. The distribution documents include the division set off to widow Chloe and an acknowledgment from Elijah and Caleb that they have received their portions. There is not a distribution document related to Elizabeth. The will is difficult to decipher in terms of Elizabeth's married name (it might be Howe or Hovey or something else altogether or maybe it is a poorly written Holt). In any event, no marriage record was located for her and no death record.

Caleb Holt and Mary Merrick had five children whose births are recorded at Willington.

i ELIZABETH HOLT, b. 29 Apr 1756. From her father's will, it seems that Elizabeth married, but the last name is unclear. It could be Howe or Hovey or some other name. No marriage record was located that would fit with the name in the will. Durrie's Holt genealogy gives her spouse as Abiel Stevens. But Abiel Stevens and Elizabeth Holt married at Andover so that does not seem right, and other sources suggest it was Elizabeth the daughter of Nathaniel Holt that married Abiel Stevens.

864) ii ELIJAH HOLT, b. 24 Oct 1757; d. 4 Jul 1817; m. 5 Nov 1783,[536] MOLLY SIMMONS, b. 1754 possibly the daughter of Paul and Mary (Isham) Simmons, but this is not confirmed; Molly d. 6 May 1814. Elijah m. 2nd, Lovina *Marcy* Dunton on 17 Aug 1815. Lovina Marcy was first married to Samuel Dunton.

767) iii CALEB HOLT, b. 23 Apr 1759; d. at Willington, 8 Sep 1826; m. at Willington, 8 Jan 1783, his second cousin, SARAH GOODALE (*Phebe Holt Goodale[4], Joshua[3], Nicholas[2], Nicholas[1]*), b. at Pomfret, 10 Jul 1760 daughter of Ebenezer and Phebe (Holt) Goodale; Sally d. 4 Oct 1831.

iv JOSHUA HOLT, b. 31 Mar 1763; d. 12 Aug 1790.

v JAMES HOLT, 24 Oct 1764; d. 25 Jan 1766.

201) NATHAN HOLT (*Abiel[3], Nicholas[2], Nicholas[1]*), b. at Windham, 18 Apr 1733 son of Abiel and Hannah (Abbott) Holt; d. 31 May 1800; m. 1st 19 Jan 1758, ABIGAIL MERRICK, b. 17 Jun 1737 daughter of John and Sarah (Parsons) Merrick; Abigail d. 1 Dec 1765. Nathan m. 2nd 26 Nov 1766, BATHSHEBA WILLIAMS, b. at Lebanon, 22 Mar 1737 daughter of Samuel and Deborah (Throope) Williams; Bathsheba d. 1 Aug 1769. Nathan m. 3rd 6 Jun 1770, LYDIA KINGSBURY, b. at Bolton, 1737 daughter of John and Deborah (Spaulding) Kingsbury; Lydia d. 22 Mar 1776.

In his will written March 1790, Nathan leaves his estate to his two children, Nathan and Abigail. In the will, Nathan is allowed use of one-half of the homestead including use of half the well (as long as he maintains it), a chamber in the house, and privilege to use of part of the cellar. The remainder of the estate is left to his daughter Abigail, both real and personal, and she is to pay her brother Nathan 50 pounds over a three-year period. Nathan and Abigail are the sole executors of the estate.[537] The will is unusual in that the daughter is bequeathed the whole estate and the son receives just use of part of the house.

Nathan Holt and Abigail Merrick had one child.

779) i NATHAN HOLT, b. 29 Aug 1761; d. at Willington, 5 Sep 1820; m. his second cousin, LOIS GOODALE (*Phebe Holt Goodale[4], Joshua[3], Nicholas[2], Nicholas[1]*), b. at Pomfret, 31 Jul 1764 daughter of Ebenezer and Phebe (Holt) Goodale; Lois d. 20 May 1842.

Nathan Holt and Bathsheba Williams had one child born at Willington.

i ABIGAIL HOLT, b. 4 Sep 1767; she was living at the time of probate of her father's estate in 1800 as Abigail Holt.

Nathan Holt and Lydia Kingsbury had two children born at Willington.

i BATHSHEBA HOLT, b. 11 Jan 1772; d. 20 Jan 1790.

ii JOHN HOLT, b. 11 Apr 1774; d. 11 Mar 1776.

202) ANNA HOLT (*Abiel[3], Nicholas[2], Nicholas[1]*), b. at Windham, 14 Jan 1735 daughter of Abiel and Hannah (Abbott) Holt; d. 10 Oct 1806; m. 29 Jan 1755, JOSEPH MERRICK, b. 17 Oct 1733 son of John and Sarah (Parsons) Merrick; Joseph d. 9 Apr 1787.

---

[535] *Connecticut Wills and Probate, 1609-1999*, Probate of Caleb Holt, Hartford, 1810, Case number 1059.

[536] "Connecticut Marriages, 1640-1939," database with images, *FamilySearch* (https://familysearch.org/ark:/61903/1:1:F7PB-68K: 11 February 2018), Elijah Holt and Molley Simons, Marriage 05 Nov 1783, Willington Tolland, Connecticut, United States; Connecticut State Library, Hartford; FHL microfilm 1,376,042.

[537] *Connecticut Wills and Probate, 1609-1999*, Probate of Nathan Holt, Hartford, 1800, Case number 1066.

Captain Joseph Merrick commanded a militia company during the Revolutionary War.

Anna Merrick's estate entered probate in 1806.[538] She did not leave a will. The personal estate was distributed with value in personal items of $56.67 to each of the heirs. There were distributions to the following heirs: Timothy Merrick, Thomas Merrick, Joseph Merrick, Caleb Merrick, Constant Merrick, Anna Hinkley, Hannah Merrick, and Elizabeth Nye.

Anna Holt and Joseph Merrick had eight children whose births are recorded at Willington.

865) i ANNE MERRICK, b. at Willington, 19 Sep 1756; d. 2 May 1809; m. 10 Jan 1782, DAVID HINCKLEY, b. 24 Feb 1754 son of John and Susannah (Harris) Hinckley; David d. 24 Jan 1835.

866) ii TIMOTHY MERRICK, b. at Willington, 31 Aug 1760; d. 4 Jan 1810; m. 29 Nov 1787, MEHITABLE ATWOOD, b. 1765 daughter of Thomas and Sarah (Fenton) Atwood; Mehitable d. 14 May 1855.

867) iii THOMAS MERRICK, b. at Willington, 6 Jan 1763; d. at Willington, 8 Sep 1840; m. 10 Jan 1790, JOANNA NOBLE, b. 8 Oct 1769 daughter of Gideon and Christian (Cadwell) Noble; Joanna d. 28 Apr 1860.

868) iv JOSEPH MERRICK, b. at Willington, 22 Feb 1765; death uncertain but about 1814 possibly by drowning; m. 21 Oct 1796, IRENA ALDEN, b. at Bellingham, MA, 24 Feb 1772 daughter of Elisha and Irene (Markham) Alden. Irena m. 2nd, Samuel Churchill; Irena d. at Pleasantville, PA, 13 Nov 1858.

869) v CALEB MERRICK, b. At Willington, 17 May 1767; d. at Vernon, CT, Jun 1822; m. 15 Sep 1791, CHARLOTTE NOBLE, b. at Willington, 19 Aug 1771 daughter of Gideon and Christian (Cadwell) Noble; Charlotte d. at Franklin, CT, 21 Nov 1805.

vi HANNAH MERRICK, b. 23 Jul 1769; d. 31 May 1842. Hannah did not marry.

870) vii CONSTANT MERRICK, b. at Willington, 14 Jan 1772; d. at Lebanon, NY, 29 Jul 1828; m. at Longmeadow, MA, 22 Sep 1796, EXPERIENCE BURT, b. 8 Aug 1776 daughter of Nathaniel and Experience (Chapin) Burt; Experience d. 1833 at Lebanon, NY, 24 Jul 1833.

871) viii ELIZABETH MERRICK, b. at Willington, 13 Jul 1774; d. at Tolland, 29 Jun 1824; m. 24 Apr 1800, as his second wife, SAMUEL NYE, b. 25 Dec 1773 son of Samuel and Abigail (Benton) Nye. Samuel m. 3rd, Anna Hatch; Samuel's first wife was Elizabeth Brewster; Samuel d. at Tolland 25 Nov 1837.

203) ISAAC HOLT (*Abiel*[3], *Nicholas*[2], *Nicholas*[1]), b. at Windham, 2 Mar 1737/8 son of Abiel and Hannah (Abbott) Holt; d. at Willington, 14 Oct 1822; m. 26 May 1762, SARAH ORCUTT, b. at Stafford, 7 Nov 1740 daughter of William and Sarah (Leonard) Orcutt; Sarah d. 30 Mar 1816.

Isaac and Sarah Holt made their home in Willington where they were admitted to full communion of the Church of Willington 12 July 1767.[539]

Isaac Holt wrote his will 8 May 1798. In the will, he makes special provision for his son Moses "being sensible that he is unable to provide for himself." The will has bequests for well beloved wife Sarah Holt, son Isaac, daughter Sarah, daughter Hannah, daughter Mary, daughter Elizabeth, son Leonard, daughter Anne, son Oliver, and son Moses. The estate entered probate 18 November 1822. Son Oliver Holt served as administrator.[540]

Isaac Holt and Sarah Orcutt had nine children whose births are recorded at Willington.

872) i ISAAC HOLT, b. at Willington, 3 Nov 1763; d. at Sharon, VT, 7 Aug 1813; m. at Sharon, 1 Jan 1789,[541] MEHITABLE ORCUTT, b. at Stafford, CT, 17 Jan 1769 daughter of Caleb and Chloe (Parker) Orcutt; Mehitable d. 12 Nov 1851.

ii MOSES HOLT, b. 28 Oct 1765; d. 7 Mar 1819.

iii SARAH HOLT, b. 22 Feb 1769; d. 13 May 1836. Sarah did not marry.

873) iv HANNAH HOLT, b. at Willington, 19 May 1771; d. likely at Clarksfield, OH before 1850;[542] m. 9 Apr 1795, ELEAZER FELLOWS, b. at Tolland, 2 Apr 1772 son of Verney and Hannah (Lathrop) Fellows; Eleazer d. after 1850 in Ohio.

874) v MARY HOLT, b. at Willington, 1 May 1773; d. at Willington, 6 Jun 1861; m. 27 Nov 1799, WILLIAM CURTIS, b. about 1774; William d. 3 Nov 1860.

---

538 *Connecticut Wills and Probate, 1609-1999*, Probate of Anna Merrick, Hartford, 1806, Case number 1476.

539 Talcott, Mary, "Records of the Church at Willington, Conn.", *New England Historical and Genealogical Register*, volume 67, 1913, p 217

540 *Connecticut Wills and Probate, 1609-1999*, Probate of Isaac Holt, Hartford, 1822, Case number 1063.

541 *Vermont, Vital Records, 1720-1908*.

542 In the 1850 U.S. Census, Eleazer Fellows, age 78, was living in Clarksfield OH; also in the home are Betsey Haskins age 43 and five children named Haskins. Betsey is the daughter of Eleazer and Hannah. Eleazer and Hannah's son Leonard also relocated to Huron County, Ohio.

875) vi OLIVER HOLT, b. 16 Jul 1775; d. 6 Mar 1869; m. 16 May 1799, MARTHA "PATTY" SIBLEY,[543] b. 9 Feb 1776 daughter of Jonathan and Patty (Brooks) Sibley; Martha "Patty" d. 16 Dec 1846.

876) vii ELIZABETH HOLT, b. at Willington, 6 Aug 1777; m. 11 Apr 1799, DANIEL GLAZIER, b. 2 Jun 1776 son of Silas and Suze (Johnson) Glazier; Daniel d. 28 Dec 1852.

877) viii LEONARD HOLT, b. at Willington, 15 Feb 1782; d. 12 Mar 1857; m. 1st, 29 Dec 1809, his first cousin once removed, ASENATH HOLT (*Lois Goodale Holt[5], Phebe Holt Goodale[4], Keturah Holt Holt[3], Henry[2], Nicholas[1]*), b. 26 Jan 1786 daughter of Nathan and Lois (Goodell) Holt; Asenath d. 13 Feb 1813. Leonard m. 2nd, about 1813, JOANNA ALDEN, b. 14 Jul 1782 daughter of Elisha and Irene (Markham) Alden; Joanna d. 30 Sep 1849.

878) ix ANNE HOLT, b. at Willington, 21 Oct 1784; d. 27 Jun 1855; m. SIMON CARPENTER, b. 13 Dec 1783 son of Elijah and Sarah (Younglove) Carpenter; Simon d. 24 Aug 1862.

204) TIMOTHY HOLT (*Abiel[3], Nicholas[2], Nicholas[1]*), b. at Windham, 2 Dec 1739 son of Abiel and Hannah (Abbott) Holt; d. 7 May 1807; m. 7 May 1761 as her 2nd husband, REBECCA CHAMBERLAIN (widow of Nathaniel Fenton);[544] Rebecca was b. about 1730 probably the daughter of Edmund and Sarah (Furbush) Chamberlain; Rebecca d. 11 Apr 1809.

The settlement of the estate of Timothy Holt in 1807 included distributions to the following persons: widow Mrs. Rebekah Holt, son Timothy Holt, and daughter Anna Crocker. The probate of the estate of Rebekah Chamberlain Fenton Holt in 1809 included distributions to the following persons: Timothy Holt, Nathaniel Fenton, Anna Crocker, Eleazer Fenton, and Rebecca Knowlton.[545] Nathaniel Fenton, Eleazer Fenton, and Rebecca Knowlton were children of Rebecca and her first husband Nathaniel Fenton.

Timothy Holt and Rebecca Chamberlain had two children whose births are recorded at Willington.

879) i ANNA HOLT, b. at Willington, 12 Feb 1762; m. 17 Nov 1785, STEPHEN CROCKER, b. 14 Dec 1760 son of Ebenezer and Hannah (Hatch) Crocker. This family was in Schoharie County, New York by about 1788.[546]

880) ii TIMOTHY HOLT, b. at Willington, 19 May 1765; d. 17 Apr 1850; m. 10 Dec 1789, ESTHER SCRIPTURE, b. 26 Aug 1765 son of John and Esther (Lee) Scripture; Esther d. 1 Aug 1841.

205) MARY HOLT (*Abiel[3], Nicholas[2], Nicholas[1]*), b. at Windham, 4 May 1742 daughter of Abiel and Hannah (Abbott) Holt; d. 13 Jan 1823; m. 27 Nov 1760, JOSEPH PERSONS, birth record not found but son of Joseph and Hannah (-) Persons; Joseph d. at Willington, 4 Nov 1812.

Joseph and Mary do not seem to have had children. Joseph's will included bequests to his wife Mary and to his siblings and their heirs. In her will, written 10 June 1819 and proved 1 Feb 1823, Mary Parsons left her entire estate to the children of Joseph and Betsy Holt. Joseph and Betsy Holt were deceased at that time; their children who were heirs were Hannah Whitaker, Esther Heath, Alva Holt, Lucy Holt, Joseph P. Holt, and Mary Holt.[547] This is the family of Joseph and Betsy (Parker) Holt. Joseph Holt was a nephew of Mary Holt Persons, the son of Mary's brother James.

This Joseph Persons is often confused (at least in "internet" trees) with Joseph Parsons of Springfield, Massachusetts who married Naomi Hitchcock and had several children in Springfield. Joseph Persons, Jr. and Mary Holt lived in Willington. They were members of the church in Willington, Joseph, Jr. and Mary admitted as members February 1777. They were also listed as members in 1806 and Joseph's death is noted in the church records in 1813.[548] It is during this same time frame that Joseph Parsons and Naomi Hitchcock were married and having children in Springfield. Adding to the confusion is that each of these Josephs had fathers named Joseph and mothers named Hannah, but they are two different people.

206) JAMES HOLT (*Abiel[3], Nicholas[2], Nicholas[1]*), b. at Windham, 27 Aug 1746 son of Abiel and Hannah (Abbott) Holt; d. 30 Sep 1818; m. 1st 20 Apr 1769, ESTHER OWENS, b. 20 Feb 1747 son of Eleazer and Jerusha (Russ) Owens; Esther d. 5 Dec 1774. JAMES m. 2nd LUCE SAWINS, b. 28 Sep 1740 daughter of George and Anne (Farrar) Sawins; Luce d. 25 Dec 1824.

James Holt wrote his will 7 February 1814 (proved 19 October 1818) and includes bequests to the following persons: well beloved wife Lucy Holt who receives one half of the personal estate which is to be at her disposal forever; sons James, Joseph, and Solomon each receive $25; daughter Esther Parker, $1; son Abiel Holt, $25; and daughter Lucy Walker, $1. These

---

[543] Connecticut, Marriage Index, 1620-1926; the handwritten marriage record confirms that the marriage is to Patty and not to her younger sister Polly.

[544] This information is confirmed by the 1809 probate record of Rebecca Holt which includes heirs from her first marriage to Nathaniel Fenton.

[545] *Connecticut Wills and Probate, 1609-1999*, Probate of Rebekah Holt, Hartford, 1809, Case number 1069.

[546] Roscoe, *History of Schoharie County*, p 316

[547] *Connecticut Wills and Probate, 1609-1999*, Probate of Mary Parsons, Hartford, 1823, Case number 1617.

[548] Ancestry.com, Connecticut, Church Record Abstracts, 1630-1920

are token money bequests as the children have previously received their full portions from the estate. The entire remainder of the estate is bequeathed to son John Holt who is also named the executor.[549]

James Holt and Esther Owens had four children whose birth are recorded at Willington, Connecticut.

881) i JAMES HOLT, b. at Willington, 12 Apr 1770; d. at Willington, 16 Jan 1856; m. 4 Dec 1794, his second cousin, MARY POOL (*Deborah Preston Pool[4], Deborah Holt Preston[3], Nicholas[2], Nicholas[1]*), b. at Willington, 14 Aug 1770 daughter of Timothy and Deborah (Preston) Pool; Mary d. 18 Jan 1853.

882) ii JOSEPH HOLT (twin of James), b. at Willington, 12 Apr 1770; d. at Willington, 29 Jan 1816; m. 6 Mar 1794, BETSY PARKER, b. at Willington, 23 Feb 1775 daughter of Jonathan and Betsy (Johnson) Parker; Betsy d. 7 May 1814.

883) iii SOLOMON HOLT, b. at Willington, 14 Apr 1772; d. in Iowa, 4 Jun 1838; m. at Franklin, CT, 7 Apr 1799, ZERVIAH ABELL, b. at Norwich, 26 Aug 1780 daughter of Thomas and Zerviah (Hyde) Abell; Zerviah d. 1845.

884) iv ESTHER HOLT, b. at Willington, 20 Nov 1774; m. 9 Jan 1800, DANIEL PARKER, b. at Willington, 5 Mar 1777 son of Jonathan and Betsy (Johnson) Parker.

James Holt and Luce Sawins had three children whose births are recorded at Willington.

885) i JOHN HOLT, b. at Willington, 11 Apr 1776; d. at Willington, 22 Apr 1841; m. 6 Sep 1804, his second cousin once removed, CLARISSA HOLT (*Philemon[5], Paul[4], Paul[3], Henry[2], Nicholas[1]*), b. 1775 (based on age at time of death) daughter of Philemon and Jemima (Eldredge) Holt; Clarissa d. 25 Feb 1840.

886) ii LUCE HOLT, b. at Willington, 11 Jun 1778; d. at Ashford, 22 Feb 1847;[550] m. at Ashford, 26 Jan 1809, AARON WALKER, b. 21 Jan 1776 son of Samuel and Alice (Case) Walker; Aaron d. at Ashford, 1 Nov 1815.

887) iii ABIEL HOLT, b. at Willington, 14 Jan 1780; d. at Mansfield, about 1826 (probate of estate in 1826); m. 30 Apr 1805, SALLY CONVERSE, b. at Stafford, 9 Mar 1781 daughter of Stephen and Zerviah (Sanger) Converse;[551] Sally's date of death is uncertain. She was alive in 1823 when her father wrote his will but there is no mention of her in the probate of Abiel's estate. The probate includes some provisions of the support of the two younger sons (Sanford and Arnold) who were underage at the time.

207) BENJAMIN PRESTON (*Deborah Holt Preston[3], Nicholas[2], Nicholas[1]*), b. at Windham, 31 Dec 1727 son of Benjamin and Deborah (Holt) Preston; d. at Ashford, 1 Dec 1798; m. at Ashford, 17 Nov 1763, BATHSHEBA SNOW, b. at Bridgewater, about 1732 daughter of Solomon and Bathsheba (Mahurin) Snow;[552] Bathsheba d. at Ashford, 22 Jan 1813.

There are records of four children of Benjamin and Bathsheba born at Ashford.

i AMOS PRESTON, b. 29 Dec 1765; d. 31 Jul 1776.

ii OLIVER PRESTON, b. 13 Feb 1768

888) iii SOLOMON PRESTON, b. at Ashford, 10 Sep 1770; d. at Ashford, 29 Sep 1851; m. at Ashford, 13 Jun 1799, SUSANNAH HAWES, b. at Medway, MA, 29 Oct 1779 daughter of Eli and Susannah (Bigelow) Hawes; Susannah d. at Ashford, 9 Sep 1860.[553]

iv BENJAMIN PRESTON, b. 26 Jun 1773

208) DANIEL PRESTON (*Deborah Holt Preston[3], Nicholas[2], Nicholas[1]*), b. at Windham, 16 Mar 1729 son of Benjamin and Deborah (Holt) Preston; m. at Windham, 4 Mar 1756, his second cousin once removed, DINAH FORD (*Dinah Holt Ford[4], George[3], Henry[2], Nicholas[1]*), b. at Windham, 17 Sep 1735 daughter of Nathaniel and Daniel (Holt) Ford.

Daniel Preston and Dinah Ford were parents of six children.

---

[549] *Connecticut Wills and Probate, 1609-1999*, Probate of James Holt, Hartford, 1818, Case number 1064.

[550] Durrie, *A Genealogy of the Holt Family*, p 50

[551] The 1823 will of Stephen Converse includes a bequest to his daughter Sally Holt.

[552] *Mayflower Families Fifth Generation Descendants, 1700-1880*. (Online database: *AmericanAncestors.org*, New England Historic Genealogical Society, 2017). John Alden, volume 16, part 3, p 207

[553] Although the marriage transcription in the Barbour collection gives her name as Susannah Harris, this seems to be an error. Other information supports that she is Susannah Hawes, for example the 1825 probate of the estate of Eli Hawes of Ashford which is administered by Solomon Preston. The "internet" reports she is daughter of Reuben Harris, but that is refuted by the 1825 will of Reuben which clearly states his daughter Susannah is unmarried.

889) i DINAH PRESTON, b. at Ashford, 13 Sep 1756; d. at Braintree, VT, 1 Jan 1836; m. at Hampton, 18 Dec 1777, STEPHEN CLARK, b. at Hampton, 15 Mar 1752 son of Stephen and Hannah (Durkee) Clark; Stephen d. at Braintree, 30 Oct 1820.

890) ii EUNICE FORD PRESTON, b. at Ashford, 12 Mar 1759; d. at Preston, NY, 31 Oct 1856; m. at Hampton, 15 Apr 1783, WILLIAM CLARK, b. at Hampton, 7 Feb 1754 son of Stephen and Hannah (Durkee) Clark; William d. at Preston, 4 Oct 1840.

891) iii CHLOE PRESTON, b. at Ashford, about 1761; d. at Ashford, 28 Nov 1839; m. at Ashford, 15 Nov 1781, JAMES BOUTELL, b. at Ashford, 30 Jul 1760 son of Jacob and Eunice (Drew) Boutell; James d. at Ashford, 13 May 1822.

892) iv DANIEL PRESTON, b. at Ashford, 4 May 1763; d. at Fly Creek, NY, 23 Aug 1849; m. at Burlington, NY, 1 Dec 1791, ESTHER CUMMINGS, b. about 1771; Esther d. at Fly Creek, 27 Nov 1862.

893) v CALVIN PRESTON, b. at Ashford, 7 Sep 1766; m. at Mansfield, 22 Jun 1785, PHILATHETA BIBBENS, b. at Mansfield, 22 Dec 1766 daughter of Hannah Bibbens, single woman.

vi Child b. at Stafford, 20 Aug 1768

209) DARIUS PRESTON (*Deborah Holt Preston*[3], *Nicholas*[2], *Nicholas*[1]), b. at Windham, 3 Mar 1731/2 son of Benjamin and Deborah (Holt) Preston; d. at Willington, 30 May 1821; m. at Willington, 15 Nov 1759, HANNAH FISKE, b. at Willington, 26 Mar 1740 daughter of William and Mary (Blancher) Fiske; Hannah D. at Willington, 12 Jan 1813.

Darius was a tanner in Willington. He and Hannah were parents of ten children.

i HANNAH PRESTON, b. at Willington, 23 Aug 1760; d. at Willington, 23 Jan 1837. Hannah did not marry.

ii Infant b. and d. same day

894) iii SARAH PRESTON, b. at Willington, 3 Mar 1764; m. at Willington, 3 Jan 1788, TIMOTHY NYE, b. at Willington, 26 Jan 1765 son of Benjamin and Phebe (West) Nye.[554]

895) iv DARIUS PRESTON, b. at Willington, 18 Dec 1766; d. at Hanover, PA, 1 Apr 1845; m. 26 Aug 1788, NAOMI HIBBARD b. at Bolton, 1770 daughter of William Bathsheba (Strong) Hibbard; Naomi d. at Wilkes-Barre.

896) v JOSHUA PRESTON, b. at Willington, 25 Sep 1768; d. at Willington, 1 Nov 1810; m. 25 Sep 1794, SARAH HOLT who has not been identified.

vi JERUSHA PRESTON, b. 18 Jun 1770; d. 13 Jul 1792. Jerusha did not marry.

897) vii CHLOE PRESTON, b. at Willington, 11 Feb 1772; d. at Corinth, NY, 9 Jun 1841; m. 10 Sep 1789, LUKE FENTON, b. at Willington, 20 Dec 1769 son of Asa and Jerusha (Hatch) Fenton; Luke d. after 1850 when he was living in Corinth with his son Darius and his family.

898) viii EUNICE PRESTON, b. at Willington, 15 Jul 1777; d. at Willington, 16 Oct 1807; m. at Willington, 6 Feb 1800, ELIJAH NYE b. at Willington, 15 Sep 1777 son of Benjamin and Mary (Crocker) Nye;[555] Elijah d. at Willington, 11 Jun 1844. Elijah was the half-brother of Timothy who married Eunice's sister Sarah.

899) ix DEBORAH PRESTON, b. at Willington, 30 Apr 1780; d. at Willington, 14 Oct 1857; m. at Willington, 10 Mar 1803, ABEL JOHNSON, b. at Willington, 28 Sep 1781 son of Abel and Eunice (Merrick) Johnson; Abel d. after 1870 when he was living at Willington.

900) x AMOS PRESTON, b. at Willington, 8 Feb 1782; d. at Willington, 6 Oct 1864; m. 4 Sep 1804, MARTHA TAYLOR, b. at Willington, 28 Jun 1779 daughter of Thomas and Experience (Freeman) Taylor; Martha d. at Willington, 7 Dec 1860.

210) JERUSHA PRESTON (*Deborah Holt Preston*[3], *Nicholas*[2], *Nicholas*[1]), b. at Windham, 29 Jul 1736 daughter of Benjamin and Deborah (Holt) Preston; m. at Ashford, 25 Aug 1767, as his third wife, JOHN PECK, b. at Uxbridge, MA, 30 Dec 1726 son of Simon and Sarah (-) Peck; John d. in VT, 1805.[556] John was first married to Mary Bowen and second married to Elizabeth Dennerson.

John Peck was born in Uxbridge and was first married there. After the death of his first wife, he relocated to Ashford and was married to Elizabeth Dennerson and after Elizabeth's death to Jerusha. There is some disagreement in the published genealogies about which wife was the mother of which children, but the five children given below are given in the Ashford

---

[554] Nye, *A Genealogy of the Nye Family*, p 217

[555] Nye, *A Genealogy of the Nye Family*, volume 2, p 218

[556] Peck, *Genealogical History of the Descendants of Joseph Peck*, p 279

records as children of Jerusha and John. The oldest son of John and Jerusha settled in Vermont and it is thought that John Peck, Sr. died there. Jerusha's death was not found, but a fourth marriage for John to a widow Hollis has been reported.[557]

901) i JOHN PECK, b. at Ashford, 8 May 1768; d. at Weston, VT, 21 Sep 1849; m. 1st about 1789, REBECCA BADGER, b. at Ashford, 1 Jan 1768 daughter of Ezekiel and Doratha (Scarborough) Badger; Rebecca d. at Cavendish, VT, about 1810. John m. 2nd about 1811, HANNAH FOSTER (widow of Phineas Austin), b. at Temple, NH, 28 Dec 1771 daughter of James and Hannah (Jewett) Foster; Hannah d. at Weston, 14 Nov 1848.

902) ii ANNA PECK, b. at Ashford, 10 Sep 1769; d. at Rushford, NY, 17 May 1855; m. at Ashford, Jan 1789, ROBERT SNOW,[558] b. at Ashford, 19 Jun 1763 son of Robert and Sarah (Chubb) Snow; Robert d. at Cavendish, VT, 13 Aug 1806.

iii EUNICE PECK, b. at Ashford, 25 Sep 1770

iv OLIVER PECK, b. at Ashford, 7 Aug 1772

903) v ELISHA PECK, b. at Ashford, 25 Mar 1777; d. at Abington, 26 Sep 1866; m. 1st at Ashford, 23 Sep 1802, SARAH BADGER, b. at Ashford, 26 Apr 1771 daughter of Ezekiel and Doratha (Scarborough) Badger; Sarah d. at Pomfret, 6 Mar 1843. Sarah had an out-of-wedlock daughter Myra Ingraham prior to her marriage to Elisha. Elisha m. 2nd 29 Oct 1844, MARY WHITMAN, b. about 1790; Mary d. at Abington, 9 Feb 1860.

211) DEBORAH PRESTON (*Deborah Holt Preston³, Nicholas², Nicholas¹*), b. at Windham, 10 Dec 1740 daughter of Benjamin and Deborah (Holt) Preston; d. at Willington, 6 Mar 1822; m. at Willington, 19 Oct 1763, TIMOTHY POOL, b. at Willington, 11 Jun 1739 son of John and Mary (Parker) Pool; Timothy d. at Willington, 16 Jul 1821.

There are records for nine children of Deborah and Timothy born at Willington.

904) i ALICE POOL, b. at Willington, 11 Dec 1765; m. at Willington, 18 Mar 1782, JOSEPH FENTON, b. at Willington, 28 Feb 1760 son of Samuel and Experience (Ingalls) Fenton; Joseph d. at Willington, 12 May 1814.

905) ii ANNA POOL, b. at Willington, 8 May 1767; d. at Willington, 12 Oct 1831; m. at Willington, 9 Apr 1795, ERASTUS EDWARDS, b. at Coventry, 1770 son of Erastus and Anna (Porter) Edwards; Erastus d. at Willington, 24 Nov 1850. Erastus was first married to Jerusha Fuller who died in 1794.

iii DEBORAH POOL, b. 26 Apr 1769; d. Jul 1771.

881) iv MARY POOL, b. at Willington, 14 Aug 1770; d. at Willington, 19 Jan 1853; m. 4 Dec 1794, her second cousin, JAMES HOLT (*James⁴, Abiel³, Nicholas², Nicholas¹*), b. at Willington, 12 Apr 1770 son of James and Esther (Owens) Holt; James d. at Willington, 16 Jan 1856.

v LOIS POOL, b. 18 Aug 1772; nothing further known.

vi TIMOTHY POOL, b. 4 Jul 1774; likely died young.

906) vii AMY POOL, b. at Willington, 7 Aug 1775; d. at Willington, about 1817;[559] m. at Willington, 24 Dec 1795, her second cousin once removed, ELIJAH SAWIN (*Mary Fenton Sawin⁵, Elizabeth Holt Fenton⁴, Abiel³, Nicholas², Nicholas¹*), b. at Willington, 31 Oct 1774 son of Isaac and Mary (Fenton) Sawin; Elijah d. at Willington, about 1814 (probate 1814).

viii SARAH POOL, b. 7 Apr 1777; d. 21 May 1777.

ix DEBORAH POOL, b. 19 Jul 1781; d. at Willington, 15 Oct 1823. Deborah did not marry.

212) DANIEL HOLT (*Daniel³, Nicholas², Nicholas¹*), b. at Windham, 5 Apr 1731 son of Daniel and Abigail (Smith) Holt; d. at Cherry Valley, NY, 21 Jan 1796; m. at Pomfret, 26 Dec 1753, KEZIA RUST, b. at Coventry, 16 Aug 1735 daughter of Noah and Kezia (Strong) Rust;[560] Kezia d. at Cherry Valley, 23 Dec 1825.

---

557 Peck, *A Genealogical History of the Descendants of Joseph Peck*, p 279

558 The marriage transcription gives the name of Abigail Peck as the wife of Robert Snow, but other records (for example the Revolutionary War pension file) establish that Robert married Anna.

559 Sawin, *Sawin: Summary Notes Concerning John Sawin*, p 38

560 The distribution of the estate of Noah Russ includes distribution to daughter Keziah Holt. Distribution is 27 December 1753 the day after the wedding of Daniel and Kezia.

Daniel and Kezia were parents of thirteen children born at Pomfret. The family relocated to Cherry Valley and the children who lived to adulthood settled in New York.

i CHLOE HOLT, b. at Pomfret, 10 Feb 1755

ii DELIA HOLT, b. 1757; d. at Pomfret, 6 May 1775.

iii LESTER HOLT, b. 1759; d. at Pomfret, 17 Sep 1764.

907) iv ABIGAIL HOLT, b. at Pomfret, 29 Mar 1761; d. after 1829; m. about 1783, WILLIAM AVERILL, b. at Windham, 19 Apr 1755 son of Stephen and Sarah (Handee) Averill;[561] William d. at Warren, NY, 1829 (probate 1829).

908) v KEZIAH HOLT, b. at Pomfret, 29 Mar 1761; d. at Buffalo, NY, 13 Jan 1820; m. at Pomfret, 8 Apr 1784, ROWLAND COTTON, b. at Pomfret, 22 Mar 1759 son of Samuel and Mary (Dresser) Cotton; Rowland d. at Attica, NY, 11 Jun 1847.

909) vi ELIJAH HOLT, b. at Pomfret, 9 Jun 1762; d. at Cherry Valley, NY, 25 Sep 1826; m. 1st ELIZABETH WILLIAMS, b. at Pomfret, 2 Apr 1768 daughter of Ebenezer and Jerusha (Porter) Williams; Elizabeth d. 16 Jan 1796. Elijah m. 2nd MARY "POLLY" ADAMS, b. at Windham, 10 Dec 1771 daughter of David and Lucy (Fitch) Adams;[562] Mary d. at Buffalo, 3 Jan 1820.

910) vii LESTER HOLT, b. at Pomfret, 21 Feb 1766; d. at Cherry Valley, NY, 11 Jan 1841; m. about 1789, CATHERINE CLYDE, b. 1769 daughter of Samuel and Catherine (Wasson) Clyde; Catherine d. at Cherry Valley, 16 May 1848.

911) viii OLIVE HOLT, b. at Pomfret, 15 Oct 1768; d. 20 Sep 1792; m. 1787, JOSEPH WHITE, b. at Chatham, CT, 26 Sep 1762 son of Joseph and Ruth (Churchill) White; Joseph d, at Cherry Valley, 3 Jun 1832. Joseph second married Olive's sister Deborah (see below).

ix JOSEPH HOLT, b. 28 Apr 1771; d. 6 Mar 1773.

912) x MARY HOLT, b. at Pomfret, 28 Apr 1771; d. at Cherry Valley, 19 Mar 1819; m. 1st about 1791, JOSEPH CLARY who has not been identified; Joseph d. about 1800. Mary m. 2nd 4 Feb 1803, JOHN DIELL, b. 1769; John d. at Cherry Valley, 19 May 1813.

913) xi MARCIA HOLT, b. at Pomfret, about 1773; m. AUGUSTUS SHARP.

911) xii DEBORAH HOLT, b. at Pomfret, 1 Feb 1775; d. at Cherry Valley, 23 Aug 1827; m. about 1793, JOSEPH WHITE who was first married to her sister Olive (see above).

914) xiii ADELIA HOLT, b. at Pomfret, 23 Jan 1778; m. CHARLES MUDGE, b. at New London, about 1770 son of Jarvis and Prudence (Treat) Mudge;[563] Charles d. of typhus at Williamsville Hospital, NY, Aug 1814 while serving in the army in the War of 1812.[564]

213) ABIGAIL HOLT (*Daniel*[3], *Nicholas*[2], *Nicholas*[1]), b. at Windham, 20 Feb 1732 daughter of Daniel and Abigail (Smith) Holt; d. at Abington, 11 Oct 1774; m. RICHARD KIMBALL, b. at Bradford, MA, 18 Jul 1722 son of Samuel and Sarah (Spofford) Kimball; Richard d. at Ames, NY, 30 Apr 1810.

There are records for six children of Abigail Holt and Richard Kimball.

915) i LIBBEUS KIMBALL, b. at Pomfret, 14 Feb 1750/1; d. at Ames, NY, 4 Sep 1839; m. at Pomfret, 7 May 1778, SARAH CRAFT, b. at Pomfret, 29 Apr 1756 daughter of Samuel and Judith (Payson) Craft; Sarah d. at Ames, 3 Aug 1831.

ii ABIGAIL KIMBALL, b. at Pomfret, 30 Nov 1754

916) iii PERSIS KIMBALL, b. at Pomfret, 5 Nov 1760; d. at Ames, NY, 6 Mar 1845; m. at Pomfret, 18 Jan 1781, GEORGE ELLIOT, b. at Voluntown, 1 Mar 1757 son of Andrew and Hannah (Palmer) Elliot; George d. at Ames, 30 Mar 1817.

---

561 Avery, *The Averill Family*, p 397

562 The 1814 will of Lucy Adams widow of David of Pomfret includes a bequest to her daughter Polly Holt wife of Elijah Holt.

563 Mudge, *Memorials: A Genealogical Account of the Name Mudge in America*, p 73

564 U.S. Army, Register of Enlistments, 1798-1914

917) iv CHESTER KIMBALL, b. at Pomfret, 19 Sep 1763; d. at New London, 2 Jan 1824; m. at New London, 8 Nov 1786; LUCIA "LUCY" FOX, b. at Chatham, CT, 19 May 1766 daughter of John and Mary (Waterman) Fox; Lucy d. at New London, 6 Apr 1855.

v FLAVEL KIMBALL, b. about 1765 and baptized at Hampton, 29 Apr 1770. Flavel had service during the Revolution. He did not marry.[565]

vi BETTY KIMBALL, b. about 1767 and baptized at Hampton, 29 Apr 1770. Nothing further found.

214) SILAS HOLT (*Daniel[3], Nicholas[2], Nicholas[1]*), b. at Windham, 29 Dec 1735 son of Daniel and Abigail (Smith) Holt; d. at Ashford, 23 Oct 1773; m. at Pomfret, 20 Jan 1757, MARY BROOKS, b. at Pomfret, 14 Oct 1735 daughter of John and Phebe (Richardson) Brooks. Mary Brooks married second, Nehemiah Howe. Mary Brooks and Nehemiah Howe had one daughter, Almira.

Silas Holt and Mary Brooks were parents of seven children.

i SILAS HOLT, b. at Pomfret, 17 Dec 1757; d. at Abington, 10 Feb 1784.

918) ii ROXLANA HOLT, b. at Pomfret, 21 Sep 1760; d. at Ashford, about 1787; m. at Ashford, 13 Jun 1782, EBENEZER SUMNER, b. at Ashford, 3 Aug 1757 son of Ebenezer and Experience (Marsh) Sumner; Ebenezer d. at Eastford, Aug 1806. Ebenezer second married Sarah Perrin on 26 May 1788.

iii ALVAH HOLT, b. at Pomfret, 10 Feb 1763; nothing further known.

iv MOLLY HOLT, b. at Pomfret, 7 Jul 1765; nothing further known.

v PERCY HOLT, b. at Pomfret, 19 Aug 1767; nothing further known. She may be the Percy who married first Roswell Babcock of Liberty, NY and married second Sampson Keyes of Ashford.

919) vi CLARINA HOLT, b. at Ashford, 6 Nov 1769; d. at Vernon, NY, 14 Nov 1845; m. at Ashford, 12 May 1793, ELIAS FRINK, b. 1770; Elias d. at Vernon, NY, 14 Apr 1854.

920) vii LUCINDA HOLT, b. at Ashford, 26 Jul 1773; d. at Ashford, 24 Mar 1847; m. at Ashford, 14 Jan 1799, DYER CLARK, b. 1772; Dyer d. at Ashford, 28 Sep 1846.

215) LOIS HOLT (*Daniel[3], Nicholas[2], Nicholas[1]*), b. at Windham, 4 Feb 1739 daughter of Daniel and Abigail (Smith) Holt; d. at Ashford, Oct 1792; m. at Pomfret, 26 Sep 1758, MOSES ROGERS, b. at Billerica, 24 Feb 1730/1 son of Nathaniel and Mary (Haggit) Rogers; Moses d. at Ashford, 1797 (probate 1797).

Lois and Moses started their family in Pomfret. They were dismissed to the church at Eastford in 1783.

Moses Rogers did not leave a will and his estate entered probate 2 May 1797 with Abel Dow (his son-in-law) as administrator. The debts of the estate exceeded the value of the personal estate to the degree that all the real estate was sold to settle the debts.[566]

921) i OLIVE ROGERS, b. at Pomfret, 7 Mar 1759; d. at Ashford, 2 Mar 1855; m. at Ashford, 28 Sep 1784, ABEL DOW, b. at Ashford, 3 Jul 1757 son of Daniel and Elizabeth (Marsh) Dow; Abel d. at Ashford, 6 Jan 1826.

ii CHESTER ROGERS, b. at Pomfret, 10 Oct 1760; nothing further definitive known. He may be one of the Chester Rogers who served from Connecticut during the Revolution. He was not administrator of his father's estate perhaps suggesting he was deceased by that time but that is not known.

iii LOIS ROGERS, b. at Pomfret, 16 Dec 1762; nothing further known.

922) iv ELISHA ROGERS, b. at Pomfret, 11 Feb 1766; d. at Springfield, VT, 24 Apr 1807;[567] m. at Springfield, 11 Jul 1788, ANNA WARD, b. 1767 daughter of Jabez Ward; Anna d. at Brownville, NY, 14 Jul 1872.[568]

923) v ABIGAIL ROGERS, b. at Pomfret, 23 Mar 1769; d. at Sherburne, NY, 29 Mar 1849; m. CYRUS DOW, b. at Ashford, 17 Jun 1764 son of Daniel and Elizabeth (Marsh) Dow; Cyrus d. at Sherburne, 23 Mar 1842 (date of death given at the proving of the will on 21 Mar 1843).

vi DANIEL ROGERS, b. 23 Mar 1769; d. 2 Apr 1769.

---

565 Morrison, *History of the Kimball Family*, p 147

566 *Connecticut State Library (Hartford, Connecticut)*; Probate Place: *Hartford, Connecticut, Probate Packets, Randall, Jonathan-Russell, Smith, 1752-1880, Case 3467, Estate of Moses Rogers*

567 The date of give is given in his widow's pension application and the family seems to have still been in Vermont at that time.

568 All the records available support that Anna did indeed live to 105. In 1838, she gave her age as 71 on a pension application and her age on the 1860 census is given as 94.

924) vii LUCIA "LUCY" ROGERS, b. at Ashford, 28 May 1771; d. at Springfield, MA, Jan 1823; m. at Ashford, 16 Nov 1797, NATHAN CROCKER, b. about 1772 son of Gershom and Ann (Fisher) Crocker;[569] Nathan d. at Springfield, 26 Jul 1817.

925) viii ALVA ROGERS, b. at Ashford, 18 Jun 1776; d. at Sherburne, NY, after 1850; m. at Ashford, 8 Sep 1803, DESIRE EATON, b. at Ashford, 29 May 1778 daughter of Ebenezer and Mary (Humphrey) Eaton; Desire d. at Sherburne, NY, Dec 1859.

216) EUNICE HOLT (*Daniel[3], Nicholas[2], Nicholas[1]*), b. at Pomfret, 22 Aug 1741 daughter of Daniel and Abigail (Smith) Holt; m. at Pomfret, 28 Nov 1760, JOSIAH WHEELER, b. at Pomfret, 21 Mar 1737/8 son of Josiah and Anna (Grosvenor) Wheeler.

There are records for ten children of Eunice and Josiah. Marriages were located for just four of the children.

926) i PERTHENE WHEELER, b. at Pomfret, 19 Sep 1762; m. 26 Oct 1783, DANIEL CHAPIN, b. at Salisbury, CT, 2 Feb 1761 son of Charles and Anna (Camp) Chapin;[570] Daniel d. at Buffalo, NY, 16 Nov 1821.

ii ESTHER WHEELER, b. at Pomfret, 6 Jan 1763

iii PERCEY WHEELER, b. at Pomfret, 9 Dec 1764

927) iv ELIJAH WHEELER, b. at Pomfret, 28 Aug 1767; d. at Great Barrington, MA, 20 Apr 1827; m. 1st MARY MATILDA MINER, b. at Woodbury, CT, 11 Apr 1773 daughter of Jehu and Sarah (Canfield) Miner; Mary d. at Great Barrington, 11 Oct 1812. Elijah m. 2nd ELIZABETH WHITING, b. 1773 likely daughter of Gamaliel and Anne (Gillette) Whiting; Elizabeth d. at Great Barrington, 21 Feb 1848.

928) v PHILADELPHIA "PHILA" WHEELER, b. at Pomfret, 28 Nov 1769; d. at East Bloomfield, NY, after 1855; m. MOSES GAYLORD, b. at West Hartford, about 1768 son of Moses and Susanna (Wells) Gaylord; Moses d. at Bloomfield, NY, 1812.[571]

929) vi RESOLVED GROSVENOR WHEELER, b. at Pomfret, 8 Mar 1772; d. at Conneaut, PA, 29 May 1839; m. N. ANNA VANDEVENTER, b. about 1785; Anna d. at Reedsburg, WI, 4 Oct 1863.

vii SARAH WHEELER, b. at Pomfret, 25 Dec 1774

viii ANNA WHEELER, b. at Pomfret, 20 Feb 1777

ix ABIGAIL WHEELER, b. at Pomfret, 20 Feb 1777

x JOSIAH WHEELER, b, at Salisbury, 22 Jan 1779

217) ASA HOLT (*Daniel[3], Nicholas[2], Nicholas[1]*), b. at Pomfret, 7 Jun 1745 son of Daniel and Abigail (Smith) Holt; d. at Springfield, VT, 1 Mar 1813; m. at Pomfret, 20 Nov 1766, MARGARET HAMMOND, baptized at Woodstock, 9 Dec 1744 daughter of Jonathan and Katherine (Davis) Hammond; Margaret d. at Springfield, 28 Sep 1834.

Asa and Margaret married at Pomfret and there are records of births of several of their children and Hartford and Winsted, Connecticut. The family was in Springfield, Vermont by 1800.

Daughter Clarissa married twice but did not have children. On 31 January 1872, Almira Tower the only surviving sibling of Clarissa declined administration of the estate and requested John Farnham be appointed. The following heirs-at-law of the estate were provided by John Farnham he having obtained this information from Almira Tower: the children of Smith Holt deceased who are Asa (known to be living) and Orin Holt, Polly Wright, and Lovina Tolcot who were living when last known of; the children of Alfleety Fasset deceased who are Perley Fasset, Abel Fasset, and Anney White; Erastus Holt is deceased many years ago and nothing is known of any family; sister Almira Tower; the children of Polly Rumrill deceased who are Serina Clark, Eliza Spafford, Polly Stone, Harvey Rumrill, Solom Rumrill, and Elmira Young; children of Asa Holt deceased who are Louisa Graves, Charles Holt, Parmely Griffin, Betsey Cleaveland, Clarissa Washburn, Mary Kennedy, Laura Holt, and Harriet Holt.[572]

Asa Holt and Margaret Hammond were parents of nine children.[573]

i ELISHA HOLT; reported in the Hammond genealogy, but no records located and has no heirs in sister Clarissa's estate settlement.

---

569 Crocker, *Crocker Genealogy*, p 93

570 Chapin, Orange, *Chapin Genealogy*

571 *Connecticut, Hale Collection of Cemetery Inscriptions and Newspaper Notices, 1629-1934*

572 *Vermont. Probate Court (Windsor District), Estate of Clarissa Taylor, 6 February 1872.*

573 Hammond, *Histories and Genealogies of the Hammond Families in America*, Volume II, Part IV, p 285. The nine children given are those listed in the Hammond genealogy. Seven of these children can be known from the probate record of daughter Clarissa.

ii ERASTUS HOLT, b. about 1769; in Clarissa's probate record, he is reported to have died "many years ago" and without family.

930) iii SMITH HOLT, b. at Hartford, about 1769; d. at Keene, NY, 28 Dec 1814; m. 26 Jan 1792, his second cousin once removed LYDIA SNOW (*Dorcas Osgood Snow[5], Mary Holt Osgood[4], Nicholas[3], Nicholas[2], Nicholas[1]*), b. 6 Oct 1769 daughter of Benjamin and Dorcas (Osgood) Snow; Lydia d. at Keene, 21 Dec 1853.

iv DANIEL HOLT, b. about 1775; d. at Springfield, VT, 24 Apr 1847; m. LYDIA who is not identified, b. about 1783 and d. at Springfield, 21 Mar 1843. The Hammond genealogy reports Daniel and Lydia had one son who died at age 19. Neither Daniel nor any heirs are mentioned in sister Clarissa's probate.

931) v ASA HOLT, b. 12 Dec 1777; d. at Rushford, NY, 1852; m. 1st at Springfield, VT, 26 Mar 1801, ELIZABETH "BETSEY" WOODWARD, b. at Springfield, 25 Oct 1782 daughter of Samuel and Eunice (Bigelow) Woodward; Betsey d. at Springfield, 2 Feb 1814. Asa m. 2nd 7 Oct 1815, POLLY ROGERS (widow of Samuel Tarbell), b. 1784 daughter of Jeremiah and Fannie (Wickes) Rogers; Polly d. at Fillmore, NY, 2 Sep 1874.

932) vi ALFREADA HOLT, b. about 1779; d. at Cavendish, VT, about 1814; m. at Springfield, 3 Jun 1799, PEARLY FASSET, b. about 1769 son of Adonijah and Anna (Copeland) Fasset; Pearly d. at Winchester, NH, 23 Feb 1826. Pearly married second Esther Gowing.

933) vii POLLY HOLT, b. 1 Jun 1782; d. at Springfield, VT, 7 Jan 1852; m. at Springfield, 9 Aug 1805, SIMEON RUMRILL, b. at New Ipswich, 12 Jun 1769 son of David and Priscilla (Corey) Rumrill; Simeon d. at Baltimore, VT, 19 Mar 1822.

viii ALMIRA HOLT, b. at Winsted, CT, 4 Apr 1790; d. at Springfield, VT, 7 Oct 1874; m. 30 Apr 1840, ABRAHAM TOWER, b. at Springfield, 11 Apr 1781 son of Isaac and Elizabeth (Stoddard) Tower; Abraham d. at Springfield, 16 Jun 1857. Almira did not have children. In her will, she left her estate to her two stepdaughters.

ix CLARISSA HOLT, b. about 1791; d. at Springfield, VT, 1872 (probate 1872); m. 1st JOHN ADAMS. Clarissa m. 2nd ARTHUR TAYLOR. Clarissa did not have children

218) LUCY HOLT (*Daniel[3], Nicholas[2], Nicholas[1]*), b. at Pomfret, 10 Oct 1747 daughter of Daniel and Abigail (Smith) Holt; d. after 1809; m. at Brooklyn, CT, 27 Nov 1770, JEDEDIAH DANA, b. at Ashford, 9 Aug 1739 son of Jedediah and Elizabeth (Barnard) Dana; d. at German Flatts, NY, 1809 (probate 31 Jan 1809).

Lucy and Jedediah resided in Ashford for much of their lives and were listed in the census there in 1790. The family relocated to German Flatts after 1790 where Jedediah died.

Jedediah Dana did not leave a will and his estate entered probate 31 January 1809. Widow Lucy declined administration of the estate and this was assumed by Jedediah Dana, Jr. with Silas Dana and Thomas Paine (a son-in-law) acting as sureties for the bond. There is an inventory of the personal estate and no real estate was reported in the inventory. In 1815, a notice was sent to Jedediah Dana, Jr. requiring him to come and show why he had not closed the administration of the estate.[574]

Jedediah Dana and Lucy Holt were parents of nine children born at Ashford.

934) i ELIZABETH DANA, b. at Ashford, 8 Jun 1771; d. at Wilbern, IL, 1840; m. at Mansfield, CT, 1 Jun 1794, AMASA OWEN, b. at Ashford, 12 Aug 1766 son of Timothy and Kezia (-) Owen; Amasa d. at Wilbern, 1842.

ii LUCY DANA, b. 8 Jul 1772

iii CLARISSA DANA, b. 14 Oct 1773

935) iv SILAS DANA, b. at Ashford, 9 Mar 1775; d. at Grove, NY, 14 Feb 1846; m. by 1800, SALLY COWEL, b. 6 Feb 1782; Sally d. at Grove, 23 Jan 1831. Silas m. 2nd, MARY who has not been identified.

936) v SALLY DANA, b. at Ashford, 23 Mar 1777; d. at German Flatts (Paine's Hollow), NY, 1 Jul 1856; m. 10 Oct 1802, THOMAS PAYN, b. at Lebanon, CT, 26 Jan 1778 son of Seth and Jerusha (Swift) Payn; Thomas d. at German Flatts, 26 Sep 1856.[575]

vi JEDEDIAH DANA, b. at Ashford, 8 Nov 1778; m. BETSEY who is not clearly identified. In 1810, Jedediah with a wife and one son under age 10 appear to be living in German Flatts, NY but nothing else definitive has been found.

---

574 New York Probate Records 1629-1971, Herkimer County, Estate Papers 1794-1838 D, Case 01842, Estate of Jedediah Dana, Sr.; accessed through family search.org.

575 Towne and Jones, "Seth Payn and Some of His Descendants", NEHGR, 1943, p 138

937) vii MARY "POLLY" DANA, b. at Ashford, 15 Jan 1781; d. at Nunda, NY, 27 Dec 1850; m. JAMES PAYN, b. at Lebanon, CT, 27 Jan 1783 son of Seth and Jerusha (Swift) Payn; James d. at Nunda, 8 Apr 1861.

viii ANNA DANA, b. 16 Sep 1783

ix DANIEL DANA, b. 3 Dec 1785

Grandchildren of Hannah Holt and Robert Gray

219) ELIZABETH GRAY (*Henry Gray³, Hannah Holt Gray², Nicholas¹*), b. at Andover, 28 Mar 1700 daughter of Henry and Mary (Blunt) Gray; d. at Pomfret, CT, 9 Jul 1765;[576] m. 8 Feb 1719/20. PAUL ABBOTT, b. at Andover, 28 Mar 1697 son of William and Elizabeth (Geary) Abbott; Paul d. at Hampton, CT, 8 May 1752.

In his will dated 20 February 1752, Paul Abbott has bequests to the following persons: beloved wife Elizabeth who receives the whole of the house in which they live plus many provisions for grain, beef, etc. to be provided by the executor; dearly beloved sons William, Nathan, Benjamin, Isaac, Asa, and Darius; and dearly beloved daughters Mary Holt, Sarah Ingalls, Elizabeth Abbott, and Hannah Abbott.[577]

Paul and Elizabeth had twelve children. The birth of the oldest child was recorded at Andover and those of the other eleven were recorded at Pomfret, Connecticut.

938) i NATHAN ABBOTT, b. 10 Apr 1721; d. unknown but he might have gone to Pennsylvania; m. 1st at Pomfret, 24 Nov 1742, EUNICE MARSH, b. at Plainfield, CT 17 Feb 1724 daughter of Thomas and Eunice (Parkhouse) Marsh; Eunice d. at Ashford 27 Oct 1760. Nathan m. 2nd HEPHZIBAH BROWN, b. about 1727; Hepzibah d. 26 May 1790 at Hampton, CT.

939) ii WILLIAM ABBOTT, b. 18 Feb 1723; d. at Pomfret 1 Nov 1805; m. 1st 9 May 1745, JERUSHA STOWELL, b. 22 Sep 1721 at Newton, MA daughter of David and Mary (Dillaway) Stowell; Jerusha d. 29 Feb 1768. William m. 2nd 4 Jun 1778, HANNAH EDMUND; Hannah d. 5 Feb 1808; nothing else is known of her at this time.

940) iii BENJAMIN ABBOTT, b. 25 Jul 1724; d. at Brookfield, VT, 21 Jun 1807;[578] m. 1st at Ashford, 16 Jan 1745/6, MARY ANN ANDREWS, b. at Windham 25 Jul 1727 daughter of John and Hannah (-) Andrews; Mary Ann d. 8 Dec 1788. Benjamin m. 2nd 30 Jun 1793 the widow HANNAH BROWN about whom nothing else is known.

iv ELIZABETH ABBOTT, b. 5 Feb 1726; d. 10 Sep 1736.

174) v MARY ABBOTT, b. 3 Mar 1728/9; d. at Windham 10 Aug 1769; m. 28 Jun 1749, JOSHUA HOLT, b. 19 Mar 1728/9 son of Joshua and Keturah (Holt) Holt. Joshua m. 2nd Susanna Goodell; Joshua d. 5 Jul 1791.

357) vi SARAH ABBOTT, b. 15 Oct 1730; d. 17 Dec 1811; m. 24 May 1749, JOSEPH INGALLS (*Phebe Farnum Ingalls⁴, John Farnum³, Elizabeth Holt Farnum², Nicholas¹*), b. at Andover, 9 Aug 1723 son of Joseph and Phebe (Farnum) Ingalls; Joseph d. 26 Oct 1790.

941) vii ISAAC ABBOTT, b. 29 Aug 1732; d. at Milford, NH about 1800;[579] m. 29 Apr 1756, MARY BARKER about whom nothing else concrete is known.[580]

645) viii DARIUS ABBOTT, b. 16 Oct 1734; d. about 1817 at Hillsborough, NH;[581] m. at Andover 1 Nov 1757, MARY HOLT, b. 30 Apr 1739 daughter of Henry and Rebecca (Gray) Holt; Mary d. about 1787.

942) ix ELIZABETH ABBOTT, b. 20 Jul 1737; d. possibly 1828;[582] m. 28 Sep 1761 as his 2nd wife, JOSEPH PHELPS, b. 27 Feb 1723/4 son of Samuel and Hannah (Dane) Phelps; Joseph d. at Andover 27 Jan 1802.

x HARRIET ABBOTT, b. 18 Sep 1740; d. 18 Sep 1740.

xi HANNAH ABBOTT, b. 24 Jun 1741; d. 18 Nov 1763.

---

576 Connecticut Town Death Records, pre-1870 (Barbour Collection).

577 Probate Records, 1747-1918; Author: Connecticut. Probate Court (Plainfield District); Probate Place: Windham, Connecticut

578 His grave site is in the Brookfield, VT cemetery. (findagrave.com)

579 1800 is the year of death used by the Daughters of the American Revolution.

580 Abbot and Abbot, *Genealogical Record of Descendants* gives her name as Sarah Barker, but the marriage record and all the birth records for the children give her name as Mary.

581 Abbot and Abbot, *Genealogical Record of Descendants*

582 Abbot and Abbot, *Genealogical Record of Descendants* gives a death date of June 1828, but I have not located a record.

xii ASA ABBOTT, b. 7 Jan 1743; d. 5 Sep 1754.

220) HENRY GRAY (*Henry Gray³, Hannah Holt Gray², Nicholas¹*), b. at Andover, 1706 son of Henry and Mary (Blunt) Gray; d. at Andover, 18 Sep 1754; m. 1736, ALICE PEABODY, b. about 1709 daughter of Jonathan and Alice (Pearl) Peabody;[583] Alice d. at Andover, 13 Nov 1797.

Henry Gray was a farmer in Andover. In his will written 12 July 1754 (probate 14 October 1754), Henry Gray bequeaths to daughter Lydia £63.6.8 to be paid to her by son Henry when she reaches age twenty-one or at marriage. His wife receives one-third part of the personal estate and improvements on one-third of the real estate while she is a widow. Son Henry receives all the lands and two-thirds of the moveable estate. If son Henry dies before age twenty-one, his part of the estate will be divided among the elder Henry's siblings: Aaron Gray, Samuel Gray, Elizabeth Abbot, Jemima Holt, Mary Foster, Hannah Foster, Rebecca Holt, and Sarah Gray. Well-beloved wife Alice is named sole executrix. Real estate was valued at £605 and personal estate at £205.2.9.[584] Son Henry died after age 21 but without marrying and daughter Lydia was the heir to the estate.

Henry Gray and Alice Peabody were parents of four children born at Andover.

i HENRY GRAY, b. 1 Feb 1737/8; d. at Andover, 1 Dec 1760. Henry died of smallpox after returning from the Army.

ii WILLIAM GRAY, b. 25 Jun 1741; d. 13 Nov 1743.

iii WILLIAM GRAY, b. 19 Nov 1744; d. 2 Jan 1745/6.

943) iv LYDIA GRAY, b. 28 May 1748; d. at Andover, 23 Feb 1821; m. at Andover, 26 Mar 1766, Dr. SYMONDS BAKER, b. at Topsfield, MA, 6 Jan 1735/6 son of Thomas and Sarah (Wade) Baker; Symonds d. at Andover, 8 Jul 1815. Symonds was first married to Susan Sargent who died in 1764.

221) MARY GRAY (*Henry Gray³, Hannah Holt Gray², Nicholas¹*), b. at Andover, about 1707 daughter of Henry and Mary (Blunt) Gray; d. likely at Pembroke; m. 26 Nov 1730, as his second wife, MOSES FOSTER, b. at Andover, 27 Sep 1696 son of Ephraim and Hannah (Eams) Foster; Moses d. at Pembroke, about 1770 (will 12 Mar 1766; probate 7 Dec 1770). Moses was first married to Elizabeth Rogers who died in 1729.

Mary and Moses had five children at Andover and a sixth child born likely in Pembroke. The family moved from Andover to Pembroke about 1742 where Moses purchased land from Samuel Gray 5 July 1742.[585]

In his will dated 12 Mar 1766 (probate 7 December 1770), Moses Foster had the following legacies: son Asa, ten shillings; son Daniel, five shillings, son Moses, five shillings; son Ephraim, five shillings; daughter Sarah Carr, five shillings; and daughter Mary Conner, five shillings. These legacies are to be paid by son Caleb. Beloved wife Mary receives two cows, four sheep, one hog and one-half of the bread corn and meat that is in his possession when he dies. She also has use of all the household stuff during her life. There are other provisions for her support. Books are to be divided equally among all the children. The remainder of the estate is bequeathed to Caleb who is named executor.[586] Sarah Carr, Asa, and Daniel are children from Moses's first marriage to Elizabeth Rogers.

944) i EPHRAIM FOSTER, b. at Andover, 30 Aug 1731; d. at Peacham, VT, 12 Nov 1803; m. about 1755, HANNAH MOOR, b. 5 Aug 1732 daughter of James and Agnes (Colbreath) Moor.[587]

ii HENRY FOSTER, b. 23 Jul 1733; d. 16 Jan 1736/7.

iii MARY FOSTER, b. 12 Jan 1735/6; d. 29 Jan 1736/7.

iv MARY FOSTER, b. at Andover, 27 Dec 1737; m. Col. SAMUEL CONNER, b. at Exeter, 2 Apr 1733 son of Samuel and Sarah (Gilman) Foster; Samuel d. at Battle of Bennington, 1777. Mary m. 2nd, at Concord, 26 Feb 1778, CALEB MOREY. No children were identified for Mary Foster.

v ELIZABETH FOSTER, b. 8 Mar 1739/40; likely died young and is not mentioned in father's will.

945) vi CALEB FOSTER, b. at Pembroke, about 1744; d. at Pembroke, 3 May 1821; m. HANNAH who has not been identified, but b. about 1737; Hannah d. at Pembroke, 28 Apr 1811.

---

[583] The 1741 probate record of Jonathan Peabody includes acknowledgment from Henry Gray and Alice Gray that they have received settlement from the estate of "our father" Jonathan Peabody.

[584] *Essex County, MA: Probate File Papers, 1638-1881.*Online database. *AmericanAncestors.org.* New England Historic Genealogical Society, 2014. Case 11604

[585] Carter, *History of Pembroke*, p 98

[586] *New Hampshire. Probate Court (Rockingham County);* Probate Place: *Rockingham, New Hampshire, volume 22, pp 337-338*

[587] Cutter, *New England Families*, volume 2, p 726

222) SAMUEL GRAY (*Henry Gray[3], Hannah Holt Gray[2], Nicholas[1]*), b. at Andover, Jul 1711 son of Henry and Mary (Blunt) Gray; d. at Amherst, NH, 3 Oct 1769;[588] m. at Andover, 8 Sep 1736, SARAH ABBOTT, b. at Andover, 25 Jan 1715/6 daughter of Ephraim and Sarah (Crosby) Abbott.[589]

Sarah and Samuel married in Andover and their first child was born there. They then moved on to New Hampshire, and the births of three children are recorded at Rumford. Samuel had some property in Pembroke that he sold to Moses Foster in 1742.[590] They settled in Amherst, New Hampshire.

No probate record was located for Samuel. Of the four children for whom there are birth records, three died in early childhood.

i SAMUEL GRAY, b. 11 Jan 1736/7; d. 15 Dec 1737.

ii SARAH GRAY, b. 25 Jan 1739; d. 10 May 1740.

iii SARAH GRAY, b. 16 Mar 1741; d. 4 Sep 1746.

946) iv MARY GRAY, b. 29 Dec 1743; d. at Amherst, NH 19 Oct 1775; m. at Amherst, 3 Dec 1762, MOSES TOWNE, b. at Topsfield, May 1739 son of Israel and Grace (Gardner) Towne; Moses d. at Milford, NH 9 Feb 1824.

223) HANNAH GRAY (*Henry Gray[3], Hannah Holt Gray[2], Nicholas[1]*), b. at Andover 4 Jan 1714/5 daughter of Henry and Mary (Blunt) Gray; m. 1st, about 1740, SAMUEL SESSIONS, b. about 1710 son of Samuel and Mary (Cox) Sessions; Samuel d. of fever,[591] at Andover, 24 Apr 1746. Hannah m. 2nd, at Andover, 31 May 1750, DAVID FOSTER, b. at Boxford, 17 Aug 1704 son of Timothy and Mary (Dorman) Foster;[592] David d. at Keene, NH 1779 (probate 1779).

Samuel Sessions was a farmer in Andover. Hannah Gray and Samuel Sessions were parents of two children born at Andover.

i SARAH SESSIONS, b. 6 Nov 1740; d. at Westminster, VT, 1 Nov 1815; m. MICHAEL GILSON, b. at Groton, 24 Feb 1730/1 son of Michael and Susannah (Sawtell) Gilson; Michael d. at Westminster, 15 Apr 1823. Michael was second married to Sally Safford. Michael Gilson served as a captain in the Vermont militia. It is not known when Sarah and Michael married, but they did not have children. In his will, Michael left the bulk of his estate to "adopted grandson" Joel Page.

947) ii JOHN SESSIONS, b. 9 Jun 1742; d. at Westminster, 1 May 1820; m. 17 Nov 1763, ANN WORSTLY, b. about 1739; Ann d. at Westminster, 12 Oct 1820.

After the death of her first husband, Hannah married David Foster of Keene. In his will 4 November 1777 (probate 14 July 1779), David Foster bequeaths to beloved wife Hannah the west lower room of the dwelling house, all the household stuff, and the use and improvement of one-third of the real estate. Daughter Hannah Bragg receives £20 in divided payments and one-half of the household items after her mother's decease. Daughter Rebecca Foster receives £80 in divided payments and the other half of the household items. Only son David receives all the real estate and the remainder of the estate and is named executor.[593] Real estate was valued at £1665 which included the 180-acre homestead valued at £1400.

Hannah Gray and David Foster were parent of three children born at Keene, New Hampshire.

948) i HANNAH FOSTER, b. at Keene, 3 Apr 1751; d. at Westminster, VT, 9 Apr 1822; m. at Keene, 14 Jun 1769, LUTHER BRAGG, b. at Wrentham, MA, 16 Feb 1742/3 son of Henry and Mary (Bennett) Bragg; Luther d. at Keene, 18 Aug 1804.

ii REBECCA FOSTER, b. at Keene, 9 Jun 1753; living and unmarried in 1777; nothing further known.

949) iii DAVID FOSTER, b. at Keene, 9 Mar 1755; d. at Keene, 7 Jan 1798; m. at Keene, 3 Jan 1781, MARY DASSANCE, b. at Norton, MA, 1 Jun 1755 daughter of Martin and Phebe (Dorman) Dassance; Mary d. at Keene, 31 Mar 1833.

---

588 Secomb, *History of the Town of Amherst*, p. 667.

589 The 1761 will of Daniel Abbott (who is a son of Ephraim Abbott and Sarah Crosby) includes a bequest to his sister Sarah Gray.

590 Carter and Fowler, *History of Pembroke*, p. 98.

591 Sessions, *History of the Sessions Family*

592 Griffin, *History of the Town of Keene*, p 599

593 *New Hampshire. Probate Court (Cheshire County)*; Probate Place: *Cheshire, New Hampshire, Estate Files, E238-E243; Estate Files, F1-F80, 1769-1808, Estate of David Foster*

224) AARON GRAY (*Henry Gray[3], Hannah Holt Gray[2], Nicholas[1]*), b. at Andover, 24 Mar 1715/6 son of Henry and Mary (Blunt) Gray; d. at Keene, NH, 30 Mar 1799; m. at Boxford, 18 Jul 1744, BETHIA PEABODY, b. at Boxford, about 1716 daughter of Jonathan and Alice (Pearl) Peabody;[594] Bethia d. 21 Jan 1788.

Aaron and Bethia started their family in Andover and relocated to Keene, New Hampshire. Gray's Hill in Keene was named for Aaron who owned property near the hill.[595]

Aaron and Bethia were parents of five children born at Andover. It is possible that other children were born after the move to Keene, but no records were located. Two of their sons, Joseph and Williams, served in the Revolution, Joseph dying of smallpox at Ticonderoga.

i AARON GRAY, b. 3 Jun 1745; d. 22 Dec 1746.

950) ii AARON GRAY, b. 16 Oct 1747; d. at Keene, 25 Feb 1812; m. about 1776, HULDAH CLARK, b. at Keene, 7 Dec 1747 daughter of Isaac and Susanna (Geer) Clark; Huldah d. at Keener, 27 Feb 1812.

iii MARY GRAY, b. 9 Sep 1751; d. at Keene, NH, 3 Mar 1812. Mary did not marry.

951) iv WILLIAM GRAY, b. 27 Dec 1753; d. at Keene, 1804 (probate 1804); m. at Keene, 25 Nov 1784, MARY "MOLLY" FISHER.

v JOSEPH GRAY, b. 10 Dec 1755; d. at Ticonderoga of smallpox, 27 Jun 1776.

225) THOMAS ABBOTT (*Hannah Gray Abbott[3], Hannah Holt Gray[2], Nicholas[1]*), b. at Andover, 3 Jan 1698/9 son of Thomas and Hannah (Gray) Abbott; d. 11 Jul 1774; m. 28 Jan 1724/5, ELIZABETH BALLARD, b. 14 Jan 1700/1 daughter of Joseph and Rebecca (Johnson) Ballard; Elizabeth d. 31 Jul 1782.

Thomas Abbott and Elizabeth Ballard lived their lives in Andover where all their children were born. However, four sons of this family relocated to Concord, New Hampshire near the time of the first settlement of Concord. Of those four, Jabez, Aaron, and Nathan, seem to have stayed in New Hampshire. Jesse seems to have returned to Massachusetts prior to his death.

No probate record was located for Thomas Abbott. Thomas Abbott and Elizabeth Ballard had ten children whose births are recorded at Andover.

i SAMUEL ABBOTT, b. 1 Nov 1725; d. 19 Nov 1725.

952) ii ELIZABETH ABBOTT, b. at Andover, 10 Jan 1726/7; d. at Andover 27 Sep 1792; m. 4 Jan 1753, as his 2nd wife, SAMUEL OSGOOD, b. 29 May 1714 son of Ezekiel and Rebecca (Wardwell) Osgood; Samuel d. 16 Mar 1774.

953) iii THOMAS ABBOTT, b. at Andover, 4 Apr 1729; d. at Andover 29 Mar 1775; m. 12 Feb 1756, LYDIA BLUNT, b. 6 Apr 1731 daughter of David and Lydia (Foster) Blunt; Lydia d. 16 Nov 1798.

954) iv JABEZ ABBOTT, b. at Andover, 18 Apr 1731; d. 7 Jan 1804 at Concord; m. 1st by 1756, his first cousin, PHEBE ABBOTT (*Edward Abbott[4], Hannah Gray Abbott[3], Hannah Holt Gray[2], Nicholas[1]*), b. 13 Feb 1732 daughter of Edward and Dorcas (Chandler) Abbott; Phebe d. 6 Jan 1770. Jabez m. 2nd 8 Aug 1772, HEPHZIBAH STEVENS, b. 28 Feb 1739/40 daughter of Samuel and Hephzibah (Ingalls) Stevens.

955) v AARON ABBOTT, b. at Andover, 17 Feb 1732/3; d. at Concord 31 Dec 1812; m. his first cousin, LYDIA ABBOTT (*Edward Abbott[4], Hannah Gray Abbott[3], Hannah Holt Gray[2], Nicholas[1]*), b. 15 Jun 1737 daughter of Edward and Dorcas (Chandler) Abbott; Lydia d. 15 Dec 1811.

vi JOSEPH ABBOTT, b. 27 Dec 1734; d. at Québec in prison Jun 1758; Joseph was taken captive by the Indians at Lake George 19 Sep 1756 and was carried to Canada and died in prison at Quebec sometime in Jan 1758. This information is recorded in the death records.[596]

480) vii NATHAN ABBOTT, b. at Andover, 7 Feb 1736/7; d. at Concord, 18 Jan 1805; m. 1766, BETTY FARNUM, b. 1743 daughter of Joseph and Zerviah (Hoit) Farnum; Betty d. 11 Nov 1821.

viii JESSE ABBOTT, b. 3 May 1740; d. 15 Jul 1740.

ix JESSE ABBOTT, b. 4 Oct 1741; d. 12 May 1808 recorded at Haverhill; m. at Andover, 27 Sep 1765, SARAH SCALES, b. 11 Sep 1743 daughter of Moses and Rebecca (Barnard) Scales; Sarah's date of death is not known. Jesse and Sarah did not have any children.

x LYDIA ABBOTT, b. 5 Oct 1743; d. 2 Jun 1749.

---

[594] Although there is not a birth record for Bethia, there is a distribution to daughter Bethia in the 1741 probate record of Jonathan Peabody.

[595] Griffin, *A History of the Town of Keene*, p 553

[596] Joseph, s. Thomas and Elizabeth, "taken Captive by the Indians at Lake George, Sept. 19, 1756, and carry'd to Canada and dyed in prison at Quebeck sometime in Jan. 1758," in his 24th y. Massachusetts: Vital Records, 1620-1850

226) EDWARD ABBOTT (*Hannah Gray Abbott[3], Hannah Holt Gray[2], Nicholas[1]*), b. at Andover, 9 Jun 1702 son of Thomas and Hannah (Gray) Abbott; d. at Concord, NH, 14 Apr 1759; m. 15 Jul 1728, DORCAS CHANDLER, b. about 1705 daughter of Thomas and Mary (Peters) Chandler; Dorcas d. 16 May 1748. Edward married 2nd, 23 Jan 1748/9, MEHITABLE EASTMAN, b. at Haverhill 17 Nov 1707 daughter of Jonathan and Hannah (Green) Eastman.

Edward Abbott was a first proprietor at Concord.[597] The births of all ten children of Edward and Dorcas are recorded at Rumford or Concord, New Hampshire.[598] No probate record was located for Edward.

956) i DORCAS ABBOTT, b. at Rumford 15 Feb 1728/9; d. 28 Sep 1797; m. 17 Jun 1746, EBENEZER HALL, b. at Bradford, 19 Sep 1721 son of Joseph and Sarah (Kimball) Hall; Ebenezer d. 24 Apr 1801. Ebenezer was the brother of Joseph Hall who married Deborah Abbott [daughter of Thomas and Hannah (Gray) Abbott].

957) ii EDWARD ABBOTT, b. 27 Dec 1730; d. 15 Sep 1801; m. about 1760 DEBORAH STEVENS, origins not certain but likely the Deborah born 1738 in Rumford, NH daughter of Aaron and Deborah (Stevens) Stevens; Aaron Stevens was an early settler at Concord; Deborah d. Nov 1817.

954) iii PHEBE ABBOTT, b. 13 Feb 1732; d. 6 Jan 1770; m. by 1756, her first cousin, JABEZ ABBOTT (*Thomas Abbott[4], Hannah Gray Abbott[3], Hannah Holt Gray[2], Nicholas[1]*), b. 18 Apr 1731 son of Thomas and Elizabeth (Ballard) Abbott. Jabez m. 2nd Hephzibah Stevens; Jabez d. 7 Jan 1804.

iv LYDIA ABBOTT, b. 7 May 1735; d. 18 Jun 1736.

955) v LYDIA ABBOTT, b. 15 Jun 1737; d. 15 Dec 1811; m. her first cousin, AARON ABBOTT (*Thomas Abbott[4], Hannah Gray Abbott[3], Hannah Holt Gray[2], Nicholas[1]*), b. 17 Feb 1732/3 son of Thomas and Elizabeth (Ballard) Abbott; Aaron d. 31 Dec 1812.

vi TIMOTHY ABBOTT, b. 21 Jul 1739; d. at Concord, 1814; no marriages or children are known for him; his probate from 1814 specifies he left no widow or children.

vii RACHEL ABBOTT, b. 31 Mar 1742; d. 26 Jul 1742.

958) viii BETSEY ABBOTT, b. 25 Aug 1743; d. 2 Oct 1827 at Goffstown, NH; m. 1759, THOMAS SALTMARSH, b. at Watertown, 2 Mar 1736 son of Thomas and Mary (Hazen) Saltmarsh; Thomas d. at Goffstown, NH 8 May 1826.[599]

ix JEMIMA ABBOTT, b. 23 Jun 1746; d. 13 Jul 1746.

x JEMIMA ABBOTT, b. 29 Apr 1748; d. 31 Jul 1748.

227) DEBORAH ABBOTT (*Hannah Gray Abbott[3], Hannah Holt Gray[2], Nicholas[1]*), b. at Andover, 1 Dec 1704 daughter of Thomas and Hannah (Gray) Abbott; d. at Concord, NH 25 Oct 1801; m. 5 Jul 1736, JOSEPH HALL, b. at Bradford 15 Dec 1707 son of Joseph and Sarah (Kimball) Hall; Joseph d. 8 Apr 1784 at Concord.[600]

Deacon Joseph Hall was from Bradford. He was deacon of the church at Concord for 40 years. Deborah is reported to have died after she lost her way while walking to pick berries, and then fell causing injuries that led to her death at the age of 97.[601]

In his will written 2 June 1783 (proved 19 May 1784), Joseph Hall bequeathed to his beloved wife Deborah the use of one-half of the dwelling house during her natural life and all the household goods, except the desk and clock, to be at her disposal. If Deborah does not make her own will, then the household items are to go to granddaughter Sarah Hall after Deborah's decease. The executor is to make suitable provisions for Deborah's support. Granddaughter Mary Wilson receives one-half of the homestead, and this will revert to granddaughter Sarah Hall if Mary does not have children. Granddaughter Sarah Hall receives the other half of the homestead, and this reverts to Mary if Sarah does not have children. Each of the granddaughters also receives three hundred and fifty dollars. Son Joseph Hall, Jr. receives the remainder of the estate. Joseph was named executor.[602]

Deborah Abbott and Joseph Hall had five children born at Concord.

i JOSEPH HALL, b. 17 Jul 1737; d. 10 Jun 1807; Joseph was a deacon and does not seem to have married or had children. His will leaves several bequests to what seem to be nieces and nephews (Wilkins and

---

597 Bouton, *The History of Concord*

598 *New Hampshire, Births and Christenings Index, 1714-1904 (accessed through ancentry.com)*

599 The graves of Elizabeth Abbott and Thomas Saltmarsh are in the Westlawn Cemetery at Goffstown with a gravestone that lists their names as Thomas Saltmarsh and Elisabeth Abbott, his wife. (accessed through findagrave.com)

600 New Hampshire Death and Disinterment Records, 1754-1947, accessed through ancestry.com

601 Bouton, *The History of Concord*

602 New Hampshire Probate Rockingham County, Estate of Joseph Hall, 19 May 1784, No. 5007

Thorndike who may be his sister Mary's children or grandchildren), a bequest to a local doctor, and he left his plot of land to the town of Concord.

ii SARAH HALL, b. 20 Sep 1738; d. 21 Oct 1746.

iii HANNAH HALL, b. 24 Nov 1740; d. 21 Oct 1746.

959) iv MARY HALL, b. 17 Mar 1743; d. 12 Dec 1773; m. THOMAS WILSON who d. at Concord 23 May 1818. After Mary's death, Thomas married Mary Hopkins Bancroft.

959a) v JEREMIAH HALL, b. 6 Jan 1746; d. 6 Oct 1770; m., 1769, ESTHER WHITTEMORE, b. 2 Aug 1752 daughter of Aaron and Abigail (Coffin) Whittemore; Esther d. 12 Jul 1803. Esther m. 2nd, Joseph Woodman.

228) GEORGE ABBOTT (*Hannah Gray Abbott[3], Hannah Holt Gray[2], Nicholas[1]*), b. at Andover, 7 Nov 1706 son of Thomas and Hannah (Gray) Abbott; d. at Concord, NH 6 Oct 1785; m. 1 Feb 1737, SARAH ABBOTT (who was his first cousin, once removed), b. Oct 1711 daughter of Samuel and Sarah (Stevens) Abbott; Sarah d. at Concord 14 Jun 1769.

George Abbott settled in Concord around 1732. He served as deacon of the church for 41 years.

In his will dated 28 February 1774, George made the following bequests: beloved son Daniel has already received his inheritance; to beloved son George, he orders that the executor provide him with a comfortable maintenance as long as he is single; beloved son Stephen receives 20 acres of land; beloved son Ezra receives a land bequest; and beloved son Joseph is named executor and also receives a parcel of land. The wording of the will suggests that son George may have had some type of disability. The inventory of his estate included real estate in Concord and Warner.[603]

George and Sarah had nine children born at Concord.

960) i DANIEL ABBOTT, b. 7 Aug 1738; d. 11 Jun 1804; m. 1st by 1761, his second cousin RACHEL ABBOTT, b. 7 Apr 1743 daughter of Nathaniel and Penelope (Ballard) Abbott; Rachel d. 13 Jun 1788. Daniel m. 2nd 1 Jan 1789 at Boscawen, MERCY KILBURN whose origins are not fully verified; she was born about 1758 based on the birth of her last child in 1799; she was living in 1830 when she was listed as a head of household in the 1830 US Census of Concord (between age 60-70).

ii GEORGE ABBOTT, b. 9 Apr 1740; d. 17 Sep 1791; George did not marry.

961) iii JOSEPH ABBOTT, b. 23 Oct 1741; d. at Concord, NH, 19 Jan 1832; m. 25 Apr 1765, his second cousin once removed, PHEBE LOVEJOY (*Henry Lovejoy[5], Henry Lovejoy[4], Mary Farnum Lovejoy[3], Elizabeth Holt Farnum[2], Nicholas[1]*), b. 20 Sep 1735 daughter of Henry and Phebe (Chandler) Lovejoy; Phebe d. 4 Jan 1789.

iv SAMUEL ABBOTT, b. 30 Mar 1743; d. 5 Nov 1761 at Crown Point during the French and Indian War.

v STEPHEN ABBOTT, b. 10 Dec 1744; d. 10 Oct 1746.

962) vi STEPHEN ABBOTT, 28 Oct 1746; d. 12 May 1811; m. 11 Apr 1778, MARY GILE, b. about 1755 (parentage not verified at this point); Mary d. Jan 1822.

vii NATHAN ABBOTT, b. 16 Nov 1748; d. 7 Mar 1749

viii NATHAN ABBOTT; b. 3 Jul 1752; d. 15 Nov 1758.

963) ix EZRA ABBOTT, b. 22 Aug 1756; d. 21 Feb 1837; m. 1st 21 Nov 1782, BETTY ANDREWS, b. 12 May 1762 daughter of Thomas and Mary (Burnham) Andrews; Betty d. 25 Aug 1794. Ezra m. 2nd 10 May 1795, ANNER CHOATE, b. at Ipswich 12 Jan 1758 daughter of Thomas and Dorothy (Proctor) Choate; Anner d. 21 Mar 1798. Ezra m. 3rd 15 Nov 1798, JANE JACKMAN, b. at Boscawen, 20 Dec 1767 daughter of Benjamin and Jane (-) Jackman; Jane d. 2 May 1847.

229) BENJAMIN ABBOTT (*Hannah Gray Abbott[3], Hannah Holt Gray[2], Nicholas[1]*), b. at Andover, 31 Mar 1710 son of Thomas and Hannah (Gray) Abbott; d. at Concord, NH 8 Mar 1794; m. 23 Jun 1742, HANNAH ABBOTT (who was his first cousin once removed), b. 30 Jul 1716 daughter of Samuel and Sarah (Stevens) Abbott; Hannah d. at Concord 27 Jul 1786.

Benjamin was also an early settler of Concord. He was renowned for his physical prowess, including a report that he hoed four acres of corn in one day when he was over the age of 80.[604]

The will of Benjamin Abbott has bequests for the following persons (although one whole page of the will appears to be missing): son Benjamin, son Isaac, and daughter Hannah. Son Isaac is named executor.[605]

Benjamin and Hannah had eight children, all born at Concord.

---

[603] *New Hampshire Wills and Probate Records 1643-1982,* Probate of George Abbott, Rockingham, 16 Oct 1785, Case number 5147.

[604] Bouton, *The History of Concord*

[605] *New Hampshire Wills and Probate Records 1643-1982,* Probate of Benjamin Abbott, Rockingham, 1 Apr 1794, Case number 5986.

964) i HANNAH ABBOTT, b. at Concord, 22 Jan 1743; d. 22 Oct 1820; m. at Hopkinton, 25 Sep 1783, JEREMIAH STORY, JR. (origins not fully verified, but perhaps the Jeremiah Story of Ipswich); d. about 1806 based on the date of probate of his estate May 1806 with widow Hannah Story as administrator.

ii ISAAC ABBOTT, b. 7 Feb 1745; d. 24 Nov 1746.

iii ISAAC ABBOTT, b. 30 Aug 1747; d. 4 Mar 1799; m. at Ipswich, 28 Feb 1771, LUCY BURNHAM of Ipswich, b. about 1738 (as reported on death record); d. 3 Sep 1826. Isaac and Lucy do not seem to have had any children. The estate of Isaac Abbott entered probate 12 March 1799 in Rockingham County, New Hampshire. Isaac did not leave a will. Lucy Abbott declined administration of the estate and requested that Isaac's brother Benjamin take on that duty. The estate had a value of $745.

965) iv BENJAMIN ABBOTT, b. 10 Feb 1750; d. 11 Dec 1815; m. 29 Jan 1778, SARAH BROWN, b. 1758 at Brunswick, ME; Sarah d. 27 Sep 1801. Benjamin m. 2nd, 17 Jun 1805, HANNAH GREENLEAF who was still living at the time of Benjamin's death.

v EPHRAIM ABBOTT, b. 15 Jun 1752; d. 30 Oct 1778; Ephraim did not marry. He was wounded at the Battle of Bennington.

vi THOMAS ABBOTT, b. 7 Oct 1754; d. 2 Sep 1773.

vii THEODORE ABBOTT; b. 7 Mar 1759; d. 22 Sep 1778.

viii SARAH ABBOTT; b. 20 Feb 1761; d. 4 Jul 1761.

230) ROBERT GRAY (*Robert Gray*[3], *Hannah Holt Gray*[2], *Nicholas*[1]), b. at Andover 1706 son of Robert and Miriam (Lovejoy) Gray; m. at Andover, 1 May 1728, his second cousin, LYDIA PEABODY (*Lydia Holt Peabody*[3], *James*[2], *Nicholas*[1]), b. at Andover, 13 Feb 1703 daughter of Samuel and Lydia (Holt) Peabody; Lydia d. at Andover, 24 Aug 1775.

Robert was a farmer in Andover. Although the death of Lydia is recorded (in 1775 as a widow), there is no record of Robert's death. Robert and Lydia were parents of seven children born at Andover.

966) i ROBERT GRAY, b. at Andover, 9 Jul 1729; d. at Andover, 19 Dec 1806 at the poorhouse; m. 1st 23 Apr 1754, MARY TUCKER who died about 1757. Robert m. 2nd, Jun 1758, ABIGAIL TAY (widow of Abijah Chandler), b. at Woburn, 1728 daughter of William and Abigail (Jones) Tay;[606] Abigail d. at Andover, 29 Jan 1790.

967) ii LYDIA GRAY, b. at Andover, 14 Nov 1732; d. at Andover, 1818 at the poorhouse; m. at Andover, 21 Nov 1751, JOHN BATCHELDER, b. at Hampton Falls, 1 Jun 1730 son of Benjamin and Rebecca (Prescott) Batchelder; John d. at Chester, NH, before 1781.

968) iii BRIDGET GRAY, b. at Andover, 5 Apr 1737; d. at Windsor, VT, 1805; m. at Billerica, 22 Jun 1758, SAMUEL PEARSON, b. about 1738 likely son of Thomas and Abigail (Lewis) Pearson; Samuel d. at Windsor, 4 Sep 1823.

iv CORNELIUS GRAY, b. 11 Dec 1738

v MERRIAM GRAY, b. at Andover, 23 Jun 1743; *possibly* m. about 1786, JOHN LOVEJOY, b. 24 Jul 1743 son of Hezekiah and Hannah (Austin) Lovejoy.[607]

vi DEBORAH GRAY, b. 8 Oct 1744

661) vii MOSES GRAY, baptized at Andover, 11 Jan 1747; d. at Tewksbury, 11 Sep 1775; m. at Tewksbury, 29 Jun 1769, MARY CLARK, b. at Tewksbury, 26 May 1745 daughter of Nathaniel and Mary (Wyman) Clark. Mary m. 2nd at Tewksbury, 30 Aug 1781, JESSE HOLT, b. at Andover, 8 Oct 1739 son of James and Mary (Chandler) Holt; Jesse d. at Tewksbury, Feb 1817.

231) ISAAC GRAY (*Robert Gray*[3], *Hannah Holt Gray*[2], *Nicholas*[1]), b. at Andover, 6 Sep 1709 son of Robert and Miriam (Lovejoy) Gray; d. at Tewksbury, 4 Oct 1770; m. at Andover, 20 Nov 1733, REBECCA FROST (widow of David Blanchard), b. at Billerica, 9 Aug 1701 daughter of Thomas and Rebecca (Farley) Frost; Rebecca d. at Tewksbury, 1 Feb 1782.[608]

Isaac Gray was a cooper. He did not leave a will and his estate entered probate 29 October 1770 with heirs widow Rebecah Gray and Mary Gray requesting that widow Rebecah French, daughter of the deceased, be allowed to administer the estate. In the distribution of the real estate on 19 November 1770, daughter widow Rebecca French, and daughter Anny Foster

---

[606] The 1781 will of William Tay includes a bequest to daughter Abigail wife of Robert Gray.

[607] Lovejoy, *The Lovejoy Genealogy*, p 66

[608] Rebecca [wid., somewhat sudden. CR1], Feb. 1, 1782, a. 81 y.

and son-in-law Isaac Foster received the distribution of the real estate. Ann and Isaac Foster were to pay sister Mary Gray £24 and Rebecca French was to pay her sister Mary £27. The widow's thirds were set off to Rebecca Gray. [609]

Isaac Gray and Rebecca Frost were parents of three children born at Andover.

969) i REBECCA GRAY, b. at Andover, 31 Aug 1734; m. at Tewksbury, 1 May 1758, JONATHAN FRENCH; Jonathan d. about 1765 (probate 1765).

ii MARY GRAY, b. at Andover, 18 Sep 1737; d. at Tewksbury, 16 Nov 1781. Mary did not marry.

970) iii ANN GRAY, b. at Andover, 30 Mar 1743; d. at Tewksbury, 9 May 1798; m. about 1762, ISAAC FOSTER, b. at Andover, 28 Apr 1737 son of John and Mary (Osgood) Foster.[610] Isaac was first married to Dorcas Jewett who died in 1762.

232) MIRIAM GRAY (*Robert Gray[3], Hannah Holt Gray[2], Nicholas[1]*), b. at Andover, 4 Sep 1713 daughter of Robert and Miriam (Lovejoy) Gray; m. at Andover, 28 Feb 1731/2, BENJAMIN FITCH, b. at Billerica, 30 Jul 1703 son of Samuel and Elizabeth (Walker) Fitch; Benjamin d. at Bedford, MA, 7 Jul 1770.

Benjamin Fitch was a mill operator on the Shawsheen River in Bedford. A colorful account of Benjamin's courting of Miriam can be found in Brown's "Glimpses of Old New England Life: Legends of Old Bedford". (Benjamin's name is given as Benjamin Fay in the account.) Brown's volume also provides an interesting account of Miriam's difficulty finding acceptance in the community due to her arriving in town wearing a red outfit and superstitions by the town members related to her having a birthmark believed to be a witch's sign.[611]

In his will written 1 December 1769 (probate 17 July 1770), Benjamin Fitch bequeathed to beloved wife Miriam the improvement of his half of the grist mill and sawmill in Bedford during her widowhood. After Miriam's death or remarriage, son David is to have the interest in the mills and David is to pay £40 to sons Benjamin, Isaac, and Abel to be equally divided among them. Son David also receives three acres of pastureland and the husbandry tools and is charged with the support of his mother. His grandchildren Hannah, Betty, John, Lydia, David, and Benjamin Tarbell the children of Hannah receive six shillings to equally divide. Daughter Miriam Fitch receives £16.13.4 and daughter Betty Wyeth of Cambridge receives £5.9.4. Daughters Louis Fitch and Eunice Fitch each receives £16.13.4. Sons Benjamin, Isaac, and Abel will divide the remaining real property except that Benjamin's portion is to be £13.6.8 as his full portion. Miriam, Louis, and Eunice may have a chamber in the house while they live unmarried. Son David Fitch was named executor.[612] James Munro blacksmith of Cambridge was named guardian for minor children Isaac and Abel.

Benjamin and Miriam were parents of eleven children born at Bedford.

971) i HANNAH FITCH, b. at Bedford, 10 Jun 1733; d. at Nottingham West, NH by 1769; m. at Bedford, 1 Aug 1751, DAVID TARBELL, b. at Salem, 15 Sep 1726 and baptized at Lynn, 25 Sep 1726 son of John and Hannah (Flint) Tarbell; David d. at Nottingham West, NH, about 1805 (will Oct 1805). David married Esther Kemp on 2 Jul 1772.

ii MIRIAM FITCH, b. at Bedford, 23 Jan 1734/5; m. 11 Sep 1788, as his second wife, TIMOTHY JAQUITH, b. at Billerica, 6 Mar 1743/4 son of Abraham and Hannah (Farley) Jaquith. Timothy was first married to Eunice Corey.

iii BENJAMIN FITCH, b. at Bedford, 6 Jan 1736/7. Benjamin was living in 1769. He is not known to have married and the wording in his father's will suggests that Benjamin may not have been fully capable. Although Benjamin was the oldest son, the bulk of the estate went to the second son David.

972) iv BETTE FITCH, baptized at Bedford, 14 Jun 1739; d. at Cambridge, 5 May 1823; m. at Bedford, 30 Mar 1763, NOAH WYETH, b. 7 Jul 1742 son of Ebenezer and Susannah (Hancock) Wyeth, Noah d. at Cambridge, 10 Sep 1811.

v LOIS FITCH, b. at Bedford, 31 Oct 1740; m. at Bedford, 2 Nov 1776, EDWARD POWERS of Boston who has not been identified. No children were identified for Lois and Edward.

973) vi DAVID FITCH, b. at Bedford, 22 May 1743; d. at Bedford, 27 Jul 1813; m. at Woburn, 3 Apr 1770, MARY FOWLE, b. 1747 whose parents have not been identified; Mary d. at Bedford, 19 Sep 1829.

vii LYDIA FITCH, b. 21 Mar 1745; d. 11 Mar 1759.

974) viii EUNICE FITCH, b. at Bedford, 26 Jul 1747; m. 29 Sep 1778, DANIEL MCNICHOL (NICHOLS)

[609] *Middlesex County, MA: Probate File Papers, 1648-1871.*Online database. *AmericanAncestors.org.* New England Historic Genealogical Society, 2014. Case 9683

[610] Pierce, *Foster Genealogy*, Part 1, p 194

[611] Brown, *Glimpses of Old New England*, pp 177-178, p 187

[612] *Middlesex County, MA: Probate File Papers, 1648-1871.*Online database. *AmericanAncestors.org.* New England Historic Genealogical Society, 2014. Case 7687

ix NATHAN FITCH, b. 27 Jan 1748/9; d. 13 May 1755.

x ISAAC FITCH, b. 18 May 1752; d. at Bedford, 24 Jul 1773.

xi ABEL FITCH, baptized 5 Oct 1755. It is not clear what became of Abel. There is an Abel Fitch who married Anne Waters and was a mariner based in Boston. That Abel Fitch died in 1787, perhaps at sea. There is a probate record in New York for Abel Fitch of Boston related to creditors of the estate. That Abel Fitch was second mate on the ship *Hope* mastered by James McGee.

233) ABIEL GRAY (*Robert Gray*[3], *Hannah Holt Gray*[2], *Nicholas*[1]), b. at Andover, 26 Jan 1714/5 son of Robert and Miriam (Lovejoy) Gray;[613] d. at Tolland, CT, 14 Apr 1805; m. 1st about 1737, ZERVIAH HATCH, b. at Tolland, 3 Oct 1715 daughter of Ichabod and Abigail (Weeks) Hatch; Zerviah d. at Tolland, 8 May 1754. Abiel m. 2nd about 1755, LOIS PALMER, b. at Stonington, 3 Mar 1721/2 daughter of Moses and Abigail (Allen) Palmer; Lois d. at West Hartford, 11 Nov 1786. Abiel m. 3rd at Hartford, 12 Nov 1787, LUCY FULLER of Willington, b. about 1735; Lucy d. at West Hartford, 16 Aug 1793.

Abiel was born in Andover, but was in Tolland by 1737 where he married Zerviah Hatch.

Son Abiel Gray did not marry and died at age twenty-eight. In his will written 6 April 1786 (probate 7 May 1786), son Abiel Gray, Jr. bequeathed to father Abiel Gray and mother Lois Gray the improvement of one-half his estate during their lives. Sisters Lucy Lothrop, Zerviah Stanley, and Comfort Gillet receive forty shillings. Sister Esther Roe and her first male child, if the child is named Abiel Gray, will receive the rest of the estate. If Esther does not have a boy and/or he does not survive to age twenty-one, then Esther will have the estate except a legacy of £16 to be paid to sister Lois Price and her three children Lois, Ebenezer, and Xerxes. Real estate was valued at £368.[614]

Abiel and Zerviah were parents of four children born at Tolland.

975) i LUCY GRAY, b. at Tolland, 29 Jan 1737/8; d. at Tolland, 25 Dec 1804; m. at Tolland, 10 Dec 1754, JOHN LOTHROP, b. at Tolland, 6 May 1732 son of John and Ann (Thatcher) Lothrop; John d. at Tolland, 24 Mar 1812.

ii JOHN GRAY, b. at Tolland, 24 Jun 1740; nothing further known. John is not mentioned in his half-brother's will. A marriage was not located for him.

976) iii ZERVIAH GRAY, b. at Tolland, 9 Jul 1742; d. at Shoreham, VT, 19 Aug 1828; m. at West Hartford, 18 Nov 1762, AMOS STANLEY, baptized at Hartford, 26 Aug 1739 son of Samuel and Anne (Bracey) Stanley; Amos d. at Becket, MA, 25 Jan 1811.

977) iv COMFORT GRAY, b. at Tolland, 25 May 1751; d. at New Hartford, 19 Apr 1841; m. at Hartford, 1 May 1768, STEPHEN GILLET, b. at Hartford, 21 Mar 1729 son of Joseph and Sarah (Burr) Gillet; Stephen d. at North Hartford, 20 May 1800.

Abiel and Lois were parents of three children born at Hartford.

978) i LOIS GRAY, b. at Hartford, about 1755; m. at West Hartford, 13 Nov 1772, EBENEZER PRICE, b. at Hartford, 13 Sep 1748 son of Ebenezer and Sarah (Ensign) Price; Ebenezer d. at South Amboy, NJ.

ii ABIEL GRAY, b. about 1758; d. at Hartford, 13 Apr 1786.

979) iii ESTHER GRAY, baptized at Hartford, 17 May 1761; d. at West Hartford, 21 Dec 1824; m. at Hartford, 15 Feb 1785, DAVID ROWE, b. about 1758 of Farmington; David d. at West Hartford, 20 Feb 1814.

234) JONATHAN GRAY (*Robert Gray*[3], *Hannah Holt Gray*[2], *Nicholas*[1]), b. at Andover, 21 Mar 1715/6 son of Robert and Miriam (Lovejoy) Gray; m. at Woburn, 20 Feb 1738, PERSIS REED, b. at Woburn, 21 Jul 1711 daughter of Timothy and Persis (Kendall) Reed.[615]

Just two children were identified for Jonathan and Persis. Jonathan's mother made a bequest in her will to her granddaughter Persis Snow, but grandson Jonathan was not mentioned suggesting he was deceased before 1767.

980) i PERSIS GRAY, b. at Woburn, 29 Mar 1740; d. at Jaffrey, NH, 27 Oct 1816; m. 1st at Woburn, 28 Dec 1756, JAMES SNOW, b. at Woburn, 7 Mar 1732 son of Zerubbabel and Elizabeth (Wyman) Snow; James d. at Woburn, 28 Jun 1783 by drowning (probate 1783). Persis m. 2nd at Jaffrey, Jan 1789, OLIVER PROCTOR, b. at Westford, 25 Feb 1729 son of John and Mary (Colesworthy) Proctor; Oliver d. at Jaffrey, 17 Jul 1809.

---

613 In the Tolland records, there is also listed Abiel's information on his birthdate giving birth as 26 Jan 1714/5 and parents as Robert and Miriam.

614 *Connecticut. Probate Court (Hartford District)*; Probate Place: *Hartford, Connecticut, volume 23, pp 206-207*

615 Jonathan Gray and Persis Reed were parents of a daughter Persis who married James Snow. She is the granddaughter Percy Snow in the will of Jonathan's mother.

ii JONATHAN GRAY, b. at Woburn, 17 Feb 1742; nothing further known and likely died before 1767.

235) DAVID GRAY (*Robert Gray*[3], *Hannah Holt Gray*[2], *Nicholas*[1]), b. at Andover, 22 Oct 1717 son of Robert and Miriam (Lovejoy) Gray; d. at Andover 1767 (by suicide); m. at Andover, 3 Jun 1756, his first cousin once removed, REBECCA HOLT (*Samuel*[4], *Samuel*[3], *Samuel*[2], *Nicholas*[1]), baptized at Andover 31 Oct 1725 daughter of Samuel and Jemima (Gray) Holt; Rebecca d. at Andover, 10 Jul 1800.

David died by suicide. Reverend Samuel Phillips delivered "A Sermon on Suicide after the death of David Gray" and is reported to have declared that David's name should be "buryd in oblivion."[616]

David Gray did not leave a will and his estate entered probate 2 Feb 1767 with Robert Gray as administrator at the request of widow Rebecca. Real estate was valued at £256.13.4 and personal estate at £184.8.2. After payment of debts and administrative costs, amount remaining was £229.10.1.[617]

David and Rebecca were parents of three children born at Andover.

i SARAH GRAY, b. at Andover, 9 May 1759; d. at Andover, 7 Sep 1836; m. at Andover, 3 Apr 1807, as his second wife, ABRAHAM SHATTUCK, b. at Pepperell, 12 Oct 1759 son of Jeremiah and Lydia (Lakin) Shattuck; Abraham d. at Washington, NH, 1841. Abraham was first married to Polly Wright.

981) ii DAVID GRAY, b. at Andover, 8 Dec 1762; d. at Andover, 7 Mar 1844; m. 1st 3 Apr 1788, SARAH CUMMINGS, b. at Andover, 21 May 1767 daughter of Jonathan and Mary (Eastman) Cummings;[618] Sarah d. at Andover, 15 Mar 1793. David m. 2nd 23 Feb 1797, REBECCA JENKINS, b. at Andover, 23 Feb 1773 daughter of Samuel and Anna (Upton) Jenkins; Rebecca d. at Andover, 9 Apr 1840.

iii CORNELIUS GRAY, b. 28 Oct 1765; d. 12 Oct 1782.

236) EDWARD GRAY (*Edward Gray*[3], *Hannah Holt Gray*[2], *Nicholas*[1]), b. at Andover, Nov 1705 son of Edward and Sarah (Osgood) Gray; d. after 1773 perhaps in Maine; m. by 1742, SARAH who has not been identified.[619]
and Sarah

Little firm information is known for this family. They had four children recorded at Andover (although one of the births occurred at Hatfield).[620] The family was in Rindge, New Hampshire briefly. Edward's son John and his wife Beulah stayed there for several years, but Edward and Sarah were there for a short time being warned out of Rindge in 1773.[621]

i EDWARD GRAY, b. 6 Oct 1742; d. 4 Aug 1747.

610) ii JOHN GRAY, b. at Andover, 26 Dec 1745; d. perhaps at Jay, ME (where youngest children were born); m. at Andover, 26 Apr 1770, his third cousin, BEULAH HOLT (*Oliver*[4], *Oliver*[3], *Henry*[2], *Nicholas*[1]), b. at Andover, 12 Apr 1744 daughter of Oliver and Susannah (Wright) Holt.

iii SARAH GRAY, b. at Hatfield, 17 Jan 1753; nothing further known.

iv EDWARD GRAY, b. at Andover, 17 Nov 1756; d. 24 May 1763.

237) HANNAH GRAY (*Edward Gray*[3], *Hannah Holt Gray*[2], *Nicholas*[1]), b. at Andover, about 1707 daughter of Edward and Sarah (Osgood) Gray; d. after 1783 (husband's will); m. at Andover, 2 Sep 1730, DANIEL COLBY, b. at Amesbury perhaps the son of John and Mary (Frame) Colby; Daniel d. at Dracut, 1785 (probate).

Hannah and Daniel had their three children in Andover, but the family was then in Dracut where Daniel purchased one-half of a ferry from Solomon Abbott in 1761. In 1768, Daniel sold his half of the ferry to Amos Bradley.[622]

In his will written 17 January 1783, Daniel Colby bequeaths to beloved wife Hannah the use and improvement of all the household items and he notes that he has procured a bond for her maintenance for her life and this is in lieu of the dower. Daughter Hannah Abbot wife of Solomon Abbot receives £3. Each of his grandchildren, the sons and daughters of Hannah, receives five English mill dollars. Grandson Solomon Abbot, Jr. the eldest son of Hannah receives the remainder of the estate and is named executor.[623]

Daniel and Hannah were parents of three children.

---

[616] Abbot, *History of Andover*

[617] *Essex County, MA: Probate File Papers, 1638-1881.*Online database. *AmericanAncestors.org.* New England Historic Genealogical Society, 2014. Case 11592

[618] The 1805 will of Jonathan Cummings includes a bequest to his granddaughter Polly Eastman Gray.

[619] It is possible that this is Sarah Coombs who married Edward Gray in Tolland, CT in 1741. Edward's first cousin Abiel Gray was in Tolland at that time and there are no other Gray families there during that period.

[620] From the Andover records: Sarah, d. Edward, jr. and Sarah, at Hatfield, Jan. 17, 1753.

[621] Stearns, *History of the Town of Rindge*, p 539

[622] Coburn, *History of Dracut*, p 261

[623] *Middlesex County, MA: Probate File Papers, 1648-1871.*Online database. *AmericanAncestors.org.* New England Historic Genealogical Society, 2014. Case 4795

i DANIEL COLBY, b. at Andover, 16 Jun 1731; d. 20 Oct 1738.

275) ii HANNAH COLBY, b. at Andover, 22 Oct 1735; m. at Andover, 3 May 1756, her third cousin, SOLOMON ABBOTT (*David Abbott[4], Sarah Farnum Abbott[3], Elizabeth Holt Farnum[2], Nicholas[1]*), b. at Andover, 14 Feb 1730/1 son of David and Hannah (Danforth) Abbott; Solomon d. 17 Dec 1797.

iii SARAH COLBY, b. 26 Dec 1742; d. 20 Oct 1747.

238) MARGERY GRAY (*Edward Gray[3], Hannah Holt Gray[2], Nicholas[1]*), b. at Andover, about 1708 daughter of Edward and Sarah (Osgood) Gray; d. at Andover, 31 Oct 1795; m. at Andover, 17 May 1739, WILLIAM WARDWELL, b. at Andover, 3 May 1709 son of William and Dorothy (Wright) Wardwell; William d. at Andover, 24 Mar 1790.

William Wardwell and his twin Thomas Wardwell who married Margery's sister Abigail Gray were grandsons of Samuel Wardwell who was hanged in Salem for witchcraft in 1692. There is little information on the family of Margery and William. There is one child known.

982) i NATHAN WARDWELL, baptized at Andover, 20 Jan 1740; d. at Andover, 14 Aug 1769; m. at Andover, 27 Dec 1763, HULDAH CHANDLER, b. at Suncook, NH, 16 Aug 1740 daughter of David and Abial (Chandler) Chandler. Huldah was second married to Stephen Stiles.

239) THOMAS GRAY (*Edward Gray[3], Hannah Holt Gray[2], Nicholas[1]*), b. at Andover, 22 Jul 1709 son of Edward and Sarah (Osgood) Gray; d. at Andover, 5 Feb 1796; m. 1st 21 Jun 1739, ELIZABETH HUTCHINSON, b. at Andover, 4 Aug 1715 daughter of John and Sarah (Adams) Hutchinson; Elizabeth d. at Andover, 22 Mar 1739/40. Thomas m. 2nd 19 Mar 1757, LYDIA GRAVES, b. at Reading, 1732 daughter of Daniel and Martha (Coats) Graves; Lydia d. at Andover, 21 Apr 1793.

Thomas Gray was a housewright in Andover. In his will written 9 April 1792 (probate 3 May 1796), Thomas Gray bequeaths to beloved wife Lydia all the household goods and furniture for and during her natural life along with a list of provisions to be provided by the executor as well as the use of his horse to ride to meetings. She also has the use and improvement end of the west end of the dwelling house. Son Thomas Gray receives £7. Daughters Sarah wife of Stephen Ayer and Phebe each receives six shilling and daughter Hannah receives three pounds. The household goods are to be divided equally among his daughters after his wife's decease. Son Daniel receives all the real estate in Andover and is named executor. Heirs signing agreement to the will on 3 March 1796 were Thomas Grey, Phebe Damon, Hannah Lacey, Amos Damon, and John Lacey. Real estate was valued at $510 and personal estate at $179.75.[624]

Thomas Gray and Elizabeth Hutchinson were parents of one child.

983) i SARAH GRAY, b. at Andover, 13 Mar 1739/40; m. at Haverhill, 18 May 1769, STEPHEN AYER, b. at Haverhill, 1 Dec 1744 son of Simon and Mary (Webster) Ayer; Stephen d. at Dunbarton, NH, 14 Dec 1825.

Thomas Gray and Lydia Graves were parents of five children.

827) i THOMAS GRAY, b. at Andover, 23 Mar 1758; d. at Andover, 5 Sep 1823; m. 7 Dec 1780, his third cousin, MARY HOLT (*Thomas[4], Thomas[3], Nicholas[2], Nicholas[1]*), b. at Andover, 11 Mar 1758 daughter of Thomas and Dorcas (Holt) Holt; Mary d. at Andover, 28 Mar 1830.

ii LYDIA GRAY, b. 3 Jun 1759; d. 26 Jan 1786.

984) iii DANIEL GRAY, b. at Andover, 20 Nov 1760; d. at Andover, 18 Jul 1833; m. at Reading, 14 Dec 1786, TABITHA ALLEN who was of Reading but not yet identified; Tabitha d. about 1847 when she last received pension payments.

985) iv PHEBE GRAY, b. at Andover, 13 Jan 1765; d. at Reading, 1 Aug 1846; m. at Reading, 9 Sep 1784, AMOS DAMON, b. at Reading, 30 Apr 1761 son of Ezra and Ruth (Bragg) Damon; Amos d. before 1846.

986) v HANNAH GRAY, b. at Andover, 10 Jun 1767; d. at Andover, 16 Dec 1827; m. at Andover, 24 Oct 1786, JOHN LACEY, b. at Danvers about 1763; John d. at Andover, 2 May 1852.

240) PRISCILLA GRAY (*Edward Gray[3], Hannah Holt Gray[2], Nicholas[1]*), b. at Andover, 10 Jan 1712/3 daughter of Edward and Sarah (Osgood) Gray; m. 4 Dec 1735, DANIEL CARLETON, b. at Andover, May 1708 son of John and Hannah (Osgood) Carleton; Daniel d. at Andover, 2 May 1795.

There is just one child known for Priscilla and Daniel.

---

[624] *Essex County, MA: Probate File Papers, 1638-1881.* Online database. *AmericanAncestors.org.* New England Historic Genealogical Society, 2014. Case 11365

987) i DANIEL CARLETON, b. at Andover, 6 Mar 1736/7; d. at Andover, 9 Dec 1801; Mar 16 Aug 1759, his first cousin, MERCY CARLETON, b. at Andover, 21 Nov 1739 daughter of Ezekiel and Mercy (Kimball) Carleton; Mercy d. at Andover, 20 Mar 1814.

241) ABIGAIL GRAY (*Edward Gray³, Hannah Holt Gray², Nicholas¹*), b. at Andover, 13 Aug 1714 daughter of Edward and Sarah (Osgood) Gray; d. at Andover, 16 Oct 1778; m. 11 Dec 1735, THOMAS WARDWELL, b. at Andover, 3 May 1709 son of William and Dorothy (Wright) Wardwell; Thomas d. at Andover, 29 Feb 1776.

Abigail and Thomas resided in Andover, their house reported as being near the center of town.[625] Thomas was a yeoman.

In his will written 24 February 1776 (probate 6 May 1776), Thomas Wardwell expresses his will that son Daniel will procure and provide for dearly beloved wife Abigail a convenient room in the dwelling house and all her necessities and comforts of life including a horse and horseman to carry her to meetings and elsewhere. These provisions are in lieu of the dower which she will receive if Daniel or his heirs neglect this duty. Oldest and well-beloved son Solomon receives twelve shillings which completes his portion and sons Jeremiah and Ezekiel receive similar bequests. Son Daniel receives all the real and personal estate and is also named executor. Real estate was valued at £362 pounds including the dwelling house with 25 acres and an additional 40 acres.[626]

Abigail and Thomas were parents of eleven children born at Andover.

i DAMARIS WARDWELL, b. 26 Apr 1737; d. 9 Nov 1767. Damaris did not marry.

ii SOLOMON WARDWELL, b. 19 Jan 1738/9; d. 24 Jan 1741/2.

iii MARY WARDWELL, b. 19 Mar 1739/40; d. 19 Apr 1745.

iv JEREMIAH WARDWELL, b. 6 Jan 1741/2; d. 4 Sep 1747.

642) v SOLOMON WARDWELL, b. at Andover, 14 Jul 1743; d. at Nelson, NH, 20 Sep 1825; m. at Andover, 29 Oct 1767, his third cousin, BETHIAH HOLT (*Benjamin⁴, Henry³, Henry², Nicholas¹*), b. at Andover, 3 Aug 1744 daughter of Benjamin and Lydia (Holt) Holt;[627] Bethiah d. at Nelson, 13 Apr 1812.

vi MARY WARDWELL, b. 3 Feb 1744/5; d. 19 Apr 1745.

vii SILVANUS WARDWELL, b. 1 Jun 1746; d. 5 Sep 1747.

988) viii JEREMIAH WARDWELL, b. at Andover, 6 Dec 1748; d. at Salisbury, NH, 9 Jan 1817; m. 21 Nov 1769, his third cousin, MOLLY LOVEJOY (*David Lovejoy⁵, Henry Lovejoy⁴, Mary Farnum Lovejoy³, Elizabeth Holt Farnum², Nicholas¹*), b. at Pembroke, NH, 29 Apr 1748 daughter of David and Elizabeth (Chandler) Lovejoy; Molly d. at Salisbury, 23 Feb 1813. After Molly's death, Jeremiah married BETSEY who has not been identified.

989) ix EZEKIEL WARDWELL, b. at Andover, 15 Feb 1750/1; d. at Andover, 16 Dec 1834; m. at Andover, 22 Nov 1783, the widow of his brother Daniel and his third cousin once removed, DAMARIS FAULKNER (*Abiel Faulkner⁵, Damaris Johnson Faulkner⁴, Thomas Johnson³, Mary Holt Johnson², Nicholas¹*), b. at Andover, 3 Nov 1753 daughter of Abiel and Mary (Poor) Faulkner; Damaris d. at Andover, 28 Mar 1826.

989) x DANIEL WARDWELL, b. at Andover, 18 Nov 1753; d. at Andover, 7 Mar 1782; m. 29 Mar 1774, DAMARIS FAULKNER (see Ezekiel just above).

xi PHEBE WARDWELL, b. 2 May 1756; d. at Andover (burial 16 Dec 1773).

242) LYDIA GRAY (*Edward Gray³, Hannah Holt Gray², Nicholas¹*), b. at Andover, 22 Aug 1716 daughter of Edward and Sarah (Osgood) Gray; d. after 1792;[628] m. 7 Apr 1737, JOHN STEVENS, b. 1711 son of Abiel and Deborah (Barker) Stevens; John d. before 1792 (when widow Lydia was dismissed from South Church to the church at Thetford).

John and Lydia were parents of eight children born at Andover.

---

[625] Stay, *Wardwell: A Brief Sketch of the Antecedents of Solomon Wardwell*, p 9

[626] *Essex County, MA: Probate File Papers, 1638-1881.*Online database. *AmericanAncestors.org.* New England Historic Genealogical Society, 2014. Case 28943

[627] There are two Bethiah Holts born five months apart, one the daughter of Ephraim Holt and Phebe Russell and one the daughter of Benjamin Holt and Lydia Holt. One of these married Thomas Russell and one married Solomon Wardwell and it is not entirely clear which is which. Ephraim Holt and Benjamin Holt were brothers. There are a couple of factors that might clarify this. The Bethiah who married Solomon Wardwell died 13 April 1812 which age at death given as 67 years 8 months which fits for Bethiah born in August 1744. Also, Solomon and Bethiah Wardwell named a son Benjamin and Bethiah and Thomas Russell named a son Ephraim.

[628] In 1792, widow Lydia Stevens (John) was dismissed from the church in Andover to church in Thetford, Vermont. Historical Manual of the South Church of Andover, p 142

i SARAH STEVENS, b. 29 Jan 1738/9; died young.

990) ii SARAH STEVENS, b. at Andover, 6 Jun 1740; m. at Andover, 13 May 1762, ISRAEL WOOD, b. at Haverhill, 14 Aug 1738 son of Richard and Sarah (Rolfe) Wood; Israel d. at Thetford, VT, 7 Apr 1818. Israel married second Sarah Young.

991) iii DEBORAH STEVENS, b. at Andover, 21 Jun 1742; d. at Andover, 2 Aug 1818; m. 1st at Andover, 6 Dec 1764, JACOB HAGGET, b. at Andover, 9 Feb 1742/3 son of Moses and Sarah (Head) Hagget; Jacob d. at Andover, 29 Jan 1769. Deborah m. 2nd 23 Feb 1775, SIMON CROSBY b. at Billerica, 14 Sep 1741 son of Solomon and Katherine (-) Crosby; Simon d. at Andover, 30 Oct 1820. Simon Crosby was first married to Dorothy Farmer.

992) iv LYDIA STEVENS, b. at Andover, 3 May 1745; d. at Brunswick, ME, Jun 1821; m. at Andover, 1 Dec 1767, JACOB ABBOTT, b. at Andover, 9 Feb 1745/6 son of Joseph and Deborah (Blanchard) Abbott; Jacob d. at Brunswick, 5 Mar 1820.

v JOHN STEVENS, b. 2 Oct 1747; d. 3 Dec 1747.

622) vi ABIEL STEVENS, b. at Andover, 24 Mar 1749/50; d. at Strafford, VT, 1806 (probate 31 Mar 1806); m. 1st at Andover, 16 Nov 1769, his third cousin, TABITHA HOLT (*Jacob4, Oliver3, Henry2, Nicholas1*), b. at Andover, 19 May 1753 daughter of Jacob and Margaret (Dolliver) Holt; Tabitha d. at Andover, 23 Sep 1778. Abiel m. 2nd 1 Jan 1779, his second cousin once removed, ELIZABETH HOLT (*Nathaniel5, Oliver4, Oliver3, Henry2, Nicholas1*), b. at Andover, 14 Nov 1752 daughter of Nathaniel and Elizabeth (Stevens) Holt; Elizabeth was living in 1806.

vii DAVID STEVENS, b. 10 Jun 1755; d. 30 Jul 1755.

viii SUSANNA STEVENS, b. 11 Jul 1756; d. 29 Mar 1757.

243) ELIZABETH GRAY (*Edward Gray3, Hannah Holt Gray2, Nicholas1*), b. at Andover, Nov 1720 daughter of Edward and Hannah (Barker) Gray; m. at Boxford, 3 Dec 1747, EPHRAIM KIMBALL, b. at Boxford, 11 Apr 1721 son of Richard and Hannah (Dorman) Kimball.[629]

Ephraim was a cooper in Boxford.[630] He sold his property there to Joshua Rea of Beverly in 1762.[631] It is not known where they relocated.

i PETER KIMBALL, b. at Boxford, 1 Jun 1749.

ii HANNAH KIMBALL, b. at Boxford, 3 Sep 1751.

iii SUSANNA KIMBALL, b. at Boxford, 24 Jun 1756.

iv ELIZABETH KIMBALL, b. at Boxford, 18 Apr 1758.

244) SARAH GRAY (*Edward Gray3, Hannah Holt Gray2, Nicholas1*), b. at Andover, 18 Mar 1723 daughter of Edward and Hannah (barker) Gray; m. 14 Jan 1747/8, THOMAS STEVENS, b. at Andover, 9 Aug 1724 son of John and Elizabeth (Chandler) Stevens; Thomas d. in PA during the Revolution on 29 Dec 1777.[632]

Thomas Stevens of Andover enlisted in the company of Capt. Samuel Johnson of Col. Wigglesworth regiment,[633] and Thomas died while in service.

Sarah and Thomas were parents of ten children born at Andover.

993) i THOMAS STEVENS, b. at Andover, 10 Oct 1748; d. at Andover, 26 Jan 1827; m. at Andover, 8 Oct 1772, SARAH INGALLS, b. at Andover, 6 Nov 1753 daughter of Ebenezer and Sarah (Kimball) Ingalls;[634] Sarah d. at Andover, 1824.

ii SARAH STEVENS, b. 4 Sep 1750; d. 23 Dec 1763.

iii ELIZABETH STEVENS, b. 26 Nov 1752; d. 16 Jan 1764.

iv EDWARD STEVENS, b. 3 Jan 1755; d. 19 Dec 1763.

---

629 Morrison and Sharples, *History of the Kimball Family in America*

630 Morrison, *History of the Kimball Family*, p 112

631 Essex Institutes Historical Collections, volumes 27-29, p 182, *The Dwellings of Boxford*

632 Thomas, "in the Continental 3 years service at Pennsylvania," Dec. 29, 1777.

633 *Massachusetts Soldiers and Sailors in the Revolution*, volume 14, p 983

634 The 1787 probate record of Ebenezer Ingalls includes Thomas Stevens signing as an heir.

597) v HEPHZIBAH STEVENS, b. at Andover, 15 Jan 1757; m. (int.) 28 Dec 1776, her third cousin, PETER HOLT (*John[4], John[3], Samuel[2], Nicholas[1]*), b. at Andover, 30 Sep 1752 son of John and Deborah (Stevens) Holt; Peter d. at the almshouse in Andover, 9 Jan 1830.

994) vi PHEBE STEVENS, b. at Andover, 6 May 1759; d. at Andover, 13 Aug 1843; m. at Andover, 22 May 1791, her first cousin once removed, NATHAN WARDWELL (*Nathan Wardwell[5], Margery Gray Wardwell[4], Edward Gray[3], Hannah Holt Gray[2], Nicholas[1]*), b. at Andover, 10 Nov 1765 son of Nathan and Huldah (Chandler) Wardwell; Nathan d. at Andover, 4 Nov 1838.

995) vii DAVID STEVENS, b. at Andover, 3 Feb 1761; d. at Andover, 29 Jan 1834; m. at Andover, 28 Dec 1784, his third cousin, SARAH ABBOTT, b. at Andover, 7 Dec 1765 daughter of Ebenezer and Lydia (Farrington) Abbott; Sarah d. at Springfield, OH, 7 Sep 1856.

996) viii SUSANNA STEVENS, b. at Andover, 3 Dec 1763; d. 10 Sep 1835; m. at Andover, 7 Jul 1785, her third cousin, ABRAHAM MOOAR (*Lydia Abbott Mooar[6], Anne Lovejoy Abbott[5], William Lovejoy[4], Mary Farnum Lovejoy[3], Elizabeth Holt Farnum[2], Nicholas[1]*), b. at Andover, 15 Jan 1761 son of Abraham and Lydia (Abbott) Mooar; Abraham d. at Peterborough, 3 Mar 1842.

ix SARAH STEVENS, b. 8 Sep 1766; nothing further known.

997) x EDWARD STEVENS, b. at Andover, 30 Sep 1768; d. at Andover, 27 Oct 1805;[635] m. 23 Feb 1791, PHEBE FRYE, b. at Andover, 4 Apr 1762 daughter of Samuel and Elizabeth (Frye) Frye.

245) BRAVITER GRAY (*Braviter Gray[3], Hannah Holt Gray[2], Nicholas[1]*), b. at Andover, 19 Jul 1717 son of Braviter and Dorothy (Abbott0 Gray; d. at Billerica, 1768 (probate 1768); m. 1st at Charlestown, 6 Jul 1743, BETHIAH HILL, b. at Billerica, 16 Jul 1718 daughter of Jonathan and Mary (Bracket) Hill; Bethiah d. at Billerica, 30 Jan 1754. Braviter m. 2nd at Billerica, 14 Jul 1757, ANNE DANFORTH, b. at Billerica, 28 Feb 1729 daughter of Jonathan and Elizabeth (Manning) Danforth; Anne d. 10 Aug 1757. Braviter m. 3rd ELIZABETH RICHARDSON (widow of John Blanchard), b. at Billerica, 9 Dec 1719 daughter of Andrew and Hannah (Jefts) Richardson; Elizabeth d. at Billerica, 1768 (probate Oct 1768).

Braviter was the eldest surviving son of Braviter and Dorothy Gray. He had inherited one-third part of his father's estate in Andover. On 28 September 1738 (recorded 7 October 1747), Braviter Gray, cordwainer of Billerica, quitclaimed his interest in the one-third part of his father's estate in Andover to his honored father-in-law Benjamin Holt for payment of eighty-five pounds.[636]

On 9 January 1743/4, Braviter Gray with his wife Bethiah of Billerica joined Francis Kidder and his wife Elizabeth of Sutton in a quitclaim of 31 acres in Billerica to Daniel Stickney.[637] This property likely related to the estate of Bethiah's father Jonathan who died in December 1743. Francis Kidder was the husband of Bethiah's sister Elizabeth Hill and Daniel Stickney was the husband of Bethiah's sister Mary Hill.

Braviter Gray did not leave a will and his estate entered probate 4 October 1768 with Joseph Gray of Fitchburg as administrator.[638] Isaac Marshal was named guardian to minor child Braviter Gray.

Also on 4 October 1768, the estate of widow Elizabeth Gray of Billerica entered probate with Isaac Marshall as administrator. Elizabeth's estate was valued at £25.5.8, £19.6.8 of that for four acres and a half of pasture in Billerica. On 27 March 1771, the property was settled on Elizabeth's son John Blanchard with John to make payment of forty-one shillings and two pence to each of his brethren and sisters: Lemuel Blanchard, Josiah Blanchard, Elizabeth Ditson, Abigail Blanchard, Hannah Blanchard, and Breveter Gray.[639]

Braviter Gray and Bethiah Hill were parents of five children born at Billerica.

i JOSEPH GRAY, b. 1 Jul 1744

ii MARY GRAY, b. 29 Oct 1745

iii TIMOTHY GRAY, b. 25 Feb 1747; d. 17 Dec 1749.

998) iv TIMOTHY GRAY, b. at Billerica, 28 Mar 1752; d. at Hillsborough, about 1827 (will proved 20 Nov 1827); m. at Hillsborough, 22 May 1781, MARTHA ROLFE, likely b. at Reading, 1752 daughter of Daniel and Mary (Lewis) Rolfe;[640] Martha was living Dec 1825 when Timothy wrote his will.

---

[635] Edward [consumption], C.R.2.], Oct. 27, 1805, a. 37 y. [and 6 m. C.R.2.]

[636] Massachusetts Land Records, Essex County, 91:76

[637] Massachusetts Land Records, Middlesex County, 48:52

[638] *Middlesex County, MA: Probate File Papers, 1648-1871.*Online database. *AmericanAncestors.org.* New England Historic Genealogical Society, 2014. Case 9677

[639] *Middlesex County, MA: Probate File Papers, 1648-1871.*Online database. *AmericanAncestors.org.* New England Historic Genealogical Society, 2014. Case 9681

[640] It seems more likely than not that Martha was the sister of Stephen Rolfe who went to Hillsborough to care for his aged father. Stephen was the son of Daniel Rolfe.

999) v JONATHAN GRAY, b. at Billerica, 3 Jan 1754; d. at Tewksbury, Jun 1817 (will 19 Nov 1816); m. at Tewksbury, 2 Mar 1786, MARY NEEDHAM, b. at Tewksbury, 14 Mar 1756 daughter of John and Prudence (Stearns) Needham; Mary d. at Tewksbury, 1833.

Braviter Gray and Elizabeth Richardson were parents of one child born at Billerica.

i BRAVITER GRAY, b. 23 May 1760; living in 1768 but nothing further known.

246) TIMOTHY GRAY (*Braviter Gray[3], Hannah Holt Gray[2], Nicholas[1]*), b. at Andover, 19 Jul 1721 son of Braviter and Dorothy (Abbott0 Gray; d. at Wilton, 17 Nov 1793; m. 1st at Andover, 3 May 1748, ELINOR BEST, b. at Boston, 25 Aug 1724 daughter of James and Mary (Frye) Best; Elinor d. at Wilton, 22 Sep 1775. Timothy m. 2nd ABIGAIL who d. at Wilton, 20 May 1801.

Timothy and Elinor started their family in Andover. Timothy purchased a lot in Wilton in 1764 and they relocated there and settled on property bought of William Vance on lot six of the fifth range and lot five of the fourth range. Timothy was a farmer, but also had a trade as a cordwainer. He served as deacon in Wilton.[641] Sons James and Jonathan died during the Revolution.

In his will written 19 March 1791 (proved 17 June 1794), Timothy Gray bequeaths to beloved wife Abigail specific provisions in accordance to their agreement prior to their marriage dated 1 May 1791. The specific provisions are to be delivered to Abigail by son Timothy within one year. Eldest son Timothy receives all the real estate including the farm in Wilton and any other lands and buildings. Timothy also receives all the money and notes, stock animals, and tools. Second son Joseph receives £27 and a firelock gun. Daughters Mary, Sarah, and Dorothy each receives £27 and one-third part of the household furniture. The bible and other valuable books are to be divided equally among the children. Timothy was named sole executor.[642]

Timothy Gray and Elinor Best were parents of nine children.

1000) i TIMOTHY GRAY, b. at Andover, 19 Feb 1749; d. at Wilton, 16 Jul 1807; m. 1st about 1770, HANNAH BLANCHARD, b. about 1750; Hannah d. at Wilton, 1 Jul 1784. Timothy m. 2nd 21 Apr 1785, RUTH BURNHAM, b. 1756 daughter of Jeremiah and Mary (Burnham) Burnham; Ruth d. at Wilton, 23 Mar 1841.

ii JAMES BEST GRAY, b. at Andover, 26 Jan 1751; d. while a prisoner at Halifax, Aug 1777.

iii ELINOR GRAY, b. 16 Mar 1753; perhaps died young as she in not in father's will.

iv JONATHAN GRAY, b. at Andover, 18 Mar 1755; d. at Wilton, 15 Sep 1775. Died of wounds received at Bunker Hill.

1001) v MARY GRAY, b. at Andover, 19 Feb 1757; d. at Francestown, 20 Apr 1841; m. at Wilton, 23 Nov 1786, SAMUEL HARTSHORN, b. at Reading, 13 Jun 1760 Thomas and Abia (-) Hartshorn; Samuel d. at Francestown, 11 Feb 1847.

1002) vi SARAH GRAY, b. at Andover, 2 Mar 1759; d. at Weston, VT, 22 Jan 1835; m. at Wilton, 8 Jan 1782, CHRISTOPHER MARTIN, b. at Andover, 31 May 1757 son of Samuel and Elizabeth (Osgood) Martin; Christopher d. at Weston, 6 Aug 1838.

1003) vii JOSEPH GRAY, b. at Andover, 9 Mar 1761; d. at Wilton, 26 Aug 1846; m. 11 Apr 1786; CHLOE ABBOTT, b. at Wilton, 4 Jun 1767 daughter of Jeremiah and Cloe (Abbott) Abbott; Chloe d. at Wilton, 19 Jul 1849.

1004) viii DOROTHY GRAY, b. at Andover, 26 Oct 1763; m. at Wilton, 3 Aug 1786, DANIEL HOLT who is not yet identified although he served from Wilton during the Revolution.

ix HENRY GRAY, b. 8 Oct 1766; d. 31 Mar 1776.

Grandchildren of James Holt and Hannah Allen

247) RHODA HOLT (*Timothy[3], James[2], Nicholas[1]*), b. at Andover, about 1707 daughter of Timothy and Rhoda (Chandler) Holt; d. likely at Concord; m. at Boston, 13 Nov 1728, ELIAS WHITTEMORE, b. likely at Malden, 1702 son of John and Ruth (Bassett) Whittemore;[643] Elias d. at Concord, NH, Dec 1792.[644]

---

641 Livermore, *History of Wilton*, p 383

642 Ancestry.com. *New Hampshire, Wills and Probate Records, 1643-1982* [database on-line]. Provo, UT, USA, *Probate Records, Vol 5-6, 1791-1796, volume 5, pp 544-546*

643 Whittemore, *A Genealogy of Several Branches of the Whittemore Family*, p 62

644 U.S., Newspaper Extractions from the Northeast, 1704-1930

Deacon Elias Whittemore and his wife Rhoda Holt had four children in Malden and Chelsea and later relocated to New Hampshire where likely their youngest child was born. They were in Pembroke by 1737[645][646] where they remained for the next 40 years and finally were in Concord. Elias Whittemore was one of the nine organizing members of the Congregational church at Pembroke where he served as deacon and Aaron Whittemore was pastor.[647]

307) i RHODA WHITTEMORE, b. at Malden, 18 Aug 1729; d. at Concord, NH, 29 Jan 1785; m. at Concord, about 1751, her third cousin, REUBEN ABBOTT (*Abigail Farnum Abbott⁴, Ralph Farnum³, Elizabeth Holt Farnum², Nicholas¹*), b. at Andover, 4 Apr 1723 son of James and Abigail (Farnum) Abbott; Reuben d. at Concord, 13 May 1822.

ii ELIAS WHITTEMORE, baptized at Chelsea, 13 Feb 1731/2; d. 31 Dec 1736.

iii TIMOTHY WHITTEMORE, baptized at Chelsea, 24 Mar 1734; d. 3 Dec 1736.

1005) iv RACHEL WHITTEMORE, b. at Malden, 17 Aug 1735; d. at Pembroke, 26 Feb 1817; m. 1757, MOSES FOSTER, b. at Andover, 26 Mar 1728 son of Moses and Elizabeth (Rogers) Foster; Moses d. at Pembroke, 21 Jan 1823.

1006) v JOHN WHITTEMORE, b. about 1737; d. at Pembroke, 1774 (probate 16 May 1774); m. about 1771, RUTH PEABODY, b. at Boxford, 10 Dec 1746 daughter of Thomas and Ruth (Osgood) Peabody; Ruth d. at Pembroke, 22 May 1828. Ruth married second Thomas Baker on 13 Feb 1776.[648]

248) PRISCILLA HOLT (*Timothy³, James², Nicholas¹*), b. at Andover, about 1708 daughter of Timothy and Rhoda (Chandler) Holt; d. at Andover, 25 Nov 1803; m. 14 May 1729, NATHAN CHANDLER, b. at Andover, 31 Jan 1708 son of John and Hannah (Frye) Chandler; Nathan d. at Andover, 31 Jul 1784.[649]

Nathan was the lieutenant of a company that marched August 15, 1757 for the relief of Fort William Henry which had come under siege from the French.[650]

In his will (probate 5 October 1784), Nathan Chandler makes bequests to the following persons: dearly beloved wife Priscilla receives use of the house from the bottom of the cellar to the top of the house and the kitchen also and the liberty of using the well; Priscilla also receives several specific provisions for her continued maintenance and the "time and improvement" of his Negro woman Flora. Other bequests are to beloved son Nathan Chandler, beloved son Isaac Chandler, daughter Hannah wife of Joshua Chandler, Mary wife of Jonathan Abbott, and Phebe wife of Isaac Abbott.[651]

There are five births recorded at Andover for Nathan Chandler and Priscilla Holt.

1007) i NATHAN CHANDLER, b. 19 Feb 1729/30 at Andover; d. at Andover, 30 Apr 1786; m. 18 Apr 1754, his third cousin, PHEBE ABBOTT, b. 14 Apr 1733 daughter of John and Phebe (Fiske) Abbott; Phebe d. 26 Jul 1812.

1008) ii ISAAC CHANDLER, b. at Andover, 8 Apr 1732; d. at Andover, 6 Mar 1817; m. 14 Apr 1757, his second cousin once removed, HANNAH BALLARD, b. 3 Jan 1732/3 daughter of Josiah and Mary (Chandler) Ballard;[652] Hannah d. 2 Oct 1824.[653]

1009) iii HANNAH CHANDLER, b. at Andover, 20 May 1735; d. at Andover, 14 Feb 1791; m. 31 Mar 1757, as his 1st wife, her first cousin, JOSHUA CHANDLER, b. 23 Jul 1732 son of Joshua and Sarah (Chandler) Chandler. Joshua m. 2nd 7 Jun 1792, Hannah Ballard the daughter of Hezekiah and Lydia (Chandler) Ballard who was the widow of Obadiah Foster; Joshua Chandler d. 15 Mar 1807.

---

645 Hurd, *History of Merrimack and Belknap Counties*, part 2, p 565

646 New Hampshire, Compiled Census and Census Substitutes Index, 1790-1890

647 Carter, *History of Pembroke*, p 322

648 The 1787 will (probate 1803) of Ruth *Osgood* Peabody Osgood includes a bequest to her daughter Ruth Baker.

649 It is generally accepted that Priscilla Holt daughter of Oliver married Nathan Chandler. However, it is more likely that Nathan's wife was Priscilla the daughter of Timothy and Rhoda (Chandler) Holt. There are no records to support that Oliver Holt had a daughter Priscilla and it is known that Timothy had a daughter Priscilla that married. In addition, Benjamin Holt son of Oliver left a will and each of his living siblings seem to be named and he names no Priscilla.

650 Chandler, *The Descendants of William and Annis Chandler*, p 139

651 *Essex County, MA: Probate File Papers, 1638-1881. Probate of Nathan Chandler, 5 Oct 1784, Case number 4962.*

652 The 1780 will of Josiah Chandler includes a bequest to his daughter Hannah the wife of Mr. Isaac Chandler.

653 This is the date of death used in *The Descendants of William and Annis Chandler*, p. 330. The deaths of both Isaac and Hannah are reported by the Chandler book as occurring in Concord, NH, but the record of Isaac's death is in the Andover records with the same specific date as the Chandler book.

276) iv MARY CHANDLER, b. 15 Jun 1740; d. 1 Apr 1824; m. 13 Nov 1759, her second cousin once removed, JONATHAN ABBOTT (*David Abbott[4], Sarah Farnum Abbott[3], Elizabeth Holt Farnum[2], Nicholas[1]*), b. 24 Oct 1739 son of David and Hannah (Danforth) Abbott; Jonathan d. 10 Apr 1817.

1010) v PHEBE CHANDLER, b. at Andover, 2 Jun 1742; d. at Andover, 1 Jul 1800; m. 22 Apr 1766, her second cousin once removed, ISAAC ABBOTT (*Phebe Lovejoy Abbott[5], William Lovejoy[4], Mary Farnum Lovejoy[3], Elizabeth Holt Farnum[2], Nicholas[1]*), b. 3 Feb 1745 son of Isaac and Phebe (Lovejoy) Abbott; Isaac d. 21 May 1836.

249) HANNAH HOLT (*Timothy[3], James[2], Nicholas[1]*), b. at Andover, 18 Dec 1709 daughter of Timothy and Rhoda (Chandler) Holt; d. at Andover, 2 Aug 1775; m. 22 Mar 1733, her second cousin once removed, BARACHIAS ABBOTT, b. at Andover, 14 May 1707 son of John and Elizabeth (Harnden) Abbott; Barachias d. at Andover, 2 Oct 1784.

The death record for Barachias lists his cause of death as cancer.[654] A probate record has not been located for Barachias. There are birth records for eleven children all born at Andover.

i BARACHIAS ABBOTT, b. 16 Jan 1733/4; d. 24 Jun 1738.

646) ii MOSES ABBOTT, b. 9 Aug 1735; d. 23 Feb 1826; m. 31 Dec 1761, his third cousin, ELIZABETH HOLT (*Henry[4], Henry[3], Henry[2], Nicholas[1]*), b. 8 Jun 1743 daughter of Henry and Rebecca (Gray) Holt; Elizabeth d. 23 Sep 1838.

403) iii HANNAH ABBOTT, b. 18 May 1737; d. Nov 1812 at Wilton, NH; m. 21 Apr 1756, her third cousin, JEREMIAH HOLT (*John[4], Samuel[3], Samuel[2], Nicholas[1]*), b. 31 Mar 1734 son of John and Mary (Lewis) Holt; Jeremiah's death record not located, but after the 1790 US Census.

822) iv BARACHIAS ABBOT, b. 22 May 1739; d. 29 Jan 1812; m. 6 Dec 1770, his third cousin, SARAH HOLT (*James[4], Nicholas[3], Nicholas[2], Nicholas[1]*), b. 7 Mar 1746/7 daughter of James and Sarah (Abbott) Holt; Sarah d. 11 Feb 1808.

1011) v ELIZABETH ABBOTT, b. at Andover, 2 Nov 1740; d. 9 Sep 1780; m. 30 Aug 1759, her second cousin, ZEBADIAH SHATTUCK, b. 26 Oct 1736 son of Joseph and Joanna (Chandler) Shattuck. Zebadiah m. 2nd 25 Dec 1781, Sarah Chandler (widow of Ralph Holbrook), b. 8 May 1751 daughter of Zebadiah and Deborah (Blanchard) Chandler; Zebadiah d. 10 Mar 1826.

660) vi PRISCILLA ABBOTT, b. 13 Feb 1742/3; d. likely at Bethel, ME; m. 16 Nov 1762, ZELA HOLT (*James[4], James[3], Henry[2], Nicholas[1]*), b. 29 Dec 1738 son of James and Mary (Chandler) Holt.

1012) vii LYDIA ABBOTT, b. at Andover, 7 Mar 1744/5; d. 11 Jul 1829; m. 15 Aug 1771, URIAH RUSSELL, b. 1743 son of Thomas and Abigail (Ballard) Russell; Uriah d. 9 Nov 1822.

viii RHODA ABBOTT, b. 23 Apr 1747; d. 11 Aug 1775; Rhoda did not marry.

ix TIMOTHY ABBOTT, b. 23 Apr 1747; d. 30 Mar 1772.

1013) x PHEBE ABBOTT, b. at Andover, 29 Aug 1749; d. 17 Apr 1809; m. 1 Feb 1774, JOHN RUSSELL, b. 1 Jul 1746 son of John and Hannah (Foster) Russell. John m. 2nd Mary Wilkins; John d. 12 Aug 1830.

1014) xi ABIGAIL ABBOTT, b.at Andover, 25 Jul 1751; d. at Greenfield, NH, 1841; m. 10 Oct 1786, as his second wife, JOHN JOHNSON, b. at Andover, 1748 *perhaps* the son of John and Lydia (Osgood) Johnson (gravestone gives his age as 85); d. at Greenfield, NH 3 Oct 1833. He was *perhaps* first married to Hannah Abbott daughter of John and Hannah (Farnum) Abbott who died in 1785 and then married Abigail.

250) JAMES HOLT (*Timothy[3], James[2], Nicholas[1]*), b. at Andover, 11 Dec 1711 son of Timothy and Rhoda (Chandler) Holt; d. at Andover, 2 Sep 1775;[655] m. 1st at Wilmington, 11 Jan 1734/5, SUSANNA NURS, b. at Reading, 14 Aug 1714 daughter of Jonathan and Abigail (Hornden) Nurs; Susanna d. at Andover, 20 Feb 1742. James m. 2nd at Wilmington, 22 Oct 1742, MARTHA WINN; Martha d. at Andover, 30 Mar 1753. James m. 3rd 6 Aug 1767, MARY CARROLL (widow of Phineas McIntire) who was his widow at the probate of his estate.

James Holt did not leave a will and his estate entered probate 7 November 1775 with widow Mary declining administration and requesting that James Holt the son of James be named administrator.[656] Real estate was valued at £193 and personal estate at £83.17.7. The dower was set off to Mary Holt.

James and Susanna were parents of five children born at Andover.

---

[654] Barachias [cancer. CR2], Oct. 2, 1784, a. 77 y. 4 m

[655] James, bur. Sept. 2, 1775, a. 63 y. CR2

[656] *Essex County, MA: Probate File Papers, 1638-1881.*Online database. *AmericanAncestors.org.* New England Historic Genealogical Society, 2014. Case 13650

i ABIGAIL HOLT, b. Feb 1736; d. 10 Feb 1749/50.

179) ii SUSANNAH HOLT, b. at Andover, 18 Apr 1737; d. at Lunenburg, 11 Jul 1801; m. at Andover, 14 Nov 1753, her second cousin once removed, JONATHAN HOLT (*Humphrey[3], Henry[2], Nicholas[1]*), b. at Andover, about 1727 son of Humphrey and Abigail (Fifield) Holt; Jonathan d. at Lunenburg, 17 Mar 1805.

1015) iii JAMES HOLT, b. at Andover, 29 Dec 1738; d. at Andover, 27 Feb 1808;[657] m. at Andover, 14 Feb 1760, DOROTHY LOVEJOY, b. at Andover, 15 Sep 1740 daughter of Ezekiel and Elizabeth (Wilson) Lovejoy; Dorothy buried at Andover, 28 May 1810.

iv JESSE HOLT, b. 1740; died young. This is a child reported in Durrie's Holt genealogy for whom no records were found.

v RHODA HOLT, b. 18 Feb 1741/2; nothing further known.

251) TIMOTHY HOLT (*Timothy[3], James[2], Nicholas[1]*), b. at Andover, 16 Apr 1714 son of Timothy and Rhoda (Chandler) Holt; d. at Andover, 27 Jul 1798; m. 13 Feb 1739, HANNAH DANE, b. at Andover, 14 Dec 1718 daughter of John and Sarah (Chandler) Dane; Hannah d. 6 Feb 1802.

Timothy and Hannah resided in Andover where Hannah was admitted to South Church on 27 June 1756 by profession of faith.[658]

In his will written 4 November 1783 (probate 3 September 1798), Timothy Holt bequeaths to beloved wife Hannah all the household stuff proper for a woman's use. Son Dane is to provide everything necessary for her comfort in health and sickness. The provisions for Hannah's support are in lieu of her thirds, but if her support is neglected, she will than have the thirds. Eldest and beloved son Dane receives all the real and personal estate except for those specific legacies in the will. Son Timothy receives some lots including one named Humphrey's pasture. Son Ezra receives a feather bed and five shillings. Daughters Hannah and Sarah each receives six shillings. Real property was valued at $2,898 and the total value of the estate was $3,681.61.[659]

Timothy Holt and Hannah Dane were parents of five children born at Andover.

1016) i DANE HOLT, b. at Andover, 1 Apr 1740; d. at Andover, 15 Dec 1818; m. 13 Dec 1763, LYDIA BALLARD, b. at Andover, 30 Jul 1742 daughter of Hezekiah and Lydia (Chandler) Ballard; Lydia d. at Andover, 28 Nov 1813.

ii HANNAH HOLT, b. at Andover, 17 Sep 1741; she is living in 1783 and given her bequest of just six shillings, it seems likely she was married; however, a clear marriage has not been located for her.

1017) iii TIMOTHY HOLT, b. at Andover, 8 Sep 1744; d. at Andover, 19 Feb 1821; m. about 1771, EDE MCINTIRE,[660] b. about 1750 (baptized at Andover 1752) daughter of Phineas and Mary (Carroll) McIntire; Ede d. 20 Jun 1824.

732) iv SARA HOLT, b. at Andover, 11 Aug 1746; m. at Andover, 26 Aug 1766, her third cousin once removed, WILLIAM ABBOTT (*Jonathan Abbott[4], Zerviah Holt Abbott[3], Henry[2], Nicholas[1]*), b. at Lunenburg, 24 Nov 1745 son of Jonathan and Mary (Lovejoy) Abbott; William d. at Wilton, NH, Oct 1807.

1018) v EZRA HOLT, b. at Andover, 20 Mar 1762; d. at Wilton, 11 May 1822; m. at Andover, 9 Oct 1794, his first cousin, DORCAS DANE, b. at Andover, 22 Apr 1771 daughter of William and Phebe (Abbott) Dane; Dorcas d. at Wilton, 30 Jun 1853.

252) JOSEPH HOLT (*Timothy[3], James[2], Nicholas[1]*), b. at Andover, 14 Feb 1718 son of Timothy and Rhoda (Chandler) Holt; d. at Wilton, Aug 1789; m. 1st 17 Jan 1744/5, DOROTHY "DOLLY" JOHNSON, b. at Andover, 3 May 1719 daughter of John and Phebe (Robinson) Johnson; Dolly d. at Andover, 30 Dec 1753. Joseph m. 2nd 1755, MARY RUSSELL, b. at Andover, 10 Feb 1728/9 daughter of John and Sarah (Chandler) Russell.

---

[657] James, jr., carbuncles, bur. Feb. 27, 1808, a. 69 y. CR2

[658] South Church of Andover, *Historical Manual*, p 136

[659] *Essex County, MA: Probate File Papers, 1638-1881.*Online database. *AmericanAncestors.org.* New England Historic Genealogical Society, 2014. Case 13701

[660] There are two Timothy Holts very close in age (born 1744 and 1746) and all published genealogies agree that the Timothy born 1744 married Ede McIntire and Timothy born in 1746 married Hannah Johnson. The basis for that conclusion is not entirely clear. The only discrepancy is that the Timothy who married Hannah Johnson died at Weston, VT in 1836 at age 93 (per death transcription) and that would fit better with the Timothy born in 1744.

Joseph Holt graduated from Harvard in 1739 and was schoolmaster in Andover. He participated in the expedition to Canada in 1758 and kept a journal of his experiences. Joseph and his wife Mary Russell moved to Wilton about 1765 where Joseph was a teacher and owned a mill. He also served as selectman.[661]

Joseph Holt served in the company of Capt. Ebenezer Jones during the expedition to Canada. His journal recounts details of the expedition including number of miles marched per day and locations on the march. The full journal is published in *The New England Historical and Genealogical Register*.[662]

Joseph Holt and Dorothy Johnson were parents of five children.

1019) i JOSEPH HOLT, b. at Andover, 28 Sep 1745; m. BETTY DALE, b. at Wilton, 2 Oct 1746 daughter of John and Mary (Ellinwood) Dale; Betty d. 10 Aug 1821.

ii RHODA HOLT, b. at Rumford, 17 Jul 1749; died young.

464) iii DOROTHY "DOLLY" HOLT, b. at Andover, 1 Oct 1751; d. at Andover, 25 Jul 1815; m. 26 Nov 1767, her second cousin, BENJAMIN FARNUM (*Timothy Farnum*[4], *Ephraim Farnum*[3], *Elizabeth Holt Farnum*[2], *Nicholas*[1]), b. at Andover, 16 Dec 1746 son of Timothy and Dinah (Ingalls) Farnum; Benjamin d. at Andover, 4 Dec 1833.

1020) iv SIMEON HOLT, b. at Andover, 22 May 1752; d. at Weld, ME, 24 Feb 1833; m. 22 Sep 1778, MARY DALE, b. at Wilton, 26 Sep 1754 daughter of John and Mary (Ellinwood) Dale; Mary d. at Weld, 29 Jan 1837.

v RHODA HOLT, b. at Andover, 30 Dec 1753; d. 8 Jun 1755.

Mary Russell and Joseph Holt were parents of eight children.

1021) i MARY HOLT, b. at Andover, 24 Nov 1755; d. at Wilton, 24 Oct 1844; m. 18 Nov 1779, EDWARD HERRICK, b. at Methuen, 9 Oct 1754 son of Edward and Mary (Kimball) Herrick; Edward d. 5 Feb 1811.

1022) ii RHODA HOLT, b. at Andover, 16 Oct 1757; d. at Wilton, 25 Jul 1799, m. 25 Nov 1778, JOHN DALE, b. 26 Jul 1748 son of John and Mary (Ellinwood) Dale; John d. at Wilton, 11 Jul 1809. After Rhoda's death, John married Lydia Lamon.

iii ESTHER HOLT, b. at Andover, 22 Mar 1760; died young, reported to have drowned.

iv Twin1 b. and d. 16 Aug 1762.

v Twin2 b. and d. 16 Aug 1762.

1023) vi VALENTINE HOLT, b. recorded at Wilton, 25 Dec 1763 and baptized at Andover 1 Jan 1764; d. at Mercer, ME, 6 Dec 1840; m. at Wilton, 13 Sep 1787, ANNA "NANCY" GOODRICH whose parents have not been identified. Nancy likely died before 1810. Valentine married second HANNAH DAY, b. about 1792. Hannah d. after 1860 when she was living with her son in Augusta, Maine.

vii JOSHUA HOLT, b. at Andover, 5 Nov 1765; nothing further known.

1024) viii ESTHER HOLT, b. at Wilton, 25 Jul 1766; d. at Lyndeborough, 14 Jul 1839; m. about 1791, EBENEZER PEARSON, b. at Reading, MA, 19 Jun 1768 son of Amos and Elizabeth (Nichols) Pearson; Ebenezer d. at Lyndeborough, 22 May 1852.

253) PHEBE HOLT (*Timothy*[3], *James*[2], *Nicholas*[1]), b. at Andover, 1 Jun 1722 daughter of Timothy and Rhoda (Chandler) Holt; d. at Tewksbury, 15 Jan 1779;[663] m. 1st 11 Feb 1742, FRANCIS PHELPS, b. at Andover, 11 Jan 1720 son of Samuel and Hannah (Dane) Phelps; Francis d. at Pepperell, 1758 (probate 1758). Phebe m. 2nd at Tewksbury, 8 Aug 1771, THOMAS MARSHALL.

Francis Phelps was a farmer, and the family was in Hollis for the births of their four children, but they later were in Pepperell. On 27 May 1756 (recorded 10 October 1763), Francis Phelps then of Hollis purchased a 30-acre tract of land in Pepperell from Robert Conant and John Conant for £130.6.8.[664]

Francis Phelps did not leave a will and his estate entered probate 15 April 1758.[665] Real estate was valued at £125 and personal estate at £133.2.10. The estate distribution included the set-off to widow Phebe and distribution of the real estate to eldest son Timothy, second son Joseph, and only daughter Phebe.

---

661 Livermore, *History of Wilton*, p 405

662 "Journals of Joseph Holt, of Wilton, N.H.", NEHGR, volume 10, 1856, pp 307-310

663 Phebe, wid. [Thomas, formerly w. Francis Phelps of Pepperell. G. R. 1; apoplexy, C. R. 1.], Jan. 15, 1779, in her 57th y.

664 Massachusetts Land Records, Middlesex County, 61:183

665 *Probate Records 1648--1924 (Middlesex County, Massachusetts)*; Author: *Massachusetts. Probate Court (Middlesex County), Probate Papers, No 17249-17365, Case 17267*

Phebe Holt and Francis Phelps were parents of four children born at Hollis, New Hampshire although the births are recorded at Hollis and in the town records at Tewksbury.

i FRANCIS PHELPS, b. at Hollis, 15 Aug 1743; died young.

1025) ii TIMOTHY PHELPS, b. at Hollis, 10 Sep 1745; d. at Shirley, MA, 26 Dec 1826; m. at Harvard, MA, 28 Jun 1768, SARAH FARNSWORTH, b. 1746; Sarah d. at Shirley, 12 Jul 1827.

1026) iii JOSEPH PHELPS, b. at Hollis, 19 Jun 1748; d. at Danvers, MA, 22 May 1835;[666] m. 1st at Tewksbury, 7 Mar 1771, RUTH FRENCH, b. at Andover, 4 May 1747 daughter of John and Phebe (Marshall) French; Ruth d. at Tewksbury, 4 May 1789. Joseph m. 2nd at Tewksbury, 28 Dec 1790, ISABEL DUTTON, b. at Tewksbury, 28 Jul 1762 daughter of Timothy and Elizabeth (Sanders) Dutton; Isabel d. at Tewksbury, 20 Mar 1824.

iv PHEBE PHELPS, b. at Hollis, 6 May 1750; d. at Tewksbury, 16 Feb 1794; m. at Tewksbury, 1 Apr 1773, JACOB FOSTER. Phebe and Jacob did not have children.

254) JOSEPH HOLT (*Joseph³, James², Nicholas¹*), b. at York, 27 Aug 1710 son of Joseph and Mary (Harmon) Holt; d. at York, 1784 (probate 11 Jun 1784); m. his second cousin once removed, MARY FARNUM (*Ralph Farnum⁴, Ralph Farnum³, Elizabeth Holt Farnum², Nicholas¹*), b. at York, 14 May 1717 daughter of Ralph and Elizabeth (Austin) Farnum; Mary d. about 1747. Joseph had a second marriage to JERUSHA HARMON (widow of Rev. Edward Pell), b. at York, 6 Mar 1716 daughter of John and Mehitable (Parker) Harmon;[667] Jerusha was living in Berwick, ME in 1798.

Joseph was a farmer in York. He did not leave a will and his estate entered probate 11 June 1784 with widow Jerusha Holt and Nicholas Sewall (a son-in-law) as administrators.[668] The total value of the estate was £893.2.8. This included 144 acres of the estate of the late Elder Joseph Holt valued at £567 but with various incumbrances and the so-called Whitney farm valued at £145 but under mortgage. The debts of the estate resulted in the estate being declared insolvent. Claims against the estate included a claim by son Ebenezer Holt for £106.15.10. The dower was set off the widow Jerusha in 1790.

Joseph Holt and Mary Farnum were parents of nine children born at York.[669]

i MARY HOLT, b. 8 Sep 1731; d. 19 Dec 1735.

ii SARAH HOLT, b. 6 Dec 1732; d. 26 Jul 1735.

iii TIMOTHY HOLT, b. 16 May 1734

iv JOSEPH HOLT, b. at York, 18 Jun 1735. Durrie's Holt Genealogy reports Joseph married Ruth Valpey in 1775 but no other information was located.

1027) v DORCAS HOLT, b. at York, 10 Apr 1737; d. at Georgetown, ME, 2 Feb 1827; m. at York, 1 Sep 1755, THOMAS DONNELL, b. at York, 29 Jul 1731 son of Nathaniel and Elizabeth (Todd) Donnell.

vi ABIGAIL HOLT, b. 29 Apr 1738

vii MIRIAM HOLT, b. at York, 23 Dec 1740; d. at York, 1811; m. at York, 1 Jan 1763, NICHOLAS SEWALL, b. at York, 17 Jan 1737/8 son of Samuel and Hannah (Kelley) Sewall; Nicholas d. at York, 17 Mar 1806. Miriam and Nicholas had two children neither of whom married. Polly was born 20 Jul 1763 and died 21 Dec 1855.[670] In 1850, Polly Sewall was living at the poorhouse in York described as insane.[671] Son John was born 12 Apr 1767 and also reported to be insane.[672]

1028) viii EBENEZER HOLT, b. at York, 29 Dec 1745; m. at York, 14 Feb 1767, CHARITY RHOADS daughter of Miles Rhoads.

ix DEBORAH HOLT, b. at York, about 1747.[673] Durrie reports Deborah married "David Eards." There is a Deborah Holt that married David Eames in Woburn in 1770, but they were both of Woburn so that may not be her. Nothing further definitive is known.

---

666 Phelps, *The Phelps Family in America*, volume 2, p 1610

667 Farnham, *Descendants of Ralph Farnum*, p 194

668 Maine, York County, Probate Estate Files, Case 9644, Estate of Joseph Holt, [Holt, J through Hooper, R]; accessed through familysearch.org

669 NEHGR, Vital Records of York, Maine, volume 111 (1957), p 25

670 Sinnett, *Sewall Genealogy*, p 58

671 *1850 United States Federal Census*, Year: 1850; Census Place: York, York, Maine; Roll: M432_274; Page: 231B; Image: 457.

672 Durrie, *Holt Genealogy*, p 129

673 Deborah is listed with the children of Joseph and Mary in the Vital Records of York, Maine, but the birth date is blank.

255) JAMES HOLT (*Joseph³, James², Nicholas¹*), b. at York, 17 Jul 1716 son of Joseph and Mary (Harmon) Holt; d. about 1742; m. about 1737, ALICE MOULTON, b. at Portsmouth, NH, 4 Jun 1715 daughter of Joseph and Abigail (Ayers) Moulton.

The 1758 will of James's father Joseph Holt included bequests to the two children of James, Samuel and Dorcas. No further information was found for these children.

i SAMUEL HOLT, b. at Portsmouth, 16 Nov 1738;[674] living in 1758.

ii DORCAS HOLT, b. at York, 18 Oct 1740; living in 1758.

256) BENJAMIN HOLT (*Joseph³, James², Nicholas¹*), b. at York, 13 Jan 1717/8 son of Joseph and Mary (Harmon) Holt; d. at York, 19 Aug 1772; m. at York, 28 Feb 1740, HANNAH MOULTON, b. at Portsmouth, NH, 7 Feb 1720 daughter of Jeremiah and Hannah (Ballard) Moulton. Hannah married second Samuel Moulton.

Benjamin Holt did not leave a will and his estate was administered by Joseph Holt, Jr. (perhaps his brother). Both Hannah Holt and Daniel Holt declined administration of the estate on 7 January 1773. The estate was insolvent. In 1789, the dower was set-off to widow Hannah, now Hannah Moulton the wife of Samuel Moulton. In 1789, it was noted that Daniel was now deceased and had a widow Sarah.[675]

Benjamin and Hannah were parents of twelve children born at York.

i DANIEL HOLT, b. at York, 23 Oct 1742; d. at York, 1788 (probate 2 Dec 1788); m. SARAH who is not yet identified but may be Sarah Pell daughter of Edward and Jerusha (Harmon) Pell. Captain Daniel Holt was a mariner. His estate was insolvent.[676] Widow Sarah administered the estate. No children are mentioned in the probate. The 1808 will of widow Sarah Holt of York (which is perhaps the will of Daniel's widow) has bequests to her brother John Pell, to Sarah Pell Moulton whose relationship is not given, and to the widow Else Moulton. (York County Case 9646)

ii BENJAMIN HOLT, b. 18 May 1744; d. 29 Jul 1744.

iii BENJAMIN HOLT, b. 20 May 1745; d. Dec 1745.

1029) iv HANNAH HOLT, b. 9 Oct 1746; m. at York, 19 Oct 1765, her first cousin, NATHANIEL RAYNES (*Hannah Holt Raynes⁴, Joseph³, James², Nicholas¹*), b. at York, about 1740 son of Nathan and Hannah (Holt) Raynes; Nathaniel d. at York, 1802 (probate 18 Oct 1802).

v JOSEPH HOLT, b. 15 Nov 1748

vi JAMES HOLT, b. 16 Oct 1750

vii JEREMIAH HOLT, b. 18 May 1752

viii MARY HOLT, b. at York, 27 Oct 1754; m. at York, 12 Jan 1776, JOSEPH JACOBS. Nothing further known.

1030) ix DORCAS HOLT, b. at York, 21 Nov 1756; d. about 1793; m. 8 Feb 1776, DANIEL MOULTON, b. at York, 31 Mar 1755 son of Abel and Judith (-) Moulton; Daniel d. at York, 1836 (probate Sep 1836). Daniel married second, Abigail Young.

x JOHN BALLARD HOLT, b. 19 Jul 1758; d. 12 Sep 1758.

xi ABIGAIL HOLT, b. at York, 24 Jul 1759; m. at York, 29 Mar 1783, JAMES GRANT, b. about 1754 son of Peter and Alice (Guptail) Grant; James d. at South Berwick, 31 May 1841. No children were identified for Abigail and James.

xii LYDIA HOLT, b. 14 Jul 1761; d. 27 Dec 1761.

257) HANNAH HOLT (*Joseph³, James², Nicholas¹*), b. at York, 4 Apr 1719 daughter of Joseph and Mary (Harmon) Holt; m. at York, 8 May 1740, NATHAN RAYNES, b. at York, 9 Jun 1712 son of Nathan and Elizabeth (Payne) Raynes; Nathan d. at York, 1774 (probate 10 Dec 1774).

Hannah and Nathan resided in York where Nathan was listed as a member of the town militia in 1757.[677]

In his will written 1 January 1772 (proved 10 December 1774), Nathan Raynes bequeaths to beloved wife Hannah, in addition to her rights of dower, one-half of the personal estate except for the "yoak chains and utensills of husbandry." Only daughter Dorcas wife of George Moore receives £20 which with what she received at marriage is her full portion. Only son Nathaniel receives all the real estate and is named sole executor.[678]

---

674 NEHGR, Vital Records of York, Maine

675 Maine, York County, Probate Estate Files, 1690-1917, Case 9641, Estate of Benjamin Holt, accessed through familysearch.org

676 Maine, York County, Probate Estate Files, 1690-1917, Case 9642, Estate of Daniel Holt, accessed through familysearch.org

677 Banks, *History of York Maine*, volume II, p 215

678 Maine, York County, Probate Estate Files, 1690-1917, Case 15708, Estate of Nathan Raynes, accessed through familysearch.org

Hannah Holt and Nathan Raynes were parents of two children born at York.

1029) i NATHANIEL RAYNES, b. at York, 1740; d. at York, 1802 (probate 18 Oct 1802); m. at York, 19 Oct 1765, his first cousin, HANNAH HOLT (*Benjamin⁴, Joseph³, James², Nicholas¹*), b. at York, 9 oct 1746 daughter of Benjamin and Hannah (Moulton) Holt.

1031) ii DORCAS RAYNES, b. at York, about 1741; d. at York, 13 Oct 1828; m. at York, 25 Nov 1760, GEORGE MOORE; George d. at York, 1816 (probate 16 May 1816).

258) LYDIA HOLT (*Joseph³, James², Nicholas¹*), b. at York, 23 Oct 1723 daughter of Joseph and Mary (Harmon) Holt; m. at York, 17 Apr 1742, EDWARD INGRAHAM, b. about 1720 son of Moses Ingraham.[679]

Edward was an innholder in York having taken over the inn from his father Moses who established the inn about 1730.[680]

Lydia Holt and Edward Ingraham were parents of eight children born at York.

i WILLIAM INGRAHAM, b. 25 Mar 1742

1032) ii ELIZABETH INGRAHAM, b. at York, 6 Aug 1743; m. at York, 26 Jan 1764, JOHN BRADBURY, b. at York, 18 Sep 1736 son of John and Abigail (Young) Bradbury; John d. at York, 1821.

iii EDWARD INGRAHAM, b. at York, 11 Jan 1746; m. at York, 21 Jun 1766, ELIZABETH JOHNSON. No further information was located for this family.

1033) iv LYDIA INGRAHAM, b. 28 Mar 1749; d. at York, 1 Dec 1824; m. 1767, ESAIAS PREBLE, b. at York, 28 May 1742 son of Samuel and Sarah (Muchmore) Preble.

1034) v JOSEPH HOLT INGRAHAM, b. at York, 10 Feb 1752; d. at Portland, ME, 4 Nov 1841; m. 1st, about 1775, ABIGAIL MILK daughter of James and Sarah (Brown) Milk;[681] Abigail d. at Portland, 17 May 1785. Joseph m. 2nd at Portland 2 Dec 1786, LYDIA STONE, b. at York, 20 Nov 1759 daughter of Benjamin and Rebecca (Littlefield) Stone; Lydia d. about 1788. Joseph m. 3rd at Portland, 26 Jul 1789, ANN TATE, b. 18 Mar 1767 daughter of Samuel and Elizabeth (-) Tate;[682] Ann d. at Portland, 27 Mar 1844.

1035) vi MARY "MOLLEY" INGRAHAM, b. at York, 14 May 1755; d. at Chesterville, ME, 28 Mar 1814; m. at York, 20 Apr 1776, JOHN WHEELER, b. 1750 perhaps in England; John d. at Wilton, ME, 23 Apr 1843.

vii RUTH INGRAHAM, b. 22 Oct 1758

1036) viii WILLIAM INGRAHAM, b. at York, 25 Sep 1761; d. at Portland, 15 Jun 1815; m. at Portland, 2 Nov 1784, SARAH TUKEY, b. at Portland, 6 Apr 1763 daughter of John and Abigail (Sweetser) Tukey; Sarah d. at Portland, 24 Sep 1803.

259) REBEKAH GROW (*Rebekah Holt Grow³, James², Nicholas¹*), b. at Andover, 21 Apr 1712 daughter of Thomas and Rebekah (Holt) Grow; d. at Pomfret, 30 Jan 1762; m. at Pomfret, 16 Jan 1734, STEPHEN INGALLS, b. at Andover, 24 Jul 1710 son of John and Sarah (Russell) Ingalls; Stephen d. at Pomfret 10 Dec 1771.

At the settlement of Stephen Ingalls's estate, the widow Mary Ingalls and the four surviving children reach an amicable agreement of the division of the estate. The children listed and agreeing to the division are sons Thomas Ingalls and Samuel Ingalls, daughter Sarah Copeland wife of James Copeland, and daughter Ruth Ingalls.[683] Real estate was valued at £167.15.0.

Rebekah and Stephen were parents of five children born at Pomfret. Son Stephen died one week before his father.

1037) i SARAH INGALLS, b. at Pomfret, 7 Nov 1735; m. at Pomfret, 26 Feb 1756, JAMES COPELAND, b. at Braintree, MA, 19 Mar 1724 son of William and Mary (Thayer) Copeland.[684]

ii STEPHEN INGALLS, b. 13 Dec 1737; d. at Pomfret, 2 Dec 1771.[685]

---

679 Son Edward Ingraham was administrator of his father Moses Ingraham's estate in 1747 in York; York County Estate Files 10110

680 Banks, *History of York Maine*, volume II, p 324

681 Willis, *The History of Portland*, p 431

682 Willis, *The History of Portland*, p 841

683 *Connecticut State Library (Hartford, Connecticut);* Probate Place: *Hartford, Connecticut, Probate Packets, Humphrey, M-Johnson, H, 1752-1880,*

684 Copeland, *The Copeland Family*, p 34

685 Stephen is not known to have married. The Ingalls genealogy suggests he might have had a wife Rebecca and lists several children of a Rebecca who died at Pomfret. However, in each case the children listed in the Ingalls book are listed as the children of Ephraim and Mary Ingalls in the Barbour Collection.

iii RUTH INGALLS, b. at Pomfret, 27 Jan 1739/40; d. at Pomfret, 1 Sep 1819. Ruth did not marry.

1038) iv THOMAS INGALLS, b. at Pomfret, 9 Dec 1742; d. at Abington, CT, 10 Jan 1816; m. 1st at Pomfret, 26 Jun 1777, SARAH BOWEN, b. about 1749; Sarah d. at Pomfret, 6 Oct 1777. Thomas m. 2nd 8 Nov 1786, RUTH WOODWORTH; Ruth d. at Pomfret, 12 Apr 1827.

1039) v SAMUEL INGALLS, b. at Pomfret, 22 Apr 1746; m. at Brooklyn, CT, 9 Nov 1769, DEBORAH MEACHAM, b. at Windham, 3 Nov 1749 daughter of Daniel and Lydia (Lillie) Meacham.

260) THOMAS GROW (*Rebekah Holt Grow3, James2, Nicholas1*), b. at Andover, 7 Nov 1714 son of Thomas and Rebekah (Holt) Grow; d. at Guilford, VT, 10 Aug 1806; m. at Pomfret, 26 Jan 1738/9, SUSANNA EATON, b. Apr 1715 daughter of Jonathan and Lydia (Starr) Eaton;[686] Susanna d. at Pomfret, 17 May 1786. Thomas m. 2nd at Hampton, 10 Nov 1786, MARTHA WINTER.

Thomas was about age sixteen when he came to Pomfret with his family. Thomas married in Pomfret and the family was well-established there, Thomas being a well-regarded deacon of the Baptist church.[687] Later in life, Thomas went to Guilford, Vermont.

In his will written 26 August 1794 at Guilford, Vermont (proved 26 August 1806), Thomas Grow bequeathed to beloved wife Martha a right in the dwelling house while she is a widow and other provisions for her support. Daughter Rebecca Jacobs receives £4; son Thomas, £60; daughter Lydia Way, £10; daughter Hannah Ransom, £4; son William, £8; son Nathaniel, £20 and the livestock from the farm; and son Ebenezer, £80. Books are to be equally divided among the children. Son Nathaniel is named executor.[688]

Thomas and Susanna were parents of nine children born at Pomfret.

1040) i REBEKAH GROW, b. at Pomfret, 16 Oct 1738; d. after 1801; m. at Pomfret, 3 Jun 1773, as his second wife, Rev. WHITMAN JACOBS, b. at Bristol, 3 May 1727 son of Nathaniel and Mary (Whitman) Jacobs; Whitman d. at Royalston, MA, 28 Mar 1801. Whitman was first married to Rebecca Rice.

ii SUSANNA GROW, b. 14 Nov 1740; d. 6 Oct 1749.

1041) iii THOMAS GROW, b. at Pomfret, 4 Apr 1743; d. at Hampton, 5 Jun 1824; m. 1st at Pomfret, 4 Jun 1767, EXPERIENCE GOODALE,[689] b. at Pomfret, 23 Apr 1747 daughter of Ebenezer and Experience (Lyon) Goodale; Experience d. at Hampton, 9 Feb 1811. Thomas m. 2nd at Hampton, 18 Aug 1811, SARAH HYDE who may have been a widow and has not been identified; Sarah d. at Hampton, 26 Dec 1819. Thomas m. 3rd at Providence, 12 Mar 1820, EXPERIENCE ABBOTT, b. at Pomfret, 21 Jan 1756 daughter of Nathan and Eunice (Marsh) Abbott; Experience d. at Hampton, 20 Apr 1835.[690]

iv LYDIA GROW, b. at Pomfret, 25 Mar 1745; m. Mr. Way who has not been identified, but perhaps Ebenezer Way who settled in Vermont. Lydia is not mentioned as an heir in the settlement of her brother Ebenezer's estate so is assumed to have died before 1827 and without children.

1042) v HANNAH GROW, b. at Pomfret, 14 Apr 1747; m. about 1777, ELISHA RANSOM, b. at Lyme, CT, 6 Feb 1746 son of Matthew and Sarah (Way) Ransom; Elisha d. at Plymouth, NY, 17 Aug 1818.

1043) vi WILLIAM GROW, b. at Pomfret, 8 Apr 1749; d. at Bridgewater, VT, 7 May 1830; m. at Windham, 30 May 1776, PRISCILLA MORSE, b. about 1752; Priscilla d. at Bridgewater, 1841.

vii TIMOTHY GROW, b. 20 Apr 1751; d. 19 Aug 1756.

1044) viii NATHANIEL GROW, b. at Pomfret, 29 May 1753; d. at Henderson, NY, 9 Jul 1838; m. at Pomfret, 16 Jan 1775, SUSANNA DOW, b. about 1752; Susanna d. at Henderson, 31 Jul 1814.

ix EBENEZER GROW, b. at Pomfret, 10 Nov 1755; d. at Hampton, 31 Oct 1827; m. CATHERINE WILLIAMS, b. at Pomfret, 16 Mar 16 Mar 1747/8 daughter of Samuel and Sarah (Paine) Williams; Catherine d. at Hampton, 22 Dec 1829. Ebenezer and Catherine do not seem to have had children. Their estates settlements are in the same file listed as Ebenezer and Catherine Grow. The distribution included heirs of Stephen Williams, heirs of Sarah Caller, heirs of Esther Chapman, and heirs of Ruth Capron who are the siblings of Catherine. The heirs of Ebenezer were listed as widow Catherine Grow (Ebenezer died before

686 Jordan, *Genealogical and Personal History of the Alleghany Valley*, volume 1, p 144

687 Larned, *History of Windham County Connecticut*, p 246

688 Ancestry.com. *Vermont, Wills and Probate Records, 1749-1999* [database on-line]. Provo, UT, USA, *Vermont. Probate Court (Marlboro District)*; Probate Place: *Windham, Vermont, volume 3, pp 243-245, Will of Thomas Grow*

689 There are two marriage transcriptions for Experience's marriage to Thomas in 1767. Early Connecticut Marriages Book I gives spouse as Thomas Grow, Jr. and the Barbour collection gives spouse as Thomas Grosvenor.

690 Grow, Experience, relict of Thomas Grow, died Dec. 20, 1835, age 80.

Catherine), heirs of William Grow, heirs of Thomas Grow, Nathaniel Grow, heirs of Rebecca Jacobs, and heirs of Hannah Ransom.

261) JOSEPH GROW (*Rebekah Holt Grow[3], James[2], Nicholas[1]*), b. at Andover, 16 Oct 1717 son of Thomas and Rebekah (Holt) Grow; d. at Newbury, VT, 3 May 1782; m. at Pomfret, 4 Feb 1741/2, ABIGAIL DANA, b. Apr 1722 daughter of Samuel and Susanna (Starr) Dana.

Joseph and Abigail were residents of Pomfret but relocated to Hartland, Vermont about 1779.[691][692] The family was in Hartland and Newbury.

Joseph and Abigail were parents of twelve children born at Pomfret.

i JOHN GROW, b. 2 Jul 1743; d. 14 Jul 1743.

ii JOSEPH GROW, b.25 Apr 1744; d. 25 Apr 1744.

1045) iii PRISCILLA GROW, b. at Pomfret, 28 Nov 1746; d. at Tolland, 14 Feb 1818; m. at Pomfret, 25 Nov 1765, THOMAS HOWARD, b. at Ipswich, 5 Sep 1742 son of Hezekiah and Sarah (Newman) Howard; Thomas d. at Tolland, 18 Oct 1805.

1046) iv JOSEPH GROW, b. at Pomfret, 13 Mar 1748; d. at Hartland, VT, 19 Mar 1813; m. 13 Dec 1770, TIRZAH SANGER, b. at Woodstock, 19 Dec 1748; d. at Hartland, about 1825.

1047) v JOHN GROW, b. at Pomfret, 9 May1750; d. at Penfield, NY, 1834; m. at Woodstock, 22 Jun 1772, DEBORAH DAVISON, b. at Mansfield, CT, 17 May 1750 daughter of Paul and Deborah (Wright) Davison; Deborah d. at Penfield, 6 Apr 1831.

1048) vi ABIGAIL GROW, b. at Pomfret, 3 Nov 1752; m. at Mansfield, CT, 20 Mar 1777, ISAAC ROYCE, b. at Mansfield, 1 Jul 1750 son of David and Hannah (Hall) Royce.

1049) vii SAMUEL GROW, b. at Pomfret, 19 Jan 1755; d. at Newbury, VT, 18 May 1842; m. about 1785, DAMARIS POWERS, b. at Lisbon, CT, 8 Jan 1761 daughter of Peter and Martha (Hale) Powers; Damaris d. at Newbury, VT, 22 Aug 1836.

1050) viii AMBROSE GROW, b. at Pomfret, 27 Jul 1756; d. at Fabius, NY, 12 Jul 1845; m. 1st at Mansfield, 18 May 1780, JEMIMA ELDRIDGE. Ambrose m. 2nd at Russell, MA, 5 Apr 1810, AMY PARSONS, b. at Springfield, MA, 20 Nov 1779 daughter of Daniel and Sarah (Ferry) Parsons; Amy d. at Fabius, after 1860. Amy was first married to Mr. Thomas.

ix ASA GROW, b. and d. 1759.

x ASA GROW, b. 25 Feb 1761; d. 13 Oct 1763.

1051) xi MARY GROW, b. at Pomfret, 8 Feb 1764; d. at West Newbury, VT, 1 Apr 1843; m. 12 Feb 1786, STEPHEN POWERS, b. at Lisbon, CT, 15 Jul 1762 son of Peter and Martha (Hale) Powers; Stephen d. at West Newbury, 22 Mar 1843.

1052) xii ANNA GROW, b. at Pomfret, 1767; d. at Newbury, VT, 16 Jun 1789; m. at Newbury, 14 Feb 1788, SAMUEL POWERS, b. about 1767 son of Peter and Martha (Hale) Powers; Samuel d. at Newbury, 21 Jan 1857.

262) RUTH GROW (*Rebekah Holt Grow[3], James[2], Nicholas[1]*), b. at Andover, 2 Aug 1720 daughter of Thomas and Rebekah (Holt) Grow; d. at Amherst, MA, after 1781; m. at Pomfret, 4 Nov 1740, JOSEPH WILLIAMS likely the son of Joseph and Mary (Goad) Williams; Joseph d. at Amherst, MA, 1781 (probate 1781).

After the births of their children in Woodstock, Ruth and Joseph were in Amherst, Massachusetts by 1766 where Joseph was a farmer and miller. Joseph served as selectman in Amherst from 1776 to 1778 and moderated the town meeting in 1779.[693]

In his will written 19 July 1781 (proved 6 November 1781), Joseph Williams bequeathed to his beloved wife Ruth the household furniture and the use of the south room in the dwelling house. Four daughters receive five shillings each: Hannah Smith, Mary Moody, Rebeckah Stimpson, and Sarah May. Daughter Ruth Dana has a bequest of thirty shillings which is crossed out. Son Ambrose Williams receives the whole of the land contained in the farm where Joseph, Sr. now lives. Son Joseph receives the land in New Pomfret, Vermont. Joseph also receives a cow when he is of lawful age and some tools. Son Ambrose is named executor.[694]

---

[691] Wells, *History of Newbury, Vermont*, p 562

[692] Dana, *The Dana Family in America*, p 57

[693] NEHGS, The Corbin Collection, volume 1, Records of Hampshire Co., MA.

[694] *Hampshire County, MA: Probate File Papers, 1660-1889.* Online database. *AmericanAncestors.org.* New England Historic Genealogical Society, 2016, 2017. Case 161-41

Ruth and Joseph were parents of ten children born at Woodstock. Three of the children, Rebecca, Ambrose, and Sarah, located in Monson after their marriages.

i HANNAH WILLIAMS, b. at Woodstock, 16 Dec 1741; m. at Amherst, MA, about 1766, CALEB SMITH who has not been identified. Not children were located to Hannah and Caleb.

ii JOSEPH WILLIAMS, b. about 1743; d. at Woodstock, 24 Nov 1760.

1053) iii MARY WILLIAMS, b. at Woodstock, 30 May 1745; d. at Amherst, MA, 27 May 1785; m. at Amherst, about 1768, LEMUEL MOODY, b. at Hadley, MA, 27 Jun 1739 son of Jonathan and Bridget (Smith) Moody; Lemuel d. at Amherst, 22 Feb 1818.

iv REBEKAH WILLIAMS, b. 20 Feb 1747; d. 18 Nov 1748.

1054) v REBEKAH WILLIAMS, baptized at Woodstock, 19 Mar 1748/9; d. at Monson, MA, Aug 1823; m. at Amherst, MA, about 1770, JOSEPH STIMSON, b. at Tolland, 12 Jan 1746/7 son of Ichabod and Margaret (Peck) Stimson; Joseph d. at Monson, 1 Jul 1810.

1055) vi SARAH WILLIAMS, baptized at Woodstock, 6 Jan 1751; d. at Homer, NY, Jul 1808; m. at Amherst, MA, by 1776, WILLIAM MAY, b. at Roxbury, MA, 21 Oct 1740 son of Eleazer and Dorothy (Davis) May; William d. at Homer, 22 Oct 1812.

1056) vii RUTH WILLIAMS, b. at Woodstock, 24 Sep 1752; d. at Amherst, MA, 16 Apr 1822; m. at Amherst, 5 Oct 1780, as his second wife, AMARIAH DANA, b. at Pomfret, 20 May 1738 son of Samuel and Mary (Sumner) Dana; Amariah d. at Amherst, 5 Oct 1830. Amariah was first married to Dorothy May who was the sister of William May who married Ruth's sister Sarah.

viii THOMAS WILLIAMS, b. 25 Jan 1754; not in father's will.

1057) ix AMBROSE WILLIAMS, b. at Woodstock, 24 Jul 1757; d. at Homer, NY, 13 Aug 1832; m. KETURAH HOAR, b. at Brimfield, 22 Aug 1755 daughter of Edmund and Hannah (Alexander) Hoar; Keturah d. at Homer, 21 May 1826.

x JOSEPH WILLIAMS, b. likely at Woodstock, about 1762. Joseph was living in 1781 and inherited land in New Pomfret, Vermont but further record of him was not located.

263) HANNAH GROW (*Rebekah Holt Grow*[3], *James*[2], *Nicholas*[1]), b. at Andover, 8 Nov 1723 daughter of Thomas and Rebekah (Holt) Grow; d. at Windham, 29 Jul 1765; m. at Pomfret, 27 Feb 1752, EPHRAIM BARKER, b. at Andover, 23 May 1730 son of William and Martha (Ingalls) Barker. Ephraim married second the widow Mary Burnham at Norwich, 21 Dec 1767.

Hannah Grow and Ephraim Barker were parents of six children.

1058) i WILLIAM BARKER, b. at Pomfret, 18 Nov 1753; d. at Madison, NY, 17 May 1826; m. about 1782, BETSEY ARMSTRONG, baptized at Norwich, 30 May 1762 daughter of Silas and Bathsheba (Worden) Armstrong;[695] Betsey d. at Madison, 29 Aug 1832.[696]

1059) ii HANNAH BARKER, baptized at Pomfret 29 Aug 1754; d. at Norwich, 1840; m. at Norwich, 20 Jan 1771, ELIJAH PITCHER,[697] b. likely at Stoughton, MA, 4 Nov 1752 son of Elijah and Tabitha (Smith) Pitcher; Elijah d. at Norwich, 14 Jun 1839.

1060) iii JOHN BARKER, b. at Pomfret, 18 Dec 1755; d. at Stoddard, NH, 15 Mar 1834; m. 1st 1786, ESTHER RICHARDSON, b. at Leominster, 9 Mar 1767 daughter of James and Hannah (House) Richardson; Esther d. at Stoddard, 17 Jul 1806. John m. 2nd 4 Dec 1806, SALLY GUILD (widow of Daniel Warner), b. at Newton, MA, 31 Jul 1775 daughter of Samuel and Sarah (Smith) Guild;[698] Sally d. at Stoddard, 19 Jan 1843.

---

[695] The 1798 will of Silas Armstrong includes a bequest to his daughter Betty wife of William Barker.

[696] Parshall's Barker genealogy provided limited information on William but included that he had married and located in Madison, NY. William and Betsey Barker had all their children in Norwich, so this marriage fits in terms of location. There is also a Revolutionary War pension file for William Barker in Madison, NY that fits this William in terms of age and location at time of enlistment.

[697] This is a supposed marriage for Hannah. The family was living in Norwich at the time of Hannah's marriage and this marriage fits for her in terms of age and location. There were not records located that firmly establish that this Hannah married Elijah Pitcher.

[698] Burleigh, *The History and Genealogy of the Guild Family*, p 45

1061) iv EPHRAIM BARKER, b. at Pomfret, 28 Feb 1759. He may be the Ephraim Barker who married at Wayland, MA, 27 Mar 1783, RUTH GOODNOW,[699] b. at Wayland, 18 Oct 1757 daughter of Silas and Jerusha (Willis) Goodnow. The Ephraim that married Ruth abandoned his family sometime between 1800 and 1805 described as "absconded to parts unknown" in a probate file for Ruth's aunt Mary Willis. Ruth Barker was listed as the head of household from 1810 on. Ruth died at Sudbury, 27 Jan 1843. Ruth inherited her aunt Mary's estate and beginning in 1813 sold off portions of the land every few years listing herself as a "free agent" in the deeds.

1062) v NATHAN BARKER, b. at Pomfret, 8 Jun 1761; d. at Palmer, MA, 10 Oct 1849; m. 11 Dec 1783, LYDIA BARKER, b. 4 Jun 1763; Lydia d. at Palmer, 2 Dec 1849.

vi Son b. 19 Mar and d. 20 Mar 1763 at Windham.

264) JAMES GROW (*Rebekah Holt Grow*[3], *James*[2], *Nicholas*[1]), b. at Andover, 25 Oct 1727 son of Thomas and Rebekah (Holt) Grow; d. at Norwich, VT, 27 Oct 1799; m. 6 Mar 1754, ANNA ADAMS, b. 9 Jan 1735; Anna d. at Greensboro, VT, 11 Feb 1813.

James and Anna lived in Abington Parish of Pomfret until about 1760 and were then in Monson and Brimfield in Hampden County, Massachusetts before finally making their way to Norwich, Vermont.[700]

In his will written 5 October 1799 (proved 23 November 1799), James Grow bequeathed to beloved wife Anna the improvement of one-third of the real estate, the use of a good horse with saddle and bridle, two cows, and five sheep to be for her sole use during her life. Son Timothy Grow receives $100; son Abisha, $5; and son James, $30. Daughters Susanna Stimpson and Sarah Hatch each receives $15. Son Marvin receives all the real estate and is named executor.[701]

James and Anna were parents of nine children.

1063) i TIMOTHY GROW, b. at Pomfret, 2 May 1755; d. at Hartland, VT, 17 May 1842; m. at Somers, CT, 25 Jan 1781, PHALLE RICHARDSON, b. at Coventry, 6 Jul 1763 son of David and Rachel (Richardson) Richardson; Phalle d. at Hartland, 29 Dec 1828.

ii ANNA GROW, b. at Pomfret, 15 Sep 1757; d. at Monson, 9 Oct 1765.

1064) iii SUSANNA GROW, b. at Pomfret, 16 Jun 1760; d. at Craftsbury, VT, 14 Sep 1841; m. at Tolland, 15 Apr 1779, JOEL STIMSON, b. at Tolland, 31 Jul 1751 son of Ichabod and Margaret (Peck) Stimson; Joel d. at Norwich, 15 Apr 1813.

iv DALINDA GROW, b. 7 Aug 1762; d. 13 Oct 1765.

v SILAS GROW, b. 11 Dec 1764; d. 12 Oct 1765.

1065) vi ABISHA GROW, b. at Monson, 1 Feb 1767; d. at Norwich, 28 Feb 1807; m. at Norwich, 19 Nov 1793, OLIVE PHELPS, b. about 1776; Olive d. at Derby, VT, 25 Aug 1825. Olive married second Abel Wilder on 8 Jan 1809.

1066) vii JAMES GROW, b. at Monson, 23 Jul 1769; d. at Thompson, CT, 17 Mar 1859; m. 1st 1 Jan 1793, ELIZABETH EDMUNDS, b. at Dudley, MA, 22 Sep 1763 daughter of Ebenezer and Hannah (Newell) Edmunds; Elizabeth d. at Thompson, 4 Nov 1835. James m. 2nd 4 Apr 1839, BETSEY TOWNE (widow of Joseph Elliott), b. at Killingly, 19 Aug 1773 daughter of Joseph and Abigail (Thompson) Towne; Betsey d. at Thompson, 8 Dec 1856.[702]

1067) viii SARAH GROW, b. at Monson, 11 Feb 1772; d. at Strafford, VT, 16 Dec 1857; m. 1st by 1799, JOEL HATCH, b. about 1768; Joel d. at Strafford, 24 Nov 1804. Sarah m. 2nd 2 Sep 1805, FREDERICK SMITH, b. at Strafford, 24 Feb 1787 son of Frederick and Sarah (Sloan) Smith; Frederick d. at Strafford, 15 Dec 1867.

1068) ix MARVIN GROW, b. at Monson, 1 Mar 1776; d. at Hardwick, VT, 20 Jan 1851 (will proved 24 Jan 1851); m. at Norwich, 28 Dec 1800, HOPE WHIPPLE, reported on death record as born at Ashford, 3 Oct 1778 perhaps the daughter of Samuel Whipple; Hope d. at Cabot, VT, Mar 1860.

Grandchildren of John Holt and Sarah Geary

699 Parshall, *The Barker Genealogy*, p 7. This Barker genealogy lists a son of this Ephraim, Silas G. Barker, who was the son of Ephraim and Ruth (Goodnow) Barker.

700 Davis, *John Grow of Ipswich*, p 32

701 *Vermont. Probate Court (Hartford District);* Probate Place: *Windsor, Vermont, Probate Records, Vol 1-3 1783-1809, volume 1, pp 202-203*

702 Age at death given as 83 years, 3 months, 20 days.

265) MOSES HOLT (*Moses[3], John[2], Nicholas[1]*), b. at Andover, 21 Oct 1716 son of Moses and Elizabeth (Russell) Holt; d. at Andover, 6 Jul 1743; m. 9 Jul 1741, his first cousin once removed, PRUDENCE RUSSELL (*Robert Russell[4], Phebe Johnson Russell[3], Mary Holt Johnson[2], Nicholas[1]*), baptized at Andover, 31 Jul 1720 daughter of Robert and Abigail (Flint) Russell; Prudence d. at Andover, 15 Nov 1745. Prudence Russell m. 2nd, 11 Mar 1744/5, her first cousin, JOHN CHANDLER (*Mehitable Russell Chandler[4], Phebe Johnson Russell[3], Mary Holt Johnson[2], Nicholas[1]*), b. 17 Andover, 19 Jan 1722 son of Joseph and Mehitable (Russell) Chandler; John d. at Andover, 11 May 1759. John Chandler m. 2nd, at Andover, 15 Oct 1747, HANNAH PHELPS, b. at Andover, 1709 daughter of Samuel and Hannah (Dane) Phelps; Hannah d. at Andover, 5 Aug 1781.

Prudence Russell and John Chandler did not have children. Moses Holt and Prudence Russell were parents of one child.

i PHINEAS HOLT, b. at Andover, 3 Mar 1741/2;[703] d. at Andover, about 1761. In 1756, Phineas made choice of his uncle Joseph Russell for his guardian. In 1761, the estate of Phineas Holt of Andover was in probate with reversion of part of his property to his grandmother Elizabeth Furbush.

John Chandler and Hannah Phelps were parents of three children.

i JOHN CHANDLER, b. 7 Jul 1748; d. 14 Mar 1749.

1069) ii JOHN CHANDLER, b. at Andover, 18 Jul 1750; d. at Princeton, MA, 26 Mar 1832; m. 1st at Lancaster, 29 Feb 1776, KATHARINE "KATY" HOLMAN, b. at Sutton, MA, 23 Mar 1753 daughter of Solomon and Sarah (Waite) Holman, Katy d. at Princeton, 18 Feb 1781. John m. 2nd at Westminster, 1 Jan 1782, MARY JACKSON, b. at Westminster, 11 Sep 1755 daughter of Josiah and Mary (Darby) Jackson; Mary d. at Princeton, 26 Jan 1836.

1070) iii JOSEPH CHANDLER, b. at Andover, 30 Jan 1753; d. at Salem, 27 Nov 1827; m. at Danvers, 12 Nov 1780, DORCAS ABBOTT, b. at Andover, 26 Oct 1755 daughter of Joseph and Anna (Peabody) Abbott; Dorcas d. at Salem, 19 Aug 1821.

---

[703] Phineas, s. Moses and Prudence, Mar. 3, 1741. [Only child. Deposition of wid. Mercy How, midwife, on Sept. 13, 1748.]

Generation Five Families

Great-Grandchildren of Elizabeth Holt and Ralph Farnum

266) BENJAMIN ABBOT (*Benjamin Abbott[4], Sarah Farnum Abbott[3], Elizabeth Holt Farnum[2], Nicholas[1]*), b. at Andover, 21 Oct 1723 son of Benjamin and Mary (Carleton) Abbott; d. at Hollis, NH, 1771;[704] m. 2 Apr 1747, his second cousin, ELIZABETH ABBOTT, b. 5 Nov 1727 daughter of George and Mary (Phillips) Abbott. Elizabeth m. 2nd, 22 Mar 1775, James Pollard.[705] Elizabeth m. 3rd, Josiah Bowers of Billerica who died in 1794. Elizabeth died about 1802 at Westford (date of will 10 Aug 1802). There is a 1790 deed from Josiah Bowers of Billerica to his son Benjamin and named in the deed record is Josiah's wife Elizabeth.[706]

There are records for nine children in this family, the oldest two recorded at Andover and the remainder at Hollis, New Hampshire.

Benjamin Abbot was active in the community of Hollis serving as selectman six times between 1752 and 1761. He also served on several committees and as the moderator of the town meeting in 1759. In 1757, he served in a regiment that participated in the French and Indian War.[707]

Elizabeth Bowers wrote her will at Westford 10 August 1802. Her will has bequests to the following persons: daughter Elizabeth Powers; daughter-in-law Lydia Abbott; granddaughter Betty Wright; Susan daughter of son Samuel Abbott; Abigail Read; and the remainder of the estate divided among "all my children" Benjamin Abbott, George Abbott, Joel Abbott, Jacob Abbott, Elizabeth Powers, and the children of daughter Polly Boynton.[708]

i BENJAMIN ABBOTT, b. 13 Apr 1748; d. 11 Jun 1748

ii BENJAMIN ABBOTT, b. 11 Apr 1749; d. at Hollis about 1838; m. by 1778, SARAH "SALLY" WRIGHT, b. 16 May 1763[709] daughter of Joshua and Abigail (Richardson) Wright.

iii ELIZABETH ABBOTT, b. 22 Feb 1751; d. at Hollis, 19 Feb 1836; m. 1st about 1770, EBENEZER NUTTING; he died at Hollis, 1773 (probate 24 Nov 1773). Elizabeth m. 2nd 4 Aug 1774, SAMPSON POWERS, b. at Hollis, 2 Apr 1748 son of Peter and Anna (Keyes) Powers; Sampson d. 2 Jan 1822 at Hollis (will written 10 Oct 1821).

iv SAMUEL ABBOTT, b. 13 Apr 1753; d. Feb 1794; m. SUSAN HUBBARD.

v MARY ABBOTT, b. 31 Dec 1754; d. 23 Jan 1755.

vi GEORGE ABBOTT, b. 29 Dec 1755; d. 15 Sep 1818; m. 29 Dec 1784, NAOMI TUTTLE, b. at Littleton, 28 Sep 1764 daughter of Samuel and Mary (Russell) Tuttle; Naomi d. about 1833.

vii JOEL ABBOTT, b. 4 Dec 1757; d. at Westford, 12 Apr 1806; m. 4 Sep 1786, LYDIA CUMMINGS, b. at Westford, 26 Nov 1769 daughter of Isaac and Elizabeth (Trowbridge) Cummings; Lydia d. at Littleton, 5 Mar 1813.

viii JACOB ABBOTT, b. 12 Apr 1760; d. at Westford, 11 Apr 1815; m. 14 Sep 1787, POLLY CUMMINGS, b. 12 Jul 1767 daughter of Thomas and Lucy (Laurence) Cummings.

ix MARY ABBOTT, b. about 1762; d. at Westford, 7 Jul 1797; m. 28 Jul 1782, ABEL BOYNTON, b. at Westford, 9 Aug 1755 son of Nathaniel and Rebekah (Barrett) Boynton. Abel m. 2nd Polly Pierce.

---

704 There is a probate record in Middlesex County, MA in 1771 related to Benjamin's estate and includes information about Benjamin being a mortgagee of Samuel Abbott. Twenty-three acres were set off to widow Elizabeth Abbott. Perley's article in the Essex Antiquarian gives a date of 5 Jan 1770.

705 This marriage may not be accurate. There is a record for a marriage in Hollis 22 Mar 1775 for "Captain Jonas Pollard" of Westford and Mrs. Elizabeth Abbott. There is a Captain James Pollard of Westford who died in 1781 with a widow Elizabeth named in the will. James Pollard was born about 1708 and he was widowed in 1774. I believe the marriage transcription in the Hollis records is an error and the spouse is James Pollard.

706 Middlesex County Deeds, 1792-1827, volumes 110-112, Images 85-86, Familysearch.org.

707 Worcester, *History of the Town of Hollis*

708 *Middlesex County, MA: Probate File Papers, 1648-1924. Will of Elizabeth Bowers, 10 Aug 1802. Case number 2269.*

709 This identification involves a young marriage for Sarah at age 15. However, her last child was born in 1807 so she would have to be very young at the time of the birth of the first child in 1778.

267) DANIEL ABBOTT (*Benjamin Abbott[4], Sarah Farnum Abbott[3], Elizabeth Holt Farnum[2], Nicholas[1]*), b. at Andover, 29 Dec 1725 son of Benjamin and Mary (Carleton) Abbott; d. Apr 1793;[710] m. 3 Apr 1756, LUCY PARKER, b. 5 Jun 1732 daughter of Thomas and Lydia (Richardson) Parker; the date of death of Lucy is not known.

The births of four children of Daniel Abbott and Lucy Parker are recorded at Dracut.

i DANIEL ABBOTT, b. 8 Sep 1757; d. at Claremont, NH, 10 Aug 1827. Daniel did not marry.

ii WILLIAM ABBOTT, b. 22 Feb 1760; d. likely at Bedford, NH; m. at Dracut, 13 Nov 1784, MARTHA "PATTY" COBURN, b. at Dracut about 1765.[711]

iii SAMUEL ABBOTT, b. 16 Feb 1765; d. at Claremont, NH, 13 Apr 1840; m. by 1794, his first cousin, ELIZABETH COTTON, b. about 1768 daughter of Rev. Samuel and Elizabeth (Parker) Cotton of Claremont; Elizabeth d. at Claremont, NH, 7 Jun 1837.[712] The mothers of Samuel Abbott and Elizabeth Cotton were sisters.

iv JONATHAN ABBOTT, b. 20 Jan 1772; d. at Litchfield, NH, 4 Jul 1855; m. 1st, 21 Feb 1795, REBECCA MASSEY, b. 24 Mar 1772 daughter of Bartholomew and Mary (Fox) Massey; Rebecca d. 19 Dec 1795. Jonathan m. 2nd, 31 Dec 1800, DOLLY PARKER, b. 12 Sep 1779.[713] Dolly died at Litchfield, 19 Sep 1824.[714] After Dolly's death, Jonathan married a widow named Miranda who d. at Claremont 23 Feb 1854.

268) MARY ABBOTT (*Benjamin Abbott[4], Sarah Farnum Abbott[3], Elizabeth Holt Farnum[2], Nicholas[1]*), b. at Andover, 21 Jul 1732 daughter of Benjamin and Abigail (Abbott) Abbott; d. at Milford, NH, 9 Aug 1798; m. 13 Nov 1759, NEHEMIAH BARKER, b. at Methuen, 11 Feb 1734 son of Ebenezer and Abigail (Morse) Barker; Nehemiah d. 20 Jan 1810.

Nehemiah Barker was an inn owner in Methuen from 1777 to 1785. He also owned one-half of an iron works. This family relocated to Milford, New Hampshire about 1785.[715] Nehemiah Barker was listed as a taxpayer in Milford in 1794.[716]

Mary Abbott and Nehemiah Barker had five children, the oldest daughter's birth recorded at Andover and the youngest four at Methuen.

i ABIGAIL BARKER, b. 24 Jan 1762; d. Jul 1793.[717]

ii JOEL BARKER, b. 11 Aug 1764; d. at Milford, 5 Dec 1832; m. at Milford, 24 Dec 1793, SARAH "SALLY" FOSTER, b. at Milford, 1774 daughter of Edward and Phebe (Pierce) Foster; Sarah d. 5 Sep 1820. Joel m. 2nd, 27 Nov 1821, CATHERINE LOVEJOY of Bow.[718]

iii MARY BARKER, b. 19 Sep 1766; d. 23 Oct 1766.

iv MARY BARKER, b. 18 Dec 1767; d. at Hollis, 3 Sep 1824; m. at Hollis, 6 Jan 1791, JACOB SPAULDING, b. at Chelmsford, 13 Dec 1767 son of Benjamin and Mary (Spaulding) Spaulding. Jacob m. 2nd, Susanna Robertson. Jacob d. at Hollis, 14 May 1838.

v DORCAS BARKER, b. 4 Sep 1770; d. at Peterborough, NH, 25 Jul 1840; m. About 1792, MERRILL PIERCE, b. at Chelmsford, 29 Jan 1764 son of Benjamin and Elizabeth (Merrill) Pierce. Merrill Pierce was the brother of Phebe Pierce (born 1748) the mother of Sarah Foster who married Dorcas's older brother Joel.

269) ABIGAIL ABBOTT (*Benjamin Abbott[4], Sarah Farnum Abbott[3], Elizabeth Holt Farnum[2], Nicholas[1]*), b. at Andover, 13 Jan 1733/4 daughter of Benjamin and Abigail (Abbott) Abbott; d. 1 Feb 1807; m. 1 Jun 1758, her second cousin, once removed, JOHN ABBOT, b. 12 Sep 1735 son of John and Phebe (Fiske) Abbott; John d. 24 Apr 1818.

John Abbot lived on the farm that he inherited from his father. He was apparently successful as he was able to pay for the college educations of three of his sons.

The estate of John Abbot entered probate 20 October 1818. His will, written 8 March 1805, has bequests for the following persons: dear and beloved wife Abigail (her yearly maintenance includes 50 pounds of good pork and 100 pounds of good beef plus all the other things she needs), eldest and well beloved son John, second and well beloved son Ezra (gets all the

[710] Abbot and Abbot, *Genealogical Record of Descendants*

[711] Coburn, *The History of Dracut*, p 130, gives Patty's parents as Jacob and Lydia, but their daughter Patty died unmarried in 1802 (at least the death record gives her name as Patty Coburn).

[712] Spofford, *Grave Stone Records: From the Ancient Cemeteries in the Town of Claremont*, p 6, Elizabeth (Cotton) Abbott wife of Samuel, June 7, 1837, 69y; Samuel Abbott, April 13, 1840, 76y

[713] Family Tree Samplers, 1759-1894. Online database. AmericanAncestors.org. New England Historic Genealogical Society, 2013. (From the collection of Dan and Marty Campanelli.) Vital records for this family are contained in a sampler stitched by Dolly Parker.

[714] Findagrave.com memorial ID 167676976

[715] Charlotte Helen Abbott, Early Records of the Barker Family of Andover. https://www.mhl.org/sites/default/files/files/Abbott/Barker%20Family.pdf

[716] Hurd, *History of Hillsborough County, New Hampshire*, published 1885

[717] Abbot and Abbot, *Genealogical Record of Descendants*, p 68

[718] Ramsdell, *History of Milford, Volume 1*, p 576

land in the town of Wilton), third and well beloved son Benjamin, eldest and well beloved daughter Abigail, well beloved daughter Elizabeth, third and well beloved daughter Phebe, youngest, and well beloved son Abiel. He notes having paid for the educations of John, Benjamin, and Abiel and that is considered part of their portion. The books are divided among the seven children. Abigail is mentioned in the will; however, she died between the time of the will and her husband's death.[719]

The births of eight children of Abigail and John Abbott are recorded at Andover.

i JOHN ABBOT, b. 8 Apr 1759; d. at Andover, 2 Jul 1843. John Abbot attended Harvard and graduated in 1784. Ill health prevented his entering the ministry which was his original plan. He was a tutor at Harvard for five years and later was a cashier at a Portland bank. He then found a position at Bowdoin College. His tenure as a professor of classical languages was rather lackluster. He was described as awkward and absentminded and fell victim to practical jokes.[720] He was criticized for his lack of scholarship. He later assumed the position of librarian which better suited him. He continued in this position at Bowdoin until 1828. He resided in Waterford, Maine. He was living with his brother in Andover at the time of his death. John did not marry.

ii EZRA ABBOTT, b. 3 Dec 1760; d. at Andover, 22 Jan 1844; m. 24 Apr 1798, his third cousin once removed, HANNAH POOR, b. 15 Jan 1770 daughter of Daniel and Hannah (Frye) Poor; Hannah d. 11 Sep 1861.

iii BENJAMIN ABBOTT, b. 17 Sep 1762; d. at Exeter, NH, 25 Oct 1849; m. 1st, HANNAH TRACY EMERY, b. at Exeter, 7 Mar 1771 daughter of John and Margaret (Gookin) Emery; Hannah d. 6 Dec 1793. Benjamin m. 2nd, at Boston, 1 May 1798, MARY PERKINS, b. at Boston, 24 May 1769 daughter of James and Elizabeth (Peck) Perkins; Mary d. at Exeter, 13 Mar 1863. Hannah Tracy Emery was mentioned in the diary of John Quincy Adams having met her on a visit to a Mr. Carter. "Miss H. Emery was there, a young lady with a beautiful countenance, an elegant person, and (I am told) an amiable mind."[721]

iv ABIGAIL ABBOTT, b. 15 Sep 1764; d. at Portland, ME, 22 Apr 1841; m. at Andover, 21 Apr 1791, WILLIAM DOUGLAS, baptized at Rutland, MA, 29 Mar 1761 son of Robert and Elinor (Fales) Douglas; William d. at Portland, 4 Dec 1827.

v ELIZABETH ABBOTT, b. 2 Aug 1766; d. at Peterborough, NH, 6 Apr 1853; m. 19 May 1796, her first cousin, ABIEL ABBOT (*Dorcas Abbott Abbott⁵, Benjamin Abbott⁴, Sarah Farnum Abbott³, Elizabeth Holt Farnum², Nicholas¹*), b. at Wilton, 14 Dec 1765 son of Abiel and Dorcas (Abbott) Abbot; Abiel d. at Cambridge, MA, 31 Jan 1859. This is a quadruple Abbott marriage; all four of the parents of this couple are Abbotts. Dr. Abiel Abbot was a distinguished minister and scholar.

vi PHEBE ABBOTT, b. 18 Nov 1768; d. at Portland, ME, 30 Apr 1852; m. 9 Apr 1789, EDWARD CARLETON, b. at Bradford, 2 Jul 1762 son of Dudley and Abigail (Wilson) Carleton; Edward d. 12 Jun 1825.

vii ABIEL ABBOT, b. 17 Aug 1770; d. at New York in transit from Cuba, 7 Jun 1828; m. at Haverhill, 19 Jul 1796, EUNICE WALES, b. at Roxbury, 21 Sep 1772 daughter of Ebenezer and Eunice (Davis) Wales; Eunice d. at Dorchester, 29 Dec 1831.

viii JACOB ABBOTT, b. 25 Jul 1771; d. Jul 1772.

270) ELIZABETH ABBOTT (*Benjamin Abbott⁴, Sarah Farnum Abbott³, Elizabeth Holt Farnum², Nicholas¹*), b. at Andover, 27 Oct 1738 daughter of Benjamin and Abigail (Abbott) Abbott; d. at Conway, NH, 12 Oct 1789;[722] m. 1st 1 Jun 1758, EBENEZER CUMMINGS, b. at Groton, 17 Apr 1735 son of William and Lucy (Colburn) Cummings; Ebenezer d. 1 Jun 1778. Elizabeth m. 2nd as his fourth wife, THOMAS MERRILL, b. at Haverhill, 5 Feb 1723/4 son of John and Lydia (Haynes) Merrill. Thomas had married as his first wife, Phebe Abbott (Family #309); Thomas Merrill d. at Conway, NH, 21 Jul 1788.

Ebenezer Cummings enlisted in the army for service in the Revolutionary War. After his death from smallpox in 1778, the town agreed to care for the widows of the Continental soldiers including Mrs. Cummings.[723]

Elizabeth Abbott and Ebenezer Cummings had eight children born at Hollis, New Hampshire.

i ELIZABETH CUMMINGS, b. 23 Nov 1759; d. 3 Oct 1812; m. 13 Jun 1780, her third cousin, HENRY LOVEJOY (*William Lovejoy⁵, Henry Lovejoy⁴, Mary Farnum Lovejoy³, Elizabeth Holt Farnum², Nicholas¹*), b. at Andover, 23 Nov 1753 son of William and Hannah (Evans) Lovejoy.

---

[719] *Essex County, MA: Probate File Papers, 1638-1881. Probate of John Abbot, 20 Oct 1818, Case number 74.*

[720] Hatch, *History of Bowdoin College*, pp 16-17

[721] John Quincy Adams, Charles Francis Adams, 1903, Life in a New England Town 1787, 1788: Diary of John Quincy Adams While a Student in the Office of Theophilus Parsons at Newburyport, p 45

[722] *New Hampshire, Death and Disinterment Records, 1754-1947*

[723] Mooar, *The Cummings Memorial*, p 100

ii EBENEZER CUMMINGS, b. 15 Sep 1761; d, about 1842;[724] m. at Surry, NH, 29 May 1787, HANNAH WASHER, b. at Amherst, about 1767 daughter of Stephen and Sarah (Wilkins) Washer; Hannah d. at Andover, VT, 6 Aug 1837.

iii ABIGAIL CUMMINGS, b. 1 Jul 1763; d. Nov 1801; m. at Conway, 8 Apr 1788, JOSEPH SEAVEY, b. 1762 son of Jonathan and Comfort (Cates) Seavey; Joseph d. about 1812.

iv BRIDGET CUMMINGS, b. 15 Jul 1765; d. 24 Jan 1786.

v LUCY CUMMINGS, b. 9 Jul 1767; d. 15 Oct 1854; m. 8 Apr 1788, PETER PEAVEY, b. at Andover, 14 Apr 1762 son of Thomas and Dorcas (Holt) Peavey; Peter d. at Greenfield, NH, 28 Jul 1836.

vi MARY CUMMINGS, b. 22 Oct 1770; d. at Francestown, NH, 6 Apr 1856; m. 8 Dec 1810, WILLIAM BIXBY, b. 4 Nov 1779 son of Edward and Lucy (Barnes) Bixby; William d. 30 Oct 1862. Mary and William had one adopted child.[725]

vii JACOB ABBOT CUMMINGS, b. 2 Nov 1772; d. at Boston, 24 Feb 1820; m. 9 Aug 1807, ELIZABETH MERRILL, b. at Haverhill, 10 Mar 1781 daughter of Gyles and Lucy (Cushing) Merrill; Elizabeth d. at Portland, ME, 24 Dec 1867.

viii SARAH CUMMINGS, b. 28 Jan 1775; d. after 1850 likely at Francestown. Sarah did not marry. At the 1850 U.S. Census, she was living with her sister Mary Bixby in Francestown.[726]

Elizabeth Abbott and her second husband Thomas Merrill had two children born at Conway, New Hampshire.

i JOHN MERRILL, b. 2 Mar 1782; d. at Portland, ME, 7 Jun 1855; m. at Portland, 26 Sep 1820, MARY SOUTHGATE BOYD, b. at Portland, 20 Jan 1797 daughter of Joseph Coffin and Isabella (Southgate) Boyd; Mary d. Apr 1861.[727]

ii BENJAMIN MERRILL, b. 15 Mar 1784; d. at Salem, MA, 30 Jul 1847.[728] Benjamin did not marry. He did graduate from Harvard in 1804 and was awarded an LLD in 1845. He worked as an attorney, practicing first in Lynn, but for most of his career practiced in Salem. In his will, he makes bequests to his siblings Jonathan A. Merrill, Sally Cummings, and John Merrill.[729] Jonathan and Sally are his half-siblings.

271) ANNA ABBOTT (*Benjamin Abbott⁴, Sarah Farnum Abbott³, Elizabeth Holt Farnum², Nicholas¹*), b. at Andover, 13 Oct 1740 daughter of Benjamin and Abigail (Abbott) Abbott; d. at Hollis, NH, 15 Jan 1810; m. Jan 1762, EPHRAIM BURGE, b. at Westford, 1 May 1738 son of Josiah and Susannah (Jaquith) Burge; Ephraim d. 20 Jul 1784.

Ephraim Burge was active in the civic life of Hollis, New Hampshire. For example, during the Revolutionary War, he was part of a 1781 committee to "class the town" which seems to have been a method of sectioning the town to answer call-ups for more soldiers for the war. He was also part of a committee charged with caring for the families of soldiers.[730]

There are records for the births of nine children at Hollis, New Hampshire.

i ANNA BURGE, b. 20 Nov 1762; d. at Dunstable, 31 Oct 1794; m. 17 Nov 1783, PHINEAS FLETCHER, b. 28 Nov 1757 son of Joseph and Elizabeth (Underwood) Fletcher. Phineas m. 2nd, Alice Ames; Phineas d. 31 Jul 1833.

ii EPHRAIM BURGE, b. 7 Jun 1764; d. at Hollis, 2 Mar 1853; m. 28 Jan 1793, PATTY BALDWIN, b. at Amherst, NH, 2 Mar 1764 daughter of Nahum and Mary (Lowe) Baldwin; Patty d. 2 Aug 1822.

iii JOSIAH BURGE, b. 15 Apr 1766; d. 25 Mar 1790. Josiah graduated from Harvard in 1787[731] and was a preacher.

iv JACOB BURGE, b. 7 Jan 1768; d. at Hollis, 10 Jun 1809. Jacob does not seem to have married.

---

724 His death is reported by several sources as occurring in Wisconsin. However, he seems to have still been in Vermont in 1839 when his son Stephen made an appeal related to his father not having received his military service pension which he first applied for in 1832. It is possible that he relocated to Wisconsin in his very last years, perhaps to be with one of his children, but that needs further investigation. There is a death record for Ebenezer's wife 6 Aug 1837 in Vermont, so Ebenezer was still in Vermont in 1837. Some of his children did relocate to Wisconsin.

725 Cochrane and Wood, *History of Francestown*, p 518

726 *1850 United States Federal Census*, Year: 1850; Census Place: Francestown, Hillsborough, New Hampshire; Roll: M432_434; Page: 37A; Image: 75.

727 Chapman, *Monograph of the Southgate Family*, p 27

728 Benja[min], b. Conway, N. H., councillor-at-law, s. Thomas [and ____ (Abbot), N. R. 9.], apoplexy, July 30, 1847, a. 73 y. Massachusetts: Vital Records, 1620-1850

729 *Essex County, MA: Probate File Papers, 1638-1881. Probate of Benjamin Merrill, 3 Aug 1847, Case number 46886.*

730 Worcester, *History of the Town of Hollis*

731 Harvard University, *Quinquennial Catalogue*, p 140

v SUSANNAH "SUKEY" BURGE, b. 21 Jul 1773; d. at Hollis, 6 Sep 1816; m. 16 Apr 1799, THOMAS FARLEY, b. 28 Dec 1769 son of Caleb and Elizabeth (Farley) Farley; Thomas d. 17 Mar 1832.

vi ABIAL BURGE, b. 27 May and d. 30 May 1775.

vii SARAH "SALLY" BURGE, b. 2 May 1777; d. at Bedford, NH, Oct 1825; m. at Hollis, 14 Apr 1821, as his second wife, Deacon STEPHEN THURSTON, b. at Rowley, 2 Jan 1770 son of Daniel and Judith (Chute) Thurston. Stephen married a third time after Sally's death; Stephen died 13 Sep 1833. Sally did not have any children.

viii SAMUEL BURGE, b. 28 Mar 1779; d. at Francestown, NH, 5 Sep 1824; m. by 1805, ANNA MAY,[732] b. 1787 (age 30 at time of death); d. 30 Oct 1817. Samuel m. 2nd, 5 Feb 1822, DEBORAH STARETT, b. 26 Dec 1782 daughter of William and Abigail (Fisher) Starett.

ix BENJAMIN BURGE, b. 5 Aug 1782; d. at Hollis, 15 Jun 1815. Benjamin attended Harvard graduating in 1805 earning a medical degree.[733] Benjamin does not seem to have married.

272) DORCAS ABBOT (*Benjamin Abbott⁴, Sarah Farnum Abbott³, Elizabeth Holt Farnum², Nicholas¹*), b. at Andover, 1 Aug 1744 daughter of Benjamin and Abigail (Abbott) Abbott; d. at Wilton, NH, 23 Feb 1829;[734] m. 20 Nov 1764, her second cousin, once removed, ABIEL ABBOT, b. 19 Apr 1741 son of John and Phebe (Fiske) Abbott; Abiel d. 19 Aug 1809.

Dorcas Abbot and Abiel Abbot were born in Andover but had their children and raised their family in Wilton, New Hampshire. Abiel served in the Revolutionary War as paymaster in Baldwin's Regiment. He was a deacon in the church at Wilton. Three of their sons attended Harvard. The total number of children in the family is not certain. There are records for the births of 12 children, and some sources report there were 16 children. In any event, ten children lived to adulthood.

Abiel Abbot wrote his will 4 August 1809. Beloved wife Dorcas Abbott receives the use of the dwelling house, $200, and a lengthy list of provisions to be provided for her support. She also receives one-third part of the pew on the lower floor of the Wilton meeting house for as long as she remains his widow. Beloved son Abiel Abbot receives a one-tenth portion of his books and clothing in addition to the expense of his education which he has already received. Beloved son Jacob receives $100 in addition to the expense of his education. Son Benjamin receives the largest bored gun in addition to the lands and utensils he has received. Son Samuel receives a portion of books plus the expense of education. Daughter Dorcas Putnam receives one-tenth of the books in addition to what she has received. Daughters Abigail Livermore, Persis Lovejoy, Rhoda Peabody receive the same bequest of one-tenth portion of the books in addition to what they have already received. Daughter Phebe Abbot receives her portion of the books and $333, one-half on interest when she reaches the age of 18 and one-half when she reaches age 21. Son Ezra receives all the lands in Wilton, Mason, and Greenfield that have not otherwise been conveyed. Ezra also receives the tools of all kinds including the husbandry and cooper tools. Ezra is named executor.[735]

There are records for the following children born at Wilton, New Hampshire.

i ABIEL ABBOT, b. 14 Dec 1765; d. at Cambridge, 31 Jan 1859; m. 19 May 1796, his first cousin, ELIZABETH ABBOTT (*Abigail Abbott Abbott⁵, Benjamin Abbott⁴, Sarah Farnum Abbott³, Elizabeth Holt Farnum², Nicholas¹*), b. 2 Aug 1766 daughter of John and Abigail (Abbott) Abbott.

ii JACOB ABBOTT, b. 7 Jan 1768; d. 2 Nov 1834; m. 11 Feb 1802, CATHERINE THAYER, b. at Hampton, 28 Sep 1779 daughter of Ebenezer and Martha (Cotton) Thayer; Catherine d. 27 Jan 1843.

iii BENJAMIN ABBOTT, b. 17 Mar 1770; d. at Temple, ME, 10 Sep 1823; m. at Andover, 17 Jan 1793, his third cousin, PHEBE ABBOTT (*Lydia Stevens Abbott⁵, Lydia Gray Stevens⁴, Edward Gray³, Hannah Holt Gray², Nicholas¹*), b. at Wilton, 25 Jun 1774 daughter of Jacob and Lydia (Stevens) Abbott; Phebe d. 18 Apr 1857.

iv EZRA ABBOT, b. 8 Feb 1772; d. at Wilton, 3 Apr 1847; m. at Coventry, CT, 6 Oct 1799, REBEKAH HALE, b. at Coventry, 9 Jan 1781 daughter of Joseph and Rebecca (Harris) Hale; Rebekah d. 5 May 1860.[736]

v DORCAS ABBOTT, b. 30 Jan 1774; died after 2 Oct 1846, the date of her will;[737] m. 3 Jan 1795, ELIPHALET PUTNAM, b. at Wilton, 23 Jan 1766 son of Nathaniel and Mary (Eastman) Putnam; Eliphalet d. 25 Feb 1826.

---

732 Cochrane's *History of Francestown, NH* suggests her name might be Charlotte Morrill. However, her gravestone gives her name as Anna wife of Samuel. In addition, the son of Samuel and Anna, Benjamin, was a graduate of Dartmouth College. Benjamin's biographical sketch for the alumni of Dartmouth College gives his mother's name as Anna May. Chapman, *Sketches of the Alumni of Dartmouth College*, p 275

733 Harvard University, *Quinquennial Catalogue*, p 151

734 *New Hampshire: Births, Deaths and Marriages, 1654-1969.* (From microfilmed records. Online database: *AmericanAncestors.org*, New England Historic Genealogical Society, 2014.)

735 *New Hampshire Wills and Probate Records 1643-1982*, will of Abiel Abbot, Hillsborough, 4 Aug 1809.

736 Abbott, *Family Tree of Ezra Abbot*. See this source of additional information.

737 *Probate Records, 1771-1921; Indexes to Probate Records, 1771-1859, 1885-1961*; Author: New Hampshire. Probate Court (Hillsborough County); *Probate Place: Hillsborough, New Hampshire*

vi Child, b. and d. 20 Apr 1776.

vii SAMUEL ABBOTT, b. 11 Jun 1777; d. 10 Jan 1782.

viii ABIGAIL ABBOTT, b. 13 Jul 1779; d. 5 Jun 1812; m. 19 May 1808, JONATHAN LIVERMORE, b. at Wilton, 10 Jul 1770 son of Jonathan and Elizabeth (Kidder) Livermore; Jonathan d. 24 Dec 1845.

ix PERSIS ABBOTT, b. 25 Dec 1781; d. at Milford, NH, 13 Nov 1859; m. 12 Jan 1804, her third cousin, HENRY LOVEJOY (*Samuel Lovejoy[6], William Lovejoy[5], Henry Lovejoy[4], Mary Farnum Lovejoy[3], Elizabeth Holt Farnum[2], Nicholas[1]*), b. 16 Aug 1781 son of Samuel and Lydia (Abbott) Lovejoy; Henry d. 23 Sep 1863.

x RHODA ABBOTT, b. 17 Mar 1784; d. at Peterborough, 19 Mar 1853; m. 14 Nov 1805, EPHRAIM PEABODY, b. at Wilton, 17 Jun 1776 son of Ephraim and Sarah (Hutchinson) Peabody; Ephraim d. 5 Jul 1816.

xi SAMUEL ABBOTT, b. 30 Mar 1786; d. 2 Jan 1839. Samuel did not marry. He attended Harvard, was admitted to the bar, but later developed an interest in chemistry.

xii PHEBE ABBOTT, b. 25 Jun 1788; d. at Jackson, ME, 25 Nov 1825, m. 25 Jun 1818, her first cousin, EZRA ABBOTT, b. at Wilton, 3 Jul 1785 son of William and Phebe (Ballard) Abbott; Ezra d. 7 Jun 1871.

273) SARAH ABBOT (*David Abbot[4], Sarah Farnum Abbott[3], Elizabeth Holt Farnum[2], Nicholas[1]*), b. at Andover, 7 Apr 1726 daughter of David and Hannah (Danforth) Abbot; d. at Bedford, 5 Mar 1814; m. 1st 30 Jan 1753, ROBERT HILDRETH, b. at Dracut, 18 May 1713 son of Ephraim and Mercy (Richardson) Hildreth; Robert d. 1760. Sarah m. 2nd 28 May 1761, JOHN LANE, b. at Bedford, 2 Oct 1720 son of Job and Martha (Ruggles) Lane; John d. 7 Dec 1789. Sarah m. 3rd 14 Jul 1791, BENJAMIN PARKER, Benjamin d. Feb 1801.

Robert Hildreth died in 1760 at Chelmsford. His estate entered probate in October 1760, and his widow Sarah requested that David Abbott of Andover be named administrator of the estate. Robert did not leave a will. Only one child was located for Sarah and Robert.

After the death of her first husband, Sarah married John Lane of Bedford. John's first wife, Ruth Bowman, had died in 1759. The births of three children were recorded for Sarah and John Lane at Bedford. A probate record was not located for John Lane. After John Lane's death in 1789, Sarah married Benjamin Parker in 1791.

Child of Sarah Abbott and Robert Hildreth:

i BENJAMIN HILDRETH, b. at Dracut, 23 Jan 1754; d. 13 Feb 1754

Children of Sarah Abbott and John Lane all born at Bedford:

i JOSIAH LANE, b. 25 Feb 1762; d. 15 Mar 1762.

ii JONATHAN LANE, b. 15 Oct 1763; d. at Bedford, 4 Mar 1808; m. 1 Feb 1787, his second cousin, HANNAH LANE, b. 26 Feb 1765 daughter of Samuel and Elizabeth (Fitch) Lane; Hannah d. at Lowell, 1848 (date of probate).

iii SARAH LANE, b. 1 Oct 1765; d. at Billerica, 11 Jun 1849; m. 1 Nov 1787, TIMOTHY STEARNS, b. at Billerica, 25 Sep 1763 son of Isaac and Sarah (Abbott) Stearns; Timothy d. 8 Aug 1816. Sarah's mother and Timothy's mother were both named Sarah Abbott.

274) DAVID ABBOT (*David Abbot[4], Sarah Farnum Abbott[3], Elizabeth Holt Farnum[2], Nicholas[1]*), b. at Andover, 28 Mar 1728 son of David and Hannah (Danforth) Abbot; d. at Billerica 1 Nov 1798; m. 28 Dec 1752, PRUDENCE SHELDON, b. at Billerica 31 Aug 1732 daughter of Samuel and Sarah[738] (Hutchinson) Richardson. A death record for Prudence was not located, although she was living at the time of her husband's death and she was on the tax rolls in Billerica for 1798.

David and Prudence had eleven children, the first ten births recorded at Andover and the youngest son born at Billerica. David owned property in Andover, Billerica, and New Suncook (now Lovell), Maine. The children in this family scattered to the four winds ending up in New Hampshire, Vermont, Maine, Ohio, and Québec.

David Abbot wrote his will 7 December 1797. Beloved wife Prudence receives the use and improvements on one-half of the dwelling house and a horse to convey her to meetings and other occasions. There are also provisions made for her support in terms of annual allotments of grains, beef, firewood, etc. Sons Josiah and Samuel receive token bequests of six shillings in addition to their portions they have already received. Son David receives all his land in New Suncook in the county of York. Son Benjamin receives all the lands in Billerica and Andover. Son Jeremiah receives $167 to make up his full portion. Daughter Elizabeth Dugles (sic) receives one pound, six shillings, and six dollars to make up the rest of her portion. Daughter Prudence

[738] The marriage record lists her name as Mary Hutchinson, but all the births of the children, including a daughter Sarah born in 1719, list the mother's name as Sarah.

Sawyer receives six shillings, daughter Parker (this is Hannah who married Aaron Parker) receives $5, daughter Olive McDole receives $30, and daughter Dorcas Abbot receives $100. Son Benjamin is named executor.[739]

i ELIZABETH ABBOTT, b. 26 Feb 1754; m. at Cavendish, VT, 19 Aug 1792, WILLIAM DOUGLASS.

ii Son, b. 7 Feb 1756; d. 2 Mar 1756.

iii PRUDENCE ABBOTT, b. 3 Oct 1757; d. at Salina, NY, 15 Dec 1839; m. 13 Oct 1778, NATHANIEL SAWYER, b. at Methuen, 16 Jun 1750 son of Josiah and Hannah (Gowing) Sawyer; Nathaniel d. 15 Oct 1807.

iv JOSIAH ABBOTT, b. 29 Dec 1759; d. Feb 1837; m. 1st, 15 May 1784, RUTH BODWELL; Ruth d. by 1790. Josiah m. 2nd, 30 Mar 1790, ANNA FURBUSH, b. Oct 1768 daughter of Charles and Sarah (Corey) Furbush.

v HANNAH ABBOTT, b. 5 Jan 1762; d. at Compton, Quebec, 1856; m. at Billerica, 21 Jan 1787, AARON PARKER, b. at Methuen, 22 Feb 1759 son of Timothy and Priscilla (Carleton) Parker; Aaron d. 1857; living in Compton in 1851 listed as 93 years old.[740]

vi SAMUEL ABBOTT, b. 27 Mar 1764; d. at Bennington, NH, 29 Mar 1833; m. 1st, at Billerica, 26 Jan 1786, his second cousin once removed, RHODA BLANCHARD, b. 17 Nov 1762 daughter of Samuel and Mary (Brown) Blanchard; Rhoda d. about 1800. Samuel m. 2nd at Hancock, NH, 22 Dec 1801, ANNA WALLACE.

vii DAVID ABBOTT, b. 4 Mar 1766; d. at Barton, VT, 11 Mar 1847; m. at Fryeburg, ME, Sep 1786, SARAH "SALLY" KEZAR;[741] Sally d. May 1816.

viii BENJAMIN ABBOTT, b. 26 Jun 1768; d. at Ashtabula, OH, 22 May 1856; m. in Vermont about 1800, BETSEY NOONING whose origins are unknown; Betsey d. 4 Sep 1854.

ix OLIVE ABBOTT, b. 24 Jul 1770; d. at Thurso, Quebec, 27 Jun 1834; m. 1st, ALEXANDER MCDOLE, b. 15 Jun 1760 son of William McDowell and Rosannah (McLaughlin) McDole; Alexander d. at Grand Isle, VT, 26 Jan 1814. Olive m. 2nd 31 Mar 1816, as his second wife, DAVID TOWN, b. 25 Jun 1762; David d. at Waterbury, VT, 4 Sep 1828.

x DORCAS ABBOTT, b. 5 Dec 1773; d. likely at Chelmsford after 1850 (still living at the 1850 U.S. Census); m. 4 Feb 1798, JOHN SNOW, b. 5 Jul 1774 son of Richard and Lydia (Wright) Snow.

xi JEREMIAH ABBOTT, b. 18 May 1776; d. in New York, 28 Mar 1835;[742] Jeremiah lived in Portland, Maine much of his adulthood. He did marry and had some children. One child has been identified, but the identity of his wife has not been found. The most likely candidate for a wife is Susanna Centre who married Jeremiah Abbott at Boston in 1797. There is a Maine death record for her for 1844 with age of 74 at time of death. There are gravestones in Portland for Jeremiah and his wife Susanna with the appropriate death years so perhaps that is this Jeremiah and Susannah.

275) SOLOMON ABBOT (*David Abbot⁴, Sarah Farnum Abbott³, Elizabeth Holt Farnum², Nicholas¹*), b. at Andover, 14 Feb 1730/1 son of David and Hannah (Danforth) Abbot; d. probably at Dracut 17 Dec 1797;[743] m. 3 May 1756, HANNAH COLBY (*Hannah Gray Colby⁴, Edward Gray³, Hannah Holt Gray², Nicholas¹*), b. 22 Oct 1735 daughter of Daniel and Hannah (Gray) Colby; Hannah's date of death is not known.

Solomon and Hannah settled in Dracut soon after the birth of their first child. In 1758, Solomon Abbott bought property and rights to a ferry in Dracut from John White. Solomon then sold half of this property to Daniel Colby in 1759 and the other half to Amos Bradley in 1761. Solomon received a deed for 100 acres from John White in 1768. Solomon Abbott is also listed on the Roll of Honor for Dracut as serving in the Revolutionary War.[744]

Seven births are recorded for Solomon Abbott and Hannah Colby, the oldest at Andover and the remainder in Dracut.

i HANNAH ABBOTT, b. 1 May 1757; d. after 1827 (living at the probate of her second husband's estate); m. 1st, 27 Feb 1776, PARKER BODWELL, b. at Methuen, 29 Oct 1750 son of Daniel and Abigail (Ladd) Bodwell; Parker d.

---

739 *Middlesex County, MA: Probate File Papers, 1648-1871. Probate of David Abbot, 1798, Case number 13.*

740 1851 Census of Canada East, Canada West, New Brunswick, and Nova Scotia; Year: 1851; Census Place: Compton, Sherbrooke County, Canada East (Quebec); Schedule: A; Roll: C_1142; Page: 89; Line: 41

741 Published genealogies give her name as Sarah Keyser, but every birth record for this couple lists her name as Sarah Parker and Parker is included as the middle name of one of their children. But the marriage of David and Sarah says Keezer.

742 Ancestry.com, *U.S., Newspaper Extractions from the Northeast, 1704-1930* (Provo, UT, USA: Ancestry.com Operations, Inc., 2014). This notice gives place of death as New York but notes that he was until recently in Portland, Maine.

743 Abbot and Abbot, *Genealogical Record of Descendants* gives this date of death; a death record or probate record was not located.

744 Coburn, *History of Dracut*

7 Aug 1795. Hannah m. 2nd, as his third wife, DAVID JONES, b. 12 Feb 1740/1 son of David and Hannah (Fox) Jones.

ii SOLOMON ABBOTT, b. 7 May 1759; d. at Dracut, 5 Jan 1842; m. about 1785, RACHEL BOWERS, b. 16 Jul 1763 daughter of John and Rachel (Varnum) Bowers; Rachel d. 7 Jan 1845.

iii SARAH ABBOTT, b. 22 Mar 1761; m. at Methuen, 16 Mar 1786, SAMUEL MORSE, b. at Methuen, 28 Mar 1759 son of Joseph and Lydia (Huse) Morse.

iv DANIEL COLBY ABBOTT, b. 26 Oct 1766; d. at Dracut, 18 Sep 1842; m. about 1792, PATIENCE COBURN, b. at Methuen, 1768 daughter of Aaron and Phebe (Harris) Coburn; Patience d. 15 Apr 1830.

v ELIZABETH DANFORTH ABBOTT, b. 11 Oct 1768; d. at Walpole, NH, 5 Jul 1856; m. 18 Sep 1793, EPHRAIM LANE, b. at Bedford, 11 Mar 1767 son of Samuel and Ruth (Davis) Lane; Ephraim d. 15 Aug 1837.

vi LYDIA ABBOTT, b. 22 May 1771; m. JOSHUA MARTIN.[745]

vii DAVID ABBOTT, b. 18 May 1775; d. at Windham, NH, 1855 (probate 8 Aug 1855); m. 1st, 13 May 1797, HANNAH CROSBY, b. 20 Sep 1773 daughter of Jonathan and Hannah (Goodhue) Crosby; Hannah d. before 1816. David m. 2nd, 21 Feb 1816, DOLLY ABBOTT, b. at Amherst, 1775 daughter of Ephraim and Dorothy (Stiles) Abbott; Dolly d. 1822. David m. 3rd, about 1827, SARAH MCKINLEY, b. 1789 daughter of Robert and Sarah (Harriman) McKinley; Sarah d. 30 Jan 1869.

276) JONATHAN ABBOT (*David Abbot⁴, Sarah Farnum Abbott³, Elizabeth Holt Farnum², Nicholas¹*), b. at Andover, 24 Oct 1739 son of David and Hannah (Danforth) Abbot; d. at Andover, 10 Apr 1817; m. 13 Nov 1759, his second cousin once removed, MARY CHANDLER (*Priscilla Holt Chandler⁴, Timothy³, James², Nicholas¹*), b. 15 Jun 1740 daughter of Nathan and Priscilla (Holt) Chandler; Mary d. 1 Apr 1824.

Captain Jonathan Abbot was part of Johnson's Regiment of Militia. This regiment was part of the first alarm that marched in response to the Lexington alarm. This regiment participated at Bunker Hill.[746]

Jonathan Abbot did not leave a will. Nathan Abbott was administrator of the estate. The widow's third is set out to widow Mary. The personal estate was sold at public auction to pay debts. Mary petitioned to the Court asking for allowances from the estate as Jonathan left ten children, two of whom are dependent on her for support. The value of the personal estate was $3,160 and the real estate value was $4,442. There was a deduction for the widow's dower of $1,480, and the debts were $7,500. The heirs-at-law signing that they agree to the administration of the estate by Nathan Abbott are as follows: Mary Abbott, Jonathan Abbott, Jr., David Abbott, Solomon Abbott, Joseph Shattuck, Benjamin Abbott, Hannah Abbott, Sarah Abbott, and Joshua Chandler signing on behalf of Abiel Chandler and Gilbert Barker.[747]

Jonathan Abbott and Mary Chandler had twelve children whose births are recorded at Andover. Two of the children died as infants. Two children did not marry. Three of the children married first cousins.

The oldest son, Jonathan Abbott, did not marry but he did leave a will that created dissension in the family. One of the heirs-at-law of the will, Benjamin Abbott, questioned its validity claiming that Jonathan was not of sound mind and memory at the time the will was made. There was a suit involving Benjamin and Jonathan Abbott, Jr. (Jonathan's nephew), and some other parties. The witnesses to the will attested that Jonathan was of sound mind. The will that Jonathan did make has bequests to the following persons: sister Mary Chandler wife of Abiel Chandler receives $100; brother Nathan, $15; brother Benjamin, $50; sister Phebe Shattuck the wife of Joseph Shattuck, $100; brother Solomon, $30; sister Hannah Barker wife of Richard Barker, $100; sister Sarah Abbott, $30; sister Priscilla Barker wife of Gilbert Barker, $30; Rebecca Shattuck, $50; nephew David Abbott receives his pasture land that adjoins his land; nephew Ezra Abbott, $200; nephew Herman Abbott, $50; niece Phebe Abbott, $20; niece Hannah Shattuck, $5; niece Phebe Abbott, $5; niece Priscilla Abbott, $20; niece Mary Abbott, $10; niece Lucinna/Susanna? Abbott, $10; nephew Nathan the son of brother David who is deceased and Joseph Shattuck receive the homestead farm in Andover; Nathan, Jr. son of Nathan, $15; nephew Gilbert Abbott, $15; nephew Jonathan Abbott receives all the residue of the estate and Jonathan is to quit-claim about three acres of property to nephew David. Nephew Jonathan is named executor.[748]

i JONATHAN ABBOT, b. 3 Mar 1760; d. 21 May 1830. Jonathan did not marry.

ii MARY ABBOTT, b. 10 Jan 1762; d. 1 May 1845; m. 17 Oct 1782, her first cousin, ABIEL CHANDLER (*Hannah Chandler Chandler⁵, Priscilla Holt Chandler⁴, Timothy³, James², Nicholas¹*), b. 28 Aug 1760 son of Joshua and Hannah (Chandler) Chandler; Abiel d. at Boston, 2 Nov 1833.

745 This is a marriage reported in Abbot and Abbot, *Genealogical Record of Descendants*. There are limited records related to this family who relocated to Hookset, New Hampshire.

746 Patrakis, Joan, "Andover in the Revolutionary War," Andover Historical Society, retrieved from http://andoverhistorical.org/explore-andover-stories-blog/andover-in-the-revolutionary-war

747 *Essex County, MA: Probate File Papers, 1638-1881. Probate of Jonathan Abbot, 6 May 1817, Case number 82.*

748 *Essex County, MA: Probate File Papers, 1638-1881. Probate of Jonathan Abbot, 1 Jun 1830, Case number 84.*

iii DAVID ABBOT, b. 11 Mar 1764; d. 1 Jun 1823; m. 26 May 1789, his first cousin, PRISCILLA CHANDLER (*Nathan Chandler*[5], *Priscilla Holt Chandler*[4], *Timothy*[3], *James*[2], *Nicholas*[1]), b. 30 Jun 1768 daughter of Nathan and Phebe (Abbott) Chandler; Priscilla d. 19 Feb 1831.

iv PHEBE ABBOTT, b. 26 Feb 1766; d 1 Dec 1848; m. 30 Mar 1790, her third cousin once removed, JOSEPH SHATTUCK, b. 8 Nov 1757 son of Joseph and Anna (Johnson) Shattuck; Joseph d. 8 Jul 1847. Joseph had first married Hannah Chandler who died in the first year of the marriage.

v NATHAN ABBOT, b. 17 May 1768; d. at Andover, 7 Apr 1850; m. 11 Dec 1792, his second cousin, HANNAH PHELPS, b. 10 Sep 1769 daughter of Joshua and Lois (Ballard) Phelps; Hannah d. 17 Dec 1853.

vi BENJAMIN ABBOTT, b. 7 Jun 1770; d. at Andover, 20 Oct 1835; m. 26 Nov 1793, his first cousin, RHODA CHANDLER (*Nathan Chandler*[5], *Priscilla Holt Chandler*[4], *Timothy*[3], *James*[2], *Nicholas*[1]), b. 2 Mar 1774/5 daughter of Nathan and Phebe (Abbott) Chandler; Rhoda d. 19 Mar 1853.

vii SOLOMON ABBOTT, b. 1 Nov 1772; d. 1 Sep 1840; m. 8 Jul 1794, his third cousin once removed, LUCY POOR FRYE (*Lucy Lovejoy Frye*[6], *Joshua Lovejoy*[5], *Henry Lovejoy*[4], *Mary Farnum Lovejoy*[3], *Elizabeth Holt Farnum*[2], *Nicholas*[1]), b. 4 Jul 1778 daughter of Theophilus and Lucy (Lovejoy) Frye; Lucy d. at Boston, 16 Jun 1854.

viii JOSHUA ABBOTT, b. 14 Nov 1774; d. 26 Mar 1775.

ix HANNAH ABBOTT, b. 14 Oct 1776; d. at Andover, 11 Jul 1840; m. 22 Dec 1818, RICHARD BARKER, b. at Methuen, 10 Dec 1775 son of John and Hannah (Dow) Barker. Hannah and Richard did not have children.

x SARAH ABBOTT, b. 9 Jul 1778; d. at Andover, 1 Jul 1860. Sarah did not marry. Sarah Abbott, age 81, single, died at the almshouse of chronic rheumatism.[749]

xi PRISCILLA ABBOTT, b. 29 Jul 1780; d. at Saugus, 23 Mar 1862; m. 30 May 1816, GILBERT BARKER, b. at Methuen, 25 Jan 1774 son of John and Hannah (Dow) Barker; Gilbert d. at Saugus, 21 Sep 1853. Priscilla and Gilbert did not have children.

xii JOSHUA ABBOTT, b. 9 Jun 1784; d. 9 Jul 1784.

277) SARAH LOVEJOY (*Sarah Farnum Lovejoy*[4], *Ralph Farnum*[3], *Elizabeth Holt Farnum*[2], *Nicholas*[1]), baptized at Andover, 30 Nov 1712 son of Henry and Sarah (Farnum) Lovejoy; d. at Andover, 11 Aug 1767; m. at Andover, 27 Nov 1736, BENJAMIN SMITH, b. about 1707 likely the son of Samuel and Sarah (-) Smith; Benjamin d. at Andover, 24 Jan 1779.

Benjamin and Sarah were parents of three children born at Andover. There is little known about this family. The marriage for daughter Sarah seems a likely marriage, but there is not firm documentation for this.

i STARLEN SMITH, b. at Andover, 22 Aug 1737

ii BENJAMIN SMITH, b. at Andover, 6 Aug 1740

iii SARAH SMITH, b. at Andover, 9 Aug 1743; d. at Canterbury, NH, 1 Mar 1808; m. about 1762, as his second wife, JOSEPH KIMBALL, b. at Exeter, NH, 29 Jan 1730/1 son of John and Abigail (Lyford) Kimball;[750][751] Joseph d. at Canterbury, NH, 6 Nov 1814. Joseph was first married to Mary Sanborn,

278) HENRY LOVEJOY (*Sarah Farnum Lovejoy*[4], *Ralph Farnum*[3], *Elizabeth Holt Farnum*[2], *Nicholas*[1]), b. at Andover, 14 Aug 1714 son of Henry and Sarah (Farnum) Lovejoy; d. at Concord, NH, 15 Mar 1793;[752] m. 1 Jan 1735, PHEBE CHANDLER, b. at Andover, 2 Jan 1714/5 daughter of John and Hannah (Frye) Chandler; Phebe d. at Concord, Jan 1805.

Phebe and Henry married in Andover and most of their children were born there. They left for Rumford, NH by 1745. Henry Lovejoy was a selectman in Concord in 1749.[753] There are records for seven children in this family, the oldest five recorded at Andover and the two youngest at Rumford, NH.

Although published genealogies report seven children in this family and there are records for the births of these seven children, it is likely there was an eighth child, Sarah, in this family. According to Bouton's *History of Concord* (p 660), Theodore Farnum of Concord married a Sarah Lovejoy and that couple had four children. Theodore Farnum was born in 1749 son of Josiah and Mary (Frye) Farnum. It is not known that Sarah Lovejoy belongs in this family, but there is no other obvious family for her in Concord at the time. The estate of Theodore Farnum entered probate in 1789 with widow Sarah as administratrix and

---

749 *Massachusetts: Vital Records, 1841-1910.* (From original records held by the Massachusetts Archives. Online database: *AmericanAncestors.org*, New England Historic Genealogical Society, 2004.)

750 Kimball, *The Joseph Kimball Family*, p 23

751 Lyford, *History of Canterbury*, p 208

752 New Hampshire, Death and Burial Records Index, 1654-1949, ancestry.com

753 Lyford, *History of Concord*, p 1339

with Chandler Lovejoy and Phineas Virgin assuming the obligation of the bond. Chandler Lovejoy is a son in this family and Phineas Virgin is likely a brother-in-law to Chandler Lovejoy.

i PHEBE LOVEJOY, b. 20 Sep 1735; d. at Concord, 4 Jan 1789; m. 25 Apr 1765, her second cousin once removed, JOSEPH ABBOTT (*George Abbott[4], Hannah Gray Abbott[3], Hannah Holt Gray[2], Nicholas[1]*), b. at Concord 23 Oct 1741 son of George and Sarah (Abbott) Abbott. Joseph married 2nd Abigail Tyler; Joseph d. at Concord 19 Jan 1832. Phebe Lovejoy and Joseph Abbott are Family 961.

ii ABIEL LOVEJOY, b. 25 Jul 1737; d. at Conway, NH 27 May 1817; m. 1764, ANNA STICKNEY, b. at Rumford, 3 Sep 1741 daughter of Jeremiah and Elizabeth (Carleton) Stickney, Anna d. 15 Jan 1815.

iii DORCAS LOVEJOY, b. 10 Sep 1739; d. likely at Rumford, ME; m. EBENEZER VIRGIN, b. at Rumford, NH 28 May 1735 son of Ebenezer and Hannah (Foster) Virgin. This family relocated to Rumford, ME where they were first settlers.[754]

iv CHANDLER LOVEJOY, b. 23 Jan 1741/2; d. at Concord 20 Nov 1827; m. MIRIAM VIRGIN, b. at Rumford 23 May 1744 daughter of Ebenezer and Hannah (Foster) Virgin. Chandler m. 2nd 28 Sep 1814, AZUBAH GRAHAM.

v HENRY LOVEJOY, b. 19 Oct 1744; died in infancy.

vi HENRY LOVEJOY, b. 27 Sep 1746; d. 18 Aug 1747.

vii HANNAH LOVEJOY, b. 26 Jan 1749; d. at Thetford, VT 29 May 1809; m. JONATHAN WEST, b. at Rumford, 20 Oct 1749 son of Nathaniel and Sarah (Burbank) West; Jonathan d. 30 Aug 1826.

viii SARAH LOVEJOY, b. 8 Jun 1752; d. at Concord, 1815; m. about 1772, her second cousin, THEODORE FARNUM (*Josiah Farnum[4], Ephraim Farnum[3], Elizabeth Holt Farnum[2], Nicholas[1]*), b. at Andover, 24 Jan 1749 son of Josiah and Mary (Frye) Farnum; Theodore d. about 1789 (probate of estate). After Theodore's death, Sarah married Jedediah Hoit.

279) DAVID LOVEJOY (*Sarah Farnum Lovejoy[4], Ralph Farnum[3], Elizabeth Holt Farnum[2], Nicholas[1]*), b. at Andover, 10 Oct 1715 son of Henry and Sarah (Farnum) Lovejoy; d. at Pembroke, NH, date unknown;[755] m. at Andover, 26 Mar 1741, ELIZABETH CHANDLER, b. at Andover, 5 Feb 1721 daughter of Zebadiah and Sarah (Abbott) Chandler.

According to the History of Pembroke, NH, David Lovejoy came to Pembroke between 1738 and 1740.[756] The births of eleven children were reported at Pembroke.

i ELIZABETH LOVEJOY, b. 10 Jan 1742; d. at Pembroke, 11 Apr 1815; m. 12 Jan 1764, JEREMIAH MORGAN, b. at Pembroke, 18 Aug 1741 son of Luther and Abigail (-) Morgan; Jeremiah d. 21 Jul 1819.

ii CHANDLER LOVEJOY, b. 9 Apr 1744; d. 15 Jul 1810; m. 9 Mar 1809, ABIGAIL DAVIS, Abigail d. 23 Mar 1831; there are no known children.

iii PRISCILLA LOVEJOY; b. 12 Mar 1746; d. 14 Apr 1832; Priscilla does not seem to have married.

iv MOLLY LOVEJOY, b. 29 Apr 1748; d. at Salisbury, NH, 23 Feb 1813; m. 21 Nov 1769, JEREMIAH WARDWELL (*Abigail Gray Wardwell[4], Edward Gray[3], Hannah Holt Gray[2], Nicholas[1]*), b. at Andover 6 Dec 1748 son of Thomas and Abigail (Gray) Wardwell; Jeremiah d. 9 Jan 1817. Jeremiah remarried to Betsy after the death of Molly.

v ABIGAIL LOVEJOY, b. 12 Sep 1750; d. 18 Mar 1833; m. about 1770, her third cousin once removed, DANIEL HOLT (*Benjamin[4], Nicholas[3], Nicholas[2], Nicholas[1]*), b. at Pembroke 14 Sep 1744 son of Benjamin and Sarah (Frye) Holt; Daniel d. 5 Dec 1813. Abigail Lovejoy and Daniel Holt are Family 809.

vi MARTHA LOVEJOY, b. 16 Aug 1752; no further record was found for Martha.

vii PHEBE LOVEJOY, b. 28 Sep 1754; d. at Pembroke, Jun 1804; m. Feb 1779, NATHANIEL AMBROSE,[757] b. about 1752 (based on age at time of death). Nathaniel m. 2nd Elizabeth (-); Nathaniel d. 24 Mar 1835 at Deerfield, NH.[758]

viii OLIVE LOVEJOY, b. 13 Nov 1756; d. Feb 1843; m. 6 Mar 1781, THOMAS KIMBALL, b. at Andover, 17 Jul 1753 son of Thomas and Penelope (Johnson) Kimball; Thomas d. 20 Oct 1825.

---

754 Lapham, *History of Rumford, Oxford County, Maine*

755 The DAR uses a death date of 18 Feb 1819, but I believe that is a different David Lovejoy.

756 Carter and Fowler, *History of Pembroke*, p 243

757 Goodhue, *History and Genealogy of the Goodhue Family*. The Goodhue Family genealogy suggests parents as Jonathan and Abigail (Goodhue) Ambrose. The Pembroke, NH history suggests parent is Robert Ambrose.

758 Nathaniel Ambrose's will was written 17 Mar 1835 and entered probate April 1835.

ix DORCAS LOVEJOY, b. 1 Oct 1758; d. 1828 in Ohio; m. 28 Jan 1783, BENJAMIN MILLS, b. at Plaistow, NH, 30 Dec 1755 son of Reuben and Mary (Howard) Mills; Benjamin d. at Scioto County, OH, 15 Jul 1829.

x ESTHER LOVEJOY, b. 8 Mar 1764; d. likely in Vermont; m. 25 Aug 1792, AMOS LAKEMAN, b. at Bradford, 7 Jan 1762 son of Samuel ad Margaret (Kimball) Lakeman; Amos d. at Woodbury, VT 20 Dec 1850.

xi DAVID LOVEJOY, b. 16 Sep 1767; d. perhaps 1819; m. 16 Sep 1790, JANE COCHRAN, b, 1766 daughter of William and Betsy (Gile) Cochran;[759] Jane d. 28 Oct 1844. David and Jane did not have children.

280) CALEB LOVEJOY (*Sarah Farnum Lovejoy[4], Ralph Farnum[3], Elizabeth Holt Farnum[2], Nicholas[1]*), b. at Andover, 28 Dec 1716 son of Henry and Sarah (Farnum) Lovejoy; d. at Pembroke, 1781;[760] m. at Andover, 26 Jan 1738, MEHITABLE CHANDLER, b. at Andover, 1717 daughter of Zebadiah and Sarah (Abbott) Chandler; Mehitable d. at Andover, 26 Jan 1786.

Six children have been located for this family. The primary information comes from the History of Pembroke, New Hampshire.[761]

i ELIZABETH LOVEJOY, b. 1738; d. after 1810 at Bow, NH;[762] m. about 1766, JOHN ROBERTSON, b. at Londonderry, 9 Jun 1732 son of Samuel and Margaret (Woodend) Robertson; John d. at Bow, NH 11 Oct 1816.

ii MEHITABLE LOVEJOY, b. 1745; d. 2 Mar 1835 at Allenstown, NH; m. JONATHAN HUTCHINSON, b. 20 Mar 1747 son of Jonathan and Theodate (Morrill) Hutchinson; Jonathan d. at Pembroke, 3 May 1830.

iii CALEB LOVEJOY, b. 1749; d. 1821 (estate probate 7 Sep 1821);[763] m. MEHITABLE KIMBALL. Caleb m. 2nd JEMIMA JUDKINS; Jemima d. 15 Sep 1853.

iv JERUSHA LOVEJOY, b. 5 Oct 1753; d. at Pembroke, 11 Oct 1841; m. 6 Jun 1775, JOHN LADD, b. at Kingston, 6 Jan 1755 son of Trueworthy and Lydia (Harriman) Ladd; John d. 8 Jun 1835.

v MARTHA LOVEJOY, b. about 1760 at Pembroke, NH; death record not found; m. at Pembroke, 21 May 1781, her third cousin, JOHN PARKER, b. 15 Aug 1760 son of Joseph and Hannah (Abbott) Parker; John d. at Pembroke 27 May 1825.

vi OBADIAH LOVEJOY, b. 1756; he is reported to have been in the Battle of Bunker Hill and is believed to have died while serving in the Army.[764] But the Lovejoy book says he married Tryphena Waugh.[765] More research needs to be done.

vii Daughter, name not known who married John Moor of Pembroke the son of James and Agnes (Colbreath) Moor. This is a daughter listed in the Lovejoy Genealogy (p 74) and the History of Pembroke but her name is not yet found. However, the children that the History of Pembroke assigned to John Moor and the unknown daughter Lovejoy have birth records that list a mother's name as Martha. As Martha Lovejoy from this family married John Parker, it is not clear how all this disparate information fits together. This is most likely just a misidentification of the wife of John Moor.

281) JOSHUA LOVEJOY (*Sarah Farnum Lovejoy[4], Ralph Farnum[3], Elizabeth Holt Farnum[2], Nicholas[1]*), b. at Andover, 2 Dec 1719 son of Henry and Sarah (Farnum) Lovejoy; d. at Andover, 2 Feb 1812; m. at Andover, 24 Mar 1742/3, LYDEA ABBOTT, b. at Andover, 10 Feb 1722/3 daughter of Henry and Mary (Platts) Abbott; Lydea d. at Andover, 11 Sep 1807.

Joshua and Lydea had six children whose births are recorded at Andover.

i JOSHUA LOVEJOY, b. 8 Jan 1743/4; d. at Sanbornton, NH 28 Jan 1832; m. 30 Apr 1769, SARAH PERKINS, b. at Middleton, 10 Mar 1744 daughter of Timothy and Phebe (Peters) Perkins; Sarah d. 3 May 1828.

ii MARY LOVEJOY, b. 13 Aug 1745; d. 15 Apr 1826; m. 24 Sep 1765, JAMES PARKER whose parentage is not entirely clear;[766] James d. 23 Oct 1801. Mary m. 2nd Jonathan Cummings. There are not any records of children for Mary and James.

---

[759] Carter and Fowler, *History of Pembroke*, p. 36

[760] This is the date of death used by the DAR; a record was not located.

[761] Carter and Fowler, *History of Pembroke, NH*

[762] She appears to still be living at the 1810 Census as a woman in her age category is in the household headed by John Robertson.

[763] Caleb's brothers-in-law Jonathan Hutchinson and John Ladd participate in the administration of the estate in addition to widow Jemima.

[764] Carter and Fowler, *The History of Pembroke, NH*

[765] Lovejoy, *The Lovejoy Genealogy*, p 105

[766] His death record from 1801 gives his age as 66 years which would mean he was born in 1735. That conflicts with most published genealogies which have him born in 1745 son of James. The death record may be wrong.

iii LYDIA LOVEJOY, b. 21 Jul 1747; d. at Haverhill, MA, 3 Jan 1838; m. 23 Jun 1767, third cousin once removed, ABIEL HOLT (*Thomas[4], Thomas[3], Nicholas[2], Nicholas[1]*), b. 3 Apr 1746 son of Thomas and Hannah (Kimball) Holt; Abiel d. 17 Nov 1824. Lydia Lovejoy and Abiel Holt are Family 832.

iv DORCAS LOVEJOY, b. 18 Aug 1749; d. 25 Jun 1843; m. about 1770, as his second wife, her second cousin once removed, BENJAMIN AMES, b. 6 Jun 1724 son of Samuel and Hannah (Stevens) Ames; Benjamin d. 10 Jan 1809.

v CHLOE LOVEJOY, b. 26 Mar 1753; d. 21 Nov 1843; m. 26 Dec 1776, her fourth cousin, JOHN POOR, b. 16 Apr 1754 son of John and Rebecca (Stevens) Poor; John d. 7 Jul 1823.

vi LUCY LOVEJOY, b. 4 Aug 1755; d. at Andover, 2 Apr 1844; m. 11 Apr 1776, THEOPHILUS FRYE, b. at Andover, 12 Oct 1753 son of Samuel and Elizabeth (Frye) Frye; Theophilus d. 2 Apr 1830.

282) WILLIAM LOVEJOY (*Sarah Farnum Lovejoy[4], Ralph Farnum[3], Elizabeth Holt Farnum[2], Nicholas[1]*), b. at Andover, 10 Apr 1723 son of Henry and Sarah (Farnum) Lovejoy; d. at Andover, 1759 (probate 13 Nov 1759); m. at Andover, 13 Feb 1744, HANNAH EVANS; Hannah was living in 1773 at the final settlement of William's estate.

William Lovejoy did not leave a will and his estate entered probate 13 November 1759 with widow Hannah as administratrix.[767] The final settlement of the estate was initiated with bond on 30 June 1772. It was determined that the estate could not be divided without prejudice to the value of the property, and the real property was settled on eldest son William. A distribution from a total amount of £64 pounds was made to the following heirs: £21.6.8 to the widow for her dower; £10.13.2 to eldest son William Lovejoy; and £5.6.7 to each of the other heirs who are sons Henry, Samuel, and David and daughters Hannah, Lowis, and Sarah.

William and Hannah were parents of eight children born in Andover. Two of the sons are believed to have died in the Revolution. Sons William and David both served in Captain Benjamin Ames's Company which saw service at Bunker Hill.

i WILLIAM LOVEJOY, b. 26 Dec 1745; d. 8 Jul 1747.

ii HANNAH LOVEJOY, b. 12 Aug 1747; d. at Wilton, NH, 31 Aug 1812; m. at Andover, 16 Jun 1768, BENJAMIN STEEL, b. at Andover, 25 Jan 1741 son of Nicholas and Phebe (Stevens) Steel; Benjamin d. at Wilton, 14 Nov 1817.

iii WILLIAM LOVEJOY, b. 24 Jun 1749; he is believed to have been captured during the Revolution and taken to Halifax where he died in prison.[768]

iv SAMUEL LOVEJOY, baptized 25 Sep 1750; d. at Wilton, 6 Oct 1801; m. about 1774, LYDIA ABBOTT, b. at Andover, 23 Oct 1753 daughter of Joseph and Anna (Peabody) Abbott; Lydia d. at Wilton, 20 Sep 1826.

v LOIS LOVEJOY, baptized 14 Jun 1752; d. at Fryeburg, ME, about 1798; m. at Wilton, 1 Jul 1784, URIAH BALLARD, b. at Andover, 7 Oct 1758 son of Uriah and Lydia (Danforth) Ballard; Uriah d. at Fryeburg, 22 Dec 1840. Uriah married second Hannah Sargent on 8 Jul 1798.

vi HENRY LOVEJOY, b. 23 Nov 1753; d. at Wilton, 14 Feb 1835; m. 13 Jun 1780, ELIZABETH CUMMINGS, b. at Hollis, 23 Nov 1759 daughter of Ebenezer and Elizabeth (Abbott) Cummings; Elizabeth d. at Wilton, 3 Oct 1812.

vii DAVID LOVEJOY, b. 8 Sep 1755; David is thought to have died during the Revolution.

viii SARAH LOVEJOY, b. 28 Nov 1758; she was living in 1773; nothing further known.

283) STEPHEN LOVEJOY (*Sarah Farnum Lovejoy[4], Ralph Farnum[3], Elizabeth Holt Farnum[2], Nicholas[1]*), b. at Andover, 7 Jun 1724 son of Henry and Sarah (Farnum) Lovejoy; m. at York, ME, 26 Jun 1749, OLIVE TRAFTON, b. at York, 4 Dec 1725 daughter of Zacchaeus and Annabel (Allen) Trafton.

Stephen served in the French and Indian Wars in the company of Capt. Joseph Holt and participated in the expedition to Lake George where he was taken ill and his father had to hire a shay to return him to Andover and eventually back to York.[769]

The births of five children are recorded at York, Maine.

i STEPHEN LOVEJOY, b. 19 May 1750

ii SAMUEL LOVEJOY, b. 27 Apr 1752

iii ANNE LOVEJOY, b. 30 Jun 1754

---

[767] *Essex County, MA: Probate File Papers, 1638-1881.*Online database. *AmericanAncestors.org.* New England Historic Genealogical Society, 2014. Case 17080

[768] Livermore, *History of Wilton*, p 440

[769] Lovejoy, *The Lovejoy Genealogy*, p 63

iv THEODORE LOVEJOY, b. 5 Apr 1756

v JOSHUA LOVEJOY, b. 17 Mar 1758

284) PHEBE FARNUM (*Henry Farnum[4], Ralph Farnum[3], Elizabeth Holt Farnum[2], Nicholas[1]*), b. at Andover, 4 Jul 1713 daughter of Henry and Phebe (Russell) Farnum; d. at Windham, 1750 (probate Apr 1750); m. at Windham, 9 May 1735, JOSEPH PRESTON, b. at Andover, 22 Aug 1713 son of Joseph and Rebecca (Preston) Preston; Joseph d. at Windham, 24 Feb 1738.

Phebe Preston did not leave a will and her estate entered probate 4 April 1750. On 3 March 1757, Henry Preston of Lebanon signed that he as only heir to the estate had received eighty-six pounds six shillings from his guardian Eliphalet Farnum as his full payment from the estate.[770]

Phebe Farnum and Joseph Preston were parents of one child.

i HENRY PRESTON, b. at Canterbury, 12 Feb 1736 and baptized at Hampton, 14 Jun 1736. Henry was living in 1757 but nothing further is known.

285) HENRY FARNUM (*Henry Farnum[4], Ralph Farnum[3], Elizabeth Holt Farnum[2], Nicholas[1]*), b. at Andover, 8 Apr 1715 son of Henry and Phebe (Russell) Farnum; d. at Sprague, CT, 20 Jun 1799; m. 3 Nov 1741, SARAH READ (widow of Joseph Knight), b. at Norwich, 28 Dec 1711 daughter of William and Ann (Stark) Read; Sarah d. at Sprague, 24 Feb 1781.

There are three known children for Henry Farnum and Sarah Read.

i HENRY FARNUM, b. at Norwich, 8 Oct 1742; d. at Lisbon, CT, about 1824 (will 1818; probate 1824); m. at Norwich, 2 Jan 1766, ABIGAIL RUDD, b. about 1746 likely the daughter of Joseph and Sarah (Moseley) Rudd; Sarah d. at Sprague, 11 Dec 1824.

ii LYDIA FARNUM, b. at Canterbury, 17 Nov 1744; d. at Ashford, 5 Dec 1785; m. 14 Jun 1764, PHINEAS BURCHARD, baptized at Norwich, 24 Sep 1738 son of John and Jane (Hyde) Burchard; Phineas d. at Ashford, 8 Jun 1811.

iii PHEBE FARNUM, b. at Canterbury, 7 Mar 1746; d. at Canterbury, 21 Dec 1808; m. at Canterbury, 16 Dec 1773, DANIEL FROST, b. at Canterbury, 6 Jul 1748 son of Daniel and Elizabeth (Bond) Frost; Daniel d. at Canterbury, 27 Aug 1839.

286) MANASSEH FARNUM (*Henry Farnum[4], Ralph Farnum[3], Elizabeth Holt Farnum[2], Nicholas[1]*) b. at Windham, 15 Feb 1717 son of Henry and Phebe (Russell) Farnum; d. at Ashford, 1768 (probate 1768); m. at Windham, 23 Apr 1739, KEZIAH FORD, b. at Windham, 27 Mar 1721 daughter of Joseph and Elizabeth (Hovey) Ford; Keziah was living in 1768.

Manasseh was a farmer in Ashford and the family were members of the church at Scotland.[771]

In his will written 20 June 1768, Manasseh Farnum bequeaths to dearly beloved wife Kezia the use of the southeast room in the dwelling house while she is a widow, one cow, and a list of provision for her maintenance to be provided by the executor. She also receives the weaving loom and other household items which after her decease will be divided equally among his daughters. Son Manasseh receives ten shillings which with the one pound that Manasseh owes his father and the twenty pounds he has received is his full portion. Daughter Elizabeth Knowlton receives five shillings in addition to the thirteen pounds she received at her marriage. Daughters Kezia, Jemima, Unice, and Hannah each receive thirteen pounds in household goods, these amounts to be paid five, ten, fifteen, and twenty years after Manasseh's decease. Son Joseph receives the whole of the buildings, lands, and livestock and is also named executor.[772] Real estate was valued at £81 and personal estate at £79.15.11.

Manasseh Farnum and Keziah Ford were parents of eight children.

i MANASSAH FARNUM, b. at Windham, 29 Jul 1739; d. at Ashford, 16 May 1808; m. 19 Apr 1758, PATIENCE BIBBINS, b. 23 Oct 1733 daughter of Arthur and Abigail (Follett) Bibbins.[773]

ii KEZIAH FARNUM, b. 6 Jan 1741; d. 24 Feb 1741.

---

[770] *Connecticut State Library (Hartford, Connecticut);* Probate Place: *Hartford, Connecticut, Probate Packets, Pettis, James-Richardson, John, 1719-1880, Estate of Phebe Preston, Case 3102*

[771] Farnham, *New England Descendants of Ralph Farnum*, p 177

[772] *Connecticut State Library (Hartford, Connecticut);* Probate Place: *Hartford, Connecticut, Probate Packets, Falshaw, S-Fuller, E, 1752-1880, estate of Manassah Farnam, town of Ashford, case 1672*

[773] The 1758 probate record of Arter Bibbins includes a receipt signed by Manasseh Farnum in 1761 stating that he has received from Mrs. Abigail Bibbins payment from the estate.

iii ELIZABETH FARNUM, b. at Windham, 10 Mar 1742; d. at Ashford, 1 Jun 1786; m. 3 Nov 1763, DANIEL KNOWLTON, b. at Boxford, 23 Dec 1738 son of William and Martha (Pinder) Knowlton; Daniel d. at Ashford, 31 May 1825. Daniel married second Rebeckah Fenton on 24 Apr 1788.

iv JOSEPH FARNUM, b. at Windham, 28 Nov 1748; d. at Enfield, 1777 (probate 1777); m. 15 Mar 1770, CATHERINE SPRING, b. at Ashford, 3 Mar 1750 daughter of Josiah and Catherine (Bicknell) Spring. Catherine married second Henry Work. Catherine likely died by 1786 as Henry Work remarried in 1787.

v KEZIAH FARNUM, b. at Windham, 28 Nov 1751; m. about 1770 (first child born 1771), JOSEPH CHAPMAN who is not yet identified.

vi JEMIMA FARNUM, baptized at Scotland, CT, 26 May 1754

vii EUNICE FARNUM, b. at Windham, 1 Feb 1757; d. at Marcellus, NY, after 1810;[774] m. at Ashford, 16 Dec 1782, SILAS SNOW, b. at Ashford 18 Apr 1761 son of Oliver and Elizabeth (Phillips) Snow;[775] Silas d. at Granby, NY, about 1835.

viii HANNAH FARNUM, baptized at Scotland, 13 Apr 1762; d. at Marcellus, NY, 2 Feb 1841; m. 13 Nov 1788, JOSHUA CHANDLER, b. at Woodstock, 19 Sep 1763 son of Moses and Frances (Lyon) Chandler; Joshua d. at Marcellus, 19 Aug 1834.

287) EPHRAIM FARNUM (*Henry Farnum[4], Ralph Farnum[3], Elizabeth Holt Farnum[2], Nicholas[1]*), b. at Windham, 20 Mar 1721 son of Henry and Phebe (Russell) Farnum; d. at Norwich, about 1750 (probate 17 Jan 1751); m. 1 Nov 1744, CHENEY ANNE WHITE, b. at Marshfield, MA, 16 Jul 1722 daughter of Ebenezer and Hannah (Doggett) White. Cheney Anne second married John Louden.

Ephraim Farnum was a farmer in Norwich. He did not leave a will and his estate entered probate on 24 January 1751 with Channey Anne Farnum as administratrix. In May 1759, John Lowdon and Chenyanna Lowdon petitioned for the sale of the real estate as was necessary to pay debts of the estate of £549.7.8.[776]

Ephraim Farnum and Cheney Anne White were parents of two children.

i EPHRAIM FARNUM, b. at Norwich, 7 Aug 1745; m. at Norwich, 7 Jan 1768, SARAH HUNN, b. about 1736 (based on age 69 at time of death); Sarah d. at Boston, 6 Nov 1805. Ephraim and Sarah's son Henry was a successful silversmith in Boston and established his business in Boston in 1800.[777]

ii EBENEZER FARNUM, b. at Norwich, 4 Dec 1747. He left for Cornwallis, Nova Scotia perhaps arriving there in 1776. He received a land grant of 100 acres in 1783 in Nova Scotia. He did marry and had a family, but the information about that has not been located.[778][779]

288) JOSHUA FARNUM (*Henry Farnum[4], Ralph Farnum[3], Elizabeth Holt Farnum[2], Nicholas[1]*), b. at Windham, 29 Mar 1723 son of Henry and Phebe (Russell) Farnum; d. at Scotland, CT, 3 Feb 1797; m. at Hampton, 6 Jun 1748, SARAH FORD, b. at Windham, 20 Dec 1714 daughter of Joseph and Elizabeth (Hovey) Ford; Sarah d. at Scotland, 28 Apr 1789.

Joshua Farnum and Sarah Ford were parents of two children.

i SARAH FARNUM, b. at Windham, 27 Mar 1749; d. 26 Aug 1758.

ii ELIZABETH FARNUM, b. at Windham, 17 Jan 1752; d. at Windham, about 1812;[780] m. at Windham, 7 Apr 1774, ASA BOTTOM,[781] b. at Norwich, 3 Aug 1748 son of David and Lucy (Read) Bottom; Asa d. at Windham, 1812 (probate 1812).

---

[774] Silas and Eunice moved from Ashford to Marcellus in 1808 (according to his pension file) and Eunice appears to be living at the 1810 census but not in 1820. Some genealogies report that Eunice died in Ashford in 1834 but that is the death record of Eunice the wife of Perley Snow.

[775] Silas provides his birth date in his Revolutionary War pension application file as 18 Apr 1761 which leads to the conclusion that his parents are Oliver and Elizabeth Snow. Also in the record is a statement in 1839 from daughter Eunice Snow applying for a payment from the pension board related to the case of her father who was then deceased.

[776] *Connecticut State Library (Hartford, Connecticut)*; Probate Place: *Hartford, Connecticut, Estate of Ephraim Farnam, Town of Norwich, Case 3762*

[777] New Hampshire Historical Society, https://www.nhhistory.org/object/973259/farnam-henry-1773-1852

[778] Nova Scotia Archives; Halifax, Nova Scotia, Canada; Census, Assesment and Poll Tax Records 1767-1827; Reference: Commissioner of Public Records Nova Scotia Archives RG 1 vol. 443 no. 38

[779] Halifax, Nova Scotia, Canada; Nova Scotia Land Petitions (1765-1800); Volume Number: 1

[780] The 1812 probate record of her husband Asa Bottom includes a separate inventory of "Mother's things" taken by administrator Walter Bottom.

[781] Asa's father was David Longbottom, but the name was shortened to Bottom. Asa's father wrote his will as David Bottom. Asa's birth transcription lists his father as David Longbottom.

289) ELIPHALET FARNUM (*Henry Farnum⁴, Ralph Farnum³, Elizabeth Holt Farnum², Nicholas¹*), b. at Windham, 21 Mar 1725 son of Henry and Phebe (Russell) Farnum; m. 1st at Canterbury, 11 Oct 1750, MARY ROGERS, possibly Mary b. at Windham, 6 Oct 1727 daughter of Hope and Esther (Meacham) Rogers; Mary d. at Canterbury, 1 May 1753. Eliphalet m. 2nd at Canterbury, 1 Feb 1757, MARY ADAMS.

Eliphalet Farnum and Mary Rogers were parents of one child.

i ELIPHALET FARNUM, b. 14 Sep 1751; d. 8 Nov 1754.

Eliphalet Farnum and Mary Adams were parents of one child.

i ELIPHALET FARNUM, b. at Canterbury, 25 Aug 1759; d. at Addison County, VT, 10 Sep 1833; m. at Keene, NH, 16 Oct 1786, HANNAH ADAMS, b. about 1762 daughter of Jonathan and Hannah (Yeamans) Adams;[782] Hannah d. at Middlebury, VT, 14 Apr 1844.

290) ELIAB FARNUM (*Henry Farnum⁴, Ralph Farnum³, Elizabeth Holt Farnum², Nicholas¹*), b. at Windham, 24 Jul 1731 son of Henry and Phebe (Russell) Farnum; d. at Otisville, NY, 9 Jun 1806; m. at Preston, 19 Jun 1754, ABIGAIL KILLAM, b. at Norwich, 19 Aug 1736 daughter of John and Abigail (Kimball) Killam; Abigail d. at Otisville, about 1782. Eliab m. 2nd EUNICE NICHOLS, b. about 1739. Eunice had two previous marriages to John Osborne and Samuel Bouton.

Eliab Farnum served during the French and Indian War as a drummer in the second Connecticut regiment commanded by Col. Nathan Whiting.[783] During the Revolution, Capt. Eliab Farnum commanded the eighth Lackaway company in the 24th regiment of Col. Nathan Denison. This regiment participated in the June 1778 Battle of Wyoming.[784]

Eliab received property on 20 May 1773 in the Delaware Purchase of what was to become Palmyra Township in Pike County, Pennsylvania.[785]

In his will written 20 March 1805, Eliab Farnum of Deer Park bequeathed to wife Eunice provisions for her support currently provided by sons Eliab and Joshua to continue after his decease. Son Russell receives one undivided half of property in Lackawack and the other half to be divided among sons George Whitfield, Jeffrey Amherst, Eliab, Stephen, and Joshua. The moveable estate is divided among his five daughters Abigail, Martha, Mary, Sarah, and Marcy.[786]

Eliab Farnum and Abigail Killam were parents of fourteen children.

i PHEBE FARNUM, b. at Preston, 10 Sep 1756; m. at Preston, 24 Mar 1774, AMOS PARKE, b. at Preston, 9 Sep 1749 son of Silas and Sarah (Ayer) Parke; Amos d. at Preston, 1 Oct 1825. Amos married second Margaret Moore. He was a physician.

ii JOSHUA FARNUM, b. at Preston, 31 Aug 1758; d. in the Wyoming Valley during the Revolution. The Farnum genealogy reports there are reports that Joshua died in the Wyoming massacre which was in July 1778. Miner's History of Wyoming records his death as 28 March 1781 during an attack on Chamber's Mills on the Delaware.[787]

iii ABIGAIL FARNUM, b. at Preston, 2 Sep 1760; m. 1st about 1778, ELEAZER OWEN, b. at Salisbury, CT, 16 Apr 1755 son of Jonathan and Patience (Vallance) Owen; Eleazer died at the Battle of Minisink, 22 Jul 1779. Abigail m. 2nd at Chemung, NY, 2 Feb 1784, ABIEL FRYE, b. at Andover, 8 Nov 1734 son of Abiel and Abigail (Emery) Frye; Abiel d. at Goshen, NY, 2 Oct 1806. A story reported by Charlotte Helen Abbott in her notes on the Frye family was that Abiel was on Washington's staff in the Revolution. While in Pennsylvania, he courted Abigail in Connecticut, but she married Eleazer Owen. When Abiel learned she widowed, he followed the family while they were moving to the Mohawk Valley and proposed to Abigail.[788]

iv MARTHA FARNUM, d. at Preston, 29 Aug 1762; b. likely at Sanford, NY, 2 Nov 1843; m. 1791, NATHAN AUSTIN, b. at Preston, 5 Apr 1764 son of Benjamin and Susanna (Burdick) Austin; Nathan d. 1847.

v MARY FARNUM, b. at Preston, 29 Aug 1762; d. at New Castle, NY, 5 Feb 1838;[789] m. an unknown PURDY.[790]

---

782 Adams, *A Genealogical History of Henry Adams of Braintree, Mass.*, volume 1, p 544

783 Guertin, Iris, Rose, comp. *Connecticut Soldiers, French and Indian War, 1755-62* [database on-line]. Provo, UT, USA: Ancestry.com Operations Inc, 2000.

784 Brewster, *History of the Certified Township of Kingston, Pennsylvania*, p 131

785 Farnham, *New England Descendants of Ralph Farnum*, p 184. A detailed description of Eliab's military and civic service can be found on pp 182-184.

786 New York Probate Records, 1629-1971, Orange County, Wills 1797-1807, Vol C, pp 349-351.

787 Miner, *History of Wyoming*, p 294

788 Abbott, Early Records of the Frye Family of Andover, https://www.mhl.org/sites/default/files/files/Abbott/Frye%20Family.pdf

789 The grave of Mary Purdy in Archer-Sarles Cemetery bears this inscription: In memory of Mary Purdy who died Feb. 5, 1838 aged 75 yrs. 6 mo. & 18 d's; Findagrave: 128537582

790 Farnham, The Descendants of Ralph Farnum

vi RUSSELL FARNUM, b. at Preston, 9 Sep 1764; d. at McClure, NY, 23 Feb 1820; m. about 1794, EUNICE VAN DEUZEN, b. about 1773; Eunice d. at McClure, 26 Oct 1834.

vii MERCY FARNUM, b. 9 Sep 1764

viii SARAH FARNUM, b. 13 Jan 1769; d. at McClure, NY, 10 Mar 1807 in childbirth; m. 26 Feb 1791, WILLIAM MACCLURE,[791] b. at Chester, NH, 1726 son of James and Jean (Andrews) MacClure; William d. at McClure, 14 Dec 1826. William married second Lydia Austin.

ix JEFFREY AMHERST FARNUM, b. at Preston, 17 Oct 1772; d. at Scipio, NY, 12 Nov 1841; m. at Big Flats, NY, Dec 1793, MERCY TRACY, b. at Norwich, 16 Sep 1775 daughter of Benjamin and Olive (Killam) Tracy; Mercy d. at Pittsford, NY, 11 May 1873.

x GEORGE WHITFIELD FARNUM, b. at Preston, 17 Oct 1772; d. after 1838[792] likely at Ledyard, NY; m. about 1800, ANNA ALLEN, b. about 1780 daughter of Gideon and Phebe (Beardsley) Allen; Anna d. after 1838.

xi ELIAB FARNUM, b. at Coventry, CT, 4 Aug 1775; d. at Benton Township, PA, 31 Mar 1855; m. at Deer Park, NY, 1 Jan 1797, HANNAH OSBORNE, b. at South Salem, NY, 24 Apr 1778 daughter of John and Eunice (Nichols) Osborne; Hannah d. 24 Aug 1835.

xii EPHRAIM FARNUM, b. 9 Nov 1777; perhaps died young

xiii STEPHEN FARNUM, b. at Deer Park, NY, 19 Oct 1779; d. at Crawford, NY, 27 Apr 1867; m. about 1810, KETURAH SAYBOTT, b. at Goshen, NY, 6 Sep 1787 daughter of Frederick and Abigail (Reeve) Saybott; Keturah d. at Hopewell, NY, 6 Dec 1872.

xiv JOSHUA FARNUM, b. at Deer Park, 8 Dec 1781; m. before 1806 PERSIS.

291) JOSEPH FARNUM (*Ralph Farnum[4], Ralph Farnum[3], Elizabeth Holt Farnum[2], Nicholas[1]*), b. at York, 20 Jun 1713 son of Ralph and Elizabeth (Austin) Farnum; d. at Lebanon, ME, 1779 (probate 6 Nov 1779); m. about 1734, MEHITABLE WEBBER, b. at York, 20 Jun 1713 daughter of Benjamin and Mehitable (Allen) Webber; Mehitable d. about 1750. Joseph m. 2nd, EUNICE who has not been identified, b. about 1729 and d. 31 May 1803.

Joseph Farnum of Lebanon did not leave a will and his estate entered probate 5 November 1779 with widow Eunice Farnham declining administration of the estate requesting that son Joseph assume this duty.[793] Real estate was valued at £1800 and the house and barn at £1400. With the inventory of the personal estate, the total value was £5214.

Joseph Farnum and Mehitable Webber were parents of eight children born at York, Maine.[794] Little information was found for the children in this family beyond their birth records.

i STARLIN FARNUM, b. 24 Jan 1734/5

ii ELIZABETH FARNUM, b. 22 Oct 1736

iii JOSEPH FARNUM, b. 10 Feb 1738; d. at Lancaster, NH, 23 Aug 1801; m. 1st at Lebanon, ME, 19 Dec 1760, MARTHA BLAISDELL, b. at York, 11 May 1743 daughter of Ephraim and Thankful (Webber) Blaisdell; Martha d. at Lebanon, ME, 26 Jul 1786. Joseph m. 2nd at Lebanon, 7 Nov 1787, HANNAH JONES.

iv MARY FARNUM, b. 24 Apr 1741

v SARAH FARNUM, b. 5 Apr 1744

vi ELIAKIM FARNUM, b. 11 Feb 1746

vii TABATHA FARNUM, b. 24 Sep 1748

viii MEHITABLE FARNUM, b. 15 Jul 1750

Joseph and Eunice Farnum were parents of four children born at Berwick.

i ALICE FARNUM, b. 1753; d. at Lebanon, ME, 14 Sep 1827; m. 1st at Lebanon, 25 Nov 1773, JOSEPH BURROUGHS, b. about 1750 son of Edward and Mary (Low) Burroughs; Joseph d. by 1818. Alice m. 2nd at Lebanon, 7 Sep 1818, NOAH LORD, b. at Berwick, 30 Apr 1748 son of Ebenezer and Martha (Emery) Lord; Noah d. at Lebanon, 19 Dec 1835. Noah was first married to Keziah Brackett.

---

[791] Transcripts of letters written by William to Sarah during his courtship of her can be seen in Farnham's Farnum genealogy.

[792] When he executed a deed

[793] Maine, York County, Probate Estate Files, Estate of Joseph Farnum, Case 5564, accessed through familysearch.org

[794] NEHGR, Vital Records of York, Maine, volume 111, p 97

ii NATHANIEL FARNUM, b. 1755; m. at Berwick, 1 Mar 1779, ELIZABETH LORD, b. at Berwick, 27 Feb 1756 daughter of Samuel and Mary (Stone) Lord.

iii MERCY FARNUM, b. 1757; d. at Lebanon, ME, 1826; m. 13 Sep 1774, SOLOMON HARTFORD, b. at Rochester, NH, 18 Feb 1758 son of Stephen and Susannah (Wentworth) Hartford;[795] Solomon d. at Lebanon, ME, 1832.

iv BARACHIAS FARNUM, b. 1760; d. at Sanbornton, NH, 27 Mar 1842; m. 1st at Lebanon, 27 Aug 1781, MARTHA STEVENS, b. 1743; Martha d. at Lebanon, 14 Dec 1786. Barachias m. 2nd 30 Sep 1787, MERIBAH GOODWIN, b. at Berwick, 1765 daughter of Elijah and Abigail (Martin) Goodwin; Meribah d. 2 Apr 1842.

292) RALPH FARNUM (*Ralph Farnum⁴, Ralph Farnum³, Elizabeth Holt Farnum², Nicholas¹*), b. at York, 21 May 1715 son of Ralph and Elizabeth (Austin) Farnum; d. at York, 1746; m. at York, 21 Aug 1742, ALICE HARRIS, b. at York, 14 Feb 1716 daughter of Joseph and Elizabeth (Donnell) Harris; Alice d. at Scarborough, ME, about 1778. Alice was second married to Thomas Curtis and third married to Samuel Bragdon.

Ralph and Alice were parents of one child.

i ELIZABETH FARNUM, b. at York, 14 Aug 1743; m. at Scarborough, ME, 15 Apr 1764, CHRISTOPHER KELLEY who has not been identified.

293) MATTHEW FARNUM (*Ralph Farnum⁴, Ralph Farnum³, Elizabeth Holt Farnum², Nicholas¹*), b. at York, 4 Aug 1719 son of Ralph and Elizabeth (Austin) Farnum; d. at Crown Point, 11 Nov 1757; m. at York, 31 Mar 1738, DOROTHY WEBBER, b. at York, 11 Feb 1719/20 daughter of Benjamin and Mehitable (Allen) Webber; Dorothy d. at Penobscot, after 1791. Dorothy was second married to John Grindle.

Matthew and Dorothy married in York, but settled in the area of Lebanon, Maine (which was incorporated in 1767). Matthew enlisted for the expedition to Crown Point where he died.[796] There are six children known for Matthew and Dorothy, the youngest child baptized at Rochester, New Hampshire shortly after the time of Matthew's enlistment.

Matthew Farnum did not leave a will and his widow Dorothy declined administration of the estate 2 April 1760 and Matthew's brother Joseph Farnum was named administrator. Real estate was valued at £71.7.[797]

i BENJAMIN FARNUM, b at Lebanon, about 1742; d. at Belgrade, ME, 12 May 1835; m. 1st at Lebanon, 17 Oct 1766, SARAH BLAISDELL, b. at Lebanon, 1746 daughter of Ephraim and Thankful (Webber) Blaisdell; Sarah d. at Lebanon, 11 May 1786. Benjamin m. 2nd about 1787, ELIZABETH MILLS, b. about 1745; Elizabeth d. at Belgrade, 31 Dec 1831.

ii DOROTHY FARNUM, b. about 1744; living in 1799 (probate of husband's estate); m. by 1761, JONATHAN DOOR, b. about 1734 son of Philip and Sarah (Child) Door; Jonathan d. at Lebanon, about Dec 1799 (probate 16 Dec 1799).

iii DAVID FARNUM, b. about 1749; d. at Lebanon, 6 Sep 1814; m. 1st at Lebanon, 26 Mar 1778, ANNA WINGATE, b. Sept 1742 daughter of Samuel Wingate; Anna d. at Lebanon, 9 Mar 1788. David m. 2nd at Berwick, ME, 24 Nov 1788, ABIGAIL DONNELL, b. at York, 7 Jul 1753 daughter of Benjamin and Sarah (Kingsbury) Donnell; Abigail d. at Lebanon, 30 Sep 1846.

iv ABIGAIL FARNUM, b. about 1750

v MATTHEW FARNUM, b. 1 Mar 1755; d. at Brooksville, ME, Jul 1821; m. about 1775, MARTHA BASTEEN, b. 1758 daughter of Joseph and Ann (Hascom) Basteen); Martha d. at Brooksville, 2 Jun 1835.

vi GERSHOM FARNUM, baptized at Rochester, NH, Apr 1757; d. at Belgrade, ME, 22 Sep 1827; m. about 1777, DOLLY MOORE, b. at York, 5 Dec 1759 daughter of David and Bethiah (Cole) Moore.

294) JONATHAN FARNHAM (*Ralph Farnum⁴, Ralph Farnum³, Elizabeth Holt Farnum², Nicholas¹*), b. at York, 11 Apr 1726 son of Ralph and Elizabeth (Austin) Farnum; d. at York, 12 Dec 1800; m. at York, 27 Dec 1750, DEBORAH DUNNING, b. at York, 9 May 1732 daughter of William and Deborah (Donnell) Dunning; Deborah d. at York, 2 Sep 1820.

Jonathan and Deborah resided in York where Jonathan fulfilled his civic duties as fence viewer, field driver, and hog reeve.[798]

Jonathan Farnham did not leave a will and his estate entered probate 20 April 1801 with Deborah Farnham as administratrix.[799] The total value of the estate was $285.19. The dower was set off to Deborah 20 December 1802. Debts of the estate were $231.27. The real estate was sold to settle the debts.

---

795 Farnham, *Descendants of Ralph Farnum*, p 362

796 Farnham, *Descendants of Ralph Farnum*, p 196

797 Maine, York County Probate, Estate Files 1690-1917, Case 5565

798 Banks, *History of York, Maine*, volume I, p 378

799 Maine, York County Probate, Estate Files 1690-1917, Case 5562

Jonathan Farnham and Deborah Dunning were parents of ten children born at York, Maine.[800]

i MARY FARNHAM, b. 12 Nov 1751; m. at York, 23 Mar 1775, WENTWORTH DOWNS. No further information was found. Wentworth Downs is not in census records for 1790 or 1800. There is a Mary Downs who died at Dayton, ME on 23 Nov 1829 at age 78 which may be this Mary.

ii MERCY FARNHAM, b. 19 May 1753; d. at York, 23 Aug 1850;[801] m. at York, 10 May 1779, RICHARD VARRELL.

iii DEBORAH FARNHAM, b. 20 Jan 1755; m. at York, 20 Oct 1774, as his second wife, JACOB PERKINS, baptized at Wells, ME, 17 Jun 1744 son of Jacob and Anna (Littlefield) Perkins.[802] Jacob was first married to Abigail Trafton.

iv JONATHAN FARNHAM, b. 29 Aug 1757; d. at York, 17 Mar 1837; m. 6 Oct 1777, LYDIA CHAPMAN; Lydia d. at York, Jun 1807.

v ELIZABETH FARNHAM, baptized 9 Dec 1759

vi RALPH FARNHAM, baptized 7 Mar 1762

vii GINNIE FARNHAM, baptized 20 May 1764

viii WILLIAM FARNHAM, baptized 7 Dec 1766; d. at Sangerville, ME, 5 Jul 1856; m. 1st about 1794, HANNAH thought to be Varnum daughter of William and Elizabeth; Hannah d. at Sangerville, 4 Nov 1815. William m. 2nd 12 Feb 1818, MARY A. EVELETH (likely a widow), born about 1774; Mary d. after 1860 when she was living in Sangerville

ix BENJAMIN FARNHAM, b. 12 Mar 1769; m. 15 Aug 1800, MARY BANE, b. about 1774; Mary d. about 1802 after the birth of her only child.

x SAMUEL FARNHAM, baptized 5 Apr 1772; d. at Bucksport, ME, after 1820; m. 1795, HANNAH H. EAMS, b. about 1776; Hannah d. at Bucksport, 1 Mar 1854.

295) NATHANIEL FARNUM (*Ralph Farnum⁴, Ralph Farnum³, Elizabeth Holt Farnum², Nicholas¹*), b. at York, 1 May 1728 son of Ralph and Elizabeth (Austin) Farnum; d. at York after 4 Dec 1802;[803] m. at York, 15 Jan 1757, MARY AUSTIN, b. at York, 11 Mar 1728/9 daughter of Joseph and Sarah (Grant) Austin.

There are seven children of Nathaniel Farnum and Mary Austin born at York.[804]

i NATHANIEL FARNUM, b. about 1757; d. at Berwick, ME, about 1847. The name of Nathaniel's first wife is unknown. He married 2nd at Berwick, 1802, LORENA "LOVE" BRAGDON,[805] b. about 1775.

ii PATIENCE FARNUM, b. about 1758; she was living and unmarried in 1820.

iii BETSEY FARNUM, b. about 1760; d. after 1820

iv HANNAH FARNUM, baptized 4 Mar 1764; m. at York, 8 Aug 1789, MOSES BUZZELL, baptized at Wells, 12 Sep 1762 son of Isaac and Hannah (Eldridge) Buzzell.

v MARY "MOLLY" FARNUM, b. 1768. There is a Molly Farnham of York who married Jacob Littlefield of Wells, ME on 10 Jul 1808, but this seems unlikely for this Molly.

vi ISABELLA FARNUM, baptized 10 Sep 1769; d. after 1850 when she was living at South Berwick in the home of her daughter Isabella and her husband Jeremiah Allen; m. at Berwick, Apr 1802, HENRY BEEDLE, b. at York, 1760 (age 80 in 1840); Henry d. at South Berwick, after 1840.

vii SAMUEL FARNUM, baptized 10 Sep 1769; d. before 1820; m. at Wells, 20 Jul 1793, SARA WEBBER, b. at Wells, 25 Sep 1769 daughter of John and Alice (Hasty) Webber.

296) PAUL FARNUM (*Ralph Farnum⁴, Ralph Farnum³, Elizabeth Holt Farnum², Nicholas¹*), b. at York, 20 Apr 1730 son of Ralph and Elizabeth (Austin) Farnum; d. at Acton, ME, 12 Apr 1820; m. at Rochester, NH, 10 Jun 1753; ELIZABETH DORR, b. about 1733 daughter of Philip and Lydia (Mason) Dorr.

---

[800] Farnham, *Descendants of Ralph Farnum*, p 202

[801] Farnham, *Descendants of Ralph Farnum*, p 202

[802] Perkins, *Jacob Perkins of Wells*, p 6

[803] This is based on the execution of a deed as reported in Farnham, *Descendants of Ralph Farnum*, p 203

[804] Farnham, *Descendants of Ralph Farnum*, p 204

[805] Maine, Marriage Records, 1713-1922, Maine State Archives; Cultural Building, 84 State House Station, Augusta, ME 04333-0084; Pre 1892 Delayed Returns; Roll Number: 35

Paul and Elizabeth resided in Rochester, New Hampshire and later in Lebanon, Shapleigh, and Acton, Maine. They were parents of six children.[806]

i MARY FARNUM, baptized at Rochester, NH, 4 Aug 1754; m. at Lebanon, ME, 22 Apr 1778, HENRY STEVENS

ii RALPH FARNHAM, b. at Rochester, 7 Jul 1756; d. at Acton, ME, 26 Dec 1860; m. about 1784, MEHITABLE BEAN, b. at Raymond, NH, 28 Aug 1765 daughter of Benjamin and Hannah (Smith) Bean; Mehitable d. at Acton, 8 Mar 1842. Ralph Farnham was the last survivor of the Battle of Bunker Hill.[807]

iii ELIZABETH "BETTY" FARNUM, b. about 1760; d. at Shapleigh, ME, 10 Aug 1819. Betty did not marry.

iv OLIVE FARNUM, b. 29 Aug 1763; d. at Lebanon, ME, 29 May 1847; m. about 1783, SAMUEL RUNNELS, b. about 1754 son of Samuel Runnels.

v PAUL FARNUM, b. 15 Jun 1766; d. at Acton, ME, 1845; m. at Berwick, ME, 2 Jan 1787, OLIVE LORD, b. 1766 daughter of Nathan and Elizabeth (Shackley) Lord; Olive d. after 1850 when she was living at Acton.

vi DUMMER FARNUM, b. at Berwick, about 1770; d. after 1830 when he was head of household at Acton, m. at Rochester, NH, 2 Dec 1790, DOROTHY HEARD, b. about 1772 daughter of Joseph Heard; Dorothy d. after 1821.

297) BETTY FARNUM (*Ralph Farnum⁴, Ralph Farnum³, Elizabeth Holt Farnum², Nicholas¹*), b. at York, 14 Aug 1732 daughter of Ralph and Elizabeth (Austin) Farnum; m.at York, 4 Oct 1753, BENJAMIN JAQUES, b. at York, 17 Oct 1731 son of Richard and Mary (Harmon) Jaques.[808]

Betty and Benjamin resided in Harpswell, perhaps relocating to Bowdoin before their deaths. Benjamin was involved in the community serving on a committee in 1764 to establish a ferry near the Narrows. He was also a member of a committee to provide assistance to those in need: "if any Chh. Members who conduct according to the Gosple, and are well reported of but by the providence of God are cast into those circumstances which necessarily call for Relief, and the committee to make it known to the Pastor, and the pastor to call the Brethren together that they may judge of their Case and according to their Liberality releive them."[809]

Betty Farnum and Benjamin Jaques were parents of seven children born at Harpswell, Maine.

i BENJAMIN JAQUES, b. 20 Mar 1758; d. at Bowdoin, ME, 27 Feb 1832; m. about 1782, ELIZABETH GRAVES, b. 19 Apr 1759 daughter of Johnson and Sarah (Staples) Graves; Elizabeth d. at Bowdoin, 15 Feb 1848.

ii JOHN JAQUES, b. 25 May 1760; d. after 1850 when he was living in Bowdoin; m. ABIGAIL ALEXANDER, b. about 1765.

iii MARY JAQUES, b. 22 Jul 1762

iv ISAAC JAQUES, b. 9 Feb 1765; d. at Bowdoin, 16 Oct 1847;[810] m. 1st about 1790, MARY, b. about 1766; Mary d. at Bowdoin, 30 Nov 1822. Isaac m. 2nd ANNA, b. about 1780; Anna d. at Bowdoin, 2 Feb 1847.

v JOSEPH JAQUES, b. 14 Jul 1767; m. about 1792, ABIGAIL RAYMOND, b. at Bowdoinham, about 1772.

vi BETTY JAQUES, b. 4 Nov 1769; d. at Topsham, 18 Jan 1828; m. 13 Dec 1792, CRISPUS GRAVES, b. at Topsham, 20 Oct 1767 son of Johnson and Sarah (Staples) Graves; Crispus d. at Topsham, 9 Mar 1850.

vii SARAH JAQUES, b. 5 Jun 1772; d. at Topsham, 6 Apt 1816; m. at Bowdoin, 22 Apr 1792, WILLIAM GRAVES, b. at Bowdoin, 4 Apr 1765 son of Johnson and Sarah (Staples) Graves; William d. at Topsham, 12 Oct 1844. William married second Katherine *Potter* Denham on 12 Mar 1817.

298) JOHN FARNUM (*Ralph Farnum⁴, Ralph Farnum³, Elizabeth Holt Farnum², Nicholas¹*), b. at York, 26 May 1735 son of Ralph and Elizabeth (Austin) Farnum; d. at Bowdoin, 24 Nov 1819; m. about 1762, ABIGAIL STOVER,[811] b. at York, 19 Sep 1732 daughter of John and Miriam (Harmon) Stover.

John Farnum and Abigail Stover were parents of eight children born at Bowdoin.[812]

i ELIZABETH "BETSEY" FARNUM, b. 31 Jan 1763; m. at Bowdoin, 8 Sep 1780, LUTHER HALL, b. at Marshfield, MA, 14 Sep 1755 son of John and Zilpha (Crocker) Hall; Luther d. at Bowdoin, 4 Oct 1826.

---

806 Farnham, *The Descendants of Ralph Farnum*, p 206

807 Appleton's Cyclopedia of American Biography 1600-1889, volume II, p 411

808 Wheeler, *History of Brunswick*, p 841

809 Wheeler, *History of Brunswick*, p 440

810 Maine, J. Gary Nichols Cemetery Collection, ca. 1780-1999

811 Some records also give the name of this family as Storer.

812 The children in this family used a variety of last name spellings: Farnham, Farnum, Varnam, and Varnum.

ii JOHN FARNUM, b. 7 Apr 1765; d. after 1850 when he was living with his daughter Catherine Farnum Wing in Litchfield, ME; m. by 1792, JUDITH who has not been identified. Judith d. before 1850.

iii WANTON STOVER VARNAM, b. 28 Aug 1767; d. at Staten Island, NY, 17 Jun 1821; m. at Bowdoin, 1796, BETSEY EATON, b. at Middleborough, MA, 20 Sep 1777 daughter of Ziba and Ruth (Leonard) Eaton; Betsey d. at Salem, MA, 1 Dec 1854.

iv ABIGAIL FARNUM, b. 27 Sep 1769; d. at Bowdoin likely between 1820 and 1830; m. 10 Oct 1792, JOHN POTTER, b. 1766 son of James and Mary (Spear) Potter; John d. at Bowdoin, 10 Dec 1855.

v MARIAM FARNUM, b. 8 Oct 1771; died young

vi MARY "POLLY" FARNUM, b. 23 May 1774; m. at Bowdoin, 12 Nov 1794, BENJAMIN WHITNEY, Jr., b. est. about 1764 (listed as over 45 at 1810 census). There are records for births of seven children of Polly and Benjamin at Bowdoin. They appear to still be living in Bowdoin in 1830 with Benjamin head of household age 60-69, female age 50-59, and four other adolescent/young adults.

vii RALPH VARNUM, b. 27 Feb 1777; d. at Bowdoinham, 2 Nov 1815; m. about 1800, EUNICE SNOW, b. at Haverhill, MA Oct 1783 (based on age 81 years 1 month at death) daughter of Isaac and Eunice (Totman) Snow;[813] Eunice d. at Lawrence, MA (buried at Bowdoin), 19 Nov 1864.[814]

viii MARIAM FARNUM, b. 1 Oct 1780

299) DANIEL FARNHAM (*Daniel Farnum⁴, Ralph Farnum³, Elizabeth Holt Farnum², Nicholas¹*), b. at York, 15 Nov 1719 son of Daniel and Hannah (Bragdon) Farnum; d. at Newburyport, MA, 18 Mar 1776; m. at Cambridge, 11 Jul 1740, SYBIL ANGIER, b. 5 Sep 1718 daughter of Samuel and Dorothy (Avery) Angier; Sybil d. at Newburyport, Jun 1797.

Daniel Farnham graduated from Harvard in 1739, was admitted to the bar, and was an attorney in Newburyport. He built a large house for his family in Newburyport and was active in town affairs. In the pre-Revolutionary period, he was a loyalist to the crown. He was outcast by friends and professional associates. He died in May 1776.[815]

Daniel Farnham did not leave a will and his estate entered probate 8 July 1776 with William Farnham as administrator. Those signing receipts in 1786 and 1787 that they received their full distribution from the estate were Micajah Sawyer and Sybil Sawyer, William Farnham signing as guardian for Katharine Hay Weld (daughter of Hannah Weld deceased), John Hay and Katharine Hay, and Josiah Smith and Dolly Smith. Real estate was valued at £1161.13.4.[816]

Daniel Farnham and Sybil Angier were parents of ten children born at Newbury.

i DANIEL FARNHAM, b. 27 Jan 1741/2; d. 29 Jan 1747.

ii WILLIAM FARNHAM, b. 26 Nov 1744; d. at Newbury, of consumption, 30 Oct 1760. William was a student at Harvard and left in his sophomore year due to illness.

iii SYBIL FARNHAM, b. 28 Nov 1746; d. at Newburyport, 8 Jul 1842; m. 25 Nov 1766, Dr. MICAJAH SAWYER, b. at Newbury, 15 Jul 1737 son of Enoch and Sarah (Pierpoint) Sawyer; Micajah d. at Newburyport, 22 Sep 1815.

iv HANNAH FARNHAM, b. 13 Feb 1748; d. at Braintree, MA, 31 Mar 1778; m. 12 Feb 1776, as his second wife, Rev. EZRA WELD, b. at Pomfret, 13 Jun 1736 son of John and Esther (Waldo) Weld; Ezra d. at Braintree, 16 Jan 1816. Ezra was a graduate of Yale. Ezra was first married to Anna Weld. After Hannah's death, Ezra had a third marriage to Abigail Greenleaf and a fourth marriage to Mary Howland.

v KATHARINE FARNHAM, b. 7 Apr 1751; d. at Boston, 17 Sep 1826; m. 6 Oct 1774, JOHN HAY who was a mariner; John d. before 1820. Catharine and John do not seem to have had children. In her will (probate 1826), Catharine had bequests to her nephew John Hay Farnham in Indiana territory and his daughter Catharine Hay, niece Louisa Dewy, niece Sibyl Lombard, niece Charlotte Farnham, niece Phebe Bliss Farnham, and grandniece Ellen Smith. The bequests to the nieces and nephews who were children of William were to be held in trust by brother William.

vi DOROTHY FARNHAM, b. Jun 1753; d. at Newburyport, 14 Sep 1801; m. at Newburyport, 22 Oct 1782, Dr. JOSIAH SMITH, b. at Ipswich, 23 Mar 1749 son of John and Hannah (Treadwell) Smith; Josiah d. at Newburyport, 9 Sep 1828. Josiah Smith was first married to Margaret Staniford and third married Mary Plummer. Dorothy and Josiah were parents of three daughters Clementina, Caroline, and Sybil Sawyer.

vii DANIEL FARNHAM, b. 22 Jul 1755; d. 16 Oct 1756.

---

813 Names of parents are given as Isaac and Eunice Snow on her death record

814 Maine, Nathan Hale Cemetery Collection, ca. 1780-1980

815 Currier, "Ould Newbury", p 130-131

816 *Essex County, MA: Probate File Papers, 1638-1881.* Online database. *AmericanAncestors.org.* New England Historic Genealogical Society, 2014. Case 9231

viii SAMUEL FARNHAM, b. 12 Sep 1757; d. 30 Oct 1757.

ix SARAH FARNHAM, b. 26 Jul 1759; d. 23 Aug 1759.

x WILLIAM FARNHAM, b. 26 Nov 1760; d. at Salem, IN, 9 Sep 1829; m. 2 Oct 1790, HANNAH BLISS EMERSON, b. at Concord, MA, 27 Jul 1770 daughter of William and Phebe (Bliss) Emerson; Hannah d. at Newburyport, 27 Mar 1807. Hannah was the aunt of Ralph Waldo Emerson.

300) ZEBADIAH FARNUM (*Daniel Farnum^4, Ralph Farnum^3, Elizabeth Holt Farnum^2, Nicholas^1*), b. at York, 19 Feb 1722 son of Daniel and Hannah (Bragdon) Farnum; m. at York, 15 Jun 1748, LUCY WEARE, b. at York, 2 Sep 1724 daughter of Elias and Elizabeth (Sayword) Weare.

Zebadiah Farnum and Lucy Weare were parents of five children born at York.

i ZEBADIAH FARNUM, b. 23 Mar 1749; d. at Newburyport, MA, 16 Jan 1832; m. at Newburyport, 10 Dec 1771, JUDITH MONTGOMERY, b. at Newbury, 24 Aug 1749 daughter of Nathaniel and Sarah (-) Montgomery; Judith d. at Newburyport, 25 Dec 1830.

ii LUCY FARNUM, b. 25 Mar 1750. Farnham's Farnum genealogy reports that Lucy married a 12-year old John Main on 10 Jan 1765. However, the 1765 marriage of John Main and Lucy Farnum was to the elder John Main born in 1720 and who died at York May 1802. This is supported by the will of John Main which names wife Lucy and includes all his children from his first marriage to Dorothy Lewis and his one child with Lucy.[817] This marriage requires that 14-year old Lucy Farnum married a man 45 years old, which although not impossible, is perhaps unlikely.

iii ELIZABETH FARNUM, b. 18 Apr 1752

iv OLIVE FARNUM, b. 31 Dec 1753; d. at Unity, ME, 21 Oct 1828; m. at Newmarket, NH, 17 Feb 1774, ROBERT JACKSON, b. perhaps at Durham, NH, 1750; Robert d. at Unity, 3 Sep 1809.

v DEBORAH FARNUM, b. 1 Jul 1757; d. at Albion, ME, 21 Oct 1839; m. at York, 3 Apr 1777, SAMUEL BAKER, b. at York, 24 Mar 1755 son of Issachar and Mary (Ellis) Baker; Samuel was living in Albion in 1840 and seems to have died about that time.

301) OLIVE FARNUM (*Daniel Farnum^4, Ralph Farnum^3, Elizabeth Holt Farnum^2, Nicholas^1*), b. at York, 5 Jul 1725 daughter of Daniel and Hannah (Bragdon) Farnum; m. at York, 11 Nov 1747, EDWARD GROW, b. at York, 27 Oct 1722 son of William and Joanna (Poor) Grow; Edward d. at York, 5 May 1785.

Col. Edward Grow was involved in maritime trade in York and was owner of a schooner *Hannah*. He was commissioned as lieutenant colonel in the 1st York Regiment of Militia on 2 December 1776 and later colonel of Frost's regiment of militia on 10 June 1778.[818]

Edward Grow did not leave a will and his estate entered probate with widow Olive as administratrix.[819] An inventory was taken in March 1786 and an order for the set off of the dower was made on 10 November 1786. Olive was apparently neglectful in her administration of the estate as on 19 June 1789, Edmund H. Quincy wrote the court regarding the delay by Mrs. Grow in presenting her accounting to the court and requesting that she be cited to appear related to this. The estate was insolvent and there was a dispute about how the sale of some of the property of the estate was handled with Olive Grow furnishing a statement on 6 July 1789 that future sales would go to the highest bidder. The case dragged on and on 14 February 1814, Thomas Savage was named administrator of the estate. On 15 April 1815, the following subscribers, heirs of the estate, gave their consent to the accounting of the estate: Olive Harmon, John Bennet for himself and wife, Bartholomew Whitman for himself and wife, Josiah Chase, and Jabez Young for himself and wife. Jabez Young who signed was the husband of Sally Grow who was the daughter of Daniel Grow and his wife Dorcas Grow.

Olive Farnum and Edward Grow were parents of nine children born at York, Maine.

i HANNAH GROW, b. 25 Aug 1748; d. at York, 22 May 1823; m. at York, 15 May 1770, JOSIAH CHASE, b. at Kittery, 1746 son of Josiah and Sarah (Tufts) Chase; Josiah d. at York, 21 Sep 1824.

ii OLIVE GROW, b. 28 Jul 1750; d. at York, 29 Oct 1838; m. at York, 14 Apr 1771, THOMAS HARMON, b. 1748 son of Nathaniel and Mary (Kingsbury) Harmon; Thomas d. at York, 11 Jun 1800.

iii EDWARD GROW, b. 24 Aug 1752

iv JOANNA GROW, b. 17 Apr 1755; d. at York, 12 Nov 1836; m. at York, 6 Jul 1778, JOHN BENNETT, b. at York, 22 May 1745 son of David and Alice (Donnell) Bennett; John d. at York, 15 Aug 1817.

---

817 Maine, York County Probate, Estate Files, Case 12510, Estate of John Main

818 Davis, *John Grow of Ipswich*, p 32

819 Maine, York County, Probate Estate Files, Case 7887, Estate of Edward Grow; accessed through familysearch.org

v ELIZABETH GROW, b. 17 Oct 1757; d. at York, likely 1844 (made a statement in 1843 related to her widow's pension and last pension payment Mar 1844); m. at York, 25 Jun 1783, BARTHOLOMEW WITHAM, b. 1754 perhaps the son of Bartholomew and Elizabeth (Hutchins) Witham; Bartholomew d. at York, 7 Mar 1826.

vi DANIEL GROW, b. 26 Sep 1761; d. at York, before 1810 (when widow is head of household); m. 7 May 1786, DORCAS GROW, b. at York, 18 Jul 1763 daughter of William and Abigail (Young) Grow; Dorcas d. at York, 8 Oct 1815. In her will, Dorcas mentions three children: daughter Eunice wife of John Lowe, daughter Sally wife of Jabez Young, and also requests that suitable gravestones be placed on her grave and that of daughter Olive.

vii THOMAS GROW, b. 17 Dec 1763; d. at sea 10 Sep 1805 (as reported by Farnham's Farnum genealogy).

viii LYDIA GROW, b. 16 Dec 1765; d. at York, 17 Feb 1852; m. at York, 9 Jun 1791, THOMAS SAVAGE, b. at Boston, 31 Mar 1770 son of John and Mary (Greenough) Savage; Thomas d. at York, 13 Sep 1838. According to Farnham's genealogy, Lydia and Thomas first attempted to marry on 4 Apr 1788, just three months before the birth of their first child, but the marriage was forbidden by Thomas's father. They finally married in 1791 six months after the birth of their second child.[820]

ix SAMUEL GROW, b. 5 Nov 1768

302) JOSHUA FARNHAM (*Daniel Farnum[4], Ralph Farnum[3], Elizabeth Holt Farnum[2], Nicholas[1]*), b. at York, Nov 1728 son of Daniel and Hannah (Bragdon) Farnum; d. at Woolwich, ME, 15 Jan 1803; m. at York, 13 Feb 1749/50, MARY GROW, b. at York, 13 Sep 1732 daughter of William and Joanna (Poor) Grow.[821]

Capt. Joshua Farnham was a land holder in Woolwich having received property in the first division. He was the town clerk of Woolwich for 37 years and was also licensed as an innholder.[822]

On 30 October 1807, heirs of Joshua Farnham, in consideration of payment of $100, conveyed to the heirs of Samuel Farnham of Woolwich all rights to the property of Joshua Farnham late of Woolwich. Those heirs conveying property were John Curtis yeoman and Mary his wife, Zebadiah Farnham mariner and Jane his wife, and John Farnham yeoman and Mary his wife all of Woolwich; John Perkins yeoman and Olive his wife of Dresden; Daniel Farnham yeoman with Mary his wife of Balltown; William Chalmers clothier and Esther his wife and Phineas Farnham and Elizabeth his wife of Fairfax; John Cook yeoman and Anna his wife of Norridgwalk; and Elizabeth Farnham widow of Bath.[823]

Joshua Farnum and Mary Grow were parents of sixteen children,[824] the births recorded at Woolwich except the oldest child Samuel recorded at Old York. The oldest child was born one month before the marriage which resulted in Mary being charged with fornication.[825]

i SAMUEL FARNHAM, b. at Old York, 22 Jan 1750; d. at Woolwich, ME, 29 May 1803; m. at Georgetown, MA, 8 Apr 1779, MARTHA ROWEL, b. about 1759 daughter of John and Mary (Reeves) Rowel.

ii DANIEL FARNHAM, b. at Woolwich, 25 May 1751; m. 1st at Georgetown, ME, 13 Jan 1776, LOIS ROWEL, b. at Georgetown, about 1755 daughter of John and Mary (Reeves) Rowel; Lois d. about 1789. Daniel m. 2nd 25 Nov 1790, MARY MCCURDY, b. at Bristol, ME, 3 Dec 1769 daughter of John and Anna (Hilton) McCurdy.

iii JOSHUA FARNHAM, b. 11 Dec 1752; likely died young

iv MARY FARNHAM, b. at Woolwich, 22 Jul 1754; m. at Woolwich, 8 Apr 1775, JOHN CURTIS, b. at Woolwich, 1750 son of John and Mary (-) Curtis; John d. at Woolwich, 2 Dec 1827.

v ESTHER FARNHAM, b. at Woolwich, 5 Jun 1756; d. at Albion, ME, 9 Aug 1826; m. at Woolwich, 20 Mar 1776, WILLIAM CHALMERS, b. 1755 son of William Chalmers; William d. at Albion, 21 Sep 1838.

vi WILLIAM FARNHAM, b. 10 Aug 1758; likely died young

vii HANNAH FARNHAM, b. at Woolwich, 1 Jul 1760; d. at Westport, ME, 26 Dec 1800; m. at Edgecomb, ME, 10 Nov 1790, as his second wife, DANIEL DUNTON, b. about 1755 son of Timothy and Elizabeth (-) Dunton; Daniel d. at Westport, 22 Mar 1813. Daniel was first married to Abigail Smith on 9 Nov 1777.

viii OLIVE FARNHAM, b. at Woolwich, 12 Feb 1762; d. at Dresden, ME, 4 Feb 1827; m. at Woolwich, 28 Sep 1786, JOHN PERKINS.

---

820 Farnham, *New England Descendants of Ralph Farnum*, p 217

821 Davis, *John Grow of Ipswich*

822 A detailed description of some of Joshua's land transactions can be found in Farnham's, *New England Descendants of Ralph Farnum*, pp 217-222.

823 Lincoln County Maine, Land Records 1761-1912. Deeds, 66:113; accessed through familysearch.org

824 Joshua Farnum was the town clerk of Woolwich and the births of his children are recorded on the second page of the town records in his own hand. Woolwich, Maine Town and Vital Records, FHL, Film 12318, image 8

825 Farnham, *The Descendants of Ralph Farnum*, p 217

ix ZEBADIAH FARNHAM, b. at Woolwich, 10 Aug 1764; d. at Woolwich, 9 Aug 1839; m. at Woolwich, 16 Dec 1788, JANE CARLETON, b. at Woolwich, 26 May 1766 daughter of John and Jane (Gilmore) Carleton; Jane d. at Woolwich, 9 Jun 1831.

x JOANNA FARNHAM (twin), b. 1 Apr 1767; d. 11 Apr 1767

xi PHINEAS FARNHAM, b. at Woolwich, 1 Apr 1767; d. at Albion, ME, 14 Dec 1837; m. at Georgetown, 5 Jan 1791, BETSEY STINSON, b. 24 Jun 1762 daughter of Robert and Mary (Paine) Stinson; Betsey d. at Woolwich, 1824. Phineas m. 2nd 4 Apr 1825, POLLY BESSEY.

xii THOMAS FARNHAM, b. at Woolwich, 30 Dec 1769; d. at Bath, ME, 12 Jan 1802; m. at Georgetown, 10 Dec 1796, ELIZABETH COUILLARD, b. at Georgetown, 29 May 1773 daughter of Charles and Margaret (Hood) Couillard.

xiii ANNA FARNHAM, b. at Woolwich, 21 Feb 1771; m. at Woolwich, 27 Jan 1791, JOHN COOK.

xiv LUCY FARNHAM, b. 26 Aug 1772; d. 1 Oct 1777.

xv JOANNA FARNHAM, b. 10 Jul 1775; d. 3 Oct 1777.

xvi JOHN FARNHAM, b. at Woolwich, 31 Aug 1779; d. at Woolwich, 28 Apr 1862; m. 1st at Woolwich, 7 Mar 1802, MARY BAGLEY, b. about 1776; d. at Woolwich, 4 Jan 1855. John m. 2nd at Woolwich, 27 Apr 1855, HANNAH WILLIAMS, b. about 1791.

303) JOHN FARNUM (*Daniel Farnum[4], Ralph Farnum[3], Elizabeth Holt Farnum[2], Nicholas[1]*), b. at Georgetown, ME, about 1735 son of Daniel and Patience (Hubbard) Farnum; d. in service and recorded at Woolwich, 7 May 1778; m. 4 Oct 1763, HANNAH CARD, b. at Georgetown, about 1746 daughter of Winchester and Elizabeth (Grow) Card; Hannah d. at Bowdoinham, Jan 1827. Hannah married second Moses Weymouth on 20 May 1788.

John and Hannah resided in Woolwich. John entered the service at Salisbury, Massachusetts on 13 February 1778 in the company of Capt. Benjamin Evans. John died while in service.[826]

There are records of four children of John Farnum and Hannah Card born at Woolwich, but they are likely parents of seven children.[827][828]

i PATIENCE FARNUM, b. 24 Jul 1764; m. at Woolwich, 18 Jan 1791, JOHN TIBBETTS. Patience and John both seem to be living in Bowdoin in 1830 with John age 60-69 and one female 60-69 and one male 15-19. John and Patience were parents of eight children born at Bowdoin.

ii DEBORAH FARNUM, b. 3 Feb 1766; d. at Bowdoinham, ME, 22 Dec 1842; m. at Woolwich, 17 Aug 1797, Maj. BENJAMIN J. BLANCHARD, b. at Woolwich, 14 May 1774 son of James and Susanna (Thompson) Blanchard; Benjamin d. at Bowdoinham, 10 Jun 1821.

iii RACHEL FARNUM, baptized 4 Oct 1767

iv ELIZABETH "BETSEY" FARNUM, b. 25 Jan 1768; d. at Bath, ME, 19 Aug 1824; m. about 1790, FRANCIS W. HODGKINS

v JANE FARNUM, b. about 1770

vi MIRIAM FARNUM, b. 5 Dec 1770; d. 9 Sep 1773.

vii HANNAH FARNUM, baptized 11 Sept 1774.

304) DAVID FARNHAM (*Daniel Farnum[4], Ralph Farnum[3], Elizabeth Holt Farnum[2], Nicholas[1]*), b. at Georgetown, ME, about 1737 son of Daniel and Patience (Hubbard) Farnum; d. at Woolwich, ME, 1 Sep 1773; m. at Woolwich, 4 Jul 1763, MARTHA CARD, b. at Georgetown, about 1743 daughter of Winchester and Elizabeth (Grow) Card; Martha d. at Woolwich, 27 May 1831. Martha m. 2nd, Sep 1780, John Soule.

David Farnham and Martha Card were parents of five children born at Woolwich.[829]

i JEREMIAH FARNHAM, b. 1 Apr 1764

---

[826] Farnham, *New England Descendants of Ralph Farnum*, p 223

[827] Farnham's *Descendants of Ralph Farnum* lists three daughters (Rachel, Jane, and Hannah) who are reported as being baptized according to Woolwich church records.

[828] Woolwich Vital Records 1756-1801, p 14; accessed through familysearch.org; https://www.familysearch.org/ark:/61903/3:1:3QS7-99N8-3ZDV?cat=64990

[829] Woolwich Vital Records 1756-1801, p 6, accessed through familysearch.org; https://www.familysearch.org/ark:/61903/3:1:3QS7-99N8-3ZZR?i=9

ii EDWARD G. FARNHAM, b. 29 Mar 1766; d. at Woolwich, 28 Oct 1849; m. at Pownalborough, ME, 26 Nov 1791, MARY "POLLY" COLBY, b. 1773; Polly d. at Woolwich, 23 May 1841.

iii JOANNA FARNHAM, b. 30 May 1768; d. at Woolwich, 20 Dec 1848; m. at Georgetown, ME, 21 Aug 1794, her stepbrother, SAMUEL SOULE, b. 18 Jan 1769 son of John and Patience (Wormall) Soule;[830] Samuel d. at Woolwich, 26 Dec 1816.

iv WINCHESTER FARNHAM, b. 25 May 1770; d. after 1843 when he was living at Jefferson, ME and conveyed property; m. m. at Pownalborough, 10 Jun 1796, MARTHA "PATTY" CLARKE.

v DAVID FARNHAM, b. 26 Aug 1772

305) ABIGAIL ABBOTT (*Abigail Farnum Abbott⁴, Ralph Farnum³, Elizabeth Holt Farnum², Nicholas¹*), b. at Andover, 1 Jan 1714/5 daughter of James and Abigail (Farnum) Abbott; d. at Charlestown about 1737; m. 13 May 1734, JOHN KIDDER, b. at Charlestown 13 Feb 1709 son of Stephen and Mary (Johnson) Kidder. John married second Anna Walker and third Mary Snow.

The Abbot genealogy[831] lists Abigail as marrying Jacob Waldron, having children Sarah, Ezra, and Elizabeth and then marrying (-) Hibbard of Charlestown. However, available records give Jacob Waldron (who was born 1743) as marrying Abigail's niece Sarah [daughter of James and Sarah (Bancroft) Abbott]. There are also three birth records for children of Jacob and Sarah named Sarah, Ezra, and Elizabeth. The only marriage of Abigail seems to be to John Kidder of Charlestown, and she seems to have died soon after the birth of her only child.

There is just one child and he likely died young as John Kidder named another son John that he had with his third wife.

i JOHN KIDDER, b. 12 Sep 1735; likely died young

306) JAMES ABBOTT (*Abigail Farnum Abbott⁴, Ralph Farnum³, Elizabeth Holt Farnum², Nicholas¹*), b. at Andover, 12 Jan 1716/7 son of James and Abigail (Farnum) Abbott; d. at Newbury, VT, 27 Dec 1803; m. about 1742, SARAH BANCROFT, b. 19 Feb 1722 daughter of Samuel and Sarah (Lampson) Bancroft; Sarah d. 1765.[832]

James Abbott and Sarah Bancroft had ten children. The oldest child's birth is recorded at Andover, and there are records of the births of some of the other children in New Hampshire. Information on other children was obtained from the Abbot genealogy, pp 28-29.[833]

i SARAH ABBOTT, b. 1 Mar 1743; death unknown; m. by 1765, JACOB WALDRON, b. at Rumford, 2 Mar 1743 son of Isaac and Susannah (Chandler) Waldron; the date or place of death is not known.

ii ABIGAIL ABBOT, b. 22 Jan 1745/6; d. at Bath, NH, 11 Feb 1815; m. 15 Apr 1767, ASA BAILEY, b. at Salem, NH, 13 May 1745 son of Edward and Elizabeth (Burbank) Bailey. Abigail divorced Asa in 1793 following years of abuse, the last straw being the sexual abuse of one of their daughters. What happened to Asa is not clear. *The Memoirs of Mrs. Abigail Bailey* recounting the events of her marriage was published in 1815 just after her death.[834]

iii MARY ABBOTT, b. 6 Feb 1748; m. 1st, 22 Oct 1773, RICHARD MINCHEN; Richard d. 1776. Mary m. 2nd, at Haverhill, NH, 22 Mar 1777, URIAH CROSS,[835] b. at Mansfield, CT, 9 Jun 1752 son of Daniel and Elizabeth (Abbe) Cross; Uriah d. at Berlin Heights, OH, 1839.[836]

iv JAMES ABBOTT, b. 10 Oct 1750; d. in Ohio 1814; m. at Groton, VT, 29 Mar 1781, ZILPHA SMITH. James m. 2nd, at Groton, VT, 25 Jul 1785, MEHITABLE HIDDEN.[837][838]

v JUDITH ABBOTT, b. 19 Feb 1753; d. at Newbury, VT, 30 Dec 1806; m. 27 Oct 1772, THOMAS BROCK, b. about 1745; Thomas d. at Newbury, 10 Jun 1811. Thomas Brock's origins are not clear at this point; he was perhaps born in Scotland.

---

[830] Ridlon, *History, Biography, and Genealogy of Families Named Sole. . .*, p 334

[831] Abbot and Abbot, *Genealogical Record of Descendants*, p 28

[832] A gravestone engraved with the names James Abbott and Sarah Bancroft is in Oxbow Cemetery in Newbury, VT.

[833] Abbot and Abbot, *Genealogical Record of Descendants*

[834] Bailey, *Memoirs of Mrs. Abigail Bailey*

[835] New Hampshire Marriage Record Index 1637-1947 (ancestry.com)

[836] There were two Uriah Cross of similar age, one born 3 Apr 1750 to Noah Cross and Mary Chamberlain and one born 9 Jun 1752 son of Daniel Cross and Elizabeth Abbe. It can be established through pension records that Uriah born 3 Apr 1750 married Ann Payne, so it is likely Uriah born 9 Jun 1752 who married Mary Abbott.

[837] Abbott Family, Groton Families in 1790, Groton Vermont Historical Society.

[838] Vermont Vital Records 1720-1908 (ancestry.com)

vi WILLIAM ABBOTT, b. 24 Apr 1755; d. at Bath, NH, 14 Jun 1807; m. 9 Dec 1777, MABEL WHITTLESEY, b. at Guilford, CT, 25 Jun 1757 daughter of Josiah and Elizabeth (Jackson) Whittlesey; Mabel d. at Haverhill, NH, 2 Nov 1836.

vii BANCROFT ABBOTT, b. 4 Jun 1757; d. at Newbury, VT, 29 Oct 1829;[839] m. 1787, LYDIA WHITE, b. at Plaistow, NH, 1 Jan 1763 daughter of Ebenezer and Hannah (Merrill) White; Lydia d. 25 Jun 1853.

viii EZRA ABBOTT, b. 8 Oct 1759; died young.

ix SUSANNAH ABBOTT, b. 3 Mar 1763; no further record.

x EZRA ABBOTT, b. 2 Jun 1765; d. in Vermont, 5 Jul 1842; m. at Newbury, VT, 8 Aug 1788, his first cousin, HANNAH ABBOTT (*Reuben Abbott5, Abigail Farnum Abbott4, Ralph Farnum3, Elizabeth Holt Farnum2, Nicholas1*), b. 29 Mar 1762 daughter of Reuben and Rhoda (Whittemore) Abbott; Hannah d. 2 Sep 1832.

307) REUBEN ABBOTT (*Abigail Farnum Abbott4, Ralph Farnum3, Elizabeth Holt Farnum2, Nicholas1*), b. at Andover, 4 Apr 1723 son of James and Abigail (Farnum) Abbott; d. at Concord, NH, 13 May 1822; m. 1st RHODA WHITTEMORE, b. at Malden, 18 Aug 1729 daughter of Elias and Rhoda (Holt) Whittemore; d. 29 Jan 1785. Reuben m. 2nd Dinah Blanchard, b. at Andover, 28 Dec 1731 daughter of Stephen and Deborah (Phelps) Blanchard; Dinah d. 11 Mar 1826. Dinah Blanchard had first been married to her cousin Joseph Blanchard.

Reuben and Rhoda had ten children whose births are recorded at Concord, New Hampshire.

i REUBEN ABBOTT, b. 18 May 1752; d. 11 Dec 1752.

ii REUBEN ABBOTT, b. 5 Feb 1754; d. 12 Dec 1834; m. 24 Sep 1776, his second cousin once removed, ZERVIAH FARNUM (*Joseph Farnum4, Ephraim Farnum3, Elizabeth Holt Farnum2, Nicholas1*), b. at Concord, about 1752 daughter of Joseph and Zerviah (Hoit) Farnum; Zerviah d. at Concord, Dec 1818.[840]

iii RHODA ABBOTT, b. 31 Dec 1755; d. at Boscawen, 31 Aug 1839; m. at Concord, 8 Jan 1778, JONATHAN JOHNSON, b. at Boscawen, 29 Dec 1753 son of John and Eleanor (Eastman) Johnson; Jonathan d. 16 Sep 1820.

iv ELIAS ABBOTT, b. 24 Oct 1757; d. at Northfield, NH, 19 Mar 1847; m. Sep 1782, ELIZABETH BUSWELL, b. at Kingston, 4 Sep 1761 daughter of James and Elizabeth (Clough) Buswell; Elizabeth d. 25 Jan 1832.[841]

v PHEBE ABBOTT, b. 14 Apr 1759; d. 4 Jul 1760.

vi PHEBE ABBOTT, b. 6 Dev 1760; d. Nov 1777.

vii HANNAH ABBOTT, b. 29 Mar 1762; d. at Vermont, 2 Sep 1832; m. at Newbury, VT, 8 Aug 1788, her first cousin, EZRA ABBOTT (*James Abbott5, Abigail Farnum Abbott4, Ralph Farnum3, Elizabeth Holt Farnum2, Nicholas1*), b. at Haverhill, 2 Jun 1765 son of James and Sarah (Bancroft) Abbott; Ezra d. 5 Jul 1842. This is the same couple as Family #137, child x.

viii RUTH ABBOTT, b. 14 Feb 1764; d. 2 Sep 1764

ix EZRA ABBOTT, b. 8 Aug 1765; d. 24 Apr 1839; m. his third cousin, MARY WALKER, b, about 1763 daughter of Joseph and Mary (Abbott) Walker; Mary d. at Concord, 22 Sep 1852.

x NATHAN ABBOTT, b. 8 Aug 1765; d. at Concord, 13 May 1849; m. his third cousin, PHEBE ABBOTT, b. 8 Aug 1764 daughter of Nathaniel and Miriam (Chandler) Abbott; Phebe d. 11 Aug 1854.

308) AMOS ABBOTT (*Abigail Farnum Abbott4, Ralph Farnum3, Elizabeth Holt Farnum2, Nicholas1*), b. at Andover, 18 Feb 1725/6 son of James and Abigail (Farnum) Abbott; d. at Concord 3 Dec 1821; m. by 1754, as her 2nd husband, REBECCA ABBOTT (widow of ABIEL CHANDLER), b. 24 Apr 1717 daughter of Nathaniel and Dorcas (Hibbert) Abbott; Rebecca d. 13 Feb 1803.

Abiel Chandler and Rebecca Abbott had four children, the first recorded at Andover and the youngest three in Rumford/Concord, New Hampshire.

i ABIEL CHANDLER, b. 27 Jun 1742; died young.

ii ABIEL CHANDLER, b. 11 May 1744; d. 27 Aug 1776 at Long Island, NY during the Revolutionary War; m. about 1766, JUDITH WALKER, b. at Rumford, 21 Dec 1744 daughter of Timothy and Sarah (Burbeen) Walker. Judith m. 2nd Nathaniel Rolfe; Judith d. at Concord 1806.

---

839 *Vermont, Vital Records, 1720-1908* (Provo, UT, USA: Ancestry.com Operations, Inc., 2013).

840 New Hampshire, Death and Disinterment Records, 1754-1947

841 Lyford, *History of the Town of Canterbury*, p 1

iii PETER CHANDLER, b. 9 Oct 1747; d. 25 Jun 1776 while serving in the Army.

iv SARAH CHANDLER, b. about 1749; Sarah is included as a child in published genealogies, but there seem to be no records related to her.

Rebecca Abbott and Amos Abbott had three children.

i AMOS ABBOTT, b. 15 Jul 1754; d. at Concord 11 Oct 1834; m. JUDITH MORSE, b. at Newburyport, 1 Mar 1766 daughter of Moses and Sarah (Hale) Morse.

ii JOHN ABBOTT, b. 23 Jun 1756; d. 31 Aug 1779. John served in the Revolutionary War.

iii REBECCA ABBOTT, b. 26 Sep 1760; d. at Loudon, NH, 24 Dec 1846; m. 9 Oct 1781, MOSES CHAMBERLAIN, b. at Hopkinton, 5 Oct 1757 son of Samuel and Martha (Mellen) Chamberlain; Moses d. 21 Oct 1811.

309) PHEBE ABBOTT (*Abigail Farnum Abbott⁴, Ralph Farnum³, Elizabeth Holt Farnum², Nicholas¹*), b. at Andover, 22 Nov 1727 daughter of James and Abigail (Farnum) Abbott; d. at Conway NH, 29 Sep 1754; m. 5 Nov 1747, as his 1st wife, THOMAS MERRILL, b. 5 Feb 1723/4 at Haverhill son of John and Lydia (Haynes) Merrill. Thomas had a total of four marriages, his 2nd to Mehitable Harriman, 3rd to Abigail Goodhue, and 4th to Elizabeth Abbott daughter of Benjamin and Abigail (Abbott) Abbott. Thomas Merrill d. at Conway 21 Jun 1788.

Phebe Abbott and Thomas Merrill had five children born at Conway, New Hampshire. Three of the sons, William, Thomas, and Amos, bought adjoining farms on the Saco River in Conway.[842] Two of the sons married two Ambrose sisters who were the daughters of Jonathan and Abigail (Goodhue) Ambrose. Abigail Goodhue Ambrose was one of the wives of Thomas Merrill making these couples, stepsiblings.

i THOMAS MERRILL, b. 31 Aug 1748; d. May 1821;[843] m. 7 Dec 1775, HANNAH AMBROSE, b, about 1750 daughter of Jonathan and Abigail (Goodhue) Ambrose.

ii WILLIAM MERRILL, b. about 1749. William did not marry.

iii ENOCH MERRILL, b. 10 Nov 1750; d. 1838; m. about 1772, MARY AMBROSE, b. at Exeter, 11 Nov 1755 daughter of Jonathan and Abigail (Goodhue) Ambrose; Mary d. at Conway, 27 Mar 1815.

iv AMOS MERRILL, b. Jul 1752; d, at Conway, 13 Mar 1840; m. 30 Dec 1779, LOIS WILLEY, b. Jan 1760; Lois d. 28 Mar 1855.

v PHEBE MERRILL, b. Dec 1753; d. at North Conway, 9 Oct 1839; m. 3 Dec 1775, her second cousin, ABIATHAR EASTMAN (*Mary Lovejoy Eastman⁵, Henry Lovejoy⁴, Mary Farnum Lovejoy³, Elizabeth Holt Farnum², Nicholas¹*), b. 29 Apr 1745 son of Richard and Mary (Lovejoy) Eastman; Abiathar d. 10 Jan 1815. Phebe Merrill and Abiathar Eastman are Family 743.

310) REBECCA ABBOTT (*Abigail Farnum Abbott⁴, Ralph Farnum³, Elizabeth Holt Farnum², Nicholas¹*), b. at Andover, 13 Aug 1730 daughter of James and Abigail (Farnum) Abbott; d. at NH date unknown; m. 1750, ENOCH EASTMAN, b. at Salisbury, 1 Jun 1725 son of Joseph and Abigail (Merrill) Eastman.
Rebecca ad Enoch were early settlers in Hopkinton. Enoch held the position of town clerk and fulfilled other civic responsibilities.[844]

Rebecca and Enoch were the parents of 12 children born in Rumford[845] and Hopkinton.[846]

i ENOCH EASTMAN, b. 22 Feb 1752; d. 14 Mar 1756 by drowning.

ii EZRA EASTMAN, b. 25 Mar 1754; died young.

iii SIMEON EASTMAN, b. 23 Oct 1755; m. about 1780, MEHITABLE PIPER.

iv ENOCH EASTMAN, b. 2 Mar 1757; no further record.

v ABIGAIL EASTMAN, b. 25 Feb 1759; d. at Hopkinton, 19 Dec 1836; m. 14 Sep 1780, MOSES COLBY, b. at Newton, NH, 7 Jun 1751 son of Moses and Mary (Sargent) Colby; Moses d. at Hopkinton, 16 Mar 1790.

---

842 Merrill, *A Merrill Memorial*, p 294
843 Merrill, *A Merrill Memorial*, p 294
844 Lord, *Life and Times in Hopkinton, N.H.*
845 Ancestry.com. *New Hampshire, Births and Christenings Index, 1714-1904*
846 Ancestry.com. *New Hampshire, Births and Christenings Index, 1714-1904*

vi SAMUEL EASTMAN, b. 13 Nov 1760; d. at Hopkinton, NH after 1840;[847] m. SARAH HARRIS.

vii REBEKAH EASTMAN, b. 10 Apr 1762; m. JAMES PUTNEY, b. at Hopkinton, 8 Feb 1761 son of John and Mary (-) Putney.

viii LUCY EASTMAN, b. 1 Dec 1763; d. 5 Jan 1816 at Tunbridge, VT; m. at Dunbarton, 16 Jan 1794, BENJAMIN ORDWAY, b. 1763 (based on age at time of death) perhaps the son of Moses and Susannah (Bly) Ordway; Benjamin d. 1 Dec 1849. After Lucy's death, Benjamin married Betsey Gilman.

ix EZRA EASTMAN, b. 15 Aug 1764; d. 14 Jun 1816; m. 28 Jun 1787, MOLLY EATON, b. 10 Aug 1769 daughter of Thomas and Molly (-) Eaton; Molly d. 11 Jan 1825.

x TAMISON EASTMAN, b. 19 Oct 1766; d. after 1850; m. SAMUEL FRENCH, b. at South Hampton, 3 Apr 1762 son of Offen and Abigail (French) French;[848] d. at Bradford, 7 Feb 1799.[849]

xi JOSEPH EASTMAN, b. 18 Sep 1768; d. at Contoocook, NH, 16 Feb 1823; m. 26 Oct 1790, BETSEY CLOUGH, b. 30 Jun 1770 daughter of James and Ruth (Webster) Clough; Betsey d. at Contoocook, NH, 1 Sep 1861.

xii SARAH EASTMAN, b. 27 Aug 1771; m. 5 Oct 1790, THOMAS EATON, b. 21 Jul 1771 son of Thomas and Molly (-) Eaton.

311) MARY ABBOTT (*Abigail Farnum Abbott⁴, Ralph Farnum³, Elizabeth Holt Farnum², Nicholas¹*), b. at Andover, 12 Oct 1732 daughter of James and Abigail (Farnum) Abbott; d, about 1780; m. by 1760 ADONIJAH TYLER, b. 26 Nov 1738[850] son of Moses and Miriam (Bailey) Tyler; Adonijah d. 12 Oct 1812 at Hopkinton, NH.

Mary Abbott and Adonijah Tyler had eight children. The births of the first six children are recorded at Henniker, New Hampshire[851] and the youngest two at Chester, New Hampshire. A probate record was not located. The family settled in Hopkinton, New Hampshire where Adonijah was a signer of the declaration of fidelity in 1776.[852]

i JAMES TYLER, b. 2 Apr 1760; d. at Thetford, VT, 20 Aug 1855;[853] m. by 1779, SARAH GOULD, b. at Hampton, 24 Jul 1760 daughter of Christopher and Abigail (Shepherd) Gould; Sarah's death record was not located.

ii RACHEL TYLER, b. 2 Mar 1762; d. in New York, Feb 1843; m. about 1782, JACOB STANLEY, b. at Hopkinton, 9 Sep 1761 son of Matthew and Mary (Putney) Stanley.

iii MIRIAM TYLER, b. 22 Mar 1764; d. Jun 1840; m. 11 May 1790, MOSES HASTINGS son of James and Mary (Foster) Hastings; Moses d. 25 Jan 1815.

iv JEREMIAH TYLER, b. 6 Apr 1766; d. at Thetford, VT, 19 Jan 1844; m. 31 Oct 1802, IRENE HEATON, b. 17 Apr 1774 daughter of William and Irene (King) Heaton; Irene died at Thetford, VT, 4 May 1840.[854]

v SIMEON TYLER, b. 22 Mar 1768; d. at Hopkinton, 24 Dec 1855; m. 14 Mar 1799, HANNAH ROWELL, b. 1776, parents unknown; Hannah d. 28 Jun 1831. Simeon m. 2nd, SUSAN PAIGE who was born about 1786 and d. 21 Mar 1865.

vi MOSES TYLER, b. 9 Apr 1770; d. at Tyler's Bridge, NH, 21 Dec 1857; m. 21 Jun 1798, BETSY MCCONNELL, b. at Pembroke, 30 Jan 1774 daughter of Samuel and Ann (Cunningham) McConnell; Betsy d. 9 Sep 1866.

vii MARY TYLER, b. 4 Jun 1773; d. 1839 at Gap Grove, IL; m. 16 Nov 1797, JACOB MARTIN, b. about 1770; Jacob d. after 1835, likely at Gap Grove.

viii SARAH TYLER, b. Mar 1775; d. at Ogle County, IL, 7 Feb 1839; m. at Hopkinton, 14 Jun 1796, ROBERT CROWELL *possibly* the son of Aaron and Elizabeth(-) Crowell; Robert d. 22 Sep 1862.[855]

312) WILLIAM FARNHAM (*William Farnum⁴, Ralph Farnum³, Elizabeth Holt Farnum², Nicholas¹*), b. at Windham, 15 Aug 1718 son of William and Anne (Flint) Farnum; d. at Windham, 29 Oct 1800; m. at Windham, 23 Jun 1742, MARTHA FULLER, b. at Windham, 7 Sep 1724 daughter of Stephen and Hannah (Moulton) Fuller; Martha d. at Hampton, 16 Apr 1792.

---

847 Ancestry.com, New Hampshire, Compiled Census and Census Substitutes Index, 1790-1890. Samuel Eastman, age 79, is recorded living at Hopkinton in 1840.
848 South Hampton Congregational Church, 1743-1801, marriages and baptisms, p 22
849 Gould & Beals, *Early Families of Bradford*, p 168
850 New Hampshire: Births, Deaths and Marriages, 1654-1969 (accessed through americanancestors.org)
851 Ancestry.com, *New Hampshire, Births and Christenings Index, 1714-1904* (Provo, UT, USA: Ancestry.com Operations, Inc., 2011).
852 Lord, *Life and Times in Hopkinton*, p 59
853 Ancestry.com, *Vermont, Vital Records, 1720-1908* (Provo, UT, USA: Ancestry.com Operations, Inc., 2013).
854 Her grave is in Post Mills Cemetery, Vermont. Findagrave Memorial ID 121161310
855 Brigham, *The Tyler Genealogy* p 237

William Farnham and Martha Fuller were parents of twelve children all but perhaps the youngest born at Canterbury, and the youngest child at Hampton. Four of the sons served in the Revolution, son William dying on a prison ship in New York Harbor.

i MARTHA FARNHAM, b. at Canterbury, 11 Nov 1743; d. at Hampton, 14 Sep 1818; m. at Windham, 3 May 1769, STEPHEN COMINS, b. about 1743; Stephen d. at Hampton, 26 Mar 1825.

ii WILLIAM FARNHAM, b. at Canterbury, 9 Feb 1745; d. on prison ship in New York Harbor, 14 Mar 1777; m. 8 May 1766, SARAH HIBBARD, b. at Windham, 2 Feb 1744 daughter of John and Martha (Durkee) Hibbard.

iii HANNAH FARNHAM, b. at Canterbury, 13 Mar 1746; d. at Yarmouth, Nova Scotia, 17 Dec 1842; m. at Canterbury, 20 Apr 1762, ELEAZER HIBBARD, b. 20 Aug 1730 son of John and Martha (Durkee) Hibbard; Eleazer d. at Yarmouth, 1798.

iv REUBEN FARNHAM, b. at Canterbury, 9 May 1748; d. at Skaneateles, NY, 25 Aug 1826; m. about 1780, LYDIA MOULTON, b. at Brimfield, MA, 30 Apr 1753 daughter of Samuel and Molly (Haynes) Moulton; Lydia d. at Marcellus, NY, 13 Mar 1826.

v ANNE FARNHAM, b. at Canterbury, 30 Apr 1750; d. at Hampton, 2 Oct 1835; m. 14 Feb 1771, BENJAMIN MOULTON, b. at Wenham, MA, 9 Mar 1742 son of Benjamin and Tabitha (Howard) Moulton; Benjamin d. at Hampton, 17 Aug 1812.

vi STEPHEN FARNHAM, b. at Canterbury, 31 May 1752. Stephen served during the Revolution. Nothing further known.

vii ABIEL FARNHAM, b. at Canterbury, 17 Apr 1754 (baptized 21 Apr 1754); d. at Hampton, 13 Feb 1818; m. at Hampton, 21 Jun 1781, CHLOE SIMMONS, b. at Windham, 18 Aug 1761 daughter of Jacob and Mehitable (Preston) Simmons; Chloe d. at Hampton, 26 Sep 1850. Abiel served in the Revolution and Chloe received a widow's pension.

viii ALICE FARNHAM, b. at Canterbury, 27 Sep 1756

ix JOHN FARNHAM, b. 21 Dec 1756; d. Jun 1783.

x JOSIAH FARNHAM, b. at Canterbury, 17 Jun 1758

xi AMASA FARNHAM, b. 6 Oct 1763; d. Jun 1785.

xii BEULAH FARNHAM, baptized at Hampton, 27 Jul 1766; d. at Hampton, 19 Jul 1838; m. at Hampton, 19 Aug 1797, ELIJAH CHENEY, b. at Pomfret, 1 May 1751 son of Oliver and Hannah (Hayward) Cheney; Elijah d. at Hampton, 26 Apr 1834.

313) ZEBADIAH FARNUM (*William Farnum[4], Ralph Farnum[3], Elizabeth Holt Farnum[2], Nicholas[1]*), b. at Windham 18 Jun 1721 son of William and Anne (Flint) Farnum; d. at Hampton, 8 Sep 1814; m. at Windham, 27 Jul 1743, MARY FULLER, b. at Windham, 9 Mar 1726/7 daughter of Stephen and Hannah (Moulton0 Fuller; Mary d. at Hampton, 20 Jul 1802.

Zebadiah Farnum served as 1st lieutenant in the 8th Connecticut militia during the Revolution. Six of his sons also served. Sons Levi and Daniel died on prison ships and sons Thomas and Ebenezer were wounded.[856]

Zebadiah Farnum and Mary Fuller were parents of twelve children born at Windham.

i MARY FARNUM, b. 19 Jul 1744; d. 22 Jun 1745.

ii ZEBADIAH FARNUM, b. 10 Jan 1745/6; m. at Canterbury, 10 Nov 1763, MARY HIBBARD

iii LEVI FARNUM, b. 13 Aug 1748; d. of starvation on a prison ship in New York harbor, 25 Dec 1776; m. 1774, DORCAS MOULTON, b. 1748 daughter of Samuel and Molly (Haynes) Moulton; Dorcas d. at Oxford, NY, 28 Jan 1838. Dorcas second Ebenezer Perry and married third Thomas Taylor. Levi and Dorcas were parents of two sons.

iv EBENEZER FARNUM, b. 17 Dec 1750; d. about 1781; m. at Windham, 3 Mar 1773, JOANNA BENJAMIN. Joanna married second Benjamin Cole.

v DANIEL FARNUM, b. 19 Jul 1752; d. in New York harbor on a prison ship, 9 Jan 1777. Daniel was a sergeant in the 17th Connecticut regiment and was taken prisoner at the Battle of Long Island. Daniel died of ship fever.

vi THOMAS FARNUM, b. 19 Nov 1754; d. at Hampton, 24 Mar 1840; m. at Hampton, 24 Dec 1797, ABIGAIL DURKEE, b. at Windham, 4 Oct 1774 daughter of Benjamin and Abigail (Durkee) Durkee; Abigail d. at Conneaut, OH, 14 Mar 1848.

---

[856] Farnham, *The New England Descendants of Ralph Farnum*, p 231

vii MARY FARNUM, b. 21 Aug 1757; d. at Hampton, 1 Jan 1839; m. at Hampton, 8 Jan 1778, SILAS SPENCER, b. at Windham, 14 Dec 1755 son of John and Mary (Simons) Spencer; Silas d. at Hampton, 24 Sep 1829.

viii ELIJAH FARNUM, b. 16 Dec 1759; d. after 1840 when he was living with his son in Fenner, NY; m. about 1782, JULIA

ix IRENA FARNUM, b. 25 Sep 1761; d. at Canterbury, 26 Dec 1830; m. at Canterbury, 29 Jan 1783, Capt. BENJAMIN BACON, b. at Canterbury, 17 Jun 1757 son of Benjamin and Deborah (Adams) Bacon; Benjamin d. at Canterbury, 22 Feb 1826.

x CALVIN FARNUM, b. 22 Oct 1763; d. at Nelson, NY, 6 Jul 1849; m. about 1790, MARTHA KINGSBURY, b. at Oxford, MA, 30 Oct 1764 daughter of Joseph and Elizabeth (Ammidown) Kingsbury; Martha d. after 1850 when she was living in Nelson.

xi OLIVE FARNUM, b. 12 Nov 1765; d. 2 Jul 1819. Olive did not marry.

xii ELISHA FARNUM, b. 24 Sep 1768; d. at Cazenovia, 7 Jan 1848; m. ANNA LATHROP, b. at Wells, VT, 1776 daughter of Samuel and Sally (Oakman) Lathrop;[857] Anna d. at Cazenovia, NY, 28 May 1842.

314) ANNA FARNUM (*William Farnum⁴, Ralph Farnum³, Elizabeth Holt Farnum², Nicholas¹*), b. at Windham, 27 Oct 1723 daughter of William and Anne (Flint) Farnum; d. at Windham, 30 Dec 1762; m. at Windham, 21 Oct 1747, JEDUTHUN ROGERS, b. at Windham, 17 Feb 1723/4 son of Hope and Esther (Meacham) Rogers; Jeduthun d. at Hampton, 19 Nov 1800. Jeduthun second married Hannah Knight on 12 Oct 1763.

Jeduthun Rogers did not leave a will and his estate entered probate 2 December 1800. On 21 October 1803, son Jeduthun Rogers signed a receipt stating he received his portion of the estate. Other receipts were signed by Hannah and Edward Pease (Hannah is from Jeduthun's second marriage), Jemima and Jabez Walcott, Anna and Ambrose Ames, Lucy and Amos Green, and Rufus Rogers (a child from the second marriage).[858]

Anna Farnum and Jeduthun Rogers were parents of nine children born at Windham.

i JEDUTHUN ROGERS, b. 24 May 1748; d. 24 Jun 1750.

ii ANNA ROGERS, b. 10 Dec 1749; d. at Mansfield, about 1832 (inventory of estate Feb 1832); m. at Mansfield, CT, 21 Jan 1770, AMBROSE AMES, b. at Mansfield, 11 Jun 1750 son of William and Abigail (Hinckley) Ames; Ambrose d. at Mansfield, 30 Mar 1811.

iii ESTHER ROGERS, b. 6 Mar 1750/1; d. 6 Sep 1753

iv JEDUTHUN ROGERS, b. 4 Mar 1753; d. at Bethel, VT, 28 Feb 1836; m. about 1784, ELIZABETH FISK, b. 1759; Elizabeth d. at Bethel, 1838.

v ESTHER ROGERS, b. 7 Jun 1755; d. 22 Jan 1756.

vi LUCY ROGERS, b. 24 Oct 1756; d. at Wales, MA, 21 Mar 1828; m. as his second wife, her first cousin, AMOS GREEN, b. at Tolland, 22 Jun 1753 son of Robert and Sarah (Rogers) Green; Amos was living in Wales in 1831 receiving a pension. Amos married third Mehitable Moulton at Wales on 11 Sep 1828. Amos was first married to Mary Nelson. Amos's mother Sarah Rogers was the sister of Lucy's father.

vii JEMIMA ROGERS, b. 19 Jul 1758; m. 1st at Windham, 21 Oct 1780, ELIPHAZ ROBINSON, b. at Windham, 19 May 1750 son of Simeon and Jerusha (Kingsley) Robinson; Eliphaz d. at Windham, 9 Oct 1785. Jemima m. 2nd JABEZ WALCOTT, b. at Windham, 10 Dec 1758 son of Elijah and Esther (Owen) Walcott.

viii ISAIAH ROGERS, b. 26 Feb 1760; d. 22 Apr 1763.

ix TABITHA ROGERS, b. 19 Nov 1761; not mentioned in the probate record.

315) SARAH FARNUM (*Nathaniel Farnum⁴, Ralph Farnum³, Elizabeth Holt Farnum², Nicholas¹*), b. at Windham, 27 Mar 1724 daughter of Nathaniel and Hannah (Preston) Farnum; d. at Hampton, 9 Sep 1813; m. at Windham, 26 Mar 1747, DAVID FISKE, b. at Windham, 17 Dec 1726 son of David and Elizabeth (Durkee) Fiske; David d. at Hampton, 3 Oct 1809.

Sarah and David resided at Hampton. They were parents of five children whose births are recorded at Windham.

i AMAZIAH FISKE, b. 6 Oct 1747; d. at Chaplin, CT, 1831; m. at Windham, 3 Jan 1771, PRISCILLA BINGHAM, b. at Mansfield, 30 Jun 1753 daughter of Nathaniel and Hannah (Wolcott) Bingham; Priscilla d. at Hampton, 16 Sep 1799.

---

857 Huntington, *Genealogical Memoir of the Lo-Lathrop Family*, p 148

858 *Connecticut State Library (Hartford, Connecticut), Probate Packets, Richardson, Josephine-Rose, Samuel, 1719-1880, Estate of Jeduthun Rogers, Case 3257*

ii SARAH FISKE, b. 13 Apr 1749; d. at Hampton, 4 Feb 1796; Sarah did not marry.

iii DAVID FISKE, b. 12 Aug 1754; d. 24 Jul 1775.

iv LUCY FISKE, b. 27 Apr 1760

v HANNAH FISKE, b. 26 Jul 1766; d. at Canton, CT, 11 Mar 1853; m. at Windham, 24 Nov 1791, JOSEPH MILLARD, b. at Windham, 7 Mar 1763 son of Joseph and Rebecca (Sawyer) Millard; Joseph d. at Bloomfield, CT, 5 Mar 1843.

316) REBEKAH FARNUM (*Nathaniel Farnum*[4], *Ralph Farnum*[3], *Elizabeth Holt Farnum*[2], *Nicholas*[1]), b. at Windham, 12 Apr 1730 daughter of Nathaniel and Hannah (Preston) Farnum; d. at Hampton, 1814; m. at Windham, 21 Jan 1748/9, JOHN ROBBINS, b. at Canterbury, 12 Jul 1721 son of Nathaniel and Elizabeth (Levins) Robbins; John d. about 1774.

Rebekah and John resided in Windham throughout their married life.

In his will dated 27 November 1773 (proved 7 January 1774), John Robbins bequeathed to wife Rebekah all the moveable estate indoor and outdoor and credits of every kind to be and remain hers forever. Rebekah also receives the use and improvement of all the real estate while she is a widow, but if she remarries, she will have use of just one-third of the real estate during her natural life. The remainder of the estate is to be divided equally among his six sons and seven daughters except for ten-pound deductions from the amounts to Mary Utley and Alice Gates. The children are sons John, Thomas, Ebenezer, Jeremiah, Nathaniel, and Rufus and daughters Mary Utley, Alice Gates, Patience, Hannah, Rebekah, Abigail, and Olive. John also directs that the labor of his three eldest sons be used to pay the debts of the estate and specifies lengths of time that their labor should go for this purpose. Beloved wife Rebekah and trusty friend Thomas Fuller were named executors. Real estate of 56 acres with dwelling house was valued at £111 and personal estate at £84.10.7.[859]

Rebekah Robbins did not leave a will and her estate entered probate 7 September 1814 with John Robbins as administrator. Her personal estate was valued at $52.09.[860]

Rebekah Farnum and John Robbins were parents of thirteen children born at Windham.

i MARY ROBBINS, b. 2 May 1748; d. likely at Rodman, NY; m. at Windham, 1 May 1766, JONATHAN UTLEY, b. at Windham, 26 Jun 1741 son of Jeremiah and Mary (Frink) Utley; Jonathan d. at Rodman, 15 Feb 1820.

ii ALICE ROBBINS, b. 31 Dec 1749; d. at Amenia, NY, 18 Aug 1774; m. at Hampton, 29 Jun 1766, NATHANIEL GATES, baptized at Hardwick, MA, 4 Apr 1744 son of Nathaniel and Anna (Robbins) Gates.[861]

iii PATIENCE ROBBINS, b. 10 Jan 1752; d. at Chaplin, CT, 4 Jan 1816; m. at Hampton, 7 May 1778, WILLIAM CLARK, b. at Lebanon, CT, 25 Aug 1752 son of Phineas and Priscilla (Case) Clark; William d. at Chaplin, 9 Jul 1839.

iv JOHN ROBBINS, b. 21 Mar 1754; m. 1st 27 Dec 1781, ELIZABETH HUTCHINSON; Elizabeth d. at Hampton, 1787. John m. 2nd at Hampton, 27 Oct 1790, ALICE WILLIAMS.

v SOLOMON ROBBINS, b. 3 Mar 1756; d. at Chaplin, CT, 23 Aug 1798; m. 19 Oct 1780, LOIS CLARK, b. about 1757 daughter of Phineas and Hannah (Swift) Clark; Lois d. at Mansfield, 19 Dec 1834.

vi EBENEZER ROBBINS, b. 24 Feb 1758; d. at Ashford, 6 Oct 1849; m. 1st at Hampton, 28 Oct 1804, ESTHER ALWORTH, b. at Pomfret, 17 Feb 1784 daughter of William and Beulah (Moseley) Alworth; Esther d. at Ashford, 26 Sep 1817. Ebenezer m. 2nd ZERRAH CARPENTER, b. 1787; Zerrah d. at Willington, 31 Jul 1855.

vii HANNAH ROBBINS, b. 10 Feb 1760; d. at Randolph, VT, 31 Oct 1819; m. at Hampton, 19 Dec 1790, JOHN SESSIONS, b. 29 Jan 1768 son of John and Martha (Neff) Sessions; John d. at Randolph, 27 Mar 1842.

viii JEREMIAH ROBBINS, b. 17 Jan 1762

ix REBEKAH ROBBINS, b. 11 Jun 1764; d. at Hampton, 15 Oct 1809; m. at Hampton, about 1790, ASAHEL SESSIONS, b. at Windham, 12 Jun 1769 son of John and Martha (Neff) Sessions; Asahel d. at Chaplin, 3 Oct 1849. Asahel married second Clarissa Robbins on 27 Mar 1810.

x NATHANIEL ROBBINS, b. 17 Dec 1766; m. at Hampton, 27 Nov 1789, his third cousin, SARAH MOSELEY (*Sarah Ford Moseley*[5], *Dinah Holt Ford*[4], *George*[3], *Henry*[2], *Nicholas*[1]), likely the Sarah b. at Mansfield, CT, 11 Mar 1773 daughter of Thomas and Sarah (Ford) Moseley. There are two sons known for Nathaniel and Sarah, Thomas Moseley Robbins and Lucius Robbins.

xi ABIGAIL ROBBINS, b. 13 Dec 1767; d. at Pompey, NY, 14 Dec 1818; m. ROBERT CAMPBELL, b. at Canajoharie, NY, 25 Sep 1764 (pension record); Robert d. at Cuba, NY, 12 Jul 1836.

---

859 *Connecticut. Probate Court (Windham District), Probate records volume 8, pp 477-479*

860 *Connecticut State Library (Hartford, Connecticut), Probate Packets, Richardson, Josephine-Rose, Samuel, 1719-1880, Case 3193*

861 Roberts, Genealogies of Connecticut Families from the NEHGR, volume 1, p 703

xii OLIVE ROBBINS, b. 1 Jun 1769

xiii RUFUS ROBBINS, b. 27 Mar 1771; d. before 1820 (when widow Esther was head of household); m. ESTHER ROATH, b. at Norwich, 12 Apr 1781 daughter of Joseph and Miriam (Killam) Roath; Esther d. at Norwich, 15 Mar 1870.

317) ASA FARNHAM (*Nathaniel Farnum⁴, Ralph Farnum³, Elizabeth Holt Farnum², Nicholas¹*), b. at Windham, 11 Nov 1731 son of Nathaniel and Hannah (Preston) Farnum; d. at Ashford, 11 Jul 1807; m. at Windham, 2 Mar 1746, LYDIA BIDLACK, b. at Windham, 8 Jan 1736/7 daughter of Benjamin and Lydia (Abbe) Bidlack; Lydia d. at Ashford, 16 Apr 1811.

Asa and Lydia resided primarily in Ashford.

In his will written 17 March 1806 (proved 1 September 1807), Asa Farnham bequeathed to beloved wife Lydia all the household furniture, the use of the east half of the dwelling house, and a comfortable and honorable support from the estate or she as an option of the use and improvement of one-third of the estate. Daughters Lydia, Sarah, and Hannah receive fifty dollars each. Daughter Bethiah receives five dollars. Son Eliasaph receives a tract of land. Son Jonathan as right to pass at the most convenient place from his now dwelling house to father's house. The remaining of the estate is to be divided equally among "my three beloved sons Solomon, Jonathan, and Eliasaph." Sons Jonathan and Eliasaph were named executors.[862] Real estate of 126 acres was valued at $2,100. The receipts in the probate packet include acknowledgments from Asa Farnham, Lydia Snell and Joseph Snell, Ephraim Spalding and Hannah Spalding, as well as several receipts from creditors of the estate.

Asa Farnum and Lydia Bidlack were parents of nine children.

i LYDIA FARNHAM, b. at Ashford, 24 Feb 1758; d. at Union, CT, 24 Aug 1819; m. about 1785, Capt. JOSEPH SNELL, b. at Windham, 3 Jun 1755 son of Thomas and Mary (Jennings) Snell; Joseph d. at Union, 30 Oct 1846. Joseph married second Margery Dunton.

ii ASA FARNHAM, b. at Ashford, 23 Jul 1760; he was not living at the time of his father's will and no heirs of his are mentioned in the will.

iii SOLOMON FARNHAM, b. at Mansfield, 17 Jun 1762; d. at Sidney, NY, 18 Jul 1811; m. at Ashford, 23 Nov 1783, SALLY AVERY, b. at Ashford, 6 Sep 1765 daughter of John and Sarah (Bicknell) Avery; Sally d. at Sidney, 13 Jan 1816.[863]

iv JOHN FARNHAM, b. 8 Apr 1765; d. 17 Mar 1767.

v JONATHAN FARNHAM, b. at Ashford, 13 Mar 1767; d. at Ashford, 15 Oct 1840; m. at Ashford, 20 Mar 1794, EUNICE SNELL, b. about 1766; Eunice d. at Ashford, 30 Aug 1841.

vi ELEASAPH FARNHAM, b. at Ashford, 25 Jul 1769; d. at Sidney, NY, 16 Jul 1828; m. about 1793, SALLY DIMMOCK, b. 12 Jun 1774 daughter of Daniel and Zilpha (Simmons) Dimmock; Sally d. at St. Joseph Township, OH, 7 Feb 1844.[864]

vii BETHIAH FARNHAM, b. estimated 1772; she is mentioned in her father's will but no other records related to her were located.

viii HANNAH FARNHAM, b. 2 Nov 1775; m. about 1802 as his second wife, EPHRAIM SPALDING, b. at Ashford, 29 Sep 1769 son of Josiah and Priscilla (Paine) Spalding;[865] Ephraim d. at Pittsfield, NY, 19 Mar 1813. Ephraim was first married to Betsey Gilbert who died 29 Mar 1801.

ix SARAH FARNHAM, b. at Ashford, 23 May 1778

318) JEREMIAH FARNUM (*Nathaniel Farnum⁴, Ralph Farnum³, Elizabeth Holt Farnum², Nicholas¹*), b. at Windham, 31 Jul 1733 son of Nathaniel and Hannah (Preston) Farnum; d. at Hampton, 18 Mar 1827; m. at Hampton, 8 Oct 1774, LUCY DURKEE, b. at Windham, 9 Aug 1747 daughter of Henry and Relief (Adams) Durkee;[866] Lucy d. at Hampton, 2 Sep 1809.

Jeremiah and Lucy resided in Hampton where their five children were born.

i RUFUS FARNUM, b. at Hampton, 8 Jul 1775; d. at Ashford, 25 Mar 1860; m. at Ashford, 26 Nov 1801, BETSEY GROVER, b. about 1779 daughter of Stephen Grover; Betsey d. at Ashford, 25 Jul 1846. Rufus m. 2nd, about 1847, LOVINA PARKER, b. 1786; Lovina d. at Ashford, 17 Nov 1868.

---

862 Connecticut Wills and Probate Records, Windham, volume 11, p 283

863 Findagrave ID: 84519816, Pioneer Cemetery, Sidney, New York

864 Findagrave ID: 20583046; Sally's burial is in the Farnham Cemetery in St. Joseph Township.

865 Spalding, *The Spalding Memorial*, p 261

866 The 1785 will of Henry Durkee includes a bequest to his daughter Lucy Farnum.

ii AARON FARNUM, b. at Hampton, 15 Nov 1776; d. at Hampton, 29 Apr 1853; m. at Hampton, 11 Aug 1803, SARAH "SALLY" ABBOTT, b. at Hampton, 20 May 1782 daughter of Henry and Sarah (Burnham) Abbott; Sally d. at Hampton, 25 Sep 1815.

iii LUCY FARNUM, b. 16 Sep 1778; d. at Hampton, 1 Dec 1864. Lucy did not marry.

iv JEREMIAH FARNUM, b. at Hampton, 5 Jan 1781; d. at Hampton, 23 Jan 1866; m. 1st at Hampton, 14 Feb 1811, CLARISSA HUGHES, b. estimated 1785 daughter of Jonathan and Eunice (Durkee) Hughes;[867] Clarissa d. 21 Apr 1820. Jeremiah m. 2nd his second cousin once removed, LUCY FARNUM (*Abiel Farnum⁶, William Farnum⁵, William Farnum⁴, Ralph Farnum³, Elizabeth Holt Farnum², Nicholas¹*), b. 15 Jul 1802 daughter of Abiel and Chloe (Simmons) Farnum; Lucy d. 15 May 1888.

v ASA FARNUM, b. 26 Apr 1783; d. 25 Dec 1785.

319) MARTHA FARNUM (*Nathaniel Farnum[4], Ralph Farnum[3], Elizabeth Holt Farnum[2], Nicholas[1]*), b. at Windham, 17 Dec 1736 daughter of Nathaniel and Hannah (Preston) Farnum; d. at Hampton, 10 Nov 1815; m. at Windham, 6 Apr 1759, JONATHAN CLARK, b. at Windham, 12 Sep 1734 son of John and Ruth (Haskell) Clark; Jonathan d. at Hampton, 21 Oct 1797.

Martha and Jonathan resided in Hampton and did not have children, or at least no children who lived to adulthood.

In his will written 29 September 1797, Jonathan Clark of Hampton bequeathed to beloved wife Martha all the household furniture, half the livestock and the use of all the lands during her natural life, although she is not to sell any of the wood and timber. Other bequests were to various kinsmen: nephew Ebenezer Robins, nephew Jonathan Clark; kinsman Jonathan Clark Brown, nephew Jonathan Farnam, and nephew John Farnam. The remainder of the estate is to be divided among his lawful heirs including the children of his niece Elizabeth Root deceased and the children of niece Mary Brown deceased. Good friend Ebenezer Moseley was named executor.[868]

320) AARON FARNUM (*Nathaniel Farnum[4], Ralph Farnum[3], Elizabeth Holt Farnum[2], Nicholas[1]*), b. at Windham, 30 May 1742 son of Nathaniel and Hannah (Preston) Farnum; d. about 1777 (perhaps at Otter Creek during the war); m. RELIEF DURKEE, b. at Windham, 3 Apr 1743 daughter of Henry and Relief (Adams) Durkee.[869]

There is one child known for Aaron Farnum and Relief Durkee.

i JOHN FARNUM, b. at Windham, about 1770; d. at Williamstown, VT, 16 Sep 1837; m. 1st at Hampton, 15 Mar 1796, MARTHA MARTIN, b. 15 Mar 1771; Martha d. at Williamstown, 21 Aug 1815. John is reported to have a second wife, but her identity has not yet been located.[870]

321) HEPHZIBAH FARNUM (*Barachias Farnum[4], Ralph Farnum[3], Elizabeth Holt Farnum[2], Nicholas[1]*), b. at Andover, 3 Oct 1723 daughter of Barachias and Hephzibah (Harnden) Farnum; d. likely at Rumford, NH, about 1744; m. about 1744, EBENEZER HALL, b. at Bradford, MA, 19 Sep 1721 son of Joseph and Sarah (Kimball) Hall; Ebenezer d. at Concord, 24 Apr 1801. Ebenezer was second married to Dorcas Abbott on 17 Jun 1746.

Hephzibah Farnum and Ebenezer Hall were parents of one child.

i EBENEZER HALL, b. at Rumford, NH, 8 Aug 1744; d. at Alfred, ME, 23 Nov 1833; m. MARY who has not been identified; Mary d. at Alfred, 8 Jun 1830.

322) RACHEL FARNUM (*Barachias Farnum[4], Ralph Farnum[3], Elizabeth Holt Farnum[2], Nicholas[1]*), b. at Andover, 31 Jan 1726/7 daughter of Barachias and Hephzibah (Harnden) Farnum; d. at Haverhill, Feb 1805; m. 1st at Haverhill, 23 Jul 1747, SAMUEL AYER, b. at Haverhill, 13 Feb 1726/7 son of Samuel and Rachel (Kimball) Ayer; Samuel d. about 1761. Rachel m. 2nd at Haverhill, 23 Nov 1762, ISAAC BRADLEY, b. at Haverhill, 10 Jan 1718/9 son of Isaac and Elizabeth (Clement) Bradley; Isaac d. at Haverhill, 14 Jan 1802. Isaac was first married to Lydia Kimball.

Rachel Farnum and Samuel Ayer were parents of six children born at Haverhill.

i HEPHZIBAH AYER, b. 17 Feb 1747/8; d. at Winslow, ME, 25 Dec 1798; m. at Haverhill, 1 Dec 1767, BENJAMIN RUNNELS, b. at Haverhill, 31 Mar 1748 son of Ebenezer and Abigail (Sollis) Runnels; Benjamin d. at Winslow, 22 Jun 1802.

ii RACHEL AYER, b. 1 Oct 1749; m. at Haverhill, 12 Nov 1767, RICHARD EMERSON, b. at Haverhill, 20 Dec 1739 son of Richard and Mary (Morse) Emerson. Richard and Rachel settled in Stoddard, NH.

---

867 The 1819 estate distribution of Jonathan Hughes includes a distribution to the representatives of Clarissa Farnham late wife of Jeremiah Farnham.

868 *Connecticut. Probate Court (Windham District), Probate Records, volume 14, p 125-126, will of Jonathan Clark*

869 The 1785 will of Henry Durkee includes a bequest to his daughter Relief Farnum which consists of forgiving the debt that her deceased husband Aaron Farnum owed to Henry.

870 Cutter, New England Families, volume 4, p 2179

iii MOLLY AYER, b. 27 Nov 1750

iv JOHN AYER, b. 21 Feb 1751; d. 16 Dec 1753.

v JOHN AYER, b. 27 Jan 1754; d. 16 Feb 1754.

vi SAMUEL AYER, b. 19 Mar 1755; d. at Haverhill, 1811 (probate 1811); m. at Haverhill, 6 Apr 1781, SARAH CHASE, b. at Haverhill, 1 Jan 1761 daughter of Anthony and Abigail (Woodman) Chase; Sarah d. at Haverhill, 4 Jan 1844.

Rachel Farnum and Isaac Bradley were parents of two children born at Haverhill.

i RUTH BRADLEY, b. 25 Aug 1763; d. 27 Aug 1764.

ii RUTH BRADLEY, b. 27 Nov 1764; m. 17 Feb 1780, JOSIAH CHASE, b. at Newbury, 18 Apr 1757 son of Nathan and Lydia (Moulton) Chase.

323) SUSANNA FARNUM (*Barachias Farnum[4], Ralph Farnum[3], Elizabeth Holt Farnum[2], Nicholas[1]*), b. at Andover, 9 Apr 1730 daughter of Barachias and Hephzibah (Harnden) Farnum; d. at Haverhill, 22 Aug 1757; m. at Haverhill, 17 Feb 1746/7, JONATHAN DUSTIN, b. at Haverhill, 4 Jul 1719 son of Jonathan and Elizabeth (Watts) Dustin; Jonathan d. at Canaan, NH, 4 July 1812. Jonathan married Ruth Perry on 15 Mar 1759.

Susanna Farnum and Jonathan Dustin were parents of six children born at Haverhill. Jonathan remarried after Susanna's death and had eight children with his second wife. About 1780, Jonathan took his family to Canaan, New Hampshire.[871]

i JESSE DUSTIN, b. 13 Sep 1747; d. at Bethel, ME, after 1820; m. at Haverhill, 12 Apr 1768, ELIZABETH SWAN, baptized at Haverhill, 18 Jan 1747 daughter of James and Mary (Smith) Swan.

ii JONATHAN DUSTIN, b. 25 Jan 1748/9; d. 17 Feb 1748/9.

iii MEHITABLE DUSTIN, b. 25 Feb 1749/50; m. 1st at Haverhill, 4 Mar 1767, THOMAS SHEPARD, b. at Haverhill, 10 Sep 1745 son of Jonathan and Joanna (Barker) Shepard; Thomas d. at Haverhill, 1771 (probate 1771). Mehitable m. 2nd at Amesbury, 5 Jul 1781, BENJAMIN BODGE. In 1789, Mehitable Bodge of Popland declined the administration of the estate of her son Jesse Shepard. Benjamin Bodge was first married to Sarah Sargent.

iv SUSANNA DUSTIN, b. 4 Jan 1753; d. at Greenwood, ME, 30 Aug 1831; m. at Haverhill, 23 Apr 1777, TIMOTHY PATCH, b. at Wenham, 17 Aug 1746 son of Timothy and Rachel (Woodbury) Patch; Timothy d. at Greenwood, 31 Dec 1832.

v TAMOR DUSTIN, b. 9 Nov 1754; at Haverhill, m. 19 Aug 1777, DAVID MORES, b. at Haverhill, 30 Jul 1757 son of Ammiruhama and Jane (Sillaway) Mores; David d. at Newbury, 14 May 1833.

vi JONATHAN DUSTIN, b. 21 Feb 1757; d. at Canaan, NH, 1813 (probate 1813); m. at Haverhill, 15 Oct 1777, HANNAH RUSSELL, b. at Haverhill, 23 Feb 1756 daughter of James and Susannah (Richardson) Russell; Hannah d. at Haverhill, 9 Mar 1801. Jonathan m. 2nd at Haverhill, 29 Jan 1802, LYDIA BRADLEY.

324) ABIGAIL FARNUM (*Barachias Farnum[4], Ralph Farnum[3], Elizabeth Holt Farnum[2], Nicholas[1]*), b. at Andover, 27 May 1734 daughter of Barachias and Hephzibah (Harnden) Farnum; m. at Haverhill, 26 Mar 1755, JOSIAH FOLSOM, b. at Exeter, NH, 1725 son of John and Mary (Sewall) Folsom. Josiah was first married to Elizabeth Bradley.

On 9 November 1767, Abigail Folsom and Josiah Folsom signed the indenture for the settlement of the estate of Abigail's father Barachias.[872]

On 7 April 1783, Josiah Folsom and his wife Abigail conveyed their property in Haverhill to Cutting Marsh of Methuen for £517. This included the Folsom's homestead property and it is assumed that the family left Haverhill at that time, but it is not clear where they went.[873] They perhaps went to Canaan, New Hampshire where two of their sons settled. Josiah Folsom does appear on the 1786 inventory of Canaan, New Hampshire.[874]

Josiah Folsom and Abigail Farnum were parents of nine children recorded at Haverhill. There is a possible tenth child, John, reported in the Folsom genealogy for whom there is no birth record.[875] Josiah also had three children by his first wife, Elizabeth Bradley.

---

[871] Wallace, *History of Canaan, New Hampshire*, p 499

[872] Massachusetts Land Records, Essex County, 125:77

[873] Massachusetts Land Records 1620-1986, Essex County Deeds, 142:23; accessed through familysearch.org

[874] Wallace, *The History of Canaan, New Hampshire*, p 687

[875] Folsom, *Genealogy of the Folsom Family*, volume I, p 190

i MARY FOLSOM, b. 3 Oct 1755; d. at Canaan, NH, Mar 1850; m. at Haverhill, 24 Aug 1774, DANIEL COLBY, b. at Haverhill, 23 Nov 1752 son of Ebenezer and Mary (Chase) Colby; Daniel d. at Grafton, 23 Jul 1853.[876]

ii SUSANNA FOLSOM, b. 23 Oct 1756; m. at Haverhill, 22 Jul 1781, JOHN WHITING

iii DOLLY FOLSOM, b. 6 Feb 1758; d. 5 Apr 1758.

iv RUTH FOLSOM, b. 22 Mar 1759; d. at Fort Covington, NY by 1821; m. 1st at Haverhill, 6 Aug 1778, JOHN BALL. Ruth m. 2nd 5 May 1783, PARRIT BLAISDELL, b. Mar 1760 son of Elijah and Mary (Sargent) Blaisdell; Parrit d. at Fort Covington, NY, 3 Aug 1836. Parrit married second Betsey Standish on 1 Jan 1822.

v JOSIAH FOLSOM, b. 8 Jan 1761; died young

vi DOLLY FOLSOM, b. 9 Oct 1762; died young

vii JOSIAH FOLSOM, b. 4 May 1764; m. LYDIA GALE

viii JOHN FOLSOM, b. about 1765; m. at Canaan, NH, 9 Jun 1791, REBECCA COLBY

ix DOLLY FOLSOM, b. 4 Sep 1766

x NELLE FOLSOM, b. 10 Jan 1768

325) SARAH FARNUM (*Barachias Farnum⁴, Ralph Farnum³, Elizabeth Holt Farnum², Nicholas¹*), b. recorded at Rumford, 20 Apr 1738 daughter of Barachias and Hephzibah (Harnden) Farnum; d. at Cabot, VT, 30 Jun 1823; m. at Plaistow, NH, 7 Mar 1759, EPHRAIM MARSH, b. at Londonderry, 2 Apr 1738 son of Ephraim and Hannah (Smith) Marsh; Ephraim d. at Cabot, 6 Nov 1825.

Sarah and Ephraim were in Chester and Salisbury, New Hampshire before arriving in Plymouth, New Hampshire in 1784.The family moved on to Cabot, Vermont in 1791.[877]

Sarah Farnum and Ephraim Marsh were parents of thirteen children.[878]

i ELIZABETH "BETTE" MARSH, b. at Plaistow, NH, 18 Feb 1760; d. at Cabot, VT, 16 Oct 1810; m. DEARBORN HEATH, b. 15 Apr 1758 son of Joshua and Hannah (Dearborn) Heath; Dearborn d. at Woodbury, VT, 22 Aug 1831. Dearborn married second Mary Hay Oct 1811.

ii SUSANNAH MARSH, b. 17 Dec 1762; reported to marry WILLIAM SEARS,[879] but if so, died soon after marriage as there is a younger child in this family named Susannah born in 1783.

iii SARAH MARSH, b. 31 Oct 1764; d. at Rumney, NH, 1806; m. at Plymouth, NH, 23 Nov 1786, DEARBORN BEAN, b. Sept 1767 son of Elisha and Ruth (-) Bean; Dearborn d. at Rumney, 24 Feb 1838. Dearborn married second Hannah Petty in 1807.

iv DANIEL MARSH, b. 3 Jan 1766; d. at Walpole, NH, 9 Aug 1857; m. 21 Dec 1794, JANE ADAMS, b. 13 Feb 1773 daughter of Edmund and Hannah (Thurston) Adams; Jane d. at Walpole, 24 Sep 1859.

v DAVID MARSH, b. at Atkinson, NH, 16 Feb 1767; d. at Haverhill, MA, 23 Dec 1840; m. at Haverhill, 28 Apr 1795, PRISCILLA, GAGE, b. at Haverhill, 12 Nov 1772 daughter of Thomas and Mary (Whittier) Gage; Priscilla d. at Haverhill, 6 Apr 1849.

vi FARNUM MARSH, b. 3 Feb 1769. He is reported in *History of Plymouth* to have gone to Pennsylvania. He appears in the census record for Cabot, VT in 1791 and may be the Vernham Marsh in the 1820 census in Kanawha County, VA (now West Virginia). The estate of Farnham Marsh of Kanawha County was sold at auction June 1830. If this is this Farnum Marsh, he married and had a household of 12 in 1820.

vii JOHN MARSH, b. 3 Jan 1771; d. at Adams, MA, 23 May 1854; m. at Walpole, NH, 18 Jan 1797, PRISCILLA POND, b. at Wrentham, MA, 1775 possibly daughter of Hezekiah and Lydia (Parkhurst) Pond; Priscilla d. at Chicopee, 9 Jan 1863.

viii MARY "POLLY" MARSH, b. 19 Jun 1773; d. at Corinth, VT, 1813; m. about 1795, DAVID HEATH, *perhaps* b. at Salem, NH, 25 Jun 1770 son of Joshua and Dorothy (Austin) Heath; David d. at Corinth, 1821. David married second Sally Batchelder.

---

[876] Daniel's gravestone gives age at death as 99 years 7 months which is one year off from the 100 years derived from birth and death record.

[877] Stearns, *History of Plymouth, New Hampshire*, p 422

[878] There are two daughters named Susannah reported in the History of Plymouth, both of whom married. As these daughters are 20 years apart in age, it would mean that the older Susannah died soon after marriage.

[879] Stearns, *History of Plymouth, New Hampshire*, volume 2, p 422

ix JAMES MARSH, b. 23 Jul 1775; d. at Cabot, VT, 8 Oct 1865; m. MIRIAM WALBRIDGE, b. at Stafford, CT, 17 Sep 1781 daughter of Eleazer and Abigail (Washburn) Walbridge; Miriam d. at Cabot, 4 Oct 1852.

x LYDIA MARSH, b. 7 Mar 1777; d. at Cabot, VT, 21 Nov 1840; m. about 1798; REUBEN CLARK, b. at Chester, NH, 4 Dec 1760 son of Joseph and Desire (Howe) Clark; Reuben d. at Cabot, 10 May 1852.

xi RUTH MARSH, b. 1 Nov 1778; d. at Cabot, VT, 15 Sep 1865; m. SOLOMON WASHINGTON OSGOOD, b. at Claremont, NH, 27 Aug 1776 son of William and Hephzibah (Dunton) Osgood; Solomon d. at Cabot, 18 Oct 1846.

xii BARACHIAS MARSH, b. 15 Apr 1781; d. at Cabot, VT, 13 May 1811; m. at Waterbury, VT, 1 Dec 1803, SUSANNAH PERRY.

xiii SUSANNAH MARSH, b. 1 May 1783; d. at Waterbury, VT, 29 Mar 1840; m. at Cabot, VT, 6 Dec 1804, JOHN DARLING, b. about 1775; John d. at Northfield, VT, 18 Aug 1857.

326) JOHN FARNUM (*Barachias Farnum⁴, Ralph Farnum³, Elizabeth Holt Farnum², Nicholas¹*), b. recorded at Rumford, 6 Apr 1740 son of Barachias and Hephzibah (Harnden) Farnum; m. at Haverhill, MA, 1762, HANNAH EASTMAN, baptized at Haverhill, Dec 1740 daughter of Jonathan and Hannah (Ingalls) Eastman.

John and Hannah resided in Haverhill, New Hampshire. John had inherited the homestead property and grist mill from his father.[880]

John Farnum and Hannah Eastman were parents of eight children. The births of seven children are recorded at Haverhill. The eighth child, James, is given in Farnham's Farnum genealogy (p 242) but with no associated records.

i BARACHIAS FARNUM, b. 5 Jan 1762; d. at Essex, VT, 1815; m. about 1800, MARY EASTMAN, b. about 1765 daughter of Thomas and Abigail (French) Eastman; Mary d. at Essex, after 1815.

ii LYDIA FARNUM, b. 29 Apr 1764

iii JONATHAN FARNUM, b. 27 May 1766; d. at Enfield, NH, 2 Dec 1854; m. HANNAH CHOATE, baptized at Ipswich, MA, 26 Apr 1772 daughter of Jacob and Hannah (Burnham) Choate; Hannah d. at Enfield, 15 Feb 1854.

iv DAVID FARNUM, b. 28 Jul 1768. David is believed to have married, but the name of his wife has not been found.

v JOHN FARNUM, b. 8 Dec 1770

vi HANNAH FARNUM, b. 24 Jun 1773

vii BENAIAH FARNUM, b. 25 Dec 1775; d. at Aurelius, NY, 6 Aug 1870; m. about 1795, SARAH; Sarah d. a Aurelius, 9 Aug 1849.

viii JAMES FARNUM, b. about 1777[881]

327) LYDIA FARNUM (*Joseph Farnum⁴, Ralph Farnum³, Elizabeth Holt Farnum², Nicholas¹*), b. at Windham, 3 Oct 1728 daughter of Joseph and Lydia (Howard) Farnum; d. at Walpole, NH, 15 Jan 1791; m. at Killingworth, 22 May 1754, as his fourth wife, JOSEPH GRISWOLD, b. at Killingworth, 22 Oct 1716 son of Joseph and Temperance (Lay) Griswold; Joseph d. at Walpole, 13 Jul 1791. Joseph was first married to Rebecca Ruttey, second married to Sarah Hurd, and third married to Sarah Jones.

Joseph Griswold and Lydia Farnum had their nine children in Killingworth, Connecticut and then relocated to Walpole, New Hampshire in 1774. Joseph was a millwright.[882] In 1774, Joseph purchased a 50-acre lot in Walpole from Benjamin Bellows and added additional property in 1777. Joseph sold his property to son Gilbert in 1784 and 1791. Part of that lot was the site of Dodge Tavern that Gilbert Griswold built in 1801.[883]

Joseph Griswold did not leave a will and his estate entered probate 7 September 1791 with Elisha Griswold as administrator and Gilbert Griswold and Ebenezer Cuhore as sureties to the bond. Personal estate was valued at £40.3.4 and debts were £37.12.10.[884]

i DANIEL GRISWOLD, b. 18 Jul 1755; m. at Walpole, 11 Jun 1779, ABIGAIL GRAVES.

ii GIDEON GRISWOLD, b. 3 Feb 1757

iii LYDIA GRISWOLD, b. 20 Mar 1759; died young

---

880 Farnham, *New England Descendants of Ralph Farnum*, p 242

881 James is a child listed in Farnham's genealogy of the Farnum family for whom no records were located

882 Frizzell, *A History of Walpole, New Hampshire*, volume 2, p 123

883 Frizzell, *A History of Walpole, New Hampshire*, volume 1, p 358

884 *New Hampshire. Probate Court (Cheshire County), Estate Files, F674-F702, 1883-1885; Estate Files, G1-G32, 1771-1793, Case 24*

iv GILBERT GRISWOLD, b. 6 Jun 1761; d. at Walpole, NH, 2 Jun 1827; m. at Saybrook, 26 Oct 1786, REBECCA NICHOLS, b. 1768; d. at Walpole, 15 Mar 1837.

v LYDIA GRISWOLD, b. 6 Dec 1763; m. at Walpole, 22 Feb 1782, JEDEDIAH DENNISON, b. Oct 1751 son of Daniel Dennison; Jedediah d. at Hartland, NY, 2 Feb 1842.

vi ELISHA GRISWOLD, b. 1 Oct 1765; d. at Charleston, VT, 9 Sep 1851; m. about 1795, LUCINDA, b. about 1773 who has not been identified; Lucinda d. 1 Mar 1843.

vii STEPHEN GRISWOLD, b. 24 Jan 1768; m. at Walpole, NH, 2 Apr 1798, ELIZABETH POOR, b. at Lancaster, MA, 13 Sep 1772 daughter of Andrew and Esther (Snow) Poor.

viii ASAHEL GRISWOLD, b. 24 Jan 1768; d. at Rochester, NY, after 1840; m. Sep 1796, PRUDENCE BLISS, b. in NH, 31 Jul 1773 daughter of Jonathan and Sarah (Preston) Bliss; Prudence d. at Rochester, 1852.

ix ETHAN GRISWOLD, b. 25 Feb 1771; d. at Walpole, 12 Oct 1799. Ethan did not marry. His brother Stephen was administrator of his estate.

328) MARY FARNUM (*Joseph Farnum⁴, Ralph Farnum³, Elizabeth Holt Farnum², Nicholas¹*), b. at Windham, 28 Jan 1729/30 daughter of Joseph and Lydia (Howard) Farnum; d. at Norwich, 13 Apr 1775; m. at Plainfield, 20 Mar 1753, JAMES LONGBOTTOM,[885] b. 27 Dec 1729 son of James and Priscilla (Lovett) Longbottom; James d. at Hanover, CT, Feb 1814. James married second Sarah Averell.

James Longbottom served in the Revolution, enlisting from Norwich and "marched at the alarm" to Boston in April 1775.[886]

In his will written 28 December 1810, James Bottom bequeathed to beloved wife Sarah one-third of the personal estate to be at her own disposal and the use and improvement of one-third of the real estate. Son Asel Bottom receives $333.34 as does son Roswell Bottom. Grandson (not named) only child and heir of Martin Bottom receives forty dollars. If the grandson dies before age twenty-one, the legacy goes to son William. Daughter Priscilla wife of Dyer Kingsley receives $33.34. The heirs of daughter Silvina late wife of Wesley Perkins receive seventy dollars. Daughter Sally wife of William Clark receives eighty-four cents. The remainder of the estate real and personal goes to son William, except if he does not pay the legacies in the will, then the estate is to be equally divided among the other children. William was named executor.[887] William and Martin, sons named in the will, and daughter Sally Clark were children from James's second marriage to Sarah Averell.

Mary Farnum and James Bottom were parents of six children born at Norwich.

i ASEL BOTTOM, b. 3 Jan 1754; d. at Lisbon, CT, 7 Oct 1838; m. at Lisbon, 29 May 1788, REBECCA PARKER.

ii PRISCILLA BOTTOM, b. 28 Feb 1755; m. at Norwich, 25 Oct 1780, DYER KINGSLEY. Dyer and Priscilla were living in Lisbon, CT in 1800. There is a Dyer Kingsley of the right age in Richmond, MA in 1810 and who dies there in 1824, but it is not clear that it is this Dyer.

iii JAMES BOTTOM, b. 30 Mar 1756; not in his father's will.

iv MARY BOTTOM, b. 26 May 1759; not in father's will.

v SILVINA BOTTOM, b. 27 Sep 1760; d. at Orwell, VT, 6 Mar 1806; m. at Norwich, 29 Sep 1784, WESLEY PERKINS, b. at Windham, Oct 1761 son of Jacob and Mary (-) Perkins; Wesley d. at Orwell, 28 May 1817.

vi ROSWELL BOTTOM, b. 2 Jan 1767; d. at Orwell, VT, 2 Oct 1853; m. 1st at Orwell, Feb 1793 OMIRA BUSH[888] who died about 1800. Roswell m. 2nd 3 Jul 1801, MERIAM CONKEY, b. at Pelham, MA, 29 Oct 1775 daughter of Asa and Margaret (Hamilton) Conkey;[889] Meriam d. at Orwell, 26 May 1863.

329) JOSEPH FARNUM (*Joseph Farnum⁴, Ralph Farnum³, Elizabeth Holt Farnum², Nicholas¹*), b. at Windham, 2 Dec 1731 son of Joseph and Lydia (Howard) Farnum; d. at Plainfield, 1803; m. at Canterbury, 10 Jul 1764, LYDIA WHEELER, b. at Plainfield, 18 Nov 1740 daughter of Benjamin and Prudence (Huet) Wheeler.

The Farnum genealogy[890] provides a summary of Joseph's will written 27 August 1798. Bequests were to wife Lydia, eldest son Benjamin, eldest daughter Olive Tanner wife of Nathan Tanner, second daughter Lucy Russell wife of Asa Russell, third daughter Polly Dyer wife of Wyllys Dyer, fourth daughter Hannah Spalding wife of Jesse Spalding, and fifth daughter Lydia Farnham. The residue of the estate was divided between sons Joseph and Stephen.

Joseph Farnum and Lydia Wheeler were parents of eight children born at Canterbury.

---

[885] James shortened his last name to Bottom which is the name used in his will and the name used by all his children.

[886] Oliver, *The Bottum (Longbottom) Family Album*, p 135

[887] *Connecticut State Library (Hartford, Connecticut), Probate Packets, Bishop, E-Bottum, James, 1748-1880, number 1316*

[888] Oliver, *The Bottum (Longbottom) Family Album*, p 136

[889] The names of Meriam's parents are given as Asa Conkey and Margaret Hamilton on her death record.

[890] Farnham, *New England Descendants of Ralph Farnum*, p 244

i OLIVE FARNUM, b. 19 Nov 1765; d. at Northampton, MA, 10 Jun 1844; m. by 1788, NATHAN TANNER, b. about 1761; Nathan d. at Northampton, 30 Dec 1839.

ii LUCY FARNUM, b. 23 May 1768; m. ASA RUSSELL who has not been identified.

iii POLLY FARNUM, b. 27 Nov 1770; m. WYLLYS DYER, b. at Canterbury, 4 Aug 1760 son of Joseph and Martha (Darbe) Dyer.

iv HANNAH FARNUM, b. 25 Mar 1773; d. at Plainfield, NH, 10 Jun 1861; m. Jan 1797, JESSE SPALDING, b. at Plainfield, CT, 12 Aug 1771 son of Jesse and Abigail (-) Spalding; Jesse d. at Plainfield, Feb 1861.

v BENJAMIN FARNUM, b. 12 Jun 1775

vi JOSEPH FARNUM, b. 25 Dec 1778; d. at Canterbury, 29 Jun 1859; m. 1st at Canterbury, 20 Oct 1803, SYBIL BALDWIN, b. 24 Mar 1782 daughter of Rufus and Hannah (Haskell) Baldwin; Sybil d. at Canterbury, 18 Jun 1837. Joseph m. 2nd 5 Dec 1837, ORINDA DAVENPORT, b. at Canterbury, 27 Jun 1791 daughter of Charles and Mabel (Wilson) Davenport; Orinda d. 29 Jun 1874.

vii STEPHEN FARNUM, b. 10 Jun 1781; d. at Plainfield, CT, 1835; m. 1st about 1804, OLIVE LEFFINGWELL, b. at Plainfield, 20 Dec 1780 daughter of Jeremiah and Sarah (Wright) Leffingwell; Olive d. at Plainfield, 1814. Stephen m. 2nd HANNAH BALDWIN, b. at Canterbury, 16 Apr 1788 daughter of Rufus and Hannah (Haskell) Baldwin; Hannah d. Apr 1828.

viii LYDIA FARNUM, b. 8 May 1784

330) SARAH FARNUM (*Joseph Farnum4, Ralph Farnum3, Elizabeth Holt Farnum2, Nicholas1*), b. at Canterbury, 28 Nov 1734 daughter of Joseph and Lydia (Howard) Farnum; d. at Jewett City, CT, 17 May 1798; m. about 1754, ELEAZER JEWETT, b. at Norwich, 31 Aug 1731 son of Eleazer and Elizabeth (Griggs) Jewett; Eleazer d. at Jewett City, CT, 7 Dec 1817. Eleazer married second Elizabeth (widow Babcock).

Eleazer is credited with being the founder of Jewett City, later incorporated as Griswold, Connecticut. He owned the first grist mill in the area and later added a sawmill.[891]

Eleazer Jewett did not leave a will and Joseph Jewett was named administrator of the estate on 6 April 1818. There were several creditors to the estate who agreed to relinquish part of their demands on the estate for the support of the widow.[892]

Sarah Farnum and Eleazer Jewett were parents of seven children born at Norwich.

i OTHNIEL JEWETT, b. 31 Aug 1754; d. 5 Feb 1757.

ii LYDIA JEWETT, b. 15 Jan 1756; d. at Norwich, 4 Dec 1794; m. at Norwich, 1 Aug 1782, Capt. JOHN WILSON, b. about 1753; John d. at Norwich, 29 Apr 1831. John married second Mary Lathrop.

iii OLIVE JEWETT, b. 22 Oct 1757; d. at Lowell, NY, 14 Feb 1836; m. 1st at Montgomery, MA, 19 Jan 1775, PHAREZ CLARK, b. at Preston, CT, 3 Nov 1749 son of Oliver and Elizabeth (Freeman) Clark; Pharez d. at Norwich 1784 (probate 3 Oct 1784). Olive m. 2nd about 1786, Lieut. JABEZ BILLS, baptized at Groton CT, 5 Aug 1742 son of Thomas Bills; Jabez d. at Lowell, NY, 22 Oct 1832.

iv ELIZABETH JEWETT, b. 11 Apr 1759; d. at Norwich, VT, 7 Mar 1843; m. about 1788, as his second wife, JONAS BOARDMAN, b. 1752 son of Elijah and Mary (Tyler0 Boardman; Jonas d. at Norwich, 16 Sep 1817. Jonas was first married to Lorana Benton.

v ELEAZER JEWETT, b. 11 Dec 1760; d. 16 Nov 1766.

vi JOSEPH JEWETT, b. 12 Dec 1762; d. at Lisbon, CT, 7 Dec 1831; m. 1st 13 Oct 1785, SALLY JOHNSON, b. 2 Jul 1764; d. 18 Nov 1786. Joseph m. 2nd 4 Mar 1790, BETSEY KING, b. 17 Jan 1767 daughter of Joseph King; Betsey d. 18 Feb 1840.

vii SALLY JEWETT, b. 8 Aug 1768; d. at Norwich, VT, 10 Dec 1790; m. 25 Jan 1790, CONSTANT MURDOCK, b. at Preston, CT, 24 Sep 1761 son of Thomas and Elizabeth (Hatch) Murdock; Constant d. at Norwich, 15 Oct 1828. Constant married second Lucy Riley.

331) BENJAMIN FARNHAM (*Joseph Farnum4, Ralph Farnum3, Elizabeth Holt Farnum2, Nicholas1*), b. at Canterbury, 3 Jan 1736 son of Joseph and Lydia (Howard) Farnum; d. at Barkhamsted, CT, 12 Nov 1809; m. at Simsbury, 8 Dec 1777, ABIGAIL ROBE, b. at Simsbury, 7 Jun 1754 daughter of Andrew and Hannah (Miller) Robe; Abigail d. at West Granby, 5 Sep 1837.

---

[891] Caulkins, *History of Norwich, Connecticut*, pp 448-449

[892892] *Connecticut State Library (Hartford, Connecticut), Estate of Eleazer Jewett, Case 5900*

Benjamin Farnham was admitted to the bar in Connecticut in 1780 and was a founding member of the Bar Association of Hartford County in 1783. He also served as town clerk of Simsbury and clerk of the Episcopal church at Turkey Hill.[893]

Benjamin Farnham did not leave a will and Abigail Farnham was named administratrix of the estate on 12 December 1809. A personal estate inventory is given with a value of $46.91.[894]

Son Julius did not marry. In his will written 23 August 1826, he bequeathed to his honored mother Abigail Farnham the use of his property in Barkhamsted for her support. His sister Matilda receives all the land he owned in Barkhamsted, reserving only that part needed for the support of his mother. Other bequests were to heirs of sister Lydia Giddings, heirs of Laura Reed, Sabrina Holcomb, Rosella Giddings, and Lucia Case.[895] The distribution of Julius's estate on 8 November 1827 included set-offs to the following heirs: widow Sabrina Holcomb, heirs of Lydia Giddings now Lydia Wilcox, heirs of Laura Reed wife of Shaylor Reed, Lucia Case wife of Levi Case, heirs of Lucinda Sharp wife of Abel Sharp, Matilda Farnham, and widow Abigail Farnham who will have use of one-half of buildings and eight acres of land during her natural life.[896]

Benjamin Farnham and Abigail Robe were parents of nine children born at Simsbury, Connecticut.

i LUCINDA FARNHAM, b. 9 Nov 1778; d. after 1850 when she was living at Wolcott, NY; reported in Farnham's genealogy as marrying Apollos____, but records were not located. Lucinda m. 2nd ABEL SHARP, b. about 1779; Abel d. after 1850.

ii JULIUS FARNHAM, b. 30 Mar 1781; d. at East Granby, 10 Sep 1826. Julius did not marry.

iii ROSELLA FARNHAM, b. 1 Feb 1783; d. at Junius, NY, about 1827; m. about 1807, *likely* IRA GIDDINGS, b. about 1780 son of Thomas and Affiah (Hayes) Giddings;[897] Ira d. at Romulus, NY, 13 Feb 1832. Ira was second married to Anna Doty.

iv SABRINA FARNHAM, b. 12 Dec 1784; d. at Bloomfield, CT, 23 Feb 1836; m. ABIEL HOLCOMB, b. at Granby, 1781 perhaps the son of Jesse and Louisa (Pinney) Holcomb; Abiel d. at Bloomfield, 20 May 1823.

v LYDIA FARNHAM, b. 18 Feb 1787; d. at Canton, CT, 25 Feb 1878; m. 1st about 1810, CHESTER GIDDINGS; Chester d. about 1826. Lydia m. 2nd about 1827, ORVILLE WILCOX, b. 11 Mar 1792 son of William and Mercy (Case) Wilcox;[898] Orville d. at Canton, 3 Sep 1864.

vi MATILDA FARNHAM, b. 26 Apr 1789; d. 24 Mar 1864; m. at Barkhamsted, 12 Aug 1828, as his second wife, GURDON TILLOTSON, b. about 1782 son of Jonathan and Martha (Spellman) Tillotson; Gurdon d. at Granby, CT, 1871 (probate 1871). Gurdon was first married to Hannah Loomis. Matilda and Gurdon resided in Granville, MA until at least 1850, but Gurdon was in Granby in 1870.

vii LAURA FARNHAM, b. 1 May 1792; d. at Granby, CT, 26 Aug 1876; m. at Barkhamsted, 21 Nov 1816, SHALOR REED, b. at Granby, 31 Aug 1797 son of Abner and Mary (Spring) Reed; Shalor d. at Granby, 3 Nov 1869.

viii LUCIA FARNHAM, b. 14 Feb 1798; d. at Granby, CT, 5 Jul 1882; m. at Barkhamsted, 11 May 1824, as his second wife, LEVI CASE, b. 1786 *likely* son of Noah and Mary (Adams) Case; Levi d. at Granby, 1 Jan 1859. Levi was first married to Anna Spencer.

332) STEPHEN FARNUM (*Joseph Farnum⁴, Ralph Farnum³, Elizabeth Holt Farnum², Nicholas¹*), b. at Canterbury, 16 Oct 1741 son of Joseph and Lydia (Howard) Farnum; d. about 1779; m. at Plainfield, 10 Mar 1768, OLIVE WHEELER, b. at Plainfield, 11 Sep 1750 daughter of Benjamin and Prudence (Huet) Wheeler; Olive d. at Hampton, 18 Oct 1835. Olive second married Philip Pearl in 1780.

There is just one child known for Stephen Farnum and Olive Wheeler.

i NATHANIEL FARNUM, b. at Plainfield, 7 Mar 1769; d. at Richfield, NY, 23 Mar 1803 (probate 6 May 1803 with Anna as administratrix); m. about 1795, ANNA HOWARD, b. about 1774; Anna d. 9 Jul 1803.[899]

333) LUCY FARNUM (*Joseph Farnum[4], Ralph Farnum[3], Elizabeth Holt Farnum[2], Nicholas[1]*), b. at Canterbury, 1 Feb 1744 daughter of Joseph and Lydia (Howard) Farnum; d. at Plainfield, 7 Apr 1766; m. at Plainfield, 9 Feb 1764, ROBERT

---

893 Farnham, *New England Descendants of Ralph Farnum*, p 246

894 *Connecticut State Library (Hartford, Connecticut)*; Probate Place: *Hartford, Connecticut, Estate of Benjamin Farnham of Barkhamsted, Case 1010*

895 *Connecticut. Probate Court (Granby District)*; Probate Place: *Hartford, Connecticut, volume 4, 55-56*

896 *Connecticut State Library (Hartford, Connecticut)*; Probate Place: *Hartford, Connecticut, Estate of Julius Farnham, Town of Granby, Case 483*

897 Giddings, *The Giddings Family*, p 181

898 Orville Wilcox is reported to have married the widow of Chester Giddings. Brown, *Genealogical History, with Short Sketches and Family Records, of the Early Settlers of West Simsbury*, p 130

899 Farnham, Genealogy of the Farnham Family, p 31

WASHBURN, b. Apr 1739 (calculated from death age of 92 years 9 days); Robert d. at Wilton, NY, 24 Apr 1831. Robert married second Adah Bennett.

Lucy Farnum and Robert Washburn were parents of one child.

i STEPHEN WASHBURN, b. at Plainfield, CT, 28 Feb 1766; m. SALINDA WETHY, b. at Preston, CT, 6 Jan 1774 daughter of Elijah and Mercy (Gates) Wethy; Salinda d. 21 Jul 1837. This family perhaps located in Schoharie County, NY.

334) JOSHUA FARNUM (*Stephen Farnum⁴, Ralph Farnum³, Elizabeth Holt Farnum², Nicholas¹*), b. at Andover, 24 Jul 1727 son of Stephen and Hannah (Richardson) Farnum; d. at Dracut about 1759 (probate 28 Jan 1760); m. about 1751, MILLICENT PERRY, likely b. at Lexington, 10 May 1726 daughter of John and Deborah (Wilson) Perry. Millicent was second married to Richard Bradden.

Joshua Farnum did not leave a will and his estate entered probate 28 January 1760 with widow Millicent as administratrix. Real estate was six acres of land with small dwelling house valued at £16.5.4 and real estate at £15.13. Debts were £25.3.7.[900]

Joshua Farnum and Millicent Perry were parents of four children born at Dracut.

i DEBORAH FARNUM, b. 28 Mar 1752. Deborah was living in 1770 when Edward Farmer of Billerica was allowed as her guardian. A marriage was not located for her.

ii JOSHUA FARNUM, b. 19 Dec 1753; d. 15 Nov 1754.

iii JOHN FARNUM, b. 19 Apr 1756; d. at Leeds and Grenville, Ontario, about 1813; m. at Wilton, NH, 9 Feb 1779, HULDAH KENNEY, b. at Middleton, 2 Jun 1755 daughter of David and Priscilla (Wilkins) Kenney.[901]

iv JOSHUA FARNUM, b. 20 Apr 1760; d. at Dublin, NH, 1 Jul 1837; m. at Dublin, 19 Dec 1782, MARY "POLLY" BORDEN, b. at Monson, MA, 21 Nov 1761;[902] Polly d. at Dublin, 18 Sep 1806. Joshua m. 2nd 27 Jan 1807 ABIGAIL BABCOCK (widow of Joel Kendall), b. 1769; Abigail d. 13 Oct 1828.

335) HANNAH FARNUM (*Stephen Farnum⁴, Ralph Farnum³, Elizabeth Holt Farnum², Nicholas¹*), b. at Andover, 17 Jan 1728/9 daughter of Stephen and Hannah (Richardson) Farnum; d. at Methuen, 5 May 1804; m. about1748, NATHAN AUSTIN, b. at Methuen, 25 Jan 1725 son of Thomas and Sarah (Lovejoy) Austin; Nathan d. at Methuen, 1755.

Hannah Farnum and Nathan Austin were parents of four children born at Methuen.

i NATHAN AUSTIN, b. 11 Jun 1748; d. at Rochester, VT, 11 Aug 1833; m. at Methuen, 27 Sep 1769, PHEBE BARKER, b. at Methuen, 4 Jun 1748 daughter of Zebadiah and Phebe (Merrill) Barker;[903] Phebe d. at Rochester, 11 Nov 1820.

ii HANNAH AUSTIN, b. 1 Feb 1749; d. 12 Nov 1753.

iii ABIJAH AUSTIN, b. 29 May 1752; d. at Methuen, 4 Mar 1780.[904]

iv PHEBE AUSTIN, b. 2 Mar 1754; m. at Methuen, 30 Jan 1772, JOHN TIPPETTS, b. at Methuen, 15 Aug 1752 son of John and Phebe (Austin) Tippetts.

336) MARTHA FARNUM (*Stephen Farnum⁴, Ralph Farnum³, Elizabeth Holt Farnum², Nicholas¹*), b. at Andover, 22 Jan 1730/1 daughter of Stephen and Hannah (Richardson) Farnum; m. at Woburn, 15 Dec 1753, ZEBULON MAY.

Martha and Zebulon were somewhat unsettled living in Woburn, perhaps Charlestown, Medford, and then in Merrimack, New Hampshire. They were twice "warned out" of Medford, in September 1759 with children Mary and Martha, and again 16 April 1764 with children Mary, Martha, Lucy, Abigail, and Zebulon. Two of the daughters were residents of Andover at the time they married. Zebulon is likely the Zebulon May enlisted at Exeter in 1776 recruited for Canada Service in Colonel Thurstone's Regiment. There are five known children of Martha and Zebulon.

i MARY MAY, b. about 1754; living in 1764 but nothing further known.

ii MARTHA MAY, b. about 1756; living in 1764 but nothing further known.

---

900 *Massachusetts, Wills and Probate Records, Middlesex County, Case 7266*

901 David Kenney of Wilton wrote his will in 1775 prior to Huldah's marriage but the will includes a bequest to daughter Huldah.

902 Farnham, The Descendants of Ralph Farnum, p. 460. The date of birth is given in the Farnum genealogy but the record of this has not been found.

903 The will of Zebadiah Barker (probate 1781) of Methuen includes a bequest to his daughter Phebe Austen.

904 Abijah, s. Nathan and Hannah, Mar. 4, 1780, a. 27 y. 11 m.

iii LUCY MAY, b. at Medford, 30 Aug 1759; d. at Merrimack, NH, 24 Feb 1812; m. at Andover, 15 Dec 1782, CHRISTOPHER RITTERBUSH, b. in (current day) Germany, about 1754; d. at Merrimack, NH, 1 Jun 1841. Christopher was a Hessian soldier who came for the Revolution and stayed.

iv ABIGAIL MAY, b. about 1761; d. at Merrimack, NH, 26 Jun 1786; m. at Andover, 4 Nov 1782, WILLIAM LONGA. Abigail had one daughter Betsey who died in infancy.

v ZEBULON MAY, b. about 1764; d. at Merrimack, NH, 18 Dec 1791.

337) STEPHEN FARNUM (*Stephen Farnum[4], Ralph Farnum[3], Elizabeth Holt Farnum[2], Nicholas[1]*), b. at Dracut, 19 Jan 1734 son of Stephen and Hannah (Richardson) Farnum; d. at Manchester, VT, 13 Jan 1813; m. at Chelmsford, 12 Feb 1765, KEZIA SKIDMORE, b. at Worcester, 23 Jul 1736 daughter of Richard and Jemima (Gould) Skidmore.

There are three children known for Stephen Farnum and Kezia Skidmore.

i PHEBE FARNUM, b. about 1768; d. at Lyndeborough, after 1830; m. at Lyndeborough, her third cousin once removed, 28 Apr 1789, as his second wife, AARON PUTNAM (*Sarah Cram Putnam[4], Sarah Holt Cram[3], Henry[2], Nicholas[1]*), b. at Lyndeborough, about 1758 son of Ephraim and Sarah (Cram) Putnam; Aaron d. after 1830. Phebe Farnum and Aaron Putnam are Family 700.

ii BENJAMIN FARNUM, b. at Wilton, 5 Oct 1770; d. at Manchester, VT, 5 Oct 1859; m. 1st at Lyndeborough, 26 Sep 1795, LOIS BARKER, b. at Wilton, 19 Apr 1775 daughter of Daniel and Bathsheba (Blanchard) Barker; Lois d. 13 Oct 1804. Benjamin m. 2nd 21 Jan 1806, SALLY WOODBURN, b. 1779; Sally d. at Peru, VT, 26 Oct 1871.

iii JAMES FARNUM, b. at Amherst, NH, 9 Apr 1776; m. about 1799, MOLLY who has not been identified. James and Molly had twins named James and Molly born 25 Apr 1800. Nothing else is known.

338) PHEBE FARNUM (*Stephen Farnum[4], Ralph Farnum[3], Elizabeth Holt Farnum[2], Nicholas[1]*), b. at Dracut, 27 Jan 1739 daughter of Stephen and Hannah (Richardson) Farnum; m. at Andover, 1 Sep 1757, THOMAS RICHARDSON, likely b. at Andover, 15 Feb 1732 son of Thomas and Elizabeth (-) Richardson.

Thomas Richardson and Phebe Farnum had their ten children in Wilton, but left Wilton between 1787 and 1790.[905] They were then likely in Lyndeborough where the two youngest daughters married. Thomas and Phebe appear to be living in Lyndeborough at the 1800 census with a household of one male over 45 and one female over 45.

Thomas Richardson and Phebe Farnum were parents of ten children born at Wilton.

i EUNICE RICHARDSON, b. 21 Sep 1758; d. 2 Nov 1758.

ii PHEBE RICHARDSON, b. 9 Dec 1759

iii HANNAH RICHARDSON, b. 9 Apr 1761; m. *likely* 1st at Lyndeborough, 20 Nov 1787, ISAAC HAGGETT; Isaac d. at Litchfield, 1798. Hannah m. 2nd, about 1799, THOMAS BOOFEE,[906] b. at Lyndeborough, 10 Apr 1750 son of Melchizedeck and Margaret (McKeen) Boofee;[907] Thomas d. at Litchfield, ME, 9 Jan 1820. Thomas was first married to Sarah Spaulding.

iv STEPHEN RICHARDSON, b. 17 Sep 1763; d. at Warren, NH, 1 Dec 1824; m. about 1784, SUSANNA who has not been identified.

v THOMAS RICHARDSON, b. 31 Oct 1764; m. at Lyndeborough, 1 Nov 1785, MARY DAVIS.

vi JOHN RICHARDSON, b. 6 Aug 1766; m. at Lyndeborough, 2 Jul 1789, LYDIA STEPHENSON, b. at Lyndeborough, 2 Dec 1772 daughter of John and Abigail (Shepherd) Stephenson.

vii WILLIAM RICHARDSON, b. 10 Aug 1768; d. after 1820 when he was living at Lyndeborough; *possibly* m. 1791, MARY PEARSON.

viii MOLLY RICHARDSON, b. 10 Jun 1770

ix RACHEL RICHARDSON, b. 22 May 1772; d. at Greenfield, NH, 28 Jul 1808; m. at Lyndeborough, 7 Jul 1791, SARGENT STRAW, later SARGENT SYMONDS, b. at Sandown, NH, 2 Jun 1772 son of John and Abigail (Sargent) Straw; Sargent d. at Acworth, NH, 6 Jan 1834. Sargent Straw changed his named to Sargent Symonds in 1829.[908] Sargent married second Sarah Gould.

---

[905] Livermore, *History of the Town of Wilton*, p 487

[906] Litchfield, *Maine, History of Litchfield*, p 68

[907] Donovan, *History of the Town of Lyndeborough*, p 665

[908] Laws of New Hampshire, Second Constitutional Period, 1829-1835, p 62

x DORCAS RICHARDSON, b. 23 Feb 1774; d. at Corinth, VT, 15 May 1854; m. at Lyndeborough, 15 Nov 1792, JOSHUA MERRILL.

339) ABIGAIL FARNUM (*Stephen Farnum⁴, Ralph Farnum³, Elizabeth Holt Farnum², Nicholas¹*), b. at Dracut, 22 Dec 1741 daughter of Stephen and Hannah (Richardson) Farnum; d. at Dracut, 5 Sep 1826; m. at Dracut, 12 Sep 1761, DANIEL CLOUGH, b. 1737 son of Daniel and Ruth (Wright) Clough; Daniel d. at Dracut, 1805 (probate 3 Dec 1805).

Daniel and Abigail resided in Dracut. As a young man, Daniel was a member of English forces that participated in the expulsion of Acadians in 1755. He also served during the Revolution, along with his son Daniel, Jr.[909]

In his will written 5 October 1788 (probate 20 November 1805), Daniel Clough bequeathed five shillings each to the following beloved children: son Solomon, son Daniel, son Benjamin, son Asa, daughter Abigail, daughter Mary, son John, daughter Martha when she arrives at age twelve years, and son Moses when he arrives at age twelve years. The remainder of the estate, real and personal, was bequeathed to beloved wife Abigail to be for her use and benefit forever. Abigail was named executrix. Widow Abigail declined to be executrix due to being of advanced years and blind and request that someone else be named to this task.[910]

On 15 March 1806 (recorded 16 August 1819), Abigail Clough sold to Moses Clough for payment of $200 the farm with buildings and all her personal estate. On 30 July 1819 (recorded 16 August 1819), Moses Clough of Dracut, for a payment of $150, sold the farm with buildings to Stephen Barker.[911]

Abigail Farnum and Daniel Clough were parents of nine children born at Dracut, although there are records for births of just four of the children. Other birth years are estimates.

i SOLOMON CLOUGH, b. 21 Oct 1761; d. at Dracut, 6 Feb 1818. Solomon does not seem to have married.

ii DANIEL CLOUGH, b. 15 Oct 1763; d. at Haverhill, MA, 24 Jun 1840; m. at Dracut, 14 Mar 1785, ABIGAIL ATWOOD, b. at Bradford, 1768 daughter of William and Jane (Hardy) Atwood; Abigail d. at Haverhill, 5 Jul 1846.

iii BENJAMIN CLOUGH, b. about 1765 (about 1769 based on age at death); d. at Sedgwick, ME, 20 Jul 1832; m. at Pelham, NH, 12 Mar 1789, RELIEF WYMAN, b. at Hudson, NH, 25 Jun 1761 daughter of Seth and Abigail (Hutchinson) Wyman;[912] Relief d. at Sedgwick, 25 May 1819.

iv ASA CLOUGH, b. about 1767; d. at Blue Hill, ME, 2 Jan 1851; m. 27 Nov 1789, ABIGAIL PECKER, b. at Bradford, MA, 27 Nov 1766 daughter of Bartholomew and Hannah (Russell) Pecker; Abigail d. at Blue Hill, 16 Mar 1854.

v ABIGAIL CLOUGH, b. 21 May 1769; d. at Dracut, 13 Jul 1854; m. at Dracut, 12 Sep 1799,[913] AQUILLA RICHARDSON, b. about 1772 son of Stephen and Mary (Chase) Richardson; Aquilla d. by drowning at Springfield, 17 Jul 1805.[914] Widow Abigail Richardson was head of household in Dracut in 1810.

vi MARY CLOUGH, b. about 1771. Mary was living in 1788.

vii JOHN CLOUGH, b. about 1773. John was living in 1788.

viii MARTHA CLOUGH, b. about 1778 (not yet 12 in 1788).

ix MOSES CLOUGH, b. 9 May 1784; d. at Pelham, NH, 26 Jul 1869; m. at Dracut, 11 Sep 1805, SUSANNA ELLINWOOD, b. about 1771 (if age at death of 77 is correct); Susanna d. at Dracut, 3 Aug 1848.

340) RACHEL FARNUM (*Stephen Farnum⁴, Ralph Farnum³, Elizabeth Holt Farnum², Nicholas¹*), b. at Dracut, 4 Mar 1746/7 daughter of Stephen and Hannah (Richardson) Farnum; d. at Andover, 8 Apr 1826; m. at Andover, 4 May 1775, JOHN STICKNEY, b. 16 May 1744 son of Moses and Hannah (Style) Stickney; John d. at Andover, 12 Aug 1807.

John Stickney did not leave a will and his estate entered probate 5 November 1807 with widow Rachel as administratrix. Real estate was valued at $430 and personal estate at $270.52. The dower third was set off to Rachel on 12 May 1809.[915]

Daughter Mary Farnum Stickney did not marry, and her estate entered probate 17 Dec 1861. House and land were valued at $200 and bank deposits, notes, and cash totaled $420.50. In her will written 16 February 1861, Mary has bequests of

909 Coburn, History of Dracut, p 112 and p 156

910 *Massachusetts, Wills and Probate Records, 1635-1991, Middlesex County, Case 4623*

911 Massachusetts Land Records, Middlesex County, 226:478, 226:479

912 The 1795 will of Seth Wyman includes a bequest to his daughter Relief wife of Benjamin Clough.

913 There is a birth of a child for Abigail and Aquilla born at Dracut in 1793, so uncertain if the marriage or birth record of this child are in error.

914 There seems to be just one Aquilla Richardson of his age in the records. In 1804, Aquilla Richardson married Margaret Parsons in Springfield and they had one child. This seems to be the same Aquilla as his widow Margaret remarried in Springfield in 1807. Perhaps Aquilla and Abigail had divorced.

915 *Essex County, MA: Probate File Papers, 1638-1881.*Online database. *AmericanAncestors.org.* New England Historic Genealogical Society, 2014. Case 26509

some furniture and personal items to her nephew Joseph Stickney; to grand-niece and grand-nephews Charlotte Schaden, Charles Schaden, and Alfred Schaden who are the children of her niece Ruth; to Mrs. Stevens wife of Warren Stevens; and to Ebenezer Ellingwood. Niece Mary Stickney receives the wearing apparel and some household items. The remainder of the estate is to be held in trust by executor Daniel Carleton and to be used for the support of niece Mary Stickney.[916] The nieces and nephew mentioned (Joseph, Ruth, and Mary) are all children of Mary's brother John Lovejoy and his wife Lucretia Lovejoy.

John Stickney and Mary Farnum were parent of seven children born at Andover.[917]

i RACHEL STICKNEY, b. 8 Mar 1777; d. 9 Mar 1777.

ii JOHN STICKNEY, b. 8 Mar 1777; d. 3 Apr 1777.

iii JOHN STICKNEY, b. 28 Aug 1778; died young.

iv JOHN STICKNEY, b. 15 Nov 1779; d. at Andover, 28 Dec 1818; m. at Andover, 8 May 1804, LUCRETIA LOVEJOY, b. at Andover, 19 Nov 1784 daughter of Isaac and Ruth (Davis) Lovejoy; Lucretia d. at Andover, 26 Jan 1825. After John's death, Lucretia married Daniel Carleton.

v MARY FARNUM STICKNEY, b. 29 Apr 1782; d. at Andover, 5 Dec 1861.

vi THOMAS STICKNEY, b. 18 Mar 1783; d. 19 Nov 1801.

vii CHARLES STICKNEY, b. 8 Dec 1784; d. 18 Sep 1802.

341) WILLIAM FARNUM (*Stephen Farnum[4], Ralph Farnum[3], Elizabeth Holt Farnum[2], Nicholas[1]*), b. at Dracut, 23 Apr 1748 son of Stephen and Hannah (Richardson) Farnum; d. after 1814;[918] m. at Pelham, 29 Oct 1772, HANNAH MARSH, b. at Bradford, MA, 13 Feb 1753 daughter of John and Martha (Rolfe) Marsh; Hannah d. 12 Mar 1821 (buried in the Marsh family plot in Pelham).

William resided in Dracut. He was a member of the militia company of Capt. Stephen Russell that marched at the alarm on 19 April 1775.[919]

On 5 Mar 1814 (deed recorded 6 Apr 1814), William transferred ownership of the homestead farm to his son Jacob Marsh Farnum for $1800.[920]

William Farnum and Hannah Marsh were parents of eight children.

i EUNICE FARNUM, b. at Dracut, 15 Dec 1773; m. at Methuen, 27 Mar 1794, BENJAMIN BARKER, b. at Methuen, 24 Jun 1767 son of Ebenezer and Hannah (Bodwell) Barker.

ii WILLIAM FARNUM, b. at Dracut, 11 Jan 1776; d. at Milton, MA, 18 Jun 1843; m. at Methuen, 25 Feb 1800, RACHEL HIBBARD, b. at Methuen, 27 Aug 1777 daughter of Nathaniel and Sarah (Bodwell) Hibbard; Rachel d. at Milton, 22 Sep 1851.

iii PATTY FARNUM, b. at Dracut, 7 Mar 1778; m. at Methuen, 28 May 1798, RICHARD SWAN MESSER, b. at Methuen, 4 Sep 1768 son of Abiel and Susanna (Swan) Messer.

iv HANNAH FARNUM, b. at Methuen, b. 23 Apr 1781; d. at Hudson, NH, 18 May 1858; m. at Methuen, 2 Apr 1816, GREENLEAF BOLES, b. at Methuen, 1788 son of Reuben and Lucy (Brown) Boles; Greenleaf d. at Hudson, 8 Mar 1871.

v POLLY FARNUM, b. at Methuen, 12 Jul 1782; d. 24 Aug 1783.

vi JOHN MARSH FARNUM, b. at Methuen, 9 Dec 1785; d. at Nashua, NH, 30 Aug 1882; m. at Methuen, 28 Jan 1810, PHEBE BOLES, b. at Methuen, about 1790 daughter of Reuben and Lucy (Brown) Boles; Phebe d. at Nashua, 19 Jul 1865.

vii EZRA MARSH FARNUM, b. at Methuen, 17 Feb 1791; d. at West Newton, MA, 22 Oct 1867; m. 1st at Salem, NH, 30 May 1809, SUSANNA EMERSON; Susanna d. at Newton, MA, 24 Jul 1842. Ezra m. 2nd at Newton, 24 Nov

---

[916] *Essex County, MA: Probate File Papers, 1638-1881.* Online database. *AmericanAncestors.org.* New England Historic Genealogical Society, 2014. Case 54308

[917] Stickney's Stickney genealogy also lists a daughter Betsey Baldwin Stickney in this family, but that seems an error. Betsey Stickney was married to John Foster and Benjamin Clark, and she was living when Mary Farnum Stickney wrote her will, but there is no mention of her (or her children) in the will of Mary Farnum Stickney.

[918] On 5 Mar 1814 (recorded 6 Apr 1814), William transferred his homestead farm to his son Jacob Marsh Farnum for $1800. Massachusetts Land Records 1620-1986, Essex County, 203:77, accessed through familysearch.org.

[919] Coburn, *History of Dracut*, p 124

[920] Massachusetts Land Records 1620-1986, Essex County, 203:77

1844, EUNICE DUNCAN (widow Eunice Crossley), b. at Kittery, ME, about 1801 daughter of Samuel and Susan (-) Duncan;[921] Eunice d. at West Newton, 5 Sep 1888.

viii JACOB MARSH FARNUM, b. at Methuen, 19 Jun 1792; d. at Harrisburg, IA, 14 Dec 1855; m. at Boston, 4 Jan 1816, HANNAH L. MITCHELL, b. at Haverhill, 3 Jun 1798 daughter of James and Hannah (Leach) Mitchell; Hannah d. at Harrisburg, 9 Dec 1855.

342) JOHN FARNUM (*John Farnum⁴, John Farnum³, Elizabeth Holt Farnum², Nicholas¹*), b. at Andover, 1 Apr 1711 son of John and Joanna (Barker) Farnum; d. at Andover, 21 Oct 1786; m. at Andover, 26 Dec 1738, SARAH FRYE, b. at Andover, 25 Mar 1721 daughter of Samuel and Sarah (Osgood) Frye); Sarah d. at Andover, 24 Jul 1816.

John Farnum was a militia captain and participated in the French wars.[922]

John Farnum did not leave a will and his estate entered probate 4 December 1786 with John Farnum as administrator. The estate of Capt. John Farnum was insolvent with the debts of the estate being £612.15.10. The dower of one-third of the real estate was set off to widow Sarah in 1787. After the set off of the dower, creditors received two-fifths of the owed amount. After Sarah's decease, there was an appraisal of the dower that reverted to the estate and was valued at $852.99. Expenses of administration were $125.41.[923]

John Farnum and Sarah Frye were parents of thirteen children born at Andover.

i NATHAN FARNUM, b. 19 May 1739; d. of illness at Fort Howard, NY during the French and Indian War on 28 Sep 1758.

ii JOHN FARNUM, b. 15 Apr 1740; d. at Andover, 5 Nov 1822; m. 13 Jan 1785, MARY FRYE, b. at Andover, 3 Oct 1758 daughter of William and Mary (Carleton) Frye; Mary d. at Andover, 1 Sep 1835. John received his bachelor's degree from Harvard in 1761.[924] He represented the town of Andover at the Massachusetts Constitutional Convention in 1779.

iii DANIEL FARNUM, b. 15 Jun 1741; d. at Andover, 10 Jul 1814; m. 22 Sep 1768, his third cousin, LYDIA PORTER (*Ruth Foster Porter⁵, Lydia Farnum Foster⁴, Samuel Farnum³, Elizabeth Holt Farnum², Nicholas¹*), b. at Boxford, 4 Nov 1745 daughter of Benjamin and Ruth (Foster) Porter.

iv ISAAC FARNUM, b. at Andover, 19 Dec 1742; d. at Andover, 8 Sep 1823; m. by 1771, MARY OSGOOD, b. at Andover, 30 Sep 1753 daughter of John and Mary (Carleton) Osgood; Mary d. at Andover, 22 May 1820.

v JEDEDIAH FARNUM, b. 10 Jan 1744/5; d. at Andover, 8 Apr 1819; m. 26 Dec 1771, REBECCA POOR, b. 1748 daughter of Timothy and Mary (Stevens) Poor; Rebecca d. at Andover, 2 Oct 1820.

vi Son b. and d. 23 May 1746

vii SAMUEL FARNUM, b. 8 Aug 1747; d. at Penobscot, ME, 13 Apr 1834; m. 22 Feb 1775, DORCAS BRAGG, b. at Andover, 4 Feb 1747 daughter of Thomas and Dorothy (Ingalls) Bragg; Dorcas d. at Penobscot, 5 May 1805.

viii JAMES FARNUM, b. 8 Aug 1750; d. at Wilton, NH, 1813; m. 1773, REBECCA INGALLS, b. at Andover, 4 Jul 1754 daughter of Henry and Sarah (Putnam) Ingalls; Rebecca d. at Salem, MA, 22 Aug 1841.[925] Rebecca's son Putnam Ingalls Farnum was a resident of Salem.

ix PETER FARNUM, b. 8 May 1752; d. at Andover, 27 May 1828; m. 1st 4 Dec 1783; SARAH DASCOMB, b. at Lunenburg, 14 May 1762 daughter of James and Elizabeth (Farrington) Dascomb; Sarah d. at Andover, 22 Nov 1788. Peter m. 2nd at Andover, 15 Sep 1789, his second cousin, CHLOE WILSON (*Hannah Frye Wilson⁵, Elizabeth Farnum Frye⁴, John Farnum³, Elizabeth Holt Farnum², Nicholas¹*), b. at Andover, 9 Feb 1766 daughter of John and Hannah (Frye) Wilson; Chloe d. at Andover, 22 Jun 1809.

x SARAH FARNUM, b. 14 Aug and d. 15 Aug 1754.

xi SIMEON FARNHAM, b. 9 Oct 1756; d. at Bangor, ME, 3 Jun 1844; m. 22 Oct 1787, ELIZABETH JOHNSON, b. at Andover, 17 Oct 1760 daughter of Samuel and Elizabeth (Gage) Johnson;[926] Elizabeth d. 22 Mar 1825. Simeon was Maj. Simeon Farnham. Elizabeth's father was Col. Samuel Johnson of Andover.

xii NATHAN FARNUM, b. 2 May 1761; d. 4 Jun 1763.

---

921 Eunice's parents are given as Samuel and Susan Dunkin at her marriage to Ezra and given as Duncan on her death record.

922 Abbott, Early Notes and Records of the Farnum Family, https://www.mhl.org/sites/default/files/files/Abbott/Farnum%20Family.pdf

923 *Essex County, MA: Probate File Papers, 1638-1881.*Online database. *AmericanAncestors.org.* New England Historic Genealogical Society, 2014. Case 9246

924 Harvard University, Quinquennial Catalogue, p 141

925 Rebecca, m., mothr of Putnam I., palsy, Aug. 23, 1841, a. 87 y.

926 The 1796 probate record of Col. Samuel Johnson of Andover includes a will with a bequest to his daughter Elizabeth Farnum.

xiii ENOCH FARNUM, b. 2 Aug 1766; d. at Andover, 13 May 1815; m. 1 May 1806, his second cousin once removed, MARY OSGOOD (*Timothy Osgood[6], Timothy Osgood[5], Mary Russell Osgood[4], Phebe Johnson Russell[3], Mary Holt Johnson[2], Nicholas[1]*), b. at Andover, 6 Aug 1776 daughter of Timothy and Chloe (Bridges) Osgood; Mary d. at Andover, 16 Jan 1848.

343) JOHANNA FARNUM (*John Farnum[4], John Farnum[3], Elizabeth Holt Farnum[2], Nicholas[1]*), b. at Andover, 1712 daughter of John and Joanna (Barker) Farnum; d. at Andover, 27 Dec 1787; m. at Andover, 2 Apr 1741, EBENEZER STEVENS, b. at Andover, 1713/4 son of Ebenezer and Sarah (Sprague) Stevens; Ebenezer d. at Andover, 6 Aug 1754.

Johanna Farnum and Ebenezer Stevens were parents of one child.

i AMOS STEVENS, b. at Andover, 22 Feb 1742/3; d. at Andover, 1 Aug 1812; m. 1st 25 Sep 1764, SARAH STEVENS, b. at Andover, 19 Mar 1743/4 daughter of Isaac and Mary (Barker) Stevens; Sarah d. at Andover, 21 Jan 1788. Amos m. 2nd at Andover, 5 Oct 1789, LYDIA BROWN; Lydia d. at Andover, 12 Feb 1815.

344) ELIZABETH FARNUM (*John Farnum[4], John Farnum[3], Elizabeth Holt Farnum[2], Nicholas[1]*), b. at Andover, 10 Oct 1714 daughter of John and Joanna (Barker) Farnum; d. at Andover, 17 Jun 1799; m. 2 Apr 1741, SAMUEL BARKER, b. at Andover, 10 Oct 1714 son of Samuel and Sarah (Gage) Barker; Samuel d. at Andover, 11 Nov 1796.

In his will written 14 March 1796 (probate 5 December 1796), Samuel Barker bequeathed to beloved wife Elizabeth the use and improvement of his share of the dwelling in which they now live, one-third part of the pew in the meeting house, and a lengthy list of annual provisions for her support. Elizabeth also receives the household furniture which will go to their two daughters after Elizabeth's death. Son Samuel receives one hundred dollars. Daughters Mehitable Barker and Abigail Barker each receives one hundred forty-three daughters. Daughters Mehitable and Abigail also have use of the east chamber, are free to go to and from the chamber without interference and have use of the well and the oven. Daughter Elizabeth wife of Phineas Tyler receives fifty dollars. Son Phineas Barker receives the remainder of the estate real and personal and is named executor.[927]

Samuel Barker and Elizabeth Farnum were parents of five children born at Andover.

i SAMUEL BARKER, b. 11 Jan 1742/3; d. at Andover, 5 Dec 1823; m. at Andover, 4 May 1766, SUSANNAH FOSTER, b. 17 Dec 1747 daughter of Joshua and Mary (Barker) Foster; Susannah d. at Andover, 7 Sep 1822.

ii PHINEAS BARKER, b. 19 Mar 1744/5; d. at Andover, 18 Mar 1817; m. 1st 23 Jun 1774, ABIGAIL FOSTER, b. at Andover, 23 Aug 1749 daughter of Stephen and Abigail (Smith) Foster;[928] Abigail d. at Andover, 22 Oct 1804. Phineas m. 2nd 26 Sep 1805, his third cousin, MARY STEVENS, b. at Andover, 17 Feb 1754 daughter of Samuel and Hephzibah (Ingalls) Stevens; Mary d. at Andover, 1 May 1821.

iii ELIZABETH BARKER, b. 27 Apr 1748; d. at Leominster, MA, 13 Jun 1820; m. at Andover, 6 Dec 1770, PHINEAS TYLER, b. at Boxford, 22 Nov 1736 son of Job and Elizabeth (Parker) Tyler; Phineas d. at Leominster, 6 Aug 1817. Phineas was first married to Hannah Foster.

iv MEHITABLE BARKER, b. 16 Dec 1752; d. at Andover, 22 May 1833. Mehitable did not marry.

v ABIGAIL BARKER, b. 16 Dec 1752; d. at Andover, 11 Nov 1815. Abigail did not marry.

345) MEHITABLE FARNUM (*John Farnum[4], John Farnum[3], Elizabeth Holt Farnum[2], Nicholas[1]*), b. at Andover, 1720 son of John and Joanna (Barker) Farnum; m. 1st 9 Sep 1742, ASA STEVENS, b. at Andover, 14 Dec 1717 son of Ebenezer and Sarah (Sprague) Stevens; Asa d. at Albany, 20 Dec 1755.[929] Mehitable m. 2nd 5 Jan 1768, SAMUEL CHICKERING, b. at Charlestown, 10 Jul 1704 son of John and Susanna (Symmes) Chickering; Samuel d. at Andover, 1787. Samuel was first married to Hannah Osgood.

Capt. Asa Stevens participated in the French war at Albany and died on the return trip home.

Asa Stevens did not leave a will and his estate entered probate 16 February 1756 with Mehitable as administratrix. There was a balance of £106.5.4 for distribution on 23 February 1767. The widow received £35.8.5 as her third part and eldest son Asa received £20.4.10. Each of the other children received £10.2.5: Simeon, William, Mehitable, Joanna, and Dorcas.[930]

In his 1757 will, Asa's father Ebenezer Stevens had bequests to his grandchildren the children of his son Asa: Asa, Simeon, Mehitable, Joanna, and Dorcas.[931] Asa's son William is not listed, but this seems an oversight as William is included in the probate distribution of the estate of his father in 1767.

---

927 *Essex County, MA: Probate File Papers, 1638-1881.*Online database. *AmericanAncestors.org.* New England Historic Genealogical Society, 2014. Case 1713

928 The 1787 will of Stephen Foster includes a bequest to his daughter Nabby wife of Phineas Barker.

929 Asa, Capt., "at Albany on his Return from Lake George," Dec. 20, 1755, a 38 y. 6 d.

930 *Essex County, MA: Probate File Papers, 1638-1881.*Online database. *AmericanAncestors.org.* New England Historic Genealogical Society, 2014. Case 26288

931 *Essex County, MA: Probate File Papers, 1638-1881.*Online database. *AmericanAncestors.org.* New England Historic Genealogical Society, 2014. Case 26324

Samuel Chickering did not leave a will and Mehitable assumed administration of the estate on 5 November 1787.[932] Mehitable Farnum and Asa Stevens were parents of seven children born at Andover.

i DORCAS STEVENS, b. 17 Nov 1742; died young.

ii ASA STEVENS, b. 30 Nov 1744; d. in ME, about 1799; m. 1st by 1775, MARY who has not been identified; Mary d. at Portland, 22 Dec 1786. Asa m. 2nd at Portland, 28 Apr 1787, DRUCILLA REED, b. at Groton, MA, 23 Dec 1766 daughter of Samuel and Mary (Tarbell) Reed; Drucilla d. at Norway, ME, 1835. Drucilla was second married to Joseph Gammon on 16 Jul 1800. Asa and Mary had four children in Andover and then were in Portland (Falmouth), ME. Asa is recorded in the 1790 census at Portland and was deceased before 1800 when his second wife remarried.

iii SIMEON STEVENS, b. 29 May 1746; d. at Salem, NH, 5 Sep 1799; m. at Billerica, 7 Feb 1771, MARIA INGALLS, b. at Billerica, 14 Dec 1749 daughter of Daniel and Sarah (Fletcher) Ingalls; Maria d. at Salem, NH, 8 Jul 1845. Simeon and Maria had several children in Billerica before relocating to Salem.

iv WILLIAM STEVENS, b. 7 Jul 1748; d. at Salem, NH, 1807 (probate 16 Dec 1807); m. at Andover, 6 Apr 1769, MARTHA CROSS, b. at Andover, 8 Feb 1749/50 daughter of Samuel and Martha (Hibbard) Cross; Martha d. after 1807.

v MEHITABLE STEVENS, b. 1 Nov 1750. It is possible that she is the Mehitable Stevens who married ITHAMAR BRADLEY at Methuen on 22 Oct 1778. Ithamar was the son of Nehemiah and Lydia (Emerson) Bradley. He died at Hollis, 9 Apr 1813.

vi JOANNA STEVENS, b. 23 Sep 1752; d. at Coventry, VT, Aug 1827; m. about 1774, DANIEL CHANDLER, b. at Andover, 9 Jul 1754 son of David and Mary (Ballard) Chandler; Daniel d. at Amherst, NH, about 1803. Serving as a captain during the Revolution did not prevent Daniel from being thrown in debtors' prison where he died.[933]

vii DORCAS STEVENS, b. 9 Oct 1755; d. before 1784 and likely with (or soon after) the birth of her child in 1780; m. 19 Jun 1780, her fourth cousin, ASA OSGOOD (*Timothy Osgood⁵, Mary Russell Osgood⁴, Phebe Johnson Russell³, Mary Holt Johnson², Nicholas¹*), b. at Andover, 22 Dec 1753 son of Timothy and Phebe (Frye) Osgood; Asa d. at Hiram, ME, 29 Jul 1833. Asa married second Lydia Hood on 22 May 1784 and married third Hannah Powers on 18 Jul 1808. Dorcas and Asa had one son Asa Osgood baptized at Andover 5 Nov 1780.

346) EBENEZER FRYE (*Elizabeth Farnum Frye⁴, John Farnum³, Elizabeth Holt Farnum², Nicholas¹*), b. at Andover, 2 Oct 1714 son of Ebenezer and Elizabeth (Farnum) Frye; d. at Lake George, 27 Sep 1755; m. at Andover, 22 Nov 1744, ELIZABETH KIMBALL, b. about 1724 (age 88 at death) who has not been identified; Elizabeth d. at Andover, 20 Oct 1812.

Ebenezer died on the expedition to Lake George. Ebenezer Frye and Elizabeth Kimball were parents of five children born at Andover.

i EBENEZER FRYE, b. 17 Sep 1754; d. at Northport, ME, 10 Mar 1828;[934] m. HANNAH BAKER, b. 30 Sep 1745 daughter of Joseph and Hannah (Lovewell) Baker; Hannah d. at Northport, 20 Mar 1824. Ebenezer Frye served as an officer during the Revolution enlisting at a rank of lieutenant and with rank of major at the close of the war.

ii DAVID FRYE, b. 17 Mar 1746/7; m. at Andover, 6 Jun 1769, TABITHA PARKER, b. at Tewksbury, 27 Jan 1742 daughter of Jonathan and Hannah (Frye) Parker.

iii ELIZABETH FRYE, b. 17 May 1749; d. at Andover, 7 Sep 1813; m. at Andover, 17 Mar 1791, as his second wife, PETER POOR, b. at Andover, 9 Jul 1726 son of Daniel and Dorothy (Kimball) Poor; Peter d. at Andover, 1802 (probate Dec 1802). Peter was first married to Sarah Wood.

iv LYDIA FRYE, b. 23 May 1752; d. at Andover, 1806 (probate 6 May 1806); m. 21 Jul 1783, her first cousin once removed, BENJAMIN STEVENS (*Hannah Farnum Stevens⁴, John Farnum³, Elizabeth Holt Farnum², Nicholas¹*), b. at Andover, 14 May 1734 son of Benjamin and Hannah (Farnum) Stevens; Benjamin d. at Andover, 6 Feb 1800. Lydia Frye and Benjamin Stevens are Family 356.

v JOHN FRYE, b. 16 Aug 1754; d. at Andover, 26 Mar 1843; m. 1st at Andover, 11 Mar 1779, his fourth cousin, LYDIA BATCHELDER (*Lydia Gray Batchelder⁵, Lydia Peabody Gray⁴, Lydia Holt Peabody³, James², Nicholas¹*), b. 1755 daughter of John and Lydia (Gray) Batchelder; Lydia d. at Andover, 19 Jan 1820. John m. 2nd at Andover,

---

932 *Essex County, MA: Probate File Papers, 1638-1881.*Online database. *AmericanAncestors.org.* New England Historic Genealogical Society, 2014. Case 5299

933 Chandler, *Descendants of William and Annis Chandler*, p 417

934 Maine, Faylene Hutton Cemetery Collection, 1780-1990

21 Jul 1821, his fourth cousin, CHLOE HOLT (*Nathaniel[5], Oliver[4], Oliver[3], Henry[2], Nicholas[1]*), baptized at Andover, 21 Sep 1766 daughter of Nathaniel and Elizabeth (Stevens) Holt; Chloe d. at Andover, 11 Apr 1855.

347) JONATHAN FRYE (*Elizabeth Farnum Frye[4], John Farnum[3], Elizabeth Holt Farnum[2], Nicholas[1]*), b. at Andover, 3 Mar 1716/7 son of Ebenezer and Elizabeth (Farnum) Frye; d. at Andover, 2 Feb 1788; m. 1st at Andover, 24 Jan 1744, SARAH WILSON who was perhaps the daughter of John and Mercy (Wright) Wilson; Sarah d. at Andover, 3 Jun 1747. Jonathan m. 2nd at Andover, 13 Nov 1753, his third cousin, SARAH PEABODY (*Moses Peabody[4], Lydia Holt Peabody[3], James[2], Nicholas[1]*), b. at Andover, 31 Mar 1729 daughter of Moses and Sarah (Holt) Peabody; Sarah d. at Andover, 12 Oct 1802.

Jonathan Frye was a blacksmith in Andover. He served as a Captain in the militia.

In his will written 31 January 1788 (probate 4 March 1788), Jonathan Frye bequeathed to beloved wife Sarah all the household goods that belong to a woman's use, all the stock of cattle, the use of one-half of the homestead land and buildings, and use of one0third of meadows and woodlands while she is a widow. What Sarah leaves will go to daughter Hannah wife of John Bowman. Daughter Sarah wife of Philip Farrington receives the value of £15 from the personal estate, the shop tools, and one-third part of the meadows which completes her portion with what she has already received. Daughter Hannah Bowman and her children receive the homelands and building and the remaining two-thirds of the meadows. Philip Farrington was named executor. Real estate was valued at £229.16 which included a dwelling house and blacksmith shop. The total value of the estate was £377.4.8. On 4 March 1789, John Bowman signed that he had received his estate distribution from executor Philip Farrington, and also noted his understanding that the just debts of the estate were to be divided between him and the said Farrington.[935]

There are records of two children of Jonathan Frye and Sarah Wilson and only daughter Sarah is in Jonathan's will.

i SARAH FRYE, b. 7 Jul 1745; d. at Andover, 30 May 1809; m. at Andover, 18 Sep 1770, PHILIP FARRINGTON, b. at Andover, 9 Apr 1749 son of Daniel and Elizabeth (Putnam) Farrington; Philip d. at Andover, 14 Mar 1829. Philip married second Judith Ingalls (1760-1827) daughter of Henry and Sarah (Putnam) Ingalls

ii PHEBE FRYE, b. 10 Feb 1746/7

There are records of four children of Jonathan Frye and Sarah Peabody born at Andover, and only daughter Hannah is in Jonathan's will.

i MARCY FRYE, b. 29 Feb 1756

ii MARY FRYE, b. 26 Jul 1759

iii REBEKAH FRYE, b. 8 Sep 1762

iv HANNAH FRYE, b. 15 Aug 1764; d. at Ashburnham, MA, 8 Jun 1841; m. at Andover, 19 Sep 1781, JOHN BOWMAN, baptized at Lexington, MA, 15 Jul 1759 son of John and Hannah (Wilson) Bowman; John d. at Ashburnham, 22 Oct 1846.[936]

348) JOHN FRYE (*Elizabeth Farnum Frye[4], John Farnum[3], Elizabeth Holt Farnum[2], Nicholas[1]*), b. at Andover, 7 Apr 1719 son of Ebenezer and Elizabeth (Farnum) Frye; d. at Royalston, MA, 19 Mar 1814; m. at Sutton, 2 Nov 1748, ELIZABETH WOODBURY, likely b. 28 Oct 1728 daughter of Benjamin and Ruth (Conant) Woodbury; Elizabeth d. at Royalston, 23 Jan 1814.

Capt. John Frye was known as the "Hero of Crown Point" for his exploits in the French and Indian War. He resided in Royalston where he filled several important civic positions including serving as town clerk from 1765 to 1781 and was delegate to the ratification of the United States constitution in 1788.[937]

John Frye and Elizabeth Woodbury were parents of nine children whose births are recorded at Royalston, Massachusetts, although the births of some of the children are also recorded at Sutton.

i JOHN FRYE, b. 27 Sep 1749; d. at Concord, VT, 3 Jan 1832; m. 1st about 1773, LUCY PIKE who d. at Royalston, 30 Mar 1786. John m. 2nd at Royalston, 14 Jun 1787, RACHEL STOCKWELL, b. at Oxford, MA, 30 Jan 1758 daughter of Joseph and Isabel (Titus) Stockwell; Rachel d. at Concord, 10 Aug 1831.

ii ELIZABETH FRYE, b. 12 Jul 1751; d. about 1780; m. 2 Mar 1769, THOMAS THOMPSON,[938] baptized at Kingston, NH, 26 Dec 1742 son of Samuel and Margaret (Clark) Thompson; Thomas d. at Keene, NH, 20 Feb 1813. Thomas m. 2nd Sarah Scott.

---

[935] *Essex County, MA: Probate File Papers, 1638-1881.*Online database. *AmericanAncestors.org.* New England Historic Genealogical Society, 2014. Case 10310

[936] The particulars of John Bowman's birth, parentage, and residence can be confirmed by his pension application file S29641

[937] Caswell, *The History of the Town of Royalston, Massachusetts*, p 186. There is a fuller biography of John Frye in this history,

[938] Barker, *Frye Genealogy*, p 57

iii EBENEZER FRYE, b. 4 Jul 1754; d. at Royalston, 8 May 1832; m. at Royalston, 11 Jun 1783, MARY WAIT, b. 1767 daughter of Benjamin and Tameson (Heard) Wait;[939] Mary d. at Royalston, 26 Aug 1798.

iv MARY FRYE, b. 18 Feb 1757; m. at Royalston, 22 Oct 1778, JOHN TOZER, b. at Southborough, MA, 23 Apr 1754 son of Richard and Mary (Belknap) Tozer; John d. at Marlborough, NH, 5 Feb 1834.

v HANNAH FRYE, b. 10 Feb 1760; d. at Maidstone, VT, 5 Dec 1815; m. at Royalston, 9 Feb 1786, NATHANIEL WAIT, b. at Gloucester, MA, Jan 1758[940] son of Benjamin and Tameson (Heard) Wait; Nathaniel d. at Maidstone, 25 Oct 1839. Nathaniel had a second marriage to Tamesin about 1820 (per information in pension file).

vi MEHITABLE FRYE, b. 2 Aug 1762; d. (buried) at Croydon, NH, 14 Jan 1842; m. at Royalston, 9 Dec 1779, BENJAMIN BARTON, b. at Sutton, MA, 21 Apr 1758 son of Bazaleel and Phebe (Carleton) Barton; Benjamin d. at Croydon, 9 Jul 1834.

vii RUTH FRYE, b. 8 Aug 1765; m. at Royalston, 13 Mar 1788, JONATHAN NICHOLS, b. at Royalston, 28 Mar 1764 son of Henry and Elizabeth (Towne) Nichols; Jonathan d. at Grantham, NH, 10 Aug 1850.

viii DAVID FRYE, b. 28 Jul 1768; d. at Croydon, NH, 15 Apr 1854; m. 1st 1 Apr 1794, LYDIA SMITH, b. 2 Apr 1769;[941] Lydia d. 24 Sep 1812. David m. 2nd at Royalston, 6 Mar 1814, REBECKAH WHEELER, b. at Templeton, 7 Apr 1783 daughter of Jonathan and Beulah (Fisk) Wheeler; Rebeckah d. at Croydon, 24 Aug 1831. David m. 3rd 9 Jun 1834, LUCY WRIGHT, b. about 1780; Lucy d. after 1850.

ix DEBORAH FRYE, b. 7 Apr 1772; d. at Royalston, 22 Nov 1851; m. 1st at Royalston, 27 Dec 1792, WILLIAM NICHOLS, b. at Sutton, 25 Apr 1771 son of William and Kezia (Fitts) Nichols; William d. at Royalston, 25 Mar 1806. Deborah m. 2nd at Royalston, 20 Aug 1809, JOSEPH WHEELER, b. 1784; Joseph d. at Royalston, 15 Oct 1822.

349) HANNAH FRYE (*Elizabeth Farnum Frye[4], John Farnum[3], Elizabeth Holt Farnum[2], Nicholas[1]*), b. at Andover, 4 Jul 1725 daughter of Ebenezer and Elizabeth (Farnum) Frye; d. at Andover, 30 Oct 1803; m. 25 Mar 1742, JOHN WILSON, b. about 1720 whose parents are not clearly identified;[942] John d. at Andover, 23 Sep 1774.

John Wilson did leave a will (although it is not in the available probate packet) and widow Hannah accepted the conditions of the will on 3 December 1774. Real estate was valued at £745.2.8 and the total estate value was £945.8.9.[943] Heirs signed that they had received their legacies from the estate in accordance with the will of John Wilson paid by the executor their brother Joshua Wilson: Sarah and Samuel Carlton, Hannah and John Barker, John Wilson, Elizabeth Wright, Mercy and Solomon Ingalls, Abiel Wilson, Simeon Wilson, Molly and Oliver Fletcher, Chloe and Peter Farnum, James Wilson, and Dorcas Wilson. These receipts were signed between 1775 and 1804.[944]

On 26 January 1779 (recorded 3 March 1801), Hannah Wilson widow of John Wilson late of Andover and five of her children, all of Andover, sold their portion of land in Bridgton that had been bequeathed to Joseph Wilson in the will of John Wilson. Joseph was now deceased. The children selling their shares were Joshua Wilson, yeoman; John Barker, Jr., joiner, and Hannah his wife; Elizabeth Wright widow of Samuel Wright; Samuel Carlton, yeoman, and Sarah his wife, and Mercy Wilson. The property was sold to Jacob Stevens of Andover for payment of £21.8.6.[945]

Hannah Frye and John Wilson were parents of fifteen children born at Andover.

i JOHN WILSON, b. 11 Jun 1742; d. 3 Oct 1747

ii JOSHUA WILSON, b. at Andover, 10 Feb 1743/4; d. at Wilton, 24 Jul 1823; m. at Andover, 15 Sep 1773, DOROTHY STEVENS, b. at Andover, 21 Apr 1751 daughter of Abiel and Dorothy (Martin) Stevens; Dorothy d. at Andover, 17 Nov 1821.

iii HANNAH WILSON, b. at Andover, 25 Jun 1746; m. at Andover, 22 Feb 1770, JOHN BARKER, b. at Andover, 6 Feb 1742/3 son of Richard and Mehitable (Barker) Barker. On 9 Jun 1783, John and Hannah Barker sold the homestead property in Andover to Philip Abbot. The dead was recorded 25 Mar 1789.[946] The family relocated to Fryeburg, Maine but the dates of death are uncertain.

---

939 The names of Mary's parents are given as Benjamin and Tameson Wait on the recording of her death.

940 Nathaniel's date of birth is given in his pension application file.

941 Barker, *Frye Genealogy*, p 71

942 John may be the son of Joshua and Mary (Wright) Wilson or John and Mercy (Wright) Wilson.

943 *Essex County, MA: Probate File Papers, 1638-1881.*Online database. *AmericanAncestors.org.* New England Historic Genealogical Society, 2014. Case 30110

944 Essex County, Massachusetts probate records, volume 371, book 71, pp 555-558, accessed through familysearch.org

945 Maine, Cumberland County Land Records, 35:179; accessed through familysearch.org

946 Massachusetts Land Records 1620-1986, Essex County, 150:44

iv ELIZABETH WILSON, b. at Andover, 6 May 1748; d. at Andover, 4 Oct 1810;[947] m. at Andover, 16 Feb 1775, SAMUEL WRIGHT perhaps the son of Samuel and Ruth (-) Wright born in 1741; Samuel perhaps d. at Andover, 16 Sep 1775. There is a record of just one child, Elizabeth born 16 Dec 1775.

v SARAH WILSON, b. at Andover, 6 Mar 1749/50; m. at Andover, 15 Oct 1772, SAMUEL CARLETON, b. at Andover, 10 Mar 1745 son of Ezekiel and Marcy (Kimball) Carleton.

vi MARCY WILSON, b. at Andover, 11 Feb 1752; d. at Nelson, NH, 4 Sep 1797; m. at Andover, 22 Apr 1779, SOLOMON INGALLS, b. at Andover, 16 Jun 1750 son of Henry and Sarah (Putnam) Ingalls; Solomon d. at Clayton, NY, 22 Sep 1840. Solomon was first married to Abigail Carleton who died in 1776 and he married third Hannah Harris.

vii JOHN WILSON, b. 29 Jan 1754. John received a lot of land in Bridgton from his father, but further information was not located.

viii JOSEPH WILSON, b. at Andover, Jan 1756; d. at Andover, 8 Jul 1776.

ix MOLLY WILSON, b. at Andover, 12 Aug 1758; d. at Lyndeborough, 12 Sep 1838; m. at Lyndeborough, 2 Sep 1790, OLIVER FLETCHER, b. at Chelmsford, 14 Jan 1751 son of Robert and Remembrance (Foster) Fletcher; Oliver d. at Lyndeborough, 20 Dec 1831.

x ABIEL WILSON, b. at Andover, 10 Jun 1760; d. at Wilton, NH, 26 Jul 1824; m. 8 Jul 1789; ABIGAIL PUTNAM, b. at Wilton, 1 Sep 1767 daughter of Philip and Hannah (Jaques) Putnam; Abigail d. at Wilton, 6 May 1831.

xi DORCAS WILSON, b. at Andover, 10 Mar 1762; d. at Andover, 4 Nov 1812. Dorcas did not marry, but she had a son CHARLES NOYES to whom she left her entire estate in her will.

xii SIMEON WILSON, b. at Andover, 28 Jun 1764. He was living in 1790 when he signed that he had received his portion of his father's estate which included land in Bridgton. Nothing further known.

xiii CHLOE WILSON, b. at Andover, 9 Feb 1766; d. at Andover, 22 Jun 1809; m. at Andover, 12 Sep 1789, her second cousin, PETER FARNUM (*John Farnum[5], John Farnum[4], John Farnum[3], Elizabeth Holt Farnum[2], Nicholas[1]*), b. at Andover, 8 May 1752 son of John and Sarah (Frye) Farnum; Peter d. at Andover, 27 Feb 1828. Peter was first married to Sarah Dascomb.

xiv PHEBE WILSON, b. at Andover, 18 Dec 1767; died young.

xv JAMES WILSON, b. at Andover, 17 Dec 1770; d. at the almshouse in Beverly, 11 Feb 1846;[948] m. 23 Aug 1794, ABIGAIL HERRICK, b. at Wenham, 8 Jul 1772 daughter of Daniel and Hannah (Trask) Herrick; Abigail d. at Beverly, 29 Nov 1845.[949]

350) JOANNA FARNUM (*James Farnum[4], John Farnum[3], Elizabeth Holt Farnum[2], Nicholas[1]*), b. at Andover, 22 May 1725 daughter of James and Johanna (Grainger) Farnum; d. at Reading, 22 Feb 1753; m. at Andover, 6 Jun 1744, JOHN FLINT, baptized at Wakefield, 30 Aug 1719 son of Ebenezer and Tabitha (Burnap) Flint; John d. at Reading, 15 Feb 1802. John married second Tamer Kimball on 30 Apr 1761.

Capt. John Flint lived on the Flint homestead in North Reading that had come down to him from his grandfather George.[950] After Joanna's death, John remarried and had two children with his second wife Tamar Kimball.

In his will written 24 February 1795 (proved 9 Mar 1802), John Flint bequeaths to beloved wife Tamer the used of all the household items and provisions for her support while she is a widow. Beloved son John, if not deeded to him beforehand, receives one-sixteenth part of the sawmill in Tewksbury. The wearing apparel to be divided among his four sons John, James, Levi, and Ebenezer. After his widow is done with the household items, these are to be divided between his two daughters Joanna and Hephzibah who each also receives twenty dollars. John, James, and Ebenezer receive no more as they have received their full portions. The remainder of the estate goes to Levi who is also named executor. Statement reporting contentment with the will was signed by Thomas and Joanna Eaton and Joshua and Hephzibah Damon. The probate file also contains a 1774 quitclaim by son James Flint giving up any claim to his father's estate in exchange for a tract of land he received of his father in the new settlement called Bridge Town. In 1793, Ebenezer quitclaimed his rights to the estate for a tract of land he received in Tewksbury. In 1773, son John Flint signed a release to his claim on the estate in consideration of land received in Tewksbury.[951] Ebenezer and Mehitable were children from John's second marriage to Tamer Kimball.

Joanna Farnum and John Flint were parents of four children born at Reading.

[947] Barker, Elizabeth [(Wilson). CR1], wid. [consumption. CR1], Oct. 4, 1810. [1811. PR61]

[948] James, widr., b. Andover, h. Abigail, consumption, at the almshouse, Feb. 11, 1846, a. 76 y.

[949] Abigail, w. James, d. Daniel Herrick, b. at Wenham, paralysis, at the Almshouse, Nov. 29, 1845, a. 73 y. [Dec. 29. dup.]

[950] Flint, *A Genealogical Register of the Descendants of Thomas Flint*, p 27

[951] *Middlesex County, MA: Probate File Papers, 1648-1871.*Online database. *AmericanAncestors.org.* New England Historic Genealogical Society, 2014. Case 8019

i JOHN FLINT, b. at Reading, 16 May 1745; d. at Lyme, NH, 31 Jul 1830; m. at Tewksbury, 19 Nov 1766, MOLLY WORCESTER, b. 18 Oct 1744 daughter of Moses and Mary (Stickney) Worcester; Molly d. at Lyme, 15 Nov 1830.

ii JOANNA FLINT, b. at Reading, 28 Dec 1746; d. at North Reading, 8 Mar 1830; m. at Reading, 21 May 1767, THOMAS EATON, b. at Reading, 30 Dec 1743 son of Thomas and Mehitable (Eaton) Eaton; Thomas d. at North Reading, 4 Dec 1829.

iii JAMES FLINT, b. at Reading, 1748; d. at Bridgton, ME, 4 Jul 1808; m. at Reading, 18 Jun 1776, ZIBAH FLINT, b. at Groton, 31 Mar 1752 daughter of Nathaniel and Hephzibah (Woodward) Flint; Zibah d. at Bridgton, 1832.

iv LEVI FLINT, b. at Reading, 13 Feb 1753; d. at Reading, 1819 (probate 10 Apr 1819); m. at Reading, 28 Sep 1780, SARAH PARKER, b. at Reading, 16 May 1754 daughter of Daniel and Sarah (Parker) Parker;[952] Sarah d. at Reading, 30 Aug 1811.

351) TABITHA FARNUM (*James Farnum*[4]*, John Farnum*[3]*, Elizabeth Holt Farnum*[2]*, Nicholas*[1]), b. at Andover, 18 Mar 1729/30 daughter of James and Johanna (Grainger) Farnum; m. at Andover, 7 Dec 1748, JACOB STEVENS, b. at Andover, 7 Nov 1725 son of Ebenezer and Sarah (Sprague) Stevens.

Tabitha and Jacob resided in Andover while their thirteen children were born. Jacob and his sons were early in Bridgton, Maine helping to establish that settlement. In 1766, Jacob was assigned to survey and mile and one-half length of what is now known as Stevens Brook to find suitable mill sites. This was the start of Bridgton being known as a mill town.[953] Jacob and his sons built a sawmill and a gristmill. Jacob and his sons were in Bridgton while Tabitha stayed in Andover with the daughters.[954] Although, Jacob seems to have made frequent trips to Andover as the youngest child in the family was born in 1773. The daughters all eventually came to Bridgton where they settled.

Jacob Stevens and Tabitha Farnum were parents of thirteen children whose births are recorded at Andover.

i JAMES STEVENS, b. at Andover, 20 Sep 1749; d. at Bridgton, ME, 2 Mar 1823; m. at Andover, 31 Aug 1773, his third cousin, HANNAH STEVENS, b. at Andover, 8 Oct 1756 daughter of Timothy and Sarah (Poor) Stevens; Hannah d. at Bridgton, 1832.

ii AARON STEVENS, b. 3 Sep 1751; d. 22 Oct 1756.

iii EBENEZER STEVENS, b. at Andover, 17 Aug 1753; d. at Andover, 29 Jan 1821; m. at Andover, 15 Jan 1793, as her third husband, ELIZABETH GARDNER, baptized at Salem, 3 Jun 1750 daughter of Samuel and Esther (Orne) Gardner; Elizabeth d. at Andover, 16 Apr 1834. Elizabeth was first married to Nathaniel Dabney and second married to James Bridges.

iv JACOB STEVENS, b. at Andover, 3 Aug 1755; d. at Sweden, ME, 22 Jan 1831; m. at Bridgton (also recorded at Rowley), OLIVE SPOFFORD, baptized at Boxford, 10 Jun 1759 daughter of William and Abigail (Perley) Spofford; Olive d. 11 Feb 1850.

v AARON STEVENS, b. at Andover, 25 Jul 1757; nothing further definitive known.

vi ESTHER STEVENS, b. at Andover, 12 Apr 1759; d. at Bridgton, ME, 10 Oct 1778; m. by 1778, ISAIAH INGALLS, b. at Andover, 13 Jul 1756 son of Francis and Eunice (Jennings) Ingalls; Isaiah d. at Bridgton, 2 Jun 1831. Isaiah was second married to Phebe Curtis.

vii ELIZABETH STEVENS, b. 15 Jan 1761; d. 7 Jul 1763.

viii CHLOE STEVENS, b. at Andover, 30 Dec 1762; m. at Gorham, ME, 26 Aug 1780, DANIEL CRAM, Jr perhaps the son of Daniel and Sarah (-) Cram. This family was living in Standish, ME in 1790.

ix ELIZABETH STEVENS, b. at Andover, 19 Nov 1764; d. at Bridgton, ME, 19 Jul 1858; m. 22 Oct 1783, PHINEAS INGALLS, b. at Andover, 14 Nov 1758 son of Francis and Eunice (Jennings) Ingalls; Phineas d. at Bridgton, 5 Jan 1844.

x PHEBE STEVENS, b. at Andover, 29 Sep 1766; nothing further known.

xi HEPHZIBAH STEVENS, b. at Andover, 2 Apr 1769; d. at Bridgton, 1 May 1846; m. at Bridgton, 2 Oct 1794, EZRA GOULD, b. at Boxford, 7 Mar 1760 son of Ambrose and Huldah (Foster) Gould; Ezra d. at Bridgton, 19 Jul 1839.

xii ASENATH STEVENS, b. at Andover, 25 Mar 1771; d. at Bridgton, 18 Apr 1840; m. 19 Aug 1794, JOHN PEABODY, b. 2 Nov 1766 son of John and Mary (Perley) Peabody; John d. at Bridgton, 20 May 1838.

---

[952] Eaton, *Genealogical History of the Town of Reading*, p 313

[953] Geraghty, Gail, "When Bridgton was a mill town" *The Bridgton News*, 5 September 2013, http://www.bridgton.com/when-bridgton-was-a-mill-town/

[954] Mitchell, *The Bridgton Town Register*, p 8

xiii SALLY STEVENS, b. at Andover, 2 Dec 1773; d. at Bridgton, 24 Jun 1829; m. WILLIAM PEABODY, b. at Andover, 12 Aug 1770 son of John and Mary (Perley) Peabody; Sally d. at Bridgton, 24 Jun 1829.

352) HANNAH STEVENS (*Hannah Farnum Stevens⁴, John Farnum³, Elizabeth Holt Farnum², Nicholas¹*), b. at Andover, 1 Oct 1720 daughter of Benjamin and Hannah (Farnum) Stevens; d. at Bradford, MA, 15 Dec 1749; m. at Andover, 16 May 1745, AARON GAGE, b. ay Bradford, 24 Feb 1717/8 son of John and Susanna (Ross) Gage; Aaron d. at Merrimack, NH, 12 Mar 1797.[955] Aaron married second Sarah Hall.

Aaron and Hannah were in Andover where their three children were born. After Hannah's death and his remarriage, Aaron relocated to Merrimack. On 12 May 1747 (acknowledged 30 March 1754 and recorded 29 May 1776), Aaron and is wife Hannah sold to Abraham Gage two tracts of land in Bradford totaling about 22 acres. On 17 March 1759, Aaron conveyed one-acre tract to Abraham. On 11 April 1776, Aaron then of Hillsborough County, New Hampshire acknowledged the deed.[956]

Hannah Stevens and Aaron Gage were parents of three children.

i ISAAC GAGE, b. at Bradford, 3 Feb 1745/6; d. at Charlestown, 11 Nov 1822; m. 16 Aug 1770, MARY WEBSTER, b. at Bradford, 19 Feb 1753 daughter of Ebenezer and Sarah (Gage) Webster; Mary d. at Charlestown, 24 Mar 1813.

ii HANNAH GAGE, b. at Bradford, 10 Nov 1747; d. at Andover, 6 Apr 1771. Hannah did not marry. "Hannah, d. Aaron and Hannah, Apr. 6, 1771."

iii AARON GAGE, b. at Bradford, 3 Aug 1749; d. at Merrimack, NH, 5 Jan 1832; m. at Andover, 30 Mar 1773, his second cousin, MARTHA STEVENS, b. at Andover, 17 Dec 1752 daughter of Abiel and Dorothy (Martin) Stevens; Martha d. at Merrimack, 19 Jun 1824.

352a ELIZABETH STEVENS (*Hannah Farnum Stevens⁴, John Farnum³, Elizabeth Holt Farnum², Nicholas¹*), b. at Andover, 12 Jan 1722/3 daughter of Benjamin and Hannah (Farnum) Stevens; d. at Andover, 5 Nov 1804; m. at Andover, Dec 1748, CHRISTOPHER CARLTON,[957] b. at Andover, 31 Dec 1717 son of Christopher and Martha (Barker) Carlton; Christopher d. at Andover, 15 Dec 1800.

On 14 February 1785, Christopher Carlton of Andover with his wife Elizabeth, Esther Johnson widow of John Johnson. John Ingalls, Jr. and Deborah Ingalls heirs of Deborah Ingalls deceased, Josiah Osgood and Sarah his wife of Methuen, and Isaac Gage and Aaron Gage, Jr. heirs of Hannah Gage deceased in consideration of £378.17, paid according to their representative interests, conveyed to Benjamin Stevens, Jr. five-sevenths parts of the real and personal estate of Benjamin Stevens late of Andover.[958]

Christopher Carlton and his brother Isaac inherited the homestead of their father Christopher. An indenture agreement was made 24 March 1770 (witnessed by John Johnson and Benjamin Stevens, 3rd) specifying the portions each received.[959]

On 23 March 1793, Christopher Carlton sold to his sons Christopher Carlton, Jr. and Phineas Carlton a thirteen-acre tract known as Osgood meadow for payment of sixty pounds. On that same date, Christopher sold a five-acre tract in Andover to son Benjamin for payment of two pounds ten shillings.[960]

In his will written 15 April 1793 (probate 4 March 1800), Christopher Carlton bequeathed to well-beloved wife Elizabeth the improvement of one-half the dwelling house and cellar. Elizabeth also received three pounds annually to be paid by the executor and is to have a cow kept for her. That part of the house shall also be improved by daughters Elizabeth and Phebe who are unmarried. The executor is to provide all needed provisions for Elizabeth's support. His executor is also to take "effectual care" and to provide for daughters Elizabeth and Phebe "who hath for a long time been visited with such bodily indispositions as render them unable to care for themselves."[961] His daughters are to have liberty of the home during their lives. They each also receive fifteen pounds. Son Benjamin receives six pounds and half the wearing apparel as he has received his portion by deed. Sons Christopher and Phinehas receive all the lands and buildings, the livestock, and the farming utensils. Christopher and Phinehas are named executors. Real estate was $2,926.67 and personal estate was $893.05.[962]Elizabeth Stevens and Christopher Carlton were parents of nine children born at Andover.

---

955 Aaron is buried at Turkey Hill Road Cemetery in Merrimack, NH.

956 Massachusetts Land Records, Essex County, 123:235 and 134:207

957 Some sources suggest that it was Elizabeth daughter of John Stevens and Elizabeth Chandler that married Christopher Carlton but there is a death record for their daughter Elizabeth (born in 1723) at about age one year. John Stevens and Elizabeth Chandler had a second daughter Elizabeth born in 1730 who married Nathaniel Holt.

958 Massachusetts Land Records, Essex County, 152:4

959 Massachusetts Land Records, Essex County, 133:176

960 Massachusetts Land Records, Essex County, 158:81, 165:189

961 Both Phebe and Elizabeth died between the time of the will and the probate of the estate.

962 Essex County, MA: Probate File Papers, 1638-1881.Online database. AmericanAncestors.org. New England Historic Genealogical Society, 2014. Case 4616

i CHRISTOPHER CARLTON, b. 7 Nov 1749; d. 18 Jun 1750.

ii CHRISTOPHER CARLTON, b. 2 May 1751; d. at Andover, 20 Dec 1822; m. at Andover, 23 Oct 1806, his second cousin once removed, MARY FARNUM, b. at Andover, 5 Mar 1785 daughter of John and Mary (Frye) Farnum; Mary d. at Andover, 5 Dec 1855.

iii ELIZABETH CARLTON, b. Jul 1753; d. at Andover, 24 Jul 1799.

iv BENJAMIN CARLTON, b. 22 Jan 1756; m. at Andover, 2 Nov 1780, his second cousin once removed, SARAH MARBLE, baptized at Andover, b. 18 Sep 1763 daughter of Cyrus and Hannah (Parker) Marble; Sarah d. at Andover, 15 Nov 1803.

v PHINEAS CARLTON, b. 28 Mar 1758; d. at Salem, 13 Dec 1831; m. at Andover, 26 May 1805, his second cousin once removed, JOANNA STEVENS, b. at Andover, 3 Dec 1779 daughter of Amos and Sarah (Stevens) Stevens; Joanna d. at Andover, 26 Dec 1827.

vi PHEBE CARLTON, b. 8 Sep 1760; d. 18 Oct 1761.

vii DAVID CARLTON, b. 15 Feb 1763; d. 17 Aug 1763.

viii DAVID CARLTON, b. 24 Dec 1764; d. 2 Sep 1765.

ix PHEBE CARLTON, b. 4 Sep 1767; d. 12 Apr 1794.

353) ESTHER STEVENS (*Hannah Farnum Stevens[4], John Farnum[3], Elizabeth Holt Farnum[2], Nicholas[1]*), b. at Andover, Feb 1724/5 daughter of Benjamin and Hannah (Farnum) Stevens; d. at Andover, 15 Apr 1803; m. at Andover, 20 Feb 1754, as his second wife, JOHN JOHNSON, b. at Andover about 1711 son of John and Phebe (Robinson) Johnson; John d. at Andover, 26 Jul 1775. John was first married to Lydia Osgood who died in 1750.

In her will dated 9 March 1803 (probate 2 May 1803), Esther Johnson bequeathed to beloved son Samuel household items including a set of curtains. The remainder of the estate goes to son Benjamin who is also named executor.[963]

In 1805, two of son Benjamin's half-siblings quitclaimed to Benjamin their interest in property in Andover left by their honored mother Esther Johnson and by their sisters Rebecca Johnson and Phebe Johnson maiden women late of Andover. Those executing quitclaims were Jonathan Lacy and his wife Lydia Lacy of Exeter, New Hampshire and Simon Frye and Hannah Frye his wife of Fryeburg, Maine. Hannah and Lydia were both children of John Johnson and his first wife Lydia Osgood.[964] In a series of transactions, Benjamin Johnson and his wife Sally sold the property in Andover including a transaction on 3 April 1805 in which the dwelling house and property was sold to John Phillips, Jr. for $4,440.[965]

Esther Stevens and John Johnson were parents of four children born at Andover.

i BENJAMIN JOHNSON, b. at Andover, 22 Sep 1755; m. at Andover, 9 May 1793, SARAH ABBOTT, b. at Andover, 30 Dec 1768 daughter of John and Sarah (Carleton) Abbott. Benjamin and Sarah seem to have moved to Hopkinton where their youngest child Samuel was born in 1811. Benjamin and Sarah sold their property including their dwelling house in Andover in a series of transactions in 1805.

ii PHEBE JOHNSON, b. 24 Mar 1759; d. at Andover, 19 Sep 1801. Phebe did not marry.

iii REBECCA JOHNSON, b. 5 Nov 1761; d. 27 Jul 1782.

iv SAMUEL JOHNSON, b. at Andover, 20 Aug 1767; d. at Andover, 25 Jan 1850; m. 17 Aug 1799, MARY POOR, b. at Andover, 17 Aug 1778 daughter of Abraham and Elizabeth (Barker) Poor.

354) DEBORAH STEVENS (*Hannah Farnum Stevens[4], John Farnum[3], Elizabeth Holt Farnum[2], Nicholas[1]*), b. at Andover, 4 Feb 1726/7 daughter of Benjamin and Hannah (Farnum) Stevens; d. at Andover, 15 Feb 1781; m. at Andover, 8 May 1755, JOHN INGALLS, b. at Andover, 25 Apr 1728 son of Henry and Hannah (Martin) Ingalls; John d. at Andover, 26 Aug 1810.

Although John died in 1810, there was a delayed probate of his estate which is dated 15 April 1817. At that time, eldest son John Ingalls stated that his father John, late of Andover, had died within the last five years and that the other children requested that he administer the estate.[966]

Deborah Stevens and John Ingalls were parents of five children born at Andover.

---

963 *Essex County, MA: Probate File Papers, 1638-1881.*Online database. *AmericanAncestors.org.* New England Historic Genealogical Society, 2014. Case 15030

964 Massachusetts Land Records, Essex County, 176:132; 176:133

965 Massachusetts Land Records, Essex County, 177:217

966 *Essex County, MA: Probate File Papers, 1638-1881.*Online database. *AmericanAncestors.org.* New England Historic Genealogical Society, 2014. Case 14527

i DEBORAH INGALLS, b. 22 Jan 1758; d. 16 Nov 1762.

ii JOHN INGALLS, b. at Andover, 11 Sep 1760; d. at Andover, 28 Mar 1836 (probate 1836). Colonel John Ingalls does not seem to have married. William Johnson, Jr. and Charles Ingalls administered the estate. The heirs of the estate signing agreement with the accounting were Jedediah Ingalls, Samuel R. Allen, Dean Carlton, Hannah Ingalls and Joseph Farnham.[967]

iii DEBORAH INGALLS, b. 24 Mar 1763; d. at Andover, 23 Mar 1823; m. 28 Dec 1786, DEAN CARLETON, b. at Andover, 28 Oct 1758 son of Peter and Elizabeth (Robinson) Carleton; Dean d. at Andover, 14 Feb 1827 "found dead in his barn."

iv HANNAH INGALLS, b. 1 Jun 1765; d. at Andover, 23 Apr 1847. Hannah did not marry.

v JEDEDIAH INGALLS, b. at Andover, 26 Jul 1768; d. (recorded both and Durham, NH and Andover) 1 Aug 1847; m. at Dirham, NH, 3 Feb 1802, ELIZABETH CURRIER, b. at Belmont, NH, 12 Jun 1782 daughter of Charles and Elizabeth (Smith) Currier;[968] Elizabeth d. at Andover, 26 Oct 1851. Dr. Jedediah Ingalls was a graduate of Dartmouth College.

355) SARAH STEVENS (*Hannah Farnum Stevens[4], John Farnum[3], Elizabeth Holt Farnum[2], Nicholas[1]*), b. at Andover, 14 Aug 1731 daughter of Benjamin and Hannah (Farnum) Stevens; d. at Methuen, 19 Dec 1803; m. at Andover, 3 Mar 1757, JOSIAH OSGOOD, b. at Andover, 20 Nov 1732 son of Josiah and Abigail (Day) Osgood; Josiah d. at Methuen, 10 Dec 1788.

Deacon Josiah Osgood did not leave a will and his estate entered probate 6 January 1789 with eldest son Josiah Osgood of Amherst, New Hampshire declining administration of the estate and widow Sarah requesting that son Benjamin be named administrator. Real estate was valued at £482 which included the home place with dwelling house and 56 acres and part of a grist mill and forge. The total value of the estate was £1746.9.10. Much of the personal estate was amounts owed to the estate in the form of notes.[969]

Sarah Stevens and Josiah Osgood were parents of ten children born at Methuen.

i JOSIAH OSGOOD, b. 18 Jan 1758; d. 5 Aug 1762.

ii JOHN OSGOOD, 27 Jul 1759; d. 8 Sep 1759.

iii SARAH OSGOOD, b. Nov 1760; d. 19 Aug 1762.

iv JOSIAH OSGOOD, b. at Methuen, 13 Nov 1762; d. at Milford, NH, 2 Apr 1813; m. at Amherst, NH, 11 Sep 1788, ELIZABETH WALTON, b. about 1766; Elizabeth d. at Milford, 11 Mar 1839.

v BENJAMIN OSGOOD, b. at Methuen, 11 Oct 1764; d. at Methuen, Apr 1837; m. at Methuen, 9 Feb 1796, MARY "POLLY" WILSON, b. at Methuen, 27 Oct 1765 daughter of James and Mary (Perkins) Wilson; Polly d. at Methuen, 20 Jan 1850.

vi JOSEPH OSGOOD, b. at Methuen, 3 Feb 1767; d. at Methuen, 14 Dec 1819; m. at Methuen, 24 Nov 1795, ABIGAIL BARKER, b. at Methuen, 25 Sep 1769 daughter of Jonathan and Abigail (Mitchell) Barker; Abigail d. at Nelson, NH, 7 Jan 1831.

vii JOHN OSGOOD, b. at Methuen, 24 Dec 1768; d. at Nelson, NH, 21 Oct 1852; m. 1st 15 May 1792, LYDIA HEALD, b. at Temple, NH, 7 Aug 1772 daughter of Oliver and Lydia (Spaulding) Heald; Lydia d. 10 Sep 1801. John m. 2nd 9 Oct 1802, BETSY RICE, b. 20 Nov 1768 daughter of David and Love (Moore) Rice;[970] Betsy d. at Nelson, 27 Oct 1843.

viii SAMUEL OSGOOD, b. at Methuen, 4 Jan 1771; d. at Sullivan, NH, 8 Dec 1826; m. 26 May 1796, LUCY HEALD, b. at Temple, 10 Jul 1770 daughter of Oliver and Lydia (Spaulding) Heald; Lucy d. at Sullivan, 19 Mar 1843.

ix NATHANIEL OSGOOD, b. at Methuen, 31 Dec 1773; d. at Sullivan, NH, 1 Apr 1852; m. at Sullivan, 13 Mar 1801, ABIGAIL WILSON, b. at Keene, 29 May 1780 daughter of Daniel and Abigail (Morse) Wilson; Abigail d. at Sullivan, 28 Feb 1865.

---

[967] *Essex County, MA: Probate File Papers, 1638-1881.*Online database. *AmericanAncestors.org.* New England Historic Genealogical Society, 2014. Case 14529

[968] The will of Charles Currier of Gilmanton written in 1810 includes a bequest to his daughter Elizabeth Ingalls.

[969] *Essex County, MA: Probate File Papers, 1638-1881.*Online database. *AmericanAncestors.org.* New England Historic Genealogical Society, 2014. Case 20238

[970] Ward, *A Genealogical History of the Rice Family*, p 96

x THADDEUS OSGOOD, b. at Methuen, 24 Oct 1775; d. at Glasgow, Scotland, 19 Jan 1852. Thaddeus did not marry. He attended Dartmouth College, studied divinity, and was ordained in 1806. He was a missionary in New York and Canada and raised money to promote education. He organized the first church in Buffalo, New York.[971]

356) BENJAMIN STEVENS (*Hannah Farnum Stevens[4], John Farnum[3], Elizabeth Holt Farnum[2], Nicholas[1]*), b. at Andover, 14 May 1734 son of Benjamin and Hannah (Farnum) Stevens; d. at Andover, 6 Feb 1800; m. at Andover, 21 Jul 1783, LYDIA FRYE, b. at Andover, 23 May 1752 daughter of Ebenezer and Elizabeth (Kimball) Frye; Lydia d. about 1806 (probate 6 May 1806).

Benjamin Stevens did not leave a will and his estate entered probate 4 March 1800 with widow Lydia declining administration and requesting that this be assumed by Ebenezer Stevens.[972] On 2 June 1800, Ebenezer informed the court that the estate was insolvent and requested the sale of all the estate except the widow's dower. On 3 March 1801, Ebenezer requested that the reversion of the widow's dower to the estate along with the other two-thirds of the estate be sold to settle the debts. A guardian bond was filed for sons Benjamin, John, and Ebenezer. Son Benjamin Stevens age sixteen years eight months and John Stevens age fourteen years eight months made choice of John Adams, Jr. as guardian. On 1 March 1806, Benjamin Stevens filed a statement that he had received the balance of his effects entrusted to his guardian John Adams and discharged him from all demands. On 5 February 1808, John Stevens also discharged John Adams from any demands.

Lydia Stevens did not leave a will and her estate entered probate 5 May 1806 with son Benjamin requesting that Capt. John Adams who was guardian to Benjamin's two brothers be named administrator.[973] Her estate was valued at $354.31.

Benjamin Stevens and Lydia Frye were parents of three sons all of whom lived to adulthood. No clear information was found for these sons beyond the time of their mother's probate.

i BENJAMIN STEVENS, b. 22 Jul 1783

ii JOHN STEVENS, b. 22 May 1785

iii EBENEZER STEVENS, b. 26 Mar 1787; he may be the Ebenezer who died at Andover, 18 Jun 1839.

357) JOSEPH INGALLS (*Phebe Farnum Ingalls[4], John Farnum[3], Elizabeth Holt Farnum[2], Nicholas[1]*), b. at Andover, 9 Aug 1723 son of Joseph and Phebe (Farnum) Ingalls; d. at Pomfret, 26 Oct 1790, his third cousin, SARAH ABBOTT (*Elizabeth Gray Abbott[4], Henry Gray[3], Hannah Holt Gray[2], Nicholas[1]*), b. at Pomfret, 15 Oct 1730 daughter of Paul and Elizabeth (Gray) Abbott; Sarah d. at Pomfret, 17 Dec 1811.

There is a 1791 probate record for Joseph Ingalls without a will. Part of the probate includes Sarah being named as the guardian of the youngest child Harvey. The estate was deemed to be insolvent. The whole of the real and personal estate was ordered to be sold, with most of the benefit of the sale to go to the creditors.[974]

There are records for twelve children of Joseph and Sarah all born at Pomfret.

i PHEBE INGALLS, b. 22 Aug 1750; d. 22 Sep 1759.

ii PETER INGALLS, b. 12 Feb 1752; d. at Pomfret, 11 Jun 1808; m. 20 Apr 1775, SARAH ASHLEY, b. at Windham, 2 Nov 1752 daughter of Joseph and Sarah (Cressy) Ashley, Sarah d. at Pomfret, 18 Nov 1811.

iii DORCUS INGALLS, b. 27 Jun 1754; no further record was located for Dorcus.

iv DARIUS INGALLS, b. 27 Jun 1754; d. likely in Vermont, 1824; m. Mar 1796, LODEMA LEE, b. at Killingly, 3 Nov 1757 daughter of Seth and Molly (Conant) Lee.

v ASA INGALLS, b. 29 Feb 1756; d. 25 Dec 1775.

vi LUTHER INGALLS, b. 24 Aug 1758; d. at Hanover, NH, 4 Jul 1855; m. 23 Jun 1781, LUCY UTLEY, born about 1760; Lucy d. 7 Jan 1831.

vii CALVIN INGALLS, b. 22 Nov 1760; d. at Stafford, Oct 1830; m. 1st, 28 Nov 1782, CATHERINE TERRINGTON; Catherine d. 31 Dec 1783. Calvin m. 2nd, 28 May 1795, MARY HORTON, b. at Union, 1 Oct 1759 daughter of Ezra and Mary (Hempstead) Horton; Mary d. 12 May 1833.

viii CHESTER INGALLS, b. 7 Aug 1762; d. at Hanover, NH, 27 May 1842; m. 4 Apr 1784, SYLVIA STEVENS, b. 25 Mar 1763 daughter of Robert and Mary (Hathaway) Stevens.

---

971 *Appleton's Cyclopedia of American Biography*, volume IV, p 601

972 *Essex County, MA: Probate File Papers, 1638-1881.*Online database. *AmericanAncestors.org.* New England Historic Genealogical Society, 2014. Case 26301

973 *Essex County, MA: Probate File Papers, 1638-1881.*Online database. *AmericanAncestors.org.* New England Historic Genealogical Society, 2014. Case 26400

974 *Connecticut Wills and Probate, 1609-1999*, Probate of Joseph Ingalls, Hartford, 1791, Case number 2280.

ix JOSEPH ROYAL INGALLS, b. 24 Aug 1764; d. 5 Sep 1783.[975]

x SARAH INGALLS, b. 18 Dec 1766; d. at Jericho, VT, 24 Apr 1833;[976] m. 22 Jan 1788, ABRAHAM FORD, b. 15 May 1764 son of Abraham and Abigail (Woodward) Ford; Abraham d. 9 Apr 1813 while on a trip to Lebanon, CT. The family settled in Vermont in 1803.

xi HANNAH INGALLS, b. 22 Aug 1769; m. 25 Jan 1791, JOSIAH INGERSOLL, *possibly* the son of Richard and Zipporah (-) Ingersoll; this family relocated to Westford, VT.

xii HARVEY INGALLS, b. 7 Jul 1775; d. 20 Dec 1833[977] at Brookfield, VT; m. ELLA FORD, b. at Windham, 6 Apr 1775 daughter of Abraham and Abigail (Woodward) Ford; Ella d. at Brookfield, 1857.

358) PHEBE INGALLS (*Phebe Farnum Ingalls*[4], *John Farnum*[3], *Elizabeth Holt Farnum*[2], *Nicholas*[1]), b. at Andover, 10 Aug 1730 daughter of Joseph and Phebe (Farnum) Ingalls; d. after 1772; m. at Andover, 20 Nov 1749, JOSHUA ABBOTT, b. at Andover, 25 Sep 1722 son of Ephraim and Sarah (Crosby) Abbott; Joshua d. at Amherst, NH, about 1772 (will 2 Mar 1772).

In his will dated 2 March 1772, Joshua Abbott orders that all his property (except his household furniture) be sold following his death. One-third of the proceeds is to be set aside for his wife Phebe. His wife is to also have her choice of one of his cows. The remainder of the proceeds are to be divided among his children: oldest son Joshua and other sons Stephen and Peter, with the sons to have £4 more than any of the daughters; daughter Phebe the wife of John Everden; daughters Elizabeth and Sarah are to have equal portions; and the youngest son Joseph to be provided for by the executor from the estate proceeds until he arrives at an age to be bound out as an apprentice. At the age of 21, Joseph will receive a cash payment for his portion.[978]

The birth of oldest daughter, Phebe, is recorded at Andover and the births of ten children are recorded at Amherst, New Hampshire.[979]

i PHEBE ABBOTT, b. 31 Aug 1750; m. about 1770, JOHN EVERDEN; the birth of one child for this couple is recorded at Amherst. John Everden seems to have seen service during the Revolution in Colonel Moses Nichols Regiment that marched from New Hampshire to Rhode Island in August 1778.[980] There is a John Everden that died 21 Aug 1837 at Winchester, NH but that may not be him.

ii SARAH ABBOTT, b. 27 Jan 1752; d. 4 Jan 1754.

iii JOSHUA ABBOTT, b. 10 May 1754. The Amherst, NH book[981] has Joshua Abbott marrying a Deborah Chandler, but I cannot find that anywhere else and there is no record of the marriage and I could not locate any possible children.

iv ELIZABETH ABBOTT, b. 12 Nov 1756.

v STEPHEN ABBOTT, b. 29 Sep 1759; m. 8 Aug 1782, SARAH LOVEJOY, b. 7 Nov 1765 daughter of Hezekiah and Hannah (Phelps) Lovejoy.[982] No children have yet been located for this couple and it is not clear where they might have settled.

vi SARAH ABBOTT, b. 19 Feb 1761; d. about 1848, Crown Point, NY; m. 29 Jan 1782, AARON NICHOLS, born about 1757; d. 13 Oct 1821 at Crown Point, NY.[983]

vii PETER ABBOTT, b. 28 Jul 1762; d. unknown but perhaps in NY; m. 23 Oct 1788, ABIGAIL FARNUM, b. at Amherst, 27 Dec 1767 daughter of Joseph and Mary (Lyon) Farnum. The children for this family are recorded in Windham, VT.

viii INFANT ABBOTT, b. and d. 16 Apr 1764.

ix INFANT ABBOTT, b. 3 Apr 1765; infant death.

---

975 Connecticut, Church Record Abstracts, 1630-1920

976 *Vermont, Vital Records, 1720-1908.*

977 The inscription on the gravestone gives exact age of 58 yrs. 5 mo. & 12 dys; Find a Grave Memorial # 92380131

978 *New Hampshire Wills and Probate Records 1643-1982,* Will of Joshua Abbot, Hillsborough, 2 Mar 1772.

979 Ancestry.com, *New Hampshire, Births and Christenings Index, 1714-1904* (Provo, UT, USA: Ancestry.com Operations, Inc., 2011).

980 "New Hampshire Revolutionary War Records, 1675-1835," database with images, *FamilySearch* (https://familysearch.org/ark:/61903/1:1:Q242-NWWR: accessed 6 February 2018), John Everden, 05 Aug 1778; citing New Hampshire, United States, Archives and Records Management, Concord.

981 Secomb, *History of the Town of Amherst*, p 478

982 The will of Hezekiah Lovejoy includes a bequest to daughter Sarah wife of Stephen Abbott.

983 Ancestry.com. *New York Pensioners, 1835* [database on-line]. Provo, UT, USA: Ancestry.com Operations Inc, 1998. Aaron Nichols who served in the Revolution in New Hampshire received a pension beginning 30 Apr 1818 in New York. Aaron Nichols is also head of household in the 1820 Census at Crown Point, Essex, NY.

x INFANT ABBOTT, b. 16 Feb 1767; infant death.

xi JOSEPH ABBOTT, b. 23 Jan 1772.

359) JOSHUA INGALLS (*Phebe Farnum Ingalls*[4], *John Farnum*[3], *Elizabeth Holt Farnum*[2], *Nicholas*[1]), b. at Andover, 13 Aug 1732 son of Joseph and Phebe (Farnum) Ingalls; d. at Andover, 1785 (probate 5 Jul 1785); m. at Andover, 9 Sep 1760, ELIZABETH STEEL, b. at Andover, 21 Feb 1737 daughter of Nicholas and Phebe (Stevens) Steel.

The will of Joshua Ingalls has bequests for the following persons: beloved wife Elizabeth, son Simeon, daughter Phebe Ingalls, and son Stephen.[984] The births of five children are recorded at Andover.

i STEPHEN INGALLS, b. 17 Jun 1761; d. about May 1794 (will written 4 Apr 1794 and probate 3 June 1794); m. 21 Sep 1786, LYDIA KIMBALL, b. 9 Mar 1761 daughter of Andrew and Esther (Barker) Kimball; Lydia d. at Andover, 16 Dec 1831.

ii ELIZABETH INGALLS, b. 2 Sep 1762; d. before 1785.

iii SIMEON INGALLS, b. 3 Sep 1764; m. 16 Jan 1787 the widow ELIZABETH FISH. The identity of Elizabeth is unknown, but she is possibly Bette Fisk who married David Fish in Andover in 1777 but just a wild guess at this point.

iv PETER INGALLS, b. 14 Jan 1766; d, before 1785.

v PHEBE INGALLS, b. 30 Dec 1768; d. at Pelham, NH, 20 Jul 1847; m. 3 Jun 1790, ELIJAH BRADSTREET, b. 4 Jul 1767 son of Samuel and Ruth (Lampson) Bradstreet; Elijah d. at Pelham, 2 Dec 1850.

360) TABITHA INGALLS (*Phebe Farnum Ingalls*[4], *John Farnum*[3], *Elizabeth Holt Farnum*[2], *Nicholas*[1]), b. at Andover, 14 Mar 1734/5 daughter of Joseph and Phebe (Farnum) Ingalls; d. at Amherst, NH, 8 May 1794; m. at Andover, 14 Feb 1755, SOLOMON KITTREDGE, b. at Billerica, 9 Jun 1736 son of Francis and Lydia (-) Kittredge;[985] Solomon d. at Amherst, 24 Aug 1792.

Solomon was a blacksmith and the family settled in Amherst, New Hampshire.[986] They reared a large family of twelve children, four of whom (Stephen, Ingalls, Asa, and Zephaniah) became physicians.

In his will written 7 May 1790 (proved 3 September 1792), Solomon Kittredge bequeathed to wife Tabitha all the household items not otherwise disposed of to be at her own disposal. There is also a list of provisions to be provided for her including two cows and four sheep. Son Josiah receives all the estate real and personal and is responsible for paying the legacies, debts of the estate, and funeral expenses. Sons Solomon and Zephaniah and daughter Tabitha wife of Benjamin Sawyer, daughter Phebe wife of Aaron Townsend, and daughter Lydia wife of Joshua Kittredge have received their full shares and will have no more. Sons Stephen and Ingalls are to receive the value of £40 pounds from the estate, and sons Peter and Asa who are minors will receive £40 as soon as they become of age. Daughters Betsy and Sally will also receive £40 in value of household items when they come of age. Son Josiah was named sole executor.[987]

Tabitha Ingalls and Solomon Kittredge were parents of twelve children.

i SOLOMON KITTREDGE, b. at Andover, 3 Aug 1755; d. at Mont Vernon, NH, 22 Oct 1845; m. 1st 27 Feb 1777, ANNA KITTREDGE, b. at Tewksbury, 23 Nov 1755 daughter of Thomas and Anna (Thorndike) Kittredge; Anna d. 2 Aug 1814. Solomon m. 2nd at Mont Vernon, 13 Apr 1815, his third cousin, ELIZABETH HOLT (*Ezekiel*[5], *Ebenezer*[4], *Samuel*[3], *Samuel*[2], *Nicholas*[1]), b. at Amherst, NH, 8 Jul 1773 daughter of Ezekiel and Mary (Stewart) Holt; Elizabeth d. 1821.

ii ZEPHANIAH KITTREDGE, b. at Tewksbury, 24 Aug 1757; d. at Mont Vernon, NH, 17 Aug 1843; m. at Tewksbury, 8 Mar 1781, ELIZABETH STICKNEY, b. at Tewksbury, 17 Mar 1761 daughter of Abraham and Sara (Kittredge) Stickney; Elizabeth d. at Mont Vernon, 6 Aug 1851.

iii TABITHA KITTREDGE, b. at Tewksbury, 28 Jul 1758; d. at Nelson, NH, 26 Nov 1845; m. 1778, BENJAMIN SAWYER, b. 19 Jun 1757 son of Josiah and Hannah (Gowing) Sawyer; Benjamin d. at Nelson, 18 Mar 1846.

iv JOSIAH KITTREDGE, b. at Tewksbury, 6 Jul 1761; d. at Mont Vernon, 23 May 1850; m. at Littleton, MA, 14 Oct 1792, MARY BAKER, b. at Littleton, 23 May 1762 daughter of Timothy and Mary (Dakin) Baker; Mary d. at Mont Vernon, 16 Sep 1828.

---

984 *Essex County, MA: Probate File Papers, 1638-1881. Probate of Joshua Ingalls, 5 Jul 1785, Case number 14535.*

985 Kittredge, *The Kittredge Family in America*, p 26

986 Kittredge, *The Kittredge Family in America*, p 26

987 *New Hampshire. Probate Court (Hillsborough County), volume 5, pp 235-237*

v PHEBE KITTREDGE, b. at Tewksbury, 5 Jun 1763; d. at Crown Point, NY, 20 Aug 1832; m. AARON TOWNSEND, b. at Charlestown, MA, 4 Aug 1763 son of Aaron and Hephzibah (Wolcott) Townsend; Aaron d. at Crown Point, 25 Apr 1856.

vi STEPHEN KITTREDGE, b. at Tewksbury, 27 Jun 1765; d. at Hancock, NH, 16 Oct 1806; m. at Amherst, 27 Nov 1788, MEHITABLE RUSSELL, b. 20 Jan 1768 daughter of Peter and Mehitable (Stiles) Russell; Mehitable d. at Charleston, ME, 4 Feb 1848. Mehitable was second married to Daniel Bickford.

vii LYDIA KITTREDGE, b. at Amherst, NH, 29 Aug 1767; d. 3 Apr 1795; m. at Amherst, 29 Nov 1787, JOSHUA KITTREDGE, b. at Tewksbury, 15 Mar 1761 son of Thomas and Anna (Thorndike) Kittredge; Joshua d. at Nelson, NH, 8 Feb 1834.

viii INGALLS KITTREDGE, b. at Amherst, NH, 10 Dec 1769; d. at Beverly, MA, 17 Jun 1856; m. 1st 26 Feb 1797, SARAH CONANT, b. 27 May 1770 daughter of Jonathan and Mercy (Lovett) Conant; Sarah d. at Beverly, 7 Oct 1833. Ingalls m. 2nd 27 Mar 1836, LYDIA SMITH, b. at Beverly, 1 Mar 1799 daughter of Ebenezer and Lydia (Ray) Smith; Lydia d. at Beverly, 22 Nov 1879.

ix BETSEY KITTREDGE, b. at Amherst, 16 Sep 1771; d. at Nelson, NH, 21 Nov 1843; m. about 1795, HENRY WHEELER, b. at Sudbury, 17 Jan 1771 son of Uriah and Anne (Smith) Wheeler; Henry d. at Nelson, 20 Jul 1840.

x PETER KITTREDGE, b. at Amherst, 25 Sep 1773; d. at Readfield, ME, 16 Jun 1857; m. at Hallowell, ME, 20 May 1795, SARAH CHURCH, b. at Little Compton, RI, May 1774 daughter of Constant and Keziah (Briggs) Church; Sarah d. at Readfield, 20 Mar 1850. Peter was a saddle and harness maker.

xi ASA KITTREDGE, b. at Amherst, 24 Mar 1776; d. at Morristown, VT, 29 Mar 1863; m. 1st at Pepperell, MA, 19 Sep 1803, SUSANNA SCOTT, b. at Townsend, MA, 31 Jan 1777 daughter of Aaron and Elizabeth (Wallis) Scott; Susanna d. at Johnson, VT, 1 Jan 1836. Asa m. 2nd at Morristown, 1836, POLLY POOR, b. at Morristown, 12 Nov 1799 daughter of George and Polly (-) Poor.

xii SALLY KITTREDGE, b. at Amherst, 19 Apr 1779; d. 28 Aug 1847; m. 15 Sep 1796, ABIEL STICKNEY, b. at Tewksbury, 5 Apr 1770 son of Samuel and Elinor (Butman) Stickney; Abiel d. at Troy, NH, 7 Feb 1854.

361) DEBORAH FAULKNER (*Deborah Farnum Faulkner⁴, John Farnum³, Elizabeth Holt Farnum², Nicholas¹*), b. at Littleton, 26 Aug 1735 daughter of Timothy and Deborah (Farnum) Faulkner; d. at Sturbridge, 31 Jul 1828; m. at Sturbridge, 11 Jul 1764, as his second wife, MOSES WELD,[988] b. at Roxbury, 27 Mar 1722 son of John and Mehitable (Child) Weld; Moses d. at Sturbridge, 10 May 1806. Moses was first married to Elizabeth Holbrook.

Deacon Moses Weld was active in the town of Sturbridge filling roles such as moderator of the town meeting. He was selected as deacon in 1764.[989]

In his will written 21 February 1797 (proved 2 September 1806), Moses Weld of Sturbridge bequeathed to his dearly beloved wife all the household furniture, two cows, six sheep, saddle and bridle, and large bible to be at her disposal. Son Timothy is to provide her a suitable home. Sons Moses and Walter receive the wearing apparel. His private library is to be divided among his six sons: John, Moses, Walter, Ebenezer, Chester, and Peleg. John, Moses, Walter, Ebenezer, and Chester each receives £45 to be paid by Timothy. As Peleg is an apprentice, he is to receive £30.10 when he reaches age 22. The children of daughter Hannah Stone receive £8, daughter Sarah receives £6, and daughter Elizabeth Stone one shilling as she has received her portion. Son Timothy receives the remainder of the estate and is named executor.[990]

In her will written 1 September 1825 (proved 22 August 1828), Deborah Weld bequeathed to son Ebenezer Weld one cent. Son Peleg Weld receives the great bible, the bedding, and all the pewter. Son Timothy receives the remainder of the estate and is named executor.[991]

Moses Weld and Deborah Faulkner were parents of six children born at Sturbridge.

i TIMOTHY WELD, b. at Sturbridge, 4 Aug 1765; d. at Sturbridge, 27 Jan 1839; m. 1st 29 May 1796, SALLY HAMMOND, b. about 1767; Sally d. at Sturbridge, 4 Jun 1813. Timothy m. 2nd ABIGAIL BOYDEN (widow of William Gilford), b. at Sturbridge, 28 Jul 1786 daughter of John and Abigail (Hobbs) Boyden; Abigail d. at Royalston, MA, 12 Oct 1870.

ii EBENEZER WELD, b. at Sturbridge, 31 Jan 1768; d. at Cornish, NH, 21 Apr 1835 (probate 22 Apr 1835). No marriage was located for Ebenezer.

---

988 The name is also spelled Wild in some records.

989 Clark, *An Historical Sketch of Sturbridge*

990 *Probate Records (Worcester County, Massachusetts); Index 1731-1881, volume 35, pp 122-123*

991 *Worcester County, MA: Probate File Papers, 1731-1881.* Online database. AmericanAncestors.org. New England Historic Genealogical Society, 2015. Case 62818

iii CHESTER WELD, b. at Sturbridge, 27 Aug 1770; d. at Berkshire, VT, 21 May 1820; m. MEHITABLE PIKE, b. at Brookfield, 30 Aug 1774 daughter of Samuel and Mehitable (Elwell) Pike; Mehitable d. at Berkshire, 2 Jul 1847. Mehitable married second Timothy Thayer in 1825.

iv ELIZABETH WELD, b. at Sturbridge, 22 Oct 1772; d. at Charlton, 20 Jul 1815; m. at Sturbridge, 29 Mar 1793, MOSES STONE, b. at Charlton, 24 Jun 1765 son of Nehemiah and Hannah (Lock) Stone; Moses d. at Holland, MA, 1798 (probate 1798).

v DEBORAH WELD, b. 16 Oct 1774; d. of consumption at Sturbridge, 12 Nov 1795.

vi PELEG WELD, b. at Sturbridge, 7 Jul 1780; d. at Cornish, NH, 30 Aug 1853; m. at Acworth, NH, 21 Apr 1808, PATTY FOSTER, b. 10 Apr 1791 daughter of Israel and Susanna (Bruce) Foster; Patty d. at Cornish, 21 Dec 1834.

362) PETER FAULKNER (*Deborah Farnum Faulkner⁴, John Farnum³, Elizabeth Holt Farnum², Nicholas¹*), b. at Andover, 5 Nov 1743 daughter of Timothy and Deborah (Farnum) Faulkner; d. at Lancaster, NH, 11 Dec 1829; m. at Sturbridge, 10 Dec 1768, his third cousin, CHLOE CRAM (*Humphrey Cram⁴, Sarah Holt Cram³, Henry², Nicholas¹*), b. at Union, CT, 25 Nov 1750 daughter of Humphrey and Hannah (Blunt) Cram.

Peter Faulkner and Chloe Cram were parents of five children born at Sturbridge.

i POLLY FAULKNER, b. 13 Jun 1772; d. 12 Sep 1775.

ii PERSIS FAULKNER, b. 14 Dec 1775; d. at St. Johnsbury, VT, 27 Jan 1872; m. 5 May 1801, her fourth cousin, RICHARD EASTMAN (*Hannah Holt Eastman⁵, Benjamin⁴, Nicholas³, Nicholas², Nicholas¹*), b. at Conway, NH, 8 Feb 1778 son of Noah and Hannah (Holt) Eastman; Richard d. at Lancaster, NH, 22 Jan 1852.

iii TIMOTHY FAULKNER, b. 19 May 1780; d. at Ashtabula, OH, 17 Dec 1853; m. SARAH MORTON, b. about 1782; Sarah d. at Ashtabula, 12 Jan 1873.[992]

iv SYLVESTER FAULKNER, b. 19 May 1780; d. at Sidney, Hastings, Ontario, 15 Aug 1863; m. at Lancaster, NH, 19 Dec 1802, his first cousin, MARY "POLLY" CRAM (*Jonathan Cram⁵, Humphrey Cram⁴, Sarah Holt Cram³, Henry², Nicholas¹*), b. at Wales, MA, about 1781 daughter of Jonathan and Anna (Webber) Cram; Mary d. at Sidney, 22 Jan 1858.

v ROXELANA FAULKNER, b. 1784;[993] d. at Conneaut, OH, 12 Apr 1868; m. at Burke, VT, 27 Dec 1806, CHAUNCEY BURRINGTON, b. about 1782, and baptized at New Hartford, CT, 25 Jan 1787 son of Ebenezer and Mary (Moultrop) Burrington; Chauncey d. after 1870 when he was living in Conneaut.

363) ISRAEL ADAMS (*Tabitha Farnum Adams⁴, John Farnum³, Elizabeth Holt Farnum², Nicholas¹*), b. at Andover, 26 Jun 1733/4 son of Israel and Tabitha (Farnum) Adams; d. at Rindge, NH, 1 Aug 1808; m. at Andover, 20 Nov 1760, his third cousin, ELIZABETH STEVENS, b. at Andover, 22 May 1738 daughter of Samuel and Hephzibah (Ingalls) Stevens; Elizabeth d. at Rindge, 9 Nov 1809.

Israel and Elizabeth had their first children in Andover and were in Rindge, New Hampshire by 1773. Israel signed the association test in Rindge, served as selectman in 1775, and was chosen constable in 1783.[994]

Although Israel died in 1809, the division of his estate was not made until 1819. Inventory was made 17 June 1819 with real estate valued at $2266. The final settlement of the estate was 20 January 1822 in which son Israel Adams as administrator agreed to make payment of $152.28 to each of the heirs: Elizabeth Adams, Samuel Adams, Israel Adams, Esther Adams, Sarah Adams, Daniel Adams, and Hannah Adams.[995]

Daughter Hannah Adams wrote her will 20 October 1851. She had bequests to her nieces of fifty dollars each: Sybil Stratton, Susanna Green, Clarissa Adams, and Louisa Hale. The wives of her nephews make chose of her wearing apparel and household furniture: Mary P. wife of Albert Adams and Ruby Adams wife of Arad Adams. She leaves her books to her brothers if they should survive her. There are other bequests to religious organizations. Levi Howe was named executor.[996]

Israel Adams and Elizabeth Stevens were parents of nine children only one of whom is known to have married.

i ELIZABETH ADAMS, b. at Andover, MA, 4 Nov 1761; d. at Rindge, NH, 28 Sep 1835. Elizabeth did not marry.

---

992 Web: Ashtabula County, Ohio, Obituary Index, 1858-2012

993 Roxelana is a presumed child of this family. There is not a recording of her birth at Sturbridge and she may have been born after the family move to New Hampshire.

994 Stearns, *History of the Town of Rindge, New Hampshire*, p 106, p 123, p 426

995 *New Hampshire. Probate Court (Cheshire County)*; Probate Place: *Cheshire, New Hampshire, Estate of Israel Adams of Rindge, Case 93*

996 *New Hampshire. Probate Court (Cheshire County)*; Probate Place: *Cheshire, New Hampshire, Estate of Hannah Adams, Rindge, Case 220.*

ii JOSHUA ADAMS, b. at Andover, 24 Aug 1763; he is thought to have died in the War of 1812 perhaps at Plattsburg.[997] Joshua was deceased before the division of his father' estate and no heirs of Joshua are included in the distribution.

iii SAMUEL ADAMS, b. at Andover, 7 Nov 1765; d. at Rindge, 5 Mar 1852. Samuel did not marry.

iv ISRAEL ADAMS, b. at Andover, 13 Jan 1768; d. at Rindge, 16 Sep 1856; m. at Rindge, 28 Aug 1796, SALLY ADAMS, b. at Ashburnham, 1771 daughter of Nathaniel Adams; Sally d. at Rindge, 3 May 1838.

v ESTHER ADAMS, b. at Andover, 26 May 1770; d. at Rindge, 26 May 1822. Esther did not marry.

vi SARAH ADAMS, b. at Rindge, 29 Mar 1773; d. at Rindge, 21 Nov 1823. Sarah did not marry.

vii DANIEL ADAMS, b. at Rindge, 10 Nov 1775; died young

viii DANIEL ADAMS, b. at Rindge, 9 Apr 1779; d. at Rodman, NY, 1871. Daniel does not seem to have married. At the initiation of the probate of his estate on 28 Apr 1871, Arad Adams a nephew appeared and requested that P. C. Williams of Rodman be named administrator it "appearing that no person has a prior right thereto."[998] Arad Adams was the son of Daniel's brother Israel.

ix HANNAH ADAMS, b. at Rindge, 20 Aug 1784; d. at Rindge, 19 Jan 1852. Hannah did not marry.

364) JOHN ADAMS (*Tabitha Farnum Adams[4], John Farnum[3], Elizabeth Holt Farnum[2], Nicholas[1]*), b. at Andover, 3 Jul 1735 son of Israel and Tabitha (Farnum) Adams; d. at Andover, 27 Jun 1813; m. 1st at Andover, 23 Nov 1758, his third cousin, HANNAH OSGOOD (*Mary Russell Osgood[4], Phebe Johnson Russell[3], Mary Holt Johnson[2], Nicholas[1]*), b. at Andover, 31 Jul 1735 daughter of Timothy and Mary (Osgood) Russell;[999] Hannah d. at Andover 22 Oct 1771.[1000] John m. 2nd at Rowley, 24 Jun 1773, HANNAH THURSTON, b. at Rowley, 25 Dec 1743 daughter of Richard and Mehitable (Jewett) Thurston; Hannah d. at Andover, 22 Jan 1774. John m. 3rd at Andover, 21 May 1776, his first cousin once removed, MARY HOLT (*Stephen[4], Nicholas[3], Nicholas[2], Nicholas[1]*), b. at Suncook, 15 Dec 1741 daughter of Stephen and Mary (Farnum) Holt; Mary d. at Andover, 9 Nov 1829.

Capt. John Adams served in the French and Indian War and was an officer during the Revolution. He served as deacon of the North Church in Andover.[1001]

In his will written 22 March 1813 (probate 6 September 1813), John Adams bequeaths to his beloved wife Mary the use and improved of the northeast room and the back part of the house while she is a widow. Mary also receives the interest on $600 annually and a lengthy list of other provisions for her support to be provided by the executor. Son Isaac Adams receives £40. Son John Adams receives the remainder of the estate real and personal and is named executor.[1002]

John Adams and Hannah Osgood were parents of five children born at Andover.

i HANNAH ADAMS, b. 26 Jul 1760; d. 30 Aug 1763.

ii SARAH ADAMS, baptized 18 Jul 1762; d. 2 Sep 1763.

iii HANNAH ADAMS, baptized 3 Jun 1764; likely died young.

iv JOHN ADAMS, b. at Andover, 26 Feb 1766; d. at Andover, 28 Sep 1839; m. 8 Dec 1789, DORCAS FAULKNER, b. at Andover, 26 Sep 1766 daughter of Joseph and Hannah (Hovey) Faulkner; Dorcas d. at Andover, 23 Sep 1847.

v ISAAC ADAMS, b. at Andover, 25 Apr 1767; d. after 1850 when he was living in Troy, MI; m. at Newburyport, MA, 7 Jun 1807, SARAH MCHARD, b. at Newburyport, 26 Apr 1777 daughter of William and Mary (-) McHard; Sarah was living in 1850. Isaac Adams attended Harvard but did not graduate. He was a physician in Newburyport. He also served as a ship master and made several foreign voyages.[1003] Isaac and Sarah were parents of six children born at Newburyport. In 1850, Isaac Adams, physician, age 82 and his wife Sarah age 70 (as on the census records) in Troy.

John Adams and Hannah Thurston were parents of one child.

i JOSEPH ADAMS, baptized at Andover, 8 May 1774; d. 22 Jun 1776.

---

[997] Adams, *A Genealogical History of Robert Adams*, p 72

[998] New York Wills and Probate Records, Jefferson County, Minutes, Orders, and Decrees, volume J, p 21; accessed through ancestry.com

[999] The 1769 will of Timothy Osgood includes a bequest to his daughter Hannah wife of John Adams.

[1000] The death transcription says 57th year of her age but this seems just an error for 37th year.

[1001] Bailey, *Historical Sketches of Andover*, p 160

[1002] *Essex County, MA: Probate File Papers, 1638-1881.*Online database. *AmericanAncestors.org.* New England Historic Genealogical Society, 2014. Case 255

[1003] Bailey, *Historical Sketches of Andover*, p 160

365) ELIZABETH ADAMS (*Tabitha Farnum Adams⁴, John Farnum³, Elizabeth Holt Farnum², Nicholas¹*), b. at Andover, 24 Dec 1737 daughter of Israel and Tabitha (Farnum) Adams; d. at Andover, 27 Sep 1779; m. at Andover, 29 Nov 1759, MICHAEL CARLTON, b. at Andover, 22 Nov 1737 son of Ezekiel and Marcy (Kimball) Carleton; Michael d. at Andover, 1785 (probate 5 Dec 1785). Michael married second the widow Phebe Porter.

In his will written 31 October 1785 (probate 5 December 1785). Michael Carlton bequeathed to beloved wife Phebe use of one-third of the real estate while she is a widow, and at her decease or remarriage this third is to be divided between his two sons Michael Carlton and Israel Carlton. Phebe also receives the household furniture she brought to the marriage and one red heifer. Daughter Elizabeth receives the whole of the household furniture that was her mother's and household items that Elizabeth has acquired. Sons Michael and Israel receive the real and personal estate divided in equal shares. Brother Samuel Carlton of Andover was named executor. Real estate was valued at £310.16.4 and stock animals at £74.12.8. The total value of the estate was £557.19.7.[1004]

Elizabeth Adams and Michael Carleton were parents of four children born at Andover.

i MICHAEL CARLTON, b. at Andover, 29 Nov 1760; d. at Andover, 26 Mar 1838; m. 1st Nov 1798, his fourth cousin, HANNAH HOLT (*Joseph⁵, Joseph⁴, Henry³, Henry², Nicholas¹*) (widow of Reuben Jones), baptized at Reading, 6 Dec 1767 daughter of Joseph and Abigail (Bean) Holt; Hannah d. at Andover, 13 Sep 1805. Michael m. 2nd SARAH KIMBALL, b. 1771; Sarah d. at Andover, 27 Jul 1847.

ii ELIZABETH CARLTON, b. at Andover, 7 Dec 1761; d. at Middleton, 2 Oct 1841; m. at Andover, 16 Dec 1786, JEREMIAH UPTON, b. at Reading, 11 Jul 1761 son of Isaac and Tabitha (-) Upton; Jeremiah d. at Middleton, 6 Dec 1825.

iii ISRAEL CARLTON, b. at Andover, 30 Jul 1763; m. at Andover, 12 Oct 1797, MARY HADLEY

iv REUBEN CARLTON, b. 19 Jan 1772; d. 25 Jul 1772.

366) DAVID ADAMS (*Tabitha Farnum Adams⁴, John Farnum³, Elizabeth Holt Farnum², Nicholas¹*), b. at Andover, 2 May 1742 son of Israel and Tabitha (Farnum) Adams; d. at Londonderry, NH, 12 Apr 1815; m. 1st 1 May 1766, ABIAH ORDWAY, b. at Methuen, 7 Mar 1744 daughter of James and Meribah (Morse) Ordway; Abiah d. 29 Jul 1776. David m. 2nd at Dracut, 20 Dec 1777, MARTHA MARSH, b. at Bradford, 12 Jan 1743 daughter of John and Martha (Rolfe) Marsh; Martha d. at Londonderry, 9 Apr 1812.

David Adams was a cordwainer and farmer. About 1783, he relocated his family to Londonderry, and the births of the youngest two children are recorded there. On 9 July 1783 (deed recorded 31 January 1785), David Adams cordwainer of Dracut sold to Nathaniel Bodwell of Methuen for £600 property in Dracut consisting of 68 acres and a dwelling house and barn.[1005]

David Adams and Abiah Ordway were parents of five children born at Dracut.

i SARAH ADAMS, b. 19 May 1767; d. 13 Nov 1801.[1006]

ii JAMES ADAMS, b. 19 Nov 1768; d. 13 Feb 1790.

iii DAVID ADAMS, b. at Dracut, 6 Apr 1771; d. at Londonderry, 21 Jan 1813; m. at Dracut, 5 Jan 1800, DELILAH COBURN, b. at Dracut, 22 Jul 1763 daughter of Jacob and Lydia (Hall) Coburn; Delilah d. at Londonderry, Aug 1818. David and Delilah did not have children. In his will, David left his estate to Delilah with Robert Adams as executor, and in her will, Delilah left her estate to her siblings and other relatives.

iv ABIAH ADAMS, b. 8 Sep 1773; d. 18 Feb 1790.

v DANIEL ADAMS, b. at Dracut, 17 Oct 1775; d. at Boxford, 2 Mar 1828; m. 24 Oct 1805, SOPHIA KIMBALL, b. at Boxford, 12 Apr 1780 daughter of Moses and Rebecca (Poor) Kimball; Sophia d. at Boxford, 24 Nov 1868.

David Adams and Martha Marsh were parents of three children.

i JOHN MARSH ADAMS, b. at Methuen, 18 Jan 1779; d. at Londonderry, 25 Apr 1815; m. at Londonderry, 6 Nov 1810, MARY "POLLY" JACKSON, b. at Merrimack, NH, 30 Aug 1785 daughter of Samuel and Mary (Hickey) Jackson; Polly d. at Monroe, MI, about 1872 (living in 1870).

1004 *Essex County, MA: Probate File Papers, 1638-1881.*Online database. *AmericanAncestors.org.* New England Historic Genealogical Society, 2014. Case 4672

1005 Massachusetts Land Records, 1620-1986, Middlesex County, 88:181

1006 This is a date reported in Adams, *A Genealogical History of Robert Adams*; no corresponding record was found. It is possible that Sarah married but that was not confirmed. One possible marriage is to James Farmer at Dracut in 1789.

ii MARTHA "PATTY" ADAMS, b. at Londonderry, 24 Nov 1781; d. at New Boston, NH, 1 Dec 1861; m. at Londonderry, 15 Dec 1808, AMOS KENDALL, b. Oct 1782 son of Jacob and Sarah (Lamson) Kendall; Amos d. at New Boston, 12 Jan 1859.

iii ROBERT ADAMS, b. at Londonderry, 13 Nov 1783; d. at Richmond, OH, 14 Feb 1865; m. at Londonderry, 7 Dec 1809, SALLY JACKSON, b. at Merrimack, 6 Jul 1789 daughter of Samuel and Mary (Hickey) Jackson; Sally d. at Richmond, OH, 4 Feb 1863.

367) RUTH FOSTER (*Lydia Farnum, Foster[4], Samuel Farnum[3], Elizabeth Holt Farnum[2], Nicholas[1]*), b. at Andover, 31 Oct 1722 daughter of David and Lydia (Farnum) Foster; d. at Boxford, 7 Nov 1760; m. at Andover, 8 Nov 1744, BENJAMIN PORTER, b. at Boxford, 6 Oct 1721 son of Benjamin and Sarah (Tyler) Porter; Benjamin d. at Boxford, 15 May 1784. Benjamin married second Mary Sherwin on 28 Apr 1763.

Ruth and Benjamin resided in Boxford, and several of their children relocated to Maine.

In his will written 18 January 1783 (probate 8 June 1784), Benjamin Porter bequeathed to beloved wife Mary the use of one-third of the real estate and use of the husbandry tools while she is a widow. Son David Foster Porter receives four good cows and £50 as well as all the notes on hand. Sons Benjamin Porter and Tyler Porter receive all the real estate to divide equally. Tyler receives the livestock and husbandry tools and all the bonds that were not given to David. Each of his three married daughters and a grandson each receives funds sufficient to purchase two good cows. The daughters are Lydia Farnum wife of Daniel Farnum, Lucy Barker wife of Asa Barker, and Sarah Kimball the wife of Solomon Kimball. The grandson is Nathan Sherwin. His three daughters Susanna Porter, Mary Porter, and Mehitable Porter each receives funds sufficient to purchase three cows. His three last named single daughters also have the privilege of living in the house while single. Tyler is charged with the duty of providing for his single sisters and he is named executor.[1007] The single daughters Mehitable, Susanna, and Mary are daughters from Benjamin's marriage to Mary Sherwin.

Ruth Foster and Benjamin Porter were parents of nine children born at Boxford.

i LYDIA PORTER, b. 4 Nov 1745; m. 22 Sep 1768, her third cousin, DANIEL FARNUM (*John Farnum[5], John Farnum[4], John Farnum[3], Elizabeth Holt Farnum[2], Nicholas[1]*), b. at Andover, 15 Jun 1741 son of John and Sarah (Frye) Farnum; Daniel d. at Andover, 10 Jul 1814.

ii MEHITABLE PORTER, b. 24 Dec 1747; d. at Boxford, about 1768; m. 26 Apr 1764, ASA SHERWIN, baptized at Boxford, 16 Dec 1744 son of Jonathan and Mary (Lurvey) Sherwin; Asa d. at Rindge, NH, 11 May 1812. Asa married second Mercy Kimball on 1 Nov 1768. Asa Sherwin was the younger brother of Mehitable's stepmother Mary Sherwin.

iii DAVID FOSTER PORTER, b. 4 Sep 1749; m. at Boxford, 17 Aug 1771, SUSANNAH TOWNE, b. at Topsfield, 19 Nov 1749 daughter of Jabez and Tryphena (Dwinell) Towne.

iv LUCY PORTER, b. 13 Oct 1751; d. at Bridgton, ME, 21 Dec 1822; m. 12 Sep 1767, ASA BARKER, b. at Andover, 10 Dec 1748 son of Timothy and Mehitable (Kimball) Barker; Asa d. at Bridgton, 18 Sep 1822.

v SARAH PORTER, b. 13 Nov 1752; d. at Deer Isle, ME, 30 Nov 1812; m. about 1778, SOLOMON KIMBALL, b. at Bradford, MA, 15 Apr 1751 son of Solomon and Martha (Graves) Kimball; Solomon d. at Belfast, ME, 1 Feb 1824. Solomon married second Mrs. Polly Tyler on 19 Mar 1814.[1008]

vi BENJAMIN PORTER, b. 29 Sep 1754; d. at Vienna, ME, 11 Apr 1837; m. 1st at Hillsborough, NH, Feb 1778, MARY SARGENT; Mary d. about 1786. Benjamin m. 2nd at Hallowell, 24 Jun 1787, PAMELIA BARTON.

vii RUTH PORTER, b. 27 Oct 1756; d. at Boxford, 15 Feb 1779.

viii TYLER PORTER, b. at Boxford, 27 Apr 1758; d. at Sebago, ME, 15 Sep 1842; m. at Boxford, 23 Dec 1779, ABIGAIL JOHNSON, b. at Andover, 21 Feb 1759 daughter of Stephen and Mary (Sessions) Johnson.[1009]

ix JONATHAN PORTER, baptized 10 Aug 1760; d. 2 Nov 1760.

368) MEHITABLE FOSTER (*Lydia Farnum, Foster[4], Samuel Farnum[3], Elizabeth Holt Farnum[2], Nicholas[1]*), b. at Andover, 21 May 1730 daughter of David and Lydia (Farnum) Foster; d. at Boxford, 25 Jan 1760; m. at Boxford, 23 Apr 1751, NATHAN ANDREWS, b. at Boxford, 25 May 1726 son of Robert and Deborah (Frye) Andrews; Nathan d. at Boxford, 29 Mar 1806. Nathan married second the widow Sarah Symonds on 6 Feb 1764.

[1007] *Essex County, MA: Probate File Papers, 1638-1881.*Online database. *AmericanAncestors.org.* New England Historic Genealogical Society, 2014. Case 22438

[1008] Morrison, *History of the Kimball Family*, volume 1, p 180

[1009] The 1802 will (probate 1814) of Stephen Johnson of Andover includes a bequest to daughter Abigail wife of Tyler Porter.

Mehitable and Nathan resided in Boxford. During the Revolution, Nathan supported the cause by allowing his horse to go in the army for which the town paid him. Nathan also served as selectman of Boxford for nine of the years from 1767 to 1790.[1010]

In his will written 7 June 1796 (probate 6 May 1806), Nathan Andrews bequeaths to beloved wife Sarah all the household goods she brought to the marriage over and above her dower of thirds. Daughters Deborah Andrews and Mehitable Knight each receives $75 which completes their full portion portions. Daughters Deborah and Mehitable and son Nathan Andrews receives the household goods to divide. Son Nathan received the whole of estate, real and personal, and is named executor. Real estate was valued at $3,520 and personal estate at $303.59.[1011]

Mehitable Foster and Nathan Andrews were parents of four children born at Boxford.

i DEBORAH ANDREWS, b. at Boxford, 19 Oct 1752; d. at Bradford, NH, 24 Oct 1831; m. at Boxford, 11 Jun 1778, JOSHUA ANDREWS, b. at Boxford, 28 Oct 1750 son of Joshua and Hannah (Wood) Andrews; Joshua d. at Bradford, 22 Aug 1837.

ii NATHAN ANDREWS, b. at Boxford, 11 Nov 1754; d. at Boxford, 17 Jun 1844; m. 1st 20 May 1783, ESTHER KIMBALL, b. at Boxford, 16 Feb 1757 daughter of John and Sarah (Barker) Kimball; Esther d. at Boxford, 11 Feb 1791. Nathan m. 2nd Nov 1792, EUNICE KIMBALL, baptized at Topsfield, 1 Nov 1761 daughter of Daniel and Hephzibah (Howe) Kimball; Eunice d. at Boxford, 28 Oct 1845.

iii LYDIA ANDREWS, b. 21 Oct 1756; not mentioned in father's will.

iv MEHITABLE ANDREWS, b. at Boxford, 23 Sep 1759; d. at Bradford, NH, Jul 1834; m. at Boxford, 23 May 1782, JONATHAN KNIGHT, b. at Middleton, 22 Apr 1755 son of Jonathan and Phebe (Perkins) Knight; Jonathan d. at Bradford, Apr 1845.

369) MARY FARNUM (*Samuel Farnum[4], Samuel Farnum[3], Elizabeth Holt Farnum[2], Nicholas[1]*), b. at Andover, 13 Aug 1731 of Samuel and Mary (How) Farnum; d. at Boxford, 29 Jun 1819; m. 2 Jan 1754, JOSEPH WOOD, b. at Boxford, 29 Mar 1734 son of Daniel and Sarah (Peabody) Wood; Joseph d. at Boxford, 4 May 1801.

In his will written 12 December 1800, Joseph Wood bequeaths to beloved wife Mary the use and improvement of all the real and personal estate while she is a widow. The following children receive one dollar each: sons Joshua, Nathan, and Joseph Wood and daughter Sarah wife of Joseph Carlton. Daughters Judah Wood and Fanny the wife of George Underwood receive forty dollars each. Daughter Deborah widow of John Buckmaster receives thirty dollars. Son Daniel receives the real and personal estate after Mary is done with the improvement of same. Mary was named executrix.[1012]

On 8 June 1804, George Underwood and his wife Fanney, for consideration of eighty dollars, quitclaimed their interest in the estate to brother Joseph.[1013] Other quitclaims to Joseph were made by Joshua of Keene, New Hampshire, Joseph and Sarah Carlton, Daniel Wood of Plainfield, New York, and Mary Wood administratrix of the estate.[1014]

Joseph Wood and Mary Farnum were parents of nine children born at Boxford.

i JOSHUA WOOD, b. 3 Jan 1754; d. at Keene, NH, 26 Oct 1820; m. ESTHER ESTY, b. about 1763 daughter of Isaac and Hannah (Smith) Esty; Esther d. at Walpole, NH, 25 Mar 1858.

ii SARAH WOOD, b. 8 Mar 1757; d. at Boxford, 20 Mar 1840; m. 28 Dec 1780, JOSEPH CARLTON, b. at Boxford, 28 Jun 1755 son of Thomas and Jane (Stickney) Carlton; Joseph d. at Boxford, 2 Nov 1829.

iii JUDITH WOOD, b. 28 Jan 1759; d. at Boxford, 18 May 1854. Judith did not marry. In her will written 25 June 1853, she made bequests to the children of her late brother Joshua Wood, children of her late brother Daniel Wood, children of late brother Nathan, Deborah Wood daughter of late brother Joseph, to Joseph Carleton, to Catherine Allen wife of Joseph F. Allen, to Mary Foster wife of Dean Foster, to Sarah Long wife of William Long, and to Timothy Stacey of Groveland. The remainder of the estate is to be divided among the daughters of her late sisters; her sisters are Sarah Carleton, Deborah Buckmister, and Fanny Underwood. The value of the estate was $672.25 which included $500 of real estate.[1015]

iv JOSEPH WOOD, b. 17 Aug 1761; d. 30 Sep 1762.

[1010] Perley, *The History of Boxford*

[1011] *Essex County, MA: Probate File Papers, 1638-1881.*Online database. *AmericanAncestors.org.* New England Historic Genealogical Society, 2014. Case 691

[1012] *Essex County, MA: Probate File Papers, 1638-1881.*Online database. *AmericanAncestors.org.* New England Historic Genealogical Society, 2014. Case 30283

[1013] Massachusetts Land Records, Essex County, 175:4

[1014] Massachusetts Land Records, Essex County, 189:280,

[1015] *Essex County, MA: Probate File Papers, 1638-1881.*Online database. *AmericanAncestors.org.* New England Historic Genealogical Society, 2014. Case 57621

v DEBORAH WOOD, b. 2 Jul 1763; d. at Boxford, 1805 (probate) 1805; m. at Boxford, 25 Nov 1789, JOHN BLAKE BUCKMASTER, baptized at Gloucester, Jan 1768 son of Richard and Judith (Lufkin) Buckmaster; John d. 1800.

vi DANIEL WOOD, b. 29 Jun 1765; d. at Seneca, NY, after 1855; m. SILENCE SHELDON who has not been identified. In 1803, Daniel Wood of Plainfield, Otsego County, NY sold his interest in his father's estate in Boxford to his brother Joseph.[1016] There is evidence of three children of Silence and Daniel. The death record of one daughter gives mother's name as Silence Sheldon, and another daughter gives mother as Charlotte Sheldon. Daniel was a housewright.

vii NATHAN WOOD, b. 17 Dec 1767; d. before 1830 (when Susanna was head of household); likely m. at Salem, MA, 25 Aug 1791, SUSANNA RUSSELL, b. at Danvers, about 1770;[1017] Susanna d. at Boston, 24 Dec 1833.

viii JOSEPH WOOD, b. 27 May 1770; d. at Boxford, 28 Sep 1834; m. at Boxford, 6 Sep 1796, POLLY FOSTER whose parents are not identified. There is just one child known for Joseph and Polly, Deborah Wood who was born 1805 and died in 1898 without marrying.

ix FANNY WOOD, b. 1 Jan 1774; d. at Salem, MA, 8 Oct 1839; m. at Boxford, 27 Jul 1799, GEORGE UNDERWOOD, b. at Salem, about 1776 son of John and Sarah (Buteman) Underwood; George d. at Salem, 2 Dec 1846. George Underwood was a mariner.

370) MARY BEVERLY (*Hannah Farnum Beverly[4], Samuel Farnum[3], Elizabeth Holt Farnum[2], Nicholas[1]*), b. at Andover, 5 Feb 1728 daughter of David and Hannah (Farnum) Beverly; m. 1st at Andover, 6 Apr 1750, ASA TOWNE, b. at Boxford, 25 Aug 1729 son of Nathan and Phebe (Curtis) Towne; Asa d. at Andover, 9 Sep 1764.

Mary Beverly and Asa Towne were parents of six children born at Andover.

i SOLOMON TOWNE, b. 8 Oct 1750; d. 30 May 1752.

ii MOLLY TOWNE, b. 8 Feb 1752; d. at Andover, 21 Jan 1820. Molly did not marry.

iii SOLOMON TOWNE, b. 9 Dec 1753

iv HULDAH TOWNE, baptized 29 Jul 1759; d. at Andover, 31 May 1787; m. at Andover, 2 May 1781, LILBORN ANDREWS, b. at Boxford, 6 Aug 1760 son of Nathaniel and Sarah (Lindal) Andrews; Lilborn d. in VT, 1838. Lilborn married second Sarah Huse.

v ASA TOWNE, b. 17 Jul 1761; d. 22 Mar 1762.

vi ASA TOWNE, b. 18 Mar 1763

371) HANNAH BEVERLY (*Hannah Farnum Beverly[4], Samuel Farnum[3], Elizabeth Holt Farnum[2], Nicholas[1]*), b. at Andover, 11 Sep 1731 daughter of David and Hannah (Farnum) Beverly; m. at Andover, 15 Oct 1755, AARON TOWNE, b. at Andover, 25 Jul 1734 son of Nathan and Phebe (Curtis) Towne; Aaron d. at Andover, 26 Feb 1822, at the almshouse.

Hannah Beverly and Aaron Towne were parents of five children born at Andover.

i MOSES TOWNE, b. 3 Jul 1756; m. 1st at Andover, 27 Mar 1780, SUSANNAH FISH, b. at Andover, 2 Nov 1754 daughter of Benjamin and Mary (Johnson) Fish; Susannah d. about 1790. Moses m. 2nd at Andover, 28 Nov 1791, HANNAH HARRIS (widow of Thomas Piper), b. 13 Sep 1759 daughter of Lawrence and Lydia (Barron) Harris; Hannah d. at Lewiston, ME, 18 mar 1851.

ii HANNAH TOWNE, b. 6 Jan 1759; d. 9 May 1764.

iii AARON TOWNE, b. 19 May 1762; d. 17 Apr 1764.

iv HANNAH TOWNE, b. 21 Oct 1764; d. at Deering, NH, Mar 1850; m. at Andover, 27 Apr 1784, THOMAS WILSON, b. at Andover, 1 May 1762 son of William and Anna (Flood) Wilson; Thomas d. at Deering, after 1850.

v AARON TOWNE, b. 25 Aug 1769; d. at Greenfield, NH between 1840 and 1850; m. 24 May 1796, PATIENCE FRETO, b. at Danvers, about 1777 *likely* daughter of William and Elizabeth (Coos) Freto; Patience d. after 1850 when she was living in Greenfield.

372) DAVID BEVERLY (*Hannah Farnum Beverly[4], Samuel Farnum[3], Elizabeth Holt Farnum[2], Nicholas[1]*), b. at Andover, 2 Aug 1739 son of David and Hannah (Farnum) Beverly; m. at Andover, 7 Jul 1763, RUTH CLOUGH.

[1016] Massachusetts Land Records, Essex County, 175:155

[1017] This marriage is speculative for Nathan but seems the most likely of the options.

Little information was found for this family. David and Ruth were both living in Andover in 1787 when they sold a piece of land to Solomon Martin.[1018] There are records for five children born at Andover and marriages for two of the children.

i JEDEDIAH BEVERLY, b. 17 Oct 1765

ii DAVID BEVERLY, b. 3 Aug 1767

iii LYDIA BEVERLY, baptized at Andover, 1 Mar 1772

iv DANIEL BEVERLY, b. 21 Aug 1775; d. at Andover, 19 Dec 1823; m. at Andover, 20 Apr 1806, his first cousin, HANNAH BEVERLY (*John Beverly[5], Hannah Farnum Beverly[4], Samuel Farnum[3], Elizabeth Holt Farnum[2], Nicholas[1]*), b. at Andover, about 1784 daughter of John and Lydia (Hildreth) Beverly.

v ASA BEVERLY, b. 9 Oct 1776; d. at Ischua, NY, 29 Dec 1852; m. about 1801, SARAH CURTIS, b. 23 Mar 1784 daughter of Solomon and Sarah (Landers) Curtis; Sarah d. at Alma, NY, 19 Feb 1868.

373) JOHN BEVERLY (*Hannah Farnum Beverly[4], Samuel Farnum[3], Elizabeth Holt Farnum[2], Nicholas[1]*), b. at Andover, 19 Apr 1744 son of David and Hannah (Farnum) Beverly; d. at Andover, 12 Dec 1811; m. at Andover, 13 Nov 1777, LYDIA HILDRETH, b. 1754 perhaps the daughter of Joseph and Lydia (Fletcher) Hildreth; Lydia d. at Andover, 5 Apr 1821.

There are likely five children of John Beverly and Lydia Hildreth born at Andover.

i LYDIA BEVERLY, b. about 1782;[1019] d. at Andover, Jan 1840; m. at Andover, 23 May 1805, ENOS DODGE, b. at Gloucester, MA, 16 Aug 1781 son of Enos and Tammy (Sawyer) Dodge; Enos d. at Andover, 17 Jul 1838.

ii HANNAH BEVERLY, b. about 1784; m. at Andover, 20 Apr 1806, her first cousin, DANIEL BEVERLY (*David Beverly[5], Hannah Farnum Beverly[4], Samuel Farnum[3], Elizabeth Holt Farnum[2], Nicholas[1]*), b. at Andover, 21 Aug 1775 son of David and Ruth (Clough) Beverly; Daniel d. at Andover, 19 Dec 1823. Hannah and Daniel were parents of at least seven children including two daughters, one who died in early childhood, named Lydia Hildreth Beverly.

iii JOHN BEVERLY,[1020] b. about 1786; d. at Andover, 2 Aug 1852; m. at Andover, 3 Apr 1822, SALLY BACON, b. about 1782; Sally d. at Andover, 20 Aug 1863. The name of Sally's mother is given as Mary Towne on the cemetery record, but her identity was otherwise not found. John and Sally had one daughter Mary Ann who died of scarlet fever at age 13. In his will, John left his entire estate to his wife Sally.

iv JOEL BEVERLY, b. 5 Mar 1794; d. at North Andover, 1 Nov 1869; m. at Andover, 6 Sep 1819, his first cousin once removed, HANNAH TOWNE (*Aaron Towne[6], Hannah Beverly Towne[5], Hannah Farnum Beverly[4], Samuel Farnum[3], Elizabeth Holt Farnum[2], Nicholas[1]*), b. about 1799 daughter of Aaron and Patience (Freto) Towne; Hannah d. at North Andover, 8 Apr 1877.

v PHEBE BEVERLY, b. 25 Aug 1798; d. at North Andover, 12 Oct 1870; m. at Andover, 25 Jul 1819, JAMES MEEDER, b. at Madbury, NH, about 1798 son of Hannah Meeder;[1021] James d. at North Andover, 19 Nov 1869.

374) SAMUEL BEVERLY (*Hannah Farnum Beverly[4], Samuel Farnum[3], Elizabeth Holt Farnum[2], Nicholas[1]*), b. at Andover, 8 Aug 1748 son of David and Hannah (Farnum) Beverly; d. after 1810 when he was living in Boscawen; m. at Salisbury, MA, 8 Apr 1775, RUTH CONNOR, b. at Salisbury, 1 Aug 1755 daughter of Gideon and Dorothy (Bracy) Connor.

Samuel and Ruth settled in Boscawen where, 1791, Samuel signed a petition requesting that the west part of Boscawen be incorporated as the town of Bristol.[1022] Samuel was living in Boscawen in 1810, but further records were not located for him. There are records for three children born at Boscawen.

i SAMUEL BEVERLY, b. 9 Dec 1786; d. at Boscawen, 10 Jul 1811.

ii MOSES G. BEVERLY, b. 21 Sep 1788; d. after Nov 1849 when he wrote his will at Union, MI; m. at Boscawen, 23 Oct 1814, MARY BARNARD. In his 1849 will, Moses leaves to his son-in-law William Daly one-third of a lot of land in Boscawen, NH that had been set off to the widow Ruth Beverly. This is a lot that was purchased by Samuel Beverly in 1791. William Daly also receives all the shoemaking tools.

iii BETSEY BEVERLY, b. 3 Mar 1791; d. at Webster, NH, 29 Mar 1861; m. BENJAMIN JACKMAN, b. at Boscawen, 14 Aug 1789 son of Joshua and Sarah (Carter) Jackman; Benjamin d. at Webster, 12 Aug 1878.

[1018] Massachusetts Land Records, 1620-1986, Essex County, 128:118

[1019] Lydia is a likely, but not confirmed, child in this family.

[1020] The names of John's parents are given as John and Lydia on his death record.

[1021] On James's death record, his place of birth is given as Madbury, NH and mother as Hannah Meeder and name of father as unknown.

[1022] Coffin, The History of Boscawen, p 138

375) ANNE LOVEJOY (*William Lovejoy[4], Mary Farnum Lovejoy[3], Elizabeth Holt Farnum[2], Nicholas[1]*), b. at Andover, 4 Nov 1711 daughter of William and Sarah (Frye) Lovejoy; d. at Andover, 5 Sep 1770; m. at Andover, 20 Jun 1728, ZEBADIAH ABBOT, b. at Andover, 6 Apr 1695 son of Nehemiah and Abigail (Lovejoy) Abbot; Zebadiah Abbot d. at Andover, 9 Sep 1767.

Anne and Zebadiah resided in Andover where Zebadiah performed civic tasks such as field driver, tithingman, and highway surveyor.[1023]

The estate of Zebadiah Abbot entered probate 5 October 1767. In his will written 21 April 1767, there are bequests to his beloved wife Anne, son Nehemiah, son Zebadiah, daughter Sarah Ballard, daughter Chloe Abbot, grandson Isaac Mooar, grandson Abraham Mooar.[1024] Daughter Chloe Abbot married Jeremiah Abbot of Wilton. The Mooar grandchildren were the children of his daughter Lydia.

Anne Lovejoy and Zebadiah Abbott were parents of seven children born at Andover.

i ANNE ABBOTT, b. 11 Dec 1729; d. 14 Apr 1738.

ii NEHEMIAH ABBOTT, b. at Andover, 24 Aug 1731; d. at Andover, 13 Oct 1808; m. 1st 11 Mar 1756, HANNAH BALLARD, b. at Andover, 8 Jun 1736 daughter of Timothy and Hannah (Chandler) Ballard; Hannah d. 27 Sep 1778. Nehemiah m. 2nd at Andover, 18 Jan 1780, LYDIA CLARK, b. at Andover, 16 Aug 1744 daughter of Dr. Parker and Lydia (Phillips) Clark; Lydia d. at Andover, 13 Feb 1814.

iii SARAH ABBOTT, b. at Andover, 3 Aug 1733; d. at Andover, 2 Aug 1809; m. at Andover, 21 Jan 1755, TIMOTHY BALLARD, b. at Andover, 1 Mar 1729/30 son of Timothy and Hannah (Chandler) Ballard; Timothy d. at Andover, 12 Jul 1768.

iv LYDIA ABBOTT, b. at Andover, 23 Jul 1735; d. at Andover, 20 Sep 1763; m. at Andover, 16 Mar 1758, ABRAHAM MOOAR, b. at Andover, 17 Jun 1728 son of Daniel and Martha (Osgood) Mooar; Abraham d. at Andover, 10 Oct 1780. Abraham Mooar married second Sarah Stevens and married third Martha Allen.

v CLOE ABBOTT, b. at Andover, 5 Nov 1737; d. at Wilton, 21 Aug 1809; m. at Andover, 16 Sep 1766, JEREMIAH ABBOTT, b. at Andover, 14 May 1743 son of John and Phebe (Fiske) Abbott; Jeremiah d. at Wilton, 2 Nov 1825.

vi ZEBADIAH ABBOTT, b. at Andover, 27 Sep 1739; d. at Andover, 24 Nov 1793; m. at Andover, 1 Oct 1765, REBECCA BALLARD, b. at Andover, 15 May 1744 daughter of Hezekiah and Lydia (Chandler) Ballard; Rebecca d. 15 Sep 1821.

vii ANNE ABBOTT, b. 27 Jul 1752; d. 8 Oct 1764.

376) PHEBE LOVEJOY (*William Lovejoy[4], Mary Farnum Lovejoy[3], Elizabeth Holt Farnum[2], Nicholas[1]*), b. at Andover, 20 Jan 1715 daughter of William and Sarah (Frye) Lovejoy; d. at Andover, 17 Dec 1751; m. at Andover, 29 Nov 1739, ISAAC ABBOT, b. at Andover, 4 Apr 1699 son of George and Dorcas (Graves) Abbott; Isaac d. at Andover, 9 Aug 1784. Isaac married second Lydia Stimson widow of Robert Calley.

Isaac Abbot attended Harvard graduating in 1723. He was deacon of South Church of Andover for 44 years.[1025] Isaac Abbot and Phebe Lovejoy had six children all born at Andover.

In his will, Isaac Abbott made bequests to the following persons: Lydia my dearly beloved wife, beloved son Isaac, beloved daughter Phebe wife of Capt. Henry Abbot, and beloved daughter Sarah wife of Timothy Abbott. Isaac is the executor of the estate.[1026]

i Son ABBOTT, b. 21 Jul 1741; d. 21 Jul 1741.

ii WILLIAM ABBOTT, b. 21 Jul 1741; d. 29 Dec 1768.

iii ISAAC ABBOTT, b. 3 Feb 1745; d. 21 May 1836; m. 22 Apr 1766, his second cousin, once removed, PHEBE CHANDLER (*Priscilla Holt Chandler[4], Timothy[3], James[2], Nicholas[1]*), b. 2 Jun 1742 daughter of Nathan and Priscilla (Holt) Chandler; Phebe d. 1 Jul 1800. Isaac Abbott and Phebe Chandler are Family 1010.

iv PHEBE ABBOTT, b. 14 Nov 1746; d. 29 Jun 1833; m. 21 Mar 1765 her first cousin, HENRY ABBOTT, b. 31 Dec 1724 son of Henry and Mary (Platts) Abbott; Henry d. 21 Feb 1805.

v SON ABBOTT; b. 12 Nov 1747; d. 14 Nov 1747.

vi SARAH ABBOTT, b. 2 Jan 1749/50; d. 2 Apr 1835; m. 2 Jan 1770, her second cousin once removed, TIMOTHY ABBOTT, b. 2 Jun 1745 son of Asa and Elizabeth (Abbott) Abbott; Timothy d. 22 Mar 1826.

1023 Abbott, *Descendants of George Abbott of Rowley*, p 153

1024 *Essex County, MA: Probate File Papers, 1638-1881.*Online database. *AmericanAncestors.org.* New England Historic Genealogical Society, 2014. Case 157

1025 Chandler, *The Descendants of William and Annis Chandler*, p. 7

1026 *Essex County, MA: Probate File Papers, 1638-1881. Probate of Isaac Abbot, 5 Oct 1784, Case number 58.*

377) HANNAH LOVEJOY (*Samuel Lovejoy[4], Mary Farnum Lovejoy[3], Elizabeth Holt Farnum[2], Nicholas[1]*), b. at Andover, 1 Mar 1717/8 daughter of Samuel and Hannah (Stevens) Lovejoy; d. at Andover, 28 Mar 1776; m. at Andover, 27 Dec 1752, as his second wife, HEZEKIAH STILES, baptized at Boxford, 1 May 1711 son of Ebenezer and Dorothy (Dalton) Stiles. Hezekiah was first married to Hannah Barnard.

Hezekiah was born in Boxford and was one of the original thirty members of the church at Middleton[1027] before settling in Andover after his marriage.

On 6 October 1771 (recorded 1783), Hezekiah sold to his son Stephen (son from his first marriage) the westerly part of his homestead in Andover for payment of £15. On 12 November 1782 (recorded 4 March 1783), Hezekiah conveyed to son Hezekiah, Jr. for the payment of £100 all his lands and buildings in Andover. On 1 November 1783, Hezekiah Stiles, Jr. and his wife Phebe conveyed this property including lands and buildings to Benjamin Ames for payment of £150.[1028]

There are records for four children of Hannah Lovejoy and Hezekiah Stiles born at Andover, but a marriage record located for just one of the children. Hezekiah had three children with his first wife Hannah Barnard.

i HANNAH STILES, b. 9 Nov 1753

ii DOROTHY STILES, b. 14 Jan 1755

iii MEHITABLE STILES, b. 18 Feb 1757

iv HEZEKIAH STILES, b. 5 Aug 1759; d. at Rindge, NH, 1791; m. 1782, PHEBE AUSTIN, b. at Lunenburg, Apr 1758 daughter of Daniel and Phebe (Lovejoy) Austin.[1029]

378) DEBORAH LOVEJOY (*Samuel Lovejoy[4], Mary Farnum Lovejoy[3], Elizabeth Holt Farnum[2], Nicholas[1]*), b. at Andover, 17 Feb 1718/9 daughter of Samuel and Hannah (Stevens) Lovejoy; d. at Hollis, NH; m. at Andover, 16 Dec 1740, JOHN PHELPS, b. at Andover, 12 Mar 1718 son of John and Sarah (Andrews) Phelps.

Deborah Lovejoy and John Phelps were parents of seven children. The births of the younger children are recorded at Dunstable, New Hampshire, although the family lived on the west end of Dunstable which ultimately became part of Hollis. John Phelps was one of the signers of a 1756 petition requesting that their sector become part of Hollis.[1030]

i DEBORAH PHELPS, b. at Andover, 15 Aug 1742; m. at Hollis, ELNATHAN BLOOD, b. likely at Hollis, 4 Dec 1744 son of Elnathan and Elizabeth (Boynton) Blood. Elnathan and Deborah had five children born in Merrimack, NH.

ii JOHN C. PHELPS, b. 20 Apr 1744; m. at Hollis,[1031] 24 Dec 1772, MARY LAKIN, b. at Groton, 31 May 1752 son of Simeon and Mary (-) Lakin

iii SARAH PHELPS, baptized at Andover, 27 Jul 1746; m. at Hollis, 19 Nov 1767, JOSEPH PIERCE.

iv NATHAN PHELPS, b. at Dunstable, 1 Sep 1749; d. at Hollis, 19 Nov 1812; m. MARY FLETCHER, b. at Chelmsford, MA, 15 Oct 1760 daughter of William and Mary (Blodgett) Fletcher; Mary d. at Hollis, 21 Apr 1822.

v HENRY PHELPS, b. at Dunstable, 8 Apr 1751; d. at Groton, NH, 7 Dec 1840; m. 1st about 1776, HANNAH NEVINS, b. about 1754 daughter of Thomas and Bridget (Snow) Nevins; Hannah d. at Groton, 11 Jan 1784. Henry m. 2nd at Plymouth, NH, 24 Jun 1784, HANNAH BLODGETT, b. 1764 daughter of James and Sarah (Snow) Blodgett;[1032] Hannah d. at Groton, 10 Oct 1843.

vi SAMUEL PHELPS, b. at Dunstable, 10 Dec 1756; d. at Hebron, NH, 7 Jan 1839; m. 6 Jun 1781, MARGARET NEVINS, b. at Hollis, 3 Feb 1760, daughter of David and Lois (Patch) Nevins

vii ABIGAIL PHELPS, b. 1757; d. at Hollis, 14 Dec 1819; m. at Hollis, 12 Apr 1781, CALEB FARLEY, b. 3 Apr 1759 son of Caleb and Elizabeth (Farley) Farley; Caleb d. at Hollis, 17 Jul 1810.

379) ISAAC LOVEJOY (*Samuel Lovejoy[4], Mary Farnum Lovejoy[3], Elizabeth Holt Farnum[2], Nicholas[1]*), b. at Andover, 9 Feb 1723 son of Samuel and Hannah (Stevens) Lovejoy; d. at Andover, 3 Dec 1799; m. at Billerica, 28 Feb 1750, DEBORAH SHELDON, b at Billerica, 23 Oct 1723 daughter of Samuel and Sarah/Mary[1033] (Hutchinson) Sheldon; Deborah d. at Andover, 25 May 1813.

1027 Guild, *The Stiles Family in America*, p 76

1028 Massachusetts Land Records, Essex County, 139:131; 153:95-96

1029 Cunningham's History of Lunenburg, p 762

1030 Worcester, *The History of the Town of Hollis*, p 77

1031 Marriage is also recorded at Groton, MA.

1032 Stearns, *History of Plymouth, New Hampshire, volume 2*, p 53

1033 Records are inconsistent in reporting the first name of Deborah's mother.

Isaac and Deborah resided in Andover. During the Revolution, Isaac served in the company of Capt. Joseph Butler enlisting 28 May 1775 serving a term of two months, eight days.[1034]

In his will written 11 April 1799 (probate 5 May 1800), Isaac Lovejoy bequeathed to beloved wife Deborah two-thirds of the lands that he holds during her natural life and all of the dwelling house, two cows and three sheep to be her own, and the use and improvement of the household furniture during her life. Deborah also has use of the clock. She is to be supported in sickness and health during her life. Son Isaac is also directed to provide support for the elder Isaac's brother James. Sons Samuel and William receive one dollar as they have received their portions. Daughter Deborah wife of Daniel Ordway receives one dollar; daughter Abigail wife of Moses Morse receives two dollars; daughter Sarah wife of Daniel Hibbard receives three dollars; daughter Percis Lovejoy receives the loom, tackling, cloth, bed and bedding, one hundred dollars, and will receive the clock after he mother's decease; and daughter Lydia wife of Palphrey Downing receives three dollars. Percis is to have liberty to live in the house during her natural life. Beloved son Isaac receives the lands, buildings, and remainder of the estate and is named executor.[1035]

Isaac Lovejoy and Deborah Sheldon were parents of nine children born at Andover.

i DEBORAH LOVEJOY, b. 1 Apr 1752; d. at Loudon, NH, 12 Apr 1801; m. at Billerica, 28 Nov 1771, DANIEL ORDWAY, b. at Methuen, 12 Oct 1745 son of James and Meribah (Morse) Ordway; Daniel d. at Loudon, 1 Mar 1834. Daniel married second Ruth Moulton.

ii SAMUEL LOVEJOY, b. 11 Sep 1753; d. at Adams, IN, 21 Sep 1822; m. Nov 1788, ESTHER MORSE, b. at Methuen, 8 Dec 1766 daughter of William and Phebe (Bodwell) Morse; Esther d. after 1850 when she was living in Adams, IN.

iii SARAH LOVEJOY, b. 18 Apr 1755; m. at Methuen, 4 Oct 1781, as his second wife, DANIEL HIBBARD, b. at Methuen, 15 Sep 1748 son of Ebenezer and Abigail (Whittier) Hibbard; Daniel d. at Methuen, 10 Oct 1800. Daniel was first married to Deborah Ingalls daughter of James and Mary (Frye) Ingalls.

iv ABIGAIL LOVEJOY, b. at Andover, 18 Apr 1755; m. at Andover, 19 Nov 1778, MOSES MORSE, b. at Methuen, 31 May 1749 son of Moses and Mary (Clark) Morse. Abigail and Moses resided in Loudon where they had a family of ten children. Abigail and Moses were living in Loudon in 1820.

v ISAAC LOVEJOY, b. 15 Mar 1757; d. at Andover, 8 Dec 1832; m. 12 Nov 1778, MARY "MOLLY" MORSE, b. at Methuen, 14 Feb 1757 daughter of William and Phebe (Bodwell) Morse; Mary d. at Andover, 17 Apr 1835.

vi WILLIAM LOVEJOY, b. 6 Jul 1759; m. at Andover, 15 Sep 1785, MARY DANE, b. at Andover, 14 Aug 1761 daughter of William and Mary (Osgood) Dane. There are records of baptisms of two children of William and Mary baptized at Andover.

vii PERSIS LOVEJOY, b. 15 Jun 1761; living and unmarried in 1799 when her father wrote his will.

viii LEMUEL LOVEJOY, b. 13 Apr 1763; d. 26 Oct 1763.

ix LYDIA LOVEJOY, b. 19 Nov 1764; d. of consumption at Andover, 31 Jan 1805; m. at Andover, 26 Apr 1785, PALFREY DOWNING, baptized at Andover, 12 Apr 1761 son of Richard and Temperance (Derby) Downing; Palfrey d. at Andover, 28 Sep 1835. Palfrey married second Abigail Barnard on 3 Dec 1805.

380) MARY LOVEJOY (*Samuel Lovejoy[4], Mary Farnum Lovejoy[3], Elizabeth Holt Farnum[2], Nicholas[1]*), b. at Andover, 23 Jul 1730 daughter of Samuel and Hannah (Stevens) Lovejoy; d. at Jaffrey, NH, 25 Oct 1802; m. at Andover, 25 Mar 1752, ISAAC BAILEY, b. at Andover, 8 Aug 1729 son of Josiah and Elizabeth (Stevens) Bailey; Isaac d. at Jaffrey, NH, 7 Jun 1812. After Mary's death, Isaac married Susannah Stevens.

Mary Lovejoy and Isaac Bailey were parents of nine children born at Lunenburg. They were discharged from the church in Lunenburg to the church in Jaffrey on 25 June 1780.[1036] They resided lot 13, range 10 in Jaffrey, and Isaac and his wife were founding member of the Church of Christ in Jaffrey when it was formed 18 May 1789.[1037]

i MARY "POLLY" BAILEY, b. 14 Feb 1753; d. at Canaan, ME; m. at Jaffrey, 12 Dec 1782, her fourth cousin, JONATHAN HOLT (*Jonathan[4], Humphrey[3], Henry[2], Nicholas[1]*), b. a Fitchburg, MA, 16 May 1756 son of Jonathan and Susanna (Holt) Holt; Jonathan d. at Canaan, 12 Dec 1832. Mary Bailey and Jonathan Holt are Family 793.

ii ISAAC BAILEY, b. 27 Feb 1757; d. at Jaffrey, 20 Sep 1826; m. 1st 1789, BETSEY WHEELOCK, b. about 1769; Betsey d. at Jaffrey, 30 Jun 1801. Isaac m. 2nd HANNAH STACEY, b. 1764; Hannah d. at Jaffrey, 3 Sep 1838.

1034 Massachusetts Soldiers and Sailors in the Revolution, volume 9, p 992

1035 *Essex County, MA: Probate File Papers, 1638-1881.*Online database. *AmericanAncestors.org.* New England Historic Genealogical Society, 2014. Case 17063

1036 Cunningham, *History of the Town of Lunenburg*, A-D, p 24

1037 Cutter, *History of the Town of Jaffrey*, p 225, p 73

iii JOHN BAILEY, b. 7 Mar 1760; m. at Jaffrey, 8 Nov 1797, REBECCA WHEELOCK.

iv BETSY BAILEY, b. 2 Jun 1762; m. at Jaffrey, Sep 1792, ABEL HODGMAN, b. at Concord, MA, 2 Aug 1759;[1038] Abel d. at Brookline, NH, after 1840.

v HANNAH BAILEY, b. 30 Jun 1764; d. at Bingham, ME, 21 Apr 1846; m. at Jaffrey, Sep 1792, CALVIN RUSSELL, b. at Lexington, MA, 12 Jan 1762 son of Ephraim and Miriam (Wheeler) Russell; Calvin d. (buried) at Bingham, ME, 1 May 1852.

vi SUSANNAH BAILEY, baptized 17 Apr 1768; d. 5 May 1769.

vii JOTHAM BAILEY, baptized 4 Feb 1770; d. 13 Jul 1770.

viii SAMUEL BAILEY, b. 12 Oct 1771; he may be the child (first name not given in the transcription) of Isaac who died at Lunenburg, 28 Mar 1776, or perhaps his younger sister Ruth died in 1776. There is no further record of him.

ix RUTH BAILEY, b. 23 Aug 1775; there is no further record of her.

381) MARY JOHNSON (*Lydia Lovejoy Johnson*[4], *Mary Farnum Lovejoy*[3], *Elizabeth Holt Farnum*[2], *Nicholas*[1]), b. at Andover, 26 Jun 1721 daughter of Caleb and Lydia (Lovejoy) Johnson; m. at Windham, 10 Oct 1739, DAVID THOMAS.

There are records of five children of Mary Johnson and David Thomas, but no further information was found for this family.

i MARY THOMAS, b. at Windham, 10 Apr 1740; d. 20 May 1741.

ii JONATHAN THOMAS, b. at Windham, 10 Sep 1742

iii HANNAH THOMAS, b. at Windham, 1 Jul 1744

iv MARY THOMAS, b. at Windham, 20 Aug 1746

v LYDIA THOMAS, b. at Willington, 20 May 1756

382) MEHITABLE JOHNSON (*Lydia Lovejoy Johnson*[4], *Mary Farnum Lovejoy*[3], *Elizabeth Holt Farnum*[2], *Nicholas*[1]), b. at Andover, 27 Jan 1725/6 daughter of Caleb and Lydia (Lovejoy) Johnson; m. 29 Apr 1747, JOSEPH SPARKS; Joseph d. at Fort La Presentation, 10 Sep 1760 (probate 24 Nov 1760).

Joseph and Mehitable resided in Tolland. Before leaving on a military campaign during the French and Indian War, Joseph deeded the bulk of his estate to his father Henry Sparks and his brother Peter Sparks. Joseph was killed in northern New York.[1039]

Joseph did not leave a will and Mehitable was named administratrix of the estate on 24 November 1760. The estate was valued at £20.2.9 and was declared insolvent on 6 July 1761.[1040]

Mehitable Johnson and Joseph Sparks were parents of eight children born at Tolland, the youngest child born after Joseph's death.

i LEMUEL SPARKS, b. 11 Sep 1747; m. 1st about 1769, JANE who has not been identified; Jane d. about 1771. Lemuel m. 2nd at Lebanon, CT, 9 Jul 1772, BATHSHEBA CLARK, b. at Lebanon, b. 26 Jun 1742 daughter of Phineas and Priscilla (Case) Clark.

ii MELVEN PERLYE SPARKS, b. 15 Feb 1749/50

iii ELIZABETH SPARKS, b. 2 Nov 1751; d. at Mansfield, CT, 1 Jun 1816; m. about 1780, PHILIP PERKINS, b. 9 Jul 1752 son of William and Elizabeth (Buck) Perkins; Philip d. at Mansfield, 19 Sep 1825.

iv URIAH SPARKS, b. 17 Apr 1752

v ISAIAH SPARKS, b. 3 Nov 1754; d. at Ashford, 7 Dec 1794; m. at Ashford, 9 Dec 1779, FELICITY DAWSET, b. at Ashford, 20 Sep 1756 daughter of Lawrence and Lucy (-) Dawset.

vi JEREMIAH SPARKS, b. Oct 1757

vii STEPHEN SPARKS, b. 24 Apr 1759; d. at Leicester, VT, 25 Jun 1827; m. 1 Jan 1783, his third cousin once removed, SARAH HOLT (*Nehemiah*[4], *George*[3], *Henry*[2], *Nicholas*[1]), b. at Windham, CT, 12 Oct 1758 daughter of Nehemiah and Anna (Farnum) Holt; Sarah d. at Leicester, 26 Sep 1843. Stephen Sparks and Sarah Holt are Family 442.

[1038] This is the date and place of birth given by Abel in his Revolutionary War pension application file.

[1039] Sparks Family Association, *The Sparks Quarterly*, volume 35, number 137b, March 1987, p 3024

[1040] *Connecticut State Library (Hartford, Connecticut)*; Probate Place: *Hartford, Connecticut, Estate of Joseph Sparks, Case 2008*

viii JOSEPH SPARKS, b. 3 Feb 1761; d. at Willington, 26 Jan 1826; m. at Willington, 24 Dec 1789, ELEANOR ORCUTT, b. at Stafford, 19 Oct 1767 daughter of Caleb and Chloe (Parker) Orcutt; Eleanor d. at Willington, 2 May 1843.

383) SARAH JOHNSON (*Lydia Lovejoy Johnson*[4], *Mary Farnum Lovejoy*[3], *Elizabeth Holt Farnum*[2], *Nicholas*[1]), b. at Windham, 29 Jul 1729 daughter of Caleb and Lydia (Lovejoy) Johnson; d. at Hartford, VT, 18 Mar 1815; m. 22 Jan 1746, NATHANIEL BUGBEE, b. at Ashford, 5 Apr 1721 son of Josiah and Sarah (Hubbard) Bugbee; Nathaniel d. at Hartford, 23 Jul 1808.

Sarah and Nathaniel were parents of eleven children born in Ashford and Enfield. About 1800, they relocated to Hartford, Vermont likely accompanying their sons Benjamin and Jonathan who settled there.[1041]

i NATHANIEL BUGBEE, b. at Ashford, 9 Mar 1747; d. 16 Sep 1749.

ii EUNICE BUGBEE, b. at Ashford, 13 Dec 1748; d. at Enfield, CT, 13 Nov 1824; m. ELI PEASE, b. at Enfield, 12 Nov 1749 son of Samuel and Zerviah (Chapin) Pease; Eli d. at Enfield, 22 Nov 1830.

iii PETER BUGBEE, b. at Ashford, 20 Jan 1750

iv HANNAH BUGBEE, b. at Ashford, 8 Sep 1751

v NATHANIEL BUGBEE, b. at Enfield, 22 Apr 1755; d. at White River Junction, VT, 1844; m. LOIS who has not been identified; Lois was b. about 1757 and d. at White River Junction, 9 Aug 1827.

vi SARAH BUGBEE, b. at Enfield, 2 Sep 1757; d. at Enfield, 30 Nov 1819; m. NAHUM KING, b. at Enfield, 9 Jan 1757 son of Benjamin and Sarah (Pease) King;[1042] Nahum d. at Enfield, 5 Mar 1812.

vii BENJAMIN BUGBEE, b. at Enfield, 8 Apr 1760; d. (buried) at White River Junction, 4 Apr 1820; m. at Enfield, 1 Jan 1784, MEHITABLE PEASE, b. at Enfield, 31 Oct 1760 daughter of Samuel and Zerviah (Chapin) Pease;[1043] Mehitable d. at Hartland, 14 May 1844.

viii JONATHAN BUGBEE, b. 1 Jun 1765; d. at Hartford, VT, 22 Apr 1849; m. 1st 1784, ESTHER COLTON, b. 9 Sep 1765 daughter of Jacob and Rachel (Marshfield) Colton; Esther d. at Hartford, 4 Mar 1793. Jonathan m. 2nd about 1794, Esther's sister ELIZABETH COLTON, b. 8 Jan 1768; Elizabeth d. at Hartford, 14 Nov 1835. Jonathan m. 3rd 10 Mar 1836, the half-sister of Esther and Elizabeth, MABEL GAINES, b. at Enfield, 17 May 1773 daughter of James and Rachel (Marshfield) Gaines; Mabel d. at Hartford, 16 Apr 1850.

ix MARY BUGBEE, b. at Enfield, 1 Nov 1767

x EBENEZER BUGBEE, b. at Enfield, 20 Feb 1770; d. at Deerfield, MA, 28 Oct 1810; m. FAITH BALL, b. 15 Feb 1772 daughter of John and Lydia (Ward) Ball; Faith d. at Deerfield, 20 May 1812.

xi PELETIAH BUGBEE, b. at Enfield, 17 Feb 1775; d. at Chelsea, VT, 2 May 1827; m. SALLY COOK, b. about 1781; Sally d. at Chelsea, 3 Apr 1846.

384) ALICE JOHNSON (*Lydia Lovejoy Johnson*[4], *Mary Farnum Lovejoy*[3], *Elizabeth Holt Farnum*[2], *Nicholas*[1]), b. at Windham, 27 Dec 1730 daughter of Caleb and Lydia (Lovejoy) Johnson; m. at Willington, 16 Apr 1752, JONATHAN ABBE, b. 1725 son of Jonathan and Mary (Johnson) Abbe.

Alice Johnson and Jonathan Abbe were parents of nine children.

i JONATHAN ABBE, b. at Willington, 26 Feb 1753; d. at Shokan, NY, 5 Oct 1807; m. 1st at Willington, 1 Nov 1774, MARY WESTON who d. at Willington, 1775. Jonathan m. 2nd at Willington, 6 May 1778, LUCY KNOX (widow of David Robbins), b. at Ashford, 8 Apr 1752 daughter of Samuel and Sarah (Hunt) Knox; Lucy d. at Shokan, 21 Jan 1828.

ii ISAAC ABBE, b. at Willington, 18 Jun 1754; m. at Ashford, 15 Sep 1776, JEMIMA KNOWLTON, b. at Ashford, 22 Apr 1759 daughter of Thomas and Bridget (Bosworth) Knowlton.

iii ALICE ABBE, b. at Willington, 20 Jun 1756

iv ANNE ABBE, b. at Willington, 26 Apr 1758; d. 30 Aug 1760.

1041 Tucker, *History of Hartford, Vermont*, p 411

1042 King, *The King Family of Suffield, Connecticut*, p 117

1043 This marriage can be established through the 1792 will of Samuel Pease which names daughter Mehitable Bugbee and the Revolutionary War pension application file of Benjamin Bugbee of Hartford, Vermont and later his widow Mehitable. Among statements in the pension file is one by Edward Pease stating he attended the wedding of Mehitable and Benjamin in Enfield.

v ANNE ABBE, b. at Willington, 11 Sep 1761

vi LYDIA ABBE, b. at Willington, 17 Dec 1762

vii PHEBE ABBE, b. at Ashford, 9 Apr 1765

viii MARY ABBE, b. at Ashford, 25 May 1767

ix STEPHEN ABBE, b. at Ashford, 2 Oct 1771; d. at Pittsfield, NY, 20 Jan 1832 (probate 1 Mar 1832); m. BETSEY who has not been identified, b. about 1772; Betsey d. at Pittsfield, 7 Oct 1848.[1044] Stephen and Betsey wither did not have children or did not have children who lived to adulthood as each of their wills leaves estates to other relatives.

385) WILLIAM JOHNSON (*Lydia Lovejoy Johnson[4], Mary Farnum Lovejoy[3], Elizabeth Holt Farnum[2], Nicholas[1]*), b. at Windham, 26 Aug 1732 son of Caleb and Lydia (Lovejoy) Johnson; d. at Willington, 6 Jun 1764; m. at Willington, 3 Jan 1754, EUNICE FISKE, b. at Willington, 29 Mar 1737 daughter of William and Mary (Blancher) Fiske.

The inventory of the estate of William Johnson was made 8 August 1764. The dower was set off to widow Eunice. Debts consumed the rest of the estate which was insolvent.[1045]

William and Eunice were parents of six children born at Willington, the youngest child born just three days before William's death. It is not known what became of this family after William's death.

i LYDIA JOHNSON, b. 14 Feb 1755

ii SARAH JOHNSON, b. 19 Jul 1757

iii BENJAMIN JOHNSON, b. 12 Dec 1758; d. 16 Mar 1759.

iv ABIGAIL JOHNSON, b. 21 May 1760

v EUNICE JOHNSON, b. 8 May 1762

vi MEHITABLE JOHNSON, b. 3 Jun 1764

386) ISAAC JOHNSON, b. at Windham, 5 Dec 1735 son of Caleb and Lydia (Lovejoy) Johnson; d. at Hadley, MA, 14 Sep 1808; m. at Willington, 15 Jul 1756, ELIZABETH BEAL, b. at Willington, 16 Jun 1734 daughter of William and Rachel (Heath) Beal; Elizabeth d. at Hadley, 5 Apr 1803.

Isaac and Elizabeth had their children in Willington and after their children reached adulthood, the family relocated to Hadley.

Isaac Johnson and Elizabeth Beal were parents of ten children born at Willington.

i CALEB JOHNSON, b. 6 Mar 1757; d. at Williamsburg, MA, 17 Jan 1823; m. about 1779, MARY who has not been identified; Mary was living in 1823.

ii ISAAC JOHNSON, b. 14 Apr 1758; d. at Willington, 3 Mar 1777.

iii AMOS JOHNSON, b. 3 Oct 1760; d. at Willington, 15 Jul 1782.

iv STEPHEN JOHNSON, b. 5 Aug 1762; d. at Hadley, MA, 1 Feb 1845; m. 26 Mar 1791, SARAH LYMAN, b. at Hadley, 12 Sep 1770 daughter of Israel and Rachel (Beals) Lyman; Sarah d. at Hadley, 19 Sep 1835.

v ELIZABETH JOHNSON, b. 26 May 1764; d. at Willington, 18 May 1783.

vi CALVIN JOHNSON, b. about 1768 and baptized at Willington, Nov 1777; d. at Columbia, NY, 7 Feb 1841; m. at Northampton, MA, 15 Jan 1795, ASENATH THAYER, b. 1772; Asenath d. at Columbia, 27 Jan 1843.

vii LUTHER JOHNSON, b. about 1770 and baptized at Willington, Nov 1777; d. at Columbia, NY, 25 Oct 1840; m. at Williamsburg, MA, 14 Jan 1796, DOLLY LUDDEN, b. at Williamsburg, 31 Aug 1774 daughter of Seth and Parnel (Smith) Ludden; Dolly d. 1819.

viii ELIJAH JOHNSON, b. 24 Dec 1771; d. at Willington, 10 Oct 1798; m. at Willington, 9 Feb 1792, CHLOE JENNINGS.

ix LYDIA JOHNSON, b. 22 Jun 1774; d. at Kingsville, OH, Nov 1824; m. at Willington, 8 Aug 1797, as his second wife, OBADIAH WARD, b. at Union, CT, Dec 1752 son of Obadiah and Esther (Ruggles) Ward; Obadiah d. at Kingsville, 12 Aug 1840. Obadiah was first married to Priscilla Eaton.

[1044] Stephen and Betsey are buried at Gardnertown Cemetery in New Lisbon, NY; findagrave ID: 59456729

[1045] *Connecticut State Library (Hartford, Connecticut)*; Probate Place: *Hartford, Connecticut, Estate of William Johnson, Town of Willington, Case 1251*

x WILLIAM JOHNSON, b. unknown; d. at Willington, 4 Sep 1785.

387) SAMUEL HOLT (*Samuel Holt⁴, Hannah Farnum Holt, Elizabeth Holt Farnum², Nicholas¹*), b. at Andover, 18 Dec 1730 son of Samuel and Jemima (Gray) Holt; d. at Andover 3 Feb 1803; m. at Andover, 14 Feb 1760, ABIGAIL BLANCHARD, b. 1734 daughter of Josiah and Sarah (Blanchard) Blanchard; Abigail d. 1 Nov 1814.

Samuel and Abigail had a farm in Andover and lived there throughout their lives. They were the owners of the now historic property at 173 Holt Road in Andover.[1046]

In his will written 8 February 1787 (probate 8 March 1803), Samuel Holt bequeathed to beloved wife Abigail all the household stuff proper for woman's use and use of west end of the dwelling house. He orders son Isaac to provide for his mother with specific provisions and if that is neglected, Abigail will receive the use and improvement of one-third of the real estate. Beloved son Samuel receives £30. Son Isaac receives all the real estate and all the personal estate. Daughter Abigail receives £15 to be paid in one year of his decease or sooner if she marries. Daughter Elizabeth receives the same bequest. The books are to be equally divided among the children. Isaac was named executor. Real estate was valued at $1,829 and personal estate at $329.[1047]

In her will written 18 November 1808 (probate 11 November 1814), Abigail Holt bequeaths to her son Samuel and daughter Elizabeth Carroll her two beds and bedding to be equally divided. Samuel also receives one of the largest platters and the great bible. Daughters Elizabeth Carroll and Abigail receive gold beads and pewter platters. Son Isaac receives one of the largest platters and the looking glass. Amos Blanchard of Andover was named executor.[1048]

Samuel Holt and Abigail Blanchard were parents of five children born at Andover.

i SAMUEL HOLT, b. at Andover, 7 Sep 1761; d. at Newton, MA, 6 Mar 1813 (probate 12 May 1813); m. at Andover, 8 May 1785, SARAH MASSEY. In his will, Samuel leaves his entire estate to his wife Sally.

ii ISAAC HOLT, b. at Andover, 21 Nov 1764; d. at Andover, 25 Jul 1843; m. 6 Dec 1789, his second cousin once removed, TABITHA BLUNT, b. at Andover, 7 Feb 1765 daughter of Isaac and Mary (Kimball) Blunt; Tabitha d. 24 Jun 1840.

iii ELIZABETH HOLT, b. at Andover, 19 May 1767; d. at Boston, 5 May 1825; m. at Boston, 18 Oct 1797, JARED CARROLL, b. at Walpole, MA, 28 Feb 1770 son of Benjamin and Judith (Ingraham) Carroll; Jared d. 13 Jul 1819.

iv ABIGAIL HOLT, b. 19 May 1767; d. at Andover, 13 May 1821; m. at Andover, 24 Nov 1788, her third cousin once removed, JOSEPH HOLT (*Thomas⁴, Thomas³, Nicholas², Nicholas¹*), b. at Andover, 29 Sep 1766 son of Thomas and Dorcas (Holt) Holt; Joseph d. at Andover, 8 Jun 1791. Abigail Holt and Joseph Holt are Family 830.

v PERSIS HOLT, b. 21 Nov 1775; buried at Andover, 24 Aug 1778.

388) DAVID HOLT (*Samuel Holt⁴, Hannah Farnum Holt, Elizabeth Holt Farnum², Nicholas¹*), b. at Andover, 28 Aug 1737 son of Samuel and Jemima (Gray) Holt; d. at Andover, 1813 (probate 8 Dec 1813); m. 26 Jun 1764, HANNAH MARTIN, b. at Andover, 11 Apr 1738 daughter of John and Hannah (Steele) Martin; Hannah d. at Andover, Aug 1831.

David and Hannah resided in Andover in the historic home at 109-R Holt Road. The home, likely built by his father Samuel, was obtained in whole by David when his brothers Jonathan and Samuel sold their portions to David.[1049]

In his will written 7 May 1807 (probate 8 December 1813), David Holt bequeathed to beloved wife Hannah the use and improvement of one-third of the real estate during her natural life, the use of a horse and a cow, and the household furnishings to be at her disposal. Sons Darius and John each receives four dollars which completes their portions. Daughter Hannah receives one hundred dollars, but this is to be held in trust by the executor and given to her as needed. Polly the wife of Samuel Hunt and Sarah the wife of Simmonds Baker each receives four dollars. Son Amos receives all the lands and buildings and is also named executor.[1050]

David Holt and Hannah Martin were parents of eight children born at Andover.[1051]

i DARIUS HOLT, b. 6 May 1765; d. at Norway, ME, 3 Jul 1854; m. 24 May 1785, his fourth cousin, CHLOE HOLT (*Abiel⁵, Thomas⁴, Thomas³, Nicholas², Nicholas¹*), b. at Andover, Apr 1768 daughter of Abiel and Lydia (Lovejoy) Holt; Chloe d. at Norway, 11 Oct 1849.

[1046] Andover Historic Preservation, 173 Holt Road, https://preservation.mhl.org/173-holt-road

[1047] *Essex County, MA: Probate File Papers, 1638-1881.*Online database. *AmericanAncestors.org.* New England Historic Genealogical Society, 2014. Case 13690

[1048] *Essex County, MA: Probate File Papers, 1638-1881.*Online database. *AmericanAncestors.org.* New England Historic Genealogical Society, 2014. Case 13618

[1049] Andover Historic Preservation, 109-R Holt Road, https://preservation.mhl.org/109-r-holt-road

[1050] *Essex County, MA: Probate File Papers, 1638-1881.*Online database. *AmericanAncestors.org.* New England Historic Genealogical Society, 2014. Case 13633

[1051] The birth dates given are those in the record transcriptions, although the births of Darius and Hannah are too close together, so there is likely some error.

ii HANNAH HOLT, b. 13 Sep 1765; d. at Andover, 12 May 1856. Hannah did not marry. She had an out-of-wedlock child, John Hovey.

iii MARY "POLLY" HOLT, b. 4 Feb 1767; d. at Cambridge of consumption, 16 Jul 1814; m. 6 Jun 1793, SAMUEL HUNT, b. at Littleton, 17 Sep 1763 son of Samuel and Jane (Scott) Hunt; Samuel d. at Cambridge, 1821 (probate Nov 1821). Samuel married second Anna Goodwin on 31 Dec 1815.

iv DAVID HOLT, b. 16 Oct 1768; d. at Andover, 28 Apr 1796.

v JOHN HOLT, b. 22 Feb 1769; d. at Andover, 21 Oct 1815; m. 25 Feb 1800, his fourth cousin, CHLOE HOLT (*Nathaniel*[5], *Oliver*[4], *Oliver*[3], *Henry*[2], *Nicholas*[1]), b. baptized at Andover, 21 Sep 1766 daughter of Nathaniel and Elizabeth (Stevens) Holt; Chloe d. at Andover, 11 Apr 1855. Chloe was first married to David Wiley and third married to John Frye.

vi ENOCH HOLT, b. 12 Sep 1770; d. at Andover, 29 May 1784.

vii SARAH HOLT, b. 27 Dec 1775; d. at Andover, 7 Jan 1865; m. at Andover, 27 May 1802, SYMONDS EPPES BAKER, b. at Andover, 17 Jan 1779 son of Dr. Symonds and Lydia (Gray) Baker; Symonds d. at Andover, 22 Mar 1819.

viii AMOS HOLT, b. 22 Apr 1777; d. at Andover, 19 Apr 1861; m. 1st 2 Jul 1802, MARTHA "PATTY" WARDWELL, b. about 1780 daughter of Simon and Ruth (Church) Wardwell; Patty d. at Andover, 9 Sep 1818. Amos m. 2nd 8 Apr 1819, EUNICE EVANS, baptized at Stoneham, 7 Nov 1790 daughter of Samuel and Ruth (Eames) Evans; Eunice d. at Andover, 24 Sep 1859.

389) DINAH HOLT (*Samuel Holt*[4], *Hannah Farnum Holt, Elizabeth Holt Farnum*[2], *Nicholas*[1]), b. at Andover, 6 Nov 1744 daughter of Samuel and Jemima (Gray) Holt; d. at Andover, 20 Nov 1780; m. 10 Sep 1765, her third cousin, ASA HOLT (*Thomas*[4], *Thomas*[3], *Nicholas*[2], *Nicholas*[1]), b. at Andover, 3 May 1742 son of Thomas and Hannah (Kimball) Holt; Asa d. at Andover, 20 Feb 1793. After Dinah's death, Asa married 5 Jul 1781, LYDIA STEVENS (widow of Elijah Patten), b. at Andover, 15 Nov 1753 daughter of Jonathan and Lydia (Felch) Stevens.

Asa Holt did not leave a will and his estate entered probate 12 April 1793 with widow Lydia as administratrix. Real estate was valued at £363.10 and personal estate at £163.7.7. Charges against the estate, including an allowance to the widow, were £125.8.0.[1052]

Son Abiel Holt married but did not have children. In his will written 14 March 1801, he bequeathed to his honored mother-in-law Molly Jones wife of Jacob Jones all the pewter and bedding items that his deceased wife brought to the marriage. He bequeathed to sister Hannah wife of William Tucker all the household stuff and furniture. Brother Asa Holt and brother-in-law William Tucker receive all the real estate and personal estate to equally divide. Brother Stephen Holt receives two hundred and fifty dollars. William Tucker was named executor.[1053]

Son Stephen Holt was a cabinetmaker who relocated to New York in 1808 and opened a boarding house on the corner of Front Street between Fulton Street and the Burling Slip. After some years as the proprietor there, he set about building the six-story Holt's Hotel, later known as United States Hotel, on Fulton Street from Pearl Street to Water Street. The hotel, constructed of white marble, opened 3 January 1833.[1054]

Dinah Holt and Asa Holt were parents of three children.

i HANNAH HOLT, b. at Andover, 20 Jun 1766; d. at Andover, 3 Mar 1852; m. 23 Oct 1788, WILLIAM TUCKER, b. at Wilmington, MA, 21 Mar 1761 son of David and Martha (Mooar) Tucker; William d. at Andover, 29 Aug 1848.

ii ASA HOLT, b. at Andover, 26 Mar 1768; m. at Wilmington, 9 Aug 1796, ABIGAIL GRIFFIN, b. at Andover, 7 Oct 1764 daughter of James and Phebe (Abbott) Griffin; Abigail d. at Middleton, 28 Jan 1859.

iii ABIEL HOLT, b. at Andover, 23 Nov 1773; d. of consumption, at Andover, 11 Apr 1801; m. 25 Aug 1793, PHEBE JONES, b. 1774 daughter of Jacob and Mary (Winn) Jones; Phebe d. at Andover, 20 Feb 1798.

Asa Holt and Lydia Stevens were parents of one child.

i STEPHEN HOLT, b. at Andover, 26 May 1782; d. at Manhattan, Sep 1852; m. 20 Mar 1803, MARY POTTER BROWN, b. 1780 daughter of Stephen and Elizabeth (Potter) Brown; Mary d. at Manhattan, 12 Apr 1853.

1052 *Essex County, MA: Probate File Papers, 1638-1881.*Online database. *AmericanAncestors.org.* New England Historic Genealogical Society, 2014. Case 13622

1053 *Essex County, MA: Probate File Papers, 1638-1881.*Online database. *AmericanAncestors.org.* New England Historic Genealogical Society, 2014. Case 13615

1054 Enton, James V., "An Old Street of New York," The American Historical Magazine, volume 3, p 70ff

390) ISAAC HOLT (*Obadiah⁴, Hannah Farnum Holt³, Elizabeth Holt Farnum², Nicholas¹*), b. at Andover, 30 Oct 1729 son of Obadiah and Rebecca (Farnum) Holt; d. 1780; m. at Danvers, 26 Dec 1757, MARY MARBLE.

Isaac Holt and Mary Marble were parents of twelve children, the older two children born at Andover, and the other children at Amherst, New Hampshire. Isaac signed the association test at Amherst in 1776.[1055]

i OBADIAH HOLT, b. 23 Mar 1758; d. at Clinton, ME, 9 Jun 1815; m. 5 May 1784, SUSANNAH JONES, b. 30 Mar 1764 daughter of Jonathan and Hannah (Hopkins) Jones;[1056] Susannah d. at Clinton, 18 Apr 1855. Susannah was second married to George Michels Dec 1816.

ii MARY HOLT, b. 14 Feb 1760; d. 26 Feb 1760.

iii MARY HOLT, b. 2 Mar 1761

iv HANNAH HOLT, b. 17 May 1763; d. at Enosburgh, VT, after 1838; m. at Amherst, 17 Aug 1786, EBENEZER CLARK, b. at Andover, MA, 28 Feb 1753 son of Timothy and Elizabeth (Abbott) Clark; Ebenezer d. at Enosburgh, 21 Apr 1836.[1057]

v ISAAC HOLT, b. 19 Oct 1765. Durrie's Holt genealogy (p 58) reports that Isaac enlisted in a company of soldiers that went to Ohio during the Indian wars and that he was never heard from again.

vi DANIEL HOLT, b. 5 Feb 1767; d. at Wells River, VT, 18 Jun 1854; m. at Amherst, NH, 22 Jul 1793, MARTHA TOWNE, b. at Amherst, 12 Nov 1771 daughter of Archelaus and Martha (Abbott) Towne; Martha d. at Wells River, 5 Oct 1845.

vii MEHITABLE HOLT, b. 19 Jan 1769; d. 31 Oct 1770.

viii JOSEPH HOLT, b. at Amherst, 3 Mar 1771; d. at Medford, MA, 27 Apr 1860; m. at Reading, 20 Nov 1794, ELIZABETH BEARD, b. at Reading, 23 May 1770 daughter of Cleveland and Elizabeth (Foster) Beard; Elizabeth d. at North Reading, 24 Oct 1859.

ix SAMUEL HOLT, b. 16 Aug 1774; d. at Wakefield, MA, 16 Sep 1848; m. at Reading, 18 Dec 1800, PHEBE RICHARDSON, b. at Reading, 16 Jan 1775daughter of Thomas and Phebe (Emerson) Richardson; Phebe d. at Wakefield, 31 Mar 1847

x ABIEL HOLT, b. about 1775. Durrie's Holt genealogy reports that Abiel married, but a record of his marriage has not been found.

xi NOAH HOLT, b. about 1777. He was a mariner who died in the West Indies.

xii SARAH HOLT, b. 1777; d. at Washington, NH, 17 Oct 1815; m. DANIEL FARNSWORTH, b. at Harvard, MA, 9 Apr 1769 son of Simeon and Lucy (Atherton) Farnsworth; Daniel d. at Washington, 28 Jul 1851. Daniel was second married to Phebe Carlisle and third married to Christiana Keyes.

391) SARAH HOLT (*Obadiah⁴, Hannah Farnum Holt³, Elizabeth Holt Farnum², Nicholas¹*), baptized at Andover, 25 Feb 1733 daughter of Obadiah and Rebecca (Farnum) Holt; d. likely at Annapolis, Nova Scotia, about 1773; m. at Andover, 30 Mar 1758, SAMUEL BANCROFT, b. at Reading, 12 Jul 1736 son of Samuel and Lydia (Parker) Bancroft. Samuel married second widow Mercy *Foster* Whitman.

Samuel and Sarah were part of the early migration to Nova Scotia arriving there about 1761 along with Samuel's brothers and sisters. It is not clear how long the family remained there, as it is reported that only Samuel's siblings Jeremiah and Hannah remained there permanently. It is likely, however, that Sarah died there as Samuel's second wife, Mercy Foster Whitman, was widowed in Annapolis in 1763.[1058]

There are six children of Sarah and Samuel noted in the diary of Samuel's father Deacon Samuel Bancroft as being the children of Samuel his son and his wife Sarah.[1059] Two additional children (William and Nathaniel) are reported for this family. It is not clear if William and Nathaniel were from Samuel's first or second marriage, and it is not known with certainty what became of them, but they are listed here.[1060]

i HANNAH BANCROFT, b. at Reading, MA, 20 Feb 1759; d. at Paradise, Nova Scotia, 19 May 1848; m. at Annapolis, Jun 1776, JOHN STARRETT, b. 1746 son of Peter and Eleanor (Armstrong) Starrett; John d. at Annapolis, 4 Oct 1829.

1055 Secomb, *History of Amherst*, p 376
1056 Bartlett, *Hugh Jones of Salem, Mass*, p 19
1057 U.S., Revolutionary War Pension and Bounty-Land Warrant Application Files, Case W15645
1058 Calnak and Savary, *History of the County of Annapolis*, p 471, p 625
1059 Bancroft, *Family Record of Deacon Samuel Bancroft*, pp 7-10
1060 Allen, John Kermott, "Thomas Bancroft of Dedham and Reading Mass., and Some of His Descendants", NEHGR, volume 96, 1942, p 50

ii SAMUEL BANCROFT, b. at Reading, 15 Apr 1761; d. at Yarmouth, Nova Scotia, about 1826; m. 31 Aug 1786, PHEBE DURKEE, b. at Wales, MA, 28 Apr 1771 daughter of Phineas and Phebe (Pearl) Durkee;[1061] Phebe d. 16 Apr 1856.

iii JEREMIAH BANCROFT, b. at Annapolis, Nova Scotia, 12 May 1763; d. at Round Hill, Nova Scotia, 25 Jul 1841; m. 1788, SARAH PAYSON, b. at Annapolis, 8 Apr 1769 daughter of Jonathan and Elizabeth (Tilestone) Payson; Sarah d. at Round Hill, 16 Apr 1854.

iv OBADIAH BANCROFT, b. at Annapolis, Nova Scotia, 29 Apr 1765; d. 8 Apr 1768.

v OBADIAH BANCROFT, b. at Annapolis, 6 Feb 1769

vi SARAH BANCROFT, b. at Annapolis, 15 Oct 1770

vii WILLIAM BANCROFT

viii NATHANIEL BANCROFT

392) JAMES HOLT (*Obadiah[4], Hannah Farnum Holt[3], Elizabeth Holt Farnum[2], Nicholas[1]*), b. at Andover, 18 Feb 1732/3 son of Obadiah and Rebecca (Farnum) Holt; m. 2 Jan 1755, his first cousin, MEHITABLE HOLT (*Ebenezer[4], Samuel[3], Samuel[2], Nicholas[1]*), b. at Andover, 3 Sep 1733 daughter of Ebenezer and Mehitable (Stevens) Holt; Mehitable d. at Andover, 4 Mar 1767. James m. 2nd 6 Aug 1767 widow MARY MCINTIRE.

There is one child known for James Holt and Mehitable Holt.[1062]

i JESSE HOLT, b. at Andover, 8 Oct 1755; m. MOLLY who has not been identified.[1063] Jesses is reported to have settled in Tewksbury.

393) MARY FARRINGTON (*Rebecca Farnum Holt[4], Thomas Farnum[3], Elizabeth Holt Farnum[2], Nicholas[1]*), b. at Andover, 31 Jan 1722/3: "Mary, d. Rebeca and "Reputed,", d. Edward Farington, jr., Jan. 31, 1722-3."[1064] Mary m. at Andover, 26 Oct 1742, JOHN GROO,[1065] *perhaps* the John born at Andover, 15 Sep 1721 (baptized in 1728), the out-of-wedlock child of Elizabeth Nichols and an unknown Mr. Grow. John d. at Dudley, MA, 17 Oct 1775.

John Grow and Mary Farrington were parents of sixteen children.

i JOHN GROO, b. at Sutton, 14 Aug 1743; m. at Thompson, 9 Oct 1766, widow PHEBE CADY.

ii HANNAH GROO, baptized at Sutton, 16 Jun 1744; died young.

iii NATHANIEL GROO, b. at Sutton, 13 Apr 1745; d. likely at Yates County, NY; m. at Killingly, 9 Nov 1769, BETTY CADY, b. at Killingly, 20 Apr 1750 daughter of Jonathan and Betty (-) Cady.

iv EDWARD GROO, b. at Sutton, 5 Mar 1746; d. at Tunbridge, VT, 25 Jan 1831; m. at Oxford, MA, 15 Nov 1774, JOANNA NICHOLS, b. at Sutton, 25 Mar 1742 daughter of Isaac and Sarah (Wilkins) Nichols; Joanna d. at Tunbridge, 17 Mar 1812.

v ELIZABETH GROO, b. at Sutton, 5 Mar 1746; d. likely at Thompson, CT; m. at Oxford, 29 Nov 1768, JONATHAN STONE, baptized at Thompson, 16 Apr 1738 son of John and Mary (-) Stone.

vi JONATHAN GROO, b. at Oxford, MA, 25 Jun 1749; d. at East Randolph, VT, Jan 1828; m. 1st 18 Mar 1773, MARY BROWN, b. at Killingly, 11 Sep 1751 daughter of Stephen and Mary (Lyon) Brown; Mary d. about 1778. Jonathan m. 2nd at Thompson, 1 Jul 1779, MARY "POLLY" TOURTELLOTTE (widow of Elisha Harris), b. 6 Jan 1747/8 daughter of Abraham and Phebe (Thornton) Tourtellotte.[1066]

vii REBEKAH GROO, b. at Oxford, 19 Nov 1751; d. at Meigs, OH, 10 Apr 1833;[1067] m. 14 Nov 1769, ISAAC SHUMWAY, b. at Oxford, 11 Nov 1742 son of Jeremiah and Experience (Learned) Shumway; Isaac d. at Meigs, 2 Oct 1822. The family lived in Chatham and Phelps, New York and in 1811 moved to Ohio.

1061 Brown, *Yarmouth, Nova Scotia Genealogies*, p 430

1062 Durrie, p 58, reports two other children: Joseph undated and Dorothy born 22 April 1764. Dorothy born in 1764 was the daughter of James Holt and Dorothy Lovejoy.

1063 This is a marriage reported in Durrie's Holt genealogy for which records have not been located.

1064 Mary is listed both as Mary Farnum and Mary Farrington in the town records.

1065 The spelling Groo is used for most of this family.

1066 The 1779 probate record of Abraham Tourtellotte contains a promise to pay from the estate to widow Mary Harris daughter of Abraham. The pension application file of son Joseph Tourtellotte includes a list of the children of Abraham and their dates of birth.

1067 Shumway, *Genealogy of the Shumway Family*, p 194

viii MARY GROW, b. at Oxford, 7 Sep 1753; d. at Williston, VT, 22 Feb 1824; m. at Douglas, MA, 13 Jun 1779, JOHN BROWN, b. at Killingly, 7 May 1758[1068] son of Nathaniel and Abiah (Leonard) Brown; John d. at Williston, 1 Sep 1855.

ix SARAH GROO, b. at Oxford, 1 Mar 1756

x SAMUEL GROO, b. at Oxford, 21 Feb 1758; d. at Neversink, NY, 30 Dec 1825; m. about 1781, SUSANNA BROOKS, b. about 1760; Susanna d. at Neversink between 1810 and 1820.

xi PHEBE GROO, b. at Oxford, 20 Sep 1759. The Grow genealogy reports that Phebe married Ebenezer Hyde of Lebanon, NH but no records were located related to that.

xii ABIGAIL GROO, b. at Oxford, 30 Sep 1761[1069]

xiii DAVID GROW, b. at Oxford, 30 Sep 1761; d. at Randolph, VT, 10 Jan 1851; m. 1st at Thompson, 21 Apr 1785, ELIZABETH BIXBY, b. at Thompson, 15 Apr 1759 daughter of Amos and Elizabeth (Stone) Bixby; Elizabeth d. at Tunbridge, 25 Mar 1807. David m. 2nd at Chelsea, VT, 11 Oct 1807, MARTHA "PATTY" HATCH, b. at Spencer, MA, 24 Mar 1777 daughter of Michael and Martha (Rice) Hatch; Martha d. at Randolph, 14 Feb 1874. David served in the Revolution for which service he received a pension as did his widow Martha.

xiv PETER GROW, b. at Oxford, 30 Apr 1763; d. at Chester, OH, 13 Mar 1837; m. 1st at Preston, CT, 29 Jan 1789, DIANA TRACY, b. at Preston, 15 Feb 1763 daughter of Samuel and Anna (Partridge) Tracy; Diana d. at Tunbridge, 9 Mar 1795. Peter m. 2nd at Tunbridge, 2 Aug 1795, Diana's sister, DEBORAH TRACY, b. at Preston, 12 Sep 1766; Deborah d. likely at Tunbridge, about 1800. Peter m. 3rd about 1804, HANNAH SHEPHARDSON (widow of Nathaniel Eddy), likely b. at Attleboro, MA, 8 May 1764 daughter of Daniel and Mary (Peck) Shephardson; Hannah d. at Chester, OH, 21 Dec 1813. Peter m. 4th at Gallia County, OH, 27 Mar 1816, EUPHEMIA BROWN who d. at Chester 1842 (probate 1842).

xv JACOB GROW, b. at Oxford, 17 Apr 1765; d. at Norwich, NY, 20 Aug 1818 (probate Sep 1818); m. at Bangall, NY, 1788,[1070] SARAH MEAD, b. about 1760 likely daughter of Jonathan and Sarah (Thompson) Mead; Sarah d. at Norwich, 30 Mar 1813.

xvi HANNAH GROW, b. at Oxford, 17 Apr 1765

394) ABIGAIL RUSSELL (*Robert Russell[4], Phebe Johnson Russell[3], Mary Holt Johnson[2], Nicholas[1]*), b. at Andover, 4 Oct 1717 daughter of Robert and Abigail (Flint) Russell; d. at Reading, 1746 (probate Sep 1746); m. at Reading, 23 Sep 1735, EBENEZER EATON; Ebenezer d. at Reading, 1738 (probate 1738).

In his will written 5 February 1738, Ebenezer bequeathed to wife Abigail all the movable estate both outdoors and household goods to be at her disposal. The remainder of the estate goes one-half to Abigail to be for her use and possession and the other half divided between daughters Abigail and Phebe. Robert Russell was named executor.[1071]

In her will written 28 May 1740 (probate Sep 1746), Abigail Eaton of Reading relict of Ebenezer bequeathed to brother Ezekiel Russell and Prudence Russell twenty pounds each when they come of age. All the remainder of the estate goes to her two daughters Abigail and Phebe to be equally divided between them. Father Robert Russell was named executor.[1072]

Abigail Russell and Ebenezer Eaton were parents of two children born at Reading.

i ABIGAIL EATON, b. about 1756; d. at Reading, Nov 1817; m. about 1755, as his second wife, JONATHAN BATCHELDER, b. at Reding, 22 Mar 1730 son of Jonathan and Sarah (Lewis) Batchelder; Jonathan d. at Reading, 6 Oct 1817. Jonathan was first married to Phebe Holt. Abigail Eaton, Jonathan Batchelder, and Phebe Holt are Family 637.

ii PHEBE EATON, b. about 1737; she was living when her mother wrote her will in 1740 but not mentioned in her grandfather Robert Russell's 1757 will.

395) EZEKIEL RUSSELL (*Robert Russell[4], Phebe Johnson Russell[3], Mary Holt Johnson[2], Nicholas[1]*), b. at Andover, 10 Jun 1722 son of Robert and Abigail (Flint) Russell; d. at Wilbraham, MA, 3 Jan 1802; m. TABATHA FLINT, b. at Reading, 18 May 1721 daughter of Ebenezer and Tabitha (Burnap) Flint; Tabitha d. at Wilbraham, 4 Jan 1808.[1073]

[1068] John Brown's pension application file includes his date of birth as 7 May 1758 at Killingly.

[1069] The Grow genealogy suggests she may have married Elijah Derby of Charlestown, NH, but that seems not correct. Elijah and Abigail married in 1799 and other information suggests Elijah was born 1774 and his wife Abigail born about 1780.

[1070] New York City, Marriages, 1600s-1800s, accessed through ancestry.com

[1071] *Middlesex County, MA: Probate File Papers, 1648-1871.*Online database. *AmericanAncestors.org.* New England Historic Genealogical Society, 2014. Case 6728

[1072] *Middlesex County, MA: Probate File Papers, 1648-1871.*Online database. *AmericanAncestors.org.* New England Historic Genealogical Society, 2014. Case 6722

[1073] Ezekiel and Tabatha are buried at the Old Hampden Cemetery in Hampden. Find A Grave 43582031 and 43582032

Ezekiel and Tabitha began their family in Ashford. The relocated to western Massachusetts about 1759 as on 20 April 1759 (recorded 21 October 1765), Ezekiel Russell of Ashford purchased a tract of land in Springfield, Massachusetts from Abraham Skinner, Jr. of Woodstock. Ezekiel was of Wilbraham when he purchased land on the east side of the Connecticut River from William King on 3 January 1771 and made an additional purchase from the inhabitants of Wilbraham on 20 May 1773.[1074] On 3 September 1782, Ezekiel sold to his son Ezekiel, Jr. several lots in Wilbraham (no. 75, 76, 78, 79, and 80) for a payment of £20. Ezekiel sold to his son Robert the homestead farm with buildings for £100.[1075]

Ezekiel Russell served in Capt. James Warriner's company of Wilbraham that marched at the alarm in April 1775 for the Battle of Lexington.[1076]

Ezekiel Russell and Tabatha Flint were parents of six children.

i TABITHA RUSSELL, b. at Ashford, CT, 19 Aug 1749; d. at Wilbraham, MA, 9 Jul 1776.

ii EZEKIEL RUSSELL, b. at Ashford, 22 Jun 1751; d. at Wilbraham, 1798 (probate 1798); m. 1st at Wilbraham, 19 Aug 1775, HEPHZIBAH HILLS, b. at Glastonbury, 10 Aug 1749; Hephzibah d. 24 Feb 1778. Ezekiel m. 2nd at Wilbraham, 2 Oct 1778, HANNAH MEACHAM; Hannah d. at Wilbraham, 27 Jan 1822.

iii ABIGAIL RUSSELL, b. at Ashford, 19 May 1755; d. at Wilbraham, 16 May 1812; m. at Wilbraham, 1 May 1782, NATHAN STEDMAN, b. 18 Jan 1751 son of Joseph and Abigail (Rockwell) Stedman; Nathan d. at Wilbraham, 27 Nov 1794. Abigail and Nathan were parents of six children, only one of whom (son Nathan) married.

iv ROBERT RUSSELL, b. at Ashford, 15 May 1757; d. at Hampden, MA, 9 Dec 1836; m. at Wilbraham, 14 Sep 1782, LYDIA BEEBE, b. 1761; Lydia d. at Hampden, 21 Aug 1837.

v BENJAMIN RUSSELL, b. at Wilbraham, 1759

vi ASA RUSSELL, b. at Wilbraham, 6 Oct 1761; m. at Wilbraham, 25 Nov 1790, THANKFUL ROOT. Asa was living in Longmeadow, MA in 1796 when he sold a piece of land to James Beebe. Another deed in 1796 includes both Asa and Thankful as signers.[1077] Nothing else is known of them and no records of children were located.

396) PHEBE RUSSELL (*Robert Russell[4], Phebe Johnson Russell[3], Mary Holt Johnson[2], Nicholas[1]*), b. at Reading, 1751 daughter of Robert and Elizabeth (-) Russell; m. at Andover, 19 Nov 1776, DAVID CHENEY, b. at Boxford, 11 Sep 1750 son of Ichabod and Rebekah (Smith) Cheney. Phebe is perhaps the widow Phebe Cheney who married John Perley in Rowley in 1805; if so, she died in 1811.

There is just one child identified for Phebe Russell and David Cheney.

i PHEBE RUSSELL CHENEY, b. about 1782 (as noted on death record); d. at Rowley, 20 Dec 1860; m. at Rowley, 1 Nov 1832, DAVID SAUNDERS, b. at Rowley, 20 May 1766 son of John and Mary (Dresser) Saunders; David d. at Rowley, 1 Dec 1847. David was first married to Priscilla Nelson.

397) ELIZABETH RUSSELL (*Robert Russell[4], Phebe Johnson Russell[3], Mary Holt Johnson[2], Nicholas[1]*), b. at Reading, 1752 daughter of Robert and Elizabeth (-) Russell; d. at Boxford, 12 Mar 1840; m. 1st at Danvers, 12 Dec 1776, ELIJAH MOULTON, b. at Danvers, 5 Dec 1748 son of Benjamin and Sarah (Smith) Moulton; Elijah d. at Danvers, 1782 (probate 7 Oct 1782). Elizabeth m. 2nd at Boxford, 10 Jun 1788, JESSE PERLEY, b. at Boxford, 20 Jun 1761 son of Nathaniel and Mehitable (Perley) Perley; Jesse d. at Boxford, 18 Apr 1846.

Elijah Mouton was a yeoman in Danvers. On 6 July 1778, Elijah and wife Elizabeth sold a tract of land of about 32 acres to John Selman of Marblehead.[1078]

Elijah Moulton's estate entered probate 7 October 1782 with Elizabeth Moulton as administratrix. The total value of the estate including some small acreage was £263.4.0.[1079]

In his will written 26 March 1842 (probate 21 April 1846), Jesse Perley, directs that his estate be sold, except for certain legacies, and the proceeds used to pay debts, funeral charges, and for the erection of appropriate gravestones for him and his late wife Elizabeth. Son Jesse Perley, Jr. receives the income from one-third of the proceeds of the estate and after Jesse, Jr.'s death, this legacy goes to his children (Elizabeth W., Sarah Jane, and Edward Payson Perley). Son Jesse also receives his choice of the stock animals and the best foreplane jointer and smoothing plane. Louisa Perley widow of son Francis received eighty dollars. His grandchildren who are the children of Francis each receives eighty dollars: Osgood Perley, Louisa Hood, Charlotte Wait, Caroline Augusta Perley, John Perley, Nathaniel Perley, and Dean Andrews Perley. Son-in-law Francis Gould receives five dollars, granddaughter Irene Gould receives one hundred-fifty dollars, grandson Francis Gould receives eighty dollars, and grandson Jesse Perley Gould receive one hundred dollars. There are additional legacies to previously named

1074 Massachusetts Land Records, Hampden County, 6:716; 11:126; 12:343

1075 Massachusetts Land Records, Hampden County, 36:435; 33:444

1076 Peck, *The History of Wilbraham*, p 138

1077 Massachusetts Land Records, Hampden County, 35:392; 35:280

1078 Massachusetts Land Records, Essex County, 136:165

1079 *Essex County, MA: Probate File Papers, 1638-1881.*Online database. *AmericanAncestors.org.* New England Historic Genealogical Society, 2014. Case 19102

grandchildren and the residue is to be equally divided among his grandchildren. Moses Dorman of Boxford was named executor.[1080]

Elizabeth Russell and Elijah Moulton were parents of two children.

i SARAH "SALLY" MOULTON, b. likely at Danvers, about 1777; d. at Rowley, MA, 19 May 1852; m. at Boxford, 1800, JONATHAN HARRIMAN, b. 1776 according to gravestone; Jonathan d. at Rowley, 1824.

ii MARY MOULTON, b. likely at Danvers, 1780; d. at Winthrop, ME, 29 Mar 1839; m. at Boxford, 1 Apr 1799, THOMAS LANCASTER, b. at Rowley, 5 May 1773 son of Paul and Mary (Gage) Lancaster; Thomas d. at Winthrop, 4 May 1864.

Elizabeth Russell and Jesse Perley were parents of four children born at Boxford.

i FRANCIS PERLEY, b. at Boxford, 19 Oct 1792; d. at Boxford, 1 Sep 1836; m. at Boxford, 18 May 1815, LOUISA GOULD, b. at Topsfield, 25 Jun 1790 daughter of Nathaniel and Hannah (Killam) Gould; Louisa d. at Topsfield, 9 Dec 1843.

ii JESSE PERLEY, b. at Boxford, 29 Oct 1795; d. at Boxford, 19 Nov 1851; m. at Boxford, 22 May 1824, SALLY GOULD, b. at Topsfield, 26 May 1800 daughter of Simon and Sarah (White) Gould; Sally d. 29 Dec 1857.

iii ANCIL PERLEY, b. 3 Jul 1798; d. at Boxford, 28 Dec 1831. Ancil does not seem to have married.

iv IRENA PERLEY, b. at Boxford, 29 Jan 1801; d. at Boxford, 28 Jul 1837; m. at Boxford, 26 Aug 1822, FRANCIS GOULD, b. at Topsfield, 5 Sep 1798 son of Nathaniel and Betty (Andrews) Gould; Francis d. at Topsfield, 13 Oct 1870. Francis Gould was the half-brother of Louisa Gould who married Irena's brother Francis.

398) WILLIAM PIERCE (*Martha Holt Pierce⁴, Hannah Farnum Holt³, Elizabeth Holt Farnum², Nicholas¹*), b. at Pomfret, 16 Mar 1727/8 son of Somers and Martha (Holt) Pierce; d. at Andover, VT, 22 Jul 1818;[1081] m. by 1750, HANNAH who has not been identified.

William and Hannah started their family in Ashford, relocated to Wilton about 1758 and remained there until just before the Revolution when he sold his Wilton homestead to Samuel Sheldon. William and Hannah then made the move to Andover, Vermont, although sons Benjamin and Timothy remained in Wilton for a time.[1082]

William and Hannah Pierce were parents of six children.

i HANNAH PIERCE, b. at Ashford, 23 May 1750; d. 24 Nov 1751.

ii HANNAH PIERCE, b. at Ashford, 31 Dec 1752

iii ASA PIERCE, b. at Ashford, 18 Apr 1757; d. 15 Sep 1776 while serving in the Continental army.[1083]

iv WILLIAM PIERCE, b. at Ashford, 28 Jun 1759; m. at Wilton, 30 Mar 1780, his second cousin once removed, SARAH HOLT (*Timothy⁴, Nicholas³, Nicholas², Nicholas¹*), b. at Andover, 31 May 1757 daughter of Timothy and Elizabeth (Holt) Holt. Sarah Holt and William Pierce are Family 600.

v BENJAMIN PIERCE, b. at Wilton, 18 May 1762; d. at Londonderry, VT, 9 May 1847; m. at Wilton, 27 Oct 1785, his third cousin once removed, DORCAS LOVEJOY (*Mary Holt Lovejoy⁴, Oliver³, Henry², Nicholas¹*), b. at Andover, MA, 16 Apr 1762 daughter of Daniel and Mary (Holt0 Lovejoy; Dorcas d. at Andover, VT, 15 Aug 1817. Dorcas Lovejoy and Benjamin Pierce are Family 628.

vi TIMOTHY PIERCE, b. at Wilton, 4 Feb 1765; m. at Wilton, 5 May 1785, PHEBE CARLETON who has not been identified.

399) EBENEZER HOLT (*Ebenezer Holt⁴, Hannah Farnum Holt³, Elizabeth Holt Farnum², Nicholas¹*), b. at Andover, 7 Sep 1730 son of Ebenezer and Mehitable (Stevens) Holt; d. at Mount Vernon, NH, Apr 1805;[1084] m. 15 Feb 1753, LYDIA PEABODY, b. 5 Jul 1731 daughter of Moses and Sarah (Holt) Peabody; Lydia's date of death is not known.

Ebenezer Holt was a farmer in Mont Vernon. *The History of the Town of Amherst, New Hampshire* lists just two children for this family (p. 636). Only a birth record for daughter Rebecca was located. There is perhaps some mis-transcription

---

[10801080] *Essex County, MA: Probate File Papers, 1638-1881.*Online database. *AmericanAncestors.org.* New England Historic Genealogical Society, 2014. Case 49908

[1081] Pierce, *Pierce Genealogy*, p 61

[1082] Livermore, *History of the Town of Wilton*, p 470

[1083] Pierce, *Pierce Genealogy*, p 61

[1084] Secomb, *History of the Town of Amherst*

with either the marriage or the birth record, as the records give the date of birth of the oldest child as three weeks after the marriage. But perhaps they are correct.

i REBECCA HOLT, b. at Amherst, NH, 7 Sep 1752; m. 14 Mar 1782, JONATHAN LAMSON, b. at Amherst, 10 Aug 1756 son of Jonathan and Mehitable (Holt) Lamson. Jonathan d. 4 Feb 1842.[1085] Jonathan's mother Mehitable Holt has not been identified in terms of her Holt ancestry.

ii SARAH HOLT, b. at Amherst, 1757; m. 25 May 1786, MOSES PEABODY, b. about 1755; Moses d. about 1842 at Mont Vernon (probate of estate 1842). Sarah and Moses do not seem to have any children, at least not any children that survived childhood. In his will, Moses mentions only wife Sarah.[1086]

400) EZEKIEL HOLT (twin) (*Ebenezer Holt⁴, Hannah Farnum Holt³, Elizabeth Holt Farnum², Nicholas¹*), b. at Andover, 7 Jul 1741 son of Ebenezer and Mehitable (Stevens) Holt; d. at Amherst, NH date unknown; m. by 1772, MARY STEWART, b. 2 Sep 1749 daughter of Samuel and Sarah (Tarbell) Stewart.

Five children have been located for this family all born at Amherst, New Hampshire. The family was then in Mont Vernon. No probate record was located.

i ELIZABETH HOLT, b. 8 Jul 1773

ii MARY HOLT, b. 11 Dec 1775; *perhaps* m. at Amherst, 25 Sep 1799, her fourth cousin, JOHN STILES PEABODY (*Samuel Peabody⁵, Moses Peabody⁴, Lydia Holt Peabody³, James², Nicholas¹*), b. at Andover, 15 Aug 1775 son of Samuel and Elizabeth (Wilkins) Peabody; John d. at New Boston, NH, 1 May 1832. John was first married to Mary Barrett who died about 1798.

iii SARAH HOLT, b. 10 Sep 1780

iv EZEKIEL HOLT, b. 19 Aug 1782; d. at Marshfield, VT, 4 Aug 1845; m. 13 Dec 1810, ABIGAIL PIKE, b. at East Montpelier, VT, 17 Sep 1791 daughter of Benjamin and Esther (Abbott) Pike; Abigail d. 24 Dec 1873.

v DAVID HOLT, b. 27 Feb 1792

401) REUBEN HOLT (*Ebenezer Holt⁴, Hannah Farnum Holt³, Elizabeth Holt Farnum², Nicholas¹*), b. at Andover, 27 Jun 1744 son of Ebenezer and Mehitable (Stevens) Holt; d. at Landgrove, VT 2 Mar 1836;[1087] m. at Amherst, NH, 6 Feb 1772, LYDIA SMALL, b. Mar 1745[1088] daughter of William and Sarah (Clark) Small; Lydia d. at Amherst, NH, 9 Mar 1795.

Reuben Holt and Lydia Small had six children born at Amherst, New Hampshire. Following the death of Lydia, Reuben relocated to Landgrove, Vermont where he was an early settler. His son Reuben accompanied him and served as the town clerk in Landgrove for many years.[1089]

i SARAH HOLT, b. 10 Nov 1772; d. 20 Oct 1851; m. 16 Nov 1797, STEPHEN TUTTLE, b. 10 Mar 1772 son of Jotham and Molly (Worthley) Tuttle; Stephen d. 1854.

ii REUBEN HOLT, b. 11 Feb 1775; d. at Landgrove, VT, 25 Nov 1836; m. 1st, 27 Dec 1798, JUDITH HILL, b. at Amherst, 31 Jan 1779; Judith d. at Landgrove, 2 Nov 1813. Reuben m. 2nd, 3 Aug 1817, SIBYL PIPER, b. at Sharon, NH, 28 Jun 1793 daughter of Thomas and Judith (Powers) Piper.

iii RACHEL HOLT, b. 2 Sep 1776; d. at Weston, VT, 4 Mar 1860; m. 30 Aug 1797, TIMOTHY HILL, b. about 1776 in Vermont;[1090] Timothy d. at Weston after 1850.

iv EBENEZER HOLT, b. 2 Jul 1778

v LYDIA HOLT, b. 19 Apr 1781

vi WILLIAM HOLT, b. 15 May 1783; d. at Landgrove, VT, 29 Mar 1811.

402) JOHN HOLT (*John⁴, Hannah Farnum Holt³, Elizabeth Holt Farnum², Nicholas¹*), b. at Andover, 16 Mar 1732 son of John and Mary (Lewis) Holt; d. at Andover, 12 Jun 1765; m. 1st 28 Nov 1753, LYDIA KIMBALL (widow of James Farnum), baptized at Wenham, 13 Dec 1730 daughter of Josiah and Elizabeth (Bragg) Kimball; Lydia d. at Andover, 7 May 1756. John m.

1085 Index to Selected Final Payment Vouchers, 1818-1864 4 Feb 1842, fold3.com

1086 *New Hampshire, Wills and Probate Records, 1643-1982*, Probate Records, 1771-1921.

1087 *Vermont, Vital Records, 1720-1908* (Provo, UT, USA: Ancestry.com Operations, Inc., 2013).

1088 Lydia was baptized at Salem but may have been born at Andover.

1089 American Series of Popular Biographies, *Biographical Sketches Massachusetts*, p 683

1090 Based on information from the 1850 U.S. Census

2nd 5 Feb 1757, RACHEL FARNUM (or Varnum) who has not been identified.[1091] Rachel was living at the probate of her husband's estate, but no information for her after that time was located. Lydia Kimball m. 1st, 27 Dec 1748, JAMES FARNUM (*James Farnum⁴, John Farnum³, Elizabeth Holt Farnum², Nicholas¹*), b. at Andover, 24 Apr 1723 son of James and Johanna (Grainger) Farnum; James d. at Andover, 27 Feb 1749/50.

John Holt did not leave a will and his estate entered probate 11 July 1765 with Barachias Abbot as administrator. Widow Rachel gave up her right of dower for a payment of £120. The total value of the estate before considering debts was £603.5.8. Claims against the estate were £516 and the creditors received a portion of what was owed.[1092]

Lydia Kimball and her first husband James Farnum did not have children. John Holt and Lydia Kimball were parents of two children born at Andover.

i JOHN HOLT, b. 16 Apr 1754; d. 12 May 1765

ii JOSIAH HOLT, b. 1 Mar 1756

John Holt and Rachel Farnum were parents of five children born at Andover.

i NEHEMIAH HOLT, b. 23 Jan 1758

ii RACHEL HOLT, b. 25 Jan 1759

iii SOLOMON HOLT, b. 14 Dec 1760

iv DANIEL HOLT, 11 Dec 1762

v JOEL HOLT, b. 4 Jul 1764; d. at Milford, NH, 28 Jun 1847; m. at Wilton, 30 Nov 1786, MARY "POLLY" COBURN, b. at Dracut, 8 Jul 1763 daughter of Amos and Mary (Parkhurst) Coburn; Mary d. at Milford, 4 Feb 1858.

403) JEREMIAH HOLT (*John⁴, Hannah Farnum Holt³, Elizabeth Holt Farnum², Nicholas¹*), b. at Andover, 31 Mar 1734 son of John and Mary (Lewis) Holt; d. at Wilton, 1816;[1093] m. at Andover, 21 Apr 1756, his third cousin, HANNAH ABBOTT (*Hannah Holt Abbott⁴, Timothy³, James², Nicholas¹*), b. at Andover, 18 May 1737 daughter of Barachias and Hannah (Holt) Abbott; Hannah d. at Wilton, Nov 1812.

Hannah Abbott and Jeremiah Holt were parents to thirteen children.

i JEREMIAH HOLT, b. at Andover, 8 Jun 1756; d. at Wilton, 3 Oct 1776.

ii BARACHIAS HOLT, b. at Wilton, 8 Feb 1758; d. at Antrim, NH, 1846; m. 14 Oct 1783, his first cousin, ELIZABETH SHATTUCK (*Elizabeth Abbott Shattuck⁵, Hannah Holt Abbott⁴, Timothy³, James², Nicholas¹*), b. at Andover, 16 Dec 1759 daughter of Zebadiah and Elizabeth (Abbott) Shattuck. A death record was not found for Elizabeth. Elizabeth is a daughter in Family 294.

iii AMOS HOLT, b. at Wilton, 16 Feb 1760; d. at Wilton, Dec 1782.

iv ENOCH HOLT, b. at Wilton, 20 Mar 1762

v ELIAS HOLT, b. at Wilton 5 May 1764; perhaps died at Sherburne, NY.

vi JOHN HOLT, b. at Wilton, 16 Sep 1766; d. at Sherburne, NY, 30 Jan 1835; m. at Lyndeborough, 3 May 1790, MARY MCKEAN, b. Deb 1762 (based on age at death); Mary d. at Sherburne, 30 May 1818.[1094]

vii ELIJAH HOLT, b. at Wilton, 30 Jul 1768; d. at Columbus, NY, 2 Sep 1850; m. Mar 1794, ANNA DICKEY, b. at Antrim, 19 Apr 1777 daughter of James and Mary (Brown) Dickey;[1095] Anna d. at Columbus, 20 Mar 1854.

viii HANNAH HOLT, b. at Wilton, 7 Jun 1770

ix PHEBE HOLT, b. at Wilton, 24 Apr 1772; d. at Columbus, NY, 28 Nov 1859.[1096]

[1091] It is possible that Rachel Farnum is the out-of-wedlock daughter of Alice Farnum, Alice being the daughter of Samuel and Hannah (Holt) Farnum.

[1092] *Essex County, MA: Probate File Papers, 1638-1881.*Online database. *AmericanAncestors.org.* New England Historic Genealogical Society, 2014. Case 13656

[1093] Death year given as 1816 in Livermore's *History of Wilton*.

[1094] Findagrave ID: 92835124; Mary wife of John Holt died May 30th1818 55 years 5 months and 26 days; Sherburne Quarter Cemetery, Sherburne, New York

[1095] Cochrane, *History of the Town of Antrim*, p 453

[1096] Durrie, *Holt Genealogy*, p 59

x RHODA HOLT, b. at Wilton, 3 Feb 1774; d. likely at Weston, VT; m. at Wilton, 30 Jan 1798, DAVID RIDEOUT, b. at Wilton, 27 Oct 1771 son of Benjamin and Sarah (Taylor) Rideout; David b. at Weston, Sep 1849.

xi TIMOTHY ABBOT HOLT, b. 3 Oct 1775; d. 22 Aug 1777.

xii JEREMIAH HOLT, b. at Wilton, 28 Mar 1778

xiii TIMOTHY ABBOT HOLT, b. at Wilton, 24 Aug 1781; Timothy d. at Washington Co, ME, 4 Mar 1858; m. his fourth cousin, SARAH SAWYER (*Prudence Abbott Sawyer*[6]*, David Abbott*[5]*, David Abbott*[4]*, Sarah Farnum Abbott*[3]*, Elizabeth Holt Farnum*[2]*, Nicholas*[1]), b. at Wilton, 25 Nov 1782 daughter of Nathaniel and Prudence (Abbott) Sawyer; Sarah d. at Marion, ME, 10 Jun 1863.

404) MARY HOLT (*John*[4]*, Hannah Farnum Holt*[3]*, Elizabeth Holt Farnum*[2]*, Nicholas*[1]), b, at Andover, 12 Apr 1737 daughter of John and Mary (Lewis) Holt; d. at Wilton, 1821; m. at Andover, 4 Nov 1756, SAMUEL PETTENGILL, b. at Andover, 16 Mar 1731/2 son of Nathaniel and Sarah (Abbott) Pettengill; Samuel died in the Ticonderoga campaign in 1776. Mary m. 2nd at Wilton, 10 Feb 1780, JOHN WRIGHT.

Mary and Samuel started their family in Andover but relocated to Wilton in 1770 where Samuel had lot 13 of the second range. Samuel served as lieutenant in Capt. Benjamin Mann's company and was at the Battle of Bunker Hill. He died during the Ticonderoga campaign.[1097] Mary and Samuel's son Benjamin also died at Ticonderoga.

Mary Holt and Samuel Pettengill were parents of nine children.

i SAMUEL PETTENGILL, b. at Andover, MA, 24 Nov 1757; d. at Andover, VT, 8 Apr 1838; m. 4 Jan 1781, MARY HOLDEN, b. about 1760; Mary d. at Andover, VT, 26 Dec 1844.

ii WILLIAM PETTENGILL, b. at Andover, 23 Aug 1759; d. at Wilton, NH, 13 Oct 1844; m. 1st at Andover, MA, 30 Sep 1765, his fourth cousin, RHODA HAGGET (*Deborah Stevens Hagget*[5]*, Lydia Gray Stevens*[4]*, Edward Gray*[3]*, Hannah Holt Gray*[2]*, Nicholas*[1]), b. at Andover, 30 Sep 1765 daughter of Jacob and Deborah (Stevens) Hagget; Rhoda d. at Wilton, 1797. William m. 2nd at Wilton, 1 Jun 1797, his fourth cousin, SARAH BALLARD (*Hannah Holt Ballard*[5]*, Jonathan*[4]*, Oliver*[3]*, Henry*[2]*, Nicholas*[1]), b. at Wilton, 13 Apr 1766 daughter of Nathan and Hannah (Holt) Ballard; Sarah d. at Wilton, 4 Jan 1856.

iii BENJAMIN PETTENGILL, b. at Andover, 7 Feb 1762; d. at Ticonderoga, 1776.

iv PETER PETTENGILL, b. at Andover, 19 Aug 1765; d. after 1830 when living at Orangeville, NY; m. at Dunstable, 21 Feb 1791, MARY MOOAR, b. at Dunstable, 10 Feb 1769 daughter of Asa and Esther (Coombs) Mooar. Mary appears to have died before the 1830 census when Peter's household was one male 60-69, one female 20-29, and one female 15-19.

v MARY PETTENGILL, b. at Andover, 11 Dec 1767; m. at Dunstable, 15 Jan 1789, THOMAS MOOAR, b. at Dunstable, 5 Feb 1766 son of Asa and Esther (Combs) Mooar.

vi JOHN PETTENGILL, b. at Andover, 11 Dec 1767; d. at Ludlow, VT, 1 Aug 1856; m. about 1797, MARY "POLLY" BARKER, b. about 1777 perhaps daughter of Phineas and Sarah (Howe) Barker; Mary d. at Ludlow, 5 May 1847.

vii SUSANNA ABBOT PETTENGILL, b. at Andover, 16 Jan 1770; d. after 1850 when she was living in Nashua; m. at Dunstable, 21 Nov 1793, SHEREBIAH HUNT, b. at Dunstable, 5 Jul 1768 son of William and Mary (Hardy) Hunt; Sherebiah d. after 1850.

viii BETTY PETTENGILL, b. at Wilton, 4 Apr 1772

ix NATHANIEL PETTENGILL, b. at Wilton, 18 Jun 1774

405) AMOS HOLT (*John*[4]*, Hannah Farnum Holt*[3]*, Elizabeth Holt Farnum*[2]*, Nicholas*[1]), b. at Andover, 9 May 1740 son of John and Mary (Lewis) Holt; d. at Wilton, NH, 29 Nov 1820; m. at Andover, 29 Jun 1762, JEMIMA INGALLS, b. at Andover, 27 Jul 1740 daughter of Francis and Lydia (Ingalls) Ingalls; Jemima d. at Wilton, 4 Dec 1816.

Amos Holt had gone to Wilton with his father and family, and he also settled there, living on the family homestead. His son Amos took over the farm after his father's death.[1098]

Son Levi planned to marry just prior to his death in 1812. He wrote his will 27 March 1812 shortly before his death. In his will, Levi bequeathed a suit of mourning apparel to his good friend Hannah Smith of Weston "to whom I had expected to be joined in marriage before this time." Mourning apparel was also bequeathed to his honored father Amos Holt, honored mother Jemima Holt, beloved brother Amos Hot, Jr., to the wife of Amos, to each of Amos's children, and to his beloved sister Cloe Bales all of Wilton; to his beloved sister Lydia Parker of Reading, Vermont; and to his beloved sisters Sally Whitney and Lois Walker of Andover, Vermont. To beloved brother Abel, he bequeaths a note he holds against him for $560 dated "Webb's Pond Township September 26, 1807" and payable January 1, 1811. He bequeathed $400 to the female asylum at Boston. The remainder of the

[1097] Livermore, *History of the Town of Wilton*, p 465

[1098] Livermore, *History of the Town of Wilton*, p 404

estate goes to Hannah Smith "whom I now own and honor as my intended wife and for whom I feel myself bound in duty and affection to make as ample provision as though our marriage had been legally solemnized. Her attention to me in my feeble state of health demands my acknowledgements." George Washington Smith of Weston was named sole executor.[1099] Levi's estate was valued at $7,576.86 almost all in the form of notes owed to him.

Amos Holt and Jemima Ingalls were parents of twelve children born at Wilton.

i LYDIA HOLT, b. about 1762; m. about 1790, JAMES PARKER who has not been identified; James d. at Reading, VT, about 1815. Lydia m. 2nd at Reading, VT, 19 Sep 1816, JERATHEMAL CUMMINGS who d. before 1820 when Lydia Cummings was head of household in Reading, VT, with the household consisting of one female over 45. There are records for two daughters of Lydia and James born at Wilton.

ii AMOS HOLT, b. 2 Oct 1764; d. 11 Aug 1767.

iii HANNAH HOLT, b. 11 Jan 1767; not mentioned in brother's will

iv AMOS HOLT, b. 20 Oct 1768; d. at Wilton, 13 Dec 1826; m. about 1790, his fourth cousin, MARY BALLARD (*Hannah Holt Ballard5, Jonathan4, Oliver3, Henry2, Nicholas1*), b. at Wilton, 8 May 1768 daughter of Nathan and Hannah (Holt) Ballard; Mary d. after 1850 when she was living in Milford, NH.

v SARAH HOLT, b. 13 Jan 1771; d. at Weston, VT, 21 Aug 1849; m. at Wilton, 3 Jun 1794, RICHARD WHITNEY, b. at Wilton, 25 Jun 1770 son of Richard and Sarah (Butterfield) Whitney; Richard d. at Weston, 30 Mar 1845.

vi ISAIAH HOLT, b. 28 Sep 1772; not mentioned in brother's will

vii PETER HOLT, b. 8 Jun 1774; d. 9 Sep 1774.

viii PETER HOLT, b. 24 Aug 1775; d. 30 Apr 1777.

ix ABEL HOLT, b. 11 Sep 1777; d. at Weld, ME, 1842 (probate Sep 1842); m. 1st at Milford, NH, 2 Dec 1802, GRACE HUBBARD, b. 26 May 1784;[1100] Grace d. at Weld, 10 Jun 1822. Abel m. 2nd about 1823, ISABELLE PRATT, b. at Turner, ME, 16 Jan 1800 daughter of Jonathan and Isabelle (Collins) Pratt; Isabelle d. after 1880 when she was living in Carthage, ME.

x LEVI HOLT, b. 28 Jun 1780; d. at Weston, MA, 10 May 1812. Levi was a trader in Boston. He was in Weston at the time of his death. He planned to marry Hannah Smith and there is a record of the marriage intention for 2 Jan 1812, but according to his will of 27 Mar 1812, they did not marry.

xi LOIS HOLT, b. 4 Jul 1782; d. at Andover, VT, 4 Dec 1862; m. JESSE WALKER, b. 1780 son of Sampson and Thankful (Pierce) Walker; Jesse d. at Andover, VT, 21 Apr 1829.

xii CHLOE HOLT, b. 4 Sep 1784; m. at Wilton, 13 Oct 1807, WILLIAM LOWTHER BALES, b. at Wilton, 13 Mar 1784 son of William and Rhoda (Keyes) Bales; William d. after 1870 when he was living in Allen, OH.

406) ELEANOR "NELLY" HOLT (*John4, Hannah Farnum Holt3, Elizabeth Holt Farnum2, Nicholas1*), b. at Andover, 27 Jun 1743 daughter of John and Mary (Lewis) Holt; m. 5 Jan 1762, AARON BLANCHARD, b. at Andover, 27 Jun 1740 son of Thomas and Elizabeth (Johnson) Blanchard; Aaron d. at Hartford, NY, 28 Oct 1801.[1101] Aaron married second Mehitable Mooar (widow of Emery Chase) on 21 Sep 1789.

Aaron Blanchard was a blacksmith. Nelly and Aaron resided in Andover where their thirteen children were born. After 1792, Aaron may have left Andover after selling his property and was perhaps in Dracut where he is buried. On 21 March 1791, Aaron Blanchard and wife Mehitable and Thomas Blanchard and wife Lois sold two lots of land in Andover to Jacob French of Tewksbury.[1102] Sons John and Aaron were first settlers in Elizabethtown, Leeds, Ontario where they had adjoining properties.[1103]

i THOMAS BLANCHARD, b. 11 Nov 1762; d. at Henderson, NY, 1 Feb 1837; m. at Andover, 12 Mar 1782, LOIS BURT, b. at Andover, 16 Jun 1763 daughter of Joseph and Abiah (Mooar) Burt; Lois d. at Henderson, 19 Sep 1814.[1104]

ii MARY BLANCHARD, b. 2 Sep 1764; d. 14 May 1786.

iii AARON BLANCHARD, b. 12 Aug 1766; d. at Greenbush, Ontario, 1843; m. MABEL LATTIMER, b. in NY, 1774; Mabel d. at Greenbush, 1861.

[1099] *Probate Records 1648--1924 (Middlesex County, Massachusetts), Probate Papers, No 11781-11878, Case 11789*

[1100] Town records of Weld, Maine

[1101] Death is recorded at Dracut but gives place of death as Hartford, NY; Aaron [h. Mehitabel], Oct. 28, 1801, a. 61, in Hartford, N. Y. G.R.6.

[1102] Massachusetts Land Records, Essex County, 153:32

[1103] Leavitt, *History of Leeds and Grenville, Ontario*, p 178

[1104] Thomas and Lois Blanchard are interred at Carpenter Cemetery in Henderson, NY; findagrave 29458615

iv SUSANNA BLANCHARD, b. 23 May 1768; d. 4 Sep 1775.

v NELLY BLANCHARD, b. 20 Apr 1770; d. 26 Sep 1775.

vi JOHN BLANCHARD, b. 1 Jun 1772; d. at Greenbush, Ontario, 22 Jun 1856; m. ABIGAIL WAITE, b. about 1781 (age 80 in 1861); Abigail d. at Greenbush, 5 Apr 1864.

vii LUCY BLANCHARD, b. 12 Sep 1774; d. 3 Sep 1775.

viii NELLE BLANCHARD, baptized at Andover, 7 Jan 1776; d. at Lynnfield, MA, 21 Jun 1854; m. 24 Aug 1795, BENJAMIN DANFORTH, b. at Lynnfield, 21 Feb 1773 son of Joshua and Keziah (Reed) Danforth; Benjamin d. at Lynnfield, 29 Jun 1854.

ix AMOS BLANCHARD, b. 1 Sep 1777; d. at Tewksbury, 3 Aug 1817; m. at Andover, 31 Jul 1798, ALICE FOSTER, b. at Tewksbury, 29 Sep 1778 daughter of Amos and Sarah (French) Foster; Alice d. at Tewksbury, 16 Dec 1837.

x LUCY BLANCHARD, b. 10 Jun 1780; d. at Danvers, 10 Mar 1845; m. at Andover, 12 Apr 1803, DANIEL MARSH, b. 1775; Daniel d. at Danvers, 15 Apr 1845.

xi SUSANNA BLANCHARD, b. 18 Jun 1782; d. 20 Aug 1783.

xii SUSANNA BLANCHARD, b. 20 Mar 1784; d. 5 Apr 1785.

xiii MARY BLANCHARD, b. 17 Mar 1786; d. 30 Jul 1786.

407) DANIEL HOLT (*John[4], Hannah Farnum Holt[3], Elizabeth Holt Farnum[2], Nicholas[1]*), b. at Andover, 10 Jan 1745/6 son of John and Mary (Lewis) Holt; d. at Wilton, 5 Nov 1777;[1105] m. about 1766, MEHITABLE PUTNAM, b. at Wilton, 25 Dec 1745 daughter of Jacob and Susannah (Stiles) Putnam; Mehitable d. at Wilton 20 Jan 1800.

Daniel Holt and Mehitable Putnam were parents of four children born at Wilton.

i MEHITABLE HOLT, b. at Wilton, 11 Sep 1768; d. at Pomfret, CT, 7 Mar 1857; m. 20 Feb 1791, JAMES ABBOTT, b. at Andover, 2 Feb 1768; James d. at Billerica, MA, Jul 1810. In her later life, Mehitable went to live with her daughter Sophronia Abbott Grosvenor in Pomfret.

ii DANIEL HOLT, b. at Wilton, 20 Oct 1769; d. at Wilton, 20 Jun 1852; m. at Wilton, 3 Feb 1795, his fourth cousin, DORCAS ABBOTT (*Chloe Abbott Abbott[6], Anne Lovejoy Abbott[5], William Lovejoy[4], Mary Farnum Lovejoy[3], Elizabeth Holt Farnum[2], Nicholas[1]*), b. at Wilton, 24 Aug 1772 daughter of Jeremiah and Chloe (Abbott) Abbott; Dorcas d. at Wilton, Jul 1847.

iii ELIZABETH HOLT, b. at Wilton, 5 Apr 1772; d. at Milford, 20 Oct 1854; m. 1792, her third cousin once removed, ABIEL HOLT (*Abiel[5], Thomas[4], Thomas[3], Nicholas[2], Nicholas[1]*), b. at Andover, Jan 1770 son of Abiel and Lydia (Lovejoy) Holt; Abiel d. at Milford, 11 Feb 1834.

iv CALEB HOLT, b. at Wilton, 16 Oct 1777; d. at Weld, ME, 19 Oct 1870; m. 1st 12 Feb 1801, his fourth cousin, ELIZABETH "BETSEY" GRAY (*Timothy Gray[5], Timothy Gray[4], Braviter Gray[3], Hannah Holt Gray[2], Nicholas[1]*), b. 12 Feb 1775 daughter of Timothy and Hannah (Blanchard) Gray; Betsey d. at Weld, 16 Jul 1809. Caleb m. 2nd 17 Jun 1810, his fourth cousin, PHEBE ABBOTT (*Chloe Abbott Abbott[6], Anne Lovejoy Abbott[5], William Lovejoy[4], Mary Farnum Lovejoy[3], Elizabeth Holt Farnum[2], Nicholas[1]*), b. at Wilton, 24 Aug 1772 daughter of Jeremiah and Chloe (Abbott) Abbott; Phebe d. after 1850. Phebe Abbott was first married to Walter Fiske.

408) SAMUEL HOLT (*John[4], Hannah Farnum Holt[3], Elizabeth Holt Farnum[2], Nicholas[1]*), baptized at Andover, 7 May 1749 son of John and Mary (Lewis) Holt; d. at Temple, NH, 5 Dec 1799;[1106] m. about 1771, LYDIA ADAMS, b. at Dunstable, NH, 27 Jul 1749 daughter of Ephraim and Thankful (Blodgett) Adams; Lydia d. at Wilton, 24 Jun 1844.

Samuel Holt was born in Andover but settled in Temple, New Hampshire around 1770 about the same time as his marriage to Lydia Adams.[1107] They were parents of ten children born at Temple.[1108][1109]

[1105] Daniel died in the 32nd year of his age according to his gravestone making it likely that it is Daniel the son of John and Mary who married Mehitable Putnam. Some sources suggest he was the son of the proposed marriage of John Holt (born 1713) and Rachel Fletcher but there are no records of that marriage or any children from that marriage.

[1106] Samuel's death record lists his parents as John and Mary Holt.

[1107] Blood, *The History of Temple, NH*, p. 226

[1108] New Hampshire Births and Christenings, 1714-1904, accessed through familysearch.org

[1109] Blood, *The History of Temple, NH*

i LYDIA HOLT, b. at Temple, 12 Nov 1771; d. at Nelson, NH, 6 Feb 1813; m. at Temple, 17 Nov 1791, ANDREW STILES, b. at Wilton, 10 Jan 1770 son of Joseph and Eunice (Wilkins) Stiles; Andrew d. at Nelson, 18 Oct 1828. Andrew married second Dorcas Beard.

ii SAMUEL HOLT, b. at Temple, 1 Apr 1773; d. at Nelson, 4 Oct 1848; m. at Temple, 1796, PHEBE PERRY, b. at Wilton, 6 Mar 1768 daughter of Abijah and Hannah (Boutwell) Perry; Phebe d. at Nelson, Dec 1822.

iii JOHN HOLT, b. 8 Nov 1775; d. 6 Nov 1776.

iv EPHRAIM ADAMS HOLT, b. at Temple, 14 Aug 1778; d. at Sullivan, NH, 31 Jul 1857; m. at Temple, 1801, RHODA RUSSELL, b. at Lyndeborough, 9 Feb 1782 daughter of Jedediah and Rhoda (Pratt) Russell; Rhoda d. at Sullivan, 28 Jun 1867.

v RACHEL HOLT, b. 9 Sep 1780; d. 9 Apr 1782.

vi DANIEL HOLT, b. 27 Sep 1782; d. at Nelson, NH, 14 Sep 1803.

vii NATHANIEL HOLT, b. at Temple, 22 May 1786; d. after 1860 when he was living in Dublin; m. 1st at Temple, 6 Dec 1805, SARAH UPHAM; Sarah d. at Temple, 18 Jul 1847. Nathaniel m. 2nd 13 Nov 1849, HANNAH BURNS, b. at Dublin, 4 Apr 1802 daughter of James and Hannah (Twitchell) Burns; Hannah d. at Dublin, 30 Nov 1871.

viii ESTHER HOLT, b. at Temple, 15 Jun 1788; d. at Weston, VT, Jun 1827; m. at Temple, 16 Mar 1806, ROBERT SMITH who has not been identified. Robert married second Sybil Fletcher on 13 Dec 1832.

ix NEHEMIAH HOLT, b. at Temple, 25 Sep 1790; d. at Milford, 20 Oct 1868; m. at Temple, 31 Dec 1812, MARY WRIGHT, b. 1792 daughter of Benjamin and Betty (Adams) Wright; Mary d. at Temple, 22 Apr 1838.

x HENRY HOLT, b. 7 Mar 1793; d. 13 Jun 1795.

409) THOMAS FARNUM (*Thomas Farnum4, Thomas Farnum3, Elizabeth Holt Farnum2, Nicholas1*), b. at Andover, 6 Sep 1734 son of Thomas and Phebe (Towne) Farnum; d. perhaps at Greenfield, NH; m. at Andover, 13 Jan 1757, LYDIA ABBOTT, b. at Andover, 28 Mar 1733 daughter of Timothy and Mary (Foster) Abbott; Lydia d. at Andover, 13 Mar 1816. Thomas death is not known but was perhaps in NH living with his grandchildren.

Lydia Abbott and Thomas Farnum had seven children whose births are recorded at Andover.

i LYDIA FARNUM, b. 10 Nov 1756; m. 27 Oct 1774, her second cousin, THOMAS HOLT (*Thomas4, Thomas3, Nicholas2, Nicholas1*), b. 15 Jun 1750 son of Thomas and Dorcas (Holt) Holt.

ii ISRAEL FARNUM, b. 14 Jun 1758; d. at Mont Vernon, NH, 1842; m. 3 Aug 1786, PHEBE SHELDON; Phebe d. 2 Feb 1824. Israel m. 2nd, 17 May 1825, SUSANNAH FARNUM, b. 22 Mar 1772 daughter of Asa and Susannah (Town) Farnum.[1110]

iii TIMOTHY FARNUM, b. 13 May 1759; m. 23 Sep 1786, SUSANNA BERRY, b. 27 Apr 1767 daughter of Nathaniel and Susanna (-) Berry; Susanna d. 16 Jul 1854.

iv PHEBE FARNUM, b. 25 Jul 1762; m. SAVAGE (according to Charlotte Helen Abbott). No records for this marriage were located, and it may be that this is the Phebe Farnum that married David Hovey.

v SARAH FARNUM, b. 21 Sep 1764; m. ENOS ABBOTT of Andover, ME, b. 7 Feb 1769 son of Jonathan and Ruth (Bragg) Abbott of The Rowley Abbott line.

vi DORCAS FARNUM, b. 27 Dec 1766; m. 25 Dec 1789, NATHAN JONES, b. 1767; Nathan d. at Andover, 14 Aug 1804.

vii MARY FARNUM, b. 1770; d. at Andover, 25 Jan 1809. Mary did not marry.

410) ASA FARNUM (*Thomas Farnum4, Thomas Farnum3, Elizabeth Holt Farnum2, Nicholas1*), b. at Andover, 11 May 1736 son of Thomas and Phebe (Towne) Farnum; m. at Topsfield, 16 Mar 1758, SUSANNAH TOWNE, b. at Topsfield, 6 Sep 1733 daughter of Benjamin and Susanna (Wilds) Towne.[1111]

On 2 September 1760, Asa Farnum for the receipt of £100 conveyed to Benjamin Towne of Topsfield and Ebenezer Farnum a piece of land of about 24 acres. This transaction also includes a statement that Asa for his debts has become bound along with Benjamin and Ebenezer to the widow Sarah Bowditch to pay her £40 with interest and an additional bond to Daniel Farrington for £40. On 15 August 1761, Asa has a further deed to Benjamin Towne and Ebenezer Farnum, this time specifying the property with the dwelling house, this transaction also related to Asa's debts and Benjamin and Abraham then assuming a

[1110] Smith, *History of Mont Vernon*, p 63

[1111] The 1772 will of Benjamin Towne includes a bequest to his daughter Susanna Varnum.

bond with Asa for four hundred good Spanish milled dollars, this being bound to Thomas Orne of Salem. The property with dwelling house was finally sold by Asa Farnum and wife Susannah to Nathan Towne for £129.6.8 on 29 June 1766.[1112]

The children in this family are something of a puzzle. There are records of either births or baptisms for four children in Andover, two of the daughters named Susannah. Smith's *History of the Town of Mont Vernon* (p. 63) states that Susannah daughter of Asa and Susannah married Israel Farnum as a second wife, but gives a birth date that varies by several years from the Andover records (reporting a birth date of 22 March 1772 for Israel's wife). Farnham's Farnum genealogy in its record for Israel gives Susannah as a daughter of Asa and Susannah with the 22 March 1772 date but then does not include her in Asa's family record. There is also a Susannah Farnum that married Jedidiah Farnum in Andover in 1797 and it seems at least possible that Susannah in this family first married Jedidiah Farnum and then Israel Farnum.

i SUSANNAH FARNUM, b. 12 Nov 1758

ii ASA FARNUM, b. 22 Nov 1760; m. at Andover, 2 Dec 1784, LUCINDA ABBOTT who has not been identified. There are records for five children of Asa and Lucinda born at Andover.

iii BENJAMIN FARNUM, baptized at Andover, 1 Apr 1764

iv SUSANNAH FARNUM, baptized at Andover, 2 Jun 1765

v SUSANNAH FARNUM, b. 22 Mar 1772;[1113] m. at Amherst, NH, 17 May 1825, as his second wife, her first cousin, ISRAEL FARNUM (*Thomas Farnum⁵, Thomas Farnum⁴, Thomas Farnum³, Elizabeth Holt Farnum², Nicholas¹*), b. at Andover, 14 Jun 1758 son of Thomas and Lydia (Abbott) Farnum; Israel d. at Mont Vernon, 1842. Israel was first married to Phebe Sheldon.

411) JOSEPH FARNUM (*Thomas Farnum⁴, Thomas Farnum³, Elizabeth Holt Farnum², Nicholas¹*), b. at Andover, 18 Jun 1745 son of Thomas and Phebe (Towne) Farnum; d. at Mont Vernon, NH, 10 May 1824; m. 1st about 1766, MARY LYON, b. about 1747 likely the daughter of Ebenezer and Abigail (Bullard) Lyon; Mary d. 1787. Joseph m. 2nd at Amherst, 17 Sep 1794, TABITHA WESTON (widow of Daniel Wilkins and Jesse Baldwin), b. at Wakefield, MA, 31 Mar 1748 daughter of Ebenezer and Mehitable (Sutherick) Weston; Tabitha d. at Mont Vernon, Jan 1820. Joseph m. 3rd, EDITH SMITH, b. about 1774; Edith d. at Mont Vernon, 12 Nov 1862.

Joseph Farnum settled in Amherst soon after its incorporation, in the area that was later Mont Vernon. He served as lieutenant in the company of Capt. John Bradford at Bennington.[1114]

On 4 July 1854 and again on 9 April 1855, Edith Farnum age eighty years of Mont Vernon, made application for a widow's pension based on her husband's service. She reported that Joseph served in the Continental army in 1776 and 1777, first as a private in the company of Capt. Shepard and later as a lieutenant under Capt. Ballard. Edith reported that in 1777 Joseph was on his way to Ticonderoga, but when troops received news of the evacuation of Ticonderoga, he returned home. Edith noted that she knew few of the details of her husband's service. The pension application was ultimately rejected.[1115]

Joseph Farnum and Mary Lyon were parents of twelve children.

i SARAH FARNUM, b. at Amherst, 22 Jun 1766

ii ABIGAIL FARNUM, b. at Amherst, 27 Dec 1767; m. 23 Oct 1788, her third cousin, PETER ABBOTT (*Phebe Ingalls Abbott⁵, Phebe Farnum Ingalls⁴, John Farnum³, Elizabeth Holt Farnum², Nicholas¹*), b. at Amherst, 28 Jul 1762 son of Joshua and Phebe (Ingalls) Abbott; Peter d. at Rome, NY, after 1815.

iii MARY FARNUM, b. at Amherst, 9 Jan 1770; d. at Claremont, NH, 5 Oct 1855; m. 24 Sep 1789, OLIVER CARLETON b. at Amherst, 23 Aug 1767 son of Oliver and Amy (Washer) Carleton; Oliver d. a Claremont, NH, 20 Feb 1860.

iv PHEBE FARNUM, b. at Amherst, 12 May 1772; m. about 1795, LAMBERT BRADFORD, b. at Amherst, 18 Mar 1775 son of William and Rachel (Small) Bradford; Lambert d. at Merrimack, NH, 12 Feb 1850.

v JOSEPH FARNUM, b. at Amherst, 4 Mar 1774; d. at Landgrove, VT, 6 Mar 1852; m. SARAH DODGE, b. 1776; Sarah d. at Landgrove, 15 May 1864.

vi SUSANNAH FARNUM, b. at Amherst, 27 Mar 1776; m. at Amherst, 10 Jan 1797, ZACCHAEUS BEMIS,[1116] b. about 1761 son of Zacchaeus and Elizabeth (Lyon) Bemis. Susannah and Zacchaeus were living in Windham, VT in 1820. The births of six children are recorded at Windham.

vii THOMAS FARNUM, b. at Amherst, 26 Jan 1778

1112 Massachusetts Land Records, 1620-1986, Essex County, 109:41; 110:34; 119:1

1113 This is as reported in Smith's *History of Mont Vernon*.

1114 Smith, *History of the Town of Mont Vernon*, p 63

1115 U. S. Revolutionary War Pension and Bounty-Land Warrant Application Files, Case R3444.

1116 Although the marriage transcription from Amherst gives his name as Zachariah, the marriage intention in Westminster gives his name as Zacchaeus Bemis, Jr. and the birth records for the children give father as Zacchaeus.

viii ASA FARNUM, b. at Amherst, 1 Feb 1780; d. after 1860 when he was living in Peru, VT; m. 14 Apr 1803, ARETHUSA LOVEJOY, b. at Amherst, 1775 daughter of Joseph and Patience (Bradford) Lovejoy; Arethusa d. after 1860.

ix HANNAH FARNUM, b. at Amherst, 3 Jul 1782

x BETTY FARNUM, b. at Amherst, 24 Mar 1784

xi LUCY FARNUM, b. at Amherst, 3 May 1786; m. 10 Jul 1811, BENJAMIN FASSETT, b. at Sherborn, MA, 7 Sep 1787 son of Asa and Margaret (Page) Fassett; Benjamin d. at Albany, NY, 9 Oct 1857.[1117] The baptisms of two children, Louisa and Joseph Farnum, are recorded at the Presbyterian church in Albany.[1118]

xii MARTHA FARNUM, b. at Mont Vernon, 1787; d. at Mont Vernon, 14 Apr 1841; m. 21 Nov 1810, SILAS WILKINS, b. 1790 son of Benjamin and Naomi (Smith) Wilkins; Silas d. at Mont Vernon, 29 Oct 1852.

Joseph Farnum and Tabitha Weston were parents of two children.

i GERA FARNUM, b. at Mont Vernon, 26 Feb 1795; d. at Roxbury, MA, 14 Apr 1864; m. at Amherst, 17 Oct 1817, SOPHRONIA BILLS, b. at Wardsboro, VT, about 1798 daughter of Ebenezer and Hannah (Bullard) Bills; Sophronia d. at Boston, 10 Apr 1886.

ii JOHN FARNUM, b. at Mont Vernon, 15 Aug 1796; d. at Brighton, MA, 30 Sep 1845; m. at Nelson, NH, 4 Oct 1821, ELIZABETH "BETSEY" ROBBINS, b. at Nelson, 14 Sep 1800 daughter of Asa and Elizabeth (Spear) Robbins

412) HANNAH FARNUM (*Ebenezer Farnum[4], Thomas Farnum[3], Elizabeth Holt Farnum[2], Nicholas[1]*), b. at Andover, 9 Sep 1733 daughter of Ebenezer and Priscilla (Ingalls) Farnum; m. at Andover, 13 Nov 1753; DANIEL FARRINGTON, b. at Andover, Jun 1732 son of Daniel and Elizabeth (Putnam) Farrington; Daniel d. at Fryeburg, ME, about 1818.

Hannah and Daniel were in Andover where their first five children were born. On 10 March 1767, Daniel and his wife Hannah sold one tract of meadow land in Andover to Daniel Lovejoy.[1119] Daniel Farrington was one of the first proprietors of Fryeburg, Maine and Hannah and Daniel settled there before 1770. Daniel obtained one of the sixty-four "rights" of property disposed of by Col. Frye.[1120]

Hannah Farnum and Daniel Farrington were parents of seven children.

i EBENEZER FARRINGTON, b. at Andover, 27 Jun 1754; d. 20 Sep 1757.

ii PUTNAM FARRINGTON, b. at Andover, 17 Jan 1756; m. SARAH PERHAM, b. at New Ipswich, NH, 10 Oct 1754 daughter of Samuel and Mary (Parker) Perham.

iii EBENEZER FARRINGTON, b. at Andover, 10 Oct 1757

iv ELIZABETH FARRINGTON, b. at Andover, 3 Feb 1759; m. at Fryeburg, 26 Feb 1781, JOHN CHARLES

v HANNAH L. FARRINGTON, b. at Andover, 9 Jul 1765; d. at North Fryeburg, 29 Nov 1825; m. about 1785, JOSEPH CHANDLER, b. at Concord, NH, 18 Nov 1760 son of John and Mary (Carter) Chandler; Joseph d. at North Fryeburg, 23 Apr 1826. Hannah and Joseph were parents of thirteen children all of whom lived to adulthood and married.

vi SARAH FARRINGTON, b. at Fryeburg, 10 Mar 1771; m. at Fryeburg, 8 Apr 1796, DAVID COLBY

vii DANIEL FARRINGTON, b. at Fryeburg, 19 Jan 1775

413) SUSANNAH FARNUM (*Ebenezer Farnum[4], Thomas Farnum[3], Elizabeth Holt Farnum[2], Nicholas[1]*), b. at Andover, 31 Aug 1735 daughter of Ebenezer and Priscilla (Ingalls) Farnum; d. at Fryeburg, ME; m. at Andover, 29 May 1753, ISAAC ABBOTT, b. at Andover, 30 Jun 1728 son of Ebenezer and Hannah (Turner) Abbott; Isaac d. at Fryeburg, after 1790.

The births of seven children are recorded at Andover. Three other children born in Maine can be reasonably placed in this family. Each of them has a record for a marriage in Fryeburg.

i SUSANNA ABBOTT, b. 29 Aug 1754;[1121] d. at Oxford County, ME, 21 Sep 1827; m. SAMUEL CHARLES, b. 28 Aug 1754 son of John and Abigail (Bliss) Charles; Samuel d. 14 Dec 1843.

[1117] Menands, New York, Albany Rural Cemetery Burial Cards, 1791-2011
[1118] Foley, *Early Settlers of New York State*, volume 1, p 165
[1119] Massachusetts Land Records, Essex County, 123:78
[1120] Barrows, *Fryeburg, Maine*, p 70
[1121] The transcription of this record indicates the record was torn and only the last letter "a" is present.

ii OLIVE ABBOTT, b. 17 Feb 1756; d. in Oxford County, ME, 27 Aug 1828; m. about 1782, as his second wife, JOHN CHARLES, b. 28 Feb 1744 son of John and Abigail (Bliss) Charles; John d. 6 Jun 1831. John was first married to Phebe Russell.

iii LUCY ABBOTT, b. 20 Mar 1759; d. at Maine about 1790; m. WILLIAM KIMBALL. William m. 2nd, BETHIAH GORDON; William d. about 1813 (date of probate).

iv EBENEZER ABBOTT, b. 7 Dec 1760.

v ISAAC ABBOTT, b. 16 Jun 1762; d. at Fryeburg, ME, 23 Jun 1861; m. SUSANNA NOYES KNIGHT, b. about 1770 daughter of Stephen and Susanna (Noyes) Knight; Susanna d. 3 Sep 1851. Isaac is likely also the father of Enoch Eaton Abbott, an out-of-wedlock child born to Sarah Eaton in 1785.

vi SIMEON ABBOTT, b. 20 May 1764; d. at Stow, ME, 7 May 1851; m. 3 Jul 1791, MARY DAY, b. Feb 1768 daughter of Moses and Hannah (-) Day; Mary d. 14 Sep 1840.

vii MICAH ABBOTT, b. 15 May 1766; d. 16 Aug 1767.

viii JAMES ABBOTT, b. 1770 (based on age 89 at death); d. at Stow, ME, Dec 1859; m. at Fryeburg, 16 Aug 1795, ELIZABETH DAY, b. 18 Jun 1773 daughter of Moses and Hannah (-) Day; Elizabeth d. 6 Nov 1857.

ix MICAH ABBOTT, b. at Fryeburg, 1 Nov 1774; d. at Stow, ME, 2 Jul 1825; m. about 1795, ALICE WILEY, b. at Stow, 20 May 1778 daughter of Benjamin and Alice (Kilgore) Wiley; Alice d. 14 Sep 1858. After Micah's death, Alice married Samuel Huntress.

x DOROTHY "DOLLY" ABBOTT, b. 16 Aug 1778; d. at Richland, MI, 11 Nov 1858; m. at Fryeburg, 26 Oct 1795, JOSEPH CHARLES, b. 7 Apr 1773 son of Abner and Sarah (Walker) Charles; Joseph d. at Wyoming County, NY, 26 Jan 1846.

414) PRISCILLA FARNUM (*Ebenezer Farnum[4], Thomas Farnum[3], Elizabeth Holt Farnum[2], Nicholas[1]*), b. at Andover, 24 Mar 1740/1 daughter of Ebenezer and Priscilla (Ingalls) Farnum; d. at Andover, 25 Oct 1784; m. 4 Sep 1760, JONATHAN BALLARD, b. 25 Nov 1729 son of Sherebiah and Lydia (Osgood) Ballard; Jonathan d. at Middleton, 1 Feb 1764.

Jonathan Ballard was a physician in Middleton. He and Priscilla were parents of three children, the youngest child born after Jonathan's death.

Dr. Jonathan Ballard did not leave a will and his estate entered probate 12 March 1764 with widow Priscilla declining administration and requesting that some fit person be named as administrator and Daniel Farrington (likely her brother-in-law) was named.[1122] The inventory included numerous medical preparations of the era such as radit-valerian and radit-gentian.

i JONATHAN BALLARD, b. at Middleton, 29 Jun 1761; d. at Temple, ME, 28 Nov 1830; m. at Andover, 17 Dec 1789, his third cousin once removed, BETTE ABBOTT (*Thomas Abbott[5], Thomas Abbott[4], Hannah Gray Abbott[3], Hannah Holt Gray[2], Nicholas[1]*), b. at Andover, 25 Jun 1763 daughter of Thomas and Lydia (Blunt) Abbott; Bette d. at Temple, 12 Feb 1842.

ii FREDERICK BALLARD, b. at Middleton, 13 Oct 1762; d. at Newry, ME, 1851; m. at Bethel, ME, 1794, HANNAH RUSSELL, b. 1775 daughter of Abraham and Sarah (Swan) Russell; Hannah d. a Newry, ME, 1848.

iii SHEREBIAH BALLARD, b. at Andover, 12 Mar 1764

415) DOROTHY "DOLLY" FARNUM (*Ebenezer Farnum[4], Thomas Farnum[3], Elizabeth Holt Farnum[2], Nicholas[1]*), b. at Andover, 21 Jan 1744/5 daughter of Ebenezer and Priscilla (Ingalls) Farnum; d. after 1820; m. at Andover, 10 Mar 1774, JOHN FOWLER, b. at Ipswich, 1748 son of Joseph and Elizabeth (Perkins) Fowler;[1123] John d. about 1778 at Mill Prison in England where he was a prisoner after being captured during the Revolution.[1124]

John and Dolly lived in Ipswich. John was a mariner and was taken by the British from the brig *Fancy* in 1777 and died in Mill Prison.[1125]

i ELIZABETH FOWLER, baptized at Ipswich, 31 Dec 1775; d. at Beverly, 25 Aug 1852; m. 7 Feb 1809, JOSEPH CHIPMAN, b. at Beverly, 26 Oct 1738 son of John and Rebecca (Hale) Chipman; Joseph d. at Beverly, 9 May 1817. Joseph Chipman was the great-great grandson of John Howland who traveled on the *Mayflower*. Joseph was first married to Elizabeth Obear. Elizabeth Fowler and Joseph Chipman were parents of two children.

1122 *Essex County, MA: Probate File Papers, 1638-1881.*Online database. *AmericanAncestors.org.* New England Historic Genealogical Society, 2014. Case 1592

1123 Stickney, *The Fowler Family*

1124 Cards Concerning Revolutionary War Service and Imprisonment, NEHGR, 1947

1125 Stickney, *The Fowler Family*, p 101

ii SARAH FOWLER, baptized at Ipswich, 9 Mar 1777; d. at Falmouth, ME, Oct 1857; m. 11 May 1799, JOSIAH BATCHELDER, b. at Beverly, 3 Jan 1776 son of Josiah and Hannah (Dodge) Batchelder; Josiah d. at Falmouth, 5 Feb 1857. Josiah Batchelder graduated from Dartmouth and Harvard Medical and was a physician in Falmouth, Maine.

416) ABIAH FARNUM (*Ebenezer Farnum*[4], *Thomas Farnum*[3], *Elizabeth Holt Farnum*[2], *Nicholas*[1]), b. at Andover, 13 Feb 1746/7 daughter of Ebenezer and Priscilla (Ingalls) Farnum; d. at Tamworth, NH, 22 Jun 1823; m. 4 Apr 1769, JOHN AYER; John d. at Pembroke, NH, 1802 (probate 19 May 1802). Abiah m. 2nd at Pembroke, 8 Nov 1810, as his third wife, Col. DAVID GILMAN, b. at Exeter, NH, 9 Jun 1735 son of Israel and Deborah (Thwing) Gilman; David d. at Tamworth, 11 May 1826. David Gilman was first married to Betsy Gilman and second married to Sarah Smith.

John Ayer was a farmer in Pembroke and signed the association test there in 1776.[1126]

In his will written 16 January 1801 (proved 19 May 1802), John Ayer bequeathed to beloved wife Abia one-third of the real and personal estate during her natural life. Daughter Abigail receives twenty-five dollars. Second daughter Polly receives one dollar as she has received her portion. Daughter Abia receives twenty-five dollars and thirty-five dollars in household furniture. Son John receives five dollars. Daughters Phebe, Sally, Betsey, and Hannah also each receive twenty-five dollars in cash and thirty-five dollars in household furniture. If any of the daughters above mentioned should not marry, they have a right to live in the home with the executor, but the executor is then under no obligation to pay the legacies to them. Son Timothy receives all the real and personal estate and is named executor.[1127] Real estate was valued at $950 and personal estate at $296.40.

Abiah Farnum and John Ayer were parents of thirteen children born at Pembroke.

i JOHN AYER, b. 10 Jan 1770; d. 21 May 1770.

ii ABIGAIL AYER, b. and d. 23 Feb 1771.

iii JOHN AYER, b. 9 Dec 1772; d. 9 May 1774.

iv ABIGAIL AYER, b. 22 Nov 1773; m. at Pembroke, 8 Nov 1796, JACOB EDDS who has not been identified. They were resident in Pembroke in 1800, but nothing further known.

v TIMOTHY AYER, b. 3 Sep 1775; d. at Pembroke, 25 Jul 1850; m. LUCINDA CRAM, b. 1776 and d. 3 Feb 1844.[1128]

vi MARY "POLLY" AYER, b. 5 Sep 1775; d. after 1855 (living at time of husband's will); m. at Pembroke, 26 Nov 1799, SAMUEL GOODHUE, b. at Deerfield, NH, 1777 son of Robert and Mary (Gilman) Goodhue; Samuel d. at Deerfield, 30 Nov 1855.

vii ABIAH AYER, b. at Pembroke, 21 Oct 1777; d. at Candia, NH, 1870; m. at Pembroke, 23 Dec 1805, JOSEPH MARTIN, b. at Candia, about 1779 son of Moses and Miriam (Wadleigh) Martin;[1129] Joseph d. at Candia, 1871.

viii JOHN AYER, b. at Pembroke, 9 Jun 1781; d. at Bristol, NH, 28 Apr 1864; m. at Pembroke, 30 Jun 1808, JUDITH MCCUTCHEON, b. at Pembroke, 1788 daughter of Phedris and Anne (Brown) McCutcheon; Judith d. at Bristol, 5 Aug 1872.

ix PHEBE AYER, b. at Pembroke, 9 Apr 1783; d. at Pembroke, 16 Feb 1848.

x EBENEZER AYER, b. 10 Jun 1785; d. 8 Feb 1787.

xi SALLY AYER, b. at Pembroke, 6 Jul 1787

xii BETSEY AYER, b. about 1789; living in 1801.[1130]

xiii HANNAH AYER, b. 15 Jul 1791; d. at Pembroke, 28 Apr 1848; m. at Pembroke, 19 Dec 1817, her fourth cousin, JOHN HOLT (*Daniel*[5], *Benjamin*[4], *Nicholas*[3], *Nicholas*[2], *Nicholas*[1]), b. at Pembroke, 14 Feb 1784 son of Daniel and Abigail (Lovejoy) Holt; John d. at Pembroke, 22 Aug 1856.

417) PHEBE FARNUM (*Ebenezer Farnum*[4], *Thomas Farnum*[3], *Elizabeth Holt Farnum*[2], *Nicholas*[1]), b. at Andover, 15 Dec 1750 daughter of Ebenezer and Priscilla (Ingalls) Farnum; likely m. about 1771, JOB ABBOTT,[1131] b. at Pembroke, about 1742 son of David and Hannah (Chandler) Abbott; Job d. at West Barnet, VT, 15 Dec 1815.

[1126] Carter, *History of Pembroke*

[1127] *New Hampshire. Probate Court (Rockingham County)*; Probate Place: *Rockingham, New Hampshire, Volume 34, p 136-137*

[1128] Carter, *History of Pembroke*, volume 2

[1129] Moore, *History of the Town of Candia*, p 481

[1130] Betsey is the only child for whom there is not a birth transcription. She is a daughter named in the will of her father.

[1131] There are at least five Phebe Farnums born in a ten-year period at Andover with little or no record evidence that would discriminate one from the other in terms of marriages. This marriage seems the most likely for this Phebe.

Job Abbott and Phebe Farnum were parents likely of ten children, the oldest six children born at Pembroke, New Hampshire and the youngest four born perhaps at Barnet, Vermont.[1132] Of the six children who married, four of them married children from newly arrived families from Scotland, three of them children of Walter and Janet (Stuart) Brock.

i SARAH ABBOTT, b. at Pembroke, 21 Mar 1772; d. at Barnet, VT, 14 Sep 1851; m. ALEXANDER STUART, b. in Scotland, 1768 son of Claudius and Janet (McFarlane) Stuart; Alexander d. at Barnet, 2 Mar 1840.

ii HANNAH ABBOTT, b. at Pembroke, 30 Dec 1773; m. JONATHAN DARLING, b. at Hampstead, NH, 20 Dec 1767 son of John and Phebe (Robards) Darling; Jonathan d. at Groton, VT, 9 Oct 1820.

iii PHEBE ABBOTT, b. at Pembroke, 28 Feb 1775; d. at Barnet, VT, 5 Oct 1873; m. JOHN BROCK, b. Glasgow, Lanarkshire, Scotland, 31 Oct 1768 son of Walter and Janet (Stuart) Brock;[1133] John d. at Barnet, 5 Nov 1852.

iv SUSANNA ABBOTT, b. at Pembroke, Dec 1778; d. at Cabot, VT, 24 Sep 1862; m. about 1798, JOSIAH DARLING, b. at Hampstead, NH, 14 Jun 1772 son of John and Phebe (Robards) Darling; Josiah d. at Ryegate about 1830. Susanna m. 2nd, Mr. Lane (or Laird) who has not been identified. Susannah m. 3rd, at Cabot, 16 Apr 1849, ANTHONY PERRY, b. at Cabot, 7 Apr 1774 son of Benjamin and Susannah (Potter) Perry; Anthony d. at Cabot, 1 Dec 1854.

v JOHN ABBOTT, b. at Pembroke, 27 Aug 1780; d. at Barnet, VT, 5 Sep 1854; m. ANNA BROCK, b. at Barnet, 1 Sep 1780 daughter of Walter and Janet (Stuart) Brock; Anna d. at Barnet, 15 Dec 1870.

vi MARY ABBOTT, b. at Pembroke, 1782; d. at Peacham, VT, 20 Jul 1864; m. at Barnet, 18 Feb 1805, JAMES BROCK, b. at Barnet, 27 Sep 1783 son of Walter and Janet (Stuart) Brock; James d. at Barnet, 27 Jul 1847.

vii JEROME JEREMIAH ABBOTT, b. about 1785; d. 1802.

viii PRISCILLA ABBOTT, b. about 1786; likely died young.

ix JOB ABBOTT, b. likely at Barnet, about 1788; reported to have "gone West" with no records located.

x JANET ABBOTT, b. about 1789; likely died young.

418) EUNICE HOLT (*Zebadiah Holt⁴, Elizabeth Farnum Holt³, Elizabeth Holt Farnum², Nicholas¹*), b. at Windham, 8 Oct 1732 daughter of Zebadiah and Sarah (Flint) Holt; d. at Ashford, 16 Feb 1776; m. at Windham, 22 Mar 1747, ISAAC BURNHAM, b. at Ipswich, Dec 1729 son of Ebenezer and Dorothy (Andrews) Burnham; Isaac d. at Ashford, 14 Oct 1807. After Eunice's death, Isaac married Rebecca who has not been identified.

In his will written 7 September 1807 (proved 28 October 1807), Isaac Burnham bequeathed to his wife Rebecca twenty dollars. Son Joseph receives $333.34 as do daughters Sarah Abbott, Eunice Hughes, Clyrama Loomis, Tryphasa Watkins, and son Isaac. The residue of the estate goes to son Roswell who is also named executor.[1134]

Isaac Burnham and Eunice Holt were parents of eight children born at Windham.

i JACOB BURNHAM, b. 19 Apr 1748; d. 20 Apr 1749.

ii SARAH BURNHAM, b. 21 Aug 1750; d. at Brookfield, VT, 18 Nov 1815; m. 1st at Windham, 20 Nov 1765, JOHN GREENSLIT, b. at Windham, 30 Jun 1741 son of John and Sarah (Manning) Greenslit; John d. at Windham, 7 Jan 1769. Sarah m. 2nd at Hampton, 7 Apr 1772, her fourth cousin, HENRY ABBOTT (*Benjamin Abbott⁵, Elizabeth Gray Abbott⁴, Henry Gray³, Hannah Holt Gray², Nicholas¹*), b. at Ashford, 3 Jun 1749 son of Benjamin and Mary Ann (Andrews) Abbott; Henry d. at Brookfield, 31 Mar 1807.

iii JOSEPH BURNHAM, b. Apr 1752; d. at Willington, 14 Mar 1837; m. at Ashford, 13 Jun 1776, ELIZABETH DURKEE, b. at Windham, 13 Jun 1754 daughter of Joseph and Elizabeth (Fiske) Durkee; Elizabeth d. at Willington, 13 Arp 1828.

iv EUNICE BURNHAM, b. 26 Aug 1754; d. after 1807; m. 1st at Windham, 18 Jan 1770, ANDREW FULLER, b. at Windham, 30 Sep 1747 son of David and Hannah (Fuller) Fuller; Andrew d. at Ashford, 17 Apr 1782. Eunice m. 2nd 16 Dec 1790, JONATHAN HUGHES, b. at Killingly, 14 Sep 1749 son of Edmund and Elizabeth (Stevens) Hughes; Jonathan d. at Willington, 21 Jan 1819. Jonathan Hughes was first married to Eunice Durkee who died 25 Apr 1789.

[1132] The four youngest children are given in the *History of Ryegate*, but not in other sources and there are no other records associated with them. Of these four youngest children, three are reported to have died in childhood and the fourth, son Job, is reported to have "gone West."

[1133] *Scotland, Select Births and Baptisms, 1564-1950.*

[1134] *Connecticut State Library (Hartford, Connecticut), Probate Packets, Buck, J-Cady, G, 1752-1880, Case 680*

v CLYRAMA BURNHAM, b. 24 Mar 1760; m. at Ashford, 18 Jan 1781, JOHN LOOMIS, b. at Windham, 4 Dec 1754 son of John and Mary (Fuller) Loomis; John d. at Ashford, 12 Mar 1828.

vi ROSWELL BURNHAM, b. 15 Nov 1761; d. at Eastford, 29 Mar 1831; m. at Ashford, 23 Oct 1783, ESTHER CHILD, b. at Woodstock, 4 Apr 1766 daughter of John and Sibyl (Bugbee) Child; Esther d. at Ashford, 27 Sep 1794.

vii ISAAC BURNHAM, b. 8 Mar 1765; d. at Parma, OH, 25 Nov 1841; m. ARTEMISSA GRIFFIN, b. at Windham, 18 Nov 1765 daughter of Ebenezer and Elizabeth (Martin) Griffin; Artemissa d. at Parma, 14 Sep 1839.

viii TRYPHOSA BURNHAM, b. 21 Aug 1767; d. at Eastford, 9 Oct 1832; m. at Ashford, 26 Aug 1792, WILLARD WATKINS, b. about 1765; Willard d. at Wales, MA, 30 Dec 1851. After Tryphosa's death, Willard went to Wales, MA where his daughter and son-in-law had settled.

419) ZEBADIAH HOLT (*Zebadiah Holt*[4], *Elizabeth Farnum Holt*[3], *Elizabeth Holt Farnum*[2], *Nicholas*[1]), b. at Windham, 13 Sep 1734 son of Zebadiah and Sarah (Flint) Holt; d. at Hampton, 15 Dec 1811; m. at Ashford, 16 Feb 1758, JEMIMA SIMONS, b. at Windham, 6 Apr 1729 daughter of Jacob and Mary (Crane) Simons;[1135] Jemima d. at Hampton, 12 May 1807.

There are records of four children of Zebadiah and Jemima, all recorded at Windham.

i JACOB HOLT, b. at Windham, 19 Mar 1760; d. at Providence, RI, 11 May 1826; m. 1st 1 Oct 1783, HANNAH JEFFORDS, b. at Pomfret, 14 Sep 1766 daughter of John and Hannah (Williams) Jeffords; Hannah d. 30 Sep 1788. Jacob m. 2nd 20 May 1790, ELEANOR HAMMOND, b. at Hampton, 19 May 1769 daughter of Hezekiah and Lucy (Griffin) Hammond; Eleanor d. at Hampton, 22 Oct 1817. Jacob m. 3rd at Providence, 22 Jun 1818, widow PENELOPE GREEN; Penelope d. at Providence, 1832.

ii TAMME HOLT, b. at Windham, 25 Dec 1765; d. at Hampton, 26 Jun 1846; m. at Windham, 24 Nov 1784, JAMES BURNHAM, b. at Windham, 21 Aug 1759 son of Eben and Martha (Hibbard) Burnham; James d. at Hampton, 5 May 1836.

iii ESTHER HOLT, b. about 1767[1136]

iv EUNICE HOLT, b. at Windham, 17 Dec 1770.

420) SARAH HOLT (*Zebadiah Holt*[4], *Elizabeth Farnum Holt*[3], *Elizabeth Holt Farnum*[2], *Nicholas*[1]), b. at Windham, 13 Feb 1737 daughter of Zebadiah and Sarah (Flint) Holt; d. at Hampton, 16 Mar 1806; m. at Windham, 15 Mar 1755, AARON FULLER, b. at Windham, 26 Jan 1734 son of Stephen and Hannah (Moulton) Fuller; Aaron d. at Hampton, 27 Feb 1809.

Aaron Fuller was a farmer in Canterbury and Hampton.[1137] Sarah and Aaron were parents of ten children.

i JONATHAN FULLER, b. at Windham, 29 Aug 1755; d. at Hampton, CT, 9 Mar 1821; m. 1st at Mansfield, 12 May 1774, EXPERIENCE HUNT, b. at Mansfield, 9 Jul 1742 daughter of Nathaniel and Experience (-) Hunt; Experience d. at Windham, 25 Dec 1776. Jonathan m. 2nd at Hampton, 28 Aug 1777, ESTHER CADY, b. about 1755; Esther d. at Hampton, 17 May 1835.

ii AARON FULLER, b. at Windham, 10 Nov 1757; d. at Windsor, MA, 30 Jun 1818; m. by 1783, ESTHER MERRILL.

iii ISAAC FULLER, b. at Windham, 17 Oct 1759; d. at Hampton, 18 Feb 1814; m. at Hampton, 27 May 1804, REBECCA DIXSON (widow of Alexander Dorrance), b. at Voluntown, 13 Apr 1765 daughter of John and Jane (Gordon) Dixson; Rebecca d. at Hampton, 16 Jun 1815. Isaac and Rebecca had one daughter, Caroline.

iv NATHAN FULLER, b. at Windham, 3 Sep 1763; d. at Scotland, CT, 25 Apr 1852; m. 8 Mar 1787, SUSANNAH LUCE, b. at Scotland, 26 Aug 1764 daughter of David and Mehitable (Dimmock) Luce; Susannah d. 15 Oct 1825.

v RUFUS FULLER, b. at Windham, 30 Aug 1766; d. at Hampton, 1 Apr 1835; m. at Norwich, 1 Dec 1793, RHODA BALDWIN, b. at Norwich, 10 Aug 1770 daughter of Oliver and Mercy (Copp) Baldwin; Rhoda d. at Hampton, 21 Nov 1837.

vi SARAH FULLER, b. at Windham, 21 Oct 1768; m. LUKE MINER.

vii JOSIAH FULLER, b. at Windham, 18 Nov 1770; d. at Plainfield, CT, 10 Apr 1841; m. 22 Apr 1799, MARY LORD, b. 21 Oct 1771 daughter of Elisha and Tamasin (Kimball) Lord; Mary d. at Plainfield, 20 May 1843. Josiah Fuller was a physician.

[1135] The 1765 estate distribution of Jacob Simonds (Simmons) includes a distribution to daughter Jemima Holt.

[1136] Esther is a child given in Durrie's Holt genealogy for whom no records were located.

[1137] Fuller, *Genealogy of the Some of the Descendants of Thomas Fuller*, p 93

viii EUNICE FULLER, b. at Windham, 5 May 1773; d. at Chaplin, 31 Dec 1846; m. 10 Sep 1809, as his third wife, her first cousin once removed, NEHEMIAH HOLT (*Nehemiah[4], George[3], Henry[2], Nicholas[1]*), b. at Windham, 28 Nov 1756 son of Nehemiah and Anna (Farnum) Holt; Nehemiah d. at Chaplin, 5 Jun 1824. Nehemiah's first two marriages were to Mary Lamphear and Sarah Dunlap. Eunice Fuller and Nehemiah Holt are Family 441.

ix DANIEL FULLER, b. at Windham, 25 Jun 1775; d. at Rocky Hill, CT, 16 Dec 1843; m. at Rocky Hill, 15 Oct 1806, MABEL ROBBINS, baptized at Rocky Hill, 16 Jun 1782 daughter of Simeon and Sarah (Rose) Robbins; Mabel d. at Rocky Hill, 21 Oct 1835. Daniel was a physician.

x LEONARD FULLER, b. at Canterbury, Oct 1781

421) ELIZABETH HOLT (*Zebadiah Holt[4], Elizabeth Farnum Holt[3], Elizabeth Holt Farnum[2], Nicholas[1]*), b. at Windham, 10 Jan 1738/9 daughter of Zebadiah and Sarah (Flint) Holt; d. at Ashford, 9 Jun 1814; m. at Windham, 19 Jan 1757, THOMAS BUTLER, b. at Windham, 23 Jun 1734 son of Thomas and Abigail (Craft) Butler; Thomas d. at Ashford, 29 Nov 1787.

Thomas Butler did not leave a will and his estate entered probate 23 February 1788 with widow Elizabeth requesting that son Zebadiah Butler be named administrator.[1138] Elizabeth Holt and Thomas Butler were parents of nine children.

i STEPHEN BUTLER, b. at Windham, 28 Aug 1757

ii ZEBADIAH BUTLER, b. at Windham, 13 Apr 1759; d. at Ashford, 16 Sep 1806; m. 1780, HANNAH WALES, b. at Ashford, 19 Jun 1760 daughter of Elisha and Mary (Abbe) Wales; Zebadiah d. at Ashford, 19 Jun 1815.

iii JEMIMA BUTLER, b. at Ashford, 28 Mar 1761; d. at Cobleskill, NY, 9 Jun 1841; m. at Ashford, 25 Oct 1787, MAVERICK JOHNSON, b. 5 Mar 1765 perhaps the son of Stephen and Sarah (Clark) Johnson; Maverick d. at Cobleskill, 2 Sep 1845.

iv ALTHEA BUTLER, b. at Ashford, 19 Feb 1763

v JOHN BUTLER, b. at Ashford, 23 Oct 1764; d. at Ashford, 17 Dec 1850; m. at Ashford, 7 Dec 1790, SALLY BROWN, b. about 1771; Sally d, at Ashford, 30 Nov 1843.

vi JOSIAH BUTLER, b. at Ashford, 14 Nov 1766

vii THOMAS BUTLER, b. at Ashford, 27 Nov 1768

viii BENJAMIN BUTLER, b. at Ashford, 8 Feb 1771; d. at Ashford, 8 Jun 1847; m. at Ashford, 12 Dec 1793, PATTY HOWE, b. about 1775; Patty d. at Ashford, 14 Feb 1841.

ix CRAFT BUTLER, b. at Ashford, 23 Sep 1776; d. at Andover, CT, 26 Oct 1834; m. at Manchester, CT, 31 Mar 1803, HULDAH JONES, b. 1783 possibly the daughter of Asa and Lucy (Parke) Jones; Huldah d. at Lebanon, CT, 14 Jan 1850.

422) MERCY HOLT (*Zebadiah Holt[4], Elizabeth Farnum Holt[3], Elizabeth Holt Farnum[2], Nicholas[1]*), b. at Windham, 14 Feb 1740/1 daughter of Zebadiah and Sarah (Flint) Holt; d. at Hampton, 15 Sep 1799; m. at Windham, 8 Sep 1763, her third cousin, WILLIAM HOLT (*William[4], Thomas[3], Nicholas[2], Nicholas[1]*), b. at Windham, 15 Jul 1743 son of William and Hannah (Holt) Holt; William d. at Hampton, 6 Aug 1815.

William Holt and Mercy Holt were parents of three children born at Hampton.

i WILLIAM HOLT, b. 22 Nov 1764; d. at Hampton, 8 May 1793; m. at Hampton, 6 Nov 1788, SARAH FULLER, b. at Hampton, 14 Jul 1768 daughter of Samuel and Sarah (Reed) Fuller.

ii MERCY HOLT, b. 7 Dec 1766; d. at Cooperstown, NY, 14 Sep 1834; m. 1788, JAMES AVERILL, b. at Ashford, 14 Dec 1763 son of James and Mary (Walker) Averill; James d. at St. Johnsville, NY, 17 Dec 1835.

iii ABIGAIL HOLT, b. 27 Sep 1774

423) SAMUEL COBURN (*Elizabeth Holt Coburn[4], Elizabeth Farnum Holt[3], Elizabeth Holt Farnum[2], Nicholas[1]*), b. at Windham, 29 Sep 1728 son of Samuel and Elizabeth (Holt) Coburn; m. at Windham, 23 Jan 1751, JUDAH WEBSTER, baptized at Beverly, MA, 8 Mar 1719 daughter of Benjamin and Ruth (Hibbard) Webster.[1139]

Samuel Coburn and Judah Webster were parents of four children.

[1138] *Connecticut State Library (Hartford, Connecticut);* Probate Place: *Hartford, Connecticut, Probate Packets, Buck, J-Cady, G, 1752-1880, Estate of Thomas Butler*

[1139] The 1762 will of Benjamin Webster of Windham includes a bequest to his daughter Judah Coburn.

i JUDITH COBURN, b. at Windham, 17 Nov 1751; d. at Braintree, VT, 7 Jul 1837; m. at Canterbury, CT, 1776, ELIJAH RANDALL, b. at Preston, CT, 10 Oct 1746 son of Peter and Keturah (Ellis) Randall; Elijah d. at Braintree, 3 May 1813.

ii CHARITY COBURN, b. at Ashford, 3 Feb 1754; d. at Hampton, 24 Aug 1838; m. at Scotland, CT, 14 Nov 1780, ZOPHAR ROBINSON, baptized at Scotland, 28 Dec 1755 son of Reuben and Esther (Palmer) Robinson; Zophar was killed in military service in 1781. Charity and Zophar had one child Chloe. Charity received a widow's pension the application being made in 1836. Her application was made by a conservator as Charity was described as insane at that time.[1140] The 1808 will of Reuben Robinson of Hampton includes a bequest to his granddaughter Chloe Robinson.

iii SAMUEL COBURN, b. at Ashford, 3 Feb 1754

iv ESTHER COBURN, b. at Canterbury, 21 Apr 1759

424) EDWARD COBURN (*Elizabeth Holt Coburn[4], Elizabeth Farnum Holt[3], Elizabeth Holt Farnum[2], Nicholas[1]*), b. at Windham, 5 Apr 1730 son of Samuel and Elizabeth (Holt) Coburn; d. at Hampton, 28 Jul 1791; m. 17 Oct 1751, PRUDENCE WEAKLEY, b. at Preston, 13 Apr 1731 daughter of William and Prudence (Randall) Weakley; Prudence d. at Windham, 19 Oct 1772. Edward m. 2nd at Windham, 22 Feb 1774, SARAH WYMAN, b. about 1736; Sarah d. at Hampton, 28 Jul 1791.

Edward Coburn and Prudence Weakley were parents of nine children.

i PRISCILLA COBURN, b. at Windham, 21 Sep 1752

ii ABIGAIL COBURN, baptized at Hampton, 15 Dec 1754

iii WILLIAM COBURN, b. 9 Oct 1756; d. 16 Oct 1756.

iv EDWARD COBURN, b. 9 Oct 1757. It is not clear what became of Edward. The Coburn genealogy reports he married Sarah Wyman in 1784, but Sarah Wyman was the second wife of his father Edward and occurred in 1774 (and the Coburn genealogy also reports Sarah Wyman as the second wife of the father). The Coburn genealogy also reports that Edward died in Sturbridge, MA in 1801. But the age at death of Edward in Sturbridge was 55 making his birth about 1746-1747. Edward Coburn in Sturbridge was married to Sarah Hobbs (widow of John Ryan) in 1781. A more likely marriage for Edward is to Eunice Hurlburt, but that has not been verified.

v PRUDENCE COBURN, b. at Windham, 27 Apr 1760

vi SAMUEL COBURN, b. and d. 25 Oct 1762

vii LUCY COBURN, b. at Windham, 9 Oct 1763

viii SUSANNAH COBURN, b. 22 Jan 1767; *perhaps* m. at Windham, 9 Sep 1789, ELLE RUDD who has not been identified. There are records of three children of Susannah and Elle born at Windham, but little else has been located. This marriage for Susannah is speculative. She was not the wife of Benjamin Saxton as is suggested in the Coburn genealogy as Benjamin's wife died in 1868 at age 93.

ix LYDIA COBURN, b. at Windham, 19 Oct 1769 and baptized at Hampton, 22 Oct 1769

Edward Coburn and Sarah Wyman were parents of one child.

i MIMA COBURN, baptized at Hampton, 15 Aug 1779

425) ZEBADIAH COBURN (*Elizabeth Holt Coburn[4], Elizabeth Farnum Holt[3], Elizabeth Holt Farnum[2], Nicholas[1]*), b. at Windham, 26 Feb 1732 son of Samuel and Elizabeth (Holt) Coburn; d. about 1814 location unknown; m. 22 Jan 1754, ELIZABETH DURKEE, b. at Hampton, 28 Nov 1737 daughter of William and Elizabeth (Ford) Durkee.[1141]

Zebadiah served in the French and Indian War and was captured 15 June 1756 twelve miles north of Osuck Fort. He was taken to Canada and held captive for thirteen months.[1142] During the Revolution, Zebadiah Farnum served as sergeant in the company of Capt. James Stedman responding to the Lexington alarm.[1143]

The family was in Windham for the births of their children and in later life were in Rutland, Vermont. Zebadiah is reported as traveling on foot from Rutland to visit his son in Troy, New York after the close of the War of 1812. Zebadiah died on his way home to Rutland.[1144]

[1140] U.S., Revolutionary War Pension and Bounty-Land Warrant Application Files, 1800-1900, Case W17564

[1141] The 1757 estate distribution of William Durkee included a set-off to daughter Elizabeth wife of Zebadiah Coburn.

[1142] Connecticut Historical Society, *Rolls of Men in the French and Indian War*, volume 9, p 133

[1143] Connecticut Men in the Revolution, Appendix A, The Lexington Alarm, p 26

[1144] Coburn, *Descendants of Edward Colburn*, p 53

Zebadiah Coburn and Elizabeth Durkee were parents of eight children born at Windham. Several of the children were settled in Ludlow, Massachusetts, at least for a time.

i ELIZABETH COBURN, b. 12 Nov 1754; m. at Windham, 16 Feb 1775, BENJAMIN BURNETT, b. at Windham, 21 Feb 1753 son of Jonathan and Elizabeth (Averill) Burnett;[1145] Benjamin d. at Coventry, NY, after 1810.

ii ZEBADIAH COBURN, b. 29 Oct 1756; d. at Homer, NY, 2 Apr 1839; m. at Ludlow, MA, 24 Feb 1783, LUNA KENDALL, b. at Ashford, 17 Sep 1762 daughter of Jacob and Prudence (Beebe) Kendall; Luna d. at Homer, 26 Mar 1831.

iii OLIVE COBURN, b. 1 Aug 1758; m. at Ludlow, MA, 9 Apr 1778, JOSEPH JENNINGS, b. at Springfield, MA, 23 Nov 1756 son of Beriah and Eunice (Stebbins) Jennings; Joseph d. at Whitestown, NY, about 1823 (will written 10 Oct 1821 and proved 14 Mar 1823). In his will, Joseph left his entire estate to son Joseph.[1146] Joseph served in the Revolution and received a pension related to his service.

iv ELIAS COBURN, b. 8 May 1760

v NATHANIEL COBURN, b. 8 Nov 1762; d. at New Brighton, PA, 6 Apr 1844; m. 1st by 1785, SALLY who is not clearly identified; Sally d. by about 1819. Nathaniel may have had a second marriage to ANN. Nathaniel served during the Revolution enlisting while in Connecticut and later applied for a pension related to his service while living in Fayette County, PA. He served in both the Connecticut line and later the Massachusetts continental forces and was at the Battle of Princeton. He served a total of three years as a fifer. He had no family living with him in 1821.[1147]

vi STEPHEN COBURN, b. 3 Nov 1764. Stephen is reported in the Coburn genealogy as marrying but the name of his wife has not been found.

vii AMAZIAH COBURN, b. 14 Jan 1768

viii WILLIAM COBURN, b. 17 May 1771; d. at Homer, NY, 1838; m. 1 Feb 1795, ABIGAIL HOTCHKISS, b. 25 Apr 1778 daughter of David and Peninah (Peck) Hotchkiss; Abigail d. at Windsor, NY, 16 Nov 1842.

426) CORNELIUS COBURN (*Elizabeth Holt Coburn⁴, Elizabeth Farnum Holt³, Elizabeth Holt Farnum², Nicholas¹*), b. at Windham, 1 Jan 1734 son of Samuel and Elizabeth (Holt) Coburn; d. at Rome, NY, 20 Jun 1824; m. 1st 20 Apr 1757, ABIGAIL GREENSLIT, b. at Preston, 17 Nov 1736 daughter of John and Sarah (Manning) Greenslit; Abigail d. at Windham, 21 Apr 1778.[1148] Cornelius m. 2nd 5 Apr 1780, RACHEL ROBINSON, b. at Windham, 30 Mar 1744 daughter of Peter and Ruth (Fuller) Robinson; Rachel d. at Rome, 12 Jun 1828.

Cornelius resided in Windham and later in Sprague. His two youngest sons Asa and Walter went to the Canterbury Hill area of Rome, New York in 1810. The following year, the sons brought their aging parents to Rome.[1149]

Cornelius Coburn and Abigail Greenslit were parents of nine children born at Windham.

i ELIPHALET COBURN, b. 2 Jan 1758; d. at Camden, NY, 1818; m. at Preston, CT, 28 Oct 1781, LOIS TRACY, likely b. at Preston, 4 Jun 1758 daughter of Isaac and Mehitable (Rudd) Tracy; Lois d. at Camden, Jan 1850.[1150]

ii EUNICE COBURN, b. 4 Aug 1760; m. at Norwich, 6 Dec 1787, ZACCHAEUS ABELL, b. at Norwich, 10 Jun 1758 son of Alpheus and Elizabeth (Griswold) Abell.[1151]

iii ASA COBURN, b. 25 Dec 1763; d. 8 Feb 1764.

iv ELIZABETH COBURN, b. 29 Dec 1764; d. at Rome, NY, 6 Jun 1835; m. at Norwich, 6 Dec 1787, DANIEL WIGHTMAN KNIGHT,[1152] b. about 1763 and baptized at Sprague, 1766 son of David and Jane (Wightman) Knight; Daniel d. at Rome, 31 May 1830.

v ELIPHAZ COBURN, b. 11 Apr 1767; d. 16 Aug 1771.

vi CLARISSA COBURN, b. 3 Nov 1770; d. 18 Oct 1776.

vii SYBIL COBURN, b. 30 Oct 1773

1145 Burnett, *The Burnett Genealogy, Supplementing the Burnap-Burnett Genealogy*, p 10

1146 New York Wills and Probate Records, Oneida County, Wills, volume 2, pp 329-330

1147 U.S. Revolutionary War Pension and Bounty-Land Warrant Application Files, Case S40856

1148 Recorded in the church record abstracts for Sprague, CT: "Cornelius, his w., d. Apr. 21, 1778, child-bed"

1149 Wager, *Our City and Its People: A Descriptive Work on the City of Rome New York*, p 21

1150 New York, U.S. Census Mortality Schedules, 1850-1880

1151 Abell, *The Abell Family in America*, p 84

1152 On some records Daniel's name is given as Daniel Whitman Knight.

viii Infant daughter d. 19 Oct 1776

ix Child stillborn 31 Mar 1778

Cornelius Coburn and Rachel Robinson were parents of three children likely born at Lisbon.

i NABBY COBURN, b. 22 Oct 1780;[1153] d. at North Rose, NY, 9 Jun 1853; m. JOSEPH PRESTON, b. about 1787; Joseph d. at Liberty Corners, WI, 15 Aug 1874.

ii ASA COBURN, b. 26 May 1782; d. at Rome, NY, 14 Apr 1868; m. 1st at Sprague, CT, 4 Nov 1804, BETSEY PORTER, b. 16 Oct 1778 daughter of Gideon and Abigail (Bottom) Porter; Betsey d. at Rome, 12 Dec 1821. Asa m. 2nd about 1822, SUSAN E. PARISH, b. 17 Aug 1800;[1154] Susan d. at Rome, 10 Jun 1870.

iii WALTER COBURN, b. 30 Nov 1784 and baptized at Sprague, 9 Jan 1785; m. at Lisbon, CT, 20 Aug 1808, ANNA SLY, b. 8 Oct 1784 likely daughter of Thomas and Anna (Jones) Sly; Anna d. at New York, NY, 28 Dec 1851.

427) SARAH COBURN (*Elizabeth Holt Coburn⁴, Elizabeth Farnum Holt³, Elizabeth Holt Farnum², Nicholas¹*), b. at Windham, 17 Apr 1736 daughter of Samuel and Elizabeth (Holt) Coburn; d. at Rutland, VT, 25 Feb 1802; m. 1756, EZEKIEL ORMSBY, b. at Hampton, 19 Mar 1738 son of John and Mehitable (Way) Ormsby; Ezekiel d. at Rutland, 26 Mar 1802.

There are just two children, twin boys, identified for Sarah Coburn and Ezekiel Ormsby.

i ELIJAH ORMSBY, b. at Canterbury, 19 Jul 1757; d. 31 Jul 1757.

ii JEREMIAH ORMSBY, b. at Canterbury, 19 Jul 1757; d. at Hebron, NY, 4 Jan 1826; m. at Windham, 14 May 1778, LUCY LILLY, b. at Windham, 22 Feb 1761 daughter of Jonathan and Hannah (Tilden) Lilly; Lucy d. at Hebron, 18 Jul 1832.

428) GEORGE COBURN (*Elizabeth Holt Coburn⁴, Elizabeth Farnum Holt³, Elizabeth Holt Farnum², Nicholas¹*), b. at Windham, 5 Sep 1737 son of Samuel and Elizabeth (Holt) Coburn; d. at Wilton, NH, 25 Jan 1812; m. 19 Nov 1764, MARY ADAMS, b. 13 Apr 1744 daughter of Ephraim and Thankful (Blodgett) Adams; Mary d. at Wilton, 28 Mar 1842.

George and Mary were in Wilton before 1768 and stayed there until their deaths. George served in the company of Capt. Nathan Ballard's company that responded to the alarm for Ticonderoga in June 1777. He also served in the company of Capt. Philip Putnam that marched from Wilton to Saratoga on 29 September 1777.[1155]

George Coburn and Mary Adams were parents of eleven children born at Wilton.

i MARY COBURN, b. 2 Sep 1765

ii LYDIA COBURN, b. 6 Mar 1767; m. 27 Nov 1788, SAMUEL HOWARD, b. at Temple, NH, 10 Sep 1763 son of Samuel and Elizabeth (Barrett) Howard; Samuel d. at Weston, VT, Aug 1813. Lydia might have had a second marriage to a Mr. Burditt as Lydia Burditt daughter of George Coburn d. at Clarendon, VT, 1833, at age 66.[1156]

iii PARTHENIA COBURN, b. 19 Feb 1770

iv JUDITH COBURN, b. 9 Sep 1772; d. at Northfield, VT, 3 May 1859; m. about 1795, JONATHAN PAIGE, b. at Weare, NH, 13 Jan 1775 son of Jonathan and Miriam (Baird) Paige. Judith and Jonathan were in Weare, NH where their oldest child was born and were then in Deering where Jonathan is thought to have died.

v LEVINA COBURN, b. 18 Aug 1774; d. at Mount Holly, VT, 10 Jun 1862; m. 16 May 1799, PHINEAS CARLETON, b. at Rindge, NH, 1 Feb 1772 son of William and Eunice (Laws) Carleton; Phineas d. at Mount Holly, 28 Oct 1852.

vi THANKFUL COBURN, b. 6 Oct 1776; d. at Hancock, NH, 26 Oct 1867; m. at Hancock, 17 Nov 1805, JAMES HILLS, b. at Hudson, NH, 8 Nov 1763 son of Elijah and Miriam (Kidder) Hills; James d. at Hudson, 19 Nov 1846.

vii GEORGE COBURN, b. 19 Sep 1778

viii JACOB COBURN, b. 9 Sep 1780; d. at Weld, ME, 25 Aug 1847; m. MILLICENT BUSS, b. at Wilton, 16 Jun 1778 perhaps the daughter of Silas and Hannah (Pierce) Buss; Millicent d. at Weld, 26 Aug 1861.

[1153] The transcription in the Barbour collection gives her mother as Abigail, but Cornelius and Rachel were married in April 1780, so if the marriage is correct, then she would be the daughter of Rachel.

[1154] The date of birth is given in the Colburn-Coburn genealogy

[1155] Livermore, *History of the Town of Wilton*, pp 351-352

[1156] U.S., Newspaper Extractions from the Northeast, 1704-1930

ix SARAH COBURN, b. 22 Aug 1782; m. at Northbridge, MA, 22 Jun 1811.

x JAMES COBURN, b. 10 Nov 1785

xi OLIVE COBURN, b. 6 Sep 1786; d. at Berlin, MA, 25 Nov 1875; m. at Berlin, MA, 10 Jun 1814, as his second wife, LEVI WHEELER, b. 1768; d. at Berlin, 27 Feb 1835. Levi was first married to Mary Carter.

429) MARY COBURN (*Elizabeth Holt Coburn*[4], *Elizabeth Farnum Holt*[3], *Elizabeth Holt Farnum*[2], *Nicholas*[1]), b. at Windham, Apr 1740 daughter of Samuel and Elizabeth (Holt) Coburn; m. at Windham, 28 Aug 1761, WILLIAM NEFF, b. at Windham, 14 May 1739 son of William and Grace (Webster) Neff; William d. at Hampton, 14 Jan 1818. William was second married to Mary Upton.

William and Mary were members of the Congregational church at Hampton. A summary of William's will given in the Neff genealogy names his wife Mary and only the children from his marriage to Mary Upton.[1157]

There are birth/baptism records (transcriptions) for six children of Mary Coburn and William Neff and Curry's Neff genealogy adds a further three children. William also had five children with his second wife.

i WILLIAM NEFF, b. at Windham, 12 Jan 1762; d. at Halfmoon, NY, 9 Dec 1820; m. at Windham, 1 Nov 1781, LUCY FORD, b. at Windham, 23 Oct 1762 daughter of Amos and Lydia (Davison) Ford; Lucy d. at Halfmoon, 22 Oct 1823.

ii DANIEL NEFF, b. at Windham, 1 Jul 1763; d. at Rutland, VT, Dec 1795; m. at Enfield, CT, 13 Jan 1785, SILENCE BRADLEY, b. at Tolland, 20 Aug 1762 daughter of Henry and Silence (Meacham) Bradley.

iii MARY NEFF, baptized at Hampton, 30 Nov 1766

iv SALATHIEL NEFF, b. at Windham, 20 Mar 1768; d. at Hampton, 20 Sep 1828; m. at Hampton, 31 Dec 1789, MARY DINGLEY MARTIN, b. at Windham, 12 Jul 1770 daughter of William and Naomi (Upton) Martin; Mary d. at Windham, 16 Jan 1856.

v RENA NEFF, baptized at Hampton, 22 Jan 1769; m. 1st at Canterbury, 23 Jun 1785, as his second wife, SAMUEL RANSOM, b. about 1755 son of William Ransom; Samuel d. about 1795 (probate 6 Jan 1795). Rena m. 2nd CALEB CRANDALL son of Peter Crandall.

vi PHILURA NEFF, baptized at Hampton, 20 Jan 1771; d. at Otsego County, NY, 1830; m. DAVID FISK, b. at Windham, 9 Jun 1770 son of Jonathan and Sarah (Leach) Fisk; David d. at Otsego County, May 1819.

vii RUFUS NEFF, b. estimate 1773; m. LUCY DEAN and was residing in Braintree, VT in 1820.

viii LUCY NEFF, b. estimate 1778; m. about 1800, ABEL FENTON MARTIN, b. at Windham, 19 Jul 1779 son of Shubael and Abigail (Flint) Martin.

ix EBENEZER NEFF, b. at Hampton, 10 May 1782; d. at Laona, NY, 23 Oct 1854; m. at Holden, MA, 7 Feb 1804, LYDIA MANNING, b. at Sterling, MA, 27 Jan 1784 daughter of Israel and Lydia (Richardson) Manning;[1158] Lydia d. at Laona, 21 Dec 1857.

430) NATHANIEL COBURN (*Elizabeth Holt Coburn*[4], *Elizabeth Farnum Holt*[3], *Elizabeth Holt Farnum*[2], *Nicholas*[1]), b. at Windham, 28 Apr 1742 son of Samuel and Elizabeth (Holt) Coburn; d. at Hampton, 6 Dec 1788; m. at Windham, 29 Nov 1764, HANNAH BURNHAM, b. at Hampton, 27 Nov 1746 daughter of Eben and Martha (Hibbard) Burnham; Hannah d. at Williamstown, VT, 17 Dec 1834.

Nathaniel and Hannah lived in Canterbury and Windham. Sometime after Nathaniel's death, at least three of the children and their mother Hannah went to Williamstown, Vermont.

In his will written 17 October 1788, Nathaniel Coburn bequeathed to beloved wife Hannah the use and improvement of all the lands, building, etc. until son Eleazer reaches age twenty-one. Eleazer inherits the real property at age twenty-one. The moveable estate is to be divided among the children. Hannah receives a list of other provisions for her support, a mare, and a sidesaddle. Daughter Parthenia Blanchard receives five shillings. Daughters Anne, Martha, Philura, and Olavia each receives thirty pounds. Eleazer receives the silver knee buckles and sleeve buckles and all the wearing apparel. Hannah was named executrix.[1159]

i PARTHENIA COBURN, b. at Canterbury, 17 Jul 1765; m. about 1788, JOHN BLANCHARD, b. at Windham, 16 Apr 1762 son of John and Lois (Cummings) Blanchard. Parthenia joined the church at Hampton, where her husband John was a member, in October 1788. Further records for this couple were not located.

[1157] Curry, *The Descendants of William Neff* (no page numbers); https://archive.org/details/descendantsofwil00curr/page/n33/mode/2up

[1158] Manning, *The Genealogical and Biographical History of the Manning Families*, p 389

[1159] *Connecticut. Probate Court (Windham District), volume 12, pp 338-339*

ii ANNE COBURN, b. at Canterbury, 29 Aug 1768

iii MARTHA COBURN, b. at Windham, 27 May 1771; d. at Williamstown, VT, 27 Oct 1844; m. at Hampton, 25 Jun 1789, JAMES MARTIN, b. at Windham, 10 Dec 1768 son of Aaron and Eunice (Flint) Martin; James d. at Williamstown, 13 Sep 1838.

iv PHYLURA COBURN, b. at Windham, 24 Sep 1773; d. at Williamstown, 29 Sep 1861; m. SHUBEL SIMONS, b. at Windham, 10 Mar 1770 son of Shubel and Tamma (Durkee) Simons; Shubel d. at Williamstown, 23 Sep 1847.

v ELEAZER COBURN, b. at Windham, 19 Oct 1778; d. at Williamstown, VT, about 1832; m. by 1813, SUSANNA STAPLES,[1160] b. in PA (likely in the Wyoming Valley), 1775 daughter of Joseph and Eleanor (Darbe) Staples; Susanna d. at Williamstown, 12 Feb 1861. Susanna married second, Jacob Jeffords on 20 Jul 1834.

vi OLIVIA COBURN, b. at Windham, 31 Jan 1780

431) HEZEKIAH COBURN (*Elizabeth Holt Coburn*[4]*, Elizabeth Farnum Holt*[3]*, Elizabeth Holt Farnum*[2]*, Nicholas*[1]), baptized at Windham, 15 Apr 1750 son of Samuel and Elizabeth (Holt) Coburn; d. at Lewis, NY, 1835; m. at Hampton, 17 Jan 1771, MARY BILL, b. at Lebanon, CT, 6 May 1750 daughter of Jonathan and Esther (Owen) Bill; Mary d. at Lewis, 1802.

On 10 January 1833, Hezekiah Coburn of Lewis, New York, age eighty-two years, made a statement related to his pension application. He enlisted in May 1775 for a period of seven months in company of Capt. Eleazer Moseley. During this term, he was at Cambridge, Massachusetts building a fort. Later he was drafted for one month at New London, Connecticut. He was also drafted for an additional six weeks of service in the following year. Following the war, he was first at Windham, Connecticut, then soon after in Williamstown, Vermont He moved to Lewis, New York, went from there to Holland Purchase for a time before returning to Lewis.[1161] On 23 March 1835, an attorney retained by son Roswell Coburn on behalf of himself and the other children of Hezekiah who was then deceased, made inquiry regarding payments from the pension. This correspondence also notes that son Eliphalet had recently died in Upper Canada.

Hezekiah Coburn and Mary Bill were parents of eight children born at Windham.

i JONATHAN COBURN, b. 17 Sep 1771; d. 18 Aug 1772.

ii JONATHAN COBURN, b. 3 Dec 1772; d. at Sheldon, NY, Aug 1830; m. about 1799, MARTHA HOPKINS, b. at Williamstown, VT, 4 Apr 1781 daughter of James and Miriam (Kent) Hopkins; Martha d. at Greenfield, PA, 2 Dec 1868. After Jonathan's death, Martha lived with her son Nathaniel. In the 1850 census, she is described as insane.[1162]

iii JOEL COBURN, b. 22 Sep 1774; d. at Berlin, VT, 25 Sep 1867; m. about 1795, ALICE JOHNSON, b. at Stafford, CT, 5 Oct 1778 daughter of Seth and Sybil (Cushman) Johnson; Alice d. 11 Mar 1844.

iv ROSWELL COBURN, b. 11 Nov 1776; d. at Lewis, NY, 18 Apr 1846; m. about 1800, JOANNA PHILLIPS, b. at Athol, MA, 10 Mar 1781 daughter of Samuel and Joanna (-) Phillips; Joanna d. at Lewis, 17 Jan 1846.

v MARY COBURN, b. at Windham, 26 Oct 1778; d. at Sheldon, NY, 28 Sep 1843; m. 26 Oct 1808, as his second wife, WILLIAM BUCKEL, b. at Hitchin, Hertfordshire, 22 Jul 1777; William d. at Redford, MI, 17 Feb 1856 while visiting his daughter. William was first married to Persis Ray. William Buckel immigrated to the United States at age nineteen and was first in New York City before settling in Orangeville, NY. William and Mary were members of the M.E. church at Orangeville. They were parents of seven children.[1163]

vi ELIPHALET COBURN, b. 25 Apr 1781; d. at Kent, Ontario, Canada, 1835; m. at Williamstown, VT, 12 Nov 1801, his third cousin once removed, ELITHEA ROBINSON (*Jemima Rogers Robinson*[6]*, Anna Farnum Rogers*[5]*, William Farnum*[4]*, Ralph Farnum*[3]*, Elizabeth Holt Farnum*[2]*, Nicholas*[1]), b. at Windham, 27 Oct 1785 daughter of Eliphaz and Jemima (Rogers) Robinson.

vii ESTHER COBURN, b. 24 Oct 1783. Esther is reported by the Coburn genealogy as marrying Mr. van Order, but no record information for this marriage has been located.

viii CLYMA COBURN, b. at Windham, 2 Feb 1786; d. after 1855 when she was living in Gerry, NY with her son John; m. JEREMIAH BENNETT, b. at Corinth, VT, 22 Jan 1784 son of William and Patience (Andrews) Bennett; Jeremiah d. after 1855.

1160 Susanna's maiden name of Staples is given on her death record as well as birthplace of Pennsylvania. Joseph Staples was killed in the Wyoming massacre in 1778.

1161 U.S., Revolutionary War Pension and Bounty-Land Warrant Application Files, 1800-1900, Case S15054

1162 Year: 1850; Census Place: Greenfield, Erie, Pennsylvania; Roll: 777; Page: 81A

1163 F. W. Beers, *History of Wyoming County, New York*, p 234

432) EBENEZER COBURN (*Elizabeth Holt Coburn[4], Elizabeth Farnum Holt[3], Elizabeth Holt Farnum[2], Nicholas[1]*), b. at Windham, 28 Jun 1752 son of Samuel and Elizabeth (Holt) Coburn; m. at Scotland, CT, 20 Nov 1777, SYBIL ROBINSON, b. at Scotland, 14 Sep 1755 daughter of Samuel and Sarah (Kimball) Robinson.

Ebenezer and Sybil started their family in Connecticut, were then in Rutland County, Vermont and when their children were still fairly young, made their way to Bristol, New York. Ebenezer and Sybil likely died in Bristol although a record was not located. Their son Ebenezer was a pioneer of DeKalb County, Indiana.[1164]

Ebenezer Coburn and Sybil Robinson were parents of four children.

i ASHER COBURN, b. perhaps at Windham, CT, 1778; d. at Bazetta, OH, 9 Aug 1852; m. ESTHER WHITNEY, b. about 1768; Esther d. at Bazetta, 3 Mar 1855.

ii EBENEZER COBURN, b. 1779; d. at Pawlet, VT, 17 Jul 1782.

iii GURDEN COBURN, b. about 1786; d. at Casnovia, MI, 17 Aug 1872; m. CYNTHIA PHILLIPS, b. about 1793; Cynthia d. after 1860 when the family was living in Concord, IN. Gurden was living with his son James in Michigan in 1870.

iv EBENEZER COBURN, b. likely at Pawlet, 8 Oct 1794; d. at Concord, IN, 9 Aug 1847; m. 1st 13 Sep 1813, PHEBE HENRY who d. 1 Jul 1815. Ebenezer m. 2nd 17 Sep 1815, DELIVERANCE WILSON, likely b. at Mendon, MA, 23 Mar 1793 daughter of Alexander and Patience (Nye) Wilson; Deliverance d. at Concord, IN, 14 May 1864.

433) STEPHEN COLBURN (*Elizabeth Holt Coburn[4], Elizabeth Farnum Holt[3], Elizabeth Holt Farnum[2], Nicholas[1]*), b. at Windham, 20 Jul 1755 son of Samuel and Elizabeth (Holt) Coburn; d at Lebanon, NH, 20 Jun 1820; m. Dec 1779, MIRIAM WOOD, b. at Mansfield, CT, 1755 daughter of Joseph and Anna (Palmer) Wood; Miriam d. at Lebanon, 21 Oct 1851.

Stephen and Miriam resided in Lebanon, New Hampshire where their ten children were born. Stephen saw service in the Revolution in 1776 and 1777.[1165]

Daughter Henrietta did not marry. In her will written 3 July 1860, Henrietta describes herself as being of Milwaukee, Wisconsin but living in Upton, Massachusetts when she wrote her will. She bequeathed one dollar each to brother Benjamin W. Colburn and sisters Sally Heath and Emily Trussel. Nieces Henrietta Maria Carlton, Almyra W. Durand, and Marietta E. Colton each receives four hundred dollars and niece Jane A. Griffith receives two hundred dollars. Nephew James W. Stoddard receives sixty dollars. There are bequests to Almira H. Rockwood and Ruammah Holbrook. Henrietta M. DeWolfe receives the real estate in Upton, partial use of the house, and four hundred dollars. She leaves two thousand dollars to the American Home Missionary Society. Sarah Whittemore receives the residue of the estate. Abram Whittemore of Milwaukee was named executor.[1166]

Stephen Colburn and Miriam Wood were parents of ten children born at Lebanon, New Hampshire.[1167]

i HENRIETTA COLBURN, b. at Lebanon, NH, 1781; d. at Upham, MA, 14 Aug 1860. Henrietta did not marry.

ii SARAH "SALLY" COLBURN, b. at Lebanon, 22 Mar 1783; d. at Bristol, NH, 1875; m. at Lebanon, 20 Jan 1814, MOSES HEATH, b. about 1777; Moses d. at New London, NH, 18 Oct 1845. Moses wrote his will in April 1821 soon after the birth of his son Louis Austin Wood Heath and he left his estate to wife Sarah and his son. The estate entered probate in Dec 1845 with Sarah as executrix. It is not clear if Moses and Sarah had other children, but they were older when they married and so perhaps had just one child. Sarah was living with her son in Bristol in 1870.

iii AMOS COLBURN, b. at Lebanon, 15 Jan 1785; d. at Waterford, VT, 2 Jul 1830; m. RUTH WOOD, b. at Lebanon, 21 Dec 1796 daughter of Ephraim and Martha (Jackson) Wood; Ruth d. at Kirby, VT, 5 Dec 1834. Ruth married second Levi S. Harrington on 24 Apr 1832.

iv ORIN COLBURN, b. at Lebanon, 11 Aug 1786; d. at Brighton, VT, 12 Dec 1850; m. SARAH COLE, b. 23 Jun 1786 daughter of Stephen and Persis (Durkee) Cole; Sarah d. at Brighton, 1 Sep 1860.

v MALENTHA COLBURN, b. at Lebanon, 17 Jul 1788; m. by 1813 ROSWELL DEWOLFE, likely b. at Otis, MA, 13 May 1786 son of Ezekiel and Beulah (Hills) DeWolfe; Roswell d. at West Fairlee, VT, about 1839 (when a guardian was named for one of his sons). This is a family that is confusing in terms of records. The Colburn genealogy reports that Malentha Colburn married Stephen DeWolfe, but the name of the father on the death records of the children is consistently given as Roswell as is the one guardianship case for a son. At least two of the sons seem to have changed their names, one using the name William R. Austin and another Lyman R. Bingham. The death record of Lyman Bingham, for example, gives his father's name as Roswell DeWolf Bingham and mother's name as Valentine Colburn. Lyman's marriage record gives the names of his parents as Roswell and

1164 Inter-State Publishing Company, *History of DeKalb County, Indiana*, pp 520-521

1165 Coburn, *Genealogy of the Descendants of Edward Coburn/Colburn*, p 54

1166 *Probate Records (Worcester County, Massachusetts); Index 1731-1881, Volume 395, pp 48-50, will of Henrietta Colburn*

1167 Most members of this family use Colburn rather than Coburn.

Melantha DeWolf. A daughter in the family, Henrietta DeWolfe, did not marry and her 1865 will and probate gives names and residences of siblings. Five children were identified for Malentha and Roswell and there may be one or two other children.

vi BENJAMIN WOOD COLBURN, b. at Lebanon, 24 Sep 1790; d. at Lebanon, 14 Jul 1882; m. 28 Jun 1820, BETSEY WOOD, b. at Lebanon, 9 Sep 1791 daughter of Ephraim and Martha (Jackson) Wood; Betsey d. at Lebanon, 27 Dec 1867.

vii AUSTIN COLBURN, b. 11 Jul 1793; d. 10 Sep 1819.

viii EMILY COLBURN, b. at Lebanon, 2 Aug 1795; d. at Wilmot, NH, 5 Feb 1882; m. at Lebanon, 8 Feb 1826, EZEKIEL R. TRUSSELL, b. at Hopkinton, 27 Sep 1795 son of Moses and Sarah (Knowlton) Trussell;[1168] Ezekiel d. at Bradford, NH, 16 Apr 1873.

ix APPHIA COLBURN, b. at Lebanon, 21 Sep 1797; d. at Upton, MA, 30 Sep 1839; m. at Upton, MA, 20 Jun 1819, LYMAN STODDARD, b. at Upton, MA, 16 Mar 1791 son of Ezekiel and Lucy (Foristall) Stoddard; Lyman d. at Wauwatosa, WI, 12 Sep 1851.

x ALPHA COLBURN, b. at Lebanon, 5 Oct 1799; d. 1838.[1169]

434) ELIZABETH FORD (*Dinah Holt Ford⁴, Elizabeth Farnum Holt³, Elizabeth Holt Farnum², Nicholas¹*), b. at Windham, 4 June 1733 daughter of Nathaniel and Dinah (Holt) Ford; d. at Windham, 1764; m. at Windham, 17 Oct 1751, JOSEPH MARTIN, b. at Windham, 29 Mar 1730 son of Ebenezer and Jerusha (Durkee) Martin. Joseph second married Elizabeth Coy at Windham on 3 Jan 1765.

Elizabeth Ford and Joseph Martin were parents of six children born at Windham.

i JOSEPH MARTIN, b. 22 Sep 1752; d. 22 Dec 1752.

ii JOSEPH MARTIN, b. 6 May 1754; d. at Chaplin, CT, 29 Aug 1828; m. at Windham, 2 Jun 1774, ABIGAIL BUTLER, b. at Windham, 12 Nov 1755 daughter of Daniel and Hannah (Parker) Butler;[1170] Abigail d. at Chaplin, 20 Aug 1833.

iii EUNICE MARTIN, b. 26 Dec 1756; d. at Chaplin, 15 May 1833; m. at Hampton, 12 Dec 1778, EBENEZER CLARK, b. at Windham, 7 Jun 1754 son of John and Elizabeth (Parker) Clark; Ebenezer d. at Chaplin, 17 Jul 1830.

iv NATHANIEL FORD MARTIN, b. 17 Oct 1759; d. at Hampton, 26 Sep 1847; m. at Windham, 1 Dec 1783, JERUSHA LINKON, b. at Windham, 15 Nov 1760 daughter of John and Anner (Martin) Linkon; Jerusha d. at Hampton, 26 Jan 1838.

v ELIZABETH MARTIN, b. 24 Dec 1761; d. at Braintree, VT, 25 Oct 1804; m. at Hampton, 1 Jan 1784, DANIEL FLINT, b. at Windham, 7 Dec 1761 son of Nathaniel and Mary (Hovey) Flint; Daniel d. at Braintree, 12 Mar 1841.

vi AMASA MARTIN, b. 31 Jul 1764; d. at Hampton, 1 Nov 1848; m. at Hampton, 14 Feb 1786, his second cousin once removed (through Martin line), URSULA UTLEY, b. at Windham, 17 May 1762 daughter of Amos and Grace (Martin) Utley; Ursula d. at Hampton, 8 Feb 1848.

435) AMOS FORD (*Dinah Holt Ford⁴, Elizabeth Farnum Holt³, Elizabeth Holt Farnum², Nicholas¹*), b. at Windham, 2 Aug 1742 son of Nathaniel and Dinah (Holt) Ford; d. at Hampton, 21 Dec 1834; m. at Windham, 25 May 1761, LYDIA DAVISON, b. at Preston, 1 Jan 1738/9 daughter of Thomas and Lydia (Herrick) Davison; Lydia d. at Hampton, 15 May 1829.

Amos was a cooper by trade. He and Lydia resided in Hampton. Amos served in the Revolution and received a pension for his service. He was in reduced circumstances in his later life and in an 1820 statement related to his pension stated that his wife Lydia was then blind and deaf.[1171]

In his will written 4 September 1815, Amos Ford left to his son John all his real estate which consisted of one-half lot in the cedar swamp. Son John Ford was named executor. A total of $56.83 was left for distribution to the heirs named as follows: Amos Ford, heirs of Lucy Neff deceased, Nathaniel Ford, John Ford, Tryphena Bradford, heirs of Eunice Fisk deceased, heirs of Lydia Ford, and Bethiah Bibbens.[1172]

Amos Ford and Lydia Davison were parents of nine children born at Windham.

1168 Stocking, *The History and Genealogy of the Knowltons of England and America*, volume 1, p 134

1169 This is a date given in Coburn, *Genealogy of the Descendants of Edward Colburn/Coburn*

1170 The 1789 estate settlement of Daniel Butler includes a distribution to Abigail Martin and Joseph Martin.

1171 NEHGR, Descendants of Andrew Ford of Weymouth, volume 120, p 48 (1966)

1172 *Connecticut State Library (Hartford, Connecticut), Probate Packets, Fitch, Eleazer-Frink, E, 1719-1889, estate of Amos Ford, number 1433*

i LUCY FORD, b. 23 Oct 1762; d. at Halfmoon, NY, 22 Oct 1823; m. at Windham, 1 Nov 1781, her second cousin, WILLIAM NEFF (*Mary Coburn Neff*[5], *Elizabeth Holt Coburn*[4], *George*[3], *Henry*[2], *Nicholas*[1]), b. at Windham, 12 Jan 1762 son of William and Mary (Coburn) Neff; William d. at Halfmoon, 9 Dec 1820.

ii AMOS FORD, b. 24 Aug 1763; d. at Chaplin, 4 Feb 1841; m. 1st 22 Jun 1786, his first cousin once removed, ANNA HOLT (*Nehemiah*[4], *George*[3], *Henry*[2], *Nicholas*[1]), b. 4 Jul 1765 daughter of Nehemiah and Anna (Farnum) Holt; Anna d. at Hampton, 10 Oct 1806. Amos m. 2nd 4 Oct 1807, ABIGAIL SNOW, b. at Windham, 2 May 1777; Abigail d. at Hampton, 6 Mar 1847. Anna Holt and Amos Ford are Family 445.

iii NATHANIEL FORD, b. 11 Jul 1765; d. at Marshall, NY, 31 Oct 1849; m. at Hampton, 27 Oct 1788, her fourth cousin, REBECCA COPELAND (*Sarah Ingalls Copeland*[5], *Rebekah Grow Ingalls*[4], *Rebekah Holt Grow*[3], *James*[2], *Nicholas*[1]), b. at Brooklyn, CT, 28 Sep 1766 daughter of James and Sarah (Ingalls) Copeland; Rebecca d. at Marshall, 2 Oct 1844.

iv TRYPHENA FORD, b. 15 Jun 1767; d. after 1830 when she was head of household at Hampton; m. at Hampton, 25 Nov 1790, JOHN BRADFORD who has not been identified; John d. at Hampton about Jan 1818 (probate Feb 1818 with Tryphena as administratrix).

v ELIZABETH FORD, b. 12 Aug 1769; d. at Hampton, 24 Apr 1790.

vi EUNICE FORD, b. 17 Nov 1771; d. at Burlington, NY, 25 Nov 1831; m. at Hampton, 3 Feb 1793, NATHAN FISK, b. at Windham, 7 Oct 1772 son of Jonathan and Sarah (Leach) Fisk; Nathan d. at Burlington, after 1855.

vii JOHN FORD, b. 10 Oct 1774; d. at Chaplin, CT, 30 Aug 1864; m. at Hampton, 2 May 1805, LUCY FOSTER, b. about 1776; Lucy d. at Chaplin, 1 Apr 1844.

viii LYDIA FORD, b. 26 Oct 1776; d. at Chaplin, 14 Apr 1830; m. 2 Apr 1799, her first cousin, STEPHEN FORD (*Jonathan Ford*[5], *Dinah Holt Ford*[4], *Elizabeth Farnum Holt*[3], *Elizabeth Holt Farnum*[2], *Nicholas*[1]), b. 24 Sep 1777 son of Jonathan and Anna (French) Ford; Stephen d. at Chaplin, 18 Dec 1864.

ix BETHIAH "THIAH" FORD, b. 7 Aug 1780; m. 21 Mar 1806, ERASTUS BIBBENS, b. about 1773 son of William and Louisa (Simons) Bibbens; Erastus d. at Windham, 28 Feb 1843.

436) ABRAHAM FORD (*Dinah Holt Ford*[4], *Elizabeth Farnum Holt*[3], *Elizabeth Holt Farnum*[2], *Nicholas*[1]), b. at Windham, 29 Aug 1744 son of Nathaniel and Dinah (Holt) Ford; d. at Brookfield, VT, 19 Mar 1832; m. at Windham, 8 Nov 1763, ABIGAIL WOODWARD, b. at Hampton, 1 May 1740 daughter of Jacob and Abigail (Flint) Woodward;[1173] Abigail d. at Brookfield, 23 Mar 1826.

Abraham and Abigail had their children in Windham County, Connecticut and relocated to Braintree, Vermont in 1801. In 1816, they sold their property in Braintree and moved to Brookfield where they both died.[1174]

In his will written 9 February 1831 (proved 5 April 1832), Abraham Ford of Brookfield bequeathed to daughter Sally Ford the sum of two hundred dollars and the right of a room in the house where her brother Elisha now lives while she remains single. Elisha is also to provide Sally a good supply of firewood and Sally also is to receive the household furniture. The heirs of son Abraham Ford deceased receive one dollar which completes their portion. Daughters Elle Ingalls and Dinah Brown each receives one dollar to complete their portions. The heirs of Jacob Ford and heirs of Hannah Flint also receive one dollar, and the same bequest is made to son Diah Ford and the heirs of daughter Nabby Ford. The remainder of the estate goes to son Elisha who is also named executor.[1175]

Abraham Ford and Abigail Woodward were parents of twelve children. The births of Abraham and Jacob are recorded at Ashford, and the births of the other children recorded at Windham.

i ABRAHAM FORD, b. 15 May 1764; d. at Lebanon, CT, 9 Apr 1813; m. at Pomfret, 22 Jan 1788, SARAH INGALLS, b. at Pomfret, 18 Dec 1766 daughter of Joseph and Sarah (Abbott) Ingalls; Sarah d. at Jericho, VT, 24 Apr 1833. Abraham was a resident of Jericho, VT at the time of his death. (his estate was probated there), but he is thought to have died in Lebanon while visiting his brother Jacob.

ii ABIGAIL FORD, b. 7 Apr 1766; d. at Randolph, VT, 4 Feb 1831; m. late in life, 7 Dec 1826, SAMSON NICHOLS, b. at Sutton, MA, 26 Apr 1759 son of Isaac and Dorcas (Sibley) Nichols; Samson d. at Braintree, VT, 23 Apr 1829.

iii JACOB FORD, b. 7 Apr 1766; d. at Lebanon, CT, 23 Jun 1824; m. 13 Sep 1788; LYDIA SMITH, b. 17 May 1761 daughter of Abijah and Bathsheba (Ladd) Smith; Lydia d. 30 Jan 1826.

iv SALLY FORD, b. 27 Nov 1764; d. at Brookfield, 15 Aug 1844. Sally did not marry. She left her estate to nieces and nephews primarily the children of her brother Elisha Ford.

1173 The 1768 estate distribution of Jacob Woodward includes a payment to Abraham Ford on behalf of his wife.

1174 Bass, *The History of Braintree, Vermont*, p 141

1175 *Vermont. Probate Court (Randolph District), Probate Place: Orange, volume 13, pp, pp 82-83*

v ALICE FORD, b. 29 Mar 1769; d. 18 May 1784.

vi DINAH FORD, b. 5 Oct 1770; d. 1 Jun 1778.

vii DIAH FORD, b. 31 Jan 1772; d. at Vernon, CT, 1848; m. at Hampton, 1 May 1794, ESTHER BURNET, b. 13 Aug 1767 daughter of Jonathan and Elizabeth (Averill) Burnet; Esther d. at Vernon, 20 Jan 1848.

viii CHLOE FORD, b. 1 Aug 1773; d. at Hampton, 6 Mar 1791.

ix ELLA FORD, b. 6 Apr 1775; d. at Brookfield, VT, 1857; m. about 1798, HARVEY INGALLS, b. at Pomfret, 7 Jul 1775 son of Joseph and Sarah (Abbott) Ingalls; Harvey d. at Brookfield, 20 Dec 1833.

x HANNAH FORD, b. 22 May 1776; d. at Williamstown, VT, 13 Jul 1821; m. 31 Mar 1803, JAMES FLINT, b. at Hampton, 10 Mar 1779 son of James and Jerusha (Lillie) Flint; James d. at Williamstown, 17 Jun 1870. James married second Sally Kelsey on 9 Jan 1822.

xi DINAH FORD, b. 27 Jul 1780; d. at Randolph, VT, 7 Mar 1868; m. at Hampton, 28 Nov 1798, HENRY BROWN, b. at Windham, 26 Apr 1772 son of Henry and Sarah (Martin) Brown; Henry d. at Randolph, 23 Jan 1855.

xii ELISHA FORD, b. 5 Jan 1785; d. at Northfield, VT, 28 Jun 1869; m. 9 Jul 1809, ASENATH SPEAR (widow of Washington Lathrop), b. at Braintree, VT, 20 Jun 1790 daughter of Nathaniel and Keziah (Stevens) Spear; Asenath d. at Brookfield, 1 Mar 1865.

437) JONATHAN FORD (*Dinah Holt Ford[4], Elizabeth Farnum Holt[3], Elizabeth Holt Farnum[2], Nicholas[1]*), b. at Windham, 20 Sep 1746 son of Nathaniel and Dinah (Holt) Ford; d. at Alexander, NY, 28 Nov 1833; m. 1st 1772, ANNA FRENCH. Jonathan m. 2nd 1782, MARY WHALING; Mary d. 23 Mar 1820.

Jonathan was a blacksmith.[1176] On 17 October 1832, Jonathan Ford of Alexander, New York made application for a pension for his Revolutionary War service. He reported enlisting as a private on 1 March 1775 from New Stratford, Connecticut in the company of Captain Zalman Reed. His enlistment term was nine months. He saw service in New York near Albany and later to St. John under the command of General Montgomery. Jonathan reported suffering greatly during the siege of the fort due to the harsh conditions. He was discharged at Ticonderoga. He reported his birth as 20 September 1746 in the town of Canada (now Hampton), Connecticut. He reported living in New Milford for about forty years before moving to Alexander about six years before his pension application.[1177]

Jonathan Ford and Anna French were parents of three children born at New Milford.

i NATHANIEL FORD, b. 12 May 1775; d. at New Milford, CT, 4 Feb 1824; m. POLLY GARLICK, b. at New Milford, about 1778 likely the daughter of Samuel and Hannah (Woods) Garlick; Polly d. at New Milford, 9 Apr 1862.

ii STEPHEN FORD, b. 24 Sep 1777; d. at Chaplin, CT, 18 Dec 1864; m. 2 Apr 1799, his first cousin, LYDIA FORD (*Amos Ford[5], Dinah Holt Ford[4], Elizabeth Farnum Holt[3], Elizabeth Holt Farnum[2], Nicholas[1]*), b. at Windham, 26 Oct 1776 daughter of Amos and Lydia (Davison) Ford; Lydia d. at Chaplin, 14 Apr 1830.

iii JONATHAN FORD, b. 22 Jun 1779; d. at New Milford, 1 Jan 1870; m. 5 Oct 1806, MABEL CLARK, b. about 1779; Mabel d. at New Milford, 11 Jan 1841.

Jonathan Ford and Mary Whaling were parents of three children born at New Milford.

i JAMES FORD, b. 3 Jul 1783; d. at Windham, NY, 29 May 1831; m. 1808, SALLY FOOTE, b. at Washington, CT, 1 Oct 1781 daughter of Aaron and Content (-) Foote.

ii BETSY FORD, b. 26 May 1788; d. at New Milford, 17 Feb 1858; m. 22 Jun 1821, ITHAMAR COLE, b. about 1791; Ithamar d. at New Milford, 21 Feb 1849.

iii ANNA FORD, b. 2 Jul 1790; d. at Alexander, NY, 1872 (probate 1 Apr 1872); m. at New Milford, 1 Nov 1807, JOHN WILKINSON, b. at New Milford, 21 Oct 1779 son of David and Dorcas (Brownson) Wilkinson; John d. likely at Alexander, NY, about 1860 (will written 1851 and proved March 1863; Federal mortality schedule gives dates of March 1860 and in the 1860 census, Anna is widowed and living with her son Henry).

1176 NEHGR, "Descendants of Andrew Ford of Weymouth", volume 120, p 50 (1966)

1177 *U.S., Revolutionary War Pension and Bounty-Land Warrant Application Files, Case S23222*

438) SARAH FORD (*Dinah Holt Ford[4], Elizabeth Farnum Holt[3], Elizabeth Holt Farnum[2], Nicholas[1]*), b. at Windham, 2 Jul 1751 daughter of Nathaniel and Dinah (Holt) Ford; m. at Hampton, 21 May 1772, THOMAS MOSELEY, b. at Windham, 7 May 1749 son of Nathaniel and Sarah (Capon) Moseley;[1178] Thomas died "in public service at New York" 8 Sep 1776.[1179]

Sarah and Thomas were parents of two children born at Mansfield. It is not known what became of Sarah after the death of her husband in 1776, other than she was admitted to the church at Hampton in 1777.

i SARAH MOSELEY, b. 11 Mar 1773; likely the Sarah that m. at Hampton, 27 Nov 1789, her third cousin, NATHANIEL ROBBINS (*Rebekah Farnum Robbins[5], Nathaniel Farnum[4], Ralph Farnum[3], Elizabeth Holt Farnum[2], Nicholas[1]*), b. at Windham, 17 Dec 1766 son of John and Rebekah (Farnum) Robbins.

ii ELIZABETH MOSELEY, b. 20 Jun 1775; d. 28 Sep 1777.

439) MARY HOLT (*George[4], Elizabeth Farnum Holt[3], Elizabeth Holt Farnum[2], Nicholas[1]*), b. at Hampton, 25 Apr 1746 daughter of George and Mary (Allen) Holt; d. at Canterbury, 20 Sep 1807; m. about 1766, JONATHAN WHEELER, b. about 1741; Jonathan d. at Canterbury, 29 Jul 1796.

In his will proved 2 August 1796, Jonathan Wheeler bequeaths to beloved wife Mary the use and improvement of his entire estate during her natural life. Eldest son receives Elisha will receive £80 in land and inventory after the decease of Mary. The remainder of the estate is to be divided among his other seven children after the death of Mary: Mary, Amy, Jonathan, Warren, William, Calvin, and Sarah. Elisha was named executor.[1180] The total value of the estate was £332.14.5.

Son William Wheeler did not marry and wrote his will 6 February 1818 which was proved 2 April 1818. He requests a gravestone such as he got for his brothers and sisters. He requests that twenty dollars be used for gravestones for his sister Copeland and her husband who died in New York. He leaves to his brother Warren Wheeler fifty dollars to cover the expense of mourning apparel for him and his family. If all of that is not needed, Warren can have what is left for his use. The rest of his estate is to be equally divided among his three brothers (Jonathan, Warren, and Calvin) and two sisters (Polly and Sally) "my own dear brothers and sisters which are all that is alive and who are equal dear to me." If his friends think it best not to move the graves of his sister Copeland and her husband into a burying ground or to take the trouble of getting the gravestones, then the twenty dollars should be divided among his brothers and sisters. Brother Warren is named executor.[1181]

Mary Holt and Jonathan Wheeler were parents of twelve children born at Canterbury.

i SALLY WHEELER, b. 16 Jan 1767; d. 6 Mar 1786.

ii MARY "POLLY" WHEELER, b. 30 Nov 1768; d. at Boonville, NY, 28 Sep 1830; m. at Canterbury, 1797, EBENEZER WHEELER, b. at Canterbury, 20 Mar 1771 son of John and Lydia (Adams) Wheeler; Ebenezer d. at Boonville, 10 Mar 1858.

iii ELISHA WHEELER, b. at Canterbury, 21 Sep 1770; d. at Canterbury, 20 Mar 1809; m. at Canterbury, 9 Feb 1797, ELIZABETH RANSFORD, b. at Canterbury, 17 Mar 1779 daughter of David and Hephzibah (Foster) Ransford; Elizabeth d. 7 May 1807.

iv AMY WHEELER, b. 21 Apr 1772; d. at Leyden, NY, 1804; m. 1791, JOSEPH COPELAND; Joseph d. at Leyden, 1803.

v BETSEY WHEELER, b. 25 Nov 1773; d. 6 Apr 1793.

vi JONATHAN WHEELER, b. 21 Sep 1775; living in 1818. Jonathan had gone to Leyden, NY along with his sisters Amy and Mary and their husbands. Jonathan is listed in the 1800 census in Leyden and in the 1803 tax lists along with his brother-in-law Ebenezer Wheeler. The census record suggests that Jonathan was married with young children in 1800, but no further clear record was found for him.

vii AZUBAH WHEELER, b. 15 Oct 1777; d. 15 Mar 1794.

viii BENJAMIN WHEELER, b. 30 Dec 1779; d. 20 Mar 1796.

ix WARREN WHEELER, b. 15 Dec 1781; d. at Canterbury, 3 Oct 1862; m. 1st by 1807, NANCY SEYMOUR, b. 25 Mar 1787 daughter of Chauncey and Isabel (Sedgwick) Seymour;[1182] Nancy d. at Canterbury, 13 Jan 1809. Warren m. 2nd 8 Apr 1812, MARY WALDO, b. at Hampton, 25 Oct 1785 daughter of John Elderkin and Beulah (Foster) Waldo;[1183] Mary d. at Canterbury, 18 Feb 1858.

[1178] The 1788 will on Nathaniel Moseley includes a bequest to his granddaughter Sarah Moseley the only heir of his son Thomas.

[1179] Dimock, *Births, Baptisms, Marriages and Deaths from the Records of the Town and Churches in Mansfield, Connecticut*, p 333

[1180] *Connecticut. Probate Court (Plainfield District);* Probate Place: *Windham, Connecticut, Probate Records, volume 9, 99 642-643*

[1181] *Connecticut State Library (Hartford, Connecticut);* Probate Place: *Hartford, Connecticut, Probate Packets, Trumbel, William-Whipple, Zebulon, 1747-1880, estate of William Wheeler*

[1182] The 1828 will of Chauncey Seymour includes a bequest to his granddaughters Caroline and Nancy Wheeler who were the daughters of Warren and Nancy.

[1183] Hall, *The Genealogy and Biography of the Waldos of America*, p 53

x WILLIAM WHEELER, b. 9 Feb 1784; d. at Canterbury, 20 Mar 1818. William was a corporal during the War of 1812.

xi CALVIN WHEELER, b. 19 Jan 1788; d. at Springfield, MA, 1851; m. CHLOE CUMMINGS, b. in CT, about 1787; Chloe d. at Springfield, 1 Apr 1879. Calvin was a physician in Springfield.

xii SARAH WHEELER, b. 9 Mar 1790; living in 1818 when her brother William wrote his will; nothing else found.

440) BENJAMIN HOLT (*George⁴, Elizabeth Farnum Holt³, Elizabeth Holt Farnum², Nicholas¹*), b. at Hampton, 8 Sep 1748 son of George and Mary (Allen) Holt; d. at Windham, 22 Jun 1809; m. about 1769, ESTHER WEBB, baptized at Scotland, CT, 28 Oct 1750 daughter of Timothy and Sarah (Howard) Webb.

Benjamin Holt did not leave a will and his estate entered probate 26 June 1809 with Benjamin Holt of Boston as administrator. Ezra Lillie (husband of daughter Esther) was one of the sureties. Inventory was $1,160.85 with debts of $565.81, $323.73 of that being owed by the estate to son Benjamin.[1184]

Benjamin Holt and Esther Webb were parents of three children likely all born at Lebanon, Connecticut.

i ESTHER HOLT, b. about 1769; d. at Scotland, CT, 19 Nov 1836; m. at Windham, 29 May 1788, EZRA LILLIE, b. at Windham, 5 Sep 1765 son of Elisha and Huldah (Tilden) Lillie; Ezra d. at Springfield, MA, 25 Jun 1852. In his later years, Ezra lived with his son Nathaniel in Springfield.

ii BENJAMIN HOLT, b. 7 Aug 1773; d. at Lancaster, MA, 9 Mar 1861; m. at Boston, 14 Jun 1802, RUTH BALDWIN, b. at Canaan, NH, 31 Aug 1783 daughter of Thomas and Ruth (Huntington) Baldwin; Ruth d. at Lancaster, 20 May 1856. Benjamin Holt was a teacher in Lancaster. He was also active in the Handel and Haydn Society of Boston serving as trustee for several years and president of the society in 1817 and 1818.[1185]

iii JERUSHA HOLT, b. about 1779; d. at Scotland, CT, 15 Jul 1800; m. at Scotland, 23 Mar 1800, LEVI JOHNSON, b. about 1773 son of Levi and Anna (Manning) Johnson; Levi d. at Windham, 17 Apr 1861. Levi married second Anne Martin.

441) NEHEMIAH HOLT (*Nehemiah⁴, George³, Henry², Nicholas¹*), b. at Windham, 28 Nov 1756 son of Nehemiah and Anna (Farnum) Holt; d. at Chaplin, CT, 5 Jun 1824; m. 1st 11 Jun 1782, MARY LAMPHEAR, b. about 1755; Mary d. at Chaplin, 11 Dec 1799. Nehemiah m. 2nd 1 Jan 1801, SARAH DUNLAP, b. 1766 daughter of Joshua and Elizabeth (Kennedy) Dunlap;[1186] Sarah d. at Chaplin, 7 Nov 1808. Nehemiah m. 3rd 10 Sep 1809, his first cousin once removed, EUNICE FULLER (*Sarah Holt Fuller⁵, Zebadiah Holt⁴, Elizabeth Farnum Holt³, Elizabeth Holt Farnum², Nicholas¹*), b. at Windham, 5 May 1773 daughter of Aaron and Sarah (Holt) Fuller; Eunice d. at Chaplin, 31 Dec 1846.

Nehemiah Holt served in the Revolution enlisted as a Sergeant in Capt. Dyer's company of Col. Durkee's regiment on the continental army. He was at the battles of Long Island, Harlem Heights, Trenton, and Princeton. After the war, he returned to Chaplin where he was a successful farmer.[1187]

In his will written 13 February 1824 (proved 14 June 1824), Nehemiah Holt of Chaplin bequeathed to his beloved wife the use of real estate in Chaplin (which is delineated in the will) until children Daniel, Almira, and Charles Austin arrive at age twenty-one. When the children are of age, his wife is to quit-claim one-sixth part of that real estate to those three children. She will then have use of the remaining one-half during her natural life as long as she keeps it in good repair. At the decease of his wife Eunice, that property will be divided into fifths with two-fifths each going to the sons and one-fifth to his daughter. Children Sally Hammond, Lucinda Lummis, Anna Kendall, and Hiram Holt receive a tract of land in Chaplin to divide equally. These last four named children are to annually pay to daughter Polly the sum of ten dollars (two dollars and fifty cents each). Daughter Polly also receives a tract of land in Chaplin. Sons Lucien, Henry and William Dunlap also receive land bequests. He also sets a piece of meadow in Chaplin for the use and support of William Dunlap during his natural life, and if that is not enough for his support some real estate may be sold to provide for William's support. After William's decease, that property is to be divided among all his children. After some individual bequests of personal items, the remaining personal estate is to be divided between William and Polly, William receiving two-thirds and Polly one-third. Rufus Lummis was named executor.[1188]

Nehemiah Holt and Mary Lamphear were parents of seven children.

i POLLY HOLT, b. at Mansfield, 28 Feb 1784; d. 26 Sep 1794.

ii SALLY HOLT, b. at Hampton, 20 Jul 1787; d. at Hampton, 20 Jan 1850; m. at Hampton, 11 Jun 1807, URIEL HAMMOND, b. at Hampton, 4 Jul 1781 son of Josiah and Elizabeth (Moseley) Hammond; Uriel d. at Hampton, 12 Nov 1868.

1184 *Connecticut State Library (Hartford, Connecticut);* Probate Place: *Hartford, Connecticut, Probate Packets, Hicks-Hovey, Elisha, 1719-1880, Case 1937*

1185 Handel and Haydn Society, *History of the Handel and Haydn Society of Boston, Massachusetts*

1186 The 1810 estate settlement of Joshua Dunlap includes payment of a legacy to Nehemiah Holt.

1187 Durrie, *Holt Genealogy*, p 38

1188 Connecticut Wills and Probate Records, Windham County, volume 18, pp 79-81; accessed through ancestry.com

iii LUCINDA HOLT, b. at Hampton, 2 Jun 1789; d. at Chaplin, CT, 20 Oct 1842; m. at Hampton, 1 Dec 1814, RUFUS LOOMIS, b. at Hampton, 11 Sep 1789 son of Jonathan and Elizabeth (Bennett) Loomis; Rufus d. at Woodstock, 30 Jul 1859. Rufus married second Amey W. Moore on 28 Mar 1844.

iv ANNA "NANCY" HOLT, b. at Hampton, 19 Apr 1791; d. at Chaplin, 20 Sep 1883; m. 1st 21 Mar 1821, SIMEON MARCY KENDALL, b. at Ashford, 18 Aug 1792 son of Isaac and Rachel (Marcy) Kendall; Simeon d. at Willington, 4 Apr 1836. Anna m. 2nd about 1839, LEVI WORK, b. at Ashford, 25 Apr 1778 son of Ingoldsby and Esther (Bugbee) Work; Levi d. at Eastford, 1846. Levi Work was first married to Lucinda Warren. Anna m. 3rd 16 Oct 1850, ELISHA BYLES, b. at Ashford, 28 Jan 1788 son of Josiah and Abigail (Clark) Byles; Elisha d. at Ashford, 23 May 1869. Elisha was first married to Sophia Huntington. Anna did not have children of her own. In her will, she made bequests to her stepson Andrew Byles and his wife Martha, to the American Board of Commissioners for Foreign Missions, to the children of John Loomis, to her other Loomis nieces and nephews who are each named, to Frank Hammond son of Charles Weld Hammond, to the children of Hiram Holt, to the children of Lucinda Loomis, to the children of Sally Hammond, and to the children of Alfred Hammond.[1189]

v ALMIRA HOLT, b. 21 Oct 1793; d. 2 Jul 1796.

vi POLLY HOLT, b. 25 Oct 1795; d. at Chaplin, 15 Mar 1842. Polly did not marry.

vii HIRAM HOLT, b. at Hampton, 31 Jan 1798; d. at Pomfret, 30 Nov 1870; m. 1st at Pomfret, 21 Feb 1828, MARIAN CHANDLER, b. at Pomfret, 15 Sep 1800 daughter of John Wilkes and Mary (Stedman) Chandler; Marian d. at Pomfret, 16 Mar 1857. Hiram m. 2nd 30 Mar 1858, MARTHA ANN MATHER (widow of Simon L. Cotton), b. 9 Jan 1827 daughter of Eleazer and Fanny (Williams) Mather; Martha d. at Providence, RI, 25 Jan 1911.

Nehemiah Holt and Sarah Dunlap were parents of four children.

i HENRY HOLT, b. at Hampton, 6 Apr 1803; d. at Cascade, MI, 15 Mar 1895; m. 1st at Herkimer County, NY, 17 Jun 1830, LORANCY POTTER, b. at Norway, NY, 1 Aug 1808 daughter of Philip and Mary (Arnold) Potter; Lorancy d. at Herkimer, 19 Apr 1835. Henry m. 2nd 19 Apr 1836, MARY DE WITT, b. 1816; Mary d. at Cascade, 13 Oct 1891.

ii ELIZABETH HOLT, b. 23 Mar 1805; d. 8 Sep 1819.

iii LUCIEN HOLT, b. at Hampton, 24 Oct 1806; d. at Willington, 7 Sep 1896; m. 2 Nov 1829, SOPHRONIA WRIGHT, b. at Mansfield, 1805 daughter of John Hyde and Lorinda (Royce) Wright;[1190] Sophronia d. at Willington, 18 Mar 1866.

iv WILLIAM DUNLAP HOLT, b. 7 Nov 1808; d. 10 Jan 1829.

Nehemiah Holt and Eunice Fuller were parents of three children.

i DANIEL HOLT, b. at Hampton, 2 Jul 1810; d. at Lowell, MA, 11 Apr 1883; m. 1st at Hampton, 6 Oct 1840, JULIETTA E. FULLER, b. at Hampton, 6 Feb 1813 daughter of Harvey and Lydia (Denison) Fuller; Julietta d. at Hampton, 14 Apr 1841. Daniel m. 2nd about 1841, ABIGAIL SARAH BROWN, b. at Glastonbury, 13 Feb 1809 daughter of Pardon and Sarah (Woodbury) Brown; Abigail d. at Lowell, 26 Feb 1852. Daniel m. 3rd 5 Jun 1861, MARY GREENLEAF DUNLAP, b. at Brunswick, ME, 29 Mar 1825 daughter of Richard T. and Mary (Greenleaf) Dunlap; Mary d. at Lowell, 25 Feb 1893. Daniel Holt graduated from Yale in 1835 and practiced as a homeopath in Lowell.[1191]

ii ALMIRA HOLT, b. at Hampton, 13 Apr 1813; d. at Chaplin, 14 Nov 1874; m. JAMES RUSSELL UTLEY, b. at Hampton, 3 Apr 1811 son of James and Phebe (Clark) Utley; Russell d. at Chaplin, 9 Aug 1896.

iii CHARLES AUSTIN HOLT, b. at Hampton, 6 Jan 1816; d. at Chaplin, 13 Jan 1894; m. 9 Jan 1837, EUNICE BENNETT, b, 6 Oct 1816 daughter of Origen and Salinda (Babcock) Bennett; Eunice d. at Chaplin, 28 Dec 1894.

442) SARAH HOLT (*Nehemiah*[4], *George*[3], *Henry*[2], *Nicholas*[1]), b. at Windham, 12 Oct 1758 daughter of Nehemiah and Anna (Farnum) Holt; d. at Leicester, VT, 26 Sep 1843. m. by 1783, her third cousin once removed, STEPHEN SPARKS (*Mehitable Johnson Sparks*[5], *Lydia Lovejoy Johnson*[4], *Mary Farnum Lovejoy*[3], *Elizabeth Holt Farnum*[2], *Nicholas*[1]), b. at Tolland, 24 Apr 1759 son of Joseph and Mehitable (Johnson) Sparks; Stephen d. at Leicester, 25 Jun 1827.

1189 Connecticut Wills and Probate Records, Ashford District Estate Files, Estate of Anna Byles, Case 51, probate 1883

1190 The names of Sophronia's parents are given on her death record as John H. and Lorinda Wright. Connecticut, Hale Collection of Cemetery Inscriptions and Newspaper Notices, 1629-1934

1191 Yale University, *Obituary Record of Graduates of Yale University, deceased from June 1870 to June 1880*, p 151

Stephen and Sarah were early settlers in Leicester, Vermont[1192] arriving there by 1785. Sarah Holt and Stephen Sparks were parents of at least nine children.

i ELIPHALET SPARKS, b. at Rutland, 30 Dec 1783; d. at Leicester, 29 Dec 1795.

ii JOSEPH SPARKS, b. at Leicester, VT, 23 Apr 1785; d. at Cambridge, WI, 11 Jan 1864; m. HANNAH who has not been identified, but according to census records born in MA about 1786. Hannah was living in 1850.

iii STEPHEN SPARKS, b. at Leicester, 13 Mar 1787; d. at Leicester, 17 Dec 1860; m. 17 Sep 1818, LUCY SAWYER, b. about 1790; Lucy d. at Leicester, 1 Jan 1860.

iv SARAH SPARKS, b. 14 Oct 1788

v ANNA SPARKS, b. 20 Oct 1790; d. at Leicester, 28 Feb 1875; m. at Leicester, 8 Nov 1814, ALEXANDER JOHNSON who has not been identified; Alexander likely died before 1840. Anna was listed as a town pauper in the 1850 and 1870 census.

vi NEHEMIAH SPARKS, b. at Leicester, 14 Mar 1792; d. after 1860 when he was living at Eagle, NY; m. 1 Jan 1815, LUCY STARKWEATHER, b. 1789; Lucy d. at Eagle, NY, 14 Jul 1858.

vii HARVEY SPARKS, b. at Leicester, 30 Nov 1794; d. at Leicester, 24 Jan 1828; m. at Leicester, 25 Jan 1821, DEBORAH ROBBINS, b. at Leicester, Sep 1798 daughter of Moses and Thirza (Dodge) Robbins; Deborah d. 26 Jun 1857.

viii ELIZA SPARKS, b. at Leicester, 16 Oct 1797; d. at Hastings, NY, 1877; m. at Pompey, NY, 20 Mar 1823,[1193] HOPESTILL HALL, b. at Middleborough, MA, 4 Sep 1797[1194] son of Jonathan and Abigail (Bisbee) Hall; Hopestill d. at Hastings, NY, 20 May 1883.

ix PATTY SPARKS, b. 1799; d. at Leicester, 28 Aug 1803.

443) MARTHA HOLT (*Nehemiah[4], George[3], Henry[2], Nicholas[1]*), b. at Windham, 20 Sep 1760 daughter of Nehemiah and Anna (Farnum) Holt; d. at Mansfield, CT, 24 Apr 1849; m. 1st 1785, JOSEPH CLARK. Martha m. 2nd 28 Apr 1791, NATHAN MARTIN, b. at Mansfield, CT, 28 Jun 1760 son of John and Hannah (Spofford) Martin; Nathan d. at Mansfield, 2 Jun 1812.

In his will written 9 March 1812 (probate 15 July 1812), Nathan Martin bequeathed to beloved wife Martha the use and improvement of all the estate for her support and for the support and benefit of his five children while she is a widow. After that, the estate is to be divided equally among his beloved children Bela, Eliphalet, Mary, Luther, and Levi. It is his intention that the division of the property take place after the decease or marriage of his beloved wife. Brother Ebenezer Martin was named executor.[1195] The estate was valued at $1,525.49 which included the homestead of 30 acres with dwelling house and barn. Debts were $54.97.

Martha Holt and Joseph Clark were parents of one child.

i ISAAC CLARK, b. at Hampton, 1786

Martha Holt and Nathan Martin were parents of five children whose births are recorded at Hampton.

i BELA MARTIN, b. 19 May 1794; d. after 1870 when he was living at Castile, NY; m. CHARRY who is not definitely identified, but b. in CT about 1791; Charry d. after 1880 when she was living in Castile at the home of her daughter and son-in-law.

ii ELIPHALET MARTIN, b. 11 Jun 1796; d. at Mansfield, 31 Jan 1873; m. at Mansfield, 31 Mar 1822, ARMINA SLATE, b. at Mansfield, 29 Aug 1803 daughter of James and Mary (Needham) Slate; Armina d. at Mansfield, 19 Jul 1873.

iii MARY "POLLY" MARTIN, b. 19 Mar 1798; d. 20 Sep 1820.

iv LUTHER MARTIN, b. 2 Sep 1801; d. at Willimantic, 21 Jul 1854; m. 27 Nov 1827, SOPHIA BUMP, b. about 1804; Sophia was living at the time of Luther's probate in 1854.

[1192] Smith, *History of Addison County, Vermont*, p 475

[1193] Ancestry.com, New York, Marriage Notices, 1800-1855

[1194] Ancestry.com, Massachusetts, Town and Vital Records, 1620-1988, Middleborough Births, Marriages, and Deaths, p 123

[1195] *Connecticut State Library (Hartford, Connecticut), Probate Packets, Manning, Eliphalet-Millard, B, 1719-1880, Estate of Nathan Martin, case 2676*

v ELI MARTIN, b. 10 Mar 1804; d. at Middletown, CT, 1 Oct 1876; m. at Middletown, 8 Oct 1827, EMELINE COE, b. at Middletown, about 1807 daughter of Ezra and Irene (Miller) Coe;[1196] Emeline d. at Middletown, 3 Apr 1868.

444) ROXERENE HOLT (*Nehemiah⁴, George³, Henry², Nicholas¹*), b. at Windham, 6 Apr 1762 daughter of Nehemiah and Anna (Farnum) Holt; d. at Leicester, VT, 13 Mar 1825; m. at Ludlow, MA, 12 May 1783, EBENEZER MORRIS HITCHCOCK, b. at Springfield, MA, 13 Nov 1762 son of Joseph and Sarah (Morris) Hitchcock; Morris d. at Leicester, 24 Oct 1833.

There are just two children known for Roxerene Holt and Ebenezer Hitchcock.

i JOSEPH HOLT HITCHCOCK, b. at Ludlow, MA, 17 Aug 1784; d. at Leicester, VT, 24 Jul 1854; m. HANNAH PARKER, b. at Westminster, MA, 28 Jun 1781 daughter of John and Olive (Temple) Parker; Hannah d. at Leicester 10 Oct 1849. There are four children known for Joseph and Hannah including a daughter Olive Temple Hitchcock.

ii ROXERENE "ROXY" HITCHCOCK, b. at Ludlow, 28 Aug 1786; d. at Malone, NY, 1871; m. EBENEZER ROBBINSON DAGGETT, b. at Leicester, VT, 22 Apr 1787 son of John and Judith (Capron) Daggett; Ebenezer d. at Malone, 6 Oct 1874.

445) ANNA HOLT (*Nehemiah⁴, George³, Henry², Nicholas¹*), b. at Windham, 6 Jul 1765 daughter of Nehemiah and Anna (Farnum) Holt; d. at Hampton, 10 Oct 1806; m. at Hampton, 22 Jun 1786, AMOS FORD, b. at Windham, 24 Aug 1763 son of Amos and Lydia (Davison) Ford. Amos married second Abigail Snow on 4 Oct 1807.

There are two children known for Anna Holt and Amos Ford.

i ANNA FORD, b. at Hampton, CT, 30 Aug 1787; d. at Girard, MI, 11 Aug 1849; m. 19 Sep 1805, LUTHER CUTLER, b. at Hampton, 12 Aug 1783;[1197] Luther d. at Girard, 17 Aug 1850.

ii PHINEAS FORD, b. at Hampton, 25 Jun 1790; d. at Batavia, NY, 7 Feb 1878; m. 27 Feb 1812, PAMELA BLISS, b. at Hatfield, MA, 9 Apr 1792 daughter of Nathan and Submit (White) Bliss; Pamela d. at Batavia, 7 Sep 1877.

446) JOSEPH ROGERS (*Priscilla Holt Rogers⁴, George³, Henry², Nicholas¹*), b. at Ashford, 4 Aug 1744 son of Ichabod and Priscilla (Holt) Rogers; m. at Wales, MA, 25 Dec 1765, SARAH JORDAN, b. at Brimfield, 30 Mar 1748 daughter of Richard and Isabel (-) Jordan.

Joseph and Sarah lived primarily in Wales, Massachusetts, but did spend some time in Stafford, Connecticut where one of the children was born. They returned to Wales, and both Joseph and Sarah are thought to have died there, although no record was found.[1198] They were parents of eleven children.

i STEPHEN ROGERS, b. 29 May 1765; m. at Wales, 28 Aug 1794, POLLY DORRAL, b. est. 1774 daughter of Thomas Dorral (ca 1748-1810).

ii JASPER ROGERS, b. 28 Jan 1767; d. at South Brimfield, 1816 (probate 2 Feb 1816); m. 6 Oct 1791, ELIZABETH "BETSEY" FENTON, b. about 1766 daughter of William and Anne (Shaw) Fenton.

iii OLIVER ROGERS, b. 10 Jun 1768; d. after 1830 when he was living in Pompey, NY; m. at Wales, 22 Apr 1790, his first cousin once removed, EUNICE ROGERS, b. at Wales, Feb 1771 daughter of Joel and Sarah (Webber) Jordan.

iv LYDIA ROGERS, b. 30 Sep 1771

v PARTHENE ROGERS, b. 28 Sep 1773; d. at West Middlebury, NY, 20 May 1836; m. 1st at Wales, 7 Aug 1788, her first cousin once removed, JOHN ROGERS, b. at Wales, 15 Mar 1767 son of Joel and Sarah (Webber) Rogers. Parthene m. 2nd, about 1830, BENJAMIN NELSON, b. 1758 son of John and Elizabeth (Nelson) Nelson; Benjamin d. (buried) at Attica, 1842. Benjamin Nelson was first married to Anne Fenton who died in 1829.

vi JOHN ROGERS, b. 25 Oct 1777; d. Oct 1782.

vii SILVANUS ROGERS, b. 11 Feb 1780; d. 6 Nov 1787.

viii JOSEPH ROGERS, b. likely at Stafford, CT, 27 Apr 1782; d. at Wales, 2 Jan 1846; m. at Union, CT, 17 Jul 1803, JANE SMALLEDGE, b. at Union, 1781 daughter of John and Mary (Goodhue) Smalledge; Jane d. at Wales, 11 Feb 1848.

1196 Bartlett, *Robert Coe, Puritan*, p 270

1197 Durrie, Holt genealogy

1198 Massachusetts, Town and Vital Records, 1620-1988, ancestry.com database, Town of Wales, Family Records, p 416

ix DOLPHUS ROGERS, b. 28 Apr 1785; d. 1 Jan 1788.

x DANIEL ROGERS, b. 29 Sep 1787; d. at Wales, 15 May 1837; m. at Wales, 14 Feb 1813, MEHITABLE DAVISON, b. at Wales, 24 Jun 1786 daughter of Dominicus and Hannah (Twist) Davison.

xi SALLY ROGERS, b. 15 Jan 1792; d. at Attica, NY, 22 Feb 1871; m. at Wales, 16 Nov 1813, IRA STEWART, b. about 1790 son of Paul and Olive (Munger) Stewart; Ira d. at Attica, 30 Sep 1880.

447) ISHMAEL ROGERS (*Priscilla Holt Rogers⁴, George³, Henry², Nicholas¹*), b. at Ashford, about 1746 son of Ichabod and Priscilla (Holt) Rogers; d. at Shaftsbury, VT, 27 Mar 1813; m. at Wales, MA, 30 Oct 1766, MARY JORDAN, b. at Brimfield, 28 Oct 1744 daughter of Richard and Isabel (-) Jordan; Mary d. at Shaftsbury, 26 Apr 1809.

Ishmael and Mary are so far something of a mystery. They were married in Wales, left there soon after. They were perhaps in Hoosick, New York for a time, but they died in Shaftsbury, Vermont. There is the record of one child born at Wales, and there were likely other children.

i DORCAS ROGERS, b. at Wales, 8 Mar 1768

448) SARAH ROGERS (*Priscilla Holt Rogers⁴, George³, Henry², Nicholas¹*), b. at Ashford, 12 Feb 1747/8 daughter of Ichabod and Priscilla (Holt) Rogers; d. at Hawley, MA, 4 Feb 1814; m. at Wales, 29 May 1768, JOHN BURROUGHS, b. at Windsor, CT, 30 Apr 1748 son of Simon and Lydia (Porter) Burroughs; John d. at Hawley, 21 Mar 1821.[1199]

Sarah and John were among the first residents of the newly incorporated town of Hawley, Massachusetts in 1792 where John was elected tythingman at the first town election.[1200] There is record of one land transaction for John Burroughs in Hawley selling a tract of land (lots 45 and 46) to Edmund Longley for £100 on 8 January 1793.[1201]

John Burroughs and Sarah Rogers were parents of nine children, the births recorded either at Williamsburg or Plainfield, Massachusetts.

i LYDIA BURROUGHS, b. at Williamsburg, MA, 21 Jun 1769; d. at Burlington, CT, 21 Sep 1854; m. at Ashfield, MA, 24 Nov 1788, ASAHEL WARNER, b. at Farmington, CT, about 1765 son of Ard and Elizabeth (Porter) Warner;[1202] Asahel d. 7 Aug 1812 (buried at Berlin, CT).

ii PORTOR BURROUGHS, b. at Williamsburg, 8 Jun 1771; d. at Otisco, NY, 10 Dec 1849; m. at Plainfield, 14 Sep 1795, ABIGAIL HAWES, b. 6 Aug 1775 daughter of Samuel and Rachel (Darlina) Hawes; Abigail d. at Otisco, 28 Jul 1843.

iii ICHABOD BURROUGHS, b. at Williamsburg, 12 Feb 1773; d. at Otisco, NY, 14 Sep 1832; m. at Plainfield, 10 Dec 1797, ELIZABETH PREBLE, b. 1775; Elizabeth d. at Otisco, 25 Feb 1855.

iv PRISCILLA BURROUGHS, b. 30 Oct 1773; d. at Bennington, VT, 15 Nov 1853; m. at Plainfield, MA, 18 May 1805, GEORGE ROBINSON, b. at Belchertown, MA, 13 Dec 1775 son of George and Mary (Robinson) Robinson; George d. at Bennington, 4 Aug 1831.

v SALLY BURROUGHS, b. at Williamsburg, MA, 21 Jun 1777; d. at Claridon, OH, 9 Dec 1853; m. 1st at Plainfield, 24 Sep 1795, NATHAN BARTON, b. at Oxford, MA, 8 Feb 1770 son of Nathan and Tamar (Barton) Barton; Nathan d. at Phelps, NY, about 1823. Sally m. 2nd at Geauga County, OH, 5 Jun 1833, JACOB WARRINER, b. at Wilbraham, MA, 18 Apr 1768 son of Isaac and Lydia (Fury) Warriner; Jacob d. at Claridon, 4 Sep 1857.

vi CATHARINE BURROUGHS, b. at Plainfield, 4 Sep 1781; d. at Okemos, MI, 5 Jan 1856; m. at Plainfield, 13 Nov 1803, JOHN JOY, b. 6 Jul 1781 son of Asa and Mary (Blanchard) Joy; John d. after 1860 when he was living at Meridian Township, MI.

vii RHODA BURROUGHS, b. 6 Nov 1783; d. at Plainfield, MA, 13 Mar 1825; m. at Plainfield, 10 Dec 1805, LEMUEL ALLIS, b. at Plainfield, 9 Jul 1784 son of Lemuel and Rebecca (Davis) Allis; Lemuel d. at Chatham, OH, 20 Oct 1855. Lemuel married second Lydia Beals.

viii MARY "POLLY" BURROUGHS, b. at Plainfield, 29 Oct 1786; d. at Phelps, NY, 12 Mar 1816; m. at Plainfield, 27 Jun 1805, her first cousin, DAVID BURROUGHS, b. at Plainfield, 20 Jul 1784 son of David and Elizabeth (Shaw) Burroughs; David d. at Allen, MI, 19 Nov 1866.

[1199] Information on this family obtained from Onondaga County Family Bible pages, in this case a transcription of the bible records of Porter Burroughs a child of Sarah and John Burroughs. http://www.rootsweb.com/~nyononda/BIBLE/BURROUGH.HTM. Information posted by Victor Burroughs who reports the original bible is in the possession of Frank Burroughs of Seneca Falls, NY.

[1200] Atkins, *History of the Town of Hawley*, p 9

[1201] Massachusetts Land Records, Franklin County, 9:141

[1202] The 1825 probate record of Ard Warner includes a distribution to the estate of Asahel Warner deceased.

ix JOHN BURROUGHS, b. 24 Dec 1788; d. 7 Aug 1794.

449) ROBERT ROGERS (*Priscilla Holt Rogers⁴, George³, Henry², Nicholas¹*), b. at Brimfield, 4 Dec 1749 son of Ichabod and Priscilla (Holt) Rogers; d. at Stafford, CT, 25 Mar 1813; m. 1st at Wales, 2 Apr 1769, ELEANOR NELSON, b. at Brimfield, 11 Feb 1743 daughter of John and Elizabeth (Nelson) Nelson; Eleanor d. at Stafford, about 1790. Robert m. 2nd about 1792, HULDAH ORCUTT, b. at Stafford, 9 May 1767 daughter of Simeon and Elizabeth (Rockwell) Orcutt; Huldah d. at Stafford, 19 Mar 1863.

Robert Rogers did not leave a will and his estate entered probate 28 April 1813 with Rufus Leonard as administrator and Nehemiah Rogers giving surety for the bond. Huldah Rogers declined administration. The total value of the estate was $526.22, $220 being the value of land and buildings. Due to debts of the estate, it was deemed insolvent and property was sold. At an estate distribution on 29 February 1816, widow Huldah Rogers was granted $17.40 for her support. Each of the children received nine dollars each: Nehemiah Rogers, Ebenezer Rogers, William Rogers, Rockwell Rogers, the wife of Thaddeus King, the wife of Benjamin Wheedon, the representatives of Lucinda Rising, and Betsey Rogers.[1203]

Robert Rogers and Eleanor Nelson were parents of five children.

i LUCINDA ROGERS, b. at Wales, MA, 8 Apr 1771; d. at Barre, VT, about 1808; m. 12 Mar 1798, PAUL RISING, b. at Suffield, CT, 28 Oct 1774 son of Paul and Ruth (Strong) Rising.

ii NEHEMIAH ROGERS, b. at Wales, 21 Mar 1774; d. at Machias, NY, 25 Apr 1852; m. at Wales, 19 Aug 1792. EUNICE MCNALL, b. 1772; Eunice d. at Cadiz, NY, 13 Jan 1861.

iii EBENEZER ROGERS, b. estimated as 1780; living in 1816.[1204]

iv EXPERIENCE ROGERS, b. at Suffield, about 1782; d. after 1850 when she was living in Suffield; m. at Suffield, 12 Jan 1804, THADDEUS KING, b. at Suffield, 25 Apr 1785 son of Thaddeus and Alice (King) King; Thaddeus d. at Suffield, 8 May 1850.

v RESINA ROGERS, b. at Stafford, about 1788; d. likely at Hudson, OH, after 1830; m. at Portage County, OH, 9 Oct 1809, as his second wife, BENJAMIN WHEEDON, b. at Branford, CT, 29 Apr 1777 son of Solomon and Sarah (Rose) Wheedon. Benjamin was first married to Deborah Merriam.

Robert Rogers and Huldah Orcutt were parents of three children.

i WILLIAM "BILLY" ROGERS, b. at Stafford, 18 May 1794; d. at Stafford, 18 Apr 1870; m. 6 Mar 1817, JULIA ORCUTT, b. 12 Mar 1798 daughter of Stephen and Molly (Washburn) Orcutt; Julia d. at Stafford, 15 Apr 1880.

ii BETSEY ROGERS, b. at Stafford, 24 Apr 1796; d. at Stafford, 15 Oct 1862; m. ROSWELL WASHBURN, b. 1794; Roswell d. at Stafford, Jun 1870.

iii ROCKWELL ROGERS, b. at Stafford, 8 Sep 1798; living in 1816; nothing further found.

450) NATHANIEL ROGERS (*Priscilla Holt Rogers⁴, George³, Henry², Nicholas¹*), b. at Brimfield, 18 May 1752 son of Ichabod and Priscilla (Holt) Rogers; d. at Stafford, CT, 23 Jun 1836; m. at Ware, 3 Nov 1773, ABIGAIL KELSEE, b. about 1756 of Ware who has not been identified; Abigail d. after 1840 when she was living at Stafford, CT.

On 15 September 1832, Nathaniel Rogers of Stafford then age eighty years, appeared to give a statement related to his pension application. He reported enlisting in the company of Capt. Jonathan Bardwell as a private on 27 April 1775 at Ware, Massachusetts where he lived at the time. He marched to Roxbury and was in the regiment of Col. Brewer and served in the regiment until August or September. The company then marched to Dorchester. He served principally on guard duty and was not in any battles. He served eight months and was discharged 1 January 1776. He then returned to Ware. He further reported that he was born on 18 May 1752 in Wales where he lived until age 22 years when he removed with his wife to Ware. The family was in Ware about four years and then moved to Williamsburg, Massachusetts for three years, and then to Belchertown for eleven years. The family then returned to Wales where Nathaniel resided with his family for about thirty-three years. John and his wife then removed to Stafford, Connecticut where they remained. On 23 January 1839, Abigail Rogers of Stafford then age 83 years, appeared to give a statement related to her widow's pension. Also giving a statement in support of Abigail's application were her son-in-law Samuel Colburn and grandson Samuel Colburn both of Stafford.[1205]

The Wales town records name five children for Nathaniel and Abigail and a sixth child can be determined from the pension file who is the wife of Samuel Colburn. Birth records were not located for any of the children.

[1203] *Connecticut State Library (Hartford, Connecticut)*; Probate Place: *Hartford, Connecticut, Probate Packets, Rockwell, N-Sessions, O, 1759-1880, estate of Robert Rogers, case 1823*

[1204] Ebenezer is a child in the estate distribution, but it is not clear whether he is a child with Eleanor Nelson or a child with Huldah Orcutt. No clear information about him was located.

[1205] U. S. Revolutionary War Pension and Bounty-Land Application Files, Case W17568

i JOSEPH ROGERS

ii POLLY ROGERS

iii ANNA ROGERS

iv SUSANNAH ROGERS, b. about 1781; d. at Stafford, CT, 1 May 1858; m. at Wales, 20 Sep 1803, SAMUEL COLBURN, b. at Stafford, about 1780 son of Samuel and Sarah (Patterson) Colburn; Samuel d. at Stafford, 7 Nov 1853.

v AMASA ROGERS

vi OLIVE ROGERS, b. about 1785; m. at Wales, 30 May 1805, JOHN SWEET who was of Strafford but has not been identified. John and Olive had two children born in Wales, and John is reported to have returned to Stafford after the death of his wife.

451) NEHEMIAH ROGERS (*Priscilla Holt Rogers⁴, George³, Henry², Nicholas¹*), b. at Wales, 7 Jul 1756 son of Ichabod and Priscilla (Holt) Rogers; d. at Wallingford, VT, 1813 (probate 1813); m. 1st at Wales, 2 Jul 1778, RHODA MUNGER, b. at Wales, about 1758 daughter of Samuel and Abigail (Bester) Munger; Rhoda d. at Wallingford, about 1801. Nehemiah m. 2nd at Wallingford, 3 Oct 1802, widow JUDITH ROUNDS who died about 1809; Nehemiah m. 3rd at Wallingford, 28 Oct 1810, MARY FULLER. Nehemiah and Mary divorced in 1812.

There is one child known for Nehemiah Rogers and Rhoda Munger.

i ELIZABETH ROGERS, b. about 1788; d. at Clarendon, VT, 18 Dec 1863; m. about 1809, FREDERICK BUTTON, b. at Clarendon, 2 Mar 1788 son of Charles F. and Hannah (Kinne) Button; Frederick d. at Clarendon, 26 May 1874.

452) EBENEZER ROGERS (*Priscilla Holt Rogers⁴, George³, Henry², Nicholas¹*), b. at Wales, 11 Apr 1759 son of Ichabod and Priscilla (Holt) Rogers; m. at Wales, 4 Dec 1777, CATHERINE RENOLDS, b. at Stafford, CT, 27 May 1757 daughter of James and Sarah (Fargo) Renolds; Catherine d. at Shaftsbury, VT, 23 Dec 1785.

Just one child is known for Ebenezer and Catherine.

i MERCY ROGERS, b. Aug 1782; d. at Québec, 1 Jul 1818; m. ISAAC V. DAVIS, b. in VT, about 1775; Isaac d. 1853. Mercy and Isaac were the parents of Ebenezer Rogers Davis who was born in Québec in 1811 and died at Jasper, MI, 9 Jan 1898.[1206]

453) ROCKSANA ROGERS (*Priscilla Holt Rogers⁴, George³, Henry², Nicholas¹*), b. at Wales, 30 Dec 1765 daughter of Ichabod and Priscilla (Holt) Rogers; d. at Monroe, MI, after 1820; m. at Wales, 31 Mar 1785, GIDEON BADGER, b. at Union, CT, 24 Feb 1765 son of Daniel and Phillipi (Hale) Badger; Gideon d. at Monroe, 26 Mar 1826.

Rocksana and Gideon married in Wales, Massachusetts and seem to be in Watervliet, New York in 1810 with a household of five persons. The family was later in Monroe County, Michigan.

Gideon enlisted 15 April 1781 from South Brimfield for a term of three years as a private in Capt. Isaac Pope's company of the 4th regiment commanded by Col. William Shepard. Gideon was then age 16 and described as 5'9" with light complexion and light hair with occupation as farmer.[1207]

On 18 June 1818, Gideon Badger of Monroe, Michigan then age fifty-four gave a statement related to his pension application. In April 1781, he enlisted from Massachusetts in the regular army in the company of Capt. Isaac Pope in the 4th regiment and served until December 1783 when he was honorably discharged. On 12 June 1820, he was living in French Town, Michigan and reported he had no real or personal property except two cows and one yearling he purchased in 1819 with the money he received that year. His sicknesses prevented his from doing his usual work as a farmer. His wife Roxana, age fifty-five, was described as infirm. Also in the home was daughter Eliza age nine. On 18 April 1822 while in Michigan, he made a statement that he planned to remove to Buffalo, New York, but on 23 October 1824 he again appeared in Michigan stating he had not accomplished his move to New York and had returned to Michigan.[1208]

There is just one child known for Gideon and Rocksana although the 1810 census suggests there are at least three other children.

i ELIZA BADGER, b. about 1811; nothing further found

[1206] *Michigan, Death Records, 1867-1952*, Michigan Department of Community Health, Division for Vital Records and Health Statistics; Lansing, Michigan; Death Records.

[1207] United State Roster of Soldiers and Sailors 1775-1783, Massachusetts, volume 1, p 433

[1208] Revolutionary War Pension and Bounty-Land Warrant Application Files, Case S34741

454) JERUSHA ROGERS (*Priscilla Holt Rogers⁴, George³, Henry², Nicholas¹*), b. at Wales, 25 Oct 1767 daughter of Ichabod and Priscilla (Holt) Rogers; m. at Wales, 17 Nov 1796, DANIEL MOULTON, b. at Wales, 17 Nov 1773 son of Jonathan Moulton.

Prior to her marriage, Jerusha had a daughter out-of-wedlock, a fact mentioned in the town records of Wales but without giving the name of the daughter. The town records reported that daughter married and settled in Stafford, Connecticut. Daniel Moulton was known as "Joffet" and the town records describe him in this unsympathetic manner: "In his features and looks he was uncomely, yes, of extreme homeliness; with great awkwardness of manners; mind rather unintelligent; the rum jug was his intimate companion if not his bedfellow."[1209] The family was in Wales until 1800 and are believed to have gone to Stafford, Connecticut.

There is a record of one child of Jerusha and Daniel.

i ROSWELL MOULTON, b. at Wales, 30 Oct 1799; d. at South Wilbraham, MA, 29 Dec 1862; m. at Stafford, CT, 5 Apr 1821, TRYPHENA COLBURN, b. at Windham, about 1800 daughter of Sylvanus Colburn; Tryphena d. at Agawam, MA, 11 Mar 1869.

455) OLIVER ROGERS (*Hannah Holt Rogers⁴, George³, Henry², Nicholas¹*), b. at Windham, 14 Apr 1748 son of Jethro and Hannah (Holt) Rogers; d. at Chaplin, Apr 1829; m. at Windham, 11 Feb 1770, HANNAH COBURN, b. at Windham, 11 Oct 1750 daughter of Robert and Mary (Gennings) Coburn.

On 2 June 1818, Oliver Rogers then age sixty-eight of the town of Mansfield, made a statement at Windham County related to his application for pension. On 15 January 1779, he enlisted for one year as a private marine on the United States Frigate Confederacy with thirty-six guns commanded by Seth Harding, Captain. He was wounded in the hand by the accidental discharge of a musket while the ship was in the mouth of the Delaware River, languished from the wound but he continued with his service. He was sent ashore to the hospital in Philadelphia in May 1779, and after his recovery was given a permit to return home. For the past thirty-one years he had received a pension related to his injury having lost use of two fingers of his hand. On 28 June at age seventy, he reported that his wife Hannah Rogers was age sixty-eight and in feeble health. He had no children who were dependent on him.[1210]

Oliver Rogers did not leave a will and his estate entered probate 30 May 1829 with Elias Sharpe as administrator. Personal estate was valued at $38.95.[1211]

There are records for six children of Oliver Rogers and Hannah Coburn born at Windham.

i LOVEWELL "LOVEL" ROGERS, b. 17 Jan 1772; d. at Lebanon, CT, 10 Nov 1833; m. before 1799, CHARLOTTE WOODWORTH, b. 1772; Charlotte d. at Lebanon, 9 Oct 1822.

ii CYNTHIA ROGERS, b. 20 Apr 1774

iii DANIEL ROGERS, b. 19 Nov 1776

iv PHILORA ROGERS, b. 23 Sep 1778

v HANNAH ROGERS, b. 26 May 1785

vi TRYPHENA ROGERS, b. 7 Dec 1788; d. at Windham, 6 May 1813.

456) BIXBEE ROGERS (*Hannah Holt Rogers⁴, George³, Henry², Nicholas¹*), b. at Canterbury, 9 Nov 1758 son of Jethro and Hannah (Holt) Rogers; d. at Galena, OH, 10 Sep 1831; m. ESTHER, b. about 1769 who has not been identified; Esther d. at Galena, 27 Nov 1817.

On 29 June 1818, Bixbee made a statement in the court at Delaware County, Ohio related to his application for pension. He enlisted in the Continental service in 1777 and served in the Connecticut line in the regiment of Col. Samuel Willis. He served a full three years and was discharged 18 May 1780. He stated he was in indigent circumstances and not able to support himself. His inventory included one yoke of oxen, one cow, and a few pigs with a total estate value of $187. In a statement in 1820, he mentioned his wife (not named) and three children living with him: James, 18; Samuel, 14; and Elizabeth, 9.[1212]

Bixbee and his family were in the census of Luzerne County, Pennsylvania from 1790 to 1810. The Rogers family traveled from Pennsylvania to Ohio about 1810. They were briefly in Knox County, Ohio but moved on to Delaware County. Bixbee was influential in the formation of the township of Genoa.[1213]

There are seven likely children of Bixbee and Esther Rogers, the oldest six children likely born in Plymouth, Pennsylvania, and the youngest child in Ohio.

i BIXBEE ROGERS, b. 1790; d. 1810.

1209 Massachusetts Town and Vital Records, Wales Family Records, p 288; ancestry.com database online

1210 Revolutionary War Pension and Bounty-Land Warrant Application Files, Case S36275

1211 *Connecticut State Library (Hartford, Connecticut), Probate Packets, Richardson, Josephine-Rose, Samuel, 1719-1880, Case 3260*

1212 Revolutionary War Pension and Bounty-Land Warrant Application Files, 1800-1900, Case S40357

1213 Perrin, *History of Delaware County and Ohio*, p 607

ii PHILOMON ROGERS, b. at Plymouth, PA, 12 Aug 1791; d. at Miami, OH, 18 Dec 1834; m. about 1815, ELIZABETH COCKRELL, b. likely in VA, 2 Mar 1796 daughter of Edward and Elizabeth (Dawson) Cockrell;[1214] Elizabeth d. at Miami, OH, 1884. Elizabeth married second William Rubert.

iii JONATHAN ROGERS, b. 1795; d. at Delaware County, OH, 1820.

iv DAVID ROGERS, b. at Plymouth, PA, 1798; d. at Genoa, OH, 1867 (probate 19 Sep 1867); m. at Delaware County, OH, 7 May 1840, SYLVIA PHELPS, b. in PA, about 1804; Sylvia d. after 1880 when she was living in Genoa with David's brother Samuel and his wife Sarah.[1215] In his will written 28 Aug 1852 and proved 19 Sep 1867, David bequeathed his entire estate to his beloved wife Sylvia "formerly Sylvia Phelps."[1216]

v JAMES ROGERS, b. 1802; d. after 1860 at Pleasant, OH, m. MATILDA COCKRELL, b. in VA, 22 Dec 1803 daughter of Edward and Elizabeth (Dawson) Cockrell; Matilda d. at Pleasant, OH, 1 Mar 1863.

vi SAMUEL ROGERS, b. 26 Aug 1804; d. at Genoa, OH, 17 Oct 1887; m. at Delaware County, OH, 27 Jun 1831, SARAH CLOSSON, b. at Luzerne County, PA, 7 Jun 1813 daughter of Daniel and Martha (Devore) Closson; Sarah d. at Genoa, OH, 13 Sep 1895.

vii ELIZABETH ROGERS, b. at Delaware County, OH, 1811; d. after 1850 when she was living at Keokuk, IA; m. at Delaware County, 26 Dec 1835, JOHN W. HOUSTON, b. in OH, about 1813; John d. at Mokelumne, CA, 30 Mar 1861 (probate 3 May 1861). Elizabeth and John had two children, Albert and Martha. Daughter Martha married Alfred J. Ross at Mokelumne Hill in 1858. "Moke Hill" was a gold rush town and it may be assumed that John went there during the gold rush. He was a carpenter. John lived in the next household from his daughter and son-in-law in 1860.[1217]

457) JOSIAH ROGERS (*Hannah Holt Rogers^4, George^3, Henry^2, Nicholas^1*), b at Canterbury, 14 Nov 1760 son of Jethro and Hannah (Holt) Rogers; d. at Washington, PA, 14 Aug 1841; m. 2 Oct 1786,[1218] RUTH HARRIS, b. at Canterbury, 26 Mar 1764 daughter of Paul and Mary (Herrington) Harris; Ruth d. at Mehoopany, PA, 22 Sep 1844.

On 4 September 1832, Josiah Rogers, aged seventy-one, at that time residing at Windham in Luzerne County, Pennsylvania made declaration related to his application for pension. In May 1779 while residing in Canterbury, he enlisted for a period of three months in a militia company under the command of Capt. Joseph Burgess. He was at Chatham and Groton serving guard duty, saw no battles at that enlistment, and returned home at the end of his term. In March 1782 he again enlisted in the state militia under Captain Daniel Allen. At that time, he enlisted as the substitute for Deacon Jacob Winters and David Dodge who were older men. Winters and Dodge paid Josiah five dollars apiece for a bounty. Josiah became sick with smallpox so did not initially march with the company but joined them about one month later at Horse Neck. The company was attached to the regiment commanded by Col. Samuel Caufield. He stayed at Horse Neck until April 1783 at the end of his term. He reported being born in Canterbury on 4 December 1760 and he resided in Canterbury until 1809 when he moved to Pennsylvania.

On 17 April 1844, widow Ruth Rogers aged eighty years appeared in Wyoming County related to her widow's pension application. She reported her marriage to Josiah occurred 2 October 1786. On 17 April 1844, daughter Lucy Arms aged fifty-four of Windham, PA made a statement in support of her mother's application. On 18 April 1844, daughter Polly Asenath Alworth aged fifty-seven of Windham township also gave a statement.

A court hearing related to payments to the survivors of Josiah and Ruth was held at Auburn, Cayuga, New York on 24 June 1846 and identified the following living children: Polly Alworth, Lucy Arms, and A. G. Rogers all of Mehoopany, PA; Ruby Miller of Washington, PA; Gustavus A. Rogers of Albany, PA; and Artemesia Estell of Burlington, PA.[1219]

There are eight children known of Josiah and Ruth. The births of the children are presumed to have occurred at Canterbury, Connecticut where the family was living before relocating to Pennsylvania about 1809.

i MARY "POLLY" ASENATH ROGERS, b. about 1787; d. at Mehoopany, PA, 3 Feb 1853; m. TIMOTHY ALWORTH, b. at Pomfret, 26 Mar 1778 son of James and Hannah (Baker) Alworth; Timothy d. at Mehoopany, 18 Nov 1842.

ii LUCY ROGERS, b. about 1789; d. after 1850 when she was living in Mehoopany; m. PHILIP R. ARMS who died at Windham, PA before 1830 when Lucy was listed as head of household.

[1214] Lombus, *Edward Cockrell's Virginia Ancestors c1630-1822*, p 27, https://www.familysearch.org/library/books/records/item/216528-edward-cockrell-s-virginia-ancestors-ca-1630-1822?viewer=1&offset=0#page=37&viewer=picture&o=info&n=0&q=

[1215] Year: 1880; Census Place: Genoa, Delaware, Ohio; Roll: 1012; Page: 409D; Enumeration District: 111

[1216] Ancestry.com. *Ohio, Wills and Probate Records, 1786-1998* [database on-line], Delaware County, Will records, volume 4, 1859-1869, pp 352-353

[1217] United States Census, 1860, California, Calaveras, Township No. 6

[1218] This is the date of marriage given by Ruth in her widow's pension application file.

[1219] U.S., Revolutionary War Pension and Bounty-Land Warrant Application Files, 1800-1900, Case W3605

iii RUBY ROGERS, b. about 1792; d. at Washington, PA between 1846 and 1850; m. about 1813 (first child born 1814), CHRISTOPHER MILLER, b. about 1788; Christopher d. after 1880 when he was living in Washington, PA.

iv RUTH ROGERS, b. about 1793; d. at Salem, PA, about 1838; m. JAMES HARRIS, b. about 1790.

v GUSTAVUS ADOLPHUS ROGERS, b. about 1795; d. after 1860 when he was living at Albany, PA; m. MARTHA "PATTY" HUMPHREY, b. about 1795.

vi ARTEMESIA ROGERS, b. about 1798; d. at Burlington, PA, 20 May 1874; m. ANDREW KING ESTELL, b. about 1795; Andrew d. at Burlington, 12 Aug 1879.

vii ALBAGANCE G. "ALBY" ROGERS, b. about 1803; d. after 1870 when he was living at Mehoopany and before 1880; m. about 1857, SARAH A., b. in PA, Mar 1820; Sarah d. after 1900 when she was living in Mehoopany.

viii THEEDA EMMA ROGERS, b. about 1808; d. before 1846; m. 7 Aug 1828, HENRY HUMPHREY.

458) JONATHAN HOLT (*Nathaniel*[4], *George*[3], *Henry*[2], *Nicholas*[1]), b. at Hampton, about 1758 and baptized on 14 Nov 1762 son of Nathaniel and Phebe (Canady) Holt; d. at Hampton, 11 Aug 1833 at age 75; m. at Hampton, 19 Oct 1780, ANNA FAULKNER,[1220] b. 23 Nov 1761 daughter of Caleb and Esther (Morse) Faulkner; Anna d. at Hampton, 31 Aug 1842.

Jonathan enlisted for a term of one year in June 1776 in the company of Capt. Benoni Cutler in a regiment commanded by Col. Andrew Ward. He was honorably discharged on 4 May 1777. He made application for a pension based on his service on 4 January 1820. On 28 June 1820, Jonathan reported he was farmer by occupation but now unable to work but little. His household at that time was his wife Anna age fifty-nine and in "pretty good health", a daughter Julia age seventeen and in good health, and a granddaughter age six in good health.

On 26 November 1836, Anna Holt, age seventy-five years and a resident of Hampton, made a statement related to her widow's pension application. Anna reported that in 1781, Benedict Arnold and British troops attacked New Haven, and that Jonathan was ordered to repair to New Haven to assist with the defense. (Arnold's attack on New Haven occurred in 1779 so there is inconsistency in Anna's report).

On 8 January 1855, Polly Faulkner a daughter of Jonathan and Anna, and then a resident of Stafford, Connecticut, provided a statement related to the pension. After relating that her mother died on 31 August 1842, she provided the following as the only living children of Jonathan and Anna: Nathaniel Holt of the State of New York; James Holt of Hampton; Lucy Kingsbury of New York; Samuel Holt of Union; Polly Faulkner of Stafford; Maxamilla Beers of Hampton; and Julia Morse of Canterbury. Children Josiah M. Holt, Caleb Holt, and Cordelia Holt were deceased. This statement was related to an increase in the amount of the pension that seemed to have not all been received and might still be due.[1221]

Jonathan Holt and Anna Faulkner were parents of eleven children born at Hampton.

i NATHANIEL HOLT, b. 24 Apr 1782; d. at De Kalb, NY, 20 Dec 1860; m. 1st his fourth cousin once removed, MARY FARNUM (*Elijah Farnum*[6], *Zebadiah Farnum*[5], *William Farnum*[4], *Ralph Farnum*[3], *Elizabeth Holt Farnum*[2], *Nicholas*[1]), b. Feb 1783 daughter of Elijah and Julia (-) Farnum; Mary d. at De Kalb, 7 May 1845. Nathaniel m. 2nd MARY ANN, b. 1808; Mary Ann d. at De Kalb, 31 Jan 1893.

ii JOSIAH HOLT, b. 10 Apr 1784; d. at Plainfield, CT, 16 Nov 1846; m. at Hampton, 11 Mar 1804, MARY PRIOR, b. about 1780 daughter of Joseph and Judith (Hutchins) Prior.

iii JAMES HOLT, b. 17 Sep 1786; d. at Hampton, 23 Dec 1864; m. at Hampton, 28 Nov 1809, ABIGAIL ASHLEY, b. at Hampton, 1 Mar 1790 daughter of Samuel and Lucy (Nye) Ashley; Abigail d. at Hampton, 24 Oct 1873.

iv LUCY HOLT, b. 17 Apr 1788; d. at Cincinnatus, NY, 30 Dec 1864; m. 1st MASON KINGSBURY, b. at Windham, 18 Jun 1788 son of Samuel and Phebe (Gennings) Kingsbury; Mason d. at Cincinnatus, 24 Aug 1849. Lucy m. 2nd widower LEWIS WARNER, b. about 1775; Lewis was living in Cincinnatus in 1865 at age 90.

v SAMUEL HOLT, b. 26 Apr 1790; d. at Union, CT, 31 Jan 1855; m. CLARISSA JENNINGS, b. at Hampton, 4 Aug 1794 daughter of Nathan and Zerviah (Richardson) Jennings;[1222] Clarissa d. at Union, 24 Sep 1861.

vi ANNA HOLT (twin of Samuel), b. and d. 26 Apr 1790.

vii MARY HOLT, b. 4 Dec 1792; d. after 1870 when she was living in Stafford; m. at Hampton, 27 Mar 1821, her first cousin, CALEB FAULKNER, b. at Brooklyn, CT, about 1802 son of Samuel and Mary (Preston) Faulkner; Caleb d. at Stafford, after 1870.

viii DILLY HOLT, b. 29 Apr 1795; d. 14 Aug 1795.

1220 Durries's Holt genealogy and other published sources state that Jonathan Holt who married Anna Faulkner was the son of Zebadiah and Sarah (Flint) Holt. But Zebadiah's son Jonathan was deceased before 1760 as evidenced by his absence from the distribution in the settlement of Zebadiah's estate.

1221 U. S. Revolutionary War Pension and Bounty-Land Application Files, Case W21360

1222 The 1823 will of Nathan Jennings of Hampton includes a bequest to his daughter Clarissa Holt.

ix MAXAMILLA HOLT, b. 11 Feb 1797; d. at Hampton, 10 Nov 1868; m. at Hampton, 7 Feb 1836, EZRA DARIUS BEERS, b. at Tyringham, MA, 1 Dec 1810 son of Ebenezer and Anne (-) Beers; Ezra d. at Hampton, 8 Nov 1870.

x CALEB FAULKNER HOLT, b. 8 Jan 1801; d. 22 Aug 1806.

xi JULIA HOLT, b. 7 Jan 1803; d. at Hampton, 11 Dec 1889; m. 27 Apr 1830, JEDEDIAH WATERMAN MORSE, b. 8 Sep 1793 son of Jedediah and Fanny (Waterman) Morse; Jedediah d. at Hampton, 12 Jun 1888.

459) CYNTHIA HOLT (*Nathaniel⁴, George³, Henry², Nicholas¹*), b. at Hampton, 27 Sep 1759 daughter of Nathaniel and Phebe (Canady) Holt; m. at Brooklyn, CT, 5 Aug 1837, ABEL STAPLES,[1223] b. at Pomfret, 30 Aug 1757 son of Jacob and Eunice (Cady) Staples; Abel d. at Brooklyn, 5 Aug 1837. Abel had a second marriage to Elizabeth who has not been identified but was his widow in the probate record.

Abel Staples served as a private in the Revolution in the company of Captain Grosvenor. In his pension application, Abel reported enlisting on 1 April 1777 for a period of seven months. He completed that seven-month term, and in October 1779 he was drafted in the Connecticut militia for a two-month term. In that tour, he was in Captain Stephen Lyon's company.[1224]

Abel Staples did not leave a will and his estate was in probate 25 August 1837 with widow Elizabeth as administratrix. The few available documents include a statement that Abel was a war pensioner.

There are records of four children for Cynthia Holt and Abel Staples born at Canterbury.

i AMOS STAPLES, b. 1 Jul 1778

ii NATHANIEL STAPLES, b. 30 Jun 1780

iii ANNA STAPLES, b. 9 Oct 1782; d. after 1870 when she was living at Hampton with her son; m. about 1807, JOHN NEWMAN BURNHAM, b. 1787 son of John N. and Sarah (Snow) Burnham; John d. at Hampton, 8 Aug 1850.

iv LUCY STAPLES, b. 20 Jan 1785

460) EPHRAIM FARNUM (*Ephraim Farnum⁴, Ephraim Farnum³, Elizabeth Holt Farnum², Nicholas¹*), b. at Rumford, 21 Sep 1733 son of Ephraim and Mary (Ingalls) Farnum; d. at Concord, 12 May 1827; m. at Bradford, MA, 23 Mar 1758, JUDITH HALL, b. at Bradford, 12 Apr 1739 daughter of David and Naomi (Gage) Hall; Judith d. at Concord, 13 Jul 1809.

Ephraim Farnum was a farmer and Concord. He and his brother Benjamin inherited the family homestead from their father.[1225] Ephraim and Judith were parents of seven children born at Concord.

i NAOMI FARNUM, b. 20 Apr 1760; d. at Boscawen, 20 Mar 1832; m. Mar 1780, JOHN CHANDLER, b. at Concord, 11 Dec 1752 son of John and Mary (Carter) Chandler; John d. at Boscawen, 24 Jan 1825.

ii JOHN FARNUM, b. 6 May 1762; d. Feb 1763.

iii JUDITH FARNUM, b. 13 Jun 1764; d. at Gorham, ME, 21 Feb 1851; m. 3 Jun 1791, JEREMIAH CHANDLER, b. at Concord, 31 Mar 1763 son of John and Mary (Carter) Chandler; Jeremiah d. at Lovell, ME, 12 Feb 1828.

iv SARAH FARNUM, b. 9 Aug 1767; m. at Boscawen, 21 Nov 1786, NATHAN CARTER, b. at Boscawen, 6 Apr 1761 son of Winthrop and Susannah (Eastman) Carter; Nathan d. at Boscawen, 25 Sep 1840.

v MOSES FARNUM, b. 20 Oct 1769; d. at Concord, 6 Mar 1840; m. 1st 13 Jun 1792, RHODA CARTER, b. 17 Feb 1771 daughter of Ezra and Phebe (Whittemore) Carter; Rhoda d. Oct 1808. Moses m. 2nd 21 Dec 1809, Rhoda's sister, ESTHER CARTER, b. 21 Feb 1778; Esther d. at Concord, 30 May 1857.

vi ESTHER FARNUM, b. 25 Oct 1772; d. at Franklin, NH, 1 Oct 1854; m. 30 Nov 1790, EBENEZER EASTMAN, b. at Concord, 19 Oct 1765 son of Moses and Elizabeth (Kimball) Eastman; Ebenezer d. at Salisbury, NH, 16 Apr 1833.

vii SUSANNAH FARNUM, b. 3 Jun 1781; d. at Boscawen, 4 May 1843; m. 29 Jan 1803, MOSES COFFIN, b. at Boscawen, 22 Jul 1779 son of Peter and Rebecca (Haseltine) Coffin; Moses d. at Boscawen, 4 Sep 1854.

461) MARY FARNUM (*Ephraim Farnum⁴, Ephraim Farnum³, Elizabeth Holt Farnum², Nicholas¹*), b. at Rumford, 8 Aug 1737 daughter of Ephraim and Mary (Ingalls) Farnum; d. at Sanbornton, NH, 14 Feb 1805; m. about 1760, JONATHAN MERRILL, b. at Rumford, 10 Feb 1733 son of John and Lydia (Haynes) Merrill; Jonathan d. at New Chester, NH, 1795 (probate 21 Feb 1795).

[1223] The 1800 will of Jonathan Holt the brother of Cynthia's father Nathaniel includes a bequest to his niece Cynthia Staples.

[1224] U.S., Revolutionary War Pension and Bounty-Land Warrant Application Files, 1800-1900; Case S14595

[1225] Bouton, *History of Concord*, p 655

Jonathan Merrill was a farmer. He and Mary were first in Concord, were in Alexandria, New Hampshire about 1773, and then in Bristol, New Hampshire.[1226]

In his will written 27 March 1794 (probate 21 February 1795), Jonathan Merrill bequeathed to his beloved wife one-third of the whole of the lands, stock, buildings, and husbandry tools during her natural life. At her decease, these items will be divided among sons John, Jonathan, and Moses. His wife is to have the household furniture which can be at her disposal. Sons John, Jonathan, and Moses receive all the lands, stock, buildings, husbandry utensils, and clothing not otherwise disposed of. Each of the other children receives £15: daughter Mary Goolding, daughter Lydia Merrill, son Stephen Merrill, daughter Sarah Merrill, son Ephraim Merrill, and daughter Abigail Merrill. These amounts were to include interest in relation to when these children had reached age 18. On 4 January 1814, estate executors John, Jonathan, and Moses Merrill exhibited payments that had been made to the heirs (although it is not clear when the payments were made): Windsor and Mary Goolden, $110; Lydia Merrill, $173; Stephen Merrill, $100; Wyman and Sally Hardy, $50; Ephraim Merrill, $50; Abigail Merrill, $50; Nathaniel Merrill, $10; Moses Merrill, $1.[1227]

Mary Farnum and Jonathan Merrill were parents of thirteen children.

i JOHN MERRILL, b. at Concord, 6 Oct 1760; died young.

ii JONATHAN MERRILL, b. 23 Dec 1761; d. 16 Mar 1763.

iii MARY MERRILL, b. at Concord, 31 Dec 1763; d. about 1800;[1228] m. about 1785, WINSOR GOOLDEN, baptized at Newbury, MA, 12 Jul 1761 daughter of Winsor and Jane (Sampson) Goolden; Winsor d. at Madrid, NY, 6 Jan 1840. Winsor was second married to Ruby who survived him.

iv SARAH MERRILL, b. 26 Apr 1766; died in childhood.

v LYDIA MERRILL, b. at Concord, 23 Nov 1767. Lydia does not seem to have married as probate records for her father refer to her as Lydia Merrill through 1814.

vi JOHN MERRILL, b. at Concord, 9 Mar 1769; d. at Hill, NH, 13 May 1831; m. 12 Nov 1794, ELIZABETH DARLING, b. 27 Apr 1771 daughter of Benjamin and Hannah (Clark) Darling; Elizabeth d. at Hill, 8 Oct 1834.

vii LUCY MERRILL, b. at Concord, 7 Feb 1771; likely died in childhood as she is not in father's will or in the payments from father's estate.

viii JONATHAN MERRILL, b. at Concord, 6 Sep 1772; d. at Hill, NH, 20 Jan 1820; m. MARY BARNARD, b. at Warner, 20 Dec 1779 daughter of Ezekiel Barnard; Mary d. at Bristol, NH, 1 Oct 1875. Mary married second Ezekiel Moore.

ix MOSES MERRILL, b. at Concord, 28 Dec 1774; d. at Alexandria, NH, 29 Oct 1841; m. 1st Mar 1810, MIRIAM BARNARD, b. about 1783 daughter of Ezekiel Barnard; Miriam d. at Alexandria, 26 Nov 1815. Moses m. 2nd about 1816, SARAH WORTHING (widow of Sherburn Sanborn), b. at Bridgewater, NH, 11 Mar 1785 daughter of Samuel and Hannah (Ingalls) Worthing; Sarah d. 1863.

x STEPHEN MERRILL, b. likely at Hill, NH, about 1776; d. at Bristol, NH, 5 Jan 1860; m. 3 Jun 1803, RUTH DARLING, b. 4 Jul 1774 daughter of Benjamin and Hannah (Clark) Darling; Ruth d. 29 Dec 1835.

xi SARAH MERRILL, b. at Hill, 14 Apr 1778; d. at Sutton, OH, 1823; m. at Hebron, NH, 7 Nov 1803, WYMAN HARDY, b. at Bow, NH, 4 Oct 1777 son of Thomas and Abigail (-) Hardy; Wyman d. at Sutton, after 1820 and before 1829.

xii EPHRAIM MERRILL, b. at Hill, 24 Nov 1779; d. at Bridgewater, NH, 15 Oct 1844; m. Apr 1808, SALLY DREW, b. at Bridgewater, NH, 28 Sep 1791 daughter of Samuel and Elizabeth (Webber) Drew; Sally d. 21 Sep 1885.

xiii ABIGAIL MERRILL, b. at Hill, 13 Mar 1782. Abigail was living and unmarried at the distribution of her father's estate; nothing further known.

462) BENJAMIN FARNUM (*Ephraim Farnum[4], Ephraim Farnum[3], Elizabeth Holt Farnum[2], Nicholas[1]*), b. at Rumford, 21 Mar 1739 son of Ephraim and Mary (Ingalls) Farnum; d. at Concord, 18 Mar 1812; m. ANNA MERRILL, b. at Rumford, 20 Dec 1743 daughter of John and Lydia (Haynes) Merrill;[1229] Anna d. at Concord, 7 Mar 1803.

Benjamin and Anna resided in Concord where Benjamin served as a surveyor of highways and hogreeve.[1230] A copy of Benjamin's will was not located, but the Farnum genealogy provides a summary of the 23 April 1806 will which lists the following heirs: beloved wife; sons Benjamin, Haines, Nathaniel, Jonathan, Abiel, and Jeremiah who each receives ten dollars;

[1226] Merrill, *A Merrill Memorial*, p 296

[1227] *New Hampshire. Court of Probate (Grafton County). Estate of Jonathan Merrill*

[1228] This is based on the pension application file for Winsor Goolden in which his second wife Ruby reports she and Winsor were married in 1801.

[1229] The 1773 will of John Merrill includes a bequest to his daughter Ann Farnham.

[1230] Bouton, *The History of Concord*

daughters Mary Hall, Lydia Conant, and Ann Wilson each receives ten dollars; daughters Abigail Farnum and Sarah Farnum each receives $110; and son Ephraim receives the residue of the estate.[1231]

Benjamin Farnum and Anna Merrill were parents of fifteen children born at Concord.

i MARY FARNUM, b. 26 Aug 1764; d. at Alfred, ME, 23 Nov 1816; m. about 1785, ABIEL HALL, b. at Rumford, NH, 31 May 1761 son of Ebenezer and Dorcas (Abbott) Hall; Abiel d. at Alfred, Oct 1829. Abiel Hall married second Anna Francis. Abiel Hall was a physician.

ii JOHN FARNUM, b. 2 Jan 1766; m. 1st about 1790, SARAH THOMPSON; Sarah d. about 1812. John m. 2nd at Warren, 3 Sep 1813, POLLY STONE (widow of John Jones), b. about 1776 likely the daughter of Uriah and Hephzibah (Hadley) Stone.

iii ANNA FARNUM, b. 18 Mar 1767; d. 18 Jun 1778.

iv BENJAMIN FARNUM, b. 10 Sep 1768; d. at Rumford, ME, 1850 (probate 26 Nov 1850); m. at Concord, 3 Jun 1790, SARAH GRAHAM, b. at Concord, 18 Feb 1770 daughter of George and Azubah (-) Graham.

v EPHRAIM FARNUM, b. 5 Apr 1770; d. at Concord, 12 Feb 1836; m. SARAH BROWN, b. 1774; Sarah d. at Concord, 24 Jul 1851.

vi HAINES FARNUM, b. 31 Oct 1771; d. at Plymouth, NH, 23 Dec 1824 (will 14 Dec 1824); m. at Pembroke, 31 Dec 1800, ELIZABETH "BETSY" WHITEHOUSE, b. at Pembroke, 23 May 1777 daughter of Solomon and Mary (Knox) Whitehouse;[1232][1233] Elizabeth d. at Plymouth, 1834 (will written 21 Jan 1832 and proved 26 Mar 1834).

vii JONATHAN FARNUM, b. 2 Aug 1773; d. 25 Jun 1778.

viii NATHANIEL FARNUM, b. 5 Apr 1775; d. at Alfred, ME, 28 Sep 1861; m. HANNAH SAYWARD, b. 20 Jan 1780 daughter of John and Elizabeth (Trafton) Sayward;[1234] Hannah d. at Alfred, 4 Jun 1846.

ix LYDIA FARNUM, b. 26 Dec 1776; d. at Alfred, ME, 28 May 1842; m. at Pembroke, 21 Jan 1796, JOHN CONANT, b. at Beverly, MA, 10 Sep 1771 son of Nathaniel and Abigail (Dodge) Conant; John d. at Alfred, 27 Feb 1850.

x JONATHAN FARNUM, b. 26 Jul 1778; d. at Alfred, ME, 11 Jan 1831; m. ESTHER PERKINS, b. at Kennebunkport, ME, 10 Jun 1787 daughter of Christopher and Esther (-) Perkins;[1235] Esther d. at Brewer, MA, 2 Jul 1885.

xi ABIEL FARNUM, b. 24 Apr 1780; d. at Alfred, ME, 29 Apr 1864; m. ADELIA CONANT, b. 1793 daughter of Joshua and Adelia (Gile) Conant; Adelia d. at Alfred, 7 Jun 1846.

xii ANNA "NANCY" FARNUM, b. 30 Jan 1783; d. at Franklin, NH, 10 Mar 1854; m. at Concord, 8 Oct 1801, Dr. JOB WILSON, b. at Belmont, NH, 25 Jan 1776 son of Nathaniel and Elizabeth (Barber) Wilson; Job d. at Franklin, 22 Sep 1851 (will proved Oct 1851).

xiii ABIGAIL FARNUM, b. 30 Oct 1783; d. at Alfred, ME, 23 Apr 1855; m. at Lyman, ME, 4 Dec 1813, Major ISSACHAR KIMBALL, b. at Lyman, 15 May 1784 son of Ezra and Lucretia (Cousins) Kimball; Issachar d. at Alfred, 3 Apr 1860.

xiv JEREMIAH FARNUM, b. 29 Jul 1785; d. at Rumford, ME, 21 Nov 1869; m. at Concord, 16 Jan 1811, SALLY HALL, b. at Concord, 11 Sep 1788 daughter of Daniel and Deborah (Davis) Hall; Sally d. at Rumford, 26 Sep 1859.

xv SARAH FARNUM, b. 29 Mar 1787; d. at Augusta, ME (burial at Alfred), 15 Oct 1864; m. at Concord, 6 Mar 1810, CHARLES P. GRIFFIN, b. at Concord, about 1786; Charles d. at Alfred, 2 Mar 1825. Sarah was hospitalized at the hospital for the insane in Augusta in 1856, was there in 1860, and is presumed to have died there. Her son William P. Griffin was her trustee.[1236]

[1231] Farnham, *The Descendants of Ralph Farnum*, p 276

[1232] The 1821 will of Solomon Whitehouse includes a bequest to his daughter Betsy Farnum. Published genealogies give Haine's wife's name as Mary Whitehouse, or as Mary Elizabeth, but that is an error. All the records located (marriage, births of children, deaths of children, probate records of her father and her husband; and Elizabeth's own will) give her name as Elizabeth or Betsy. Solomon Whitehouse also had a daughter Mary who married Jonathan Freeman.

[1233] Carter, *History of Pembroke*, p 315

[1234] Sayward, *The Sayward Family*, p 100

[1235] Esther's place of birth and names of parents are given on her death record.

[1236] Maine, York County Probate Estate Files, Estate of Sarah Griffin, Case 7861

463) SARAH FARNUM (*Ephraim Farnum⁴, Ephraim Farnum³, Elizabeth Holt Farnum², Nicholas¹*), b. at Concord, 26 Jul 1747 daughter of Ephraim and Mary (Ingalls) Farnum; d. at Fryeburg, ME, Mar 1829; m. about 1765, WILLIAM EATON, b. at Hampstead, NH, 21 Apr 1743 son of Jeremiah and Hannah (Osgood) Eaton; William d. about 1780.

Sarah Farnum and William Eaton were parents of seven children born at Fryeburg, Maine.

i WILLIAM EATON, b. 3 Mar 1766; d. at Chatham, NH, 27 May 1852; m. at Fryeburg, 26 Nov 1795, NANCY FARRINGTON, b. 1779; Nancy d. at Chatham, 28 Jul 1858.[1237]

ii OSGOOD EATON, b. 6 Mar 1768; d. at Rumford, ME, 1 Jul 1836; m. at Concord, 10 Sep 1793, BETHIAH VIRGIN, b. at Concord, 23 Feb 1775 daughter of William and Mehitable (Stickney) Virgin; Bethiah d. at Rumford, 18 Dec 1857.

iii SARAH EATON, b. 20 Dec 1769; d. at Fryeburg, 2 Oct 1854; m. as his second wife, JOSEPH F. CHASE son of Josiah and Mehitable (Frye) Chase. Joseph Chase was first married to Mehitable Day. Sarah is likely the Sarah Eaton who gave birth to an out-of-wedlock child with Isaac Abbott (1762-1861), Enoch Eaton Abbott (b. 1785).

iv HANNAH EATON, b. 31 Jan 1772; m. at Concord, 4 Oct 1796, DAVID BLANCHARD, b. at Concord, 4 Dec 1771 son of John and Eleanor (Stevens) Blanchard; David d. at Concord, 10 Jan 1805.

v JEREMIAH EATON, b. 8 Mar 1774

vi MARY EATON, b. 2 Jul 1776; d. at Waterford, ME, 20 Jun 1849; m. at Eddington, ME, 29 Jan 1795, DAVID WHITCOMB, b. at Bolton, MA, 13 Apr 1764 son of Levi and Sarah (Gates) Whitcomb; David d. at Waterford, 27 Apr 1835.

vii SUSANNAH EATON, b. 21 Jan 1778; m. at Concord, 1 Mar 1803, JEREMIAH WARDWELL, baptized at Andover, 22 Jan 1771 son of Joshua and Mary (Saunders) Wardwell. Susannah and Jeremiah were living at Sidney, ME in 1850.

464) BENJAMIN FARNUM (*Timothy Farnum⁴, Ephraim Farnum³, Elizabeth Holt Farnum², Nicholas¹*), b. at Andover, 16 Dec 1746 son of Timothy and Dinah (Ingalls) Farnum; d. at Andover, 4 Dec 1833; m. 26 Nov 1767, his second cousin, DOROTHY "DOLLY" HOLT (*Joseph⁴, Timothy³, James², Nicholas¹*) perhaps the daughter of Joseph and Dolly (Johnson) Holt;[1238] Dolly d. at Andover, 25 Jul 1815.

Capt. Benjamin Farnum received his commission as a captain in the regiment of Col. James Frye in May 1775. He was wounded at the Battle of Bunker Hill on 17 June 1775. He was a captain in the 11th Massachusetts regiment in November 1776. Later, he had a dispute over his rank, and he ultimately resigned his commission which was effective 28 March 1779.[1239] Capt. Farnum kept a diary of his experiences during the war from 1775 to 1778.[1240]

In his will written 20 November 1833 (probate 7 January 1834), Benjamin Farnum bequeaths to daughter Dolly the widow of Moody Spofford one dollar, which with the fifteen hundred dollars she has received completes her portion. Son Benjamin also receives one dollar to complete his portion. His grandchildren the children of his daughter Phebe Worcester deceased wife of Osgood Worcester likewise receive one dollar each which completes the portion with the fifteen hundred dollars previously given. Daughter Mary wife of Amos Town of Norway receives one dollar as does daughter Cloe wife of John Carlton of Andover and daughter Hannah wife of Uriah Holt, Esq. of Norway. His four daughters and the children of daughter Phebe receive all the household furniture to divide. Grandchildren Jacob Farnum and Elizabeth Storer who are the children of son Jacob deceased also receive one dollar. The remainder of the estate goes to grandson Jacob Farnum son of Benjamin and Jacob is named executor.[1241] The probate record also includes a statement from Benjamin's physician Joseph Kittredge attesting that Benjamin left no widow and that the children named in the will (Benjamin Farnum, Dolly Spofford, Mary Town, Chloe Carlton, and Hannah Holt) are the only surviving children.

Benjamin Farnum and Dolly Holt were parents of fourteen children born at Andover.

i DOLLY FARNUM, b. 18 Aug 1768; d. at Andover, 18 Nov 1843; m. 8 Sep 1788, MOODY SPOFFORD, b. at Andover, 19 Apr 1755 son of Thomas and Roxby (Moody) Spofford; Moddy d. at Andover, 31 Mar 1833.

ii ABIAH FARNUM, b. 6 May 1770; d. at Andover, 22 Oct 1793. Abiah did not marry.

1237 The dates of death for both William and Nancy are given in pension records. Pension file W3666

1238 These are the parents of Dolly identified in the History of Wilton and in Durrie's Holt genealogy. However, the Dolly daughter of Joseph and Dolly is reported as born in 1751 and Dolly the wife of Benjamin Farnum died in 1815 at age 68 giving her a birth year of 1747. No other Dolly Holt was identified who might fit better, so it will be left as is.

1239 National Archives, Founders Online, letter from George Washington to Col. Benjamin Tupper references Capt. Benjamin Farnum and the dispute over rank; https://founders.archives.gov/documents/Washington/03-19-02-0300

1240 A short excerpt from this diary can be found in Gardner, "Colonel James Frye's Regiment", *The Massachusetts Magazine: Devoted to Massachusetts History, Genealogy, and Biography*, volume 3, p 187

1241 *Essex County, MA: Probate File Papers, 1638-1881.*Online database. *AmericanAncestors.org.* New England Historic Genealogical Society, 2014. Case 9228

iii BENJAMIN FARNUM, b. 1 Mar 1772; d. at Andover, 8 Feb 1844; m. at Andover, 15 May 1794, RUTH SALTMARSH, b. at Bedford, MA, 29 Mar 1774 daughter of Seth and Ruth (Bowman) Saltmarsh.

iv JACOB FARNUM, b. 10 Oct 1774; d. at Andover "drowned in the great pond" 19 Aug 1801; m. 20 Dec 1798, ELIZABETH FOSTER LOVEJOY, b. at Andover, 6 Aug 1780 daughter of Nathaniel and Elizabeth (Brandon) Lovejoy; Elizabeth d. at West Newbury, 3 Apr 1866. Elizabeth married second Dean Robinson on 21 Apr 1811.

v PHEBE FARNUM, b. 18 Jun 1776; d. 17 Aug 1778.

vi PHEBE FARNUM, b. 3 Feb 1779; Phebe d. at Andover, 31 Mar 1818; m. at Andover, 27 Dec 1798, OSGOOD WORCESTER, b. at Tewksbury, 16 Feb 1772 son of Eldad and Rebecca (Osgood) Worcester; Osgood d. at Andover, 2 Sep 1838.

vii MARY "MOLLY" FARNUM, b. 18 Oct 1780; d. at Norway, ME, 21 Oct 1847; m. at Andover, 30 Jan 1806, AMOS TOWNE, b. at Andover, 28 May 1779 son of Peter and Rebekah (Sheldon) Towne; Amos d. at Norway, 8 Jan 1837.

viii Daughter, b. and d. 3 Dec 1782.

ix CHLOE FARNUM, b. 21 Nov 1783; d. at Andover, 16 Feb 1846;[1242] m. 24 Dec 1807, JOHN CARLETON, b. at Andover, 30 Mar 1775 son of Peter and Sarah (Ingalls) Carleton; John d. at Andover, 21 Jul 1845.[1243]

x Stillborn child 13 Jun 1785

xi Daughter b. and d. 11 Jun 1786

xii RHODA FARNUM, b. 27 Jul 1787; d. 18 Jan 1788.

xiii HANNAH FARNUM, b. 27 Aug 1789; d. at Norway, ME, 4 Feb 1835; m. 4 Feb 1808, her fourth cousin once removed, URIAH HOLT (*Jacob⁵, Jacob⁴, Oliver³, Henry², Nicholoas¹*), b. at Andover, 25 May 1775 son of Jacob and Rhoda (Abbott) Holt; Uriah d. at Norway, 21 Jun 1849.

xiv Stillborn child 17 Apr 1791

465) JOHN FARNUM (*James Farnum⁴, Ephraim Farnum³, Elizabeth Holt Farnum², Nicholas¹*), b. at Concord, 1 Aug 1753 son of James and Elizabeth (Wilson) Farnum; d. at Salisbury, NH, 17 Feb 1820; m. 22 May 1772, his first cousin, SARAH PETERS (*Elizabeth Farnum Peters⁴, Ephraim Farnum³, Elizabeth Holt Farnum², Nicholas¹*), b. about 1750 daughter of James and Elizabeth (Farnum) Peters; Sarah d. at Salisbury, 7 Oct 1818.

John Farnum and Sarah Peters were parents of ten children;[1244] birth years are estimated based on date of marriage, age at death, and census records. The family was in Concord at least until 1787 and were in Salisbury, New Hampshire after that time.

i JOHN FARNUM, b. about 1773; d. likely at Corinth, VT; m. at Salisbury, 16 Aug 1798, SALLY PHILBRICK, b. about 1778 daughter of Jonathan Philbrick.

ii BETSY FARNUM, b. about 1774; d. at Corinth, VT, 24 Jul 1860; m. 1st about 1794, Mr. J. Tucker who is not yet identified; he died by 1810. Betsy m. 2nd at Topsham, VT, Jun 1811, as his second wife, AMOS AVERY, b. at Lyme, CT, about 1760 son of Andrew and Martha (-) Avery; Amos d. at Corinth, 25 Dec 1825. Amos was first married to Arthena Rowland.

iii WILLIAM FARNUM, b. about 1776; d. perhaps at Hill, NH, m. at Warner, NH, 25 Nov 1802, ELIZABETH TUCKER.

iv JOSEPH FARNUM, b. about 1778; d. at Salisbury, 15 Aug 1839; m. 12 May 1806, SALLY PETERS, b. at Salisbury, Jun 1785 daughter of John and Hannah (Usher) Peters; Sally d. at Salisbury, 13 Dec 1843.

v JACOB FARNUM, b. about 1782; d. at Salisbury, 31 Oct 1820; m. about 1816, NANCY TAPPAN, b. about 1798 of Corinth, VT; Nancy d. at Salisbury, 16 Oct 1820. Jacob and Nancy were parents of three children. Jacob's estate entered probate 15 Nov 1820 with brother Ebenezer Farnum as administrator. This includes a statement that Jacob left no widow, father or mother but had three minor children.[1245]

vi EBENEZER FARNUM, b. about 1784; d. at Salisbury, 1824 (probate 1824); m. about 1805, DOROTHY TUCKER, b. about 1784; Dorothy d. after 1860 when she was living in Salisbury.

[1242] Carlton, Chloe, w. John [wid. CR1], fits [disease of the heart. CR1], Feb. 16, 1846, a. 62 y. 2 m. 25 d.

[1243] Carleton, John, m., farmer, s. Peter and Sarah, dropsy [consumption. CR1], July 21, 1845, a. 68 y. [a. 67 y. CR1]

[1244] Farnham, *The Descendants of Ralph Farnum*, p 289

[1245] *New Hampshire. Probate Court (Hillsborough County), volume 30, p 135*

vii SEABORN FARNUM, b. about 1786; d. at Topsham, VT, Jun 1837; m. at Corinth, VT, 14 Nov 1809, MARTHA AVERY, b. about 1790 daughter of Andrew and Eunice (Rowland) Avery; Martha d. after 1850 when she was living at Topsham.

viii HANNAH FARNUM, b. about 1792; m. at Salisbury, 12 Jul 1814, as his second wife, JOHN FIFIELD, b. about 1770 son of Joseph and Anne (Badger) Fifield; John d. at Salisbury, 1847. John was first married to Elizabeth Pettengill.

ix SARAH FARNUM, b. about 1793; d. at Salisbury, NH, 1863; m. 18 Mar 1823, as his second wife, NATHAN TUCKER, b. at Salisbury, 31 May 1794 son of Nathan and Lydia (Stevens) Tucker; Nathan d. at Salisbury, 23 Mar 1861. Nathan was first married to Mary Fellows.

x BENJAMIN FARNUM is reported to have died in Massachusetts. It is possible that he is the Benjamin Farnum who ran the poor house in Georgetown, MA. That Benjamin was born at Salisbury, NH about 1799 and died at Georgetown between 1865 and 1870. If so, he married in 1833, ELIZABETH C. WILKINS daughter of Samuel and Lucy (Peabody) Wilkins.

466) PRISCILLA RUSS (*Priscilla Farnum Russ[4], Ephraim Farnum[3], Elizabeth Holt Farnum[2], Nicholas[1]*), b. at Rumford, 3 Jun 1733 daughter of John and Priscilla (Farnum) Russ; d. at Andover, 1 Aug 1818; m. 1st at Andover, 17 Nov 1757, THOMAS BLANCHARD, b. at Andover, 20 Jan 1734/5 son of Thomas and Elizabeth (Johnson) Blanchard; Thomas d. at Lake George, 9 Oct 1758. Priscilla m. 2nd at Andover, 10 Jan 1760, EBENEZER RAND, b. about 1731 *perhaps* the son of Waffe and Elizabeth (Orne) Rand of Boston; Ebenezer d. at Andover, 18 Apr 1813 (probate 1813).

Priscilla and Ebenezer did not have children of their own but raised Priscilla's niece Eunice Russ (see Deborah Russ just below).

Ebenezer Rand did not leave a will and his estate entered probate 6 May 1813 with widow Priscilla requesting that Josiah Brown of Tewksbury be named administrator. Real estate was valued at $2,100 and personal estate at $4,328.93. The dower was set off to widow Priscilla.[1246]

467) DEBORAH RUSS (*Priscilla Farnum Russ[4], Ephraim Farnum[3], Elizabeth Holt Farnum[2], Nicholas[1]*), b. at Andover, 30 Apr 1744 daughter of John and Priscilla (Farnum) Russ; m. 1st about 1765 in a Native American ceremony, Almonoch (aka Peter Bridges) of the Narragansett tribe; reported as having divorced.[1247] Deborah m. 2nd at Tewksbury, 23 Jun 1768, JOHN HOYT; John d. at Tewksbury, 6 Mar 1769 when felling a tree.[1248] Deborah m. 3rd at Tewksbury, 12 Mar 1778, Lt. EBENEZER KITTREDGE, b. at Billerica, 1732 son of James and Elizabeth (-) Kittredge. Ebenezer was first married to Abigail Russell.

There is one child of Deborah Russ and Peter Bridges/Almonoch.

I EUNICE RUSS, b. at Andover, 23 May 1766; d. at West Roxbury, MA, 24 Feb 1864; m. at Andover, 24 Nov 1784, PRINCE AMES, b. about 1759; Prince d. at Andover 21 Apr 1817.[1249] Prince Ames is described as mulatto. He served in the Revolution entering the service as a substitute for Benjamin Ames. His widow Eunice received a pension based on his service. Prince Ames served in the company of Capt. John Abbot from February 1777 through December 1780. Eunice was raised by her aunt Priscilla Russ and her husband Ebenezer Rand.

Deborah Russ and John Hoyt were parents of one child.

i HANNAH HOYT, b. at Tewksbury, 10 Jan 1769; m. at Andover, 17 Apr 1788, JESSE HAGGETT, b. at Andover, 23 Jan 1765 son of Thomas and Susannah (Adams) Haggett;[1250] Jesse d. at Massena, NY, 5 Jul 1839.

468) TIMOTHY FARNHAM (*Zebadiah Farnum[4], Ephraim Farnum[3], Elizabeth Holt Farnum[2], Nicholas[1]*), b. at Concord, about 1739 son of Zebadiah and Mary (Walker) Farnum; m. at Hopkinton, NH, 8 May 1763, SUSANNAH SCALES, b. at Canterbury, NH, 26 Oct 1744 daughter of Rev. James and Susannah (Hovey) Scales.[1251]

Timothy and Susannah resided in Hopkinton, New Hampshire where there are records for three children.

1246 *Essex County, MA: Probate File Papers, 1638-1881.*Online database. *AmericanAncestors.org.* New England Historic Genealogical Society, 2014. Case 23205

1247 Abbott, Abbott Genealogies, Russ Family of Andover

1248 John, "with ye fall of a tree," Mar. 6, 1769. CR1

1249 This is the date of death given by Eunice in the pension application file. The Andover records have a date of 21 Apr 1816.

1250 Abbott, The Haggett Family of Andover, https://www.mhl.org/sites/default/files/files/Abbott/Haggett%20Family.pdf

1251 Although published genealogies report her name as Searles, she seems to be the daughter of Rev. James Scales. For example, a deed from James *Seals* to Timothy and Susannah Farnham mentions the education that has been provided to James's son Stephen and this would be Rev. Stephen Scales. Rev. Scales and his wife Susannah were living in Hopkinton where James was the long-time minister.

i JOHN S. FARNHAM, b. at Hopkinton, 9 Sep 1763; d. at Harmony, OH, 8 Apr 1822; m. about 1799, MINDA ATKINS, b. 23 May 1779 daughter of David and Mindwell (Butler) Atkins; Minda was living in 1822 when John wrote his will.

ii ANNA FARNHAM, b. at Hopkinton, May 1768; d. 5 Apr 1784.

iii ZEBADIAH FARNHAM, baptized at Hopkinton, 20 Oct 1771.

469) SAMUEL FARNUM (*Zebadiah Farnum⁴, Ephraim Farnum³, Elizabeth Holt Farnum², Nicholas¹*), b. at Concord, 10 Feb 1743 son of Zebadiah and Mary (Walker) Farnum; d. at Essex, NY, 25 Jan 1813; m. at Hopkinton, NH, 1 Dec 1764, SARAH ABBOTT, b. at Concord, 3 Dec 1748 daughter of Nathaniel and Penelope (Ballard) Abbott; Sarah d. at Elizabethtown, NY, 2 Apr 1841.

On 17 December 1840, widow Sarah Farnum, then of Westford, New York, made application for a pension based on the service of her husband Samuel. She related that while living in Corinth, Vermont, Samuel enlisted as private in the militia company of Capt. Green in 1776 for a period of one year. He had additional periods of enlistment, although Sarah's recollection of this service was limited. A separate source document that Samuel appeared on the rolls of Capt. Simeon Stevens for one year of service. He also appeared in the 1781 campaign on the rolls of Capt. Nehemiah Kimball in Vermont from July through November, Sarah also provided information on the date and place of marriage and the place and date of Samuel's death as 25 January 1813 in Essex, New York. Sarah also provided a bible page which listed the date of marriage and the births of eight children in the family. Sarah's nephew Nathaniel Abbott provided a statement that his father's sister Sarah married Samuel Farnum. Samuel and Sarah lived in Concord, New Hampshire after their marriage, were then in Corinth, Vermont, and later moved to Westport, New York. Abiel Walker who married Sarah's sister Ruth also provided a statement. On 20 November 1840, grandson Joseph Farnum of Elizabethtown, New York provided a statement that he had cared for his grandmother Sarah for the past ten years and that he was now administrator of her estate. There is also a statement that Sarah was extremely poor and spent some time in the Essex County poor house before going to live with her grandson Joseph who was also very poor.[1252]

The pension file provides record of births of eight children. The oldest children may have been born at Concord, but the younger children likely born at Corinth, Vermont.

i MEHITABLE FARNUM, b. 15 Sep 1765; d. 24 Feb 1781

ii SAMUEL FARNUM, b. 1767; likely the Samuel who at Reber in Essex County, NY at age 46 on 12 Feb 1813; m. FREELOVE WILSON, b. 1780 and d. at Lewis, NY on 6 May 1856.

iii ZEBADIAH FARNUM, b. in Vermont, 31 Mar 1769; d. at Watkins, OH, 13 Oct 1854; m. JANE MCNINCH, b. 13 Oct 1763; Jane d. 18 Mar 1853.

iv SARAH FARNUM, b. 19 Apr 1771

v POLLY FARNUM, b. 31 Aug 1774

vi Child (possibly Chloe) FARNUM, b. 17 Mar 1781

vii JOHN FARNUM, b. 5 Jul 1784

viii JOSEPH FARNUM, b. 1 Feb 1786

470) JOHN FARNUM (*Zebadiah Farnum⁴, Ephraim Farnum³, Elizabeth Holt Farnum², Nicholas¹*), b. at Concord, 1 Feb 1750 son of Zebadiah and Mary (Walker) Farnum; d. likely at Rumford, ME; m. about 1772, SARAH "SALLY" WEST, b. at Concord, 8 Nov 1745 daughter of Nathaniel and Sarah (Burbank) West; Sally d. at Concord, 17 Dec 1800.

John Farnum and Sally West were parents of nine children born at Concord.

i BETTY FARNUM, b. 1 Nov 1772

ii SARAH FARNUM, b. 29 Mar 1774[1253]

iii MARY FARNUM, b. 22 Oct 1776

iv DEBORAH FARNUM, b. 21 Jul 1777

v JOHN WEST FARNUM, b. 25 Jun 1779; d. at Sumner, ME, 5 Mar 1843; m. at Concord, 18 Dec 1806, SARAH KNOWLES, b. about 1779; Sarah d. at Sumner, 4 Sep 1851.

[1252] U. S. Revolutionary War and Bounty-Land Pension Application Files, Case W16982

[1253] Farnham's Farnum genealogy reports that Sarah married Zebadiah Abbott who was born in 1769. However, Zebadiah married Sarah Farrington daughter of Benjamin and Sarah (Batchelder) Farrington.

vi ZEBADIAH FARNUM, b. 4 Mar 1781; d. after 1850 when he was living at Hollis, ME; m. at Concord, 19 Dec 1809, his second cousin, CHLOE ABBOTT (*Nathan Abbott[5], Thomas Abbott[4], Hannah Gray Abbott[3], Hannah Holt Gray[2], Nicholas[1]*), b. at Concord, 10 Jun 1783 daughter of Nathan and Betty (Farnum) Abbott; Chloe d. after 1850.

vii NATHANIEL FARNUM, b. 1 Mar 1783; d. after 1850 when he was living in Concord; m. about 1805; DEBORAH SHEPARD, b. at Strafford, VT, 9 Jun 1785 daughter of Thomas and Lydia (-) Shephard; Deborah d. after 1860.

viii SAMUEL FARNUM, b. 10 Apr 1786; died young

ix SAMUEL FARNUM, b. 10 Jun 1788; d. at Rumford, ME, 10 Apr 1870; m. 19 Mar 1812, BETSEY GODWIN, b. at Chandler's Mills, ME, 1793 daughter of William and Rachel (Harper) Godwin; Betsey d. at Rumford, 6 Apr 1861.

471) LYDIA FARNUM (*Zebadiah Farnum[4], Ephraim Farnum[3], Elizabeth Holt Farnum[2], Nicholas[1]*), b. at Concord, about 1756 daughter of Zebadiah and Mary (Walker) Farnum; m. at Pembroke, 14 Oct 1783, ASA HARDY.

Bouton's History of Concord (p 659) reports that Lydia and Asa resided at Horse hill and gives the names of five children in this family.

i ABIGAIL HARDY

ii SAMUEL HARDY

iii ZEBADIAH HARDY, b. about 1791; d. at Rumford, ME, 17 Jun 1862; m. about 1812, SARAH who has not been identified, but born 1796; Sarah d. after 1860 when she was living at Rumford.

iv POLLY HARDY

v ASA HARDY, b. about 1795; m. at Concord, 2 Jun 1818, JUDITH COLBY, b. about 1784. Asa was living in Sutton, NH in 1850.

472) ANN FARNUM (*Zebadiah Farnum[4], Ephraim Farnum[3], Elizabeth Holt Farnum[2], Nicholas[1]*), b. at Concord, about 1758 daughter of Zebadiah and Mary (Walker) Farnum; d. at Bow, NH, before 1834 (not living at husband's will); m. 1st about 1780, NOAH WEST, b. at Rumford, 1 Oct 1756 son of Nathaniel and Sarah (Fairbank) West; Noah d. about 1785. Ann m. 2nd at Pembroke, 6 Feb 1787, JONATHAN CLOUGH, b. 8 Oct 1749 son of Elisha and Mary (Welch) Clough;[1254] Jonathan d. at Bow, 7 Jun 1835. Jonathan Clough was first married to Abigail Buswell.

In his will dated 27 January 1834 (proved June 1835), Jonathan Clough made the following bequests: son Jonathan, one dollar; son William, twenty-five dollars; children of daughter Sally Jones, deceased, seven dollars; son Levi, twenty-five dollars; daughters Abigail Walker, Ruth Palmer, and Anna Clough, one dollar each plus the household furniture; children of daughter Martha Flanders deceased, four dollars; son Isaac, one hundred seventy-five dollars; son Manley receives all the real and personal estate after the payment of legacies. Son Isaac Clough was named executor.[1255] Children Sally, William, Jonathan, and Abigail are from Jonathan's first marriage to Abigail Buswell.

Ann Farnum and Noah West were parents of one child born at Concord.

i SALLY WEST, b. at Concord (and noted in the Bow town records), 11 Nov 1782

Ann Farnum and Jonathan Clough were parents of eight children born at Bow.[1256]

i LEVI CLOUGH, b. 13 Dec 1787; d. at Manchester, NH, 6 Feb 1849; m. at Concord, 24 Jan 1811, LUCINDA HOUGHTON who has not been identified but who is *perhaps* the daughter of Nahum and Sarah (Hazeltine) Houghton. In 1850, Lucinda was living with her son Nahum in Westbrook, ME.

ii NOAH CLOUGH, b. 27 Feb 1788; d. at Bow, 24 Dec 1833. Noah did not marry.

iii MANLEY CLOUGH, b. 10 Oct 1790; d. at Bow, after 1850; m. 27 Jun 1813, his third cousin once removed, BETSEY CHANDLER (*John Chandler[6], Isaac Chandler[5], Priscilla Holt Chandler[4], Timothy[3], James[2], Nicholas[1]*), b. 21 Sep 1796 daughter of John and Dorothy (Ballard) Chandler; Betsey d. at Bow, after 1870.

iv ISAAC CLOUGH, b. 1 Oct 1792; d. 6 Jul 1794.

[1254] Speare, *The Genealogy and Descendants of John Clough of Salisbury*, p 91

[1255] *New Hampshire. Probate Court (Merrimack County), volume 8, p 342*

[1256] Bow, NH, *The Town Book of Bow*, p 229

v ANNA CLOUGH, b. 18 Jun 1794; d. at Lyme, NH, 29 Mar 1860; m. at Bow, 31 Mar 1814, her first cousin, ELISHA CLOUGH, b. at Bow, 18 Apr 1788 son of David and Hannah (Winslow) Clough; Elisha d. at Lyme, 20 Oct 1861.

vi RUTH CLOUGH, b. 5 Sep 1796; d. at Bow, 4 Feb 1841; m. at Bow, 28Nov 1822, NATHAN P. PALMER who has not been identified. The births of four children of Ruth and Nathan are recorded at Bow.

vii MARTHA CLOUGH, b. 1 Jun 1798; d. at Bow, 18 Jul 1832; m. at Pembroke, 6 Nov 1817, JAMES FLANDERS "of Bow" who has not been identified. Martha and James had four children whose births are recorded at Bow.

viii ISAAC CLOUGH, b. 1 Aug 1800; d. after 1860 when he was living in Bow. Isaac did not marry.

473) JOSIAH FARNUM (*Josiah Farnum⁴, Ephraim Farnum³, Elizabeth Holt Farnum², Nicholas¹*), b. at Andover, 4 Aug 1739 son of Josiah and Mary (Frye) Farnum; d. at Concord, 1809; m. 1st at Andover, 25 Sep 1766, MEHITABLE KIMBALL, b. at Andover, 4 May 1738 daughter of Daniel and Mehitable (Ingalls) Kimball; Mehitable d. about 1779. Josiah m. 2nd, 29 Feb 1780, SARAH SAWYER,[1257] b. about 1747 (based on age 80 at death); Sarah d. at Concord, 16 Jul 1827. Sarah married second Capt. Benjamin Emery on 17 Dec 1812 (his first wife Sarah Bailey died in 1811).

There is little known in terms of the children of Josiah and Mehitable. There is record evidence for just two children both born at Concord.

i MEHITABLE FARNUM, b. at Concord, 5 Jul 1771

ii EPHRAIM FARNUM, b. about 1773; d. at Concord, 13 Sep 1803.[1258]

474) THEODORE FARNUM (*Josiah Farnum⁴, Ephraim Farnum³, Elizabeth Holt Farnum², Nicholas¹*), b. at Andover, 24 Jan 1748/9 son of Josiah and Mary (Frye) Farnum; d. at Concord, 1789 (probate 18 Feb 1789); m. about 1772, SARAH LOVEJOY, b. at Rumford, 8 Jun 1752 daughter of Henry and Phebe (Chandler) Lovejoy; Sarah d. at Concord, 1815. Sarah second married Jedediah Hoit on 28 Feb 1796.

Theodore and Sarah resided in Concord where Theodore signed the association test in 1776 and was part of Starks' brigade at Bennington in August 1777.[1259]

The estate of Theodore Farnum entered probate 18 February 1789 with widow Sarah as administratrix. Real estate was valued at £150 and personal estate at £48.18.3.[1260] Sarah was named as guardian for minor children Enoch, Dorcas, Rebecca, and Phebe.

Theodore Farnum and Sarah Lovejoy were parents of four children born at Concord.

i ENOCH FARNUM, b. 27 Feb 1773; d. at Concord, 3 Jun 1820; m. at Concord, 13 Nov 1802, DORCAS DAVIS, b. at Concord, about 1781 daughter of Samuel and Lydia (Merrill) Davis; Lydia d. at Concord, 14 Oct 1830.

ii DORCAS FARNUM, b. 11 May 1775; d. at Concord, 1822;[1261] m. at Concord, 7 Aug 1799, JOSEPH ELLIOT, b. at Concord, about 1775 son of Joseph and Lydia (Goodwin) Elliot.

iii REBECCA FARNUM, b. 9 Jun 1782; d. after 1850 when living in Concord; m. at Concord, 28 Feb 1811, SAMUEL ELLIOT SCALES, b. at Concord, 24 Oct 1785 daughter of Mehitable Elliot and unknown Scales (only mother's name is on the birth transcription); Samuel d. after 1850.

iv PHEBE FARNUM, b. 21 Apr 1785; d. after 1833 when dismissed from Congregational church; m. at Concord, 19 Jun 1804, CHARLES ELLIOT, b. at Concord, 22 Sep 1780 son of Jonathan and Mary (Collins) Elliot.

475) EPHRAIM FARNUM (*Josiah Farnum⁴, Ephraim Farnum³, Elizabeth Holt Farnum², Nicholas¹*), b. at Andover, 13 Oct 1751 son of Josiah and Mary (Frye) Farnum; d. at Concord, 19 Sep 1803; m. at Concord, 3 Oct 1776, ABIGAIL STEVENS; Abigail d. after 1815 when she transferred property to her two daughters.

Ephraim Farnum and Abigail Stevens were parents of three children born at Concord.

i PETER CHANDLER FARNUM, b. 18 Mar 1778; d. at Concord, 4 May 1816; m. 27 Mar 1804, PHEBE ABBOTT, b. at Concord, 17 May 1779 daughter of Reuben and Zerviah (Farnum) Abbott; Phebe d. after 1860 when she was living in Concord with her daughter Mary and her husband James K. Page.

1257 Farnham, *The Descendants of Ralph Farnum*, p 293. The Farnum genealogy states she was the widow of Benjamin Emery, but that seems to be the other way around and Sarah married Capt. Benjamin Emery in 1812 after Josiah's death. It is not clear that her name was Sarah Sawyer.

1258 Recorded as Ephraim Farnum, Jr. son of Josiah.

1259 Lyford, *History of Concord*, volume 1, pp 281-282

1260 *New Hampshire. Probate Court (Rockingham County)*; Probate Place: *Rockingham, New Hampshire, Estate of Theodore Farnum, Case 5419*

1261 The NH vital records give 1822; the Congregational church records give death as 1834. Reed and Thorne, History and Manual of the First Congregational Church, Concord, p XII

ii NAOMI FARNUM, b. about 1780; d. after 1850 when she was living in Concord with her husband; m. at Concord, 17 Nov 1803, MOSES SWETT, b. about 1778 (census records); Moses d. after 1850.

iii SALLY FARNUM, b. about 1783; d. at Concord, age 61, 15 Oct 1844; m. about 1813, MOSES SHUTE, b. at Concord, about 1790 (census records); Moses d. at Concord, 13 Mar 1858. Moses married second Sophia Dunckley on 11 Jun 1846.

476) EBENEZER FARNUM (*Josiah Farnum⁴, Ephraim Farnum³, Elizabeth Holt Farnum², Nicholas¹*), b. at Andover, 4 Aug 1754 son of Josiah and Mary (Frye) Farnum; d. at Concord, 11 Mar 1829; m. about 1776, DOROTHY "DOLLY" CARTER, b. about 1755; Dolly d. at Concord, 2 Dec 1827.

Little concrete is known of this family and three children are attributed to this family likely all born at Concord.[1262]

i MEHITABLE FARNUM, b. about 1777; m. at Concord, 15 Nov 1804, DAVID ELLIOT, b. at Concord, about 1779 son of Joseph and Lydia (Goodwin) Elliot.

ii EZEKIEL FARNUM, b. about 1782; d. at Concord, 3 Nov 1826. Ezekiel does not seem to have married.

iii JANE FARNUM, b. about 1783

477) JOANNA FARNUM (*Josiah Farnum⁴, Ephraim Farnum³, Elizabeth Holt Farnum², Nicholas¹*), b. at Andover, 27 Sep 1757 daughter of Josiah and Mary (Frye) Farnum; d. at Concord, 17 Nov 1832; m. about 1781, JOSEPH RUNNELS, b. at Boxford, 19 Oct 1758 son of Samuel and Joanna (Platts) Runnels; Joseph d. at Concord, 18 Dec 1843.

Joseph resided in Boxford before his marriage, and it is likely that he is the Joseph Runnels of Boxford who at age 20 in 1779 served in Capt. Robertson's company of Col. Johnson's regiment of the Continental army for a term of nine months. He is described as 5 feet 7 inches with dark hair.[1263]

Soon after his service, Joseph was in Concord where he and Joanna married and resided in the Horse Hill area.[1264] Joseph had received property from his grandfather near Horse Hill on 21 September 1780.[1265]

Joanna Farnum and Joseph Runnels were parents of ten children born at Concord. Children Joseph, Josiah, Sarah, and Dorcas lived together in Concord.

i JOSEPH RUNNELS, b. 27 Mar 1782; d. at Concord, 14 Aug 1863. Joseph did not marry.

ii ISAAC RUNNELS, b. 27 Nov 1784; d. at Concord, 16 Dec 1851; m. 9 Aug 1821, his first cousin, ANNA RUNNELS, b. at Concord, 17 Aug 1803 daughter of Samuel and Anna (Hardy) Runnels; Anna d. at Concord, 4 Apr 1878.

iii THEODORE RUNNELS, b. 2 Apr 1786; d. at Bradford, MA, 25 Sep 1869; m. at Bradford, 22 Jun 1816, MEHITABLE "HITTY" PHILLIPS, b. at Bradford, 3 Apr 1788 daughter of Samuel and Mehitable (Hagget) Phillips; Mehitable d. at Beverly, 9 Jul 1863.

iv SARAH RUNNELS, b. 2 May 1788; d. at Concord, 4 Aug 1881. Sarah did not marry.

v JONATHAN RUNNELS, b. 28 Mar 1790; d. at LeBouef, PA, 29 Jul 1873; m. at Bridgewater, NH, 11 Oct 1812, LYDIA PRESSY, b. 17 Mar 1795;[1266] Lydia d. at LeBouef, 29 Jul 1861.

vi JOSIAH RUNNELS, b. 10 Apr 1792; d. at Concord, 24 Apr 1873. Josiah did not marry.

vii FARNUM RUNNELS, b. 1 Mar 1794; d. 3 Mar 1794.

viii FARNUM RUNNELS, b. 25 Jan 1795; d. at Hopkinton, NH, 19 Jun 1891; m. 1st 27 Mar 1823, JERUSHA WEBBER, b. at Hopkinton, 23 Aug 1802 daughter of Jeremiah and Lydia (Flanders) Webber; Jerusha d. at Hopkinton, 4 Jul 1848. Farnum m. 2nd 11 Jun 1850, GRACE TRUSSELL, b. at Hopkinton, 13 Aug 1801 daughter of John and Jemima (Colby) Trussell; Grace d. at Hopkinton, 18 Mar 1881.

ix DORCAS RUNNELS, b. 9 Jul 1797; d. at Concord, 14 Jan 1887. Dorcas did not marry. Her brother Farnum administered her estate as she left no husband or child.

x HAZEN RUNNELS, b. 21 Sep 1801; d. at Concord, 27 Jun 1859; m. 1st 5 Apr 1832, SARAH BLANCHARD FISK, b. at Concord, 8 Jun 1805 daughter of Ebenezer and Sarah (Blanchard) Fisk; Sarah d. at Concord, 30 Oct 1840.

1262 Farnham, *The Descendants of Ralph Farnum*, p 296

1263 Massachusetts Soldiers and Sailors in the Revolution, volume 13, p 666

1264 Bouton, *History of Concord*, p 660

1265 Runnels, *A Genealogy of the Runnels and Reynolds Families*, p 48

1266 Lydia's date of birth is given in the Runnels' genealogy.

Hazen m. 2nd, 19 Apr 1842, SARAH E. CORLISS, b. at Concord, 24 Nov 1810 daughter of John and Deborah (Sargent) Corliss; Sarah d. at Concord, 17 Jan 1870.

478) JOSEPH FARNUM (*Joseph Farnum⁴, Ephraim Farnum³, Elizabeth Holt Farnum², Nicholas¹*), b. at Rumford, NH, 27 Nov 1740 son of Joseph and Zerviah (Hoit) Farnum; d. at Concord, 1 Nov 1837;[1267] m. about 1768, RUTH WALKER, b. about 1750 whose parents have not been identified; Ruth d. at Concord, 15 Jun 1829.

Joseph served in the French and Indian War. He was known as Capt. Joseph Farnum.

On 5 September 1832, Joseph Farnum, then age ninety-one and of Concord, gave a statement related to his application for a pension. His first enlistment during the Revolution was in December 1775 as a corporal in Capt. Benjamin Emery's company of Starks' regiment of the New Hampshire line. In June 1776, he served six months as a sergeant under Capt. Shepard. He reported he was born in Concord in 1740 and resided there his entire life.[1268]

Joseph Farnum and Ruth Walker were parents of four children born at Concord.

i BETSEY FARNUM, b. 27 Jan 1770; d. at Northfield, NH, 12 Feb 1855; m. at Boscawen, 25 Jan 1787, JOSEPH CLEASBY,[1269] b. at Marlborough, MA, 9 Sep 1765[1270] son of Joseph and Sarah (Williams) Cleasby; Joseph d. at Northfield, 3 Nov 1855.

ii HANNAH FARNUM, b. 2 Apr 1773; d. after 1850 when she was living with her daughter Hephzibah (wife of Asaph Abbott) in Concord; m. at Concord, 29 Dec 1793, JOSEPH DOW, b. about 1769 son of Ebenezer and Elizabeth (Wilson) Dow; Joseph d. at Concord, Jan 1817.

iii HEPHZIBAH FARNUM, b. 6 Apr 1777; d. at Concord, 13 Feb 1855; m. at Concord, 21 Sep 1796, ISAAC DOW, b. 1774 son of Ebenezer and Elizabeth (Wilson) Dow; Isaac d. at Concord, 17 Feb 1851.

iv SUSANNA FARNUM, b. 2 Jun 1779; d. at East Concord, 7 Dec 1825; m. at Concord, 27 Sep 1803, REUBEN GOODWIN, b. at Concord, 27 May 1778 son of Samuel and Elizabeth (Bancroft) Goodwin; Reuben d. at East Concord, 19 Aug 1852. Reuben married second Betsey Webber on 26 Dec 1826.

479) STEPHEN FARNUM (*Joseph Farnum⁴, Ephraim Farnum³, Elizabeth Holt Farnum², Nicholas¹*), b. at Rumford, NH, 24 Aug 1742 son of Joseph and Zerviah (Hoit) Farnum; d. at Concord, 15 Feb 1832; m. at Bradford, MA, 25 Sep 1766, MARTHA HALL, b. at Bradford, 27 Dec 1743 daughter of David and Naomi (Gage) Hall; Martha d. at Concord, 25 Aug 1825.

Stephen resided in Concord where he fulfilled civic duties such as hogreeve and surveyor of highways. He lived on the homestead farm with his father.[1271]

Stephen Farnum and Martha Hall were parents of seven children born at Concord.

i DAVID FARNUM, b. 24 Dec 1767; d. at Rumford, ME, 1839; m. DORCAS WHEELER, b. at Concord, 4 Feb 1771 daughter of Jeremiah and Keziah (Blanchard) Wheeler; Dorcas d. at Rumford, 1 Dec 1864.

ii STEPHEN FARNUM, b. 20 Sep 1771; d. at Rumford, ME; m. SUSAN JACKMAN, b. at Boscawen, 19 Mar 1775 daughter of George and Martha (Webster) Jackman.

iii PHEBE FARNUM, b. 14 Oct 1774; d. at Hopkinton, after 1860; m. at Concord, 15 Nov 1798, JOSHUA MORSE, b. at Newbury, NH, 14 Dec 1766 son of Joshua and Rebecca (Patten) Morse; Joshua d. at Hopkinton, 14 Mar 1826. Joshua was a cabinetmaker in Hopkinton.[1272]

iv ISAAC FARNUM, b. 1 Dec 1776; d. 20 Apr 1778.

v ISAAC FARNUM, b. 1 Dec 1778; d. at Concord, after 1870; m. at Concord, 10 Jan 1803, HANNAH MARTIN, b. at Concord, 6 Sep 1781 daughter of Henry and Esther (Kimball) Martin; Hannah b. at Concord, 2 Apr 1868.

vi SIMEON FARNUM, b. 14 Jan 1782; d. at Concord, 1864; m. 1st at Hopkinton, 1 Jul 1811, MARY SMITH, b. at Hopkinton, 14 Mar 1789 daughter of Moody and Hannah (Quimby) Smith; Mary d. at Concord, 1819. Simeon m. 2nd 15 Feb 1820, Mary's sister CLARISSA SMITH, b. at Hopkinton, 29 Jul 1794; Clarissa d. at Concord, 29 Jun 1879.

[1267] *American Almanac and Useful Knowledge for the Year 1839*, p 283; obituary notice for Capt. Joseph Farnum of Concord, age 97; soldier in the French and Indian War

[1268] U. S. Revolutionary War Pension and Bounty-Land Application Files, S16791

[1269] Joseph's name is spelled Clisby on the grave monument but is spelled Cleasby in most records.

[1270] Joseph's date of birth is given in his Revolutionary War pension application file. The names and births of the eleven children of Betsey and Joseph are also given in the pension file.

[1271] Bouton, *History of Concord*

[1272] U.S., Craftperson Files, 1600-1995

vii JUDITH FARNUM, b. 28 Apr 1784; d. at Hopkinton, 27 Mar 1859; m. at Concord, 28 Mar 1803, JEREMIAH STORY, b. at Hopkinton, NH, 25 Mar 1775 son of Jeremiah and Mary (Burnham) Story; Jeremiah d. 13 May 1859.

480) BETTY FARNUM (*Joseph Farnum⁴, Ephraim Farnum³, Elizabeth Holt Farnum², Nicholas¹*), b. at Concord, about 1743; d. at Concord, 11 Nov 1821; m. about 1766, NATHAN ABBOTT, b. at Andover, 7 Feb 1736/7 son of Thomas and Elizabeth (Ballard) Abbott; Nathan d. at Concord, 18 Jan 1805.

Nathan Abbott and Betty Farnum had ten children whose births are recorded at Concord.

i BETTY ABBOTT, b. 2 Jul 1767; d. 1774.

ii JACOB ABBOTT, b. 16 Jan 1769; d. 13 Jan 1838; m. 1802, BETSEY KNAPP, b. 4 Mar 1782; Betsey d. at Rumford, ME, 18 Mar 1831.

iii ASA ABBOTT, b. 11 Nov 1770; d. 11 Feb 1843. Asa did not marry.

iv DAVID ABBOTT, b. 22 Sep 1772. The Abbot genealogy reports he went to New York in 1794 and left no trace after that. He was a house-joiner. The Rutherford County Tennessee Historical Society suggests that this David Abbott made his way to Tennessee and died in Gibson County, TN in 1856. The historical society has prepared a summary on David and reports he married Elizabeth Cummins 15 Oct 1811.[1273] David Abbott owned a mill and received a pension for service in the War of 1812.[1274] There is an 1850 U.S. Census Record for Fall Creek, Rutherford, TN which lists David Abbott born about 1772 in NH as head of the household.[1275] He wrote a will in 1855 that was in probate in Gibson County, TN in 1857.[1276]

v HENRY ABBOTT, b. 22 Sep 1774; d. at Rumford, ME, 1 Feb 1862; m. 1 Jun 1798, his second cousin once removed, SUSANNAH HALL (*Stephen Hall⁶, Dorcas Abbott Hall⁵, Edward Abbott⁴, Hannah Gray Abbott³, Hannah Holt Gray², Nicholas¹*), b. at Concord, 13 Nov 1781 daughter of Stephen and Patience (Flanders) Hall; Susannah d. 20 Mar 1867.

vi ANNA ABBOTT, b. 7 Jun 1776; died young.

vii BETTY ABBOTT, b. 19 Apr 1778; d. 24 May 1831; m. 3 Jun 1816, JEREMIAH EASTMAN. Betty and Jeremiah did not have children.

viii ANNA ABBOTT, b. 8 Jan 1781; m. Feb 1806, her third cousin once removed, EDMUND BLANCHARD, b. at Canterbury, NH, 27 Jan 1778 son of Jonathan and Hannah (Chadwick) Blanchard; Edmund d. in Vermont, 29 Nov 1836.[1277]

ix CHLOE ABBOTT, b. 10 Jun 1783; d. at Hollis, ME, after 1850; m. 19 Dec 1809, ZEBADIAH FARNUM, b. at Concord, 4 Mar 1781 son of John and Sally (West) Farnum; Zebadiah d. at Hollis, after 1850.

x ESTHER ABBOTT, b. 19 May 1789; d. at Concord after 1850. At the 1850 U.S. Census she was living with her nephew Asa Blanchard in Concord.

481) ABNER FARNUM (*Joseph Farnum⁴, Ephraim Farnum³, Elizabeth Holt Farnum², Nicholas¹*), b. at Concord about 1746 son of Joseph and Zerviah (Hoit) Farnum; d. at Concord, 2 Aug 1820; m. 1st about 1769, REBECCA MERRILL, b. at Rumford, 16 Aug 1751 daughter of John and Rebecca (Abbott) Merrill; Rebecca d. about 1777. Abner m. 2nd about 1778, SARAH ELLIOT, b. about 1743 (age at death 73); Sarah d. at Concord, 13 Dec 1816.

Abner resided in Concord where he signed the association test in 1776. He served as field driver for the town. In 1777, he enlisted for one year in the company of Capt. Daniel Livermore of the 3rd New Hampshire regiment.[1278]

Abner Farnum and Rebecca Merrill were parents of three children born at Concord.

i THOMAS FARNUM, b. 31 Dec 1769; d. at Concord, 7 Sep 1793.

ii JOHN FARNUM, b. about 1772; died young.

1273 Rutherford County Tennessee Historical Society, "Some of the Earliest People in Rutherford County by Their Date of Birth Prior to 1800," retrieved from http://rutherfordtnhistory.org/wp-content/uploads/2017/10/Pioneers-before-1800.pdf

1274 National Archives, War of 1812 Pension and Bounty Land Warrant Application Files, www.fold3.com/image/270301070?xid=1945

1275 Year: 1850; Census Place: Fall Creek, Rutherford, Tennessee; Roll: M432_894; Page: 164B; Image: 321

1276 Tennessee Wills and Probate Records, 1779-2008, Gibson County, TN, Will Books Vol D-F, 1846-1862, Will of David Abbott.

1277 *Vermont, Vital Records, 1720-1908*.

1278 Bouton, *History of Concord*, p 752

iii MOSES FARNUM, b. about 1774; d. at Cornish, NH, 19 Sep 1828; m. at Lebanon, NH, 30 Oct 1800, REBECCA DEAN, b. about 1773; Rebecca d. at Cornish, 27 Oct 1828.

There are records of seven children of Abner Farnum born at Concord whose mother is likely Sarah Elliot.[1279]

i JOHN FARNUM, b. 5 Dec 1779; d. at Concord, 23 Nov 1843; m. at Concord, 14 Dec 1814, MIRIAM DIMOND, b. at Concord, 1788 daughter of John and Sarah (Emerson) Dimond; Miriam d. after 1850 when she was living in Concord.

ii POLLY FARNUM, b. 25 Aug 1781

iii ABNER FARNUM, b. 5 Mar 1782; d. at Concord, 29 Aug 1830; m. at Concord, 10 Mar 1808, MARY MARTIN, b. at Concord, 1785 daughter of Henry and Esther (Kimball) Martin; Mary d. at Concord, 9 Dec 1841.

iv JACOB FARNUM, b. 3 Jan 1785; d. at Concord, 17 Feb 1804.

v JOSEPH FARNUM, b. 31 Mar 1787; d. at Salem, 4 Oct 1858; m. at Salem, 31 Mar 1811, ELIZABETH HOBBS, b. at Boxford, 17 Nov 1783 daughter of Jonathan and Rachel (Foster) Hobbs; Elizabeth d. at Salem, 4 Mar 1867.

vi JEDEDIAH FARNUM, b. 9 Feb 1789; d. at Quincy, MA, 18 Mar 1845; m. about 1826, MARTHA MORGAN, b. at Sedgwick, ME, 31 May 1803 daughter of Daniel and Elizabeth (Allen) Morgan; Martha d. at Dorchester, 16 Jan 1875. Jedediah and Martha lived in Orland, Maine until after 1830 and then relocated to Quincy. They were parents of eight children.

vii NATHAN FARNUM, b. 19 Feb 1791; d. at Salem, MA, 21 Mar 1850;[1280] m. at Wenham, 1 Nov 1818, LYDIA HOBBS, b. 13 Sep 1792 daughter of Jonathan and Rachel (Foster) Hobbs;[1281] Lydia d. at Salem, 28 Apr 1851.

482) ZERVIAH FARNUM (*Joseph Farnum⁴, Ephraim Farnum³, Elizabeth Holt Farnum², Nicholas¹*), b. at Concord, 1752 daughter of Joseph and Zerviah (Hoit) Farnum; d. at Concord, Dec 1818; [1282] m. 24 Sep 1776, her second cousin once removed, REUBEN ABBOTT (*Reuben Abbott⁵, Abigail Farnum Abbott⁴, Ralph Farnum³, Elizabeth Holt Farnum², Nicholas¹*), b. at Concord, 5 Feb 1754 son of Reuben and Rhoda (Whittemore) Abbott; Reuben d. at Concord, 12 Dec 1834.

Reuben Abbott was a farmer in Concord. He and wife Zerviah Farnum had seven children born at Concord.

i RUTH ABBOTT, b. 25 Apr 1777; d. at Concord, 20 Feb 1849; m. 11 Mar 1798, her fourth cousin, HENRY CHANDLER (*Isaac Chandler⁵, Priscilla Holt Chandler⁴, Timothy³, James², Nicholas¹*), b. at Andover, 16 Jul 1766 son of Isaac and Hannah (Ballard) Chandler; Henry d. at Concord, 3 Apr 1856.

ii PHEBE ABBOTT, b. 17 May 1779; d. at Boscawen, NH, 25 Apr 1816; m. 27 Mar 1804, PETER CHANDLER FARNUM, b. at Concord, 18 Mar 1778 son of Ephraim and Abigail (Stevens) Farnum; Peter d. at Boscawen, 4 May 1816.

iii REBECCA ABBOTT, b. 13 May 1781; d. at Newbury, VT, 30 Oct 1872; m. at Concord, 6 Feb 1803, her second cousin, THOMAS ROBINSON BROCK (*Judith Abbott Brock⁶, James Abbott⁵, Abigail Farnum Abbott⁴, Ralph Farnum³, Elizabeth Holt Farnum², Nicholas¹*), b. at Newbury, 5 Dec 1775 son of Thomas and Judith (Abbott) Brock; Thomas d. at Newbury, 19 Jan 1839.

iv SUSANNAH ABBOTT, b. 20 Jun 1785; death unknown. Bouton's History of Concord reports that she did not marry.

v ZERVIAH ABBOTT, b. 20 Dec 1785; d. at Concord, 1 Jul 1841; m. 13 Sep 1808, JESSE CARR TUTTLE, b. at Concord, 1779 son of Stephen and Jane (Carr) Tuttle; Jesse d. at Concord, Dec 1835.

vi POLLY ABBOTT, b. 2 Mar 1789; d. at Concord, Sep 1859; m. 8 Dec 1825, HENRY MARTIN, b. at Concord, 7 Aug 1779 son of Henry and Esther (Kimball) Martin, Henry d. at Concord, 1860.

[1279] The Concord records list the mother as Rebecca, but the consensus from published sources is that these were children with Abner's second wife Sarah Elliot. And for those children in this group for whom there are death records that list parents, Sarah is listed as the mother. The Farnum genealogy lists three further children for Abner and Sarah (Thomas #2, Isaac, and Betsey) but there were no records located for these children and they are not included here.

[1280] Names of parents are given as Abner and Sarah on his death record.

[1281] Lydia's parents are named as Jonathan and R Hobbs on her death record.

[1282] New Hampshire, Death and Disinterment Records, 1754-1947

vii REUBEN ABBOTT, b. 23 Oct 1790; d. at Concord, 27 Jun 1869; m. 16 Mar 1815, his third cousin once removed, HANNAH ABBOTT (*Daniel Abbott⁵, George Abbott⁴, Hannah Gray Abbott³, Hannah Holt Gray², Nicholas¹*), b. at Concord, 28 Oct 1791 daughter of Daniel and Mercy (Kilburn) Abbott; Hannah d. at Concord, 13 Sep 1876.

483) SUSAN FARNUM (*Joseph Farnum⁴, Ephraim Farnum³, Elizabeth Holt Farnum², Nicholas¹*), b. at Concord, about 1759 daughter of Joseph and Zerviah (Hoit) Farnum; d. at Loudon, NH, 23 Oct 1850; m. about 1786, WILLIAM WHEELER, b. at Concord, MA, 31 Mar 1760 son of Jeremiah and Esther (Russell) Wheeler; William d. at Loudon, NH, 26 Nov 1852.

After her marriage, Susan resided with her husband in Loudon. William served for three years from May 1777 through May 1780 as a private in the company of Capt. Edmund Monroe in Col. Bigelow's regiment of the Massachusetts line. He was at the Battle of Monmouth where his captain was killed and was at the taking of Burgoyne. William provided a statement on 22 June 1819 related to his pension application. He was allowed a pension.[1283]

Susan Farnum and William Wheeler were parents of three children born at Loudon.

i RUSSELL WHEELER, b. 7 Jan 1788; d. at Loudon, 4 Sep 1864; m. at Chichester, NH, 2 Jul 1818, NANCY PERKINS, b. Jan 1796; Nancy d. at Loudon, 19 Oct 1873.

ii SUSANNAH WHEELER, b. 7 Jun 1789; d. at Loudon, 1 Jul 1884. Susannah did not marry.

iii CATHERINE WHEELER, b. 25 Mar 1792; d. at Loudon, 13 Sep 1829. Catherine did not marry.

484) JACOB FARNUM (*Joseph Farnum⁴, Ephraim Farnum³, Elizabeth Holt Farnum², Nicholas¹*), b. at Concord, about 1758 son of Joseph and Zerviah (Hoit) Farnum; d. at Rumford, ME, 1 Sep 1836; m. about 1794, BETSEY WHEELER, b. at Concord, MA, 7 Mar 1766 daughter of Jeremiah and Esther (Russell) Wheeler; Betsey d. at Rumford, 8 Nov 1858.

Jacob Farnum was an early settler of Rumford, Maine having a property on the north side of what was known as the Great River (likely a reference to the Androscoggin River). Jacob was the town treasurer from 1806 to 1808.[1284]

Jacob Farnum and Betsey Wheeler were parents of six children born at Rumford, Maine.

i ESTHER FARNUM, b. 23 Apr 1794; d. at Canton, ME, 30 Nov 1862; m. at Rumford, 2 Sep 1813, JOEL AUSTIN, b. at Mexico, ME, 26 Apr 1789 son of Peter and Deborah (Gage) Austin; Joel d. at Canton, 8 Dec 1862.

ii CATHARINE "CATY" FARNUM, b. 14 Dec 1796; d. at Hanover, ME, 10 Feb 1890; m. at Rumford, 17 Feb 1820, EBEN ABBOTT, b. at Rumford, ME, 30 Jan 1792 son of John and Ruth (Lovejoy) Abbott; Eben d. at Hanover, 30 Jan 1874. Eben served in the army during the War of 1812 serving in Capt. Wheeler's company of the Massachusetts militia from September to November 1814.[1285]

iii DANIEL FARNUM, b. 22 Apr 1799; d. at Rumford, ME, 14 Mar 1893; m. at Rumford, 24 Feb 1833, his first cousin once removed, MARY W. VIRGIN (*Daniel Virgin⁷, Dorcas Lovejoy Virgin⁶, Henry Lovejoy⁵, Henry Lovejoy⁴, Mary Farnum Lovejoy³, Elizabeth Holt Farnum², Nicholas¹*), b. 1809 daughter of Daniel and Mary (Wheeler) Virgin; Mary d. at Rumford, 23 Aug 1856. Daniel m. 2nd, 28 Mar 1861, MARTHA JANE SILVER, b. at Rumford, 26 Jul 1833 daughter of Nathan and Sally (Swain) Silver; Martha d. at Rumford, 9 Jul 1907. Martha Silver was first married to Anson Bowker whom she divorced in Aug 1859. After Daniel's death, Martha married William Crawford Richmond in 1896.

iv HANNAH FARNUM, b. 28 Aug 1801; d. at Canton, ME, 14 Dec 1902; m. at Rumford, 2 May 1826, HENRY H. CHILDS, b. 1798 likely son of Daniel and Phebe (Parks) Childs; Henry d. at Canton, 18 Sep 1871.

v LYDIA FARNUM, b. 23 Dec 1803; d. at Rumford, 5 Nov 1864; m. at Rumford, 26 Aug 1832, JOHN E. SEGAR, b. at Bethel, 4 Mar 1803 son of Nathaniel and Mary (Russell) Segar; John d. at Rumford, 30 Oct 1882.

vi SUSANNA FARNUM, b. 19 Jul 1806; d. at Rumford, 30 Jan 1896; m. at Rumford, 22 Mar 1827, AARON MOORE ELLIOTT, b. at Rumford, 10 Aug 1802 son of Cotton and Gratia (Moore) Elliott; Aaron d. at Rumford, 10 May 1880.

485) WILLIAM PETERS (*Elizabeth Farnum Peters⁴, Ephraim Farnum³, Elizabeth Holt Farnum², Nicholas¹*), b. at Rumford, 7 Dec 1740 son of James and Elizabeth (Farnum) Peters; d. at Henniker, 5 Jul 1775 when a tree fell on him; m. at Hopkinton, NH, 25 Oct 1766, SARAH JEWELL; Sarah d. at Henniker, 1812.

There is a record for one child of William Peters and Sarah Jewell.

1283 U. S. Revolutionary War Pension and Bounty-Land Warrant Application Files, Case S24001

1284 Lapham, *History of Rumford, Oxford County, Maine*

1285 War of 1812 Pension Application Files Index, 1812-1815

i JACOB PETERS, b. 17 Apr 1772; d. at Henniker, 19 Sep 1845; m. 1st 3 Dec 1793, SARAH WOOD EAGER, b. at Oakham, MA, 3 Feb 1772 daughter of Joseph and Hannah (Wood) Eager; Sarah d. 26 Jul 1814. Jacob m. 2nd at Henniker, 7 Sep 1815, ANNA COCHRAN.

Great-Grandchildren of Mary Holt and Thomas Johnson

486) MARY HARNDEN (*Mary Johnson Harnden4, Mary Johnson Johnson3, Mary Holt Johnson2, Nicholas1*), b. at Andover, 1702 daughter of Barachias and Mary (Johnson) Harnden; d. at Medfield, 1798; m. at Boston, 6 Sep 1722, THOMAS MASON, b. at Medfield, 22 Aug 1699 son of Ebenezer and Hannah (Clark) Mason; Thomas d. at Medfield, 26 Dec 1789.

Mary and Thomas resided in Medfield where Thomas was selectman in 1743, 1748, and 1757.[1286]

In his will written 9 June 1774 (probate 2 February 1790), Thomas Mason bequeathed to beloved wife Mary the use of half his real estate and the southwest part of the dwelling house while a widow, and the moveable estate to be hers forever. Son Barachias Mason, daughter Olive How, daughter Caroline Clark, and daughter Catherine Cutler each receives five shillings. Grandson Simeon Smith receives twenty shillings. Sons Sady Mason and Thomas Mason receive the wearing apparel. Son Silas receives all the real estate, husbandry tools, armory, and stock animals. Silas is also charged with provisioning his mother and paying the debts and legacies. Silas was also named executor. Real estate was valued at £233.3.0[1287]

Mary Harnden and Thomas Mason were parents of ten children born at Medfield.

i BARACHIAS MASON, b. 10 Jun 1723; d. at Medfield, 19 Mar 1795; m. by 1766, LOVE WHITNEY (widow of Jonathan Battle), b. at Hopkinton, MA, 21 Nov 1727 daughter of Mark and Tabitha (-) Whitney; Love d. at Medfield, 1802. Barachias graduated from Harvard in 1742. He taught school and singing in Medfield and well as being an innkeeper. Her served as selectman for five years.

ii OLIVE MASON, b. 9 Jul 1724; d. at Medfield, 25 Sep 1807; m. 1st 1745, JOSEPH MORSE, b. at Medfield, 1721 son of Joshua and Mary (-) Morse; Joseph d. in Nova Scotia. Olive m. 2nd WILLIAM HOW of Nova Scotia. After William's death, Olive returned to Medfield.[1288]

iii LOIS MASON, b. 22 Jun 1726; d. in childbirth, at Natick, 24 Mar 1757; m. 2 May 1756, NATHANIEL SMITH. Nathaniel married second Tamason Adams on 27 Apr 1758. Lois had one son Simeon born on 24 Mar 1757.

iv THOMAS MASON, b. 4 Aug 1728; d. Feb 1731.

v JOSEPH MASON, b. 4 Nov 1729; d. 1729.

vi SADEY MASON, b. 1 Nov 1730; d. at Princeton, MA, 3 Sep 1804; m. at Rutland, 16 Oct 1756, SARAH ELLIS, b. at Medfield, 13 Sep 1734 daughter of James and Tabitha (Mason) Ellis;[1289] Sarah d. at Princeton, Feb 1823.

vii THOMAS MASON, b. 14 Jun 1733; d. at Princeton, MA, 28 Nov 1814; m. at Medfield, 31 Aug 1763, MARY BAXTER, b. at Medfield, 15 Apr 1737 daughter of John and Rebecca (Fisher) Baxter; Mary d. at Medfield, 8 Apr 1824.

viii CAROLINE MASON, b. 28 Jan 1735; d. at Medfield, 2 Aug 1830; m. at Medfield, 20 Jan 1757, JOSEPH CLARK, b. at Medfield, 30 Sep 1735 son of Joseph and Hannah (Dwight) Clark; Joseph d. at Medfield, 31 Jan 1816.

ix SILAS MASON, b. 17 Jun 1740; d. at Medfield, Oct 1792; m. at Medfield, 27 Jan 1762, PRISCILLA WHEELOCK, b. at Medfield, 25 Jun 1743 daughter of Ephraim and Experience (Bullard) Wheelock; Priscilla d. at Medfield, 13 Nov 1834.

x CATHERINE MASON, b. 23 Jul 1743; d. at Medfield, 8 Feb 1817; m. 1767 as his second wife, SIMEON CUTLER, b. at Medfield, 1734 son of John and Hannah (Plimpton) Cutler; Simeon d. at Medfield, 13 Oct 1815.

487) MARY PELTON (*Jemima Johnson Pelton4, Mary Johnson Johnson3, Mary Holt Johnson2, Nicholas1*), b. at Canterbury, 21 Oct 1706 daughter of John and Jemima (Johnson) Pelton; d. at Middletown, CT, 12 Dec 1740; m. at Middletown, 11 Dec 1735, THOMAS MCCLAVE son of Scottish immigrants John and Joanna (McCornach) McClave; Thomas d. at Middletown, 23 Mar 1756, Thomas married second Mary Burr on 9 Jul 1741 and had a third wife Elizabeth Bigelow.

Mary and Thomas resided in Middletown, Connecticut where their three children were born. Thomas also had one child with Mary Burr and two children with Elizabeth Bigelow.

1286 Tilden, *History of the Town of Medfield*, p 429

1287 *Suffolk County, MA: Probate File Papers.* Online database. *AmericanAncestors.org.* New England Historic Genealogical Society, 2017-2019. Case 19434

1288 Tilden, *History of the Town of Medfield*, p 441

1289 James Ellis's widow Hannah quitclaimed her rights to his estate and one of the named heirs (or heir representative) was Sadey Mason.

In his will written 22 March 1756 (proved 30 April 1756), Thomas McClave bequeathed to beloved wife Elizabeth the use of one-half of the dwelling house and one-third of the lands. His two eldest sons Robert and Thomas each receives fifteen acres of land in the home lot. Third son Josiah receives ten acres in the home lot. Sons John and Timothy also receive lots of land and daughter Mary receives pewter plates, five cows, and five sheep. The other moveable estate is to be divided among his five sons. Trusty friend John McComb is named executor.[1290]

i ROBERT MCCLAVE, b. 23 Aug 1736; d. unknown but may be the Robert McClave of Middletown whose estate was probated in 1790; m. at Chatham, 17 Feb 1762, HANNAH SMITH. The family was living in Chatham at least until 1771 when one of their children was born there.

ii THOMAS MCCLAVE, b. 15 Feb 1737/8; d. at Lyme, NH, 1815; m. at Chatham, 29 May 1765, SUSANNA STEVENSON, baptized at Portland, CT, 19 Jul 1743 daughter of John and Susannah (Savage) Stevenson; Susanna d. at Lyme, 1798.

iii JOSIAH MCCLAVE, b. 5 Dec 1740. He may be the Josiah who died in 1777 (probate 9 June 1777 for Middletown). There is no record of a marriage.

488) JOHN PELTON (*Jemima Johnson Pelton[4], Mary Johnson Johnson[3], Mary Holt Johnson[2], Nicholas[1]*), b. at Canterbury, 29 Feb 1708 son of John and Jemima (Johnson) Pelton; d. at Saybrook, 29 Jan 1786; m. 1st at Saybrook, 9 Dec 1731, ELIZABETH CHAMPION, b. at Lyme, 13 Mar 1710 daughter of Thomas and Elizabeth (Wade) Champion; Elizabeth d. at Saybrook, 10 Jul 1755. John m. 2nd, 1756, MARTHA SHIPMAN. b. about 1733 daughter of John and Ruth (Hungerford) Shipman; Martha d. at Essex, CT, 4 Sep 1787.[1291] After John's death, Martha married Dr. Joseph Bishop on 28 Sep 1786.

John resided in Saybrook on his father's homestead.[1292] He had a total of twenty-two children.

In his will written 15 April 1775 (proved 27 June 1786), John Pelton bequeathed to beloved wife Martha use of one-third of the real estate during her natural life and one-third of the moveable estate to be at her disposal. Sons John, Nathan, and Ethemar each receives five shillings to be paid by son William. Son Josiah receives ten pounds. Daughters Leze and Luce also receive five shillings to be paid in kind. Son William receives all the lands on the west side of the highway and the remainder of the movable estate after the debts are paid. Son Joseph receives five shillings in lawful money. Daughters Ruth, Martha, Priscilla, Mary, and Elizabeth receives five shillings each in the form of household items, this to be paid within two years or as they arrive at age eighteen. His other three sons, Phinnias, Jonathan, and David receive all the land on the east side of the highway. The remainder of the estate goes to son William who is also named executor. At the time of the probate, Josiah Pelton assumed administration and the estate was represented as insolvent.[1293]

John Pelton and Elizabeth Champion were parents of eleven children born at Saybrook, Connecticut.

i Son b. and d. 11 Sep 1732

ii ELIZABETH PELTON, b. 7 Oct 1733; d. Feb 1750.

iii JOHN PELTON, b.7 Nov 1735; d. at Portland, CT, 17 Apr 1819; m. about1764, ABIGAIL MILLER; Abigail d. at Portland, 3 Apr 1812.

iv NATHAN PELTON, b. 2 May 1738; d. at East Windsor, 16 May 1813; m. 1st 23 May 1763, RUTH THOMPSON, b. 1 Jun 1740 daughter of James and Jennet (Scott) Thompson;[1294] Ruth d. at East Windsor, 21 Jun 1789. Nathan m. 2nd 30 Sep 1790 the widow MARY WATERS.

v ITHAMAR PELTON, b. 20 Nov 1740; d. at Middlefield, MA, 16 Mar 1826; m. about 1764, ASENATH PRATT, b. at Haddam, 20 Sep 1741 daughter of Hezekiah and Anna (Kirtland) Pratt;[1295] Asenath d. at Middlefield, 2 Mar 1825.

vi LUCY PELTON, b. 5 Mar 1743; d. 2 May 1748.

vii JOSIAH PELTON, b. 13 Aug 1745; d. at Gustavus, OH, 3 Sep1818; m. 10 Dec 1767, MARY GRISWOLD, b. 18 Apr 1747 daughter Giles and Mercy (Chatfield) Griswold; Mary d. at Gustavus, 7 Mar 1811. Josiah m. 2nd 20 Aug 1811, the widow CHLOE GILDER.

viii WILLIAM PELTON, b. 2 Dec 1747; d. at Pulteney, NY, 25 May 1825; m. 1790, LOIS HARVEY, b. at East Haddam, 24 Aug 1750 daughter of John and Elizabeth (-) Harvey; Lois d. at Pulteney, 1823.

1290 *Connecticut State Library (Hartford, Connecticut);* Probate Place: *Hartford, Connecticut, Probate Packets, Lyman, H-Miller, Ambrose, 1752-1880, Estate of Thomas McClave, Case 2249*

1291 Connecticut, Church Record Abstracts, 1630-1920

1292 Pelton, *Genealogy of the Pelton Family*, p 59

1293 *Connecticut. Probate Court (Saybrook District);* Probate Place: Hartford; Case 1695, estate of John Pelton

1294 The 1771 will of James Thompson (probate 1777) includes a bequest to his daughter Ruth Pelton.

1295 The 1781 will of Hezekiah Pratt (probate 1786) includes a bequest to his daughter Asenath Pelton.

ix ELIZA "LESE" PELTON, b. 26 Feb 1749; d. at Essex, CT, 20 Apr 1786; m. about 1770, ROBERT DENISON, b. at Saybrook, 1745 son of Jabez and Dorothy (Cogswell) Denison; Robert d. at Essex, 12 Jan 1813.

x LUCY PELTON, b. 11 Sep 1752; m. 7 Oct 1779, as his second wife, WILLIAM MILLER, b. at Middletown, CT, 19 Jul 1744 son of William and Eunice (Clark) Miller;[1296] William d. at Middletown, 2 Nov 1795. William was first married to Chloe Martin.

xi SARAH PELTON, b. 2 Jan 1755; died young

John Pelton and Martha Shipman were parents of eleven children.

i JOSEPH PELTON, b. 25 Nov 1756; d. at Lyme, NH, 15 Jun 1837; m. at Portland, CT, 3 Nov 1781, his first cousin, PRUDENCE PELTON (*Josiah Pelton⁵, Jemima Johnson Pelton⁴, Mary Johnson Johnson³, Mary Holt Johnson², Nicholas¹*), b. 1755 daughter of Josiah and Hannah (Churchill) Pelton; Prudence d. at Lyme, 2 May 1822.

ii RUTH PELTON, b. 17 Jan 1758; d. unknown but before 1810; m. about 1780, THEOPHILUS LORD, b. at Lyme, CT, 16 Sep 1756 son of Samuel and Catherine (Ransom) Lord; Theophilus d. after 1830 when he was living in Lyme. Theophilus had a second married to Abigail (per his pension application).

iii MARTHA PELTON, b. 24 Aug 1759; d. at Springwater, NY, 16 Feb 1846; m. about 1782, her first cousin, JOHN PELTON (*Josiah Pelton⁵, Jemima Johnson Pelton⁴, Mary Johnson Johnson³, Mary Holt Johnson², Nicholas¹*), b. 9 Mar 1759 son of Josiah and Hannah (Churchill) Pelton; John d. at Springwater, 28 Aug 1848.

iv PRISCILLA PELTON, b. 10 Sep 1761; m. at Middletown, CT, 27 Mar 1782, TIMOTHY BUTLER who has not been identified. Nothing further was found for this couple, other than they seem to be living in Middletown in 1790.

v PHINEAS PELTON, b. 5 Dec 1763; d. at Pulteney, NY, 5 Mar 1847; m. 6 May 1784, MARGARET TUCKER, b. at Saybrook, 5 Apr 1764 daughter of Noah and Annah (Williams) Tucker; Margaret d. at Bradford, NY, May 1850.[1297]

vi SARAH PELTON, b. 1 Jan 1766; d. at Monroe, NH, 21 Aug 1862; m. 3 Mar 1785, SAMUEL SIMMONS, b. at Middletown, 22 Sep 1756 son of Samuel and Anna (Prior) Simmons; Samuel d. at Hanover, NH, 15 Oct 1841.

vii JONATHAN PELTON, b. 21 May 1768; d. at Waterville, NY, 3 Dec 1850; m. about 1789, ELIZABETH BAKER, b. in MA, 1771; Elizabeth d. at Waterville, 1859.

viii ELIZABETH PELTON, b. 5 Oct 1771; d. at New Hartford, CT, 23 May 1837; m. by 1795, BENJAMIN TUCKER, b. about 1771; Benjamin d. at New Hartford, 17 Jun 1855.

ix DAVID PELTON, b. 30 Dec 1773; d. at Lyme, NH, 22 Aug 1821; m. at Fitzwilliam, NH, 15 Jun 1796, LUCY STONE, b. at Framingham, MA, 17 Apr 1771 daughter of Abner and Lucy (Mellen) Stone.[1298] Lucy married second Simeon Fillmore on 18 Mar 1828.

x ISRAEL PELTON, b. 1 Apr 1775; d. at Clinton, CT, 20 Mar 1829; m. about 1807, LOIS WRIGHT, b. at Old Saybrook, 1775 daughter of Josiah and Lydia (Whittlesey) Wright; Lois d. at Clinton, 18 Apr 1815.

xi JEMIMA PELTON, b. 3 Aug 1779; d. at Essex, CT, 8 Feb 1852; m. at Essex, 24 Sep 1801, RUSSELL POST, b. at Essex, 13 Sep 1778 son of David and Deborah (Ward) Post; Russell d. at Essex, Nov 1876.

489) JAMES PELTON (*Jemima Johnson Pelton⁴, Mary Johnson Johnson³, Mary Holt Johnson², Nicholas¹*), b. at Canterbury, 21 Jul 1710 son of John and Jemima (Johnson) Pelton; d. at Haddam, 1795 (probate 1795); m. at Middletown, 14 Jan 1735/6, ELIZABETH BURR, b. at Middletown, 23 Apr 1719 daughter of Jonathan and Abigail (Hubbard) Burr; Elizabeth d. at Haddam, 12 Nov 1804.

James was a farmer in Haddam, his homestead being close to the line of Guilford.

In his will proved 27 April 1795, James Pelton bequeathed to his beloved wife Elizabeth all of the personal estate to be hers, forever. He notes that he has already disposed of all his real estate. He bequeathed his wearing apparel to the children of his son John Pelton. As he has already provided for his children, he gives them his blessing. These children are James, John, Benjamin, Phineas, Elizabeth, Jemimah who is deceased, Sarah, Martha, and Abigail. Son James was named executor.[1299]

[1296] Miller, *A Genealogy of Reminiscences. . . of the Family Miller*, p 72

[1297] U.S. Census Mortality Schedules, New York, 1850-1880; New York State Education Department, Office of Cultural Education; Albany, New York; Year: 1850; Roll: M2; Line Number: 1

[1298] Norton, *History of Fitzwilliam*, p 729

[1299] *Connecticut State Library (Hartford, Connecticut), Probate Packets, Parsons, J-Plum, R, 1752-1880, Case 2553*

There are nine known children of James Pelton and Elizabeth Burr.[1300]

i ELIZABETH PELTON, b. at Middletown, 5 Aug 1738; d. at Haddam, 29 Jan 1827; m. 30 Apr 1761, STEPHEN JOHNSON, baptized at Middleton, 10 Jul 1740 son of Stephen and Elizabeth (Brainard) Johnson.

ii JAMES PELTON, b. at Middletown, 3 Apr 1741; d. Aug 1808 in Hartford, NY while on a visit to one of his brothers;[1301] m. at Haddam, 19 Nov 1767, RUTH JOHNSON, b. at Middletown, 16 Sep 1744 daughter of Stephen and Elizabeth (Brainard) Johnson; Ruth d. at Essex, VT, 1829.

iii JEMIMA PELTON, baptized at East Hampton, 30 Oct 1743; d. before 1795; nothing further known.

iv JOHN PELTON, b. about 1745; d. at Hartford, NY, 12 Aug 1803; m. at Middletown, 24 Jul 1769, HULDAH JOHNSON, b. 23 Jul 1746 daughter of Stephen and Elizabeth (Brainard) Johnson; Huldah d. at Hartford, NY, 25 Apr 1794. John m. 2nd PATIENCE who was the wife named in John's 28 Oct 1802 will. Patience has not been identified.

v BENJAMIN PELTON, b. 1753; d. at Portland, CT, 24 Aug 1821; m. at Haddam, 9 Sep 1775, HANNAH SNOW, b. about 1753; Hannah d. at Guilford, OH, Oct 1844. Benjamin served a three-year term in the Connecticut continental line during the Revolution and suffered great hardship. In later life, he was thought to be mentally unstable and took to wandering from his home in Pawlet, Vermont back to his original home in Connecticut where he died at the home of a cousin.[1302]

vi SARAH PELTON, b. about 1755; d. at Chester, CT, 22 Jan 1853; m. at Madison, CT, 29 Aug 1776, FRANCIS LEWIS, b. at Haddam, 21 Aug 1749 son of Nathan and Sarah (Arnold) Lewis; Francis d. at Haddam, 10 Aug 1814.

vii PHINEAS PELTON, b. 1758; d. at South Gower, Leeds, Ontario, 17 Jan 1850; m. at Madison, CT, Jun 1778, RUTH JOHNSON, b. about 1760 daughter of Nathaniel Johnson.

viii MARTHA PELTON, b. about 1760; m. at Haddam, Aug 1784, DAVID JOHNSON who has not been identified.

ix ABIGAIL PELTON, b. estimate 1762; d. after 1795. Nothing further is known.

490) PHINEAS PELTON (*Jemima Johnson Pelton[4], Mary Johnson Johnson[3], Mary Holt Johnson[2], Nicholas[1]*), b. about 1712 son of John and Jemima (Johnson) Pelton; d. at Chatham, 30 May 1799; m. at Middletown, 22 May 1740, MARY MCKEE, b. about 1724 daughter of Andrew and Jerusha (-) McKee;[1303] Mary d. at Portland, CT, 28 Sep 1749. Phineas did remarry, but the name of his second wife has not been found.

Phineas resided in Chatham although part of the property was in Portland. Of the few available records for this family, the baptismal records are in the records of the church at Portland.[1304]

Phineas Pelton and Mary McKee were parents of three children.

i MARY PELTON, b. at Middletown, Sep 1741

ii ITHAMAR PELTON, baptized 19 May 1744; d. at Portland, CT, 22 Jan 1806; m. 23 Jul 1767, ELIZABETH HALL, b. about 1748; Elizabeth d. at Portland, 26 Aug 1815.

iii JESSE PELTON, baptized at Portland, 21 Jun 1747; died young

Phineas and his second wife, whose name is not known, were parents of two children.

i JESSE PELTON, baptized at Portland, CT, 8 Dec 1751

ii LUCY PELTON, baptized at Portland, 8 Dec 1755; *perhaps* m. 11 Nov 1772, SAMUEL STANNARD.

491) JOSIAH PELTON (*Jemima Johnson Pelton[4], Mary Johnson Johnson[3], Mary Holt Johnson[2], Nicholas[1]*), b. about 1714 son of John and Jemima (Johnson) Pelton; d. at Portland, CT, 2 Feb 1792; m. HANNAH CHURCHILL, b. at Portland, Apr 1731 daughter of John and Bethiah (Stocking) Churchill;[1305] Bethiah d. 12 Jun 1810.

1300 The Pelton genealogy adds a daughter Lucy who married Samuel Stannard to this family, but as Lucy is not in James's will that seems unlikely. Lucy who married Samuel Stannard may be the daughter of Phineas Pelton.

1301 Pelton, *Genealogy of the Pelton Family*, p 228

1302 Pelton, *Genealogy of the Pelton Family*, p 254

1303 The 1765 will of Andrew McKee includes bequests to his grandchildren Ithamar and Mary Pelton.

1304 Connecticut Church Record Abstracts, 1630-1920, volume 091, Portland, pp 136-138

1305 Roberts, Genealogies of Connecticut Families: From the New England Historical and Genealogical Register, volume 1, p 410

Josiah was a farmer in Chatham in the part of the town later set off as Portland.[1306] Two of the sons, Moses and Josiah, were involved in trade through the West Indies and South America. The sons jointly owned a vessel that was confiscated by Spaniards during the Mexican war of independence. Josiah was commanding the vessel at the time it was captured and Josiah was held captive for three years. After his release, Josiah took his family to Ohio.[1307]

Josiah Pelton and Hannah Churchill were parents of ten children born at Chatham/Portland.

i JEMIMA PELTON, b. 1751; d. 14 May 1774.

ii JOSIAH PELTON, b. 1753; d. 23 Oct 1771.

iii PRUDENCE PELTON, b. 1755; d. at Lyme, NH, 2 May 1822; m. at Chatham, 3 Nov 1781, her first cousin, JOSEPH PELTON (*John Pelton[5], Jemima Johnson Pelton[4], Mary Johnson Johnson[3], Mary Holt Johnson[2], Nicholas[1]*), b. 25 Nov 1756 son of John and Martha (Shipman) Pelton; Joseph d. at Lyme, 15 Jun 1837.

iv Child b. and d. 1757

v JOHN PELTON, b. 9 Mar 1759; d. at Springwater, NY, 28 Aug 1848; m. about 1782, his first cousin, MARTHA PELTON (*John Pelton[5], Jemima Johnson Pelton[4], Mary Johnson Johnson[3], Mary Holt Johnson[2], Nicholas[1]*), b. 24 Aug 1759 daughter of John and Martha (Shipman) Pelton; Martha d. at Springwater, 16 Feb 1846.

vi HANNAH PELTON, b. 1760; d. at Glastonbury, 20 May 1799; m. at Portland, 12 May 1788, ELISHA CLARK, b. at Preston, 31 Oct 1763 son of Ebenezer and Eunice (Calkins) Clark; Ebenezer was a mariner, lost at sea in 1796. Hannah m. 2nd, about 1798, as the second of his three wives, CHARLES TREAT, b. at Glastonbury, 1 Jun 1759 son of Jonathan and Ruth (House) Treat; Charles d. at Glastonbury, 5 Apr 1825. Charles was first married to Dorothy Fox and third married to Hannah's sister Phebe (see below).

vii MOSES PELTON, b. 4 Mar 1762; d. at Otisco, NY, 5 Feb 1842; m. at Marlborough, CT, 14 May 1791, MINDWELL HORSFORD, b. 1761 daughter of Daniel Horsford; Mindwell d. at Otisco, 31 Oct 1841.

viii PHEBE PELTON, b. 4 Jul 1764; d. at Glastonbury, CT, 8 Jan 1844; m. 1st at Portland, 11 Aug 1782, STEPHEN HURLBURT, b. 1757 son of Elijah and Elizabeth (Belding) Hurlburt; Stephen was a mariner (captain) who died in the West Indies, 24 Nov 1794. Phebe m. 2nd at Glastonbury, 5 Jan 1800, CHARLES TREAT, b. at Glastonbury, 1 Jun 1759 son of Jonathan and Ruth (House) Treat; Charles d. at Glastonbury, 5 Apr 1825. Charles was first married to Dorothy Fox and second married to Phebe's sister Hannah (see above).

ix MARSHALL PELTON, b. 10 Oct 1768; d. at Portland, CT, 4 Jun 1852; m. at Cromwell, CT, 3 Jan 1793, BETSEY SAGE, baptized at Cromwell, 1 Dec 1771 daughter of Lewis-Samuel and Deborah (Ranney) Sage; Betsey d. at Portland, 1 Sep 1855.

x JOSIAH PELTON, b. 5 Mar 1772; d. at Vermilion, OH, 9 Jul 1834; m. at Portland, 15 Dec 1793, LUCY SHEPARD, b. 1774; Lucy d. at Euclid, OH, 2 Sep 1815.

492) JOHNSON PELTON (*Jemima Johnson Pelton[4], Mary Johnson Johnson[3], Mary Holt Johnson[2], Nicholas[1]*) (twin of Josiah), b. about 1714 son of John and Jemima (Johnson) Pelton; d. at Portland, CT, 13 Dec 1804; m. at Chatham, 3 Mar 1748, KEZIAH FREEMAN, b. about 1724; Keziah d. at Chatham, Mar 1814.

Johnson Pelton lived in Portland, Connecticut on a homestead based on an inheritance from his father.[1308] Johnson Pelton and Keziah Freeman were parents of nine children likely all born at Portland, Connecticut.

i HANNAH PELTON, b. 10 Jan 1749; d. 28 May 1753.

ii SUSANNAH PELTON, b. 9 Aug 1750

iii EUNICE PELTON, b. 12 Apr 1753

iv JOHNSON PELTON, b. 3 Dec 1754; d. at Portland, CT, 7 Feb 1839; m. 17 Feb 1780, RACHEL PENFIELD, b. at Chatham, 14 Nov 1756 daughter of John and Ruth (Stocking) Penfield; Rachel d. at Portland, 6 Mar 1843.

v HANNAH PELTON, B. 7 Nov 1756

vi FREEMAN PELTON, b. 2 Jan 1759; d. at Plymouth, VT, 13 Jan 1847; m. 30 Nov 1783, PRUDENCE RUSSELL, b. at Middletown, CT, 3 Jun 1763 daughter of Noadiah and Lois (Bliss) Russell; Prudence d. at Plymouth, 12 Sep 1861.

[1306] Pelton, *Genealogy of the Pelton Family*, p 320
[1307] Pelton, *Genealogy of the Pelton Family*, p 341
[1308] Pelton, *Genealogy of the Pelton Family*, p 307

vii JESSE PELTON, b. 8 Feb 1761; d. at Hartford, 1795 (probate 20 Apr 1795); m. 23 Sep 1784, PHEBE PENFIELD, b. at Chatham, CT, 5 Dec 1760 daughter of John and Ruth (Stocking0 Penfield. Phebe was living in Chatham as head of household in 1800.

viii SAMUEL PELTON, b. 7 Aug 1767; d. at Hartford, CT, 17 Apr 1814; m. at West Hartford, 20 Oct 1791, JOANNA MERRILL, baptized at West Hartford, 17 May 1772 daughter of Abraham and Joanna (Brace) Merrill.

ix SETH PELTON, b. 12 Jul 1770; d. at Litchfield, NY, 19 Apr 1855; m. at West Hartford, 17 May 1792, ABIGAIL HOOKER BRACE, baptized at West Hartford, 13 Feb 1774 daughter of Henry and Abigail (Hooker) Brace; Abigail d. at Litchfield, 24 Apr 1849.

493) JEMIMA PELTON (*Jemima Johnson Pelton*[4], *Mary Johnson Johnson*[3], *Mary Holt Johnson*[2], *Nicholas*[1]), b. about 1716 daughter of John and Jemima (Johnson) Pelton; m. at Saybrook, Jan 1732/3, GIDEON BUCKINGHAM, b. at Saybrook, 22 Feb 1707/8 son of Hezekiah and Sarah (Lay) Buckingham.[1309]

The births of seven children of Jemima and Gideon are recorded at Saybrook.

i JEMIMA BUCKINGHAM, b. 10 Jan 1734/5; d. at Saybrook, CT, 10 Nov 1813; m. at Saybrook, 24 Dec 1786, as his second wife, ROBERT DENISON, b. at Saybrook, 1745 son of Jabez and Dorothy (Cogswell) Denison. Robert was first married to Eliza Pelton. Jemima Buckingham and Eliza Pelton were first cousins.

ii GIDEON BUCKINGHAM, b. 19 Apr 1737; likely died young

iii SAMUEL BUCKINGHAM, b. 20 Jul 1740; d. at Old Saybrook, 30 Jan 1815; m. 1st 1773, ELISABETH HARVEY. Samuel m. 2nd about 1783, PHILENA WILLIAMS.

iv SARAH BUCKINGHAM, b. 16 Mar 1741/2; d. at Old Saybrook, 2 Apr 1787. Sarah did not marry.

v JARED BUCKINGHAM, b. 9 Mar 1743/4; m. at Lyme, 3 May 1770, LUCY MATHER, b. at Lyme, May 1751 daughter of Timothy and Sarah (Lay) Mather; Lucy d. at Lyme, 26 May 1831.

vi REUBEN BUCKINGHAM, b. 29 Aug 1745; d. at Otselic, NY, 4 Feb 1828; m. 1st about 1770, MABEL BALL. Reuben m. 2nd 1809, PHILENA CHAPIN, b. at Springfield, MA, 15 Dec 1772 daughter of William and Martha (Chapin) Chapin. Reuben served in the Revolution and received a pension related to his service.

vii KETURAH BUCKINGHAM, b. 8 Apr 1747

494) SARAH PELTON (*Jemima Johnson Pelton*[4], *Mary Johnson Johnson*[3], *Mary Holt Johnson*[2], *Nicholas*[1]), b. about 1718 daughter of John and Jemima (Johnson) Pelton; d. at Saybrook, 20 Sep 1745; m. at Saybrook, 18 Jan 1738/9, DANIEL COMSTOCK, b. at Saybrook, 20 Sep 1713 son of Samuel and Martha (Pratt) Comstock. Daniel married second Annah Brockway.

Sarah Pelton and Daniel Comstock were parents of four children born at Saybrook. Daniel also had five children with his second wife.

i Daughter, b. 1 Sep 1739 and d. 3 Sep 1739.

ii DANIEL COMSTOCK, 30 Sep 1740

iii ASA COMSTOCK, b. 6 Mar 1742/3

iv SARAH COMSTOCK, b. 8 Sep 1745; d. 20 Sep 1745.

495) ELIZABETH PELTON (*Jemima Johnson Pelton*[4], *Mary Johnson Johnson*[3], *Mary Holt Johnson*[2], *Nicholas*[1]), b. about 1720 daughter of John and Jemima (Johnson) Pelton; d. at Lyme, CT, 3 Dec 1771; m. 1745, BENJAMIN HARVEY, b. at Lyme, 28 Jul 1722 son of John and Sarah (-) Harvey; Benjamin d. at Plymouth, PA, 27 Nov 1795.

For a detailed biography of Benjamin Harvey, the reader is referred to *The Harvey Book*, pages 609-680.[1310]

In his will written 19 November 1795 (proved 16 December 1795), Benjamin Harvey bequeaths to his wife Catherine provisions necessary for her support and income from one-third of the real estate which is bequeathed to son-in-law Abraham Tillberry. He bequeaths to daughter Lucy Tillberry the sawmill and the necessaries belonging thereto and likewise the gristmill. She also receives all the land on the side of the creek that turns the mills. Son Elisha Harvey receives all the tract of land beginning at the mouth of the creek and all the buildings on those lands. Elisha also receives the moveable estate. Daughter Lois Sweet widow receives the land in the town of Plymouth. Grandson Benjamin Harvey receives 540 acres lying in the township of Huntington. Nephew John Harvey receives a tract of land in Haverland. Any residue of the estate goes to Elisha. Elisha and trusty friend Roswell Wells are named executors.[1311]

1309 Chapman, *Buckingham Family*, p 149

1310 Harvey, *The Harvey Book*; available on archive.org; https://archive.org/details/harveybookgiving00harv/page/608/mode/2up

1311 Wills 1787-1916; Indexes 1787-1918; Author: Luzerne County (Pennsylvania). Register of Wills; Probate Place: Luzerne, Pennsylvania, pp 15-16

Benjamin Harvey and Elizabeth Pelton were parents of eight children born at North Lyme.

i MARY HARVEY, b. 1746; d. 27 Oct 1767.

ii BENJAMIN HARVEY, b. 1747; d. Mar 1777. Benjamin did not marry.

iii SETH HARVEY, b. 1749; d. 10 Dec 1771.

iv ABIGAIL HARVEY, b. 1752; d. 22 Nov 1769.

v SILAS HARVEY, b. 1754; d. 3 Jul 1778.

vi LOIS HARVEY, b. 1756; d. at Halfmoon, NY, 1808; m. at Beekmantown, 1779, ELNATHAN SWEET, b. at Exeter, RI, 24 Jun 1755 son of Elnathan and Abiah (Jenkins) Sweet; Elnathan d. at Beekmantown before 1790.

vii ELISHA HARVEY, b. 1758; d. at Plymouth, PA, 14 Mar 1800; m. ROSANNA JAMESON daughter of Robert and Agnes (Dixon) Jameson; Rosanna d. 17 Jan 1840.

viii LUCY HARVEY, b. 1760; m. ABRAHAM TILLBURY, baptized at Walpack, NJ, 19 Dec 1762 son of John and Lena (Verweye) Tillbury;[1312] Abraham d. at Plymouth, PA, after 1817.

496) JOSEPH PELTON (*Jemima Johnson Pelton[4], Mary Johnson Johnson[3], Mary Holt Johnson[2], Nicholas[1]*), b. 15 Apr 1722 son of John and Jemima (Johnson) Pelton; d. at Portland, CT, 31 Dec 1804; m. at Middletown, 27 Sep 1744, ANNA PENFIELD, b. at Middletown, 26 Oct 1728 daughter of John and Anne (Cornwell) Penfield; Anna d. at Portland, 19 May 1797.

Joseph Pelton was a farmer in Chatham, Connecticut now known as Portland. Joseph Pelton and Anna Penfield were parents of thirteen children.[1313][1314]

i ELIZABETH PELTON, b. at Middletown, 19 Nov 1745; d. 28 Sep 1749.

ii SARAH PELTON, b. 15 Jan 1748; d. at Portland, CT, 21 Aug 1841; m. at Portland, 21 Jan 1773, JONATHAN BROWN, b. about 1749; Jonathan d. at Portland, 9 Mar 1826.

iii JONATHAN PELTON, b. 23 Mar 1750; d. 16 Sep 1750.

iv JOSEPH PELTON, b. 15 Nov 1751; d. 3 Dec 1751.

v JOSEPH PELTON, b. 19 Oct 1752; d. at Great Barrington, MA, 13 May 1820; m. 1st Feb 1776, MARY SHEPHARD, b. at Chatham, 30 Jan 1758 daughter of Daniel and Sarah (Cornwell) Shephard; Mary d. at Portland, CT, 8 Sep 1797. Joseph m. 2nd Mar 1798, the widow LUCINDA (KNEELAND) BIDWELL.

vi ABNER PELTON, b. 4 Mar 1755; d. at Portland, CT, 17 Jan 1846; m. 1st 8 May 1775, SARAH BIDWELL, b. at Middletown, 12 Mar 1753 daughter of Daniel and Agnes (Abbe) Bidwell;[1315] Sarah d. at Portland, 8 Dec 1795. Abner m. 2nd 28 Apr 1796 the widow DOROTHY BAGLEY, b. about 1754; Dorothy d. at Portland, 2 Mar 1844.

vii ANNA PELTON, b. 25 Mar 1757; d. at Cromwell, CT, 8 Apr 1833; m. at Chatham, 15 Nov 1774, CHARLES DAVIS, baptized at Middletown, 7 Feb 1752 son of John Davis [perhaps John and Sybil (Robberds) Davis]; Charles d. at Cromwell, 13 Nov 1840.

viii JONATHAN PELTON, b. 10 Jun 1759; d. at Euclid, OH, 22 Sep 1830; m. at Chatham, 4 Dec 1782, ELIZABETH DOANE, b. at Middletown, 10 May 1761 daughter of Seth and Mercy (Parker) Doane; Elizabeth d, at Euclid, 30 Mar 1840.

ix ELIZABETH PELTON, b. 13 Jun 1762; d. at Sheffield, MA, 10 Jan 1849; m. at Chatham, 17 Nov 1785, MOSES STOCKING, b. at Chatham, 12 Jun 1760 son of Benjamin and Phebe (Washburn) Stocking; Moses d. at Pittsford, NY, 14 Aug 1829.

x AZUBA PELTON, b. at Middletown, 24 Jul 1764; d. at Fayette, NY, 3 Aug 1841; m. at Chatham, CT, 4 Nov 1783, AMOS NATHANIEL ROBERTS, b. at Middletown, 25 Nov 1759 son of Daniel and Ruth (Clark) Roberts; Nathaniel d. at Fayette, 1 Nov 1846.[1316]

[1312] *U.S., Dutch Reformed Church Records in Selected States, 1639-1989*, Holland Society of New York; New York, New York; Walpeck NJ, Book 78.

[1313] Pelton, Genealogy of the Pelton Family in America

[1314] The births of the youngest three children are recorded at Gill, MA but the baptisms are in Chatham (later named Portland), Connecticut which is where the family was living. The older children's births are recorded at Middletown, Connecticut.

[1315] The 1790 will of Daniel Bidwell of Chatham includes a bequest to his daughter Sarah wife of Abner Pelton.

[1316] Azuba and Nathaniel are interred at the West Fayette Church Cemetery; findagrave ID: 130157402

xi ASAHEL PELTON, b. at Chatham, 17 Jun 1768; d. at Portland, CT, 26 Jul 1843; m. 5 Dec 1790, ABIGAIL RANNEY, baptized 24 Sep 1769 daughter of George and Hannah (Sage) Ranney; Abigail d. at Portland, 12 Mar 1839.

xii RUEL PELTON, b. at Chatham, 30 May 1770; d. at Sherman, NY, 1 Nov 1851; m. 9 Apr 1792, LUCY BARNES, b. at Middletown, 31 May 1770 daughter of Giles and Katharine (Stow) Barnes; Lucy d. at Sherman, 24 Jun 1851.

xiii HATSEL PELTON, b. at Chatham, 23 Oct 1772; d. at Woodstock, VT, Sep 1806; m. about 1793, HANNAH STILES, b. at Hebron, 7 Oct 1769 daughter of Benjamin and Damaris (Brown) Stiles;[1317] Hannah was living in Woodstock in 1810 as head of household.

497) MEHITABLE CHANDLER (*Mehitable Russell Chandler⁴, Phebe Johnson Russell³, Mary Holt Johnson², Nicholas¹*), b. at Andover, about 1709 daughter of Joseph and Mehitable (Russell) Chandler; d. at Townsend, MA, Jul 1768;[1318] m. 1st at Andover, 7 Feb 1731/2, ROBERT CROSBY, b. at Billerica, 20 Jul 1711 son of Joseph and Sarah (French) Crosby; Robert d. at Townsend, 10 Feb 1743. Mehitable m. 2nd 26 Nov 1745, ANDREW SPALDING, b. at Chelmsford, 8 Dec 1701 son of Andrew and Abigail (Waring) Spalding. Andrew was first married to Hannah Wright.

After her first marriage, Mehitable settled in Townsend with her first husband Robert Crosby. After his death, Mehitable married Andrew Spalding. Andrew had been a resident of that part of Chelmsford that was set off as Westford. He also was one of the grantees of the 1750 Masonian charter of New Ipswich.[1319] Andrew also intervened by making application to the General Court on behalf of his "son-in-law" Joel Crosby. Joel was taken captive at Halfway Brook near Lake George on 20 June 1758.[1320]

Mehitable Chandler and Robert Crosby were parents of six children born at Townsend.

i ROBERT CROSBY, b. at Townsend, 13 Sep 1732; m. at Dunstable, 5 Mar 1760, SUSANNAH SHERWIN, b. at Boxford, 28 Aug 1734 daughter of Ebenezer and Hephzibah (Cole) Sherwin; Susannah d. at Winslow, ME, 7 May 1807. This family resided in New Ipswich.

ii JONAH CROSBY, b. about 1736; d. at Albion, ME, 24 Apr 1814; m. 22 Dec 1757, LYDIA CHANDLER, b. 10 Dec 1735 daughter of William and Susanna (Burge) Chandler; Lydia d. at Albion, 18 Dec 1814.

iii PHEBE CROSBY, baptized 10 Dec 1738; d. at Shirley, MA, 22 Jul 1826; m. at Westford, 7 Jul 1757, JABEZ KEEP, b. at Westford, 13 Dec 1736 son of Jabez and Sarah (Leonard) Keep; Jabez d. at Sheffield, MA, 21 Jan 1821. Phebe and Jabez had one son and five daughters. Phebe took the daughters and joined a Shaker village. Jabez remarried the widow Elizabeth Rogers about 1785.[1321]

iv JOEL CROSBY, baptized 29 Jun 1740; d. at Winslow, ME, 27 Mar 1775; m. at Chelmsford, 30 Mar 1763, HANNAH STEVENS, b. at Chelmsford, 22 Jun 1737 daughter of Samuel and Ruth (Wright) Stevens; Hannah d. at Winslow, 28 Mar 1828. Hannah married second William Richardson.

v JOSIAH CROSBY, b. about 1741. He was living in New Ipswich in 1763 but nothing further found.[1322]

vi MARAH CROSBY, b. unknown; d. at Townsend, 18 Mar 1743.

Mehitable Chandler and Andrew Spalding were parents of five children born at Westford.

i RUTH SPALDING, b. 25 Dec 1746; died young.

ii SOLOMON SPALDING, b. 28 Sep 1748; d. at Westford, 6 Aug 1826; m. 3 May 1780, JEMIMA REED, b. at Westford, 19 Nov 1761 daughter of Thomas and Susanna (Dutton) Reed; Jemima d. 3 Mar 1845.

iii HENRY SPALDING, b. 5 Jul 1750; d. likely at Clinton, ME where he was living in 1810; m. about 1776, BETSEY TAGART.

iv RUTH SPALDING, b. 15 May 1752; d. at Temple, NH, 8 May 1790; m. at Westford, 3 Dec 1772, ISAAC BUTTERFIELD, b. 1 Nov 1750;[1323] Isaac d. at Wilton, ME, 12 Oct 1812. Isaac married second Ruth Butterfield on 22 Jul 1790.

1317 Guild, *The Stiles Family in America*

1318 Mehetabel Spalding the wife of Andrew Spalding deceast this life July the . . . 1768 (Townsend, MA town records)

1319 Chandler, *The History of New Ipswich*, p 54

1320 Chandler, The Descendants of William and Annis Chandler, p 112.

1321 Best, *John Keep of Longmeadow, Massachusetts*, p 25, pp 38-39; available on familysearch.org

1322 Chandler, Descendants of William and Annis Chandler, p 112

1323 Maine, Nathan Hale Cemetery Collection, 1780-1980; date of birth is given on the cemetery record

v ABIGAIL SPALDING, b. 3 Jun 1754; d. at Dunstable, MA, 19 Jan 1830; m. 1st at Westford, 28 Nov 1774, THOMAS RICHARDSON, b at Westford, 8 Jan 1751 son of Abiel and Sarah (Boynton) Richardson; Thomas d. at Temple, NH, 8 Apr 1786. Abigail m. 2nd 30 Dec 1794, OLIVER TAYLOR, b. 1 May 1746 son of Samuel and Susannah (Perham) Taylor; Oliver d. 13 Oct 1823. Oliver Taylor was first married to Bridget Blodgett.

498) THOMAS CHANDLER (*Mehitable Russell Chandler4, Phebe Johnson Russell3, Mary Holt Johnson2, Nicholas1*), b. at Andover, 22 Apr 1711 son of Joseph and Mehitable (Russell) Chandler; d. of smallpox, at Andover, about 1761 (probate 13 Sep 1761); m. at Andover, 15 Feb 1739, ELIZABETH WALCOTT perhaps the daughter of Ebenezer and Elizabeth (Wiley) Walcott.[1324]

Thomas and Elizabeth owned the property in Andover that is now the site of the historic home at 102 Gould Road. Thomas originally obtained the land from Elizabeth's father Ebenezer. Elizabeth sold the property in 1777 to Joel and Martha Jenkins.

Thomas Chandler did not leave a will and his estate entered probate 13 April 1761 with Elizabeth as administratrix. The real estate was sold to settle the debts of the estate. There was remaining £128.2.7 for distribution to the children. Eldest son Ebenezer received £32.8 and the other children received £16.4. Those children were Thomas, Elijah, Peter, Joseph, Asa, and Elizabeth.[1325]

Thomas Chandler and Elizabeth Walcott were parents of ten children born at Andover.

i ELIZABETH CHANDLER, b. 17 Dec 1739; d. 15 Jan 1740.

ii ELIZABETH CHANDLER, b. 13 Mar 1741/2; living in 1761.

iii BRIDGET CHANDLER, b. 2 Apr 1744; d. before 1761.

iv EUNICE CHANDLER, b. 12 Feb 1745/6; d. 20 May 1749.

v EBENEZER CHANDLER, b. 14 May 1749; d. at Wilton, NH, 15 Sep 1823; m. 1st at Reading, MA, 29 Nov 1768, MARY BURNAP, likely b. at Reading, 1744 daughter of John and Ruth (Smith) Burnap; Mary d. at Wilton, 22 Oct 1778. Ebenezer m. 2nd 25 May 1779, SARAH AVERILL (widow of James Hutchinson), b. at Andover, 30 Nov 1751 daughter of Thomas and Sarah (Kneeland) Averill; Sarah d. at Wilton, 19 Jun 1794. Ebenezer m. 3rd REMEMBRANCE FLETCHER (widow of Levi Pierce), b. at Chelmsford, 23 Dec 1752 daughter of Robert and Remembrance (Foster) Fletcher; Remembrance d. at Temple, NH, 30 Nov 1833.

vi THOMAS CHANDLER, b. 22 Oct 1751; d. about 1767.

vii ELIJAH CHANDLER, b. 6 Aug 1753; d. 1775 reported by the Chandler genealogy as dying at Bunker Hill, but this was not confirmed.

viii PETER CHANDLER, b. 25 Mar 1755; d. at Nelson, NH, 14 Jul 1819; m. 6 Mar 1787, MERCY INGALLS, b. at Andover, 29 Apr 1761 daughter of David and Priscilla (Howe) Ingalls; Mercy d. at Wilton, 12 Feb 1842.

ix JOSEPH CHANDLER, b. 22 Dec 1756; reported to have died in military service.

x ASA CHANDLER, b. 25 Apr 1759; d. at Stoddard, NH, 7 Dec 1822 (will 6 Dec 1822); m. 20 Nov 1781, ELEANOR RICHARDSON, b. 22 Jul 1753; Eleanor d. 6 Dec 1834.[1326]

499) JOSEPH CHANDLER (*Mehitable Russell Chandler4, Phebe Johnson Russell3, Mary Holt Johnson2, Nicholas1*), b. at Andover, 13 Feb 1716/7 son of Joseph and Mehitable (Russell) Chandler; m. 30 Dec 1741, SARAH RICHARDSON, b. at Bradford, 26 Sep 1719 daughter of Joseph and Hannah (Nelson) Richardson.[1327]

It is not known where Joseph died. The Chandler genealogy reports that he moved to Readsboro, Vermont about 1765 and after that was in either Ware, Massachusetts or Weare, New Hampshire.[1328] This family apparently moved frequently as there are records related to their children at Andover, Groton, Ware in Massachusetts and at Willington, Connecticut.

i JOSEPH CHANDLER, b. at Andover, 1 Apr 1743; died young

ii REUBEN CHANDLER, b. at Andover, 6 Dec 1744; may be the Reuben son of Joseph whose death is recorded at Ashford, CT, 7 May 1751.

[1324] The historic property at 102 Gould Road in Andover is reported as being obtained by Thomas Chandler from Ebenezer Walcott. https://preservation.mhl.org/102-gould-rd

[1325] *Essex County, MA: Probate File Papers, 1638-1881.*Online database. *AmericanAncestors.org.* New England Historic Genealogical Society, 2014. Case 4977

[1326] Chandler, *Descendants of William and Annis Chandler*

[1327] The 1746 will of Joseph Richardson of Bradford includes a bequest to his daughter Sarah wife of Joseph Chandler.

[1328] Chandler, *Descendants of William and Annis Chandler*, p 114

iii THOMAS CHANDLER, b. at Groton, 20 Jan 1746. Thomas married but the name of his wife is not known. He is reported as dying of spotted fever about 1800.

iv JOHN CHANDLER, b. at Groton, MA, 29 May 1749; d. at Westhampton, MA, about 1824; m. 1st at Sutton, MA, 8 Jun 1775, ELIZABETH ESTY; Elizabeth d. at Lunenburg, 19 Apr 1812. John m. 2nd at Easthampton, 26 May 1815, REBEKAH ALVORD, b. about 1768 daughter of Zebadiah and Rebecca (Searle) Alvord; Rebekah d. at Easthampton, 7 May 1820.

v SARAH CHANDLER, b. about 1750; m. JAMES STURTEVANT and resided in Eaton, Québec

vi SALMON CHANDLER, b. about 1753; m. at Warren, MA, 27 Jan 1776, EXPERIENCE WOLCOTT

vii HANNAH CHANDLER, b. about 1754; d. at Willington, CT, 30 Dec 1755.

viii JOSEPH CHANDLER, b. at Willington, CT, 3 Apr 1756; d. at Ballston Spa, Saratoga (as reported in the Chandler genealogy).

500) PETER OSGOOD (*Mary Russell Osgood⁴, Phebe Johnson Russell³, Mary Holt Johnson², Nicholas¹*), b. at Andover, 14 Nov 1717 son of Timothy and Mary (Russell) Osgood; d. at Andover, 17 Nov 1801; m. at Andover, 8 Sep 1743, SARAH JOHNSON, b. at Andover, Nov 1719 daughter of Timothy and Katherine (Sprague) Johnson; Sarah d. at Andover, 1 Aug 1804.

Capt. Peter Osgood and Sarah Johnson raised their family in Andover. Peter was a successful merchant and served as magistrate. He also served as representative to the General Court and the state convention for the adoption of the constitution 9 January 1783. Son Samuel Osgood graduated from Harvard in 1770 and served as the first Postmaster General of the United States.[1329] Son Isaac was a successful entrepreneur in Andover and his estate included a mill, a homestead of 104 acres valued at $10,000, an additional eight dwelling houses, and a machine shop.[1330]

In his will written 15 September 1800 (probate 7 December 1801), Peter Osgood bequeathed to beloved wife Sarah the use of the dwelling house she now possesses and what is necessary for her comfortable maintenance. Son Peter receives a piece of woodland and fifty dollars. Son Samuel receives five dollars which completes his portion. Daughter Susanna receives fifty dollars and half the stock in the Union Bank, and "considering her husband's industry, prudence, and fame in his profession" his income is such that his family is in better circumstances that some of his other children, that will be her full portion. Son Isaac receives five dollars to complete his portion. The remainder of the estate goes to son Timothy.[1331] Son Peter named in the will died 5 January 1801 between the time of the will and the time of probate.

Peter Osgood and Sarah Johnson were parents of ten children born at Andover.

i ISAAC OSGOOD, b. 27 Jan 1744; d. 17 Oct 1753.

ii PETER OSGOOD, b. at Andover, 24 Jun 1745; d. at Andover, 5 Jan 1801; m. at Andover, 24 Nov 1788, HANNAH PORTER, b. about 1762 at Boxford (according to her death record); Hannah d. at Andover, 18 Sep 1854.

iii SAMUEL OSGOOD, b. at Andover, 3 Feb 1748; d. at New York, NY, 12 Aug 1813; m. 1st at Cambridge, 4 Jan 1775, MARTHA BRANDON, b. about 1752 likely the daughter of Benjamin and Elizabeth (Foxcroft) Brandon; Martha d. at Andover, 13 Sep 1778. Samuel m. 2nd at New York, 24 May 1786, MARIA BOURNE (widow of Walter Franklin), b. about 1754 daughter of Daniel Bourne;[1332] Maria d. at New York, Oct 1814.

iv SARAH OSGOOD, b. 11 Feb 1750; d. 24 Oct 1762.

v JOSEPH OSGOOD, b. 3 Dec 1751; d. 14 Oct 1753.

vi SUSANNA OSGOOD, b. at Andover, 23 Oct 1754; d. at Andover, 28 Apr 1840; m. at Andover, 7 Nov 1771, Dr. THOMAS KITTREDGE, b. at Andover, 13 Jul 1746 son of John and Sarah (Merriam) Kittredge; Thomas d. at Andover, 16 Oct 1818.

vii ISAAC OSGOOD, b. at Andover, 15 Jul 1755; d. at Andover, 30 Sep 1847; m. 1st at Salem, 12 Oct 1790, SALLY PICKMAN, b. at Salem, 7 Jun 1771 daughter of Clarke Gayton and Sarah (Orne) Pickman; Sally d. at Salem 10 Aug 1791. Isaac m. 2nd, Sally's sister, REBECCA TAYLOR PICKMAN, b. at Salem, about 1772; Rebecca d. at Salem, 29 Aug 1801. Isaac m. 3rd at Salem, 28 Jun 1803, MARY PICKMAN, b. at Salem, 20 Sep 1765 daughter of Benjamin and Mary (Toppan) Pickman; Mary d. at North Andover, 7 Sep 1856.

viii JOSEPH OSGOOD, b. 30 May 1758; d. 17 Oct 1762.

1329 Osgood, *A Genealogy of the Descendants of John, Christopher, and William Osgood*, pp 85-86

1330 *Essex County, MA: Probate File Papers, 1638-1881.*Online database. *AmericanAncestors.org.* New England Historic Genealogical Society, 2014. Case 48886, Estate of Isaac Osgood, 1847.

1331 *Essex County, MA: Probate File Papers, 1638-1881.*Online database. *AmericanAncestors.org.* New England Historic Genealogical Society, 2014. Case 20256

1332 The will of Walter Franklin of Long Island makes mention of his father-in-law Daniel Bourne. His name is also given in some sources as Daniel Browne.

ix LYDIA OSGOOD, b. 22 Mar 1760; d. 22 Feb 1763.

x TIMOTHY OSGOOD, b. at Andover, 17 Mar 1763; d. at Andover, 13 Dec 1842; m. 13 Nov 1788, his second cousin once removed, SARAH "SALLY" FARNUM (*Isaac Farnum⁶, John Farnum⁵, John Farnum⁴, John Farnum³, Elizabeth Holt Farnum², Nicholas¹*), b. at Andover, 10 Mar 1771 daughter of Isaac and Mary (Osgood) Farnum.

501) TIMOTHY OSGOOD (*Mary Russell Osgood⁴, Phebe Johnson Russell³, Mary Holt Johnson², Nicholas¹*), b. at Andover, 27 Aug 1719 son of Timothy and Mary (Russell) Osgood; d. at Andover, 31 Aug 1753; m. 6 Jan 1742, PHEBE FRYE, b. at Andover, 19 Mar 1721 daughter of Nathan and Hannah (Bridges) Frye; Phebe d. at Andover, after 1783 (living at time of daughter's will).

Timothy Osgood was a farmer in Andover. He did not leave a will and his estate entered probate 22 October 1823 with widow Phebe as administratrix. Dower was set off to the widow on 26 April 1756. The value of the estate not set off to the widow was £491.2.6. The division of the estate was made 10 October 1765 with the two-thirds of the real estate not set off as dower going to eldest son Timothy on condition that he pay £35.2.5 each to brother Asa and sisters Phebe and Abiah.[1333]

Daughter Phebe did not marry and in her will written 18 February 1783, she left bequests of six shillings each to her mother, brother Timothy Osgood, and brother Asa Osgood. The remainder of her estate was bequeathed to sister Abiah Osgood who was also named executrix.[1334]

Timothy Osgood and Phebe Frye were parents of seven children born at Andover, the youngest child born two months after Timothy's death. Timothy and three of the children died in the fall/winter of 1753, Timothy and his son James dying on the same day.

i TIMOTHY OSGOOD, b. 27 Jul 1743; d. at Andover, 16 Aug 1816; m. at Andover, 13 Mar 1765, his first cousin once removed (through the Bridges line), CHLOE BRIDGES, b. at Andover, 28 Dec 1743 daughter of James and Mary (Abbott) Bridges; Chloe d. at Andover, 5 Dec 1798.

ii ASA OSGOOD, b. Oct 1744; d. 1 Dec 1753.

iii PHEBE OSGOOD, b. 29 Apr 1746; d. at Andover, 4 Mar 1783. Phebe did not marry.

iv ABIAH OSGOOD, b. 13 Dec 1747; d. at Dracut, 17 Sep 1825; m. at Dracut, 24 Nov 1801, PARKER VARNUM, b. about 1746 son of John and Phebe (Parker) Varnum; Parker d. at Dracut, 18 Dec 1824.

v JAMES OSGOOD, b. 26 Dec 1749; d. 31 Aug 1753.

vi MARY OSGOOD, b. 24 Mar 1752; d. 16 Oct 1753.

vii ASA OSGOOD, b. 22 Dec 1753; d. at Hiram, ME, 29 Jul 1833; m. 1st 19 Jun 1780, his fourth cousin, DORCAS STEVENS (*Mehitable Farnum Stevens⁵, John Farnum⁴, John Farnum³, Elizabeth Holt Farnum², Nicholas¹*), b. at Andover, 9 Oct 1755 daughter of Asa and Mehitable (Farnum) Stevens; Dorcas d. 1780. Asa m. 2nd at Methuen, 22 May 1784, Mrs. LYDIA HOOD; Lydia d. 1807. Asa m. 3rd 18 Jul 1808, HANNAH POWERS; Hannah d. 25 Dec 1853.

502) THOMAS OSGOOD (*Mary Russell Osgood⁴, Phebe Johnson Russell³, Mary Holt Johnson², Nicholas¹*), b. at Andover, 2 Nov 1721 son of Timothy and Mary (Russell) Osgood; d. at Andover, 3 Nov 1798; m. 3 Dec 1747, SARAH HUTCHINSON, b. at Andover, 24 Sep 1719 daughter of John and Sarah (Adams) Hutchinson; Sarah d. 3 Nov 1798.

In his will dated 5 June 1793 (probate 3 December 1798), Thomas Osgood bequeaths the use of one-third part of his real estate and one-half of stock animals to beloved wife Sarah. After her decease, any remaining goes to his grandchildren children of his deceased daughter Sarah wife of Jonathan Bradley and to his daughter Molly the wife of Joseph Bradley to be equally divided between them. The six children of his daughter Sarah are to receive one-half of the real estate which will be in trust with their father Jonathan Bradley. Son-in-law Jonathan Bradley receives one-quarter part of the stock animals. Daughter Molly Bradley receives the other half of the real estate. His two sons-in-law were named executors.[1335]

Thomas Osgood and Sarah Hutchinson were parents of three children born at Andover.

[1333] *Essex County, MA: Probate File Papers, 1638-1881.*Online database. *AmericanAncestors.org.* New England Historic Genealogical Society, 2014. Case 20283

[13341334] *Essex County, MA: Probate File Papers, 1638-1881.*Online database. *AmericanAncestors.org.* New England Historic Genealogical Society, 2014. Case 20257

[1335] *Essex County, MA: Probate File Papers, 1638-1881.*Online database. *AmericanAncestors.org.* New England Historic Genealogical Society, 2014. Case 20280

i SARAH OSGOOD, b. 3 Dec 1759; d. at Andover, 14 Sep 1790; m. at Haverhill, 11 Feb 1773, JONATHAN BRADLEY, b. at Haverhill, 14 Feb 1744/5 son of William and Mehitable (Emerson) Bradley;[1336] Jonathan d. at Andover, 23 Feb 1818. Jonathan m. 2nd at Haverhill, 14 Apr 1791, Sarah Ayer.

ii THOMAS OSGOOD, b. 28 Oct 1751; nothing further known, but not living and without heirs at the time of father's will.

iii MARY "POLLY" OSGOOD, b. at Andover, 1755; d. at Andover, 10 Aug 1840; m. at Haverhill, 28 Mar 1781, JOSEPH BRADLEY, b. at Haverhill, 14 Feb 1744/5 son of William and Mehitable (Emerson) Bradley; Joseph d. at Andover, 21 Mar 1802.

503) ISAAC OSGOOD (*Mary Russell Osgood[4], Phebe Johnson Russell[3], Mary Holt Johnson[2], Nicholas[1]*), b. at Andover, 4 Aug 1724 son of Timothy and Mary (Russell) Osgood; d. at Haverhill, 17 May 1791; m. 18 Jun 1752, ABIGAIL BAILEY, b. at Haverhill, 10 Jan 1730 daughter of Joshua and Elizabeth (Johnson) Bailey; Abigail d. at Haverhill, 25 Jan 1801 of black jaundice.

Isaac Osgood graduated from Harvard College in 1744[1337] and was a merchant in Haverhill. Sons Joshua and Isaac also attended Harvard.

Isaac Osgood did not leave a will and his estate entered probate 23 July 1791 with widow Abigail declining administration and requesting that son Timothy be named administrator. There were some conflicts in the settlement of the estate related to claims against the estate some of which were disputed. The estate was declared insolvent and some real estate needed to be sold to settle the estate. Real property was valued at £1640.3.3 which included a wharf, brew house, malt house, and a stone and cooper shop. There was other substantial real estate that had been mortgaged for more than it was worth. No distribution was included with the probate documents.[1338]

Isaac Osgood and Abigail Bailey were parents of eight children born at Haverhill.

i JOSHUA BAYLEY OSGOOD, b. at Haverhill, 29 Apr 1753; d. at Boston (although resident of Fryeburg), 30 May 1791; m. May 1780, ELIZABETH BROWN, b. at Haverhill, 26 Apr 1757 daughter of Henry Young and Elizabeth (Lovejoy) Brown; Elizabeth d. at Fryeburg, 30 Jun 1790. Joshua graduate from Harvard in 1772. He was a merchant in Fryeburg. He served as a Colonel of a regiment that was part of the Canada expedition.[1339]

ii ISAAC OSGOOD, b. 29 Sep 1754; d. at Haverhill, 27 Jan 1799. Dr. Isaac Osgood graduated from Harvard in 1775. He spent some years in Madagascar before returning to Haverhill where he died. Isaac did not marry.

iii MARY OSGOOD, b. 3 Jul 1756; d. 1 May 1758.

iv TIMOTHY OSGOOD, b. 13 Apr 1758; d. 1 Aug 1759.

v TIMOTHY OSGOOD, b. at Haverhill, 2 Dec 1759; d. at Portland, 22 Aug 1839; m. at Portland, 24 May 1812, SARAH "SALLY" CODMAN, b. 1765 daughter of Richard and Sarah (Smith) Codman; Sally d. at Portland, 16 Nov 1838. Timothy did not have children.

vi WILLIAM OSGOOD, b. 23 May 1761; d. at Haverhill, 16 Jul 1792. William did not marry.

vii PETER OSGOOD, b. at Haverhill, 5 Aug 1764; d. at Haverhill, 28 Sep 1856; m. at Haverhill, 13 Jul 1796, MARY WILLIS, b. about 1774 daughter of Benjamin and Mary (Ball) Willis; Mary d. at Haverhill, 23 Oct 1825.

viii JOSEPH OSGOOD, b. 21 Jun 1767; d. 12 Jul 1767.

504) DEBORAH OSGOOD (*Mary Russell Osgood[4], Phebe Johnson Russell[3], Mary Holt Johnson[2], Nicholas[1]*), b. at Andover, 28 Apr 1730 daughter of Timothy and Mary (Russell) Osgood; d. about 1793; m. 2 Jan 1759, OBADIAH WOOD, b. about 1734 likely the son of Nathaniel and Elizabeth (Powell) Wood; Obadiah d. at Andover, 23 Oct 1810. Obadiah m. 2nd 8 May 1794 widow Lydia Blanchard.

Obadiah Wood did not leave a will and his estate entered probate 6 November 1810 with widow Lydia as administratrix. The personal estate was valued at $151.19.[1340]

There are just two children known for Deborah Osgood and Obadiah Wood. Neither daughter married. In her will dated 9 February 1824, Susanna Wood single lady of Andover expressed that Mr. Timothy Osgood in whose family she resides

---

[1336] Crane, *Historic Homes and Institutions and Personal Memoirs of Worcester County, Massachusetts*, volume 1, p 367. One oddity in the records is that the twin sons of William and Mehitable Bradley are listed as stillborn on 14 Feb 1744/5 but then they were baptized on 17 Feb 1744/5. The 1780 probate of William Bradley of Haverhill includes a will that has as heirs sons Jonathan and Joseph (among other children).

[1337] Harvard University, Quinquennial Catalogue, p 101

[1338] *Essex County, MA: Probate File Papers, 1638-1881.*Online database. *AmericanAncestors.org.* New England Historic Genealogical Society, 2014. Case 20205

[1339] Osgood, *A Genealogy of the Descendants of John, Christopher and William Osgood*, p 92

[1340] *Essex County, MA: Probate File Papers, 1638-1881.*Online database. *AmericanAncestors.org.* New England Historic Genealogical Society, 2014. Case 30303

should have proper compensation for his attention to her. She bequeaths to sister Deborah the dwelling house in which Deborah now resides. Deborah should also receive $60 per year from the estate. The remainder of the estate goes to Timothy Osgood who is also named executor.[1341] It is possible that Timothy Osgood mentioned is her first cousin son of Peter and Sarah (Johnson) Osgood.

i SUSANNA WOOD, b. at Andover, 5 Nov 1759; d. at Andover, 13 Feb 1824. Susanna did not marry.

ii DEBORAH WOOD, b. about 1772; d. at Andover, 30 Mar 1852. Deborah did not marry.[1342]

505) PHEBE OSGOOD (*Mary Russell Osgood*[4], *Phebe Johnson Russell*[3], *Mary Holt Johnson*[2], *Nicholas*[1]), b. at Andover, 26 May 1733 daughter of Timothy and Mary (Russell) Osgood; d. at Methuen, 2 Mar 1797;[1343] m. about 1757, THOMAS POOR, b. at Andover 19 Jul 1732 son of Thomas and Mary (Adams) Poor; Thomas d. at Methuen, 23 Sep 1804. Thomas married second Miriam Sargent.

Thomas Poor was the captain of a company of Minute Men in Col. James Frye's regiment and marched at the alarm 19 April 1775. He received promotion to Major in May 1775. He was commissioned as Colonel on 13 May 1778 and was in command of a regiment raised for service at Peekskill.[1344]

In his will written 11 September 1804, Thomas Poor bequeathed to beloved wife Miriam use of part of the house and provisions for her support to be provided annually, and the household furniture that was hers at the time of marriage. Son Stephen received five dollars which completes his full portion. Son Caleb receives one-sixty-eighth part of the land of the original Shelburne grant and a 100-acre lot number fifteen and one undivided half-part of lot twenty-eight and additional parcels. Daughter Polly Lovejoy wife of Abiel Lovejoy receive 100 acres in East Andover. Daughter Hannah Whittier wife of William Whittier receives 100 acres also in East Andover and daughter Phebe Plummer wife of Moses Plummer receives a similar bequest. Daughter Sarah receives use and occupancy of a chamber in the house and other provisions for her support while she is unmarried. Daughter Nancy Frye wife of Robinson Frye receives a 58-acre lot and daughter Suzee Frye wife of Daniel Frye receives a 100-acre lot. The remaining household items is to be equally divided among the daughters. The remaining outlands are to be sold and what is owed him collected and the remainder to be divided among the children except Stephen who has received his full amount. Sons Enoch and Thomas receive the remainder of the estate real and personal to divide equally and they are also named executors. After the sale of the outlands, the total value of the personal estate was $3,294.10.[1345]

On 8 July 1806, son Stephen, then of Andover, sold his property in Methuen to his brothers Enoch and Thomas for $400. On 8 June 1815, Enoch and Thomas along with Thomas's wife Prudence sold 48 acres of property to Asa Currier for $400.[1346]

Phebe Osgood and Thomas Poor were parents of ten children. Sons Enoch and Caleb settled in North Carolina, although Enoch returned to Massachusetts.

i MARY POOR, b. at Andover, 23 Dec 1757; d. likely at Andover, ME; m. at Andover, 30 Apr 1776, ABIEL LOVEJOY, b. at Andover, 28 Apr 1749 son of Christopher and Anne (Mooar) Lovejoy; Abiel d. at Andover, ME, about 1820.[1347]

ii HANNAH POOR, b. at Andover, 4 Dec 1759; d. at Methuen, 11 Mar 1835; m. 19 Mar 1789, as his second wife, WILLIAM WHITTIER, b. at Methuen, 26 Sep 1752 son of Richard and Elizabeth (Bodwell) Whittier; William d. at Methuen, 25 Aug 1812. William was first married to Lydia Haseltine.

iii PHEBE POOR, b. at Andover, 3 Jul 1761; m. at Andover, 22 Nov 1796, as his second wife, MOSES PLUMMER, b. at Rowley, 24 Jan 1744/5 son of Thomas and Bethiah (Tenney) Plummer. Moses was first married to Hannah Hale.

iv STEPHEN POOR, b. at Andover, 16 Feb 1763; d. at Newburyport, 17 Jul 1812; m. 1st at Andover, 25 Oct 1795, ELIZABETH DUSTIN, b. at Windham, NH, 8 Sep 1773 daughter of Peter and Betty (Sawyer) Dustin;[1348] Elizabeth d. about 1800. Stephen m. 2nd 24 Aug 1801, MARY PLUMMER, b. about 1782 (based on age at time of death); Mary d. at Andover, 2 Dec 1845. Mary married second Joseph Cummings at Andover on 19 Dec 1815.

v ENOCH POOR, b. at Andover, 20 Apr 1765; d. at Methuen, 17 Mar 1834; m. at Rowan County, NC, 1794 (bond 8 Apr 1794), PRUDENCE BREVARD, b. in NC, 4 Jan 1772 daughter of Robert and Sarah (Craig) Brevard;

1341 *Massachusetts, Essex County, Probate Records; Author: Massachusetts. Supreme Judicial Court (Essex County), Probate Records, Wood, N-Wood, S, 1828-1991*

1342 Deborah Wood described as a "single lady" daughter of Obadiah and as born at North Andover.

1343 Charlotte Helen Abbott in her notes of the Poor Family of Andover reports that Phebe died by suicide.

1344 Massachusetts Soldiers and Sailors in the Revolution, volume 12, p 562

1345 *Essex County, MA: Probate File Papers, 1638-1881.*Online database. *AmericanAncestors.org.* New England Historic Genealogical Society, 2014. Case 22391

1346 Massachusetts Land Records, Essex County, 178:280-281; 207:9-10

1347 Poor, "History of Andover, Maine"

1348 The 1825 will of Peter Dustin includes a bequest to his granddaughter Eliza Poor, now Eliza Osborne.

Prudence d. at Methuen, 29 Jul 1850. Enoch and Prudence had five children in North Carolina and the Enoch returned to Methuen where a sixth child was born.

vi CALEB POOR, b. at Andover, 28 Mar 1767; d. after 1813 (living in Morganton, NC in 1810); m. Jul 1796, POLLY MIRA AVERY, b. at Burke County, NC, 24 Aug 1779 daughter of Waightstill and Leah (Probart) Avery;[1349] Polly Mira d. at Henderson County, NC, 20 Feb 1857. Caleb and Polly divorced in 1813.[1350] Polly Mira married second Jacob Summey in 1823.

vii NANCY POOR, b. about 1771; d. at Methuen, 9 Jan 1855; m. at Methuen, 25 Oct 1797, ROBINSON FRYE, b. at Methuen, 28 May 1771 son of James and Mehitable (Robinson) Frye; Robinson d. at Methuen, 5 Dec 1816.

viii SARAH POOR, b. about 1772 (based on age 65 at time of death); d. at Andover, 16 Dec 1837; m. at Andover, 29 Sep 1825, as his third wife, ISAAC MOOAR, b. at Andover, 16 Feb 1759 son of Abraham and Lydia (Abbott) Mooar; Isaac d. at Andover, 12 Jan 1832. Isaac was first married to Sarah Abbott and second married to Lydia Cawley.

ix THOMAS POOR, baptized at Andover, 27 Mar 1774; d. at Methuen 20 Oct 1815. Thomas does not seem to have married. His estate was administered by Enoch Poor. The accounting of the estate includes costs of Enoch Poor for providing boarding, support, and a nurse for Thomas from 4 Nov 1811 through 25 oct 1815.

x SUSANNAH POOR, b. at Methuen, 14 Jan 1778; d. at Methuen, 5 Feb 1834; m. at Methuen, 17 Dec 1795, DANIEL FRYE, b. at Methuen, 7 Jun 1773 son of James and Mehitable (Robinson) Frye; Daniel d. at Methuen, 14 Oct 1837. After Susannah's death, Daniel married Phebe Carleton.

506) PELETIAH RUSSELL (*Peter Russell[4], Phebe Johnson Russell[3], Mary Holt Johnson[2], Nicholas[1]*), b. at Andover, 27 Dec 1727 son of Peter and Deborah (Crosby) Russell; d. in Nova Scotia in 1757 during the French and Indian War; m. about 1752, OLIVE MOORE, b. at Westford, 27 Dec 1729 daughter of Samuel and Deborah (Butterfield) Moore; Olive d. at Bath, NH, 11 Oct 1807. Olive m. 2nd Timothy Barron.

As a child, Peletiah went with his family to Litchfield, New Hampshire. He and his wife Olive had five children there. From 24 April 1755 to 1 November 1755, he served as a sergeant in Capt. Tash's company of Col. Blanchard's regiment which was stationed at Fort Edward. In 1757 he participated in the Crown Point expedition serving as second lieutenant in Capt. Emery's company. Peletiah was wounded near Lake George and was taking to Nova Scotia where he died of his injuries.[1351]

i REUBEN RUSSELL, b. 1 Nov 1749; d. Nov 1753.

ii OLIVE RUSSELL, b. 1751

iii PELETIAH RUSSELL, b. 1753; d. at Groton, MA, 21 Jan 1831; m. at Groton, 30 May 1780, SARAH DERUMPLE, b. at Groton, 23 Mar 1753 daughter of William and Elizabeth (Shed) Derumple; Sarah d. at Groton, 21 Apr 1795.

iv JOHN RUSSELL, b. 7 Sep 1753; d. at Richmond, VT, 26 Dec 1814; m. at Haverhill, NH, SARAH HAZELTINE, b. about 1760; Sarah d. at Burlington, VT, 26 Aug 1848.

v MOOR RUSSELL, b. 30 Oct 1757; d. at Holderness, NH, 29 Aug 1851; m. at Plymouth, NH, 23 Dec 1790, ELIZABETH WEBSTER, b. at Plymouth, NH, 8 Jul 1773 daughter of David and Elizabeth (Clough) Webster;[1352] Elizabeth d. at Holderness, 4 Jun 1839.

507) RACHEL RUSSELL (*Peter Russell[4], Phebe Johnson Russell[3], Mary Holt Johnson[2], Nicholas[1]*), b. at Andover, 1 Nov 1730 daughter of Peter and Deborah (Crosby) Russell; d. 28 Nov 1802; m. about 1747; TIMOTHY UNDERWOOD, b. about 1725 son of Joseph and Susannah (Parker) Underwood; Timothy d. at Putney, VT, about 1804.

Timothy Underwood was a captain of a company of minutemen in the regiment of Col. William Prescott. Timothy and Rachel moved their family from Westford to Putney, Vermont in 1776.[1353]

Rachel Russell and Timothy Underwood were parents of eleven children born at Westford.

i RACHEL UNDERWOOD, b. 21 May 1747; d. at Shrewsbury, 21 Dec 1810; m. at Shrewsbury, 1 Mar 1775, SAMUEL BRIGHAM, b. at Shrewsbury, 1 Jul 1741 son of John and Susannah (Fiske) Brigham; Samuel d. at Shrewsbury, 28 Feb 1836.

ii TIMOTHY UNDERWOOD, b. 15 Aug 1749; d. 30 May 1759.

1349 The 1823 will of Waightstill Avery includes a bequest to his daughter Polly Mira Poor.

1350 Insooe, Slavery and the Sectional Crisis in Western North Carolina, p 119

1351 Stearns, *Genealogical and Family History of the State of New Hampshire*, volume 2, p 732

1352 Stearns, *Genealogical and Family History of the State of New Hampshire*, volume 1, p 26

1353 Underwood, *The Underwood Families of America*, volume 1, p 50

iii JOSEPH UNDERWOOD, b. 8 Sep 1751; died young.

iv DEBORAH UNDERWOOD, b. 19 Sep 1754; d. at Putney, VT, Dec 1840; m. at Shrewsbury, 24 Jun 1773, ABNER MILES, b. at Shrewsbury, 12 Jan 1744/5 son of Joseph and Jemima (Lee) Miles; Abner d. at Putney, 1803.

v JOSEPH UNDERWOOD, b. 1 Aug 1757; d. at Putney, VT, 30 May 1818; m. at Putney, 4 Oct 1781, ELIZABETH REYNOLDS, b. Dec 1758 daughter of Grindall and Sarah (Searle) Reynolds; Elizabeth d. at Putney, Oct 1817.

vi TIMOTHY UNDERWOOD, b. 30 Nov 1759; d. at Northborough, MA, 18 Dec 1824; m. at Shrewsbury, 6 Aug 1791, MARY "POLLY" ADAMS, b. at Shrewsbury, 12 Sep 1761 daughter of Jonathan and Hephzibah (Baker) Adams;[1354] Mary d. at Northborough, 13 Sep 1805. Timothy m. 2nd at Northborough, MA, 26 Jul 1807, Polly's sister, HEPHZIBAH ADAMS, b. at Shrewsbury, 20 Nov 1768; Hephzibah d. at Northborough, 2 Jan 1814.

vii SUSANNA UNDERWOOD, b. 6 May 1762; m. at Putney, VT, 31 Jul 1785, JOHN MOORE

viii PHINEAS UNDERWOOD, b. 18 Mar 1764; d. at Virginia, IL, 2 Apr 1843; m. SARAH who has not been identified.

ix RUSSELL UNDERWOOD, b. 16 Aug 1766; m. at Shrewsbury, 1 Jan 1789, ELIZABETH "BETTY" ALLEN, b. at Shrewsbury, 13 Mar 1765 daughter of Elnathan and Thankful (Hastings) Allen.[1355]

x MARY "MOLLY" UNDERWOOD, b. 10 Aug 1768; d. at Shrewsbury, 6 Oct 1789; m. 20 Dec 1786, HUMPHREY BIGELOW, b. at Shrewsbury, 4 Sep 1761 son of Samuel and Phebe (Rand) Bigelow; Humphrey d. at Shrewsbury, 2 Oct 1842. Humphrey married second Hannah Whipple.

xi JAMES UNDERWOOD, b. 7 Mar 1771; d. at Swanzey, NH, 4 Feb 1832; m. at Westmoreland, NH, 25 Apr 1793, HANNAH AMSBURY, b. at Westmoreland, 30 Jun 1775 daughter of Israel and Anna (-) Amsbury; Hannah d. at Rockingham, VT, 22 Jan 1809.

508) PHEBE RUSSELL (*Peter Russell*[4]*, Phebe Johnson Russell*[3]*, Mary Holt Johnson*[2]*, Nicholas*[1]), b. at Andover, 16 May 1736 daughter of Peter and Deborah (Crosby) Russell; d. at Goffstown, NH, Nov 1836; m. 1st about 1752, JOHN BUTTERFIELD, b. at Chelmsford, 20 Feb 1731 son of John and Anne (Hildreth) Butterfield; John d. at Goffstown, 1765. Phebe m. 2nd, 774, SAMUEL ROBIE, b. at Hampton, NH, 17 Oct 1717 son of Ichabod and Sarah (Cass) Robie; Samuel d. at Goffstown, 18 Oct 1793. Samuel was first married to Mary Perkins.

John and Phebe settled in Goffstown, New Hampshire and they were parents of five children. John Butterfield died of wounds he received when accidentally shot at a blacksmith shop.[1356] Phebe remarried to Samuel Robie who was a widower. Phebe and Samuel were in Goffstown by 1779, and their homestead was on what became known as Robie Hill. Samuel served as selectman and served on a committee to formulate a plan of government.[1357]

Phebe Russell and John Butterfield were parents of five children.

i JOHN BUTTERFIELD, b. at Litchfield, 7 Sep 1753; d. at New Boston, NH, 10 Oct 1828, m. about 1772, NAOMI STEVENS, b. at Plaistow, 24 Oct 1751 daughter of Thomas and Prudence (Merrill) Stevens; Naomi d. at Goffstown, 9 Jan 1816.

ii PETER BUTTERFIELD, b. 22 Dec 1754; d. at Goffstown, 22 Oct 1838; m. 1st at Goffstown, 1 Oct 1776, HANNAH GUY who died at Goffstown, 1803. Peter m. 2nd 19 Aug 1810, RACHEL RICHARDS (widow of David Greer), b. 1767 daughter of Benjamin and Susannah (Eaton) Richards; Rachel d. at Goffstown, 21 Oct 1851.

iii SARAH BUTTERFIELD, b. 1758; d. at Goffstown, 2 Sep 1850; m. at Goffstown, 21 Dec 1785, ELIPHALET RICHARDS, b. at Goffstown, 1761 son of Benjamin and Susannah (Eaton) Richards; Eliphalet d. 8 Oct 1846.

iv PHEBE BUTTERFIELD, b. 1760; d. 1839 at unknown location;[1358] m. 9 Dec 1779, NATHANIEL GLIDDEN, b. at Exeter, 1747 son of Nathaniel and Anna (Lord) Glidden; Nathaniel d. at Chester, NH, 26 Apr 1814.

v DEBORAH BUTTERFIELD, b. at Goffstown, 11 Jan 1762; d. at Goffstown, 11 Sep 1840; m. at Goffstown, 25 Dec 1781, JONATHAN BELL, b. at Pelham, 23 Apr 1755 son of William and Abigail (Kittredge) Bell; Jonathan d. at Goffstown, 10 Jun 1844.

Phebe Russell and Samuel Robie were parents of three children

[1354] The 1801 will of Jonathan Adams of Shrewsbury includes a bequest to his daughter Mary Underwood.

[1355] The 1800 will of Elnathan Allen of Shrewsbury includes a bequest to his daughter Betty Underwood.

[1356] Hadley, *History of the Town of Goffstown*, p 61

[1357] Hadley, *History of the Town of Goffstown*, p 433

[1358] The Butterfield cemetery monument notes Phebe wife of Nathaniel Glidden as living 1760-1839 but location of her death is unknown.

i SAMUEL ROBIE, b. 1777; d. at Goffstown, 8 Jul 1865; m. DEBORAH MOORE, b. 27 Mar 1776 daughter of Abraham and Esther (Walker) Moore; Deborah d. at Manchester, NH, 8 May 1868.

ii THOMAS R. ROBIE, b. at Goffstown, 1779; d. at Goffstown, 12 Sep 1811; m. at Goffstown, 8 Feb 1803, RACHEL BARRON, b. at Merrimack, NH, 25 Feb 1776 daughter of William and Rebecca (Fassett) Barron; Rachel d. 23 April 1839.

iii MARY ROBIE, b. at Goffstown, 1782; d. at Goffstown, 22 Mar 1829; m. BENJAMIN WALKER PATTEE, b. 9 Jun 1781 son of John and Mary (Hadley) Pattee; Benjamin d. 17 Nov 1849.

508a) PETER RUSSELL (*Peter Russell*[4], *Phebe Johnson Russell*[3], *Mary Holt Johnson*[2], *Nicholas*[1]), b. at Litchfield, NH, 6 Aug 1738 son of Peter and Deborah (Crosby) Russell; d. at Peeling (later Woodstock), NH, 20 Aug 1815; m. about 1760, MEHITABLE STILES, b. at Middleton, MA, 10 Jun 1739 daughter of Caleb and Sarah (Walton) Stiles; Mehitable d. at Peeling, NH, 27 May 1811.

Peter and Mehitable settled in Lyndeborough where was Mehitable was admitted as a church member in 1780. It is believed that Peter served in the same company as his brother Peletiah Russell during the French and Indian War.[1359] He is likely the Peter Russell of Lyndeborough who did "half a turn" of service as sergeant during the Revolution for the Ticonderoga campaign in 1776.[1360]

Peter and Mehitable were parents of seven children including an unnamed infant who died soon after birth.[1361]

i PETER RUSSELL, d. about age 24 without marrying

ii SARAH RUSSELL, b. estimate 1763; *perhaps* the Sally Bickford who d. at Dover, NH, Mar 1850 at age 90;[1362] m. at Amherst, 17 Aug 1786, JOSIAH BICKFORD. No records of children were located.

iii MEHITABLE RUSSELL, b. 20 Jan 1768; d. at Charleston, ME, 4 Feb 1848; m. 1st at Amherst, 27 Nov 1788, STEPHEN KITTREDGE, b. at Tewksbury, 27 Jun 1765 son of Solomon and Tabitha (Ingalls) Kittredge; Stephen d. at Hancock, NH, 16 Oct 1806. Mehitable m. 2nd, 17 Sep 1811, DANIEL BICKFORD, b. 13 Feb 1765 son of Edmond and Elizabeth (Clough) Bickford; Daniel d. at Charleston, ME, 22 Mar 1834.

iv JOSEPH RUSSELL, b. about 1770; d. at Peeling, NH, about 1826; m. about 1795, MARY ROBBINS, b. at Plymouth, NH, about 1770 daughter of Jonathan and Mary (Fletcher) Robbins; Mary d. at Woodstock, NH, 17 Mar 1844. Mary married second John Gray on 14 Oct 1827.

v BETSEY RUSSELL, b. about 1776; d. at Hancock, NH, 21 Nov 1843; m. at Peeling, NH, 7 Feb 1805, ASA SIMONDS, b. at Groton, MA, 5 Apr 1776 son of Joseph and Mehitable (Cummings) Simonds; Asa d. at Hancock, 18 Jul 1858. Asa married Clarissa Newell on 7 May 1845.

vi MARY "POLLY" RUSSELL; b. estimate 1780; d. about 1835; m. at Woodstock, NH, 9 Mar 1809, Col. JOHN PALMER, b. at Salisbury, NH, 26 Dec 1783 son of Dudley and Rebecca (Pingry) Palmer; John d. at Meredith, NH, 8 Mar 1861.[1363] John Palmer married second Betsey *Cate* Batchelder in 1837. Mary Russell and John Palmer were parents of four children.

509) DEBORAH RUSSELL (*Peter Russell*[4], *Phebe Johnson Russell*[3], *Mary Holt Johnson*[2], *Nicholas*[1]), b. at Litchfield, NH, 3 Jun 1740 daughter of Peter and Deborah (Crosby) Russell; d. at Merrimack, NH, 9 Sep 1820; m. about 1758, JONATHAN CUMMINGS, b. at Dunstable, 5 Jun 1729 son of Jonathan and Elizabeth (Blanchard) Cummings; Jonathan d. at Merrimack, 10 Jul 1787.

Deborah and Jonathan resided in Merrimack, New Hampshire where Jonathan filled numerous civic duties such as fence viewer, field driver, constable, and surveyor of highways.[1364]

Deborah Russell and Jonathan Cummings were parents of sixteen children born at Merrimack, New Hampshire.[1365]

i JONATHAN CUMMINGS, b. 4 Mar 1759; m. at Merrimack, 28 Jun 1785, LYDIA HILLS, b. at Merrimack, 13 Jul 1761 daughter of Ebenezer and Elizabeth (-) Hills.

[1359] Stearns, *History of Plymouth, New Hampshire*, volume 2, p 594

[1360] Donovan, *History of Lyndeborough*, p 199

[1361] Stearns, *History of Plymouth, New Hampshire*, volume 2, p 594

[1362] New Hampshire State Library; Concord, New Hampshire; U.S. Census Mortality Schedules, New Hampshire, 1850-1880; Archive Roll Number: 3; Census Year: 1850; Census Place: Dover, Strafford, New Hampshire

[1363] This is a marriage reported in the History of Plymouth. However, the marriage is in 1809 and that would be a relatively late marriage for Mary. On the other hand, there are only four children in this family all born before 1817. The death records for at least two of the children of John and Mary Palmer give mother's place of birth as Lyndeborough which would fit for Mary in this family.

[1364] Merrimack Historical Society, History of Merrimack, New Hampshire, p 226

[1365] The three youngest children are given in Mooar's *Cummings Memorial*, pp 58-59.

ii DEBORAH CUMMINGS, b. 14 Jun 1761; m. at Merrimack, 12 Apr 1781, JAMES COOMBS, b. at Merrimack, 5 Jul 1760 son of John and Margaret (Alld) Coombs.

iii SYBIL CUMMINGS, b. 8 May 1763; d. at Merrimack, 17 Apr 1811; m. at Merrimack, 12 Oct 1783, as the second of his three wives, SAMUEL BARRON, b. at Bedford, NH, 26 Feb 1757 son of Moses and Lucy (Parker) Barron; Samuel d. at Merrimack, 3 Oct 1836. Lt. Samuel Barron was first married to Mary Arbuckle and third married to Jenny Moore.

iv THOMAS CUMMINGS, b. 15 Dec 1764; d. at White Pigeon, MI, 28 Nov 1838; m. 25 Oct 1792, as her second husband, ANNA GIBSON (widow of Samuel May), b. at Lyme, 1769 daughter of Samuel and Elizabeth (Stewart) Gibson;[1366] Anna d. at Hinesburg, VT, 3 Sep 1845.

v REBECCA CUMMINGS, b. 28 Sep 1767; d. 13 Jun 1782.

vi SUSANNAH CUMMINGS, b. 7 Sep 1768; m. 7 Jan 1793, JOHN STACY. There are records for births of two children of Susannah and John born at Poland, Maine. Their son John settled in Minot, Maine.

vii JENNE CUMMINGS, b. 30 Sep 1770; d. 6 Sep 1775.

viii ELIZABETH CUMMINGS, b. 12 Sep 1772; d. at Waterville, ME, 8 Feb 1858.[1367] Elizabeth did not marry. In 1850, she was living with her sister Rebecca and her husband Stephen Benson.

ix JOSEPH CUMMINGS, b. 29 Mar 1774; d. 16 May 1774.

x BENJAMIN CUMMINGS, b. 29 Mar 1774; d. 24 May 1774.

xi RACHEL CUMMINGS, b. 12 May 1775

xii CYRUS CUMMINGS, b. 21 May 1777; d. at Newport, VT, 11 Feb 1858; m. ABIGAIL DAVIS, b. at Poland, ME, 17 Nov 1780 daughter of Moses and Olive (Bodwell) Davis;[1368] Abigail d. at Newport, 9 Feb 1854.

xiii MARY CUMMINGS, b. 2 Jun 1779; d. at Merrimack, 3 Mar 1830; m. 26 Mar 1823, Dr. ABEL GOODRICH, b. at Lunenburg, MA, 19 Sep 1761 son of Philip and Jane (Boynton) Goodrich;[1369] Abel d. at Merrimack, 12 Jan 1841.

xiv SARAH CUMMINGS, b. 1781; m. by 1799, JOSIAH HODGMAN, b. at Merrimack, 28 Jan 1778 son of Josiah and Rebecca (Foster) Hodgman.

xv REBECCA CUMMINGS, b. 6 Apr 1783; d. at Waterville, ME, 14 Dec 1857; m. Dec 1800, STEPHEN BENSON, b. at Middleborough, 8 Jun 1777 son of Ichabod and Abigail (Griffith) Benson;[1370] Stephen d. at Waterville, 27 Aug 1852.

xvi RUTH W. CUMMINGS, b. 13 Jul 1785

510) JAMES RUSSELL (*Peter Russell[4], Phebe Johnson Russell[3], Mary Holt Johnson[2], Nicholas[1]*), b. at Litchfield, 31 May 1746 son of Peter and Deborah (Crosby) Russell; d. at Belpre, OH, 1821; m. 1st about 1774, MARY FRENCH, b. at Dunstable, NH, 18 Oct 1755 daughter of Benjamin and Mary (Lovewell) French; Mary d. at Woodstock, VT, about 1790. James m. 2nd at Ross, OH, 9 Aug 1814 the widow JUDAH O'NEAL.

James Russell enlisted for military service on 28 April 1775 with the rank of second lieutenant. He later achieved the rank of captain in Colonel Brooks's regiment. After the war, the family moved from Litchfield, New Hampshire to Woodstock, Vermont. Mary died there about 1790. After Mary's death, James went to Ohio where his older sons had settled.[1371]

The children of James and Mary are not well documented. There are three known sons and perhaps a fourth. There were perhaps two daughters in this family, but no certain information has been found for them. The three likely sons are given here.

i ROBERT RUSSELL, b. likely at Litchfield, 30 Jan 1782; d. at Columbus, OH, 28 Apr 1860; m. about 1808, MARY ANN KEAN, b. in VA, about 1792; Mary Ann d. at Columbus, 7 Jul 1850.

ii JAMES RUSSELL, b. about 1785; d. at Ross County, OH, about 1819; m. at Ross County, 27 Apr 1813, as her second husband, SOPHIA PARMENTER, b. 9 Oct 1793 daughter of Artemus and Lucy (Grant) Parmenter; Sophia d. at Ross County, 9 Dec 1845. Sophia was first married to Abiasher Rogers about 1809 and third married to Thomas Bradford on 5 Jul 1820.

1366 The 1811 will (probate 1823) of Samuel Gibson of Merrimack includes a bequest to his daughter Anna Cummings.

1367 Maine, Nathan Hale Cemetery Collection, 1780-1980

1368 NEHGR, Early Vital Records of Poland, Maine, 1934, vol 88, p 60

1369 Cunningham, *History of the Town of Lunenburg*, volume E-H, p 313

1370 NEHGR, Early Vital Records of Poland, Maine, 1934, vol 88, p 155

1371 DAR, *Ohio Early State and Local History*, p 180

iii FREDERICK AUGUSTUS RUSSELL, b. 13 Mar 1787; d. at Vevay, IN, 30 Apr 1866; m. 1st at Newburyport, MA, 28 Nov 1810, ANNA BARTLETT who died about 1814. Frederick m. 2nd at Washington, DC, 13 May 1815, THEODOSIA GUSTINE, b. at Culpepper, VA, 1792 daughter of Joel Trumbull and Anne (Greene) Gustine; Theodisia d. at Washington, 25 Jul 1828. Frederick m. 3rd 10 Mar 1846, ANTOINETTE DEROLODS, b. in Spain, about 1827. Antoinette d. at Vevay, 1 Sep 1898.

511) THOMAS RUSSELL (*Joseph Russell4, Phebe Johnson Russell3, Mary Holt Johnson2, Nicholas1*), b. at Andover, 5 Jun 1732 son of Joseph and Hepsibah (Eaton) Russell; d. at Wilton, 30 Mar 1818; m. at Andover, 15 May 1760, his second cousin, BETHIAH HOLT (*Ephraim4, Henry3, Henry2, Nicholas1*), b. at Andover, 20 Mar 1743 daughter of Ephraim and Phebe (Russell) Holt; Bethiah d. at Wilton, 20 Aug 1817.

Thomas and Bethiah started their family in Andover and relocated to Wilton in 1769. They were parents of eleven children.

i BETHIAH RUSSELL, b. at Andover, 20 Apr 1761; d. 25 Apr 1761.

ii BETHIAH RUSSELL, b. at Andover, 7 Jan 1763; d. likely at Dublin, NH, after 1820; m. 1st at Wilton, 18 Apr 1782, DANIEL SIMONDS; Daniel d. at Dublin, about 1805. Bethiah m. 2nd at Dublin, 5 Jan 1809, DRURY MORSE, b. at Holliston, MA, 16 Aug 1757 son of Micah and Mary (Fairbanks) Morse; Drury d. at Dublin, 16 Nov 1820. Drury was first married to Mary Adams.

iii THOMAS RUSSELL, b. at Andover, 5 Jun 1765; d. at Temple, ME, 9 Jul 1863; m. 10 Feb 1789, his fourth cousin once removed, LYDIA ABBOTT (*Lydia Stevens Abbott5, Lydia Gray Stevens4, Edward Gray3, Hannah Holt Gray2, Nicholas1*), b. at Wilton, 1 May 1771 daughter of Jacob and Lydia (Stevens) Abbott; Lydia d. at Temple, 20 Jun 1855.

iv HANNAH RUSSELL, b. at Andover, 23 Sep 1767; d. at Weld, ME, Nov 1850; m. at Wilton, 23 Aug 1787, her first cousin, JAMES HOUGHTON (*Phebe Holt Houghton5, Ephraim4, Henry3, Henry2, Nicholas1*), b. at Andover, 16 Jun 1756 son of James and Phebe (Holt) Houghton; James d. at Weld, 21 Dec 1835.

v DANIEL RUSSELL, b. at Andover, 7 Nov 1769; d. at Wilton, 3 Jan 1841; m. at Wilton, 25 Nov 1794, ELIZABETH DASCOMB, b. at Wilton, 20 Jan 1771 daughter of James and Elizabeth (Farrington) Dascomb; Elizabeth d. at Wilton, 18 Oct 1852.

vi PHEBE RUSSELL, b. at Wilton, 13 Sep 1772; d. at Weld, ME, 13 Sep 1852; m. about 1811, DAVID BARRETT, b. at Mason, NH, 1782 son of Reuben and Sarah (Fletcher) Barrett; David d. at Weld, 12 Feb 1864.

vii MOLLY RUSSELL, b. at Wilton, 4 Jun 1775; d. at Peterborough, NH, 4 Jun 1864; m. 1st at Wilton, 20 Dec 1804, THOMAS EATON, b. about 1775; Thomas d. at Wilton, Aug 1812. Molly m. 2nd 4 Feb 1817, as his second wife, SAMUEL EDES, b. at Needham, MA, 15 Oct 1753 son of Nathan and Sarah (-) Edes; Samuel d. at Peterborough, 10 Jul 1846.

viii ABEL RUSSELL, b. at Wilton, 5 Feb 1778; d. at Weld, ME, 10 Jun 1859; m. at Royalston, MA, 2 Jan 1806, NANCY CLEMENT, b. at Petersham, MA, 2 Sep 1780 daughter of Thomas and Mary (Smith) Clement; Nancy d. at Weld, 25 Feb 1862.

ix JOSEPH RUSSELL, b. at Wilton, 6 May 1780; d. at Weld, ME, 28 Jun 1858; m. 1st about 1802, HANNAH DASCOMB, b. at Wilton, about 1779 daughter of James and Elizabeth (Farrington) Dascomb;[1372] Hannah d. at Weld, 17 Dec 1806. Joseph m. 2nd 8 Jan 1809, his fourth cousin, SARAH HOLT (*Simeon5, Joseph4, Timothy3, James2, Nicholas1*), b. at Wilton, 21 Sep 1780 daughter of Simeon and Mary (Dale) Holt; Sarah d. at Weld, 13 Mar 1857.

x EPHRAIM RUSSELL, b. at Wilton, 16 Jul 1783; d. at Readfield, ME, 3 Dec 1875; m. 6 Apr 1809, REBECCA IRELAND, b. at Canaan, ME, 1789 daughter of Abraham and Betsey (Wyman) Ireland; Rebecca d. at Weld, ME, 2 Apr 1833.

xi ASENATH RUSSELL, b. at Wilton, 31 May 1786; d. at Weld, ME, 17 May 1868. Asenath did not marry.

512) HEPHZIBAH RUSSELL (*Joseph Russell4, Phebe Johnson Russell3, Mary Holt Johnson2, Nicholas1*), baptized at Andover, 30 Jun 1734 daughter of Joseph and Hepsibah (Eaton) Russell; m. at Andover, 26 Feb 1756, her first cousin once removed, JOSEPH RUSSELL, b. at Andover, 8 Jan 1719/20 son of John and Sarah (Chandler) Russell; Joseph d. at Andover, 31 Aug 1783.

[1372] Cunningham, *History of Lunenburg*, volume A-D, p 178

Joseph Russell did not leave a will and his estate entered probate 4 November 1783 with widow Hephzibah as administratrix.[1373] Personal estate was valued at £97.1.10. No real estate was listed in the inventory, but the personal inventory included carpentry and wheelwright tools.

The births of seven children are recorded at Andover, and marriages can be confirmed for two of the children both of whom settled in Bethel, Maine.

i HEPHZIBAH RUSSELL, b. 18 Jun 1756

ii JOSEPH RUSSELL, b. 8 Jul 1758

iii SIMEON RUSSELL (twin), b. 24 Jul 1761

iv HANNAH RUSSELL (twin), b. 27 Jul 1761

v LYDIA RUSSELL, b. at Andover, 17 May 1764; d. at Bethel, ME, 12 Sep 1847; m. 7 Jun 1787, her third cousin once removed, JOHN HOLT (*Humphrey[4], Humphrey[3], Henry[2], Nicholas[1]*), b. at Andover, 12 May 1764 son of Humphrey and Mary (Holton) Holt; John d. at Bethel, 16 Jul 1830. Lydia Russell and John Holt are Family 792.

vi ELIJAH RUSSELL, b. 1 Nov 1768. There is an Elijah Russell who was a printer in Concord, NH who married Polly Davis, but it is not clear that this is that Elijah.

vii CHANDLER RUSSELL, b. at Andover, 20 Sep 1775; d. at Bethel, ME, 8 Jun 1846; m. at Bethel, 14 Dec 1803, BETSEY DUSTON, b. 12 Jul 1782 daughter of Jesse and Elizabeth (Swan) Duston; Betsey d. after 1850 when she was living in Bethel.

513) JONATHAN RUSSELL (*Joseph Russell[4], Phebe Johnson Russell[3], Mary Holt Johnson[2], Nicholas[1]*), b. at Andover, 14 Oct 1749 son of Joseph and Hannah (Perkins) Russell; d. after 1820 when he was living in Pamelia; m. at Middleton, 17 Jan 1771, RUTH HUTCHINSON, baptized 16 Sep 1750 daughter of Josiah and Sarah (Dean) Hutchinson; Ruth d. after 1820.

Jonathan and Ruth married and started their family in Middleton where Ruth's family lived. Three children were born in Middleton, and they then relocated to Wendell where their remaining children were born. Jonathan and Ruth remained in Wendell until 2 January 1816 when they sold "the farm on which I now live" consisting of about 75 acres to Fester Foster of Petersham for $450.[1374] They were then in Pamelia, Jefferson County, New York where several of their children were also located. In the 1820 census, Jonathan Russell above age 45 with one female above age 45 were living in Pamelia. Living next to them was son James and his young family. Nearby were daughter Hannah and her husband Stephen Farr and daughter Rachel and her husband Curtis Goulding.[1375] Daughter Phebe and her husband Reuben Locke also settled in Pamelia.

Jonathan and Ruth were parents of eleven children.[1376]

i JOSEPH RUSSELL, b. at Middleton, 19 Jul 1771; d. at Alexandria, NY (burial Orleans Four Corners), 23 Oct 1853; m. at Montague, MA, 1 Apr 1795, POLLY W. BENJAMIN, b. likely at Hardwick, MA, 1775 daughter of Abel and Susannah (Carpenter) Benjamin; Polly d. after 1850 when she and Joseph were living with their daughter and son-in-law in Alexandria.

ii BETSY RUSSELL (twin), b. at Middleton, 18 Sep 1773; d. after 1870 when she was living (age 97) at the home of her son Lyman in Pamelia, NY; m. at Warren, MA, 1 Dec 1796, ROBERT WHITE, b. at Warren, MA, 26 May 1774 son of William and Janet (Marr) White; Robert d. at Pamelia, 30 Oct 1851.

iii RUTH RUSSELL (twin), b. at Middleton, 18 Sep 1773; d. at Wendell, 2 Aug 1790.

iv SARAH RUSSELL, b. at Wendell, 7 Feb 1780

v HANNAH RUSSELL, b. at Wendell, 3 Jan 1782; m. at Wendell, 18 Feb 1806, STEPHEN FARR, b. 14 Aug 1781 son of Stephen and Lois (Randall) Farr; Stephen d. at Clayton, NY, 1874 (probate 23 Mar 1874). It is not clear when Hannah died, but Stephen has at least one additional wife with children born in 1837 and 1839.

vi RACHEL RUSSELL, b. at Wendell, 17 Oct 1783; d. at Pamelia, 21 Mar 1871; m. at Wendell, 1805, CURTIS GOULDING, b. at Holliston, MA, 10 Aug 1776 son of Joseph and Kezia (Parker) Goulding; Curtis d. at Pamelia, 10 Jul 1857.

vii PHEBE RUSSELL, b. at Wendell, 19 Oct 1785; d. at Pamelia, NY, 27 Jan 1856; m. at Wendell, 28 Jan 1805, REUBEN LOCKE, b. at Shutesbury, MA, 6 Apr 1783 son of Ebenezer and Hannah (Randall) Locke; Reuben d. at Pamelia, 30 Oct 1855.

[1373] *Essex County, MA: Probate File Papers, 1638-1881.*Online database. *AmericanAncestors.org.* New England Historic Genealogical Society, 2014. Case 24406

[1374] Massachusetts Land Records, 1620-1986, Franklin County, Deed 1815-1816 volume 35, pp 517-519

[1375] 1820 U S Census; Census Place: Pamelia, Jefferson, New York; Page: 456; NARA Roll: M33_72; Image: 248

[1376] Vital Records of Wendell, 1760-1896, p 33 and p 262; accessed through familysearch.org

viii JONATHAN RUSSELL, b. at Wendell, 12 Sep 1786; d. 30 Jul 1808.

ix Son twin b. and d. 30 Nov 1790

x Daughter twin b. and d. 30 Nov 1790

xi JAMES RUSSELL, b. at Wendell, 27 Jul 1793; d. after 1870 when he was living in Pea Ridge, IL at the home of his daughter Harriet and her husband; m. MINERVA who has not been identified.

514) SARAH RUSSELL (*Joseph Russell[4], Phebe Johnson Russell[3], Mary Holt Johnson[2], Nicholas[1]*), b. at Andover, 29 Oct 1750 daughter of Joseph and Hannah (Perkins) Russell; d. at Middleton, MA, 2 Jan 1844; m. at Middleton, 12 Aug 1772, NEHEMIAH WILKINS, b. at Middleton, 14 Aug 1752 son of Ichabod and Mary (Clark) Wilkins; Nehemiah d. at Middleton, 17 Jun 1811.

Nehemiah Wilkins served in the Revolution as a private in the company of Capt. Stephen Wilkins from 1 July 1776 to 7 January 1777. In 1837, Sarah applied for and received a widow's pension.

In September 1776, Nehemiah wrote the following letter to Sarah from Camp Ticonderoga: "Dear wife and parents and all ther friends I take this my opportunity to inform you of my Estate hoping thes Lines will find you and our Children and my parents and all other of my friends well through the Goodness of god. I my Self have been very poorley but I am betor so I leave our fetague is Very Hard so that wee cant Hardly get time to cook. It is very sickly, There was to of men fired on by the Ingines yesterday between ground pint and Ticonderoga but made there Escape with out being hurt there was a party of Ingines seen by the mils and wee espect the Regulers very. Out alowans is very poore sum times half a pund of meat and a pound and a half of bread and sum times a pound of meat and one pound of bread no saus nor no pint only when upon fetague then we have half a glas of rum, Rum is one doler per quart shugar and cheas two shillings per pound. I beg you to write to me so send said to ware receive this. I still remain your Loving Husband till Deth shall part, Nehemiah Wilkins."

On 26 September 1776, Sarah wrote this letter to her husband: "Thes lines comes with my love to you hoping that by the blessing of God that tha will find you in good health as has left me and the children and I shall be glad that you would come home when your time is oute, and your father and mother is well and all your friends so nomore at prissent but I remain your faithful wife, Sary Wilkins."[1377]

On 21 February 1803, Nehemiah Wilkins conveyed to Nehemiah Wilkins, Jr., mariner, a tract of land in Middleton consisting of seven and one-half acres for $175.[1378] On 15 April 1806, Nehemiah Wilkins, for $480, conveyed to Ephraim Wilkins the farm in Middleton with buildings. For an additional $228.32, Nehemiah sold to Ephraim a lengthy list of household items and tools including four beds, thirteen chairs, kitchen items, axe, and two candlesticks.[1379]

Sarah Russell and Nehemiah Wilkins were parents of ten children born at Middleton.

i SARAH WILKINS, b. 18 Mar 1774; d. likely at Danvers, 1816;[1380] m. likely 15 Mar 1804, EBENEZER GOODHUE, b. at Bradford, 20 Mar 1783 son of Phineas and Hannah (Parsons) Goodhue; Ebenezer d. at Middleton, 20 Mar 1843. Ebenezer married second Sarah's sister Mary.

ii LUCY WILKINS, b. 20 Oct 1775; d. at Topsfield, 9 Dec 1868; m. at Middleton, 20 May 1802, MOSES PERKINS, b. at Topsfield, 21 Aug 1775 son of Oliver and Lucy (Gould) Perkins; Moses d. at Topsfield, 18 Oct 1858.

iii ABIGAIL WILKINS, b. 7 Sep 1777; d. at Middleton, 8 May 1806; m. at Middleton, 13 May 1798, JOSEPH WRIGHT, b. about 1770; Joseph d. at Middleton, 5 Nov 1836.

iv NEHEMIAH WILKINS, b. 16 Dec 1779; likely the mariner Nehemiah lost at sea, Nov 1803. "Nehemiah, mariner in the schooner Friendship, sailed from Winyan, Nov. —, 1803, lost at sea, ____. P. R. 82."

v EPHRAIM WILKINS, b. 13 Sep 1781; d. at Middleton, 22 Feb 1827; m. at Middleton, 6 Apr 1806, HANNAH DIXEY, baptized at Marblehead, 8 Jul 1787 daughter of Richard and Rebecca (Homan) Dixey; Hannah d. at Middleton, 4 Sep 1831.

vi MARY WILKINS, b. 31 Oct 1783; d. at Middleton, 7 Mar 1861; m. at Middleton, 28 Sep 1816, EBENEZER GOODHUE (see sister Sarah above).

vii JAMES WILKINS, b. 1 Nov 1785; d. at Middleton, 23 Jul 1875; m. 1 May 1817, BETSEY WILKINS, b. at Middleton, 21 Jan 1793 daughter of Samuel and Sarah (Fuller) Wilkins;[1381] Betsey d. at Middleton, 21 Jun 1872.

viii ROBERT CLARK WILKINS, b. 5 Mar 1788; d. at Middleton, 21 Aug 1827. Robert does not seem to have married.

1377 Revolutionary War Pension and Bounty-Land Warrant Application Files, Case W26086. The two letters are included in the pension application file.

1378 Massachusetts Land Records, Essex County, 171:180

1379 Massachusetts Land Records, Essex County, 177:213; 177:214

1380 U.S., Newspaper Extractions from the Northeast, 1704-1930

1381 The names of Betsey's parents are given as Samuel Wilkins and Sarah Fuller on her death record.

ix NANCY WILKINS, b. 18 Mar 1790; d. at Danvers, 26 Aug 1874; m. at Middleton, 22 Oct 1812, WILLIAM GIFFORD, b. at Danvers, 27 Feb 1784 son of William and Lydia (Putnam) Gifford; William d. at Middleton, 2 Jan 1849.

x JESSE WILKINS, b. 8 Mar 1792; d. at Middleton, 27 Jan 1827; m. at Middleton, 10 Oct 1810, PEGGY PEABODY, b. 14 Dec 1791 daughter of Benjamin and Hannah (Black) Peabody; Peggy d. at Middleton, 21 Dec 1840.

515) JAMES RUSSELL (*Joseph Russell[4], Phebe Johnson Russell[3], Mary Holt Johnson[2], Nicholas[1]*), b. at Andover, 7 Jan 1753 son of Joseph and Hannah (Perkins) Russell; d. at Boxford, 24 Apr 1830; m. about 1782, REBECCA PEABODY, b. at Middleton, 24 Mar 1763 daughter of Joseph and Mary (-) Peabody; Rebecca d. at Middleton, 11 Oct 1844.

James and Rebecca started their family in Middleton but moved to Boxford in 1784. In 1824, James conveyed the homestead farm to his sons Perkins and Peabody.[1382]

James Russell and Rebecca Peabody were parents of eleven children, the oldest child born at Middleton and the remainder at Boxford.

i JOSEPH RUSSELL, b. 14 Mar 1783; d. at Lyndeborough, NH, 14 Mar 1827; m. at Lyndeborough, 13 Jan 1805, NAOMI WILKINS, b. at Amherst, NH, 16 May 1783 daughter of Aaron and Lydia (Smith) Wilkins; Naomi d. at Lyndeborough, 2 Jun 1869.[1383]

ii REBECCA RUSSELL, b. 14 Apr 1785; d. at Londonderry, about 1811 (husband's remarriage); m. at Londonderry, 21 May 1804, ELIJAH DWINELL. Elijah married Emilia Eastman on 7 Mar 1812.

iii JAMES RUSSELL, b. 4 Oct 1787; d. of cholera at Lowell, 5 Sep 1849; m. at Lyndeborough, 18 Aug 1816, HANNAH PEABODY, b. at Middleton, 6 Feb 1793 daughter of Nathaniel and Ruth (Elliott) Peabody; Hannah d. at Lowell, 12 Feb 1881.

iv PERKINS RUSSELL, b. 2 Dec 1789; d. at Boxford, 14 Aug 1857; m. at Salem, 27 Aug 1848, ANN PERKINS who has not been identified. Perkins married late in life and did not have children. At the probate, widow Ann stated he had no issue and she was the only one entitled to the estate. Although married, Perkins and Ann were not living together in either the 1850 or the 1855 census at which time Perkins was living with other relatives.

v PEABODY RUSSELL, b. 2 Dec 1789; d. at Boxford, 14 Aug 1846; m. at Middleton, 17 Jan 1817, DOLLY KENNEY, b. at Middleton, 6 Nov 1785 daughter of Archelaus and Elizabeth (-) Kenney; Dolly d. at Boxford, 1 Jul 1845.

vi POLLY RUSSELL, b. 15 Apr 1792; d. at North Reading, 11 Oct 1884; m. at Middleton, 30 Oct 1813, FRANCIS PEABODY, b. at Middleton, 12 Feb 1793 son of Francis and Lucy (Masury) Peabody; Francis d. at Middleton, 16 Feb 1866.

vii ALMOODY RUSSELL, b. 25 Apr 1794; nothing further found.

viii DANIEL RUSSELL, b. 15 Oct 1796; d. at Boxford, 1819.

ix SAMUEL RUSSELL, b. 27 May 1799; d. at Salem, 19 Apr 1831; m. at Salem, 26 May 1822, LYDIA BRIDGES PICKETT, b. at Rowley, 14 May 1798 daughter of Benjamin Scudder and Sarah (Bridges) Pickett; Lydia d. at Boston, 18 Apr 1841.

x IRA RUSSELL, b. 21 Apr 1802; d. at Manchester, NH, 1 Mar 1859; m. at Lowell, 14 Nov 1831, MARY JANE ALLEN, b. 1809; Mary Jane d. at Manchester, 3 Apr 1883.

xi PETER RUSSELL, b. 3 Oct 1805; d. at Danvers, 14 Apr 1843; m. at Danvers, 20 Dec 1832, MEHITABLE P. DWINELL, b. at Danvers, 22 May 1805 daughter of Stephen and Mehitable (Putnam) Dwinell; Mehitable d. at Danvers, 5 Feb 1880.

516) RACHEL RUSSELL (*Joseph Russell[4], Phebe Johnson Russell[3], Mary Holt Johnson[2], Nicholas[1]*), b. at Andover, 23 Feb 1757 daughter of Joseph and Hannah (Perkins) Russell; m. at Middleton, 29 Jan 1784, JONATHAN DWINELLS,[1384] b. at Lynn, 4 May 1759 son of David and Keziah (Ramsdell) Dunnel; Jonathan d. after 1830. Rachel and Jonathan were living in Hillsborough, New Hampshire in 1830 (male and female each age 70-79 in the 1830 census).

[1382] Perley, *The Dwellings of Boxford*, p 137

[1383] Donovan, *The History of the Town of Lyndeborough*, p 848

[1384] Jonathan's last name has multiple spellings. On his birth record it is Dunnell, but Dwinell at marriage, but the name to has settled as Dwinells which is the spelling used by the children, although some use Dwinnells.

Rachel and Jonathan were in Middleton for the first years of their marriage and three children were born there. They were in Hillsborough, New Hampshire in 1790 where two more children were born.[1385] They were still living in Hillsborough in 1830, but not record of their deaths was found.

i CATHERINE DWINELLS, b. at Middleton, 1 Jan 1786; nothing further found.

ii LYDIA SYMONDS DWINELLS, b. at Middleton, 28 Sep 1787; d. at Hillsborough, 27 Sep 1874; m. at Hillsborough, 25 Deb 1817, ADAM D. MILLS, b. at Deering, about 1790 son of Robert and Margaret (Dinsmoor) Mills;[1386] Adam d. at Deering, 30 Sep 1866.

iii CHARLOTTE DWINELLS, b. at Middleton, 26 May 1789; d. after 1870 when she was living with her son Hiram at Hinsdale, NY; m. at Hillsborough, 8 Sep 1808, DANIEL WILEY who is not yet identified. Charlotte was a widow at least by 1855 and likely much before. Only one son Hiram was found for Charlotte and Daniel.

iv JONATHAN DWINELLS, b. at Hillsborough, 10 Sep 1795; d. at Yorkshire, NY, 15 Sep 1881; m. about 1823, ELIZABETH "BETSEY" ATWOOD, b. about 1795; Betsey d. at Yorkshire, 27 Sep 1880.

v JAMES DWINELLS, b. at Hillsborough, 28 Jun 1800; d. at West Canaan, NH, 17 Dec 1859; m. at Hillsborough, 22 Feb 1832, LOUISA R. CRAIN, b. at Hillsborough, 24 Mar 1806 daughter of Joshua and Sarah (Giddings) Crain; Louisa d. at West Canaan, 18 Oct 1857. Louisa's father Dr. Joshua Crain was a physician and surgeon in Hillsborough.[1387]

517) HANNAH RUSSELL (*Joseph Russell*[4], *Phebe Johnson Russell*[3], *Mary Holt Johnson*[2], *Nicholas*[1]), b. at Andover, 11 Oct 1760 daughter of Joseph and Hannah (Perkins) Russell; d. at Newburyport, 24 Aug 1840; m. at Middleton, 10 May 1784, CALEB PUTNAM, b. at Danvers, 24 Nov 1763 son of Archelaus and Abigail (Goodrich) Putnam; Caleb d. at Newburyport, 6 Mar 1826.

Hannah Russell and Caleb Putnam were parents of at least seven children. There are perhaps one or two other children who died in childhood, but records are scant. The family seems to have been mostly in Newburyport but were also in Maine and New Hampshire. They were in Topsham, Maine in the 1790 census and in Newburyport in 1820. The two oldest children settled in Mississippi.

i JAMES RUSSELL PUTNAM, b. at Topsham, ME, 11 Nov 1789; d. at Vicksburg, MS, 1 Apr 1843; m. in Davidson County, TN, 24 May 1822, SOPHIA ANN PERKINS,[1388] b. about 1802; Sophia d. at New Orleans, 1851. James R. Putnam was a physician.

ii CHARLES CALEB PUTNAM, b. about 1790; d. at Canton, MS, 1862; m. at Washington, DC, MARGARET MURDOCH, b. 4 Jul 1805 daughter of John and Ann (Corby) Murdoch;[1389] Margaret d. at Orleans, LA, 13 Apr 1886. Charles Putnam was an attorney.

iii ABIGAIL PUTNAM, b. perhaps at Lyme, NH, about 1793; m. at Hallowell, ME, 4 Apr 1813, JOHN KINSMAN GILMAN, b. at Exeter, NH, 14 Aug 1787 son of Samuel and Martha (Kinsman) Gilman.

iv HANNAH RUSSELL PUTNAM, b. at Lyme, about 1795; d. at Stoneham, MA (although resident of Newburyport), 12 Sep 1874. Hannah did not marry.

v DEBORAH PUTNAM, b. at Lyme, about 1797; d. at Newburyport, 1 Sep 1877; m. at Newburyport, 24 May 1825, WILLIAM GREELEY.

vi BENJAMIN FRANKLIN PUTNAM, b. about 1800; d. at Boston, 5 Jan 1845; m. at Portsmouth, NH, 14 May 1824, NANCY MELCHER, b. at Portsmouth, about 1799 daughter of Nathaniel and Elizabeth (Ward) Melcher;[1390] Nancy d. at Boston, 6 Jul 1856.

vii JOHN PUTNAM, b. 1802; d. at Newburyport, 20 Sep 1805.

518) SARAH HUNT (*Jemima Russell Hunt*[4], *Phebe Johnson Russell*[3], *Mary Holt Johnson*[2], *Nicholas*[1]), b. at Billerica, 23 Dec 1725 daughter of Joseph and Jemima (Russell) Hunt; m. at Westford, 7 Mar 1750, JOSIAH JOHNSON, b. at Lancaster, 5 Jun 1726 son of Josiah and Annis (Chandler) Johnson.

[1385] Browne, *The History of Hillsborough*, p 186
[1386] Adam's death record gives the names of his parents as Robert and Margaret Mills.
[1387] Browne, *The History of Hillsborough*, p 154
[1388] Tennessee, Marriage Records, 1780-2002
[1389] The 1820 will of John Murdoch of Washington, DC gives Margaret's date of birth and the maiden name of her mother.
[1390] The names of Nancy's parents are given as Nathaniel and Elizabeth Melcher on her death record.

Records are scant for this family. An account of son Jeremiah Johnson states he had two brothers and three sisters and suggests that one of Jeremiah's sisters married a Kimball and another married a Bingham.[1391]

i JOSIAH JOHNSON, b. at Leominster, 20 Jan 1752

ii HANNAH JOHNSON, b. at Westford, 1754[1392]

iii JEMIMA JOHNSON, b. at Montague, 2 May 1757; *perhaps* m. at Newton, NH, 5 Apr 1784, ARCHELAUS COLBY, b. at Newton, 24 Mar 1762 son of Moses and Mary (Sargent) Colby.

iv JOSEPH JOHNSON, b. at Montague, 21 Jan 1761; m. 1st about 1785, MARY HUNT; Mary d. at Charlestown, NH, about 1796. Joseph m. 2nd about 1797, ANNA who has not been identified.

v JEREMIAH JOHNSON, b. at Montague, 16 Sep 1763; d. at Reading, VT, 2 Dec 1847; m. 1st at Charlestown, NH, THOMAZIN "FANNY" BLANCHARD, b. at Quincy, MA, 20 Sep 1765 daughter of Nehemiah and Mary (Gibson) Blanchard; Fanny d. at Reading, 10 Dec 1824. Jeremiah m. 2nd about 1826, SYBIL KIMBALL; Sybil d. at Mineral Point, WI, 1852 where she had been living with her son Solon Kimball Johnson.

vi SARAH JOHNSON, b. at Montague, 24 Apr 1766; m. at Springfield, VT, 19 Dec 1787, HORATIO BINGHAM, b. about 1765. Sarah and Horatio were parents of nine children and were living in Springfield, VT in 1830.

519) ROBERT HUNT (*Jemima Russell Hunt⁴, Phebe Johnson Russell³, Mary Holt Johnson², Nicholas¹*), b. at Billerica, 20 Jan 1731/2 son of Joseph and Jemima (Russell) Hunt; m. at Canaan, CT, 26 Dec 1753, REBEKAH PECK, b. at Litchfield, 15 Dec 1736 daughter of Isaac and Ruth (Tomlinson) Peck; Rebekah d. at Salisbury, CT, 1812.

Robert Hunt and Rebekah Peck were parents of twelve children born at Canaan, Connecticut.

i AMOS HUNT, b. 14 Jul 1754; d. at Canaan, 8 Jun 1768.

ii RUSSELL HUNT, b. 11 Mar 1756; d. at Canaan, 26 Aug 1831; m. ESTHER BEEBE, b. 1763 daughter of Asahel and Rebecca (Wright) Beebe;[1393] Esther d. at Canaan, 8 Jul 1850.

iii CHLOE HUNT, b. 7 Feb 1759; d. at Sherburne, NY, 3 Jan 1822; m. at Canaan, 18 Nov 1777, AARON MILLS, b. at Staatsburg, NY, 1754[1394] son of Daniel and Jerusha (Steele) Mills; Aaron d. at Sherburne, 18 Apr 1835.

iv SAMSON ROBERT HUNT, b. 23 Feb 1761; d. at Glastonbury, CT, 30 Jul 1826; m. 1st about 1782, CHARITY DUTCHER, b. at Glastonbury, 30 Jan 1764 daughter of Rufus and Jane (Ashley) Dutcher; Charity d. at Glastonbury, 23 Feb 1807. Samson m. 2nd at Glastonbury, 23 Oct 1807, POLLY BIDWELL, b. at Glastonbury, 4 Apr 1785 daughter of Jonathan and Hannah (Matson) Bidwell.[1395]

v SARAH HUNT, b. 11 Jun 1763; d. at Canaan, 1 Oct 1832; m. RUFUS LANDON, b. at Salisbury, CT, 4 Feb 1759 son of John and Katherine (-) Landon;[1396][1397] Rufus d. at Canaan, 17 Jan 1848.

vi MILO HUNT, b. 11 Oct 1765; d. at Montague, MA, 16 Mar 1815; m. LYDIA ROWE, b. at Montague, 15 Jan 1770 daughter of Daniel and Lucretia (Austin) Rowe; Lydia d. of typhus, at Montague, 6 Dec 1818.

vii JOHN HUNT, b. 11 Dec 1767; d. at Glastonbury, 28 Feb 1831; m. at Glastonbury, 18 Feb 1790, ELIZABETH PULSIFER, b. at Glastonbury, 21 Feb 1773 daughter of Sylvester and Huldah (Hollister) Pulsifer; Elizabeth d. at New Haven, 28 Sep 1820.[1398]

viii EMMA HUNT, b. 19 Dec 1769; d. at Great Barrington, MA, 17 Oct 1862; m. 1st EZRA TUPPER, b. at Stafford, CT, 19 Mar 1766 son of Solomon and Abiah (West) Tupper. Emma m. 2nd at Sherburne, NY, 17 Feb 1815, as his second wife, JOHN WOODWARD DEWEY, b. at Lebanon, CT, 31 Dec 1762 son of John and Rhoda (Gillett) Dewey; John d. at Hamilton, Canada West while visiting his daughter, 15 Nov 1839.[1399] John W. Dewey was first married to Abigail Rudd.

[1391] Johnson, *The Johnson Memorial: Jeremiah Johnson and Thomazin Blanchard Johnson, His Wife*, p 25

[1392] Hannah is a possible daughter in this family.

[1393] The 1806 probate distribution for the estate of Asahel Bugbee includes a distribution to daughter Hester Hunt.

[1394] U. S. Revolutionary War Pension and Bounty-Land Application Files, Case S13927

[1395] The name of Polly's father as Jonathan is given on the marriage transcription. The 1810 will of Jonathan Hunt of Glastonbury includes a bequest to his daughter Polly Hunt.

[1396] Date and place of birth are given in Rufus's Revolutionary War pension application file.

[1397] *Salisbury, CT: Vital Records, 1720-1914.* (Online Database, NewEnglandAncestors.org. New England Historic Genealogical Society, 2010.) p 54

[1398] *U.S., Newspaper Extractions from the Northeast, 1704-1930.*

[1399] Dewey, *Life of George Dewey and Dewey Family History*, p 441

ix FREDERICK HUNT, b. 29 Feb 1772; perhaps m. at Canaan, 27 Feb 1793, JERUSHA LOWREY, b. at Canaan, 21 Feb 1774 daughter of Nathaniel and Jerusha (Newell) Lowrey.

x ELIZABETH "BETSEY" HUNT, b. 29 May 1774; m. *perhaps* SOLOMON BEEBE son of Asahel and Rebecca (Wright) Beebe.

xi REBECCA HUNT, b. 13 Aug 1778; d. after 1870 when she was living at Albany, IL; m. about 1800, SALMON KNICKERBOCKER, b. 28 Feb 1773 son of Lawrence and Catherine (Dutcher) Knickerbocker.

xii AMOS HUNT, b. 17 Jul 1780. Amos married, but the name of his wife is unknown. Amos had one son Salmon born about 1823.

520) RUSSELL HUNT (*Jemima Russell Hunt*[4], *Phebe Johnson Russell*[3], *Mary Holt Johnson*[2], *Nicholas*[1]), b. at Billerica, about 1733 son of Joseph and Jemima (Russell) Hunt; d. at Canaan, CT, 18 Oct 1806; m. at Canaan, 3 May 1758, LYDIA PECK, b. about 1738 likely the daughter of Isaac and Ruth (Tomlinson) Peck; Lydia d. at Canaan, 18 Feb 1818.

Russell Hunt did not leave a will and the estate entered probate 11 November 1806 with Amos Hunt and Salmon Hunt providing the administrative bond. The total value of his estate was $3,043.44 in an inventory made 10 December 1806. The widow's dower was set off to Lydia 11 May 1807.[1400]

Russell Hunt and Lydia Peck were parents of eight children born at Canaan.

i ISAAC HUNT, b. 9 Apr 1759

ii RUSSELL HUNT, b. 11 Oct 1762; d. at Canaan, 20 Jan 1839; m. about 1785, LUCY SWIFT who has not been identified.

iii SALMON HUNT, b. 23 Jan 1765; d. at Canaan, 28 Apr 1839; m. REUBY WHITNEY, b. at Canaan, about 1765 daughter of John and Elizabeth (Adams) Whitney;[1401] Reuby d. at Canaan, 10 Feb 1837.

iv DAVID HUNT, b. 22 Apr 1767; d. at Canaan, 22 Feb 1834; m. 1st at Canaan, 1791, HANNAH JOHNSON, b. about 1768; Hannah d. at Canaan, 2 Feb 1806. David m. 2nd 1807, WEALTHY ANN BURRALL, b. 16 Oct 1775 daughter of William and Elizabeth (Morgan) Burrall;[1402] Wealthy d. 9 Apr 1840.

v CYRUS HUNT, b. 25 Sep 1769

vi LYDIA HUNT, b. 18 Feb 1772; d. at South Danby, NY, 6 Jul 1826; m. WILLIAM HUGG, b. at Canaan, CT, 18 Dec 1764 son of William and Margaret (Johnson) Hugg; William d. at South Danby, 10 Jun 1826.

vii AMOS HUNT, b. 6 May 1774; d. (buried at South Canaan), 13 Jul 1851; m. MARY LOWRY, b. 1779 daughter of Nathaniel and Jerusha (Newell) Lowry; Mary d. at Canaan, 19 Aug 1863.

viii JEMIMA HUNT, b. 1777; d. at Cornwall, CT, 7 Apr 1832; m. JOSEPH WILCOX, b. 1769; Joseph d. at Cornwall, 23 Mar 1852.

521) JAMES RUSSELL (*James Russell*[4], *Phebe Johnson Russell*[3], *Mary Holt Johnson*[2], *Nicholas*[1]), b. at North Yarmouth, 7 Aug 1737 son of James and Rhoda (Chandler) Russell; m. at North Yarmouth, 5 Jun 1760, LYDIA MITCHELL.

James Russell and Lydia Mitchell were parents of six children born at North Yarmouth.

i PHEBE RUSSELL, b. 2 Sep 1760

ii LYDIA RUSSELL, b. 12 Mar 1762; m. SOLOMON VEASEY JORDAN, b. at Randolph, MA, 31 Aug 1746 son of Elijah and Joanna (Veasey) Jordan; Solomon d. at Brokenstraw, PA, 4 Mar 1846.

iii TEMPERANCE RUSSELL, b. 27 Apr 1764; d. at South Waterford, ME, 18 Jan 1831; m. DAVID JORDAN, b. 1759 son of Elijah and Joanna (Veasey) Jordan; David d. at South Waterford, 30 May 1847.

iv JANE "JENNY" RUSSELL, baptized 10 Jun 1770; d. at Norway, ME, 1 Mar 1856; m. at New Gloucester, ME, 4 Jun 1791, as his second wife, JAMES LEBARON, b. at Middleborough, MA, 30 Nov 1759 son of James and Hannah (Turner) LeBaron;[1403] James d. at Paris, ME, 9 Jun 1836. James was first married to Elizabeth Washburn.

1400 *Connecticut State Library (Hartford, Connecticut)*; Probate Place: *Hartford, Connecticut, Probate Packets, Hull-Kilmer, 1755-1880, Russell Hunt, Case 1739*

1401 The 1793 estate of John Whitney of Canaan includes a distribution to Ruby and Salmon Hunt.

1402 Morgan, *James Morgan of New London, Conn. and His Descendants*

1403 Lapham and Maxim, *History of Paris, Maine*, p 659

v EUNICE RUSSELL, b. 1772; d. at New Gloucester, ME, 24 Dec 1825; m. about 1794, ENOCH MORSE, b. 3 Jul 1772 son of John and Sarah (Sander) Morse. Eunice and Enoch were parents of ten children.

vi NATHANIEL RUSSELL, b. about 1774 (based on age 68 at death); d. at Oxford, ME, 10 Nov 1842; m. SARAH MORSE, b. at Oxford, ME, 26 Sep 1774 daughter of John and Sarah (Sanders) Morse; Sarah d. at Norway, ME, 20 Jul 1861.

522) THOMAS CHANDLER RUSSELL (*James Russell[4], Phebe Johnson Russell[3], Mary Holt Johnson[2], Nicholas[1]*), b. at Cumberland, 9 Oct 1740 son of James and Rhoda (Chandler) Russell; m. about 1767, SARAH GOOCH, b. 17 Oct 1751 daughter of John and Elizabeth (Boothbay) Gooch.[1404]

There are records of fifteen children of Thomas C. Russell and Sarah Gooch all born (recorded) at Cumberland, Maine.[1405]

i BETSY RUSSELL, b. at Cumberland, 23 Jun 1768; d. at Hartford, ME, 14 May 1857; m. 1st at North Yarmouth, Dec 1785, DANIEL BROWN, b. at Cumberland, 10 Dec 1756 son of Jacob and Lydia (Weare) Brown; Daniel d. at Yarmouth, Oct 1797. Betsy m. 2nd 11 Mar 1800, her first cousin, JEREMIAH RUSSELL (*Joseph Russell[5], James Russell[4], Phebe Johnson Russell[3], Mary Holt Johnson[2], Nicholas[1]*), b. at Yarmouth, 3 Apr 1772 son of Joseph and Miriam (Brown) Russell; Jeremiah d. at Hartford, ME, 30 Nov 1843.[1406] Daniel Brown served in the Revolution and was prisoner of war in 1779.

ii RHODA RUSSELL, b. at Cumberland, 10 Mar 1770; d. at West Boylston, MA, 13 Dec 1852; m. at Cumberland, 1787, SAMUEL LAWRENCE, b. at Cumberland, 6 Jul 1766 son of Joseph and Abigail (Brown) Lawrence; Samuel d. at West Boylston, 31 Mar 1824.

iii JAMES RUSSELL, b. 3 Dec 1771; d. at North Yarmouth, 5 Jul 1859; m. at Cumberland, 20 Dec 1796, JOANNA TRUE, b. at Cumberland, 22 Aug 1777 daughter of William and Susannah (Brown) True; Joanna d. at North Yarmouth, 27 Feb 1863.

iv SARAH RUSSELL, b. 14 Nov 1773; d. after 1850 when she was living in Somersworth, NH with her two daughters; m. at Cumberland, 18 Jun 1795, THOMAS THOMPSON, b. at Scarborough, ME, about 1768; Thomas d. after 1830 when the family was living in Parsonsfield, ME. There is record evidence for two daughters of Sarah and Thomas, Sarah and Susan. Neither daughter married and her 1865 will daughter Sarah left her entire estate to her sister Susan. Susan's 1884 death record gives the names of her parents as Sarah Russell and Thomas Thompson and father's place of birth as Scarborough.

v JOSEPH RUSSELL, b. 17 Dec 1775; likely m. at Cumberland, 8 Jan 1801, RACHEL PRATT, b. at Cumberland, 23 Apr 1778 daughter of Sherebiah and Anna (Millett) Pratt. Births of seven children of Joseph and Rachel Russell are recorded at Cumberland.

vi MIRIAM RUSSELL, b. 23 May 1777; m. at Cumberland, 1801, JAMES RUSSELL

vii JOANNA RUSSELL, b. at Cumberland, 23 Apr 1779; d. at Yarmouth, 20 Jan 1848; m. 28 Jan 1808, ASA S. TRUE, b. at Cumberland, 28 Feb 1780 son of William and Susannah (Brown) True; Asa d. at Yarmouth, 13 Nov 1848.

viii JOHN RUSSELL, b. 30 Apr 1781

ix PHEBE RUSSELL, b. 16 May 1783; d. at Parsonsfield, ME, 29 Jan 1858; m. 1800, JOHN F. HUNTRESS, b. at Newington, NH, 7 Nov 1775 son of Nathan and Susanna (Chick) Huntress; John d. at Parsonsfield, 13 Sep 1852.

x MARY RUSSELL, b. 14 May 1784; d. at Yarmouth, 4 Jan 1857; m. at Cumberland, 30 Mar 1803, DAVID PRATT, b. at Cumberland, 3 May 1776 son of Sherebiah and Anna (Millett) Pratt; David d. at Yarmouth, 28 Feb 1850.

xi HANNAH RUSSELL, b. 15 May 1786

xii DORCAS RUSSELL, b. 7 May 1789; d. at Hartford, ME, May 1860; m. BENJAMIN THOMAS, b. at Middleborough, MA, 25 Dec 1785 son of Perez and Sarah (Wood) Thomas; Benjamin d. at Hartford, 1867 (probate 1867).

xiii RACHEL RUSSELL, b. 29 Nov 1790

1404 Gooch, *The History of a Surname, with some Account of the Line of John Gooch*, p 87

1405 Bennett, Vital Records of Cumberland, Maine 1701-1892, https://digitalmaine.com/cumberland_books/1

1406 U. S. Revolutionary War Pension and Bounty-Land Application, Case W22129

xiv JACOB MITCHELL RUSSELL, b. 18 Aug 1792; d. after 1860 when he was living in Aroostook County, ME; m. by 1828, MARGARET E. who has not been identified, but born about 1805. Jacob and Margaret were parents of at least eight children.

xv DESIRE RUSSELL, b. at Cumberland, 16 May 1794; d. at Melrose, MA, 5 Jun 1882; m. at Hartford, ME, 22 Aug 1813, MARTIN ELLIS, b. 15 Sep 1791 son of Perez and Mary (Hathaway) Ellis; Martin d at Canton, ME, 14 May 1871. Martin served in the War of 1812.

523) JOSEPH RUSSELL (*James Russell[4], Phebe Johnson Russell[3], Mary Holt Johnson[2], Nicholas[1]*), b. about 1742 son of James and Rhoda (Chandler) Russell; d. 1775; m. at Cumberland, 22 Oct 1765, MIRIAM BROWN, b. at Cumberland, 10 Jun 1746 daughter of Jacob and Lydia (Weare) Brown.

Joseph Russell and Miriam Brown were parents of five children born at Cumberland.

i RHODA RUSSELL, b. 10 Feb 1766

ii ANDREW RUSSELL, b. 13 Apr 1768

iii JOSEPH RUSSELL, b. 26 May 1770

iv JEREMIAH RUSSELL, b. 3 Apr 1772; d. at Hartford, ME, 30 Nov 1843; m. 11 Mar 1800, his first cousin, BETSY RUSSELL (*Thomas C. Russell[5], James Russell[4], Phebe Johnson Russell[3], Mary Holt Johnson[2], Nicholas[1]*), b. at Cumberland, 23 Jun 1768 daughter of Thomas Chandler and Sarah (Gooch) Russell; Betsy d. at Hartford, 14 May 1857. Betsy was first married to Daniel Brown.

v SARAH RUSSELL, b. 26 Nov 1773

524) LYDIA DANFORTH (*Tabitha Johnson Danforth[4], John Johnson[3], Mary Holt Johnson[2], Nicholas[1]*), b. at Westborough, 29 Jun 1729 daughter of John and Tabitha (Johnson) Danforth; m. at Andover, 24 Jan 1754, her first cousin once removed, URIAH BALLARD, b. at Andover, 28 Apr 1715 son of Uriah and Elizabeth (Henshaw) Ballard; Uriah d. at Wilton, 1803. Uriah was first married to Sarah Dane and second married to Mehitable Barker.

Lydia and Uriah had their children in Andover, and at unknown time relocated to Wilton where Uriah died.

Lydia Danforth and Uriah Ballard were parents of three children born at Andover. Uriah had one child with Sarah Dane (Joseph Ballard 1739-1739) and one child with Mehitable Barker (Sarah Ballard 1745-1819).

i LYDIA BALLARD, b. at Andover, 9 Aug 1756; nothing further known.

ii URIAH BALLARD, b. at Andover, 7 Oct 1758; d. at Fryeburg, ME, 22 Dec 1840; m. 1st, at Wilton, 1 Jul 1784, LOIS LOVEJOY *possibly* the daughter of William and Hannah (Evans) Lovejoy; Lois d. about 1798. Uriah m. 2nd, at Fryeburg, ME, 8 Jul 1798, HANNAH SARGENT, b. 1775 daughter of William and Hannah (Frye) Sargent; Hannah d. at Fryeburg, 2 Dec 1821.

iii MEHITABLE BALLARD, b. at Andover, 26 Mar 1761; nothing further known.

525) JOHN DANFORTH (*Tabitha Johnson Danforth[4], John Johnson[3], Mary Holt Johnson[2], Nicholas[1]*), b. at Westborough, 25 Mar 1731 son of John and Tabitha (Johnson) Danforth; d. at Greenbush, 29 Sep 1758;[1407] m. 6 Mar 1755, ELIZABETH WILSON, likely b. at Billerica, 10 Oct 1732 daughter of John and Jemima (Shed) Wilson; Elizabeth d. at Concord, NH, 27 Jun 1804. Elizabeth married second Ebenezer Dow on 12 Jun 1760.

John served in the French and Indian War and died at Greenbush.

In his will written 3 May 1758 (probate 13 November 1758), John Danforth bequeathed to dear and well-beloved wife Elizabeth the use and improvement of all the estate while she is a widow, and Elizabeth is to pay the debts of the estate and support children Elizabeth and Hannah. Honored mother Tabatha Danforth receives £13 in case her own estate does not support her. There is also a bequest to Lydia daughter of his sister Lydia Ballard. The remainder of the estate goes to children Elizabeth and Hannah.[1408] On 5 July 1774, Hannah and Elizabeth made choice of Nathan Bailey as guardian. On 28 May 1781(recorded 12 May 1785), Hannah Danforth sold her half of the land inheritance of her father to Elijah Haseltine and his wife for a price of £59.[1409]

John Danforth and Elizabeth Wilson were parents of two children.

i ELIZABETH DANFORTH, b. in Andover, 22 Oct 1755; m. at Tewksbury, 2 May 1776, ELIJAH HASELTINE, b. at Tewksbury, 1 May 1747 son of Samuel and Sarah (Bixby) Haseltine.

[1407] John, at Greenbush, Sept. 29, 1758.

[1408] *Essex County, MA: Probate File Papers, 1638-1881.*Online database. *AmericanAncestors.org.* New England Historic Genealogical Society, 2014. Case 7140

[1409] Massachusetts Land Records, Essex Count, 143:135

ii HANNAH DANFORTH, b. at Andover, 26 Jun 1757; d. at Andover, 17 Sep 1817; m. at Andover, 25 Mar 1806, as his second wife, WILLIAM BAILEY, b. at Tewksbury, 13 Feb 1747/8 son of Joseph and Sarah (Goss) Bailey; William d. at Andover, 12 Mar 1836. William was first married to Rebecca Hildreth and third married to Anna Frye.

526) HANNAH JOHNSON (*Zebadiah Johnson⁴, John Johnson³, Mary Holt Johnson², Nicholas¹*), b. at Andover, 31 Mar 1724 daughter of Zebadiah and Hannah (Robbins) Johnson; d. about 1773; m. at Andover, 29 May 1744, MOSES THURSTON, b. about 1721 son of Abner and Shua (Gilman) Thurston; Moses d. at Hollis, 6 Apr 1800. Moses was second married to Katherine Emerson.

Moses Thurston was a hatter and deacon of the Congregational church in Hollis.[1410] Hannah Johnson and Moses Thurston were parents of perhaps thirteen children.[1411]

i HANNAH THURSTON, b. at Andover, 10 Sep 1744; d. at Pepperell, 5 Sep 1758.

ii MOSES THURSTON, b. at Andover, 7 Jul 1746; d. at Westminster, MA, 29 Jul 1809; m. at Westminster, 21 Apr 1768, ESTHER BIGELOW, b. at Watertown, 22 Mar 1744 daughter of Eleazer and Mary (Fiske) Bigelow; Esther d. at Cambridge, VT, 24 Oct 1831.

iii CHLOE THURSTON, b. at Hollis, NH, 15 Jul 1748; d. at Vershire, VT, 13 Dec 1807; m. 7 Dec 1780, STEPHEN RUNNELLS, b. at Haverhill, MA, 3 Jul 1754 son of Ebenezer and Abigail (Sollis) Runnells; Stephen d. at Vershire, 1798.

iv SHUA THURSTON, b. (recorded) at Andover, 15 Jul 1748; d. at Haverhill, NH, 19 Feb 1827; m. ANDREW SAVAGE CROCKER, b. at Newbury, 28 May 1743 son of John and Mary (Savage) Crocker; Andrew d. at Haverhill, NH, 17 Jul 1821.

v GILMAN THURSTON, b. at Hollis, NH, 19 Jul 1750

vi MARY THURSTON, b. at Hollis, 29 Jul 1752; d. 6 Jun 1753.

vii MARY THURSTON, b. at Hollis, estimated 1755; reported as marrying a Presbyterian minister Rev. Spofford, but records related to that were not located.

viii LYDIA THURSTON, b. at Hollis, 6 Jul 1756; d. 28 Oct 1757.

ix LYDIA THURSTON, b. at Pepperell, estimated 1759; reported as marrying Mr. Johnson who has not been found.

x PETER THURSTON, baptized at Pepperell, 16 Nov 1760; d. at Granville, OH, 29 Aug 1827; m. 1st at Boxford, 22 Apr 1787, EUNICE CHADWICK, b. about 1759 *perhaps* the daughter of William and Eunice (Goss) Chadwick; Eunice d. at Fletcher, VT, 1 Aug 1802. Peter m. 2nd HANNAH BUTLER (widow of Zalmon Wheeler), b. at Fairfield, CT, 18 Aug 1772 daughter of Thomas and Jane (White) Butler; Hannah d. at Centerburg, OH, 28 May 1866.

xi JOSEPH THURSTON, baptized at Pepperell, 2 Jun 1763; m. POLLY MELVIN. He is reported to have gone to Canada, but returned to Colchester, VT where he died.

xii PHEBE THURSTON, b. at Pepperell, 14 Feb 1765; d. at Vershire, VT, 29 Oct 1856; m. at Vershire, 7 Oct 1788, Rev. STEPHEN FULLER, b. at North Mansfield, CT, 3 Dec 1756 son of David and Desire (Hopkins) Fuller; Stephen d. at New Haven, VT, 12 Apr 1816. Rev. Stephen Fuller attended Dartmouth College and was the first settled minister at Vershire, VT.[1412]

xiii HANNAH THURSTON, b. at Pepperell, estimate 1767; m. 21 Sep 1788, JOHN WHEELER, b. at Charlestown, NH, 31 Oct 1768 son of Moses and Elizabeth (Holden) Wheeler;[1413] John d. at Granville, OH, 12 May 1813.

527) LYDIA JOHNSON (*Zebadiah Johnson⁴, John Johnson³, Mary Holt Johnson², Nicholas¹*), b. at Andover, 27 Feb 1735/6 daughter of Zebadiah and Hannah (Robbins) Johnson; d. at Temple, NH, 13 Sep 1774; m. at Andover, 13 Aug 1752, ABRAHAM DINSMORE, b. at Bedford, NH, 22 Feb 1730 son of Thomas and Hannah (Whitaker) Dinsmore.

1410 Thurston, *Thurston Genealogies*, p 44

1411 The children for this family are somewhat uncertain. The Thurston genealogy reports ten children, but three of the daughters who are reported as marrying (Hannah, Lydia, and Mary) are recorded as dying in childhood. Perhaps there were replacements children for each of these childhood deaths, so I have listed here thirteen children to account for the proposed marriages for daughters Hannah, Lydia, and Mary, although that may not be correct.

1412 Child, *Gazetteer of Orange County Vermont,* Town of Vershire, p 498

1413 Wheeler, *Genealogical and Encyclopedic History of the Wheeler Family*, p 552

Lydia and Abraham married in Andover but were soon after in Hollis where their oldest six children were born. They were then in Temple, New Hampshire where Abraham was thythingman in 1771 and the constable in 1779.[1414]

Lydia and Abraham were parents of ten children.

i ABRAHAM DINSMORE, b. at Hollis, 17 Jan 1753; d. at Royalton, VT, 10 Jun 1839;[1415] m. 26 Nov 1776, LOVE LEMAN, b. at Hollis, 1 Nov 1752 daughter of Samuel and Love (Wheeler) Leman.

ii ZEBADIAH DINSMORE, b. at Hollis, 17 Jan 1755; d. at Pittsfield, VT, 24 Dec 1814; m. at Temple, NH, 13 Mar 1777, ELIZABETH TODD, b. 1755; Elizabeth d. at Pittsfield, 22 Jan 1827.

iii LYDIA DINSMORE, b. at Hollis, 24 Jan 1757

iv HANNAH DINSMORE, b. at Hollis, 2 Mar 1759

v PHEBE DINSMORE, b. at Hollis, 17 May 1761

vi THOMAS DINSMORE, b. at Hollis, 14 Aug 1763; d. at Alstead, NH, 21 Apr 1836; m. SALLY WALLACE, b. 1763; Sally d. at Alstead, 17 Jul 1834.

vii JOHN DINSMORE, b. at Temple, 23 Nov 1765

viii AMOS DINSMORE, b. at Temple, 25 Feb 1768; m. at Temple, 5 Jan 1794, RACHEL STONE who has not been identified but may be Rachel Cutter widow of David Stone.

ix ABEL DINSMORE, b. at Temple, 14 Jun 1770; d. at Chelsea, VT, 10 Aug 1831; m. at Groton, MA, 20 Aug 1789, RACHEL FISKE, b. at Groton, 11 Mar 1772 daughter of Peter and Rachel (Kemp) Fiske; Rachel d. at Chelsea, 7 Dec 1849.

x MARY DINSMORE, b. at Temple, 16 Aug 1772; m. at Temple, 25 Nov 1788, ASA SEVERANCE, b. about 1761; Asa d. at Alstead, NH, 20 Apr 1854.

528) ZEBADIAH JOHNSON (*Zebadiah Johnson[4], John Johnson[3], Mary Holt Johnson[2], Nicholas[1]*), b. at Andover, 20 Sep 1742 son of Zebadiah and Hannah (Robbins) Johnson; d. likely at Temple, NH; m. at Reading, 1 Sep 1761, LYDIA BANCROFT, b. at Reading, 8 Sep 1738 daughter of Samuel and Lydia (Parker) Bancroft.[1416]

Zebadiah Johnson and Lydia Bancroft were parents of eight children.

i SAMUEL JOHNSON, b. at Andover, 1 Jul 1762; d. 27 Mar 1776.

ii LYDIA JOHNSON, b. at Andover, 4 Aug 1764

iii NATHANIEL JOHNSON, b. at Andover, 8 Jul 1761; d. at Northwood, NH, 1828 (probate Feb 1828); m. at Boston, 2 Aug 1787, CATHERINE AMIEL, perhaps b. 1771 daughter of John and Elizabeth (Farquhar) Amiel. Catherine died before 1828. Nathaniel and Catherine were parents of eleven children. Most of the children were born in Boston, but Nathaniel relocated to Hillsborough and finally to Northwood just before his death. His estate included real estate valued at $7,640.[1417]

iv ZEBADIAH JOHNSON, b. at Andover, 25 Mar 1769; d. at Boston, 2 Sep 1793; m. at Boston, 30 Mar 1791, ELIZABETH KNEELAND, b. 1768 daughter of Nathaniel and Sarah (Hastings) Kneeland; Elizabeth d. at Boston, Sep 1795.

v HANNAH JOHNSON, b. at Temple, NH, 16 Jan 1771

vi GEORGE JOHNSON, b. at Temple, NH, 7 May 1773; d. at Boston, Aug 1797; m. at Boston, 1794, OLIVE BODGE, b. at Haverhill, 17 Sep 1775 daughter of Nathaniel and Hannah (Holliman) Bodge.

vii JOEL JOHNSON, b. at Temple, 13 Mar 1775; m. at Holden, MA, 7 Feb 1808, ELEANOR FALES, b. at Holden, 16 Dec 1777 daughter of Lemuel and Elizabeth (White) Fales; Eleanor d. at Henderson, NY, 9 May 1833.

[1414] Blood, *The History of Temple, New Hampshire*, pp 188-189

[1415] Revolutionary War Pension and Bounty-Land Warrant Application Files 2007, Case S12777

[1416] Zebadiah is not mentioned in his father's 1769 will, although he was clearly living at that time. It may be that Zebadiah had received already his portion. There may also have been a family falling out. The family records of Lydia's father, Deacon Samuel Bancroft of Reading, makes note on 5 Mar 1769 of traveling to Andover: "Monday 5 up this day to Andover: Johnson haveing again abused his wife. I reconciled them again. Came home at Eleven at Night." Bancroft, *Family Record of Dea. Samuel Bancroft*, p 23. It was about this time (1769-1770) that Zebadiah and his wife Lydia relocated to Temple, New Hampshire.

[1417] *New Hampshire. Probate Court (Rockingham County), Estate Papers, No 11518-11596, 1827-1828, Estate of Nathaniel Johnston*

viii SAMUEL JOHNSON, b. at Temple, NH, 14 Mar 1777; d. at Burlington, OH, 1859; m. MARY WHEELER, b. at Fairfield, VT, 23 Apr 1788 daughter of Zalmon and Hannah (Butler) Wheeler; Mary d. at Millerton, IA, 20 May 1868.

529) JOHN JOHNSON (*Zebadiah Johnson[4], John Johnson[3], Mary Holt Johnson[2], Nicholas[1]*), baptized at Andover, 28 Jun 1747 son of Zebadiah and Hannah (Robbins) Johnson; m. at Reading, 9 Jul 1767, MARGARET MCINTIRE

There are records for two children of John and Margaret, but it is not known what became of this family.

i MARY JOHNSON, baptized at Andover, 20 Nov 1768

ii JOHN JOHNSON, b. at Reading, 29 May 1769

530) ABIEL FAULKNER (*Damaris Johnson Faulkner[4], Thomas Johnson[3], Mary Holt Johnson[2], Nicholas[1]*), b. at Andover, 30 Oct 1728 son of Joseph and Damaris (Johnson) Faulkner; d. at Andover, 4 Jul 1756; m. at Andover, 4 Mar 1752, MARY POOR, b. at Andover, 6 Apr 1734 daughter of Thomas and Mary (Adams) Poor; Mary d. at Andover, 20 Apr 1791.

Abiel and Mary were parents of two children before Abiel's early death.

i DAMARIS FAULKNER, b. at Andover, 3 Nov 1753; d. at Andover, 28 Mar 1826; m. 1st 29 Mar 1774, her third cousin once removed, DANIEL WARDWELL (*Abigail Gray Wardwell[4], Edward Gray[3], Hannah Holt Gray[2], Nicholas[1]*), b. at Andover, 18 Nov 1743 son of Thomas and Abigail (Gray) Wardwell; Daniel d. at Andover, 7 Mar 1782. Damaris m. 2nd 22 Nov 1783, Daniel's brother EZEKIEL WARDWELL, b. at Andover, 15 Feb 1750/1; Ezekiel d. at Andover, 16 Dec 1834. Damaris Faulkner and Ezekiel Wardwell are Family 989.

ii ABIEL FAULKNER, b. at Andover, 4 Sep 1755; d. at Andover, 26 Nov 1818; m. 1st 16 Feb 1777, his fourth cousin, HANNAH ABBOTT (*Thomas Abbott[5], Thomas Abbott[4], Hannah Gray Abbott[3], Hannah Holt Gray[2], Nicholas[1]*), b. at Andover, 5 May 1759 daughter of Thomas and Lydia (Blunt) Abbott; Hannah d. at Andover, 14 Nov 1789. Abiel m. 2nd 20 Dec 1791, his fourth cousin, LYDIA OSGOOD (*Elizabeth Abbott Osgood[5], Thomas Abbott[4], Hannah Gray Abbott[3], Hannah Holt Gray[2], Nicholas[1]*), b. at Andover, 31 May 1754 daughter of Samuel and Elizabeth (Abbott) Osgood; Lydia d. at Andover, 2 Oct 1816. Abiel m. 3rd 29 May 1817, CLARISSA DILLAWAY who was born about 1775 and died 1827. Abiel was a musical instrument maker.

531) JOHN WRIGHT (*Hannah Johnson Wright[4], Thomas Johnson[3], Mary Holt Johnson[2], Nicholas[1]*), b. at Andover, 9 Apr 1726 son of John and Hannah (Johnson) Wright; d. at Woolwich, ME, 19 May 1809; m. at Andover, 7 Apr 1748, MARY ELLOYT; Mary d. about 1751. John m. 2nd, by 1754, MARY BOWEN, b. about 1737 and d. at Woolwich, ME, 1798.

John Wright and Mary Elloyt were parents of two children.

i JOHN WRIGHT, b. at Andover, 3 May 1749; d. 11 Oct 749.

ii HANNAH WRIGHT, b. at Georgetown, ME, 2 Dec 1750; d. at Woolwich, ME, 16 Sep 1771.

John Wright and Mary Bowen were parents of seven children.[1418]

i MARY WRIGHT, b. at Georgetown, 7 Mar 1754; m. at Woolwich, 28 Jan 1773, DANIEL SMITH, b. at Woolwich, 5 Jun 1749 son of Ebenezer and Hannah (Motherwell) Smith.

ii ELIZABETH WRIGHT, b. at Georgetown, 13 Jul 1755; d. 8 Nov 1771.

iii SARAH WRIGHT, b. at Georgetown, 12 Jul 1757

iv JOHN WRIGHT, b. at Georgetown, Aug 1759; d. at Woolwich, 2 Feb 1847; m. at Georgetown, 21 Dec 1780, LUCY BROOKINGS, b. at Woolwich, 24 Jun 1760 daughter of Josiah and Anna (Revis) Brookings; Lucy d. at Woolwich, Mar 1847.

v JOSEPH WRIGHT, b. at Georgetown, 4 Jan 1762; d. at Woolwich, 24 Jun 1841; m. at Georgetown, 16 Dec 1788, MARY "MOLLY" BROOKINGS, b. at Woolwich, 8 Nov 1764 daughter of Josiah and Anna (Revis) Brookings; Mary d. at Woolwich, 30 Mar 1809.

vi JANE WRIGHT, b. at Georgetown, 22 Aug 1764; d. at Bowdoinham, ME, after 1837; m. at Georgetown, 21 Aug 1790, JAMES BUKER, b. at Bowdoinham, 22 Feb 1768 son of James and Ruth (Sargent) Buker;[1419] James d. 1837 (probate Feb 1837).

1418 Georgetown Historical Society, geargetownhistoricalsociety.org/genealogy

1419 Georgetown Historical Society, geargetownhistoricalsociety.org/genealogy

vii MEHITABLE WRIGHT, b. at Woolwich, 15 Dec 1766; m. at Georgetown, 14 Dec 1786, JABEZ BOWEN, b. at Rehoboth, MA, 21 Oct 1765 son of Jabez and Patience (Millard) Bowen.

532) SARAH WRIGHT (*Hannah Johnson Wright[4], Thomas Johnson[3], Mary Holt Johnson[2], Nicholas[1]*), b. at Andover, 25 Jan 1735/6 daughter of John and Hannah (Johnson) Wright; d. at Pelham, NH, about 1774; m. at Andover, 26 Apr 1757, URIAH ABBOTT, b. at Andover, 29 Sep 1735 son of Uriah and Sarah (Mitchell) Abbott; Uriah d. at Pelham, about 1808 (probate 1808). Uriah married second Sarah Perry.

Uriah Abbott was a housewright in Pelham, New Hampshire. Her served in the French and Indian War participating the expedition to Crown Point. He also served as a sergeant in Capt. Elisha Woodbury's company in 1775.[1420]

Uriah Abbott did not leave a will and on 17 August 1808, the following heirs, who were children of the deceased, were notified Jonathan Gage, a creditor of the estate, had petitioned to assume administration of the estate as the heir had neglected to do so: Dudley Abbott, Benjamin Abbott, Joseph Abbott, and Lydia Abbott. On 3 November 1808, Dudley Abbott of Beverly signed that he had been notified to appear related to the estate. The total value of the estate, both real and personal, was $195.16. The estate was insolvent. Dudley was a son of Uriah with his first wife Sarah Wright and the others named were from Uriah's second marriage.[1421]

Sarah Wright and Uriah Abbott were parents of three children. Uriah also had eight children with his second wife Sarah Perry.

i SARAH ABBOTT, b. at Pelham, 17 Apr 1758; died young.

ii URIAH ABBOTT, b. at Pelham, 20 Feb 1762; died young.

iii DUDLEY ABBOTT, b. at Pelham, 12 Jun 1767; d. after 1820 when he was living in Beverly; m. at Beverly, 2 Jun 1791, ANNA "NANCY" POLAND, baptized at Ipswich, 13 Nov 1769 daughter of Nathan and Anna (Whipple) Poland; Nancy d. at Amesbury, 4 Jan 1854.

533) JONATHAN JOHNSON (*Andrew Johnson[4], James Johnson[3], Mary Holt Johnson[2], Nicholas[1]*), b. at Andover, 27 Jan 1731/2 son of Andrew and Hannah (Chandler) Johnson; d. at Westford, MA, 1789 (probate 12 Nov 1789); m. 11 Jul 1754, SARAH BATES, b. at Westford, 29 Aug 1733 daughter of Edward and Mary (Snow) Bates;[1422] Sarah d. at Westford, 27 Feb 1813.

Jonathan Johnson was a hatter. The family resided in Hollis where six children were born, but later returned to Westford where marriages of three of the children are recorded. Baptisms of two additional children likely of this family are recorded at Westford, although the time and place of their births is not known.

Jonathan Johnson did not leave a will and the inventory of his estate was made 30 Nov 1789 and only personal estate is given appraised at £6.3.2.[1423]

Jonathan Johnson and Sarah Bates were parents of eight children. Their son Jonathan served during the Revolution and was captured by Indians and received harsh treatment. He has his comrades were later ransomed by British forces, taken to Québec, and held as prisoners of war until 1783.[1424]

i ELIZABETH JOHNSON, b. at Hollis, 4 Aug 1754

ii SARAH JOHNSON, b. at Hollis, 30 May 1756. She may have married a Mr. Proctor, but this has not been verified.

iii MARY JOHNSON, b. at Hollis, 29 Apr 1758; d. at Bolton, NY, 6 Jan 1840; m. at Westford (also recorded at Dunstable), 7 May 1778, SAMUEL FRENCH, b. 1755; Samuel d. at Bolton, 21 Mar 1833.[1425]

iv JONATHAN JOHNSON, b. at Hollis, 4 Jun 1760; d. at Hatley, Stanstead, Québec, 1830;[1426] m. 1st at Westford, 22 Jun 1773, ESTHER WRIGHT; Esther d. at Westford, 26 Apr 1792. Jonathan m. 2nd at Westford, 6 Nov 1792, SUSANNA HEALD, b. at Westford, 28 Jun 1767 daughter of Gershom and Hannah (Blood) Heald; Susanna d. at Hatley, 1834.

v HANNAH JOHNSON, b. at Hollis, 4 Jun 1762; m. at Westford, 12 Apr 1781, JOSEPH BRABROOK. There are records of two children of Joseph and Hannah Brabrook at Chelmsford.

1420 Abbott, *Descendants of George Abbott of Rowley*, p 185

1421 *New Hampshire. Probate Court (Rockingham County);* Probate Place: *Rockingham, New Hampshire, Estate Papers, No 8000-8076, 1808-1809, Case 8036*

1422 In 1781, Jonathan Johnson served as administrator of the estate of Edward Bates of Westford.

1423 *Middlesex County, MA: Probate File Papers, 1648-1871.*Online database. *AmericanAncestors.org.* New England Historic Genealogical Society, 2014. Case 12695

1424 Hubbard, *Forests and Clearings*, pp 62-63

1425 U.S. Revolutionary War Pension and Bounty-Land Warrant Application Files, Case W24239

1426 Hubbard, *Forests and Clearings*, p 274

vi DAVID JOHNSON, b. at Hollis, 4 Jul 1764

vii ARATHUSA JOHNSON, b. estimated 1770 and baptized at Westford, 13 Oct 1782

viii DELIVERANCE "DILLY" JOHNSON, b. about 1772 and baptized at Westford, 13 Oct 1782; d. at Westford, 1 Mar 1839; m. at Westford, 10 May 1794, JONAS HILDRETH, b. at Westford, 25 Jun 1766 son of Zachariah and Elizabeth (Prescott) Hildreth; Jonas d. at Westford, 14 Jan 1808.

534) ELIZABETH JOHNSON (*Andrew Johnson*[4], *James Johnson*[3], *Mary Holt Johnson*[2], *Nicholas*[1]), b. at Andover, 18 Apr 1737 daughter of Andrew and Hannah (Chandler) Johnson; d. about 1777; m. at Andover, 30 May 1765, SAMUEL FARLEY, b. at Reading, 1 May 1741 son of Samuel and Mary (Adams) Farley; Samuel d. after 1820 when he was living in Scipio, NY. Samuel married second Hannah Chandler on 5 Mar 1778.

Samuel and Elizabeth had three children in Andover and then relocated to Pepperell where a fourth child was born. After Elizabeth's death, Samuel married Hannah Chandler daughter of David and Abial (Chandler) Chandler and had five more children. Samuel then was in several locations including Springfield, Hampden, and finally in Scipio, New York.[1427]

On 10 October 1820, Samuel Farley of Scipio, New York then age seventy-nine gave a statement related to his pension application. He first enlisted in 1776 in the company of Capt. John Nutting and he had a second enlistment in the Spring 1777 for a period of three years. Samuel served two years of his enlistment himself but hired a substitute for the third year. He originally was granted a pension in 1818. He reported being a blacksmith by trade, but his infirmities prevented his being able to do this work. In 1820, his household consisted of one daughter living with him. The value of his estate in 1820 was $79.01.[1428]

Elizabeth Johnson and Samuel Farley were parents of four children.

i ELIZABETH FARLEY, b. at Andover, 11 Aug 1766; d. at Charlestown, MA, 12 Dec 1858; m. at Groton, 16 Sep 1784, JOSHUA PARKER, b. at Groton, 26 May 1764 son of Ephraim and Azubah (Farnsworth) Parker; Joshua d. at Groton, 15 Sep 1843.

ii SAMUEL FARLEY, b. at Andover, 2 Jan 1769

iii MARY FARLEY, b. at Andover, 11 May 1771; m. at Brimfield, 23 Dec 1800, SOLOMON DUNHAM, b. at Brimfield, 17 Dec 1770 son of Joseph and Sarah (Davis) Dunham; Solomon d. at Brimfield, 1836.[1429]

iv HANNAH FARLEY, b. at Pepperell, 15 Oct 1776

535) EPHRAIM JOHNSON (*Andrew Johnson*[4], *James Johnson*[3], *Mary Holt Johnson*[2], *Nicholas*[1]), b. at Andover, 31 Mar 1742 son of Andrew and Hannah (Chandler) Johnson; d. at Wilton, NH, 27 Dec 1834; m. (intention) 23 Mar 1765, MARY FARLEY, b. at Reading, 28 Apr 1743 daughter of Samuel and Mary (Adams) Farley; Mary d. at Wilton, 24 Apr 1834.

Ephraim and Mary resided in Wilton where their seven children were born.

On 1 April 1818 in the seventy-sixth year of his age, Ephraim Johnson made a declaration related to his application for pension. He related that he was a minute man and was in Lexington soon after the battle in April 1775. Immediately after, he enlisted in Capt. Benjamin Ames's company in the regiment of Col. James Frye in the 1st regiment of the Massachusetts line for eight months. Following that term, he immediately re-enlisted in in Capt. Southbridge's company in Col. Poor's regiment for one year. He was honorably discharged at Trenton, New Jersey. He was at the battles of Bunker Hill and Trenton. He noted that he was poor and relied on his benevolent neighbors for assistance. On 4 July 1820, Ephraim Johnson of Wilton aged seventy-eight provided a statement that members of his family were wife age seventy-seven and daughter Elizabeth age thirty-three. Personal estate was valued at $29.00 verified by the selectman of Wilton. He had been a laborer but "was now past labouring." A letter from Edmund Parker dated 15 August 1835 related to possible arrears of the pension noted that the pensioner was deceased leaving four children one of whom lived in Canada.[1430]

Daughter Elizabeth did not marry, and on 4 June 1839 the administration of her estate was assigned to Jonathan Burton of Wilton. The administration order notes the Elizabeth died "leaving no children nor Father nor Mother, but a Brother residing in the Province of Canada and two sisters who declined administration of said estate."[1431]

i ANDREW JOHNSON, b. at Reading, 3 Jul 1766; died young

ii EPHRAIM JOHNSON, b. at Reading, 19 Jul 1769

iii JOSIAH JOHNSON, b. at Wilton, 14 Aug 1774; d. after 1852, at St. Armand, Québec; m. at Rockingham, VT, 3 Aug 1797, ELIZABETH WHITNEY, b. 1776 likely daughter of John and Elizabeth (Sawtell) Whitney of Rockingham, VT.

[1427] Stuart, "Some Descendants of George Farley", NEHGR, 1982, volume 136, p 138

[1428] Revolutionary War Pension and Bounty-Land Warrant Application Files, 1800-1900, Case 43541

[1429] Dunham, *Dunham Genealogy*, p 203

[1430] U. S. Revolutionary War Pension and Bounty-Land Warrant Application Files, Case S44464

[1431] *New Hampshire. Probate Court (Hillsborough County)*; Probate Place: *Hillsborough, New Hampshire, volume 44, p 69*

iv ANDREW JOHNSON, b. at Wilton, 4 Sep 1778; d. at Ludlow, VT, 15 Jun 1825 (probate 28 Sep 1825); m. about 1802, ELIZABETH "BETSEY" DAY, b. about 1780 daughter of Robert Day; Elizabeth d. at Ludlow, 2 Jul 1857.

v MARY JOHNSON, b. at Wilton, 1782; m. at Wilton, 25 Oct 1810, DAVID MCINTIRE, b. about 1776.

vi HANNAH JOHNSON, b. at Wilton, 1783; d. at Bedford, MA, 30 Jul 1842; m. at Wilton, 1 Jan 1809, OBED POLLARD, b. at Bedford, MA, 18 Oct 1783 son of Oliver and Mary (Hill) Pollard; Obed d. at Lexington, MA, 11 Mar 1846.

vii ELIZABETH JOHNSON, b. at Wilton, 1787; d. at Wilton, 3 May 1839. Elizabeth did not marry.

536) JAMES JOHNSON (*Andrew Johnson⁴, James Johnson³, Mary Holt Johnson², Nicholas¹*), b. at Andover, 15 Oct 1743 son of Andrew and Hannah (Chandler) Johnson; m. at Andover, 16 Aug 1768, ANNIS COREY, b. at Chelmsford, 4 Nov 1735 daughter of Ephraim and Hannah (Merrill) Corey.

James Johnson resided in west parish of Andover and had the nickname "general." He served in the French and Indian War and in the Revolution, described as becoming "het up" in battled from which he never fully recovered.[1432]

He is likely the James Johnson of Andover who was a private in Capt. Benjamin Ames's company of minute men who marched at the alarm on 19 April 1775. He had several short periods of enlistment followed by a three-year term from 7 March 1777 to 7 March 1780.[1433]

There are three children known for James Johnson and Annis Corey born at Andover.

i JAMES JOHNSON, b. 26 Mar 1769. He perhaps settled in New Boston, New Hampshire.[1434]

ii ANNIS JOHNSON (twin), b. 3 Dec 1772; d. at Haverhill, MA, 12 Jan 1858; m. at Andover, 12 Dec 1797, DUDLEY TROW, b. at Beverly, about 1773 son of John and Hannah (Dodge) Trow; Dudley d. at Haverhill, 11 Jul 1856.

iii HANNAH JOHNSON (twin), b. 3 Dec 1772; d. at Andover, Feb 1849; m. 1st at Andover, 3 Jul 1800, HENRY LUSCOMBE; Henry d. about 1803. Hannah m. 2nd at Andover, 14 May 1807, JOHN BAILEY, b. about 1751; John d. at Tewksbury, 18 Oct 1807. Hannah m. 3rd at Andover, 17 Jul 1826, JOHN HARDY. John Bailey was first married to Sarah Hunt. Hannah had one son, Henry Luscombe born 1800, from her first marriage, and a daughter Cynthia born 16 Dec 1807 from her marriage to John Bailey.[1435]

537) OBADIAH JOHNSON (*Obadiah Johnson⁴, James Johnson³, Mary Holt Johnson², Nicholas¹*), b. at Andover, 20 Nov 1725 son of Obadiah and Hannah (Osgood) Johnson; m. 29 Dec 1748, LYDEA BALLARD, b. at Andover, 12 Mar 1727/8 daughter of Josiah and Mary (Chandler) Ballard; Lydea d. at Andover, 6 Jul 1779.

Obadiah Johnson and Lydea Ballard were parents of seven children born at Andover.

i OBADIAH JOHNSON, b. 14 Nov 1749

ii JOSIAH JOHNSON, b. 28 Dec 1751

iii LYDIA JOHNSON, b. 30 Aug 1754

iv MARY JOHNSON, baptized 3 Oct 1756

v DEBORAH JOHNSON, b. 6 Jan 1760

vi HANNAH JOHNSON, baptized 19 Sep 1762; d. at Hatley, Québec, 2 Mar 1809; m. at Andover, 2 Sep 1784, JEREMIAH LOVEJOY, b. at Andover, 29 Oct 1761 son of Jeremiah and Dorothy (Ballard) Lovejoy; Jeremiah d. at Hatley, 17 Jul 1810.[1436]

vii JAMES JOHNSON, baptized 25 Aug 1765; d. at Andover, 2 May 1789.

538) JACOB JOHNSON (*Obadiah Johnson⁴, James Johnson³, Mary Holt Johnson², Nicholas¹*), b. at Andover, 19 May 1727 son of Obadiah and Hannah (Osgood) Johnson; d. at Andover, 31 May 1803 at age 86; m. at Andover, 16 May 1758, SARAH DOLIVER, b. about 1740; Sarah d. at Andover, 4 Apr 1807 at age 67 years, 6 months.

Jacob was a blacksmith in Andover following in his father's footsteps. On 26 December 1786 (recorded 5 December 1788), Jacob conveyed to his son Isaac for £150 three pieces of land in Andover including the blacksmith shop. On 26 November

---

1432 Abbott, Early Records of the Johnson Family of Andover, p 11, https://www.mhl.org/sites/default/files/files/Abbott/Johnson%20Family.pdf

1433 Massachusetts Soldiers and Sailors in the Revolution, volume 8, p 837

1434 Abbott, Early Records of the Johnson Family of Andover, p 11

1435 Cynthia, d. John, deceased, and Hannah, Dec. 16, 1807. Cynthia was born at Andover.

1436 Hubbard, *Forests and Clearings*, p 283

1788, for £85, Isaac Johnson conveyed to Stephen Osgood of Tewksbury the three tracts of land, half the dwelling house, and half the blacksmith shop.[1437]

In his will written 5 November 1802 (probate 28 June 1803), Jacob Johnson bequeathed to beloved wife Sarah the improvement of one-third of the real estate during her natural life as well as the best bed and the household furniture except that given to his two daughters as long as she is a widow. Sarah also receives provisions for her support. Sons Isaac, Joseph, and David each receives one dollar to complete their portions. Daughter Sarah receives the second bed and the furniture belonging to the same and the use of a room in the house while she is single. Daughter Elizabeth receives the third bed and furniture and also may remain in the house while she is single. Jacob further states that his wife is not to bring any man or family into his house without the consent of son Osgood. After Sarah's death, the furniture is divided between daughters Sarah and Elizabeth but reverts to Osgood if they die without children. Son Osgood receives all the lands and buildings and is also named executor.[1438]

Jacob Johnson and Sarah Doliver were parents of ten children born at Andover. Sons Joseph and David settled in Bradford, Vermont and son Isaac likely also settled there.

i JACOB JOHNSON, b. 28 Jul 1759; d. at Andover, of "putrid fever" 17 May 1790.

ii PHINEAS JOHNSON, b. 1 Sep 1761; d. at Andover of consumption, 28 Oct 1791.

iii ISAAC JOHNSON, b. 28 July 1763. Isaac seems to have gone to Bradford, VT with his brothers Joseph and David and he may be the Isaac listed there in the 1820 census with what seems a large family, but the name of his wife has not been found.

iv JOSEPH JOHNSON, b. 1 Apr 1765; d. likely at Orange County, VT, 1827; m. at Andover, 12 Feb 1795, ELIZABETH BICKFORD, baptized at Salem, 24 Jul 1768 daughter of Jonathan and Sarah (King) Bickford; Elizabeth d. at Roxbury, MA, 15 Aug 1854.

v SARAH JOHNSON, b. at Andover, 22 Feb 1767. Sarah did not marry; she may be the Sally Johnson who died at Andover, 6 May 1826.

vi ELIZABETH JOHNSON, baptized at Andover, 29 Oct 1769. Elizabeth did not marry; she perhaps died at Andover, 13 Apr 1824.

vii DAVID JOHNSON, b. 11 Jul 1772; d. after 1830 at Bradford, VT; m. at Andover, 15 Dec 1796, ABIGAIL AMES, b. at Andover, 4 Oct 1779 daughter of Benjamin and Dorcas (Lovejoy) Ames;[1439] Abigail d. at Bradford, after 1850.

viii DOLIVAR JOHNSON, baptized 11 Sep 1774; d. 20 Aug 1779.

ix OSGOOD JOHNSON, b. 24 Jun 1777; d. of consumption at Andover, 23 Dec 1808; m. at Andover, 25 Nov 1802, FANNY ABBOTT, b. at Andover, 30 Mar 1779 daughter of Jeduthun and Hannah (Poor) Abbott; Fanny d. at Andover, 19 Jul 1829.

x HANNAH BLANCHARD JOHNSON, baptized 20 Jun 1782; d. 27 Nov 1784.

539) DEBORAH JOHNSON (*Obadiah Johnson[4], James Johnson[3], Mary Holt Johnson[2], Nicholas[1]*), b. at Andover, 5 Jul 1742 daughter of Obadiah and Deborah (Ruse) Johnson; d. at Haverhill, 30 Mar 1812; m. at Andover,12 Nov 1761, NATHAN BAILEY, b. at Bradford, 17 Jul 1740 son of Nathan and Mary (Palmer) Bailey; Nathan d. at Haverhill, 25 Aug 1806.

Nathan Bailey had a farm in Andover, but when the family relocated to Haverhill, he kept a public house. He served as a captain in the militia.[1440]

In his will written 9 July 1806 (probate 1 October 1806), Nathan Bailey bequeaths to beloved wife Deborah and to her heirs and assigns forever all the real estate in Haverhill. She also has the improvement of all the personal estate during her natural life. Each of the following heirs receives a bequest of one dollar: son Nathan, son Obadiah, daughter Deborah Dane, daughter Dolly Ordway, daughter Anna Whittier, daughter Hannah Osgood, daughter Mary, daughter Phebe, and granddaughter Rhoda Merrill. Daughters Mary and Phebe will receive all the household furniture at the decease of their mother. Deborah was named executrix. Real estate was valued at $700, $550 of that being the dwelling house with lot in Haverhill. Personal estate was valued at $376.38. On 5 October 1813, son Nathan was named administrator as his mother had died before the full administration of the estate.[1441] Deborah Bailey did not leave a will and her estate entered probate 8 May 1812.[1442] Son Nathan was named administrator. Real estate was valued at $520 and personal estate at $475.11.

[1437] Massachusetts Land Records, 1620-1986, Essex County, 149:131, 149:132

[1438] *Essex County, MA: Probate File Papers, 1638-1881.*Online database. *AmericanAncestors.org.* New England Historic Genealogical Society, 2014. Case 15049

[1439] The will of Captain Benjamin Ames (probate 1809) includes a bequest to his daughter Abigail wife of David Johnson.

[1440] Cutter, *Genealogical and Personal Memoirs Relating to the Families of Boston and Eastern Massachusetts*, Volume 2, p 1045

[1441] *Essex County, MA: Probate File Papers, 1638-1881.*Online database. *AmericanAncestors.org.* New England Historic Genealogical Society, 2014. Case 1374

[1442] *Essex County, MA: Probate File Papers, 1638-1881.*Online database. *AmericanAncestors.org.* New England Historic Genealogical Society, 2014. Case 1307

Deborah Johnson and Nathan Bailey were parents of nine children born at Andover.

i DEBORAH BAILEY, b. at Andover, 2 Jan 1763; d. at Greenfield, NH, 13 Dec 1838; m. at Andover, 8 May 1783, JOHN DANE, b. at Newburyport, 27 Aug 1762 son of John and Mary (Moody) Dane; John d. at Greenfield, 28 May 1841.

ii HANNAH BAILEY, b. at Andover, 21 Dec 1765; d. at Blue Hill, ME, 10 Jul 1829; m. at Andover, 31 May 1785, her fourth cousin, JOSEPH OSGOOD (*Elizabeth Abbott Osgood[5], Thomas Abbott[4], Hannah Gray Abbott[3], Hannah Holt Gray[2], Nicholas[1]*), b. at Andover, 5 Oct 1760 son of Samuel and Elizabeth (Abbott) Osgood; Joseph d. at Blue Hill, 15 Mar 1854.

iii MARY BAILEY, b. 2 Jan 1767; d. at Haverhill, 19 May 1851. Mary did not marry. She was living with her sister Dorothy in 1850.

iv ANNA BAILEY, b. at Andover, 10 Feb 1769; m. at Haverhill, 22 Jul 1798, WILLIAM WHITTIER, b. at Haverhill, 30 Jul 1778 son of Job and Mercy (Lufkin) Whittier; William d. at Haverhill, 21 Aug 1850.

v NATHAN BAILEY, b. at Andover, 2 Apr 1771; d. at Haverhill, 9 May 1857; m. at Haverhill, 10 May 1803, JEMIMA EMERSON, b. at Salem, NH, 9 Feb 1778 daughter of T. Webster and Hannah (Maxfield) Emerson; Jemima d. before 1850. Nathan was living at the poor farm in Haverhill in 1855.

vi CHLOE BAILEY, b. at Andover, 22 Apr 1773; d. at Haverhill, 28 Dec 1803; m. at Haverhill, 23 Dec 1790, SAMUEL MERRILL, b. at Haverhill, 6 Jan 1761 son of Samuel and Abigail (Eaton) Merrill. Samuel was first married to Rhoda Bailey who died in 1789.

vii OBADIAH BAILEY, b. at Andover, 31 May 1775; d. at Haverhill, 15 Sep 1829; m. at Haverhill, May 1800, MIRIAM LUFKIN, b. at Haverhill, about 1780; Miriam d. at Haverhill, 24 May 1848.

viii DOROTHY BAILEY, b. at Andover, 10 Dec 1777; d. at Haverhill, 9 Feb 1865; m. 1st 27 Nov 1800, AMOS ORDWAY, b. at Haverhill, 8 Nov 1770 son of Benjamin and Rebecca (Massey) Ordway; Amos d. at Haverhill, 13 Aug 1828. Dorothy m. 2nd 19 Nov 1837, BENJAMIN PUTNAM, b. at Danvers, 20 Mar 1782 son of Benjamin and Miriam (Flint0 Putnam; Benjamin d. at Haverhill, 20 Aug 1850.

ix PHEBE BAILEY, b. at Andover, 9 Sep 1781; Phebe did not marry.

540) PETER JOHNSON (*Obadiah Johnson[4], James Johnson[3], Mary Holt Johnson[2], Nicholas[1]*), b. at Andover, 26 Jul 1749 son of Obadiah and Dorothy (Ballard) Johnson; d. of consumption at Andover, 3 Nov 1798; m. at Andover, 26 Aug 1773, EUNICE BLANCHARD, b. at Andover, 12 Aug 1755 daughter of Samuel and Ruth (Tenney) Blanchard; Eunice d. at Wayland, MA, 6 Oct 1846.[1443]

Peter Johnson had inherited from his father Obadiah all the lands, dwelling house, barn, and other buildings in Andover.[1444]

Peter Johnson and Eunice Blanchard were parents of eleven children born at Andover. Children 2-5 were all baptized on the same day, 9 June 1782.

Daughter Eunice married Nathaniel Coverly, Jr. who had followed his father into the printing business. The company had financial reverses and a bankruptcy case in 1803 stripped Eunice and Nathaniel of all but their essential possessions. The business, however, resumed and Eunice continued the pamphlet shop as her own after the decease of her husband in 1824.[1445]

i EUNICE JOHNSON, b. 2 Feb 1774; d. at Wayland, MA, 6 Aug 1863; m. at Boston, 10 Feb 1800, NATHANIEL COVERLY, b. about 1775 son of Nathaniel and Susanna (Cowell) Coverly; Nathaniel d. at Boston, 14 Sep 1824.

ii DOROTHY "DOLLY" JOHNSON, b. about 1776 and baptized at Andover, 9 Jun 1782

iii MARY BLANCHARD JOHNSON, b. about 1778 and baptized 9 Jun 1782; d. at Wayland, MA, 4 Sep 1863; m. JOHN ALLEN, b. at Medfield, MA, 9 Aug 1767 son of Nathan and Thankful (Hartshorn) Allen;[1446] John d. at Wayland, 3 Feb 1859.

iv FANNY JOHNSON, b. estimated 1779 and baptized 9 Jun 1782

v PETER JOHNSON, baptized 9 Jun 1782; d. at Charlestown, MA, 18 Jan 1848; m. at Marblehead, 14 Aug 1803, PRISCILLA PROCTOR, b. at Marblehead, 9 Jan 1785 daughter of Joseph and Nancy (Broughton) Proctor.

[1443] Eunice, b. Andover, wid. Peter, dropsy, Oct. 6, 1846, a. 91.

[1444] *Essex County, MA: Probate File Papers, 1638-1881.*Online database. *AmericanAncestors.org.* New England Historic Genealogical Society, 2014. Case 15104

[1445] A detailed account of the Coverly family printing business and financial reverses can be found in Keller, Kate van Winkle, "Nathaniel Coverly and Son, Printers, 1767-1825." Proceedings of the American Antiquarian Society, April 2007, volume 117, part 1, pp 211-252

[1446] Father's name of Nathan is given on John's death record.

vi HANNAH JOHNSON, baptized 6 Jul 1783

vii OBADIAH JOHNSON, baptized 8 Oct 1785

viii JOSEPH JOHNSON, baptized 24 May 1789

ix SAMUEL JOHNSON, baptized 27 Feb 1791

x DAVID JOHNSON, baptized 26 May 1793

xi PAMELA JOHNSON, baptized 26 Jun 1796

541) HANNAH JOHNSON (*Obadiah Johnson⁴, James Johnson³, Mary Holt Johnson², Nicholas¹*), b. at Andover, 8 Feb 1753 daughter of Obadiah and Dorothy (Ballard) Johnson; m. at Andover, 8 Apr 1773, her third cousin, TIMOTHY HOLT (*Elizabeth Holt Holt⁴, John³, Samuel², Nicholas¹*), b. at Andover, 19 May 1746 son of Timothy and Elizabeth (Holt) Holt;[1447] Timothy d. at Weston, VT, 3 May 1836.

Hannah and Timothy were in Andover, members of South Church admitted on profession of faith on 22 August 1775 and were dismissed to the church at Wilton on 25 June 1780.[1448] It is not known how long the family was in Wilton, but they were in Weston, Vermont by 1810.[1449] Timothy over age 45 was head of household and Hannah appears to be deceased by 1810.

There are just three children known for Hannah Johnson and Timothy Holt.

i HANNAH HOLT, b. at Andover, 29 Jun 1773

ii ELIZABETH HOLT, baptized at Andover, 24 Sep 1775; d. at Brookline, VT, 24 Nov 1874;[1450] m. at Wilton, 27 Nov 1794, her first cousin, ISRAEL WHITNEY (*Hannah Holt Whitney⁵, Timothy⁴, Nicholas³, Nicholas², Nicholas¹*), b. at Wilton, 4 Jul 1774 son of Richard and Hannah (Holt) Whitney; Israel d. at Brookline, 14 Dec 1850.

iii TIMOTHY HOLT, b. at Andover, 7 Sep 1777; d. at Weston, VT, 31 May 1860; m. 16 Oct 1804, HANNAH TYLER, b. at Rindge, NH, 20 Oct 1786 daughter of Parker and Hannah (Flint) Tyler; Hannah d. at Unity, NH, 10 Sep 1874.

542) ELIZABETH CHAMBERLAIN (*Mary Johnson Chamberlain⁴, James Johnson³, Mary Holt Johnson², Nicholas¹*), b. at Billerica, 5 Apr 1720 daughter of Joseph and Mary (Johnson) Chamberlain; d. at Mansfield, CT, 19 Mar 1809; m. 30 Mar 1738, PETER DIMMOCK[1451], baptized at Mansfield, 15 Sep 1717 son of Benjamin and Mary (Thatcher) Dimmock; Peter d. at Mansfield, 30 Jul 1810.

Elizabeth Chamberlain and Peter Dimmock were parents of ten children born at Mansfield, Connecticut.[1452]

i DINAH DIMMOCK, b. 16 Mar 1740; d. at Mansfield, 16 Jan 1767; m. at Mansfield, 31 Oct 1765, Capt. AMARIAH WILLIAMS, b. at Watertown, MA, 9 Feb 1729 son of William and Elizabeth (Wilson) Williams; Amariah d. at Mansfield, 26 Mar 1802. Amariah married second Mary Royce.

ii PETER DIMMOCK, b. 6 Mar 1741/2; died young

iii ELIZABETH DIMMOCK, b. 10 Feb 1744; d. at Mansfield, 10 Jun 1773; m. 25 Dec 1760, Capt. JACOB HOVEY, baptized at Mansfield, 10 Aug 1740 son of Joseph and Thankful (Learned) Hovey; Jacob d. 22 Dec 1807. Joseph married second Abial Smith on 5 May 1777.

iv JOSEPH DIMMOCK, b. 27 Feb 1745; d. at Bridgewater, VT, 26 Feb 1820; m. PRUDENCE DEWOLFE, b. 1750; Prudence d. at Bridgewater, 29 Sep 1824.

v SYBIL DIMMOCK, b. 10 Oct 1749

vi ABIGAIL DIMMOCK, b. 10 Jun 1751; d. 19 Dec 1771; m. at Mansfield, 20 Jul 1768, ELEAZER DUNHAM, b. at Mansfield, 2 Jul 1744 son of Ebenezer and Phebe (Ladd) Dunham. Eleazer married second Elizabeth.

vii BENJAMIN DIMMOCK, b. 24 Feb 1753

viii RUTH DIMMOCK, b. 3 Feb 1757

[1447] There are two Timothy Holts of similar age, one who married Hannah Johnson and one who married Ede McIntire. It is generally accepted in published genealogies (Durrie's Holt genealogy and Littlefield's Weston genealogies) that this Timothy married Hannah Johnson. However, the Timothy Holt who died at Weston in 1836 was 93 years at time of death which fits better with Timothy Holt born 8 Sep 1744 son of Timothy and Hannah (Dane) Holt, and it may well be Timothy born 1744 who married Hannah Johnson.

[1448] South Church, *Historical Manual of South Church of Andover*

[1449] Year: 1810; Census Place: Weston, Windsor, Vermont; Roll: 65; Page: 468; Image: 00335; Family History Library Film: 0218669

[1450] Death record gives father as Timothy Holt and age at death as 99 years, 2 months, 7 days

[1451] Dimock has multiple spellings including Dimick and Dimmick and the name spelling is not consistent in records.

[1452] Dimock, *Births, Baptisms, Marriages and Deaths . . . of Mansfield, Connecticut*, p 64

ix MIRIAM DIMMOCK, b. 24 Sep 1759; m. about 1779, JAMES WILLS.

x PETER DIMMOCK, b. 11 Aug 1761; d. at Paris, NY, 1838. Peter served in the Revolution entering in service in 1779 as a substitute for his father who had been drafted. He had a second enlistments as a substitute for his brother Joseph. After the war, he resided in Mansfield until about 1813 when he went to Paris, NY and was later in Kirkland. By 1836, he had returned to Paris, NY where he likely died in 1838 (last time of pension payment). Peter had much difficulty obtaining a pension due to confusion in the records, and he finally obtained a pension of $20 per year by a special act of Congress approved 28 June 1836 making payment retroactive to 1831.[1453] Peter's petition to Congress pleads for consideration of his case as "his head is whitened for the grave and his feet are ready to enter the dark and gloomy valley, that they will not suffer him to depart, uncheered by his country's bounty, but that he may yet, while among his compatriots of the Revolution for the few short days yet allotted to him, be permitted to take a little of that bounty and thereby be able to join with his old associates in arms in celebrating the glory & gratitude of his country." Peter does seem to have married and there is a record for one daughter who died at Tolland 18 Apr 1794 at age two. The name of his wife was not found.

543) JOSEPH CHAMBERLAIN (*Mary Johnson Chamberlain[4], James Johnson[3], Mary Holt Johnson[2], Nicholas[1]*), b. at Billerica, 24 Feb 1721/2 son of Joseph and Mary (Johnson) Chamberlain; m. at Stafford, CT, 3 Jul 1744, ELIZABETH DELANO, b. at Dartmouth, MA, 15 May 1722 daughter of Jonathan and Amy (Hatch) Delano.[1454]

Joseph Chamberlain and Elizabeth Delano were parents of three children.

i SUSANNAH CHAMBERLAIN, b. at Tolland, 16 Jul 1745; m. at Amenia, NY, 16 Sep 1773, DANIEL HUNTER

ii JOEL CHAMBERLAIN, b. at Tolland, 4 Oct 1747

iii ABNER CHAMBERLAIN, b. at Coventry, CT, 14 Nov 1751

544) MEHITABLE CHAMBERLAIN (*Mary Johnson Chamberlain[4], James Johnson[3], Mary Holt Johnson[2], Nicholas[1]*), b. at Lebanon, CT, 19 Aug 1727 daughter of Joseph and Mary (Johnson) Chamberlain; likely d. at Surry, NH; m. at Tolland, 25 Mar 1751, ELIJAH BENTON, b. at Tolland, 30 Jun 1728 son of Daniel and Mary (Skinner) Benton; Elijah d. at Surry, NH, 1786 (probate 1786).

Mehitable and Elijah had their twelve children in Tolland but were in Surry, New Hampshire by 1772 when Elijah purchased land. He sold half his land to son Abijah in 1774 and the other half of the property to Gideon Tiffany also in 1774.[1455]

Elijah's estate was in probate 26 March 1786 with Barnabas Delano as administrator. Personal estate was valued at £5.13.9.[1456]

Elijah Benton and Mehitable Chamberlain were parents of twelve children born at Tolland. Sons Adoniram and Elijah both served in Revolution for which service they received pensions.[1457]

i ABIJAH BENTON, b. 25 Feb 1752; d. at Surry, NH, 26 May 1823; m. 29 Mar 1774, REBECCA FIELD, b. 13 Aug 1752 daughter of Moses and Anna (Dickinson) Field; Rebecca d. at Surry, 28 Dec 1816.

ii LYDIA BENTON, b. 6 Jun 1753

iii LOIS BENTON, b. 4 Apr 1755; m. at Alstead, 3 Dec 1776, GIDEON DELANO, b. at Tolland, 27 Nov 1742 son of Barnabas and Ruth (Pack) Delano; Gideon d. at Alstead, 4 Jul 1809.

iv MEHITABLE BENTON, b. 14 Aug 1756; d. at Vershire, at age 58, 5 Jul 1814; m. at Alstead, NH, 12 Nov 1795, JONATHAN AUSTIN.

v ADONIRAM BENTON, b. 27 Mar 1758; d. 29 Oct 1760.

vi ELIJAH BENTON, b. 17 Apr 1760; d. at Stewartstown, NH, 14 Oct 1841; m. 20 Oct 1793, SALLY SELLINGHAM, b. 1773 daughter of Henry and Amy (Brainard) Sellingham; Sally d. after 1844.

vii ADONIRAM BENTON, b. 21 May 1761; d. at Surry, NH, 29 Aug 1842; m. 1st RUTH, b. about 1770; Ruth d. at Keene, NH, 10 Nov 1815. Adoniram m. 2nd at Surry, 5 Jun 1816 widow BETSEY GRIFFIN, b. about 1772; Betsey d. at Surry, 5 Aug 1859.

viii JOSEPH BENTON, b. 5 Aug 1763

1453 U. S. Revolutionary War Pension and Bounty-Land Application Files, case S23197

1454 The March 1751 will of Jonathan Delano of Tolland includes bequests to his wife Amy and to his daughter Elizabeth Chamberlain.

1455 Kingsbury, *History of the Town of Surry*, p 309

1456 *New Hampshire. Probate Court (Cheshire County)*; Probate Place: *Cheshire, New Hampshire, Estate Files, Case B56*

1457 Benton, *David Benton, Jr. and Sarah Bingham: Their Ancestors and Descendants*, p 28

ix MARY BENTON, b. 5 Aug 1763; d. at Surry, NH, 20 Jan 1825; m. 22 Apr 1783, LEVI FULLER, b. at Bolton, 1762 son of Joshua and Joanna (Taylor0 Fuller; Levi d. at Surry, 12 Mar 1822.

x RUHAMMAH BENTON, b. 24 Aug 1765; d. 24 May 1766.

xi ENOCH BENTON, b. 3 Sep 1767; d. 13 Sep 1767.

xii WILLIAM BENTON, b. 16 Jan 1770; d. at Lebanon, NH, 6 May 1829; m. at Wrentham, MA, 22 Jan 1792, CYNTHIA RICHARDSON, b. 1770; Cynthia d. at Lebanon, 27 Mar 1853.

545) JOHN CHAMBERLAIN (*Mary Johnson Chamberlain[4], James Johnson[3], Mary Holt Johnson[2], Nicholas[1]*), baptized at Tolland, 21 Jun 1730 son of Joseph and Mary (Johnson) Chamberlain; m. 1st about 1758, MARGARET, b. about 1733 who has not been identified;[1458] Margaret d. at Amenia, 29 Dec 1772. John m. 2nd about 1773, ABIGAIL FENTON (widow of Abiel Abbot), b. at Willington, 27 Aug 1730 daughter of Francis and Ann (Berry) Fenton; Abigail d. at Amenia, 14 Aug 1776. John m. 3rd about 1777, LYDIA LATHROP (widow of Timothy Delano), b. at Tolland, 21 Jun 1736 daughter of John and Ann (Thatcher) Lathrop.

John Chamberlain was early in Amenia and signed the association test there in 1776. He was a physician who practice for a time in Poughkeepsie.[1459] He was a member of the Dutchess County militia "associated exempts" company of Capt. Abraham Schenck.[1460]

John and Margaret Chamberlain were parents of seven children born at Amenia.[1461][1462] Sons Joseph, Jabez and David were physicians.

i JOHN CHAMBERLAIN, baptized 24 Nov 1759

ii JABEZ CHAMBERLAIN, baptized 18 Oct 1761; died young

iii JACOB CHAMBERLAIN, baptized 17 Apr 1763

iv JOSEPH CHAMBERLAIN, baptized 21 Apr 1765; m. HANNAH CHAMBERLAIN.

v JABEZ CHAMBERLAIN, b. 10 Apr 1767; d. at Asylum, PA, 30 Sep 1848; m. 1st about 1792, JANE WILSON. Jabez m. 2nd 9 Jul 1795, IRENE GILBERT, b. at Lyme, CT, 14 Apr 1772 daughter of Samuel and Mary (Dodge) Gilbert; Irene d. at Asylum, PA, 6 Jan 1867. Jabez was a physician who came to Frenchtown about 1792, returned for a time to New York, and finally settled in Asylum, PA where he died.[1463]

vi DAVID CHAMBERLAIN, baptized 20 Aug 1769

vii MATILDA CHAMBERLAIN, baptized 26 Jan 1772; d. 28 Jul 1772

546) ABIAL CHAMBERLAIN (*Mary Johnson Chamberlain[4], James Johnson[3], Mary Holt Johnson[2], Nicholas[1]*), b. at Mansfield, CT, Mar 1732 daughter of Joseph and Mary (Johnson) Chamberlain; d. at Mansfield, 15 May 1771; m. at Mansfield, 10 Dec 1751, JAMES ROYSE, baptized at Mansfield, 15 Apr 1722 son of James and Mehitable (Arnold) Royse. James was first married to Abigail Scripture on 10 Dec 1742 and third married on 12 Nov 1771 to Rachel Kidder (widow of Jesse Dimmock).

Abial Chamberlain and James Royse were parents of eight children born at Mansfield.[1464]

i SOLOMON ROYSE, b. at Mansfield, 7 Jun 1752; d. at Mansfield, 17 Aug 1823; m. 1777, LYDIA ATWOOD, b. about 1759; Lydia d. at Mansfield, 18 Jul 1824.

ii ABIAL ROYSE, b. at Mansfield, 22 Aug 1753; d. at Pawlet, VT, 24 Jan 1835; m. at Amenia, NY, 9 Nov 1775, SIMEON REED, b. at Norwalk, CT, 21 Apr 1752 son of Eliakim and Sarah (Richards) Reed; Simeon d. at Pawlet, 24 Jul 1840.

1458 Although not certain, it is possible that Margaret is Margaret Delano, b. at Tolland in 1733 daughter of Jabez and Prudence (Hibbard) Delano. Jabez Delano died in 1752 prior to the marriage of his daughters so his will does not reference married names. Margaret Delano is of the right age and the use of the name Jabez for the second son of Margaret and John Chamberlain fits with this identification. This would also fit with the kinship network in this portion of the tree as there are several Delanos specifically related to Jonathan and Amy (Hatch) Delano marrying into this Chamberlain section. Margaret Delano is the granddaughter of Jonathan and Amy (Hatch) Delano. John Chamberlain's third wife Lydia Lathrop was the widow of Timothy Delano who was the son of Jonathan and Amy (Hatch) Delano.

1459 Reed, *Early History of Amenia*, p 57 and p 139

1460 New York in the Revolution, volume 1, p 154

1461 *New York, Genealogical Records, 1675-1920*, The New York Genealogical and Biographical Record (quarterly-1904) - Extracts; Publication Place: New York; Publisher: New York Genealogical and Biographical Society; Page Number: 205.

1462 World Chamberlain Society, William of Woburn, Fourth Generation, http://worldchamberlaingenealogy.org/dcc_fgr/dccfgr/ln08648.pdf

1463 Heverly, *History and Geography of Bradford County, Pennsylvania*, p 286

1464 Dimock, *Births, Baptisms, Marriages and Deaths. . . Mansfield, Connecticut*, pp 149-150

iii MEHITABLE ROYSE, b. at Mansfield, 8 Sep 1756; d. at Aurora, NY, 10 Sep 1849; m. at Mansfield, 24 May 1781, ELISHA DUNHAM, b. at Mansfield, 24 Sep 1754 son of Ebenezer and Eunice (Atwood) Dunham; Elisha d. at Pawlet, VT, Jan 1828.

iv UZZIEL ROYSE, b. at Mansfield, 4 Aug 1758; d. at Thompson, NY, 23 May 1833; m. at Tolland, 23 Nov 1786, EXPERIENCE PETTIS who has not been identified.

v ANNA ROYSE, b. at Mansfield, 7 Apr 1760; d. at Mansfield, 5 May 1802; m. at Mansfield, 22 Oct 1778, SYLVANUS CONANT, b. at Mansfield, 10 Feb 1750 son of Malachi and Sarah (Freeman) Conant; Sylvanus d. at Storrs, 2 Sep 1843. Sylvanus was second married to Elizabeth Utley.

vi DINAH ROYSE, b. 30 Jun 1763

vii LOIS ROYSE, b. 25 Nov 1765

viii JOSEPH CHAMBERLAIN ROYSE, b. at Mansfield, 16 Jul 1768; d. at Wales, MA, 1 Dec 1845; m. at Mansfield, 10 Nov 1794, MATILDA UPHAM, b. at Mansfield, 20 Jul 1774 mother of Joseph and Mary (Fletcher) Upham; Matilda d. at Wales, 9 Apr 1853.

547) JAMES CHAMBERLAIN (*Mary Johnson Chamberlain[4], James Johnson[3], Mary Holt Johnson[2], Nicholas[1]*), b. at Mansfield, 11 Feb 1734 son of Joseph and Mary (Johnson) Chamberlain; d. at Amherst, MA, 28 Apr 1812; m. 27 Jan 1757, ABIGAIL BOYNTON (widow of John Palmer), b. at Coventry, 17 Jun 1729 daughter of Zachariah and Sarah (Wyckham) Boynton; Abigail d. at Amherst, 5 Mar 1814.

Capt. James Chamberlain headed a Connecticut militia calvary company in Col. Chapman's regiment in the Revolution.[1465]

On 19 May 1812, widow Abigail requested that her son James be named administrator of James's estate. Personal estate was valued at $1801.85. Real estate was valued at $3,256 and one-third was set off to the widow. On 29 April 1814, after the reversion of the dower, a distribution was made to the following heirs: heirs of son James, daughter Naomi Hilliard, daughter Sarah Paine, and heirs of daughter Mary Cleveland.[1466]

James Chamberlain and Abigail Boynton were parents of six children, the birth of the oldest child recorded at Coventry and the others either at Coventry or Tolland.[1467] The family was in Amherst, Massachusetts in later years.

i JOSEPH CHAMBERLAIN, b. at Coventry, 4 Nov 1757; d. (buried) at Tolland, 12 Jun 1759.

ii MARY CHAMBERLAIN, b. 7 Aug 1759; d. at Winsted, CT, 15 Nov 1807; m. at Ellington, 9 Sep 1779, RUFUS CLEVELAND, b. at Canterbury, 15 Jun 1756 son of Benjamin and Rachel (-) Cleveland; Rufus d. at Winsted, 22 Feb 1838. Rufus married second Alice Jenkins.

iii SARAH CHAMBERLAIN, b. 12 Aug 1761; d. at Hadley, MA, 25 Jun 1835; m. at Ellington, 1782, ROSWELL PAINE, b. at North Bolton, CT, 24 Feb 1756 son of Stephen and Deborah (Skinner) Paine; Roswell d. at Amherst, MA, 7 Mar 1806.

iv JOSEPH CHAMBERLAIN, b. 1763; d. at Tolland, 3 Jun 1766.

v JAMES CHAMBERLAIN, b. 24 Jul 1766; d. at Amherst, MA, 22 Feb 1814; m. at East Windsor, CT, 25 Jun 1788, ANNAH WATKINS BABCOCK, b. at Ashford, 28 Dec 1767 daughter of Elijah and Elizabeth (Bassett) Babcock; Annah d. at Portland, ME, 2 Oct 1804.

vi NAOMI CHAMBERLAIN, b. 19 Nov 1769; d. at Colebrook, NH, 26 Apr 1867; m. at East Windsor, 1787, JOSEPH HILLIARD, b. 18 Aug 1765 son of Miner and Miriam (Barnes) Hilliard; Joseph d. at Colebrook, 22 Nov 1830.

548) PHEBE CHAMBERLAIN (*Mary Johnson Chamberlain[4], James Johnson[3], Mary Holt Johnson[2], Nicholas[1]*), baptized at Mansfield, 7 Aug 1737 daughter of Joseph and Mary (Johnson) Chamberlain; m. at Amenia, NY, 4 Mar 1762, ELIHU BEARDSLEY, baptized at Stratford, CT, 31 Oct 1736 son of David and Sarah (Wells) Beardsley;[1468] d. after 1800 when he was in Amenia.

There are records for two children of Phebe Chamberlain and Elihu Beardsley.

i SARAH BEARDSLEY, baptized at Milford, CT, 29 May 1763 but likely born at Amenia; m. 18 Feb 1787, her first cousin, CONRAD CHAMBERLAIN (*Colbe Chamberlain[5], Mary Johnson Chamberlain[4], James Johnson[3], Mary*

1465 Cole, *History of Tolland County, Connecticut*, volume 1, p 459

1466 *Hampshire County, MA: Probate File Papers, 1660-1889.* Online database. *AmericanAncestors.org.* New England Historic Genealogical Society, 2016, 2017. Case 26-26

1467 Cleveland, *A Genealogy of Benjamin Cleveland*, pp 186-187

1468 Holt, *Beardsley Genealogy*, p 40

Holt Johnson[2], Nicholas[1]), b. at Amenia, 17 Dec 1767 son of Colbe and Catherine (Winegar) Chamberlain; Conrad d. at Chenango, NY, 1829 (probate 29 Dec 1829). Conrad Chamberlain is a child in the next family below.

ii WILLIAM BEARDSLEY, b. at Milford, 25 May 1766

549) COLBE CHAMBERLAIN (*Mary Johnson Chamberlain[4], James Johnson[3], Mary Holt Johnson[2], Nicholas[1]*), b. at Tolland, 2 Dec 1738 son of Joseph and Mary (Johnson) Chamberlain; d. at Amenia, NY, 11 Sep 1796; m. at Amenia, 14 Nov 1765, CATHERINE WINEGAR, b. 2 Mar 1749 daughter of Conrad and Ann (Rauh) Winegar; Catherine d. at Amenia, 26 May 1808.

During the Revolution, Colbe Chamberlain served as 1st lieutenant in the Dutchess County 3rd militia company of Capt. Joshua Laselle.[1469] Col. Colbe Chamberlain was a town supervisor in Amenia in 1781.[1470]

Colbe Chamberlain and Catherine Winegar were parents of ten children born at Amenia.[1471]

i MARY CHAMBERLAIN, b. 13 Jul 1766; d. at Whitney Point, NY, 1 Nov 1836; m. by 1786, BENJAMIN HUBBARD FULLER, b. at Kent, CT, 1755; Benjamin d. at Whitney Point, 16 Aug 1816.

ii CONRAD CHAMBERLAIN, b. 17 Dec 1767; d. at Chenango, NY, 1829 (probate 29 Dec 1829); m. 18 Feb 1787, his first cousin, SARAH BEARDSLEY (*Phebe Chamberlain Beardsley[5], Mary Johnson Chamberlain[4], James Johnson[3], Mary Holt Johnson[2], Nicholas[1]*), baptized at Milford, 29 May 1763 daughter of Elihu and Phebe (Chamberlain) Beardsley. Sarah is a child in the family just above.

iii ELIZABETH CHAMBERLAIN, b. 13 Jul 1769; d. at Amenia, 27 Aug 1796; m. DANIEL HIBBARD, b. at Amenia, 1 Jun 1766 son of Robert and Lydia (Hebard) Hibbard; Daniel d. at Amenia, 6 Jan 1841. Daniel was second married to Elizabeth' s sister Letitia.

iv COLBE CHAMBERLAIN, b. 31 May 1771; d. at Westfield, MA, 2 Feb 1849; m. HANNAH PLATT, b. at Brookfield, CT, 1777 daughter of Jeremiah and Mary (Merwin) Platt; Hannah d. at Westfield, 28 Apr 1857.

v MARGARET CHAMBERLAIN, b. 10 Jan 1773; m. MOSES WALTHAM

vi JOSEPH H. CHAMBERLAIN, b. 14 Aug 1775; d. at Brooklyn, NY, 21 Feb 1857;[1472] m. LAURA BOSWORTH, b. at Washington, CT, 10 May 1783; Laura d. at Brooklyn, 29 Dec 1839.

vii LETITIA CHAMBERLAIN, b. 17 Sep 1777; m. as his second wife DANIEL HIBBARD who was first married to Letitia's sister Elizabeth (see above).

viii SUSANNAH CHAMBERLAIN, b. 21 Feb 1779; d. at Amenia, 20 Feb 1852; m. about 1811, as his second wife, SAMUEL SNYDER WINEGAR, b. 24 Apr 1776 son of Hendrick and Alice (Spooner) Winegar; Samuel d. at Amenia, 20 Feb 1852. Samuel was first married to Margaret Boyd.

ix HENRY C. CHAMBERLAIN, b. 21 Jul 1783; d. at Fort Wayne, IN, 11 Aug 1851; m. LORANA JACKSON, b. in CT, about 1785; Lorana d. at Fort Wayne, 1852.

x CATHERINE CHAMBERLAIN, b. 7 Jun 1786; d. at Amenia, 29 Jul 1816; m. JOHN J. HOLLISTER, b. 1777 son of David and Sarah (Landers) Hollister; John d. at Sharon, CT, 24 Sep 1834.

550) WILLIAM CHAMBERLAIN (*Mary Johnson Chamberlain[4], James Johnson[3], Mary Holt Johnson[2], Nicholas[1]*), b. at Tolland, 25 Jan 1744/5 son of Joseph and Mary (Johnson) Chamberlain; d. at Amenia, 27 Nov 1810; m. at Amenia, 12 Mar 1767, ABIGAIL HATCH, b. at Kent, CT, Dec 1742 daughter of Barnabas and Phebe (Cushman) Hatch;[1473] Abigail d. at Amenia, 4 Apr 1812.

Capt. William Chamberlain served with the 3rd regiment of Dutchess County militia and was at the Battle of Bennington.[1474] He also served on the Committee of Safety in Amenia.[1475] Abigail and William were early settlers of the Amenia district, and their nine children were born there.

i ISAAC CHAMBERLAIN, b. 12 Mar 1768; d. at Amenia, 3 Sep 1783.

ii SYBIL CHAMBERLAIN, b. 19 Jan 1770; d. at Amenia, 25 Dec 1843; m. SOLOMON FREEMAN, b. at Amenia, Feb 1767 son of Robert and Anna (Wentfield) Freeman, Solomon d. at Amenia, 16 Jan 1840.

1469 Reed, *Early History of Amenia*, p 63

1470 Smith, *History of Dutchess County, New York*, Part I, p 344

1471 Amenia Town Records, Records of the Town Clerk of Amenia Precinct, 1749-1868, "Michael Hopkins Record Book"

1472 The gravestone monument for Joseph and his wife Laura includes their dates of birth. Findagrave ID: 135498835

1473 The 1778 will of Barnabas Hatch includes a bequest to his daughter Abigail Chamberlain.

1474 New York State Comptroller's Office, *New York in the Revolution as Colony and State*, volume 1, p 139

1475 Reed, *Early History of Amenia*, p 68

iii WILLIAM CHAMBERLAIN, b. 12 Nov 1771; d. at Chenango, NY, 12 Jun 1850; m. LUCY PARK, b. at Amenia, 7 Oct 1776 daughter of Ebenezer and Bathsheba (Smith) Park; Lucy d. at Chenango, 14 Aug 1853.

iv JAMES CHAMBERLAIN, b. 6 Dec 1773; nothing further definitive known; he perhaps married Hannah.

v PHEBE CHAMBERLAIN, b. 8 Nov 1775; d. at Windham, NY, 20 Mar 1843; m. ROSWELL BUMP, b. 25 Oct 1772 son of Jedediah and Dimis (Chapman) Bump; Roswell d. at Windham, 13 Jan 1845.

vi ABIGAIL CHAPMAN, b. 31 Aug 1778; d. at Amenia, 23 Jun 1859; m. GILBERT BOYD, b. at Amenia and baptized at Sharon, 13 Nov 1791 son of John and Elizabeth (Winegar) Boyd; Gilbert d. at Amenia, 30 Aug 1832.

vii EPHRAIM CHAMBERLAIN, b. 23 Jan 1781; d. 8 Oct 1807.

viii REBECKAH CHAMBERLAIN, b. 8 Feb 1783; d. at Binghamton, NY, 27 Oct 1832; m. about 1803, ARCHIBALD MONTGOMERY ALLERTON, b. at Canterbury, 3 Dec 1780 son of David and Janet (Montgomery) Allerton; Archibald d. at Binghamton, 11 Apr 1863. Archibald was second married to Bathsheba Park.

ix OLIVER EDGERTON CHAMBERLAIN, b. 12 Sep 1785; d. at Amenia, 5 Aug 1843; m. HELENA ROW[1476], b. at Amenia, 1789 daughter of Conrad and Sybil (Goodrich) Row; Helena d. at Amenia, 5 Jan 1863.

551) REBECCA CHAMBERLAIN (*Mary Johnson Chamberlain⁴, James Johnson³, Mary Holt Johnson², Nicholas¹*), b. at Tolland, 25 Jan 1744/5 daughter of Joseph and Mary (Johnson) Chamberlain; d. at Amenia, 10 Dec 1777; m. at Amenia, 25 Jan 1765, SOLOMON CHASE, b. at Groton, MA, 9 Sep 1743 son of Benjamin and Rachel (Hartwell) Chase; Solomon d. at Westerlo, NY, 4 Nov 1828. Solomon married Mercy Oldridge on 18 Aug 1779. Solomon may also have married Mary Lapham in 1778 who died soon after.

Rebecca Chamberlain and Solomon Chase were parents of eight children.[1477]

i RACHEL CHASE, baptized at Amenia, 19 Jan 1766;[1478] m. JACOB DORMAN, b. about 1758; Jacob d. at Westerlo, NY, 1816 (probate 9 May 1816).

ii SOLOMON CHASE, b. at Amenia 20 Oct 1767; d. at New Milford, CT, 2 Jul 1808; m. 9 May 1790, ESTHER EVERETT, b. 31 Jul 1775; Esther d. at Kent, CT, 9 May 1824.

iii REBECCA CHASE, b. 31 Mar 1769; d. at Amenia, 15 Aug 1772.[1479]

iv STEPHEN CHASE, b. at Amenia, 20 Jul 1770; d. at Green Bay, WI, 20 Feb 1866; m. about 1800, ANNA BURCH, b. 18 Mar 1782 daughter of Joshua and Ann (Champlin) Burch; Anna d. at Port Huron, MI, 1854.[1480]

v MEHITABLE CHASE, b. at Amenia, 13 Mar 1772; d. at Amenia, 23 Oct 1795.

vi MARY CHASE, b. at Amenia, 1 Mar 1774; Mary does not seem to have married.

vii JOHN CHASE, b. at Amenia, 1 Jul 1775; d. at Warehouse, CT, 26 Dec 1852; m. about 1806, JANE ABBE, b. at Enfield, 6 Jan 1778 daughter of Obadiah and Jane (McLester) Abbe; Jane d. at Warehouse Point, 15 Jul 1863.

viii CHARLES YOUNG CHASE, b. at Amenia, 4 Oct 1777; d. at Corinth, VT, 14 Aug 1830; m. at Sharon, CT, 27 Mar 1808, BETSEY PATCHEN, b. 31 Oct 1778 daughter of Abel and Rebecca (Gay) Patchen; Betsey d. at Sharon, CT, 10 Dec 1853.

552) CHRISTOPHER HUNTINGTON (*Mehitable Johnson Huntington⁴, James Johnson³, Mary Holt Johnson², Nicholas¹*), b. at Mansfield, CT, 7 Jul 1738 son of Thomas and Mehitable (Johnson) Huntington; d. at Compton, Québec, 14 Dec 1810; m. at Mansfield, 7 May 1761, MARY DIMOCK, b. at Mansfield, 9 Oct 1739 son of Perez and Mary (Bailey) Dimock; Mary d. 1833.[1481]

Christopher and Mary were from Mansfield, but relocated first to Norwich, Vermont and then to Roxbury, Vermont in 1789. He was a preacher of the doctrine of universal salvation. His last years were spent in Canada East.[1482]

Christopher Huntington and Mary Dimock were parents of ten children born at Mansfield.[1483]

1476 The name is also spelled Rauh or Rau.

1477 Several of the births of the children are recorded in the Kent, CT records but may have occurred in Amenia.

1478 *New York, Genealogical Records, 1675-1920*, The New York Genealogical and Biographical Record (quarterly-1904) - Extracts

1479 *Connecticut Town Death Records, pre-1870 (Barbour Collection)*. The death transcriptions notes she died at age 3.The Chase genealogy reports that Rebecca married Azariah Darrow and died in 1872, but that is a different Rebecca Chase as Rebecca and Azariah Darrow were having children 1812-1815.

1480 Chase, *Seven Generations of the Descendants of Aquila and Thomas Chase*

1481 Huntington Family Association, *The Huntington Family in America, p 308*

1482 Huntington Family Association, *The Huntington Family in America, p 308*

1483 Dimock, *Births, Baptisms, Marriages and Deaths from the Records of the Town and Churches of Mansfield, Connecticut*

i CHRISTOPHER HUNTINGTON, b. 11 Nov 1761; d. at Richmond, PA, 11 Nov 1854; m. 6 Feb 1785, EUNICE SHADDOCK, b. 14 Mar 1762; Eunice d. at Richmond, after 1856.[1484]

ii ELIJAH HUNTINGTON, b. 21 Aug 1763; d. at Braintree, VT, 24 Jun 1828; m. 1st about 1792, SARAH FIELD who has not been identified.[1485] Elijah m. 2nd at Braintree, VT, 9 Jun 1801, LYDIA PARMALEE, b. at Newtown, CT, 6 Aug 1779;[1486] Lydia d. at Braintree, 27 May 1851.

iii JEDIDIAH HUNTINGTON, b. 9 Aug 1765; d. at Brighton, NY, 25 Feb 1852; m. at Brookfield, VT, 20 Mar 1794, SARAH RICHARDSON, b. at Washington, VT, 6 Nov 1768.

iv THOMAS HUNTINGTON, b. 10 Jun 1767; d. at Compton, Québec, 6 May 1811; m. Sep 1795, SUBMIT HUNTINGTON, b. at Hartford, VT, about 1769 daughter of James and Hannah (Marsh) Huntington.[1487]

v PEREZ HUNTINGTON, b. 26 Jun 1769; d. at Compton, Québec, Sep 1834; m. in VT, 19 Sep 1802, ABIGAIL HATCH, b. at Willington, CT, 23 Mar 1781 daughter of Herman and Eunice (Broughton) Hatch; Abigail d. at Lowell, MA, 19 Jul 1847.

vi BENJAMIN HUNTINGTON, b. 5 Jul 1771; d. at Compton, Québec, 25 Feb 1841; m. at Roxbury, VT, 30 Apr 1801, CATHARINE GUSTIN, b. at Marlow, NH, 12 Apr 1779 daughter of Josiah and Margaret (Wardner) Gustin; Catharine d. at Compton, 6 Aug 1854.

vii MARY HUNTINGTON, b. 21 Nov 1774; d. at Hatley, Québec, 6 Jul 1850; m. about 1812, as his second wife, JAPHET LE BARON, b. at Sheffield, MA, 11 Jul 1767 son of Joshua and Grace (Bush) Le Baron; Japhet d. at Hatley, 10 Feb 1845. Japhet was first married to Betsey Prouty.

viii LYDIA HUNTINGTON (twin of Mary), b. 21 Nov 1774; d. at Roxbury, VT, Jun 1792.

ix GIDEON HUNTINGTON, b. 25 Apr 1777; d. at 1860 when living in Norwich, VT; m. at Compton, 16 Jun 1815, AVIS BLISS (widow of Sylvester Day), b. at Strafford, VT, about 1781 daughter of Samuel and Olive (Pinnock) Bliss; Avis d. at Norwich, 12 Jun 1859.

x MEHITABLE HUNTINGTON, b. 28 May 1780; d. at Compton, Québec, Jan 1816.

553) JEMIMA NORCROSS (*Jemima Abbot Norcross⁴, Jemima Johnson Abbot⁴, Mary Holt Johnson², Nicholas¹*), b. at Watertown, 24 May 1720 daughter of Nathaniel and Jemima (Abbot) Norcross; d. at Cambridge by 1776; m. at Watertown, 30 Apr 1741, ELIPHALET ROBBINS, baptized at Cambridge, 16 Jan 1718 son of John and Abigail (Adams) Robbins; Eliphalet d. at Cambridge, 1795 (probate 1795). Eliphalet was second married to Mrs. Sarah Whiting on 13 Mar 1777.

Eliphalet Robbins of Cambridge served as 2nd lieutenant in the regiment of Col. William Brattle in 1763 during the French and Indian War.[1488]

Eliphalet Robbins did not leave a will and his estate entered probate 9 April 1795 with widow Sarah declining administration due to her advanced years. Mary Draper and Joseph Draper asked that Mr. Eliphalet Robbins be named administrator of the estate of their honored father Eliphalet Robbins. Nathaniel and Jemima Kingsbury also declined administration. Eliphalet Robbins of Newton was named administrator. Personal estate was valued at £31.17.0 and additional inventory of notes owed the estate and interest was £51.5.6. In October 1796, there was a warning issued to Eliphalet Robbins to appear at probate court with an accounting of the estate. Eliphalet Robbins was removed as administrator in November 1799 due to his neglect of the trust of administration and Aaron Hill was appointed administrator. A new inventory conducted 13 May 1800 found the estate to be insolvent with claims against the estate of $157.96.[1489]

Eliphalet Robbins and Jemima Norcross were parents of five known children born at Cambridge.

i MOSES ROBBINS, b. at Cambridge, 6 Jul 1742; d. at Cambridge, 12 Sep 1797; m. at Cambridge, 31 Oct 1765, SARAH DANA, b. at Cambridge, 16 Apr 1743 daughter of William and Mary (Greene) Dana.[1490]

ii NATHANIEL ROBBINS, b. at Cambridge, 3 Sep 1745; m. at Cambridge, 19 Apr 1768, MARY COOLIDGE, b. at Watertown, 8 Oct 1743 daughter of David and Mary (Mixer) Coolidge.[1491]

1484 U.S., Revolutionary War Pension and Bounty-Land Warrant Application Files, 1800-1900. Eunice gives her maiden name as Eunice Shaddock and her birth date as 14 March 1762 in her widow's pension application.

1485 This is a marriage reported by the Huntington Family Association; records related to Sarah Filed were not located.

1486 Huntington Family Association, *The Huntington Family in America*

1487 Huntington Family Association, *The Huntington Family in America*

1488 Colonial Soldiers and Officers in New England, 1620-1775 (Online database, americanancestors.org), Massachusetts Officers in the French and Indian War 1748-1763, p 305

1489 *Middlesex County, MA: Probate File Papers, 1648-1871.*Online database. *AmericanAncestors.org.* New England Historic Genealogical Society, 2014. Case 19239

1490 The 1769 will of William Dana of Cambridge includes a bequest to his daughter Sarah Robbins.

1491 The 1772 probate record of David Coolidge of Watertown includes heirs signing the settlement, Mary Robbins and Nathaniel Robbins.

iii JEMIMA ROBBINS, b. at Cambridge, 30 Mar 1747; d. at Dedham, 19 Jul 1814; m. 1st at Cambridge, 10 Dec 1765, ISRAEL WHITNEY, b. at Watertown, 6 Aug 1741 son of Daniel and Dorothy (Tainter) Whitney; Israel d. at Watertown, 11 Sep 1774. Jemima m. 2nd at Dedham, 3 Aug 1776, ABNER ELLIS, b. at Dedham, 21 Jan 1731/2 son of Joseph and Hannah (-) Ellis; Abner d. at Dedham, 10 Oct 1781. Abner's first wife Meletiah Ellis died 18 Aug 1775. Jemima m. 3rd at Dedham, 12 Dec 1783, NATHANIEL KINGSBURY, b. at Walpole, MA, 1749 son of Benjamin and Abigail (Baker) Kingsbury; Nathaniel d. at Medfield, 21 Mar 1846. Jemima had children with each of her three husbands. After Jemima's death, Nathaniel married Lavina Morse.

iv ELIPHALET ROBBINS, b. about 1750; d. after 1800 when he was living in Newton; m. at Newton, 15 Mar 1777, MARTHA DURANT, b. at Newton, 22 Oct 1755 daughter of Edward and Mary (Allen) Durant.[1492]

v MARY ROBBINS, b. at Cambridge, 2 May 1760; d. at Dedham, 21 Aug 1827; m. at Cambridge, 2 Jun 1779, as his second wife, JOSEPH DRAPER, b. 2 Mar 1740 son of Daniel and Rachel (Pond) Draper; Joseph d. at Dedham, 28 Nov 1823 (probate 1824). Joseph was first married to Hannah Whiting.

554) MERCY NORCROSS (*Jemima Abbot Norcross[4], Jemima Johnson Abbot[4], Mary Holt Johnson[2], Nicholas[1]*), baptized at Watertown, 9 Aug 1730 daughter of Nathaniel and Jemima (Abbot) Norcross; d. at Cambridge, MA (now Brighton), 28 Jun 1791; m. at Cambridge, 3 May 1749, JOHN STRATTON, b. at Cambridge, 9 Aug 1727 son of Ebenezer and Lydia (Fuller) Stratton; John d. at Cambridge, 21 Nov 1791.

Mercy and John resided in Cambridge on the south side of the Charles River, the area that later became the Brighton area of Boston.[1493]

In his will written 5 May 1791 (probate 6 December 1791), John Stratton of Cambridge bequeaths to beloved wife Mercy all the personal estate during her natural life. Daughter Abigail Richards receives half of all the real estate. Good friend Nathaniel Champney who was brought up in his family receives the other half of the real estate. Son-in-law Silas Robbins receives £3 and each of his Robbins grandchildren receives £12: John, Aaron, George, Lucy, and Mercy. Son-in-law William Richards and Nathaniel Champney were named executors. Personal estate was valued at £212.8.7 and real estate at £496 including the homestead containing ten acres.[1494]

There are five children known for Mercy Norcross and John Stratton.

i MARY STRATTON, b. at Cambridge, 29 Apr 1752; d. about 1779; m. at Cambridge, 7 Mar 1772, SILAS ROBBINS *likely* b. at Lancaster, 24 Nov 1746 son of Roger and Lucy (-) Robbins; Silas d. at Harvard, 13 Mar 1825 (probate 1825 with son-in-law Stephen Bacon [husband of Lucy named in John Stratton's will] as administrator).

ii ABIGAIL STRATTON, baptized 11 May 1755; d. at Dover, MA, 3 May 1832; m. at Cambridge, 27 Oct 1774, WILLIAM RICHARDS, b. at Dedham, 12 Aug 1746 son of Ebenezer and Thankful (Stratton) Richards; William d. at Dover, 26 Dec 1835.

iii LYDIA STRATTON, baptized 27 Feb 1757; likely died young.

iv JOHN STRATTON, baptized 13 Apr 1759; likely died young.

v WILLIAM STRATTON, b. at Cambridge, 11 Jul 1762; nothing further known but deceased before time of father's will.

555) URIAH NORCROSS (*Jemima Abbot Norcross[4], Jemima Johnson Abbot[4], Mary Holt Johnson[2], Nicholas[1]*), b. at Watertown, 23 Jul 1732 son of Nathaniel and Jemima (Abbot) Norcross; d. at Boston, 23 Jun 1797; m. 1st at Boston, 15 Apr 1754, MERCY WATTS, b. at Hull, MA, 19 Jan 1734/5 daughter of Joseph and Hannah (Paine) Watts; Mercy d. at Boston, 6 Jan 1779.[1495][1496] Uriah m. 2nd at Boston, 25 Aug 1779, ABIGAIL DINSDALE who has not been identified.

Uriah and Mercy resided in Boston. After Mercy's death, guardians were assigned the minor children on 19 November 1779 to represent their interests in the estate of Mercy's father Joseph Watts. The minor children were Elisha under 14, Hannah above 14, Joseph above age 14, Nathaniel under age 14, Rebecca under 14, Uriah above 14, and William under 14.[1497]

Mercy Watts Norcross had been the heir of one undivided third part of her father's estate. When Mercy died intestate in 1779 this triggered a dispute related to the division of the estate of Joseph Watts. Four of the children of Uriah and Mercy brought suit to obtain four-sevenths part of their mother's inheritance with the case finally settled in 1805 after a hearing at the

---

1492 The 1781 will of Edward Durant of Newton includes a bequest to his daughter Martha wife of Eliphalet Robbins.

1493 Stratton, *A Book of Strattons*, volume 2, p 28

1494 *Middlesex County, MA: Probate File Papers, 1648-1871.*Online database. *AmericanAncestors.org.* New England Historic Genealogical Society, 2014. Case 21850

1495 Reports of Cases Argued in the Supreme Judicial Court of the Commonwealth of Massachusetts, volume I, p 324; date of death of Mercy Watts is given in part of court case documents related to a dispute of the estate of Mercy Watts's father.

1496 There is a 1779 guardianship case for the minor children of Uriah Norcross who are the grandchildren of Joseph Watts related to his estate.

1497 *Suffolk County, MA: Probate File Papers.*Online database. *AmericanAncestors.org.* New England Historic Genealogical Society, 2017-2019. (From records supplied by the Massachusetts Supreme Judicial Court Archives., Case 17104

Massachusetts Supreme Judicial Court. These four children were John Gordon and Hannah his wife in her right, Nathaniel Cross, Elisha Cross, and Jonas Woods and Rebecca his wife in her right.[1498]

Uriah Norcross and Mercy Watts were parents of nine children born at Boston.

i MERCY NORCROSS, b. at Boston, 31 Mar 1755; d. at Bellows Falls, VT, 13 Nov 1836; m. at Boston, 7 Jul 1776, NATHANIEL CLARK, b. 12 Mar 1749 son of John and Hannah (Cutting) Clark;[1499] Nathaniel d. at Bellows Falls, 9 Apr 1836.

ii MARY NORCROSS, b. at Boston, 22 Dec 1757; d. after 1832 (living at probate of husband's estate); m. at Cambridge, 3 Apr 1776, HENRY COOLIDGE, baptized at Cambridge, 3 Jun 1750 son of Henry and Phebe (Dana) Coolidge; Henry d. at Waterford, ME, about 1832 (probate 1832).

iii JOSEPH WATTS NORCROSS, b. at Boston, 4 Aug 1760; d. at Boston, 1790 (probate Apr 1790); m. at Boston, 8 Mar 1784, JANE "JENNY" TRUMAN, baptized at Boston, 15 Dec 1765 daughter of William and Sarah (-) Truman;[1500] Jane d. at Boston, Dec 1793. Jane married second Thomas Whitman on 17 Sep 1790.

iv HANNAH NORCROSS, b. at Boston, 16 Jul 1762; m. at Boston, 5 Mar 1781, JOHN GORDON who is not identified but may be the John b. at Boston, 28 Oct 1738 son of John and Content (Newcomb) Gordon.

v URIAH NORCROSS, b. at Boston, 9 Jan 1765

vi WILLIAM NORCROSS, b. at Boston, 25 Mar 1765[1501]

vii NATHANIEL NORCROSS, b. at Boston, 22 Jul 1769; m. at Boston, 1 Aug 1791, JUDITH DAY, baptized at Gloucester, 18 Aug 1765 daughter of David and Bethiah (Dimmock) Day; Judith d. at Boston, 13 Sep 1849.

viii REBECCA NORCROSS, b. at Boston, about 1771; d. at Acton, MA, 23 Feb 1855; m. at Boston, 22 May 1796, JONAS WOOD, b. 1772; Jonas d. at Acton, 6 Jan 1842.

ix ELISHA NORCROSS, b. at Boston, 1776; d at New York, NY, 28 Nov 1846; m. 1st at Charlestown, 23 Apr 1797, POLLY HOLMAN, b. 1771; Polly d. at New York by 1821. Elisha m. 2nd at New York, 7 Mar 1822, MARGARET M. ANNIN, b. at Basking Ridge, NJ, 7 Mar 1799 daughter of Alexander and Margaret (Miller) Annin; Margaret d. at Newark, NJ, 19 Oct 1876.

556) JOSIAH NORCROSS (*Jemima Abbot Norcross[4], Jemima Johnson Abbot[4], Mary Holt Johnson[2], Nicholas[1]*), b. at Watertown, about 1734 son of Nathaniel and Jemima (Abbot) Norcross; d. at Newton, 13 Dec 1801; m. at Watertown, 6 Jan 1757, ELIZABETH CHILD, b. at Watertown, 1 Jan 1737/8 daughter of Jonathan and Elizabeth (-) Child; Elizabeth d. at Newton, 30 Jul 1801.

In his will written 13 October 1801 (probate 6 April 1802), Josiah Norcross bequeathed to son Moses one-half of his chaise, a feather bed, and bolster and pillows. The remainder of the estate both real and personal goes to his sons Nathaniel, John, and Josiah, daughter Jemima Coolidge, and daughter Abigail Dana with some exceptions. John's portion is to have $385 deducted which is an amount he already received. Son Josiah has the privilege of living in and improving the house. John receives one-half of the chaise. The $385 deducted from John's portion is to be divided among the other children except Moses who has received his full portion. Sons Nathaniel Norcross of Newton and John Norcross of Cambridge were named executors.[1502] Heirs signing their satisfaction with the will were Moses Norcross, Joshua Coolidge, Aaron Dana, and Josiah Norcross. The personal estate was valued at $587.82 and the real estate at $4,704.82.

Josiah Norcross and Elizabeth Child were parents of nine children born at Watertown.

i NATHANIEL NORCROSS, b. at Watertown, 30 Jun 1757; died young.

ii ELIZABETH NORCROSS, b. at Watertown, 16 Jun 1760; died young.

iii JOSIAH NORCROSS, b. at Watertown, 22 Apr 1762; m. 1st at Newton, 6 Sep 1798, ELIZABETH "BETSY" CARKHAM.[1503]

[1498] Reports of Cases Argued in the Supreme Judicial Court of the Commonwealth of Massachusetts, volume I, p 323ff

[1499] Clark, *Records of the Descendants of Hugh Clark*, p 45

[1500] The 1808 will of William Truman of Boston includes a bequest to his grandchildren, the children of his daughter Jenny deceased: Joseph Norcross and Marcy Low wife of Samuel Low.

[1501] The births of Uriah and William are recorded in the transcriptions available as occurring three months apart which obviously is not correctt, but this is what is in the records.

[1502] *Middlesex County, MA: Probate File Papers, 1648-1871.*Online database. *AmericanAncestors.org.* New England Historic Genealogical Society, 2014. Case 16029

[1503] There appear to be two different Josiah Norcross, one who was in Sutton and one in Shrewsbury. The Josiah who died in Shrewsbury in 23 Dec 1862 (at age 85 years, 11 months, 7 days) was the son of Nathaniel and Mary Norcross (according to the death record).

iv NATHANIEL NORCROSS, b. at Watertown, 22 Apr 1764; m. 1st at Newton, 22 May 1783, ANNA WARD, b. at Newton, 11 Feb 1762 daughter of George and Abigail (Merrick) Ward; Anna d. about 1805. Nathaniel m. 2nd at Boston, 22 Mar 1806, FANNY WINCHESTER, b. at Newton, 4 Mar 1768 daughter of Stephen and Hannah (*Hastings* Aspinwall) Winchester; Fanny d. at Newton, Sep 1846.

v JEMIMA NORCROSS, b. at Watertown, 14 May 1766; d. at Watertown, 18 Aug 1849; m. 11 Dec 1783, JOSHUA COOLIDGE, b. at Watertown, 11 Sep 1759 son of Joseph and Eunice (Stratton) Coolidge; Joshua d. at Watertown, 30 May 1835.

vi ELIZABETH NORCROSS, b. at Watertown, 10 Apr 1768; nothing further known but deceased before 1801.

vii JOHN NORCROSS, baptized 27 May 1770; d. at Brighton, 13 Jun 1823; m. at Cambridge, 8 Aug 1799, MARGARET "PEGGY" EVERETT, b. at Dedham, 26 May 1765 daughter of Israel and Sarah (Metcalf) Everett; Peggy d. (buried) at Cambridge, Dec 1843.

viii ABIGAIL NORCROSS, baptized 28 Jun 1772; d. at Watertown, 20 Nov 1813; m. at Newton, 13 Jun 1798, AARON DANA, b. at Newton, 17 Jun 1762 son of John and Abigail (Smith) Dana; Aaron d. at Watertown, 20 Jan 1809.

ix MOSES NORCROSS, baptized 14 Aug 1774; d. at Northborough, MA, 22 Jan 1823; m. at Newton, 26 May 1799, MARY "POLLY" WINCHESTER, b. at Newton, 24 Mar 1770 daughter of Stephen and Hannah (*Hastings* Aspinwall) Winchester.[1504]

557) MARY NORCROSS (*Jemima Abbot Norcross⁴, Jemima Johnson Abbot⁴, Mary Holt Johnson², Nicholas¹*), baptized at Watertown, 16 Apr 1738 daughter of Nathaniel and Jemima (Abbot) Norcross; m. at Cambridge, 1 Jun 1755, DANIEL ROBBINS, b. at Newton, 10 Jan 1733 son of Daniel and Hannah (Trowbridge) Robbins.

Mary and Daniel resided in Lancaster, Massachusetts where Daniel was town clerk. He was captain of a militia company in the regiment of Col. Asa Whitcomb that marched to Cambridge at the alarm on 19 April 1775 with fourteen days of service.[1505]

In two transactions, Daniel Robbins and his wife Mary conveyed land to daughter Hannah and her husband Moses Newhall. On 9 April 1774 (recorded 25 February 1779), Daniel and Mary conveyed to Hannah Newhall for her use and for her heirs, a piece of land on Daniel's farm of one acre and twenty-three rods for payment of £10. On 21 April 1778 (recorded 25 February 1779), Daniel and Mary conveyed to Moses Newall a tract of 33 acres in Lancaster for payment of £33.6.8.[1506]

Mary Norcross and Daniel Robbins were parents of seven children born at Lancaster, Massachusetts.

i HANNAH ROBBINS, b. 8 Jul 1756; d. at Sterling, MA, 6 Oct 1821; m. at Lancaster, 18 Nov 1773, MOSES NEWHALL, b. at Lynn, 10 Dec 1751 son of Moses and Susanna (Bowden) Newhall;[1507] Moses d. at Sterling, 1820 (probate 7 Nov 1820).

ii MARY ROBBINS, b. 27 Jan 1758

iii SUSANNAH ROBBINS, b. 17 Apr 1760; d. at Wilbraham, 30 Jun 1788; m. at Wilbraham, 28 Apr 1782, DANIEL COTTON, b. at Brimfield, 31 Mar 1756 son of Benjamin and Abiah (Cooley) Colton.

iv JEMIMA ROBBINS, b. 17 Jul 1762; d. at Sterling, 17 Jul 1819; m. at Wilbraham, 8 Nov 1783, JOSHUA EDDY, b. at Gloucester, RI, 2 Nov 1749 son of James and Anne (Burch) Eddy; Joshua d. at Sterling, 12 Dec 1819. Joshua was first married to Margaret Scott.

v ELIZABETH ROBBINS, b. 2 Apr 1764

vi DANIEL ROBBINS, b. 1 Feb 1769

vii SARAH ROBBINS, b. 5 Jun 1774; d. at Wilbraham, 17 Oct 1835; m. 6 Apr 1795, MOSES BURT, b. 4 Jul 1773 son of Moses and Esther (Ely) Burt;[1508] Moses d. at Wilbraham, 28 May 1869. Moses was second married to Betsey Sessions Flynt.

558) ASA NORCROSS (*Jemima Abbot Norcross⁴, Jemima Johnson Abbot⁴, Mary Holt Johnson², Nicholas¹*), b. at Watertown, 9 Mar 1740/1 son of Nathaniel and Jemima (Abbot) Norcross; d. at Holliston, MA, 25 Aug 1830; m. 1st at Newton, MA, 20 Apr 1760, ELIZABETH GREENWOOD, b. at Newton, 21 Nov 1740 daughter of Josiah and Phebe (Stearns) Greenwood; Elizabeth d. by 1774. Asa m. 2nd 10 Nov 1774, ELIZABETH FAIRBANKS, b. at Medway, MA, 11 Aug 1749 daughter of George and Jerusha (Twitchell) Fairbanks; Elizabeth d. at Holliston, Sep 1829.

1504 Hotchkiss, *Winchester Notes*, p 78

1505 Marvin, *History of the Town of Lancaster, Massachusetts*, volume I, pp 294-295

1506 Massachusetts Land Records, Worcester County, 81:171; 81:172

1507 Waters, *The Newhall Family of Lynn*, p 72

1508 Burnham, *Genealogical Records of Henry and Ulalia Burt*, p 99

Asa and his first wife Elizabeth Greenwood resided in Dublin, New Hampshire and seven children were born there. They lived on lot 7, range 6.[1509] After the death of his first wife, Asa remarried and relocated to Holliston, Massachusetts where he died.

On 11 January 1776 (recorded 4 October 1783), Asa Norcross of Dublin purchased a lot of land in Holliston from Willard Hunt, also of Dublin, for a sum of £196.[1510]

Asa Norcross did not leave a will and his estate was in probate 21 October 1830 with Elisha Cutter named as administrator at the request of grandson Asa G. Norcross who declined the administration. The homestead in Holliston was appraised at $800 and personal estate at $20.46. Claims against the estate were $356. After the selling of real estate and settling of debts, $265.82 remained for distribution. The heirs if the estate were Lucy Twitchell, Phebe Mason, and Sally Mason; Maynard Bragg only child of Sybil Bragg deceased; thirteen children of daughter Ama Leland deceased;[1511] grandson Asa G. Norcross son of Asa deceased and Asa G.'s three children Ellis, Sylvia, and Sarah.[1512]

Asa Norcross and Elizabeth Greenwood were parents of seven children born at Dublin.

i LUCY NORCROSS, b. 1 Jun 1760; d. at Windham, VT, 13 Sep 1845; m. 27 May 1779. STEPHEN TWITCHELL, b. at Sherborn, MA, 25 Jun 1753 son of Gershom and Hannah (Sawin) Twitchell; Stephen d. at Windham, 12 Sep 1845.

ii PHEBE NORCROSS, b. 30 Jun 1764; d. at Dublin, 1 Jul 1841; m. 27 Jun 1783, BENJAMIN MASON, b. at Sherborn, 28 May 1760 son of Benjamin and Martha (Fairbanks) Mason; Benjamin d. at Dublin, 16 May 1840.

iii ELIZABETH NORCROSS, b. 6 Apr 1766; likely died young

iv SARAH NORCROSS, b. 10 Jun 1768; d. at Sullivan, NH, 12 Mar 1846; m. 12 May 1785, BELA MASON, b. at Dublin, 1 Oct 1764 son of Benjamin and Martha (Fairbanks) Mason; Bela d. at Sullivan, 6 Jan 1841.

v ASA NORCROSS, b. 25 May 1770; d. at Bellingham, MA, 31 May 1823; m. at Bellingham, 16 Nov 1797, SILVIA THAYER, b. at Bellingham, 13 Sep 1771 daughter of Silas and Lydia (Thayer) Thayer; Silvia d. at Bellingham, 30 Dec 1824.

vi MOSES NORCROSS, b. 5 Feb 1772; d. 5 Apr 1773.

vii MOSES NORCROSS, b. 5 Aug 1773; d. 12 Apr 1774.

Asa Norcross and Elizabeth Fairbanks were parents of three children born at Holliston.

i AMA NORCROSS, b. 10 Jul 1776; d. at East Otto, NY, 1828; m. at Holliston, 17 Feb 1794, ASA LELAND, b. at Holliston, 15 Feb 1770 son of Asa and Lois (Marshall) Leland; Asa d. at East Otto, 1832.

ii SYBIL NORCROSS, b. 6 Apr 1779; d. 16 Jul 1798; m. at Holliston, 1 Sep 1796, Col. ARIAL BRAGG, b. at Wrentham, MA, 30 Jul 1772 son of Arial and Sarah (Fisher) Bragg; Arial d. at Milford, MA, 26 Oct 1855. Arial was second married to Elizabeth Chamberlain and third married to Nancy Mellen.

iii MOSES NORCROSS, b. 23 Aug 1784; likely died young.

559) NEHEMIAH NORCROSS (*Jemima Abbot Norcross⁴, Jemima Johnson Abbot⁴, Mary Holt Johnson², Nicholas¹*), baptized at Watertown, 7 Feb 1741/2 son of Nathaniel and Jemima (Abbot) Norcross; m. at Roxbury, 26 Jun 1764, RUTH BUGBEE.

Nehemiah Norcross and Ruth Bugbee were parents of four children, three of these children in the Charlestown records.[1513]

i NEHEMIAH NORCROSS, b. 29 Aug 1765; d. at Boston, 7 Jun 1804; m. at Boston, 1 Mar 1787, ANNA SIMPSON; Anna d. at Boston, 13 Mar 1837.

ii JOHN NORCROSS, b. 8 May 1767; died young

iii JOHN NORCROSS, b. 1 Apr 1770

iv NANCY NORCROSS, b. 1 Jan 1774; d. at Boston, Aug 1797; m. at Boston, 19 Jan 1794, HAZAEL SIMONDS, b. 1773 son of Hazael and Mary (Tidd) Simonds.

[1509] Mason, *History of Dublin, N.H.*

[1510] Massachusetts Land Records 1620-1986, Middlesex County, 84:643

[1511] Ama Leland's children (all last name Leland) are Moses, Asa, Eliza, Lois, Tuttle, Joseph R., Achsah, Sarah, Meriam, Harrison, Abigail, Dexter, and Laura.

[1512] *Middlesex County, MA: Probate File Papers, 1648-1871.*Online database. *AmericanAncestors.org.* New England Historic Genealogical Society, 2014. Case 16023

[1513] The second son John is given in Norcross, *The History and Genealogy of the Norcross Family*, p 24; accessed through NEHGS digital collections

560) SUSANNAH NORCROSS (*Jemima Abbot Norcross[4], Jemima Johnson Abbot[4], Mary Holt Johnson[2], Nicholas[1]*), b. at Watertown, 27 Jul 1746 daughter of Nathaniel and Jemima (Abbot) Norcross; m. 10 Oct 1765, JONATHAN WHITNEY, b. at Watertown, 12 Apr 1743 son of Joseph and Mary (Child) Whitney; Jonathan d. at Watertown, 3 Jun 1802.[1514]

Jonathan Whitney and Susannah Norcross were parents of five children born at Watertown.

i SUSANNAH WHITNEY, b. 23 May 1766. Susannah gave birth on 6 Oct 1799 to Samuel Fowle, an out-of-wedlock child of SAMUEL FOWLE, b. at Watertown, 18 Dec 1762 son of Edmund and Abigail (Whitney) Fowle. The son Samuel Fowle died at Medford, MA 8 May 1865.

ii MARY WHITNEY, b. 10 Jan 1767; d. at Weston, MA, 30 Apr 1830; m. at Lincoln, MA, 1 Sep 1793, JOHN DUDLEY, b. at Marlborough, 27 Apr 1770 son of Benjamin and Mary (Stratton) Dudley; John d. at Weston, 20 Sep 1848.

iii JONATHAN WHITNEY, b. 15 Dec 1769; d. 1829; m. 9 Apr 1793, LUCY PARKS, b. at Lincoln, 10 Dec 1774 daughter of Daniel and Lydia (Priest) Parks; Lucy d. after 1840 when she was head of household in Watertown.

iv JOSEPH WHITNEY, b. 16 Jun 1774; d. at Watertown, 29 Dec 1821; m. at Watertown, 25 Jun 1798, REBECCA PRIEST, *likely* b. at Groton, 4 Oct 1768 daughter of Timothy and Sarah (Butterfield) Priest.

v SAMUEL WHITNEY, b. 6 May 1776

561) JOHN ABBOTT (*John Abbott[4], Jemima Johnson Abbot[4], Mary Holt Johnson[2], Nicholas[1]*), b. at Stow, MA, 2 Apr 1724 son of John and Elizabeth (Phipps) Abbott; d. at Sempronius, NY, 21 May 1814; m. at Lyme, CT, 1747, SARAH BAKER; Sarah d. at Hoosick, NY, 1777. John had a second marriage the Mrs. Hawley, a widow.

Lemuel Abbott's *Descendants of George Abbott or Rowley* contains a detailed biography of John Abbott (pp 205-209), summarized here. John was born in Massachusetts, apprenticed for a time in Connecticut, ran away from his apprenticeship due to mistreatment, and then bought out and worked-off his apprenticeship. John married Sarah Baker in Connecticut and likely all their children were born there. The family was then in Pawlet, Vermont where John was a carpenter, trader, and farmer. In 1777, Pawlet was overrun by Indian troops working with the British and John and family fled eventually arriving in Hoosick, New York. In 1779, he served as captain of a company of "associated exempts" and later held the rank of colonel.

John Abbott and Sarah Baker were parents of nine children. Daughters Betsey and Eunice married respectively Samuel Stewart and Eden Johnson. Stewart and Johnson started the first permanent settlement of Bristol, Vermont in the spring of 1786. In 1786, Eden and his wife Eunice had already two children. Eden and Eunice went from Bristol to Plattsburgh and then were on to Upper Canada (later Ontario) where they died, Eden drowning in the Grand River when his canoe overturned.[1515]

i JOHN ABBOTT, b. at Colchester, 17 Jul 1748 and baptized 25 Dec 1748; d. at Niles, NY, 30 Mar 1835, m. about 1780, SUSANNA MEACHAM, b. at Warren, MA, 23 Nov 1756 daughter of Isaac and Lydia (Blanchard) Meacham; Susanna d. at Niles, NY, 12 May 1833.

ii SARAH ABBOTT, baptized at Colchester, 27 May 1750; d. at Cambridge, NY, 4 Sep 1775; m. about 1770, JAMES GREEN, b. in Ireland, 15 Nov 1740 son of Thomas and Sarah (McConnell) Green; James d. at Cambridge, 5 Jan 1812. James married second Mary who has not been identified.

iii SAMUEL ABBOTT, b. at Salisbury, CT, 1752; d. at Ira, NY, 9 Apr 1835; m. about 1785, DESIRE GIBBS, b. at 1766; Desire d. at Ira, NY, 7 Nov 1832.

iv JOEL ABBOTT, b. about 1754; d. at Athens, OH where he is listed in the 1820 census. Joel married but the name of his wife has yet to be found. He served as a 1st lieutenant in Yates regiment during the Revolution.

v CHAUNCEY ABBOTT, b. about 1755; d. about 1772.

vi EUNICE ABBOTT, b. 30 Sep 1756; d. at Upper Canada (Ontario); m. about 1776, likely at Pawlet, VT, EDEN JOHNSON; Eden d. 4 Nov 1809 when he drowned in the Grand River.

vii ELIZABETH "BETSY" ABBOTT, b. 1759; d. at North Royalton, OH, 4 Feb 1836; m. SAMUEL STEWART, b. at Londonderry, 23 Feb 1749; Samuel d. at North Royalton, 8 Aug 1827.

viii PHEBE ABBOTT, b. about 1765; d. at Sherburne, NY, 19 May 1833; m. about 1785, JOSEPH GUTHRIE, b at Ancient Woodbury, 1760 son of James and Abigail (Betts) Guthrie; Joseph d. at Sherburne, 6 Jan 1845.

1514 Bartley, "Watertown, Massachusetts, Marriages, Deaths, and Other Events, 1797-1837," NEHGR, volume 165, 2011, p 202

1515 Child, *Gazetteer and Business Directory for Addison County, Vt. 1881-82*, pp 84-86

ix DANIEL ABBOTT, b. 4 Jun 1768; d. at Hamburg, NY, 1838 (probate 6 Apr 1838 with widow Orpha); m. 1st at Pawlet, VT, by 1786, SUSAN SCOTT, b. 1770 daughter of John Scott; Susan d. at Exeter, NY, perhaps about 1795. Daniel m. 2nd at Buffalo, 1830, ORPHA SMITH who survived him.

562) SAMUEL ABBOTT (*John Abbott4, Jemima Johnson Abbot4, Mary Holt Johnson2, Nicholas1*), b. at Windham, CT, 18 Sep 1726 son of John and Elizabeth (Phipps) Abbott; d. at Norwich, 1788; m. at Norwich, 4 Oct 1749, PHEBE EDGERTON, b. at Norwich, 8 Feb 1732 daughter of John and Phebe (Harris) Edgerton; Phebe d. at Norwich, 1793.

Col. Samuel Abbott served as lieutenant in the Colonial forces in 1758. He was lieutenant colonel and then colonel of the 20th regiment of Connecticut infantry during the Revolution. He was a prominent man in Norwich where he resided.[1516]

Samuel's estate entered probate 20 August 1788 with widow Phebe choosing not to take administration of the estate and request that son Daniel take this role. The distribution of the real estate was made on 14 October 1789 with two-sixth parts to eldest son Daniel with his portion valued at £236.3.4. First daughter Eunice Hobart, second daughter Phebe Baker; third daughter Betsey Abbott, and to youngest son Phipps Abbott each received one-sixth part.[1517]

Samuel Abbott and Phebe Edgerton were parents of ten children born at Norwich.

i DANIEL ABBOTT, b. at Norwich, 22 Sep 1751; d. at Norwich, 22 Oct 1810; m. about 1774, SALLY REYNOLDS b. about 1753 daughter of Elisha and Sarah (Smiley) Reynolds.

ii JEDEDIAH ABBOTT, b. 1 Mar 1755; d. 18 Nov 1760.

iii JOHN ABBOTT, b. 8 Aug 1757; d. before 1788.

iv PHEBE ABBOTT, b. 22 Feb 1760; d. 18 Jan 1764.

v EUNICE ABBOTT, b. 5 Mar 1762; m. JOSHUA HOBART. Eunice and Joshua are report as residing in New York, but records were not located.[1518]

vi PHEBE EDGERTON ABBOTT, b. 28 Mar 1764; d. likely at Salisbury, CT, by 1808; m. about 1788, EPHRAIM BAKER, b. at Windham, 3 Dec 1766 son of Samuel and Lydia (Smith) Baker; Ephraim d. at Catskill, NY, after 1812. Ephraim married second, about 1809, Mary Kelsey.

vii SAMUEL ABBOTT, b. 28 May 1766; d. 6 Jun 1766.

viii ELIZABETH ABBOTT, baptized at Norwich, 3 Jan 1768; died young.

ix ELIZABETH "BETTY" ABBOTT, b. at Norwich, 1 Sep 1775; d. at Holly, MI, 9 Oct 1848; m. 2 Jun 1799, ADONIJAH BAKER, b. at Windham, 29 Apr 1777 son of Samuel and Chloe (Silsby) Baker; Adonijah d. at Holly, 29 Feb 1852. Adonijah Baker was the half-brother of Ephraim who married Betty's sister Phebe.

x PHIPPS ABBOTT, baptized at Norwich, 4 Apr 1779 (but perhaps born in 1777); d. at Canaan, 1800.

563) JEMIMA ABBOTT (*John Abbott4, Jemima Johnson Abbot4, Mary Holt Johnson2, Nicholas1*), b. perhaps at Windham, 23 Mar 1729 daughter of John and Elizabeth (Phipps) Abbott; d. at Bridgeport, VA (current WVA), 1815; m. at Windham, 14 Mar 1751, JOHN WALDO, b. at Windham, 18 Oct 1728 son of Edward and Thankful (Dimock) Waldo; John d. at Bridgeport, 23 Aug 1814.

Jemima and John lived in Windham, but by the late 1760's they were in Albany County, New York. They accompanied their son Rev. John J. Waldo to Bridgeport in what was then Virginia about 1795.[1519]

Jemima Abbott and John Waldo were parents of nine children, the oldest six recorded at Windham and the youngest three children perhaps born in Albany County, New York.

i PHIPPS WALDO, b. 21 Jan 1752; d. during the Revolution at a court-house gathering on the Mohawk River on 18 Jan 1776.[1520]

ii OLIVE WALDO, b. 23 Nov 1753; d. at Granville, NY, about 1848; m. 13 Dec 1774, PETER HARTWELL, b. about 1750 son of Peter and Mary (Coleman) Hartwell; Peter d. at Granville, after 1830 when he was head of household.

iii GAMALIEL WALDO, b. 28 Aug 1755; d. at Middletown Springs, VT, 29 Apr 1829; m. 19 Dec 1779, MARY CAMPBELL (widow of Charles Gardner), b. 1749; Mary d. at Middletown Springs, 20 Nov 1839.

iv ANN WALDO, b. 24 Nov 1758; m. 19 Dec 1779, BENJAMIN WAITE, b. at Newport, RI, 3 Sep 1753 son of William and Mary (Nichols) Waite; Benjamin d. at Brockville, Ontario, 22 Nov 1830.

1516 Baker, *Genealogical Record of Rev. Nicholas Baker*, p 39

1517 *Connecticut State Library (Hartford, Connecticut)*; Probate Place: *Hartford, Connecticut, Estate of Samuel Abbott of Norwich, Case 10*

1518 Abbott, *Descendants of George Abbott of Rowley*, p 214

1519 Lincoln, *Genealogy of the Waldo Family*, volume I, p 143

1520 Hall, *Genealogy and Biography of the Waldos in America*, p 97

v ZERVIAH WALDO, b. 2 Feb 1760; d. at Clarksburg, WV, 17 Jan 1857; m. 8 Dec 1785, JOB GOFF, b. at Coventry, RI, 22 Nov 1760 son of Nathan and Mary (Potter) Goff; Job d. at Clarksburg, 8 Dec 1845.

vi Rev. JOHN J. WALDO, b. 16 Feb 1762; d. at Bridgeport, VA (WV), 10 Dec 1840; m. 15 Jan 1786, PEACE BULL, b. at Hoosick Falls, NY, 2 Nov 1767 daughter of Isaac and Amy (Chase) Bull; Peace d. at Shinnston, VA (WV), 4 Nov 1841.

vii DANIEL WALDO, b. 24 May 1764; m. 1786 SUSANNA who is not clearly identified. Daniel and Susanna lived in Hebron, NY and were parents of three known children: John Abbott Waldo, Betsey Waldo, and Jemima Waldo.

viii JEMIMA WALDO, b. 26 May 1766; b. at Amsterdam, NY, 19 Sep 1840; m. HENRY LAKE, b. at Harlingen, NJ, 11 Apr 1761 son of Thomas Lake; Henry d. at Ames, NY, 25 Sep 1851.

ix JEDEDIAH WALDO, b. 19 Oct 1772; d. at Shinnston, WV, 20 Jan 1858; m. 1st 30 Nov 1794, POLLY POTTER, b. at Hoosick Falls, NY, 15 Apr 1776; Polly d. at Harrison County, WV, 13 Apr 1816. Jedediah m. 2nd at Harrison County, 19 Jun 1817, SARAH SHINN, b. 1777 daughter of Levi and Elizabeth (Smith) Shinn; Sarah d. at Shinnston, 26 Jul 1851. Sarah Shinn was first married to Samuel Wamsley.

564) MARY WHEELER (*Mary Abbott Wheeler[4], Jemima Johnson Abbot[4], Mary Holt Johnson[2], Nicholas[1]*), b. at Norwich, 12 Jun 1728 daughter of Nathan and Mary (Abbott) Wheeler; d. at Tolland, about 1808;[1521] m. at Tolland, 3 Nov 1747, DANIEL BENTON, b. at Tolland 6 Jan 1723/4 son of Daniel and Mary (Skinner) Benton; Daniel d. at Tolland, 4 Dec 1777.

Mary and Daniel resided in Tolland where their twelve children were born.

Daniel Benton did not leave a will and his estate entered probate 2 February 1778 with widow Mary Benton as administratrix. The widow's dower was set off the Mary 12 May 1779. The children heirs at the initial distribution on 12 May 1779 were eldest son Daniel Benton, second son Jacob Benton, third son William Benton, fourth son Nathan Benton, fifth son Silas Benton, daughter Mary Hatch, and daughter Sarah Benton. A division of real property was made in 1800 which included sons Daniel Benton and Jacob Benton and Joshua Griggs who had purchased the rights of some of the heirs. The final distribution of the estate was ordered 24 May 1808 after the reversion of the dower to the estate after the death of Mary.[1522]

i ELISHA BENTON, b. at Tolland, 9 Aug 1748; d. at Stafford, 21 Jan 1777. Elisha did not marry.

ii DANIEL BENTON, b. at Tolland, 29 Apr 1752; d. at Tolland, 6 Jul 1805; m. at Somers, 18 Feb 1779, BETSEY RICHARDSON, likely b. at Lebanon, CT, 21 Mar 1754 daughter of David and Rachel (Richardson) Richardson; Betsey d. at Tolland, 24 May 1827.

iii MARY BENTON, b. at Tolland, 31 Aug 1750; d. at Milton, NY, 1822; m. at Tolland, 28 Apr 1777, as his second wife, JONATHAN HATCH, b. at Tolland, 24 Sep 1743 son of Joseph and Mary (Clarke) Hatch; Jonathan d. at Milton, 1820. Jonathan was first married to Bathsheba West.

iv AZARIAH BENTON, b. at Tolland, 29 Mar 1754; d. on a prison ship in New York Harbor, 29 Sep 1776.

v JACOB BENTON, b. 22 Apr 1754; d. at Tolland, 9 Jun 1843; m. 1st 14 Mar 1782, SARAH WESTON, b. at Lebanon, 20 Aug 1755 daughter of John and Elizabeth (Goodwin) Weston;[1523] Sarah d. at Stafford, 23 Sep 1787. Jacob m. 2nd 1 Jul 1789, SARAH LADD, b. at Tolland, 27 Apr 1760 daughter of Jonathan and Anna (Tyler) Ladd; Sarah d. at Tolland, 23 Mar 1844.

vi HANNAH BENTON, b. 3 May 1756; d. 18 Oct 1757.

vii HANNAH BENTON, b. 18 Feb 1758; d. 22 Sep 1775.

viii WILLIAM BENTON, b. 13 Apr 1760

ix NATHAN BENTON, b. 3 May 1764

x SILAS BENTON, b. 6 Jun 1766

xi SARAH BENTON, b. estimated at 1768. Sarah is an heir in the 1779 estate distribution, but no other record was found of her.

xii JERUSHA BENTON, b. 9 Sep 1770; d. 19 Sep 1775.

1521 The final division of the estate of Daniel Benton could not be made until the decease of the widow Mary and the division was made in October 1808. There is a death record for a widow Mary Benton in Tolland in July 1808 although the transcription says she is the widow of Jacob.

1522 *Connecticut State Library (Hartford, Connecticut)*; Probate Place: *Hartford, Connecticut, Probate Packets, Badger, Joshua-Billings, J, 1759-1880, Case 147*

1523 The 1788 probate of John Weston of Willington includes a distribution to the heirs of daughter Sarah Benton.

565) ELIJAH WHEELER (*Mary Abbott Wheeler[4], Jemima Johnson Abbot[4], Mary Holt Johnson[2], Nicholas[1]*), b. at Norwich, 22 Feb 1731 son of Nathan and Mary (Abbott) Wheeler; d. at Amenia, 3 Sep 1774; m. at Kent, CT, 27 Nov 1760, SARAH MARSH, b. at Kent, 9 Feb 1740/1 daughter of Cyrus and Margaret (Kinsman) Marsh.

Elijah Wheeler resided in Amenia and was named one of the overseers of the poor in 1772.[1524]

In his will written 2 September 1774, Elijah Wheeler of Amenia bequeathed to beloved wife Sarah all his lands until his eldest son Nathan A. Wheeler arrives at age twenty-one. If Nathan should die, then she will hold the lands until next son Robert K. Wheeler reaches twenty-one. After that, Sarah is to have use of one-half of the house and one-third of the estate real and moveable for her natural life. Daughters Joanna Wheeler and Elizabeth Wheeler each receives one cow and £50 to be paid at age eighteen. The remainder of the estate is to be equally divided among his sons Nathan A., Robert K., Elijah, Cyrus M., and William except that eldest son Nathan is to have an additional £50. If any of his sons should be disposed to a liberal education in the learned professions, then the executor is authorized to sell the portion of the estate necessary for that. Well-beloved brother Eliphalet and wife Sarah were jointly named executors. Although the will was written the day before Elijah's death, it was not presented at probate until 3 August 1779. The inventory was made November 1774.[1525]

Elijah Wheeler and Sarah Marsh were parents of seven children likely all born at Amenia, New York.

i NATHAN ABBOTT WHEELER, b. 1761

ii JOANNA WHEELER

iii ROBERT KINSMAN WHEELER. Robert appears to be living in Virgil, NY in 1830 with a family.

iv ELIZABETH WHEELER

v ELIJAH WHEELER

vi CYRUS MARSH WHEELER, b. about 1772; d. at Northwest, NY; 13 Jul 1838; m. SARAH SCOTT, b. 1776; Sarah d. at Northwest, 3 Sep 1854.

vii WILLIAM WHEELER, b. 1774

566) ELIPHALET WHEELER (*Mary Abbott Wheeler[4], Jemima Johnson Abbot[4], Mary Holt Johnson[2], Nicholas[1]*), b. at Tolland, 3 Jul 1738 son of Nathan and Mary (Abbott) Wheeler; d. at Amenia, NY, 5 Sep 1788 (probate 8 May 1789); m. 10 Nov 1767, ABIGAIL COLE, b. at Sharon, 10 Sep 1751 daughter of Caleb and Anne (St. John) Cole.

There is one known child and one possible child of Eliphalet Wheeler and Abigail Cole, although there may be others.

i ANNA WHEELER,[1526] b. 1769; d. 25 Apr 1843; m. ROGER DELANO, b. at Amenia, 1766 son of Jethro and Elizabeth (Lathrop) Delano; Roger d. at Clarkson, NY, 1850.

ii DANIEL A. WHEELER, b. at Sharon, CT, 1770; d. at Whitney Point, NY, 12 May 1823. The name of Daniel's first wife is unknown but married about 1797. There are children Eliphalet Wheeler and Abigail Wheeler from his first marriage. Daniel m. 2nd, RHODA who has not been identified, b. about 1783. Dr. Daniel Wheeler was a physician in Broome County, NY. He also built a grist mill and served as president of the medical society at Chenango Point from 1806 to 1812.[1527]

567) HANNAH CADY (*Hannah Abbott Cady[4], Jemima Johnson Abbott[3], Mary Holt Johnson[2], Nicholas[1]*), b. at Tolland, 24 Jun 1732 daughter of John and Hannah (Abbott) Cady; d. at Chesterfield, NH, 21 Jun 1803; m. Nov 1753, WILLIAM SHURTLEFF, b. at Plympton, MA, 7 Apr 1730 son of John and Sarah (Lucas) Shurtleff; William d. at Chesterfield, 25 Dec 1801.

Hannah and William resided in Connecticut first in Tolland the then in Windsor. In 1787, they made the move to Chesterfield, New Hampshire.[1528]

Hannah Cady and William Shurtleff were parents of nine children.[1529][1530]

i JOHN SHURTLEFF, b. at Tolland, 6 Sep 1755; d. (buried in Milwaukee, WI),[1531] 28 May 1839; m. at Ellington, 25 May 1781, PATIENCE CHUBBUCK, likely b. at Wareham, MA, 6 Aug 1757 daughter of Ebenezer and Mary (Burgess) Chubbuck; Patience was living in 1806 when she was dismissed from the church in Somers, CT to the

---

1524 Reed, *Early History of Amenia*, p 48

1525 *Wills and Administrations (New York County, New York), volume 0033, pp 146-147*

1526 Anna is a possible child in this family.

1527 Smith, *History of Broome County, New York*, p 135, p 360

1528 Randall, *History of Chesterfield*, p 433

1529 Connecticut Town Birth Records, pre-1870 (Barbour Collection)

1530 Shurtleff, Descendants of William Shurtleff

1531 National Cemetery Administration, U.S. Veterans' Gravesites, ca.1775-2006

church in Chesterfield, NH.[1532] John is reported to have had a second marriage to Mrs. Hines who has not been identified.

ii ASAHEL SHURTLEFF, b. at Tolland, 25 May 1757; d. at Swanzey, NH, 24 Mar 1830; m. at Ellington, 8 Nov 1781, SARAH DEWEY, b. at Lebanon, CT, 13 May 1759 daughter of Solomon and Anna (Downer) Dewey; Sarah d. at Rindge, NH, 21 Mar 1837.

iii SUSANNAH SHURTLEFF, b. at Tolland, 19 Apr 1759; d. at Brookfield, VT, 14 Oct 1810. Susannah did not marry.

iv AMOS SHURTLEFF, b. 1761; d. 1768.

v HANNAH SHURTLEFF, b. 1763; d. 1764.

vi HANNAH SHURTLEFF, b. at Windsor, CT, 9 Jul 1765; d. at Stanstead, Québec, 25 Jun 1845; m. at Sharon, VT, 10 Feb 1785, ZADOK STEELE, b. at Tolland, 17 Dec 1758 son of James and Abigail (Huntington) Steele; Zadok d. at Stanstead, 23 May 1845.

vii SARAH SHURTLEFF, b. at Windsor, 15 Nov 1767; d. at Sharon, VT, 19 Oct 1859; m. at Randolph, VT, 12 Feb 1787, SAMUEL STEELE, b. at Tolland, 10 May 1761 son of James and Abigail (Huntington) Steele; Samuel d. at Sharon, 29 Jan 1849.

viii BETSEY SHURTLEFF, b. at Windsor, 4 Jul 1770; d. at Brookfield, VT, 22 Jul 1848; m. at Brookfield, 23 Dec 1812, as his second wife, ELIPHALET WALCOTT, b. at Windham, 3 Oct 1760 son of Elijah and Esther (Owen) Walcott; Eliphalet d. at Brookfield, 27 Feb 1849. Eliphalet was first married to Anna Coburn.

ix ROSWELL SHURTLEFF, b. at Windsor, 29 Aug 1773; d. at Hanover, NH, 4 Feb 1851; m. at Spencer, MA, 2 Sep 1810, ANNA POPE, b. at Spencer, 16 Feb 1784 daughter of Joseph and Anna (Hammond) Pope; Anna d. at Hanover, 3 Mar 1826. Roswell graduated from Dartmouth graduating in 1799 and ultimately obtained the Doctor of Divinity degree from the University of Vermont in 1834. He was a theologian and professor emeritus at Dartmouth.[1533]

568) ELIZABETH CADY (*Hannah Abbott Cady[4], Jemima Johnson Abbott[3], Mary Holt Johnson[2], Nicholas[1]*), b. at Tolland, 6 Jun 1736 daughter of John and Hannah (Abbott) Cady; d. at Columbia, CT, 5 Sep 1813; m. 30 Aug 1770, SOLOMON DEWEY, b. at Lebanon, 29 Apr 1724 son of Josiah and Sarah (Hutchinson) Dewey; Solomon d. at Columbia, CT, 2 May 1819. Solomon was first married to Anna Downer.

Solomon Dewey was a cabinetmaker and farmer in Lebanon, Connecticut, the family homestead being at Chestnut Hill.[1534]

In his will written 1 Jul 1803 (proved 31 May 1819), Solomon Dewey bequeaths to beloved wife Elizabeth the use of one-third part of his real estate during her life. Sons Solomon and Andrew receive the wearing apparel and $33.34. Sons Asahel and Eleazer receive the remainder of the estate to divide. Daughters Anna Woodworth, Sarah Shurtliff, Molly Scovel, and Betty Newel each receives $60. Granddaughter Jerusha Hunt also receives $60. Eleazer and Asahel were named executors. Real estate was valued at $1,495 being one-half of the farm where the deceased last lived.[1535] Sons Solomon and Andrew and daughters Anna, Sarah, and Molly are children from Solomon's first marriage to Anna Downer.

Elizabeth Cady and Solomon Dewey were parents of four children born at Lebanon, Connecticut.

i BETSY DEWEY, b. at Lebanon, 4 Jun 1771; d. at Ellington, 11 Aug 1826; m. at Ellington, 18 Dec 1794, NATHANIEL NEWELL, b. 17 Mar 1766 son of Nathaniel and Abigail (Aborn) Newell; Nathaniel d. at Ellington, 1 Aug 1842. Nathaniel married second Eunice Green.

ii HANNAH DEWEY, b. at Lebanon, 20 Sep 1773; d. at Columbia, CT, 5 Jun 1803; m. 1798, DARIUS HUNT, b. about 1770 son of Eldad and Jerusha (West) Hunt.

iii ASAHEL DEWEY, b. at Lebanon, 13 Jun 1775; d. at Columbia, CT, 26 Apr 1846; m. at Lebanon, 8 Mar 1798, LUCINA FULLER, b. at Lebanon, 10 Apr 1777 daughter of Bezaleel and Phebe (Sprague) Fuller; Lucina d. at Columbia, 14 Dec 1826.

1532 Connecticut, Church Record Abstracts, 1630-1920

1533 Chapman, *Sketches of the Alumni of Dartmouth College*, p 99

1534 A more detailed description of Solomon Dewey including reminiscences of his granddaughter can be found in Dewey, *The Life of George Dewey, Rear Admiral, USN*, pp 406-407

1535 *Connecticut State Library (Hartford, Connecticut)*; Probate Place: *Hartford, Connecticut, Probate Packets, Decker, Joseph-Durkee, M, 1719-1880, Case 1124*

iv ELEAZER DEWEY, b. at Lebanon, 4 Dec 1778; d. at Columbia, CT, 11 May 1872 "the oldest man in town"; m. about 1801,[1536] REBECCA LITTLE, b. 17 Jun 1770 daughter of Consider and Rebekah (Buckingham) Little; Rebecca d. at Columbia, 5 Jun 1866.

569) NAHUM CADY (*Hannah Abbott Cady⁴, Jemima Johnson Abbott³, Mary Holt Johnson², Nicholas¹*), b. at Tolland, 14 Mar 1743 son of John and Hannah (Abbott) Cady; d. at East Windsor, 14 Oct 1834; m. Jan 1771, DEBORAH FITCH, b. about 1752 likely the daughter of Elisha and Priscilla (Patten) Fitch; Deborah d. at South Windsor, 17 Apr 1826.

Nahum was a farmer in Tolland for most of his life but relocated to Vernon late in life. Nahum Cady and Deborah Fitch were parents of eight children born at Tolland.

i PRISCILLA CADY, b. 18 Jun 1771; d. at Champion, NY, 23 May 1854; m. at West Hartford, 28 Jul 1792, THOMAS FRANCIS, b. 1766 likely son of Hezekiah and Deborah (Blinn) Francis;[1537] Thomas d. at Champion, 10 Jan 1835.

ii ASAHEL CADY, b. 8 Sep 1774; d. at Manchester, CT, 30 Aug 1844; m. 2 Apr 1800, MABEL SMITH, b. about 1764; Mabel d. at Manchester, 25 Aug 1834.

iii ELIJAH CADY, b. 9 Mar 1777; d. at South Windsor, CT, 3 Feb 1853; m. SABRA LOOMIS, b. 1783 daughter of John and Sabra (Bissell) Loomis;[1538] Sabra d. at Olmsted Falls, OH, 27 Mar 1861.[1539]

iv DEBORAH CADY, b. 28 Feb 1780; d. after 1850 when she was living in Byron, NY; m. 25 Dec 1804, THOMAS STUDLEY.

v BETTY CADY, b. 20 May 1782; d. at Champion, NY, 6 Sep 1870; m. 6 Oct 1803, MINER MERRILL, b. 25 Aug 1781 son of Moses and Waitstill (Heath) Merrill; Miner d. at Champion, 9 Mar 1860.

vi LYDIA CADY, b. 20 Sep 1784; d. at East Windsor, 15 May 1837; m. at East Windsor, 7 Jan 1821, JARED BISBEE, b. at Tolland, 29 Aug 1776 son of Joseph and Libiah (-) Bisbee.

vii OLIVE CADY, b. 2 Aug 1787; d. at Saranac, MI, 16 Feb 1862; m. JERRY PECK, b. 1788; Jerry d. at Saranac, 12 Jan 1862.

viii EUNICE CADY, b. 27 Jul 1790; d. at Champion, NY, 1 Sep 1862; m. DANIEL DOWD MERRIAM, b. 22 May 1783 son of Marshal and Mary (Driggs) Merriam; Daniel d. at Champion, 20 Jul 1860.

570) AMOS CADY (*Hannah Abbott Cady⁴, Jemima Johnson Abbott³, Mary Holt Johnson², Nicholas¹*), b. at Tolland, 3 Sep 1747 son of John and Hannah (Abbott) Cady; d. at Vernon, CT, 5 Aug 1843;[1540] m. 1st 16 Jul 1771, HANNAH KINGSBURY, b. at Tolland, 5 Apr 1752 daughter of Simon and Deliverance (Cady) Kingsbury;[1541] Hannah d. 7 Nov 1786. Amos m. 2nd 10 Dec 1789, ESTHER TUTHILL, b. in Maryland, about 1757 daughter of Moses and Martha (Edwards) Tuthill;[1542] Esther d. at Vernon, 27 Jan 1857.

Amos Cady and Hannah Kingsbury were parents of seven children born at Tolland.

i SARAH CADY, b. 16 Jan 1772; d. at Vernon, CT, 4 Jun 1798; m. 16 Jun 1796, SAMUEL LYMAN, b. Feb 1772 son of James Lyman; Samuel d. at Vernon, 11 Apr 1845.[1543]

ii JOHN CADY, b. 12 Oct 1773; d. after 1855 when he was living in Franklinville, NY; m. BETSEY, b. in CT about 1780 who has not been identified; Betsey was living in 1855.

iii SIMON CADY, b. 21 Mar 1776; d. 24 May 1776.

iv RUSSELL CADY, b. 20 Jun 1777; d. at Vernon, 20 Dec 1861; m. 1st 26 Nov 1812, BETSEY CHAPMAN, b. 1782 daughter of Thomas and Rebecca (Dart) Chapman;[1544] Betsey d. at Andover, CT, 23 Sep 1830. Russell m. 2nd SOPHIA HUTCHINS, baptized at Bolton, CT, 1 May 1791 daughter of Joshua and Rhoda (Newton) Hutchins; Sophia d. at Vernon, 16 Jun 1883.

[1536] Eleazer and wife Rebecca were admitted to the church at Columbia in 1801.
[1537] Francis, *Descendants of Robert Francis*, p 99
[1538] The 1824 final estate distribution of John Loomis (who died in 1787) includes heirs Sabra Cady and Elijah Cady.
[1539] Connecticut, Deaths and Burials Index, 1650-1934. Sabra died at Olmstead Falls, OH and was buried at South Windsor, CT.
[1540] *Hale Collection of Cemetery Inscriptions and Newspaper Notices, 1629-1934,* Amos Cady died at age 97.
[1541] The 1793 will of Simon Kingsbury includes a bequest to the heirs of daughter Hannah Cady deceased.
[1542] Goodwin, *Genealogical Notes: or Contributions to the Family History of Some of the First Settlers of Connecticut and Massachusetts*, p 57
[1543] Connecticut, Hale Collection of Cemetery Inscriptions and Newspaper Notices, 1629-1934; Samuel Lyman died at age 72.
[1544] The 1817 will of Thomas Chapman of Vernon includes a bequest to his daughter Betsy Cady.

v AMOS CADY, b. 11 May 1779; d. at Guilford, CT, 3 Sep 1826; m. at Amherst, MA, 6 Aug 1807, HANNAH KELLOGG, b. at Amherst, MA, 14 Jul 1786 daughter of Martin and Hannah (Crocker) Kellogg;[1545] Hannah d. at New London, 14 Feb 1839.

vi DILLA CADY, b. 5 Jun 1781; d. 27 Mar 1801.

vii SIMON CADY, b. 27 Jun 1783; d. at East Windsor, 1824;[1546] m. about 1810, LUCINDA LOOMIS, b. at East Windsor, about 1786 daughter of John and Sabra (Bissell) Loomis;[1547] Lucinda d. at Hartford, 9 Apr 1856.

Amos Cady and Esther Tuthill were parents of two children born at Tolland.

i HANNAH CADY, b. 1 Oct 1790; d. after 1850 when she was living with her mother in Vernon. Hannah did not marry.

ii JAMES CADY, b. 19 Aug 1793; nothing further known.

571) ANNIS CHURCH (*Annis Johnson Church[4], Josiah Johnson[3], Mary Holt Johnson[2], Nicholas[1]*), b. at Lancaster, 6 Jul 1731 daughter of Joshua and Annis (Johnson) Church; d. at Sterling, 6 Apr 1807; m. at Harvard, 16 Nov 1749, CALEB WHITNEY, b. at Lancaster, 4 Oct 1729 son of Jonathan and Alice (Willard) Whitney; Caleb d. at Sterling, 28 Mar 1822.

Caleb Whitney was a farmer in Worcester County, Massachusetts. In his will written 8 December 1794 (proved 21 May 1822), Caleb bequeaths to beloved wife Anes all the household furniture, one-third of the house, and the improvement of one-third of the farm while she is a widow. Eldest daughter Elizabeth Pierce receives one pound which completes her portion. Son Joshua Whitney receives six pounds and son Joseph receives eight pounds to complete their portions. Daughter Annis Holman receives five pounds. Son Hezekiah receives eight pounds. The remainder of the estate including the husbandry tools goes to son Jonathan who is also named executor.[1548]

Annis Church and Caleb Whitney were parents of twelve children some of the births recorded in Harvard and some at Shutesbury, and some at both places. The family seems to be in Harvard and then Shutesbury before a final move to Sterling.

i JOSHUA WHITNEY, b. 4 Jan 1750; d. at Harvard, 24 Jan 1750.

ii ELIZABETH WHITNEY, b. at Harvard, 27 Jun 1751; d. at Jaffrey, NH, 23 Oct 1823; m. at Lancaster, 13 Mar 1778, her third cousin once removed, SAMUEL PIERCE (*Daniel Pierce[4], Dinah Holt Pierce[3], Henry[2], Nicholas[1]*), b. at Harvard, 21 May 1749 son of Daniel and Sarah (Buck) Pierce; Samuel d. at Jaffrey, 27 Dec 1824. Samuel was first married to Abigail Carter. Elizabeth Whitney and Samuel Pierce are Family 712.

iii ANNIS WHITNEY, b. 20 Jun 1753; died young.

iv JOSHUA WHITNEY, b. at Harvard, 18 Feb 1754; d. at Gardner, 2 Jul 1812; m. at Sterling, 30 Nov 1781, his first cousin, VASHTI KNIGHT (*Prudence Church Knight[5], Annis Johnson Church[4], Josiah Johnson[3], Mary Holt Johnson[2], Nicholas[1]*), b. at Lancaster, 23 Dec 1760 daughter of Ebenezer and Prudence (Church) Knight; Vashti d. at Gardner, 29 Oct 1832.[1549]

v ANNIS WHITNEY, b. 9 May 1756; d. 31 Jan 1758.

vi CALEB WHITNEY, b. 23 Jun 1758; d. at Albany, 1 Feb 1778. Caleb enlisted for a three-year term in the company of Capt. Joseph Hodgkins during the Revolution and died in service. He was reported sick at Albany on 10 Dec 1777 where he died reported as 1 Feb 1778 in military records.[1550]

vii JOSEPH WHITNEY, b. at Harvard, 9 Jul 1760; d. at Hubbardston, 24 Sep 1840; m. ESTHER CRITTENDEN, baptized at Middletown, CT, 11 Feb 1781 daughter of Gideon and Esther (Cone) Crittenden; Esther d. at Orange, MA, 25 Jan 1862.

viii ANNIS WHITNEY, b. 29 Jun 1763; m. about 1790, JOHN HOLMAN, b. at Sutton, 26 Dec 1761 son of David and Lucy (Thurston) Holman; John d. at Hague, NY, 1842. This family was is Sterling, relocated to Princeton for a short period, were in Leicester, Vermont where their youngest child was born and were then in Hague, NY. John

---

[1545] Hopkins, *The Kelloggs in the Old World and the New*, volume 1, p 142

[1546] Connecticut, Hale Collection of Cemetery Inscriptions and Newspaper Notices, 1629-1934

[1547] John Loomis died in 1787 and a guardian was appointed for daughter Lucinda of about two years. The final distribution of his estate was 6 Feb 1824 and included heirs Lucinda Cady and Simon Cady.

[1548] *Worcester County, MA: Probate File Papers, 1731-1881.* Online database. AmericanAncestors.org. New England Historic Genealogical Society, 2015. Case 64743

[1549] Joshua, a soldier of the Revolution, July 2, 1812, a. 58. G.S.2.

[1550] Compiled Service Records of Soldiers Who Served in the American Army During the Revolutionary War, Records of 15th Massachusetts Regiment

received a pension for his service in the Revolution and the file notes his movements from Sutton to Vermont and then to Hague.[1551]

ix LUCY WHITNEY, b. at Shutesbury, 20 Apr 1765; d. 16 May 1765.

x HEZEKIAH WHITNEY, b. at Shutesbury, 16 Aug 1766; d. at Mexico, NY, 21 May 1842; m. at Templeton, MA, 10 Dec 1793, SUSANNA WHITE; Susanna d. at Mexico, 14 Oct 1847.

xi JONATHAN WHITNEY, b. at Shutesbury, 8 Sep 1768; d. at Sterling, 18 Feb 1847; m. at Gardner, 7 Nov 1793, LUCY WHEELER, b. at Gardner, 31 May 1771 daughter of Josiah and Lucy (Graves) Wheeler; Lucy d. at Sterling, 2 Jan 1856.

xii LUCY WHITNEY, b. 25 Sep 1770; d. 7 Sep 1771.

572) PRUDENCE CHURCH (*Annis Johnson Church[4], Josiah Johnson[3], Mary Holt Johnson[2], Nicholas[1]*), b. at Lancaster, MA, 5 Apr 1739 daughter of Joshua and Annis (Johnson) Church; m. at Harvard, 19 Oct 1758, EBENEZER KNIGHT, b. at Lancaster, 12 Jan 1730/1 son of Amos and Elizabeth (Kendall) Knight; Ebenezer d. at Lancaster, 1776 (probate 5 Apr 1776).

Ebenezer Knight was a farmer in Lancaster. He did not leave a will and his estate entered probate 5 April 1776 with Prudence Knight as administratrix and Jonathan Knight providing surety for the bond.[1552] The total value of the estate was £42.14.11.

Prudence Church and Ebenezer Knight were parents of eight children born at Lancaster.

i PRUDENCE KNIGHT, b. 3 May 1759; d. at Packersfield, NH, about 1800; m. at Templeton, MA, 10 Jan 1782, JOSIAH ATWOOD, b. at Templeton, 24 Jan 1760 son of John and Elizabeth (Lawrence) Atwood; Josiah d. at Nelson, NH, 26 Nov 1841. Josiah married second Lydia White on 17 May 1802.

ii VASHTI KNIGHT, b. 23 Dec 1760; d. at Gardner, MA, 29 Oct 1832; m. at Sterling, 30 Nov 1781, her first cousin, JOSHUA WHITNEY (*Annis Church Whitney[5], Annis Johnson Church[4], Josiah Johnson[3], Mary Holt Johnson[2], Nicholas[1]*), b. at Harvard, 18 Feb 1754 son of Caleb and Annis (Church) Whitney; Joshua d. at Gardner, 2 Jul 1812.

iii ABEL KNIGHT, b. 16 Dec 1763

iv TALMON KNIGHT, b. 29 Mar 1766; d. at Troy, NH, 1843 (probate 1843); m. at Templeton, 15 Mar 1791, HANNAH SAWYER whose parents have not been identified. Talmon and Hannah do not seem to have had children. In his will written 1836, Talmlon allows use of the estate to Leonard and Nancy Cobb, with the estate ultimately going to the Cobb children when they are of age. There is also a provision for the support of his sister Eliza Knight if she is still living at his decease. Leonard Cobb and his wife Nancy Osborne were residents of Troy and lived on Talmon's farm after his death.[1553]

v PHEBE KNIGHT, b. 2 Mar 1768; d. at Templeton, 8 Mar 1852; m. at Templeton, 8 Jan 1793, JOHN SAWYER, b. likely b. at Lancaster, 21 Feb 1767 son of Jotham and Dinah (Weeks) Sawyer; John d. at Templeton, 25 Feb 1842.

vi RUTH KNIGHT, b. 26 Mar 1770

vii ELIZABETH KNIGHT, b. 7 Apr 1772; living in 1836 when her brother Talmon wrote his will. Elizabeth did not marry.

viii ANNIS KNIGHT, baptized at Lancaster, 14 Aug 1774; d. at Winchendon, MA, 24 Nov 1862; m. 1st at Marlborough, NH, 22 Oct 1799, as his second wife, ELKANAH LANE, b. at Norton, MA, 14 Jan 1745 son of Elkanah and Hannah (Tingley) Lane; Elkanah d. at Swanzey, NH, 21 Oct 1811. Annis m. 2nd at Swanzey, 3 Jan 1816, WILLIAM BRIDGE, b. at Worcester, 21 Feb 1767 son of Samuel and Mary (Goodwin) Bridge; William d. at Swanzey, 8 Mar 1825. Elkanah Lane was first married to Esther Dinsmore. William Bridge was first married to Abigail Carter.

573) CALEB CHURCH (*Annis Johnson Church[4], Josiah Johnson[3], Mary Holt Johnson[2], Nicholas[1]*), b. at Lancaster, 3 Jun 1741 son of Joshua and Annis (Johnson) Church; m. 1st at Harvard, 11 May 1762, TAMER WARNER, b. at Harvard, 3 Dec 1738

[1551] Holman's Holman genealogy states that this John married Sally Stone, and perhaps he did in 1786, but Annis is listed as the mother of his children including the six children born in Sterling and one child born in Leicester. And the Holman genealogy notes that this John's children all have a mother listed as Annis. The John Holman who is the son of David and Lucy is clearly the John who was in Hague, NY based on details in his pension file. But that John's movements also match the movements of John and Annis and the births of their children. There are four John Holmans born in Sutton in a four-year period all of whom would have been of an age to marry either Sally Stone or Annis Whitney.

[1552] *Worcester County, MA: Probate File Papers, 1731-1881.* Online database. AmericanAncestors.org. New England Historic Genealogical Society, 2015. Case 35651

[1553] Caverly, *An Historical Sketch of Troy*, p 166

daughter of Nathan and Nathan (Goodenough) Warner; Tamer d. at Harvard, 22 Feb 1763. Caleb m. 2nd, at Bolton, 11 Jul 1764, ELIZABETH WALKER.

Caleb Church and Tamer Warner had one infant who died 18 Feb 1763 and Tamer died four days later. There are records for three children of Caleb Church and Elizabeth Walker.

i HANNAH CHURCH, b. at Templeton, MA, 17 Feb 1765; d. at Salisbury, VT, 1 Aug 1814; m. SAMUEL TAYLOR, b. at Ellington, CT, 1759 son of Stephen and Sarah (Hadlock) Taylor; Stephen d. at Salisbury, 12 Mar 1822. This family was in Grantham, NH after their marriage before settling in Salisbury about 1795.

ii DANIEL CHURCH, b. at Bolton, MA, 11 Oct 1766; m. at Leicester, VT, 13 Dec 1792, PRUDENCE STONE, b. at Dublin, NH, 19 Oct 1775daughter of Silas and Elizabeth (Russell) Stone.

iii SILAS CHURCH, baptized at Lancaster, MA, 6 Jan 1771; m. at Grantham, NH, Jan 1791, JOANNE JENNE who has not been identified.

574) JOSHUA CHURCH (*Annis Johnson Church4, Josiah Johnson3, Mary Holt Johnson2, Nicholas1*), b. at Lancaster, 6 Apr 1743 son of Joshua and Annis (Johnson) Church; d. at Chester, VT, about 1829; m. at Lancaster, 21 Feb 1765, KEZIAH GOSS.

Joshua and Keziah married in Lancaster, and the births of their first two children are recorded there. Joshua seems to have been earlier in Chester where he was one of those petitioning New York for a patent for the town of Chester which was granted. He had property in Chester that he sold to Thomas Chandler, but then bought back from Thomas Chandler 116 acres in 1770. Joshua was perhaps back and forth between Chester and Worcester County, but the family seemed finally settled in Chester in 1775.[1554]

On 10 April 1818, Joshua Church, age seventy-three and a resident of Chester, gave a statement related to his application for a pension. He enlisted from Charlestown, New Hampshire in March 1776 in a company commanded by Capt. Estabrook. He was discharged November 1776 and had a second enlistment March 1777 in the regiment of Col, Cilley. In that enlistment, he served as quartermaster for the regiment and was discharged in May 1780. He had a further period of service in defense of the frontier, in this enlistment with the rank of lieutenant, and continued until December 1783 when he was discharge at Bethel, Vermont. He was at the Battle of the Cedars, the Battle of Saratoga, Battle of Newtown, and with the expedition of General Sullivan against the Indians. On 1 August 1820, Joshua made a further statement that he had not property and no family.[1555]

Joshua Church and Keziah Goss were parents of five children.[1556]

i JOSHUA CHURCH, b. at Lancaster, MA, 8 Apr 1765; d. at Chester, VT, 3 Aug 1840; m. 1st at Chester, VT, 7 Mar 1790, ABIAH DAVIS, b. at Templeton, MA, 12 Jun 1769 daughter of Eleazer and Abiah (Ward) Davis; Abiah d. about 1812. Joshua m. 2nd 8 Feb 1813, BETSEY LELAND, b. at Holliston, MA, 3 Jul 1780 daughter of Asa and Lois (Marshall) Leland; Betsey d. at Chester, 2 Sep 1819. Joshua m. 3rd 9 Mar 1823, SARAH KIBLING, b. at Claremont, NH, 1 Mar 1785 daughter of John and Elizabeth (Fisher) Kibling; Sarah d. at Chester, 21 Feb 1877.

ii KEZIAH CHURCH, b. at Lancaster, 6 May 1767; d. at Chester, VT, 25 Mar 1844; m. at Chester, Jun 1789, ANTHONY WILLIAMS, b. in RI, about 1764; Anthony d. at Chester, 31 Aug 1853.

iii LUCY CHURCH, b. at Leominster, MA, 29 Aug 1769

iv CATHERINE CHURCH, b. at Templeton, MA, 13 Nov 1771; d. at Eden, NY, 11 Aug 1845; m. at Chester, 29 Nov 1789, JONATHAN CARYL, baptized at Hopkinton, MA, 22 Mar 1761 son of Jonathan and Ann (Clark) Caryl; Jonathan d. at Eden, NY, 12 Nov 1832.

v NATHAN CHURCH, b. at Chester, VT, 25 Mar 1775; d. at Massena, NY, 1855; m. at Chester, VT, 15 Jul 1798, SUSANNAH CHASE, baptized at Shirley, MA, 14 Nov 1779 daughter of Joshua and Susannah (Fitch) Chase; Susannah d. at Massena, NY, 1856.

575) OLIVE CHURCH (*Annis Johnson Church4, Josiah Johnson3, Mary Holt Johnson2, Nicholas1*), baptized at Harvard, 10 Apr 1748 son of Joshua and Annis (Johnson) Church; d. at Templeton, 2 Jul 1822; m. at Templeton, 29 Nov 1764, JOSHUA WRIGHT, b. about 1737 (age 74 at death); Joshua d. at Templeton, 27 Nov 1811.

Olive and Joshua resided in Templeton throughout their marriage. Joshua owned considerable property in Templeton and was involved in multiple land transactions. Joshua sold a 340-acre tract of land in Templeton to his son Rufus for a payment of $1,000 on 13 June 1809 (recorded 8 May 1811).[1557] In March 1806, Joshua Wright had conveyed a property to his son-in-law Jonathan Whitcomb and Milla Whitcomb. On 10 July 1812, widow Olive Wright, for a payment of $1,000,

---

1554 *Early Vermont Settlers, 1700-1784.* (Original Online Database: *AmericanAncestors.org*, New England Historic Genealogical Society, 2015. (By Scott Andrew Bartley, Lead Genealogist.) Joshua Church of Chester

1555 U.S. Revolutionary War Pension and Bounty-Land Warrant Application Files, Case S40833

1556 *Early Vermont Settlers, 1700-1784.* (Original Online Database: *AmericanAncestors.org*, New England Historic Genealogical Society, 2015. (By Scott Andrew Bartley, Lead Genealogist.) Joshua Church of Chester

1557 Massachusetts Land Records, Worcester County, 179:290

quitclaimed any right of dower to that property, granting this to Silas Church acting as guardian for the heirs of Jonathan Whitcomb.[1558]

On 25 March 1811, a petition was filed by the selectman of Templeton requesting that a guardian be appointed for Joshua Wright as due to age and infirmity he had become *non compos mentis* and was not longer able to manage his affairs. Leonard Stone was named guardian.[1559] Joshua died just six months later.

Joshua did not leave a will and his estate entered probate 29 January 1812. Widow Olive Wright and heirs Rus Wright, James F. Robbins, and Milla Robbins all declined to administer the estate and requested that Thomas Fisher be named administrator. The personal estate had a value of $274.46, and after expenses were deducted, payments of $111.07 were made to each of the heirs, Rufus Wright and James Robbins. Real estate was valued at $1,497.55.[1560]

Joshua Wright and Olive Church were parents of three children born at Templeton.

i RUFUS WRIGHT, b. 15 Sep 1765; d. at Templeton, 30 Oct 1817; m. at Templeton, 5 Mar 1786, ELIZABETH KENDALL, b. 1763; Elizabeth d. at Templeton, 27 Aug 1839.

ii ANNIS WRIGHT, 1 Jul 1767

iii MILLIE WRIGHT, b. 6 Aug 1770; d. at Templeton, 26 Dec 1854; m. 1st at Templeton, 25 May 1790, JONATHAN WHITCOMB son of William and Mercy (Wetherbee) Whitcomb; Jonathan d. at Templeton, 1 May 1809. Millie m. 2nd 2 May 1811, JAMES F. ROBBINS. James F. Robbins had a guardian appointed in 1826 due to being a spendthrift.

576) SILAS CHURCH (*Annis Johnson Church[4], Josiah Johnson[3], Mary Holt Johnson[2], Nicholas[1]*), b. at Harvard, 23 Oct 1751 son of Joshua and Annis (Johnson) Church; d. at Templeton, 27 Oct 1845; m. at Lancaster, 25 Nov 1771, MARY OSGOOD, b. at Lancaster, 23 Apr 1751 daughter of Jonathan and Asenath (Sawyer) Osgood; Mary d. at Templeton, 16 Feb 1817. Silas m. 2nd 1 Aug 1817 ASENATH WILDER, b. about 1746; Asenath d. at Templeton, 22 Feb 1824.

Silas was a farmer in Templeton. In his will written 15 December 1830 (probate 2 December 1845), Silas Church bequeathed to son Silas the bed and bedding "he now sleeps on." Son Elijah Church received twenty dollars. Daughter Asenath Church receives all the household furniture except Silas's bed and all the money and notes except the twenty dollars for Elijah, as long as she remains unmarried. If Asenath marries, the money should be divided equally among Silas Church, Joseph Church, Asenath Church, and Joshua Church. Daughter Asenath and son Joshua receive the chaise and sleigh and his half of the pew in the meeting house. Son Artemas receives one dollar. Grandson Charles Church receives the gun, baronet, and cartridge box. The real estate is to be held by sons Silas and Joseph as they have heretofore possessed it. Joseph was named executor.

Son Silas did not marry, and in his will written 7 December 1841 (probate 1 August 1846), Silas made bequests of either one dollar or five dollars to brothers Joseph, Elijah, and Artemas and to sister Asenath Osgood. The remainder of the estate went to brother Joshua Church who was also named executor.[1561]

Silas Church and Mary Osgood were parents of nine children born at Templeton.

i SILAS CHURCH, b. 31 Dec 1774; d. at Templeton, 24 Jun 1846. Silas did not marry.

ii JOSEPH CHURCH, b. 3 Jun 1777; d. at Templeton, 13 Nov 1864; m. 7 Feb 1805, LYDIA PATCH, b. at Stow, 3 Mar 1780 daughter of Samuel and Lydia (Walcott) Patch; Lydia d. at Templeton, 22 Sep 1867.

iii ASENATH CHURCH, b. 18 Oct 1779; d. at Sterling, 2 Jan 1865; m. 2 Feb 1832, as his third wife, TYLER PATCH OSGOOD, b. at Templeton 14 Aug 1774 the out-of-wedlock child of Hannah Hill and Elias Patch. Tyler was adopted by Samuel and Thankful (Matthews) Osgood and inherited the estate of Samuel Osgood. Tyler d. at Sterling, 14 Apr 1851. Tyler was married to Asenath's sister Annis who was his second wife. Tyler was first married to Betsey Stockwell.

iv ELIJAH CHURCH, b. 5 Oct 1781; d. at Corinna, ME, 7 Sep 1872; m. about 1813, HANNAH T. BURRELL[1562] possibly the daughter of Noah and Olive (-) Burrell b. at Freeport, ME, 18 Sep 1787; Hannah d. at Corinna, 19 Jun 1872.

[1558] Worcester County deeds, 205:348

[1559] *Worcester County, MA: Probate File Papers, 1731-1881.* Online database. AmericanAncestors.org. New England Historic Genealogical Society, 2015. Case 67783

[1560] *Worcester County, MA: Probate File Papers, 1731-1881.* Online database. AmericanAncestors.org. New England Historic Genealogical Society, 2015. Case 67784

[1561] *Worcester County, MA: Probate File Papers, 1731-1881.* Online database. AmericanAncestors.org. New England Historic Genealogical Society, 2015. Case 11812

[1562] Hannah's name is given as Hannah Burrell on the death record of one of the children. She died at age 84 years 9 months which would fit with the birth date of Hannah the daughter of Noah.

v ARTEMAS CHURCH, b. 27 Feb 1784; d. at Sturbridge, MA, 19 Jan 1859; m. 1st 31 Mar 1821, ELIZABETH SEAVER[1563] (widow of James Cheney), b. about 1785 daughter of Joseph and Esther (Lamb) Seaver; Elizabeth d. at Templeton, 27 Sep 1830. Artemas m. 2nd 6 Apr 1832, MEHITABLE MARSH (widow of Reuben Young), b. at Athol, 1785; Mehitable d. at Athol, 28 Jan 1879.

vi JONATHAN CHURCH, b. 29 Mar 1786; d. 31 Aug 1788.

vii ANNIS CHURCH, b. 15 Jan 1790; d. at Sterling, 5 Feb 1829; m. at Templeton, 8 Nov 1825, as his second wife, TYLER PATCH OSGOOD (see sister Asenath above).

viii JOSHUA CHURCH, b. 3 Jun 1791; d. at East Templeton, 11 Jan 1851; m. 4 May 1820, his first cousin once removed, BETSEY WHITNEY (*Jonathan Whitney⁶, Annis Church Whitney⁵, Annis Johnson Church⁴, Josiah Johnson³, Mary Holt Johnson², Nicholas¹*), b. at Sterling, 16 Nov 1798 daughter of Jonathan and Lucy (Wheeler) Whitney; Betsey d. at Templeton, 21 Mar 1876.

ix JONATHAN CHURCH, b. 18 Jan 1795; d. 19 Jan 1795.

577) HULDAH CHURCH (*Annis Johnson Church⁴, Josiah Johnson³, Mary Holt Johnson², Nicholas¹*), b. at Harvard, 20 Apr 1754 daughter of Joshua and Annis (Johnson) Church; m. at Templeton, 20 Oct 1769, JOSEPH OSGOOD, b. at Lancaster, 18 Oct 1742 son of Jonathan and Asenath (Sawyer) Osgood; Joseph d. at Canaan, ME, 29 May 1822.

Joseph Osgood was a farmer in Templeton. Huldah and Joseph reared their children in Templeton but moved to Canaan later in life. Huldah Church and Joseph Osgood were parents of five children born at Templeton.

i JOSEPH OSGOOD, b. 10 Sep 1770; d. by 1804 likely in VT; m. at Templeton, 3 Nov 1792, RACHEL HOLBROOK, b. 1775 likely daughter of Moses Holbrook; Rachel d. at Brighton, MI, about 1860. Rachel was remarried by 1805 to Barnard Kelley as their first child, Aaron Holbrook Kelley, was born in 1805 in Vermont.

ii HULDAH OSGOOD, b. 22 Feb 1773; m. at Templeton, 26 Dec 1798, JASON SPRAGUE, b. at Templeton, 12 May 1775 son of William and Tryphena (Fisher) Sprague; Jason d. at South Wardsboro, VT, 2 Nov 1818.

iii ANNIS OSGOOD, b. 11 Feb 1775; d. at Canaan, ME, 8 Nov 1848; m. at Templeton, 6 Nov 1793, JOSEPH BARRETT, b. at Westford, May 1769 son of Nathaniel and Martha (Wheeler) Barrett; Joseph d. at Canaan, 19 Jan 1817.

iv THANKFUL OSGOOD, b. 29 Nov 1778; d. at Waterville, ME, 14 Jan 1868; m. at Templeton, 30 Nov 1797, ABEL WHEELER, b. at Templeton, 31 Dec 1774 son of Thomas and Mary (Child) Wheeler; Abel d. at Waterville, 12 Mar 1857.

v SILAS OSGOOD, b. 29 Sep 1781; d. at Parma, NY, 11 Feb 1851; m. at Templeton, 24 Nov 1802, ASENATH "SENEY" WHITCOMB; Seney d. at Parma, 3 Jan 1849.

578) LUCY JOHNSON (*David Johnson⁴, Josiah Johnson³, Mary Holt Johnson², Nicholas¹*), b. at Lancaster, 21 Oct 1739 daughter of David and Mary (Warner) Johnson; d. at Wendell, 16 Feb 1833; m. at Leominster, 5 Oct 1763, HENRY SWEETSER, b. at Malden, 25 Mar 1738 son of Phillips and Mary (Green) Sweetser; Henry d. at Wendell, 18 Jun 1827.

Henry Sweetser served in the Revolution as 2nd Lieutenant in the company of Capt. Aaron Osgood in the Hampshire County Regiment commanded by Lt. Col. Samuel Williams. Lt. Sweetser received his commission on 10 May 1776.[1564] He later held the rank of captain.

On 17 June 1793 (deed recorded 15 August 1827), Henry Sweetser of Wendell conveyed to his son Nathan, for the payment of twenty shillings, all the land in his possession along with all the houses, outhouses, barns, and buildings.[1565]

Capt. Henry Sweetser and Lucy Johnson were parents of five children as given in the Wendell town family records.[1566]

i LUCY SWEETSER, b. 14 Sep 1764; d. at Wendell, 21 Apr 1835; m. at Wendell, 29 Dec 1788, ZEDEKIAH FISKE, b. at Waltham, 23 Jul 1763 son of Daniel and Sarah (Kendall) Fiske; Zedekiah d. at Wendell, 5 Aug 1844.

ii NATHAN SWEETSER, b. 1 Mar 1768; d. at Wendell, 8 May 1842; m. 1st at Wendell, 27 Jun 1796, BEULAH FISKE, b. at Waltham, 4 Mar 1770 daughter of Daniel and Sarah (Kendall) Fiske; Beulah d. at Wendell, 1 Aug 1797. Nathan m. 2nd at Ashby, 1 Sep 1800, LYDIA JOHNSON, b. at Acton, about 1776 daughter of William and Sarah (-) Johnson;[1567] Lydia d. at New Braintree, 12 Feb 1872.

iii MARY SWEETSER, b. 12 Apr 1771

1563 The death record of daughter Maria gives mother's name as Elizabeth Seaver.

1564 *Massachusetts Soldiers and Sailors in the Revolutionary War*, volume 15, p 302

1565 Massachusetts Land Records, Franklin County, 66:168

1566 Holbrook, Jay Mack, Massachusetts Vital Records, Wendell, 1763-1893, p 21, accessed through ancestry.com

1567 The names of Lydia's parents are given as William Johnson and Sarah Johnson on her death record.

iv ANNIS SWEETSER, b. 20 Dec 1778; d. at Carlisle, NY, 19 Jan 1852; m. at Wendell, 11 Jun 1800, JOSEPH GUNN, b. at Montague, 19 Oct 1772 son of Israel and Mary (Root) Gunn; Joseph d. at Carlisle, 22 Jun 1845.

v ELIZABETH SWEETSER, b. 20 Apr 1782

579) ELIZABETH JOHNSON (*David Johnson[4], Josiah Johnson[3], Mary Holt Johnson[2], Nicholas[1]*), b. at Leominster, 5 Mar 1744 daughter of David and Mary (Warner) Johnson; d. at Dunbarton, NH, 1818; m. at Leominster, 29 Sep 1766, SAMUEL EVANS, b. at Woburn, 1742 son of Andrew and Mary (Richardson) Evans; Samuel d. at Leominster, 9 Dec 1811.

Elizabeth and Samuel were first in Reading. On 30 March 1776 (deed recorded 23 April 1777), Samuel Evans, yeoman, then of Danvers purchased a 77-acre tract of land in north Leominster from Nathaniel Wyman for £194. On 9 May 1805, Samuel transferred his property including half of the house and cellar to his son Elias for a payment of $500.[1568]

In his will written 27 May 1811 (proved 7 January 1812), Samuel Evans bequeaths to beloved wife Elizabeth the use of the west room in house and cellar, one-half of the household furniture, and a lengthy list of annual provisions for her support to be provided by son Elias Evans. Eldest son Eliab receives a feather bed and $169 which completes his portion. Eldest daughter Elizabeth Cleveland receives a feather bed and $24 to complete her portion. Youngest daughter Lucy Sayles receives $14 to complete her portion. Son Elias is responsible for paying the legacies and receives the remainder of the estate. Elias is also named executor.[1569]

Elizabeth Johnson and Samuel Evans were parents of nine children.

i ELIZABETH EVANS, b. at Reading, 5 Sep 1767; d. at Dunbarton, NH, 1829; m. 1st at Reading, 9 Jan 1794, as his second wife Rev. JOHN CLEVELAND, b. at Canterbury, 1750 son of John and Mary (Dodge) Cleveland; John d. at Wrentham, MA, 31 Jan 1815. John was first married to Abigail Adams. Elizabeth m. 2nd at Wrentham, 27 Dec 1815, Rev. WALTER HARRIS, b. at Lebanon, CT, 8 Jan 1761 son of Nathaniel and Grace (Lyman) Harris; Walter d. at Dunbarton, about 1843.

ii SAMUEL EVANS, b. at Reading, 3 Apr 1769; d. at Leominster, 3 Sep 1790. "Samuel, s. Samuel, Sept. 3, 1790, a. 21. Bilious fever."

iii ELIAB EVANS, b. at Reading, 4 Jan 1772; d. at Danvers, MA, 12 Nov 1845; m. at Danvers, 21 Dec 1797, BETSY NICHOLS, b. at Danvers, 6 Jun 1777 daughter of Andrew and Eunice (Nichols) Nichols; Betsy d. at Danvers, 27 Mar 1845.

iv ELIAS EVANS, b. at Reading, 4 Jan 1772. This Elias likely died young.

v MARY EVANS, b. at Leominster, 25 Dec 1773; nothing further known and not living at father's will.

vi LUCY EVANS, b. 8 Jan 1776; d. 2 Sep 1778.

vii ELIAS EVANS, b. at Leominster, about 1777;[1570] d. at Leominster, 23 Jan 1837; m. 1st at Leominster, 20 Dec 1798, LUCY GLOVER, b. 2 Jul 1780 daughter of John and Rachel (Littlefield) Glover; Lucy d. by 1806.[1571] Elias m. 2nd at Leominster, 17 Oct 1806, SARAH DEANE CASWELL, b. about 1784 daughter of Samuel and Sarah (Hutchinson) Caswell;[1572] Sarah d. of Fitchburg, 1 Feb 1862.

viii LUCY EVANS, b. at Leominster, 8 Jul 1780; d. at Wrentham, 1836; m. 1st at Wrentham, 8 Nov 1807, ARIEL SAYLES, b. at Franklin, MA, 15 Jun 1780 son of Elisha and Catherine (Ballou) Sayles; Ariel d. at Wrentham, 15 Sep 1814. Lucy m. 2nd at Wrentham, 18 Jun 1818, as his second wife, LUTHER FISHER, b. at Wrentham, 25 Apr 1772 son of James and Jemima (Whiting) Fisher; Luther d. at Wrentham, 23 Mar 1824. Luther was first married to Betsy Smith.

ix JESSE EVANS, b. at Leominster, 24 Nov 1783; nothing further known and not living at father's will.

580) JOSIAH JOHNSON (*David Johnson[4], Josiah Johnson[3], Mary Holt Johnson[2], Nicholas[1]*), b. at Leominster, 7 Mar 1746 son of David and Mary (Warner) Johnson; d. at Buckland, 21 Feb 1827;[1573] m. 1774, MARTHA TAYLOR, b. 21 Dec 1756 daughter of Orthniel and Martha (Arms) Taylor; Martha d. 27 Oct 1825.

Josiah Johnson was a farmer in Buckland, although he also owned a gristmill for a short period.[1574]

1568 Massachusetts Land Records, Worcester County, 78:54; 159:465

1569 *Worcester County, MA: Probate File Papers, 1731-1881.* Online database. AmericanAncestors.org. New England Historic Genealogical Society, 2015. Case 19375

1570 There is not a birth record, and it is possible that it is the twin Elias of Eliab who reaches adulthood. However, his age at death in 1837 is given as age 60 and the wording of the will suggests he is a younger son.

1571 Glover, *Glover Memorials and Genealogies*, p 522

1572 The names of Sarah's parents are given as Samuel Caswell and Sarah Hutchinson on her death record.

1573 Josiah [Lt. N. R. 1.], h. Martha (Taylor), and s. David and Mary (Warner), Feb. .21, 1827. P. R. 39. [a. 80 y. G. R. 2.]

1574 Johnson, *Records of the Descendants of David Johnson of Leominster*, p 6

Josiah Johnson did not leave a will and the estate entered probate 13 March 1827 with Othniel Johnson named administrator. The farm and building were appraised at $900. Distribution of the real estate was made 12 July 1828 to the following heirs: Mary the wife of David White; Martha the wife of Josiah Hathaway; Susannah the wife of Henry Woodward; Lydia wife of Bildad Woodward; Rufus Johnson; Abigail Johnson; Leander Johnson; Othniel Johnson; Lovice wife of Hezekiah Brainerd; Josiah Johnson; and Sylvia wife of Ebenezer Woodward.[1575]

Josiah Johnson and Martha Johnson were parents of fourteen children born at Buckland.[1576]

i DAVID JOHNSON, b. 24 Jul 1775; d. 12 Aug 1777.

ii MARTHA JOHNSON, b. 31 Oct 1776; d. 14 Aug 1777.

iii OTHNIEL JOHNSON, b. 4 Apr 1778; d. at Buckland, 5 Mar 1851; m. at Buckland, Mary 1801, ANNA ELMER, b. at Buckland, 23 Sep 1783 daughter of Gad and Anna (Phillips) Elmer; Anna d. at Buckland, 19 Sep 1867.

iv RUFUS JOHNSON, b. 21 Jul 1779; d. recorded at Buckland, 2 Dec 1843;[1577] m. at Buckland, 4 Feb 1802, RUTH PHILLIPS, b. 6 Feb 1779; Ruth d. at Black Township, IN, 27 Dec 1842.

v JOSIAH JOHNSON, b. 28 Feb 1781; d. at Northfield, OH, 11 Dec 1856; m. at Buckland, 5 Dec 1801, BETSY ELMER, b. at Buckland, 7 Jun 1785 daughter of Gad and Anna (Phillips) Elmer; Betsy d. at Northfield, 27 Nov 1870.

vi MARY JOHNSON, b. 15 Oct 1782; d. at Heath, MA, 13 Oct 1852; m. 1st at Montague, 2 Dec 1802, DAVID NICHOLS, b. at Charlemont, 9 Mar 1779 son of Thomas and Elizabeth (Pierce) Nichols; David d. at Charlemont, 11 May 1812. Mary m. 2nd at Charlemont, 30 Aug 1822, DAVID WHITE, b. at Heath, 26 May 1785 son of Benjamin and Abigail (Wilder) White; David d. at Heath, 5 Mar 1862.

vii DAVID JOHNSON, b. 18 Jun 1784; d. 14 Mar 1788.

viii MARTHA JOHNSON, b. 10 Mar 1786; d. at Buckland, 20 Apr 1834; m. at Buckland, 14 Jul 1809, JOSIAH HATHAWAY, b. about 1782 son of Josiah and Tryphena (-) Hathaway; Josiah d. at Buckland, 20 Aug 1829.

ix LEANDER JOHNSON, b. 17 Feb 1787; d. at Canandaigua, NY, 13 Jun 1852; m. 1st SUSANNA who has not been identified but may be Susanna Rosencranz; Susanna d. at Canandaigua, 12 May 1823. Leander m. 2nd OLIVE who is not identified but might be Olive Standish, b. in NY about 1805 (based on census records). Leander perhaps also had a first marriage.

x SYLVIA JOHNSON, b. 22 Sep 1789; d. at Champion, NY, 1870; m. at Buckland, 17 Sep 1812, EBENEZER WOODWARD, b. at Taunton, 17 Oct 1787 son of Spencer and Abigail (Thayer) Woodward; Ebenezer d. at Champion, 2 Jun 1874.

xi ABIGAIL JOHNSON, b. 2 Apr 1791; d. at Buckland, 4 Feb 1871; m. at Montague, 22 Nov 1832, as his second wife, SAMUEL ALLIS, b. at Buckland, 27 Mar 1787 son of Stephen and Thankful (Munn) Allis; Samuel d. at Buckland, 30 Jul 1856. Samuel was first married to Sarah Boyden.

xii SUSANNAH JOHNSON, b. 7 Mar 1793; d. after 1865 when she was living in Rutland, NY; m. at Buckland, 21 Feb 1815, HENRY WOODWARD, b. at Taunton, 10 Apr 1789 son of Henry and Azubah (Thayer) Woodward; Henry d. after 1865.

xiii LYDIA JOHNSON, b. 28 Jan 1798; d. at Antwerp, NY, 13 Dec 1874; m. at Buckland, 27 Dec 1818, BILDAD WOODWARD, b. at Buckland, 7 Mar 1793 son of Spencer and Abigail (Thayer) Woodward; Bildad d. at Antwerp, 14 Aug 1877.

xiv LOVICE JOHNSON, b. 19 Nov 1799; d. at Chester, OH, 1859; m. HEZEKIAH BRAINERD, b. at Haddam, CT, 2 Aug 1795 son of Jesse and Mary (Thomas) Brainerd; Hezekiah d. at Chester, OH, 25 Apr 1890.[1578][1579] Hezekiah married second Mary Talbot.

581) ANNIS JOHNSON (*David Johnson⁴, Josiah Johnson³, Mary Holt Johnson², Nicholas¹*), b. at Leominster, 28 Mar 1750 daughter of David and Mary (Warner) Johnson; d. at Leominster, 5 Apr 1777; m. at Leominster, 17 Jan 1771, DAVID KENDALL, b. at Leominster, 5 Dec 1746 son of Amos and Mary (Hart) Kendall; David d. at Leominster, 15 Sep 1825. David married second Prudence.

1575 Massachusetts Wills and Probate Records, Franklin County, Estate of Josiah Johnson, Case 2621

1576 There is also a baptism record only for a possible fifteenth child Harrietta, baptized 23 Feb 1800 at Buckland. This baptism is just three months after the birth of another of the children and there is no further record of her. It is possible that the baptismal record is an error and is for another child in the family.

1577 Rufus relocated to Posey County, Indiana in 1822 and it seems more likely that he died there although the death is recorded at Buckland.

1578 Brainard, *Genealogy of the Brainerd Family, Part 1 Descendants of Daniel, James, and Joshua Brainerd*, p 90

1579 Ohio, Soldier Grave Registrations, 1804-1958; the grave registration gives both birth and death dates

David Kendall did not leave a will and his estate entered probate 20 September 1825.[1580] The following children and heirs signed a request that William Perry of Leominster be named executor: Nathaniel Low and Lorinda Low of Leominster, Martin Kendall and Prudence Kendall of Gardner, and Abigail Cummings, Polly Stearns, and David Kendall of Boston. Prudence Kendall, Abigail Cummings, Polly Stearns, and David Kendall were children of David Kendall's second marriage to Prudence.

Annis Johnson and David Kendall were parents of two children.

i ANNIS KENDALL, b. at Leominster, 28 Oct 1771; d. at Lancaster, MA, 11 Mar 1821; m. at Leominster, 19 Dec 1793, NATHANIEL LOW, b. at Amesbury, 3 Aug 1766 son of Nathaniel and Hannah (Ring) Low; Nathaniel d. at Lancaster, 29 Apr 1827.

ii DAVID KENDALL, b. 25 Aug 1773; died young

582) LUKE JOHNSON (*David Johnson⁴, Josiah Johnson³, Mary Holt Johnson², Nicholas¹*), b. at Leominster, 26 Aug 1755 son of David and Mary (Warner) Johnson; d. at Leominster, 26 Feb 1828; m. 1st 26 Nov 1789, SARAH BOWERS ROGERS, b. at Leominster, 6 Jun 1762 daughter of John and Relief (Prentice) Rogers; Sarah d. 2 Jul 1794. Luke m. 2nd 5 Mar 1796, BEULAH LELAND, b. at Holliston, 17 May 1754 daughter of Asaph and Beulah (Littlefield) Leland; Beulah d. at Leominster, 16 Sep 1831.

Luke was a farmer in Leominster. He did not leave a will and his estate entered probate 21 March 1828.[1581] Widow Beulah Johnson and son-in-law Rufus Kendall declined administration and described themselves as the only heirs within the county. They requested that William Perry, a chief creditor of the estate, be named administrator. A statement by William Perry describes the estate as completely insolvent and also notes there is a son that lives in Germantown near Philadelphia.

Luke Johnson and Sally Rogers were parents of three children born at Leominster.

i SALLY JOHNSON, b. 9 Feb 1791; d. at Leominster, 27 Apr 1815. Sally did not marry.

ii MARY "POLLY" JOHNSON, b. 5 Mar 1792; d. at Leominster, 13 Jun 1836; m. at Leominster, 7 Jun 1815, RUFUS KENDALL, b. at Leominster, 4 Oct 1785 son of John and Rebecca (Hills) Kendall; Rufus d. at Leominster, 13 Sep 1842.

iii WALTER ROGERS JOHNSON, b. 12 Jun 1794; d. at Washington, DC, 26 Apr 1852; m. at Medfield, MA, 2 Sep 1823, NANCY MARIA DONALDSON, b. at New York, 28 Dec 1794 daughter of Lothario and Mary (Rider0 Donaldson; Nancy d. at Washington, DC, 22 Apr 1890. Walter R. Johnson graduated from Harvard in 1819. He was chemist, principal of an academy in Germantown, PA, professor of physics and chemistry at the University of Pennsylvania, and the first secretary of the American Association for the Advancement of Science.[1582]

583) DAVID JOHNSON (*David Johnson⁴, Josiah Johnson³, Mary Holt Johnson², Nicholas¹*), b. at Leominster, 8 Apr 1758 son of David and Mary (Warner) Johnson; d. at Sempronius, NY, 22 Jun 1840;[1583] m. about 1787, PRUDENCE COLBURN, b. at Buckland, 13 Nov 1765 daughter of Ebenezer and Prudence (Carter) Colburn; Prudence d. 12 Feb 1849.

David had several periods of service during the Revolution with total time of service of about five years. The first enlistment was 17 May 1776 in the company of Capt. William Warner. His enlistments included a three-year term in the continental army. He received an honorary badge for faithful service.[1584]

In his will written 22 May 1838 (proved 10 November 1840) at Niles, Cayuga County, New York, David Johnson bequeathed to beloved wife Prudence all the household furniture to dispose of as she thinks best amongst her children and grandchildren. Abraham van Oten receives seventy-five dollars to hold in trust for granddaughter Clarissa L.W. Brinkenhoof and this to be paid to Clarissa at age twenty-one or earlier if she marries. Three-fourths of all monies and notes are to be divided among his grandchildren living at the time of his death. Wife Prudence receives the other one-fourth of the money. Son Roswell receives all the real estate which is the farm on which David now resides. Prudence receives the use of one-third part of the farm as dower while she is a widow. Wife Prudence, Abraham van Otten, and Roswell Johnson are named executors.[1585]

David Johnson and Prudence Colburn were parents of nine children all born at Buckland, Massachusetts except the youngest child.

1580 *Worcester County, MA: Probate File Papers, 1731-1881.* Online database. AmericanAncestors.org. New England Historic Genealogical Society, 2015. Case 34543

1581 *Worcester County, MA: Probate File Papers, 1731-1881.* Online database. AmericanAncestors.org. New England Historic Genealogical Society, 2015. Case 33526

1582 Appleton's Cyclopedia of American Biography, volume III, p 451

1583 David's death is recorded in the Buckland records but noted as having occurred at Sempronius.

1584 Massachusetts Soldiers and Sailors in the Revolutionary War, volume 8, p 821

1585 Ancestry.com. *New York, Wills and Probate Records, 1659-1999* [database on-line]., Cayuga County, *Record of Wills, Vol D-F, 1838-1844, volume D, pp 453-454*

i FANNY JOHNSON, b. 25 Jun 1788; d. at Moravia, NY, 29 Mar 1856; m. THOMAS WEST, b. in MA, about 1780 perhaps the son of William and Joanna (Peckham) West; Thomas d. at Moravia, 9 Mar 1868.

ii CLARISSA JOHNSON, b. 1790; d. 1800.

iii OSMOND JOHNSON, b. Jun 1792; d. at Northumberland County, VA, 1825; m. at Westmoreland, VA, 16 Feb 1821, ANNA H. PAYNE CRASK.[1586] Osmond was a mariner who obtained his seaman's protection certificate at Salem on 18 Mar 1813.[1587] He later settled in Virginia. Osmond and Anna were parents of two children.

iv HENRY SWEETSER JOHNSON, b. 24 Jul 1794; d. at Dexter, MI, 31 Jul 1847; m. 7 Mar 1816, OLIVE ARMSTRONG FILLMORE, b. Bennington, VT, 16 Dec 1797 daughter of Nathaniel and Phebe (Millard) Fillmore; Olive d. at Dexter, 10 Apr 1883. Olive was the sister of President Millard Fillmore.

v DAVID JOHNSON, b. 1796; perhaps died young

vi HARRIET JOHNSON, b. 27 Apr 1799; d. at Alabama, NY, 3 Nov 1863; m. 1st 3 Oct 1821, JACOB BRINKERHOFF, b. 17 Aug 1795 daughter of Jacob and Annatie (Demarest) Brinkerhoff;[1588] Jacob d. 25 Aug 1823. Harriet m. 2nd 1 Mar 1828, JACOB LUND, b. 13 Nov 1796;[1589] Joseph d. at Alabama, NY, 18 Oct 1887.

vii CLARISSA JOHNSON, b. 5 Nov 1801; d. at Owasco, NY, 16 Dec 1883; m. 27 Mar 1829, ABRAHAM VAN ETTEN, b. 30 Mar 1800; Abraham d. 23 Jun 1882.

viii ROSWELL JOHNSON, b. and d. 1804

ix ROSWELL JOHNSON, b. at Sempronius, NY, 19 Sep 1806; d. at Auburn, NY, 29 May 1887; m. 18 May 1836, MARY S. PALMER, b. 29 May 1816;[1590] Mary d. 16 May 1881.

584) MARY KNIGHT (*Mary Johnson Knight*[4]*, Josiah Johnson*[3]*, Mary Holt Johnson*[2]*, Nicholas*[1]), b. at Lancaster, 1 Apr 1748 daughter of Jonathan and Mary (Johnson) Knight; m. at Lancaster, 18 Sep 1766, WILLIAM KENDALL *possibly* the son of Jonathan and Admonition (Tucker) Kendall; William d. after 1822 when he was living in Westmoreland.

Mary and William were first in Lancaster but were in Westmoreland, New Hampshire by 1788. William Kendall and Mary Knight were parents of eleven children.[1591]

i MARY KENDALL, b. at Lancaster, 3 Jan 1767; d. at Lancaster, about 1796; m. at Lancaster, 3 Nov 1784, EZRA WILLARD, b. at Lancaster, 19 Mar 1761 son of Simon and Elizabeth (-) Willard; Ezra d. at Rome, NY, 6 May 1851. Ezra married second Susannah Tenney on 14 Nov 1798.

ii ANNIS KENDALL, b. at Lancaster, 4 Dec 1769; m. at Westmoreland, 6 May 1799, DANIEL LISAM who has not been identified.

iii RUFUS KENDALL, baptized at Lancaster, 22 Nov 1772; m. at Westmoreland, 6 May 1799, MARY "POLLY" DUDLEY, b. at Harvard, 29 Aug 1773 daughter of John and Sybil (Russell) Dudley. Rufus was a physician.

iv LUTHER KENDALL, baptized at Lancaster, 19 Feb 1775; d. after 1850 when he was living Newfane, NY; m. at Middletown, VT, 21 Nov 1802, JEMIMA WALDO, b. at Middletown, VT, 7 Jun 1783 daughter of Gamaliel and Mary (Campbell) Waldo; Jemima d. after 1850.

v WILLIAM KENDALL, baptized at Lancaster, 27 Jul 1777; d. at Roxbury, VT, 11 Nov 1828; m. at Westmoreland, 15 Jan 1804, LYDIA RUSSELL, b. at Walpole, NH, 18 Dec 1779 daughter of Jeduthun and Susannah (Glazier) Russell; Lydia d. at Roxbury, 26 May 1866.

vi SEWELL KENDALL, baptized at Lancaster, 5 Mar 1780; d. at Bethel, VT, 5 Apr 1864; m. at Westmoreland, 19 Mar 1801, LUCY LOCKE, b. at Whately, MA, 13 Sep 1780 daughter of John and Ruth (Faxon) Locke; Lucy d. after 1870.

vii CEPHAS KENDALL, baptized at Lancaster, 21 Jul 1782; d. at Derby, VT, 30 Jul 1859; m. CLOTILDA YOUNG, b. at Weathersfield, VT, 4 Jul 1780 daughter of Ichabod and Martha (Huntley) Young; Clotilda d. at Derby, 5 Jan 1860.

viii EUSEBIA KENDALL, b. at Lancaster, 6 Mar 1785

[1586] Ancestry.com, Virginia Marriages before 1824

[1587] US, New England Seamen's Protection Certificate Index, 1796-1871

[1588] Brinkerhoff, *The Family of Joris Dircksen Brinkerhoff*, 1638, p 53

[1589] Date of birth is engraved on gravestone

[1590] Johnson, *Johnson Genealogy*, p 36

[1591] Westmoreland Historical Committee, *History of Westmoreland*, p 474

ix ALPHEUS KENDALL, baptized at Westmoreland, 13 Apr 1788; d. at Brookfield, VT, before 1850; m. 1st 4 Dec 1808, IRENA PULSIPHER, b. at Rockingham, VT, 20 Dec 1786 daughter of David and Priscilla (Russell) Pulsipher; Irena d. at Rockingham, 27 May 1809. Alpheus m. 2nd at Weathersfield, 8 Mar 1810, LUCY YOUNG, b. at Weathersfield, 21 Aug 1784 daughter of Ichabod and Martha (Huntley) Young; Lucy d. at Brookfield, 25 Aug 1873.

x CYNTHIA KENDALL (twin), b. at Westmoreland, 1791

xi SCINDA KENDALL (twin), b. at Westmoreland, 1791

585) ANNIS KNIGHT (*Mary Johnson Knight4, Josiah Johnson3, Mary Holt Johnson2, Nicholas1*), baptized at Lancaster, 24 Mar 1751 daughter of Jonathan and Mary (Johnson) Knight; d. at Canton, PA, 14 Sep 1833; m. 29 May 1770, JOSEPH BROWN, b. at Lancaster, MA, 5 Jul 1746 son of Josiah and Prudence (Prentice) Brown.

Annis and Joseph were first in Lancaster, but were later in Walpole, New Hampshire and Ira, Vermont. Annis Knight and Joseph Brown were parents of at least twelve children. Several of the children settled in Canton in Bradford County, Pennsylvania.

i ARETHUSA BROWN, b. at Lancaster, MA, 22 Dec 1770

ii DAMARIS BROWN, b. at Lancaster, 15 Dec 1772

iii ANNIS BROWN, b. perhaps at Ira, VT, about 1774; m. DAVID LINDLEY, b. at Litchfield, CT, 10 Nov 1772 son of Solomon and Mindwell (Peck) Lindley; David d. at Canton, PA, 27 May 1833. Annis and David settled in East Canton.[1592]

iv JOHN PRENTICE BROWN, b. at Ira, VT, 1775; d. at Fort Ann, NY, 22 Aug 1838; m. POLLY EARL, b. 1781; Polly d. at Fort Ann, 11 Jun 1860.

v JOSEPH BROWN, b. at Walpole, NH, 14 Dec 1777; d. at Tinmouth, VT, 9 Jan 1863; m. at Woodstock, CT, MARY "POLLY" WHITE, b. in CT, 1783; Polly d. at Poultney, VT, 11 Oct 1882.

vi JONATHAN BROWN, b. at Walpole, NH, 28 Jan 1780; d. at Edwards Township, NY, 12 Dec 1817 when he was shot and killed;[1593] m. at Middletown, VT, 4 Jul 1805, ACHSAH HAYNES, b. at Middletown, 10 Jan 1786 daughter of Jonathan and Lydia (Haskins) Haynes; Achsah d. at Fine, NY 1860. Achsah married second Oliver Hutchins.

vii SYBIL BROWN, b. at Walpole, NH, 22 Jun 1782; d. at Middletown Springs, VT, 18 Mar 1861; m. at Middletown, 15 May 1802, HEZEKIAH HAYNES, b. at Middletown, 12 Feb 1780 son of Jonathan and Lydia (Haskins) Haynes; Hezekiah d. at Middletown Springs, 26 Sep 1860.

viii LUCINDA BROWN, b. 25 May 1784; d. at Granville, PA (buried at Canton), 18 Jan 1874; m. EPHRAIM E. KENDALL, b. 27 May 1784 son of Ephraim and Elizabeth (Knight) Kendall; Ephraim d. at Granville, 15 Jun 1871.

ix SOLOMON BROWN, b. at Clarendon, VT, 20 Jul 1788; d. at Canton, PA, 7 Sep 1856; m. at Wells, VT, 6 Dec 1810, LUSANNA GLASS, b. at Wells, 28 Mar 1790 daughter of Rufus and Huldah (Fuller) Glass; Lusanna d. at Canton, 14 Jun 1853.[1594]

x BETSEY BROWN, b. at Ira, VT, 29 Mar 1790

xi AMANDA BROWN, b. at Ira, VT, 29 Mar 1792; d. at Canton, PA, 22 Dec 1875; m. at Middletown VT, 21 Sep 1811, ELIAS WRIGHT, b. in CT about 1790; Elias d. at Canton, 27 Jan 1868.

xii ORILLA BROWN, b. at Ira, VT, 26 Aug 1794

586) RUTH KNIGHT (*Mary Johnson Knight4, Josiah Johnson3, Mary Holt Johnson2, Nicholas1*), b. at Lancaster, 18 Jan 1753 daughter of Jonathan and Mary (Johnson) Knight; d. at Chester, VT, 6 Aug 1826; m. at Leominster, 15 May 1773, JOSEPH WHITMORE, b. at Leominster, 6 Jun 1749 son of Joseph and Mary (Marion) Whitmore;[1595] Joseph d. at Chester, VT, 30 Aug 1830.

Ruth Knight and Joseph Whitmore were parents of seven children whose births are recorded at Chester, Vermont.

1592 Heverly, Pioneer and Patriot Families of Bradford County, Pennsylvania, volume 2, p 168

1593 Hutchins, *Genealogy of Thomas Hutchins of Salem*, p 643

1594 Heverly, Pioneer and Patriot Families of Bradford County, Pennsylvania, volume 2, p 223

1595 Stearns, *History of Ashburnham*, p 954

i LUCY WHITMORE, b. 30 Apr 1775; m. at Chester, VT, 20 Oct 1799, NATHAN WINN, b. at Rindge, NH, 22 Mar 1774 son of Caleb and Hannah (Demaray) Winn; Nathan d. at Middletown, VT, 28 Sep 1857.

ii JOSEPH WHITMORE, b. 15 Jun 1778; m. 1st at Chester, 20 Feb 1800, ESTHER HOLDEN, b. at Barre, MA, 10 Apr 1778 daughter of Aaron and Rachel (Richardson) Holden; Esther d. by 1813. Joseph m. 2nd at Middletown, VT, 20 Sep 1813. HANNAH HASKINS, b. at Middletown, 5 Oct 1786 daughter of Richard and Elizabeth (Corbin) Haskins.

iii SYLVANUS WHITMORE, b. 30 Dec 1779; d. at Sinclairville, NY, 7 Apr 1841; m. at Middletown, VT, 24 May 1801, JEMIMA HASKINS, b. at Middletown, 3 Jun 1783 daughter of Benjamin and Deliverance (Fillmore) Haskins; Jemima d. at Sinclairville, 22 Jun 1873.

iv HULDAH WHITMORE, b. 30 May 1782; d. at Henderson, NY, 25 Jun 1871; m. 1st at Middletown, 27 Feb 1803, JOHN FILLMORE, b. at Middletown, VT, 25 Sep 1781 son of Luther and Eunice (Haskins) Fillmore; John d. at Middletown, 23 Feb 1822. Huldah m. 2nd, about 1829, as his second wife, EZRA NUTTING, b. at Jaffrey, NH, 22 Mar 1783 son of Simeon and Dorothy (Hudson) Nutting; Ezra d. at Henderson, NY, 11 Jan 1863. Ezra was first married to Abigail Hall (1790-1828).

v EDMUND WHITMORE, b. 29 Jun 1784; d. at Ira, VT, 16 Oct 1832; m. about 1810, CHLOE WILMARTH, b. at Rehoboth, MA, 13 Dec 1786 daughter of Nathaniel and Lydia (Carpenter) Wilmarth; Chloe d. at Ira, 11 Oct 1865.

vi JONATHAN WHITMORE, b. 2 Jun 1786; d. after 1860 and before 1870 at Jackson, MI; m. by 1809, REBECCA ALLEN, b. at Whiting, VT, 26 Apr 1793 daughter of Ezra and Rebecca (Johnson) Allen; Rebecca d. at Jackson, MI. 23 Mar 1872.

vii REBECCA WHITMORE, b. 27 Sep 1792

587) ELIZABETH KNIGHT (*Mary Johnson Knight[4], Josiah Johnson[3], Mary Holt Johnson[2], Nicholas[1]*), b. at Lancaster, 10 Apr 1756 daughter of Jonathan and Mary (Johnson) Knight; d. 1801; m. 30 May 1775, EPHRAIM KENDALL, b. at Lancaster, 16 Feb 1756 son of Jonathan and Admonition (Tucker) Kendall, Ephraim d. at Sandy Creek, NY, 1842. Ephraim m. 2nd Experience Coleman.

Elizabeth Knight and Ephraim Kendall were parents of at least five children.

i LUKE KENDALL, b. at Lancaster, MA, 16 Mar 1776; d. at Dummerston, VT, 1 May 1849; m. ANNA WILDER, b. recorded at Dummerston, 23 Jan 1782 daughter of Joshua and Lois (Haws) Wilder; Anna d. 20 Aug 1867.

ii APPHIA KENDALL, baptized at Lancaster 12 Apr 1778; d. at Sandy Creek, NY, 23 Mar 1870; m. AHOLIAB WILDER, b. at Wendell, MA, 7 Jan 1782 son of Aholiab and Joanna (Perry) Wilder; Aholiab d. at Sandy Creek, 20 Jan 1865.

iii EPHRAIM E. KENDALL, b. 27 May 1784; d. at Canton, PA, 18 Jan 1874;[1596] m. his first cousin, LUCINDA BROWN (*Annis Knight Brown[5], Mary Johnson Knight[4], Josiah Johnson[3], Mary Holt Johnson[2], Nicholas[1]*), b. 25 May 1784 daughter of Joseph and Annis (Knight) Brown; Lucinda d. at Canton, 18 Jan 1874. Ephraim served in the War of 1812.

iv SYBIL KENDALL, b. at Dummerston, VT, 13 Jun 1791; d. at Dummerston, 16 Apr 1823; m. at Dummerston, 25 Feb 1812, SETH HUDSON, b. at Dummerston, 12 Jul 1792 son of Enos and Patty (Brown) Hudson; Seth d. at Dummerston, 6 Jan 1851. Seth was second married to Lydia Miller.

v SAMUEL KENDALL, b. at Dummerston, 1794; d. at St. Clair, MI, 24 Aug 1878; m. HANNAH PIGSLEY, b. at Gloucester, RI, about 1798 daughter of Welcome and Abigail (Place) Pigsley; Hannah d. at Fort Gratiot, MI, 20 May 1873.

588) SIBBEL KNIGHT (*Mary Johnson Knight[4], Josiah Johnson[3], Mary Holt Johnson[2], Nicholas[1]*), b. at Lancaster, 22 Aug 1759 daughter of Jonathan and Mary (Johnson) Knight; m. at Lancaster, 16 Jul 1776, HENRY WILLARD FARMER, b. at Worcester, 7 Feb 1753 son of William and Ruth (Willard) Farmer; Henry d. at Herkimer, NY, about 1814 (probate 8 Jan 1814)

Sibbel and Henry were in Lancaster just after their marriage, were in Chester, Vermont before 1790 and in Herkimer, New York by 1800.

On 26 September 1789 (recorded 1792), Henry W. Farmer, yeoman of Chester, and Jonathan Knight, Jr., physician of Westmoreland, New Hampshire, sold a 50-acre lot in Chester to Malachi Greene of Warwick, Rhode Island for a payment of £35.[1597]

1596 Pennsylvania Historical and Museum Commission; Harrisburg, Pennsylvania; Pennsylvania Veterans Burial Cards, 1929-1990; Series Number: Series 2

1597 Vermont, Town Clerk Records, Windsor County, Chester, volume A-B, volume B, p 461; accessed through familysearch.org

Henry Farmer did not leave a will and administration of his estate was granted to Sibbel Knight and Nathan Ainsworth on 8 January 1814.[1598]

Sibbel Knight and Henry Willard Farmer were parents of at least four children, although there are likely others.

i WILLIAM FARMER, baptized at Lancaster, 1 Feb 1778

ii JONATHAN FARMER, baptized at Lancaster, 21 Mar 1779; d. at Fowler, NY, 1866; m. LUSEBA DEWITT, b. about 1786 daughter of Benjamin and Molly (Larkin) DeWitt; Luseba d. about 1866.

iii LEMUEL FARMER, b. about 1796; d. at Bolingbrook, IL, 26 Jan 1861; m. ROXANA RATHBUN, b. about 1801; Roxana d. at Bolingbrook, 11 Oct 1863.[1599] Lemuel and Roxana lived in Marcellus, NY until 1855 before relocating to Illinois.

iv ANNIS FARMER, b. at Herkimer, NY, 1804; d. at Lansing, MI, 15 Sep 1891; m. JOHN H. HOFFMAN, b. 20 Jan 1802; John d. at Delhi, MI, 25 Sep 1861.

589) JONATHAN KNIGHT (*Mary Johnson Knight[4], Josiah Johnson[3], Mary Holt Johnson[2], Nicholas[1]*), b. at Lancaster, 12 Jan 1761 son of Jonathan and Mary (Johnson) Knight; d. at Piermont, NH, 15 Dec 1836; m. 1st OBEDIENCE ROOT, b. 1755; Obedience d. 12 Feb 1789. Jonathan m. 2nd, ELIZABETH DUDLEY, b. at Groton, MA, 31 Oct 1763 daughter of John and Sybil (Russell) Dudley; Elizabeth d. at Westmoreland, NH, 29 Apr 1866.

Jonathan Knight was a physician in Westmoreland. His second wife Betsey lived to age 102 reported as still with her full mental faculties.[1600]

Jonathan Knight and Obedience Root were parents of three children born at Walpole, New Hampshire.

i JERUSHA KNIGHT, b. 7 May 1782; m. at Westmoreland, 29 May 1803, JONATHAN SMITH SKINNER, b. at Surry, 13 May 1777 son of Abner and Susannah (Smith) Skinner. Jerusha and Jonathan seem to be living in Westmoreland in 1820. No children were identified.

ii OBEDIENCE KNIGHT, b. 2 Sep 1784; d. at Roxbury, VT, 17 Jun 1856; m. at Westmoreland, 19 Mar 1801, HENRY LOCKE, baptized at Whately, MA, 8 Aug 1778 son of John and Ruth (Faxon) Locke; Henry d. at Roxbury, 13 Sep 1856.

iii SYBIL KNIGHT, b. 28 May 1786

Jonathan Knight and Elizabeth Dudley were parents of four children born at Westmoreland, New Hampshire.

i JONATHAN KNIGHT, b. 25 Oct 1790; d. at Manchester, NH, 1 May 1879; m. at Stoddard, 14 Jan 1817, DOROTHY JOSLIN, b. at Stoddard, 10 Apr 1796 daughter of David and Rebecca (Richardson) Joslin; Dorothy d. at Manchester, 11 Nov 1873. Jonathan and Dorothy resided in Piermont, NH but were in Manchester in their later years. Jonathan Knight was a physician.

ii JOSIAH KNIGHT, b. 8 Mar 1792; d. at St. Charles, IA, 16 Mar 1882; m. 1st 20 Apr 1815, BETSEY JOSLIN, b. 1 Jan 1789 daughter of Peter and Sarah (Kidder) Joslin; Betsey d. at Charles City, IA, 24 Dec 1858. Josiah m. 2nd about 1860, ELEANOR COCHRANE (widow of Simeon Avery), b. at Bradford, VT, Jan 1808 daughter of John and Agnes (Wilson) Cochrane; Eleanor d. at Newbury, VT, 13 Jan 1909.[1601]

iii CURTIS KNIGHT, b. 15 Apr 1794; d. at Kaneville, IL, 19 Jun 1854; m. at Cornish, NH, 26 Dec 1814, BETSEY ATWOOD, b. at Pelham, 8 Oct 1798 daughter of Joshua and Sarah (McAdams) Atwood; Betsey d. at Elkhart, IN, 27 Feb 1888 where she was living with her daughter Maria and her husband William Forward. This family lived in Fairlee, Vermont for much of their lives and moved West with their children later in life.

iv PRENTISS KNIGHT, b. 21 Jan 1797; d. at Medina, NY, 25 Mar 1874; m. 2 Jan 1822, MELINDA GOULD, b. at Hanover, NH, 7 Nov 1800 daughter of Ralph W. and Anne (Smith) Gould; Melinda d. at Bradford, VT, 5 Dec 1872.

590) ISAAC JOHNSON (*Isaac Johnson[4], Josiah Johnson[3], Mary Holt Johnson[2], Nicholas[1]*), b. at Leominster, 9 Nov 1746 son of Isaac and Lydia (-) Johnson; m. at Walpole, NH, 21 Dec 1771, MARY MESSER, b. at Willington, 9 Nov 1748 daughter and Timothy and Hannah (Marble) Messer.

1598 New York Wills and Probate Records, Herkimer County, Letters of Administration, Book C, p 17

1599 Findagrave ID: 61875153

1600 Wells, *History of Newbury, Vermont*, p 611

1601 Vermont State Archives and Records Administration; Montpelier, Vermont, USA; User Box Number: PR-01922; Roll Number: S-30782; Archive Number: M-2033182. Death record gives Eleanor's age as 101.

Little is known of this family other than there were six children born at Walpole, New Hampshire and the family seems to have left there. It is possible that the daughter Lydia married Abraham Edson and settled in Vermont, but that cannot be certain.

i STEPHEN JOHNSON, baptized at Walpole, 18 Apr 1773; died young

ii MARY JOHNSON, baptized at Walpole, 9 Apr 1775; died young

iii STEPHEN JOHNSON, baptized at Walpole, Jan 1778

iv MARY JOHNSON, baptized at Walpole, 20 Feb 1780

v LYDIA JOHNSON, baptized at Walpole, 29 Jun 1783

vi ABIGAIL JOHNSON, baptized at Walpole, 25 May 1788

591) SARAH JOHNSON (*Isaac Johnson*[4], *Josiah Johnson*[3], *Mary Holt Johnson*[2], *Nicholas*[1]), b. at Leominster, 18 Apr 1749 daughter of Isaac and Lydia (-) Johnson; d. at Walpole, NH, 26 Dec 1787; m. about 1769, as his second wife, ISAAC BUNDY, b. at Preston, CT, 9 Jun 1745 son of James and Sarah (Jameson) Bundy; Isaac d. at Columbia, NH, 1825.[1602] Isaac was married first to Mehitable Brown in 1768[1603] who died soon after and married third the widow Amelia Fowler.

Sarah and Isaac resided in Walpole, New Hampshire. Isaac had received his farm in Walpole from his father and he remained there on the farm until 1794,[1604] a few years after Sarah's death. Isaac then relocated to Columbia, New Hampshire. Isaac participated in the civic affairs of Walpole, for example serving on a committee to draw up plans for a new meeting house in 1786. Isaac Bundy who served as sergeant in Bellow's regiment of militia during the Revolution.[1605]

Sarah Johnson and Isaac Bundy were parents of ten children born at Walpole, New Hampshire.

i MARY "POLLY" BUNDY, b. 1770 and baptized 1 Jun 1771; m. 2 Sep 1793, TIMOTHY HOLMES, b. at Walpole, 3 May 1763 son of Lemuel and Abigail (Bicknell) Holmes.

ii SUSANNA BUNDY, b. 19 Dec 1771; d. at Norway, ME, 30 Oct 1851; m. 16 May 1794, TITUS OLCOTT BROWN, b. at Tolland, CT, 25 Aug 1764 son of Elias and Abigail (Olcott) Brown; Titus d. at Norway, 23 Feb 1855.

iii SOPHRONIA BUNDY, b. 1772[1606]

iv ISAAC BUNDY, b. 5 Jun 1774; d. at Burke, VT, 9 Nov 1854; m. 1st 20 Feb 1799, ANNA HOLMES, b. at Walpole, 20 Jan 1773 daughter of Lemuel and Abigail (Bicknell) Holmes; Anna d. at Surry, 1 Jul 1807. Isaac m. 2nd 31 Dec 1807, ABIGAIL WETHERBEE, b. at Chesterfield, NH, 15 Aug 1781 daughter of Joab and Abigail (Houghton) Wetherbee; Abigail d. at Burke, 12 Mar 1867.

v EUNICE BUNDY, b. 25 May 1777; d. at Walpole, 10 Feb 1785.

vi DAVID BUNDY, baptized 21 Nov 1779; d. at Columbia, NH, 18 Feb 1847; m. 1800, his fourth cousin, HANNAH ROSEBROOK (*Sarah Cram Rosebrook*[5], *Humphrey Cram*[4], *Sarah Holt Cram*[3], *Henry*[2], *Nicholas*[1]), baptized at Holland, MA, 26 Dec 1781 daughter of John and Sarah (Cram) Rosebrook; Hannah d. at Columbia, 29 Oct 1852.

vii ELISHA BUNDY, b. 1782; d. at Elmira, NY, 28 Nov 1834; m. about 1803, SARAH WHIPPLE who has not been identified. Elisha and Sarah had five daughters one of whom, Clarissa, married an early abolitionist Sylvester Gardiner Andrus. Elisha was known as Judge Bundy and operated a tavern called the Mansion House in Elmira.[1607]

viii REBECCA BUNDY, b. at Walpole, 1783; d. at Stratford, NH, 8 Jan 1864; m. at Westmoreland, 12 Apr 1802, EPHRAIM H. MAHURIN, b. at Westmoreland, 11 Mar 1780 son of Ephraim and Beulah (Howe) Mahurin; Ephraim d. at Stratford, 3 Mar 1859.

ix SARAH BUNDY, baptized 10 Jul 1785

x SAMUEL BUNDY, baptized 28 Dec 1787; d. at Ithaca, NY, 11 Apr 1831;[1608] m. ELIZABETH TERRY, b. about 1790; Elizabeth d. at Ithaca, 3 Sep 1838.

1602 There is a headstone for Sgt. Isaac Bundy in the Walpole Village Cemetery placed in 1925; *Applications for Headstones for U.S. Military Veterans, 1925-1941.* It is not clear that Isaac died in Walpole. He was living in Coos County, NH in 1810.

1603 New Hampshire, Marriage and Divorce Records, 1659-1947

1604 Frizzell, *A History of Walpole*, p 307

1605 *U.S., Revolutionary War Rolls, 1775-1783*

1606 As reported in the History of Walpole

1607 Towner, *Our County and Its People*, p 136

1608 NYGBR, "Town of Ithaca: Ithaca Cemetery", volume 53, 1922, p 289

592) LYDIA JOHNSON (*Isaac Johnson⁴, Josiah Johnson³, Mary Holt Johnson², Nicholas¹*), b. at Leominster, 22 Oct 1751 daughter of Isaac and Lydia (-) Johnson; d. at Westminster, VT, 11 Feb 1787; m. at Walpole, NH, 21 Dec 1771, EPHRAIM RANNEY, b. at Middletown, CT, 27 Oct 1749 son of Ephraim and Silence (Wilcox) Ranney; Ephraim d. at Westminster, 30 Jul 1835. Ephraim married second Rhoda Harlow.

Ephraim Ranney was born in the "Upper Houses" section of Middletown which later was incorporated as Cromwell, Connecticut. He was one of the first settlers in Westminster.[1609]

Lydia Johnson and Ephraim Ranney were parents of four children born at Westminster, Vermont.

i LYDIA RANNEY, b. 28 Sep 1772; d. at Westminster, VT, 20 Jul 1859; m. EBENEZER GOODHUE, b. at Dunstable, MA, 12 Aug 1767 son of Josiah and Elizabeth (Fletcher) Goodhue); Ebenezer d. at Neenah, WI, 6 Mar 1854.

ii REBECCA RANNEY, b. 22 Dec 1777; d. at Westminster, Aug 1841; m. 20 Jan 1799, GIDEON WARNER, b. recorded at Westminster, 19 Dec 1767 son of Gideon and Freelove (-) Warner; Gideon d. after 1850 when he was living in Westminster.

iii EPHRAIM RANNEY, b. 25 Jan 1781; d. at Westminster, 3 Jun 1826; m. 9 Oct 1800, MERCY CLARK, b. at Harwich, MA, 30 Nov 1780 daughter of Scotto and Sarah (Griffiths) Clark; Mercy d. at Coventry, VT, 29 Jan 1848.

iv CALVIN RANNEY, b. 4 Nov 1784; d. at Algona, IA, 7 Oct 1873; m. at Brattleboro, 20 Oct 1803, ANNA BRADLEY ROOT, b. in VT about 1783 whose parents have not been identified; Anna d. at Westminster, 2 Aug 1870. After his wife's death, Calvin went to Iowa to live with one of his sons.

593) DAVID JOHNSON (*Isaac Johnson⁴, Josiah Johnson³, Mary Holt Johnson², Nicholas¹*), b. at Montague, MA, 16 Feb 1757 son of Isaac and Lydia (-) Johnson; d. at Saratoga, NY, 22 Feb 1839; m. at Walpole, NH, 14 Nov 1783, MARY JOINER likely daughter of William and Hannah (Bowker) Joiner[1610] who were in Walpole in the 1770's; Mary d. at Day Center, NY, 5 Jan 1844.

David Johnson went with his parents to Walpole, New Hampshire and as a young man entered the continental forces serving for five year. After the war, he married Mary Joiner and the first of their children were born in Walpole. The family was in Vermont for a time before moving to Hadley, New York and finally Day Center.

On 18 April 1818, David Johnson then age fifty-nine and living at Hadley, New York, made application for a pension related to his service during the Revolution. He enlisted from Walpole, New Hampshire on 16 February 1777 in the New Hampshire line and was finally discharged in July 1782 at Windsor, New York. He served in the regiment of Col. Joseph Cilley. He was at the battles of Saratoga and Stillwater. He received a pension based on his service. An 1820 statement declared his personal estate with a value of $21.87, His household at that time was his wife Mary age 60 and an eleven-year-old boy, Samuel Waldo, who was not able to support himself. On 28 August 1839, son John Johnson then age forty-four and living at Day, New York, provided a statement related to his mother's application for a widow's pension. In her statement, Mary reported that she was married to David Johnson on 14 November 1783 and prior to marriage her name was Mary Joiner.[1611]

Frizzell's *History of Walpole* names of eight children of David Johnson and Mary Joiner and those eight are listed here. The oldest children may have been born in Walpole, the family was then in Vermont where the younger children were born, and finally at Day Center in Saratoga County, New York. Most birth dates are estimated.

i HANNAH JOHNSON, b. at Walpole, about 1784; d. at Hubbardston, MI, 23 Feb 1877; m. 1st about 1803, ASA GILBERT, b. at Brookfield, MA, 3 Oct 1779 son of Asa and Hannah (Barnes) Gilbert; Asa d. in Washtenaw County, MI, about 1830. Hannah m. 2nd at Washtenaw County, 3 Mar 1842, as his second wife, JACOB DUBOIS, b. at Marbletown, NY, 15 Dec 1771 son of Conrad and Mary DeLamater DuBois; Jacob d. at Mason, MI, 11 Sep 1844. Jacob was first married to Sarah Buck.

ii LUKE JOHNSON, estimated 1786

iii LYDIA JOHNSON, estimated 1788

iv ANNIS JOHNSON, estimated 1790

v SALLY JOHNSON, b. 9 Mar 1791; d. at Hadley, NY, 29 Dec 1844; m. ABNER WAIT, b. 7 Jan 1785 son of Abner and Susannah (Buffington) Wait; Abner d. at Day, NY, 17 Oct 1850.

vi LOIS JOHNSON, b. about 1793; m. JOHN DEAN, b. 1789 likely son of Alexander and Sage (Prouty) Dean; John d. at Stony Creek, NY, 29 Nov 1856.

1609 Adams, *Middletown Upper Houses*, p 198

1610 Frizzell, *History of Walpole*, p 163

1611 U.S. Revolutionary War Pension and Bounty-Land Warrant Application Files, Case W21465

vii JOHN JOINER JOHNSON, b. 1796; d. at Day, NY, 23 May 1864; m. FALLY ALLEN, b. in RI, 1799 daughter of David and Amey (Shrieve) Allen; Fally d. at Edinburgh, NY, 5 Sep 1885.

viii ORRA JOHNSON, b. 3 Sep 1797; d. at Courtland, MI, 28 Aug 1872; m. ALEXANDER DEAN, b. 28 May 1793 son of Alexander and Sage (Prouty) Dean;[1612] Alexander d. at Courtland, 6 Aug 1871.

594) LUCRETIA JOHNSON (*Isaac Johnson[4], Josiah Johnson[3], Mary Holt Johnson[2], Nicholas[1]*), baptized at New Salem, 13 Jun 1762 daughter of Isaac and Lydia (-) Johnson; d. at Cambridge, VT, 9 Mar 1841; m. at Walpole, NH, 20 Aug 1780, THOMAS PARKER , b. at Salem, NH, 20 Mar 1754 son of Samuel and Sarah (Messer) Parker; Thomas d. at Cambridge, VT, 29 Jun 1829.

Thomas Parker served in the Revolution and made application for a pension on 1 April 1818 while a resident of Chelsea, Vermont. He enlisted in January 1776 in the company of Capt. Jason Wait of the New Hampshire line. He mustered at Charleston, New Hampshire, marched to Québec and was then in Ticonderoga. After serving one year, he was discharged at Ticonderoga. In 1780 while a resident at Royalton, Vermont, he served another period of four to five weeks. At application, he reported an estate value of $159 and $240 in debts. In 1820, his household consisted of himself, wife Lucretia age 58 and described as feeble, daughter Harriet age 19 who had been confined to her bed most of the past four years, and daughter Polly age 16. Following Thomas's death, Lucretia continued with a widow's pension.[1613]

Thomas and Lucretia were parents of eight children born at Chelsea, Vermont.

i SARAH PARKER, b. 7 Dec 1781

ii THOMAS PARKER, b. 29 Jul 1784

iii EUNICE PARKER, b. 25 Feb 1790; d. at Chelsea, 21 Feb 1820. Eunice did not marry.

iv LUCRETIA J. PARKER, b. 14 Dec 1792; d. at Hanover, NH, 22 Oct 1879; m. OLIVER H. PERRY, b. at Pomfret, VT, 21 Jun 1786 son of William and Lucy (Holmes) Perry; Oliver d. at Woodstock, VT, 28 Sep 1836.

v MARIA PARKER, b. 28 Apr 1785

vi FANNY PARKER, b. 5 Nov 1798; d. at Plainfield, NH, 21 Aug 1885; m. at Chelsea, 8 Feb 1820, LYMAN WELLS, b. 1795; Lyman d. at Plainfield, 19 Sep 1874.

vii HARRIET PARCE PARKER, b. 9 Jun 1801; d. at Springfield, MA, 10 Mar 1867; m. DON CARLOS HATCH, b. at Brookfield, VT, 4 Apr 1800 son of Asher and Lydia (Story) Hatch; Don Carlos d. at Springfield, 1 Jul 1875.

viii MARY DANA PARKER, b. 5 Oct 1803; d. at Sigourney, IA, 23 Mar 1862; m. 18 Sep 1825, her third cousin once removed, SOLLIS RUNNELLS (*Chloe Thursten Runnells[6], Hannah Johnson Thurston[5], Zebadiah Johnson[4], John Johnson[3], Mary Holt Johnson[2], Nicholas[1]*), b. 1797 son of Stephen and Chloe (Thursten) Runnells; Sollis d. at Sigourney, 15 Jul 1877.

595) ELISHA JOHNSON (*Isaac Johnson[4], Josiah Johnson[3], Mary Holt Johnson[2], Nicholas[1]*), baptized at Ervings Grant, MA, 18 Jun 1764 son of Isaac and Lydia (-) Johnson; d. at Shrewsbury, VT, 15 Sep 1845; m. at Walpole, NH, 5 Nov 1789, OLIVE ASHLEY, b. 1765 likely the daughter of Martin and Sarah (Root) Ashley; Olive d. at Shrewsbury, 4 Apr 1813. Elisha m. 2nd at Shrewsbury, ELIZABETH KILBURN (widow of Willard Colburn), b. at Walpole, 3 Feb 1770 daughter of John and Content (Carpenter) Kilburn; Elizabeth d. at Shrewsbury, 4 Aug 1826. Elisha m. 3rd BETSEY who has not been identified and who d. at Shrewsbury, 3 Apr 1865. Betsey is likely Betsey Marsh of Henniker (perhaps Betsey Hartshorn widow of Joseph Marsh). Elisha Johnson of Shrewsbury married Betsey Marsh of Henniker on 4 Dec 1828.

Elisha and Olive were married in Walpole but were soon after in Shrewsbury, Vermont where they were early settlers. After Olive's death, Elisha married the widow Elizabeth Kilburn Colburn. Two of the sons of Elisha and Olive married their stepsisters the children of Elizabeth Colburn and her first husband Willard Colburn.

Elisha Johnson and Olive Ashley were parents of nine children born at Shrewsbury, Vermont.

i OLIVE JOHNSON, b. 9 Apr 1790; d. at Ludlow, VT, 23 Sep 1881. Olive did not marry.

ii ELISHA JOHNSON, b. 3 Oct 1791; d. at Ludlow, 11 Feb 1868; m. at Shrewsbury, 12 Feb 1818, his stepsister, REBECCA COLBURN, b. at Shrewsbury, 16 Jan 1796 daughter of Willard and Elizabeth (Kilburn) Colburn; Rebecca d. at Ludlow, 15 Mar 1869.

iii DAVID JOHNSON, b. 28 Jun 1793; d. at Shrewsbury, 26 May 1876; m. at Shrewsbury, 1 Feb 1822, his stepsister, MARY ANN COLBURN, b. at Shrewsbury, 14 Mar 1800 daughter of Willard and Elizabeth (Kilburn) Colburn; Mary Ann d. at Sherburne, VT, 1 Aug 1869.

iv LUCINDA JOHNSON, b. 16 Apr 1795

1612 The names of Alexander's parents are given on his death record.

1613 U.S. Revolutionary War Pension and Bounty-Land Warrant Application Files, Case W18728

v JOSIAH JOHNSON, b. about 1797[1614]

vi JOHN JOHNSON, b. about 1799

vii RHODA JOHNSON, b. 29 May 1801; d. at Shrewsbury, 3 Feb 1866; m. at Shrewsbury, 16 Nov 1831, ELI PIERCE, b. at Shrewsbury, 25 Feb 1802 son of Ephraim and Sarah (Pollard) Pierce. Eli d. at Shrewsbury, 15 May 1873.

viii DANIEL JOHNSON, b. 1803; d. at Woodstock, VT, 31 Jul 1875; m. at Shrewsbury, 23 Dec 1828, JULIA COLBURN, b. at Shrewsbury, 25 Nov 1802 daughter of Moses and Julia (Colburn) Colburn; Julia d. at Shrewsbury, 11 Jun 1848.

ix CALEB JOHNSON, b. 1807; d. at Bolton, MA, 14 Apr 1887; m. at Lancaster, MA, 4 Apr 1833, MARY WHITCOMB GOSS, b. at Lancaster, 4 Jun 1807 daughter of John and Mary (Fuller) Goss; Mary d. at Lancaster, 2 Jun 1885.

Elisha Johnson and Elizabeth Kilburn were parents of one child.

i WILLARD JOHNSON, b. 10 May 1817; d. at Ludlow, VT, 3 Feb 1889; m. 1st, about 1840, FREELOVE PRATT, b. at Mount Holly, VT, 1819 daughter of Laban and Tamer (Aldrich) Pratt; Freelove d. at Ludlow, 18 Sep 1877. Willard m. 2nd 6 Jun 1878 SALLY SUSANNAH KNIGHT (widow of Philip Lord), b. at Shrewsbury, 14 Mar 1821 daughter of Luther and Sarah (Saunders) Knight; Sally d. at Shrewsbury 3 Jul 1889.

596) ANNIS JOHNSON (*Isaac Johnson⁴, Josiah Johnson³, Mary Holt Johnson², Nicholas¹*), b. at Ervings Grant, MA, 27 Oct 1766 daughter of Isaac and Lydia (-) Johnson; d. at Putney, VT, 20 May 1851; m. 26 Oct 1788, THEOPHILUS CRAWFORD, b. at Union, CT, 25 Apr 1764 son of James and Grace (Carpenter) Crawford; Theophilus d. at Putney, 10 Jan 1856.

Theophilus and Annis arrived in Putney, Vermont in 1799 coming from Westminster, and a colorful account of Theophilus's history can be found in "People of Putney 1753-1953." Theophilus purchased 217 acres in Putney and in 1808 built a brick house now known as Hickory Ridge House and on the National Register of Historic Places. His land holdings expanded to 500 acres by the time of his death.[1615]

Annis Johnson and Theophilus Crawford were parents of ten children whose births are recorded at Putney, Vermont, although the older children were likely born in Westminster as the family arrived in Putney in 1799.

i DAVID CAMPBELL, b. 6 Aug 1789; d. at Putney, 1 Mar 1871; m. at Putney, 14 Nov 1822, NANCY CAMPBELL, b. at Putney, 14 Jul 1795 daughter of Alexander and Jerusha (Wilder) Campbell; Nancy d. at Putney, 27 Sep 1863. In the War of 1812, David held the rank of Brigadier Major. He was also a member of the Vermont state constitutional convention.[1616]

ii SALLY CRAWFORD, b. 6 Jun 1791; d. at Montpelier, VT, 7 Mar 1852; m. at Putney, 15 Dec 1811, ABEL CARTER, b. recorded at Lancaster, NH, 10 Mar 1786 son of Elijah and Sarah (Bridge) Carter; Abel d. at Lowell, MA, 9 Jan 1869.

iii HENRY CRAWFORD, b. 22 Sep 1793; d. at Buffalo, NY, 26 Mar 1836; m. at Westminster, VT, 8 Dec 1819, WEALTHY D. WALES, b. at Westminster, 2 Sep 1798 daughter of Aaron and Eunice (Edwards) Wales;[1617] Wealthy d. at Springfield, 14 Feb 1867. Wealthy married second Daniel Adams on 1 Mar 1838. Henry attended Middlebury College where he graduated in 1815. He was an attorney in Walpole, NH and Buffalo, NY.[1618]

iv GRATIA CRAWFORD, b. 9 Dec 1795; d. at Johnson, VT, 7 Oct 1849; m. at Putney, 18 Feb 1822, CORNELIUS LYNDE, b. at Williamstown, VT< 19 Jun 1797 son of Cornelius and Rebecca (Davis) Lynde; Cornelius d. at River Falls, WI, 17 May 1873.

v JAMES CRAWFORD, b. 6 Mar 1798; d. at Dubuque, IA, 2 Nov 1846; m. 1st at Putney, 25 Nov 1828, TIRZAH MARIA WHITE, b. at Putney, 2 Apr 1804 daughter of Phineas and Esther (Stevens) White; Tirzah d. at Putney, 15 Nov 1837. James m. 2nd in 1838, MARY BROWN BELLOWS (widow of Pliny Dickinson), b. at Walpole, NH, 6 Jan 1800 daughter of Caleb and Marie (Hartwell) Bellows; Mary d. at Monticello, IA, 16 Feb 1885. After James's death, Mary married George King Smith.

[1614] Josiah and John are children given in the History of Rutland, but for whom there are no associated birth records.

[1615] Forthnightly Club of Putney, VT, "People of Putney 1753-1953" pp 15-16; accessed through American Ancestors digital collections; http://digitalcollections.americanancestors.org/cdm/ref/collection/p15869coll33/id/3322

[1616] Forthnightly Club of Putney, VT, "People of Putney 1753-1953" p 16

[1617] The 1832 will of Aaron Wales includes a bequest to his daughter Wealthy D. Crawford.

[1618] Middlebury College, Catalogue of Officers and Students of Middlebury College, 1800-1915, p 35, class of 1815

vi MARK A. CRAWFORD, b. 20 Oct 1800; d. at Putney, 10 May 1861; m. at Adams, MA, 3 Dec 1828, JUDITH HUNT MASON, b. at Woodstock, CT, 3 Jul 1807 daughter of John and Huldah (-) Mason; Judith d. at Putney, 23 Aug 1884.

vii FANNY CRAWFORD, b. 6 Feb 1803; d. at Ripon, WI, 26 Sep 1871; m. 29 Jul 1828, ZEBULON PERKINS BURNHAM, b. at Brookfield, VT, 30 Aug 1796 son of Walter and Submit (Smith) Burnham; Zebulon d. at Ripon, 25 Feb 1861.

viii LYDIA CRAWFORD, b. 15 Feb 1805; d. at Putney, after 1870; m. about 1832, as his second wife, JOHN CAMPBELL, b. at Putney, 1 Jan 1793 son of Alexander and Jerusha (Wilder) Campbell; John d. at Putney, 4 Jun 1866. John was first married to Catherine Houghton on 4 Feb 1827.

ix THEOPHILUS CRAWFORD, b. 28 Apr 1807; d. after 1870 when he was living in Vernon, IA; m. about 1836, ELIZA MARIA CAMPBELL, b. at Putney, 11 Jan 1815 daughter of Alexander and Jerusha (Wilder) Campbell; Eliza d. after 1880 when she was widowed and living in Vernon.

x ANNIS CRAWFORD, b. 11 Feb 1811; d. at Lowell, MA, 17 Feb 1888; m. 8 Feb 1831, WALTER BURNHAM, b. at Brookfield, VT, 12 Jan 1808 son of Walter and Submit (Smith) Burnham; Walter d. at Lowell, 16 Jan 1883.

Great-Grandchildren of Samuel Holt and Sarah Allen

597) PETER HOLT (*John⁴, John³, Samuel², Nicholas¹*), b. at Andover, 30 Sep 1752 son of John and Deborah (Stevens) Holt; d. at Andover, 9 Jan 1830; m. 28 Dec 1776, HEPHZIBAH STEVENS, b. at Andover, 15 Jan 1757 daughter of Thomas and Sarah (Gray) Stevens.

Peter and Hephzibah Holt were parents of eight children born at Andover. Peter died at the almshouse in Andover.[1619]

i PETER HOLT, b. 5 Dec 1776; d. 6 Oct 1780.

ii HEPHZIBAH HOLT, b. 30 Sep 1778; nothing further known.

iii THOMAS HOLT, baptized at Andover, 10 Sep 1780; nothing further known.

iv PETER HOLT, b. 10 Jun 1783; d. at Chelsea, MA, 11 Apr 1837; m. at Chelsea, 6 Jun 1811, SUSANNA GREEN, b. at Chelsea, 10 Dec 1782 daughter of Joseph and Susanna (Pratt) Green; Susanna d. at Chelsea, 6 Jan 1861.

v PHEBE HOLT, b. Jul 1785; d. at Chelsea, 26 May 1859; m. 4 Jul 1821, JOSEPH GREEN, b. at Chelsea, 6 Jun 1784 son of Joseph and Susanna (Pratt) Green; Joseph d. at Chelsea, 15 Jan 1848.

vi JOEL HOLT, b. 29 Aug 1787; d. at Woburn, 17 May 1861; m. at Reading, 25 Nov 1813, NANCY MCINTIRE, b. at Reading, 14 Jul 1795 daughter of Ebenezer and Lydia (Jeffrey) McIntire.

vii SUSANNA HOLT, b. 12 Oct 1790; d. at Andover, 13 Feb 1821; m. at Andover, 29 Nov 1808, EZRA HATCH, b. at Wells, ME, about 1785 son of Francis and Huldah (Hatch) Hatch; Ezra d. at North Andover, 30 Jul 1862. Ezra married second Tammy Larrabee on 4 Jul 1822.

viii JOHN HOLT, b. 15 Jul 1796; d. 30 Nov 1799.

598) ELIZABETH HOLT (*Elizabeth Holt Holt⁴, John³, Samuel², Nicholas¹*), b. at Andover, 25 Nov 1748 daughter of Timothy and Elizabeth (Holt) Holt; m. 1 Jun 1769, ISAAC FRYE, b. at Andover, 6 Feb 1748 son of Abiel and Abigail (Emery) Frye; Isaac d. at Wilton, NH, 3 Nov 1791.

Elizabeth and Isaac were in Wilton soon after their marriage arriving there in 1771 or 1772.

Isaac Frye distinguished himself in the Revolution. He was quartermaster in the third New Hampshire regiment of Col. James Reed in 1775 and was at the Battle of Bunker Hill. He received his commission as captain on 1 January 1776. Capt. Frye was the muster-master at Amherst in 1782. Following the war, he was breveted with the rank of major on 27 Nov 1783.[1620]

Elizabeth Holt and Isaac Frye were parents of ten children.

i ISAAC FRYE, baptized at Andover, 17 Dec 1769; d. at Wilton, 14 Sep 1814; m. at Wilton, 19 Jun 1794, HANNAH PHELPS, b. at Andover, 18 Jan 1774 daughter of Joseph and Abigail (Smith) Phelps; Hannah d. at Wilton, 28 Oct 1861.

ii TIMOTHY FRYE, b. at Wilton, 21 Sep 1773; d. 17 Mar 1776.

[1619] Peter, at the almshouse, Jan. 9, 1830, a. 80 y.

[1620] Livermore, *History of the Town of Wilton*, p 106

iii ABIEL FRYE, b. at Wilton, 28 Jul 1774; d. at Wilton, about 1820. Abiel did not marry.

iv JOHN FRYE, b. at Wilton, 23 Aug 1775; d. at Edinboro, PA, 11 Sep 1851; m. LUCY WELLMAN, b. in VT, 1782 daughter of Timothy and Lucy (Skinner) Wellman;[1621] Lucy d. at Edinboro, 1867.

v TIMOTHY HOLT FRYE, b. at Wilton, 27 Oct 1777; d. at Weld, ME, 7 Jan 1830; m. 8 Jan 1809, his fourth cousin, RACHEL HOLT (*Simeon*[5]*, Joseph*[4]*, Timothy*[3]*, James*[2]*, Nicholas*[1]), b. at Wilton, 7 Feb 1783 daughter of Simeon and Mary (Dale) Holt; Rachel d. after 1860 when she was living in Weld.

vi JOSHUA FRYE, b. at Wilton, 21 Dec 1779; d. at Wilton, 20 Jun 1864; m. 1st about 1805, LOIS FARRINGTON, b. at Hubbardston, MA, 4 Mar 1783 daughter of Elijah and Elizabeth (Sawin) Farrington; Lois d. at Athens, VT, 17 Aug 1815. Joshua m. 2nd 19 May 1831, LUCY JONES, b. at Hillsborough, NH, 27 Apr 1787 daughter of Joel and Mary (Bishop) Jones; Lucy d. at Wilton, 17 Dec 1875.

vii BETSY FRYE, b. at Wilton, 21 Dec 1781; d. at Wilton, 9 Jun 1862. Betsy did not marry. In 1860, she was living with her brother Joshua and his wife Lucy.

viii HANNAH FRYE, b. at Wilton, 30 May 1785; d. at Wilton, 31 Oct 1863; m. 26 Oct 1813, BENJAMIN BLANCHARD, b. at Wilton, 5 Apr 1781, Benjamin and Sarah (Griffin) Blanchard; Benjamin d. 12 Jul 1855.

ix ALFRED FRYE, b. at Wilton, 28 Feb 1787; d. at Wilton, 25 Sep 1867; m. 1st 19 Aug 1817, LUCY FARRINGTON, b. at Hubbardston, MA, 29 Apr 1787 daughter of Elijah and Elizabeth (Sawin) Farrington; Lucy d. at Wilton, 12 Dec 1835. Alfred m. 2nd about 1836, BETSEY BLANCHARD, b. at Milford, NH, 9 Jul 1801 daughter of Phineas and Sarah (Stevens) Blanchard; Betsey d. at Wilton, 11 Feb 1863.

x SARAH "SALLY" FRYE, b. at Wilton, 20 Sep 1790; d. at Wilton, 18 May 1835. Sally did not marry.

599) HANNAH HOLT (*Elizabeth Holt Holt*[4]*, John*[3]*, Samuel*[2]*, Nicholas*[1]), b. at Andover, 18 Jan 1754 daughter of Timothy and Elizabeth (Holt) Holt; d. at Brookline, VT, Apr 1833; m. about 1774, as his second wife, RICHARD WHITNEY, b. at Oxford, MA, 22 Apr 1743 son of Israel and Hannah (Blodgett) Whitney Richard d. at Brookline, 20 Apr 1816. Richard was first married to Sarah Butterfield who died in 1773.

Hannah and Richard were in Wilton, New Hampshire where Richard served one term as selectman in 1780.[1622] The family then settled in Brookline, Vermont where they were one of the early families.[1623] They settled in area that was known as Whitney hill.

Hannah Holt and Richard Whitney were parents of ten children, the first nine children born at Wilton and the youngest child born perhaps at Brookline, Vermont.

i ISRAEL WHITNEY, b. 4 Jul 1774; d. at Brookline, VT, 14 Dec 1850; m. at Wilton, 27 Nov 1794, his first cousin, ELIZABETH HOLT (*Timothy*[5]*, Timothy*[4]*, Nicholas*[3]*, Nicholas*[2]*, Nicholas*[1]), b. at Andover, 17 Sep 1775 daughter of Timothy and Hannah (Johnson) Holt;[1624] Elizabeth d. at Brookline, 24 Nov 1874.

ii TIMOTHY HOLT WHITNEY, b. 21 Nov 1776; d. at Athens, VT, 16 Mar 1859; m. 1st 11 Feb 1800, ABIGAIL BLANCHARD, b. at Wilton, 11 Jun 1777 daughter of Benjamin and Sarah (Griffin) Blanchard; Abigail d. at Athens, 27 Apr 1843. Timothy m. 2nd about 1844, ARATHUSA BARTLETT, b. at Newfane, VT, about 1794 daughter of William and Arathusa (Gibson) Bartlett; Arathusa d. at Newfane, 1 Oct 1868.

iii EBENEZER WHITNEY, b. 3 Jul 1778; d. at Brookline, VT, 12 Apr 1869; m. DEBORAH JOY whose parents are not identified, b. about 1778; Deborah d. at Brookline, 20 Sep 1850.

iv ABRAM WHITNEY, b. 8 Jan 1780; d. at Lindley, NY, Mar 1860; m. BETSEY who has not been identified, b. in VT, about 1783; Betsey d. after 1865 when she was living in Hornby, NY.

v ISAAC WHITNEY, b. 21 Jan 1782; d. at Weston, VT, 22 Nov 1860; m. at Chester, VT, Dec 1806, ABIGAIL EDSON.

vi JACOB WHITNEY, b. 15 Jan 1784; d. 9 Jul 1785.

vii HANNAH WHITNEY, b. 15 Aug 1785; d. at Newfane, VT, 27 Jan 1871; m. 1st about 1810, JAMES CAMPBELL. Hannah m. 2nd JOSEPHUS ORVIS, b. 28 Feb 1780 son of Waitstill and Elizabeth (Church) Orvis; Josephus d. at South Newfane, 24 Dec 1855.

[1621] Wellman, *Descendants of Thomas Wellman*, p 213

[1622] Livermore, *History of the Town of Wilton*, p 50

[1623] Stickney, *The Local History of Brookline, Vermont*, p 6

[1624] Elizabeth's death record gives her father as Timothy and age at death of 99 years, 2 months, 7 days which corresponds to the birth of Elizabeth daughter of Timothy and Hannah.

viii SARAH BUTTERFIELD WHITNEY, b. 1 Nov 1787; d. at Brookline, VT, 17 Sep 1873; m. JOEL HARWOOD, b. about 1786; Joel d. at Brookline, 11 Dec 1849.

ix SOLOMON WHITNEY, b. 26 Aug 1790; d. at Austinburg, OH, 1862 (probate 1862); m. SARAH, b. in NY, about 1784; Sarah d. after 1862.

x CHLOE WHITNEY, b. 22 Nov 1795; d. after 1870 when she was living in Putney, VT; m. DAVID KIDDER, b. at Oxford, MA, 11 May 1797 son of David and Sarah (Fressenden) Kidder; David d. after 1870.

600) SARAH HOLT (*Elizabeth Holt Holt^4, John^3, Samuel^2, Nicholas^1*), b. at Andover, 31 May 1757 daughter of Timothy and Elizabeth (Holt) Holt; m. at Wilton, 30 Mar 1780, her second cousin once removed, WILLIAM PIERCE (*William Pierce^5, Martha Holt Pierce^4, Hannah Farnum Holt^3, Elizabeth Holt Farnum^2, Nicholas^1*), b. at Ashford, CT, 28 Jun 1759 son of William and Hannah (-) Pierce of Wilton, NH.[1625][1626]

Sarah Holt and William Pierce were parents of ten children,[1627][1628] the older children likely born at Wilton and the younger children at Weston, Vermont.

i SARAH PIERCE, b. 1782; d. at Weston, VT, 22 Jan 1857; m. at Weston, 2 May 1813, JOHN KIMBALL, b. about 1785; John d. at Weston, after 1820.

ii HANNAH PIERCE, b. about 1783; d. at Springfield, VT, about 1820; m. at Weston, 23 Aug 1803, CHARLES LOCKWOOD, b. at Springfield, VT, 28 Dec 1780 son of Abraham and Lydia (Pollard) Lockwood. Charles married second Lucy Lewis on 20 Jan 1821.

iii WILLIAM PIERCE, b. 20 Sep 1785; d. at Salem, NY, 26 May 1867; m. about 1815, MARY MONCRIEF, b. 4 Oct 1786;[1629] Mary d. at Salem, 5 Jan 1847.

iv ASA PIERCE, b. 6 Dec 1788; d. at Weston, 3 Feb 1874; m. at Jamaica, VT, 13 May 1817, HANNAH HIGGINS, b. at Jamaica, 30 Mar 1798 daughter of Ichabod and Elizabeth (Young) Higgins; Hannah d. at Clarendon, VT, 30 Dec 1872.

v ELIZABETH "BETSEY" PIERCE, b. estimate 1790. Betsey is reported as marrying Mr. Lockwood, but no further information has been located.

vi LYDIA PIERCE; m. AARON BLANCHARD.[1630] There are no clear records for this family. They may be the Aaron and Lydia who died at Norfolk, NY with burial in the Bixby Cemetery. Lydia Blanchard died there 3 Jan 1848.

vii PHEBE PIERCE, b. 1793; d. at Weston, 4 Nov 1834.

viii POLLY PIERCE, b. about 1795

ix CALVIN PIERCE, b. about 1797

x ROXANA PIERCE, b. 2 Jul 1801; d. at Weston, 17 May 1874; m. 15 Nov 1832, WILLIAM CAMPBELL, b. at Andover, VT, 16 Apr 1811 son of Hezekiah and Betsey (-) Campbell; William d. at Weston, 8 Nov 1859.

601) ISAAC HOLT (*Joshua^4, John^3, Samuel^2, Nicholas^1*), b. at Andover, 15 May 1752 son of Joshua and Ruth (Burnap) Holt; d. at Andover, 11 Oct 1821; m. at Andover, 8 Jan 1778, HANNAH STEVENS, b. at Andover, 22 May 1754 daughter of Samuel and Hannah (Shattuck) Stevens; Hannah d. at Andover, 15 Jun 1814.

Little information is available for this family. No probate or land transaction records were located. There are baptisms of two children, but no further information on those children.

i HANNAH HOLT, baptized at Andover 3 Aug 1783

ii ISAAC HOLT, baptized at Andover 7 Jul1793

602) HANNAH HOLT (*Joshua^4, John^3, Samuel^2, Nicholas^1*), b. at Andover, 17 Mar 1764 daughter of Joshua and Ruth (Burnap) Holt; d. at Salem by 1792; m. 4 Jan 1781, WILLIAM PHELPS, b. 1747 perhaps the son of Jonathan and Judith (Cox) Phelps;[1631] William d. at Salem, 8 Sep 1812. William second married Sally Punchard on 29 Dec 1792.

1625 Livermore, *History of Wilton*, p 470
1626 Littlefield, *Genealogies of the Early Settlers of Weston*
1627 Pierce, *Pierce Genealogy*, p 104
1628 Littlefield, *Genealogies of the Early Settlers of Weston, p 306*
1629 Pierce, *Pierce Genealogy*, p 180. Mary is perhaps the daughter of Hugh Moncrief of Scotland who was in Salem, NY at this time. William Moncrief was also there, but his daughter Mary was Mary Safford.
1630 Littlefield, *Genealogies of Early Settlers of Weston*, p 306
1631 Phelps, *The Phelps Family of America*, volume 2, p 1593

William and Hannah lived in Salem where William was a blacksmith. There are just two children known for this family.

i WILLIAM PHELPS, b. and d. 1781

ii WILLIAM PHELPS, b. 1783; d. at Salem, 16 Oct 1875; m. 1st at Beverly, 19 Aug 1804, BETSEY RICHARDSON, b. about 1786 daughter of Philip and Sarah (Smith) Richardson;[1632] Betsey d. at Salem, 7 Jan 1822. William m. 2nd at Salem, 18 Sep 1822, ELIZABETH BOWEN, b. about 1785; Elizabeth d. at Salem, 1858. William m. 3rd 20 Mar 1859, PHILADELPHIA CATT (widow of Thomas Pepper), b. at Lewis, Sussex, England in 1795; Philadelphia d. at Salem, 5 Sep 1887.

603) UZZIEL HOLT (*Joshua⁴, John³, Samuel², Nicholas¹*), b. at Andover, 12 Apr 1766 son of Joshua and Ruth (Burnap) Holt; d. at Sharon, VT, after 1840; m. by 1801, SARAH who may be SARAH STILES, b. at Lyndeborough, 24 Mar 1762 daughter of Moses and Sarah (-) Stiles. It is known from the 1811 will of Moses Stiles that his daughter Sarah married a Holt and no other marriage was found for her. It is speculation at this point that Uzziel is the Holt that she married. Sarah Stiles was third cousin once removed of Uzziel Holt.

Uzziel served in the Vermont militia during the War of 1812 as a private and suffered a broken leg. He ultimately received a pension due to disability.[1633] Uzziel Holt, age 75 and a veteran, was living in Sharon, VT in 1840.

There is a record of one child for Uzziel and Sarah Holt.

i JACOB H. HOLT, b. at Lyndeborough, Aug 1801; m. at Norwich, VT, 13 Mar 1832, BETSEY PARKER, b. in VT about 1807. There are at least nine children of Jacob and Betsy Holt.

604) MEHITABLE HOLT (*Daniel⁴, John³, Samuel², Nicholas¹*), b. at Lunenburg, 20 Sep 1751 daughter of Daniel and Mehitable (Holt) Holt; d. at Amherst, NH, 1827; m. about 1778, BENJAMIN STEARNS, b. at Lunenburg, 3 Dec 1754 son of Benjamin and Ann (Taylor) Stearns; Benjamin d. at Amherst, NH, 1808.

Mehitable Holt and Benjamin Stevens were parents of two children.

i BENJAMIN STEARNS, b. at Amherst, NH, 2 May 1786

ii SHUAH STEARNS, b.at Amherst, NH, 1791; d. at Mont Vernon, NH, 1835; m. at Francestown, 18 Dec 1817, JONATHAN STEVENS, b.at Chelmsford, 10 Mar 1794 son of Jonathan and Thankful (Foster) Stevens; Jonathan d. at Mont Vernon, 26 Aug 1839.

605) ABIGAIL HOLT (*Daniel⁴, John³, Samuel², Nicholas¹*), b. at Lunenburg, 9 Mar 1753 daughter of Daniel and Mehitable (Holt) Holt; m. at Townsend, 28 Oct 1776, WILLIAM BLOOD, b. at Pepperell, 14 Sep 1748 son of William and Lucy (Fletcher) Blood.

William Blood and Abigail Holt were parents of seven children born at Pepperell.

i DANIEL BLOOD, b. 22 Apr 1777; d. 15 Oct 1777.

ii JONATHAN BLOOD, b. 10 Apr 1778. It is not clear what became of Jonathan. He may be the Jonathan Blood who married Rebecca Squires at Townsend on 12 Feb 1799.

iii WILLIAM BLOOD, b. 14 Feb 1783; d. at Pepperell, 3 Jan 1826. William does not seem to have married.

iv DANIEL BLOOD, b. 14 Jun 1786; d. at Pepperell, 27 Feb 1871; m. at Pepperell, 6 May 1813, ANNA STEVENS, b. 1790; Anna d. at Pepperell, 21 Oct 1866.

v LEONARD BLOOD, b. 29 Aug 1788; d. at Ware, MA, 8 May 1870; m. at Pepperell, 1813, ABIGAIL BLOOD, b. at Pepperell, 4 Jul 1786 daughter of Moses and Abigail (Shattuck) Blood; Abigail d. at Ware, 21 Apr 1859.

vi ABIGAIL BLOOD, b. 11 May 1792; d. at Pepperell, 9 Oct 1833. Abigail did not marry.

vii GARDNER BLOOD, b. 18 Aug 1795; d. at Gloversville, NY, 18 Jun 1873; m. 1st a Pepperell, 27 Apr 1820, LYDIA BLOOD. Gardner m. 2nd MARIAH, b. about 1806 who died at Johnstown, NY between 1850 and 1855.

606) DANIEL HOLT (*Daniel⁴, John³, Samuel², Nicholas¹*), b. at Lunenburg, 26 Mar 1756 son of Daniel and Mehitable (Holt) Holt; d. at Townsend, while felling a tree, 31 Aug 1798;[1634] m. at Townsend, 13 Dec 1781, his third cousin once removed, MARY BUTTERFIELD, b. at Townsend, 17 Jan 1756 daughter of Eleazer and Mary (Wright) Butterfield; Mary d. at Lunenburg, 29 Jun 1849. Mary second married, at Townsend, 28 Apr 1803, SILAS CARLY who d. at Townsend in 1805.

1632 The 1808 will of Philip Richardson of Beverly includes a bequest to his daughter Betsey Phelps.

1633 *War of 1812 Pension Application Files Index, 1812-1815.*

1634 Holt, Daniel, "was instantly killed by the fall of a tree", Aug. 31, 1798, a. 43y.

Daniel's estate entered probate on 4 September 1798 with widow Mary requesting that Seth Lewis be named administrator as her children were all young. Real estate was sixty acres of land with buildings valued at $800. Claims against the estate were $852.32.[1635]

In her will, Mary Carly bequeathed one hundred dollars to each of her daughters: Mary Lewis, Betsy Holt, Chloe Holt, and Emily Holt. She bequeathed ten dollars to be used for books for Sabbath school libraries for the destitute. To the heirs of her son Levi Holt late of Townsend, she does not leave anything "as I have done for them heretofore all that I ever calculated to do." Daughters Mary Lewis and Chloe Holt received the residue of the estate who are named executrices.[1636]

Daniel Holt and Mary Butterfield were parents of seven children born at Townsend.

i LEVI HOLT, b. 6 Jan 1783; d. at Townsend, 26 Jan 1847; m. at Billerica, 8 Aug 1805, SARAH STEARNS, b. about 1787; Sarah d. at Townsend, age 48, 1 Aug 1835. Levi was a blacksmith and died as a pauper at the poor farm.

ii MARY "POLLY" HOLT, b. 14 Sep 1786; d. at Lunenburg, 8 Sep 1851; m. at Billerica, 29 Jun 1806, ISAAC LEWIS, b. 14 Sep 1786 son of Samuel and Betty (Parker) Lewis.[1637]

iii BETSEY HOLT, b. 5 Apr 1789; d. at Townsend, 5 May 1859. Betsey did not marry.

iv DANIEL HOLT, b. 11 Nov 1790; d. at Townsend, 13 Apr 1827; Daniel did not marry.

v CHLOE HOLT, b. 22 Jun 1793; d. at Townsend, 31 Aug 1882. Chloe did not marry.

vi LUKE HOLT, b. 5 Jun 1796; d. at Townsend, 28 May 1833; m. at Dracut, 10 Sep 1825, LUCIA PALMER, b. at Townsend, 26 Sep 1801 daughter of David and Chloe (Kingsley) Palmer; Lucia d. at Somerville, 5 Sep 1863. Lucia married second William Thomson in 1840. Luke Holt did not leave a will and his estate was administered by his widow Lucia. No children are known for Luke and Lucia.

vii EMILY P. HOLT, b. 6 Oct 1798; d. at Townsend, 2 Mar 1872. Emily did not marry. She was a nurse.[1638]

607) SARAH HOLT (*Daniel*[4], *John*[3], *Samuel*[2], *Nicholas*[1]), b. at Lunenburg, 2 Sep 1762 daughter of Daniel and Mehitable (Holt) Holt; d. at Townsend, 2 May 1837; m. at Townsend, Dec 1783, JONATHAN BAILEY, b. at Bradford, MA, 27 Aug 1758 son of Nathaniel and Mary (Spofford) Bailey; Jonathan d. at Townsend, 27 Dec 1844.[1639]

Jonathan Bailey, then age seventy-four, made a statement of 6 November 1832 related to his pension application. In 1776, he served for two months in the company of Capt. Job Shattuck and was in Cambridge building a fort. He served further terms of six months in the company of Capt. Minot in the vicinity of Boston and another two-month service in Rhode Island and was discharged in 1777.[1640]

Sarah Holt and Jonathan Bailey were parents of eight children born at Townsend.

i LUCY BAILEY, b. 11 Jun 1785; d. at Townsend, 24 Mar 1854. Lucy did not marry.

ii JOEL BAILEY, b. 20 Mar 1787; d. at Rubicon, WI, 3 Jun 1862. The name of his first wife was not found. He was second married to ALVIRA who was born in NH about 1809.

iii ELDAD BAILEY, b. 17 Feb 1791; d. at Townsend, 29 Dec 1880; m. 1st at Littleton, 12 Dec 1813, REBECCA DOLE, b. at Littleton, about 1789 daughter of Lemuel and Rebecca (Warren) Dole; Rebecca d. at Townsend, 3 Feb 1852. Jonathan m. 2nd at Lunenburg, 8 Dec 1853, ASENATH CHAFFIN (widow of Ebenezer Jones), b. at Littleton, 31 Jul 1812 daughter of Asaph and Anna (Reed0 Chaffin; Asenath d. at Townsend, 29 Feb 1892.

iv SARAH BAILEY, b. 22 Oct 1793; d. at Lunenburg, 24 Mar 1870; m. 10 Apr 1832, NATHANIEL PARKER, b. 23 Apr 1808 son of Nathaniel and Sarah (Adams) Parker; Nathaniel d. at Lunenburg, 25 Feb 1885.

v MEHITABLE BAILEY, b. 8 Jan 1796; d. at Townsend, 5 Nov 1861; m. at Lunenburg, 17 Oct 1817, EBENEZER SANDERS, b. at Townsend, 28 Apr 1791 son of Solomon and Lydia (Levistone) Sanders; Ebenezer d. at Townsend, 28 Jun 1874.

vi ELISHA BAILEY, b. 22 Aug 1798; d. at Townsend, 30 Oct 1857; m. 1st at Lunenburg, 17 Mar 1825, FAIRANDA B. FITTS, b. at Royalston, MA, 4 Mar 1802 daughter of Isaac and Mehitable (Bishop) Fitts; Fairanda d. about

---

1635 *Middlesex County, MA: Probate File Papers, 1648-1871.*Online database. *AmericanAncestors.org.* New England Historic Genealogical Society, 2014. Case 11774

1636 *Worcester County, MA: Probate File Papers, 1731-1881.* Online database. AmericanAncestors.org. New England Historic Genealogical Society, 2015. Case 10003

1637 Lewis, *Edmund Lewis of Lynn, Massachusetts*, p 52

1638 Emily's name is given as Pamela in the 1799 guardianship case but is called Emily in her mother's will and is Emily on her death record. She is listed as Emily P. Holt on some census records.

1639 Jona Bailey; Male; Widower; Age 86; Laborer; Died Dec 27 1844; Buried in Townsend; Old Age; (A Pauper).

1640 U. S. Revolutionary War Pension and Bounty-Land Application Files, Case S28994

1831. Elisha m. 2nd at Lunenburg, 17 Nov 1832, Fairanda's sister, PHEBE FITTS, b. at Winchendon, about 1806; Phebe d. at Townsend, 5 Nov 1859.

vii PATTY BAILEY, b. 19 Oct 1800; d. at Townsend, 28 Nov 1863; m. at Townsend, 27 Dec 1821, ASA SANDERS. Patty and Asa did not have any surviving children.

viii ESTHER BAILEY, b. 12 Sep 1805; d. at Fitchburg, 15 Feb 1901; m. 5 Jan 1825, JONATHAN WYETH, b. at Groton, 20 Jan 1802 son of Jonathan and Elizabeth (Warren) Wyeth; Jonathan d. at Lunenburg, 5 Feb 1876.

Great-Grandchildren of Henry Holt and Sarah Ballard

608) NATHANIEL HOLT (*Oliver⁴, Oliver³, Henry², Nicholas¹*), b. at Andover, 23 Nov 1725 son of Oliver and Susannah (Wright) Holt; d. at Andover, Feb 1806; m. 1 Aug 1751, ELIZABETH STEVENS, b. at Andover, 21 Oct 1730 daughter of John and Elizabeth (Chandler) Stevens; Elizabeth d. Dec 1807.

Nathaniel and Elizabeth resided in Andover where they were admitted to South Church on 7 October 1764 by profession of faith.[1641] They were parents of six children born at Andover.

i ELIZABETH HOLT, b. 14 Nov 1752; m. likely at Andover, 7 Jan 1779, as his second wife, her second cousin once removed, ABIEL STEVENS (*Lydia Gray Stevens⁴, Edward Gray³, Hannah Holt Gray², Nicholas¹*),[1642] b. at Andover, 24 Mar 1749/50 son of John and Lydia (Gray) Stevens; Abiel d. at Stafford, VT, 1806. Abiel was first married to Tabitha Holt daughter of Jacob and Mary (Dolliver) Holt. Elizabeth Holt and Abiel Stevens are Family 622.

ii SUSANNAH HOLT, b. 11 May 1755; m. 18 Apr 1776; CARLETON PARKER, baptized at Reading, 1750 son of Timothy and Priscilla (Carleton) Parker; Carleton d. at Andover, 23 Dec 1809.

iii URIAH HOLT, b. 13 Sep 1757; d. 13 Feb 1761.

iv NATHANIEL HOLT, b. 19 Dec 1759; d. 16 Mar 1761.

v CHLOE HOLT, baptized 21 Sep 1766; d. at Andover, 11 Apr 1855; m. 1st at Andover, 20 Apr 1789, DAVID WILEY who d. by about 1799. Chloe m. 2nd 25 Feb 1800, her fourth cousin, JOHN HOLT (*David⁵, Samuel⁴, Samuel³, Samuel², Nicholas¹*), b. at Andover, 22 Feb 1769 son of David and Hannah (Martin) Holt; John d. at Andover, 21 Oct 1815. Chloe m. 3rd 21 Jul 1821, her fourth cousin, JOHN FRYE (*Ebenezer Frye⁵, Elizabeth Farnum Frye⁴, John Farnum³, Elizabeth Holt Farnum², Nicholas¹*), b. at Andover, 16 Aug 1754 son of Ebenezer and Elizabeth (Kimball) Frye; John d. 26 Mar 1843. John Frye was first married to Lydia Batchelder.

vi NATHANIEL HOLT, b. 6 Apr 1769; d. at Andover, 24 May 1829; m. at Andover, 3 Mar 1791, MEHITABLE FOSTER, b. at Andover, 17 Sep 1772 daughter of Dudley and Rachel (Steel) Foster; Mehitable d. at Andover, 16 Aug 1859.

609) OLIVER HOLT (*Oliver⁴, Oliver³, Henry², Nicholas¹*), b. at Andover, 24 Jan 1739/40 son of Oliver and Susannah (Wright) Holt; m. at Andover, 8 Oct 1761, EUNICE RAYMOND, b. at Beverly, 30 Apr 1744 daughter of Boanerges and Jemima (Meacham) Raymond.

Oliver and Eunice lived in Wilton, New Hampshire and were parents of two known children.

i EUNICE HOLT, b. at Wilton, 25 Jul 1764; d. at Andover, VT, 18 Jun 1798; m. at Wilton, 18 Dec 1794, JOSEPH FULLER, b. at Middleton, MA, 21 Jul 1760 son of Amos and Hannah (Putnam) Fuller.

ii OLIVER HOLT, b. at Wilton, 13 Feb 1776; d. at Ellenburg, NY, 24 Jun 1837; m. at Andover, VT, 16 Apr 1804, PHEBE HASELTINE, b. about 1786; Phebe d. after 1850 when she was living in Ellenburg with her son Raymond and his family.

610) BEULAH HOLT (*Oliver⁴, Oliver³, Henry², Nicholas¹*), b. at Andover, 12 Apr 1744 daughter of Oliver and Susannah (Wright) Holt; m. at Andover, 26 Apr 1770, JOHN GRAY, b. at Andover, 26 Dec 1745 son of Edward and Sarah (-) Gray.

Beulah Holt and John Gray were parents of six children who were all baptized in Salem, Massachusetts on 13 May 1787. It is not clear when or where they were each born. The couple married in Andover and then were in Milton, New Hampshire. They moved from Milton to Rindge in February 1773 with their son Eliphalet.[1643] John signed the association test at

[1641] South *Church, Historical Manual*, p 12

[1642] Durrie's Holt genealogy gives Elizabeth Holt born in 1756 daughter of Caleb and Mary (Merrick) Holt as the second wife of Abiel Stevens. However, Caleb Holt's will written in 1793 names his daughter as Elizabeth Howe.

[1643] Stearns, *History of the Town of Rindge*, p 539

Rindge in 1776 and served in the regiment of Col. Enoch Hale in 1778. When the children were baptized at Salem, they were described as being of Andover. Two of the sons in the family were in Jay, Maine in their adulthood. Marriages were located for just two of the children.

i ELIPHALET GRAY, b. about 1771 perhaps at Milton, NH and baptized at Salem, MA, 13 May 1787; m. MARY COOLIDGE, b. at Watertown, MA, 5 Sep 1767 daughter of Simon and Mary (Jennison) Coolidge.[1644] Eliphalet was in Jay, Maine in 1810 but is thought to have gone to Carthage after that.

ii JOHN GRAY baptized at Salem 13 May 1787

iii SUSANNA WRIGHT GRAY baptized at Salem 13 May 1787

iv OLIVE GRAY baptized at Salem 13 May 1787

v FREDERICK GRAY baptized at Salem 13 May 1787

vi URIAH HOLT GRAY, b. about 1784 and baptized 13 May 1787; d. at Jay, ME, after 1840; m. ANNA DAVENPORT, b. at Winthrop, ME, 13 Jul 1786 daughter of Ebenezer and Mary (Crane) Davenport;[1645] Anna d. at Jay, 1866.

611) SARAH HOLT (*Uriah⁴, Oliver³, Henry², Nicholas¹*), b. at Lancaster, 18 Mar 1727 daughter of Uriah and Sarah (Wright) Holt; d. at Harvard, 29 Oct 1769; m. at Harvard, 27 Nov 1746, JONATHAN WHITNEY, b. 1724 son of Jonathan and Alice (Willard) Whitney;[1646] Jonathan d. at Harvard, 20 Jan 1770.

Jonathan Whitney did not leave a will and his estate entered probate 30 January 1770. The total value of the estate was £161.5.0. In the estate settlement 20 April 1771, land of about 35 acres was settled on son Phineas and he was to pay to each of his sisters or their guardians or representatives the sum of £26.6.11. Those sisters were Sarah, Relief, Abigail, and Rachel.[1647]

Sarah Holt and Jonathan Whitney were parents of ten children born at Harvard.

i PHINEAS WHITNEY, b. 3 Jul 1747; d. at Norway, ME, 21 May 1830; m. at Harvard, 31 Oct 1765, KEZIAH FARNSWORTH, likely b. at Harvard, 1 Jun 1742 daughter of Phineas and Azubah (Burt) Farnsworth; Keziah d. after 1820 when she is mentioned in the pension application file of Phineas.

ii JONATHAN WHITNEY, b.1 Jul 1749; d. 27 Oct 1756.

iii SARAH WHITNEY, b. 5 Aug 1751; d. at Deerfield, NH, 12 Jul 1827; likely m. at Harvard, 26 Aug 1771; JOHN MEAD, b. 1743; John d. at Deerfield, 15 Jun 1831.

iv RELIEF WHITNEY, b. 21 May 1754; d. 15 Aug 1756.

v RELIEF WHITNEY, b. 13 Nov 1758; d. at Harvard, 17 Apr 1818; m. at Harvard, 2 Jul 1780, JONAS WHITNEY, b. at Harvard, 3 Mar 1756 son of Jonas and Zebudah (Davis) Whitney; Jonas d. at Harvard, 26 Nov 1803.

vi ANNAS WHITNEY, b. 26 Feb 1761; d. 1 Jun 1761.

vii ABIGAIL WHITNEY, b. 29 Jan 1763; m. at Harvard, 17 Nov 1789, BENJAMIN HOAR (later Benjamin Whitney), b. at Leominster, MA, 21 Sep 1757 son of Oliver and Silence (Houghton) Hoar. On 3 March 1815, a special act was passed by the State of New York allowing Benjamin Hoar and each of the members of his family to legally change their name to Whitney. The family included Benjamin, his wife Abigail, and children Theophilus, Abel, Silence, Oliver, Polly, and Abigail. The family were residents of Cambridge, NY at that time.[1648]

viii OLIVER WHITNEY, b. 29 Jan 1763; d. 29 Mar 1763.

ix ANNAS WHITNEY, b. 30 Mar 1765; d. 23 Jan 1768.

x RACHEL WHITNEY, b. 19 Sep1767; d. at Harvard, Aug 1825; m. at Harvard, 7 Nov 1793, SALMON WILLARD, baptized at Harvard, 15 Jul 1770 son of Benjamin and Hannah (Godfrey) Willard; Salmon d. at Lancaster, MA, 10 Jul 1860. Salmon was second married to Mercy Kelly.

612) URIAH HOLT (*Uriah⁴, Oliver³, Henry², Nicholas¹*), b. at Lancaster, 7 Feb 1729 son of Uriah and Sarah (Wright) Holt; d. at Woodstock, VT, 1812; m. at Harvard, 20 Feb 1752, ANNESS WILLARD, b. at Harvard, 20 Jun 1730 daughter of Henry and

---

1644 Bond, *Genealogies of the Families and Descendants of the Early Settlers of Watertown*, p 175

1645 Stackpole, *History of Winthrop, Maine*, p 343

1646 Although there is not a birth record for Jonathan, he can be established as the son of Jonathan and Alice through probate records.

1647 *Worcester County, MA: Probate File Papers, 1731-1881.* Online database. AmericanAncestors.org. New England Historic Genealogical Society, 2015. Case 64948

1648 New York State, Laws of the State of New York: Revised and Passed at the Thirty-sixth Session of the Legislature, volume 3, p 60

Abigail (Fairbanks) Willard; Anness d. at Ashburnham, 28 Nov 1779. Uriah m. 2nd, at Ashburnham, 6 Jun 1785, SARAH GOODRIDGE.

Uriah and Anness resided in Harvard for about twenty years after their marriage and then were in Ashburnham where Anness died. Uriah continued in Ashburnham for a few more years but was in Woodstock, Vermont by 1790.

There are records for ten children of Uriah and Anness.

i JOSHUA HOLT, b. at Harvard, 23 Jun 1753. Joshua "marched at the alarm" on 19 April 1775 from Ashburnham in the company of Capt. Jonathan Gates.[1649]

ii URIAH HOLT, b. at Harvard, 10 May 1755. He is perhaps the Uriah "marched at the alarm" in the company of Capt. Deliverance Davis.

iii ANNESS HOLT, b. at Harvard, 1 Sep 1757; m. at Ashburnham, 30 Oct 1780, JONATHAN BENJAMIN, b. at Ashburnham, 30 Jul 1760 son of William and Sarah (Child) Benjamin; Jonathan d. at Woodstock, VT, 24 Apr 1834.

iv JACOB HOLT, b. 23 Jun 1759; d. after 1830 at Woodstock, VT; m. at Ashburnham, 5 Jul 1781, ANNA MELVIN, b.at Ashburnham, 8 Nov 1760 daughter of Nathan and Anna (Foster) Melvin.

v SARAH HOLT, baptized at Harvard, 20 Sep 1761; died young

vi JONATHAN HOLT, baptized at Harvard, 9 Sep 1764; died young

vii LEMUEL HOLT, baptized at Harvard, 1 Nov 1767; d. at Hartland, VT, 8 Mar 1848; m. ABIGAIL HODGMAN, b. 1774; Abigail d. at Hartland, 26 Oct 1839.

viii SARAH HOLT, baptized at Harvard, 15 Jul 1770

ix JONATHAN HOLT, baptized at Ashburnham, 14 Jun 1772; d. at Berlin Corners, VT, 1 Nov 1843; m. SARAH LAKE, b. at Woodstock, VT, 22 Feb 1777 son of George and Sarah (Lovejoy) Lake; d. at Berlin Corners, 8 Dec 1857.

x OLIVER HOLT, baptized at Ashburnham, 1 Oct 1775; d. 1 Feb 1779.

613) MARY HOLT (*Uriah[4], Oliver[3], Henry[2], Nicholas[1]*), b. at Lancaster, 5 Apr 1740 daughter of Uriah and Sarah (Wright) Holt; m. at Harvard, 7 Sep 1764, THOMAS DARBY, b. at Harvard, 22 Sep 1739 son of Simon and Mercy (Wilson) Darby; Thomas d. at Westminster, VT, 7 Dec 1833.[1650]

Thomas and Mary started their family in Harvard, but were in Chesterfield, Vermont about 1771. They disappear from records in Chesterfield in 1804[1651] and were after in Westminster, Vermont. There are records of four children in this family although there may well be others.

i MOLLY DARBY, b. at Harvard, 10 May 1765

ii OLIVER DARBY, baptized at Harvard, 24 May 1767; m. 29 Nov 1788, LOVINA STOCKWELL *perhaps* the daughter of Abel and Patience (Thomas) Stockwell. Oliver and Lovina seem to have gone to Essex County, New York before heading west to Washtenaw County, MI where they were living in 1840. So far, just one daughter Lovina born in New York about 1810, has been located.

iii LYDIA DARBY, b. at Chesterfield, 30 Oct 1776

iv ASA DARBY, b. at Chesterfield, 16 Jan 1782

614) SARAH HOLT (*David[4], Oliver[3], Henry[2], Nicholas[1]*), b. at Andover, 20 Nov 1733 daughter of David and Sarah (Russell) Holt; d. at Andover, 30 Sep 1769; m. 26 May 1757, JAMES BARNARD, b. at Andover, 24 Sep 1727 son of James and Abigail (Wilson) Barnard. James m. 2nd, 11 Mar 1775 widow Mary Barker.

Sarah Holt and James Barnard were parents of five children born at Andover, only two of whom are known to have lived to adulthood. Daughter Abigail Barnard Downing did not leave a will and her estate entered probate 29 November 1836. The nearest next of kin listed as living in the commonwealth were first cousins.[1652]

i DAVID BARNARD, b. 18 Nov 1758; nothing further known.

1649 Stearns, *History of Ashburnham*, p 142

1650 Thomas Darby, age 95, born about 1738, died 7 Dec 1833.

1651 Randall, *History of Chesterfield*, p 265

1652 *Essex County, MA: Probate File Papers, 1638-1881.*Online database. *AmericanAncestors.org.* New England Historic Genealogical Society, 2014. Case 8255

ii SARAH BARNARD, baptized 2 Aug 1761; died young.

iii SARAH BARNARD, b. 10 Jun 1764; d. 8 Nov 1774.

iv ABIGAIL BARNARD, b. 21 Feb 1767; d. at Andover, 18 Nov 1836; m. at Andover, 3 Dec 1805, as his second wife, PALFREY DOWNING, baptized at Andover, 12 Apr 1761 son of Richard and Temperance (Derby) Downing; Palfrey d. at Andover, 28 Sep 1835. Palfrey was first married to Lydia Lovejoy daughter of Isaac and Deborah (Sheldon) Lovejoy.

v JAMES BARNARD, b. 27 Jun 1769; d. at Andover, 10 Dec 1811; m. at Andover, 6 Sep 1791, HANNAH HAWLEY, baptized at Marblehead, 1 Mar 1772 daughter of Joseph and Hannah (Pearce) Hawley.[1653]

615) DORCAS HOLT (*David⁴, Oliver³, Henry², Nicholas¹*),[1654] baptized at Andover 31 Jul 1737 daughter of David and Sarah (Russell) Holt; m. at Andover, 22 Mar 1759, THOMAS PEAVEY, b. at Andover, 14 Mar 1736 son of Peter and Esther (Barker) Peavey.

Dorcas Holt and Thomas Peavey were parents four children born at Andover who are known to have reached adulthood. There may be two or three other children who died in childhood, but the records for this are not clear.

i PETER PEAVEY, b. 14 Apr 1762; d. at Greenfield, NH, 28 Jul 1836; m. 8 Apr 1788, LUCY CUMMINGS, b. at Hollis, 9 Jul 1767 daughter of Ebenezer and Elizabeth (Abbott) Cummings; Lucy d. 15 Oct 1854.

ii THOMAS PEAVEY, b. about 1765; m. by 1795, LYDIA ABBOTT, b. at Wilton, 22 Oct 1768 daughter of Jeremiah and Cloe (Abbott) Abbott; Lydia d. at Peterborough, NH, 1 Sep 1832.

iii HANNAH PEAVEY, b. about 1773; m. at Andover, 10 Sep 1795, PETER JOHNSON who has not been identified. Nothing further is known of this family at this time.

iv DORCAS PEAVEY, b. about 1774, d. at Salem, MA, 30 Jun 1855; m. at Andover, 12 Mar 1794, as his second wife, GEORGE SMITH, b. about 1758; George d. at Salem, 12 Sep 1843. George Smith was first married to Mary Greg. Dorcas does not seem to have had children. In her will, she has bequests to several grandchildren, but these are the children of her stepchildren Andrew Smith and Mary Smith Frye.

616) DAVID HOLT (*David⁴, Oliver³, Henry², Nicholas¹*), b. at Andover, 4 Jul 1740 son of David and Sarah (Russell) Holt; m. at Andover, 22 Jun 1769, REBECCA OSGOOD, b. at Andover, 6 Feb 1739/40 daughter of Samuel and Dorothy (Wardwell) Osgood; Rebecca d. at Andover, 21 May 1790.

David Holt and Rebecca Osgood were parents of five children born at Andover.

i REBECCA HOLT, b. 10 Dec 1770; d. 23 Nov 1774.

ii SARAH HOLT, b. 12 Sep 1773; d. 3 Nov 1774.

iii REBECCA HOLT, b. 25 Aug 1776; m. at Andover, 1 Apr 1800, her third cousin once removed, NATHAN KIMBALL HOLT (*Abiel⁵, Thomas⁴, Thomas³, Nicholas², Nicholas¹*), baptized at Andover, 30 Aug 1778 son of Abiel and Lydia (Lovejoy) Holt; Nathan d. at Boscawen, NH, 10 Nov 1836.

iv SARAH HOLT, b. 12 Jul 1779

v DORCAS HOLT, b. 20 Nov 1781; d. at Andover, 24 Mar 1842; m. 23 Sep 1803, her third cousin, HENRY ABBOTT (*Moses Abbott⁵, Hannah Holt Abbott⁴, Timothy³, James², Nicholas¹*), b.at Andover, 22 Sep 1778 son of Moses and Elizabeth (Holt) Abbott; Henry d. at Andover, 24 Sep 1845.

617) JONATHAN HOLT (*Jonathan⁴, Oliver³, Henry², Nicholas¹*), b. at Andover, 29 Sep 1738 son of Jonathan and Lydia (Blanchard) Holt; d. at Albany, ME, 1810 (probate 1810); m. at Andover, 31 Dec 1761, RUTH KIMBALL, baptized 30 Mar 1739 daughter of Josiah and Elizabeth (Bragg) Kimball;[1655] Ruth d. at Albany, ME, 5 Mar 1823.

Jonathan and Ruth had their children in Andover. They relocated to Albany, Maine in 1803 where Jonathan served as deacon.

[1653] Hawley, *Genealogy of the Hawley Family of Marblehead*, p 5, https://archive.org/details/genealogyofhawle00hawl_0

[1654] Although sources (Durrie's Holt genealogy and Charlotte Helen Abbott's Andover notes) state that Dorcas who married Thomas Peavey was the daughter of Ephraim Holt and Phebe Russell, there is no evidence that Ephraim and Phebe had a daughter Dorcas. The 1759 distribution of the estate of Ephraim Russell has only the following children as heirs: eldest son Ephraim, Phebe Houghton, Bethiah Holt, Asenath Holt, and Mastin Holt. These are also the only children of Ephraim and Phebe for whom there are birth records.

[1655] Morrison and Sharples, *History of the Kimball Family*, p 113

Jonathan Holt did not leave a will and his estate entered probate 15 December 1810 with widow Ruth requesting that Uriah Holt of Norway be named administrator. The real estate was ordered to be sold to satisfy the debts of the estate. The dower was set off to widow Ruth on 22 December 1810.[1656] Uriah Holt was a cousin of Jonathan.

Jonathan Holt and Ruth Kimball were parents of seven children born at Andover.

i JONATHAN HOLT, b. 29 Jun 1763; d. 22 Mar 1764.

ii BETTY HOLT, b. 25 Aug 1767; d. at Andover, 7 Feb 1827; m. at Andover, 4 Sep 1794, WILLIAM GRIFFIN, b. 1767 son of William and Mary (Howard) Griffin; William d. at Andover, 24 May 1830.

iii LYDIA HOLT, b. 15 May 1770; d. at Albany, ME, 12 Jan 1834; m. at Andover, 22 Nov 1795, SAMUEL TOWNE, b. at Andover, 26 Mar 1769 son of Nathan and Mary (Curtis) Towne; Samuel d. at Albany, 1 Nov 1850.

iv MOSES HOLT, b. 3 Sep 1773; m. 28 Jun 1796, MARY AUSTIN, b. at Andover, 15 Aug 1771 daughter of Daniel and Eunice (Kimball) Austin.

v AMY HOLT, b. 25 Jul 1776; d. at Andover, 29 Sep 1803, of consumption; m. at Andover, 23 Oct 1798, DAVIS FOSTER, b. at Reading, 15 Aug 1771 son of Jonathan and Sarah (Townsend) Foster. Davis married second widow Nancy (Johnson) Russell the widow of Stephen Russell.

vi NANCY HOLT, b. 22 Jul 1779; m. likely at Andover, 21 Oct 1800, CHARLES NEWELL who has not been identified. The family seems to be living in Andover in 1810 with three children.

vii RUTH KIMBALL HOLT, b. 18 Apr 1782; d. 11 Apr 1799.

618) HANNAH HOLT (*Jonathan[4], Oliver[3], Henry[2], Nicholas[1]*), b. at Andover, 19 Dec 1745 daughter of Jonathan and Lydia (Blanchard) Holt; d. at Concord, NH, 1 Dec 1818; m. at Andover, 1763, her third cousin, NATHAN BALLARD, b. at Andover, 1 Nov 1744 son of Timothy and Hannah (Chandler) Ballard; Nathan d. at Concord, 14 Jan 1835.

Nathan and Hannah moved from Andover to Wilton soon after their marriage. Nathan was a farmer there from 1765-1782. He served in the Revolution in Captain Benjamin Taylor's Company in 1775 and in 1777 in the company that marched from Wilton and Amherst to Ticonderoga. He was a selectman of Wilton for several years. After 1782, the family relocated to Concord where they were first settlers at Little Pond at Concord.[1657]

Nathan and Hannah Ballard were parents of nine children, the oldest daughter born at Andover and the other children at Wilton.

i HANNAH BALLARD, b. at Andover, 12 May 1764; d. about 1809; m. at Wilton, 28 Mar 1793, DAVID MCINTIRE, b. about 1762 of undetermined origins; David's death is unknown.

ii SARAH BALLARD, b. 13 Apr 1766; d. at Wilton, 4 Jan 1856; m. at Wilton, 1 Jun 1797, WILLIAM PETTENGILL, b. at Andover, 23 Aug 1759 son of Samuel and Mary (Holt) Pettengill; William d. at Wilton, 13 Oct 1844.

iii MARY BALLARD, b. 8 May 1768; d. at Milford, after 1850; m. about 1790, her fourth cousin, AMOS HOLT (*Amos[5], John[4], Samuel[3], Samuel[2], Nicholas[1]*), b. 20 Oct 1768 son of Amos and Jemima (Ingalls) Holt; Amos d. at Wilton, 13 Dec 1826.

iv BETSEY BALLARD, b. 19 Aug 1771; d. at Peterborough, 5 Nov 1856; m. at Wilton, 13 May 1794, RICHARD TAYLOR BUSS, b. at Wilton, 7 Sep 1772 son of Stephen and Phebe (Keyes) Buss; Richard d. at Peterborough, 20 Oct 1862.

v PHEBE BALLARD, b. 30 Apr 1773; d. at Wilton, 15 Nov 1840; m. at Concord, 23 Feb 1794, JOHN GUTTERSON, b. at Andover, 27 Aug 1766 son of Samuel and Lydia (Stevens) Gutterson; John d. at Milford, 13 Dec 1841.

vi NATHAN BALLARD, b. 21 Feb 1775; d. at Concord, 5 Jul 1856; m. HANNAH BUSS, b. at Wilton, 3 Dec 1774 daughter of Stephen and Phebe (Keyes) Buss; Hannah d. 1857.

vii JOHN BALLARD, b. 22 Feb 1778; d. at Wilton, 28 Sep 1855; m. at Wilton, 20 Jan 1808, RHODA BALES, b. at Wilton, 16 May 1779 daughter of William and Rhoda (Keyes) Bales; Rhoda d. at Wilton, 15 Jan 1839.

viii EZRA BALLARD, b. 2 Feb 1780; d. 16 Sep 1781.

ix TIMOTHY BALLARD, b. 1 Jan 1782; d. 14 Jan 1782.

[1656] *Maine. Probate Court (Oxford County)*; Probate Place: *Oxford, Maine, Estate Files, Timothy Gibson-Daniel Leavitt, Pre 1820, Estate of Jonathan Holt*

[1657] Livermore, *History of Wilton*, p 304

619) JACOB HOLT (*Jacob⁴, Oliver³, Henry², Nicholas¹*), b. at Andover, 29 Mar 1739 son of Jacob and Mary (Osgood) Holt; d. at Albany, ME, 12 May 1816; m. at Andover, 22 Mar 1764, RHODA ABBOTT, b. at Andover, 22 Jun 1741 daughter of Ephraim and Hannah (Phelps) Abbott; Rhoda d. at Albany, 12 Jan 1821.

Rhoda Abbott and Jacob Holt had their twelve children in Andover, and then in 1795 went north to the new settlement of Oxford Township in Maine.

i JACOB HOLT, b. 15 Feb 1765; d. at Charlestown, MA, 22 Sep 1800; m. at Andover, 11 May 1787, his third cousin once removed, ABIGAIL HOLT (*Joseph⁵, Joseph⁴, Henry³, Henry², Nicholas¹*), b. at Reading, Sep 1765 daughter of Joseph and Abigail (Bean) Holt; Abigail d. at Charlestown, 16 Jun 1851.

ii NEHEMIAH HOLT, b. 25 Dec 1767; d. at Bethel, ME, 26 Mar 1846; m. 24 Jan 1793, ABIGAIL TWIST, b. at Reading, about 1768; Abigail d. at Bethel, 31 Jan 1853.

iii EPHRAIM HOLT, b. 19 Mar 1769; d. at Greenfield, NH, 24 Oct 1836; m. at Andover, 27 Nov 1794, his third cousin, HANNAH HOLT (*Joshua⁴, Nicholas³, Nicholas², Nicholas¹*), b. at Andover, Jun 1771 daughter of Joshua and Phebe (Farnum) Holt; Hannah d. at Greenfield, 21 Apr 1842. Ephraim Holt and Hannah Holt are Family 873.

iv STEPHEN HOLT, b. 7 Jun 1771; d. at Norway, ME, 25 Sep 1817; m. at Albany, VT, 1 Jul 1806, his fourth cousin, MOLLY BRAGG, b. at Andover, 29 Apr 1779 daughter of Ingalls and Molly (Frye) Bragg; Molly d. at Norway, 17 Aug 1823.

v RHODA HOLT, b. 5 Jul 1772; d. before 1773.

vi RHODA HOLT, b. 13 Jul 1773; d. 1 Apr 1850 (burial at Albany, ME); m. 1803, JOHN LOVEJOY, b. at Andover, 24 Mar 1773 son of Joseph and Mary (Gorden) Lovejoy; John d. at Albany, ME, 8 Nov 1832.

vii URIAH HOLT, b. 25 May 1775; d. at Norway, ME, 21 Jun 1849; m. 4 Feb 1808, HANNAH FARNUM, b. at Andover, 27 Oct 1789 daughter of Benjamin and Dolly (Holt) Farnum; Hannah d. 4 Feb 1835.

viii MARY OSGOOD HOLT, b. 21 Apr 1777; d. at Andover, 11 Feb 1856; m. 22 Dec 1802, her second cousin once removed, ZACHARIAH CHICKERING, b. at Andover, 19 May 1764 son of Samuel and Mary (Dane) Chickering; Zachariah d. at Andover, 30 Jun 1841.

ix TABITHA HOLT, b. 11 Aug 1779; d. likely at Waterford, ME; m. at Waterford, 19 Jun 1798, THOMAS GREENE, b. at Rowley, 17 Mar 1775 son of Thomas and Lydia (Kilburn) Greene; Thomas d. at Waterford, Oct 1809 (probate 12 Dec 1809).

x HANNAH HOLT, b. 17 Jul 1781; d. at Albany, ME, 23 Dec 1856; m. 1 Oct 1801, PARSONS HASKELL, b. at Falmouth, ME, 27 Oct 1777 son of Benjamin and Lydia (Freeman) Haskell; Parsons d. at Albany, 6 Jul 1829.

xi DAVID HOLT, b. 21 Aug 1783; d. at Andover, 3 Oct 1836; m. 2 Jul 1820, his second cousin, SARAH ABBOTT (*Ruth Holt Abbott⁶, Joseph⁵, Benjamin⁴, Henry³, Henry², Nicholas¹*), b. at Andover, 11 Jul 1787 daughter of Abner and Ruth (Holt) Abbott; Sarah d. at Andover, 26 Jul 1874.

xii SARAH ABBOTT HOLT, b. 19 May 1786; d. at Phillipston, MA, 23 Jun 1845; m. Jun 1817, JOSEPH CHICKERING, b. at Dedham, 30 Apr 1780 son of Jabez and Hannah (Balch) Chickering; Joseph d. at Phillipston, 27 Jan 1844.

620) NEHEMIAH HOLT (*Jacob⁴, Oliver³, Henry², Nicholas¹*), b. at Andover, 24 Oct 1740 son of Jacob and Mary (Osgood) Holt; d. at Salem, MA, 1786 (probate 1786); m. at Salem, 21 Jul 1771, ESTHER VARNUM, b. 21 May 1747; Esther d. at Salem, 12 Feb 1822.

Nehemiah Holt did not leave a will and his estate entered probate 12 July 1786 with widow Esther as administratrix. Claims exceeded the assets and the estate was declared insolvent. Esther Holt was named as guardian for the three minor children: Nehemiah age thirteen, Molley age eight, and Esther age four.[1658]

In her will written 14 June 1821 (probate 2 April 1822), Esther Varnum Holt bequeathed to her daughter Esther Andrews one dollar and the remainder of her estate went to her other daughter Mary Proctor who was also named executrix. Real estate was valued at $550 and personal estate at $78.55.[1659]

Nehemiah Holt and Esther Varnum were parents of seven children born at Salem. Son Nehemiah was a mariner and died at Alexandria while on a voyage. Daughter Mary's first husband died while at sea and age 29 and it is possible that her second husband also died at sea.

[1658] *Essex County, MA: Probate File Papers, 1638-1881.*Online database. *AmericanAncestors.org.* New England Historic Genealogical Society, 2014. Case 13678

[1659] *Essex County, MA: Probate File Papers, 1638-1881.*Online database. *AmericanAncestors.org.* New England Historic Genealogical Society, 2014. Case 13639

i NEHEMIAH HOLT, baptized at Salem, 6 Dec 1772; d. at Alexandria, 25 Apr 1798.

ii HANNAH HOLT, baptized at Salem, 13 Jun 1773; died young.

iii ESTHER HOLT, b. 2 Jul 1775; d. 23 Sep 1777.

iv MARY "MOLLY" HOLT, b. 9 Sep 1777; d. at Salem, 7 Dec 1856; m. 1st at Salem, 22 Jun 1794, JOSHUA FOSTER, b. about 1766; Joshua d. at the West Indies, 6 Dec 1795.[1660] Mary m. 2nd at Salem, 17 Oct 1800, DANIEL PROCTOR, b. at Danvers, 12 Jul 1768 son of Benjamin and Keziah (Littlefield) Proctor.

v VARNUM HOLT, b. 13 Nov 1779; d. 28 Dec 1783.

vi ESTHER HOLT, b. 9 Dec 1781; d. at Salem, 31 Mar 1874; m. at Salem, 20 Sep 1807, DANIEL ANDREWS, b. at Salem, 23 Sep 1779 son of Nehemiah and Catherine (Seamore) Andrews; Daniel d. at Salem, 25 Dec 1820.

vii JACOB HOLT, b. 24 Aug 1783; d. 3 Feb 1784.

621) ELIZABETH HOLT (*Jacob⁴, Oliver³, Henry², Nicholas¹*), b. at Andover, 24 Jan 1747/8 daughter of Jacob and Margaret (Dolliver) Holt; d. at Chelmsford, 8 Aug 1794; m. at Andover, 28 Feb 1771, FRANCIS BOWERS, baptized at Chelmsford, 22 Jul 1744 son of Jonathan and Mary (Grimes) Bowers. Francis married second Mrs. Rachel Harwood on 6 Dec 1797.

Francis Bowers was a blacksmith in Chelmsford. After Elizabeth's death Francis sold his property (deed recorded 1 October 1795) in Chelmsford including the dwelling house, about fifty acres of land, and blacksmith shop to Cyrus Baldwin of Billerica for £200. On 13 August 1794 (deed recorded 1803), Francis conveyed one acre of his property to the Middlesex Canal for £6, this property to be used for the building of the canal.[1661] Francis's place and date of death were not found, but on 5 January 1800, Rachel Bowers was dismissed from the church in Chelmsford to the church in Greenfield.[1662]

Elizabeth Holt and Francis Bowers were parents of five children born at Chelmsford.

i FANNY BOWERS, baptized at Chelmsford, 13 Jun 1773; d. at Peterborough, NH, 18 Apr 1828; m. 1799, her third cousin once removed, STEPHEN HOLT (*Joshua⁴, Nicholas³, Nicholas², Nicholas¹*), baptized at Andover, 2 May 1773 son of Joshua and Phebe (Farnum) Holt; Stephen d. at Greenfield, NH, 26 Mar 1868. Stephen was second married to Margaret Batchelder. Fanny Bowers and Stephen Holt are Family 841.

ii FRANCIS BOWERS, b. 20 May 1775; d. at Peterborough, NH, 15 Oct 1835; m. at Andover, 23 Oct 1798, his third cousin once removed, CHLOE HOLT (*Joshua⁴, Nicholas³, Nicholas², Nicholas¹*), baptized at Andover, 4 Jun 1775 daughter of Joshua and Phebe (Farnum) Holt; Chloe d. at Peterborough, 6 Nov 1849. Francis Bowers and Chloe Holt are Family 842.

iii DAVID BOWERS, b. 13 Apr1777

iv TABITHA BOWERS, b. 24 Dec 1780; d. 14 Jan 1781.

v BENJAMIN BOWERS, b. 8 Mar 1783

622) TABITHA HOLT (*Jacob⁴, Oliver³, Henry², Nicholas¹*), b. at Andover, 19 May 1753 daughter of Jacob and Margaret (Dolliver) Holt; d. at Andover, 23 Sep 1778; m. at Andover, 16 May 1769, her third cousin, ABIEL STEVENS (*Lydia Gray Stevens⁴, Edward Gray³, Hannah Holt Gray², Nicholas¹*), b. at Andover, 24 Mar 1749/50 son of John and Lydia (Gray) Stevens; Abiel d. at Strafford, VT, 1806 (probate 31 Mar 1806). Abiel m. 2nd 7 Jan 1779, his second cousin once removed, ELIZABETH HOLT (*Nathaniel⁵, Oliver⁴, Oliver³, Henry², Nicholas¹*), b. at Andover, 14 Nov 1752 daughter of Nathaniel and Elizabeth (Stevens) Holt.

Abiel Stevens resided in Andover and all his children were born there. Later in life, he and his second wife Elizabeth relocated to Strafford, Vermont where his son Jacob had settled.

The estate of Abiel Stevens of Strafford entered probate on 31 March 1806 with Elizabeth Stevens as administratrix, but the inventory or distribution were not in the available probate records.[1663]

Tabitha Holt and Abiel Stevens were parents of four children born at Andover.

i ABIEL STEVENS, b. 10 Oct 1770; d. at East Bethany, NY, 7 Sep 1853; m. 1st about 1793, EUNICE who has not been identified; Eunice d. at Strafford, 5 May 1804. Abiel m. 2nd about 1804, MARCY HASKELL, b. 1777 daughter of Job and Isabel (Winship) Haskell; Marcy d. at East Bethany, 27 Jun 1837.

ii TABITHA STEVENS, b. 1774; d. 26 Aug 1775.

[1660] Joshua, native of Ipswich, h.____ (Holt), mate of a vessel, Capt. Patten, at the West Indies, fever, Dec. 6, 1795, a. 29 y. C. R. 4.

[1661] Massachusetts Land Records. Middlesex County, 120:4; 150:58

[1662] Massachusetts, Town and Vital Records, 1620-1988, Chelmsford church records

[1663] Ancestry.com. *Vermont, Wills and Probate Records, 1749-1999* [database on-line]. Orange County

iii JACOB STEVENS, b. 12 Mar 1776; d. at East Bethany, NY, 26 Mar 1856; m. at Strafford, VT, 17 Mar 1779, DINAH NORTON (widow of Jonathan Frary), b. about 1773 daughter of Elihu and Dinah (Snow) Norton; Dinah d. at Strafford, 16 Feb 1803. Jacob had a second marriage, but the name of his second wife has not been found.

iv NEHEMIAH STEVENS, baptized 3 May 1778

Abiel Stevens and Elizabeth Holt were parents of three children born at Andover.

i URIAH HOLT STEVENS, baptized 31 Oct 1779; d. at Strafford, VT, 17 May 1845; m. SALLY ELVINA BLAISDELL, b. about 1785 daughter of Harvey and Elizabeth (Sargent) Blaisdell;[1664] Sally d. after 1850 when she was living in Strafford.

ii DAVID STEVENS, baptized 16 Sep 1781; d. at Clymer, NY, 29 Jun 1842; m. at Strafford, 6 Dec 1804, RUTH BLAISDELL, b. 11 Jan 1785 daughter of Harvey and Elizabeth (Sargent) Blaisdell; Ruth d. at Clymer, 30 Apr 1837.

iii LEONARD STEVENS, baptized 25 Jun 1785

623) THOMAS HOLT (*Thomas[4], Oliver[3], Henry[2], Nicholas[1]*), b. at Lancaster, 1 Mar 1749 son of Thomas and Susannah (Parker) Holt; d. at Bolton, Sep 1808; m. at Bolton, Dec 1770, MARY COREY, b. about 1748;[1665] Mary d. at Bolton, 18 Jan 1803. Thomas m. 2nd 20 May 1806, ABIGAIL FLETCHER.

Thomas Holt was a blacksmith. He died at Bolton and the probate of his estate was in Bolton, but he states he is of Marlborough at the time he wrote his will.

In his will written 24 September 1807 (probate 14 September 1808), Thomas Holt bequeathed to beloved wife Abigail the lawful interest on five hundred dollars to be paid annually and all the household goods and items she brought to the marriage this to be in full of her dower and portion in the estate. In a codicil written the same day as the will, he added thirty dollars to the bequest to Abigail. Sons Thomas Holt and John Holt, both of Boston, each receives one thousand dollars. Thomas and John are responsible for purchasing gravestones for Thomas and his first wife. "Faithful and affectionate" daughter Sally receives one hundred dollars. Daughter Mary Hunt wife of Solomon Hunt receives five dollars as does daughter Lucy Saunders "wife of the late Jonathan A. Saunders." The remainder of the estate is to be divided among Thomas Holt, John Holt, Mary Hunt, and Sally Holt. Son Thomas Holt was named executor. The personal estate was valued at $2601.56 most of that in the form of notes owed to the estate.[1666]

There are five children known of Thomas Holt and Mary Corey. The dates of birth and order of birth are not known but are estimated based on age at death and year of marriage. Sons Thomas and John were merchants in Boston.

i LUCY HOLT, b. about 1771; m. JONATHAN A. SAUNDERS. Lucy was living and widowed in 1807 but nothing further is known.

ii MARY "POLLY" HOLT, b. 1772; m. at Boxborough, 2 Apr 1794,[1667] SOLOMON HUNT, b. at Tewksbury, 28 Jan 1772 son of Nathaniel and Sarah (Kittredge) Hunt.

iii SARAH HOLT, b. about 1776; Sarah was living and unmarried in 1808.

iv THOMAS HOLT, b. about 1777; d. at Boston, 30 Apr 1838; m. at Cambridge, 3 Apr 1800, HEPHZIBAH BROWN who has not been identified.

v JOHN HOLT, b. about 1779; d. at Boston, 1819 (probate 21 Jun 1819 leaving widow Sarah); m. at Boston, 22 May 1808, SARAH "SALLY" OAKMAN[1668] who has not been identified.

624) DANIEL LOVEJOY (*Mary Holt Lovejoy[4], Oliver[3], Henry[2], Nicholas[1]*), b. at Methuen, 28 May 1749 son of Daniel and Mary (Holt) Lovejoy; d. at Wilton, NH, Apr 1808 (will Mar 1808; probate May 1808); m. at Andover, 25 Jul 1770, ABIGAIL CUMMINS whose parents have not been identified; Abigail was living in 1808.

Daniel and Abigail were in Andover for the births of their first three children and were in Wilton by about 1778. Daniel was chosen deacon of the church at Wilton on 25 July 1793.[1669]

1664 The 1826 will of Harvey Blaisdell of Strafford has bequests to daughter Elvina Stevens and daughter Ruth Stevens

1665 Mary Corey's parents are not known by me, but Thomas's father had as his second wife Dinah Fowler who was the widow of Samuel Corey. One possibility is that Mary was a daughter of Samuel and Dinah Corey making Mary Thomas's stepsister.

1666 *Worcester County, MA: Probate File Papers, 1731-1881.* Online database. AmericanAncestors.org. New England Historic Genealogical Society, 2015. Case 30677

1667 The location of the marriage is unclear as the marriage intention and/or marriage is recorded at Boxborough, Chelmsford, Tyngsboro, and Tewksbury.

1668 The marriage intentions give her name as Oakman, and I think that is correct, although the marriage transcription says Oakes.

1669 Livermore, *History of the Town of Wilton*, p 440

In his will written 3 March 1808 (probate 3 May 1808), Daniel Lovejoy bequeathed to beloved wife Abigail the use and improvement of all the real estate during her natural life. Son Daniel receives one-half of the farming tools and one-third of the wearing apparel. Son Phineas receives $150 to be paid to him by son Isaac. Phineas also receives one-third of the apparel. Son Isaac receives all the stock animals, one-half of the farming tools, and will receive all the real estate at the decease of his mother. The three sons will divide the household furniture at the decease of their mother.[1670]

Daniel Lovejoy and Abigail Cummins were parents of seven children.

i HANNAH LOVEJOY, baptized at Andover, 13 Sep 1772; d. 16 Sep 1775.

ii LOIS LOVEJOY, baptized at Andover, 6 Jun 1773; d. 18 Sep 1775.

iii PHEBE LOVEJOY, baptized at Andover, 9 Jul 1775; d. 3 Jan 1777.

iv HANNAH LOVEJOY, b. at Wilton, 18 Mar 1778; nothing further known and not living at the time of her father's will.

v DANIEL LOVEJOY, b. at Wilton, 25 Apr 1779; m. at Wilton, 16 Feb 1804, his first cousin, PHEBE LOVEJOY (*Jonathan Lovejoy*[5], *Mary Holt Lovejoy*[4], *Oliver*[3], *Henry*[2], *Nicholas*[1]), b. at Amherst, NH, 22 Feb 1783 daughter of Jonathan and Tabitha (Upton) Lovejoy; Phebe d. at Nashua, NH, 4 Sep 1871.

vi PHINEAS LOVEJOY, b. at Wilton, 19 Nov 1781; m. at Landgrove, VT, 17 Sep 1807, HANNAH TUTHILL, b. at Landgrove, 7 Sep 1787 daughter of Daniel and Sarah (Brailey) Tuthill.

vii ISAAC LOVEJOY, b. at Wilton, 27 Dec 1783; m. 1st 11 Feb 1808, DORCAS PEABODY, b. at Wilton, 1784 daughter of Ephraim and Sarah (Hutchinson) Peabody; Hannah d. at Wilton, Aug 1809. Isaac m. 2nd 25 Feb 1810, Dorcas's sister, HANNAH PEABODY, b. 1786; Hannah d. at Wilton, 1812.

625) MOSES LOVEJOY (*Mary Holt Lovejoy*[4], *Oliver*[3], *Henry*[2], *Nicholas*[1]), b. at Methuen, 9 Sep 1751 son of Daniel and Mary (Holt) Lovejoy; d. at Wilton, 19 Mar 1807; m. at Andover, 25 Nov 1773, his third cousin, DORCAS HOLT (*Thomas*[4], *Thomas*[3], *Nicholas*[2], *Nicholas*[1]), b. at Andover, 19 Mar 1753 daughter of Thomas and Dorcas (Holt) Holt.

Moses and Dorcas settled in Wilton. Moses served in the Revolution in the company of Capt. Philip Putnam which saw service at Saratoga as part of the continental army.[1671]

Moses Lovejoy and Dorcas Holt were parents of six children born at Wilton.

i MOSES LOVEJOY, b. Feb 1776; died young.

ii MOSES LOVEJOY, b. 29 Mar 1778; d. at Wilton, 13 Nov 1846; m. at Mason, NH, 6 Nov 1807, NANCY TARBELL, b. at Mason, 4 Jun 1786 daughter of Samuel and Anna (Heldrick) Tarbell; Nancy d. at Mason, 16 Oct 1851.

iii DORCAS LOVEJOY, b. 30 May 1780; d. at Wilton, 8 Jul 1859. Dorcas did not marry.

iv HENRY LOVEJOY, b. 14 May 1782; d. at Weston, VT, 15 May 1848; m. 1st about 1807, BETSEY PEASE, b. at Weston, 31 Oct 1788 daughter of Augustus and Tirzah (Hall) Pease; Betsey d. at Weston, 16 Jan 1819. Henry m. 2nd 2 Dec 1819, SALLY AUSTIN, b. at Weston, 11 Jun 1798 daughter of David and Dorcas (Barker) Austin; Sally d. at Weston, 17 Jul 1868.

v EZEKIEL LOVEJOY, b. 14 Nov 1784; d. at Weston, VT, 30 Jan 1840; m. at Wilton, 15 Feb 1810, EUNICE GAGE, b. at Pelham, 7 Apr 1786 daughter of Pierce and Eunice (Eaton) Gage; Eunice d. at Weston, 7 Aug 1872.

vi HANNAH LOVEJOY, b. 22 Jun 1787; d. at Weld, ME, 5 Nov 1843; m. about 1808, her first cousin, STEPHEN HOLT (*William*[5], *Thomas*[4], *Thomas*[3], *Nicholas*[2], *Nicholas*[1]), b. at Andover, 11 Apr 1786 son of William and Elizabeth (Jones) Holt; Stephen d. at Weld, 7 Dec 1855. Stephen m. 2nd 1846, PHEBE ESTES (widow of Abijah Douglas).

626) JONATHAN LOVEJOY (*Mary Holt Lovejoy*[4], *Oliver*[3], *Henry*[2], *Nicholas*[1]), b. at Methuen, 11 Apr 1754 son of Daniel and Mary (Holt) Lovejoy; d. at Milford, NH, 3 Jun 1830; m. at Andover, 31 Jul 1777, TABITHA UPTON, b. at Reading, 26 Jul 1751 daughter of Isaac and Tabitha (-) Upton; Tabitha d. 12 Apr 1824.

Jonathan was a farmer in Milford he and Tabitha locating there in 1778[1672] just after their marriage. Jonathan and Tabitha raised their seven children in Milford.

[1670] *New Hampshire. Probate Court (Hillsborough County)*; Probate Place: *Hillsborough, New Hampshire, Probate Records volume 16, pp 34-35*

[1671] Livermore, *History of the Town of Wilton*, p 439

[1672] Ramsdell, *History of Milford*, volume 1, p 822

i TABITHA LOVEJOY, b. 15 Sep 1778; d. after 1850 when she was living in Sheffield, OH; m. 1st at Milford, 20 Mar 1806, EDMUND HARRIS whose parents have not been identified; Edmund d. in VT by 1809. Tabitha m. 2nd at Cavendish, VT, 16 Jan 1810, JONATHAN TAYLOR, b. in MA, about 1770; Jonathan d. after 1850. Tabitha and Jonathan named their eldest son Edmund Harris Taylor.

ii MARTHA "PATTY" LOVEJOY, b. 25 Dec 1780; d. at Milford, 13 Nov 1823; m. 22 May 1806, JOSEPH COLBURN, b. at Dracut, 19 Jun 1783 son of Job and Hannah (Hildreth) Colburn; Joseph d. at Milford, 14 Aug 1861.

iii PHEBE LOVEJOY, b. 22 Feb 1783; d. at Nashua, 4 Sep 1871; m. at Wilton, 16 Feb 1804, her first cousin, DANIEL LOVEJOY (*Daniel Lovejoy5, Mary Holt Lovejoy4, Oliver3, Henry2, Nicholas1*), b. at Wilton, 25 Apr 1779 son of Daniel and Abigail (Cummins) Lovejoy.

iv ISAAC UPTON LOVEJOY, b. 10 Mar 1785; d. at Milford, 13 Dec 1831; m. 1813, MARY HOWE, b. at Milford, 8 Oct 1787 daughter of Stephen and Hannah (Duncklee) Howe; Mary d. at Dunstable, 24 Jul 1855.

v CHLOE LOVEJOY, b. 8 May 1787; d. at Nashua, 9 Apr 1870. Chloe did not marry.

vi MARY "POLLY" LOVEJOY, b. 5 Aug 1789; d. at Nashua, 18 Mar 1874; m. 1st 8 Nov 1821, DANIEL GILSON, b. 1756; Daniel d. at Brookline, NH, 10 Jul 1839. Polly m. 2nd 22 Jun 1852, AMOS FLETCHER, b. at New Ipswich, about 1785; Amos d. at Hollis, 2 Nov 1853. White she was widowed, Polly and her sister Chloe lived together in Nashua.

vii JONATHAN LOVEJOY, b. 19 Mar 1793; d. at Milford, 20 Jan 1826; m. 20 Nov 1817, SARAH WILLOBY, b. at Hollis, 11 May 1794 daughter of Oliver and Sarah (Bailey) Willoby; Sarah d. at Hollis, 21 May 1886. After Jonathan's death, Sarah married Timothy Hodgman.

627) SARAH LOVEJOY (*Mary Holt Lovejoy4, Oliver3, Henry2, Nicholas1*), b. at Methuen, 5 Jun 1759 daughter of Daniel and Mary (Holt) Lovejoy; d. at Temple, NH, 19 Jun 1830; m. at Amherst, NH, 19 Apr 1781, SILAS KEYES, b. at Shrewsbury, 7 Aug 1757 son of John and Abigail (-) Keyes; Silas d. 18 Aug 1840. Silas married second Asenath Dodge on 2 Apr 1834.

Sarah and Silas were married in Amherst and their eldest child was born in Wilton. The family was then in Princeton, Massachusetts, but settled finally in Temple, New Hampshire where their youngest children were born. Silas served as church deacon and was a thythingman for several years in Temple.[1673]

In his will written 24 July 1839 (proved 1 September 1840), Silas Keyes bequeathed to beloved wife Asenath, one hundred dollars, the large bible, and the household furniture she brought to the marriage. Sons Silas, Ephraim, Jonathan, and Warren each receives three hundred dollars. The daughters each receive two dollars: Phebe wife of Moses Tyler, Joanna wife of Hubbard C. Courier, Persis wife of Azor Maynard, and Abigail wife of William R. Stacy. Grandchildren James and Joanna Howard receive one dollar each. The residue of the estate is to be divided among children and grandchildren with sons a proportion of three dollars each, daughters two dollars each, and grandchildren one dollar each.[1674] Son Jonathan Keyes of Wilton was named executor.

Sarah Lovejoy and Silas Keyes were parents of ten children.

i SARAH KEYES, b. at Wilton, 1 May 1782; d. at Temple, NH, Jun 1819. Sarah did not marry.

ii JEMIMA KEYES, b. at Princeton, MA, 16 Feb 1784; d. at Boston, 9 Jan 1834; m. at Temple, NH, 4 Jul 1820, Dr. NATHANIEL HOWARD, b. at Temple, 21 Mar 1783 son of Samuel and Elizabeth (Barrett) Howard; Nathaniel d. at Marlborough, MA, 8 Aug 1852. After Jemima's death, Nathaniel married Olive Cole.

iii SILAS KEYES, b. at Princeton, 29 Dec 1785; d. at Temple, NH, 25 Nov 1858; m. at Temple, 18 Sep 1832, REBECCA PRATT, b. at New Ipswich, NH, 16 Nov 1802 daughter of Phineas and Joanna (Bucknam) Pratt; Rebecca d. at Temple, 12 Jan 1856.

iv PHEBE KEYES, b. at Princeton, 17 Aug 1787; d. at Boston, 17 May 1846; m. at Boston, 28 Nov 1810, MOSES TYLER "of Boston".

v EPHRAIM KEYES, b. at Princeton, 21 Mar 1789; d. at Fenner, NY after 1840 and before 1850; m. about 1814, BATHSHEBA BARNES, b. in NY, about 1788; Bathsheba d. after 1860 when she was living at Hamilton, NY.

vi JONATHAN KEYES, b. at Princeton, 6 Mar 1791; d. at Wilton, 7 Apr 1864; m. at Temple, NH, 30 Sep 1819, MIRIAM TYLER, b. 23 Jan 1798 daughter of Parker and Hannah (Flint) Tyler; Miriam d. at Wilton, 17 Dec 1839.

1673 Blood, *The History of Temple, New Hampshire*

1674 There may be an error in the copy of the will into the will book as it states the residue is to be divided in the same proportions as the main legacies and the proportions are given as 3, 2, 1. The legacies are written as three hundred dollars, two dollars, and one dollar so perhaps the "hundred" was omitted in the legacies to daughters and grandchildren. *New Hampshire. Probate Court (Hillsborough County), Volume 48, pp 53-54*

vii JOANNA KEYES, b. at Northborough, MA, 7 Feb 1793; m. at Boston, 25 Jan 1828, HUBBARD C. CURRIER who was of Bow, NH. Joanna and Hubbard live in the Boston area where Hubbard was a peddler.

viii PERSIS KEYES, b. at Northborough, 15 Feb 1795; d. at Boston, 12 Nov 1882; m. at Princeton, MA, 24 May 1823, as his second wife, Capt. AZOR MAYNARD, b. at Northborough, 1787 son of Holland and Mary (Moore) Maynard; Azor d. at Cambridge, 6 Mar 1860. Azor was first married to Mary Richardson.

ix ABIGAIL KEYES, b. at Northborough, 11 May 1797; d. at Cambridge, 14 Aug 1862; m. at Boston, 20 May 1827, WILLIAM RAND STACY, b. at Boston; 1800 son of Philemon and Polly (possibly Hooper) Stacy; William d. at Boston, 13 Nov 1874.

x WARREN KEYES, b. at Northborough, 23 Jun 1799; d. at Temple, NH, 14 Sep 1876; m. at Temple, 6 Nov 1823, LUCY WHEELER CUMMINGS, b. at Temple, 16 Nov 1800 daughter of Archelaus and Polly (Edwards) Cummings; Lucy d. at Temple, 20 Jan 1893.

628) DORCAS LOVEJOY (*Mary Holt Lovejoy⁴, Oliver³, Henry², Nicholas¹*), b. at Methuen, 16 Apr 1762 daughter of Daniel and Mary (Holt) Lovejoy; d. at Andover, VT, 15 Aug 1817; m. at Wilton, 27 Oct 1785, BENJAMIN PIERCE, b. at Wilton, 18 May 1762 son of William and Hannah (-) Pierce; d. at Londonderry, VT, 9 May 1847. Benjamin married second Mrs. Abigail *Frink* Dodge on 8 Feb 1820.

Benjamin Pierce was a shoemaker by trade and he and Dorcas resided in Wilton for the first ten years of their marriage and then relocated to Andover, Vermont.

Benjamin served during the Revolution as a member of the Commander-in-Chief's Guard. He enlisted from Wilton of 27 February 1781 as a private in the company of Capt. Isaac Frye. He transferred 16 June 1783 into the Commander-in-Chief's guard commanded by Lieutenant Commandant William Colfax. He served until his discharge on 20 December 1783.[1675]

Benjamin Pierce and Dorcas Lovejoy were parents of nine children. Benjamin also had four children with his second wife.

i DORCAS PIERCE, b. at Wilton, 22 Jan 1786; d. at Londonderry, VT, 7 Sep 1853; m. THOMAS HALL, b. at Andover, VT, 5 Aug 1785 son of Henry and Abigail (Keyes) Hall; Thomas d. at Londonderry, 13 Jul 1835.

ii POLLY PIERCE, b. at Wilton, 29 Apr 1787; d. at Weston, VT, 20 Dec 1857; m. DANIEL DODGE, b. at Hancock, NH, 22 Nov 1791 son of Joseph and Molly (Ritter) Dodge; Daniel d. at Weston, 19 Sep 1842.

iii JAMES PIERCE, b. at Wilton, 17 Aug 1789; d. at Weston, 12 Apr 1813; m. 5 Dec 1811, MARY WALKER

iv ABIEL PIERCE, b. at Wilton, 21 Mar 1791; d. at Vernon, WI, 30 Nov 1871; m. 1st about 1814, his fourth cousin, NANCY HOLT (*Dorothy Gray Holt⁵, Timothy Gray⁴, Braviter Gray³, Hannah Holt Gray², Nicholas¹*), b. at Lyndeborough, about 1794 daughter of Daniel and Dorothy (Gray) Holt; Nancy d. at Andover, VT, 13 Jan 1828. Abiel m. 2nd 1829, HANNAH ROBINSON MANNING, b. at Andover, VT, 4 Sep 1792 daughter of Samuel and Amy (Gorham) Manning; Hannah d. at Waukesha, WI, 1 Jan 1878.

v ASA PIERCE, b. at Wilton, 17 Mar 1794; d. at Fort Wayne, IN, 7 Dec 1858; m. BETSEY DODGE, b. at Andover, VT, 29 Dec 1798 daughter of Joseph and Elizabeth (Putnam) Dodge; Betsey d. at Fort Wayne, 7 Feb 1882.

vi ALVA PIERCE, b. at Andover, VT, 6 Oct 1796; d. at Andover, 22 Sep 1818; m. 1817, DOLLY BAKER, b. at Nelson, NH, about 1795 daughter of Thomas and Sarah (Temple) Baker;[1676] Dolly d. at Londonderry, VT, 17 Aug 1879. Dolly married second Oliver Atwood.

vii NANCY PIERCE, b. at Andover, VT, 2 Dec 1798; d. at Lyndeborough, NH, 1 Aug 1862; m. at Londonderry, VT, 30 Dec 1830, her fourth cousin twice removed, ISAAC JEWETT (*Mary Chandler Jewett⁷, Ebenezer Chandler⁶, Thomas Chandler⁵, Mehitable Russell Chandler⁴, Phebe Johnson Russell³, Mary Holt Johnson², Nicholas¹*), b. at Nelson, NH, 18 Feb 1794 son of Isaac and Mary (Chandler) Jewett; Isaac d. at Wilton, 26 Jan 1853. Nancy m. 2nd about 1854, as the fourth of his five wives, her third cousin, DAVID PUTNAM (*David Putnam⁵, Sarah Cram Putnam⁴, Sarah Holt Cram³, Henry², Nicholas¹*), b. at Lyndeborough, 19 Jan 1790 son of David and Abigail (Carleton) Putnam; David d. at Lyndeborough, 10 Jun 1870.

viii ALANSON PIERCE, b. at Andover, VT, 27 Aug 1801; d. at Weathersfield, VT, 1851 (probate 17 Jun 1851); m. 1 May 1825, HANNAH BURTON, b. at Simonsville, VT, 13 Dec 1799 daughter of Samuel and Hannah (Putnam) Burton; Hannah d. at Weathersfield, 22 Jun 1892.

ix ABEL PIERCE, b. at Andover, VT, 1 Apr 1804; d. at Londonderry, VT, 1832; m. at Andover, 8 May 1825, HARRIET DODGE, b. at Andover, VT, 1 Aug 1808 daughter of John and Abigail (Frink) Dodge.

[1675] Godfrey, *The Commander-in-Chief's Guard, Revolutionary War*, p 225

[1676] The names of Dolly's parents are given on her death record.

629) DOROTHY LOVEJOY (*Mary Holt Lovejoy⁴, Oliver³, Henry², Nicholas¹*), b. at Andover, MA, 26 Sep 1764 daughter of Daniel and Mary (Holt) Lovejoy; d. at Andover, VT, 4 Aug 1807; m. at Wilton, NH, 5 Feb 1793, JACOB SHELDON, b. at Wilton, about 1764 son of Samuel and Sarah (Wellman) Sheldon.[1677]

Dorothy and Jacob married in Wilton but soon after were in Andover, Vermont. They settled on a farm in Andover where they remained.

Their grandson, Lawson Sheldon son of Joel, was a prominent citizen of Cass County, Nebraska where he owned 3,000 acres of land divided into ten farms. He also owned a sawmill.[1678]

Dorothy Lovejoy and Jacob Sheldon were parents of six children.

i JACOB SHELDON, b. at Nelson, NH, 19 May 1794; d. at Pittsford, VT, 5 Aug 1851; m. 1st at Pittsford, 18 Jan 1816, JOANNA HAWLEY, b. at Chittenden, VT, 2 Jul 1791 daughter of Nathan and Abigail (Churchill) Hawley; Joanna d. at Pittsford, 22 Apr 1821. Jacob m. 2nd 20 Oct 1822, LOUISA TINKHAM, b. about 1790; Louisa d. at Pittsford, 7 Aug 1859.

ii SARAH "SALLY" SHELDON, b. at Andover, VT, 22 Aug 1796; d. at Plymouth, VT, 25 Dec 1862; m. at Plymouth, VT, 5 Sep 1847, as his second wife, OLIVER WOODWARD, b. in NH, about 1782; Oliver d. after 1860.

iii JOHN SHELDON, b. at Andover, VT, 2 Dec 1798; d. at Sheldon, VT, 7 Jul 1872; m. 1st about 1822, AMY who is possibly Amy Rawson daughter of Leonard and Lydia (Hitchcock) Rawson; Amy d. at Sheldon, 21 Jun 1841. John m. 2nd about 1842, HONOR HITCHCOCK (widow of Thomas Adams), b. 12 Jul 1805 daughter of Chapman and Chrissy (Hill) Hitchcock;[1679] Honor d. at Sheldon, 10 Oct 1864. John m. 3rd at Montpelier, VT, 12 Mar 1867, MARY D. CHASE, b. about 1807; Mary was living in 1870.

iv JOSEPH SHELDON (twin), b. at Andover, VT, 2 Feb 1801. Joseph is reported as residing in White Pigeon, MI but nothing further found.[1680]

v JOEL SHELDON (twin), b. at Andover, VT, 2 Feb 1801; d. at Nehawka, NE, 19 Mar 1875; m. FIDELIA PETTIGREW, b. at Ludlow, VT, 4 May 1806 daughter of Andrew and Ruth (Ross) Pettigrew; Fidelia d. at Nehawka, 21 Feb 1896.

vi DOROTHY SHELDON, b. at Reading, VT, 19 Jan 1804; d. at Pittsford, VT, 11 Nov 1838; m. NATHAN HAWLEY CHURCHILL, b. at Chittenden, 11 Jun 1803 son of Caleb and Sarah (Hawley) Churchill; Nathan d. at Brandon, VT, 12 Jan 1884. Nathan second married Nancy Lyon.

630) WILLIAM HOLT (*William⁴, Oliver³, Henry², Nicholas¹*), b. at Lyndeborough, 23 Mar 1760 son of William and Beulah (-) Holt; m. about 1784, BETSEY SPAULDING, b. at Lyndeborough, 18 Nov 1759 daughter of Levi and Anna (Burns) Spaulding.

There are records of five children of William and Betsey Holt born at Lyndeborough.

i LEVI SPAULDING HOLT, b. 28 Nov 1784

ii BEULAH HOLT, b. 13 Jan 1787; d. at Peterborough, NH, 1 Oct 1850; m. by 1814, SETH PERKINS who has not been identified; Seth d. before 1850. This family lived in Plainfield, NY and their children were born there. The family relocated to Peterborough after Seth's death.

iii OLIVER HOLT, b. 16 May 1789; d. at Greenfield, NH, 2 Jul 1881; m. MARY REYNOLDS, b. about 1788; Mary d. at Greenfield, 18 Feb 1865.

iv BETTY HOLT (twin), b. 23 Jan 1791

v WILLIAM HOLT (twin), b. 23 Jan 1791; d. 6 Feb 1791.

631) OLIVER HOLT (*William⁴, Oliver³, Henry², Nicholas¹*), b. at Lyndeborough, about 1761 son of William and Beulah (-) Holt; d. at Lyndeborough, after 1850;[1681] m. at Lyndeborough, 31 Dec 1789, JANE KARR, b. 1768; Jane d. at Goshen, 1 Sep 1844.

Oliver Holt and Jane Karr were parents of eight children born at Lyndeborough.

i JACOB HOLT, b. 27 Aug 1790; d. 27 Sep 1790.

ii THEODORE KARR HOLT, b. 10 Jan 1792; d. at Lyndeborough, 12 Nov 1836, m. about 1815, SALLY MESSER

1677 The death date of Jacob Sheldon is uncertain. One biography of his son Joel reports that Jacob lived to be age 87. Chapman Brothers, Portrait and Biographical Album of Otoe and Cass Counties, Nebraska, part 2, p 1232

1678 Portrait and Biographical Album of Otoe and Cass Counties, Nebraska, Part II, p 1231

1679 Hitchcock, *Genealogy of the Hitchcock Family*, p 26

1680 Sheldon, The Sheldon Magazine, No. 1-4, p 96

1681 Oliver was living with his son David in Lyndeborough in 1850.

iii JANE HOLT, b. 28 Apr 1794; d. at Cambridge, MA, 8 Aug 1884; m. at Lempster, NH, 1 Dec 1814, ARRONET GUNNISON, b. at Goshen, NH, 2 Jan 1789 son of Daniel and Ruth (Richman) Gunnison; Arronet d. at Cambridge, 3 Nov 1849.

iv OLIVER HOLT, b. 30 Oct 1796; d. at Alstead, NH, 15 Dec 1876; m. HARRIET WILEY, b. 1 Aug 1799 daughter of Reuben and Sarah (Hall) Wiley; Harriet d. at Alstead, 22 Dec 1877.

v JOANNA HOLT, b. 16 Dec 1798; d. at Wilton, 6 Dec 1885; m. 6 May 1818, JOHN LEWIS, b. at Henniker, about 1795 son of John Lewis; John d. at Wilton, 25 Oct 1888.

vi PARKER HOLT, b. 6 Nov 1801; d. 21 Aug 1802.

vii DAVID HOLT, b. 9 Jun 1804; d. at Lyndeborough, 22 Oct 1884; m. 1st 20 Jan 1829, BETHIAH WILSON, b. about 1807; Bethiah d. at Lyndeborough, 5 Jan 1837. David m. 2nd 18 Jun 1837, ANN COCHRAN, b. at Antrim, 2 Mar 1802 daughter of Andrew and Jennet (Wilson) Cochran; Ann d. at Lyndeborough, 13 Apr 1870. David m. 3rd 4 Aug 1879, JULIA THOMPSON (widow of William L.S. Clark), b. in CT, Sep 1834; Julia d. after 1900 when she was living at Woonsocket, RI at the home of one of her daughters.

viii CALVIN HOLT, b. about 1806; d. after 1880 when he was living at Harrisville, OH; m. MARGARET ORDWAY, b. in NH about 1807; Margaret d. after 1880. Calvin and Margaret do not seem to have had children.

632) BENJAMIN HOLT (*William⁴, Oliver³, Henry², Nicholas¹*), b. at Lyndeborough, about 1765 son of William and Beulah (-) Holt; m. at Lyndeborough, 19 Aug 1788, BATHSHEBA BARKER, b. at Wilton, 6 Sep 1769 daughter of Daniel and Bathsheba (Blanchard) Barker.

Just three children have been identified for Benjamin Holt and Bathsheba Barker.

i HANNAH HOLT, b. at Lyndeborough, about 1792; d. at Lyndeborough, 15 Dec 1865. Hannah did not marry.

ii MARY HUSE HOLT, b. about 1801; d. at Bennington, NH, 15 Jan 1880; m. at Hancock, NH, 26 Apr 1831, JOHN COLBY, b. perhaps at Bennington, 1 Apr 1801 son of John and Eunice (Dane) Colby; John d. at Bennington, 5 Nov 1849.

iii JOHN FLETCHER HOLT, b. at Lyndeborough, 12 Nov 1807; d. at Lyndeborough, 17 Apr 1883; m. 1st Nov 1834, his third cousin once removed, ABIGAIL HARWOOD (*Rebecca Cram Harwood⁶, Jacob Cram⁵, Jonathan Cram⁴, Sarah Holt Cram³, Henry², Nicholas¹*), b. at Lyndeborough, 20 Jun 1805 daughter of Andrew and Rebecca (Cram) Harwood; Abigail d. at Lyndeborough, 29 Nov 1869. John m. 2nd at Nashua, 19 Oct 1871, MARY A. BROWN, b. at Milford, 1825 daughter of Jacob and Betty (Coburn) Brown; Mary d. at Lyndeborough, 29 Jan 1897.

633) MARY HOLT (*William⁴, Oliver³, Henry², Nicholas¹*), b. at Lyndeborough, about 1767 daughter of William and Beulah (-) Holt; m. at Lyndeborough, 9 Aug 1790, MOSES STILES, b. at Lyndeborough, 6 Jun 1765 son of Moses and Sarah (-) Stiles.

Mary and Moses were married at Lyndeborough by Rev. Sewell Goodrich. They were parents of seven children all born at Lyndeborough.[1682] The small township of Stilesville, Indiana was named for their son Jeremiah Stiles who was a pioneer there.[1683]

i WILLIAM HOLT STILES, b. at Lyndeborough, 18 Dec 1790; d. at Winhall, VT, 1870; m. LYDIA STORY, b. about 1790; Lydia d. at Winhall, Dec 1865.

ii REUBEN STILES, b. about 1792; m. *perhaps* ABIGAIL WYMAN, b. at Woburn, MA, 3 Sep 1795.

iii JEREMIAH STILES, b. at Lyndeborough, about 1795; d. at Savannah, MO; m. at Weathersfield, VT, 7 Jan 1816, SIBYL PHILBRICK, b. at Deering, NH, 11 Dec 1793 daughter of David and Jerusha (Mills) Philbrick;[1684] Sibyl d. at Stilesville, IN, 16 Jan 1827.

iv DANIEL STILES

v RHODA STILES

vi OLIVE STILES

vii JANE HOLT STILES, b. at Lyndeborough, 17 Aug 1807; d. at Jamaica, VT, 7 Apr 1872; m. ISAAC NEWTON PIKE, b. at Somerset, VT, 14 Feb 1803 son of William Grant and Myranda (Scott) Pike; Isaac d. at Jamaica, 6 May 1884.

[1682] Guild, *The Stiles Family in America*, p 484

[1683] Baker, *From Needmore to Prosperity: Hoosier Place Names in Folklore and History*, p 213

[1684] Chapman, *A Genealogy of the Philbrick and Philbrook Families*, p 95

634) JUDITH HOLT (*William⁴, Oliver³, Henry², Nicholas¹*), b. at Lyndeborough, about 1769 daughter of William and Beulah (-) Holt; d. at Northfield, VT, 28 Sep 1843; m. at Lyndeborough, 12 Nov 1793, her second cousin once removed, ABIEL CRAM (*John Cram⁵, John Cram⁴, Sarah Holt Cram³, Henry², Nicholas¹*), b. at Wilton, 28 Aug 1770 son of John and Susanna (Fuller) Cram; Abiel d. at Tunbridge, VT between 1820 and 1830.[1685]

Judith and Abiel lived in Tunbridge and just two children are known. In 1830, Judith's household consisted of herself and one female age 20-29. In the 1820 census, the household was Abiel, female over 45, a female 16-25, and one female under 10.

i SUSAN CRAM, b. about 1803; d. at Northfield, VT, 21 Jun 1838. Susan did not marry.

ii DANIEL CRAM, b. about 1807; d. at Tunbridge, 21 Jun 1870; m. HANNAH HACKETT, b. at Tunbridge, about 1808 daughter of Ephraim and Mary (Corvin) Hackett;[1686] Hannah d. at Tunbridge, 20 Nov 1889.

635) JOSEPH HOLT (*Joseph⁴, Henry³, Henry², Nicholas¹*), b. at Andover, 16 Jan 1726/7 son of Joseph and Abigail (Rich) Holt; d. at Reading, 1787 (probate 1787); m. ABIGAIL BEAN (or Bourn), b. about 1730; Abigail was living in 1787.

Joseph Holt did not leave a will and his estate entered probate 1 December 1787 with widow Abigail requesting that son Joseph be named administrator. Real estate of lands and buildings part in Reading and part in Andover were valued at £187.10.0, Daughter Sarah Holt and Esther Holt, minors over age fourteen, made choice of Benjamin Jenkins of Andover as their guardian.[1687]

Joseph Holt and Abigail Bean were parents of ten children born at Reading.

i JOSEPH HOLT, b. about 1753; d. at North Reading, 21 Mar 1821; m. at Wilmington, MA, 9 Dec 1779, MARY EATON CARTER, b. at Wilmington, 22 Apr 1756 daughter of Nathan and Martha (Jones) Carter; Mary d. at Reading, 26 Feb 1853.

ii ZERVIAH HOLT, baptized 1754

iii BENJAMIN HOLT, baptized 1755

iv LYDIA HOLT, baptized 1760; d. at Reading, 21 Aug 1822; m. at Reading, 27 May 1783, NATHANIEL EATON, b. about 1756; Nathaniel d. at Reading, 11 Mar 1823.

v ABRAHAM HOLT, baptized 19 Jun 1763

vi ABIGAIL HOLT, baptized 22 Sep 1765; d. at Charlestown, MA, 16 Jun 1851; m. at Andover, 11 May 1787, her third cousin, JACOB HOLT (*Jacob⁵, Jacob⁴, Oliver³, Henry², Nicholas¹*), b. at Andover, 11 Feb 1765 son of Jacob and Rhoda (Abbott) Holt; Jacob d. at Charlestown, 22 Sep 1800.

vii HANNAH HOLT, baptized 6 Dec 1767; d. at Andover, 13 Sep 1805;[1688] m. 1st at Reading, 2 Dec 1790, REUBEN JONES, b. 1765, son of Jacob and Mary (Winn) Jones; Reuben d. by 1798. Hannah m. 2nd Nov 1798, MICHAEL CARLTON, b. at Andover, 29 Nov 1760 son of Michael and Elizabeth (Adams) Carlton; Michael d. at Andover, 26 Mar 1838. Michael married Sarah Kimball on 15 Nov 1812.

viii ELIZABETH HOLT, baptized 8 Oct 1769

ix SARAH HOLT, baptized 11 Aug 1771; m. at Lynnfield, 11 Apr 1793, JOSEPH BROWN, b. at Reading (also recorded at Lynnfield), 11 Jul 1766 son of Joseph and Mary (Eaton) Brown.[1689]

x ESTHER HOLT, baptized 25 Sep 1773; m. at Reading, 24 Apr 1794, JOHN PERRY

636) ABIGAIL HOLT (*Joseph⁴, Henry³, Henry², Nicholas¹*), b. at Andover, 16 Jan 1726/7 daughter of Joseph and Abigail (Rich) Holt; d. at Andover, 12 Dec 1767; m. at Andover, 15 Jul 1749, OBED JOHNSON, b. at Haverhill, 30 Dec 1727 son of Cornelius and Lydia (Clement) Johnson; Obed d. at Reading, Dec 1773 (probate 20 Dec 1773). Obed was second married to Eleanor Upton but died a few months after his second marriage.

On 1 May 1763, Obed Johnson of Andover, with the consent of his wife Abigail relinquishing her right of dower to the parcel, sold 19 acres with buildings to William Goldsmith of Ipswich for £82.13.4.[1690]

1685 In the 1820 census, Abiel Cram is head of household in Tunbridge. In the 1830 census, the head of household is widow Judith Cram.

1686 The names of Hannah's parents are given as Ephraim Hackett and Mary Corvin on her death record.

1687 *Middlesex County, MA: Probate File Papers, 1648-1871.*Online database. *AmericanAncestors.org.* New England Historic Genealogical Society, 2014. Case 11786 and Case 11787

1688 Hannah, w. Michael, Sept. 13, 1805, a. 38 y.

1689 Perley, The Essex Antiquarian, volume 13, p 139

1690 Massachusetts Land Records, 1620-1986, Essex County, volume 113:31; accessed through familysearch.org

Obed Johnson did not leave a will and his estate entered probate 20 December 1773. Widow Eleanor declined administration of the moveable estate and requested that her son-in-law Obed Johnson assume this duty. The personal estate inventory was £68.2.3 and charges against the estate were £32.8.5.[1691]

Births of three children are recorded at Andover.

i OBED JOHNSON, b. at Andover, 18 Dec 1750; d. at Blue Hill, ME, 8 Oct 1841; m. about 1778, JOANNA WOOD, b. at Beverly, MA, 11 Sep 1760 daughter of Joseph and Ruth (Haskell) Wood; Joanna d. at Blue Hill, 7 Aug 1826. Obed and Joanna were parents of nine children.

ii SAMUEL JOHNSON, b. 30 Dec 1753

iii ABIGAIL JOHNSON, b. 19 Apr 1756

637) PHEBE HOLT (*Joseph[4], Henry[3], Henry[2], Nicholas[1]*), b. at Reading, 22 Jun 1731 daughter of Joseph and Abigail (Rich) Holt; d. at Reading, 3 Nov 1754; m. at Reading, about 1751, JONATHAN BATCHELDER, b. at Reading, 22 Mar 1730 son of Jonathan and Sarah (Lewis) Batchelder; Jonathan d. at Reading, 6 Oct 1817. Jonathan m. 2nd, 1755, ABIGAIL EATON (*Abigail Russell Eaton[5], Robert Russell[4], Phebe Johnson Russell[3], Mary Holt Johnson[2], Nicholas[1]*), b. at Reading, about 1736 daughter of Ebenezer and Abigail (Russell) Eaton; Abigail d. at Reading, Nov 1817.

In his will written 2 February 1795 (probate 4 November 1817), Jonathan Batchelder bequeathed to beloved wife Abigail the use of all the household stuff during her natural life, the use of a room in the house and access to the cellar, and a lengthy list of specific provisions to be provided annually by the executor. After Abigail's decease, daughter Sarah is to have one bed and the residue of the household items are to be divided among his three youngest daughters Abigail, Sarah, and Lydia. Wearing apparel is to be divided among his three sons Jonathan, Ebenezer, and John. The executor is to pay within twelve months £4 to daughters Abigail, Sarah, and Lydia and to the children of daughter Phebe deceased. The remainder of the estate goes to son John Batchelder who is also named executor.[1692]

Jonathan Batchelder were parents of three children. Phebe died giving birth to twin daughters.

i JONATHAN BATCHELDER, b. at Reading, 11 Nov 1752; d. at Mason, NH, 7 Apr 1838 (probate 2 May 1838); m. at Reading, 11 Mar 1784, MARY "POLLY" DIX, b. at Reading, 7 Aug 1758 daughter of John and Mary (-) Dix.[1693]

ii PHEBE BATCHELDER, b. at North Reading, 3 Nov 1754; d. at Blue Hill, ME, 3 Nov 1790; m. at Reading, 26 Nov 1782, her third cousin once removed, NICHOLAS HOLT (*Nicholas[4], Nicholas[3], Nicholas[2], Nicholas[1]*), b. at Andover, Feb 1756 son of Nicholas and Lois (Phelps) Holt; Nicholas d. at Blue Hill, 27 Mar 1838. Nicholas m. 2nd at Blue Hill, 13 Apr 1795, MOLLY WORMWOOD. Nicholas Holt and Phebe Batchelder are Family 820.

iii HANNAH BATCHELDER, twin of Phebe, b. 3 Nov 1754; likely died young.

Jonathan Batchelder and Abigail Eaton were parents of six children born at Reading.

i ABIGAIL BATCHELDER, b. 28 Sep 1756; m. at Reading (intention) 5 Mar 1776, DANIEL GOWING, b. at Wilmington, 5 Jul 1764 son of Daniel and Sarah (Burnett) Gowing; Daniel d. at Wilmington, 13 May 1819.

ii EBENEZER BATCHELDER, b. 27 Jun 1758; m. BETTY DIX, b. at Reading, 12 Jan 1769 son of John and Mary(-) Dix;[1694] Betty d. at Lyndeborough, NH, 11 Oct 1838.

iii JOHN BATCHELDER, b. 24 Nov 1759; died young.

iv JOHN BATCHELDER, b. about 1761; d. at North Reading, 16 Mar 1840; m. MARY EAMES, b. 29 Apr 1765 daughter of John and Hannah (Cornell) Eames; Mary d. at North Reading, 3 Apr 1845.

v SARAH BATCHELDER, b. 22 Sep 1764

vi LYDIA BATCHELDER, b. about 1766; m. TIMOTHY EATON, b. 1767 son of William and Rebecca (Flint) Eaton.

638) ELIZABETH HOLT (*Joseph[4], Henry[3], Henry[2], Nicholas[1]*), b. about 1733 daughter of Joseph and Abigail (Rich) Holt; d. at Kingston, NH, after 1774; m. 1st, about 1750, EDMUND DAMON, b. at Reading, 1728 son of Ebenezer and Elizabeth (-) Damon; Edmund d. at Reading, 23 Jun 1754. Elizabeth m. 2nd, at Reading, 22 Sep 1757, PETER ABBOTT, b. at Andover, 8 May 1734 son of Ephraim and Sarah (Crosby) Abbott; Peter d. at Kingston, 18 Apr 1774.

[1691] *Middlesex County, MA: Probate File Papers, 1648-1871.*Online database. *AmericanAncestors.org.* New England Historic Genealogical Society, 2014. Case 12740

[1692] *Middlesex County, MA: Probate File Papers, 1648-1871.*Online database. *AmericanAncestors.org.* New England Historic Genealogical Society, 2014. Case 600

[1693] The 1805 will of John Dix of Reading includes a bequest to his daughter Polly Bacheler.

[1694] The 1806 will of John Dix includes a bequest to his daughter Betty Bachelor.

Elizabeth Holt and Edmund Damon were parents of two sons born at Reading. It is not known what became of these children.

i EDMUND DAMON, b. 2 Jan 1752

ii BENJAMIN DAMON, b. 25 Nov 1753

The family of Elizabeth and Peter Abbott was beset by tragedy. Four children ranging in age from three years to seven years old died between 2 March and 6 March 1765.

Peter Abbott did not leave a will, but his estate entered probate 25 May 1774 at Kingston, New Hampshire. Widow Elizabeth declined administration of the estate. David Clifford assumed the bond for the probate. There was an inventory in 1774 and an additional inventory 29 March 1777. The debts against the estate were £150 and the value of the personal estate was £106. There is nothing in the probate papers to suggest there are heirs other than the mention of the widow. There is no settlement to heirs included in the record; there is just a list of creditors against the estate.[1695]

There are seven births recorded for this family. The two oldest, twins Peter and Edmund, were recorded at Andover. The third child is recorded at Concord, and the youngest four are recorded at Kingston, New Hampshire.

i PETER ABBOTT, b. 22 Jun 1758; d. at Chester, NH Nov 1828; m. 7 Mar 1782, PHEBE SPRATT[1696] who was "of Deerfield" but parents not located; Phebe d. at Chester 16 Feb 1846. Peter and Phebe were parents of seven children born at Rockingham

ii EDMUND ABBOTT, b. 22 Jun 1758; d. 2 Mar 1765.

iii BENJAMIN ABBOTT, b. Sep 1760; d. 4 Mar 1765.

iv DANIEL ABBOTT, b. 7 Jun 1762; d. 6 Mar 1765.

v BETTY ABBOTT, b. 7 Jun 1762; d. 4 Mar 1765.

vi EPHRAIM ABBOTT, b. 16 Dec 1764; no further record located.

vii BETTY ABBOTT, b. 15 Dec 1766; no further record located.

639) RACHEL HOLT (*Joseph⁴, Henry³, Henry², Nicholas¹*), b. about 1740 daughter of Joseph and Abigail (Rich) Holt; m. at Billerica, 9 Apr 1764, JAMES UPTON, b. 26 Mar 1733 son of William and Hannah (Felton) Upton.

Little is known of this family. The birth of one child is recorded in Reading. Rachel was living in 1773 when her father wrote his will and she is described as the wife of James Upton (rather than widow) so James is assumed to also be living in 1773. The one son that is known settled in Dublin, New Hampshire before moving on the Westminster, Vermont.

i JAMES UPTON, b. at Reading, 1 Feb 1766; d. at Westminster, VT, 21 Sep 1842; m. at Dublin, NH, 24 Jul 1788, REBECCA WHITNEY, b. about 1758 (based on age 62 at time of death); Rebecca d. at Westminster, 21 Nov 1820.[1697]

640) JOSEPH HOLT (*Benjamin⁴, Henry³, Henry², Nicholas¹*), b. at Andover, 20 Aug 1740 son of Benjamin and Lydia (Holt) Holt; d. at Andover, 15 Dec 1801; m. at Andover, 1 Jun 1762, RUTH JOHNSON, b. at Haverhill, 27 Oct 1744 daughter of Cornelius and Eleanor (Currier) Johnson;[1698] Ruth d. at Andover, 18 May 1827.[1699] She was living in 1814 when her brother James wrote his will.[1700]

Joseph and Ruth resided in Andover. Joseph is called lieutenant on his death record. He is likely the Joseph Holt of Andover who served as Sergeant in the company of Capt. Henry Abbot that marched at the alarm on 19 April 1775.[1701]

Joseph received the homestead property of his father Benjamin by deed.[1702]

1695 *New Hampshire Wills and Probate Records 1643-1982,* Probate of Peter Abbott, Rockingham, 25 May 1774, Case number 4103.

1696 Some sources give her name as Pratt, but the marriage record and the birth records for the children give her name as Phebe Spratt.

1697 Vinton's Upton Memorial suggests that James had a first wife Mary Whitney married in 1788 and second wife Rebecca unknown. However, the marriage transcription for the 1788 marriage lists the bride as Rebecca Whitney. The transcriptions for the births of each of the three children of James gives the mother's name as Rebecca.

1698 The 1774 will (probate 1796) of Cornelius Johnson of Concord, New Hampshire includes a bequest to his daughter Ruth Holt. New Hampshire Probate, Rockingham County, volume 32, pp 172-173

1699 The transcription of the death record incorrectly gives her as the widow of Henry. However, her probate record establishes she was widow of Joseph.

1700 New Hampshire Probate, Rockingham County, will of James Johnson, volume 42, p 106

1701 Massachusetts Soldiers and Sailors in the Revolutionary War, volume 8, p 193

1702 Massachusetts Land Records, Essex County, 110:159, 117:62

In his will written 9 October 1798 (probate 1 February 1802), Joseph Holt bequeathed to beloved wife Ruth all the "household stuff proper for woman's use" excepting the clock which is Henry's. She also receives two good cows and one good hog to be at her disposal. Ruth also has use of the two east lower rooms, porch, and garret over the rooms. She also has other specified access and use of the property. She also receives the use and improvement of one-third of the lands and barn. Son Henry is to provide his mother with a suitable horse and horseman to take her to meetings and to doctors and nurses while she is widow. Son Henry receives all the real estate in Andover and Wilton. Henry also receives all the personal estate. Son Abner receives one-third of the lands "for quality and quantity" lying in township number five, now called Oxford, in the county of York. Sons Joseph and Paul with have the first choice of their thirds of the lands in Oxford. Joseph also receives $150 and a good pair of three-year-old steer which he will receive at age twenty-one, and he also has the benefit of his own labor after age twenty. Son Paul receives $50 and the benefit of his own labor at age twenty-one. Daughters Ruth and Lydia each receives one dollar which completes their shares. Daughter Elinor and Hannah each receives $133.33 at age twenty-one or on the day of marriage. Son Henry is ordered to take care of Joseph's brother Benjamin "in health and sickness during the term of his natural life."[1703] Daughter Hannah is to have the comfortable privilege of living in that portion of the house reserved for Ruth while Hannah is unmarried. Ruth has use of the great bible during her life, and it then goes to Joseph. Joseph receives the firelock, bayonet, and cartridge box and Paul receives the swords. Henry is named executor. Real estate was valued at $5,685.[1704]

In her will written 15 November 1822 (probate 5 June 1827), Ruth Holt bequeathed to her grandchildren Henry Holt, Herman Holt, Eliza Holt, and Mary Holt the children of her son Henry the sum of one dollar "by reason of what they received from the estate of their late father Henry Holt deceased do not stand in need of my bounty." She releases her son-in-law Abner Abbot of Albany, Maine from a promissory note for $21.66. One dollar each was bequeathed to the following grandchildren: Ruth Williams wife of Thomas Williams of Boston, Sarah Holt wife of David Holt of Andover, Obed Abbot, Stephen Abbot, and Mary Phillips wife of Edwin Phillips of Boston. Household furniture and wearing apparel was bequeathed to her daughters to equally divide between them: Lydia Holt wife of Timothy Holt of Greenfield, New Hampshire, Eleanor Flint wife of Ephraim Flint of Albany, Maine, and Hannah Faulkner wife of John Faulkner of Andover. One-tenth part of the remainder of the estate was left to son Abner Holt of Albany. Three-tenths part is left to Job Abbot to hold in trust with interest used for the support of son Joseph Holt and his family. A further three-tenths is to be held in trust by Job Abbot for the support of son Paul Holt and his family. The remaining three-tenths was bequeathed to daughter Hannah Faulkner. Job Abbot was named executor.[1705]

Joseph Holt and Ruth Johnson were parents of twelve children born at Andover.

i HENRY HOLT, b. 20 Aug 1763; d. at Andover, 24 Feb 1821; m. 1st 22 Jun 1790, MEHITABLE BLUNT, b. at Andover, 4 Jan 1769 daughter of Isaac and Mary (Kimball) Blunt; Mehitable d. at Andover, 1 Sep 1802. Henry m. 2nd 27 Jan 1803, Mehitable's sister, ANNA BLUNT, b. 9 May 1763; Anna d. at Andover, 13 Jun 1840.

ii RUTH HOLT, b. 25 Feb 1765; d. at Albany, ME, 17 Nov 1806; m. at Andover, 29 Jan 1784, ABNER ABBOTT, b. at Andover, 29 Jan 1761 son of Stephen and Mary (Abbott) Abbott; Abner d. at Albany, 16 Sep 1833. Abner married second Dorcas J. Jason on 10 Mar 1808.

iii LYDIA HOLT, b. 18 Apr 1767; d at Peterborough, NH, 22 Nov 1825; m. at Andover, 7 Nov 1793, her second cousin once removed, TIMOTHY HOLT (*Joshua⁴, Nicholas³, Nicholas², Nicholas¹*), b. at Andover, Apr 1767 son of Joshua and Phebe (Farnum) Holt; Timothy d. at Peterborough, 22 Oct 1856. Timothy married second on 11 Mar 1830, Charity Savage. Lydia Holt and Timothy Holt are Family 838.

iv JOSEPH HOLT, b. 16 Apr 1769; d. 8 Sep 1775.

v ABNER HOLT, b. 6 Oct 1771; d. at Albany, ME, 14 Dec 1854; m. 1st 29 Mar 1795, his second cousin, ABIGAIL FLINT (*Asenath Holt Flint⁵, Ephraim⁴, Henry³, Henry², Nicholas¹*), b. at Reading, about 1772 daughter of Ebenezer and Asenath (Holt) Flint; Abigail d. 21 May 1798. Abner m. 2nd 20 Jun 1799, ELIZABETH CHANDLER, b. at Andover, 1 Jun 1777 daughter of William and Elizabeth (Chandler) Chandler; Elizabeth d. at Albany, ME, 1 Nov 1816. Abner m. 3rd 1 Feb 1819, Mrs. DELILAH PIPIN who died at Albany, 16 Jul 1821. Abner m. 4th 12 Jan 1822, ABIGAIL SHEA, b. about 1782; Abigail d. at Albany, 13 May 1856.

vi OBED HOLT, b. 25 Nov 1773; d. 8 Sep 1775.

vii HANNAH HOLT, b. 28 Sep 1775; d. 7 Jul 1778.

viii ELEANOR HOLT, b. 3 Nov 1777; d. at Albany, ME, 23 Jun 1858; m. 21 Jan 1799, her second cousin, EPHRAIM FLINT (*Asenath Holt Flint⁵, Ephraim⁴, Henry³, Henry², Nicholas¹*), b. at Reading, 4 Sep 1773 son of Ebenezer and Asenath (Holt) Flint; Ephraim d. at Albany, 13 Oct 1859.

ix JOSEPH HOLT, b. 5 Nov 1780; d. at Andover, 18 Jul 1860; m. 13 Jan 1803, LYDIA JONES, b. at Londonderry, 6 Oct 1780 daughter of Josiah and Rebecca (Jenkins) Jones; Lydia d. at Andover, 14 Jul 1858.

[1703] Joseph's brother Benjamin had been found *non compos mentis*.

[1704] *Essex County, MA: Probate File Papers, 1638-1881.*Online database. *AmericanAncestors.org.* New England Historic Genealogical Society, 2014. Case 13664

[1705] *Essex County, MA: Probate File Papers, 1638-1881.*Online database. *AmericanAncestors.org.* New England Historic Genealogical Society, 2014. Case 13686

x PAUL HOLT, b. 11 Jan 1783; d. at Lowell, MA, 15 Oct 1868; m. 12 Apr 1805, ELIZABETH "BETTY" BELL, b. at Tewksbury, 1 Nov 1784 daughter of John and Hannah (Peacock) Bell;[1706] Elizabeth d. at Lowell, 1 Oct 1867.

xi TABITHA HOLT, b. 22 May 1785; d. 12 Nov 1789.

xii HANNAH HOLT, b. 7 Apr 1787; d. at Lawrence, MA, 22 Jan 1873; m. at Andover, 14 Jun 1812, JOHN FAULKNER, b. at Andover, 7 Mar 1785 son of Abiel and Hannah (Abbott) Faulkner; John d. at Andover, 27 Jan 1823.

641) ALICE HOLT (*Benjamin⁴, Henry³, Henry², Nicholas¹*), b. at Andover, 13 Nov 1742 daughter of Benjamin and Lydia (Holt) Holt; d. at Morrisville, NY, 7 Mar 1826; m. at Andover, 3 Dec 1761, her first cousin, DANIEL HOLT (*Thomas⁴, Thomas³, Nicholas², Nicholas¹*), b. at Andover, 11 Sep 1740 son of Thomas and Hannah (Kimball) Holt.

Daniel and Alice Holt had their six children in Lunenburg, but they were then in Wilton, New Hampshire. Daniel served in the Revolution beginning in 1777 and was present at the Battle of Bennington. He was in a unit from New Hampshire that joined the Continental army in Rhode Island. He had another enlistment from Wilton on 13 July 1779 and was stationed at West Point. He had a further three-year enlistment on 27 February 1781. Following the war, Daniel and Alice moved to Packersfield (Nelson) and were there until about 1809. Their final move was to Madison County, New York.[1707]

Alice and Daniel Holt were parents of six children born at Lunenburg.

i HANNAH HOLT, b. 15 Feb 1763

ii THOMAS HOLT, b. 25 Nov 1764; d. at Morrisville, NY, 14 Mar 1847; m. at Westford, MA, 26 Jan 1785; POLLY BEVINS, b. 1762; Polly d. at Morrisville, 2 Oct 1840.

iii LYDIA HOLT, b. 29 Aug 1767

iv ENOCH HOLT, b. 15 Aug 1770

v LOIS HOLT, b. 19 Sep 1772; d. at Morrisville, NY, 28 May 1826; m. at Nelson, NH, 24 Oct 1793, ABIATHAR GATES, b. at Bolton, MA, 20 Aug 1769 son of Cyrus and Ruth (Bruce) Gates.

vi DORCAS HOLT, baptized 17 Dec 1775; d. at Hanover, NY, 7 May 1850; m. at Andover, MA, 17 Apr 1796, her fourth cousin once removed, DANIEL FARNUM (*Lydia Porter Farnum⁶, Ruth Foster Porter⁵, Lydian Farnum Foster⁴, Hannah Holt Farnum³, James², Nicholas¹*), b. at Andover, 13 Apr 1770 son of Daniel and Lydia (Porter) Farnum; Daniel d. at Hanover, NY, 25 Nov 1847.

642) BETHIAH HOLT (*Benjamin⁴, Henry³, Henry², Nicholas¹*), b. at Andover, 3 Aug 1744 daughter of Benjamin and Lydia (Holt) Holt; d. at Nelson, NH, 13 Apr 1812; m. at Andover, 20 Oct 1767, her third cousin, SOLOMON WARDWELL (*Abigail Gray Wardwell⁴, Edward Gray³, Hannah Holt Gray², Nicholas¹*),[1708] b. at Andover, 14 Jul 1743 son of Thomas and Abigail (Gray) Wardwell; Solomon d. at Nelson, 20 Sep 1825.

Solomon Wardwell was a cabinetmaker and had a shop in Andover. The family was in Andover until 1777 when Solomon purchased a farm in Hollis, and Solomon was a selectman there in 1783. The family moved on to Packersfield, which was later Nelson, in 1784. Solomon was selectman in Packersfield in 1786 and served as delegate to the Constitutional Convention in 1791.

Solomon was a member of Capt. Henry Abbot's company of Minute Men in Andover and marched on 19 April 1775, but as news of the day developed including that the British had fallen back, Wardwell and some others turned back at Bedford.[1709]

Bethiah Holt and Solomon Wardwell were parents of nine children.[1710][1711]

i SOLOMON WARDWELL, b. at Andover, 3 Feb 1768; d. at Nelson, NH, 19 Feb 1789.

ii BENJAMIN WARDWELL, b. at Andover, 6 Aug 1769; d. at Salem, 4 Jun 1832; m. at Danvers, 20 Oct 1797, SUSAN "SUKEY" HAMMOND, baptized at Danvers, 26 Nov 1780 daughter of Benjamin and Susanna (Elledge)

[1706] Elizabeth's parents are given as John and Hannah Bell on her death record.

[1707] Nelson Picnic Association, *Celebration of the Town of Nelson*, p 92

[1708] There are two Bethiah Holts near in age, one of whom married Solomon Wardwell and one who married Thomas Russell. There do not seem to be any records that clearly establish which was which, and I have chosen this arrangement: Bethiah daughter of Benjamin married Solomon Wardwell and Bethiah daughter of Ephraim Holt and Phebe Russell married Thomas Russell. It could well be the other way around.

[1709] Nelson Picnic Association, *Celebration of the Town of Nelson*, pp 148-149

[1710] Published genealogies give nine children of Bethiah Holt and Solomon Wardwell. There are two areas of conflict in records. First, there is a record for a daughter Anna born 25 July 1779 and in published genealogies this child is given as Amos. This may simply be a transcription error as there are no other records for a daughter Anna. Second, there is the record of a baptism for a daughter Chloe at Andover on 1 September 1771. As there was a son Abiel born on 25 Aug 1771, this may again just be a transcription error. There are no other records related to a daughter Chloe.

[1711] Stay, *Wardwell: A Brief Sketch of the Antecedents of Solomon Wardwell*, pp 10-11

Hammond. Benjamin m. 2nd at Salem, 1 Jun 1801, DOROTHY MOULTON. Benjamin Wardwell's estate was administered by his son-in-law Aaron Perkins whose wife Susan was the only heir to the estate.

iii ABIEL WARDWELL, b. at Andover, 25 Aug 1771; d. Jan 1821 at Charleston, SC (he was a mariner resident in Salem); m. 1st at Salem, 28 Apr 1800, HANNAH ELLEDGE, b. about 1779 daughter of Richard and Hannah (Mullett) Elledge; Hannah d. at Salem, 18 Oct 1805. Abiel m. 2nd at Salem, 20 Jan 1811, his third cousin, ESTHER ANDREWS (*Mary Holt Andrews^5, James^4, James^3, Henry^2, Nicholas^1*), b. at Boxford, 16 Dec 1777 daughter of Jacob and Mary (Holt) Andrews; Esther d. at Salem, 5 Jun 1861.

iv EZRA WARDWELL, b. at Andover, 24 Aug 1773; d. at Sullivan, NH, 3 Jun 1845; m. at Packersfield, 28 Jan 1800, LOIS WHITNEY, b. at Packersfield, 15 Mar 1781 daughter of Josiah and Anna (Scollay) Whitney; Lois d. at Sullivan, 16 Jan 1859.

v EZEKIEL WARDWELL, b. at Andover, 17 Aug 1777; d. at Baltimore, MD, 1 Jan 1803.[1712]

vi AMOS WARDWELL, b. at Hollis, 25 Jul 1779; d. at Sullivan, NH, 1 Dec 1843; m. 1st at Corinth, VT, 8 Jun 1807, LODICE CORLISS, b. 1781; d. at Sullivan, 17 Oct 1807. Amos m. 2nd at Sullivan, 6 Sep 1808, BETSEY WILDER, b. at Lancaster, MA, 22 Feb 1777 daughter of Phineas and Bridget (Bailey) Wilder; Betsey d. at Sullivan, 31 Mar 1859.

vii BETHIAH WARDWELL, b. at Hollis, 2 Feb 1782; d. at Andover, 2 Mar 1855. Bethiah did not marry. Her probate lists heirs all of whom are nieces and nephews as she was the last surviving sibling. Those nieces and nephews were Lois Beals, Suzy Buckminster, Ichabod N. Wardwell, Henry Wardwell, Granville Wardwell, Amos Wardwell, George Wardwell, Lodica Wardwell, Betsey Hubbard, William H. Wardwell, Octavia S. Wardwell, Nathaniel A. Wardwell, Harriet Sims, and Susan W. Perkins.[1713]

viii DANIEL WARDWELL, b. at Hollis, 11 Jan 1784; d. at Andover, 14 Apr 1851; m. at Andover, 24 Sep 1816, his fourth cousin, SARAH OSGOOD (*Timothy Osgood^6, Peter Osgood^5, Mary Russell Osgood^4, Phebe Johnson Russell^3, Mary Holt Johnson^2, Nicholas^1*), b. at Andover, 9 Sep 1789 daughter of Timothy and Sarah (Farnum) Osgood; Sarah d. at Andover, 8 Jun 1867. Daniel Wardwell was a physician.

ix JOEL WARDWELL, b. at Nelson, NH, 29 May 1787; d. at Andover, 8 Jan 1813. Joel was studying to be a physician at the time of his death.

643) MARY HOLT (*Benjamin^4, Henry^3, Henry^2, Nicholas^1*), b. at Andover, 19 Sep 1751 daughter of Benjamin and Lydia (Holt) Holt; m. at Andover, 13 Apr 1772, JAMES LARRABEE[1714] described as "of Lynn" *perhaps* the son of Joseph and Elizabeth (Trask) Larrabee.

There is one child known for Mary and James.

i JAMES HOLT LEATHERBEE,[1715] b. at Andover, 17 Jul 1772; d. at Boston, 6 May 1821; m. at Boston, 17 Aug 1792, RACHEL WILLIAMS, b. at Medford, 14 Sep 1766 daughter of John and Rachel (Tufts) Williams; Rachel d. at Boston, 14 Apr 1823.

644) MARTHA HOLT (*Benjamin^4, Henry^3, Henry^2, Nicholas^1*), b. at Andover, 15 Oct 1754 daughter of Benjamin and Lydia (Holt) Holt; d. at Smithville, NY, 9 Oct 1829; m. at Andover, 23 Nov 1775, JONATHAN FELT, b. at Temple, NH, 8 Apr 1753 son of Aaron and Mary (Wyatt) Felt; Jonathan d. at Packersfield (Nelson), NH, 17 Feb 1807 (probate 1807).

Martha and Jonathan settled at Packersfield, New Hampshire prior to 1775 and their twelve children were born there. Jonathan was a signer of the Association Test and also had one month of service from 28 September to 24 October 1777 in the company of Capt. James Lewis that marched to Saratoga.[1716]

In his will written 4 February 1807, Jonathan Felt notes that he made a deed to son Jonathan on 8 December last, but this was put in the hands of Samuel Griffin for one year. Jonathan wants the deed to be held by Samuel Griffin after his decease and to keep the bond that Jonathan took of Jonathan, Jr. and this is to be used for the support of his wife and his minor children. He has given sons Jonathan and Benjamin each $300 and wills that sons Joseph, Henry, and Amos receive the same when they come of age. Each of his daughters Patty, Mary, and Milla are to be set out with household furniture equal to daughters Lydia and Polly, which he estimates as $150 of value each, at their marriages. The remainder of the estate is to be divided among his sons and daughters, the sons each receive two shares and daughter one share.[1717]

[1712] This is per Stay's Wardwell genealogy

[1713] *Essex County, MA: Probate File Papers, 1638-1881.*Online database. *AmericanAncestors.org.* New England Historic Genealogical Society, 2014. Case 56330

[1714] Name is also spelled Leatherby

[1715] The spelling of the last name shifts from Larrabee used by the father to Leatherbee used by the son.

[1716] Nelson Picnic Association, *Celebration of the Town of Nelson*, p 71

[1717] *New Hampshire. Probate Court (Cheshire County), wills volume 76, pp 123-124*

i JONATHAN FELT, b. 6 Nov 1776; d. at Adams, NY, 17 Dec 1862; m. 27 Apr 1802, ABIGAIL HUNTING, b. 5 Aug 1780 daughter of Jonathan and Mary (Sawin) Hunting; Abigail d. at Adams, 21 May 1836.

ii LYDIA FELT, b. 20 Sep 1778; d. at Nelson, 4 Feb 1827; m. 12 Apr 1796, NOAH ROBBINS, b. at Temple, NH, 23 Apr 1771; Noah d. at Nelson, 1841 (probate 1841).

iii BENJAMIN FELT, b. 31 Jul 1780; d. at Granby, NY, 19 Sep 1827; m. 1st 14 Dec 1802, NANCY PETTS; Nancy d. at Granby, 1821. Benjamin m. 2nd about 1825, as her second husband, SALLY HUTCHINS, b. at Lyndon, 18 Jun 1797 daughter of John and Elizabeth (Russell) Hutchins; Sally d. at Fremont, OH, 23 Dec 1898. Sally Hutchins was first married to John Babcock and was third married to John Allen.

iv MARTHA "PATTY" FELT, b. 28 Sep 1783; d. at Cleveland, OH, 1 Mar 1863; m. at Rodman, NY, 7 Apr 1807, JOHN SEYMOUR HALE, b. at Leominster, MA, 9 Dec 1779 son of Ephraim and Hannah (Spofford) Hale; John d. at Solon, OH, 10 Feb 1852.

v POLLY FELT, b. 14 Jul 1785; d. at Newark, OH, 15 Mar 1855; m. at Nelson, NH, 12 Feb 1806, JESSE SMITH, b. 25 Feb 1784 son of Ezra and Phebe (Walcott) Smith; Jesse d. at Peru, IN, 7 Jun 1867.

vi JOSEPH FELT, b. 14 Jul 1787; d. at Peterborough, NH, 16 Oct 1874; m. at Peterborough, 5 May 1816, BETSEY NAY, b. 21 Jun 1796 daughter of John and Betsey (Puffer) Nay;[1718] Betsey d. at Peterborough, 2 Oct 1852. After Betsey's death, Joseph married Nancy who has not been identified.

vii SOLOMON FELT, b. 15 Apr 1789; d. 14 Sep 1801.

viii HENRY FELT, b. 18 Aug 1791; d. at Adams, NY, 29 Feb 1872; m. about 1820, MALINDA MORSE, b. at Adams, NY, 17 Jun 1799 daughter of Alpheus and Melinda (Thompson) Morse; Malinda d. at Lorraine, NY, 31 Oct 1888.

ix MARCY FELT, b. 6 Jul 1793; d. at Porter, NY, 9 May 1873; m. about 1814, ZIBA HENRY, b. at Stoddard, NH, 14 Mar 1791 son of Ziba and Sarah (-) Henry; Ziba d. at Porter, NY, 11 Sep 1859.

x MILLY FELT, b. 3 Sep 1795; d. 18 Aug 1814.

xi BETSY FELT, b. 27 Oct 1797; d. 24 Jan 1798.

xii AMOS FELT, b. 11 May 1799; d. 19 Mar 1812.

645) MARY HOLT (*Henry⁴, Henry³, Henry², Nicholas¹*), b. at Andover, 30 Apr 1739 daughter of Henry and Rebecca (Gray) Holt; d. at Amherst, NH, 1787; m. at Andover, 1 Nov 1757, her first cousin, DARIUS ABBOTT (*Elizabeth Gray Abbott⁴, Henry Gray³, Hannah Holt Gray², Nicholas¹*), b. at Pomfret, CT, 16 Oct 1734 son of Paul and Elizabeth (Gray) Abbott; Darius d. 1817.

Darius Abbott was born at Pomfret and married Mary Holt of Andover. Darius was a housewright and likely the builder of the historic Andover home at 142 Hidden Road. The property on which this home was built was purchased from the Holt family in 1760 and 1763 by Darius Abbott and Samuel Holt. Darius Abbott sold the homestead land with the dwelling to Jacob Jones 16 April 1776 with the deed recorded 17 March 1778.[1719]

The births of the first nine children of this family are recorded at Andover. The four youngest children were likely born at either Amherst or Hillsborough. The family went first to Amherst before finally settling at Hillsborough.[1720]

i ANNA ABBOTT, b. 31 Aug 1758; d. 14 Oct 1775.

ii HENRY ABBOTT, b. 1 Jun 1761; no further record.

iii ELIZABETH ABBOTT, b. 23 Mar 1763; according to the Holt genealogy, Elizabeth married but not known to whom; she lived in Holderness, NH.[1721]

iv HANNAH ABBOTT, b. Mar 1765; d. 11 Sep 1775.

v PAUL ABBOTT, b. 18 Mar 1767; death date not known but in NH; m. about 1795, NAOMI CARR whose origins are unknown.

vi TRYPHENA ABBOTT, b. 23 Feb 1769; d. at Putney, VT, Jun 1836; m. 2 Jun 1790, JOHN WALLACE, b. at Bedford, NH, 12 May 1764 son of John and Sarah (Woodburn) Wallace; John d. 1834 (probate 25 Nov 1834).

vii CALVIN HOLT ABBOTT, b. 15 Apr 1771; d. at Barre, VT, 14 Aug 1841; m. 10 Apr 1800, LUCY DUTTON, b. 16 May 1781 daughter of John and Elizabeth (Spaulding) Dutton; Lucy d. 15 Apr 1851.

1718 The names of Betsey's parents are given on the marriage record of Betsey and Joseph.

1719 Andover Preservation Commission, 142 Hidden Road, https://preservation.mhl.org/142-hidden-road

1720 Stearns, *Genealogical and Family History of the State of New Hampshire, volume 1*, p 360

1721 Durrie, *Genealogical History of the Holt Family*

viii LUTHER ABBOTT, b. May 1773; d. 14 Sep 1773.

ix ASA ABBOTT, b. Sep 1774; d. 12 Sep 1775.

x LUTHER ABBOTT, twin of Hannah, b. about 1778; no further record.

xi MARY ABBOTT, b. about 1780; no further record.

xii NANCY ABBOTT, b. about 1780; m. 23 Apr 1804, JOEL JONES (see Hannah below).

xiii HANNAH ABBOTT, b. 1783 (baptized 4 May 1783);[1722] d. about 1803; m. about 1800, JOEL JONES, *possibly* the son of Joel and Mary (Bishop) Jones b. at Hillsborough, 7 Aug 1783. Joel m. 2nd, Hannah's sister Nancy (see above).

646) ELIZABETH HOLT (*Henry⁴, Henry³, Henry², Nicholas¹*), b. at Andover, 8 Jun 1743 daughter of Henry and Rebecca (Gray) Holt; d. at Andover, 25 Sep 1838; m. at Andover, 31 Dec 1761, her third cousin, MOSES ABBOTT (*Hannah Holt Abbott⁴, Timothy³, James², Nicholas¹*), b. at Andover, 9 Aug 1735 son of Barachias and Hannah (Holt) Abbott; Moses d. at Andover, 23 Feb 1826.

Moses Abbot served as a Lieutenant in the French and Indian War and later held the rank of Captain in the militia. He was a yeoman, surveyor, and schoolmaster in Andover. His homestead, which was divided between his sons Noah and Enoch, became the sites of two historic homes in Andover, 6 Stinson Road and 22 Stinson Road. The home at 6 Stinson Road was nominated to the National Register of Historical Places.[1723]

The estate of Moses Abbot entered probate 18 Apr 1826. His will, written 19 March 1814, has a bequest to well-beloved wife Elizabeth who receives all the household items "proper for woman's use" to be at her own disposal. His wife and unmarried daughters also have use of and improvements of the east lower room, bedroom, and well room. The lands not bequeathed to his sons Enoch and Noah are also to be used for her support. The will includes bequests to five sons (Enoch, Noah, Moses, Henry, and Jacob) and seven daughters (Rebecca, Elizabeth, Hannah, Rhoda, Anna, Abigail, and Phebe). The bulk of the real estate goes to Enoch and Noah, although all the sons receive land bequests. Sons Moses, Henry, and Jacob also receive $300. Each of the daughters receive $150 and a cow. Moses, Noah, and Enoch are named joint executors.[1724]

Moses and Elizabeth had thirteen children whose births are recorded at Andover.

i REBECCA ABBOTT, b. 2 Jan 1763; d. at Andover, 21 Jan 1844; m. 28 Jun 1798, her fourth cousin, JOSEPH PHELPS, b. at Pomfret, 17 Oct 1756 son of Joseph and Lydia (Osgood) Phelps; Joseph d. at Andover, 12 Sep 1835. Which Joseph Phelps married Rebecca Abbott is uncertain. Charlotte Helen Abbott speculates that it was Joseph son of Joseph and Ruth (French) Phelps born in 1774 and died in 1858 (although she also proposed a Joseph Phelps born in 1750 son of Thomas, but that family went to New Hampshire). Rebecca Phelps is described as a widow at her death in 1844. Joseph Phelps born in Pomfret did die in Andover in 1835 at the age of 79 and he fits better in terms of age. The family of Joseph who was born in Pomfret had returned to Andover where Joseph's father died in 1802. In addition, Joseph Phelps (son of Joseph and Ruth) born in Tewksbury in 1774 resided in Danvers (according to his Mason membership card), and there is a Joseph Phelps in Danvers married to Eunice Gardner and having children during this same period.

ii MOSES ABBOTT, b. 30 Nov 1765; d. at Andover, 9 Mar 1859; m. 1st, 5 Feb 1799, MARTHA "PATTY" FRYE, b. at Andover, 22 Mar 1772 daughter of Benjamin and Elizabeth (Clark) Frye; Martha d. at Salem, 15 Sep 1804. Moses m. 2nd, as her second husband, PRISCILLA FLINT, b. at Reading, 1784 daughter of Daniel and Priscilla (Sawyer) Flint; Priscilla d. at Andover 5 Apr 1811. Priscilla was first married to James Nelson.

iii ELIZABETH ABBOT, b. 8 May 1768; d. at Andover, 12 Feb 1829. Elizabeth did not marry.

iv NOAH ABBOTT, b. 11 May 1770; d. at Andover, 13 Jul 1849; m. 18 Feb 1806, his second cousin, HANNAH HOLT (*Dane⁵, Timothy⁴, Timothy³, James², Nicholas¹*), b. 16 Apr 1771 daughter of Dane and Lydia (Ballard) Holt; Hannah d. 14 Jun 1862.

v HANNAH ABBOTT, b. about 1771; d. 15 Mar 1772

vi HANNAH ABBOTT, b. Apr 1772; d. at Andover, 13 Apr 1840. Hannah did not marry.

vii ENOCH ABBOTT, b. 8 Apr 1774; d. at Andover, 26 Sep 1842; m. 4 Jul 1799, NANCY FLINT, b. at Danvers, 19 Sep 1777 daughter of Samuel and Ede (Upton) Flint;[1725] Nancy d. at Andover 1 Feb 1851.

viii RHODA ABBOTT, 8 Sep 1776; d. at Andover, 6 Feb 1850. Rhoda did not marry.

[1722] Historical Society of Amherst, Transcriptions of Baptisms of Children from Volume I of the Congregational Church of Amherst, New Hampshire, http://www.hsanh.org/Baptisms%202.htm

[1723] Andover Historic Preservation, 6 Stinson Road, retrieved from https://preservation.mhl.org/6-stinson-road

[1724] *Essex County, MA: Probate File Papers, 1638-1881. Probate of Moses Abbott, 18 Apr 1826, Case number 99*

[1725] The 1812 will of Ede Upton Flint Dane includes a bequest to her daughter Nancy Abbott.

ix ANNA ABBOTT, b. 8 Sep 1776; d. at Andover, 27 Jul 1834. Anna did not marry.

x HENRY ABBOTT, b. 22 Sep 1778; d. at Andover, 22 Sep 1845; m. 23 Sep 1803, his third cousin, DORCAS HOLT (*David*[5], *David*[4], *Oliver*[3], *Henry*[2], *Nicholas*[1]), b. 20 Nov 1781 daughter of David and Rebecca (Osgood) Holt; Dorcas d. 24 Mar 1842.

xi JACOB ABBOTT, b. 30 Jun 1781; d. at Andover, 12 May 1836; m. 1 Jan 1808, BETSEY BULLARD, b. at Needham, 12 Sep 1782 daughter of Nathaniel and Sarah (Saunders) Bullard; Betsey d. 28 Jul 1858.

xii ABIGAIL ABBOTT, b. 22 Dec 1783; d. 9 Aug 1827; m. 21 Dec 1811, JONATHAN PHELPS, b. at Tewksbury, 1 Sep 1780 son of Joseph and Ruth (French) Phelps;[1726] Jonathan d. at Andover, 1 Mar 1866.

xiii PHEBE ABBOTT, b. Mar 1786; d. at Andover, 6 Aug 1864. Phebe did not marry. Her estate entered probate 11 Oct 1864. The estate was valued at $500 real property and $10 personal property. Her will includes bequests to the following persons: brother Moses Abbot, Eliza Moore wife of Richard Moore, Jonathan Edwin Phelps, Eliza H. Phelps, Belinda Jane Phelps, Hannah H. Phelps, and George Herbert Gutterson. George Gutterson is named executor.[1727]

647) SAMUEL PEABODY (*Sarah Holt Peabody*[4], *Henry*[3], *Henry*[2], *Nicholas*[1]), b. at Andover, 1 Sep 1741 son of Moses and Sarah (Holt) Peabody; d. at Mont Vernon, NH, 6 Aug 1814; m. at Reading, 26 Sep 1765, ELIZABETH WILKINS, baptized at Middleton, 1743 daughter of Joseph and Abigail (Burtt) Wilkins.

Samuel and Elizabeth were parents of nine children who were likely all born at Andover where most of the children were baptized, several of them on the same date of 12 Oct 1777, so the year of birth for some of the children is an estimate. The family was then in Mont Vernon, New Hampshire about 1785.[1728]

i MOSES PEABODY, b. about 1765 and baptized 12 Oct 1777; d. at Mont Vernon, NH, Nov 1842 (probate 6 Dec 1842); m. 25 May 1786, his first cousin, SARAH HOLT (*Ebenezer*[5], *Ebenezer*[4], *Samuel*[3], *Samuel*[2], *Nicholas*[1]), b. at Amherst, NH, 1757 daughter of Ebenezer and Lydia (Peabody) Holt; Sarah d. at Mont Vernon, 25 May 1845. Moses and Sarah do not seem to have had children, or at least no children who survived childhood. In his will, Moses mentions only his wife Sarah.

ii SAMUEL PEABODY, b. about 1769 and baptized 12 Oct 1777; d. at Boxford, MA, 7 Jun 1824; m. 11 Jun 1790, HULDAH STILES, baptized at Boxford, 8 Apr 1759 daughter of John and Hannah (Deney) Stiles; Huldah, d. 23 Sep 1819. Huldah's father John Stiles was first married to Hannah Holt daughter of Oliver and Susannah (Wright) Holt.

iii JOSEPH PEABODY, b. 30 Oct 1770; d. at Middleton, 6 Nov 1853; m. 1st 4 Sep 1800, OLIVE BERRY who d. 5 Oct 1803. Joseph m. 2nd 22 Oct 1805, ANNA FLINT, b. Jun 1780 daughter of Jeremiah and Sarah (Elliot) Flint; Anna d. at Middleton, 19 Dec 1852.

iv JOHN STILES PEABODY, b. 15 Aug 1775; d. at New Boston, NH, 1 May 1832; m. 1st about 1795, MARY BARRETT, b. about 1779 daughter of Jonathan and Abigail (Raymond) Barrett; Mary d. about 1798. John m. 2nd at Amherst, NH, 25 Sep 1799, MARY HOLT, *perhaps* his fourth cousin, b. at Amherst, 11 Dec 1775 daughter of Ezekiel and Mary (Stewart) Holt.

v AARON PEABODY, baptized 12 Oct 1777; d. at Mont Vernon, NH, 1854;[1729] m. at Amherst, 7 Sep 1802, EDITH WILKINS,[1730] b. about 1783; Edith d. at the poor house in Mont Vernon in 1863. Aaron and Edith did not have children. In 1850 and 1860, Edith is listed at the poor house in Mont Vernon. Aaron is not listed there in 1850 and it is not known where he was living.

vi JACOB PEABODY baptized 25 Jun 1780; d. after 1850 when he was living in New Boston, NH; m. SARAH WILKINS, b. about 1784; Sarah d. after 1850.

vii HENRY PEABODY, baptized at Andover 27 May 1781

viii SARAH PEABODY, b. about 1782; d. at Marshfield, VT, 2 Mar 1862; m. at Mont Vernon, 29 Feb 1804, DANIEL DAMON, b. about 1777; Daniel d. at Plainfield, VT, 11 Mar 1825.

ix JOEL PEABODY, b. 23 May 1785; d. at Danvers, MA, 17 May 1829; m. 8 Feb 1807, ELIZABETH WILKINS, b. at Middleton, MA, 21 Mar 1782 daughter of Benjamin and Hannah (Upton) Wilkins; Elizabeth d. at Middleton, 1 Sep 1871.

[1726] The death record of Jonathan Phelps lists parents Joseph and Ruth. Ancestry.com. *Massachusetts, Town and Vital Records, 1620-1988*

[1727] *Essex County, MA: Probate File Papers, 1638-1881. Probate of Phebe Abbott, 11 Oct 1864, Case number 30887.*

[1728] Smith, *History of Mont Vernon*, p 121

[1729] This is the year of death reported in the *History of Mont Vernon*

[1730] The marriage transcription gives her name as Judith Wilkins, but she is Edith in census records.

648) PHEBE HOLT (*Ephraim⁴, Henry³, Henry², Nicholas¹*), b. at Andover, Apr 1735 daughter of Ephraim and Phebe (Russell) Holt; m. at Andover, 11 Sep 1755, JAMES HOUGHTON, b. at Pomfret, 13 Sep 1728 son of Edward and Abigail (Coy) Houghton.

Phebe and James started their family in Andover but were soon after in Union, Connecticut where seven of their eight children were born. The family with one of the sons and the five daughters moved on the Dublin, New Hampshire where they were by 1781.[1731] Son James remained in Connecticut but came to Dublin about five years after his father. Son Silvanus remained in Connecticut. Two of the children relocated to Bethel, Maine after marriage and some of the children returned to Connecticut where they married and settled.

i JAMES HOUGHTON, b. at Andover, MA, 16 Jun 1756; d. at Weld, ME, 21 Dec 1835;[1732] m. at Wilton, 23 Aug 1787, his first cousin, HANNAH RUSSELL (*Thomas Russell⁵, Joseph Russell⁴, Phebe Johnson Russell³, Mary Holt Johnson², Nicholas¹*), b. at Andover, 23 Sep 1767 daughter of Thomas and Bethiah (Holt) Russell; Phebe d. at Weld, Nov 1850.

ii EPHRAIM HOUGHTON, b. at Union, 18 May 1759; d. at Woodstock, CT, 6 May 1840; m 1st at Thompson, ABIGAIL "NABBY" HOLBROOK, b. at Woodstock, 26 Apr 1770 daughter of Thomas and Abigail (Adams) Holbrook; Nabby d. at Woodstock, 23 Sep 1815. Ephraim m. 2nd Mar 1817,[1733] MARY "POLLY" NICHOLS (widow of Benjamin Skinner), b. at Thompson, 3 May 1773 daughter of Jonathan and Mary (Sibley) Nichols; Polly d. at Woodstock, 4 Aug 1855.

iii PHEBE HOUGHTON, b. at Union, 11 Aug 1762; d. at Thompson, 25 Feb 1800; m. at Thompson, 6 Jan 1789, EBENEZER ORMSBEE, b. at Killingly, 17 Mar 1764 son of Thomas and Hannah (Carpenter) Ormsbee; Ebenezer d. at Thomson, 1806 (probate 1806 with widow Experience). Ebenezer married second Phebe's sister Experience (see below).

iv SILVANUS HOUGHTON, b. at Union, 21 Jun 1765; d. at Thompson, 7 Feb 1816; m. at Thompson, 15 Jan 1795, BETSEY HOLBROOK, b. at Woodstock, 24 Oct 1774 daughter of Thomas and Abigail (Adams) Holbrook; Betsey d. at Thompson, 27 Sep 1820.

v ORINDA HOUGHTON, b. at Union, 14 Feb 1768; d. at Wilton, ME, 9 May 1843; m. at Dublin, NH, about 1790, BENJAMIN LEARNED, b. at Dublin, 23 Sep 1767 son of Benjamin and Elizabeth (Wilson) Learned; Benjamin d. at Wilton, ME, 16 Sep 1853. After Orinda's death, Benjamin married widow Jane Hardy.

vi BETHIAH HOUGHTON, b. at Union, 8 Mar 1771; d. at Gilead, ME, 21 Apr 1846; m. at Dublin, 16 Jan 1789, JOHN MASON, b. at Dublin, 8 May 1769 son of Moses and Lydia (Knapp) Mason; John d. at Gilead, 19 Sep 1844.

vii ASENATH HOUGHTON, b. at Union, CT, 29 Nov 1775; d. at Thompson, CT, 30 Dec 1860; m. about 1796, WILLIAM JORDAN, b. at Dudley, MA, 5 Dec 1774 son of William and Comfort (Palmer) Jordan; William d. at Thompson, 27 Jun 1849 (probate 1849 with widow Asenath).

viii EXPERIENCE HOUGHTON, b. at Union, 8 Feb 1777; m. about 1801, EBENEZER ORMSBEE who was first married to her sister Phebe (see above). Experience was living in Thompson in 1810 but nothing is known after that.

649) EPHRAIM HOLT (*Ephraim⁴, Henry³, Henry², Nicholas¹*), b. at Andover, Jan 1736/7 son of Ephraim and Phebe (Russell) Holt; d. at Holden, MA, 25 May 1816;[1734] m. at Boxford, 7 Jan 1762, SARAH BLACK, baptized at Boxford, 24 Jul 1743 daughter of Daniel and Sarah (Symonds) Black.[1735]

On 13 May 1799, Ephraim Holt and Sarah his wife in her right, and all the other of Sarah's siblings, quitclaimed to John Black rights in property left by the will of Sarah's father Daniel Black.[1736]

Ephraim and Sarah were parents of eight children born at Holden.

i EPHRAIM HOLT, b. 3 Dec 1762; d. at Hubbardston, 3 Jun 1844; m. at Middleton, 24 Feb 1795, JERUSHA "RUSHA" KENNEY, b. at Middleton, 5 May 1769 daughter of Simeon and Jerusha (Johnson) Kenney; Jerusha d. at Grafton, MA, 2 Nov 1857.

[1731] Leonard, *History of Dublin, NH*, p 179 and p 630

[1732] Abstract of Graves of Revolutionary Patriots; Volume: 2

[1733] U.S., Revolutionary War Pension and Bounty-Land Warrant Application Files, 1800-1900; Case W2550, widow's pension application of Mary Houghton

[1734] U.S., Newspaper Extractions from the Northeast, 1704-1930

[1735] Perley, *Essex Antiquarian*, volume 9, p 187

[1736] Massachusetts Land Records, Worcester County, 165:40

ii SARAH HOLT, b. 23 Aug 1764; d. at Holden, Jul 1859; m. at Holden, 29 Mar 1792, ISRAEL DAVIS, b. at Holden, 29 Oct 1766 son of Israel and Rebecca (Hubbard) Davis; Israel d. at Hubbardston, 24 Aug 1848.

iii SAMUEL HOLT, b. 2 Oct 1767

iv PHEBE HOLT, b. 30 Mar 1770; d. 3 Jun 1773.

v DANIEL HOLT, b. 20 Jan 1774; d. 3 Apr 1774.

vi DANIEL HOLT, b. 27 Mar 1775

vii JOHN HOLT, b. 22 Jan 1777; d. at Troy, NH, 1 Apr 1836; m. at Holden, 24 Nov 1803, HANNAH WRIGHT, b. at Holden, 29 Apr 1781 daughter of Judah and Tabitha (Hartwell) Wright; Hannah d. at West Boylston, MA, 8 Jan 1857.

viii PHEBE HOLT, b. 28 Jun 1779; d. at Keene, NH, 11 Apr 1867; m. at Holden, 20 Jan 1803, ZALMON HOW, b. at Winchendon, MA, 23 Feb 1775 son of Jotham and Dorothy (Smith) How; Zalmon d. at Fitzwilliam, NH, 1855.

650) ASENATH HOLT (*Ephraim⁴, Henry³, Henry², Nicholas¹*), b. at Andover, 31 Mar 1743 daughter of Ephraim and Phebe (Russell) Holt; d. at Reading, 8 Nov 1785; m. at Reading, 7 Jun 1764, EBENEZER FLINT, b. at Reading, 17 Jun 1742 son of Ebenezer and Abigail (Sawyer) Flint; Ebenezer d. at Wilton, 29 Apr 1829. After Asenath's death, Ebenezer married Mary Damon (widow Mrs. Taylor) on 29 Nov 1789.

Ebenezer Flint, Jr. was a member of the company of Capt. John Flint that marched at the alarm on 19 April 1775. He was also listed on 15 May 1775 in the 3rd Reading company commanded by Capt. Flint.[1737]

Ebenezer Flint and Asenath Holt were parents of nine children born at Reading.

i EBENEZER FLINT, b. 13 May 1765; d. at Hillsborough, NH, 14 Mar 1833; m. at Andover, 14 Mar 1793, his third cousin once removed, DORCAS LUFKIN (*Mehitable Holt Lufkin⁵, Thomas⁴, Thomas³, Nicholas², Nicholas¹*), b. at Andover, 1776 (baptized 23 May 1779) daughter of Samuel and Mehitable (Holt) Lufkin); Dorcas d. at Hillsborough, 26 Apr 1848.

ii DANIEL FLINT, b. 27 Mar 1767; d. at Hillsborough, 27 Jun 1853; m. at Andover, 28 Jan 1795, his fourth cousin (through Abbott lines) LYDIA SHATTUCK, b. at Andover, 27 Apr 1765 daughter of Joseph and Anna (Johnson) Shattuck; Lydia d. at Hillsborough, 1 Apr 1843.

iii ASENATH FLINT, b. 4 Mar 1769; d. at Temple, NH, 8 Dec 1817; m. 21 Mar 1792, EDWARD PRATT, b. at Reading, 25 Apr 1765 son of Daniel and Abigail (Humphrey) Pratt; Edward d. at Temple, 17 Nov 1829. Edward married second Hannah Emerson in 1819.

iv ABIGAIL FLINT, b. 30 Jun 1771; d. 21 May 1798; m. 29 Mar 1795, her second cousin, ABNER HOLT (*Joseph⁵, Benjamin⁴, Henry³, Henry², Nicholas¹*), b. at Andover, 6 Oct 1771 son of Joseph and Ruth (Johnson) Holt; Abner d. at Albany, ME, 14 Dec 1854. Abner had three further marriages.

v EPHRAIM FLINT, b. 4 Sep 1773; d. at Albany, ME, 13 Oct 1859; m. 21 Jan 1799, his second cousin, ELEANOR HOLT (*Joseph⁵, Benjamin⁴, Henry³, Henry², Nicholas¹*), b. at Andover, 3 Nov 1777 daughter of Joseph and Ruth (Johnson) Holt; Eleanor d. at Albany, 23 Jun 1858.

vi JOHN FLINT, b. 4 Apr 1776; d. 4 Sep 1778.

vii AMOS FLINT, b. 16 Apr 1778; d. at Francestown, 27 Apr 1873; m. 3 Feb 1803, ABIGAIL MORSE, b. at Francestown, 1 Aug 1787 daughter of Timothy and Abigail (Dean) Morse; Abigail d. at Francestown, 1 Mar 1885.

viii JOHN FLINT, b. 23 Feb 1780; d. at Wilton, NH, 30 May 1847; m. 13 Feb 1803, his fourth cousin once removed, SARAH FLINT (*Levi Flint⁶, Joanna Farnum Flint⁵, James Farnum⁴, John Farnum³, Elizabeth Holt Farnum², Nicholas¹*), b. at Reading, 25 Nov 1783 daughter of Levi and Sarah (Parker) Flint; Sarah d. at Wilton, 6 Oct 1863.

ix PHEBE FLINT, b. 4 May 1782; d. 30 May 1797.

651) MARSTIN HOLT (*Ephraim⁴, Henry³, Henry², Nicholas¹*), b. at Andover, 13 Aug 1747 son of Ephraim and Phebe (Russell) Holt; m. at Holden, 13 Feb 1772, ABIGAIL WHEELER, b. at Holden, 20 Sep 1746 daughter of Moses and Abigail (Godin) Wheeler.

Marstin and Abigail had three children in Holden, Massachusetts and relocated to Dublin, New Hampshire 2 February 1779[1738] where their two youngest children were born. Abigail seems to have died before 1800 as in 1800, Marstin and

[1737] Massachusetts Soldiers and Sailors in the Revolution, volume 5, p 792

[1738] Leonard, *The History of Dublin*, p 795

his two daughters seem to be in Barre, Vermont.[1739] Marstin does not appear on the census records after that. Daughter Abigail married in nearby Berlin, Vermont in 1810 and daughter Phebe lived single in Berlin where she was in 1860.[1740] Phebe was living alone and head of household in Berlin in 1840. She worked as a washerwoman.

i MOSES HOLT, b. at Holden, 4 Dec 1772; d. at Boston, 25 Apr 1823; m. 31 Mar 1796, AZUBA HUBBARD, b. at Holden, 13 Aug 1776 daughter of Elisha and Mercy (Hubbard) Hubbard; Azuba d. at Hubbardston, 9 Apr 1857.

ii AMOS SHELDON HOLT, b. at Holden, 17 Jul 1774; d. at Holden, 7 Apr 1855; m. 1st at Princeton, 29 Dec 1794, SALLY WOOLEY, b. at Princeton, 16 Dec 1774 daughter of David and Sarah (Porter) Wooley; Sally d. at Holden, 14 Dec 1814. Amos m. 2nd at Ashburnham, 4 Oct 1818, SALLY LINDAL, b. at Pepperell, 24 Nov 1794 daughter of James and Abigail (Collins) Lindal; Sally d. at Holden, 1838.

iii AARON HOLT, b. at Holden, 7 Oct 1776; d. at Troy, NH, 21 Oct 1826 after being kicked by a horse; m. at Holden, 28 Nov 1799, DOROTHY HOW, b. at Holden, 13 Sep 1780 daughter of Jotham and Dorothy (Smith) How; Dorothy d. at Holden, 21 Jul 1873. Dorothy married second John Hall on 22 Nov 1849.

iv ABIGAIL HOLT, b. at Dublin, NH, 2 Nov 1782; m. at Berlin, VT, 14 Jun 1810, MOSES BATCHELDER whose parents have not been identified. Moses d. at Dunham, Québec, Oct 1843.[1741] In the 1825 census Canada, there were twelve persons living in the household.[1742]

v PHEBE HOLT, b. at Dublin, NH, 13 Feb 1785; d. at Berlin, VT, after 1860. Phebe did not marry.

652) KETURAH STEWART (*Keturah Holt Stewart⁴, Henry³, Henry², Nicholas¹*), baptized at Andover, 16 Sep 1744 daughter of John and Keturah (Holt) Stewart; m. about 1773, AMOS GREEN, b. at Reading, 16 May 1740 son of Thomas and Mary (Green) Green.

Amos Green was a joiner and farmer. Amos settled in the west part of Amherst, New Hampshire about 1770.[1743] Keturah and Amos had seven children there.

i HANNAH GREEN, b. at Amherst, 27 Sep 1773; d. at Amherst, Aug 1801; m. at Amherst, 3 Sep 1797, AMOS UPHAM, b. at Amherst, 15 Oct 1771 son of Phineas and Ruth (Green) Upham; Amos d. at Amherst, 24 Nov 1826.

ii AMOS GREEN, b. at Amherst, 22 Nov 1776; d. at Amherst, 1 Feb 1860; m. RUTH HASTINGS, b. 26 Mar 1787 daughter of William and Dorothy (Stearns) Hastings;[1744] Ruth d. at Amherst, 22 Apr 1847.

iii NATHAN GREEN, b. at Amherst, 15 Jul 1778; d. at Littleton, MA, 15 Jan 1857; m. at Mont Vernon, 10 Mar 1812, HANNAH TROW, b. at Mont Vernon, 1786 daughter of Joseph and Martha (Dodge) Trow;[1745] Hannah d. at Boston, 8 Sep 1863. At the time of his marriage, Nathan was a resident of Barre, VT and later was in Plattsburg, NY.

iv MARY "POLLY" GREEN, b. at Amherst, 23 Aug 1781; d. at Barre, VT, 6 Jun 1865; m. at Amherst, 28 Nov 1799, WILLIAM BRADFORD, b. at Amherst, about 1780 son of William and Hannah (Hopkins) Bradford; William d. at Barre, 3 Mar 1866.

v ELIZABETH "BETSEY" GREEN, b. at Amherst, 15 Oct 1783; d. at Mont Vernon, 18 Dec 1868; m. at Amherst, 17 Mar 1806, LUTHER ODELL, b. at Amherst, 9 Sep 1785 son of William and Susannah (Lovejoy) Odell; Luther d. at Amherst, 6 Jul 1862.

vi SUSANNAH GREEN, b. at Amherst, 10 Oct 1786; m. 1st JOSEPH ROBINSON. Susannah m. 2nd Mr. Myatt who has not been identified.

vii MARTHA "PATTY" GREEN, b. at Amherst, 23 Jun 1788

653) WILLIAM STEWART (*Keturah Holt Stewart⁴, Henry³, Henry², Nicholas¹*), baptized at Andover, 9 Aug 1747 son of John and Keturah (Holt) Stewart; d. at Londonderry, VT, 12 May 1837; m. SARAH KIMBALL,[1746] b. 1752; Sarah d. at Londonderry, 28 Feb 1828.

1739 Year: 1800; Census Place: Barre, Orange, Vermont; Series: M32; Roll: 51; Page: 483; Image: 273; Family History Library Film: 218688; household on one male 45 and over, one female 10 to 15, and one female 26 to 44.

1740 Year: 1860; Census Place: Berlin, Washington, Vermont; Roll: M653_1324; Page: 706; Family History Library Film: 805324

1741 Institut Généalogique Drouin; Montreal, Quebec, Canada; Drouin Collection; Author: Gabriel Drouin, comp.

1742 1825 Census of Lower Canada

1743 Secomb, *History of the Town of Amherst*, p 609

1744 The 1832 will of William Hastings includes a bequest to daughter Ruth Green wife of Amos Green.

1745 The names of Hannah's parents are given as Joseph and Martha on her death record.

1746 Sarah's last name is given as Kimball on the death record of her son Robert Stewart (1793-1865).

William was a carpenter by trade. The family was first in Amherst, New Hampshire and later in Londonderry, Vermont. During the Revolution, he enlisted in April 1776 and served nine months in Col. Gilman's regiment of the New Hampshire line. He applied for a pension based on his service. In a statement made on 20 June 1820, William reported that he had no land or personal property except a set of carpenter's tools and household furniture for upholding life. His household consisted of his wife age 66 and two daughters and a son who depended on him. Daughter Betsy Wyman aged 39 years "is delirious", Hannah Stewart aged 28 years is of "feeble constitution", and Hiram Steward age 11 years old fell from the barn and broke his thigh.[1747][1748]

There are three children known for William and Sarah, although there may well be others.

i ELIZABETH "BETSEY' STEWART, b. at Amherst, about 1781; d. at Londonderry, VT, 7 Jan 1868; m. about 1800, Capt. NATHAN WYMAN who seems to be the Nathan b. 1775 son of Timothy and Elizabeth (Shattuck) Wyman and who d. at Jamaica, VT in 1854. If so (and it seems likely as the Nathan who died in 1854 is also Capt. Nathan Wyman), that would mean that Betsey and Nathan divorced by about 1820. Betsey was living in her father's household in 1820 and in the home of her son Nathan in 1850 and 1860. Capt. Nathan was with another wife Patty in 1850.

ii HANNAH STEWART, b. about 1783; d. at Londonderry, 4 Mar 1852. Hannah did not marry but *perhaps* had an out-of-wedlock child, Hiram, who was born in Londonderry in 1808 and who died in 1888. Hiram Stewart married Mehitable How.

iii ROBERT STEWART, b. about 1793; d. at Londonderry, 24 May 1865; m. MARY MASON, b. about 1805; Mary d. at Londonderry, 26 May 1842.

654) SIMPSON STEWART (*Keturah Holt Stewart⁴, Henry³, Henry², Nicholas¹*), baptized at Andover, 5 Feb 1749 son of John and Keturah (Holt) Stewart; d. at Berlin, VT, 13 Jun 1841; m. about 1774, HANNAH,[1749] b. about 1752 who has not been clearly identified; Hannah d. at Berlin, VT, 13 Jan 1813.

Simpson and Hannah were first in Amherst, New Hampshire and relocated to Jaffrey about 1780, and the family made a final move to Berlin, Vermont about 1795.[1750] In 1950, the house built by Simpson Stewart was the oldest building standing in Berlin, Vermont.[1751]

During the Revolution, Simpson served two terms of enlistment in the regiment of Col. Moses Nichols. He was at the Battle of Bennington.[1752]

Simpson and Hannah Stewart were parents of eleven children.

i JOHN STEWART, b. at Amherst, NH, 10 Apr 1774; d. at Berlin, VT, 27 Sep 1847; m. 11 May 1806, TAMOR HUBBARD, b. at Putney, VT, 21 Sep 1781 daughter of Elisha and Tamor (Moore) Hubbard; Tamor d. at Berlin, 3 May 1860.

ii SIMPSON STEWART, b. at Amherst, NH, 11 Feb 1776; m. Phebe who has not been identified.

iii HANNAH STEWART, b. at Amherst, NH, 31 Aug 1778; m. at Berlin, VT, 20 Aug 1797, JOHN BLACK, b. at Holden, MA, 11 Sep 1770 son of John and Hannah (Davis) Black.

iv EPHRAIM HOLT STEWART, b. 2 Jan 1781; d. 7 Nov 1783.

v WILLIAM H. STEWART, b. at Jaffrey, NH, 17 May 1783; d. at Kingsbury, NY, 1 Jul 1878; m. about 1805, REBECCA VAUGHAN, b. about 1791; Rebecca d. at Hudson Falls, NY, 29 Jun 1836.

vi EPHRAIM HOLT STEWART, b. at Jaffrey, 13 Apr 1785; m. at Kingsbury, NY, about 1815, CHARLOTTE MIX, b. about 1791; Charlotte d. at London, MI, Oct 1880.

vii ELIZABETH STEWART, b. at Jaffrey, 5 Jan 1788

viii LUTHER STEWART, b. at Jaffrey, 6 Jan 1790

ix SARAH STEWART, b. at Berlin, about 1791; m. Mr. Reynolds who has not been identified.

x MARY STEWART, b. at Berlin, about 1793; d. at Berlin, 24 May 1814.

xi TERZIAH STEWART, b. at Berlin, VT, about 1795; d. at Berlin, about 1825.

[1747] Although Hiram is described as a son, it is more likely that he is a grandson.

[1748] U. S., Revolutionary War Pension and Bounty-Land Warrant Application Files, Case S41150

[1749] Hannah's name is variously reported as Hannah Rollins or Hannah Delano but no record of a marriage for Simpson and Hannah has been located.

[1750] Edson, *Stewart Clan Magazine*, p 192

[1751] Nye, *Early History of Berlin, Vermont*, p 83

[1752] Edson, *Stewart Clan Magazine*, p 192

655) HENRY STEWART (*Keturah Holt Stewart⁴, Henry³, Henry², Nicholas¹*), baptized at Andover, 8 Mar 1752 son of John and Keturah (Holt) Stewart; d. at Kingsbury, NY, 16 May 1835 (probate 1835); m. 1st, about 1772, SARAH who has not been identified; Sarah d. at Dublin, NH, 5 Jan 1785. Henry m. 2nd, MARTHA WEATHERBY who was living in 1827 when Henry wrote his will.

Henry Stewart and his first wife Sarah were in Amherst, New Hampshire before locating to Dublin in 1779. After Sarah's death, Henry took his children to New York and settled in Washington County.[1753] Henry died at Kingsbury and is buried in the cemetery on Kingsbury Street.[1754]

In his will written 25 June 1827 (proved 16 June 1835), Henry Stewart of Kingsbury bequeathed to beloved wife Martha her wearing apparel, the household furniture, two good cows, and one good horse to be hers, forever. Grandson James H. S. M'Farling (also referred to as Henry in the will) receives the farm on which the elder Henry now lives with certain provision for the use of part of the property by Henry and Martha until their deaths. He leaves to his four daughters the farm in Fort Ann which consists of about 200 acres. His daughters are Sally wife of William Smith, Lucy wife of Layton Bentley, Polly the wife of James Allcock, and Rene the wife of Thomas Kinsler. Samuel Andrews was named executor.[1755]

The five children of Henry and Sarah are recorded at Dublin, although the births of the older children were likely at Amherst.

i SARAH STEWART, b. 2 Sep 1772; m. WILLIAM SMITH; nothing further has yet been found.

ii LUCY STEWART, b. 3 Sep 1776; d. at Kingsbury, NY, 2 Oct 1855; m. LAYTON BENTLEY, b. at Kent, CT, 10 Sep 1775 son of Benjamin and Deborah (Baker) Bentley; Layton d. at Kingsbury, 1 Mar 1849.

iii MARY "POLLY" STEWART, b. 1 Nov 1778; d. at Deering, NH, 11 Aug 1827; m. at Hillsborough, 7 Oct 1798, JAMES ALCOCK, b. at Deering, 27 Apr 1777 son of Robert and Elizabeth (Marong) Alcock; James d. at Deering, 12 Jun 1847.

iv RHENY STEWART, b. 1 Apr 1781; d. at Kingsbury, NY, 1862 (will proved 21 Jul 1862); m. 1st at Hillsborough, NH, 25 Nov 1800, JAMES MCFARLAND, b. at Goffstown, about 1773 son of Daniel and Martha (Steele) McFarland. Rheny m. 2nd about 1815, THOMAS KINSLER, b. in Ireland, about 1785; Thomas d. after 1875 when he was living in Kingsbury with his daughter Mary Ann. Rheny and James were parents of two children, Betsey McFarland who married Oliver Dickey and James Henry Stewart McFarland who is named in the will of Henry Stewart.[1756] The birth of James Henry Stewart McFarland is recorded at Irasburg, VT, 31 Mar 1808. Rheny and Thomas Kinsler had one daughter, Mary Ann who married William H. Young. In her will, Rheny Kinsler bequeathed her entire estate to her daughter Mary Ann Young with the provision that she care for Thomas Kinsler during his natural life.[1757]

v HENRY STEWART, b. 4 Jan 1785; d. 5 Feb 1785.

656) MARTHA STEWART (*Keturah Holt Stewart⁴, Henry³, Henry², Nicholas¹*), baptized at Andover, 6 Nov 1757 daughter of John and Keturah (Holt) Stewart; d. at Reading, MA, 19 Apr 1843; m. 1st, about 1775, JAMES HARTSHORN, b. at Amherst, 17 Mar 1755 son of James and Tabitha (Pratt) Hartshorn; James d. about 1780. Martha m. 2nd, at Amherst, AMOS ELLIOTT, b. at Amherst, 17 Jun 1755 son of Francis and Phebe (Wilkins) Elliott; Amos d. at Amherst, 7 Apr 1807. Martha m. 3rd, at Reading, MA, 2 Feb 1812, JONATHAN WESTON, b. 1 Mar 1757 son of Jonathan and Ruth (Flint) Weston; Jonathan d. at Reading, 23 Apr 1839.

Martha resided in Amherst, New Hampshire, Her first husband, James Hartshorn, served in the Revolution in the company of Capt. David Wilkins and was one of those captured at the Cedars and died about 1780. Martha received a widow's pension of $20 half-yearly based on her husband's service.[1758] Her second husband, Amos Elliott, was for many years a deacon of the Congregationalist church in Amherst.[1759]

James Hartshorn and Martha Stewart were parents of one child.

i MARTHA HARTSHORN, b. at Amherst, 14 Oct 1775; m. at Amherst, 29 Oct 1795, ABIJAH SPAFFORD of Reading at the time of marriage, perhaps the son of Abijah and Mary (Town) Spafford.

Martha Stewart and Amos Elliott were parents of four children born at Amherst.

[1753] Leonard, *History of Dublin, NH*, p 905

[1754] Edson, *Stewart Clan Magazine*, volumes 1-8, p 195

[1755] *New York, Wills and Probate Records, 1659-1999, Washington County, Wills, Vol A2-B2, 1830-1845, pp 87-89, accessed through ancestry.com*

[1756] Cochrane, *History of the Town of Antrim*, p 597; Hadley, *History of the Town of Goffstown*, p 302

[1757] *New York, Wills and Probate Records, 1659-1999, Washington County, volume J, pp 54-55*

[1758] U. S. Revolutionary War Pensions, Widows Pensions, Massachusetts

[1759] Secomb, *History of the Town of Amherst*, p 578 and p 614

i AMOS ELLIOTT, b. 1782; d. at Amherst, 27 Apr 1826; m. at Amherst, 4 Aug 1803, MARGARET WILEY, b. about 1784; Margaret d. at Somersworth, NH, 26 Jun 1869.

ii BETSY ELLIOTT, b. 1783; d. at Lancaster, MA, 25 Oct 1861; m. at Amherst, 12 Nov 1807, JOHN WILEY, b. about 1788; John d. at Amherst, 19 Mar 8 Mar 1839.[1760]

iii HANNAH ELLIOTT, b. 1788; d. at Berlin, MA, 18 Oct 1867; m. at Reading, 2 Dec 1815, LEVI HARTSHORN, b. at Amherst, 1789 son of Edward and Lucy (Elliott) Hartshorn; Levi d. at Amherst, 27 Sep 1819.

iv LUTHER ELLIOTT, b. Feb 1794; d. at Amherst, 1 Apr 1876; m. 22 Sep 1818, ESTHER DAMON, b. at Reading, 30 Jun 1793 daughter of Aaron and Lucy (Emerson) Damon; Esther d. at Amherst, 14 Feb 1891.

657) HENRY PEABODY (*Mary Holt Peabody⁴, Henry³, Henry², Nicholas¹*), b. at Boxford, 25 May 1749 son of Joseph and Mary (Holt) Peabody; d. 1776 while serving in the Army (probate 5 Mar 1776); m. 17 Apr 1769, LYDIA REA, b. at Beverly, 8 Oct 1750 daughter of Joshua and Sarah (Prince) Rea.[1761] Lydia's date of death not found, but she was living in 1783 and had not remarried.

Henry and Lydia resided in Boxford. They were parents of two children. Henry did not leave a will and his estate entered probate 5 March 1776 with widow Lydia as administratrix. Real estate was valued at £26.13.4 and personal estate at £27.6.0.[1762]

i JOSEPH PEABODY, b. at Boxford, 17 Sep 1770; m. at Wilmington, 17 Nov 1796, ELIZABETH JENKINS, b. at Wilmington, 13 Dec 1765 daughter of Joseph and Sarah (Barron) Jenkins.

ii JAMES REA PEABODY, b. 1773

658) MARY HOLT (*James⁴, James³, Henry², Nicholas¹*), baptized at Andover, 18 May 1735 daughter of James and Mary (Chandler) Holt; d. after 1811; m. 1st, 3 Sep 1754, NATHANIEL ANDREWS likely the son of Thomas and Ruth (Bixbee) Andrews; Nathaniel d. at Boxford, 1759 (probate 1759). Mary m. 2nd, 19 Nov 1761, JACOB ANDREWS; Jacob d. at Boxford, 1786 (probate 3 Oct 1786).

Nathaniel Andrews did not leave a will and his estate entered probate 24 September 1759 with widow Mary as administratrix. The dower was not set off to the widow until 1811 after Mary petitioned to the court noting that the dower was never set off to her. This request followed the death of her son Jacob in 1811 and the timing seems related to that.[1763]

Jacob Andrews did not leave a will and his estate entered probate 3 October 1786 with son Jacob as administrator. The total value of the estate was £91.13.4 with the only real estate being 3 acres of upland and 26 acres of pasture. Debts were £148.8.4.[1764]

Mary Holt and Nathaniel Andrews were parents of one child born at Boxford.

i JOHN ANDREWS, b. 7 Nov 1758

Mary Holt and Jacob Andrews were parents of nine children born at Boxford.

i JACOB ANDREWS, b. 9 Aug 1762; d. at Boxford 1811[1765] (probate 21 Jan 1811 with widow Jane as administratrix); m. at Topsfield, 1 Apr 1792, JANE GOULD, b. at Topsfield, 30 Jul 1746 daughter of Simon and Jane (Palmer) Gould; Jane d. at Boxford, 24 Feb 1837.

ii MARY ANDREWS, b. 27 Feb 1764; d. at Boxford, 13 Jan 1810; m. at Boxford, 18 Apr 1794, OLIVER WHITE, baptized at Wenham, 3 Sep 1758 son of Thomas and Lucy (Fiske) White.

iii NATHANIEL ANDREWS, b. 5 Sep 1765

iv BETTY ANDREWS, b. 30 Mar 1767; d. at Topsfield, 7 Oct 1851; m. at Topsfield, 3 Mar 1791, NATHANIEL GOULD, b. at Topsfield, 16 Jul 1753 son of Thomas and Mary (Gould) Gould; Nathaniel d. at Topsfield, 3 Jul 1842. Nathaniel was first married to Hannah Killam.

1760 The parents of John Wiley who married Betsy and Margaret Wiley who married Amos have not been found, but I wonder if they might be children of John and Dorcas (Abbott) Wiley.

1761 The 1783 will of Joshua Rea includes a bequest to his daughter Lydia Peabody.

1762 *Essex County, MA: Probate File Papers, 1638-1881.*Online database. *AmericanAncestors.org.* New England Historic Genealogical Society, 2014. Case 20832

1763 *Essex County, MA: Probate File Papers, 1638-1881.*Online database. *AmericanAncestors.org.* New England Historic Genealogical Society, 2014. Case 693

1764 *Essex County, MA: Probate File Papers, 1638-1881.*Online database. *AmericanAncestors.org.* New England Historic Genealogical Society, 2014. Case 635

1765 Andrews, Jacob, -, 1811, a. 48 y. P. R. 29.

v HANNAH ANDREWS, b. 15 Jun 1769; d. at Newburyport, 8 Dec 1829; m. at Boxford, 27 Dec 1792, JOHN DORMAN, b. at Boxford, 18 Jun 1763 son of John and Hannah (Jackson) Dorman; John d. at Newburyport, 25 Dec 1857.

vi DOLLY ANDREWS, b. 25 Dec 1770; d. at Boxford, 1811 (probate Oct 1811 with Seth Saltmarsh as administrator). Dolly did not marry.

vii ANNA ANDREWS, b. 23 Feb 1774; d. at Cambridge, 11 Apr 1844 (although resident of Salem at time of death); m. at Boxford, 18 Oct 1803, SETH SALTMARSH, b. at Andover, 12 Apr 1778 son of Seth and Ruth (Bowman) Saltmarsh; Seth d. at Salem, 19 Jan 1836.

viii JOSHUA ANDREWS, b. 30 Nov 1775

ix ESTHER ANDREWS, b. 16 Dec 1777; d. at Salem, 5 Jun 1861; m. at Salem, 20 Jan 1811, her third cousin, ABIEL WARDWELL (*Solomon Wardwell*[5], *Abigail Gray Wardwell*[4], *Edward Gray*[3], *Hannah Holt Gray*[2], *Nicholas*[1]), b. at Andover, 25 Aug 1771 son of Solomon and Bethiah (Holt) Wardwell; Abiel d. of consumption at Charleston, SC, 30 Jan 1821 (probate 3 Apr 1821). Captain Abiel Wardwell was a master mariner and captained the brig *Britannia*. Other vessels he captained were the *Betsey*, *Astrea*, and *Eunice*.[1766] Abiel was first married to Hannah Elledge.

659) BRIDGET HOLT (*James*[4], *James*[3], *Henry*[2], *Nicholas*[1]), baptized at Andover, 16 Jan 1737 daughter of James and Mary (Chandler) Holt; m. at Boxford, 16 Oct 1757, as his second wife, LEVI ANDREWS, b. at Boxford, 27 Aug 1727 son of Thomas and Ruth (Bixbee) Andrews. Levi was first married to Sarah Towne.

Bridget and Levi started in Boxford, were in Hudson, New Hampshire for a time before finally settling in Nottingham West before 1775.

Bridget Holt and Levi Andrews were parents of eight children.

i LYDIA ANDREWS, b. at Boxford, 14 Jan 1758

ii MARY ANDREWS, baptized at Boxford 15 Nov 1761

iii LETITIA ANDREWS, b. at Nottingham, 20 Aug 1762; m. EBENEZER CUMMINGS

iv JOEL ANDREWS, b. at Nottingham, NH, 3 Sep 1764

v LEVI ANDREWS, b. at Nottingham, 2 Oct 1766; d. at Greenfield, NH, 29 Nov 1825; m. about 1788, BETSEY COLBY, b. about 1768.[1767]

vi JAMES ANDREWS, b. 12 Oct 1768

vii THOMAS ANDREWS, b. at Nottingham, 2 May 1771; d. at Hudson, NH, 4 Apr 1847; m. about 1795, HANNAH MARSHALL, b. at Nottingham, 4 Oct 1774 daughter of John and Susannah (Smith) Marshall; Hannah d. 16 Feb 1800.

viii HANNAH ANDREWS, b. at Nottingham, 3 Jan 1780; m. JOHN ESTEY.

660) ZELA HOLT (*James*[4], *James*[3], *Henry*[2], *Nicholas*[1]), b. at Andover, 29 Dec 1738 son of James and Mary (Chandler) Holt; d. likely at Bethel, ME; m. at Andover, 16 Nov 1762, his second cousin, PRISCILLA ABBOTT (*Hannah Holt Abbott*[4], *Timothy*[3], *James*[2], *Nicholas*[1]), b. at Andover, 13 Feb 1742/3 daughter of Barachias and Hannah (Holt) Abbott.

Priscilla Abbott and Zela Holt married in Andover, were for a time in Wilton, New Hampshire where some of their children were born, and finally settled in Bethel, Maine around 1790.[1768][1769] Their six children were likely born in Wilton, although the birth of one child is recorded in Bethel and the baptism of the youngest child was recorded at Andover.

i CALVIN HOLT, b. 26 Aug 1763; d. 27 Mar 1795.

ii JAMES HOLT, b. about 1765; d. perhaps at Bethel; m. at Reading, MA, 28 Feb 1793, MEHITABLE EATON, b. at Reading, Jul 1773 daughter of Timothy and Mehitable (Burnup) Eaton.

iii PRISCILLA HOLT, b. at Wilton, 2 Jan 1768; d. at Bethel, 4 Jan 1848; m. 23 May 1791, JOHN STEARNS, b. Aug 1762 son of John and Martha (Harrington) Stearns; John d. at Bethel, 14 Dec 1826.

[1766] Salem and Beverly, Massachusetts, Crew Lists and Shipping Articles, 1797-1934; accessed through familysearch.org

[1767] The family bible of Levi Andrews and Betsey Colby, including three pages of family births, deaths, and marriages, is extant and can be seen at the following site: https://www.heirloomsreunited.com/2018/06/bible-of-levi-andrews-and-betsey-colby.html

[1768] Lapham, *History of Bethel*, p 563

[1769] Livermore, *History of Wilton*, p 407

iv TIMOTHY ABBOT HOLT, b. 15 Aug 1773; d. at Bethel, 1856; m. at Andover, 17 Jan 1799, ANNA STEVENS, b. at Andover, 5 Jul 1774 daughter of Peter and Abigail (Johnson) Stevens; Anna d. at Bethel, 1861.

v MARY HOLT, b. about 1775; d. 18 Feb 1790.

vi BRIDGET HOLT, baptized Mar 1777; d. at Bethel, after 1850. Bridget did not marry. In 1850, she was living with her brother Timothy in Bethel.

661) JESSE HOLT (*James[4], James[3], Henry[2], Nicholas[1]*), b. at Andover, 8 Oct 1739 son of James and Mary (Chandler) Holt; d. of consumption, at Tewksbury, Feb 1817; m. at Tewksbury, 30 Aug 1781, MARY CLARK, b. at Tewksbury, 26 May 1745 daughter of Nathaniel and Mary (Wyman) Clark. Mary was first married at Tewksbury, 29 Jun 1769 to MOSES GRAY (*Robert Gray[4], Robert Gray[3], Hannah Holt Gray[2], Nicholas[1]*), baptized at Andover, 11 Jan 1747 son of Robert and Lydia (Peabody) Gray; Moses d. at Tewksbury, 11 Sep 1775.

Jesse married Mary Clark Gray a widow with three children. Mary was first married to Nicholas Holt descendant Moses Gray. Moses Gray and Mary Clark were parents of three children born at Tewksbury.

i MOSES GRAY, b. 20 Jan 1770; d. at Hancock, NH, 24 Mar 1847; m. at Tewksbury, 26 Jul 1791, MARY SCARLETT, b. at Tewksbury, 26 Aug 1767 daughter of Newman and Betty (Peacock) Scarlett; Mary d. at Hancock, 10 Apr 1832.

ii HENRY GRAY, b. 25 Jul 1772; d. 24 Feb 1810 when crushed by his cartwheel on the road from Boston to Tewksbury;[1770] m. at Tewksbury, 20 Oct 1797, SYBIL FARMER, b. at Tewksbury, 3 Dec 1774 daughter of Peter and Ednah (Hardy) Farmer; Sybil d. after 1850 when she was living in Tewksbury.

iii JOHN GRAY, b. 10 Aug 1775; d. at Tewksbury, 3 Nov 1837; m. at Tewksbury, 11 Aug 1796, LUCY FLETCHER, b. at Shirley, 2 Jul 1776 daughter of Oliver and Sarah (Fletcher) Fletcher; Lucy d. at Chelmsford, 1 Aug 1858.

Jesse Holt and Mary Clark were parents of one child.

i MOLLY HOLT, b. at Tewksbury, 29 Sep 1784; m. at Tewksbury, 22 Apr 1810, LOAMMI KITTREDGE, b. at Tewksbury, 14 Jun 1785 son of John and Abigail (Dutton) Kittredge. Loammi and Mary were living in Tewksbury in 1820 with what appear to be three young children. No further record was found for them.

662) ABEL HOLT (*Barzillai[4], James[3], Henry[2], Nicholas[1]*), b. at Marlborough, 14 Jun 1740 son of Barzillai and Elizabeth (Goss) Holt; d. at Boylston, MA, Feb 1815; m. 21 Oct 1765, EUNICE KEYES, b. at Shrewsbury, 19 Apr 1745 daughter of Henry and Ruth (Moore) Keyes; Eunice d. 21 Oct 1840.

Abel and Eunice were first in Shrewsbury where Abel purchased property from William Thomas in 1766. The family moved to Boylston about 1788. On 1 December 1788, Abel Holt purchased an 89-acre tract of land from David Child of Boylston for £50.[1771]

In May 1804, Abel and wife Eunice conveyed to Jonas Holt a tract of land in Boylston for a payment of $58. On 16 June 1813, Abel and Eunice conveyed land in Boylston to Henry Keyes Holt for a payment of $44.[1772]

In his will written 20 February 1811 (proved 14 March 1815), Abel Holt bequeathed to beloved wife Eunice the use and improvement of all the real and personal estate, after the payment of debts and legacies, during her natural life. He bequeathed one dollar each to children Lois Drury, Amasa Holt, Asa Holt, Jonas Holt, Eunice Prescott, Henry Keyes Holt, and Tyler Holt. Fifty cents each was bequeathed to Lucy Holt and Jarvis Holt the children of son Abel who was deceased. Lucy and Jarvis will receive an additional four dollars and fifty cents each after the decease of Eunice. Eunice was named executrix, a duty she declined due to her advanced age and requested William Drury be named. The heirs signing their agreement with the will were Lois Drury, Amasa Holt, Asa Holt, Jonas Holt, Eunice Prescott, Henry K. Holt, and Tyler Holt.[1773]

Abel Holt and Eunice Keyes were parents of eight children, the oldest five children born at Shrewsbury and the youngest children at Boylston.

i LOIS HOLT, b. 11 May 1767; d. at Holden, about 1819 (husband remarried 1820); m. at Holden, 6 Sep 1787, WILLIAM DRURY, b. in Shrewsbury, 11 Jan 1758;[1774] William d. at Holden, 20 Jan 1850. William married Hannah How in 1820. He likely also is the William Drury who married Lucy Drury in 1782.

1770 Henry, coming from Boston fell under the wheel of his wagon and was instantly killed, Feb. 24, 1810, a. 35 y. C. R. 1. [a. 34 y. G. R. 2.]

1771 Massachusetts Land Records, Worcester County, 57:6, 106:226

1772 Massachusetts Land Records, Worcester County, 183:280; 186:402

1773 *Worcester County, MA: Probate File Papers, 1731-1881.* Online database. AmericanAncestors.org. New England Historic Genealogical Society, 2015. Case 30608

1774 William's place and date of birth are given in the Holden records but without the names of parents. The History of Shrewsbury is not much help in identifying his parents.

ii AMASA HOLT, b. 24 Apr 1772; d. at Berlin, MA, 3 Nov 1815; m. 1st at Berlin, MA,[1775] 25 Jun 1799, "NABBY" NOURSE, b. at Berlin, MA, about 1777 (based on age 30 at death) daughter of Benjamin Sybil (Bailey) Nourse;[1776] Nabby d. at Berlin, 7 Jul 1807. Amasa m. 2nd at Berlin, 12 Apr 1808, HANNAH MOORE whose parents have not been identified; Hannah d. at Berlin, 8 Sep 1843 (probate 1843). Hannah married Daniel Holbrook on 21 Dec 1828.

iii ASA HOLT, b. 11 Jan 1775; d. at Boylston, 10 Aug 1847; m. at Southborough, 18 Dec 1801, NANCY PIERCE, b. at Southborough, about 1783 daughter of Jonathan and Lydia (Bowman) Pierce;[1777] Nancy d. at West Boylston, 10 Sep 1863.

iv ABEL W. HOLT, b. 22 Jun 1776; d. at Holden, 1802 (probate 1802 with widow Sally as administratrix); m. at Boylston, 16 Jan 1799, SARAH "SALLY" STRATTON,[1778] b. at Rutland, 30 Apr 1776 daughter of Samuel and Mary (Eaton) Stratton;[1779] Sally d. at West Boylston, 15 Feb 1852. Sally second married David Fairbank in 1804. Abel and Sally had two children, Lucy and Jarvis.

v JONAS HOLT, b. 22 Oct 1779; d. at West Boylston, 9 Oct 1853; m. at Boylston, 17 Apr 1802, ANNA READ,[1780] b. about 1780 daughter of Simeon and Anna (Read); Anna d. at West Boylston, 6 Sep 1845.

vi EUNICE HOLT, b. 21 Oct 1782; d. at West Boylston, 22 Dec 1870; m. at Holden, 19 Apr 1807, BRIGHAM PRESCOTT, b. at Shrewsbury, 1783 son of Jonathan and Mary (Brigham) Prescott; Brigham d. at West Boylston, 20 Nov 1865.

vii HENRY KEYES HOLT, b. 2 Jul 1788; d. at West Boylston, 8 Sep 1828; m. at West Boylston, 16 Nov 1813, LYDIA FAIRBANK, b. at Sterling, 19 Sep 1788 daughter of Seth and Relief (Sawyer) Fairbank; Lydia d. at Leominster, 23 Feb 1875. Lydia married second Nathaniel Davenport on 25 Sep 1844.

viii TYLER HOLT, b. 2 Sep 1790; d. at West Boylston, 8 Nov 1866; m. 1 Oct 1812, ARETHUSA FAIRBANK, b. about 1792 daughter of William and Keziah (Houghton) Fairbank;[1781] Arethusa d. at Sterling, 16 Aug 1837.

663) BARZILLAI HOLT (*Barzillai⁴, James³, Henry², Nicholas¹*), b. at Marlborough, 12 May 1745 son of Barzillai and Elizabeth (Goss) Holt; d. at Plattsburgh, NY, 1819; m. at Shrewsbury, 9 Nov 1770, LUCY WILLIAMS, b. about 1748 of undetermined parents.

Barzillai Holt and Lucy Williams were parents of eight children born at Shrewsbury.[1782]

i BARZILLAI HOLT, b. 30 Jan 1773; d. at Plattsburgh, NY, 28 Dec 1833; m. 4 Mar 1798, JANE HOLLENBECK, b. 1777 daughter of Jacob Hollenbeck; Jane d. at Plattsburgh, 29 Nov 1812.

ii JAMES HOLT, b. 16 Dec 1774; d. at Boylston, MA, 5 Apr 1855; m. at Boylston, 29 May 1800, EUNICE LOVELL, b. at Worcester, 11 Aug 1780 daughter of Jonathan and Mercy (Raymond) Lovell; Eunice d. at Holden, MA, 1 Dec 1865.

iii LUCY HOLT, b. 8 Mar 1777; d. at Boylston, 27 Jan 1855; m. at Boylston, 28 Sep 1797, ROBERT ANDREWS, b. at Shrewsbury, 15 Sep 1776 son of Robert and Dorothy (Goodenow) Andrews; Robert d. at Boylston, 2 Nov 1862.

iv BETSEY HOLT; m. JESSE SOPER

v LEVI HOLT; m. 1st CATHERINE MCLANE. Levi m. 2nd IRENE BARBER.

vi SUSAN HOLT; m. WILLIAM EMORY.

vii DOROTHY HOLT; m. JAMES EMORY.

viii NAHUM HOLT. Nahum did not marry.[1783]

1775 There is a 1798 marriage intention for Amasa Holt of Boylston and Thankful Fairbanks, but it is not clear that his is his marriage or if the marriage occurred.

1776 Houghton, *History of the Town of Berlin*, p 444

1777 The names of Nancy's parents are given as Jonathan Peirce and Lydia Bowman on her death record.

1778 Durrie's Holt genealogy states that Abel married Hannah Wright daughter of Judah and Tabitha Wright, but it was Abel's third cousin John Holt that married Hannah Wright the daughter of Judah and Tabitha.

1779 Sally's father's name is given as Samuel Stratton on her death record.

1780 Anna's last name is not entirely clear in the records. The transcription of the marriage record says "Wren" and her death record lists parents as Simeon and Anna and what looks like Rood or might be Read or even Rand. This needs further investigation.

1781 The 1841 probate of William Fairbank includes the children of Tyler Holt as heirs.

1782 The marriages for the children are those that are given in Durrie's Holt genealogy (p 78), but records were not located for several of them.

1783 Durrie, Holt Genealogy, p 79

664) SILAS HOLT (*Barzillai[4], James[3], Henry[2], Nicholas[1]*), b. at Marlborough, about 1752 son of Barzillai and Elizabeth (Goss) Holt; d. at Sempronius, NY, 1 Jan 1823;[1784] m. at Lunenburg, 25 Jan 1772, SARAH HARRINGTON, b. at Westminster, MA, 10 Nov 1752 daughter of Seth and Abigail (-) Harrington. Silas m. 2nd HEPHZIBAH who has not been identified.

The family was in Westminster, Massachusetts, then in Brandon, Vermont in 1790, and afterwards in Sempronius, New York.

In his pension application made 27 April 1818, Silas Holt of Sempronius reported he enlisted on 1 January 1780 from Westminster, Massachusetts in the company of Capt. John Lillie in Col. Cram's artillery regiment and he served until 2 May 1782 at which time he hired Oliver Fullum as a substitute. Silas was discharged at West Point. In a statement made 10 October 1820, Silas, then age 67, stated he was a carpenter by trade but was then too infirm to work in his trade. Part of his infirmity related a broken leg he received while in the army, His household at that time consisted of himself and his wife Hepsy who was 51 and described as a cripple. He reported the value of his personal estate as $22.88.[1785]

i SETH HOLT, b. at Westminster, MA, 25 Apr 1776; d. 8 Nov 1812 at Manchester near the Niagara River, NY during the War of 1812;[1786] m. at Brandon, VT, 5 Dec 1799, ABIGAIL CHENEY, b. in VT, 20 Jun 1781 daughter of Edward and Abigail (Hale) Cheney; Abigail d. after 1860 when she was living in Fairhaven, IL. Abigail married second Daniel Galusha on 17 Jan 1817. Seth Holt served as a lieutenant in the light infantry. Abigail received a widow's pension based on Seth's service after the death of her second husband. Seth and Abigail had eight children five of whom died in early infancy.

ii ABIGAIL HOLT, b. at Westminster, MA, 31 Jan 1778

iii SARAH HOLT, b. about 1778; m. 1st BENJAMIN SPRINGER and 2nd Mr. Sneather.[1787] There is a Benjamin Springer, Jr. and a young wife (both age 16-25) in Sempronius in 1810 which is where Seth Holt lived, and that may be this couple, but that would make Sarah's date of birth nearer 1785.

665) ELIZABETH HOLT (*Barzillai[4], James[3], Henry[2], Nicholas[1]*), b. at Marlborough, 29 Aug 1753 daughter of Barzillai and Elizabeth (Goss) Holt; d. at Shutesbury, MA, 28 Feb 1842; m. 1st at Lancaster, 10 Feb 1772, JEDEDIAH BOYNTON, baptized at Rowley, 22 Jan 1743/4 son of Ephraim and Sarah (Stewart) Boynton; Jedediah d. at Royalston, 1774 (probate 15 Jun 1774). Elizabeth m. 2nd JOSIAH WHITE BEAMAN, b. at Lancaster, 4 Oct 1752 son of Phineas H. and Joanna (White) Beaman; Josiah d. at Shelburne, MA, 2 Dec 1841.

Jedidiah Boynton did not leave a will and his estate entered probate 16 June 1774 with widow Elizabeth requesting that John Boynton of Winchendon as administrator.[1788] Real estate was valued at £113.6.2 and the total value of the estate was £160.10.9 and after payment of claims against the estate of £120.0.5 with £40.10.4 left to the estate. Part of the payments did include £15 to Elizabeth Boynton. John Boynton was named guardian to Lucy Boynton. On a date that cannot be read, Lucy Brown and Simeon Brown of Springfield, Vermont acknowledged that Lucy Boynton now Brown, heir to the estate, had received from the estate £145 for her full share from the estate.

After her first husband's death, Elizabeth married Josiah White Beaman, a carpenter by trade. Josiah also served as deacon in Shutesbury. The family lived in Sterling for a time prior to settling in Shutesbury.

Josiah Beaman enlisted 1 April 1777 from Winchendon in the company of Captain Set Oaks. Josiah was at the Battle of Brandywine with the baggage wagon and wintered at Valley Forge. He was discharged the end of March 1778. He received a pension for his service.[1789]

On 12 March 1827 (deed recorded in 1836), Josiah Beaman and wife Elizabeth for fifteen hundred dollars conveyed to Isaiah Beaman property in Shutesbury including the dwelling house. Josiah and Elizabeth reserved for themselves use of part of the house during their natural lives.[1790]

Elizabeth Holt and Jedediah Boynton were parents of one child.

i LUCY BOYNTON, b. at Lancaster, MA, 30 May 1773; m. by 1793 SIMEON BROWN of Springfield, VT who has not been identified. The births of four children of this couple are recorded at Springfield and the death of a son there in 1815. Simeon is referred to as Doctor Simeon Brown in one record. Dr. Simeon Brown was the town treasurer of Springfield 1795-1796.[1791]

Three likely children have been identified for Elizabeth Holt and Josiah Beaman.

1784 U.S., The Pension Roll of 1835, Volume 2, New York, p 514

1785 Revolutionary War Pension and Bounty-Land Warrant Application Files, Case S44937

1786 War of 1812 Pension and Bounty Land Warrant Application Files, File 13231, file of Abigail Galusha widow of Seth Holt

1787 Sarah and her husbands are given in Durrie's Holt genealogy, but records have not been located. No person with the name of Sneather was found in census records from 1800 through 1820.

1788 *Worcester County, MA: Probate File Papers, 1731-1881.* Online database. AmericanAncestors.org. New England Historic Genealogical Society, 2015. Case 6791 and Case 6802

1789 U. S. Revolutionary War pension application file

1790 Massachusetts Land Records, Franklin County, volume 96, pp 66-67

1791 Hubbard, *History of the Town of Springfield, Vermont*

i PHINEAS BEAMAN, b. about 1776; d. at West Boylston, 16 Sep 1795.

ii JOSIAH BEAMAN, b. about 1785; d. at Shutesbury, 18 Dec 1868; m. 1st at Sterling, MA, 14 Mar 1806, NANCY FAIRBANK, b. about 1785; Nancy d. at Shutesbury, 24 Feb 1813. Josiah m. 2nd at Shutesbury, 3 Oct 1813, ABIAH CONANT, b. at Oakham, 1789 daughter of Luther and Susannah (Allen) Conant; Abiah d. at Prescott, MA, 31 Jan 1879.

iii ISAIAH BEAMAN, b. about 1790; d. at Shutesbury, 5 Jan 1842; m. at Shutesbury, 21 Apr 1811, SOPHIA FAIRBANK, b. about 1786; Sophia d. at Shutesbury, 14 Sep 1844.

666) ABIEL HOLT (*Barzillai*[4], *James*[3], *Henry*[2], *Nicholas*[1]), b. at Marlborough, 11 May 1763 son of Barzillai and Lois (Pike) Holt; d. at West Boylston, 29 Jun 1845; m. at Sterling, 16 Nov 1785, DOLLY FAIRBANK, b. at Lancaster, 8 Feb 1769 daughter of Silas and Lydia (Prouty) Fairbank. Abiel married 2nd at Grafton, 27 Feb 1828, MIRIAM WOOD (widow of Reuben Jenks), b. at Grafton, 4 Nov 1779 daughter of Dr. Joseph and Miriam (Collester) Wood; Miriam d. at West Boylston, 14 Dec 1842.

Abiel and Dolly married at Sterling and the birth of their first child was recorded at Lancaster. After that, they were settled in West Boylston. On 15 January 1841, Abiel Holt of West Boylston and is wife Miriam in her own right conveyed to Asa Boynton a tract of land in West Boylston for a payment of $400.[1792]

Abiel and Dolly were parents of ten children.

i DOLLY FAIRBANK HOLT, b. at Lancaster, 1786; d. at West Boylston, 15 Dec 1841; m. 30 May 1809, ASA BOYNTON, b. at Sterling, 31 Jul 1786 son of Abiel and Lois (Raymond) Boynton; Asa d. at West Boylston, 23 Mar 1843.

ii SILAS HOLT, b. at Lancaster, 1788; d. at West Boylston, 1812 (probate Oct 1812). Silas did not marry.

iii SOPHIA HOLT, b. at Boylston, Aug 1792 (age 88 years, 4 months, 10 days at death); d. at Clinton, MA, 17 Dec 1880. Sophia did not marry.

iv CLARISSA HOLT, b. at West Boylston, 1795; d. at Worcester, 30 Aug 1867; m. at Sterling, 12 Mar 1815, ARTEMUS FAIRBANK, b. at Sterling, 1791 son of Oliver and Susanna (Gates) Fairbank; Artemus d. at West Boylston, 15 Dec 1836.

v ELIZA HOLT, b. at West Boylston, about 1797; d. at Brookfield, 15 Sep 1838; m. 1st at Oakham, 27 Oct 1816, JOSHUA BRIMHALL, b. 1792 son of Samuel and Eunice (Humphrey) Brimhall; Joshua d. at Oakham, 4 May 1817. Eliza m. 2nd at Oakham, 8 Apr 1823, JONAS BELLOWS, b. at Paxton, 16 Nov 1796 son of Jonas and Sarah (Bridges) Bellows; Jonas d. at Brookfield, 8 Jun 1886. Jonas married second Calista Morey on 2 Apr 1840.

vi IRENE HOLT, b. at West Boylston, 1799; d. at Worcester, 7 Apr 1840; m. at Sterling, 29 May 1825, THOMAS HART RICE, b. at Auburn, MA, 10 Mar 1803 son of Peter and Mary (Hart) Rice; Thomas d. at West Boylston, 8 Jun 1892. Thomas married second Abigail Hubbard on 1 Oct 1840.

vii CATHERINE HOLT, b. about 1801; Catherine did not marry.

viii ABIEL CARTER HOLT, b. about 1803; died young.

ix PARKMAN HOLT, b. at West Boylston, 1809; d. at West Boylston, 21 Jun 1841; m. at West Boylston, 21 Sep 1830, MARTHA CLEVELAND, b. at Medfield, 21 Sep 1808 daughter of Zimri and Eunice (Clark) Cleveland; Martha d. at West Boylston, 23 Jul 1879.

x EPHRAIM MERRICK HOLT, b. at West Boylston, 1811; d. at West Boylston, 29 Sep 1838; m. at West Boylston, 28 Sep 1836, ZILPHA BRUCE, b. at Berlin, MA, 1816 daughter of John and Prudence (Priest) Bruce; Zilpha d. at Oxford, 18 May 1893. Zilpha married second Jason Knowlton and married third David Wait.

667) JOTHAM HOLT (*Barzillai*[4], *James*[3], *Henry*[2], *Nicholas*[1]), b. at Lancaster, 10 Jan 1765 son of Barzillai and Lois (Pike) Holt; d. at Barre, NY, 3 Jan 1839; m. at Sterling, 3 Jan 1788, LYDIA FAIRBANK, b. at Lancaster, 3 Mar 1770 daughter of Silas and Lydia (Prouty) Fairbank; Lydia d. at Pitcher, NY, 23 Sep 1856.

Jotham Holt, age sixty-eight and resident of Truxton, appeared at the court of common pleas of Cortland County on 25 September 1832 to provide a statement related to his application for a pension. In February or March 1781, he enlisted as a private in the company of Capt. Ring in a regiment of the Massachusetts line commanded by Col. Brooks. The company mustered at Lancaster and then went to Leicester and Springfield. Then in the company of Capt. Smith marched to Peekskill, New York. They then marched to West Point and a place called Gallows hill and remained until the winter. He was then in New Burgh, again to West Point, and in New York and took possession of the city the day the British evacuated on 25 November 1783. After three weeks in New York, they returned to winter quarters and he was discharged in December. He reported he was born in 1765 in Lancaster.

[1792] Massachusetts Land Records, Worcester County, 356:195

On 6 October 1840, Alexander A. Holt of Barre made a statement in support of his mother Lydia's widow's pension application. Alexander reported he was born in 1792, that his mother and father were married throughout his memory, his father died on 3 January 1839, and his mother was currently living in the home of John Lansing in Barre. Statements were also made by Justus Crandall and Barzillai Holt. On 23 March 1855, widow Lydia Holt then age eighty-five appeared in Chenango County to obtain a warrant related to bounty-land. The pension claim also contains limited information on some of the children: Sally born 13 December 1789, Jotham, Jr. born 1791, Andrew A. born in 1792, and Barzillai and James with ages not given.[1793]

In his will, Jotham Holt bequeathed to beloved wife Lydia all the real estate in his possession during her natural life. After the death of Lydia, the estate is to be divided equally among his legal heirs except the heirs of daughter Betsey now deceased formerly the wife of William Prout. Betsey's heirs receive the sum of five dollars. James Holt was named executor.[1794]

On 4 January 1839, executor of the will James Holt presented the will and provided the following list of all the heirs-at-law of the estate: widow Lydia Holt; James Holt, Andrew A. Holt, Cyrus Holt, Silas Holt, Barzillai Holt, Aminda Lansing wife of John Lansing, and Semantha Congdon wife of Alva Congdon all of the town of Barre in the county of Orleans; Sally Prout wife of Daniel Prout residing in Bloomingville, Huron County, Ohio; Jotham Holt residing in Calhoun County, Michigan; Amasa Holt residing in Cortlandville, Cortland County, New York; Lydia Crandall wife of Justus Crandall residing in the town of Pitcher, Chemung County, New York; Lois Hopkins wife of David M. Hopkins residing in Sheldon, Genesee County, New York; and Isaac Prout, Thomas M. Prout, and Silas Prout children of Betsey Prout deceased residing in Jackson County, Michigan. The final settlement of the estate was 1 March 1841 with the heirs of Betsey Prout receiving five dollars and each of the other heirs receiving $44.16.[1795]

Jotham Holt and Lydia Fairbank were parents of thirteen children as given in the probate record. The movements of the family and places of birth are not clear. On census records, daughter Sarah's place of birth is given as Connecticut, Jotham and Andrew in Massachusetts, and children starting with Amasa born in New York.

i SARAH HOLT, b. about 1790; d. at Castalia, OH, 11 Jan 1873; m. DANIEL PROUT, b. 3 Aug 1787 son of Degory and Jemima (Sherwood) Prout;[1796] Daniel d. at Castalia, 30 Jul 1865.

ii JOTHAM HOLT, b. about 1790; d. at Fredonia. MI, 2 May 1854; m. OLIVE HIX, b. in NH, about 1798; Olive d. 24 Nov 1861.

iii ANDREW A. HOLT, b. 1 Nov 1792; d. at Barre, NY, 14 May 1873; m. at Phelps, NY, 13 Jul 1812, PHEBE SWAN, b. 1794; Phebe d. at Barre, 25 Sep 1854.

iv ELIZABETH "BETSEY" HOLT, b. about 1795; d. at Romulus, NY, 1826; m. about 1815, WILLIAM PROUT, b. at Romulus, 4 Feb 1785 son of Degory and Jemima (Sherwood) Prout; William d. at Quincy, MI, 20 Jul 1871. William married second, Nancy Wing.

v AMASA B. HOLT, b. about 1796; d. after 1860 when he was living at Cortlandville, NY; m. 1st ANNA, b. about 1796 and d. about 1853. Amasa m. 2nd SARAH COBB.

vi JAMES HOLT, b. about 1798; d. at Barre, NY, 4 Apr 1848; m. CHARLOTTE, b. about 1800; Charlotte d. at Albion, NY, 1864.

vii LYDIA HOLT, b. about 1801; d. at Pitcher, NY, 13 Feb 1859; m. about 1817, JUSTUS B. CRANDALL, b. 1792 son of Elisha and Hannah (Burdick) Crandall;[1797] Justus d. at Pitcher, 13 May 1855.

viii CYRUS HOLT, b. about 1802; d. at Marion, MI, 30 Mar 1882; m. POLLY VEDDER, b. at Cortland, NY, 8 Jul 1802 (calculated from age at death); Polly d. at Marion, MI, 26 Sep 1875.

ix SILAS HOLT, b. about 1802; d. at Bunker Hill, MI, 22 Dec 1879; m. about 1825, EMILY HICKS, b. at Pomfret, CT, 13 Jul 1804 daughter of Zephaniah and Polly (Preston) Hicks; Emily d. at Bunker Hill, 17 Sep 1869.

x BARZILLAI HOLT, b. 12 May 1804; d. at Howell, MI, 12 May 1872; m. 1st SARAH VEDDER. Barzillai m. 2nd MARY, b. 6 Jun 1813 and d. 5 Sep 1863. Barzillai m. 3rd widow EMMA C. WOOD, b. 1826; Emma d. 19 Apr 1878.

xi LOIS HOLT, b. estimate 1805; m. DAVID M. HOPKINS

xii AMANDA HOLT, b. about 1809; d. after 1880 when she was living in Calhoun, MI; m. about 1828, JOHN P. LANSING, b. in NY, about 1806; John was living in 1880.

xiii SAMANTHA HOLT, b. estimate 1812; m. ALVAH CONGDON, b. estimate 1810. In the 1840 census, Alvah Congdon lived next to James Holt in Barre with a household of one male 20-29, one female 20-29, one male under five, and one female 70-79.

1793 U. S. Revolutionary War Pension and Bounty-Land Warrant Application Files, Case W18059

1794 *Probate Records, 1825-1920; Index to Probate Records, 1825-1926;* Author: *New York. Surrogate's Court (Orleans County), Volume A, p 180*

1795 New York Probate Record, Orleans County, Order Book, volume 2, pp 305-306; Order Book, volume 3 pp 230-231

1796 Gable, *Historic Tales of Seneca County*, p 103

1797 Crandall, *Elder John Crandall of Rhode Island*, p 151

668) JONATHAN CRAM (*Jonathan Cram⁴, Sarah Holt Cram³, Henry², Nicholas¹*), b. at Wilmington, MA, 8 Jun 1733 son of Jonathan and Mary (Chamberlain) Cram; d. at Wilton, NH, 24 Oct 1810; m. about 1759, SARAH PUTNAM, b. at Salem, 28 Jun 1736 daughter of Jacob and Susannah (Stiles) Putnam; Sarah d. at Wilton, 26 May 1805.

Jonathan and Sarah lived in Wilton where Jonathan served as town treasurer. He was also involved in providing schooling for the town.[1798]

Son Philip did not marry. In his will written 4 January 1832, he bequeathed one thousand dollars to be divided among his siblings: Jonathan Cram, Mary Gage, Susannah Smith, Mehitable Cram, Zerviah Carleton, and the children of deceased sister Sarah Jaquith. He also bequeathed to sister Mehitable and to Mary Carleton the daughter of sister Zerviah the right and privilege of residing in his dwelling house in Wilton. Mehitable is also to receive provision from the executor for her support. David Cram of Wilton receives all the lands and buildings and was named executor.[1799][1800]

In her will written 4 May 1841, Mehitable Cram had bequests of household items or small amounts of money to Philip Putnam Carleton, Saviah Thayer, Susan Smith and Sarah Smith who are daughters of Otis Smith, and niece Mary M. Carleton. Niece Mary M. Carleton receives all the real estate and the remainder of the personal estate. David Cram, gentleman of Wilton, was named executor.[1801]

Jonathan Cram and Sarah Putnam were parents of seven children born at Wilton.

i SARAH CRAM, b. 21 Feb 1760; d. at Andover, VT, Dec 1824; m. at Wilton, 2 Jan 1787, JOSHUA JAQUITH, b. about 1764 possibly the son of Joshua and Hannah (Beard0 Jaquith; Joshua d. at Andover, VT, 15 Dec 1840.

ii JONATHAN CRAM, b. 18 Nov 1764; d. at Andover, VT, Nov 1857; m. at Wilton, 22 May 1787, MARY GREELEY, b. at Hudson, NH, 15 Oct 1760 daughter of Samuel and Abigail (Blodgett) Greeley; Mary d. at Andover, 11 Apr 1857.

iii PHILIP CRAM, b. 24 Feb 1766; d. at Wilton, 7 Jan 1832. Philip did not marry.

iv SUSANNAH CRAM, b. 26 Jun 1769; d. at Wilton, 28 Oct 1837; m. 1st about 1789, ABIEL BRIDGES, perhaps b. at Andover, MA, 14 May 1767 son of John and Mary (Spaulding) Bridges; Abiel d. at Wilton, 7 Nov 1801. Susannah m. 2nd 7 Feb 1804, as his second wife, URIAH SMITH, b. about 1745 likely the son of Zachariah and Lydia (Hastings) Smith; Uriah d. at Wilton, 4 Mar 1829. Uriah was first married to Lydia Keyes. Uriah and Lydia (Keyes) Smith were the parents of Betsey Smith who married Joseph Holt (1792-1864).

v MARY CRAM, b. 27 Jan 1769; d. after 1832 (living at brother's will); m. at Wilton, 12 Jun 1794, JOSEPH GAGE, b. at Pelham, NH, 20 Aug 1769 son of Peirce and Mary (Bodwell) Gage.

vi MEHITABLE CRAM, b. 14 Jul 1772; d. at Wilton, 7 Oct 1842. Mehitable did not marry.

vii ZEVIAH CRAM, b. 20 Sep 1775; d. at Wilton, 10 Feb 1859; m. 21 Feb 1799, DAVID CARLETON, b. about 1772; David d. at Wilton, 15 Aug 1851.

669) DAVID CRAM (*Jonathan Cram⁴, Sarah Holt Cram³, Henry², Nicholas¹*), b. at Wilmington, MA, 26 Jun 1737 son of Jonathan and Mary (Chamberlain) Cram; d. at Lyndeborough, NH, 25 Jun 1825; m. about 1760, MARY BADGER, b. 1739 daughter of John and Mary (McFarland) Badger; David d. at Lyndeborough, 10 Mar 1825.

David and Mary resided in Lyndeborough about a mile east of South Lyndeborough village. David did not serve in the Revolution but hired Hezekiah Dunklee to do service for him at Bennington. David served functions in the town as surveyor of highways, and he was one of those who participated in the system in which the poor of the town were sent to live ("vendue") to the lowest bidder.[1802]

David Cram and Mary Badger were parents of ten children.

i MARY CRAM, b. at Wilton, 29 Dec 1761; m. at Groton, MA, 23 Sep 1784, AMBROSE LAKIN, b. at Groton, 22 Sep 1756 son of Ambrose and Dorothy (Gilson) Lakin.

ii ELIZABETH CRAM, b. at Lyndeborough, 2 Jan 1764; d. at Williamstown, VT, 26 Feb 1845; m. 14 Oct 1789, ISAAC LEWIS, b. at Pepperell, 4 Feb 1766 son of Jonathan and Persis (Crosby) Lewis;[1803] Isaac d. at Williamstown, 27 Jul 1824.

iii LOUISA CRAM, b. at Lyndeborough, 14 Sep 1765; m. DARIUS JEFFRIES.[1804]

[1798] Livermore, *History of the Town of Wilton*, p 355 and p 75

[1799] It seems likely that David Cram mentioned in the will was Philip's first cousin once removed son of David and Sarah (Putnam) Cram.

[1800] New Hampshire Wills and Probate Records, Hillsborough County, 39:235-236

[1801] New Hampshire Wills and Probate Records, Hillsborough County, 48:213

[1802] Donovan, *History of the Town of Lyndeborough*, p 711, p 181, and p 273

[1803] Essex Institute Historical Collections, volume 43, p 321, "Edmund Lewis of Lynn and Some of His Descendants"

[1804] This is a marriage reported in the History of Lyndeborough; not further records were found for this couple.

iv DAVID CRAM, b. at Lyndeborough, 26 May 1767; m. 25 Oct 1792, her second cousin, SARAH PUTNAM (*Ephraim Putnam⁵, Sarah Cram Putnam⁴, Sarah Holt Cram³, Henry², Nicholas¹*), b. at Lyndeborough, 16 Jan 1773 daughter of Ephraim and Lucy (Spalding) Putnam; Sarah d. at Roxbury, VT, 5 May 1813.

v HANNAH CRAM, b. at Lyndeborough, 26 May 1769; d. after 1832 when she was at Amherst, NH; m. 1st SAMUEL ROGERS who d. at Keene, NH, 1827 (probate 1827 with Gideon Cram as executor of the will). Hannah m. 2nd at Lyndeborough, 8 Dec 1829, WILLIAM HASTINGS, b. about 1759; William d. at Amherst, 20 Apr 1832.

vi GIDEON CRAM, b. at Lyndeborough, 25 Feb 1771; d. at Lyndeborough, 17 Jun 1837; m. about 1799, his second cousin, AMY PUTNAM (*David Putnam⁵, Sarah Cram Putnam⁴, Sarah Holt Cram³, Henry², Nicholas¹*), b. at Lyndeborough, 6 Mar 1779 daughter of David and Abigail (Carleton) Putnam; Amy d. at Lyndeborough, 17 Dec 1866.

vii DEBORAH CRAM, b. at Lyndeborough, 21 Jul 1773; d. at Roxbury, VT, 5 Jun 1863; m. at Wilton, 6 Jun 1799, AMBROSE HUTCHINSON, b. at Wilton, 12 Feb 1773 son of George and Elizabeth (Bickford) Hutchinson;[1805] Ambrose d. at Brookfield, VT, 28 Aug 1836.

viii ROBERT CRAM, b. 27 Jun 1776; d. at Roxbury, VT, 23 Sep 1854; m. 19 Jan 1801, HANNAH WEBSTER, b. 1775; Hannah d. at Roxbury, VT, 24 Feb 1863.

ix JONATHAN CRAM, b. 9 Mar 1779; d. at Williamstown, VT, 21 Mar 1869; m. 15 Mar 1804, LYDIA SMITH, b. 1783; Lydia d. at Williamstown, 7 Sep 1840.

x REBECCA CRAM, b. 27 Feb 1782; d. 10 Sep 1782.

670) JACOB CRAM (*Jonathan Cram⁴, Sarah Holt Cram³, Henry², Nicholas¹*), b. at Wilmington, 4 Oct 1739 son of Jonathan and Mary (Chamberlain) Cram; d. at Lyndeborough, 1819 (probate 6 Aug 1819); m. about 1762, ISABELLA HUTCHINSON,[1806] b. Dec 1739; Isabella d. at Lyndeborough, 3 Feb 1812.

Jacob and Isabella resided in Lyndeborough but relocated to Litchfield, Maine about 1793.[1807]

In his will written 3 July 1815 (proved 6 August 1819), Jacob Cram bequeathed to son Zebulon one dollar and seventy-five cents and a bequest of one dollar and seventy-five cents goes to Rebecca wife of Andrew Harwood. The remainder of the estate is to be equally divided among son John Cram, heirs of son Jacob Cram deceased, daughter Olive Cram wife of John Cram, daughter Rachel wife of William Fuller, and daughter Sarah wife of Jesse Fales. Daughter Sarah Fales receives an additional payment of one hundred dollars, a just debt to her for services to the family. Jotham Hildreth of Lyndeborough was named executor.[1808]

Jacob and Isabella Cram were parents of seven children born at Lyndeborough.

i JOHN CRAM, b. 4 Nov 1763; d. at Lyndeborough, 30 Aug 1833; m. at Lyndeborough, 4 May 1786, his second cousin, HULDAH WOODWARD (*Hannah Putnam Woodward⁵, Sarah Cram Putnam⁴, Sarah Holt Cram³, Henry², Nicholas¹*), b. at Lyndeborough, 23 Jun 1765 daughter of Eleazer and Hannah (Putnam) Woodward; Huldah d. 14 Jan 1853.

ii JACOB CRAM, b. 23 Nov 1765; d. at Litchfield, ME, 16 Jan 1815; m. at Lyndeborough, 24 Sep 1787, MARTHA DOAK,[1809] b. about 1771; Martha d. at Litchfield, 16 Feb 1835.

iii OLIVE CRAM, b. 6 Oct 1769; d. at Gardiner, ME, 16 Mar 1851; m. 25 Nov 1788, her second cousin, JOHN CRAM (*John Cram⁵, John Cram⁴, Sarah Holt Cram³, Henry², Nicholas¹*), b. at Wilton, 16 Oct 1768 son of John and Susanna (Fuller) Cram; John d. at Hallowell, ME, 4 Jan 1818.

iv ZEBULON CRAM, b. 29 Mar 1772; d. at Litchfield, ME, 11 Feb 1852; m. 21 Jun 1799, ANICE HUTCHINSON, b. 19 Jun 1775; Anice d. at Litchfield, 22 Dec 1844.

v RACHEL CRAM, b. 5 Jul 1777; d. at Irasburg, VT, 19 Jun 1850; m. 30 Mar 1799, WILLIAM FULLER, baptized at Ipswich, MA, 12 Feb 1775 son of William and Mary (Holland) Fuller;[1810] William d. at Chester, MN, about 1862. William went to Minnesota to live with his son William after the death of Rachel.

vi SARAH CRAM, b. 25 Aug 1781; d. at Litchfield, ME, 27 Aug 1869; m. Dec 1813, JESSE FALES, b. at Walpole, MA, 24 Jan 1782 son of Moses and Rebecca (Bullard) Fales; Jesse d. at Mount Vernon, ME, 8 Apr 1852.

1805 Perley, *The Hutchinson Family*, p 28

1806 Litchfield, Maine, *The History of Litchfield, Maine* gives her name as Isabella Cunningham

1807 Donovan, History of the Town of Lyndeborough, p 717

1808 *New Hampshire. Probate Court (Hillsborough County), Probate Records, volume 29, pp 249-250*

1809 Martha is not the daughter of James and Jenet Doak born in 1773. Their daughter Martha married John McDuffee which can be verified by the 1812 will of James Doak.

1810 "John Fuller of Ipswich, Mass." NEHGR, volume 53, p 339

vii REBECCA CRAM, b. 9 Mar 1784; d. at Lyndeborough, 11 Sep 1867; m. 1804, ANDREW HARWOOD, b. at Mont Vernon, NH, 1777 son of John and Abigail (Hastings) Harwood; Andrew d. at Lyndeborough, 2 Dec 1859. Two of the children of Rebecca and Andrew married Holts. Daughter Abigail Harwood married John Fletcher Holt and Alice Harwood married David Kendall Holt.

671) ELIZABETH CRAM (*Jonathan Cram⁴, Sarah Holt Cram³, Henry², Nicholas¹*), b. at Wilmington, 4 Nov 1741 daughter of Jonathan and Mary (Chamberlain) Cram; d. at Lyndeborough, 10 Nov 1829; m. about 1764, JOHN CARKIN, b. at Nottingham, 18 Dec 1735 son of John and Esther (Wines) Carkin; John d. at Lyndeborough, 2 Mar 1799.

John Carkin was a farmer. He and Elizabeth settled in Lyndeborough after their marriage and their four children were born there.

In his will written 20 August 1791 (proved 16 April 1799), John Carkin bequeathed to beloved wife Elizabeth the use of the household furniture during her natural life and a comfortable maintenance to be provided by son Aaron. Beloved son Aaron receives the farm and is responsible for the debts of the estate. Beloved daughters Elizabeth and Prudence each receives £6.13.4 and will divide the household items after their mother's decease. Son Aaron was named executor.[1811]

i JOHN CARKIN, b. 9 Sep 1765; d. at Lyndeborough, 9 Jul 1777.

ii AARON CARKIN, b. 30 Mar 1767; d. at Lyndeborough, 19 Feb 1852; m. at Lyndeborough, 15 Dec 1791, ELIZABETH "BETSEY" DUNCKLEE, b. 7 May 1768;[1812] Betsey d. at Lyndeborough, 30 Nov 1845.

iii ELIZABETH CARKIN, b. 24 Jul 1770; m. at Lyndeborough, 6 Nov 1794, her second cousin, EPHRAIM PUTNAM (*Ephraim Putnam⁵, Sarah Cram Putnam⁴, Sarah Holt Cram³, Henry², Nicholas¹*), b. at Lyndeborough, 20 Oct 1768 son of Ephraim and Lucy (Spalding) Putnam; Ephraim was living in Lyndeborough in 1850 at the poor farm.

iv PRUDENCE CARKIN, b. 2 Sep 1774; d. at Lyndeborough, 29 Nov 1814. Prudence did not marry.

672) RACHEL CRAM (*Jonathan Cram⁴, Sarah Holt Cram³, Henry², Nicholas¹*), b. at Lyndeborough, 16 Apr 1744 daughter of Jonathan and Mary (Chamberlain) Cram; d. at Lyndeborough, 29 Apr 1833; m. 1769, EPHRAIM PUTNAM, b. at Salem, 30 Sep 1744 son of Archelaus and Mehitable (Putnam) Putnam; Ephraim d. at Lyndeborough, 11 May 1821.

Rachel and Ephraim resided in Lyndeborough where their eight children were born.

i JONATHAN PUTNAM, b. 14 Sep 1769; d. at Lyndeborough, 27 Sep 1843; m. at Lyndeborough, 24 Nov 1791, MARY HILDRETH, b. 1772 (died at age 74) of Lyndeborough;[1813] Mary d. at Lyndeborough, 15 Apr 1846.

ii MEHITABLE PUTNAM, b. 6 Dec 1772; d. after 1850 when she was living in Peterborough; m. 20 Feb 1801, ROBERT RITCHEY, b. at Peterborough, 3 Dec 1763 son of William and Mary (Waugh) Ritchey; Robert d. at Peterborough, 23 Nov 1832.[1814]

iii ARCHELAUS PUTNAM, b. 6 Mar 1775; d. 4 Mar 1839. Archelaus did not marry.

iv EPHRAIM PUTNAM, b. 7 Jan 1778; d. 20 Feb 1785.

v ABIJAH PUTNAM, b. 30 Nov 1780; d. 16 Feb 1785.

vi EPHRAIM PUTNAM, b. 30 Apr 1785; d. at Lyndeborough, 11 Jun 1862; m. at Lyndeborough, 8 Feb 1814, his fourth cousin, ESTHER PEARSON (*Esther Holt Pearson⁵, Joseph⁴, Timothy³, James², Nicholas¹*), b. at Wilton, 11 Nov 1792 daughter of Ebenezer and Esther (Holt) Pearson; Esther d. at Lyndeborough, 12 Mar 1856.

vii NATHANIEL PUTNAM, b. 22 Aug 1788; d. at Lyndeborough, 19 Mar 1843. Nathaniel did not marry. At the probate of his estate, his brothers Jonathan Putnam and Ephraim Putnam described as his nearest kin both declined administration of the estate.

viii AMOS PUTNAM, b. 25 Jul 1791; d. 1795.

673) SOLOMON CRAM (*Jonathan Cram⁴, Sarah Holt Cram³, Henry², Nicholas¹*), b. at Lyndeborough, about 1746 son of Jonathan and Mary (Chamberlain) Cram; d. at Lyndeborough, 1 May 1825; m. about 1771, MARY, b. about 1740; Mary d. at Lyndeborough, 21 Apr 1819.

In his will written 24 December 1824 (proved 31 May 1825), Solomon Cram of Lyndeborough bequeathed to the Baptist Church and Society of Milford, fifty dollars. Son James Cram receives one dollar as he has received his portion. Timothy

---

1811 *New Hampshire. Probate Court (Hillsborough County), Volume 8, pp 219-221, will of John Carkin*

1812 Elizabeth's date of birth is on her gravestone; Johnson Corner Cemetery, Lyndeborough, findagrave ID 50827315

1813 Although not certain, it is possible that the parents of Mary Hildreth are Ephraim and Elizabeth (Ellenwood) Hildreth and that she was born in Amherst 12 Jan 1772.

1814 Robert Ritchey's date and place of birth and names of parents are given on his death record.

Putnam, Esq. receives all the stock animals, farming tools, and household items to be at his disposal and also to pay any debts of the estate. Benjamin Goodridge of Lyndeborough was named executor.

Solomon and Mary Cram were parents of four children born at Lyndeborough.

i MARY CRAM, b. 1772; d. 3 Oct 1777.

ii SARAH CRAM, b. 1774; d. 23 Sep 1777.

iii JAMES CRAM, b. Aug 1777; d. at Lyndeborough, 3 Oct 1860. James did not marry. His occupation is listed as teacher on his death record.

iv MARY CRAM, b. 1779; d. 24 Sep 1781.

674) URIAH CRAM (*Jonathan Cram[4], Sarah Holt Cram[3], Henry[2], Nicholas[1]*), b. about 1750 son of Jonathan and Mary (Chamberlain) Cram; d. at Lyndeborough, 2 Oct 1831; m. about 1779, EUNICE ELLENWOOD, b. 1745; Eunice d. at Lyndeborough, 1 Dec 1831.

Uriah and Eunice resided in Lyndeborough. Uriah seems to have done not active service during the Revolution but hired Jacob Dutton for three months of service.[1815]

Uriah Cram and Eunice Ellenwood were parents of five children born at Lyndeborough.

i HENRY CRAM, b. 1780; d. at Lyndeborough, 30 Nov 1848; m. about 1806, RHODA CARLETON, b. at Lyndeborough, 29 Jun 1783 daughter of Jeremiah and Lois (Hoyt) Carleton; Rhoda d. 8 Oct 1855.

ii JOSEPH CRAM, b. 22 Apr 1784; d. at Lyndeborough, 21 Jul 1858; m. at Billerica, 24 Dec 1818, ELIZABETH BROWN, b. at Billerica, 30 Sep 1790 daughter of Samuel and Elizabeth (Noyes) Brown; Elizabeth d. at Lyndeborough, 18 May 1878.

iii EUNICE CRAM, b. 31 Aug 1785; d. at Lyndeborough, 29 Feb 1868; m. 1st about 1809, WILLIAM ABBOTT, b. at Chelmsford, 3 Nov 1787 son of Jeremiah and Susannah (Baldwin) Abbott; William d. at Lyndeborough, 14 Jan 1824. Eunice remained a widow for 12 years and then married WILLIAM STRAFFORD 25 Jul 1836. In 1850, Eunice Strafford was the head of her household in Lyndeborough with her children from her marriage to William Abbott. In 1860, she was using the name Eunice Abbott and living with her son Calvin, and her death record is in the name Abbott. Nothing else was found for William Strafford.

iv JAMES CRAM, b. 13 Mar 1788; d. at Lyndeborough, 29 Jun 1861; m. at Billerica, 11 Dec 1828, LUCY BROWN, b. at Billerica, 1 Feb 1804 daughter of Samuel and Elizabeth (Noyes) Brown; Lucy d. 1 Nov 1884.

v LYDIA CRAM, b. 27 Jun 1790; d. 3 Aug 1794.

675) DINAH CRAM (*Humphrey Cram[4], Sarah Holt Cram[3], Henry[2], Nicholas[1]*), b. at Windham, 10 Dec 1737 daughter of Humphrey and Hannah (Blunt) Cram; d. at Hartland, VT, 13 Oct 1821; m. 1st at Windham, 1 May 1755, THOMAS PARKE ROOD, b. 23 May 1732 son of David and Joanna (Parke) Rood; Thomas d. at Hartland, 10 Oct 1795. Dinah m. 2nd about 1796, WILLIAM BENJAMIN, b. at Watertown, 16 Jun 1738 son of Jonathan and Hannah (Cunnable) Benjamin; William d. at Hartland, Dec 1816. William's first wife was Sarah Child.

Dinah Cram and Thomas Rood were parents of six children, the oldest child born at Montpelier and the other likely at Hartland, Vermont.

i JOANNA ROOD, b. at Montpelier, 20 Jul 1757; d. 14 Jun 1758.

ii HUMPHREY ROOD, b. at Hartland, 8 Aug 1761; d. at Hartland, Nov 1833; m. at Ashburnham, MA, 19 Jan 1785, ELIZABETH "BETSEY" KIBLINGER, b. at Ashburnham, 24 Apr 1763 daughter of John and Catherine (Wolfe) Kiblinger; Betsey d. at Morrisville, VT, 17 Jan 1852.

iii BETSEY ROOD, b. Jun 1764; d. 5 Nov 1766.

iv DAVID ROOD, b. 11 Aug 1768; d. 23 Jan 1773

v SARAH ROOD, b. 6 May 1771; d. 17 Apr 1774.

vi MIRANDA ROOD, b. 20 Sep 1775; d. 12 May 1778.

676) SARAH CRAM (*Humphrey Cram[4], Sarah Holt Cram[3], Henry[2], Nicholas[1]*), b. at Hampton, about 1740 daughter of Humphrey and Hannah (Blunt) Cram; m. at Union, CT, 10 Apr 1760, JOHN ROSEBROOK, b. at Grafton, 24 May 1738 son of James and Margaret (MacCoy) Rosebrook; John d. at Fabyan, NH, 25 Sep 1817.

[1815] Donovan, *History of the Town of Lyndeborough*, p 164

John Rosebrook served in the Revolution as 2nd Lieutenant in Capt. Nehemiah May's company of Hampshire County militia.[1816]

John Rosebrook and Sarah Cram were parents of nine children. Births of seven of the children are recorded at Wales, Massachusetts and two further children are recorded in baptismal records at Holland, Massachusetts. The family then relocated to Lancaster, New Hampshire where John served on a committee related to building a new meeting house.[1817]

i PERSIS ROSEBROOK, b. at Wales, 16 Sep 1760; d. at Holland, 15 Oct 1830; m. at Wales, 7 Apr 1782, DAVID WALLIS, b. at Woodstock, 13 Sep 1758 son of David and Mary (Freeland) Wallis; David d. at Holland, 11 Jul 1843.

ii MARGARET ROSEBROOK, b. at Wales, 14 Apr 1762. Margaret is not listed with the other children all baptized at Holland in 1781.

iii SARAH ROSEBROOK, b. at Wales, 18 Jun 1764; m. at Holland, 5 Feb 1789, EZRA REEVE, b. at Holland, 11 Aug 1760 son of Ezra and Mary (Landon) Reeve.

iv CHARLES ROSEBROOK, b. at Wales, 18 Mar 1766; d. at Holland, MA, 30 Jul 1838; m. at Holland, 10 Feb 1799, MARGARET "PEGGY" REEVE, b. at Holland, 9 Feb 1763 daughter of Ezra and Mary (Landon) Reeve; Peggy d. Oct 1812.

v JOHN ROSEBROOK, b. about 1768; m. at Holland, MA, 1 Jan 1792, MEHITABLE REEVE, b. at Holland, 7 Feb 1767 daughter of Ezra and Mary (Landon) Reeve.

vi JONATHAN ROSEBROOK, b. at Wales, 19 Aug 1771; d. at Lancaster, NH, about 1799 (remarriage of his widow); m. at Lancaster, 17 Jul 1796, MARY "POLLY" MONROE, b. 14 Mar 1775 (death age 61 years 4 days); Mary d. at Guildhall, VT, 18 Mar 1836. Widow Polly Rosebrook married Joshua Hopkinson at Lancaster on 1 Sep 1799.

vii IRENA ROSEBROOK, b. at Wales, 8 Jan 1774; m. at Lancaster, NH, 31 Dec 1797, HOPE BROWN, b. at Alstead, NH, 22 Apr 1775 son of Elias and Abigail (Olcott) Brown.

viii URIAL ROSEBROOK, b. at Wales, 9 Sep 1776; m. at Lancaster, 15 Jul 1800, SUSANNA FOWLER

ix HANNAH ROSEBROOK, b. at Holland, 1780; d. at Columbia, NH, 29 Oct 1852; m. about 1800, DAVID BUNDY, b. at Walpole, NH, 1779 son of Isaac and Sarah (Johnson) Bundy; David d. at Columbia, 18 Feb 1847.

677) MEHITABLE CRAM (*Humphrey Cram⁴, Sarah Holt Cram³, Henry², Nicholas¹*), b. at Union, CT, 15 Apr 1745 daughter of Humphrey and Hannah (Blunt) Cram; d. at Milton, VT, about 1781; m. at Union, 29 Nov 1764, JONAH LOOMIS, b. at Windsor, CT, 5 May 1743 son of Daniel and Sarah (Enos) Loomis; Jonah d. at Georgia, VT, 22 Apr 1813. Jonah was second married to Martha Post.

Mehitable Cram and Jonah Loomis were parents of six children likely all born at Milton, Vermont.

i SARAH LOOMIS, b. 9 Jul 1767; d. at Warren, VT, 22 Jul 1826; m. about 1786, DANIEL MUNSELL, b. at Stafford, CT, 1765 son of Samuel and Eunice (Downer) Munsell; Daniel d. at Warren, 31 Mar 1813.

ii WILLIAM LOOMIS, b. 2 Dec 1769; d. at East Roxbury, VT, 7 Mar 1813; m. 1795, ANNA PROUTY, b. Jul 1779 daughter of Jacob and Rachel (Eddy) Prouty; Anna d. at East Roxbury, 23 Oct 1857. Anna married second Bernard Blanchard.

iii ELIZABETH LOOMIS, b. 22 Jun 1774; d. at Jefferson County, NY, 20 Dec 1847; m. ELIJAH GROUT, b. at Petersham, MA, 26 May 1767 son of Joel and Sarah (Hudson) Grout; Elijah d. at Fall River, WI, 17 Oct 1854. After Elizabeth's death, Elijah went to live with their son Elijah Loomis Grout.

iv CHARLES LOOMIS, b. 1776; d. at Hiram, OH, 22 Sep 1848; m. OLIVE HATCH, b. at Willington, CT, 1774 daughter of Herman and Eunice (Broughton) Hatch; Olive d. at Hiram, 20 Dec 1859.

v ENOS LOOMIS, b. 1778; d. at Jersey, OH, 23 Apr 1839; m. about 1811, ELSABETH SMEDLEY, b. about 1790; Elsabeth d. at Lafayette, IN, 7 Aug 1849. Elsabeth went to live with her son Enos after her husband's death.

678) JONATHAN CRAM (*Humphrey Cram⁴, Sarah Holt Cram³, Henry², Nicholas¹*), b. at Union, 9 Mar 1746 son of Humphrey and Hannah (Blunt) Cram; d. of smallpox,[1818] at Lancaster, NH, 28 Aug 1811; m. at Wales, MA, 15 Jan 1770, ABIGAIL WEBBER, b. at Brimfield, 15 May 1749 daughter of Edward and Abigail (Haynes) Webber.

[1816] Massachusetts Soldiers and Sailors in the Revolution, volume 13, p 578

[1817] Somers, *History of Lancaster, New Hampshire*, p 177

[1818] Somers, *History of Lancaster, New Hampshire*, p 327

Jonathan Cram and Abigail Webber were parents of eight children likely all born at Wales. The family was in Lancaster, New Hampshire at the time the children married. Three of the children remained in Lancaster, but the others scattered to Illinois, Kentucky, and Canada.

i HUMPHREY CRAM, b. at Wales, 1772; d. a Lancaster, NH, 17 Mar 1813; m. 5 Jul 1797, his fourth cousin once removed, PHEBE EASTMAN (*Abiah Holt Eastman[5], Benjamin[4], Nicholas[3], Nicholas[2], Nicholas[1]*), b. 21 Oct 1773 daughter of Richard and Abiah (Holt) Eastman; Phebe d. at North Conway, NH, 14 May 1866.

ii FRANCIS CRAM, b. at Wales, 29 Nov 1773; d. at Lenox, Upper Canada (Québec), 3 Nov 1810;[1819] m. at Lancaster, NH, 13 Feb 1797, POLLY GUSTIN, b. 1777; Polly d. at Rochester, NY, 16 Dec 1863. Polly was married second to Elijah Harlow.

iii EDWARD CRAM, b. at Wales, 11 Apr 1776; d. at Sidney, Ontario, 19 Dec 1851. Edward does not seem to have married.

iv AMBROSE CRAM, b. at Wales, 26 Apr 1778; d. at Campbell, KY, about 1825; m. at Newport, NH, 21 Oct 1805, FANNY HURD, b. at Newport, 27 Mar 1783 daughter of Stephen and Abigail (Glidden) Hurd;[1820] Fanny d. at Pendleton, KY, 23 Oct 1854.

v MARY "POLLY" CRAM, b. at Wales, about 1781; d. at Sidney, Hastings, Ontario,[1821] 22 Jan 1858; m. at Lancaster, 19 Dec 1802, her first cousin, SYLVESTER FAULKNER (*Peter Faulkner[5], Deborah Farnum Faulkner[4], John Farnum[3], Elizabeth Holt Farnum[2], Nicholas[1]*), b. at Sturbridge, MA, 19 May 1780 son of Peter and Chloe (Cram) Faulkner; Sylvester d. at Sidney, 15 Aug 1863.

vi JONATHAN CRAM, b. 1785; d. at Lancaster, 1813; m. at Lancaster, 9 Aug 1807, KATY C. CHAPMAN

vii ABIGAIL CRAM, b. about 1787; d. at DeKalb, IL, 3 Aug 1861; m. about 1808, ESDRAS ROSBROOK, b. 31 Aug 1782 son of Eleazer and Hannah (Haynes) Rosbrook; Esdras d. at DeKalb, 19 Feb 1875.

viii SELENDA CRAM, b. about 1790; d. at Lancaster, NH, 19 Feb 1830; m. at Lancaster, 14 Oct 1813, WARREN PORTER, b. at Charlestown, NH, 1 Jun 1792 son of Chandler and Jerusha (Downer) Porter; Warren d. at Lancaster, 4 Apr 1878.

679) MOSES STILES (*Phebe Cram Stiles[4], Sarah Holt Cram[3], Henry[2], Nicholas[1]*), b. at Ashford, 17 Oct 1735 son of Moses and Phebe (Cram) Stiles; d. at Greenfield, NH, 1811 (probate 1811); m. by 1761, SARAH who has not been identified.

Moses came from Connecticut and settled in Lyndeborough.[1822] He was in Greenfield at the time of his death.

In his will written 28 March 1811 (proved 18 June 1811), Moses Stiles of Greenfield bequeathed one dollar to his son Aaron Stiles. Daughter Sarah Holt received the plain chest and table, one pewter platter, and three pewter plates. His other two sons Moses Stiles and Samuel Stiles have received their shares and signed acquittances. Niece Rachel Taylor receives the rest of the estate real and personal provided she lives with and cares for Moses for Moses's natural life. Joseph Ellingwood of Greenfield was named executor.[1823]

Moses and Sarah Stiles were parents of seven children born at Lyndeborough. Three of the children died in the same week in September 1777.

i SARAH STILES, b. 24 Mar 1762; m. *perhaps* by 1801, UZZIEL HOLT (*Joshua[4], John[3], Samuel[2], Nicholas[1]*), b. at Andover, 12 Apr 1766 son of Joshua and Ruth (Burnap) Holt; Uzziel d. after 1840 when he was living in Sharon, VT, age 75. From her father's will, it is known that Sarah married a Holt and a child of Uzziel and Sarah Holt is recorded at Lyndeborough in 1801. However, it is speculation that Uzziel is the Holt that she married. Sarah Stiles and Uzziel Holt are Family 603.

ii MOSES STILES, b. 6 Jun 1765; m. at Lyndeborough, 9 Aug 1790, his second cousin once removed, MARY HOLT (*William[4], Oliver[3], Henry[2], Nicholas[1]*), b. at Lyndeborough, about 1767 daughter of William and Beulah (-) Holt. Moses Stiles and Mary Holt are Family 633.

[1819] Institut Généalogique Drouin; Montreal, Quebec, Canada; *Drouin Collection.* Francis Cram of the County of Lenox, age about thirty-six years, died on the third and buried on the fourth day of November 1810

[1820] The 1813 will of Stephen Hurd of Newport, NH includes a bequest to his daughter Fanny Cram.

[1821] *1851 Census of Canada East, Canada West, New Brunswick, and Nova Scotia*, Year: 1851; Census Place: Sidney, Hastings County, Canada West (Ontario); Schedule: A; Roll: C_11727; Page: 24; Line: 37. Mary Faulkner, age 69. Also listed are Sylvester Faulkner, age 71, Sylvester age 28 and what seems his wife Adelaide and children age 5 and 3.

[1822] Guild, *The Stiles Family in America*, p 472

[1823] *New Hampshire. Probate Court (Hillsborough County), Probate Records volume 17, pp 291-292*

iii AARON STILES, b. 18 Sep 1767; d. at Lyndeborough before 1840 (when his widow was head of household); m. ABIAH SLADER,[1824] b. about 1775 daughter of (-) and Sally (Dustin) Slader; Abiah d. after 1860 when she was living with her daughter in Peterborough.

iv MARY STILES, b. 14 Jun 1770; d. 8 Sep 1777.

v PHEBE STILES, b. 22 Jun 1774; d. 5 Sep 1777.

vi SAMUEL STILES, b. 15 Sep 1776; d. 9 Sep 1777.

vii SAMUEL STILES, b. 19 Apr 1779; d. after 1850 when living in Warren, VT; m. BETSY CRAM, b. about 1778; Betsy d. after 1850. Samuel and Betsy did not have children but adopted a son William Stiles.

680) ASAHEL STILES (*Phebe Cram Stiles⁴, Sarah Holt Cram³, Henry², Nicholas¹*), b. at Ashford, 21 May 1739 son of Moses and Phebe (Cram) Stiles; d. at Addison, NY; m. by 1768, SARAH DUTTON, b. at Nottingham, NH, 18 Apr 1744 daughter of Josiah and Sarah (Parker) Dutton.

Asahel and Sarah resided in Lyndeborough until about 1787 when they relocated to Addison, New York where they are believed to have died.[1825]

Asahel served during the Revolution performing one-third of a term of service on his own behalf and one-third of a term each for Solomon Cram and Capt. Jonathan Cram. Asahel participated in the Ticonderoga campaign.[1826]

Asahel Stiles and Sarah Dutton were parents of nine children.

i DANIEL STILES, b. at Lyndeborough, 21 Oct 1768; d. at Quincy, OH, 27 Jan 1839; m. about 1795, LOIS MORSE, b. at Guilford, CT, 14 Nov 1776 daughter of John and Deborah (Lines) Morse.[1827]

ii ESTHER STILES, b. 25 Aug 1770; d. 27 Mar 1785.

iii SARAH STILES, b. at Lyndeborough, 17 Mar 1773; m. TIMOTHY SEARL, b. 17 Apr 1774 son of Reuben and Mercy (Allis) Searl; Timothy d. at DePue, IL, 17 Sep 1837.

iv HANNAH STILES, b. at Lyndeborough, 27 Feb 1775; d. at McArthur, OH, 9 Dec 1840; m. JOHN WYMAN, b. at Oxford, MA, 27 Nov 1763 son of John and Anna (Town) Wyman; John d. at McArthur, 26 Mar 1839.[1828]

v RHODA STILES, b. at Lyndeborough, 8 Sep 1778; d. at Quincy, OH, 17 May 1849; m. URIAH MARTIN; Uriah d. at Bath, OH, 1829 (probate Nov 1829).

vi REUBEN STILES, b. at Lyndeborough, 30 Dec 1780; d. at Troupsburg, NY, 5 Aug 1832; m. at Lyndeborough, 1804, his first cousin, PHEBE DUTTON, b. at Lyndeborough, 22 Aug 1786 daughter of Ezra and Phebe (Gould) Dutton; Phebe d. at Troupsburg, 3 Dec 1863. Phebe married second John Coffin.

vii ASAHEL STILES, b. at Lyndeborough, 20 Oct 1783; d. at Quincy, OH, 27 Jan 1860; m. URANA JOHNSON, b. 13 Aug 1786 daughter of Daniel and Sarah (Jones) Johnson; Urana d. at Quincy, 8 Apr 1863.

viii ESTHER STILES, b. at Lyndeborough, 7 Jul 1786; d. at Elk, OH, Jam 1858; m. about 1804, JOSHUA GREEN, b. 1782; Joshua d. at Lynden, MN, 26 Nov 1869. Joshua married second Jane Akin on 28 Jul 1858.

ix BENJAMIN STILES, b. at Steuben County, NY, about 1788;[1829] d. at Bath, OH, 29 Jul 1860; m. HANNAH HELMER, b. 1789; Hannah d. at Bath, 17 Feb 1864.

681) JOHN STILES (*Phebe Cram Stiles⁴, Sarah Holt Cram³, Henry², Nicholas¹*), b. at Ashford, 19 Aug 1740 son of Moses and Phebe (Cram) Stiles; m. at Pepperell, 30 Sep 1774, SUSANNAH CHAMBERLAIN, b. at Pepperell, 1752 daughter of Phineas and Lydia (Williams) Chamberlain.

John and Susannah lived in Lyndeborough in the area of town that was later annexed by Francestown. He served two months in the Revolution in the company of Capt. Peter Clark and was at Bennington.[1830]

There are ten children reported for John Stiles and Susannah Chamberlain likely all born at Lyndeborough.[1831]

i JOHN STILES, b. 22 Oct 1778; d. 16 Apr 1786.

1824 It is not certain that her last name is Slader; Staton has also been suggested.

1825 Guild, *The Stiles Family in America*, p 475

1826 Donovan, *The History of Lyndeborough*, volume 1, p 201

1827 Morse and Leavitt, *Morse Genealogy*, p 146

1828 Ohio, Soldier Grave Registrations, 1804-1958; gives both birth date and date of death

1829 Guild, *The Stiles Family in America*, p 477

1830 Donovan, *History of the Town of Lyndeborough*, volume 1, p 163, p 201

1831 Guild, *The Stiles Family in America*, p 473

ii SUSANNAH STILES, b. 4 Oct 1780; d. 12 May 1786.

iii BETTY STILES (twin), b. 20 Jan 1783; d. 10 Feb 1783.

iv MESECH WEIR STILES (twin), b. 20 Jan 1783; d. at Washington County, NY, 1843; m. at Winhall, VT, 9 Oct 1812, his fourth cousin twice removed, SUSANNA GOWING (*Abigail Batchelder Gowing⁷, Abigail Eaton Batchelder⁶, Abigail Russell Eaton⁵, Robert Russell⁴, Phebe Johnson Russell³, Mary Holt Johnson², Nicholas¹*), b. at Wilmington, MA, 27 Apr 1783 daughter of Daniel and Abigail (Batchelder) Gowing; Susanna d. after 1850 when she was living at Jackson, NY.

v JOHN STILES, b. at Lyndeborough, 17 May 1786; d. at Winhall, VT, 1845; m. at Wilmington, MA, 24 Sep 1807, his fourth cousin twice removed, HANNAH GOWING (*Abigail Batchelder Gowing⁷, Abigail Eaton Batchelder⁶, Abigail Russell Eaton⁵, Robert Russell⁴, Phebe Johnson Russell³, Mary Holt Johnson², Nicholas¹*), b. at Wilmington, 7 Jun 1787 daughter of Daniel and Abigail (Batchelder) Gowing; Hannah d. at Winhall, 16 Oct 1855.

vi SUSANNAH STILES, b. 2 May 1787; d. at Greenfield, NH, 10 Aug 1860; m. at Winhall, VT, 4 Oct 1814, JESSE CUDWORTH, b. at Greenfield, NH, 9 Jun 1786 son of Samuel and Hannah (Boyden) Cudworth; Jesse d. at Greenfield, 5 May 1876.

vii ASAHEL STILES, b. 23 Nov 1789; d. at Randolph, VT, 27 Sep 1834; m. at Tunbridge, 12 Nov 1812, NANCY BRADFORD, b. 1788 daughter of Timothy and Edith (Howe) Bradford; Nancy d. at Randolph, 6 Jul 1861. A grandson of Asahel and Nancy, Maynard F. Stiles, was a prominent attorney in West Virginia.[1832]

viii MOSES STILES, b. about 1791; d. at Boston, 1830; m. at Boston, 24 Feb 1816, MARY DOBIE, b. about 1784; Mary d. at Charlestown, MA, 5 Mar 1856. Moses and Mary did not have children.

ix DAVID STILES, d. about age 22[1833]

x BETSEY STILES

682) SARAH STILES (*Phebe Cram Stiles⁴, Sarah Holt Cram³, Henry², Nicholas¹*), b. at Ashford, 24 Jul 1747 daughter of Moses and Phebe (Cram) Stiles; m. by 1770, BENJAMIN DUTTON, b. at Nottingham, 27 Apr 1743 son of Josiah and Sarah (Parker) Dutton; Benjamin d. at Lyndeborough, 3 Sep 1803.

Benjamin was one of four brothers who came to Lyndeborough, Benjamin arriving about 1769.[1834] Benjamin Dutton and Sarah Stiles were parents of nine children born at Lyndeborough.

i BENJAMIN DUTTON, b. 17 Jul 1770; m. at Francestown, 29 Apr 1794, LYDIA CLARK, b. at Danvers, MA, 4 Feb 1770 daughter of Hugh and Lydia (Gardner) Clark.[1835] Benjamin and Lydia were parents of nine children born at Chester, VT.

ii SARAH DUTTON, b. 15 May 1772; died young

iii REUBEN STILES DUTTON, b. 26 Aug 1774; m. 1st about 1797, ANNA "NANCY" CLARK, b. perhaps at Merrimac, 1773 daughter of Hugh and Lydia (Gardner) Clark; Anna d. at Lyndeborough, about 1821. Reuben m. 2nd at Peterborough, 21 Nov 1822, LYDIA DIAMOND (widow of Aaron Avery), b. at Peterborough, 6 May 1797 daughter of William and Rebecca (Symonds) Diamond.

iv JACOB DUTTON, b. 26 Sep 1776; d. 2 Dec 1779.

v SARAH DUTTON, b. 19 Mar 1779; d. 31 Dec 1785.

vi AMY DUTTON, b. 24 Jul 1781; d. 6 Jul 1782.

vii DAIDAMIA DUTTON, b. 29 Apr 1784; d. at Peterborough, 28 Jul 1864; m. her second cousin, JOSIAH DUTTON CRAM (*Nathan Cram⁵, Benjamin Cram⁴, Sarah Holt Cram³, Henry², Nicholas¹*), b. at Lyndeborough, 27 Mar 1780 son of Nathan and Rachel (Dutton) Cram; Josiah d. at Peterborough, 7 Nov 1847.

viii LOIS DUTTON, b. 10 Sep 1786; d. 1 Dec 1803.

ix MOSES DUTTON, b. 24 Mar 1789; d. at Paw Paw, MI, 9 Apr 1879; m. at Lyndeborough, 6 Feb 1812, DOLLY STEARNS, b. in MA, about 1796.

683) ABIGAIL WOODWARD (*Huldah Cram Woodward⁴, Sarah Holt Cram³, Henry², Nicholas¹*), b. at Canterbury, 24 Mar 1742/3 daughter of Ephraim and Huldah (Cram) Woodward; d. at Brooklyn CT, 28 May 1786; m. at Canterbury, 28 Apr 1768,

---

[1832] Miller and Maxwell, *West Virginia and its People*, volume 1, p 46

[1833] Stiles, *The Stiles Family in America*, p 475

[1834] Donovan, *History of the Town of Lyndeborough*, vol 2, p 735

[1835] Clark, *Records of the Descendants of Hugh Clark*, p 39

PETER DAVISON, b. at Pomfret, 15 May 1739 son of Joseph and Mary (Warner) Davison; Peter d. at Brooklyn, CT, 29 May 1800. Peter married second Susannah Hammett (widow of Benjamin Weaver) on 6 Nov 1786.

Peter Davison did not leave a will. At the distribution of the estate on 23 July 1801, it was considered that some of the heirs lived out of state, some of the heirs-at-law were minors, and that the real estate, consisting of thirty-six acres, could not reasonably be divided without impacting its value. Therefore, the real estate was settled on Peter Davison, the only heir living in the state capable of assuming the estate. Peter was to make proportional payments to the other heirs-at-law. The heirs of the estate listed were heirs of Ebenezer Davison, Ephraim Davison, Peter Davison, Huldah Carpenter, Bariah Davison, Alpheus Davison, and Abigail Davison.[1836] Abigail mentioned in the probate was Peter's daughter with his second wife Susannah.

Abigail Woodward and Peter Davison were parents of six children.[1837]

i EBENEZER DAVISON, b. at Canterbury, 17 Oct 1769; d. before 1801 when his father's estate was settled. The "heirs of Ebenezer" are mentioned in the estate file but not named.

ii EPHRAIM DAVISON, b. at Canterbury, 5 Dec 1772; m. 1st at Brooklyn, CT, 12 Mar 1795, his stepsister, ANNA WEAVER, b. at Ashford, about 1774 daughter of Benjamin and Susannah (Hammett) Weaver; Anna d. by 1807. Ephraim m. 2nd at Francestown, NH, 17 Nov 1808, his first cousin, DELIA WOODWARD (*Ithamar Woodward[5], Huldah Cram Woodward[4], Sarah Holt Cram[3], Henry[2], Nicholas[1]*), b. at Lyndeborough, 9 Jul 1779 daughter of Ithamar and Huldah (Sharp) Woodward; Delia d. at Francestown, 16 Mar 1846.

iii PETER DAVISON, b. at Canterbury, 23 Jun 1775; d. at Brooklyn, CT, 1847. Peter did not marry. In his will, he left his estate primarily to his half-sister Abigail Davison and to Betsey Weaver (likely his stepsister). He also mentions dividing any residue among any of his living brothers and sisters but does not name them.

iv HULDAH CARPENTER, b. at Canterbury, 9 Apr 1778; d. at Eastford, CT, 14 Mar 1863; m. 1st at Ashford, 15 Apr 1800, JOSEPH TITUS CARPENTER, b. at Ashford, 2 Jun 1774 son of Jonah and Zerviah (Whittemore) Carpenter; Joseph d. at Ashford, 11 Apr 1805. Huldah m. 2nd at Ashford, 26 Nov 1807, JOHN GRIGGS, b. at Ashford, 5 Oct 1775 son of Joseph and Rebecca (Chaffee) Griggs; John d. at Pomfret, 1 Jun 1866. Joseph T. Carpenter died the day before Huldah gave birth to twins.

v BERIAH DAVISON, b. at Canterbury, 12 Jul 1780; d. at Brooklyn, CT, 24 Oct 1853; m. 2 Apr 1807, MARY UTLEY, b. at Hampton, 30 Jan 1789 daughter of Thomas and Abigail (Hodgkins) Utley; Mary d. at Brooklyn, Jan 1879. Beriah and Mary's son George Luther Davison was a silversmith.[1838]

vi ALPHEUS DAVISON, b. at Brooklyn, CT, 20 May 1786; d. at Monson, ME, 18 Oct 1866; m. at Westminster, VT, 21 Feb 1817, POLLY HITCHCOCK, b. 10 Mar 1793 daughter of Heli and Tryphena (Goodell) Hitchcock; Polly d. at Monson, ME, 8 May 1867. Alpheus was a physician in Westminster, Vermont and later in Monson, Maine.

684) ITHAMAR WOODWARD (*Huldah Cram Woodward[4], Sarah Holt Cram[3], Henry[2], Nicholas[1]*), b. at Canterbury, 21 Jan 1748/9 son of Ephraim and Huldah (Cram) Woodward; d. at Francestown, NH, 9 Jan 1839; m. at Canterbury, 23 Nov 1773, HULDAH SHARP, b. at Pomfret, 3 Oct 1749 daughter of Solomon and Sarah (Goodell) Sharp; Huldah d. at Francestown, 12 Jun 1823.

Ithamar and Huldah lived in Lyndeborough but in that part of the town that was annexed by Francestown in 1792. Ithamar served in the Revolution enlisting from Lyndeborough on 26 September 1776 in the company of Capt. McConnell. He was at the Battle of White Plains.[1839]

Ithamar did not leave a will and administration of his estate was granted to eldest son Daniel on 5 February 1839. Inventory of the estate was made 5 March 1839 with real estate valued at $1600 and personal estate at $178.88. The personal estate was insufficient to settle the debts and a portion of the real estate was licensed to be sold. After payment of debts and expenses, the balance left in the estate was $36.38.[1840]

Ithamar and Huldah were parents of eight children born at Lyndeborough.

i ELIPHALET WOODWARD, b. 16 Nov 1774; d. at Marshfield, VT, 4 Mar 1830; m. 4 Mar 1802, PATTY BUTTERFIELD, b. at Francestown, 4 Jul 1781 daughter of Isaac and Sarah (Webster) Butterfield; Patty d. at Marshfield, 23 Sep 1861.

1836 Connecticut Wills and Probate Records; Plainfield Probate District, Estate of Peter Davison of Brooklyn, Case 608

1837 There are inconsistencies in the Barbour vital records transcriptions related to this family. For example, the transcriptions report that Abigail died in 1781 and Peter remarried in 1781. But it can be established through probate records, death records, etc. that Peter's second wife was not widowed until 1785 and so they cannot have married until 1786. Also, other record information for son Alpheus is consistent with his being born in 1786, so it seems more likely that the transcriptions are just in error and the dates given as 1781 are 1786.

1838 American Silversmiths; https://www.americansilversmiths.org/makers/silversmiths/257922.htm

1839 Donovan, *History of the Town of Lyndeborough*, volume 1, p 205

1840 New Hampshire County Probate Records, Hillsborough, Ithamar Woodward, Case 09933, 44:57, 43:438, 37:479, 49:113; accessed through familysearch.org

ii DANIEL WOODWARD, b. at Lyndeborough, 30 Jan 1777; d. at Francestown, 25 Jun 1867; m. 1st 29 Dec 1803, LUCY BURNHAM, b. about 1780; Lucy d. at Lyndeborough, 19 Aug 1830. Daniel m. 2nd, 1 May 1848, his first cousin, HANNAH WOODWARD (*John Woodward5, Huldah Cram Woodward4, Sarah Holt Cram3, Henry2, Nicholas1*), b. at Lyndeborough, 20 Jan 1791 daughter of John and Judith (Foster) Woodward; Hannah d. 16 Nov 1853. Daniel m. 3rd about 1854, his first cousin once removed, HANNAH W. WOODWARD (*Israel Woodward6, Hannah Putnam Woodward5, Sarah Cram Putnam4, Sarah Holt Cram3, Henry2, Nicholas1*), b. at Lyndeborough, 11 Jul 1812 daughter of Israel and Hannah (Hardy) Woodward; Hannah W. d. at Hudson, NH, 12 Jan 1894.

iii DELIA WOODWARD, b. at Lyndeborough, 9 Jul 1779; d, at Francestown, 16 Mar 1846; m. at Francestown, 14 Nov 1808, as his second wife, her first cousin, EPHRAIM DAVISON (*Abigail Woodward Davison5, Huldah Cram Woodward4, Sarah Holt Cram3, Henry2. Nicholas1*), b. at Canterbury, CT, 5 Dec 1772 son of Peter and Abigail (Woodward) Davison. Ephraim was first married to Anna Weaver.

iv ELIJAH WOODWARD, b. at Lyndeborough, 21 Feb 1782; d. at Landgrove, VT, 25 Jan 1852; m. at Francestown, 17 Nov 1808, RHODA AUSTIN, b. 20 Jan 1786 daughter of Jonathan and Hannah (Charles) Austin; Rhoda d. at Landgrove, 18 Feb 1863.[1841]

v LUCY WOODWARD, b. at Lyndeborough, 9 Sep 1784; d. at Francestown, 28 Jun 1840; m. at Francestown, 7 Apr 1808, her first cousin, EPHRAIM PUTNAM WOODWARD (*Ward Woodward5, Huldah Cram Woodward4, Sarah Holt Cram3, Henry2. Nicholas1*), b. at Brooklyn, CT, 2 Jun 1784 son of Ward and Rebecca (Putnam) Woodward; Ephraim d. somewhere in New York, 1822. The story is that Ephraim had gone to New York to settle a new place and then send for his family, but he died soon after his arrival in 1822.

vi BENJAMIN WOODWARD, b. at Lyndeborough, 12 May 1789; d. at Francestown, 21 Jul 1859; m. BETSEY BIXBY, b. at Francestown, 11 May 1786 daughter of Asa and Elizabeth (Dane) Bixby; Betsey d. at Francestown, 19 Jul 1862.

vii AARON WOODWARD, b. at Lyndeborough, 19 Dec 1792; d. at Francestown, 20 Dec 1866. Aaron did not marry.

viii HULDAH WOODWARD, b. at Lyndeborough, 2 Aug 1795; d. at Jasper, NY, 26 Jan 1885; m. 19 Apr 1827, OLIVER WHITING, b. at Lyndeborough, 3 Apr 1798 son of Oliver and Hannah (Marshall) Whiting; Oliver d. at Jasper, 10 Oct 1886.

685) WARD WOODWARD (*Huldah Cram Woodward4, Sarah Holt Cram3, Henry2, Nicholas1*), b. at Canterbury, 5 Apr 1751 son of Ephraim and Huldah (Cram) Woodward; d. at Brooklyn, CT, 12 Apr 1810; m. 19 Oct 1780, his first cousin, REBECCA PUTNAM (*Sarah Cram Putnam4, Sarah Holt Cram3, Henry2, Nicholas1*), b. at Lyndeborough, 17 Mar 1761 daughter of Ephraim and Sarah (Cram) Putnam; Rebecca d. 18 Oct 1848.

Ward and Rebecca resided in Brooklyn, Connecticut. Capt. Ward Woodward served in the continental army during the Revolution.[1842]

Ward Woodward did not leave a will and his estate entered probate 1810 with the inventory taken 25 June 1810. Real estate was valued at $2604 and the value of personal estate and debts were both listed as 1139.84. The distribution on 8 February 1814 included the dower set off to widow Rebecca and heirs Aaron Woodward, Sewall Woodward, Ephraim P. Woodward, Ward Woodward, Duodemia Woodward, Eleazer Woodward, Nabby Woodward, David Woodward, and Augustus Woodward.[1843]

Rebecca Putnam and Ward Woodward were parents of eleven children born at Brooklyn, Connecticut.

i AARON WOODWARD, b. 20 Sep 1781; d. at Nashville, NH, 16 Jul 1845; m. 15 Oct 1807, his first cousin, ELIZABETH WOODWARD (*Hannah Putnam Woodward5, Sarah Cram Putnam4, Sarah Holt Cram3, Henry2, Nicholas1*), b. at Lyndeborough, 31 Aug 1781 daughter of Eleazer and Hannah (Putnam) Woodward; Elizabeth d. at Hollis, 27 Jan 1879.

ii SEWELL WOODWARD, b. 8 Feb 1783; d. at Brooklyn, CT, 26 Apr 1847.

iii EPHRAIM PUTNAM WOODWARD, b. 2 Jun 1784; d. in NY, 1822;[1844] m. at Francestown, 7 Apr 1808, his first cousin, LUCY WOODWARD (*Ithamar Woodward5, Huldah Cram Woodward4, Sarah Holt Cram3, Henry2, Nicholas1*), b. at Lyndeborough, 9 Sep 1784 daughter of Ithamar and Huldah (Sharp) Woodward; Lucy d. at Francestown, 29 Jun 1840.

1841 Cochrane and Wood, *History of Francestown*, p 486

1842 Donovan, *The History of the Town of Lyndeborough*, p 894

1843 *Connecticut State Library (Hartford, Connecticut);* Probate Place: *Hartford, Connecticut, Probate Packets, Whipple, Zebulon-Z, Misc, 1747-1880. Estate of Ward Woodward, Case 2353*

1844 It is believed that Ephraim went to NY to settle a new place but died soon after his arrival there about 1822.

iv WARD WOODWARD, b. 12 Sep 1785; d. after 1830 when he was living at Sempronius, NY; m. SARAH YORK who has not been identified.

v DEIDAMIA WOODWARD, b. 8 Oct 1787; d. at Brooklyn, CT, 5 Nov 1855. Deidamia did not marry.

vi ELEAZER WOODWARD, b. 11 Jul 1790; d. at Locke, NY, before 1850; m. HENRIETTA INGRAHAM, b. at Killingly, 17 Jan 1794 daughter of Remember and Zimroude (Bicknell) Ingraham; Henrietta d. at Henry County, OH, 11 Mar 1856.

vii ABIGAIL WOODWARD, b. 11 Jan 1792; d. at Danville, NY, 31 Aug 1859; m. at Brooklyn, CT, 5 Jan 1815, JOSEPH AUSTIN, b. at Coventry, RI, 15 Sep 1789 son of Joseph and Elizabeth (Wait) Austin; Joseph d. at Moravia, NY, 20 Jul 1846 (probate 29 Sep 1846).

viii DAVID WOODWARD, b. 12 Nov 1793; d. at Brooklyn, CT, 30 Jan 1866; m. 1st at Lyndeborough, 23 Jan 1817, his first cousin once removed, HANNAH PUTNAM WOODWARD (*Ephraim Woodward6, Hannah Putnam Woodward5, Sarah Cram Putnam4, Sarah Holt Cram3, Henry2, Nicholas1*), b. about 1795 daughter of Ephraim and Hannah (Badger) Woodward; Hannah d. 4 May 1846. David m. 2nd at Brooklyn, 14 Jan 1849, Mrs. NANCY LITTLEHALE of Northbridge, MA, b. 24 Oct 1811; Nancy d. at Brooklyn, 17 Dec 1864.

ix SALLY WOODWARD, b. 1 Apr 1796; d. 8 Sep 1797.

x ARTEMUS WOODWARD, b. 19 Feb 1800; d. Nov 1810.

xi AUGUSTUS WOODWARD, b. 24 Jun 1804; d. at Brooklyn, CT, 17 Dec 1880; m. at Canterbury, 17 Sep 1829, CAROLINE WHEELER, b. about 1807 daughter of Warren and Nancy (Seymour) Wheeler; Carolyn d. at Brooklyn, 26 Feb 1865.

686) JOHN WOODWARD (*Huldah Cram Woodward4, Sarah Holt Cram3, Henry2, Nicholas1*), b. at Canterbury, CT, 10 Jun 1753 son of Ephraim and Huldah (Cram) Woodward; d. at Lyndeborough, 14 Oct 1825; m. about 1777, JUDITH FOSTER, b. 13 Nov 1753; Judith d. at Lyndeborough, 1 Jun 1835.

John traveled from Canterbury to Lyndeborough where he married Judith Foster. The oldest child may have been born in Canterbury, but the family then settled permanently in Lyndeborough.[1845]

i SAMUEL WOODWARD, b. (recorded at Lyndeborough), 9 Nov 1778; d. at Lyndeborough, after 1850; m. about 1802, his second cousin, ELIZABETH CHAMBERLAIN (*Jonathan Chamberlain5, Elizabeth Cram Chamberlain4, Sarah Holt Cram3, Henry2, Nicholas1*), b. at Lyndeborough, 3 Jun 1776 daughter of Jonathan and Margaret (Cram) Chamberlain; Lydia d. at Lyndeborough, 1852.

ii JOHN WOODWARD, b. at Lyndeborough, 10 Jan 1782; d. at Lyndeborough, 21 Aug 1858; m. by 1807, ANNA THOMPSON, b. about 1785 daughter of John and Esther (Redington) Thompson; Anna d. at Lyndeborough, 18 Jul 1829.

iii LUCY WOODWARD, b. at Lyndeborough, 26 Mar 1784; d, at Unadilla, NY, 11 Nov 1828; m. at Lyndeborough, 29 Jan 1818, DANIEL MARR, b. at Alstead, NH, 4 Sep 1790 son of James and Sarah (Barker) Marr; Daniel d. at Unadilla, 23 Jun 1850.

iv ABIGAIL WOODWARD, b. at Lyndeborough, 17 Mar 1786; d. after 1850 when she was living at Ripley, OH; m. by about 1812, ZEBADIAH BARKER, b. at Temple, NH, 1 Mar 1784 son of David and Sarah (Barker) Barker; Zebadiah d. at Fitchville, OH, 16 Sep 1847. Four children have been identified for Abigail and Zebadiah who were born in Skaticook (near Lansingburgh), New York; there may be more.

v DANIEL WOODWARD, b. at Lyndeborough, 26 Mar 1787; m. HANNAH PUTNAM who has not been identified. The History of Lyndeborough reports David and Hannah went to Ohio. They have not yet been found there.

vi EPHRAIM WOODWARD, b. at Lyndeborough, 4 Jun 1788; d. at Findlay, OH, 11 Mar 1865; m. MARY "MOLLY" MARR, b. at Alstead, NH, 5 Feb 1792 daughter of James and Sarah (Barker) Marr; Molly d. at Findlay, 8 Aug 1877.

vii HANNAH WOODWARD, b. at Lyndeborough, 20 Jan 1791; d. at Lyndeborough, 16 Nov 1853; m. 1 May 1848, as his second wife, her first cousin, DANIEL WOODWARD (*Ithamar Woodward5, Huldah Cram Woodward4, Sarah Holt Cram3, Henry2, Nicholas1*), b. at Lyndeborough, 30 Jan 1777 son of Ithamar and Huldah (Sharp) Woodward; Daniel d. at Francestown, 25 Jun 1867. Daniel was first married to Lucy Burnham and third married to Hannah W. Woodward.

[1845] Donovan, *The History of the Town of Lyndeborough*, p 896

viii JUDITH WOODWARD, b. at Lyndeborough, 18 Mar 1793; d. at Nashua, NH, 29 Mar 1872; m. 1st 26 Apr 1821, CHARLES HADLEY, b. at Lyndeborough, 12 Feb 1798 son of Joshua and Betsey (Giddings) Hadley; Charles d. at Andover, MA, 22 Sep 1825. Judith m. 2nd at Andover, 1 Mar 1838, as his second wife, SAMUEL FERSON, b. at Francestown, 16 Aug 1795 son of James and Mary (Starrett) Ferson; Samuel d. at Nashua, NH, 18 Dec 1877. Samuel was first married to Fanny Bixby.

687) JOHN CRAM (*John Cram4, Sarah Holt Cram3, Henry2, Nicholas1*), b. at Wilton, 28 Sep 1743 son of John and Sarah (-) Cram; m. 1st by 1767, SUSANNA who is *likely* SUSANNA FULLER, b. at Middleton, MA, 11 Mar 1747 daughter of Amos and Hannah (Putnam) Fuller; Susanna d. at Wilton, 1779. John m. 2nd at Wilton, 9 Dec 1779, MARY JAQUITH.

John Cram resided in Wilton and all his children were born there. A death record was not located. He is perhaps the John Cram who served with a rank or corporal in Evans' Regiment of Militia.[1846]

John and Susanna Cram were parents of eight children born at Wilton.

i SUSANNA CRAM, b. and d. 15 Nov 1767

ii JOHN CRAM, b. 16 Oct 1768; d. at Hallowell, ME, 4 Jan 1818; m. 25 Nov 1788, his second cousin, OLIVE CRAM (*Jacob Cram5, Jonathan Cram4, Sarah Holt Cram3, Henry2, Nicholas1*), b. at Lyndeborough, 6 Oct 1769 daughter of Jacob and Isabella (-) Cram; Olive d. at Gardiner, ME, 16 Mar 1851.

iii ABIEL CRAM, b. 28 Aug 1770; d. at Tunbridge, VT, before 1830 (when Judith was head of household); m. at Lyndeborough, 12 Nov 1793, his second cousin once removed, JUDITH HOLT (*William4, Oliver3, Henry2, Nicholas1*), b. at Lyndeborough, about 1769 daughter of William and Beulah (-) Holt; Judith d. at Northfield, VT, 28 Sep 1843. Abiel Cram and Judith Holt are Family 634.

iv SUSANNA CRAM, b. 2 Feb 1772; d. at Marlow (burial Stoddard), NH, 9 Dec 1828; m. at Stoddard, NH, 5 Apr 1795, LUTHER PHELPS, b. at Leominster, MA, 4 Apr 1768 son of Edward and Martha (Farnsworth) Phelps; Luther d. at Marlow, 23 Apr 1855. The farm owned by Luther was in Marlow but just adjacent to Stoddard.[1847]

v DANIEL CRAM, b. 6 Mar 1774

vi ANDREW CRAM, b. 24 Oct 1775; d. at Marlow, 10 Sep 1868; m. 1st at Stoddard, 30 Sep 1805, SALLY TOWNE who died before 1842. Andrew m. 2nd at Stoddard, 9 Nov 1842, MARY GREEN (widow of John P, Henshaw), b. about 1794 daughter of John and Mary (-) Green;[1848] Mary d. at Marlow, 3 Apr 1878.

vii SARAH CRAM, b. 26 Jan 1778; d. 3 Nov 1778

viii ARCHELAUS CRAM, b. 26 Jun 1779; d. after 1850 when he was living at Maine, NY; m. 1st at Stoddard, 11 Feb 1808, BEULAH KENNEY, b. at Stoddard, 27 Oct 1785 daughter of Isaac and Anna (Adams) Kenney. Archelaus m. 2nd, about 1817, CATHARINE LEWIS, b. about 1800; Catharine d. after 1855 when she was living at Cortlandville, NY.

John Cram and Mary Jaquith were parents of three children born at Wilton.

i SARAH CRAM, b. 10 May 1781

ii MARY "POLLY" CRAM, b. 30 Dec 1783; d. at Stockholm, NY, 2 Jun 1851; m. at Stoddard, 7 Apr 1802, PEARLEY SEAVER, b. at Westminster, MA, 17 Dec 1781 son of Samuel and Sarah (Cutter) Seaver; Pearley d. at Stockholm, 26 May 1842.

iii PHEBE CRAM, b. 8 Aug 1786

688) ASA CRAM (*John Cram4, Sarah Holt Cram3, Henry2, Nicholas1*), b. at Wilton, 4 Apr 1746 son of John and Sarah (-) Cram; d. 16 Jul 1775; m. 25 Jul 1771, SYBIL MCLANE, b. at Chelmsford, 22 Mar 1749 daughter of Charles and Susanna (Farmer) McLane.

Asa and Sybil resided in Wilton. Asa enlisted 23 April 1775 in Capt. William Walker's company of Col. Reed's regiment. Asa was wounded at the Battle of Bunker Hill and died of his wounds 16 Jul 1775.[1849]

Asa Cram and Sybil McLane were parents of two children born at Wilton.

i ASA CRAM, b. 22 Apr 1772; d. 6 Aug 1776.

1846 U.S., Revolutionary War Rolls, 1775-1783

1847 Gould, *History of Stoddard*, p 120

1848 The names of Mary's parents are given as John and Mary Green on her death record.

1849 Livermore, History of the Town of Wilton, p 354

ii NATHAN CRAM, b. 18 Nov 1774; d. at Peru, VT, 1817; m. at Goffstown, 19 Mar 1795, AMELIA KEMP, b. about 1775 and baptized at Groton, MA, 10 May 1778 daughter of Joseph and Lucy (-) Kemp; Amelia d. at Braintree, VT, 26 Jul 1873. Amelia was second married to Benjamin Killam on 8 Mar 1818.

689) JOSEPH CRAM (*John Cram⁴, Sarah Holt Cram³, Henry², Nicholas¹*), b. at Wilton, 21 Apr 1748 son of John and Sarah (-) Cram; d. after 1810 when he was living at Andover, VT; m. 13 Dec 1773, ABIGAIL FARMER.

Joseph and Abigail started their family in Wilton and relocated to Andover, Vermont by 1779. They were parents of five children.

i ABIGAIL CRAM, b. at Wilton, 23 Feb 1775

ii JOSEPH CRAM, b. at Wilton, 24 Feb 1777; d. at Andover, VT, 12 Apr 1782.

iii LUCY CRAM, b. at Andover, VT, 21 Feb 1779; d. 17 Jul 1800.

iv BETSEY CRAM, b. at Andover, VT, 12 Aug 1781; d. 13 Oct 1784.

v JOSEPH CRAM, b. 6 At Andover, VT, Jun 1791. At age 23, Joseph enlisted from Andover, VT on Jul 1814 in Capt. Smead's company.[1850]

690) LYDIA CRAM (*John Cram⁴, Sarah Holt Cram³, Henry², Nicholas¹*), b. at Wilton, 28 May 1750 daughter of John and Sarah (-) Cram; d. at Andover, VT, 2 Jul 1818; m. NATHANIEL GREELEY, b. at Hudson, 28 Oct 1744 son of Samuel and Abigail (Blodgett) Greeley; Nathaniel d. at Andover, VT, 16 Dec 1819.

Nathaniel and Lydia resided in Wilton and fourteen children were born there. They relocated to Andover, Vermont before 1810 where they both died.

i LYDIA GREELEY, b. 22 Jun 1769; d. at Andover, VT, after 1850. Lydia did not marry.

ii ABIGAIL GREELEY, b. 11 Nov 1770; d. at Andover, VT, 1 Jan 1857; m. at Andover, VT, 28 Mar 1819, as his third wife, DAVID BURTON, b. at Wilton, 7 Jan 1759 son of John and Rebekah (Gage) Burton; David d. at Andover, 27 Aug 1822. David was first married to Hannah Haseltine and second married to Mary Rogers.

iii NATHANIEL GREELEY, b. 18 Aug 1772; d. 25 Jun 1776.

iv SAMUEL GREELEY, b. 27 Apr 1774; m. 4 Jul 1797, OLIVE HAMBLET, b. at Hudson, NH, 28 Feb 1786 daughter of Hezekiah and Mehitable (Greeley) Hamblet; Olive d. after 1850 when she was living in Oswegatchie, NY with her son Samuel.

v SARAH GREELEY, b. 4 Jan 1776

vi EUNICE GREELEY, b. 16 Apr 1777; d. at Fairview, PA, 26 Aug 1847; m. at Weston, VT, 27 Jan 1801, WALTER BUTLER, b. 1767; Walter d. at Fairview, 24 Apr 1833.

vii ESTHER GREELEY, b. 29 Dec 1778

viii NATHAN GREELEY, b. 15 Feb 1781

ix ABEL GREELEY, b. 1 Apr 1783; d. at Ellsworth, WI, 1872; m. at Andover, VT, 29 Aug 1805, SARAH WARNER, b. at Andover, VT, 13 Mar 1785 daughter of Moses Warner; Sarah d. at Weston, VT, 27 Sep 1849. After Sarah's death, Abel went to Wisconsin with his son Julius.

x JOHN GREELEY, b. 8 Jan 1785; d. at Andover, VT, 18 Mar 1816; m. about 1811, LUCY ABBOTT, b. at Andover, VT, 1793 daughter of Joseph and Lucy (King) Abbott; Lucy d. at Andover, VT, 7 May 1880. Lucy married second Asa Parker on 5 Dec 1819.

xi JOSEPH GREELEY, b. 31 Dec 1786; d. at Perry Township, OH, 5 Mar 1879; m. at Andover, VT, 6 Mar 1817, his first cousin, POLLY CRAM (*Jonathan Cram⁶, Jonathan Cram⁵, Jonathan Cram⁴, Sarah Holt Cram³, Henry², Nicholas¹*), b. at Wilton, 15 Dec 1788 daughter of Jonathan and Mary (Greeley) Cram; Polly d. at Perry Township, Jul 1853.

xii CYRUS GREELEY, b. 28 Sep 1788; d. in OH, 22 Feb 1838; m. 7 May 1809, NANCY MARSH, b. at Andover, VT, 19 May 1793 daughter of John and Louis (Marsh) Marsh; Nancy d. at Cox Creek, IA, 11 Jan 1860.

xiii HIRAM GREELEY, b. 16 May 1790; d. at Mount Tabor, VT, 17 Aug 1856; m. at Landgrove, 2 Nov 1815, BETSEY DAVIS, b. at Merrimack, NH, 6 Apr 1794 daughter of Gideon and Martha (Patten) Davis; Betsey d. at Mount Tabor, 28 Aug 1858.

[1850] U.S. Army, Register of Enlistments, 1798-1914

xiv SOLOMON GREELEY, b. 7 Mar 1793; d. at Bristol, IA, 1870; m. at Weston, 14 Jan 1828, CHARITY ARVILLA CHAFFEE, b. about 1812; Charity d. at Exeter, WI, Aug 1850.

691) EBENEZER CRAM (*John Cram[4], Sarah Holt Cram[3], Henry[2], Nicholas[1]*), b. at Wilton, 19 Sep 1754 son of John and Sarah (-) Cram; d. at Chester, VT, 23 Feb 1835 (probate April 1835); m. about 1775, his second cousin, RACHEL HOLT (*Jonathan[4], Humphrey[3], Henry[2], Nicholas[1]*), b. at Lunenburg, 20 Apr 1753 daughter of Jonathan and Rachel (Taylor) Holt; Rachel d. about 1820. Ebenezer married second SARAH who has not been identified but who was his widow at probate.

Ebenezer and Rachel lived in Wilton until the mid-1780's and then relocated to Chester, Vermont.

On 19 September 1832, Ebenezer Cram then residing in Chester and his seventy-seventh year made a statement related to his Revolutionary War pension application. While living in Wilton, he entered the service in October 1775 in the company of Capt. Benjamin Taylor. That first enlistment ended mid-January 1776 and he re-entered the service in July 1777 for three months. He gave his birth date as 19 September 1754. He was born in Wilton and lived there for several years after the war and then relocated to Chester. Ebenezer's brother Zebulon, then of Clarendon, made a statement is support of the application on 21 July 1832. The pension was rejected at that time due to not meeting the six-month service requirement. On 8 November 1854, widow Sarah Cram made a statement related to the widow's pension.[1851]

Ebenezer Cram did not leave a will and inventory of his estate was made 8 April 1835 with a total value of $92.66, and the estate was declared insolvent.[1852]

There are five confirmed children of Rachel Holt and Ebenezer Cram and there are perhaps several other children.

i RACHEL TAYLOR CRAM, b. at Wilton, 6 May 1774

ii ASA CRAM, b. at Wilton, 10 Jun 1776; m. about 1803, ABIGAIL who has not been identified. There are records of two children of Asa and Abigail born at Wilton.

iii LEVI CRAM, b. 9 Aug 1778

iv SARAH CRAM, b. 10 Sep 1780

v ABIGAIL CRAM, b. at Wilton, 1786; d. at Alstead, NH, 19 Aug 1879; m. 1st, at Fitchburg, 30 Nov 1809, NATHAN BENNETT, who died at Fitchburg in 1814 (probate 1814). Abigail seems to have had a second marriage to Mr. Wheeler who has not been identified as she was Abigail Wheeler when she married at Fitchburg, 9 Nov 1832, JONATHAN BLOOD, b. 1795 son of Daniel and Sarah (Putnam) Blood; Jonathan d. at Alstead, 31 Mar 1872.

692) ZEBULON CRAM (*John Cram[4], Sarah Holt Cram[3], Henry[2], Nicholas[1]*), b. at Wilton, 30 Jun 1760 son of John and Sarah (-) Cram; d. at Clarendon, VT, 27 Jan 1850; m. about 1783, ESTHER who has not been identified.

On 20 July 1832, Zebulon Cram of Rutland County, Vermont then age seventy-two gave a statement related to his application for a Revolutionary War pension. In 1777 while living in Wilton, he enlisted in the militia under Capt. Bowman. He served guarding the ferry near New Castle and was there until the end of October. He re-entered service in July 1778 under Capt. Mann and marched to Rhode Island and was there until being discharged in September. He had a third enlistment in 1780 under Capt. Barns in Col. Nichols regiment. They marched to West Point where he remained until discharged in October. He also related that he was born in Wilton on 30 June 1760 and he stayed there after the war until 1805 at which time he went to Andover, Vermont. He was in Andover until about 1829 when he went to Clarendon.[1853]

There are records for nine children of Zebulon and Esther born at Wilton.

i ESTHER CRAM, b. 17 Oct 1784; d. at Londonderry, VT, 28 Feb 1821; m. WILLIAM STEVENS, b. 1783; William d. at Londonderry, 7 May 1856.

ii NANCY CRAM, b. 25 Sep 1786; d. at Cavendish, VT, 12 Aug 1873; m. at Andover, VT, 26 Dec 1816, as his second wife, ERASTUS BENTON, b. at Surry, NH, 10 Apr 1775 son of Abijah and Rebecca (Field) Benton. Erastus was first married to Permelia Hathorn.

iii BETSEY CRAM, b. 15 Jul 1788; d. 25 May 1795.

iv CHLOE CRAM, b. 28 Mar 1790

v CHARLOTTE CRAM, b. 21 May 1792

vi OLIVE CRAM, b. 2 May 1794; d. at Granville, OH, Mar 1870; m. at Andover, VT, 17 Jan 1815, SIMEON REED, b. at Rutland County, VT, 1 Jan 1792 son of Simeon and Sarah (Cummings) Reed; Simeon d. at Granville, 20 Sep 1855.

1851 U.S., Revolutionary War Pension and Bounty-Land Warrant Application Files, 1800-1900, Rejected pension of Ebenezer Cram

1852 *Vermont. Probate Court (Windsor District)*; Probate Place: *Windsor, Vermont, Estate of Ebenezer Cram*

1853 U.S. Revolutionary War Pension and Bounty-Land Warrant Application Files, Case S22705

vii LUCINDA CRAM, b. 1 Nov 1796; m. 1st at Andover, VT, 19 Sep 1819, OLIVER RICHARDSON; Oliver d. at Clarendon, VT, 28 Mar 1829. Lucinda m. 2nd at Woodstock, VT, 29 Mar 1832, MORRIS LAMB.

viii Son, b. 21 Mar 1800 and d. 29 Mar 1800.

ix BETSEY CRAM, b. 17 May 1801

693) HANNAH CRAM (*John Cram4, Sarah Holt Cram3, Henry2, Nicholas1*), b. at Wilton, 5 Jun 1764 daughter of John and Sarah (-) Cram; d. at Wallingford, VT, 16 Jun 1840; m. 19 Jun 1782, DAVID HASELTINE, b. at Haverhill, MA, 15 Dec 1759 son of Nathan and Elizabeth (Follensbee) Haseltine; d. at Wallingford, VT, 17 Apr 1840.

On 13 April 1818, David Haseltine of Andover, Vermont made a declaration related to his application for a pension. He enlisted from the town of Wilton on 14 June 1777 for a term of three years in the company commanded by Capt. Isaac Frye on the New Hampshire line. He was in the Battle of Saratoga, at the surrender of Burgoyne, in a battle with the Indians at Genesee County, and with General Sullivan's expedition. On 31 July 1820, he provided additional information in that he was so afflicted with rheumatism that he was no longer able to earn his living by labor. His wife, age fifty-six, was in feeble health. He had no property of any kind. In a statement dated just March 18th, grandson Henry C. Burton inquired whether the heirs of his grandfather were entitled to any payments. Henry noted that his grandfather died 17 April 1840 and his grandmother on 15 June 1840.[1854]

There are six likely children of David Haseltine and Hannah Cram.[1855]

i DAVID HASELTINE, b. at Lyndeborough, 13 Aug 1782; d. at Andover, VT, 5 Feb 1864; m. at Andover, 18 May 1803, RACHEL MCINTIRE, b. at Charlton, MA, 11 Apr 1781 daughter of Caleb and Elizabeth (Harwood) McIntire; Rachel d. at Ludlow, VT, 15 Nov 1864.

ii JAMES HASELTINE, b. about 1784; d. at Mt. Tabor, VT, 4 Oct 1862; m. at Andover, VT, 7 Dec 1809, POLLY PARKHURST

iii PENINAH HASELTINE, b. at Andover, VT, about 1786; d. at Andover, 26 Aug 1859; m. 10 May 1808, ROBERT GRAHAM, b. at Townsend, MA, 20 Dec 1778 son of John and Margaret (Sloan) Graham; Robert d. at Andover, 26 Aug 1863.

iv HANNAH HASELTINE, b. at Andover, 9 Aug 1789; d. at Wallingford, VT, 16 Aug 1872. Hannah had an out-of-wedlock child, Matilda Boutwell, born at Andover, 9 Aug 1789. Hannah m. about 1831, as his second wife, ISAAC BROWN, b. 26 Apr 1778 son of Isaac and Hannah (Hill) Brown; Isaac d. at Wallingford, 28 Jun 1862. Isaac was first married to Sally.

v JOHN SULLIVAN HASELTINE, b. 8 Sep 1791; d. at Watson, MI, 10 Jan 1880; m. DEBORAH PAGE EATON, b. at Cavendish, VT, 2 Aug 1798 daughter of Kimball and Mary (Page) Eaton; Deborah d. at Watson, 18 Feb 1873.

vi MARY HASELTINE, b. about 1794; d. at Wallingford, VT, 10 Feb 1873; m. at Andover, 26 Mar 1812, her first cousin, BENJAMIN BURTON, b. about 1790 son of David and Hannah (Haseltine) Burton.

694) HANNAH PUTNAM (*Sarah Cram Putnam4, Sarah Holt Cram3, Henry2, Nicholas1*), b. at Lyndeborough, 9 Mar 1742/3 daughter of Ephraim and Sarah (Cram) Putnam; d. at Lyndeborough, 5 Oct 1811; m. about 1764, ELEAZER WOODWARD, b. at Brooklyn, CT, 8 Jan 1738 son of Ephraim and Hannah (Williams) Woodward; Eleazer d. at Lyndeborough, 19 Dec 1815.

Hannah Putnam was reported to be the first white child born in Salem-Canada which was later known as Lyndeborough. Hannah was a professional midwife. Her husband Eleazer came from Brooklyn, Connecticut and was one of the first settlers in Salem-Canada.[1856] Eleazer in 1770 was the first builder on the land that became known as the "Old Town Farm" and was later used as the poor farm.

Eleazer Woodward and Hannah Putnam were parents of nine children born at Lyndeborough.

i HULDAH WOODWARD, b. 23 Jun 1765; d. at Lyndeborough, 14 Jan 1853; m. at Lyndeborough, 4 May 1786, her second cousin, JOHN CRAM (*Jacob Cram5, Jonathan Cram4, Sarah Holt Cram3, Henry2, Nicholas1*), b. at Lyndeborough, 4 Nov 1763 son of Jacob and Isabella (Hutchinson) Cram; John d. at Lyndeborough, 30 Aug 1833.

ii HANNAH WOODWARD, b. 1 Feb 1767; d. 15 Jul 1788.

iii EPHRAIM WOODWARD, b. 18 Mar 1768; buried at Lyndeborough, 8 Feb 1859; m. 1st 17 Jan 1791, HANNAH BADGER, b. 19 Dec 1770 daughter of David and Rachel (-) Badger; Hannah d. at Lyndeborough, 22 Jan 1830. Ephraim m. 2nd 17 Mar 1831, JANE REED (widow of Ebenezer Barrett). Ephraim m. 3rd, at Greenfield, 5 Oct 1852, the widow MARY HYDE.

[1854] U. S. Revolutionary War Pension and Bounty-Land Warrant Application Files, Case S39639

[1855] There may be one or two other children in this family, possibly Betsey Haseltine who married Daniel Shedd at Andover VT in 1811.

[1856] Donovan, *The History of the Town of Lyndeborough*, p 890

iv ELEAZER WOODWARD, b. 5 Oct 1771; d. at Lyndeborough, 4 Jan 1855; m. 15 Nov 1797, RACHEL HOUSTON, b. at Lyndeborough, 22 Oct 1779 daughter of Samuel and Mary (-) Houston; Rachel d. at Lyndeborough, 2 Apr 1843.

v ISRAEL WOODWARD, b. 17 May 1773; d. at Lyndeborough, 29 Mar 1858; m. 18 Nov 1804, HANNAH HARDY who is *perhaps* the Hannah b. at Wilmington, MA, 14 Nov 1781 daughter of David and Hannah (Worcester) Hardy; Hannah d. at Lyndeborough, 6 Jul 1845.

vi WARD WOODWARD, b. 31 Aug 1776; d. at Homer, NY, 24 Oct 1850; m. 16 Nov 1797, ELIZABETH DAY, b. at Lyndeborough, 8 Jul 1779 daughter of Isaac and Susannah (Clough) Day; Elizabeth d. at Homer, 10 Nov 1856.

vii SARAH WOODWARD, b. 6 Feb 1779; d. at Boston, about 1805; m. 16 Jul 1799, her second cousin, BENJAMIN CRAM (*Olive Chamberlain Cram*[5]*, Elizabeth Cram Chamberlain*[4]*, Sarah Holt Cram*[3]*, Henry*[2]*, Nicholas*[1]), b. at Lyndeborough, 8 Mar 1774 son of Benjamin and Olive (Chamberlain) Cram; Benjamin d. at New Ipswich, NH, 12 Apr 1835. Benjamin married second Polly Vose at Stoughton on 1 Dec 1805.

viii ELIZABETH WOODWARD, b. 31 Aug 1781; d. at Hollis, 27 Jan 1879; m. 15 Oct 1807, her first cousin, AARON WOODWARD (*Ward Woodward*[5]*, Huldah Cram Woodward*[4]*, Sarah Holt Cram*[3]*, Henry*[2]*, Nicholas*[1]), b. at Brooklyn, CT, 20 Sep 1781 son of Ward and Rebecca (Putnam) Woodward; Aaron d. at Nashville, NH, 16 Jul 1845.

ix DAVID WOODWARD, b. 18 Jan 1787; d. at Jasper, NY, 15 Mar 1852; m. 1st 29 Mar 1810, POLLY KIDDER, b. about 1790 daughter of Joseph and Polly (Epps) Kidder; Polly d. about 1818. David m. 2nd 20 Mar 1819, ELIZABETH DANFORTH, b. at Hillsborough, 15 Dec 1794 daughter of Jonathan and Sarah (Chandler) Danforth; Elizabeth d. at Jasper, 28 May 1870.

695) EPHRAIM PUTNAM (*Sarah Cram Putnam*[4]*, Sarah Holt Cram*[3]*, Henry*[2]*, Nicholas*[1]), b. at Danvers, 15 Jun 1744 son of Ephraim and Sarah (Cram) Putnam; d. at Lyndeborough, 2 Mar 1799; m. about 1767, LUCY SPALDING.

Ephraim and Lucy were parents of six children born at Lyndeborough.

i EPHRAIM PUTNAM, b. 20 Oct 1768; d. after 1850 when he was living at Lyndeborough; m. at Lyndeborough, 6 Nov 1794, ELIZABETH CARKIN, b. at Lyndeborough, 24 Jul 1770 daughter of John and Elizabeth (Cram) Carkin.

ii DANIEL PUTNAM, b. 2 Sep 1770; d. at Lyndeborough, 12 Dec 1841; m. at Lyndeborough, 28 Aug 1794, HANNAH JOHNSON, b. at Lyndeborough, 18 Feb 1777 daughter of John and Abigail (Carleton) Johnson; Hannah d. at Lyndeborough, 9 Aug 1872.

iii SARAH PUTNAM, b. 16 Jan 1773; d. at Roxbury, VT, 5 May 1813; m. 25 Oct 1792, her second cousin, DAVID CRAM (*David Cram*[5]*, Jonathan Cram*[4]*, Sarah Holt Cram*[3]*, Henry*[2]*, Nicholas*[1]), b. at Lyndeborough, 26 May 1767 son of David and Mary (Badger) Cram.

iv ELIZABETH PUTNAM, b. 4 Feb 1775

v ESTHER PUTNAM, b. 9 Apr 1777

vi JOHN PUTNAM, b. 15 Jul 1781

696) SARAH PUTNAM (*Sarah Cram Putnam*[4]*, Sarah Holt Cram*[3]*, Henry*[2]*, Nicholas*[1]), b. at Lyndeborough, 8 Jun 1746 daughter of Ephraim and Sarah (Cram) Putnam; d. at Hancock, NH, 27 Apr 1822; m. about 1768, JOHN BRADFORD, b. 1744 son of Andrew and Rebecca (Cole) Bradford;[1857][1858] John d. at Hancock, 27 Jun 1836.

Capt. John Bradford commanded a militia company during the Revolution and participated in the Battle of Bennington.[1859]

Sarah and John were parents of eight children, the births of the first five children recorded at Amherst and likely the younger children at Hancock.

i SARAH BRADFORD, b. 16 Jul 1769; d. at Warner, NH, 15 Nov 1856; m. 1786, SOLOMON ANDREWS, b. at Concord, 4 Apr 1759 son of Isaac and Lucy (Perkins) Andrews; Solomon d. at Windsor, NH, 29 Mar 1840.

ii THOMAS BRADFORD, b. 8 Jun 1771; d. at Lyndeborough, 14 Sep 1852; m. 1st at Hillsborough, 26 Mar 1795, ABIGAIL MERRILL; Abigail d. at Lyndeborough, 14 Jan 1797. Thomas m. 2nd 2 Oct 1799, MARTHA "PATTY"

[1857] Hayward, *The History of Hancock*, p 385
[1858] Browne, *History of Hillsborough*, p 77
[1859] Hayward, The History of Hancock, p 385

COBURN, b. at Dracut, 31 Oct 1769 daughter of Amos and Mary (Parkhurst) Coburn; Patty d. at Lyndeborough, 15 Oct 1849.

iii JOHN BRADFORD, b. 9 Jul 1773; d. after 1850 when he was living at Peterborough; m. at Amherst, NH, Apr 1798, MARY LANGDELL, b. at Mont Vernon, 27 Apr 1776 daughter of Joseph Langdell; Mary d. at Peterborough, 21 Oct 1860.

iv EPHRAIM PUTNAM BRADFORD, b. 26 Dec 1776; d. at New Boston, NH, 14 Dec 1845; m. at Amherst, 1 Sep 1806, MARY MANNING BARKER, b. 9 Oct 1785 daughter of Ephraim and Mary (-) Barker; Mary d. at New Boston, 8 May 1874.

v BETTY BRADFORD, b. 29 Jan 1779; d. at Milford, NH, 29 May 1868; m. 25 Jan 1797, MOSES BURNS, b. at Milford, 10 Sep 1768 son of John and Elizabeth (Jones) Burns; Moses d. at Milford, 28 Jan 1841.

vi THATCHER BRADFORD, b. 1781; d. at Hancock, NH, 18 Oct 1848; m. at Hancock, 6 Mar 1806, MERCY FOSTER, b. at Hancock, 30 Mar 1786 daughter of John and Sarah (Taylor) Foster; Mercy d. at Hancock, 17 Mar 1871.

vii REBECCA BRADFORD, b. about 1782; d. at Antrim, NH, Jan 1864; m. at Hancock, 25 Dec 1808, JACOB WHITTEMORE, b. at Greenfield, about 1781 son of Amos and Molly (Taylor) Whittemore; Jacob d. at Antrim, 14 Oct 1860.

viii WILLIAM BRADFORD, b. 1784; d. at Hancock, Aug 1800.

697) HULDAH PUTNAM (*Sarah Cram Putnam*[4], *Sarah Holt Cram*[3], *Henry*[2], *Nicholas*[1]), b. at Lyndeborough, 15 May 1748 daughter of Ephraim and Sarah (Cram) Putnam; d. at Lyndeborough, 13 Jan 1778; m. at Lyndeborough, 26 Nov 1768, JONAS KIDDER, b. at Hudson, NH, 16 Nov 1743 son of Jonas and Hannah (Proctor) Kidder; Jonas d. at Hudson, 1 Nov 1837. Jonas was second married to Alice Taylor on 20 May 1778 and third to Abigail Carleton on 5 Jul 1827. Abigail Carleton was the widow of Huldah's brother David.

Capt. Jonas Kidder and Huldah Putnam had their five children in Lyndeborough where Huldah died two months after the birth of her fifth child. The house that Jonas built in Lyndeborough housed a tavern.

During the Revolution, Jonas initially paid a bounty to John Purple to serve a one-year term in the Continental army for him. He enlisted as a private in 1778 and was serving as lieutenant by 1779. He was commissioned as a captain in 1780 in the regiment of Col. Moses Nichols.[1860]

Huldah Putnam and Jonas Kidder were parents of five children born at Lyndeborough.

i AARON KIDDER, b. 8 May 1769; m. at Lyndeborough, 8 Dec 1791, PAMELIA FULLER, b. at Lyndeborough, 12 Mar 1770 daughter of Andrew and Mary (Putnam) Fuller; Pamelia d. at West Fairlee, VT, 20 Dec 1816.[1861]

ii JONAS KIDDER, b. 8 Jan 1771; d. at Lyndeborough, 17 Aug 1817. A marriage was not located for Jonas.

iii HANNAH KIDDER, b. 11 Mar 1773; d. at Hudson, NH, 13 Dec 1862; m. at Lyndeborough, 23 Oct 1792, LEVI CROSS, b. about 1767 son of John and Elizabeth (Dakin) Cross; Levi d. at Hudson, 25 Dec 1838.

iv DAVID KIDDER, b. 6 Jan 1775; d. at West Fairlee, VT, 14 Oct 1849; m. at Lyndeborough, 14 Jan 1796, BETSY FULLER, b. at Lyndeborough, 6 Feb 1776 daughter of Andrew and Mary (Putnam) Fuller; Mary d. at West Fairlee, 3 Nov 1817.

v EPHRAIM KIDDER, b. 19 Nov 1777; d. 6 Apr 1778.

698) DAVID PUTNAM (*Sarah Cram Putnam*[4], *Sarah Holt Cram*[3], *Henry*[2], *Nicholas*[1]), b. at Lyndeborough, 6 May 1753 son of Ephraim and Sarah (Cram) Putnam; d. at Lyndeborough, 3 Jul 1826; m. at Lyndeborough, 18 Jun 1778, ABIGAIL CARLETON, b. about 1751 daughter of Jeremiah and Eunice (Taylor) Carleton; Abigail d. at Lyndeborough, 5 Jan 1835. Abigail was first married to Adam Johnson who died during the Revolution and was third married to Jonas Kidder who had been married to David's sister Huldah.

David Putnam and Abigail Carleton were parents of five children born at Lyndeborough.

i AMY PUTNAM, b. 6 Mar 1779; d. at Lyndeborough, 16 Dec 1866; m. about 1799, her second cousin, GIDEON CRAM (*David Cram*[5], *Jonathan Cram*[4], *Sarah Holt Cram*[3], *Henry*[2], *Nicholas*[1]), b. at Lyndeborough, 25 Feb 1771 son of David and Mary (Badger) Cram; Gideon d. at Lyndeborough, 17 Jun 1837.

ii TIMOTHY PUTNAM, b. 20 May 1782; d. at Lyndeborough, 11 Jun 1847; m. 1807, RACHEL DASCOMB, b. 15 Nov 1785 daughter of Jacob and Rachel (Dale) Dascomb; Rachel d. at Lyndeborough, 14 Apr 1838.

[1860] Donovan, *History of the Town of Lyndeborough*, p 190

[1861] Stafford, *Genealogy of the Kidder Family*, p 49 reports that Aaron Kidder died at Kingsbury, NY.

iii ABIGAIL PUTNAM, b. 1 Jun 1785; d. at Lyndeborough, 30 Jul 1836. Abigail did not marry.

iv DAVID PUTNAM, b. 19 Jun 1790; d. at Lyndeborough, 10 Jun 1870; m. 1st at Lyndeborough, 7 Feb 1815, TRYPHENA BUTLER, b. at Lyndeborough, 2 Apr 1792 daughter of Jonathan and Lois (Kidder) Butler; Tryphena d. at Lyndeborough, 31 Jan 1831. David m. 2nd, 1831, SARAH FLETCHER, b. at Lyndeborough, 30 Oct 1794 daughter of Oliver and Molly (Wilson) Fletcher; Sarah d. at Lyndeborough, 21 Jun 1847. David m. 3rd about 1848, his fourth cousin, ABIGAIL FOSTER (*Mary Holt Foster5, Joshua4, Nicholas3, Nicholas2, Nicholas1*), b. at Greenfield, 1799 daughter of Isaac and Mary (Holt) Foster; Abigail d. at Lyndeborough, 7 Mar 1853. David m. 4th about 1854, NANCY PIERCE (widow of Isaac Jewett), b. at Andover, VT, 2 Dec 1798 daughter of Benjamin and Dorcas (Lovejoy) Pierce; Nancy d. at Lyndeborough, 4 Aug 1862. David m. 5th 13 Oct 1862, SARAH BROWN (widow of James C. Bradford), b. at Mont Vernon, Oct 1806 daughter of Jeremiah and Sarah (perhaps Lovejoy) Brown; Sarah d. 15 Sep 1888.

v SARAH PUTNAM, b. 19 Aug 1793; d. at Lyndeborough, 30 May 1890; m. 16 Dec 1817, JONATHAN CLARK, b. 4 Jul 1795 son of William and Sarah (Barron) Clark; Jonathan d. at Lyndeborough, 23 Oct 1879.

699) KETURAH PUTNAM (*Sarah Cram Putnam4, Sarah Holt Cram3, Henry2, Nicholas1*), b. at Lyndeborough, 29 Jun 1756 daughter of Ephraim and Sarah (Cram) Putnam; m. about 1776, JOHN SMITH, b. at Amherst, NH, 8 Dec 1751 son of John and Ann (Davis) Smith.

John and Keturah resided in Lyndeborough where John participated in the "vendue" system of the town for the care of the poor. In this system, the town paid the lowest bidder for taking the poor into their homes.[1862]

Keturah Putnam and John Smith were parents of nine children born at Lyndeborough, New Hampshire. Three of the daughters did not marry and lived together in Needham. The occupation of two of the sisters, Pamelia and Rachel, was listed as "maiden lady" in the 1860 census.

i BENJAMIN SMITH, b. 3 Jul 1777

ii JOHN SMITH, b. 20 Jun 1779; m. 1st about 1800, HANNAH HALL who d. about 1810. John m. 2nd at Washington, NH, 10 Jul 1811, ABIGAIL FOSTER, b. at Washington, NH, 30 Jul 1789 daughter of Elijah and Molly (Severance) Foster; Abigail d. about 1818. John m. 3rd at Shipton, Québec, 1819, RACHEL WALTON (widow of Benjamin Bragdon).

iii SARAH SMITH, b. 9 Aug 1781; d. at Needham, MA, 26 Oct 1854. Sarah did not marry.

iv HULDAH PUTNAM SMITH, b. 12 Oct 1784

v KETURAH SMITH, b. 3 Feb 1787; d. after 1850 when she was living at Knox County, IL at the home of her daughter Elizabeth; m. at Washington, NH, 9 Oct 1815, MOODY HUDSON

vi EPHRAIM SMITH, b. 18 Apr 1789; d. at Unadilla, NY, 1 Aug 1862; m. at Hancock, NH, 30 Jan 1817, his fourth cousin, BETSEY KIMBALL (*Abiah Holt Kimball5, Joshua4, Nicholas3, Nicholas2, Nicholas1*), b. at Hancock, 1 Apr 1793 daughter of Daniel and Abiah (Holt) Kimball; Betsey d. at Unadilla, 6 Mar 1872.

vii PAMELA "MILLY" SMITH, b. 21 May 1791; d. at Needham, MA, 8 Apr 1872. Milly did not marry.

viii RACHEL SMITH (twin), b. 5 May 1794; d. at Needham, 19 Oct 1876. Rachel did not marry.

ix JACOB SMITH 9twin), b. 5 May 1794; d. at Manchester, VT, 16 Jun 1869; m. at Manchester, 4 Sep 1822, ROXANA ELLIOTT, b. at Mason, NH, about 1798 daughter of John A. and Elizabeth (Glidden) Elliott; Roxana d. at Manchester, 27 Nov 1867.

700) AARON PUTNAM (*Sarah Cram Putnam4, Sarah Holt Cram3, Henry2, Nicholas1*), b. about 1758 son of Ephraim and Sarah (Cram) Putnam; m. 1st at Lyndeborough, 28 Dec 1780, SARAH LEE who has not been identified. Aaron m. 2nd at Lyndeborough, 28 Apr 1789, his third cousin once removed, PHEBE FARNUM (*Stephen Farnum5, Stephen Farnum4, Ralph Farnum3, Elizabeth Holt Farnum2, Nicholas1) likely* b. about 1768 daughter of Stephen and Kezia (Skidmore) Farnum.[1863]

There are records for two children of Aaron Putnam and Sarah Lee.[1864]

i WARD PUTNAM, b. at Lyndeborough, 4 Dec 1781; d. at Danvers, MA, 10 Nov 1852; m. 1st at Danvers, MA, before 1807, the widow SALLY LARRABEE, b. 24 Jun 1783. Ward m. 2nd at Danvers, 29 Jan 1807, SARAH SHAW, b. at

[1862] Donovan, *History of the Town of Lyndeborough*, p 273

[1863] Farnham, *The New England Descendants of the Immigrant Ralph Farnum*

[1864] There may be other children of Aaron but given here are children for whom there are records.

Danvers, 24 Jun 1781 daughter of William and Lydia (Harwood) Shaw;[1865] Sarah d. after 1850 when she was living in Danvers.

ii NANCY PUTNAM, b. at Lyndeborough, 28 Jun 1783

There are records of three children of Aaron Putnam and Phebe Farnum.

i ALICE PUTNAM, b. at Lyndeborough, 7 Dec 1792; d. at Lyndeborough, 25 Oct 1832; m. 18 Apr 1813, ELIJAH UPTON, b. at Wilmington, MA, 6 Nov 1785 son of Paul and Jerusha (Richardson) Upton; Elijah d. at Lyndeborough, 4 Feb 1835.

ii ISRAEL PUTNAM, b. at Lyndeborough, 1797. It is possible that Israel married, but firm information on this is not yet located.

iii EPHRAIM TOWN PUTNAM, b. at Lyndeborough, 13 Jan 1803; d. after 1850 when he was living in the Nashville district of Nashua; m. MARY

701) JOHN PUTNAM (*Sarah Cram Putnam[4], Sarah Holt Cram[3], Henry[2], Nicholas[1]*), b. at Lyndeborough, about 1762 son of Ephraim and Sarah (Cram) Putnam; d. at Hyde Park, VT, 5 Nov 1837; m. at Lyndeborough, 30 Nov 1784, OLIVE BARRON, b. at Lyndeborough, 17 Feb 1765 daughter of William and Olive (Johnson) Barron; Olive d. at Hartford, VT, 24 May 1858.

John and Olive were in Lyndeborough but relocated to Bradford, Vermont. In the War of 1812, John and his sons John and Ephraim enlisted. John served as lieutenant and regimental adjutant.[1866]

John Putnam and Olive Barron were parents of eleven children, their oldest child born at Lyndeborough and the remainder of the children at Bradford, Vermont.[1867]

i OLIVE PUTNAM, b. at Lyndeborough, 22 May 1785; d. at Pittsford, MI, 8 Apr 1861; m. at Bradford, VT, 1 Dec 1799, MOSES H. COLLINS, b. at Bradford, about 1799 son of Ichabod and Ruth (Martin) Collins; Moses d. at Pittsford, after 1860. Olive and Moses were parents of fifteen children.

ii SARAH PUTNAM, b. at Bradford, about 1787; d. after about 1840 likely at Emerald Grove, WI; m. at Bradford, 25 Sep 1803, EBER JONES CHAPIN, b. 1778 son of Luther and Dinah (Jones) Chapin; Eber d. at South Newbury, VT, 1838 (probate Feb 1839). Sarah went to live with her daughter and son-in-law, Sarah and John Cummings, who were in Emerald Grove.

iii JONATHAN PUTNAM, b. at Bradford, 19 Jun 1789; d. at Bradford, 21 May 1855; m. at Newport, VT, 9 Apr 1810, MARY "POLLY" STOCKWELL, b. about 1790; Polly d. at Bradford, 16 Mar 1870.

iv REBEKAH PUTNAM, b. at Bradford, 8 Ju; 1790; d. at Danville, Estrie Region, Québec, 9 May 1865; m. at Newport, VT, 19 Oct 1809, ISAAC STOCKWELL, b. at Putney, VT, 11 Aug 1786 son of Moses and Sarah (Pierce) Stockwell; Isaac d. at Danville, 26 Oct 1853.

v JOHN PUTNAM, b. at Bradford, 21 May 1793; d. at Johnstown Center, WI, 19 Aug 1857; m. at Bradford, 28 Mar 1819, MARY PECKETT, b. at Bradford, 1798; Mary d. at Johnstown Center, 28 Jun 1877. John was a wealthy farmer in Wisconsin. He was killed in an accident with a reaping machine.[1868]

vi MICAH BARRON PUTNAM, b. about 1794; d. about 1796.

vii HANNAH PUTNAM, b. at Bradford, 17 Mar 1795; d. at Holyoke, MA, 25 Jul 1888; m. 1817, JOHN PEARSONS, b. at Lyndeborough, 29 Aug 1792 son of Daniel and Patience (Kimball) Pearsons; John d. at Bradford, 30 Oct 1857.

viii EPHRAIM PUTNAM, b. at Bradford, 30 Jul 1797; d. at Bradford, 1837; m. at Boston, 15 May 1822, RACHEL C. STODDARD, b. at Boston, 15 Mar 1797 daughter of Abner and Elizabeth (Low) Stoddard; Rachel d. at Boston, 21 Sep 1874.

ix ELIZABETH PUTNAM, b. at Bradford, 22 Feb 1802; d. at Boston, 8 Mar 1850; m. at Fairlee, VT, 8 Mar 1827, ISRAEL PRESCOTT, b. 1802 son of Joseph and Sarepta (Olmstead) Prescott; Israel d. at West Newbury, VT, 6

[1865] The 1815 probate of William Shaw of Danvers includes a distribution to daughter Sarah Putnam. Although the marriages of Ward are listed as to two different Sarahs, it seems that these *could* represent the same person. The Danvers list a birth date of the widow Sarah Larrabee as 24 Jun 1783 and the birth date of Sarah Shaw is recorded as 24 Jun 1781. The transcription for the marriage to Sally Larrabee states just before 1807.

[1866] McKeen, *History of Bradford, Vermont*, p 266.

[1867] The information on this family found in McKeen's *A History of Bradford, Vermont* (pp 266-267) was provided by a daughter in this family, Hannah Putnam Pearsons.

[1868] McKeen, *A History of Bradford, Vermont*, p 267

Aug 1879. Israel married second Sarah Carleton in 1850. Isaac was a carpenter and chair maker and for a time had a shop in Newbury with Isaac H. Olmstead.[1869]

x LUCY PUTNAM, b. at Bradford, 1804; d. at New Oregon, IA, 1871; m. at Fairlee, VT, 7 Dec 1826, SAMUEL PHELPS BLISS, b. 1803 son of Samuel and Orenda (Phelps) Bliss; Samuel d. at New Oregon, 25 Dec 1870.

xi WILLIAM BARRON PUTNAM, b. at Bradford, 23 Aug 1807; d. at Auburn, WI, 6 Jan 1887; m. 1st at West Fairlee, VT, 21 Nov 1830, ESTHER BROWN, b. at West Fairlee, 27 Jul 1809 daughter of Solomon and Sally (House) Brown; Esther d. at Auburn, 6 Feb 1869. William m. 2nd at Tunnel City, WI, 24 Sep 1871, EUNICE WHEELER (widow of Nathan Winship), b. 1825 daughter of John and Rhoda (Osgood) Wheeler; Eunice d. 23 Dec 1912.

702) JONATHAN CHAMBERLAIN (*Elizabeth Cram Chamberlain[4], Sarah Holt Cram[3], Henry[2], Nicholas[1]*), b. (recorded at Lyndeborough but likely at Chelmsford), 23 Feb 1743/4 son of Jonathan and Elizabeth (Cram) Chamberlain; d. at Lyndeborough, 26 Apr 1815; m. 13 Jul 1768, his first cousin, MARGARET CRAM (*Benjamin Cram[4], Sarah Holt Cram[3], Henry[2], Nicholas[1]*), b. at Lyndeborough, 1748 daughter of Benjamin and Elizabeth (-) Cram.

Jonathan and Margaret resided in Lyndeborough. Jonathan, along with his father, enlisted in the company of Capt. Peter Clark that marched to Ticonderoga in July 1777. Jonathan was also at the Battled of Saratoga.[1870]

Jonathan Chamberlain and Margaret Cram were parents of eleven children born at Lyndeborough.

i BENJAMIN CHAMBERLAIN, b. 7 Apr 1770; d. at Clinton, ME, 17 Feb 1849; m. JOANNA HERRICK, b. 1779; Joanna d. at Clinton, 10 Nov 1864.

ii JONATHAN CHAMBERLAIN, b. 17 Mar 1772; m. at Pittston, ME, 20 Jun 1801, ELIZABETH "BETSEY" JEWELL, b. at Gardiner, ME, 9 Mar 1780 daughter of Henry and Sarah (Greeley) Jewell.[1871]

iii JOHN CHAMBERLAIN, b. 26 Mar 1774; d. after 1850 when he was living in Hallowell, ME; m. at Packersfield, 4 Mar 1800, ABIGAIL BROWN, b. at Packersfield, 13 May 1778 daughter of Abijah and Deliverance (Breed) Brown; d. after 1850.

iv ELIZABETH CHAMBERLAIN, b. 3 Jun 1776; d. at Lyndeborough, 1852; m. about 1802, her second cousin, SAMUEL WOODWARD (*John Woodward[5], Huldah Cram Woodward[4], Sarah Holt Cram[3], Henry[2], Nicholas[1]*), b. at Lyndeborough, 9 Nov 1778 son of John and Judith (Foster) Woodward; Samuel d. after 1850.

v DAVID CHAMBERLAIN, b. 3 Dec 1778

vi DANIEL CHAMBERLAIN, b. 6 Mar 1781; d. at Woburn, MA, 5 May 1874; m. at Lyndeborough, 29 Dec 1812, HANNAH PEARSONS, b. at Lyndeborough, 1788 daughter of Daniel and Patience (Kimball) Pearsons; Hannah d. at Lyndeborough, 29 Jul 1873.

vii MARGARET CHAMBERLAIN, b. 28 Dec 1783; d. at West Gardiner, ME, 21 Aug 1856; m. ABEL FARRAR COLE, b. at Concord, MA, 6 Sep 1779 son of John and Mary (Dudley) Cole; Abel d. at West Gardiner, 13 Jan 1835.

viii OLIVE CHAMBERLAIN, b. 4 Aug 1788; d. at Jasper, NY, 25 Mar 1865; m. at Lyndeborough, 25 Sep 1817, her second cousin once removed, EPHRAIM WOODWARD (*Ephraim Woodward[6], Hannah Putnam Woodward[5], Sarah Cram Putnam[4], Sarah Holt Cram[3], Henry[2], Nicholas[1]*), b. at Lyndeborough, 25 Nov 1792 son of Ephraim and Hannah (Badger) Woodward; Ephraim d. at Jasper, 23 Sep 1879.

ix NATHANIEL CHAMBERLAIN, b. 3 Mar 1791; d. at Toledo, OH, 20 Mar 1857; m. 1816, MARY "POLLY" KNAPP, b. at Hanover, NH, 7 Sep 1795 daughter of Peter and Priscilla (Owen) Knapp; Mary d. 10 Jan 1839.

x ASA CHAMBERLAIN, b. 10 Apr 1793; d. at Hanover, NH, 24 Jul 1858; m. at Lyndeborough, 27 Jan 1818, SALLY PRATT RUSSELL, b. at Lyndeborough, 20 Jun 1796 daughter of Jedediah and Rhoda (Pratt) Russell; Sally d. after 1860.

xi JOSEPH CHAMBERLAIN, b. 12 Nov 1795; d. at Mason, NH, 28 Nov 1874; m. 25 Apr 1823, LUCINDA BURTON, b. at Andover, VT, 6 May 1796 daughter of John and Eunice (Heald) Burton; Lucinda d. at Mason, NH, 12 Feb 1863.

703) SAMUEL CHAMBERLAIN (*Elizabeth Cram Chamberlain[4], Sarah Holt Cram[3], Henry[2], Nicholas[1]*), b. 4 Apr 1745 (recorded at Chelmsford) son of Jonathan and Elizabeth (Cram) Chamberlain; d. at Lyndeborough, about 1812;[1872] m. 1st about

[1869] U.S., Craftperson Files, 1600-1995

[1870] Donovan, *History of the Town of Lyndeborough*, p 180

[1871] Jewell, *The Jewell Register*, p 14

[1872] Donovan, *The History of the Town of Lyndeborough, NH*, volume II, p. 180

1774, HANNAH ABBOTT, b. at Amherst, NH, 18 Sep 1755 daughter of Josiah and Hannah (Hobbs) Abbott; Hannah d. at Lyndeborough, 25 Sep 1784. Samuel m. 2nd 8 Nov 1785, NAOMI RICHARDSON, b. about 1762; Naomi d. about 1850.[1873]

Samuel Chamberlain enlisted 7 December 1776 in Captain William Walker's company and served three months in Fishkill. He had additional service in the regiment of Colonel Samuel McConnell.[1874]

Samuel and Hannah Chamberlain had five children born at Lyndeborough.

i HANNAH CHAMBERLAIN, b. 28 Apr 1775; d. at Greenfield, NH after 1850 (seems to be listed in the 1850 Census); m. at Hancock, Nov 1801, JONATHAN BURNHAM, origins unknown; Jonathan died at Greenfield, 1827 (probate 5 Jun 1827).[1875]

ii ELIZABETH CHAMBERLAIN, b. 20 May 1777; d. 13 Jun 1780.

iii SAMUEL CHAMBERLAIN, b. 4 May 1779; death not known but thought to be in Ohio or Michigan; m. 1st about 1809, OLIVE whose identity is not known. Olive died about 1818. Samuel m. 2nd, 6 May 1819, HEPHZIBAH RUSSELL, b. at 28 Oct 1783 daughter of Jedediah and Rhoda (Pratt) Russell. Hannah Russell was first married to Herman Ladd Sargent.

iv AMY CHAMBERLAIN, b. 14 Feb 1781; d. at Lyndeborough, 15 Jan 1850. Amy did not marry.

v BETSEY CHAMBERLAIN, b. 18 Apr 1783; d. at Lyndeborough, 26 Dec 1853. Betsey did not marry.

Samuel Chamberlain and Naomi Richardson were parents of ten children born at Lyndeborough.

i BENJAMIN CHAMBERLAIN, b. 30 Jan 1786; m. MARY ORDWAY.[1876] Records have not been located for this couple.

ii RACHEL CHAMBERLAIN, b. 6 Oct 1787; d. at Columbus, NY, 23 Apr 1847; m. THOMAS DUTTON, b. at Lyndeborough, 14 Dec 1783 son of Ezra and Phebe (Gould) Dutton; Thomas d. at Columbus, NY, 6 Jun 1870.

iii JOSEPH CHAMBERLAIN, b. 12 Dec 1789; d. at Lyndeborough, 30 Aug 1862; m. 27 Dec 1817, SALLY ABBOTT, baptized at Chelmsford, MA, 1 Apr 1792 daughter of Jeremiah and Susannah (Baldwin) Abbott; Sally d. at Lyndeborough, 31 May 1857.

iv PETER CHAMBERLAIN, b. 9 Nov 1791

v NAOMI CHAMBERLAIN, b. 25 Nov 1793

vi SILAS CHAMBERLAIN, b. 20 Feb 1797; d. at Hollis, NH, 1854; m. at Lyndeborough, 18 Mar 1821, ROXANA BURTON, b. about 1796 daughter of John and Eunice (Heald) Burton;[1877] Roxana d. at Hollis, 12 Oct 1872.

vii SARAH CHAMBERLAIN, b. 10 Apr 1800

viii PHINEAS CHAMBERLAIN, b. 4 Apr 1802; d. 10 Mar 1803.

ix LEVI CHAMBERLAIN, b. 29 Jun 1804; d. at New Boston, NH, 28 Mar 1858; m. at New Boston, 23 Nov 1828, LUCINDA DODGE, b. at New Boston, 8 Aug 1804 daughter of Antipas and Jerusha (Dodge) Dodge; Lucinda d. at New Boston, 5 Nov 1878.

x OLIVE CHAMBERLAIN, b. 5 Oct 1807

704) OLIVE CHAMBERLAIN (*Elizabeth Cram Chamberlain⁴, Sarah Holt Cram³, Henry², Nicholas¹*), b. recorded at Chelmsford, 16 Aug 1750 daughter of Jonathan and Elizabeth (Cram) Chamberlain; m. about 1774, her first cousin, BENJAMIN CRAM (*Benjamin Cram⁴, Sarah Holt Cram³, Henry², Nicholas¹*), b. at Lyndeborough, 1754 son of Benjamin and Elizabeth (-) Cram; Benjamin d. at Lyndeborough, 31 Jul 1836.

There are just two children known for Olive Chamberlain and Benjamin Cram born at Lyndeborough.

i BENJAMIN CRAM, b. 8 Mar 1774; d. at New Ipswich, NH, 12 Apr 1835; m. 1st 16 Jul 1799, his second cousin, SARAH WOODWARD (*Hannah Putnam Woodward⁵, Sarah Cram Putnam⁴, Sarah Holt Cram³, Henry², Nicholas¹*), b. at Lyndeborough, 6 Feb 1779 daughter of Eleazer and Hannah (Putnam) Woodward; Sarah d. at Boston, about 1805. Benjamin m. 2nd at Stoughton, MA, 1 Dec 1805, POLLY VOSE, b. at Stoughton, 14 Jun 1780 daughter of Jeremiah and Hannah (Holmes) Vose; Polly d. at New Ipswich, 8 Jan 1836.

1873 Donovan, *History of Lyndeborough*, p 692

1874 Donovan, *History of Lyndeborough*, volume II, p 180

1875 Probate includes the set-off of the dower to widow Hannah. Hillsborough County, NH probate records, volume 30 p 523 and volume 35 p 480.

1876 Donovan, *History of the Town of Lyndeborough*, volume II, p 692

1877 The 1834 will of John Burton of Wilton includes a bequest to daughter Roxana wife of Silas Chamberlain.

ii DANIEL CRAM, b. 6 Jan 1778; d. about 1795.[1878]

705) MOLLY CHAMBERLAIN (*Elizabeth Cram Chamberlain[4], Sarah Holt Cram[3], Henry[2], Nicholas[1]*), b. recorded at Chelmsford, 10 May 1756 daughter of Jonathan and Elizabeth (Cram) Chamberlain; d. at Albion, ME; m. at Lyndeborough, 18 Jan 1780, JOHN KIDDER, b. at Lyndeborough, 4 Mar 1757 son of John and Tryphena (Powers) Kidder.

John and Molly started their family in Lyndeborough, were in Temple, New Hampshire for a time before finally settling in Albion, Maine.[1879] Molly Chamberlain and John Kidder were parents of nine children. The children may have been born in Lyndeborough, although their births are recorded in the Albion, Maine records.

i SAMUEL KIDDER, b. 19 May 1780; d. at Albion, 23 Mar 1849; m. at Temple, NH, 23 Sep 1802, REBECCA BILLINGS, b. at Temple, 31 Oct 1781 daughter of Daniel and Lydia (Wheeler) Billings.

ii BENJAMIN KIDDER, b. 22 Feb 1782; d. at Albion, 7 Feb 1867; m. at Albion, 13 Jun 1808, SALLY STRATTON, b. a New Ipswich, 7 Feb 1786 daughter of Nehemiah and Sarah (Prichard) Stratton; Sally d. at Albion, 12 Jan 1864.

iii REBECCA KIDDER, b. 29 Mar 1784; d. at Hodgdon, ME, 3 Aug 1850; m. about 1804, BENJAMIN TARBELL, b. at Billerica, 2 Oct 1778 son of William and Elizabeth (French) Tarbell; Benjamin d. at Hodgdon, 1869.

iv MARY "POLLY" KIDDER, b. 14 Sep 1785; d. at Albion, 1826; m. at Albion, 1807, WILLIAM COLLEY, b. Jan 1788; William d. at Belfast, ME, 23 Nov 1879.[1880] William married second Esther Johnson on 23 May 1829.

v SARAH KIDDER, b. 7 May 1787; d. at Albion, 27 Feb 1852; m. SAMUEL WEBB REED, b. 5 May 1787 son of Joel and Eunice (Webb) Reed; Samuel d. at Albion, 13 Aug 1876.

vi JOHN KIDDER, b. 13 Jun 1789; d. at Pike Township, IN, 14 May 1858; m. at Albion, Oct 1815, SARAH BURROUGHS, b. at Lyndeborough, NH, 9 Aug 1798 daughter of Asa and Lois (Butler) Burroughs; Sarah d. at Pike Township, 4 Oct 1875.

vii JONATHAN KIDDER, b. 15 Dec 1794; d. by 1832; m. about 1825, SARAH EATON, b. about 1801; Sarah d. at Malden, MA, 12 May 1886. Sarah married second Artemas Cutter of Malden on 19 Oct 1833 at Westbrook, ME. A record was found for one son of Jonathan and Sarah named Albion Kidder who was born at Gorham, ME in 1829 and died at Malden in 1855.

viii RACHEL KIDDER, b. 6 Oct 1796; d. after 1860 when she was living at Albion, m. JAMES STRATTON, b. at Albion, 21 Nov 1794 son of Nehemiah and Lois (Newell) Stratton; James d. after 1860.

ix LIVINA KIDDER, b. 12 Feb 1804; m. at Albion, 18 Sep 1853, as his second wife, ZENAS COLBY, b. about 1799 son of Benjamin and Rebecca (Thompson) Colby.

706) JOHN CHAMBERLAIN (*Elizabeth Cram Chamberlain[4], Sarah Holt Cram[3], Henry[2], Nicholas[1]*), b. recorded at Chelmsford, 16 Sep 1759 son of Jonathan and Elizabeth (Cram) Chamberlain; d. at Waterford, VT, about 1825 (probate Feb 1826); m. about 1782, MOLLY POWERS, b. at Acton, MA, 7 Feb 1762 daughter of Elliot and Mary (Cragin) Powers.[1881]

In his will written 10 December 1825 (proved February 1826), John Chamberlain of Waterford bequeaths to beloved wife Molly all the household furniture. He bequeaths to son John two notes that he holds dated 16 November 1822 with a total value of seven hundred dollars this securing the support of Molly on his real estate and John providing her with a cow and three sheep. Son John also receives the mare, two cows, and eight sheep. Daughter Mary Beman receives five dollars; Sarah Persons, one dollar; Lydia Badger, one dollar; Chloe Richardson, one dollar; Abigail Campbell, one dollar, and Betsy Carpenter, one dollar. Son John is to pay the legacies. If wife Molly does not live to spend all the property, then daughter Mary is to have one hundred dollars. The remainder of the estate goes to son John who is also named executor.[1882] Personal estate was valued at $721.51 which included $626.71 in notes owed by son John.

John Chamberlain and Molly Powers were parents of eleven children born at Lyndeborough.

i MARY "MOLLY" CHAMBERLAIN, b. 27 Mar 1783; m. a Mr. Beman who has not been identified. A Mary Chamberlain married James Beeman at Peterborough on 19 Jan 1823, but it is not clear that this is her marriage. Nothing further is known, although the provisions of her father's will would suggest she was in reduced circumstances or needed extra support.

[1878] Donovan, *History of Lyndeborough*, p 720

[1879] Stafford, *A Genealogy of the Kidder Family*, p 87

[1880] War of 1812 Pension Application Files Index, 1812-1815

[1881] Powers, *The Powers Family*, p 36

[1882] *Vermont. Probate Court (Caledonia District), Probate Records, volume 10, pp 63-64, will of John Chamberlain*

ii JOHN CHAMBERLAIN, b. 18 Apr 1785; d. at Johnson, VT, Sep 1845; m. 15 Feb 1812, LUCY MASON, b. at Walpole, NH, 7 Jul 1790 daughter of Joseph and Lucy (Flint) Mason;[1883] Lucy d. at Johnson, 16 Aug 1845.

iii SARAH CHAMBERLAIN, b. 30 May 1787; m. TIMOTHY PEARSON who is not yet identified. Records were found for three children born in Roxbury, VT.

iv MARTHA CHAMBERLAIN, b. 28 Mar 1789; not living at time of father's will.

v ABIGAIL CHAMBERLAIN, b. 25 Jun 1791; d. at Roxbury, VT, 19 Jan 1854; m. at Lyndeborough, 26 Nov 1812, HENRY CAMPBELL, b. in NH, about 1789; Henry d. at Northfield, VT, 9 Sep 1868.

vi ELIOT CHAMBERLAIN, b. 1 Feb 1793; d. 12 Jan 1796.

vii ELIZABETH CHAMBERLAIN, b. 21 Feb 1795; d. at Concord, VT, before 1850; m. by 1824, JEDEDIAH CARPENTER, b. at Surry, NH, 10 Mar 1802 son of Aaron and Mary (Thompson) Carpenter;[1884] Jedediah d. at Vermillion, SD, 1886.

viii JONATHAN CHAMBERLAIN, b. and d. Fen 1797.

ix LYDIA CHAMBERLAIN, b. 10 Apr 1798; d. at Nauvoo, IL, 4 Sep 1844; m. by 1824, JOHN BADGER, b. at Waterford, 11 Sep 1800 son of James and Hannah (Sawyer) Badger.

x CHLOE CHAMBERLAIN, b. 5 Aug 1800; d. at Waterford, VT, 2 Jan 1852; m. FRANCIS RICHARDSON, b. at Waterford, 12 Jan 1799 son of Abiel and Rebecca (Chase) Richardson; Francis d. at Concord, VT, 17 Mar 1876.

xi ELIOT CHAMBERLAIN, b. 12 May 1802; d. 10 Oct 1802.

707) NATHAN CRAM (*Benjamin Cram[4], Sarah Holt Cram[3], Henry[2], Nicholas[1]*), b. at Lyndeborough, 5 Apr 1752 son of Benjamin and Elizabeth (-) Cram; d. at Hancock, NH, 21 Jan 1851; m. by 1775, RACHEL DUTTON, b. at Nottingham, NH, 9 Sep 1757 daughter of Joseph and Sarah (Dutton); Rachel d. at Hancock, 15 Aug 1835.

Nathan and Rachel were in several locations in New Hampshire. They started their family in Lyndeborough, were in Greenfield where the births of several children were recorded, then in Antrim, and finally Hancock.

Nathan Cram and Rachel Dutton were parents of fifteen children. Several of the children made their way west, three of them settling in Jo Daviess County, Illinois. Three of the children settled in Peterborough.

i RACHEL CRAM, b. at Lyndeborough, 1 Jun 1775; d. at Peterborough, 13 Oct 1833; m. 30 Nov 1797, WILLIAM STUART, b. at Peterborough, 1771 son of William and Elizabeth (White) Stuart; William d. at Peterborough, 25 May 1822.

ii NATHAN CRAM, b. at Lyndeborough, 9 Sep 1778; d. at Belfast, ME, 8 Oct 1815; m. at Peterborough, 8 Nov 1802, ELIZABETH "BETSEY" WHITE, b. at Peterborough, 27 Oct 1781 daughter of John and Hannah (Miller) White; Betsey d. at Peterborough, 9 Feb 1858. Betsey was the sister of Sally who married Nathan's brother Joseph.

iii JOSIAH DUTTON CRAM, b. at Lyndeborough, 27 Mar 1780; d. at Peterborough, 7 Nov 1847; m. his second cousin, DAIDAMIA DUTTON (*Sarah Stiles Dutton[5], Phebe Cram Stiles[4], Sarah Holt Cram[3], Henry[2], Nicholas[1]*), b. at Lyndeborough, 29 Apr 1784 daughter of Benjamin and Sarah (Stiles0 Dutton; Daidamia d. at Peterborough, 28 Jul 1864.

iv HULDAH ANN CRAM, b. at Lyndeborough, 30 Jan 1782; d. at New London, IN, 5 Apr 1859; m. at Hancock, NH, 27 Nov 1804, GILBERT MCCOY, b. at Sharon, NH, 3 Dec 1781 son of Gilbert and Elizabeth (Stewart) McCoy; Gilbert d. at West Milton, OH, 12 Sep 1825.

v SARAH PARKER CRAM, b. at Lyndeborough, 9 Sep 1783; d. at Dublin, NH, 18 Dec 1863; m. 19 May 1804, JOSEPH TYRRELL, b. 12 Mar 1775 son of Samuel and Mary (McInnes) Tyrrell; Joseph d. at Hancock, NH, 3 May 1850.

vi BETSEY CRAM, b. 5 Mar 1786; d. 7 Sep 1805.

vii POLLY CRAM, b. 9 May 1788; m. at Hancock, 18 Mar 1806, JONATHAN BARNARD. Nothing further was found for this couple.

viii JOSEPH CRAM, b. at Greenfield, 26 Mar 1789; d. at Brattleboro, VT, 30 Nov 1874; m. 4 Jul 1817, SALLY WHITE, b. at Peterborough, NH, 2 Oct 1788 daughter of John and Hannah (Miller) White;[1885] Sally d. at Peterborough, 19 Aug 1864. After Sally's death, Joseph went to Brattleboro with children.

[1883] Mason, *Descendants of Capt. Hugh Mason*, p 494
[1884] Kingsbury, *History of Surry*, p 504
[1885] Smith and Morison, *History of the Town of Peterborough*, p 337

ix BENJAMIN CRAM, b. at Greenfield, 26 Mar 1789; d. at Berreman, IL, 22 Mar 1876; m. 1st at Thorndike, ME, 19 Apr 1814, JANE ALEXANDER, b. about 1791 daughter of Alexander and Mary (-) Alexander; Jane d. at Thorndike, 5 Jul 1841. Benjamin m. 2nd about 1842, RUTH NUTT, b. about 1798. After Ruth's death, Benjamin went to Illinois where he lived with his sister Phebe and her fourth husband William Blair. Jane's father, Alexander Alexander, was born in Scotland.

x ANNA B. CRAM, b. at Greenfield, 25 Jun 1791; d. at Stockton, IL, 22 Mar 1876; m. at Hancock, NH, 29 May 1810, SAMUEL TYRRELL, b. 12 Nov 1779 son of Samuel and Mary (McInnes) Tyrrell; Samuel d. at Jo Daviess County, IL, 27 Jul 1845.

xi ABIGAIL SARAH CRAM, b. at Greenfield, 3 Jul 1793; m. 1 Dec 1836, as his third wife, FRANCIS THOMPSON, b. at Halifax, MA, 2 Aug 1785 son of Ephraim and Joanna (Thayer) Thompson; Francis d. at Hancock, NH, 27 Mar 1837. Francis was first married to Jane Beal and second married to Sarah Beal. Abigail is reported to have gone to Ohio after the death of her husband.[1886]

xii EZRA DUTTON CRAM, b. at Greenfield, 10 Jun 1795; d. at Brooks, ME, 11 Nov 1868; m. LUCY CILLEY, b. at Brooks, ME, 2 Aug 1805 daughter of Benjamin and Sally (Newt) Cram; Lucy d. at Lowell, MA, 29 Jan 1891.

xiii PHEBE CRAM, b. at Greenfield, NH, 21 Apr 1797; d. at Berreman, IL, 6 May 1881; m. 1st at Antrim, 8 Oct 1816, MESHACH TAYLOR, b. at Hancock, NH, 22 Jul 1793 son of Daniel and Lucy (Shattuck) Tenney; Meshach d. at Faribault, MN, 15 Apr 1870. Phebe and Meshach divorced about 1819.[1887] Phebe m. 2nd 9 Jun 1821, JOHN GATES, b. 26 Oct 1777;[1888] John d. at Bremen, IL, 18 Aug 1847. Phebe m. 3rd at Carroll, IL, 18 Jan 1848, WILLIAM "TUTTY" BAKER, b. in KY, 2 Apr 1793 son of James and Margaret (Morrissett) Baker; William d. at Freeport, IL, 14 Jul 1855. Tutty Baker was the founder of Freeport, IL. He was first married to Elizabeth Baker. Phebe m. 4th, 4 Oct 1860, WILLIAM BLAIR, b. 23 Jun 1787 son of James and Anna (Brayfield) Blair; William d. at Berreman, IL, 5 Sep 1870. William Blair was first married to Lucinda Harris.

xiv EPHRAIM CRAM, b. at Antrim, 25 Mar 1800; d. 5 Sep 1800.

xv SAMUEL WHITE CRAM, b. at Antrim, 9 Sep 1802; d. between 1843 and 1850 likely at Antrim; m. at Lowell, 24 Mar 1831, SARAH ANN WHEELER, b. at Concord, MA, 1811 daughter of Phineas and Sarah (Smith) Wheeler; Sarah d. at Bradford, MA, 2 Sep 1875. Samuel and Sarah were parents of five children. Their son Samuel H. Cram served in the Civil War.

708) HANNAH PIERCE (*Thomas Pierce⁴, Dinah Holt Pierce³, Henry², Nicholas¹*), b. at Wilmington, 16 Dec 1733 daughter of Thomas and Hannah (Thompson) Pierce; d. at Marblehead, 23 Jul 1797; m. at Wilmington, 7 Feb 1754, PETER DOLIVER[1889], b; at Marblehead, 1726 son of Peter and Mary (Dennis) Doliver; Peter d. at Marblehead, 28 Sep 1807. Peter married second Jane Girdler (widow of Joseph Doliver) on 13 Jul 1800.

Peter Doliver did not leave a will and his estate entered probate 20 January 1808 with widow Jane as administratrix. Real estate was valued at $995 and personal estate at $539.89. The dower was set off to the widow 30 April 1808.[1890]

Hannah Pierce and Peter Doliver were parents of seven children.

i PETER DOLIVER, b. at Wilmington, MA, 29 Apr 1755; d. at Mount Desert, ME, after 1820; m. at Marblehead, 7 Feb 1778, MARGARET STANLEY, baptized at Marblehead, 31 Oct 1756 daughter of John and Margaret (LaCroix) Stanley;[1891] Margaret d. before 1820.

ii HANNAH DOLIVER, b. at Wilmington, 21 Feb 1757; d. at Marblehead, 3 May 1806; m. at Marblehead, 27 Jan 1776, JOHN BROWN. There are records for six children of Hannah and John born at Marblehead.

iii THOMAS PIERCE DOLIVER, b. at Wilmington, 2 Jun 1759; m. at Marblehead, 11 Apr 1783, MARY HINES (widow of William Burrows).

iv AMOS DOLIVER, b. at Wilmington, 1 May 1761

v SARAH DOLIVER, b. at Wilmington, 1 Nov 1762; d. at Northeast Harbor, ME, 28 Dec 1851; m. at Marblehead, MA, 7 Dec 1786, JOHN SAVAGE; John d. at Northeast Harbor, 27 Feb 1816.

[1886] Hayward, *The History of Hancock*, p 923

[1887] Some sources report that he died leaving Phebe with one child, but Meshach apparently lived on and had a second wife and sixteen children.

[1888] Chapman Brothers, Portrait and Biographical Album of Jo Daviess County, IL, p 245

[1889] Name is also given as Doliber.

[1890] *Essex County, MA: Probate File Papers, 1638-1881.*Online database. *AmericanAncestors.org.* New England Historic Genealogical Society, 2014. Case 8123

[1891] In 1820, Peter's household consisted of himself and his 83-year old mother-in-law Margaret Stanley (pension application file).

vi MARY DOLIVER, baptized at Marblehead, 14 Aug 1768; d. at Marblehead, 21 Nov 1865; m. 1st at Marblehead, 24 Feb 1788, JOHN SEAWOOD; John d. about 1821. Mary m. 2nd at Marblehead, 8 Sep 1822, JOHN BROWN, b. about 1751; John d. at Marblehead, 1 Jul 1827.

vii JOSEPH DOLIVER, baptized at Marblehead, 14 Aug 1768; m. 1st at Marblehead, 12 Mar 1797, MIRIAM DENNIS; Miriam d. 1807. Joseph m. 2nd at Marblehead, 10 Jan 1808, SARAH GIRDLER.

709) ESTHER PIERCE (*Thomas Pierce⁴, Dinah Holt Pierce³, Henry², Nicholas¹*), b. at Wilmington, 27 Aug 1741 daughter of Thomas and Hannah (Thompson) Pierce; d. at Wilmington, 6 Sep 1821; m. 1st at Wilmington, 26 Dec 1759, JOSEPH HARNDEN;[1892] Joseph d. about 1777 (probate 3 Feb 1778).[1893] Esther m. 2nd 18 Feb 1778, SAMUEL EAMS, b. at Wilmington, 14 Oct 1755 son of John and Mary (Jaquith) Eams; Samuel d. at Wilmington, 21 Jan 1834. After Esther's death, Samuel married Rebecca Butters.

Joseph Harnden did not leave a will and his estate entered probate 3 February 1778 with Esther as administratrix. Real estate was valued at £977 which included house and barn, one-fourth of a sawmill and homestead farm of 173 acres. Personal estate was valued at £371.1.4. Dower was set off to widow Esther on 10 April 1778. Daughters Molly and Esther, minors above age fourteen, selected Capt. John Harnden of Wilmington as their guardian on 3 November 1778. On 2 November 1778, Deacon Samuel Thompson of Woburn was named as guardian for children under age fourteen, Joseph Harnden, Rachel Harnden, and Hannah Harnden, as was the desire of Samuel Eames and Esther Eames. On 2 March 1785, Joseph Harnden Rachel Harnden, then over fourteen, selected Joshua Harnden as guardian.[1894]

Samuel Eams did not leave a will and his estate entered probate 6 February 1834 with widow Rebecca declining administration and Jonathan Jaquith, the husband of daughter Tirzah was initially named administrator. After Jonathan's death in 1836, administration was assumed by William Blanchard. Real estate was valued at $7,060 which included a 140-acre homestead. Personal estate was valued at $503.49. The heirs of the estate included grandchildren John Eams son of son Samuel, Aaron Pearson who was the husband of Samuel's daughter Dolly, and Silvester Eams and Abigail Eams who were represented by guardian Henry Carter.[1895]

Esther Pierce and Joseph Harnden were parents of seven children born at Wilmington.

i MOLLY HARNDEN, b. 23 Jan 1761; d. at Tewksbury, 3 Jan 1829; m. at Tewksbury, 20 Mar 1782, EPHRAIM KENDALL, b. 5 Feb 1753 son of Ezra and Ruth (Frost) Kendall; Ephraim d. at Tewksbury, 19 Oct 1821.

ii ESTHER HARNDEN, b. 10 Apr 1763; d. at Wilmington, 1 Jun 1836; m. 1st 2 May 1783, REUBEN BUCK, b. at Wilmington, 27 Jun 1759 son of Zebadiah and Mary (Butter) Buck; Reuben d. at Wilmington, 30 Nov 1805. Esther m. 2nd 6 Aug 1809, SAMUEL JAQUES, b. at Wilmington, 26 Sep 1753 son of Samuel and Keziah (Thompson) Jaques; Samuel d. at Wilmington, 20 Oct 1830. Samuel was first married to Ruth Wyman.

iii RACHEL HARNDEN, b. 29 Jun 1765; d. at Andover, 2 May 1853; m. at Wilmington, 11 May 1786, SIMEON FURBUSH, b. at 1758 and baptized at Andover, 22 Jul 1764 son of Charles and Sarah (Corey) Furbush; Simeon d. at Andover, 10 Jul 1835.

iv JOSEPH HARNDEN, b. 11 Apr 1770; d. likely at Denmark, ME, after 1820; m. at Wilmington, 12 May 1791, POLLY JAQUITH; Polly d. 1810 (recorded at Wilmington). Joseph and Polly had five children born at Wilmington and four children born in Oxford County, Maine.

v HANNAH HARNDEN, b. 3 May 1772; d. at Wilmington, 4 Apr 1850. Hannah did not marry.

vi THIRZA HARNDEN, b. 28 Aug 1774; d. Oct 1777.

vii ABIGAIL HARNDEN, b. 23 Jan 1777; d. Dec 1777.

Esther Pierce and Samuel Eams were parents of two children born at Wilmington.

i THIRZA EAMS, b. 25 Sep 1778; d. at Wilmington, 11 Nov 1855; m. at Wilmington, 28 Nov 1799, JONATHAN JAQUITH, b. at Wilmington, 23 Nov 1775 son of Jonathan and Lydia (Johnson) Jaquith; Jonathan d. at Wilmington, 2 Feb 1836.

ii SAMUEL EAMS, b. 11 Jun 1780; d. at Wilmington, 2 Aug 1829; m. 1800, DOROTHY "DOLLY" GIBSON, b. at Lunenburg, 28 Feb 1782 daughter of Timothy and Sarah (Foster) Gibson; Dolly d. at Wilmington, 24 Mar 1815.

1892 Joseph might be the son of John and Mary (Jaquith) Harnden born in 1736. One issue is discrepancies in dates. The death transcription for Joseph son of John and Mary is Dec 1775. The last child of Joseph and Esther was Jan 1777 and the probate of his estate was Feb 1778.

1893 The probate case and the guardianship cases for the children are in 1778 two weeks before Esther's second marriage.

1894 *Middlesex County, MA: Probate File Papers, 1648-1871.*Online database. *AmericanAncestors.org.* New England Historic Genealogical Society, 2014. Case 10361 and Case 10362

1895 *Middlesex County, MA: Probate File Papers, 1648-1871.*Online database. *AmericanAncestors.org.* New England Historic Genealogical Society, 2014. Case 6715

Samuel m. 2nd at Wilmington, 14 Feb 1816, ABIGAIL JONES, b. 20 Apr 1777 daughter of Enoch and Abigail (Foster) Jones; Abigail d. at Wilmington, 23 Sep 1848.

710) DANIEL PIERCE (*Daniel Pierce⁴, Dinah Holt Pierce³, Henry², Nicholas¹*), b. at Harvard, 3 Oct 1742 son of Daniel and Sarah (Buck) Pierce; d. at St. Johnsbury, VT, 16 Jul 1821; m. at Leominster, 11 Dec 1766, MARCY GATES, b. about 1747 likely the daughter of Paul and Submit (Howe) Gates; Marcy d. 1827.[1896]

Daniel Pierce and Marcy Gates were married in Leominster and their oldest child was born there. On 23 March 1769, Daniel Pierce of Leominster and his wife Marcy sold to James Richardson for twenty-seven pounds, six shillings a piece of land containing sixteen acres and three-quarter acres, this land running on the road from Leominster to Lancaster west of the land of Elijah Fairbanks and along the land of the heirs of Daniel Pierce, and being the whole of the land set off to Daniel from the estate of his honored father.[1897] At the estate division of father Daniel Pierce, eldest son Daniel had received sixteen acres and seventy rods on the west side of the road starting at the corner of Elijah Fairbank's land.[1898] Daniel and Marcy then moved to Westmoreland where nine children were born. In later life, Daniel and Marcy relocated to St. Johnsbury, Vermont where they died.

Daniel served in the Revolution. In 1789, he held a rank of Captain likely as a member of the militia.[1899]

Daniel Pierce and Marcy Gates were parents of ten children.

i DANIEL PIERCE, b. at Leominster, MA, 27 Jan 1768; d. at St. Johnsbury, 3 Nov 1839; m. at Putney, VT, 2 Apr 1789, ABIGAIL GILSON, b. at Groton, MA, 11 Jun 1766 daughter of Daniel and Apphia (Kent) Gilson; Abigail d. 1847.

ii ARETAS PIERCE, b. at Westmoreland, NH, 2 Jun 1770; d. at Murray, NY, 31 Aug 1840; m. REBECCA BLOOD, b. 1775; Rebecca d. at Murray, 2 Dec 1850.

iii MARCY PIERCE, b. at Westmoreland, 6 Aug 1771; d. at Westmoreland, 29 Jun 1850; m. about 1792, as his second wife, PHINEAS DAGGETT, b. 22 Aug 1764 son of William and Thankful (Gleason) Daggett; Phineas d. at Westmoreland, 5 Oct 1842. Phineas was first married to Betsey Wilson.

iv SARAH PIERCE, b. at Westmoreland, 10 Jun 1773; d. at Chicago, 11 Mar 1864; m. before 1800, THOMAS PECK, b. at Rehoboth, MA, 30 Apr 1774 son of Ebenezer and Sarah (Brown) Peck; Thomas d. at Saint-Andre-d'Argenteuil, Laurentides Region, Québec, 11 Feb 1823. Thomas Peck was a merchant. The family was in Portland, Maine but went to Montréal by 1808 where the children were baptized in 1810. Son Ebenezer Peck was an attorney and a member of parliament from Stansted. Ebenezer left Québec in 1837 and was an attorney and later a claims court judge in Chicago.[1900] Sarah went with her son to Chicago where she died.

v BETTY PIERCE, b. and d. 17 Feb 1775

vi NATHANIEL PIERCE, b. at Westmoreland, 8 Aug 1777; m. about 1806, BETSEY MCMANUS, b. at Dummerston, VT, 9 Feb 1786 daughter of Patrick and Grace (-) McManus. Betsey's father Patrick McManus was an Irish soldier with British forces who was surrendered by General Burgoyne.[1901]

vii LEVI PIERCE, b. at Westmoreland, 24 May 1779; d. at St. Johnsbury, VT, 1829; m. at Surry, NH, 10 Feb 1803, POLLY FOWLER, b. at Surry, 9 Oct 1780 daughter of Joshua C. and Lydia (Stearns) Fowler; Polly d. at Lyndon, VT, Aug 1865.

viii ABEL PIERCE, b. 12 Aug 1781; d. at St. Johnsbury, 10 Jan 1863; m. MERCY ALLEN, b. 1783; Mercy d. at St. Johnsbury, 30 Jan 1850.

ix REUBEN PIERCE, b. at Westmoreland, 25 May 1783; d. at St. Johnsbury, 25 Jul 1855; m. at St. Johnsbury, 24 Dec 1807, ABIGAIL COBB, b. 1788; Abigail d. at Irasburg, VT, 26 Sep 1867.

1896 Pierce's *Pierce Genealogy* varies from this information in two ways. First, Pierce states this son of Daniel was named David and married Sarah Mainer but that is not correct. This son is clearly Daniel which can be established with birth, probate, and land records. A David Pierce did marry Sarah Mainer but that is another person. Secondly, Pierce states it was Daniel a son of John Pierce that married Marcy Gates and that Daniel was a resident of New Hampshire at the time of his marriage. However, the Leominster records clearly state that Daniel and Marcy were both residents of Leominster at the time of marriage. Their first child was born in Leominster in 1768. On 5 Nov 1768, Daniel Pierce and wife Marcy of Leominster sold the lands set off to him from his honored father's estate, the description of the land being the same as the land distributed to Daniel Pierce eldest son of Daniel Pierce, to James Richardson, and after that time Daniel and Marcy were in Westmoreland where their other children were born.

1897 Massachusetts Land Records 1620-1986, Worcester County, 60:247, accessed through familysearch.org

1898 *Worcester County, MA: Probate File Papers, 1731-1881.* Online database. AmericanAncestors.org. New England Historic Genealogical Society, 2015. Case 46616

1899 Westmoreland Historical Committee, *History of Westmoreland*, p 520

1900 Assemble Nationale Du Québec, Ebenezer Peck, http://www.assnat.qc.ca/en/deputes/peck-ebenezer-4795/biographie.html

1901 Westmoreland Historical Committee, *History of Westmoreland*, p 520

x LOIS PIERCE, b. at Westmoreland, 16 Jul 1785; d. at St. Johnsbury, 31 Jan 1868; m. about 1802, NAHUM STILES, b. 18 Jan 1777 son of John and Keziah (Divoll) Stiles; Nahum d. at St. Johnsbury, 23 Feb 1840.

711) REUBEN PIERCE (*Daniel Pierce⁴, Dinah Holt Pierce³, Henry², Nicholas¹*), b. at Harvard, 17 Mar 1747 son of Daniel and Sarah (Buck) Pierce; d. at Leominster, 30 Dec 1801;[1902] m. at Leominster, 1 Jan 1771, MARY WOOD, b. about 1748 *perhaps* the daughter of Nehemiah and Mary (Johnson) Wood; Mary d. at Jaffrey, 22 Aug 1833.

Reuben Pierce did not leave a will and his estate entered probate 18 May 1802 with Simeon Tyler as administrator at the request of widow Mary Peirce. On 9 May 1805, the following heirs of the estate request the division of the two-thirds of the estate that had never been divided: Mary Peirce, Simeon Tyler, Mary Tyler, Elijah Fairbanks signing as guardian for Sarah Peirce and Zebadiah Peirce and Simeon Tyler signing as guardian for Abijah Peirce. On 4 January 1806, a document was presented to court stating that Simeon Tyler and Mary his wife and Sarah Peirce had quitclaimed their rights to the premises to Zebadiah Peirce who was then of age and that a payment was to be made to Abijah Peirce. Real estate was valued at $658.33.[1903]

Reuben Pierce and Mary Wood were parents of eight children born at Leominster. Three of the children died in a nine-day period in February 1778.

i MARY PIERCE, b. 20 Sep 1771; d. at Leominster, 15 Oct 1814; m. at Leominster, 14 Feb 1794, SIMEON TYLER, b. at Boxford, 15 Aug 1771 son of Phineas and Elizabeth (Barker) Tyler; Simeon d. at Leominster, 12 Feb 1858. Simeon married second Mrs. Alice Woods on 16 Feb 1816.

ii SARAH PIERCE, b. 28 Aug 1773; d. 7 Feb 1778.

iii ABIGAIL PIERCE, b. 2 Oct 1774; d. 9 Feb 1778.

iv REUBEN PIERCE, b. 3 Feb 1778; d. 16 Feb 1778.

v REUBEN PIERCE, b. 10 Sep 1779; nothing further known and not in father's estate distribution.

vi SARAH PIERCE, b. 4 Sep 1781; d. at Jaffrey, NH, 29 Sep 1837. Sarah did not marry.

vii ZEBADIAH PIERCE, b. 23 Dec 1784; d. at Jaffrey, NH, 12 Mar 1828; m. at Leominster, 17 Sep 1807, PHEBE KIMBALL TYLER, b. at Rindge, NH, 6 Sep 1785 daughter of Joshua and Ismenia (Kimball) Tyler; Phebe d. at Jaffrey, 13 Jul 1869.

viii ABIJAH PIERCE, b. 7 Oct 1788; d. at Jaffrey, 23 Oct 1870; m. 1st 20 Feb 1817, SALLY MAYNARD, b. at Jaffrey, 4 Oct 1799 daughter of Parker and Peggy (Taggart) Maynard; Sally d. at Jaffrey, 6 Oct 1840. Abijah m. 2nd, Sally's sister, ELVIRA MAYNARD (widow of Ezra Jewett), b. 23 Jul 1806; Elvira d. at Jaffrey, 2 Aug 1888.

712) SAMUEL PIERCE (*Daniel Pierce⁴, Dinah Holt Pierce³, Henry², Nicholas¹*), b. at Harvard, 21 May 1749 son of Daniel and Sarah (Buck) Pierce; d. at Jaffrey, 27 Dec 1824; m. 1st 10 Jun 1774, ABIGAIL CARTER, b. at Leominster, 23 Feb 1750/1 daughter of Oliver and Beulah (Wilder) Carter; Abigail d. 28 Feb 1777. Samuel m. 2nd at Lancaster, 13 Mar 1778, his third cousin once removed, ELIZABETH WHITNEY (*Annis Church Whitney⁵, Annis Johnson Church⁴, Josiah Johnson³, Mary Holt Johnson², Nicholas¹*), b. at Harvard, 27 Jun 1751 daughter of Caleb and Annis (Church) Whitney; Elizabeth d. at Jaffrey, 23 Oct 1823.

Samuel Pierce and Abigail Carter were parents of two children.

i ASAPH PIERCE, b. at Leominster, 9 Jul 1774; d. at Moretown, VT, 9 Feb 1840; m. 10 Feb 1797, HANNAH STICKNEY, b. at Pembroke, NH, 22 Oct 1773 daughter of Lemuel and Rebecca (Kimball) Stickney; Hannah d. at Moretown, 29 Dec 1837.

ii SAMUEL PIERCE, b. at Jaffrey, 9 May 1776; d. at Jaffrey, 8 Apr 1858; m. at Jaffrey, 21 Feb 1806, MEHITABLE "HITTY" BROOKS, b. at Jaffrey, 26 Dec 1777 daughter of Joseph and Abigail (Perry) Brooks; Hitty d. at Jaffrey, 7 Apr 1866.

Samuel Pierce and Elizabeth Whitney were parents of eight children.

i ELIZABETH "BETSEY" PIERCE, b. 29 Mar 1779; d. at Jaffrey, 10 Mar 1823; m. 18 Jan 1818, her first cousin, JACOB PIERCE (*Jacob Pierce⁵, Daniel Pierce⁴, Dinah Holt Pierce³, Henry², Nicholas¹*), b. at Jaffrey, 28 Apr 1778 son of Jacob and Rebecca (Whitcomb) Pierce; d. at Alstead, NH, 18 May 1828 (probate 1828 in Cheshire County). Jacob had three other marriages (see in the next family below).

1902 Reuben, Dec. 30, 1801. [While lifting at a stick of timber, sallied away, fell down, and expired without any struggle. C.R.]

1903 *Worcester County, MA: Probate File Papers, 1731-1881.* Online database. AmericanAncestors.org. New England Historic Genealogical Society, 2015. Case 46838

ii CALEB PIERCE, b. at Jaffrey, 30 Jan 1781; d. at Flint, MI, 13 Aug 1850; m. 20 Feb 1805, LUCY GALE, b. at Princeton, MA, 19 Dec 1786 daughter of Abraham and Abigail (Rice) Gail; Lucy d. at Grand Blanc, MI, 12 May 1873. After Caleb's death, Lucy was living with her son Silas in Grand Blanc.

iii ANNIS PIERCE, b. at Jaffrey, 12 Apr 1783; d. at Dublin, 28 Oct 1834; m. 18 Dec 1806, BENJAMIN FROST, b. 1 Dec 1778 son of Benjamin and Rachel (Kimball) Frost; Benjamin d. at Dublin, NH, 9 Mar 1825.

iv ABIGAIL PIERCE, b. at Jaffrey, 9 Oct 1785; m. 17 Feb 1812, JUDE CARTER, b. 17 Jan 1781 (gravestone); Jude d. at St. Johns, MI, 27 Jan 1857.

v SARAH PIERCE, b. at Jaffrey, 30 Sep 1787; d. at Wilton, 20 Feb 1836; m. 1st 12 Mar 1812, JOEL FISK, b. at Jaffrey, 14 Jan 1787 son of Thomas and Sarah (Shipley) Fisk; Joel d. at Jaffrey, 19 Jan 1823. Sarah m. 2nd 10 Sep 1825, JAMES BRIDGES, b. at Wilton, 27 Nov 1778 son of John and Mary (Spaulding) Bridges; James d. at Wilton, 6 Mar 1846. James was first married to Mary Eams. James and Mary (Eams) Bridges were the parents of Anna Bridges who married Samuel Holt son od Daniel and Dorcas (Abbott) Holt.

vi LUCY PIERCE, b. and d. 28 Nov 1789.

vii JOSEPH PIERCE, b. at Jaffrey, 23 Mar 1792; d. at Jaffrey, 22 Apr 1860; m. 18 Dec 1821, ESTHER JAQUITH, b. at Jaffrey, 9 Mar 1794 daughter of Samuel and Lois (Mower) Jaquith; Esther d. at Providence, RI, 29 Mar 1866. Esther was first married to Joseph's brother Silas (see just below).

viii SILAS PIERCE, b. at Jaffrey, 4 Jan 1795; d. at Jaffrey, 25 Jul 1819; m. 7 May 1818, ESTHER JAQUITH (see brother Joseph just above).

713) JACOB PIERCE (*Daniel Pierce⁴, Dinah Holt Pierce³, Henry², Nicholas¹*), b. at Harvard, 2 Aug 1751 son of Daniel and Sarah (Buck) Pierce; d. at Jaffrey, 9 Aug 1826; m. at Leominster, 19 Feb 1777, REBECCA WHITCOMB, b. at Leominster, 19 Mar 1754 daughter of Benjamin and Dorothy (White) Whitcomb; Rebecca d. at Jaffrey, 3 Mar 1843.

Jacob Pierce was a farmer in Jaffrey. He served in the Revolution and is reported to have been at the Battle of Bunker Hill and is called Lieutenant in Jaffrey records,[1904] although his rank is given as Sergeant in Rebecca's pension application file. In her widow's pension application made 10 November 1838, Rebecca stated that Jacob enlisted for eight months in 1775 and immediately following that served an additional three months.[1905]

Jacob Pierce and Rebecca Whitcomb were parents of thirteen children whose births are recorded at Jaffrey, New Hampshire.

i JACOB PIERCE, b. 28 Apr 1778; d. at Alstead, NH, 18 May 1828 (probate 1828 in Cheshire County); m. 1st 27 Nov 1800, MARY SAWTELLE, b. at Shirley, MA, 27 Aug 1778 daughter of Obadiah and Sarah (Fletcher) Sawtelle; Mary d. at Alstead, 7 Oct 1812. Jacob m. 2nd at Charlestown, NH, 2 Nov 1813, ELECTA EVANS, b. 20 Feb 1795; Electa d. at Alstead, 1 Apr 1817. Jacob m. 3rd 18 Jan 1818, his first cousin, ELIZABETH "BETSEY" PIERCE (*Samuel Pierce⁵, Daniel Pierce⁴, Dinah Holt Pierce³, Henry², Nicholas¹*), b. at Jaffrey, 29 Mar 1779 daughter of Samuel and Elizabeth (Whitney) Pierce; Betsey d. 10 Mar 1823. Jacob m. 4th about 1824, SALLY GARFIELD, b. 1782 daughter of Samuel and Sally (Harris) Garfield;[1906] Sally d. at Langdon, NH, 4 Sep 1872.

ii REBECCA PEIRCE, b. 2 Dec 1780; d. at Jaffrey, 13 Dec 1823. Rebecca did not marry.

iii BENJAMIN PIERCE, b. 3 Feb 1782; d. at Richland, NY, 16 May 1864; m. at Winchester, NH, 1 Aug 1813, SALLY ERSKINE, b. at Winchester, 3 Jun 1782 daughter of John and Phebe (Robinson) Erskine; Sally d. at Richland, 27 Dec 1851.

iv KEZIA PIERCE, b. 29 Sep 1783; d. at Winchester, 12 Nov 1824; m. 6 Feb 1806, ALVAN JEWELL, b. at Winchester, 6 Oct 1784 son of Asahel and Hannah (Wright) Jewell; Alvan d. at Winchester, 9 May 1856. Alvan married second Kezia's sister Deborah (see below).

v DEBORAH PIERCE, b. 4 Oct 1785; d. at Winchester, 29 Nov 1838; m. 19 Oct 1826, ALVAN JEWELL (see above).

vi REUBEN PIERCE, b. 4 Sep 1787; d. at North Bloomfield, NY, 26 Jun 1857; m. 1st 9 Mar 1814, LYDIA HOLDEN, b. at Hancock, NH, 19 Nov 1785 daughter of Asa and Dorcas (Sawtelle) Holden; Lydia d. 15 Jan 1823. Reuben m. 2nd 21 May 1823, FLORILLA SWETLAND, b. at Waterville, NY, 25 Aug 1805 daughter of Benjamin and Rosanna (Hancock) Swetland; Florilla d. at West Bloomfield, 20 Jun 1905.

vii MARIAM PIERCE, b. 6 Jul 1789; d. at Jaffrey, 26 Apr 1863; m. 29 Nov 1812, BENJAMIN HALE, b. at Rindge, NH, 19 Sep 1790 son of Moses and Sybil (Adams) Hale; Benjamin d. at Jaffrey, 12 Feb 1832.

1904 Cutter, *History of Jaffrey*

1905 U.S., Revolutionary War Pension and Bounty-Land Warrant Application Files, 1800-1900, Case W16681

1906 The 1843 probate of Samuel Garfield of Alstead includes Sally Pierce as an heir.

viii DANIEL PIERCE, b. 2 Apr 1791; d. 22 Apr 1808.

ix MOSES PIERCE, b. 22 Jan 1793; d. after 1854 when he was living in Uxbridge, MA;[1907] m. BETSEY JEWETT, b. 1796; Betsey d. after 1870 when she was living in Merrimac, WI.

x JOSIAH PIERCE, b. 5 Mar 1795; d. 11 Apr 1795.

xi NANCY PIERCE, b. 10 Jul 1796; d. at Fitchburg, MA, 11 Jan 1866; m. 24 Apr 1823, SEWELL HOSMER, b. at Concord, MA, 13 Jan 1798 son of Reuben and Lydia (Powers) Hosmer; Sewell d. at Fitchburg, 9 Jan 1884.

xii JOSIAH PIERCE, b. 17 Jun 1798; d. 1886 (will proved 16 Apr 1886 at Oswego County, NY);[1908] m. 9 Feb 1824, PAULINE ERSKINE, b. at Winchester, NH, 25 Dec 1801 daughter of John and Phebe (Robinson) Erskine; Paulina d. at Mexico, NY, Jun 1901.

xiii TRIPHOSA PIERCE, b. 15 Apr 1800; d. 10 May 1802.

714) MERIAH PIERCE (*John Pierce⁴, Dinah Holt Pierce³, Henry², Nicholas¹*), b. at Harvard, 19 Oct 1748 daughter of John and Hannah (Houghton) Pierce; d. at Harvard, 12 Apr 1781; m. at Bolton, 30 Nov 1768, ELISHA HOUGHTON, baptized at Harvard, 5 Jun 1748 son of Ephraim and Sarah (-) Houghton; Elisha d. at Shaftsbury, VT, 18 Nov 1826. Elisha married second Elizabeth Rice, intention 28 Sep 1781 and he married third Relief who was his widow at probate.

Elisha Houghton enlisted at Harvard in May 1778 in the company of Capt. Joshua Brown and served in the 15th infantry regiment under the command of Col. Timothy Bigelow. He served a three-year enlistment and was discharged in May 1781 at West Point. He participated in battles at Bunker Hill, Stillwater, Monmouth, and Newport. In 1820, he reported no family living with him. He was allowed a pension for his service.[1909]

In his will written 7 February 1826, Elisha Houghton of Shaftsbury bequeathed his entire estate to his wife Relief except one dollar which he bequeathed to his beloved son Timothy. Trusty friend Caleb Vaughn was named executor. The value of the estate was $38.97.[1910]

There are records for one child of Meriah and Elisha.[1911] Elisha has one known child, Timothy, from his second marriage to Elizabeth Rice.

i ELISHA HOUGHTON, b. at Harvard, 15 Jan 1775; d. 15 May 1777.

715) HANNAH PIERCE (*John Pierce⁴, Dinah Holt Pierce³, Henry², Nicholas¹*), b. at Harvard, 25 Aug 1751 daughter of John and Hannah (Houghton) Pierce; m. at Bolton, 28 Jun 1769, LEMUEL BURNHAM.

There are records for two children of Hannah Pierce and Lemuel Burnham, although it is possible there are other children.

i HANNAH BURNHAM, baptized at Bolton, MA, 12 Aug 1770; m. at Bolton, 9 Nov 1800, THOMAS COLBURN. There are records of two children of Hannah and Thomas baptized at Bolton.

ii ACHSAH BURNHAM, baptized at Bolton, 1 Oct 1772; d. at Harvard, 18 Apr 1852; m. at Harvard, 30 Nov 1797, LUTHER SAWYER, b. at Harvard, 18 Apr 1773 son of Manasseh and Lydia (Fairbank) Sawyer; Luther d. at Harvard, 5 Sep 1834.

716) JOHN PIERCE (*John Pierce⁴, Dinah Holt Pierce³, Henry², Nicholas¹*), b. at Bolton, 22 May 1759 son of John and Hannah (Houghton) Pierce; d. at Harvard, 12 Sep 1828; m. 1st 16 May 1799, DINAH SAWYER, b. 1772; Dinah d. at Harvard, 12 Jun 1825.

John and Dinah resided in Harvard. John Pierce did not leave a will and his estate entered probate 23 September 1828. John Pierce, the only son who had arrived at age twenty-one, declined administration and requested that Cephas Houghton be named. Personal estate was valued at $352.53 and real estate at $1,350.[1912]

[1907] In Jan 1854 while living in Uxbridge, Moses Pierce signed a power-of-attorney related to claims related to his mother's widow pension. Several genealogies report that Moses died in Wisconsin, and his wife did die there. Moses died before 1860 and perhaps he made the move to Wisconsin before his death, or perhaps his wife traveled to Wisconsin with her children after Moses died.

[1908] Josiah and his family lived in Mexico, NY throughout their lives, but in 1880 Josiah, wife Paulina, and their unmarried daughter Aurilla were living in Federalsburg, MD next to Stephen Emery who was a son-in-law. Although his probate was in Mexico, he may have died in Maryland. Paulina was living in Mexico at the time of her death last living in the home of Stephen Emery.

[1909] U.S., Revolutionary War Pension and Bounty-Land Warrant Application Files, 1800-1900, Case S39725

[1910] *Vermont. Probate Court (Bennington District), Probate Estate Files, Hill, Rachael-Houghton, James, 1781-1884, Estate of Elisha Houghton*

[1911] There is a daughter Moriah born in Harvard on 2 May 1777 who has been suggested as a daughter in this family, but the town records give this child as Maria daughter of Elijah and Maria Houghton. There was an Elijah Houghton son of Thomas and Meriah Houghton in Harvard at that time; he was married to Mercy Whitney. Although it is possible Moriah is a daughter of Elisha, given that he names only a son Thomas in his will, she is not listed with the family.

[1912] *Worcester County, MA: Probate File Papers, 1731-1881.* Online database. AmericanAncestors.org. New England Historic Genealogical Society, 2015. Case 46728

John Pierce and Dinah Sawyer were parents of three children born at Harvard.

i ELIZA PIERCE, b. 17 Apr 1800; d. at Harvard, 16 Jun 1818. "Eliza, only d. John and Dinah, June 16, 1818, a. 18 y. 2 m. GR1"

ii JOHN PIERCE, b. 13 Oct 1803; d. at Boston, 21 Dec 1883; m. 1st at Groton, 8 Dec 1828, SARAH PARKER who is not identified;[1913] Sarah d. by 1845. John m. 2nd at Arrowsic, ME, 3 Nov 1845, LOUISA PERCY, b. at Phippsburg, ME, 12 Jun 1810 daughter of James and Sarah (Wyman) Percy;[1914] Louisa d. at Boston, 1 May 1895.

iii STILLMAN PIERCE, b. 23 Apr 1809; d. at Derby, VT, 17 Jun 1872; m. at Woburn, 12 Nov 1834, SARAH S. FRENCH, b. at Randolph, MA, about 1815 daughter of Caleb and Joanna (-) French;[1915] Sarah d. at Cambridge, 19 Jul 1866.

717) CALVIN PIERCE (*John Pierce⁴, Dinah Holt Pierce³, Henry², Nicholas¹*), b. at Bolton, 1 Mar 1766 son of John and Hannah (Houghton) Pierce; d. at Bolton, after 1832; m. 1st 12 Jan 1786, BETSEY BROWN, b. 1771; Betsey d. at Bolton, 1817. Calvin m. 2nd 31 Mar 1818, Mrs. LUCY BRIDE of Berlin, MA; Lucy d. after 1832.

On 17 December 1832, Calvin Pierce and his wife Lucy, for a payment of $900, conveyed (mortgaged) to Stephen P. Gardner of Bolton trustee of Margaret B. Blanchard wife of Ira H.T. Blanchard, the farm with dwelling house and 100 acres. However, if Calvin pays Stephen P. Gardner $900 plus lawful interest within a year, then the deed is void.[1916] The mortgage on the property was not discharged until 1847 and that involved two other parties.

Calvin and Betsey were parents of nine children born at Bolton.

i JOHN PIERCE, b. 23 Mar 1786; d. at Jaffrey, NH, 28 Apr 1853; m. at Bolton, 1 Jul 1814, SALLY BRIGHAM, b. about 1791; Sally d. at Jaffrey, 28 Feb 1873.

ii ELIZABETH "BETSEY" PIERCE, b. about 1788; m. at Bolton, 22 Oct 1807, THORNDIKE CHASE, b. at Lynn, 1 Mar 1782 son of Samuel and Alice (Mower) Chase; Thorndike d. at Chelsea, MA, 20 Mar 1863.

iii CALVIN PIERCE, b. about 1790

iv MARY PIERCE, b. about 1793; d. at Bolton, before 1817 (husband's remarriage); m. at Bolton, 10 Aug 1813, JOHN CHASE, b. at Lynn, 26 Mar 1792 son of Samuel and Alice (Mower) Chase; John d. at Lynn, 2 Oct 1875. John was second married to Esther Myrick and third married to Sarah Lakeman.

v LOUISA PIERCE, b. about 1795

vi SOPHIA PIERCE, b. about 1797

vii SOPHRONIA PIERCE, b. 13 May 1806; d. at Bolton, 23 Jul 1883; m. at Bolton, 29 Jun 1830, LUTHER WILLARD HOUGHTON, b. at Bolton, 26 Nov 1809 son of Thomas and Asenath (Whitney) Houghton; Luther d. at Bolton, 3 Apr 1875.

viii DANIEL PIERCE, d. at Bolton, 1827

ix RUFUS PIERCE, d. at Bolton, 1819

Calvin Pierce and Lucy Bridge were parents of one child.

i LUCY PIERCE, b. about 1819

718) EPHRAIM STONE (*Kezia Pierce Stone⁴, Dinah Holt Pierce³, Henry², Nicholas¹*), b. at Harvard, 22 Jan 1745 son of Isaac and Kezia (Pierce) Stone; d. at Brome, Québec, 15 Jun 1820; m. 12 Aug 1768, LUCINDA CHAMBERLAIN, b. at Bridgewater, MA, 20 Mar 1751 daughter of Henry and Susannah (Hinds) Chamberlain; Lucinda d. at Brome, 1 Apr 1821.

Ephraim Stone served in the Revolution first participating at the campaign in Ticonderoga in 1777. He served as Captain in periods of service in 1779 and 1780. Although Ephraim Stone was a Revolution patriot, his son-in-law Jacob Ball was from a loyalist family that fled to Canada during the period of the Revolution.[1917] The family was in Brome by 1797.

Ephraim Stone and Lucinda Chamberlain were parents of ten children.[1918]

[1913] The Pierce genealogy gives her date of birth as 4 Jan 1803 which would make her a likely daughter of Joshua and Elizabeth (Farley) Parker born 21 Jan 1803 in Groton.

[1914] The names of Louisa's parents are given on her death record and James Percy and Sarah Wyman.

[1915] Names of Sarah's parents are given as Caleb and Joanna French on her death record.

[1916] Massachusetts Land Records, Worcester County, 289:511

[1917] Taylor, *History of Brome County, Quebec*, p 278

[1918] Much of the information for this family was obtained from worldchamberlaingenealogy.org of the World Chamberlain Society; record for Lucinda Chamberlain and Ephraim Stone, http://worldchamberlaingenealogy.org/dcc_fgr/dccfgr/ln01132.pdf

i SYLVANUS STONE, b. 1769; d. at Brome, Québec, 1809; m. ROWENA CHAMBERLAIN, b. at Westmoreland, NH, 27 Nov 1771 daughter of John and Eunice (Edson) Chamberlain.

ii ELIZABETH STONE, b. 6 May 1771; d. at Brome, 10 Aug 1865; m. 1787, JACOB BELL, b. at Newfane, VT, 28 May 1764 son of Jacob and Deborah (Belknap) Bell; Jacob d. at Knowlton, Québec, 9 Nov 1831.

iii EPHRAIM STONE, b. 1773; d. 1855; m. at Dunham, Québec, 1834, MARY WELLS, b. 1818 daughter of Peter and Abigail (Sweet) Wells.

iv HANNAH STONE, b. about 1775. Hannah is reported as having two marriages, to Mr. Baker and Mr. Blake, but records have not been located related to this.

v ISAAC STONE, b. about 1777; d. at Brome, 1864; m. his first cousin, ARTHUSIA STONE (*Daniel Stone⁵, Kezia Pierce Stone⁴, Dinah Holt Pierce³, Henry², Nicholas¹*), b. at Westmoreland, NH, 23 Sep 1788 daughter of Daniel and Abigail (Ellis) Stone; Arthusia d. at Brome, 1860.

vi PHILENA STONE, b. 1779; d. at Knowlton, Québec, 8 Apr 1850; m. at Franklin, VT, 11 Feb 1809, LEVI KNOWLTON, b. at Templeton, MA, 4 Dec 1768 son of Ezekiel and Anna (Miles) Knowlton; Levi d. at Knowlton, 21 Apr 1842.

vii LYDIA STONE, b. 1780; d. at Brome, 16 Aug 1846; m. THOMAS STOW.

viii SUSAN STONE, b. 1783; d. likely at Bolton, Québec, 1852; m. Oct 1806, JOHN DIAMOND, b. at Georgia, VT, 27 May 1783 son of Reuben and Elizabeth (Sweasy) Diamond.

ix JACOB STONE, b. 1785; m. about 1815, FANNY DIAMOND.

x EDWARD STONE, b. at Canada East, 1801; d. at Brome, 27 Apr 1882; m. at Dunham, Québec, ELIZABETH WELLS, b. 1804 daughter of Peter and Abigail (Sweet) Wells; Elizabeth d. at Brome, 30 Jun 1890.

719) DINAH STONE (*Kezia Pierce Stone⁴, Dinah Holt Pierce³, Henry², Nicholas¹*), b. at Harvard, 3 Aug 1749 daughter of Isaac and Kezia (Pierce) Stone; d. at Westmoreland, NH, 26 Oct 1811; m. at Westmoreland, 25 Dec 1766, MOSES WHITE, b. at Brookfield, MA, 2 Aug 1743 son of Cornelius and Hannah (Gilbert) White; Moses d. at Westmoreland, 6 Mar 1829. Moses married second Silence Blaisdell on 17 Jun 1813 and Silence died 30 Apr 1821.

Moses was a farmer in Westmoreland and served as church deacon. He built his homestead about 1771 on what is now Glebe Road in Westmoreland. Moses had received 200 acres in Westmoreland by deed of gift from his father Cornelius. The property passed to son Calvin and stayed in the White family until 1890.[1919]

In his will written 6 February 1826 (probate 10 March 1829), Moses White bequeathed one dollar to each of the following heirs: daughter Sarah wife of Benjamin Puffer; heirs of son Solomon who is deceased; heirs of son Bethuel; son Samuel; and daughter Eunice wife of John Ingalls. Son Calvin receives a piece of land containing about 25 acres. Son John receives ten acres and some stock animals. Daughter Cynthia receives ten acres of land, one cow, and four sheep. Daughter Orpha also receives ten acres. Daughter Hannah wife of David French and daughter Cynthia receive all the household furniture. Son Calvin receives the farming utensils and the residue of the estate and is named executor. In a codicil dated 13 February 1826, he adds a one-dollar bequest to the heirs of his daughter Dinah.[1920]

Dinah and Moses were parents of twelve children born at Westmoreland.

i SARAH WHITE, b. 14 Nov 1767; d. at Richford, VT, 1826; m. at Westmoreland, 27 Oct 1794, BENJAMIN PUFFER, b. at Framingham, 6 Apr 1765 son of Jabez and Rachel (Morse) Puffer; Benjamin d. at Westfield, VT, 24 Aug 1859.

ii SOLOMON WHITE, b. 7 Oct 1769; d. at Grafton, NH, 1810; m. at Littleton, NH, 29 Jan 1806, MERCY MERRILL, b. 1779; Mercy d. at Stockton, NY, 5 Sep 1855. Mercy married second Nathaniel Crissey on 18 Mar 1819. Nathaniel Cressey was married to Solomon's sister Dinah White (see Dinah below).

iii BETHUEL WHITE, b. 1 Dec 1771; d. at Haverhill, OH, Aug 1819; m. 1st at Littleton, 25 Feb 1796, MARGERY DANIELS, b. at Littleton, 12 Nov 1773 daughter of Increase and Elona (Thayer) Daniels; Margery d. a Littleton, 23 Nov 1808. Bethuel m. 2nd 21 Dec 1809, RUTH GATES WHIPPLE, b. 1780 daughter of Thomas and Lydia (Gates) Whipple; Ruth d. at Scioto County, 1815. Bethuel m. 3rd 4 Aug 1816, LUCY HARD, b. at Arlington, VT, 23 Jan 1780 daughter of Elijah and Lucy (Benedict) Hard; Lucy d. at Haverhill, OH, 12 Jun 1822.

iv CALVIN WHITE, b. 29 Jun 1774; d. at Westmoreland, 11 Apr 1843; m. at New Castle, NH, 23 Aug 1797, SARAH RICHARDSON, b. at Chesterfield, NH, 5 Sep 1779 daughter of Silas and Silence (Daniels) Richardson; Sarah d. at Westmoreland, 21 Sep 1853.

[1919] Westmoreland Historical Committee, *History of Westmoreland (Great Meadow) New Hampshire*, p 159

[1920] *New Hampshire. Probate Court (Cheshire County)*; Probate Place: *Cheshire, New Hampshire, Estate Files, W393-W448, 1825-1829, Case W444*

v HANNAH WHITE, b. 3 Oct 1777; d. at Keene, NH, 26 Jan 1857; m. at Westmoreland, 11 Sep 1799, as his second wife, DAVID FRENCH, b. at Mendon, MA, 26 Nov 1755 son of Abijah and Joanna (Holbrook) French; David d. at Westmoreland, 19 Feb 1836. David was first married to Lydia Twitchell.

vi DINAH WHITE, b. 14 Nov 1779; d. about 1818; m. 17 Jun 1812, NATHANIEL CRISSEY, b. at Southington, CT, 26 Jan 1768 son of John and Martha (Davenport) Crissey; Nathaniel d. at Stockton, NY, 23 May 1852. Nathaniel was first married to Hannah Bishop and third married to Mercy Merrill (widow of Solomon White).

vii SAMUEL WHITE, b. 28 Feb 1782; d. at Alabama, NY, 2 Jul 1863; m. at Littleton, 18 Oct 1807, BETSY ROGERS, b. 5 Apr 1784 (calculated from age 94 years, 6 months, 25 days at death); Betsy d. at Alabama, NY, 30 Oct 1878.

viii CORNELIUS WHITE, baptized 21 Sep 1784; d. 4 Dec 1784.

ix CYNTHIA WHITE, b. 1 Jun 1786; d. at Clayton, NY, after 1865; m. about 1829, as his second wife, JOHN INGALLS who was first married to Cynthia's sister Eunice (see below).

x ORPHA WHITE, b. 30 Jun 1789. Orpha was living in 1826 and given her bequest of land in her father's will seems to be unmarried at that time, but that is not certain.

xi EUNICE WHITE, b. 31 Aug 1791; d. about 1828; m. 20 Oct 1813, JOHN INGALLS, b. at Nelson, NH, 27 Feb 1788 son of Solomon and Marcy (Wilson) Ingalls; John d. at Clayton, NY, after 1865. John married second Eunice's sister Cynthia (see above).

xii JOHN WHITE, b. 12 Jun 1796; d. at Boston, 26 Jul 1861; m. 7 Jun 1821, HARRIET CARROLL, b. at Thompson, CT, 1796 daughter of Elijah and Patience (Smith) Carroll; Harriet d. at North Brookfield, MA, 20 Apr 1880.

720) DANIEL STONE (*Kezia Pierce Stone[4], Dinah Holt Pierce[3], Henry[2], Nicholas[1]*), b. at Harvard, 10 Jul 1754 son of Isaac and Kezia (Pierce) Stone; d. at Lower Canada, 9 May 1842; m. 27 Oct 1779, ABIGAIL ELLIS, b. at Keene, NH, 1 May 1755 daughter of Gideon and Elizabeth (Metcalf) Ellis; Abigail d. at Lower Canada, 20 Jul 1847.

Daniel was born at Harvard, and when about twelve years old went with his family to Westmoreland. Daniel and Abigail married there, and their oldest five children were born there. The family traveled from Westmoreland to Cavendish, Vermont and finally to Lower Canada.[1921]

In statement made 27 July 1833 for his pension application, Daniel Stone, then age seventy-eight and residing in Brome, Lower Canada, reported that he enlisted from Keene, New Hampshire in April 1775. He marched on 21 April 1775 to Massachusetts and was under the command of Capt. Jeremiah Stiles for eight months. He was in the Battle of Bunker Hill and was stationed in Cambridge until January 1776. He enlisted again in 1777 from Westmoreland in the company of Capt. John Cole and was at Otter Creek in Vermont and then at Charlestown. He reported being born in Harvard in 1755, was a resident of Keene at his first enlistment, then at Westmoreland, and finally at Brome in Lower Canada. Abigail Stone appeared to make her widow's pension application on 25 November 1844 then age eighty-nine and residing in Brome. She reported she married Daniel on 27 October 1779. Son Daniel Stone, age forty-eight in 1844, provided a family record with births and deaths of children in the family. The record gives the birth of father Daniel Stone as 10 July 1754 and mother Abigail Ellis as 1 May 1755 and also gives the births of seven children as well as the deaths of daughter Anna and son Bethuel.[1922]

Daniel Stone and Abigail Ellis were parents of seven children, the oldest five births recorded at Westmoreland and the youngest two children recorded at Cavendish, Vermont.

i ANNA STONE, b. at Westmoreland, 19 Nov 1780; d. at Brome, Québec, 4 Aug 1816.

ii KEZIA STONE, b. at Westmoreland, 2 Jun 1782; m. 8 Jul 1804, EBENEZER CHAMBERLAIN, b. 2 Jun 1782 son of Ebenezer and Martha (Howe) Chamberlain; Ebenezer d. at Knowlton's Landing, Québec, 21 Mar 1849.

iii ISAAC STONE, b. at Westmoreland, 1 Jul 1784

iv BETHUEL STONE, b. at Westmoreland, 14 Oct 1786; d. at Brome, 20 Sep 1813.

v ARTHUSIA STONE, b. at Westmoreland, 23 Sep 1788; d. at Brome, 1860; m. her first cousin, ISAAC STONE (*Ephraim Stone[5], Kezia Pierce Stone[4], Dinah Holt Pierce[3], Henry[2], Nicholas[1]*), b. 1777 son of Ephraim and Lucinda (Chamberlain) Stone; Isaac d. at Brome, 1864.[1923]

vi ABIGAIL STONE, b. 22 Jun 1792; d. at Knowlton, Québec, 10 Oct 1856; m. at Dunham, Québec, JAMES BALL, b. at South Hero, VT, 24 Dec 1787 son of Jacob and Elizabeth (Stone) Ball; James d. at Brome, 8 Jan 1885.

vii DANIEL STONE, b. at Cavendish, VT, 12 Apr 1796; m. at Dunham, Québec, 3 Apr 1821, THIRZA WESTOVER, b. at Bas Canada, about 1797; Thirza d. after 1871 when she was living at Brome.

1921 Bartlett, *Simon Stone Genealogy*, p 195

1922 Revolutionary War Pension and Bounty-Land Warrant Application Files, Case W25118

1923 *Quebec, Canada, Vital and Church Records (Drouin Collection), 1621-1968*, Institut Généalogique Drouin; Montreal, Quebec, Canada

721) JACOB STONE (*Kezia Pierce Stone⁴, Dinah Holt Pierce³, Henry², Nicholas¹*), b. at Harvard, 26 Jul 1756 son of Isaac and Kezia (Pierce) Stone; d. likely at Ogdensburg, NY; m. about 1782, ABIGAIL HOWE, b. at Sudbury, 28 Mar 1751 daughter of Edward and Lois (Maynard) Howe.[1924]

Jacob Stone went with his parents to Westmoreland. He enlisted in the militia and served two three-month terms and participated in the Battle of Bennington. After the war, Jacob married Abigail Howe and moved to Charlotte, Vermont where their children were born. The family was later in Ogdensburg, New York where he kept an inn.[1925]

Daughter Lois married and adopted one child. In her will written 8 December 1847 (proved 10 November 1851), Lois Hemphill of Troy bequeathed to adopted daughter Mercy W. Richardson the sum of $500. She bequeathed $300 to Mercy S. Salisbury wife of Orrin Salisbury. There were other bequests to sister Mary Bigelow, the children of sister Sarah Canfield deceased, and brothers Solomon Stone and Daniel Stone. There were also several other bequests to members of the Hemphill family.[1926]

Jacob Stone and Abigail Howe were parents of five children likely born at Charlotte, Vermont.

i LOIS STONE, b. about 1781; d. at Troy, NY, 5 Sep 1851; m. ANDREW HEMPHILL, b. at Windham, NH, 22 Jul 1772 son of Nathaniel and Agnes (Park) Hemphill; Andrew d. at Troy, 17 Feb 1844.

ii SALLY STONE, b. about 1783; d. at Potsdam, NY, 3 Sep 1835; m. about 1805, THOMAS CANFIELD, b. about 1773; Thomas d. at Potsdam, 1846.

iii SOLOMON STONE, b. 1787; d. at Kalamazoo, MI, 3 Feb 1872; m. ELEANOR CLINTON, b. at Barkhamsted, CT, 26 May 1788 daughter of Henry and Eleanor (Darrow) Clinton; Eleanor d. at Gulls Prairie, MI, 13 Nov 1836.

iv DANIEL STONE, b. 29 May 1789; d. at Potsdam, NY, 7 Oct 1866; m. at Potsdam, 26 Mar 1816, SALLY CLINTON, b. at Ferrisburgh, VT, 13 Jan 1800 daughter of Henry and Eleanor (Darrow) Clinton; Sally d. at Broadhead, WI, 13 Jan 1886.

v MARY "POLLY" STONE, b. 1791; d. at ClintoOnville, NY, 23 Mar 1854; m. about 1815, SAMUEL BIGELOW, b. at Winchendon, MA, 11 Sep 1787 son of Roger and Mary (Child) Bigelow; Samuel d. at Clintonville, 7 Aug 1856.

722) ABIGAIL STONE (*Kezia Pierce Stone⁴, Dinah Holt Pierce³, Henry², Nicholas¹*), b at Harvard, 19 Feb 1765 daughter of Isaac and Kezia (Pierce) Stone; m. at Westmoreland, 11 Dec 1783, SETH GARY, b. 1764 son of Seth and Hannah (Briggs) Gary;[1927] Seth was living in Charlotte, VT in 1810.

Seth and Abigail were settled in Colchester, Vermont by 1800 and were in nearby Charlotte, Vermont in 1810. Seth served in the War of 1812.[1928] Seth relocated again to Potsdam, New York[1929] by 1815.

There are records for four children of Abigail Stone and Seth Gary recorded at Westmoreland, New Hampshire.

i PHILENA GARY, b. 4 Oct 1784; m. 1809, CALEB HOUGH, b. at Barkhamsted, CT, 23 Jun 1782 son of Caleb and Rebecca (Andrews) Hough; Caleb d. at Potsdam, 8 Jun 1836.

ii POLLY GARY, b. 8 Apr 1787

iii ELNATHAN GARY, b. 6 Mar 1789; d. after 1830 when he was living at Potsdam; m. RHODA GOODRICH, b. 11 Aug 1789 daughter of Nathan and Rhoda (Allen) Goodrich.

iv ELI BUSH GARY, b. 29 Aug 1791; d. at Oshkosh, WI, 19 May 1867; m. at Potsdam, NY, 19 Jan 1817, FRANCES O. EASTON, b. at Weybridge, VT, 9 Nov 1798 daughter of Joel and Mabel (Bidwell) Easton; Frances d. at Chicago (buried at Oshkosh), 25 Dec 1878.

723) ABIGAIL KINGSBURY (*Abigail Holt Kingsbury⁴, Paul³, Henry², Nicholas¹*), b. at Hampton, CT, 17 May 1742 daughter of Jonathan and Abigail (Holt) Kingsbury; d. at Lima, NY, 1791; m. 1st, at Windham, 13 Nov 1759, JOHN GOULD, baptized at Ipswich 28 Mar 1731 son of Henry and Rebecca (Cole) Gould; John d. at Hampton, 29 Oct 1764 (probate Nov 1764). Abigail m. 2nd, at Hampton, 11 Sep 1770, JOHN ABBOTT. On 14 Mar 1791, Abigail filed for divorce from John Abbott on grounds of desertion.[1930]

1924 Westmoreland Historical Committee, *History of Westmoreland*, p 459

1925 Bartlett, *Simon Stone Genealogy*, p 196

1926 New York Wills and Probate Records, Rensselaer County, volume 41, pp 339-340

1927 Brainerd, *Gary Genealogy*, p 174

1928 Rann, *History of Chittenden County, Vermont*, p 557

1929 Brainerd, *Gary Genealogy*, p 174

1930 Knox and Ferris, Connecticut Divorces: Superior Court Records for the Counties of Tolland, New London & Windham 1719-1910, p 259; John, Wrentham, MA m. Abigail Gould, Windham, 11 Sep 1770; desertion 14 Mar 1791

John Gould did not leave a will and his estate entered probate November 1764 with the inventory taken 8 March 1765. Real estate was valued at £111 and personal estate at £59. The settlement on 24 November 1766 included a set-off to widow Abigail Gould, sons John and Jonathan and daughters Abigail and Sally.[1931]

Abigail Kingsbury and John Gould were parents of four children, the youngest child born after John's death. No children were identified for Abigail Kingsbury and John Abbott. After her divorce from John Abbott, Abigail went with her children to Lima, New York but Abigail died soon after arrival.

i ABIGAIL GOULD, b. at Windham, 14 Feb 1760; d. at Lima, NY, 16 May 1852; m. 3 Jul 1782, JEDEDIAH WATKINS, b. at Ashford, 5 Oct 1739 son of William and Mehitable (Humphrey) Watkins; Jedediah d. at Lima, 19 Aug 1832.

ii JOHN GOULD, b. at Windham, 12 Oct 1761; living in 1766 but nothing further known that is definite.

iii JONATHAN GOULD, b. at Windham, 28 Apr 1763; d. at Livonia, NY, 3 Mar 1816; m. 1st at Ashford, 1 Jan 1795, PATIENCE DYER; Patience d. at Lima, NY, 1811. Jonathan m. 2nd RACHEL who has not been identified; Rachel d. at Livonia, 7 Mar 1830.

iv SALLY GOULD, b. at Windham, 8 Jul 1765; d. at Lima, NY, 19 Oct 1844; m. 1785, PAUL DAVISON, b. at Ashford, 1765; Paul d. at Lima, NY, 19 Feb 1805.

724) JONATHAN KINGSBURY (*Abigail Holt Kingsbury⁴, Paul³, Henry², Nicholas¹*), b. at Hampton, CT, 25 Apr 1745 son of Jonathan and Abigail (Holt) Kingsbury; d. at Hampton, 25 Sep 1802; m. 1st, 14 Jan 1768, ANNE GEER, b. at Preston, 22 Dec 1745 daughter of Aaron and Mercy (Fisher) Geer;[1932] Anne d. 23 Oct 1773. Jonathan m. 2nd, 21 Jun 1775, LODEMA RANSOM, b. at Kent, 8 Mar 1752 daughter of John and Bethia (Lewis) Ransom;[1933] Lodema d. 24 Mar 1814.

Jonathan Kingsbury was educated at Yale graduating in 1767. He was a farmer in Hampton and owned considerable property. He represented the tow of Hampton in the General Assembly during three sessions 1789-1791.[1934]

In his will written 6 May 1801 (proved 30 November 1802), Jonathan Kingsbury bequeathed to beloved wife Lodema one-third of the household furniture, one-third of the farming tools, and two hundred dollars-worth of neat stock for her own use and disposal forever. She also receives the use and improvement of one-third part of the home farm which consists of about 450 acres but excludes the Holt farm and the so-called Ashford farm. Daughter Anna Rindge receives one-fourteenth part of the estate real and personal. Second daughter Lora Hammond, third daughter Artimesia Wallace, fourth daughter Rhoda Kingsbury, fifth daughter Lodema Kingsbury, and youngest daughter Amie Kingsbury also receive one-fourteenth part each. Sons Lewis, Lester, Ransom, and Jonathan each receives one-seventh of the estate. Grandson Jonathan Rindge receives thirty dollars at age twenty-one. Trusty friend Daniel Dennison was named executor. The total value of the estate was $12,029.96. The home farm of 450 acres was valued at $6,600.[1935]

Jonathan Kingsbury and Anne Geer were parents of three children.

i ANNA KINGSBURY, b. at Hampton, 21 Nov 1768; d. at Hampton, 15 May 1857; m. at Hampton, 22 Dec 1787, THOMAS RINDGE, b. about 1763; Thomas d. at Hampton, Oct 1819.[1936] Thomas served as a private in the Revolution and Anna received a widow's pension based on his service. Thomas Rindge enlisted for one year in June 1780 and served in the Connecticut line. He enlisted for a second term in April 1782 and was discharged 19 March 1783 at West Point.

ii LORA KINGSBURY, b. at Windham, 8 Sep 1771; d. at Bolton, CT, 17 Jan 1810; m. LEMUEL HAMMOND, b. at Bolton, 4 Nov 1766 son of Nathaniel and Dorothy (Tucker) Hammond; Lemuel d. at Bolton, 31 Oct 1805.

iii MERCY KINGSBURY, b. 9 Oct 1773; d. 12 May 1774.

Jonathan Kingsbury and Lodema Ransom were parents of eight children born at Hampton.[1937]

i ARTIMISSA KINGSBURY, b. 15 Jun 1776; d. at Ann Arbor, MI, 9 Dec 1835; m. Mr. Wallace who has not been identified. Their son, Jonathan Kingsbury Wallace, lived in Ann Arbor.

[1931] *Connecticut State Library (Hartford, Connecticut)*; Probate Place: *Hartford, Connecticut, Probate Packets, Geer, J-Gurley, 1719-1880, Estate of John Gould, Case 1644*

[1932] The 1797 will of Aaron Geer includes a bequest to the heirs of Anne Kingsbury wife of Jonathan Kingsbury.

[1933] The 1791 will of John Ransom of Kent includes a bequest to his daughter Lodema Kingsbury.

[1934] Dexter, *Biographical Sketches of the Graduates of Yale College: May 1763-July 1778*, p 234

[1935] *Connecticut, Wills and Probate Records, 1609-1999, Windham, Volume 15, pp 39-42*

[1936] This is the death date given in the pension application file and the estate was in probate in 1820.

[1937] Kingsbury, The Genealogy of the Descendants of Henry Kingsbury, p 173

ii RHODA KINGSBURY, b. 31 Mar 1778; d. at Hampton, 6 Jun 1852; m. at Hampton, 20 Oct 1801, JOHN TWEEDY, b. at Danbury, 16 Mar 1774 son of Samuel and Anna (Smith) Tweedy; John d. at Hampton, 18 Apr 1852.

iii LODEMA KINGSBURY, b. 24 Feb 1780; d. in West Virginia while traveling to handle affairs related to husband's estate who had died in Kentucky; m. Mr. Nettleton who has not been identified, but is perhaps Henry Nettleton whose brother William Nettleton, of both Connecticut and Kentucky, died in 1837 and left his entire estate to his brother Henry.

iv AMY KINGSBURY, b. 13 Aug 1783; m. ROBERT DURKEE, b. at Hampton, 23 Feb 1779 son of Andrew and Mary (Benjamin) Durkee; Robert d. at Perry, Feb 1867.

v LEWIS KINGSBURY, b. 5 Mar 1785; d. at Batavia, MI, about 1846 (probate 1846). Lewis does not seem to have married. No widow or children are mentioned in his probate file. His estate was sold to settle debts of the estate.

vi LESTER KINGSBURY, b. 28 May 1787; d. at Dansville, NY, 30 Mar 1837; m. 1813, ANNE SPENCER, b. at Litchfield, CT, 1796 son of Samuel and Lucretia (Parsons) Spencer; d. 14 Feb 1877.

vii RANSOM KINGSBURY, b. 10 Mar 1789; m. 1st at Mansfield, 28 Apr 1813, MARIA FRANCIS, b. 1794; Maria d. at Willington, 24 May 1834. Ransom m. 2nd at Willington, 5 Nov 1834, HANNAH CROCKER (widow of Ira Heath), b. 1794; Hannah d. at Fillmore, NY, Mar 1881.

viii JONATHAN KINGSBURY, b. 15 Apr 1794; d. at Livonia, NY, 5 Nov 1869; m. ARTEMISIA CLARK, b. at Brooklyn, 20 Feb 1794 daughter of Moses and Millicent (Skinner) Clark;[1938] d. at Livonia, 1 Oct 1887.

725) PAUL HOLT (*Paul⁴, Paul³, Henry², Nicholas¹*), b. at Windham, 4 Jan 1742/3 son of Paul and Mehitable (Chandler) Holt; d. at Hampton, 26 Oct 1827; m. 1st, 20 Aug 1767, SARAH WELCH, b. at Norwich, 6 Jul 1742 daughter of Joseph and Lydia (Rudd) Welch; Sarah d. 26 Dec 1784. Paul m. 2nd, 15 Jan 1789, PHEBE WELCH CADY, b. 1754 daughter of Gideon and Sarah (Hutchins) Cady;[1939] Phebe d. at Hampton, 31 May 1800. Paul m. 3rd, 27 Nov 1800, his second cousin, DINAH HOLT (*Joshua⁴, Joshua³, Nicholas², Nicholas¹*) (widow of Seth Stowell), b. at Windham, 22 Mar 1750 daughter of Joshua and Mary (Abbott) Holt; Dinah d. 21 Feb 1826. DINAH HOLT 1st m. 30 Jun 1778, SETH STOWELL, b. 29 May 1742 son of Nathaniel and Margaret (Trowbridge) Stowell; Seth d. about 1798 (when estate went to probate).

Paul Holt served in the Revolution in the Connecticut militia and is reported to have been at the Battle of Bunker Hill.[1940]

Paul Holt and Sarah Welch were parents of ten children.

i THOMAS HOLT, b. at Windham, 3 Sep 1768; d. at Hampton, 13 Sep 1831; m. at Hampton, 12 Jun 1792, EDE MARTIN, b. at Hampton, 30 Sep 1766 daughter of Benjamin and Lucy (Clark) Martin; Ede d. at Hampton, 28 Jan 1844.

ii VINE HOLT, b. at Windham, 16 Feb 1770; d. at Bristol, CT, 9 Apr 1828; m. at Brooklyn, CT, 28 Oct 1793, SUSAN KNOWLES who has not been identified.

iii ZIBA HOLT, b. at Windham, 25 Aug 1771; d. at Delphi, IN, 6 May 1860; m. 1st at Gallatin County, KY, 1 Dec 1804, PENELOPE KING, b. 1778; Penelope d. 1811. Ziba m. 2nd at Gallatin County, Oct 1811, LUCINDA WOOD, b. 1793; Lucinda d. 15 Mar 1825.[1941]

iv MEHITABLE HOLT, b. at Hampton, 7 Jun 1773; *perhaps* d. at Webster, MA, 5 Nov 1848; m. by 1797, OLIVER RICHMOND, b. at Killingly, 2 May 1765 son of Philip and Abilene (-) Richmond.

v SARAH HOLT, b. at Hampton, 3 Mar 1775; d. at Chaplin, CT, 10 Feb 1833; m. at Hampton, 15 Jan 1797, STEPHEN UTLEY, b. at Windham, 21 Nov 1762 son of Samuel and Hannah (Abbott) Utley; Stephen d. at Chaplin, 1 Mar 1841.

vi CHANDLER HOLT, b. at Hampton, 17 Jan 1777; d. at Paris, NY, 1797.[1942]

vii ERASTUS HOLT, b. at Hampton, 8 Sep 1778; d. at Pittsfield, VT, 28 Mar 1875; m. 1 Jun 1800, SARAH PARMENTER, b. at Oakham, MA, about 1782 daughter of Isaiah and Lydia (Hayden) Parmenter; Sarah d. at Pittsfield, 28 Dec 1863.

[1938] The 1862 will of Moses Clark of Brooklyn, CT includes a bequest to his daughter Artemisia Kingsbury

[1939] The 1799 will of Gideon Cady includes a bequest to his daughter Phebe Holt.

[1940] Durrie, *Genealogical History of the Holt Family*, p 89

[1941] Stewart, *Recollections of the Early Settlement of Carroll County, Indiana*, pp 106-110; this source has a lengthy, colorful biography of Col. Ziba Holt.

[1942] Durrie, Holt genealogy

viii LYDIA HOLT, b. at Hampton, 7 Oct 1780; m. ZACHARIAH YOUNG; Lydia and Zachariah were living in Greenfield, PA in 1840.

ix RUFUS HOLT, b. at Hampton, 1 Feb 1783; d. at Willington, 22 Dec 1852; m. at Willington, 12 Jan 1809, BETSEY HORTON, b. at Ashford, 5 Apr 1785 daughter of Moses and Silence (Wilson) Horton.

x ABIGAIL HOLT, b. at Hampton, 17 Dec 1784. (Durrie in his Holt genealogy reports that Abigail did not marry, although I wonder if she is the Abigail that married Benjamin Minor in 1804 at Hampton).

Paul Holt's third wife, Dinah Holt, was first married to Seth Stowell. Seth participated in the Revolution as one of those who helped buy and equip a privateer.[1943] Seth did not leave a will and his estate entered probate 5 May 1798 with widow Dinah as administratrix. Heirs of the estate were Olive, Keziah, Artimissa, and Mardin.[1944]

Dinah Holt and Seth Stowell were parents of four children.

i OLIVE STOWELL, b. at Pomfret, 2 Apr 1779; d. at New Woodstock, NY, 13 Jun 1829; m. at Woodstock, 6 Feb 1803, LUTHER CORBIN, b. at Woodstock, 18 Feb 1775 son of Silas and Anna (Fisk) Corbin; Luther d. at New Woodstock, 5 Aug 1848.

ii KEZIA STOWELL, b. at Pomfret, 4 Sep 1781; living in 1798 but nothing further known.

iii ARTEMESIA STOWELL, b. at Pomfret, 7 Nov 1784; d. at New Woodstock, NY, 25 Jan 1853; m. at New Woodstock, 1 Jan 1806, ABIEL AINSWORTH, b. at Woodstock, 10 May 1777 son of Nathan and Phebe (Kinsley) Ainsworth; Abiel d. at New Woodstock, 4 Nov 1866.

iv MARVIN CHARLES STOWELL, b. at Union, CT, 15 Mar 1789; d. at Cazenovia, NY; m. at Pomfret, 17 Jan 1813, LUCY HOUGHTON, *likely* the Lucy b. at Woodstock, 20 Jul 1790 daughter of Jonas and Sarah (Abbott) Houghton.

726) PHILEMON HOLT (*Paul⁴, Paul³, Henry², Nicholas¹*), b. at Hampton, 22 Jun 1744 son of Paul and Mehitable (Chandler) Holt; d. at Willington, 31 Jul 1818; m. at Willington, 27 Aug 1771, JEMIMA ELDREDGE, b. at Willington, 28 Mar 1755 daughter of Jesse and Abigail (Smith) Eldredge; Jemima d. at Willington, 3 Oct 1821.

The estate of Philemon Holt entered probate 17 October 1818 with Jemima Holt and Amasa Holt as administrators. The distribution of the personal estate included one-third to widow Jemima Holt and the remainder in four equal shares to each of the following heirs: son Jerome Holt, one share to daughter Clarissa Holt wife of John Holt, one share to son Amasa Holt, and one share to representatives of Lucinda Fenton deceased late wife of Abiel Fenton.[1945]

There is evidence for five children of Philemon and Jemima likely all born at Windham.[1946]

i JEROME HOLT, b. unknown. He is the first child listed in the distribution but his brother Amasa was administrator of the estate. Nothing else is known of him.

ii MATILDA HOLT, b. at Windham, 14 Feb 1773; likely died young.

iii CLARISSA HOLT, b. about 1775; d. at Willington, 25 Feb 1840; m. at Willington, 6 Sep 1804, her first cousin once removed, JOHN HOLT (*James⁴, Abiel³, Nicholas², Nicholas¹*), b. at Willington, 11 Apr 1776 son of James and Luce (Sawins) Holt; John d. at Willington, 22 Apr 1841. Clarissa Holt and John Holt are Family 885.

iv LUCINDA HOLT, b. at Windham, 30 Apr 1775; d. at Willington, 15 Dec 1816; m. at Willington, 27 Jun 1791, ABIEL FENTON, b. at Willington, 27 May 1767 son of Eleazer and Elizabeth (Davis) Fenton; Abiel d. at Willington, 30 May 1822.

v AMASA HOLT, b. about 1781; d. at Willington, 22 Jun 1850; m. BETSEY who has not been identified; Betsey was b. about 1777 and d. at Willington, 3 Oct 1851.

727) EBENEZER HOLT (*Paul⁴, Paul³, Henry², Nicholas¹*), b. recorded at Windham, 23 Feb 1745/6 son of Paul and Mehitable (Chandler) Holt; m. at Somers, 29 Aug 1771, MARY COLLINS.

Ebenezer Holt and Mary Collins were parents of six children born at Hampton, Connecticut. The movements of this family are not clear after the births of their children, but Ebenezer perhaps went to Pittsfield, Vermont with his brother Stephen.

[1943] Stowell, *The Stowell Genealogy*, p 107

[1944] *Connecticut State Library (Hartford, Connecticut);* Probate Place: *Hartford, Connecticut, Probate Packets, Spencer, Hulda-Thompson, Calvin, 1759-1880*, case 4169, Seth Stowell

[1945] *Connecticut State Library (Hartford, Connecticut);* Probate Place: *Hartford, Connecticut, Philemon Holt estate*

[1946] Durrie's Holt genealogy reports eight children (not named), but evidence was found for just one child beyond the four in the probate.

i EBENEZER HOLT, b. 1772; died young

ii MOLLY HOLT, b. 29 Jun 1773

iii CHLOE HOLT, b. 6 Apr 1775; d. 7 Apr 1776

iv CHLOE HOLT, b. 24 Feb 1777

v LEVI HOLT, b. 17 Apr 1779; d. at South Wilbraham, MA, 1814 (probate 6 Jun 1814); m. at Somers, CT, 2 Mar 1807, LUCINDA JONES, b. at Somers, 4 Apr 1787 daughter of Issachar and Eleanor (Hunt) Jones. Lucinda married second Elisha Russ on 17 Apr 1817.

vi JUSTIN HOLT, b. about 1781; died young[1947]

728) STEPHEN HOLT (*Paul⁴, Paul³, Henry², Nicholas¹*), b. at Hampton, 12 Mar 1748 son of Paul and Mehitable (Chandler) Holt; d. at Pittsfield, VT, 31 Dec 1838; m. 20 Nov 1774, HANNAH GEER, b. 2 Nov 1755 daughter of Aaron and Mercy (Fisher) Geer;[1948] Hannah d. at Chaplin, CT, 1858.

Stephen and Hannah began their family in Windham and moved to Pittsfield, Vermont in 1787 and erected a sawmill in 1797. He was as one of the first selectmen when the town of officially organized in 1793.[1949]

Stephen and Hannah were parents of eight children.

i STEPHEN HOLT, b. at Windham, 2 Oct 1775; d. 15 Feb 1779.

ii ELISHA HOLT, b. at Windham, 8 Oct 1778; d. at Worthington, OH, 9 Oct 1857; m. 1st at Pittsfield, 19 Jan 1803, SAREPTA HOSINGTON, b. about 1783; Sarepta d. at Pittsfield, about 1812. Elisha m. 2nd at Pittsfield, 29 May 1815, LOUISA B. HARRISON, b. at Chittenden, VT, about 1785 daughter of Samuel and Rebecca (Keeler) Harrison; Louisa d. at Worthington, OH, 1841. Elisha m. 3rd about 1842, EMILY M. who has not been identified but born in PA about 1812.

iii HANNAH HOLT, b. at Windham, 13 Nov 1780; d. at Pittsfield, VT, 27 Jan 1868; m. 20 Mar 1800, ROBERT CROSSMAN, b. at Sutton, MA, 29 Sep 1778 son of Jacob and Anne (Claflin) Crossman;[1950] Robert d. at Pittsfield, 13 May 1859.

iv STEPHEN HOLT, b. at Windham, 12 Sep 1783; d. at Pittsfield, VT, 7 Feb 1856; m. at Pittsfield, 23 Mar 1806, REBECCA PARMENTER, b. 1783 daughter of Thomas and Mary (Walker) Parmenter; Rebecca d. at Pittsfield, 15 Sep 1856.

v JOSIAH HOLT, b. at Windham, 20 May 1786; d. at Stockbridge, VT, 5 Dec 1871; m. at Pittsfield, 28 May 1815, LUCINDA CHASE, b. at Ticonderoga, NY[1951] about 1791; Lucinda d. at Stockbridge, 5 Dec 1871.

vi CLARISSA HOLT, b. likely at Pittsfield, 27 Jul 1789; d. at Pittsfield, 18 Jan 1822; m. at Pittsfield, 28 Feb 1814, MOSES RICE, b. 1787; Moses d. after 1850 when he was living at Leicester, VT. Moses was second married to Edna Hubbard on 24 Feb 1823.

vii AMOS HOLT, b. at Pittsfield, VT, 16 Mar 1795; d. 8 Sep 1796.

viii AMOS HOLT, b. at Pittsfield, 16 Mar 1799; d. at Brandon, VT, 30 Apr 1874; m. about 1825, ANNA E. GAINES, b. at Pittsfield, 1806 daughter of Asa and Annah (Doyle) Gaines; Anna d. at Brandon, 28 Apr 1860.

729) JAMES HOLT (*Paul⁴, Paul³, Henry², Nicholas¹*), b. at Hampton, 21 May 1750 son of Paul and Mehitable (Chandler) Holt; d. at Bristol, CT, 29 Mar 1826; m. 1st, 31 Dec 1769, HULDAH STILES, b. at Hampton, 18 Sep 1736 daughter of Samuel and Huldah (Durkee) Stiles; Huldah d. at Hampton, 12 Jul 1799.[1952] James m. 2nd, 29 Jun 1800, CHLOE STILES (niece of Huldah), b. 4 May 1781 daughter of Isaac and Abigail (Case) Stiles. Chloe Holt was living in Bristol in 1850 with her son James.

James Holt and Huldah Stiles were parents of two children.

i LYDIA HOLT, b. at Hampton, 28 Jan 1770; m. at Hampton, 12 Aug 1792, NATHANIEL SWEET NILES, b. at Warwick, RI, 1759 son of Benjamin and Ruth (Niles) Niles; Nathaniel d. likely at Pomfret, 16 Nov 1832.[1953]

ii HULDAH HOLT, b. at Hampton, 9 Sep 1772; d. 28 Sep 1775.

1947 Durrie, Holt genealogy

1948 The 1797 will of Aaron Geer includes a bequest to daughter Hannah Holt wife of Stephen Holt.

1949 Smith, *History of Rutland County, Vermont*, p 603 and p 720

1950 The names of Robert's parents are given as Jacob and Ann on his death record.

1951 Lucinda's place of birth is given on the death record of one of her children.

1952 Huldah the wife of James Holt died at age 63.

1953 U.S., The Pension Roll of 1835

James Holt and Chloe Stiles were parents of one child.

i JAMES HOLT, b. at Willington, 13 Oct 1801; d. at Bristol, CT, 13 Dec 1890. James did not marry. He owned a sawmill in Bristol.

730) MEHITABLE HOLT (*Paul⁴, Paul³, Henry², Nicholas¹*), b. at Windham, 1 May 1757 daughter of Paul and Mehitable (Chandler) Holt; d. at Hampton, 27 Oct 1819; m. at Pomfret, 27 Nov 1789, JEREMIAH PHELPS, b. at Hebron, 13 Jul 1729 son of Timothy and Hannah (Calkins) Phelps.[1954]

The estate of Mehitable Phelps entered probate 1 November 1819 with Ziba H. Phelps as administrator. Proceeds of the sale of the personal estate were $368.88 which was not sufficient for the claims against the estate of $597.34 and a portion of the real estate was sold to settle the estate. Heirs were Zibha H. Phelps, Lucy Martin, Josiah H. Phelps and John Phelps.[1955]

Mehitable Holt and Jeremiah Phelps were parents of four children.

i LUCY PHELPS, b. at Pomfret, 27 Jun 1790; likely d. at Hartford, 28 May 1871; m. at Hampton, 19 Jan 1817, ASA U. MARTIN, b. 8 Feb 1792 son of Amasa and Ursula (Utley) Martin.

ii ZIBA HOLT PHELPS, b. at Pomfret, 14 Oct 1793; d. at Hampton, 16 Jan 1878; m. at Hampton, 1 Jan 1818, BETSEY GRIFFIN, b. about 1798 likely daughter of Ebenezer and Mary (Fuller) Griffin; Betsey d. at Hampton, 4 Dec 1866.

iii JOSIAH H. PHELPS, b. at Pomfret, 7 Oct 1795;[1956] d. at Manhattan, KS, 30 Jan 1885; m. RUTH, b. at Rochester, VT, 14 May 1801; Ruth d. at Manhattan, KS, 15 May 1865. Josiah m. 2nd at Manhattan, KS, 10 Nov 1878, a woman 55 years his junior, MARY MATILDA PAXTON, b. in NY, about 1851. Josiah attended Yale and was a physician in Rochester, VT and later in Manhattan, KS. In his will written in 1879, he left his entire estate to his wife Mary M. Phelps. No children are mentioned in the will. The Hampton, CT records from the Barbour collection mention a son Peter but without year of birth and without the name of mother.

iv JOHN PHELPS, b. about 1797; d. at Tolland, 26 Sep 1847; m. at Hampton, 30 Nov 1818, BETSEY ROBINSON, b. at Windham, 26 Dec 1793 daughter of Asa and Olive (Huntington) Robinson; Betsey d. at Tolland, 3 Feb 1832.

731) JONATHAN ABBOT (*Jonathan Abbot⁴, Zerviah Holt Abbott³, Henry², Nicholas¹*), b. at Lunenburg, 20 Aug 1740 son of Jonathan and Martha (Lovejoy) Abbot; d. at Andover, 26 Dec 1821; m. 1st, about 1762, his third cousin, MEHITABLE ABBOTT, b. at Andover 11 Aug 1736 daughter of Ephraim and Hannah (Phelps) Abbott; Mehitable d. 1 Jan 1777. Jonathan m. 2nd, 17 Dec 1778, his third cousin, DORCAS ABBOTT, b. 23 Sep 1758 daughter of Stephen and Mary (Abbott) Abbott; Dorcas d. 3 Mar 1844.

Jonathan Abbot served in the Revolutionary War with the rank of Sergeant in the company commanded by Capt. Henry Abbott. He was a farmer and lived on the homestead inherited from his father.

In his will (probate 1 January 1822), Jonathan Abbot made bequests to the following persons: beloved wife Dorcas, beloved son Stephen, beloved son Jonathan, daughters Mehitable, Sarah, Zurviah, Nabby, and Hannah, daughter Dorcas, daughter Phebe, grandson Stephen son of Stephen, and each of his grandsons named Jonathan. Son Stephen was the sole executor.[1957] The grandsons named Jonathan each receives a firelock for their bequest. Wife Dorcas is to be cared for in terms of all her needs with provisions procured by his executor and delivered to her and she is to be cared for in health and in sickness as long as she is a widow. In consideration of this care and support, Dorcas forgoes her right of dower. But if the executor fails in his responsibilities to her, then her right of dower is reinstated.

Mehitable and Jonathan Abbot were parents of six children born at Andover.

i MEHITABLE ABBOTT, b. 29 Sep 1764; d. at Newry, ME, 6 Sep 1858; m. at Andover, 20 Sep 1787, BENJAMIN RUSSELL, b. at Andover, 28 Jul 1763 son of Benjamin and Mary (Feaver) Russell; Benjamin d. at Newry, 21 Aug 1842.

ii SARAH ABBOTT, b. 22 Jun 1766; d. at Frelighsburg, Québec, 25 Jul 1845; m. at Andover, 11 Jun 1793, JONATHAN STICKNEY, b. at Rowley, 29 Jul 1763 son of Jonathan and Mary (March) Stickney; Jonathan d. at Frelighsburg, 12 Sep 1839.[1958]

[1954] Phelps and Servin, *The Phelps Family in America*, volume 1, p 211

[1955] *Connecticut State Library (Hartford, Connecticut);* Probate Place: *Hartford, Connecticut, Estate of Mehitable Phelps, Case 3023*

[1956] Josiah's birthdate, and that of his wife Ruth, is engraved on his tombstone.

[1957] Essex County, MA: Probate File Papers, 1638-1881.Online database. AmericanAncestors.org. New England Historic Genealogical Society, 2014. Case 83

[1958] *Quebec, Canada, Vital and Church Records (Drouin Collection), 1621-1968*

iii ZERVIAH ABBOTT, b. 19 Mar 1768; d. at Bethel, ME, 18 Oct 1847; m. at Andover, 29 Dec 1789, JOHN ELLENWOOD, b. at Amherst, NH, 19 Sep 1765 son of Joseph and Sarah (-) Ellenwood; John d. at Bethel, 19 Jun 1847.

iv ABIGAIL ABBOTT, b. 30 Jul 1770; d. at Bethel, ME, 2 Jun 1810; m. at Andover, 17 Sep 1789, THEODORE RUSSELL, b. at Andover, 6 Dec 1765 son of Benjamin and Mary (Feaver) Russell; Theodore, d. at Bethel, 4 Jun 1821.

v HANNAH ABBOTT, b. 18 Nov 1774; d. at Bethel, ME, 5 Aug 1854; m. 16 Aug 1795, SIMEON TWITCHELL, b. at Bethel, 18 Feb 1770 son of Eleazer and Martha (Mason) Twitchell; Simeon d. at Bethel, 4 May 1844.

vi JONATHAN ABBOTT, b. 11 Jun 1776; d. at Bethel, ME, 7 Jan 1843; m. 27 Jan 1799, his third cousin once removed, BETSY BATCHELDER, b. at Wilton, 4 Aug 1777 daughter of Daniel and Rebecca (Abbott) Batchelder; Betsy d. at Bethel, 18 Nov 1864. Jonathan Abbott and Betsy Batchelder are Family 1079.

Jonathan Abbot and Dorcas Abbott were parents of four children born at Andover.

i STEPHEN ABBOTT, b. 30 Dec 1779; d. at Andover, 1 Oct 1835; m. at Andover, 13 Aug 1801, his third cousin, HANNAH RUSSELL (*Phebe Abbott Russell[5], Hannah Holt Abbott[4], Timothy[3], James[2], Nicholas[1]*), b. at Andover, Sep 1778 daughter of John and Phebe (Abbott) Russell; Hannah d. at Andover, 3 Jan 1840.

ii DORCAS ABBOTT, b. 26 Mar 1782; d. at Salem, 18 Apr 1841; m. 14 Oct 1810, JOSEPH SIBLEY, b. at Salem, 13 Dec 1783; Joseph d. at Salem, 1826.

iii PHEBE ABBOTT, b. 17 Jan 1788; d. at Andover, 14 Apr 1870; m. 13 Nov 1810, her third cousin once removed, JOSHUA BALLARD, b. at Andover, 3 Jan 1785 son of Hezekiah and Mary (Chandler) Ballard; Joshua d. at Andover, 4 Feb 1871.

iv POLLY ABBOTT, b. 9 Jun 1790; d. 1 Feb 1796.

732) WILLIAM ABBOT (*Jonathan Abbot[4], Zerviah Holt Abbott[3], Henry[2], Nicholas[1]*), b. at Lunenburg, 24 Nov 1745 son of Jonathan and Martha (Lovejoy) Abbot; d. Wilton, NH, Oct 1807;[1959] m. 26 Aug 1766, his third cousin, SARA HOLT (*Timothy[4], Timothy[3], James[2], Nicholas[1]*), b. 11 Aug 1746 daughter of Timothy and Hannah (Dane) Holt.

William Abbot and Sarah Holt were parents of six children.

i HANNAH ABBOTT, b. at Andover, 11 Jun 1767; d. at Temple, NH, 13 Mar 1858; m. at Temple, 10 Feb 1791, DANIEL HEALD, b. at Temple, 5 Sep 1761 son of Oliver and Lydia (Spaulding) Heald; Daniel d. at Temple, 26 Aug 1836.

ii SARAH ABBOTT, b. at Andover, 3 Jun 1769; m. EZRA UPTON. Sarah and Ezra did not have children.[1960]

iii MARTHA ABBOTT, b. at Wilton, 11 Dec 1772; d. at Temple, 15 Dec 1861; m. 17 Feb 1795, ELISHA CHILD, b. at Groton, MA, 31 Oct 1767 son of Moses and Sarah (Stiles) Child; Elisha d. at Temple, 1 Apr 1853.

iv MARY ABBOTT, b. at Wilton, 5 Apr 1775; d. 20 Aug 1777.

v WILLIAM ABBOTT, b. at Wilton, 7 Jan 1779; d. at Malden, MA, 15 Jan 1843; m. 1st, at Wilton, 29 Jan 1799, his third cousin once removed, REBECCA BATCHELDER, b. at Wilton, 20 Dec 1775 daughter of Daniel and Rebecca (Abbott) Batchelder; Rebecca d. 1805. William m. 2nd, 4 Jun 1806, APPHIA TYLER, b. 22 Nov 1784; Apphia d. 29 Sep 1806. William m. 3rd, 29 Sep 1807, ABIGAIL SAWTELL, b. at Groton, 31 Jul 1779 daughter of Richard and Elizabeth (Bennett) Sawtell; Abigail d. at Lynn, 14 Nov 1864.

vi MOLLY ABBOTT, b. at Wilton, 23 Apr 1782; d. at Boston, Jun 1806; m. at Malden, 15 Sep 1805, SAMUEL TUFTS, b. at Malden, 1 Apr 1783 son of Samuel and Martha (Upham) Tufts; Samuel d. at Cleveland, OH, Dec 1863. Samuel married second Sarah F. Loring and third Clarissa Pool.

733) MARTHA ABBOT (*Jonathan Abbot[4], Zerviah Holt Abbott[3], Henry[2], Nicholas[1]*), b. at Andover, 23 Jan 1749/50 daughter of Jonathan and Martha (Lovejoy) Abbot; d. at Temple, NH, 10 Jan 1842; m. 3 May 1774; OLIVER WHITING, b. at Pelham, NH, 6 Apr 1750 son of Eleazer and Dorothy (Crosby) Whiting; Oliver d. 28 Sep 1829.

Oliver Whiting saw service in the New Hampshire militia during the Revolution serving for six weeks in 1779.[1961] Oliver and Martha married in Andover but were soon after in Temple where they remained.

1959 Livermore, *History of the Town of Wilton*, p 550; no death record was located to support this information.

1960 This is a marriage reported by the Abbot genealogical register for which records have not yet been located.

1961 Compiled Service Records of Soldiers Who Served in the American Army During the Revolutionary War 1775-1785

Oliver Whiting and Martha Abbot were parents of nine children, the oldest child born at Andover and the remainder at Temple, New Hampshire.

i PATTY WHITING, b. 22 Jul 1775; d. at Temple, 9 Aug 1778.

ii OLIVER WHITING, b. 5 Jan 1778; d. at Wilton, 9 Aug 1849; m. at Temple, 2 Jan 1800, FANNY STILES, b. at Temple, 30 Mar 1778 daughter of Asa and Hannah (Bixby) Stiles;[1962] Fanny d. at Wilton, 25 May 1866.

iii PATTY WHITING, b. 13 Feb 1780; d. at Temple, 17 Jan 1800; m. 1799, EPHRAIM BLOOD, b. at Concord, MA, 6 Mar 1779 son of Francis and Elizabeth (Spaulding) Blood. Ephraim married second Rebecca Maynard and third Mrs. Goldsmith.

iv SALLY WHITING, b. 1 Jul 1782; d. 3 Jun 1785.

v HANNAH WHITING, b. 8 Oct 1784; d. at Temple, 9 Dec 1817; m. 28 Mar 1804, ELIAS BOYNTON, b. at Temple, 15 May 1782 son of Elias and Elizabeth (Blood) Boynton. After Hannah's death, Elias married Mary Ferguson 16 Jul 1817.

vi NATHAN ABBOT WHITING, b. 20 Apr 1787; d. at Cicero, NY, after 1860; m. at Temple, 2 Apr 1811, BETSEY BLOOD, b. 1793 daughter of Francis and Rebecca (Parlin) Blood; Betsey d. at Cicero, after 1855.

vii BENJAMIN WHITING, b. 13 Apr 1789; d. at Temple, 23 Jan 1856; m. 18 Jun 1811, REBECCA BLOOD, b. at Temple, about 1792 daughter of Francis and Rebecca (Parlin) Blood.

viii GEORGE WHITING, b. 16 Feb 1791; d. at Temple, 13 Sep 1822; m. 1813, ELIZABETH SEARLE, b. at Temple, 13 Aug 1794 daughter of Daniel and Hannah (Blood) Searle. After George's death, Elizabeth married Josiah Stickney on 9 Aug 1824.

ix DAVID WHITING, b. 22 Apr 1793; d. at Temple, 7 Feb 1827; m. 1 Jun 1815, POLLY FARRAR, b. at Temple, 1795 daughter of Simon and Mehitable (Thompson) Farrar.

734) HANNAH ABBOT (*David Abbot⁴, Zerviah Holt Abbott³, Henry², Nicholas¹*), b. at Pembroke, 7 Sep 1743 daughter of David and Hannah (Chandler) Abbott; d. at Pembroke, 17 Mar 1813; m. her third cousin, BENJAMIN HOLT (*Benjamin⁴, Nicholas³, Nicholas², Nicholas¹*), b. 28 Feb 1741 son of Benjamin and Sarah (Frye) Holt.

In his will written 7 January 1811 and proved 1 March 1826, Benjamin Holt directs that his executor David Holt pay the legacies in the will. Beloved wife Hannah receives a full one-third part of the real estate and full use of all the household furniture during her natural life. Son Nicolas receives twenty-two dollars which completes his portion. Son David receives all the real and personal estate except Benjamin reserves one yoke of oxen. To complete their full portions daughter Sarah Chandler receives twenty-two dollars, daughters Hannah Mason, Molly Russell, Mehitable Shannon, and Phebe Chandler each receive twenty-five dollars, and daughter Dolly Shannon twenty-two dollars. Daughter Betty Holt receives one hundred dollars. Granddaughter Hannah Norris with what she has received is her full share. Daughter Betty Holt and granddaughter Hannah Norris receive use of part of the house while they remain unmarried. Hannah and Betty will also share equally in the household furniture after his wife's demise.[1963]

Hannah Abbot and Benjamin Holt were parents of eleven children likely all born at Pembroke.

i SARAH HOLT, b. 23 Jan 1764; d. at Danbury, NH, after 1830; m. at Pembroke, 17 Apr 1787, JOSIAH CHANDLER, b. 1763 of undetermined parents;[1964] Josiah d. at Danbury, after 1830. Josiah served as a private in the Revolution and received a pension as an invalid.

ii NICHOLAS HOLT, b. 4 Aug 1766; d. at Danbury, NH, 24 Jun 1816; m. at Concord, 9 Jun 1790, ACHSAH RUSSELL, b. at Haverhill, MA, 14 Sep 1758 daughter of Edward and Mary (Page) Russell; Achsah d. at Warrensburg, NY, 26 May 1851.

iii HANNAH HOLT, b. 15 Sep 1768; d. at Pembroke, 22 Aug 1831; m. 18 Oct 1789, ISAAC MORRISON, b. at Nottingham, NH, 3 Feb 1760 son of James and Martha (White) Morrison; Isaac d. at Pembroke, 9 Jan 1846.

iv MOLLY HOLT, b. 7 Apr 1770; m. 3 Mar 1791, JOHN RUSSELL, *perhaps* b. at Haverhill, MA, 16 Jun 1767 son of James and Susannah (Richardson) Russell. Molly and John had seven children born at New London, NH, but have not located clear information on their deaths.

[1962] Gould, *The Stiles Family in America*, p 84

[1963] New Hampshire County Probate Records, 1660-1973, Merrimack, case 282, probate of Benjamin Holt, 1:211, 6:523. Accessed through familysearch.org

[1964] There is another Josiah Chandler born 1762 son of David and Mary (Ballard) Chandler who married Margaret Aiken.

v PHEBE HOLT, b. 14 Jul 1772; d. at Lovell, ME, 1 Jun 1850; m. 13 Nov 1798, her fourth cousin, TIMOTHY CHANDLER, b. at Andover, Sep 1775 son of Timothy and Mary (Walker) Chandler; Timothy d. at Lovell, 29 Nov 1854.

vi DAVID HOLT, b. 12 May 1774; d. at Rumford, ME, 1 Feb 1859; m. 10 Nov 1795, his fourth cousin, CHLOE CHANDLER, b. at Andover, 30 Aug 1771 daughter of Timothy and Mary (Walker) Chandler; Chloe d. at Rumford, 17 Mar 1859.

vii MEHITABLE HOLT, b. 28 Jul 1776; d. 16 Jan 1778.

viii MEHITABLE HOLT, b. 17 Jul 1778; d. at Cottage, NY, 28 Jan 1855; m. 1st, at Pembroke, NH, Sep 1798, as his second wife, JOHN SHANNON, b. 1 Feb 1769;[1965] John d. at Perrysburg, NY, about 1840. Mehitable m. 2nd, about 1842, AZARIAH DARBEE, b. in CT, 1762 son of Jedediah and Lucretia (Cleveland) Darbee; Azariah d. at Dayton, NY, 18 Aug 1851. John Shannon was first married to Ruth Whittemore daughter of Benjamin and Abigail (Abbott) Whittemore. Azariah Darbee was first married to Susannah Phelps.

ix ELIZABETH HOLT, b. 7 May 1780; d. at Chichester, NH, after 1844; m. at Pembroke, 12 Feb 1835, as his third wife, JONATHAN LEAVITT, b. at Chichester, 17 Nov 1772 son of Jonathan and Anna (Tilton) Leavitt; Jonathan d. at Chichester, 24 Dec 1844. Jonathan was first married to Rebecca Lake and second married to Hannah Perkins.

x DORCAS HOLT, b. 7 May 1783; d. 27 Feb 1810.

xi DOLLY HOLT, b. 1 May 1785; d. at Leon, NY, 1851; m. Mar 1802, SAMUEL SHANNON, b. 1774;[1966] Samuel d. at Leon, NY, 1 Oct 1849.

735) BRIDGET ABBOT (*David Abbot[4], Zerviah Holt Abbott[3], Henry[2], Nicholas[1]*), b. at Pembroke, about 1761 daughter of David and Hannah (Chandler) Abbot; m. 24 Dec 1787, her third cousin, PHINEAS AMES, b. 7 Sep 1764 son of Samuel and Elizabeth (Stevens) Ames; Phineas d. about 1792. Bridget m. 2nd, 17 Dec 1793, STEPHEN HARRIMAN, b. at Haverhill, 10 Mar 1757 son of Stephen and Sarah (Mascraft) Harriman; Stephen d. at Lisbon, OH, 25 Feb 1828. Stephen was first married to Lucy Story.

No children were identified for Bridget Abbot and Phineas Ames. Following the death of Phineas, Bridget married Stephen Harriman who was also widowed and had four children from his first marriage. After spending time in Tunbridge, Vermont the family relocated to Clark County, Ohio.

Stephen Harriman did not leave a will and a report on the inventory of the estate was made 22 April 1828 with the final settlement in March 1834. George W. Harriman was administrator. The heirs-at-law, in addition to George W. Harriman, were Bridget Harriman, Noah and Sarah Norton, Isaac and Mary Chamberlain, Stephen Harriman, Ira Harriman, James and Betty Hackett, Thomas Harriman, John and Sophronia Lasky, and Flanders children (Lucy, Charlotte, Walter, James, Stephen, Sarah, William, and Arthur). The real estate was sold to settle the debts of the estate. The sale of the property brought $3,465 and $1,033.97 was paid to creditors.[1967] Sarah Norton, Mary Chamberlain, Stephen Harriman, and the Flanders grandchildren are heirs from Stephen Harriman's first marriage to Lucy Story.

Bridget Abbot and Stephen Harriman had four children who were living at the time of the probate of Stephen's estate in 1828. There are birth records in Tunbridge, Vermont for three of the children. It is possible there were other children who died before adulthood.

i IRA HARRIMAN, b. 24 Nov 1795; d. at Madison, OH, 7 Jul 1857; m. at Ashtabula, OH, 16 Jan 1823, LOEY BROWN, b. 18 Sep 1803 daughter of Solomon and Lydia (Walton) Brown; Loey d. at Madison, OH, 24 May 1884.

ii SOPHRONIA HARRIMAN, b. at Tunbridge, 18 Sep 1800; m. 1st, at Clark County, OH, 14 Jun 1829, JOHN LASKY; John d. before 1850. Sophronia m. 2nd, at Kane, IL, 27 May 1850, EDWARD GRAY, b. in Germany, about 1790; Edward d. before 1857. Sophronia m. 3rd, at Houston, MN, 14 Jun 1857, GEORGE HOLLIDAY, b. in England, about 1815.

iii THOMAS JEFFERSON HARRIMAN, b. at Tunbridge, 25 May 1801; *perhaps* m. at Champaign, OH, 20 May 1830, MARGERY ALEXANDER.

iv GEORGE WASHINGTON HARRIMAN, b. at Tunbridge, 2 Sep 1803; d. at Garnett, KS, 16 Feb 1875; m. 1st, at Clark County, OH, 22 Nov 1835, ELIZABETH MORRIS, b. likely at Clark County, about 1815 daughter of Joseph

[1965] John's birth date is from a family bible record.

[1966] John Shannon and Samuel Shannon are likely brothers, but they do not seem to be the children of Samuel and Lydia (Leavitt) Shannon. The 1817 probate of Samuel Shannon of Rockingham County, NY (a Revolutionary War pensioner with widow Lydia) includes a statement that Lydia Taber Shannon, Thomas Shannon, and Sarah Shannon are the only children of the deceased.

[1967] Ohio Probate Records, Clark County, Administration Records 1828-1836, pp 62-63; Settlements 1827-1844, volume 1, pp 327-329

and Lavina (Drake) Morris;[1968] Elizabeth d. before 1850. George m. 2nd, 23 Aug 1851, SARAH ANN CAMPBELL, b. in OH, Apr 1835 of undetermined parents; Sarah was still living in 1900 in Indianapolis with her daughter Ida and her husband.

736) EPHRAIM BLUNT (*Zerviah Abbott Blunt⁴, Zerviah Holt Abbott³, Henry², Nicholas¹*), b. at Danville, VT, 20 Jun 1754 son of Ephraim and Zerviah (Abbott) Blunt; d. at Danville, 15 Feb 1829; m. 21 Nov 1776, MARTHA ORDWAY, b. at Amesbury, 28 Mar 1753 daughter of Moses and Anna (-) Ordway.

Ephraim Blunt and Martha Ordway were parents of eight children born at Danville, Vermont.

i DAVID BLUNT, b. 7 Jun 1777; d. at Shefford, Québec, 13 Aug 1839; m. at Danville, 13 Sep 1801, POLLY DAVIS *perhaps* the daughter of Dudley and Mary (Straw) Davis; Polly d. at Shefford, 1831.[1969]

ii EPHRAIM BLUNT, b. 10 Nov 1778; d. at Danville, 27 Oct 1845; m. 1st, about 1807, LYDIA MORRILL, b. at Londonderry, 9 Sep 1787 daughter of Samuel and Sally (Blunt) Morrill; Lydia d. at Danville, 25 Aug 1814. Ephraim m. 2nd, BETSEY PEABODY, b. in NH, 1790; Betsey d. at Danville, 25 Mar 1875.

iii ANNA BLUNT, b. 27 Aug 1780; m. at Danville, 3 Oct 1808, JOSIAH BATCHELDER.

iv MARTHA BLUNT, b. 31 May 1782; died young.

v MOSES BLUNT, b. 6 Dec 1783; d. at Stanstead, Québec, 12 Sep 1834; m. LYDIA BOYNTON, b. 15 Aug 1791 daughter of John and Lydia (Dow) Boynton;[1970] Lydia d. likely at Stanstead, after 1871.[1971]

vi MARTHA BLUNT, b. 24 Oct 1785; m. ISAAC WHEELER STANTON, b. 10 Apr 1781 son of Isaac and Ruth (Ayer) Stanton; Isaac d. at Danville, 26 Oct 1870.

vii ASA BLUNT, b. 13 Nov 1787; d. at Stanstead, Québec, 1819; m. about 1814, NANCY BOYNTON, b. 11 Oct 1794 daughter of John and Lydia (Dow) Boynton; Nancy d. at Derby, VT, 23 Mar 1878. After Asa's death, Nancy married Heman Lindsey.

viii SARAH BLUNT, b. 26 Mar 1790

737) ZERVIAH BLUNT (*Zerviah Holt Abbott³, Henry², Nicholas¹*), b. at Suncook, NH, 1759 daughter of Ephraim and Zerviah (Abbott) Blunt;[1972] d. at Calais, VT, 18 Jan 1860; m. at Canterbury, NH, 26 Feb 1778, AARON HARTSHORN, b. at Reading, 1754 son of Thomas and Abia (-) Hartshorn; Aaron d. at Danville, VT, 19 Jun 1799.

During the Revolution, Aaron Hartshorn served as a private in the company of Capt. Batchelder and additional service in the company of Capt. Abbot. Periods of service were claimed from December 1775 and in 1776 and 1777 and a total of eight months service were allowed. Widow Zerviah Hartshorn received a pension of $26.66 per annum related to Aaron's service. In 1855 at age 96 years, Zerviah made a claim for bounty land and was determined to be entitled to 160 acres.[1973]

The obituary for Zerviah Hartshorn included the following information. Mrs. Hartshorn was born in Suncook, Massachusetts. The family came to Danville, Vermont in 1787. Aaron died at the young age of 40 leaving his widow with ten children. Zerviah remained a widow for 61 years. She was an active member of the Free Will Baptist church.[1974]

The pension file includes a summary of the 19 July 1800 probate of Aaron Hartshorn in which the real estate was divided among the following heirs: widow Zerviah Hartshorn and children Thomas, Aaron, Susan, Ephraim, Zerviah, Mary S., Sarah, Abigail, Abraham S., and Charles C. P. Hartshorn.

Zerviah Blunt and Aaron Hartshorn were parents of twelve children born in Vermont and the youngest seven children at Danville.

i SUSANNAH HARTSHORN, b. 30 Sep 1779; d. at Danville, 20 Jan 1881; m. 1st, at Danville, 18 Mar 1804, DANIEL SMITH; Daniel d. at Danville, 6 Jul 1823. Susannah m. 2nd, at Danville, 17 Jun 1827, EBENEZER EATON, b. at Mansfield, CT, 1777 son of Nathaniel and Sarah (Johnson) Eaton; Ebenezer d. at Danville, 31 Jan 1859.

[1968] At the 1850 Census, the three young children of George and Elizabeth Harriman were living with Lavina Morris Murray and her husband George Murray. Lavina Morris is the daughter of Joseph and Lavina (Drake) Morris. It might be assumed that the children went to live with their aunt after mother's death. In 1850, G. W. Harriman was living with his elderly mother Bridget.

[1969] *Quebec, Canada, Vital and Church Records (Drouin Collection), 1621-1968*, Institut Généalogique Drouin

[1970] Boynton, *The Boynton Family*, p 40

[1971] Lydia was living in Stanstead at the 1871 Canada census.

[1972] Zerviah Hartshorn's death record lists her parents as Zerviah Blunt and Ephraim "Hartshorn" although this seems just to be a confusion of the name of her spouse and the name of her father. Her age on the death record is 100 years, 11 months, 21 days. *Vermont Vital Records 1720-1908*

[1973] Revolutionary War Pension and Bounty-Land Warrant Application Files, 1800-1900, Case W19694

[1974] *The Caledonian*, St. Johnsbury, Vermont, February 3, 1860. "Death of a Centenarian"

ii THOMAS HARTSHORN, b. 1780; d. at Danville, 1802.

iii AARON HARTSHORN, b. 1781; d. at Middlesex County, Ontario, Canada, 6 Feb 1847; m. at Danville, 12 Jan 1806, HANNAH PEASLEY, b. at Danville, 1787 daughter of Jedediah and Judith (Hunt) Peasley; Hannah d. in Middlesex County, 1843.

iv Son (name not known), b. about 1783; d. before 1800.[1975]

v EPHRAIM HARTSHORN, b. 1785; d. at McHenry, IL, Feb 1849; m. at Danvers, MA, 25 May 1807, MARTHA "PATTY" CROWELL, b. at Danvers, 12 Dec 1780 daughter of John and Mary (Masury) Crowell; Martha d. at Danville, 1 Jul 1877.

vi BENJAMIN HARTSHORN, b. 1787; d. at Danville, Dec 1798.

vii ZERVIAH HARTSHORN, b. 1789; d. at St. Johnsbury, VT, 19 Feb 1851; m. 15 Apr 1812, PETER KNAPP, b. at Duanesburg, NY, 15 Apr 1793 son of Peter and Priscilla (Owen) Knapp; Peter d. at Barnet, VT, 12 Jul 1861. After Zerviah's death, Peter married Electa Sayre.

viii MARY SHORT HARTSHORN, b. 1790; d. at Danville, 6 Mar 1826; m. NATHAN FULLER, b. 1778; Nathan d. at Danville, 24 Oct 1839. After Mary's death, Nathan married Freelove Fuller.

ix SARAH HARTSHORN, b. about 1792; d. at Claremont, NH, 15 Jun 1869; m. at Danville, 9 Oct 1814, BENNAGER RODGERS, b. in CT, 3 Oct 1782 son of Joseph and Lois (Hall) Rodgers; Bennager d. at Claremont, 31 Mar 1864.

x ABIGAIL HARTSHORN, b. 3 Sep 1793; d. at Danville, 8 Sep 1862; m. 1816, JOHN FARNSWORTH, b. at Washington, NH, 3 Jun 1787 son of Manassah and Charity (Rounsevel) Farnsworth; John d. at Danville, 1 Apr 1837.

xi ABRAHAM SILVER HARTSHORN, b. 1795; d. at Moira, NY, 25 Apr 1869; m. at Danville, 9 Feb 1818, SARAH GREEN, b. at Danville, 1800; Sarah d. at Moira, 22 Oct 1885.

xii CHARLES COTESWORTH PINKEY HARTSHORN, b. 1799; d. at Danville, 4 Apr 1887; m. at Danville, 11 Feb 1823, HANNAH WEST, b. 1791; Hannah d. at Danville, 22 1876. Charles m. 2nd, 4 Jun 1878, ABIGAIL SANBORN (widow Parker).

738) SARAH ABBOTT (*Job Abbott4, Zerviah Holt Abbott3, Henry2, Nicholas1*), b. 1751 at Suncook daughter of Job and Sarah (Abbott) Abbott; d. at Temple, NH, 9 Oct 1854 (age at death inscribed as 103 years, 2 months, 25 days on her gravestone);[1976] m. 25 Nov 1773, her third cousin, ABIEL HOLT (*Joseph4, Thomas3, Nicholas2, Nicholas1*), b. at Lunenburg, 14 Jul 1748 son of Joseph and Mary (Abbott) Holt; Abiel d. 7 Jan 1811.

Abiel Holt was a farmer in Temple. He and Sarah Abbott were parents of five children born at Temple, New Hampshire.

i ABIEL HOLT, b. 25 Nov 1774; d. at Temple, 11 Mar 1839; m. 31 Jan 1799, ELIZABETH "BETSEY" HOWARD, b. at Temple, NH, 15 May 1776 daughter of Samuel and Elizabeth (Barrett) Howard; Betsey d. at Temple, 30 Dec 1847.

ii ABIGAIL HOLT, b. 22 May 1779; d. at Waterford, ME, about 1806; m. 1799, JONATHAN KIMBALL, b. at Waterford, 1773 son of Isaac and Abigail (Raymond) Kimball. Jonathan Kimball married Elizabeth Bowers 26 Feb 1807.

iii JOSEPH HOLT, b. 23 Feb 1782; d. at Temple, 19 Jul 1835; m. ANNA P.,[1977] b. about 1780; Ruth d. at Tempe 12 Feb 1872. Joseph and Anna did not have children.

iv EMELIA HOLT, b. 11 Jun 1784; d. at Temple, 26 Sep 1834. Emelia did not marry.

v NATHAN ABBOT HOLT, b. about 1790; d. at Temple, 25 Mar 1839; m. at Temple, 7 Dec 1815, BETSY PARKHURST, b. at Temple, 10 Oct 1788 daughter of William Parkhurst; Betsy d. at Temple, 29 Dec 1875.

739) NATHAN ABBOTT (*Job Abbott4, Zerviah Holt Abbott3, Henry2, Nicholas1*), b. at Pembroke 4 Sep 1753 son of Job and Sarah (Abbott) Abbott; d. at Andover 1801 (probate of will 31 Mar 1801); m. 8 May 1777, his third cousin, SARAH BALLARD, b. 28 Dec 1755 daughter of Hezekiah and Lydia (Chandler) Ballard; Sarah d. 20 Aug 1825.

[1975] The gravestone for Hartshorn in Danville has three unmarried sons on the stone: Benjamin, Thomas, and a third son whose name is broken off; this son is not in the estate distribution of his father and so is deceased before 1800.

[1976] Gravestone inscription: Aged 103 yrs. 2 ms. & 25 ds.

[1977] The will of Joseph Holt includes a bequest to his wife Anna P. Holt.

Nathan was raised by his uncle Nathan and his wife Abigail Ames who did not have children. The younger Nathan inherited all his uncle's real estate.[1978] Nathan and Sarah resided in Andover where Nathan served as deacon.

Deacon Nathan Abbot wrote his will 29 December 1800 and his estate entered probate 31 March 1801.[1979] Beloved wife Sarah receives "all my household stuff and furniture proper for a woman." She also receives use and improvement of one-third part of the dwelling and son Job to provide a list of specific provisions for her support as long as she remains a widow. She also receives use of the clock while she is a widow. If she decides to remarry, she is to receive one hundred-fifty dollars so long as she quits to son Job her right in the real estate. Beloved son Nathan receives one hundred-fifty dollars. Son Job receives all the real estate, but as each of his younger brothers reaches age twenty-one, they are to receive the offer of a lot of land that Nathan owns in Oxford, York County. The selection of the value of the lots is in decreasing order starting with two hundred dollars for the first lot down to twenty dollars each for the fifth and last two lots. Each of the younger sons also receives two hundred-fifty dollars and a cow. Those beloved sons are Able, Pascal, Jeremiah, Joshua, and Amos. If any of the younger sons chooses a trade, they receive only two hundred dollars and a cow. Beloved daughters Sally and Lydia each receive one hundred thirty-three dollars and eighty-four cents when they reach age twenty-one or on the day of their marriage. Job is also responsible for the expense of the upbringing of the children who are still underage and to pay for their common schooling. Job is also to provide for Nathan's Aunt Abigail Abbot. Wife Sarah Abbot is named sole executrix. The value of the real estate was $6,058.52. This included the homestead with a cider house and lots of various types and sizes in Boston, Wilmington, Temple, and Oxford.

Nathan Abbott and Sarah Ballard were parents to twelve children born at Andover.[1980] Three of the sons in the family relocated to Dexter, Maine.

i NATHAN ABBOTT, b. 25 Aug 1778; d. at Andover, 13 Feb 1837; m. 10 Nov 1801, his third cousin, HANNAH RUSSELL (*Lydia Abbott Russell[5], Hannah Holt Abbott[4], Timothy[3], James[2], Nicholas[1]*), b. at Andover, Apr 1780 daughter of Uriah and Lydia (Abbott) Russell; Hannah d. at Andover, 16 Nov 1832. Hannah Russell is child in Family 297.

ii Son, b. 11 Jun 1780 and d. 16 Jun 1780

iii Son, b. 2 Mar 1781 and d. 1781

iv JOB ABBOTT, b. 7 Aug 1782; d. at Andover, 15 Dec 1859; m. 9 Oct 1807, his first cousin, LUCY CHANDLER (*Nathan Chandler[6], Nathan Chandler[5], Priscilla Holt Chandler[4], Timothy[3], James[2], Nicholas[1]*), b. at Andover, 30 Nov 1785 daughter of Nathan and Lucy (Ballard) Chandler; Lucy d. at Andover, 19 Jul 1872.

v JOSHUA ABBOTT, b. 29 Jun 1784; d. 29 Jan 1796.

vi ABEL ABBOTT, b. 7 Sep 1786; d. at Andover, 3 Jul 1862; m. 1st, 29 Sep 1811, his first cousin, SARAH ABBOTT (*Job Abbott[5], Job Abbott[4], Zerviah Holt Abbott[3], Henry[2], Nicholas[1]*), b. at Wilton, NH, 7 Apr 1789 daughter of Job and Anna (Ballard) Abbott; Sarah d. at Andover, 1 Dec 1821. Abel m. 2nd, 28 Dec 1822, his fourth cousin, MARY JONES, b. at Andover, 29 Jul 1786 daughter of Ebenezer and Elizabeth (Abbott) Jones; Mary d. at Andover, 9 Dec 1869.

vii PASCHAL ABBOTT, b. 23 Jul 1788; d. at Dexter, ME, 30 May 1859; m. 1st, at Andover, 10 Oct 1810, his first cousin, MARY FOSTER ABBOTT (*Job Abbott[5], Job Abbott[4], Zerviah Holt Abbott[3], Henry[2], Nicholas[1]*), b. at Wilton, 18 Apr 1791 daughter of Job and Anna (Ballard) Abbott; Mary d. at Andover, 28 Oct 1828. Paschal m. 2nd, at Greenfield, NH, 22 Jun 1829, HANNAH FOSTER (*Mary Holt Foster[5], Joshua[4], Nicholas[3], Nicholas[2], Nicholas[1]*), b. at Greenfield, 18 Jun 1796 daughter of Isaac and Mary (Holt) Foster; Hannah d. at Tilton, NH, 17 Oct 1885.

viii JEREMIAH ABBOTT, b. 14 Aug 1790; d. at Dexter, ME, 21 Jul 1879; m. at Dexter, 19 Mar 1826, LUCY SAFFORD, b. at Washington, NH, 30 Dec 1802 daughter of John and Olive (Puffer) Stafford; Lucy d. at Dexter, 26 Sep 1866.

ix SARAH ABBOTT, b. 20 Dec 1792; d. at Andover, 20 Sep 1846; m. 17 Jun 1813, her third cousin, ABIEL RUSSELL (*Lydia Abbott Russell[5], Hannah Holt Abbott[4], Timothy[3], James[2], Nicholas[1]*), b. at Andover, Mar 1789 son of Uriah and Lydia (Abbott) Russell; Abiel d. at Andover, 14 Jan 1881.

x AMOS ABBOTT, b. 13 Mar 1795; d. at Dexter, ME, 24 Dec 1865; m. at Dexter, 7 Sep 1823, MEHITABLE SAFFORD, b. at Washington, NH, 13 Jul 1798 daughter of John and Olive (Puffer) Safford; Mehitable d. at Dexter, 1870.

[1978] *Essex County, MA: Probate File Papers, 1638-1881.*Online database. *AmericanAncestors.org.* New England Historic Genealogical Society, 2014. Case 103

[1979] *Essex County, MA: Probate File Papers, 1638-1881.*Online database. *AmericanAncestors.org.* New England Historic Genealogical Society, 2014. Case 104

[1980] Perley, "Abbot Notes," *Essex Antiquarian*, volume 2, p 100 was use for some of the information on the marriages of the children.

xi JOSHUA ABBOTT, b. 22 Apr 1797; d. at Topeka, KS, 5 Jun 1855;[1981] m. 1st, at Andover, 13 Oct 1820, his first cousin, LYDIA ABBOTT (*Job Abbott5, Job Abbott4, Zerviah Holt Abbott3, Henry2, Nicholas1*), b. at Wilton, 18 Oct 1800 daughter of Job and Anna (Ballard) Abbott; Lydia d. at Dexter, ME, 11 May 1826. Joshua m. 2nd, at Dexter, 12 Oct 1826, MARY WOOD BAKER, b. at Dexter, 25 Jul 1810 daughter of Samuel and Hannah P. (-) Baker; Mary d. at Boston, 3 Apr 1870.

xii LYDIA ABBOTT, b. 4 Nov 1800; d. at Tewksbury, 19 Oct 1883; m. at Andover, 1 May 1823, THOMAS P. KENDALL, b. at Andover, 16 Nov 1799 son of Ephraim and Molly (Harnden) Kendall; Thomas d. at Tewksbury, 27 Jun 1857.

740) JOB ABBOTT (*Job Abbott4, Zerviah Holt Abbott3, Henry2, Nicholas1*), b. about 1755 at Pembroke son of Job and Sarah (Abbott) Abbott; d. at Wilton 12 Jul 1805; m. at Andover, 12 Dec 1780, his third cousin once removed, ANNA BALLARD (*Sarah Abbott Ballard6, Anne Lovejoy Abbott5, William Lovejoy4, Mary Farnum Lovejoy3, Elizabeth Holt Farnum2, Nicholas1*), b. 15 Nov 1762 daughter of Timothy and Sarah (Abbott) Ballard; Anna d. at Wilton, 7 Apr 1805.[1982]

Job Abbott and Anna Ballard were parents of thirteen children born at Wilton. Both parents died in 1805 and the children seem to have gone to Andover after that. Three of the children married their first cousins, children of Nathan and Sarah (Ballard) Abbott.

i SAMUEL ABBOTT, b. 14 May 1781; d. Apr 1782.

ii SAMUEL ABBOTT, b. 15 Jul 1783; d. at Dexter, ME, 22 Apr 1862; m. about 1808, SARAH PALMER, b. 14 Jul 1783; Sarah d. at Dexter, 29 Jul 1868.[1983]

iii ANNA ABBOTT, b. 28 Jul 1785; d. at Andover, MA, 9 May 1828. Anna did not marry.

iv JAMES ABBOTT, b. 14 Mar 1787; d. at Andover, 6 May 1807.

v SARAH ABBOTT, b. 7 Apr 1789; d. at Andover, 1 Dec 1821; m. at Andover, 29 Sep 1811, her first cousin, ABEL ABBOTT (*Nathan Abbott5, Job Abbott4, Zerviah Holt Abbott3, Henry2, Nicholas1*), b. at Andover, 7 Sep 1786 son of Nathan and Sarah (Ballard) Abbott; Abel d. at Andover, 3 Jul 1862. Abel m. 2nd, 28 Dec 1822, MARY JONES, b. at Andover, 29 Jul 1786 daughter of Ebenezer and Elizabeth (Abbott) Jones; Mary d. at Andover, 9 Dec 1869.

vi MARY FOSTER ABBOTT, b. 18 Apr 1791; d. at Andover, 28 Oct 1828; m. 10 Oct 1810, her first cousin, PASCHAL ABBOTT (*Nathan Abbott5, Job Abbott4, Zerviah Holt Abbott3, Henry2, Nicholas1*), b. at Andover, 23 Jul 1788 son of Nathan and Sarah (Ballard) Abbott; Paschal d. at Dexter, ME, 30 May 1859. Paschal m. 2nd, at Greenfield, 22 Jun 1829, HANNAH FOSTER (*Mary Holt Foster5, Joshua4, Nicholas3, Nicholas2, Nicholas1*), b. at Greenfield, 18 Jun 1796 daughter of Isaac and Mary (Holt) Foster; Hannah d. at Tilton, NH, 17 Oct 1885.

vii WILLIAM BALLARD ABBOTT, b. 9 Jul 1793; d. at Andover, 19 May 1840; m. 9 Dec 1816, LUCINDA FLINT, b. at Andover, 30 Oct 1796 daughter of John and Ruth (Upton) Flint; Lucinda d. at Andover, 25 Aug 1861.

viii JOB ABBOTT, b. 15 Aug 1795; d. at Andover, 15 Oct 1819.

ix TIMOTHY BALLARD ABBOTT, b. 14 Aug 1797; d. at Andover, 22 Nov 1820; m. at Wilton, 6 Apr 1819, ABIGAIL WILSON, b. at Wilton, 8 Jan 1799 daughter of Abiel and Abigail (Phillips) Wilson; Abigail d. at Wilton, 4 Jan 1831.

x ABIGAIL ABBOTT, b. 5 Jan 1799; d. at Andover, 15 Jul 1822.

xi LYDIA ABBOTT, b. 18 Aug 1800; d. at Dexter, ME, 11 May 1826; m. at Andover, 13 Oct 1820, her first cousin, JOSHUA ABBOTT (*Nathan Abbott5, Job Abbott4, Zerviah Holt Abbott3, Henry2, Nicholas1*), b. at Andover, 22 Apr 1797 son of Nathan and Sarah (Ballard) Abbott; Joshua d. at Topeka, KS, 5 Jun 1855. Joshua m. 2nd, at Dexter, Joshua m. 2nd, 12 Oct 1826, Mary Wood Baker.

xii FANNY ABBOTT, b. 7 Jan 1802; d. at Bradford, MA, 26 Nov 1887; m. at Andover, 13 Apr 1822, BENJAMIN ROBERT DOWNES, b. at Newburyport, 15 Sep 1798 son of Robert and Sarah Coffin (Knapp) Downes; Benjamin d. at Bradford, 6 Jul 1871.

xiii Son b. and d. 1804.

[1981] ABBOTT, JOSHUA, late of Dexter, Me., aged 58 yrs., d. Topeka, June 5, 1855, of dysentery. (Lawrence, Herald of Freedom, June 9), Death Notices from Kansas Territorial Newspapers, 1854-1861 by Alberta Pantle August 1950 (Vol. 18, No. 3), pages 302 to 323, Transcribed by Trudy Thurgood; digitized with permission of Kansas State Historical Society.

[1982] Date of death obtained from her gravestone which has the following inscription: Erected to the memory of Mrs. Anne Abbott, consort of Mr. Job Abbott, who died April 7, 1805, in the 43 year of her age. Findagrave Memorial ID: 34218725

[1983] Age at time of death given as 85 years, 15 days. Maine, Nathan Hale Cemetery Collection.

741) ABIGAIL ABBOTT (*Job Abbott[4], Zerviah Holt Abbott[3], Henry[2], Nicholas[1]*), b. about 1757 daughter of Job and Sarah (Abbott) Abbott; d. 1 May 1845 at Lovell, ME;[1984] m. by 1778, STEPHEN DRESSER, b. at Andover, 25 Oct 1754 son of Jonathan and Sarah (Foster) Dresser; Stephen d. at Frye, ME, 28 Sep 1829.

Stephen served in the Revolution enlisting from Fryeburg in Bedel's Regiment.[1985] Abigail Abbott and Stephen Dresser were parents of eleven children born at Lovell, Maine.[1986]

i BETSY DRESSER, b. 14 Oct 1778; d. at Stow, ME, 2 Nov 1825; m. about 1797, SAMUEL FARRINGTON, b. 22 Jun 1776 son of John and Mary (Stevens) Farrington; Samuel d. at Stow, 14 Mar 1838.

ii STEPHEN DRESSER, b. 8 Apr 1781; d. at Stow, 19 Aug 1858; m. 1st, about 1801, ABIGAIL KILGORE, b. at Lovell, about 1785 daughter of James and Abigail (-) Kilgore; Abigail d. at Lovell, 1817. Stephen m. 2nd, at Fryeburg, 19 Apr 1817, his fourth cousin, MEHITABLE ABBOTT (*Micah Abbott[6], Susannah Farnum Abbott[5], Ebenezer Farnum[4], Thomas Farnum[3], Elizabeth Holt Farnum[2], Nicholas[1]*) , b. at Fryeburg, 1797 daughter of Micah and Alice (Wiley) Abbott; Mehitable d. at Stow, 9 Apr 1884.

iii SARAH DRESSER, b. 1 Feb 1783; d. 9 Mar 1783.

iv ABIGAIL DRESSER, b. 1785; d. at Lovell, 1819; m. about 1805, JONATHAN FARRINGTON, b. 1780 son of John and Mary (Stevens) Farrington; Jonathan d. at Lovell, 19 Jun 1818.

v JOB ABBOTT DRESSER, b. 5 Mar 1787; d. at Lovell, 24 Apr 1882; m. at Lovell, 1 Oct 1810, HANNAH HALL, b. 18 Mar 1785; Hannah d. at Lovell, 29 May 1864.

vi MARY "POLLY" DRESSER, b. 8 May 1790; d. at Chatham, NH, 26 Aug 1879; m. at Lovell, 10 Sep 1807, JOSEPH GORDON, b. 1781; Joseph d. at Chatham, 7 Nov 1871.

vii SARAH DRESSER, b. 6 Aug 1792; d. at Lovell, May 1874; m. 19 Feb 1810, her fourth cousin, JOSEPH KIMBALL (*Lucy Abbott Kimball[6], Susannah Farnum Abbott[5], Ebenezer Farnum[4], Thomas Farnum[3], Elizabeth Holt Farnum[2], Nicholas[1]*), b. at Fryeburg, 20 Aug 1788 son of William and Lucy (Abbott) Kimball; Joseph d. at Lovell, 2 Mar 1859.

viii JONATHAN FOSTER DRESSER, b. 19 Jul 1794; d. at Chatham, before 1850; m. 20 Oct 1817, BETSY WILEY, b. about 1798.

ix SUSANNA DRESSER, b. 10 Jul 1796; m. at Lovell, 22 Nov 1814, her first cousin, JAMES EASTMAN (*Daniel Eastman[6], Sarah Abbott Eastman[5], Abigail Farnum Abbott[4], Ralph Farnum[3], Elizabeth Holt Farnum[2], Nicholas[1]*), b. at Lovell, 25 Dec 1788 son of Daniel and Sarah (Whiting) Eastman; James d. at Lovell, 21 Feb 1870.

x EMILIAH HOLT DRESSER, b. 30 Jul 1799; d. at Lovell, 7 Apr 1835; m. 1817, MOSES HUTCHINS, b. at Fryeburg, 10 Dec 1791 son of Moses and Rose (Whittier) Hutchins; Moses d. at Lovell, 24 May 1872.

xi CHLOE DRESSER, b. 18 Apr 1801; d. at Lovell, 2 Oct 1835. Chloe did not marry.

742) MARY EASTMAN (*Mary Lovejoy Eastman[5], Henry Lovejoy[4], Mary Farnum Lovejoy[3], Elizabeth Holt Farnum[2], Nicholas[1]*), b. at Pembroke, 22 May 1742 daughter of Richard and Mary (Lovejoy) Eastman; d. at Andover, 26 Jul 1801; m. at Andover, 4 Jul 1766, JONATHAN CUMMINGS, b. at Topsfield, 14 Oct 1743 son of David and Sarah (Goodhue) Cummings; Jonathan d. at Andover, 1805. After Mary's death, Jonathan m. 30 Dec 1802, MARY LOVEJOY (*Joshua Lovejoy[5], Henry Lovejoy[4], Mary Farnum Lovejoy[3], Elizabeth Holt Farnum[2], Nicholas[1]*) (widow of James Parker), b. at Andover, 13 Aug 1745 daughter of Joshua and Lydea (Abbott) Lovejoy; Mary Lovejoy d. at Andover, 15 Apr 1826. Mary Lovejoy and her first husband James Parker did not have children.

Jonathan Cummings was a blacksmith in Andover and also had extensive land holdings. He was owner of the historic property at 42 Wildwood Road in Andover.[1987] He was the proprietor of the Cummings Purchase and Gore in Norway, Maine which was settled and developed by his son Jonathan.[1988]

In his will written 31 December 1800 (probate 5 August 1805), Jonathan Cummings bequeathed to beloved wife Mary all the household stuff for woman's use to be at her own disposal. Mary also receives a lengthy list of provisions to be provided by the executor while she is a widow. Beloved son Jonathan receives a lot of land in Norway, Cumberland County. Son Daniel receives all the real property in Andover. Sons Jonathan, Stephen, and Amos are to equally divide the lands in the district of Maine. Son Amos also receives a tract in land in Norway. Son Abiather receives land in Norway, stock animals and one hundred

[1984] Ancestry.com, *U.S., Find A Grave Index, 1600s-Current* (Provo, UT, USA: Ancestry.com Operations, Inc., 2012).
[1985] Compiled Service Records of Soldiers Who Served in the American Army During the Revolutionary War 1775-1785
[1986] Many of the vital records for this family were obtained from Lovell Historical Society Online Collections Database, http://lovell.pastperfectonline.com/byperson?keyword=Dresser%2C+Stephen+Lt.+%281754-1829%29
[1987] Andover Historic Preservation; https://preservation.mhl.org/24-wildwood-road
[1988] Lapham, *Centennial History of Norway, Oxford County, Maine*, p 409

dollars. Beloved daughter Mary receives land in Oxford, York County and with what she has received this completes her portion. Beloved daughter Betty receives land in Oxford and two hundred dollars. Granddaughter Polly Eastman Gray also receives a tract of land in Oxford and a cow to be delivered to her by son Daniel when she is age twenty-one. Son Daniel is named executor.[1989] Real estate was valued at $19,223 including the homestead farm with 111 acres valued at $5,000. On 5 August 1806, the following heirs and legatees signed that they had received from Daniel everything due to them from the estate: Bernard Douglas and Betsey Douglas; Jonathan Cummings and Joanna Cummings; Amos Cummings and Abigail Cummings; Stephen Cummings and Eleanor Cummings; Solomon Holt and Mary Holt.

Jonathan Cummings and Mary Eastman were parents of eleven children born at Andover.

i SARAH CUMMINGS, b. 21 May 1767; d. at Andover, 15 Mar 1793; m. at Andover, 3 Apr 1788, her third cousin twice removed, DAVID GRAY (*David Gray⁴, Robert Gray³, Hannah Holt Gray², Nicholas¹*), b. at Andover, 8 Dec 1762 son of David and Rebecca (Holt) Gray; David d. at Andover, 7 Mar 1844. David married second Rebecca Jenkins. Sarah Cummings and David Gray are Family 981.

ii MARY CUMMINGS, b. 25 Aug 1768; d. 21 Sep 1768.

iii JONATHAN CUMMINGS, b. 5 Feb 1771; d. at Norway, ME, 12 Jul 1820; m. about 1803, JOANNA COBB, b. 6 Mar 1783 daughter of Jedediah and Abigail (Jordan) Cobb; Joanna d. (buried at) Gray, ME, 30 Jun 1844. Joanna married second Charles Barbour.

iv STEPHEN CUMMINGS, b. 12 Jan 1773; d. at Cape Elizabeth, ME, 2 Mar 1854; m. 1794, ELEANOR HEALD, b. at Temple, NH, 6 Feb 1775 daughter of Ephraim and Sarah (Conant) Heald; Eleanor d. at Portland, 31 May 1824. Stephen was a physician

v Child b. and d. Nov 1773 (buried 1 Dec 1773).

vi MARY CUMMINGS, b. 1 Nov 1774; d. at Andover, 8 Oct 1852; m. 22 May 1798, her third cousin once removed, SOLOMON HOLT (*Joshua⁴, Nicholas³, Nicholas², Nicholas¹*), b. at Andover, Dec 1768 son of Joshua and Phebe (Farnum) Holt; Solomon d. at Andover, 15 Apr 1830. Mary Cummings and Solomon Holt are Family 839.

vii DANIEL CUMMINGS, b. 6 Dec 1776; d. 25 Jun 1778.

viii DANIEL CUMMINGS, b. 2 Sep 1778; d. at Maidstone, VT, 26 Dec 1827; m. 30 Jun 1801, his fifth cousin, HANNAH AMES (*Phebe Chandler Ames⁶, Nathan Chandler⁵, Priscilla Holt Chandler⁴, Timothy³, James², Nicholas¹*), b. at Andover, 19 Jul 1781 daughter of Benjamin and Phebe (Chandler) Ames; Hannah d. after 1860 when she was living in Haverhill, MA. Hannah married second Leonard White.

ix AMOS CUMMINGS, b. 2 Jul 1781; d. likely at Boston, 30 Apr 1852;[1990] m. 1st at Andover, 25 Jan 1803, ABIGAIL JUDKINS who has not been identified. Amos m. 2nd at Boston, 3 Nov 1841, CLARISSA WALDIN (widow of William Woods), b. at Belfast, ME, about 1805 daughter of John and Catherine (Chadbourne) Waldin; Clarissa d. at Somerville, 31 Jan 1897.

x BETSY CUMMINGS, b. 13 Oct 1783; d. at Conway, NH, 1 Apr 1860; m. at Andover, 2 Sep 1806, as his second wife, BARNARD DOUGLAS, b. at Rutland, MA, 24 Apr 1763 son of Robert and Elinor (Fales) Douglas; Barnard d. at Conway, 21 Sep 1849.

xi ABIATHAR EASTMAN, b. 22 Sep 1786; d. at Andover, of consumption, 8 Oct 1802.

743) ABIATHAR EASTMAN (*Mary Lovejoy Eastman⁵, Henry Lovejoy⁴, Mary Farnum Lovejoy³, Elizabeth Holt Farnum², Nicholas¹*), b. at Pembroke, 29 Apr 1745 son of Richard and Mary (Lovejoy) Eastman; d. at North Conway, 10 Jan 1815; m. at Conway, 3 Dec 1775, his second cousin, PHEBE MERRILL (*Phebe Abbott Merrill⁵, Abigail Farnum Abbott⁴, Ralph Farnum³, Elizabeth Holt Farnum², Nicholas¹*), b. at Conway, Dec 1753 daughter of Thomas and Phebe (Abbott) Merrill; Phebe d. at North Conway, 9 Oct 1839.

Abiathar Eastman was a farmer in Conway where he served as a church deacon. He was in the Revolutionary War and had a rank of Sergeant. The Eastman genealogy reports that he was absent from duty at Chelsea in September 1785 and found unfit for duty by order of Major Watson.[1991]

Abiathar and Phebe Eastman had seven children born at Conway.

i SAMUEL EASTMAN, b. 19 Jan 1777; d. 25 Jun 1802.

[1989] *Essex County, MA: Probate File Papers, 1638-1881.*Online database. *AmericanAncestors.org.* New England Historic Genealogical Society, 2014. Case 6716

[1990] Amos Cummings age 70 years, 10 months at death and born at Andover which corresponds exactly to his birth date

[1991] Rix, *History and Genealogy of the Eastman Family*, p 174

ii LYDIA EASTMAN, b. 4 Sep 1779; d. at Bartlett, NH, 21 Apr 1872; m. 26 May 1801, her fourth cousin once removed, FRYE HOLT (*Nathan⁵, Benjamin⁴, Nicholas³, Nicholas², Nicholas¹*), b. 15 Sep 1779 son of Nathan and Sarah (Chamberlain) Holt; Frye d. at North Conway, 8 Apr 1850.

iii ABIATHAR EASTMAN, b. 17 Apr 1784; d. at Plattsburgh, Dec 1813 during the War of 1812; m. at Conway, 1802, SUSAN DURGIN, b. at Conway, 17 Apr 1784 daughter of Benjamin and Sarah (Runnels) Durgin; Susan d. at Sweden, ME, 19 Apr 1853.

iv HENRY EASTMAN, b. 29 Jul 1786; d. at North Conway, 3 Jul 1838; m. 1815, ESTHER EASTMAN, b. 14 Aug 1788 daughter of Noah and Hannah (Holt) Eastman.

v THOMAS EASTMAN, b. 18 Jul 1788; d. at North Conway, 7 Aug 1846; m. 18 Apr 1816, EUNICE HILL, b. at Conway, 19 Apr 1797 daughter of Leavitt and Sarah (Russell) Hill; Eunice d. at North Conway, 24 Jan 1862.

vi CALEB EASTMAN, b. 12 Aug 1790; d. 1 Jul 1791.

vii CALEB EASTMAN, b. 12 Mar 1793; d. at York, ME, 12 May 1872; m. at York, 8 May 1833, ADALINE TAPLY, b. 28 Feb 1810;[1992] Adaline d. at Portland, ME, 15 Mar 1888.

744) RICHARD EASTMAN (*Mary Lovejoy Eastman⁵, Henry Lovejoy⁴, Mary Farnum Lovejoy³, Elizabeth Holt Farnum², Nicholas¹*), b. at Pembroke, 20 Apr 1747 son of Richard and Mary (Lovejoy) Eastman; d. at North Conway, NH (buried at Conway), 6 Dec 1826; m. 1st about 1766, his third cousin once removed, ABIAH HOLT (*Benjamin⁴, Nicholas³, Nicholas², Nicholas¹*), b. about 1747 daughter of Benjamin and Sarah (Frye) Holt; Abiah d. at North Conway, 1 May 1790. Richard m. 2nd 27 Aug 1791, SUSANNAH RUNNELS (widow of Benjamin Durgin), b. 1765 daughter of Jonathan and Keziah (Carter) Runnels;[1993] Susannah d. at North Conway, 29 May 1849.

Richard Eastman had gone from Pembroke to Conway with his father and they were among first settlers there. Richard and Abiah's son Jonathan is reported as the first white child born in Conway.[1994] Richard built his first house in a low-lying tract of land but were forced to move to higher ground following spring floods in 1785.[1995]

Susannah Runnels and her first husband Benjamin Durgin had two daughters both of whom married descendants of Nicholas Holt. Susan Durgin married Abiathar Eastman (*Abiathar Eastman⁶, Mary Lovejoy Eastman⁵, Henry Lovejoy⁴, Mary Farnum Lovejoy³, Elizabeth Holt Farnum², Nicholas¹*) and Lydia Durgin married Job Eastman (*Hannah Holt Eastman⁵, Benjamin⁴, Nicholas³, Nicholas², Nicholas¹*).

Richard Eastman and Abiah Holt were parents of eleven children.

i SALLY EASTMAN, b. (recorded) at Conway, 2 Jun 1766; d. at Conway, 19 Feb 1801; m. 24 Apr 1788, her second cousin, ABIEL LOVEJOY (*Abiel Lovejoy⁶, Henry Lovejoy⁵, Henry Lovejoy⁴, Mary Farnum Lovejoy³, Elizabeth Holt Farnum², Nicholas¹*), b. at Concord, 10 Aug 1763 son of Abiel and Anna (Stickney) Lovejoy; Abiel d. at Lancaster, NH, 2 Nov 1837. Abiel married second Betsey White daughter of Nathaniel and Betsy (Martin) White.

ii JONATHAN EASTMAN, b. at Conway, 18 Jul 1770; d. at North Conway, 11 May 1868; m. 18 Apr 1793, his second cousin, PHEBE LOVEJOY (*Abiel Lovejoy⁶, Henry Lovejoy⁵, Henry Lovejoy⁴, Mary Farnum Lovejoy³, Elizabeth Holt Farnum², Nicholas¹*), b. at Conway, 26 Jul 1774 daughter of Abiel and Anna (Stickney) Lovejoy; Phebe d. at North Conway, 6 May 1852.

iii POLLY EASTMAN, b. at Conway, 17 Feb 1772; d. at North Conway, 19 Aug 1859; m. 22 Jul 1790, AMOS BARNES, b. at Groton, MA, 9 Jan 1757 son of Joseph and Sarah (Melvin) Barnes; Amos d. at North Conway, 6 Dec 1840.

iv PHEBE EASTMAN, b. 21 Oct 1773; d. at North Conway, 14 May 1866; m. 5 Jul 1797, her fourth cousin, HUMPHREY CRAM (*Jonathan Cram⁵, Humphrey Cram⁴, Sarah Holt Cram³, Henry², Nicholas¹*), b. at Wales, MA, 1772 son of Jonathan and Abigail (Webber) Cram; Humphrey d. at Lancaster, NH, 17 Mar 1813.

v ABIAH EASTMAN, b. 26 Jan 1776; d. 6 Oct 1776.

vi HANNAH EASTMAN, b. at Conway, 25 Feb 1778; d. at Conway, 6 Jul 1876; m. 18 Dec 1803, ISAAC MERRILL, b. at Fryeburg, ME, 19 Apr 1775 son of Nathaniel and Ann (Walker) Merrill; Isaac d. at Conway, 17 Aug 1843.

vii RICHARD EASTMAN, b. 18 Apr 1780; d. at Ogden, KS, 13 May 1876; m. 1st ELMIRA MORRILL who has not been identified. Richard m. 2nd, LOUISA MORRILL, b. at Falmouth, ME, 31 Jan 1798; Louisa d. at Ogden, 14 Oct 1874.

1992 Adaline's date of birth is engraved on her gravestone; findagrave ID: 98508457

1993 Runnels, *Genealogy of the Runnels and Reynolds Families in America*, p 131

1994 Rix, *History and Genealogy of the Eastman Family*, p 175

1995 Merrill, *History of Carroll County, New Hampshire*, p 845

viii ABIAH EASTMAN, b. at Conway, 6 Apr 1782; d. at North Conway, 19 Nov 1840; m. at Conway, 24 Jun 1806, WILLIAM CHURCH FORD, b. at Cornwall, CT, 19 Mar 1776 son of Hezekiah and Deborah (Chandler) Ford.

ix WILLIAM EASTMAN, b. at Conway, 18 Apr 1784; d. at Jackson, NH, 25 Mar 1872; m. 1st ANNA "NANCY" LOVEJOY, b. at Conway, 16 Apr 1785 daughter of Abiel and Anna (Stickney) Lovejoy; Anna d. at Conway, 19 Mar 1827. William m. 2nd, at Adams, NH, 10 Apr 1828, RUTH B. ELKINS (widow of James C. Trickey), b. at Jackson, about 1801 daughter of Daniel and Hannah (Gray) Elkins; Ruth d. at Jackson, 2 Mar 1880.

x DORCAS EASTMAN, b. at Conway, 4 Jun 1786; d. at Conway, 7 Nov 1873; m. SAMUEL MERRILL, b. at Fryeburg, ME, 19 Dec 1780 son of Nathaniel and Ann (Walker) Merrill.

xi MARTHA "PATTY" EASTMAN, b. at Conway, 22 Jun 1788; d. at Brownfield, ME, 20 Feb 1887; m. JONATHAN STICKNEY, b. at Conway, 4 Mar 1784 son of John and Mary (Evans) Stickney; Jonathan d. at Brownfield, 11 Feb 1832.

Richard Eastman and Susannah Runnels were parents of seven children.

i KEZIAH EASTMAN, b. at Conway, 5 Oct 1792; d. at Leeds, ME, Mar 1881; m. at Conway, 26 Dec 1813, HENRY TUCKER, b. at Falmouth, Cornwall, England, 1 May 1789; Henry d. at Conway, 18 Aug 1830.

ii ELISABETH "BETSEY" EASTMAN, b. at Conway, 11 May 1795; d. at Conway, 9 Nov 1891; m. 6 Dec 1821, as his second wife, her first cousin once removed, JOHN HILL (*Sarah Russell Hill*^{7}, *Sarah Eastman Russell*^{6}, *Mary Lovejoy Eastman*^{5}, *Henry Lovejoy*^{4}, *Mary Farnum Lovejoy*^{3}, *Elizabeth Holt Farnum*^{2}, *Nicholas*^{1}), b. at Conway, 27 Apr 1791 son of Leavitt and Sarah (Russell) Hill; John d. at Conway, 24 Apr 1870. John was first married to Polly Freeman.

iii AMOS EASTMAN, b. at Conway, 28 Aug 1797; d. at Conway, 30 Jan 1854; m. 16 Feb 1822, BETSEY E. MERRILL, b. at Fryeburg, 14 Nov 1790 daughter of Nathaniel and Ann (Walker) Merrill; Betsey d. at North Conway, 1 Apr 1876.

iv CLARISSA EASTMAN, b. at Conway, 28 Oct 1799; d. at Conway, 12 Jul 1869; m. about 1842, STEPHEN MERRILL, b. 14 Oct 1793 son of Enoch and Mary (Ambrose) Merrill; Stephen d. at North Wolfeboro, NH, 23 Jun 1860. Stephen Merrill was first married to Mary Hoit Gilman who died in 1841.

v HARRIET EASTMAN, b. at Conway, 18 Apr 1803; d. at Jackson, NH, 18 Apr 1893; m. 1 May 1821, GEORGE PENDEXTER MESERVE, b. at Jackson, 11 Apr 1798 son of Jonathan and Alice (Pendexter) Meserve; George d. at Jackson, 19 Sep 1884.

vi JOHN LANGDON EASTMAN, b. at Conway, 12 Mar 1805; d. at North Conway, 28 Mar 1885; m. at Portland, ME, 18 Nov 1834, his first cousin once removed MARGARET DOUGLAS (*Betsy Cummings Douglas*^{7}, *Mary Eastman Cummings*^{6}, *Mary Lovejoy Eastman*^{5}, *Henry Lovejoy*^{4}, *Mary Farnum Lovejoy*^{3}, *Elizabeth Holt Farnum*^{2}, *Nicholas*^{1}), b. at Portland, 10 Jan 1812 daughter of Barnard and Betsey (Cummings) Douglas; Margaret d. at North Conway, 28 Apr 1885.

vii IRENA EASTMAN, b. at Conway, 22 Mar 1815; d. at North Conway, 19 Dec 1902; m. at Conway, 20 May 1839, JONATHAN E. CHASE, b. at Concord, 1 Oct 1811 son of Stephen and Esther (Eastman) Chase; Jonathan d. at Conway, 24 Aug 1883.

745) SARAH EASTMAN (*Mary Lovejoy Eastman*^{5}, *Henry Lovejoy*^{4}, *Mary Farnum Lovejoy*^{3}, *Elizabeth Holt Farnum*^{2}, *Nicholas*^{1}), b. at Pembroke, 6 May 1749 daughter of Richard and Mary (Lovejoy) Eastman; d. at Conway, 29 Dec 1836; m. 1767, THOMAS RUSSELL, b. at Andover, 12 Feb 1746/7 son of Thomas and Abigail (Ballard) Russell; Thomas d. at Conway, 15 Jul 1823.

Sarah and Thomas started their family in Andover but were in Conway, New Hampshire in 1771 where Thomas was an original proprietor. Thomas signed the association test there on 9 June 1776. He served as selectman in 1795.[1996]

Sarah Eastman and Thomas Russell were parents of thirteen children.

i THOMAS RUSSELL, b. at Andover, 22 Feb 1768; d. at Bartlett, NH, 1853; m. 19 Jul 1798, RUTH HARRIMAN, b. at Concord, 12 Mar 1774 daughter of Philip and Hannah (Eastman) Harriman; Ruth d. 1850.

ii SARAH RUSSELL, b. at Andover, 2 Jan 1770; d. at Conway, 4 Dec 1852; m. 17 Nov 1790, LEAVITT HILL, b. 2 Mar 1770 son of Charles and Sarah (Prentice) Hill;[1997] Leavitt d. at Conway, 4 Dec 1843.

[1996] Merrill, *History of Carroll County, New Hampshire*, p 822, p 818, p 918

[1997] Binney, *History and Genealogy of the Prentice Family*, p 25

iii JAMES RUSSELL, b. at Conway, 4 Mar 1772; died young.

iv RICHARD RUSSELL, b. at Conway, 2 Feb 1774

v ABIGAIL RUSSELL, b. at Conway, 22 Mar 1776; d. at Hanover, NH, 21 Dec 1856; m. at Conway, 12 Oct 1806, as his second wife, ASA CROSBY, b. 15 Jul 1765 son of Josiah and Sarah (Fitch) Crosby; Asa d. at Hanover, 12 Apr 1836. Asa was first married to Betsey Hoit. Asa Crosby was a physician.

vi JAMES RUSSELL, b. at Conway, 5 May 1778; d. at Albany, NH, 30 Sep 1861; m. SARAH ALLEN, b. in ME, about 1788; Sarah d. at Conway, 17 Feb 1859.

vii ESTHER RUSSELL, b. at Conway, 4 May 1780; d. at Conway, 4 Sep 1807; m. at Conway, 1 May 1800, JONATHAN PHILBRICK, b. 5 Aug 1775 son of Jonathan and Hannah (Gilman) Philbrick;[1998] Jonathan d. at Lawrenceburg, IN, after 1850. Jonathan married second Jane Hardy.

viii MARY RUSSELL, b. at Conway, 7 Aug 1782; d. at Freehold, NJ, 3 Mar 1859; m. at Conway, 1 Feb 1809, JONATHAN FREEMAN, b. at Hanover, NH, 21 Mar 1783 son of Otis and Ruth (Bicknell0 Freeman; Jonathan d. at Freehold, 11 Sep 1871.

ix ELIZABETH RUSSELL, b. at Conway, 20 May 1785; d. at Conway, 28 Sep 1865. Eliza did not marry.

x PRISSILLA RUSSELL, b. at Conway, 25 May 1787

xi URIAH B. RUSSELL, b. at Conway, 9 Aug 1791; m. 1st BETSEY PALMER, b. at Eaton, NH, about 1797; Betsey d. at Lowell, 13 Nov 1844. Uriah m. 2nd at Lowell, 24 Jul 1845, BETSEY GREENOUGH, b. about 1804.

xii JONATHAN E. RUSSELL, b. at Conway, 7 Jul 1793

xiii ALVAH RUSSELL, b. at Conway, 9 Dec 1796; d. at Conway, 15 Jul 1856; m. at Eaton, NH, 28 Mar 1833, ASENATH DAVIS, b. at Eaton, NH, 17 Apr 1812 daughter of Nathaniel and Nancy (March) Davis;[1999] Asenath d. at Laconia, NH, 11 Feb 1893. Asenath married second, James S. Hoit.

746) NOAH EASTMAN (*Mary Lovejoy Eastman[5], Henry Lovejoy[4], Mary Farnum Lovejoy[3], Elizabeth Holt Farnum[2], Nicholas[1]*), b. at Pembroke, 20 Mar 1753 son of Richard and Mary (Lovejoy) Eastman; d. 28 Aug 1829; m. his third cousin once removed, HANNAH HOLT (*Benjamin[4], Nicholas[3], Nicholas[2], Nicholas[1]*), b. 28 Feb 1758 daughter of Benjamin and Sarah (Frye) Holt; Hannah d. 15 Apr 1820.

Noah and Hannah resided in Conway. Noah served as selectman in 1795-1796, 1798, and 1800. He was the miller of North Conway for fifty years.[2000]

Noah Eastman and Hannah Holt were parents of thirteen children whose births are recorded at Conway, New Hampshire.[2001]

i BENJAMIN EASTMAN, b. 28 Dec 1775; d. at North Conway, 30 Apr 1846; m. about 1815, APPHIA STEVENS, b. at Norway, ME, 1786 daughter of Joseph and Elizabeth (Hammond) Stevens.[2002]

ii RICHARD EASTMAN, b. 8 Feb 1778; d. at Lancaster, NH, 22 Jan 1852; m. 5 May 1801, his fourth cousin, PERSIS FAULKNER (*Peter Faulkner[5], Deborah Farnum Faulkner[4], John Farnum[3], Elizabeth Holt Farnum[2], Nicholas[1]*), b. at Sturbridge, MA, 14 Dec 1775 daughter of Peter and Chloe (Cram) Faulkner; Persis d. at St. Johnsbury, VT, 27 Jan 1872.

iii NOAH EASTMAN, b. 7 May 1780; died young

iv JOB EASTMAN, b. 3 Jun 1782; d. at Bartlett, NH, 5 Feb 1869; m. at Conway, 11 Feb 1803, LYDIA DURGIN, b. at Conway, 18 Oct 1785 daughter of Benjamin and Susannah (Runnels) Durgin; Lydia d. 13 Oct 1841. Job m. 2nd 19 May 1842, MARY A. LANG; Mary d. at Bartlett, 24 May 1888.

v NOAH EASTMAN, b. 15 Oct 1784; d. at North Conway, 15 Oct 1857; m. at Conway, 14 Nov 1816, SALLY DOLLOFF, b. at Conway, 16 Jun 1781 daughter of Josiah and Jene (Knox) Dolloff; Sally d. at Somerville, MA, 13 Sep 1855.

[1998] Chapman, *A Genealogy of the Philbrick Family*, p 92

[1999] The names of Asenath's parents are given as Nathaniel Davis and Mary Williams on her death record and as Nathaniel Davis and Nancy March on the record of her second marriage to James Hoit. The death record of one of Asenath's siblings gives parents as Nathaniel Davis and Nancy March.

[2000] Merrill, *History of Carroll County, New Hampshire*, p 840, p 846

[2001] New Hampshire, Birth Records, 1659-1900, accessed through ancestry.com

[2002] Lapham, *Centennial History of Norway, Oxford County, Maine*, p 603

vi SUSANNA "SUKEY" EASTMAN, b. 12 May 1786; d. at Intervale, NH, 29 May 1844; m. at Conway, 8 Oct 1806, JOHN PENDEXTER, b. 29 Jul 1784 son of John and Martha (Jackson) Pendexter;[2003] John d. at Intervale, 21 May 1840.

vii ESTHER EASTMAN, b. 14 Aug 1788; d. at North Conway, 1876; m. 1815, her first cousin, HENRY EASTMAN (*Abiathar Eastman^6, Mary Lovejoy Eastman^5, Henry Lovejoy^4, Mary Farnum Lovejoy^3, Elizabeth Holt Farnum^2, Nicholas^1*), b. at Conway, 29 Jul 1786 son of Abiathar and Phebe (Merrill) Eastman; Henry d. at North Conway, 3 Jul 1838.

viii FRY HOLT EASTMAN, b. 12 Aug 1790; d. at Bartlett, NH, 15 May 1874; m. 25 Aug 1812, HANNAH UPTON HENLEY, b. at Norway, ME, Aug 1795 daughter of John and Sarah (Upton) Henley; Hannah d. recorded at Bartlett, 31 Mar 1878.

ix DANIEL EASTMAN, b. 6 Sep 1792; d. at Conway, 22 Aug 1885; m. MARTHA LEWIS CHADBOURNE, b. at Conway, 12 May 1793 daughter of William and Martha (McMillan) Chadbourne; Martha d. at Conway, 21 Dec 1879.

x JOHN EASTMAN, b. 25 Nov 1794; d. at Saco, ME, 1854; m. about 1819 ELIMIRA STEVENS, b. at Norway, ME, 1794 daughter of Joseph and Elizabeth (Hobbs) Stevens; Elmira d. 5 Jan 1863.

xi HANNAH EASTMAN, b. 22 Jun 1796; d. at Bartlett, 13 Aug 1887; m. 12 Sep 1816, JOHN DINSMORE, b. at Conway, 11 Nov 1792 son of Stephen and Mehitable (Frye) Dinsmore; John d. at Bartlett, 4 Feb 1879.

xii PHEBE B. EASTMAN, b. 27 Aug 1799; d. at Conway, 1 Jan 1893; m. DEAN CARBY, b. at Lunenburg, VT, about 1807 son of Thaddeus and Sally (Reed) Carby; Dean d. at Conway, 11 Nov 1882.

xiii POLLY CUMMINGS EASTMAN, b. 7 Dec 1801; d. at Conway, 12 Nov 1855; m. 21 Oct 1822, her third cousin once removed, JEREMIAH CHANDLER, b. at Newmarket, NH, 23 Mar 1794 son of Moses and Sally (Goodwin) Chandler; Jeremiah d. at Conway, 16 May 1864.

747) ESTHER EASTMAN (*Mary Lovejoy Eastman^5, Henry Lovejoy^4, Mary Farnum Lovejoy^3, Elizabeth Holt Farnum^2, Nicholas^1*), b. at Pembroke, 6 May 1761 daughter of Richard and Mary (Lovejoy) Eastman; d. at Sherbrooke, Québec, 30 Dec 1846; m. 26 Oct 1781, EPHRAIM ABBOTT, b. at Andover, 18 Mar 1759 son of Ebenezer and Lydia (Farrington) Abbott; Ephraim d. at Sherbrooke, 1 Jan 1834.[2004]

Ephraim Abbott enlisted from Andover October 1775 as a private in Colonel Enoch Poor's Regiment of the Massachusetts line. His regiment was in New London, New York, Albany, Crown Point, and St. Johns. Ephraim became ill and was sent home October 1776. He enlisted again in 1777 for three months and served in New Jersey. He had an enlistment in April 1778 in the Continental line and in 1780 a further enlistment in the militia. He was present at the capture of Burgoyne. He was credited with eighteen months of service and received a pension for his service which was continued by his widow Esther.[2005]

In his pension application of 1832, Ephraim stated he was born in Andover, moved to Conway, New Hampshire when he was about 21 years old, remained there for about twenty years and then relocated to Eaton, Lower Canada.

Ephraim and Esther were parents of perhaps eleven children, although there are birth records for three children. The oldest nine children were likely born at Conway and the two youngest children at Eaton. The children who married all married in Eaton or Ascot.

i ESTHER ABBOTT, b. 29 Aug 1782; d. at Cookshire,[2006] Québec, 18 Aug 1869; m. about 1802, JOHN COOK, b. at Wallingford, CT, 20 Nov 1770 son of David and Lois (Moss) Cook; John d. at Eaton, 28 May 1819.

ii POLLY ABBOTT, b. 23 May 1784; d. at Massena, NY, 1859; m. 1804, SAMUEL BRIGHAM HUDSON, b. 1777 son of Elisha and Susanna (Brigham) Hudson; Samuel d. 1853.

iii ANNA ABBOTT, b. 1785; d. at Phelps, NY, 6 May 1822; m. at Eaton, Nov 1807, CHARLES HUDSON, b. in MA, 7 Apr 1785 son of Elisha and Susanna (Brigham) Hudson; Charles d. at Arcadia, NY, after 1850.

iv LYDIA ABBOTT, b. about 1790; nothing further known.

v SUSAN ABBOTT, b. 1792; d. at Stanstead, 13 Jan 1840; m. at Ascot, 1824, JOSEPH GRIFFIN, b. about 1790.

vi SARAH ABBOTT, b. about 1793; d. at Québec, after 1861; m. about 1811, CHARLES WARD, b. 26 Aug 1790 son of Henry and Priscilla (Bixby) Ward; Charles d. at Stanstead, before 1851.

[2003] New Hampshire Historical Society, John Pendexter, https://www.nhhistory.org/object/253007/pendexter-john

[2004] *Quebec, Canada, Vital and Church Records (Drouin Collection), 1621-1968.*

[2005] Revolutionary War Pension and Bounty-Land Warrant Application Files

[2006] Cookshire-Eaton is the present name

vii PATTI ABBOTT, b. about 1794; nothing further known.

viii SOPHIA ABBOTT, b. 1795; d. at Stanstead, 17 May 1887; m. 1st, at Eaton, 21 Mar 1820, HIRAM WILCOX, b. 1795; Hiram d. at Ascot, 25 Aug 1820. Sophia m. 2nd, about 1822, JOHN CHAMBERLAIN, b. about 1788; John d. at Stanstead, 24 Nov 1847. Sophia m. 3rd, 1850, ALVIN FLINT, b. at Westmoreland, NH, 4 Aug 1786 son of Jonas and Eunice (Gardner) Flint; Alvin d. at Stanstead, 6 Feb 1862. Alvin Flint was married to Joanna Barney.

ix EBENEZER ABBOTT, b. 23 Aug 1800; d. at Saratoga, MN, 23 Oct 1890; m. about 1827, CAROLINE CASWELL, b. at Eaton, 11 Oct 1807 daughter of Apthorp and Amarilla (Holden) Caswell; Caroline d. at Oshawa, Ontario, 1853.

x PHEBE ABBOTT, b. about 1802; d. in VT, 16 Jan 1851; perhaps m. at Ascot, 1825, HORACE BLODGETT.

xi SAMUEL EASTMAN ABBOTT, b. 1804; d. at Sand Hill, Québec, 11 Feb 1872; m. 1827, SALLY CHASE, b. Dec 1806; Sally d. at Sand Hill, 25 Jan 1867.

748) SAMUEL ABBOTT (*Samuel Abbott[1], Zerviah Holt Abbott[3], Henry[2], Nicholas[1]*), b. at Pembroke, 16 Apr 1750 son of Samuel and Miriam (Stevens) Abbott; d. at North Pembroke, 11 Mar 1836; m. 22 Mar 1781, LYDIA PERRIN, b. about 1752 (based on age at time of death) parents not yet certain; Lydia d. 1 Apr 1829.

Samuel Abbott was a farmer in Pembroke.[2007] He and Lydia Perrin were parents of seven children born at Pembroke.

i EBENEZER ABBOTT, b. 22 Dec 1780; d. at Northfield, NH, after 1850; m. COMFORT SIMONDS, b. at Northfield, 25 Apr 1786 daughter of John and Dorothy (Batchelder) Simonds; Comfort d. after 1860.

ii AMOS ABBOTT, b. 6 Feb 1783; m. at Belmont, NH, 21 Nov 1811, DEBORAH BUSWELL, b. at East Kingston, NH, 12 Dec 1792 daughter of James and Ruth (Lord) Buswell; Deborah d. at Monroe, MO, about 1870.

iii JOB ABBOTT, b. about 1785; died young.

iv JOHN ABBOTT, b. 2 Nov 1788; d. at Peabody, MA, 15 Dec 1872; m. 1st, at Pembroke, 2 Jun 1814, SALLY DAVIS, b. about 1792 and d. about 1815. John m. 2nd, at Danvers, MA, Dec 1815, LYDIA CARRIAGE, b. at Danvers, 21 Dec 1800 daughter of William and Elizabeth (Fairn) Carriage; Lydia d. at Lynn, Sep 1821. John m. 3rd, at Danvers, 20 Oct 1822, ANNA LARRABEE, b. at Lynn, about 1791 daughter of Joseph and Lydia (Collis) Larrabee; Anna d. at Danvers, 5 May 1864.

v BETSY ABBOTT, b. 3 Jan 1790; m. at Epping, NH, 17 Jun 1813, BENJAMIN BROWN son of Benjamin Brown.

vi HANNAH ABBOTT, b. 23 Nov 1792; m. A STEVENS who has not been identified.[2008]

vii JOB ABBOTT, b. about 1794; m. at Manchester, NH, 16 Oct 1817, CHARLOTTE "LOTTIE" MERRILL, b. about 1795 "of Manchester."

749) ABIGAIL ABBOTT (*Samuel Abbott[1], Zerviah Holt Abbott[3], Henry[2], Nicholas[1]*), b. at Pembroke, 6 Sep 1753 daughter of Samuel and Miriam (Stevens) Abbott; d. likely at Salisbury, NH; m. 23 Nov 1773, BENJAMIN WHITTEMORE, b. 4 Dec 1750 son of Aaron and Abigail (Coffin) Whittemore.

The History of Salisbury reports that Benjamin Whittemore, known as Button Whittemore, was often in legal disputes including once with his son who had his father jailed. The family was in Salisbury after 1791 when Benjamin purchased property there, and later relocated to Danbury. Benjamin is reported to have had a second wife, but that information is not clear.[2009]

Abigail Abbott and Benjamin Whittemore were parents of ten children born at Pembroke.[2010]

i RUTH WHITTEMORE, b. 15 Sep 1775; d. Oct 1797; m. at Salisbury, 18 Aug 1795, JOHN SHANNON, b. at Canterbury, 1 Feb 1769;[2011] John d. at Perrysburg, NY, about 1840. John m. 2nd, Sep 1798, MEHITABLE HOLT (*Benjamin[5], Benjamin[4], Nicholas[3], Nicholas[2], Nicholas[1]*), b. 17 Jul 1778 daughter of Benjamin and Hannah (Abbott) Holt; Mehitable d. at Cottage, NY, 28 Jan 1855.

ii JOHN WHITTEMORE, b. 7 Feb 1776; d. at Dixville, NH, 19 Jan 1846; m. 1st, 1 Jan 1799, BETSEY PILLSBURY, b. at Salisbury, 24 Apr 1779 daughter of Samuel and Elizabeth (Pingrey) Pillsbury; Betsey d. at Dixville, 15 Dec

---

2007 Carter, *History of Pembroke, Genealogies*, p 2

2008 Carter, *History of Pembroke, Genealogies*, p 2

2009 Dearborn, *History of Salisbury*, p 857. The two names of second wives suggested by Dearborn, Ruth D. and Sarah Sawyer, were the wives of Benjamin's son Benjamin.

2010 *The History of Salisbury* suggests there were 16 children, but record evidence was found just for these ten

2011 The is a transcription of a birth at Canterbury, but no names of parents on the card.

1815. John m. 2nd, at Stewartstown, 3 Feb 1834, OLIVE BRAINERD, b. at Rumney, NH, 5 Dec 1790 daughter of Barzillai and Hannah (Blodgett) Brainerd;[2012] Olive d. at Colebrook, 17 Sep 1860.

iii EBENEZER WHITTEMORE, b. 2 Feb 1778; d. at Springfield, NH, 30 Oct 1863; m. at Boscawen, 20 Feb 1800, LYDIA S. RICHARDS, b. 1778 daughter of Daniel and Eunice (Somerby) Richards; Lydia d. at North Wilmot, NH, 13 Jul 1845.

iv JUDITH WHITTEMORE, b. 6 Feb 1780; d. about 1813; m. 8 Aug 1799, JOSEPH ADAMS, b. at Newbury, 1 May 1779 *likely* the son of Abraham and Mary (Bricket) Adams; Joseph d. at Bright, IN, 12 Mar 1843. After Judith's death, Joseph married Sarah Judd on 29 Jan 1814.

v BENJAMIN WHITTEMORE, b. 29 Sep 1782; d. at Concord, NH, 19 May 1871; m. 1st, 27 Sep 1821, RUTH D. HILDRETH, b. about 1799; Ruth d. at Salisbury, 15 Jul 1828. Benjamin m. 2nd, at Andover, NH, 4 Oct 1829, SARAH SAWYER, b. at Hopkinton, about 1790 daughter of Samuel and Lucy (Perley) Sawyer;[2013] Sarah d. at Concord, 8 Sep 1880.

vi AMOS WHITTEMORE, b. 22 Aug 1785; d. at Princeton, IL, before 1855; m. 1st, at Salisbury, 28 Nov 1822, JUDITH CAMP (or Kemp), b. about 1796; Judith d. at Salisbury, 14 Mar 1835. Amos m. 2nd, 22 Aug 1841, MEHITABLE MARCH (widow of John Quimby), b. at Springfield, NH, 1 Jul 1799 daughter of David and Eunice (Persons) March; Mehitable was still living in 1860 in Concord, IL.

vii ESTHER WHITTEMORE, b. Jul 1788; d. at Salisbury, 22 Jun 1825. Esther did not marry.

viii AMELIA WHITTEMORE, b. 1790; nothing further known.

ix SAMUEL WHITTEMORE, b. 10 Nov 1792; d. at Charleston, IL, before 1860; m. 10 Jan 1821, MARTHA PERRIN, b. at Salisbury, about 1796 daughter of Stephen and Achsah (Heath) Perrin.[2014]

x SARAH WHITTEMORE, b. 8 Jul 1795; d. 1799.

750) JEREMIAH ABBOTT (*Samuel Abbott[1], Zerviah Holt Abbott[3], Henry[2], Nicholas[1]*), b. at Pembroke, 9 May 1757 son of Samuel and Miriam (Stevens) Abbott; d. at Montville, ME, 27 Jan 1816; m. 29 Nov 1787, ELIZABETH "BETSEY" FRYE, b. 18 Feb 1767 daughter of Ebenezer and Hannah (Baker) Frye; Betsey d. at Montville, 27 Aug 1841.

Jeremiah Abbott served as a private during the Revolution initially in Colonel Wingate's regiment of New Hampshire militia. He saw other service in Colonel Thomas Stickney's regiment under General Stark and was at the Battle of Bennington. He served a total of 21 months and 6 days for which his widow Betsey received a pension of $70.66 per annum. As part of the pension application, son Joel Abbott made an affidavit giving the date of his father's death and that his mother Betsey Abbott was now living in Montville with Joel.[2015]

The family started in New Hampshire, were in Vermont for a time where at least one child was born, and were lastly in Montville, Maine. Five children have been identified for Jeremiah Abbott and Betsey Frye. There are no birth records, but the children are identified through death records giving Jeremiah Abbott and Betsey Frye as parents and from information in the pension application file. The information is consistent with census records as the siblings lived with each other off and on during their adult years. Given that the first child known was born ten years after the marriage, there may well be other children who have not been identified.

i JOEL ABBOTT, b. in VT, about 1797; d. after 1870 perhaps at China, ME; m. at Montville, 11 Mar 1824, JANE CARTER, b. at Montville, 11 Oct 1804 daughter of Thomas and Joanna (Perkins) Carter; Jane d. at Montville, after 1880.

ii HANNAH A. ABBOTT, b. in NH (according to census records), 1804; d. at Montville, ME, 23 Jul 1890; m. before 1833, REUBEN G. BLAKE, b. in ME, Apr 1803;[2016] Reuben d. at Montville, 4 May 1887.

iii EBENEZER GUY ABBOTT, b. in ME, 1808; d. at Morrill, ME, 12 Jan 1892; m. at Knox, ME, 29 Nov 1849, DESIRE BLAKE, b. about 1810; Desire d. after 1880.

iv LEONARD W. ABBOTT, b. about 1810; d. at Montville, 16 Mar 1814.

[2012] Brainard, *Descendants of Daniel, James and Joshua Brainerd*, p 79

[2013] The names of Sarah's parents are given on her death record. Other census and probate records establish her siblings which further confirms parents.

[2014] Dearborn, *History of Salisbury*, p 687

[2015] Revolutionary War Pension and Bounty-Land Warrant Application Files

[2016] It is possible that Reuben Blake who married Hannah Abbott and Desire Blake who married Ebenezer Guy Abbott are siblings and the children of Moses and Hannah (Mayo) Blake.

v LYDIA FRYE ABBOTT, b. at Montville, Jan 1811; d. at Montville, 14 May 1901; m. about 1847, as his second wife, HATHERLY VARNEY, b. about 1810; Hatherly d. at Levant, ME, 5 Aug 1851. Hatherly was first married to Adeline Smith.

751) SARAH ABBOTT (*Samuel Abbott[1], Zerviah Holt Abbott[3], Henry[2], Nicholas[1]*), b. at Pembroke, 21 Jul 1759 daughter of Samuel and Miriam (Stevens) Abbott; m. 4 Nov 1790, as his second wife, JEREMIAH WHEELER, b. at Concord, MA, Feb 1745 son of Jeremiah and Esther (Russell) Wheeler; Jeremiah d. at Concord, NH, 17 Oct 1827. Jeremiah was first married to Keziah Blanchard.

Sarah and Jeremiah resided in Concord, New Hampshire. Jeremiah fulfilled civic duties such as surveyor of highways and tythingman. He signed the 1776 association test.[2017]

Jeremiah Wheeler had seven children with his first wife Keziah Blanchard. Sarah Abbott and Jeremiah Wheeler were parents of seven children born at Concord.

i LYDIA WHEELER, b. 8 Jan 1791; nothing further known.

ii KEZIAH BLANCHARD WHEELER, b. 25 Feb 1793; d. at Rumford, ME, 26 Nov 1873; m. at Concord, 13 Mar 1814, COLMAN GODWIN, b. 6 May 1782 son of William and Rachel (Harper) Godwin; Colman d. at Rumford, 24 Aug 1852.

iii JOHN WHEELER, b. 25 Feb 1793; d. at Concord, after 1870; m. 1st, 19 Feb 1817, MAHALA COCHRAN, b. at Pembroke, 1 Feb 1797 daughter of James and Lettice (Duncan) Cochran; Mahala d. at Concord, 24 Oct 1832. John m. 2nd, about 1834, MARY who has not been identified, but described as "of Warner" in the death record of one of the children; Mary d. by 1841. John m. 3rd, at Sanbornton, 3 Apr 1842, EUNICE HILLIARD, b. at Sanbornton, about 1814 daughter of Daniel and Polly (Eaton) Hilliard; Eunice d. at Concord, 26 Oct 1885. Eunice Hillard was first married to Edwin D. Fogg.

iv JEREMIAH WHEELER, b. 15 Feb 1795; d. at Manchester, NH, 27 Jan 1873; m. at Concord, 28 Mar 1820, SARAH WHIDDEN, b. in NH, about 1798 daughter of Josiah and Polly (Currier) Whidden.

v RUTH W. WHEELER, b. 4 Jan 1799; d. at Concord, 19 Mar 1880; m. at Concord, 16 Feb 1829, ANDREW MOODY, b. at Penobscot, ME, 2 Nov 1796 son of William and Mary (Dresser) Moody; Andrew d. at Concord, 10 Jan 1881.

vi JUDITH WHEELER, b. 10 Aug 1802; d. at Manchester, NH, after 1850; m. at Concord, 13 Feb 1823, SAINT LUKE MORSE, b. in NH, 11 Dec 1797 son of Benjamin and Dolly (George) Morse; Saint Luke d. after 1850.

vii MIRIAM WHEELER, b. 21 Jun 1805; may have died young.

752) LYDIA ABBOTT (*Samuel Abbott[1], Zerviah Holt Abbott[3], Henry[2], Nicholas[1]*), b. at Pembroke, 14 Jul 1761 daughter of Samuel and Miriam (Stevens) Abbott; d. at Bethel, VT, 9 Dec 1840; m. 29 Mar 1787, NATHANIEL MORRILL, b. at South Hampton, NH, 11 Jan 1761 son of Paul and Martha (Worthen) Morrill; Nathaniel d. at Bethel, 17 Nov 1832.

This family was in Chichester, New Hampshire and Tunbridge, Vermont, and finally in Bethel, Vermont. Lydia and Nathaniel were parents of ten children.[2018]

i WILLIAM MORRILL, b. 1788; d. at Macon, MO, 1865; m. at Pembroke, 11 Feb 1813, MARY MARTIN, b. at Pembroke, 27 Jul 1790 daughter of Robert and Abigail (McCriss) Martin.

ii JUDITH MORRILL, b. at Chichester, 16 Aug 1789; d. at Royalton, VT, 3 Sep 1869; m. at Tunbridge, 11 Jan 1811, THOMAS RUSS, b. at Royalton, 31 Mar 1789 son of Jeremiah and Eunice (Moxley) Russ; Thomas d. at Royalton, 29 Apr 1868.

iii ABIGAIL MORRILL, b. 1791; d. at Royalton, 20 Apr 1836; m. 3 Dec 1812, JOHN GOULD DUTTON, b. at Clarendon, VT, 18 Nov 1789 son of Amasa and Sarah (Parmalee) Dutton;[2019] John d. at Northfield, VT, 7 Nov 1877.

iv SARAH "SALLY" MORRILL, b. 1792; d. at Tunbridge, after 1860; m. about 1817, LYMAN WIGHT, b. about Tunbridge, about 1792; Lyman d. at Randolph, VT, 1 May 1869.

v NATHANIEL MORRILL, b. 28 Jan 1795; d. at Concord, MI, 14 Oct 1865; m. at Canaan, NH, 8 Mar 1820, HANNAH MARTIN, b. at Pembroke, 15 Dec 1792 daughter of Robert and Abigail (McCriss) Martin; Hannah d. at Concord, MI, 14 Jun 1873.

[2017] Bouton, History of Concord, p 332, p 271

[2018] Smith, *Morrill Kindred in America*, volume 2, p 39.

[2019] Lovejoy, *History of Royalton*, part 2, p 776

vi JEREMIAH MORRILL, b. 1796; d. at Danville, VT, 17 Aug 1859; m. SARAH MORRILL, b. in VT, 25 Jul 1805 daughter of Jacob and Abigail (-) Morrill; Sarah d. at Lowell, MA, 8 Dec 1870.

vii SAMUEL MORRILL, b. 1799; d. at Orleans, VT, 14 Aug 1872; m. at Bethel, 1820, ACHSAH PEARSON, b. at Randolph, VT, 9 Jan 1804 daughter of John T. and Polly (-) Pearson; Achsah d. at Troy, VT, 18 Sep 1873.

viii LYDIA MORRILL, b. 1801; d. at Walcott, VT, 10 Feb 1885; m. ZIBA GIFFORD, b. at Tunbridge, 23 Aug 1792 son of Ziba and Sarah (McKnight) Gifford; Ziba d. at Walcott, 1 May 1870.

ix EZEKIEL MORRILL, b. 1803; d. at Tunbridge, 2 Jan 1836.

x SUSAN MORRILL, b. 1809; d. at Troy, VT, 1 Mar 1876; m. at Tunbridge, 8 Jan 1843, DANIEL KELSEY, b. at Tunbridge, 8 Apr 1797 son of James and Parmelia (Pratt) Kelsey; Daniel d. at Troy, VT, 22 May 1875.

753) EZRA ABBOTT (*Samuel Abbott[1], Zerviah Holt Abbott[3], Henry[2], Nicholas[1]*), b. at Pembroke, 4 Aug 1763 son of Samuel and Miriam (Stevens) Abbott; d. at Sanbornton, NH, 16 Nov 1824; m. 30 Nov 1794, MOLLY BROWN daughter of William and Ruth (McDuffee) Brown;[2020] Molly d. at Cabot, VT, 1836.

Ezra Abbott and Molly Brown made the move from Pembroke to Sanbornton soon after their marriage and their five children were born in Sanbornton.

i SARAH ABBOTT, b. 23 Aug 1795; d. at Sanbornton, 16 May 1817; m. at Sanbornton, 14 Dec 1815, JOHN ABRAMS, b. at Sanbornton, 18 Jan 1793 son of John and Mehitable (Harriman) Abrams; d. at sea, 4 Jul 1853.[2021] John was second married to Nancy Rollins and third married to Ruth Sanborn.

ii JOHN ABBOTT, b. 30 Apr 1797; d. at Allenstown, NH, 21 Dec 1855; m. 31 Dec 1818, his fourth cousin once removed, MARY BUNTIN (*Betsey Hutchinson Buntin[7], Mehitable Lovejoy Hutchison[6], Caleb Lovejoy[5], Henry Lovejoy[4], Mary Farnum Lovejoy[3], Elizabeth Holt Farnum[2], Nicholas[1]*), b. at Pembroke, 25 Feb 1795 daughter of Robert and Betsy (Hutchinson) Buntin; Mary d. at Allenstown, 9 Feb 1858.

iii MARY ABBOTT, b. 5 Sep 1798; d. at Sanbornton, 27 Jun 1827; m. 28 Dec 1819, ASAHEL QUIMBY, b. at Sanbornton, 20 Jun 1797 son of Harper and Hannah (Thompson) Quimby; Asahel d. at Hill, NH, 25 Jul 1849. Asahel married second Sarah Bennett.

iv WILLIAM ABBOTT, b. 21 Feb 1800; d. at Medford, MN, 1862; m. at Hebron, 30 Dec 1824, LOIS SAWYER, b. at Newport, NH, 19 Dec 1801 daughter of Richard K. and Mary B. (Bean) Sawyer;[2022] Lois d. at Medford, 20 Jun 1863.

v CHAUNCEY ABBOTT, b. about 1802. He is reported to have left Sanbornton for New York in 1832 with nothing further heard of him.[2023]

754) WILLIAM ABBOTT (*Samuel Abbott[1], Zerviah Holt Abbott[3], Henry[2], Nicholas[1]*), b. at Pembroke, 10 Sep 1765 son of Samuel and Miriam (Stevens) Abbott; d. at Pembroke, 22 Jul 1838; m. his third cousin, DORCAS PARKER, b. at Andover, 17 Feb 1769 daughter of Joseph and Hannah (Abbott) Parker; Dorcas d. 9 Nov 1853.

William Abbott and Dorcas Parker were parents of nine children born at Pembroke.

i NATHANIEL ABBOTT, b. 10 Feb 1793; d. 27 Aug 1814.

ii WILLIAM ABBOTT, b. 15 Aug 1794; d. at Chichester, 23 May 1874; m. 1st, 22 Oct 1816, ESTHER FOWLER, b. at Pembroke, 16 Mar 1797 daughter of Benjamin and Mehitable (Ladd) Fowler; Esther d. at Pembroke, 31 Dec 1831. William m. 2nd, at Epsom, 5 Feb 1833, NANCY D. CAMPBELL, b. at Pembroke, about 1815 daughter of David and Deborah (Goss) Campbell; Nancy d. at Dover, NH, 22 Sep 1890.

iii HANNAH ABBOTT, b. 10 Jul 1796; d. at Pembroke, 3 Apr 1863; m. at Pembroke, 12 Sep 1828, her fourth cousin once removed, HERMAN ABBOT OSGOOD (*Christopher Osgood[6], Elizabeth Abbott Osgood[5], Thomas Abbott[4], Hannah Gray Abbott[3], Hannah Holt Gray[2], Nicholas[1]*), b. at Pembroke, 20 Jul 1797 son of Christopher and Anna (Abbott) Osgood; Herman d. at Pembroke, 12 Feb 1858.

2020 Chase, *History of Old Chester*, p 478

2021 According to the History of Sanbornton, John died on a return trip from Oregon where he had been for two years; died when crossing the Gulf of Mexico.

2022 Dearborn, *History of Salisbury*, p 470

2023 Runnels, *History of Sanbornton, Genealogies*, p 1

iv MIRIAM ABBOTT, b. 3 Mar 1798; d. at Worcester, VT, 17 Apr 1873; m. 24 Dec 1816, her first cousin, SAMUEL KELLEY (*Rachel Abbott Kelley[5], Samuel Abbott[1], Zerviah Holt Abbott[3], Henry[2], Nicholas[1]*), b. at Pembroke, 23 Sep 1792 son of John and Rachel (Abbott) Kelley; Samuel d. at Worcester, VT, 2 Apr 1871.

v MARY ABBOTT, b. 29 Jan 1800; d. at Pembroke, 20 Aug 1845; m. 15 Dec 1841, JONATHAN ROBINSON, b. at Epsom, 27 Jun 1785 son of David and Hannah (Fowler) Robinson; Jonathan d. at Pembroke, 19 Sep 1853.

vi ADRIAN ABBOTT, b. 21 Dec 1802; d. at Beddington, ME, 18 Apr 1881; m. about 1836, FANNY SCHOPPE, b. at Beddington, 23 Sep 1814 daughter of John and Eliza (Weston) Schoppe; Fanny d. at Pittsburg, NH, 28 Oct 1902.

vii LAVINIA ABBOTT, b. 12 Apr 1807; d. at North Pembroke, 25 Oct 1880; m. at Pembroke, 12 Mar 1824, JOHN LADD FOWLER, b. at Pembroke, 1 Aug 1801 son of Benjamin and Mehitable (Ladd) Fowler; John d. at North Pembroke, 27 Mar 1871.

viii SAVALLA ABBOTT, b. 24 Aug 1809; d. at Goffstown, after 1860; m. 1st, 16 Mar 1830, NATHAN LIBBEY, b. at Epsom, 25 Jun 1808 son of Nathan and Abigail (Fowler) Libbey; Nathan d. at Philadelphia, PA, 15 Oct 1874. It is possible that Savalla and Nathan Libbey divorced. In 1860, Savalla was in Goffstown listed as Savalla Thrasher with some of the children from her marriage to Nathan Libbey living with her. In 1860, Nathan Libbey was living in Philadelphia with what seems to be a new wife. If Savalla married a Mr. Thrasher, he was not in the home with her in 1860.

ix Stillborn child, 26 Aug 1811.

755) RACHEL ABBOTT (*Samuel Abbott[1], Zerviah Holt Abbott[3], Henry[2], Nicholas[1]*), b. at Pembroke, 15 Jun 1768 daughter of Samuel and Miriam (Stevens) Abbott; d. at Pembroke, 28 Dec 1854; m. 30 Dec 1789, JOHN KELLEY, b. 22 Jul 1764 son of Samuel and Sarah (Barker) Kelley; John d. at Pembroke, 1 Jan 1817.

John Kelley was a farmer and he and Rachel raised their family in Pembroke. John did not leave a will and his estate entered probate 15 January 1817. His widow declined administration and this duty was assumed by son John Kelley. Real estate was valued at $800 and personal estate at $282.68.[2024]

Rachel Abbott and John Kelley were parents of ten children born at Pembroke.

i MIRIAM KELLEY, b. 23 Aug 1790; d. at Epsom, NH, 26 Sep 1879; m. at Pembroke, 30 Nov 1830, LEVI BAKER, b. at Pembroke, 22 Feb 1798 son of Joseph and Hannah (Haggett) Baker; Levi d. at Pembroke, 7 Oct 1844.

ii SAMUEL KELLEY, b. 23 Sep 1792; d. at Worcester, VT, 2 Apr 1871; m. 24 Dec 1816, his first cousin, MIRIAM ABBOTT (*William Abbott[5], Samuel Abbott[1], Zerviah Holt Abbott[3], Henry[2], Nicholas[1]*), b. at Pembroke, 3 Mar 1798 daughter of William and Dorcas (Parker) Abbott; Miriam d. at Worcester, 17 Apr 1873.

iii JOHN KELLEY, b. 10 Dec 1794; d. at Pembroke, 23 Apr 1864; m. 1st at Chichester, 10 Dec 1818, PHEBE STEVENS, b. 1802 daughter of Phebe and Olive (Locke) Stevens; Phebe d. at Pembroke, about 1851. John m. 2nd, 13 Aug 1856, ABIGAIL TIBBETTS (widow of William Caldwell), b. at Madbury, NH, about 1802; Abigail d. at Pembroke, 18 Apr 1877.

iv ALVA KELLEY, b. 14 Feb 1797; d. at Boston, MA, 4 May 1872; m. at Charlestown, 20 Jun 1824, LUCY BEAVERSTOCK, b. at Charlestown, 1 Jun 1800 daughter of Samuel and Olive (Read) Beaverstock; Lucy d. at Boston, 19 Dec 1878.

v HEPHZIBAH KELLEY, b. 6 Mar 1799; d. at Epsom, 24 Jan 1881; m. 20 Nov 1823, STEPHEN BAKER, b. at Pembroke, 4 May 1796 son of Joseph and Hannah (Haggett) Baker; Stephen d. at Epsom, 30 May 1869.

vi DAVID KELLEY, b. 10 Mar 1801; d. at Boston, 20 Jul 1846; m. at Charlestown, 25 Jan 1827, OLIVE BEAVERSTOCK, b. at Charlestown, 17 May 1809 daughter of Samuel and Olive (Reed) Beaverstock.

vii JASON ABBOTT KELLEY, b. 16 Feb 1803; d. at West Bridgewater, MA, 22 Feb 1882; m. at Chichester, 13 May 1830, MARINDA GILES DEARBORN, b. at Pembroke, 30 Apr 1805 daughter of Joseph and Sally (Bellamy) Dearborn; Marinda d. at Concord, 29 Dec 1867.

viii SALLY KELLEY, b. 17 Nov 1804; d. at Pembroke, 17 Jan 1878; m. 19 Aug 1828, MALACHI HAINES, b. at Chichester, 29 Oct 1802 son of Malachi and Sally (Fife) Haines; Malachi d. at Chichester, 1 Apr 1863.

ix BENAIAH KELLEY, b. 10 Dec 1807; d. at Hillsboro, IL, 17 Oct 1888; m. 1st at Montgomery County, IL, 10 Oct 1841, SARAH ANN MCADAMS, b. in IL, about 1820; Sarah d. at Hillsboro, about 1875. Benaiah m. 2nd, at Montgomery County, 23 Oct 1879, CYNTHIA E. KING, b. about 1839.

2024 *New Hampshire. Probate Court (Rockingham County)*; Probate Place: *Rockingham, New Hampshire, Estate Papers, No 9415-9493, 1816-1817*, Case 9460

x MEHITABLE KELLEY, b. 12 Aug 1809; d. at North Pembroke, 23 Jan 1895; m. 21 Jan 1834, DARIUS SNELL, b. at Barnstead, NH, 15 Apr 1808 son of Thomas and Hannah (Merrill) Snell; Darius d. at North Pembroke, 16 Jan 1892.

756) MARIAM ABBOTT (*Samuel Abbott¹, Zerviah Holt Abbott³, Henry², Nicholas¹*), b. at Pembroke, 5 Sep 1771 daughter of Samuel and Miriam (Stevens) Abbott; d. at Randolph, VT, 21 Jun 1820; m. JOHN MORRILL, b. 17 Jan 1759 son of Paul and Martha (Worthen) Morrill; John d. at Randolph, 21 Sep 1849.

John Morrill and Mariam Abbott settled in Randolph, Vermont soon after their marriage. They had a farm there and were the parents of eleven children all born at Randolph.[2025]

i NANCY MORRILL, b. 5 Aug 1794; d. at Hampton, MN, 5 Mar 1860; m. at Randolph, 22 Feb 1815, WILLIAM PERRIN, b. at Royalton, VT, 11 Feb 1793 son of Greenfield and Sally (Ashcroft) Perrin;[2026] William d. at Hampton, 13 Feb 1865.

ii BETSEY MORRILL, b. 6 Feb 1796; d. at Chelsea, VT, 20 Jul 1852; m. 31 Mar 1818, PETER M. LOUGEE, b. Jan 1791;[2027] Peter d. at Randolph, 10 Dec 1857. Peter married second Betsey Worthley.

iii IRA MORRILL, b. 5 Sep 1797; d. at Randolph, VT, after 1870; m. 1st, at Randolph, 3 Jan 1822, MARY PICKENS, b. about 1799; Mary d. at Randolph, 25 Feb 1839. Ira m. 2nd, 22 Jun 1839, MARY B. SMITH, b. about 1810; Mary d. after 1870.

iv MARIAM MORRILL, b. 19 Sep 1799; d. at Randolph, 17 Mar 1833; m. 4 Feb 1854, ASAHEL BRAINERD, b. at Randolph, 15 Nov 1798 son of Asahel and Lydia (Loveland) Brainerd; Asahel d. at Randolph, 5 Aug 1851.

v JOHN MORRILL, b. 1 Jun 1801; d. at Randolph, 1852 (probate 19 Nov 1852); m. 1827, ABIAH OSGOOD, b. at Randolph, 11 Dec 1804 daughter of Abijah and Betsey (Sprague) Osgood; Abiah d. 29 Oct 1853.

vi MARY "POLLY" MORRILL, b. 15 Apr 1802; d. at Wolcott, VT, Nov 1885; m. 1 Dec 1825, PHILANDER SMITH, b. at Randolph, about 1805 son of Jonathan and Abigail (Edgerton) Smith; Philander d. at Wolcott, 24 May 1875.

vii MARTHA MORRILL, b. 15 May 1805; d. at Wolcott, VT, 25 May 1900; m. Feb 1827, IRA WALBRIDGE, b. at Cabot, VT, 25 Aug 1799 son of Oliver and Elizabeth (Smith) Walbridge; Ira d. at Wolcott, 29 Jun 1877.

viii Son, b. 10 Jun 1807

ix Son, b. 20 Aug 1809

x WILLIAM MORRILL, b. 11 Jan 1811; d. at Lewiston, WI, 2 Oct 1893; m. ANNA FOLSOM, b. at Tunbridge, 4 Aug 1808 daughter of John and Anna (Fifield) Folsom; Anna d. at Briggsville, WI, 28 Jan 1892.

xi GILBERT MORRILL, b. 11 Feb 1812; d. at Randolph, 3 Dec 1893; m. 1837, SALLY SPRAGUE, b. at Randolph, 2 Feb 1817 daughter of John and Sally (Story) Sprague; Sally d. at Randolph, 29 Mar 1886.

757) ALICE PEARL (*Dinah Holt Pearl⁴, Keturah Holt Holt³, Henry², Nicholas¹*), b. at Willington, 6 Jul 1748 daughter of Timothy and Dinah (Holt) Pearl. The birth transcription says 6 Jul 1743, but this seems an error and Durrie's Holt genealogy says 1748; her age at death in 1826 was 76. Alice d. Dec 1826; m. at Willington, 10 Oct 1767, ELEAZER SCRIPTURE, b. at Willington, 10 May 1742 son of John and Hannah (Wells) Scripture; Eleazer d. at Willington, 1813 (estate inventory 13 Oct 1813).

Eleazer Scripture did not leave a will and his estate entered probate October 1813 with Alpheus Scripture as administrator. The widow's dower was set off to Alice Scripture. The estate was insolvent and sold to pay debts.[2028]

Alice Pearl and Eleazer Scripture were parents of ten children born at Willington.

i ROSWELL SCRIPTURE, b. 18 Apr 1768; d. at Stafford, CT, 8 Feb 1839; m. SOPHIA DANA, b. 1777 daughter of James and Elizabeth (Whittemore) Dana; Sophia d. at Cobleskill, NY, 17 Dec 1861.

ii HIRAM SCRIPTURE, b. 2 Apr 1772; d. at Westmoreland, NY, 17 Apr 1849; m. ELIZABETH PARKER, b. about 1773; Elizabeth d. at Westmoreland, 23 Aug 1862.

iii ZEVINAH SCRIPTURE, b. 24 Dec 1774; nothing further known.

[2025] Nickerson and Cox, *Illustrated Historical Souvenir of Randolph, Vermont*, p 79

[2026] Aldrich and Holmes, *History of Windsor County, Vermont*, p 783

[2027] Birth date is given on his death record.

[2028] *Connecticut State Library (Hartford, Connecticut)*; Probate Place: *Hartford, Connecticut, Probate Packets, Rockwell, N-Sessions, O, 1759-1880*, probate of Eleazer Scripture, 1813, case number 1893

iv ALPHEUS SCRIPTURE, b. 1 Sep 1777; d. at Willington, 23 Oct 1846; m. ELIZABETH, b. 1777; Elizabeth d. at Willington, 21 Sep 1865.

v IRENE SCRIPTURE, b. 24 Mar 1779; d. at Willington, 31 Aug 1861; m. RUFUS FISK, b. at Willington, 10 Feb 1773 son of Rufus and Dorcas (Gleason) Fisk; Rufus d. at Willington, 22 Sep 1848.

vi ELIZABETH SCRIPTURE, b. 14 Oct 1781; d. at Rushville, NY, 1 Jan 1864; m. PORTER HINKLEY, b. at Willington, 19 Oct 1781 son of John and Ann (Whipple) Hinkley; Porter d. at Gorham, NY, 6 Jun 1849.

vii ELEAZER SCRIPTURE, b. 24 Mar 1783. What became of Eleazer is not clear. On 2 September 1805, Eleazer Scripture born in Connecticut was convicted in Oneida County of grand larceny and sentenced to one year in Newgate Prison. Eleazer's older brother Hiram was in Oneida County at this time, so perhaps that is this Eleazer. There is also an Eleazer Scripture from Connecticut who died in Pewaukee, IL, after 1855. That Eleazer was married to Susan Saunders who was born in RI in 1796 daughter of Thomas and Elizabeth (Cross) Saunders.

viii CYRREL SCRIPTURE, b. 17 Mar 1785; d. at Willington, 15 Feb 1853; m. ABIGAIL HALL, b. 1788; Abigail d. at Willington, 15 Apr 1845.

ix LOIS SCRIPTURE, b. 11 Sep 1788; d. at Rushville, NY, 17 Sep 1846; m. at Willington, 17 Jul 1808, STEPHEN CARD, b. 1785 who has not been identified.

x ALLICE SCRIPTURE, b. 14 Jul 1790; d. at Tolland, 3 Mar 1863; m. at Willington, 27 Oct 1808, ISAAC NILES, b. at Willington, 9 Mar 1786 son of James and Mary (Fenton) Niles; Isaac d. at Tolland, 7 Oct 1858.

758) OLIVER PEARL (*Dinah Holt Pearl*[4], *Keturah Holt Holt*[3], *Henry*[2], *Nicholas*[1]), b. at Willington, 9 Oct 1749 son of Timothy and Dinah (Holt) Pearl; d. at Willington, 4 Nov 1831; m. 1st, 1 Jan 1772, MERCY HINCKLEY, b. 1749 daughter of John and Susanna (Harris) Hinckley;[2029] Mercy d. at Willington, 15 Nov 1781. Oliver m. 2nd, 24 Apr 1782, his second cousin, HANNAH HOLT (*Abiel*[4], *Abiel*[3], *Nicholas*[2], *Nicholas*[1]), b. 14 Mar 1756 daughter of Abiel and Mary (Downer) Holt; Hannah d. 20 Nov 1832.

Oliver Pearl and Mercy Hinckley were parents of five children born at Willington.

i ALICE PEARL, b. 15 Dec 1772; d. 30 Mar 1773.

ii OLIVER PEARL, b. 14 Sep 1774; d. 6 Apr 1775.

iii OLIVER PEARL, b. 15 May 1776; d. 16 Oct 1786.

iv DANIEL PEARL, b. 1779; d. 14 Jul 1779.

v DANIEL PEARL, b. 29 May 1780; d. before 1850; m. at Willington, 5 Mar 1806, POLLY HORTON, b. about 1783; Polly d. at Owego, NY, after 1860.

Hannah Holt and Oliver Pearl were parents of six children born at Willington.

i HANNAH PEARL, b. 29 Apr 1783; d. 23 Nov 1786.

ii MARCY PEARL, b. 18 Aug 1785; m. 1st, at Ashford, 1 Jan 1810, WILLIAM BUFFINGTON, b. at Ashford, 21 Jun 1789 son of William and Candace (Salisbury) Buffington; William d. at Ashford, 20 Jan 1814. Marcy m. 2nd, about 1815, LOREN FULLER.[2030]

iii OLIVER PEARL, b. 10 Nov 1788; d. at Berlin Heights, OH, 26 May 1835; m. about 1811, MARY SEXTON, b. at Ellington, 5 Dec 1795 daughter of William and Docia (Emerson) Sexton; Mary d. at Berlin Heights, 15 May 1884.

iv WALTER PEARL, b. 15 Sep 1791; m. at Mansfield, CT, 24 Nov 1814, MARIA DAVIS, b. at Mansfield, 9 Jul 1794 daughter of Thomas and Patience (Dennison) Davis.[2031]

v HANNAH PEARL, b. 17 May 1794; d. at Berlin Heights, OH, 26 Oct 1849; m. 1822, PHILIP SEELY BAKER, b. in CT, 22 Jul 1790; Philip d. at Berlin Heights, 12 May 1889. Philip married second the widow Lavinia Decker.

vi CYREL PEARL, b. 16 Sep 1797; d. at Lounsberry, NY, 20 Jul 1837; m. 29 May 1820, ROSANNAH FARMER, b. 24 Jun 1804 daughter of Thomas and Rosannah (Thompson) Farmer; Rosannah d. at Lounsberry, 17 Jun 1875.

2029 The 1788 Connecticut probate record of John Hinckley (widow Susanna) includes as heirs grandsons Daniel Pearl and Oliver Pearl the children of Mercy who is deceased.

2030 Gay, *Historical Gazetteer of Tioga County, part I*, p 370

2031 Dimock, *Births, Baptisms, Marriages, and Deaths: From the Records of the Town and Churches in Mansfield, Connecticut*, p 59

759) JOSHUA PEARL (*Dinah Holt Pearl[4], Keturah Holt Holt[3], Henry[2], Nicholas[1]*), b. at Willington, 15 Sep 1752 son of Timothy and Dinah (Holt) Pearl; d. at Vernon, 11 Oct 1837; m. 14 Jan 1773, DEBORAH MARSHALL, b. at Bolton, 1755 daughter of John and Eunice (Kingsbury) Marshall; Deborah d. at Vernon, 11 May 1818.

Joshua Pearl and Deborah Marshall were parents of eleven children, nine of the births recorded at Bolton, Connecticut and two additional children whose parents are identified on death records.

i JOHN MARSHALL PEARL, b. at Bolton, 28 Apr 1774; d. at Belchertown, MA, 26 Apr 1853; m. 1797, ACHSAH FENTON, b. at Willington, 10 Aug 1773 daughter of Eleazer and Elizabeth (Davis) Fenton; Achsah d. at Belchertown, 17 Jan 1863.

ii TIMOTHY PEARL, b. at Bolton, 19 Jul 1776; d. at Belchertown, 10 Dec 1837; m. SALLY PERRY, b. about 1774 daughter of Joseph Perry; Sally d. at Belchertown, 30 Oct 1837.

iii JOSHUA PEARL, b. at Bolton, 8 Nov 1778; d. at Vernon, CT, 27 Jan 1817; m. 14 May 1801, EUNICE STEDMAN who has not been identified. Eunice was living in Vernon in 1830 as head of household.

iv ELIZABETH PEARL, b. at Bolton, 24 Oct 1780; no further information.

v LYDIA PEARL, b. at Bolton, 6 Mar 1783; d. at Vernon, 6 Nov 1841; m. at Vernon, 27 Oct 1808, ELIJAH CHAPMAN, likely the Elijah b. 1783 who d. at Vernon, 31 Aug 1872.

vi EUNICE PEARL, b. 13 Jan 1786; d. 13 Mar 1797.

vii WALTER PEARL, b. 6 Mar 1788; d. 16 Feb 1789.

viii CYRIL PEARL, b. 1790; d. 11 Mar 1797.

ix POLLY PEARL, b. likely at Bolton, 1792; d. at Belchertown, 24 Sep 1857; m. at Vernon, 12 May 1825, as his second wife, ISRAEL COWLES, b. at Belchertown, 5 Nov 1788 son of Josiah and Chloe (Mehuren) Cowles; Israel d. at Belchertown, 11 Feb 1857. Israel was first married to Lois Dunton.

x ACHSAH PEARL, b. at Bolton, 15 May 1795; d. at Vernon, 13 Dec 1857; m. about 1816, ANSON ROGERS, b. likely at Vernon, about 1790; Anson d. at Vernon, 22 Dec 1872.

xi EUNICE PEARL, b. at Vernon, 1798; d. at Belchertown, 4 Jan 1873;[2032] m. as his second wife, HORATIO RICE, b. at Belchertown, 5 Feb 1787 son of Timothy and Elizabeth (Howe) Rice; Horatio d. at Belchertown, 9 Mar 1871. Horatio was first married to Elizabeth Allen.

760) LOIS PEARL (*Dinah Holt Pearl[4], Keturah Holt Holt[3], Henry[2], Nicholas[1]*), b. at Willington, 21 Apr 1753 daughter of Timothy and Dinah (Holt) Pearl; d. at Willington, 15 Jul 1788; m. 6 Aug 1771, SAMUEL DUNTON, b. at Wrentham, MA, 10 Nov 1748 son of Samuel and Sarah (Bennet) Dunton; Samuel d. at Willington, 1 May 1813. After Lois's death, Samuel married Lovina Marcy.

Samuel Dunton served as a Sergeant during the Revolution in Wadsworth Brigade.[2033]

In his will written 21 February 1810 (probate 6 November 1813), Samuel Dunton notes that his five first children namely Amasa, Josiah, Leonard, Sally, and Lois have received £40 each, except Josiah received £33 10 shillings; Josiah will receive an amount to bring his up to £40. Sons Amasa, Josiah, and Leonard also receive land in Willington. Two oldest daughters, Sally Stewart and Lois Eldridge, each receives $33 to bring their portion to £50 which is their full portion of the estate. His two youngest daughters, Lodicia and Eliza, each receives one dollar and the remainder of the estate both real and personal goes to his beloved wife Lovina. Wife Lovina Dunton was named executrix.[2034]

Lois Pearl and Samuel Dunton were parents of seven children born at Willington. Samuel had three children with his second wife Lovina Marcy.

i AMASA DUNTON, b. 5 Jan 1772; d. at Earlville, NY, 11 Apr 1836; m. at Willington, 9 Apr 1793. MERCY TAYLOR, b. at Mansfield, CT, 21 Jun 1777 daughter of Thomas and Experience (Freeman) Taylor; Mercy d. at Earlville, 5 Mar 1848.

ii LEONARD DUNTON, b. 20 Mar 1774; d. 29 Oct 1775.

iii JOSIAH DUNTON, b. 20 Nov 1777; d. at Cambridge, NY, 24 Nov 1866; m. SARAH CROCKER, b. 4 Mar 1779 daughter of Seth and Mary (Hinckley) Crocker;[2035] Sarah d. at Cambridge, NY, 10 May 1863.

2032 The death record of Eunice Rice gives parents names as Joshua and Deborah.

2033 Eldredge, *Eldredge Genealogy*, p 11

2034 *Connecticut. Probate Court (Stafford District);* Probate Place: *Tolland, Connecticut, Probate Records, Vol 7-8, 1809-1815*, volume 8, pp 98-100

2035 The 1806 will of Seth Crocker of Cambridge, NY includes a bequest to his daughter Sarah Dunton.

iv SARAH "SALLY" DUNTON, b. 8 Dec 1779; b. at Fort Edward, NY, after 1850; m. by 1810, JOSEPH STEWART, b. 14 Mar 1778 son of Joseph and Rosanna (Harmon) Stewart;[2036] Joseph d. after 1850.

v LEONARD DUNTON, b. 2 Jul 1782; d. at Rome, NY, Jan 1832; m. at Ellington, CT, 4 Nov 1806, ROSINA MCKINSTRY, b. at Ellington, 25 Jan 1783 daughter of Ezekiel and Rosina (Chapman) McKinstry; Rosina d. at Rome, 1 Sep 1847.

vi LOIS DUNTON, b. 4 Oct 1784; d. likely at Syracuse; m. at Willington, 8 Oct 1804, ZOETH ELDRIDGE, b. 1 Apr 1782 son of Zoeth and Bethiah (Hinkley) Eldridge; Zoeth d. at Syracuse, 1844.

vii SAMUEL DUNTON, b. 13 Dec 1787; d. 2 Jun 1798.

761) ELIZABETH PEARL (*Dinah Holt Pearl⁴, Keturah Holt Holt³, Henry², Nicholas¹*), b. at Willington, 15 Jan 1756 daughter of Timothy and Dinah (Holt) Pearl; d. at Willington, 8 Jan 1779; m. 6 Aug 1771, ZOETH ELDRIDGE, b. at Willington, about 1751 son of Jesse and Abigail (Smith) Eldridge; Zoeth d. at Willington, 18 Mar 1828. Zoeth m. 2nd, Bethiah Hinkley.[2037]

Zoeth Eldridge was a farmer in Willington. He served in the Revolution first as part of the Minute Men militia and later in the Second Connecticut Regiment which participated in the siege of Boston.

Elizabeth Pearl and Zoeth Eldridge were parents of five children born at Willington. Zoeth's son with his second wife Bethiah Hinkley (Zoeth) married Elizabeth's niece Lois Pearl.

i ZOETH ELDRIDGE, b. 29 Jan 1772; d. 6 Sep 1780.

ii TIMOTHY ELDRIDGE, b. 8 Sep 1773; d. 3 Jul 1775.

iii ERASTUS ELDRIDGE, b. 30 Apr 1775; d. at Springfield, MA, 6 May 1820; m. at Enfield, CT, 1 Nov 1795, RUBY ALLEN, b. at Enfield, 14 May 1778 daughter of Moses and Mary (Adams) Allen; Ruby d. at Whitehall, NY, 15 Sep 1844.

iv TIMOTHY ELDRIDGE, b. 16 Feb 1777; d. likely in western New York; m. by 1804, CLARISSA HAZEN, b. at Hartford, VT, 9 Nov 1784 daughter of Solomon and Theodore (Pease) Hazen; Clarissa d. at Greenville, IL, about 1857.[2038] Timothy and Clarissa were in Hartford, Vermont for about twenty years where they had nine children.

v ELIJAH ELDRIDGE, b. 26 Dec 1778; d. at sea, 1799. He shipped from Boston on the *Pickering* 15 Feb 1799 and was never heard from again.[2039]

762) SARAH PEARL (*Dinah Holt Pearl⁴, Keturah Holt Holt³, Henry², Nicholas¹*), b. at Willington, 16 Nov 1758 daughter of Timothy and Dinah (Holt) Pearl; d. at Willington, 11 Oct 1826; m. 17 Nov 1776, SAMUEL JOHNSON, b. 1751 (based on age 92 at time of death); Samuel d. at Willington, 22 Mar 1843. Samuel is likely the son of Daniel and Keziah (Dodge) Johnson born at Lebanon, CT 10 Jun 1751.

Samuel Johnson and Sarah Pearl were parents of ten children born at Willington. Marriages were identified for just two of the children.

i DINAH JOHNSON, b. 1 May 1777

ii DAVID JOHNSON, b. 15 Jan 1779; d. 4 Jun 1785.

iii KETURAH JOHNSON, b. 8 Jan 1781

iv JOHN JOHNSON, b. 28 Nov 1782

v SAMUEL JOHNSON,[2040] b. 21 Oct 1784; d. at Medfield, MA, 28 Jan 1840; m. 1st, at Medfield, 31 Mar 1812, BETSEY FISHER; Betsey d. at Medfield, 12 Dec 1814. Samuel m. 2nd, 28 Mar 1816, CATHERINE HARTSHORN, b. at Medfield, 1 Sep 1792 daughter of Moses and Catherine (Clark) Hartshorn; Catherine d. at Medfield, 27 Dec 1860.

vi DAVID JOHNSON, b. 15 Sep 1786

vii DANIEL JOHNSON, b. 29 Sep 1788

viii SARAH JOHNSON, b. 11 Jun 1791

2036 Stewart Clan Magazine, volume 1, number 3, 1922, p 28, Stewarts of Londonderry, NH

2037 Eldredge, *Eldredge Genealogy*, p 8

2038 Hazen, *The Hazen Family in America*, p 290

2039 Eldredge, *Eldredge Genealogy*, p 9. The Eldridge genealogy suggests the Pickering was a pirate ship, but it was the USS Pickering and there is no information on the history of that ship that suggests it was a pirate ship.

2040 Tilden, *History of the Town of Medfield*, reports that Samuel Johnson was born in 1784 and came from Ashford, CT. He was a stagecoach driver. The death record of one of his children gives Samuel's place of birth as Willington.

ix IRA JOHNSON, b. 3 Nov 1794; d. at Willington, 15 Aug 1878; m. 21 Oct 1819, CYNTHIA SWIFT CUSHMAN, b. at Willington, 29 Mar 1797 daughter of Joab and Hannah (Swift) Cushman; Cynthia d. at Willington, 23 Sep 1892.

x RALPH JOHNSON, b. 27 Jun 1798; d. at Willington, 6 Oct 1826.

763) TIMOTHY PEARL (*Dinah Holt Pearl[4], Keturah Holt Holt[3], Henry[2], Nicholas[1]*), b. at Willington, 6 Jun 1760 son of Timothy and Dinah (Holt) Pearl; d. at Willington, 2 Jul 1834; m. 9 Jan 1783, LOIS CROCKER, b. 9 Dec 1763 daughter of Joseph and Anne (Fenton) Crocker; Lois d. 24 Sep 1850.

Timothy Pearl did not leave a will and his estate entered probate 15 July 1834. There was a $150 surety provided by Austin Pearl as principal and Chloe Pearl both of Willington.[2041]

Timothy Pearl and Lois Crocker were parents of five children born at Willington.

i ELIJAH CROCKER PEARL,[2042] b. 18 Jun 1783; d. at Georgetown, WV, 21 Mar 1864; m. at Willington, 6 Dec 1804, POLLY ELDRIDGE, b. at Willington, 29 Jun 1786 daughter of Zoeth and Bethiah (Hinkley) Eldridge; Polly d. at Amsterdam, NY, 23 Jun 1874.

ii LOIS PEARL, b. 23 Aug 1785; d. at Willington, 19 Sep 1807.

iii CHLOE PEARL, b. 24 Jan 1792; d. at Willington, 1 Jun 1835. Chloe did not marry.

iv ANNA PEARL, b. 24 Apr 1794; d. 1 Jan 1800.

v AUSTIN PEARL, b. 21 Aug 1798; d. at Willington, 14 Jul 1863; m. at Willington, 24 Oct 1824, SOPHRONIA ELDRIDGE, b. at Willington, 11 Dec 1799 daughter of Zoeth and Bethiah (Hinkley) Eldridge; Sophronia d. at Brookfield, MA, 6 Aug 1882.

764) PHEBE PEARL (*Dinah Holt Pearl[4], Keturah Holt Holt[3], Henry[2], Nicholas[1]*), b. at Willington, 27 Nov 1765 daughter of Timothy and Dinah (Holt) Pearl; d. at Willington, 10 Apr 1816; m. 24 Mar 1785, ZEBADIAH MARCY, b. at Woodstock, 2 Jul 1761 son of Zebadiah and Priscilla (Morris) Marcy; Zebadiah d. at Willington, 24 Sep 1851. Zebadiah married second Mary "Polly" Britt.

Phebe Pearl and Zebadiah Marcy were parents of eleven children born at Willington. Zebadiah also had several children with his second wife.

i PRISCILLA MARCY, b. 29 Nov 1786; d. at Worcester, MA, 4 Aug 1874; m. 1st, about 1808, JESSE OAKLEY. Priscilla m. 2nd, JONAS GREEN, b. in MA, about 1784; Jonas d. at Tolland, 1860.

ii ELIZABETH MARCY, b. 14 Feb 1788; m. at Willington, 1 Sep 1804, JOHN GIPSON.

iii PHEBE MARCY, b. 12 Oct 1789; d. at Webster, NY, 11 Jun 1871; m. at Willington, 28 Apr 1808, her third cousin, ALPHEUS CROCKER (*Sarah Holt Crocker[5], Abiel[4], Abiel[3], Nicholas[2], Nicholas[1]*), b. at Willington, 3 Jul 1787 son of Zebulon and Sarah (Holt) Crocker; Alpheus d. at Webster, 24 Nov 1873.

iv LOIS MARCY, b. 7 Aug 1791; d. at Franklin, IL, 20 Dec 1860; m. PETER STOLP, b. at Claverack, NY, 19 Aug 1791 son of Johannes Pieter and Catrina (Chrysler) Stolp;[2043] Peter d. at Franklin, 17 Oct 1853.

v LUCY MARCY, b. 21 Apr 1793; d. at Concord, NY, 19 Mar 1859; m. at Skaneateles, NY, 1 Jan 1816, ABIJAH SIBLEY, b. at Willington, 1 Nov 1788 son of Jonathan and Patty (Brooks) Sibley; Abijah d. at Concord, NY, 3 Jun 1856.

vi HANNAH MARCY, b. 21 Aug 1795

vii SARAH MARCY, b. 2 Sep 1797

viii THOMAS J. MARCY, b. 16 Sep 1780; d. at Coventry, CT, 16 Jul 1866; m. at Somers, 9 Dec 1824, AMELIA KIBBE, b. in CT, about 1805; Amelia d. at Coventry, 11 Sep 1866.

ix TIMOTHY MARCY, b. 6 Aug 1803; d. at Willimantic, CT, 6 Sep 1858; m. ANGELINE GAGER, b. 1805 daughter of Samuel and Fanny (Woodworth) Gager; Angeline d. at Willimantic, 5 Jun 1891.

x ZEBADIAH MARCY, b. 26 Jan 1806; d. at Riverhead, NY, 1878; m. at Willington, 5 Nov 1827, ABIGAIL STILES, b. at Willington, 7 Feb 1795 daughter of Isaac and Abigail (Case) Stiles.

[2041] *Connecticut State Library (Hartford, Connecticut);* Probate Place: *Hartford, Connecticut, Probate Packets, Kimball, N-Warren, H, 1827-1895*

[2042] *Biographical Review: This Volume Contains Biographical Sketches of Leading Citizens of Clinton and Essex Counties, New York, Part 1*, p 479, Biographical Review Publishing Company, 1896; details on Elijah's biography and business ventures can be found at this source.

[2043] Peter's date of birth is on his gravestone; findagrave: 7580071

xi LUCINDA MARCY, b. 30 Nov 1808; d. at West Haven, CT, 13 Sep 1881; m. at Hartford, 9 Jan 1825, ELIAS H. SNOW, b. in CT, about 1797; Elias d. after 1870 when he was living in New Haven.

765) MARY HOLT (*Joshua⁴, Keturah Holt Holt³, Henry², Nicholas¹*), b. at Windham, 11 Jul 1752 daughter of Joshua and Mary (Abbott) Holt; d. at Hampton, 23 Oct 1824; m. 7 Nov 1771, JOSEPH FULLER, b. at Ipswich, 1738[2044] son of John and Hannah (Lord) Fuller; Joseph d. 29 Jan 1805.

Joseph Fuller and Mary Holt were parents of seven children born at Hampton.

i MARY "POLLY" FULLER, b. 13 Oct 1772; d. at Middlefield, NY, 29 Oct 1851; m. THOMAS FULLER, b. at Windham, 21 Jul 1765 son of Thomas and Sarah (Griffin) Fuller; Thomas d. at Middlefield, 11 Jul 1837.

ii CHLOE FULLER, b. 11 Dec 1774; d. at Cooperstown, NY, 24 Aug 1854;[2045] m. 21 Nov 1803, TRUMBULL DORRANCE, b. about 1774 son of George and Alice (Trumbull) Dorrance; Trumbull d. at Dalton, MA, 9 Aug 1824.

iii ELIJAH FULLER, b. 21 Apr 1777; d. at Chenango County, NY, 30 Apr 1864; m. 5 Dec 1803, RUTH ROBINSON, b. at Tolland, CT, 10 Jan 1781 daughter of Joshua and Sybil (Webb) Robinson; Ruth d. at Chenango County, 12 Feb 1849.

iv JOSEPH FULLER, b. 6 Jan 1779; m. at Canterbury, Dec 1809, ELIZABETH FISH, b. at Canterbury, 14 Mar 1782 daughter of Darius and Sarah (Howard) Fish.

v ELISHA FULLER, b. 30 Jan 1782; d. at Hampton, 25 May 1837; m. at Hampton, 29 Oct 1805, PHEBE BURNHAM, b. 24 Apr 1788 daughter of Jedediah and Phebe (Martin) Burnham; Phebe, d. 30 Oct 1820.

vi HARVEY FULLER, b. 13 Sep 1784; d. at Hampton, 21 Apr 1860; m. 16 Dec 1810, LYDIA DENISON, b. at Hampton, 20 Jul 1789 daughter of Daniel and Lydia (Clark) Denison; Lydia d. 4 Feb 1838.

vii DANIEL FULLER, b. 14 Feb 1789; d. at Philadelphia, 12 Mar 1856; m. 1821, MARY ANN BIRD, b. at Philadelphia, 1792 daughter of William and Mary (Ross) Bird;[2046] Mary Ann d. at Philadelphia, 23 Dec 1859.

766) URIAH HOLT (*Joshua⁴, Keturah Holt Holt³, Henry², Nicholas¹*), b. at Windham, 23 Mar 1754 son of Joshua and Mary (Abbott) Holt; d. at West Springfield, MA, 22 Sep 1828; m. at Ashford, 11 Nov 1779, MARGARET MASON, b. at Ashford, 13 Aug 1754 daughter of Ebenezer and Mehitable (Holmes) Mason; Margaret d. 1817. Uriah m. 2nd, at West Springfield, 15 Oct 1818, EUNICE CHAPIN (widow of Charles Ferry), b. at Springfield, 22 Feb 1769 daughter of Elisha and Eunice (Jones) Chapin; Eunice d. at West Springfield, 1843.

Uriah and Margaret started their family in Ashford and relocated to West Springfield after the births of their first two children.

The estate of Uriah Holt was probated in 1829.[2047] Rodney Holt was administrator of the estate. The value of the estate was $230.85 and debts against the estate totaled $477.83. Widow Eunice requested relief as the value of the estate was not enough to support her in her infirm condition.

Uriah Holt and Margaret Mason were parents of seven children.

i SALLY HOLT, b. at Ashford, 18 Sep 1780; d. 9 Oct 1848; m. at Northampton, MA, 9 Apr 1803, WILLIAM SHELDON, b. at Northampton, 2 Jun 1768 son of Benjamin and Elizabeth (Hunt) Sheldon.

ii MARY "POLLY" HOLT, b. at Ashford, 2 Mar 1782; d. 1 Jun 1842; m. at West Springfield, 14 Nov 1805, ALPHEUS STEBBINS, b. at Wilbraham, 28 Jul 1780 son of Eldad and Ann (Badger) Stebbins;[2048] Alpheus d. at Wilbraham, 25 Sep 1857.

iii CLARISSA HOLT, b. at West Springfield, 11 Mar 1784; d. 4 Feb 1813. Clarissa did not marry.

iv BETSEY HOLT, b. at West Springfield, 7 May 1786; d. at Kirkland, NY, after 1865; m. 1812, as his second wife, STEPHEN BUSHNELL, b. in Connecticut, 4 Aug 1781;[2049] Stephen d. at Kirkland, 20 Jul 1862. Stephen was first married to Thankful Wilcox.

2044 Fuller, *Genealogy of Descendants of Captain Matthew Fuller*, p 216

2045 U.S., Newspaper Extractions from the Northeast, 1704-1930; Mrs. C. Dorrance wid of the late Dr. Trumbull Dorrance of Pittsfield, Mass.

2046 The 1903 SAR application of William A.M. Fuller, grandson of Daniel Fuller gives the names of his grandparents and names the parents of his grandmother Mary Ann Bird and William Bird and Mary Ross.

2047 *Probate Records, 1809-1881, Hampden County, Massachusetts;* Author: *Massachusetts. Probate Court (Hampden County);* Probate Place: *Hampden, Massachusetts*. Probate of Uriah Holt, 1829, Case number 5783.

2048 Badger, *Giles Badger and His Descendants*, p 28

2049 Stephen's date of birth is on his gravestone. Findagrave: 69227383

v RODNEY HOLT, b. at West Springfield, 18 Jun 1788; d. at Springfield, 25 Sep 1862; m. at West Springfield, 18 Apr 1822, CHLOE FOSTER, b. at Barkhamsted, CT, 15 Jan 1799 daughter of Eli and Catherine (Barker) Foster;[2050][2051] Chloe d. at Springfield, 9 Dec 1886.

vi JOHN HOLT, b. at West Springfield, 5 Dec 1792; d. at West Springfield, 21 Aug 1825; m. 16 May 1821, TAMAR LEONARD, b. at West Springfield, 2 Jan 1795 daughter of Rufus and Betsey (Flower) Leonard; Tamar d. at West Springfield, 1825.

vii PERLEY HOLT, b. at West Springfield, 21 Apr 1795; d. at New York, NY, after 1868 (listed in the city directory); m. at Simsbury, CT, 1824,[2052] LYDIA E. OWEN, b. in CT, about 1798 daughter of Isaac and Zerviah (Cornish) Owen;[2053] Lydia d. after 1860. Perley was a tobacco merchant in New York.

767) LEMUEL HOLT (*Joshua⁴, Keturah Holt Holt³, Henry², Nicholas¹*), b. at Windham, 28 Feb 1756 son of Joshua and Mary (Abbott) Holt; d. at Lyme, NH, 1 Aug 1836; m. 1778, his first cousin, MARY ABBOTT (*Isaac Abbott⁵, Elizabeth Gray Abbott⁴, Henry Gray³, Hannah Holt Gray², Nicholas¹*), b. 20 Jan 1757 daughter of Isaac and Mary (Barker) Abbott; Mary d. 8 Sep 1849.

Lemuel Holt and Mary Abbott were parents of seven children.

i LESTER HOLT, b. at Windham, CT, 27 Aug 1779; d. at Lyme, 3 May 1869; m. at Hollis, 14 Feb 1809, LYDIA FRENCH, b. at Bedford, NH, 24 May 1784 daughter of David and Lydia (Parker) French; Lydia d. at Lyme, 5 Jan 1852.

ii DOROTHY "DOLLY" HOLT, b. at Windham, 3 Oct 1781; d. at Lyme, 18 Jun 1861; m. 17 Nov 1808, NATHAN PUSHEE; Nathan, b. at Lunenburg, 5 Aug 1784 son of David and Susanna (Pierce) Pushee; Nathan d. at Lyme, 16 Dec 1810. Dolly m. 2nd, May 1824, FREEMAN JOSSELYN, b. at Pembroke, MA, 25 Aug 1778 son of Joseph and Mercy (Waterman) Josselyn; Freeman d. at Lyme, 15 Dec 1868. Freeman Josselyn was first married to Deborah Turner who died in 1822. When Nathan Pushee died, David Pushee was appointed guardian of Nathan's two daughters, Debby and Dolly.

iii DEBORAH HOLT, b. at Lyme, 3 Oct 1781; d. at Lyme, 4 May 1866. Deborah did not marry.

iv HARVEY HOLT, b. at Hanover, 27 Sep 1785; d. at Lyme, 23 Oct 1842; m. 21 Jun 1819, HANNAH CUMMINGS, b. at Cornish, NH, 4 Jun 1789 daughter of Isaac and Abigail (Kimball) Cummings; Hannah d. at Bradford, VT, 5 Mar 1885.

v ISAAC HOLT, b. at Hanover, 18 Nov 1792; d. at Piermont, NH, 4 Jun 1851; m. 1st, at Thetford, VT, 7 Mar 1822, RACHEL FLETCHER. Isaac m. 2nd, at Corinth, VT, PHEBE PAGE. Isaac m. 3rd, at Orange, VT, 10 Mar 1847, SALLY DINSMOOR.

vi MARY HOLT, b. at Lyme, 22 Oct 1795; d. at Lyme, 9 Aug 1884. Mary did not marry.

vii CHLOE HOLT, b. at Lyme, 30 Nov 1797; d. before 1860; m. 27 Nov 1825, ALBERT BALCH, b. at Lyme, 5 Sep 1802 son of Isaac and Elizabeth (Bell) Balch;[2054] Albert d. at Whitewater, WI, 8 Mar 1879. After Chloe's death, Albert went to Wisconsin and married Alice who has not been identified.

768) KETURAH HOLT (*Joshua⁴, Keturah Holt Holt³, Henry², Nicholas¹*), b. at Windham, 21 Aug 1758 daughter of Joshua and Mary (Abbott) Holt; d. at Randolph, VT, 25 Jul 1839;[2055] m. 29 Jan 1784, JONATHAN AMIDON, b. 7 Feb 1759 son of Henry and Sarah (Doubleday) Amidon; Jonathan d. at Randolph, 15 Apr 1838.

Jonathan Amidon served in the Revolutionary War with enlistments in 1777 and 1779 as a private. His war service included the battle of White Marsh and spending the winter at Valley Forge.[2056]

Jonathan Amidon did not leave a will and his estate entered probate 1 May 1838. J. K. Parish was named administrator at the request of widow Keturah Amidon. The real estate was sold for $566.00 and after the settlement of all the debts, there was $119 to be distributed to the heirs.[2057]

[2050] Chloe's parents are given as Eli and Catherine Foster on her death record.

[2051] Chapin, *Sketches of the Old Inhabitants of Old Springfield*, p 218

[2052] U.S., Newspaper Extractions from the Northeast, 1704-1930

[2053] The 1825 will of Isaac Owen in Connecticut includes a bequest to daughter Lydia wife of Perly Holt.

[2054] Balch, *Genealogy of the Balch Families*, p 138

[2055] Ancestry.com, *Vermont, Vital Records, 1720-1908* (Provo, UT, USA: Ancestry.com Operations, Inc., 2013).

[2056] Best, *Amidon Family*, p 27

[2057] *Vermont. Probate Court (Randolph District)*; Probate Place: *Orange, Vermont, Folder 45, Abbott, Benjamin-Brown, Enoch, 1832-1841*, probate of Jonathan Amidon, 1 May 1838

Jonathan Amidon and Keturah Holt were parents of eight children, the first two children born at Willington and the other children at Randolph, Vermont.

i HANNAH AMIDON, b. 28 Oct 1784; d. at Randolph, VT, after 1850; m. SAMUEL BRUCE, b. in Massachusetts, 1770 (census records); Samuel d. at Randolph, after 1850.

ii ELIJAH AMIDON, b. 1 Jul 1786; d. at Bernardston, MA, 7 Nov 1863; m. at Randolph, VT, 19 Oct 1809, REBECCA AVERILL, b. about 1793 daughter of Samuel and Molly (Barnes) Averill;[2058] Rebecca D. at Monson, MA, 30 Nov 1870.

iii ALFRED AUGUSTUS AMIDON, b. 16 May 1789; d. at Onondaga County, NY, 8 Dec 1817; m. at Barnard, VT, 1 Dec 1815, BERTHA STEVENS, b. at Barnard, about 1792 daughter of Andrew and Sarah (Clark) Stevens;[2059] Bertha d. at Barnard, 19 Apr 1837.

iv JACOB AMIDON, b. 26 Sep 1791; d. at Northfield, VT, 5 May 1866; m. 1st, 22 Apr 1816, MERCY COLE WHITTEN, b. at Cornish, NH, 31 Mar 1794 daughter of Samuel and Rebecca (-) Whitten; Mercy d. at Northfield, 9 Oct 1833. Jacob m. 2nd, 4 Dec 1834, ARMENIA RICHMOND, b. at Barnard, 4 Apr 1807 daughter of Paul and Fanny (Udall) Richmond;[2060] Armenia d. at Northfield, 22 Oct 1887.

v DYER AMIDON, b. 7 Mar 1794; d. at Richfield, MI, 26 Aug 1853; m. at Brookfield, VT, 23 Aug 1814, SABRA M. SMITH, b. 1795 daughter of Shubal and Mary (Parish) Smith; Sabra d. at Richfield, 9 Jul 1872.

vi MARY AMIDON, b. 18 Aug 1796; d. at Randolph, 18 Sep 1819.

vii SARAH AMIDON, b. about 1800; d. at Brookfield, VT, 31 Mar 1873; m. 2 Dec 1820, her second cousin, WALTER ABBOTT (*Benjamin Abbott⁶, Benjamin Abbott⁵, Elizabeth Gray Abbott⁴, Henry Gray³, Hannah Holt Gray², Nicholas¹*), b. at Brookfield, 10 Jul 1796 son of Benjamin and Lucy (Flint) Abbott; Walter d. at Brookfield, 2 Jan 1879.

viii LUCINDA AMIDON, b. 1804; d. at Moretown, VT, 3 Nov 1883; m. SOLOMON TUBBS, b. about 1800 son of Ananias Tubbs; Solomon d. at Northfield, 14 Mar 1865.

769) SARAH HOLT (*Joshua⁴, Keturah Holt Holt³, Henry², Nicholas¹*), b. at Windham, 26 Oct 1761 daughter of Joshua and Mary (Abbott) Holt; d. at Stockbridge, VT, 19 Feb 1813; m. 1783, JOHN DURKEE, b. at Windham, 2 Jul 1762 son of Joseph and Elizabeth (Fiske) Durkee; John d. at Stockbridge, 2 May 1838. After Sarah's death, John married second Polly Webber and third Jemima Strong.

John Durkee served in the Revolution in from Connecticut in Captain Robbins's company. John and his brother Eben Durkee served in the same company. His widow Jemima was granted 160 acres of bounty land related to this service.[2061]

In his will written 14 March 1838 (probate 4 July 1838), John Durkee bequeathed to beloved wife Jemima one hundred eighty-five dollars payable in one cow and in household furniture she brought to the marriage. Jemima also receives the use of one-half of the farm and buildings in Stockbridge while she is a widow. Eunice Durkee widow of son John Durkee receives five dollars in addition to what John received during his life. Son Oren Durkee receives five dollars in addition to what he has received. Daughters Sally Morgain, Polly Bloss, and Elisa Whitcomb each receive five dollars. Harriet Durkee daughter of Harvy Durkee receives five dollars in addition to what her father received from the estate. Youngest son Fisk Durkee receives one-half of the farm and will receive the whole farm after the decease of Jemima. Justin Morgain was named sole executor.[2062]

Sarah Holt and John Durkee were parents of seven children born at Stockbridge, Vermont.

i JOHN DURKEE, b. 20 Nov 1784; d. at Stockbridge, 17 Aug 1836; m. about 1807, EUNICE RANNEY, b. at Chester, VT, 12 Dec 1784 daughter of Daniel and Eunice (Gile) Ranney; Eunice d. at Elk Grove, IL, after 1850.

ii OREN DURKEE, b. 5 Nov 1786; d. at Stockbridge, 14 Oct 1862; m. at Bethel, VT, 7 Oct 1813, PHILENA RICH, b. at Bethel, 1 Apr 1791 daughter of Justus and Mary (Tufts) Rich; Philena d. 8 Mar 1849.

iii SALLY DURKEE, b. Jun 1789; d. at Stockbridge, 18 Apr 1879; m. at Rochester, VT, 25 Mar 1814, JUSTIN MORGAN, b. at West Springfield, MA, 15 Mar 1786 son of Justin and Mary (Day) Morgan; Justin d. at Stockbridge, 4 May 1853.

2058 Avery, *The Averell Family*, p 301

2059 The 1839 will of Andrew Stevens of Barnard includes bequests to grandson Alfred Amidon and granddaughter Harriet Rand.

2060 Richmond, *The Richmond Family*, p 150

2061 Revolutionary War Pension and Bounty-Land Warrant Application Files

2062 *Vermont. Probate Court (Hartford District)*; Probate Place: *Windsor, Vermont, Probate Records, Vol 12-13 1835-1840*, vol 13, pp 85-86

iv MARY DURKEE, b. 29 Mar 1791; d. at Middlesex, VT, 28 Mar 1873; m. 1811, BENJAMIN BLOSS, b. likely at Killingly, 19 Nov 1784 son of Richard and Sarah (Barrett) Bloss;[2063] Benjamin d. 23 Sep 1862.

v ELIZABETH DURKEE, b. 26 Jun 1794; d. at Claridon, OH, 21 Oct 1872; m. 1st, at Stockbridge, VT, 17 Mar 1836, JAMES WHITCOMB, b. at Hardwick, MA, 1781 son of Lot and Lydia (Nye) Whitcomb; James d. at Burton, OH, 10 Nov 1844. Elizabeth m. 2nd, about 1848, NERI WRIGHT, b. at Westminster, VT, 1 Nov 1785 son of Medad and Mary (Willard) Wright; Meri d. at Claridon, 28 Nov 1864.

vi HARVEY DURKEE, b. 21 Dec 1797; d. at Pittsfield, 28 Nov 1826; m. 22 May 1825, HARRIET GAY, b. 1804; Harriet d. at Pittsfield, 3 Dec 1835. After Harvey's death, Harriet m. Horace Rice.

vii FISK DURKEE, b. 7 May 1803; d. at Stockbridge, 13 Feb 1885; m. 20 May 1841, ABBY S. EVERETT, b. at Stockbridge, about 1820 daughter of Ebenezer and Lucy (Kinch) Everett; Abby d. at Stockbridge, 20 Feb 1896.

770) HANNAH HOLT (*Joshua⁴, Keturah Holt Holt³, Henry², Nicholas¹*), b. at Windham, 24 May 1764 daughter of Joshua and Mary (Abbott) Holt; d. (buried at North Craftsbury, VT, last resided in Westford, VT), 7 Aug 1855; m. at Clarendon, VT, 21 Jan 1788, AARON CARPENTER, b. at Rehoboth, 9 May 1763 son of Jabez and Abigail (Dyer) Carpenter; Aaron d. at Milton, VT 26 Sep 1836.[2064]

Hannah and Aaron resided in Milton, Vermont and were first members of the Congregational church when it was organized 21 September 1804.[2065]

In his will written 4 June 1836, Aaron Carpenter bequeathed to beloved wife Hannah the rents and profits on one-third part of the real estate during her life. She also has use of specified rooms in the house and cooking privileges. Daughters Patty Dorance, Hannah Brigham, and Dorcas Meers and son Harvey Carpenter receive one hundred dollars each. Daughter Sally Collins receives sixty dollars (as she already received forty) and daughters Polly Carpenter and Abigail Carpenter each receive one hundred dollars. Fifty dollars of each legacy is to be paid in cattle and a schedule is set out for the payments. Polly and Abigail will continue to have a room in the house. Son Alfred Carpenter receives the remainder of the estate and is responsible to pay the legacies. Alfred is named executor. Real estate, a 234-acre home farm, was valued at $3,252.50 and personal estate at $798.59. Claims against the estate were $121.33.[2066]

Aaron Carpenter and Hannah Holt were parents of eight children born at Milton, Vermont.

i PATTIE CARPENTER, b. 5 Nov 1788; d. at Irasburg, VT, 4 Mar 1864; m. ELISHA DORRANCE, b. about 1775; Elisha d. at Colchester, 10 Dec 1846.

ii SALLY CARPENTER, b. 21 Apr 1793; d. at Craftsbury, VT, 1885; m. about 1814, NATHAN COLLINS, b. at Ira, VT, 17 May 1792 son of Nathan and Keziah (Carpenter) Collins; Nathan d. at Craftsbury, 23 Jan 1887.

iii POLLY CARPENTER, b. 5 Mar 1797; d. at Milton, 12 May 1863. Polly did not marry. In 1850, she was living with her sister Abigail.

iv HANNAH CARPENTER, b. 1 May 1799; d. at Monroe, OH, 3 Aug 1859; m. 1st, about 1829, HIRAM BRIGHAM, b. at Milton, Nov 1800 son of Leonard and Abigail (Forbush) Brigham; Hiram d. at Croton, OH, 1838. Hannah m. 2nd, at Licking, OH, 6 May 1841, ALLEN WILLIAMS, b. in NJ, about 1803; Allen d. at Robinson, IL, after 1880. Allen was first married to Elizabeth Stadden in 1825 and third married to Emeline.

v ALFRED CARPENTER, b. 6 Jun 1801; d. at Milton, 29 Mar 1863; m. 1st, 19 Oct 1835, MARY EASTMAN, b. at Westford, VT, 12 Oct 1806 daughter of Caleb and Dorcas (Faxon) Eastman; Mary d. at Milton, 14 Sep 1841. Alfred m. 2nd, 20 Apr 1842, HANNAH FULLINGTON, b. 19 Aug 1802 daughter of Ephraim and Hannah (Patten) Fullington; Hannah d. at Milton, 24 Sep 1866.

vi HARVEY CARPENTER, b. 6 Feb 1804; d. at Hartford, OH, 31 Aug 1856; m. about 1828, ALTHEA THOMAS, b. at Colchester, VT, 9 Jan 1810; Althea d. at Hartford, OH, 1891. Althea married second David Weaver.

vii ABIGAIL CARPENTER, b. 29 Jul 1807; d. at Milton, 4 Oct 1866; m. about 1838, WARREN HOLMES, b. at Westford, VT, 1810 son of Manley and Sarah (Howe) Holmes; Warren d. at Westford, 31 Mar 1884. Warren second married Anna Eliza Tucker about 1867.

viii DORCAS CARPENTER, b. about 1810; d. at Willis, KS, 1 Jan 1892; m. about 1835, TIMOTHY VILLERY MEARS, b. at Milton, 10 Feb 1812 son of Stephen and Hannah (Crittenden) Mears; Timothy d. at Willis, 5 Jan 1892.

2063 Lovejoy, *History of Royalton*, p 690

2064 Ancestry.com, Vermont, Vital Records, 1720-1908

2065 Rann, *History of Chittenden County, Vermont*, p 653

2066 *Vermont. Probate Court (Chittenden District)*; Probate Place: *Chittenden, Vermont, Estate Files, Box 9, Files #914-941, 1813-1841*

771) DORCAS HOLT (*Joshua⁴, Keturah Holt Holt³, Henry², Nicholas¹*), b. at Windham, 30 Mar 1767 daughter of Joshua and Mary (Abbott) Holt; d. at Middlebury, VT, 1 Jul 1800; m. JOSIAH FULLER, b. 30 Oct 1764 son of David and Hannah (Fuller) Fuller; Josiah d. Potsdam, NY, 4 Dec 1835. Josiah was first married to Deliverance and third married to Olivia Moore.

Dorcas and Josiah had two children one of whom died in childhood and no further information on the second child.

i LUDOPHICUS FULLER, b. about 1797; d. at Middlebury, 11 Aug 1802.

ii MERTIA FULLER, b. at Middlebury, 4 Jul 1799; nothing further known.

772) SAMUEL HOLT (*Joshua⁴, Keturah Holt Holt³, Henry², Nicholas¹*), b. at Windham, 16 May 1771 son of Joshua and Susanna (Goodell) Holt; d. at Hampton, 22 Jun 1846; m. at Hampton, 28 Nov 1799, HANNAH BENNETT, b. at Windham, 5 Jan 1775 daughter of Isaac and Sarah (Cady) Bennett;[2067] Hannah d. at Hampton, 5 Oct 1862.

In 1860, Hannah Bennett Holt was living in Hampton with her three single daughters Anna, Mary, and Louisa. Hannah died in 1862, and two of the daughters later married. Daughter Louisa married a man about twenty years her junior. In 1870, daughter Mary was living with Louisa and her husband.

Samuel Holt and Hannah Bennett were parents of eleven children all born at Hampton. There are not records of the births for most of the children and year of birth for several children is estimated from census records and death records. Six of the children (Daniel Cady, Susanna, Samuel Bennett, Fidelia, Hannah, and Louisa) were baptized at Hampton on 15 November 1825.

i SUSANNAH HOLT, b. 22 Sep 1800; d. at Hampton, 25 Dec 1856. Susannah did not marry.

ii SARAH "SALLY" HOLT, b. 20 Nov 1801; d. at Monson, MA, 16 Nov 1861; m. about 1822, HARVEY HORTON, b. at Willington, 27 Nov 1799 son of Moses and Silence (Wilson) Horton;[2068] Harvey d. at Monson, 27 Apr 1886.

iii ANNA HOLT, b. 1803; d. at Hampton, 27 Jun 1897; m. about 1861, as his second wife, LEWIS FULLER, b. at Hampton, 20 Oct 1797 son of Benjamin and Joanna (Trowbridge) Fuller; Lewis d. at Hampton, 1 Nov 1883. Lewis was first married on 2 Dec 1819 to ELIZA HOLT (*Jacob⁶, Zebadiah⁵, Zebadiah⁴, George³, Henry², Nicholas¹*), b. at Hampton, 18 Sep 1800 daughter of Jacob and Eleanor (Hammond) Holt; Eliza d. at Hampton, 20 May 1860.

iv LESTER HOLT, b. 13 Oct 1804; d. at Hampton, 18 Jul 1880; m. 29 Mar 1829, CLARISSA JOHNSON, b. about 1806; Clarissa d. at Hampton, 16 May 1880.

v MARY HOLT, b. about 1806; d. at Hampton, 2 Nov 1879. Mary did not marry. Her estate was administered by Lester Holt.

vi SAMUEL BENNETT HOLT, b. about 1807; d. at Hampton, 29 Dec 1844; m. at Hampton, 24 May 1842, ABIGAIL WHITMORE, b. 11 Jul 1815 daughter of John and Anna (Strong) Whitmore; Abigail did not remarry and died at Hamilton, NY, 9 Apr 1907.

vii ELISHA HOLT, b. 6 Jun 1811; d. at Elba, WI, after 1870; m. about 1838, CORNELIA DUTCHER, b. in NY, about 1816 daughter of James Dutcher; Cornelia d. after 1880 when she was living at Elba.

viii FIDELIA HOLT, b. 5 May 1812; d. after 1880 when she was living in Milford, WI; m. 8 Jul 1845, ELISHA BENNETT, b. in NY, about 1802; Elisha d. at Milford, after 1870.

ix HANNAH HOLT, b. 23 Aug 1814; d. at Brooklyn, CT, 4 Feb 1892; m. 11 May 1840, PERRIN SCARBOROUGH, b. at Brooklyn, CT, 12 Sep 1808 son of Samuel and Mary (Cleveland) Scarborough; Perrin d. at Brooklyn, 26 Apr 1874.

x DANIEL CADY HOLT, b. about 1815; d. at Monson, MA, 23 Dec 1888; m. 1st SARAH GRIFFIN who has not been identified.[2069] Daniel m. 2nd at Hampton, 4 Apr 1847, SOPHIA PARSONS, b. 12 Jan 1826 daughter of Reuben and Lydia (Thurston) Parsons; Sophia d. at Monson, 8 Mar 1914.

xi LOUISA HOLT, b. about 1821; d. at Hampton, 28 Jan 1879; m. after 1860, OLIVER F. BENNETT, b. about 1837 (per census records).

773) OLIVER HOLT (*Joshua⁴, Keturah Holt Holt³, Henry², Nicholas¹*), baptized at Windham, 9 May1773 son of Joshua and Susanna (Goodell) Holt; d. at Pomfret, CT, 1 Nov 1821; m. at Eastford, 26 May 1803, SIDNEY BEDOLPH CLAPP, b. 1784 daughter of Seth and Charlotte (Borden) Clapp;[2070] Sidney d. at Pomfret, 6 Sep 1837.

Oliver Holt was a blacksmith in Pomfret.

2067 The 1817 probate of Isaac Bennett includes a distribution to Hannah Holt and spouse Samuel Holt.

2068 Harvey's parents are named as Moses and Silence on his death record.

2069 This is marriage given in Durrie's Holt genealogy; records were not located.

2070 Clapp, *The Clapp Memorial*, p 165

Oliver Holt did not leave a will and his estate entered probate 28 February with widow Sidney Holt as administratrix. Real estate consisted of a dwelling house with two and three-quarters acres valued at $450 and personal estate of $159.79. Debts were $555.84 and included $180.81 due to Charlotte Clapp secured by mortgage. The estate was declared insolvent. The widow's dower was set off to Sidney which included a portion of the house.[2071]

Oliver Holt and Sidney Clapp were parents of nine children born at Pomfret.[2072]

i CHARLES HOLT, b. about 1805; d. at Vineland, NJ, 20 Mar 1874; m. at Pomfret, 28 May 1828, NANCY INGALLS, b. at Pomfret, 23 Nov 1796 daughter of Lemuel and Dorothy (Sumner) Ingalls; Nancy d. at Pomfret, 17 Dec 1840.

ii LOUISA HOLT, b. about 1806; d. at Stockbridge, WI, 6 Apr 1871; m. at Pomfret, 26 Oct 1835, LEMUEL GOODELL, b. at Pomfret, 27 Nov 1800 son of Richard and Marcy (Parkhurst) Goodell; Lemuel d. at Stockbridge, 9 Apr 1897.

iii HIRAM HOLT, b. about 1808; d. at Stockbridge, WI, 22 Jun 1856; m. at Hanover, NH, 5 Jan 1835, ELVIRA RICHARDSON,[2073] b. in VT (according to census records), about 1808; Elvira d. at Stockbridge, 23 Mar 1857.

iv OLIVER HOLT, b. 2 Feb 1809; d. at Hartland, VT, 22 Aug 1883; m. at Woodstock, CT, 16 Mar 1835, ELIZA CLAPP BROWN, b. at Woodstock, 14 Nov 1802 daughter of Azor and Abigail (Clapp) Brown; Eliza d. after 1870.

v GEORGE W. HOLT, b. at Pomfret, 18 Apr 1811; d. at Scriba, NY, 27 Dec 1877; m. 31 May 1833, ELIZABETH WEST, b. in NY, 10 Oct 1815 daughter of Samuel and Ruth (-) West; Elizabeth d. after 1880.

vi ALBERT HOLT, b. 1813; d. at Stockbridge, WI, 6 May 1889; m. at Boone, IL, 17 Feb 1841, LAURA STORY, b. in NY, 1819; Laura d. after 1870.

vii SUSAN HOLT, b. at Pomfret, 7 May 1815; d. at Stockbridge, WI, 21 May 1892; m. 16 Sep 1837, THOMAS CRAFT CLEVELAND, b. at Hartland, VT, 5 Sep 1811 son of Thomas and Anna (Craft) Cleveland; Thomas d. at Stockbridge, Feb 1874.

viii LEMUEL HOLT, b. about 1817; living in Tehama, CA in 1866. He may have married Clarissa Davis at Jackson, MI, 4 Nov 1844.

ix JOSEPH W. HOLT, b. about 1819; d. at Saint Charles, MI, 31 Jul 1887; m. CAROLINE C. WOODRUFF, b. in NY, 12 Nov 1830 daughter of Nelson Woodruff; Caroline d. at Saint Charles, 14 Dec 1906.

774) ZILPHA HOLT (*Joshua*[4], *Keturah Holt Holt*[3], *Henry*[2], *Nicholas*[1]), b. at Windham, 2 Fen 1776 and baptized at Hampton, 28 Apr 1776 daughter of Joshua and Susanna (Goodell) Holt; d. at Stockbridge, VT, 8 Mar 1830; m. at Stockbridge, VT, 17 Mar 1808, as the third of his four wives, JONATHAN WHITNEY, b. at Willington, 20 Feb 1766 son of Peter and Marcy (Case) Whitney; Jonathan d. at Tunbridge, VT, 12 Apr 1853. Jonathan was first married to Eunice Story, second married to Dora Marsh, and fourth married to Betsey Goodell.

Jonathan Whitney was born in Connecticut and went to Vermont in 1787 originally as a surveyor. After working as a surveyor, he settled in Tunbridge about 1790. He was a schoolteacher for about eighteen years, although he had no formal education and was self-taught.[2074]

Zilpha Holt and Jonathan Whitney were parents of five children born at Tunbridge, Vermont.

i REBECCA WHITNEY, b. 25 Jun 1811; died in infancy.

ii LAURA FISKE WHITNEY, b. 24 Jul 1813; d. after 1880 when she was living at Bloomingdale, IL; m. DANIEL N. BROWN, b. in VT, about 1810; Daniel d. after 1880.

iii ROSWELL WHITNEY, b. Oct 1815; died young

iv ALBERT GALLATIN WHITNEY, b. 27 Jul 1817; d. at Tunbridge, 30 Jan 1901; m. 1st at Northfield, VT, 19 May 1844, ADELINE D.M. LEONARD, b. at Berlin, VT, 1823 daughter of John and Eliza (Lougee) Leonard; Adeline d. at Northfield, 19 Aug 1865. Albert m. 2nd at Worcester, VT, WEALTHY CONNOR, b. at Shelburne, 8 Jul 1841 daughter of Milton J. and Mary (Blair) Connor; Wealthy d. at Worcester, VT, 8 Jul 1872.

[2071] *Connecticut State Library (Hartford, Connecticut), Probate Packet, Oliver Holt, Town of Pomfret, Case 2153*

[2072] These are children as given in several published genealogies including Holton's *Winslow Memorial*. Durrie's Holt genealogy does not include son Lemuel.

[2073] Although published sources including the Cleveland genealogy give her name as Almira Cleveland or a Cleveland, the marriage transcription states Elvira Richardson, her gravestone states Elvira, and the death record for daughter Louise P. Holt Scott gives the names of parents as Hiram Holt and Elvira Richardson. Ancestry.com. *Cook County, Illinois, Deaths Index, 1878-1922* [database on-line]. Provo, UT, USA: Ancestry.com Operations, Inc., 2011.

[2074] Pierce, *Whitney: The Descendants of John Whitney*, p 206

v JAMES MONROE WHITNEY, b. 4 Nov 1820; d. at Tunbridge, 18 Oct 1905; m. at Royalton, VT, 21 May 1843, ELIZA COZZENS, b. at Bethel, VT, 1819; Eliza d. at Tunbridge, 10 Mar 1895.

775) CHLOE GOODALE (*Phebe Holt Goodale⁴, Keturah Holt Holt³, Henry², Nicholas¹*), b. at Pomfret, 28 Dec 1755 daughter of Ebenezer and Phebe (Holt) Goodale; d. at New Haven, Oct 1833;[2075] m. at Willington, 25 May 1775, her second cousin, FRANCIS FENTON (*Elizabeth Holt Fenton⁴, Abiel³, Nicholas², Nicholas¹*), b. at Willington, 13 Feb 1750/1 son of Francis and Elizabeth (Holt) Fenton.

Francis Fenton and Chloe Goodale were parents of six children born at Willington.

i ELIZABETH FENTON, b. 27 Mar 1777

ii OLIVER FENTON, b. 1 Nov 1778; d. 22 Nov 1781.

iii CHLOE FENTON, b. 20 May 1780; d. at South Windsor, CT, 19 Feb 1823; m. ELLIOT GRANT, b. at Windsor, CT, 23 Apr 1762 son of Edward and Hannah (Foster) Grant; Elliot d. at East Windsor, 7 Jun 1846.

iv CHESTER FENTON, b. 11 Mar 1782; d. 5 Mar 1783.

v PHEBE FENTON, b. 1 Sep 1783

vi LEISTER FENTON, b. 26 Jun 1786

776) RHODA GOODALE (*Phebe Holt Goodale⁴, Keturah Holt Holt³, Henry², Nicholas¹*), b. at Pomfret, 28 Feb 1758 daughter of Ebenezer and Phebe (Holt) Goodale; d. at South Windsor, CT, 17 Nov 1841; m. at Willington, JOSEPH ELDREDGE, b. at Willington, 28 Feb 1759 son of Joseph and Abigail (Smith) Eldredge;[2076] Joseph d. at Willington, 14 Dec 1830.

Rhoda and Joseph resided in Willington, and after Joseph's death, Rhoda lived in South Windsor.

On 25 December 1839, Rhoda Eldridge of East Windsor, then age eighty-two, provided a statement related to her application for a widow's pension. She related that Joseph served in the company of Capt. Jonathan Parker from 20 June 1776 to 1 January 1777. Joseph served a further two months in 1778 when he was drafted to go to New London. The master role of the company of Capt. Jonathan Parker is included in the pension packet. The pension file includes a statement made 5 December 1839 by Abigail Green, age fifty-three of Windsor, in support of the application, given her relationship with the family as "well acquainted."[2077]

Rhoda Goodale and Joseph Eldredge were parents of seven children born at Willington.[2078] A marriage is known for just one of the children.

i RHODA ELDREDGE, b. 26 Mar 1780; d. 5 Oct 1782.

ii ELIZABETH ELDREDGE, b. 23 Sep 1781

iii RHODA ELDREDGE, b. 5 May 1784

iv ABIGAIL ELDREDGE, b. 19 Sep 1786. It is *possible* that Abigail is the Abigail Green who made a statement in Rhoda's widow's pension application. If so, she married Asahel Green and she died at South Windsor in 1868.

v CALISTA ELDREDGE, b. 22 Nov 1788

vi CHESTER ELDREDGE, b. 12 Jun 1790

vii FREEMAN ELDREDGE, b. 10 Nov 1792; d. at Greenville, NY, 6 May 1861; m. at Greenville, 10 Oct 1819, LANA SCHREIBER, b. in NY, about 1800 daughter of Peter E. Schreiber; Lana d. at Greenville, 1881 (probate 2 Jul 1881).

777) SARAH GOODALE (*Phebe Holt Goodale⁴, Keturah Holt Holt³, Henry², Nicholas¹*), b. at Pomfret, 10 Jul 1760 daughter of Ebenezer and Phebe (Holt) Goodale; d. at Willington, 4 Oct 1831; m. at Willington, 8 Jan 1783, her second cousin, CALEB HOLT (*Caleb⁴, Abiel³, Nicholas², Nicholas¹*), b. at Willington, 23 Apr 1759 son of Caleb and Mary (Merrick) Holt; Caleb d. at Willington, 8 Sep 1826.

Caleb Holt was a tanner and currier, and had a large, successful farm in Willington. He owned enough land to be able to give each of his four sons a farm.[2079]

Caleb Holt and Sally Goodale had five children born at Willington.

2075 Connecticut, Deaths and Burials Index, 1650-1934

2076 Eldredge, *Eldredge Genealogy*

2077 U.S. Revolutionary War Pension and Bounty-Land Warrant Application Files, Case W17756

2078 The births of the children are provided by Rhoda Eldredge in her application for a widow's pension in the form of a page taken from the family bible.

2079 J. H. Beers, 1903, *Commemorative Biographical Record of Tolland and Windham*, volume I, p 221

i HORACE HOLT, 29 Aug 1784; d. at Norwich, 30 Jan 1863; m. his second cousin, POLLY HOLT (*James*[5], *James*[4], *Abiel*[3], *Nicholas*[2], *Nicholas*[1]), b. at Willington, 7 Sep 1798 daughter of James and Mary (Pool) Holt; Polly d. at Willington, 24 Jan 1853.

ii ROYAL HOLT, b. 2 Dec 1786; d. at Willington, 20 Feb 1864; m. at Willington, 13 Aug 1809, LOVINA LAMB, b. at Randolph, VT, 17 Jan 1791 daughter of Joseph and Darias (Marcy) Lamb; Lovina d. at Willington, 5 May 1856.

iii JOSHUA HOLT, b. 17 Apr 1782; d. at Willington, 8 Nov 1834; m. 27 Oct 1831, DALUKA LEONARD, of Ashford, b. about 1806; Daluka d. at Willington, 17 Mar 1885.

iv RALPH HOLT, b. 10 Oct 1794; d. at Willington, 22 Feb 1873; m. 1819, SALLY RIDER, b. at Willington, 18 Nov 1796 daughter of Joseph and Ruanna (-) Rider; Sally d. at Willington, 26 Jun 1868.

v JULIANNA HOLT, b. 25 Apr 1796; d. at Willington, 4 Nov 1862; m. 2 Nov 1823, as his second wife, ROBERT SHARP, b. about 1791 likely the son of Solomon and Rebecca (Perkins) Sharp; Robert d. at Willington, 1 Nov 1874. Robert was first married to CELINDA HOLT (*James*[5], *James*[4], *Abiel*[3], *Nicholas*[2], *Nicholas*[1]), b. at Willington, 16 Jan 1796 daughter of James and Mary (Pool) Holt; Celinda d. at Willington, 20 May 1823.

778) CHESTER GOODALE (*Phebe Holt Goodale*[4], *Keturah Holt Holt*[3], *Henry*[2], *Nicholas*[1]), b. at Pomfret, 3 Sep 1762 son of Ebenezer and Phebe (Holt) Goodale; d. at Egremont, MA, 29 Jan 1835; m. at Richmond, MA, 10 Jul 1790, ASENATH COOK, b. at Goshen, CT, 11 Oct 1769 daughter of Walter and Ruhamah (Collins) Cook;[2080] Asenath d. at Egremont, 7 May 1858.

On 15 August 1832, Chester Goodale, then age sixty-nine and resident of Egremont, made a statement related to his application for pension. While living in Willington, he enlisted in July 1777 as a substitute for Ebenezer Goodale. He was in the company of Capt. Jedediah Amidown in Col. Root's regiment, and they marched to New London where he was stationed. Later in the same year, he enlisted as a substitute for a Cushman and was stationed at a place called Sandy Beach. He had a further enlistment from 1 April 1780 to 1 January 1781 in the company of Capt. Joshua Bottom. At that enlistment, he was at Peekskill and Horse Neck and was in the battle in November 1780 at Horse Neck. In 1781, he did two months as a substitute for James Holt of Willington. He further stated that he was born in Pomfret in 1762 and that he lived in Willington until he went into service. On 12 January 1839, widow Asenath Goodale made a statement related to her widow's pension. She stated that after their marriage, she and Chester resided at Stockbridge, Becket, Great Barrington, and Egremont. Son Chester Goodale provided a statement on 12 February 1839.[2081]

Son Samuel Goodale graduated from Union College in 1836 and obtained his master's degree in 1839. He obtained his doctorate from Union Theological Seminary in 1839 giving the commencement address and was a member of Phi Beta Kappa. He was a professor of natural science at Nebraska College and was throughout his career an Episcopal minister. He was chaplain of the Nebraska Senate from 1871-1872. He was a founding member of Psi Upsilon fraternity.[2082]

Chester and Asenath were parents of five children.[2083]

i CHESTER GOODALE, b. 24 Apr 1791; d. at Egremont, MA, 31 Jan 1884; m. at Sheffield, MA, 9 May 1821, SOPHIA BUSHNEL, b. at Sheffield, 1800 daughter of Samuel and Lucretia (Hubbard) Bushnel; Sophia d. at Egremont, 3 Jun 1871.

ii LAURA GOODALE, b. at New Salem, MA, 12 Mar 1793; d. at Egremont, 4 Feb 1855; m. at Richmond, MA, 17 Nov 1811, STEPHEN HADLEY, b. at Gardner, MA, 14 Nov 1785 son of Joseph and Naomi (Pierce) Hadley; Stephen d. at Egremont, 30 Jan 1869.

iii ASENATH GOODALE, b. 24 May 1795

iv PHEBE GOODALE, b. at West Stockbridge, MA, 15 Jul 1804; d. at Egremont, MA, 28 Jun 1860; m. ALFORD C. BELL, b. 1808; Alford d. at Ballston, NY, 1 Apr 1851.

v SAMUEL GOODALE, b. 23 Dec 1813; d. at Columbus, NE, 8 Dec 1898; m. 1st 1843, REBECCA KIMBALL, b. about 1827; Rebecca d. at Kalamazoo, MI, 9 Dec 1850. Samuel m. 2nd at Wilbraham, MA, 6 Aug 1852, ROXANNA STARKWEATHER MERRICK, b. at Wilbraham, 16 Mar 1826 daughter of Samuel F. and Mary (Starkweather) Merrick; Roxanna d. at Columbus, 2 Apr 1918.

779) LOIS GOODALE (*Phebe Holt Goodale*[4], *Keturah Holt Holt*[3], *Henry*[2], *Nicholas*[1]), b. at Pomfret, 31 Jul 1764 daughter of Ebenezer and Phebe (Holt) Goodale; d. at Willington, 20 May 1842; m. at Willington, 6 Feb 1783, her second cousin, NATHAN

2080 Hibbard, *A History of the Town of Goshen*, p 450

2081 U. S. Revolutionary War Pension and Bounty-Land Warrant Application Files, Case W19522

2082 Psi Upsilon Fraternity, *The Twelfth Annual Catalogue of the Psi Upsilon Fraternity*, p 2

2083 Daughter Laura completed a sampler with the family births. This sampler was included in the pension application file, but the original sampler has been removed from the file and is now held in the National Archives. A facsimile of the sampler is in the pension packet.

HOLT (*Nathan[4], Abiel[3], Nicholas[2], Nicholas[1]*), b. at Windham, 29 Aug 1761 son of Nathan and Abigail (Merrick) Holt; Nathan d. at Willington, 5 Sep 1820.

Nathan Holt and Lois Goodale were parents of seven children all born at Willington.

i LOIS HOLT, b. 9 May 1784; d. 20 Feb 1821; m. about 1806, ASA CURTIS, b. 1785 *likely* the son of Ransom and Alice (Whitten) Curtis; Asa was living in Black Hawk, IL in 1860.

ii ASENATH HOLT, b. 26 Jan 1786; d. at Willington, 13 Feb 1813; m. 29 Dec 1809, LEONARD HOLT (*Isaac[4], Abiel[3], Nicholas[2], Nicholas[1]*), b. at Willington, 15 Feb 1782 son of Isaac and Sarah (Orcutt) Holt; Leonard d. at Willington, 12 Mar 1857. Leonard m. 2nd, about 1813, JOANNA ALDEN, b. at Stafford, 14 Jul 1782 daughter of Elisha and Irene (Markham) Alden; Joanna d. at Willington, 30 Sep 1849. Asenath Holt and Leonard Holt are Family 877.

iii CONSTANT HOLT, b. 11 Dec 1787; d. at Webster, NY, 15 Nov 1835; m. 1st, 9 Apr 1812, SALLY DART, b. at Manchester, CT, 1789 daughter of Joseph and Sybil (Loomis) Dart; Sally d. 8 Oct 1813. Constant m. 2nd, 13 Feb 1815, Sally's sister SYBIL DART, b. 1787; Sybil d. 12 Aug 1822. Constant m. 3rd, at Willington, 2 Feb 1823, POLLY SIBLEY, b. at Willington, 26 Mar 1781 daughter of Jonathan and Patty (Brooks) Sibley; Polly d. at Penfield, NY, 17 Dec 1858. Polly Sibley married second David Baker 24 Oct 1841.

iv BATHSHEBA HOLT, b. 13 Feb 1792; d. at Willington, 25 Sep 1880. Bathsheba did not marry.

v PHEBE HOLT, b. 12 Aug 1795; d. at Jewett City, 5 Dec 1844; m. 28 Dec 1814, STEPHEN BARROWS, b. 24 Nov 1789 son of Isaac and Rebecca (Turner) Barrows; Stephen d. at Jewett City, 28 Feb 1878. Stephen married second Hannah Hazard.

vi EBENEZER GOODALE HOLT, b. 24 Jul 1798; d. at Auburn, NY, 17 Oct 1835; m. about 1822, ANN F. WHITE, b. in NY, about 1805 daughter of Jonas White; Anna d. after 1850.

vii MARILDA HOLT, b. 19 Nov 1802; d. at Willington, 31 Mar 1868; m. at Hartford, 27 Oct 1844, RICHARD SALE, b. about 1800; Richard d. at Willington, 1856 (probate 21 Jun 1856). Richard and Marilda lived in Brooklyn, NY although they seem to have been in Willington at the time of Richard's death as his will and probate are in Connecticut. They did not have children.

780) WALTER GOODALE (*Phebe Holt Goodale[4], Keturah Holt Holt[3], Henry[2], Nicholas[1]*), b. at Pomfret, 6 Apr 1766 son of Ebenezer and Phebe (Holt) Goodale; d. at South Windsor, 20 Jul 1820; m. about 1787, SABRA BISSELL (widow of John Loomis), b. at Windsor, 25 May 1763 daughter of Hezekiah and Sabra (Trumbull) Bissell; Sabra d. at East Windsor, 17 Nov 1834.

Sabra Bissell had two daughters with her first husband John Loomis, both of whom married Nicholas Holt descendants. Sabra Loomis married Elijah Cady (*Nahum Cady[5], Hannah Abbott Cady[4], Jemima Johnson[3], Mary Holt Johnson[2], Nicholas[1]*) son of Nahum and Mary (Fitch) Cady. Lucinda Loomis married Simon Cady (*Amos Cady[5], Hannah Abbott Cady[4], Jemima Johnson[3], Mary Holt Johnson[2], Nicholas[1]*) son of Amos and Hannah (Kingsbury) Cady.

Walter Goodale did not leave a will and his estate entered probate 27 October 1820 with Walter Goodale as administrator and John L. Goodale providing surety for the bond. Inventory was made 2 November 1820 with personal estate valued at $489.99 which included $178 in the form of shocks of rye, hay stalks, corn, and flour. Debts were $504.13.[2084]

There are four children known for Walter Goodale and Sabra Bissell likely born at South Windsor.

i JOHN L. GOODALE, b. about 1788; d. between 1840 and 1850;[2085] m. 1st at East Hartford, 1 May 1822, BETSEY TREAT, b. about 1798 daughter of Thomas and Jemima (Calkins) Treat; Betsey d. at East Windsor, 1824. John m. second, at East Windsor, 1 Jan 1828, HANNAH LOOMIS, b. 1800 daughter of Gideon and Margaret (Witherhill) Loomis; Hannah d. at South Windsor, 28 May 1867. John does not seem to have had children.

ii NANCY GOODALE, b. about 1790; d. at Manchester, CT, 20 Jul 1880; m. WHITING RISLEY, baptized at East Hartford, 13 Aug 1786 son of Nehemiah and Mary (Beaumont) Risley; Whiting d. at Manchester, 8 Aug 1853.

iii WALTER GOODALE, b. about 1794; d. at South Windsor, 7 Oct 1835; m. about 1823 LAURA who is likely LAURA AVERY, b. 20 Oct 1793 daughter of Amos and Abigail (Loomis) Avery; Laura d. at Bloomfield, CT, 13 Mar 1886. Laura was the widow at the probate of Walter's estate. At the time of the estate distribution in 1847, she was Laura "now wife of Alexander Hills" and she received one-third for the dower and the other two-thirds of the estate was distributed to Walter A. Goodale.[2086] Laura married Alexander Hills in 1842, but by 1850 he was

---

2084 *Connecticut State Library (Hartford, Connecticut), East Windsor Probate District, Estate of Walter Goodale of East Windsor, Case 1309*

2085 John L. Goodale is on the 1840 census at East Windsor with household of one male 40-49 and one female 40-49. His wife is on the 1850 census but not John.

2086 *Connecticut State Library (Hartford, Connecticut)*; Probate Place: *Hartford, Connecticut, East Windsor Probate District, Estate of Walter Goodale, 1835, Case 1310*

out of the picture and Laura was using the name Laura Goodale and living with Walter A. and his wife Esther in Manchester, Connecticut.

iv RALPH T. GOODALE, b. about 1802; d. at East Windsor, 29 Apr 1834; m. at East Windsor, 28 Nov 1828, MARY E. SKINNER, b. about 1806; Mary d. at Manchester, CT, 8 Aug 1875. Mary married second Martin Risley on 16 Nov 1836.

781) WILLARD GOODALE (*Phebe Holt Goodale⁴, Keturah Holt Holt³, Henry², Nicholas¹*), b. at Pomfret, 8 Mar 1768 son of Ebenezer and Phebe (Holt) Goodale; d. at Perry, NY, 11 Nov 1858; m. MARY ANN MCLEAN, b. 1772; Mary Ann d. at Perry, 2 Oct 1752.

Willard and Mary Ann were parents of five children.

i HORACE GOODALE, b. 1800; d. at Perry, NY, about 1837 (probate 9 Jun 1837). Horace does not seem to have married and his father Willard was administrator of his estate.

ii HECTOR MCLEAN GOODALE, b. 1801; d. of consumption, at Perry, NY, Jan 1850;[2087] m. ELIZA SILVER, b. in VT, 1803; Eliza d. at Perry, 1877.[2088]

iii LAURA GOODALE, b. Aug 1804; d. at Decatur, IL, 20 Mar 1868; m. Dec 1826, ADMIRAL ROE, b. at Seneca, NY, 25 Nov 1800 son of Thomas Roe;[2089] Admiral d. after 1880 when he was living in Oshkosh, WI.

iv WILLIAM GOODALE, b. at East Windsor, CT, 16 Sep 1806; d. at Perry, NY, 29 Apr 1843; m. LUCINDA GIBBS, b. at Triangle, NY, 19 Mar 1807. LUCINDA GIBBS, b. 1807; Lucinda d. at Rochester, NY, 7 Sep 1889.[2090]

v GEORGE WILLARD GOODALE, b. 1808; d. at Perry, NY, 13 Feb 1890; m. SALLY SILVER, b. in VT, about 1816 daughter of Levi and Susannah (Nichols) Silver; Sally d. at Perry, 26 Nov 1897.

782) PHEBE GOODALE (*Phebe Holt Goodale⁴, Keturah Holt Holt³, Henry², Nicholas¹*), b. at Willington, 29 Aug 1775 daughter of Ebenezer and Phebe (Holt) Goodale; d. at South Windsor, 6 Nov 1856; m. as his third wife, GUSTAVUS GRANT, b at East Windsor, 1759 son of Samuel Rockwell and Mabel (Loomis) Grant;[2091] Gustavus d. at South Windsor, 11 Mar 1841. Gustavus was first married to Lucina Grant and second married to Electa Goodwin.

Gustavus Grant was a farmer and innkeeper in Windsor. He also served civic duties as selectman, constable and sheriff.[2092]

In his will written 17 October 1836, Gustavus Grant bequeathed to beloved wife Phebe the use of part of the dwelling house, all the household furniture, and three acres of woodland. After Phebe's decease, the land is to go to son Lucius. Son Marvin receives two plots of land that adjoin Marvin's land. Grandson Sheldon Grant also receives a land bequest as does son Randolph. Sons Frank, William, Willis, and Lucius also receive land bequests. The sons are responsible to pay money legacies to the daughters: Electa Johnson, Marilda Hosmer, Roxey Noble, Lucina, and Phebe Grant. Frank Grant was named executor.

Phebe Goodale and Gustavus Grant were parents of eleven children born at East Windsor. Gustavus also had five children with his wife Lucina Grant.[2093]

i ELECTA GRANT, b. 28 Feb 1800; d. at South Windsor, 3 Apr 1839; m. at East Windsor, 15 Oct 1820, HENRY JOHNSON, b. 2 Jul 1791 son of John and Olive (Morgan) Johnson;[2094] Henry d. at South Windsor, 27 Nov 1878. Henry was second married to Phebe Barber on 5 Nov 1840.

ii MARILDA GRANT, b. 16 Mar 1801; d. at Hartford, 29 Mar 1882; m. at East Windsor, 21 Jul 1820, HORACE HOSMER, b. at East Windsor, 8 Sep 1794 son of Joseph and Miriam (Newbury) Hosmer; Horace d. at East Windsor, 12 Sep 1860.

iii MARVIN GRANT, b. 27 Sep 1802; d. at South Windsor, 2 Sep 1867; m. ABIGAIL BELCHER, b. at East Windsor, 12 Apr 1807 daughter of Elijah Dean and Beersheba (Hosmer) Belcher; Abigail d. at South Windsor, 3 Mar 1889.

iv FRANK GRANT, b. 19 Jan 1804; d. at South Windsor, Apr 1880; m. 5 Jan 1842, ELECTA MCLEAN, b. at Glastonbury, 12 Dec 1816 daughter of James and Ruth (Hollister) McLean' Electa d. at South Windsor, 1885..

2087 New York, U.S. Census Mortality Schedules, 1850-1880

2088 Burial at Prospect Hill Cemetery, Perry Center, findagrave ID: 64554328

2089 Torrey, *David Roe of Flushing, NY and Some of His Descendants*

2090 New York Department of Health; Albany, NY; *NY State Death Index, Year 1889*

2091 Cutter, *New England Families, Genealogical and Memorial*, volume 3, p 1304

2092 Grant, *The Grant Family*, p 48

2093 Stiles, *Families of Ancient Windsor*, p 330

2094 The names of Henry's parents and his date of birth are given on his death record.

v GUSTAVUS GRANT, b. 4 Mar 1805; d. at Wapping, CT, 12 Jul 1867. Gustavus did not marry. In 1850, he was living with his mother Phebe.

vi ROXY GRANT, b. 11 Jan 1807; d. at Pittsfield, MA, 18 Nov 1869; m. at East Windsor, 29 Mar 1834, WILLIAM NOBLE, b. at Washington, MA, 23 Sep 1804 son of William and Mary (Smith) Noble;[2095] William d. at Pittsfield, 18 Aug 1868.

vii RANDOLPH GRANT, b. 26 Aug 1808; d. at South Windsor, 3 May 1885; m. at East Windsor, 6 Jan 1835, his first cousin once removed, NANCY GRANT (*Chloe Fenton Grant⁶, Francis Fenton⁵, Elizabeth Holt Fenton⁴, Abiel³, Nicholas², Nicholas¹*), b. 11 May 1811 daughter of Elliot and Chloe (Fenton) Grant; Nancy d. at Wapping, CT, 28 Mar 1886.

viii LUCIUS GRANT, b. 18 Sep 1810; d. at South Windsor, 1 Sep 1846; m. at East Windsor, 22 Nov 1838, MARY FOSTER, b. Dec 1816 daughter of Abel and Irena (Olcott) Foster; Mary d. after 1900 when she was living in Hartford.

ix LUCINA GRANT, b. 11 Jan 1813; d. at South Windsor, 19 Nov 1884; m. at East Windsor, 6 Jan 1835, her first cousin once removed, HORACE GRANT (*Chloe Fenton Grant⁶, Francis Fenton⁵, Elizabeth Holt Fenton⁴, Abiel³, Nicholas², Nicholas¹*), b. about 1807 son of Elliot and Chloe (Fenton) Grant; Horace d. at South Windsor, 15 Mar 1851.

x PHEBE GRANT, b. 16 Jul 1814; m. OTIS BUCKINGHAM of Coventry.[2096] Records were not located for this couple.

xi WEALTHY GRANT, b. 8 Feb 1816; d. at Hartford, 6 Nov 1899; m. at East Windsor, 21 Jun 1844, WILLIAM SMITH SIMMONS, b. 24 Sep 1813 son of William Smith and Nancy (Sherman) Simmons; William d. at Hartford, 4 Jan 1867.

783) FIFIELD HOLT (*Fifield⁴, Humphrey³, Henry², Nicholas¹*), b. at Andover, 29 Oct 1744 son of Fifield and Abigail (Taylor) Holt; d. at Hollis, 6 Apr 1819; m. ANNA LAKIN, b. at Groton, MA, 16 Jan 1746 daughter of Robinson and Hannah (Dodge) Lakin; Anna d. at Hollis, 29 Jun 1811.

Fifield Holt and Anna Lakin were parents of seven children born at Wilton.

i NATHAN TAYLOR HOLT, b. 2 Aug 1773; d. 12 Nov 1774.

ii NATHAN TAYLOR HOLT, b. 23 Feb 1775; d. at Hollis, after 1855; m. at Hollis, 12 May 1799, SYBIL PHELPS, b. at Amherst, NH, 30 Nov 1777 daughter of John C. and Mary (Lakin) Phelps; Sybil d. at Hollis, 24 Nov 1857.

iii FIFIELD HOLT, b. 17 Nov 1776; died young

iv EDMOND HOLT, b. 7 Mar 1778

v BETSEY HOLT, b. 19 Nov 1780; d. at Hollis, 12 Jul 1798.

vi POLLY HOLT, b. 3 Aug 1782; m. at Hollis, 9 Jan 1805, THOMAS RICHARDSON.

vii FIFIELD HOLT, b. 27 Mar 1784; d. at Bloomfield, ME, 1830; m. at Westmoreland, NH, 10 Jul 1814, GRATIA BURT, b. at Westmoreland, 16 Jan 1786 daughter of Joseph and Ruth (*Warner* Howe) Burt; Gratia d. at New Sharon, ME, 14 Feb 1874. Rev. Fifield Holt graduated from Middlebury College in 1810 and attended Andover Theological Seminary.[2097]

784) WILLIAM HOLT (*William⁴, Humphrey³, Henry², Nicholas¹*), b. at Lunenburg, 16 Feb 1744 son of William and Mary (Martin) Holt; d. at New Salem, MA, 7 Jan 1805; m. at Lunenburg, 2 Mar 1769, HANNAH PIKE, b. at Newbury, 17 Sep 1748 daughter of Thomas and Lois (Perley) Pike.

William Holt and Hannah Pike were parents of nine children. Cunningham's History of Lunenburg reports the oldest child was born in Lunenburg, but the others were born in Royalston, Vermont.[2098] William returned to Massachusetts to New Salem where he died. Sons William and Thomas both died during the War of 1812.

2095 The names of William's parents are given as William and Mary on his death record. Also, History and Genealogy of the Family of Thomas Noble, p 538

2096 Stiles, *Families of Ancient Windsor*

2097 Hanson, *History of the Old Towns, Norridgewock and Canaan*, p 289

2098 Cunningham, *Cunningham's History of the Town of Lunenburg*, E-H, p 417

i WILLIAM HOLT, b. 2 Oct 1769; d. about 1813 during the War of 1812; m. about 1804, ELIZABETH "BETSEY" COLLOCH[2099] who has not been identified. On 5 Feb 1823, Betsey Holt of Northfield, MA was named guardian for son William Holt then under age fourteen. Son William was "only heir of William Holt, who was a soldier in the late war with Great Britain, and was killed in said service, late of Massena in the state of New York." On 20 Dec 1825, William Holt then over age fourteen made choice of Jonathan Robbins of Northfield as his guardian.

ii MOSES PIKE HOLT, b. 24 Apr 1771, d. at Hartford, CT, 11 Mar 1826; m. at Enfield, 23 Apr 1806, HANNAH CHAFFEE, b. about 1780 daughter of William and Mary (Whipple) Chaffe.

iii HANNAH HOLT, b. 8 Jul 1773; d. at Deerfield, MA, 19 Aug 1861. Hannah did not marry.

iv PARLEY HOLT, b. 15 Jul 1776; d. at Derby, VT, Sep 1827; m. at Derby, 3 Apr 1806, HANNAH SARGENT, b. about 1777; Hannah d. at Derby, 14 May 1829.

v SARAH HOLT, b. 10 Feb 1779; d. at Crete, IL, 24 Apr 1853; m. at Montague, 18 Nov 1809, QUARTUS MARSH, b. at Montague, 17 Aug 1782 son of Jonathan and Freedom (Taylor) Marsh; Quartus d. at Crete, Jan 1850.

vi SAMUEL HOLT, b. 15 Apr 1781; d. at New Salem, MA, 15 Mar 1845; m. 1st at Waltham, 15 Aug 1813, LUCY SHED, b. at Medford, 21 Jul 1776 daughter of Zacharias and Lydia (Spring) Shed; Lucy d. at New Salem, 28 Oct 1824. Samuel m. 2nd at New Salem, 17 Oct 1825, MARY "POLLY" WINSHIP (who may have been a widow), b. about 1783 and d. at New Salem, 10 Oct 1864. Samuel did not have children. In his will, in addition to bequests for his wife, there was a bequest for his nephew Horatio Nelson Marsh son of Quartus and Sally Marsh. Samuel served in the War of 1812.

vii MARY HOLT, b. 26 Oct 1783; d. at Templeton, MA, 1 Feb 1869; m. at Winchendon, 23 Aug 1807, JAMES DYER, b. 1776; James d. at Templeton, 2 Jan 1866.

viii THOMAS HOLT, b. 31 Aug 1785; died in the War of 1812.

ix LOIS HOLT, b. 6 Feb 1788; d. at Deerfield, MA, 16 Dec 1873; m. 12 Jan 1818, STEPHEN SMITH, b. at Deerfield, 5 Aug 1790 son of Abner and Sybil (Rose) Smith; Stephen d. at Deerfield, 29 Jan 1877.

785) DAVID HOLT (*William[4], Humphrey[3], Henry[2], Nicholas[1]*), b. at Lunenburg, 26 Sep 1746 son of William and Mary (Martin) Holt; d. at New Salem, 1792; m. at Lancaster, 30 Oct 1770, HANNAH KENDALL, b. at Lancaster, 10 Dec 1747 daughter of Ebenezer and Hannah (Thompson) Kendall.

In his will written 5 Aug 1792 (probate 6 November 1792), David Holt bequeathed to true and loving wife Hannah the use of one-third of the real estate during her natural life specifying that this was one-third as it is now before deductions for debts and charges. The remainder of the estate was left to his six children Hannah Turner, Jain Holt, David Holt, Azubah Holt, Lydia Holt, and Kendall Holt specifying that the sons would receive one-quarter more than the daughters. Real estate was valued at £175. The widow's dower was set off the Hannah on 5 April 1793. The final settlement was 16 January 1794 with the distribution of the remaining £30.7.5 after the deduction of the widow's allowance, debts, and expenses to the six children of the deceased: Hannah Tuner, Janie Holt, Azubah Holt, Lydia Holt, the legal heirs of David Holt who died since his father, and Kendall Holt.[2100]

David Holt and Hannah Kendall were parents of six children born at New Salem, Massachusetts.

i HANNAH HOLT, b. about 1772; d. 22 Dec 1845; m. at New Salem, 31 Aug 1791, ZADOCK TURNER, b. about 1762 son of Micah and Mary (Eaton) Turner; Zadock d. at Northfield, MA, 11 Feb 1828. Zadock served in the Revolution for which service he received a pension, and later Hannah a widow's pension.

ii DAVID HOLT, b. 26 Aug 1776; drowned at South Hadley Falls, 15 Jul 1793.

iii JANE HOLT, b. 1778; d. about 1799; m. at New Salem, 10 Mar 1796, JONATHAN MORTON, b. 1765 son of Benjamin and Mary (Dexter) Morton;[2101] Jonathan d. at Annsville, NY, 8 Mar 1853. Jonathan married second Esther Bennett in 1800.

iv AZUBA HOLT, b. 27 May 1779; d. after 1850 when she was living at Warwick, MA; m. 1st at Northfield, 1818, SAMUEL BARNS who died shortly after the marriage. Azuba m. 2nd 7 Dec 1829 (intention at Montague), DANIEL WHITTEMORE (or Whitmore), b. in CT about 1775; Daniel d. at Warwick, 17 Dec 1854.

2099 This is the name given in Durrie's Holt genealogy

2100 *Hampshire County, MA: Probate File Papers, 1660-1889.* Online database. *AmericanAncestors.org.* New England Historic Genealogical Society, 2016, 2017. Case 73-23

2101 Warden and Dexter, *Genealogy of the Dexter Family in America*, p 53

v LYDIA HOLT, b. 4 Aug 1781; d. at Wendell, MA, 28 Aug 1863; m. 7 Mar 1811, BENJAMIN DAVIS, b. at Lebanon, CT, 1 Nov 1769 son of Daniel and Abigail (Bridges) Davis;[2102] Benjamin d. at Orange, MA, 27 Aug 1851.

vi KENDALL HOLT, b. 7 Aug 1784; d. at Cambridge, 27 Jan 1826; m. at Cambridge, 2 Jan 1806, SARAH "SALLY" SMITH, b. at Cambridge, about 1788; Sally d. at Cambridge at the almshouse, 12 Feb 1870. Sally married second John Ellison in Jan 1828 at Cambridge.

786) JONATHAN HOLT (*William[4], Humphrey[3], Henry[2], Nicholas[1]*), b. at Lunenburg, 22 Jan 1748 son of William and Mary (Martin) Holt; d. at New Salem, MA, 22 Sep 1831; m. at New Salem, 12 Dec 1772, MARIA WHEELER, baptized at New Salem, 28 Oct 1750 daughter of Samuel and Ruth (Wheeler) Wheeler; Maria d. at New Salem, 29 Mar 1813.

Jonathan Holt was a cooper by trade and served 64 days in the War of 1812. The family lived in New Salem.[2103] Jonathan Holt and Maria Wheeler were parents of six children born at New Salem.

i MARY "POLLY" HOLT, b. about 1774; d. at Jamaica, VT, 13 May 1829; m. at New Salem, 15 Mar 1798, PETER CHASE, b. at Petersham, MA, 24 Feb 1770 son of Henry and Abigail (Stratton) Chase; Peter d. at Jamaica, 18 Aug 1851.

ii MARTIN HOLT, b. 4 Mar 1778; d. at Lykens, OH, 5 Aug 1848; m. MARGARET SLOAN, b. 1788 daughter of William and Sarah (Nelson) Sloan; Margaret d. at Lykens, 28 Nov 1865. Martin and Margaret were in western New York, but around 1836 they located in Lykens, OH where their son Nelson Holt settled in 1836.[2104]

iii DANIEL HOLT, b. 7 Apr 1782; d. 2 Apr 1800.

iv SAMUEL HOLT, b. 9 Jun 1785; d. at New Salem, 16 Apr 1851; m. at New Salem, 13 Feb 1814, SARAH ROSS, b. at Templeton, 11 Feb 1783 daughter of Roger and Hannah (Robinson) Ross; Sarah d. at New Salem, 19 Jul 1857. Sarah married second Thomas Hatstat in 1855.

v SARAH HOLT, b. 9 Jun 1785; m. at New Salem, 25 Jun 1809, AARON HAGAR, b. 1789 son of Aaron and Rachel (Stone) Hagar; Aaron d. at New Salem, 11 May 1822.

vi EBENEZER HOLT, b. about 1787; d. at Athol, MA, 3 Jul 1835; m. at New Salem, 18 Oct 1813, ARETHUSA HAGAR, b. at New Salem, about 1794 daughter of Aaron and Rachel (Stone0 Hagar; Arethusa d. at Athol, 2 Apr 1883.

787) HUMPHREY HOLT (*William[4], Humphrey[3], Henry[2], Nicholas[1]*), b. at Lunenburg, 1 Jan 1750 son of William and Mary (Martin) Holt; m. likely EDITH CHASE, b. at Sutton, MA, 27 Aug 1753 daughter of Ambrose and Thankful (Robbins) Chase.

The movements of this family are unclear, partially related to record loss.[2105] The family is thought to have been in New Salem, Massachusetts where the children were born and then moved on to New Hampshire. Humphrey may have died in Middlesex, Vermont in 1808 with probate administered by son Amos Holt. The name Noah is also given on one of the folders of the probate.[2106] The names of children as given in Cunningham's History of Lunenburg are given here (Noah, Susannah, Amos, Humphrey, Rhoda, and Edith). The names of Noah and Amos turn up in records related to Middlesex, Vermont, and it may be that those sons belong to this family. Records related to children Humphrey and Rhoda are found in Barre. This is supported by other secondary information.[2107] What is given here should be considered speculative.

i NOAH HOLT, b. 11 Aug 1779 (birth date given on death record); d. at East Calais, VT, 22 Jun 1844; m. about 1802, ROSANNAH AINSWORTH, b. at Calais, about 1785 daughter of Moses and Margaret (McKnowland) Ainsworth; Rosannah d. 19 Dec 1870.[2108]

ii SUSANNAH HOLT. There is a Susan Holt that married William Bridge in 1812 at Woodstock, Vermont.

iii AMOS HOLT, b. at New Salem, 31 Oct 1783; d. at Moretown, VT, 13 Feb 1853; m. at Barre, VT, 1 Jan 1805, HOPY HOWLAND, b. about 1787 daughter of Abraham and Mary (White) Howland; Hopy d. at Middlesex, VT, 12 Dec 1881.[2109]

[2102] Stoughton, *History of the Town of Gill*, volumes 3 and 4, published by the Holbrook Research Institute, 1987

[2103] Cunningham, *Cunningham's History of the Town of Lunenburg*, E-H, p 419

[2104] Baskin & Beatty, *History of Crawford County and Ohio*

[2105] Cunningham, *History of the Town of Lunenburg*, E-H, p 419

[2106] Vermont Probate Files, 1800-1921, Chittenden County, Holt, Humphrey (1808, Box 2 File 192); accessed through familysearch.org

[2107] For example, The Gazetteer of Washington County, Vermont, 1783-1889, Part First, p 403 reports that Amos Holt came to Montpelier with his father Humphrey from New Hampshire at an early date.

[2108] Parker, *Genealogy of the Ainsworth Families in America*, p 36

[2109] Child and Adams, *The Gazetteer of Washington County, Vermont, 1783-1889*, Part First, p 525

iv RHODA HOLT, b. about 1790; d. at Barre, VT, about 1824; *perhaps* the Rhoda Holt who m. at Barre, VT, 3 Dec 1812, ESECK HOWLAND, b. at Middletown, MA, about 1789 son of Eseck and Phebe (Sears) Howland; Eseck d. at East Montpelier, 3 Jun 1872. Eseck was second married to Laura Holden on 20 Oct 1824.

v EDITH HOLT

vi HUMPHREY HOLT, b. about 1794; d. at Barre, VT, 5 Aug 1864; m. about 1823, PHILENA HOLDEN, b. at Barre, 2 Feb 1805 daughter of Eli and Hannah (Persons) Holden; Philena d. at Barre, 13 Apr 1842.

788) MARY HOLT (*William⁴, Humphrey³, Henry², Nicholas¹*), b. at Winchendon, 8 Nov 1754 daughter of William and Mary (Martin) Holt; d. at Royalston, MA, 26 Jan 1847; m. JONATHAN BOSWORTH, b. at Bellingham, MA, Sep 1748 son of Jonathan and Susanna (Chilson) Bosworth; Jonathan d. at Royalston, 1 Dec 1818.

Jonathan Bosworth served in the Revolution as a private in the company of Capt. Oliver Capron. He was a yeoman and the family resided in Royalston.[2110]

Jonathan Bosworth did not leave a will and his estate entered probate 8 April 1819 with Samuel Simonds as administrator as widow Mary declined administration. The estate was declared insolvent 28 June 1819.[2111]

Mary Holt and Jonathan Bosworth were parents of fifteen children born at Royalston.[2112]

i Son b. 5 Mar and d. 6 Mar 1773.

ii JONATHAN BOSWORTH, b. 17 Feb 1774; d. 4 Jul 1774.

iii SUSANNAH BOSWORTH, b. 9 May 1775; d. at Ossian, NY, 6 Aug 1870; m. at Royalston, 15 Sep 1796, JOHN BARRETT, b. At Winchendon, 26 Apr 1773 son of Thornton and Abigail (Bowker) Barrett; John d. at Ossian, 22 Aug 1856.

iv WALSINGHAM BOSWORTH, b. 17 Mar 1777; d. at Winchendon, 5 Apr 1821; m. at Royalston, 1 Jul 1798, MARY "POLLY" PIPER, b. at Acton, 20 May 1769 daughter of Josiah and Sarah (Davis) Piper;[2113] Mary d. at Winchendon, 1 Sep 1846.

v Son b. and d. 16 Dec 1778.

vi Son b. and d. 10 Nov 1779.

vii JONATHAN BOSWORTH, b. 27 Nov 1780; d. at Royalston, 19 Apr 1830; m. at Royalston, 31 Oct 1802, ELIZABETH WAIT, b. at Grafton, MA, 2 Jul 1785 daughter of Simon and Mercy (Flagg) Wait.[2114]

viii WILLIAM HOLT BOSWORTH, b. 6 Apr 1783; d. at Winchendon, 13 May 1846; m. at Templeton, 24 Sep 1809, LUCY BACON, b. at Rowley, about 1788 daughter of Samuel and Ruth (Plummer) Bacon;[2115] Lucy d. at Winchendon, 21 Apr 1851. William and Lucy do not seem to have had children.

ix JOHN BOSWORTH, b. 27 Feb 1785; d. at Winchendon, 3 May 1849; m. at Winchendon, 14 Aug 1809, LUCINDA FLAGG, b. at Winchendon, 13 Sep 1792 daughter of John and Betsey (Blanchard) Flagg.

x CHILSON BOSWORTH, b. 27 May 1787; d. at Royalston, 22 Mar 1871; m. 1st at Royalston, Dec 1809, CHLOE SIBLEY, b. at Grafton, 26 May 1791 daughter of William and Abigail (Fay) Sibley; Chloe d. at Royalston,10 Aug 1850. Chilson m. 2nd, 5 Jun 1853, SARAH TRASK (widow Sarah Palkey), b. at Windsor, ME, about 1795 daughter of Edward and Sarah (-) Trask;[2116] Sarah d. at Royalston, 30 Jul 1870.

xi MARY BOSWORTH, b. 12 Sep 1789; d. after 1850 when she was living in Byron, ME; m. at Royalston, 14 Dec 1817, JOHN GILCREAS, b. at Dracut 25 Feb 1795 son of John and Abigail (Downing) Gilcreas; John d. at Peru, ME, 16 May 1872. John had a second marriage to Achsah Smith in 1855, but it may be that Mary and John divorced rather than he was widowed.

2110 Lainhart and Fiske, *Mayflower Families Through Five Generations*, Volume Twenty-three, Part Two, Family of John Howland, p 303

2111 *Worcester County, MA: Probate File Papers, 1731-1881.* Online database. AmericanAncestors.org. New England Historic Genealogical Society, 2015. Case 6303

2112 Massachusetts Town Clerk Records 1626-2001, Worcester, Royalston, Births, Marriages, Deaths 1772-1843, p 15, https://www.familysearch.org/ark:/61903/3:1:3QS7-L979-49SL-1?i=12

2113 The 1823 will of Josiah Piper of Royalston includes a bequest to daughter Mary widow of Walsingham Bosworth.

2114 The 1822 estate distribution of Simon Wait of Royalston includes heirs Elizabeth Bosworth and Jonathan Bosworth.

2115 The 1836 will of Samuel Bacon includes a bequest to daughter Lucy wife of William Bosworth

2116 The names of Sarah's parents are given on her death record as Edward and Sarah Trask.

xii JOSEPH BOSWORTH, b. 9 Jan 1792; d. at Royalston, 28 Jul 1867; m. 13 Apr 1819, ABIGAIL SAUNDERS BEMIS, b. at Royalston, about 1796 of undetermined parents;[2117] Abigail d. at Royalston, 7 Feb 1864.

xiii BENJAMIN BOSWORTH, b. 14 Mar 1794; d. after 1880 when he was living at Pittstown, NY; m. 1st 11 Apr 1826, ESTHER BALL (or perhaps Ballou) described as of Richmond, NH, b. about 1790;[2118] Esther d. at Royalston, 8 Feb 1827 at age 37. Benjamin m. 2nd, 1 Nov 1828, BETSEY BOWKER; Betsey d. at Winchendon, 14 May 1834. Benjamin m. 3rd, ELIZA who has not been identified, b. about 1821, and living in 1891 when she was living at the almshouse in Pittstown.

xiv HANNAH BOSWORTH, b. 29 Jan 1797; d. at Royalston, 10 Jul 1836. Hannah did not marry.

xv MEHITABLE "HARRIET" BOSWORTH, b. 12 Jul 1799; d. at Winchendon, 19 Mar 1880; m. at Royalston, 4 Apr 1825, HOSEA BISHOP, b. at Fitzwilliam, NH, 3 Jul 1802 son of William and Betsey (Jesoph) Bishop; Hosea d. after 1870 when he was living in Westminster, MA.

789) SIMEON HOLT (*Humphrey⁴, Humphrey³, Henry², Nicholas¹*), b. at Andover, 26 Jan 1747 son of Humphrey and Elizabeth (Kimball) Holt; d. at Andover, 5 Jan 1828; m. at Wilmington, 31 Mar 1767, SARAH READ who has not been identified; Sarah d. at Andover, 20 Aug 1827. Both Simeon and Sarah died at the almshouse.

Simeon Holt and Sarah Read were parents of twelve children born at Andover. Marriages were located for only three of the children. Sons Frederick and Loammi also died at the almshouse in Andover.

i FREDERICK REED HOLT, b. 23 Jan 1768; d. at Andover at the almshouse, 26 Feb 1830.

ii SARAH HOLT, baptized 22 Oct 1769

iii SIMEON HOLT, b. 18 May 1771

iv BETTY KIMBALL HOLT, b. 23 Jul 1773; d. 9 Sep 1778.

v MOLLY HOLT, b. 23 Jul 1773; d. at Carlisle, MA, 7 Jan 1853; m. at Billerica, 1 Oct 1794, JOHN R. BLANCHARD, b. at Billerica, 17 May 1773 son of John and Sarah (Dickson) Blanchard; John d. at Carlisle, 19 Nov 1855.

vi LOAMMI B. HOLT, b. 23 Jul 1775; d. at Andover at the almshouse, 11 Jan 1827; m. at Andover, 12 Jan 1797, MARY "POLLY" HARRIS, b. about 1779 daughter of William and Mary (Mooar) Harris.[2119] Loammi and Mary lived in Gloucester and Andover and were parents of seven children. Only one child, William Harris Holt, is known to have lived to adulthood and married. William Harris Holt married Clarissa Emmons.

vii MARTHA "PATTY" HOLT, baptized 27 Jul 1777; d. at Danvers, 7 Jan 1865; m. at Danvers, 31 Mar 1795, JOHN HUTCHINSON, b. at Danvers, 25 Apr 1767 son of John and Lydia (Goodell) Hutchinson; John d. at Danvers, 10 Jul 1850.

viii JONATHAN HOLT, baptized 27 Jul 1777;[2120] d. 7 May 1778.

ix BETTY KIMBALL HOLT, baptized 21 Nov 1779

x ABIGAIL HOLT, baptized 18 Nov 1781

xi JONATHAN HOLT, baptized, 11 Jan 1784

xii JACOB HOLT, b. 7 Mar 1787

790) HUMPHREY HOLT (*Humphrey⁴, Humphrey³, Henry², Nicholas¹*), baptized at Andover, 18 Feb 1753 son of Humphrey and Mary (Holton) Holt; d. at Londonderry, NH, 1826 (probate 5 Sep 1826); m. 1st at Andover, 12 May 1774. PHEBE CURTIS (widow Fish). Humphrey m. 2nd, perhaps in Maine, JERUSHA who has not been identified. Humphrey m. 3rd at Londonderry, 11 Sep 1817, SARAH BATCHELDER who survived him.

In his will written 25 October 1820 and proved 5 September 1826, Humphrey Holt of Londonderry bequeathed to wife Sarah all the household furniture she brought with her. The estate is to be divided in equal parts and distributed to the following children: Phebe Nichols wife of Phineas Nichols, Polly Morse wife of Isaac Morse, Sally Gordon wife of Wells Gordon, Esther Darrah wife of John Darrah, Eliza Manter wife of Jabez Manter, Margaret C. H. Ordway, Joseph Holt, William Holt,

---

2117 The Mayflower descendants book gives Abigail's parents as Jason Bemis and Mercy Piper. Abigail's death record gives her parents as Luke and Mary Bemis. There is not a daughter Abigail in either the 1831 will of Jason Bemis or in the 1841 will of Luke Bemis.

2118 Esther's parentage is undetermined.

2119 The 1820 will of Mary Harris includes a bequest of one dollar to her daughter Mary Holt.

2120 Jonathan and his sister Patty are reported in the records as being triplets, but a record was not located for the third triplet.

and John Holt. Margaret C. H. Ordway is his granddaughter the child of his daughter Margaret Clark Holt and James Ordway.[2121]

Humphrey Holt and Phebe Curtis were parents of two children.

i PHEBE HOLT, b. at Andover, 14 Oct 1775; m. by 1795, PHINEAS NICHOLS, perhaps b. 1765 son of Phineas and Anna (Sanders) Nichols; Phineas d. (recorded at Tewksbury), 23 Oct 1854. Phebe and Phineas were parents of ten children four of whom were born in Lovell, Maine, some recorded as Salem, New Hampshire, and the youngest children in Massachusetts. Phineas was living with his son Humphrey Holt Nichols in Groveland, MA in 1850.

ii JOSEPH HOLT, b. at Andover, 7 Jul 1778. Joseph was living in 1820 when his father wrote his will. He may be the Joseph Holt who married Miriam Smith in 1808 in North Hampton, NH, but that is not clear.

Humphrey and Jerusha Holt were parents of seven children. The oldest four children may have been born in Eastern River Township, Maine and the youngest three children in Londonderry, New Hampshire. The older children were baptized at Eastern River Township.[2122]

i MARGARET CLARK HOLT, b. 1784; d. at Methuen, MA, about 1808; m. at Methuen, 30 Mar 1806, JAMES ORDWAY, b. at Methuen, 30 Sep 1781 son of James and Mary (Martain) Ordway; James d. at Methuen, 24 Feb 1814. James married second Elizabeth Mitchell on 25 Nov 1810.

ii MARY "POLLY" HOLT, b. 1788 and baptized 12 Sep 1790; d. at Methuen, 8 Aug 1876; m. at Methuen, 13 Jan 1809, ISAAC MORSE, b. at Methuen, 3 Feb 1781 son of Paine and Martha (Sprague) Morse; Isaac d. at Methuen, 15 May 1845 (probate 15 May 1845). Mary and Isaac were parents of eight children born at Methuen.

iii SARAH "SALLY" HOLT, b. 1790 and baptized 12 Sep 1790; d. at Carmel, ME, 2 Jan 1842; m. at Londonderry, NH, 13 Mar 1812, WELLS GORDON, b. at Salem, NH, 9 Mar 1779 son of Alexander and Hannah (Stanley) Gordon.

iv WILLIAM HOLT, b. about 1790; m. at Londonderry, 16 Feb 1814, HANNAH ANDREWS.

v ESTHER HOLT, b. about 1792; m. at Londonderry, 15 Sep 1810, JOHN DARRAH, b. about 1791; John d. at Manchester, NH, 22 Oct 1854.

vi ELIZA HOLT, b. about 1795; m. at Londonderry, 22 Mar 1816, JABEZ MANTER, b. about 1796 son of Grafton and Lydia (Leach) Manter; Jabez d. at Litchfield, NH, 1846.

vii JOHN HOLT, b. about 1796; d. at Beaver Dam, WI, 9 Mar 1858; m. at Londonderry, 25 Mar 1819, RACHEL SAWYER, b. in MA, about 1795; Rachel d. at Beaver Dam, 18 Mar 1865.

791) WILLIAM HOLT (*Humphrey⁴, Humphrey³, Henry², Nicholas¹*), b. at Tewksbury, 29 Jul 1761 son of Humphrey and Mary (Holton) Holt; d. at Fryeburg, ME, 4 May 1827; m. about 1792, ESTHER FRYE, b. at Fryeburg, 11 Jul 1773 daughter of Simon and Hannah (Johnson) Frye;[2123] Esther d. at Fryeburg, 21 Jan 1863.

William Holt served in the Revolution as a fifer. After the war, he went to Fryeburg where he settled.[2124]

On 18 June 1863, Thomas K. Holt of Fryeburg, "only son" of Esther Holt declined administration of his mother's estate.[2125]

William and Esther were parents of nine children likely all born at Fryeburg.[2126]

i MARY HOLTON HOLT, b. 15 Jun 1793; perhaps m. at Lovell, 10 Aug 1819, ISAAC F. HODGDON. Mary was of Fryeburg at the time of the marriage. The young couple was in Lovell in 1820 and several children are recorded at Lebanon, ME for Isaac and Mary Hodgdon.

ii SARAH HOLT, b. 1795; d. at Fryeburg, 9 Aug 1812.

iii SOPHIA HOLT, b. about 1800; d. at Bethel, ME, 9 Dec 1868; m. SIMEON BROWN, b. at Bethel, ME, 27 Apr 1798 son of Benjamin and Hannah (Russell) Brown; Simeon d. at Bethel, 18 Mar 1886.

iv WILLIAM H. HOLT, b. about 1797; d. before 1850; m. CAROLINE FARRINGTON, b. 1799; Caroline d. at San Rafael, CA, 16 Dec 1897.

2121 *New Hampshire. Probate Court (Rockingham County);* Probate Place: *Rockingham, New Hampshire, Probate Records volume 49, p 145*

2122 Records of the Baptist Church of Kenduskeag, Maine, accessed through familysearch.org

2123 The 1819 will of Simon Frye (probate 1822) includes a bequest to daughter Esther wife of William Holt.

2124 Durrie, *Genealogical History of the Holt Family*, p 40

2125 *Maine. Probate Court (Oxford County), Notices of Administrators, Petitions for Administration, 1857-1866, p 265*

2126 *Biographical Review of Leading Citizens of Oxford and Franklin Counties, Maine*, 1897, p 275 lists names of seven children, omitting Sarah who died at age 17 and Lydia F. Holt who is a likely child in this family.

v ESTHER HOLT, b. about 1804; d. at Wabasha County, MN, 8 Feb 1875; m. DANIEL R. BRYANT, b. 1807 son of Christopher and Susanna (Swan) Bryant; Daniel d. at Greenwood, ME, 18 Dec 1856[2127] (probate May 1857).

vi LYDIA F. HOLT, b. about 1805; d. after 1860 when she was living at Bethel, ME; m. JOHN SHATTUCK SWAN, b. about 1796, likely at Bethel, son of James and Hannah (Shattuck) Swan; John d. after 1870 when he was living at Bethel.

vii JOSEPH HOLT, b. 25 Nov 1808; d. at Denmark, ME, 25 Mar 1861; m. MEHITABLE MILLER, b. 18 Feb 1812;[2128] Mehitable d. at Denmark, 1 Jan 1888.

viii JOHN H.F. HOLT, b. 1811; d. at Fryeburg, 14 Jul 1833.

ix THOMAS K. HOLT, b. 5 Mar 1814; d. at Fryeburg, 25 Sep 1888; m. 1st about 1840, ELIZABETH "ELIZA" BRICKETT, b. at Fryeburg, Aug 1811 daughter of Jonathan and Martha (Brackett) Brickett; Eliza d. at Fryeburg, 7 Apr 1854. Thomas m. 2nd about 1855, PARTHENA R. JOHNSON, b. at Brownfield, 14 Jul 1824 daughter of James and Esther (Wood) Johnson; Parthena d. at Fryeburg, 27 Jun 1906.

792) JOHN HOLT (*Humphrey⁴, Humphrey³, Henry², Nicholas¹*), b. at Andover, 12 May 1764 son of Humphrey and Mary (Holton) Holt; d. at Bethel, ME, 16 Jul 1830; m. 7 Jun 1787, his third cousin once removed, LYDIA RUSSELL (*Hephzibah Russell Russell⁵, Joseph Russell⁴, Phebe Johnson Russell³, Mary Holt Johnson², Nicholas¹*), b. at Andover, 17 May 1764 daughter of Joseph and Hephzibah (Russell) Russell; Lydia d. at Bethel, 12 Sep 1847.

John Holt went to Bethel where he cleared his property before returning to Andover to marry Lydia Russell and then returning with his bride to Bethel. John served as a Captain in the militia at Bethel and was deacon of the Baptist church. He served for three years during the Revolution.[2129]

John Holt did not leave a will and his estate entered probate October 1830 with son Hiram Holt as administrator at the request of widow Lydia Holt. At the time of his death, John had no real estate and personal estate was valued at $206.79.[2130]

John Holt and Lydia Russell were parents of nine children born at Bethel.

i JOHN HOLT, b. 1 Jun 1788; d. 22 Jan 1789.

ii HARMON HOLT, b. 12 Nov 1789; d. at Medford, ME, May 1861; m. 10 Nov 1810, SALLY DUSTIN, b. about 1790; Sally d. after 1860 (living at 1860 census).

iii WILLIAM HOLT, b. 4 Feb 1792; d. at Bethel, 6 Dec 1868; m. 4 May 1814, MARY STEARNS, b. at Bethel, 18 Apr 1795 daughter of Thomas and Lois (Colby) Stearns; Mary d. at Bethel, 5 Jan 1875.

iv JOSEPH R. HOLT, b. at Bethel, 28 Feb 1795; d. at Bethel, 22 Sep 1878; m. 4 Dec 1817, SUSAN STEARNS, b. at Bethel, 30 Dec 1797 daughter of Thomas and Lois (Colby) Stearns; Susan d. at Bethel, 28 Feb 1873.

v MARY HOLT, b. 20 Jan 1797; d. 20 Oct 1802.

vi NATHAN HOLT, b. 20 Mar 1799; d. 6 Aug 1802.

vii HASKELL HOLT, b. 3 Jun 1801; d. 30 Sep 1802.

viii HIRAM HOLT, b. at Bethel, 21 Jul 1803; d. likely at Bethel, after 1870; m. 9 Jun 1826, ELOHE VARRIL, b. 6 Nov 1801 daughter of Samuel and Sarah (Prince) Varril; Elohe was living in 1870. Hiram Holt was the postmaster of East Bethel.

ix LYDIA HOLT, b. at Bethel, 17 Nov 1805; d. at Bethel, 1891; m. 9 Jun 1832, HUMPHREY BEAN, b. at Bethel, 22 Jan 1802 son of Amos and Huldah (Kimball) Bean; Humphrey d. at Bethel, 1884.

793) JONATHAN HOLT (*Jonathan⁴, Humphrey³, Henry², Nicholas¹*), b. at Lunenburg, 16 May 1756 son of Jonathan and Susanna (Holt) Holt; d. at Clinton, ME, 12 Dec 1832; m. at Jaffrey, NH, 12 Dec 1782, MARY "POLLY" BAILEY, b. at Lunenburg, 14 Feb 1753 daughter of Isaac and Mary (Lovejoy) Bailey.

Jonathan Holt had several periods of service during the Revolution initially enlisting as a private in Capt. Josiah Stearn's company in Col. Ephraim Doolittle's 24th regiment. This initial service was eight days. He had additional service of six months in 1779 and six months in 1780 in the Continental army with a final discharge of 12 December 1780.[2131]

2127 Maine, J. Gary Nichols Cemetery Collection, ca. 1780-1999

2128 Maine, J. Gary Nichols Cemetery Collection, ca. 1780-1999. Mehitable's date of birth is given on her cemetery record.

2129 Lapham, *History of Bethel*, p 424

2130 *Maine. Probate Court (Oxford County)*; Probate Place: *Oxford, Maine, Estate Files, Drawer H52, Hamlin, Cyrus-Howe, Jacob, 1820-1834, Estate of John Holt*

2131 Massachusetts Office of the Secretary of State, *Massachusetts Soldiers and Sailors of the Revolutionary War*, volume 8, p 192

Jonathan and Mary began their family in Lunenburg, and the births of their five children may have occurred in Lunenburg[2132] although they are recorded in the town records at Jaffrey, New Hampshire. From Jaffrey, the family moved on the Canaan, Maine where both Jonathan and Polly died. All four sons in the family served in the War of 1812.

i ISAAC HOLT, b. 9 Aug 1783; d. after 1863 when he was in Canaan, but perhaps died in Clinton; m. 1st 13 Mar 1811, ELEANOR KIMBALL; Eleanor d. at Canaan, 8 Jul 1829. Isaac m. 2nd 3 Jan 1830, MEHITABLE who d. 24 Oct 1838. Isaac m. 3rd 14 Feb 1841, HANNAH who d. at Canaan, 10 Nov 1851.

ii MARY "POLLY" HOLT, b. 6 May 1785; d. at Canaan, ME, 10 Sep 1868; m. about 1809, SAMUEL WHEELER, b. at Canaan, 1789 son of Daniel and Mary (Pollard) Wheeler; Samuel d. at Canaan, 28 Jan 1855.

iii ALVA HOLT, b. 16 Nov 1787; d. after 1870 when he was in Canaan, ME; m. RHODA WALKER, b. about 1793; Rhoda d. at Canaan, 22 Sep 1866.

iv ASA HOLT, b. 23 Apr 1790; d. at Canaan, 10 Jun 1881; m. MARGARET "PEGGY" NELSON, b. at Dover, NH, 5 May 1794 daughter of Daniel and Polly (Granville) Nelson; Margaret d. at Canaan, 1 Jul 1877.

v JONATHAN HOLT, b. 31 Oct 1793; d. at Canaan, 28 Mar 1882; m. BETSEY BAILEY, b. about 1801; Betsey d. 22 Aug 1890.

794) SUSANNA HOLT (*Jonathan⁴, Humphrey³, Henry², Nicholas¹*), b. at Lunenburg, 29 May 1758 daughter of Jonathan and Susanna (Holt) Holt; m. at Leominster, MA, 26 Nov 1779, COTTON WHITING, b. at Concord, MA, 27 Oct 1752 son of Stephen and Mary (Grover) Whiting; Cotton d. at Chester, VT, 1815 (probate 6 Apr 1815).

Cotton Whiting did not leave a will and his estate entered probate 6 April 1815 with Rufus Bruce appointed administrator as Susannah Whiting and John Whiting declined administration. Real estate was valued at $460 with total value of $631.41. The real estate was mortgaged and was later sold to settle the estate. Those signing they reviewed the probate accounting were James Ellison, John Whiting, and Susannah Whiting. The dower was set off to widow Susannah on 21 December 1815.[2133]

There are four children known for Susanna Holt and Cotton Whiting.

i SUSANNA WHITING, baptized at Leominster, 20 May 1781.

ii ELIZABETH "BETSEY" WHITING, baptized at Leominster, 20 May 1781; d. at Chester, VT, 14 Jul 1857; m. at Chester, 29 May 1800, MARCH GOWING, b. about 1777; March d. at Chester, 24 Jun 1855.

iii MARY "POLLY" WHITING, b. about 1784; m. at Chester, 26 Jul 1802, JAMES ELLISON.

iv JOHN WHITING, b. about 1785; m. at Chester, 29 Aug 1813, LUCINDA GLEASON.

795) ELIJAH HOLT (*Jonathan⁴, Humphrey³, Henry², Nicholas¹*), b. at Lunenburg, 23 Oct 1759 son of Jonathan and Susanna (Holt) Holt; d. at Jamaica, VT, before 1815; m. at Oakham, 1 Feb 1781, LUCY PARMENTER, b. 1757 daughter of Solomon and Elizabeth (Craig) Parmenter;[2134] d. at Elk Creek, PA, after 1840 (female over age 80 living in the family of Elijah Holt at Elk Creek, PA).

Elijah Holt served a six-month period of service in the Revolution from 26 June 1778 to 1 January 1779 in Capt. Benjamin Edgell's company. He had an earlier period of service in 1777 at Bennington.[2135]

Elijah and Lucy married in Oakham and were living there in 1790 and were later in Jamaica, Vermont where Elijah died between 1810 and 1815. There is a record for daughter Lucy born at Fitchburg and Elijah is a likely second child.[2136]

i LUCY HOLT, b. at Fitchburg, 16 Mar 1782; d. at Elk Creek, PA, 31 Dec 1850; m. THOMAS KIDDER, b. at Sutton, MA, 13 Nov 1780 son of Francis and Mary (Chase) Kidder; Thomas d. at Elk Creek, 6 Oct 1860.

ii ELIJAH HOLT, b. likely at Oakham, MA, about 1786; d. unknown but perhaps after 1870; m. at Windham County, VT, 11 Oct 1810, PHEBE BAKER AMES, b. about 1788; Phebe d. about 1840. Elijah may have had a second marriage to Amelia.

796) WILLIAM HOLT (*Jonathan⁴, Humphrey³, Henry², Nicholas¹*), b. at Lunenburg, 11 Apr 1761 son of Jonathan and Susanna (Holt) Holt; d. at Chester, VT, 27 Jul 1827; m. 20 Apr 1782, ELIZABETH HUTCHINSON, b. at Lunenburg, 22 Oct 1763 daughter of Samuel and Elizabeth (Fessenden) Hutchinson; Elizabeth d. after 1851 when she was living in Plymouth, VT.

2132 Cunningham, *History of the Town of Lunenburg*, E-H, p 412

2133 *Vermont. Probate Court (Windsor District)*; Probate Place: *Windsor, Vermont, Estate of Cotton Whiting*

2134 The will of Solomon Parmenter includes a bequest to his daughter Lucy Holt wife of Elijah Holt.

2135 Fitchburg Historical Society, Proceedings of the Fitchburg Historical Society, "Fitchburg Soldiers of the Revolution", p 198

2136 Thomas, *Once Upon a Time*, p 44. This brief volume includes a biography of Elijah Holt (presumed son of Elijah and Lucy) describing him as a brother-in-law of Thomas Kidder who was the husband of Lucy Holt.

William Holt enlisted in the Continental army as part of the quota from Fitchburg. He served in the regiment of Col. Timothy Bigelow from 25 April 1777 to 25 April 1780.[2137] On 11 April 1818, William Holt of Chester, Vermont age fifty-seven, appeared and gave a statement related to his application for a Revolutionary War pension. He enlisted as a private on 25 April 1777 in the company of Capt. Sylvanus Smith and served in the Massachusetts line and was discharged at West Point on 25 April 1780. On 25 September 1820, William valued his estate at $74.86. At that time, family dependent on him for support were his wife age 59, daughter Roxanna age 19, daughter Mary age 21, and daughter Charlotte age 16 who for the past year had been afflicted by fits. William stated his usual work was as a farmer but had little ability to do that because of his declining health. He worked out as a day laborer.

On 22 December 1837 in Sullivan County, New Hampshire, widow Elizabeth Holt appeared to make her statement related to the widow's pension. She related that she and William lived in Lunenburg after their marriage and moved to Cavendish, Vermont about 1786. William and Elizabeth lived in Cavendish, Chester, and Ludlow and were in that area for forty years. In December 1830, Elizabeth moved to Marlow, New Hampshire with her son. In 1839, she returned to Vermont when her son returned there. On 19 October 1850, Elizabeth then a resident of Plymouth, Vermont appeared in order to request an increase in her pension that was due her due to a resolution in July 1848 related to the widows' pensions. She appeared again on 28 March 1851 again requesting an increase in her pension.

On 28 February 1838, Lincoln Stiles of Cavendish made a statement related to Elizabeth's application recalling that he had known William Holt and Elizabeth Hutchinson since childhood. William and Elizabeth were playmates as children and "there was manifestly a mutual attachment between the said William and the said Elizabeth which eventually resulted in their marriage."[2138]

There are four children known for William Holt and Elizabeth Hutchinson, although it seems likely there were other children as the oldest known child was born ten years after the marriage.

i ASA HOLT, b. likely at Cavendish, about 1792; d. at Plymouth, VT, 25 May 1862; m. 28 Jun 1812, JERUSHA PUTNAM, b. at Lyndeborough, 1796 (according to death record); Jerusha d. at Bridgewater, VT, 13 May 1874.

ii MARY HOLT, b. about 1799; living in 1820

iii ROXCENA HOLT, b. about 1801; d. at Lempster, NH, 4 May 1860; m. at Chester, VT, 2 Dec 1824, EPHRAIM JENNINGS, b. at Marlborough, NH, 1797 son of Ebenezer and Dorcas (Pope) Jennings; Ephraim d. at Lempster, 16 May 1881.

iv CHARLOTTE HOLT, b. about 1804; Charlotte was living in Plymouth, VT in 1860 and was unmarried.

797) JAMES HOLT (*Jonathan[4], Humphrey[3], Henry[2], Nicholas[1]*), b. at Lunenburg, 2 May 1764 son of Jonathan and Susanna (Holt) Holt; d. at Warsaw, NY, 22 Jul 1837; m. at Jaffrey, 28 Jan 1783,[2139] OLIVE DEAN, b. at Wilmington, MA, 27 Aug 1755[2140] daughter of William and Sarah (Underwood) Dean; Olive was living in Attica, NY in 1848.

James Holt served during the Revolution and made application for a pension based on his service. On 15 October 1832, giving his age as seventy on the past 2 May and then living in Warsaw, James stated that he enlisted from Worcester County on 10 May 1780. The company mustered at Leicester and marched to West Point. His unit was along the Hudson River, in New Jersey, and at Stoney Point. On 11 January 1781, he received a discharge signed by Col. Michael Jackson. James reported he was born in Fitchburg, moved to Jaffrey about a year after his army service and stayed there four years, and from there went to Chester, Vermont. He moved every few years after that and lived in Londonderry, Brooklyn, Manchester, and Shaftsbury, Vermont and was then off to New York where he lived in Cambridge, then towns in Chenango County, Cayuga County, and finally in Genesee County about 1817 or 1818. He also reported there was a record of his birth in a bible in the possession of his daughter and that he married in January 1782 in the twentieth year of his age. As part of her widow's pension application, Olive Holt provided the family bible page giving a date of marriage of James Holt and Olive Dean as 28 January 1783. The page provided also records the birth and death of the oldest daughter Olive. A deposition was also provided by Ephraim Dinsmore, son-in-law of Olive Holt who noted that Olive had lived in his household since the death of her husband. James Holt was granted a pension in 1832 and Olive later received the widow's pension.[2141]

There are two children known of James Holt and Olive Dean

i OLIVE HOLT, b. 7 Feb 1784; d. 17 May 1784.

ii OLIVE HOLT, b. in VT, 16 Nov 1792; d. after 1870 when she was living in Eden, IL; m. 1st about 1811, JARED SIMONDS who has not been identified; Jared d. about 1825. Olive m. 2nd about 1827, EPHRAIM DINSMORE, b. about 1785 son of Abraham and Love (Leeman) Dinsmore; Ephraim d. at Warsaw, NY, 9 Nov 1847. Ephraim Dinsmore was first married to Sarah Graves Whitney.

2137 Proceedings of the Fitchburg Historical Society, 1908, volume IV, "Fitchburg Soldiers in the Revolution", p 199

2138 Revolutionary War Pension and Bounty-Land Warrant Application Files, 1800-1900, Case W18029

2139 This is the date of marriage given by Olive Dean Holt in the pension application file of James Holt. It varies by five years from the transcription at Jaffrey, NH, but the daughter in this family was born in 1784 according to the family bible records.

2140 Olive Dean Holt gives her birth date as August 1755 in the pension application file of James Holt.

2141 U.S., Revolutionary War Pension and Bounty-Land Warrant Application Files, 1800-1900. Case 19799

798) RHODA HOLT (*Jonathan⁴, Humphrey³, Henry², Nicholas¹*), b. at Lunenburg, 22 Feb 1768 daughter of John and Susanna (Holt) Holt; d. at Norridgewock, ME, 21 Sep 1848; m. 1st at Fitchburg, 12 Oct 1784, NATHAN TAYLOR, b. at Dorchester, MA, 18 Feb 1760[2142] son of Nathan and Submit (Blackman) Taylor; Nathan d. at Canaan, ME by drowning on 10 Jun 1804. Rhoda m. 2nd 19 Jul 1812, Capt. ASA LONGLEY, b. at Groton, Jul 1762; Asa d. at Corinna, ME, 21 May 1845. Asa Longley was first married to Betsey Parker who died in 1811.

On 8 June 1847, Rhoda Longley of Corrina, Maine then age seventy-nine appeared at Somerset County court to provide a statement related to her application for a widow's pension based on the service of her late husband Nathan Taylor. Among the materials provided to the court were two pages from the family bible, one listing the marriages in the family and the other listing the births of Nathan, Rhoda, and each of their children. Rhoda reported that Nathan had served during the Revolution at various times from 1777 through its close in 1784. He enlisted from Hillsborough, New Hampshire in February 1777 in Capt. Bradford's company of Col. Reed's regiment. He was discharged and then re-enlisted for the three-year term in the same company. He had a third enlistment in April 1781 and served as orderly sergeant in Capt. Morrison's company for a further term of three years. He was finally discharged in the spring of 1784.

The couple was married in Fitchburg by Rev. Payson on 12 October 1784. After their marriage, Rhoda and Nathan lived in Fitchburg and Lunenburg, were then in Jaffrey, New Hampshire until 1800 when the family moved to Canaan, Maine. It was there that Nathan died by drowning in the Kennebec River on 10 June 1804. Rhoda later married Asa Longley and Asa died 21 May 1845.

On 1 September 1847, Nathan's brother James, then eighty years old and residing in Southwick, Massachusetts, gave a statement in support of Rhoda's application confirming his brother's years of service. Nathan and Rhoda's son Amasa, a minister of the gospel then living in New Salem, Massachusetts, recalled that his father died when Amasa was seventeen. His grandfather's name was Nathan and his grandfather lived in Antrim or Amherst and lived several years longer that Nathan the younger.[2143]

Rhoda Holt and Nathan Taylor were parents of eight children, as recorded in the family bible. It is not clear where the children were born, and at least the oldest children were born in Massachusetts, perhaps in Fitchburg or Lunenburg (on census records birthplace is given as Massachusetts). The youngest, twins Nathan and Rhoda, were born after Nathan's death.

i AUGUSTUS TAYLOR, b. 4 Aug 1785; d. 14 Nov 1789.

ii AMASA TAYLOR, b. 9 Jul 1787; d. at New Salem, MA, 18 Oct 1860; m. at Weston, VT, 22 Jan 1815, MARY "POLLY" WAITE, b. at Mason, NH, 1792 daughter of John and Jemima (Scripture) Waite; Mary d. at Petersham, MA, 6 Feb 1880.

iii AUGUSTUS TAYLOR, b. 21 Aug 1790; m. 21 Jan 1812, MARY who has not been identified. Augustus and Mary Taylor divorced in Somerset County, Maine in Jun 1822 with Augustus as plaintiff and Mary as defendant.[2144]

iv SUSANNA HOLT TAYLOR, b. 4 Jan 1794; d. after 1880 when she was living with a daughter in Corinna, ME; m. 28 Feb 1815, DAVID PARKMAN, b. about 1792; d. at Corinna, 4 Dec 1864 (probate Jan 1865).

v ELIZABETH WHITNEY TAYLOR, b. 16 Aug 1796; d. at Norridgewock, ME, 7 Aug 1827; m. 10 Oct 1815, JOSEPH BAKER, b. 27 Aug 1793 son of Abner and Elizabeth (Young) Baker;[2145] Joseph d. at Norridgewock, 1871. Joseph married second Charity Blackwell.

vi SUBMIT BLACKMAN TAYLOR,[2146] b. 1 Oct 1798; d. at Van Buren, AK, 29 Oct 1888; m. 16 Jan 1823, BENJAMIN FRANKLIN JUDKINS, b. at Athens, ME, 19 Mar 1801 son of Hill and Betsey (Shaw) Judkins; Benjamin d. at Medina, WI, 30 Mar 1881. Submit and Benjamin lived in Maine where Benjamin was a farmer and carpenter. In 1849, they made their way to Wisconsin in the area of Milwaukee. After her husband's death, Submit was with family in Arkansas where she died.[2147]

vii RHODA TAYLOR (twin), b. 4 Sep 1804

viii NATHAN TAYLOR (twin), b. 4 Sep 1804; d. 19 Dec 1804.

799) ROXANNA HOLT (*Jonathan⁴, Humphrey³, Henry², Nicholas¹*), b. at Lunenburg, 10 Jul 1802 daughter of Jonathan and Azuba (Butterfield) Holt; d. at Mercer County, IL, after 1870; m. at Mason, NH, 15 Mar 1820, JAIRUS ROBINSON, b. at Weathersfield, VT, 7 Aug 1793 son of Benjamin and Ruth (Johnson) Robinson; Jairus d. at Weathersfield, 28 May 1828.

2142 The family bible record gives the date as 18 Feb 1759, but the Dorchester records give the date as 18 Feb 1760.

2143 Revolutionary War Pension and Bounty-Land Warrant Application Files, Case W24571

2144 Maine, Divorce Records, 1798-1891, ancestry.com

2145 Litchfield, Maine, *History of Litchfield*, p 44

2146 Her name is given as Submitta in the family bible records, but Submit in other records and on her gravestone

2147 Chapman Brothers, *Portrait and Biographical Album of Otoe and Cass Counties, Nebraska, Part II*, p 867

i ROXANA SAMANTHA ROBINSON, b. about 1820; m. CARTER R. PIPER, b. about 1819 son of John and Polly (Butterfield) Piper.[2148]

ii SUSAN A. ROBINSON, b. about 1822; d. at Redwood Falls, MN, 26 Nov 1885; m. at Stoughton, MA, 12 May 1839, WILLIAM PITTS TENNEY, b. 17 Nov 1816 son of William and Mary (Butterfield) Tenney; William d. by suicide at Redwood Falls, 1 Aug 1893.

iii GEORGE HUBBARD ROBINSON, b. at Weathersfield, VT, 5 May 1825; d. at Massena, IA, 21 May 1904; m. MARY JANE WEST, b. at Belmont County, OH, 13 May 1840 daughter of Cornelius and Margaret (Major) West; Mary Jane d. 18 Aug 1890.

iv IRA HOLT ROBINSON, b. at Weathersfield, 23 Mar 1827; d. at Brandon, IA, 29 Apr 1918; m. MAHALA JANE HUFFMAN, b. at Burton, IL, 13 Feb 1843 daughter of James and Hannah (Heskett) Huffman; Mahala d. Preemption, IL, 13 Jan 1911.

800) IRA HOLT (*Jonathan[4], Humphrey[3], Henry[2], Nicholas[1]*), b. at Lunenburg, 21 Mar 1805 son of Jonathan and Azuba (Butterfield) Holt; d. at Arlington, MA, 14 May 1880; m. 13 May 1827, HANNAH ROBBINS, b. at Windsor, NH, about 1807 daughter of Abram and Hannah (Elliott) Robbins; Hannah d. at Newton, MA, 24 Apr 1894..

Ira Holt was a successful businessman who dealt in tinwork and stoves. The family lived in New Ipswich, Hillsborough, Fitchburg, and finally Arlington.

In his will written 16 April 1880, Ira Holt bequeathed to beloved wife Hannah eight thousand dollars and all the household furniture she may wish to keep. Son Henry Harrison Holt receives the gold-headed cane, grandson Clark Morris Holt receives the old pocketbook that belonged to Ira's grandfather, and Ira Gilbert Holt receives his watch and chain. The remainder of the personal estate is to be divided among his four children: Almira Jane Hackett of St. Paul, Minnesota; Sarah Mariah Jernegan of Arlington, Massachusetts; Martha Ann Tolman of Boston, Massachusetts; and Henry Harrison Holt of Kalama, Washington Territory. His real estate including two houses and land in Arlington and Fitchburg and land along the turnpike from New Ipswich to Jaffrey in New Hampshire is to be sold when the majority of the children agree to sell and the money equally divided among the children. Adams K. Tolman was named executor.[2149] Real estate was valued at $10,400 and personal estate consisting primarily of bonds and notes at $18,773.16. The grandsons mentioned in the will, Ira Gilbert Holt and Clark Morris Holt, were sons of Henry Harrison Holt.

Ira Holt and Hannah Robbins were parents of four children.

i ALMIRA "MYRA" JANE HOLT, b. at New Ipswich, NH, 19 Nov 1829; d. at St, Paul, MN, 1910; m. at Fitchburg, 12 Dec 1853, CHARLES WESLEY HACKETT, b. at Lyndeborough, 1831 son of Ephraim and Lois (Butler) Hackett; Charles d. at St, Paul, 21 Mar 1903.

ii SARAH MARIAH HOLT, b. at New Ipswich, 22 Apr 1832; d. at Walnut Creek, CA, 8 Jan 1923; m. at Fitchburg, 10 Dec 1855, THOMAS A. JERNEGAN, b. at Edgartown, MA, 5 Nov 1831 son of Nathan and Prudence (Norton) Jernegan; Thomas d. at Cambridge, MA, 7 May 1909.

iii MARTHA ANN HOLT, b. at Hillsborough, 30 Apr 1837; d. at Newton, MA, 9 Jun 1919; m. at Fitchburg, 29 Nov 1860, ADAMS K. TOLMAN, b. at Boston, 31 Aug 1837 son of Thomas and Susan R. (Adams) Tolman; Adams d. at Newton, 14 May 1893.

iv HENRY HARRISON HOLT, b. at Townsend, MA, 22 Aug 1843; d. at Tacoma, WA, 4 Aug 1920; m. at Winona, MN, 16 May 1864, WELTHE RUGGLES TUCKER, b. at Meteghan, Digby, Nova Scotia, 20 Jan 1838 daughter of Gilbert and Eveline (Snyder) Tucker; Welthe d. at Sunshine Station, WA, 11 Jul 1927.

801) GEORGE HOLT (*Shuah Holt Holt[4], Humphrey[3], Henry[2], Nicholas[1]*), b. at Andover, 21 Feb 1756 son of Jonathan and Shuah (Holt) Holt; m. NANCY FISH, b. at Andover, 6 Jan 1758 daughter of Benjamin and Mary (Johnson) Fish.

i GEORGE HOLT, b. at Andover, 21 Feb 1781; m. at Kingston, NH, 16 Nov 1800, REBECCA DURANT of Exeter, NH; Rebecca d. at Andover, 10 Oct 1824. George and Rebecca had eight children whose births are recorded at Andover.

ii NANCY HOLT, b. at Andover, 26 Sep 1782; m. at Andover, 23 Jun 1808, DAVID PACE, b. at Methuen, 12 Nov 1782 son of Thomas and Susanna (Jennings) Pace; David d. at North Andover, 11 Jan 1858.

iii WILLIAM HOLT, b. at Andover, 27 May 1785; d. at Andover, 23 Dec 1810 (probate May 1811 with widow Sarah as administratrix); m. at Andover, 26 Mar 1807, SARAH MITCHELL. William and Sarah had three daughters, one who died in infancy and the youngest daughter born after William's death.

2148 The 1860 estate settlement of John Piper of Baltimore, VT lists Carter R. Piper as an heir.

2149 *Middlesex County (Mass.) probate packets (1 - 4702) (second series) 1872-1967 (and 4703 - 19,935), Probate Packets, No. 5368 – 5437, Case of Ira Holt*

iv AMOS HOLT, b. 5 Jun 1787; d. at Andover, 26 Jul 1811. His death is recorded at Andover, but he was living in Salem at the time of his death. George Holt was administrator of the estate.

v PHEBE HOLT, b. at Andover, 28 Jul 1789; d. at Dunbarton, NH, 24 Aug 1878; m. at Salem, MA, 23 Jul 1812, JOHN DUKE, b. at Bordeaux, France, 11 Jul 1779; John d. at Dunbarton, 16 Jan 1864.

vi MARY HOLT, b. at Andover, 7 Jul 1791; d. at Dunbarton, 28 Nov 1835; m. 11 Aug 1809, JAMES ALLISON, b. at Dunbarton, 24 May 1784 son of Samuel and Molly (Barr) Allison; James d. at Goffstown, 2 Feb 1867. James married second Mary Ireland on 8 Mar 1837.

vii REBECCA HOLT, b. at Andover, 25 May 1793; d. at Andover, 14 Jan 1878; m. at Andover, 3 Apr 1817, JOHN GOODHUE, b. at Bradford, MA, 23 May 1786 son of Phineas and Hannah (Parsons) Goodhue; John d. at North Andover, 13 Apr 1856.

viii ENOCH HOLT, b. at Andover, 5 Sep 1795; d. at Melrose, 20 Dec 1855; m. at Andover, 25 Dec 1817, SARAH W. DAVISON, b. at Concord, NY (per death record), 1797; d. at Melrose, 2 Oct 1858.

ix ELIZA HOLT m. CHARLES HOLMES.[2150]

x JONATHAN HOLT, b. at Andover, 1 May 1798; d. at Ipswich, 2 Jan 1863; m. 1st at Ipswich, 28 Jan 1821, HANNAH HOBBS, b. at Ipswich, 11 Mar 1798 daughter of Abraham and Mary (Story) Hobbs; Hannah d. Ipswich, 6 Jan 1852. Jonathan m. 2nd at Rowley, 3 Jan 1855, FRANCES "FANNY" LORD (widow of Nehemiah Jewett), b. at Bridgton, ME about 1807 daughter of Thomas and Priscilla (Harmon) Lord; Fanny d. at Hamilton, MA, 10 Sep 1894.

xi LEVINA HOLT, b. at Andover, 2 Aug 1800; *perhaps* she is the Levina who married at Andover, 25 Mar 1820, DAVID E. CHAPMAN of Gilmanton, NH.

802) SARAH HOLT (*Shuah Holt Holt[4], Humphrey[3], Henry[2], Nicholas[1]*), b. at Andover, 3 Feb 1757 daughter of Jonathan and Shuah (Holt) Holt; d. at Sullivan, NH, 12 Apr 1844; m. at Andover, 21 May 1776, JONATHAN BAKER, b. at Topsfield, 25 Jun 1749 son of Thomas and Sarah (Wade) Baker; Jonathan d. at Sullivan, 12 Oct 1833.

Sarah and Jonathan started their family in Topsfield but were in Sullivan, New Hampshire in 1777 where they remained.[2151] In his will (probate 23 October 1833), Jonathan Baker bequeathed to his beloved wife Sarah all his pasture and wild land lying to the west and adjoining the land of Stephen Foster to be hers and to her heirs and assigns forever. He bequeathed twenty-five cents to each of his children: Betsy, Sally, Jonathan, Polly, Phebe, Aaron, Thomas, Rebecca, Abigail, Mahala, George, David, William, Emerson, and Elijah. The rest of the personal estate including the pew in the meeting house is bequeathed to wife Sarah to be of her own use and benefit forever. Samuel Locke was named executor.[2152] In her will written 15 June 1841, Sarah Baker bequeathed to son Elijah the pastureland and wild land. Daughter Rebecca Baker received all the household furniture and the pew in the meeting house. Daughters Phebe and Abigail received the residue of the personal estate. To her remaining children, she had "nothing to give": Betsy, Sally, Jonathan, Aaron, Mahala, David, William, and Emerson, and the heirs of Thomas, Polly, and George who are deceased.[2153]

Sarah and Jonathan were parents of fifteen children, all but the oldest born at Gilsum (later Sullivan), New Hampshire. Five of the children settled in Jefferson County, New York.

i BETSEY BAKER, b. at Topsfield, 4 Jul 1776; m. at Sullivan, 2 Sep 1798, WILLIAM THOMPSON, b. at Northbridge, MA, 13 Jul 1776 son of William and Lydia (Dyer) Thompson; William d. at Surry, NH, 16 Apr 1864.

ii SARAH BAKER, b. at Sullivan, 25 Apr 1778; d. at Pittsford, VT, 21 Jan 1871; m. at Sullivan, 7 Mar 1796, THOMAS POWELL, b. at Litchfield, NH, 13 Mar 1772; d. at Pittsford, VT, 25 Aug 1842.

iii JONATHAN BAKER, b. at Sullivan, 5 Aug 1779; d. at Watertown, NY, 28 Oct 1863; m. DORCAS FELLOWS, b. at Shelburne, MA, 2 Sep 1787 daughter of Willis and Sarah (Hart) Fellows;[2154] Dorcas d. at Watertown, 24 Aug 1877.

iv MARY "POLLY" BAKER, b. at Sullivan, 3 Dec 1781; d. 12 Apr 1839[2155] and this is confirmed by her mother's will of 1841 with Polly listed as deceased. It is not known if she married or where she died.

v PHEBE BAKER, b. at Sullivan, 22 Apr 1784; d. at Hopkinton, NY, 8 Apr 1880; m. at Sullivan, 4 Jul 1807, JOSEPH SMITH, b. 1783 son of Dudley and Mary (Baker) Smith; Joseph d. at Hopkinton, 1867.

2150 Eliza is a child given in Durrie's Holt genealogy for whom no records were found.

2151 Seward, *A History of the Town of Sullivan*, p 826

2152 *New Hampshire. Probate Court (Cheshire County);* Probate Place: *Cheshire, New Hampshire, Estate Files, B475-B532, 1829-1834, will of Jonathan Baker*

2153 *New Hampshire. Probate Court (Cheshire County);* Probate Place: *Cheshire, New Hampshire, Wills, volume 78, p 421*

2154 Oakes, *Genealogical and Family History of the County of Jefferson, New York*, volume 2

2155 Seward, *A History of the Town of Sullivan, New Hampshire*

vi AARON BAKER, b. at Sullivan, 10 Jul 1786; d. at Columbia Cross Roads, PA, 8 May 1847; m. 29 Mar 1814, MARY HAVEN, b. at Marlborough, NH, 23 Jun 1788 daughter of John and Abigail (Tay) Haven; Mary d. at Columbia Cross Roads, 25 Sep 1873.

vii THOMAS BAKER, b. at Sullivan, 30 Apr 1788; d. at Watertown, NY, 10 Feb 1841; m. 27 Apr 1817, BETSEY TOLMAN, b. at Marlborough, NH, 2 Jun 1788 daughter of Ebenezer and Mary (Clark) Tolman; Betsey d. at Watertown, 24 Dec 1866.

viii REBECCA BAKER, b. at Sullivan, 27 Apr 1790; d. at Sullivan, 18 Jul 1875; m. at Sullivan, 15 Sep 1840, as his second wife, SOLOMON SMITH, b. at Ipswich, MA, 9 Nov 1777 son of Dudley and Mary (Baker) Smith; Solomon d. at Sullivan, 15 Oct 1859.

ix ABIGAIL BAKER, b. at Sullivan, 27 Apr 1790; d. at Jay, NY, 30 Dec 1869; m. ZIBA NYE, b. at Barre, MA, 15 Oct 1781 son of Sylvanus and Mary (Banks) Nye; Ziba d. at Jay, 2 Oct 1860.

x MAHALA BAKER, b. at Sullivan, 9 Nob 1792; d. at Henderson, NY, 28 Mar 1867; m. JOEL JOHNSON who has not been identified; Joel was living in Henderson, NY in 1865.

xi GEORGE BAKER, b. at Sullivan, 1 Feb 1794; d. at Sullivan, 16 Oct 1835; m. 26 Nov 1815, EUNICE WHITTEMORE, b. at New Ipswich, NH, 2 May 1783 daughter of Samuel and Elizabeth (Brown) Whittemore; Eunice d. at Peterborough, NH, 14 Jun 1866.

xii DAVID BAKER, b. at Sullivan, 11 Jun 1796; d. at Dexter, NY, 5 Sep 1879 (probate 1879 with nephew John L. Baker of Watertown as executor); m. REBECCA GOTHAM, b. at NH, about 1797; Rebecca d. at Dexter, 28 Feb 1863. David and Rebecca had one son Andrew.

xiii WILLIAM BAKER, b. at Sullivan, 27 Oct 1797; d. at Westmoreland, NH, 27 May 1871; m. at Keene, 28 Aug 1831, CHARLOTTE BALCH, b. 1808.

xiv EMERSON BAKER, b. at Sullivan, 25 Mar 1799; d. at Polk City, IA, 26 Dec 1870; m. 1st 3 Nov 1824, CHLOE WRIGHT, b. at Packersfield, NH, 14 May 1801 daughter of John and Phebe (Stoddard) Wright; Chloe d. at Rodman, NY, 16 Feb 1834.Emerson m. 2nd DORCAS, b. 1 Apr 1805; Dorcas d. at Polk City, 9 Sep 1879.

xv ELIJAH BAKER, b. at Sullivan, 20 Oct 1800; d. at Dalton, NH, 15 Feb 1887; m. 9 Feb 1826, LAURA MASON, b. at Dublin, NH, 16 Dec 1801 daughter of John and Mary (Haven) Mason; Laura d. at Dalton, 6 Apr 1887.

803) ZEBADIAH HOLT (*Shuah Holt Holt*[4], *Humphrey*[3], *Henry*[2], *Nicholas*[1]), b. at Andover, 28 Jul 1759 son of Jonathan and Shuah (Holt) Holt; d. 15 Mar 1817; m. at Billerica, 23 Dec 1784, SARAH LEWES. Sarah married second Jotham Blanchard.

Zebadiah Holt served during the Revolution for seven years from 1775 through 1783. His final rank was sergeant major. He was at the Battle of Bunker Hill, the taking of Burgoyne, and in the retreat through New Jersey.[2156] He is called Capt. Zebadiah Holt in Andover records and in his probate record.

Zebadiah Holt did not leave a will and his estate entered probate 15 April 1817 with Amasa Holt as administrator as Sarah declined administration. The total estate value was $107.85 and consisted only of personal estate. On 21 April 1818, Sarah petitioned that the whole of the residue of the personal estate be granted to her due to her destitute condition.[2157]

Zebadiah Holt and Sarah Lewis were parents of seven children born at Andover.

i AMASA HOLT, b. at Andover, 30 Dec 1785; d. at Lynn, 26 Aug 1844; m. 21 Sep 1817, his fourth cousin once removed, LUCRETIA PARKER (*Elizabeth Farley Parker*[6], *Elizabeth Johnson Farley*[5], *Andrew Johnson*[4], *James Johnson*[3], *Mary Holt Johnson*[2], *Nicholas*[1]), b. at Groton, 11 Jan 1787 daughter of Joshua and Elizabeth (Farley) Parker;[2158] Lucretia d. at Lynn, 13 Aug 1868.

ii ZEBADIAH HOLT, b. at Andover, 5 Apr 1787; d. at Canton, MA, 19 Jul 1870; m. 1st at Milford, NH, his third cousin, BETSEY HOLT (*Abiel*[6], *Abiel*[5], *Thomas*[4], *Thomas*[3], *Nicholas*[2], *Nicholas*[1]), b. at Milford, 12 Apr 1797 daughter of Abiel and Elizabeth (Holt) Holt; Betsey d. at Milford, 8 May 1826. Zebadiah m. 2nd at Chelmsford, 11 Nov 1833, PHILENA I. HARRINGTON, b. at Worcester, 1814; Philena d. at Canton, 11 Mar 1854 of consumption.

iii SALLY LEWIS HOLT, b. at Andover, 5 Apr 1789; d. at Andover, 19 Oct 1837. Sally did not marry.

iv ASA LEWIS HOLT, b. at Andover, 1 Jun 1791; d. at Andover, 29 Mar 1825; m. at Tewksbury, Apr 1818, ALETHENIA FISK. Alethenia married second Joseph Parker on 4 Feb 1830. There is a record for one daughter for Asa and Alethenia.

2156 Durrie, Holt genealogy

2157 *Essex County, MA: Probate File Papers, 1638-1881.*Online database. *AmericanAncestors.org.* New England Historic Genealogical Society, 2014. Case 13706

2158 The names of Lucretia's parents are given as Joshua and Elizabeth on her death record.

v JONATHAN HOLT, b. at Andover, 17 Jun 1793; d. at Andover, 1 Dec 1827; m. at Andover, 3 Jan 1817, MARY MERRILL. Jonathan and Mary were parents of five children.

vi ELIZABETH GOULD HOLT, b. at Andover, 13 Jun 1795; d. at Milford, NH, 3 Jan 1869; m. 9 Dec 1827, EZEKIEL MILLS, b. at Mont Vernon, NH, 22 Feb 1800 son of Ebenezer and Hannah (Upton) Mills; Ezekiel d. at Milford, 28 Jun 1881.

vii CHARLES HOLT, b. at Andover, 30 Apr 1797; m. ELIZABETH, b. at Eden, ME, about 1784; Elizabeth d. at Charlestown, MA, 23 Feb 1855. Charles and Elizabeth had one daughter, Elizabeth, who married Thomas Armitage.

804) PHEBE HOLT (*Shuah Holt Holt⁴, Humphrey³, Henry², Nicholas¹*), b. at Andover, 31 Jan 1761 daughter of Jonathan and Shuah (Holt) Holt; d. 20 Sep 1848; m. at Chelmsford, 11 Jan 1790, LEVI FLETCHER, b. at Chelmsford, 3 Mar 1757 son of William and Mary (Blodgett) Fletcher; Levi d. at Lowell, 2 Nov 1832.

Phebe Holt and Levi Fletcher were parents of five children.

i WILLIAM FLETCHER, b. at Chelmsford, 2 Sep 1791; d. at Lowell, 2 Nov 1881. William did not marry.

ii PHEBE FLETCHER, b. at Chelmsford, 1 Apr 1794; d. at Lowell, 24 Aug 1864. Phebe did not marry.

iii SHUAH HOLT FLETCHER, b. at Chelmsford, 24 Mar 1796; d. at Lowell, 20 Sep 1881; m. at Chelmsford, 21 Jan 1826, JOSEPH FLETCHER, b. at Chelmsford, 9 May 1793 son of Joseph and Lucy (Proctor) Fletcher; Joseph d. at Francestown, NH, 26 Nov 1866.

iv ZACCHAEUS FLETCHER, b. at Chelmsford, 9 Aug 1798; d. at Mansfield, MA, 6 May 1881; m. at Andover, 31 Dec 1823, ADELINE AUSTIN, b. at Andover, 4 May 1801 daughter of Samuel and Dorcas (Marble) Austin; Adeline d. at Foxborough, MA, 25 Jul 1890. Zacchaeus served as a colonel in the militia.

v RELIEF FLETCHER, b. at Lowell, 28 Mar 1802; d. at Lowell, 29 Jan 1883. Relief did not marry.

Great-Grandchildren of Nicholas Holt and Mary Russell

805) JAMES PARKER (*Phebe Ingalls Parker⁴, Mary Holt Ingalls³, Nicholas², Nicholas¹*), b. at Andover, 30 Aug 1746 son of James and Phebe (Ingalls) Parker; d. at Livermore, ME, 26 Apr 1815;[2159] m. at New Gloucester, ME, 16 Aug 1783, PHEBE NOYES, b. 13 Apr 1763 daughter of Simon and Elizabeth (Eaton) Noyes; Phebe d. at Livermore, 23 Jul 1848.

James's father died in 1782 and the following year, James married Phebe Noyes in New Gloucester, Maine. On 11 February 1784, James Parker then of a new township called Bakerstown[2160] in Cumberland County, Commonwealth of Massachusetts, sold to Samuel Johnson for £60 his property in Andover including the dwelling house. This sale was made with consent and approval of his mother Phebe Parker and of his sister Anna Bragg who relinquished their rights as heirs to the property.[2161]

James and Phebe had ten children, the first nine births recorded at Poland, Maine and the tenth at Livermore. James is listed in Poland in the 1800 census. In 1800, the family relocated to Livermore where James for a time owned the grist mill at Gibbs Mills.[2162] James seems to have been in Livermore only a few years before his death.[2163] He sold his mill interest to Eli Putnam, but the date of the transaction is not given in Washburn's Livermore notes. Phebe is buried at Livermore where her son Alfred resided.

i JAMES PARKER, b. 23 Apr 1784; d. after 1850 when he was living at Sedgwick, ME; m. about 1830, MARY TAY,[2164] b. about 1805; Mary d. after 1870 when she was living at St. George, ME.

ii PHEBE PARKER, b. 17 Feb 1786

iii ALFRED PARKER, b. 23 Feb 1788; d. at Livermore, ME, 1876; m. about 1815, RUTH PRAY,[2165] b. at Oxford, MA, 23 Mar 1796 daughter of Ebenezer and Deborah (Leonard) Pray; Ruth d. after 1870.

2159 Livermore Vital Records, p 269; accessed through familysearch,org

2160 The Bakerstown Plantation was later to be Poland, Maine.

2161 Massachusetts Land Records, 1620-1986, Essex County, 142:233, accessed through familysearch.org.

2162 Monroe, *History of the Town of Livermore*, p 188

2163 Washburn, *Notes Historical, Descriptive, and Personal of Livermore*, p 45

2164 Mary's maiden name is given as Mary Tay on the death record of her son Marcellus.

2165 Washburn, *Notes Historical, Descriptive, and Personal of Livermore*, p 45

iv NANCY PARKER, b. 15 Mar 1790

v SIMON PARKER, b. 26 Jul 1792

vi SARAH PARKER, b. 5 Feb 1794

vii ELIZABETH PARKER, b. 11 Jul 1797

viii BENJAMIN PARKER, b. 13 Jun 1800; m. 1st ANNA, b. about 1800 who has not been identified and who d. likely at Dracut about 1851. Benjamin m. 2nd at Lowell, MA, 25 Nov 1852, EUNICE THURSTON, b. perhaps in Canada (census record), about 1826 daughter of Nathaniel and Martha (-) Thurston.

ix JESSE PARKER, b. 13 Jun 1800; d. at East Vassalboro, ME, 23 Mar 1885; m. 6 Jun 1826, CLEMENTINE ELDRIDGE CHANDLER, b. at Monmouth, ME, 1 Aug 1805 daughter of Daniel R. and Sally C. (Maloon) Chandler; Clementine d. at Vassalboro, 4 Oct 1860.

x CHARLES PARKER, b. at Livermore, 21 Aug 1804.[2166]

806) WILLIAM HOLT (*Benjamin⁴, Nicholas³, Nicholas², Nicholas¹*), b. at Andover, Oct 1737 son of Benjamin and Sarah (Frye) Holt; d. at Allenstown, NH, 28 Aug 1816; m. at Andover, 2 Sep 1769, ELIZABETH "BETSEY" AMES, perhaps b. at Andover, 13 Jan 1744/5 daughter of Samuel and Elizabeth (Stevens) Ames.

William Holt and Betsey Ames resided in Pembroke and were parents of seven children.[2167]

i WILLIAM HOLT, b. at Pembroke, 1775; d. at Pembroke, 29 Dec 1801.

ii DORCAS HOLT, b. at Pembroke, about 1776; d. at Bradford, MA, 19 Aug 1853; m. FRANCIS KIMBALL, b. at Bradford, 10 May 1777 son of Francis and Betsey (Head) Kimball; Francis d. at Bradford, 1 Dec 1843.

iii OLIVE HOLT, b. about 1777

iv ENOCH HOLT, b. at Pembroke, about 1780; d. at Salem, MA, 5 Dec 1873; m. at Pembroke, 25 Apr 1805, SALLY MORGAN, b. at Pembroke, 31 May 1781 daughter of Jeremiah and Elizabeth (Lovejoy) Morgan; Sally d. at Bow, NH, 15 Mar 1848.

v BETSEY HOLT, b. 1781; d. 8 Jul 1801.

vi FANNY HOLT, b. at Allenstown, about 1782; reported in the History of Pembroke to marry a Clark but no records have yet been found.

vii BENJAMIN HOLT, b. at Allenstown, about 1783; d. after 1870 when he was living at Alexandria, NH; m. about 1805, BETSEY EVANS.

807) SARAH HOLT (*Benjamin⁴, Nicholas³, Nicholas², Nicholas¹*), b. at Andover, about 1738 daughter of Benjamin and Sarah (Frye) Holt; m. about 1756, STEPHEN COFFIN, b. at Newbury, 6 Aug 1729 son of Daniel and Lydia (Moulton) Coffin.

Stephen Coffin was an early settler in Alfred, Maine following there after his brother Simeon was a first settler.[2168] Sarah Holt and Stephen Coffin were likely parents of seven children according to the Coffin genealogy.[2169] One further child, James, seems a likely child in this family.[2170]

i SARAH COFFIN, b. 1756; d. at South Berwick, ME, 15 Oct 1836; m. at Berwick, 9 Oct 1773, BENJAMIN KNIGHT, b. 21 Sep 1757 son of John and Olive (Hamilton) Knight; Benjamin d. at South Berwick, 16 Apr 1843.

ii PETER COFFIN, b. about 1758; d. at Gilead, ME, 1 Nov 1843; m. 1st 7 Feb 1782, SARAH WALKER, b. about 1758 daughter of Timothy and Martha (Colby) Walker; Sarah d. at Conway, NH, 31 Aug 1803. Peter m. 2nd at

---

2166 Livermore Vital Records, p 269; accessed through familysearch,org

2167 Carter, *History of Pembroke*, p 148

2168 Parsons, *Centennial History of Alfred, York County*, Maine, p 8

2169 Appleton, *Gatherings toward a Genealogy of the Coffin Family: Five Generations of Descendants of Tristram Coffin of Newbury and Nantucket*, https://www.ancestry.com/search/collections/16038/

2170 Information from the Lovell Historical Society summarizing notes and original correspondence between Ms. Charlotte Hobbs and Dr. Leslie Coffin (personal communication from Marianne Grant who provided copies of the original Hobbs notes and letters). Four further children have been suggested as belonging to this family. Boyle in his *Early Families of Alfred, Maine*, p 61 reports on the proposal by Gardner in *The Gardner Family of Maine* that there are sons Hezekiah, Josiah and Grindall in this family. However, the sources for that information are not clear. In addition, Grindall Coffin was born 7 April 1785 which would require that Sarah had 30 years of childbearing, which although not impossible, does require additional verification. An oldest son Stephen born 12 August 1754 has also been suggested, but that is not clear, and The History of Bethel suggests that Stephen Coffin born in 1754 was likely a son of Benjamin Coffin.

Carroll, NH, 12 Aug 1804, JANE ORDWAY (widow of John Evens), b. at Goffstown, NH, 8 May 1770 daughter of Joseph and Mehitable (Abbott) Ordway; Jane d. at Stoneham, ME, 6 Dec 1854.

iii MARY COFFIN, b. at Kittery, ME, 8 May 1763; d. at Knox, ME, 22 Sep 1842; m. 1782, PAUL WENTWORTH, b. 1759 *possibly* son of Paul and Patience (Abbott) Wentworth; Paul d. at Knox, 4 Sep 1833.

iv ABIAH COFFIN, b. about 1764; d. after 1840 at Waterboro, ME; m. about 1790, JONATHAN KNIGHT, b. 1762 son of John and Olive (Hamilton) Knight; Jonathan d. at Waterboro, 1848.

v NICHOLAS COFFIN, b. 5 Apr 1765; d. at Lincoln, ME, 14 Feb 1850; m. 10 Jun 1788, POLLY HEATH, b. about 1768 daughter of Joshua Heath; Polly d. about 1808; Nicholas m. 2nd 14 Aug 1810, LYDIA LEEMAN,[2171] b. about 1789; Lydia d. after 1855 when she was living at Lincoln, ME.

vi LYDIA COFFIN, b. about 1768; m. at Conway, NH, 17 Mar 1791, JAMES STERLING, b. 1767 son of Hugh and Isabel (Stark) Sterling.[2172]

vii BENJAMIN COFFIN, b. about 1769; d. likely before 1850. He is perhaps the Benjamin Coffin who m. at Conway, 13 Nov 1792, HANNAH BURBANK, b. at Conway, 26 Jan 1774 daughter of Ebenezer and Hannah (Dolloff) Burbank; Hannah d. after 1850 when she was living at Lowell, ME.

viii JAMES COFFIN, b. at Alfred, ME, 5 Jun 1771;[2173] d. at Lovell, ME, 11 Jan 1829; m. about 1794, MARY "POLLY" STEPHENS, b. at Fryeburg, 10 Mar 1776 daughter of John Stephens; Polly d. at Lovell, 4 Apr 1860.

808) NATHAN HOLT (*Benjamin[4], Nicholas[3], Nicholas[2], Nicholas[1]*), b. at Andover, about 1740 son of Benjamin and Sarah (Frye) Holt; d. at Pembroke, NH, 3 Mar 1818; m. at Pembroke, 1762, SUSANNAH BLANCHARD, b. about 1742; Susannah d. at Pembroke, 28 Aug 1837.

Nathan Holt served in the Revolution and was wounded at Bunker Hill by a musket ball passing through his right thigh.[2174][2175] Nathan enrolled in Capt. Daniel Moore's company of Col. John Stark's regiment on 1 May 1775.[2176] He received a pension as an invalid commencing 4 March 1795 related to his service.[2177] The allowed payment was a one-fourth pension.

On 31 January 1846, Phebe Holt, then age sixty-eight and resident of Concord, appeared to give a statement related to the pension and receiving possible payments due. Her deceased mother Susannah Holt had been the widow of Nathan Holt. Her parents were married at Pembroke in 1762 by Rev. Aaron Whittemore. Her father Nathan died 3 March 1818 and her mother died at Pembroke on 28 August 1837. On 19 February 1846, Calvin Ainsworth register of probate for Merrimack County, New Hampshire stated that satisfactory evidence had been presented to support that Susannah Holt died 28 August 1837 and the only surviving children were Stephen Holt of Pembroke, Frye Holt of Concord, Phebe Holt of Concord, Sally Goodwin wife of James Goodwin, and Mary Wheeler widow of Jonas Wheeler.

Nathan's sister Dorcas Emery provided a statement on 13 February 1846. Dorcas, then age eighty-three and resident of Pembroke, reported she was the youngest of thirteen children in the family. Her brother Nathan married Susannah Blanchard and they had a family of nine children five of whom were currently living. George W. Dow, town clerk of Pembroke, on 13 February 1846, provided a statement that he examined the town records from 1767 forward and could find no record of the marriage or the births of the children, but noted that the records were irregular and that some of the records of the town had been destroyed by fire.

On 20 September 1847, Arthur Fletcher contacted the pension board regarding possible payment that may be due to surviving children based on the widow's pension of their mother Susan who died in 1836. A payment of arrears was allowed in October 1847 to the "only children": Stephen Holt, Frye Holt, Phebe Holt, Sally Goodwin, and Mary Wheeler.[2178]

Nathan and Susannah lived in Pembroke throughout their married lives. Nathan with his son Nathan, Jr. built a grist mill on Great Brook about 1800.[2179]

Nathan Holt did not leave a will and his estate entered probate 20 May 1818 with William Holt as administrator. Real estate of about 20 acres in the 7th range was valued at $200 and personal estate was valued at $83.62.[2180]

Nathan Holt and Susannah Blanchard were parents of eleven children[2181] born at Pembroke.

2171 U. S. Revolutionary War Pension and Bounty-Land Warrant Application Files, Case W8189

2172 Sterling, *The Sterling Genealogy*, volume 2, p 1103

2173 This is the date and place of birth given in correspondence between Dr. Leslie Coffin and Ms. Charlotte Hobbs, and the correspondence suggests that James was a son of Stephen. The information is reported as coming from a family bible record although the bible pages or the transcription of the bible pages are not given.

2174 U S. Revolutionary War Pension and Bounty-Land Warrant Application Files, Case W15913

2175 Carter, *History of Pembroke*, volume II, p 147

2176 *U.S., Revolutionary War Rolls, 1775-1783* [database on-line]. Provo, UT, USA: Ancestry.com Operations, Inc., 2007. *Reeds Regiment, 1775 (Folder 136) - Waldron's Regiment, 1776 (Folder 159)*

2177 U.S. Pension Roll of 1835, New Hampshire Pension Roll

2178 U. S. Revolutionary War Pension and Bounty-Land Warrant Application Files, Case W15913

2179 Carter, *History of Pembroke*, volume I

2180 *New Hampshire. Probate Court (Rockingham County), Estate Papers, No 9686-9748, 1818, Case 9731*

2181 In the pension file, Nathan's sister Dorcas states that Nathan and Susannah had nine children and perhaps that is a misstatement, or perhaps there is still more to learn about the children in this family.

i NATHAN HOLT, b. 1762; d. at North Pembroke, 11 Apr 1841; m. at Pembroke, 16 Jul 1783, SARAH BLACK, perhaps b. at Haverhill, MA, 11 Feb 1762 daughter of Edmund and Sarah (Lufkin) Black; Sarah d. at North Pembroke, 9 Apr 1854 at age 92.

ii ABIAH HOLT, b. 1765; d. at Pembroke, 2 Nov 1835; m. at Pembroke, 5 May 1790, as his second wife, JAMES FIFE, b. 1742 son of John and Jane (Garvin) Fife; James d. at Pembroke, after 1820.

iii ESTHER HOLT, b. about 1766; d. at North Pembroke, 30 Oct 1824; m. 28 Dec 1797, ROBERT FIFE, b. at Pembroke, Feb 1766 son of William and Phebe (White) Fife; Robert d. at North Pembroke, 9 Jun 1854.

iv SUSANNAH BALLARD HOLT, b. 1771; d. at Pembroke, 16 Jul 1843; m. at Pembroke, 29 Dec 1806, as his second wife, SAMUEL GARVIN, b. at Bow, NH, 15 Sep 1777 son of James and Deborah (-) Garvin; Samuel d. at Pembroke, 22 April 1837. Samuel was first married at Pembroke, 26 Nov 1799 to MEHITABLE LOVEJOY (*Caleb Lovejoy⁶, Caleb Lovejoy⁵, Henry Lovejoy⁴, Mary Farnum Lovejoy³, Elizabeth Holt Farnum², Nicholas¹*), b. at Pembroke, 11 Feb 1781 daughter of Caleb and Mehitable (Kimball) Lovejoy; Mehitable d. 1804.

v STEPHEN HOLT, b. 1773; d. at Pembroke, 11 May 1856. Stephen did not marry. In his will proved May 1856, Stephen Holt left his entire estate to his niece Almira Blake wife of Stephen Blake "to her sole and separate use free from the interference and control of her husband" during her natural life. At Almira's decease the estate goes to her children Louisa H. Blake and Henry F. Blake. If Almira's children both die with heirs, then the estate goes to Phillip F. Holt.[2182] Almira Holt Blake was a daughter of Frye Holt and his wife Lydia Eastman.

vi WILLIAM HOLT, b. about 1776; d. at Pembroke, 25 May 1843; m. SARAH FIFE, b. about 1785 daughter of William and Phebe (White) Fife; Sarah d. at Pembroke, 3 Mar 1865.

vii PHEBE HOLT, b. about 1778; d. after 1846 when she was living at Concord and unmarried.

viii FRYE HOLT, b. 15 Sep 1779; d. at North Conway, 8 Apr 1850; m. 26 May 1801, his fourth cousin once removed, LYDIA EASTMAN (*Abiathar Eastman⁶, Mary Lovejoy Eastman⁵, Henry Lovejoy⁴, Mary Farnum Lovejoy³, Elizabeth Holt Farnum², Nicholas¹*), b. at Conway, 4 Sep 1779 daughter of Abiathar and Phebe (Merrill) Eastman; Lydia d. at Bartlett, NH, 21 Apr 1872.

ix MARY "POLLY" HOLT, b. about 1780; d. after 1850; m. about 1798, JONAS WHEELER, b. estimated 1772; Jonas d. before 1847.

x SARAH "SALLY" HOLT, b. about 1780; d. after 1850 when she was living at Concord; m. 9 Mar 1826, JAMES GOODWIN, b. at Merrimack, 23 Jan 1784 son of Alpheus and Abiah (Heath) Goodwin; James d. after 1850.

xi OLIVE HOLT, b. about 1785; d. at Pembroke, 6 Jul 1818.

809) DANIEL HOLT (*Benjamin⁴, Nicholas³, Nicholas², Nicholas¹*), b. at Pembroke, 14 Sep 1744 son of Benjamin and Sarah (Frye) Holt; d. at Pembroke, 5 Dec 1813; m. about 1770, ABIGAIL LOVEJOY, b. at Pembroke, 12 Sep 1750 daughter of David and Elizabeth (Chandler) Lovejoy; Abigail d. at Pembroke, 18 Mar 1833.

In his will written 18 October 1813, Daniel Holt bequeaths to beloved wife Abigail one-third of the real and personal estate while she is a widow. Children Abigail Little, Jedediah Holt, Benjamin Holt, Stephen Holt, Esther Johnson, and John Holt each receive one dollar exclusive of what they have already received. Sons Richard Holt and Daniel Holt receive all the real and personal estate in Pembroke and elsewhere not otherwise disposed of. Son Richard Holt was named executor.[2183]

Abigail Lovejoy and Daniel Holt were parents of eight children all born at Pembroke.[2184]

i ABIGAIL HOLT, b. 14 Apr 1771; m. at unknown date Mr. Little. Nothing else is known.[2185]

ii JEDEDIAH HOLT, b. 12 Aug 1774; d. at Dorchester, NH, 25 Oct 1850; m. at Concord, 1805, MARTHA "PATTY" NOYES, b. at Bow, 28 Mar 1787 daughter of John and Mary (Fowler) Noyes.

iii BENJAMIN HOLT, b. 4 Dec 1776; d. at Loudon, 15 Jun 1867; m. at Pembroke, 28 Nov 1805, ANNA KNOX, b. at Pembroke, 12 Aug 1782 daughter of William and Elinor (McDaniel) Knox; Anna d. at Loudon, 10 Oct 1867.

iv STEPHEN HOLT, b. 16 Sep 1779; d. at Pembroke, 28 Jun 1839; m. 6 Mar 1814, POLLY KNOX, b. 15 Aug 1792 daughter of John and Mary Ann (Knox) Knox; Polly d. at Pembroke, 10 Oct 1849.

2182 *New Hampshire. Probate Court (Merrimack County), volume 25, p 652*

2183 *New Hampshire. Probate Court (Rockingham County)*; Probate Place: *Rockingham, New Hampshire, Probate Records, Vol 41-42, 1812-1815*, vol 42, p 52, will of Daniel Holt

2184 Durrie's Holt genealogy also reports a set of twins, unnamed, who died in early infancy.

2185 The Holt genealogy and History of Pembroke report that Abigail married twice and did not have children. No records related to her marriages have been located.

v RICHARD HOLT, b. 12 Feb 1782; d. at Pembroke, 18 Aug 1836; m. 2 Mar 1834, MARY ANN KNOX, b. 11 Aug 1796 daughter of Daniel and Rachel (McClintock) Knox; Mary Ann d. at Pembroke, 13 Aug 1865.

vi JOHN HOLT, b. 14 Feb 1784; d. at Pembroke, 22 Aug 1856; m. 19 Dec 1817, HANNAH AYER, b. at Pembroke, 15 Jul 1791 daughter of John and Abia (-) Ayer; Hannah d. at Pembroke, 22 Apr 1848.

vii ESTHER HOLT, b. 7 Jun 1787; d. at Allenstown, NH, about 1843; m. 4 Feb 1809, JOHN JOHNSON, b. at Allenstown, about 1786. By 1850, John was apparently married to Mary with whom he had a six-year child.

viii DANIEL LOVEJOY HOLT, b. 14 Jun 1791; d. at Pembroke, after 1870; m. 23 Apr 1815, SALLY HOLT, b. at Pembroke, 16 Apr 1789 daughter of Nathan and Sarah (Black) Holt; Sally d. at Pembroke, 16 Apr 1841.

810) FRYE HOLT (*Benjamin⁴, Nicholas³, Nicholas², Nicholas¹*), b. at Pembroke, about 1746 son of Benjamin and Sarah (Frye) Holt; m. about 1770, MARY POOR who has not been identified.

This is a family for which there is little firm information. Both Durrie's Holt genealogy and History of Pembroke list fifteen children but little else in terms of births, deaths, and marriages and little was located in records. Frye is reported to have gone to Hull, Canada late in life.[2186] The order of the children is not known.

i SALLY HOLT, b. about 1773; m. at Pembroke, 25 Jan 1793, her first cousin, NICHOLAS GILMAN (*Mary Holt Gilman⁵, Benjamin⁴, Nicholas³, Nicholas², Nicholas¹*), b. at Pembroke, 21 Apr 1773 son of Nathaniel and Mary (Holt) Gilman; Nicholas d. at Dorchester, NH, 29 Mar 1817.

ii JOSEPH HOLT

iii ELIZABETH "BETSEY" HOLT, b. about 1782 (age 68 in 1850); d. after 1850; m. at Dorchester, NH, 24 Mar 1801, DAVID HUTCHINS, b. about 1769 son of Hezekiah and Anna (Merrill) Hutchins;[2187] David d. after 1850 when he was living in Rumford, ME.

iv FRYE HOLT, b. estimate 1788 (age 40-49 in 1830); m. at Bristol, NH, 11 Jul 1822, HANNAH DODGE, b. estimate 1802. The family was living in Bristol, NH in 1830 with a total household of five.[2188]

v NANCY HOLT, d. at age 20 years.

vi ENOCH HOLT

vii PHEBE HOLT

viii DOLLY HOLT

ix DANIEL HOLT; died young

x CLARISSA HOLT

xi HARRIET HOLT

xii ABIGAIL HOLT

xiii CHARLOTTE HOLT

xiv MOSES HOLT

xv LUCINDA HOLT; d. at age 5 years.

811) MARY "MOLLY" HOLT (*Benjamin⁴, Nicholas³, Nicholas², Nicholas¹*) b. at Pembroke, about 1752 daughter of Benjamin and Sarah (Frye) Holt; m. about 1770, NATHANIEL GILMAN, b. at Exeter, NH, 29 Aug 1748 son of Peter and Abigail (-) Gilman.[2189]

Mary and Nathaniel were parents of eight children as reported in *The Story of the Gilmans*. There are records for six of the children.[2190]

i EZEKIEL GILMAN, b. at Pembroke, NH, 27 Apr 1771; d. at Deerfield, NH, 1804 (probate 1804); m. at Candia, NH, 28 Nov 1799, SALLY BEAN, b. likely at Candia, about 1780 daughter of Nathan and Hannah (Buswell)

2186 Carter, *History of Pembroke*, p 149

2187 Lapham, *History of Rumford, Oxford County, Maine*, p 356

2188 1830; Census Place: Bristol, Grafton, New Hampshire; Series: M19; Roll: 75; Page: 91; Family History Library Film: 0337928; 1 male 40-49, 2 females 20-29, 1 male under 5, and 1 female under 5

2189 Ames, *The Story of the Gilmans*, p 110

2190 New Hampshire Births and Christenings 1714-1904

Bean. Sally m. 2nd by about 1809, Woodin Norris (b. 1763). Son of Sally and Woodin Norris, Ezekiel Gilman Norris, was born 1809.

ii NICHOLAS GILMAN, b. at Pembroke, 21 Apr 1773; d. at Dorchester, NH, 29 Mar 1817; m. at Pembroke, 25 Jan 1798, his first cousin, SALLY HOLT (*Frye5, Benjamin4, Nicholas3, Nicholas2, Nicholas1*), b. about 1773 daughter of Frye and Mary (Poor) Holt.

iii ABIGAIL GILMAN, b. at Groton, 22 Mar 1777; d. at Waterville, VT, 12 Feb 1851; m. STEVENS REDDING, b. at Middleborough, MA, 27 Oct 1780 son of Moses and Priscilla (Rider) Redding; Stevens d. at Bangor, WI, 24 Dec 1868.

iv SALLY GILMAN, b. at Groton, 25 May 1779

v JOHN GILMAN, b. at Groton, 7 Feb 1782

vi PHEBE GILMAN, b. about 1783; d. at Canaan, NH, 26 Oct 1868; m. 14 Jun 1805, JOHN R. DUSTIN, b. about 1784; John d. after 1850 when he was living at Canaan.

vii POLLY GILMAN

viii DOLLY GILMAN

812) DORCAS HOLT (*Benjamin4, Nicholas3, Nicholas2, Nicholas1*), b. at Pembroke, about 1764 daughter of Benjamin and Sarah (Frye) Holt; d. at Pembroke, 17 Sep 1850; m. 16 Sep 1787, JOSEPH EMERY, b. 19 Dec 1764 son of Joseph and Hannah (Stickney) Emery; Joseph d. 8 Jun 1830.

Dorcas and Joseph resided in Pembroke where Joseph was selected as constable in 1805. They were members of the south meeting house church in Pembroke.[2191]

Dorcas Holt and Joseph Emery were parents of nine children born at Pembroke.

i PHEBE EMERY, b. 28 Apr 1788; d. at Pembroke, 18 Oct 1818; m. 11 Dec 1817, CHARLES KING WILLIAMS, b. 1 Sep 1780 son of Jonathan and Elizabeth (King) Williams; Charles d. at Pembroke, 12 Apr 1861. After Phebe's death, Charles married her sister Abigail (see below).

ii SARAH "SALLY" EMERY, b. 14 Feb 1790; d. after 1855 when she was living in Somerville, MA; m. 8 Aug 1811, JOHN BUSS, b. at Boston, about 1790; John d. at Boston, of intemperance, 8 Sep 1828. Sarah and John had five daughters two of whom died in early childhood.

iii DORCAS EMERY, b. 28 Sep 1791; d. at Pembroke, Sep 1852; m. at Pembroke, 12 Sep 1826, as his second wife, JOHN PARKER, b. at Andover, MA, 20 May 1783 son of John and Joanna (Bailey) Parker; John d. at Pembroke, 18 Jan 1862. John married first Esther Baker.

iv JOSEPH EMERY, b. Sep 1793; d. 24 Dec 1796.

v HANNAH EMERY, b. 5 Jul 1795; d. at Pembroke, 6 May 1883; m. 29 Dec 1824, as his third wife, STEPHEN BATES, b. at Hingham, MA, 4 Sep 1784 son of Stephen and Susanna (Trufont) Bates; Stephen d. at Pembroke, 20 Sep 1872. Stephen was first married to Anne Thurston and second married to Anna Shattuck.

vi ABIGAIL EMERY, b. 10 Sep 1797; d. at Pembroke, 3 Jan 1859; m. about 1822, as his second wife CHARLES KING WILLIAMS who was first married to Abigail's sister Phebe (see above).

vii JOSEPH EMERY, b. 13 Sep 1799; d. at Pembroke, 22 Sep 1886; m. 16 Sep 1829, HANNAH MORRILL, b. at Epping, 28 Apr 1809 daughter of Nathaniel and Hannah (Rowell) Morrill; Hannah d. at Pembroke, 2 Aug 1859.

viii FANNY EMERY, b. 21 Sep 1801; d. 4 Nov 1802.

ix MELINDA EMERY, b. 18 Jun 1805; d. 10 Jul 1827.

813) STEVENS CHANDLER (*Mary Holt Chandler Osgood4, Nicholas3, Nicholas2, Nicholas1*), b. at Andover, 15 Dec 1738 son of William and Mary (Holt) Chandler; d. at Andover, Nov 1814 (buried 10 Nov 1814); m. 1st at Ashford, about 1762, ALICE SNOW, b. at Ashford, 23 Sep 1741 daughter of Joseph and Sarah (Cornell) Snow; Alice d. at Ashford, 17 Jan 1782. Stevens m. 2nd at Ashford, Jun 1784, MARY PRESTON; Mary d. 10 Mar 1787. Stevens m. 3rd at Ashford, 3 Jul 1790, SARAH ROGERS; Sarah d. at the almshouse in Andover, 26 Aug 1817.

Stevens Chandler lived in Connecticut for most of his adult life but returned to Andover by 1814 when he was received into the church at South Andover 15 May 1814. He was a tailor by trade. He was living at the almshouse in Andover at the time of his death.[2192] Two of his daughters, Lois and Alice, also died at the almshouse in Andover.[2193]

[2191] Carter, *History of Pembroke*, p 162, p 252

[2192] Chandler, *Descendants of William and Annis Chandler*, p 212

[2193] Massachusetts Vital Records Project, Andover

Stevens Chandler and Alice Snow were parents of six children.

i JAMES CHANDLER, b. at Ashford, 25 Jul 1763

ii JOEL CHANDLER, b. at Ashford, 10 Mar 1765

iii MARY CHANDLER, b. at Willington, 22 Apr 767

iv WILLIAM CHANDLER, b. at Willington, 14 Jan 1771; d. about 1800; m. MATILDA BURT

v ELIZABETH CHANDLER, b. at Willington, 9 Apr 1774; d. after 1850 when she was living at the poor house in Dedham; m. at Dedham, MA, 29 Oct 1809, THOMAS COLBURN, b. at Dedham, 28 Feb 1753 son of Samuel and Mercy (Dean) Chandler; Thomas d. at Dedham, 22 Feb 1836.

vi STEVENS CHANDLER, b. recorded at Ashford, 12 Nov 1781; d. at Cortlandville, NY, Oct 1850; m. POLLY WINCHESTER, b. 6 Jun 1779 daughter of Amariah Winchester;[2194] Polly d. at Homer, NY, 14 Jan 1844.

Stevens Chandler and Mary Preston were parents of one child.

i BENJAMIN CHANDLER, b. at Ashford, 31 May 1785; d. of illness near Fort Niagara, 21 Sep 1813 during the War of 1812; m. CHARITY CARPENTER, b. at Tolland, 27 Oct 1783 daughter of Simeon and Abigail (Cushman) Carpenter.

Stevens Chandler and Sarah Rogers were parents of two children.

i ALICE CHANDLER, b. at Ashford, 27 Nov 1791; d. at Andover, 11 Oct 1833.

ii LOIS CHANDLER, b. at Ashford, 18 Oct 1797; d. at Andover, 13 Feb 1811.

814) MARY CHANDLER (*Mary Holt Chandler Osgood⁴, Nicholas³, Nicholas², Nicholas¹*), b. at Andover, 8 Feb 1740/1 daughter of William and Mary (Holt) Chandler; d. at Ashford, 11 Mar 1787; m. at Ashford, 18 Nov 1762, JOSEPH SNOW, b. at Ashford, 15 Nov 1738 son of Joseph and Sarah (Cornell) Snow. Joseph married second Desire Swift on 1 Jan 1788. Joseph d. at Ashford, about 1801 (notice of insolvent estate given 1802).

Joseph Snow and Mary Chandler were parents of eight children born at Ashford.

i SIMEON SNOW, b. 1 Sep 1763; m. by 1788, LYDIA BILLINGS

ii AMOS SNOW, b. 20 Sep 1765; d. at Ashford, 13 Sep 1805; m. at Ashford, 27 Jun 1797, his fourth cousin once removed, EUNICE BURNHAM (*Joseph Burnham⁶, Eunice Holt Burnham⁵, Zebadiah⁴, George³, Henry², Nicholas¹*) b. at Ashford, 25 May 1777 daughter of Joseph and Elizabeth (Durkee) Burnham.

iii MARY SNOW, b. 18 Mar 1768

iv JUSTUS SNOW, b. 26 Mar 1769; m. about 1796, his third cousin once removed, SABRA HOLT (*Nehemiah⁴, George³, Henry², Nicholas¹*), b. at Windham, 12 Jan 1768 daughter of Nehemiah and Anna (Farnum) Holt.

v JOSEPH SNOW, b. 31 Mar 1772

vi LEMUEL SNOW, b. 22 Jul 1777

vii CHLOE SNOW, b. 7 Apr 1780

viii ELIPHALET SNOW, b. 7 Jul 1784; d. after 1850 when he was living at Mansfield, CT; m. at Mansfield, 24 May 1807, ANNA ROBINSON, b. about 1788; Anna d. after 1850.

815) DORCAS OSGOOD (*Mary Holt Chandler Osgood⁴, Nicholas³, Nicholas², Nicholas¹*), b. at Andover, 11 Aug 1748 daughter of Jeremiah and Mary (Holt) Osgood; d. at Westport, NY, 31 Aug 1811; m. at Ashford, CT, 5 Jul 1764, BENJAMIN SNOW, b. at Ashford, 23 Jan 1743/4 son of Joseph and Sarah (Cornell) Snow.

There are records for two children of Dorcas and Benjamin born at Ashford.

i JESSE SNOW, b. 3 Jan 1765

ii LYDIA SNOW, b. 6 Oct 1769; d. at Keene, NY, 21 Dec 1853; m. 26 Jan 1792, her second cousin once removed, SMITH HOLT (*Asa⁴, Daniel³, Nicholas², Nicholas¹*), b. at Hartford, about 1769 son of Asa and Margaret (Hammond) Holt; Smith d. at Keene, 28 Dec 1814. Smith Holt and Lydia Snow are Family 930.

[2194] Chandler, *Descendants of William and Annis Chandler*

816) JEDEDIAH HOLT (*Stephen[4], Nicholas[3], Nicholas[2], Nicholas[1]*), b. at Suncook, 23 Feb 1743/4 son of Stephen and Mary (Farnum) Holt; d. at Andover, 12 Feb 1790; m. at Andover, 19 Jun 1766, PHEBE BARKER, b. at Andover, 2 Jan 1749/50 daughter of Samuel and Sarah (Robinson) Barker.

Jedediah Holt served as a sergeant during the Revolution in Peter Poor's company. He "marched on the alarm" to Cambridge on 19 April 1775.[2195]

Jedediah Holt did not leave a will and the estate entered probate 7 June 1790. Widow Phebe Holt was named administratrix. The heirs signing their agreement with the plan for inventory of the estate were Phebe Holt also signing as the guardian for Samuel Holt and Stephen Holt, Nathan Barker signing on behalf of his wife, and Phebe Holt. Real estate was valued at £455.12.4 and personal estate at £398.7.10. The children receiving distributions from the estate were Samuel Holt, Stephen Holt, Phebe Holt, and Sarah Barker.[2196]

Phebe Barker and Jedediah Holt were parents of five children born at Andover.

i SARAH HOLT, b. 16 Jan 1768; d. at Boxford, 9 Jul 1843; m. at Andover, 12 Aug 1788, NATHAN BARKER, b. at Andover, 12 Aug 1768 son of Samuel and Susannah (Foster) Barker; Nathan d. at Boxford, 17 Dec 1821.

ii PHEBE HOLT, b. 18 Feb 1771; d. at Andover, 23 Jan 1844; m. at Andover, 1805, WILLIAM FOSTER, b. about 1772 son of William and Mehitable (Fuller) Foster; William d. at Andover, 14 Nov 1833.

iii MOLLY HOLT, b. 2 Jul 1773; d. 18 Apr 1784.

iv SAMUEL HOLT, b. 24 Jan 1778; d. at Winthrop, ME, 1819 (probate 21 Dec 1819); m. at Andover, 10 May 1803, LYDIA FARNUM, b. at Andover, 14 Jul 1780 daughter of Jedediah and Rebecca (Poor) Farnum.

v STEPHEN HOLT, b. 4 Feb 1786; d. before 1850; m. *likely*, 2 Mar 1809, ABIGAIL DOLE, b. about 1790 daughter of Greenleaf and Mary (Moore) Dole; Abigail d. after 1850.[2197]

817) HANNAH HOLT (*Nicholas[4], Nicholas[3], Nicholas[2], Nicholas[1]*), b. at Andover, 16 Nov 1741 daughter of Nicholas and Hannah (Osgood) Holt; d. at Blue Hill, ME, 31 Dec 1826; m. at Andover, 15 Sep 1763, JONATHAN DARLING, baptized at Salem, 11 Jul 1742 son of Jonathan and Sarah (Wardwell) Darling; Jonathan d. at Blue Hill, 26 Feb 1828.

Jonathan participated in the siege of Louisburg in 1759. He came to Blue Hill about 1762-1763 and settled at what became known as Darling's Point. He was involved in civic affairs of the town.[2198]

Jonathan Darling kept a diary and an abstract of the diary can be found in Maine Historical Magazine, volume 2, starting on page 76. In the diary, Jonathan notes the death of his father at Louisburg in 1746 and his mother's death in 1755. He recounts some of the details of his participation in the expedition to Louisburg in 1759-1760. The walls at Louisburg were fully blown up on 8 November 1760 for which "the Governor gave us four days' pay, and a pint of rum a man for our good behavior." He also recounts his selection of a property in Blue Hill on which to settle. The diary continues through 1773.

Hannah Holt and Jonathan Darling were parents of nine children. The birth of the oldest child is recorded at Andover although the "Families of the Early Settlers of Blue Hill Maine" reports this child as the first while male child born in Blue Hill. It may be that the second child Jonathan was the first white male child born at Blue Hill.

i JONATHAN DARLING, possibly b. at Blue Hill, 25 Nov 1763; d. 7 Mar 1765.

ii JONATHAN DARLING, b. at Blue Hill, 17 Oct 1765; d. at Enfield, ME, 17 Dec 1848; m. 28 Dec 1797, MIRIAM GRAY, b. at Sedgwick, ME, 22 May 1777 daughter of John and Hannah (Getchell) Gray; Miriam d. at Enfield, 9 Feb 1858.

iii HANNAH DARLING, b. Mar 1767; d. 6 Jul 1767.

iv HANNAH DARLING, b. 12 Jun 1768; d. 13 Dec 1768.

v SARAH "SALLY" DARLING, b. at Blue Hill, 30 Jun 1770; d. at Blue Hill, 16 Oct 1836; m. 13 Sep 1794, PETER PARKER, b. at Andover, 17 Oct 1769 son of Peter and Phebe (Marble) Parker; Peter d. at Blue Hill, 30 Apr 1855.

vi MARY DARLING, b. at Blue Hill, 8 Aug 1774; d. at Lowell, ME, 7 Jun 1849; m. 15 Dec 1796, STEPHEN MESSER, b. at Andover, 10 May 1773 son of Stephen and Ann (Barker) Messer; Stephen d. at Lowell, 10 Dec 1833.

[2195] *Massachusetts Soldiers and Sailors in the Revolution*, volume 8, p 191

[2196] Essex County, MA: Probate File Papers, 1638-1881.Online database. AmericanAncestors.org. New England Historic Genealogical Society, 2014. Case 13654

[2197] Abigail Dole daughter of Greenleaf did marry a Stephen Holt. This is confirmed by the 1829 will of Greenleaf Dole which includes a bequest to daughter Abigail wife of Stephen Holt. The question is whether it is this Stephen Holt. The two other Stephen Holts (born 1782 and 1786) in Andover of an appropriate age can be accounted for as having other spouses. But this marriage should be considered tentative.

[2198] "Families and Early Settlers of Blue Hill Maine," The Maine Historical Magazine, volume 5, p 187

vii PHEBE DARLING, b. at Blue Hill, 26 Feb 1776; d. at Enfield, ME, 3 Oct 1851; m. 5 Mar 1810, ELISHA GUPTILL, b. at Steuben, ME, 1 May 1791 son of William and Jane (Downs) Guptill; Elisha d. at Bradley, ME, 1 Nov 1867.

viii SAMUEL DARLING, b. at Blue Hill, 28 Jul 1781; d. at Patten, ME, 1859; m. 1st 29 Jul 1805, his second cousin, HANNAH OSGOOD (*Joseph Osgood⁶, Elizabeth Abbott Osgood⁵, Thomas Abbott⁴, Hannah Gray Abbott³, Hannah Holt Gray², Nicholas¹*), b. at Andover, May 1786 daughter of Joseph and Hannah (Bailey) Osgood; Hannah d. at Blue Hill, 6 Jun 1806. Samuel m. 2nd MARY "POLLY" JELLISON, b. 1792 daughter of William and Martha (Hopkins) Jellison; Polly d. at Patten, 1871.

ix JEDEDIAH DARLING, b. at Blue Hill, 24 Jul 1784; d. at Blue Hill, 30 Dec 1862; m. 2 Nov 1807, LYDIA STINSON, b. 4 Apr 1788; Lydia d. at Blue Hill, 27 Feb 1881.

818) PHEBE HOLT (*Nicholas⁴, Nicholas³, Nicholas², Nicholas¹*), b. at Andover, 29 Jan 1752 daughter of Nicholas and Lois (Phelps) Holt; d. at Blue Hill, 12 Feb 1831; m. about 1769, ISRAEL WOOD, b. at Beverly, MA, 17 Oct 1744 son of Joseph and Ruth (Haskell) Wood; Israel d. at Blue Hill, 13 Nov 1800.

Israel Wood came to Blue Hill, Maine with his father in 1763. He there married Phebe Holt and their nine children were born there. Israel lived in the property established by his father across from the schoolhouse in Blue Hill.[2199]

Israel Wood did not leave a will and widow Phebe requested that Phineas Pillsbury be named administrator. The heirs-at-law in addition to wife Phebe were Phebe wife of Phineas Pillsbury, Lois wife of Ezra Parker, Anna single woman, Ruth single woman, Joseph age 16, Hannah age 14, Samuel Holt age 10, and Israel age 19. The dower was set off to widow Phebe. Real estate was valued at $1,075 which include the homestead valued at $365 and 100 acres of land valued at $500. At the time of the estate settlement on 6 May 1802, daughter Phebe was deceased, and her portion was paid to her heirs.[2200]

Phebe Holt and Israel Wood were parents of nine children born at Blue Hill.[2201]

i PHEBE WOOD, b. at Blue Hill, 22 Apr 1769; d. at Blue Hill, 14 Sep 1801; m. 21 Oct 1788, PHINEAS PILLSBURY, b. at Bradford, MA (baptized at Newburyport), 18 Feb 1767 son of Parker and Aphhia (Jaques) Pillsbury; Phineas d. at Greene, ME, 4 Nov 1859. Phineas married second Sarah T. Larrabee.

ii ANNA WOOD, b. 13 Apr 1771; d. 16 Dec 1776.

iii LOIS WOOD, b. at Blue Hill, 6 Feb 1774; d. at Blue Hill, 31 Dec 1861; m. 17 Dec 1791, EZRA PARKER, b. 15 Jul 1767; Ezra d. 14 Jul 1818.

iv ANNA WOOD, b. at Blue Hill, 24 Dec 1776; d. at Blue Hill, 11 Mar 1841. Anna did not marry.

v RUTH WOOD, b. at Blue Hill, 15 Nov 1779; d. at Blue Hill, 28 Nov 1865; m. 7 Mar 1811, JAMES SAVAGE, b. at Sharon, MA, 29 Jun 1781 son of Nathan and Remember (Tupper) Savage;[2202] James d. at Blue Hill, 3 Jun 1847.

vi ISRAEL WOOD, b. at Blue Hill, 20 Jul 1782; d. at Blue Hill, 25 May 1831; m. 1st 15 Dec 1808, JOANNA PARKER, b. at Blue Hill, 7 May 1784 daughter of Peter and Phebe (Marble) Parker; Joanna d. at Blue Hill, 4 Mar 1820. Israel m. 2nd, BETSEY BRIGGS HATCH, b. at Pembroke, MA, 31 Jan 1796 daughter of Briggs and Betsey (Hatch) Hatch. After Israel's death, Betsey married Benjamin Herrick.

vii JOSEPH WOOD, b. 1 Apr 1785; d. at Blue Hill, 20 Jan 1834; m. 1st 4 Nov 1813, HANNAH JOHNSON, b. at Penobscot, 30 Jul 1787 daughter of Giles and Elizabeth (Brooks) Johnson; Hannah d. at Blue Hill, 17 Apr 1817. Joseph m. 2nd about 1819, JOANNA HINCKLEY, b. at Blue Hill, 6 Mar 1792 daughter of Isaiah and Annie (Horton) Hinckley; Joanna d. at Blue Hill, 27 Aug 1846.

viii HANNAH WOOD, b. at Blue Hill, 27 Jan 1788; d. at Orland, ME, 30 Oct 1846; m. 21 Dec 1815, as his second wife, ISAAC PERRY, b. about 1775; Isaac d. after 1850 when he was living in Orland. Isaac was first married to Rhoda Burnham.

ix SAMUEL HOLT WOOD, b. at Blue Hill, 19 Jul 1791; d. at Blue Hill, 2 May 1826.

819) JEDEDIAH HOLT (*Nicholas⁴, Nicholas³, Nicholas², Nicholas¹*), b. at Andover, 12 Mar 1754 son of Nicholas and Lois (Phelps) Holt; d. at Blue Hill, 17 Aug 1847; m. at Beverly, 24 Feb 1778, SARAH THORNDIKE, b. at Beverly, Sep 1751 (baptized 4 Jul 1756) daughter of Hezekiah and Sarah (Prince) Thorndike; Sarah d, at Blue Hill, 15 Jan 1836.

Jedediah had gone to Blue Hill with his father. At the outbreak of the Revolution, the British occupied nearby Castine. Citizens of Blue Hill were compelled to sign a loyalty oath to the king. When a second oath was required, Jedediah fled to

---

2199 Candage, *Historical Sketches of Bluehill, Maine*, p 23

2200 *Maine, Wills and Probate Records, 1584-1999, Hancock, Maine, Estate Files, No 484-563, 1790-1915, Estate of Israel Wood*

2201 "Families and Early Settlers of Blue Hill Maine," The Maine Historical Magazine, volume 5

2202 Cochrane, History of Francestown, p 909

Beverly where he remained until the end of the war. His two oldest children were born there and after the war, the family returned to Blue Hill.[2203]

Jedediah Holt did not leave a will, and there seemed to be a delay in the probate of the estate as the administrator's bond was signed on 11 April 1849 with son Jonah as administrator. Real estate was valued at $1,333 for the homestead property and $10 for 5 acres of wild sand and personal estate at $43.32.[2204]

Jedediah Holt and Sarah Thorndike were parents of six children.

i JEDEDIAH HOLT, b. at Beverly, MA, 3 Mar 1779; d. at Blue Hill, ME, 5 Aug 1842; m. 11 Oct 1802, MARY VILES, b. at Orland, ME, 28 Nov 1782 daughter of Joseph and Hannah (Horton) Viles; Mary d. at Blue Hill, 22 Jan 1843.

ii JEREMIAH THORNDIKE HOLT, b. at Beverly, 12 May 1781; d. at Blue Hill, Apr 1832 (probate 5 Jul 1832); m. Nov 1808, his fourth cousin once removed, ELIZABETH OSGOOD (*Joseph Osgood[6], Elizabeth Abbott Osgood[5], Thomas Abbott[4], Hannah Gray Abbott[3], Hannah Holt Gray[2], Nicholas[1]*), b. at Andover, Nov 1789 daughter of Joseph and Hannah (Bailey) Osgood; Elizabeth d. at Blue Hill, 4 Feb 1858.

iii JONAH HOLT, b. at Blue Hill, 4 Nov 1783; d. at Blue Hill, 19 Feb 1860; m. 27 Feb 1811, his fourth cousin once removed, ELIZABETH OSGOOD STEVENS (*Dorcas Osgood Stevens[6], Elizabeth Abbott Osgood[5], Thomas Abbott[4], Hannah Gray Abbott[3], Hannah Holt Gray[2], Nicholas[1]*), b. at Blue Hill, 8 Dec 1793 daughter of Theodore and Dorcas (Osgood) Stevens; Elizabeth d. at Blue Hill, 20 Nov 1847. Jonah m. 2nd about 1848, ALMIRA WILCOX, b. about 1821; Almira was living in 1860.

iv SAMUEL P. HOLT, b. at Blue Hill, 8 Jul 1785; d. at Blue Hill, 29 Sep 1827; m. 4 Nov 1813, LYDIA LOWELL, b. 2 Feb 1789 daughter of Eliphalet and Elizabeth (Haney) Lowell;[2205] Lydia d. at Blue Hill, 7 May 1857.

v STEPHEN HOLT, b. at Blue Hill, 10 May 1788; d. at Blue Hill, 16 May 1830; m. about 1818, EDITH PARKER, b. at Blue Hill, 2 Mar 1795 daughter of Robert and Ruth (Wood) Parker; Edith d. after 1860 when she was living in Rockland, ME.

vi SALLY P. HOLT, b. at Blue Hill, 3 Jul 1793; d. at Blue Hill, 1 Nov 1803.

820) NICHOLAS HOLT (*Nicholas[4], Nicholas[3], Nicholas[2], Nicholas[1]*), b. at Andover, Feb 1756 son of Nicholas and Lois (Phelps) Holt; d. at Blue Hill, 8 Mar 1833;[2206] m. 1st at Reading, 26 Nov 1782, his third cousin once removed, PHEBE BATCHELDER (*Phebe Holt Batchelder[5], Joseph[4], Henry[3], Henry[2], Nicholas[1]*), b. at North Reading, 3 Nov 1754 daughter of Jonathan and Phebe (Holt) Batchelder; Phebe d. at Blue Hill, about 1790. Nicholas m. 2nd at Blue Hill 13 Apr 1795, MARY "MOLLY" WORMWOOD, b. about 1765; Molly d. at Blue Hill, 30 Nov 1831.

Nicholas Holt served in the Revolution and applied for a pension, but this was rejected as he had not served for the required six-month period for a pension.[2207] In his pension application, Nicholas reported enlisting in 1780 from Reading in Capt. Flint's company in Col. Jackson's regiment of the Continental line. He joined the army at West Point. He left the service on 1 January 1781 after serving nine months. In 1852, son Joseph applied for the payment of the pension which had not been drawn by his father.[2208]

Nicholas Holt and Phebe Batchelder were parents of two children born at Blue Hill, Maine.

i LEVI HOLT, b. at Blue Hill, 16 Aug 1785; d. at Hampden, ME, 5 Mar 1879; m. at Blue Hill, 4 Apr 1809, BETSEY STEVENS, b. at Andover, 14 May 1782 daughter of Benjamin and Hannah (Varnum) Stevens; Betsey d. at Hampden between 1850 and 1860 (in the 1850 census but Levi is widowed in 1860).

ii JONATHAN HOLT, b. at Blue Hill, 15 Aug 1787; d. at Bangor, ME, 9 Oct 1818; m. CYNTHIA EMERY.

Nicholas Holt and Molly Wormwood were parents of three children born at Blue Hill.

i PHEBE BATCHELDER HOLT, b. at Blue Hill, 28 Jan 1796; m. NATHAN FISH.[2209]

ii HANNAH HOLT, b. at Blue Hill, 6 May 1798

[2203] Durrie, Holt genealogy, p 43

[2204] Hancock Maine Estate Files, Estate of Jedediah Holt

[2205] Lowell, *The Historic Genealogy of the Lowells of America*, p 69

[2206] The dates of death for Nicholas Holt and Molly Wormwood are those given by son Joseph Holt in the pension application file.

[2207] Rejected or Suspended Applications for Revolutionary War Pensions

[2208] U.S., Revolutionary War Pension and Bounty-Land Warrant Application Files, 1800-1900, Case R5186

[2209] Durrie, Holt genealogy

iii JOSEPH HOLT, b. at Blue Hill, 21 Jul 1801; d. at Blue Hill, 1885; m. 10 Feb 1825, MARGARET MORSE, b. 31 Oct 1799 daughter of Samuel and Elizabeth (Candage) Morse;[2210] Margaret d. at Blue Hill, 30 May 1869.

821) ABIGAIL HOLT (*James⁴, Nicholas³, Nicholas², Nicholas¹*), b. at Andover, 18 Jun 1758 daughter of James and Sarah (Abbott) Holt; d. 2 Oct 1824; m. 7 Dec 1780, her fourth cousin, ISAAC CHANDLER, b. 4 Oct 1754 son of William and Rebecca (Lovejoy) Chandler; Isaac d. 12 Jan 1832. After Abigail's death, Isaac married Elizabeth Upton.

Isaac Chandler was a farmer and the family lived on the farm that had belonged to Abigail Holt's maternal grandfather Benjamin Abbott.[2211] The property owned by Isaac Chandler is the site of 17 Hidden Road in Andover. The house on the property was built by David Hidden, a son-in-law of Isaac and Abigail Chandler.[2212] The house was built in 1812 on Isaac's property and half the house was deeded to David Hidden in 1828. The house passed into the hands of the two children of David and Mary (Chandler) Hidden, Mary Elizabeth Hidden and David Isaac Chandler Hidden.

Isaac Chandler wrote his will 9 November 1831. Wife Elizabeth receives a bequest of $300 and is allowed all the household property that she brought to the marriage providing that Elizabeth quit claim and release the estate from her right of dower. Beloved granddaughter Sarah Ann Chandler receives $100 in addition to what she has already received. Beloved daughter Mary Hidden wife of David Hidden receives one-fourth part of the estate. Beloved daughter Abigail Chandler receives the remaining three-fourths of the estate. Captain Timothy Flagg was named sole executor. The real property of the estate was valued at $3,230.00 including the homestead valued at $2,200.00. The personal estate was valued at $96.33. The heirs-at-law requested that the executor publish that the probate hearing be held in Salem as this was more convenient. Those signing are Elizabeth Chandler, David Hidden, Mary Hidden, Abigail Chandler, and Sally Chandler signing as guardian for Sarah Ann Chandler.[2213]

Abigail Holt and Isaac Chandler were parents of five children born at Andover.

i ABIGAIL CHANDLER, b. 13 Dec 1781; d. 20 Sep 1788.

ii ISAAC CHANDLER, b. at Andover, 11 Jun 1784; d. at Andover, 28 Sep 1813; m. 7 Nov 1812, SALLY THOMPSON, b. at Wilmington, 18 Jul 1789 daughter of Benjamin and Susanna (Jaquith) Thompson; Sally d. at Wilmington, 19 Sep 1853. Isaac and Sally had one daughter Sarah Ann Chandler who married Albert Bond.

iii MARY CHANDLER, b. at Andover, 5 Jun 1786; d. at Andover, 9 Sep 1855; m. at Andover, 1 Jul 1816, DAVID HIDDEN, b. at Newbury, 21 Sep 1784 son of David and Elisabeth (Stickney) Hidden; David d. at Andover, 5 Jun 1861.

iv ABIGAIL CHANDLER, b. at Andover, 3 Sep 1794; d. at Andover, 22 Oct 1866. Abigail did not marry.

v HANNAH CHANDLER, b. 10 Jan 1798; d. 1 May 1807.

822) SARAH HOLT (*James⁴, Nicholas³, Nicholas², Nicholas¹*), b. at Andover, 7 Mar 1746/7 daughter of James and Sarah (Abbott) Holt; d. 11 Feb 1808; m. 6 Dec 1770, her third cousin, BARACHIAS ABBOTT (*Hannah Holt Abbott⁴, Timothy³, James², Nicholas¹*), b. 22 May 1739 son of Barachias and Hannah (Holt) Abbott; Barachias d. 29 Jan 1812.

Barachias and Sarah had their seven children in Andover, but then relocated to Wilton about 1786. Barachias owned property there which he previously cleared and established a farm. Barachias Abbot served as a selectman in Wilton 1791-1792.[2214] One of the children died in infancy. The two daughters did not marry and remained in Wilton. Sons Timothy and Joel remained in Wilton, Timothy living with his father. Barachias, the oldest son, moved on to Landgrove, Vermont. Barachias and Sarah perhaps returned to Andover in their later years as both their deaths are recorded there, as well as the death of their son Timothy.

i BARACHIAS ABBOTT, b. 20 Dec 1771; d. at Landgrove, VT, 23 Mar 1855; m. at Temple, NH, 18 Jan 1798, ANNA COLBURN, b. at Temple, 20 Feb 1777 daughter of Elias and Mehitable (Wheeler) Colburn. Anna d. at Landgrove, 1 May 1856.[2215] There are twelve children recorded for this family.

ii TIMOTHY ABBOTT, b. 30 Mar 1773; death recorded at Andover, 1 Jan 1837; m. at Montague, MA, 22 Sep 1801, MARY "POLLY" BANCROFT, b, about 1778 likely the daughter of Kendall and Susanna (Ewers) Bancroft;[2216] Polly's death is recorded at Wilton, 13 Feb 1852. Polly was living with her son Henry in Chelmsford at the 1850

2210 "Families and Early Settlers of Blue Hill Maine," The Maine Historical Magazine, volume 5, p 200

2211 Chandler, *Descendants of William and Annis Chandler*, p 422

2212 "17 Hidden Road," https://preservation.mhl.org/17-hidden-road

2213 Essex County, MA: Probate File Papers, 1638-1881. Probate of Isaac Chandler, 21 Feb 1832, case number 4934.

2214 Livermore, *History of Wilton*

2215 The graves of Barachias and Anna are in the Old Landgrove Cemetery in Landgrove, VT; FIndagrave memorial ID 184633891

2216 Kendall Bancroft lived in Montague where he died in 1806. His will includes a daughter Mary, although the will does not give the last names of any of the children. One of the children of Timothy and Polly was named Kendall Bancroft Abbott.

U.S. Census. Timothy and Polly had seven children. Son Henry married Caroline Abbott, Nancy Abbott from whom he was divorced,[2217] and Harriet Robinson.

iii JOEL ABBOTT, b. 29 Apr 1775; d. 7 May 1775

iv JOEL ABBOTT, b. 10 Oct 1776; d. at Wilton, 26 Mar 1863; m. 24 Mar 1803, his third cousin once removed, JUDITH RAY BATCHELDER, b. 21 Jun 1779 daughter of Daniel and Rebecca (Abbott) Batchelder. Joel and Judith are the parents in Family 1072.

v SARAH ABBOTT, b. 10 Oct 1779; d. at Wilton, 19 Oct 1858. Sarah did not marry. In the 1850 U.S. Census, Sarah was living in the household next to her brother Joel in Wilton but living on her own.

vi JAMES ABBOTT, b. 30 Mar 1780; d. at Andover, 4 Oct 1858. m. 31 May 1806, MARY FOSTER, b. at Greenfield, NH, about 1784 perhaps the daughter of Isaac and Mary (Holt) Foster;[2218] Mary d. at Andover 20 Feb 1862. Isaac Foster and Mary Holt are Family 869.

vii ELIZABETH ABBOTT, b. 14 Sep 1784; d. at Wilton, 9 Apr 1854. Elizabeth did not marry.

823) SARAH HOLT (*Nathan⁴, Nicholas³, Nicholas², Nicholas¹*), b. at Danvers, 29 Oct 1758 daughter of Nathan and Sarah (Abbott) Holt; d. 17 Sep 1841; m. at Danvers, 2 Dec 1777, WILLIAM FROST, b. at New Castle, NH, 15 Nov 1754 son of William and Elizabeth (Prescott) Frost; William d. at Andover 28 Sep 1836. Sarah and William are second great grandparents of Robert Frost.

William Frost served as a lieutenant in the Continental Army during the Revolution.[2219] He was also deacon of the Congregational Church.[2220]

Sarah Holt and William Frost had twelve children all born at Andover.

i NATHAN HOLT FROST, b. 4 Sep 1778; d. 9 Jun 1784.

ii SALLY FROST, b. 28 Dec 1779; d. at Newburyport, 3 May 1863; m. at Andover, 16 Nov 1802, SAMUEL DRAKE, b. at Epping, about 1775 son of Simon and Judith (Perkins) Drake; Samuel d. at Newburyport, 27 Jun 1845.

iii BETSEY FROST, b. 21 Aug 1781; d. at Andover, 9 Aug 1819. Betsey did not marry.

iv WILLIAM FROST, b. 28 Mar 1783; d. 12 Apr 1784.

v DOROTHY CLIFFORD FROST, b. 1 Mar 1785; d. at Northwood, NH, 20 Apr 1822; m. at Andover, 7 Oct 1806, DUDLEY LEAVITT, b. about 1772 (based on age at death); Dudley d. at Northwood, 5 Feb 1838. After Dorothy's death, Dudley married her sister Mary.

vi MARY "POLLY" FROST, b. 18 Jan 1787; d. at Northwood, 17 Apr 1846; m. 5 Aug 1823, DUDLEY LEAVITT (see sister Dorothy).

vii NATHAN HOLT FROST, b. Jan 1789; d. at Rutherford County, TN, 19 Mar 1866;[2221] m. at Charlotte County, VA, 20 Nov 1817, MARTHA HEWETT JOHNSON,[2222] b. in Virginia about 1791; Martha d. at Rutherford County, 24 Oct 1873. Nathan attended Phillips Academy in Andover graduating in 1808.[2223] He was a merchant who was in Virginia from about 1810 to 1826 and then relocated to Tennessee.

viii HARRIET HOLT FROST, b. 29 Mar 1791; d. at Andover, 11 Dec 1818; m. at Salem, 29 Aug 1814, ROBERT CROWELL, b. at Salem, 9 Dec 1787 son of Samuel and Lydia (Woodbury) Crowell; Robert d. at Essex, 10 Nov 1855. After Harriet's death, Robert married Hannah Choate.

ix WILLIAM FROST, b. 12 Jun 1793; d. at Andover, 28 Mar 1866; m. 1st, 11 Dec 1823, LUCY FOSTER, b. 17 Nov 1800 daughter of Charles and Lucy (Austin) Foster; Lucy d. 4 Nov 1838. William m. 2nd, 18 Mar 1840, MARY WOMSTEAD MEAD, b. 23 Apr 1804 daughter of Levi and Susannah (Hilton) Mead; Mary d. 11 Dec 1866.

2217 *New Hampshire, Marriage and Divorce Records, 1659-1947*, New England Historical Genealogical Society; New Hampshire Bureau of Vital Records, Concord, New Hampshire; New Hampshire, Marriage and Divorce Records, 1659–1947. Married in 1854 and divorced 1864

2218 There is a possibility that Mary Foster was the daughter of Isaac's first wife Mary Hartwell. All published genealogies say mother is Mary Holt who was the second wife. Isaac Foster married Mary Hartwell in 1779 and she died in 1781, and this may be too early of a birth date for Mary Foster, but there is no birth record for Mary Foster. This is offered as an option as Mary Foster and James Abbott named one of their sons Hartwell Barachias Abbott which would be a name that honored father's father and mother's mother.

2219 Compiled Service Records of Soldiers Who Served in the American Army During the Revolutionary War 1775-1785, accessed through fold3

2220 Frost, *The Nicholas Frost Family*, p 23

2221 Year: 1860; Census Place: Murfreesboro, Rutherford, Tennessee; Roll: M653_1271; Page: 83; Family History Library Film: 805271

2222 Virginia, Compiled Marriages, 1740-1850

2223 Biographical catalogue of the trustees, teachers, and students of Phillips Academy, Andover, 1778-1830.

x SAMUEL ABBOTT FROST, b. 11 Jun 1795; d. at Brentwood, NH, 11 Jan 1848; m. at Eden, ME, 10 Oct 1821, MARY "POLLY" BLUNT, b. at New Castle, NH, 28 Jun 1787 daughter of William and Mary (Fernald) Blunt; Mary d. 14 Jan 1875.

xi LUCY FROST, b. 28 Nov 1798; d. at Andover, 26 Feb 1842; m. at Leicester, MA, 23 Feb 1820, JOHN RICHARDSON, b. about 1789; John d. at Andover, 3 Oct 1841.

xii BENJAMIN PRESCOT FROST, b. 17 Nov 1800; d. at Andover, 25 Jun 1827.

824) MARY HOLT (*Nathan[4], Nicholas[3], Nicholas[2], Nicholas[1]*), b. at Danvers, 3 Oct 1761 daughter of Nathan and Sarah (Abbott) Holt; d. at Beverly, 7 Jan 1850; m. 1 Nov 1781, ROBERT ENDICOTT, b. 29 Oct 1756 son of John and Elizabeth (Jacobs) Endicott; Robert d. at Beverly, 6 Mar 1819.

Mary Holt married Robert Endicott a descendant of Governor John Endicott. They settled in Beverly where they had a family of seven children. The Endicott family was instrumental in the shipping industry in Salem and three of the sons of Robert and Mary were mariners.

Son Robert Endicott went to sea at age 20,[2224] and although he did not die at sea, he died at age 28 of "decline." Son Nathan Holt Endicott went to sea at age 16 and was chief mate when he died of fever aboard the ship *Glide* in Calcutta. A son-in-law, John Ellingwood, also died at sea. He was first officer of the ship *Bramin* when he died in the Bay of Bengal.[2225]

Third oldest son, Captain Samuel Endicott, was a shipmaster in command of the ship *George* for several years. The ship *George* was built in Salem in 1814 and was part of a large fleet of merchant vessels owned by Joseph Peabody. This ship made annual trips to Calcutta and the round trip took nearly a year. The average outbound trip was 115 days and the average return took 103 days.[2226] After his seafaring days, Samuel was president of the bank in Beverly.

Youngest son, William, lived to be 99 years 10 months old. He was a successful business owner having a mercantile and drug store at the corner of Cabot and Washington Streets in Beverly.[2227]

Robert and Mary Endicott had seven children born at Beverly.

i MARY ENDICOTT, b. 29 Jul 1782; d. at Beverly, 8 Jan 1813; m. at Beverly, 18 Oct 1808, JOHN ELLINGWOOD, b. at Beverly, 20 Dec 1783 son of John and Hannah (Glover) Ellingwood; John d. aboard ship in Calcutta, 7 Nov 1816.

ii ROBERT ENDICOTT, b. 5 May 1785; d. at Beverly, 29 Aug 1813 of "decline." Robert did not marry. He was a mariner.

iii NATHAN HOLT ENDICOTT, b. 31 Jan 1788; d. aboard ship at the Bay of Bengal, 2 Jul 1816. Nathan did not marry. He died from a fever.

iv Daughter, b. 7 Jun 1790 and d. 10 Jun 1790

v SAMUEL ENDICOTT, b. 18 Jul 1793; d. at Beverly, 28 Jan 1872; m. 1st, 11 Jun 1820, his first cousin, HANNAH HOLT (*Peter[5], Joshua[4], Nicholas[3], Nicholas[2], Nicholas[1]*), b. at Epping, NH, 4 May 1794 daughter of Peter and Hannah (Holt) Holt; Hannah d. 14 Mar 1825. Samuel m. 2nd, 21 May 1826, Hannah's sister, SARAH FARNUM HOLT, b. at Epping, 12 Feb 1809; Sarah d. 23 Aug 1847. Samuel m. 3rd, 7 Jun 1852, MARY THORNDIKE LEECH, b. at Beverly, 3 Aug 1803 daughter of William and Ruth (Lee) Leech. Mary T. Leech had first married ship captain John Giddings. Mary d. 20 Dec 1881.

vi Daughter, b. 7 Sep 1796 and d. 11 Sep 1796

vii WILLIAM ENDICOTT, b. 11 Mar 1799; d. just two months before his 100th birthday on 8 Jan 1899; m. 26 Sep 1824, JOANNA LOVETT RANTOUL, b. at Beverly, 13 Jan 1803 daughter of Robert and Joanna (Lovett) Rantoul; Joanna d. 26 Jun 1863.[2228]

825) PETER HOLT (*Joshua[4], Nicholas[3], Nicholas[2], Nicholas[1]*), b. at Andover, 12 Jun 1763 son of Joshua and Phebe (Farnum) Holt; d. at Greenfield, 25 Apr 1851; m. 23 Jan 1793, his first cousin, HANNAH HOLT (*Nathan[4], Nicholas[3], Nicholas[2], Nicholas[1]*), b. at Danvers, 11 May 1769 daughter of Nathan and Sarah (Abbott) Holt; Hannah d. at Beverly, 26 Jul 1857.

Reverend Peter Holt graduated from Harvard in 1790.[2229] He was installed at the Presbyterian Church in Peterborough and Greenfield.[2230]

2224 Web: US, New England Seamen's Protection Certificate Index, 1796-1871

2225 Ancestry.com, U.S., Newspaper Extractions from the Northeast, 1704-1930

2226 Essex Institute, *Old-Time Ships of Salem*

2227 Hurd, *History of Essex County, Massachusetts*

2228 Joanna Endicott's death is recorded in the Beverly records but noted as occurring in St. Louis.

2229 Quinquennial Catalogue of the Officers and Graduates of Harvard University

2230 The Quarterly Christian Spectator, volume 1, 1827, p 336

In his will written 26 November 1847 and proved 6 May 1851, Peter Holt bequeaths to beloved wife Hannah all his household furniture and all the farming tools to be at her own use and disposal. He notes that he has prospects of an inheritance from England, and if that occurs and it is a large amount, then he wishes for a reasonable amount of that sum to be divided among the families of his deceased brothers and the families of his deceased brothers-in-law. He also wishes that something be given to his daughter-in-law Henrietta Adams. The reside of the estate he bequeaths to his wife during her lifetime. Following that, the estate is to be divided equally between his beloved daughter Mary E. W. Holt and his beloved son-in-law Samuel Endicott.[2231]

Peter Holt and Hannah Holt were parents of seven children all born at Epping, New Hampshire. Two of the daughters of Hannah and Peter married Samuel Endicott son of Mary Holt and Robert Endicott.

i HANNAH HOLT, b. 4 May 1794; d. at Beverly, MA, 14 Mar 1825; m. at Beverly, 11 Jun 1820, her first cousin, SAMUEL ENDICOTT (*Mary Holt Endicott[5], Nathan[4], Nicholas[3], Nicholas[2], Nicholas[1]*), b. at Beverly, 18 Jul 1793 son of Robert and Mary (Holt) Endicott; Samuel d. at Beverly, 28 Jan 1872. Samuel Endicott was second married to Hannah's sister Sarah Farnum Holt and third married to Martha Thorndike Leech.

ii NATHAN HOLT, b. 16 Aug 1795; d. 23 Jul 1807.

iii PETER HOLT, b. 20 Feb 1802; d. 16 Jul 1817.

iv JEREMIAH HOLT, b. 5 Sep 1803; d. 20 Nov 1817.

v JOSHUA HOLT, b. 9 Mar 1805; married at unknown date, Henrietta about whom nothing else in known at this time. Henrietta is the daughter-in-law Henrietta Adams referred to in Peter Holt's will.

vi SARAH FARNUM HOLT, b. 12 Feb 1809; d. at Beverly, 23 Aug 1847; m. 21 May 1826, SAMUEL ENDICOTT (refer to sister Hannah above).

vii MARY E. W. HOLT, b. 27 May 1812; d. at Beverly, 19 Aug 1887. Mary did not marry.

826) JAMES HOLT (*Nathan[4], Nicholas[3], Nicholas[2], Nicholas[1]*), b. at Danvers, 1772 son of Nathan and Sarah (Abbott) Holt; d. in India, Aug 1807;[2232] m. 30 Aug 1796, LUCY WHIPPLE, b. 8 Mar 1778; Lucy d. at Danvers, 6 Mar 1839. Although James's death is reported as August 1807, the probate of his estate was April 1807.

James Holt was a seaman who died on a voyage to India leaving a widow with three small children. Lucy Holt was administratrix of his estate which entered probate 20 April 1807. The value of the personal estate was $61.65. After expenses of the estate, the allowance to Lucy was $45.65.[2233]

James Holt and Lucy Whipple were parents of four children born at Danvers.

i JAMES HOLT, b. 25 Feb 1797; d. at Danvers, 12 Nov 1856; m. 6 Apr 1819, MERCY SMITH, b. at Danvers, 9 Oct 1796 daughter of Israel and Margaret (-) Smith (mother was the widow Margaret Standly); Mercy d. at Danvers, 6 Nov 1856.

ii STEPHEN HOLT, b. 24 Jan 1799; d. 2 Oct 1800.

iii LUCY ANN HOLT, b. 29 Aug 1801; d. at Danvers, 28 Sep 1829; m. at Danvers, 15 May 1823, GILMAN PARKER, b. at Topsfield, 19 Sep 1802 son of Edmund and Jane (Pingrey) Parker; Gilman d. 3 Jun 1866. After Lucy's death, Gilman married Abigail Welch.

iv LYDIA HOLT, b. 27 Jan 1804; d. at Danvers, 3 Apr 1889; m. at Danvers, 28 Dec 1824, SAMUEL HARRIS, b. at Ipswich, 3 Apr 1799 son of Daniel and Sarah (Emmons) Harris; Daniel d. at Danvers, 7 Dec 1877.

826a) THOMAS HOLT (*Dorcas[4], Nicholas[3], Nicholas[2], Nicholas[1]*), b. at Andover, 15 Jun 1750 son of Thomas and Dorcas (Holt) Holt; d. after 1794 when living at Lyndeborough; m. 27 Oct 1774, his second cousin, LYDIA FARNUM (*Thomas Farnum[5], Thomas Farnum[4], Thomas, Farnum[3], Elizabeth Holt Farnum[2], Nicholas[1]*), b. 10 Nov 1756 daughter of Thomas and Lydia (Abbott) Farnum.

Thomas and Lydia married in Andover and baptisms of three children are recorded there. The family was then in Amherst, New Hampshire. In 1779, Thomas Holt of Andover purchased property in Amherst from Isaac and Hannah Holt of

2231 New Hampshire, County Probate Records, 1660-1973, Hillsborough, 57:213, will of Peter Holt

2232 James, h. Lucy (Whipple), at India, Aug. —, 1807.

2233 Essex County, MA: Probate File Papers, 1638-1881.Online database. AmericanAncestors.org. New England Historic Genealogical Society, 2014. Case 13651

Andover. Thomas and Lydia sold their property in Amherst in 1793 and 1794 and were of Lyndeborough in 1794 when they sold the last of their property in Amherst. They perhaps were next in Greenfield, but that is not known.[2234]

Thomas Holt's household was six persons in Amherst in 1790: two males 16 and over, one male under 16, and three females.[2235] Three children were identified for Thomas Holt and Lydia Farnum.

i STEPHEN HOLT, baptized at Andover, 27 Apr 1777

ii LYDIA HOLT, baptized at Andover, 12 Jul 1778; d. at Greenfield, NH, 25 Nov 1869; m. at Lyndeborough, 30 Apr 1793, JOHN SAVAGE, b. at Marblehead, MA, 13 Sep 1771 son of John and Mary (Jackson) Savage; John d. at Greenfield, 5 Oct 1850.

iii PHEBE HOLT, baptized 11 Jun 1780; *perhaps* m. at Andover, 15 Mar 1805, SAMUEL EATON, b. at Reading, 17 Oct 1782 son of Samuel Phillips and Sarah (Evans) Eaton; Samuel d. at Lynn, 14 Nov 1871.

827) MARY HOLT (*Dorcas⁴, Nicholas³, Nicholas², Nicholas¹*), b. at Andover, 11 Mar 1758 daughter of Thomas and Dorcas (Holt) Holt; d. at Andover, 20 Mar 1830; m. at Andover, 7 Dec 1780, her third cousin, THOMAS GRAY (*Thomas Gray⁴, Edward Gray³, Hannah Holt Gray², Nicholas¹*), b. at Andover, 23 Mary 1758 son of Thomas and Lydia (Graves) Gray; Thomas d. at Andover, 5 Sep 1823.[2236]

Thomas and Mary resided in Andover where Thomas was a farmer. On 2 May 1821 (recorded 7 May 1821), Thomas Gray conveyed to his son Jacob for $1,200 several tracts of land in Andover plus all the household furniture, farming utensils, and stock animals and all his goods and chattels of every description.[2237]

Mary Holt and Thomas Gray were parents of seven children born at Andover.

i AMOS GRAY, b. Nov 1781; d. at Andover, 13 Nov 1856; m. 4 Nov 1806, LUCY LOVEJOY, b. at Andover, 1 Sep 1780 daughter of Isaac and Ruth (Davis) Lovejoy; Lucy d. at Andover, 1 Mar 1864.

ii PHEBE GRAY, b. 20 Mar 1783; d. at Andover, 13 Aug 1861; m. 3 Jan 1806, JOEL JENKINS, b. at Andover, 23 Oct 1780 son of Joel and Patty (Carter) Jenkins; Joel d. at Andover, 28 Mar 1832.

iii HANNAH GRAY, baptized 16 May 1784

iv ABIAH GRAY, b. 20 Apr 1786; d. at Andover, 17 Dec 1843; m. 24 May 1804, ORLANDO LOVEJOY, b. at Andover, 23 Nov 1782 son of Isaac and Ruth (Davis) Lovejoy; Orlando d. at Andover, 3 Jul 1869.

v SARAH "SALLY" GRAY, b. 26 Jul 1788; d. at Andover, 17 Dec 1863; m. 16 May 1822, SAMUEL GUNNISON, baptized at Salem, 13 May 1787 son of John and Susannah (-) Gunnison; Samuel d. from senility at the asylum in Ipswich, 9 Jul 1868.

vi JACOB GRAY, b. 16 Nov 1792; m. at Andover, 10 Jan 1822, ELIZABETH B. "BETSEY" LEAVITT.

vii NOAH GRAY, b. 31 Jan 1797; d. at Kalamazoo, MI, 20 Sep 1851; m. 1st at Malden, 8 Jun 1817, ELIZABETH SIMPSON, b. about 1800; Elizabeth d. at Malden, 20 Dec 1847. Noah m. 2nd about 1849, LYDIA PENNELL (widow of John L. Shakespeare), b. in PA, 1814 daughter of James and Eleanor (Inman) Pennell; Lydia d. at Kalamazoo, 29 Jan 1895.

828) LOIS HOLT (*Dorcas⁴, Nicholas³, Nicholas², Nicholas¹*), b. at Andover, 29 Oct 1760 daughter of Thomas and Dorcas (Holt) Holt; d. at Andover, 17 Apr 1852; m. 4 Jan 1785, MOSES PEARSON, b. at Wilmington, 6 Nov 1750 son of Nathan and Mary (Wilson) Pearson; Moses d. recorded at Andover 11 Aug 1836 (1835).[2238] Moses Pearson was first married to Hephzibah Jones.

Moses Pearson served in the Revolution as a private first enlisting in September 1776 in the militia company of Captain Putnam of Wilton, New Hampshire. In his pension application, Moses reported he was living in Amherst, New Hampshire at the time of his enlistment. He saw service at White Plains, New York. He had another enlistment for nine months in 1778 and marched to Fishkill for two months and was later in Hampstead, Connecticut. The total period of service was credited at twelve months. Moses and later his widow Lois received a pension related to his service.[2239]

2234 New Hampshire Land Records, Hillsborough County, 8:179, 30:450, 30:452, 35:272

2235 Year: 1790; Census Place: Amherst, Hillsborough, New Hampshire; Series: M637; Roll: 5; Page: 227; Image: 144; Family History Library Film: 0568145

2236 Durrie's Holt genealogy lists Mary as the Mary Holt that married John Adams in 1776 (his third marriage). However, John Adams's Mary died in 1829 at age 89, meaning she was born about 1740 so that is not this Mary.

2237 Massachusetts Land Records, Essex County, 226:109

2238 The transcription of the death record says 1835 but the pension application and the gravestone say 1836.

2239 U.S., Revolutionary War Pension and Bounty-Land Warrant Application Files, 1800-1900

Moses and Lois lived in Wilmington (although their deaths are recorded in Andover) and they were parents of nine children all born at Wilmington.

i THOMAS PEARSON, b. 28 Oct 1785; d. at Haverhill, 1 Aug 1863; m. at Andover, 24 Nov 1811, LUCY TROW, b. at Beverly, 1786 daughter of John and Hannah (Dodge) Trow; Lucy d. at Haverhill, about 1863.

ii NATHAN PEARSON, b. 20 Aug 1787; d. at Wilmington, 20 Feb 1855; m. LYDIA ANN HOWE.

iii HEPHZIBAH PEARSON, b. 28 Mar 1790; d. at North Andover, 29 Aug 1880; m. at Wilmington, 30 Nov 1815, WILLIAM TUCKER, b. at Wilmington, 10 Aug 1789 son of William and Hannah (Holt) Tucker; William d. 26 Mar 1861.

iv JOSEPH J. PEARSON, b. 5 Sep 1792; d. at Andover, 15 Jul 1841; m. at Andover, 23 Oct 1814, SARAH FOSTER, b. at Ashby, about 1790; Sarah d. at Andover, 11 Feb 1853.

v ABIEL PEARSON, b. 8 Jun 1795; d. at Wilmington, 9 Nov 1851; m. at Reading, 18 Apr 1822, JERUSHA DAMON, b. about 1804 perhaps the daughter of Edmund and Lucy (Flint) Damon; Lucy d. at Andover, 21 Feb 1884.

vi JABEZ PEARSON, b. 1 Aug 1797; d. at Boston, 28 Apr 1850; m. at Andover, 15 Sep 1823, OLIVE P. TUCKER.

vii JAMES PEARSON, b. 21 Dec 1799. Nothing further certain is known, but it is possible he was the James Pearson who married ELIZA ANN BRADLEY in Boston 6 Dec 1827. James's brother Jabez was in Boston. This is speculation at this point. If so, James died in Boston in 1836 (probate May 1836) leaving two sons, James Bradley Pearson and Joel F. Pearson.

viii AMOS PEARSON, b. 5 oct 1802; d. at Haverhill, MA, 3 Jul 1866; m. at Boston, 13 Feb 1836, ANNIS TROW, b. at Andover, 10 May 1800 daughter of Dudley and Annis (Johnson) Trow; Annis d. at Medford, 20 Apr 1873.

ix KENDALL PEARSON, b. 30 Jan 1805; d. recorded at Andover, 16 May 1824.

829) WILLIAM HOLT (*Dorcas^{4}, Nicholas^{3}, Nicholas^{2}, Nicholas^{1}*), b. at Andover, 7 Sep 1763 son of Thomas and Dorcas (Holt) Holt; d. at Wilton, 23 Dec 1810; m. 29 Jul 1784, ELIZABETH JONES, b. at Andover, about 1763 daughter of Jacob and Mary (Winn) Jones;[2240][2241] Elizabeth d. at Weld, ME, 1829.

William Holt and Elizabeth Jones were parents of eight children, the oldest six at Andover and youngest two at Wilton, New Hampshire.

i JACOB HOLT, b. 13 Dec 1784; d. by suicide in Boston Harbor, Dec 1817; m. at Beverly, 19 Oct 1806, HANNAH RAYMOND, b. at Beverly, 19 Mar 1781 daughter of David and Hannah (Giles) Raymond. Jacob was a sea captain. He committed suicide by jumping into Boston Harbor.[2242]

ii STEPHEN HOLT, b. 11 Apr 1786; d. at Weld, ME, 7 Dec 1855; m. 1st, about 1815, his first cousin, HANNAH LOVEJOY (*Moses Lovejoy^{5}, Mary Holt Lovejoy^{4}, Oliver^{3}, Henry^{2}, Nicholas^{1}*), b. at Wilton 22 Jun 1787 daughter of Moses and Dorcas (Holt) Lovejoy; Hannah d. at Weld, 5 Nov 1843. Stephen m. 2nd, about 1846, PHEBE DOUGLAS.

iii WILLIAM HOLT, b. 6 Mar 1788; d. at sea, 22 Oct 1820; m. 28 Nov 1812, LUCY WOODBURY, b. at Beverly, 31 May 1789 daughter of Thomas and Jane (Homan) Woodbury; Lucy d. at Beverly, 19 Aug 1870. William was master of a ship out of Beverly and died while on voyage.

iv ELIZABETH HOLT, b. 12 Mar 1790; d. Mar 1797.

v JOSEPH HOLT, b. 28 Jan 1792; d. at Wilton, 20 Jun 1864; m. at Wilton, 31 Jan 1813, BETSEY SMITH, b. at Wilton, 9 Jan 1791 daughter of Uriah and Lydia (Keyes) Smith; Betsey d. at Wilton, 8 Sep 1869.

vi ASA HOLT, b. 5 May 1794; d. at Weld, ME, 12 Jul 1825; m. at Brattleboro, VT, 24 Jul 1822, SYBIL BUTTERFIELD, b. at Brattleboro, 5 Apr 1792 daughter of Benjamin and Lois (Herrick) Butterfield; Sybil d. at Weld, 22 Dec 1830. After Asa's death Sybil married Joshua Eaton.

vii ELIZABETH HOLT, b. about 1798; d. at Weld, ME, 23 Mar 1867; m. at Andover, MA, 16 Feb 1818, BENJAMIN HOUGHTON, b. at Dublin, NH, 1789 son of James and Hannah (Russell) Houghton; Benjamin d. at Weld, 6 Mar 1882.

[2240] A birth record was not located for Elizabeth, but the will of Jacob Jones includes a bequest to his daughter Betty.

[2241] Bartlett, *Hugh Jones of Salem*, p 18

[2242] Newspaper Extractions from the Northeast, 1704-1930

viii NATHAN HOLT, b. about 1801; d. at Weld, ME, after 1880; m. Nov 1824, PHEBE SEVERY, b. in ME, 5 Dec 1803 daughter of Aaron and Phebe (Tucker) Severy; Phebe d. 16 Nov 1884.

830) JOSEPH HOLT (*Dorcas⁴, Nicholas³, Nicholas², Nicholas¹*), b. at Andover, 29 Sep 1766 son of Thomas and Dorcas (Holt) Holt; d. at Andover, 8 Jun 1791; m. 27 Nov 1788, his third cousin once removed, ABIGAIL HOLT (*Samuel⁵, Samuel⁴, Samuel³, Samuel², Nicholas¹*), b. 19 May 1767 daughter of Samuel and Abigail (Blanchard) Holt; Abigail d. 13 May 1821.

Joseph Holt died at the young age 24 of nervous fever.[2243] Joseph and Abigail had two children at Andover, the younger child born after Joseph's death.

i JOSEPH HOLT, b. 20 Jan 1790; d. at Andover, 4 Jul 1866; m. 18 Oct 1821, ELIZABETH BRADDOCK, b. in ME, 1792 daughter of John Braddock; Elizabeth d. at Andover, 3 Dec 1875.

ii SAMUEL HOLT, b. 24 Sep 1791; d. 1 Apr 1802.

831) MEHITABLE HOLT (*Thomas⁴, Thomas³, Nicholas², Nicholas¹*), b. at Andover, 8 Feb 1743/4 daughter of Thomas and Hannah (Kimball) Holt; d. at Hillsborough, 20 Oct 1816; m. 1st 28 May 1761, SAMUEL LUFKIN son of Samuel Lufkin; Samuel d. 30 Apr 1777. Mehitable m. 2nd at Andover, 14 Jul 1785, ABNER WILKINS, b. 1 Jul 1743; Abner d. at Middleton, 17 Aug 1820. Abner was first married to Eunice Smith.

Mehitable Holt and Samuel Lufkin were parents of five children for whom there are records. There may be a sixth child who died before 1779. The birth dates and locations are uncertain. Mehitable had all her children baptized at Andover on 23 May 1779.

i SAMUEL LUFKIN, b. 25 Mar 1762; d. at Acworth, NH, 30 Jul 1838; m. at Billerica, 19 Dec 1786, SARAH LIVINGSTON, b. at Billerica, 18 Feb 1766 daughter of Seth and Mary (Sprague) Livingston; Sarah d. at Acworth, 15 Jul 1849.

ii MEHITABLE LUFKIN, b. at Chelmsford, 1767; d.at Jaffrey, NH, 24 Feb 1804; m. at Amherst, NH, 16 Jul 1787, JACOB DANFORTH, b. at Billerica, 27 Feb 1766 son of David and Joanna (Shed) Danforth; Jacob d. at Amherst, 15 Nov 1851.

iii SARAH LUFKIN, b. about 1769; d. at Hillsborough, 26 Jan 1848; m. at Amherst, NH, 31 Aug 1790, GEORGE DASCOMB, b. at Northfield, MA, 16 Oct 1764 son of James and Elizabeth (Farrington) Dascomb; George d. at Hillsborough, 21 Jun 1842.

iv JONATHAN LUFKIN, b. about 1774; m. Mar 1801, JANE DAVIDSON

v DORCAS LUFKIN, b. 1776; d. at Hillsborough, 26 Apr 1848; m. at Andover, 14 Mar 1793, her fourth cousin, EBENEZER FLINT (*Asenath Holt Flint⁵, Ephraim⁴, Henry³, Henry², Nicholas¹*), b. at Reading, MA, 13 May 1765 son of Ebenezer and Asenath (Holt) Flint; Ebenezer d. at Hillsborough, 14 Mar 1833.

832) ABIEL HOLT (*Thomas⁴, Thomas³, Nicholas², Nicholas¹*), b. at Andover, 3 Apr 1746 son of Thomas and Hannah (Kimball) Holt; d. at Andover, 17 Nov 1824; m. 23 Jun 1767, his third cousin once removed, LYDIA LOVEJOY (*Joshua Lovejoy⁵, Henry Lovejoy⁴, Mary Farnum Lovejoy³, Elizabeth Holt Farnum², Nicholas¹*), b. at Andover, 21 Jul 1747 daughter of Joshua and Lydea (Abbott) Lovejoy; Lydia d. at Haverhill, 3 Jan 1838.

Abiel Holt served in the Revolution as a private in Colonel Tupper's Regiment of the Massachusetts line. He received a pension related to his service. An inventory of his estate related to his pension conducted in 1820 found that he had no real estate and had personal property valued at $26.59. Abiel was then seventy-six years old and a laborer, although he reported recent palsy rendered him unable to go out. Living in the home was his wife aged 73, daughter Hannah age 28, and a grandchild aged 6 years, "a sickly feeble race totally unable to support themselves, they have been assisted by the town for the last six years."[2244]

Lydia Holt widow of Abiel died at Haverhill, Massachusetts. She did not leave a will, and the heirs at the time of her decease named in the probate record were Daniel Holt of Norway, Maine, Joshua Holt of Haverhill, Thomas Holt of Andover, Chloe Holt of Bethel, Maine, and Hannah Holt of Nashua, New Hampshire.[2245]

Lydia Lovejoy and Abiel Holt were the parents of nine children all born at Andover.

[2243] Joseph, jr., nervous fever, bur. June 8, 1791, a. 24 y. 9 m. CR2

[2244] Revolutionary War Pension and Bounty-Land Warrant Application Files, 1800-1900

[2245] *Essex County, MA: Probate File Papers, 1638-1881.*Online database. *AmericanAncestors.org.* New England Historic Genealogical Society, 2014. Case 13670, estate of Lydia Holt, 17 Apr 1838

i CHLOE HOLT, baptized 10 Apr 1768; d. at Norway, ME, 11 Oct 1849; m. 24 May 1785, her fourth cousin, DARIUS HOLT (*David[5], Samuel[4], Samuel[3], Samuel[2], Nicholas[1]*), b. at Andover, 6 Mar 1765 son of David and Hannah (Martin) Holt; Darius d. at Norway, 3 Jul 1854.

ii ABIEL HOLT, baptized 10 Jan 1770; d. at Milford, NH, 11 Feb 1834; m. 1792, his third cousin once removed, ELIZABETH HOLT (*Daniel[5], John[4], Samuel[3], Samuel[2], Nicholas[1]*), b. at Wilton, 5 Apr 1772 daughter of Daniel and Mehitable (Putnam) Holt; Elizabeth d. at Milford, 20 Oct 1854.

iii HANNAH HOLT, baptized 19 Jan 1772; d. 18 Sep 1775.

iv SIMEON KIMBALL HOLT, b. about 1774; d. 23 Sep 1775.

v NATHAN KIMBALL HOLT, baptized 30 Aug 1778; d. at Boscawen, NH, 10 Nov 1836; m. at Andover, 1 Apr 1800, his third cousin once removed, REBECCA OSGOOD HOLT (*David[5], David[4], Oliver[3], Henry[2], Nicholas[1]*), b. at Andover, 25 Aug 1776 daughter of David and Rebecca (Osgood) Holt.

vi DANIEL HOLT, baptized 30 Sep 1781; d. at Norway, ME, 15 Sep 1851; m. 1802, MARY "POLLY" HALE, b. in MA, about 1783 daughter of Israel and Esther (Taylor) Hale;[2246] Polly d. at Norway, 4 Nov 1851.

vii JONATHAN LOVEJOY HOLT, b. Jul 1784; d. at Haverhill, MA, 12 Apr 1848; m. at Andover, 9 May 1808, JANE KIMBALL, b. at Andover, 25 Jul 1789 daughter of Moses and Jane (Gordon) Kimball; Jane d. at Lowell, 20 Aug 1861.

viii THOMAS HOLT, b. 15 Jan 1790; d. at Andover, after 1858; m. 1812, RUTH BEARD, b. at Wilmington, MA, about 1789 daughter of Jacob and Anna (Evans) Beard; Ruth d. at Andover, 1 Sep 1858.

ix HANNAH KIMBALL HOLT, b. 4 Jun 1792; d at Lowell, 2 Apr 1842. Hannah did not marry.

833) PHEBE HOLT (*Joshua[4], Nicholas[3], Nicholas[2], Nicholas[1]*), b. at Andover, 28 Nov 1756 daughter of Joshua and Phebe (Farnum) Holt; d. at Greenfield, 1849; m. 11 Dec 1778, JOSEPH BATCHELDER, b. 6 Mar 1748 son of Joseph and Judith (Rea) Batchelder; Joseph d. 1826.

This family started in Andover, were in Lyndeborough where at least one child was born, and were in Greenfield by about 1786. Joseph was a deacon in Greenfield. Phebe Holt and Joseph Batchelder were parents of ten children.[2247]

i ANNA CARLTON BATCHELDER, b. at Andover, 2 Apr 1781; d. after 1850 when she and Hezekiah were living in Lyndeborough; m. 25 Feb 1813, HEZEKIAH DUNCKLEE, b. at Greenfield, 16 Feb 1784 son of Hezekiah and Mehitable (White) Duncklee; Hezekiah d. at Francestown, 16 Nov 1863.

ii PHEBE BATCHELDER, b. at Lyndeborough, 2 Nov 1782; d. at Mont Vernon, NH, 20 Feb 1866; m. Apr 1820, WILLIAM RICHARDSON, b. at Billerica, MA, 20 Aug 1778 son of Jacob and Sarah (Brown) Richardson; William d. at Mont Vernon, 16 Mar 1863.

iii FANNY BATCHELDER, b. 30 Aug 1784

iv JOSEPH BATCHELDER, b. 13 Mar 1786; d. at Peoria, IL, 27 Nov 1849; m. 1st, at Athol, MA, 20 May 1819, MARY TILESTON HUMPHREY, b. at Athol, 5 Jul 1795 daughter of John and Hannah (Brinton) Humphrey; Mary d. at Athol, 20 Aug 1825. Joseph m. 2nd, 5 Jan 1832, RACHEL STONE, b. at Jericho, NY, 26 Sep 1796 daughter of William and Tamson (Graves) Stone;[2248] Rachel d. at Peoria, 22 Aug 1842.

v CHLOE BATCHELDER, b. at Greenfield, 22 Feb 1788; d. at Tioga, NY, after 1870; m. 30 Mar 1817, MOSES CARLETON, b. at Lyndeborough, 7 Sep 1792 son of Jeremiah and Lois (Hoyt) Carleton; Moses d. at Tioga, after 1860.

vi BETSEY BATCHELDER, b. 29 May 1789; d. at Greenwood, NY, 4 Aug 1856; m. 30 Dec 1813, her third cousin once removed, JOHN JOHNSON HOLT (*Simeon[5], Joseph[4], Timothy[3], James[2], Nicholas[1]*), b. at Wilton, 21 Jul 1787 son of Simeon and Mary (Dale) Holt; John d. at Jasper, NY, after 1870.

vii JOHN BATCHELDER, b. 7 May 1791; d. 27 May 1792.

viii PERSIS BATCHELDER, b. 6 May 1793

ix JUDITH BATCHELDER, b. 19 May 1795

x LUCY BATCHELDER, b. 3 Jul 1797

2246 The 1841 will of Israel Hale includes a bequest to his daughter Polly Holt.

2247 Pierce, Batchelder Genealogy, p 410

2248 Stone, The Family of John Stone, p 27 (This genealogy was written by William Leete Stone who was Rachel's brother.)

834) JOSHUA HOLT (*Joshua⁴, Nicholas³, Nicholas², Nicholas¹*), b. at Andover, 17 Jan 1758 son of Joshua and Phebe (Farnum) Holt; d at Greenfield, 14 Mar 1835; m. 31 Oct 1782,[2249] HANNAH INGALLS, b. 20 Feb 1759 daughter of David and Priscilla (Howe) Ingalls; Hannah d. 1 Dec 1838.

Joshua served in the Revolutionary War. After the war, he settled in New Hampshire in the area later known as Greenfield on land his father had purchased prior to 1780.[2250][2251] He received a pension of thirty-six dollars per year for his war service.[2252]

In his will dated 13 March 1835, left five dollars each to his children Joshua, Farnum, Hannah Balch, and Mary. His son Herman, who "has been absent for many years," also receives five dollars whenever he returns. All the remainder of the estate is bequeathed to his beloved wife Hannah and it is to be at her entire use and disposal. Executors of the estate are Hannah and Joshua's brother Stephen Holt.[2253]

Hannah Ingalls Holt did not leave a will. Her estate was probated in 1839 when Stephen Holt petitioned to be administrator as her "several children" had not stepped forward to administer the estate. The total value of her estate was $1722 which included real estate valued at $850 being one undivided half of the old Holt farm consisting of 170 acres and buildings.[2254]

Joshua Holt and Hannah Ingalls had six children born at Greenfield.

i JOSHUA HOLT, b. 13 Jun 1788; d. at Roseville Park, IA, 21 Jun 1848;[2255] m. at Antrim, 11 May 1815, ISABELLA READ NESMITH, b. at Antrim, 16 Oct 1784 daughter of James and Elizabeth (Brewster) Nesmith; Isabella d. at Indianapolis, after 1850. Joshua graduated from Dartmouth in 1814 and was a teacher in Harrisburg, PA and later in Indianapolis.[2256] Durrie's Holt genealogy describes him as having superior intellect "but intemperance wrought his ruin."[2257]

ii FARNUM HOLT, b. 15 Apr 1791; d. at Greenfield, 27 Feb 1865; m. 14 Jun 1816, his fourth cousin, LUCY CUMMINGS PEAVEY (*Peter Peavey⁶, Dorcas Holt Peavey⁵, David⁴, Oliver³, Henry², Nicholas¹*), b. at Greenfield, 3 Jul 1792 daughter of Peter and Lucy (Cummings) Peavey; Lucy d. at Milford, 13 Feb 1874.

iii NATHAN HOLT, b. and d. 1792 at age 11 weeks.

iv HERMAN HOLT, b. 4 Apr 1793. According to the Holt genealogy, he went to Mississippi. No records were located for him and he does not show up in any census records.

v HANNAH HOLT, b. 3 May 1796; d, at Francestown, 7 Oct 1856; m. about 1832, as his second wife, MASON BALCH, b. at Francestown, 23 Oct 1800 son of Isiah and Elizabeth (Epps) Balch; Mason d. at Greenfield, 21 Jul 1873. Mason was first married to Sabrina Holmes, and after Hannah's death, he married Elizabeth Gould (the widow Elizabeth Stiles).

vi MARY HOLT, b. 19 Aug 1798; d. at Greenfield, 23 Mar 1856. Mary was a teacher. She did not marry.

835) MARY HOLT (*Joshua⁴, Nicholas³, Nicholas², Nicholas¹*), b. at Andover, 5 Dec 1759 daughter of Joshua and Phebe (Farnum) Holt; d. at Greenfield, 9 Jul 1819; m. 26 Aug 1784, ISAAC FOSTER, b. 23 Dec 1751 son of Jacob and Abigail (Frost) Foster. Isaac Foster was first married to Mary Hartwell who died in 1781.

Isaac Foster had his first marriage in Andover and his wife Mary Hartwell died there; they did not have children. Isaac Foster and Mary Holt married in Andover, although Mary's family was already in Greenfield. Isaac and Mary settled in Greenfield where their nine children were born.

i MARY FOSTER, b. about 1785; d. at Andover, 20 Feb 1862; m. 31 May 1806, her second cousin, JAMES ABBOTT (*Barachias Abbott⁵, Hannah Holt Abbott⁴, Timothy³, James², Nicholas¹*), b. at Andover, 30 Mar 1780 son of Barachias and Sarah (Holt) Abbott; James d. at Andover, 4 Oct 1858.

ii DORCAS FOSTER, b. about 1787; d. at Greenfield, 8 May 1879; m. about 1838, JOSIAH TAYLOR, b. at Boxborough, MA, 3 Mar 1778 son of Silas and Mary (Wilkins) Taylor; Josiah d. at Temple, NH, 4 Oct 1850. Josiah Taylor was first married to Elizabeth Sargent.

[2249] This is the marriage date given by Hannah in her widow's pension application.
[2250] Durrie, Holt Genealogy, p 44
[2251] Hurd, *History of Hillsborough County, NH*, p 344
[2252] Revolutionary War Pension and Bounty-Land Warrant Application Files, fold3
[2253] New Hampshire, County Probate Records, 1660-1973, Hillsborough, 41:65, 37:255, 41:116, 41:285, Probate of Joshua Holt
[2254] New Hampshire, County Probate Records, 1660-1973, Hillsborough, 44:66, 43:499, 27:385, 46:212, probate of Hannah Holt
[2255] Joshua was living in Indianapolis at the time of his death but was on a trip to Iowa when he died.
[2256] Chapman, *Sketches of the Alumni of Dartmouth College*, p 172
[2257] Durrie, Holt Genealogy, p 94

iii ISAAC H. FOSTER, b. 1789; d. at Greenfield, 8 Mar 1882; m. about 1847, LUCINDA WOODWARD, b. at Lyndeborough, 1812 daughter of Ephraim and Hannah (Badger) Woodward; Lucinda d. at Bennington, NH, 29 Oct 1887.

iv TIMOTHY FOSTER, b. 1790; d. at Greenfield, 19 Nov 1863. Timothy did not marry.

v AMOS FOSTER, b. 31 Jul 1794; d. at Greenfield, 10 Oct 1882; m. 1st, about 1823, BETSEY PRATT, b. at Easthampton, MA, 13 Feb 1800 daughter of Joshua and Sylvia (Smith) Pratt;[2258] Betsey d. at Greenfield, 10 Dec 1853. Amos m. 2nd, about 1854, MARY M. DYKE, b. at Greenfield, 1810 daughter of Gideon and Mary (Fuller) Dyke; Mary d. at Peterborough, 29 Dec 1905. Mary Dyke was first married to Samuel Gould.

vi HANNAH FOSTER, b. 18 Jun 1796; d. at Tilton, NH, 17 Oct 1885; m. at Greenfield, 22 Jun 1829, her fourth cousin once removed, PASCHAL ABBOTT (*Nathan Abbott5, Job Abbott4, Zerviah Holt Abbott3, Henry2, Nicholas1*), b. at Andover, 23 Jul 1788 son of Nathan and Sarah (Ballard) Abbott; Paschal d. at Dexter, ME, 30 May 1859. Paschal Abbott was first married to his first cousin, MARY FOSTER ABBOTT (*Job Abbott5, Job Abbott4, Zerviah Holt Abbott3, Henry2, Nicholas1*) (1791-1828) daughter of Job and Anna (Ballard) Abbott.

vii ABIGAIL FOSTER, b. 1799; d. at Lyndeborough, 7 Mar 1853; m. about 1848 as the third of his five wives, DAVID PUTNAM, b. at Lyndeborough, 19 Jun 1790 son of David and Abigail (Carleton) Putnam; David d. at Lyndeborough, 10 Jun 1870. David Putnam's other marriages were to Tryphena Butler, Sarah Fletcher, Nancy Pierce, and Sarah Brown.

viii PHEBE FOSTER, b. 1802; d. at Andover, 2 May 1886; m. at Brentwood, NH, as his second wife, JOSEPH CUMMINGS, b. at Andover, 6 Dec 1792 son of Stephen and Deborah (Peabody) Cummings; Joseph d. at Andover, 10 Oct 1860. Joseph was first married to Mary Poor.

ix ANN FOSTER, b. about 1805; d. at Medford, MA, 7 Mar 1869; m. at Medford, 1 Jan 1837, as his second wife, THOMAS OLIVER PRATT, b. at Chelsea, 26 Apr 1792 son of Daniel and Abigail (Wilcott) Pratt; Thomas d. at Medford, 24 Jun 1870. Thomas was first married to Phebe Hudson.

836) ABIAH HOLT (*Joshua4, Nicholas3, Nicholas2, Nicholas1*), b. at Andover, 16 Apr 1761 daughter of Joshua and Phebe (Farnum) Holt; d. at Hancock, NH, 4 May 1841; m. 21 Jun 1791, as his second wife, DANIEL KIMBALL, b. at Ipswich, 20 Oct 1755 son of Daniel and Hephzibah (Howe) Kimball; d. 24 May 1843. Daniel's first wife was Elizabeth Osgood.

Daniel Kimball and Abiah Holt made their home in Hancock, New Hampshire where Daniel served as a deacon and selectman. He had served in the Revolution and worked at a powder mill making gunpowder for the Continental army.[2259]

Daniel had three children with his first wife Elizabeth Osgood. Daniel and Abiah Kimball were parents of eight children all born at Hancock.

i BETSEY KIMBALL, b. 1 Apr 1793; d. at Unadilla, NY, 6 Mar 1872; m. at Hancock, NH, 30 Jan 1817, EPHRAIM SMITH, b. 18 Apr 1789 son of James and Keturah (Putnam) Smith; Ephraim d. at Unadilla, 1 Aug 1862.

ii PHEBE KIMBALL, b. 28 Mar 1795; d. at Andover, 18 Jan 1836; m. at Andover, 20 Oct 1814, RALPH HOLBROOK CHANDLER, b. at Andover, 17 Feb 1791 son of John and Mary (King) Chandler; Ralph d. at Andover, Aug 1861. After Phebe's death, Ralph married Phebe's sister Mary (see below).

iii HANNAH KIMBALL, b. 17 Nov 1796; d. at Hancock, 1881; m. 16 Sep 1818, LUKE BOWERS, b. at Hancock, 25 Oct 1792 son of John and Elizabeth (Boutelle) Bowers; Luke d. at Hancock, 11 Aug 1834.

iv ANNA KIMBALL, b. 23 Jul 1798; d. Nov 1800.

v JOSEPH KIMBALL, b. 6 Dec 1799; d. Nov 1800.

vi JOSEPH KIMBALL, b. 21 Jan 1801; d. at Somerville, MA, Sep 1864; m. 20 Oct 1831, LUCY BOYD, b. at Antrim, 6 Oct 1802 daughter of James and Fanny (Baldwin) Boyd; Lucy d. at Antrim, 10 Feb 1879.

vii BENJAMIN KIMBALL, b. 8 Feb 1803; d. at Hancock, 18 Mar 1877; m. 27 Oct 1829, SALLY MATTHEWS, b. 5 Jan 1804 daughter of Thomas and Sally (Goodhue) Matthews; Sally d. at Hancock, 31 Mar 1887.

viii MARY KIMBALL, b. 14 Oct 1805; d. at Andover, 28 Jul 1891; m. at Hancock, 20 Oct 1836, RALPH HOLBROOK CHANDLER who was first married to Mary's sister Phebe (see above).

[2258] Pratt, *The Pratt Family: A Genealogical Record of Matthew Pratt*, p 54
[2259] Hayward, *History of Hancock*, p 694

837) JOHN HOLT (*Joshua⁴, Nicholas³, Nicholas², Nicholas¹*), b. at Andover, 12 Jan 1765 son of Joshua and Phebe (Farnum) Holt; d. at Greenfield, 11 Feb 1835; m. 6 Jan 1792, his third cousin, DORCAS ABBOTT, b. Dec 1766 daughter of George and Hannah (Lovejoy) Abbott; Dorcas d. 15 Mar 1841.

Dorcas Abbott and John Holt married in Andover, but were soon after in Greenfield, New Hampshire where they reared their family.

In his will written 17 April 1827, John Holt bequeaths to beloved wife Dorcas use of one-half of the dwelling house while she remains a widow and all the household furniture not otherwise disposed of the be at her own disposal. There are also several specific provisions for the continued care and support of Dorcas. This includes provisions for medical care if needed, annual supplies of staple goods, and $200 in cash. Daughter Dorcas wife of Peter Pevey receives $50; daughter Sarah wife of Francis Dunkley, $50; daughter Tamesin, $250; daughter Phebe, $250; daughter Martha, $250; and daughter Elizabeth, $250. He also provides that the four unmarried daughters can remain in the mother's household if they choose to do so. He also wills that the four daughters, if employed, should pay some moderate amount to continue to live in the home and this is to be paid to their brother John. His only son John receives all the estate real and personal not otherwise disposed of. The wearing apparel is to be divided equally between John and his brothers-in-law. John is named sole executor.[2260]

Dorcas Abbott and John Holt were parents of eight children born at Greenfield.

i DORCAS HOLT, b. 12 Jan 1793; d. at Greenfield, 4 Jan 1856; m. about 1815, PETER PEAVEY, b. at Wilton, 27 Jul 1788 son of Peter and Lucy (Cummings) Peavey; Peter d. at Greenfield, 26 Oct 1879. After Dorcas's death, Peter married her sister Tamesin (see below).

ii SARAH HOLT, b. 10 Mar 1795; d. at Francestown, 4 Jun 1885; m. at Greenfield, 28 Feb 1817, FRANCIS DUNCKLEE, b. at Greenfield, 1791 son of Hezekiah and Mehitable (White) Duncklee; Francis d. at Francestown, 14 Feb 1859.

iii HANNAH HOLT, b. 15 Sep 1797; d. at Greenfield, 10 Nov 1821.

iv JOHN HOLT, b. 9 Aug 1799; d. at Greenfield, 16 Apr 1869; m. 1st, 1836, his first cousin, PHEBE HOLT (*Hannah Holt Holt⁵, Joshua⁴, Nicholas³, Nicholas², Nicholas¹*), b. 9 Jun 1797 daughter of Ephraim and Hannah (Holt) Holt; Phebe d. at Greenfield, 8 May 1862. John m. 2nd, about 1863, MARY R. HOLT, b. 1823 (based on census records) whose parents are not identified; Mary d. at Greenfield, 24 Aug 1868.

v TAMESIN HOLT, b. 23 Nov 1803; d. at Greenfield, 4 Jan 1896; m. about 1857, PETER PEAVEY who was first married to her sister Dorcas (see above).

vi PHEBE FARNUM HOLT, b. 1806; d. at Bennington, NH, 31 Oct 1880; m. 30 Apr 1844, as his second wife, FRANCIS BURNHAM. b. at Greenfield, 13 Jan 1784 son of Nathaniel and Mary (-) Burnham; Francis d. at Greenfield, 27 Mar 1870. Francis was first married to Mary Fletcher.

vii MARTHA HOLT, b. 24 Apr 1808; d. at Portsmouth, NH, 10 Mar 1895; m. about 1837, as his second wife, ARNOLD B. HUTCHINSON, b. at Lyndeborough, 17 Apr 1808 son of Ebenezer and Thomasin (Griffin) Hutchinson; Arnold d. at Portsmouth, 30 Jul 1888. Arnold was first married to Clarissa Fuller.

viii ELIZABETH HOLT, b. 2 Apr 1811; d. 20 Jun 1830.

838) TIMOTHY HOLT (*Joshua⁴, Nicholas³, Nicholas², Nicholas¹*), b. at Andover, Apr 1767 son of Joshua and Phebe (Farnum) Holt; d. at Peterborough, 1856; m. 7 Nov 1793, his second cousin once removed, LYDIA HOLT (*Joseph⁵, Benjamin⁴, Henry³, Henry², Nicholas¹*), b. 18 Apr 1767 daughter of Joseph and Ruth (Johnson) Holt; Lydia d. 22 Nov 1825. Timothy m. 2nd, 11 Mar 1830, CHARITY SAVAGE, b. 1779 and d. at Peterborough, 28 Feb 1846.

Timothy and Lydia Holt located in Peterborough immediately after their marriage. Their farm was at East Mountain on the border of Peterborough and Greenfield. Timothy was deacon at the Congregational Church in Greenfield.[2261]

In his will written 29 April 1847 (proved 5 November 1856), Timothy Holt bequeathed to son Timothy Holt ten dollars. Daughter Chloe Baldwin wife of Ziba Baldwin and Ruth Hovey wife of Timothy Hovey each receive five dollars. Daughters Lydia Holt and Tabitha Holt have the privilege of occupying the southeast chamber, but if the executor disposes of the dwelling, they are to be paid five dollars each. Son Joseph Holt receives all the real estate and all the residue of the personal estate and is named executor.[2262]

Timothy and Lydia were parents of eight children. The births of the three oldest children are recorded at Andover, although the births may have occurred in Peterborough.

i LYDIA HOLT, b. 19 Apr 1795; d. at Peterborough, 5 Nov 1867. Lydia did not marry.

[2260] *New Hampshire. Probate Court (Hillsborough County)*; Probate Place: *Hillsborough, New Hampshire, Probate Records, Vol 40-41, 1833-1835*, pp 32-34

[2261] Smith and Morison, *History of Peterborough: Genealogy and History of Peterborough Families*, p 117

[2262] *New Hampshire. Probate Court (Hillsborough County)*; Probate Place: *Hillsborough, New Hampshire, Probate Records, Vol 68, 1856-1869*, p 62

ii CHLOE HOLT, b. 30 Mar 1797; d. at Peterborough, 1876; m. 1834, ZIBA BALDWIN, b. at Milford, 1787 son of Jeremiah Baldwin; Ziba d. at Peterborough, 28 Oct 1872. Ziba was first married to Eliza Morse who died in 1831.

iii TABITHA HOLT, b. 16 Sep 1799; d. at Peterborough, 22 Jan 1855. Tabitha did not marry.

iv TIMOTHY HOLT, b. 16 Mar 1802; d. at Concord, 22 Apr 1867; m. 1825, MARY JACKMAN, b. at Boscawen, 12 Nov 1802 daughter of Nehemiah and Ruth (Flanders) Jackman; Mary d. at Concord, 12 Mar 1884.

v JOSEPH HOLT, b. 4 Apr 1804; d. at Peterborough, 13 Dec 1861; m. at Peterborough, 17 Jan 1832, MARY JANE MILLER, b. 1806 daughter of Adams and Ann (Robertson) Miller; Mary Jane d. at Lowell, 16 Jul 1870.

vi JOSHUA HOLT, b. 17 Mar 1807; d. 6 Jul 1811.

vii RUTH HOLT, b. 8 Feb 1809; d. 18 Jul 1811.

viii RUTH HOLT, b. 19 May 1812; d. at Peterborough, 29 Jul 1874; m. at Peterborough, 17 Nov 1836, TIMOTHY L. HOVEY, b. at Peterborough, 9 Aug 1813 son of Richard and Asenath (Baxter) Hovey; Timothy d. at Peterborough, 31 Mar 1887. After Ruth's death, Timothy married Myra Parker (widow of Charles Hutchinson) daughter of Jonathan and Alice (Gutterson) Parker.

839) SOLOMON HOLT (*Joshua⁴, Nicholas³, Nicholas², Nicholas¹*), b. at Andover, Dec 1768 son of Joshua and Phebe (Farnum) Holt; d. 15 Apr 1830; m. 22 May 1798, MARY CUMMINGS, perhaps b. at Andover, 1 Nov 1774 daughter of Jonathan and Mary (Eastman) Cummings;[2263] Mary d. 8 Oct 1852.

Solomon Holt inherited the homestead from his father Joshua Holt. The historic home is at 111 Reservation Road in Andover. Solomon served as a deacon of the newly formed West Parish church in Andover.[2264]

In his will written 24 Feb 1830, Solomon Holt bequeaths to beloved wife Mary the use and improvement of one-third part of the homestead farm in Andover and several provisions for her support. Son Solomon is to furnish his mother with a horse and chaise. Sons Solomon and Nathan each receive $450. Son Abiathar receives his support including board and tuition to prosecute his studies "till he is fitted to enter college" and his executor is to furnish this support to Abiathar out of the estate. When he enters college, Abiathar will receive $450, and if he does not enter college, he will receive that amount when he is age twenty-one. Son Stephen will also receive $450 at age twenty-one, and until that time he is to labor on the farm for son Solomon, and Solomon will provide his support. Daughters Mary and Phebe C. each receive $200 and the improvements on the northeast chamber as long as they remain single. Mary and Phebe each receive a seat in the pew at the west parish meeting house. His wearing apparel is to be divided among his five sons, the books are to be equally divided among all the children, and his military equipment goes to Solomon. The remainder of the estate goes to Solomon who is also named executor.[2265]

Solomon Holt and Mary Cummings were parents of eight children born at Andover.

i SOLOMON HOLT, b. 1799; d. at Andover, 3 Apr 1883; m. 25 May 1824, his fourth cousin, PHEBE ABBOTT (*Benjamin Abbott⁶, Jonathan Abbott⁵, David Abbott⁴, Sarah Farnum Abbott³, Elizabeth Holt Farnum², Nicholas¹*), b. at Andover, 27 Nov 1798 daughter of Benjamin and Rhoda (Chandler) Abbott; Phebe d. at Andover, 18 Oct 1872.

ii MARY HOLT, b. 8 Mar 1801; d. 17 Feb 1803.

iii JOSHUA HOLT, b. 6 Mar 1804; d. at Haverhill, 24 Sep 1886; m. 1st, 26 Nov 1829, REBECCA BAILEY, b. at Andover, 19 Nov 1804 daughter of William and Rebecca (Gillson) Bailey; Rebecca d. 4 Sep 1834. Joshua m. 2nd, 2 Apr 1836, CHARLOTTE GAGE, b. at Andover, 18 Jun 1806 daughter of Nathaniel and Betsey (Kimball) Gage; Charlotte d. at Bradford, 30 Nov 1846. Joshua m. 3rd, 25 Oct 1848, his first cousin once removed, SARAH ABBOTT (*James Abbott⁶, Barachias Abbott⁵, Hannah Holt Abbott⁴, Timothy³, James², Nicholas¹*), b. at Andover, 23 Jul 1814 daughter of James and Mary (Foster) Abbott; Sarah d. at Bradford, 10 Jul 1857. Joshua m. 4th, 7 Apr 1859, MARY A. SARGENT, b. at Walton, NH, about 1811 daughter of William and Susan (Stackpole) Sargent; Mary d. at Lawrence, 26 Sep 1891. Mary Sargent was first married to Charles Gault.

iv MARY HOLT, b. 20 Feb 1806; d. at Lyndon, VT, 23 Feb 1900; m. at Andover, 6 Jun 1837, as his second wife, SAMUEL READ HALL, b. at Croydon, NH, 27 Oct 1795 son of Samuel Read and Elizabeth (Hall) Hall; Samuel d. at Brownington, VT, 24 Jun 1877. Samuel was first married to Mary Dascomb.

v NATHAN HOLT, b. 18 Apr 1808; d. at Lawrence, MA, 26 Dec 1891; m. at Andover, 21 Aug 1832, ABIGAIL COCHRAN, b. at Andover, 13 Apr 1812 daughter of Samuel and Mary (Bailey) Cochran; Abigail d. at Lawrence, 5 Sep 1892.

2263 Durrie's Holt genealogy gives Mary's parents as Justin and Mary (-) Cummings.

2264 Andover Historic Preservation, 111 Reservation Road, https://preservation.mhl.org/111-reservation-road

2265 Essex County, MA: Probate File Papers, 1638-1881.Online database. AmericanAncestors.org. New England Historic Genealogical Society, 2014. Case number 13695, probate of Solomon Holt

vi PHEBE CUMMINGS HOLT, b. 30 Apr 1810; d. at Andover, Aug 1858; m. at Andover, 19 Oct 1835, TIMOTHY DWIGHT PORTER STONE, b. at Cornwall, CT, 21 Jul 1811 son of Timothy and Mary (Merwin) Stone; Timothy d. at Andover, 11 Apr 1887. After Phebe's death, Timothy married Susan Margaret Dickinson.

vii ABIATHER HOLT, b. 31 Jan 1813; d. at Lowell, 18 Aug 1846; m. at Andover, 15 Sep 1836, ELIZABETH PLUNKETT, b. at Belfast, Ireland, 8 Feb 1814 daughter of John and Elizabeth (Keenan) Plunkett; Elizabeth d. at Matagorda, TX, 7 Jan 1887.[2266] Elizabeth immigrated with her parents around 1830.[2267] Abiather was a manufacturer in Lowell.

viii STEPHEN P. HOLT, b. 12 Feb 1816; d. at Andover, 17 Nov 1860; m. at Andover, 2 Dec 1847, JEANETTE M. SMITH, b. at Andover, 14 May 1824 daughter of Peter and Rebecca (Bartlett) Smith; Jeanette d. at Andover, 23 May 1872.

840) HANNAH HOLT (*Joshua*[4], *Nicholas*[3], *Nicholas*[2], *Nicholas*[1]), b. at Andover, Jun 1771 daughter of Joshua and Phebe (Farnum) Holt; d. at Greenfield, 21 Apr 1842; m. 27 Nov 1794, her third cousin once removed, EPHRAIM HOLT (*Jacob*[5], *Jacob*[4], *Oliver*[3], *Henry*[2], *Nicholas*[1]), b. 19 Mar 1769 son of Jacob and Rhoda (Abbott) Holt; Ephraim d. 24 Oct 1836.

Ephraim and Hannah lived in Greenfield where Ephraim was a selectman from 1811 to 1827 and a representative to the General Court from 1829 to 1832.[2268]

Ephraim and Hannah Holt were parents of seven children born at Greenfield.

i HANNAH HOLT, b. 19 Oct 1795; d. at Peterborough, 15 Nov 1879. Hannah did not marry.

ii PHEBE HOLT, b. 9 Jun 1797; d. at Greenfield, 8 May 1862; m. 1836, her first cousin, JOHN HOLT (*John*[5], *Joshua*[4], *Nicholas*[3], *Nicholas*[2], *Nicholas*[1]), b. 9 Aug 1799 son of John and Dorcas (Abbott) Holt; John d. at Greenfield, 19 Apr 1869. After Phebe's death, John married Mary R. Holt, b. 1823 and d. at Greenfield, 24 Aug 1868.

iii EPHRAIM HOLT, b. 2 Jul 1799; d. 26 Apr 1801.

iv JACOB HOLT, b. 23 Apr 1801; d. 26 Apr 1811.

v EPHRAIM HOLT, b. 12 Dec 1803; d. at Greenfield, 26 Aug 1867; m. SELINDA HILL, b. 26 May 1809 daughter of Job and Betsey (Perry) Hill; Selinda d. at Peterborough, 25 Aug 1891.

vi RHODA HOLT, b. 26 Dec 1809; d. 1 Jul 1811.

vii RHODA HOLT, b. 7 Aug 1815; d. at Pepperell, MA, 15 Feb 1849; m. 7 Oct 1845, JOHN VARNUM AMES, b. at Pepperell, 16 Jul 1821 son of John and Jane (Varnum) Ames; John d. after 1865. After Rhoda's death, John married Jane M. Wolcott in 1852 and Harriet R. Perry in 1855.

841) STEPHEN HOLT (*Joshua*[4], *Nicholas*[3], *Nicholas*[2], *Nicholas*[1]), b. at Andover, May 1773 son of Joshua and Phebe (Farnum) Holt; d. at Greenfield, 26 Mar 1868; m. 1799, his third cousin once removed, FANNY BOWERS (*Elizabeth Holt Bowers*[5], *Jacob*[4], *Oliver*[3], *Henry*[2], *Nicholas*[1]), b. at Chelmsford, Jun 1773 daughter of Francis and Elizabeth (Holt) Bowers; Fanny d. 18 Apr 1828. Stephen married in 1831, MARGARET BATCHELDER, b. Sep 1784 and d. at Greenfield, 17 Aug 1867.

Stephen and Fanny Holt resided in Greenfield, New Hampshire where Stephen was a selectman in 1805 and 1806. Son Stephen Holt, Jr. operated the first steam mill in Greenfield.[2269]

In his will dated 2 September 1867, Stephen Holt bequeaths to Jane Bradford wife of Robert Bradford all the household furniture her mother brought "at the time of our marriage." The remaining household items, books, and wearing apparel are to be divided among the following heirs: son Stephen Holt, Jr., daughter Mary Jaquith wife of Benjamin Jaquith, daughter Ann Jaquith widow of Ambrose Jaquith, and Benjamin F. Jaquith and Fannie Hardy children of daughter Fannie Jaquith deceased. All the rest and residue of the estate real and personal is to be divided among the same heirs with the addition of the children of daughter Rhoda Dane who is deceased. The children of Rhoda are Maria, Moses, and Dexter. He also directs the erection of gravestones for deceased family members. Ephraim Holt of Greenfield, New Hampshire was named executor.[2270]

Stephen Holt and Fanny Bowers were parents of eight children all born at Greenfield.

2266 *Texas, Death Certificates, 1903-1982*, Texas Department of State Health Services; Austin Texas, USA.

2267 "John Plunkett" Veteran Biographies, San Jacinto Museum of History, https://www.sanjacinto-museum.org/Library/Veteran_Bios/Bio_page/?id=677&army=Texian

2268 Hurd, *History of Hillsborough County, New Hampshire*

2269 Hurd, *History of Hillsborough County, New Hampshire*

2270 *New Hampshire. Probate Court (Hillsborough County)*; Probate Place: *Hillsborough, New Hampshire, Probate Records, Vol 81-84, 1865-1890*, p 218, will of Stephen Holt

i FANNY HOLT, b. 3 Jun 1800; d. at Greenfield, 20 Nov 1834; m. at Lyndeborough, 26 Dec 1826, BENJAMIN JAQUITH, b. at Wilmington, MA, 13 Apr 1798 son of Benjamin and Phebe (Ames) Jaquith; Benjamin d. at Greenfield, 8 Dec 1881. Benjamin married second, Fanny's sister MARY BOWERS HOLT (see below). After Mary's death, Benjamin married Hannah Marshall.

ii BETSEY HOLT, b. 11 Jun 1802; d. 1816.

iii STEPHEN HOLT, b. 4 Mar 1804; d. 12 Mar 1804.

iv MARY BOWERS HOLT, b. 5 Jul 1805; d. at Greenfield, 1870; m. 1835, BENJAMIN JAQUITH (see sister Fanny above).

v RHODA HOLT, b. 11 Sep 1807; d. at Lowell, MA, 2 Apr 1846; m. MOSES DANE, b. about 1800 son of John and Deborah (Bailey) Dane; Moses d. at Cedar, IA, 24 Mar 1888. After Rhoda's death, Moses married Lavina Lane.

vi STEPHEN HOLT, b. 24 Apr 1810; d. at Francestown, NH, 24 Nov 1879; m. 2 Jun 1839, SARAH A. SPAULDING, b. at Lyndeborough, 2 Jan 1820 daughter of Henry and Lucy (Duncklee) Spaulding; Sarah d. at Francestown, 30 Mar 1890.

vii ANNA DANDRIDGE HOLT, b. 13 Jul 1812; d. at Peterborough, 17 Jan 1895; m. AMBROSE JAQUITH, b. 1810 son of Benjamin and Phebe (Ames) Jaquith; Ambrose d. at Greenfield, 6 Jan 1864.

viii BENJAMIN HOLT, b. 25 Nov 1816; d. 19 Apr 1827.

842) CHLOE HOLT (*Joshua*[4], *Nicholas*[3], *Nicholas*[2], *Nicholas*[1]), b. at Andover, Jun 1775 daughter of Joshua and Phebe (Farnum) Holt; d. at Peterborough, 6 Nov 1849; m. 23 Oct 1798, her first cousin once removed, FRANCIS BOWERS (*Elizabeth Holt Bowers*[5], *Jacob*[4], *Oliver*[3], *Henry*[2], *Nicholas*[1]), b. at Chelmsford, 20 May 1775 son of Francis and Elizabeth (Holt) Bowers; Francis d. 15 Oct 1835.

Francis Bowers and Chloe Holt came to Peterborough about 1800. He had a homestead farm, but from about 1820 to 1835 he operated what was known as Holmes' Mills.[2271]

Francis Bowers did not leave a will. His widow declined administration, and this was assumed by Samuel Miller December 1835. On 18 June 1836, an allowance of one hundred-fifty dollars was made to the widow for her support. Real estate was valued at $1,075 and personal estate $1,483.97.[2272]

Francis Bowers and Chloe Holt were parents of eight children born at Peterborough.

i CHLOE BOWERS, b. 15 Jan 1799; d. at Francestown, 7 Oct 1844; m. JOHN DANE, b. at Andover, 22 Nov 1786 son of John and Deborah (Bailey) Dane; John d. at Francestown, 8 Jul 1850.

ii RUTH D. BOWERS, b. 20 Jan 1803; d. at Lowell, MA, 10 Dec 1883; m. 1831, SAMUEL MILLER, b. at Peterborough, about 1796 son of Hugh and Jane (Templeton) Miller; Samuel d. at Peterborough, 9 May 1872.

iii BENJAMIN BOWERS, b. 16 Mar 1807; d. 16 Mar 1811.

iv PHEBE F. BOWERS, b. 18 Apr 1809; d. 28 Feb 1811.

v FRANCIS H. BOWERS, b. 24 Feb 1811; d. at Billerica, MA, 5 Feb 1864; m. at Lowell, 16 Jan 1845, MARTHA A. SHERBURN, b. at Epsom, NH, about 1825 daughter of John and Abigail (Page) Sherburn; Martha d. at Somerville, MA, 23 Feb 1904.

vi HANNAH BOWERS, b. 11 Jun 1812; d. at Carrollton, MN, 11 May 1886; m. 1st, about 1835, EZRA DANE, b. at Greenfield, about 1802 son of John and Deborah (Bailey) Dane; Ezra d. before 1866. Hannah m. 2nd, at Lowell, 5 Aug 1867, LUKE MILLER, b. at Wakefield, NH, 18 Aug 1815 son of Andrew and Jenny (Ames) Miller; Luke d. at Lanesboro, MN, 5 Sep 1881. Luke Miller was first married to Abby D. Lovell.

vii BETSEY H. BOWERS, b. 28 Nov 1820; d. at Peterborough, 15 Oct 1861. Betsey did not marry. She lived with her sister Ruth and her husband.

viii PHEBE F. BOWERS, b. 12 Oct 1823; d. at Lowell, 19 Apr 1910; m. at Lowell, 29 Nov 1883, NATHANIEL GAY, b. at Raymond, ME, 22 Apr 1814 son of Luther and Mary (Cash) Gay; Nathaniel d. at Lowell, 30 Jun 1889.

843) DANIEL HOLT (*Daniel*[4], *Nicholas*[3], *Nicholas*[2], *Nicholas*[1]), b. at Andover, Dec 1761 son of Daniel and Hannah (Holt) Holt; d. at Fitchburg, 27 Nov 1830; m. 5 Jan 1790, MARY JONES, b. at Andover, about 1769 daughter of Jacob and Mary (Winn) Jones.[2273]

2271 Smith and Morison, *History of Peterborough: Genealogy and History of Peterborough Families*, p 21

2272 New Hampshire, County Probate Records, 1660-1973, Hillsborough, 37:272, 41:229, 41:1, 27:308, probate of Francis Bowers, 1835

2273 The will of Jacob Jones includes a bequest to his granddaughter Mary Holt the child of his daughter Mary who is deceased.

Daniel and Mary Holt had one daughter and Mary likely died soon after that. Deacon Daniel Holt lived in Fitchburg and does not seem to have remarried.

Daniel Holt did not leave a will and John Andrews assumed administration of the estate. Debts exceeded the value of the estate, the estate was sold, and creditors received eighty cents on the dollar.[2274]

i MARY "POLLY" HOLT, b. at Fitchburg, 14 Mar 1792; d. at Fitchburg, 19 Oct 1818; m. at Fitchburg, 7 Aug 1810, JOHN ANDREWS, b. at Ipswich, about 1786 son of Daniel and Susan (Choate) Andrews; John d. at Fitchburg, 1 Apr 1874. After Mary's death, John married Zoa Lawrence.

844) ABIEL HOLT (*Daniel⁴, Nicholas³, Nicholas², Nicholas¹*), b. at Andover, 8 Jun 1765 son of Daniel and Hannah (Holt) Holt; d. at Rindge, NH, 18 Jun 1825; m. 26 Jul 1791, PHEBE PUTNAM, b. at Fitchburg, 20 Sep 1770 daughter of Daniel and Rachel (-) Putnam; Phebe d. at Fitchburg, 12 Nov 1827.

Abiel and Phebe Holt spent their early married life in Fitchburg where four children were born. They relocated to Rindge, New Hampshire in 1806 where a fifth child was born. Abiel died in Rindge and Phebe seems to have returned to Fitchburg.[2275]

Abiel Holt did not leave a will. Widow Phebe Holt declined administration of the estate and requested oldest son Abiel to be named administrator. This document is also signed by Nathan Holt and Edah Holt. On 15 October 1825, widow Phebe Holt was allowed to take $150 from the estate account. A committee was named to set off the dower to widow Phebe.[2276]

i ABIEL HOLT, b. 16 Aug 1791; d. at Winthrop, MA, 10 Jun 1864; m. at Rindge, NH, Nov 1815, EDAH DARLING, b. at Rindge, 14 Apr 1792 daughter of Amos and Ede (Stone) Darling; Edah d. at Ashburnham, 30 Oct 1864.

ii DANIEL HOLT, b. about 1795. The History of Rindge reports that Daniel went to New York, had a family there, and died 1871. A tentative marriage is being suggested for him. Only one Daniel Holt of the correct age was found in the census records in the state of New York. That Daniel was married in Worcester County, MA which would fit for him. Daniel Holt, m. at Warren, MA, 16 Sep 1820, FRANCES BRIGHAM, b. at Brookfield, 27 Nov 1798 daughter of Tilly and Rachel (Walker) Brigham. Daniel Holt who married Frances was a grocer in New York. He died in New York City, 1866 (probate Sep 1866). Frances d. after 1870. Daniel and Frances Holt had two daughters, Sarah and Maria.

iii NATHAN HOLT, b. about 1798; d. 25 Oct 1827. Nathan did not marry.

iv EDAH PUTNAM HOLT, b. at Lunenburg, 29 Sep 1804; d. at Fitchburg, 9 Jul 1861; m. at Fitchburg, 18 Sep 1859, WILLIAM BASCOM PHELPS, b. at Fitchburg, 2 Mar 1811 son of Samuel and Elizabeth (Hartwell) Phelps; William d. at Fitchburg, 2 Apr 1882.

v LIBERTY HOLT, b. at Rindge, 9 Nov 1813; d. at Ashburnham, 29 Jun 1887; m. 1st, at Westminster, MA, 7 Nov 1837, LUCY WHEELER, b. at Westminster, 5 Oct 1812 daughter of Haman and Sally (Wheeler) Wheeler; Lucy d. at Fitchburg, 18 Jul 1863. Liberty m. 2nd, at Ashburnham, 30 Oct 1864, SARAH WHEELER, b. at Sudbury, about 1813 daughter of Nathan and Dolly (-) Wheeler; Sarah d. at Ayer, MA, 12 Sep 1899. Sarah Wheeler was first married to Elnathan Haynes.

845) MARY HOLT (*Joseph⁴, Thomas³, Nicholas², Nicholas¹*), b. 17 Aug 1745 daughter of Joseph and Mary (Abbott) Holt; m. 26 Jun 1766, BENJAMIN DARLING, b. 28 Apr 1728 son of John and Lois (Gowing) Darling; Benjamin d. at Lunenburg, about 1783 based on date of probate.

In his young adult life, Benjamin was a mariner, but returned home and married Mary Holt. He inherited property in Lunenburg form his father and settled there.[2277]

Benjamin Darling did not leave a will. The personal estate was insufficient to pay the debts and widow Mary Darling petitioned the Court to be allowed to sell as much of the real estate as was needed to pay his debts.[2278]

Mary Abbott and Benjamin Darling were parents of seven children born at Lunenburg.

i PATIENCE DARLING, b. 28 Mar 1767; m. at Lunenburg, 1785, JOHN DARLING, b. at Lunenburg, 13 Aug 1759 son of Timothy and Joanna (Blood) Darling.

2274 Worcester County, MA: Probate File Papers, 1731-1881. Online database. AmericanAncestors.org. New England Historic Genealogical Society, 2015. Case 30625

2275 Stearns, *History of the Town of Rindge*, p 556

2276 *New Hampshire. Probate Court (Cheshire County)*; Probate Place: *Cheshire, New Hampshire, Estate Files, H324-H374, 1822-1826*, probate of Abiel Holt

2277 Weeks, *The Darling Family in America*, p 14

2278 Worcester County, MA: Probate File Papers, 1731-1881. Online database. AmericanAncestors.org. New England Historic Genealogical Society, 2015. Case Number 15392

ii MOLLY DARLING, b. 11 Jun 1769; d. at Temple, ME; m. at Lunenburg, 22 May 1792, MITCHELL RICHARDS, b. at Lunenburg, 1759 likely the son of Mitchel and Esther (Mitchell) Richards; Mitchell d. at Temple, 2 May 1845.

iii LOIS DARLING, b. 29 Aug 1771; nothing further known.

iv EUNICE DARLING, b. 13 Apr 1774; d. at Jaffrey, NH, 27 Jul 1834; m. at Jaffrey, 25 Nov 1811, RUFUS SAWYER, b. at Lancaster, MA (baptized 20 Jul 1760) son of Bezeleel and Lois (Lawrence) Sawyer; Rufus d. at Jaffrey, 29 Sep 1845.

v BENJAMIN DARLING, b. 11 Dec 1775; d. at Northfield, MA, 4 Nov 1840; m. FANNY AMES, *perhaps* b. at Hollis, 5 Sep 1773 daughter of Jonathan Robbins and Fanny (Powers) Ames; Fanny d. at Northfield, 18 Dec 1859.

vi JAMES DARLING, b. 5 Dec 1779; d. at Northfield, 5 May 1811; m. at Lunenburg, 3 Oct 1801, OLIVE READ, b. at Westford, MA, 30 Jun 1781 daughter of Abel and Rebekah (Farrar) Read.

vii LEVI DARLING, b. 8 May 1782; d. at Northfield, after 1821. Levi may not have married. In 1821, he was being supported by the town of Northfield.[2279]

846) SARAH HOLT (*Joseph⁴, Thomas³, Nicholas², Nicholas¹*), baptized at Lunenburg 14 Dec 1746 daughter of Joseph and Mary (Abbott) Holt; m. at Lunenburg, 1 Feb 1767, BARNABAS WOOD, b. at Lunenburg, 21 May 1746 son of Jonathan and Sarah (Whitney) Wood; Barnabas d. at Windsor, VT, 5 Apr 1822.

Sarah and Barnabas were first in Lunenburg where their first two children were baptized.[2280] They were in Jaffrey, New Hampshire by 1782 where Barnabas was highway surveyor in 1782 and 1785.[2281] The family was in Westminster, Vermont for a time before being finally in Windsor, Vermont.

There are four likely children for Sarah and Barnabas, although there may well be other children.

i OLIVE WOOD, baptized at Lunenburg, 25 Jun 1769; d. at Springfield, VT, 21 Jan 1815; m. 1st at Rockingham, VT, 10 May 1791, ISAIAH EDSON; Isaiah d. about 1798. Olive m. 2nd at Springfield, VT, 8 Jul 1799, EBENEZER SHED, b. at Lunenburg, about 1777 son of Solomon and Elizabeth (Boynton) Shed; Ebenezer d. at Springfield, 30 Jul 1860.

ii JONATHAN BRADSTREET WOOD, baptized at Lunenburg, 7 Jan 1771; d. at Springfield, VT, 19 Mar 1805; m. at Rockingham, VT, 6 Dec 1792, RELIEF STICKNEY likely b. at Holden, 13 May 1775 daughter of Moses and Abigail (Hale) Stickney; Relief d. at Springfield, 24 Jan 1842.

iii BAZALEEL WOOD, b. 1780; d. at Springfield, VT, 1849; m. at Chester, VT, 19 Apr 1821, HANNAH LOVELL, b. 1793; Hannah d. at Springfield, 19 Mar 1853.

iv JOHN WOOD, b. at Rockingham, VT, 1788; d. at West Rutland, VT, 3 Feb 1861; m. LUCY PHIPPEN, b. at Westminster, VT, 5 Dec 1786 daughter of Joseph and Lilie (Paul) Phippen; Lucy d. at West Rutland, 27 Sep 1828.

847) JOSEPH HOLT (*Joseph⁴, Thomas³, Nicholas², Nicholas¹*), b. at Lunenburg, 18 Dec 1752 son of Joseph and Dorcas (Boynton) Holt; d. at Fitchburg, 3 Sep 1803 (suicide by hanging); m. 30 Jan 1777, ELIZABETH STRATTON.

Joseph died by suicide on 3 September 1803. The following account was given of his death: "He was found dead hanging with a pair of bridle rains by his neck upon the limb of a small chestnut tree half after ten in the Evening, they had a Jury on the body, & their verdict was that he was insane."[2282]

Joseph Holt did not leave a will and his estate entered probate 22 September 1803 with son Abiel Holt as administrator at the request of widow Elisabeth Holt and eldest son Joseph Holt. The home farm was valued at $850 with a total real estate value of $1,063.33 and personal estate of $363.34.[2283] On 23 January 1804, Ephraim Gibson of Fitchburg was named as guardian to represent the interests of the minor children Dolly and Sally. On 10 September 1803, son Joseph then of Lunenburg quitclaimed his right to the property of his honored father Joseph to his brother Abiel Holt.

Joseph Holt and Elizabeth Stratton were parents of six children born at Fitchburg.[2284]

i BETSEY HOLT, b. 23 Sep 1777; d. at Ashby, MA, 9 Jun 1844; m. at Fitchburg, 28 Oct 1797, JACOB BARNARD, b. at Harvard, 16 Apr 1769 son of Jotham and Lucy (Wetherbee) Barnard; Jacob d. at Ashby, 2 Feb 1854. Betsey and Jacob were in Schenectady for several years and later returned to Massachusetts. The 1808 probate of

---

2279 Cunningham, *Cunningham's History of the Town of Lunenburg*, p 178

2280 Cunningham, *Cunningham's History of the Town of Lunenburg*, p 828

2281 Cutter, *History of the Town of Jaffrey*, p 521

2282 Davis, *The Old Records of the Town of Fitchburg*, p 345

2283 *Worcester County, MA: Probate File Papers, 1731-1881.* Online database. AmericanAncestors.org. New England Historic Genealogical Society, 2015. Case 30654

2284 Davis, *The Old Records of the Town of Fitchburg*, pp 345-346

Jacob's father Jotham includes a statement that son Jacob was living out of the Commonwealth. Jacob is on the 1810 census at Schenectady and Betsy and Jacob's daughter Eliza was born there in 1807.

ii JOSEPH HOLT, b. 22 Jul 1779; d. at Chesterfield, NH, 9 Mar 1832; m. at Fitchburg, 9 Feb 1802, BETSEY OSBORN, b. at Fitchburg, 9 Mar 1779 daughter of Ephraim and Sarah (-) Osborn; Betsey d. at Chesterfield, 18 Dec 1838.

iii ABIEL HOLT, b. 29 Aug 1781; d. before 1841 (wife died as a widow); m. at Fitchburg, 21 Jan 1807, CATHERINE GOODRICH, b. at Fitchburg, 7 Sep 1786 daughter of Abijah and Eunice (Martin) Goodrich; Catherine d. at Fitchburg, 18 Feb 1841.

iv SALLY HOLT, b. 10 Sep 1785; d. at Lunenburg, 18 Feb 1847;[2285] m. 1st 3 Dec 1807, ZACHARIAH WHITNEY, b. at Lunenburg, 1781 son of Zachariah and Betty (Wetherbee) Whitney; Zachariah d. at Lunenburg, 5 Jul 1812. The 1828 will of Zachariah's father Zachariah includes bequests to his three grandchildren the children of Zachariah deceased: Joseph H. and Josiah B. Whitney and Lavina Eaton widow of John Eaton. Sally Holt m. 2nd 6 Aug 1828, as his second wife, AARON PATCH, b. at Ipswich 1768 son of John Patch; Aaron d. at Holden, 6 Dec 1859.

v DOLLY HOLT, b. 1 Jul 1787

vi DORCAS HOLT, b. 4 Mar 1791; d. at Malden, 24 Sep 1868; m. at Fitchburg, 2 Jun 1814, NATHAN HOLDEN, b. 1786; Nathan d. at Malden, 12 Jan 1829.

848) ALICE HOLT (*William⁴, Thomas³, Nicholas², Nicholas¹*), b. 26 Apr 1747 at Windham daughter of William and Hannah (Holt) Holt; d. at Stockbridge, VT, 28 Nov 1814;[2286] m. 13 Nov 1764, her second cousin, ROBERT LYON (*Sarah Holt Lyon⁴, Robert³, Nicholas², Nicholas¹*), b. at Pomfret, 30 Sep 1743 son of Peletiah and Sarah (Holt) Lyon; Robert d. 12 Feb 1809.

Robert Lyon and Alice Holt were parents of five children born at Hampton, Connecticut. They relocated to Stockbridge, Vermont after the births of their children.

i ROBERT LYON, b. 23 Dec 1765; d. at Stockbridge, VT, 17 Mar 1844; m. at Stockbridge, 26 Nov 1789, KATHERINE BURNET, b. about 1762; Katherine d. at Stockbridge, 4 Apr 1833.

ii RUFUS LYON, b. 24 Apr 1767; d. at Stockbridge, 30 Jan 1841; m. at Stockbridge, 5 Oct 1792, LOVINA WILLARD, b. in VT, about 1775; Lovina d. at Stockbridge, Aug 1852.

iii ALICE LYON, b. 14 Jun 1769; d. at Braintree, VT, 1804; *perhaps* m. about 1795, her fourth cousin, WILLARD COPELAND (*Sarah Ingalls Copeland⁵, Rebekah Grow Ingalls⁴, Rebekah Holt Grow³, James², Nicholas¹*), baptized at Brooklyn, CT, 4 Dec 1768 son of James and Sarah (Ingalls) Copeland; Willard d. at Braintree, VT, 20 Feb 1852. Willard married second Rebecca White on 12 Dec 1805. There are records of two children of Alice Lyon and Willard Copeland: James born at Mansfield, CT in 1799 and Clarissa born at Brooklyn, CT in 1802. Neither James nor Clarissa married.

iv ROSWELL LYON, b. 2 Oct 1770; d. at Stockbridge, 8 Nov 1814; m. at Stockbridge, 27 Aug 1795, LYDIA ROBERTS, b. 1778; Lydia d. at Stockbridge, 19 Jul 1859.

v CHESTER LYON, b. 25 May 1772; d. at Braintree, VT, 17 Mar 1812; m. about 1795, THIRZA POOLER, b. at Pomfret, 10 Nov 1772 daughter of Amasa and Hannah (Cady) Pooler; Thirza d. at Braintree, 18 Oct 1843.

849) SARAH HOLT (*William⁴, Thomas³, Nicholas², Nicholas¹*), b. at Windham, 21 Jun 1748 daughter of William and Hannah (Holt) Holt; d. at Hampton, 7 Apr 1777; m. 16 Nov 1769, HENRY DURKEE, b. 29 Sep 1749 son of Henry and Relief (Adams) Durkee. Henry m. 2nd, Sarah Loomis; Henry d. 22 Apr 1820.

Sarah Holt and Henry Durkee were parents of three children born at Hampton.

i HENRY DURKEE, b. 25 Aug 1770; m. at Hampton, 25 Sep 1794, SALLY RUSSELL, b. at Ashford, 28 Feb 1774 daughter of Benjamin and Phebe (Smith) Russell; Sally d. at Pittsfield, MA, 23 Dec 1833.

ii ABIEL DURKEE, b. 14 Mar 1774; d. 8 Feb 1778.

iii SARAH DURKEE, b. 18 Jan 1777; d. at Hampton, 2 Jan 1806; m. 22 Dec 1796, AZEL GOODWIN, b. at Lebanon, CT, 31 Aug 1769 son of Jonathan and Anna (Clark) Goodwin; Azel d. at Coventry, 14 Apr 1829. Azel married second Clarissa Hunt.

[2285] Cunningham's History of Lunenburg

[2286] *Vermont, Vital Records, 1720-1908.*

850) ABIGAIL BARNARD (*Alice Holt Barnard⁴, Thomas³, Nicholas², Nicholas¹*), b. at Andover, 15 May 1744 daughter of John and Alice (Holt) Barnard; m. at Andover, 22 Mar 1764, SAMUEL DOWNING, baptized at Salem, 2 May 1742 son of Richard and Temperance (Derby) Downing; Samuel d. at Minot, ME, 13 Dec 1812.

Abigail and Samuel had their ten children in Andover. After the Revolution, Samuel obtained a land grant in Minot, Maine based on his service.[2287] In 1798, Samuel Downing was listed at lot 81 of Auburn (Minot), son Samuel, Jr. at lot 79, and Thomas Downing also on lot 81.[2288]

i SAMUEL DOWNING, b. 3 Jan 1765; d. at Minot, 30 Sep 1847; m. at Andover, 25 Aug 1789, ELIZABETH BAILEY, b. at Andover, 6 Jul 1768 daughter of Moses and Elizabeth (Mooar) Bailey; Elizabeth d. at Minot, 1830. Samuel m. 2nd 15 Jun 1833, LUCY MERRILL, b. 6 Apr 1785 daughter of Moses and Mary (True) Merrill; Lucy d. at New Gloucester, ME, 9 May 1862. He may be the Samuel Downing who was paid a bounty by Capt. Benjamin Ames, Chairman of Class No. 13 of the town of Andover to serve in the Continental army for the three-year term.[2289]

ii JOHN DOWNING, b. 1 Feb 1766; d. at Auburn, ME, 12 Sep 1852; m. 14 Nov 1788, RUTH EMERY, b. 29 May 1769 daughter of Moses and Ruth (Bodwell) Emery; Ruth d. at Monmouth, ME, 26 Oct 1864.

iii ABIGAIL DOWNING, b. 29 Sep 1768; d. at Dracut, 8 Apr 1814; m. at Andover, 26 Nov 1793, JOHN GILCREASE, b. at Dracut, 23 Jun 1770 son of John and Martha (-) Gilcrease; John d. at Dracut, Aug 1826 (probate 26 Sep 1826).

iv THOMAS DOWNING, b. 24 Jul 1770; d. at Cambridge, ME, 1 Apr 1852; m. at New Gloucester, 27 Apr 1791, ABIGAIL BAYLEY, b. at Newbury, MA, 6 Apr 1772 daughter of Edmund and Abigail (West) Bayley; Abigail d. at Cambridge, ME, 24 Mar 1849.

v SALLY DOWNING, b. 9 Aug 1772; d. at Andover, 6 Aug 1854; m. at Andover, 12 Jan 1794, THEODORE POOR, b. at Andover, 24 Jan 1766 son of Timothy and Mary (Stevens) Poor; Theodore d. at Andover, 13 May 1851.

vi MOLLY DOWNING, b. 13 Aug 1774

vii ALICE DOWNING, b. 8 Jul 1778; d. at Auburn, 4 Sep 1820; m. 1799, REUBEN MERROW, b. at Dover, NH, 24 May 1776 son of Thomas and Hannah (Woodbury) Merrow; Reuben d. at Auburn, 8 Jan 1864. Reuben married second Catherine Verrill.

viii HANNAH DOWNING, b. 20 Aug 1780; d. at Minot, 18 Apr 1867; m. at Minot, 23 Jun 1798, BENJAMIN FRANKLIN LANE, b. 1777; Benjamin d. at Minot, 4 Oct 1846.

ix AMOS DOWNING, b. 13 Jul 1783; d. at Oxford, ME, 24 Sep 1856; m. RUTH WOLCOTT, b. at Methuen, 7 Nov 1780 daughter of Solomon and Lydia (Bodwell) Wolcott; Ruth d. at Oxford, Mar 1856.

x RICHARD DERBY DOWNING, b. 31 Mar 1785; d. at Auburn, ME, 2 Nov 1875; m. 1810, ELIZABETH "BETSEY" RICE, b. at Yarmouth, Nova Scotia, 1787 daughter of Jessie and Sarah (Cann) Rice; Betsey d. at Auburn, 4 May 1838.

851) LYDIA BARNARD (*Alice Holt Barnard⁴, Thomas³, Nicholas², Nicholas¹*), b. at Andover, 23 Jan 1745/6 daughter of John and Alice (Holt) Barnard; d. at Sharon, NH, 9 Feb 1829; m. at Andover, 3 Sep 1767, JOSIAH SAWYER, b. at Reading, 17 Sep 1744 son of Josiah and Hannah (Gowing) Sawyer; Josiah d. at Sharon, 3 Oct 1829.

Josiah Sawyer and Lydia Barnard were parents of eight children. [2290]

i LYDIA SAWYER, baptized at Andover, 21 Feb 1768; d. at Peterborough, 28 Aug 1850; m. WILLIAM NAY, b. Mar 1763 son of William and Betsy (Russell) McNay;[2291] William d. at Sharon, NH, 1 Jun 1813 (probate 7 Jun 1813).

ii JOSIAH SAWYER, baptized at Methuen, 24 Jun 1770; d. at Peterborough, NH, 23 Apr 1800; m. about 1795, MARTHA "PATTY" WYMAN.

iii HANNAH SAWYER, b. at Methuen, 10 Feb 1772; d. at Lowell, MA, 27 Sep 1860; m. 1st by 1793, SIMEON BASS who has not been identified; Simeon d. by 1808. Hannah m. 2nd at Deering, 3 Nov 1808, PHINEAS EVERETT, b. at Rutland, MA, 22 Apr 1776 son of Phineas and Mary (Clapp) Everett; Phineas d. at Bradford, NH, 30 Jul 1830. Phineas was first married to Lydia Bullard.

[2287] Maine, Revolutionary War Land Grants, 1776-1780. Both Samuel and his son Samuel, Jr. had lots of land in Androscoggin County, Maine, and it is not clear if the land bounty is for Samuel or his son. However, the son Samuel's pension file (the application of his widow Lucy) states there was not previously obtained land bounty.

[2288] Drew, History of Androscoggin County, Maine, p 602

[2289] Massachusetts Soldiers and Sailors in the Revolution, volume 4, p 931

[2290] Some children are as given in Smith, *History of the Town of Peterborough*, p 242

[2291] Smith, *History of the Town of Peterborough*, p 213

iv MOSES SAWYER, b. 1774; d. at Sharon, NH, 1851; m. 1st by 1797, HEPHZIBAH HARTSHORN, b. 28 Nov 1771 (Sharon town records); Hephzibah d. at Sharon, 25 Jun 1816. Moses m. 2nd SARAH INGALLS, b. at Rindge, NH, 28 Aug 1782 daughter of Josiah and Sarah (Bowers) Ingalls; Sarah d. at Rindge, 16 Nov 1871.

v JACOB SAWYER, b. 1779; d. at Murray, NY, 2 Jul 1841; m. at Townsend, MA, 18 Jan 1803, ANNA FOSTER, b. at Pepperell, 9 Jul 1781 daughter of Leonard and Lucy (Wetherbee) Foster; Anna d. at Murray, 6 Sep 1858.

vi ALICE SAWYER, b. at Sharon, 1781; d. at Peterborough, 4 Sep 1849; m. 24 Nov 1801, GEORGE SHEDD, b. at Billerica, 28 Feb 1778 son of Reuben and Sybil (Bullard) Shedd; George d. at Peterborough, 30 Oct 1855.

vii REBECCA SAWYER, b. at Sharon, about 1783; d. at Wilton, 24 Dec 1869; m. at Peterborough, 22 Nov 1810, her fourth cousin once removed, WILLIAM PETTENGILL (*Rhoda Hagget Pettengill[6], Deborah Stevens Hagget[5], Lydia Gray Stevens[4], Edward Gray[3], Hannah Holt Gray[2], Nicholas[1]*), b. at Wilton, 12 Nov 1785 son of William and Rhoda (Hagget) Pettengill; William d. at Wilton, 13 Oct 1865.

viii ABIAL SAWYER, b. 25 Apr 1784; d. at Peterborough, 23 Oct 1870; m. SYBIL BUSS, b. at Sharon, 16 Jan 1787 daughter of Silas and Hannah (Pierce) Buss; Sybil d. at Peterborough, 26 Feb 1866.

852) ABIGAIL KENDALL (*Abigail Holt Kendall[4], Robert[3], Nicholas[2], Nicholas[1]*), b. at Windham, 21 Oct 1742 daughter of David and Abigail (Holt) Kendall; d. at Ashford, 8 Nov 1781; m. 28 May 1771, ENOS PRESTON, b. at Windham, 7 Jun 1737 son of John and Sarah (Foster) Preston. Enos married second Hannah Stiles on 12 Nov 1783.

Abigail Kendall and Enos Preston were parents of three children born at Ashford.

i ABRAHAM PRESTON, b. 5 Aug 1771; d. at Perry, OH, 1860; m. LOVINA HAVENS, b. at Ashford, 27 Jan 1774 daughter of Simon and Elizabeth (Vincent) Havens;[2292] Lovina d. at Worthington, OH, 1 Mar 1869. After their marriage, Abraham and Lovina were in Otsego County, NY before moving to Franklin County, OH in 1817.[2293]

ii ALLIS PRESTON, b. 12 Oct 1773

iii ALVAH PRESTON, b. 9 Mar 1779; d. at Ellington, NY, 30 Mar 1852; m. LYDIA POWERS, b. at Lancaster, MA, 12 Nov 1774 daughter of Oliver and Lydia (Winn) Powers; Lydia d. at Ellington, 20 Feb 1843.

853) DAVID KENDALL (*Abigail Holt Kendall[4], Robert[3], Nicholas[2], Nicholas[1]*), b. at Windham, 13 Nov 1744 son of David and Abigail (Holt) Kendall; d. at Ashford, after 1820; m. at Ashford, 23 Feb 1775, MEHITABLE STILES, b. at Windham, 15 Nov 1740 daughter of Samuel and Huldah (Durkee) Stiles; Mehitable d. at Ashford, 27 Jan 1827.

David and Mehitable were admitted to the church at Ashford 24 February 1799 and two of their children, Eunice and Daniel, were baptized on 12 May 1799.[2294]

David and Mehitable were parents of four children born at Ashford.

i SARAH KENDALL, b. 27 Oct 1776

ii LUCY HOLT KENDALL, b. 26 Mar 1779; d. at Ashford, 11 Jul 1786.

iii EUNICE KENDALL, b. 19 Jul 1784; d. at Ashford, 4 Feb 1856; m. at Ashford, 28 Jan 1844, as his second wife, BENJAMIN WHEATON, b. at Swansea, 30 Oct 1775 son of James and Sarah (Slade) Wheaton; Benjamin d. at Ashford, 30 Mar 1852. Benjamin was first married to Annah Lyon.

iv DANIEL KENDALL, b. 29 May 1785 and baptized at Ashford 12 May 1799; nothing further definitive found.

854) SETH TRUESDELL (*Mary Holt Truesdell[4], Robert[3], Nicholas[2], Nicholas[1]*), b. at Pomfret, 23 Mar 1746 son of Joseph and Mary (Holt) Truesdell; d. at Pomfret, 19 Oct 1776; m. at Pomfret, 10 Jan 1771, ESTHER WEST, likely b. at Tolland, 17 Mar 1754 daughter of Solomon and Abigail (Strong) West.

Seth Truesdell and Esther West were parents of four children born at Pomfret.

i RUTH TRUESDELL, b. 10 Aug 1771

ii JOSEPH TRUESDELL, b. 20 Dec 1772; d. 1 Sep 1777.

iii SAMUEL TRUESDELL, b. 22 Sep 1774; d. at Thompson, 30 Jan 1842; m. about 1800, LOIS FAY RICHARDS, b. at Killingly, 21 Sep 1777 daughter of Israel and Lois (Holmes) Richards; Lois d. at Thompson, 10 Mar 1832. Samuel m. 2nd at Thompson, 29 Sep 1833, NANCY NICHOLS (widow of Sylvester Stanley), b. 1782 daughter of Jonathan and Rebecca (Swift) Stanley; Nancy d. at Putnam, CT, 23 Oct 1851.

2292 The 1816 will of Simon Havens of Ashford includes a bequest to his daughter Lovina Preston.

2293 Williams Brothers, History of Franklin and Pickaway Counties, Ohio, p 378

2294 *Connecticut, Church Record Abstracts, 1630-1920, volume 001, Ashford*

iv JERUSHA TRUESDELL, b 6 Apr 1776; m. at Pomfret, 10 Apr 1796, her second cousin once removed, OLIVER GOODALE (*Phebe Holt Goodale*[4]*, Joshua*[3]*, Nicholas*[2]*, Nicholas*[1]), b. at Willington, about 1774 son of Ebenezer and Phebe (Holt) Goodale.

855) JEDUTHUN TRUESDELL (*Mary Holt Truesdell*[4]*, Robert*[3]*, Nicholas*[2]*, Nicholas*[1]), b. recorded at Killingly, 21 Jan 1748 son of Joseph and Mary (Holt) Truesdell; d. at Pomfret, 12 Apr 1801; m. at Pomfret, 20 Jan 1774; ABIGAIL WHITE.

Jeduthun Truesdell and Abigail White were parents of seven children born at Pomfret. Four of the children died in childhood.

i SILAS TRUESDELL, b. 2 Nov 1774; d. 17 Nov 1774.

ii SILAS TRUESDELL, b. 27 Mar 1777; d. 7 May 1787.

iii JOSEPH TRUESDELL, b. 27 Aug 1779; *possibly* m. at Pomfret, 30 Sep 1804, BETSEY INGALLS, b. at Pomfret, 22 May 1780 daughter of Benjamin and Eunice (Woodworth) Ingalls.

iv ELISHA TRUESDELL, b. 28 Apr 1782; d. at Harpursville, NY, 16 Oct 1849; m. SARAH CARPENTER, b. at Tolland, 11 Nov 1787 daughter of Simeon and Abigail (Cushman) Carpenter; Sarah d. at Harpursville, 1857.

v HARVEY TRUESDELL, b. 28 Dec 1783; d. 29 Aug 1789.

vi SARAH TRUESDELL, b. 11 Aug 1787; d. 5 Sep 1789.

vii JEDUTHUN TRUESDELL, b. 25 Dec 1789

856) DARIUS TRUESDELL (*Mary Holt Truesdell*[4]*, Robert*[3]*, Nicholas*[2]*, Nicholas*[1]), b. at Pomfret, 16 Jan 1752 son of Joseph and Mary (Holt) Truesdell; d. at Woodstock, 6 May 1808; m. at Woodstock, 10 Oct 1772, RHODA CHAFFEE, b. at Woodstock, 10 May 1751 daughter of Thomas and Dorcas (Abbott) Chaffee; Rhoda d. at Woodstock, 19 Nov 1834.

Rhoda had an out-of-wedlock child, daughter Annice Corbin born at Woodstock, 18 May 1771. Nothing further is known regarding Anice.

Rhoda Chaffee and Darius Truesdell were parents of nine children born at Woodstock.

i ASA TRUESDELL, b. 17 Jul 1773; nothing further known.

ii DARIUS TRUESDELL, b. 1 Aug 1775; d. at Hartford, 16 Mar 1814; m. at Chester, MA, 14 Sep 1794, RACHEL SIZER, b. at Middletown, CT, 12 Mar 1772 daughter of William and Abigail (Wilcox) Sizer; Rachel d. at Fishkill, NY, 16 Dec 1853.

iii RHODA TRUESDELL, b. 31 Jan 1778; d. at Colrain, MA, 26 Mar 1795. From the Colrain, MA records: "Truesdale, Rhode, drowned while crossing North River on a log. She was on a visit from Connecticut at the house of Ephraim Manning, Mar. 26, 1795."

iv SILAS CHAFFEE TRUESDELL, b. 14 Jan 1784; nothing further known.

v CYRUS TRUESDELL, b. about 1785; d. at Woodstock, 6 Jan 1815.

vi JOHN TRUESDELL, b. 25 Jul 1786; d. at Killingly, CT, 17 May 1860; m. at Sturbridge, MA, 4 Sep 1808, SOPHIA BAYLIS, b. at Taunton, 2 Jul 1784 daughter of Frederick and Hannah (Brown) Baylis; Sophia d. at Putnam, CT, 24 Oct 1833.

vii THOMAS TRUESDELL, b. 10 Jul 1789; d. at Montclair, NJ, 20 Mar 1874; m. 1st, at Providence, RI, 14 Oct 1811, HARRIET LEE, b. at Providence, 10 Jul 1786 daughter of William and Abigail (Kinnicutt) Lee; Harriet d. at Brooklyn, NY, 30 Jun 1862. Thomas m. 2nd, 1865, JESSIE MARGERY GUNN, b. at Thurso, Caithness, Scotland, 4 Feb 1827; Jessie d. at Caldwell, NJ, 1888.

viii SARAH TRUESDELL, b. 29 Jul 1791; d. at Woodstock, 19 Jan 1815.

ix POLLY TRUESDELL, b. 5 Feb 1794; d. at Jefferson, OH, after 1850; m. at Woodstock, about 1815, JEREMIAH C. OLNEY, b. 1 Jun 1792 son of Ithamar and Anne (Cady) Olney; Jeremiah d. at Jefferson, OH, 1860.

857) REUBEN RICHARDSON (*Martha Holt Richardson*[4]*, Robert*[3]*, Nicholas*[2]*, Nicholas*[1]), b. at Windham, 7 Dec 1754 son of John and Martha (Holt) Richardson; m. at Yarmouth, 24 Aug 1775, MARY BURGESS daughter of Joshua Burgess.

Reuben Richardson and Mary Burgess were parents of five children born at Yarmouth, Nova Scotia.[2295]

2295 Trask, *Early Vital Records of the Township of Yarmouth, Nova Scotia*, p 10

i SARAH RICHARDSON, b. 21 Dec 1776; d. at Yarmouth, Oct 1823; m. about 1798, EBENEZER CROSBY, b. 1772 son of Ebenezer Crosby; Ebenezer d. at Yarmouth, 13 Dec 1863.

ii MARY RICHARDSON, b. 11 Oct 1778; m. LEVI HERSEY, b. at Yarmouth, 30 Dec 1780 son of Levi and Chloe (Day) Hersey.

iii STEPHEN RICHARDSON, b. 21 Aug 1780

iv REUBEN RICHARDSON, b. 11 Jul 1782

v JOHN RICHARDSON, b. 10 Nov 1784

858) STEPHEN RICHARDSON (*Martha Holt Richardson⁴, Robert³, Nicholas², Nicholas¹*), b. at Pomfret, 26 Sep 1759 son of John and Martha (Holt) Richardson; d. at Middletown, VT, 3 Jan 1834;[2296] m. at Norwich, CT, 21 Dec 1786, HANNAH RUDD, b. about 1767; Hannah d. at Middletown, about 1848.

Stephen Richardson served in the Revolution being drafted from Norwich, Connecticut in 1777. He was in the Battle of Stillwater and the capture of Burgoyne. In 1778, he enlisted and was discharged at the beginning of 1779. He entered the service as a private with a final rank of first sergeant. In his pension application file, Stephen reported he was born 24 September 1759 in Abington and he moved to Vermont around the end of the war and was in Bennington. At the time of his pension application in 1832, he was living in Rutland. Stephen married Hannah Rudd in Connecticut in 1786. In 1842, Hannah Richardson made application for her pension as a widow. Daughter Clarissa Burnum and son Harvey Richardson made statements in support of their mother's application.[2297]

The only two children located for this family are the two children identified in the pension file. Little in the way of records was located.

i CLARISSA RICHARDSON, b. at Middletown, 24 Oct 1795; m. at Middletown, 28 Nov 1816, ORSON BURNUM.

ii HARVEY RICHARDSON, b. at Middletown, about 1801; d. at Middletown Springs, 10 Jan 1885; m. 1st about 1825, MIRIAM AMES[2298] who has not been identified. Harvey m. 2nd about 1842, LAURA who is not identified but may be Laura Leonard.[2299]

859) MARY FENTON (*Elizabeth Holt Fenton⁴, Abiel³, Nicholas², Nicholas¹*), b. at Willington, 13 Apr 1749 daughter of Francis and Elizabeth (Holt) Fenton; d. at Willington, 14 Apr 1822; m. 1st, 21 May 1770, ISAAC SAWIN, b. 23 Sep 1748 son of George and Anna (Farrar) Sawin; Isaac d. 29 Oct 1776. Mary m. 2nd, 2 Jul 1778, as his second wife, JAMES NILES, b. at Braintree, 2 Apr 1747 son of John and Dorothy (Reynolds) Niles; James d. 18 Jan 1822. James Niles was first married to Elizabeth Vinton.

Isaac Sawin did not leave a will. The inventory of his estate was completed 5 February 1777 with a total value of £126 including house and land valued at £80. George Sawin was named guardian for three-year-old Elijah. The distribution of the estate includes a set-off of one-third part for widow Mary and the remaining two-thirds to only child Elijah.[2300]

After Isaac's death, Mary married James Niles and had four children. James had three children with his first wife, Elizabeth Vinton. James Niles wrote his will 8 June 1819 and the estate entered probate 1822. In his will, beloved wife Mary receives one cow, four sheep, the use of a west room of the house and provisions to be provided by the executors. Five of the children will divide the household items after their mother's decease (Elizabeth, Phebe, Isaac, Joshua Holt, and Molly). Oldest son James receives $50. There are in-kind bequests to Elizabeth, Phebe, and Molly. Son Isaac receives the house Isaac is living in and the land it stands upon. Son Joshua Holt receives his father's house. Sons Isaac and Joshua Holt are named executors.[2301] Children James, Elizabeth, and Phebe are children from James Niles's marriage to Elizabeth Vinton.

Mary Fenton and Isaac Sawin had two children born at Willington.

i ELIZABETH SAWIN, b. 16 Dec 1770; d. 8 Feb 1771.

ii ELIJAH SAWIN, b. 31 Oct 1774; d. at Willington, 1814 (date of probate); m. at Willington, 24 Dec 1795, AMEY POOL, b. at Willington, 7 Aug 1775 daughter of Timothy and Deborah (Presson) Pool. Amey's date and place of death are not known. Some of the children seem to have relocated to Massachusetts and perhaps Amey traveled there also.

2296 *U.S., Revolutionary War Pension and Bounty-Land Warrant Application Files, 1800-1900* [database on-line].

2297 U.S., Revolutionary War Pension and Bounty-Land Warrant Application Files, 1800-1900, Case W26386

2298 Miriam Ames is given as the name of the mother of James Richardson on his death record. He is the one known son of Harvey from his first marriage.

2299 There is not a clear record of the name of Harvey's second wife. The two census records give her name as Laura, the death record of one of the children says her name was Lucy Leonard and one says her name was Smith.

2300 *Connecticut Wills and Probate, 1609-1999*, Probate of Isaac Sawin, Tolland, 1777, Case number 1879.

2301 *Connecticut Wills and Probate, 1609-1999*, Probate of James Niles, Stafford District, 1822, Case number 1554.

Mary Fenton and James Niles had four children born at Willington.

i JOHN NILES, b. 2 Oct 1779; d. 26 Jun 1803.

ii MOLLY NILES, b. 3 Oct 1782. No birth or death record was located for Molly, but she was living in 1819 at the time of her father's will.

iii ISAAC NILES, b. 9 Mar 1786; d. at Tolland, 7 Oct 1858; m. at Willington, 27 Oct 1808, his third cousin, ALLICE SCRIPTURE (*Alice Pearl Scripture⁵, Dinah Holt Pearl⁴, Joshua³, Nicholas², Nicholas¹*), b. at Willington, 14 Jul 1790 daughter of Eleazer and Alice (Pearl) Scripture; Allice d. 3 Mar 1863.

iv JOSHUA HOLT NILES, b. 6 Sep 1790; d. at Willington, 10 Apr 1850; m. at Willington, 3 Dec 1812, SIBYL HUGHES, b. at Ashford, 4 May 1795 daughter of Jonathan and Eunice (Fuller) Hughes; Sibyl d. at Willington, 29 May 1873.

860) SARAH HOLT (*Abiel⁴, Abiel³, Nicholas², Nicholas¹*), b. at Willington, 8 Dec 1757 daughter of Abiel and Mary (Downer) Holt; d. at Willington, 1856;[2302] m. 24 Oct 1782, ZEBULON CROCKER, b. at Willington, 5 Mar 1757 son of Ebenezer and Hannah (Hatch) Crocker; Zebulon d. at Willington, 17 Jan 1826.

The estate of Zebulon Crocker was probated in 1826 with son Zebulon Crocker as administrator. The inventory was completed 27 January 1826 with a total value of $2,081.88. The distribution of the dower was made to widow Sarah Crocker on 4 October 1826. The distribution agreement included the following children as heirs: Candace Crocker, Alpheus Crocker, Bethiah Crocker, Ira Heath and Hannah his wife, and Zebulon Crocker.[2303]

Zebulon and Sarah Crocker had six children born at Willington.

i ALPHEUS CROCKER, b. 3 Sep 1783; d. 23 May 1784.

ii CANDACE CROCKER, b. 6 Jun 1785; d. at Willington, 11 Jan 1849. Candace did not marry.

iii ALPHEUS CROCKER, b. 3 Jul 1787; d. 24 Nov 1873; m. at Willington, 28 Apr 1808, his third cousin, PHEBE MARCY (*Phebe Pearl Marcy⁵, Dinah Holt Marcy⁴, Joshua³, Nicholas², Nicholas¹*), b. at Willington, 12 Oct 1789 daughter of Zebadiah and Phebe (Pearl) Marcy; Phebe d. at Webster, NY, 11 Jun 1871. This family lived in Webster, NY.[2304]

iv BETHIAH CROCKER, b. 1 Jun 1791; d. at Willington, 10 Dec 1860; m. at Willington, 3 Oct 1832, JOSEPH HULL, b. at Willington, 16 Feb 1788 son of Hazard and Abigail (-) Hull; Joseph d. at Willington, 26 Mar 1871.

v HANNAH CROCKER, b. 9 Apr 1796; m. about 1815, IRA HEATH, b. at Willington, 13 Oct 1793 son of David and Abigail (Scripture) Heath. There have been found just two records for children in this family and it is uncertain what became of Hannah and Ira. One of the sons settled in New York, so perhaps they will be found there, although there is no evidence of them in census records after 1820.

vi Reverend ZEBULON CROCKER, b. 8 Mar 1802; d. at Middletown, CT, 14 Nov 1847; m. at East Windsor, 11 Oct 1830, ELIZABETH "BETSY" PORTER, b. about 1799 daughter of Daniel and Ann (Allyn) Porter;[2305] Betsy d. at Cromwell, 25 Feb 1877. Zebulon and Betsy do not seem to have had any children. Zebulon's will leaves the entire estate to Betsy.

861) MARY HOLT (*Abiel⁴, Abiel³, Nicholas², Nicholas¹*), b. at Willington, 8 Dec 1760 daughter of Abiel and Mary (Downer) Holt; d. at Dracut, 6 Nov 1833;[2306] m. at Charlton, MA, 17 Feb 1783,[2307] DANIEL NEEDHAM possibly the son of Daniel and Hannah (Allen) Needham; Daniel d. at Paxton, MA 1801 (date of probate 6 Oct 1801; will written 4 Mar 1801).

The will of Daniel Needham written 4 March 1801 includes a bequest of the widow's third to his wife Mary, and the equal division of the remainder of the estate among his four children namely Polly, Parsons, Rachel, and Sally.[2308]

Daniel Needham and Mary Holt were parents of five children the births reported either at Paxton or Charlton.

[2302] In the 1850 U.S. Census, 92-year old widow Sarah Crocker was living at the home of her daughter Bethiah Hull. Probate of estate was 1856 with Joseph Hull as administrator.

[2303] Ancestry.com. *Connecticut, Wills and Probate Records, 1609-1999* [database on-line]. Case number 545, Probate of Zebulon Crocker

[2304] Year: 1870; Census Place: Webster, Monroe, New York; Roll: M593_971; Page: 447B; Family History Library Film: 552470

[2305] Betsy's parents are confirmed by the 1833 probate of Dr. Daniel Porter that includes a distribution to daughter Betsy Crocker.

[2306] Mary, w. Daniel, Nov. 6, 1833, a. 73.

[2307] *Massachusetts, Compiled Marriages, 1633-1850*. Daniel and Mary Holt of Willington, int. Feb. 17, 1783.

[2308] Worcester County, MA: Probate File Papers, 1731-1881. Online database. AmericanAncestors.org. New England Historic Genealogical Society, 2015.

i MARY "POLLY" NEEDHAM, b. at Paxton, 31 Mar 1784; m. at Danvers, 30 Sep 1807[2309], JOHN NEEDHAM who has not been identified.

ii JOHN NEEDHAM, baptized at Charlton, 16 Apr 1786; d. before his father's will in 1801.

iii JOSEPH PARSONS NEEDHAM, baptized at Charlton, Jun 1788; d. at Buffalo, NY, after 1865; m. at Medway, MA, 1 Feb 1815, JOANNA WIGHT, b. at Medway, 22 Jan 1794 daughter of Aaron and Jemima (Rutter) Wright; Joanna d. after 1865.

iv RACHEL NEEDHAM, b. at Paxton, 14 Dec 1791; d. at Perinton, NY, 12 Apr 1887; m. at Salem, JOSEPH BLOOD, b. 24 Jun 1787 perhaps the son of Joseph and Priscilla (French) Blood; Joseph d. 14 Sep 1840.

v SARAH NEEDHAM, baptized at Charlton, 14 Oct 1798; d. at Dracut, 22 Oct 1880; m. 26 Aug 1821, JOEL FOX, b. at Dracut, 12 Aug 1784 son of Joel and Hannah (Cheever) Fox; Joel d. at Lowell, 21 Dec 1861.

862) ABIEL HOLT (*Abiel⁴, Abiel³, Nicholas², Nicholas¹*), b. at Willington, 12 Jul 1762 son of Abiel and Mary (Downer) Holt; d. at Fairfax, VT, 6 Jun 1829; m. by 1787, MARY MOSHER, b. 21 Jul 1762 daughter of Nathaniel and Elizabeth (Crandall) Mosher; Mary d. 6 Sep 1827.

Abiel Holt served in the Revolution as a private in Captain Abner Robinson's company.[2310] Abiel Holt and Mary Mosher were parents of eight children.

i PHEBE HOLT, b. at Fairfax, 14 Oct 1787; d. at Sharon, VT, 11 May 1851; m. at Sharon, 19 Feb 1818, JOSEPH ROICE, b. about 1792; Joseph d. at Sharon, 7 Apr 1827.

ii LUCINDA HOLT, b. at Fairfax, 14 Oct 1789; d. at Fairfax, 24 Mar 1849; m. at Sharon, 1 Feb 1820, IRA FARNSWORTH, b. at Fairfax, 27 Nov 1799 son of Thomas and Chloe (Balch) Farnsworth; Ira d. at Fairfax, 5 Dec 1860.

iii ABIEL HOLT, b. at Sharon, 9 Sep 1791; d. at Boston, NY, 9 Dec 1869; m. at Albany, 20 Jan 1817, his third cousin, MARY ABBOTT, b. at Colden, NY, 8 Mar 1798 daughter of Caleb and Hannah (Wheat) Abbott;[2311] Mary d. at Colden, NY, 16 Oct 1879.

iv ARNOLD HOLT, b. at Sharon, 5 Jul 1794; d. at Moline, IL, about 1869 (probate Jan 1870); m. 1st, 22 Nov 1815, RUEY AUSTIN, b. at Milton, VT, 2 Jul 1797 daughter of David and Judith (Hall) Austin; Ruey d. at Colden, NY, 21 Oct 1841. Arnold m. 2nd, 19 Oct 1842, HANNAH MILLINGTON, b. in VT, 18 Sep 1819 daughter of John and Mary (Gardiner) Millington; Hannah d. at Washington, IA, 27 Sep 1906.

v ZEBINA HOLT, b. at Sharon, 7 Sep 1797; d. at Salem, MN, 19 Feb 1871; m. about 1820, his third cousin, ORINDA ABBOTT, b. at Colden, 21 Aug 1803 daughter of Caleb and Hannah (Wheat) Abbott; Orinda d. at Salem, MN, 10 Mar 1880.

vi WORSTER HOLT, b. at Sharon, 19 Nov 1799; d. at Salem, MN, 17 Sep 1881; m. NANCY LEWIS, b. in VT, 1814; Nancy d. at Concord, NY, before 1870.

vii NICHOLAS MOSHER HOLT, b. at Sharon, 16 Mar 1801; d. at Brecksville, OH, 1866; m. at Burlington, VT, 1 Jan 1827, ANN REYNOLDS, b. in MA, 1804; Ann d. at Brecksville, after 1880.

viii ELIZABETH HOLT, b. at Sharon, 16 Mar 1801; d. at Springville, NY, 2 Aug 1848; m. about 1823, ALVA DUTTON, b. at Fairfax, 29 Jan 1798 son of Reuben and Polly (Farnsworth) Dutton; Alva d. at Springville, 25 Jun 1878. Alva married second Martha Ann Jewett.

863) ABEL HOLT (*Abiel⁴, Abiel³, Nicholas², Nicholas¹*), b. at Willington, 1770 son of Abiel and Eunice (Kingsbury) Holt; m. 1st, 17 Nov 1793, ANNA ABEL, b. at Norwich, 8 Jul 1771 daughter of Thomas and Zerviah (Hyde) Abel; Anna d. at Sharon, VT 13 Apr 1798. Abel m. 2nd, by 1798, RUTH KING, b. at Wilbraham, MA, 13 Feb 1779 daughter of Oliver and Ruth (Cooley) King.

Abel Holt and Anna Abel had one child.

i THOMAS ABEL HOLT, b. at Sharon, VT, 23 Jul 1796; d. at Sharon, 26 Aug 1815.

Abel Holt and Ruth King were parents of nine children, the first eight children born at Sharon, Vermont and the youngest child at Burlington, Vermont. After the births of their children, the family relocated to Oneida, New York.

[2309] From Danvers vital records: Needham, Mary, of Charlton, and John Needham, Sept. 30, 1807.

[2310] Connecticut Revolutionary War Military Lists, 1775-83

[2311] Durrie, Holt Genealogy, p 100; Abbot, Genealogical Register, p 62

i ANNA HOLT, b. 1 Oct 1798; m. at Sharon, 25 Oct 1824, THOMAS MOREHOUSE, b. about 1801; Thomas d. at Sharon, 6 Jun 1825.

ii RUTH HOLT, b. 22 Sep 1801; d. 11 Jul 1820.

iii EUNICE HOLT, b. 18 Jan 1804; d. at Sharon, 13 Sep 1819.

iv SAMUEL KING HOLT, b. 2 May 1806

v HORACE HOLT, b. 5 May 1808

vi CHARLES HOLT, b. 9 Aug 1810

vii ORAMEL HOLT, b. 17 Jan 1813; d. at Whittaker, MI, 5 Nov 1893; m. ELECTA GEER, b. about 1815 daughter of Thomas and Laura (-) Geer; Electa d. at Augusta, MI, 2 Nov 1875.

viii THOMAS ABEL HOLT, b. 10 Aug 1815

ix EMILY HOLT, b. 16 Feb 1818; d. at Willowvale, NY, 9 Jun 1883; m. 2 Feb 1837, AMOS ROGERS, b. at Laurens, NY, 24 Oct 1815 son of Oliver Glason and Deborah (Lewis) Rogers;[2312] Amos d. at New Hartford, NY, 2 Dec 1879.

864) ELIJAH HOLT (*Caleb*[4], *Abiel*[3], *Nicholas*[2], *Nicholas*[1]), b. at Willington, 24 Oct 1757 son of Caleb and Mary (Merrick) Holt; d. 4 Jul 1817; m. 5 Nov 1783,[2313] MOLLY SIMMONS, b. 1754 possibly the daughter of Paul and Mary (Isham) Simmons, but this is not confirmed; Molly d. 6 May 1814. Elijah m. 2nd, Lovina *Marcy* Dunton on 17 Aug 1815. Lovina Marcy was first married to Samuel Dunton. Lovina was b. at Ashford, 27 Jan 1763 daughter of Zebadiah and Priscilla (Morris) Marcy; Lovina d. at Willington, 10 Nov 1840.

Elijah Holt's estate was probated in 1817. He did not leave a will. The total value of the estate was $4898.49. The distribution of the estate was made equally between Chloe wife of Chester Carpenter and Mary wife of Chester Burnham. Widow Lovina Holt received a distribution of $300 in accordance with the pre-marriage contract.[2314] The pre-marriage contract provided that Lovina would retain all the property she brought to the marriage. She had inherited real estate from her father Zebadiah Marcy and her first husband Samuel Dunton.

Elijah Holt and Molly Simmons had four children born at Willington.

i CHLOE HOLT, b. 2 Jul 1788; d. at Willington, 24 Oct 1819; m. at Willington, 16 Mar 1815, CHESTER CARPENTER, b. at Ashford, 3 Jul 1780 Jonah and Zerviah (Whittemore) Carpenter; Chester d. 3 Apr 1868. After Chloe's death, Chester married Betsey Kilbourn.

ii MARY HOLT, b. 14 Sep 1790; d. at Willington, 25 Feb 1851; m. 30 Mar 1813, CHESTER BURNHAM, b. at Ashford, 28 Jun 1788 son of Roswell and Esther (Child) Burnham; Chester d. 25 Oct 1857.

iii ELIJAH HOLT, b. 23 Apr 1792; d. 8 Mar 1809.

iv CALEB HOLT, b. 30 Jun 1798; d. 16 Sep 1811.

865) ANNE MERRICK (*Anna Holt Merrick*[4], *Abiel*[3], *Nicholas*[2], *Nicholas*[1]), b. at Willington, 19 Sep 1756 daughter of Joseph and Anna (Holt) Merrick; d. 2 May 1809; m. 10 Jan 1782, DAVID HINCKLEY, b. 24 Feb 1754 son of John and Susannah (Harris) Hinckley; David d. 24 Jan 1835.

In his will written 18 February 1830, David Hinckley left his entire estate, real and personal, to his daughter Joanna Hinckley. But if son Benjamin was living when David died, Benjamin was to have the wearing apparel. After the payment of debts, Joanna at her discretion, might divide what was left between herself and David's other two daughters Hannah Hinckley and Betsey Torrey. Joanna was named executrix of the estate.[2315]

Anne and David Hinckley had six children whose births are recorded at Willington.

[2312] Rogers, *James Rogers of New London, CT*, p 404

[2313] "Connecticut Marriages, 1640-1939," database with images, *FamilySearch* (https://familysearch.org/ark:/61903/1:1:F7PB-68K: 11 February 2018), Elijah Holt and Molley Simons, Marriage 05 Nov 1783, Willington Tolland, Connecticut, United States; Connecticut State Library, Hartford; FHL microfilm 1,376,042.

[2314] Ancestry.com. *Connecticut, Wills and Probate Records, 1609-1999* [database on-line]. Provo, UT, USA: Ancestry.com Operations, Inc., 2015. Original data: Connecticut County, District and Probate Courts, Stafford Probate District. Probate of Elijah Holt, Case number 1062, 1817

[2315] *Connecticut, Wills and Probate Records, 1609-1999*, Author: Connecticut State Library (Hartford, Connecticut); Probate Place: Hartford, Connecticut.

i BENJAMIN HINCKLEY, b. 23 Nov 1782; d. at Hiram, OH, 1835 (probate 1835); m. at Willington, 10 Feb 1806, SUSANNA DAVIS, b. about 1782 daughter of Avery and Amy (Lillibridge) Avery;[2316] Susanna d. at Hiram, 8 Jan 1873.

ii HANNAH HINCKLEY, b. 14 Aug 1786. Her death is uncertain, but she was living and unmarried in 1830 when her father wrote his will. It is believed she traveled with her sister Joanna and brother Benjamin to Ohio.

iii CALEB HINCKLEY, b. 3 Jun 1790; d. 26 Jul 1790.

iv EBER HINCKLEY, b. 17 Oct 1791; d. 9 May 1796.

v BETSEY HINCKLEY, b. 28 Jul 1796; d. at Union, IA, 21 Feb 1879; m. at Tolland, 21 Jun 1826, DAVID B. TORREY, b. about 1784 in Connecticut; David d. at Burlington, IA, 3 Dec 1863.

vi JOANNA HINCKLEY, b. 12 Mar 1799; d. at Windsor, OH, 19 Apr 1857; m. at Portage County, OH, 20 Jun 1840, as his second wife, Rev. RUSSELL DOWNING, b. in New York 20 Nov 1796; Russell d. at Windsor, 8 Apr 1881.[2317]

866) TIMOTHY MERRICK (*Anna Holt Merrick[4], Abiel[3], Nicholas[2], Nicholas[1]*), b. at Willington, 31 Aug 1760 son of Joseph and Anna (Holt) Merrick; d. 4 Jan 1810; m. 29 Nov 1787, MEHITABLE ATWOOD, b. 1765 daughter of Thomas and Sarah (Fenton) Atwood; Mehitable d. 14 May 1855.

Timothy was a farmer in Willington. The Merrick genealogy reports he built one of the more pretentious houses in Willington at the time. He was respected in the town, often serving as the moderator of the town meeting.[2318]

Timothy Merrick did not leave a will and the estate entered probate 5 February 1810. The total value of the estate was $2,438 with the 101-acre homestead farm with buildings valued at $1,628.[2319]

There are two children known for Timothy and Mehitable both born at Willington.

i JOSEPH MERRICK, b. 2 Jul 1789; d. at Willington, 5 Jan 1854; m. 10 Apr 1814, LODICIA DUNTON, b. at Willington, 22 Sep 1794 daughter of Samuel and Lovina (Marcy) Dunton; Lodicia d. at Willington, 1 Sep 1857.

ii ANNE MERRICK, b. 26 Feb 1791; d. at Willington, 28 Oct 1817; m. CYREL JAMES, b. at Willington, 21 Sep 1791 son of Amos and Christian (Noble) James.

867) THOMAS MERRICK (*Anna Holt Merrick[4], Abiel[3], Nicholas[2], Nicholas[1]*), b. at Willington, 6 Jan 1763 son of Joseph and Anna (Holt) Merrick; d. at Willington, 8 Sep 1840; m. 10 Jan 1790, JOANNA NOBLE, b. 8 Oct 1769 daughter of Gideon and Christian (Cadwell) Noble; Joanna d. 28 Apr 1860.

Thomas Merrick was a farmer in Willington. He and his wife Joanna Noble were parents of five children born at Willington.

i LOVISA MERRICK, b. 22 Mar 1791; d. at Willington, 14 May 1863; m. 14 Nov 1827, ELEAZER ROOT, b. about 1790 *likely* the son of Eleazer Root; Eleazer d. at Willington, Mar 1837 (probate 13 Mar 1837).

ii GIDEON NOBLE MERRICK, b. Jan 1793; d. at Willington, 24 Jan 1862; m. 16 Apr 1820, POLLY NILES, b. at Willington, 5 Oct 1798 daughter of James and Polly (Woodward) Niles; Polly d. at Willington, 2 Mar 1869.

iii HARRIET MERRICK, b. 24 Jan 1795; d. at Willington, 9 May 1860; m. at Willington, 22 Sep 1831, JONATHAN CASE WALKER, b. at Ashford, 5 Jan 1799 son of Samuel and Alice (Case) Walker; Jonathan d. at Willington, 2 Nov 1863.

iv MARILDA MERRICK, b. Mar 1801; d. at Wintonbury, CT, 26 Jul 1872; m. at Willington, 15 Jun 1821, RALPH R. GRIGGS, b. at Tolland, 31 Jan 1798 son of Stephen and Betsey (Lathrop) Griggs; Ralph d. at Wintonbury, 22 Aug 1874.

v HARVEY MERRICK, b. 2 May 1808; d. at Bristol, CT, 17 Aug 1887; m. at Willington, 23 Apr 1838, his second cousin once removed, ESTHER CHILDS BURNHAM (*Mary Holt Burnham[6], Elijah[5], Caleb[4], Abiel[3], Nicholas[2], Nicholas[1]*), b. at Willington, 13 Feb 1816 daughter of Chester and Mary (Holt) Burnham; Esther d. at Bristol, 7 Feb 1905.

[2316] Susanna's parents are confirmed by the 1836 Connecticut probate record of father Avery Davis and the 1859 will of brother Avery Davis which includes a bequest to sister Susan Hinckley.

[2317] Web: Ashtabula County, Ohio, Obituary Index, 1858-2012

[2318] Merrick, *Genealogy of the Merrick Family*, p 284

[2319] *Connecticut State Library (Hartford, Connecticut)*; Probate Place: *Hartford, Connecticut, Probate Packets, McKinney, H-Nash, S, 1759-1880*, Probate of Timothy Merick, Case 1480

868) JOSEPH MERRICK (*Anna Holt Merrick^{4}, Abiel^{3}, Nicholas^{2}, Nicholas^{1}*), b. at Willington, 22 Feb 1765 son of Joseph and Anna (Holt) Merrick; death uncertain but about 1814 possibly by drowning; m. 21 Oct 1796, IRENA ALDEN, b. at Bellingham, MA, 24 Feb 1772 daughter of Elisha and Irene (Markham) Alden. Irena m. 2nd, Samuel Churchill; Irena d. at Pleasantville, PA, 13 Nov 1858.

Joseph Merrick and Irene Alden were parents of five children all born at Willington.

i IRENE MERRICK, b. 21 Aug 1797; d. at Willington, 29 Apr 1814.

ii LODICA MERRICK, b. 14 Dec 1798; d. at Oil Creek, PA, 1 Aug 1863; m. at Longmeadow, MA, 15 Sep 1821, AMOS HALL, b. 5 Mar 1790;[2320] Amos d. at Oil Creek, 9 Mar 1863.

iii ELISHA ALDEN MERRICK, b. 3 Apr 1800; d. at Belvidere, IL, 13 Aug 1839; m. about 1827, JERUSHA TENANT, b. at Colchester, 21 Aug 1807 daughter of John and Hannah (Atwell) Tenant; Jerusha d. at Huntington, WV, 15 Oct 1904. Jerusha married second James McClintock.

iv AUSTIN MERRICK, b. 13 Sep 1801; d. at Pleasantville, PA, 6 Aug 1876; m. 1st, 5 Feb 1839, SYLVIA WITCHER, b. at Rochester, VT, 6 May 1808 daughter of Stephen and Esther (Emerson) Witcher; Sylvia d. 1849. Austin m. 2nd, about 1851, ELIZA, b. about 1812 who has not been identified; Eliza d. 1869.

v LAURA MERRICK, b. 14 Nov 1803; d. at Adams, NE, 2 Sep 1885; m. about 1830, her second cousin, WILLIAM CURTIS (*Mary Holt Curtis^{5}, Isaac^{4}, Abiel^{3}, Nicholas^{2}, Nicholas^{1}*), b. at Willington, 20 May 1802 son of William and Mary (Holt) Curtis; William d. a Adams, 17 Mar 1879..

869) CALEB MERRICK (*Anna Holt Merrick^{4}, Abiel^{3}, Nicholas^{2}, Nicholas^{1}*), b. At Willington, 17 May 1767 son of Joseph and Anna (Holt) Merrick; d. at Vernon, CT, Jun 1822; m. 15 Sep 1791, CHARLOTTE NOBLE, b. at Willington, 19 Aug 1771 daughter of Gideon and Christian (Cadwell) Noble; Charlotte d. at Franklin, CT, 21 Nov 1805.
Dr. Caleb Merrick had a practice in Willington and Franklin, Connecticut.[2321]

Caleb and Charlotte had five children.

i WEALTHY MERRICK, b. at Willington, 20 Sep 1792; d. at Ellington, 12 Oct 1861; m. Mar 1818, BUELL NYE, b. at Tolland, 7 Mar 1790 son of Hezekiah and Asenath (Buell) Nye; Buell d. at Springfield, MA, 10 Apr 1833.[2322]

ii MARK MERRICK, b. at Amherst, MA, 14 Nov 1794; d. at Vernon, 18 Apr 1853; m. HANNAH SPARKS, b. at Vernon, 8 May 1794 daughter of Jonas and Olive (Smith) Sparks;[2323] Hannah d. after 1870 at Chatham, NJ (living at Chatham at the 1870 Census).

iii SOPHRONIA MERRICK, b. at Amherst, 1 Apr 1797; d. at Willington, 14 May 1843; m. at Willington, 20 Nov 1814, SPAFFORD BRIGHAM, b. 1782 son od Stephen and Hannah (Field) Brigham;[2324] Spafford d. at Ellington, 26 Sep 1866.

iv LEANDER MERRICK, b. at Tolland, 31 May 1799; d. at Amherst, 24 May 1856; m. 1st, 2 Dec 1824, HARRIET HODGE, b. 1798 daughter of John and Sarah (Dickinson) Hodge; Harriet d. at Amherst, 3 May 1825. Leander m. 2nd, 27 Nov 1827, HARRIET ELVIRA MORTON, b. 3 Feb 1808 daughter of Ebenezer and Hannah (Ingram) Morton; Harriet d. at Amherst, 18 Jun 1882.

v CHARLOTTE MERRICK, b. at Willington, 29 Jan 1802; d. at Willington, 1818.

870) CONSTANT MERRICK (*Anna Holt Merrick^{4}, Abiel^{3}, Nicholas^{2}, Nicholas^{1}*), b. at Willington, 14 Jan 1772 son of Joseph and Anna (Holt) Merrick; d. at Lebanon, NY, 29 Jul 1828; m. at Longmeadow, MA, 22 Sep 1796, EXPERIENCE BURT, b. 8 Aug 1776 daughter of Nathaniel and Experience (Chapin) Burt; Experience d. 1833 at Lebanon, NY, 24 Jul 1833.

Dr. Constant Merrick was a physician, but like many individuals in this era also maintained a farm. After Constant and Experience married, they relocated to Madison County, New York about 1800.[2325] The family lived near Billings Hill in Madison County and then settled in the village of Lebanon about 1806 where Dr. Merrick was the second physician in the village.[2326]

[2320] Birth date is calculated from age at death of 73 years, 4 days. Bell, *History of Venango County*, 9 734

[2321] Merrick, *Genealogy of the Merrick Family*, p 285

[2322] Nye, *Genealogy of the Nye Family*, p 354

[2323] Hannah's parents are confirmed by the 1823 Connecticut probate of Jonas Sparks which includes a distribution to daughter Hannah Merrick.

[2324] Brigham, *History of the Brigham Family*, p 169

[2325] Merrick, *Genealogy of the Merrick Family*, p 286

[2326] Smith, *Our County and Its People. . .Madison County*, p 371

Constant Merrick and Elizabeth Burt had nine children the oldest in Longmeadow and the other children at Lebanon, New York.

i ELIZA MERRICK, b. at Longmeadow, 27 Apr 1797; d. at Lebanon, NY, 9 Jan 1815; m. 17 Apr 1814, JAMES KNAPP BENEDICT, b. 3 Feb 1790 son of Czar and Elizabeth (Knapp) Benedict;[2327] James d. at Lebanon, 9 May 1864. After Eliza's death, James married Pamelia Sweet. Eliza did not have children.

ii LAURA MERRICK, b. 17 Mar 1799; d. at Longmeadow, MA, 7 Sep 1875; m. at Lebanon, 12 Sep 1821, SAMUEL COLTON STEBBINS, b. at Longmeadow, 27 Jun 1796 son of Benjamin and Lucy (Colton) Stebbins; Samuel d. at Longmeadow, 12 Dec 1873.

iii EXPERIENCE MERRICK, b. 27 Feb 1801; d. 11 Mar 1801.

iv NATHANIEL BURT MERRICK, b. 5 Mar 1802; d. at Hudson, NY, 18 Jan 1877; m. 12 Jun 1832, LAURA H. HAMILTON, b. about 1810 daughter of Samuel and Mehitable (Bemis) Hamilton; Laura d. 27 Jan 1840. Nathaniel m. 2nd, Mar 1841, MARTHA M. BURCHARD who was "of Rochester;" Martha d. at Rochester, 7 Mar 1897.

v CONSTANT MERRICK, b. 14 Apr 1804; d. 16 Aug 1805.

vi EXPERIENCE MERRICK, b. at Lebanon, 28 Jul 1806; d. at Earlville, NY, 1870; m. 10 Jun 1830, DAVID CLARK, b. 1800 in Connecticut of as yet undetermined origins; David d. at Earlville, 1873.

vii CONSTANT MERRICK, b. at Lebanon, 22 Nov 1808; d. at Lebanon, 3 Apr 1834.

viii ANNA MERRICK, b. at Lebanon, 1 Sep 1810; d. at Chicago, 21 Jan 1886; m. 10 Jun 1830, GORDON HYDE, b. at Columbus, NY, 10 Feb 1801 son of Ambrose and Phebe (Hyde) Hyde; Gordon d. at Hamilton, NY, 1885.

ix JERUSHA MERRICK, b. at Lebanon, 8 Jun 1819; d. at Norwich, NY, 1874; m. 2 Sep 1840, ISAAC FOOTE, b. 28 May 1817 son of Isaac and Harriet (Hyde) Foote; Isaac d. at Norwich, 1893.

871) ELIZABETH MERRICK (*Anna Holt Merrick⁴, Abiel³, Nicholas², Nicholas¹*), b. at Willington, 13 Jul 1774 daughter of Joseph and Anna (Holt) Merrick; d. at Tolland, 29 Jun 1824; m. 24 Apr 1800, as his second wife, SAMUEL NYE, b. 25 Dec 1773 son of Samuel and Abigail (Benton) Nye. Samuel m. 3rd, Anna Hatch; Samuel's first wife was Elizabeth Brewster; Samuel d. at Tolland 25 Nov 1837.

Samuel Nye wrote his will 24 December 1836[2328] and entered probate 29 Nov 1837. Beloved wife Ann receives the use and improvement of one-third of the real estate during her natural life. Ann also receives two shares in the Tolland County Bank. He makes other provisions for her support, and she also receives the clock. Daughter Harriet Brigham receives one hundred dollars. Son Horace and daughters Harriet and Anne receiving the wearing apparel except the cloak. The remainder of the personal estate goes to two grandchildren Buey (?) Nye and Samuel Nye. The remainder of the estate goes to son-in-law William Holman who is also named executor. Conspicuously absent from the will is Chester Nye, Samuel's son from his first marriage. Chester was living at the time the will was written. The two grandchildren mentioned are William B. Nye and Samuel Nye who were sons of Horace.

Elizabeth Merrick and Samuel Nye had four children all born at Tolland.

i HARRIET NYE, b. 15 Aug 1801; d. at Coventry, CT, 21 Mar 1879; m. 29 Nov 1827, URIAH BRIGHAM, b. at Coventry, 26 Aug 1793 son of Cephas and Amelia (Robertson) Brigham; Uriah d. at Coventry, 2 May 1860. Uriah was first married to Emily Wright who died in 1827.

ii HORACE NYE, b. 22 Aug 1803; death unknown; m. Apr 1827, BETSEY BRIGHAM, b. at Mansfield, CT, about 1805 daughter of Stephen and Huldah (Freeman) Brigham; Betsey d. at Mansfield, 17 Sep 1872.

iii SUSANNA NYE, b. 16 Feb 1805; d. 7 Feb 1828.

iv ANNA NYE, b. 12 Aug 1810; d. at Tolland, 15 Mar 1870; m. 26 Mar 1833, WILLIAM HOLMAN, b. at Ashford, 24 Oct 1811 son of Abraham and Polly (Converse) Holman; William d. at East Hoosick, MA, 8 Oct 1887.

872) ISAAC HOLT (*Isaac⁴, Abiel³, Nicholas², Nicholas¹*), b. at Willington, 3 Nov 1763 son of Isaac and Sarah (Orcutt) Holt; d. at Sharon, VT, 7 Aug 1813; m. at Sharon, 1 Jan 1789,[2329] MEHITABLE ORCUTT, b. at Stafford, CT, 17 Jan 1769 daughter of Caleb and Chloe (Parker) Orcutt; Mehitable d. 12 Nov 1851.

2327 Benedict, *Genealogy of the Benedicts*, p 270

2328 Connecticut State Library (Hartford, Connecticut); Probate Place: Hartford, Connecticut, Probate Packets, Kimball, N-Warren, H, 1827-1895, Probate of Samuel Nye, case number 700.

2329 *Vermont, Vital Records, 1720-1908.*

Isaac and Mehitable were married in Connecticut and moved soon after to Sharon, Vermont where their three children were born. Little information has been located for this couple. Probate records were not found.

i FREEMAN HOLT, b. 19 Apr 1790; d. at Sharon, 14 Jun 1865; m. 1st, LUCY PAGE, b. at Sharon, 13 Aug 1797 daughter of Samuel and Elizabeth (Mosher) Page; Lucy d. at Sharon, 10 Oct 1859. Freeman m. 2nd, 9 Jul 1860 at Gloucester, MA, MARY BRADLEY (widow Cressy), b. at Rumney, NH, 11 Feb 1801 daughter of Ebenezer and Sarah (Hall) Bradley; Mary d. at Haverhill, MA, 30 Mar 1885.

ii CALEB HOLT, b. 28 Oct 1791; d. at Sharon, 29 Jan 1880; m. 1st, at Sharon 16 Jan 1822, CLARISSA PARKER, b. at Sharon, 28 Jul 1797 daughter of James and Kezia (Wetherbee) Parker; Clarissa d. 6 Oct 1852. Caleb m. 2nd, at Rumney 20 May 1853, MARY P. HERRICK, b. at Londonderry, 17 May 1808 daughter of Nehemiah and Sarah (Day) Herrick; Mary d. at Sharon, 6 Apr 1874.

iii HANNAH HOLT, b. 11 Sep 1793; d. likely at Bethel, VT after 1850; m. at Sharon, 3 Nov 1833, as his third wife, ELISHA TERRY, b. at Bethel, 22 Nov 1786 son of Ephraim and Lucinda (Bugbee) Terry; Elisha d. at Bethel after 1850. Hannah and Elisha were both living at the 1850 Census but not located after that.

873) HANNAH HOLT (*Isaac⁴, Abiel³, Nicholas², Nicholas¹*), b. at Willington, 19 May 1771 daughter of Isaac and Sarah (Orcutt) Holt; d. likely at Clarksfield, OH before 1850;[2330] m. 9 Apr 1795, ELEAZER FELLOWS, b. at Tolland, 2 Apr 1772 son of Verney and Hannah (Lathrop) Fellows; Eleazer d. after 1850 in Ohio.

Hannah and Eleazer had their children in Willington. In 1849, perhaps after the death of Hannah, Eleazer followed his son Eleazer to Clarksfield, Ohio. He bought ten acres of land there and lived with his daughter Betsey and her family.[2331]

Eleazer Fellows and Hannah Holt were parents of three children born at Willington.

i LEONARD FELLOWS, b. 23 Oct 1800; d. at Clarksfield, OH, Aug 1849; m. 24 Nov 1824, ARMINDA JOHNSON, b. at Sweden, NY, 10 Jun 1807;[2332] Arminda d. at Marion, MN, 18 Nov 1893.

ii LOTHROP FELLOWS, b. 4 Nov 1803; d. at Lockport, NY, 2 Jan 1845; m. 5 Dec 1827, MELINDA FISKE PARSONS, b. at Lockport, 16 Jun 1809 daughter of Seth and Achsah (Tenney) Parsons;[2333] Melinda d. at Milwaukee, 10 Mar 1891.

iii BETSEY PRIOR FELLOWS, b. 13 May 1806; m. about 1831, Mr. HASKINS, not identified but perhaps Jarius Haskins. Their youngest child was born about 1845. Weeks in *Pioneer History of Clarksfield* reports that Mr. Haskins died, and Betsey married Mr. Lang but continued to use the name Haskins and she is the head of household in census records in Clarksfield. She was living in 1860.

874) MARY HOLT (*Isaac⁴, Abiel³, Nicholas², Nicholas¹*), b. at Willington, 1 May 1773 daughter of Isaac and Sarah (Orcutt) Holt; d. at Willington, 6 Jun 1861; m. 27 Nov 1799, WILLIAM CURTIS, b. about 1774; William d. 3 Nov 1860.

In his will written 7 February 1852, William leaves his entire estate to children Sarah H. Curtis and Wilson W. Curtis stating that he has already provided for his other children (who are not named). "The said Wilson W. Curtis and Sara H. Curtis shall well and truly provide for support and maintain myself and my wife Mary Curtis during the whole period of each of our natural lives and at the death of each myself and my said wife Mary Curtis to give to each of us a decent christian burial."[2334]

Daughter Sarah Holt Curtis did not marry. In her will dated 1 August 1874, Sarah bequeaths twenty-five dollars to her brother Selden; to Chiara Ann wife of George Plimpton and daughter of her brother Oliver H. Curtis she leaves a string of gold beads to be solely her property; to brother Alfred Curtis, twenty dollars; and the remainder of the estate goes to brother Wilson W. Curtis who is also named executor.[2335]

Mary and William Curtis had nine children born at Willington. This family illustrates a pattern for this generation: a new wave of migration with children heading to the western territories, western New York, and western Massachusetts.

i SANFORD CURTIS, b. 7 Nov 1800; d. 9 May 1807.

2330 In the 1850 U.S. Census, Eleazer Fellows, age 78, was living in Clarksfield OH; also in the home are Betsey Haskins age 43 and five children named Haskins. Betsey is the daughter of Eleazer and Hannah. Eleazer and Hannah's son Leonard also relocated to Huron County, Ohio.

2331 Weeks, *Pioneer History of Clarksfield*, p 130

2332 Date of birth is on her cemetery record. Dalby, John. *Minnesota Cemetery Inscription Index, Select Counties* [database on-line]. Provo, UT, USA: Ancestry.com Operations Inc, 2003.

2333 Parsons, *Parsons Family: Descendant of Cornet Joseph Parsons*, p 164

2334 *Connecticut State Library (Hartford, Connecticut);* Probate Place: *Hartford, Connecticut, Probate Packets, Carpenter, Comfort-Kimball, J, 1833-1880*, Case number 222, accessed through ancestry.com

2335 *Connecticut State Library (Hartford, Connecticut);* Probate Place: *Hartford, Connecticut, Probate Packets, Carpenter, Comfort-Kimball, J, 1833-1880*, Case 221

ii WILLIAM CURTIS, b. 20 May 1802; d. at Adams, NE, 17 Mar 1879; m. about 1803, his second cousin, LAURA MERRICK (*Joseph Merrick[5], Anna Holt Merrick[4], Abiel[3], Nicholas[2], Nicholas[1]*), b. at Willington, 14 Nov 1803 daughter of Joseph and Irene (Alden) Merrick; Laura d. at Adams, 2 Sep 1885.

iii HORACE CURTIS, b. 9 Feb 1804; d. at Buchanan, MI, 31 Dec 1887;[2336] m. SALLY M. CLARK, b. in Pennsylvania, 3 Dec 1814 daughter of Benjamin and Esther (-) Clark; Sally d. at Buchanan, 24 Mar 1899.

iv SARAH HOLT CURTIS, b. 24 Oct 1805; d. at Willington, 30 Sep 1874. Sarah did not marry.

v ALFRED CURTIS, b. 7 Jun 1809; d. at Westfield, NY, 2 Dec 1878; m. at Willington, 5 Dec 1831, EUNICE RIDER, b. 9 Dec 1812 of undetermined parents;[2337] Eunice d. at Westfield, 3 Sep 1892.

vi OLIVER HOLT CURTIS, b. 30 Mar 1811; d. at Amherst, MA, 27 Feb 1899; m. at Tolland, 14 Nov 1837, EMILY HILLS, b. at Ellington, 12 Mar 1811 daughter of Leonard and Mary (Ladd) Hills; Emily d. at Amherst, 27 Mar 1888.

vii WILSON WHITING CURTIS, b. 25 Feb 1813; d. at Willington, 10 Aug 1890; m. at Willington, 12 Feb 1852, SARAH ELDREDGE, b. at Willington, 14 Feb 1813 daughter of Elijah and Sally (Hunt) Eldridge; Sarah d. at Willington, 13 Feb 1887.

viii SELDEN CURTIS, b. 1 Dec 1815; d. at Willington, 18 Feb 1902; m. 1st, 28 Mar 1841, MARY ELIZABETH PARSONS, b. at Somers, CT, 24 Feb 1821 daughter of Rufus and Chloe (Weston) Parsons;[2338] Mary d. at Willington, 21 Oct 1852. Selden m. 2nd, at Ashford, 5 Jun 1853, MARTHA AURELIA SKINNER, b. 14 Mar 1822 daughter of Ezekiel and Sarah (Mott) Skinner; Martha d. at Willington, 21 Sep 1892. Martha was first married to Richard Boon.

ix HENRY CURTIS, b. 1 Jun 1818; d. 3 Aug 1846.

875) OLIVER HOLT (*Isaac[4], Abiel[3], Nicholas[2], Nicholas[1]*), b. 16 Jul 1775 son of Isaac and Sarah (Orcutt) Holt; d. 6 Mar 1869; m. 16 May 1799, MARTHA "PATTY" SIBLEY,[2339] b. 9 Feb 1776 daughter of Jonathan and Patty (Brooks) Sibley; Martha "Patty" d. 16 Dec 1846.

There are records for five children of Oliver and Patty Holt all born at Willington.

i MARCIA HOLT, b. 22 Feb 1800; d. 1 Mar 1831. Marcia did not marry.

ii SUSANNAH HOLT, b. 4 Feb 1802; d. at Mansfield, CT, 2 May 1874; m. at Willington, 18 Jun 1827, EBER DUNHAM, b. at Mansfield, 23 Jan 1798 son of Jonathan and Betty (Babcock) Dunham; Eber d. at Mansfield, 21 Oct 1878.

iii MARIAH HOLT, b. 16 Aug 1806; d. at Mansfield, 4 Jun 1867; m. 1 Jan 1846, CHAUNCEY DUNHAM, b. at Mansfield, about 1798 of undetermined parents; Chauncey d. at Mansfield, 11 Jul 1850.

iv MARTHA SIBLEY HOLT, b. 15 May 1810; d. at Tamaroa, IL, 18 Jul 1864; m. at Willington, 20 Oct 1834, BENAJAH GUERNSEY "B.G." ROOTS, b. at Fabius, NY, 20 Apr 1811 son of Peter and Elizabeth (Keep) Roots; B.G. d. at Tamaroa, 9 May 1888. After Martha's death, B.G. married Elizabeth Reynolds. Benajah Guernsey Roots was an abolitionist and is believed to have been active in the Underground Railroad.[2340]

v ELIZA HOLT, b. 7 Feb 1821; d. at Tamaroa, IL, 7 Dec 1870; m. 13 Sep 1840, her second cousin once removed, NELSON HOLT *(Constant Holt[6], Nathan Holt[5], Nathan Holt[4], Abiel[3], Nicholas[2], Nicholas[1])*, b. at Penfield, NY, 6 Jan 1816 son of Constant and Sibyl (Dart) Holt;[2341] Nelson d. at Tamaroa, 29 Oct 1900.

876) ELIZABETH HOLT (*Isaac[4], Abiel[3], Nicholas[2], Nicholas[1]*), b. at Willington, 6 Aug 1777 daughter of Isaac and Sarah (Orcutt) Holt; m. 11 Apr 1799, DANIEL GLAZIER, b. 2 Jun 1776 son of Silas and Suze (Johnson) Glazier; Daniel d. 28 Dec 1852.

[2336] *Michigan, Death Records, 1867-1950*, Michigan Department of Community Health, Division for Vital Records and Health Statistics; Lansing, Michigan. The death record includes parents as William and Mary and birthplace as Connecticut. The death record for Sally Clark includes names of parents as Benjamin and Esther.

[2337] Eunice's birth date is on her gravestone; findagrave ID: 87772382

[2338] Parsons, *Parsons Family*, volume 2, p 319

[2339] Connecticut, Marriage Index, 1620-1926; the handwritten marriage record confirms that the marriage is to Patty and not to her younger sister Polly.

[2340] National Park Service. "Network to Freedom." https://www.nps.gov/subjects/ugrr/ntf_member/ntf_member_details.htm?SPFID=4068809&SPFTerritory=NULL&SPFType=NULL&SPFKeywords=NULL

[2341] Durrie, *Holt Genealogy*, p 164

In his will written 10 September 1852, Daniel Glazier bequeaths to beloved wife Mary all the furniture she brought to the marriage, all the furniture obtained since their marriage (except the secretary), $850, and the use of one-third part of the house as long as she remains a widow; grandson Daniel Johnson Glazier, $150 over what he has received; grandson Isaac Glazier receives 10 shares of bank stock; Elizabeth Spalden and Sarah R. Glazier receive all of his furniture (except the secretary) and $4000 to be divided equally between them; grandson Hiram Rider receives a piece of land; and son Orlen Glazier receives the remainder of the estate and is named executor.[2342] Elizabeth Spalden and Sarah R. Glazier are daughters of son Isaac. Daniel Johnson Glazier is the son of Isaac. Hiram Rider is the son of daughter Sarah.

There are records for four children of Daniel and Elizabeth Glazier. The Willington Historical Society states there were five children, but records for that child were not found and perhaps there was a fifth child that died before adulthood.

i SARAH GLAZIER, b. 17 Apr 1800; d. at Willington, 1850; m. at Willington, 3 May 1818, HIRAM RIDER, b. at Willington, 28 Apr 1790 son of Joseph and Jane (Poole) Rider; Hiram d. at Willington, 26 Sep 1851.

ii ISAAC GLAZIER, b. 19 Jan 1803; d. at Willington, 4 Feb 1835; m. 7 Mar 1824, LUCIA SNOW, b. at Ashford, 23 Nov 1804 daughter of Amos and Eunice (Burnham) Snow; Lucia d. at Willington, 30 Sep 1849.

iii ORLAN GLAZIER, b. 12 May 1805; d. at Willington, 13 Apr 1857; m. 2 Aug 1836, SOPHRONIA JOHNSON, b. at Willington, 4 Apr 1814 daughter of Abel and Deborah (Preston) Johnson; Sophronia d. at Hartford, 25 Mar 1898.

iv ELIZA GLAZIER, b. 1814; d. 2 Mar 1815.

877) LEONARD HOLT (*Isaac⁴, Abiel³, Nicholas², Nicholas¹*), b. at Willington, 15 Feb 1782 son of Isaac and Sarah (Orcutt) Holt; d. 12 Mar 1857; m. 1st, 29 Dec 1809, his first cousin once removed, ASENATH HOLT (*Nathan⁵, Nathan⁴, Abiel³, Nicholas², Nicholas¹*), b. 26 Jan 1786 daughter of Nathan and Lois (Goodell) Holt; Asenath d. 13 Feb 1813. Leonard m. 2nd, about 1813, JOANNA ALDEN (widow of Josiah Converse), b. 14 Jul 1782 daughter of Elisha and Irene (Markham) Alden; Joanna d. 30 Sep 1849.

Leonard Holt and his three children are somewhat of a mystery. His son William married twice, and one child has been identified for William. Leonard's two children by his second wife, Asenath Frances and Oliver A., led lives out of the ordinary. Oliver and Asenath lived with their father until after 1850. Asenath and her father Leonard were excommunicated from the church in Willington 31 December 1852[2343] but the reasons for this are not known. After that, Asenath attended Thetford Academy in Vermont[2344] and worked as a teacher for the remainder of her life. Oliver A. Holt married Nancy Abbe in 1853 and they had one son Leonard O. Holt who died of croup at age two years. After the birth of Leonard O., Oliver relocated to Tamaroa, IL and that is where his son Leonard O. died. Oliver lived in Tamaroa the remainder of his life, but his wife Nancy lived in Connecticut with her family. They do not seem to have divorced, and after Oliver's death, Nancy listed herself as the widow of Oliver in town registers. Asenath went to Tamaroa and was living with her brother in 1860 and she was there as a single head of household in 1880.[2345] Asenath spent her later years in Washington, D.C. where she died in 1904, although she was buried in Tamaroa.

Leonard Holt did not leave a will and the only probate document available was the administration bond given by Oliver A. Holt and Eber Dunham.

Leonard Holt and Asenath Holt had one child.

i WILLIAM HOLT, b. at Willington, 6 May 1811; d. at Willington, 5 Feb 1878; m. 1st, 21 Mar 1836, CAROLINE DELAURA CARPENTER, b. at Waterford, VT, 23 Mar 1811 daughter of Isaiah and Caroline (Bugbee) Carpenter; Caroline d. at Willington, 29 Feb 1864. William m. 2nd, at Waterford, VT, 13 Oct 1864, MARY B. PARKER, b. at New Hampton, NH, 22 Feb 1822 daughter of Ezra and Hannah (Burleigh) Parker; Mary d. at Newbury, VT, 23 Mar 1900.

Leonard and Joanna Holt had two children.

i OLIVER A. HOLT, b. at Willington about 1817; d. at Tamaroa, IL, 27 Aug 1876; m. 10 Oct 1853, NANCY AMELIA ABBE, b. at Enfield, 16 Oct 1830 daughter of Harvey C. and Mary A. (Gowdy) Abbe; Nancy d. at Bristol, CT, 5 Apr 1917.

ii ASENATH FRANCES HOLT, b. at Willington, Sep 1820; d. at Washington, D. C., 28 Jun 1904.

2342 *Connecticut State Library (Hartford, Connecticut);* Probate Place: *Hartford, Connecticut, Probate Packets, Carpenter, Comfort-Kimball, J, 1833-1880*, probate of Daniel Glazier, case number 354

2343 Connecticut, Church Record Abstracts, 1630-1927, volume 127 Willington

2344 *U.S., High School Student Lists, 1821-1923.* Asenath F. Holt of Willington, CT sponsored by Leonard Holt, Thetford Academy

2345 Saints, *1880 United States Federal Census*, Year: 1880; Census Place: Tamaroa, Perry, Illinois; Roll: 241; Page: 8C; Enumeration District: 071.

878) ANNE HOLT (*Isaac⁴, Abiel³, Nicholas², Nicholas¹*), b. at Willington, 21 Oct 1784 daughter of Isaac and Sarah (Orcutt) Holt; d. 27 Jun 1855; m. SIMON CARPENTER, b. 13 Dec 1783 son of Elijah and Sarah (Younglove) Carpenter; Simon d. 24 Aug 1862.

Simon Carpenter did not leave a will. Lucien H. Carpenter and Elisa A. Carpenter signed the administrator's bond. Anne and Simon had two children neither of whom married. The two children lived together in Willington throughout their lives.

i LUCIEN HOLT CARPENTER, b. 21 May 1817; d. at Willington, 6 Aug 1889.

ii ELIZA A. CARPENTER, b. about 1823; d. at Willington, 31 Dec 1880.

879) ANNA HOLT (*Timothy⁴, Abiel³, Nicholas², Nicholas¹*), b. at Willington, 12 Feb 1762 daughter of Timothy and Rebecca (Chamberlain) Holt; m. 17 Nov 1785, STEPHEN CROCKER, b. 14 Dec 1760 son of Ebenezer and Hannah (Hatch) Crocker. This family was in Schoharie County, New York by about 1788.[2346]

Anna and Stephen Crocker went to Rhode Island following their marriage where at least one child was born. The family was in Schoharie County by 1788 and settled in Carlisle. Stephen seems to still be living at the time of the 1820 census as the head of household, male over age 45. If so, Anna had died before that as the female in the household was age 26-44 and there are two children under age 10 in the household.

There are just three children identified for Anna and Stephen, although there may well be other children.

i BERIAH CROCKER, b. 1785; d. at Sloansville, NY, 19 Jan 1874; m. at Reformed Protestant Church, Nassau, NY, 31 Oct 1813,[2347] SARAH GARRISON, b. about 1795; Sarah d. at Sloansville, 1 Oct 1868.

ii HANNAH CROCKER, b. about 1786; m. New London, CT, 8 Jan 1801, JOSEPH WEEKS, b. at New London, 26 May 1771 son of Joseph and Elizabeth (Grant) Weeks; Joseph d. at New London, 31 Jul 1809.

iii EDEY CROCKER, b. in RI, 1794; d. at Sloansville, NY, 23 Jan 1876; m. JACOB TEEPLE, b. 1791 son of John and Lanah (Vosseller) Teeple; Jacob d. at Sloansville, 1866.

880) TIMOTHY HOLT (*Timothy⁴, Abiel³, Nicholas², Nicholas¹*), b. at Willington, 19 May 1765 son of Timothy and Rebecca (Chamberlain) Holt; d. 17 Apr 1850; m. 10 Dec 1789, ESTHER SCRIPTURE, b. 26 Aug 1765 son of John and Esther (Lee) Scripture; Esther d. 1 Aug 1841.

Timothy and Esther Holt lived in Willington throughout their lives and were parents to three children.

i NORMAN HOLT, b. 6 Aug 1791; d. 12 Apr 1792.

ii ORRIN HOLT, b. 13 Mar 1793; d. at Willington, 20 Jun 1855; m. 24 Sep 1819, ELIZA DUNTON, b. at Willington, 12 Apr 1801 daughter of Samuel and Lovina (Marcy) Dunton; Eliza d. at Willington, 8 Apr 1850. Orrin was a member of the Connecticut state legislature and elected to the twenty-fourth U.S. Congress as a Jacksonian. He was re-elected as a Democrat to the twenty-fifth Congress with total period of service in the U.S. Congress 1836-1839. He held positions within the Connecticut state militia up to the rank of Inspector General.[2348]

iii REBECCA HOLT, b. 1 May 1797; d. at Willington, 14 Feb 1857. Rebecca did not marry.

881) JAMES HOLT (*James⁴, Abiel³, Nicholas², Nicholas¹*), b. at Willington, 12 Apr 1770 son of James and Esther (Owens) Holt; d. at Willington, 16 Jan 1856; m. 4 Dec 1794, his second cousin, MARY POOL (*Deborah Preston Pool⁴, Deborah Holt Preston³, Nicholas², Nicholas¹*), b. at Willington, 14 Aug 1770 daughter of Timothy and Deborah (Preston) Pool; Mary d. 18 Jan 1853.

James Holt and Mary Pool were parents to five children born at Willington.

i CELINDA HOLT, b. 16 Jan 1796; d. at Willington, 20 May 1823; m. 18 Nov 1816, ROBERT SHARP, b. about 1791 likely the son of Solomon and Rebecca (Perkins) Sharp; Robert d. at Willington, 1 Nov 1874. After Celinda's death, Robert married Julianna Holt (see Family 681).

ii POLLY HOLT, b. 7 Sep 1798; d. at Willington, 24 Jan 1853; m. her second cousin, HORACE HOLT (*Caleb⁵, Caleb⁴, Abiel³, Nicholas², Nicholas¹*), b. at Willington, 29 Aug 1784 son of Caleb and Sarah (Goodale) Holt; Horace d. at Willington, 30 Jan 1863.

[2346] Roscoe, *History of Schoharie County*, p 316

[2347] New York Marriages 1686-1980, familysearch.org

[2348] Biographical Directory of the United States Congress, Orrin Holt, http://bioguide.congress.gov/scripts/biodisplay.pl?index=H000748

iii TIMOTHY HOLT, b. 12 Jul 1801; d. at Willington, 29 Dec 1864; m. 1st, at Mansfield, CT, 2 Mar 1827, THANKFUL WILSON, b. at Mendon, MA, 8 May 1801 daughter of Reuben and Joanna (Taft) Wilson; Thankful d. at Willington, 6 Dec 1835. Timothy m. 2nd, at Mansfield, 4 Mar 1836, ALMIRA A. PERKINS, b. about 1809 daughter of Ransom and Huldah (Montgomery) Perkins; Almira d. at Willington, 29 Apr 1874.

iv JAMES HOLT, b. 15 Aug 1804; d. at Webster, MA, 22 Sep 1851; m. at Willington, 5 May 1830, PHILEA WILSON, b. at Mendon, 24 Nov 1803 daughter of John and Leah (Darling) Wilson; Philea d. at Webster, 26 Apr 1858.

v ALMIRA HOLT, b. 30 Aug 1810; d. 3 Nov 1813.

882) JOSEPH HOLT (*James⁴, Abiel³, Nicholas², Nicholas¹*) (twin of James), b. at Willington, 12 Apr 1770 son of James and Esther (Owens) Holt; d. at Willington, 29 Jan 1816; m. 6 Mar 1794, BETSY PARKER, b. at Willington, 23 Feb 1775 daughter of Jonathan and Betsy (Johnson) Parker; Betsy d. 7 May 1814.

The probate record for Joseph Holt includes few documents as the documents are damaged and not able to be digitally rendered. There was not a will. The surety bond for the administration was $10,000 suggesting a substantial estate. There are six guardian bonds, although the documents are not available; only folder sheets are available for minors Lucy, Mary, and Alvah.[2349] There are birth records for six children which do not include Mary, but there are six minor children at the time of probate, and son Thomas was deceased in 1814.

There is evidence for seven children of Joseph Holt and Betsy Parker, all born at Willington.

i HANNAH HOLT, b. 16 Jan 1795, no further record

ii ESTHER HOLT, b. 27 Jan 1797; no further record

iii THOMAS HOLT, b. 27 May 1799; d. at Willington, 5 May 1814.

iv ALVAH HOLT, b. 14 Aug 1801; d. at Hartford, 30 Mar 1876; m. 13 Feb 1823, BETSEY KELSEY, b. at Hartford, 18 Mar 1794 daughter of Levi and Sarah (Burkett) Kelsey;[2350] Betsey d. at Hartford, 2 Jun 1869.

v LUCY HOLT, b. 22 Jan 1804; d. at Willington, 3 Feb 1868; m. 24 Nov 1825, ELI ELDREDGE, b. at Ashford, 18 Apr 1803 son of Elijah and Bethiah (Chapman) Eldredge; Eli d. at Willington, 31 May 1864.

vi JOSEPH PARSONS HOLT, b. 19 Jul 1806; d. at Northfield, MN, 8 May 1886; m. 23 Nov 1834, JULIA CUSHMAN, of Stafford, b. about 1817; Julia d. at Northfield, 3 Apr 1892.[2351]

vii MARY HOLT, b. about 1808; only known through guardian record and no further record.

883) SOLOMON HOLT (*James⁴, Abiel³, Nicholas², Nicholas¹*), b. at Willington, 14 Apr 1772 son of James and Esther (Owens) Holt; d. in Iowa, 4 Jun 1838; m. at Franklin, CT, 7 Apr 1799, ZERVIAH ABELL, b. at Norwich, 26 Aug 1780 daughter of Thomas and Zerviah (Hyde) Abell; Zerviah d. 1845.

Solomon and Zerviah were married in Connecticut, but were in Exeter, New York by 1810. After 1830, they relocated to Iowa City, Iowa. Solomon Holt and Zerviah Abell were parents of eight children born at Exeter, New York.[2352]

i ESTHER HOLT, b. 16 Jun 1804; d. at Lebanon, NY, 31 May 1882; m. DANIEL ABBOTT, b. 3 Nov 1805 son of Daniel and Sally (Bellows) Abbott; Daniel d. at Lebanon, 1891. Daniel Abbott is a descendant of George Abbott of Rowley.

ii AUSTIN HOLT, b. about 1807; d. at Jefferson County, KY, about 1839; m. at Jefferson County, 17 Dec 1833, SUSANNAH WARWIC, b. about 1810. Susannah married second James Hamilton on 13 Sep 1840.

iii DIODATE HOLT, b. about 1809; d. after 1870 when he was living in Elizabethtown, KY; m. at Jefferson County, KY, 7 Mar 1834, ELIZABETH OWINGS TOY, b. in Maryland, Dec 1811 daughter of Joseph and Sarah (Owings) Toy; Elizabeth d. after 1900 when she was living in Elizabethtown, KY.

2349 Connecticut State Library (Hartford, Connecticut); Probate Place: Hartford, Connecticut, Probate Packets, Holt, Clarisa-Hunt, O, 1759-1880, case number 1064

2350 Barbour, *Families of Early Hartford, Conn.*, p 354

2351 Neill, *History of Rice County*

2352 There are baptism records for children of Solomon and Zerviah Holt at the Congregational Church at Exeter: Austin, Diodate, Harvey, Eunice Hitchcock, Mary Calista, and James Thompson all on 27 March 1825. Presbyterian Historical Society; Philadelphia, Pennsylvania; *U.S., Presbyterian Church Records, 1701-1907;* Book Title: *1825 – 1861.* The names of Esther's parents, Solomon and Zeviah, are engraved on her gravestone. The younger Harvey is listed on the 1850 census as born about 1830. There may be another child born before Esther, but that information is not determined.

iv HARVEY HOLT, b. about 1813; d. before 1828. He was baptized in 1825 but there seems to be a second son Harvey born by 1828.

v EUNICE HITCHCOCK HOLT, b. about 1816; d. at Johnson County, IA, 22 Mar 1869; m. 20 Jul 1851, DAVID WRAY, b. at Hamilton County, OH, 15 Oct 1815 son of Richard and Catherine (Buford) Wray; David d. at Johnson County, 27 Sep 1872. David Wray was first married to Maria Alt.[2353]

vi MARY CALISTA HOLT, b. about 1820; m. at Johnson County, IA, 12 Jan 1845, JAMES M. PRICE; James d. before 1850.

vii JAMES THOMPSON HOLT, b. 22 Nov 1822; d. at Berwick, IA, 2 Mar 1901; m. 1850, PHEBE E. DUNKLE, b. in OH, 5 Nov 1832; Phebe d. at Berwick, 19 Feb 1917.

viii HARVEY HOLT, b. about 1828; d. after 1850 when he was living in Iowa City, IA with his sisters Eunice Holt and Mary C. Price.

884) ESTHER HOLT (*James[4], Abiel[3], Nicholas[2], Nicholas[1]*), b. at Willington, 20 Nov 1774 daughter of James and Esther (Owens) Holt; m. 9 Jan 1800, DANIEL PARKER, b. at Willington, 5 Mar 1777 son of Jonathan and Betsy (Johnson) Parker.

Esther Holt and Daniel Parker were parents of seven children born at Willington. They then made the trip west and were in Ashtabula County, Ohio by 1820.

i JONATHAN PARKER, b. 1 Feb 1801; d. at Madison, OH, after 1850; m. at Ashtabula County, 14 Mar 1827, ABIGAIL DEVAN, b. 1802 daughter of Talcott and Temperance (-) Devan; Abigail d. at Montville, OH, 18 Mar 1838.

ii KEZIAH PARKER, b. 16 Oct 1802; d. at Geneva, OH, 5 Jul 1833; m. at Ashtabula County, 24 Feb 1820, EZEKIEL ARNOLD, b. at Ontario, NY, 1797; Ezekiel d. at Geneva, 5 Jun 1880.

iii DANIEL PARKER, b. 2 Mar 1805; d. 7 Apr 1805.

iv HANNAH PARKER, b. 1 Mar 1806; d. at Sycamore, IL, 15 Jul 1883; m. MARSHALL CALL, b. at Randolph, VT, 24 Feb 1800 son of Rufus and Lydia (Ellis) Call; Marshall d. at Sycamore, 26 May 1873.

v NEHEMIAH PARKER, b. 2 Jun 1808; d. at Orwell, OH, 13 Mar 1871; m. 1st, at Ashtabula County, 6 Apr 1836, CHLOE SAMANTHA COOK, b. 1817 daughter of Zera and Chloe (Loomis) Cook; Chloe d. 12 Jun 1847. Nehemiah m. 2nd, 16 Nov 1848, ZILPHA FENTON, b. 1813; Zelpha d. at Orwell, 4 Jan 1898. After Nehemiah's death, Zelpha married Ichabod Clapp 27 May 1880.

vi ESTHER PARKER, b. 2 Jun 1810. Esther's marriage is uncertain, but most likely m. at Madison, OH, 14 Mar 1826, DAVID MORSE, b. in NY, about 1800 and d. at Thompson, OH, 1851. If this is Esther's marriage, she died at Thompson, OH, 20 May 1883.

vii BETSY PARKER, b. 18 Aug 1812; nothing further known.

885) JOHN HOLT, b. at Willington, 11 Apr 1776 son of James and Lucy (Sawins) Holt; d. at Willington, 22 Apr 1841; m. 6 Sep 1804, his first cousin once removed, CLARISSA HOLT, b. 1775 (based on age at time of death) daughter of Philemon and Jemima (Eldredge) Holt; Clarissa d. 25 Feb 1840.

There is little information on this family. Three children are known, all born at Willington.

i MATILDA HOLT, b. 13 Jun 1805; d. at Willington, 26 Jun 1834. Matilda did not marry.

ii JOHN HOLT, b. 15 Mar 1809; d. at Colchester, CT, 1851 (probate 15 Oct 1851 with widow Waity Holt declining administration); m. at Willington, 29 Aug 1832, WAITY MOORE, b. in Rhode Island about 1812; Waity d. at Willington, 22 Jan 1868. After John's death, Waity married Lester Carew, 29 Mar 1859.

iii LAUNDA HOLT, b. 5 Sep 1813; no further record.

886) LUCE HOLT (*James[4], Abiel[3], Nicholas[2], Nicholas[1]*), b. at Willington, 11 Jun 1778 daughter of James and Lucy (Sawins) Holt; d. at Ashford, 22 Feb 1847;[2354] m. at Ashford, 26 Jan 1809, AARON WALKER, b. 21 Jan 1776 son of Samuel and Alice (Case) Walker; Aaron d. at Ashford, 1 Nov 1815.

Luce did not remarry after Aaron's death and in the 1830 U.S. Census at Ashford, she is listed as Mrs. Lucy Walker with the household consisting of one female age 50-59 and one female 15-19.[2355]

[2353] Iowa City, *History of Johnson County, Iowa*, p 955

[2354] Durrie, *A Genealogy of the Holt Family*, p 50

[2355] 1830; Census Place: Ashford, Windham, Connecticut; Series: M19; Roll: 11; Page: 176; Family History Library Film: 0002804

The estate of Aaron Walker entered probate 1815 and the inventory was completed 29 November 1815 with a total value of $2,016.81 which included the value of the home farm and buildings of $1,164. Claims against the estate totaled $755.07. The administration of the estate included a consideration of the part of the estate which was still part of the widow's portion of Aaron's mother Alice Walker Wilson.[2356]

Luce and Aaron had two daughters whose births are recorded at Ashford.

i MARIA TRUMBULL WALKER, b. 11 Jul 1810; d. 18 May 1812.[2357]

ii LUCY MAIN WALKER, b. 11 Nov 1813; d. at Ashford, 5 May 1881; m. at Willington, 8 Apr 1840, GEORGE WHITON, b. at Ashford, 8 Jun 1816 son of Abner and Amy (Chaffee) Whiton; George d. at Ashford, 22 Sep 1887.

887) ABIEL HOLT (*James[4], Abiel[3], Nicholas[2], Nicholas[1]*), b. at Willington, 14 Jan 1780 son of James and Lucy (Sawins) Holt; d. at Mansfield, about 1826 (probate of estate in 1826); m. 30 Apr 1805, SALLY CONVERSE, b. at Stafford, 9 Mar 1781 daughter of Stephen and Zerviah (Sanger) Converse;[2358] Sally's date of death is uncertain. She was alive in 1823 when her father wrote his will but there is no mention of her in the probate of Abiel's estate. The probate includes some provisions of the support of the two younger sons (Sanford and Arnold) who were underage at the time.

Abiel and Sally had three children whose birth are recorded at Ashford.

i ALFRED CONVERSE HOLT, b. 25 Feb 1806; d. at Hillsdale County, MI, 17 Mar 1852; m. 29 Mar 1830, ADELINE L. HURLBUT, b. at Bozrah, CT, about 1810 daughter of Asa and Salome (Arnold) Hurlbut;[2359] Adeline d. at Reading, MI, 24 Aug 1887. After Alfred's death, Adeline married Herman C. Hawse who was first married to Elvira Bacon. At the 1860 U.S. Census for Butler, MI, Adeline and H. C. Hawse are living in a household that includes two Hawse children and 10-year old Amos C. Holt.[2360]

ii SANFORD HOLT, b. 5 Feb 1815; d. at Haverhill, MA, 22 Oct 1886; m. at Willington, 30 Aug 1835, FIDELIA STUDLEY, b. 1t Mansfield, 12 Jan 1816 daughter of Ebenezer and Fidelia (Hodges) Studley. Fidelia d. at West Boylston, MA, 15 Nov 1882. After Fidelia's death, Sanford married Lydia P. Sawyer on 28 Nov 1883. Lydia Sawyer was the daughter of Timothy Sawyer and Nancy Porter Pendleton.

iii ARNOLD HOLT, b. 24 Sep 1816; d. at Hartford, 21 Dec 1862; m. at Hartford, 7 May 1838, JULIA CURTISS, b. about 1816 daughter of Lyman Curtiss. Arnold and Julia did not have children.

888) SOLOMON PRESTON (*Benjamin Preston[4], Deborah Holt Preston[3], Nicholas[2], Nicholas[1]*), b. at Ashford, 10 Sep 1770; d. at Ashford, 29 Sep 1851 son of Benjamin and Bathsheba (Snow) Preston; m. at Ashford, 13 Jun 1799, SUSANNAH HAWES, b. at Medway, MA, 29 Oct 1779 daughter of Eli and Susannah (Bigelow) Hawes; Susannah d. at Ashford, 9 Sep 1860.[2361]

There are three children known for Solomon Preston and Susannah Hawes.

i CLARISSA PRESTON, b. at Ashford, 16 Apr 1800; d. at Ashford, 30 Jul 1853. Clarissa did not marry.

ii ERMINA PRESTON, b, at Ashford, 16 Aug 1801; d. at Ashford, 2 Jul 1886; Ermina m. 1st 27 Mar 1829, ELIPHALET BROWN, b. at Windham, 18 Oct 1801 son of John and Olive (Martin) Brown; Eliphalet d. 5 Oct 1834. Ermina m. 2nd 4 Apr 1854, LUCIUS HORTON, b. at Willington, 15 Dec 1804 son of Moses and Silence (Wilson) Horton; Lucius d. at Ashford, 14 Sep 1884. Lucius Horton was first married to Huldreth Thayer. Ermina and Eliphalet were parents of Theron Brown a noted minister and author of his day.

iii MINERVA PRESTON, b. at Ashford, 5 Aug 1807; d. at Ashford, 3 Nov 1848; m. at Ashford, 24 May 1837, ALFRED CHAFFEE, b. 1811 son of Carpenter and Lois (Lyon) Chaffee;[2362] Alfred d. at Ashford, 13 Jul 1866. Alfred was second married to Almira Dean.

889) DINAH PRESTON (*Daniel Preston[4], Deborah Holt Preston[3], Nicholas[2], Nicholas[1]*), b. at Ashford, 13 Sep 1756 daughter of Daniel and Dinah (Ford) Preston; d. at Braintree, VT, 1 Jan 1836; m. at Hampton, 18 Dec 1777, STEPHEN CLARK, b. at Hampton, 15 Mar 1752 son of Stephen and Hannah (Durkee) Clark; Stephen d. at Braintree, 30 Oct 1820.

2356 *Connecticut Wills and Probate, 1609-1999*, Probate of Aaron Walker, Hartford, 1815, Case number 4184.

2357 Durrie, *A Genealogy of the Holt Family*, p 103

2358 The 1823 will of Stephen Converse includes a bequest to his daughter Sally Holt.

2359 Hurlbut, *The Hurlbut Genealogy*, p 151

2360 Year: 1860; Census Place: Butler, Branch, Michigan; Roll: M653_538; Page: 1041; Family History Library Film: 803538

2361 Although the marriage transcription in the Barbour collection gives her name as Susannah Harris, this seems to be an error. Other information supports that she is Susannah Hawes, for example the 1825 probate of the estate of Eli Hawes of Ashford which is administered by Solomon Preston. The "internet" reports she is daughter of Reuben Harris, but that is refuted by the 1825 will of Reuben which clearly states his daughter Susannah is unmarried.

2362 Chaffee, *The Chaffee Genealogy*, p 140

Dinah and Stephen started their family in Hampton and relocated to Braintree, Vermont after 1800. Stephen served as a private in the Revolution in Captain James Stedman's company. He marched from Windham for the relief of Boston in April 1775.[2363]

Son Fielder Clark married but did not leave any children. In his will written 18 May 1869 (proved 22 April 1875), he bequeathed his estate to his beloved wife Mary with the exception of two hundred dollars to be used for gravestones. Following his wife's death, his estate is to be divided among the children of or the legal heirs of the children of his brothers and sisters. The brothers and sisters are named as Hosea Clark, Eli Clark, Orilla Spear, Sophia Wiley, Phebe Wiley, and Permelia Fisk. Edson Martin of Williamstown was named executor, or if he is not able, then Myron J. Pratt.[2364]

Dinah Preston and Stephen Clark were parents of eleven children. The births of the first six children are recorded at Hampton, and the younger five children may also have been born there.

i ABEL CLARK, b. 10 Jan 1779; d. 11 Sep 1790.

ii PERMELIA CLARK, b. 28 May 1781; d. at Brookfield, VT, 8 Oct 1866; m. CHARLES FISK, b. at Hampton, about 1782 son of John and Eunice (Jennings) Fisk; Charles d. at Brookfield, 1 Dec 1868.

iii ARASTUS CLARK, b. 6 May 1783; d. at Randolph, VT, 7 Feb 1857; m. EUNICE BLODGETT, b. at Randolph, 23 Sep 1793 daughter of Henry and Abigail (Parmalee) Blodgett; Eunice d. at Randolph, 10 Oct 1854. Arastus and Eunice do not seem to have had children.

iv PHEBE CLARK, b. 3 Apr 1786; d. at Williamstown, VT, 29 Mar 1854; m. JONATHAN WILEY, b. at Dublin, NH, 6 Feb 1796 son of Benjamin and Abigail (Townsend) Wiley.

v AUGUSTUS CLARK, b. 20 Mar 1788; d. 10 Nov 1790.

vi WILLARD CLARK, b. 1790; d. 9 Oct 1790.

vii FIELDER CLARK, b. 1792; d. at Randolph, VT, 19 Apr 1875; m. MARY "POLLY" SPEAR, b. at Braintree, 15 May 1790 daughter of Elias and Mary (Dyer) Spear; Polly d. at Braintree, 4 Feb 1876.

viii ELI K. CLARK, b. 1799; d. at Andover, OH, 14 Aug 1868; m. 1st EUNICE BROWN, b. 1799; Eunice d. at Andover, OH, 30 Apr 1852. Eli m. 2nd at Ashtabula, OH, 22 Sep 1853, BETSEY SMITH.

ix SOPHIA CLARK, b. 1797; d. at Roxbury, VT, 8 Jun 1843; m. JAMES WILEY who has not been identified.

x ORILLA CLARK, b. 1799; d. at Stowe, VT, 12 Dec 1881; m. at Braintree, 6 Mar 1817, ELIAS SPEAR, b. at Braintree, 28 Jan 1795 son of Elias and Mary (Dyer) Spear.

xi HOSEA CLARK, b. 25 Apr 1801; d. 24 at Northfield, VT, Dec 1874; m. HULDAH WORTHINGTON, b. at Williamstown, VT, 31 Jul 1801 daughter of Daniel and Mary (Fisk) Worthington; Huldah d. at Northfield, VT, 15 Sep 1874.

890) EUNICE FORD PRESTON (*Daniel Preston[4], Deborah Holt Preston[3], Nicholas[2], Nicholas[1]*), b. at Ashford, 12 Mar 1759 daughter of Daniel and Dinah (Ford) Preston; d. at Preston, NY, 31 Oct 1856; m. at Hampton, 15 Apr 1783, WILLIAM CLARK, b. at Hampton, 7 Feb 1754 son of Stephen and Hannah (Durkee) Clark; William d. at Preston, 4 Oct 1840.

In his pension application file, William reported that he enlisted for six months in a militia company from Hampton, Connecticut. The regimental commander was Colonel John Chester. The troops were shipped to New York where he participated in the Battle of Long Island. He was also in White Plains and Morristown. In the fall of 1777, he enlisted for another month again in the militia. He reported he was born in Hampton 7 February 1754. After the war, he stayed in Hampton until 1795 and then went to Burlington, New York. He was in Burlington about thirty years before moving to Preston, New York. Following William's death in 1840, Eunice F. Clark made her application for widow's pension. Eunice reported she and William married 15 April 1783. In 1844, children Eunice Nicholson of Preston and Alfred Clark of Preston made depositions in support of their mother's application.

There are three children known for Eunice F. Preston and William Clark, born at Hampton, Connecticut.

i ALFRED CLARK, b. 22 May 1784; d. 1 Nov 1787.

ii EUNICE CLARK, b. 19 Jan 1786; d. at Preston, NY, after 1844; m. WILLIAM NICHOLSON, b. at Preston, CT, 7 Jul 1789 son of William Beard and Marvel (Palmer) Nicholson. William was living in the almshouse in Preston in 1873.

iii ALFRED CLARK, b. 19 Jun 1789; d. at Preston, NY, 10 Feb 1880; m. SUSAN MINER, b. about 1791; Susan d. at Norwich, NY, 17 Dec 1862.

2363 Record of Service of Connecticut Men in the War of the Revolution,

2364 *Vermont. Probate Court (Randolph District), Folder 113, Bugbee, Isaac-Currier, Jacob, 1875-1886, will of Fielder Clark*

891) CHLOE PRESTON (*Daniel Preston[4], Deborah Holt Preston[3], Nicholas[2], Nicholas[1]*), b. at Ashford, about 1761 daughter of Daniel and Dinah (Ford) Preston; d. at Ashford, 28 Nov 1839; m. at Ashford, 15 Nov 1781, JAMES BOUTELL, b. at Ashford, 30 Jul 1760 son of Jacob and Eunice (Drew) Boutell; James d. at Ashford, 13 May 1822.

In 1852, daughter Marcia Robinson, then of Ashford and age fifty-five, made application for pension benefits that may have been due her mother Chloe Boutell deceased. On 25 May 1852, the judge of probate court for Ashford in Windham County stated that sufficient evidence had been presented to support that James Boutell was a Revolutionary soldier enlisting in 1776 in the company of Capt. Reuben Marcy, and at the time of his enlistment he was a minor under age twenty-one. James was the son of Jacob Boutell who was a corporal in the same company. James Boutell married Chloe Preston on 15 November 1781. James died on 13 May 1822 at age sixty-two and Chloe died on 28 November 1839 at age seventy-six. In 1852, there were still living the following children: Jacob Boutell, Marcia Robinson, Sally Boutell, and James Boutell. Niece Mary Franklin, formerly Mary Boutell, also provided a statement in 1852 confirming information about her uncle including the four surviving children. Mary's husband William Franklin also provided a statement. The pension documents include a statement by Benjamin C. Simmons, town clerk of Ashford, reporting records for the marriage of Jacob Boutell and Eunice Drew on 20 June 1759 and the birth of their son James on 30 July 1760. James Boutell and Chloe Preston were joined in marriage 15 November 1781.[2365]

James and Chloe were parents of nine children born at Ashford.

i IRA BOUTELL, b. 20 Jan 1785; d. *perhaps* at Batavia, NY, before 1852;[2366] m. about 1810, ELIZABETH BROWN, b. about 1785; Elizabeth d. at Batavia, 7 Oct 1828. Ira m. 2nd about 1829, HARRIET JANE KETCHAM, b. about 1793; Harriet d. at Batavia, 28 Jan 1858.

ii JOHN BOUTELL, b. 1 Sep 1789

iii JACOB BOUTELL, b. 17 Oct 1791; d. at Eastford, CT, 15 Jan 1886; m. at Ashford, 24 Oct 1827, SYBIL SNOW, b. about 1795 likely daughter of Araunah and Sarah (Hovey) Snow; Sybil d. at Eastford, 10 Apr 1876.

iv WILLARD BOUTELL, b. 20 Aug 1794; d. at Logan County, OH, about 1850; m. MARY who is not clearly identified, b. about 1793; Mary d. at Logan County, May 1850.[2367]

v MARCIA BOUTELL (twin), b. 12 Sep 1797; d. at Ashford, 15 Mar 1869; m. at Ashford, 1 Jun 1835, as his second wife, AMASA ROBINSON, b. at Woodstock, 31 Dec 1764 son of Timothy and Keziah (Goodell) Robinson; Amasa d. at Ashford, 28 Sep 1843. Amasa was first married to Hannah Chubb.

vi LUSHA BOUTELL (twin), b. 12 Sep 1797; d. 7 Sep 1800.

vii JAMES BOUTELL, b. 25 Feb 1800; d. at Wrentham, MA 16 Aug 1879; m. at Ashford, 22 Mar 1824, JULIA ANN PRESTON, b. at Ashford, 6 Jun 1797 daughter of Zera and Hannah (Smith) Preston; Julia d. at Wrentham, 2 Feb 1878.

viii LUCIUS BOUTELL, b. 14 May 1805; d. 27 Apr 1817.

ix SALLY BOUTELL, b. 16 Apr 1807; d. after 1852 when she was living in Wrentham, MA (according to information in the pension file for her father). Sally did not marry.

892) DANIEL PRESTON (*Daniel Preston[4], Deborah Holt Preston[3], Nicholas[2], Nicholas[1]*), b. at Ashford, 4 May 1763 son of Daniel and Dinah (Ford) Preston; d. at Fly Creek, NY, 23 Aug 1849; m. at Burlington, NY, 1 Dec 1791, ESTHER CUMMINGS, b. about 1771; Esther d. at Fly Creek, 27 Nov 1862.

On 16 October 1832, Daniel Preston, aged seventy years and a resident of Otsego, appeared in the court of common pleas to provide information for his pension application. He reported enlisting from Mansfield, Connecticut in January 1778 for a period of three months in the company of Capt. Benjamin Clark. He marched to Providence where he served mostly garrison duty. He enlisted again in August 1779 and was then at Fort Griswold. He had a third enlistment for a period of six months in June 1780 and marched to West Point and from there to Stoney Point. In the pension file, he also reports his birth as 4 May 1762. He lived in various locations in Connecticut until about forty years ago (about 1792) and then moved to Butternuts in Otsego County where he lived about one year. He then moved on to Burlington where he stayed for four years and was then in the town of Otsego where he currently resided. On 18 October 1849, widow Esther Preston then aged seventy-nine years appeared at court to provide information for the widow's pension. She reported she and Daniel were married on 4 December in 1790 or 1791 in the town of Burlington, New York. She reported that six children were still living the oldest being now fifty-four years old. Others making statements in support of the application were daughter Abigail and her husband Leander Plumb. In a statement on 13 September 1851, Abigail Plumb stated she had a sister living and another sister who if still living would be fifty-five. She has brothers living named Alson, Leander, and Daniel. A statement was made by son Alson on 13 September

[2365] U.S. Revolutionary War Pension and Bounty-Land Warrant Application File, Case W20740

[2366] Ira's date of death is most often reported as 20 July 1861 and there is an Ira Boutell living in Batavia in 1860, but that is perhaps a different person. There are statements from three family members in the pension file of James Boutell that there were only four children living in 1852: Jacob, Marcia, James, and Sally. It may be that the marriages I have reported are for a different Ira Boutell, but this is yet to be determined.

[2367] U.S., Federal Census Mortality Schedules Index, 1850-1880

1851, then age forty-eight. He reported having two older sisters still living and the eldest was fifty-five. Names of other children given in the pension record were Edward, Marcia, Lavina, and Juliann.[2368]

Daniel and Esther were parents of nine children all born in Otsego County, New York. Birth dates are not known for most of the children and are estimated.

i RUFUS PRESTON, b. about 1794; d. at Fly Creek, NY, 26 Mar 1837; m. OLIVE HECOX, b. at Otsego County, 1798 daughter of Samuel and Elizabeth (-) Hecox; Olive d. at Fly Creek, 12 Jul 1830.

ii MARCIA PRESTON, b. about 1795; d. before 1851.

iii EDWARD PRESTON, b. about 1796; d. before 1851.

iv ABIGAIL PRESTON, b. about 1798; d. at Fly Creek, NY, 19 Jul 1871; m. LEANDER PLUMB, b. about 1796; Leander d. at Fly Creek, 3 Oct 1876. Three children, Electa, Maria, and Orville, are named in Leander's will.

v ALSON PRESTON, b. 9 May 1803; d. at Cooperstown, NY, 12 Feb 1877; m. LUCY CARPENTER, b. 1804; Lucy d. at Cooperstown, 30 Aug 1875.

vi JULIANN PRESTON, b. estimated 1805; d. before 1851.

vii DANIEL PRESTON, b. 22 Apr 1810; d. at Fly Creek, 27 Jun 1885; m. LAVINA, b. about 1811 who is not firmly identified but may be Lavina Sherwood; Lavina was living in 1880.

viii LAVINA PRESTON, b. about 1815; d. after 1865 when she was living in Otsego; m. Mr. Brown who has not been identified. Lavina was apparently widowed before 1850 when she was living with her brother Daniel. There were no children living with her.

ix LEANDER PRESTON, b. 9 Mar 1818; d. at Dodge, WI, 4 Sep 1901; m. 1843, EUNICE BLOOMFIELD, b. in NY, Feb 1820 daughter of Samuel and Sarah (Wheeler) Bloomfield; Eunice d. at Waupun, WI, 27 Jun 1913.

893) CALVIN PRESTON (*Daniel Preston[4], Deborah Holt Preston[3], Nicholas[2], Nicholas[1]*), b. at Ashford, 7 Sep 1766 son of Daniel and Dinah (Ford) Preston; m. at Mansfield, 22 Jun 1785, PHILATHETA BIBBENS, b. at Mansfield, 22 Dec 1766 daughter of Hannah Bibbens, single woman.[2369]

Calvin and Philatheta were parents of four children born at Mansfield, Connecticut.

i ZALMON PRESTON, b. 3 Sep 1785; m. by 1808, ANNA BUTRICK, baptized at Windsor, MA, 16 Sep 1787 daughter of Oliver and Patience (Sabin) Butrick.

ii FIDELIA PRESTON, b. 22 Sep 1786; d. at Caton, NY, 20 Apr 1872; m. 8 Dec 1805, CHRISTOPHER TOBEY, b. at Conway, MA, 20 Nov 1784 son of Zacchaeus and Mary (Gifford) Tobey; Christopher d. at Caton, 8 Nov 1867.

iii AMELIA PRESTON, b. 4 Mar 1788

iv CHARLES PRESTON, b. 24 Jul 1789; d. at Corning, NY, 18 Jan 1872; m. about 1812, BETSEY BLANDIN, b. in VT, about 1794.

894) SARAH PRESTON (*Darius Preston[4], Deborah Holt Preston[3], Nicholas[2], Nicholas[1]*), b. at Willington, 3 Mar 1764 daughter of Darius and Hannah (Fiske) Preston; m. at Willington, 3 Jan 1788, TIMOTHY NYE, b. at Willington, 26 Jan 1765 son of Benjamin and Phebe (West) Nye.[2370]

Little information was located for this family. There is a birth record for one child, and it seems that Timothy and Sarah went to Richfield, New York and had other children. However, records related to that are not yet found.

i CHLOE NYE, b. at Willington, 22 Jan 1792

895) DARIUS PRESTON (*Darius Preston[4], Deborah Holt Preston[3], Nicholas[2], Nicholas[1]*), b. at Willington, 18 Dec 1766 son of Darius and Hannah (Fiske) Preston; d. at Hanover, PA, 1 Apr 1845; m. 26 Aug 1788, NAOMI HIBBARD b. at Bolton, 1770 daughter of William Bathsheba (Strong) Hibbard; Naomi d. at Wilkes-Barre.

Darius and Naomi moved from Connecticut to Hanover, Pennsylvania prior to 1790 and lived in what was known as Back Road near Ashley.[2371]

Darius Preston and Naomi Hibbard were parents of seven children.[2372]

[2368] Revolutionary War Pension and Bounty-Land Warrant Application Files, Case W5581
[2369] Dimock, *Birth, Baptisms, Marriages and Deaths. . . Mansfield, Connecticut*, p 31
[2370] Nye, *A Genealogy of the Nye Family*, p 217
[2371] Plumb, *History of Hanover Township*, p 465
[2372] The marriages as are given in Plumb, *History of Hanover Township*, p 465

i HIBBARD PRESTON, b. at Willington, 18 Mar 1790; d. at Wilkes-Barre, PA, 20 Mar 1870; m. MARGARET PEASE, b. 11 Mar 1794 (on gravestone) daughter of Samuel and Lydia (-) Pease; Margaret d. at Wilkes-Barre, 3 Feb 1875.

ii HANNAH PRESTON, b. about 1792; m. DAVID PEASE son of Samuel and Lydia (-) Pease

iii JERUSHA PRESTON, b. about 1796; d. at Susquehanna, PA, Apr 1870; m. JACOB RUDOLPH who has not been identified.

iv ISABELLA PRESTON, b. about 1798; m. HENRY BARKMAN, b. about 1789. Isabella and Henry were living in Wilkes-Barre in 1860.

v ASENATH PRESTON, b. at Wilkes-Barre, 29 May 1801; d. at New Haven, CT, 3 May 1875; m. DANIEL S. BARNES, b. 1798; Daniel d. at New Haven, 15 Mar 1883.

vi WILLISTON PRESTON, b. about 1803; d. after 1875; m. RACHEL KREIDLER, b. about 1810; Rachel d. at Wilkes-Barre, 12 Aug 1875.

vii CYPRIAN PRESTON, b. about 1814; d. at Bellevue, PA, 19 Jul 1877; m. CHRISTIANA WILEY, b. about 1820; Christiana d. at likely at Cranford, NY (burial at Pittsburgh), 1881. Christiana was living in New Jersey with her children in 1880.

896) JOSHUA PRESTON (*Darius Preston[4], Deborah Holt Preston[3], Nicholas[2], Nicholas[1]*), b. at Willington, 25 Sep 1768 son of Darius and Hannah (Fiske) Preston; d. at Willington, 1 Nov 1810; m. 25 Sep 1794, SARAH HOLT who has not been identified.

Joshua and Sarah were parents of two children born at Willington.

i FLORINDA PRESTON, b. 26 Aug 1799; d. at Chaplin, CT, 16 Feb 1869; m. 31 Mar 1824, ORRIN WITTER, b. at Brooklyn, CT, 15 Jul 1797 son of Jacob B. and Olive (Brown) Witter. Orrin d. at Chaplin, 2 Feb 1869.

ii AUSTIN PRESTON, b. 5 Nov 1803; d. at Saugerties, NY, 23 Jan 1886; m. at Hampton, 10 Jan 1825, HARRIET BURNHAM, b. at Hampton, 23 Jun 1806 daughter of Jedediah and Phebe (Martin) Burnham; Harriet d. at Hampton, 15 Apr 1888.

897) CHLOE PRESTON (*Darius Preston[4], Deborah Holt Preston[3], Nicholas[2], Nicholas[1]*), b. at Willington, 11 Feb 1772 daughter of Darius and Hannah (Fiske) Preston; d. at Corinth, NY, 9 Jun 1841; m. 10 Sep 1789, LUKE FENTON, b. at Willington, 20 Dec 1769 son of Asa and Jerusha (Hatch) Fenton; Luke d. after 1850 when he was living in Corinth with his son Darius and his family.[2373]

Chloe and Luke Fenton were parents of twelve children.

i CHLOE FENTON, b. 17 Feb 1790; d. 29 Oct 1790.

ii ORRIN FENTON, b. 13 Apr 1791; d. 1 May 1791.

iii LUKE FENTON, b. 23 Aug 1792; d. at Luzerne, NY, 7 Nov 1848; m. about 1818, ANNA CHURCH, b. about 1800 who has not been identified.

iv WELTHY FENTON, b. 3 Jan 1795; d. at Moriah, NY, 15 Apr 1887; m. EZRA H. BOARDMAN, b. at Corinth, NY, 31 Aug 1791 son of Daniel and Electa (Hickok) Boardman; Ezra d. at Schroon, NY, 19 Apr 1831.

v ORRIN FENTON, b. 23 Apr 1797

vi EUNICE FENTON, b. 21 Aug 1799

vii DARIUS FENTON, b. 20 Oct 1801; d. at Corinth, NY, 12 Feb 1885; m. SARAH EGGLESTON, b. 10 Mar 1801 daughter of John and Lucinda (Standish) Eggleston; Sarah d. at Corinth, 21 Nov 1877.

viii LYMAN FENTON, b. 3 Mar 1804; d. at Rockford, IL, 1884 (will 28 Apr 1884); m. FANNY ROBERTS, b. about 1810 and d. Dec 1877. Lyman and Fanny seem not to have had children. In his will, Lyman left his estate to his housekeeper (his house, all the furnishings and $5,000) and the residue to any of his brothers and sisters now living who came forward within a year and proved their identity.

ix LEWIS FENTON, b. 12 Jan 1806

2373 There is a gravestone in Corinth that gives his death as 1848, but he does seem to be the Luke Fenton listed at age 80 in 1850 in the household of Darius Fenton in Corinth.

x LOUISA FENTON, b. 20 Mar 1809; reported in the Fenton genealogy as marrying Mr. Angle who has not been identified but may be Samuel Smith Angle.

xi HORACE FENTON, b. 12 Mar 1812; d. at Saratoga, NY, 5 Feb 1850; m. about 1839, CAROLINE D. HAMMOND, b. 1819 daughter of George and Nancy (Taber) Hammond;[2374] Caroline d. at Saratoga, 22 Mar 1853.

xii ALMIRA FENTON, b. 27 Mar 1818

898) EUNICE PRESTON (*Darius Preston⁴, Deborah Holt Preston³, Nicholas², Nicholas¹*), b. at Willington, 15 Jul 1777 daughter of Darius and Hannah (Fiske) Preston; d. at Willington, 16 Oct 1807; m. at Willington, 6 Feb 1800, ELIJAH NYE b. at Willington, 15 Sep 1777 son of Benjamin and Mary (Crocker) Nye;[2375] Elijah d. at Willington, 11 Jun 1844. Elijah was the half-brother of Timothy who married Eunice's sister Sarah.

Eunice Preston and Elijah Nye were parents of four children born at Willington.

i POLLY NYE, b. 28 Apr 1801; d. at Willington, 13 May 1875. Polly did not marry.

ii JERUSHA NYE, b. 5 May 1803; d. at Elyria, OH, 19 Oct 1877; m. at Lee, MA, 4 Jul 1825, JOSEPH INGERSOLL, b. at Lee, 25 Dec 1796 son of William and Mercy (Crocker) Ingersoll; Joseph d. at Elyria, 23 Jan 1861.

iii ELIJAH CROCKER NYE, b. 22 May 1805; d. at Somers, 19 Dec 1848; m. at Ellington, 26 Nov 1843, JULIA ANN MCKINNEY, b. at Ellington, 22 Sep 1817 daughter of John and Sarah (Denison) McKinney; Julia d. at Tolland, 25 Jan 1896. Julia was second married to Mr. Eaton.

iv PHEBE NYE, b. 10 Apr 1807; d. at Andover, CT, 25 Mar 1879; m. at Willington, 18 Oct 1835, as his second wife, NATHAN BURNAP, b. 1798; Nathan d. at Coventry, CT, 25 Mar 1886.

899) DEBORAH PRESTON (*Darius Preston⁴, Deborah Holt Preston³, Nicholas², Nicholas¹*), b. at Willington, 30 Apr 1780 daughter of Darius and Hannah (Fiske) Preston; d. at Willington, 14 Oct 1857; m. at Willington, 10 Mar 1803, ABEL JOHNSON, b. at Willington, 28 Sep 1781 son of Abel and Eunice (Merrick) Johnson; Abel d. after 1870 when he was living at Willington.

Abel Johnson was a farmer is Willington. Deborah and Abel were parents of eleven children born a Willington.

i EUNICE JOHNSON, b. 22 Jan 1804; d. 23 Sep 1805.

ii ELISHA JOHNSON, b. 22 Jul 1805; d. at Hartford, CT, 12 Dec 1873; m. at Tolland, 19 Nov 1832, HANNAH CUSHMAN, b. at Willington, 1 Aug 1813 daughter of Joan and Hannah (Swift) Cushman; Hannah d. at Wethersfield, CT, 2 Feb 1899.

iii TRUMAN PRESTON, b. 11 Jan 1807; d. at Willington, 11 Feb 1822.

iv MERRICK JOHNSON, b. 15 Apr 1809; d. at Willimantic, CT, 25 Apr 1895; m. at Willington, 25 Sep 1837, CELINDA GLAZIER, b. at Willington, 25 Jun 1818 daughter of David and Fanny (-) Glazier; Celinda d. at Willimantic, 16 Jan 1896.

v MARCUS JOHNSON, b. 15 Dec 1811; d. at Willington, 27 Aug 1852; m. at Willington, 13 Sep 1834, BETHIAH B. MARTIN, b. 29 Aug 1812 daughter of Elisha Martin; Bethiah d. at Willington, 12 Feb 1875.

vi EUNICE JOHNSON, b. 11 Aug 1812; d. at Westfield, MA, 2 Nov 1890; m. at Willington, 28 Sep 1830, SETH DUNHAM GRIGGS, b. at Tolland, 1 May 1809 son of Roswell and Sarah (Dunham) Griggs; Seth d. at Westfield, 1 Nov 1890.

vii SOPHRONIA JOHNSON, b. 4 Apr 1814; d. at Hartford, CT, 25 Mar 1898; m. at Willington, 2 Aug 1836, her third cousin, ORLAN GLAZIER (*Elizabeth Holt Glazier⁵, Isaac⁴, Abiel³, Nicholas², Nicholas¹*), b. at Willington, 12 May 1805 son of Daniel and Elizabeth (Holt) Glazier; Orlan d. at Willington, 13 Apr 1857.

viii ELIZA JOHNSON, b. 5 Feb 1816; d. 6 Feb 1818.

ix ELIZA JOHNSON, b. 3 Jan 1818; d. (burial at Willington), 3 Jul 1894; m. at Wethersfield, 15 Oct 1849, JOSEPH WALKER PRATT, b. at Hebron, NH, 29 Mar 1821 son of Joseph S. and Sarah (Walker) Pratt; Joseph d. 25 Apr 1898.

x ABEL JOHNSON, b. 15 Dec 1819; d. at Willington, 28 Jul 1861; m. at Willington, 25 Apr 1843, his third cousin once removed, SARAH G. HOLT (*Royal⁶, Caleb⁵, Caleb⁴, Abiel³, Nicholas², Nicholas¹*), b. 6 Nov 1819 daughter of Royal and Lovina (Lamb) Holt; Sarah d. at Willington, Oct 1890.

[2374] The 1839 probate of George Hammond includes heir Caroline Fenton wife of Horace Fenton.

[2375] Nye, *A Genealogy of the Nye Family*, volume 2, p 218

xi TRUMAN JOHNSON, b. 1822; d. at Willington, 30 Nov 1851; m. at Willington, 4 Mar 1844, EMILY FRANCES MERRICK, b. at Willington, 21 Nov 1824 daughter of Gideon N. and Polly (Niles) Merrick; Emily d. at Willington, 21 Apr 1895.

900) AMOS PRESTON (*Darius Preston^4, Deborah Holt Preston^3, Nicholas^2, Nicholas^1*), b. at Willington, 8 Feb 1782 son of Darius and Hannah (Fiske) Preston; d. at Willington, 6 Oct 1864; m. 4 Sep 1804, MARTHA TAYLOR, b. at Willington, 28 Jun 1779 daughter of Thomas and Experience (Freeman) Taylor; Martha d. at Willington, 7 Dec 1860.

Amos Preston was a tanner and lived at Willington Hollow.[2376] There are records of eleven children of Amos and Martha.

i ALMIRA PRESTON, b. 6 Aug 1805; d. at Willington, 30 Jul 1869. Almira did not marry.

ii SALINA PRESTON, b. 22 Dec 1806; d. at Willimantic, CT, 17 Dec 1861; m. at Willington, 23 Mar 1829, ORIGEN B. HALL, b. at Mansfield, CT, 4 Dec 1806 son of Nathan and Philomela (Fisk) Hall; Origen d. at Willimantic, 16 Jul 1888. Origen married second Almira Barrows on 22 Jan 1863.

iii SYLVESTER TAYLOR PRESTON, b. 5 Aug 1808; d. at Willington, 15 Mar 1887; m. at Willington, 16 Sep 1833, FEAR GLAZIER, b. at Willington, 25 Nov 1813 daughter of David and Cylinda (Marcy) Glazier; Fear d. at Willington, 23 Mar 1891.

iv FLORINDA PRESTON, b. 19 Feb 1810; d. at Brooklyn, CT, 20 Oct 1880; m. at Willington, 6 Mar 1833, CALEB DAVIS WILLIAMS, b. at Brooklyn, CT, 12 Oct 1802 son of John and Sukey (Farrington) Williams; Caleb d. at Brooklyn, 21 May 1878.

v OLIVIA PRESTON, b. 5 Oct 1811; d. at Stafford, CT, 7 Jun 1865; m. at Willington, 14 May 1832, JOHN FULLER, b. at Willington, 17 May 1803 son of John and Azubah (Vinton) Fuller; John d. at Stafford, 14 May 1871.

vi JOSHUA PRESTON, b. 15 Jul 1813; d. at Hartford, CT, Apr 1900; m. at Willington, 3 Mar 1835, CAROLINE ELDRIDGE, b. at Willington, 6 Feb 1816 daughter of Arial and Betsey (Dimmock) Eldridge; Caroline d. at Chicago, 27 Apr 1882.

vii HARRIET PRESTON, b. 8 Jan 1815; d. at Windham, 24 Feb 1884; m. at Willington, 1 Feb 1837, ANDREW H. FULLER, b. 19 Oct 1811 son of Daniel and Zernah (Hall) Fuller; Andrew d. at Windham, 27 Apr 1891.

viii LUCIUS PRESTON, b. 12 May 1816; d. at Willington, 23 Dec 1899; m. at Willington, 19 Feb 1839, OLIVIA A. DIMOCK, b. at Tolland, 12 Sep 1815 daughter of Otis and Wealthy (Kinney) Dimock; Olivia d. at Willington, 10 Sep 1888.

ix LOUISA PRESTON, b. 13 Feb 1819; d. at Willington, 6 Apr 1896; m. at Willington, 6 Jul 1841, CHARLES FRANCIS MORRISON, b. at Hebron, 15 Aug 1815 son of Jon and Betsey (Palmer) Morrison; Charles d. at Willington, 12 Sep 1882.

x ORREN PRESTON, b. Mar 1821; d. 22 Jul 1821.

xi CHARLES PRESTON, b. 1822; d. at age 6 years 6 months, 10 Feb 1829.

901) JOHN PECK (*Jerusha Preston Peck^4, Deborah Holt Preston^3, Nicholas^2, Nicholas^1*), b. at Ashford, 8 May 1768 son of John and Jerusha (Preston) Peck; d. at Weston, VT, 21 Sep 1849; m. 1st about 1789, REBECCA BADGER, b. at Ashford, 1 Jan 1768 daughter of Ezekiel and Doratha (Scarborough) Badger; Rebecca d. at Cavendish, VT, about 1810. John m. 2nd about 1811, HANNAH FOSTER (widow of Phineas Austin), b. at Temple, NH, 28 Dec 1771 daughter of James and Hannah (Jewett) Foster; Hannah d. at Weston, 14 Nov 1848.

John Peck and Rebecca Badger were parents of eight children.

i OLIVER PECK, b. at Ashford, CT, 13 Sep 1789; died young.

ii OLIVE PECK, b. at Cavendish, VT, about 1791; d. at Proctorsville, VT, 8 Nov 1840; m. 8 Dec 1808, JOSEPH BALDWIN, b. at Cavendish, VT, 22 Feb 1783 son of Joseph and Elizabeth (Danforth) Baldwin; Joseph d. at Proctorsville, 9 Mar 1860.

iii PALMER PECK, b. at Cavendish, 7 Dec 1793; d. 1816.

iv DOLLY PECK, b. at Cavendish, 15 Jan 1794; d. at Weston, 15 Feb 1870; m. 3 Oct 1818, EPHRAIM KILE, b. at Reading, VT, 16 Sep 1789 son of William and Ruth (Sherwin) Kile; Ephraim d. at Weston, 22 Mar 1872.

2376 Preston, *Descendants of Roger Preston*, p 161

v OLIVER PECK, b. at Cavendish, 24 Jan 1797; d. at Stockbridge, VT, 20 Dec 1878; m. 31 Mar 1819, his stepsister, LUCY AUSTIN, b. 1801 daughter of Phineas and Hannah (Foster) Austin;[2377] Lucy d. at Westminster, 7 Apr 1889.

vi OREN A. PECK, b. at Cavendish, 4 Jul 1799; d. at Weston, 18 Feb 1880; m. 4 Dec 1823, SARAH SHATTUCK, b. 29 Jan 1799 daughter of Parker and Sarah (Spofford) Shattuck; Sarah d. 18 Sep 1884. Sarah married second Lemuel Abbott.

vii EZEKIEL PECK, b. at Cavendish, 24 Jan 1801; d. at Keene, NH, 28 Apr 1891; m. 3 Mar 1831, SINA FENN, b. at Ludlow, VT, 1 Sep 1805 daughter of Austin and Hannah (Ives) Fenn; Sina d. at Troy, NH, 11 Sep 1885.

viii RHODA PECK, b. at Cavendish, 1 Jul 1804; d. 1808.

John Peck and Hannah Foster were parents of two children.

i JAMES FOSTER PECK, b. at Cavendish, 28 Jul 1812; d. at Weston, 31 Jan 1880; m. 1st 29 Apr 1841, PHEBE RHODES, b. 22 Jun 1817 daughter of Amasa and Olive (-) Rhodes; Phebe d. at Weston, 12 Jul 1856. James m. 2nd 16 Oct 1856, MARY BARRETT WINSHIP, b. at Weston, 27 Jun 1828 daughter of John and Sally (Richardson) Winship; Mary d. at Malden, MA, 21 Jun 1895.

ii DANIEL DENNISON PECK, b. at Cavendish, 14 Feb 1817; d. at Weston, 15 Jan 1852; m. 5 Dec 1842, JANE STEVENS, b. at Cambridge, NY,[2378] 28 Feb 1826 daughter of David and Lydia (Fletcher) Stevens; Jane d. at Troy, NH, 20 Apr 1896. Jane married second John H. Condon.

902) ANNA PECK (*Jerusha Preston Peck[4], Deborah Holt Preston[3], Nicholas[2], Nicholas[1]*), b. at Ashford, 10 Sep 1769 daughter of John and Jerusha (Preston) Peck; d. at Rushford, NY, 17 May 1855; m. at Ashford, 29 Jan 1789, ROBERT SNOW,[2379] b. at Ashford, 19 Jun 1763 son of Robert and Sarah (Chubb) Snow; Robert d. at Cavendish, VT, 13 Aug 1806.

On 5 February 1839, Anna Snow of Rushford aged seventy-one appeared before the court of common pleas to provide information related to her application for a widow's pension. She stated that Robert Snow served five years during the Revolution, part of the time with the militia and part of the time in the regular army. One of the enlistments was as substitute for Oliver Utley. He was in two engagements, one of those at White Plains. Anna and Robert married at Ashford 29 January 1789 and soon after moved to Cavendish, Vermont where Robert died on 18 August 1806. For the past seven years (since 1832), Anna resided in Rushford, New York. On 17 March 1855, Anna made application for bounty land to which she might be entitled.[2380] Anna did not leave a will and administration of her estate was granted to her son-in-law Samuel White on 16 June 1856.[2381]

Robert Snow did not leave a will and his estate entered probate 5 September 1806 with David Chubb and Anna Snow as administrators. Anna Snow was allowed as guardian to Clary Snow, who was over fourteen, Anna agreeing to pay to Clary what was due from the estate "when she shall arrive at full age." Anna was also named guardian to Alden, Warren, Percy, Nancy, and Sybil on 5 September 1806. Later, Reuben Chapman was allowed as guardian for Alden and Anna continued as guardian to the other children. On 15 June 1809, it was determined that the personal estate was not sufficient to cover the debts and a portion of the real estate needed to be sold. Clary signed a statement that she had no objection to the sale of part of the real estate for the support of the family.[2382]

Robert and Anna were parents of seven children born at Cavendish, Vermont.

i CLARY SNOW, b. about 1790. Clary was living in 1809 but nothing further known.

ii ALDEN SNOW, b. 1 Feb 1793; d. at Mount Vernon, OH, 26 Mar 1880; m. 1st at Geauga County, OH, 19 Jul 1827, RUTH PARKER who d. at Mount Vernon about 1849. Alden m. 2nd at Knox, OH, 20 May 1851, MATILDA T. CRUTCHLY, b. in MD about 1805; Matilda d. at Mount Vernon, 1889.

iii WARNER SNOW, b. 10 Apr 1795; d. at Rushford, NY, about 1840; m. about 1828, his third cousin, ALMIRA RUMRILL (*Polly Holt Rumrill[5], Asa[4], Daniel[3], Nicholas[2], Nicholas[1]*), b. about 1808 daughter of Simeon and Polly (Holt) Rumrill; Almira d. at Rushford, 26 Aug 1894. Polly married second Winthrop G. Young.

iv PERCY SNOW, b. 8 Nov 1798; d. at Rushford, NY, 20 Sep 1875; m. 26 Nov 1818, SAMUEL WHITE, b. at Cavendish, VT, 16 Jan 1795 son of Thomas and Betsey (Lincoln) White; Samuel d. at Rushford, 15 May 1874.

2377 Lucy's parents' names are given as Phineas and Hannah Austin on her death record.

2378 Jane's place of birth is given as Cambridge, NY on her death record.

2379 The marriage transcription gives the name of Abigail Peck as the wife of Robert Snow, but other records (for example the Revolutionary War pension file) establish that Robert married Anna.

2380 Revolutionary War Pension and Bounty-Land Warrant Application Files, 1800-1900, Case W25041

2381 *Record of Wills, Other Miscellaneous Surrogate Records, 1807-1930;* Author: *New York. Surrogate's Court (Allegany County);* Probate Place: *Allegany, New York, Letter of Administration, volume 001, p 125*

2382 *Vermont. Probate Court (Windsor District);* Probate Place: *Windsor, Vermont, Estate of Robert Snow*

v JEFFERSON SNOW, b. 18 Mar 1801; nothing further known. Jefferson was not part of the guardianship case for the other children.

vi NANCY SNOW, b. 18 Apr 1803; d. at Otho, IA, 19 May 1891; m. at Rushford, 18 Aug 1826, BENJAMIN J. CHENEY, b. 3 Apr 1803 son of Benjamin and Eunice (Hubbard) Cheney; Benjamin d. at Otho, 30 Mar 1882.

vii SYBIL SNOW, b. May 1806

903) ELISHA PECK (*Jerusha Preston Peck*[4], *Deborah Holt Preston*[3], *Nicholas*[2], *Nicholas*[1]), b. at Ashford, 25 Mar 1777 son of John and Jerusha (Preston) Peck; d. at Abington, 26 Sep 1866; m. 1st at Ashford, 23 Sep 1802, SARAH BADGER, b. at Ashford, 26 Apr 1771 daughter of Ezekiel and Doratha (Scarborough) Badger; Sarah d. at Pomfret, 6 Mar 1843. Sarah had an out-of-wedlock daughter Myra Ingraham prior to her marriage to Elisha. Elisha m. 2nd 29 Oct 1844, MARY WHITMAN, b. about 1790; Mary d. at Abington, 9 Feb 1860.

Elisha Peck and Sarah Badger were parents of three children.[2383]

i POLLY PECK, b. at Ashford, 29 Jul 1803; d. 2 Apr 1805.

ii ALANSON PECK, b. at Pomfret, 30 Jun 1805; d. at Ashford, 10 Dec 1886; m. 13 Apr 1829, ABIGAIL CARPENTER, b. 19 Dec 1802 daughter of Joseph Titus and Huldah (Davison) Carpenter; Abigail d. at Ashford, 14 May 1889.

iii MINERVA PECK, b. at Ashford, 19 Apr 1809; d. after 1880 when she was living in Eastford; m. at Pomfret, 2 Apr 1839, CYREL W. KENT, b. in Rhode Island, about 1815 son of James and Betsy (Whittaker) Kent; Cyrel d. at Eastford, about 1900 (probate 1900).

904) ALICE POOL (*Deborah Preston Pool*[4], *Deborah Holt Preston*[3], *Nicholas*[2], *Nicholas*[1]), b. at Willington, 11 Dec 1765 daughter of Timothy and Deborah (Preston) Pool; m. at Willington, 18 Mar 1782, JOSEPH FENTON, b. at Willington, 28 Feb 1760 son of Samuel and Experience (Ingalls) Fenton; Joseph d. at Willington, 12 May 1814.

Joseph Fenton did not leave a will and the dower was set off to widow Alice on 11 July 1814. The settlement of Joseph Fenton's estate on 14 July 1817 included distributions to the following heirs: son Nathan Fenton, son Joseph Fenton, son Alva Fenton, son Miner Fenton, daughter Julia King, daughter Amy Fenton, daughter Lois Fenton, daughter Experience Badcock, and daughter Alice Fenton.[2384]

Alice Pool and Joseph Fenton were parents of eleven children born at Willington.

i LOIS FENTON, b. at Willington, 7 Feb 1783; d. at Charleston, PA, after 1860; m. at Willington, 6 Feb 1800, ELIJAH FENTON, b. at Willington, 18 Oct 1778 son of Asa and Jerusha (Hatch) Fenton; Elijah d. at Charleston, after 1850.

ii EXPERIENCE FENTON, b. at Willington, 17 Nov 1784; d. at Tolland, 6 Jan 1846; m. at Tolland, 24 Nov 1803, CHESTER BABCOCK, b. at Mansfield, CT, 8 Jun 1781 son of Elijah and Ruth (King) Babcock; Chester d. at Tolland, 12 Dec 1864. Chester married second the widow Olive D. Fuller on 20 Sep 1846.

iii DEBORAH FENTON, b. 26 Apr 1769; d. Jul 1771.

iv MARY "POLLY" FENTON, b. 17 Aug 1790; d. at Willington, 13 Apr 1814.

v AMY FENTON, b. at Willington, 23 Oct 1792; d. at Homer, NY, 3 Mar 1867; m. 20 Nov 1817, WILLIAM MARTIN HIBBARD, b. at Mansfield, CT, 9 Sep 1795 son of Andrew and Ruth (Loomis) Hibbard; William d. at Homer, 7 Jun 1861.

vi JULIA FENTON, b. at Willington, 1 Jan 1795; d. at Mansfield, CT, 13 Sep 1850; m. ALVA KING, b. about 1793; Alva d. at Mansfield, 10 Jun 1852.

vii NATHAN FENTON, b. at Willington, 5 May 1797; d. at Hartford, 4 Dec 1873; m. LUCINDA HUGHES, b. 1798; Lucinda d. at Hartford, 1870.

viii JOSEPH FENTON, b. at Willington, 17 Dec 1801. It is possible that he married Mary Parker and relocated to Pennsylvania, but that is not certain.

ix ALBRAY FENTON, b. 13 Sep 1803; likely died young.

[2383] Peck's *Genealogical History of the Descendants of Joseph Peck*, p 281, reports daughters Jerusha born in 1795 and Betsey born in 1796, but these births are several years before the marriage of Elisha Peck and Sarah Badger. Perhaps Elisha had an earlier marriage but that would require his marrying before age eighteen which would not be typical for this period.

[2384] *Connecticut State Library (Hartford, Connecticut)*; Probate Place: *Hartford, Connecticut, Probate Packets, Enos-Foskit, John, 1759-1880, Estate of Joseph Fenton, Case 768*

x ALVA FENTON, b. at Willington, 4 Apr 1806; d. at Windsor, CT, 23 Apr 1891; m. 1830, ELIZABETH B. PORTER, b. 10 Mar 1809 daughter of William and Mary (Burt) Porter.

xi MINER FENTON, b. at Willington, 22 Nov 1808; d. at Enfield, CT, 18 Oct 1870; m. 1st at Stafford, 8 Dec 1834, EMILY STROUD who died about 1836. Miner m. 2nd at Stafford, 6 Nov 1836, CAROLINA CARPENTER.

905) ANNA POOL (*Deborah Preston Pool⁴, Deborah Holt Preston³, Nicholas², Nicholas¹*), b. at Willington, 8 May 1767 daughter of Timothy and Deborah (Preston) Pool; d. at Willington, 12 Oct 1831; m. at Willington, 9 Apr 1795, ERASTUS EDWARDS, b. at Coventry, 1770 son of Erastus and Anna (Porter) Edwards; Erastus d. at Willington, 24 Nov 1850. Erastus was first married to Jerusha Fuller who died in 1794.

Anna Pool and Erastus Edwards were parents of five children born at Willington.

i JERUSHA EDWARDS, b. 19 Jul 1796; d. at Willington, 31 Jul 1829. Jerusha did not marry.

ii ANNA EDWARDS, b. 22 Jul 1798; nothing further known.

iii ERASTUS EDWARDS, b. 4 Oct 1801; d. at Willington, 4 Nov 1880; m. at Thompson, 27 Feb 1837, MARY ANN CHILDS, b. at Woodstock, 1807 daughter of Cyril and Mary (Bartholomew) Childs; Mary Ann d. at Woodstock, 8 Dec 1883.

iv AMOS PORTER EDWARDS, b. 3 Sep 1804; d. at Thompson, CT, 13 Aug 1843; m. at Thompson, 8 Dec 1828, CAROLINE CORBIN, b. at Thompson, 5 May 1806 daughter of Alpheus and Lucy (Prince) Corbin;[2385] Caroline d. at Worcester, 3 Jun 1893.

v DEBORAH EDWARDS, b. 19 Apr 1807; d. at Worcester, MA, 30 Sep 1887; m. about 1860, as his second wife, HEZEKIAH ELDREDGE, b. at Ashford, 2 Nov 1796 son of Elijah and Bethiah (Chapman) Eldredge; Hezekiah d. 11 Dec 1881. Hezekiah was first married to Laura Chapman.

906) AMY POOL (*Deborah Preston Pool⁴, Deborah Holt Preston³, Nicholas², Nicholas¹*), b. at Willington, 7 Aug 1775 daughter of Timothy and Deborah (Preston) Pool; d. at Willington, about 1817;[2386] m. at Willington, 24 Dec 1795, her second cousin once removed, ELIJAH SAWIN (*Mary Fenton Sawin⁵, Elizabeth Holt Fenton⁴, Abiel³, Nicholas², Nicholas¹*), b. at Willington, 31 Oct 1774 son of Isaac and Mary (Fenton) Sawin; Elijah d. at Willington, about 1814 (probate 1814).

Isaac, son of Amy and Elijah, provided some communication for the preparation of Sawin's *Summary Notes Concerning John Sawin*. He reported that his father Elijah was the only child of his father Isaac and was orphaned when his father died in the war. The family lived in Willington. In 1851, son Isaac reported he was the only child still living and that he then resided in North Bergen. His brother operated a tavern in Massachusetts.[2387]

Elijah Sawin did not leave a will and Amy Sawin was named administratrix. Real estate included 54 acres with buildings valued at $500 but still incumbered by the dower thirds of Elijah's mother Mary Fenton Sawin Niles. The widow thirds were set off to Amy on 1 November 1815. The remainder of the estate real and personal was equally divided among the children Isaac, Ephraim, Elizabeth, and Lucy with the sons receiving their shares from the real property as far as the estate would allow.[2388]

Amy Pool and Elijah Sawin were parents of six children born at Willington.

i ELIZABETH SAWIN, b. 5 Jun 1797; living in 1815.

ii ROENA SAWIN, b. 22 Oct 1800; d. 11 Mar 1801.

iii ISAAC SAWIN, b. at Willington, 2 Mar 1804; d. at Sherwood, MI, 12 May 1898; m. ELEANOR HAMMOND, b. in CT, 11 Feb 1806 daughter of Eli and Olivia (Howard) Hammond; Eleanor d. at Sherwood, 21 Jan 1887. This family was in Bergen, NY before relocating to Michigan.

iv EPHRAIM SAWIN, b. at Willington, 21 Mar 1806; d. at Ludlow, MA, 22 Jan 1835 (probate 3 Mar 1835); m. at Springfield, MA, 12 Oct 1831, ELIZA HAYDEN. After Ephraim's death, Eliza married David Pease of Ludlow on 9 Apr 1840.

v MANERVA SAWIN, b. 23 Aug 1808; died young.

[2385] The names of Caroline's parents are given as Alpheus Corbin and Lucy Prince on her death record.

[2386] Sawin, *Sawin: Summary Notes Concerning John Sawin*, p 38

[2387] Sawin, *Sawin: Summary Notes Concerning John Sawin*, p 38

[2388] *Connecticut State Library (Hartford, Connecticut)*; Probate Place: *Hartford, Connecticut, Probate Packets, Rockwell, N-Sessions, O, 1759-1880, Estate of Elijah Sawin, Case 1877*

vi LUCY SAWIN, b. at Willington, 11 Oct 1812; d. at Alabama, NY, 20 Jun 1849; m. at Bergen, about 1840, HIRAM HOTCHKISS, b. perhaps at New Haven, 1815 son of Moses and Lucy (Griswold) Hotchkiss;[2389] Hiram d. at Alabama, NY, 11 Jan 1848. Lucy had gone to Bergen, NY with her brother Isaac.

907) ABIGAIL HOLT (*Daniel[4], Daniel[3], Nicholas[2], Nicholas[1]*), b. at Pomfret, 29 Mar 1761 daughter of Daniel and Kezia (Rust) Holt; d. after 1829; m. about 1783, WILLIAM AVERILL, b. at Windham, 19 Apr 1755 son of Stephen and Sarah (Handee) Averill;[2390] William d. at Warren, NY, 1829 (probate 3 Oct 1829).

William and Abigail stated their family in Pomfret but were in Montgomery County, New York by 1790 and later in Warren, New York.[2391]

In his will written 5 May 1828 (proved 3 October 1829), William Averill bequeaths to beloved wife Abigail one-third of the real estate and all the money in his possession at the time of his decease. He also notes that he is due a legacy from his father Stephen's estate, and if that is not received before his death, that legacy is to go to Abigail. If Abigail accepts the legacy from Stephen Averill's estate that is in lieu of her dower. Son Charles receives two hundred dollars in addition to what he has received. Other children receiving two hundred dollars are son Elijah Averill, daughter Arminda wife of Michael Mann, daughter Sophia wife of Robert Henry, and daughter Betsey wife of John Shepherd. These legacies are to be paid is six annual installments. The remainder of the estate goes to daughter Mira wife of Timothy Green and Mira also receives the other one-third of the real estate after the decease of her mother. Mira is responsible for paying the debts and the legacies. Executors named were wife Abigail, Timothy Green, and Muzo White. In a codicil likely 25 April 1829 (although in the will book written as 25 April 1828), William made some adjustments to the legacy providing a lot of land for the benefit of the children of his son Elijah. There were other adjustments made based on payments made or received from his children. Of specific interest was the lot of land which at that time was in the hands of John Shepherd husband of daughter Betsey and there had been agreement that John would place that property in trust, but he had not done so.[2392] Son Elijah was still living at that time and so this may represent that William saw a special need for Elijah's children.

Abigail Holt and William Averill were parents of six children.

i ARMINDA AVERILL, b. likely at Pomfret, about 1783; d. at Detroit, after 1852; m. MICHAEL D. MANN

ii CHARLES HOLT AVERILL, b. 7 Oct 1786; d. at Niagara, NY, 28 Jan 1858; m. AGNES B. MARSH, b. 4 Feb 1781; Agnes d. at Niagara, 7 Sep 1858.

iii ELIJAH AVERILL, b. (recorded) at Pomfret, 2 Jul 1788; d. after 1830 when he was living at Warren, NY; m. 26 Nov 1812, SUSAN SLAYTON, b. at Chester, MA, 27 Jan 1789 daughter of Reuben and Mary (Moore) Slayton; Susan d. after 1875 when she was living at Minden, NY.

iv SOPHIA AVERILL, b. about 1791; m. ROBERT HENRY

v BETSEY AVERILL, b. about 1794; m. JOHN SHEPHARD

vi ALMIRA "MIRA" AVERILL, b. about 1796; d. after 1855 when she was living in Warren, NY; m. TIMOTHY GREEN, b. in NY about1791; Timothy d. after 1855.

908) KEZIAH HOLT (*Daniel[4], Daniel[3], Nicholas[2], Nicholas[1]*), b. at Pomfret, 29 Mar 1761 daughter of Daniel and Kezia (Rust) Holt; d. at Buffalo, NY, 13 Jan 1820; m. at Pomfret, 8 Apr 1784, ROWLAND COTTON, b. at Pomfret, 22 Mar 1759 son of Samuel and Mary (Dresser) Cotton; Rowland d. at Attica, NY, 11 Jun 1847.

Rowland Cotton, through a series of enlistments, served for the entire period of the Revolution in the Continental army increasing in rank from private to first sergeant by the end of the war. He was at the battles of Trenton, Harlem Heights, at the crossing of the Delaware with George Washington, the battles of Princeton, Germantown, and Fort Mifflin, and wintered at Valley Forge. In the War of 1812 beginning 16 December 1813, he served as captain and acting brigade quartermaster under General Timothy S. Hopkins. Rowland was wounded in the knee during the retreat from Black Rock on 30 December 1813 and was discharged 26 January 1814 due to his injury. He was allowed pension with a starting date of 27 January 1814. He was also allowed pension based on his service in the Revolution.

Following the wars, Rowland was in Buffalo in 1817 and had relocated to Attica before 1832. In 1851, inquiry was made by the children regarding possible payments. The children living in 1851 were Lester H. cotton of Milwaukee, Wisconsin; Samuel Cotton of Jackson County, Iowa; Mary Cotton of Wyoming County, New York; Daniel H. Cotton of Erie County, New York, and Elijah H. Cotton of Wyoming County, New York.[2393]

Rowland did not leave a will and Elijah H. Cotton was named administrator on 5 October 1847.[2394] Keziah Holt and Rowland Cotton were parents of five children.

[2389] Beers, *Gazetteer and Biographical Record of Genesee County, NY, 1788-1890*, p 130

[2390] Avery, *The Averill Family*, p 397

[2391] Avery, *The Averill Family*, p 397

[2392] Ancestry.com. *New York, Wills and Probate Records, 1659-1999* [database on-line]. *Wills, Vol E-F, 1828-1841, volume E, pp 56-58*

[2393] U.S. Revolutionary War Pension and Bounty-Land Warrant Application Files, Case S11170

[2394] New York Wills and Probate Records, Wyoming County, Miscellaneous Records, volume 1, p 169

i SAMUEL COTTON, b. likely at Cherry Valley, about 1788; d. at Cottonville, IA, 3 Sep 1866; m. about 1820, MARY BEMUS, b. about 1789 daughter of Jotham and Asenath (Andress) Bemus;[2395] Mary d. at Cottonville, 27 Nov 1865.

ii MARY COTTON, b. about 1790 (based on age 68 at time of death); d. at Attica, NY, 16 Oct 1858. Mary did not marry. She resided with her brother Elijah in 1850. In her will written 23 August 1847, Mary bequeathed to her brother Elijah H. Cotton and Clarissa his wife all her estate in Attica for their use during their natural lives. After their decease, the estate is to be divided among the heirs of Elijah and Clarissa and brothers Lester H., Samuel, and Daniel H. Cotton.[2396]

iii DANIEL H. COTTON, b. 8 Feb 1794; d. at Cottonville, IA, 5 Jul 1881; m. 13 Jan 1822, CEMANTHA DODGE, b. 7 Mar 1804 daughter of Alvan and Mary (Blount) Dodge; Cemantha d. at Cottonville, 1 Oct 1861.

iv ELIJAH H. COTTON, b. at Cherry Valley, 21 Jul 1800; d. at Pavilion, NY, 31 Jul 1882; m. at Clarkson, NY, 21 Sep 1825, CLARISSA KENNEDY, b. about 1805; Clarissa d. at Pavilion, 10 May 1886.

v LESTER HOLT COTTON, b. at Canandaigua, NY, 4 Sep 1804; d. at Detroit, MI, 4 Jan 1878 (probate Wayne County, MI, 1878); m. 1st at Monroe, MI, 3 Jul 1833, MARY ANNA WHITE, b. at Troy, NY, 1814 daughter of Marvin and Abigail (Dexter) White; Mary Anna d. at Milwaukee, WI, 18 Jan 1849. Lester m. 2nd 1850, the widow SARAH L. CULLY, b. in NY, about 1822; Sarah d. at Detroit, 26 Aug 1880.

909) ELIJAH HOLT (*Daniel⁴, Daniel³, Nicholas², Nicholas¹*), b. at Pomfret, 9 Jun 1762 son of Daniel and Kezia (Rust) Holt; d. at Cherry Valley, NY, 25 Sep 1826; m. 1st ELIZABETH WILLIAMS, b. at Pomfret, 2 Apr 1768 daughter of Ebenezer and Jerusha (Porter) Williams; Elizabeth d. 16 Jan 1796. Elijah m. 2nd at Woodstock, 20 Feb 1797, MARY "POLLY" ADAMS, b. at Windham, 10 Dec 1771 daughter of David and Lucy (Fitch) Adams;[2397] Mary d. at Buffalo, 3 Jan 1820.

Known as General Elijah Holt, Elijah was active in military affairs of Cherry Valley, New York. He was representative to the General Assembly of New York in 1798 and served as a justice in Cherry Valley.[2398]

Elijah Holt and Elizabeth Williams were parents of four children.

i OLIVE HOLT, b. 1787; d. at Buffalo, NY, 13 Apr 1837; m. ELISHA ENSIGN, b. 5 Feb 1785 son of Elisha and Sally (Gay) Ensign; Elisha d. at Buffalo, 12 Sep 1852.

ii JERUSHA WILLIAMS HOLT, b. at Cherry Valley, 30 Jan 1791; d. at Cherry Valley, 24 Dec 1834; m. at Cherry Valley, 1809, ERASTUS JOHNSON, b. at Middletown, CT, 9 Apr 1786 son of Jesse and Mary (Stevenson) Johnson;[2399] Erastus d. at Cherry Valley, 25 Mar 1837.

iii ELIZABETH HOLT, b. about 1792; reported to have died accidentally during childhood.[2400]

iv WILLIAMS HOLT, b. at Cherry Valley, 12 Jul 1795; d. at Winnebago, IL, 18 May 1876; m. LOUISA VIBBARD, b. about 1809 daughter of Leonard and Elizabeth (Klumph) Vibbard;[2401] Louisa d. at Winnebago, 20 Oct 1875.

Elijah Holt and Mary Adams were parents of seven children likely all born at Cherry Valley.

i DAVID ADAMS HOLT, b. at Cherry Valley, 6 May 1800; d. at Winnebago, IL, 13 Jul 1839; m. SILVIA HAWKS, b. 20 Nov 1801 daughter of Joseph and Nancy (Alvord) Hawks; Silvia d. at Winnebago, 3 Jan 1889. David Adams and Silvia were in Winnebago County, IL by 1835.[2402]

ii MARY HOLT; m. (per Durrie's Holt genealogy), Rev. WILLIAM PARSONS. Records were not located for this couple.

iii ELIZA WILLIAMS HOLT, b. about 1804; d. at Westfield, 10 Mar 1858; m. 1st (according to Durrie) an unknown Mr. Higgins. Eliza m. 2nd 1838, ABRAM DIXON, b. at Manchester, VT, 23 Jul 1787 son of Joseph and Mercy Raymond Dixon; Abram d. at Westfield, 19 Apr 1875. Abram was first married to Caroline Pelton.

2395 Mary's mother Asenath Bemus was living with Samuel and Mary Cotton in Richland, IA in 1850.
2396 New York Wills and Probate Records, Wyoming County, Wills volume 3, pp 380-381
2397 The 1814 will of Lucy Adams widow of David of Pomfret includes a bequest to her daughter Polly Holt wife of Elijah Holt.
2398 Sawyer, *History of Cherry Valley, New York*, p 51, p 59, and p 63
2399 Cutter, *Genealogical and Family History of Central New York*, volume 2, p 844
2400 Durrie, Holt Genealogy
2401 Klumph, *Klumph Genealogy and Early Klumph History*, p 33
2402 H.F. Kett, History of Winnebago County, Illinois, p 236

iv HARRIET HOLT, b. about 1808; d. after 1875 when she was living at Westfield, NY; m. 1st Dr. PETER CANER, b. at Herkimer County, NY, 15 Dec 1800;[2403] Peter d. at Warsaw, NY, 2 Apr 1854. Harriet m. 2nd ELAM CHAFFEE BLISS, b. at Skaneateles, NY, 13 Nov 1802 son of Edward Upham and Mary (Chaffee) Bliss; Elam d. at Westfield, 6 May 1882. Elam Bliss was first married to Mary Harmon. Dr. Peter Caner attended Fairfield Medical College and had a successful practice in Warsaw.

v HORATIO NELSON HOLT, b. 8 Jan 1811; d. at Brooklyn, NY (buried at Buffalo), 19 May 1894;[2404] m. at Buffalo, 24 Jul 1839, ABBY GOODMAN SEYMOUR, b. 19 Jun 1815 daughter of Henry R. and Elizabeth (Selden) Seymour; Abby d. at Brooklyn, 7 Feb 1865.

vi GEORGE WASHINGTON HOLT, b. 25 Nov 1813; d. at Westfield, NY, 4 Jan 1889; m. 1863, AMELIA BENTON HARRINGTON, b. at Westfield, 1 Mar 1839 daughter of Jonas and Ruby (Benton) Harrington; Amelia d. at Westfield, 20 May 1904.[2405]

vii ELIJAH HOLT, b. 1817; d. at Edinboro, PA, 1888; m. about 1843, LAURA CONANT, b. about 1820 daughter of Origen and Mary (Butler) Conant;[2406] Laura d. at Edinboro, 1895.

910) LESTER HOLT (*Daniel[4], Daniel[3], Nicholas[2], Nicholas[1]*), b. at Pomfret, 21 Feb 1766 son of Daniel and Kezia (Rust) Holt; d. at Cherry Valley, NY, 11 Jan 1841; m. about 1789, CATHERINE CLYDE, b. 1769 daughter of Samuel and Catherine (Wasson) Clyde; Catherine d. at Cherry Valley, 16 May 1848.

Major Lester Holt served in the War of 1812.

In his will written 13 Aug 1839 (probate 31 May 1841), Lester Holt of Cherry Valley bequeathed to beloved wife Catherine ten shares of the Central Bank, all the household furnishings, use of the house, and provisions for her support to be provided by Horatio Holt. This bequest is in lieu of her dower. He gives to the executors the lot of land and house in Fort Plain currently occupied by son Daniel. The executors are to use this for the support of Daniel's children and after Daniel's death, the property will go to Daniel's children. Son Daniel also receives $300 in cash which goes to the executors to give to Daniel in small amounts as needed. Daughter Morgiana Danforth wife of Thomas P. Danforth of Middleburgh receives fifteen shares in the Central Bank. Son Lester Holt receives two thousand dollars charged upon the land and property that is being devised to him. Son Horatio receives the property in Cherry Valley where Lester now lives. Son Henry receives property of the west side of Alden Street in Cherry Valley. Henry also receives ten shares of bank stock and the value of a judgment owed to Lester in the amount of $560. Daughter Lucia Marvin wife of Dan Marvin receives fifteen shares of bank stock and $200. Son William Holt receives thirty shares in the Schenectady and Utica railroad. Granddaughter Catherine Jane Magher receives $100. Son Horatio Holt and Horace Lathrop of Cooperstown were named executors.

There are the following heirs noted in the probate: a widow, Horatio Holt of Cherry Valley; William W. Holt of Cherry Valley; Daniel Holt of Fort Plain; Kezia Stewart wife of Alvan Stewart of Utica; Morgiana Danforth wife of Thomas P. Danforth of Middleburgh; Lucia Marvin wife of Dan Marvin of the city of New York; Henry Holt of Fort Brady, Michigan; Lester J. Magher of Michigan City, Indiana, and Catherine J. Magher of unknown location children of Jane Magher deceased; Catherine M. Holt, Martha Holt, Horatio H. Holt, and Chester Holt children of Lester Holt deceased of Mount Hope in Lawrence County, Alabama. Benjamin Davis of Cherry Valley was named special guardian to look after the interests of Lester's children and Peter Magher was special guardian for Jane's children.[2407] Daughter Kezia is not mentioned in the will but is listed as one of the heirs-at-law.

Lester Holt and Catherine Clyde were parents of eleven children likely all born at Cherry Valley, New York.

i JANE CLYDE HOLT, b. 1790; d. at Cherry Valley, NY, 4 May 1835; m. 25 Nov 1810, PETER MAGHER, b. about 1777; Peter d. at Cooperstown, 16 Jun 1854.

ii DANIEL HOLT, b. 1 Dec 1792; d. at Fort Plain, NY, 1866; m. 20 Jun 1828, ANN BECKER, b. Oct 1807; Ann d. 7 Apr 1841.

iii KEZIA HOLT, b. about 1793; d. at New York, NY, 2 Dec 1854; m. 1819, ALVAN STEWART, b. at Granville, NY, 1 Sep 1790 son of Uriel and Anna (Holgate) Stewart; Alvan d. at New York, 14 May 1850.

iv LESTER HOLT, b. about 1797; d. at Mount Hope, AL, Sep 1840; m. at Lawrence County, AL, 29 Mar 1832, MARY E. CLEERE who has not been firmly identified. Mary married second R. C. Oglesby on 16 Nov 1843. Lester had some type of medical practice in Mount Hope as his estate inventory includes medical supplies. Lester was also postmaster.

[2403] Young, *History of the Town of Warsaw, New York*, p 244

[2404] New York, New York, Death Index, 1862-1948

[2405] The family relationships are confirmed by the DAR application of the daughter of George W. and Amelia Holt, Alice E. Holt.

[2406] Conant, *A History and Genealogy of the Conant Family*, p 547

[2407] *Wills and Administrations, 1792-1902;* Author: *New York. Surrogate's Court (Otsego County), Wills and Administrations, Book 0005-0007, 1840-1846, pp 61-76*

v MORGIANNA HOLT, b. about 1800; d. at Middleburgh, NY, 1873 (probate 1873); m. 10 Oct 1838, as his fourth wife, THOMAS PAINE DANFORTH, b. 20 Jun 1781 son of Jonathan and Judah (Spalding) Danforth; Thomas d. at Middleburgh, 1865. Thomas was a Judge. He was first married to Nancy Wager, second married to Sarah Donolly and third married to Angeline Hathaway.

vi CHARLES HOLT, b. 1802; d. at Fort St. Philip, LA, 24 Sep 1824. Charles graduated from West Point and had rank of 2nd Lieutenant, July 1823.

vii HORATIO HOLT, b. 12 Apr 1803; d. at Cherry Valley, 30 Jun 1859. Horatio did not marry.

viii CATHERINE HOLT, b. 1805; d. at Cherry Valley, 29 May 1834 of consumption.

ix HENRY HOLT, b. about 1810; d. at Washington, DC, after 1881. Henry was an army surgeon stationed at Fort Brady, Michigan and later in Washington, DC. He is likely the Henry C. Holt (a physician) who married at Norfolk, VA, 22 May 1843, SARAH JANE TUCKER (widow of Andrew McD. Jackson), b. in Virginia about 1811. Sarah was living in 1880.

x WILLIAM W. HOLT, b. 12 May 1812; d. at Middletown, CT (burial at Cherry Valley), 2 Feb 1885; m. MARIA FANNING, b. about 1832 daughter of John and Clarissa (Hoyt) Fanning; Maria d. at Brooklyn, 17 May 1910.

xi LUCIA L. HOLT, b. 5 Dec 1813; b. at Brooklyn, NY, 29 Nov 1880; m. 25 Feb 1835, DAN MARVIN, b. at Fairfield, NY, 17 Dec 1808 son of Reinold and Mabel (Bushnell) Marvin;[2408] Dan d. 17 Oct 1884.

911) OLIVE HOLT (*Daniel⁴, Daniel³, Nicholas², Nicholas¹*), b. at Pomfret, 15 Oct 1768 daughter of Daniel and Kezia (Rust) Holt; d. 20 Sep 1792; m. 1787, JOSEPH WHITE, b. at Chatham, CT, 26 Sep 1762 son of Joseph and Ruth (Churchill) White; Joseph d, at Cherry Valley, 3 Jun 1832. Joseph second married Olive's sister DEBORAH HOLT, b. at Pomfret, 1 Feb 1775; Deborah d. at Cherry Valley, 23 Aug 1827.

Dr. Joseph White served in the Revolution in Captain Rudd's Company in August and September 1778. He was a physician in Cherry Valley. He served as state senator 1796-1797 and was county judge of Otsego County for twenty-one years beginning in 1800.[2409]

In this will written 30 May 1832 (proved 7 July 1832), Joseph White, M.D. bequeathed to son Delos White, M.D., in addition to what he has received, all the securities that he holds against him including mortgages and notes. He also receives dividends of 100 shares from the Central Bank during his natural life and the shares to revert to grandson Joseph L. White and granddaughter Lavantia White. Delos also receives one thousand dollars. Son Menzo White, M.D. receives all the medical books and instruments, fifty shares in the Central Bank, all the shares of stock in the Albany turnpike, and 209 acres of land known as the Clyde farm. Daughter Lavantia the wife of Jacob Livingston, in addition to the part of the home farm she has received, receives the remainder of the farm to be held in trust for grandson Joseph W. Livingston and granddaughter Lavantia Livingston until they reach age twenty-five. Daughter Lavantia also receives one hundred shares of stock in Central Bank and all the domestic animals and husbandry utensils. Son Joseph White receives $9000 in bonds and mortgages. Son George receives 250 shares in Central Bank and the lands in Cary's patent. The remainder of the estate is to be divided among children Menzo White, Lavintia Livingston, Joseph White, and George White except his gold watch which goes to granddaughter Lavintia Livingston. Joseph White, Jacob Livingston, and Horace Lathrop were named executors.[2410]

Olive Holt and Joseph White were parents of one child.

i DELOS WHITE, b. at Cherry Valley, about 1790; d. at Cherry Valley, 18 Mar 1835; m. ELIZA OLIVIA LITTLE, b. at Springfield, MA, 9 Nov 1795 daughter of David and Alice (Loomis) Little; Eliza d. at Cherry Valley, 15 Jan 1862.

Deborah Holt and Joseph White were parents of four children.

i MENZO WHITE, b. at Cherry Valley, 19 Oct 1793; d. at Cherry Valley, 16 Jan 1858. Menzo did not marry.

ii LEVANTIA WHITE, b. at Cherry Valley, 15 Nov 1795; d. at Cherry Valley, 6 Sep 1889; m. at Cherry Valley, 26 Jun 1821, as his second wife, JACOB LIVINGSTON, b. 1780 son of John and Mary Anne (LeRoy) Livingston; Jacob d. at Cherry Valley, 19 May 1865. Jacob was first married to Catherine De Peyster.

iii JOSEPH WHITE, b. at Cherry Valley, 26 Nov 1801; d. at Westfield, NY, 22 Sep 1840. Joseph did not marry.

iv GEORGE WASHINGTON WHITE, b. at Cherry Valley, 9 Aug 1809; d. at Cherry Valley, 1867; m. May 1834, MARY PHELON, b. at Litchfield, CT, 3 Sep 1815 daughter of Joseph and Alcena (Denslow) Phelon; Mary d. at Cherry Valley, 1878.

2408 Marvin, *Descendants of Reinold and Matthew Marvin*, p 184

2409 Williams, Descendants of Thomas White of Weymouth

2410 *New York, Wills and Probate Records, 1659-1999, Otsego County, Wills and Administrations, Book 0001-0002, 1830-1836, pp 176-178*

912) MARY HOLT (*Daniel⁴, Daniel³, Nicholas², Nicholas¹*), b. at Pomfret, 28 Apr 1771 daughter of Daniel and Kezia (Rust) Holt; d. at Cherry Valley, 19 Mar 1819; m. 1st about 1791, JOSEPH CLARY who has not been identified; Joseph d. about 1800. Mary m. 2nd 4 Feb 1803, JOHN DIELL, b. 1769; John d. at Cherry Valley, 19 May 1813.

Mary and her family resided primarily in Cherry Valley, New York. John Diell was a merchant in Cherry Valley was granted a license to keep a public house and inn in 1800.[2411]

In his will written 20 August 1812 (proved 7 June 1813), John Diell bequeathed to beloved wife Mary the use and occupation of all the estate, real and personal, during the time she is a widow. This is expressing so that Mary is able to provide for, maintain, and educate their children. Mary also receives the household furniture except the articles that he received by his first wife; those items are to go to his daughter Elisa. He directs that his children be educated in the following manner. Son John is to have a collegiate education and afterward to be educated in such profession as he may choose. Daughters Elisa, Nancy Ann, and their youngest not yet named daughter are to have a good English education, and when they are sufficiently advanced in their school, they are to have the advantage of a year of school abroad. John also directs that his mother is to have a comfortable living out of the estate. He names the following children: daughter Elisa from his former wife; Mary Ann, John, and a young daughter not yet named; and the children of Mary with her former husband, Salena, Joseph, and Betsey.[2412]

Mary Holt and Joseph Clary were parents of three children. Their oldest child, Joseph, was admitted as an attorney on 14 February 1821 and he became the first law partner of Millard Fillmore in 1830.[2413]

i JOSEPH CLARY, b. at Paris, NY, 1 Nov 1792; d. at Buffalo, NY, 11 Aug 1842; m. at New York, NY, 1 Feb 1830, MARIA THERESA RATHBUN, b. at Charlemont, MA, 28 Feb 1801 daughter of Samuel and Polly (Turner) Rathbun; Maria d. at Buffalo, 3 Aug 1875. Joseph was an attorney and Millard Filmore's first law partner.

ii SELENA CLARY, b. at Cherry Valley, about 1794; living in 1812.

iii BETSEY CLARY, b. at Cherry Valley, about 1796; living in 1812.

Mary Holt and John Diell were parents of three children.

i MARY ANN DIELL, b. at Cherry Valley, about 1804; living in 1812.

ii JOHN DIELL, b. at Cherry Valley, Aug 1808; d. at sea on voyage from Hawaii, 18 Jan 1841; m. at Plattsburgh, NY, 18 Jul 1832, CAROLINE ADRIANCE PLATT, b. at Plattsburgh, 1 Jul 1807 daughter of Isaac and Anne (Tredwell) Platt; Caroline d. at Adriance, VA, 16 Jan 1901. Rev. John Diell was First Chaplain of the American Seaman's Friend Society at Honolulu and served in that position for nine years. He died aboard ship on his voyage home with his wife and children.[2414] John attended Hamilton College in Buffalo and Auburn Theological Seminary in Cherry Valley.

iii CELINDA DIELL, b. at Cherry Valley, 23 Sep 1811; d. at Cherry Valley, 11 Mar 1890; m. at Cherry Valley, 9 Apr 1829,[2415] EDWIN JUDD, b. at Cherry Valley, 5 Feb 1805 son of Oliver and Elizabeth (Belden) Judd);[2416] Edwin d. at Cherry Valley, 28 Nov 1873.

913) MARCIA HOLT (*Daniel⁴, Daniel³, Nicholas², Nicholas¹*), b. at Pomfret, about 1773 daughter of Daniel and Kezia (Rust) Holt; m. AUGUSTUS SHARP.

Marcia and Augustus are reported in Durrie's Holt genealogy as settling in Buffalo and having two children. There is an Augustus Sharp in Buffalo in 1820 with a household of male age 26-44, female age 26-44, 2 males under 10, and 1 female under 10. Nothing else was found.

914) ADELIA HOLT (*Daniel⁴, Daniel³, Nicholas², Nicholas¹*), b. at Pomfret, 23 Jan 1778 daughter of Daniel and Kezia (Rust) Holt; m. CHARLES MUDGE, b. at New London, about 1770 son of Jarvis and Prudence (Treat) Mudge;[2417] Charles d. of typhus at Williamsville Hospital, NY, Aug 1814 while serving in the army in the War of 1812.[2418]

2411 Sawyer, *History of Cherry Valley, New York*, p 52

2412 New York Probate Records, 1629-1971, Otsego County, Wills and Administrations 1792-1813, volumes A-D, volume D, pp 112-114

2413 "Sketch of Joseph Clary: Millard Fillmore's First Law Partner", Buffalo Historical Society, Publications of the Buffalo Historical Society, volume 11, pp 98-105. A detailed biography of Joseph Clary can be found in this article.

2414 Findagrave ID: 35335542

2415 Marriages from the Cherry Valley Gazette 1818-1834 (provided by New Horizons Genealogy, http://www.newhorizonsgenealogicalservices.com/ny-genealogy/otsego-county/cherry_valley_gazette_marriages.htm)

2416 Judd, *Thomas Judd and His Descendants*, p 59

2417 Mudge, *Memorials: A Genealogical Account of the Name Mudge in America*, p 73

2418 U.S. Army, Register of Enlistments, 1798-1914

Charles Mudge was trader in Cherry Valley and relocated to Buffalo where he built one of the first homes. Adelia and Charles's home was burnt during the War of 1812.[2419] Charles served in the War of 1812 in Capt. Burbank's company of the 21st Regiment of Infantry of Massachusetts.

Adelia Holt and Charles Mudge were parents of three children.

i HIRAM MUDGE, b. about 1798 and d. about 1812 at age 14.

ii DEBORAH MUDGE, b. about 1803; d. at Palmyra, NY, 1849; m. at Palmyra, 2 Jan 1821, ERASTUS COLE

iii MARY MUDGE, b. about 1803; m. JOHN JOHNSON

915) LIBBEUS KIMBALL (*Abigail Holt Kimball[4], Daniel[3], Nicholas[2], Nicholas[1]*), b. at Pomfret, 14 Feb 1750/1 son of Richard and Abigail (Holt) Kimball; d. at Ames, NY, 4 Sep 1839; m. at Pomfret, 7 May 1778, SARAH CRAFT, b. at Pomfret, 29 Apr 1756 daughter of Samuel and Judith (Payson) Craft; Sarah d. at Ames, 3 Aug 1831.

Libbeus Kimball served as a private during the Revolution and made declaration related to his pension application on 6 August 1832. He was then age eighty-one and resident of Canajoharie. In June 1775, he enlisted from Pomfret and marched seventy miles to Boston and was discharged. In 1776, he enlisted when there was a call for soldiers to go to Lake Champlain and he was then in the company of Capt. Elijah Sharpe. He was in battles at Skenesborough and Fort Anne. He suffered great hardships during these campaigns. He had an additional enlistment in 1781 to go to New London. After the close of the war, he moved to Canajoharie where he still resided.[2420]

Libbeus Kimball and Sarah Craft were parents of three children born at Pomfret.

i MATILDA KIMBALL, b. at Pomfret, 23 Nov 1780; d. at Ames, NY, 1 Feb 1848; m. at Florida, NY, 5 Aug 1795, RUFUS MORRIS, b. at Scituate, RI, 4 Feb 1772 son of Lemuel and Lydia (Wilkinson) Morris;[2421] Rufus d. 25 Sep 1848.

ii SYLVESTER KIMBALL, b. at Pomfret, 27 May 1783; d. at Ames, NY, 28 May 1830; m. 26 Feb 1812, LYDIA ATWATER, b. 27 Aug 1792 daughter of Caleb Atwater; Lydia d. at Cherry Valley, NY, 24 May 1881. Lydia married second Waitstill Crumb.

iii CRAFTS PAYSON KIMBALL, b. at Pomfret, 14 Jan 1788; d. at Rutland, NY, 7 Nov 1872; m. 14 Jan 1814, JULIANA PORTER, b. at Clinton, NY, 3 Jun 1796 daughter of Raphael and Mercy (Hamlin) Porter; Juliana d. at Rutland, 21 Apr 1868.

916) PERSIS KIMBALL (*Abigail Holt Kimball[4], Daniel[3], Nicholas[2], Nicholas[1]*), b. at Pomfret, 5 Nov 1760 daughter of Richard and Abigail (Holt) Kimball; d. at Ames, NY, 6 Mar 1845; m. at Pomfret, 18 Jan 1781, GEORGE ELLIOT, b. at Voluntown, 1 Mar 1757 son of Andrew and Hannah (Palmer) Elliot; George d. at Canajoharie, 22 Mar 1817.

Rev. George Elliot was a Freewill Baptist minister who served as pastor of the church at Bowman's Creek, New York (later known as Ames). He was ordained 6 February 1794 at Florida, New York.[2422]

George Elliot served in the Revolution and was wounded. On 25 September 1838, Percy Elliot of Canajoharie, then age seventy-eight, appeared to make a statement related to her application for a widow's pension. She reported that she and George were married at Pomfret on 30 January 1781 (although reported by the town clerk as 18 January 1781) at the home of her brother Libeus Kimball. She reported that her husband George died at their residence in Canajoharie on 22 March 1817. Percy further stated that she and George grew up in the same neighborhood. She had known that he served in the Northern campaign during the war. He served for six months at that time and returned in the Fall of the year about the time her brother Libeus returned. George was later drafted into service and went to Rhode Island. At that time, she was under promise of marriage to George. She heard that he was wounded and in the hospital. When he came home, he had a wound over his left eye from being shot and Percy dressed the wound. Persis's brother Libeus also made a statement in support of his sister's application. In 1851, son Elijah Elliot wrote questioning the amount of pension his mother had received, his thought being she was eligible for a larger pension than she had received. In that same letter, Elijah also inquired related to the eligibility of a pension for his sister who was the widow of Charles Morris. His sister married Charles Morris as his second wife on 4 October 1810.[2423]

Persis Kimball and George Elliot were parents of four children.

i SARAH ELECTA ELLIOT, b. about 1782; d. at Canajoharie, NY, 27 Feb 1861; m. 4 Oct 1810, as his second wife, CHARLES MORRIS, b. at Killingly, 24 Apr 1762 son of Lemuel and Lydia (Wilkinson) Morris; Charles d. at Canajoharie, 7 Jun 1838. Charles was first married to Miriam Nichols.

2419 Mudge, *Memorials: A Genealogical Account of the Name Mudge in America*, p 97

2420 U.S. Revolutionary War Pension and Bounty-Land Warrant Application Files, Case S16179

2421 Morris, *A Genealogical and Historical Register of the Descendants of Edward Morris*, p 188

2422 Burgess & Ward, Free Baptist Cyclopaedia, p 183

2423 Revolutionary War Pension and Bounty-Land Warrant Application Files, Case 25612

ii RELECTY ELLIOT, b. 10 Oct 1795; d. at Ames, NY, 15 Feb 1875; m. 1840, as his second wife, JOHN WHITE, b. 1786; John d. after 1875 when he was living in Canajoharie with his daughter. John was first married to Catherine Jones.

iii ELIJAH ELLIOT, b. 1797; d. at Ames, NY, 9 Jul 1873; m. 1st about 1820, ANN SMITH, b. about 1800; Ann d. at Ames, 12 Feb 1828. Elijah m. 2nd, SALLY who has not been identified and who died at Ames, 3 Jul 1844.

iv ETHELWINA ELLIOT, b. about 1804; d. at Ames, 23 Jan 1887. Ethelwina did not marry. In 1870, she was living with her brother Elijah who was widowed at that time.

917) CHESTER KIMBALL (*Abigail Holt Kimball⁴, Daniel³, Nicholas², Nicholas¹*), b. at Pomfret, 19 Sep 1763 son of Richard and Abigail (Holt) Kimball; d. at New London, 2 Jan 1824; m. at New London, 8 Nov 1786; LUCIA "LUCY" FOX, b. at Chatham, CT, 19 May 1766 daughter of John and Mary (Waterman) Fox; Lucy d. at New London, 6 Apr 1855.

Chester resided in New London where he was a dealer in marble and stone.[2424] He also served on the common council for New London from 1810 through 1819.[2425]

Chester Kimball and Lucy Fox were parents of eleven children born at New London.

i GURDON KIMBALL, b. 29 Jan 1788; d. at New Haven, 17 May 1871; m. 19 Nov 1809, LUCY WAY HOLT, b. at New Haven, 29 Jun 1793 daughter of Jonathan and Abiah (Dunton) Holt; Lucy d. at New Haven 31 Dec 1865. Lucy Holt is a descendant of William Holt of New Haven.

ii CHESTER KIMBALL, b. 31 Jan 1790; d. at New London, 15 Jan 1823; m. at New London, 5 Nov 1809, LUCRETIA "LUCY" COIT, b. at New London, 28 Sep 1792 daughter of John and Lucy (Smith) Coit; Lucy d. at New York, NY, 10 Nov 1843.

iii JOHN KIMBALL, b. 23 Mar 1792; d. 5 Dec 1793.

iv RICHARD KIMBALL, b. 30 Jan 1794; d. at Savannah, GA, 23 Jan 1818.[2426] Richard was a merchant.

v LUCY KIMBALL, b. 17 Mar 1796; d. at New London, 15 Jun 1882; m. 1 Dec 1814, GURDON BISHOP, b. at New Haven, 26 Jul 1789 son of Jonathan and Anne (Allen) Bishop; Gurdon d. at Waterford, 28 Apr 1865.

vi MARY WATERMAN KIMBALL, b. 15 Oct 1798; d. at New London, 9 Dec 1828; m. 14 May 1823, ZEBADIAH C. BAKER, b. 6 May 1802 son of Lemuel and Bethiah (Comstock) Baker; Zebadiah d. 2 Oct 1840. Zebadiah married second Mercy Crandall.

vii JOHN KIMBALL, b. 4 Nov 1800; d. 2 Nov 1816.

viii ABIGAIL HOLT KIMBALL, b. 8 Mar 1803; d. at New London, 30 Jun 1835; m. Sep 1822, JAMES BLOYD LYMAN, b. at Lebanon, CT, Nov 1799 son of Elisha and Abigail (Bloyd) Lyman; James d. at Norwich, 3 oct 1865. James married second Abigail's sister Charlotte (see below).

ix HARRIET KIMBALL, b. 31 Jul 1805; d. at New London, 9 Feb 1834; m. 27 Aug 1829, GURDON TRACY BISHOP, b. at New London, 21 Jul 1804 son of Moses and Elizabeth (Starr) Bishop; Gurdon d. at New London, 1877.

x EDWIN KIMBALL, b. 4 Nov 1808; d. 22 Jun 1827.

xi CHARLOTTE ELIZABETH KIMBALL, b. 11 Sep 1810; d. at New London, 9 Jan 1901; m. 2 May 1836, JAMES BLOYD LYMAN who was first married to Charlotte's sister Harriet (see above).

918) ROXLANA HOLT (*Silas⁴, Daniel³, Nicholas², Nicholas¹*), b. at Pomfret, 21 Sep 1760 daughter of Silas and Mary (Brooks) Holt; d. at Ashford, about 1787; m. at Ashford, 13 Jun 1782, EBENEZER SUMNER, b. at Ashford, 3 Aug 1757 son of Ebenezer and Experience (Marsh) Sumner; Ebenezer d. at Eastford, Aug 1806. Ebenezer second married Sarah Perrin on 26 May 1788.

Roxlana Holt and Ebenezer Sumner were parents of two children.

i MYRA SUMNER, b. at Ashford, 17 Apr 1783

ii ROXALANA SUMNER, b. about 1785; d. at Burlington, NY, 22 Mar 1873; m. DANIEL BOLTON, b. at Stafford, CT, 15 Nov 1783 son of Daniel and Alice (Leach) Bolton;[2427] Daniel d. at Burlington, 5 Apr 1851.

2424 Morrison, *History of the Kimball Family*, p 279

2425 Caulkins, *History of New London*, p 619

2426 Savannah, Georgia Vital Records, 1803-1966, accessed through ancestry.com

2427 Bolton, *Nathaniel Bolton, a Forgotten New England Poet*, p 25

919) CLARINA HOLT (*Silas⁴, Daniel³, Nicholas², Nicholas¹*), b. at Ashford, 6 Nov 1769 daughter of Silas and Mary (Brooks) Holt; d. at Vernon, NY, 14 Nov 1845; m. at Ashford, 12 May 1793, ELIAS FRINK, b. 1770; Elias d. at Vernon, NY, 14 Apr 1854.

Clarina and Elias were members of the church at West Hartford where Elias served in the post of collector from 1800 to 1811.[2428] The family was later in Vernon, New York. Census records note that Elias was a shoemaker and also deaf, at least in his later years.

There are four children known for Clarina Holt and Elias Frink.

i LUCIA FRINK, b. about 1795 and baptized at West Hartford, 21 Jul 1803; d. after 1850 when she was living with her father and sister Mary in Vernon, NY. Lucia did not marry.

ii SILAS HOLT FRINK, b. about 1797 and baptized at West Hartford, 21 Jul 1803; d. at Jackson, MI, 17 Dec 1876; m. SOPHRONIA WILSON, b. in NY 1808; Sophronia d. at Detroit, 12 Nov 1890.

iii MARY TIFFANY FRINK, b. about 1801 and baptized at West Hartford, 21 Jul 1803; d. at Vernon, NY, 18 Mar 1865. Mary did not marry.

iv CLARINA FRINK, baptized at West Hartford, 4 Jun 1809; nothing further found.

920) LUCINDA HOLT (*Silas⁴, Daniel³, Nicholas², Nicholas¹*), b. at Ashford, 26 Jul 1773 daughter of Silas and Mary (Brooks) Holt; d. at Ashford, 24 Mar 1847; m. at Ashford, 14 Jan 1799, DYER CLARK, b. 1772; Dyer d. at Ashford, 28 Sep 1846.

Lucinda Holt and Dyer Clark were parents of five children born at Ashford.

i SABRINA HOWE CLARK, b. 3 Nov 1799; d. at Ashford, 14 Feb 1839; m. at Ashford, 15 Jun 1819, CLARK GRANT, b. at Willington, 28 Feb 1793 son of Miner and Eunice (Swift) Grant; Clark d. at Ashford, 16 Apr 1826.

ii LUCINDA HOWE CLARK, b. 30 Jul 1802; d. at Ashford, 12 Nov 1860; m. at Ashford, 19 Feb 1829, JOSEPH BURNHAM SIMMONS, b. at Ashford, 12 Oct 1801 son of Alva and Tryphena (Burnham) Simmons; Joseph d. at Ashford, 12 Feb 1835. Lucinda m. 2nd at Ashford, 14 Apr 1841, GEORGE CADY.

iii NEHEMIAH HOWE CLARK, b. 13 Jun 1805; d. at Ashford, 15 Oct 1812.

iv ANDREW JUDSON CLARK, b. 11 Apr 1809

v DYER HOWE CLARK, b. 23 May 1817; d. at Ashford, 13 Dec 1897; m. at West Springfield, MA, 13 Sep 1837, AUGUSTA A. SAUNDERS, b. about 1820 daughter of Ezekiel and Betsey (Potter);[2429] Augusta d. at East Hartford, 18 Sep 1884.

921) OLIVE ROGERS (*Lois Holt Rogers⁴, Daniel³, Nicholas², Nicholas¹*), b. at Pomfret, 7 Mar 1759 daughter of Moses and Lois (Holt) Rogers; d. at Ashford, 2 Mar 1855; m. at Ashford, 28 Sep 1784, ABEL DOW, b. at Ashford, 3 Jul 1757 son of Daniel and Elizabeth (Marsh) Dow; Abel d. at Ashford, 6 Jan 1826.

Olive and Abel lived in Ashford where their four children were born.

In his will written 21 December 1825, Abel Dow bequeathed to wife Olive use of one-third of the real estate during her natural life and one-third of the personal estate to be at her disposal. Grandson Maro Austin, son of Sally and Joseph Austin late of Woodstock deceased, receives twenty dollars. The remainder of the estate, including the dower thirds at the decease of Olive, are to be equally divided between his two daughters Lois H. Carpenter and Laura Hicks. Samuel H. Carpenter and his wife Lois were named executors.[2430]

i SALLY DOW, b. at Ashford, 28 Nov 1785; d. at Woodstock, 27 Apr 1809; m. JOSEPH AUSTIN who has not been identified. Joseph was second married to Polly.

ii WILLIAM DOW, b. at Ashford, 6 Mar 1788; d. at Ashford, 25 Dec 1816. William did not marry. In his will written 20 August 1814, he bequeathed to uncles Nathan Crocker and Alva Rogers the obligations that William holds against them. There are also bequests to nephew Maro Austin, cousin Horatio Dow, Asaph Smith, his mother, sisters Lois and Laura, and his father.[2431]

iii LOIS DOW, b. at Ashford, 1 Dec 1790; d. at Ashford, 25 May 1882; m. SAMUEL HAYWARD CARPENTER, b. at Ashford, 26 Jan 1788 son of Comfort and Priscilla (Hayward) Carpenter; Samuel d. at Ashford, 30 Dec 1850.

2428 Connecticut Church Record Abstracts, volume 122, Part I, West Hartford

2429 Augusta's parents are given in the Connecticut death index as Ezek Saunders and Betsey Potter.

2430 *Connecticut State Library (Hartford, Connecticut)*; Probate Place: *Hartford, Connecticut, Estate of Abel Dow, Case 1496*

2431 *Connecticut. Probate Court (Pomfret District)*; Probate Place: *Windham, Connecticut, volume 12, p 308*

iv LAURA DOW, b. at Ashford, 16 Jun 1796; d. at Ashford, 1875; m. 1st 10 Feb 1813, AMOS TROWBRIDGE, b. 16 Oct 1790 son of James and Mary (Kendall) Trowbridge; Amos d. 25 Feb 1822. Laura m. 2nd at Ashford, 30 Sep 1824, ABRA HICKS, b. at Pomfret, 17 Dec 1800 son of Israel and Phebe (Grow) Hicks; Abra d. at Ashford, 1887.

922) ELISHA ROGERS (*Lois Holt Rogers4, Daniel3, Nicholas2, Nicholas1*), b. at Pomfret, 11 Feb 1766 son of Moses and Lois (Holt) Rogers; d. perhaps at Springfield, VT, 24 Apr 1807;[2432] m. at Springfield, 11 Jul 1788, ANNA WARD, b. 1767 daughter of Jabez Ward; Anna d. at Brownville, NY, 14 Jul 1872.[2433]

Elisha Rogers served as a private in the continental army, Connecticut line in the company of Capt. Daniel Allen. Elisha served two three-year enlistments. On 10 September 1838 while living in Lyme, New York, widow Anna Rogers made application for a widow's pension. The probate documents include the date of marriage, the name of Anna's father as Jabez, and the date of Elisha's death. In 1855 while living at Brownville, Anna, then age eighty-eight, made a follow-up statement. In 1855, son Riley Rogers then age sixty-six provide a statement in support of his mother's pension.[2434]

Elisha Rogers and Anna Ward were parents of four children.

i RILEY ROGERS, b. at Springfield, VT, 15 Dec 1788; d. at Brownville, NY, 20 Oct 1874; m. LORENA KELLOGG, b. 1792 whose parents have not been identified; Lorena d. at Brownville, 19 May 1858.

ii NAMAH ROGERS, b. 27 Nov 1790

iii RALPH H. ROGERS, b. at Springfield, VT, 29 Sep 1792; d. at Lyme, NY, 30 Sep 1866; m. ELIZA HORTON, b. 7 Dec 1799 daughter of Henry and Abigail (Cook) Horton;[2435] Eliza d. at Lyme, 2 Jul 1890.

iv GEORGE ROGERS, b. at Springfield, 12 Oct 1794; d. at Brownville, NY, 19 Mar 1844; m. ELIZABETH "BETSY" HANCOCK. Elizabeth was living at the time of George's death and in the 1860 census at Brownville with three of her children. Nine children were listed as heirs of the estate. Although Elisha died in 1844 (which is verified in the probate), in 1847 one of the creditors of the estate, Henry W. Hills, was allowed as administrator of the estate.[2436]

923) ABIGAIL ROGERS (*Lois Holt Rogers4, Daniel3, Nicholas2, Nicholas1*), b. at Pomfret, 23 Mar 1769 daughter of Moses and Lois (Holt) Rogers; d. at Sherburne, NY, 29 Mar 1849; m. CYRUS DOW, b. at Ashford, 17 Jun 1764 son of Daniel and Elizabeth (Marsh) Dow; Cyrus d. at Sherburne, 23 Mar 1842 (date of death given at the proving of the will on 21 Mar 1843).

In his will written 24 June 1841 (proved 21 March 1843), Cyrus Dow of Sherburne bequeathed his personal estate to wife Nabby to be at her disposal. She also receives the income from all the real property during her life. After Nabby's decease, all the real property goes to son Cyrus M. Dow on condition that he pay four hundred dollars to daughter Almira Daniels within two years. Cyrus M. Dow was named executor.[2437] At the proving of the will, Cyrus M. Dow gave a statement that the only heirs were widow Nabby Dow, Cyrus M. Dow of Sherburne, and Almira Daniels wife of James Daniels of Columbus, Pennsylvania.

Two children are known for Abigail Rogers and Cyrus Dow.

i ALMIRA DOW, b. about 1798 (age 77 at death); d. at Columbus, PA, 8 Jun 1875; m. JAMES DANIELS, b. in CT, about 1796; James d. at Columbus, 14 Feb 1877. James Daniels was a wagon maker.

ii CYRUS MARSH DOW, b. about 1809; d. at Sherburne, NY, 14 Jan 1873; m. 1st SAMANTHA D. GREEN, b. 1812; Samantha d. at Sherburne, 11 Apr 1842. Cyrus m. 2nd PHILENA, b. about 1818 and d. at Sherburne, 26 Feb 1853. Cyrus m. 3rd SUSAN D. SMITH (widow of Thomas Jefferson King), b. about 1810 daughter of Isaac and Susan (Densmore) Smith; Susan d. at Sherburne, Feb 1767. Cyrus m. 4th MARY, b. about 1817.

924) LUCIA "LUCY" ROGERS (*Lois Holt Rogers4, Daniel3, Nicholas2, Nicholas1*), b. at Ashford, 28 May 1771 daughter of Moses and Lois (Holt) Rogers; d. at Springfield, MA, Jan 1823; m. at Ashford, 16 Nov 1797, NATHAN CROCKER, b. about 1772 son of Gershom and Ann (Fisher) Crocker;[2438] Nathan d. at Springfield, 26 Jul 1817.

Lucy Rogers and Nathan Crocker were parents of nine children, the oldest born at Ashford and the other children born at Springfield, Massachusetts.

2432 The date of give is given in his widow's pension application and the family seems to have still been in Vermont at that time.

2433 All the records available support that Anna did indeed live to 105. In 1838, she gave her age as 71 on a pension application and her age on the 1860 census is given as 94.

2434 U. S. Revolutionary War Pension and Bounty-Land Warrant Application Files, 1800-1900, Case W22116

2435 The 1857 will of Henry Horton includes a bequest to his daughter Eliza Rogers.

2436 *Minutes, Orders and Decrees, 1830-1910;* Author: *New York. Surrogate's Court (Jefferson County), Minutes, Vol B, 1847-1853, pp 41-42*

2437 *New York. Surrogate's Court (Chenango County);* Probate Place: *Chenango, New York, Wills Volume E 1840-1848, pp 318-319*

2438 Crocker, *Crocker Genealogy*, p 93

i LUCY CROCKER, b. at Ashford, 18 Aug 1798; d. at La Harpe, IL, 1 Dec 1888; m. at Springfield, 13 Nov 1815, HENRY COMSTOCK, b. at Old Saybrook, CT, 11 Jan 1794 son of Josiah and Lucy (Pratt) Comstock; Henry d. at La Harpe, 22 Jan 1879.

ii FANNY CROCKER, b. at Springfield, 15 Jul 1800; m. at Springfield, 21 Oct 1819, WILLIAM WRIGHT, b. in NY. Fanny and William were in Chatham, NY in 1832 where one of their children was born, but where they were after has not been found.

iii CLARISSA CROCKER, b. at Springfield, 1 Sep 1802; d. at Union, ME, 1865; m. at Springfield, 1 Sep 1824, JOHN R. POST, b. about 1801; John d. at Union after 1840 and before 1850. There are four known children of Clarissa and John.

iv WILLIAM DOW CROCKER, b. at Springfield, 31 Mar 1805; m. at Springfield, 23 Nov 1825, MARY STANNARD, b. about 1805; Mary d. at Springfield, 16 Oct 1831.

v NATHAN F. CROCKER, b. at Springfield, 25 Nov 1807; d. at West Orange, NJ, 8 Jan 1890; m. at Springfield, 20 Sep 1833, LORRAINE KELLOGG, b. in CT, 31 Jul 1805 daughter of Ichabod and Pamelia (Betts) Kellogg; Lorraine d. Feb 1885.

vi HARVEY CROKER, b. about 1808; d. at Springfield, 30 Sep 1829.

vii EDWIN CROCKER (twin), b. at Springfield, 24 May 1812

viii ELIZA CROCKER (twin), b. at Springfield, 24 May 1812

ix MARY CROCKER, b. at Springfield, 3 Oct 1814

925) ALVA ROGERS (*Lois Holt Rogers⁴, Daniel³, Nicholas², Nicholas¹*), b. at Ashford, 18 Jun 1776 son of Moses and Lois (Holt) Rogers; d. at Sherburne, NY, after 1850; m. at Ashford, 8 Sep 1803, DESIRE EATON, b. at Ashford, 29 May 1778 daughter of Ebenezer and Mary (Humphrey) Eaton; Desire d. at Sherburne, NY, Dec 1859.

Alva Rogers and Desire Eaton were parents of five children.

i LEISCTER HOLT ROGERS, b. at Ashford, 4 Jan 1804; d. at Sherburne, NY, 23 Jul 1827.

ii JARVIS ROGERS, b. at Ashford, 13 Sep 1805; d. at Sherburne, NY, 17 Jul 1857; m. HANNAH, b. about 1807; Hannah living at Sherburne in 1865. Hannah married second Henry A. Poultney.

iii MARY HUMPHREY ROGERS, b. at Ashford, 10 Sep 1807; d. at Norwich, NY, 1 Feb 1865; m. about 1831, as his second wife, BENJAMIN TALBOT LYON, b. at Foster, RI, 26 Nov 1796 son of Benjamin and Hannah (Talbot) Lyon; Benjamin d. at Norwich, 31 May 1864. Benjamin was first married to Mary Comstock.

iv HARLOW ROGERS, b. at Sherburne, NY, 20 Apr 1816; d. at Clear Lake, WI, 20 Apr 1908; m. HARRIET M. THAYER, b. at Sherburne, 27 Feb 1818 son of Alanson and Jerusha (Baker) Thayer; Harriet d. at Clear Lake, 15 Feb 1885.

v ALVA ROGERS, b. at Sherburne, 1820; d. at Clear Lake, WI, 3 Nov 1880; m. ANN ELIZABETH CARR, b. 1822; Ann d. after 1880 when she was living at Clear Lake.

926) PERTHENE WHEELER (*Eunice Holt Wheeler⁴, Daniel³, Nicholas², Nicholas¹*), b. at Pomfret, 19 Sep 1762 daughter of Josiah and Eunice (Holt) Wheeler; m. 26 Oct 1783, DANIEL CHAPIN, b. at Salisbury, CT, 2 Feb 1761 son of Charles and Anna (Camp) Chapin;[2439] Daniel d. at Buffalo, NY, 16 Nov 1821.

Dr. Daniel Chapin attended Yale and was a physician in Buffalo from about 1805.[2440] He was also a member of the New York state assembly in 1801-1802.[2441] He served as judge in the court of common pleas in Niagara. The family lived in Bloomfield before setting in Buffalo. Perthene and Daniel were parents of six children. Birth dates of the children, for the most part, are estimates based on age at death, census records, etc.

i WILLIAM WHITING CHAPIN, b. about 1785; d. at Buffalo, 20 Jun 1857; m. about 1815, MARY NOBLE, b. in CT, about 1785; Mary d. at Buffalo, 13 May 1862.

ii THOMAS CHAPIN, b. about 1788. The Chapin genealogy reports that Thomas married and had three children, but records related to his family were not located.

[2439] Chapin, Orange, *Chapin Genealogy*

[2440] Hill, *Municipality of Buffalo, 1720-1923*, volume 1, p 392

[2441] Daniel Chapin, politicalgraveyard. com

iii ELIZA CHAPIN, b. 11 Jan 1790; d. at Hamburg, NY, 1 Mar 1852; m. at Buffalo, 1 Nov 1812, DAVID BEARD, b. at Derby, CT, 13 Jun 1770 son of James and Ruth (Holbrook) Beard;[2442] David d. at Buffalo, 29 Nov 1838.

iv JAMES CHAPIN, b. about 1793; d. about 1825. James did not marry.[2443]

v SOPHIA CHAPIN, b. 1795; d. at Buffalo, 18 Mar 1860; m. about 1820, WALTER NORTON, b. 1786 son of Samuel and Ruth (Kenney) Norton; Walter d. at Buffalo, 21 Feb 1849 (probate 2 Mar 1849).

vi CLARISSA CHAPIN, b. 1806; d. at St. Catharines, Niagara, Ontario, 2 May 1867; m. about 1825, ELEAZER WILLIAMS STEPHENSON, b. at Springfield, MA, 1798 son of Erastus and Elizabeth (Murphy) Stephenson; Eleazer d. at St, Catharines, 28 Apr 1867. Col. Eleazer Williams Stephenson took his family to St. Catharines about 1825. He had a successful livery stable and established the first Royal mail stage-coach line. He was killed by runaway horses. He was also a promotor of building the Welland canal.[2444] In 1851, Stephenson was elected to the town council and was chosen mayor.[2445]

927) ELIJAH WHEELER (*Eunice Holt Wheeler*[4], *Daniel*[3], *Nicholas*[2], *Nicholas*[1]), b. at Pomfret, 28 Aug 1767 son of Josiah and Eunice (Holt) Wheeler; d. at Great Barrington, MA, 20 Apr 1827; m. 1st MARY MATILDA MINER, b. at Woodbury, CT, 11 Apr 1773 daughter of Jehu and Sarah (Canfield) Miner; Mary d. at Great Barrington, 11 Oct 1812. Elijah m. 2nd ELIZABETH WHITING, b. 1773 likely daughter of Gamaliel and Anne (Gillette) Whiting; Elizabeth d. at Great Barrington, 21 Feb 1848.

Rev. Elijah Wheeler was from Pomfret. He was a physician and practiced medicine in South Britain (Southbury), Connecticut. He later entered the ministry and settled in Great Barrington, Massachusetts in 1805 where he was minister of the congregational church from 1806 to 1823 when he left the position due to failing health.[2446]

In his will (probate 15 August 1827), Elijah Wheeler, who describes himself as minister of the gospel, bequeathed to beloved wife Elizabeth the improvement on one-third of the real estate while she is a widow and all the household furniture as her own property. Beloved son Russel Canfield receives five dollars which completed his portion and son Josiah William receives $420. Any estate remaining after payment of debts is to be divided among his wife and two sons while Elizabeth is a widow and then divided between the two sons. Trusty friend Deacon George Beckwith was named executor.[2447] The probate record specifies that in addition to widow Elizabeth, Russel C. Wheeler of New York City and Josiah W. Wheeler of Albany, New York are the only two heirs.

Elijah Wheeler and Mary Miner were parents of two children. The two sons married sisters who were also their second cousins through the Wheeler line.[2448][2449]

i RUSSELL CANFIELD WHEELER, b. at Southbury, NY, 1 Dec 1795; d. at Brooklyn, NY, 13 Aug 1847; m. 23 Oct 1833, THEODOSIA MARY DAVENPORT, b. at Stamford, CT, 8 Nov 1810 daughter of John Alfred and Eliza Maria (Wheeler) Davenport; Theodosia d. at New Haven, 14 Sep 1883. Russell graduated from Yale in 1816 and practice law in New York until illness forced his retirement.

ii JOSIAH WILLIAM WHEELER, b. perhaps at Red Hook, NY, 5 Apr 1807; d. at Brooklyn, Mar 1882; m. 15 Oct 1835, MARY BORMAN DAVENPORT, b. at Stamford, 7 Aug 1814 daughter of John Alfred and Eliza Maria (Wheeler) Davenport; Mary d. at Brooklyn, 30 Apr 1896. Josiah graduated from Williams College in 1825.

928) PHILADELPHIA "PHILA" WHEELER (*Eunice Holt Wheeler*[4], *Daniel*[3], *Nicholas*[2], *Nicholas*[1]), b. at Pomfret, 28 Nov 1769 daughter of Josiah and Eunice (Holt) Wheeler; d. at East Bloomfield, NY, after 1855; m. about 1791, MOSES GAYLORD, b. at West Hartford, about 1768 and baptized 17 Jul 1768 son of Moses and Susanna (Wells) Gaylord; Moses d. at Bloomfield, NY, 1812.[2450]

Phila and Moses resided in Bloomfield, New York where Moses was licensed as an inn and tavern keeper.[2451] Moses did not leave a will and his brother Flavel was appointed administrator of his estate on 19 February 1813.[2452]

Names of children have been suggested, but little firm information. Four children in this family can be tracked through cemetery and census records.

2442 Beard, *A Genealogy of the Descendants of Widow Martha Beard*, p 22

2443 Chapin, *The Chapin Book of Genealogical Data*, p 172

2444 A Cyclopedia of Canadian Biography, volume 1, p 645

2445 Dictionary of Canadian Biography, volume IX, http://www.biographi.ca/en/bio/stephenson_eleazer_williams_9E.html

2446 Taylor, *History of Great Barrington*, p 387

2447 *Probate Records, 1761-1917;* Author: *Massachusetts. Probate Court (Berkshire County), Probate Records, Vol 30-31, 1826-1827, volume 31, pp 231-233*

2448 Dexter, *Biographical Notices of Graduates of Yale College*

2449 Davenport, *A History and Genealogy of the Davenport Family*

2450 *Connecticut, Hale Collection of Cemetery Inscriptions and Newspaper Notices, 1629-1934*

2451 Aldrich, *History of Ontario County, New York*, p 131

2452 New York Wills and Probate Records, Ontario County, Records of Wills, Volume 0006, pp 132-133

i ELIZA GAYLORD

ii DELIA GAYLORD

iii EDWIN GAYLORD

iv HECTOR GAYLORD, about1798; d. at East Bloomfield, 11 Jan 1848; m. about 1823, HANNAH SMITH, b. in CT, about 1804; Hannah d. after 1850 when she and her children were living with her brother-in-law George in East Bloomfield.

v HOMER GAYLORD

vi SARAH E. GAYLORD, b. about 1800; d. at East Bloomfield, 23 May 1843; m. ASAHEL HUNTINGTON, b. at Franklin, CT, 10 Sep 1795 daughter of Azariah and Parnel (Chamption) Huntington; Asahel d. 22 Oct 1822.

vii GEORGE GAYLORD, b. about 1803; d. after 1875 when he was living in East Bloomfield as a boarder. George did not marry. After the death of his brother Hector, he took in Hector's children for several years.

viii WELLS MOSES GAYLORD, b. about 1804; d. at Rochester, NY, 4 Nov 1846; m. MARY ANN KENDALL, b. in MA, about 1804; Mary d. at Rochester, 23 Sep 1895.[2453]

929) RESOLVED GROSVENOR WHEELER (*Eunice Holt Wheeler*[4], *Daniel*[3], *Nicholas*[2], *Nicholas*[1]), b. at Pomfret, 8 Mar 1772 son of Josiah and Eunice (Holt) Wheeler; d. at Conneaut, PA, 29 May 1839; m. N. ANNA VANDEVENTER, b. about 1785; Anna d. at Reedsburg, WI, 4 Oct 1863.

Resolved G. Wheeler was a wanderer and seems to have been in Lempster, New Hampshire before his marriage, in Clarence, Erie County, New York in 1802,[2454] later in Canada where some of the children were born, in Lempster, New Hampshire in the 1810 and 1820 census, back in New York at Pembroke for the 1830 census, and finally in Conneaut, Pennsylvania. He was named lieutenant in the Genesee County, New York militia in April 1803.[2455]

There are likely eight children in this family.

i MARY WHEELER, b. 1804; d. 1819.

ii AMANDA EMELINE WHEELER, b. 20 Aug 1805; d. at Reedsburg, WI, 14 Sep 1886; m. SAMUEL HALL CHASE, b. at East Machias, ME, 1804 son of Eleazer and Alice (Hall) Chase; Samuel d. at Reedsburg, 29 Jan 1890.

iii CHRISTOPHER VANDEVENTER WHEELER, b. 11 Oct 1807; d. at Bedford, IA, 30 Jul 1882; m. EMILY WEAVER, b. at Willington, CT, 11 Dec 1811 daughter of Thomas and Sarah (Lee) Weaver; Emily d. at Wester, NE, 18 Jun 1902 where she was living at the home of her daughter.

iv ELIJAH G. WHEELER, b. 27 Nov 1812; d. at Yankton, Dakota Territory, 26 Jul 1880; m. 1st about 1833, HARRIET who has not been identified, b. 1816 and d. 1856. Elijah m. 2nd at Allegan County, MI, 15 Jan 1857, HARRIET A. BOGART, b. in PA, 1833; Harriet d. after 1915 when she was living in San Jose, CA.

v SARAH ANN WHEELER, b. in Canada, 1818; d. after 1885 when she was living in Vinton, IA; m. 1858, as his second wife, WILLIAM P. STEWART, b. in OH, 1814; William d. at Vinton, IA, 7 Jul 1893. William was first married to Isabel Logan and third married to Sarah P. Morton on 19 Jun 1893 shortly before his death. In 1850, Sarah Wheeler and her mother Ann were living in Baraboo, WI.

vi PETER VANDEVENTER WHEELER, b. in Canada, 18 Aug 1820; d. at Urbana, IA, 9 Jan 1903; m. ELECTA A. WHITFORD, b. in NY, 8 Feb 1827 daughter of Oliver and Phebe (Laampman) Whitford; Electa d. at Vinton, IA, 7 Jul 1916.[2456]

vii JOHN G. WHEELER, b. in New York, 4 Apr 1822; d. at Milwaukee, WI, 9 May 1913; m. ELLA WAITE, b. in NY 1826; Ella d. at Fairfield, IA, about 1870. John was admitted to the Milwaukee Home for Disabled Volunteer Soldiers in 1896.[2457]

viii WILLIAM H. WHEELER, b. 8 Feb 1826; d. at Douglas, CO, 6 Apr 1892; m. at DeKalb, IL, 10 Oct 1849, JANE H. KENDALL, b. in NY, 30 May 1830; Jane d. at Glendale, CO, 10 Feb 1918.[2458]

[2453] Presbyterian Historical Society; Philadelphia, Pennsylvania; U.S., Presbyterian Church Records, 1701-1907; Book Title: Church Register 1832-1903; Accession Number: V MI46 R5894r v.2

[2454] White, *Our County and Its People*, volume 1, p 516

[2455] Military Minutes of the Council of Appointment of the State of New York, 1783-1821, volume 1, p 692

[2456] Iowa, Deaths and Burials, 1850-1990. Electa's date of birth and names of her parents are given on her death record.

[2457] U.S. National Homes for Disabled Volunteer Soldiers, 1866-1938, Milwaukee

[2458] The dates of birth for William and Jane are given on their gravestones. Graves are in Fairmount Cemetery, Denver, CO. findagrave ID: 13472092

930) SMITH HOLT (*Asa⁴, Daniel³, Nicholas², Nicholas¹*), b. at Hartford, about 1769 son of Asa and Margaret (Hammond) Holt; d. at Keene, NY, 28 Dec 1814; m. 26 Jan 1792, his second cousin once removed LYDIA SNOW (*Dorcas Osgood Snow⁵, Mary Holt Osgood⁴, Nicholas³, Nicholas², Nicholas¹*), b. 6 Oct 1769 daughter of Benjamin and Dorcas (Osgood) Snow; Lydia d. at Keene, 21 Dec 1853.

After the births of their first seven children, Smith and Lydia moved their family to what became Keene, New York along the Ausable River valley arriving there in 1806.[2459]

Smith Holt and Lydia Snow were parents of ten children, the oldest seven children born in Connecticut, likely at Ashford, and the three youngest in Keene, New York.

i ALVA SMITH HOLT, b. 1793; d. at Keene, NY, 16 May 1879; m. MARY "POLLY" PEASE, b. 28 Jan 1795 daughter of Augustus and Tirzah (Hall) Pease; Polly d. at Keene, 29 Oct 1872.

ii ORRIN HOLT, b. 1796; d. at Scotland, Ontario, Canada, 12 Oct 1887, m. at Townsend, Ontario, 7 Feb 1831,[2460] LORETTA DUDBRIDGE, b. in Ontario, about 1813; d. at Townsend, Ontario between 1871 and 1881.

iii LOIS C. HOLT, b. 1797; d. at Keene, NY, 3 Oct 1876; m. ORRIN DIBBLE, b. in VT, 1795; d. at Keene, NY, 14 Sep 1860.

iv POLLY HOLT, b. 20 May 1799 (on gravestone); d. at Williston, VT, 28 Aug 1881; m. JOHN WRIGHT, b. at Williston, 8 Oct 1797 son of Elisha and Asenath (Brigham) Wright; John d. at Williston, 28 Oct 1881.

v LODISA HOLT, b. 1801; d. at Williston, VT, 19 Oct 1887; m. ROSWELL TALCOTT, b. 24 Aug 1798 son of Jonathan and Jerusha (Morton) Talcott; Roswell d. at Williston, 1 Sep 1893.

vi JAMES SMITH HOLT, b. 1804; d. at Keene, NY, 17 Jul 1878; m. HARRIET SEAMON, b. in NY, about 1807; Harriet d. at Keene, 16 Aug 1874.

vii JASON HOLT, b. 1805; d. at Sombra, Lambton, Ontario, 26 Apr 1893; m. CHARLOTTE WARD, b. 3 Aug 1810 daughter of Nathan and Charlotte (Beach) Ward;[2461] Charlotte d. at Sombra, 30 Apr 1874. After Charlotte's death, Jason married Ellen (1849-1892) who has not been identified.

viii HARVEY HOLT, b. at Keene, 4 Mar 1808; d. at Keene, NY, 14 Jan 1893; m. MARIA CHASE, b. 8 Nov 1819 daughter of Ebenezer and Sarah (Cheney) Chase; Maria d. at Keene, 2 Dec 1906.

ix NEWMAN HOLT, b. 1811; d. at Keene, NY, 1812.

x LYDIA HOLT, b. at Keene, 1813; d. at Williston, VT, 17 Jan 1841; m. HIRAM MURRAY, b. at Williston, 1807; Hiram d. at Williston, 3 Oct 1864.

931) ASA HOLT (*Asa⁴, Daniel³, Nicholas², Nicholas¹*), b. likely at Hartford, 12 Dec 1777 son of Asa and Margaret (Hammond) Holt; d. at Rushford, NY, 1852; m. 1st at Springfield, VT, 26 Mar 1801, ELIZABETH "BETSEY" WOODWARD, b. at Springfield, 25 Oct 1782 daughter of Samuel and Eunice (Bigelow) Woodward;[2462] Betsey d. at Springfield, 2 Feb 1814. Asa m. 2nd 7 Oct 1815, POLLY ROGERS (widow of Samuel Tarbell), b. 1784 daughter of Jeremiah and Fannie (Wickes) Rogers; Polly d. at Fillmore, NY, 2 Sep 1874.

Asa settled in Springfield, Vermont where he took the freeman's oath in 1802[2463] shortly after his first marriage. Asa resided in Springfield through the births of his children but was in Rushford, New York in later life.

Asa Holt and Betsey Woodward were parents of six children born at Springfield, Vermont.[2464]

i LOUISA HOLT, b. 28 Dec 1801; d. at Cuba, NY, 1882; m. at Springfield, VT, 18 Nov 1824, LEWIS GRAVES, b. at Springfield, 26 Jun 1801 son of Selah and Sabra (Graves) Roundy; Lewis d. at Cuba, NY, 1891.

ii CHARLES HOLT, b. 12 Dec 1803; d. at Springfield, 11 Sep 1888; m. 1st, at Springfield, 30 Jan 1830, BETSEY PARKER, b. at Rockingham, VT, 9 Dec 1800 daughter of Leonard and Abigail (Parker) Parker; Betsey d. at Springfield, 24 Feb 1862.

iii PERMELIA HOLT, b. 8 Jan 1806; d. at Waterford, NY, 21 Sep 1892; m. about 1827, JASPER GRIFFIN, b. at Jericho, VT, 26 Nov 1806 son of Jasper and Lydia (Lane) Griffin; Jasper d. at Jericho, 1844.

2459 Donaldson, *History of the Adirondacks*, p 31

2460 Witnesses of the marriage were John Dudbridge and Barton Becker.

2461 Charlotte was baptized in Sombra as an adult in 1868 and names of parents on given as Nathan and C. on the baptism record.

2462 Hubbard, *History of Springfield, Vermont*, p 511

2463 Hubbard, *History of Springfield, Vermont*, p 528

2464 The five oldest children, including twins Morris L. and Lewis M., are recorded together in the Springfield town records kept by S. M. Lewis. Vermont Town Clerk Records, Springfield, volume 3, p 22, https://www.familysearch.org/ark:/61903/3:1:3QS7-L999-24KX?i=16&cc=1987653&cat=693475

iv LEWIS M. HOLT (twin), b. 10 Aug 1808; d. at Pampas, IL, 11 Aug 1850; m. about 1832, BETSEY A. CAMPBELL, b. in MA, 1812; d. (buried), at Centerville, WI, 11 Aug 1886. Betsey was second married to James D. Kincaid.

v MORRIS L. HOLT (twin), b. 10 Aug 1808; d. at Pike, NY, 28 May 1871; m. LUCINDA CAMPBELL, b. 15 Jul 1814 daughter of William and Elizabeth (Pool) Campbell; Lucinda d. at Pike, 21 Feb 1894.

vi ELIZABETH HOLT, b. 30 Aug 1810; d. at McKean, PA, 22 Jul 1875; m. 1 Jul 1836, as his second wife, PLINNY CLEVELAND, b. at Stockbridge, VT, 7 Jul 1801 son of William Darbee and Phebe (Abbott) Cleveland;[2465] Plinny d. at McKean, 20 Aug 1867. Plinny was first married to Rachel Ketchum.

Asa Holt and Polly Rogers were parents of four children likely all born at Springfield, Vermont.

i LAURA ANN HOLT, b. 4 Apr 1816; d. at Perry, OH, 3 Nov 1903; m. about 1833, ASAPH W. MORGAN, b. at Springfield, VT, 21 May 1809 son of Isaac and Anna (Wood) Morgan; Asaph d. at Perry, 20 Feb 1898.

ii CLARISSA HOLT, b. 23 May 1818; d. at Caneadea, NY, 20 Feb 1895; m. 1st SAMUEL MORGAN, b. about 1810; Samuel d. at Almond, NY, 2 Jan 1847. Clarissa m. 2nd about 1848, as his second wife, WILLIS FOX, b. in CT, about 1800; Willis d. at Yorkshire, NY, 1852 (probate 6 Apr 1852). Clarissa m. 3rd ABEL WASHBURN, b. 1817;[2466] Abel d. at Caneadea, 6 Jan 1892.

iii HARRIET HOLT, b. 2 Feb 1823; d. at Tacoma, WA, 13 Dec 1885; m. before 1850, REUBEN HENRY CRITTENDEN, b. at Savoy, MA, 23 Nov 1823 son of Amos and Mehitable (Thomas) Crittenden; Reuben d. at Tacoma, 20 Sep 1898.

iv MARY HOLT, b. 1826; d. at Fillmore, NY, 1914; m. NOAH KENNEDY, b. in VT, Aug 1808;[2467] Noah d. at Caneadea, NY, 25 Dec 1881.

932) ALFREADA HOLT (*Asa*[4], *Daniel*[3], *Nicholas*[2], *Nicholas*[1]), b. about 1779 daughter of Asa and Margaret (Hammond) Holt; d. at Cavendish, VT, about 1814; m. at Springfield, 3 Jun 1799, PEARLY FASSET, b. about 1769 son of Adonijah and Anna (Copeland) Fasset; Pearly d. at Winchester, NH, 23 Feb 1826. Pearly married second Esther Gowing.

In his will written 7 February 1826, Pearly Fasset bequeaths one dollar to each of his children: eldest son Perley Fasset, eldest daughter Alfreada Fasset, second daughter Anna Fasset, second son Abel Hammond Fasset, and third son Amos Twitchell Fasset. The remainder of the estate is left to wife Esther Fasset and Esther Fasset and Joseph Gowing are named executors.[2468]

Alfreada Holt and Pearly Fasset were parents of five children.

i PEARLY FASSET, b. at Cavendish, 16 Nov 1800; d. at Plymouth, NH, 4 Sep 1884; m. SUSAN L. GREEN, b. at Andover, VT, about 1816 daughter of Thomas and Jerusha (Hardy) Green;[2469] Susan d. at Reading, VT, 28 May 1871.

ii ALFREADA FASSET, b. about 1803; living in 1826 but nothing further known.

iii ANNA FASSET, b. at Cavendish, 14 Jul 1804; d. at Springfield, VT, 10 Feb 1873; m. at Springfield, 1 Apr 1829, ABEL PRESCOTT WHITE, b. at Mason, NH, 23 Jul 1804 son of Abel and Ruth (Prescott) White; Abel d. at Springfield, 20 Sep 1893.

iv ABEL HAMMOND FASSET, b. at Cavendish, 24 Aug 1806; d. at Winchester, NH, 1 Feb 1886; m. at Keene, NH, 4 Mar 1840, EUNICE EVERDEN, b. at Winchester, Aug 1803 daughter of John and Mary (Wright) Everden; Eunice d. at Winchester, 22 Dec 1886.

v AMOS TWITCHELL FASSET, b. about 1809

933) POLLY HOLT (*Asa*[4], *Daniel*[3], *Nicholas*[2], *Nicholas*[1]), b. 1 Jun 1782 daughter of Asa and Margaret (Hammond) Holt; d. at Springfield, VT, 7 Jan 1852; m. at Springfield, 9 Aug 1805, SIMEON RUMRILL, b. at New Ipswich, 12 Jun 1769 son of David and Priscilla (Corey) Rumrill; Simeon d. at Baltimore, VT, 19 Mar 1822. Simeon was married to Dolly Clark before his marriage to Polly.

2465 Cleveland, *Genealogy of the Cleveland and Cleaveland Families*, p 705

2466 In 1870, Polly Holt, then age 87, was living with her daughter Clarissa and her husband Abel Washburn in Caneadea, New York

2467 Mary's mother Polly Holt was living with Mary and Noah Kennedy in the 1860 census of Genesee Falls, NY, Polly then age 77.

2468 *New Hampshire. Probate Court (Cheshire County)*; Probate Place: *Cheshire, New Hampshire, Estate Files, F206-F255, 1826-1836, Estate of Pearly Fasset, Case 208*

2469 The names of Susan's parents are given as Thomas Green and Jerusha on her death record.

Polly and Simeon live in Weathersfield, Vermont but in a section that was annexed to the school district of Baltimore, Vermont. Simeon bought property in Baltimore from Benjamin Page in 1811.[2470]

Simeon Rumrill did not leave a will and his estate entered probate 19 April 1822 with Benjamin Page as administrator and the request of widow Polly and son John L. Rumrill (who is a son from Simeon's first marriage). The personal estate was not sufficient to pay the debts and the whole of the farm was sold for $505.[2471]

Polly and Simeon were parents of ten children.

i HARVEY H. RUMRILL, b. at Weathersfield, VT, 2 Oct 1806; d. at Midland, MI, 1 May 1883; m. 1st 6 Mar 1831, SARAH MILLER, b. 1811 daughter of Jeremy and Sarah (Hodgeman) Miller; Sarah d. at Midland, about 1849. Harvey m. 2nd about 1850 RUTH ANN MYERS, b. 1816 daughter of Surzardus and Maria (-) Myers; Ruth d. at Midland, 18 Feb 1894. After Harvey's death, Ruth married Ephraim Allen on 7 Jun 1884.

ii ALMIRA RUMRILL, b. 1808; d. at Rushford, NY, 26 Aug 1894; m. 1st WARNER SNOW who was perhaps her third cousin, Warner b. at Cavendish 10 Apr 1795 son of Robert and Anna (Peck) Snow, but that is not certain. Almira m. 2nd WINTHROP G. YOUNG, b. 1810 son of Jospehus and Esther (Gary) Young; Winthrop d. at Rushford, 30 Mar 1877.

iii ALVA HOLT RUMRILL, b. 1810; d. at Springfield, VT, 21 Apr 1823

iv CLARISSA RUMRILL, b. 1811; d. at Springfield, 4 May 1828.

v HARRIET RUMRILL, b. 1 Jul 1813; d. at Springfield, 17 Jan 1837.

vi SARINA RUMRILL, b. 8 Aug 1815; d. at Wallingford, VT, 5 Nov 1888; m. WILLIAM CLARK, b. about 1818; William d. at Wallingford, 11 Nov 1889.[2472]

vii SOLON B. RUMRILL, b. at Springfield, 11 Dec 1817; d. at Sterling Center, MN, 19 Feb 1878; m. at Weathersfield, 11 Mar 1849, ROSINA DE WOLF, b. at Pomfret, VT, 11 Nov 1827 daughter of Daniel Shays and Mary (Hodges) De Wolf; Rosina d. at Spokane, WA, 9 Jul 1909.

viii ELIZA M. RURMRILL, b. at Baltimore, VT, 20 Feb 1820; d. at Chester, VT, 13 Feb 1884; m. 1 Jan 1837, WILLIAM HULL SPAFFORD, b. at Weathersfield, 13 Sep 1812 son of Abel and Mathilda (Grout) Spafford; William d. at Rutland, 4 Jun 1893.

ix MARY H. RUMRILL, b. at Baltimore, VT, 11 Mar 1822; d. at Springfield, VT, 16 Oct 1904; m. 1846, CHESTER HUBBARD STONE, b. at Troy, VT, Jul 1822 son of Walter and Nancy (Dexter) Stone; Chester d. at Springfield, 25 Sep 1907.

934) ELIZABETH DANA (*Lucy Holt Dana⁴, Daniel³, Nicholas², Nicholas¹*), b. at Ashford, 8 Jun 1771 daughter of Jedediah and Lucy (Holt) Dana; d. at Wilbern, IL, 1840; m. at Mansfield, CT, 1 Jun 1794, AMASA OWEN, b. at Ashford, 12 Aug 1766 son of Timothy and Kezia (-) Owen;[2473] Amasa d. at Wilbern, 1842.

Elizabeth and Amasa resided in Mansfield, Connecticut until 1819 when they located in Scioto County, Ohio. They later lived in Bureau, Illinois.

Elizabeth Dana and Amasa Owen were parents of ten children born at Mansfield, Connecticut.

i WILLIAM DANA OWEN, b. 6 Jan 1795; d. after 1850 when he was living in Randolph, PA; m. SARAH who has not been identified; Sarah b. about 1788 and d. at Guys Mills, PA, 15 Feb 1858.

ii LUCY OWEN, b. 8 Oct 1796

iii TIMOTHY OWEN, b. 11 Mar 1799; d. at Lacon, IL, 3 May 1886; m. at Scioto County, OH, 2 Mar 1825, JANE DEVER, b. 1804; Jane d. at Lacon, 5 Mar 1883.

iv HIRAM OWEN, b. 1 Apr 1801; d. after 1870 when he was living at Hennepin, IL; m. 1st by 1835, MINERVA who has not been identified, but born in NY about 1806 and died after 1850 when the family was living in Washington, PA. Hiram m. 2nd at Woodford, IL, 11 Jul 1858, the widow SARAH A. WATKINS, b. in PA, about 1820.

2470 Pollard, *The History of the Town of Baltimore, Vermont*, p 10 and p 168

2471 Vermont Wills, Windsor County, Estate Files, Estate of Simeon Rumrill

2472 On William Clark's death record, the name of his father is given as Mayor Clark.

2473 Dana, *Dana Family in America*, p 273

v RODERICK OWEN, b. 24 May 1803; d. at Tiskilwa, IL, 19 Apr 1861; m. at Scioto County, OH, 22 Sep 1821, NANCY ADAMS, b. at Elmira, NY, 1806 daughter of Joseph and Abigail (Reike) Adams;[2474] Nancy d. at Tiskilwa, 25 Sep 1849.

vi JEDEDIAH OWEN, b. 28 May 1805; d. at Lee's Summit, MO, Sep 1881; m. at Tazewell County, IL, 1 May 1831, ELIZABETH SOWARD who died before 1850.

vii MARIAM ELIZA OWEN, b. 10 Mar 1808; d. at Bolivar, MO, 22 Jan 1873; m. at Scioto County, OH, 15 Jan 1824, SAMUEL HARDIN HADLOCK, b. 1801 likely son of David and Elizabeth (Hardin) Hadlock; Samuel d. at Bolivar, 9 Apr 1886.

viii LUCY OWEN, b. 1 Oct 1812; d. at Bolivar, MO, 21 Jun 1884; m. at Tazewell County, IL, 1 Jul 1838, CARVER GUNN, b. at Montague, MA, 12 Jul 1799 son of Elisha and Mindwell (Carver) Gunn; Carver d. at Bolivar, 20 Apr 1885.

ix EMELINE OWEN, b. 1811; d. at Marshall County, IL, 7 Mar 1850; m. 1st at Tazewell County, IL, 19 Jun 1831, FRAZIER SOWARDS, b. 1807 son of Solomon and Sophia (Fuller) Sowards; Frazier d. at Marshall County, about 1839. Emeline m. 2nd at Tazewell, IL, 10 Sep 1840, Frazier's brother, JAMES SOWARDS, b. about 1818; James d. at Lacon, IL, 16 Sep 1882. James was second married to Mary Jones.

x LUCY OWEN, b. 1 Oct 1812; d. at Bolivar, MO, 21 Jun 1884; m. at Tazewell County, IL, 1 Jul 1838, CARVER GUNN, b. at Montague, MA, 12 Jul 1799 son of Elisha and Mindwell (Carver) Gunn; Carver d. at Bolivar, 20 Apr 1885.

935) SILAS DANA (*Lucy Holt Dana[4], Daniel[3], Nicholas[2], Nicholas[1]*), b. at Ashford, 9 Mar 1775 son of Jedediah and Lucy (Holt) Dana; d. at Grove, NY, 14 Feb 1846; m. by 1800, SALLY COWEL, b. 6 Feb 1782; Sally d. at Grove, 23 Jan 1831. Silas m. 2nd, MARY who has not been identified.

In his will written 15 January 1846 (proved 4 March 1846), Silas Dana bequeaths to wife Mary one-third of his real estate, two good cows, one horse worth fifty dollars, one good bed and bedding and bedstead to have and to hold the said real estate during her natural life. Lucy Cowel receives one-third of the real estate to use during her natural life as well as a good bed. Daughter Mary Ann receives the use of the last third of the real estate. The household furniture is to be divided among his wife Mary, Lucy Cowel, and daughter Mary Ann. The remainder of the estate is to be divided among his son and daughters. At the decease of his wife, Lucy Cowel, and Mary Ann, the estate is to be sold and divided among his son and daughters (who are not named). Wife Mary and Reuben Ward, Jr. are named executors.[2475] At the proving of the will on 4 March 1846, Reuben Ward presented the will and provided the following list of heirs: widow Mary Dana living in Grove; one son Lester Dana in Bolivar, NY; and four daughters who are Eliza the wife of James White of Grove; Wealthy the wife of Franklin Smith of Castile, Wyoming County; Mary Ann Dana of Grove; Clarissa the wife of William Huffman supposed to reside in the state of Ohio; and the children of Elijah and Lucy White who are James White, Sarah White, Elijah White, Jr., Lucinda White, Joseph White, Albert White, and John White with the last five named children being minors and residing in Grove.[2476] Lucy Cowel is likely a relative, perhaps sister, of Sally Cowel.

There are six known children of Silas Dana and Sally Cowel perhaps all born at Grove, New York.

i LUCY DANA, b. about 1801; d. at Grove, NY, about 1841; m. at Grove, 1822, ELIJAH WHITE, b. in NY, about 1799; Elijah d. after 1870 when he was living at Grove.

ii ELIZA DANA, b. about 1803; d. after 1865 when she was living at Bolivar; m. by 1825, JAMES WHITE, b. about 1801; James was living in 1865.

iii LESTER H. DANA, b. about 1805; d. after 1880 when he was living at East Tawas, MI; m. MARY "POLLY" WHITE.

iv CLARISSA DANA, b. about 1808; d. after 1860 when she was living at Steuben, IN; m. WILLIAM HUFFMAN, b. in PA, about 1798; William was living at Steuben in 1860.

v MARY ANN DANA, b. about 1808; d. after 1865 when she was living at Bolivar, NY with her sister Eliza. Mary Ann did not marry.

vi WEALTHY ANN DANA, b. 6 Sep 1822; d. at Oklahoma City, OK, 8 Jun 1892; m. BENJAMIN FRANKLIN SMITH, b. at Gorham, NY, 16 Apr 1821 son of Isaac Adams and Lydia (Wright) Smith; Benjamin d. at Minco, OK, 4 Feb 1910.

2474 Obituary of Mrs. Nancy Owen, "Western Christian Advocate", Cincinnati, OH, 21 November 1849, p 4

2475 *Record of Wills, Other Miscellaneous Surrogate Records, 1807-1930;* Author: *New York. Surrogate's Court (Allegany County), Probate of Wills, Vol 0002-0003, 1840-1865, volume 0003, pp 391-392*

2476 *Record of Wills, Other Miscellaneous Surrogate Records, 1807-1930;* Author: *New York. Surrogate's Court (Allegany County), Orders, Minutes, Decrees, Vol A, E, 1807-1851, p 266*

936) SALLY DANA (*Lucy Holt Dana[4], Daniel[3], Nicholas[2], Nicholas[1]*), b. at Ashford, 23 Mar 1777 daughter of Jedediah and Lucy (Holt) Dana; d. at German Flatts (Paine's Hollow), NY, 1 Jul 1856; m. 10 Oct 1802, THOMAS PAYN, b. at Lebanon, CT, 26 Jan 1778 son of Seth and Jerusha (Swift) Payn; Thomas d. at German Flatts, 26 Sep 1856.[2477]

Sally Dana and Thomas Payn were parents of five children likely all born at Paine's Hollow, New York and all of whom used Paine as spelling for their last name.[2478]

i THOMAS ALMIREN PAINE, b. 25 Mar 1805; d. at Manistee, MI, 28 Nov 1867; m. 1st about 1828, CAROLINE ALLEN, b. about 1806; Caroline d. at Paine's Hollow, NY, 31 Mar 1832.Thomas m. 2nd, about 1833, MARY GOLDEN, b. in NY, 23 Feb 1810; Mary d. at Manistee, 26 Dec 1892.

ii WILLIAM DANA PAINE, b. 9 Aug 1809; d. Nunda, NY, 1873; m. SAMANTHA RICE, b. 15 Feb 1815 daughter of Elijah and Anna (Price) Rice; Samantha d. at Nunda, 8 Sep 1903.

iii CARLOS GRANT PAINE, b. 20 Feb 1811; d. at Nunda, NY, 1882; m. 1st 1835, JERUSHA SWIFT, b. at Mansfield, CT, 25 Jan 1812 daughter of Philip and Fanny (Russ) Swift; Jerusha d. at Nunda, about 1855. Carlos m. 2nd, about 1855, NANCY SWEET (widow of Abraham Burdick), b. 1817; Nancy d. at Nunda, 1901.

iv PHILANDER ALONZO PAINE, b. 28 Nov 1814; d. (buried at) Richland, IA, 13 Apr 1884;[2479] m. SALLY FILKINS, b. in NY, about 1817; Sally d. 4 Nov 1887 and is also buried at Richland, although living at South Fork, IA in 1885.

v SALLY AMANDA PAINE, b. 10 Sep 1817; d. at Paine's Hollow, 29 May 1839;[2480] m. at Herkimer County, NY, 19 Aug 1838, DELOS L. FILER, b. 27 Sep 1817 son of Alanson and Polly (Dodge) Filer; Delos d. at Milwaukee, WI, 26 Jul 1879. Delos was second married to Juliet Golden and third married to Mary Pierce.

937) MARY "POLLY" DANA (*Lucy Holt Dana[4], Daniel[3], Nicholas[2], Nicholas[1]*), b. at Ashford, 15 Jan 1781 daughter of Jedediah and Lucy (Holt) Dana; d. at Nunda, NY, 27 Dec 1850; m. JAMES PAYN (PAINE), b. at Lebanon, CT, 27 Jan 1783 son of Seth and Jerusha (Swift) Payn; James d. at Nunda, 8 Apr 1861.

James Paine was the first permanent settler (although not the first "pioneer") in Nunda, New York arriving there from Herkimer County on 15 March 1817 with their two oldest sons.[2481] They were parents of four children.

i EARL JUDSON PAINE, b. at Paine's Hollow, 24 Mar 1807; d. at Nunda, NY, 23 Aug 1881; m. CATHERINE GRIMES, b. 10 Nov 1803 daughter of Richard and Anna (Phillips) Grimes; Catherine d. at Nunda, 25 Feb 1879.

ii LUCIUS F. PAINE, b. at Paine's Hollow, about 1810; d. at Nunda, 12 Feb 1883; m. EMELINE HOPKINS, b. about 1811 daughter of Charles and Emma (Adams) Hopkins; Emeline d. at Nunda, 23 Apr 1889.

iii JAMES ALMIRON PAINE, b. at Nunda, 12 Nov 1819; d. at 31 Mar 1899; m. 1st LUCRETIA PUTNAM, b. about 1823. James m. 2nd ESTHER GREENWOOD, b. in England, Aug 1845 daughter of James and Mary (-) Greenwood; Esther d. after 1900 when she was living in Nunda.

iv MARY ALMIRA PAINE, b. at Nunda, 12 Nov 1819; d. at Nunda, 30 Mar 1857; m. Dec 1853, Rev. LYMAN STILSON, b. at Meredith, NY, 29 Jan 1805 son of Cyrenus and Sarah (Baldwin) Stilson; Lyman d. at Jefferson, IA, 23 Mar 1886.

Great-Grandchildren of Hannah Holt and Robert Gray

938) NATHAN ABBOTT (*Elizabeth Gray Abbott[4], Henry Gray[3], Hannah Holt Gray[2], Nicholas[1]*), b. 10 Apr 1721 son of Paul and Elizabeth (Gray) Abbott; d. unknown but he might have gone to Pennsylvania; m. 1st at Pomfret, 24 Nov 1742, EUNICE MARSH, b. at Plainfield, CT 17 Feb 1724 daughter of Thomas and Eunice (Parkhouse) Marsh; Eunice d. at Ashford 27 Oct 1760. Nathan m. 2nd HEPHZIBAH BROWN, b. about 1727; Hepzibah d. 26 May 1790 at Hampton, CT.

Nathan Abbott and Eunice Marsh had nine children whose births are recorded in Windham County, the oldest two children at Ashford and the remining six children at Pomfret. Five of the children are known to have died in early childhood,

[2477] Towne and Jones, Seth Payn and Some of His Descendants, NEHGR, 1943, p 138

[2478] Towne and Jones, Seth Payn and Some of His Descendants, NEHGR, 1943, p 138

[2479] Philander was living at South Fork, IA in 1880 but burial was in Richland. Iowa, Cemetery Records, 1662-1999

[2480] Sally's only child, Sally Amanda Filer was born 20 May 1839.

[2481] Hand, *Centennial History of the Town of Nunda*, p 120

four of the children dying in a two-week period in 1754. In 1754, there were outbreaks of "throat distemper" and "malignant fever" in various locations in the New England colonies.[2482]

i NATHAN ABBOTT, b. 18 May 1744; d. at Woodstock, 19 Jan 1794;[2483] m. JUDITH STODDARD, b. 24 Sep 1749 daughter of Ebenezer and Anna (Stowell) Stoddard. There is a probate record for Nathan Abbott from 1794 that names wife Judith as administrator of the estate with Ebenezer Stoddard as co-signer on the surety bond.[2484]

ii EUNICE ABBOTT, b. 20 Nov 1746; no further record. There is a Eunice Abbott as head of household in the 1790 US Census in Fairfield, but there is no reason to believe that is this Eunice.

iii GIDEON ABBOTT, b. 3 Jun 1748; d. 5 Sep 1754.

iv HANNAH ABBOTT, b. 25 Mar 1750; d. 27 Aug 1754.

v PAUL ABBOTT, b. 11 Feb 1753; d. 30 Aug 1754.

vi ELIZABETH ABBOTT, b. 12 Feb 1754; d. 11 Sep 1754.

vii EXPERIENCE ABBOTT, b. 21 Jan 1756; d. at Hampton, 20 Dec 1835; m. 12 Mar 1820, as his third wife, THOMAS GROW, b. at Pomfret, 4 Apr 1743 son of Thomas and Susanna (Eaton) Grow.

viii STEPHEN ABBOTT, b. 20 Oct 1757; d. at North Providence, RI, 24 Jul 1813;[2485][2486] m. 28 Jun 1781, ESTHER INGALLS, b. 26 Nov 1762 daughter of Zebadiah and Esther (Goodell) Ingalls; Esther d. 4 Feb 1851.

ix RUFUS ABBOTT, b. 18 Sep 1759; d. 1 Mar 1760.

939) WILLIAM ABBOTT (*Elizabeth Gray Abbott[4], Henry Gray[3], Hannah Holt Gray[2], Nicholas[1]*), b. 18 Feb 1723 son of Paul and Elizabeth (Gray) Abbott; d. at Pomfret 1 Nov 1805; m. 1st 9 May 1745, JERUSHA STOWELL, b. 22 Sep 1721 at Newton, MA daughter of David and Mary (Dillaway) Stowell; Jerusha d. 29 Feb 1768. William m. 2nd 4 Jun 1778, HANNAH EDMUND; Hannah d. 5 Feb 1808; nothing else is known of her at this time.

There are four births records at Pomfret for William Abbott and his first wife Jerusha Stowell.

i ANNA ABBOTT, b. 29 Jun 1748; d. at Pomfret, 5 Nov 1791. Anna does not seem to have married.

ii WILLIAM ABBOTT, b. 27 May 1752; d. at Lisle, NY, 1806 (probate 15 Jul 1806); m. 8 Jul 1776, HANNAH SNOW, b. at Ashford, 2 Jul 1754 daughter of Samuel and Hannah (Mason) Snow.

iii ELIZABETH ABBOTT, b. 3 Mar 1758; d. 31 Dec 1769.

iv RHODA ABBOTT, b. 27 Jul 1761; d. likely in New York. The Abbot genealogy states she married and went to New York with her brother, but a spouse was not suggested. There was a Rhoda Abbott who married DAVID HEACOCK the son of David and Sarah (DeWulf) Heacock. Some sources suggest it was a daughter Rhoda of Jesse and Johannah (Kellogg) Abbott of the Rowley Abbott line, and that family was in Putnam County, NY where David Heacock also shows up. Remains an area for further research.

940) BENJAMIN ABBOTT (*Elizabeth Gray Abbott[4], Henry Gray[3], Hannah Holt Gray[2], Nicholas[1]*), b. 25 Jul 1724 son of Paul and Elizabeth (Gray) Abbott; d. at Brookfield, VT, 21 Jun 1807;[2487] m. 1st at Ashford, 16 Jan 1745/6, MARY ANN ANDREWS, b. at Windham 25 Jul 1727 daughter of John and Hannah (-) Andrews; Mary Ann d. 8 Dec 1788. Benjamin m. 2nd 30 Jun 1793 the widow HANNAH BROWN about whom nothing else is known.

Benjamin Abbott and Mary Ann Andrews had ten children whose births are recorded at several towns in Windham County including Ashford, Pomfret, and Windham. The Abbot genealogy[2488] lists a daughter named Isabel in this family but omits the daughter Louisa; there are records for Louisa but not for Isabel, so she is not included here. This may just be a matter of the name being confused.

[2482] Caulfield, Ernest. "The Pursuit of a Pestilence." In *Proceedings of the American Antiquarian Society*, vol. 60, no. 1, p. 21. American Antiquarian Society., 1950.

[2483] *Connecticut, Hale Collection of Cemetery Inscriptions and Newspaper Notices, 1629-1934*. Newspaper notice gives age at death as 49, and states he was in the Revolutionary War.

[2484] *Connecticut Wills and Probate, 1609-1999*, Probate of Nathan Abbott, Hartford, 1794, Case number 4.

[2485] Ancestry.com, Rhode Island, Vital Extracts, 1636-1899

[2486] There is a Rhode Island probate record for Col. Stephen Abbott from August 1813 that contains an inventory and provides for widow Esther to administer the estate. Probate Files, Early to 1885 (Pawtucket, R.I.); Author: Pawtucket (Rhode Island). Court of Probate; Probate Place: Providence, Rhode Island

[2487] His grave site is in the Brookfield, VT cemetery. (findagrave.com)

[2488] Abbot and Abbot, *Genealogical Record of Descendants*

i HENRY ABBOTT, b. 12 Nov 1746; d. 27 Jan 1749.

ii HENRY ABBOTT, b. 3 Jun 1749; d. at Vermont, 31 Mar 1807; m. at Hampton, 7 Apr 1772, a fourth cousin, SARAH BURNHAM (*Eunice Holt Burnham*[5], *Zebadiah*[4], *George*[3], *Henry*[2], *Nicholas*[1]), b. 21 Aug 1750 daughter of Isaac and Eunice (Holt) Burnham. Sarah had married first John Greenslit with whom she had two children.

iii STEPHEN ABBOTT, b. 23 May 1751; d. 21 Aug 1754.

iv BENJAMIN ABBOTT, b. 21 Jan 1753; d, 21 Aug 1754.

v MARY ABBOTT, b. 4 Aug 1754; d. at Brookfield, VT, 28 Feb 1811; m. 17 May 1781, THOMAS ADAMS, b. at Canterbury, CT, 24 Apr 1757 son of Eliphalet and Mary (Frost) Adams; Thomas d. at Brookfield, 1803 (distribution of estate 5 Aug 1803).

vi ASA ABBOTT, b. 25 May 1756; d. at Hampton, 1834 (will dated 10 Apr 1834); m. by 1783, SARAH BIDLACK, b. at Hampton, 30 Sep 1756 daughter of James and Mehitable (Durkee) Bidlack. Sarah was first married to STEPHEN FULLER son of Stephen and Mary (Abbott) Fuller. Stephen died at the Battle of Wyoming.

vii HANNAH ABBOTT, b. 10 Feb 1759; m. at Hampton, 24 May 1775, JOSIAH COLLINS, b. about 1749 (based on age 63 at time of death); Josiah d. at Hampton, 24 Feb 1812.

viii TRYPHENA ABBOTT, b. 22 Sep 1760; d. at Stafford, 21 Nov 1835; m. May 1781, ABNER ASHLEY, b. at Hampton, 19 Jan 1754 son of Abner and Mary (Crossley) Ashley; Abner d. at Tolland 1837 (will proved 2 January 1838).

ix LOUISA ABBOTT, b. 24 Dec 1762; d. at New York, 16 Mar 1806; m. at Canterbury, 1 Sep 1785, SAMUEL PRESTON, b. 19 Feb 1763 son of Jacob and Mary (Butts) Preston.

x BENJAMIN ABBOTT, b. 2 Oct 1764; d. at Brookfield, VT, 12 Sep 1829;[2489] m. about 1786, LUCY FLINT, b. 10 Jun 1767 daughter of Nathaniel and Lucy (Martin) Flint; Lucy d. 24 Sep 1839.

941) ISAAC ABBOTT (*Elizabeth Gray Abbott*[4], *Henry Gray*[3], *Hannah Holt Gray*[2], *Nicholas*[1]), b. 29 Aug 1732 son of Paul and Elizabeth (Gray) Abbott; d. at Milford, NH about 1800;[2490] m. 29 Apr 1756, MARY BARKER about whom nothing else concrete is known.[2491]

Isaac Abbott was a farmer. He was born in Pomfret and there married Mary (although some sources say Sarah) Barker who was also from Pomfret, but her parentage is not known. The births of their first seven children are recorded at Pomfret, but there is also a recording of these births at Princeton, Massachusetts. The young family left Pomfret by 1769, were for a time in Princeton where they were early settlers recorded there in 1769,[2492] and finally settled in Milford, New Hampshire where they were about 1778.[2493] Isaac Abbott served as a private in the company of Colonel Stickney during the Revolutionary War.

Isaac Abbott and Mary Barker had twelve children, the oldest seven recorded at Pomfret, the births of four children recorded at Princeton, and the youngest child whose birthplace is unknown. This youngest child died in Milford.

i MARY ABBOTT, b. at Pomfret, 20 Jan 1757; d. at Lyme, NH, 8 Sep 1849; m. 9 Dec 1778, her first cousin, LEMUEL HOLT (*Joshua*[4], *Joshua*[3], *Nicholas*[2], *Nicholas*[1]), b. at Windham, 28 Feb 1756 son of Joshua and Mary (Abbott) Holt; Lemuel d. 1 Aug 1836. Mary Abbott and Lemuel Holt are Family 767.

ii HANNAH ABBOTT, b. at Pomfret, 2 Aug 1758; d. at Stoddard, NH, 9 Mar 1847; m. at Amherst, NH, 25 May 1781, ISRAEL TOWNE, b. at Stoddard, NH, 17 Jun 1761 son of Israel and Lydia (Hopkins) Towne; Israel d. 2 May 1848.

iii CHLOE ABBOTT, b. at Pomfret, 7 Aug 1760; d. at Lyme, 1835. Chloe is reported to have married twice, but the name of her first husband has not been found. She m. 2nd, about 1801, WILLIAM PORTER, b. 1761 son of William and Esther (Carpenter) Porter. William was a widower with several children, his wife Phebe Kingsbury having died in 1800. William d. 3 Mar 1847. Chloe did not have children.

iv SARAH "SALLY" ABBOTT, b. at Pomfret, 14 Oct 1762; d. at Mason, NH, 1846; m. at Amherst, 25 Oct 1795, JAMES BROWN.

v METYLDA ABBOTT, b. at Pomfret, 29 Aug 1764.

2489 Benjamin's estate entered probate in Orange County, VT in 1830.

2490 1800 is the year of death used by the Daughters of the American Revolution and in Ramsdell's *History of Milford, volume 1*.

2491 Abbot and Abbot, *Genealogical Record of Descendants* gives her name as Sarah Barker, but the marriage record and all the birth records for the children give her name as Mary.

2492 Blake, *The History of the Town of Princeton*, p 81

2493 Ramsdell, *The History of Milford, volume 1*, p 560

vi ISAAC ABBOTT, b. at Pomfret, 17 Jul 1766; d. at Milford, NH, 1 Sep 1831; m. 15 Oct 1793, RUTH AMES, b. at Wilmington, MA, 31 Jul 1776 daughter of Caleb and Mary (Harvey) Ames/Eams; Ruth d. at Milford, 29 Jul 1844.

vii ESTHER ABBOTT, b. at Pomfret, 28 Jun 1768.

viii FIDELIA ABBOTT, b. at Princeton, 29 May 1770.

ix OLIVE ABBOTT, b. at Princeton, 28 Oct 1772. It is possible that she married Isaac Parker 6 Feb 1794 at Amherst. The Olive Abbott that married Isaac was of Milford and she died 2 Jan 1862 at age 89 which fits for this Olive. Isaac Parker was b. at Monson, NH, 2 Mar 1769 son of Josiah and Hannah (Parkis) Parker.

x DOROTHY ABBOTT, b. at Princeton, 10 Sep 1774; d. at Milford, 16 Aug 1802.

xi DEBORAH ABBOTT, b. at Princeton, 10 Sep 1774; d. at Milford, 22 May 1806.

xii STEPHEN ABBOTT, b. 1778; d. at Milford, 9 Jul 1792.

942) ELIZABETH ABBOTT (*Elizabeth Gray Abbott[4], Henry Gray[3], Hannah Holt Gray[2], Nicholas[1]*), b. 20 Jul 1737 daughter of Paul and Elizabeth (Gray) Abbott; d. possibly 1828;[2494] m. 28 Sep 1761 as his 2nd wife, JOSEPH PHELPS, b. 27 Feb 1723/4 son of Samuel and Hannah (Dane) Phelps; Joseph d. at Andover 27 Jan 1802.

Elizabeth Abbott married Joseph Phelps after he was widowed and with two small children. His first wife was Lydia Osgood who died at Pomfret 20 July 1761. Just two months later, Elizabeth and Joseph married. Elizabeth and Joseph had six children, the oldest two born at Pomfret. The family then returned to Massachusetts settling in Princeton in Worcester County where their youngest four children were born. In later life, the couple returned to their roots in Andover.

The will of Joseph Phelps includes bequests to the following persons: beloved wife Elisabeth, beloved son Joseph gets some oxen and a yoke to make up the rest of his part, beloved son Elisha gets carpenter tools to make up the rest of his part, and beloved daughters Hannah, Elisabeth, Lydia, and Tryphenea get one dollar each (which is in addition to what he has already given them). Legacies at the final settlement are to Hannah Adams, Elizabeth Harrington, Lydia Whittemore, Tryphena Russell, Elisha Phelps, and Joseph Phelps. Elizabeth Phelps also receives a payment.[2495] Joseph Phelps and Hannah Adams are Joseph's children from his marriage to Lydia Osgood.

i ELIZABETH PHELPS, b. 1 Mar 1765; d. at Lexington, 26 Jun 1835; m. about 1787, NATHAN HARRINGTON, b. at Lexington, 29 Apr 1762 son of Daniel and Anna (Munroe) Harrington; Nathan d. 30 Jun 1837.

ii LYDIA PHELPS, b. 5 Feb 1767; d. at Cambridge, 10 Nov 1834; m. PHILIP CARTERET WHITTEMORE, b. at Arlington, 1 Sep 1766 son of William and Abigail (De Carteret) Whittemore; Philip d. 30 Jun 1855.

iii TRYPHENA PHELPS, b. 28 Sep 1769; d. at Woburn, 8 Oct 1818; m. at Woburn, 19 Jun 1791, WILLIAM "BILL" RUSSELL, b. 4 May 1763 son of Jesse and Elizabeth (Whipple) Russell. After Tryphena's death, Bill Russell married Mrs. Phebe Dorman. Bill Russell d. at Billerica, 4 Jul 1842.

iv ELISHA PHELPS, b. 10 Oct 1771; d. at Andover, 27 Jan 1823; m. at Woburn, 28 Oct 1795, RHODA TAY, b. at Wilmington, 19 Nov 1770 daughter of Benjamin and Sybil (Marion) Tay; Rhoda d. 16 Oct 1841. Elisha and Rhoda do not seem to have had any children. Elisha died at the almshouse in Andover.[2496]

v SAMUEL PHELPS, b. 5 Aug 1773; d. 19 Aug 1778.

vi POLLY PHELPS, b. 8 Oct 1775; d. 11 Aug 1778.

943) LYDIA GRAY (*Henry Gray[4], Henry Gray[3], Hannah Holt Gray[2], Nicholas[1]*), b. 28 May 1748; d. at Andover, 23 Feb 1821 daughter of Henry and Alice (Peabody) Gray; m. at Andover, 26 Mar 1766, Dr. SYMONDS BAKER, b. at Topsfield, MA, 6 Jan 1735/6 son of Thomas and Sarah (Wade) Baker; Symonds d. at Andover, 8 Jul 1815. Symonds was first married to Susan Sargent who died in 1764.

Lydia Gray was the only heir to her father's estate. She married Symonds Baker was a physician in Methuen and Andover.

In his will written 4 June 1813 (probate 1 August 1815), Symonds Baker bequeathed to beloved wife Lydia all the household items not otherwise disposed of in the will. He leaves not more to Lydia as she received an estate from her father sufficient for her support. Daughter Susannah Frye wife of Joseph Frye receives ten dollars with what she has received is her full portion. His three grandchildren Thomas Baker, Deborah Poor, and Priscilla Frye each receives five dollars. Rebecca Holt, for her long a faithful service to the family, receives the use and improvement of the east chamber as long as she is single. She is also to have a decent maintenance from the estate if she shall need it. By this he means that she is to reside with the family of son Symonds, but if the circumstances of his son's family make that not comfortable, Rebecca is to be provided for out of the

2494 Abbot and Abbot, *Genealogical Record of Descendants* gives a death date of June 1828, but I have not located a record.
2495 *Essex County, MA: Probate File Papers, 1638-1881. Probate of Joseph Phelps, 10 Mar 1802, Case number 21650.*
2496 *Massachusetts, Town and Vital Records, 1620-1988.*

estate rather than be a charge of the town. Son Symonds receives several specific furniture items including the eight-day clock. Symonds receives the residue of the personal estate. He also has the use and improvement of the real estate, but after son Symonds decease, the real estate goes to his grandson David Baker.[2497]

In her will written 18 May 1816 (probate 3 April 1821), Lydia Gray Baker bequeathed to daughter-in-law Sally Baker wife of Symonds, granddaughter Deborah Poor, and granddaughter Priscilla Frye each one pewter platter. She leaves in trust with the executor, one hundred dollars and the interest from that amount is to be paid annually to Sally Baker for her sole and separate use during the life of Symonds E. Baker. If Sally outlives Symonds, then at his decease the whole of the principal is to be paid to Sally. If Symonds outlives Sally, then the money goes to his children. Daughter Susanna Frye receives the household furniture. Son Symonds receives the use and improvement of a piece of land and the property goes to grandson David after Symonds' decease. Lydia makes a number of other provisions related to daughter Susannah and her children and for the sale of portions of the estate. David Gray was named executor. Real estate was valued at $4,152.41.[2498]

Lydia Gray and Symonds Baker were parents of three children. Dr. Baker had three children with his first wife Susan Sargent, but those children all died of canker rash.

i HENRY GRAY BAKER, b. 1 Apr 1767; d. at Andover, 10 Mar 1802; m. 21 Sep 1786, DEBORAH AMES, b. at Groton, 6 Apr 1768 daughter of Nathan and Deborah (Bower) Ames; Deborah d. at Andover, 7 Dec 1819. Deborah was second married to Caleb Abbott.

ii SUSANNA SARGENT BAKER, b. 10 Apr 1769; d. at Andover, 12 Jul 1856; m. 18 Sep 1799, JOSEPH FRYE, b. at Andover, 6 Nov 1767 son of Benjamin and Elizabeth (Clark) Frye; Joseph is reported to have been executed in Canada for horse smuggling about 1820.[2499]

iii SYMONDS EPPES BAKER, b. 17 Jan 1779; d. at Andover, 22 Mar 1819; m. 27 May 1802, his second cousin, SARAH HOLT (*David*[5], *Samuel*[4], *Samuel*[3], *Samuel*[2], *Nicholas*[1]), b. at Andover, 27 Dec 1775 daughter of David and Hannah (Martin) Holt; Sarah d. at Andover, 7 Jan 1865.

944) EPHRAIM FOSTER (*Mary Gray Foster*[4], *Henry Gray*[3], *Hannah Holt Gray*[2], *Nicholas*[1]), b. at Andover, 30 Aug 1731 son of Moses and Mary (Gray) Foster; d. at Peacham, VT, 12 Nov 1803; m. about 1755, HANNAH MOOR, b. 5 Aug 1732 daughter of James and Agnes (Colbreath) Moor.[2500]

Known as Capt. Ephraim Foster, Ephraim was involved in the military affairs of the town of Bow. He fulfilled civis duties such as serving as selectman and moderator of the town meeting.[2501]

The records for this family are incomplete, but Ephraim Foster and Hannah Moor are likely parents of six children born at Bow, New Hampshire.[2502]

i EPHRAIM FOSTER, b. about 1758; m. 1st about 1790, JERUSHA MINER, baptized at Woodbury, CT, 26 May 1771 daughter of Reuben and Beulah (Root) Miner; Jerusha d. at Peacham, VT, 23 Mar 1813. Ephraim m. 2nd about 1814, SARAH HERRICK, b. at Hopkinton, NH, about 1778 daughter of Jonathan and Rachel (Allen) Herrick; Sarah d. at Peacham, 21 Sep 1825.

ii ANNA FOSTER, b. about 1760; d. at Hardwick, VT, 28 Feb 1853; m. at Concord, NH, 15 Oct 1780, TIMOTHY HALL,[2503] b. at Rumford (Concord), NH, 5 Jun 1757 son of Ebenezer and Dorcas (Abbott) Hall; Timothy d. at Irasburg, VT, 16 Jul 1832.

iii DANIEL FOSTER, b. estimate 1762

iv MARY FOSTER, b. about 1763; m. about 1780, MOODY MORSE, b. at Chester, NH, 12 Jan 1753 son of Thomas and Mary (Bartlett) Morse; Moody d. at Peacham, VT, 13 Mar 1822.

v MOSES FOSTER, b. estimate 1764

vi Daughter (name unknown) who married Mr. Clark (according to Pierce's Foster Genealogy).

vii ENOCH FOSTER, b. 27 Apr 1770; d. at Walden, VT, 30 May 1854; m. 1st about 1792, MARY "POLLY" GUY, b. 1776; Mary d. at Peacham, 7 Jan 1809. Enoch m. 2nd at Walden, VT, 26 Mar 1810, SUSANNAH MUDGETT

2497 *Essex County, MA: Probate File Papers, 1638-1881.* Online database. *AmericanAncestors.org.* New England Historic Genealogical Society, 2014. Case 1497

2498 *Essex County, MA: Probate File Papers, 1638-1881.* Online database. *AmericanAncestors.org.* New England Historic Genealogical Society, 2014. Case 1469

2499 Abbott, Early Records of the Frye Family of Andover, https://www.mhl.org/sites/default/files/files/Abbott/Frye%20Family.pdf

2500 Cutter, *New England Families*, volume 2, p 726

2501 Bow, NH, *The Town Book of Bow*, volume 1

2502 Pierce's Foster genealogy gives children Enoch, Ephraim, Daniel, and Moses and two unnamed daughters. Carter's *History of Pembroke* (volume 2, p 99) gives known children as Ann, Daniel, and Moses.

25032503 This marriage is substantiated by the Revolutionary War pension fie of Timothy Hall who married Anna Foster of Bow, (widow of Edward Gould), b. at Walden, 7 Nov 1771 daughter of Edward and Sarah (Smith) Mudgett;[2504] Susannah d. at Peacham, 15 Dec 1832.

945) CALEB FOSTER (*Mary Gray Foster⁴, Henry Gray³, Hannah Holt Gray², Nicholas¹*), b. about 1744 son of Moses and Mary (Gray) Foster; Caleb d. at Pembroke, NH, 3 May 1821; m. HANNAH who has not been identified, but born about 1737 (based on age at death); Hannah d. at Pembroke, 28 Apr 1811.[2505]

Caleb Foster and Hannah Foster were parents of three children born at Pembroke.

i HANNAH FOSTER, b. 16 Aug 1768

ii ELIZABETH FOSTER, b. 10 Dec 1770

iii CALEB FOSTER, b. 3 Feb 1777; m. at Pembroke, 6 Mar 1798, BETSEY FOSTER who has not been identified.

946) MARY GRAY (*Samuel Gray⁴, Henry Gray³, Hannah Holt Gray², Nicholas¹*), b. at Rumford, 29 Dec 1743 daughter of Samuel and Sarah (Abbott) Gray; d. at Amherst, NH 19 Oct 1775; m. at Amherst, 3 Dec 1762, MOSES TOWNE, b. at Topsfield, May 1739 son of Israel and Grace (Gardner) Towne; Moses d. at Milford, NH 9 Feb 1824.

Mary Gray and Moses Towne were parents of six children all born at Amherst.

i SARAH TOWNE, b. 10 Dec 1762; d. at Hopkinton, NH, 18 Feb 1805; m. about 1785, her first cousin, JOSEPH TOWNE, b. at Amherst, 30 Sep 1758 son of Thomas and Hannah (Boutelle) Towne. Joseph married second Margaret Barker in 1806.

ii SAMUEL GRAY TOWNE, b. 25 May 1764; d. at Nashua, NH, 24 Sep 1848. Samuel did not marry.

iii MOSES TOWNE, b. 21 Oct 1766; d. at Nashua, 14 Aug 1854; m. SARAH TAYLOR, b. about 1767; Sarah d. at Nashua, 17 Apr 1851.

iv MARY TOWNE, b. 14 Sep 1768; d. at Amherst, 1 Mar 1777.

v ELIZABETH TOWNE, b. 27 Oct 1770; d. at Hopkinton, 27 Aug 1822; m. at Amherst, 20 Oct 1794, TRUEWORTHY GILMAN, b. 1769 son of Trueworthy and Elizabeth (Bartlett) Gilman; Trueworthy d. at Hopkinton, 6 Jan 1799.

vi LEMUEL TOWNE, b. 17 Jun 1773; d. 8 Oct 1775.

947) JOHN SESSIONS (*Hannah Gray Sessions Foster⁴, Henry Gray³, Hannah Holt Gray², Nicholas¹*), b. at Andover, 9 Jun 1742 son of Samuel and Hannah (Gray) Sessions; d. at Westminster, 1 May 1820; m. 17 Nov 1763, ANN WORSTLY, b. about 1739; Ann d. at Westminster, 12 Oct 1820.

John Sessions was a farmer in Westminster where he served as deacon of the Congregational church and a judge of the county court. At one time, he was a member of the Colonial Congress that met in New York.[2506]

Johns Sessions and Ann Worstly were parents of three children born at Westminster, Vermont.

i ANNA SESSIONS, b. 20 Jul 1765; d. at Putney, VT, 3 Aug 1861; m. 2 Dec 1784, DAVID FOSTER, likely b. at Boxford, MA, 23 Aug 1756 son of Jeremiah and Bridget (Wood) Foster; David d. at Westminster, 26 Jul 1818.

ii JOHN SESSIONS, b. 30 Jul 1768; d. at Lunenburg, VT, 25 Jan 1852; m. 16 Oct 1793, LUCINDA WASHBURN, b. at Middletown, CT, 14 May 1770 daughter of Joseph and Ruth (Wetmore) Washburn;[2507] Lucinda d. at Lunenburg, 11 Mar 1820.

iii SAMUEL SESSIONS, b. 25 Jun 1773; d. at Westminster, 9 Jan 1824; m. at Westminster, 5 Nov 1817, his first cousin, HANNAH BRAGG (*Hannah Foster Bragg⁵, Hannah Gray Foster⁴, Henry Gray³, Hannah Holt Gray², Nicholas¹*), b. at Keene, 5 Jan 1787 daughter of Luther and Hannah (Foster) Bragg; Hannah d. at Westminster, 9 Mar 1827. Samuel's father and Hannah's mother were half-siblings.

948) HANNAH FOSTER (*Hannah Gray Sessions Foster⁴, Henry Gray³, Hannah Holt Gray², Nicholas¹*), b. at Keene, 3 Apr 1751 daughter of David and Hannah (Gray) Foster; d. at Westminster, VT, 9 Apr 1822; m. at Keene, 14 Jun 1769, LUTHER BRAGG, b. at Wrentham, MA, 16 Feb 1742/3 son of Henry and Mary (Bennett) Bragg; Luther d. at Keene, 18 Aug 1804.

2504 The 1823 will of Edward Mudgett includes a bequest to his daughter Susannah Foster.

2505 Pierce, *Foster Genealogy*, part 1, p 164

2506 Sessions, *Materials for a History of the Sessions Family*, p 73

2507 The 1810 will of Joseph Washburn of Orleans County, VT includes a bequest to his daughter Lucinda Sessions.

Luther and Hannah resided in Keene where Luther signed the association test in 1776 and a member of the Keene, New Hampshire company of foot.[2508]

In his will written 15 June 1804, Luther Bragg bequeaths to beloved wife Hannah one-third of the real estate and all of the household furniture. There are other provisions for her support. Eldest son Calvin Bragg receives one-third of the real estate and one-half of the personal estate. Calvin is charged with paying one-half the debts and one-half the legacies and providing one-half of the support for son Luther who is not capable of caring for himself. Son Henry Bragg receives one-third of the real estate and one-half the personal estate with the same provisions as Calvin. Henry will also receive the one-third that will be used by his mother after her decease. Sons Luther, David, Ambrose, Enos, and James receive one dollar each. Son James is to be well-schooled until age fourteen and son shall have the benefit of his earnings as he is of age nineteen. Daughter Lavina Ladd receives one dollar and one-fourth of the household furniture after her mother's decease. Daughter Sarah Bragg receives one hundred dollars and daughters Hannah Bragg and Grata Bragg receive seventy-five dollars and these three daughters each also receive one-fourth of the household furniture. Sons Calvin and Henry were named executors.[2509]

Luther Bragg and Hannah Foster were parents of thirteen children born at Keene.

i CALVIN BRAGG, b. 10 Dec 1769; d. at Keene, 10 Mar 1810; m. 13 Jun 1798, his second cousin, SALLY GRAY (*Aaron Gray[5], Aaron Gray[4], Henry Gray[3], Henry Holt Gray[2], Nicholas[1]*), b. at Keene, 11 Jun 1779 daughter of Aaron and Huldah (Clark) Gray; Sally d. at Keene, 1 Aug 1840. Sally married second Aaron Gary.

ii LEVINA BRAGG, b. 28 Jul 1771; d. after 1860 when she was living in Lunenburg, VT; m. TIMOTHY LADD, b. at Chesterfield, NH, 22 Feb 1773 son of Timothy and Rachel (Spencer) Ladd; Timothy d. at Lunenburg, 18 Apr 1825.

iii LUTHER BRAGG, b. 28 Mar 1773; d. at Keene, 2 May 1842. Luther did not marry.

iv DAVID BRAGG, b. 19 Jan 1776; d. at Keene, 20 Aug 1804; m. at Keene, 10 Jul 1803, PRISCILLA WOODARD, b. at Marlborough, NH, 23 Aug 1780 daughter of Solomon and Priscilla (Holmes) Woodard.

v SARAH BRAGG, b. 16 Feb 1778; d. at Lunenburg, VT, 5 May 1869; m. ASAHEL PERRY, b. about 1773 (based on age at time of death); Asahel d. at Lunenburg, 22 Aug 1845.

vi HENRY BRAGG, b. 6 Apr 1780; m. at Keene, 15 Nov 1804, MARY FELT, b. at Nelson, NH, 8 May 1780 daughter of Joshua and Hannah (Stocker) Felt.

vii ASA BRAGG, b. 5 Apr 1782; d. 17 Apr 1782.

viii JAMES BRAGG, b. 19 Apr 1783; d. 5 Oct 1785.

ix AMBROSE BRAGG, b. 15 May 1785; d. after 1860 when he was living in Warrensville, OH. Ambrose may not have married.

x HANNAH BRAGG, b. 5 Jan 1787; d. at Westminster, VT, 9 Mar 1827; m. at Westminster, 5 Nov 1817, her first cousin, SAMUEL SESSIONS (*John Sessions[5], Hannah Gray Sessions[4], Henry Gray[3], Hannah Holt Gray[2], Nicholas[1]*), b. 25 Jun 1773 son of John and Ann (Worstly) Sessions; Samuel d. at Westminster, 9 Jan 1824.

xi ENOS BRAGG, b. 6 Jul 1789. Enos enlisted in the army during the War of 1812 on 14 May 1812 and was reported as deserted at Grand River, OH in 1813. It is not clear what became of him.

xii GRATIA BRAGG, b. 28 Apr 1792; d. at Westminster, VT, 9 Aug 1824. Gratia did not marry. In her will written 12 May 1824, Gratia made bequests of one dollar each to the heirs of brother Calvin and brothers Luther, Daniel, Henry, Ambrose, and James. There were bequests of personal and household items to sister Lavina wife of Timothy Ladd, sister Sarah wife of Asahel Perry, sister Hannah wife of Samuel Sessions, and Mary wife of brother Henry Bragg. There are other bequests to her nieces and nephews each named.[2510]

xiii JAMES BRAGG, b. 14 Nov 1794; likely the James who d. at Sacramento, CA, 16 Jan 1853;[2511] m. at Berrien County, MI, ABIGAIL HART, baptized at Berlin, CT, 3 Dec 1803 daughter of Gideon and Cynthia (Langdon) Hart;[2512] Abigail d. at Bainbridge, MI, 25 Apr 1861. James likely went to California to the gold rush with his nephew Justus. After his death, Abigail and children are living with Justus in Berrien County in 1860.[2513]

[2508] Griffin, *The History of Keene, New Hampshire*, p 162, p 205

[2509] *New Hampshire. Probate Court (Cheshire County)*; Probate Place: *Cheshire, New Hampshire, Estate Files, B139-B197, 1803-1811, estate at Luther Bragg*

[2510] New Hampshire Will and Probate, Cheshire County, Estate of Gratia Bragg, Case 407

[2511] California State Library Mortuary Records (Northern California), 1849-1900; Sacramento, California; Microfilm Reel #: 2

[2512] Hooker, *The Descendants of Rev. Thomas Hooker*, p 127

[2513] 1860 United States Federal Census; Census Place: Bainbridge, Berrien, Michigan; Roll: M653_537; Page: 54; Family History Library Film: 803537

949) DAVID FOSTER (*Hannah Gray Sessions Foster[4], Henry Gray[3], Hannah Holt Gray[2], Nicholas[1]*), b. at Keene, 9 Mar 1755 son of David and Hannah (Gray) Foster; d. at Keene, 7 Jan 1798; m. at Keene, 3 Jan 1781, MARY DASSANCE, b. at Norton, MA, 1 Jun 1755 daughter of Martin and Phebe (Dorman) Dassance;[2514] Mary d. at Keene, 31 Mar 1833.

Mary's father was from Paris, France. David and Mary resided in Keene and were the parents of six children.

David did not leave a will and his estate entered probate 2 February 1798 with Thaddeus Metcalf as administrator at the request of widow Mary. Personal estate was valued at $529.10 and after payments of claims there was $262.76 left with the widow.[2515]

i SAMUEL FOSTER, b. 8 Nov 1781; d. at Keene, 3 Dec 1848. Samuel did not marry, and the probate of his estate was in Cheshire County, New Hampshire in 1849. Brother David of Whitesboro, Oneida, New York was administrator of the estate and stated that Samuel had no widow or children and David was the only heir of the estate.[2516]

ii BETSEY FOSTER, b. 28 Oct 1783; d. at Keene, 10 Nov 1810. Betsey did not marry.

iii DAVID FOSTER, b. 21 Feb 1786; d. at Whitestown, NY, Jan 1863 (probate 31 Mar 1863); m. 1st 11 May 1812, MARY FIELD daughter of Thomas Field of Keene;[2517] Mary d. at Whitestown, 1 Mar 1841. David m. 2nd MARGARET who has not been identified and was his widow at his probate.

iv POLLY FOSTER, b. 16 Mar 1791; d. at Keene, 26 Apr 1848. Polly did not marry.

v NANCY FOSTER, b. 30 Jan 1794; d. at Keene, 17 Nov 1824.

vi SALLY FOSTER, b. 16 Nov 1796; d. at Keene, 24 Aug 1798.

950) AARON GRAY (*Aaron Gray[4], Henry Gray[3], Hannah Holt Gray[2], Nicholas[1]*), b. at Andover, 16 Oct 1747 son of Aaron and Bethia (Peabody) Gray; d. at Keene, 25 Feb 1812; m. about 1776, HULDAH CLARK, b. at Keene, 7 Dec 1747 daughter of Isaac and Susanna (Geer) Clark; Huldah d. at Keener, 27 Feb 1812.

Aaron, along with his father, was a member of the "alarm" militia company established in Keene in 1773. Aaron was also a signer of a petition in 1776 related to an outbreak of smallpox in the area. Members of the community felt the epidemic was being improperly managed which they attributed to the early practice of inoculation, purposefully injecting the material from pustules in belief that this would prevent infection.[2518]

Aaron Gray and Huldah Clark were parents of seven children born at Keene.[2519]

i BETSEY GRAY, b. 4 Oct 1776; d. at Glover, VT, 27 Dec 1830; m. at Keene, 16 Feb 1800, ASA BROWN, b. about 1775; Asa d. after 1850 when he was living at Glover.

ii SALLY GRAY, b. 11 Jun 1779; d. at Keene, 1 Aug 1840; m. 13 Jun 1798, her second cousin, CALVIN BRAGG (*Hannah Foster Bragg[5], Hannah Gray Foster[4], Henry Gray[3], Hannah Holt Gray[2], Nicholas[1]*), b. at Keene, 14 Dec 1769 son of Luther and Hannah (Foster) Bragg; Calvin d. at Keene, 10 Mar 1810.

iii JOSEPH GRAY, b. 15 Jun 1780; d. at Glover, VT, 3 Oct 1860; m. at Keene, 13 Dec 1803, ABIGAIL "NABBY" LEONARD, b. at Warwick, MA, 26 Apr 1781 daughter of Noah and Bethia (Wetherell) Leonard;[2520] Nabby d. at Glover, 28 Nov 1846.

iv ELI GRAY, b. 15 Dec 1782; d. 25 May 1785.

v ISAAC GRAY, b. 15 Feb 1785; d. at Keene, 22 Sep 1865; m. at Keene, 12 Feb 1810, ABIAH BARKER, b. about 1792; Abiah d. at Keene, 2 Mar 1851.

vi ELI GRAY, b. 11 Jul 1787; d. after 1855 when he was living at Fort Edward, NY; m. 25 Oct 1813, ROXALANA JOY, b. at Alstead, NH, 14 Sep 1798 daughter of Nathaniel and Sarah (Ward) Joy; Roxalana d. after 1855. Eli and Roxalana were in Poultney and then Middletown, Vermont but are listed in the 1855 census at Fort Edward. Eli was a carpenter.

[2514] Mayflower Families Fifth Generation Descendants, John Alden, volume 16, part 4, p 261; accessed through americanancestors.org

[2515] New Hampshire Wills and Probate Records, Cheshire County, Estate Files, Case 51

[2516] *New Hampshire. Probate Court (Cheshire County);* Probate Place: *Cheshire, New Hampshire, Estate Files, F297-F360, 1843-1851, Case 343, estate of Samuel Foster*

[2517] Pierce, *Foster Genealogy*, Part I, p 284

[2518] Griffin, *History of the Town of Keene*, p 214

[2519] Whitcomb, *Vital Statistics of the Town of Keene*, volume 1, p 31

[2520] Glover Historical Society, Glover History, vol. 19, no. 1, 2010, http://www.gloverhistoricalsociety.org/ghs/wp-content/uploads/2012/07/GHSnews2010winter1.pdf

vii DANIEL "DAN" GRAY, b. 3 Nov 1789; d. at Glover, VT, 9 May 1875; m. at Keene, 4 Jan 1815, MARY "POLLY" FISKE, b. at Lexington, MA, about 1795 daughter of David and Sarah (Hadley) Fiske;[2521] Mary d. at Glover, 25 Apr 1877.

951) WILLIAM GRAY (*Aaron Gray⁴, Henry Gray³, Hannah Holt Gray², Nicholas¹*), b. at Andover, 27 Dec 1753 son of Aaron and Bethia (Peabody) Gray; d. at Keene, 1804 (probate 1804); m. at Keene, 25 Nov 1784, MARY "MOLLY" FISHER.

William Gray enlisted on 15 May 1775 in Col. Stark's regiment and was present at the Battle of Bunker Hill. He also signed the 1776 association test.[2522]

William Gray did not leave a will and his estate entered probate 19 October 1804 with widow Mary declining administration and requesting that this duty be assumed by Capt. Abel Blake. Personal estate was valued at $778.84 and after debts and costs paid there was a balance of $424.62. On 27 October 1809, the guardian for the heirs signed that he had received $424.62 from administrator Abel Blake for all the balance due on the inventory of the personal estate. Real estate was valued at $825.[2523]

There are records of seven children of William Gray and Molly Fisher born at Keene.

i HEPHZIBAH GRAY, b. 20 Feb 1785; d. at Keene, 3 May 1818. Hephzibah did not marry.

ii HENRY GRAY, b. 10 Jan 1787; d. at Keene, 16 Jan 1850. He left a widow Sela who declined administration of his estate. Sela has not been identified.

iii MOLLY GRAY, b. 27 Mar 1789; d. 3 Jul 1790.

iv MOLLY GRAY, b. 5 Feb 1791; d. at Keene, 29 Sep 1821. Molly did not marry.

v DANIEL GRAY, b. 7 Jan 1794

vi JOEL GRAY, b. 4 Feb 1798; d. at Keene, 27 Sep 1833.

vii ABIGAIL GRAY, b. 9 Aug 1801; d. 25 Nov 1817.

952) ELIZABETH ABBOTT (*Thomas Abbott⁴, Hannah Gray Abbott³, Hannah Holt Gray², Nicholas¹*), b. at Andover, 10 Jan 1726/7 daughter of Thomas and Elizabeth (Ballard) Abbott; d. at Andover 27 Sep 1792; m. 4 Jan 1753, as his 2nd wife, SAMUEL OSGOOD, b. 29 May 1714 son of Ezekiel and Rebecca (Wardwell) Osgood; Samuel d. 16 Mar 1774. Samuel was first married to Dorothy Wardwell.

Samuel Osgood did not leave a will. His widow Elizabeth was administrator of the estate. The value of the estate was £1,085. The probate records contain the details of the portion that Elizabeth received but does not have the other distributions.[2524] Elizabeth Osgood also did not leave a will and her estate entered probate 6 Nov 1792. The value of her estate was £42. Thomas Osgood was the administrator of Elizabeth's estate.[2525]

Elizabeth Abbott and Samuel Osgood had eight children whose births are recorded at Andover.

i LYDIA OSGOOD, b. 31 May 1754; d. at Andover, 2 Oct 1816; m. 20 Dec 1791, as the second of his three wives, ABIEL FAULKNER, b. at Andover, 4 Sep 1755 son of Abiel and Mary (Poor) Faulkner; Abiel d. 26 Nov 1818. His first marriage was to Hannah Abbott who was Lydia Osgood's first cousin. Abiel's third marriage was to Clarissa Dillaway. Lydia did not have children.

ii ELIZABETH OSGOOD, b. 17 Dec 1755; d. 16 Sep 1764.

iii SARAH OSGOOD, b. 14 Sep 1758; d. 21 Oct 1764.

iv JOSEPH OSGOOD, b. 5 Oct 1760; d. at Blue Hill, ME, 15 Mar 1854; m. 31 May 1785, HANNAH BAILEY, b. at Andover, 21 Dec 1765 daughter of Nathan and Deborah (Johnson) Bailey; Hannah d. 10 Jul 1829.

v DORCAS OSGOOD, b. Mar 1763; d. at Blue Hill, ME, 27 Apr 1832; m. at Andover, 4 Oct 1791, THEODORE STEVENS, b. 12 Jul 1763 son of Benjamin and Hannah (Varnum) Stevens; Theodore d. 15 May 1820.

vi JOHN OSGOOD, b. 7 Sep 1765; d. at Allenstown, NH, Dec 1829; m. Oct 1802, MARY SLATER daughter of Benjamin and Mary (Henley) Slater.[2526] No children have been identified for this couple.

2521 The 1820 probate of David Fiske of Lexington includes a payment to Daniel Gray on behalf of his wife Polly heir of David Fiske.

2522 Griffin, *History of the Town of Keene*, p 177, p 204

2523 *New Hampshire. Probate Court (Cheshire County), Estate Files, G33-G100, 1793-1813, Case 56*

2524 *Essex County, MA: Probate File Papers, 1638-1881. Probate of Samuel Osgood, 5 Jul 1774, Case number 20268.*

2525 *Essex County, MA: Probate File Papers, 1638-1881. Probate of Elizabeth Osgood, 6 Nov 1792, Case number 20192.*

2526 Her father's name is given in a Massachusetts Supreme Court Case involving a property dispute, not directly involving Mary, but concerning a property of her father Benjamin (a seaman who was an alien and never naturalized). She is listed as a daughter of Benjamin, Mary the wife of John Osgood. Massachusetts Reports: Cases Argued and Determined in the Supreme Judicial Court of Massachusetts, Volume 32, p 346

vii THOMAS OSGOOD, b. 11 Jun 1767; d. at Charlestown, MA, 21 Mar 1818; m. 15 Mar 1792, HANNAH STEVENS, b. at Andover, 23 May 1770 daughter of Bimsley and Rebecca (-) Stevens; Hannah d. 1 Sep 1830.

viii CHRISTOPHER OSGOOD, b. 25 Apr 1769; d. at Suncook, 3 Oct 1841; m. 1st 7 Nov 1793, his third cousin once removed, ANNA ABBOTT (*Zebadiah Abbott6, Anne Lovejoy Abbott5, William Lovejoy4, Mary Farnum Lovejoy3, Elizabeth Holt Farnum2, Nicholas1*), b. Sep 1767 daughter of Zebadiah and Rebecca (Ballard) Abbott; Anna d. 26 Dec 1827. Christopher m. 2nd at Derry, NH, 17 Feb 1829, his first cousin, ANNA ABBOTT (*Thomas Abbott5, Thomas Abbott4, Hannah Gray Abbott3, Hannah Holt Gray2, Nicholas1*), b. at Andover, 28 Feb 1769 daughter of Thomas and Lydia (Blunt) Abbott; Anna d. at Pembroke, 31 May 1847.

953) THOMAS ABBOT (*Thomas Abbott4, Hannah Gray Abbott3, Hannah Holt Gray2, Nicholas1*), b. 4 Apr 1729 son of Thomas and Elizabeth (Ballard) Abbott; d. at Andover 29 Mar 1775; m. 12 Feb 1756, LYDIA BLUNT, b. 6 Apr 1731 daughter of David and Lydia (Foster) Blunt; Lydia d. 16 Nov 1798.

Thomas was a farmer in Andover having inherited the homestead as the oldest son in his family of origin.

Thomas Abbot wrote his will 24 Mar 1775. The will includes a request that his honored mother be well provided for. Thomas's father died in 1774 and as executor of his father's estate, Thomas would have been charged with the care of his mother. In his will, Thomas bequeaths to eldest son Thomas £80 or that value in land when he reaches age 21. Son Joel receives £60. Daughters Lydia, Hannah, Betty, Ane, and Chloe each receive £40. Dearly beloved wife Lydia receives all the remainder of the estate trusting that she in the future will make a just distribution of the estate. Lydia is also named executor of the estate.[2527]

Thomas and Lydia had seven children whose births are recorded at Andover. The Andover record transcriptions contain a baptism in November 1771 for a daughter "Eleanor" but this is the same month as the birth of daughter Chloe; as there is Chloe, but not Eleanor, in the will, this is either an error in the records or there was a twin who died very young.

i LYDIA ABBOTT, b. 10 Apr 1757; d. at Deering, NH, 12 Nov 1826; m. at Andover, 4 May 1779, THOMAS ELIPHALET MERRILL, b. at South Hampton, NH, 25 Oct 1751 son of Eliphalet and Mary (Clough) Merrill; Thomas d. at Weare, NH, 19 Oct 1830.

ii HANNAH ABBOTT, b. 5 May 1759; d. 14 Nov 1789; m. at Andover, 16 Feb 1777, ABIEL FAULKNER, b. at Andover, 4 Sep 1755 son of Abiel and Mary (Poor) Faulkner; Abiel d. 26 Nov 1818.

iii THOMAS ABBOTT, b. 25 May 1761; d. at Providence, 11 Jun 1826;[2528] m. at Providence, 5 Jan 1800, RUTH OWEN, b. 21 Feb 1766 daughter of Joseph and Mary (Tripp) Owen; Ruth d. 26 Apr 1849.

iv BETTE ABBOTT, b. 25 Jun 1763; d. at Temple, ME, 12 Feb 1842; m. 17 Dec 1789, JONATHAN BALLARD, b. May 1761; Jonathan d. 28 Nov 1830.

v JOEL ABBOTT, b. 22 Nov 1765; d. at Andover, Dec 1826. He does seem to have married and had a son Joel. The identity of his wife has not yet been found. There is not any specific information about the son Joel.

vi ANNA ABBOTT, b. 28 Feb 1769; d. 31 May 1847; m. at Derry, NH, 17 Feb 1829, CHRISTOPHER OSGOOD, b. at Andover, 25 Apr 1769 son of Samuel and Elizabeth (Abbott) Osgood. Christopher was first married to another Anna Abbott.

vii CHLOE ABBOTT, b. 4 Nov 1771; d. at Melbourne, Québec; m. 19 Jan 1799, PETER FRYE, b. about 1771; Peter d. at Melbourne, Québec, 29 Jul 1843.[2529]

954) JABEZ ABBOTT (*Thomas Abbott4, Hannah Gray Abbott3, Hannah Holt Gray2, Nicholas1*), b. 18 Apr 1731 son of Thomas and Elizabeth (Ballard) Abbott; d. 7 Jan 1804 at Concord; m. 1st by 1756, his first cousin, PHEBE ABBOTT (*Edward Abbott4, Hannah Gray Abbott3, Hannah Holt Gray2, Nicholas1*), b. 13 Feb 1732 daughter of Edward and Dorcas (Chandler) Abbott; Phebe d. 6 Jan 1770. Jabez m. 2nd 8 Aug 1772, HEPHZIBAH STEVENS, b. 28 Feb 1739/40 daughter of Samuel and Hephzibah (Ingalls) Stevens.

Jabez participated in some civic duties in Concord including serving as a highway surveyor. He also signed a 1776 resolution related to pledging loyalty to the revolutionary cause: *We, the Subscribers, do solemnly engage and promise, that we will, to the utmost of our Power, at the Risque of our Lives and Fortunes, with ARMS, oppose the Hostile Proceedings of the British Fleet and Armies against the United American Colonies.*[2530]

Jabez Abbott and Phebe Abbott had four children whose births are recorded at Concord.

[2527] *Essex County, MA: Probate File Papers, 1638-1881. Probate of Thomas Abbot, 6 May 1776, Case number 141.*

[2528] *Rhode Island, Vital Extracts, 1636-1899.*

[2529] Ancestry.com, *Quebec, Canada, Vital and Church Records (Drouin Collection), 1621-1968* (Provo, UT, USA: Ancestry.com Operations, Inc., 2008), Institut Généalogique Drouin; Montreal, Quebec, Canada; Author: Gabriel Drouin, comp..

[2530] Bouton, *History of Concord*, p 270

i JOSEPH ABBOTT, b. 22 Apr 1757; d. 21 Nov 1758.

ii JOSEPH ABBOTT, b. 5 Aug 1759; d. at Boscawen, NH, 7 Oct 1837; m. at Salisbury, 3 Apr 1794, MOLLY MELOON, b. at Salisbury, 25 Jan 1769 daughter of Nathaniel and Bathsheba (Tucker) Meloon; Molly d. 17 Dec 1847.

iii PHEBE ABBOTT, b. 29 Oct 1762; d. at Boscawen, 14 Sep 1819; m. 29 Dec 1791, PAUL CLARK, b. at Newbury, 23 May 1762 son of Daniel and Mehitable (Hale) Clark;[2531] Paul d. 11 Jan 1808.

iv NATHAN ABBOTT, b. 29 Jun 1765; d. at Concord, 19 Mar 1844; m. 24 Feb 1801, RHODA BRICKETT, b. at Newbury, MA, 24 Jul 1769 daughter of Thomas and Mary (Noyes) Brickett.

Jabez Abbott and Hephzibah Stevens had four children whose births are recorded at Concord.

i LYDIA ABBOTT, b. 10 Jun 1773; d, 23 Mar 1841; m. at Concord, 27 Oct 1796, CHRISTOPHER ROWELL, b. at Hampstead, 22 Aug 1769 son of Christopher and Ruth (Moors) Rowell.

ii HEPHZIBAH ABBOTT, b. 1 Feb 1780; d. at Concord, 23 Jan 1817. Hephzibah did not marry.

iii DYER ABBOTT, b. 18 Jun 1778; d. at Henniker, 8 Mar 1832; m. at Boscawen, 1 Oct 1807, SARAH ATKINSON, b. at Boscawen, 19 Jul 1785 daughter of Benjamin and Jane (Varney) Atkinson.

iv ASENATH ABBOTT, b. 3 Oct 1781; d. at Pembroke, NH after 1850;[2532] m. 24 Feb 1801, THOMAS BRICKETT, b. at Pembroke, 7 Aug 1778 son of Thomas and Mary (Noyes) Brickett; Thomas d. about 1855 (probate of estate 25 Sep 1855).

955) AARON ABBOTT (*Thomas Abbott*[4], *Hannah Gray Abbott*[3], *Hannah Holt Gray*[2], *Nicholas*[1]), b. 17 Feb 1732/3 son of Thomas and Elizabeth (Ballard) Abbott; d. at Concord 31 Dec 1812; m. his first cousin, LYDIA ABBOTT (*Edward Abbott*[4], *Hannah Gray Abbott*[3], *Hannah Holt Gray*[2], *Nicholas*[1]), b. 15 Jun 1737 daughter of Edward and Dorcas (Chandler) Abbott; Lydia d. 15 Dec 1811.

There are perhaps eight children (according to the Abbot genealogy) but only two survived childhood.[2533] There were no records located for the six children who died in childhood, so they are just listed here: Betsey, Betsey2, Samuel, Samuel2, Joseph, and Thomas. The two children who lived to adult age are listed below.

i LYDIA ABBOTT, b. 4 Apr 1771; m. at Concord, 17 Apr 1811, as his second wife, her first cousin, TIMOTHY ABBOTT (*Edward Abbott*[5], *Edward Abbott*[4], *Hannah Gray Abbott*[3], *Hannah Holt Gray*[2], *Nicholas*[1]), b. 12 Mar 1769 son of Edward and Deborah (Stevens) Abbott; Timothy d. 23 Jan 1819. Lydia and Timothy did not have children. Timothy was first married to Sarah Bradley.

ii AARON ABBOTT, b. at Concord, 11 Apr 1778; d. at Bethel, ME, 8 Sep 1856; m. 1 Jan 1800, his second cousin, SARAH ABBOTT (*Stephen Abbott*[5], *George Abbott*[4], *Hannah Gray Abbott*[3], *Hannah Holt Gray*[2], *Nicholas*[1]), b. at Concord, 26 Jun 1780 daughter of Stephen and Mary (Gile) Abbott; Sarah d. at Bethel, 1853.

956) DORCAS ABBOTT (*Edward Abbott*[4], *Hannah Gray Abbott*[3], *Hannah Holt Gray*[2], *Nicholas*[1]), b. at Rumford 15 Feb 1728/9 daughter of Edward and Dorcas (Chandler) Abbott; d. at Concord, 28 Sep 1797; m. 17 Jun 1746, EBENEZER HALL, b. at Bradford, 19 Sep 1721 son of Joseph and Sarah (Kimball) Hall; Ebenezer d. 24 Apr 1801; Ebenezer was the brother of Joseph Hall who married Deborah Abbott [daughter of Thomas and Hannah (Gray) Abbott]. Ebenezer Hall was first married to Hephzibah Farnum.

Ebenezer Hall was a farmer in Concord and served as selectman. Dorcas Abbott is believed to be the "first white girl born in Concord."[2534]

Ebenezer Hall wrote his will 8 June 1791. Beloved wife Dorcas receives the income from one-half of his real estate and one-half of the cattle during her natural life and all the household items. Beloved son Ebenezer receives a 60-acre lot in Warner. Beloved daughter Hephzibah Hazeltine receives £3. Well beloved son Obadiah receives six shillings. Beloved daughter Dorcas Carter receives £3. Beloved daughter Sarah Hazeltine also receives £3. Beloved sons Daniel, Timothy, and Abiel each receive six shillings. Daughter Lydia Cavis receives $8 as does daughter Deborah Barker. Beloved son Stephen receives the whole of the real estate in Concord. Son Stephen is also the sole executor of the estate. The 7 July 1801 inventory of the estate

---

[2531] Hale, *Genealogy of the Descendants of Thomas Hale*, p 248

[2532] She and her husband Thomas Brickett are both listed in the 1850 U.S. Census living at Pembroke.

[2533] Abbot and Abbot, *Genealogical Record of Descendants*, p 88

[2534] Hurd, *History of Merrimack and Belknap Counties*, Part 2, p 540

of Ebenezer Hall included real estate valued at $3,475.[2535] The son Ebenezer Hall mentioned in the will is Ebenezer's son from his first marriage to Hephzibah Farnum.

Dorcas Abbott and Ebenezer Hall were parents to twelve children.

i HEPHZIBAH HALL, b. at Rumford, 29 Mar 1747; d. at Concord, 23 Nov 1817; m. about 1765, RICHARD HAZELTINE, b. 5 Apr 1742 son of Richard and Sarah (Barnes) Hazeltine; Richard d. 21 Apr 1817.

ii OBADIAH HALL, b. at Rumford, 13 Oct 1748; d. 24 Mar 1831; m. 3 Nov 1770, MARY PERHAM, b. 3 May 1749; Mary d. 27 Feb 1822. After Mary's death, Obadiah married Abigail Morrison.

iii DORCAS HALL; b. 13 Jan 1751; d. 5 Sep 1813 (or 1823); m. EPHRAIM CARTER, b. at Concord, 21 Oct 1746 son of Ezra and Ruth (Eastman) Carter.

iv SARAH HALL, b. at Rumford, 4 Feb 1753; d. May 1845; m. by 1774, WILLIAM HAZELTINE, b. at Rumford, 16 Jun 1744 son of Richard and Sarah (Barnes) Hazeltine; William d. at Canterbury, Jan 1826.

v DANIEL HALL, b. at Rumford, 13 Jan 1755; d. at Concord, 18 Feb 1835; m. 26 Sep 1775, DEBORAH DAVIS, b. at Concord, 15 Jul 1757 daughter of Robert and Sarah (Walker) Davis; Deborah d. 31 Oct 1822.

vi TIMOTHY HALL, b. at Rumford, 5 Jun 1757; d. at Irasburg, VT, 16 Jul 1832; m. at Concord, 15 Oct 1780, ANNA FOSTER of Bow, born about 1760; d. at Hardwick, VT, 28 Feb 1853.[2536][2537]

vii STEPHEN HALL, b. at Concord, 13 May 1759; d. at Concord, 23 Nov 1808; m. PATIENCE FLANDERS, b. at Boscawen, 9 Oct 1758 daughter of Ezekiel and Sarah (Bishop) Flanders; Patience d. 17 Feb 1834.

viii ABIEL HALL, b. at Rumford, 31 May 1761; d. 13 Oct 1829 at Alfred, ME; m. 1st, MARY FARNUM, b. at Concord, 26 Aug 1764 daughter of Benjamin and Anna (Merrill) Farnum; Mary d. 23 Nov 1816. Abiel m. 2nd, 1819, ANNA FRANCIS (widow of Edward Grant); Anna d. 11 Dec 1857.

ix HANNAH HALL, b. 1 Nov 1764; d. 16 Nov 1765.

x HANNAH HALL, b. 2 Oct 1766; died young.

xi LYDIA HALL, b. at Concord, 10 Oct 1767; d. at Bow, NH, 30 Mar 1855; m. 5 Jan 1788, NATHANIEL CAVIS, b. 25 Dec 1761; Nathaniel d. 10 Sep 1842.

xii DEBORAH HALL, b. at Concord, 18 Sep 1769; d. 25 Oct 1791; m. at Hillsborough, 26 Oct 1787, DANIEL BARKER. Daniel perhaps married Anna Lathrop 19 Mar 1792.

957) EDWARD ABBOTT (*Edward Abbott⁴, Hannah Gray Abbott³, Hannah Holt Gray², Nicholas¹*), b. 27 Dec 1730 son of Edward and Dorcas (Chandler) Abbott; d. 15 Sep 1801; m. about 1760 DEBORAH STEVENS, origins not certain but likely the Deborah born 1738 in Rumford, NH daughter of Aaron and Deborah (Stevens) Stevens. Aaron Stevens was an early settler at Concord. Deborah d. Nov 1817.

Edward Abbott and Deborah Stevens had nine children.

i MARY ABBOTT, b. 1761; d. 1843; m. by 1780, THOMAS CAPEN, b. at Charlestown, 19 Apr 1762 son of Thomas and Mary (Wyman) Capen;[2538] Thomas died at sea in 1808. This family settled in New Pennacook, Maine.

ii MEHITABLE ABBOTT, b. 23 Apr 1763; d. 16 Sep 1838;[2539] m. by 1786, BENJAMIN LUFKIN, b. at Ipswich, 8 Apr 1763;[2540] Benjamin d. at Roxbury, ME, Nov 1844.

iii SUSANNA ABBOTT, b. 1765; d. 25 Feb 1841; m. by 1786, JOHN WEEKS, b. at Portsmouth, NH, 23 Jun 1757; John d. at Concord, 6 Apr 1836.

iv EDWARD ABBOTT, b. about 1767; d. about 1784?

v TIMOTHY ABBOTT, b. 12 Mar 1769; d. 23 Jan 1819; m. 1st, SARAH BRADLEY daughter of Abraham and Sarah (-) Bradley; Sarah d. 1810.[2541] Timothy m. 2nd, his first cousin, LYDIA ABBOTT (*Aaron Abbott⁵, Thomas Abbott⁴,*

[2535] *New Hampshire Wills and Probate Records 1643-1982,* Probate of Ebenezer Hall, Rockingham, 5 May 1801, Case number 6818.

[2536] Revolutionary War Pension and Bounty-Land Warrant Application Files

[2537] Anna Hall was living with her daughter Judith Kellogg at the 1850 census.

[2538] Hayden and Tuttle, *The Capen Family*, p 137

[2539] Mehitable Lufkin's death is reported in the records of the First Congregational Church of Concord. (Reed and Thorne, History and Manual of the First Congregational Church)

[2540] Lapham, *History of Rumford*, p 369

[2541] Ancestry.com, New Hampshire, Death and Disinterment Records, 1754-1947

Hannah Gray Abbott³, Hannah Holt Gray², Nicholas¹), b. 4 Apr 1771 daughter of Aaron and Lydia (Abbott) Abbott. Aaron and Lydia Abbott are Family 220.

vi SAMUEL ABBOTT, b. 8 Apr 1771; m. at Pembroke, 4 Mar 1792, MARY "POLLY" CURRIER, b. at Concord, 13 Oct 1776 daughter of William and Mary (Carter) Currier.[2542] Samuel was a carpenter and relocated to Buffalo, New York. Later, the family moved to Switzerland County, Indiana where both Samuel and Polly died in 1820.

vii DEBORAH ABBOTT, b. and d. 1773.

viii DEBORAH ABBOTT, b. at Concord, 29 May 1774; d. at Rumford, ME, 20 Apr 1861; m. PHINEAS HOWE, b. at Bolton, MA, 25 Mar 1769 son of Phineas and Experience (Pollard)[2543] Howe; Phineas d. 27 Dec 1847.

ix ESTHER ABBOTT, b. 1777; d. 1824; m. at Concord, 13 Mar 1800, TRUEWORTHY KILGORE. Esther and Trueworthy did not have children.

958) BETSEY ABBOTT (*Edward Abbott⁴, Hannah Gray Abbott³, Hannah Holt Gray², Nicholas¹*), b. 25 Aug 1743 daughter of Edward and Dorcas (Chandler) Abbott; d. 2 Oct 1827 at Goffstown, NH; m. 1759, THOMAS SALTMARSH, b. at Watertown, 2 Mar 1736 son of Thomas and Mary (Hazen) Saltmarsh; Thomas d. at Goffstown, NH 8 May 1826.[2544]

Betsey Abbott and Thomas Saltmarsh had ten children born in New Hampshire with some births recorded at Concord. Birth records for every child were not located and the Abbot genealogy was used to supplement information.[2545]

i MEHITABLE SALTMARSH, b. at Concord, 12 Apr 1762; d. at Gilford, NH, 25 Oct 1814; m. at Goffstown, 9 Feb 1784, JAMES HOYT, b. at Kingston, 28 Mar 1762 son of Eliphalet and Mary (Peaslee) Hoyt; James d. 1834. After Mehitable's death, James married Abigail Whittier in 1815 and Huldah Fifield in 1822.

ii JOHN SALTMARSH, b. at Concord, 21 May 1764; d. after 1850 (living in Bedford at the 1850 U.S. Census); m. at Goffstown, 22 Nov 1785, SUSAN BURNHAM, b. at Ipswich, 1756 daughter of Samuel and Martha (Story) Burnham.

iii MARY "POLLY" SALTMARSH, b. at Concord, 28 Aug 1766; d. at Peterborough, 21 Apr 1848; m. at Goffstown, 31 Mar 1791, SAMUEL VOSE, b. at Bedford, 23 May 1759 son of Samuel and Phebe (Vickery) Vose; Samuel d. at Antrim, NH, 8 Aug 1830.

iv EDWARD ABBOTT SALTMARSH, b. 1768 likely at Goffstown; d. at Hookset, NH, 11 Mar 1851; m. at Goffstown, 19 Oct 1791, SARAH "SALLY" STORY, b. 1773 (based on age at time of death) daughter of Nehemiah and Sarah (Gold) Story; Sally d. 19 May 1860.

v THOMAS SALTMARSH, b. 1771; d. at Saco, ME, 1804; m. at Wolfeboro, 7 Jun 1799, BETSY EVANS, b. 21 May 1780 daughter of Benjamin and Lydia (Browne) Evans.

vi SALLY SALTMARSH, b. 1773.

vii SAMUEL SALTMARSH, b. 1775; d. at Goffstown, 1844; m. 28 May 1800, BETSY BURNHAM, b. about 1780; Betsy d. at Goffstown, 1840.

viii CATHERINE SALTMARSH, b. 1777; d. after 1850 (still living at the 1850 U.S. Census); m. her first cousin, THOMAS SALTMARSH, b. at Bedford, MA, 22 Aug 1772 son of Seth and Ruth (Bowman) Saltmarsh; Thomas d. at Gilford, NH, 18 Sep 1823.

ix ISAAC SALTMARSH, b. 1779; d. at Antrim, NH, 13 Mar 1823; m. at Bradford, NH, 13 Nov 1805, PHEBE STRATTON, b. at Marlboro, MA, 27 Feb 1790 daughter of Jonathan and Abigail (Barnes) Stratton; Phebe d. 13 Sep 1872.

x HAZEN SALTMARSH, b. 1781; d. 1805.

959) MARY HALL (*Deborah Abbott Hall⁴, Hannah Gray Abbott³, Hannah Holt Gray², Nicholas¹*), b. 17 Mar 1743 daughter of Joseph and Deborah (Abbott) Hall; d. 12 Dec 1773; m. THOMAS WILSON who d. at Concord 23 May 1818. Thomas m. 2nd, Mary Hopkins Bancroft.

Thomas Wilson wrote his will 20 May 1818. In his will, he directs that his estate be divided equally among his five children (four children living and the children of his son Thomas who is deceased). First named is Mary Thorndike wife of John

---

2542 Currier and Currier, *The Genealogy of Richard Currier*, p 26. The Abbot and Abbot genealogy gives her name as Ruth Currier, but the Currier genealogy says Mary Currier and the marriage record says Polly Currier.

2543 The division of William Pollard's estate in 1763 includes a disbursement to his daughter Elizabeth wife of Phineas Howe.

2544 The graves of Elizabeth Abbott and Thomas Saltmarsh are in the Westlawn Cemetery at Goffstown with a gravestone that lists their names as Thomas Saltmarsh and Elisabeth Abbott, his wife. (accessed through findagrave.com)

2545 Abbot and Abbot, *Genealogical Record of Descendants*, p 101

Thorndike. However, if John Thorndike brings any demand against the estate, that amount is to be deducted from Mary's share. Second named is daughter Eliza Flagg. Next named is daughter Rebecca Wilson. Then named are the children of his son Thomas. Lastly, is daughter Ruth Wilson who is to pay Eliza what she owes her.[2546] Just the oldest child named, Mary Thorndike, is from Thomas's marriage to Mary Hall.

Mary Hall and Thomas Wilson had two children born at Concord.

i JEREMIAH HALL WILSON, b. at Concord 1770; d. 10 Apr 1775

ii MARY "MOLLY" WILSON, b. 23 Jul 1772; m. 1st, 25 Mar 1792, JOHN THORNDIKE, b. at Beverly, 30 Nov 1768 son of Larkin and Ruth (Woodbury) Thorndike. Dr. John Thorndike died at Concord, 1821. Mary m. 2nd, 27 Nov 1823, her third cousin, ABIEL WALKER, b. 5 Jul 1766 son of James and Ruth (Abbott) Walker. Abiel was first married to Judith Davis.

959a) JEREMIAH HALL (*Deborah Abbott Hall⁴, Hannah Gray Abbott³, Hannah Holt Gray², Nicholas¹*), b. at Concord, 6 Jan 1746 son of Joseph and Deborah (Abbott) Hall; d. 6 Oct 1770; m., 1769, ESTHER WHITTEMORE, b. 2 Aug 1752 daughter of Aaron and Abigail (Coffin) Whittemore; Esther d. 12 Jul 1803. Esther m. 2nd, Joseph Woodman.

Jeremiah Hall and Esther Whittemore were parents of one child.

i SARAH HALL, b. at Concord, 29 Aug 1770; d. at Concord, 16 Feb 1826; m. at Concord, 3 Jul 1787, JONATHAN WILKINS, b. at Marlborough, MA, 19 Jun 1755 son of Josiah and Lois (Bush) Wilkins; Jonathan d. at Concord, 9 Mar 1830.

960) DANIEL ABBOT (*George Abbott⁴, Hannah Gray Abbott³, Hannah Holt Gray², Nicholas¹*), b. 7 Aug 1738 son of George and Sarah (Abbott) Abbott; d. 11 Jun 1804; m. 1st by 1761, his second cousin RACHEL ABBOTT, b. 7 Apr 1743 daughter of Nathaniel and Penelope (Ballard) Abbott; Rachel d. 13 Jun 1788. Daniel m. 2nd 1 Jan 1789 at Boscawen, MERCY "MARY" KILBURN whose origins are not fully verified, although she is likely the daughter of Jedediah and Hannah (Platts) Kilburn. She was born about 1758 based on the birth of her last child in 1799. Mercy was living in 1830 when she was listed as a head of household in the 1830 US Census of Concord (between age 60-70).

The will of Daniel Abbot has bequests for the following persons: beloved wife Mary, beloved sons Beriah, Jeremiah, Daniel, George, Thomas, Abiel, Peter Hazeltine, Benjamin, daughters Judith, Sarah, Hannah, Lois, Susanna, son Nathan Kilburn, and son Samuel who is appointed executor along with Thomas.[2547]

Children of Daniel Abbot and Rachel Abbott were born at Concord. There are birth records for all the children except the oldest child Beriah.

i BERIAH ABBOTT, b. about 1758; d. at Pomfret, VT, 13 Mar 1832;[2548] m. about 1785 the widow MARY ANDREWS FAIRFIELD. Mary d. 29 Jul 1813; Beriah m. 2nd, MARTHA GRISWOLD, b. about 1759 and d. at Randolph, VT, 28 Jan 1841.

ii SARAH ABBOTT, b. 19 Jul 1761; d. 21 Jan 1774.

iii SAMUEL ABBOTT, b. 26 Mar 1764; d. at Concord, 1 Dec 1849; m. 17 Nov 1787, MARY T. "POLLY" STORY, b. 16 Oct 1764 daughter of Jeremiah and Mary "Polly" (Burnham) Story; Polly d. 21 Dec 1849.

iv JEREMIAH ABBOTT, b. 21 Feb 1766; d. at Pomfret, VT, 10 Feb 1811; m. 15 Jan 1795, CLARISSA PERRY, b. at Ashford, CT, 31 Mar 1770 daughter of Robert and Sarah (Hodges) Perry;[2549] Clarissa d. 10 Oct 1826.

v DANIEL ABBOTT, b. 21 Feb 1768; d. 19 Sep 1769.

vi DANIEL ABBOTT, b. 7 Mar 1770; d. unknown; m. 29 Jan 1794, LUCY HARVEY, b. at Gilsum, NH, 15 Dec 1768 daughter of Thomas and Grace (Willey) Harvey; Lucy d. 8 Feb 1849.

vii GEORGE ABBOTT, b. 12 May 1772; m. BETSY EASTMAN.

viii THOMAS ABBOTT, b. 5 Jul 1776; d. at Concord, NH, 1845; m. 14 Apr 1801, ANNA EATON, b. in NH about 1781; d. at Concord after 1850 (living with her daughter Dorcas and her family at the 1850 census). Her parentage is not verified but she is *possibly* the daughter of Ephraim and Eunice (-) Eaton.

2546 *New Hampshire Wills and Probate Records 1643-1982,* Probate of Thomas Wilson, Rockingham, 20 May 1818, Case number 9739.

2547 *New Hampshire Wills and Probate Records 1643-1982,* Probate of Daniel Abbott, Rockingham, 27 Aug 1804, Case number 7284.

2548 Ancestry.com, *Vermont, Vital Records, 1720-1908* (Provo, UT, USA: Ancestry.com Operations, Inc., 2013).

2549 Robert Perry was an early settler of Windsor County, Vermont. Aldrich and Holmes, *History of Windsor County, Vermont*, p 969

ix ABIEL ABBOTT, b. 19 Mar 1778; d. at Waldo, ME, 1 Aug 1836;[2550] m. at Lincolnville, ME, 2 Feb 1809, SARAH COMBS,[2551] "of Georgetown (ME)". She is SARAH HINKLEY, b. at Georgetown, 14 Aug 1774 daughter of John and Hannah (Oliver) Hinkley[2552] and the widow of Leonard Coombs. Sarah d. at Waldo, 4 Nov 1865 (age 91 years, 3 months at time of death).[2553] The death record of daughter Harriet gives the maiden name of mother as Sarah Hinkley.

x PETER HAZELTINE ABBOTT, b. 28 Feb 1780; d. after 1860 (listed in the 1860 Census living with his son Asaph); m. 9 Mar 1815, his first cousin once removed, SARAH ABBOTT, b. 10 Sep 1781 daughter of Moses and Mary (Batchelder) Abbott; Sarah d. 10 Aug 1846.

xi BENJAMIN ABBOTT, b. 29 Mar 1782; m. ESTHER CURRIER, b. 5 Nov 1787 daughter of Nathaniel Currier.

xii JUDITH ABBOTT, b. 4 Apr 1784; d. 18 Apr 1831; m. JOHN CARPENTER.

xiii CHILD ABBOTT, b. and d. 12 Jun 1788.

Children of Daniel Abbott and Mercy Kilburn: In the 1850, 1860, and 1870 U.S. Census, Sarah, Lois, and Nathan were living together in Concord and it seems none of them married. Nathan is listed as single on his death record. Susannah also does not seem to have married.

i SARAH ABBOTT, b. 4 Apr 1790; d. after 1870.[2554]

ii HANNAH ABBOTT, b. 28 Oct 1791; d. 13 Sep 1876; m. 16 Mar 1815, her third cousin once removed, REUBEN ABBOTT (*Zerviah Farnum Abbott*[5], *Joseph Farnum*[4], *Ephraim Farnum*[3], *Elizabeth Holt Farnum*[2], *Nicholas*[1]), b. at Concord, 23 Oct 1790 son of Reuben and Zerviah (Farnum) Abbott; Reuben d. 27 Jun 1869.

iii LOIS ABBOTT, b. 31 Oct 1793; d. at Concord, 18 Dec 1881.

iv SUSANNAH ABBOTT, b. 23 May 1797; d. 22 Jun 1847.[2555]

v NATHAN KILBURN ABBOTT, b. 30 Aug 1799; d. at Concord 14 Jun 1878.

961) JOSEPH ABBOTT (*George Abbott*[4], *Hannah Gray Abbott*[3], *Hannah Holt Gray*[2], *Nicholas*[1]), b. 23 Oct 1741 son of George and Sarah (Abbott) Abbott; d. at Concord, NH, 19 Jan 1832; m. 25 Apr 1765, his second cousin once removed, PHEBE LOVEJOY (*Henry Lovejoy*[5], *Henry Lovejoy*[4], *Mary Farnum Lovejoy*[3], *Elizabeth Holt Farnum*[2], *Nicholas*[1]), b. 20 Sep 1735 daughter of Henry and Phebe (Chandler) Lovejoy; Phebe d. 4 Jan 1789. Joseph m. 2nd, ABIGAIL TYLER.

Joseph Abbott and Phebe Lovejoy had ten children born at Concord.

i PHEBE ABBOTT, b. 22 Feb 1766; d. at Woodbury, VT, 31 May 1837;[2556] m. her third cousin, JOSEPH BLANCHARD, b. at Dunstable, NH, 24 Nov 1761 son of John and Eleanor (Stevens) Blanchard; Joseph d. 19 Feb 1839.

ii MOLLY ABBOTT, b. 20 Jul 1767; d. at Concord, 15 Aug 1791; m. 22 May 1785, ISAAC HOUSTON, b. at Bedford, NH, 1760 son of James and Mary (Mitchell) Houston. Isaac m. 2nd, Ruth Gale. Isaac d. at Hanover, NH, 25 Mar 1833.

iii HANNAH ABBOTT, b. 3 Jan 1769; d. 31 Oct 1810; m. 10 Dec 1795, DAVID KIMBALL, b. at Rumford, 10 Oct 1757 son of Reuben and Miriam (Collins) Kimball.

iv SARAH ABBOTT, b. 3 Jan 1769; d. at Concord, 27 Jan 1857; m. Nov 1787, her second cousin, TIMOTHY CHANDLER, b. at Rumford, 25 Apr 1762 son of Timothy and Elizabeth (Copp) Chandler; Timothy d. 9 Aug 1848.

v LOIS ABBOTT, b. 29 Mar 1771; d. 14 Mar 1790.

[2550] Ancestry.com, Maine, Death Records, 1761-1922

[2551] "Maine Marriages, 1771-1907," database, *FamilySearch* (https://familysearch.org/ark:/61903/1:1:F4DX-WLN: 10 February 2018), Abial Abbot and Sarah Combs, 02 Feb 1809; citing Lincolnville, Waldo, Maine, reference vol 1; FHL microfilm 11,351.

[2552] "Maine Births and Christenings, 1739-1900," database, *FamilySearch* (https://familysearch.org/ark:/61903/1:1:F4HY-ZPV: 10 February 2018), Sarah Hinkley, 14 Aug 1774; citing GEORGETOWN, SAGADAHOC, MAINE; FHL microfilm 873,976.

[2553] Maine State Archives; Cultural Building, 84 State House Station, Augusta, ME 04333-0084; Pre-1892 Delayed Returns; Roll Number: 1; Maine State death records 1761-1922

[2554] She is listed in the 1870 US Census living with Lois Abbot and Nathan K. Abbot. There is no record of her after that.

[2555] Abbot and Abbot, *Genealogical Record of Descendants*, p 105

[2556] *Vermont, Vital Records, 1720-1908.*

vi RACHEL ABBOTT, b. 2 Mar 1773; d. at Fryeburg, ME, 2 Mar 1837; m. 29 Nov 1797, JONATHAN WARD, b. at Concord, 17 Aug 1774 son of Stephen and Elizabeth (Copp) Ward; Jonathan d. 5 Feb 1822. Jonathan's mother, Elizabeth Copp, was first married to Timothy Chandler who was Rachel Abbott's first cousin, once removed.

vii DORCAS ABBOTT, b. 20 Dec 1774; d. 6 Oct 1788.

viii ISAAC ABBOTT, b. 10 Apr 1777; d. Jan 1800.

ix NATHAN ABBOTT, b. 27 Aug 1779; d. 26 Aug 1839; m. ELIZABETH "BETSEY" COLBY, b. 1786 daughter of John and Ann (Carter) Colby; Betsey d. 14 Dec 1819.

x RUTH ABBOTT, b. 8 May 1782; d. after 1850. Ruth did not marry. She was living alone in Concord at the 1850 U. S. Census.[2557]

962) STEPHEN ABBOTT (*George Abbott[4], Hannah Gray Abbott[3], Hannah Holt Gray[2], Nicholas[1]*), b. at Concord, 28 Oct 1746 son of George and Sarah (Abbott) Abbott; d. 12 May 1811;[2558] m. 11 Apr 1778, MARY GILE, b. about 1755 (parentage not verified at this point); Mary d. Jan 1822.

Stephen Abbott and Mary Gile had seven children born at Concord.

i EPHRAIM ABBOTT, b. 5 Feb 1779; d. Jan 1822. Ephraim did not marry.

ii SARAH ABBOTT, b. 20 Jun 1780; d. at Bethel, ME, 1853; m. 1 Jan 1800, her second cousin, AARON ABBOTT (*Aaron Abbott[5], Thomas Abbott[4], Hannah Gray Abbott[3], Hannah Holt Gray[2], Nicholas[1]*), b. at Concord, 11 Apr 1778 son of Aaron and Lydia (Abbott) Abbott; Aaron d. 8 Sep 1856.

iii POLLY ABBOTT, b. at Concord, 26 Apr 1782; d. after 1850 at Bethel, ME (still living at the 1850 U.S. Census); m. about 1804, JOSEPH TWITCHELL, b. at Bethel, 28 Mar 1782 son of Eleazer and Martha (Mason) Twitchell; Joseph d. after 1870.

iv THEODORE ABBOTT, b. 23 Feb 1784; d at George's Mill, NH, 8 May 1855; m. at New London, NH, 25 Jun 1809, MARY "POLLY" BURPEE, b. 29 Sep 1791 daughter of Thomas and Sarah (Smith) Burpee.

v STEPHEN ABBOTT, b. 19 May 1786; d. likely at Portland, ME; m. at Portland, 11 Jul 1819, the widow ABIGAIL WEBB, b. about 1787; Abigail d. 26 Aug 1846. Stephen and Abigail did not have children.

vi LUCY ABBOTT, b. 24 Jan 1789; m. at Springfield, NH, 2 Oct 1816, BENJAMIN HASELTINE, b. about 1785 "of Wendell."

vii SAMUEL ABBOTT, b. 14 May 1791; d. at Montpelier, VT, 4 May 1861; m. 5 Mar 1813, JANE DAY, b. at Boscawen, 20 Jul 1794 daughter of Daniel and Jane (Cass) Day.

963) EZRA ABBOTT (*George Abbott[4], Hannah Gray Abbott[3], Hannah Holt Gray[2], Nicholas[1]*), b. 22 Aug 1756 son of George and Sarah (Abbott) Abbott; d. 21 Feb 1837; m. 1st 21 Nov 1782, BETTY ANDREWS, b. 12 May 1762 daughter of Thomas and Mary (Burnham) Andrews; Betty d. 25 Aug 1794. Ezra m. 2nd, 10 May 1795, ANNER CHOATE, b. at Ipswich 12 Jan 1758 daughter of Thomas and Dorothy (Proctor) Choate; Anner d. 21 Mar 1798. Ezra m. 3rd, 15 Nov 1798, JANE JACKMAN, b. at Boscawen, 20 Dec 1767 daughter of Benjamin and Jane (Woodman) Jackman; Jane d. 2 May 1847.

Ezra Abbott served several campaigns during the Revolutionary War.[2559] He was taken prisoner at Fort Cedars 19 May 1779. He was also at Ticonderoga in 1777 serving in the regiment of Colonel Thomas Stickney.

Ezra and his first wife Betty Andrews had four children whose births are recorded at Concord.

i LUCY ABBOTT, b. 5 Apr 1784; d. at Warner, Nov 1869; m. 17 Feb 1835, OBADIAH/DIAH HUTCHINSON, b. 2 Nov 1776 son of Jonathan and Mehitable (Lovejoy) Hutchinson; Diah d. at Warner, NH, 22 Aug 1843. Lucy did not have any children.

ii HARRIET B. ABBOTT, b. 12 Apr 1786; d. at Hartford, VT, 1 Apr 1862; m. 20 Jun 1816, JOHN CHAMPION, b. at South Lyme, CT, 12 Dec 1792 son of Ezra and Lucretia (Tubbs) Champion;[2560] John d. at Hartford, VT, 27 Oct 1879.

iii ROBERT BURNHAM ABBOTT, b. 27 Apr 1791; d. at Concord, 22 Aug 1830; m. 1st, at Hopkinton, 25 Dec 1817, RACHEL BURNHAM, b. 2 Sep 1796; Rachel d. 19 Jun 1823. Robert m. 2nd, 11 May 1823, ELIZABETH FOX, b. 2

[2557] Year: 1850; Census Place: Concord, Merrimack, New Hampshire; Roll: M432_435; Page: 61A; Image: 124. Ruth Abbott, age 68, as the only member of the household.

[2558] *New Hampshire, Death and Disinterment Records, 1754-1947.*

[2559] Bouton, *History of Concord*, p 623

[2560] Trowbridge, *The Champion Genealogy*, p 121

Jun 1794; Elizabeth d. 7 Apr 1840. Robert did not have children. His will leaves his estate to his wife Elizabeth and to his sister Champion, sister Lucy, and sister Rose Dimond.[2561]

iv ROSE B. ABBOTT, b. 26 Oct 1796; d. after 1860 (still living at the 1860 U.S. Census, but deceased before 1870); m. 11 Dec 1816, JACOB DIMOND, b. at Concord about 1790 son of Reuben and Mary (Currier) Dimond; Jacob d. at Concord, 28 Apr 1879.[2562]

Ezra and Anner Choate had one child.

i ANNER ABBOTT, b. 2 Mar 1798; d. 12 Jun 1798.

Ezra and his third wife Jane Jackman had six children whose births are recorded at Concord.

i BETSY ABBOTT, b. 9 Aug 1799; d. 8 Aug 1856; m. Apr 1822, AMOS HOIT, b. 20 Feb 1800 son of Joseph and Polly (Elliot) Hoit. Amos m. 2nd, 6 Apr 1858, Asaneth Swain widow of Henry Swain.

ii ANNER ABBOTT, b. 8 Feb 1801; d. 23 Jan 1872; m. 13 Jun 1827, SAMUEL RUNNELS, b. at Boxford, 6 Dec 1796 son of Samuel and Anna (Hardy) Runnels; Samuel d. at Concord, 22 Nov 1864.

iii GEORGE B. ABBOTT, b. 27 Jan 1803; d. 8 May 1887; m. 1st, 22 Aug 1836, ELIZA DIDO SPAULDING, b. 6 Dec 1807 daughter of John and Elizabeth (Wheeler) Spaulding; Eliza d. 11 Oct 1856. George m. 2nd, 31 Dec 1861, CLARISSA CARTER, b. about 1815; Clarissa d. 14 Mar 1882.

iv JANE WOODMAN ABBOTT, b. 15 Sep 1805; d. at Warner, 30 Nov 1891; m. 9 Oct 1850, as his second wife, STEPHEN SANBORN, b. 21 Jun 1807 son of Daniel and Betsey (Whitcomb) Sanborn; Stephen d. 24 Jul 1869. Jane did not have children.

v BENJAMIN JACKMAN ABBOTT, b. 4 Feb 1808; d. 4 Mar 1869; m. about 1833, DOROTHY TEWKSBURY, b. about 1813 possibly the sister of Daniel who married Sarah, but no records have been located.

vi SARAH ABBOTT, b. 22 Jan 1815; d. at Stewartstown, 26 Feb 1889; m. DANIEL TEWKSBURY, b. at Warner, 1 Oct 1810 son of Stephen and Sally (Flanders) Tewksbury; Daniel d. 6 Mar 1874.

964) HANNAH ABBOTT (*Benjamin Abbott[4], Hannah Gray Abbott[3], Hannah Holt Gray[2], Nicholas[1]*), b. at Concord, 22 Jan 1743 daughter of Benjamin and Hannah (Abbott) Abbott; d. 22 Oct 1820; m. Sep 1783, JEREMIAH STORY (origins not fully verified, but perhaps the Jeremiah Story of Ipswich); d. at Concord, about 1806 based on the date of probate of his estate May 1806 with widow Hannah Story as administrator.

Jeremiah Story did not leave a will. His widow Hannah was administratrix of the estate. The inventory of the estate gave a value of $1,000 for real estate which included a lot in Concord, a 36-acre wood lot in Hopkinton, and a 100-acre lot in Groton in Grafton County.[2563]

Just two children have been identified in this family.

i HANNAH STORY, b. 6 Sep 1784; d. after 1850 likely at Concord; m. 1st, 27 Feb 1806, BENNING NOYES, b. at Bow, 9 Dec 1780 son of Benjamin and Hannah (Thompson) Noyes; Benjamin d. 2 Nov 1814. Hannah m. 2nd, at Montague, 13 Apr 1816, as his second wife, EPHRAIM UPHAM, b. at Weston, 3 Nov 1778 son of Thomas and Martha (Williams) Upham; Ephraim d. 29 Mar 1844. Ephraim was first married to Hannah Cushman.

ii SARAH STORY, b. May 1787; died young.

965) BENJAMIN ABBOT (*Benjamin Abbott[4], Hannah Gray Abbott[3], Hannah Holt Gray[2], Nicholas[1]*), b. at Concord, 10 Feb 1750 son of Benjamin and Hannah (Abbott) Abbott; d. at Concord, 11 Dec 1815; m. 29 Jan 1778, SARAH BROWN, b. at Kingston, NH, 13 Feb 1758 daughter of Daniel and Ruth (Morrill) Brown; Sarah d. 27 Sep 1801. Benjamin m. 2nd, 17 Jun 1805, HANNAH GREENLEAF who was still living at the time of Benjamin's death.

Benjamin Abbot served in the Revolutionary War with the rank of Sergeant under the commands of Captain Gordon Hutchins and Colonel John Stark.[2564] He participate in the Battle of Bunker Hill.

Benjamin Abbot wrote his will 19 October 1815. His beloved wife Hannah receives the improvements of one-third part of the real and personal estate. Son Ephraim Abbot and daughter Hannah Hall each receive one dollar. Daughter Ruth Morrill Hall receives two dollars as does daughter Sarah Noyes. Son Isaac receives ten dollars and daughter Abigail Baker receives five

---

2561 Probate Records, 1832-1972; Probate Indexes, 1823-1973; Author: New Hampshire Probate Court (Merrimack County): Probate Place: Merrimack, New Hampshire. Will of Robert B. Abbott, 5 Jun 1830.

2562 Ancestry.com, New Hampshire, Death and Burial Records Index, 1654-1949

2563 *New Hampshire Wills and Probate Records 1643-1982,* Probate of Jeremiah Story, Rockingham, 19 Mar 1806, Case number 7548.

2564 Rolls of Soldiers in the Revolutionary War, Volume 14, p 63, 181, 186

dollars. Daughter Permelia receives fifty dollars and son Theodore Thomas Abbot receives four dollars. Son Benjamin Abbot receives all the remainder of the estate and is also named executor.[2565]

Benjamin Abbot and Sarah Brown had nine children whose births are recorded at Concord, although some of the births occurred elsewhere.

i EPHRAIM ABBOTT, b. 28 Sep 1779; d. at Westford, MA, 21 Jul 1870; m. 1st, at Andover, 5 Jan 1814, MARY HOLYOKE PEARSON, b. 10 Mar 1782 daughter of Eliphalet and Priscilla (Holyoke) Pearson; Mary d. 15 Jul 1829. Ephraim m. 2nd, 21 Jan 1830, ABIGAIL WHITING BANCROFT, b. at Groton, 1797 daughter of Amos and Abigail (Whiting) Bancroft; Abigail d. at Groton, 17 May 1886.

ii HANNAH ABBOTT, b. 9 Mar 1782; d. at Westford, MA, 5 Apr 1869; m. 15 Nov 1803, her second cousin once removed, EBENEZER HALL (*Daniel Hall[6], Dorcas Abbott Hall[5], Edward Abbott[4], Hannah Gray Abbott[3], Hannah Holt Gray[2], Nicholas[1]*), b. 9 May 1778 son of Daniel and Deborah (Davis) Hall; Ebenezer d. 14 Oct 1853.

iii RUTH MORRILL ABBOTT, b. 27 Jun 1784; d. after 1860 (living in Concord at the 1860 U.S. Census); m. 26 Nov 1805, her second cousin once removed, JAMES HALL (*Daniel Hall[6], Dorcas Abbott Hall[5], Edward Abbott[4], Hannah Gray Abbott[3], Hannah Holt Gray[2], Nicholas[1]*), b. 1784 son of Daniel and Deborah (Davis) Hall.

iv BENJAMIN ABBOTT, b. 23 Sep 1786; d. at Whiteside, IL, 28 Feb 1854; m. 17 Sep 1807, DORCAS NOYES, b. at Bow, NH, 22 Aug 1785 daughter of Enoch and Eunice (Kinsman) Noyes; Dorcas d. 17 Feb 1877.

v SARAH ABBOTT, b. 3 Oct 1788; d. at Hartland, VT, 27 Jul 1878; m. 12 Sep 1805, STEPHEN NOYES, b. at Bow, NH, 5 Jul 1783 son of Enoch and Eunice (Kinsman) Noyes; Stephen d. 27 Feb 1868.

vi ABIGAIL LAWRENCE ABBOTT, b. 20 May 1791; d. at Chicopee, MA, 5 Dec 1856; m. 9 Feb 1809, SETH BAKER, b. at Pembroke, 21 May 1783 son of Thomas and Ruth (Peabody) Baker; Seth d. 30 Apr 1865.

vii ISAAC ABBOTT, b. 3 Aug 1793; d. 12 Nov 1840; m. 7 May 1817, SUSAN ELA, b. at Hooksett, 7 Jan 1797 daughter of Israel and Zebiah (Martin) Ela.[2566] Susan was still living in 1880 when she was living with her daughter Fanny and her husband Leonard Beard.[2567]

viii PARMELIA ABBOTT, b. 1 Feb 1796; d. at Pewaukee, WI, 1872; m. 7 Nov 1816, NATHANIEL GOSS, b. at Greenland, NH, 3 Nov 1788 son of Nathaniel and Mary (Nye) Goss; Nathaniel d. at Pewaukee, 7 Jul 1855.

ix THEODORE THOMAS ABBOTT, b. 22 Mar 1799; d. at Lunenburg, MA, 23 Mar 1887; m. at Lowell, 7 Aug 1826, MEHITABLE FROST GREENOUGH, b. at Newburyport, 1 Jan 1800 daughter of John and Elizabeth "Betsy" (March) Greenough; Mehitable d. 28 Mar 1887.

966) ROBERT GRAY (*Robert Gray[4], Robert Gray[3], Hannah Holt Gray[2], Nicholas[1]*), b. at Andover, 9 Jul 1729 son of Robert and Lydia (Peabody) Gray; d. at Andover, 19 Dec 1806 at the poorhouse;[2568] m. 1st 23 Apr 1754, MARY TUCKER who died about 1757. Robert m. 2nd, Jun 1758, ABIGAIL TAY (widow of Abijah Chandler), b. at Woburn, 1728 daughter of William and Abigail (Jones) Tay;[2569] Abigail d. at Andover, 29 Jan 1790.

Although Robert Gray died at the poorhouse, his son Rev. Robert Gray graduated from Harvard in 1786 and was a minister in Dover, New Hampshire.[2570]

There are no children known for Robert Gray and Mary Tucker. There are two children known for Robert Tucker and Abigail Tay.

i CORNELIUS GRAY, baptized at Andover, 10 Jun 1759; nothing further known.

ii ROBERT GRAY, b. at Andover, 2 Jun 1761; d. at Wolfeboro, NH, 25 Aug 1822; m. 1st at Medford, 22 Mar 1787, LYDIA TUFTS, b. at Medford, 13 Jun 1762 daughter of Peter and Anna (Adams) Tufts; Lydia d. at Dover, NH, 31 Aug 1801. Robert m. 2nd at Lincoln, MA, 24 Aug 1802, SUSANNA HOAR, b. at Lincoln, 22 Feb 1774; Susanna d. at Lincoln, 8 Feb 1858.

967) LYDIA GRAY (*Robert Gray[4], Robert Gray[3], Hannah Holt Gray[2], Nicholas[1]*), b. at Andover, 14 Nov 1732 daughter of Robert and Lydia (Peabody) Gray; d. at Andover, 1818 at the poorhouse; m. at Andover, 21 Nov 1751, JOHN BATCHELDER, b. at Hampton Falls, 1 Jun 1730 son of Benjamin and Rebecca (Prescott) Batchelder; John d. at Chester, NH, before 1781.

There are two children known for Lydia and John.

2565 *New Hampshire Wills and Probate Records 1643-1982,* Probate of Benjamin Abbott, Rockingham, 17 Jan 1816, Case number 9209.

2566 Ela, *Genealogy of the Ela Family*, p 17

2567 Year: 1880; Census Place: Lancaster, Coos, New Hampshire; Roll: 762; Page: 153C; Enumeration District: 040

2568 Robert, at the poorhouse, Dec. 19, 1806. [a. 78 y. CR2].

2569 The 1781 will of William Tay includes a bequest to daughter Abigail wife of Robert Gray.

2570 Wadleigh, *Notable Events in the History of Dover*, p 174

i JOHN PRESCOTT BATCHELDER, b. at Chester, about 1753

ii LYDIA BATCHELDER, b. at Chester, about 1755; b. at Andover, MA, 19 Jan 1820; m. at Andover, 11 Mar 1779, JOHN FRYE, b. at Andover, 16 Aug 1754 son of Ebenezer and Elizabeth (Kimball) Frye; John d. at Andover, 26 Mar 1843.

968) BRIDGET GRAY (*Robert Gray⁴, Robert Gray³, Hannah Holt Gray², Nicholas¹*), b. at Andover, 5 Apr 1737 daughter of Robert and Lydia (Peabody) Gray; d. at Windsor, VT, 1805; m. at Billerica, 22 Jun 1758, SAMUEL PEARSON, b. about 1738 likely son of Thomas and Abigail (Lewis) Pearson; Samuel d. at Windsor, VT, 4 Sep 1823.

Bridget and Samuel were in Wilmington, Massachusetts immediately after their marriage but then relocated to Windsor, Vermont where they died.

The children of Bridget and Samuel are uncertain, but nine children are proposed. The only child for whom a birth record was located was Bridget, but other of the children can be identified through deeds or other histories.

i BRIDGET PEARSON, b. at Wilmington, MA, 26 Apr 1759; m. at Lyndeborough, 1779, ASA BOUTWELL, b. at Lyndeborough, 17 Feb 1761 son of James and Mary (Johnson) Boutwell; Asa d. at Barre, VT, Aug 1820.

ii HANNAH PEARSON, b. 18 Jul 1761; d. at Windsor, VT, 27 Dec 1844; m. at Rochester, NH, 17 May 1781, WILLIAM PEARSON, b. at Wilmington, MA, 27 Sep 1757 son of William and Mary (Jaquith) Pearson; William d. at Windsor, 22 Sep 1836.

iii SAMUEL PEARSON, b. 1 Apr 1763; d. 3 Nov 1847; m. about 1786, HANNAH who is possibly Hannah Montgomery.

iv CHLOE PEARSON, b. about 1766; d. at Reading, VT, about 1799; m. about 1783, DANIEL PEABODY, b. at Boxford, MA, 3 Jan 1766 son of Daniel and Anna (Stickney) Peabody;[2571] Daniel d. at Reading, 22 Apr 1813. Daniel married second at Reading, 30 Jan 1800, Abigail Reading.

v OLIVE PEARSON, b. about 1767; d. at Granville, NY, 15 May 1845; m. about 1787, SCOTTOWAY "SCOTTER" WHITCOMB, b. at Warren, MA, 10 Jul 1766 son of Scottoway and Mary (Sheldon) Whitcomb; Scotter d. at Granville, 24 Dec 1840.

vi CORNELIUS GRAY PEARSON, b. 1768; d. at Ellisburg, NY, 6 Aug 1849; m. MARY "POLLY" BENJAMIN, b. at Ashburnham, 7 Jul 1773 daughter of William and Sarah (Child) Benjamin;[2572] Polly d. at Ellisburg, 4 May 1849.

vii RHODA PEARSON, b. about 1771; d. at Windsor, VT, 1806; m. at Reading, 17 Feb 1799, OLIVER DAVIS, b. about 1774; Oliver d. at Windsor, about 1808.

viii JOHN LEWIS PEARSON, b. about 1773; d. at West Windsor, VT, 14 Mar 1822; m. by about 1797, REBECCA CADY, b. 1777 daughter of John and Hannah (-) Cady (death record); Rebecca d. at West Windsor, 20 Feb 1865.

ix LUCY PEARSON, b. 1775; d. at Reading, 30 Apr 1854; m. at Windsor, VT, 21 Jul 1799, JESSE HOLDEN, b. at Barre, MA, 21 Aug 1779 son of Benjamin and Abigail (Bacon) Holden; Jesse d. at Reading, 7 May 1845.

969) REBECCA GRAY (*Isaac Gray⁴, Robert Gray³, Hannah Holt Gray², Nicholas¹*), b. at Andover, 31 Aug 1734 daughter of Isaac and Rebecca (Frost) Gray; m. at Tewksbury, 1 May 1758, JONATHAN FRENCH; Jonathan d. 1765 (probate 1765).

In his will written 1 June 1765 (probate 8 October 1765), Jonathan French bequeathed to beloved wife Rebecca all his lands and buildings and movable estate to be at her disposal and to allow her to bring up his beloved daughter Rebecca. At age twenty-one or at marriage, Rebecca is to receive £40. Wife Rebecca was named executrix. Real estate was valued at £150.[2573]

Rebecca Gray and Jonathan French were parents of two children.

i REBECCA FRENCH, b. at Tewksbury, 4 Mar 1759; d. at Tewksbury, 1 Apr 1829; m. 22 Apr 1777, BENJAMIN MACE, b. at Newbury, 25 Nov 1746 son of Daniel and Priscilla (Annis) Mace; Benjamin d. at Tewksbury, 30 Nov 1828.

ii JONATHAN FRENCH, b. 25 Oct 1760; d. 1 Nov 1760.

2571 Peabody, *Peabody Genealogy*, p 52

2572 Bicha and Brown, *The Benjamin Family in America*, p 144

2573 *Middlesex County, MA: Probate File Papers, 1648-1871.*Online database. *AmericanAncestors.org.* New England Historic Genealogical Society, 2014. Case 8506

970) ANN GRAY (*Isaac Gray⁴, Robert Gray³, Hannah Holt Gray², Nicholas¹*), b. at Andover, 30 Mar 1743 daughter of Isaac and Rebecca (Frost) Gray; d. at Tewksbury, 9 May 1798; m. about 1762, ISAAC FOSTER, b. at Andover, 28 Apr 1737 son of John and Mary (Osgood) Foster.[2574] Isaac was first married to Dorcas Jewett.

Isaac Foster served in the French and Indian War in the company of Lt. Col. James Frye. Isaac was captured by Ottawa on 19 September 1756 near Lake George and taken to a lake known as Almipagon which was 150 miles north of Lake Superior. Isaac was held there for two years, and later was taken to a place called Detroit where he was ransomed by a Frenchman but had to work off the ransom with labor. After fourteen months, he was taken to Crown Point where there was a late exchange of prisoners. He was not able to return home until three years two months after his departure in 1756. He later petitioned for financial relief related to his long and multiple hardships.[2575]

Ann Gray and Isaac Foster were parents of eight children born at Tewksbury. Isaac also had one son with his first wife Dorcas Jewett.

i ABIAL FOSTER, b. 25 May 1763; d. at Fitzwilliam, NH, 23 Jan 1833; m. 1st at Billerica, 23 Nov 1788, SARAH WHITING whose parents are not certain; Sarah d. by 1817. Abial m. 2nd at Richmond, NH, 27 Jul 1817, LYDIA WHITNEY, b. at Fitzwilliam, 21 Oct 1787 daughter of Joel and Lydia (Willard) Whitney; Lydia d. at Fitchburg, MA, 29 Aug 1846. Lydia married second at Brattleboro, VT, 1839, Moses Towne.

ii MARY FOSTER, b. 19 Dec 1764

iii EZRA FOSTER, b. 20 Mar 1767; d. at Littleton, NH, 22 Feb 1856; m. at Lancaster, NH, 25 Nov 1795, ABIGAIL GARLAND, b. 1777; Abigail d. at Littleton, 13 Apr 1859.

iv SOLOMON FOSTER, b. 6 May 1769

v ISAAC GRAY FOSTER, b. 22 Jun 1771; d. at Tewksbury, 20 Nov 1850. Isaac was living at the poor house in Tewksbury in 1850. It is not known if he married.

vi JOHN FOSTER, b. 15 May 1773; d. at Albany, ME, 20 Jun 1806; m. at Andover, 26 Jul 1796, BETSEY BALDWIN STICKNEY, b. about 1776; Betsey d. at Albany, 18 Dec 1861. Betsey married second Benjamin Clark on 15 Oct 1807.

vii JOEL FOSTER, b. 16 Mar 1776; d. at Hancock, NH, 20 Feb 1841 (probate 3 Mar 1841); m. 1st at Tewksbury, 9 Sep 1802, REBECCA HUNT, b. at Tewksbury, 8 Mar 1769 daughter of Nathaniel and Sarah (Kittredge) Hunt; Rebecca d. at Hancock, 27 Aug 1811. Joel m. 2nd 26 Dec 1811, AGNES NANCY TYRRELL, b. at Bedford, NH, 11 Nov 1781 daughter of Samuel and Mary (McInnes) Tyrrell; Nancy d. at Hancock, 20 Apr 1835.

viii ANNA FOSTER, b. 2 Nov 1781; d. 14 Jun 1800.

971) HANNAH FITCH (*Miriam Gray Fitch⁴, Robert Gray³, Hannah Holt Gray², Nicholas¹*), b. at Bedford, 10 Jun 1733 daughter of Benjamin and Miriam (Gray) Fitch; d. at Nottingham West, NH by 1769; m. at Bedford, 1 Aug 1751, DAVID TARBELL, b. at Salem, 15 Sep 1726 and baptized at Lynn, 25 Sep 1726 son of John and Hannah (Flint) Tarbell; David d. at Nottingham West, NH, about 1805 (will Oct 1805). David married Esther Kemp on 2 Jul 1772.

Hannah and David were in Billerica in their early marriage but were later in Nottingham, New Hampshire.

In his will written 14 October 1805, David Tarbell bequeathed to beloved wife Esther two cows, a heifer, three sheep, all the household furniture, and all the personal estate not otherwise disposed of to be at her disposal. Three daughters Hannah Spaulding, Betsy Woods, and Lydia Shipley receive five shillings each. Son David receives one dollar. Daughter Mary receives a chest with drawers and a bed. Daughter Esther Tarbell receives the loom. Daughter Rhoda Roby receives five shillings. Son John Tarbell receives five shillings and son Samuel the oxen and farming tools. Wife Esther Tarbell and Samuel Marsh of Nottingham were named executors.[2576] Mary, Esther, Rhoda, John, and Samuel were David's children from his second marriage to Esther Kemp.

Hannah Fitch and David Tarbell were parents of seven children.

i HANNAH TARBELL, baptized at Billerica, 19 Jan 1752; died young.

ii HANNAH TARBELL, baptized at Billerica, 29 Sep 1754; m. 1st at Dunstable, 22 Jun 1773, JEREMIAH FARMER; Jeremiah d. at Groton, 1801 (probate 21 Apr 1801). Hannah m. 2nd at Groton, 6 May 1801, EPHRAIM SPAULDING.

iii BETTY TARBELL, baptized at Billerica, 30 Jun 1757; d. at Dunstable, about 1837; m. at Groton, 7 Jul 1778, AMOS WOODS, b. at Groton, 17 Dec 1748 son of Amos and Hannah (Nutting) Woods; Amos d. 28 Nov 1829.[2577]

iv JOHN TARBELL, b. about 1760; died young.

[2574] Pierce, *Foster Genealogy*, part 1, p 194

[2575] Pierce, Foster Genealogy, part 1, p 194; see this source for the full transcript of the petition and a 1757 petition by his father John Foster.

[2576] *New Hampshire. Probate Court (Hillsborough County)*; Probate Place: *Hillsborough, New Hampshire, Probate Records, volume 11, pp 335-336*

[2577] Revolutionary War Pension Application File

v LYDIA TARBELL, b. about 1766; d. at Groton, 20 Jun 1820; m. at Groton, 20 Sep 1787, WILLIAM SHEPLE, b. at Groton, 1762 son of William and Agnes (Storman) Sheple; William d. at Groton, 11 Aug 1828.

vi DAVID TARBELL, b. at Nottingham, 14 Oct 1767; d. after 1830 when he was living at Nottingham West; m. at Dunstable, 6 Apr 1804, ANNA SPRAKE daughter of Samuel and Anna (Sprake) Sprake.[2578]

vii BENJAMIN TARBELL, b. about 1769; died young.

972) BETTE FITCH (*Miriam Gray Fitch*[4], *Robert Gray*[3], *Hannah Holt Gray*[2], *Nicholas*[1]), baptized at Bedford, 14 Jun 1739 daughter of Benjamin and Miriam (Gray) Fitch; d. at Cambridge, 5 May 1823; m. at Bedford, 30 Mar 1763, NOAH WYETH, b. 7 Jul 1742 son of Ebenezer and Susannah (Hancock) Wyeth, Noah d. at Cambridge, 10 Sep 1811.

Bette and Noah resided in Cambridge. Noah served in the militia and "marched at the alarm" 19 April 1775.[2579]

In his will written 19 August 1807 (probate 12 November 1811), Noah Wyeth bequeathed to beloved wife Betty the income and improvement of all the real estate while she is a widow. She also receives all the household furniture, except the clock, to be at her disposal. Son Job Wyeth receives the clock, but he is not to remove from the house during the life of his mother. Son Job receives all the real estate and the remainder of the personal estate at the death or remarriage of his mother. Job is to pay fifty dollars each to his sisters Elizabeth, Lydia, and Rhoda, to the children of his sister Dorcas deceased late the wife of Samuel Hill, and to the children of his brother Noah Wyeth deceased.[2580]

Bette Fitch and Noah Wyeth were parents of seven children born at Cambridge.

i NOAH WYETH, b. at Cambridge, 24 Jun 1763; d. 1805 (probate 29 Jan 1806); m. at New York, 25 Dec 1795, HANNAH THOMAS, baptized at Andover, 8 Oct 1775 daughter of Alexander and Mary (Kemble) Thomas. Captain Noah Wyeth was master of the brig *Pallas* which sailed from New York.

ii ELIZABETH WYETH, b. at Cambridge, 4 Mar 1765; d. at Brooklyn, 1829; m. at Cambridge, 14 Feb 1785, ANDREW NEWELL, baptized at Charlestown, 10 Feb 1750/1 son of David and Mary (-) Newell; Andrew d. at New York, NY, 1798 (probate 13 Nov 1798).

iii LYDIA WYETH, b. at Cambridge, 3 Feb 1766; d. at Cambridge, 22 Oct 1843; m. at Cambridge, 26 Sep 1804, NATHANIEL WOODWARD.

iv RHODA WYETH, b. at Cambridge, 18 May 1768; d. at Lempster, NH, 17 Feb 1866; m. at Mason, NH, 23 Oct 1794, ARTEMAS MANNING, b. at Lancaster, MA, 13 Aug 1766 son of John and Prudence (Houghton) Manning; Artemas d. at Washington, NH, 8 May 1838.

v DORCAS WYETH, b. at Cambridge, 21 Nov 1770; d. at Mason, NH, 19 Jan 1807; m. SAMUEL HILL, b. at Cambridge, 1764 son of Samuel and Sarah (Cutler) Hill; Samuel d. at Mason, 23 May 1813.

vi ISAAC WYETH, b. 10 Feb 1773; d. 6 Sep 1779.

vii JOB WYETH, b. at Cambridge, 24 Jun 1776; d. at Cambridge, 5 Jun 1840; m. at Cambridge, 31 Jan 1804, LYDIA CONVERS FRANCIS, b. 1778 daughter of Benjamin and Sarah (Hall) Francis; Lydia d. at Cambridge, 4 Jan 1850.

973) DAVID FITCH (*Miriam Gray Fitch*[4], *Robert Gray*[3], *Hannah Holt Gray*[2], *Nicholas*[1]), b. at Bedford, 22 May 1743 son of Benjamin and Miriam (Gray) Fitch; d. at Bedford, 27 Jul 1813; m. at Woburn, 3 Apr 1770, MARY FOWLE, b. 1747 whose parents have not been identified; Mary d. at Bedford, 19 Sep 1829.

David Fitch was a miller in Bedford. In his will written 8 February 1813, David Fitch bequeathed to beloved wife Mary the use and improvement of half the dwelling house, use of all the furnishings, and the pew in the meeting house as well as specific provisions for her support while she is a widow. Daughters Polly Wheeler and Lydia Page each receives $100. Beloved son David receives the remainder of the estate and is named executor.[2581] Real estate was valued at $2,527 and personal estate at $828.96.

David Fitch and Mary Fowle were parents of four children born at Bedford, Massachusetts.

[2578] The 1826 will (probate Feb 1837) of Samuel Sprake of Nottingham (death at Hudson) includes a bequest to his daughter Anna Tarbell wife of David Tarbell.

[2579] Paige, *History of Cambridge*, p 409

[2580] *Middlesex County, MA: Probate File Papers, 1648-1871.*Online database. *AmericanAncestors.org.* New England Historic Genealogical Society, 2014. Case 25825

[2581] *Middlesex County, MA: Probate File Papers, 1648-1871.*Online database. *AmericanAncestors.org.* New England Historic Genealogical Society, 2014. Case 7689

i POLLY FITCH, b. at Bedford, 20 Oct 1770; d. at Concord, NH, 27 Apr 1818; m. at Billerica, 4 Nov 1794, BENJAMIN WHEELER, b. at Monson, NH, 18 Aug 1768 son of Daniel and Amy (Morse) Wheeler;[2582] Benjamin d. at Concord, 11 Dec 1848. Benjamin married second Hannah Clement.

ii LYDIA FITCH, b. at Bedford, 7 Dec 1772; d. at Bedford, 24 Jan 1852; m. 10 Sep 1801, NATHANIEL PAGE, b. at Bedford, 25 Oct 1775 son of Nathaniel and Sarah (Brown) Page; Nathaniel d. 30 Aug 1858.

iii DAVID FITCH, b. at Bedford, 28 Jun 1777; d. at Bedford, 24 May 1860; m. 1st 12 Nov 1799, HANNAH PROCTOR, b. 7 Feb 1779 daughter of Peter and Molly (Putnam) Proctor; Hannah d. at Bedford, 22 Dec 1803. David m. 2nd 8 Jan 1805, OLIVE SIMONDS, b. at Burlington, MA, 12 Nov 1783 daughter of Jonathan and Phebe (Cummings) Simonds; Olive d. 20 Sep 1859. David m. 3rd 29 Feb 1860, SUSAN DODGE (widow of Amos Adams), b. 18 May 1804 daughter of David and Polly (Stevens) Dodge; Susan d. at Billerica, 20 Mar 1878.

iv ISAAC FITCH, b. 15 Jan 1782; d. 5 Feb 1797.

974) EUNICE FITCH (*Miriam Gray Fitch⁴, Robert Gray³, Hannah Holt Gray², Nicholas¹*), b. at Bedford, 26 Jul 1747 daughter of Benjamin and Miriam (Gray) Fitch; m. 29 Sep 1778, DANIEL MCNICHOL (NICHOLS)

A record of one child of Eunice and Daniel was located.

i BETTY NICHOLS, b. at Amesbury, 1 Aug 1779

975) LUCY GRAY (*Abiel Gray⁴, Robert Gray³, Hannah Holt Gray², Nicholas¹*), b. at Tolland, 29 Jan 1737/8 daughter of Abiel and Zerviah (Hatch) Gray; d. at Tolland, 25 Dec 1804; m. at Tolland, 10 Dec 1754, JOHN LOTHROP, b. at Tolland, 6 May 1732 son of John and Ann (Thatcher) Lothrop;[2583] John d. at Tolland, 24 Mar 1812.

John Lothrop and Lucy Gray were parents of twelve children born at Tolland.

i DESIRE LOTHROP, b. and d. 11 Nov 1755

ii ANNA LOTHROP, b. 19 Oct 1756; d. 23 Nov 1756

iii LUSCALLA LOTHROP, b. 23 Nov 1757; d. at Tolland, 30 Nov 1827; m. 1st 14 Jan 1779. ELIAB LADD, b. at Tolland, 21 Apr 1754 son of Jonathan and Anna (Tyler) Ladd; Eliab d. at Tolland, 15 Dec 1800. Luscalla m. 2nd, 1808, as his second wife, JESSE MEACHAM, b. at Somers, 24 Aug 1751 son of Joseph and Hannah (Horton) Meacham; Jesse d. at Somers, 1 Jun 1822. Jesse was first married to Sarah Bush.

iv Son, b. and d. 6 Dec 1759

v PRESCINDA LOTHROP, b. 30 Jan 1761; d. at Watertown, NY, 20 Mar 1810; m. 1783, WILLIAM D. HUNTINGTON, b. at Tolland, 19 Sep 1757 son of John and Mehitable (Steele) Huntington; William d. at Watertown, 11 May 1842. William married second Prescinda's sister Elvira (see below).

vi JOHN LOTHROP, b. 24 Apr 1763; killed in battle at Horse Neck, 10 Dec 1780.

vii ELIZABETH LOTHROP, b. 23 Aug 1765; d. at Brookfield, VT, 16 Sep 1837; m. at Tolland, 17 Aug 1785, ANDREW STEELE, b. at Tolland, 25 Dec 1763 son of James and Abigail (Huntington) Steele; Andrew d. at Brookfield, 18 Feb 1811.

viii ELVIRA LOTHROP, b. 13 Jun 1768; d. at Watertown, NY, 5 Dec 1836; m. 1st about 1793, ALANSON DRESSER, b. at Pomfret, 11 Jun 1768 son of John and Sarah (Dresser) Dresser; Alanson d. at Watertown, 26 Oct 1808. Elvira m. 2nd, about 1811, WILLIAM D. HUNTINGTON who was first married to Elvira's sister Prescinda (see above).

ix ROWLAND LOTHROP, b. 10 Mar 1771; d. at Tolland, 14 Sep 1844; m. 1st at Tolland, 1 Jan 1799, HANNAH CRAFTS, b. at Pomfret, 13 Jul 1777 daughter of Benjamin and Anna (Richardson) Crafts; Hannah d. at Tolland, 15 Oct 1820. Rowland m. 2nd at Tolland, 28 Feb 1821, HANNAH CLEAVELAND, b. at Hartland, VT, 20 Sep 1794 daughter of Thomas and Ann (Crafts) Cleaveland; Hannah d. at Tolland, 4 Feb 1868. Hannah Cleaveland was the niece of Rowland's first wife Hannah Crafts.

x LUCY LOTHROP, b. 5 Nov 1774; d. at Tolland, 31 Aug 1807; m. at Tolland, 4 Sep 1793, ERASTUS RAWDON, b. at Tolland, 19 Dec 1766 son of Thomas and Lydia (Bozworth) Rawdon; Erastus d. at Windsor, OH, 14 Aug 1826.

xi JONATHAN LOTHROP, b. 17 Feb 1776; d. 13 May 1776.

[2582] Wheeler, *The Genealogical and Encyclopedic History of the Wheeler Family*, p 51

[2583] Huntington, *A Genealogical Memoir of the Lo-Lathrop Family*, p 92

xii MARY "MOLLY" LOTHROP, b. 12 Sep 1779; d. at Delaware, OH, 1854; m. 1st Mr. Woodward who has not been identified. Mary m. 2nd at Bethel, VT, 3 Jun 1819, as his second wife, EZRA WEST TORREY, b. at Stafford, CT, 14 Sep 1780 son of David and Anna (Lillie) Torrey; Ezra d. at Delaware, OH, 1841. Ezra was first married to Dorcas Adye.

976) ZERVIAH GRAY (*Abiel Gray[4], Robert Gray[3], Hannah Holt Gray[2], Nicholas[1]*), b. at Tolland, 9 Jul 1742 daughter of Abiel and Zerviah (Hatch) Gray; d. at Shoreham, VT, 19 Aug 1828; m. at West Hartford, 18 Nov 1762, AMOS STANLEY, baptized at Hartford, 26 Aug 1739 son of Samuel and Anne (Bracey) Stanley; Amos d. at Becket, MA, 25 Jan 1811.

Zerviah and Amos were married in Connecticut and started their family there. They relocated to Lenox, Massachusetts and then to Becket where Amos died. After her husband's death, Zerviah went with her son Amos to Shoreham, Vermont where she died.

In his will written 4 June 1802 (proved 7 July 1812), Amos Stanley of Becket bequeathed to beloved wife Zerviah one-third of the real and personal estates during her life and the great bible. Son John G. Stanley receives a piece of land in Lenox which was reasonably deeded to Amos by Calvin Burnham and also another lot of land on which John G. now lives. John G. is to pay $840, the amount of a note John owes to his father, to the other children to be equally divided among them: Amos Stanley, Jr., Zerviah Weeks, and Amanda Falley. The remainder of the estate both real and personal is to be equally divided among Amos, Zerviah, and Amanda. Son John G. Stanley was named executor. Real estate was valued at $1,810.[2584]

Zerviah Gray and Amos Stanley were parents of five children.

i ZERVIAH STANLEY, b. at West Hartford, about 1763; d. at Castalia, OH, 25 May 1838; m. 1st about 1782, CURTIS LEWIS; Curtis d. at Lenox, MA, about 1791. Zerviah m. 2nd Mr. Weeks who is not yet identified.

ii AMOS STANLEY, baptized at Hartford, 8 Jun 1766; d. at Shoreham, VT, 29 Jul 1830; m. about 1790, ANNA NORTHRUP, b. at Lenox, MA, 1770 daughter of Samuel and Phebe (Beecher) Northrup; Anna d. at Shoreham, 19 Dec 1862. Anna married second Ezekiel Gardner.

iii AMANDA STANLEY, b. at Lenox, MA, 18 Aug 1771; d. at Margaretta, OH, 29 Nov 1850; m. about 1794, RICHARD FALLEY, b. at Westfield, MA, 15 Sep 1768 son of Richard and Margaret (Hitchcock) Falley; Richard d. at Castalia, OH, 28 Feb 1835.

iv JOHN GRAY STANLEY, b. at Lenox, 30 Sep 1778; d. at Lenox, 25 Oct 1835; m. at Peru, MA, 27 Jan 1803, ORILLA BREWSTER, b. at Becket, 27 Jan 1782 daughter of Oliver and Jerusha (Badger) Brewster; Orilla d. at Lenox, 21 Sep 1860.

v ABIEL HATCH STANLEY, b. at Lenox, Feb 1785; d. Mar 1785.

977) COMFORT GRAY (*Abiel Gray[4], Robert Gray[3], Hannah Holt Gray[2], Nicholas[1]*), b. at Tolland, 25 May 1751 daughter of Abiel and Zerviah (Hatch) Gray; d. at New Hartford, 19 Apr 1841; m. at Hartford, 1 May 1768, STEPHEN GILLET, b. at Hartford, 21 Mar 1729 son of Joseph and Sarah (Burr) Gillet; Stephen d. at North Hartford, 20 May 1800.

Stephen Gillet did not leave a will and his estate entered probate 7 July 1800 with Joseph Gillet as administrator. Real estate was valued at $367.62 which included one-fourth of a sawmill valued at $84. Debts against the estate rendered the estate insolvent. The dower was set off to widow Comfort.[2585]

There are records for six children of Comfort Gray and Stephen Gillet likely all born at New Hartford.[2586]

i STEPHEN GILLET, b. 1769 and baptized 12 Dec 1773; d. at New Hartford, 3 Oct 1776.

ii JOSEPH GILLET, b. 1773 and baptized 7 Oct 1776; d. at New Hartford, 10 Oct 1776.

iii ZERVIAH GILLET, baptized at New Hartford, 12 Dec 1773; d. at Barkhamsted, CT, 30 Apr 1844; m. 3 Oct 1791, NEHEMIAH ANDRUS, b. 1767 son of Nehemiah and Phebe (Benham) Andrus; Nehemiah d. at Barkhamsted, 2 Aug 1844.

iv STEPHEN GILLET, b. 1776 and baptized 3 Aug 1777; d. at New Hartford, Sep 1796 at age 20.

v JOSEPH GILLET, baptized at New Hartford, 10 Sep 1780; d. at New Hartford, 1857 (probate 1857); m. 1st BETHIAH BACON, b. at Burlington, CT, 27 Jul 1782 daughter of Moses and Rosanna (Rust) Bacon;[2587] Bethiah

---

2584 *Berkshire County, MA: Probate File Papers, 1761-1917.*Online database. *AmericanAncestors.org.* New England Historic Genealogical Society, 2017. Case 2923

2585 *Connecticut State Library (Hartford, Connecticut);* Probate Place: *Hartford, Connecticut, Probate Packets, Gaylord, C-Goodwin, Sarah, 1769-1880, Estate of Stephen Gillet*

2586 Connecticut, Church Record Abstracts, 1630-1920, New Hartford. Only baptism and other church records were located for birth information and in several cases the children seem to have been baptized several years after birth.

2587 The final estate division of the estate of Moses Bacon of Burlington (probate 1829, division 1832) includes a distribution to Joseph R. Gillette; Connecticut Probate Records, Hartford, Farmington District, 9:548

d. at New Hartford, 25 Jul 1820Joseph m. 2nd SABRINA who has not been identified; Sabra d. at New Hartford, 17 Nov 1749. Joseph m. 3rd ABIGAIL LOOMIS (marriage contract of 8 Mar 1850 noted in Joseph's will), b. 4 Jan 1795 daughter of Joseph and Mary (Crissey) Loomis; Abigail d. 11 Oct 1871. Joseph was father of four children.

vi URSULA GILLET, baptized at New Hartford, 19 Sep 1793; nothing further found.

978) LOIS GRAY (*Abiel Gray4, Robert Gray3, Hannah Holt Gray2, Nicholas1*), b. at Hartford, about 1755 daughter of Abiel and Lois (Palmer) Gray; m. at West Hartford, 13 Nov 1772, EBENEZER PRICE, b. at Hartford, 13 Sep 1748 son of Ebenezer and Sarah (Ensign) Price; Ebenezer d. at South Amboy, NJ.

Ebenezer Price was one of the first permanent settlers in Sayreville borough of South Amboy. The home of Ebenezer and Lois was located on what was known as Roundabout Landing on a point of land between the Raritan and South rivers.[2588] Ebenezer and his sons Ebenezer, Jr. and Xerxes made stoneware and pottery using the clay from what is known as Morgan's clay banks at South Amboy.[2589]

Lois and Ebenezer were parents of three children. In his will written 6 April 1786, Lois's brother Abiel left a legacy of £16 to be paid to his sister Lois Price and her three children Lois, Ebenezer, and Xerxes.[2590]

i LOIS PRICE, b. at Hartford, CT, 1 Aug 1774; d. at Tennent, NJ, 29 Mar 1853; m. HENRY FRENCH; Henry d. at South Amboy, 1847.

ii EBENEZER PRICE, b. about 1776; d. at South Amboy, 1820 (probate 1820); m. MARY BROWN.

iii XERXES PRICE, b. at Hartford, about 1777; d. at South Amboy, 24 Oct 1845; m. NANCY LETTS, b. 1779 daughter of Francis and Mary (van Deventer) Letts; Nancy d. 8 Aug 1829.

979) ESTHER GRAY (*Abiel Gray4, Robert Gray3, Hannah Holt Gray2, Nicholas1*), baptized at Hartford, 17 May 1761 daughter of Abiel and Lois (Palmer) Gray; d. at West Hartford, 21 Dec 1824; m. at Hartford, 15 Feb 1785, DAVID ROWE, b. about 1758 of Farmington; David d. at West Hartford, 20 Feb 1814.

There are records of five children of Esther Gray and David Rowe born/baptized at West Hartford.[2591]

i ABIEL GRAY ROWE, baptized 23 May 1787; married at West Hartford, 2 Apr 1820, EUNICE LANDER. Abiel was living in Farmington, CT in 1820 but nothing further was found.

ii Son, b. 1789 and d. 31 Oct 1790.

iii LUCY ROWE, baptized 23 Oct 1790

iv Child, d. at West Hartford, 15 Sep 1792.

v LUMAN ROWE, b. 1794 and baptized 10 May 1802; d. at West Hartford, 28 Feb 1814 at age 20.

980) PERSIS GRAY (*Jonathan Gray4, Robert Gray3, Hannah Holt Gray2, Nicholas1*), b. at Woburn, 29 Mar 1740 daughter of Jonathan and Persis (Reed) Gray; d. at Jaffrey, NH, 27 Oct 1816; m. 1st at Woburn, 28 Dec 1756, JAMES SNOW, b. at Woburn, 7 Mar 1732 son of Zerubbabel and Elizabeth (Wyman) Snow; James d. at Woburn, 28 Jun 1783 by drowning (probate 1783). Persis m. 2nd at Jaffrey, Jan 1789, OLIVER PROCTOR, b. at Westford, 25 Feb 1729 son of John and Mary (Colesworthy) Proctor; Oliver d. at Jaffrey, 17 Jul 1809. Oliver was first married to Elisabeth Proctor.

In 1775, a guardian was appointed for James due to *non compos mentis*. Persis requested that Samuel Thompson be named guardian for James. James Snow did not leave a will and on 4 November 1783, widow Persis requested that Samuel Thompson be named administrator. Real estate was valued at £79.8.3 and claims against the estate were £59.3.2.[2592]

James Snow and Persis Gray were parents of eight children born at Woburn.

i JAMES SNOW, b. 21 Feb 1757

ii JESSE SNOW, b. 3 Apr 1760; d. at Brandon, VT, 4 Apr 1833; m. 1st at Jaffrey, NH, Jan 1789, BETSEY WYMAN. Jesse m. 2nd at Brandon, 20 Mar 1827, MERCY CHURCHILL.

iii JONATHAN SNOW, b. 3 Aug 1762

iv PERSIS SNOW, b. 28 Mar 1765; d. 22 Nov 1785.

2588 Wall, *History of Middlesex County, New Jersey*, volume 2, p 469

2589 New Jersey Geological Survey, *Report on the Clay Deposits of Woodbridge*, p 1

2590 *Connecticut. Probate Court (Hartford District);* Probate Place: *Hartford, Connecticut, volume 23, pp 206-207*

2591 Connecticut, Church Record Abstracts, 1630-1920, Volume 122, Part 3, West Hartford

2592 *Middlesex County, MA: Probate File Papers, 1648-1871.*Online database. *AmericanAncestors.org.* New England Historic Genealogical Society, 2014. (From records supplied by the Massachusetts Supreme Judicial Court Archives. Case 20817 and Case 20818

v HANNAH SNOW, b. 27 May 1767

vi ASA SNOW, b. 24 Jun 1769; m. at Lynnfield, 27 Nov 1789, BETSEY MANSFIELD, b. at Lynnfield, MA, about 1772 daughter of William and Elizabeth (Townsend) Mansfield;[2593] Betsey d. at Danvers, 13 Mar 1851.

vii JOSIAH SNOW, b. 1 Aug 1772; d. before 1820 when Azubah was head of household; m. at Billerica, 14 May 1797, AZUBAH HILL, b. at Billerica, 1 Mar 1768 daughter of Jonathan and Mary (Lane) Hill;[2594] Azubah was head of household in the 1840 census at Billerica.

viii JOSEPH SNOW, b. 12 Jul 1774

981) DAVID GRAY (*David Gray⁴, Robert Gray³, Hannah Holt Gray², Nicholas¹*), b. at Andover, 8 Dec 1762 son of David and Rebecca (Holt) Gray; d. at Andover, 7 Mar 1844; m. 1st 3 Apr 1788, SARAH CUMMINGS, b. at Andover, 21 May 1767 daughter of Jonathan and Mary (Eastman) Cummings;[2595] Sarah d. at Andover, 15 Mar 1793. David m. 2nd 23 Feb 1797, REBECCA JENKINS, b. at Andover, 23 Feb 1773 daughter of Samuel and Anna (Upton) Jenkins; Rebecca d. at Andover, 9 Apr 1840.

David Gray was the builder of the small house currently standing as the historic property at 232 Salem Street in Andover. David had been a member of the South Church but is reported as being excommunicated in 1830 due to being a Universalist.[2596]

In his will written 4 August 1840 (probate 16 April 1844), David Gray bequeathed to son Henry J, Gray the sum of fifteen hundred dollars which is to be held in trust by Henry and his successors and used for the benefit of son David Gray, Jr. After the decease of David, Jr., any principal and interest remaining is to be divided equally among David Jr.'s children. His express design in creating the trust is that David and his children will have the benefit of the legacy. Second son Samuel receives land of about 10 acres with buildings which was purchased from Ezra Holt where Samuel formerly lived. Samuel also receives fifteen hundred dollars. To daughter Mary Eastman Eaton wife of William Eaton of Reading partly in consideration of the "attachment of her mother to my person, and the highly dutiful and affectionate manner in which the said Mary has conducted toward me since her mother's decease, the recollection of which I shall carry with me to the grave, the sum of two thousand dollars." The remainder of the estate goes to son Henry Jenkins Gray who is named executor. Heirs signing assent to the probate of the will with Henry J. Gray as executor were Mary E. Eaton, David Gray, and Samuel Gray.[2597]

David Gray and Sarah Cummings were parents of one child.

i MARY EASTMAN GRAY, baptized at Andover, 1 Apr 1791; d. at Reading, 3 Apr 1847; m. at Andover, 3 Jul 1814, WILLIAM EATON, baptized at Reading, 15 Nov 1781 son of Jeremiah and Hannah (Wardwell) Eaton; William d. at Reading, 24 Apr 1845.

David Gray and Rebecca Jenkins were parents of four children born at Andover.

i DAVID GRAY, b. at Andover, 15 Mar 1798; d. at Andover, 20 Aug 1870; m. 1st 28 Apr 1825, AMELIA "EMILY" ABBOTT, b. at Andover, 6 Apr 1805 daughter of Caleb and Deborah (Ames) Abbott; Amelia d. 1 Sep 1833. David m. 2nd 20 Mar 1834, SARAH PETERS, b. at Andover, 5 Jun 1800 daughter of Joseph and Mehitable (Adams) Peters; Sarah d. 31 May 1836. David m. 3rd 11 Jun 1837, MARIA MERRILL (widow of Myron Bailey), likely b. at Bradford, 29 Oct 1814 daughter of Jesse and Betsey (Carleton) Merrill; Maria d. 21 Nov 1843. David m. 4th 12 Sep 1845, his third cousin once removed, SOPHRONIA ABBOTT (*Enoch Abbott⁶, Moses Abbott⁵, Hannah Holt Abbott⁴, Timothy³, James², Nicholas¹*), b. at Andover, 18 Feb 1803 daughter of Enoch and Nancy (Flint) Abbott; Sophronia d. at Andover, 6 Dec 1898.

ii REBECCA GRAY, baptized at Andover, 24 Mar 1799; d. 27 May 1802.

iii SAMUEL GRAY, b. at Andover, 30 Jan 1803; d. at Andover, 29 Sep 1880; m. 12 Jul 1831, MARTHA LOVEJOY ABBOTT, baptized at Andover, 9 Sep 1804 daughter of Stephen and Hannah (Russell) Abbott; Martha d. at Andover, 10 Dec 1856.

iv HENRY JENKINS GRAY, b. at Andover, 17 Dec 1806; d. at Andover, 6 Jul 1881; m. 14 May 1851, LYDIA SAWYER, b. at Rindge, NH, 5 Apr 1813 daughter of Francis and Lydia (Hibbert) Sawyer; Lydia d. at Andover, 12 Aug 1887. Lydia was first married to Asa Sawyer.

2593 The 1809 will of William Mansfield includes bequests to daughter Betty Snow and to her children Betsey Snow, Daniel Snow, Amone Snow, and Arethusa Snow.

2594 On 15 May 1797, Azubah Snow signed that she had received her full portion of the estate of her father Jonathan Hill. In Jonathan Hill's 1795 will, his daughter Zuba was unmarried.

2595 The 1805 will of Jonathan Cummings includes a bequest to his granddaughter Polly Eastman Gray.

2596 Andover Historic Preservation, 232 Salem Street, https://preservation.mhl.org/232-salem-st

2597 *Essex County, MA: Probate File Papers, 1638-1881.*Online database. *AmericanAncestors.org.* New England Historic Genealogical Society, 2014. Case 40840

982) NATHAN WARDWELL (*Margery Gray Wardwell⁴, Edward Gray³, Hannah Holt Gray², Nicholas¹*), baptized at Andover, 20 Jan 1740 son of William and Margery (Gray) Wardwell; d. at Andover, 14 Aug 1769; m. at Andover, 27 Dec 1763, HULDAH CHANDLER, b. at Suncook, NH, 16 Aug 1740 daughter of David and Abial (Chandler) Chandler. Huldah was second married to Stephen Stiles.

Huldah and Nathan Wardwell had two children before Nathan's death at age 28. Huldah then married Stephen Stiles, and after the births of their three children, the family relocated to New Hampshire finally settling in Hillsborough. Huldah's children with Stephen Stiles were Huldah (1773-1859), Stephen (1777-1852), and Moses (1781-1868).

Children of Nathan and Huldah Wardwell:

i NATHAN WARDWELL, b. at Andover, 10 Nov 1765; d. at Andover, 4 Nov 1838; m. at Andover, 22 May 1791, his first cousin once removed, PHEBE STEVENS (*Sarah Gray Stevens⁴, Edward Gray³, Hannah Holt Gray², Nicholas¹*), b. at Andover, 6 May 1759 daughter of Thomas and Sarah (Gray) Stevens; Phebe d. 13 Aug 1843 (age at death given as 85). Phebe Stevens and Nathan Wardwell are Family 994.

ii OLIVE WARDWELL, b. at Andover, 3 Jul 1768; d. at Salem, 7 Jan 1849; m. at Andover, 9 Nov 1794, SIMEON TOWNE. Simeon's identity is uncertain. He is described as Simeon, Jr. on the marriage transcription, but he is likely Simeon Towne born in 1751 who was first married to Hannah Symonds.

983) SARAH GRAY (*Thomas Gray⁴, Edward Gray³, Hannah Holt Gray², Nicholas¹*), b. at Andover, 13 Mar 1739/40 daughter of Thomas and Elizabeth (Hutchinson) Gray; m. at Haverhill, 18 May 1769, STEPHEN AYER, b. at Haverhill, 1 Dec 1744 son of Simon and Mary (Webster) Ayer; Stephen d. at Dunbarton, NH, 14 Dec 1825.

Sarah and Stephen started their family in Haverhill, Massachusetts but relocated to Dunbarton by 1773. Stephen served as constable of Dunbarton in 1788.[2598] He also served during the Revolution in the company of Capt. Eliphalet Daniels enlisting 18 March 1776.[2599] Stephen was a tanner by trade.

Sarah Gray and Stephen Ayer were parents of seven children. Son Thomas served in the 11th infantry in the War of 1812, and when he died in 1860, he was the oldest person living in Dunbarton at age 91.[2600]

i THOMAS AYER, b. at Haverhill, 18 Apr 1770; d. at Dunbarton, May 1860; m. 1st 20 Jul 1790, MARY "MOLLY" PARKER of Goffstown; Mary d. by 1815. Thomas m. 2nd 29 Oct 1815, widow SALLY CILLEY.

ii ANNE AYER, b. at Haverhill, 28 Jun 1771

iii ELIZABETH AYER, b. at Dunbarton, 16 Jun 1773; d. at Hillsborough, 2 Jul 1797; m. at Dunbarton, 13 Feb 1794, JAMES MCCALLEY, b. at Hillsborough, 2 Aug 1765 son of James and Jane (Stark) McCalley.[2601] James married second Eunice Huntley on 9 Apr 1799.

iv PETER AYER, b. at Dunbarton, 23 Dec 1774

v STEPHEN AYER, b. at Dunbarton, 7 Jun 1776; d. at St. Johnsbury, VT, 6 Apr 1859; m. 1st at Goffstown, 26 Oct 1802, RUTH MIRICK; Ruth d. by 1805 and perhaps after the birth of twins in Oct 1803. Stephen m. 2nd about 1806, TRYPHENA who has not been identified; Tryphena d. before 1850. Stephen and Tryphena were parents of at least seven children.

vi SARAH AYER, b. at Dunbarton, 9 Apr 1778

vii SUSANNAH AYER, b. at Dunbarton, 1 Jan 1781; d. at Dunbarton, 29 Dec 1864; m. at Dunbarton, 24 Apr 1800, JONATHAN CLIFFORD, b. at Dunbarton 23 Sep 1775 son of Israel and Achsah (Stevens) Clifford; Jonathan d. at Dunbarton, 12 Feb 1863.

984) DANIEL GRAY (*Thomas Gray⁴, Edward Gray³, Hannah Holt Gray², Nicholas¹*), b. at Andover, 20 Nov 1760 son of Thomas and Lydia (Graves) Gray; d. at Andover, 18 Jul 1833; m. at Reading, 14 Dec 1786, TABITHA ALLEN who was of Reading but not yet identified; Tabitha d. about 1847 when she last received pension payments.

Daniel Gray resided on the family homestead in Andover.

In his pension application file, Daniel reported that he enlisted at Andover in June or July 1779 in the company of Captain Silas Clark and Colonel Tupper's regiment. He served nine months. The inventory taken as part of his 1818 application showed real estate of 23 acres valued at $330 and personal estate of $82.98 and debts of $203 for a mortgage on the real estate. His widow Tabitha received a pension following Daniel's death.[2602]

2598 Stark, *History of the Town of Dunbarton*, p 268

2599 National Archives; Washington, D.C.; *Compiled Service Records of Soldiers who Served in the American Army During the Revolutionary War*; Record Group Title: *War Department Collection of Revolutionary War Records*; Record Group Number: *93*; Series Number: *M881*; NARA Roll Number: *560*

2600 Stark, *History of the Town of Dunbarton*

2601 Browne, *The History of Hillsborough, Biography and Genealogy*, p 385

2602 U.S., Revolutionary War Pension and Bounty-Land Warrant Application Files, 1800-1900

Daniel Gray and Tabitha Allen were parents of eight children born at Andover.

i TABITHA GRAY, b. at Andover, 1 Dec 1787; d. at Andover, 15 Jun 1867; m. 1st 6 Nov 1806, ELIJAH STILES, b. at Middleton, 4 Mar 1784 son of Daniel and Sarah (Averill) Stiles; Elijah d. at Andover, 11 Aug 1850. Tabitha m. 2nd 12 Oct 1863, as his third wife, JONATHAN F. RUSSELL, b. at Mason, NH, 1781 son of John and Ruhamah (Frost) Russell; Jonathan d. at Methuen, 31 Dec 1866.

ii DANIEL GRAY, b. at Andover, 15 Aug 1789; m. ABIGAIL. Daniel enlisted for the War of 1812 on 13 Apr 1813 for a period of five years or the duration of the war. He was discharged at Sackett's Harbor 17 May 1815.[2603] According to Charlotte Helen Abbot's notes, Daniel did not return after the war and was last heard of in 1847 as being in Robinson, KY.

iii MARTHA "PATTY" GRAY, b. at Andover, 18 Apr 1791; d. at North Andover, 8 Aug 1877; m. 7 Jan 1812, JOHN TOWNE, b. at Andover, 26 Mar 1786 son of Nathan and Mary (Curtis) Towne; John d. at Andover, 25 May 1854.

iv ISRAEL GRAY, b. at Andover, 4 Apr 1793; m. at Andover, 18 Jun 1818, his first cousin, LYDIA G. LACEY (*Hannah Gray Lacey5, Thomas Gray4, Edward Gray3, Hannah Holt Gray2, Nicholas1*), b. at Andover, 27 Nov 1789 daughter of John and Hannah (Gray) Lacey.

v BENJAMIN GRAY, b. at Andover, 12 Apr 1795; d. at North Andover, 31 May 1865; m. at Nottingham, NH, 1 Nov 1818, HANNAH SIMPSON, b. at Nottingham, about 1789; Hannah d. at Andover, 27 Sep 1855.

vi HENRY GRAY, b. at Andover, 3 Feb 1797; d. at Reading, 3 May 1852; m. at Wakefield, 18 Dec 1823, NANCY WHITE, b. at Reading, 6 May 1800 daughter of John and Judith (Green) White; Nancy d. at Wakefield, 24 Oct 1869.

vii CORNELIUS GRAY, b. at Andover, 29 Apr 1799; d. at North Andover, 26 Jul 1873; m. 1st at Andover, 9 May 1822, MARY MARETTA, b. about 1804 (based on age 45 at death); Mary d. at Andover, 19 Jun 1849. Cornelius m. 2nd 5 Mar 1850, BETSEY BODWELL, b. at Methuen, 1802 daughter of Henry and Sarah (Lowell) Bodwell.

viii LYDIA GRAY, b. at Andover, 7 Oct 1807

985) PHEBE GRAY (*Thomas Gray4, Edward Gray3, Hannah Holt Gray2, Nicholas1*), b. at Andover, 13 Jan 1765 daughter of Thomas and Lydia (Graves) Gray; d. at Reading, 1 Aug 1846 (as a widow); m. at Reading, 9 Sep 1784, AMOS DAMON, b. at Reading, 30 Apr 1761 son of Ezra and Ruth (Bragg) Damon; Amos d. before 1846.

Phebe and Amos were parents of four children born at Reading.

i AMOS DAMON, b. at Reading, 13 Aug 1786; m. at Reading, 30 May 1814, NANCY STANDISH.

ii EZRA DAMON, b. at Reading, 19 Dec 1787; d. at Reading, 4 Jan 1867. Ezra did not marry.

iii MICAH DAMON, b. at Reading, 19 Dec 1792

iv INGALLS DAMON, b. at Reading, 26 Aug 1795; d. at North Reading, 13 Feb 1867; m. at Reading, 16 Apr 1830, his fourth cousin twice removed, HANNAH HOLT (*Benjamin7, Joseph6, Joseph5, Joseph4, Henry3, Henry2, Nicholas1*), b. at Reading, 12 Jan 1807 daughter of Benjamin and Hannah (Sheldon) Holt; Hannah d. Jan 1833.

986) HANNAH GRAY (*Thomas Gray4, Edward Gray3, Hannah Holt Gray2, Nicholas1*), b. at Andover, 10 Jun 1767 daughter of Thomas and Lydia (Graves) Gray; d. at Andover, 16 Dec 1827; m. at Andover, 24 Oct 1786, JOHN LACEY, b. at Danvers about 1763; John d. at Andover, 2 May 1852.

Hannah Gray and John Lacey were parents of six children born at Andover.

i THOMAS LACEY, b. 9 Mar 1787; d. 11 Mar 1787.

ii LYDIA G. LACEY, b. 27 Nov 1789; m. at Andover, 18 Jun 1818, her first cousin, ISRAEL GRAY (*Daniel Gray5, Thomas Gray4, Edward Gray3, Hannah Holt Gray2, Nicholas1*), b. at Andover, 4 Apr 1793 son of Daniel and Tabitha (Allen) Gray.

iii HANNAH LACEY, b. at Andover, 31 Dec 1797; d. at Andover, 21 Jul 1838; m. at Andover, 16 Nov 1816, her third cousin once removed, ISAAC HOLT (*Isaac6, Samuel5, Samuel4, Samuel3, Samuel2, Nicholas1*), b. at Andover, 22 Nov 1794 son of Isaac and Tabitha (Blunt) Holt; Isaac d. at Andover, 29 Jan 1848. Isaac married second Mary Dale on 17 Feb 1839.

iv JOHN LACEY, b. 4 Jun 1801; d. at Springfield, MA, 8 Dec 1880; m. at Wilbraham, 31 Mar 1836, NABBY ELVIRA CHAFFEE, b. at South Wilbraham, 14 Aug 1814 daughter of Norman and Nabby (Davis) Chaffee; Elvira

2603 U. S. Army, Register of Enlistments, 1798-1914; Daniel Gray enlisted from Andover as a Corporal; age 25; occupation, shoemaker

d. at Palmer, MA, 14 Feb 1888. John and Elvira divorced in 1860[2604] and Elvira remarried to John Giles in 1865. John was a veterinarian according to his death record.

v THOMAS LACEY, b. 1 Jan 1804; d. 6 Jan 1804.

vi PHEBE LACEY, b. 22 Jul 1806; d. 31 Jul 1806.

987) DANIEL CARLETON (*Priscilla Gray Carleton[4], Edward Gray[3], Hannah Holt Gray[2], Nicholas[1]*), b. at Andover, 6 Mar 1736/7 son of Daniel and Priscilla (Gray) Carleton; d. at Andover, 9 Dec 1801; Mar 16 Aug 1759, his first cousin, MERCY CARLETON, b. at Andover, 21 Nov 1739 daughter of Ezekiel and Mercy (Kimball) Carleton; Mercy d. at Andover, 20 Mar 1814.

"Elder" Daniel Carleton did not leave a will and his estate entered probate 31 March 1802 with Daniel Carleton as administrator.[2605] The dower was set off to widow Mercy Carleton on 13 April 1808. Real estate was appraised at $6,230 and personal estate at $638.66. In her will dated 3 October 1812 (probate 5 May 1814), Mercy Carleton makes bequests to her grandchildren and great-grandchildren. Her grandchildren the sons and daughters of her son Daniel each receives eighty-four cents: Daniel Carlton, Timothy Carlton, Jacob Carlton, Kimball Carlton, Mercy the wife of Enoch Wilson, Hannah the wife of Jonathan Johnson, Phebe the wife of Joseph Hadley, and Molly Carlton. Granddaughter-in-law Hannah Carlton widow of grandson Amos and her two daughters, Hannah Farnum Carlton and Mary Carlton, receive her wearing apparel. Great-grandsons the sons of grandson Amos receive bequests: James Farnum Carlton, the desk; Amos Carlton, the large chest with three drawers; and Daniel, the small chest with the case for bottles. Other furniture bequests were made to her two great-granddaughters and the residue of the estate to be divided among her five great-grandchildren. Abijah Fuller was named executor. Personal estate was valued at $160.48.[2606]

Daniel and Mercy Carleton were parents of two children born at Andover.

i DANIEL CARLETON, b. 22 May 1760; d. at Andover, 23 May 1807; m. 15 Oct 1778, MARY KIMBALL, b. about 1762 of undetermined parents; Mary d. 7 Nov 1828.

ii MERCY CARLETON, b. 3 May 1776; not living at time of mother's will.

988) JEREMIAH WARDWELL (*Abigail Gray Wardwell[4], Edward Gray[3], Hannah Holt Gray[2], Nicholas[1]*), b. at Andover, 6 Dec 1748 son of Thomas and Abigail (Gray) Wardwell; d. at Salisbury, NH, 9 Jan 1817; m. 21 Nov 1769, his third cousin, MOLLY LOVEJOY (*David Lovejoy[5], Henry Lovejoy[4], Mary Farnum Lovejoy[3], Elizabeth Holt Farnum[2], Nicholas[1]*), b. at Pembroke, NH, 29 Apr 1748 daughter of Daniel and Elizabeth (Chandler) Lovejoy; Molly d. at Salisbury, 23 Feb 1813. After Molly's death, Jeremiah married BETSEY who has not been identified.

Jeremiah Wardwell served as a private in Captain Benjamin Ames's Company of Minutemen who "marched at the alarm" 19 April 1775 and in Waldron's New Hampshire Regiment.[2607]

Jeremiah and Molly had their children at Pembroke and then relocated to Salisbury about 1804 where they had a farm.[2608]

In his will dated 10 May 1814 (proved 5 March 1817), wife Betsy receives a portion of the house for her use which is detailed including her right to access the cellar. She also receives twenty acres, one cow, and four sheep, and she is to have the increase of these so long as she is a widow and no longer. If she marries, she has all the furniture she brought to the marriage and all the bedding and clothing she now has. She is also to have use of a horse. Son Isaac receives all the wearing apparel and one dollar. Sons Amos, Abial, John, and Jesse each receives two dollars. Daughters Polly Hutchinson, Phebe Wester, and Sally Adams each receives two dollars. Son Abial also receives half of the household furniture. Son Reuben receives all the lands, buildings, and tenements and the right to carry on the dowry of his mother-in-law as she and he shall agree until she have done with it and then it is the be exclusively his property. Reuben also receives a specific list of household items including the eight-day clock and the farming utensils, and all the cattle, the horse, and sheep. Reuben was also named executor.[2609]

Jeremiah Wardwell and Molly Lovejoy were parents of ten children born at Pembroke.

i AMOS WARDWELL, b. 17 Oct 1770; d. at Grafton, NH, 19 Apr 1817; m. Anna who has not been identified. Amos and Anna did not have children. In his will, Amos has bequests to each of his brothers and sisters and leaves the remainder of the estate to his wife Anna.

2604 Index for 1798-1890 Divorce judgments found in Hartford County, Superior Court Civil Case Records, compiled by Mel E. Smith, Reference Librarian, Connecticut State Library History & Genealogy Unit, 2015

2605 *Essex County, MA: Probate File Papers, 1638-1881.*Online database. *AmericanAncestors.org.* New England Historic Genealogical Society, 2014. Case 4620

2606 *Essex County, MA: Probate File Papers, 1638-1881.*Online database. *AmericanAncestors.org.* New England Historic Genealogical Society, 2014. Case 4670

2607 U.S. Compiled Revolutionary War Military Service Records, 1775-1783

2608 Dearborn, *History of Salisbury*, p 820

2609 *New Hampshire. Probate Court (Hillsborough County)*; Probate Place: *Hillsborough, New Hampshire, Probate Records, Vol 25-26, 1815-1818*, p 640, will of Jeremiah Wardwell

ii MARY "POLLY" WARDWELL, b. 28 Aug 1772; d. at Merrimack, NH, 31 Aug 1850; m. JONATHAN HUTCHINSON, b. at Pembroke, 24 Apr 1771 son of Jonathan and Mehitable (Lovejoy) Hutchinson; Jonathan d. at Pembroke, 17 Jan 1843.

iii ISAAC WARDWELL, b. 22 Nov 1774; d. at Lebanon, NH, 9 Jun 1848; m. at Lebanon, 16 May 1813, MARY CUSHING, b. about 1791 but not otherwise identified; Mary d. after 1860 at Brookfield, VT (living with her son in Brookfield in 1860).

iv ABIEL WARDWELL, b. 25 Nov 1777; d. at Pembroke, 9 Feb 1860; m. at Salisbury, 8 Nov 1813, SALLY WEBSTER, b. at Salisbury, 27 Aug 1779 daughter of Israel and Elizabeth (Rolfe) Webster.

v PHEBE WARDWELL, b. 29 Apr 1780; d. at Salisbury, 20 Jan 1847; m. at Pembroke, 22 Jan 1801, JEREMY WEBSTER, b. at Hampton, 19 Jun 1775 son of Jeremiah and Anna (Sleeper) Webster; Jeremy d. at Salisbury, 20 Aug 1841.

vi SALLY WARDWELL, b. 11 Feb 1783; d. 31 Mar 1855; m. 2 Mar 1813; JEREMIAH ADAMS, b. at New London, NH, 15 Apr 1793 son of Benjamin and Judith (Adams) Adams; Jeremiah d. at New London, 22 Aug 1832.

vii JOHN WARDWELL, b. 14 Sep 1785; d. after 1850 at Meredith, NH; m. about 1812, CLARISSA DAVIS, b. about 1794 but not identified; Clarissa d. at Laconia, after 1860.

viii JOSEPH WARDWELL, b. 3 Jul 1788; d. at Boston, 3 Feb 1814. Joseph graduated from Dartmouth College in 1813 and was a teacher.[2610] He did not marry.

ix JESSE WARDWELL, b. 3 Dec 1790; d. at sea, 1821 (probate 4 Jan 1822). Jesse was a mariner lost at sea. He served as a private in the First New Hampshire Regiment in the War of 1812.[2611]

x REUBEN WARDWELL, b. 23 Apr 1795; d. at Salisbury, 15 Apr 1838; m. at Newburyport, MA, 21 May 1815, MARY "POLLY" WEBSTER, b. at Salisbury, 23 Apr 1790 daughter of Israel and Elizabeth (Rolfe) Webster); Mary d. at Salisbury, 22 Sep 1836.

989) EZEKIEL WARDWELL (*Abigail Gray Wardwell[4], Edward Gray[3], Hannah Holt Gray[2], Nicholas[1]*), b. at Andover, 15 Feb 1750/1 son of Thomas and Abigail (Gray) Wardwell; d. at Andover, 16 Dec 1834; m. at Andover, 22 Nov 1783, the widow of his brother Daniel and his third cousin once removed, DAMARIS FAULKNER (*Abiel Faulkner[5], Damaris Johnson Faulkner[4], Thomas Johnson[3], Mary Holt Johnson[2], Nicholas[1]*), b. at Andover, 3 Nov 1753 daughter of Abiel and Mary (Poor) Faulkner; Damaris d. at Andover, 28 Mar 1826. Damaris m. 1st 29 Mar 1774, DANIEL WARDWELL, b. at Andover, 18 Nov 1753; d. at Andover, 7 Mar 1782.

Brothers Ezekiel and Daniel each married Damaris Faulkner who is also a Nicholas Holt descendant. Daniel died at age 28 leaving three young children. The next year, Damaris married his older brother Ezekiel and the family lived in Andover.

Daniel Wardwell and Damaris Faulkner were parents of five children born at Andover.

i MARY WARDWELL, b. 28 Nov 1774; d. at Andover, 6 Dec 1866; m. 6 Dec 1798, her fourth cousin once removed, DANE HOLT (*Dane[5], Timothy[4], Timothy[3], James[2], Nicholas[1]*), b. at Andover, 11 Mar 1768 son of Dane and Lydia (Ballard) Holt; Dane d. at Andover, 27 Nov 1839.

ii DANIEL WARDWELL (twin of Mary), b. 28 Nov 1774; died young

iii JOSEPH WARREN WARDWELL, b. 21 Sep 1775; d. 17 Sep 1781.[2612]

iv DANIEL WARDWELL, b. 27 Aug 1776; d. at Andover, 16 Oct 1844; m. at Methuen, 29 May 1800, LYDIA MORSE, baptized at Methuen, 2 Jul 1775 daughter of Joseph Morse; Lydia d. at Andover, 1 Sep 1843 at age 69.

v ENOCH WARDWELL, b. 19 Apr 1778; d. 13 Jul 1798.

Ezekiel Wardwell and Damaris Faulkner were parents of five children born at Andover.

i JOSEPH WARDWELL, b. 27 Jul 1784; d. at Andover, 15 Aug 1841; m. 8 Apr 1813, LUCINDA WOOD, b. at Andover, 3 Mar 1796 daughter of John A. and Esther (Nickerson) Wood; Lucinda d. at Andover, 8 Jun 1865.

ii ELIZABETH WARDWELL, b. at Andover, 4 Apr 1787; d. at Enfield, NY, 1872; m. 1st 10 May 1804, AMOS LOVEJOY, b. at Andover, 24 Sep 1780 son of Joseph and Mary (Gordon) Lovejoy; Amos d. at Andover, 15 Apr 1806. Elizabeth m. 2nd at Andover, 17 Feb 1811, SAMUEL LOOMIS, b. about 1786; Samuel d. at Enfield, 1873.

[2610] Chapman, *Sketches of the Alumni of Dartmouth College*, p 169

[2611] *U.S., War of 1812 Service Records, 1812-1815* [database on-line]. Provo, UT, USA: Ancestry.com Operations Inc, 1999.

[2612] Wardwell, Joseph Warren, s. Daniel, bur. Sept. 17, 1781, a. 6 y. wanting 4 d. C.R.2.

iii SAMUEL WARDWELL, b. 15 Jun 1790; d. 28 May 1796.

iv PAMELIA WARDWELL, b. 6 May 1792; m. at Andover, 10 May 1812, her fourth cousin, ELI HOLT (*Timothy[5], Timothy[4], Timothy[3], James[2], Nicholas[1]*), b. at Andover, 6 Apr 1786 son of Timothy and Ede (McIntire) Holt.

v AMOS WARDWELL, b. 25 Jul 1796; m. at Andover, 3 Dec 1818, ANNA SHATTUCK, b. at Otisfield, ME, 6 Sep 1800 daughter of William and Abigail (Foster) Shattuck; Anna d. at Andover, 25 Jan 1869.

990) SARAH STEVENS (*Lydia Gray Stevens[4], Edward Gray[3], Hannah Holt Gray[2], Nicholas[1]*), b. at Andover, 6 Jun 1740 daughter of John and Lydia (Gray) Stevens; d. about Thetford, VT, about 1796; m. at Andover, 13 May 1762, ISRAEL WOOD, b. at Haverhill, 14 Aug 1738 son of Richard and Sarah (Rolfe) Wood; Israel d. at Thetford, VT, 7 Apr 1818. Israel married second Sarah Young.

Sarah and Israel had their eleven children in Andover where they were members of South Church. They were dismissed to the church at Thetford, Vermont on 10 April 1788.[2613]

i ISRAEL WOOD, b. 22 Jan 1763; d. at Stanstead, Québec, 1815; m. at Dracut, 14 Dec 1786, ABIGAIL CURTIS, b. at Dracut, 20 Feb 1765 daughter of Ephraim and Abigail (Williams) Curtis; Abigail d. at Stanstead, 1814. Israel was a Loyalist and went to Stanstead about 1793. He was Captain of the Calvary in 1811 and served in the War of 1812.[2614]

ii RICHARD WOOD, b. 11 Mar 1764; d. 22 Mar 1764.

iii DAVID WOOD, b. 1 Feb 1765; d. at Hancock, NH, 19 Dec 1834; m. at Wilton, 15 Apr 1790, ANNA ABBOTT, b. at Wilton, 15 Jul 1770 daughter of Jeremiah and Cloe (Abbott) Abbott; Anna d. at Hancock, 19 Mar 1844.

iv ABIEL WOOD, b. 6 Mar 1767; d. at Thetford, 22 Dec 1840; m. at Loudon, NH, 18 Mar 1790, SARAH MOULTON.

v SARAH WOOD, b. 7 Jun 1769; d. at Thetford, VT, 4 Apr 1803; m. about 1793, SIMON CLOSSON, b. at Thetford, 19 Apr 1767 son of John and Sabra (Alger) Closson; Simon d. at Thetford, 18 Sep 1835. Simon had subsequent marriages to Hannah Elle and Ruth Young.

vi LYDIA WOOD, b. 21 Apr 1771

vii JOSEPH WOOD, baptized 7 Nov 1773

viii JACOB WOOD, b. 30 Mar 1774; d. at Thetford, 11 Mar 1801; m. about 1798, but his wife's name is unknown, although it might be CLARISSA.

ix BETHIAH WOOD, b. 7 Mar 1777; d. at Thetford, 16 Jun 1795.

x MOSES WOOD, b. 16 May 1779; d. at Newark, NJ, 5 Apr 1867; m. 1st at Wilton, NH, 20 Oct 1807, BETSEY ABBOTT, b. at Wilton, 21 Oct 1778 daughter of Jeremiah and Cloe (Abbott) Abbott; Betsey, d. at Andover, 20 Jul 1835. Moses m. 2nd 3 Apr 1836, PAMELIA LADD SHEPARD (widow of Jesse Powers), b. at Montpelier, VT, 1796 daughter of Horace and Martha (-) Shepard; Pamelia d. at Newark, 24 Aug 1881.

xi SAMUEL WOOD, baptized 19 May 1782

991) DEBORAH STEVENS (*Lydia Gray Stevens[4], Edward Gray[3], Hannah Holt Gray[2], Nicholas[1]*), b. at Andover, 21 Jun 1742 daughter of John and Lydia (Gray) Stevens; d. at Andover, 2 Aug 1818; m. 1st at Andover, 6 Dec 1764, JACOB HAGGET, b. at Andover, 9 Feb 1742/3 son of Moses and Sarah (Head) Hagget; Jacob d. at Andover, 29 Jan 1769. Deborah m. 2nd 23 Feb 1775, SIMON CROSBY b. at Billerica, 14 Sep 1741 son of Solomon and Katherine (-) Crosby; Simon d. at Andover, 30 Oct 1820. Simon Crosby was first married to Dorothy Farmer.

Jacob Hagget did not leave a will and his estate entered probate 3 April 1769 with Deborah Hagget as administratrix.[2615] Real property was valued at £413.6.8 including the homestead of about 100 acres and 10 acres of woodland. The dower was set off to the widow Deborah Hagget now Crosby on 20 October 1781. Deborah was appointed guardian for two minor children Rhoda and Phebe in 1769. When the daughters reached age fourteen, they each selected Deacon Ezra Kendall as guardian.

Deborah Stevens and Jacob Hagget were parents of two children.

i RHODA HAGGET, b. at Andover, 30 Sep 1765; d. at Wilton, NH, 1797; m. at Andover, 28 Feb 1782, her fourth cousin, WILLIAM PETTENGILL (*Mary Holt Pettengill[5], John[4], Hannah Farnum Holt[3], Elizabeth Holt Farnum[2], Nicholas[1]*), b. at Andover, 23 Aug 1759 son of Samuel and Mary (Holt) Pettengill; William d. at Wilton, 13 Oct

[2613] Historical Manual of the South Church in Andover

[2614] Hubbard, *Forests and Clearings*, p 116

[2615] *Essex County, MA: Probate File Papers, 1638-1881.*Online database. *AmericanAncestors.org.* New England Historic Genealogical Society, 2014. Case 12055

1844. William m. 2nd at Wilton, 1 Jun 1797, his fourth cousin, SARAH BALLARD (*Hannah Holt Ballard5, Jonathan4, Oliver3, Henry2, Nicholas1*), b. at Wilton, 13 Apr 1766 daughter of Nathan and Hannah (Holt) Ballard; Sarah d. at Wilton, 4 Jan 1856.

ii PHEBE HAGGET, b. at Andover, 7 May 1767; d. at Milford, 24 Aug 1849; m. at Andover, 14 Oct 1784, BARTHOLOMEW HUTCHINSON, b. at Amherst, NH, 10 Feb 1759 son of Nathan and Rachel (Stearns) Hutchinson; Bartholomew d. at Milford, 23 Sep 1841.

992) LYDIA STEVENS (*Lydia Gray Stevens4, Edward Gray3, Hannah Holt Gray2, Nicholas1*), b. at Andover, 3 May 1745 daughter of John and Lydia (Gray) Stevens; d. at Brunswick, ME, Jun 1821; m. at Andover, 1 Dec 1767, JACOB ABBOTT, b. at Andover, 9 Feb 1745/6 son of Joseph and Deborah (Blanchard) Abbott; Jacob d. at Brunswick, 5 Mar 1820.

Jacob began his adult life as a farmer, but sold his farm in Wilton, New Hampshire to his brother in 1776. He lived in the town of Wilton involved in trade goods. He also built the first mill on the Souhegan River. He returned to Andover for a time and served on the board of Phillips Academy. He returned to New Hampshire and was later in Maine where he served on the board of Bowdoin College.[2616]

Jacob and Lydia's grandson, Jacob Abbott (1803-1879), was a writer of children's books, the most well-known being the Rollo books.

Jacob and Lydia had ten children, five of whom died in childhood. A sixth child, John, graduated Harvard in 1801 but died in 1809.

i LYDIA ABBOTT, b. and d. 1 Jun 1769

ii LYDIA ABBOTT, b. 1 May 1771; d. at Temple, ME, 20 Jun 1855; m. 10 Feb 1789, a fourth cousin, THOMAS RUSSELL (*Thomas Russell5, Joseph Russell4, Phebe Johnson Russell3, Mary Holt Johnson2, Nicholas1*), b. at Andover, 5 Jun 1765 son of Thomas and Bethia (Holt) Russell; Thomas d. 9 Jul 1863.

iii HANNAH ABBOTT, b. 31 Jul 1772; d. 10 May 1786.

iv PHEBE ABBOTT, b. 25 Jun 1774; d. 18 Apr 1857 (buried at Andover); m. at Andover, 17 Jan 1793, her third cousin once removed, BENJAMIN ABBOTT (*Dorcas Abbott5, Benjamin Abbott4, Sarah Farnum Abbott3, Elizabeth Holt Farnum2, Nicholas1*), b. at Wilton, 17 Mar 1770 son of Abiel and Dorcas (Abbott) Abbott; Benjamin d. at Temple, ME, 10 Sep 1823.

v JACOB ABBOTT, b. 20 Oct 1776; d. at Farmington, ME, 21 Jan 1847; m. at Hallowell, ME, 8 Apr 1798, his second cousin, BETSY ABBOTT, b. at Concord, NH, 6 Aug 1773 daughter of Joshua and Eliza (Chandler) Abbott; Betsy d. 30 Jul 1846.

vi DORCAS ABBOTT, b. 6 Sep 1778; d. 29 Dec 1778.

vii SALVA ABBOTT, b, 6 Sep 1778; d. 16 Sep 1778.

viii JOHN S. ABBOTT, b. 25 Sep 1779; d. 9 Jun 1809. John graduated from Harvard in 1801.

ix LUCY ABBOTT, b. 19 Apr 1781; d. at Grafton, NH, 1 Apr 1866; m. DANIEL CAMPBELL, born about 1777 whose origins are not yet known; Daniel d. Oct 1849. Lucy and Daniel did not have children. In his will, Daniel left his estate to his wife Lucy as long as she was his widow and also had bequests to his brothers.

x DORCAS HIBBERT ABBOTT, b. 21 Feb 1784; d. 14 Aug 1784.

993) THOMAS STEVENS (*Sarah Gray Stevens4, Edward Gray3, Hannah Holt Gray2, Nicholas1*), b. at Andover, 10 Oct 1748 son of Thomas and Sarah (Gray) Stevens; d. at Andover, 26 Jan 1827; m. at Andover, 8 Oct 1772, SARAH INGALLS, b. at Andover, 6 Nov 1753 daughter of Ebenezer and Sarah (Kimball) Ingalls;[2617] Sarah d. at Andover, 1824.

There are six children known for Thomas Stevens and Sarah Ingalls all born at Andover.

i THOMAS STEVENS, b. 17 Feb 1774. Nothing further definite known.

ii SARAH STEVENS, b. 7 Jan 1776

iii JEDEDIAH STEVENS, b. 1778; d. at Andover, 27 Mar 1813. "Jedediah, s.Tho[ma]s, at the almshouse, Mar. 27,1813."

[2616] Abbot and Abbot, *Genealogical Record of Descendants*, p 131

[2617] The 1787 probate record of Ebenezer Ingalls includes Thomas Stevens signing as an heir.

iv PHEBE KIMBALL STEVENS, b. 28 Jul 1787; d. at Boston, 3 Aug 1815;[2618] m. at Andover, 9 Jul 1809,[2619] ROBERT CAIN, a resident of Boston, b. in Ireland, about 1780 son of Patrick Cain; Robert d. at Boston, 21 Oct 1831. Robert's will establishes a trust and makes other specific provisions for his only child Elizabeth who was his daughter with Phebe born 1811. Robert's widow was Elizabeth (likely Elizabeth Bates), so he had remarried after Phebe's death.

v ABIEL STEVENS, b. 30 Sep 1789; d. at Lawrence, MA, 30 Sep 1869; m. at Salem, 7 Jul 1811, ABIGAIL ARCHER, b. at Salem, about 1793 daughter of Benjamin and Abigail (Woodman) Archer;[2620] Abigail d. at Methuen, 27 Nov 1874.

vi SAMUEL INGALLS STEVENS, b. 19 Jul 1792. Samuel was a mariner and obtained his seaman's certificate in 1811 from the Port of Salem.[2621] Nothing further is known.

994) PHEBE STEVENS (*Sarah Gray Stevens⁴, Edward Gray³, Hannah Holt Gray², Nicholas¹*), b. at Andover, 6 May 1759 daughter of Thomas and Sarah (Gray) Stevens; d. at Andover, 13 Aug 1843; m. at Andover, 22 May 1791, her first cousin once removed, NATHAN WARDWELL (*Nathan Wardwell⁵, Margery Gray Wardwell⁴, Edward Gray³, Hannah Holt Gray², Nicholas¹*), b. at Andover, 10 Nov 1765 son of Nathan and Huldah (Chandler) Wardwell; Nathan d. at Andover, 4 Nov 1838.

Phebe Stevens and Nathan Wardwell were parents of five children born at Andover.

i NATHAN WARDWELL, b. 28 Apr 1792; d. at Methuen, 8 Dec 1833; m. 30 Dec 1813, HANNAH MORSE, b. at Methuen, 1 May 1788 daughter of Daniel and Hannah (Baker) Morse; Hannah d. at Methuen, 30 Mar 1845.

ii PHEBE WARDWELL, b. 18 Oct 1793; d. at Andover, 1 Oct 1875; m. at Andover, 28 Jun 1812, THOMAS CHADWICK MASON, baptized at Reading, 19 Sep 1790 son of Robert and Elizabeth (McIntire) Mason; Thomas d. at Andover, 26 Nov 1861.

iii ISAAC WARDWELL, b. 29 Sep 1795; d. at Danvers, 17 Dec 1861; m. at Andover, 26 Jan 1828, DOLLY SMITH, b. 19 May 1805;[2622] Dolly d. at Danvers, 14 Nov 1858.

iv SALLY WARDWELL, b. 29 Jun 1798; d. at Andover, 10 Sep 1845; m. at Andover, Jul 1820, her fourth cousin once removed, HERMAN JONES (*Dorcas Farnum Jones⁶, Thomas Farnum⁵, Thomas Farnum⁴, Thomas Farnum³, Elizabeth Holt Farnum², Nicholas¹*), b. at Andover, 27 Oct 1793 son of Nathan and Dorcas (Farnum) Jones; Herman d. at Andover, 9 Feb 1869.

v MARY WARDWELL, b. 6 Jul 1800; d. at Andover, 24 Feb 1856; m. 27 Sep 1818, her third cousins once removed, JAMES HOVEY (*Hannah⁶, David⁵, Samuel⁴, Samuel³, Samuel², Nicholas¹*), b. at Andover about 1792 the son of Hannah Holt and an unknown Hovey; James d. at Andover, 29 Jan 1869.

995) DAVID STEVENS (*Sarah Gray Stevens⁴, Edward Gray³, Hannah Holt Gray², Nicholas¹*), b. at Andover, 3 Feb 1761 son of Thomas and Sarah (Gray) Stevens; d. at Andover, 29 Jan 1834; m. at Andover, 28 Dec 1784, his third cousin, SARAH ABBOTT, b. at Andover, 7 Dec 1765 daughter of Ebenezer and Lydia (Farrington) Abbott; Sarah d. at Springfield, OH, 7 Sep 1856.[2623][2624]

David Stevens served in the Revolutionary War and received a pension of $96 per year. He was a wheelwright. He struggled with alcoholism and a guardian was appointed for him in 1819 due to drunkenness and being a spendthrift. Joseph Holt, Jr. was named his guardian. This guardianship continued until David's death in 1834.[2625]

David Stevens enlisted from Andover as a private 5 July 1779 and was discharged 10 April 1780. He served in Colonel Tupper's Massachusetts Continental Regiment of Foot Soldiers and marched to West Point.[2626]

David Stevens and Sarah Abbott were parents of seven children born at Andover.

i DAVID STEVENS, b. 27 Jul 1784; d. 26 Jun 1794.

[2618] Recorded as "Mrs. Phoebe Caine, age 28"

[2619] Robert, resident in Boston, and Phebe [K. int.] Stevens, July 9, 1809. C. R. 2.*

[2620] The names of Abigail's parents are given as Benjamin and Abigail Archer on her death record.

[2621] US, New England Seamen's Protection Certificate Index, 1796-1871

[2622] Dolly's date of birth is given in the Danvers records but without location or parents.

[2623] Sarah was still living at the time of the probate of her husband's estate. Sarah traveled to Ohio to live with her son Ebenezer and his wife Lucy Herrick and was living with them in 1850.

[2624] The Revolutionary War pension file of David Stevens includes an 1855 statement of widow Sarah Stevens who was then living in Hamilton County, Ohio.

[2625] Essex County, MA: Probate File Papers, 1638-1881.Online database. AmericanAncestors.org. New England Historic Genealogical Society, 2014. Case 26319, Case 26320, Case 26321

[2626] Revolutionary War Pension and Bounty-Land Warrant Application Files, 1800-1900 Case W 4823

ii EBENEZER STEVENS, b. 25 Aug 1787; d. at Mt. Wealthy, OH, 11 Jun 1857; m. at Topsfield, MA, 10 Feb 1811, LUCY HERRICK, b. at Boxford, 11 Mar 1790 daughter of Edmund and Mehitable (Curtice) Herrick; Lucy d. at Mt. Healthy, 2 Feb 1883.

iii EPHRAIM STEVENS, b. 2 Feb 1790; nothing further known.

iv JACOB STEVENS, b. 26 Jul 1792; d. at Cincinnati, 10 Oct 1874; m. at Medway, MA, 10 Sep 1823, OLIVE BEALS, b. at Medfield, 25 Feb 1800 daughter of Asa and Olive (Cheney) Beals; Olive d. at Cincinnati, 10 May 1879.

v DAVID STEVENS, b. 9 Oct 1794; nothing further known.

vi SARAH STEVENS, b. 26 Apr 1797; nothing further known.

vii HERMAN ABBOT STEVENS, b. 18 Oct 1802; d. at Cincinnati, 14 Apr 1881; m. about 1829, SARAH W. BEAZY,[2627] b. at Freedom, ME, Jun 1800; Sarah d. at Cincinnati, 8 Apr 1871.

996) SUSANNA STEVENS (*Sarah Gray Stevens[4], Edward Gray[3], Hannah Holt Gray[2], Nicholas[1]*), b. at Andover, 3 Dec 1763 daughter of Thomas and Sarah (Gray) Stevens; d. 10 Sep 1835; m. at Andover, 7 Jul 1785, her third cousin, ABRAHAM MOOAR (*Lydia Abbott Mooar[6], Anne Lovejoy Abbott[5], William Lovejoy[4], Mary Farnum Lovejoy[3], Elizabeth Holt Farnum[2], Nicholas[1]*), b. at Andover, 15 Jan 1761 son of Abraham and Lydia (Abbott) Mooar; Abraham d. at Peterborough, 3 Mar 1842.[2628]

Susanna and Abraham were married in Andover but were soon after in Wilton where at least their two oldest children were born. Abraham was finally in Peterborough. They were parents of six children.

i ABRAHAM MOOAR, b. at Wilton, 11 Apr 1787; d. at Peterborough, 13 Nov 1866; m. 26 Jan 1808, BETSY MOORS, b. 17 Feb 1788 daughter of Timothy and Sibyl (Cummings) Moors; Betsy d. 27 Aug 1840.

ii ISAAC ABBOT MOOAR, b. at Wilton, 20 Nov 1787; d. at Hancock, NH, 19 Feb 1875; m. MARY FOGG, b. at Hancock, 4 Sep 1789 daughter of Jeremiah and Hannah (Eastman) Fogg; Mary d. at Hancock, 19 Aug 1867.

iii SUSAN MOOAR, b. 15 Sep 1789; d. 21 Mar 1795.

iv SUSAN MOOAR, b. 10 May 1796; d. at Peterborough, 2 Jun 1821; m. at Peterborough, 9 Apr 1818, JOHN PUFFER, b. 13 Mar 1791 son of Elijah and Elizabeth (Jackson) Puffer;[2629] John d. at Madison, IN, 7 Feb 1862. John married second Mary Wood.

v JACOB MOOAR, b. 21 Jan 1798; d. 5 Sep 1800.

vi JACOB MOOAR, b. 2 Mar 1802; d. perhaps at Maryland, IL, 17 Jul 1860;[2630] m. at Peterborough, 16 Nov 1826, MARTHA "PATTY" MCCRILLIS, b. at Lempster, NH, 23 Feb 1807 daughter of Michael and Sarah (Hancock) McCrillis.

997) EDWARD STEVENS (*Sarah Gray Stevens[4], Edward Gray[3], Hannah Holt Gray[2], Nicholas[1]*), b. at Andover, 30 Sep 1768 son of Thomas and Sarah (Gray) Stevens; d. at Andover, 27 Oct 1805;[2631] m. 23 Feb 1791, PHEBE FRYE, b. at Andover, 4 Apr 1762 daughter of Samuel and Elizabeth (Frye) Frye.

Edward Stevens and Phebe Frye were parents of five children born at Andover.

i PATTY STEVENS, b. 1792; d. 18 Aug 1792.

ii ENOCH STEVENS, b. 18 Nov 1796; d. at Haverhill, 28 Dec 1860; m. at Andover, 25 Jun 1819, HANNAH PERRY, b. at Bradford, 13 Sep 1799 daughter of John and Sally (Woodward) Perry; Hannah d. at Haverhill, 13 Feb 1866.

iii EDWARD STEVENS, b. 2 Jan 1799; d. at Charlestown, 4 May 1858; m. at Charlestown, 13 Dec 1829, SARAH S. BOLTON, b. about 1803 who has not been identified; widow Sarah Stevens was living in Charlestown in 1872. Edward was a ship's carpenter and joiner. He died at the almshouse in Charlestown described as insane. In 1850, Edward and Sarah were living in Charlestown with no children in the home.

iv CYNTHIA STEVENS, b. 10 Sep 1801; d. 22 Sep 1812.

v AMELIA STEVENS, b. 20 Mar 1805; d. 1821.

2627 The name of Sarah's parent is given as "Beazy" on the cemetery record as well as the place of birth as Freedom, Maine.

2628 Mooar, *Mooar Genealogy*, p 44

2629 Smith, *History of the Town of Peterborough*, p 229

2630 The Mooar genealogy reports this death date and location as Illinois; Jacob appears to be in Maryland, Ogle County, IL in the 1855 census.

2631 Edward [consumption], C.R.2.], Oct. 27, 1805, a. 37 y. [and 6 m. C.R.2.]

998) TIMOTHY GRAY (*Braviter Gray⁴, Braviter Gray³, Hannah Holt Gray², Nicholas¹*), b. at Billerica, 28 Mar 1752 son of Braviter and Bethiah (Hall) Gray; d. at Hillsborough, about 1827 (will proved 20 Nov 1827); m. at Hillsborough, 22 May 1781, MARTHA ROLFE, likely b. at Reading, 1752 daughter of Daniel and Mary (Lewis) Rolfe;[2632] Martha was living Dec 1825 when Timothy wrote his will and Martha Gray is listed as head of household in Hillsborough in 1830 aged 70-79.

In his will written 1 December 1825 (proved 20 November 1827), Timothy Gray bequeathed to his beloved wife Martha the use of two-thirds of the real estate during her natural life, but then clarifies that he has deeded one-half of the real estate to son Timothy and Martha has not signed the deed. He intends Martha to have use of two-thirds of one-half the estate, not two-thirds of the whole. Martha also receives two cows, four sheep, and all the household furniture. Martha also has a room and the house and kitchen use for her natural life. The executor is also to provide her comfortable maintenance. Son Braviter receives the wearing apparel. Daughter Mary wife of John Cresey receives five dollars. Daughter Betsy receives two cows and four sheep while she remains single and a room in the house. She also receives a small plot of land for a garden. Son Timothy receives all the real and personal estate and is named executor.[2633]

Timothy Gray and Martha Rolfe were parents of six children born at Hillsborough.

i TIMOTHY GRAY, b. 13 May 1781; d. 10 Feb 1782.

ii TIMOTHY GRAY, b. 25 Oct 1782; d. at Hillsborough, 1841 (probate 2 Mar 1841); m. at Washington, NH, 16 Nov 1806, MARTHA (or Betsey) GRAVES, b. at Washington, NH.[2634] The probate administration for Timothy Gray states he left no widow and just one child Catherine wife of John Hartwell who was living in another state.

iii MARY "POLLY" GRAY, b. 24 Feb 1784; d. at Bradford, NH before 1830 (no longer shows in census records; she is in the 1810 census as female age 16-26); likely m. 1st about 1804, JACOB PARMENTER, b. 24 Oct 1780 son of Nathaniel and Lydia (Nutting) Parmenter; Jacob d. at Hillsborough, 9 Nov 1806.[2635] Mary m. 2nd at Bradford, 11 Aug 1807, JOHN CRESSY, b. Jun 1773 son of Daniel and Abigail (Allen) Cressy;[2636] John d. at Bradford, NH, 2 Apr 1849. John was first married to Polly Lovett. John Cressy and Mary Gray had one son Enoch who studied at Hopkinton Academy and was a teacher in Kentucky where he died in 1843.

iv BRAVERTER GRAY, b. 24 Oct 1785; d. at Hillsborough, 25 May 1875; m. at Bradford, NH, 13 Nov 1808, SALLY PARMENTER, b. at Hillsborough, 5 Apr 1785 daughter of Nathaniel and Lydia (Nutting) Parmenter; Sally d. at Hillsborough, 15 Jan 1877.

v BETSY GRAY, b. 22 Jan 1788; d. 17 Jun 1788.

vi BETSY GRAY, b. 4 Mar 1789. Betsy was living and unmarried in Dec 1825 and likely the adult female age 40-49 living with Martha Gray in the 1830 census.

999) JONATHAN GRAY (*Braviter Gray⁴, Braviter Gray³, Hannah Holt Gray², Nicholas¹*), b. at Billerica, 3 Jan 1754 son of Braviter and Bethiah (Hall) Gray; d. at Tewksbury, Jun 1817 (will 19 Nov 1816); m. at Tewksbury, 2 Mar 1786, MARY NEEDHAM, b. at Tewksbury, 14 Mar 1756 daughter of John and Prudence (Stearns) Needham; Mary d. at Tewksbury, 1833.

Jonathan Gray was a farmer in Tewksbury. The home of Jonathan and Mary was built about 1789 and is now an historic building at 30 East Street in Tewksbury.[2637]

Jonathan Gray was a Minute Man and participated in the battle at Merriam's Corner near Lexington 19 April 1775.[2638]

In his will written 19 November 1816, Jonathan Gray bequeaths to beloved wife Mary the use of all the real estate during her natural life. After Mary's death, the estate is to be equally among his surviving children or their heirs; the children are Jonathan Gray, Bravity Gray, William Gray, Timothy Gray, and Mary Jaques. Wife Mary is named executrix and she also receives all the personal estate to be at her disposal.[2639]

[2632] It seems more likely than not that Martha was the sister of Stephen Rolfe who went to Hillsborough to care for his aged father. Stephen was the son of Daniel Rolfe.

[2633] *New Hampshire. Probate Court (Hillsborough County), Probate Records, volume 35, pp 574-577*

[2634] Gage, *History of Washington, New Hampshire*, p 454 gives her name as Betsy Graves and parents as William and Lucy (Wheeler) Graves. Published genealogies give her name as Martha Graves, but the marriage record says Betsy Graves. Timothy and his wife had a daughter Catherine Gray who married John Hartwell. Catherine's death record gives her mother's name as Maria. There is a Martha Graves born in Washington of likely the right age who was the daughter of Thaddeus and Mary (Mann) Graves.

[2635] This is a deduction. Polly Parmenter of Hillsborough married John Cressy of Bradford in 1807. Jacob Parmenter was the brother of Braverter Gray's wife Sally Parmenter. A marriage record was not found for Jacob Parmenter and Mary Gray.

[2636] Gould and Beals, Bradford Historical Society, *Early Families of Bradford*

[2637] Massachusetts Historical Commission, https://www.tewksbury-ma.gov/sites/tewksburyma/files/file/file/tew_11_east_30_formb_0.pdf

[2638] Massachusetts Historical Commission

[2639] *Middlesex County, MA: Probate File Papers, 1648-1871.*Online database. *AmericanAncestors.org.* New England Historic Genealogical Society, 2014. Case 9685

In her will written 8 August 1829, Mary Gray made bequests to son Jonathan who received the bedstead and daughter Mary Jaques who received the gold necklace and the wearing apparel. The personal estate including the farm animals and farm produce went to son Timothy. Timothy was named executor.[2640]

Jonathan Gray and Mary Needham were parents of seven children born at Tewksbury.

i JONATHAN GRAY, b. 9 May 1786; d. of cholera at Tewksbury, 13 Aug 1845; m. 1st at Reading, 22 Apr 1813, MARY BATCHELDER, baptized at Reading 28 Jun 1789 daughter of John and Mary (Eams) Batchelder; Mary d. before 1826. Jonathan m. 2nd, Mary's sister, PHEBE BATCHELDER, baptized at Reading 1 Jun 1807; Phebe d. at Medford, 8 Jun 1860.

ii MARY GRAY, b. 10 Feb 1788; d. at Tewksbury, 17 May 1878; m. at Tewksbury, 20 Oct 1808, JOHN JAQUES, b. at Tewksbury, 15 Nov 1783 son of John and Hannah (Eams) Jaques; John d. at Tewksbury, 15 Oct 1853.

iii BRAVITY GRAY, b. 11 Jun 1789; d. at Tewksbury, 29 Nov 1858; m. 1st at Tewksbury, 4 Dec 1817, SARAH CARTER, b. about 1794; Sarah d. at Tewksbury, 17 Sep 1818. Bravity m. 2nd at Tewksbury, 27 Apr 1824, SARAH BROWN, b. at Tewksbury, 22 Apr 1797 daughter of Joseph and Sarah (Foster) Brown; Sarah d. at Methuen, 12 Apr 1887.

iv WILLIAM GRAY, b. 4 Aug 1792; d. at Tewksbury, 3 Oct 1868; m. at Billerica, 1 Jan 1846, ABIGAIL ALLEN RICHARDSON, b. at Billerica, 17 Oct 1821 daughter of John O. and Nancy (Allen) Richardson; Abigail d. at Woburn, 29 Apr 1898.

v LUCY GRAY, b. 27 Nov 1794; d. 12 Oct 1802.

vi JULIA GRAY, b. 17 Mar 1796; d. 17 Oct 1802.

vii TIMOTHY GRAY, b. 23 Dec 1797; d. at Tewksbury, 27 Sep 1840; m. at Tewksbury, Apr 1832, SARAH WEBSTER, b. in ME, 29 May 1809 (calculated from death at age 58 years, 6 months, 17 days), her mother listed on record for Sarah's second marriage as Betsy Richard; Sarah d. at Tewksbury, 16 Dec 1867. Sarah married second Stephen D. Kenny in 1845.

1000) TIMOTHY GRAY (*Timothy Gray[4], Braviter Gray[3], Hannah Holt Gray[2], Nicholas[1]*), b. at Andover, 19 Feb 1749 son of Timothy and Elinor (Best) Gray; d. at Wilton, 16 Jul 1807; m. 1st about 1770, HANNAH BLANCHARD, b. about 1750; Hannah d. at Wilton, 1 Jul 1784. Timothy m. 2nd 21 Apr 1785, RUTH BURNHAM, b. 1756 daughter of Jeremiah and Mary (Burnham) Burnham; Ruth d. at Wilton, 23 Mar 1841.

Timothy Gray was a farmer in Wilton. He saw service in the Revolution in the companies of Capt. Taylor and Capt. Nathan Ballard.[2641]

In his will written 28 May 1807 (proved 20 October 1807), Timothy Gray bequeathed to Ruth his well-beloved wife the great bible and two good cows to be at her disposal, and the cows are to be maintained by the executor while Ruth is a widow. Ruth also has use of the books and the improvement of a portion of the house (described in detail) and privileges for use of certain parts of the house. There is also a lengthy list of annual supplies for Ruth, including two gallons of new rum, to be provided by the executor. There are also contingencies given related to Ruth's remarriage when she would continue to receive seventeen dollars per year, and if her second husband dies then Timothy's estate would resume her maintenance if needed. These bequests to Ruth are in lieu of her dower thirds from the estate. Well-beloved daughter Hannah Blanchard receives $57.42 in one year and $25 after the decease of Ruth which completes her full portion. Daughter Elizabeth Holt receives $60 in two years and $25 after the decease of Ruth. Daughter Elenor Shelden receives $51.74 in three years which completes her portion. The executor is to pay son Henry Gray $110 at age twenty-one and he is also to receive $90 which is to come from Abiel Guttman and $50 after his mother's deceased. The estate is also responsible for his clothing. Son Abel receives $200 at age twenty-one, $100 at age twenty-two, and $50 at his mother's decease. Son Abiel Gray also receives $200 at twenty-one, $100 at twenty-two, and $50 at his mother's decease. Daughter Lucy Burnham Gray receives one-third of the household furniture and enough money to make a total of $150 when she reaches twenty-one and $25 after her mother's decease, and well-beloved daughter Ruth Gray receives the same bequest. Well-beloved son Timothy receives all the lands and buildings in Wilton as well as the husbandry tools and stock animals. Son Timothy Gray and Timothy Abbott, Jr. are named executors.[2642]

Daughter Ruth Gray did not marry and her will written 16 January 1858 includes bequests to the following persons: brothers Timothy, Henry, and Abel; niece Sarah Ann Gray daughter of brother Abiel; sister Lucy B. G. Chandler, and Fanny G. Crosby wife of Caleb Crosby.[2643]

Timothy Gray and Hannah Blanchard were parents of seven children born at Wilton.[2644]

2640 *Middlesex County, MA: Probate File Papers, 1648-1871.*Online database. *AmericanAncestors.org.* New England Historic Genealogical Society, 2014. Case 9686

2641 Livermore, *History of the Town of Wilton*, p 383

2642 *New Hampshire. Probate Court (Hillsborough County), Probate Records Volume 15, pp 140-144, will of Timothy Gray*

2643 *Middlesex County, MA: Probate File Papers, 1648-1871.*Online database. *AmericanAncestors.org.* New England Historic Genealogical Society, 2014. Case 33035

2644 *New Hampshire, Births and Christenings Index, 1714-1904, accessed through ancestry.com*

i HANNAH GRAY, b. 4 Jul 1770; d. 18 Aug 1770.

ii TIMOTHY GRAY, b. 30 Sep 1771; d. 1 Dec 1776.

iii HANNAH GRAY, b. 13 Jun 1773; d. at Ferrisburgh, VT in late 1807 or early 1808; m. 9 Apr 1795, ABIEL BLANCHARD, b. at Andover, Mar 1773 son of Daniel and Jerusha (Eaton) Blanchard; Abiel d. at Clermont County, OH, 1821. Abiel m. 2nd Patience Varney on 31 May 1808.

iv ELIZABETH GRAY, b. 12 Feb 1775; d. at Weld, ME, 16 Jul 1809; m. 12 Feb 1801, her fourth cousin, CALEB HOLT (*Daniel5, John4, Hannah Farnum Holt3, Elizabeth Holt Farnum2, Nicholas1*), b. at Wilton, 16 Oct 1777 son of Daniel and Mehitable (Putnam) Holt; Caleb d. at Weld, 19 Oct 1870. Caleb married second Phebe Abbott (widow of Walter Fiske) daughter of Jeremiah and Cloe (Abbott) Abbott.

v TIMOTHY GRAY, b. 21 Jan 1778; d. 26 Sep 1781.

vi ELEANOR GRAY, b. 5 Aug 1779; d. at Andover, VT, 3 May 1847; m. at Wilton, 15 Nov 1804, UZZIEL SHELDON, b. about 1776 son of Samuel and Sarah (Wellman) Sheldon; Uzziel d. at Andover, VT, 3 Jun 1864.

vii JAMES BEST GRAY, b. 26 May 1781; d. 4 Oct 1795.

Timothy Gray and Ruth Burnham were parents of six children born at Wilton.

i TIMOTHY GRAY, b. 14 May 1787; d. at Wilton, 4 Aug 1867; m. 1st 21 Aug 1808, FANNY BURTON, b. at Wilton, 2 Feb 1790 daughter of Abraham and Elizabeth (Dale) Burton; Fanny d. 3 Nov 1810. Timothy m. 2nd at Milford, 14 Apr 1812, NANCY SMITH, b. at Milford, 4 Apr 1787 daughter of Daniel and Ruhammah (Cutter) Smith; Nancy d. at Wilton, 16 Apr 1866.

ii HENRY GRAY, b. 1 Oct 1789; d. at Wilton, 23 Oct 1862; m. by 1813, SUSAN MERRILL, b. at Amherst, NH, 17 Jun 1791 daughter of Nathan and Susanna (Bacon) Merrill; Susan d. at Wilton, 17 Apr 1868.

iii ABEL GRAY, b. 13 Oct 1791; d. at Olney, IL, 22 Apr 1862; m. Jul 1813, his third cousin once removed, BETSEY PETTENGILL (*William Pettengill6, Mary Holt Pettengill5, John4, Samuel3, Samuel2, Nicholas1*), b. at Wilton, 21 Aug 1792 daughter of William and Ruth (Hagget) Pettengill; Betsey d. at Olney, 7 Feb 1859.

iv ABIEL GRAY, b. 25 Jul 1793. He is known to have had at least one daughter Sarah Ann Gray, but information on his wife or other children was not located. There is an Abiel Gray born in NH in 1793 in the 1850 census in Wards Grove, Illinois and there is a daughter Sarah Ann Gray age 28 and born in NY in the household. There is also a wife Jerusha (whose maiden name is Jerusha Davis) age 44 with several children age 13 and under. It is not known for certain if the census record is for this Abiel Gray. However, I think it is more likely than not this Abiel. In which case, he was married first to Sarah Gates and married second to Jerusha Davis. If so, the daughter Sarah Ann Gray mentioned in her aunt Ruth's will was living in Saline, NE in 1880.

v LUCY BURNHAM GRAY, b. 18 Sep 1795; d. at Weare, 22 Jun 1871; m. 19 Feb 1818, her fourth cousin once removed, JOEL CHANDLER (*Ebenezer Chandler6, Thomas Chandler5, Mehitable Russell Chandler4, Phebe Johnson Russell3, Mary Holt Johnson2, Nicholas1*), b. at Wilton, 19 Jun 1794 son of Ebenezer and Sarah (Averill) Chandler; Joel d. at Weare, 22 Aug 1860.

vi RUTH GRAY, b. 24 May 1800; d. at Lowell, MA, 7 Mar 1858. Ruth did not marry. She lived in Wilton until 1850 and was in Lowell by 1855.

1001) MARY GRAY (*Timothy Gray4, Braviter Gray3, Hannah Holt Gray2, Nicholas1*), b. at Andover, 19 Feb 1757 daughter of Timothy and Elinor (Best) Gray; d. at Francestown, 20 Apr 1841; m. at Wilton, 23 Nov 1786, SAMUEL HARTSHORN, b. at Reading, 13 Jun 1760 Thomas and Abia (-) Hartshorn; Samuel d. at Francestown, 11 Feb 1847.

Samuel was a farmer in Wilton and raised their family of six children there. In later life, they lived in Francestown at the home of their daughter Anna and her husband William Parker.[2645]

In his will written 24 April 1846 (proved 7 April 1847), Samuel Hartshorn bequeathed all his wearing apparel to his son Thomas. Daughters Anna Parker and Abiah Hayward receive all the household furniture. The children of his deceased daughter Mary Batchelder receive one hundred dollars to equally divide. The remainder of the estate is to be equally divided among son Thomas and daughters Anna and Abiah except sixty dollars is to be deducted from Thomas's portion for a payment her received 9 February 1846. The children of his deceased son Samuel receive no bequest as Samuel received his full portion during his lifetime. William Parker of Francestown was named executor.[2646]

[2645] Livermore, *History of the Town of Wilton*, p 392

[2646] *New Hampshire. Probate Court (Hillsborough County), Probate Record Volume 55, pp 287-288*

i SAMUEL HARTSHORN, b. 18 Feb 1788; d. at Wilton, 3 Dec 1832; m. 6 Mar 1817, POLLY TARBELL, b. at Mason, NH, 9 Feb 1793 daughter of Samuel and Anna (Heldrick) Tarbell; Polly d. at Wilton, 27 Sep 1876.

ii THOMAS HARTSHORN, b. 25 Dec 1789; d. at Francestown, 19 Oct 1855 (probate 20 Jan 1856; will Oct 1855); m. 1st about 1820, ELIZA ROBERTS, b. 1800 daughter of daughter of Thaddeus and Lucy (Hitchcock) Roberts;[2647] Eliza d. at Keene, NY, 3 May 1848. Thomas m. 2nd about 1849, ABIAH INGALLS, b. 27 Apr 1789 daughter of Caleb and Mary (Chatsey) Ingalls;[2648] Abiah d. at Keene, NY, 4 Jul 1851.

iii JACOB HARTSHORN, b. 20 Jun 1791; d. 26 Nov 1798.

iv MARY HARTSHORN, b. 20 Jan 1793; d. at Mason, NH, 5 Dec 1838; m. at Mason, 2 Jun 1817, her fourth cousin once removed, JOHN BATCHELDER (*Jonathan Batchelder[6], Phebe Holt Batchelder[5], Joseph[4], Henry[3], Henry[2], Nicholas[1]*), b. at Mason, 4 Dec 1789 son of Jonathan and Mary (Dix) Batchelder; John d. at Mason, 3 Jun 1869.

v ANNA HARTSHORN, b. 6 Feb 1796; d. at Wilton, 13 Oct 1887; m. 11 Apr 1820, as his second wife, WILLIAM PARKER, b. at Wilton, 1790 son of Hananiah and Hephzibah (Warren) Parker; William d. at Wilton, 18 Oct 1859. William was first married to Hannah Fitch Hayward.

vi ABIAH HARTSHORN, b. 10 Nov 1798; d. at Francestown, 26 Dec 1856; m. about 1825 as his second wife, JOSEPH HAYWARD, b. at Concord, 22 Nov 1772 son of Joseph and Rebecca (Prescott) Hayward; Joseph d. at Dublin, NH, 14 Mar 1846. Joseph was first married to Sally Minot. Joseph Hayward was the brother of William Parker's first wife Hannah Fitch Hayward (see Anna Hartshorn above).

1002) SARAH GRAY (*Timothy Gray[4], Braviter Gray[3], Hannah Holt Gray[2], Nicholas[1]*), b. at Andover, 2 Mar 1759 daughter of Timothy and Elinor (Best) Gray; d. at Weston, VT, 22 Jan 1835; m. at Wilton, 8 Jan 1782, CHRISTOPHER MARTIN, b. at Andover, 31 May 1757 son of Samuel and Elizabeth (Osgood) Martin; Christopher d. at Weston, 6 Aug 1838.

Christopher and Sarah started their family in Wilton, but relocated to Weston, Vermont. They were parents of six children.

In his pension application declaration made 9 May 1827, Christopher Martin, aged seventh and a resident of Weston, stated he enlisted from Wilton in March 1777 for a term of three years in the Continental in the company of Capt. Isaac Frye. He served the three-year term and was discharged at West Point. He reported an earlier period of service enlisting at Cambridge soon after Bunker Hill for a period of eighteen months during which time he was with General Sullivan at the retreat from Canada. He was at the Battle of Princeton and the surrender of Burgoyne. The total value of his property reported in 1827 was $58.53 most of that the value of one heifer and ten sheep. His wife was age sixty-eight in 1827.[2649]

i HENRY MARTIN, b. at Wilton, 1 May 1782

ii SALLY MARTIN, b. at Wilton, 15 May 1784; d. at Ludlow, VT, 20 Jun 1857; m. at Weston, 29 Mar 1821, ANDRUS COLEMAN, b. 6 Mar 1793 son of Solomon and Hephzibah (Davis) Coleman; Andrus d. at Ludlow, VT, 4 Dec 1873.

iii LUTHER MARTIN, b. 1789; d. at Weston, 10 Jan 1797.

iv ABIGAIL MARTIN, b. 1792; d. at Londonderry, VT, 8 Jan 1873. Abigail did not marry.

v LUTHER MARTIN, b. 1799; d. at Londonderry, VT, 3 Jun 1869; m. 12 Jan 1826, POLLY PATTERSON, b. at Londonderry, 23 Nov 1802 daughter of John and Betridge (Morrison) Patterson;[2650] Polly d. at Ludlow, 7 Oct 1883.

vi LUCY MARTIN, b. 1800; d. at Weston, 17 Sep 1810.

1003) JOSEPH GRAY (*Timothy Gray[4], Braviter Gray[3], Hannah Holt Gray[2], Nicholas[1]*), b. at Andover, 9 Mar 1761 son of Timothy and Elinor (Best) Gray; d. at Wilton, 26 Aug 1846; m. 11 Apr 1786; CHLOE ABBOTT, b. at Wilton, 4 Jun 1767 daughter of Jeremiah and Cloe (Abbott) Abbott; Chloe d. at Wilton, 19 Jul 1849.

Joseph Gray enlisted in the service in 1777 when just age 16. He served in the company of Capt. Isaac Frye in Col. Scammell's regiment.[2651] He was a farmer in Wilton and Joseph and Chloe were parents of twelve children all born in Wilton.

[2647] Eliza Hartshorn and two of her children (Solon and James P.) are interred in the same plot (s253) as Thaddeus and Lucy Roberts; Norton Cemetery, Keene, NY, Find a Grave 74762238

[2648] Burleigh, *Genealogy and History of the Ingalls Family in America*, p 65; Abiah's date of birth is given in the Revolutionary War Pension Application File of her father Caleb Ingalls, Case R5476

[2649] Revolutionary War Pension and Bounty-Land Warrant Application Files, Case S40972

[2650] Sausaman, *Nathan Alldredge (1739-1826) of North Carolina and Tennessee*, p 60

[2651] Joseph's detailed narrative of his experiences during the war are contained in Livermore, *History of the Town of Wilton*, pp 246-251

i JOSEPH GRAY, b. 14 Aug 1787; d. 13 Oct 1865; m. Apr 1815, MARY "POLLY" SPAULDING, b. at Wilton, 11 Feb 1789 daughter of Abijah and Mary (Wyman) Spaulding;[2652] Mary d. at Wilton, 25 Dec 1852.

ii CHLOE GRAY, b. 3 Nov 1789; d. at Wilton, 29 Mar 1819; m. 26 Oct 1813, OLIVER FLETCHER, b. at Wilton, 22 Apr 1785 son of Oliver and Sarah (Dale) Fletcher; Oliver d. at Wilton, 31 Mar 1816.

iii SALLY GRAY, b. 11 Jul 1791; d. at Leominster, MA, 4 Apr 1834; m. SETH PAYSON TYLER, b. at Sterling, 29 Apr 1791 son of Parker and Hannah (Flint) Tyler; Seth d. at Leominster, 24 Aug 1868. Seth married second Susan Wheeler in 1836.

iv ANNA ABBOTT GRAY, b. 7 Apr 1793; m. 1 Jun 1817, ASA PERHAM, b. at Lyndeborough, 12 Aug 1795 son of Oliver and Anna (Pierce) Perham; Asa d. at Lyndeborough (probate 3 Oct 1848). Anna was living in 1848.

v LYDIA GRAY, b. 5 Mar 1795; m. at Wilton, 5 Feb 1822, as his second wife, RUSSELL UPTON, b. 4 Jul 1788 son of Paul and Jerusha (Richardson) Upton; Russell d. at Lyndeborough, 27 Sep 1841. Russell was first married to Susan who died at Lyndeborough in 1821.

vi JAMES BEST GRAY, b. 21 Apr 1797; d. at Milford, 6 Dec 1867; m. 1st 12 Dec 1822, his fifth cousin once removed, SARAH BURNS (*Betty Bradford Burns⁶, Sarah Putnam Bradford⁵, Sarah Cram Putnam⁴, Sarah Holt Cram³, Henry², Nicholas¹*), b. 9 Jan 1803 daughter of Moses and Betty (Bradford) Burns; Sarah d. at Wilton, 8 Nov 1843. James m. 2nd 14 Mar 1844, his fourth cousin once removed, ADELINE GUTTERSON (*Phebe Ballard Gutterson⁶, Hannah Holt Ballard⁵, Jonathan⁴, Oliver³, Henry², Nicholas¹*), b. at Milford, 7 Jul 1813 daughter of John and Phebe (Ballard) Gutterson; Adeline d. at Milford, 19 Mar 1886.

vii BETSY GRAY, b. 21 Jun 1799; d. at Milford, 6 Oct 1869; m. 25 Sep 1827, ABBOT SMITH, b. at Groton, MA, 22 Dec 1798 son of Sylvanus and Abigail (Farley) Smith; Abbot d. at Milford, 28 Dec 1852.

viii CALVIN GRAY, b. 28 Oct 1801; d. at Wilton, 15 Dec 1856; m. 11 Apr 1826, CLARISSA KING, b. at Wilton, 7 Mar 1804 daughter of Benning and Abigail (Morgan) King; Clarissa d. at Wilton, 8 Aug 1885.

ix HENRY NEWTON GRAY, b. 1 Sep 1804; d. (buried) at Wilton, 8 Sep 1826.

x MATILDA GRAY, b. 24 Jul 1807; d. at Milford, 23 Nov 1835; m. 26 Jan 1832, AMOS GUTTERSON, b. at Milford, 17 Apr 1797 son of John and Phebe (Ballard) Gutterson; Amos d. at Milford, 12 Nov 1859.

xi ELVIRA GRAY, b. 20 Dec 1808; d. at Wilton, 3 Apr 1881; m. 28 Nov 1833, SAMUEL FRENCH, b. at Wilton, 2 Jun 1809 son of Burleigh and Tamar (Sheldon) French; Samuel d. at Wilton, 26 Nov 1878.

xii EMELINE GRAY, b. 11 Oct 1811; d. at Lyndeborough, 3 Jun 1891 (probate Nov 1891); m. 12 Dec 1849, as his second wife, her third cousin once removed, Dr. ISRAEL HERRICK (*Mary Holt Herrick⁵, Joseph⁴, Timothy³, James², Nicholas¹*), b. at Wilton, 9 Jul 1794 son of Edward and Mary (Holt) Herrick; Israel d. at Lyndeborough, 18 Feb 1866. Israel was first married to Eliza H. Burns.

1004) DOROTHY GRAY (*Timothy Gray⁴, Braviter Gray³, Hannah Holt Gray², Nicholas¹*), b. at Andover, 26 Oct 1763 daughter of Timothy and Elinor (Best) Gray; m. at Wilton, 3 Aug 1786, DANIEL HOLT who is not yet identified although he served from Wilton during the Revolution.

There is one child known for Dorothy Gray and Daniel Holt.

i DOROTHEA HOLT, b. at Lyndeborough, 28 May 1791

[2652] Spalding, *Spalding Memorial*, p 206

Great-Grandchildren of James Holt and Hannah Allen

1005) RACHEL WHITTEMORE (*Rhoda Holt Whittemore[4], Timothy[3], James[2], Nicholas[1]*), b. at Malden, 17 Aug 1735 daughter of Elias and Rhoda (Holt) Whittemore; d. at Pembroke, 26 Feb 1817; m. 1757, MOSES FOSTER, b. at Andover, 26 Mar 1728 son of Moses and Elizabeth (Rogers) Foster; Moses d. at Pembroke, 21 Jan 1823.

There is just one child known for Rachel and Moses.

i RUTH FOSTER, b. at Pembroke, 1757; d. at Pembroke, 26 Nov 1836; m. AMOS GILE, b. at Haverhill, 10 Jun 1749 son of Samuel and Sarah (Emerson) Gile; Amos d. at Pembroke, 25 Sep 1833.

1006) JOHN WHITTEMORE (*Rhoda Holt Whittemore[4], Timothy[3], James[2], Nicholas[1]*), b. likely at Pembroke, about 1737 son of Elias and Rhoda (Holt) Whittemore; d. at Pembroke, 1774 (probate 16 May 1774); m. about 1771, RUTH PEABODY, b. at Boxford, 10 Dec 1746 daughter of Thomas and Ruth (Osgood) Peabody; Ruth d. at Pembroke, 22 May 1828. Ruth married second Thomas Baker on 13 Feb 1776.[2653]

John Whittemore died at age 37 leaving two small children. He did not leave a will and his estate entered probate 16 May 1774 with widow Ruth as administratrix. Real estate was valued at £384 and personal estate at £123.13.5[2654] The widow's thirds were set off to Ruth on 23 December 1774. The final settlement of the estate was not until 1794 when Timothy Baker and Ruth his wife as administratrix reported that the debts of the estate exceeded the value of the personal estate and petitioned for the sale of the real estate. Part of the expenses of the estate were the maintenance of two children. In 1775, there had been an initial order allowing the sale of part of the estate due to debts.

John Whittemore and Ruth Peabody were parents of two children born at Pembroke.

i ELIAS WHITMORE, b. 2 Mar 1772; d. at Windsor, NY, 26 Dec 1853; m. 12 Aug 1812, ANNA NICHOLS, b. 5 Feb 1786 daughter of Eli and Elizabeth (Ruggles) Nichols; Anna d. at Windsor, 15 Oct 1848. Elias Whittemore was a U. S. Congressman from 4 Mar 1825 to 3 Mar 1827 representing New York's 21st district. He was a merchant in Windsor, NY.[2655]

ii THOMAS WHITTEMORE, b. 27 Jan 1774; d. at Pembroke, 22 Jul 1845; m. at Pembroke, 15 Nov 1798, MARGARET "PEGGY" CUNNINGHAM, b. at Pembroke, 23 Jan 1779 daughter of James and Elizabeth (Duncan) Cunningham.

1007) NATHAN CHANDLER (*Priscilla Holt Chandler[4], Timothy[3], James[2], Nicholas[1]*), b. at Andover, 19 Feb 1729/30 son of Nathan and Priscilla (Holt) Chandler; d. at Andover, 30 Apr 1786; m. 18 Apr 1754, his third cousin, PHEBE ABBOTT, b. 14 Apr 1733 daughter of John and Phebe (Fiske) Abbott; Phebe d. 26 Jul 1812.

Phebe and Nathan lived in West Parish of Andover on part of the farm that had been owned by Nathan's grandfather John Chandler.[2656]

In his will, Nathan left beloved wife Phebe his clock. She also has use of the northwest room of the home as long as she remains his widow. The will also notes that Nathan's mother is still living, and she is apparently living with the family, as wife Phebe will have full use of the kitchen after the decease of his mother. Phebe will have the full use of the kitchen as long as she does not interfere with Nathan's son using the kitchen. Phebe also is to have use of the well and a spot for a garden. Nathan also provides a lengthy list of provisions for her continued support to be provided by the executor. Only and well-beloved son Nathan receives all the lands and buildings. Daughter Phebe wife of Benjamin Ames receives five shillings and one-sixth of the household goods. Daughters Lucy the wife of Zebadiah Chandler and Mary wife of William Ballard receive similar bequests. In addition to the same bequest as her sisters, daughter Elizabeth has continued use of the house as long as she is unmarried. Daughters Priscilla and Rhoda receive twenty-five pounds, thirteen shillings, and four pence when they reach age 21. To beloved daughter Chloe he leaves ten shillings and "considering the difficulties she labours under not likely to be capable of taking care of herself I commit the care of her to my son Nathan." He also orders that his daughters Priscilla and Rhoda be raised in his house until they are of age. Nathan also specifies that son Nathan is to carry out all the bequests of the will "as I think I have given him the wherewith out of my estate to do it." Son Nathan Chandler declined to be executor writing to Judge Benjamin Greenleaf 3 July 1786 that "I utterly refuse" this responsibility. However, Judge Greenleaf responded to Nathan in a letter 6 November 1786 ordering him to assume the administration of the estate which Nathan then did carry out.[2657] I can only imagine the younger Nathan's situation. He was just 30 years old, newly married, and just had his first child. As the only son

---

2653 The 1787 will (probate 1803) of Ruth *Osgood* Peabody Osgood includes a bequest to her daughter Ruth Baker.

2654 *New Hampshire. Probate Court (Rockingham County), Estate Papers, No 3989-4128, 1773-1774, Case 4102*

2655 Whitmore, Elias, Biographical Directory of the United States Congress, https://bioguideretro.congress.gov/Home/MemberDetails?memIndex=W000423

2656 Chandler, *Descendants of William and Annis Chandler*, p 329

2657 *Essex County, MA: Probate File Papers, 1638-1881.*Online database. *AmericanAncestors.org. Probate of Nathan Chandler, 6 Jul 1786, case number 4963.*

in the family, he had responsibility for his widowed mother and grandmother, a disabled sister, and two sisters still underage who were living in Andover.

Phebe and Nathan Chandler had nine children whose births are recorded at Andover.[2658]

i PHEBE CHANDLER, b. 18 Oct 1754; d. at Andover, 19 Jun 1798; m. 30 Apr 1772, her second cousin once removed, BENJAMIN AMES, b. at Andover, 9 Nov 1749 son of Benjamin and Hephzibah (Chandler) Ames; Benjamin d. 23 Nov 1813.

ii NATHAN CHANDLER, b. 16 Jun 1756; d. at Andover, 27 Jun 1837; m. 27 Nov 1782, his first cousin once removed, LUCY BALLARD, b. at Andover 4 Apr 1760 daughter of Hezekiah and Lydia (Chandler) Ballard; Lucy d. 29 Jun 1827.

iii LUCE CHANDLER, b. 26 Jun 1758; d. at Andover, 6 Oct 1841; m. 16 Aug 1774, ZEBADIAH CHANDLER, b. at Andover, 11 Nov 1752 son of Zebadiah and Deborah (Blanchard) Chandler; Zebadiah d. 5 Feb 1835.

iv EZRA CHANDLER, b. 20 Jun 1761; d. 10 Sep 1778. Ezra "died coming out of ye army."

v ELIZABETH CHANDLER, b. 15 May 1763; d. at Andover, 22 Sep 1848. Elizabeth did not marry.

vi MARY CHANDLER, b. 18 May 1766; d. at Peterborough, 12 Sep 1819; m. 11 Nov 1783, WILLIAM BALLARD, b. at Andover, Jun 1764 son of William and Hannah (How) Ballard; William d. about 1807. Mary m. 2nd, DANIEL ABBOTT "of Andover" (according to the Chandler genealogy) but I do not know what Abbott family he belongs to.

vii PRISCILLA CHANDLER, b. 30 Jun 1768; d. at Andover, 19 Feb 1831; m. 26 May 1789, her first cousin, DAVID ABBOTT (*Jonathan Abbott⁵, David Abbott⁴, Sarah Farnum Abbott³, Elizabeth Holt Farnum², Nicholas¹*), b. at Andover, 11 Mar 1764 son of Jonathan and Mary (Chandler) Abbott; David d. 1 Jun 1823. Priscilla Chandler and David Abbott are Family 843.

viii CHLOE CHANDLER, b. 30 Jun 1771; d. at Andover 24 Aug 1821. Chloe did not marry. She died at the almshouse.

ix RHODA CHANDLER, b. 2 Mar 1774; d. at Andover, 19 Mar 1853; m. at Andover, 26 Nov 1793, her first cousin, BENJAMIN ABBOTT (*Jonathan Abbott⁵, David Abbott⁴, Sarah Farnum Abbott³, Elizabeth Holt Farnum², Nicholas¹*), b. at Andover, 7 Jun 1770 son of Jonathan and Mary (Chandler) Abbott; Benjamin d. at Andover, 20 Oct 1835. "Benjamin, Oct. 20, 1835, a. 65 y."

1008) ISAAC CHANDLER (*Priscilla Holt Chandler⁴, Timothy³, James², Nicholas¹*), b. at Andover, 8 Apr 1732 son of Nathan and Priscilla (Holt) Chandler; d. at Andover, 6 Mar 1817; m. 14 Apr 1757, his second cousin once removed, HANNAH BALLARD, b. 3 Jan 1732/3 daughter of Josiah and Mary (Chandler) Ballard;[2659] Hannah d. 2 Oct 1824.[2660]

Isaac Chandler served one and half days at the Lexington alarm in the Company of Captain Joseph Holt.[2661] Isaac Chandler and Hannah Ballard were the parents of eight children born at Andover.

i ISAAC CHANDLER, b. 28 Jan 1758; d. at Hamilton, MA, 30 Jan 1839; m. at Wilmington, 10 Dec 1783, ABIGAIL "NABBY" BOUTWELL, b. at Wilmington, 19 Jan 1762 daughter of Jonathan and Abigail (Eams) Boutwell; Abigail d. at Hamilton, 19 Sep 1836.

ii JOHN CHANDLER, b. 21 Nov 1759; d. at Bow, NH, Sep 1819; m. 17 Apr 1783, his first cousin once removed, DOROTHY BALLARD, b. at Andover, 12 Dec 1757 daughter of Timothy and Hannah (Chandler) Ballard; Dorothy d. likely at Bow, after 1820.

iii JAMES CHANDLER, b. 28 Nov 1761; d. at Andover, 1 Dec 1835; m. 29 Apr 1783, his third cousin, PHEBE DANE, b. at Andover, 14 May 1762 daughter of Joseph and Elizabeth (Wyman) Dane; Phebe d. at Andover, 10 Dec 1843.

iv SAMUEL CHANDLER, b. 25 Jan 1764; d. at Antrim, NH, 12 Jan 1842; m. 21 Apr 1790, SARAH JAQUES, b. at Pelham, NH, 25 Jul 1767 daughter of Nehemiah and Lucy (Colburn) Jaques;[2662] Sarah d. at Hillsborough, 20 May 1858.

[2658] Massachusetts Vital Records Project. http://ma-vitalrecords.org

[2659] The 1780 will of Josiah Chandler includes a bequest to his daughter Hannah the wife of Mr. Isaac Chandler.

[2660] This is the date of death used in *The Descendants of William and Annis Chandler*, p. 330. The deaths of both Isaac and Hannah are reported by the Chandler book as occurring in Concord, NH, but the record of Isaac's death is in the Andover records with the same specific date as the Chandler book.

[2661] Chandler, *The Descendants of William and Annis Chandler*, p 330

[2662] New Hampshire, Births and Christenings Index, 1714-1904

v HENRY CHANDLER, b. 16 Jul 1766; d. at Concord, 3 Apr 1856; m. 11 Mar 1798, his fourth cousin, RUTH ABBOTT (*Zerviah Farnum Abbott*[5], *Joseph Farnum*[4], *Ephraim Farnum*[3], *Elizabeth Holt Farnum*[2], *Nicholas*[1]), b. at Concord, 25 Apr 1777 daughter of Reuben and Zerviah (Farnum) Abbott; Ruth d. at Concord, 20 Feb 1849.

vi BENJAMIN CHANDLER, b. 17 Jan 1768; d. at Lancaster, MA, 24 Feb 1847; m. Nov 1802, ELIZABETH PRATT, b. 31 Dec 1780 daughter of James and Zerviah (Rugg) Pratt; Elizabeth d. at Lancaster, 3 Jun 1857.

vii HANNAH CHANDLER, b. 12 Jan 1771; d. 12 Apr 1818; m. at Hillsborough, 18 Oct 1791, SAMUEL BRADFORD, b. at Hillsborough, 29 Sep 1768 son of Samuel and Anna (Washer) Bradford.[2663] According to the Chandler genealogy (p 619) in 1802, Samuel went on a cattle drive from Hillsborough and was never heard from again.

viii MARY CHANDLER, b. Nov 1773; d. at Hillsborough, 16 Jun 1850; m. at Hillsborough, 14 Oct 1794, ABRAHAM ANDREWS, b. at Hillsborough, 25 Jan 1772 son of Isaac and Lucy (Perkins) Andrews; Abraham d. 23 Mar 1845.

1009) HANNAH CHANDLER (*Priscilla Holt Chandler*[4], *Timothy*[3], *James*[2], *Nicholas*[1]), b. at Andover, 20 May 1735 daughter of Nathan and Priscilla (Holt) Chandler; d. at Andover, 14 Feb 1791; m. 31 Mar 1757, as his 1st wife, her first cousin, JOSHUA CHANDLER, b. 23 Jul 1732 son of Joshua and Sarah (Chandler) Chandler. Joshua m. 2nd 7 Jun 1792, Hannah Ballard the daughter of Hezekiah and Lydia (Chandler) Ballard who was the widow of Obadiah Foster; Joshua Chandler d. 15 Mar 1807.

In his will written 24 February 1806, Joshua Chandler has bequests to the following persons: beloved wife Hannah Chandler, beloved son Abiel Chandler, beloved daughter Hannah Chandler (who is under 18 at the time of the will), and beloved son Joshua Chandler. Son Joshua is named executor. Hannah Chandler is Joshua's daughter from his marriage to Hannah Ballard.[2664]

Joshua Chandler and Hannah Chandler were parents of three children born at Andover.

i JOSHUA CHANDLER, b. 18 Aug 1758; d. at Andover, 26 Nov 1817; m. at Andover, 18 Oct 1798, his second cousin, DORCAS FOSTER, b. at Andover, Jun 1777 daughter of Obadiah and Hannah (Ballard) Foster; Dorcas d. at Andover, 21 Dec 1830. Joshua and Dorcas were stepsiblings.

ii ABIEL CHANDLER, b. 28 Aug 1760; d. at Boston, 2 Nov 1833; m. at Andover, 17 Oct 1782, his first cousin, MARY ABBOTT (*Jonathan Abbott*[5], *David Abbott*[4], *Sarah Farnum Abbott*[3], *Elizabeth Holt Farnum*[2], *Nicholas*[1]), b. at Andover, 10 Jan 1762 daughter of Jonathan and Mary (Chandler) Abbott; Mary d. 1 May 1845.

iii HANNAH CHANDLER, b. 13 Oct 1764; d. at Andover, 30 Aug 1785; m. at Andover, 1 Jun 1784, JOSEPH SHATTUCK, b. at Andover, 8 Nov 1757 son of Joseph and Anna (Johnson) Shattuck; Joseph d. at Andover, 8 Jul 1847. Joseph m. 2nd, 30 Mar 1790, PHEBE ABBOTT, b. at Andover, 22 Feb 1766 daughter of Jonathan and Mary (Chandler) Abbott; Phebe d. at Andover, 31 Dec 1848.

1010) PHEBE CHANDLER (*Priscilla Holt Chandler*[4], *Timothy*[3], *James*[2], *Nicholas*[1]), b. at Andover, 2 Jun 1742 daughter of Nathan and Priscilla (Holt) Chandler; d. at Andover, 1 Jul 1800; m. 22 Apr 1766, her second cousin once removed, ISAAC ABBOT (*Phebe Lovejoy Abbott*[5], *William Lovejoy*[4], *Mary Farnum Lovejoy*[3], *Elizabeth Holt Farnum*[2], *Nicholas*[1]), b. 3 Feb 1745 son of Isaac and Phebe (Lovejoy) Abbot; Isaac d. 21 May 1836.

Isaac Abbot served in the Revolutionary War and was wounded at Bunker Hill.[2665] He served as a deacon and was also the first postmaster of Andover. He lost his eyesight several years prior to his death.

Isaac Abbot made the following bequests in his will which was written 14 September 1833. His granddaughter Mrs. Mary Shattuck of Andover received one silver tablespoon, six silver teaspoons and $10. Daughter-in-law Mrs. Mary Abbot widow of his son Isaac received a clock and $10. Grandchildren Josiah F., Samuel, and Isaac Abbot children of son Isaac received $10 each. His wearing apparel was divided among William, Isaac, and Moses Abbot who are the children of his son William Abbot of Concord. Granddaughter Phebe Abbot daughter of son William received the dictionary, the bible, and the umbrella. Granddaughter Rebekah Abbot daughter of William received the looking glass. All the named grandchildren received $10 each. His dwelling house and all the remainder of the estate is bequeathed to son William Abbot of Concord.[2666]

Isaac and Phebe had four children whose births are recorded at Andover.

i PHEBE ABBOT, b. 27 May 1767; d. 8 Nov 1772.

ii ISAAC ABBOT, b. 9 Dec 1768; d. 27 Dec 1806; m. 1st, 5 Jul 1798, HEPHZIBAH FISKE, b. 21 Apr 1773 daughter of John and Hephzibah (-) Fiske; Hephzibah d. 22 Mar 1800. Isaac m. 2nd, 7 Oct 1801, MARY MOULTON, b. at Danvers, 16 Mar 1775 daughter of Ebenezer and Elizabeth (Curtis) Moulton; Mary d. 19 Aug 1851.

2663 Browne, *History of Hillsborough*, volume I, p 81

2664 *Essex County, MA: Probate File Papers, 1638-1881.*Online database. *AmericanAncestors.org.* New England Historic Genealogical Society, 2014. Case 4954

2665 The Essex Antiquarian, volume 1, Abbot Genealogy, p 80

2666 *Essex County, MA: Probate File Papers, 1638-1881. Probate of Isaac Abbot, 7 Jun 1836, Case number 60.*

iii PRISCILLA ABBOT, b. 1 Jun 1770; d. 10 Feb 1830; m. 6 Jun 1820, as his third wife, JOHN KNEELAND, b. at Boston, 14 Oct 1748 son of John and Sarah (Mulberry) Kneeland. John married a fourth time after Priscilla's death; John d. 4 Sep 1831. John Kneeland was the stepson of Samuel Abbot who was Priscilla's first cousin once removed. Priscilla married late in life and did not have children.

iv WILLIAM ABBOT, b. 30 Oct 1772; d. at Concord, NH about 1856 (probate date 24 Jun 1856); m. 14 May 1801, his third cousin once removed, REBECCA BAILEY, b. 10 Apr 1781 daughter of Moses and Elizabeth (Mooar) Bailey; Rebecca was still living in 1860 when she was living in Concord with her son Moses.[2667]

1011) ELIZABETH ABBOTT (*Hannah Holt Abbott⁴, Timothy³, James², Nicholas¹*), b. at Andover, 2 Nov 1740 daughter of Barachias and Hannah (Holt) Abbott; d. 9 Sep 1780; m. 30 Aug 1759, her second cousin, ZEBADIAH SHATTUCK, b. 26 Oct 1736 son of Joseph and Joanna (Chandler) Shattuck. Zebadiah m. 2nd 25 Dec 1781, Sarah Chandler (widow of Ralph Holbrook), b. 8 May 1751 daughter of Zebadiah and Deborah (Blanchard) Chandler; Zebadiah d. 10 Mar 1826.

Zebadiah Shattuck was a farmer in Andover. He served during the war with the French.[2668]

Elizabeth Abbott and Zebadiah Shattuck had six children born at Andover. Zebadiah Shattuck had two children with his second wife, Sarah Chandler (Sarah Shattuck who married Richard Trow and Zebadiah Shattuck who married Sarah Durant).

i ELIZABETH SHATTUCK, b. 16 Dec 1759; d. at Antrim, NH; m. 14 Oct 1783, her first cousin, BARACHIAS HOLT (*Jeremiah⁵, John⁴, Samuel³, Samuel², Nicholas¹*), b. at Wilton, NH, 8 Feb 1758 son of Jeremiah and Hannah (Abbott) Holt; Barachias d. at Antrim, 1846.

ii HANNAH SHATTUCK, b. Dec 1761; d. at Bethel, ME, m. at Andover, 17 May 1787, JAMES SWAN, b. at Methuen, 2 Dec 1760 son of James and Mary (Smith) Swan; James d. at Bethel, about 1844 (probate 1844).

iii DOROTHY SHATTUCK, b. 14 Apr 1764; d. at Bethel, ME, 24 Jan 1852; m. 1st, at Andover, 26 Feb 1784, JACOB RUSSELL, b. at Andover, Jan 1761 son of John and Hannah (Foster) Russell; Jacob d. 1799. Dorothy m. 2nd, at Bethel, 2 Nov 1803, INGALLS BRAGG, b. at Andover, 24 Jun 1753 son of Thomas and Dorothy (Ingalls) Bragg; Ingalls d. at East Andover, ME, 1 Jan 1808. After Ingalls's death, Dorothy married BENJAMIN GAGE.

iv PHEBE SHATTUCK, b. Feb 1766; d. at Plainfield, VT, 16 Jun 1856; m. at Andover, 25 Jul 1786, her first cousin, ABIEL SHATTUCK, b. at Andover, 8 Aug 1762 son of Joseph and Anna (Johnson) Shattuck; Abiel d. at Plainfield, 29 Apr 1834.

v JOHN SHATTUCK, b. 23 Oct 1768; no further record

vi RHODA SHATTUCK, b. 1 Sep 1776; m. about 1798, SAMUEL CLARK

1012) LYDIA ABBOTT (*Hannah Holt Abbott⁴, Timothy³, James², Nicholas¹*), b. at Andover, 7 Mar 1744/5 daughter of Barachias and Hannah (Holt) Abbot; d. at Andover, 11 Jul 1829; m. 15 Aug 1771, URIAH RUSSELL, b. 1743 son of Thomas and Abigail (Ballard) Russell; Uriah d. 9 Nov 1822.

Uriah Russell wrote his will 31 March 1818 and his estate entered probate 7 January 1823.[2669] His beloved wife Lydia is to have the improvements on all the household furniture during her lifetime, and after her decease, the household items will pass to his two daughters. The executor is to see that she is comfortably provided for. Sons James, Thomas, and Abiel each receives $125. The two daughters, Hannah Abbot the wife of Nathan Abbot and Lydia Faulkner wife of Joseph Faulkner, each receives $15. Son Joel Russell receives all the residue of the estate, both real and personal, and is named executor.

There are records for eleven children born at Andover. There is a daughter Phebe for which there is only a baptismal record. The oldest son died of yellow fever at Curacao.

i URIAH RUSSELL, b. Sep 1773; d. of yellow fever at Curacao, 1799.[2670]

ii THOMAS RUSSELL, b. Dec 1774; d, Sep 1775.

iii HANNAH RUSSELL, b. Sep 1775; d. 9 Oct 1776.

iv JAMES RUSSELL, b. Nov 1777; d. about 1861 in Oxford County, ME;[2671] m. at East Andover, ME, 13 Aug 1804, his first cousin once removed, DOLLY RUSSELL (*Dorothy Shattuck Russell⁶, Elizabeth Abbott Shattuck⁵, Hannah Holt Abbott⁴, Timothy³, James², Nicholas¹*), b. about 1784 daughter of Jacob and Dorothy (Shattuck) Russell; Dolly d. at Beverly, MA, 20 Sep 1863.

[2667] Year: *1860;* Census Place: *Concord Ward 7, Merrimack, New Hampshire;* Roll: *M653_675;* Page: *945;* Family History Library Film: *803675*

[2668] Shattuck, *Memorials of the Descendants of William Shattuck*, p 150

[2669] *Essex County, MA: Probate File Papers, 1638-1881. Probate of Uriah Russell, 7 Jan 1823, Case number 24434.*

[2670] Uriah, jr., yellow fever, at Curacoa, —— —, 1799. CR2

[2671] James Russell was living at the time of the 1860 U.S. Census; his wife was a widow when she died in 1863.

v THOMAS RUSSELL, b. Nov 1777 (twin of James); d. at Andover, 18 Jan 1849; m. by 1812, ABIGAIL BELL, b. at Tewksbury about 1786 of not yet verified parents; Abigail d. at Andover 10 Oct 1833. Abigail's maiden name of Bell is given on the death record of one of her children.

vi HANNAH RUSSELL, b. Apr 1780 (based on age at death); d. at Andover, 16 Nov 1832; m. 10 Nov 1801, her third cousin, NATHAN ABBOTT (*Nathan Abbott⁵, Job Abbott⁴, Zerviah Holt Abbott³, Henry², Nicholas¹*), b. at Andover, 25 Aug 1778 son of Nathan and Sarah (Ballard) Abbott; Nathan d. 13 Feb 1837.

vii LYDIA RUSSELL, b. Sep 1782; d. Oct 1782.

viii JOEL RUSSELL, b. Aug 1783; d. at Andover, 22 Jul 1871; m. 2 Apr 1805, SARAH CURTIS, b. at Middleton, 16 Oct 1782 daughter of Israel and Elizabeth (Wilkins) Curtis; Sarah d. at Andover, 6 Feb 1857.

ix LYDIA RUSSELL, b. 5 Dec 1785; d. at Andover, 2 Dec 1865; m. 13 Jun 1809, her third cousin once removed, JOSEPH FAULKNER (*Abiel Faulkner⁶, Abiel Faulkner⁵, Damaris Johnson Faulkner⁴, Thomas Johnson³, Mary Holt Johnson², Nicholas¹*), b. at Andover, 30 Jul 1783 son of Abiel and Hannah (Abbott) Faulkner; Joseph d. 5 Aug 1831.

x PHEBE RUSSELL, baptized 29 Jan 1786; no further record and likely died young.

xi ABIEL RUSSELL, b. Mar 1789; d. at Andover, 14 Jan 1881; m. 17 Jun 1813, his third cousin, SARAH ABBOTT (*Nathan Abbott⁵, Job Abbott⁴, Zerviah Holt Abbott³, Henry², Nicholas¹*), b. at Andover, 20 Dec 1792 daughter of Nathan and Sarah (Ballard) Abbott; Sarah d. 20 Sep 1846.

1013) PHEBE ABBOTT (*Hannah Holt Abbott⁴, Timothy³, James², Nicholas¹*), b. at Andover, 29 Aug 1749 daughter of Barachias and Hannah (Holt) Abbot; d. at Andover, 17 Apr 1809; m. 1 Feb 1774, JOHN RUSSELL, b. 1 Jul 1746 son of John and Hannah (Foster) Russell. John m. 2nd Mary Wilkins; John d. at Andover, 12 Aug 1830. Mary Wilkins was first married to Nathaniel Sherman.

The estate of John Russell was probated 17 August 1830.[2672] The will of John Russell has bequests to the following persons: beloved wife Mary; grandson John Russell (oldest male heir with the name Russell), daughters Phebe Lovejoy, Hannah Abbot, Betsy Smith, Sally Loring, the heirs of daughter Dolly Lovejoy who is deceased, and heirs of daughter Nancy Woodbridge who is deceased; daughter-in-law Phebe Russell (this to be in the hands of a trustee);[2673] and grandchildren John Russell, William Russell, Edward Russell, Phebe Russell, and Joseph Russell. Benjamin Jenkins is named executor and trustee.

Phebe Abbott and John Russell had eight children born at Andover.

i JOHN RUSSELL, b. 10 Oct 1774; d. at Andover, May 1818; m. at Andover, 21 Jul 1799, DIANA BRAY, b. at Gloucester, Oct 1775 daughter of Edward and Edith (Doane) Bray; Diana d. at Andover, 4 Mar 1858.[2674]

ii PHEBE RUSSELL, b. 1776; d. at Andover, 2 Dec 1858; m. 2 Nov 1794, her third cousin, EBENEZER LOVEJOY, b. at Andover, 16 Feb 1773 son of Jeremiah and Dorothy (Ballard) Lovejoy; Ebenezer d. at Andover, Jun 1834.

iii HANNAH RUSSELL, b. Sep 1778; d. at Andover, 3 Jan 1840; m. 13 Aug 1801, her third cousin, STEPHEN ABBOTT (*Jonathan Abbott⁵, Jonathan Abbott⁴, Zerviah Holt Abbott³, Henry², Nicholas¹*), b. at Andover, 30 Dec 1779 son of Jonathan and Dorcas (Abbott) Abbott; Stephen d. at Andover, 1 Oct 1835.

iv BETTY RUSSELL, b. 1780; d. at Andover, 7 Nov 1866; m. 27 Sep 1804, THOMAS SMITH, b. at Andover, 13 Mar 1781 son of Thomas and Mary (Harris) Smith; Thomas d. at Andover, 18 Sep 1832.

v SALLY RUSSELL, b. 1783; d. at Andover, 10 Jun 1848; m. at Andover, 23 Oct 1806, THOMAS LORING, born in NH, about 1780 son of John and Sarah (Foster) Loring; Thomas d. at New Orleans, 1826. Thomas was a machinist and he placed the machinery in the first steamboat to go down the Ohio River. He died of spotted fever in New Orleans.[2675][2676]

vi DOLLY RUSSELL, b. Sep 1783; d. at Andover, 26 Jun 1809; m. 19 May 1808, her third cousin, JOHN LOVEJOY, b. at Andover, 25 Jul 1780 son of Jeremiah and Dorothy (Ballard) Lovejoy; John d. at Andover, 26 Feb 1817. After Dolly's death, John married PERSIS BAILEY, b. at Andover, 25 May 1783 daughter of William and Rebecca (Hildreth) Bailey; Persis d. at Andover, 18 Feb 1816.

vii WILLIAM RUSSELL, b. 1785; d. 21 Nov 1788.

2672 *Essex County, MA: Probate File Papers, 1638-1881.* Online database. *AmericanAncestors.org.* New England Historic Genealogical Society, 2014. Case number 24400

2673 It has not been determined who daughter-in-law Phebe Russell is.

2674 Diana's death record confirms Gloucester as her place of birth making Edward and Edith her likely parents.

2675 *New Hampshire, Death and Burial Records Index, 1654-1949.*

2676 Charlotte Helen Abbott, The Loring Family

viii NANCY RUSSELL, b. Aug 1790; d. at Arlington, MA, 29 Dec 1818; m. 1812, SAMUEL WOODBRIDGE, b. at Marblehead, 13 Jan 1788 son of Dudley and Sara (Brock) Woodbridge; Dudley d. at Cambridge, 28 Jan 1867. After Nancy's death, Samuel married, 30 Sep 1821, DORCAS RUSSELL (*Mehitable Abbott Russell⁶, Jonathan Abbott⁵, Jonathan Abbott⁴, Zerviah Holt Abbott³, Henry², Nicholas¹*), b. at Bethel, ME, 8 Apr 1796 daughter of Benjamin and Mehitable (Abbott) Russell; Dorcas d. at Boston, 29 Nov 1877.

1014) ABIGAIL ABBOTT (*Hannah Holt Abbott⁴, Timothy³, James², Nicholas¹*), b. at Andover, 25 Jul 1751 daughter of Barachias and Hannah (Holt) Abbot; d. at Greenfield, NH 1841; m. 10 Oct 1786, as his second wife, JOHN JOHNSON, b. at Andover, 1748 *perhaps* the son of John and Lydia (Osgood) Johnson (gravestone gives his age as 85); d. at Greenfield, NH 3 Oct 1833. John was *perhaps* first married to Hannah Abbott daughter of John and Hannah (Farnum) Abbott who died in 1785 and then married Abigail. It is speculation that the same John Johnson married both Hannah Abbott and Abigail Abbot.

There are two children known for Abigail Abbott and John Johnson born at Greenfield.

i JOSEPH JOHNSON, b. 1787; d. at Greenfield, 20 Apr 1860; m. at Peterborough, 13 May 1812, MARY DIAMOND, b. at Lexington, MA, 1789 daughter of William and Rebecca (Symonds) Diamond;[2677] Mary d. at Greenfield, 7 May 1858. Mary's father William was the drummer at the Battles of Lexington and Bunker Hill.

ii PHEBE JOHNSON, b. 1792; d. at West Windsor, VT, 12 May 1879; m. 1822, ROYAL SAWIN, b. at Windsor, 1798 son of Munning and Melissa (Powers) Sawin; Royal d. at West Windsor, 13 Sep 1875.

1015) JAMES HOLT (*James⁴, Timothy³, James², Nicholas¹*), b. at Andover, 29 Dec 1738 son of James and Susanna (Nurs) Holt; d. at Andover, 27 Feb 1808;[2678] m. at Andover, 14 Feb 1760, DOROTHY LOVEJOY, b. at Andover, 15 Sep 1740 daughter of Ezekiel and Elizabeth (Wilson) Lovejoy; Dorothy buried at Andover, 28 May 1810.

James Holt did not leave a will and his estate entered probate 8 March 1808 with widow Dorothy as administratrix. The widow's thirds were set off to Mrs. Dorothy Holt on 2 June 1808. Real estate was appraised at $2,803.62 including the homestead of 63 acres with buildings. Personal estate was valued at $163.[2679]

On 16 June 1808 (recorded 22 October 1808, Dorothy Riggs wife of Asa Riggs conveyed her portion of the real estate inherited from her honored father James Holt to Ebenezer Perry of Andover for $360, excepting that portion set aside for her mother's dower. Also on 16 June 1808, Benjamin Wiggin of Tuftonboro and his wife Hannah conveyed Hannah's portion of the estate to Ebenezer Perry also for $360.[2680] Ebenezer Perry was the husband of daughter Elizabeth.

James and Dorothy were parents of four children born at Andover.[2681]

i DOROTHY HOLT, b. 22 Apr 1764; m. at Andover (also recorded at Gloucester), 13 Nov 1787, ASA RIGGS, b. at Gloucester, 28 Jan 1760 son of George and Rachel (Elwell) Griggs; Asa d. at the workhouse in Gloucester, 10 Mar 1821. Dorothy and Asa do not seem to have children as they were just two adults over 45 in the household in the 1810 census at Gloucester.

ii ENOCH HOLT, b. 1769; d. of smallpox at Woburn, 23 Nov 1792. "Enoch, s. James, jr., smallpox, at Woburn, bur. Nov. 23, 1792, a. 23 y. CR2"

iii ELIZABETH HOLT, b. estimate 1770; m. at Andover, 15 May 1803, EBENEZER PERRY of Reading who has not been identified.

iv HANNAH HOLT, baptized 29 Jun 1777; d. at Sutton, MA, Oct 1849;[2682] m. at Andover, 14 Jun 1798, BENJAMIN WIGGINS.

1016) DANE HOLT (*Timothy⁴, Timothy³, James², Nicholas¹*), b. at Andover, 1 Apr 1740 son of Timothy and Hannah (Dane) Holt; d. at Andover, 15 Dec 1818; m. 13 Dec 1763, his third cousin once removed, LYDIA BALLARD, b. at Andover, 30 Jul 1742 daughter of Hezekiah and Lydia (Chandler) Ballard; Lydia d. at Andover, 28 Nov 1813.

Dane Holt served in the Revolutionary War in Captain Henry Abbott's Andover Company. This company "marched at the alarm" 19 April 1775.[2683]

[2677] Smith and Morison, *History of Peterborough*, p 55

[2678] James, jr., carbuncles, bur. Feb. 27, 1808, a. 69 y. CR2

[2679] *Essex County, MA: Probate File Papers, 1638-1881.*Online database. *AmericanAncestors.org.* New England Historic Genealogical Society, 2014. Case 13652

[2680] Massachusetts Land Records, Essex County, 185:173

[2681] Some sources (Durrie and Charlotte Helen Abbott) report a daughter Susannah baptized 9 Nov 1760, but that seems to be Susannah daughter of James and Sarah (Abbott) Holt who was born 27 Oct 1760 and died 26 Nov 1760.

[2682] Hannah, wid. Benjamin, Oct. 1849, a. 73, dysentery; born in Andover

[2683] Bailey, *Historical Sketches of Andover*, p 302

Dane Holt wrote his will 8 January 1806 and the estate entered probate 5 January 1819.[2684] "I give to Lydia my beloved wife all my household stuff and furniture proper for woman's use to be entirely at her own disposal excepting my clock which I give to my son Dane." Lydia also receives the use and improvement of the easterly end of the dwelling house and other specific provisions for her support. Beloved son Dane receives all the real estate and the personal estate that is not otherwise disposed of. Beloved daughter Lydia receives $105 and daughter Hannah receives $75. Beloved son Jacob receives $250. The wearing apparel to be equally divided between his two sons Dane and Jacob. Son Dane is named executor. Heirs signing in 1819 that they have received notification of the probate from executor Dane Holt are Lydia Cummings and Asa Cummings, Hannah Abbot and Noah Abbot, and Jacob Holt. Dane Holt's wife Lydia died in 1813 and son Dane Holt assumed administration of the estate.

Dane Holt and Lydia Ballard had four children born at Andover.

i LYDIA HOLT, b. 12 Aug 1765; d. at Albany, ME, 18 Mar 1853; m. at Andover, 25 May 1797, as his second wife, ASA CUMMINGS, b. at Ipswich, 18 Sep 1759 son of Thomas and Anne (Kittell) Cummings; Asa d. at Albany, ME, 22 May 1845. Asa was first married to Hannah Peabody.

ii DANE HOLT, b. 11 Mar 1768; d. at Andover, 27 Nov 1839; m. 6 Dec 1798, his fourth cousin, MARY WARDWELL (*Daniel Wardwell[5], Abigail Gray Wardwell[4], Edward Gray[3], Hannah Holt Gray[2], Nicholas[1]*), b. at Andover, 28 Nov 1774 daughter of Daniel and Damaris (Faulkner) Wardwell; Mary d. at Andover, 6 Dec 1866.

iii HANNAH HOLT, b. 16 Apr 1771; d. at Andover, 14 Jun 1862; m. 18 Feb 1806, her second cousin, NOAH ABBOTT (*Moses Abbott[5], Hannah Holt Abbott[4], Timothy[3], James[2], Nicholas[1]*), b. at Andover, 11 May 1770 son of Moses and Elizabeth (Holt) Abbott; Noah d. at Andover, 13 Jul 1849.

iv JACOB HOLT, b. 7 Jun 1780; d. at Merrimack, NH, 30 Mar 1847; m. 2 Apr 1807, MARY FRYE, b. at Andover, 12 Mar 1788 daughter of John and Betsy (Noyes) Frye; Mary d. at Merrimack, 19 Sep 1825. After Mary's death, Jacob married LUCY KIMBALL, b. at Lunenburg, Apr 1791 daughter of Samuel and Mary (Goodridge) Kimball; Lucy d. at Lowell, 11 Apr 1875 but is buried at Merrimack. Jacob graduated from Dartmouth College in 1803. He was a schoolteacher and later ordained as a minister. He was ordained in 1827 and was minister of the Congregational Church of Brookline from 1827 to 1832.[2685]

1017) TIMOTHY HOLT (*Timothy[4], Timothy[3], James[2], Nicholas[1]*), b. at Andover, 8 Sep 1744 son of Timothy and Hannah (Dane) Holt; d. at Andover, 19 Feb 1821; m. about 1771, EDE MCINTIRE,[2686] b. about 1750 (baptized at Andover 1752) daughter of Phineas and Mary (Carroll) McIntire;[2687] Ede d. 20 Jun 1824.

Timothy and Ede were parents of eleven children whose births are recorded at Andover.

i NEHEMIAH HOLT, b. at Andover, 1 Apr 1773; d. 22 Aug 1775.

ii TIMOTHY HOLT, b. at Andover, 20 Aug 1775.[2688] Perhaps he is the Timothy Holt that married Susannah Burgess at Salem in 1797.

iii DOROTHY "DOLLY" HOLT, b. at Temple, NH, 27 Jan 1776; d. at Temple, ME, 30 Dec 1827; m. 17 Nov 1805, THOMAS CHANDLER, b. at Wilton, 8 Jan 1783 son of Ebenezer and Sarah (Averill) Chandler; Thomas d. at Temple, ME, 26 Jan 1856. Thomas married second Sally Averill on 14 Oct 1828.

iv EDE HOLT, b. at Temple, NH, 14 Jan 1777; d. at Amherst, 26 Jun 1825; m. MOSES T. TRUELL, b. at Amherst, 27 Apr 1783 perhaps son of Amos Truell; Moses d. at Hollis, 13 Aug 1867. Moses married second Ruth Lawrence Fowle.

v NEHEMIAH HOLT, b. at Andover, 22 Jan 1779; d. at Temple, NH, Apr 1849; m. by 1807, RHODA who is not yet identified; Rhoda d. at Amherst, NH, 6 Feb 1835.

vi HANNAH HOLT, b. at Andover, 6 Apr 1781; m. JOSEPH FIELDS.[2689]

[2684] *Essex County, MA: Probate File Papers, 1638-1881. Probate of Dane Holt, 5 Jan 1819, case number 13629.*

[2685] Chapman, *Sketches of the Alumni of Dartmouth College*, p 111

[2686] There are two Timothy Holts very close in age (born 1744 and 1746) and all published genealogies agree that the Timothy born 1744 married Ede McIntire and Timothy born in 1746 married Hannah Johnson. The basis for that conclusion is not entirely clear. The only discrepancy is that the Timothy who married Hannah Johnson died at Weston, VT in 1836 at age 93 (per death transcription) and that would fit better with the Timothy born in 1744.

[2687] McIntire, *Descendants of Philip McIntire*, p 26

[2688] Most genealogies report that he is Timothy Abbot Holt who married Anna Stevens and lived in Bethel. But it is much more likely that the Timothy Abbot Holt who married Anna Stevens was the son of Zela and Priscilla (Abbott) Holt. Timothy Abbot Holt son of Zela was born in Bethel. Timothy A. and Anna (Stevens) Holt named two of their children Zela and Priscilla.

[2689] McIntire, *Descendants of Philip McIntire*, p 26. This is a marriage reported in genealogies for which no records were located.

vii SARAH HOLT, b. at Andover, 16 Aug 1783; d. at Francestown, 3 Feb 1858; m. JOSEPH KILLAM, b. at Wilmington, MA, 4 Mar 1764 son of Benjamin and Sarah (Foster) Killam; Joseph d. at Francestown, 18 Jan 1861. Sarah and Joseph did not have children. In his will written in 1858 just after the death of Sarah and of Sarah's brother Stephen, Joseph Killam left his estate to his sister-in-law Polly Holt (Stephen's widow) and to her children. He also made nominal bequests to his two sisters Sarah Stiles and Lidia Foster.[2690] Joseph Killam had at least one earlier marriage.

viii ELI HOLT, b. at Andover, 6 Apr 1786; d. at Nashville, NH, 17 Feb 1844; m. at Andover, 10 May 1812, his fourth cousin, PAMELIA WARDWELL (*Ezekiel Wardwell⁵, Abigail Gray Wardwell⁴, Edward Gray³, Hannah Holt Gray², Nicholas¹*), b. at Andover, 6 May 1792 daughter of Ezekiel and Damaris (Faulkner) Wardwell; Pamelia d. between 1833 (birth of youngest child) and 1844 (not living at husband's probate). Eli and Pamelia were parents of one son and nine daughters born in Lyndeborough.

ix EZRA HOLT, b. at Andover, 11 Sep 1788; d. at Andover, 14 Apr 1859; m. 22 Apr 1812, ELIZABETH GAGE WARDWELL, b. at Andover 1789 and baptized 10 Jul 1791 daughter of Simon and Ruth (Church) Wardwell; Elizabeth d. at Andover, 3 Sep 1868.

x PHEBE HOLT, b. at Andover, 8 Jan 1793; d. at Amherst, NH, 27 Oct 1847; m. LILLY EATON BOUTELL, b. at Amherst, 1796; Lilly d. at Amherst, 25 Jul 1829.

xi STEPHEN C. HOLT, b. at Andover, 22 Jul 1798; d. at Francestown, NH, 2 Jan 1858; m. about 1820, MARY C. "POLLY" CRAGIN, b. at Temple, NH, 18 Jun 1800 daughter of Francis and Sarah (Cummings) Cragin; Mary d. at Francestown, 15 Feb 1890.[2691] Stephen Holt was a shoemaker.

1018) EZRA HOLT (*Timothy⁴, Timothy³, James², Nicholas¹*), b. at Andover, 20 Mar 1762 son of Timothy and Hannah (Dane) Holt; d. at Wilton, 11 May 1822; m. at Andover, 9 Oct 1794, his first cousin, DORCAS DANE, b. at Andover, 22 Apr 1771 daughter of William and Phebe (Abbott) Dane; Dorcas d. at Wilton, 30 Jun 1853.

Dorcas and Ezra started their family in Andover and then settled in Wilton. Ezra Holt was a farmer in Wilton where he lived on lot 6 of the ninth range.[2692] Ezra Holt and Dorcas Dane were parents of seven children.

i EZRA HOLT, b. at Andover, 9 Aug 1795; d. at Milford, NH, 7 Apr 1860; m. 1st, at Dracut, 13 Feb 1821, JOANNA MARSHALL, b. at Dracut, 30 Aug 1797 daughter of Joshua and Esther (Moors) Marshall; Joanna d. at Wilton, 20 Dec 1839. Ezra m. 2nd, at Mont Vernon, NH, 28 May 1840, DOLLY B. GOULD, b. at Alstead, 3 Jan 1812;[2693] Dolly d. at Lexington, MA, 11 Feb 1897.

ii DORCAS HOLT, b. at Andover, 24 Dec 1797; d. at Wilton, 11 Nov 1869. Dorcas did not marry.

iii SARAH ABBOT HOLT, b. 1 Sep 1800; d. 26 Aug 1801.

iv JOSEPH HOLT, b. at Andover, May 1803; d. at Wilton, after 1870; m. Oct 1840, his third cousin once removed, BETSEY FRYE (*Joshua Frye⁶, Elizabeth Holt Frye⁵, Timothy⁴, Nicholas³, Nicholas², Nicholas¹*), b. in VT, about 1808 daughter of Joshua and Lois (Farrington) Frye; Betsey d. at Wilton, 5 Jun 1885.

v HERMAN HOLT, b. at Wilton, 1807; d. at Wilton, 21 Jun 1836.

vi DANE HOLT, b. at Wilton, 1810; d. at Wilton, 23 Dec 1858; m. Dec 1839, ESTHER BLANCHARD, b. at Milford, 5 May 1816 daughter of Phineas and Sarah (Stevens) Blanchard; Esther d. at Milford, 21 Feb 1893.

vii MARY HOLT, b. at Wilton, 1816; d. at Wilton, 11 Feb 1853. Mary did not marry.

1019) JOSEPH HOLT (*Joseph⁴, Timothy³, James², Nicholas¹*), b. at Andover, 28 Sep 1745 son of Joseph and Dorothy (Johnson) Holt; d. at Wilton, after 1815 (when he was selectman at Wilton); m. by 1772, BETTY DALE, b. at Wilton, 2 Oct 1746 daughter of John and Mary (Ellinwood) Dale; Betty d. at Wilton, 10 Aug 1821.

Joseph and Betty resided in Wilton where their nine children were born. Their property was on lot number ten of the eighth range. Joseph served as selectman of Wilton for 14 years from 1796-1808 and again in 1815.[2694]

i JOSEPH HOLT, b. 17 Aug 1772; d. at Landgrove, VT, 27 Jun 1818; m. at Wilton, 18 Jul 1793, TRYPHENA PERRY, b. at Wilton, 29 Sep 1771 daughter of Abijah and Phebe (Boutwell) Perry; Tryphena d. at Landgrove, 29 May 1810.

2690 *New Hampshire. Probate Court (Hillsborough County), Probate Records, Vol 68, 1856-1869, pp 509-510*

2691 The names of Polly Cragin's parents and her date of birth are given on her burial card.

2692 Livermore, *History of the Town of Wilton*, p 407

2693 Ramsdell, *History of Milford*, volume 1, p 749

2694 Livermore, *History of the Town of Wilton*, p 50 and p 408

ii JOHN DALE HOLT, b. 9 May 1774; d. at Weston, VT, 26 Apr 1862; m. 20 Jun 1798, SARAH HALL, b. at Wilton, 26 Apr 1778 daughter of Timothy and Sarah (Keyes) Hall; Sarah d. at Weston, 27 Nov 1844.

iii SIMEON HOLT, b. 23 Feb 1776; d. at Wilton, 13 Feb 1847; m. about 1801, ESTHER D. BROOKS, b. at Dublin, NH, 1780 daughter of Joseph and Abigail (Perry) Brooks; Esther d. at Wilton, 1878.

iv BETTY HOLT, b. 28 Nov 1777; d. 15 Dec 1777.

v DOROTHY JOHNSON "DOLLY" HOLT, b. 18 Dec 1778; d. at Landgrove, VT; m. at Wilton, 18 Feb 1802, NATHAN FISKE, b. at Pepperell, 3 Jan 1769 son of Daniel and Elizabeth (Varnum) Fiske; Nathan d. at Landgrove, 1831.

vi BETSY HOLT, b. 3 Mar 1781; d. at Andover, VT, 27 Sep 1825; m. at Wilton, 13 Nov 1800, DANIEL PEABODY, b. at Wilton, 4 Jan 1778 son of Isaac and Miriam (Putnam) Peabody; Daniel d. at Andover, VT, 9 Nov 1853. Daniel married second Lucinda Wightman.

vii ANNA HOLT, b. 11 Apr 1783; d. 25 Mar 1784.

viii ANNA DALE HOLT, b. 4 Mar 1785; d. at New Ipswich, NH, 6 Dec 1851; m. at Wilton, 31 Dec 1805, JOHN WILSON, b. at New Ipswich, 28 May 1780 son of Supply and Susanna (Cutter) Wilson; John d. at New Ipswich, 3 Apr 1869.

1020) SIMEON HOLT (*Joseph⁴, Timothy³, James², Nicholas¹*), b. at Andover, 22 May 1752 son of Joseph and Dorothy (Johnson) Holt; d. at Weld, ME, 24 Feb 1833; m. 22 Sep 1778, MARY DALE, b. at Wilton, 26 Sep 1754 daughter of John and Mary (Ellinwood) Dale; Mary d. at Weld, 29 Jan 1837.[2695]

Simeon and Mary resided in Wilton for most of their lives, but in 1825 relocated to Weld, Maine where they lived with their daughter Sarah and her husband Joseph Russell.[2696]

Simeon Holt and Mary Dale were parents of eight children born at Wilton.

i MARY HOLT, b. 26 Dec 1778

ii SARAH HOLT, b. 21 Sep 1780; d. at Weld, ME, 13 Mar 1857; m. 8 Jan 1809, as his second wife, her fourth cousin, JOSEPH RUSSELL (*Bethiah Holt Russell⁵, Ephraim⁴, Henry³, Henry², Nicholas¹*), b. at Wilton, 6 May 1780 son of Thomas and Bethiah (Holt) Russell; Joseph d. at Weld, 28 Jun 1858. Joseph was first married to Hannah Dascomb.

iii RACHEL HOLT, b. 7 Feb 1783; d. after 1860 when she was living in Weld; m. 8 Jan 1809, her fourth cousin, TIMOTHY HOLT FRYE (*Elizabeth Holt Frye⁵, Timothy⁴, Nicholas³, Nicholas², Nicholas¹*), b. at Wilton, 27 Oct 1777 son of Isaac and Elizabeth (Holt) Frye; Timothy d. at Weld, 7 Jan 1830.

iv ABIAH HOLT, b. 30 Mar 1785; d. at Weld, ME, 17 Feb 1869; m. at Wilton, 23 May 1819, ANDREW PARKHURST, b. at Temple, NH, 14 Oct 1786 son of Andrew and Lydia (Chandler) Parkhurst; Andrew d. at Weld, 21 Nov 1871.

v JOHN JOHNSON HOLT, b. 21 Jul 1787; d. after 1870 when he was living at Steuben, NY; m. 30 Dec 1813, his fourth cousin, BETSEY BATCHELDER (*Phebe Holt Batchelder⁵, Joshua⁴, Nicholas³, Nicholas², Nicholas¹*), b. 29 May 1789 daughter of Joseph and Phebe (Holt) Batchelder; Betsey d. at Greenwood, NY, 4 Aug 1856.

vi JACOB HOLT, b. 3 Feb 1790; d. 24 Jan 1796.

vii DOLLY HOLT, b. 17 May 1793; d. 31 Jan 1796.

viii DOLLY HOLT, b. 26 Aug 1797

1021) MARY HOLT (*Joseph⁴, Timothy³, James², Nicholas¹*), b. at Andover, 24 Nov 1755 daughter of Joseph and Mary (Russell) Holt; d. at Wilton, 24 Oct 1844; m. at Wilton, 18 Nov 1779, EDWARD HERRICK, b. at Methuen, 9 Oct 1754 son of Edward and Mary (Kimball) Herrick; Edward d. at Wilton, 5 Feb 1811.

Edward and Mary located in Wilton at the time of their marriage, Edward arriving there in 1779. Edward purchased part of the estate of Caleb Putnam and also owned the mills at Barnes's Falls. Edward served as a Sergeant during the Revolution and was afterwards a Lieutenant in the New Hampshire militia.[2697]

In his will written 2 February 1811 (proved 9 April 1811), Edward Herrick bequeathed to son Benjamin thirty-eight dollars in addition to what he has received. Daughter Mary wife of John Putnam receives two dollars and thirty-three cents. Son George receives eight dollars. Son Edward receives three dollars and daughter Sarah Herrick, ten dollars. Daughter Anna Herrick receives eighty-eight dollars in one year or at the time of marriage if she marries earlier. Son Israel receives eighty-

2695 Foster, "Early Settlers of Weld," The Maine Historical and Genealogical Recorder, 1884, volume 1, p 123

2696 Foster, "Early Settlers of Weld," The Maine Historical and Genealogical Recorder, 1884, volume 1, p 123

2697 Livermore, *History of the Town of Wilton*, p 398

eight dollars at age twenty-one. Son Larkin receives sixty-eight dollars. To beloved wife Mary, he bequeaths all the real and personal estate to have and to hold to her Mary Herrick and her heirs forever. Mary is responsible to pay the debts and legacies and is named executrix.[2698]

Mary Holt and Edward Herrick were parents of nine children born at Wilton.

i BENJAMIN HERRICK, b. 13 Dec 1780; m. at Boston, 22 Jul 1807, ELCY NUGENT, b. at Stonington, CT, about 1781.

ii MARY HERRICK, b. 13 Apr 1782; d. at Dexter, ME, 16 Jun 1882; m. 7 Jul 1803, JOHN PUTNAM, b. at Wilton, 27 Nov 1774 son of Jacob and Abigail (Burnap) Putnam; John d. at Nashua, NH, 16 Mar 1835. Mary died in her 100th year believed to be, at that time, the longest living native of Wilton.[2699]

iii GEORGE HERRICK, b. 12 Feb 1784; d. at Wilton, after 1840; m. about 1808, his third cousin once removed, MARY "POLLY" HOLT (*Joel[6], John[5], John[4], Samuel[3], Samuel[2], Nicholas[1]*), b. at Wilton, 17 Apr 1787 daughter of Joel and Mary (Coburn) Holt; Mary d. after 1850 when she was living with her son Daniel H. Herrick in Wilton. George and Mary lived in Weston, VT just after their marriage and their oldest two children were born there. They then returned to Wilton and George is last noted on the 1840 census.

iv EDWARD HERRICK, b. 29 Oct 1785; d. at Wilton, 9 Dec 1873; m. 1st 27 Dec 1810, NANCY BARRETT, b. at Westford, MA, 28 Dec 1790 daughter of Ebenezer and Jane (Reed) Barrett; Nancy d. 27 Nov 1824. Edward m. 2nd 22 Nov 1825, his second cousin once removed, MARY ANDREWS (*Mary Chandler Andrews[6], Isaac Chandler[5], Priscilla Holt Chandler[4], Timothy[3], James[2], Nicholas[1]*), b. at Hillsborough, 1 Jan 1796 daughter of Abraham and Mary (Chandler) Andrews.[2700]

v SARAH HERRICK, b. 27 Dec 1788; d. at Norridgewock, ME, 17 Mar 1866; m. 8 Sep 1814, JOSIAH PEET, b. at Bethlehem, CT, 21 Jun 1780 son of Benjamin and Elizabeth (Hendee) Peet; Josiah d. at Norridgewock, 17 Feb 1852. Rev. Josiah Peet was a minister at Norridgewock; he was the subject of a memoir written by David Shepley.[2701]

vi ANNA HERRICK, b. 6 Dec 1790; d. at Wilton, 7 Oct 1873; m. at Wilton, 6 Oct 1814, ELIJAH STOCKWELL, b. at Westborough, MA, 14 May 1784 son of Daniel and Rebecca (Warren) Stockwell; Elijah d. at Wilton, 26 Jul 1852.

vii ISRAEL HERRICK, b. 9 Jul 1794; d. at Lyndeborough, 18 Feb 1866; m. 1st at Milford, 28 Nov 1822, ELIZA H. BURNS, b. at Milford, 24 Nov 1802 son of Samuel and Abigail (Jones) Burns;[2702] Eliza d. at Milford, 28 Nov 1848. Israel m. 2nd 12 Dec 1849, his third cousin once removed, EMELINE GRAY (*Joseph Gray[5], Timothy Gray[4], Braviter Gray[3], Hannah Holt Gray[2], Nicholas[1]*), b. at Wilton, 11 Oct 1811 daughter of Joseph and Chloe (Abbott) Gray; Emeline d. at Lyndeborough, 3 Jun 1891. Israel graduated from the medical school at Dartmouth College and was a homeopathic physician.[2703]

viii DIADAMIA HERRICK, b. 1 Jan 1797; d. 6 Feb 1797.

ix LARKIN HERRICK, b. 16 Dec 1799; d. at Wilton, 6 Nov 1866; m. at Wilton, 17 May 1827, SARAH SHELDON, b. at Wilton, 19 Jul 1804 daughter of Samuel and Phebe (Keyes) Sheldon; Sarah d. at Lebanon, NH, 2 May 1891.

1022) RHODA HOLT (*Joseph[4], Timothy[3], James[2], Nicholas[1]*), b. at Andover, 16 Oct 1757 daughter of Joseph and Mary (Russell) Holt; d. at Wilton, 25 Jul 1799, m. 25 Nov 1778, JOHN DALE, b. 26 Jul 1748 son of John and Mary (Ellinwood) Dale; John d. at Wilton, 11 Jul 1809. After Rhoda's death, John married Lydia Lamon.

John Dale was a farmer in Wilton living on the family homestead. He served during the Revolution at Winter Hill and at White Plains.[2704]

In his will written 20 May 1809 (proved 10 August 1809), John Dale bequeathed to beloved wife Lydia a list of annual provisions to be provided by the executor and other specified support which were in lieu of her thirds. Daughter Rhoda wife of Ebenezer Hutchinson receives five dollars. Daughter Abigail wife of Abel Fiske receives $21.75. Daughter Polly receives $200 in five years or earlier if she marries. Daughters Anna, Betsey, and Sally also each receive $200 within a specified number of years or at the time of marriage. Son Lemon received $200 when he arrives at age twenty-one and daughter Lydia receives $130. Sons John and Ebenezer receive all the real and personal estate to be equally divided. They are responsible for the maintenance Mrs. Dale and their unmarried sisters. John and Ebenezer were named executors.[2705] Lamon and Lydia were children from John's second marriage to Lydia Lamon.

[2698] *New Hampshire. Probate Court (Hillsborough County), Probate Records volume 17, pp 210-211*

[2699] Livermore, *History of the Town of Wilton*, p 480

[2700] Chandler, *Descendants and William and Annis Chandler*, p 619

[2701] Shepley, David, Memoir with Sermons of Rev. Josiah Peet, 1854; New York: NY, John F. Trow, Printer

[2702] Ramsdell, *History of Milford*, p 612

[2703] Livermore, *History of the Town of Wilton*, p 399

[2704] Livermore, *History of the Town of Wilton*, p 357

[2705] *New Hampshire. Probate Court (Hillsborough County), Probate Records volume 16, pp 263-266*

Rhoda Holt and John Dale were parents of eleven children born at Wilton.

i JOHN DALE, b. 6 Jan 1779; d. 7 Jan 1779.

ii RHODA DALE, b. 15 Feb 1780; d. at Weld, ME, 27 Jun 1852; m. 22 Dec 1803, EBENEZER HUTCHINSON, b. at Wilton, 18 Sep 1780 son of Ebenezer and Phebe (Sawtell) Hutchinson; Ebenezer d. at Weld, 23 Jan 1845.

iii ABIGAIL DALE, b. 7 Nov 1781; d. at Wilton, 26 Jan 1852; m. 12 Apr 1804, ABEL FISKE, b. at Wilton, 24 Jul 1784 son of Abel and Anna (Spaulding) Fiske; Abel d. at Wilton, 25 Sep 1877.

iv MARY DALE, b. 10 Sep 1783; d. after 1860 when she was living in Wilton; m. 8 Aug 1811, FREDERICK HUTCHINSON, b. at Wilton 10 Jul 1783 son of Samuel and Mary (Wilkins) Hutchinson; Frederick d. at Wilton, 18 Dec 1850.

v JOHN DALE, b. 3 Aug 1785; d. at Wilton, 12 Apr 1843; m. 1st about 1824, NANCY BEEDE, b. at Sandwich, NH, 1796 son of John and Sarah (Sleeper) Beede;[2706] Nancy d. at Wilton, 7 Oct 1825. John m. 2nd at New Boston, 3 May 1827, MARY ANN COCHRAN, b. at New Boston, about 1805 daughter of James and Jane (Crombie) Cochran;[2707] Mary d. at New Boston, 4 Oct 1876.

vi EBENEZER DALE, b. 17 Mar 1788; d. at Sandwich, NH, 1 Sep 1862; m. about 1824, MEHITABLE BEEDE, b. at Sandwich, 12 Apr 1800 daughter of John and Sarah (Sleeper) Beede; Mehitable d. at Sandwich, 14 Aug 1861.

vii ANNA DALE, b. 20 Nov 1789; d. at Francestown, 16 Sep 1862; m. 22 Jan 1834, as his second wife, ABNER BLANCHARD, b. at Wilton, 31 May 1787 son of Benjamin and Sarah (Griffin) Blanchard; Abel d. 24 Mar 1855. Abner was first married to Hannah Tarbell.

viii SALLY DALE, b. 3 Dec 1791; d. 6 Jun 1796.

ix BETSEY DALE, b. 10 Jul 1793; d. at Milford, NH, Mar 1852; m. 7 Dec 1815, JESSE RAYMOND, b. at Mont Vernon, 1792 son of Nathaniel and Phebe (Dodge) Raymond;[2708] Jesse d. at Milford, 14 Jul 1864.

x SUMNER DALE, b. 20 Jun 1795; d. 25 Jun 1796.

xi SARAH DALE, b. 4 Aug 1797; d. at Weld, ME, 17 May 1862; m. 25 Dec 1817, JOHN BURTON, b. at Wilton, 25 Oct 1796 son of Abraham and Elizabeth (Dale) Burton; John d. at Weld, 24 Feb 1873.

1023) VALENTINE HOLT (*Joseph⁴, Timothy³, James², Nicholas¹*), b. at Andover (recorded at Wilton), 25 Dec 1763 and baptized at Andover 1 Jan 1764 son of Joseph and Mary (Russell) Holt; d. at Mercer, ME, 6 Dec 1840; m. at Wilton, 13 Sep 1787, ANNA "NANCY" GOODRICH whose parents have not been identified. Nancy likely died before 1810. Valentine married second HANNAH DAY, b. about 1792. Hannah d. after 1860 when she was living with her son in Augusta, Maine.

Valentine was born in Andover but went with his family to Wilton. He married and had eight children there with his first wife. It is not known if Anna died before or after the family move to Maine, but Valentine and his family were in Maine about 1803. There Valentine had a second marriage to Hannah Day and there is record evidence for five children from his second marriage.

On 10 March 1840, Valentine Holt then aged seventy-six of Mercer, Maine (where he had lived for about thirty-seven years), made a statement related to his application for a pension. He enlisted 5 February 1777 in Capt. Benjamin Farnham's company of Col. Tupper's regiment of the Massachusetts line. He served as a waiter for Capt. Farnham who was his brother-in-law.[2709] He served more than nine months and was discharged the end of November 1777. He reported being born in Andover 25 December 1763 and then moving with his father's family to Wilton, which is where he resided at his enlistment. His father Joseph had a man with a sleigh carry him from Wilton to Worcester where Valentine met Capt. Farnham. The company went to Danbury for winter quarters and in the spring went to Fishkill, then to Newburgh on the North River, and from there to Saratoga. Capt. Farnham then sent Valentine to Andover and on to Wilton on business where Valentine stayed four or five days. At that time, there was need of militia due to the advance of General Burgoyne and Valentine joined the company of Capt. Goff and was at the Battle of Bennington. He then re-joined with Capt. Farnham and was at Stillwater for five days before being sent to West Point for discharge. In June 1780, he enlisted in the New Hampshire line in the company of Capt. William Barron for three months. He then marched to Hudson, New York. After the desertion of General Arnold, Valentine was sent to West Point where he was discharged October 1780. Valentine went on to say that he sought assistance of Capt. Vose about six years previously to obtain his pension, but Capt. Vose died, and Valentine heard no more about it. The pension application was rejected as the service as a waiter was not provided for unless he had been previously enlisted and detached from the ranks to

[2706] The 1841 will of John Beede of Sandwich includes bequests to his granddaughter Nancy B. Dale child of his deceased daughter and to his daughter Mehitable Dale (who married Ebenezer Dale).

[2707] Mary Ann's parents are given as James and Jane Cochran on her death record.

[2708] Smith, *History of the Town of Mont Vernon*, Genealogies, p 128

[2709] Capt. Benjamin Farnum was married to Valentine's half-sister Dolly Holt.

be a waiter. He was not enlisted and paid as a soldier. His service of three months, sixteen days in 1780 was not long enough to qualify for a pension.[2710]

Children of Valentine Holt and Anna Goodrich:

i NANCY HOLT, b. at Wilton, 13 Mar 1788; m. at Charlestown, MA, 31 May 1812, JAMES WHITTIER who is not yet identified.

ii AMMI RUHAMA HOLT, b. at Wilton, 8 Jun 1789; d. at Clayton, NY, 1827; m. MARTHA ABBOTT, b. about 1800; Martha d. at Clayton, 28 Jan 1850.

iii LYDIA PORTER HOLT, b. 17 Aug 1791; d. 28 Jul 1792.

iv LYDIA PORTER HOLT, b. at Wilton, 13 May 1793; d. at Barre, VT, 9 Feb 1868; m. at Lyndeborough, 25 May 1815, ROBERT PARKER, b. 1789; Robert d. at Barre, 7 Apr 1831.

v HANNAH GOODRICH HOLT, b. at Wilton, 15 May 1795; m. at Charlestown, MA, 7 Oct 1818, JOHN SYLVESTER, b. about 1788; John d. at Charlestown, 14 Dec 1848.

vi SAMUEL GOODRICH HOLT, b. 14 Apr 1797

vii ISRAEL HOLT, b. 1 Aug 1799

viii ROBERT GOODRICH HOLT, b. at Wilton, 15 Jan 1802; m. at Lyndeborough, 10 Sep 1822, LUCY LAKIN, b. at Lyndeborough, about 1802 daughter of Thomas and Lucy (Burton) Lakin.

Children of Valentine Holt and Hannah Day:

i VALENTINE HOLT, b. 18 Nov 1812; d. at Chelsea, ME, 22 Jan 1899; m. about 1836, MARY ANN MORRILL, b. about 1814; Mary Ann d. at Augusta, ME, after 1870 and before 1880.

ii SARAH D. HOLT, b. about 1818;[2711] d. at Boston, 28 Feb 1874; m. HENRY D. BROWN, b. in ME, about 1818; Henry d. during the Civil War, enlisted 29 Feb 1864 and did not survive the war. Sarah and Henry lived in Maine where Henry was a blacksmith. They were parents of eight children.

iii MARY HARRICK HOLT, b. at Rome, ME, 23 Apr 1818; d. at Chelsea, MA, 1 Jan 1906; m. at Lowell, MA, 1 Aug 1842, SAMUEL ALDEN RICH, b. 25 Aug 1812 son of Ezekiel and Elizabeth (Brown) Rich; Samuel d. at Chelsea, MA, 5 Aug 1890.

iv ANNA T. HOLT, b. at Mercer, ME, about 1819; d. at Charlestown, MA, 6 Aug 1873; m. 1st at Hallowell, ME, 4 Jun 1842, HENRY C. SLADE. Anna m. 2nd C. C. FOSTER who is not yet identified.

v WESLEY RUSSELL HOLT, b. at Mercer, 10 Aug 1829; d. at South Gardiner, ME, 28 Jan 1902; m. at Somersworth, NH, 4 Apr 1850, ANN WITHAM, b. 1830; Ann d. at Hallowell, ME, 31 Aug 1869.

1024) ESTHER HOLT (*Joseph[4], Timothy[3], James[2], Nicholas[1]*), b. at Wilton, 25 Jul 1766 daughter of Joseph and Mary (Russell) Holt; d. at Lyndeborough, 14 Jul 1839; m. about 1791, EBENEZER PEARSON, b. at Reading, MA, 19 Jun 1768 son of Amos and Elizabeth (Nichols) Pearson; Ebenezer d. at Lyndeborough, 22 May 1852.

There are four children known for Esther Holt and Ebenezer Pearson with the births recorded at Wilton or Lyndeborough. The family lived in Lyndeborough.

i ESTHER PEARSON, b. at Wilton, 11 Nov 1792; d. at Lyndeborough, 12 Mar 1856; m. 8 Feb 1814, EPHRAIM PUTNAM, b. at Lyndeborough, 30 Apr 1785 son of Ephraim and Rachel (Cram) Putnam; Ephraim d. at Lyndeborough, 11 Jun 1862.

ii EBENEZER PEARSON, b. at Lyndeborough, 11 Jan 1797; d. at Hancock, NH, 6 Aug 1864; m. 1824, JOANNA KARR, b. at Lyndeborough, 6 Apr 1803 daughter of James and Sarah (Huse) Karr; Joanna d. at Hancock, 5 Aug 1874.

iii ABIGAIL PEARSON, b. at Wilton, 16 Aug 1800; d. at Lyndeborough, 26 Jun 1879; m. 10 Nov 1844, as his second wife, MARK HADLEY, b. at Lyndeborough, 19 Apr 1793 son of Joshua and Betsey (Giddings) Hadley; Mark d. at Lyndeborough, 26 Mar 1858. Mark was first married to Elizabeth Herrick.

[2710] U.S. Revolutionary War Pension and Bounty-Land Application Files, Case R5188

[2711] Names of parents are given as Valentine Holt and Hannah on her death record.

iv WILLARD PEARSON, b. at Lyndeborough, 21 May 1806; d. at Woburn, MA, 31 Mar 1841; m. 7 Jul 1833, ANN P. CHILD, b. at Medford, MA, 15 Dec 1810 daughter of Aaron and Catherine (Floyd) Child;[2712] Ann d. at Woburn, 21 Nov 1886.

1025) TIMOTHY PHELPS (*Phebe Holt Phelps⁴, Timothy³, James², Nicholas¹*), b. at Hollis, 10 Sep 1745 son of Francis and Phebe (Holt) Phelps; d. at Shirley, MA, 26 Dec 1826; m. at Harvard, MA, 28 Jun 1768, SARAH FARNSWORTH, b. 1746; Sarah d. at Shirley, 12 Jul 1827.

There are records for three children of Timothy Phelps and Sarah Farnsworth.[2713]

i JOHN PHELPS, b. at Harvard, MA, 8 Mar 1769; d. before 1829 (wife's remarriage); m. at Shirley. MA, 13 Mar 1794, MARY "POLLY" BROWN, b. at Shirley, 19 Mar 1775 daughter of Joseph and Mary (Longley) Brown; Mary d. at Wilbraham, 4 Apr 1851. Mary married second Richard Firmin on 1 Feb 1829.

ii SALLY PHELPS, baptized at Harvard, 4 Oct 1772; d. at Shirley, 1 Jan 1848; m. at Shirley, 17 Nov 1796, WILLIAM CONANT, b. at Ashburnham, 17 Aug 1765 son of Jonathan and Eunice (Farwell) Conant; William d. at Shirley, 5 Aug 1846.

iii JACOB PHELPS, b. at Harvard, 8 May 1775; d. at Shrewsbury, 29 Aug 1857; m. 29 Nov 1798, SUSIE DICKINSON, b. at Shirley, 6 Sep 1774 daughter of James and Priscilla (Harris) Dickinson; Susie d. at Shirley, 10 Dec 1855.

1026) JOSEPH PHELPS (*Phebe Holt Phelps⁴, Timothy³, James², Nicholas¹*), b. at Hollis, 19 Jun 1748 son of Francis and Phebe (Holt) Phelps; d. at Danvers, MA, 22 May 1835;[2714] m. 1st at Tewksbury, 7 Mar 1771, RUTH FRENCH, b. at Andover, 4 May 1747 daughter of John and Phebe (Marshall) French; Ruth d. at Tewksbury, 4 May 1789. Joseph m. 2nd at Tewksbury, 28 Dec 1790, ISABEL DUTTON, b. at Tewksbury, 28 Jul 1762 daughter of Timothy and Elizabeth (Sanders) Dutton; Isabel d. at Tewksbury, 20 Mar 1824.

Joseph Phelps was a farmer and he lived primarily in Tewksbury where the births of all his children are recorded, but later relocated to Danvers. On 25 March 1830, Joseph Phelps of Tewksbury, for the payment of twenty-five dollars, conveyed property of Francis Phelps of Danvers.[2715]

Son Theodore Phelps did not have children and his estate probate listed the following heirs, in addition to his widow Betsey, on 7 April 1863: brothers Jonathan Phelps and Joel Phelps of Andover; brother Samuel Phelps, if living, of unknown residence; brother Henry Phelps of Tewksbury; Nathan Mears, Edwards Mears, and Abner Frost all nephews of Tewksbury; Elizabeth C. Phelps, Sarah Phelps, and Abigail Moulton wife of Benjamin Moulton all nieces of Lynn; Hannah Phelps of niece of South Danvers; Junius Phelps a nephew of parts unknown; brother Timothy Phelps of Dedham; Joel, Francis, David and several unknown children of Elisha Phelps, a brother, who is deceased; Jacob Sheldon a nephew and Mary Bailey a niece of Salem, New Hampshire; Francis A. Phelps a nephew of Reading; and George Phelps a nephew of Chelsea.[2716]

Joseph Phelps and Ruth French were parents of eleven children born at Tewksbury.

i RUTH PHELPS, b. 30 Aug 1771; d. at Tewksbury, 28 Apr 1853; m. at Tewksbury, 26 Sep 1803, EPHRAIM FROST, b. at Tewksbury, 25 Sep 1768 son of Ephraim and Mary (Patton) Frost; Ephraim d. at Tewksbury, 15 Aug 1826.

ii FRANCIS PHELPS, b. 30 Nov 1772; d. at Danvers, 15 Jan 1836; m. at Danvers, 1 May 1802, HANNAH DUNCKLEE, b. at Danvers, 5 Jan 1779 daughter of Hezekiah and Katharine (Marsh) Duncklee; Hannah d. at Danvers, 23 Dec 1842.

iii JOSEPH PHELPS, b. 3 Apr 1774; d. at Salem, 7 Jan 1858; m. at Danvers, 19 Jan 1804, EUNICE GARDNER, b. at Danvers, 28 Sep 1772 daughter of Thomas and Mary (Buffington) Gardner; Eunice d. at Danvers, 2 Aug 1811.

iv HANNAH PHELPS, b. 17 Oct 1775; d. 10 Nov 1775.

v ISAAC PHELPS, b. 5 Mar 1777; d. 22 Sep 1778.

vi ISAAC PHELPS, b. 30 Dec 1778; d. at the West Indies, 27 Jul 1800. "Isaac, s. Joseph and Ruth (French), on his passage from the West Indies, July 27, 1800. PR8"

2712 The names of Ann's parents are given as Aaron and Catharine on her death record.

2713 The Phelps genealogy gives daughter Rachel who married Ephraim Pollard in 1793 as a child in this family. Rachel Pollard died in 1793 just after her marriage in the 27th year of her age making her born in 1766 two years before the marriage of Timothy and Sarah. There was not a birth or baptism record located for a daughter Rachel.

2714 Phelps, *The Phelps Family in America*, volume 2, p 1610

2715 Massachusetts Land Records, Middlesex County, 297:70

2716 *Essex County, MA: Probate File Papers, 1638-1881.* Online database. *AmericanAncestors.org.* New England Historic Genealogical Society, 2014. Case 50067

vii JONATHAN PHELPS, b. 1 Sep 1780; d. at Andover, 1 Mar 1866; m. at Andover, 21 Dec 1811, his second cousin, ABIGAIL ABBOTT (*Moses Abbott⁵, Hannah Holt Abbott⁴, Timothy³, James², Nicholas¹*), b. at Andover, 22 Dec 1783 daughter of Moses and Elizabeth (Holt) Abbott; Abigail d. at Andover, 9 Aug 1827.

viii SAMUEL PHELPS, b. 12 Mar 1782; d. at Lexington, MA, 31 Mar 1863; m. at Lunenburg, SALLY BROOKS, b. at Plymouth, 11 Feb 1782 daughter of Samuel and Hephzibah (-) Brooks;[2717] Sally d. at Cambridge, 28 Feb 1875.

ix ELISHA PHELPS, b. 18 Aug 1784; d. at Northfield, NH, 19 Aug 1836; m. at Tewksbury, 7 Feb 1814, MARY FRENCH, *perhaps* b. at Salisbury, MA, 19 Feb 1792 daughter of Moses and Elizabeth (-) French; Mary d. at Northfield, 9 Dec 1869.

x MARY PHELPS, b. 30 Jun 1786; d. at Salem, NH (according to brother's probate record); m. at Tewksbury, 8 Oct 1815, AMOS SHELDON, b. at Danvers, 20 Mar 1791 son of Amos and Polly (Foster) Sheldon; Amos d. at Danvers, 1 Dec 1836.

xi JACOB PHELPS, b. 8 Aug 1788; d. at Danvers, 12 Apr 1834; m. at Boston, 15 Dec 1811, REBECCA REED, likely b. at Danvers, 4 Apr 1790 daughter of William and Elizabeth (Manning) Reed.

Joseph Phelps and Isabel Dutton were parents of six children born at Tewksbury.

i LYDIA PHELPS, b. 22 Aug 1791. Lydia is not mentioned in the probate of her brother Theodore either as living or as having heirs. There is an entry in the Tewksbury records for a daughter of Joseph dying in 1818 but with the name torn or not readable for the transcription and *perhaps* this refers to Lydia. "———, d. Joseph, ——— , 1818. CR1"

ii TIMOTHY PHELPS, b. 11 May 1793; d. at Dedham, 24 Mar 1883; m. at Bedford, 5 Oct 1823, DORCAS CHAMBERLAIN, b. at Bedford, MA, 6 Dec 1797 daughter of Phineas and Dorcas (Varnum) Chamberlain; Dorcas d. at Dedham, 2 Nov 1881.

iii THEODORE PHELPS, b. 9 Aug 1795; d. at Salem (although resident of Danvers), 6 Mar 1863; m. at Danvers, 21 Apr 1824, BETSEY FOSTER SHELDON, b. at Danvers, 14 Feb 1795 daughter of Amos and Polly (Foster) Sheldon; Betsey d. at Middleton, 9 May 1881.

iv JOEL PHELPS, b. 12 Jun 1798; d. at Andover, 14 Jun 1872; m. at Andover, 23 Dec 1824, LYDIA A. THOMPSON of Charlestown, b. 18 Mar 1800 (on gravestone); Lydia d. at Andover, 1 Nov 1841.

v HANNAH PHELPS, b. 12 Jun 1801; d. at Medford, 5 Jun 1860; m. at Tewksbury, 12 May 1826, RUSSELL MEARS, b. at Tewksbury, about 1800 son of Russell and Susanna (Dutton) Mears; Russell d. at Medford, 18 Jun 1860.

vi HENRY PHELPS, b. 17 Jul 1806; d. at Tewksbury, 16 May 1886; m. at Tewksbury, 21 Feb 1828, BETSEY FOSTER, b. at Tewksbury, about 1800 daughter of Joseph and Sarah (Frost) Foster;[2718] Betsey d. at Tewksbury, 1 Sep 1883.

1027) DORCAS HOLT (*Joseph⁴, Joseph³, James², Nicholas¹*), b. at York, 10 Apr 1737 daughter of Joseph and Mary (Farnum) Holt; d. at Georgetown, ME, 2 Feb 1827; m. at York, 1 Sep 1755, THOMAS DONNELL, b. at York, 29 Jul 1731 son of Nathaniel and Elizabeth (Todd) Donnell.

Thomas Donnell was a first settler of Donnell Island, Maine which is now known as MacMahan Island. Thomas Donnell built his house on the island in 1761. The name of the island changed to MacMahan after two of the Donnell daughters married two McMahan brothers.[2719]

Dorcas Holt and Thomas Donnell were parent of four children, two of the births at Georgetown and two at York.

i MARY DONNELL, b. at Georgetown, 30 Oct 1756; d. at Georgetown, 29 Dec 1807; m. at Georgetown, 24 Aug 1788, TIMOTHY MCMAHAN, b. at Georgetown, 21 May 1762 son of Torrence and Elizabeth (Donnell) McMahan; Timothy d. at Georgetown, 5 Apr 1849.

ii SARAH DONNELL, b. at Georgetown, 27 Jan 1758; d. at Georgetown, 25 Jun 1825; m. at Georgetown, 6 Fen 1778, DANIEL MCMAHAN, b. at Georgetown, 22 Jun 1750 son of Torrence and Elizabeth (Donnell) McMahan; Daniel d. at Georgetown, 1 Dec 1835.

iii TIMOTHY DONNELL, b. at York, 12 Oct 1759; m. at York, 23 Oct 1779, ALICE HARRIS. There is a record of one child of Timothy and Alice born at York.

[2717] Sally's parents are given and Samuel and Hephzibah Brooks on her death record and place of birth is given as Plymouth.

[2718] The names of Betsey's parents are given as Joseph and Sarah on her death record.

[2719] Reynolds, *Images of America: Georgetown*, p 8

iv DEBORAH DONNELL, b. at York, 12 Jun 1761; d. at Westport, ME, 5 Jun 1852; m. 2 Jan 1793, THOMAS BROOKS, b. 10 Jul 1768 son of Charles and Hannah (Rowell) Brooks; Thomas d. at Westport, 24 Feb 1833.

1028) EBENEZER HOLT (*Joseph⁴, Joseph³, James², Nicholas¹*), b. at York, 29 Dec 1745 son of Joseph and Mary (Farnum) Holt; m. at York, 14 Feb 1767, CHARITY RHOADS daughter of Miles Rhoads.

There are two children known for Ebenezer Holt and Charity Rhoads.

i TIMOTHY HOLT, b. at York, 28 Dec 1768

ii JOSEPH HOLT, b. at York, 9 Apr 1770; *perhaps* m. at Boston, 7 Dec 1800, PHEBE ABORN

1029) HANNAH HOLT (*Benjamin⁴, Joseph³, James², Nicholas¹*), b. at York, 9 Oct 1746 daughter of Benjamin and Hannah (Moulton) Holt; m. at York, 19 Oct 1765, her first cousin, NATHANIEL RAYNES (*Hannah Holt Raynes⁴, Joseph³, James², Nicholas¹*), b. at York, about 1740 son of Nathan and Hannah (Holt) Raynes; Nathaniel d. at York, 1802 (probate 18 Oct 1802).

In his will written 7 July 1802 (proved 18 October 1802), Nathaniel Raynes bequeathed to wife Hannah, in addition to her dower in the real estate, the use and improvement of all the household furniture and indoor movables. Hannah also has the use of two cows which are to be wintered and summered on the farm by son Stephen. Daughter Dorcas the wife of Obadiah Gerrish receives five dollars which completes her full portion. Sons Benjamin Raynes and Jotham Raynes each receives one dollar to complete their portions. Son Nathan Raynes receives six acres of land in York which is a property that was purchased from Elder Joseph Holt. Daughter Hannah receives a bed and bedding, and the use of all the furniture in the room she occupies and use of the room while she is single. Son John receives one dollar to complete his portion. Son Stephen Raynes receives the homestead farm in York and the remainder of the estate. Stephen is also named executor.[2720]

Hannah Holt and Nathaniel Raynes were parents of seven children born at York.

i DORCAS RAYNES, b. about 1767; d. at York, 1849; m. at York by Rev Isaac Lyman on 6 Jun 1793, OBADIAH GERRISH, *perhaps* the Obadiah baptized a Kittery, Jul 1766 son of Benjamin and Elizabeth (Hill) Gerrish; Obadiah d. at York, 1824 (probate 9 Aug 1824). In 1830, widow Dorcas Gerrish was head of household in York with no others in the household. Dorcas and Obadiah seem not to have had children as in his will written 12 April 1809, Obadiah leaves his entire estate to his wife Dorcas to be hers forever.

ii BENJAMIN RAYNES, b. about 1769; d. before 1818 (probate 1818); m. at York, 18 Nov 1791, ELIZABETH PAYNE who was his widow at probate. Benjamin was a mariner.

iii JOTHAM RAYNES, b. 22 Mar 1772; d. at Vienna, ME, Oct 1816 (probate 1816); m. 1st ABIGAIL who is not identified, but who died at Vienna 5 Jan 1811. Jotham m. 2nd DAMARIS, b. about 1778 and d. at Parkman, ME, 19 Nov 1857. Jotham's will names two sons, Robert and Jotham. There is a record for a third son, Gerish, who was born 22 Aug 1810 and died 22 Nov 1811.

iv NATHAN RAYNES, b. estimate 1774; m. 24 Mar 1802, HANNAH HAMMOND, b. at Kittery, about 1780 daughter of George and Mary (Weeks) Hammond.[2721] Nathan and Hannah resided in York.

v HANNAH RAYNES, b. estimate 1777; living and unmarried in 1802.

vi JOHN RAYNES, b. 27 Apr 1780; d. at Moscow, IN, 12 Dec 1861; m. Jan 1803, LUCY MORRILL, b. at Salisbury, MA, 4 Oct 1786 daughter of Daniel and Betsey (Osgood) Morrill; Lucy d. at Moscow, 6 Apr 1834.

vii STEPHEN RAYNES, b. about 1782; d. at York, Jan 1850; m. MARY SWETT.[2722]

1030) DORCAS HOLT (*Benjamin⁴, Joseph³, James², Nicholas¹*), b. at York, 21 Nov 1756 daughter of Benjamin and Hannah (Moulton) Holt; d. about 1793; m. 8 Feb 1776, DANIEL MOULTON, b. at York, 31 Mar 1755 son of Abel and Judith (-) Moulton; Daniel d. 1836 (probate 13 Sep 1836). Daniel married second, Abigail Young.

Daniel and Dorcas resided in York where Daniel was a farmer. He also served captain in a company of the state militia.[2723]

In his will written 5 September 1833 (probate 13 Sep 1836), Daniel Moulton of York bequeaths to beloved wife Abigail, in addition to her dower, one cow, two sheep, half the household furniture and indoor movables except for one bed which will go to his granddaughter. Son Josiah Moulton receives one undivided half of the real and personal estate in York as well as another strip of land that adjoins his dwelling house. But Josiah is to relinquish any claim to George of another strip of land. Son George receives the dwelling house, salt marsh which he purchased from Abel Moulton, and one-eighth part of the sawmill which is Daniel's part of the mill. George receives the other undivided half of the real and personal estate. Daughter Hannah Goodwin receives fifteen dollars and daughter Dorcas Moulton receives ten dollars. Daughter Abigail Moulton receives the other half of

---

[2720] Maine, York County, Probate Estate Files, 1690-1917, case 15710

[2721] Fogg, "Early Families of Eliot and Kittery, Maine", Old Eliot, 1902, vol. 5, no 1, p 23

[2722] Mary Swett is giving as the mother's name on the death record of Stephen's daughter Mary Ann.

[2723] Little, *Genealogical and Family History of the State of Maine*, volume 1, p 416

the household furniture, the use of a room in the house, and yearly provisions to be provided by Josiah. Granddaughter Dorcas Moulton, daughter of George, receives a bed. George was named sole executor. In a codicil written 23 April 1835, Daniel notes that his wife has died and that the personal estate that had gone to his wife will now go to George, except for a silver tankard which had come from his wife Abigail's father Samuel Young. The tankard is to go to daughter Abigail. Further, there has been a change in the future prospects of son Josiah, so that George will now be responsible for the debts and legacies, and George will also receive all the real and personal property that had gone to Josiah. The heirs signing consent to the will and codicil on 6 August 1836 were Josiah Moulton, Abigail Moulton, Abel Moulton, Jr., Dorcas Moulton, John Goodwin, and Hannah Goodwin.[2724]

Dorcas Holt and Daniel Moulton were parents of seven children born at York. Daniel also had a daughter Abigail from his second marriage.

i NOAH MOULTON, baptized 7 May 1777; he was a mariner and lost at sea.[2725]

ii DORCAS MOULTON, baptized 4 August 1778; died young.

iii JOSIAH MOULTON, baptized 9 Jun 1782; d. after 1850 when he was living at York; m. 1st about 1811, OLIVE LOWE. Josiah m. 2nd MARIA BRADBURY.

iv HENRY MOULTON, baptized 19 Sep 1784; died young.

v GEORGE MOULTON, baptized 14 Oct 1787; d. at York, 3 Mar 1859; m. 1st at York, 10 Sep 1806, NANCY MOULTON, b. at York, 20 Apr 1788 daughter of Ebenezer and Anne (Bradbury) Moulton; Nancy d. at York, 30 Jul 1822. George m. 2nd 12 Mar 1823, SALLY MYRICK, b. 1787; Sally d. at York, 4 Jul 1857.

vi HANNAH MOULTON, b. 25 Mar 1790; m. at York, 30 Nov 1811, EBENEZER GRANT; Ebenezer d. at York, 1823 (probate 24 Nov 1823). Hannah m. 2nd at York, 14 Jun 1831, JOHN GOODWIN.

vii DORCAS MOULTON, b. 16 Nov 1792; d. at York, 18 Jan 1879; m. at York, Sep 1813, ABEL MOULTON, b. at York, 10 Nov 1785 son of John and Lydia (Grant) Moulton; Abel d. at York, 14 Sep 1852.

1031) DORCAS RAYNES (*Hannah Holt Raynes⁴, Joseph³, James², Nicholas¹*), b. at York, about 1741 daughter of Nathan and Hannah (Holt) Raynes; d. at York, 13 Oct 1828; m. at York, 25 Nov 1760, GEORGE MOORE; George d. at York, 1816 (probate 16 May 1816).

George Moore did not leave a will. Inventory of his estate was made 4 June 1816 with real estate valued at $2,000 and personal estate at $452.21. George also held notes of money owed him totaling about $1,200. On 19 July 1816, the following heirs singed that they have received their distribution from the estate: Joseph Moor, Hannah Sewell, Betsey Moore, Samuel Payne, and Nancy Payne.[2726]

There are five children known for Dorcas Raynes and George Moore.

i JOSEPH MOORE, b. estimate 1765; m. at York, 1 Sep 1793, SUSANNAH ALLEN.

ii HANNAH MOORE, b. at York, 10 Jun 1766; d. at York, 15 Jun 1834; m. at York, 15 Dec 1800, NATHANIEL SEWALL, b. at York, 29 Apr 1760 son of John and Joanna (Stone) Sewall; Nathaniel d. at Alfred, ME, 9 Jan 1814.

iii BETSEY MOORE, unmarried in 1816.

iv GEORGE MOORE, b. 14 May 1777; d. at York, 2 Nov 1828 (probate 1829); m. about 1802, BETSEY HARRIS, b. at York, 19 Oct 1779 daughter of Joseph and Elizabeth (Raynes) Harris; Betsey d. at York, 14 Nov 1841.[2727]

v NANCY MOORE, b. about 1784 (based on census); d. after 1850 when she was living at York; m. at York, 18 Jan 1809, SAMUEL PAYNE, b. about 1777; Samuel d. after 1850.

1032) ELIZABETH INGRAHAM (*Lydia Holt Ingraham⁴, Joseph³, James², Nicholas¹*), b. at York, 6 Aug 1743 daughter of Edward and Lydia (Holt) Ingraham; m. at York, 26 Jan 1764, JOHN BRADBURY, b. at York, 18 Sep 1736 son of John and Abigail (Young) Bradbury; John d. at York, 1821.

John Bradbury served as lieutenant in Capt. Moulton's company on the expedition to Lake George in 1760-1761. He served as deacon of Christ Church of York.[2728]

There are records of twelve children for Elizabeth and John born at York.

[2724] Maine, York County, Probate Estate Files, 1690-1917, Estate of Daniel Moulton, Case 13665, accessed through familysearch.org

[2725] Moulton, *Moulton Annals*, p 189

[2726] Maine, York County, Probate Estate Files, 1690-1917, Estate of George Moore, Case 13426, accessed through familysearch.org

[2727] Maine, Nathan Hale Cemetery Collection, 1780-1980

[2728] Encyclopedia of Virginia Biography, volume 5, p 909 (a grandson of Elizabeth and John Bradbury settled in Petersburg, Virginia). John Bradbury kept a diary from 1762 through 1813 which is in the archives of the Maine Historical Society.

i JOHN BRADBURY, b. 29 Oct 1764; d. at Chesterville, ME, 24 Jul 1851; m. at York, 10 Apr 1788, PRISCILLA BURBANK, b. 2 Aug 1764 daughter of Benjamin and Jane (Sewall) Burbank; Priscilla d. at Chesterville, 8 Apr 1831.

ii WILLIAM BRADBURY, b. 18 Jan 1766; d. at Chesterville, 22 Nov 1846; m. ANNA MITCHELL, b. at Bath, ME, 1 Dec 1760 daughter of Jonathan and Keziah (Libby) Mitchell; Anna d. at Chesterville, 13 Nov 1827.

iii LYDIA BRADBURY, b. 27 Aug 1767; d. at after 1850 when she was living at Hallowell; m. at Hallowell, 4 Oct 1790, THOMAS DAVENPORT, b. at Hallowell, 27 Nov 1764 son of Jonathan and Susanna (White) Davenport; Thomas d. at Hallowell, 1845.

iv JOANNA BRADBURY, b. 6 Nov 1768; d. at Hallowell, 1 May 1838; m. 9 Feb 1801, JONATHAN DAVENPORT, b. at Hallowell, 14 Dec 1775 son of Jonathan and Susanna (White) Davenport; Jonathan d. at Chelsea, ME, 29 Aug 1857.

v SAMUEL BRADBURY, b. 9 Feb 1771; d. at York, 10 Nov 1849;[2729] m. 1st at York, 11 Jul 1802, DORCAS REMICK, b. about 1770 daughter of Nathaniel and Susanna (-) Remick;[2730] Dorcas d. about 1806.Samuel m. 2nd 15 Mar 1815, SARAH LEIGHTON (widow of William Harrold), b. at Eliot, ME, 13 Aug 1782 daughter of William and Miriam (Fernald) Leighton; Sarah d. at Dorchester, MA, 16 Dec 1863.

vi ELIZABETH BRADBURY, b. 25 Jun 1773; d. at Boston, 30 Aug 1856; m. SAMUEL LINSCOTT, b. at Chesterville, ME, 26 May 1782 son of Samuel and Dorcas (Dunning)Linscott; Samuel d. 1844.

vii MARY BRADBURY, b. 8 Nov 1774

viii JOSEPH BRADBURY, b. 9 Nov 1776; died young

ix JOSEPH BRADBURY, b. 24 Mar 1779; d. at Wilton, ME, 11 Jun 1860; m. about 1806, ABIGAIL CHANEY, b. at Dunstable, MA, 26 Apr 1786 daughter of John and Abigail (Blodgett) Chaney; Abigail d. at Wilton, 25 Jan 1860.

x DORCAS BRADBURY, b. 8 May 1781; d. after 1870 when she was living at York; m. at York, 2 Oct 1813, RUFUS SIMPSON, b. at York, 22 Jul 1790 son of Peletiah and Mary (Donnell) Simpson

xi JOTHAM BRADBURY, b. 8 Jul 1783

xii DAVID BRADBURY, b. 5 Jun 1785; m. at York, 8 Jun 1812, SOPHIA CHASE, b. about 1788 daughter of Josiah and Hannah (Chase) Grow; Sophia d. at Montclair, NJ, 24 Jun 1867.

1033) LYDIA INGRAHAM (*Lydia Holt Ingraham[4], Joseph[3], James[2], Nicholas[1]*), b. 28 Mar 1749 daughter of Edward and Lydia (Holt) Ingraham; d. at York, 1 Dec 1824; m. 1767, ESAIAS PREBLE, b. at York, 28 May 1742 son of Samuel and Sarah (Muchmore) Preble.

Esaias Preble was captain of a company of Minute Men at Cambridge in 1775. He was a member of the Massachusetts Convention to ratify the constitution as a representative from York.[2731]

Son William Pitt Preble graduated from Harvard in 1808 and in 1813 was appointed U.S. District Attorney for Maine. He was a strong advocate for the removal of Maine from Massachusetts. In 1820, he was named as a judge of the state supreme court.[2732]

Daughter Hannah did not marry. In her will written 14 June 1851 (probate July 1864), she first left instructions that her gravestone should be plain white marble with the inscription "Hannah daughter of Esaias and Lydia Preble" with the date of her death. She also included directions for head stones and foot stones for the graves of her parents. She bequeathed to her brother William Pitt a plain gold ring which was to be of standard quality and full weight and should bear the inscription on the inside "Hannah to William" and she requests that William wear this ring for her sake "as a token of my affectionate remembrance of all his acts of thoughtful kindness for me." Niece Olive (?) Moody receives a gold diamond ring to be selected and presented to her by her father. The remainder of the estate is left to Charles Moody and Sarah Moody his wife, Charles being the child of her sister Lydia and her husband Samuel Moody.[2733]

Lydia Ingraham and Esaias Preble were parents of fifteen children born at York.

i ESAIAS PREBLE, b. 27 Sep 1767; d. at York, 1776.

[2729] Maine State Archives; Augusta, Maine; U.S. Census Mortality Schedules, Maine, 1850-1880; Archive Collection: 1; Census Year: 1849; Census Place: York, York, Maine

[2730] Remick, *Remick Genealogy*, p 177

[2731] Sons of the American Revolution, Maine Society, *Maine in War*, p 155

[2732] Preble, *Genealogical Sketch of the First Three Generations of Prebles*, p 20

[2733] Maine, York County, Probate Estate Files, Estate of Hannah Preble, Case 15456

ii SARAH PREBLE, b. 19 Feb 1769; d. at Portland, ME, 27 Aug 1840; m. at York, 7 Mar 1795, WILLIAM MCLELLAN, b. at Gorham, ME, 7 May 1771 son of Alexander and Margaret (Johnson) McLellan; William d. at Portland, 5 Oct 1863.

iii LYDIA PREBLE, b. 27 Sep 1770; d. at York, 9 May 1842; m. SAMUEL MOODY, b. at York, 4 Jan 1762 son of Joseph and Elizabeth (Moore) Moody; Samuel d. at York, 1 Dec 1847.

iv THEODOCIA PREBLE, b. 15 Sep 1772; d. at York, 24 Sep 1849; m. at York, Nov 1791, ROBERT ROSE MOODY, b. 9 Mar 1770 son of Joseph and Elizabeth (Moore) Moody; Robert d. at York, 18 May 1824.

v HEPHZIBAH PREBLE, b. 27 Feb 1774

vi SAMUEL PREBLE, b. 8 Dec 1775

vii ESAIAS PREBLE, b. 16 Dec 1776; d. at Boston, 26 Feb 1856; m. 1807, MARY A. BELL, b. at New Castle, NH, 24 Dec 1789 daughter of George and Sarah (-) Bell; Mary d. at Boston, 16 Jul 1866.

viii JOANNA PREBLE, b. Jan 1779; m. 1826, as his second wife, JOHN BURLEIGH HILL. John was first married to Mary Libbey Maloon.

ix HANNAH PREBLE, b. Jan 1781; d. at York, 22 Mar 1861. Hannah did not marry.

x RUTH PREBLE, b. 8 Apr 1782; d. at Eastport, ME, 26 Aug 1851; m. JOHN LANGDON STORER, b. at Wells, 24 Dec 1784 son of John and Hannah (-) Storer; John d. at Eastport, 3 Dec 1844.

xi WILLIAM PITT PREBLE, b. 27 Nov 1783; d. at Portland, ME, 11 Oct 1857; m. at York, 6 Sep 1810, NANCY GALE TUCKER, b. at York, 16 Sep 1786 daughter of Joseph and Mary (Stone) Tucker; Nancy d. at Portland, 17 Oct 1848.

xii HARRIET PREBLE, b. 27 Sep 1785; d. at Lubec, ME, 28 Dec 1848; m. at Wells, 27 Jul 1804, STEPHEN THACHER, b. at Lebanon, CT, 9 Jan 1774; Stephen d. at Rockland, ME, 19 Feb 1859. Stephen Thacher was a Yale graduate and held a number of state and federal offices including postmaster and probate judge. He once penned a letter of admiration to President Thomas Jefferson.[2734]

xiii STATIRA PREBLE, b. 28 Mar 1788; d. at Darksville, MO, 23 Jun 1854; m. at Portland, 31 Jan 1813, JOHN HANCOCK HALL, b. at Portland, ME, 21 Jan 1781 son of Stephen and Mary (Cotton) Hall; John d. at Darksville, 26 Feb 1841.

xiv RUFUS PREBLE, b. 4 Mar 1790; d. at New Castle, NH, 27 Apr 1827; m. at New Castle, NH, 31 Jul 1815, ELIZABETH BELL, b. at New Castle, 9 Aug 1788 daughter of George and Sarah (-) Bell; Elizabeth d. New Castle, 19 Aug 1844.

xv ADOLPHUS PREBLE, b. 24 Jul 1793; m. at Washington County, IN, 4 Dec 1823, DELIVERANCE LITTLE. Adolphus served in the War of 1812 and received a land grant related to his service.

1034) JOSEPH HOLT INGRAHAM (*Lydia Holt Ingraham⁴, Joseph³, James², Nicholas¹*), b. at York, 10 Feb 1752 son of Edward and Lydia (Holt) Ingraham; d. at Portland, ME, 4 Nov 1841; m. 1st, about 1775, ABIGAIL MILK daughter of James and Sarah (Brown) Milk;[2735] Abigail d. at Portland, 17 May 1785. Joseph m. 2nd at Portland 2 Dec 1786, LYDIA STONE, b. at York, 20 Nov 1759 daughter of Benjamin and Rebecca (Littlefield) Stone; Lydia d. about 1788. Joseph m. 3rd at Portland, 26 Jul 1789, ANN TATE, b. 18 Mar 1767 daughter of Samuel and Elizabeth (-) Tate;[2736] Ann d. at Portland, 27 Mar 1844.

Joseph Holt Ingraham was a silversmith in Portland and his residence was on Fore Street in Portland. The family became first members of the second parish church of Portland when it was established in 1788.[2737] Joseph H. served as representative to the General Court of Massachusetts from 1810 to 1815 and again in 1817. He was responsible for building a large portion of the commercial wharf in Portland which was originally named for him.[2738] He built a home at 51 State Street in 1801 which is currently listed on the National Register of Historic Places.

Joseph H. Ingraham and Abigail Milk were parents of three children.

i EDWARD INGRAHAM, d. at Portland, 30 Jun 1777

ii EDWARD INGRAHAM, b. 1778; d. 17 Aug 1779.

2734 Jefferson, Thomas, *The Papers of Thomas Jefferson: 11 July to 15 November 1803*, p 266

2735 Willis, *The History of Portland*, p 431

2736 Willis, *The History of Portland*, p 841

2737 Willis, *The History of Portland*, p 468, p 778

2738 Smith, Extracts from the Journals Kept by the Reverend Thomas Smith, p 106 and p 250

iii JAMES MILK INGRAHAM, b. at Portland, 6 Jan 1781; d. at Biddeford, ME, 2 Jun 1856; m. at Portland, 25 Nov 1804, ELIZA "BETSY" THURSTON, b. at Hampton, NH, 6 Jun 1787 daughter of Benjamin and Sarah (Phillips) Thurston; Betsy d. at Biddeford, 22 May 1856.

Child of Joseph H. Ingraham and Lydia Stone:

i WILLIAM F. INGRAHAM, b. at Portland, 22 Oct 1787

There are records for ten children of Joseph H. Ingraham and Ann Tate born at Portland.

i ELIZABETH R. INGRAHAM, b. 17 Sep 1791; d. at Portland, Mar 1880.[2739] Elizabeth did not marry.

ii JOHN HENNIKER INGRAHAM, b. at Portland, 11 Jun 1793; d. at Augusta, ME, 13 Apr 1864; m. at Augusta, 1818, ABIGAIL GUILD CONY, b. at Augusta, 17 Jan 1791 daughter of Daniel and Susannah (Curtis) Cony; Abigail d. at Bangor, 20 Nov 1875. Rev. John H. Ingraham was ordained at the Congregational Church of Thomaston on 15 October 1817 and served in that capacity until 1 January 1829.[2740]

iii GEORGE TATE INGRAHAM, b. at Portland, 11 Sep 1795; d. at Portland, 30 Dec 1875; m. 1st at Portland, 1 Oct 1821, SARAH "SALLY" LEAVITT, b. 1802 daughter of John and Jemima (Crabtree0 Leavitt; Sally d. at Portland, 1832. George m. 2nd at Portland, 10 May 1834, MARTHA RUSSELL, b. 1802; Martha d. at Portland, 2 May 1890.

iv SAMUEL P. INGRAHAM, b. at Portland, 2 Nov 1796; d. at Portland, 26 Jun 1863; m. at Hallowell, 20 May 1825, MARY ADAMS, b. 1798; Mary d. at Portland, 4 Feb 1876.

v EDWARD T. INGRAHAM, b. 3 Sep 1798

vi HOLT INGRAHAM, b. at Portland, 22 May 1800; d. at Portland, 2 Aug 1877; m. SARAH ANN INGRAHAM, b. at Portland, 12 Nov 1806 daughter of Edward and Mary (Daley) Ingraham; Sarah d. at Portland, 12 Nov 1869.

vii ANN T. INGRAHAM, b. at Portland, 23 Mar 1802; d. at Portland, 18 Oct 1866; m. at Portland, 15 May 1825, EDWIN BAILEY, b. at Hanover, MA, 7 May 1798 son of Calvin and Sarah (Jacobs) Bailey; Edwin d. Aug 1828.[2741] Ann and Edwin had one child who died in 1828.

viii JOSEPH W. INGRAHAM, b. 18 Jan 1804

ix MARY LITTLE INGRAHAM, b. at Portland, 13 Sep 1806; d. at Portland, 1 Apr 1895; m. at Portland, 19 Nov 1834, DANIEL BRAZIER, b. at Portland, 29 Dec 1809 son of Harrison and Abigail (Riggs) Brazier; Daniel d. at Boston, 12 Jan 1849.

x NATHANIEL DEERING INGRAHAM. The birth record for Nathaniel only gives 4 Jan 180_. Joseph H. Ingraham was an owner with Nathaniel Deering in Deering's Wharf, which is the likely origin of son Nathaniel Deering Holt's name.

1035) MARY "MOLLEY" INGRAHAM (*Lydia Holt Ingraham⁴, Joseph³, James², Nicholas¹*), b. at York, 14 May 1755 daughter of Edward and Lydia (Holt) Ingraham; d. at Chesterville, ME, 28 Mar 1814; m. at York, 20 Apr 1776, JOHN WHEELER, b. 14 May 1750[2742] perhaps in England; John d. at Wilton, ME, 23 Apr 1843. John married second Elizabeth Teague who was the widow of Samuel Hiscock.

John and Molley Wheeler came to Chesterville, Maine from York about 1793. John was a tailor by trade, the first in the town. There was an outbreak of typhus fever in the town in 1814 and Molley died in March 1814, daughter Mary Wheeler Chandler died in May, and daughter Sally died in June.[2743] Son Edward's wife Phebe Chandler also died in the epidemic in May 1814.

John Wheeler served in the Navy during the Revolution. On 22 April 1818, at age sixty-eight while living at Wilton, Maine, John made application for a pension. He reported that in September 1777 from Portsmouth, New Hampshire, he shipped as quartermaster on the Continental sloop of war *Ranger* with Paul Jones, Commander.[2744] Before sailing, word was received of the capture of Burgoyne, and the passage was delayed in order to take word of the capture to France. John was moved to a ship that they captured during the passage and traveled on that ship to Bordeaux and then rejoined the *Ranger* at L'Orient. They sailed in the company of a French frigate to the Isle of Man. The *Ranger* captured another ship that was carrying furniture of

---

2739 Maine State Archives; Augusta, Maine; U.S. Census Mortality Schedules, Maine, 1850-1880; Archive Collection: 4; Census Year: 1880; Census Place: Portland, Cumberland, Maine; Page: 2

2740 Congregational Churches in Maine, *Minutes of the General Conference of the Congregational Churches*, volume 1, p 33

2741 Bailey, *Bailey Genealogy*, p 351

2742 John's birth date is recorded in the Chesterville town records.

2743 Sewall, *History of Chesterville, Maine*, p 33

2744 This refers to Captain John Paul Jones.

the Lord Lieutenant of Ireland, and they took this captured ship to Brest. They then encountered the British war ship *Drake* with twenty guns and had a hard fight, but the *Ranger* captured the *Drake*.[2745] They returned to Portsmouth and he was verbally discharged with honor having served fifteen months, although he had only signed on for six months. In a further statement in 1820, his household consisted of himself and wife Betsey age fifty-four.[2746]

There are records of ten children of Molley and John Wheeler.[2747] All the births are recorded in the Chesterville records, and births of several of the children are also recorded at York, and it is likely that all but the youngest two children were born at York.

i JOHN WHEELER, b. at York, 15 Mar 1777; d. at Chesterville, 2 Dec 1855; m. 1798, CHARITY LINSCOTT, b. at Harpswell, ME, 23 Dec 1776 daughter of Samuel and Dorcas (Dunning) Linscott;[2748] Charity d. at Chesterville, 23 May 1865.

ii POLLY WHEELER, b. at York, 20 Apr 1778; d. at Chesterville, 15 May 1814.

iii EDWARD INGRAHAM WHEELER, b. at York, 16 Jul 1780; d. at Pittsfield, ME, 13 May 1862; m. 1st about 1804, PHEBE CHANDLER, b. at Winthrop, ME, about 1783 daughter of Samuel and Rebecca (Walton) Chandler; Phebe d. at Chesterville, ME, May 1814. Edward m. 2nd 1815, MERCY MYRICK, b. 1784 daughter of John and Elizabeth (Palmer) Merrick; Mercy d. at Pittsfield, 27 Feb 1868.

iv LYDIA WHEELER, b. 6 Oct 1782; d. 23 Sep 1783.

v ABIGAIL MILK WHEELER, b. at York, 12 Aug 1784; d. at Columbus, IL, 20 Oct 1873; m. at Chesterville, ME, 11 Mar 1804, JABEZ WHITNEY, b. 1780 likely son of Phineas and Anna (Morton) Whitney; Jabez d. in Adams County, IL, 10 Jun 1839.

vi ELCY WHEELER, b. at York, 16 Feb 1787

vii GEORGE WHEELER, b. at York, 16 Dec 1789; d. at Farmington, ME, 29 Oct 1865; m. 28 Dec 1814, HANNAH CHANDLER, b. at Farmington, 4 Apr 1786 daughter of Moses and Sarah (Berry) Chandler; Hannah d. at Farmington, 12 Apr 1870.

viii WILLIAM LYMAN WHEELER, b. at York, 2 Apr 1792; d. at Portland, ME, 30 Dec 1876; m. at Farmington, ME, 3 May 1813, MARY JORDAN, b. 1794; Mary d. at Norridgewock, ME, 13 Mar 1846. William and Mary were parents of six sons.

ix SALLY WHEELER, b. at Chesterville, 9 Jul 1794; d. at Chesterville, 9 Jun 1814.

x JENNY SEWALL WHEELER, b. at Chesterville, 15 Apr 1797; d. at Wilton, ME, 20 Apr 1844; m. at Wilton, ME, 14 May 1818, her stepbrother, JESSE S. HISCOCK, b. at Nobleboro, ME, 18 Dec 1794 son of Samuel and Elizabeth (Teague) Hiscock; Jesse d. at Wilton, 15 Nov 1842.

1036) WILLIAM INGRAHAM (*Lydia Holt Ingraham⁴, Joseph³, James², Nicholas¹*), b. at York, 25 Sep 1761 son of Edward and Lydia (Holt) Ingraham; d. at Portland, 15 Jun 1815; m. at Portland, 2 Nov 1784, SARAH TUKEY, b. at Portland, 6 Apr 1763 daughter of John and Abigail (Sweetser) Tukey;[2749] Sarah d. at Portland, 24 Sep 1803.

William Ingraham and Sarah Tukey were parents of seven children born at Portland, Maine.[2750]

i EDWARD INGRAHAM, b. 27 Jun 1785; d. at Portland, 11 Aug 1874; m. 1st 13 Jul 1806, MARY DALEY, b. at Portland, 1 Jan 1788 daughter of Emor and Mary (Bailey) Daley; Mary d. 16 Feb 1824. Edward m. 2nd 13 Sep 1824, MARY F. ASPINWALL (widow of Edward Grueby), b. 25 Feb 1786 daughter of Caleb and Elizabeth (Freeman) Aspinwall; Mary d. at Portland, 16 Apr 1876.

ii JOSEPH INGRAHAM, b. 15 Aug 1787; d. at Charlestown, MA, 4 Feb 1867; m. at Portland, 28 May 1812, BETSEY CLARK, b. at Saco, about 1789 daughter of Joel and Elizabeth (-) Clark;[2751] Betsey d. at Charlestown, 13 Oct 1878.

iii NATHANIEL M. INGRAHAM, b. 21 Jun 1790; d. at Boston, 16 Dec 1869; m. about 1812, HARRIET LILLIE, b. at Eastport, about 1794 daughter of John and Elizabeth (-) Lillie;[2752] Harriet d. at Boston, 8 Jun 1881.

2745 The naval duel of the *Ranger* and *Drake* took place in the North Channel on 24 April 1778.

2746 Revolutionary War Pension and Pension and Bounty-Land Warrant Application Files, Case S37540

2747 Maine Births and Christenings 1739-1900; accessed through familysearch.org. Chesterville Vital Records 1788-1907, p 45

2748 Chesterville Vital Records, p 14

2749 Willis, *The History of Portland*, p 847

2750 Munsell, American Ancestry, volume XI, p 195

2751 Betsey's parents are given as Joel and Elizabeth Clark in her death record and her place of birth as Saco.

2752 Names of parents are as given on her death record.

iv WILLIAM INGRAHAM, b. 22 Jan 1793, d. 22 Aug 1794.

v WILLIAM INGRAHAM, b. 14 Jun 1795; d. at Portland, Jun 1827; m. at Portland, 9 Nov 1818, MARY KIMBALL, b. at Portland, 22 Jul 1795 daughter of Jeremiah and Mary (Tucker) Kimball; Mary d. at Portland, 12 Jan 1867.

vi THOMAS INGRAHAM, b. 8 Sep 1797; d. at Portland, after 1834 and likely before 1840; m. at Portland, 18 Jan 1818, MARY WATERHOUSE, b. 1800 daughter of William and Hannah (Pierce) Waterhouse; Mary d. at Portland, 4 Aug 1877. Thomas and Mary were parents of five children four of whom died in childhood. Only son William W. Ingraham lived to adulthood and married.

vii LOUISA G. INGRAHAM, b. 13 Mar 1803; d. at Lewiston, ME, 26 Nov 1872; m. at Portland, 18 Apr 1820, SAMUEL BRACKETT, b. at Portland, 8 Jun 1796 son of Nathaniel and Elizabeth (Lewis) Brackett;[2753] Samuel d. at Lewiston, 14 Sep 1883.

1037) SARAH INGALLS (*Rebekah Grow Ingalls[4], Rebekah Holt Grow[3], James[2], Nicholas[1]*), b. at Pomfret, 7 Nov 1735 daughter of Stephen and Rebekah (Grow) Ingalls; m. at Pomfret, 26 Feb 1756, JAMES COPELAND, b. at Braintree, MA, 19 Mar 1724 son of William and Mary (Thayer) Copeland.[2754]

Sarah and James resided in Pomfret for the births of three children and were later in Brooklyn, Connecticut where an additional eight children were born (baptized).[2755]

i PHEBE COPELAND, b. 19 Nov 1756

ii AMASA COPELAND, b. 22 Apr 1758; d. at Abington, CT, 18 Aug 1852; m. at Pomfret, 24 Jan 1788, TRYPHENA LISCOMB, b. at Pomfret, 7 Oct 1759 daughter of Thomas and Sarah (Parkhurst) Liscomb;[2756] Tryphena d. at Hampton, 2 Apr 1834.

iii SARAH COPELAND, b. at Pomfret, 4 May 1760; m. at Pomfret, 9 Nov 1783, RICHARD RINDGE. There are records for the births of eight children of Sarah and Richard at Hampton, CT and they were living there in 1800. Richard is likely the Revolutionary War pensioner in Glover, VT in 1818. He died at Calais, VT, 27 Aug 1843. At the time of a pension declaration in 1820, the only family member with him was daughter Polly then age 20. Sarah and Richard's youngest child Polly was born in Hampton on 19 Dec 1799. Richard's pension application includes details of his being taken prisoner while serving as a mariner. He also reported losing his left leg in about 1787.

iv JOSEPH COPELAND, baptized at Brooklyn, 19 Aug 1764.

v REBECCA COPELAND, baptized at Brooklyn, 28 Sep 1766; d. at Marshall, NY, 2 Oct 1844; m. at Hampton, CT, 27 Oct 1788, her fourth cousin, NATHANIEL FORD (*Amos Ford[5], Dinah Holt Ford[4], Elizabeth Farnum Holt[3], Elizabeth Holt Farnum[2], Nicholas[1]*), b. at Windham, 11 Jul 1765 son of Amos and Lydia (Davison) Ford; Nathaniel d. at Marshall, 31 Oct 1849.

vi WYLLYS COPELAND, baptized at Brooklyn, 4 Dec 1768; d. after 1850 when he was living in Killingly, CT. Census records suggest that Wyllys did marry and had at least one child, but the name of his wife is not found. In 1850, he was living with a family headed by David Darby.

vii WILLARD COPELAND, baptized at Brooklyn, 4 Dec 1768; d. at Braintree, VT, 20 Feb 1852;[2757] m. 1st about 1795, Alice Lyon *likely* his fourth cousin, ALICE LYON (*Alice Holt Lyon[5], William[4], Thomas[3], Nicholas[2], Nicholas[1]*), b. at Hampton, 14 Jun 1769 daughter of Robert and Alice (Holt) Lyon; Alice d. at Braintree, 1804. Willard m. 2nd at Braintree, 12 Dec 1805, REBECCA WHITE, b. at Braintree, MA, 30 May 1766 daughter of Micah and Susanna (Eager) White; Rebecca d. at Randolph, VT, 1 Aug 1856.[2758] Willard and Alice were parents of two children, James and Clarissa. Willard and Rebecca had one son, Abel Wyllys Willard. None of his children married, although they all lived fairly long lives, James dying at age 94.

viii LYDIA COPELAND, baptized at Brooklyn, 4 Aug 1771

ix MOLLY COPELAND, baptized at Brooklyn, 25 Jul 1773

[2753] McLellan, *History of Gorham, ME*, p 410

[2754] Copeland, *The Copeland Family*, p 34

[2755] Coon, "The Children of James and Sarah (Ingalls) Copeland", *Mayflower Quarterly Magazine*, 2019. This recently published article documents baptisms of seven children not previously identified for this family.

[2756] The 1802 probate of Thomas Liscomb of Pomfret includes a distribution to daughter Triphena Copeland.

[2757] Bass, *History of Braintree, Vermont*, p 127

[2758] Bass, *History of Braintree, Vermont*

x STEPHEN COPELAND, baptized at Brooklyn, 3 Mar 1776. He may be the Stephen Copeland born in CT, living in Conneaut, PA in 1860 with his son Joseph and his family.

xi JOHN COPELAND, baptized at Brooklyn, 21 Sep 1778

1038) THOMAS INGALLS (*Rebekah Grow Ingalls*[4], *Rebekah Holt Grow*[3], *James*[2], *Nicholas*[1]), b. at Pomfret, 9 Dec 1742 son of Stephen and Rebekah (Grow) Ingalls; d. at Abington, CT, 10 Jan 1816; m. 1st at Pomfret, 26 Jun 1777, SARAH BOWEN, b. about 1749; Sarah d. at Pomfret, 6 Oct 1777. Thomas m. 2nd 8 Nov 1786, RUTH WOODWORTH; Ruth d. at Pomfret, 12 Apr 1827.

Thomas's first wife Sarah died just four months after their marriage. Thomas and Ruth had two daughters born at Pomfret. Both daughters lived single. Daughter Nancy was a spinner and weaver in Abington.

i ROXY INGALLS, b. at Pomfret, 19 Nov 1788; d. at Pomfret, 21 Jul 1857.

ii NANCY INGALLS, b. at Pomfret, 16 Nov 1790; d. at Abington, 7 Dec 1847. "Nancy, spinner & weaver, of Abington Soc., d. Dec. 7, 1847, age 57."

1039) SAMUEL INGALLS (*Rebekah Grow Ingalls*[4], *Rebekah Holt Grow*[3], *James*[2], *Nicholas*[1]), b. at Pomfret, 22 Apr 1746 son of Stephen and Rebekah (Grow) Ingalls; m. at Brooklyn, CT, 9 Nov 1769, DEBORAH MEACHAM, b. at Windham, 3 Nov 1749 daughter of Daniel and Lydia (Lillie) Meacham.

There are records of four children of Samuel and Deborah born at Pomfret.

i SAMUEL INGALLS (twin), b. 24 Aug 1770; d. at Dunkley's Grove, IL, Oct 1839; m. DIANA DODGE, b. 1778; Diana d. at Pelham, MA, 3 Dec 1833.

ii LEMUEL INGALLS (twin), b. 24 Aug 1770; m. at Belchertown, MA, 1 Oct 1802, LOUISA PRENTISS. Louisa and Lemuel had nine children born at Belchertown.

iii STEPHEN INGALLS, b. 10 Sep 1772

iv ALICE INGALLS, b. 21 Feb 1775

1040) REBEKAH GROW (*Thomas Grow*[4], *Rebekah Holt Grow*[3], *James*[2], *Nicholas*[1]), b. at Pomfret, 16 Oct 1738 daughter of Thomas and Susanna (Eaton) Grow; d. after 1801; m. at Pomfret, 3 Jun 1773, as his second wife, Rev. WHITMAN JACOBS, b. at Bristol, 3 May 1727 son of Nathaniel and Mary (Whitman) Jacobs; Whitman d. at Royalston, MA, 28 Mar 1801. Whitman was first married to Rebecca Rice.

Rev Whitman Jacobs was the first settled pastor of the Baptist church in Royalston, Massachusetts, installed there 13 December 1770. For twenty years prior to that, he had a pastorate in Thompson, Connecticut. Rev. Jacobs was dismissed as pastor at Royalston in 1786 reportedly as he took the government's side related to Shay's rebellion and most of the church congregation sided with Shay.[2759]

In his will written 15 July 1800, after first noting that he has settled his real estate by deed of gift, Whitman Jacobs bequeathed to beloved wife Rebecah all the household furniture except two beds. There are other bequests to daughter Rebeckah Haven and to sons Elnathan, John, Simeon, Whitman, and Joseph. Son Ely and daughter Metcalf have received their full shares. Son Thomas receives a colt and a pair of yearlings.[2760] The children named in the will, with the exception of Thomas, were the children of Whitman and his first wife Rebecca Rice.

On 15 July 1800 (recorded 4 February 1806), the same date as the will, Whitman Jacobs of Royalston "for the consideration of love and good will that I bear to my beloved wife Rebecah Jacobs and to my son Thomas Jacobs both of Royalston" conveyed to Rebecah and Thomas the whole of his half of the buildings on the farm he now owned along with 50 acres of land.[2761]

Rebekah Grow and Whitman Jacobs were parents of one child.

i THOMAS JACOBS, b. at Athol, MA, 1780; d. at Royalston, MA, 24 Nov 1849; m. at Royalston, 1 Jan 1805, ELIZABETH BENNETT, b. at Fitzwilliam, NH, 1784 daughter of Joseph and Elizabeth (-) Bennett;[2762] Elizabeth d. of consumption at Royalston, 15 Jul 1857.

[2759] Caswell, *The History of the Town of Royalston*, p 67

[2760] *Worcester County, MA: Probate File Papers, 1731-1881.* Online database. AmericanAncestors.org. New England Historic Genealogical Society, 2015. Case 32865

[2761] Massachusetts Land Records, Worcester County, 161:369

[2762] Names of parents and place of birth are given on Elizabeth's death record with age at death of 73 years, 3 months, 15 days.

1041) THOMAS GROW (*Thomas Grow⁴, Rebekah Holt Grow³, James², Nicholas¹*), b. at Pomfret, 4 Apr 1743 son of Thomas and Susanna (Eaton) Grow; d. at Hampton, 5 Jun 1824; m. 1st at Pomfret, 4 Jun 1767, EXPERIENCE GOODALE,[2763] b. at Pomfret, 23 Apr 1747 daughter of Ebenezer and Experience (Lyon) Goodale; Experience d. at Hampton, 9 Feb 1811. Thomas m. 2nd at Hampton, 18 Aug 1811, SARAH HYDE who may have been a widow and has not been identified; Sarah d. at Hampton, 26 Dec 1819. Thomas m. 3rd at Providence, 12 Mar 1820, EXPERIENCE ABBOTT, b. at Pomfret, 21 Jan 1756 daughter of Nathan and Eunice (Marsh) Abbott; Experience d. at Hampton, 20 Apr 1835.[2764]

Thomas Grow resided in Hampton, Connecticut on a homestead farm of 180 acres. He served as a private in the company of Capt. Hyde during the Revolution.[2765]

Thomas Grow did not leave a will and his estate entered probate 14 June 1824 with Thomas Grow as administrator. The distributions from the personal estate were made to the following heirs: daughter Dille Bacon, daughter Olive Hovey, daughter Lois Burnham, daughter Chloe Bennet, daughter Phebe Hicks, daughter Hannah Rindge, daughter Rhoda Bennet, son David Grow, heirs of daughter Anna Darby deceased, and Nelson Clark only surviving heir of daughter Experience Clark deceased. The remaining real estate was set out to Dille Bacon, Olive Hovey, Lois Burnham, Chloe Bennet, Phebe Hicks, Hannah Rindge, and Rhoda Bennet. Not real estate was set out to sons Elisha Grow, Joseph Grow, and Thomas Grow as they had previously received more than their shares.[2766]

Thomas Grow and Experience Goodale were parents of fourteen children.

i DILLE GROW, b. at Pomfret, 14 Sep 1768; d. at Charlton, MA, 16 Feb 1829; m. 1st at Pomfret, 12 Jan 1792, AARON NICHOLS, b. at Thompson, 14 Feb 1764 son of Jonathan and Mary (Sibley) Nichols; Aaron d. at Thompson, 18 Apr 1807. Dille m. 2nd at Charlton, 12 Jun 1808, as the second of his three wives, DANIEL BACON, b. about 1760; Daniel d. at Charlton, 9 Mar 1834. Dille and Aaron did not have children.

ii OLIVE GROW, b. at Pomfret, 27 Jan 1770; d. at Hampton, 20 Aug 1858; m. at Hampton, 1 Jan 1789, Dr. JACOB HOVEY, b. at Hampton, 16 May 1760 son of Nathaniel and Ruth (Parker) Hovey; Jacob d. at Hampton, 24 Aug 1830.

iii LOIS GROW, b. at Windham, 6 Mar 1771; d. at Scotland, CT, 22 Nov 1843; m. at Windham, 3 Dec 1790, WILLIAM BURNHAM, b. at Windham, 5 Mar 1764 son of Andrew and Jane (Bennett) Burnham; William d. at Scotland, 20 Apr 1847.

iv PHEBE GROW, b. at Pomfret, 2 Apr 1772; d. at Pomfret, 6 Jan 1853; m. at Pomfret, 3 Dec 1795, ISRAEL HICKS, b. 18 Jun 1766 son of Israel and Elizabeth (Bowen) Hicks; Israel d. at Pomfret, 15 Sep 1839.

v CHLOE GROW, b. at Windham, 18 Oct 1773; d. at Cortland, NY, 21 Oct 1862; m. at Mansfield, CT, 17 Mar 1803, ASA BENNETT, b. at Mansfield, 10 Jul 1778 son of Asa and Mary (Barrows) Bennett; Asa d. at Homer, NY, 9 Nov 1825.

vi HANNAH GROW, b. at Pomfret, 31 Aug 1775; d. at Homer, NY, 16 Nov 1853; m. ISAAC RINDGE, b. a Windham, 28 May 1773 son of Isaac and Mercy (Quarles) Rindge; Isaac d. at Homer, 24 Nov 1832.

vii ANNA GROW, b. at Windham, 15 Sep 1777; d. at Homer, NY, 30 Jun 1806; m. 10 May 1796 JOSEPH DARBY, b. at Canterbury, 22 Aug 1772 son of Eleazer and Anna (Doubleday) Darby; Joseph d. at Homer, 22 May 1835.

viii ELISHA GROW, b. at Pomfret, 9 Feb 1779; d. at Waterford, MI, 22 Aug 1850; m. 25 Dec 1801, LOIS PALMER, b. at Hampton, 7 Mar 1784 daughter of Abel and Lois (Palmer) Palmer; Lois d. at Waterford, 5 Sep 1850.

ix RHODA GROW, b. at Pomfret, 6 Sep 1780; d. at Homer, NY, 24 Dec 1874; m. about 1802, ALFRED BENNETT, b. at Mansfield, CT, 26 Sep 1780 son of Asa and Mary (Barrows) Bennett; Alfred d. at Homer, 10 May 1861.

x THOMAS GROW, b. at Pomfret, 19 Oct 1782; d. at Hampton, CT, 25 Dec 1852; m. 1st at Hampton, 17 Jan 1811, POLLY BENNETT, b. at Mansfield, CT, 25 Jul 1789 daughter of Nathaniel and Edna (Little) Bennett; Polly d. at Hampton, 20 Nov 1830. Thomas m. 2nd 20 Apr 1831, JERUSHA WALES, b. at Windham, 11 Dec 1798 daughter of Nathan and Rosamond (Robinson) Wales; Jerusha d. at Hampton, 12 Dec 1881.

xi EXPERIENCE "SPEEDY" GROW, b. at Pomfret, 8 Jul 1784; d. at Chaplin, CT, 19 Feb 1810; m. about 1805, DANIEL CLARK, b. at Hampton, 28 Aug 1781 son of Daniel and Mehitable (Slate) Clark; Daniel d. at Coudersport, PA, 4 Mar 1829. Daniel married second Lucy Bennet.

2763 There are two marriage transcriptions for Experience's marriage to Thomas in 1767. Early Connecticut Marriages Book I gives spouse as Thomas Grow, Jr. and the Barbour collection gives spouse as Thomas Grosvenor.

2764 Grow, Experience, relict of Thomas Grow, died Dec. 20, 1835, age 80.

2765 Davis, *John Grow of Ipswich*, p 35

2766 *Connecticut State Library (Hartford, Connecticut), Estate of Thomas Grow, Case 1706*

xii JOSEPH GROW, b. at Hampton, 11 Sep 1787; d. at Ashford, 17 Mar 1827; m. at Hampton, 8 Dec 1808, BETSEY ROBBINS, b. at Voluntown, 1787 daughter of Samuel and Zerviah (Cook) Robbins;[2767] Betsey d. at Glenwood, PA, 28 Jul 1863.

xiii DAVID GROW, b. at Hampton, 2 Oct 1791; d. 13 Dec 1846. David did not marry. The distribution from his estate on 12 June 1847 included payments to the following heirs: Thomas Grow, Olive Hovey, Phebe Hicks, Chloe Bennet, Hannah Rindge, Rhoda Bennet, Elisha Grow, heirs of Lois Burnham, heirs of Anna Darbee, heirs of Joseph Grow, and heirs of Experience Clark.[2768]

xiv JOHN GROW, b. 23 Dec 1793; d. 4 Jan 1810.

1042) HANNAH GROW (*Thomas Grow[4], Rebekah Holt Grow[3], James[2], Nicholas[1]*), b. at Pomfret, 14 Apr 1747 daughter of Thomas and Susanna (Eaton) Grow; m. about 1777, ELISHA RANSOM, b. at Lyme, CT, 6 Feb 1746 son of Matthew and Sarah (Way) Ransom; Elisha d. at Plymouth, NY, 17 Aug 1818.

Elisha Ransom was the first minister of the north parish Baptist church of Woodstock, Vermont when the parish was formed in July 1780.[2769]

Hannah Grow and Elisha Ransom were parents of five children born at Woodstock, Vermont.

i LYDIA RANSOM, b. 21 Jan 1778

ii HANNAH RANSOM, b. 17 Apr 1780; d. at Shiawassee County, MI, 24 Nov 1876; m. at Reading, VT, 1 Apr 1800, JOHN FARRAR SWAIN, b. at Reading, 28 May 1776 son of Nathaniel and Mary (Emerson) Swain; John d. at North Norwich, NY, 3 May 1811.

iii THOMAS GROW RANSOM, b. 27 Feb 1782

iv IRENE RANSOM, b. 29 Feb 1784

v ELISHA RANSOM, b. 1786; d. at Smyrna, NY, 1852; m. ELECTA JOHNSON, b. in CT, 1798; Electa d. at Harmony, NY, 26 Aug 1860.

1043) WILLIAM GROW (*Thomas Grow[4], Rebekah Holt Grow[3], James[2], Nicholas[1]*), b. at Pomfret, 8 Apr 1749 son of Thomas and Susanna (Eaton) Grow; d. at Bridgewater, VT, 7 May 1830; m. at Windham, 30 May 1776, PRISCILLA MORSE, b. at Woodstock, CT 1752 daughter of John and Elizabeth (Bugbee) Morse; Priscilla d. at Bridgewater, 6 Oct 1841.

William and Priscilla started their family in Pomfret, Connecticut and were then in Woodstock, Vermont. Elder William Grow served as the minister of the Baptist church in Woodstock starting in 1788 following his brother-in-law Elisha Ransom. William's leadership of the church was characterized as having incidents of "imprudence" which led to decline in membership of the church. This imprudence consisted of accusations of "immoral conduct" which led to his being deposed as minister.[2770] The family was later in Bridgewater, Vermont.

In his will written 5 October 1818 (proved 17 May 1830), William Grow of Bridgewater bequeathed to beloved wife Priscilla the real and personal estate for her use and comfort during her life. He bequeaths to children two dollars each: eldest son Jedediah, Timothy, Oliver, heirs of Polly deceased, second daughter Susanna Smith, third daughter Esther Field, and youngest daughter Dilly Brown. Son William receives all the real and personal estate after his mother's death and is responsible to pay the legacies.[2771] At the inventory 24 June 1830, personal estate was valued at $716.54, about half that amount in the form of a note owed by Timothy Grow. William had apparently disposed of his real property as what remained was one-half of an eleven-acre lot valued at $27.50.

William Grow and Priscilla Morse were parents of nine children.

i POLLY GROW, b. at Windham, CT, 10 Oct 1775; d. at Craftsbury, VT, 2 Apr 1812; m. 1802, LEONARD MORSE, b. at Woodstock, CT, 10 Oct 1775 son of Calvin and Sophia (Nason) Morse;[2772] Leonard d. at Craftsbury, 27 Aug 1847. Leonard married second Betsey White.

ii JEDEDIAH GROW, b. 1778; d. at Hounsfield, NY, 1828; m. at Woodstock, VT, 31 May 1802, ABIGAIL LUCAS, b. in MA, 1774 (per census records); Abigail d. after 1850 when she was living in Watertown, NY with her daughter.

iii SUSANNA GROW, b. at Pomfret, 19 Apr 1781; d. at Bridgewater, VT, 18 Feb 1853; m. at Bridgewater, 14 Nov 1799, ELIHU SMITH, b. at Woodstock, VT, 17 Dec 1773 son of Beriah and Penelope (Montague) Smith; Elihu d. at Bridgewater, 1854 (probate 1854).

[2767] The 1839 will of Samuel Robbins of Voluntown includes a bequest to his daughter Betsy Grow widow of Joseph Grow.

[2768] *Connecticut State Library (Hartford, Connecticut), Estate of David Grow, Case 237*

[2769] Dana, *History of Woodstock, Vermont*, p 373

[2770] Dana, *History of Woodstock, Vermont*, p 399

[2771] *Vermont. Probate Court (Hartford District), Probate Records volume 10, p 327*

[2772] Morse, *Morse Genealogy*, p 215

iv ESTHER GROW, b. at Pomfret, 26 Aug 1782; d. at Hounsfield, NY, May 1860; m. at Bridgewater, VT, 9 Feb 1811, PHILIP FIELD, b. at Woodstock, VT, 15 Jun 1778 son of Elijah and Tamesin (Crain) Field; Philip d. at Hounsfield, 16 Mar 1860.

v BETSEY GROW, b. at Pomfret, CT, 20 Nov 1784; not mentioned in father's will.

vi TIMOTHY GROW, b. 1787; d. at Woodstock, VT, 21 Feb 1857; m. about 1808, OCTAVIA FRENCH, b. at Bridgewater, VT, 28 Apr 1790 daughter of Ephraim C. and Rhoda (Dike) French; Octavia d. at Woodstock, VT, 12 Dec 1862.

vii OLIVER GROW, b. about 1788; d. at Hounsfield, NY, 20 Nov 1861; m. 1st 1810, SUSAN WARREN, b. 1788; Susan d. at Hounsfield, 10 Mar 1824. Oliver m. 2nd CLARISSA, b. in NH, about 1798 (per census records) who has not been identified; Clarissa d. after 1860 when she was living in Hounsfield.

viii WILLIAM GROW, b. at Bridgewater, VT, 15 Oct 1791; d. at New Haven, VT, 7 Oct 1866; m. ANNA SANDERSON, b. at Woodstock, VT, 8 Aug 1786 daughter of Phinehas and Lucy (Burke) Sanderson; Anna d. at New Haven, 9 Apr 1856.

ix ADEHLIA "DILLY" GROW, b. at Bridgewater, VT, 1 Feb 1799; d. at Saint Charles, MN, 3 Jun 1873; m. JOSEPH BROWN, b. at Middleborough, MA, 21 Apr 1791 son of Thomas and Hannah (Lovell) Brown; Joseph d. at Saratoga, MN, 5 Oct 1874.[2773]

1044) NATHANIEL GROW (*Thomas Grow4, Rebekah Holt Grow3, James2, Nicholas1*), b. at Pomfret, 29 May 1753 son of Thomas and Susanna (Eaton) Grow; d. at Henderson, NY, 9 Jul 1838; m. at Pomfret, 16 Jan 1775, SUSANNA DOW, b. about 1752; Susanna d. at Henderson, 31 Jul 1814.

Nathaniel and Susanna resided in Pomfret, Connecticut but relocated to Henderson, New York about 1807. Nathaniel Grow and Susanna Dow were parents of seven children.

i TIMOTHY GROW, b. at Pomfret, 28 Oct 1775; d. 9 Jun 1779.

ii REBECCA GROW, b. at Pomfret, 4 May 1777; d. at Lorraine, NY, 7 Jan 1845; m. 1st 9 Mar 1797, JOHN STOWELL, b. at Guilford, VT, 7 Nov 1774 son of John and Sarah (-) Stowell;[2774] John is reported to have "gone west" and was never again heard from. Rebecca m, 2nd at Ellisburg, NY, 24 Dec 1824, HUBBARD RANDALL, b. at Colchester, CT, 7 May 1775 son of Benjamin and Amy (Avery) Randall; Hubbard d. at Redfield, NY, 12 Apr 1859. Hubbard was first married to Mary Jennings.

iii LUCINDA GROW, b. at Pomfret, 27 Dec 1778; d. at Smithville, NY, 16 Mar 1854; m. at Guilford, VT, 14 Mar 1799, ELISHA CHASE, b. at Guilford, VT, 23 Apr 1778 son of Paul and Elizabeth (Kinnicutt) Chase.

iv SALLY GROW, b. at Pomfret, 27 Mar 1781; d. at Adams, NY, 3 Dec 1840; m at Guilford, 22 Jun 1799, JOHN BARNEY, b. at Guilford, 6 Oct 1775 son of John and Mary (Grove) Barney; John d. at Waukesha, WI, 7 Jan 1863.

v ABIGAIL GROW, b. at Pomfret, 18 Feb 1783

vi ALVAH GROW, b. at Pomfret, 13 Jul 1785; d. at Henderson, NY, 8 May 1856; m. at Guilford, VT, 6 Feb 1812, POLLY BOYDEN, b. at Guilford, VT, 12 May 1790 daughter of Joseph and Mary (Knowlton) Boyden; Polly d. at Henderson, 25 Jun 1850.

vii EATON GROW, b. at Hampton, 16 Jul 1788; d. after 1860 when he was living in New Haven WI; m. about 1812, LEAH WHEELER, b. at Chesterfield, NH, 23 Jun 1792 daughter of James and Rachel (-) Wheeler; Leah d. after 1860.

1045) PRISCILLA GROW (*Joseph Grow4, Rebekah Holt Grow3, James2, Nicholas1*), b. at Pomfret, 28 Nov 1746 daughter of Joseph and Abigail (Dana) Grow; d. at Tolland, 14 Feb 1818; m. at Pomfret, 25 Nov 1765, THOMAS HOWARD, b. at Ipswich, 5 Sep 1742 son of Hezekiah and Sarah (Newman) Howard; Thomas d. at Tolland, 18 Oct 1805.

Thomas Howard was a tanner and currier by trade. He also farmed and had a 72-acre homestead farm in Pomfret.[2775]

In his will written 12 October 1805 (proved 9 November 1805), Thomas Howard bequeathed to beloved wife Priscilla us of one-third of the real and personal estate while she is a widow. Son Asa Howard receives £50; daughters Priscilla Williams and Lois Sowle each receives £5; sons Thomas, Harvey, and Stephen have each received their full share, so the remainder of the estate is to be divided among sons Joseph, Benjamin, Hezekiah, and Ralph. Sons Thomas and Joseph were named executors.[2776]

2773 Aged 83 yrs., 5 mos., 14 days at death which exactly corresponds with birth record.

2774 Stowell, *The Stowell Genealogy*, p 87

2775 Howard, *Howard Genealogy*, p 41

2776 *Connecticut State Library (Hartford, Connecticut), Estate of Thomas Howard, Case 1103*

Priscilla's estate was administered by Hezekiah Nye and was deemed to be insolvent.[2777]
Priscilla Grow and Thomas Howard were parents of fourteen children.

i ASA HOWARD, b. at Pomfret, 2 Apr 1766; d. at Tolland, 7 Dec 1843; m. 17 Jun 1790, MARY STEELE, b. at Tolland, 25 Jul 1765 daughter of Stephen and Hannah (Chapman) Steele; Mary d. at Tolland, 25 Nov 1843.

ii SAMUEL HOWARD, b. at Pomfret, 1 Oct 1767; d. 27 Oct 1785.

iii PRISCILLA HOWARD, b. at Pomfret, 22 May 1769; d. at Unadilla, NY, 8 Dec 1861; m. 1st, as his second wife, ISRAEL WILLIAMS (widower of Temperance Holmes), b. at Pomfret, 19 Nov 1763 son of David and Elizabeth (Dana) Williams; Israel d. at Franklin, NY, Oct 1807. Priscilla m. 2nd 26 Mar 1812, ASAHEL PACKARD, b. 1761 and d. at Unadilla, 28 Jun 1846. Asahel was first married to Martha French.

iv THOMAS HOWARD, b. at Pomfret, 2 Dec 1770; d. 3 Mar 1772.

v THOMAS HOWARD, b. at Pomfret, 27 Feb 1772; d. at Preble, NY, 29 Oct 1841; m. 2 Apr 1795, ABIGAIL BARTLETT, b. at Wilbraham, MA, 25 Aug 1774 daughter of Moses and Abigail (-) Bartlett; Abigail d. at Preble, 19 Oct 1852.

vi HARVEY HOWARD, b. at Pomfret, 18 Apr 1773; d. at Preble, NY, 29 Aug 1830; m. 12 Jun 1794, SARAH GRIGGS, b. at Tolland, 1775 daughter of Ichabod and Mercy (Hatch) Griggs; Sarah d. at Preble, 25 Dec 1851.

vii HEZEKIAH HOWARD, b. at Pomfret, 1 Feb 1776; d. 27 Aug 1782.

viii STEPHEN HOWARD, b. at Pomfret, 16 Jul 1777; d. at Stafford, CT, 29 May 1813; m. 25 Jun 1800, MELINDA DIMICK, b. 2 Mar 1781 daughter of Edward and Rebecca (Lathrop) Dimick; Melinda d. at Stafford, 27 Nov 1815.

ix LOIS HOWARD, b. at Pomfret, 3 Apr 1779; d. at Abington, MA, 4 May 1842; m. at Tolland, 26 Feb 1805, THOMAS SOULE, b. at Ware, MA, 1 Jul 1783 son of Constant S. and Jemima (Jenkins) Soule; Thomas d. at Duxbury, MA, 23 Oct 1819.

x JOSEPH HOWARD, b. at Tolland, 16 Nov 1780; d. at South Windsor, 18 Feb 1865; m. 29 Oct 1804, DELANA REED, b. at Tolland, 9 Jan 1782 daughter of Samuel and Lydia (Pierce) Reed; Delana d. at Tolland, 7 Sep 1823.

xi BENJAMIN HOWARD, b. at Tolland, 12 Mar 1782; d. at Tolland, 28 Sep 1826; m. 17 Apr 1803, DELIVERANCE CASWELL, b. at Tolland, 8 Dec 1782 daughter of Lemuel and Deliverance (Chubbuck) Caswell; Deliverance d. at Tolland, 4 Sep 1826.

xii HEZEKIAH HOWARD, b. at Tolland, 10 Apr 1784; d. at Franklin, PA, 26 Sep 1878; m. at Franklin, NY, 31 Dec 1807, MARGARET SPRING, b. at Stephentown, NY, 24 Oct 1784 daughter of Ephraim Spring; Margaret d. at Rockdale, PA, 14 Jul 1851.

xiii SAMUEL DANA HOWARD, b. at Tolland, 19 Dec 1785; d. 24 Jul 1800.

xiv RALPH HOWARD, b. at Tolland, 21 Feb 1788; d. at Halifax, Nova Scotia, 7 Feb 1815; m. at Windsor, VT, 31 Jan 1812, RHODA HOISINGTON, b. at Windsor, 24 Feb 1791 daughter of Aaron and Hannah (Wilson) Hoisington, Rhoda d. at Windsor, VT, Aug 1842.

1046) JOSEPH GROW (*Joseph Grow⁴, Rebekah Holt Grow³, James², Nicholas¹*), b. at Pomfret, 13 Mar 1748 son of Joseph and Abigail (Dana) Grow; d. at Hartland, VT, 19 Mar 1813; m. 13 Dec 1770, TIRZAH SANGER, b. at Woodstock, 19 Dec 1748 daughter of Nathaniel and Mary (Roth) Sanger; d. at Hartland, about 1825.

Joseph and Tirzah had their first child in Pomfret, Connecticut and were then in Fitzwilliam, New Hampshire where their other children were born. Joseph and Tirzah were admitted to the church at Fitzwilliam 17 December 1772. Joseph served as selectman of Fitzwilliam in 1773.[2778] After six years in Fitzwilliam, they left for Hartland, Vermont where they were first members of the Congregational church.[2779]

Joseph Grow and Tirzah Sanger were parents of twelve children.

i JOHN MARSHALL GROW, b. at Pomfret, CT, 15 Nov 1771; d. at Derby, VT, 26 Feb 1853; m. 1st at Hartland, VT, 4 Dec 1794, POLLY STOWELL, b. at Pomfret, 3 May 1771 daughter of Elisha and Jerusha (Sabin) Stowell; Polly d. at Hartland, 3 Mar 1813. John m. 2nd at Hartland, 12 May 1813, OLIVE BLAKE (widow of Charles Fitch), b. at Keen, NH, 16 Dec 1777 daughter of Asahel and Ithamar (-) Blake; Olive d. at Johnson, VT, 16 Nov 1873.

ii SAMUEL PORTER GROW, b. at Fitzwilliam, NH, 23 Mar 1773; m. at Hartland, VT, 14 Mar 1799, JERUSHA STOWELL, b. at Pomfret, 28 Nov 1777 daughter of Elisha and Jerusha (Sabin) Stowell.

[2777] *Connecticut State Library (Hartford, Connecticut), Estate of Priscilla Howard*

[2778] Norton, *The History of Fitzwilliam*, p 253 and p 590

[2779] Davis, *John Grow of Ipswich*, p 40

iii JOSEPH GROW, b. at Fitzwilliam, NH, 3 Nov 1774; d. at Hartland, VT, 12 Feb 1813; m. LOIS COATS

iv JAMES REED GROW, b. at Fitzwilliam, 2 Oct 1776; d. at Holyoke, MA, 12 Mar 1857; m. at Hinsdale, NH, 5 Jul 1802, SOPHIA SANGER, b. 1784 daughter of Benjamin and Theena (Shattuck) Sanger;[2780] Sarah d. at Brownington, VT, 15 Mar 1825.

v LUCRETIA GROW, b. at Fitzwilliam, 17 Sep 1778; d. at Alden, NY, 25 Jul 1856 (probate 10 Mar 1857); m. 1st at Hartland, VT, 4 Apr 1799, OLIVER UDELL, b. about 1799; Oliver d. at Alden, 1822. Lucretia m. 2nd, about 1826, NATHAN TUTTLE (whose first wife was Polly Taylor), b. about 1771; Nathan d. at Darien, NY, 1855.

vi NATHANIEL GROW, b. at Hartland, VT, 5 May 1780; d. at Hartland, 6 Jun 1838; m. at Hartland, 20 May 1806, SALLY BURK, b. at Hartland, 6 Jan 1789 daughter of Joseph and Judith (Barrell) Burk.

vii TIRZAH GROW, b. at Hartland, 18 Jul 1782; d. at Hartland, 19 Nov 1853; m. about 1798, EBENEZER COTTON, b. at Pomfret, 5 May 1768 son of Thomas and Sarah (Holbrook) Cotton; Ebenezer d. at Hartland, 26 Sep 1819.

viii LUCY GROW, b. at Hartland, 20 Aug 1785; d. at Ionia, MI, 5 Nov 1867; m. 20 Sep 1810, SULLIVAN RUST, b. at Hartland, 23 Jan 1780 son of Oliver and Lucy (Buttrick) Rust; Sullivan d, at Darien, NY, 6 Oct 1842.

ix POLLY GROW, b. 2 Mar 1787; d. 20 Jan 1788.

x GEORGE GROW, b. at Hartland, 17 Nov 1788; d. at Nashua, NH, 29 Apr 1844; m. ABIGAIL MATHEWS, b. at Hartland, 11 Jan 1792 daughter of Samuel and Abigail (Sumner) Mathews; Abigail d. at Boston, 30 Jun 1885.

xi POLLY GROW, b. 17 Nov 1790; d. at Hartland, 27 Sep 1875; m. at Hartland, 27 Jan 1808, JONATHAN BURK, b. at Hartland, 25 Oct 1784 son of Joseph and Judith (Barrell) Burk; Jonathan d. at Hartland, 23 Oct 1861.

xii OTIS GROW, b. at Hartland, 25 Jul 1793; d. at Cavendish, VT, 13 Dec 1876; m. 1st 24 Aug 1815, JERUSHA BRYANT, b. about 1793; Jerusha d. at Chester, VT, 15 Nov 1853. Otis m. 2nd 29 Sep 1856, PRISCILLA GRIFFIN, b. at Nelson, NH, 13 Jun 1800 daughter of Samuel and Sophia (Foster) Griffin; Priscilla d. at Windham, VT, 7 Jan 1873.

1047) JOHN GROW (*Joseph Grow⁴, Rebekah Holt Grow³, James², Nicholas¹*), b. at Pomfret, 9 May1750 son of Joseph and Abigail (Dana) Grow; d. at Penfield, NY, 1834; m. at Woodstock, 22 Jun 1772, DEBORAH DAVISON, b. at Mansfield, CT, 17 May 1750 daughter of Paul and Deborah (Wright) Davison; Deborah d. at Penfield, 6 Apr 1831.

John and his wife Deborah were in Pomfret and Canterbury in the early part of their marriage but spent thirty years of their married life in Vermont. Later in life, they were in several locations in New York.

On 2 October 1832, John Grow of Penfield, New York, then age eighty-two, appeared to make a statement related to his application for a pension. He reported being born at Pomfret on 9 May 1750. On 1 June 1776, he enlisted in the company of Capt. Asa Bacon in the regiment of Col. John Chester for seven months but was discharged after six months eight days "on account of being sick." While in the service, he went from Canterbury, where he was living at the time, to New York and then on to Long Island and then to New York City. He was at the battle of Long Island. Following the war, he moved from Canterbury back to Pomfret, In February 1779, he went to Vermont and was in Hartland until 1794 when he relocated to Littleton now known as Waterford, Vermont. In 1813, he went to Galen, New York and in 1815 to Victor, New York, and in 1820 arrived in Penfield where he remained.[2781]

John and Deborah were parents of ten children.

i ASA GROW, b. at Pomfret, 24 Jun 1772; d. at Tecumseh, MI, 1851; m. likely at Waterford, VT, about 1800, MARY HOLBROOK.

ii ABIGAIL GROW, b. at Pomfret, 27 Dec 1773; d. at Waitsfield, VT, 28 May 1829; m. 1st about 1794, JAMES PETRIE, b. about 1765; James d. at Hartland, 5 Dec 1825. Abigail m. 2nd at Waitsfield, 15 Jan 1827, ELIAS TAYLOR, b. at Williamstown, MA, 27 Jun 1756 son of Samuel and Anne (Alexander) Taylor;[2782] Elias d. at Waitsfield, 26 May 1829. Elias was first married to Mercy Goss and second married to Azubah Child.

iii JOHN GROW, b. at Canterbury, 31 Jul 1775; d. at Yates, NY, Mar 1843; m. 1st 11 Aug 1804, SARAH BROWN, b. May 1786 daughter of Isaac and Huldah (Walker) Brown; Sarah d. at Ridgeway, NY, 6 Dec 1833. John m. 2nd about 1835, CYRENA MCDOWAL, b. in MA, Jan 1787 (computed from age 77 years 2 months at death); Cyrena d. at Yates, 21 Mar 1864.

iv AMBROSE GROW, b. at Pomfret, 29 Oct 1777; m. 1st at Waterford, 7 Jan 1803, HANNAH GRAVES, b. at Athol, MA, 23 Mar 1778 daughter of Nathaniel and Mercy (Paige) Graves; Hannah d. at Junius, NY, 1820. Ambrose m. 2nd 2 Jan 1821, SARAH GODFREY.

[2780] James R. Grow was the administrator of the 1816 probate of the estate of Benjamin Sanger of Hinsdale.

[2781] U.S. Revolutionary War Pension and Bounty-Land Warrant Application Files, Case S13211

[2782] Jones, *History of the Town of Waitsfield, Vermont*, p 481

v EREPTA GROW, b. at Hartland, 8 Jan 1780; d. at Reading, NY, 12 Dec 1842; m. at Waterford, VT, 4 Jul 1798, Rev. ASA CARPENTER, b. at Ashford, CT, 10 Oct 1770 son of Jonah and Zerviah (Whittemore) Carpenter; Asa d. at Penfield, NY, 10 Sep 1826.

vi SUSAN SMITH GROW, b. at Hartland, 29 Oct 1782; d. at Waterford, VT, 31 Mar 1866; m. at Waterford, 12 May 1799, AMOS KINNE,[2783] b. at Pomfret, CT, 1 Feb 1774 son of Amos and Esther (Utley) Kinney; Amos d. at Waterford, 22 Jun 1849.

vii ELIAS GROW, b. at Hartland, 7 Apr 1785; d. at Penn Yen, NY, 1830; m. at Junius, NY, 15 May 1809, HULDAH DRYER, b. at West Stockbridge, MA, 7 Sep 1789 daughter of John and Keziah (French) Dryer.

viii SALLY GROW, b. at Hartland, 12 Apr 1787; d. at Beaver Dam, WI, 30 Nov 1862; m. at Hartland, 12 Feb 1804, VINE TAYLOR, b. at Hartland, 8 Feb 1780 son of Oliver and Abigail (Sprague) Taylor; Vine d. at Beaver Dam, 9 Feb 1859.

ix OLIVER H. GROW, b. at Hartland, 11 Jan 1790; d. at Victor, NY, 15 Apr 1877; m. 30 Apr 1813, PERMELIA "MILLY" DRYER, b. 8 Nov 1791 daughter of Samuel and Philena (Robbins) Dryer; Milly d. at Victor, 5 Aug 1872.

x ABIEL GROW, b. at Hartland, 14 Dec 1792; d. at Ottawa, IL, 3 Dec 1870; m. 25 Dec 1813, SARAH SEELY, b. at Stockbridge, MA, 1 Sep 1793 daughter of Jonas and Sarah (Slater) Seely; Sarah d. at Ottawa, 18 Dec 1868.

1048) ABIGAIL GROW (*Joseph Grow[4], Rebekah Holt Grow[3], James[2], Nicholas[1]*), b. at Pomfret, 3 Nov 1752 daughter of Joseph and Abigail (Dana) Grow; d. after 1840 when she was living in Homer, NY with her son Joseph;[2784] m. at Mansfield, CT, 20 Mar 1777, ISAAC ROYCE, b. at Mansfield, 1 Jul 1750 son of David and Hannah (Hall) Royce.

Isaac Royce is reported as serving in the Revolution, but the pension application of his widow Abigail was rejected as the service could not be verified.[2785] Despite this denial of claim, a biography of Harrison D. Hyde, who married Abigail and Isaac's granddaughter Mary M. Royce, claims that Isaac was a Revolutionary War hero. This biography also reports that Abigail was nearly captured by the British during the war at the bombardment of Boston. Abigail lived to age ninety-two.[2786]

Abigail Grow and Isaac Royce were parents of four children born at Mansfield, Connecticut.

i ALBA GROW ROYCE, b. at Mansfield, 10 May 1778; d. between 1838 (birth of youngest child) and 1850; m. by about 1822, ALMIRA GREEN, b. 2 Jul 1799; Almira d. at Pioneer, OH, 6 Sep 1868.[2787]

ii TIRZAH GROW, b. at Mansfield, 19 Jan 1780.

iii JOSEPH ROYCE, b. at Mansfield, 8 Apr 1782; d. after 1840 when he was living in Homer, NY and before 1850; m. by 1825, SALLY CROSS, b. 1794; Sally d after 1850 when she was living at Deerfield, MI.

iv LESTER ROYCE, baptized at Mansfield, CT, 17 Jul 1785; d. after 1850 when he was living at Cortland, NY;[2788] m. DELIGHT WARNER, b. at Ashford, 24 Mar 1789 daughter of Eleazer and Joanna (Hale) Warner;[2789] Delight d. after 1850.

1049) SAMUEL GROW (*Joseph Grow[4], Rebekah Holt Grow[3], James[2], Nicholas[1]*), b. at Pomfret, 19 Jan 1755 son of Joseph and Abigail (Dana) Grow; d. at Newbury, VT, 18 May 1842; m. about 1785, DAMARIS POWERS, b. at Lisbon, CT, 8 Jan 1761 daughter of Peter and Martha (Hale) Powers; Damaris d. at Newbury, VT, 22 Aug 1836.

Samuel and Damaris lived in Hartland, Vermont until 194 when they moved to Newbury. They are credited with building the first framed house in the area. The were members of first church of Newbury.[2790]

i HALE GROW, b. at Hartland, 8 Aug 1786; d. at Topsham, VT, 8 Mar 1865; m. about 1809, JUDITH DUSTIN, b. at Atkinson, NH, 15 Apr 1789 daughter of Nathaniel and Judith (Knight) Dustin; Judith d. at Newbury, VT, 28 Mar 1886.

ii MOODY GROW, b. at Hartland, 1 Nov 1787; d. at Prairie du Sac, WI, 10 Apr 1871; m. 1st at Springfield, MA, 11 Jan 1812, CLARISSA PARSONS, b. at Springfield, 9 Jul 1790 daughter of Daniel and Sarah (Ferry) Parsons;

[2783] The Kinne name is also spelled Kinney.

[2784] The 1840 Census for the household of Joseph Royce includes a female age 80-89.

[2785] U. S. Revolutionary War and Bounty-Land Warrant Application Files, Case R9056

[2786] *Biographical Album of Oakland County, Michigan*, 1891, Chapman Brothers, p 261

[2787] Almira's date of birth is engraved on her gravestone (findagrave ID 202249626). Her maiden name is given as Almira Green on the death record of one of her daughters, but no other record of her maiden name was located.

[2788] Both Lester and his wife Delight seem to have died between 1850 in 1855. In the 1850 census, Lester and Delight and daughters Sophronia and Joanna were living together. In 1855, Sophronia and Joanna, both still single, were in their own household.

[2789] Warner, *The Descendants of Andrew Warner*, p 209

[2790] Wells, *History of Newbury, Vermont*, p 562

Clarissa d. at Newbury, VT, 17 Dec 1813. Moody m. 2nd about 1814, HANNAH PARKER, b. about Nov 1790 (based on age 76 years 11 months at death); Hannah d. at Prairie du Sac, 26 Oct 1867.

iii CHARLES GROW, b. at Hartland, 12 May 1790; d. at Topsham, VT, 16 Jun 1886; m. 4 Jul 1816, LYDIA SAWYER, b. about 1795; Lydia d. at Neponset, IL, 9 Jan 1876 at age 81.

iv ELIZA GROW, b. at Hartland, 17 Jun 1794; d. at Rutland, VT, 23 Jul 1872; m. at Newbury, 18 Apr 1816, JESSE PUTNAM, b. at Upham, MA, 21 Dec 1790 son of Israel and Susannah (Heath) Putnam; Jesse d. at Rutland, 3 Mar 1868.

v SAMUEL GROW, b. at Newbury, VT, 20 Oct 1799; d. at Corinth, VT, 28 Nov 1883; m. about 1829, RELIEF EMERSON, b. at Newbury, 14 Jan 1804 daughter of John and Abigail (Duty) Emerson; Relief, d. at Newbury, 10 Mar 1859.

1050) AMBROSE GROW (*Joseph Grow[4], Rebekah Holt Grow[3], James[2], Nicholas[1]*), b. at Pomfret, 27 Jul 1756 son of Joseph and Abigail (Dana) Grow; d. at Fabius, NY, 12 Jul 1845; m. 1st at Mansfield, 18 May 1780, JEMIMA ELDRIDGE. Ambrose m. 2nd at Russell, MA, 5 Apr 1810, AMY PARSONS, b. at Springfield, MA, 20 Nov 1779 daughter of Daniel and Sarah (Ferry) Parsons; Amy d. at Fabius, after 1860. Amy was first married to Mr. Thomas.

On 11 September 1832, Amme Grow of the town of Fabius, New York appeared to give a statement related to her application for a widow's pension. The statement relates that Ambrose enlisted in May 1776 for a term of seven months and was discharged on 25 December 1776. He served a three-month term from September to December 1777 and a third enlistment for three months in 1778. After this, Ambrose moved to Hartland, Vermont and from there enlisted for eight months on 1 May 1779. He was involved in the pursuit of enemy forces after the burning of Royalston. He was also present at the battles of Long Island and Rhode Island. One of Amy's children form her first marriage, Lovewell Thomas, provided a statement in support of his mother's application.[2791]

Ambrose Grow and Jemima Eldridge were parents of ten children.[2792] There are birth records for only two of the children. The order of birth and dates of birth are estimated based on dates of marriage and dates of death.

i LORA GROW, b. at Hartland, VT, 19 May 1782; d. at Phelps, NY, about 1805; m. about 1801, WILLIAM INGERSOLL but is likely of Lee, MA as their eldest child was born there.

ii JEMIMA GROW, b. likely at Salisbury, CT, 1786; d. at Hartland, VT, 9 Mar 1878; m. at Hartland, 1 Jul 1804, JAMES BURNHAM, b. 1782 son of James and Martha (Sanborn) Burnham;[2793] James d. at Woodstock, VT, 18 May 1845.

iii PERMELIA GROW, b. about 1789; d. at Enfield, CT, 23 May 1869; m. about 1810, DAVID HALE, b. at Enfield, about 1777 son of David and Ruth (Pease) Hale; David d. at Enfield, 6 Sep 1863.

iv MINERVA GROW, b. at Salisbury, about 1790; d. at West Hartford, VT, 1852; m. 1st at Norwich, VT, 7 Dec 1812; JOHN BALDWIN, b. at Norwich, 11 Dec 1788 son of Levi and Anna (Waterman) Baldwin; John d. at Norwich, 27 Aug 1823. Minerva m. 2nd at Norwich, 10 Jun 1825, ORANGE BARTLETT, b. at Norwich, 16 Dec 1789 son of Elliott and Abigail (Wright) Bartlett; Orange d. at West Hartford, 1867.

v ARVILLA GROW, b. at Salisbury, about 1791; d. at Barnard, VT, 14 Mar 1863; m. 1st about 1810, STEPHEN WATKINS, b. at Pomfret, VT, 18 May 1782 son of John and Mary (Scarborough) Watkins; Stephen d. at Pomfret, 1813 (probate 1813 with will naming wife Arvilla, son William, and mother Polly). Arvilla m. 2nd at Pomfret, 11 Sep 1814, PHINEAS CHURCHILL, b. 28 Apr 1793 son of Isaac and Elizabeth (Raymond) Churchill; Phineas d. at Royalton, VT, 27 Aug 1886.

vi POLLY GROW, b. 1793; d. at Salisbury, 29 Dec 1796.

vii GIRDEN GROW, b. about 1795; d. at Schenectady, NY before 1840 when widow Mary was head of household; m. MARY who has not been identified, b. about 1805 and living as a widow in Schenectady in 1871.

viii PORNTON GROW, b. about 1796; d. at Bellona, NY, 11 Nov 1848; m. RUTH BAKER, b. about 1796; Ruth d. at Bellona, 16 Feb 1865.

ix WILLIAM GROW, b. at Salisbury, 19 Jun 1799; d. at Summit, NJ, 25 Sep 1881; m. (according to the Grow genealogy), LEAH DE LANE who has not been identified. William appears to have had a second wife Mary.

x MARY GROW, b. about 1800.[2794]

[2791] U. S. Revolutionary War Pension and Bounty-Land Warrant Application Files, Case W1416

[2792] Davis, *John Grow of Ipswich*, p 43

[2793] Heath and Lusk, *Genealogical Records of Deacon John Burnham*, Third Edition, p 175

[2794] Mary is a child given in the Grow genealogy and she is said to have died unmarried. No records were located for her.

Ambrose Grow and Amy Parsons were parents of two children whose births are recorded at Springfield, Massachusetts although the births may have occurred in New York.

i SARAH PARSONS GROW, b. 19 Nov 1812; d. at Gaines, NY, 4 Mar 1896; m. at Fabius, NY, 3 Oct 1835, JOHN GIFFORD HATCH, b. at Falmouth, MA, 28 Feb 1805 son of Job and Achsah (Gifford) Hatch; John d. at East Bloomfield, NY, 24 Dec 1883.

ii ALMERIN GROW, b. 10 Mar 1816; d. at San Francisco, 10 Jan 1908. Almerin was an interesting character. He had at least five marriages and he moved frequently being in Illinois, Ohio, Syracuse, NY, Utah, and California. He was involved with the Mormons for a period of time. On census records, he describes himself variously as a physician and dentist and minister and preacher. His first wife seems to be ELIZA who was born in Kentucky about 1823 and who was the mother of children Ambrose and Amy. Almerin married MARY H. TRUMBULL at Union, IL on 29 Jul 1853. He married MARY ANN TROTTER at Hamilton, OH on 18 Mar 1859. He married SARAH WILCOX at Hamilton, OH on 20 Feb 1868 and at Sacramento, CA on 7 Nov 1877, NELLIE STOCKHAM. It is possible he had two other marriages, one of them to Mary Donnelly.

1051) MARY GROW (*Joseph Grow⁴, Rebekah Holt Grow³, James², Nicholas¹*), b. at Pomfret, 8 Feb 1764 daughter of Joseph and Abigail (Dana) Grow; d. at West Newbury, VT, 1 Apr 1843; m. 12 Feb 1786, STEPHEN POWERS, b. at Lisbon, CT, 15 Jul 1762 son of Peter and Martha (Hale) Powers; Stephen d. at West Newbury, 22 Mar 1843.

Stephen and Mary settled in West Newbury, Vermont where they kept a farm and raised their eleven children.[2795]

i PETER POWERS, b. at Newbury, 17 Apr 1787; d. at Corinth, VT, 25 Jun 1857; m. about 1806, RUTH ROGERS (widow of Aaron Ferrin), b. at Hampton, 3 Apr 1778 daughter of Josiah and Hannah (Woodman) Rogers; Ruth d. at Corinth, 9 Aug 1876.

ii MARTHA POWERS, b. 18 Aug 1788; d. 3 Mar 1790.

iii MARTHA POWERS, b. at Newbury, 23 May 1790; d. at Newbury, 14 Sep 1880; m. at Newbury, 23 Jan 1819, JOHN BAILEY, b. at Newbury, 14 Jul 1791 son of Joshua and Anna (Fowler) Bailey; John d. at Newbury, 21 Aug 1879.

iv JONATHAN POWERS, b. at Newbury, 8 Mar 1792; d. at Sutton, VT, 2 Jul 1873; m. at Bradford, VT, 21 Mar 1820, HARRIET CORLISS, b. about 1798 perhaps daughter of Emerson Corliss; Harriet d. at Sutton, 5 Feb 1854.

v ANNA POWERS, b. at Newbury, 12 May 1792; d. at Newbury, 1 Sep 1841; m. 17 Sep 1812, THOMAS ABBOTT, b. at Newbury, 8 Jun 1788 son of Bancroft and Lydia (White) Abbott; Thomas d. at Georgetown, NY, 1855 (probate 1855). Thomas married second, Anna's sister Abigail Powers on 23 Dec 1841.

vi POLLY POWERS, b. 5 Dec 1795; d. 12 Oct 1823.

vii ABIGAIL POWERS, b. 7 Sep 1797; d. at Newbury, 24 Nov 1862; m. 23 Dec 1841, THOMAS ABBOTT who was first married to Abigail's sister Anna (see above).

viii STEPHEN POWERS, b. at Newbury, 16 Jul 1799; d. at Dorchester, MA, 16 Dec 1868; m. about 1822, MARY STEPHENS, b. at Hampstead, NH, 14 Sep 1802 daughter of Joseph and Betsy (Heath) Stephens;[2796] Mary d. at Boston, 9 May 1891.

ix JOHN POWERS, b. 30 Jul 1802; d. 13 Jul 1803.

x BETSEY POWERS, b. at Newbury, 6 Jun 1804; d. at Newbury, 25 Dec 1877; m. 27 Nov 1826, her first cousin, JOHN HALE POWERS (*Anna Grow Powers⁵, Joseph Grow⁴, Rebekah Holt Grow³, James², Nicholas¹*), b. at Newbury, 26 Jan 1789 son of Samuel and Anna (Grow) Powers; John d. at Newbury 10 Dec 1866.

xi ELECTA D. POWERS, b. 13 Dec 1806; d. at Bradford, VT, 9 Nov 1888; m. 21 Jan 1837, her first cousin, JONATHAN POWERS, b. at Deer Isle, ME, 12 Nov 1808 son of Moody and Elizabeth (Eaton) Powers; Jonathan d. at Bradford, 28 Jan 1882.

1052) ANNA GROW (*Joseph Grow⁴, Rebekah Holt Grow³, James², Nicholas¹*), b. at Pomfret, 1767 daughter of Joseph and Abigail (Dana) Grow; d. at Newbury, VT, 16 Jun 1789; m. at Newbury, 14 Feb 1788, SAMUEL POWERS, b. about 1767 son of Peter and Martha (Hale) Powers; Samuel d. at Newbury, 21 Jan 1857. Samuel married second Sarah Ford and married third Mary White.

Samuel and Anna resided in Newbury, Vermont. Anna died six months after the birth of her only child. Samuel also had two children with his second wife.

[2795] Wells, *History of Newbury, Vermont*, p 660

[2796] The names of Mary's parents are given as Joseph Stephens and Betsy Heath on her death record.

i JOHN HALE POWERS, b. at Newbury, 26 Jan 1789; d. at Newbury, 10 Dec 1866; m. 27 Nov 1826, his first cousin, BETSEY POWERS (*Mary Grow Powers⁵, Joseph Grow⁴, Rebekah Holt Grow³, James², Nicholas¹*), b. at Newbury, 6 Jun 1804 son of Stephen and Mary (Grow) Powers; Betsey d. at Newbury, 25 Dec 1877.

1053) MARY WILLIAMS (*Ruth Grow Williams⁴, Rebekah Holt Grow³, James², Nicholas¹*), b. at Woodstock, 30 May 1745 daughter of Joseph and Ruth (Grow) Williams; d. at Amherst, MA, 27 May 1785; m. at Amherst, about 1768, LEMUEL MOODY, b. at Hadley, MA, 27 Jun 1739 son of Jonathan and Bridget (Smith) Moody; Lemuel d. at Amherst, 22 Feb 1818.

In his will written 23 March 1809 (probate 6 April 1818), Lemuel Moody bequeathed to son William Moody and to daughter Mary Thurston one dollar each. The remainder of the estate went to son Lemuel who was also named executor.[2797]

Mary Williams and Lemuel Moody were parents of three children born at Amherst, Massachusetts.

i WILLIAM MOODY, b. 1769; d. at Hawley, MA, 1 Aug 1850; m. at Amherst, Aug 1795, PAMELIA "MILLEY" FAIRBANKS, b. about 1759; Pamelia d. at Hawley, 27 Nov 1848 (age 89 years 10 months).

ii LEMUEL MOODY, b. about 1772; d. at Amherst, MA, 31 Oct 1831 (probate Feb 1823); m. Nov 1802, SALLY HANKS, b. about 1782.

iii MARY MOODY, b. about 1780; m. at Amherst, 9 Oct 1806, PAUL THURSTON, b. at Belchertown, 8 Dec 1776 son of Thomas and Elizabeth (Larmon) Thurston; Paul d. at Pelham, MA, 12 Oct 1829.

1054) REBEKAH WILLIAMS (*Ruth Grow Williams⁴, Rebekah Holt Grow³, James², Nicholas¹*), baptized at Woodstock, 19 Mar 1748/9 daughter of Joseph and Ruth (Grow) Williams; d. at Monson, MA, Aug 1823; m. at Amherst, MA, about 1770, JOSEPH STIMSON, b. at Tolland, 12 Jan 1746/7 son of Ichabod and Margaret (Peck) Stimson; Joseph d. at Monson, 1 Jul 1810.

Rebekah and Joseph started their family in Tolland where the oldest children were born and were afterwards in Monson, Massachusetts.

In his will written 15 March 1810 (proved 19 Jul 1810), Joseph Stimson bequeathed to beloved wife Rebecca the use of all the household goods during her natural life. The following bequests were made to his children: Enos Stimson, twenty dollars; Joseph Stimson, thirty dollars and half the wearing apparel; Rufus Stimson, one dollar; Noah Stimson, one dollar; Ira Stimson, half the property and half the wearing apparel; son Jeremy the other half of the property; daughters Polly Truesdell and Rebecca Stimson, the household goods after the decease of their mother; and to granddaughter Serepta Truesdell daughter of Polly, four dollars. Son-in-law Perley Truesdell was named executor.[2798]

Rebekah Williams and Joseph Stimson were parents of eight children.

i ENOS STIMSON, b.at Tolland, 24 Jun 1772; d. at Homer, NY, 1853 (probate 1853); m. by 1800, DESIRE BIXBY, b. at Stafford, CT, 27 Jan 1777 daughter of Abijah and Anna (Corbin) Bixby.

ii REBECCA STIMSON, b. at Tolland, 4 Dec 1774. Rebecca was living and unmarried in 1810.

iii JOSEPH STIMSON, b. at Monson, 24 Apr 1778; d. at Port Leyden, NY, 30 Aug 1851; m. 1801, CATHERINE SMITH, b. 31 Aug 1777 and baptized at Haddam, Oct 1777 daughter of Lewis and Ann (Hubbard) Smith; Catherine d. at Port Leyden, 21 Mar 1860.

iv RUFUS STIMSON, b. 20 Feb 1781; d. at Palmer, MA, 18 Jan 1821; m. POLLY FULLER, b. at Monson, 1780 daughter of Eleazer and Rachel (Bartlett) Fuller; Polly d. at Monson, 15 Jan 1863.

v NOAH STIMSON, b. at Monson, 19 Jan 1783; d. at Palmer, MA, 13 Aug 1872; m. 1st 1806, HANNAH BUSH, b. at Monson, 23 Oct 1787 daughter of Stephen and Zilpha (Thresher) Bush; Hannah d. 5 Oct 1849. Noah m. 2nd at Brookfield, MA, 5 Mar 1851, CHLOE GARDNER.

vi Rev. IRA STIMSON, b. 18 May 1785; d. at Maquoketa, IA, 13 Jan 1852; m. ANNA S., b. 18 Mar 1788 (per gravestone) who has not been identified; Anna d. at Maquoketa, 16 May 1868. Anna is perhaps Anna Merriman b. at Southington, CT, 18 Mar 1788 daughter of N. Mansfield and Mary (Wadsworth) Merriman.

vii POLLY STIMSON, b. about 1787; d. at Monson, 11 Dec 1862; m. about 1805, PEARLEY TRUESDELL, b. at Monson, 17 Jun 1771 son of Thomas and Rhoda (Curtis) Truesdell; Pearley d. at Monson, 7 Oct 1843.

viii JEREMIAH STIMSON, b. about 1791; d. at Fredericksburg, IA, 26 Sep 1871; m. BETSY BUSH, b. 1792 daughter of Stephen and Zilpha (Thresher) Bush; Betsy d. at Fredericksburg, 1857.

2797 *Hampshire County, MA: Probate File Papers, 1660-1889.* Online database. *AmericanAncestors.org.* New England Historic Genealogical Society, 2016, 2017. Case 100-8

2798 *Massachusetts, Wills and Probate Records, 1635-1991, Hampshire County, volume 26, pp 287-288*

1055) SARAH WILLIAMS (*Ruth Grow Williams⁴, Rebekah Holt Grow³, James², Nicholas¹*), baptized at Woodstock, 6 Jan 1751 daughter of Joseph and Ruth (Grow) Williams; d. at Homer, NY, Jul 1808; m. at Amherst, MA, about 1775, WILLIAM MAY,[2799] b. at Roxbury, MA, 21 Oct 1740 son of Eleazer and Dorothy (Davis) Mary; William d. at Homer, 22 Aug 1812.

Sarah and William married at Amherst by 1776 and William was a farmer in Amherst in 1776. The births of eight children for this couple are recorded at Monson. Two of Sarah's siblings also settled in Monson. The family moved on to Homer, New York where Sarah and William are buried at Glenwood Cemetery in Homer as is their oldest son Eleazer.[2800]

William served short periods during the Revolution serving with the militia for 11 days in 1775 on the Lexington alarm. He served an additional four days with the militia in August 1777 at New Providence and was at Stillwater in September 1777.[2801]

On 27 April 1791, William May of Monson conveyed to Eleazer May and Ithamar May of Pomfret a lot of land containing thirty-nine acres for payment of eighteen pounds.[2802] Eleazer and Ithamar are most likely William's two brothers who resided in Pomfret. It may be about this time that Sarah and William made the move to Homer.

There are records of eight children of Sarah Williams and William May born at Monson, Massachusetts.[2803]

i ELEAZER MAY, b. at Monson, 4 Sep1776; d. at Homer, NY, 7 Sep 1867; m. at Tolland, 29 Nov 1798, DOROTHY "DOLLY" PELTON, b. at Somers, 1 Jul 1780 daughter of Moses and Dorothy (Benton) Pelton;[2804] Dolly d. at Homer, 1 May 1861.

ii ABIGAIL MAY, b. 25 Apr 1779

iii WILLIAM MAY, b. at Monson, 28 Jun 1781; d. at Hinsdale, NY, 11 May 1839; m. RHODA ANDREWS, b. at Wolcott, CT, 10 Feb 1788 daughter of Ebenezer and Abigail (Sperry) Andrews;[2805] Rhoda d. at Hinsdale, 6 Apr 1844.

iv SARAH MAY, b. 22 May 1784

v MARY SABIN MAY, b. at Monson, 1 May 1786; d. at Lowell, MA, 19 Sep 1848; m. at Thompson, CT, 17 Nov 1811; BENJAMIN GREENE, b. at Warwick, RI, 14 Nov 1784 son of Caleb and Polly (Remington) Greene;[2806] Benjamin d. at Lowell, 30 Jul 1863. Benjamin Greene was first married to Nancy Henry who died in 1810.

vi DOLLY MAY, b. at Monson, 7 Apr 1788; d. after 1850 when she was living in Auburn, OH; m. ENOCH BECKETT ANDREWS, b. at Wolcott, 4 Dec 1784 son of Ebenezer and Abigail (Sperry) Andrews; Enoch d. at Bainbridge, OH, 11 Feb 1872.

vii BELA MAY, b. at Monson, 24 Oct 1790; d. after 1870 when he was living at Kingsville, OH; m. LOVINA, b. in NY about 1801 who has not been identified; Lovina d. after 1880 when she was living in Kingsville with her unmarried daughter Jane.

viii LORIN RUEL MAY, b. at Monson, 9 Sep 1794; d. at Hinsdale, NY, 2 Mar 1879; m. ASENATH R., b. in NH, about 1800 who has not been identified; Asenath d. at Hinsdale, 10 May 1881.

1056) RUTH WILLIAMS (*Ruth Grow Williams⁴, Rebekah Holt Grow³, James², Nicholas¹*), b. at Woodstock, 24 Sep 1752 daughter of Joseph and Ruth (Grow) Williams; d. at Amherst, MA, 16 Apr 1822; m. at Amherst, 5 Oct 1780, as his second wife, AMARIAH DANA, b. at Pomfret, 20 May 1738 son of Samuel and Mary (Sumner) Dana; Amariah d. at Amherst, 5 Oct 1830. Amariah was first married to Dorothy May.

Ruth and Amariah resided in Amherst, Massachusetts where Amariah was the schoolmaster for a time. Amariah served in the Revolution and was at the taking of Ticonderoga.[2807] He was also one of the incorporators of the second parish in Amherst. Mariah was also a participant in Shay's rebellion following which he was required to take an oath of allegiance which he did in February or March 1787.[2808]

Ruth Williams and Amariah Dana were parents of eight children born at Amherst, Massachusetts. Amariah also had eight children with his first wife Dorothy May.

i JOHN DANA, b. and d. 14 Jun 1783

[2799] Vital Records of Amherst, Massachusetts, http://dunhamwilcox.net/ma/0-index_amherst.htm
[2800] Findagrave ID 182910792
[2801] Vital Records of Amherst, Massachusetts, NEHGR Corbin Collection, http://dunhamwilcox.net/ma/0-index_amherst.htm
[2802] Massachusetts Land Records, 1620-1986, Hampden County, 31:19
[2803] Massachusetts Births and Christenings, 1639-1915, accessed through familsearch.org
[2804] Pelton, *Genealogy of the Pelton Family*, p 474
[2805] Andrews, *Genealogical History of John and Mary Andrews*, p 131
[2806] Greene, *The Greenes of Rhode Island*, p 220
[2807] Dana, *The Dana Family in America*, p 67
[2808] Carpenter, *History of the Town of Amherst, Massachusetts*, p 133 and p 606

ii RUTH DANA, b. 8 Jun 1784; d. after 1860 when she was living in Hardwick with her son William; m. at Hardwick, 17 May 1804; JOHN TERRY, b. 1783 son of John and Sarah (Ramsdell) Terry; John d. 1843.

iii HANNAH DANA, b. 27 Oct 1786; d. at South Amherst, 5 Jan 1861; m. DAVID DICKINSON, b. at Amherst, 4 Aug 1785 son of Waitstill and Lucretia (Montague) Dickinson; David d. at South Amherst, 19 Nov 1833.

iv AMARIAH DANA, b. 14 Nov 1787; d. at Minerva, NY, 7 Jul 1864; m. likely in VT, HANNAH, b. about 1794 who is not definitely identified; Hannah d. at Minerva, after 1865.

v SAMUEL DANA, b. 26 Mar 1790; d. at Russell, NY, 11 Jul 1882; m. at Amherst, 15 Jan 1815, JULIA MOODY, b. 4 Nov 1791 daughter of Elihu and Rachel (Moody) Moody; Julia d. at Massena, NY, 22 Jul 1880.

vi SARAH DANA, b. 14 Dec 1791; d. at Amherst, 7 Jun 1870; m. 2 May 1820, as his second wife, ELIJAH CHURCH, b. at Amherst, 18 Nov 1780 son of Giles and Lois (Billings0 Church; Elijah d. at Amherst, 21 Nov 1843. Elijah was first married to Mehitable Williams.

vii SYLVIA DANA, b. 1 Jun 1793; d. at Amherst, 26 Apr 1850. Sylvia did not marry.

viii JOSEPH DANA, b. 14 Mar 1795; d. at Amherst, 27 Apr 1874; m. 28 Oct 1824, CLARISSA BENTON, b. at Tolland, CT, 14 Aug 1792 daughter of Timothy and Sarah (West) Benton; Clarissa d. at Amherst, 27 Aug 1876.

1057) AMBROSE WILLIAMS (*Ruth Grow Williams*[4], *Rebekah Holt Grow*[3], *James*[2], *Nicholas*[1]), b. at Woodstock, 24 Jul 1757 son of Joseph and Ruth (Grow) Williams; d. at Homer, NY, 13 Aug 1832; m. by 1782, KETURAH HOAR, b. at Brimfield, 22 Aug 1755 daughter of Edmund and Hannah (Alexander) Hoar; Keturah d. at Homer, 21 May 1826.

Ambrose served as a private in the company of Capt. Reuben Dickinson serving as a Minuteman. He lived in Amherst until about 1783 when he moved to Monson where Ambrose and Keturah's eight children were born. The family relocated to Homer about 1804.

On 9 April 1782 (recorded 7 May 1784), Ambrose Williams, then of Amherst, in consideration of £180 received, conveyed two tracts of land to William Kellogg of Amherst. This deed is also signed by Keturah Williams and Ruth Williams. Ruth would be Ambrose's mother Ruth Grow Williams as this land may have comprised a portion of her dower.[2809] The probate of Ambrose's father was in 1781 and these tracts likely represent part of his inheritance from his father.

Ambrose and Keturah were parents of eight children likely all born at Monson as the family was living in Monson in 1800.

i THOMAS WILLIAMS, b. 11 Mar 1783; d. at Homer, NY, 2 May 1851; m. 1807, OLIVE BLODGETT, b. at Stafford, CT, 16 Jul 1788 daughter of Paul and Hannah (Vinton) Blodgett; Olive d. at Homer, 25 Aug 1860.

ii POLLY WILLIAMS, b. 7 Jun 1785; d. at Cortland, NY, 22 Jun 1847; m. STEPHEN STORY, b. in VT, 1785; Stephen d. at Cortland, 1877 (probate 13 May 1877). There are two children known for Polly and Stephen, Sarah and Huldah. Huldah was the administratrix of her father's estate.

iii ELIZABETH "BETTY" WILLIAMS, b. 4 Jul 1787

iv ZEBINA WILLIAMS, b. 11 Jul 1792; d. at Homer, NY, 8 Jun 1862; m. PHEBE ANN ALVORD, b. 1804; Phebe d. at Homer, 30 Apr 1875.

v HANNAH WILLIAMS, b. 22 Feb 1795; d. at Homer, 22 Jan 1874; m. WOODIN HULL, b. 1789; Woodin d. at Homer, 12 Dec 1843.

vi CYRUS WILLIAMS, b. 18 Mar 1797; d. at Dixon, IL, 2 Aug 1866; m. LYDIA DODGE, b. in Canada, 1806; Lydia d. at Dixon, 1879.

vii CALVIN WILLIAMS, b. 28 Jun 1799; d. at Prophetstown, IL, 7 Oct 1884; m. about 1822, SALLY HILL, b. in VT, 1791; Sally d. at Prophetstown, 17 Aug 1844.

viii LOUIS WILLIAMS, b. 1800; d. at Homer, 1811.

1058) WILLIAM BARKER (*Hannah Grow Barker*[4], *Rebekah Holt Grow*[3], *James*[2], *Nicholas*[1]), b. at Pomfret, 18 Nov 1753 son of Ephraim and Hannah (Grow) Barker; d. at Madison, NY, 17 May 1826; m. about 1782, BETSEY ARMSTRONG, baptized at Norwich, 30 May 1762 daughter of Silas and Bathsheba (Worden) Armstrong;[2810] Betsey d. at Madison, 29 Aug 1832.[2811]

On 9 June 1818, William Barker of Madison, New York then age sixty-six, appeared in the court of common pleas and made declaration related to his application for a pension. On 1 May 1775, he enlisted as a private from Norwich, Connecticut in

[2809] Massachusetts Land Records 1620-1986, Hampden County, 22:668

[2810] The 1798 will of Silas Armstrong includes a bequest to his daughter Betty wife of William Barker.

[2811] Parshall's Barker genealogy provided limited information on William but included that he had married and located in Madison, NY. William and Betsey Barker had all their children in Norwich, so this marriage fits in terms of location. There is also a Revolutionary War pension file for William Barker in Madison, NY that fits this William in terms of age and location at time of enlistment.

the company of Capt. William Gale. He enlisted for an initial term of eight months but prior to the end of that enlistment he enlisted for an additional year. He served in the Connecticut line until 1 January 1777. He was in the Battle of Long Island just prior to the "great retreat" and at the Battle of White Plains. In June 1820, he had no real estate and a few personal items. His household consisted of his wife Betsey age fifty-eight.[2812]

There are records of eight children of William Barker and Betsey Armstrong born at Norwich. Marriages were located for just two of the children.

i HANNAH BARKER, b. 8 Feb 1783

ii SILAS BARKER, b. 28 Nov 1784; d. at Caneadea, NY, 17 Jan 1868; m. at Madison, NY, 18 Sep 1811,[2813] HARRIET HALL,[2814] b. 31 Oct 1784 and d. after 1875 when she was living with son William at Grove, NY.

iii ASA BARKER, baptized at Norwich, 10 Oct 1788

iv MARTIN BARKER, baptized at Norwich, 10 Oct 1788

v JOSEPH BARKER, b. 25 May 1790

vi LYDIA BARKER, b. 11 Jul 1794

vii LUCRETIA BARKER, b. 16 Jun 1797; d. at Koshkonong, WI, 15 Sep 1896; m. JOHN CHADWICK, b. 1793; John d. at Koshkonong, 17 Feb 1858.

viii JOHN BARKER, b. 28 Jun 1799

1059) HANNAH BARKER (*Hannah Grow Barker⁴, Rebekah Holt Grow³, James², Nicholas¹*), baptized at Pomfret 29 Aug 1754 daughter of Ephraim and Hannah (Grow) Barker; d. at Norwich, 1840; m. at Norwich, 20 Jan 1771, ELIJAH PITCHER,[2815] b. likely at Stoughton, MA, 4 Nov 1752 son of Elijah and Tabitha (Smith) Pitcher; Elijah d. at Norwich, 14 Jun 1839.

Hannah Barker and Elijah Pitcher were parents of ten children born at Norwich.

i ELIJAH PITCHER, b. 25 Jul 1771; d. at Norwich, 26 Apr 1843; m. at Norwich, 24 Jun 1798, HANNAH LATHROP, b. at Norwich, 22 Sep 1772 daughter of Zephaniah and Hannah (Lathrop) Lathrop; Hannah d. at Norwich, 24 Dec 1813.

ii ELISHA PITCHER, b. 2 May 1773; d. at Mexico, NY, 18 Nov 1850; m. at Preston, CT, 16 Mar 1794, JANE COOMBS, b. at Preston, 1774 daughter of Thomas and Abigail (Sealey) Coombs; Jane d. at Mexico, 1843.

iii WILLIAM PITCHER, b. 26 Aug 1775; d. at Norwich, 18 Jul 1835; m. 1797, LUCY DARBY, b. at Norwich, 1769 daughter of Blanchard and Priscilla (Longbottom) Darby; Lucy d. at Norwich, 1813.

iv DAVID PITCHER, b. 6 Nov 1777; d. at Norwich, 10 Mar 1857; m. 1st at Norwich, 20 Jun 1802, MARY GIBBONS, b. 1781 daughter of Gerard Gibbons; Mary d. at Norwich, 8 May 1834. David m. 2nd 11 Apr 1835, MARY HURLBUT, b. 3 Sep 1794 daughter of Asa and Betsey (Kelley) Hurlbut;[2816] Mary d. at Lebanon, CT, 7 Feb 1859.

v EPHRAIM PITCHER, b. 22 Feb 1780; d. at Johnston, OH, 25 Feb 1858; m. 1st at Norwich, 28 May 1805, DESIRE BROWN, b. 1786; Desire d. at Norwich, 30 Jan 1822. Ephraim m. 2nd at Lisbon, CT, 9 May 1822, CHARLOTTE W. CROCKER, b. at Bozrah, CT, 27 Sep 1791 daughter of Asa and Lois (Crocker) Crocker; Charlotte d. at Johnston, 29 Jun 1860.

vi DANIEL PITCHER, b. 22 Nov 1782; d. at Norwich, 12 Oct 1822; m. 1803, BETSEY ELLIS, b. at Norwich, 13 May 1785 daughter of William and Ann (Edgerton) Ellis; Betsey d. at Warren, PA, 19 Sep 1874. Betsey married second Parley Coburn.

vii GURDON PITCHER, b. 15 May 1785; b. by 1844 (wife's remarriage); m. 1st about 1806, REBECCA HARRIS, b. about 1782; Rebecca d. at Avon, CT, 4 Dec 1825. Gurdon m. 2nd at Harlem, 1826, CHARLOTTE BIGELOW, b. at Hartford, Sep 1798 daughter of James and Anne (Spencer) Bigelow; Charlotte d. after 1870 when she was living in Brooklyn with her son. Charlotte married Samuel H. Ames on 14 Jul 1844.

[2812] Revolutionary War Pension and Bounty-Land Warrant Application Files, Case S45223

[2813] War of 1812 pension file; W.O. 6264; W.C. 5940

[2814] The death record of son William gives the names of his parents as Silas Barker and Harriet Benjamin. The 1812 pension index gives her maiden name as Harriet Hall and Harriet's statement in the application gives her name as Harriet Hall. War of 1812 Pension Application Files Index, 1812-1815

[2815] This is a supposed marriage for Hannah. The family was living in Norwich at the time of Hannah's marriage and this marriage fits for her in terms of age and location. There were no records located that firmly establish that this Hannah married Elijah Pitcher.

[2816] Hurlbut, *The Hurlbut Genealogy*, p 152

viii ASHER PITCHER, b. Sep 1788; d. at Norwich, 6 May 1870; m. at Norwich, 27 Feb 1814, BETHIAH ELLIS, b. at Franklin, CT, 15 Mar 1790 daughter of William and Ann (Edgerton) Ellis; Bethiah d. at Norwich, 19 Feb 1863.

ix HANNAH PITCHER, b. June 1791; d. at Norwich, 12 Feb 1796.

x JERUSHA PITCHER, b. 11 Oct 1797; d. at Norwich, 29 Aug 1884; m. at Norwich, 9 Oct 1825, ERASTUS WATERS, b. 1798 perhaps son of Levi and Hannah (Bottom) Waters; Erastus d. at Norwich, 10 May 1848.

1060) JOHN BARKER (*Hannah Grow Barker⁴, Rebekah Holt Grow³, James², Nicholas¹*), b. at Pomfret, 18 Dec 1755 son of Ephraim and Hannah (Grow) Barker; d. at Stoddard, NH, 15 Mar 1834; m. 1st at Leominster, 9 Jul 1786, ESTHER RICHARDSON, b. at Leominster, 9 Mar 1767 daughter of James and Hannah (House) Richardson; Esther d. at Stoddard, 17 Jul 1806. John m. 2nd 4 Dec 1806, SALLY GUILD (widow of Daniel Warner), b. at Newton, MA, 31 Jul 1775 daughter of Samuel and Sarah (Smith) Guild;[2817] Sally d. at Stoddard, 19 Jan 1843.

John Barker resided in the area of Stoddard, New Hampshire known as Leominster Corner as there were several settlers in this area that came from Leominster.[2818] John married Esther Richardson in Leominster and their first children were born there.

During the Revolution, John served as a private and an orderly sergeant. He was present at the Battle of Bunker Hill, on the Quebec expedition with Benedict Arnold, and was a Fort Ticonderoga in 1776. An engraved powder horn that belonged to John Barker sold at auction for $9,000 in 2018.[2819]

In his will written 4 April 1825 (probate 7 June 1834), John Barker bequeathed to daughter Loency, fifty dollars; son Albemarle, twenty dollars; son Ephraim, sixty dollars; daughter Almira, seventy dollars; sons Cephas, Cicero, and Franklin and daughter Sally, one dollar; daughter Betsey, six dollars; sons John and William to equally divided the money owed by son Franklin in a note; and beloved wife Sally receives use of all the estate during her life. After Sally's death, the estate is to be divided among her children "according to her will and pleasure." These children are Samuel Guile, Luman, Mary and Harriet Newel. Wife Sally Barker was named sole executrix.[2820]

John Barker and Esther Richardson were parents of fourteen children.

i JOHN BARKER, b. at Leominster, 24 Jan 1787; d. at Stoddard, 14 Jul 1829; m. at Leominster (intention), 24 Jan 1812, SUSAN BIGELOW, b. at Leominster, 17 Sep 1792 daughter of Nathaniel and Anne (Rider) Bigelow;[2821] Susan d. at Stoddard, 18 May 1860.

ii WILLIAM BARKER, b. at Leominster, 20 Oct 1788; d. at Syracuse, NY, 30 Apr 1854; m. 1st about 1813, PHEBE ROSE, b. 1797 daughter of William and Mary (Dewitt) Rose; Phebe d. at Syracuse, 14 Jan 1819 at age 22. William m. 2nd 1819, ESTHER RIGGS ORTON, b. 6 Dec 1796 daughter of Arunah and Lois (Gibbs) Orton; Esther d. at Syracuse, 1 Feb 1881.

iii FRANKLIN BARKER, b. at Leominster, 12 Jul 1790; d. at Stoddard, NH, 12 Apr 1799.

iv SALLY BARKER, b. at Leominster, 15 Jul 1792; d. at Leominster, 29 Apr 1859; m. 8 Leominster, 8 Feb 1820, HORACE RICE, b. at Leominster, 1796 son of John and Anne (Bigelow) Rice; Horace d. at Leominster, 21 Sep 1877.

v CEPHAS BARKER, b. at Leominster, 15 Dec 1793; b. at Berkshire, NY, 10 Aug 1857; m. 1821, MARY JEWETT, b. at Berkshire, 8 Apr 1802 daughter of Ezekiel and Sarah (Blackman) Jewett; Mary d. at Berkshire, 16 Feb 1864.

vi CICERO BARKER, b. at Leominster, 15 Dec 1793; d. at Onondaga, NY, 22 Jun 1870; m. MARY SATTERLY, b. at Windsor, NY, 20 Feb 1790 daughter of Samuel and Hannah (Woodhull) Satterly; Mary d. at Onondaga, 16 Sep 1881.

vii BETSEY BARKER, b. at Stoddard, 4 Jul 1795; d. at Dalton, MA, 30 May 1877; m. at Leominster, 9 Dec 1819, MOODY TYLER, b. at Leominster, 24 Feb 1789 son of Phineas and Tabitha (Hartwell) Tyler; Moody d. at Dalton, 3 Jul 1870.

viii ALBEMARLE BARKER, b. at Stoddard, 11 Jun 1797; d. at Newton, MA, 22 Apr 1848; m. at Lexington, MA, 20 Jun 1824; ABIGAIL A. FRANCIS, b. at Marblehead, 1800 daughter of Richard and Elizabeth (Adams) Francis;[2822] Abigail d. at Lowell, 5 May 1891.

ix LOUISE BARKER, b. and d. 16 Jan 1799

x LOENCY BARKER, b. at Stoddard, 16 Jan 1799; d. at Newton, MA, 20 Jul 1845. Loency did not marry.

2817 Burleigh, *The History and Genealogy of the Guild Family*, p 45

2818 Gould, *History of Stoddard*, p 120

2819 Morphy Auctions; https://auctions.morphyauctions.com/LotDetail.aspx?inventoryid=448012

2820 *New Hampshire. Probate Court (Cheshire County), Wills, Volume 77, pp 513-154*

2821 Howe, *The Bigelow Family*, p 126

2822 The names of Abigail's parents are given on her death record as Richard and Elizabeth Adams.

xi EPHRAIM BARKER, b. at Stoddard, 10 Feb 1801; d. at Walpole, NH, 6 Sep 1876; m. at Amherst, MA, 26 Sep 1825, LYDIA VINTON, b. at Granby, 27 Aug 1804 daughter of Simeon and Roxanna (Church) Vinton; Lydia d. at Walpole, 1871.

xii FRANKLIN BARKER, b. at Stoddard, 11 Apr 1803; d. at Syracuse, NY, 1859 (probate 18 Mar 1859); m. at Stoddard, 13 Apr 1826, BETSEY BLOOD, b. at Gilsum, NH, 16 Nov 1808 daughter of Levi and Polly (Whipple) Blood; Betsey d. at Clinton, IA, 23 Feb 1894.

xiii ALMIRA BARKER, b. at Stoddard, 8 Dec 1804; d. at Falmouth, MA, 3 Feb 1885;[2823] m. at Leominster, 23 May 1834, DANIEL RUSSELL, b. at Boston, 1803 son of John and Sarah (Stedman) Russell; Daniel d. at Newton, 10 Oct 1856.

xiv NATHAN BARKER, b. 25 Jun 1806; d. 21 Jul 1806.

John Barker and Sarah Guild were parents of four children.

i SAMUEL GUILE BARKER, b. at Stoddard, 6 Oct 1807; d. at Syracuse, 8 Jan 1892; m. 1st at Stoddard, 18 May 1837, SARAH TOWNE, b. at Marlow, NH, 4 Jan 1803 daughter of Andrew and Anna (-) Towne;[2824] Sarah d. at Syracuse, 9 Jun 1864. Samuel m. 2nd PHEBE MYERS (widow of Waterman Sears)

ii LUMAN BARKER, b. at Stoddard, 8 Jul 1809; m. MARY ANN POWERS

iii MARY BARKER, b. at Stoddard, 2 Dec 1811; d. after 1880 when she was living at Brunswick, Maine with her daughter's family; m at Stoddard, 18 Apr 1837, ELIPHALET FOX, b. 10 Feb 1802 son of Samuel and Sarah (Duncan) Fox; Eliphalet d. at Antrim, 11 Oct 1862.

iv HARRIET NEWELL BARKER, b. at Stoddard, 7 Jun 1819; d. at Marlborough, NH, 3 Sep 1889; m. at Stoddard, 16 Jun 1842, CHARLES WORCESTER, b. at Stoddard, 1813 son of Nathaniel and Lucy (Fay) Worcester; Charles d. at Keene, NH, 10 May 1903.

1061) EPHRAIM BARKER (*Hannah Grow Barker[4], Rebekah Holt Grow[3], James[2], Nicholas[1]*), b. at Pomfret, 28 Feb 1759 son of Ephraim and Hannah (Grow) Barker. He may be the Ephraim Barker who married at Wayland, MA, 27 Mar 1783, RUTH GOODNOW,[2825] b. at Wayland, 18 Oct 1757 daughter of Silas and Jerusha (Willis) Goodnow; Ruth d. at Sudbury, 27 Jan 1843.

Ephraim abandoned his family sometime between 1800 and 1805 described as "absconded to parts unknown" in a probate file for Ruth's aunt Mary Willis.[2826] Ruth Barker was listed as the head of household from 1810 on. Ruth inherited her aunt Mary's estate and beginning in 1813 sold off portions of the land every few years listing herself as a "free agent" in the deeds.[2827]

Ephraim Barker and Ruth Goodnow were parents of seven children born at Sudbury.

i SILAS GOODNOW BARKER, b. 15 Nov 1784; d. at Chester, VT, 1858 (probate 30 Sep 1858); m. at Dorchester, MA, 19 Nov 1808, POLLY MARSHALL, b. about 1781; Polly d. at Chester, 8 Sep 1856.

ii EPHRAIM BARKER, b. 23 Aug 1786; d. at Halifax, MA, 16 Sep 1830; m. at Boston, 5 Nov 1809, LUCY S. WATERMAN, b. at Halifax, 6 Nov 1788 daughter of Isaac and Lucy (Samson) Waterman;[2828] Lucy d. at Halifax, 14 May 1877.

iii LEWIS BARKER, b. 13 Jul 1788; d. at Baton Rouge, 19 Dec 1820. Lewis Barker of Sudbury, age 31, enlisted in the army for a term of five years on 3 Feb 1820. He died at Baton Rouge the night of 19/20 Dec 1820.[2829]

iv SEWEL BARKER, b. 27 Sep 1791

2823 Almira was living at the home of her daughter Emily Russell Beal at the time of her death.

2824 The 1885 will (probate 1865) of Andrew Towne of Marlow includes a bequest to his daughter Sally Barker. There are inconsistencies in records about the name of her mother. The birth record says mother is Anna, and Anna is listed as mother of the other children in the family except one that gives mother as Sarah Spaulding. The 1802 marriage record for Andrew says wife is Sarah Spaulding.

2825 Parshall, *The Barker Genealogy*, p 7. This Barker genealogy lists a son of this Ephraim, Silas G. Barker, who was the son of Ephraim and Ruth (Goodnow) Barker.

2826 *Middlesex County, MA: Probate File Papers, 1648-1871.*Online database. *AmericanAncestors.org.* New England Historic Genealogical Society, 2014. Probate of Mary Willis, Case 25077. The probate of Mary Willis's estate was in 1805. The will or Mary Willis was written in 1779 prior to Ruth's marriage to Ephraim Barker. In her will, Mary Willis left her estate to her niece Ruth Goodnow single woman.

2827 Massachusetts Land Records, Middlesex County, 204:512, 208:270, 223:65

2828 Waterman, *The Waterman Family, Volume 1*, p 439

2829 U.S. Army, Register of Enlistments, 1798-1914

v NATHAN BARKER, b. 25 Nov 1792; d. at Medford, 11 Apr 1852; m. at Malden, 19 Aug 1815, HANNAH WAIT TOWNSEND, b. at Malden, 9 Sep 1793 daughter of John and Ann (Ramsdell) Townsend; Hannah d. at Medford, 28 Apr 1881.

vi GEORGE BARKER, b. 23 Sep 1794; d. at Sudbury, 13 Oct 1860; m. at Medford, 13 Sep 1818, REBECCA LYMAN, b. 1798; Rebecca d. at Somerville, 4 Jan 1882.

vii MARY W. BARKER, b. 4 Mar 1797; d. at Sudbury, 6 Oct 1889; m. at Sudbury, 16 Dec 1817, CYRUS TAYLOR, b. at Sudbury, 1797 son of John and Mary (Conant) Taylor;[2830] Cyrus d. at Sudbury, 16 Jan 1872.

1062) NATHAN BARKER (*Hannah Grow Barker[4], Rebekah Holt Grow[3], James[2], Nicholas[1]*), b. at Pomfret, 8 Jun 1761 son of Ephraim and Hannah (Grow) Barker; d. at Palmer, MA, 10 Oct 1849; m. 11 Dec 1783, LYDIA BARKER, b. 4 Jun 1763; Lydia d. at Palmer, 2 Dec 1849.

Nathan and Lydia were in Ashford from 1801 to 1818. The children were baptized in Ashford, the oldest of them all baptized on 10 June 1802. Nathan was deacon of the church at Ashford from 1810 to 1818 when they were dismissed and recommended to the church at Palmer.[2831] Nathan and Lydia were parents of eleven children[2832] and the birth locations are not certain. The youngest children were born at Ashford, but the older children may have been born in western Massachusetts before the family was admitted to the church at Ashford in 1801. The death record of one of the older children gives his place of birth as Lenox, Massachusetts.

i JAMES BARKER, b. 5 Mar 1785; d. 6 May 1788.

ii ELISHA BARKER, b. 13 Dec 1786; d. at Wilbraham, 23 Jul 1870. Elisha did not marry. He lived with his sister Lydia at least from 1850 to the time of his death.

iii CALVIN BARKER, b. 24 Jan 1789; d. at Millbury, MA, 30 Dec 1852; m. 1st at Millbury, 28 Nov 1825, LUCY WASHBURN WOODWARD, b. at Millbury, 8 Sep 1801 daughter of Josiah and Lois (Chapin) Woodward; Lucy d. at Millbury, 6 Nov 1833. Calvin m. 2nd 12 Mar 1836, LUCY BLISS, b. at Springfield, 10 Apr 1803 daughter of Gaius and Temperance (Leonard) Bliss; Lucy d. at Millbury, 3 Mar 1888.

iv DOLLY BARKER, b. 3 Dec 1790; d. at Ashford, 29 Mar 1812.

v ROXANNA BARKER, b. 26 Dec 1792; d. at Wilbraham, 17 Jun 1884; m. at Palmer, 8 May 1820, ROYAL RINDGE, b. at Wilbraham, 10 Apr 1795 son of William and Hannah (Utley) Rindge; Royal d. at Wilbraham, 12 Feb 1878.

vi NATHAN BARKER, b. 14 Apr 1795; d. at Cortland, NY, 18 Nov 1865; m. at Wilbraham, 18 Jul 1818, EUNICE AUSTIN, b. 1800 daughter of Daniel and Eunice (Allen) Austin; Eunice d. at Cortland, 18 May 1865.

vii SITNAH BARKER, b. 25 Feb 1797; d. at Springfield, MA, 3 Jul 1870; m. 1st at Palmer, 23 Nov 1820, ALANSON BURR, b. at Wilbraham, 22 Sep 1794 son of Timothy and Naomi (Walden) Burr; Alanson d. at Wilbraham, 25 Dec 1823. Sitnah m. 2nd at Wilbraham, 7 Oct 1824, Alanson's brother, ELISHA BURR, b. at Wilbraham, 11 Aug 1782; Elisha d. at Wilbraham, 16 Jan 1863. Elisha was first married to Hannah Learned.

viii GILBERT BARKER, b. 13 Mar 1799; d. at Palmer, 2 Oct 1883; m. at Palmer, 23 Oct 1824, PERSIS KING, b. at Palmer, 23 Feb 1805 daughter of John and Betsey (Shearer) King; Persis d. at Palmer, 30 Jun 1887.

ix CYRUS GROW BARKER, b. 13 May 1801; d. at Clinton, WI, 27 Sep 1870; m. at Palmer, 13 Jan 1826, ELIZA KING, b. at Palmer, 8 Jun 1802 daughter of John and Betsey (Shearer) King; Eliza d. at Clinton, 28 Mar 1887.

x LYDIA BARKER, b. 2 May 1803; d. at Wilbraham, 23 May 1884; m. at Palmer, 28 Aug 1828, SYLVESTER HILLS, b. 1800 son of Elijah and Olive (Rider) Hills; Sylvester d. at Palmer, 26 May 1830. Lydia did not remarry.

xi WILLIAM SEDGWICK BARKER, b. 29 Jun 1807; d. at Springfield, 6 Apr 1855; m. at Palmer, 3 Feb 1831, HERSEY KNOWLTON, b. 6 Jun 1804 daughter of Nathan and Lydia (Leonard) Knowlton; Hersey d. at Springfield, 2 Oct 1867.

1063) TIMOTHY GROW (*James Grow[4], Rebekah Holt Grow[3], James[2], Nicholas[1]*), b. at Pomfret, 2 May 1755 son of James and Anna (Adams) Grow; d. at Hartland, VT, 17 May 1842; m. at Somers, CT, 25 Jan 1781, PHALLE RICHARDSON, b. at Coventry, 6 Jul 1763 son of David and Rachel (Richardson) Richardson; Phalle d. at Hartland, 29 Dec 1828.

Timothy and Phalle were in Somers for just a brief period after their marriage and were in Hartland, Vermont by 1782. Timothy was a Baptist deacon and preacher in Hartland and Hartford, Vermont. He lost his sight in his later years.[2833]

2830 Parents' names are given as John Taylor and Mary Conant on his death record.

2831 Connecticut, Church Record Abstracts, 1630-1920

2832 Temple, *History of the Town of Palmer*, p 426. The dates of birth of the children are given in the town history.

2833 Davis, *John Grow of Ipswich*, p 44

Timothy Grow and Phalle Richardson were parents of twelve children.

i DALINDA GROW, b. at Somers, CT, 3 Nov 1781; d. at East Hardwick, VT, 14 Oct 1854; m. at Hartland, 3 Dec 1801, ELIHU BRUNSON, b. at Westfield, MA, 19 May 1779 son of Nathaniel and Sarah (Wetmore) Bronson; Elihu d. at East Hardwick, 3 Dec 1863.

ii PERSIS GROW, b. at Hartland, 17 Jun 1783; d. at Tuscola, MI, 29 Dec 1877; m. at Hartland, 14 Jan 1805, JOHN SLAFTER, b. at Norwich, VT, 31 Oct 1776 son of John and Elizabeth (Hovey) Slafter; John d. 21 Nov 1856.

iii CANDACE GROW, b. at Hartland, 19 Jul 1785; d. at Barre, 25 Feb 1806.

iv AMELIA GROW, b. at Hartland, 15 May 1787; d. at Bloomington, WI, 22 Apr 1872; m. 18 Jan 1820, as his second wife, DAVID FROST SLAFTER, b. 1 Mar 1784 son of Anthony and Experience (Frost) Slafter; David d. at Cabot, VT, 31 May 1866. David was first married to Dimmis Baldwin.

v OLIVE GROW, b. 26 Dec 1788; d. 17 Apr 1790.

vi OLIVE GROW, b. at Hartland, 24 Jun 1791; d. at Lawrence, NY, 21 Apr 1854; m. 26 Jan 1809, ELIJAH SLAFTER, b. at Hartland, 9 Jan 1784 son of John and Elizabeth (Hovey) Slafter; Elijah d. at Genesee, MI, 29 Jul 1864.

vii DAVID GROW, b. at Hartland, 9 Mar 1793; d. at Collinsville, CT, 16 Dec 1858; m. 30 Dec 1817, LYDIA TINKHAM, b. 1787 daughter of Seth and Sarah (Nichols) Tinkham;[2834] Lydia d. at Springfield, MA, 17 Jan 1881.

viii SILAS GROW, b. at Hartland, 12 Mar 1795; d. at St. Johnsbury, VT, 29 Aug 1862; m. 10 Mar 1822, SAMSILLE WALLBRIDGE,[2835] b. 15 Oct 1799 daughter of Asa and Relief (Dickinson) Wallbridge; Samsille d. at St. Johnsbury, 16 Dec 1868.

ix DUSTIN GROW, b. at Hartland, 15 Jun 1797; d. at Clinton, WI, 25 Aug 1874; m. at Windsor, 17 Jan 1822, SARAH G. LAMSON, b. at Randolph, VT, 22 Apr 1800 daughter of Samuel and Polly (Bragg) Lamson; Sarah d. at Clinton, 7 Mar 1866.

x LEVINA GROW, b. at Hartland, 17 Jul 1799; d. at New Rochelle, NY, 6 Oct 1854; m. 28 Dec 1819, EDMUND CLARK HOVEY, b. at Norwich, 16 Oct 1791 son of Isaac and Elizabeth (Clark) Hovey; Edmund d. at Craftsbury, VT, 28 Nov 1846. Levina m. 2nd at Derby, VT, THOMAS BALDWIN, b. at Westminster, VT, 10 May 1783 son of Thomas and Mary (Lovejoy) Baldwin; Thomas d. at Coventry, VT, 5 May 1861. Thomas was first married to Mary Rice who died 19 Jan 1848.[2836]

xi RACHEL GROW, b. at Hartland, 7 Apr 1801; d. at Tuscola, MI, 22 Oct 1871; m. 16 Jan 1822, NEWELL HUTTSON LAMSON, b. at Randolph, VT, 6 Apr 1798 son of Samuel and Polly (Bragg) Lamson; Newell d. at Tuscola, 8 Dec 1863.

xii CHRISTIANA GROW, b. at Hartland, 7 Jun 1804; d. at Lawrence, NY, May 1882; m. 25 Feb 1839, as his second wife, Deacon GEORGE TAYLOR, b. about 1804; George d. at Lawrence, 24 May 1858. George was first married to Harriet who died in 1835.

1064) SUSANNA GROW (*James Grow⁴, Rebekah Holt Grow³, James², Nicholas¹*), b. at Pomfret, 16 Jun 1760 daughter of James and Anna (Adams) Grow; d. at Craftsbury, VT, 14 Sep 1841; m. at Tolland, 15 Apr 1779, JOEL STIMSON, b. at Tolland, 31 Jul 1751 son of Ichabod and Margaret (Peck) Stimson; Joel d. at Norwich, 15 Apr 1813.

During the Revolution, Joel served as a fifer in the company of Capt. Solomon Will. Joel married Susanna in Tolland, but they were soon after in Norwich, Vermont where the births of their nine children are recorded. They were active church members, Joel serving as a chorister. Joel was also a tithingman.[2837]

i Child b. and d. 10 May 1780

ii SEBA STIMSON, b. 8 Aug 1781; d. at Craftsbury, VT, 23 Feb 1862; m. 1st at Craftsbury, 3 Jan 1805, PHILABE ALLEN, b. at Craftsbury, 10 Mar 1786 daughter of Elijah and Hannah (Hamilton) Allen; Philabe d. at Craftsbury, 7 Feb 1842. Seba m. 2nd 21 Sep 1842, MARY HOLBROOK, b. about 1792; Mary d. at Craftsbury, 27 Apr 1845. Seba m. 3rd by 1850, POLLY BURR, b. in MA, about 1789; Polly d. at Craftsbury, 31 Jan 1866.

iii ALBA STIMSON, b. 10 May 1783; d. at Thetford, VT, 15 Mar 1864; m. at Norwich, 16 Mar 1809, PHEBE BURTON, b. 1789 daughter of Pierce and Phebe (Stoddard) Burton; Phebe d. at Norwich, 7 Feb 1859.

[2834] The names of Lydia's parents are given on her death record.

[2835] Her name is also given as LaMoille, but Samsille is engraved on her gravestone (as well as her date of birth). Findagrave ID: 100084968

[2836] "Baldwin Bible Records", NEHGR, 1937, volume 91, p 389

[2837] Goddard and Partridge, *A History of Norwich Vermont*, p 71, pp 246-247

iv SAREPTA STIMSON, b. 31 Aug 1785; d. at Cheshire, MI, 14 Aug 1868; m. at Greensboro, VT, 12 Oct 1812, GUSTAVUS HEYWOOD, b. at Charlestown, NH, 23 Apr 1786 son of William and Joanna (Wetherbee) Heywood; Gustavus d. a Cheshire, 14 Apr 1868.

v ANNA STIMSON, b. 2 May 1788; d. at Hardwick, VT, 17 Mar 1853; m. 1st at Norwich, 6 Jan 1813, PIERCE BURTON, b. at Norwich, 15 May 1787 son of Pierce and Phebe (Stoddard) Burton; Pierce d. of consumption at Norwich, 2 May 1815. Anna m. 2nd at Norwich, 1 Jan 1818, ALPHA WARNER, b. at Hardwick, MA, 6 Dec 1770 son of Daniel and Mary (Wright) Warner; Alpha d. at Chillicothe, OH, 6 Jan 1854. Alpha was first married to Lydia Cobb who died 27 May 1816. Col. Alpha Warner was an innkeeper in Hardwick. Anna and Alpha had four children all of whom died by age 20.

vi CLARISSA STIMSON, b. 23 May 1791; d. at Norwich, 8 Nov 1830. Clarissa did not marry.

vii JOEL STIMSON, b. 9 Apr 1793; d. at Oakwood, MI, 8 Oct 1848; m. BETSEY PERRY, b. 1804; Betsey d. at Hadley Township, MI, 20 Sep 1877.

viii ENOS STIMSON, b. 21 Feb 1795; d. at Montpelier, VT, 27 Dec 1882; m. 1821, MARGERY SPENCER, b. in VT, about 1798; Margery d. after 1870 when she was living in Montpelier.

ix HORACE STIMSON, b. 29 Jan 1798; d. at Allegan, MI, 3 Aug 1857; m. at Kalamazoo, MI, 1 Mar 1837, CYNTHIA MARIA HAINES, b. at Morristown, NJ, 10 Apr 1804 daughter of Stephen and Mary (Cook) Haines;[2838] Cynthia d. at Lansing, MI, 16 May 1889. Cynthia was first married to Dr. Seth J. Porter.

1065) ABISHA GROW (*James Grow*[4], *Rebekah Holt Grow*[3], *James*[2], *Nicholas*[1]), b. at Monson, 1 Feb 1767 son of James and Anna (Adams) Grow; d. at Norwich, 28 Feb 1807; m. at Norwich, 19 Nov 1793, OLIVE PHELPS, b. about 1776; Olive d. at Derby, VT, 25 Aug 1825. Olive married second Abel Wilder on 8 Jan 1809.

Abisha Grow and Olive Phelps were parents of five children born at Norwich, Vermont.

i ANNA GROW, b. 7 Jul 1794; reported to have died in Smithland, KY.[2839]

ii LAURA GROW, b. 2 Feb 1796; d. at Waterbury, VT, 12 Nov 1836. Laura did not marry.

iii SARAH GROW, b. 14 Jan 1799; d. at Waukon, IA, 7 Aug 1866; m. 14 Jan 1819, EZRA PITT BUTLER, b. at Waterbury, VT, 25 Aug 1796 son of Ezra and Tryphena (Diggins) Butler; Ezra d. at Battle Creek, MI, 7 Oct 1875. Sarah and Ezra were in Waterbury until 1850 and then headed west. Ezra's father Ezra Butler was Governor of Vermont from 1826-1828.

iv FANNY GROW, b. 28 Mar 1801; d. at Charleston, VT, 9 Feb 1884; m. 1 Jun 1823, DANIEL BROWN, b. at Corinth, VT, 12 Sep 1800 son of Daniel and Susannah (Durgin) Brown; Daniel d. at Charleston, 9 Dec 1865.

v JAMES GROW, b. 9 Aug 1803; d. unknown (Grow genealogy reports 1838); m. at Waterbury, VT, 20 Apr 1826, MIRANDA KINGSBURY who has not been identified. Two daughters were located for this family born in 1830 and 1834. The older daughter Jane gives her birthplace as Antwerp, New York in some records. The younger daughter Ellen is listed as born in Vermont. Jane married in Craftsbury in 1856. Both James and Miranda seem to be deceased before 1850.

1066) JAMES GROW (*James Grow*[4], *Rebekah Holt Grow*[3], *James*[2], *Nicholas*[1]), b. at Monson, 23 Jul 1769 son of James and Anna (Adams) Grow; d. at Thompson, CT, 17 Mar 1859; m. 1st 1 Jan 1793, ELIZABETH EDMUNDS, b. at Dudley, MA, 22 Sep 1763 daughter of Ebenezer and Hannah (Newell) Edmunds; Elizabeth d. at Thompson, 4 Nov 1835. James m. 2nd 4 Apr 1839, BETSEY TOWNE (widow of Joseph Elliott), b. at Killingly, 19 Aug 1773 daughter of Joseph and Abigail (Thompson) Towne; Betsey d. at Thompson, 8 Dec 1856.[2840]

In 1782, at age thirteen, James went to Hartland, Vermont where he resided with his sister Susanna and her husband Joel Stimson. In 1783, James's parents were also in Norwich where the family purchased a farm. About 1790, James returned to Pomfret where he was a schoolteacher and a farmer. In 1798, James took up preaching and was later a Baptist minister.[2841]

James Grow and Elizabeth Edmunds were parents of six children born at Pomfret.

i MARVIN GROW, b. 28 Nov 1794; d. 9 Dec 1797.

ii ANNE GROW, b. 2 Sep 1796; d. at Pomfret, 31 Oct 1815.

iii HANNAH GROW, b. 21 May 1799; d. at Pomfret, 14 Dec 1822.

2838 Porter, A Genealogy of the Descendants of Richard Porter, p 131

2839 Davis, *John Grow of Ipswich*, reports Anna did not marry and died in Kentucky. The reason for her being in Kentucky was not found.

2840 Age at death given as 83 years, 3 months, 20 days.

2841 Davis, *John Grow of Ipswich*, pp 45-46. This source also provides a lengthy biography of James on pp 46-48.

iv ELIZABETH "BETSEY" GROW, b. 28 Mar 1801; d. at Thompson, CT, 10 Jul 1881; m. at Thompson, 19 Mar 1828, GEORGE DAVIS, b. at Thompson, 28 Mar 1806 son of Thomas and Rebecca (Brackett) Davis; George d. at Thompson, 2 Apr 1879.

v DALINDA GROW, b. 31 Mar 1803; d. at Thompson, 25 Dec 1888; m. at Thompson, 4 Jan 1827, WILLIAM BATES, b. at Thompson, 30 Nov 1800 son of Tyler and Mary (Kimberly) Bates; William d. at Thompson, 9 Oct 1882.

vi JEMIMA GROW, b. 26 Aug 1806; d. at Thompson, 18 Oct 1851; m. at Thompson, 2 Apr 1829, WELCOME BATES, b. at Thompson, 2 May 1804 son of Tyler and Mary (Kimberly) Bates; Welcome d. at Thompson, 8 Aug 1882.

1067) SARAH GROW (*James Grow⁴, Rebekah Holt Grow³, James², Nicholas¹*), b. at Monson, 11 Feb 1772 daughter of James and Anna (Adams) Grow; d. at Strafford, VT, 16 Dec 1857; m. 1st by 1799, JOEL HATCH, b. at New Haven, about 1768 and baptized 12 Jan 1772 son of Nathaniel and Achsah (Parmalee) Hatch; Joel d. at Strafford, 24 Nov 1804. Sarah m. 2nd 2 Sep 1805, FREDERICK SMITH, b. at Strafford, 24 Feb 1787 son of Frederick and Sarah (Sloan) Smith; Frederick d. at Strafford, 15 Dec 1867.

Sarah Grow and Joel Hatch were parents of four children whose births are recorded at Strafford where the family was living by 1800. The final division of the estate of Joel Hatch was ordered on 9 June 1820, and after the set off of the widow's thirds, there were distributions to the following heirs: Royal Hatch, Lucia Hatch, Harriet Hatch, and Adaline Hatch.[2842]

i LUCIA HATCH, b. 16 Nov 1799; d. at Strafford, 30 Mar 1887; m. at Strafford, 18 Jun 1821, WILLIAM SANBORN, b. at Strafford, 10 Feb 1797 son of Moses and Sarah (Marden) Sanborn; William d. at Strafford, 16 Nov 1876.

ii ROYAL HATCH, b. 15 Mar 1801; d. at Strafford, 29 Oct 1862; m. 9 Jan 1831, MARIAN CHANDLER, b. at Woodstock, CT, 5 Apr 1811 daughter of John and Deborah (Eddy) Chandler; Marian d. at Strafford, 28 May 1851.

iii HARRIET HATCH, b. 17 Sep 1802; d. at Strafford, 28 Jul 1882; m. at Strafford, 3 Jun 1824, Dr. GREENLEAF FIFIELD, b. a Wheelock, VT, 27 Oct 1801 son of Edward and Sarah (Bean) Fifield; Greenleaf d. at Conneaut, OH, 27 Jun 1851. Greenleaf attended Middlebury College and was a physician in Ohio.

iv SARAH ADALINE HATCH, b. 24 Aug 1804; d. at Strafford, 10 Dec 1866; m. 26 Oct 1825, SAMUEL S. KIBLING, b. at Ashburnham, 26 Mar 1800 son of Jacob and Sarah (Coolidge) Kibling; Samuel d. at Strafford, 5 Sep 1862.

Sarah Grow and Frederick Smith were parents of five children born at Strafford.

i EMELINE SMITH, b. at Strafford, VT, 10 Jul 1806; d. at Claremont, NH, 22 Jul 1860; m. 26 Dec 1825, THOMAS JEFFERSON HARRIS, b. at Plainfield, NH, 30 Aug 1801 son of John and Elizabeth (Hyde) Harris;[2843] Thomas d. at Claremont, 9 Sep 1880.

ii WEALTHY A. SMITH, b. at Strafford, 6 Aug 1808; d. at Kaneville, IL, 13 Dec 1881;[2844] m. at Strafford, 20 Jan 1831, JOHN D. BUZZELL, b. at Strafford, 3 Dec 1804 son of Aaron and Miriam (Flanders) Buzzell; John d. after 1860 when he was living in Strafford and before 1870 when Wealthy was living with her daughter in Ohio.

iii SIDNEY HATCH SMITH, b. 23 Mar 1810; d. 20 Jan 1813.

iv EDNA SAMANTHA SMITH, b. at Strafford, 1 Jan 1813; d. at Charlotte, VT, 4 May 1879; m. at Strafford, 14 May 1837, JOHN CHANDLER WILDER, b. at Charlotte, 1 Aug 1802 son of Daniel and Persis (Chandler) Wilder; John d. at St. Albans, VT, 20 Jan 1894.

v MARIA LOUISA SMITH, b. at Strafford, 27 Jun 1815; d. at Weybridge, VT, 6 Nov 1870; m. 6 Oct 1840, CYRUS BRYANT DRAKE, b. at Weybridge, 18 Aug 1812 son of Asaph and Louisa (Belding) Drake; Cyrus d. at Royalton, VT, 21 Apr 1878.

1068) MARVIN GROW (*James Grow⁴, Rebekah Holt Grow³, James², Nicholas¹*), b. at Monson, 1 Mar 1776 son of James and Anna (Adams) Grow; d. at Hardwick, VT, 20 Jan 1851 (will proved 24 Jan 1851); m. at Norwich, 28 Dec 1800, HOPE WHIPPLE, reported on death record as born at Ashford, 3 Oct 1778 perhaps the daughter of Samuel Whipple; Hope d. at Cabot, VT, Mar 1860.

2842 *Vermont. Probate Court (Bradford District)*; Probate Place: *Orange, Vermont, Probate Records, Box 74110, Eastman, Charles-Humphrey, Josiah, 1830-1840, Warrant to divide the estate of Joel Hatch; accessed through Ancestry.com.*

2843 The names of Thomas's parents are given as John Harris and Elizabeth Hyde on his death record.

2844 Web: Illinois, Select Deaths Index, 1877-1916

Marvin was another of his family that settled in Vermont being first at Hartland and later at Hardwick. And as his brothers were, he was active in the Baptist faith and for a time was a preacher in Greensboro, Vermont.[2845]

In his will written 13 March 1838 (probate 24 January 1851), Marvin Grow bequeathed to beloved wife Hope the use of his real estate of six acres and a dwelling house during her natural life. After her death, the property is to be divided equally between his two daughters, Philabe Sanborn and Betsey Page. Son-in-law George H. Page was named executor.[2846]

Marvin Grow and Hope Whipple were parents of two children.

i PHYLABE GROW, b. at Hardwick, 9 Jan 1802; d. at Greeley, CO, 3 Jun 1880; m. at Hardwick, 1 Jan 1824, WILLIAM SANBORN, b. at Hardwick, 3 Jan 1798 son of Israel and Sally (Cheever) Sanborn; William b. at Greeley, 6 Sep 1886.

ii BETSEY GROW, b. at Hardwick, 15 Jun 1803; d. at Greensboro, VT, 3 Nov 1848; m. 11 Mar 1827, GEORGE HAMMER PAIGE, baptized at Hardwick, MA, Jun 1805 son of Paul and Pennianah (Hammer) Paige; George d. at Cabot, VT, 7 Apr 1873.

Great-Great-Grandchildren of Mary Holt and Thomas Johnson

1069) JOHN CHANDLER (*John Chandler[5], Mehitable Russell Chandler[4], Phebe Johnson Russell[3], Mary Holt Johnson[2], Nicholas[1]*), b. at Andover, 18 Jul 1750 son of John and Hannah (Phelps) Chandler; d. at Princeton, MA, 26 Mar 1832; m. 1st at Lancaster, 29 Feb 1776, KATHARINE "KATY" HOLMAN, b. at Sutton, MA, 23 Mar 1753 daughter of Solomon and Sarah (Waite) Holman, Katy d. at Princeton, 18 Feb 1781. John m. 2nd at Westminster, 1 Jan 1782, MARY JACKSON, b. at Westminster, 11 Sep 1755 daughter of Josiah and Mary (Darby) Jackson; Mary d. at Princeton, 26 Jan 1836.

John Chandler and Katharine Holman were parents of two children born at Princeton, Massachusetts.

i JOHN CHANDLER, b. 22 May 1777; d. at Peru, VT, 6 Feb 1859; m. at Chelsea, MA, 8 Nov 1804, MARY WYMAN, b. at Chelsea, 15 Jul 1782; Mary d. at Peru, 23 Jan 1846.

ii JOSEPH CHANDLER, b. 20 Mar 1780; d. at Hartland, 7 Apr 1854; m. at Charlestown, 17 Dec 1809, SARAH "SALLY" BENNETT, b. at Lunenburg, 31 May 1778 daughter of James Bennett; Sally d. at Hartland, 20 Jan 1851.

John Chandler and Mary Jackson were parents of two children born at Princeton.

i EPHRAIM H. CHANDLER, b. 9 Jun 1783; d. at Princeton, 30 Oct 1856; m. at Princeton, 19 Apr 1810, MARY POWERS, b. 3 Dec 1790 daughter of John Powers; Mary d. at Princeton, 16 Jun 1854.

ii MARY "POLLY" CHANDLER, b. 31 May 1795; d. at Salisbury, VT, 21 Dec 1842; m. at Sterling, MA, 26 Apr 1815, SILAS HOLMAN, b. at Sterling, 17 Apr 1790 son of Samuel and Sarah (Davis) Holman; Silas d. at Salisbury, VT, 17 Mar 1839.

1070) JOSEPH CHANDLER (*John Chandler[5], Mehitable Russell Chandler[4], Phebe Johnson Russell[3], Mary Holt Johnson[2], Nicholas[1]*), b. at Andover, 30 Jan 1753 son of John and Hannah (Phelps) Chandler; d. at Salem, 27 Nov 1827; m. at Danvers, 12 Nov 1780, his fourth cousin, DORCAS ABBOTT, b. at Andover, 26 Oct 1755 daughter of Joseph and Anna (Peabody) Abbott; Dorcas d. at Salem, 19 Aug 1821.

Joseph worked for Elias Hasket Derby in Salem, one of the wealthiest merchants of the era and a pioneer in trade with China. Joseph later worked for Elias's son John Derby.[2847]

In his will dated 28 March 1826, Joseph Chandler named son-in-law Jonathan Kenney as executor. Son Joseph Abbot Chandler had debts to the father totaling $219.34, and the bequest to Joseph Abbot is to include this owed amount. Joseph Abbot Chandler will receive a one-third part of the estate, but this is to be held by Jonathan Kenney and all the profit from this third is to be paid to Joseph's wife Deborah as long as she remains his wife or his widow. After Deborah's decease, that third of the estate is to go to grandson Joseph T. Chandler. The remaining two-thirds of the estate goes to daughter Dorcas Chandler and daughter Hannah Kenney. The real estate was valued at $1,325.00 and the personal estate was $1,939.15 which included about $1,700 in cash, notes, and bank deposits. The heirs-at-law providing their assent to the presentation of the will were Joseph A. Chandler and his wife Deborah Chandler, Dorcas Chandler, and Hannah Kenney.[2848]

2845 Davis, *John Grow of Ipswich*, p 48

2846 *Vermont. Probate Court (Caledonia District);* Probate Place: *Caledonia, Vermont, Volume 20, pp 275-276*

2847 McKey, Richard Haskayne. "Elias Hasket Derby, Merchant of Salem, Massachusetts, 1739-1799." PhD diss., Clark University, 1961.

2848 Essex County, MA: Probate File Papers, 1638-1881.Online database. AmericanAncestors.org. New England Historic Genealogical Society, 2014. Case number 4951, Probate of Joseph Chandler

Daughter Dorcas did not marry. In her will dated 28 January 1843, Dorcas Chandler made bequests to Mrs. Hannah Kenney of one hundred dollars, her niece Dorcas Kenney to receive silver spoons, and her brother Joseph A. Chandler receives fifty dollars. There are several small bequests to what seem other relations and friends. One-half of the remainder of the estate goes to her nephew Joseph T. Chandler who is to hold this in trust and pay to his father Joseph A. Chandler the interest on the estate annually. At the decease of Joseph A. Chandler, that part of the estate is to go to Susan E. Chandler. The other half of the estate is to be equally divided among her nieces and nephews.[2849] The value of the real estate was $1,200 for a house and lot and personal estate valued at $828.

Dorcas Abbott and Joseph Chandler had four children born at Danvers.

i HANNAH CHANDLER, b. 15 Dec 1781; d. at Salem, 21 Dec 1856; m. at Salem, 20 Oct 1805, JONATHAN KENNEY, b. at Middleton, 23 Aug 1771 son of Simeon and Jerusha (Johnson) Kenney; Jonathan d. at Salem, 29 Dec 1847.

ii DORCAS CHANDLER, b. 11 Jun 1785; d. at Salem, 1 Feb 1843. Dorcas did not marry.

iii JOSEPH ABBOT CHANDLER, b. 28 Dec 1789; d. at Salem, 25 Nov 1861; m. at Salem, 24 May 1812, DEBORAH SYMONDS, b. at Salem, 1796 daughter of Thorndike and Betsey (Gurley) Symonds; Deborah d. at Salm, 3 Nov 1832. Joseph was a saddler for a time and also worked as a butcher.

iv JOHN CHANDLER, b. 21 Jun 1795; d. 27 Sep 1803.

[2849] *Essex County, Massachusetts, Probate Records and Indexes 1638-1916;* Author: *Massachusetts. Probate Court (Essex County);* Probate Place: *Essex, Massachusetts, Probate Records, Vol 412-414, Book 112-114, 1843-1847*

Master List of Families

This list gives the names of parents who head the covered families for whom there are children, followed by the Family#. For the purposes of this list, all the surnames that have multiple spellings have been incorporated in one spelling (all Abbott/Abbot are Abbott; all Farnum/Farnham are Farnum, etc.).

Name	Family#
Abbe, Jonathan and Alice Johnson	384
Abbott, Aaron and Lydia Abbott	955
Abbott, Abiel and Dorcas Abbott	272
Abbott, Abigail and Benjamin Abbott	53
Abbott, Abigail and Benjamin Whittemore	749
Abbott, Abigail and John Abbott	269
Abbott, Abigail and John Johnson	1014
Abbott, Abigail and John Kidder	305
Abbott, Abigail and Stephen Dresser	741
Abbott, Amos and Rebecca Abbott	308
Abbott, Anna and Ephraim Burge	271
Abbott, Barachias and Hannah Holt	249
Abbott, Barachias and Sarah Holt	822
Abbott, Benjamin and Abigail Abbott	53
Abbott, Benjamin and Elizabeth Abbott	266
Abbott, Benjamin and Elizabeth Abbott	53
Abbott, Benjamin and Hannah Abbott	229
Abbott, Benjamin and Mary Andrews	940
Abbott, Benjamin and Mary Carleton	53
Abbott, Benjamin and Sarah Brown	965
Abbott, Benjamin and Sarah Farnum	10
Abbott, Betsey and Thomas Saltmarsh	958
Abbott, Bridget and Stephen Harriman	735
Abbott, Chloe and Joseph Gray	1003
Abbott, Daniel and Lucy Parker	267
Abbott, Daniel and Mercy Kilburn	960
Abbott, Daniel and Rachel Abbott	960
Abbott, Darius and Mary Holt	645
Abbott, David and Hannah Chandler	169
Abbott, David and Hannah Danforth	54
Abbott, David and Prudence Sheldon	274
Abbott, Deborah and Joseph Hall	227
Abbott, Dorcas and Abiel Abbott	272
Abbott, Dorcas and Ebenezer Hall	956
Abbott, Dorcas and John Holt	837
Abbott, Dorcas and Jonathan Abbott	731
Abbott, Dorcas and Joseph Chandler	1070
Abbott, Dorcas and Nicholas Holt	37
Abbott, Dorothy and Braviter Gray	47
Abbott, Edward and Deborah Stevens	957
Abbott, Edward and Dorcas Chandler	226
Abbott, Elizabeth and Benjamin Abbott	266
Abbott, Elizabeth and Benjamin Abbott	53
Abbott, Elizabeth and Ebenezer Cummings	270
Abbott, Elizabeth and Joseph Phelps	942
Abbott, Elizabeth and Samuel Osgood	952
Abbott, Elizabeth and Thomas Merrill	270
Abbott, Elizabeth and Zebadiah Shattuck	1011
Abbott, Ephraim and Esther Eastman	747
Abbott, Ezra and Anna Choate	963
Abbott, Ezra and Betty Andrews	963
Abbott, Ezra and Jane Jackman	963
Abbott, Ezra and Molly Brown	753
Abbott, George and Sarah Abbott	228
Abbott, Hannah and Abiel Holt	40
Abbott, Hannah and Benjamin Abbott	229
Abbott, Hannah and Benjamin Holt	734
Abbott, Hannah and Jeremiah Holt	403
Abbott, Hannah and Jeremiah Story	964
Abbott, Hannah and John Cady	126
Abbott, Hannah and Samuel Chamberlain	703
Abbott, Isaac and Mary Barker	941
Abbott, Isaac and Phebe Chandler	1010
Abbott, Isaac and Phebe Lovejoy	376
Abbott, Isaac and Susannah Farnum	413
Abbott, Jabez and Hephzibah Stevens	954
Abbott, Jabez and Phebe Abbott	954
Abbott, Jacob and Lydia Stevens	992
Abbott, James and Abigail Farnum	59
Abbott, James and Sarah Bancroft	306
Abbott, Jemima and John Waldo	563
Abbott, Jemima and Nathaniel Norcross	123
Abbott, Jeremiah and Elizabeth Frye	750
Abbott, Job and Anna Ballard	740
Abbott, Job and Phebe Farnum	417
Abbott, Job and Sarah Abbott	171
Abbott, John and Abigail Abbott	269
Abbott, John and Elizabeth Phipps	124
Abbott, John and Jemima Johnson	24
Abbott, John and Sarah Baker	561
Abbott, Jonathan and Dorcas Abbott	731
Abbott, Jonathan and Martha Lovejoy	168
Abbott, Jonathan and Martha Lovejoy	282
Abbott, Jonathan and Mary Chandler	276
Abbott, Jonathan and Mehitable Abbott	731
Abbott, Jonathan and Zerviah Holt	33
Abbott, Joseph and Phebe Lovejoy	961
Abbott, Joshua and Mary Abbott	174
Abbott, Joshua and Phebe Ingalls	358
Abbott, Lydea and Joshua Lovejoy	281
Abbott, Lydia and Aaron Abbott	955
Abbott, Lydia and Nathaniel Morrill	752
Abbott, Lydia and Thomas Farnum	409
Abbott, Lydia and Uriah Russell	1012
Abbott, Martha and Oliver Whiting	733
Abbott, Mary and Adonijah Tyler	311
Abbott, Mary and Joseph Holt	191
Abbott, Mary and Joshua Abbott	174
Abbott, Mary and Lemuel Holt	767
Abbott, Mary and Nathan Wheeler	125
Abbott, Mary and Nehemiah Barker	268
Abbott, Mehitable and Jonathan Abbott	731
Abbott, Miriam and John Morrill	756
Abbott, Moses and Elizabeth Holt	646
Abbott, Nathan and Betty Abbott	480
Abbott, Nathan and Eunice Marsh	938
Abbott, Nathan and Sarah Ballard	739
Abbott, Paul and Elizabeth Gray	219
Abbott, Peter and Elizabeth, Holt	638
Abbott, Phebe and Jabez Abbott	954
Abbott, Phebe and John Russell	1013
Abbott, Phebe and Nathan Chandler	1007
Abbott, Phebe and Thomas Merrill	309
Abbott, Priscilla and Zela Holt	660

Master List of Families

Family	No.
Bean, Abigail and Joseph Holt	635
Beardsley, Elihu and Phebe Chamberlain	548
Bennett, Hannah and Samuel Holt	772
Benton, Daniel and Mary Wheeler	564
Benton, Elijah and Mehitable Chamberlain	544
Best, Elinor and Thomas Gray	246
Beverly, David and Hannah Farnum	75
Beverly, David and Ruth Clough	372
Beverly, Hannah and Aaron Towne	371
Beverly, John and Lydia Hildreth	373
Beverly, Mary and Asa Towne	370
Beverly, Samuel and Ruth Connor	374
Bibbens, Philatheta and Calvin Preston	893
Bidlack, Lydia and Asa Farnum	317
Bissell, Sabra and Walter Goodale	780
Black, Sarah and Ephraim Holt	649
Blanchard, Aaron and Eleanor Holt	406
Blanchard, Abigail and Samuel Holt	387
Blanchard, Eunice and Peter Johnson	540
Blanchard, Hannah and Timothy Gray	1000
Blanchard, Lydia and Jonathan Holt	139
Blanchard, Susannah and Nathan Holt	808
Blood, William and Abigail Holt	605
Blunt, Ephraim and Martha Ordway	736
Blunt, Ephraim and Zerviah Abbott	170
Blunt, Hannah and Humphrey Cram	154
Blunt, Lydia and Thomas Abbott	953
Blunt, Mary and Henry Gray	43
Blunt, Zerviah and Aaron Hartshorn	737
Bosworth, Jonathan and Mary Holt	788
Boutell, James and Chloe Preston	891
Bowen, Mary and John Wright	531
Bowen, Sarah and Thomas Ingalls	1038
Bowers, Fanny and Stephen Holt	841
Bowers, Francis and Chloe Holt	842
Bowers, Francis and Elizabeth Holt	621
Boynton, Abigail and James Chamberlain	547
Boynton, Dorcas and Joseph Holt	191
Boynton, Jedediah and Elizabeth Holt	665
Bradbury, John and Elizabeth Ingraham	1032
Bradford, John and Sarah Putnam	696
Bragdon, Hannah and Daniel Farnum	58
Bragg, Luther and Hannah Foster	948
Bride, Lucy and Calvin Pierce	717
Bridges, Peter and Deborah Russ	467
Brooks, Mary and Silas Holt	214
Brown, Betsey and Calvin Pierce	717
Brown, Joseph and Annis Knight	585
Brown, Miriam and Joseph Russell	523
Brown, Molly and Ezra Abbott	753
Brown, Sarah and Benjamin Abbott	965
Buch, Sarah and Daniel Pierce	163
Buckingham, Gideon and Jemima Pelton	493
Bugbee, Nathaniel and Sarah Johnson	383
Bugbee, Ruth and Nehemiah Norcross	559
Bundy, Isaac and Sarah Johnson	591
Burge, Ephraim and Anna Abbott	271
Burgess, Mary and Reuben Richardson	857
Burnap, Ruth and Joshua Holt	134
Burnham, Hannah and Nathaniel Coburn	430
Burnham, Isaac and Eunice Holt	418
Burnham, Lemuel and Hannah Pierce	715
Burnham, Ruth and Timothy Gray	1000
Burr, Elizabeth and James Pelton	489
Burroughs, John and Sarah Rogers	448
Burt, Experience and Constant Merrick	870
Butler, Thomas and Elizabeth Holt	421
Butterfield, Azuba and Jonathan Holt	179
Butterfield, John and Phebe Russell	508
Butterfield, Mary and Daniel Holt	606
Cady, Amos and Esther Tuthill	570
Cady, Amos and Hannah Kingsbury	570
Cady, Elizabeth and Solomon Dewey	568
Cady, Hannah and William Shurtleff	567
Cady, John and Hannah Abbott	126
Cady, Nahum and Deborah Fitch	569
Canady, Phebe and Nathaniel Holt	95
Card, Hannah and John Farnum	303
Card, Martha and David Farnum	304
Carkin, John and Elizabeth Cram	671
Carleton, Abigail and David Putnam	698
Carleton, Christopher and Elizabeth Stevens	352a
Carleton, Daniel and Mercy Carleton	987
Carleton, Daniel and Priscilla Gray	240
Carleton, Mary and Benjamin Abbott	53
Carleton, Mercy and Daniel Carleton	987
Carleton, Michael and Elizabeth Adams	365
Carpenter, Aaron and Hannah Holt	770
Carpenter, Simon and Anne Holt	878
Carter, Abigail and Samuel Pierce	712
Carter, Dorothy and Ebenezer Farnum	476
Chaffee, Rhoda and Darius Truesdell	856
Chamberlain, Abial and James Royse	546
Chamberlain, Colbe and Catherine Winegar	549
Chamberlain, Elizabeth and Peter Dimmock	542
Chamberlain, James and Abigail Boynton	547
Chamberlain, John and Margaret	545
Chamberlain, John and Molly Powers	706
Chamberlain, Jonathan and Elizabeth Cram	159
Chamberlain, Jonathan and Margaret Cram	702
Chamberlain, Joseph and Elizabeth Delano	543
Chamberlain, Joseph and Mary Johnson	121
Chamberlain, Lucinda and Ephraim Stone	718
Chamberlain, Mehitable and Elijah Benton	544
Chamberlain, Mehitable and Jonathan Cram	153
Chamberlain, Molly and John Kidder	705
Chamberlain, Olive and Benjamin Cram	704
Chamberlain, Phebe and Elihu Beardsley	548
Chamberlain, Rebecca and Solomon Chase	551
Chamberlain, Rebecca and Timothy Holt	204
Chamberlain, Samuel and Hannah Abbott	703
Chamberlain, Samuel and Naomi Richardson	703
Chamberlain, Susannah and John Stiles	681
Chamberlain, William and Abigail Hatch	550
Champion, Elizabeth and John Pelton	488
Chandler, Annis and Josiah Johnson	25
Chandler, Dorcas and Edward Abbott	226
Chandler, Elizabeth and David Lovejoy	279
Chandler, Hannah and Andrew Johnson	119
Chandler, Hannah and David Abbott	169
Chandler, Hannah and Joshua Chandler	1009
Chandler, Huldah and Nathan Wardwell	982
Chandler, Isaac and Abigail Holt	821
Chandler, Isaac and Hannah Ballard	1008
Chandler, John and Hannah Phelps	265
Chandler, John and Katharine Holman	1069
Chandler, John and Mary Jackson	1069
Chandler, Joseph and Dorcas Abbott	1070
Chandler, Joseph and Mehitable Russell	108
Chandler, Joseph and Sarah Richardson	499

References

Abbot, Abiel. 1829. *History of Andover: From its Settlement to 1829.* Andover, MA: Flagg and Gould.

Abbot, Abiel, and Ephraim Abbot. 1847. *Genealogical Register of the Descendants of George Abbot of Andover, George Abbot of Rowley, Thomas Abbot of Andover, Arthur Abbot of Ipswich, Robert Abbot of Branford, CT, and George Abbot of Norwalk, CT.* Boston: James Munroe and Company.

Abbott, Charlotte Helen. n.d. "Abbott Genealogies." http://www.mhl.org/abbott-genealogies.

Abbott, Lemuel Abijah. 1906. *Descendants of George Abbott of Rowley, Mass., of His Joint Descendants of George Abbott, Sr., of Andover, Mass. . .* Boston: Published by the compiler, T. R. Marvin Printing.

Abbott, Stanley Hale. 1961. *The Family Tree of Ezra Abbot.* Hastings, NE: Stanley Hale Abbott.

Adams, Andrew N. 1898. *A Genealogical History of Henry Adams, of Braintree, Mass., and His Descendants; also John Adams, of Cambridge, Mass., 1632-1897.* Rutland, VT: The Tuttle Company, printers.

Adams, Charles Collard. 1908. *Middletown Upper Houses: A History of the North Society of Middletown, Connecticut, from 1650 to 1800, with Genealogical and Biographical Chapters on Early Families and a Full Genealogy of the Ranney Family.* New York, NY: Grafton Press.

Adams, John Quincy, and Charles Francis Adams. 1903. *Life in a New England Town, 1787, 1788: Diary of John Quincy Adams While a Student in the Office of Theophilus Parsons at Newburyport.* Newburyport, MA: Little, Brown.

Aldrich, George. 1880. *Walpole As It Was and As It Is.* Claremont, NH: Claremont Manufacturing.

Aldrich, Lewis Case, and George S. Conover. 1893. *History of Ontario County, New York.* Syracuse, NY: D. Mason & Co.

Aldrich, Lewis Cass, and Frank R. Holmes. 1891. *History of Windsor County, Vermont.* Syracuse, NY: D. Mason and Co.

Ames, Constance Le Neve (Gilman). 1950. *The Story of the Gilmans and a Gilman Genealogy of the Descendants of Edward Gilman of Hingham, England, 1550-1950.* Yakima, WA: Printed for the author.

Anderson, Robert Charles. 1999-2011. *The Great Migration: Immigrants to New England 1634-1635.* Boston, MA: Great Migration Study Project.

Andrews, Alfred. 1872. *Genealogical History of John and Mary Andrews, Who Settled in Farmington, Conn., 1640.* Chicago, IL: A. H. Andrews.

Appleton, W. S. 1896. *Gatherings toward a Genealogy of the Coffin Family: Five Generations of Descendants of Tristram Coffin of Newbury and Nantucket.* Boston, MA: Press of David Clapp & Son.

Atkins, William Giles. 1887. *History of the Town of Hawley, Franklin County, Massachusetts: From its First Settlement in 1771 to 1887, with Family Records and Biographical Sketches.* West Cummington, MA: Published by the author.

Avery, Clara Arlette. 1914. *The Averell-Averill-Avery Family: A Record of the Descendants of William and Abigail Averell of Ipswich, Mass.* Cleveland, OH: Evangelical Publishing House.

Badger, John Cogswell. 1909. *Giles Badger and His Descendants.* Manchester, NH: J.B. Clarke Printers.

Bailey, Abigail Abbot. 1815. *Memoirs of Mrs. Abigail Bailey, Who Had Been the Wife of Major Asa Bailey.* Boston: Samuel T. Armstrong.

Bailey, Hollis, Gertrude Bailey, and Abbie Ellsworth. 1899. *Bailey Genealogy: James John, and Thomas, and Their Descendants: In Three Parts.* Bailey/Bayley Family Association.

Bailey, Sarah Loring. 1880. *Historical Sketches of Andover: Comprising the Present Towns of Andover and North Andover.* Boston: Houghton.

Baker, Fred A. 1917. *Genealogical Record of Rev. Nicholas Baker.* Detroit, MI: Printed for the author.

Balch, Galusha Burchard. 1897. *Genealogy of the Balch Families in America.* Salem, MA: E. Putnam.

Bancroft, Samuel, and Frank D. Andrews. 1922. *Family Record of Dea. Samuel Bancroft, 1715-1782: of Reading, Mass., with His Journal of an Expedition of Soldiers, August 1757, Commanded to Report to Gen. Pepperrell at Springfield.* Vineland, NJ: Privately printed. https://archive.org/details/familyrecordofde00banc/mode/2up.

Banks, Charles Edward. 1967. *History of York Maine in Three Volumes.* Baltimore, MD: Regional Publishing Company.

Barbour, Lucius Barnes. 1982. *Families of Early Hartford, Connecticut.* Baltimore, MD: Genealogical Publishing Company .

Barker, Elizabeth Frye. 1920. *Frye Genealogy: Adrian of Kittery, Me., John of Andover, Mass., Joshua of Virginia, Thomas of Rhode Island.* New York: T. A. Wright.

Barrows, John Stuart. 1938. *Fryeburg, Maine: An Historical Sketch.* Fryeburg, ME: Pequawket Press.

Bartlett, Joseph Gardner. 1908. *Hugh Jones of Salem, Mass., and His Descendants.* Boston, MA: New England Historic Genealogical Society.

—. 1911. *Robert Coe, Puritan: His Ancestors and Descendants, 1340-1910, with Notices of Other Coe Families.* Boston, MA: Published by author.

—. 1926. *Simon Stone Genealogy: Ancestry and Descendants of Deacon Simon Stone Watertown, Mass., 1320-1926.* Boston, MA: Stone Family Association.

Baskin & Beatty. 1881. *History of Crawford County and Ohio.* Chicago, IL: Baskin & Beatty.

Bass, Henry Royce. 1883. *The History of Braintree, Vermont, Including a Memorial of Families that have Resided in Town.* Rutland, VT: Tuttle & Co.

Beard, Ruth, and John Gunn Baird. 1915. *A Genealogy of the Descendants of Widow Martha Beard of Milford, Conn.* Ansonia, CT: Emerson Publishing.

Beers, Frederick W. 1890. *Gazetteer and Biographical Record of Genesee County, N.Y., 1788-1890.* Syracuse, NY: J. W. Vose.

—. 1880. *History of Wyoming County, N.Y., with Illustrations, Biographical Sketches and Portraits of Some Pioneers and Prominent Residents.* New York, NY: F. W. Beers.

Belknap, Henry Wyckoff. 1925. *The Burnap-Burnett Genealogy.* Salem, MA: Essex Institute Historical Collection.

Benedict, Henry Marvin. 1870. *The Genealogy of the Benedicts in America.* Albany: J Munsell.

Benton, John Hogan. 1906. *David Benton, Jr. and Sarah Bingham: Their Ancestors and Descendants.* Boston, MA: Press of David Clapp & Son.

Best, Frank Eugene. 1904. *Amidon Family: A Record of the Descendants of Roger Amadowne of Rehoboth, Mass.* Chicago, IL: F. E. Best.

Bicha, Gloria Wall, and Helen Benjamin Brown. 1977. *The Benjamin Family in America.* https://archive.org/details/benjaminfamilyin00bich/mode/2up.

Binney, Charles J.F. 1883. *The History and Genealogy of the Prentice, or Prentiss Family, in New England.* Boston, MA: Published by the editor.

Biographical Review. 1896. *Biographical Review: This Volume Contains Biographical Sketches of Leading Citizens of Clinton and Essex Counties, New York.* Boston, MA: Biographical Review Publishing Company.

Blake, Francis E. 1915. *History of the Town of Princeton in the County of Worcester and the Commonwealth of Massachusetts.* Princeton, MA: Published by the town.

Blood, Henry Ames. 1860. *The History of Temple, N. H.* Boston, MA: George C. Rand and Avery, printers.

Bolton, Charles Knowles. 1932. *Nathaniel Bolton, a Forgotton New England Poet.* Worcester, MA: American Antiquarian Society.

Bond, Henry. 1860. *Genealogies of the Families and Descendants of the Early Settlers of Watertown, Massachusetts.* Boston, MA: NEHGS.

Bouton, Nathaniel. 1856. *The History of Concord from Its First Grant in 1725 to the Organization of the City Government in 1853.* Concord, NH: Benning W. Sanborn.

Bow, NH. n.d. *The Town Book of Bow, 1760-1877.* https://www.americanancestors.org/databases/bow-nh-the-town-book-of-bow-new-hampshire-1760-1877/.

Boyle, Frederick. 2006. *Early Families of Alfred, Maine.* Portsmouth, NH: Peter E. Randall.

Boynton, John Farnham, and Caroline Harriman Boynton. 1897. *The Boynton Family. A Genealogy of the Descendants of William and John Boynton, who Emigrated from Yorkshire, England, in 1638, and Setted at Rowley, Essex County, Massachusetts.* Groveland, MA.

Brainard, Lucy Abigail. 1908. *The Genealogy of the Brainerd-Brainard Family in America, 1649-1908.* Hartford Press.

Brainerd, Lawrence. 1918. *Gary Genealogy: The Descendants of Arthur Gary of Roxbury, Massachusetts, with an Account of the Posterity of Stephen Gary of Charlestown, Massachusetts, and also of a South Carolina Family of this Name.* Boston, MA: T.R. Marvin & Sons, Printers.

Brewster, William. 1930. *History of the Certified Township of Kingston, Pennsylvania, 1769 to 1929: Together with a Short Account of the Fourteenth Commonwealth.* Wilkes-Barre, PA: Smith-Bennett Corporation.

Brigham, Emma Elisabeth. 1927. *The History of the Brigham Family: Second Volume.* Rutland, VT: The Tuttle Company.

Brigham, Willard. 1907. *The History of the Brigham Family: A Record of Several Thousand Descendants of Thomas Brigham the Emigrant, 1603-1653.* New York: The Grafton Press.

Brinkerhoff, Richard. 1887. *The Family of Joris Dircksen Brinckerhoff, 1638.* New York, NY: R. Brinkerhoff.

Brown, Abiel. 1856. *Genealogical History, with Short Sketches and Family Records, of the Early Settlers of West Simsbury, now Canton, Conn.* Hartford, CT: Press of Case, Tiffany & Co.

Brown, Abram English. 1892. *Glimpses of Old New England Life: Legends of Old Bedford.* Boston, MA: Published by the author.

Brown, George Stayley. 1993. *Yarmouth, Nova Scotia, Genealogies: Transcribed from the Yarmouth Herald.* Genealogical Publishing Company.

Browne, George Waldo. 1921-22. *The History of Hillsborough, New Hampshire, 1735-1921.* Manchester, NH: John B. Clarke.

Burgess, G. A., and J. T. Ward. 1889. *Free Baptist Cyclopaedia.* Free Baptist Cyclopaedia Company.

Burleigh, Charles. 1887. *The Genealogy and History of the Guild, Guile and Gile Family.* Portland, ME: B. Thurston & Co.

Burnett, Edgar Albert. 1941. *The Burnett Genealogy, Supplementing the Burnap-Burnett Genealogy (1925) by Henry Wycoff Belknap.* Lincoln, NE: Brown Printing Service.

Burnham, Roderick H. 1892. *Genealogical Records of Henry and Ulalia Burt, the Emigrants who Early Settled at Springfield, Mass., and Their Descendants Through Nine Generations, from 1640 to 1891.* Warwick, NY: Miss Elizabeth Burt.

Calnek, W. A., and A. W. Savary. 1897. *History of the County of Annapolis: Including Old Port Royal and Acadia* . Toronto: William Briggs.

Campbell, John Roy. 1876. *A History of the County of Yarmouth, Nova Scotia.* Saint John, NB: J & A McMillan.

Candage, Rufus George Frederick. 1905. *Historical Sketches of Bluehill, Maine.* Ellsworth, ME: Hancock County Publishing Company, printers.

Carpenter, Edward Wilson. 1896. *The History of the Town of Amherst, Massachusetts.* Amherst, MA: Press of Carpenter & Morehouse.

Carter, Nathan Franklin, and Trueworthy Ladd Fowler. 1895. *History of Pembroke, N. H. 1730-1895.* Concord, NH: Republican Press Association.

Caswell, Lilley Brewer, and Fred Wilder Cross. 1917. *The History of the Town of Royalston, Massachusetts.* Athol, MA: The Town of Royalston.

Caulfield, Ernest. 1950. "The Pursuit of a Pestilence." *Pocessdings of the American Antiquarian Society* 60 (1): 21-52.

Caulkins, Frances Manwaring. 1866. *History of Norwich, Connecticut: From its Possession by the Indians, to the Year 1866.* Hartford, CT: Published by the author.

Caulkins, Frances Manwaring, and Cecilia Griswold. 1895. *History of New London, Connecticut, from the First Survey of the Coast in 1612 to 1860.* New London, CT: H. D. Utley.

Caverly, A. M. 1858. *An Historical Sketch of Troy [N.H.] and Her Inhabitants, from the First Settlement of the Town, in 1764, to 1855.* Keene, NH: Sentinel Office.

Chaffee, William Henry. 1909. *The Chaffee Genealogy.* New York: Grafton Press.

Chandler, Charles Henry, and Sarah Fiske Lee. 1914. *The History of New Ipswich, New Hampshire, 1735-1914: With Genealogical Records of the Principal Families.* Fitchburg, MA: Sentinel Printing Company.

Chandler, George. 1883. *The Descendants of William and Annis Chandler who Settled in Roxbury, Mass., 1637.* Worcester: Press of C. Hamilton.

Chapin, Charles Wells. 1893. *Sketches of the Old Inhabitants and Other Citizens of Old Springfield of the Present Century.* Springfield, MA: Springfield Printing and Binding Company.

Chapin, Gilbert Warren. 1924. *The Chapin Book of Genealogical Data.* Hartford, CT: Chapin Family Association.

Chapin, Orange. 1862. *The Chapin Genealogy: Containing a Very Large Proportion of the Descendants of Dea. Samuel Chapin.* Northapmton, MA: Printed by Metcalf and Co.

Chapman Brothers. 1885. *Portrait and Biographical Album of Otoe and Cass Counties, Nebraska.* Chicago, IL: Chapman Brothers.

Chapman, F. W. 1872. *Buckingham Family: or the Descendants of Thomas Buckingham.* Hartford, CT: Press of Case, Lockwood & Brainard.

Chapman, George T. 1867. *Sketches of the Alumni of Dartmouth College, from the First Graduation in 1771 to the Present Time, with a Brief History of the Institution.* Cambridge, MA: Riverside Press.

Chapman, Jacob. 1886. *A Genealogy of the Philbrick and Philbrook Families.* Exeter Gazette Steam Printing House.

Chapman, Leonard Bond. 1907. *Monograph on the Southgate Family of Scarborough, Maine: Their Ancestors and Descendants.* Portland, ME: H. W. Bryant.

Chase, Benjamin. 1869. *History of Old Chester.* Auburn, NH: Published by the author.

Chase, George Wingate. 1861. *The History of Haverhill, Massachusetts, from its First Settlement, in 1640, to the Year 1860.* Haverhill, MA: Published by the author.

Child, Hamilton. 1882. *Gazetteer and Business Directory of Addison County, Vt., for 1881- 82.* Syracuse, NY: Printed at the Journal Office.

—. 1888. *Gazetteer of Orange County, VT. 1762-1888, Part First.* Syracuse, NY: Syracuse Journal Company, Printers.

Child, Hamilton, and William Adams. 1889. *The Gazetteer of Washington County, Vermont, 1783-1889.* Syracuse, NY: Syracuse Journal Company.

Clapp, Ebenezer. 1876. *The Clapp Memorial: Record of the Clapp Family in America, Containing Sketches of the Original Six Emigrants, and a Genealogy of Their Descendants Bearing the Name.* Boston, MA: D. Clapp.

Clark, John. 1866. *Records of the Descendants of Hugh Clark, of Watertown, Mass. 1640-1866.* Boston, MA: Printed for the author.

Clark, Joseph Sylvester. 1838. *An Historical Sketch of Sturbridge, Mass., from its Settlement to the Present Time.* Brookfield, MA: E. and L. Merriam, Printers.

Cleveland, Edmund Janes. 1899. *The Genealogy of the Cleveland and Cleaveland Families.* Hartford, CT: Printed for the subscribers.

Cleveland, Horace Gillette. 1879. *A Genealogy of Benjamin Cleveland, a Great-grandson of Moses Cleveland, of Woburn, Mass.* Chicago, IL: Printed for the compiler.

Coburn, Silas Roger. 1922. *History of Dracut, Massachusetts, Called by the Indians Augumtoocooke and before Incorporation, the Wildernesse North of the Merrimac. First Permanment Settlement in 1669 and Incorporated as a Town in 1701.* Lowell, MA: Press of the Courier-Citizen.

Coburn, Silas Roger, and George Augustus Gordon. 1913. *Genealogy of the Descendants of Edward Colburn/Coburn; Came from England, 1635.* Lowell, MA: W. Coburn.

Cochrane, Warren Robert. 1880. *History of the Town of Antrim, New Hampshire, from its Earliest Settlement to June 27, 1877, with a Brief Genealogical Record of all the Antrim Families.* Manchester, NH: Mirror Steam Printing Press.

Cochrane, Warren Robert, and George K. Wood. 1895. *History of Francestown, N. H., from its Earliest Settlement April, 1758, to January 1, 1891: With a Brief Genealogical Record of all the Francestown Families.* Nashua, NH: Published by the town.

Coffin, Charles Carleton. 1878. *The History of Boscawen and Webster [N.H.] from 1733 to 1878.* Concord, NH: Republican Press Association.

Cogswell, Leander Winslow. 1880. *History of the Town of Henniker, Merrimack County, New Hampshire, from the Date of the Canada Grant by the Province of Massachusetts, in 1735, to 1880; with a Genealogical Register of the Families of Henniker.* Concord, NH: Republican Press Association.

Coldham, Peter Wilson. 1987. *The Complete Book of Emigrants: 1607-1660.* Baltimore, MD: Genealogical Publishing Company.

Cole, J. R. 1888. *History of Tolland County, Connecticut.* New York, NY: W. W. Preston.

Conant, Frederick Odell. 1887. *A History and Genealogy of the Conant Family in England and America, Thirteen Generations, 1520-1887.* Portland, ME: Private printing by the press of Harris & Williams.

Coon, Deborah J. 2019. "The Children of James and Sarah (Ingalls) Copeland: Sixth Generation Descendants of John Alden." *The Mayflower Quarterly Magazine* 85 (1): 34-35.

Copeland, William Turner. 1937. *The Copeland Family: A Copeland Genealogy.* Rutland, VT: Tuttle Publishing.

Crandall, John Cortland. 1931. *Elder John Crandall of Rhode Island and His Descendants* . New Woodstock, NY: J. C. Crandall.

Crane, Ellery Bicknell. 1907. *Historic Homes and Institutions and Genealogical and Personal Memoirs of Worcester County, Massachusetts, with a History of Worcester Society of Antiquity.* New York: Lewis Publishing Company.

Crocker, James Russell, and William Adolph Walter. 1967. *Crocker Genealogy.* San Diego, CA: Published by the authors.

Cunningham, George Alfred. n.d. *Cunningham's History of the Town of Lunenburg: from the Original Grant, December 7th 1719 to January 1st, 1866.* https://dp.la/search?q=Cunningham%27s+history+of+the+town+of+Lunenburg.

Currier, Harvey Lear, and John McNabb Currier. 1910. *Genealogy of Richard Currier of Salisbury and Amesbury, Massachusetts (1616--1686-7) and Many of His Descendants.* Newport, VT: Orleans County Historical Society.

Currier, John J. 1896. *"Ould Newbury": Historical and Biographical Sketches.* Boston, MA: Damrell and Upham.

—. 1902. *History of Newbury, Mass. 1635-1902.* Boston, MA: Damrell and Upton.

Curry, Dorothy Neff. 1958. *The Descendants of William Neff who married Mary Corliss, January 23, 1665, Haverhill, Massachusetts.* https://archive.org/details/descendantsofwil00curr/mode/2up.

Cutter, Daniel Bateman. 1881. *History of the Town of Jaffrey, New Hampshire, from the Date of the Masonian Charter to the Present Time, 1749-1880.* Concord, NH: Printed by the Republican Press Association.

Cutter, William Richard. 1912. *Genealogical and Family History of Central New York: A Record of the Achievements of Her People in the Making of a Commonwealth and the Building of a Nation, Volume 2.* New York, NY: Lewis Historical Publishing Company.

—. 1908. *Genealogical and Personal Memoirs Relating to the Families of Boston and Eastern Massachusetts.* Boston, MA: Lewis Historical Publishing Company.

—. 1915. *New England Families, Genealogical and Memorial: a Record of the Achievements of Her People in the Making of Commonwealths and the Founding of a Nation, Volumes 1-4.* New York: Lewis Historical Publishing Co.

Dana, Elizabeth Ellery. 1956. *The Dana Family in America.* Cambridge, MA: Wright and Potter Printing Company.

Dana, Henry Swan. 1889. *History of Woodstock, Vermont.* Boston, MA: Houghton, Mifflin and Company.

Davenport, A. B. 1851. *A History and Genealogy of the Davenport Family in England and America 1086-1850.* New York, NY: S. W. Benedict.

Davis, George Whitefield. 1913. *John Grow of Ipswich: John Groo (Grow) of Oxford.* G. W. Davis.

Davis, Walter Alonzo, City Clerk. 1899. *The Old Records of the Town of Fitchburg, Massachusetts.* Fitchburg, MA: Published by authority of the city council.

Dearborn, John Jacob. 1890. *The History of Salisbury, New Hampshire: From Date of Settlement to the Present Time.* Manchester, NH: Printed by W.E. Moore.

Dewey, Adelbert Milton, Louis Marinus Dewey, William Tarbox Dewey, and Orville C. Dewey. 1898. *Life of George Dewey, Rear Admiral, U.S.N.; and Dewey Family History: Being an Authentic Historical and Genealogical Record of More Than Fifteen Thousand Persons in the United States by the Name of Dewey, and Their Descendants.* Westfield, MA: Dewey Publishing Company.

Dimock, Susan Whitney. 1898. *Births, Baptisms,Mmarriages and Deaths, from the Records of the Town and Churches in Mansfield, Connecticut, 1703-1850.* New York, NY: The Baker and Taylor Company.

Donaldson, Alfred Lee. 1921. *A History of the Adirondacks.* New York, NY: Century Co.

Donovan, Dennis. 1906. *The History of the Town of Lyndeborough, New Hampshire.* Tufts College Press.

Dow, Joseph, and Lucy Ellen Dow. 1893. *History of the Town of Hampton, New Hampshire, from its Settlement in 1638 to the Autumn of 1892.* Salem, MA: L. E. Dow.

Dunham, Isaac Watson. 1907. *Dunham Genealogy: Emglish and American Branches of the Dunham Family.* Bulletin Print.

Durrie, Daniel S. 1864. *A Genealogical History of the Holt Family in the United States More Particularly the Descendants of Nicholas Holt of Newbury and Andover, Mass.* Albany: Munsell.

Dwight, Benjamin Woodbridge. 1871. *The History of the Descendants of Elder John Strong.* Albany, NY: Joel Munsell.

Eaton, Lilley. 1874. *Genealogical History of the Town of Reading, Mass., Including the Present Towns of Wakefield, Reading, and North Reading, with Chronological and Historical Sketches, from 1639 to 1874.* Boston, MA: A. Mudge & Son.

Edson, George Thomas. 1922. *Stewart Clan Magazine, Volumes 1-8.* Filley, NE: T. G. Edson.

Ela, David Hough. 1896. *Genealogy of the Ela Family: Descendant of Israel Ela, of Haverhill, Mass.* Manchester, CT: Elwood S. Ela, Printer.

Eldredge, Zoeth Skinner. 1896. *Eldredge Genealogy.* Boston: D. Clapp Printers.

Elliot, Hazem Tracy. 1947. *The Hazen Family in America.* Thomaston, CT: R. Hazen.

Essex Institute. 1922. *Old-Time Ships of Salem, 2nd Edition.* Salem, MA: Nichols Press Printers.

Farnham, John Marshall Willoughby. 1889. *Genealogy of the Farnham Family.* New York, NY: Baker & Taylor.

Farnham, Russell Clare. 1999. *The New England Descendants of the Immigrant Ralph Farnum of Rochester, Kent County, England, and Ipswich, Massachusetts.* Peter Randall Publishing.

Flint, John, and John H. Stone. 1860. *A Genealogical Register of the Descendants of Thomas Flint, of Salem: With a Copy of the Wills and Inventories of the Estates of the First Two Generations.* Andover, MA: Printed by W. F. Draper.

Fogg, William. 1902. "Early Families of Eliot and Kittery, Maine." *Old Eliot: A Monthly Magazine of the History and Biography of the Upper Parish of Kittery, now Eliot,* 1-61.

Foley, Janet Wethy. 1993. *Early Settlers of New York State: Their Ancestors and Descendants.* Baltimore, MD: Genealogical Publishing Company.

Folsom, Elizabeth Knowles. 1938. *Genealogy of the Folsom Family.* Rutland, VT: The Tuttle Publishing Company.

Forthnightly Club of Putney, Vt. 1953. "People of Putney 1753-1953." Putney, VT. http://digitalcollections.americanancestors.org/cdm/ref/collection/p15869coll33/id/3322.

Foster, E. J. 1884. "Early Settlers of Weld." *The Maine Historical and Genealogical Recorder* 1-2: 119 ff.

Francis, Charles E. 1906. *Francis: The Descendants of Robert Francis of Weathersfield, Conn.* New Haven, CT: The Tuttle, Morehouse & Taylor Company.

Frizzell, Martha McDanolds. 1963. *A History of Walpole, New Hampshire.* Walpole, NH: Walpole Historical Society.

Frost, John Eldridge. 1943. *The Nicholas Frost Family.* Milford, NH: Cabinet Press.

Fuller, William Hylsop. 1914. *Genealogy of Some Descendants of Captain Matthew Fuller, John Fuller of Newton, John Fuller of Lynn, John Fuller of Ipswich, Robert Fuller of Dorchester and Dedham.* Printed for the Compiler.

Fuller, William Hyslop. 1919. *Genealogy of Some Descendants of Thomas Fuller of Woburn.* Palmer, MA: C. B. Fiske.

Gable, Walter. 2017. *Historic Tales of Seneca County, New York.* Charlestown, SC: History Press.

Gage, George N. 1886. *History of Washington, New Hampshire, from the First Settlement to the Present Time, 1768-1886.* Claremont, NH: The Claremont Manufacturing Company.

Gay, William Burton. 1887. *Historical Gazetteer of Tioga County, New York, 1785-1888.* Syracuse, NY: W. B. Gay & Co.

Giddings, Minot Samuel. 1882. *The Giddings Family: or, The Descendants of George Giddings, who Came from St. Albans, England, to Ipswich, Mass., in 1635.* HArtford, CT: Press of the Case, Lockwood & Brainard Co.

Glover, Anna. 1867. *Glover Memorials and Genealogies: An Account of John Glover of Dorchester.* Boston, MA: D. Clapp.

Goddard, M. E., and Henry V. Partridge. 1905. *A History of Norwich Vermont.* Hanover, NH: The Dartmouth Press.

Godfrey, Carlos E. 1904. *The Commander-in-Chief's Guard, Revolutionary War.* Washington, DC: Stevenson-Smith Co.

Gooch, Frank Austin. 1926. *The History of a Surname, with some Account of the Line of John Gooch in New England.* New Haven, CT: Printed for the author.

Goodhue, Jonathan Elbridge. 1891. *History and Genealogy of the Goodhue Family : In England and America to the Year 1890.* Rochester, NY: E. R. Andrews.

Goodwin, Nathaniel. 1856. *Genealogical Notes: or Contributions to the Family History of Some of the First Settlers of Connecticut and Massachusetts.* Hartford, CT: F. A. Brown.

Gould, Isaiah. 1897. *History of Stoddard, Cheshire County, N.H.* Keene, NH: W. L. Metcalf, printer.

Gould, Sherry L, and Kathleen C. Beals. 2004. *Early Families of Bradford, NH.* Bradford, NH: Bradford Historical Society.

Grant, Arthur Hastings. 1898. *The Grant Family: A Genealogical History of the Descendants of Matthew Grant, of Windsor, Conn.1601-1898.* Poughkeepsie, NY: A. V. Haight.

Greene, George Sears. 1903. *The Greenes of Rhode Island: With Historical Records of English Ancestry.* New York, NY: The Kickerbocker Press.

Greven, Philip. 1970. *Four Generations: Population, Land, and Family in Colonial Andover, Massachusetts.* Ithaca: Cornell University Press.

Griffin, Simon G. 1904. *A History of the Town of Keene from 1732, When the Township Was Granted by Massachusetts, to 1874, When it Became a City.* Keene, NH: Sentinel Printing Company.

Guild, Mary Stiles Paul. 1892. *The Stiles Family in America: Genealogies of the Massachusetts Family, Descendants of Robert Stiles of Rowley, Mass. 1659-1891. And the Dover, N. H., Family, Descendants of William Stiles of Dover, N. H., 1702-1891.* Albany, NY: Joel Munsell's Sons.

H. F. Kett and Company. 1877. *The History of Winnebago County, Illinois.* Chicago, IL: H. F. Kett & Co.

Hadley, George Plummer. 1924. *History of the Town of Goffstown 1733-1920.* Goffstown, NH: Published by the town.

Hale, Robert Safford. 1889. *Genealogy of Descendants of Thomas Hale of Walton, England, and of Newbury, Mass.* Albany, NY: Weed, Parsons, and Co.

Hall, Joseph Davis. 1883. *The Genealogy and Biography of the Waldos of America from 1650 to 1883.* Danielsonville, CT: Press of Scofield and Hamilton.

Hammond, Charles. 1893. *The History of Union, Conn.* New Haven: Price, Lee & Adkins.

Hammond, Frederick Stam. 1904. *Histories and Genealogies of the Hammond Families in America.* Oneida, NY: Ryan and Burkhart, Printers.

Hand, H. Wells. 1908. *1808-1908. Centennial History of the Town of Nunda.* Rochester Herald Press.

Hanson, John Wesley. 1849. *History of the Old Towns, Norridgewock and Canaan, Comprising Norridgewock, Canaan, Starks, Skowhegan, and Bloomfield, from their Early Settlement to the Year 1849; Including a Sketch of the Abnakis Indians.* Boston, MA: Published by the author.

Harmon, Artemas C. 1920. *The Harmon Genealogy, Comprising all Branches in New England.* Washington, DC: Printed by Gibson Bros.

Harvard University. 1905. *Quinquennial Catalogue of the Officers and Graduates of Harvard University.* Cambridge, MA: Harvard University.

Harvey, Oscar Jewell. 1899. *The Harvey Book: Giving the Genealogies of Certain Branches of the American families of Harvey, Nesbitt, Dixon and Jameson.* Wilkes Barre, PA: E. B. Yordy & Company.

Hatch, Louis C. 1920. *History of Bowdoin College.* Portland, ME: Loring, Short, and Harmon.

Hayden, Charles Albert, and Jessie Hale Tuttle. 1929. *The Capen Family: Descendants of Bernard Capen of Dorchester, Mass.* Minneapolis, MN: Augsburg Publishing House.

Hayward, William Willis. 1889. *The History of Hancock, New Hampshire, 1764-1889.* Lowell, MA: Vox Populi Press.

Heath, Florence Burnham, Mildred Windsor Burnham Lusk, and Roderick Henry Burnham. n.d. *Genealogical Records of Deacon John Burnham and his Descendants.* Digital Publisher, FamilySearch International.

Heverly, Clement F. 1924. *History and Geography of Bradford County, Pennsylvania 1615-1924.* Bradford County Historical Society.

—. 1915. *Pioneer and Patriot Families of Bradford County, Pennsylvania 1800-1825, volume II.* Towanda, PA: Bradford Star Print.

Hibbard, Augustine George. 1897. *History of the Town of Goshen, Connecticut, with Genealogies and Biographies Based upon the Records of Deacon Lewis Mills Norton, 1897.* Hartford, CT: Press of the Case, Lockwood & Brainard Co.

Hill, Henry Wayland. 1922. *Municipality of Buffalo, New York: A History 1720-1923, volume I.* New York, NY: Lewis Historical Publishing.

Hitchcock, Mrs. Edward. 1894. *The Genealogy of the Hitchcock Family: Who are Descended from Matthias Hitchcock of East Haven, Conn., and Luke Hitchcock of Wethersfield, Conn.* Amherst, MA: Press of Carpenter and Morehouse.

Holman, David Emery. 1909. *The Holmans in America: Concerning the Descendants of Solaman Holman who Settled in West Newbury, Massachusetts, in 1692-3.* New York, NY: The Grafton Press.

Holt Association of America. 1930. *The First Three Generations of Holts in America.* Newburgh, NY: Moore Printing Company.

Holt, Nellie Beardsley. 1950. *Beardsley Genealogy: The Family of William Beardsley One of The First Settlers of Stratford Connecticut.* https://archive.org/details/BeardsleyGenealogyTheFamilyOfWilliamBeardsleyOneOfTheFirstSettlersOfStratfordCon.

Hooker, Edward, and Margaret Huntington Hooker. 1909. *The Descendants of Rev. Thomas Hooker, Hartford, Connecticut, 1586-1908.* Rochester, NY: Printed for Margaret Huntington Hooker.

Hopkins, Timothy. 1903. *The Kelloggs in the Old World and the New.* San Francisco, CA: Sunset Press.

Hotchkiss, Fanny Winchester. 1912. *Winchester Notes.* New Haven, CT: Tuttle, Morehouse & Taylor.

Houghton, William Addison. 1895. *History of the Town of Berlin, Worcester County, Mass., from 1784 to 1895.* Worcester, MA: F. S. Blanchard & Co., Printers.

Howard, Jarvis Cutler. 1884. *Howard Genealogy: A Genealogical Record Embracing all the Known Descendants in this Country, of Thomas and Susanna Howard, who have Borne the Family Name or have Married into the Family.* Hartford, CT: Published by the compiler.

Howe, Gilman Bigelow. 1890. *Genealogy of the Bigelow Family of America, from the Marriage in 1642 of John Biglo and Mary Warren to the Year 1890.* Worcester, MA: Charles Hamilton.

Hoyt, David Webster. 1871. *A Genealogical History of the Hoyt, Haight, and Hight Families: With Some Account of the Earlier Hyatt Families, a List of the First Settlers of Salisbury and Amesbury, Mass.* Providence, RI: Printed for the author.

Hubbard, Benjamin F. 1874. *Forests and Clearings: The History of Stanstead County, Province of Quebec.* Montreal: Printed for the author.

Hubbard, Charles Horace, and Justus Dartt. 1895. *History of the Town of Springfield, Vermont.* Boston: G. H. Walker.

Huntington Family Association. 1915. *The Huntington Family in America: A Genealogical Memoir of the Known Descendants of Simon Huntington from 1633 to 1915.* Hartford, CT: Huntington Family Association.

Huntington, Elijah Baldwin. 1884. *A Genealogical Memoir of the Lo-Lathrop Family in this Country: Embracing the Descendants, as far as Known, of the Rev. John Lothropp, of Scituate and Barnstable, Mass., and Mark Lothrop, of Salem and Bridgewater, Mass.* Ridgefield, CT: Mrs. Julia Huntington.

Hurd, Duane Hamilton (Ed.). 1885. *History of Merrimack and Belknap Counties, New Hampshire.* Philadelphia: J. W. Lewis.

Hurd, Duane Hamilton. 1888. *History of Essex County, Massachusetts: With Biographical Sketches of Many of Its Pioneers and Prominent Men, Volume 1.* Philadelphia: J. W. Lewis.

—. 1885. *History of Hillsborough County, New Hampshire.* Philadephia: J. W. Lewis.

Hurlbut, Henry Higgins. 1888. *The Hurlbut Genealogy: Or, Record of the Descendants of Thomas Hurlbut, of Saybrook and Wethersfield, Conn.* Albany, NY: Joel Munsell's Sons.

Hutchins, Jack Randolph. 1972. *Genealogy of Thomas Hutchins of Salem, Massachusetts, with a History of Allied Families.* Washington, DC: Goetz Press.

Iowa City, Iowa. 1883. *History of Johnson County, Iowa.* Iowa City, IA: Published by the town.

Jewell, Pliny, and Joel Jewell. 1860. *The Jewell Register: Containing a List of the Descendants of Thomas Jewell, of Braintree, Near Boston, Mass.* Hartford, CT: Case, Lockwood.

Johnson, James Bowen. 1895. *The Johnson Memorial: Jeremiah Johnson and Thomazin Blanchard Johnson, His Wife.* Washington, DC: Howard University Print.

Johnson, William Wallace. 1892. *Johnson Genealogy: Records of the Descendants of John Johnson, of Ipswich and Andover, Mass., 1635-1892.* North Greenfield, WI: Published by the compiler.

—. 1876. *Records of the Descendants of David Johnson of Leominster.* Milwaukee, WI: Printed by Godfrey & Crandall.

Jones, Matt Bushnell. 1909. *History of the Town of Waitsfield, Vermont, 1782-1908, with Family Genealogies.* Boston, MA: G. E. Littlefield.

Jordan, John Woolf. 1913. *Genealogical and Personal History of the Allegheny Valley, Pennsylvania, under the Editorial Supervision of John W. Jordan.* New York, NY: Lewis Historical Publishing Company.

Judd, Sylvester. 1856. *Thomas Judd and His Descendants.* Northampton: J & L Metcalf, Printers.

Kimball, John. 1885. *The Joseph Kimball Family: A Genealogical Memoir of the Ascendants and Descendants of Joseph Kimball of Canterbury, N. H.* Concord, NH: Printed by the Republican Press Association.

King, Cameron Haight. 1908. *The King Family of Suffield, Connecticut.* San Francisco, CA: Press of the Walter N. Brunt Co,.

Kingsbury, Frank B. 1925. *History of the Town of Surry, Cheshire County, New Hampshire: From Date of Severance from Gilsum and Westmoreland, 1769-1922, with a Genealogical Register and Map of the Town.* Surry, NH: Published by the town.

Kingsbury, Fred J. 1905. *The Genealogy of the Descendants of Henry Kingsbury.* Hartford, CT: Author.

Kittredge, Mabel Thorndike Hodges. 1936. *The Kittredge Family in America.* Rutland, VT: Tuttle Publishing.

Klumph, Richard Amidon. 1960. *Klumph Genealogy and Early Klumph History.* Kalamazoo, MI: Published by the author.

Lapham, William Berry. 1886. *Centennial History of Norway, Oxford County, Maine, 1786-1886.* Portland, ME: B. Thurston.

—. 1891. *History of Bethel, Formerly Sudbury, Canada, Oxford County, Maine, 1768-1890.* Augusta, ME: Press of the Maine Farmer.

—. 1890. *History of Rumford, Oxford County, Maine, from Its First Settlement in 1779, to the Present Time.* Augusta, ME: Press of the Maine Farmer.

Lapham, William Berry, and Silas Packard Maxim. 1884. *History of Paris, Maine, from its Settlement to 1880, with a History of the Grants of 1736 & 1771, Together with Personal Sketches, a Copious Genealogical Register and an Appendix.* Paris, ME: Printed for the authors.

Larned, Ellen Douglas. 1874. *History of Windham County, Connecticut.* Worcester, MA: Published by the author.

Leavitt, Thaddeus William Henry. 1879. *History of Leeds and Grenville Ontario, from 1749 to 1879.* Recorder Press, Brockville.

Leonard, Levi Washburn, and Josiah Lafayette Seward. 1920. *The History of Dublin, N.H.: Containing the Address by Charles Mason, and the Proceedings at the Centennial Celebration, June 17, 1852, with a Register of Families.* Dublin, NH: Published by the town.

Lewis, George Harlan. 1908. *Edmund Lewis, of Lynn, Massachusetts, and Some of HIs Descendnats.* Salem, MA: Essex Institute.

Lincoln, Waldo. 1902. *Genealogy of the Waldo Family: A Record of the Descendants of Cornelius Waldo, of Ipswich, Mass., from 1647 to 1900.* Worcester, MA: Press of Charles Hamilton.

Little, George Thomas, Henry S. Burrage, and Albert Roscoe Stubbs. 1909. *Genealogical and Family History of the State of Maine.* New York, NY: Lewis Historical Publishing.

Littlefield, Peter F., and Karl Pfister. 2001. *Genealogies of the Early Settlers of Weston, Vermont, Second Edition.* Weston, VT: Weston Historical Society.

Livermore, Abiel Abbot, and Putnam Sewall. 1888. *History of the Town of Wilton, Hillsborough County, New Hampshire, with a Genealogical Register.* Lowell, MA: Marden and Rowell.

Lord, Charles Chase. 1890. *Life and Times in Hopkinton, N.H.* Concord, NH: Republican Press.

Lovejoy, Clarence Earle. 1930. *The Lovejoy Genealogy with Biographies and History.* New York: Published by the author.

Lovejoy, Mary Elevyn Wood. 1911. *History of Royalton, Vermont, with Family Genealogies, 1769-1911.* Burlington, VT: Free Press Printing Company.

Lovering, Martin, and Ursula N. McFarland Chase. 1915. *History of the Town of Holland, Massachusetts.* Rutland, VT: The Tuttle Company.

Lowell, Delmar Rial. 1899. *The Historic Genealogy of the Lowells of America from 1639 to 1899.* Published by the author.

Lyford, James Otis. 1896. *History of Concord, New Hampshire: From the Original Grant in Seventeen Hundred and Twenty-five to the Opening of the Twentieth Century.* Canterbury, NH: Rumford Press.

—. 1912. *History of the Town of Canterbury, New Hampshire, 1727-1912.* Concord, NH: Rumford.

Manning, William Henry. 1902. *The Genealogical and Biographical History of the Manning Families of New England and Descendants.* Salem, MA: Salem Press.

Marvin, Abijah Perkins. 1879. *History of the Town of Lancaster, Massachusetts: From the First Settlement to the Present Time, 1643-1879.* Lancaster, MA: Published by the town.

Marvin, George Franklin. 1904. *Descendants of Reinold and Matthew Marvin of Hartford, Ct., 1638 and 1635, Sons of Edward Marvin, of Great Bentley, England.* Boston, MA: T. R. Marvin & Son.

Mason, Edna Warren. 1937. *Descendants of Capt. Hugh Mason in America.* New Haven, CT: Tuttle, Morehouse & Taylor.

May, John Joseph. 1902. *Danforth Genealogy: Nicholas Danforth and William Danforth.* Boston, MA: Charles H. Pope.

McIntire, Robert Harry. 1941. *Descendants of Philip McIntire, a Scottish Highlander who was Deported by Oliver Cromwell Following the Battle of Dunbar, September 3, 1650, and Settled at Reading, Mass., about 1660.* Lancaster, PA: Lancaster Press.

McKeen, Silas. 1875. *A History of Bradford, Vermont.* Montpelier, VT: J. D. Clark & Son.

McLellan, Hugh Davis. 1903. *History of Gorham, Me.* Gorham, ME: Portland, Smith & Sale.

Merrick, George Byron. 1902. *Genealogy of the Merrick--Mirick--Myrick Family of Massachusetts.* Madison, WI: Tracy, Gibbs & Company.

Merrill, Georgia Drew. 1891. *History of Androscoggin County, Maine.* Boston, MA: W. A. Ferguson & Co.

—. 1889. *History of Carroll County, New Hampshire.* Boston, MA: W. A. Ferguson.

Merrill, Samuel. 1917-1928. *A Merrill Memorial: An Account of the Descendants of Nathaniel Merrill, an Early Settler of Newbury, Massachusetts.* Cambridge, MA.

Miller, Frank E. 1925. *A Genealogy of Reminiscences, Sketches of History, Births, Deaths, Marriages, Occupation. . . of the Family Millers .* Syracuse, NY: Printed by the Syracuse Press.

Miller, Thomas Condit, and Hu Maxwell. 1913. *West Virginia and its People, Volume I.* New York, NY: Lewis Historical Publishing.

Miner, Charles. 1845. *History of Wyoming, in a Series of Letters, from Charles Miner, to His Son William Penn Miner.* Philadelphia, PA: J Crissy.

Mitchell, Harry Edward, O. M. Bean, and Charles S. Hartford. 1904. *The Bridgton Town Register, 1905.* Brunswick, ME: H. E. Mitchell Company.

Monroe, Ira Thompson. 1932. *History of the Town of Livermore, Androscoggin County, Maine: From its Inception in 1735 and its Grant of Land in 1772 to its Organization and Incorporation in 1795 up to the Present Time, 1928.* Lewiston, ME: Printed by the Lewiston Journal Printshop.

Mooar, George. 1901. *Mooar (Moors) Genealogy: Abraham Mooar of Andover, and His Descendants.* Boston: Press of David Clapp.

—. 1903. *The Cummings Memorial: A Genealogical History of the Descendants of Isaac Cummings, an Early Settler of Topsfield, Massachusetts.* New York: B. F. Cummings.

Moore, Jacob Bailey. 1893. *History of the Town of Candia, Rockingham County, N.H.: From its First Settlement to the Present Time.* Manchester, NH: G. W. Browne.

Morris, Jonathan Flynt. 1887. *A Genealogical and Historical Register of the Descendants of Edward Morris of Roxbury, Mass. and Woodstock, Conn.* Hartford, CT: Case, Lockwood & Brainard.

Morrison, Leonard Allison, and Stephen Paschall Sharples. 1897. *History of the Kimball Family in America, from 1634 to 1897 : and of its Ancestors the Kemballs or Kemboldes of England; with an Account of the Kembles of Boston, Massachusetts.* Boston: Damrell & Upham.

Morse, J. Howard, and Emily W. Leavitt. 1903. *Morse Genealogy: Comprising the Descendants of Samuel, Anthony, William, and Joseph Morse and John Moss: Being a Revision of the Memorial of the Morses, Volumes 1-2.* New York, NY: Morse Society.

Moulton, Henry William, and Claribel Moulton. 1906. *Moulton Annals.* Chicago, IL: Edward A. Claypool.

Mudge, Alfred. 1868. *Memorials: Being a Genealogical, Biographical and Historical Account of the Name of Mudge in America from 1638 to 1868.* Boston, MA: Printed by Alfred Mudge & Son, for the family.

Munsell, Frank. 1898. *American Ancestry: Giving the Name and Descent, in the Male Line, of Americans Whose Ancestors Settled in United States Previous to the Declaration of Independence, A.D. 1776, volume XI.* Albany, NY: Joel Munsell's Sons.

Neill, Edward D. 1882. *History of Rice County, Including Explorers and Pioneers of Minnesota.* Minneapolis, MN: Minnesota Historical Company.

Nelson Picnic Association. 1917. *Celebration of the Town of Nelson, New Hampshire.* New York, NY: Evening Post job printing office.

Nickerson & Cox. 1895. *Illustrated Historical Souvenir of Randolph, Vermont.* Randolph, VT: Nickerson & Cox.

Norton, John Foote. 1888. *The History of Fitzwilliam, New Hampshire, from 1752-1887.* New York, NY: Burr Printing House.

Nye, George Hyatt. 1907. *A Genealogy of the Nye Family.* Cleveland, OH: The Nye Family of America Association.

Nye, Mary Greene. 1951. *Early History of Berlin, Vermont 1763-1820.* Montpelier, VT: Norbert J. Towne and H. J. Dodge; Agent, Vermont Historical Society.

Oakes, Rensselaer Allston. 1905. *Genealogical and Family History of the County of Jefferson, New York.* New York, NY: Lewis Publishing Company.

Oliver, Rebekah Deal. 1970. *The Bottum (Longbottom) Family Album: The Descendants of Daniel (-1732) and Elizabeth (Lamb) Longbottom of Norwich, Connecticut.* Denver, CO: W. Kelly Oliver.

Osgood, Ira. 1894. *A Genealogy of the Descendants of John, Christopher and William Osgood, Who Came from England and Settled in New England Early in the Seventeenth Century.* Salem, MA: Salem Press.

Paige, Lucius Robinson. 1877. *History of Cambridge, Massachusetts. 1630-1877: With a Genealogical Register.* Boston, MA: H. O. Houghton.

Parker, Francis Jewett. 1894. *Genealogy of the Ainsworth Families in America.* Boston, MA: Printed for the compiler.

Parshall, James C. 1897. *The Barker Genealogy: Giving the Names and Descendants of Several Ancestors, who Settled in the United States Previous to the Declaration of Independence, A.D. 1776.* Middletown, NY: Printed for the author.

Parsons, Henry. 1912. *Parsons Family: Descendants of Cornet Joseph Parsons, Springfield, 1636--Northampton,1655; Volume 2.* New York: Frank Allaben Genealogical Company.

Parsons, Usher. 1872. *A Centennial History of Alfred, York County, Maine.* Philadelphia, PA: Sanford, Everts & Co.

Peabody, Selim Hobart. 1909. *Peabody Genealogy.* Boston, MA: Charles H. Pope.

Peck, Chauncey Edwin. 1914. *The History of Wilbraham, Massachusetts.* Town of Wilbraham.

Peck, Ira Ballou. 1868. *A Genealogical History of the Descendants of Joseph Peck.* Boston, MA: A. Mudge.

Pelton, Jeremiah M. 1892. *Genealogy of the Pelton Family in America.* Albany, NY: Joel Munsell's Sons.

Perkins, Thomas Allen. 1947. *Jacob Perkins of Wells, Maine and his Descendants, 1583-1936.* Haverhill, MA: Record Publishing Company.

Perley, Derby. 1870. *The Hutchinson Family: or, The Descendants of Barnard Hutchinson, of Cowlam, England.* Salem, MA: Essex Institute Press.

Perley, Sidney. 1893. *The Dwellings of Boxford, Essex County, Mass.* Salem, MA: The Essex Institute.

—. 1880. *The History of Boxford, Essex County, Massachusetts, from the Earliest Settlement Known to the Present Time.* Boxford, MA: Published by the author.

Perrin, William Henry. 1880. *History of Delaware County and Ohio.* Chicago, IL: Baskin & Co.

Phelps, Oliver Seymour, and Andrew Tinkey Servin. 1899. *The Phelps Family of America and Their English Ancestors.* Pittsfield, MA: Eagle Publishing.

Pierce, Frederic Beech. 1882. *Pierce Genealogy: Being the Record of the Posterity of Thomas Pierce, an Early Inhabitant of Charlestown, and Afterwards Charlestown Village (Woburn), in New England.* Worcester, MA: Press of C. Hamilton.

Pierce, Frederick Clifton. 1898. *Batchelder, Batcheller Genealogy. Descendants of Rev. Stephen Bachiler, of England ... Who Settled the Town of New Hampton, N.H., and Joseph, Henry, Joshua and John Batcheller of Essex Co., Mass.* Chicago: W. B. Conkey.

—. 1899. *Foster Genealogy, Part I.* Chicago: Published by the author, Press of W. B. Conkey.

—. 1895. *Whitney: The Descendants of John Whitney, who Came from London, England, to Watertown, Massachusetts, in 1635.* Chicago, IL: Published by the author; press of W. B. Conkey.

Plumb, Henry Blackman. 1885. *History of Hanover Township: Including Sugar Notch, Ashley, and Nanticoke Boroughs.* Wilkes-Barre, PA: R. Baur. Printer.

Pollard, Annie M. 1954. *The History of the Town of Baltimore, Vermont.* Montpelier, VT: Vermont Historical Society.

Poor, Henry V. 1904. "History of Andover, Maine: Purchase of theTtownship and Distribution of the Land." *The Rumford Falls Times*, Aug 13: 1-16.

Porter, Joseph Whitcomb. 1878. *A Genealogy of the Descendants of Richard Porter, Who Settled at Weymouth, Mass., 1635, and Allied Families.* Bangor, ME: Burr & Robinson.

Powers, Amos H. 1884. *The Powers Family: A Genealogical and Historical Record of Walter Power, and some of his Descendants to the Ninth Generation.* Chicago. IL: Fergus Printing.

Pratt, Francis G. Salem, MA. *The Pratt Family: A Genealogical Record of Mathew Pratt of Weymouth, Mass., and his American Descendants, 1623-1889.* 1890: Higginson Genealogical Books.

Preston, Charles Henry. 1931. *Descendants of Roger Preston of Ipswich and Salem Village.* Salem, MA: The Essex Institute.

Ramsdell, George Allen, and William P. Colburn. 1901. *The History of Milford, Volume 1.* Milford, NH: Rumford Press.

Randall, Oran Edmund. 1882. *History of Chesterfield, Cheshire County, N.H., from the Incorporation of "Township Number One," by Massachusetts, in 1736, to the Year 1881.* Brattleboro, VT: D. Leonard.

Rann, William S. 1886. *History of Chittenden County, Vermont.* Syracuse, NY: D. Mason & Co.

Reed, Newton. 1875. *Early History of Amenia.* Amenia, NY: De Lacey & Wiley, Printers.

Remick, Oliver Philbrick, and Winifred Lovering Holman. 1933. *Remick Genealogy: Compiled from the Manuscript of Lieutenant Oliver Philbrick Remick for the Maine Historical Society by Winifred Lovering Holman.* Concord, NH: Rumford Press.

Reynolds, Gene. 2014. *Images of America: Georgetown.* Charleston, SC: Arcadia Publishing.

Richmond, Joshua Bailey. 1897. *The Richmond Family, 1594-1896, and Pre-American Ancestors, 1040-1594.* Boston, MA: Published by the compiler.

Ridlon, Gideon Tibbetts. 1926. *A Contribution to the History, Biography and Genealogy of the Families Named Sole, Solly, Soule, Sowle, Soulis.* Lewiston, ME: Journal Press, published by the author.

Rix, Guy Scoby. 1901. *History and Genealogy of the Eastman Family of America: Containing Biographical Sketches and Genealogies of both Males and Females.* Concord, NH: I. C. Evans.

Roberts, Gary Boyd. 1983. *Genealogies of Connecticut Families from The New England Historical and Genealogical Register In Three Volumes.* Genealogical Publishing Company.

Rogers, James Swift. 1902. *James Rogers of New London, Ct: And His Descendants.* Boston, MA: Published by the compiler.

Roscoe, William E. 1882. *History of Schoharie County, New York, with Illustrations and Biographical Sketches of Some of its Prominent Men and Pioneers.* Syracuse, NY: D. Mason & Co.

Runnels, Moses Thurston. 1873. *A Genealogy of Runnels and Reynolds Families in America.* Boston, MA: Alfred Mudge & Son.

—. 1882. *History of Sanbornton, New Hampshire, Volume II.* Boston, MA: Mudge.

Sausaman, William Amel. 1971. *Nathan Alldredge (1739-1826) of North Carolina and Tennessee and His Descendants.* Springfield, IL: Published by the author.

Sawin, Thomas E. 1866. *Sawin: Summary Notes Concerning John Sawin, and His Posterity.* Wendell, MA: T. E. Sawin.

Sawyer, John. 1898. *History of Cherry Valley [N.Y.] from 1740 to 1898.* Cherry Valley, NY: Gazette Print.

Sayward, Charles Augustus. 1890. *The Sayward Family: Being the History and Genealogy of Henry Sayward of York, and His Descendants.* Ipswich, MA: Independent Press, E. G. Hull.

Secomb, Daniel F. 1883. *History of the Town of Amherst, Hillsborough County, New Hampshire.* Concord, NH: Evans, Sleeper, and Woodbury.

Sessions, Francis Charles. 1890. *Materials for a History of the Sessions Family in America: The Descendants of Alexander Sessions of Andover, Mass., 1669.* Albany, NY: Joel Munsell's Sons.

Seward, Josiah Lafayette. 1921. *A History of the Town of Sullivan, New Hampshire, 1777-1917.* Keene, NH: J. L. Seward.

Shattuck, L'emuel. 1855. *Memorials of the Descendants of William Shattuck, the Progenitor of the Families in America that Have Borne His Name.* Boston: Dutton and Wentworth, printed for the family.

Sheldon, Henry Olcott. 1857. *The Sheldon Magazine, No. 1-4.* Sydney, OH.

Shurtleff, Benjamin. 1912. *Descendants of William Shurtleff of Plymouth and Marshfield, Massachusetts.* Revere, MA: Published by the author.

Sinnett, Charles Nelson. 1926. "The Sewall Genealogy." Unpublished manuscript. Accessed October 14, 2019. https://archive.org/details/sewallgenealogyw00sinn/page/n5.

Smith, Albert, and John Hopkins Morison. 1876. *History of the Town of Peterborough, Hillsborough County, New Hampshire.* Boston: Press of G.H. Ellis.

Smith, Annie Elizabeth Morrill. 1914-1931. *Morrill Kindred in America.* New York, NY: Lyons Genealogical Company.

Smith, Charles James. 1907. *History of the Town of Mont Vernon, New Hampshire.* Boston: Blanchard Printing Company.

Smith, Henry Perry. 1886. *History of Addison County Vermont.* Syracuse, NY: D. Mason & Co.

—. 1885. *History of Broome County: With Illustrations and Biographical Sketches of Some of its Prominent Men and Pioneers.* Syracuse, NY: D. Mason & Co.

Smith, James Hadden. 1882. *History of Duchess County, New York: With Illustrations and Biographical Sketches of Some of its Prominent Men and Pioneers.* Syracuse, NY: D. Mason & Co.

Smith, John E. 1899. *Our County and Its People: A Descriptive and Biographical Record of Madison County, New York.* Boston: Boston History Company.

Smith, Thomas, Samuel Deane, Samuel Freeman, and William Willis. 1849. *Journals of the Rev. Thomas Smith, and the Rev. Samuel Deane, Pastors of the First Church in Portland: with Notes and Biographical Notices: and a Summary History of Portland.* Portland, ME: J. S. Bailey.

Somers, Amos Newton. 1899. *History of Lancaster, New Hampshire.* Concord, NH: Rumford Press.

South Church of Andover. 1859. *Historical Manual of the South Church in Andover, Mass.* Edited by George Mooar. Andover, MA: Printed by Warren F. Draper.

Spalding, Charles Warren. 1897. *The Spalding Memorial: A Genealogical History of Edward Spalding of Virginia and Massachusetts Bay and His Descendants.* Chicago, IL: American Publishers Association.

Speare, Eva Augusta. 1952. *The Genealogy of the Descendants of John Clough of Salisbury, Massachusetts.* John Clough Genealogical Society.

Spofford, Charles B. 1896. *Grave Stone Records: From the Ancient Cemeteries in the Town of Claremont, New Hampshire, with Historical and Biographical Notes.* Claremont, NH: G. I Putnam.

Stackpole, Everett Schemerhorn. 1925. *History of Winthrop, Maine with Genealogical Notes.* Auburn, ME: Press of Merrill and Webber.

Stafford, Morgan Hewitt. 1941. *A Genealogy of the Kidder Family Comprising the Descendants in the Male Line of Ensign James Kidder, 1626-1676, of Cambridge and Billerica in the Colony of Massachusetts Bay.* Rutland, VT: Tuttle Publishing.

Stark, Caleb. 1860. *History of the Town of Dunbarton, Merrimack County, New-Hampshire, from the Grant by Mason's Assigns, in 1751, to the Year 1860.* Concrd: G. Parker Lyon.

Stay, Elizabeth Wardwell. 1905. *Wardwell: A Brief Sketch of the Antecedents of Solomon Wardwell, with the Descendants of his Two Sons, Ezra and Amos, who Died in Sullivan, N.H.* Greenfield, MA: Press of E. A. Hall & Co.

Stearns, Ezra S. 1875. *History of the Town of Rindge, New Hampshire, from the Date of the Rowley Canada or Massachusetts Charter, to the Present Time, 1736-1874, with a Genealogical Register of the Rindge Families.* Boston: G. H. Ellis.

Stearns, Ezra S., William F. Witcher, and Edward E. Parker. 1908. *Genealogical and Family History of the State of New Hampshire: A Record of the Achievements of Her People in the Making of a Commonwealth and the Founding of a Nation.* New York: Lewis Publishing.

Stearns, Ezra Scollay. 1887. *History of Ashburnham, Massachusetts, from the Grant of Dorchester Canada to the Present Time, 1734-1886; with a Genealogical Register of Ashburnham Families.* Ashburnham, MA: Published by the town.

Stearsns, Ezra Scollay, and Moses Thurston Runnels. 1906. *History of Plymouth, New Hampshire: Vol. I. Narrative--vol. II. Genealogies.* Plymouth, NH: Printed for the town by University Press.

Sterling, Albert Mack, and Sterling Edward Boker. 1909. *The Sterling Genealogy, Vol II.* New York: Grafton Press.

Stewart, James Harvey. 1872. *Recollections of the Early Settlement of Carroll County, Indiana.* Cincinnati, OH: Printed for the author by Hitchcock and Walden.

Stickney, Charles Perham, John B. Stebbins, and Abby Maria Hemenway. 1886. *The Local History of Brookline, Vt.: The General History of the Town.* Chicago, IL: Written for Volume V of the Vermont Historical Magazine.

Stickney, Matthew Adams. 1869. *A Genealogical Memoir of the Descendants of William and Elizabeth Stickney.* Salem, MA: Author.

—. 1883. *The Fowler Family: A Genealogical Memoir of the Descendants of Philip and Mary Fowler, of Ipswich, Mass.* Salem, MA: Printed for the author.

—. 1867. *The Stickney Family: A Genealogical Memoir.* Salem, MA: Printed for the Author, Essex Institute Press.

Stiles, Henry R. 1999/1892. *Families of Ancient Windsor, Connecticut: Consisting of Volume II of the History and Genealogies of Ancient Windsor, Connecticut, Including East Windsor, South Windsor, Bloomfield.* Clearfield Company; Reprinted by Genealogical Publishing Company.

Stocking, Charles Henry Wright. 1897. *The History and Genealogy of the Knowltons of England and America.* New York, NY: Kinckerbocker Press.

Stone, William Leete. 1888. *The Family of John Stone: One of the First Settlers of Guilford, Conn.* Albany, NY: J. Munsell's Sons.

Stoughton, Ralph M. 1978. *History of the Town of Gill, Franklin County, Massachusetts, 1793-1943.* Gill, MA: Published by the town.

Stowell, William Henry Harrison. 1922. *The Stowell Genealogy: A Record of the Descendants of Samuel Stowell of Hingham, Mass.* Rutland, VT: Tuttle Company.

Stratton, Harriet Russell. 1918. *A Book of Strattons: Being a Collection of Stratton Records from England and Scotland, and a Genealogical History of the Early Colonial Strattons in America, with Five Generations of their Descendants.* New York, NY: Grafton Press.

Taylor, Charles James. 1882. *History of Great Barrington, Berkshire County, Massachusetts.* Great Barrington, MA: C. W. Bryan.

Taylor, Ernest Manly. 1908. *History of Brome County, Quebec, from the Date of Grants of Land Therein to the Present Time, with Records of Some Early Families.* Montreal: Lovell.

Temple, Josiah Howard. 1889. *History of the Town of Palmer, Massachusetts, Early Known as the Elbow Tract: Including Records of the Plantation, District and Town. 1716-1889. With a Genealogical Register.* Springfield, MA: Published by the town of Palmer.

Thomas, Marion. 1976. *Once Upon a Time.* Silver Creek, NY: The Fortnightly Club.

Thurston, Brown. 1892. *Thurston Genealogies.* Portland, ME: Brown Thurston.

Tilden, William Smith. 1887. *History of the Town of Medfield, Massachusetts, 1650-1886.* Boston, MA: G. H. Ellis.

Torrey, Clarence Almon, and Charles Harvey Roe. 1958. *David Roe of Flushing, New York and Some of His Descendants, Second Edition.* Unpublished manuscript. https://archive.org/details/davidroeofflushi00torr_0/page/n3/mode/2up.

Towne, Edwin Eugene. 1901. *The Descendants of William Towne.* Newtonville, MA: Published by the author.

Towne, Philip William, and Roderick Bissell Jones. 1743. "Seth Payn of Lebanon, Conn., and Paines Hollow, N.Y., and Some of His Descendants." *The New England Historical and Genealogical Register* 134.

Towner, Ashburn. 1892. *Our County and Its People: A History of the Valley and County of Chemung, from the Closing Years of the Eighteenth Century.* Syracuse, NY: D. Mason & Co.

Trask, Gwen Guiou. 1982. *Early Vital Records of the Township of Yarmouth, Nova Scotia, 1762-1811.* Yarmouth County Historical Society.

Trowbridge, Francis Bacon. 1891. *The Champion Genealogy: A History of the Descendants of Henry Champion, of Saybrook and Lyme, Connecticut, Together with Some Account of Other Families of the Name.* New Haven, CT: Printed for the author by Tuttle, Morehouse & Taylor.

Tucker, William Howard. 1889. *History of Hartford, Vermont, July 4, 1761-April 4, 1889.* Burlington, VT: The Free Press Association.

Van Wagenen, Avis Stearns. 1901. *Genealogy and Memoirs of Isaac Stearns and His Descendants.* Syracuse, NY: Currier Printing.

Vinton, John Adams. 1874. *The Upton Memorial: A Genealogical Record of the Descendants of John Upton, of North Reading, Mass. ... Together with Short Genealogies of the Putnam, Stone and Bruce Families.* E. Upton and Sons.

Wadleigh, George. 1913. *Notable Events in the History of Dover, New Hampshire, from the First Settlement in 1623 to 1865.* Dover, NH.

Wager, Daniel E. 1896. *Our City and Its People: A Descriptive Work on the City of Rome New York.* Boston History Company.

Wall, John Patrick, and Harold E. Pickersgill. 1921. *History of Middlesex County, New Jersey, 1664-1920, Volume 1.* New York, NY: Lewis Historical Publishing.

Wallace, William Allen. 1910. *The History of Canaan, New Hampshire.* Concord, NH: Rumford Press.

Ward, Andrew Henshaw. 1858. *A Genealogical History of the Rice Family.* Boston, MA: C. B. Richardson.

Warden, William A, and Robert L. Dexter. 1905. *Genealogy of the Dexter Family in America: Descendants of Thomas Dexter.* Worcester, MA: Published by the authors.

Warner, Lucien C., and Josephine Genung Nichols. 1919. *The Descendants of Andrew Warner.* New Haven, CT: Tuttle, Morehouse & Taylor.

Washburn, Israel. 1874. *Notes, Historical, Descriptive, and Personal, of Livermore, in Androscoggin (Formerly in Oxford) County, Maine.* Portland, ME: Bailey & Noyes.

Waterman, Edgar Francis. 1939. *The Waterman Family, Volume I: Descendants of Robert Waterman of Marshfield, Massachusetts.* New Haven, CT: Edgar F. Waterman.

Waters, Henry Fitzgilbert. 1882. *The Newhall Family of Lynn, Massachusetts.* Salem, MA: Printed for Essex Institute.

Weaver, William L. 1867. *A Genealogy of the Fenton Family : Descendants of Robert Fenton, an Early Settler of Ancient Windham, Conn. (Now Mansfield).* Willimantic, CT.

Weeks, Frank Edgar. 1908. *Pioneer History of Clarksfield.* Clarksfield, OH: Published by the author.

Weeks, Lyman Horace. 1913. *The Darling Family in America: Being an Account of the Founders and First Colonial Families, an Official List of the Heads of Families of the Name Darling, Resident in the United States in 1790, and a Bibliography.* New York, NY: W. W. Clemens.

Wellman, Joshua Wyman, George Walter Chamberlain, and Arthur Holbrook Wellman. 1918. *Descendants of Thomas Wellman of Lynn, Massachusetts.* Boston, MA: A. H. Wellman.

Wells, Frederic Palmer. 1902. *History of Newbury, Vermont, from the Discovery of the Coös Country to Present Time. With Genealogical Records of Many Families.* St. Johnsbury, VT: The Caledonian Company.

Westmoreland Historical Committee. 1976. *History of Westmoreland (Great Meadow) New Hampshire: 1741-1970, and Genealogical Data.* Westmoreland, NH: Westmoreland Historical Committee.

Wheeler, Albert Gallatin. 1914. *The Genealogical and Encyclopedic History of the Wheeler Family in America.* Boston, MA: American College of Genealogy.

Wheeler, George Augustus. 1878. *History of Brunswick, Topsham, and Harpswell, Maine, Including the Ancient Territory Known as Pejepscot.* Boston, MA: A. Mudge & Sons, printers.

Whitcomb, Frank H. 1905. *Vital Statistics of the Town of Keene, New Hampshire.* Keene, NH: Sentinel Printing Company.

White, Truman C. 1898. *Our County and its People: A Descriptive Work on Erie County, New York.* Boston, MA: The Boston History Company.

Whitman, Charles Foster. 1924. *A History of Norway, Maine: From its Earliest Settlement to the Close of the Year 1922.* Lewiston, ME: Published by the town of Norway.

Whittemore, Bernard Bemis. 1890. *A Genealogy of Several Branches of the Whittemore Family, Including the Original Whittemore family of Hitchin, Hertfordshire, England.* Nashua, NH: F. P. Whittemore.

Williams Brothers. 1890. *History of Franklin and Pickaway Counties, Ohio, with Illustrations and Biographical Sketches of Some of the Prominent Men and Pioneers.* Cleveland, OH: Williams Brothers.

Williams, C. S. 1907. *Descendants of Thomas White of Weymouth.* New York, NY: Privately printed.

Willis, William. 1833. *The History of Portland, from its First Settlement, Part II From 1700 to 1833.* Portland, ME: Charles Day & Co. Printers.

Worcester, Samuel T. 1879. *History of the Town of Hollis, New Hampshire, from its First Settlement to the Year 1879: with Many Biographical Sketches of its Early Settlers, Their Descendants, and Other Residents.* Boston: A. Williams.

Young, Andrew W. 1869. *History of the Town of Warsaw, New York.* Buffalo, NY: Press of the Sage, Sons & Co.

Name Index

Naomi 1770-. 135, 528
Rachel 1777-1851. 210
Sarah 1744-.......... 196
William M. 1795-1861 533
HICKS
Abra 1800-1887.... 543
Emily 1804-1869.. 397
Israel 1766-1839 .. 611
HIDDEN
David 1784-1861 .. 492
Mehitable 192
HIGGINS
Hannah 1798-1872 361
HILDRETH
Benjamin 1754-1754 174
Jonas 1766-1808 .. 322
Lydia 1754-1821.... 57, 231
Mary 1772-1846 ... 400
Robert 1713-1760.. 42, 174
Ruth D. 1799-1828450
HILL
Azubah 1768- 575
Bethiah 1718-1754 36, 154
Eunice 1797-1862. 445
John 1791-1870.... 446
Judith 1779-1813 . 245
Leavitt 1770-1843 446
Sally 1791-1844.... 621
Samuel 1764-1813 571
Selinda 1809-1891 504
Timothy 1776-1850 245
HILLIARD
Eunice 1814-1885. 451
Joseph 1765-1830. 329
HILLS
Emily 1811-1888 .. 520
Hephzibah 1749-1778 243
James 1763-1846 . 260
Lydia 1761- 307
Sylvester 1800-1830 625
HINCKLEY
Benjamin 1782-1835 516
Betsey 1796-1879. 516
Caleb 1790-1790... 516
David 1754-1835 . 132, 515
Eber 1791-1796.... 516
Hannah 1786- 516
Joanna 1792-1846 490
Joanna 1799-1857 516
Mercy 1749-1781. 114, 455
HINES
Mary 421
HINKLEY
Porter 1781-1849 . 455
Sarah 1774-1865 .. 565
HISCOCK
Jesse S. 1794-1842608
HITCHCOCK
Ebenezer M. 1762-1833 .... 68, 271
Honor 1805-1864.. 375
Joseph H. 1784-1854 271
Polly 1793-1867.... 406
Roxerene 1786-1871 271
HIX
Olive 1798-1861 ... 397
HOAR
Benjamin 1757-.... 365
Keturah 1755-1826 .... 165, 621
Susanna 1774-1858 568
HOBART
Joshua 338
HOBBS
Elizabeth 1783-1867 290
Hannah 1798-1852 480
Lydia 1792-1851 .. 290
HODGDON
Isaac F................. 474
HODGE
Harriet 1798-1825 517
HODGKINS
Francis W............ 191
HODGMAN
Abel 1759- 235
Abigail 1774-1839 366
Josiah 1778- 308
HOFFMAN
John H. 1802-1861354
HOISINGTON
Rhoda 1791-1842 . 614
HOIT
Zerviah 1720-1794 15, 73
HOIT/see also HOYT
Amos 1800-........... 567
HOLBROOK
Abigail 1770-1815 386
Betsey 1774-1820. 386
Mary 615
Rachel 1775-1860. 347
HOLCOMB
Abiel 1781-1823 ... 206
HOLDEN
Esther 1778-1813. 353
Jesse 1779-1845 ... 569
Lydia 1785-1823 .. 425
Mary 1760-1844 ... 247
Nathan 1786-1829 508
Philena 1805-1842 472
HOLLENBECK
Jane 1777-1812.... 394
HOLLIDAY
George 1815- 438
HOLLISTER
John J. 1777-1834 330
HOLMAN
John 1761-1842.... 343
Katharine 1753-1781 .... 167, 629
Polly 1771-1821.... 334
Silas 1790-1839.... 629
William 1811-1887518
HOLMES
Anna 1773-1807 ... 355
Charles 480
Timothy 1763- 355
Warren 1810-1884 462
HOLT
Aaron 1686-.............. 8
Aaron 1776-1826 .. 388
Abel 1740-1815 ... 101, 393
Abel 1770- 130, 514
Abel 1777-1842 248
Abel W. 1776-1802394
Abiah 1747-1790 . 112, 121, 445
Abiah 1761-1841 . 126, 501
Abiah 1765-1835 .. 485
Abiah 1785-1869 .. 597
Abiather 1813-1846 504
Abiel 1698-1772 . 6, 30
Abiel 1718-1744 29
Abiel 1727-1785 .... 30, 130
Abiel 1746-1824 .. 125, 180, 498
Abiel 1748-1811 .. 112, 127, 440
Abiel 1755- 127
Abiel 1762-1829 .. 130, 514
Abiel 1763-1845 .. 101, 396
Abiel 1765-1825 .. 126, 506
Abiel 1770-1834 .. 249, 499
Abiel 1773-1801 ... 239
Abiel 1774-1839 ... 440
Abiel 1775- 240
Abiel 1780-1826 .. 134, 525
Abiel 1781- 508
Abiel 1791-1864 ... 506
Abiel 1791-1869 ... 514
Abiel C. 1803-....... 396
Abigail 1688-17425, 6, 25
Abigail 1706-1716 .. 23
Abigail 1716-1749 . 25, 109
Abigail 1719- 29
Abigail 1722- .. 29, 128
Abigail 1727-1767 . 97, 377
Abigail 1732-1774 . 31, 137
Abigail 1736-1750 158
Abigail 1738- 160
Abigail 1748- 116
Abigail 1753- ... 65, 92, 362
Abigail 1758-1824123, 492
Abigail 1759- 161
Abigail 1761- 137, 535
Abigail 1765-1851369, 377
Abigail 1766- 119
Abigail 1767- 131
Abigail 1767-1821125, 238, 498
Abigail 1771- 485
Abigail 1774- 257
Abigail 1778- 395
Abigail 1779-1806 440
Abigail 1781- 473
Abigail 1782- 388
Abigail 1784- 433
Abner 1771-1854. 380, 387
Abraham 1763- 377
Adelia 1778-. 137, 539
Albert 1813-1889 . 464
Alfreada 1779-1814 .... 140, 548
Alfred Converse 1806-1852 525
Alice 1722-1762..... 29, 128
Alice 1742-1826..... 98, 125, 381
Alice 1747-1814... 127, 129, 508
Almira 1790-1874 140
Almira 1793-1796 269
Almira 1810-1813 523
Almira 1813-1874 269
Alva 1787- 476
Alva S. 1793-1879 547
Alvah 1763- 138
Alvah 1801-1876 .. 523
Amanda 1809- 397
Amasa 1759-1847 128
Amasa 1769-1770 119
Amasa 1772-1815 394
Amasa 1781-1850 433
Amasa 1785-1844 481
Amasa B. 1796- 397
Ambrose 1742- 60
Ammi R. 1789-1827 600
Amos 1740-1820.... 63, 247
Amos 1760-1782... 246
Amos 1764-1767... 248
Amos 1768-1826.. 248, 368
Amos 1777-1861... 239
Amos 1783-1853... 471

Temperance 1764-1831 315
Theodore 1765-1821 436
Thomas 1663-1731 .. 3, 16
Thomas 1687- 16
Thomas 1732-1818 79, 99, 309
Thomas 1747-1823 .... 112, 446
Thomas 1765-1863 .... 309, 581
Thomas 1768-1853446
Thomas 1775-1775592
Thomas 1777-1849593
Thomas C. 1740- ... 80, 316
Timothy 1733-1818 62
Uriah 1743-1822 . 157, 592
Uriah 1773-1799 .. 592
Uriah B. 1791- 447
William 1763- 554
William 1785-1788593

RUST
Kezia 1735-1825.... 31, 136
Sullivan 1780-1842 615

SADEY
Samuel 1681-1744. 16, 74

SAFFORD
Lucy 1802-1866.... 441
Mehitable 1798-1870 441

SAGE
Betsey 1771-1855 . 296

SALE
Richard 1800-1856467

SALTMARSH
Catherine 1777- ... 563
Edward Abbott 1768-1851 563
Hazen 1781-1805 . 563
Isaac 1779-1823 ... 563
John 1764- 563
Mary 1766-1848 ... 563
Mehitable 1762-1814 563
Ruth 1774- 282
Sally 1773- 563
Samuel 1775-1844 563
Seth 1778-1836 392
Thomas 1736-1826 .... 145, 563
Thomas 1771-1804563
Thomas 1772-1823563

SANBORN
Abigail 440
Stephen 1807-1869 567
William 1797-1876628
William 1798-1886629

SANDERS
Asa 364
Ebenezer 1791-1874 363

SANDERSON
Anna 1786-1856 ... 613

SANGER
Sophia 1784-1825. 615
Tirzah 1748-1825 164, 614

SARGENT
Hannah 1775-1821 317
Hannah 1777-1829 470
Mary -1786 228
Mary A. 1811-1891 503

SATTERLY
Mary 1790-1881 ... 623

SAUNDERS
Augusta A. 1820-1884 542
David 1766-1847 .. 243
Jonathan A. 371

SAVAGE
Charity 1779-1846 .... 126, 502
James 1781-1847 . 490
John 1771-1850.... 496
John -1816 421
Thomas 1770-1838190

SAWIN
Elijah 1774-1814 . 136, 512, 534
Elizabeth 1770-1771 512
Elizabeth 1797- 534
Ephraim 1806-1835 534
Isaac 1748-1776 .. 129, 512
Isaac 1804-1898 ... 534
Lucy 1812-1849.... 535
Manerva 1808- 534
Roena 1800-1801 .. 534
Royal 1798-1875... 594

SAWINS
Luce 1740-1824 ..... 30, 133

SAWTELL
Abigail 1779-1864 436

SAWTELLE
Mary 1778-1812 ... 425

SAWYER
Abial 1784-1870 ... 510
Alice 1781-1849.... 510
Benjamin 1757-1846 223
Dinah 1772-1825. 108, 426
Hannah 344
Hannah 1772-1860 509
Jacob 1779-1841 ... 510
John 1767-1842.... 344
Josiah 1744-1829 128, 509
Josiah 1770-1800 . 509
Lois 1801-1863 452
Lucy 1790-1860.... 270
Luther 1773-1834 426
Lydia 1768-1850 .. 509
Lydia 1795-1876 .. 617
Lydia 1813-1887 .. 575
Micajah 1737-1815188
Moses 1774-1851.. 510
Nathaniel 1750-1807 175
Rachel 1795-1865. 474
Rebecca 1783-1869510
Rufus 1760-1845 .. 507
Sarah 1747-1827 ... 73, 286
Sarah 1782-1863 .. 247
Sarah 1790-1880 .. 450

SAYBOTT
Keturah 1787-1872 184

SAYLES
Ariel 1780-1814.... 348

SAYWARD
Hannah 1780-1846 280

SCALES
Samuel E. 1785- ... 286
Sarah 1743- 144
Susannah 1744- 72, 283

SCARBOROUGH
Perrin 1808-1874 . 463

SCARLETT
Mary 1767-1832 ... 393

SCHOPPE
Fanny 1814-1902 . 453

SCHREIBER
Lana 1800-1881 ... 465

SCOTT
Sarah 1776-1854 .. 340
Susan 1770-1795.. 338
Susanna 1777-1836 224

SCRIPTURE
Allice 1790-1863.. 455, 513
Alpheus 1777-1846 455
Cyrrel 1785-1853 . 455
Eleazer 1783- 455
Elizabeth 1781-1864 455
Esther 1765-1841 133, 522
Hiram 1772-1849 . 454
Irene 1779-1861 ... 455
Lois 1788-1846 455
Roswell 1768-1839454
Zevinah 1774- 454

SEAMON
Harriet 1807-1874 547

SEARL
Timothy 1774-1837 404

SEARLE
Elizabeth 1794- 437

SEARS
William 202

SEAVER
Elizabeth 1785-1830 347
Pearley 1781-1842 409

SEAVEY
Joseph 1762-1812 172

SEAWOOD
John -1821 422

SEELY
Sarah 1793-1868.. 616

SEGAR
John E. 1803-1882 291

SELLINGHAM
Sally 1773- 327

SESSIONS
Abiah -1811 30
Anna 1765-1861 ... 556
Asahel 1769-1849. 198
John 1742-1820 ... 143, 556
John 1768-1842.... 198
John 1768-1852.... 556
Samuel 1710-1746 32, 143
Samuel 1773-1824 .... 556, 557
Sarah 1740-1815.. 143

SEVERANCE
Asa 1761-1854...... 319

SEVERY
Phebe 1803-1884.. 498

SEWALL
Nathaniel 1760-1814 604
Nicholas 1738-1806 160

SEXTON
Mary 1795-1884 ... 455

SEYMOUR
Abby G. 1815-1865537
Nancy 1787-1809 . 267

SHADDOCK
Eunice 1762- 332

SHANNON
John 1769-1840 ... 438, 449
Samuel 1774-1849 438

SHARP
Augustus 137, 539
Huldah 1749-1823 .... 103, 406
Robert 1791-1874 466, 522

SHATTUCK
Abiel 1762-1834 ... 592
Abraham 1759-1841 150
Anna 1800-1869 ... 580

Eunice 1825-1912. 417
George 1789-1865 608
Henry 1771-1840.. 224
Jenny S. 1797-1844 608
Jeremiah 1745-1827 .... 113, 451
Jeremiah 1795-1873 451
Jerusha 1734-......... 86
Joanna.................. 340
John 1750-1843... 162, 607
John 1768-1813.... 318
John 1777-1855.... 608
John 1793-........... 451
John G. 1822-1913 546
Jonas 1772- 485
Jonathan 1741-1796 .... 67, 267
Jonathan 1775- 267
Joseph 1784-1822. 215
Josiah 1738- ... 32, 139
Josiah 1779- 139
Josiah W. 1807-1882 545
Judith 1802- 451
Keziah B. 1793-1873 451
Leah 1792- 613
Levi 1768-1835..... 261
Lucy 1771-1856.... 344
Lucy 1812-1863.... 506
Lydia 1740- 49, 204
Lydia 1782-1783... 608
Lydia 1791- 451
Maria 1750-1813. 117, 471
Mary 1726- 86
Mary 1728-1808 .... 86, 339
Mary 1768-1830 ... 267
Mary 1788-1868 ... 320
Mary 1804-1819 ... 546
Miriam 1805- 451
Nathan 1700-1766 19, 86
Nathan 1730- 86
Nathan A. 1761-... 340
Olive 1750-1835 .... 50, 206
Percey 1764- 139
Perthene 1762- 139, 544
Peter V. 1820-1903 546
Philadelphia 1769- 139, 545
Polly 1778-1814.... 608
Rebeckah 1783-1831 215
Resolved G. 1772-1839 .... 139, 546
Robert K. 340
Russell 1788-1864 291
Russell C. 1795-1847 545
Ruth W. 1799-1880 451
Sally 1767-1786.... 267
Sally 1794-1814.... 608
Samuel 1789-1855 476
Sarah 1774- 139
Sarah 1790- 268
Sarah 1813-1899.. 506
Sarah A. 1811-1875 421
Sarah A. 1818- 546
Susannah 1789-1884 291
Warren 1781-1862 267
William 1760-1852 74, 291
William 1774- 340
William 1784-1818 268
William H. 1826-1892 546
William L. 1792-1876 608
WHEELOCK
Betsey 1769-1801. 234
Priscilla 1743-1834 292
Rebecca 235
WHIDDEN
Sarah 1798- 451
WHIPPLE
Hope 1778-1860 .. 166, 628
Ruth G. 1780-1815 428
Sarah.................... 355
WHITCOMB
Asenath -1849 347
David 1764-1835 .. 281
James 1781-1844 . 462
Jonathan -1809 346
Rebecca 1754-1843 .... 108, 425
Scotter 1766-1840 569
WHITE/see also WIGHT
Abel P. 1804-1893 548
Abigail.......... 129, 511
Anna F. 1805-....... 467
Bethuel 1771-1819 428
Calvin 1774-1843 . 428
Cheney Anne 1722-44, 182
Cornelius 1784-1784 429
Cynthia 1786- 429
David 1785-1862 .. 349
Delos 1790-1835 ... 538
Dinah 1779-1818.. 429
Elijah 1799- 550
Elizabeth 1781-1858 420
Eunice 1791-1828. 429
George W. 1809-1867 538
Hannah 1777-1857 429
John 1786- 541
John 1796-1861.... 429
Joseph 1762-1832 137, 538
Joseph 1801-1840 538
Levantia 1795-1889 538
Lydia 1763-1853 .. 193
Mary 1783-1882 ... 352
Mary Anna 1814-1849 536
Menzo 1793-1858 . 538
Moses 1743-1829. 109, 428
Nancy 1800-1869 . 577
Oliver 1758- 391
Orpha 1789- 429
Rebecca 1766-1856 609
Robert 1774-1851. 310
Sally 1788-1864 ... 420
Samuel 1782-1863 429
Samuel 1795-1874 532
Sarah 1767-1826.. 428
Solomon 1769-1810 428
Susanna -1847 344
Tirzah M. 1804-1837 358
WHITEHOUSE
Eizabeth 1777-1834 280
WHITFORD
Electa A. 1827-1916 546
WHITING
Benjamin 1789-1856 437
Cotton 1752-1815 118, 476
David 1793-1827 .. 437
Elizabeth 1773-1848 .... 139, 545
Elizabeth 1781-1857 476
George 1791-1822 437
Hannah 1784-1817 437
John 202
John 1785- 476
Mary 1784- 476
Nathan A. 1787-... 437
Oliver 1750-1829. 111, 436
Oliver 1778-1849.. 437
Oliver 1798-1886.. 407
Patty 1775-1778... 437
Patty 1780-1800... 437
Sally 1782-1785 ... 437
Sarah -1817.......... 570
Susanna 1781- 476
WHITMAN
Mary 1790-1860 .. 136, 533
WHITMORE
Abigail 1815-1907 463
Edmund 1784-1832 353
Elias 1772-1853 ... 589
Huldah 1782-1871 353
Jonathan 1786- 353
Joseph 1749-1830 .. 89
Joseph 1778- 353
Lucy 1775- 353
Rebecca 1792- 353
Sylvanus 1779-1841 353
WHITNEY
Abigail 1763- 365
Abram 1780-1860. 360
Albert G. 1817-1901 464
Annas 1761-1761 . 365
Annas 1765-1768 . 365
Annis 1753- 343
Annis 1756-1758 .. 343
Annis 1763- 343
Benjamin 1764- 188
Betsey 1798-1876. 347
Caleb 1729-1822 ... 87, 343
Caleb 1758-1778 .. 343
Chloe 1795- 361
Ebenezer 1778-1869 360
Elizabeth 1751-1823 ....107, 343, 424
Elizabeth 1776- 322
Esther 1768- 263
Hannah 1785-1871 360
Hezekiah 1766-1842 344
Isaac 1782-1860 ... 360
Israel 1741-1774 .. 333
Israel 1774-1850 . 326, 360
Jabez 1780-1839 .. 608
Jacob 1784-1785 .. 360
James M. 1820-1905 465
Jonathan 1724-1770 .... 93, 365
Jonathan 1743-1802 .... 86, 337
Jonathan 1749-1756 365
Jonathan 1766-1853 .... 115, 464
Jonathan 1768-1847 344
Jonathan 1769-1829 337
Joseph 1760-1840 343
Joseph 1774-1821 337
Joshua.................. 119
Joshua 1750-1750 343
Joshua 1754-1812 343, 344